The Top 7000 Charities in England and Wales

Charities with income exceeding £1,000,000

dp

First Edition

Summer 2018

ISBN-13: 978-1-912736-00-3

ISBN-10: 1-912736-00-4

Printed in 8pt Nimbus Sans L

Designed by URW++ Design and Development GmbH

Dellam Publishing Limited

2 Heath Drive, Sutton, Surrey, SM2 5RP

Fax: 020 8770 7478   email: enquiries@dellam.com

Acknowledgements

This is a long and detailed publication containing thousands of facts and figures. It is only to be expected, despite continuous and repeated editing and checking, that errors may occur. In such cases, once we are aware of any, we publish a correction on our website.

Readers are encouraged to check regularly at www.dellam.com/books for any corrections and updates.

Although we take extreme care to ensure accuracy and being up-to-date, we cannot accept responsibility for any errors or omissions.

Contains public sector information licensed under Open Government Licence v3.0. from The Charity Commission (England and Wales) and The Charity Commission for Northern Ireland.
© Crown Copyright and database right (2018).

Contains information from the Scottish Charity Register supplied by the Office of the Scottish Charity Regulator and licensed under the Open Government Licence v.2.0.
© Crown Copyright and database right (2018).

Contains OS data © Crown copyright and database right (2017)
Contains Royal Mail data © Royal Mail copyright and database right (2017)
Contains National Statistics data © Crown copyright and database right (2017)
Contains HM Land Registry data © Crown copyright and database right (2017).

Contains Parliamentary information licensed under the Open Parliament Licence v3.0.

Contains Companies House data supplied under section 47 and 50 of the Copyright, Designs and Patents Act 1988 and Schedule 1 of the Database Regulations (SI 1997/3032).

We appreciate your interest in our publications, and your comments and suggestions are always welcome. Please contact us at enquiries@dellam.com.

Introduction

Although charities have existed since before biblical times, and many current religious charities date back many centuries, they were only required by be publicly registered under the Charities Act 1960.

The Charities Act 2011 lists the purposes for establishing a charity: the prevention or relief of poverty; the advancement of education; religion; health or the saving of lives; citizenship or community development; arts, culture, heritage or science; amateur sport; human rights, conflict resolution or reconciliation or the promotion of religious or racial harmony or equality and diversity; environmental protection or improvement; animal welfare; the relief of those in need because of youth, age, ill-health, disability, financial hardship or other disadvantage; and the promotion of the efficiency of the armed forces of the Crown or of the efficiency of the police, fire and rescue services or ambulance services.

There are tax advantages for charities: no corporation tax is paid, no income tax is paid by the trustees, eligible for 80% mandatory relief on business rates. In addition, they can reclaim the income tax paid on donations through GiftAid and gifts are exempt from inheritance tax.

The sector is characterised by large number of volunteers without whose dedication the relief that their respective charities provide would be diminished. Trustees, apart from expenses, normally receive no payment for their services. The charity sector is dependent on good people, but perhaps more importantly, given their large incomes, people with strong financial and management skills.

This study looks at all charities registered with the Charity Commission for England and Wales and where their income is more than £1 million.

The aim of this study is to provide an overview of the key movers and shakers in the charity sector. Only key data has been isolated, particularly the last five years' income, but also the date registered, their address, activities, telephone number, web address, number of employees and number of volunteers.

Some charities, mainly for historic reasons, have long names. We have used these in the profile section but have abbreviated them in the league table. Thus, The College of The Holy and Undivided Trinity in the University of Oxford of The Foundation of Sir Thomas Pope, next to Blackwell's bookshop in Broad Street, is referred to as 'Trinity College'.

Standard cataloguing guidelines for charity names in the profile section have been used, but there will be occurrences when the name may not be strictly alphabetical. A certain licence was adopted where it was felt that strictly alphabetical could lead to improper cataloguing. Some charity names have been shortened in the league tables for aesthetic reasons.

John D Blackburn
Editor

Charity Names Abbreviated

Association of Chief Executives of Voluntary Organisations - ACEVO	Assoc of Chief Executives of Voluntary Organisations
The British Academy for The Promotion of Historical Philosophical and Philological Studies	The British Academy
British Association for Behavioural and Cognitive Psychotherapies	Association for Behavioural & Cognitive Psychotherapies
The British Isles Province of The Congregation of Sisters of Charity of Jesus and Mary	Congregation of Sisters of Charity of Jesus and Mary
Charitable Trusts of The Congregation of Franciscan Missionaries of The Divine Motherhood	Franciscan Missionaries of The Divine Motherhood
Charity for Roman Catholic Purposes Administered in Connection with the Congregation of Our Lady of The Missions	Congregation of Our Lady of The Missions
Charity for Roman Catholic Purposes Administered in Connection with the English Province of The Community of The Religious of Jesus and Mary	The Community of The Religious of Jesus and Mary
Charity for Roman Catholic and Other Charitable Purposes Administered in Connexion with the Society of The Holy Child Jesus	Society of the Holy Child Jesus
The Charity of The Order of The Marist Sisters Province of England	The Charity of The Order of The Marist Sisters
Chesterfield and District Society for People with a Learning Disability	Chesterfield Society for People with a Learning Disability
Christ's College Cambridge in the University of Cambridge First Founded By King Henry VI of England and After His Death	Christ's College, Cambridge
The College of All Souls of The Faithful Departed, of Oxford	All Souls College, Oxford
College of Corpus Christi and Of The Blessed Virgin Mary in the University of Cambridge	Corpus Christi College, Cambridge
The College of Saint Mary of Winchester in Oxford, Commonly Called New College	New College, Oxford
The College of St Mary Magdalen in the University of Oxford	Magdalen College, Oxford

The College of St Mary Magdalene in the University of Cambridge	Magdalene College, Cambridge
The College of St Peter Le Bailey in the University of Oxford	St Peter's College, Oxford
The College of The Holy and Undivided Trinity in the University of Oxford of The Foundation of Sir Thomas Pope	Trinity College, Oxford
The College of The Lady Frances Sidney Sussex in the University of Cambridge	Sidney Sussex College, Cambridge
The College or Hall of Valence Mary Commonly Pembroke College in the University of Cambridge	Pembroke College, Cambridge
The Community of St Edmund of The English Congregation of The Order of St Benedict Established at Douai Abbey, Woolhampton, Berkshire	The Order of St Benedict Established at Douai Abbey
Congregation of Sisters of Our Lady of Sion or Order of Our Lady of Sion	Congregation of Sisters of Our Lady of Sion
The Congregation of The Little Sisters of The Poor - English Province	Congregation of The Little Sisters of The Poor
Construction Industry Relief, Assistance and Support for The Homeless and Hospices Limited	Construction Industry Relief
The Dean and Chapter of The Cathedral Church of Christ in Oxford of The Foundation of King Henry VIII	Christ Church, Oxford
The Education and Training Trust of The Chartered Insurance Institute	The Education and Training Trust of The CII
Eglwys Bresbyteraidd Cymru - The Presbyterian Church of Wales	The Presbyterian Church of Wales
The English Benedictine Order of Oulton Abbey Near Stone, Staffs	English Benedictine Order of Oulton Abbey
The English Province of The Congregation of Our Lady of Charity of The Good Shepherd CIO	Our Lady of Charity of The Good Shepherd
The English Province of The Institute of Franciscan Missionaries of Mary	The Institute of Franciscan Missionaries of Mary
The English Province of The Sisters of Saint Joseph of Annecy	The Sisters of Saint Joseph of Annecy

The English Region of The Sisters of Charity of St Jeanne Antide	The Sisters of Charity of St Jeanne Antide
European Renal Association-European Dialysis and Transplant Association	European Renal Association-European Dialysis
The Faculty of Pharmaceutical Medicine of The Royal Colleges of Physicians of The United Kingdom	Faculty of Pharmaceutical Medicine of The RCP of UK
Faculty of Public Health of The Royal Colleges of Physicians of The United Kingdom	Faculty of Public Health of The RCP of UK
Faculty of Sexual and Reproductive Healthcare of The Royal College of Obstetricians and Gynaecologists	Faculty of Sexual & Reproductive Healthcare RCOG
The Foundation of Sir John Percyvale in Macclesfield of 1502, Re-Founded By King Edward VI in 1552	Foundation of Sir John Percyvale in Macclesfield
The Gemmological Association and Gem Testing Laboratory of Great Britain	The Gemmological Association
Girls Not Brides: The Global Partnership To End Child Marriage	Girls Not Brides
Godolphin International Thoroughbred Leadership Programme Limited	Godolphin International Leadership Programme
Gonville and Caius College in the University of Cambridge Founded in Honour of The Annunciation of The Blessed Mary The Virgin	Gonville and Caius College, Cambridge
The Incorporated Bishop's Stortford College Association	Bishop's Stortford College Association
Institute of The Blessed Virgin Mary Commonly Called The Sisters of Loreto	The Sisters of Loreto
Institute of The Religious of The Sacred Heart of Mary Immaculate Virgin	Institute of Sacred Heart of Mary Immaculate Virgin
International Association of Teachers of English as a Foreign Language	International Association of Teachers of TOEFL
International Network for The Availability of Scientific Publications	Int Network for the Availability of Scientific Publications
International Non-Governmental Organisation Training and Research Centre	International NGO Training and Research Centre

International Society for Influenza and Other Respiratory Diseases	International Society for Influenza
Jesus College Within The University and City of Oxford of Queen Elizabeth's Foundation	Jesus College, Oxford
The King's College of Our Lady and Saint Nicholas in Cambridge	King's College, Cambridge
The Kynge's College of Our Ladye of Eton Besyde Windesore	Eton College
Learning on Screen - The British Universities and Colleges Film and Video Council	Learning on Screen - Film and Video Council
The Library and Museum Charitable Trust of The United Grand Lodge	Library & Museum Charitable Trust of Grand Lodge
The Lincolnshire and Nottinghamshire Air Ambulance Charitable Trust	The Lincs and Notts Air Ambulance Charitable Trust
Lucy Cavendish College in the University of Cambridge	Lucy Cavendish College, Cambridge
The Keepers and Governors of The Free Grammar School of John Lyon	John Lyon's Charity
Management Accounting for Non Governmental Organisations	Management Accounting for NGOs
The Master Fellows and Scholars of Emmanuel College in the University of Cambridge	Emmanuel College, Cambridge
The Master and Fellows of Darwin College in the University of Cambridge	Darwin College, Cambridge
The Master and Fellows of The College of The Great Hall of The University Commonly Called University College in the University of Oxford	University College, Oxford
The Master and Fellows of The College or Hall of Saint Catharine The Virgin in the University of Cambridge	St Catharine's College, Cambridge
The Master and Scholars of Balliol College in the University of Oxford	Balliol College, Oxford
Mid Warwickshire Society for Mentally Handicapped Children and Adults	Mid Warwicks Society for Mentally Handicapped

National Confidential Enquiry Into Patient Outcome and Death	National Confidential Enquiry Into Patient Outcome
The National Federation of Women's Institutes of England, Wales, Jersey, Guernsey and The Isle of Man	The National Federation of Women's Institutes
The National Society for The Prevention of Cruelty To Children	NSPCC
The Nuffield Trust for Research and Policy Studies in Health Services	Nuffield Trust for Research in Health Services
The Parochial Church Council of St Mary Abbots, Kensington	St Mary Abbots, Kensington
The Parochial Church Council of The Eccesiastical Parish of Ashtead	Parish of Ashtead
The Parochial Church Council of The Ecclesiastical Parish of All Saints Woodford Wells	All Saints Woodford Wells
The Parochial Church Council of The Ecclesiastical Parish of All Souls, Langham Place, London	All Souls, Langham Place, London
The Parochial Church Council of The Ecclesiastical Parish of Bath Abbey with St James, Bath	Bath Abbey with St James, Bath
The Parochial Church Council of The Ecclesiastical Parish of Brighton, St Peter	Brighton, St Peter
The Parochial Church Council of The Ecclesiastical Parish of Emmanuel, South Croydon	Emmanuel, South Croydon
The Parochial Church Council of The Ecclesiastical Parish of Fulwood Christ Church, Sheffield	Fulwood Christ Church, Sheffield
The Parochial Church Council of The Ecclesiastical Parish of Great Chesham	Parish of Great Chesham
The Parochial Church Council of The Ecclesiastical Parish of Greyfriars Reading	Greyfriars, Reading
The Parochial Church Council of The Ecclesiastical Parish of Holy Trinity, Cambridge	Holy Trinity, Cambridge
The Parochial Church Council of The Ecclesiastical Parish of Holy Trinity, Cheltenham	Holy Trinity, Cheltenham
The Parochial Church Council of The Ecclesiastical Parish of Howell Hill with Burgh Heath	Parish of Howell Hill with Burgh Heath

The Parochial Church Council of The Ecclesiastical Parish of St Aldates, Oxford	St Aldates, Oxford
The Parochial Church Council of The Ecclesiastical Parish of St Barnabas Woodside Park	St Barnabas, Woodside Park
The Parochial Church Council of The Ecclesiastical Parish of St Ebbe with Holy Trinity and St Peter Le Bailey, Oxford	Holy Trinity and St Peter Le Bailey, Oxford
The Parochial Church Council of The Ecclesiastical Parish of St Helen, Bishopsgate	St Helen, Bishopsgate
The Parochial Church Council of The Ecclesiastical Parish of St James Gerrards Cross with St James Fulmer	St James Gerrards Cross with St James Fulmer
The Parochial Church Council of The Ecclesiastical Parish of St James, Westminster	St James, Westminster
The Parochial Church Council of The Ecclesiastical Parish of St John The Baptist, Burford	St John The Baptist, Burford
The Parochial Church Council of The Ecclesiastical Parish of St Martin-in-the-Fields, London	St Martin-in-the-Fields, London
The Parochial Church Council of The Ecclesiastical Parish of St Mary Magdalene, Richmond with St Matthias and St John The Divine	St Mary Magdalene, Richmond with St Matthias
The Parochial Church Council of The Ecclesiastical Parish of St Marylebone with Holy Trinity St Marylebone	St Marylebone with Holy Trinity St Marylebone
The Parochial Church Council of The Ecclesiastical Parish of St Michael & All Angels, Summertown	St Michael & All Angels, Summertown
The Parochial Church Council of The Ecclesiastical Parish of St Nicholas, Sevenoaks	St Nicholas, Sevenoaks
The Parochial Church Council of The Ecclesiastical Parish of St Paul, Hammersmith	St Paul, Hammersmith
The Parochial Church Council of The Ecclesiastical Parish of Uxbridge	Parish of Uxbridge
The Parochial Church Council of The Ecclesiastical Parish of Wimbledon	Parish of Wimbledon
The Parochial Church Council of The Ecclesiastical Parish of Woking Christ Church	Woking Christ Church

Powys Association of Voluntary Organisations Cymdeithas Mudiadau Gwirfoddol Powys	Powys Association of Voluntary Organisation
The President and Fellows of Murray Edwards College, Founded as New Hall, in the University of Cambridge	Murray Edwards College, Cambridge
The President and Fellows of Wolfson College in the University of Cambridge	Wolfson College, Cambridge
Principal Fellows and Scholars of Hertford College in the University of Oxford	Hertford College, Oxford
The Principal and Fellows of Mansfield College in the University of Oxford	Mansfield College, Oxford
The Principal and Fellows of St Hugh's College in the University of Oxford	St Hugh's College, Oxford
The Principal and Fellows of The College of The Lady Margaret in the University of Oxford	Lady Margaret Hall, Oxford
The Principal and Fellows of The Manchester Academy and Harris College in the University of Oxford	Harris Manchester College, Oxford
The Priory for Wales of The Most Venerable Order of The Hospital of St John of Jerusalem	Priory for Wales of Most Venerable Order of St John
The Provost and Scholars of the House of the Blessed Mary the Virgin in Oxford, commonly called Oriel College, of the Foundation of Edward the Second of famous memory, sometime King of England	Oriel College, Oxford
The Queens' College of Saint Margaret and Saint Bernard in the University of Cambridge	Queen's College, Cambridge
The Rector and Scholars of Exeter College in the University of Oxford	Exeter College, Oxford
Roman Catholic Purposes Administered in Connection with the Society of African Missions	Society of African Missions
Roman Catholic Purposes in Connection with the Congregation of The Most Holy Redeemer	The Congregation of The Most Holy Redeemer
The Royal Foundation of The Duke and Duchess of Cambridge and Prince Harry	Royal Foundation of Duke & Duchess of Cambridge

The Royal Institution of Chartered Surveyors' Benevolent Fund Limited	The RICS' Benevolent Fund Limited
Royal Society for The Prevention of Cruelty To Animals Bath and District Branch	RSPCA Bath and District Branch
Royal Society for The Prevention of Cruelty To Animals Bristol and District Branch	RSPCA Bristol and District Branch
Royal Society for The Prevention of Cruelty To Animals Bury Oldham and District Branch	RSPCA Bury Oldham and District Branch
Royal Society for The Prevention of Cruelty To Animals Central, West & North East London Branch	RSPCA Central, West & North East London Branch
Royal Society for The Prevention of Cruelty To Animals Halifax, Huddersfield and District Branch	RSPCA Halifax, Huddersfield and District Branch
Royal Society for The Prevention of Cruelty To Animals Hillingdon, Slough, Windsor, Kingston and District Branch	RSPCA Hillingdon, Slough, Windsor, Kingston
Royal Society for The Prevention of Cruelty To Animals Isle of Wight Branch	RSPCA Isle of Wight Branch
Royal Society for The Prevention of Cruelty To Animals Leicestershire Branch	RSPCA Leicestershire Branch
Royal Society for The Prevention of Cruelty To Animals Middlesex North West Branch	RSPCA Middlesex North West Branch
Royal Society for The Prevention of Cruelty To Animals Norwich and Mid-Norfolk Branch	RSPCA Norwich and Mid-Norfolk Branch
Royal Society for The Prevention of Cruelty To Animals Sheffield Branch	RSPCA Sheffield Branch
Royal Society for The Prevention of Cruelty To Animals Solent Branch	RSPCA Solent Branch
Royal Society for The Prevention of Cruelty To Animals Sussex Brighton and East Grinstead Branch	RSPCA Sussex Brighton and East Grinstead Branch
Royal Society for The Prevention of Cruelty To Animals	RSPCA
Royal Society for The Prevention of Cruelty To Animals, Llys Nini Branch - Cardiff To Swansea	RSPCA Llys Nini Branch - Cardiff To Swansea

The Royal United Services Institute for Defence and Security Studies	Royal United Services Institute for Defence
Saint John Baptist College in the University of Oxford	St John's College, Oxford
Society of Jesus Trust of 1929 for Roman Catholic Purposes	Society of Jesus Trust of 1929
The South London Church Fund and Southwark Diocesan Board of Finance	Southwark Diocesan Board of Finance
Spina Bifida, Hydrocephalus, Information, Networking, Equality - Shine	Shine - Spina Bifida, Hydrocephalus, Information
Stockport, East Cheshire, High Peak, Urmston & District Cerebral Palsy Society	Stockport, E Cheshire, High Peak, Cerebral Palsy
Swansea and Brecon Diocesan Board for Social Responsibility	Swansea & Brecon Diocesan Board for Soc Resp
Trust Property Held ICW The English Province of The Congregation of The Sisters of The Presentation of The Blessed Virgin Mary	Sisters of The Presentation of Blessed Virgin Mary
Trust Property Held in Connection with the English Province of The Congregation of Christian Brothers	The Congregation of Christian Brothers
Trust Property Held in Connexion with the Sisters of The Holy Family of Bordeaux	Sisters of The Holy Family of Bordeaux
WESC Foundation - The Specialist Centre for Visual Impairment	WESC Foundation
The Warden and Scholars of The House or College of Scholars of Merton in the University of Oxford	Merton College, Oxford
Westminster Roman Catholic Diocesan Trust and Other Trust Funds Administered By The Westminster Roman Catholic Diocesan Trustee	Westminster Roman Catholic Diocesan Trust

Charity Profiles

1610 Limited
Registered: 5 Jun 2009 *Employees:* 487
Tel: 07480 228766 *Website:* 1610.org.uk
Activities: Education, training; advancement of health or saving of lives; arts, culture, heritage, science; amateur sport; economic, community development, employment; recreation
Address: 12 Upper Holway Road, Taunton, Somerset, TA1 2HD
Trustees: Dr Jonathan Michael Sladden, Mrs Rebecca Elizabeth Bevins, Mr Malcolm Winlow
Income: £7,514,029 [2017]; £7,967,054 [2016]; £8,180,960 [2015]; £7,473,567 [2014]; £6,270,801 [2013]

1st Place Children and Parents' Centre Ltd
Registered: 18 Jul 2007 *Employees:* 124 *Volunteers:* 17
Tel: 020 7740 8070 *Website:* 1stplace.uk.com
Activities: Education, training; advancement of health or saving of lives; arts, culture, heritage, science; environment, conservation, heritage; economic, community development, employment
Address: 1st Place Children and Parents' Centre, Chumleigh Street, Burgess Park, London, SE5 0RN
Trustees: Ms Sarah McCarthy, Mr Mark Devlin, Nigel Lloyd, Ms Ana Rita Brito, Ms Heather Elizabeth Munn, Mr Douglas Buist, Ms Mollie Sunshine McClelland Morris, Mr Philip Wilkins, Ms Lucy Brazener, Ms Amanda Leat, Ms Lucia Adams, Ms Sophia Yunlu Zhang, Ms Anna Ruby Jenkins
Income: £2,379,848 [2017]; £2,001,112 [2016]; £1,846,278 [2015]; £1,927,903 [2014]; £1,471,411 [2013]

The 29th May 1961 Charity
Registered: 27 Jun 1961
Tel: 020 7024 9034
Activities: General charitable purposes
Address: Ryder Court, 14 Ryder Street, London, SW1Y 6QB
Trustees: Mr Vanni Emanuele Treves, Mr Andrew Charles Jones, Mr Paul Varney, Mrs Elizabeth Celia Rantzen
Income: £3,791,323 [2017]; £3,381,798 [2016]; £3,499,191 [2015]; £3,416,822 [2014]; £3,257,791 [2013]

42nd Street - Community Based Resource for Young People Under Stress
Registered: 21 Mar 1990 *Employees:* 39
Tel: 0161 228 7321 *Website:* 42ndstreet.org.uk
Activities: General charitable purposes; advancement of health or saving of lives; human rights, religious or racial harmony, equality or diversity
Address: 42nd Street, 89-91 Great Ancoats Street, Manchester, M4 5AG
Trustees: Miss Harriet Gibson, Ms Jaqui Cotton, Mr Richard Hawkins, Mr Hywel Thomas, Mr Richard Spearing, Ms Elizabeth Allen, Mr Kevin Jones, Ms Nikki Nazran
Income: £1,829,058 [2017]; £1,191,225 [2016]; £1,103,400 [2015]; £1,084,144 [2014]; £951,813 [2013]

4children
Registered: 20 Feb 1984 *Employees:* 1,253
Tel: 020 7131 4000
Activities: General charitable purposes; education, training; economic, community development, employment; other charitable purposes
Address: Smith & Williamson, 25 Moorgate, London, EC2R 6AY
Trustees: Jo Cleary, Jon McLeod, Gary Walker, Debbie Sorkin, Sally Rees, Wendy Fabbro
Income: £29,482,285 [2015]; £26,039,306 [2014]; £21,263,744 [2013]

The 5BEL Charitable Trust
Registered: 18 Jan 2010 *Employees:* 1 *Volunteers:* 2
Tel: 07733 327244 *Website:* brightonbelle.com
Activities: Environment, conservation, heritage; economic, community development, employment
Address: 52-55 Trafalgar Street, Brighton, BN1 4EB
Trustees: Denis Dunstone, Mr Michael Clifford Hart, Mr Douglas Stuart Lindsay, Stuart Wilkinson, Mr Arthur John Gordon Rushton, Rev Stephen Richard Baxter
Income: £1,771,313 [2016]; £1,571,783 [2015]; £988,691 [2014]; £739,988 [2013]; £426,241 [2012]

7 Hills Leisure Trust
Registered: 6 Feb 2013 *Employees:* 463
Tel: 0114 223 3600
Activities: Education, training; advancement of health or saving of lives; arts, culture, heritage, science; amateur sport; recreation
Address: Don Valley Stadium, Worksop Road, Sheffield, S9 3TL
Trustees: Mr Roderick Howard Plews, Mr Alexander William Pettifer MBE, Mr Stuart Britland, Mr Neale Gibson, Mr Patrick Abel, Mr Graham Moore, Mr John Barron Swain, Mr Peter Taylor, Ms Elizabeth Winders
Income: £10,542,697 [2017]; £12,790,000 [2016]; £6,970,000 [2015]; £4,746,000 [2014]

A C O R D
Registered: 30 Sep 1981 *Employees:* 335
Tel: 020 7324 4698 *Website:* acordinternational.org
Activities: General charitable purposes; education, training; advancement of health or saving of lives; prevention or relief of poverty; overseas aid, famine relief; environment, conservation, heritage; economic, community development, employment
Address: Acord, The Grayston Centre, 28 Charles Square, London, N1 6HT
Trustees: Ms Jacqueline Williams, Ms Bonnie Campbell, Ms Hussainatu Jummai Adbullah, Ms Naana Otoo-Oyortey, Jocelyne Vokouma, Ms Ngone Diop, Mr David Munthali, Dr Alioune Sall, Jean-Francois Curtis
Income: £7,833,000 [2016]; £8,720,000 [2015]; £10,057,000 [2014]; £8,654,000 [2013]; £9,790,000 [2012]

A New Direction London Limited
Registered: 8 Oct 2008 *Employees:* 24
Tel: 020 7608 2132 *Website:* anewdirection.org.uk
Activities: General charitable purposes; education, training; disability
Address: Third Floor, 20-26 Brunswick Place, London, N1 6AD
Trustees: Marc Jaffrey, Mr Neil Harris, Professor Maggie Atkinson, Mr Eylan Ezekial, Ms Gabriella Cala-Lesina, Ms Keely Williams, Mr Matthew Dolton, Ms Hilary Ann Ewing, Ms Charlotte Louise Hillenbrand
Income: £2,589,751 [2017]; £2,383,328 [2016]; £1,792,632 [2015]; £2,102,114 [2014]; £1,549,542 [2013]

A W Charitable Trust
Registered: 14 Oct 1981
Tel: 0161 740 0116
Activities: General charitable purposes; education, training; advancement of health or saving of lives; prevention or relief of poverty; overseas aid, famine relief; religious activities
Address: 66 Waterpark Road, Salford, M7 4JL
Trustees: Rabbi Aubrey Weis, Mr Sir Weis, Mrs Rachel Weis
Income: £15,023,560 [2017]; £14,954,623 [2016]; £12,826,601 [2015]; £12,764,848 [2014]; £13,644,873 [2013]

The A1 Steam Locomotive Trust
Registered: 21 Jun 1993 *Employees:* 1 *Volunteers:* 45
Tel: 01481 256943 *Website:* a1steam.com
Activities: Environment, conservation, heritage
Address: Ramili, Rue Cohu, Castel, Guernsey, GY5 7SX
Trustees: Mr Mark Colin Allatt, Mr Graeme Bunker, Mr David Andrew Elliott, Mr Paul Bruce, Mr David Burgess, Mr Rob Morland, Mr James Christopher Walker, Mr Graham Langer
Income: £1,407,373 [2017]; £955,700 [2016]; £928,727 [2015]; £812,174 [2014]; £1,064,452 [2013]

AAGBI Foundation
Registered: 30 Jan 1986 *Employees:* 32 *Volunteers:* 10
Tel: 020 7631 1650 *Website:* aagbi.org
Activities: Education, training; advancement of health or saving of lives
Address: 21 Portland Place, London, W1B 1PY
Trustees: Dr Rachel Collis, Dr Paul Clyburn, Ms Paula Keats, Dr Kathleen Ferguson, Dr Michael Nathanson, Dr Andrew Klein, Dr Gerard Michael Anthony Keenan, Dr Archie Kennedy Naughton, Elizabeth McGrady, Dr Sally El-Ghazali, Dr William Fawcett, Dr Matthew Davies, Dr Mathew Patteril, Dr Upma Misra, Dr Isabeau Walker, Dr Samantha Shinde, Dr Nancy Redfern, Dr Paul Barker, Dr Guy Jackson, Dr Timothy Meek, Tei Sheraton, Dr Ravijit Singh Gill, Dr Craig Bailey, Dr Ravishankar Rao Baikady, Dr Ann Harvey, Dr Deirdre Conway
Income: £4,115,747 [2017]; £7,628,276 [2016]; £3,852,776 [2015]; £3,145,597 [2014]; £2,760,362 [2013]

ABC Awards
Registered: 7 Jun 2001
Tel: 0115 854 1316 *Website:* abcawards.co.uk
Activities: Education, training
Address: ABC Awards, Robins Wood House, Robins Wood Road, Nottingham, NG8 3NH
Trustees: Mrs Eileen Mary Hartley, Ms Helen Kathryn Richardson, Skills and Education Group Limited, Mr John Yarham, Mrs Jill Elizabeth Lanning
Income: £1,390,112 [2016]; £1,754,217 [2015]; £1,894,561 [2014]; £2,409,910 [2013]; £2,219,858 [2012]

The ABC Trust
Registered: 11 Nov 2008 *Employees:* 3
Tel: 020 8211 7935
Activities: General charitable purposes; education, training; prevention or relief of poverty; religious activities; arts, culture, heritage, science
Address: 79 Wargrave Avenue, London, N15 6TU
Trustees: Mr Joseph Paneth, Mr Chaim Solomon Goldman, Mr Jacob Jakobovits
Income: £3,954,385 [2017]; £4,211,013 [2016]; £2,139,460 [2015]; £1,121,263 [2014]; £1,241,507 [2013]

The ABDO College of Education
Registered: 3 Jul 2001 *Employees:* 20
Tel: 01227 733901 *Website:* abdocollege.org.uk
Activities: Education, training
Address: Godmersham Park, Godmersham, Canterbury, Kent, CT4 7DT
Trustees: Ms Kim Devlin FBDO, Mr John Antony Luke Hardman FBDO, Mr Clive Marchant FBDO, Mr Daryl Newsome FBDO, Ms Angela McNamee FBDO, Mrs Fiona Anderson FBDO, Ms Gaynor Foulkes Foulkes-Taylor FBDO, Mrs Gerardine Dynan FBDO
Income: £2,539,378 [2016]; £2,353,658 [2015]; £1,796,232 [2014]; £1,527,469 [2013]; £1,461,890 [2012]

ABF The Soldiers' Charity
Registered: 15 Mar 2012 *Employees:* 82 *Volunteers:* 1,000
Tel: 0845 241 4833 *Website:* soldierscharity.org
Activities: Armed forces, emergency service efficiency
Address: Mountbarrow House, 6-20 Elizabeth Street, London, SW1W 9RB
Trustees: Mr Simon Richard Martin, Major General Robert Nitsch, Mr James Rous, Mr Paul Joseph Hearn, Ms Mary Catherine Fagan, Ms Amanda Metcalfe, Major General Malcolm David Wood CBE, Mr Damien Edward Francis, Mr Peter Baynham, Mr Glenn John Haughton, Lt Gen Philip Jones CB CBE, Ms Lisa Christine Worley
Income: £19,371,465 [2017]; £22,842,918 [2016]; £20,371,444 [2015]; £14,454,275 [2014]; £13,195,915 [2013]

ACE (Action in Caerau and Ely)
Registered: 10 Jan 2013 *Employees:* 27 *Volunteers:* 300
Tel: 029 2000 3132 *Website:* aceplace.org
Activities: General charitable purposes; education, training; prevention or relief of poverty; economic, community development, employment
Address: ACE Our Place: Dusty Forge, 460 Cowbridge Road West, Cardiff, CF5 5BZ
Trustees: Ms Jean O'Keefe, Mrs Patricia O'Regan, Mr Melvin Witherden, Miss Marian Dixey, Mrs Helen McCarthy, Mrs Gloria Yates, Mr Gareth Pierce, Mr Carl Meredith, Mr Martin Hulland, Mrs Tracy Cazenave
Income: £1,191,705 [2017]; £1,037,042 [2016]; £1,070,806 [2015]; £834,292 [2014]

ADS (Addiction Dependency Solutions)
Registered: 22 Feb 1990 *Employees:* 194 *Volunteers:* 140
Tel: 0161 831 2400 *Website:* adsolutions.org.uk
Activities: Education, training; advancement of health or saving of lives; accommodation, housing; other charitable purposes
Address: ADS, 135-141 Oldham Street, Manchester, M4 1LN
Trustees: Mr Janusz Karczewski-Slowikowski, Mr David Black, Ms Moira Stevenson, Mr Michael Murphy, Ms Christine Green, Mr Peter Elton, Stephanie Mullenger, Mr Alan Watson, Mr Anthony Williams
Income: £11,161,405 [2017]; £13,661,649 [2016]; £13,227,640 [2015]; £7,314,141 [2014]; £8,192,449 [2013]

AECC University College
Registered: 29 Apr 1980 *Employees:* 202 *Volunteers:* 2
Tel: 01202 436337 *Website:* aecc.ac.uk
Activities: Education, training; advancement of health or saving of lives
Address: AECC University College, Parkwood Campus, Parkwood Road, Ferndown, Dorset, BH5 2DF
Trustees: Mr Edgar Newcomb, Dr Martin Copp, Professor Haymo Thiel, Professor Christopher Stephens, Mr Peter Roberts, Mr Philip Hume, Mr Adrian Wild, Dr Mark Gurden, Ms Judith Worthington, Mr Peter Dingley, Mr Adrian Simpson, Mr Daniel Sullivan
Income: £9,167,799 [2017]; £8,709,100 [2016]; £7,891,324 [2015]; £7,476,633 [2014]; £7,682,967 [2013]

The AES Tring Park School Trust
Registered: 22 Aug 1994 *Employees:* 135
Tel: 01442 821678 *Website:* tringpark.com
Activities: Education, training; arts, culture, heritage, science; environment, conservation, heritage
Address: Tring Park School for The Performing Arts, The Mansion, Tring, Herts, HP23 5LX
Trustees: Mrs Juliet Anne Thackeray Murray, Ms Mary Patricia Bonar, Mr Michael Geddes, Mr John Michael Harper, Carol Atkinson, Ms Janet Rosalind Mitchell, Mr Mark Andrew Hewitt, Eric Pillinger, Mrs Angela Odell, June Taylor, Alice Cave, Mr Daniel Joseph Zammit
Income: £9,131,049 [2016]; £8,445,105 [2015]; £8,052,208 [2014]; £7,027,964 [2013]; £7,090,104 [2012]

AIM Awards
Registered: 20 Apr 2004 *Employees:* 27
Tel: 01332 861999 *Website:* aimawards.org.uk
Activities: Education, training
Address: 10 Newmarket Court, Newmarket Drive, off Ascot Drive, Derby, DE24 8NW
Trustees: Mrs Pauline Christiane Riley, Lindsay Cooper, Mrs Patricia Ann Harman, Mrs Teresa Karen Flowers, Mr Ian George Bond, Ms Leslie Jean Atkin, Mr Robin Webber-Jones, Mr Simon Martin, Mrs Susan Hopewell, Mr Gerald Philip Willmore, Miss Liza-Jo Guyatt
Income: £1,763,274 [2017]; £1,353,198 [2016]; £1,265,615 [2015]; £1,183,030 [2014]; £1,221,187 [2013]

The AIM Foundation
Registered: 23 Nov 1971 *Employees:* 39
Tel: 01392 667000
Activities: The advancement of health or saving of lives; economic, community development, employment
Address: Francis Clark, Vantage Point, Pynes Hill, Exeter, EX2 5FD
Trustees: Mr Nicholas John Marks, Miss Caroline Daphne Marks, Mrs Joanna Muriel Precious, Mr Ian Roy Marks CBE DL, Mrs Angela Daphne Marks, Mrs Philippa Gillian Bailey
Income: £4,322,949 [2016]; £3,775,476 [2015]; £446,737 [2014]; £301,478 [2013]; £300,213 [2012]

AKO Foundation
Registered: 29 Apr 2013
Tel: 020 7070 2400
Activities: General charitable purposes; education, training; arts, culture, heritage, science
Address: c/o Ako Capital LLP, 61 Conduit Street, London, W1S 2GB
Trustees: Mr David Woodburn, Mr Martin Byman, Ms Katja Nissen Tangen, Mr Henrik Syse, Mr Nicolai Tangen
Income: £8,897,072 [2017]; £11,951,992 [2016]; £15,146,590 [2015]; £6,468,312 [2014]; £19,592,697 [2013]

ALRA
Registered: 20 Feb 2002 *Employees:* 69
Tel: 020 8870 6475 *Website:* alra.co.uk
Activities: Education, training; arts, culture, heritage, science
Address: Academy of Live & Recorded Arts, Royal Victoria Patriotic Building, John Archer Way, London, SW18 3SX
Trustees: Tony Bradshaw, Carolyn Lloyd-Davies, Mr Luke Adamson, Michael Lyle, Mr Harry Alan Cowd, Mr Clive Lynch, Susie Parriss
Income: £2,445,082 [2017]; £2,282,981 [2016]; £2,402,176 [2015]; £2,309,115 [2014]; £2,299,497 [2013]

AOUK
Registered: 27 Mar 2002
Tel: 01904 787767 *Website:* aouk.org
Activities: Education, training; advancement of health or saving of lives
Address: AOUK, Marlborough House, York Business Park, York, YO26 6RW
Trustees: Mr Mark Jackson, Mr Matthew Pead, Ian Pallister, Mr Jonathan Dwyer, Sat Parmar, Mr Shaun O'Brien
Income: £1,273,014 [2016]; £1,287,479 [2015]; £919,807 [2014]; £978,256 [2013]; £1,020,403 [2012]

AQA Education
Registered: 15 Jan 1999
Tel: 0161 953 1180 *Website:* aqa.org.uk
Activities: Education, training
Address: Devas Street, Manchester, M15 6EX
Trustees: Sir Michael Griffiths, Mr Mark Bramwell, Professor Mark Smith, Mr Jovan Trkulja, Professor Jonathan Phillips, Ms Jan Smith, Mr Paul Nesbitt, Ms Elizabeth Kitcatt, Mr Martin Guy Turner, Mr Nigel Walkey, Mr Grenville Jackson, Ms Susan Moore, Professor Toby Dominic Brodigan Salt, Mr Justin Van Wijngaarden, Ms Philippa Hird, Mr Mike Nicholson, Mr Nadeem Kiyani
Income: £169,091,000 [2017]; £150,847,000 [2015]; £144,511,000 [2014]; £152,814,000 [2013]; £155,327,000 [2012]

ARP Charitable Services
Registered: 25 Mar 1987 *Employees:* 45
Tel: 020 7234 9740 *Website:* phoenix-futures.org.uk
Activities: Education, training; advancement of health or saving of lives; accommodation, housing; other charitable purposes
Address: 68 Newington Causeway, London, SE1 6DF
Trustees: Ms Sue Ellenby, Susan Kinnaird, Mr James Cook, Phoenix House
Income: £1,940,000 [2017]; £4,247,000 [2016]; £5,942,000 [2015]; £6,044,000 [2014]; £7,614,677 [2013]

ASCB Charitable Fund
Registered: 23 Apr 2008 *Employees:* 4
Tel: 01252 787057 *Website:* armysportcontrolboard.org
Activities: Amateur sport; other charitable purposes
Address: MacKenzie Building, Fox Lines, Queens Avenue, Aldershot, Hants, GU11 2LB
Trustees: Mr David Rowe, Mrs Suzanne Anderson, Brigadier James Medley Woodham, Mr Nicholas Jonathon Wright, Brigadier Neil David Sexton, Brigadier Stephen John Vickery, Brigadier Robert Jason Walton-Knight, Major General Duncan Francis Capps CBE, Brigadier Timothy John Seal
Income: £4,662,945 [2017]; £3,727,114 [2016]; £3,132,731 [2015]; £4,637,054 [2014]; £3,183,556 [2013]

ASDAN
Registered: 17 Dec 1997 *Employees:* 51
Website: asdan.org.uk
Activities: Education, training; prevention or relief of poverty
Address: Wainbrook House, Hudds Vale Road, St George, Bristol, BS5 7HY
Trustees: Ms Alison Delyth, Mr John Simpson, Mrs Sandra Slocombe, Mr Peter Andrew Scholey, Mr David Brockington, Mr Christopher William Kerry Smith, Mrs Julie Dyer, Mr Gary Williams, Asher Craig, Mrs Linda Peck, Mr Paul Jacobs
Income: £3,175,536 [2017]; £3,582,977 [2016]; £3,626,501 [2015]; £4,117,683 [2014]; £5,131,591 [2013]

ASIST
Registered: 19 Jul 1995 *Employees:* 38 *Volunteers:* 6
Tel: 01782 845584 *Website:* asist.co.uk
Activities: Education, training; advancement of health or saving of lives; disability; other charitable purposes
Address: Winton House, Stoke Road, Stoke on Trent, Staffs, ST4 2RW
Trustees: Mr Michael Creek, Ms Pamela Trudy Edwards, Dr Susan Cheryl Read, Mr Mark Steven Granger Ashton, Mr Simon Christopher Harris, Mr Jason Lancaster
Income: £1,010,537 [2017]; £986,031 [2016]; £949,002 [2015]; £1,079,709 [2014]; £1,153,604 [2013]

ATG Training
Registered: 10 Jul 2002 *Employees:* 38
Tel: 01865 551225 *Website:* atg-training.co.uk
Activities: Education, training
Address: Activate Learning, Oxpens Road, Oxford, OX1 1SA
Trustees: Mr Stephen Ball, Ms Cheri Ashby, Ms Sally Anne Sheila Dicketts
Income: £2,690,281 [2017]; £3,092,620 [2016]; £2,782,106 [2015]; £3,524,634 [2014]; £3,542,896 [2013]

Abberley Hall Ltd
Registered: 8 Jul 1963 *Employees:* 110
Tel: 01684 892666 *Website:* abberleyhall.co.uk
Activities: General charitable purposes; education, training
Address: Kendall Wadley LLP, Granta Lodge, 71 Graham Road, Malvern, Worcs, WR14 2JS
Trustees: Mr Andrew Grant Duncan, The Hon David Piers Carlis Legh DL, Mr Mark Turner, Mrs Catharine Hope, Mr Anthony Goddard, Mr Vernon Taylor, Mr Richard D'A Samuda, Mr Andrew Richard Manning Cox, Dr Jamie McManus, Mr James Jonathan Tanner
Income: £3,827,913 [2016]; £3,695,452 [2015]; £3,836,927 [2014]; £4,028,428 [2013]; £4,097,688 [2012]

The Abbey School, Reading
Registered: 28 Sep 1962 *Employees:* 348 *Volunteers:* 9
Tel: 0118 987 6911 *Website:* theabbey.co.uk
Activities: Education, training
Address: 20 St Patricks Avenue, Charvil, Reading, Berks, RG10 9RA
Trustees: Dr Carole Print, Rev Ann Joyce Templeman, Sue Colebrook, Mrs Elizabeth Ann Harrison, Mrs Katie Lane, Mr Paramjit Uppal, Lady Louise Bell, Dr Ian Kemp, Mrs Juliet Anderson, Mrs Julie Cornell, Mr Michael Emmanuel, Mr Simon Dimmick, Mr Nigel David Hopes
Income: £16,045,105 [2016]; £15,651,887 [2015]; £14,820,436 [2014]; £14,120,566 [2013]; £13,519,812 [2012]

Abbeycroft Leisure
Registered: 5 Dec 2006 *Employees:* 156 *Volunteers:* 122
Tel: 01440 702548 *Website:* acleisure.com
Activities: General charitable purposes; education, training; advancement of health or saving of lives; amateur sport; recreation
Address: Haverhill Leisure Centre, Lordscroft Lane, Haverhill, Suffolk, CB9 0ER
Trustees: David Howells, Mr Terry Clements, Mrs Sarah Howard, Diane Saunders, Mr Simon Burton, Ian Charles Runnacles, Mrs Anne Margaret Greenfield, Mr Anthony Preece, Mrs Lois Caroline Wreathall
Income: £8,540,295 [2017]; £7,794,543 [2016]; £4,262,793 [2015]; £4,213,044 [2014]; £4,224,986 [2013]

The Abbeyfield (Maidenhead) Society Limited
Registered: 16 Aug 1974 *Employees:* 95 *Volunteers:* 1
Tel: 01628 675408
Activities: Accommodation, housing
Address: 5 The Ridings, Maidenhead, Berks, SL6 4LU
Trustees: Tony Jesseman, Mr David Cager, Mr Howard McBrien, Mr Kenneth Jackson, Mr Yash Maudgil
Income: £2,266,218 [2017]; £2,353,651 [2016]; £2,372,118 [2015]; £2,878,928 [2014]; £4,003,036 [2013]

The Abbeyfield (St Albans) Society Limited
Registered: 18 Feb 1963 *Employees:* 50
Tel: 07711 696417 *Website:* abbeyfieldstalban.co.uk
Activities: Accommodation, housing
Address: 9 Upper Lattimore Road, St Albans, Herts, AL1 3UD
Trustees: Mr Derek Farr, Mr John Thomson, Jill Elek, Mr Keith Faulkner, Mr Steve Gore, Mr Malcolm Wooster
Income: £1,543,760 [2017]; £1,538,177 [2016]; £1,345,393 [2015]; £1,359,350 [2014]; £1,303,017 [2013]

Abbeyfield Braintree, Bocking and Felsted Society Limited
Registered: 12 Feb 1969 *Employees:* 59
Tel: 01376 344385 *Website:* abbeyfieldatbraintree.co.uk
Activities: Accommodation, housing
Address: Great Bradfords House, 159 Coggeshall Road, Braintree, Essex, CM7 9GD
Trustees: Mr Anthony Michael St John Cramphorn, Mr Roy Hackett, Ronnie Hackett, Mr Martin Quaife, Mr David Summersgill, Ian Norgett, Mrs Barbara Guest
Income: £1,028,556 [2017]; £759,239 [2016]; £775,548 [2015]; £786,710 [2014]; £708,528 [2013]

Abbeyfield Bristol and Keynsham Society
Registered: 19 Dec 1968 *Employees:* 30 *Volunteers:* 20
Tel: 0117 973 6997 *Website:* abbeyfield-bristol.co.uk
Activities: Accommodation, housing
Address: c/o Frances Stretton, 29 Alma Vale Road, Bristol, BS8 2HL
Trustees: Mr John Kane, Mrs Jean Pitt, Mrs Sara Touzel, Mrs Susan Hopkins, Mrs Gill Oakhill, Michael Innes, Mr Roger Spooner
Income: £1,239,262 [2016]; £1,294,339 [2015]; £1,540,270 [2014]; £928,506 [2013]

The Abbeyfield Hoylake and West Kirby Society Ltd
Registered: 18 Jun 1964 *Employees:* 50 *Volunteers:* 5
Tel: 0151 625 1092 *Website:* abbeyfieldwestkirby.co.uk
Activities: Accommodation, housing
Address: Abbeyfield Society, Seafield House, Darmonds Green, Wirral, Merseyside, CH48 5DT
Trustees: Lesley Guratsky, Ms Jane Hyndman, Mr Christopher Stringer, Mr Anthony Graham Aldwinckle, Mrs Anne-Marie Swift
Income: £1,036,892 [2017]; £911,155 [2016]; £924,010 [2015]; £835,244 [2014]; £871,979 [2013]

The Abbeyfield Ilkley Society Limited
Registered: 3 Feb 1969 *Volunteers:* 105
Tel: 01943 886000 *Website:* abbeyfieldthedales.co.uk
Activities: Accommodation, housing
Address: Abbeyfield Grove House, 12 Riddings Road, Ilkley, W Yorks, LS29 9BF
Trustees: Mrs Frances Johnson, Mr Stephen Robert Davidson, Mrs Amanda Louise Ashby, Mr David Roger Binns, Mr Dale Smith
Income: £2,833,648 [2017]; £2,780,492 [2016]; £3,410,939 [2015]; £2,622,319 [2013]; £2,420,722 [2012]

The Abbeyfield Loughborough Society Limited
Registered: 11 Dec 1964 *Employees:* 65 *Volunteers:* 25
Tel: 01509 266605 *Website:* abbeyfieldloughborough.co.uk
Activities: Accommodation, housing
Address: 44 Westfield Drive, Loughborough, Leics, LE11 3QL
Trustees: David Hogg, Mr Brian Robert Bunn, Mrs Jaqueline Stephens, Mrs Ruth Johnson, Mr Roderick Jonathan Pearson, Mrs Pamela Carol Dickson, Mr Frank Fay, Mr Sean Hale, Ms Priscilla Lapworth
Income: £1,379,924 [2017]; £1,437,766 [2016]; £1,352,342 [2015]; £1,281,648 [2014]; £1,260,131 [2013]

The Abbeyfield Newcastle upon Tyne Society Limited
Registered: 22 Aug 1963 *Employees:* 57 *Volunteers:* 19
Tel: 0191 285 7174 *Website:* abbeyfieldnewcastle.org.uk
Activities: Accommodation, housing
Address: The Abbeyfield Newcastle upon Tyne Society Ltd, Registered Office, 40a The Grove, Gosforth, Newcastle upon Tyne, NE3 1NH
Trustees: Mr Anthony Kay, Mrs Carole Eke, Mrs Vee Wilkinson, Mr Brian Duell, Mrs Marion Anderson, Mr Raymond Mackintosh
Income: £1,749,788 [2017]; £2,081,660 [2016]; £1,712,861 [2015]; £1,582,728 [2014]; £1,518,668 [2013]

Abbeyfield Reading Society Ltd
Registered: 23 Mar 1964 *Employees:* 30 *Volunteers:* 10
Tel: 0118 962 3721
Activities: Accommodation, housing
Address: 21 Bulmershe Road, Reading, Berks, RG1 5RH
Trustees: Ms Stella Margaret Tyers, Mr Roderick John Symonds MBE, Mr Norman Pitcher, Mr Ronald Cummins, Mr Christopher John Widdows, Mr David Brian Cox, Mr Paul Alexander Barton
Income: £1,073,552 [2017]; £1,004,058 [2016]; £941,287 [2015]; £905,385 [2014]; £948,733 [2013]

The Abbeyfield Society
Registered: 22 Sep 1962 *Employees:* 1,080 *Volunteers:* 4,000
Tel: 01727 857536 *Website:* abbeyfield.com
Activities: Accommodation, housing
Address: Abbeyfield Society, St Peters House, 2 Bricket Road, St Albans, Herts, AL1 3JW
Trustees: William Ian David Plaistowe, Mr Christopher John Addison Smith, Ms Jenny Lawrence, Ms Sara Jayne Beamand, Mr Norman Alistair Greville, Mr Cedric Meiring, Mr Brian Owen Williams, Mr Jeffrey Medlock, Mrs Elizabeth Amanda Houlihan, Rev Stephen Venner, Andre Decraene, Mr Andrew De Hochepied Larpent, Mr Ken Staveley
Income: £54,653,000 [2017]; £43,070,000 [2016]; £50,969,000 [2015]; £44,056,000 [2014]; £49,390,000 [2013]

Abbeyfield South Downs Limited
Registered: 6 Mar 1963 *Employees:* 34 *Volunteers:* 24
Tel: 01435 866539 *Website:* abbeyfield.com
Activities: General charitable purposes; accommodation, housing
Address: 9 Meadway Crescent, Hove, E Sussex, BN3 7NJ
Trustees: Mr David Byrne, Mrs Lynne Elizabeth Phair, Mr David James Carver, Mr William Francis Rendall, Mr Malcolm Paris, Mr Ian Arthur Thomas, Ms Joanne Kathleen Sorenson, Mr Anthony Tallents Davy
Income: £3,841,846 [2017]; £787,388 [2016]; £785,877 [2015]; £727,107 [2014]; £564,441 [2013]

The Abbeyfield Southend Society Limited
Registered: 16 Jan 1970 *Employees:* 49 *Volunteers:* 7
Website: abbeyfieldsouthend.co.uk
Activities: Accommodation, housing
Address: 29 Turner Close, Shoeburyness, Essex, SS3 9TL
Trustees: Ted Speakman, Mr Geoff Salmon JP, Mr Ernest Terence Martin, Mr Ian Phillip Carey JP, Mr Roger Calton, Gina Reames, Janice Price
Income: £1,576,997 [2017]; £1,506,545 [2016]; £1,510,726 [2015]; £1,368,300 [2014]; £1,303,384 [2013]

Abbeyfield Southern Oaks
Registered: 6 Apr 1966 *Employees:* 19 *Volunteers:* 102
Tel: 020 8394 0050 *Website:* abbeyfieldsouthernoaks.org
Activities: General charitable purposes; accommodation, housing
Address: Abbeyfield, The Old House, Epsom Road, Epsom, Surrey, KT17 1JZ
Trustees: Mr John Anthony Shelton, Ms Janet Fisher, Mr William Scott, Mr Graham Walker, Ms Lynette Maggs, Mrs Margaret Angus, Dr John Flower, Dr Andrew Hoy, Mr Nigel MacDonald, Mr Maurice Pagella, Dr Malcolm Wakerley, Mrs Susanna Walker, Mr Charles Nicholas Shore, Mr Jim Ratliff, Mrs Mary Boorman
Income: £1,071,511 [2016]; £616,851 [2015]; £139,981 [2014]; £119,547 [2013]; £115,372 [2012]

Abbeyfield The Dales Limited
Registered: 30 Jan 2015 *Employees:* 146
Tel: 01943 886000 *Website:* abbeyfieldthedales.co.uk
Activities: Accommodation, housing
Address: Abbeyfield Grove House, 12 Riddings Road, Ilkley, W Yorks, LS29 9BF
Trustees: Mr David Roger Binns, Councillor Dale Smith, Mr Arthur Francis, Martin Carter, Mr Mark Harman, Dr Eileen Mary Senior, Mr Nigel Peter Hopkins, Ms Nora Whitham MBE, Mr Mohamed Amin Valli
Income: £3,992,173 [2017]; £278,103 [2016]

Abbeyfield Wessex Society Limited
Registered: 29 Oct 1963 *Employees:* 26 *Volunteers:* 10
Tel: 01202 762051 *Website:* abbeyfieldwessex.org
Activities: Accommodation, housing
Address: Office, Westbourne House, 22 Poole Road, Bournemouth, BH4 9DS
Trustees: Mr Keith Millman, Mr Steven Arundel, Brenda Biddle, Dr Christopher Williams, Anastasia Turner
Income: £1,327,831 [2016]; £1,472,830 [2015]; £1,471,513 [2014]; £1,675,657 [2013]; £1,359,714 [2012]

Abbeyfield Wey Valley Society Limited
Registered: 12 Jul 2016 *Employees:* 132 *Volunteers:* 65
Tel: 01252 733507 *Website:* abbeyfieldweyvalley.co.uk
Activities: The advancement of health or saving of lives
Address: Abbeyfield Society, Wey Valley House, Mike Hawthorn Drive, Farnham, Surrey, GU9 7UQ
Trustees: Peter Duffy, Brian Thomas, Gillian Ward, Tim Shepherd, Mr Desmond Hutchinson, Ms Sarah MacKenzie, Paul Whitlock, Chris Tibbott, Peter Newman, Mr Ian Thomson, Mr Derek Ansell
Income: £3,970,223 [2017]

Abbot's Hill Limited
Registered: 15 Feb 1963 *Employees:* 167 *Volunteers:* 2
Tel: 01442 839140 *Website:* abbotshill.herts.sch.co.uk
Activities: Education, training
Address: Abbots Hill School, Bunkers Lane, Hemel Hempstead, Herts, HP3 8RP
Trustees: Mrs Janet Mark, Mr Neil James, Dr Linda Summerton, Mr Jonathan Gillespie, Dr Shori Thakur, Mr Nigel Chadwick, Mr Martin Hart, Mr Alan Lees, Mr Gordon James, Mrs Jill Myers
Income: £8,027,387 [2017]; £7,371,304 [2016]; £6,819,501 [2015]; £6,304,946 [2014]; £5,834,858 [2013]

Abbots Bromley School for Girls Limited
Registered: 21 Apr 2004 *Employees:* 99
Tel: 01283 841850 *Website:* abbotsbromleyschool.com
Activities: Education, training
Address: Abbots Bromley School for Girls, High Street, Abbots Bromley, Rugeley, Staffs, WS15 3BW
Trustees: Simon Davis, Mrs Pauline Norvall, Mr Richard Knight, Mrs Susan Goff, Mr Ray Mansell, Mr Steven Bourne, Mrs Heather Graham, Mr Simon Roderick James
Income: £4,266,935 [2016]; £2,400,235 [2015]; £3,216,510 [2014]; £3,281,619 [2013]; £3,675,348 [2012]

Abbotsholme School
Registered: 23 Apr 1965 *Employees:* 120
Tel: 01666 822671 *Website:* abbotsholme.com
Activities: Education, training; disability; arts, culture, heritage, science; amateur sport
Address: 59 High Street, Malmesbury, Wilts, SN16 9AH
Trustees: Dr Paul Kirtley, Miss Jenny Richardson, Mr Derrick Cantrell, Mrs Stephanie Jayne Walker, Mr Christopher Hall, Mr Jan Bladen, Mrs Catherine Margaret Jamieson, Mr Paul Stokes
Income: £4,752,235 [2016]; £5,798,425 [2015]; £5,014,664 [2014]; £4,865,632 [2013]; £5,066,608 [2012]

The William Scott Abbott Trust
Registered: 15 Apr 1964 *Employees:* 23 *Volunteers:* 65
Website: sacrewell.org.uk
Activities: Education, training; animals; environment, conservation, heritage; economic, community development, employment; recreation
Address: Manor Farm, Manor Road, Sutton, Peterborough, PE5 7XG
Trustees: Mr Duncan Pickering, Mr Stuart A Bish, Ms Sarah Jane Bell, Jane K Scriven, Ms Rachel Mary Wild
Income: £1,032,963 [2016]; £1,610,509 [2015]; £1,275,874 [2014]; £834,286 [2013]; £858,732 [2012]

Aberdour School Educational Trust
Registered: 30 Jul 1971 *Employees:* 67
Website: aberdourschool.co.uk
Activities: Education, training
Address: Maurice Andrews Chartered Accountants, Grove House, 25 Upper Mulgrave Road, Sutton, Surrey, SM2 7BE
Trustees: Mr Colin Denis Wright, Mr Nicholas Henry Keene Mallett, Mrs Rosena Mary Monaghan, Mr Donald Davie, Mr Richard Nicol, Mrs Carole Joyce Strutt, Mr Michael Charles Farmer, Mr Peter John Dickerson
Income: £3,988,681 [2017]; £3,907,789 [2016]; £3,732,140 [2015]; £3,348,327 [2014]; £3,107,972 [2013]

Aberglasney Restoration Trust
Registered: 17 Feb 1995 *Employees:* 23 *Volunteers:* 35
Tel: 01558 668998 *Website:* aberglasney.org
Activities: Environment, conservation, heritage
Address: Aberglasney Gardens, Llangathen, Carmarthen, SA32 8QH
Trustees: Mrs Gwyneth Hayward, Gethin Lewis, Martin Presdee Jones, Peter Burgess, Roderick Evans, Mr Robert Pugh, Ms Helen Scutt, Ian Howell, Tom Lloyd, Mr David Roger Evans, Phillip Ratcliffe
Income: £1,239,993 [2017]; £696,316 [2016]; £1,838,645 [2015]; £541,053 [2014]; £798,823 [2013]

Abertawe Bro Morgannwg University LHB Charitable Fund and Other Related Charities
Registered: 15 Feb 2008
Tel: 01639 683676
Activities: The advancement of health or saving of lives
Address: Abertawe Bro Morgannwg University, Local Health Board, 1 Talbot Gateway, Seaway Parade, Baglan, Port Talbot, SA12 7BR
Trustees: Abmu Lhb
Income: £1,794,000 [2017]; £2,384,000 [2016]; £1,341,000 [2015]; £1,531,000 [2014]; £1,614,000 [2013]

Aberystwyth University Students' Union
Registered: 23 Jan 2013 *Employees:* 13
Tel: 01970 621708 *Website:* abersu.co.uk
Activities: Education, training; amateur sport; recreation
Address: Aberystwyth University Students' Union, Penglais, Aberystwyth, Dyfed, SY23 3DX
Trustees: Ms Olympia Petrou, Mr Peter Curran, Mr Gwion Llwyd Williams, Miss Emma Beenham, Miss Molly-Jean Longden, Mr Alan Roberts, Mr Ryan Beasley, Mr Bruce Wight, Miss Jessica Williams, Mr Richard Matthews
Income: £1,823,394 [2017]; £2,530,714 [2016]; £2,738,871 [2015]; £2,781,599 [2014]

Abilities Limited
Registered: 7 Jul 1994 *Employees:* 83 *Volunteers:* 5
Tel: 01305 771327 *Website:* abilities.org.uk
Activities: Education, training; disability; prevention or relief of poverty; economic, community development, employment
Address: Abilities Ltd, Waverley Road, Weymouth, Dorset, DT3 5HL
Trustees: Mrs Jenny Price, Mr Mark Cowling
Income: £1,370,905 [2016]; £1,591,678 [2015]; £1,428,631 [2014]; £1,318,935 [2013]

Ability Housing Association
Registered: 17 Jun 1976 *Employees:* 121
Tel: 01784 495624 *Website:* ability-housing.co.uk
Activities: Accommodation, housing
Address: The Coach House, Cresham Road, Staines upon Thames, Middlesex, TW18 2AE
Trustees: Mr Vince Mewitt, Ms Nicola Philp, Mrs Sally Reay, Mrs Gina Small, Ms Karen Hillhouse, Mr Ian Lines, Mrs Jane Harrison
Income: £13,671,352 [2016]; £8,871,201 [2015]; £8,753,596 [2014]; £8,732,225 [2013]; £8,915,095 [2012]

AbilityNet
Registered: 23 Jan 1998 *Employees:* 53 *Volunteers:* 235
Website: abilitynet.org.uk
Activities: Education, training; disability; other charitable purposes
Address: c/o Microsoft Ltd, Microsoft Campus, Thames Valley Park, Reading, Berks, RG6 1WG
Trustees: Mr David Barnett, Mr David Morriss, Mr Alan Brooks, Ms Aileen Thompson, Mrs Suzie Woodhams, IBM UK Ltd, The Information Technologists' Company, Miss Nishita Sharma, Mr Bill Brown, Mr Kush Kanodia, Miss Rhianna Kinchin, Mike Bernard, Microsoft Ltd
Income: £3,650,394 [2016]; £2,664,486 [2015]; £2,596,914 [2014]; £3,707,953 [2013]; £3,492,061 [2012]

Abingdon School
Registered: 2 Sep 1998 *Employees:* 335 *Volunteers:* 33
Tel: 01235 849060 *Website:* abingdon.org.uk
Activities: Education, training
Address: Abingdon School, Park Road, Abingdon, Oxon, OX14 1DE
Trustees: Mrs Olga Senior, Mr Andrew Saunders-Davies, Mr Mark Lascelles, Professor Michael Stevens, Mr Kenneth Welby, Mr Jonathan Aspull Carroll, Mrs Glynne Butt, Ms Penny Chapman, Mr Damien Tracey, Mr Matthew Tate, Mr Robert Nicholas Barr
Income: £27,530,000 [2017]; £25,101,000 [2016]; £23,490,000 [2015]; £23,406,000 [2014]; £20,952,000 [2013]

About with Friends
Registered: 26 Oct 2015 *Employees:* 42 *Volunteers:* 25
Tel: 01263 515230 *Website:* aboutwithfriends.co.uk
Activities: General charitable purposes; disability; economic, community development, employment
Address: About with Friends, 22d Holt Road, Cromer, Norfolk, NR27 9JW
Trustees: Sarah Hall, Mr Andrew Davies, Neil Foley, Ms Alison Mackway, Tracey Hicks
Income: £1,510,037 [2017]

Above Bar Church
Registered: 12 Aug 2009 *Employees:* 20 *Volunteers:* 375
Website: abovebarchurch.org.uk
Activities: Education, training; prevention or relief of poverty; overseas aid, famine relief; religious activities
Address: Above Bar Church, Above Bar Street, Southampton, SO14 7FE
Trustees: Mrs Hannah Chanter, Anthony Watkins, Mr Daniel Deacon, Dr Olanrewaju Akinyegun, Richard Collins, Nicholas Berryman, Mr John Neil Risbridger, Prof Ian Castro, Mr Jonathan Paul Webber, Mr Paul Derek Zealey, Roger Bishop
Income: £1,072,049 [2017]; £980,319 [2016]; £1,043,006 [2015]; £736,795 [2014]; £719,039 [2013]

Above The Stag Theatre
Registered: 2 Oct 2013 *Employees:* 2 *Volunteers:* 2
Tel: 020 3488 2815 *Website:* abovethestag.com
Activities: Education, training; arts, culture, heritage, science
Address: Arch 17, Miles Street, London, SW8 1RZ
Trustees: Ms Katherine Patricia Ives, Mr Peter Anthony Bull, Mr Matthew Joseph Baldwin Smith
Income: £1,424,207 [2017]; £382,071 [2016]; £344,156 [2015]

Edward Penley Abraham Research Fund
Registered: 30 Mar 1967 *Employees:* 1
Tel: 01865 275573
Activities: Education, training; advancement of health or saving of lives
Address: University of Oxford, Sir William Dunn School of Pathology, South Parks Road, Oxford, OX1 3RE
Trustees: Professor Sir Richard Gardner FRS, Professor Henry Woudhuysen, Professor Gillian Griffiths, Professor Matthew Freeman, Professor Mark Irwin Greene
Income: £2,453,425 [2017]; £2,074,194 [2016]; £2,023,989 [2015]; £3,109,489 [2014]; £2,223,792 [2013]

Absolute Return for Kids (Ark)
Registered: 9 Jan 2003 *Employees:* 34
Tel: 020 3116 0784 *Website:* arkonline.org
Activities: General charitable purposes; education, training; advancement of health or saving of lives; prevention or relief of poverty; overseas aid, famine relief
Address: Absolute Return for Kids, 65 Kingsway, London, WC2B 6TD
Trustees: Mr Ian Gerald Patrick Wace, Mr Paul Roderick Clucas Marshall, Mr Anthony Williams, Mr Kevin Roy Gundle, Lord Stanley Fink
Income: £12,938,000 [2016]; £13,006,000 [2015]; £9,503,000 [2014]; £12,959,000 [2013]; £17,247,000 [2012]

Absolutely Cultured Limited
Registered: 15 Jun 2015 *Employees:* 39 *Volunteers:* 2,527
Tel: 01482 318882 *Website:* hull2017.co.uk
Activities: Arts, culture, heritage, science
Address: Pacific Court, 36a-40 High Street, Hull, HU1 1NQ
Trustees: Dr Tapan Mahapatra, Mr Neil Hodgkinson, Mr Stephen Liddle, Matt Jukes, Ms Lee Corner, Ms Karen Okra, Mrs Sameera Anwar West, Professor Glenn Burgess, Councillor Stephen Brady
Income: £12,965,101 [2017]; £2,850,272 [2016]

Absolutely Leisure
Registered: 7 Aug 2009 *Employees:* 115
Tel: 01753 894764 *Website:* absolutely-group.co.uk
Activities: Amateur sport
Address: 20 Ashcroft Court, Burnham, Slough, SL1 8JT
Trustees: Mr Richard Andrew Hodgson, Brett Edwards, Alison Taylor, Mrs Jacqueline Gillan
Income: £4,502,622 [2017]; £4,705,555 [2016]; £4,322,726 [2015]; £3,375,579 [2014]; £2,290,334 [2013]

Abu Bakr Trust
Registered: 3 Mar 2005 *Employees:* 49 *Volunteers:* 87
Tel: 07720 384628 *Website:* www.abubakrgirlschool.org
Activities: Education, training; religious activities; economic, community development, employment
Address: 154-160 Wednesbury Road, Walsall, W Midlands, WS1 4JJ
Trustees: Mr Mohammad Luqman, Mrs Ummekulsoom Luqman, Mr Mohammed Ramzan, Mr Dawood Rashid
Income: £2,153,858 [2016]; £1,576,842 [2015]; £1,218,956 [2014]; £1,080,992 [2013]; £901,711 [2012]

Academy Concerts Society

Registered: 27 Apr 1984 *Employees:* 11 *Volunteers:* 2
Website: asmf.org
Activities: Education, training; arts, culture, heritage, science
Address: The Griffin Building, 83 Clerkenwell Road, London, EC1R 5AR
Trustees: Alan Kerr, Harvey De Souza, Bernard Oppetit, Rachel Ingleton, Ms Fiona Bonds, Mr William Schofield, Simon Haslam, Ms Charlotte Richardson, Evelyne Dube, Anthony O'Carroll, Mr Andrew Stephen Marriner
Income: £2,845,412 [2017]; £3,469,324 [2016]; £2,711,255 [2015]; £3,014,277 [2014]; £2,606,275 [2013]

Academy for Contemporary Circus and Physical Theatre

Registered: 16 Jul 1996 *Employees:* 33 *Volunteers:* 16
Tel: 0117 947 7288 *Website:* circomedia.com
Activities: Education, training; arts, culture, heritage, science; amateur sport
Address: Circomedia, Britannia Road, Kingswood, Bristol, BS15 8DB
Trustees: Ms Elizabeth Dunn, Claire Williams, Ms Bethan Touhig-Gamble, Ms Lynn Barlow, Caroline Hadley, Ms Sophina Iqbal Rumbles, Ann-Marie Leighton
Income: £1,024,888 [2017]; £954,738 [2016]; £886,307 [2015]; £922,404 [2014]; £773,518 [2013]

The Academy of Ancient Music

Registered: 12 Mar 2001 *Employees:* 8
Tel: 01223 301509 *Website:* aam.co.uk
Activities: Education, training; arts, culture, heritage, science
Address: 11B King's Parade, Cambridge, CB2 1SJ
Trustees: Mr Graham Beattie Nicholson, Mr Hugh Burkitt, Mr Terence Sinclair, John David Reeve, Mr Philip Edward Jones, Mr Matthew Ferrey, Mrs Janet Helen Unwin, Mrs Madeleine Virginia Tattersall
Income: £1,144,873 [2016]; £2,597,220 [2015]; £1,650,019 [2014]; £1,617,984 [2013]; £1,190,749 [2012]

The Academy of Medical Royal Colleges

Registered: 3 Jul 1996 *Employees:* 14
Tel: 020 7490 6810 *Website:* aomrc.org.uk
Activities: The advancement of health or saving of lives
Address: Academy of Medical Royal Colleges, 10 Dallington Street, London, EC1V 0DB
Trustees: Ms Pamela Charlwood, Professor Alan Boyd, Dr Suzy Lishman, Mr Charles Winstanley, Ms Suzanne McCarthy, Professor Carol Seymour, Dr Carrie McEwen, Mr Miller McLean
Income: £1,792,187 [2017]; £1,511,046 [2016]; £1,511,046 [2015]; £1,823,191 [2014]; £1,350,007 [2013]

Academy of Medical Sciences

Registered: 21 Jul 1998 *Employees:* 34 *Volunteers:* 400
Tel: 020 3176 2151 *Website:* acmedsci.ac.uk
Activities: Education, training; advancement of health or saving of lives
Address: The Academy of Medical Sciences, 41 Portland Place, London, W1B 1QH
Trustees: Professor Elizabeth Mary Claire Fisher, Professor Sir Stephen O'Rahilly FRS FMedSci, Dr James Smith FRS FMedSci, Professor Julie Williams, Prof George Griffin FMedSci, Professor Sir Robert Lechler FMedSci, Prof Philippa Saunders FMedSci, Professor Sir Douglas Matthew Turnbull, Professor Fiona Mary Watt, Professor Paul Michael Stewart, Prof Anne Dell CBE FRS FMedSci, Professor Sir Rory Collins FRS FMedSci, Professor Edward Thomas Bullmore, Dr Fiona Marshall, Professor Annette Dolphin FRS FMedSci, Professor Frances Mary Platt, Professor Dame Jessica Corner, Professor Hilary Octavia Dawn Critchley
Income: £11,077,414 [2017]; £8,110,122 [2016]; £5,799,261 [2015]; £4,329,442 [2014]; £4,641,728 [2013]

The Academy of Youth Limited

Registered: 15 Mar 1997 *Employees:* 72 *Volunteers:* 2
Tel: 0121 766 8077 *Website:* ufa.org.uk
Activities: Education, training
Address: The Academy of Youth Ltd, The Bond, 180-182 Fazeley Street, Birmingham, B5 5SE
Trustees: Mrs Thelma Probert, Dr John Robert Lloyd, Mr Paul Davies, Mr James Robinson, Mr Gideon White, Jason R Smith, Mr Michael Burgess, Mrs Gill Gregory, Ms Hamira Sultan
Income: £3,266,215 [2017]; £3,530,350 [2016]; £3,046,281 [2015]; £2,235,584 [2014]; £984,714 [2013]

Access - The Foundation for Social Investment

Registered: 19 Dec 2014 *Employees:* 5
Tel: 020 7084 6834 *Website:* access-socialinvestment.org.uk
Activities: General charitable purposes; education, training; economic, community development, employment
Address: Access Foundation Social Investment, New Fetter Place, 8-10 New Fetter Lane, London, EC4A 1AZ
Trustees: Mr Arvinda Gohil, Ms Victoria Jane Hornby, Ms Annika Elisabeth Small, Mr Martin John Rich, Mr John Gordon Kingston OBE, Mr David Alan Curtis, Mrs Lorraine Ann Oldroyd, Mrs Susan Cooper
Income: £1,881,000 [2016]; £36,574,421 [2015]

Access Community Trust

Registered: 26 Apr 2010 *Employees:* 76 *Volunteers:* 34
Tel: 01502 527200 *Website:* accessct.org
Activities: Education, training; prevention or relief of poverty; accommodation, housing; arts, culture, heritage, science; economic, community development, employment
Address: Access Community Trust, 113-114 High Street, Lowestoft, Suffolk, NR32 1HN
Trustees: Mr David Ellis, Ms Janet Catherine Sutton, Mr Graham Jermyn, Mrs Penelope Walker, Mr John Bunyard, Mr Steven Wright, Mr Darren Steel
Income: £2,809,821 [2016]; £2,207,721 [2015]; £2,344,789 [2014]; £2,448,098 [2013]; £2,231,448 [2012]

The Access Project
Registered: 21 Jul 2011 Employees: 32 Volunteers: 920
Tel: 020 7601 1939 Website: theaccessproject.org.uk
Activities: Education, training; recreation
Address: The Access Project, Bastion House, 140 London Wall, London, EC2Y 5DN
Trustees: Mr Neil McIntosh, Ms Catherine Clark, Mr Jimmy Daboo, Mr James Toop, Ms Katie Brewis, Mr John Kelly-Jones, Mr Matthew Thomas Wood, Ms Jane Newman, Ms Mary Curnock Cook, Mr Neil Cosgrove, Mr Peter Denison-Pender, Mr Andrew Burns
Income: £1,489,917 [2017]; £1,012,150 [2016]; £786,971 [2015]; £524,219 [2014]; £371,237 [2013]

Access Sport CIO
Registered: 28 Apr 2014 Employees: 25 Volunteers: 6
Tel: 020 7993 9883 Website: accesssport.org.uk
Activities: Education, training; disability; amateur sport; recreation
Address: Access Sport, 3 Durham Yard, London, E2 6QF
Trustees: Paul Lee, Grace Clancey, Tina Kokkinos, John Baker, Martin McPhee, Tim Jones, Phil Veasey, Mark Burgess, Preston Rabl
Income: £1,142,622 [2017]; £1,061,277 [2016]; £1,331,305 [2015]

The Access To Justice Foundation
Registered: 3 Oct 2008 Employees: 4 Volunteers: 50
Tel: 020 7092 3973 Website: accesstojusticefoundation.org.uk
Activities: The prevention or relief of poverty; other charitable purposes
Address: The Access To Justice Foundation, P O Box 64162, London, WC1A 9AN
Trustees: Bob Nightingale MBE, Steve Johnson, Mr Lance Dominic Piers Ashworth QC, Mr Toby Brown, Ms Frances Edwards, Mr Laurence Harris, Dame Janet Hilary Smith, Lord Goldsmith QC, Ms Nicola Sawford, Mr Jeffrey Forrest
Income: £2,232,516 [2016]; £1,987,935 [2015]; £925,913 [2014]; £220,405 [2013]; £188,023 [2012]

Access for Living
Registered: 7 Feb 1994 Employees: 87
Tel: 020 8297 6659 Website: accessforliving.org.uk
Activities: Disability
Address: Access for Living, Unit 9, Southbrook Mews, London, SE12 8LG
Trustees: Ms Joan Toovey, Magda Moorey, Mr Ron Dixon
Income: £2,455,936 [2017]; £2,556,775 [2016]; £2,516,243 [2015]; £2,633,203 [2014]; £2,597,546 [2013]

Accessible Transport Group Limited
Registered: 30 Jun 1988 Employees: 921
Tel: 0121 327 8128 Website: wmsnt.org
Activities: Education, training; disability; other charitable purposes
Address: 80 Park Road, Aston, Birmingham, B6 5PL
Trustees: Mr Paul Beecham, Ms Jacqueline Robinson, Nick Hall-Palmer, Mr William Coffin, Mr Richard Brooks, Mrs Jane Robson, Mr Frank Green
Income: £22,281,438 [2017]; £21,839,726 [2016]; £20,994,553 [2015]; £19,551,867 [2014]; £18,330,604 [2013]

Ace Africa (UK)
Registered: 13 Sep 2005 Employees: 4 Volunteers: 6
Tel: 020 7933 2994 Website: ace-africa.org
Activities: Education, training; advancement of health or saving of lives; prevention or relief of poverty; overseas aid, famine relief; economic, community development, employment
Address: Ace-Africa (UK), c/o Lockton Companies LLP, The St Botolph Building, 138 Houndsditch, London, EC3A 7AG
Trustees: Francis Howard, David Montgomery, Ms Lucy Demery, Mr David James Whitworth, Christopher Rowse, Genevieve Lloyd, Mr Simon Curtis
Income: £1,220,222 [2016]; £1,181,986 [2015]; £1,011,528 [2014]; £843,195 [2013]; £414,859 [2012]

The Ace Centre-North
Registered: 13 Nov 2001 Employees: 23
Tel: 01457 829444 Website: acecentre.org.uk
Activities: Education, training; disability
Address: Ace Centre North, Hollinwood Business Centre, Albert Street, Oldham, Lancs, OL8 3QL
Trustees: Mr Leslie George Coop, Mr Phil Woolas MP, Juliet Linda Goldbart PhD, Mrs Jean Jones, Mr Michael Ruane, Mrs Jennifer Malone, Mr Robert Oldham, Mr Andrew Raymond Walker, Mr Terry Waller, Mr David Reay, Mr John Devlin
Income: £3,792,532 [2017]; £3,582,190 [2016]; £1,425,077 [2015]; £636,861 [2014]; £1,130,690 [2013]

Achieve Lifestyle
Registered: 31 Mar 2011 Employees: 82
Tel: 01784 437695 Website: achievelifestyle.co.uk
Activities: Arts, culture, heritage, science; amateur sport
Address: Egham Leisure Centre, Vicarage Road, Egham, Surrey, TW20 8NL
Trustees: Mr Paul Tuley, Andrea Boyd, Dr Lara Tarocco, Mr Jeremy Taylor, Mr Warren Hubbard, Ms Hazel Aitken, Keith Heal, Mrs Gillian Warner, Ms Katie Jane Wills, Mr John Joseph Dalton
Income: £1,683,807 [2017]; £1,773,214 [2016]; £1,881,140 [2015]; £1,843,884 [2014]; £1,780,763 [2013]

Achievement for All (3as)
Registered: 27 May 2011 Employees: 162
Website: afaeducation.org
Activities: General charitable purposes; education, training; economic, community development, employment; human rights, religious or racial harmony, equality or diversity; other charitable purposes
Address: Achievement for All 3as, St Anne's House, Oxford Square, Oxford Street, Newbury, Berks, RG14 1JQ
Trustees: Professor Sonia Blandford, Mrs Stephanie Morgan Tyrer, Mr Andrew Foster, Mrs Charlotte Warner, Mr Brian Lamb, Mr Douglas McPhee, Mrs Penny Hubbard
Income: £4,571,496 [2017]; £6,065,734 [2016]; £7,224,523 [2015]; £8,923,890 [2014]; £6,487,839 [2013]

Achisomoch Aid Company Limited
Registered: 5 Sep 1979
Tel: 020 8731 8988 Website: achisomoch.org
Activities: General charitable purposes; education, training; advancement of health or saving of lives; prevention or relief of poverty; overseas aid, famine relief; religious activities
Address: 26 Hoop Lane, London, NW11 8BU
Trustees: Mr Maurice Levenson, Mr Jack Emanuel, Mr Isaac Katz
Income: £26,671,948 [2017]; £17,088,490 [2016]; £15,216,093 [2015]; £11,257,478 [2014]; £9,375,178 [2013]

Acis Group Limited

Registered: 1 Apr 2011 *Employees:* 207
Tel: 0800 027 2057 *Website:* acisgroup.co.uk
Activities: Education, training; advancement of health or saving of lives; disability; prevention or relief of poverty; accommodation, housing
Address: ACIS House, 57 Bridge Street, Gainsborough, Lincs, DN21 1GG
Trustees: Graham Ward, Mr Nigel Robert Whitaker, Ms Denise Maguire, Mr Paul Satchwell, Mr Michael Kay, Mrs Kathryn Smart, Mr Ronan O'Hara
Income: £34,105,899 [2017]; £31,777,838 [2016]; £30,271,456 [2015]; £27,619,464 [2014]; £22,924,516 [2013]

Ackworth School

Registered: 21 Sep 1966 *Employees:* 143 *Volunteers:* 3
Tel: 01977 624302 *Website:* ackworthschool.com
Activities: Education, training
Address: 7 Grange Drive, Emley, Huddersfield, W Yorks, HD8 9SF
Trustees: Mr Andrew Whiteley, Mr Digby Swift, Mrs Zephyrine Barbarachild, Mrs Katharine Napier, Mr Christopher P Jones, Mr Charles Nicholas Seed, Mr Stewart Huntington, Pat Golding, Mrs Carol Rayner, Mrs Anne Telford-Kenyon, Mr Aidan Mortimer, Mr David Bunney, Mr Christopher Daviid Allen, Mr Kirk Dyson, Mr Robert Lincoln, Mrs Gwyneth Elizabeth Lindley-Jones
Income: £7,406,422 [2017]; £7,217,367 [2016]; £7,513,840 [2015]; £7,015,622 [2014]; £7,442,415 [2013]

Acorn Early Years Foundation

Registered: 16 Dec 2011 *Employees:* 222 *Volunteers:* 3
Tel: 01908 510309 *Website:* acornchildcare.co.uk
Activities: Education, training
Address: Unit C, Lincoln Lodge, Castlethorpe, Milton Keynes, Bucks, MK19 7HJ
Trustees: Mrs Marion Ruth Stone, Mrs Katherine Boyd, Mr Giles Ashley Chilton, Mrs Carolyn Ann Norfolk, Mrs Hannah Evans
Income: £5,109,977 [2017]; £2,930,038 [2016]; £1,805,142 [2015]; £1,204,154 [2014]; £944,737 [2013]

Acorn Recovery Projects

Registered: 24 Jul 1997 *Employees:* 79 *Volunteers:* 100
Tel: 0800 169 2407 *Website:* acorntreatment.org
Activities: Education, training; advancement of health or saving of lives; disability; accommodation, housing
Address: Calico Homes Ltd, Centenary Court, Croft Street, Burnley, Lancs, BB11 2ED
Trustees: Grahame Elliott, Mr Jonathan Rowe Foster, Ms Andrea Dixon, Keith Hyde, Mrs Helen Robertshaw, Mr Stuart Higgins Dr
Income: £2,707,500 [2017]; £3,263,166 [2016]; £3,679,004 [2015]; £1,723,583 [2014]; £3,254,878 [2013]

Acorn Villages Limited

Registered: 8 May 1972 *Employees:* 191 *Volunteers:* 50
Tel: 01206 394124 *Website:* acornvillages.com
Activities: Education, training; disability; accommodation, housing
Address: Acorn Villages Ltd, Mistley Hall, Clacton Road, Mistley, Manningtree, Essex, CO11 2NJ
Trustees: Mrs M I Green, Mr Colin Daines, Mr Jerry Gray, Mr Robert John Finch, Mrs Judith Anne Owens, Mr Keith Jordan, Mr John Derek Whittaker, Mr Keith Henry Burrows, Rev Derek Lang, Mrs Brenda Elizabeth Eyers
Income: £3,654,920 [2017]; £3,517,865 [2016]; £4,404,258 [2015]; £4,185,744 [2014]; £4,197,215 [2013]

Acorns Children's Hospice Trust

Registered: 15 Nov 1988 *Employees:* 481 *Volunteers:* 1,713
Tel: 01564 825000 *Website:* acorns.org.uk
Activities: The advancement of health or saving of lives; disability
Address: Acorns Childrens Hospice Trust, Drakes Court, 302 Alcester Road, Wythall, Birmingham, B47 6JR
Trustees: Mr Robert Judges, Mr David Butcher, Mr James McCarthy, Mrs Avril Hitchman, Professor Timothy Geoffrey Barrett, Mr Mark Hopton, Ms Penny Dison, Mr Riley Philip, Mr David Widdas, Dr Sarinder Singh Sahota, Mrs Vivien Cooper, Mr David Watts, Miss Anne Kennaugh, Mr Royston Foster, Mr Chris Sallnow, Mr Robert Leonhardt, Mr Graham Muth
Income: £15,271,000 [2017]; £15,193,000 [2016]; £14,227,000 [2015]; £16,435,000 [2014]; £13,880,000 [2013]

Acre Housing

Registered: 24 Apr 1992
Tel: 0118 951 6200 *Website:* acrehousing.org.uk
Activities: Education, training; disability; prevention or relief of poverty; accommodation, housing
Address: Field Seymour Parkes, Solicitors, No 1 London Street, Reading, Berks, RG1 4QW
Trustees: Mr Kenneth Nelson Templeton, Jennifer Pozzoni, Mr Andrew Stuart Bryan, Lady Jan Hart Thomson, Simon Tearle
Income: £1,068,436 [2017]; £838,782 [2016]; £1,045,709 [2015]; £822,962 [2014]; £4,967,511 [2013]

The Act Foundation

Registered: 13 Mar 1998 *Employees:* 136
Tel: 01753 753900 *Website:* theactfoundation.co.uk
Activities: General charitable purposes
Address: The Act Foundation, 61 Thames Street, Windsor, Berks, SL4 1QW
Trustees: Mr Michael Anthony Street, Mr Andrew Ross, Mr Denis Taylor, Mr Russell Peter Meadows, Mr Stephen Charles O'Sullivan, Mr John Joseph O'Sullivan, Mr Robert Frederick White, Mrs Christine Margaret Erwood, Mr Colin John Clarkson
Income: £24,472,915 [2017]; £21,416,845 [2016]; £19,871,633 [2015]; £19,570,057 [2014]; £16,981,142 [2013]

Actes Trust

Registered: 8 Jan 2008 *Employees:* 38 *Volunteers:* 14
Tel: 01642 856030 *Website:* actes.co.uk
Activities: General charitable purposes; education, training; advancement of health or saving of lives; prevention or relief of poverty; accommodation, housing; amateur sport; environment, conservation, heritage; economic, community development, employment; recreation; other charitable purposes
Address: West Middlesbrough Neighbourhood, 99-101 Acklam Road, Middlesbrough, Cleveland, TS5 5HR
Trustees: Mr James Cooper, Mrs Sharon Stuttard, Mr Geoffrey Donald Payne, Charlie Rooney
Income: £1,109,894 [2017]; £904,883 [2016]; £897,613 [2015]; £763,995 [2014]; £601,635 [2013]

Action 4 Youth

Registered: 23 Feb 1994 *Employees:* 39 *Volunteers:* 26
Website: action4youth.org
Activities: Education, training; arts, culture, heritage, science; amateur sport; other charitable purposes
Address: 5 Smeaton Close, Aylesbury, Bucks, HP19 8UN
Trustees: Mr Edward Herbert Weston JP, Mr Richard Stansfield, Mr Lewis Duncan Oldreive, Mrs Camilla Rose Soames, Mr Kenneth Birkby, Mrs Vivien Salisbury, Mr Martin Reed
Income: £1,389,767 [2017]; £1,209,080 [2016]; £1,379,351 [2015]; £1,038,295 [2014]; £1,165,882 [2013]

Action Against Hunger
Registered: 27 Jun 1995 *Employees:* 166 *Volunteers:* 36
Tel: 020 8293 6190 *Website:* actionagainsthunger.org.uk
Activities: The advancement of health or saving of lives; prevention or relief of poverty; overseas aid, famine relief
Address: First Floor, Rear Premises, 161-163 Greenwich High Road, London, SE10 8JA
Trustees: Mr Francois Danel, Mrs Frances Pasteur, Mrs Pilar Junco, Mr Paul Wilson, Mr Tim Wright, Mr Nicolas Sarkis
Income: £26,382,148 [2016]; £16,871,941 [2015]; £12,523,575 [2014]; £10,466,324 [2013]; £8,289,186 [2012]

Action Against Medical Accidents
Registered: 19 Apr 1988 *Employees:* 24 *Volunteers:* 61
Tel: 020 8688 9555 *Website:* avma.org.uk
Activities: Education, training; advancement of health or saving of lives
Address: AVMA, Freedman House, Christopher Wren Yard, 117 High Street, Croydon, Surrey, CR0 1QG
Trustees: Dr Suzanne Shale, Ms Rachael Vasmer, Mr Nigel Donald Holland, Ms Caroline Browne, Ms Linda Kenward, Ms Hilary Scott, Dr Angela Brown, Mr Jonathan Hazan, Mike Andersson
Income: £1,143,296 [2017]; £1,147,016 [2016]; £1,221,360 [2015]; £1,137,015 [2014]; £1,196,994 [2013]

Action Deafness
Registered: 29 Sep 2015 *Employees:* 24 *Volunteers:* 12
Tel: 0844 593 8440 *Website:* actiondeafness.org.uk
Activities: Education, training; disability; other charitable purposes
Address: Action Deafness, Peepul Centre, Orchardson Avenue, Leicester, LE4 6DP
Trustees: Alison Lewis, Karen Read, Ben Stephens, Helen Foulkes, Roland Hilton, Andy Palmer, Emma Allen
Income: £1,726,461 [2016]

Action Homeless (Leicester) Limited
Registered: 17 Nov 1989 *Employees:* 52 *Volunteers:* 93
Tel: 0116 221 1881 *Website:* actionhomeless.org.uk
Activities: Accommodation, housing; economic, community development, employment; other charitable purposes
Address: Action Homeless Ltd, Ridgeway House, Newton Lane, Wigston, Leics, LE18 3SE
Trustees: Mr Roy Christopher Roberts, Mr Anthony John Harrop, Mr Stephen De Looze, Mr Nicholas Paul David Winks, Mr Steven John Malcherczyk, Alex Payton, Mrs Claire Hurst, Mr David John Ireland
Income: £2,323,119 [2017]; £1,946,225 [2016]; £2,212,220 [2015]; £2,009,636 [2014]; £1,802,910 [2013]

Action Housing and Support Limited
Registered: 21 Apr 1981 *Employees:* 125 *Volunteers:* 51
Tel: 01709 821251 *Website:* actionorg.uk
Activities: Education, training; accommodation, housing
Address: 6 Genesis Business Park, Sheffield Road, Rotherham, S Yorks, S60 1DX
Trustees: Mr Atholl Stott, Mr Ian Knowles, Miss Danielle Wray, Mr Andrew Hopton, Mrs Paula Louise Warnock
Income: £5,312,910 [2017]; £5,774,650 [2016]; £6,230,109 [2015]; £6,198,411 [2014]; £6,167,878 [2013]

Action Medical Research
Registered: 12 Dec 1962 *Employees:* 50 *Volunteers:* 1,000
Tel: 01403 210406 *Website:* action.org.uk
Activities: Education, training; advancement of health or saving of lives; disability
Address: Vincent House, 31 North Parade, Horsham, W Sussex, RH12 2DP
Trustees: Mrs Valerie Anne Remington-Hobbs, Professor Sarah Bray BA MPhil PhD, Mr Nick Peters, Professor David Edwards, Mr Richard Duncan Wild, Mr Philip A Hodkinson, Ms Esther Alderson, Mr Luke George Batchelor Bordewich, Professor Nigel Jonathan Klein, Mrs Kathy Lynn Harvey
Income: £6,822,953 [2016]; £7,467,871 [2015]; £7,455,221 [2014]; £7,929,189 [2013]; £6,946,837 [2012]

Action Together CIO
Registered: 10 Feb 2016 *Employees:* 44 *Volunteers:* 130
Tel: 0161 339 4985 *Website:* actiontogether.org.uk
Activities: General charitable purposes; other charitable purposes
Address: Action Together CIO, 95-97 Penny Meadow, Ashton under Lyne, Lancs, OL6 6EP
Trustees: Mr Jonathan Yates, Mr Simon Walker, Mrs Anne Parkes, Mr Martin Collett, Mr John Mellor, Revd Roger Farnworth, Clr Maria Bailey, Mr Adrian Ball, Mr Philip Spence, Ms Camilla Guereca, Mr Mustak Mustafa, Miss Victoria Strang
Income: £1,832,967 [2017]

Action for Blind People
Registered: 22 Sep 1962 *Employees:* 767 *Volunteers:* 1,835
Tel: 020 7635 4838 *Website:* actionforblindpeople.org.uk
Activities: General charitable purposes; education, training; disability; prevention or relief of poverty; amateur sport; economic, community development, employment
Address: Action for Blind People, 105 Judd Street, London, WC1H 9NE
Trustees: Dr Mike Nussbaum, Ms Sandi Esther Wassmer, Alan Tinger
Income: £22,567,000 [2017]; £27,938,000 [2016]; £14,124,000 [2015]; £20,416,000 [2014]; £21,530,000 [2013]

Action for Carers (Surrey)
Registered: 9 Nov 2006 *Employees:* 54
Tel: 01483 302748 *Website:* actionforcarers.org.uk
Activities: Education, training; advancement of health or saving of lives; prevention or relief of poverty; economic, community development, employment
Address: Astolat, Coniers Way, Burpham, Guildford, Surrey, GU4 7HL
Trustees: Ms Margaret Hicks, Geoff Martin, Ms Patricia Adams, Ms Leanda Hargreaves, Ms Nicola Walsh, Mr David Perry, Mr Christopher Crook, Ms Laura Dennett, Ms Henrietta Griffiths
Income: £1,907,473 [2017]; £1,659,093 [2016]; £1,530,818 [2015]; £1,416,270 [2014]; £1,327,631 [2013]

Action for Children

Registered: 11 Jun 2003 *Employees:* 5,013 *Volunteers:* 1,688
Tel: 01923 361500 *Website:* actionforchildren.org.uk
Activities: General charitable purposes; education, training; disability
Address: 3 The Boulevard, Ascot Road, Watford, Herts, WD18 8AG
Trustees: Mr John O'Brien, Mr Daleep Mukarji OBE, Mr Les Clifford, Ms Kate Guthrie, Ms Tracy Griffin, Mrs Fiona Talitha Flora Thorne, Miss Evelyn Patricia Gordon, The Reverend Doctor Sheryl Anderson, Mr Richard Cryer, Ms Yvette Stanley, Mr Markus Ruetimann, Ms Deborah Morgan, Ms Josephine Larbie, Mrs Gillian Ellis
Income: £159,830,000 [2017]; £160,884,000 [2016]; £173,070,000 [2015]; £179,670,000 [2014]; £180,029,000 [2013]

Action for Deafness

Registered: 4 Feb 2008 *Employees:* 24 *Volunteers:* 12
Tel: 01444 415582 *Website:* actionfordeafness.org.uk
Activities: Disability
Address: Action for Deafness, 5a Hazelgrove Road, Haywards Heath, W Sussex, RH16 3PH
Trustees: Mr Roger Hewitt, Simon Hesselberg, Mr Eamonn Sean Skyrme, Mr Mark Clark, John Taylor, Ann Rees
Income: £2,054,338 [2017]; £1,781,938 [2016]; £1,781,938 [2015]; £2,074,994 [2014]; £1,392,134 [2013]

Action for Family Carers

Registered: 12 Dec 2008 *Employees:* 65 *Volunteers:* 63
Tel: 01621 856297 *Website:* affc.org.uk
Activities: General charitable purposes
Address: 23 Essex Road, Maldon, Essex, CM9 6JQ
Trustees: Rebecca Loader, Mr Colin Bennett, Ms Denise Fielding, Paul Osman, Theresa Byles, Mrs Judy Spiceley, Mr Colin Philpott, Sue Bailey, Ms Pauline Haggerty, Mr Tony Dixon
Income: £1,622,367 [2017]; £1,626,194 [2016]; £904,729 [2015]; £674,455 [2014]; £599,669 [2013]

Action for Kids Charitable Trust

Registered: 25 Mar 1998 *Employees:* 34 *Volunteers:* 44
Tel: 020 8347 8111 *Website:* my-afk.org
Activities: Education, training; advancement of health or saving of lives; disability; economic, community development, employment
Address: Action for Kids, 15a Tottenham Lane, London, N8 9DJ
Trustees: Mr Mike Harry, Ms Belinda Jane Blank, Miss Caroline Samantha Anne Hattersley, Mr Peter Mitchell, Mr Benjamin Joseph Cavanagh, Mr Mark David Lewis BA, Ms Susan Jane Baldwin, Mr Gurmeet Singh Dhillon, Tina Brivati, Mr Milos Ilic-Miloradovic
Income: £2,236,161 [2017]; £2,308,622 [2016]; £2,652,721 [2015]; £2,546,828 [2014]; £2,191,735 [2013]

Action on Addiction

Registered: 15 Feb 2007 *Employees:* 144 *Volunteers:* 10
Website: actiononaddiction.org.uk
Activities: Education, training; advancement of health or saving of lives; prevention or relief of poverty; economic, community development, employment
Address: Head Office, East Knoyle, Tisbury, Salisbury, Wilts, SP3 6SR
Trustees: Mr Edward John Lloyd, Dr Angela Spatharou, Mr Robert Fox, Mr Hugo De Ferranti, Mrs Tanya Farrell, Mrs Melanie Falk Vere Nicoll, Dr Henrietta Bowden-Jones, Ms Frances Gibb, Mr James Robert Drummond Smith, Professor Gerald William Libby
Income: £6,020,808 [2017]; £6,888,220 [2016]; £7,125,157 [2015]; £7,640,643 [2014]; £6,773,847 [2013]

Action on Disability and Development

Registered: 18 Nov 1986 *Employees:* 101
Tel: 01373 473064 *Website:* add.org.uk
Activities: Education, training; disability; prevention or relief of poverty; overseas aid, famine relief; economic, community development, employment
Address: Action on Disability & Development, The Old Church School, Butts Hill, Frome, Somerset, BA11 1HR
Trustees: Mr Robert Andrew Niven, Mr Stuart McKinnon-Evans, Mrs Deborah Jane Botwood Smith, Ms Sarah Jane Dyer, Ms Louise James, Mr Kieran Breen, Mr Kenneth James Jones, Dr Mary Catherine Keogh, Mr Venkatesh Balakrishna, Ms Sally Neville, Mr David Ezra Ruebain, Mr Kudakwashe Dube, Ms Jillian Emma Popkins, Mr Phillimon Simwaba, Mr Matthew David Jackson
Income: £2,990,112 [2016]; £3,178,291 [2015]; £2,962,122 [2014]; £3,360,035 [2013]; £3,526,583 [2012]

Action on Disability

Registered: 4 Apr 2002 *Employees:* 24 *Volunteers:* 20
Tel: 020 7385 2098 *Website:* actionondisability.org.uk
Activities: General charitable purposes; education, training; disability; amateur sport; economic, community development, employment
Address: Action on Disability, c/o Normand Croft School, Lillie Road, London, SW6 7SR
Trustees: Mrs Angeleca Jane Louise Silversides, Ms Gabriella Maria Zahzouh, Mr Peter Harden, Ms Amy Susannah Rait, Miss Victoria Susan Brignell, Mr Patrick McVeigh, Mrs Kate Betteridge, Mr Michael Gannon
Income: £1,203,995 [2017]; £1,044,598 [2016]; £1,027,159 [2015]; £1,222,230 [2014]; £1,235,584 [2013]

Action with Communities in Rural England (Acre)

Registered: 26 Mar 1997 *Employees:* 3
Tel: 01285 653477 *Website:* acre.org.uk
Activities: Education, training; prevention or relief of poverty; environment, conservation, heritage; economic, community development, employment
Address: Corinium Suite, Unit 9 Cirencester Office Park, Tetbury Road, Cirencester, Glos, GL7 6JJ
Trustees: Mr Jeremy John Leggett, Mr Charles Coats, Mrs Janet Mary Thornton, Professor Mark Shucksmith, Ms Dorothy Florence Pollard, John Rose, Ivan Annibal, Louise Beaton, David Emerson, Mr Dominic Driver
Income: £3,050,082 [2017]; £3,011,695 [2016]; £2,734,276 [2015]; £2,701,904 [2014]; £3,452,282 [2013]

ActionAid

Registered: 28 Oct 1972 *Employees:* 196 *Volunteers:* 15
Website: actionaid.org.uk
Activities: Education, training; prevention or relief of poverty; overseas aid, famine relief; environment, conservation, heritage; economic, community development, employment; human rights, religious or racial harmony, equality or diversity
Address: ActionAid, 33-39 Bowling Green Lane, London, EC1R 0BJ
Trustees: Ms Patricia Whaley, Ms Gemma Peters, Mr John Monks, Mrs Joanna Maycock, Mr Alexander Cobham, Miss Noelie Audi-Dor, Helen Pankhurst, Mr Giles Fernando, Mr David Todd, Catharine Brown, Miss Sophie Healy-Thow
Income: £60,406,000 [2016]; £65,331,000 [2015]; £62,791,000 [2014]; £63,660,000 [2013]; £59,454,000 [2012]

Activate Community and Education Services
Registered: 27 Mar 2008 *Employees:* 48
Website: activateces.org.uk
Activities: Education, training; disability; economic, community development, employment
Address: 34 Shamrock Road, Birkenhead, Merseyside, CH41 0EQ
Trustees: Mr David Lees Barlow, Mrs Kim Marie Thompson, Mrs Christy Ryder, Mr Ken Siviter
Income: £1,412,120 [2017]; £1,270,140 [2016]; £986,080 [2015]; £886,361 [2014]; £488,753 [2013]

Active Communities Network Limited
Registered: 15 Oct 2007 *Employees:* 51 *Volunteers:* 1,300
Tel: 01923 771977 *Website:* activecommunities.org.uk
Activities: General charitable purposes; education, training; arts, culture, heritage, science; amateur sport; economic, community development, employment
Address: Langwood House, 63-81 High Street, Rickmansworth, Herts, WD3 1EQ
Trustees: Mr James Thomas Orr Atkinson, Mr Gerard David Devlin, Mr John Hadley, Miss Joanne Elizabeth Calvino
Income: £2,702,018 [2017]; £2,427,085 [2016]; £1,810,150 [2015]; £1,476,167 [2014]; £1,646,178 [2013]

Active Humber Ltd
Registered: 25 Feb 2014 *Employees:* 19
Tel: 01482 244344 *Website:* activehumber.co.uk
Activities: Education, training; advancement of health or saving of lives; amateur sport; recreation
Address: Humber Sports Partnership, Unit 2 Health Annex, Diadem Grove, Hull, HU9 4AL
Trustees: Mr Richard Smith, Mrs Larissa Friese Greene, Mr Stephen Pinus, Dr Nicolas Tupper, Mr Christopher Harry Adams
Income: £1,027,757 [2017]; £913,073 [2016]; £835,602 [2015]

Active Lancashire Limited
Registered: 7 Jan 2015 *Employees:* 31 *Volunteers:* 788
Tel: 01772 299830 *Website:* activelancashire.org.uk
Activities: The advancement of health or saving of lives; disability; amateur sport; recreation
Address: Lancashire Sport Partnership, Offices 3 & 4 Farington House, Lancashire Enterprise Business Park, Leyland, Lancs, PR26 6TW
Trustees: Mrs Julie Bell, Mr David Edmundson, Mr Charles Geoffrey Bean, Ms Clare Elizabeth Platt, Ms Lesley Lloyd, Mr Christopher George Standish, Ms Margaret Still, Adrian Ibbetson, Superintendent Andrea Jane Barrow
Income: £1,648,423 [2017]; £1,591,878 [2016]

Active Life Limited
Registered: 3 Jan 2003 *Employees:* 106
Tel: 01227 264444 *Website:* activelifeltd.co.uk
Activities: Education, training; advancement of health or saving of lives; disability; arts, culture, heritage, science; amateur sport; recreation
Address: 4 Ravensbourne Avenue, Herne Bay, Kent, CT6 7ET
Trustees: Mr Paul Montgomery, John Gaskell, Mr Keith Hooker, Mr Ian Wild, Mrs Christine Elizabeth Longmire, Mr James Anthony Connelly, Gerald Knox, Mr Simon Paul Jones, Mr Nicholas Edward John Wells, Ann Taylor, Mr Robert James Thomas, Mrs Rosalind Barley
Income: £5,241,520 [2016]; £5,133,460 [2015]; £4,963,666 [2014]; £4,642,587 [2013]; £4,421,749 [2012]

Active Luton
Registered: 25 Oct 2005 *Employees:* 184
Tel: 01582 400272 *Website:* activeluton.co.uk
Activities: Education, training; amateur sport
Address: Luton Borough Council, Active Luton, Community Centre & Pavilion, Eaton Green Road, Wigmore Valley Park, Luton, Beds, LU2 9JB
Trustees: Mr Colin Michael Mayes, Mr Clive Anthony Robbins, Ms Patricia Anne Wilson, Mr Mark Cattle, Mrs Siobhan Rooney, Mr Paul Seath, Mrs Glynis Yates, Mrs Claire Ovenell, Mr Clive Richard Mead, Mr David Jonathan Williets, Mr Mahmood Hussain, Mr Mohammed Kabir, Mr John Victor Young, Mrs Morag Stewart, Mrs Lynne McMulkin
Income: £9,519,772 [2017]; £9,534,816 [2016]; £9,361,432 [2015]; £9,859,899 [2014]; £9,536,323 [2013]

Active Nation UK Ltd
Registered: 5 Jul 1995 *Employees:* 362 *Volunteers:* 124
Tel: 07887 896684 *Website:* activenation.org.uk
Activities: Education, training; advancement of health or saving of lives; disability; amateur sport; recreation
Address: 1B Hatton Rock Business Centre, Hatton Rock, Stratford upon Avon, Warwicks, CV37 0NQ
Trustees: Mr Barry James, Mr Anthony Gerard Majakas, Mr David Hughes, Mr Timothy Cleveland Hewett
Income: £14,158,021 [2017]; £13,759,851 [2016]; £15,041,605 [2015]; £16,547,734 [2014]; £16,526,181 [2013]

Active Northumberland
Registered: 1 Aug 2013 *Employees:* 986
Tel: 01670 519489 *Website:* activenorthumberland.org.uk
Activities: Amateur sport; recreation
Address: 8 Bamburgh Drive, Pegswood, Morpeth, Northumberland, NE61 6TT
Trustees: David Hall, Mr Tony Gates, Mr Ken Dunbar, Councillor Cath Homer, Ms Judith Stonebridge, James Murray
Income: £20,090,541 [2017]; £23,573,493 [2016]; £10,839,823 [2015]

ActiveNewham
Registered: 30 May 2014 *Employees:* 352 *Volunteers:* 595
Tel: 020 3770 4444 *Website:* activenewham.org.uk
Activities: The advancement of health or saving of lives; arts, culture, heritage, science; amateur sport; recreation
Address: Unit SF10, Stratford Office Village, 14-30 Romford Road, London, E15 4BZ
Trustees: Mr Timothy John Davies, Mr Forhad Hussain, Miss Alia Harris, Jaine Stannard, Sion O'Connor, Mr Mark Sands, Mr Richard John Charles Hunt, Mr Ken Clark, Bob Heaton, Mr Stephen Gillatt
Income: £9,293,018 [2017]; £8,028,883 [2016]; £8,062,891 [2015]

The Actors' Benevolent Fund
Registered: 28 Jun 1963 *Employees:* 3 *Volunteers:* 25
Tel: 020 7836 6378 *Website:* actorsbenevolentfund.co.uk
Activities: General charitable purposes; advancement of health or saving of lives; disability; prevention or relief of poverty
Address: Actors Benevolent Fund, 6 Adam Street, London, WC2N 6AD
Trustees: Mr Philip Lowrie, Milton Johns, Rosalind Shanks, Mr Alex Michael Jennings, Mr Brian Murphy, Dawn Keeler, Mr James Bolam, Mr Julien Colhoun Ball, Peter Bourke, Mr William Charles Anthony Gaunt, Mr Clifford Rose, Ms Patricia Marmont, Mr Nicholas Peter Simons, Ms Amanda Holt, Dame Sian Phillips, Miss Josephine Tewson, Mr Colin Bennett, Barbara Whatley, Mr Christopher David Luscombe, Irene Sutcliffe, Ms Josie Kidd, Dame Penelope Keith, John Gale, Ms Lucy Briers, Ms Karen Gledhill, Mr Peter Harding, Mr John Burrell, Ms Linda Regan
Income: £1,675,230 [2016]; £1,262,303 [2015]; £1,690,245 [2014]; £923,128 [2013]; £1,086,936 [2012]

The Harper Adams University Students' Union
Registered: 9 Jun 2014 *Employees:* 73 *Volunteers:* 14
Tel: 00-353-87-688 7307 *Website:* harpersu.com
Activities: General charitable purposes; arts, culture, heritage, science; amateur sport; recreation
Address: 16 The Sycamore, Elmfield, Leopardstown, Dublin 18
Trustees: Mr George Robert Barbour, Mr David Andrew Johns, Mr Jonathan Dymond, Miss Sue Bryan, Mr Steve Bolton, Miss Charlotte Garbutt
Income: £1,367,240 [2017]; £1,157,413 [2016]; £799,541 [2015]

Harper Adams University
Registered: 15 Jun 2012 *Employees:* 504
Tel: 01952 820280 *Website:* harper-adams.ac.uk
Activities: General charitable purposes; education, training
Address: Harper Adams University College, Edgmond, Newport, TF10 8NB
Trustees: Mr Campbell Tweed, Dr David George Llewellyn, Heather Jenkins, Mr Michael James Lewis, Dr John Donaldson, Dr Julia Pointon, Mr Martin Thomas, Professor Mark Ormerod, Dr Moira Harris, Mr Sandy Graham, Mr Jonathan Garnham, Mr Stephen Vickers, Mr Mark Roach, Mr Colin Bailey, Colonel Richard Hambleton, Mrs Christine Snell, Mr Peter Cowdy, Mr Peter Nixon, Mr Dominic Wong, Ms Lavinia Moroz-Hale
Income: £42,685,000 [2017]; £39,082,821 [2016]; £38,412,570 [2015]; £38,269,332 [2014]; £34,396,672 [2013]

Adcote School Educational Trust Limited
Registered: 23 Apr 1965 *Employees:* 71
Tel: 01939 261392 *Website:* adcoteschool.co.uk
Activities: Education, training
Address: Adcote School, Little Ness, Shrewsbury, Salop, ST4 1JY
Trustees: Mr Ian Galliers, Mr Mark Fairbrother, Mr Davis John Knight, Mr Robert Ryan Jervis, Mrs Anne Elizabeth Hughes, Mrs Anita Roberts
Income: £3,879,384 [2015]; £2,128,412 [2014]; £1,872,018 [2013]; £1,660,410 [2012]

Addaction
Registered: 19 Feb 1991 *Employees:* 1,431 *Volunteers:* 810
Tel: 020 7251 5860 *Website:* addaction.org.uk
Activities: Education, training; advancement of health or saving of lives; prevention or relief of poverty; accommodation, housing; economic, community development, employment
Address: Addaction, 67-69 Cowcross Street, London, EC1M 6PU
Trustees: Lord Alex Carlile, Mr Ronald Finlay, Mr Nigel McCorkell, Mark Beaumont, Ms Anne Chapman, Dr Gwen Adshead, Mr Richard Gould, Miss Debbie Simpson, Mrs Jane Winehouse, Dr Susanne Ludgate, Mr William David Willis
Income: £78,857,000 [2017]; £74,779,000 [2016]; £64,773,000 [2015]; £57,819,000 [2014]; £50,961,000 [2013]

Addiction Recovery Agency Ltd
Registered: 14 Mar 1991 *Employees:* 42 *Volunteers:* 30
Tel: 0117 930 0282 *Website:* addictionrecovery.org.uk
Activities: Education, training; advancement of health or saving of lives; prevention or relief of poverty; accommodation, housing
Address: Kings Court, King Street, Bristol, BS1 4EF
Trustees: Mr David Shattock, Ms Louise Marie Davies, Mr Simon Charles Goodman, Ms Jayne Dilys Mary Tucker, Ms Patsy Elliott Hudson, Mr Paul Francis Bullivant, Mr Andrew Carruthers, Mr David Wynne Thomas
Income: £2,098,224 [2017]; £2,090,571 [2016]; £2,511,636 [2015]; £2,234,237 [2014]; £2,286,652 [2013]

Addysg Oedolion Cymru / Adult Learning Wales
Registered: 27 Aug 1998 *Employees:* 145 *Volunteers:* 58
Tel: 0330 058 0845 *Website:* addysgoedolion.cymru
Activities: Education, training
Address: Addysg Oedolion Cymru/Adult Learning Wales, 7 Coopers Yard, Curran Road, Cardiff, CF10 5NB
Trustees: Mr Dafydd Gwyrfai Bowen Rhys, Mr Christopher Franks, Mr Nick Taylor, Mrs June Jeremy, Ms Cathrine Clark, Dr John Graystone, Ms Sonia Reynolds, Mr Iwan Hywel, Ms Julie Cook, Ms Gayle Hudson, Ms Gerry Jenson, Mr Toni Schiavone, Mr David Elis-Williams, Mr Guy Smith, Ms Heather Willbourn, Ms Caroline Davies
Income: £7,229,000 [2017]; £6,885,000 [2016]; £6,480,000 [2015]; £7,579,000 [2014]; £3,513,468 [2013]

The Adolescent and Children's Trust
Registered: 19 Mar 1993 *Employees:* 154
Tel: 020 8695 8135 *Website:* tactcare.org.uk
Activities: General charitable purposes; education, training; advancement of health or saving of lives; disability
Address: TACT, 303 Hither Green Lane, London, SE13 6TJ
Trustees: Mr Geoffrey Drayson Knox, Ms Gillain Louise Santi, Ms Anne Lee, Ms Lisa Joann Waterman-Glasgow, Mr Matthew Doyle, Ms Joan Lawton, Mr Jonathan Peter Fayle, Mr Phillip Woodman, Mr Michael David Thomas
Income: £21,762,808 [2017]; £23,355,980 [2016]; £23,366,905 [2015]; £23,146,662 [2014]; £21,760,607 [2013]

Adoption Matters
Registered: 16 Mar 1983 *Employees:* 58 *Volunteers:* 100
Tel: 01244 390938 *Website:* adoptionmatters.org
Activities: Other charitable purposes
Address: Adoption Matters, 14 Liverpool Road, Chester, CH2 1AE
Trustees: Mr Annesley Wright, David Cracknell, Mr David Champness, Mrs Sara Juliet Winstanley, Mr Joseph James McArdle, Mrs Carolyn Ann Johnson, Mr David Shield, Mrs Elizabeth Harlow
Income: £2,810,799 [2017]; £3,231,206 [2016]; £2,575,438 [2015]; £2,250,177 [2014]; £1,635,163 [2013]

Adoption UK Charity
Registered: 26 Feb 2015 *Employees:* 15 *Volunteers:* 125
Tel: 01295 752245 *Website:* adoptionuk.org
Activities: General charitable purposes; education, training
Address: Adoption UK, Units 11 & 12 Vantage Business Park, Bloxham Road, Banbury, Oxon, OX16 9UX
Trustees: Mary Greenwood, Barry Catchpole, Eleanor Bradford, Mr Tony Breslin, Jane Game, Ms Anita Bharucha, Mr Peter Seymour, PAC-UK
Income: £1,774,153 [2017]; £2,197,532 [2016]

Adref Ltd
Registered: 19 Jul 1990 *Employees:* 44 *Volunteers:* 28
Tel: 01685 878755 *Website:* adref.org.uk
Activities: Education, training; accommodation, housing; economic, community development, employment
Address: Adref Ltd, 54-55 Bute Street, Aberdare, Rhondda Cynon Taf, CF44 7LD
Trustees: Mr Richard Clive Bennett, Mr Bryn Davies, Mrs Geraldine Margaret Jones
Income: £2,157,376 [2017]; £2,056,553 [2016]; £2,000,063 [2015]; £1,738,462 [2014]; £1,619,961 [2013]

Adult Placement Services
Registered: 26 Jul 1995 *Employees:* 332
Tel: 01423 530053 *Website:* avalongroup.org.uk
Activities: Education, training; disability; accommodation, housing; other charitable purposes
Address: Avalon Group, 6 Grove Park Court, Harrogate, N Yorks, HG1 4DP
Trustees: Miss Elizabeth Anne O'Hare, Mr Ian Lawson, Mr Stephen Fox, Mrs Louise Nicola Drake, Mrs Wendy Ramshaw, Mrs Angela Waddingham
Income: £9,455,221 [2017]; £9,126,688 [2016]; £8,547,296 [2015]; £7,415,951 [2014]; £7,115,997 [2013]

Adult Training Network Limited
Registered: 30 Aug 2002 *Employees:* 34 *Volunteers:* 20
Tel: 020 8574 9588 *Website:* adult-training.org.uk
Activities: Education, training; economic, community development, employment
Address: Unit 3 Triangle Centre, 399 Uxbridge Road, Southall, Middlesex, UB1 3EJ
Trustees: Ms Satvinder Bahad, Mr Inderjit Singh Ubbey, Mr Lee Heavens
Income: £1,037,995 [2016]; £1,160,435 [2015]; £1,434,240 [2014]; £1,883,898 [2013]; £1,559,961 [2012]

Adults Supporting Adults (ASA Lincs)
Registered: 12 May 2004 *Employees:* 43 *Volunteers:* 7
Tel: 01529 416270 *Website:* asaorg.co.uk
Activities: The advancement of health or saving of lives; other charitable purposes
Address: ASA, Railton House, East Road, Sleaford, Lincs, NG34 7EQ
Trustees: Mr Keith Phillips, Mrs Pamela Elizabeth Railton, Mr Howard Sanders, Mr Niall Armstrong, Mr Nigel Horner, Mr Nigel Maurice Dickens
Income: £1,660,726 [2017]; £1,767,817 [2016]; £1,987,305 [2015]; £2,504,698 [2014]; £1,912,404 [2013]

Adur Community Leisure Limited
Registered: 11 Nov 2005 *Employees:* 166
Website: impulseleisure.co.uk
Activities: Education, training; advancement of health or saving of lives; arts, culture, heritage, science; amateur sport; recreation
Address: Blackshots Leisure Centre, Blackshots Lane, Grays, Essex, RM16 2JU
Trustees: Philip Pickard, Mrs Margaret Woolacott, Mr Stephen Francis Kibblewhite, Malcolm Roberts, Mr Kevin Boram, Dr Peter Wilson, Mr J R Seymour, Mr Leonard Victor Saunders, Mrs Carol Ann Albury
Income: £3,056,772 [2017]; £3,654,398 [2016]; £2,486,921 [2015]; £2,434,464 [2014]; £2,498,696 [2013]

Advance Advocacy and Non-Violence Community Education
Registered: 1 Jun 2001 *Employees:* 41 *Volunteers:* 2
Tel: 020 8237 5590 *Website:* advancecharity.org.uk
Activities: General charitable purposes; education, training; advancement of health or saving of lives; human rights, religious or racial harmony, equality or diversity; other charitable purposes
Address: 150 King Street, Hammersmith, London, W6 0QU
Trustees: Ruth Fuller Sessions, Rebecca Egan, Emily Midwood, Christine Mullin, Ms Helen Arbon, Ms Swatee Jasoria, Christine Losecaat, Elizabeth Jones, Tallulah Perez-Sphar, Miss Pria Rai, Ms Louise Finer, Ms Maria Sookias
Income: £2,164,289 [2017]; £1,583,043 [2016]; £1,346,268 [2015]; £1,537,238 [2014]; £1,450,896 [2013]

Advance HE
Registered: 19 Jan 2004 *Employees:* 93
Tel: 01904 717521 *Website:* heacademy.ac.uk
Activities: Education, training
Address: The Higher Education Academy, Innovation Way, York Science Park, York, YO10 5BR
Trustees: Professor Eunice Angela Simmons, Ms Rebecca Mary Bunting, Professor Janice Kay, Mr Amatey Doku, Professor Nigel Seaton, Mr Nigel Carrington, Professor Colin Riordan, Mr Stephen Marston, Mr Geoffrey Mark Layer
Income: £9,326,000 [2017]; £12,168,000 [2016]; £16,231,000 [2015]; £18,544,000 [2014]; £20,008,000 [2013]

Advanced Life Support Group
Registered: 20 Jan 2003 *Employees:* 30 *Volunteers:* 11,460
Tel: 0161 794 1999 *Website:* alsg.org
Activities: Education, training
Address: Advanced Life Support Group, 29-31 Ellesmere Street, Swinton, Manchester, M27 0LA
Trustees: Dr Barbara Phillips, Mr Peter Driscoll, Mr Kim Hinshaw, Mrs Kathy Doyle, Dr Martin Samuels, Prof Terence Wardle, Mr Alan Charters, Prof Kevin Mackway-Jones, Dr Peter-Marc Fortune, Dr Christopher Vallis
Income: £1,770,022 [2016]; £1,659,643 [2015]; £1,760,366 [2014]; £1,603,961 [2013]; £1,554,672 [2012]

Adventist Development and Relief Agency - UK
Registered: 30 Mar 1999 *Employees:* 9 *Volunteers:* 3,000
Website: adra.org.uk
Activities: General charitable purposes; education, training; advancement of health or saving of lives; disability; prevention or relief of poverty; overseas aid, famine relief; environment, conservation, heritage; economic, community development, employment
Address: Adra-UK, Stanborough Park, Watford, Herts, WD25 9JZ
Trustees: Ms Jennifer Phillips, Mr Tristan Simmons, Mr John Rees-Stoner, Mr Earl Ramharacksingh, Mr Ian Sweeney, Dr Stephen Logan, Mr John Surridge
Income: £1,992,962 [2016]; £1,663,139 [2015]; £1,723,318 [2014]; £1,826,656 [2013]; £1,949,717 [2012]

Adventure Hyndburn
Registered: 14 Jul 2003 *Employees:* 49 *Volunteers:* 4
Tel: 01254 387757 *Website:* surestarthyndburn.co.uk
Activities: Education, training; advancement of health or saving of lives; disability; prevention or relief of poverty; economic, community development, employment
Address: The Park Child & Family Centre, Norfolk Grove, Church, Accrington, Lancs, BB5 4RY
Trustees: Mr Munsif Dad, Jane Makey, Judith Helen Addison, Mrs Maureen Askew, Richard Hooper, Rebecka Southworth, Sharon Lesley Shahili, Zabina Rahman
Income: £1,312,306 [2017]; £1,524,277 [2016]; £1,456,684 [2015]; £1,459,675 [2014]; £1,382,726 [2013]

The Adventure Learning Charity
Registered: 4 Dec 2013 *Employees:* 40
Website: alfcharity.org
Activities: Education, training; advancement of health or saving of lives; amateur sport; environment, conservation, heritage; recreation
Address: Buckinghamshire Green Park Centre, Green Park, Aston Clinton, Aylesbury, Bucks, HP22 5NE
Trustees: Mr James Lee, Mrs Carina Keen, Mr Steve Bowles, Mr Nicholas Hooper, Mr Mervyn Ramsay, Mr Edward Plunket, Mr Stephen Dannan
Income: £1,521,476 [2016]; £968,425 [2015]; £1,378,599 [2014]

Adventure Plus
Registered: 8 Jun 2000 *Employees:* 14 *Volunteers:* 60
Tel: 01993 703308 *Website:* adventureplus.org.uk
Activities: Education, training; religious activities; amateur sport
Address: Adventure Plus, Main Street, Clanfield, Bampton, Oxon, OX18 2SN
Trustees: Mr Christopher Dean Compston, Mr Kevin Stewart Ashman, Mr Brian Foxton City & Guilds Fabrication NRSWA ACC, Mrs Helen Leighton, Mr James Peter Gould, Mr Richard Mark Bach, Mr Nicholas John Stevens, Ms Donna Williams BA(Psych) HDipEd, Tim Lawson-Cruttenden, Mr Mark Richard Hellawell
Income: £1,110,067 [2016]; £1,092,283 [2015]; £909,428 [2014]; £425,569 [2013]; £332,741 [2012]

Advice UK
Registered: 1 Jun 1988 *Employees:* 16
Tel: 0300 777 0107 *Website:* adviceuk.org.uk
Activities: General charitable purposes; education, training; prevention or relief of poverty; economic, community development, employment
Address: 101e Universal House, 88-94 Wentworth Street, London, E1 7SA
Trustees: Ms Simin Azimi, Graham Richard Elliott Smith, Ms Hayley Kendall, Ms Naomi Wayne, Mr Baljit Basheda, Ms Alene Wilton
Income: £2,182,751 [2017]; £2,014,798 [2016]; £1,806,860 [2015]; £2,050,058 [2014]; £2,752,067 [2013]

Advising Communities
Registered: 4 Mar 1997 *Employees:* 26 *Volunteers:* 85
Tel: 0300 030 1121 *Website:* advisingcommunities.uk
Activities: The prevention or relief of poverty
Address: Advising Communities, 6-8 Westmoreland Road, London, SE17 2AX
Trustees: Mr Chris Snow, Miss Magdelena Nikolova, Ms Denise Owusu-Ansah, Dr Alexandra Xanthaki, Mr Andrew Boaden, Dr Chris Sanford, Mr Andrew Brookes
Income: £1,275,324 [2017]; £1,193,014 [2016]; £1,028,246 [2015]; £1,011,849 [2014]; £1,013,089 [2013]

Adviza Partnership
Registered: 19 Oct 2009 *Employees:* 137 *Volunteers:* 231
Tel: 0118 402 7170 *Website:* adviza.org.uk
Activities: Education, training; disability; economic, community development, employment
Address: Adviza Partnership, Ocean House, The Ring, Bracknell, Berks, RG12 1AX
Trustees: Mr Terry Arthur Stock, Mrs Katharine Mary Horler, Mr David Charles Lunn, Mr Peter Thorn, Mrs Elaine Mary Barnes, Mr Timothy Parry, Campbell Christie CBE, Jonathan Olafoe, Nonie Zaremba, Mr Bruce Arthur Edward Laurie, Mrs Alison Frances Mihail, Sue Gale, Ms Sue Ormiston, Mrs Hilary Elizabeth Omissi, Mr Kieran O'Brien, Mrs Ruth Irene Spellman, Les Windows, Louise Sarginson
Income: £6,934,233 [2017]; £9,613,456 [2016]; £9,088,901 [2015]; £8,731,528 [2014]; £8,247,089 [2013]

Advocacy Focus
Registered: 12 Apr 2001 *Employees:* 43 *Volunteers:* 27
Tel: 0300 323 0965 *Website:* advocacyfocus.org.uk
Activities: Education, training; advancement of health or saving of lives; disability
Address: First Floor, Advocacy Focus, The Old Tannery, Eastgate, Accrington, Lancs, BB5 6PW
Trustees: Mr Alan Clarkin, Ms Christine Marie Southworth, Miss Michelle Gray, Mrs Denise Bond, Mr Simon Burrows, Mr Graham Bruce Campbell
Income: £1,446,469 [2017]; £1,004,136 [2016]; £716,551 [2015]; £708,346 [2014]; £599,386 [2013]

The Advocacy Project
Registered: 13 Dec 2000 *Employees:* 58 *Volunteers:* 3
Tel: 020 8969 3000 *Website:* advocacyproject.org.uk
Activities: General charitable purposes; education, training; advancement of health or saving of lives; disability
Address: The Advocacy Project, 73 St Charles Square, London, W10 6EJ
Trustees: Mr Paul Kitchener, Dr Dele Olajide, Mr Adam Antonio, Mr Michael Hagan, Ms Jacqueline Sheila McKinlay, Ms Kate Ferguson, Ms Sue Page, Ms Claire Starza-Allen, Ms Tsatsa Janiashvili
Income: £1,195,560 [2017]; £1,199,632 [2016]; £1,216,968 [2015]; £1,350,691 [2014]; £1,029,169 [2013]

Advocacy Support in Cymru Ltd
Registered: 19 May 2011 *Employees:* 60
Tel: 029 2054 0444 *Website:* ascymru.org.uk
Activities: General charitable purposes; advancement of health or saving of lives; disability
Address: Charterhouse 1, Links Business Park, Fortran Road, St Mellons, Cardiff, CF3 0LT
Trustees: Mr Graham Oliver, Mr Norman Francis, Ms Colleen Forse, Ms Eileen Wareham
Income: £1,797,843 [2017]; £1,913,049 [2016]; £1,498,224 [2015]; £1,300,904 [2014]; £1,643,305 [2013]

Advocacy for All
Registered: 14 Oct 1997 *Employees:* 61 *Volunteers:* 30
Website: advocacyforall.org.uk
Activities: Disability
Address: The Civic Centre, St Mary's Road, Swanley, Kent, BR8 7BU
Trustees: Mr Brian James, Mr John Anthony Watts, Mrs Sigrun Asa Danielsson
Income: £1,395,792 [2017]; £1,254,449 [2016]; £990,197 [2015]; £961,770 [2014]; £748,864 [2013]

Advonet
Registered: 2 Oct 2008 *Employees:* 68 *Volunteers:* 91
Tel: 0113 244 0606 *Website:* advonet.org.uk
Activities: Education, training; advancement of health or saving of lives; disability; prevention or relief of poverty; economic, community development, employment; human rights, religious or racial harmony, equality or diversity
Address: Advonet, Unity Business Centre, 26 Roundhay Road, Leeds, LS7 1AB
Trustees: Mr Reinhard Beck, Ms Sabine Dufeutrelle, Mr Ralph Porter, Ms Victoria Anderson, Mr Arash Manouchehri, Mr Ivan Nip, Mr Mau Yip, Ms Helen Bradley, Mr Kirti Tandel, Ms Hazel June Woodcock
Income: £1,638,834 [2017]; £2,062,672 [2016]; £1,055,112 [2015]; £1,092,580 [2014]; £84,593 [2013]

Aegis Trust
Registered: 13 Oct 2000 *Employees:* 125 *Volunteers:* 15
Website: aegistrust.org
Activities: Education, training; advancement of health or saving of lives; overseas aid, famine relief; economic, community development, employment; human rights, religious or racial harmony, equality or diversity
Address: 15 Bridge Street, Newark, Notts, NG24 1EE
Trustees: Dr James Michael Smith, Ms I Maxine Marcus, Mrs Ruth Messenger, Mr John Noland Ryan Montgomery, Mr David Thomas Ormesher Jr, Mrs Louise Harris
Income: £1,301,069 [2016]; £3,102,273 [2015]; £4,829,130 [2014]; £4,529,960 [2013]

Affinity Trust
Registered: 18 Jan 2011 *Employees:* 1,904 *Volunteers:* 15
Tel: 01844 267800 *Website:* affinitytrust.org
Activities: Disability; accommodation, housing
Address: 1 St Andrews Court, Wellington Street, Thame, Oxon, OX9 3WT
Trustees: Mr Andrew Taylor, Mr Malcolm Roger Thomas, Mrs Margaret Elizabeth Moody, Mr Timothy Tamblyn, Mrs Anne Anketell, Mr Keith Gordon Cameron, Mr John William Hawthorne, Dr Sue Ross, Mr David Walden, Ms Jennifer Edwards CBE
Income: £45,237,885 [2016]; £42,726,388 [2015]; £37,960,429 [2014]; £35,426,270 [2013]; £30,694,674 [2012]

Afghan Ekta Cultural/Religious Community Centre
Registered: 27 Sep 2001 *Volunteers:* 35
Website: gurunanakdarbar.org.uk
Activities: General charitable purposes; education, training; religious activities; arts, culture, heritage, science
Address: 96 Balmoral Drive, Hayes, Middlesex, UB4 0BY
Trustees: Mr Popander Singh, Mr Kultar Singh Kapoor, Mr Gurmeet Singh, Mr Davinder Singh Prit
Income: £1,044,185 [2016]; £1,255,017 [2015]; £1,704,918 [2014]; £1,151,357 [2013]; £1,243,813 [2012]

Afghanaid
Registered: 29 Mar 1995 *Employees:* 166 *Volunteers:* 10
Website: afghanaid.org.uk
Activities: Education, training; prevention or relief of poverty; overseas aid, famine relief; animals; economic, community development, employment
Address: Afghanaid, 56-64 Leonard Street, London, EC2A 4LT
Trustees: Mr David Page, Ms Mary Catherine Mountain, Mr Christopher William Kinder, Mr Shirazuddin Siddiqi, Ms Orzala Ashraf Nemat, Ms Pauline Maria Hayes CBE, Ms Elizabeth Margaret Winter OBE, Dr Martin Greeley, Mr Stephen Turner, Mr Anthony Ralph Fitzherbert, Dr Brian Stanley Pratt, Mr Mark Rainer Bowden
Income: £6,530,430 [2016]; £5,911,007 [2015]; £6,562,026 [2014]; £5,049,749 [2013]; £8,011,785 [2012]

Africa Educational Trust
Registered: 17 Dec 1963 *Employees:* 15 *Volunteers:* 3
Tel: 020 7841 1072 *Website:* africaeducationaltrust.org
Activities: General charitable purposes; education, training; disability; prevention or relief of poverty; overseas aid, famine relief; human rights, religious or racial harmony, equality or diversity
Address: Africa Educational Trust, 88 Kingsway, London, WC2B 6AA
Trustees: Ms Jill Landymore, Ms Sally Healy, Professor Francis Katamba, Ms Sarah Hughes, Mr Robert Strang, Professor Richard Hodder-Williams, Prof Cisco Magagula, Prof Lynn Davies, Mr Russell Levy
Income: £3,657,617 [2017]; £3,937,239 [2016]; £3,804,559 [2015]; £3,710,136 [2014]; £4,316,501 [2013]

Africa Inland Mission International
Registered: 5 Mar 2003 *Employees:* 84 *Volunteers:* 35
Website: aimint.org
Activities: Education, training; advancement of health or saving of lives; prevention or relief of poverty; religious activities
Address: Aim, Halifax Place, Nottingham, NG1 1QN
Trustees: Mr Tim Oglesby, Nick Waring, Mr John Byrne, Dr Elizabeth Hill, Kola Kehinde, Heather Potts, Mrs Ruth Elizabeth Hyde, Mr Peter Collison, Rev Henry Curran
Income: £2,845,406 [2016]; £2,638,771 [2015]; £2,433,743 [2014]; £2,576,745 [2013]; £2,171,647 [2012]

African Agricultural Technology Foundation
Registered: 7 Jan 2005 *Employees:* 49
Website: aatf-africa.org
Activities: General charitable purposes; prevention or relief of poverty; overseas aid, famine relief; environment, conservation, heritage; economic, community development, employment; other charitable purposes
Address: P O Box 30709, Nairobi, Kenya
Trustees: Mr Kwame Akuffo-Akoto, Mr Rory Radding, Dr Stanford Blade, Mr Justin Rakotoarisaona, Professor Jennifer Ann Thompson, Anne Glover, Dr Denis Kyetere, Dr Larry Beach, Dr Johnson Irungu Waithaka, Mr McLean Sibanda, Dr Ousmane Badiane, Dr Jeremy Tinga Ouedraogo
Income: £24,547,499 [2016]; £13,751,420 [2015]; £16,654,528 [2014]; £12,029,780 [2013]; £11,492,361 [2012]

African Enterprise International
Registered: 3 May 2012 *Employees:* 9
Tel: 01285 841900 *Website:* aeint.org
Activities: Education, training; advancement of health or saving of lives; prevention or relief of poverty; overseas aid, famine relief; religious activities; economic, community development, employment; human rights, religious or racial harmony, equality or diversity
Address: The Trust Partnership LLP, 6 Trull Farm Buildings, Trull, Tetbury, Glos, GL8 8SQ
Trustees: Mr James Catford, Jeffrey Collett, Rev David Carpenter, Ms Charity Kivengeri, Professor William Ogara, Dr John Senyonyi, Mr Absalom Gatsi, Rev Nii Amoo Darku, Rev Grace Masalakulangwa
Income: £1,092,179 [2016]; £1,128,931 [2015]; £1,205,553 [2014]; £1,445,066 [2013]; £1,632,145 [2012]

African Foundation for Development Afford
Registered: 1 Jul 2004 *Employees:* 9 *Volunteers:* 13
Tel: 020 3326 3750 *Website:* afford-uk.org
Activities: General charitable purposes; education, training; prevention or relief of poverty; amateur sport; economic, community development, employment
Address: African Foundation for Development, Rich Mix Building, 35-47 Bethnal Green Road, London, E1 6LA
Trustees: Gibril Faal, Olayinka Ewuola, Ndidi Njoku, Mr Francis Weboko Inyundo, Martin Osengor, Mr Adeyemi Olusegun Daramy
Income: £1,272,953 [2017]; £740,456 [2016]; £497,558 [2015]; £408,423 [2014]; £364,198 [2013]

The African Institute for Mathematical Sciences - Next Einstein Initiative Foundation (UK)
Registered: 19 Oct 2010 *Employees:* 2
Tel: 020 7637 4847 *Website:* nexteinstein.org
Activities: Education, training; economic, community development, employment
Address: De Morgan House, 57-58 Russell Square, London, WC1B 4HS
Trustees: Professor Neil Turok, Professor Fernando Quevedo, Mr Mohammed Jouade Gharbi, Mr Cheikh Tidiane Mbaye, Ms Lucy Quist, Professor K Moffatt, Dr Howard Alper, Ms Mpule Kwelagobe, Ms Lydie Hakizimana
Income: £8,331,726 [2017]; £7,440,347 [2016]; £9,268,542 [2015]; £7,460,587 [2014]; £3,983,821 [2013]

African Prisons Project
Registered: 30 Nov 2007 *Employees:* 33 *Volunteers:* 20
Tel: 020 8408 1548 *Website:* africanprisons.org
Activities: Education, training; advancement of health or saving of lives; prevention or relief of poverty; overseas aid, famine relief; human rights, religious or racial harmony, equality or diversity
Address: The Generator Business Centre, 95 Miles Road, Mitcham, Surrey, CR4 3FH
Trustees: Dr Anne Merriman, Mr Richard Reed, Mr Jonathan Price, Prof Nicholas Johnson, Miss Aisha Kaweesi, Mr Paul Francis Cavadino, Mrs Lyn Margaret McLean, Ms Siobhan Bryant, Mr George Daly, Mrs Shirlene OH
Income: £2,020,312 [2016]; £773,310 [2015]; £492,900 [2014]; £405,549 [2013]; £150,877 [2012]

Afrikids Limited
Registered: 24 Mar 2011 *Employees:* 7 *Volunteers:* 3
Tel: 020 7269 0740 *Website:* afrikids.org
Activities: Education, training; overseas aid, famine relief; economic, community development, employment
Address: Afrikids, 21 Southampton Row, London, WC1B 5HA
Trustees: Mr John Hickman, Ms Georgina Fienberg, Mr Martin Ott, Mr Duncan Spencer, Mr Jason Haines, Ms Frances Cleland Bones
Income: £2,815,318 [2016]; £1,727,830 [2015]; £1,588,332 [2014]; £1,851,737 [2013]

After Adoption
Registered: 7 Nov 1990 *Employees:* 97 *Volunteers:* 18
Tel: 0161 839 4932 *Website:* afteradoption.org.uk
Activities: General charitable purposes
Address: After Adoption, Unit 5 Citygate, 5 Blantyre Street, Manchester, M15 4JJ
Trustees: Mr Brian Latham, Mr David Tomlinson, Ms Patricia Carol Franklin-Bruce, Ms Heather Ottaway, Mr Andrew Houghton, Lady Rhona Bradley, Dr Hugh McLaughlin, Mr Neil Langford McArthur, Mr Julian Waring
Income: £4,954,026 [2017]; £4,851,443 [2016]; £4,857,838 [2015]; £4,209,432 [2014]; £3,278,562 [2013]

Aga Khan Foundation (United Kingdom)
Registered: 4 Dec 1973 *Employees:* 17
Tel: 020 7383 9090 *Website:* akf.org.uk
Activities: Education, training; advancement of health or saving of lives; prevention or relief of poverty; overseas aid, famine relief; arts, culture, heritage, science; environment, conservation, heritage
Address: 210 Euston Road, London, NW1 2DA
Trustees: Prince Amyn Mohamed Aga Khan, His Highness Prince Karim Aga Khan, Mr Guillaume De Spoelberch
Income: £27,983,000 [2016]; £73,525,000 [2015]; £25,947,000 [2014]; £15,688,000 [2013]; £18,272,000 [2012]

The Against Malaria Foundation
Registered: 5 Aug 2004 *Employees:* 3 *Volunteers:* 20
Tel: 020 7371 8735 *Website:* againstmalaria.com
Activities: Education, training; advancement of health or saving of lives
Address: Against Malaria Foundation, c/o PWC, 10 Bricket Road, St Albans, Herts, AL1 3JX
Trustees: Mr Peter Robert Sherratt, Mr Robert Keith Hamilton Mather, Mr Guy Davis, Mr Jeremy James Schwartz, Professor Richard Paul Lane, Mr Jonathan Calascione, Mr Arthur Boler, Ms Stephanie Cook
Income: £36,192,981 [2017]; £36,650,322 [2016]; £9,022,372 [2015]; £2,483,076 [2014]; £5,356,437 [2013]

Agape Ministries Ltd
Registered: 25 Apr 1969 *Employees:* 101 *Volunteers:* 180
Tel: 0121 765 4404 *Website:* agape.org.uk
Activities: Overseas aid, famine relief; religious activities
Address: Agape, 167 Newhall Street, Birmingham, B3 1SW
Trustees: Mr Javier Garcia, Mr Ian Johnson, Rev Richard
Boothroyd, Mr Gary Palmer, Sally Taylor, Mrs Lisbet Diers
Income: £2,622,345 [2016]; £2,530,494 [2015]; £2,516,328 [2014];
£2,519,960 [2013]; £2,417,455 [2012]

Age Concern (Herne Bay)
Registered: 30 Jun 1995 *Employees:* 33 *Volunteers:* 130
Tel: 01227 749570 *Website:* ageukhernebay.org.uk
Activities: General charitable purposes; education, training;
disability
Address: 16 Reculver Road, Herne Bay, Kent, CT6 6LE
Trustees: Mr David Bowley, Dr Roger Wheeldon, Mr Ronald
Charles Woodward, Mr Christopher Jones, Mr Ian Valentine,
Mrs Jenni Bedford, Mrs Evelyn Denham, Mr Timothy Goodwin,
Miss Larissa Shisharkina, Mr William Wright
Income: £1,108,849 [2017]; £933,973 [2016]; £1,034,291 [2015];
£843,238 [2014]; £839,218 [2013]

Age Concern Bedfordshire
Registered: 12 Feb 2002 *Employees:* 129 *Volunteers:* 24
Tel: 01234 216002 *Website:* ageukbedfordshire.org.uk
Activities: General charitable purposes
Address: Age Concern, 78-82 Bromham Road, Bedford,
MK40 2QH
Trustees: Mrs Marjorie Stephenson, Mrs Sally Harrison, Mr Michael
Tuffnell, Mrs Anne Teresa Powis, Mrs Janet Wilkins, Ms Rita
Beaumont, Mrs Wendy Annabel Davies
Income: £1,198,513 [2017]; £1,080,050 [2016]; £1,070,654 [2015];
£963,203 [2014]; £979,915 [2013]

Age Concern Birmingham
Registered: 20 Mar 1987 *Employees:* 53 *Volunteers:* 92
Tel: 0121 362 3650 *Website:* ageconcernbirmingham.org.uk
Activities: General charitable purposes; prevention or relief of
poverty
Address: Age Concern, 76-78 Boldmere Road, Sutton Coldfield,
W Midlands, B73 5TJ
Trustees: Mrs Margaret Patricia Birkett, Dr Jay Chauhan, Mr Antony
Denis Cannon, Dr Peter Michael Kevern, Mr Michael Malpas
Income: £1,516,377 [2017]; £1,270,001 [2016]; £1,481,318 [2015];
£2,141,802 [2014]; £2,111,845 [2013]

Age Concern Bromley
Registered: 26 Feb 1997 *Employees:* 68 *Volunteers:* 439
Website: ageukbromleyandgreenwich.org.uk
Activities: General charitable purposes
Address: Age UK Bromley & Greenwich, Community House,
South Street, Bromley, Kent, BR1 1RH
Trustees: Mrs Lynda Stimson, Mr Gordon Hayward, Mrs Morgan
Vine, Mr John Pannett, Margaret Lewis, Mr Barry John Styles,
Mrs Christina Parry, Mrs Judy Lyons, Mrs Teresa McMahon,
Ms Lorna Blackwood
Income: £1,580,225 [2017]; £1,273,798 [2016]; £1,480,002 [2015];
£1,941,123 [2014]; £1,456,294 [2013]

Age Concern Cambridgeshire
Registered: 12 Jan 2005 *Employees:* 58 *Volunteers:* 336
Tel: 01354 696650 *Website:* ageuk.org.uk
Activities: General charitable purposes; prevention or relief of
poverty
Address: 2 Victoria Street, Chatteris, Cambs, PE16 6AP
Trustees: Hazel Williams, Amelia Everitt, David Bruch
Income: £1,237,042 [2016]; £1,122,529 [2015]; £1,210,811 [2014];
£1,076,382 [2013]

Age Concern Camden
Registered: 22 Jan 1986 *Employees:* 112 *Volunteers:* 400
Website: ageukcamden.org.uk
Activities: General charitable purposes; prevention or relief of
poverty
Address: Age UK Camden, Tavis House, 1-6 Tavistock Square,
London, WC1H 9NA
Trustees: Virendra Ahuja, Ms Barbara Louise Hughes MBE,
Ms Marika Freris, Miss Dorothy May, Mr Mohammad Shah-Goni
Khan, Beatris Salvatore Januaro, Ms Janet Guthrie, Dr Thomas
Fitzgerald, Mrs Mary Patricia Burd, Mr David Michael Mitchell,
Mr Jacob John Coy
Income: £3,109,406 [2017]; £3,022,665 [2016]; £2,231,123 [2015];
£2,114,959 [2014]; £2,191,483 [2013]

Age Concern Cardiff and The Vale of Glamorgan
Registered: 6 Sep 2010 *Employees:* 53 *Volunteers:* 270
Tel: 029 2083 8902 *Website:* ageconnectscardiff.org.uk
Activities: General charitable purposes
Address: Age Concern Cardiff and The Vale of Glamorgan, Unit
4 Cleeve House, Lambourne Crescent, Cardiff, CF14 5GP
Trustees: Mr Colin Harvey, Mrs Jo McGill, Mrs Anna Eckersley,
Mrs Audrey Violet Males OBE, Mr David Hughes, Mr Stuart Young
Income: £1,294,990 [2017]; £1,366,609 [2016]; £1,335,384 [2015];
£1,460,996 [2014]; £2,058,983 [2013]

Age Concern Cheshire
Registered: 12 Apr 2002 *Employees:* 115 *Volunteers:* 232
Tel: 01606 881660 *Website:* ageukcheshire.org.uk
Activities: General charitable purposes
Address: 314 Chester Road, Hartford, Northwich, Cheshire,
CW8 2AB
Trustees: Mr Craig Haslam Cawthorn, Mr Alan Derrick Smith,
Mrs Susan Harrison, Mr Thamir K Al-Jorani, Ms Nicola Brooks,
Mr Michael Stewart, Mrs Rita Hollens, Mr John Llewellyn Townsend,
Miss Sarah Twibell, Mr John Howard Webb, Professor Margaret
Andrews, Ms Sheila Wentworth
Income: £3,087,221 [2017]; £2,912,984 [2016]; £2,063,978 [2015];
£1,833,644 [2014]; £1,980,159 [2013]

Age Concern Durham County
Registered: 17 Dec 2007 *Employees:* 23 *Volunteers:* 134
Tel: 0191 386 3856 *Website:* ageukcountydurham.org.uk
Activities: General charitable purposes; education, training;
advancement of health or saving of lives; prevention or relief of
poverty; arts, culture, heritage, science; economic, community
development, employment
Address: Mrs Harriet Gibbon, Age UK House, Belmont Business
Park, Durham, DH1 1TW
Trustees: Mrs Annie Elizabeth Hitchman, Mr David Martin,
Ms Heather Joan Scott, Mr David Robert Haw, Mr Tony Armstrong,
Mr Ivan Halliday Wood, Mrs Pauline Una York, Mrs Natalie
Davison-Terranova
Income: £1,539,028 [2017]; £991,148 [2016]; £1,123,603 [2015];
£1,149,541 [2014]; £1,366,021 [2013]

Age Concern East Cheshire
Registered: 18 Jan 2002 *Employees:* 52 *Volunteers:* 159
Tel: 01625 612958 *Website:* ageukcheshireeast.org
Activities: General charitable purposes
Address: Age Concern East Cheshire, New Horizons Centre, Henderson Street, Macclesfield, Cheshire, SK11 6RA
Trustees: Mrs Sharon Brearley, Mr Ian Ross, Mrs Genevieve Powrie, Arthur Dicken, Mr Michael Strutt, Ms Tricia Grierson
Income: £1,566,084 [2017]; £1,760,717 [2016]; £1,549,427 [2015]; £1,464,693 [2014]; £1,559,751 [2013]

Age Concern East Sussex
Registered: 22 Dec 2010 *Employees:* 54 *Volunteers:* 194
Tel: 01273 476704 *Website:* ageuk.org.uk
Activities: General charitable purposes
Address: Age Concern, 54 Cliffe High Street, Lewes, E Sussex, BN7 2AN
Trustees: Mr Antony Stephen Caulfield, Mr Ralph Henry Chapman, Ms Pauline Jackson, Ms Joan Winifred Fraser, Ms Rebecca Haywood, Mr John Merchant, Mr Eric William Mayne, Mr Roger Bury Howarth, Ms Susan Hayward, Mr Martin Burke
Income: £2,125,495 [2017]; £1,980,672 [2016]; £1,781,499 [2015]; £1,652,500 [2014]; £1,262,992 [2013]

Age Concern Enfield
Registered: 30 Jul 1997 *Employees:* 54 *Volunteers:* 133
Tel: 020 8373 4120 *Website:* ageuk.org.uk
Activities: General charitable purposes
Address: Ponders End Library, High Street, Enfield, Middlesex, EN3 4EY
Trustees: Mr Enver Cavit Kannur, Miss Ruth Mary Baker, Mrs Sandra Kirwan, Ms Androulla Pallikarou, Mrs Maria Aranjo, Miss Andreea Hausmann, Mr Rasheed Sadegh-Zadeh, Mrs Beryl Antoinette De Souza, Mr John Mitchell Cherry QC, Mrs Jacqueline Frances Wood, Mrs Rasheeda Ali-Selvaratnam
Income: £1,176,974 [2017]; £1,147,375 [2016]; £1,309,806 [2015]; £1,238,180 [2014]; £1,216,429 [2013]

Age Concern Essex
Registered: 12 Mar 2002 *Employees:* 534 *Volunteers:* 338
Website: ageukessex.org.uk
Activities: General charitable purposes; advancement of health or saving of lives; disability; prevention or relief of poverty
Address: Widford Hall, Widford Hall Lane, Chelmsford, Essex, CM2 8TD
Trustees: Mrs Vera Eleanor Sinclair, Mr Christopher Ignatowicz, Mrs Heather Plaxton, Mrs Jill Fletcher, Mr Dan Crease, Mr Peter Bland, Mrs Christine Plampin, Mr Michael Mahoney, Mr Nigel Rodliffe, Mr Christopher Stephen Kelly, Mr Adam Willis, Dr Ann Naylor, Mrs Gabrielle Spray
Income: £4,299,677 [2017]; £4,130,644 [2016]; £3,384,120 [2015]; £3,167,312 [2014]; £2,923,628 [2013]

Age Concern Gloucestershire
Registered: 21 Oct 2005 *Employees:* 40 *Volunteers:* 130
Tel: 01452 422660 *Website:* ageconcernglos.org.uk
Activities: General charitable purposes; education, training; disability; prevention or relief of poverty
Address: Age Concern, 26 Station Road, Gloucester, GL1 1EW
Trustees: Mr Lawrence David Boyd, Mr John Cullen, Mr Christopher John Gardiner, Mr Adam Barry Vines, Mrs Patricia Le Rolland, Ms Eileen Morrison, Mr Alan Charles Machin, Mr Nigel Foster Burton, Ms Sonia Dyer, Mr Tony Hoffman
Income: £1,205,988 [2017]; £1,345,770 [2016]; £1,666,024 [2015]; £1,578,635 [2014]; £1,487,275 [2013]

Age Concern Hampshire
Registered: 22 Jan 1985 *Employees:* 156 *Volunteers:* 420
Tel: 01962 868545 *Website:* ageconcernhampshire.org.uk
Activities: General charitable purposes; education, training; advancement of health or saving of lives; disability; prevention or relief of poverty; accommodation, housing; human rights, religious or racial harmony, equality or diversity; recreation
Address: 2nd Floor, St Georges House, 18 St Georges Street, Winchester, Hants, SO23 8BG
Trustees: Age Concern Hampshire Corporate Trustee Limited
Income: £3,118,256 [2017]; £2,649,694 [2016]; £2,982,648 [2015]; £2,717,983 [2014]; £2,553,444 [2013]

Age Concern Herefordshire & Worcestershire
Registered: 3 May 2000 *Employees:* 91 *Volunteers:* 159
Tel: 01905 740950 *Website:* ageukhw.org.uk
Activities: General charitable purposes; education, training; advancement of health or saving of lives; prevention or relief of poverty; economic, community development, employment
Address: Age Concern Herefordshire & Worcestershire, Malvern Gate, Bromwich Road, Worcester, WR2 4BN
Trustees: Keith Trafford, Mark Richardson, Michael Newitt, Hannah Solway, Eric Brooker, Charlotte Marie Wood, Trish Haines, Robert Rankin, Margaret Wheatley, Matthew Burke, Caroline Irvine
Income: £1,607,248 [2017]; £1,681,215 [2016]; £1,602,777 [2015]; £1,574,991 [2014]; £1,539,471 [2013]

Age Concern Hillingdon
Registered: 4 Jan 1996 *Employees:* 52 *Volunteers:* 330
Tel: 020 8756 3040 *Website:* ageukhillingdon.org.uk
Activities: General charitable purposes; advancement of health or saving of lives; prevention or relief of poverty; arts, culture, heritage, science
Address: Age Concern, Unit 2 Chapel Court, 126 Church Road, Hayes, Middlesex, UB3 2LW
Trustees: Mrs Christine Beatty, Mr Roger Calverley, Mr Neil Frankln, Mr Hiran Weereratne, Mr Anthony Valentine, Mr Ian Edwards, Anne Marie Horgan-Smith, Mrs Raminder Jeet Manget
Income: £1,837,130 [2017]; £1,875,590 [2016]; £2,086,372 [2015]; £1,725,648 [2014]; £1,620,670 [2013]

Age Concern Isle of Wight
Registered: 5 Apr 2007 *Employees:* 139 *Volunteers:* 600
Tel: 01983 525282 *Website:* ageukiw.org.uk
Activities: General charitable purposes; education, training; prevention or relief of poverty; economic, community development, employment
Address: 147 High Street, Newport, Isle of Wight, PO30 1TY
Trustees: Ms Dorothy Moir, Mrs Vilma Barraclough, Mr Edgar Elsom, Mr Richard Evans, Mrs Jane Patterson, Mrs Dawn Eileen Berryman, Mrs Sheila Johnston Evans, Mr Stuart Robert Fraser
Income: £2,344,910 [2017]; £2,397,872 [2016]; £1,219,408 [2015]; £1,188,326 [2014]; £815,056 [2013]

Age Concern Islington
Registered: 6 Apr 1995 *Employees:* 32 *Volunteers:* 100
Tel: 020 7281 6018 *Website:* ageukislington.org.uk
Activities: General charitable purposes; education, training; advancement of health or saving of lives; disability; prevention or relief of poverty; recreation
Address: 6-9 Manor Gardens, London, N7 6LA
Trustees: Ms Kathrin Louise Meyrick, Mr Clive Bowman, Ms Monica Douglas-Parris, Mr Howard Sharman, Mr Chris Bulford, Mr Mark Warwick, Ms Marie Marjorie Thiman, Ms Hilary Nathan
Income: £1,660,799 [2017]; £1,291,677 [2016]; £938,382 [2015]; £889,036 [2014]; £917,914 [2013]

Age Concern Kensington and Chelsea
Registered: 28 Sep 2000 *Employees:* 99 *Volunteers:* 442
Tel: 020 8969 9105 *Website:* aukc.org.uk
Activities: General charitable purposes; education, training; advancement of health or saving of lives; disability; prevention or relief of poverty; arts, culture, heritage, science
Address: 1 Thorpe Close, London, W10 5XL
Trustees: Mrs Christine Vigars, Moya Denman, Martin Pendry, Ms Christine Ann Blewett, Mrs Barbara Ilias, Mrs Susan Cornish, Mr Timothy James Nicholls, Mr John Neville Hilton Cox
Income: £2,586,283 [2017]; £2,343,503 [2016]; £2,221,050 [2015]; £1,561,856 [2014]; £1,409,678 [2013]

Age Concern Kingston upon Thames
Registered: 24 Aug 1988 *Employees:* 106 *Volunteers:* 250
Tel: 020 8942 8256 *Website:* staywellservices.org.uk
Activities: General charitable purposes; disability; prevention or relief of poverty; other charitable purposes
Address: Raleigh House, 14 Nelson Road, New Malden, Surrey, KT3 5EA
Trustees: Mrs Anne Cann, Elizabeth Aitchison, Mr Afzal Ashraf, Mr Rowan Cole, Dr Deborah Stinson
Income: £2,414,718 [2017]; £2,044,402 [2016]; £1,764,011 [2015]; £1,399,731 [2014]; £1,071,377 [2013]

Age Concern Liverpool & Sefton
Registered: 30 Oct 1986 *Employees:* 130 *Volunteers:* 200
Tel: 0151 330 5678 *Website:* ageconcernliverpool.org.uk
Activities: General charitable purposes
Address: Age Concern Liverpool & Sefton, The Poppy Centre, 179 Townsend Lane, Clubmoor, Liverpool, L13 6DY
Trustees: Mrs Elsie Cliff, Ken Ravenscroft, Mr Andrew Booth, Mrs Mary McOnie, Mr Rupert William Whitaker Lowe, Mrs Elizabeth Powell, Mr Roger Pontefract, Mr Keith Cawdron, Mrs Michelle Wood
Income: £2,272,290 [2017]; £2,338,946 [2016]; £2,393,870 [2015]; £1,758,774 [2014]; £2,750,007 [2013]

Age Concern London
Registered: 24 May 2002 *Employees:* 31 *Volunteers:* 8
Tel: 020 7820 6770 *Website:* ageuklondon.org.uk
Activities: General charitable purposes
Address: 6th Floor, Tavis House, 1-6 Tavistock Square, London, WC1H 9NA
Trustees: Mr David Goldsmith, Kate James, Mr John Cole, Ronald Marcus Jacobson, Mr David Muir, Ms Imogen Clark
Income: £1,847,025 [2017]; £1,422,663 [2016]; £1,633,217 [2015]; £1,673,263 [2014]; £1,931,322 [2013]

Age Concern Manchester
Registered: 8 Nov 2000 *Employees:* 212 *Volunteers:* 134
Tel: 0161 817 2351 *Website:* ageuk.org.uk
Activities: General charitable purposes; advancement of health or saving of lives; disability; prevention or relief of poverty; arts, culture, heritage, science; economic, community development, employment
Address: 20 St Ann's Square, Manchester, M2 7HG
Trustees: Dr Sean Lennon, Mr Brian Green, Mr Richard Zoltie, Mr Colin Daniel Fall
Income: £3,528,673 [2017]; £3,454,364 [2016]; £3,663,422 [2015]; £3,561,704 [2014]; £3,384,386 [2013]

Age Concern Mid Mersey
Registered: 19 Jul 1991 *Employees:* 48 *Volunteers:* 181
Tel: 01744 752644 *Website:* ageuk.org.uk
Activities: General charitable purposes; education, training; disability; prevention or relief of poverty; arts, culture, heritage, science; economic, community development, employment; other charitable purposes
Address: Mansion House, Victoria Park, City Road, St Helens, Merseyside, WA10 2UE
Trustees: Prof Michael Thomas BSc MA, Mr John Chapman, Dr Ivan Camphor, Mr Peter Stubbs, Mr Raymond Travies, Ms Denny Balmer, Mrs Susan Haden
Income: £1,206,476 [2017]; £1,243,426 [2016]; £2,534,356 [2015]; £1,442,249 [2014]; £1,251,339 [2013]

Age Concern Newcastle upon Tyne
Registered: 22 Sep 1994 *Employees:* 111 *Volunteers:* 200
Tel: 0191 255 7000
Activities: General charitable purposes; prevention or relief of poverty
Address: RSM, 1 St James Gate, Newcastle upon Tyne, NE1 4AD
Trustees: Mrs Veena Soni, Mary Nicholls, John Peacock, Prof Philip Thomas, Barry Speker, Mr Mark Curry, Jo Geary, Ms Charlotte Carpenter
Income: £2,030,213 [2016]; £2,755,866 [2015]; £2,845,831 [2014]; £2,814,877 [2013]

Age Concern Norfolk
Registered: 20 Aug 1999 *Employees:* 139 *Volunteers:* 283
Tel: 01603 787111 *Website:* ageuk.org.uk
Activities: Education, training; advancement of health or saving of lives; disability; prevention or relief of poverty; economic, community development, employment
Address: 300 St Faiths Road, Old Catton, Norwich, NR6 7BJ
Trustees: Mr Stephen Bernard Burke, Mrs Helen Mary Jones, Mr Paul Stephen Slyfield, Roy Stanley Dickinson, Mr Surjait Malhi Singh, Judith Mary Garvey, Mr Jeffrey Prosser, Mr Stephen Drake, Graham Robinson, Judith Ann Wildig, David John Stonehouse
Income: £2,714,559 [2017]; £2,720,706 [2016]; £3,074,969 [2015]; £3,267,302 [2014]; £3,096,693 [2013]

Age Concern Salford
Registered: 7 Sep 2004 *Employees:* 73 *Volunteers:* 51
Tel: 0161 788 7300 *Website:* ageconcernsalford.org.uk
Activities: General charitable purposes
Address: 108 Church Street, Eccles, Manchester, M30 0LH
Trustees: Mr Haydn Worrall, Mrs Christine Hudson, Mr Bob Boyd, Ms Elaine Kenney, Mr Norman Owen, Mr Alan Clague, Mr Peter Griffin, Eve Murphy, Mr Ken Whittick
Income: £1,252,026 [2017]; £1,261,770 [2016]; £1,255,077 [2015]; £1,150,791 [2014]; £1,313,222 [2013]

Age Concern Slough and Berkshire East
Registered: 22 Mar 2000 *Employees:* 59 *Volunteers:* 310
Tel: 01753 497888 *Website:* ageconcernsabe.org.uk
Activities: General charitable purposes; education, training; advancement of health or saving of lives; disability; prevention or relief of poverty; economic, community development, employment; human rights, religious or racial harmony, equality or diversity; other charitable purposes
Address: The Village, 102-110 High Street, Slough, Berks, SL1 1HL
Trustees: Mr Raj Dhokia, Mr Antony Cannings, Mr Gregory Ian Sinclair, Ms Paula Grevett, Mr Gareth Pountain, Mr Bharat Bhushan Mittal
Income: £2,089,070 [2017]; £2,870,291 [2016]; £3,258,776 [2015]; £3,530,137 [2014]; £2,767,003 [2013]

Age Concern Solihull

Registered: 5 Jun 1996 *Employees:* 77 *Volunteers:* 325
Tel: 0121 704 7840 *Website:* ageuksolihull.org.uk
Activities: General charitable purposes
Address: Age UK Solihull, The Core, Central Library Building, Solihull, W Midlands, B91 3RG
Trustees: David Mattocks JP, Peter Oakley JP, Allan Steer, David Bowyer, Sally Tomlinson, Nicola Robinson, Eric Bourne JP, John Baynton, Salim Ahmed, Mark Way, Amanda Copsey
Income: £1,384,212 [2017]; £1,347,215 [2016]; £1,376,874 [2015]; £1,090,955 [2014]; £1,107,810 [2013]

Age Concern Tyneside South

Registered: 17 Aug 2016 *Employees:* 36 *Volunteers:* 93
Tel: 0191 456 6903 *Website:* ageconcerntynesidesouth.org.uk
Activities: General charitable purposes; education, training; advancement of health or saving of lives; disability; prevention or relief of poverty
Address: Age Concern, 29 Beach Road, South Shields, Tyne & Wear, NE33 2QU
Trustees: Mr Ian Johnson, Mr Joseph Edward Tiernan, Cameron Ward, Mrs Helen Louise Tranter, Mr Steven Peter Duckworth, Mr Raymond Staward
Income: £1,289,710 [2017]

Age Concern Wigan Borough

Registered: 2 Apr 2004 *Employees:* 63 *Volunteers:* 90
Tel: 01942 241972 *Website:* ageuk.org.uk
Activities: Education, training; prevention or relief of poverty; amateur sport; economic, community development, employment
Address: Age Concern, Pennyhurst Mill, Haig Street, Wigan, Lancs, WN3 4AZ
Trustees: Mr Bryan Shepherd, Mr Matthew Thomas Hothersall, Mr Reginald William Nash, Mr James Walton Maloney, Lady Joy Lesley Smith BSc, Dr Bridget Diann Whittell
Income: £1,111,026 [2017]; £1,127,587 [2016]; £1,149,669 [2015]; £1,031,673 [2014]; £1,081,026 [2013]

Age Concern Wirral

Registered: 4 Mar 1994 *Employees:* 119 *Volunteers:* 703
Tel: 0151 653 4404 *Website:* ageukwirral.org.uk
Activities: General charitable purposes; advancement of health or saving of lives
Address: The Devonshire Resource Centre, 141 Park Road North, Birkenhead, Wirral, Merseyside, CH41 0DD
Trustees: Mr Michael Anthony Jones, Mrs Ruth Rogers, Mr Keith Andrew Bailey, Mr Brian Lawrence Williams, Mrs Patricia Crocker, Mr Russell Steven Beddoe, Dr George Kerr Rennie, Mr Paul Smith, Frances Elizabeth White, Mr Malcolm Pimbley
Income: £2,601,922 [2017]; £2,717,975 [2016]; £2,834,434 [2015]; £2,572,120 [2014]; £2,788,855 [2013]

Age Concern York

Registered: 13 Mar 2007 *Employees:* 117 *Volunteers:* 400
Tel: 01904 627995 *Website:* ageukyork.org.uk
Activities: General charitable purposes; disability
Address: Age Concern, 70 Walmgate, York, YO1 9TL
Trustees: Dr Rosemary Jennifer Suttill, Dr Helen Vos, Mr Gareth Alan Wigdahl, Mr Derek Bottomley, Mrs Hilary Henderson
Income: £1,538,765 [2017]; £1,265,504 [2016]; £1,127,891 [2015]; £1,089,019 [2014]; £1,015,437 [2013]

Age Concern in Cornwall and The Isles of Scilly

Registered: 12 Jul 1990 *Employees:* 71 *Volunteers:* 620
Tel: 01872 266388 *Website:* ageukcornwall.org.uk
Activities: General charitable purposes; other charitable purposes
Address: Boscawen House, Chapel Hill, Truro, Cornwall, TR1 3BN
Trustees: Mrs Val Jenner, Mrs Sarah Painter, Mr Mike Smith, Ms Louise Southwell, Mrs Sarah Hancock, Kate Gammon, Mr Arthur Nicholls, Mr Andrew Burdall, Mrs Margaret Ford, Mr Ivan Perry, Mr Colin Garrick
Income: £3,181,253 [2017]; £3,545,001 [2016]; £3,401,771 [2015]; £3,482,946 [2014]; £2,714,192 [2013]

Age Cymru Gwent

Registered: 21 Feb 2014 *Employees:* 120 *Volunteers:* 110
Tel: 01633 763330 *Website:* agecymrugwent.org
Activities: General charitable purposes; advancement of health or saving of lives; disability; prevention or relief of poverty
Address: 12 Baneswell Road, Newport, NP20 4BP
Trustees: Mr Philip Brabon, Mr Clifford Edwards, Mrs Susan Elizabeth Gregory, Mr William John Hudson Clark, Mr John Rogers, Mr John Arthur Grimes, Dr Carolyn Ann Wallace, Mr Lyn Morgan James, Mrs Betsi Knight
Income: £1,721,208 [2017]; £1,970,585 [2016]; £2,332,084 [2015]

Age Cymru Gwynedd A Mon

Registered: 30 Aug 2011 *Employees:* 61 *Volunteers:* 170
Tel: 01286 677711 *Website:* agecymrugwyneddamon.co.uk
Activities: General charitable purposes; disability; prevention or relief of poverty; economic, community development, employment; recreation
Address: Age Cymru, Gwynedd A Mon, Ty Seiont, Ffordd Santes Helen, Caernarfon, Gwynedd, LL55 2YD
Trustees: Mr Dafydd Iwan, Mr Robert Cledwyn Williams Cledwyn, Mr Gwilym Ellis Evans Gwilym, Mr V Wynne Williams, Mrs Meinir Owen, Mr Alwyn Jones Alwyn, Anwen Hughes, Mr John Pritchard
Income: £1,224,233 [2017]; £944,385 [2016]; £914,482 [2015]; £941,337 [2014]; £946,850 [2013]

Age Cymru Swansea Bay Limited

Registered: 29 Mar 2011 *Employees:* 50 *Volunteers:* 70
Tel: 01792 641164 *Website:* agecymruswanseabay.org.uk
Activities: General charitable purposes
Address: Age Cymru Swansea Bay, Ty Davies, Tawe Business Village, Swansea Enterprise Park, Swansea, SA7 9LA
Trustees: Professor Dame June Clark, Mr Craig Lawton, Mrs Caroline Byrt, Mr Melvyn Clifford Rayner
Income: £1,481,169 [2017]; £1,236,215 [2016]; £1,183,793 [2015]; £3,002,076 [2014]; £1,195,936 [2013]

Age Cymru

Registered: 5 Mar 2009 *Employees:* 62 *Volunteers:* 151
Website: agecymru.org.uk
Activities: Education, training; advancement of health or saving of lives; disability; prevention or relief of poverty; arts, culture, heritage, science; human rights, religious or racial harmony, equality or diversity
Address: 93 Harriet Street, Cardiff, CF24 4BX
Trustees: Mr Lyn James, Mr Keith Martin Jones, Mr Peter John Hamilton, Mr Desmond Perkins, Ms Margaret Hewlett, Mr Hugh Irwin, Ms Sian Callaghan, Mr Steven George Milsom, Mr Stephen Findlay-Saunders, Miss Maria Jeanne Coggins
Income: £2,914,122 [2017]; £3,850,173 [2016]; £4,117,370 [2015]; £3,319,501 [2014]; £3,139,707 [2013]

Age UK Barnet
Registered: 26 Apr 2000 Employees: 28 Volunteers: 180
Tel: 020 8368 0059 Website: ageukbarnet.org.uk
Activities: General charitable purposes
Address: 37 Brunswick Grove, London, N11 1ED
Trustees: Mr Dale Bevington, Mr Jonathan Gabriel Fenton, Mr Peter Falk, Dr Catherine Loveday, Mr Martin Benton, Ms Lynette Ruth Webb
Income: £1,000,477 [2017]; £1,011,945 [2016]; £935,329 [2015]; £854,569 [2014]; £663,624 [2013]

Age UK Birmingham Limited
Registered: 4 Oct 2010 Employees: 37 Volunteers: 117
Tel: 0121 437 0033 Website: ageukbirmingham.org.uk
Activities: General charitable purposes; advancement of health or saving of lives; disability; prevention or relief of poverty; accommodation, housing
Address: Age UK, 55 Alcester Road South, Birmingham, B14 7JG
Trustees: Mr Peter Cornell, Mr Gary Stephen Allmark, Mr Bruce Moore, Mr John Ellis, Mrs Sarah A Elizabeth Phillips MBE, Dr Rashda Tabassum
Income: £1,310,807 [2017]; £1,087,575 [2016]; £1,007,830 [2015]; £1,048,630 [2014]; £1,044,638 [2013]

Age UK Blackburn with Darwen
Registered: 15 Sep 2011 Employees: 44 Volunteers: 114
Tel: 01254 266620 Website: ageukbwd.org.uk
Activities: General charitable purposes; education, training; disability; prevention or relief of poverty; recreation
Address: Age UK, 4 King Street, Blackburn, BB2 2DH
Trustees: Mrs Marion Ramsbottom, Mr Ian Woolley, Mr Christopher John Porter, Mr Faizal Patel, Mr Peter Watkins, Mrs Judith Isherwood, Mr John Leonard Thomas, Mr Anthony Hedley
Income: £1,077,187 [2017]; £1,313,016 [2016]; £1,432,086 [2015]; £1,234,746 [2014]; £1,104,919 [2013]

Age UK Bradford & District
Registered: 13 Sep 1993 Employees: 55 Volunteers: 410
Tel: 01274 395144 Website: ageuk.org.uk
Activities: Education, training; advancement of health or saving of lives; prevention or relief of poverty; arts, culture, heritage, science; economic, community development, employment
Address: 13 Sunbridge Road, Bradford, BD1 2AY
Trustees: Mr Jonathan Wright, Joan Robertshaw, Mrs Sharon Wears, Mr Akhtar Malik, Mrs Pamela James, Mr Neal Heard, Mrs Penny Coulthard, Masoud Khan
Income: £1,412,132 [2017]; £1,357,113 [2016]; £1,310,074 [2015]; £1,446,863 [2014]; £1,310,679 [2013]

Age UK Brighton & Hove
Registered: 11 Jun 2014 Employees: 61 Volunteers: 90
Tel: 01273 720603 Website: ageuk-bh.org.uk
Activities: Education, training; advancement of health or saving of lives; prevention or relief of poverty
Address: Age UK, 29-31 Prestonville Road, Brighton, BN1 3TJ
Trustees: Linda Dyos, Mr Simon Dowe, Ms Linda Hawkins, Christopher Heathcote, Amanda Latham, Mr Ben Smitton, Mehvish Durrani, Mr Peter James Worster, Ms Karin Divall
Income: £1,271,118 [2017]; £2,629,194 [2016]

Age UK Bristol
Registered: 6 Dec 1994 Employees: 32 Volunteers: 53
Tel: 0117 928 1547 Website: ageukbristol.org.uk
Activities: General charitable purposes
Address: Age UK Bristol, Canningford House, 38 Victoria Street, Bristol, BS1 6BY
Trustees: Mrs Susan Mary Perry, Mrs Joan Robertson Cox, Mr Peter Scott, Mr Alan Paul Carpenter, Mina Elizabeth Malpass, Mr Hung-Yuan Cheng, Mr Geoffrey Clements, Dr Graham Pegg, Mrs Patricia Robinson, Ms Omobola Adeola Olatunde, Mr Karl Ashley Jones, Caroline Adriana Jane Bolhoven
Income: £1,464,133 [2017]; £1,041,375 [2016]; £758,322 [2015]; £752,348 [2014]; £731,336 [2013]

Age UK Calderdale & Kirklees
Registered: 10 Feb 2004 Employees: 140 Volunteers: 130
Website: ageuk.org.uk
Activities: General charitable purposes
Address: 4-6 Square, Woolshops, Halifax, W Yorks, HX1 1RJ
Trustees: Mrs Angela Kathryn Riley, Mr Mike Walker, Mr Anthony John Hillyard, Lis Boulton, Mr Anthony Flowers, Mrs Stacey Martine Porter, Mr William Andrew Waite BComm, Mr Michael Felton, Mrs Susan Ellis, Mr Peter Spark, Mrs Lorraine Hill, Mrs Catherine Smyth
Income: £2,222,944 [2017]; £2,354,129 [2016]; £2,134,336 [2015]; £2,238,424 [2014]; £2,258,139 [2013]

Age UK Cambridgeshire and Peterborough
Registered: 3 Mar 2016 Employees: 171 Volunteers: 510
Tel: 01354 691895
Activities: General charitable purposes; disability; prevention or relief of poverty
Address: AgeUK Cambridgeshire & Peterborough, 2 Victoria Street, Chatteris, Cambs, PE16 6AP
Trustees: Hazel Williams, David Bruch, Mr John Holdich, Clive Adkin, Mr Yusufali Bandali, Mr Jeremy Alexander, Mr Peter Clements, Mr Michael Bond, Mr Brian Parsons, Mrs Alison Reid, Adrian Kirby
Income: £2,919,793 [2017]

Age UK Coventry
Registered: 21 Feb 2003 Employees: 74 Volunteers: 412
Website: ageukcoventry.org.uk
Activities: General charitable purposes
Address: 15 River Drive, Atherstone, Warwicks, CV9 3SR
Trustees: Mr Harry Hall, Moira Coates, Margaret Egrot, Mr Graham Barnetson, Mr Roger Wagstaff, Mr Laurence Tennant, Ms Parmjeet Jassal
Income: £2,163,811 [2017]; £1,951,733 [2016]; £1,653,140 [2015]; £1,654,764 [2014]; £1,450,708 [2013]

Age UK Croydon
Registered: 2 Jun 2000 Employees: 86 Volunteers: 79
Tel: 020 8683 7100 Website: ageukcroydon.org.uk
Activities: General charitable purposes
Address: 81 Brigstock Road, Thornton Heath, Surrey, CR7 7JH
Trustees: Ms Brenda Scanlan, Mrs Samantha Kismet Naraine, Robert Silk, Mrs Patricia Robinson, Mr Oumaduth Sauba, Ms Deborah McCluskey, Mrs Nicole Harris, Mrs Bushra Ahmed, Miss Philippa Brooks, Mrs Victoria Emily Trevillion
Income: £1,569,872 [2017]; £1,090,210 [2016]; £972,856 [2015]; £725,420 [2014]; £631,489 [2013]

Age UK Derby & Derbyshire
Registered: 11 Mar 1998 *Employees:* 71 *Volunteers:* 200
Tel: 01773 768240 *Website:* ageuk.org.uk
Activities: General charitable purposes
Address: 29A Market Place, Heanor, Derbys, DE75 7EG
Trustees: Mrs Alison Johnson, Ms Lynda Done, Mrs Hilary Campbell, Mr James Matthews, Mr Clive Newton, Mr David Brown, Mr John Holdridge
Income: £1,712,069 [2017]; £1,337,158 [2016]; £1,362,009 [2015]; £1,335,166 [2014]; £1,378,191 [2013]

Age UK Doncaster
Registered: 9 Sep 1999 *Employees:* 131 *Volunteers:* 40
Tel: 01302 812345 *Website:* ageuk.org.uk
Activities: General charitable purposes
Address: Age UK Doncaster, Unit 1, Ten Pound Walk, Doncaster, S Yorks, DN4 5HX
Trustees: Sarah Rogerson, Mrs Daphne Yolander Richards, Christine Ellingworth, Mrs Gail Margaret Stafford, Dr Lis Rodgers, Mr Anthony Hudson
Income: £1,750,759 [2017]; £1,736,804 [2016]; £1,616,670 [2015]; £1,748,090 [2014]; £2,164,043 [2013]

Age UK East London
Registered: 4 Nov 2011 *Employees:* 91 *Volunteers:* 232
Tel: 020 8981 7124 *Website:* ageuk.org.uk
Activities: Education, training; advancement of health or saving of lives; disability; prevention or relief of poverty; human rights, religious or racial harmony, equality or diversity
Address: Age UK, 82 Russia Lane, London, E2 9LU
Trustees: Mr Andrew Bassett Phillips, Mr Glyn Kyle, Mrs Lucy Bracken, Miss Emma Catherine Whitby, Miss Fiona Speak, Mr Mark Ian Harvey, Mr Kevin Rigg, Dr Mary Flatley, Ms Rosanna Clare Hardwick
Income: £1,968,827 [2017]; £2,135,548 [2016]; £1,633,459 [2015]; £1,469,245 [2014]; £1,705,484 [2013]

Age UK Exeter
Registered: 7 May 1992 *Employees:* 49 *Volunteers:* 340
Tel: 01392 202092 *Website:* ageukexeter.org.uk
Activities: General charitable purposes; advancement of health or saving of lives; disability; prevention or relief of poverty; arts, culture, heritage, science; amateur sport
Address: Age Concern, 138 Cowick Street, Exeter, EX4 1HS
Trustees: Dr John Vincent, Dr Vaughan Pearce, John Cartridge, Mrs Lesley Robson, Mrs Margaret Clark, Ms Kay Eldergill, Dr Gillian Mary Fenwick, Mr Norman Shiel, Mr Richard Halstead, Mr Tim Borton, Rachael Whitson
Income: £1,388,209 [2017]; £2,029,750 [2016]; £1,381,630 [2015]; £1,241,400 [2014]; £1,188,567 [2013]

Age UK Faversham and Sittingbourne
Registered: 31 May 2013 *Employees:* 115 *Volunteers:* 70
Tel: 01227 749570 *Website:* ageukfaversham.org.uk
Activities: General charitable purposes; prevention or relief of poverty
Address: Age UK Herne Bay, 16 Reculver Road, Herne Bay, Kent, CT6 6LE
Trustees: Ted Wilcox, Mrs Rosemary Madgwick, Tony Mogridge, Mr David North, Pam Brookes, Doreen Shaw, Miss Louise Wilson
Income: £1,776,736 [2017]; £1,873,909 [2016]; £1,851,468 [2015]; £2,189,806 [2014]

Age UK Hertfordshire
Registered: 7 Nov 2006 *Employees:* 402 *Volunteers:* 528
Tel: 01707 323272 *Website:* ageuk.org.uk
Activities: General charitable purposes
Address: Age UK Hertfordshire, 1 Silver Court, Watchmead, Welwyn Garden City, Herts, AL7 1LT
Trustees: Ms Penny Butler, Mr John Newman, Mr Subhash Bakhai, Mr Paul Neale, Ms Maria Ball, Mr Johnson Wong, Mr John Ellis, Mr Glenn Taylor
Income: £3,383,044 [2017]; £3,237,527 [2016]; £3,294,192 [2015]; £3,834,156 [2014]; £2,810,360 [2013]

Age UK Lambeth
Registered: 18 Jul 1997 *Employees:* 24 *Volunteers:* 181
Tel: 020 7733 0528 *Website:* ageuklambeth.org.uk
Activities: General charitable purposes
Address: Third Floor, 336 Brixton Road, London, SW9 7AA
Trustees: Diana Kahn, Kate Woollcombe, Katie Stone, Mr Owen Davies, Mr Bernard Nawrat, Carolyn Cripps OBE, Mr Yawar Choudhry, Lisa Hoong, Mr Colin Adamson
Income: £1,464,847 [2017]; £1,461,993 [2016]; £976,512 [2015]; £1,265,575 [2014]; £1,333,560 [2013]

Age UK Lancashire
Registered: 7 Jun 2011 *Employees:* 198 *Volunteers:* 800
Website: ageuklancs.org.uk
Activities: General charitable purposes; advancement of health or saving of lives; prevention or relief of poverty
Address: Suite 22, Railway House, Railway Road, Chorley, Lancs, PR6 0HW
Trustees: Mr David Acklam, Mr David Clifford Baker, Mr Jonathan Ashworth Lenney, Ms Vivien Mumford, Julie Diane Edmonds, Mr Mark Johnson
Income: £3,704,099 [2017]; £4,327,440 [2016]; £5,043,698 [2015]; £5,233,212 [2014]; £5,116,095 [2013]

Age UK Leeds
Registered: 13 Feb 1976 *Employees:* 51 *Volunteers:* 55
Website: ageukleeds.org.uk
Activities: General charitable purposes
Address: Rumples Croft, Lower Brockholes, Halifax, W Yorks, HX2 8XQ
Trustees: Mr Thomas Wade Morrish, Aisha Butt, Mr Dennis Patrick Holmes, Mrs Holly Smith, Barry Seal, Indra Barathan, Mrs Janet Marian Fletcher
Income: £1,392,385 [2017]; £1,284,669 [2016]; £1,078,007 [2015]; £907,968 [2014]; £771,545 [2013]

Age UK Leicester Shire & Rutland Home Help Limited
Registered: 31 May 2001 *Employees:* 113
Tel: 07971 453113 *Website:* ageukleics.org.uk
Activities: General charitable purposes
Address: 39 Lychgate Close, Burbage, Hinckley, Leics, LE10 2ES
Trustees: Margaret Watts, Barbara Freestone, David Hodgen, Mr Malcolm Lindsey, Mr Graham Andrew Frank Smith, Dr Neil Kilpatrick, Dr Narayanasamy Vijayakumar, Mr David Illingworth, Bernard Greaves, Mr Christopher Saul, Mrs Gillian Ruth Austen, Mr Simon Lindley, Mr Paul Richards, Dr Peter George Neville, Mr Stephen Hunt
Income: £1,344,379 [2017]; £1,169,331 [2016]; £1,190,633 [2015]; £1,758,141 [2014]; £1,380,079 [2013]

Age UK Leicester Shire and Rutland Limited
Registered: 28 Mar 2012 *Employees:* 402 *Volunteers:* 1,100
Tel: 0116 299 2245 *Website:* ageukleics.org.uk
Activities: Education, training; advancement of health or saving of lives; disability; prevention or relief of poverty; human rights, religious or racial harmony, equality or diversity; recreation
Address: Age UK Leicestershire & Rutland, Lansdowne House, 113 Princess Road East, Leicester, LE1 7LA
Trustees: Ms Margaret Watts, Mr Christopher Saul, Mrs Gillian Ruth Austen, Mr Simon Richard Lindley, Mr Graham Smith, Dr Neil Kilpatrick, Dr Narayanasamy Vijayakumar, Mr David Illingworth, Mr Bernard Greaves, Mr David Robert Hodgen, Mr Malcolm Lindsey, Mr Paul Richards, Mrs Barbara Freestone, Dr Peter George Neville, Mr Stephen Hunt
Income: £7,493,597 [2017]; £7,502,772 [2016]; £7,892,292 [2015]; £8,176,777 [2014]; £3,669,276 [2013]

Age UK Lewisham and Southwark
Registered: 12 Jun 1987 *Employees:* 81 *Volunteers:* 200
Tel: 020 7701 9700 *Website:* ageuklands.org.uk
Activities: General charitable purposes; advancement of health or saving of lives; disability; prevention or relief of poverty; overseas aid, famine relief; religious activities; human rights, religious or racial harmony, equality or diversity
Address: Stones End Day Centre, 11 Scovell Road, London, SE1 1QQ
Trustees: Mr Leon Kreitzman, John Hodgett, Mr John Veness, Mr Ray Boyce, Mr Connor Mark Lambourne, Miss Caroline Brown, Ms Marcia Purnell, Ms Miny Jansen, Ms Irene Payne, Mr Rowan Charles Benoit Adams, Ms Sharron Nestor
Income: £2,210,817 [2017]; £2,296,024 [2016]; £1,912,141 [2015]; £1,820,918 [2014]; £1,191,316 [2013]

Age UK Lincoln and Kesteven
Registered: 10 Dec 1999 *Employees:* 146 *Volunteers:* 200
Tel: 01522 696000 *Website:* ageuklincoln.org.uk
Activities: General charitable purposes; education, training; disability; prevention or relief of poverty; arts, culture, heritage, science; amateur sport
Address: Age UK Lincoln, 36 Park Street, Lincoln, LN1 1UQ
Trustees: Mrs Patricia Parker, Mr Brian Cropley, Mr Richard Hare, Mr Herman Kok, Councillor Clive Ronald Oxby, Mr Stewart Featherby, Mrs Jasmit Phull, Ms Alison Hurton
Income: £3,715,070 [2017]; £4,084,438 [2016]; £4,011,148 [2015]; £2,611,375 [2014]; £2,375,106 [2013]

Age UK Lindsey
Registered: 3 Mar 2000 *Employees:* 148 *Volunteers:* 120
Tel: 01507 524242 *Website:* ageuk.org.uk
Activities: General charitable purposes; advancement of health or saving of lives; disability; prevention or relief of poverty
Address: Age UK Lindsey, The Old School House, Manor House Street, Horncastle, Lincs, LN9 5HF
Trustees: Canon John Thorold, Ms Rose Dobbs, Mrs Claire Parker, Mr Paul Steiger, Mr Owen Bierley, Mr Hugh Thomson, Mr Graham Marsh
Income: £1,139,777 [2017]; £1,198,307 [2016]; £1,254,616 [2015]; £1,271,860 [2014]; £1,263,443 [2013]

Age UK Maidstone
Registered: 6 Jun 1997 *Employees:* 67 *Volunteers:* 150
Tel: 01622 753618 *Website:* ageuk.org.uk
Activities: General charitable purposes
Address: 7 Mill Street, Maidstone, Kent, ME15 6XW
Trustees: Mrs Carol Vizzard, Mr Michael Yates, Mr Bryan Vizzard, Mr Arif Shivji, Mr James Owen, Mrs Kim Bannister, Mr Ken Hesketh
Income: £1,104,019 [2017]; £1,063,265 [2016]; £1,150,536 [2015]; £1,113,845 [2014]; £967,279 [2013]

Age UK Medway
Registered: 1 Dec 2009 *Employees:* 112 *Volunteers:* 120
Tel: 01634 572616 *Website:* ageuk.org
Activities: General charitable purposes; advancement of health or saving of lives; prevention or relief of poverty; other charitable purposes
Address: The Admirals Offices, Main Gate Road, Chatham Historic Dockyard, Chatham, Kent, ME4 4TZ
Trustees: Susan Robinson, Mr Terry Reginald Lucy, Mr Robert Wilson, Mrs Tania Blackmore, Mrs Julia Burton-Jones, Mrs Ann West, Mr Alan John Bates, Mrs Katrina Festorazzi, Ms Karen Williams, Mrs Sarah Llewellyn
Income: £2,145,824 [2017]; £1,982,194 [2016]; £2,024,039 [2015]; £1,726,261 [2014]; £1,432,470 [2013]

Age UK Milton Keynes
Registered: 9 Mar 2000 *Employees:* 69 *Volunteers:* 513
Tel: 01908 550700 *Website:* ageukmiltonkeynes.org.uk
Activities: General charitable purposes
Address: The Peartree Centre, 1 Chadds Lane, Peartree Bridge, Milton Keynes, Bucks, MK6 3EB
Trustees: Mrs Meg Bates, Mr John David Goodman, Mr Peter James Lazard, Mr Stewart Robert Jones, Jan McMeekin, Mrs Diana Surtees Payne, Miss Susan Joy Graham, Dr Anthony Watson, Mrs Janet Deeley, Mr Michael Malget
Income: £2,217,242 [2017]; £2,222,988 [2016]; £2,340,189 [2015]; £2,361,582 [2014]; £2,744,917 [2013]

Age UK North Tyneside
Registered: 3 Oct 1995 *Employees:* 275 *Volunteers:* 217
Tel: 0191 280 8484 *Website:* ageuk.org.uk
Activities: General charitable purposes
Address: Bradbury Centre, 13 Saville Street West, North Shields, Tyne & Wear, NE29 6QP
Trustees: Mr Bob Morton Chartered Accountant, Mrs Carole Pitkeathley, Ms Tracy Harrison, Mr William John Booth, Mr Christopher Swan, Mr Richard Adams Chair Person, Mr David Sharp, William Carr, Miss Julie Gillson
Income: £4,733,668 [2017]; £4,469,682 [2016]; £4,480,000 [2015]; £4,332,000 [2014]; £4,201,992 [2013]

Age UK North West Kent
Registered: 22 Sep 2011 *Employees:* 89 *Volunteers:* 45
Tel: 01474 564898 *Website:* ageuk.org.uk
Activities: General charitable purposes; advancement of health or saving of lives; disability; prevention or relief of poverty; recreation; other charitable purposes
Address: The Fleming Resource Centre, Clarence Row, Gravesend, Kent, DA12 1HJ
Trustees: Mr M J Munn, Mr John Hill, Miss Julie Hall, Mrs Jan Elizabeth Stanton, Mr Graham John Cole, Mrs Ann Allen, Mr John Burden, Mrs Elizabeth Agnes Haggart, Mr Anthony Roy Pritchard
Income: £1,385,873 [2017]; £1,386,241 [2016]; £1,379,888 [2015]; £1,341,529 [2014]; £1,266,820 [2013]

Age UK Northamptonshire

Registered: 13 Jan 1997 *Employees:* 127 *Volunteers:* 555
Tel: 01604 611200 *Website:* ageuk.org.uk
Activities: General charitable purposes; education, training; advancement of health or saving of lives; disability; prevention or relief of poverty; accommodation, housing
Address: Age Concern, Upton House, 31 Billing Road, Northampton, NN1 5DQ
Trustees: Mr Anthony Douglas Lainsbury, Mr Peter Newham, Mr Andrew Graham Rees, Mrs Julia Faulkner, Mr Robert Wootton, Mrs Anne Goodman MBE, Mr Clive Richard Dobbs, Mrs Lee Mason, Dr Ann Judith Robinson, Mrs Jackie Haynes, Mr Barry Lilley
Income: £4,027,457 [2017]; £4,426,749 [2016]; £3,439,032 [2015]; £3,498,711 [2014]; £3,242,523 [2013]

Age UK Northumberland

Registered: 11 Nov 1998 *Employees:* 287 *Volunteers:* 200
Tel: 01670 784800 *Website:* ageuk-northumberland.org.uk
Activities: General charitable purposes; education, training
Address: Age UK, The Round House, Lintonville Parkway, Ashington, Northumberland, NE63 9JZ
Trustees: Mr Ralph Firth, Mr Parry Jenkins, Mr George Brown Hall, Miss Antonia Sintra Brindle, Ms Patricia Jane Grahamslaw, Mr Andrew Alexander Marsh, Ms Sophie Clare Milliken, Mrs Anu Kaura, Mr Graeme Martin James
Income: £5,407,416 [2017]; £5,031,943 [2016]; £4,919,200 [2015]; £5,057,625 [2014]; £5,488,009 [2013]

Age UK Nottingham and Nottinghamshire

Registered: 30 Jan 1998 *Employees:* 68 *Volunteers:* 337
Tel: 0115 844 0011 *Website:* ageuknotts.org.uk
Activities: General charitable purposes; education, training; advancement of health or saving of lives; disability; prevention or relief of poverty; other charitable purposes
Address: Age UK Nottingham & Nottinghamshire, Bradbury House, 12 Shakespeare Street, Nottingham, NG1 4FQ
Trustees: Mr Nigel Cullen Solicitor, Mrs Sandra Warzynska, Mr Michael Williamson, Mrs Jacqueline Louise Lewis LLB Hons, Dr Graham Cox, Mr Anil Ghelani, Mr Brian Burdus, Mr Leonard Christopher Simmonds, Mr Terence Thomas Brown
Income: £3,045,254 [2017]; £2,983,647 [2016]; £2,839,040 [2015]; £2,846,764 [2014]; £3,247,688 [2013]

Age UK Oldham Limited

Registered: 21 Dec 2011 *Employees:* 107 *Volunteers:* 350
Tel: 0161 633 0213 *Website:* ageuk.org.uk
Activities: General charitable purposes; advancement of health or saving of lives; prevention or relief of poverty; arts, culture, heritage, science
Address: Age UK Oldham, 10 Church Lane, Oldham, Lancs, OL1 3AN
Trustees: Mr Alex Boyd, Mrs Jill Read, Mr John Thomson, Mrs Zoe Ashton, Ms Jennifer White, Mr Stuart Bailey, Mr Clint Edward Elliott
Income: £2,548,832 [2017]; £2,524,374 [2016]; £2,201,206 [2015]; £2,488,501 [2014]; £1,978,825 [2013]

Age UK Oxfordshire

Registered: 5 Apr 2002 *Employees:* 160 *Volunteers:* 345
Tel: 0345 450 1276 *Website:* ageuk.org.uk
Activities: General charitable purposes; education, training; advancement of health or saving of lives; disability; prevention or relief of poverty; arts, culture, heritage, science; amateur sport; economic, community development, employment
Address: 9 Napier Court, Barton Lane, Abingdon, Oxon, OX14 3YT
Trustees: Mrs Davina Jessie Logan, Miss Sara Fernandez, Dr Stuart William Herbertson, Mr Adam Ogilvie-Smith, Mr David Patrick Ryan, Mr Niven Greenhalf, Dr Judith Frances Wardle, Esther Jackson, Ms Kerry Rogers, Miss Amber Pavey
Income: £2,919,944 [2017]; £3,978,256 [2016]; £2,618,191 [2015]; £2,330,341 [2014]; £2,988,204 [2013]

Age UK Portsmouth

Registered: 31 Dec 1996 *Employees:* 84 *Volunteers:* 83
Tel: 023 9286 2121 *Website:* ageukportsmouth.org.uk
Activities: General charitable purposes; education, training; advancement of health or saving of lives; prevention or relief of poverty; arts, culture, heritage, science; amateur sport; other charitable purposes
Address: Age UK Portsmouth, The Bradbury Centre, 16-18 Kingston Road, Portsmouth, PO1 5RZ
Trustees: Mrs Jean Evans, Mrs Margaret Geary, Mr Timothy Ian Gamester, Reverend Bob White, Mr Thomas Jack, Mr Paul Hummel-Newell
Income: £1,030,602 [2017]; £976,652 [2016]; £954,521 [2015]; £708,488 [2014]; £491,978 [2013]

Age UK Richmond upon Thames

Registered: 20 Dec 2000 *Employees:* 30 *Volunteers:* 130
Website: ageukrichmond.org.uk
Activities: General charitable purposes; disability; prevention or relief of poverty
Address: 51 Godwin Road, Bromley, Kent, BR2 9LG
Trustees: Dr Jane Young, Mr Geoffrey Boyes, Mr Denis Palmer, Mr Michael Anthony Styles, Miss Sandra Aldridge, Mrs Rachel Veronica Schroter, Carmel Bamford, Charlotte Cornish, Mr Don Barrett
Income: £1,351,536 [2017]; £1,352,412 [2016]; £1,279,005 [2015]; £1,082,996 [2014]; £1,025,740 [2013]

Age UK Sheffield

Registered: 3 Mar 2005 *Employees:* 59 *Volunteers:* 48
Tel: 0114 250 2850 *Website:* ageuksheffield.org.uk
Activities: General charitable purposes; education, training; disability; prevention or relief of poverty
Address: South Yorkshire Fire & Rescue, 1st Floor, Age UK Sheffield, 197 Eyre Street, Sheffield, S1 3FG
Trustees: Mary Butler, Mr David Campbell, Ms Melinda Riley, Mr Paul Harriman, Jo Roy, Ms Melanie Perkins, Mr Timothy Furness
Income: £1,502,672 [2017]; £1,462,195 [2016]; £1,161,503 [2015]; £1,319,479 [2014]; £1,307,728 [2013]

Age UK Shropshire Telford & Wrekin
Registered: 6 Feb 2002 *Employees:* 226 *Volunteers:* 847
Tel: 01743 233123 *Website:* ageukshropshireandtelford.org.uk
Activities: General charitable purposes; disability; prevention or relief of poverty
Address: Age Concern, 3 Mardol Gardens, Shrewsbury, Salop, SY1 1PR
Trustees: Mrs Anne Wignall, Mrs Margaret Ann Lewis, Ms Sally Hampson, Mr Dennis Cook, Mr Peter Cates, Mrs Susan Robson, David Bell, Mrs Geraldine Parkin
Income: £2,361,007 [2017]; £2,323,494 [2016]; £2,052,972 [2015]; £2,084,351 [2014]; £1,817,643 [2013]

Age UK South Lakeland
Registered: 13 Apr 2011 *Employees:* 54 *Volunteers:* 281
Tel: 01539 728118 *Website:* ageuksouthlakeland.org.uk
Activities: General charitable purposes
Address: Age Concern, 17 Finkle Street, Kendal, Cumbria, LA9 4AB
Trustees: Mrs Susan Newell, Mr John Bateson, Mr Peter Smith, Ms Sarah Senior, Ms Janet McLeod, Mr Peter Clarke, Ms Jan Wright
Income: £2,011,373 [2017]; £1,847,148 [2016]; £1,580,814 [2015]; £1,400,469 [2014]; £1,433,534 [2013]

Age UK South Staffordshire
Registered: 15 Jul 1998 *Employees:* 154 *Volunteers:* 151
Tel: 01785 788478 *Website:* ageuk.org.uk
Activities: General charitable purposes; prevention or relief of poverty
Address: Age UK, The Roller Mill, Teddesley Road, Penkridge, Stafford, ST19 5BD
Trustees: Mr Gareth Roberts, Kevin Dobson, Mr David Walton, Mr Richard Beresford, Nicola Sawyer
Income: £2,405,935 [2017]; £2,213,730 [2016]; £2,157,241 [2015]; £1,993,780 [2014]; £1,935,886 [2013]

Age UK Stockport
Registered: 29 Dec 2010 *Employees:* 65 *Volunteers:* 88
Tel: 0161 480 1211 *Website:* ageukstockport.org.uk
Activities: General charitable purposes; advancement of health or saving of lives; prevention or relief of poverty
Address: Age Concern, 56 Wellington Street, Stockport, Cheshire, SK1 3AQ
Trustees: Susan Chapman, Mrs Susan Helen Carpentier Alting, Ms Nichola Joanne Booth, Mrs Carol Mitchell, Mr Paul Miles Carter, Mr Stephen Andrew Clarke, Ms Kirstie Elizabeth Clegg
Income: £1,542,474 [2017]; £1,509,253 [2016]; £1,209,586 [2015]; £1,345,916 [2014]; £1,551,550 [2013]

Age UK Suffolk
Registered: 29 Mar 2001 *Employees:* 265 *Volunteers:* 533
Tel: 01473 359911 *Website:* ageuksuffolk.org
Activities: General charitable purposes
Address: Age UK Suffolk, Unit 14 Hillview Business Park, Old Ipswich Road, Claydon, Ipswich, Suffolk, IP6 0AJ
Trustees: Mr John Robinson, Mr Peter Jones, Mrs Helen Thomas, Mrs Melanie Chew, Mr David Chenery, Mr Anthony Sheppard, Mrs Emma Woollard, Mrs Nicola Bradford
Income: £3,137,818 [2017]; £3,864,724 [2016]; £4,261,391 [2015]; £4,361,765 [2014]; £4,177,512 [2013]

Age UK Sunderland
Registered: 12 Jun 2001 *Employees:* 89 *Volunteers:* 341
Tel: 0191 514 1131 *Website:* ageuksunderland.org.uk
Activities: General charitable purposes; education, training; disability; prevention or relief of poverty
Address: Age UK, Bradbury Centre, Grange House, Stockton Road, Sunderland, Tyne & Wear, SR2 7AQ
Trustees: Mr Ged McCormack, Mrs Ann Lorna Lawson-Mclean, Mr Graham Burt, Mrs Susan Amanda Ritchie, Mrs Dianne Hutchinson, Mrs Patricia Robinson, Mrs Carol Harries, Councillor Graeme Miller, Mr David Teasdale
Income: £2,206,215 [2017]; £1,857,647 [2016]; £1,835,361 [2015]; £1,493,902 [2014]; £1,501,758 [2013]

Age UK Surrey
Registered: 19 Apr 1994 *Employees:* 51 *Volunteers:* 268
Tel: 01483 503414 *Website:* ageuk.org.uk
Activities: General charitable purposes; education, training; advancement of health or saving of lives; disability; prevention or relief of poverty; amateur sport; recreation
Address: Rex House, William Road, Guildford, Surrey, GU1 4QZ
Trustees: Mr Leslie James Mussett, Mr Barry Seymour, Ms Emma Jane Sarah Walker, Dr Khim Horton, Mr John Burbridge, Ms Alison Hurst Baker, Mr Philip Andrew James Currie
Income: £1,625,000 [2017]; £1,395,000 [2016]; £1,192,000 [2015]; £1,095,000 [2014]; £1,116,000 [2013]

Age UK Sutton
Registered: 28 Mar 2001 *Employees:* 34 *Volunteers:* 511
Tel: 020 8770 4098 *Website:* ageuksutton.org.uk
Activities: General charitable purposes; education, training; advancement of health or saving of lives; disability; prevention or relief of poverty; recreation; other charitable purposes
Address: Civic Offices, 2 Lower Square, St Nicholas Way, Sutton, Surrey, SM1 1EA
Trustees: Ms Catherine James, Mr Charles Lister OBE, Mr Kumar Ghosh, Mr Richard Jones, Mr Tim Howe, Mr Steven Kohn
Income: £1,034,400 [2017]; £1,080,546 [2016]; £877,882 [2015]; £706,881 [2014]; £503,383 [2013]

Age UK Wakefield District
Registered: 13 Mar 2003 *Employees:* 73 *Volunteers:* 150
Tel: 01977 552114 *Website:* ageukwd.org.uk
Activities: General charitable purposes; education, training
Address: Age UK, 7 Bank Street, Castleford, W Yorks, WF10 1JD
Trustees: Mr Ulric Murray, Mrs Andrea Wooffindin, Mr Alan Warwick Burnley, Bill Barker, Mrs Bridget Sowerby, Mrs Barbara Lyn Burnley
Income: £1,617,523 [2017]; £1,456,889 [2016]; £942,787 [2015]; £710,773 [2014]; £495,554 [2013]

Age UK Warwickshire
Registered: 9 Jan 2002 *Employees:* 109 *Volunteers:* 552
Tel: 01926 458100 *Website:* ageukwarwickshire.org.uk
Activities: General charitable purposes; advancement of health or saving of lives; disability; prevention or relief of poverty
Address: 8 Clemens Street, Leamington Spa, Warwicks, CV31 2DL
Trustees: Mr Christopher Long-Leather, Ms Grace Hampson, Mr Robert Perkins, Mr Mark Harris, Ms Joanne Tilley, Mr Stuart Bayliss
Income: £3,098,104 [2017]; £3,480,212 [2016]; £2,671,942 [2015]; £2,282,345 [2014]; £2,289,315 [2013]

Age UK West Cumbria
Registered: 19 Dec 2007 *Employees:* 110 *Volunteers:* 447
Tel: 01946 66669 *Website:* ageuk.org.uk
Activities: General charitable purposes
Address: Age UK West Cumbria, Old Customs House, West Strand, Whitehaven, Cumbria, CA28 7LR
Trustees: Mrs Lesley Toole, Mrs A E Prowse, Mrs Susan Gallagher, Mr Steve Donaldson, Geraldine Lancaster, Dr R T Proudfoot, Mr John Winter
Income: £2,283,372 [2017]; £2,060,091 [2016]; £2,199,564 [2015]; £2,234,124 [2014]; £2,328,006 [2013]

Age UK West Sussex
Registered: 26 Apr 2001 *Employees:* 100 *Volunteers:* 350
Tel: 01903 731800 *Website:* ageuk.org.uk
Activities: General charitable purposes; education, training; advancement of health or saving of lives; prevention or relief of poverty; arts, culture, heritage, science; recreation
Address: Suite 2, 1st Floor, Diane Henderson, Anchor Springs, Littlehampton, W Sussex, BN17 6BP
Trustees: Mr Bob Page, Mr John Dixon, Mr David Turner, George Moise, Mr Len Barnett, Mr Joe Ashton, Andrew Machin, Julie Tidbury
Income: £2,658,599 [2017]; £2,455,137 [2016]; £2,045,835 [2015]; £1,921,175 [2014]; £1,970,330 [2013]

Age UK
Registered: 25 Feb 2009 *Employees:* 1,548 *Volunteers:* 7,500
Tel: 0800 169 8080 *Website:* ageuk.org.uk
Activities: General charitable purposes; education, training; advancement of health or saving of lives; prevention or relief of poverty; overseas aid, famine relief; accommodation, housing; other charitable purposes
Address: Tavis House, 1-6 Tavistock Square, London, WC1H 9NA
Trustees: Sir Brian Pomeroy, Ms Sharon Jane Allen, Ms Anna Bradley, Mr David Edgar Hunter, Mr Stuart Purdy, Ms Suzanna Taverne, Mr Mark Lunney, Mr Andrew Michael Morley Dixon, Nick Wilkinson
Income: £149,697,000 [2017]; £168,071,000 [2016]; £174,575,000 [2015]; £166,629,000 [2014]; £158,900,000 [2013]

Agored Cymru
Registered: 23 Jul 2004 *Employees:* 36
Tel: 01248 670011 *Website:* agored.cymru
Activities: Education, training
Address: Agored Cymru, 3 Purbeck House, Lambourne Crescent, Llanishen, Cardiff, CF14 5GJ
Trustees: Mr Robert Clapham, Mr Brenig Davies, Mr Alexander Martin, Mr John Sexton, Mr Alan Smith, Mrs Kathleen Nancy Burns, Dr John Graystone, Dr Hywel Davies, Dr Zbig Sobiesierski, Mr Paul Martin, Mrs Carys Swain
Income: £1,384,547 [2016]; £1,381,193 [2015]; £2,254,033 [2014]; £2,378,736 [2013]; £3,123,387 [2012]

Ahavat Shalom Charity Fund
Registered: 30 Oct 1981
Tel: 020 8357 2727
Activities: General charitable purposes; education, training; religious activities
Address: Lynwood House, 373-375 Station Road, Harrow, Middlesex, HA1 2AW
Trustees: Mr Elan Shasha, Mr Avraham Hillel, Mr Eliyahu Hillel, Mr Abraham Simon Abraham, Mrs Anne Abrahams
Income: £4,033,545 [2016]; £2,017,889 [2015]; £3,255,966 [2014]; £2,962,197 [2013]

Ahavath Chessed Charitable Association Limited
Registered: 16 Mar 1962
Tel: 020 8557 9557
Activities: General charitable purposes; religious activities
Address: 23 Overlea Road, London, E5 9BG
Trustees: Heinrich Feldman, Mrs Dvora Feldman, Shulom Feldman
Income: £3,633,612 [2017]; £2,305,128 [2016]; £1,083,864 [2015]; £3,669,705 [2014]; £3,081,725 [2013]

Ahmadiyya Muslim Association United Kingdom
Registered: 11 May 1988 *Employees:* 218 *Volunteers:* 9,000
Tel: 020 8874 5836 *Website:* loveforallhatredfornone.org
Activities: Education, training; prevention or relief of poverty; religious activities
Address: 53 Melrose Road, London, SW18 1LX
Trustees: Dr Chaudhry Nasir Ahmad, Dr Shabir Ahmed Bhatti, Mr Ahmad Salam, Mr Mohamed Arshad Ahmedi, Mr Mohammed Nasser Khan, Mr Shakeel Rahman Butt, Dr Ch Ijaz Ur Rehman, Mr Masroor Ahmad, Mr Nisar Ahmad Orchard, Mr Sheikh Tariq Mahmood, Mr Irfan Chaudhry, Mr Sultan Lone, Mr Irfan Ahmed Quraishi, Mr Mubashar Ahmed, Dr Munawar Ahmad, Dr Tariq Anwar Bajwa, Mr Mansoor Ahmed Shah, Mr Mohammed Akram Ahmedi, Mr Rafiq Ahmed Hayat, Mr Fareed Ahmad, Mr Fahim Anwer, Mr Malik Abdul Haleem Khan, Mr Noman Hanif Raja, Mr Mirza Abdul Rasheed, Mr Abdullah Jheengoor, Mr Mirza Waqas Ahmad, Mr Mujib Ahmad Mirza
Income: £18,557,799 [2017]; £16,997,538 [2016]; £15,257,728 [2015]; £13,910,600 [2014]; £14,012,813 [2013]

Ahmadiyya Muslim Jamaat International
Registered: 30 Mar 2004 *Employees:* 181
Tel: 020 8544 7602 *Website:* amjinternational.org
Activities: General charitable purposes; education, training; advancement of health or saving of lives; disability; prevention or relief of poverty; overseas aid, famine relief; accommodation, housing; religious activities; animals; environment, conservation, heritage; economic, community development, employment; human rights, religious or racial harmony, equality or diversity; other charitable purposes
Address: 22 Deer Park Road, London, SW19 3TL
Trustees: Mr Abdul Majid Tahir, Mr Munir Ud Din Shams, Mr Shajar Ahmad Farooqi, Mr Lodewijk Verhagen, Mr Mubarak Ahmad, Mr Naseer Ahmad Qamar, Mr Abdullah Uwe Wagishauser, Mr Lal Khan Malik
Income: £30,944,000 [2016]; £26,714,000 [2015]; £26,086,000 [2014]; £25,074,000 [2013]; £20,308,000 [2012]

The Ahoy Centre
Registered: 14 Dec 2000 *Employees:* 18 *Volunteers:* 23
Tel: 020 8691 7502 *Website:* ahoy.org.uk
Activities: Education, training; disability; amateur sport
Address: The Ahoy Centre, Borthwick Street, Deptford, London, SE8 3JY
Trustees: Mrs Anne Wheeler, Ms Giovanna Pomilio, Mr Anthony Desmond Ballantyne Clarke, Mr Malcolm Graham Chumbley, Ms Vivien Burnett, Ms Sandra Short, Michael Rees
Income: £1,021,874 [2016]; £727,670 [2015]; £622,742 [2014]; £644,597 [2013]; £663,395 [2012]

Aid to The Church in Need (United Kingdom)
Registered: 12 Jun 2003 *Employees:* 30 *Volunteers:* 15
Tel: 020 8642 8668 *Website:* acnuk.org
Activities: Religious activities
Address: 12-14 Benhill Avenue, Sutton, Surrey, SM1 4DA
Trustees: Mr Philipp Habsburg-Lothringen, Mr Timothy Church, Lord David Alton, Mr Graham Hutton, Mr John Marsden
Income: £14,926,432 [2016]; £10,055,178 [2015]; £8,655,243 [2014]; £7,589,989 [2013]; £6,875,797 [2012]

The Aimwell Charitable Trust
Registered: 13 Jul 1994
Activities: General charitable purposes
Address: 3rd Floor, Baystone Associates, 52 Conduit Street, London, W1S 2YX
Trustees: Mr Isaac Kaye, Mr Steven Kaye, Mr Warren Roiter, Mrs Myrna Kaye, Mr Geoffrey Jayson
Income: £1,867,620 [2017]; £1,219,582 [2016]; £2,348,332 [2015]; £1,877,730 [2014]; £2,778,124 [2013]

The Air Ambulance Service
Registered: 5 Aug 2003 *Employees:* 230 *Volunteers:* 888
Tel: 0300 304 5999 *Website:* theairambulanceservice.org.uk
Activities: The advancement of health or saving of lives; armed forces, emergency service efficiency
Address: Clifton House, Butlers Leap, Rugby, Warwicks, CV21 3RQ
Trustees: Mr Michael Burgoyne, Mr Paul Wilson, Mr Royston Jones, Mr Neil Bandtock, Mr John Leonard Williams, Mr Chris Faircliffe, Mr Philip Holdcroft
Income: £16,306,000 [2016]; £14,694,000 [2015]; £11,930,000 [2014]; £11,152,000 [2013]; £9,397,000 [2012]

The Air Training Corps General Purposes Fund Charitable Incorporated Trust CIO
Registered: 16 Mar 2015 *Volunteers:* 12,000
Tel: 01400 267632 *Website:* raf.mod.uk
Activities: General charitable purposes; education, training; amateur sport; armed forces, emergency service efficiency
Address: Royal Air Force, Cranwell, Sleaford, Lincs, NG34 8HB
Trustees: Air Cdre D McCafferty, Mr G Bowerman, Gp Capt J Lawlor, Mr A Irvine
Income: £1,475,332 [2017]; £4,714,968 [2016]

Airedale Voluntary Drug and Alcohol Agency known as Project 6
Registered: 23 Jun 1989 *Employees:* 38 *Volunteers:* 31
Tel: 0114 258 7553 *Website:* project6.org.uk
Activities: Education, training; advancement of health or saving of lives
Address: Sheffield Alcohol Advisory Service, 644-646 Abbeydale Road, Sheffield, S7 2BB
Trustees: Ms Enid Feather, Ms Pamela Essler, Ms Dawn Townend, Ms Jenni Farrow
Income: £1,294,533 [2017]; £1,261,513 [2016]; £1,136,598 [2015]; £1,321,044 [2014]; £1,136,710 [2013]

Aish Hatorah UK Limited
Registered: 6 Apr 1998 *Employees:* 42 *Volunteers:* 30
Tel: 020 8457 4444 *Website:* aish.org.uk
Activities: General charitable purposes; education, training; arts, culture, heritage, science; other charitable purposes
Address: Aish Hatorah, 379 Hendon Way, London, NW4 3LP
Trustees: Mr Adrian Cohen, Mr Jeremy Newman, Mr Simon Fine, Jacqueline Rashbass, Mr Anthony Moshal
Income: £2,925,805 [2016]; £2,934,183 [2015]; £3,600,957 [2014]; £3,165,318 [2013]; £3,896,357 [2012]

Akshar Educational Trust
Registered: 13 Jul 1993 *Employees:* 104 *Volunteers:* 200
Tel: 020 8965 8381
Activities: Education, training
Address: 260 Brentfield Road, Neasden, London, NW10 8HE
Trustees: Mr Jayendra Patel Patel, Arvind P Patel, Mr Jm Patel, Vh Patel, Mr Kishorekant Bhattessa, Mahesh Patel, Rk Patel
Income: £4,325,382 [2017]; £4,348,718 [2016]; £4,482,439 [2015]; £4,095,855 [2014]; £4,266,048 [2013]

Al Badr Islamic Trust
Registered: 29 Mar 1995 *Employees:* 52 *Volunteers:* 5
Tel: 01524 389595 *Website:* jamea.co.uk
Activities: Education, training; religious activities
Address: Ashton Road, Lancaster, LA1 5AJ
Trustees: Mr Fazl Wadee, Mr Ziaooddin Satia, Huzayfa Wadee
Income: £1,830,446 [2016]; £1,482,273 [2015]; £1,617,775 [2014]; £1,422,923 [2013]; £1,414,134 [2012]

Al-Ayn Social Care Foundation
Registered: 23 Sep 2015 *Employees:* 2 *Volunteers:* 120
Website: alayn.co.uk
Activities: The advancement of health or saving of lives; prevention or relief of poverty
Address: Al Ayn Social Care Foundation, Unit 5 Watling Gate, 297-303 Edgware Road, Colindale, London, NW9 6NB
Trustees: Mrs Aliya Azam, Mr Mohamad Baqer Al-Yassin, Mrs Rabab Kleit, Mr Ahmed Al-Khaja, Mr Mustafa M A Mohamed
Income: £9,733,067 [2016]

Al-Imdaad Foundation UK
Registered: 2 Feb 2011 *Employees:* 5 *Volunteers:* 103
Tel: 01254 698771 *Website:* alimdaad.co.uk
Activities: General charitable purposes; education, training; advancement of health or saving of lives; disability; prevention or relief of poverty; overseas aid, famine relief; accommodation, housing; environment, conservation, heritage; economic, community development, employment; other charitable purposes
Address: 185 Audley Range, Blackburn, Lancs, BB1 1TH
Trustees: Mr Ahad Miah, Mr Muhammad Nurullah Shikder, Mr Yacoob Ebrahim Vahed, Mr Ziyaad Patel, Mr Zubair Miah, Mr Mahmood Miah, Mr Moulana Ahmed Suleman Chohan
Income: £3,956,742 [2017]; £3,590,570 [2016]; £6,858,023 [2015]; £3,441,935 [2014]; £1,747,033 [2013]

Al-Khair Foundation
Registered: 19 Nov 2008 *Employees:* 154 *Volunteers:* 395
Tel: 020 8649 9964 *Website:* alkhair.org
Activities: General charitable purposes; education, training; advancement of health or saving of lives; disability; prevention or relief of poverty; overseas aid, famine relief; accommodation, housing; religious activities; arts, culture, heritage, science; amateur sport; environment, conservation, heritage; economic, community development, employment; human rights, religious or racial harmony, equality or diversity; other charitable purposes
Address: Al Khair Foundation, 109-117 Cherry Orchard Road, Croydon, Surrey, CR0 6BE
Trustees: Dr M J H Qureshi, Mr Mohmed Ayyub Shaikh, Mr Thomas Richard Swift, Imam Qasim Rashid Ahmad, Mr Basil Nader
Income: £20,146,030 [2017]; £19,062,279 [2016]; £21,963,666 [2015]; £21,350,569 [2014]; £17,197,212 [2013]

The Al-Khoei Benevolent Foundation
Registered: 23 Aug 1989 *Employees:* 8 *Volunteers:* 7
Tel: 020 7372 4049 *Website:* al-khoei.org
Activities: General charitable purposes; education, training; prevention or relief of poverty; overseas aid, famine relief; religious activities; human rights, religious or racial harmony, equality or diversity; other charitable purposes
Address: 11 Coverdale Road, London, NW2 4DB
Trustees: Mr Sayed Saheb Khoei, Seyed Mohammad Hassan Faghihe-Mousavi, Seyed Fazel Hosseini Milani, Mrs Zahra Gharavi Naeini
Income: £1,885,110 [2016]; £3,384,561 [2015]; £1,796,048 [2014]; £1,715,760 [2013]; £4,401,154 [2012]

Al-Mahdi Institute
Registered: 31 May 2000 *Employees:* 20
Tel: 0121 446 5047 *Website:* almahdi.edu
Activities: Education, training; religious activities
Address: Weoley Park Road, Selly Oak, Birmingham, B29 6RB
Trustees: Mr Arif Abdulhussain, Mr Abbas Ali Datoo, Mr Meboob Ladak
Income: £1,273,865 [2017]; £1,022,605 [2015]; £983,981 [2014]; £444,810 [2013]; £444,810 [2012]

Al-Muntada Al-Islami Trust
Registered: 13 Jan 1986 *Employees:* 31 *Volunteers:* 34
Tel: 020 7471 8264 *Website:* almuntadatrust.org
Activities: General charitable purposes; education, training; advancement of health or saving of lives; prevention or relief of poverty; overseas aid, famine relief; religious activities; arts, culture, heritage, science; amateur sport
Address: 7 Bridges Place, Fulham, London, SW6 4HW
Trustees: Mr Abdul Hakeem Montague, Dr Saeed Alghade, Abdullah Alfaiz
Income: £2,500,853 [2016]; £1,891,961 [2015]; £3,276,738 [2014]; £2,952,522 [2013]

Al-Shirkatul Islamiyyah
Registered: 10 Oct 1986 *Employees:* 9 *Volunteers:* 240
Tel: 020 8544 7600 *Website:* alshirkat.org
Activities: Education, training; religious activities
Address: ASI, 22 Deer Park Road, London, SW19 3TL
Trustees: Mr Abdul Baqi Arshad, Mr Mubarak Ahmad, Mr Naseer Ahmad Qamar, Mr Mirza Mahmood Ahmad, Mr Abdul Hafeez Shahid, Mr Abdul Majid Tahir, Mr Munir Ud Din Shams, Rafiq Ahmad Hayat, Mr Fateh Ahmad Khan Dahri
Income: £5,558,823 [2017]; £5,441,621 [2016]; £8,589,199 [2015]; £5,998,163 [2014]; £4,709,764 [2013]

Alabare Christian Care Centres
Registered: 29 Nov 1991 *Employees:* 162 *Volunteers:* 315
Tel: 01722 344480 *Website:* alabare.co.uk
Activities: Education, training; disability; prevention or relief of poverty; accommodation, housing; religious activities
Address: Riverside House, 2 Watt Road, Salisbury, Wilts, SP2 7UD
Trustees: Mr Malcolm Cassells, Rev John Anthony Proctor, Mrs Alicia Proctor, Mrs Christine Robinson, Mr Martin Clark, Mr Richard Holman, Reverend Canon David Michael Karl Durston MA, Mr David Lawes, Mr Phil Davis, Mr Don Alexander, Mr John Hunter
Income: £7,558,967 [2017]; £7,989,694 [2016]; £6,783,694 [2015]; £7,872,629 [2014]; £6,556,715 [2013]

The Albany 2001 Company
Registered: 15 Dec 2005 *Employees:* 50 *Volunteers:* 57
Tel: 020 8692 0231 *Website:* thealbany.org.uk
Activities: Arts, culture, heritage, science; economic, community development, employment
Address: The Albany, Albany Centre & Theatre, Douglas Way, London, SE8 4AG
Trustees: Miss Claire Pritchard, Mr Kurban Haji, Mike Harris, Mrs Tabitha Siklos, Beres Williams, Ms Camille Dawson, Ms Linda Bernhardt, Ms Lisa Mead, Tricia Jenkins, Ms Vicki Amedume, Mrs Joan Ruddock, Karla Sally Barnacle-Best, Ms Olivia Douglass
Income: £2,902,886 [2017]; £2,649,769 [2016]; £2,670,456 [2015]; £2,377,574 [2014]; £1,794,463 [2013]

The Albert Hunt Trust
Registered: 10 Mar 1979
Tel: 0345 304 2424
Activities: General charitable purposes
Address: The Albert Hunt Trust, Wealth Advisory Services, 440 Strand, London, WC2R 0QS
Trustees: Mrs Breda Mary McGuire, Mr Ian Fleming, Mr Stephen Ernest Harvey, Coutts & Co
Income: £1,624,516 [2017]; £1,666,114 [2016]; £1,695,190 [2015]; £1,687,499 [2014]; £1,392,278 [2013]

The Albert Kennedy Trust
Registered: 16 Sep 2002 *Employees:* 17 *Volunteers:* 179
Tel: 020 7831 6562 *Website:* akt.org.uk
Activities: Education, training; accommodation, housing
Address: Albert Kennedy Trust, 48 Chocolate Studios, 7 Shepherdess Place, London, N1 7LJ
Trustees: Paul Bates, Mr Terry Stacy, Ms Lesley Brook, Mr Stephen Crocker, Ms Susan Eastoe, Mr Richard Bayly, Ms Sally Hill, Mr Gavin Wills, Ms Katherine Cowan, Simon O'Hara, Ms Sharon Pearce, Ms Helen Johnston
Income: £1,035,814 [2017]; £1,040,485 [2016]; £1,013,225 [2015]; £1,028,002 [2014]; £589,505 [2013]

Albert Memorial College
Registered: 26 May 2006 *Employees:* 301
Tel: 01728 723789 *Website:* framlinghamcollege.co.uk
Activities: Education, training
Address: Framlingham College, College Road, Framlingham, Woodbridge, Suffolk, IP13 9EY
Trustees: Mr Peter Moorhouse, Mr John Kelsall, Mrs Mary Amanda Makey BA, Dr Simon Rudland, Air Vice-Marshal Bill Rimmer, The Right Hon Lord Smith of Finsbury, Mr Peter Howard-Dobson, Sir Amyas Morse, Mr Peter Lawrence, Mr John Ellerby, Mrs Sue Ashurst, Mr Richard John Sayer, Mr James Powell MA FCA, Air Vice-Marshal Simon Dougherty OStJ MSc MBBS FRCP FFOM DAvMed DObs, Mrs Penelope Mhairi Creasy, Rev Graeme Knowles CVO FKC, Mr Mark Slater, Mr Peter Over, Mrs Lucy Rowan-Robinson, Mr Charles Packshaw, Mr Ian Fulcher
Income: £15,308,282 [2017]; £14,006,932 [2016]; £13,568,411 [2015]; £13,512,568 [2014]; £13,109,346 [2013]

The Albion Foundation
Registered: 9 Aug 2000 *Employees:* 58 *Volunteers:* 62
Tel: 0871 271 9840 *Website:* thealbionfoundation.co.uk
Activities: General charitable purposes; education, training; amateur sport
Address: The Albion Foundation, Ford Street, Smethwick, W Midlands, B67 7QY
Trustees: Mr Brendon Batson, Mrs Preet Kaur Gill MP, Mr Martin Charles Swain, Mr Simon King, Mr Ninder Johal, Mr Martin Swain, Mr Ninder Johal, Mr Simon Topper
Income: £2,258,456 [2017]; £1,870,483 [2016]; £1,791,717 [2015]; £1,704,887 [2014]; £1,676,281 [2013]

Albion in the Community
Registered: 22 Aug 2005 *Employees:* 190 *Volunteers:* 50
Tel: 01273 878255 *Website:* albioninthecommunity.org.uk
Activities: General charitable purposes; education, training; advancement of health or saving of lives; disability; amateur sport; economic, community development, employment
Address: American Express, Community Stadium, Village Way, Falmer, Brighton, BN1 9BL
Trustees: Mr Marc Louis Sugarman, Mr David Andrew Jones, Mr Martin Perry, Mr Paul Mullen, Mr Alan Roy McCarthy, Mr Philip Charles Frier, Mrs Judith Richards, Mrs Sarah Sheehan
Income: £3,507,315 [2017]; £3,342,025 [2016]; £3,238,871 [2015]; £3,064,891 [2014]; £3,125,951 [2013]

The Alcohol and Drug Service
Registered: 15 Mar 2005 *Employees:* 81 *Volunteers:* 18
Tel: 01482 320606 *Website:* ads-uk.org
Activities: General charitable purposes; education, training; advancement of health or saving of lives
Address: 82 Spring Bank, Hull, HU3 1AB
Trustees: Adele Wilkinson, Mr Andrew Charles Cooke, Mrs Denise White, Mrs Lorna Wakefield, Jon Boddy, Andy Smith, Mr Kevin Yorath
Income: £2,510,649 [2017]; £1,524,643 [2016]; £2,084,836 [2015]; £2,031,892 [2014]; £2,031,503 [2013]

Aldeburgh Music Endowment Fund
Registered: 3 Jul 1981
Tel: 01728 687100 *Website:* snapemaltings.co.uk
Activities: Arts, culture, heritage, science
Address: Snape Maltings Concert Hall, Snape Bridge, Snape, Saxmundham, Suffolk, IP17 1SP
Trustees: Mrs Sarah Anne Zins, Simon Robey, Stephen Swift, Mr David Robbie, Garth Pollard
Income: £1,679,264 [2017]; £687,277 [2016]; £4,422,024 [2015]; £658,100 [2014]; £549,189 [2013]

The Aldenham Foundation
Registered: 24 Nov 1987 *Employees:* 245
Tel: 01923 858122 *Website:* aldenham.com
Activities: Education, training
Address: Aldenham School, Aldenham Road, Elstree, Borehamwood, Herts, WD6 3AJ
Trustees: Mr Ian Andrew Dewar, Mr Stephen Nokes, Jonathan Smith, Dr Deborah Nicholes, Mr Anthony John Bingham, Mr Torquil Sligo-Young, Mr Tom Wells, Mr David Stephen Lambert, Mr Trevor Barton, Mr David Tidmarsh, Mr Alan Day, Mrs Vandana Shah, Mr Anthony Hellman, Michael O'Dwyer, Andrew Cox, Mr Ronak Mashru
Income: £16,778,042 [2017]; £16,326,490 [2016]; £15,505,494 [2015]; £15,753,565 [2014]; £14,233,806 [2013]

Alder Hey Children's Charity
Registered: 26 Feb 2015 *Employees:* 20 *Volunteers:* 50
Tel: 0151 252 5666 *Website:* alderheycharity.org
Activities: The advancement of health or saving of lives
Address: Alder Hey Children's Charity, Eaton Road, West Derby, Liverpool, L12 2AP
Trustees: Sir Malcolm Thornton, Mrs Elizabeth Craig, Mrs Helen Dearden, Mrs Eileen Jones, Mr John Carson, Dame Josephine Williams, Mrs Shalni Arora, Mrs Jeannie France-Hayhurst, Mrs Glynis Johnston, Ms Nicola Collins
Income: £4,937,000 [2017]; £14,466,000 [2016]

Alderley Edge School for Girls
Registered: 6 Dec 1991 *Employees:* 113 *Volunteers:* 15
Tel: 01260 277436 *Website:* aesg.co.uk
Activities: Education, training; religious activities
Address: 33 Crompton Close, Congleton, Cheshire, CW12 2DR
Trustees: The Revd Canon Brendan Clover MA LTCL, Mrs Shirley Herring, Mrs Katherine Doyle, Mr Keith Ronald Lowe, Mrs Caroline Lowe, Mr Christopher Trueman, Mr Graham Tyson, Mr Peter Ainsworth, Prov Superior Janet Arrowsmith, Dr Robert Dwyer Nolan, Sister Catherine Joy, Mrs Joanna Claire Rostron, Ms Tracy Pollard, Mrs Deborah Summerfield
Income: £5,082,923 [2017]; £5,146,931 [2016]; £4,806,852 [2015]; £4,674,047 [2014]; £4,408,730 [2013]

The Aldingbourne Trust
Registered: 21 Aug 1978 *Employees:* 224 *Volunteers:* 120
Tel: 01243 544607 *Website:* aldingbournetrust.co.uk
Activities: General charitable purposes; education, training; disability; accommodation, housing; arts, culture, heritage, science; economic, community development, employment; human rights, religious or racial harmony, equality or diversity
Address: The Aldingbourne Trust, Blackmill Lane, Norton, Chichester, W Sussex, PO18 0JP
Trustees: Mr John Hugh Shipstone Shippam, Mr David Godsmark, Miss Frances Russell, Mr David Hilditch, Mr Andrew John Pitts, Mrs Jackie Williscroft, Mr Alistair Bath, Mr John Douglas Dixon, Mr Richard Bunker
Income: £6,299,818 [2017]; £5,383,473 [2016]; £4,943,727 [2015]; £4,572,920 [2014]; £4,560,808 [2013]

The Rodney Aldridge Charitable Trust
Registered: 24 Feb 2004 *Employees:* 6
Website: aldridgefoundation.com
Activities: Education, training; amateur sport; economic, community development, employment
Address: Aldridge Foundation, 30 Millbank, London, SW1P 4DU
Trustees: Sir Rodney Aldridge, Mr Richard Benton, Mr Tom Ilube, Lady Carol Aldridge, Mr Brent Thomas, Mr James Sporle, Mrs Jennifer Lavender
Income: £1,921,508 [2017]; £1,377,585 [2016]; £3,191,942 [2015]; £2,545,901 [2014]; £676,549 [2013]

Aldro School Educational Trust Limited
Registered: 10 Jun 1969 *Employees:* 74 *Volunteers:* 30
Tel: 01483 810266 *Website:* aldro.org
Activities: Education, training
Address: Aldro School, Lombard Street, Shackleford, Godalming, Surrey, GU8 6AS
Trustees: Mr Brian Kirkpatrick, Mr Garth Taylor Williams, Mr Edward Reid, Mrs Sarah Louise Hunt, James Geffen, Mr Jonathan F Perry, Rev Philip Vernon Parker, Rev Margot Spencer, Tim Woodhouse, Tim Johns
Income: £3,755,211 [2017]; £3,896,823 [2016]; £4,076,221 [2015]; £4,261,969 [2014]; £4,041,812 [2013]

Aldwickbury School Trust Ltd
Registered: 19 May 1969 *Employees:* 107
Tel: 01582 760575 *Website:* aldwickbury.org.uk
Activities: Education, training
Address: Aldwickbury School, Wheathampstead Road, Harpenden, Herts, AL5 1AD
Trustees: Stuart Westley, Mr J G Bromfield, Mrs Alexandra Virginia Louise Beaty BA, Dr Roger Leonard Axworthy, Mr C S Boothby, Mr Christian Mark Dinwoodie, Mr A D Coley, Mr J P Cavanagh QC MA (Oxon) LLM (Cantab), Mr E Bond, Mr J Hodgson, Miss J Bryant, Mr Andrew Charles Hine
Income: £5,622,919 [2017]; £5,790,906 [2016]; £4,849,504 [2015]; £4,500,272 [2014]; £4,239,644 [2013]

The Alexander Mosley Charitable Trust
Registered: 15 Jul 2011
Tel: 020 7465 4300
Activities: General charitable purposes
Address: 10 New Square, Lincoln's Inn, London, WC2A 3QG
Trustees: Mr Horatio Edmund Mortimer, Mrs Emma Maria Maitland Mosley, Mr Max Patrick Mosley, Mr Max Rufus Mosley
Income: £4,759,871 [2017]; £4,624,734 [2016]; £3,524,861 [2015]; £3,224,876 [2014]; £622,137 [2013]

Alexandra Park and Palace
Registered: 25 Mar 1981 *Employees:* 123 *Volunteers:* 70
Tel: 020 8365 4310 *Website:* alexandrapalace.com
Activities: Amateur sport; environment, conservation, heritage; recreation
Address: Alexandra Park and Palace Trust, Alexandra Palace, Alexandra Palace Way, London, N22 7AY
Trustees: Mr Bob Hare, Ms Sarah Williams Vice Chair, Mr Erdel Dogan, Ms Anne Stennett, Ms Dana Carlin, Mr Nick Da Costa
Income: £14,389,000 [2017]; £40,935,000 [2016]; £61,139,000 [2015]; £10,551,000 [2014]; £8,921,000 [2013]

Alexian Brothers of The Province of The Sacred Heart
Registered: 18 Feb 1964 *Employees:* 97 *Volunteers:* 10
Tel: 020 7969 5500
Activities: General charitable purposes; accommodation, housing; religious activities
Address: Haysmacintyre, Fairfax House, 15 Fulwood Place, London, WC1V 6AY
Trustees: Brother Finbar Butler, Brother Fidelis, Brother Dermot
Income: £2,220,269 [2016]; £2,139,405 [2015]; £2,080,856 [2014]; £2,411,168 [2013]; £2,180,789 [2012]

Alfanar
Registered: 22 Jul 2004 *Employees:* 11 *Volunteers:* 5
Website: alfanar.org.uk
Activities: Education, training; advancement of health or saving of lives; prevention or relief of poverty; economic, community development, employment
Address: 38 Artillery Lane, London, E1 7LS
Trustees: Julia Middleton, Lubna Olayan, Cynthia Oakes, Mrs Charlotte Boyle, Mr Sherif Foda, Nadia Plumbly, Mr Amjad Adnan Nureddin Bseisu, Hakeem Iguodala Belo-Osagie, Dr Laila Eskander
Income: £1,010,821 [2016]; £1,084,580 [2015]; £805,932 [2014]; £721,403 [2013]; £444,907 [2012]

Alfurqan Education Trust
Registered: 8 Jul 2011 *Employees:* 41 *Volunteers:* 15
Tel: 020 8432 9477 *Website:* alfurqaneducationtrust.org
Activities: Education, training; religious activities
Address: 6 Lampton Road, Hounslow, Middlesex, TW3 1JL
Trustees: Mr Ismail Abdisamad Mohamud, Mr Mukhtar Ali Abdi, Mr Ali Hussein Hassan, Mr Ahmed Abdulle Abdi, Abdulsatar Abdi, Mohamed Qalalid, Mr Mohamed Hussein Hassan, Mr Ahmed Sharif Jibril
Income: £1,119,324 [2016]; £3,050,741 [2015]; £241,811 [2014]; £188,610 [2013]

The Alice Ellen Cooper-Dean Charitable Foundation
Registered: 29 Sep 1978
Tel: 01305 251333
Activities: General charitable purposes
Address: Unity Chambers, 34 High East Street, Dorchester, DT1 1HA
Trustees: Mrs Linda Jean Bowditch, Rupert Edwards Esq, Mr John Robert Barrett Bowditch, Mr Douglas James Edward Neville-Jones, Mrs Emma Jane Blackburn, Mr Alastair Edward Cowen
Income: £1,327,738 [2017]; £1,252,359 [2016]; £1,200,448 [2015]; £1,076,512 [2014]; £1,089,119 [2013]

Alive Church Lincoln
Registered: 15 Feb 2011 *Employees:* 22 *Volunteers:* 600
Tel: 01522 533535 *Website:* alivechurch.org.uk
Activities: General charitable purposes; religious activities
Address: 22 Newland, Lincoln, LN1 1XG
Trustees: Mr Paul Benger, Jamie Clark, Mr Stuart Bell, Irene Bell, Mr Stephen A Campbell, Miss Lynsey Norris
Income: £1,202,935 [2017]; £1,093,006 [2016]; £1,036,393 [2015]; £966,078 [2014]; £721,581 [2013]

Alive Leisure
Registered: 8 Apr 2014 *Employees:* 254
Tel: 01553 818016 *Website:* aliveleisure.co.uk
Activities: General charitable purposes; education, training; advancement of health or saving of lives; arts, culture, heritage, science; amateur sport; recreation
Address: Lynnsport, Columbia Way, King's Lynn, Norfolk, PE30 2NB
Trustees: Dr Ian Mack, Mr Ian Trundley, Mr Peter Lemon, Abigail Louise Panks, Mr Michael Andrews, Mr Nigel Maggs-Oosterhagen
Income: £5,559,270 [2017]; £5,158,349 [2016]; £3,424,319 [2015]

All Aboard Shops Limited
Registered: 11 Aug 2008 *Employees:* 66 *Volunteers:* 220
Website: allaboardshops.com
Activities: General charitable purposes; education, training; advancement of health or saving of lives; prevention or relief of poverty; environment, conservation, heritage
Address: 27 Elsworthy Road, London, NW3 3BT
Trustees: Mr Howard Brecker, Mr Robert Lionel Lipson, Mr Michael Howard Wernicke, Miss Henrietta Klug, Mr Brian Anthony Finch, Mr Harvey John Rose, Mr Neil Richard Kelsey
Income: £2,147,061 [2016]; £2,236,511 [2015]; £2,315,729 [2014]; £2,161,420 [2013]

All Hallows (Cranmore Hall) School Trust Limited
Registered: 18 Sep 1962 *Employees:* 114 *Volunteers:* 1
Tel: 01749 881600 *Website:* allhallowsschool.co.uk
Activities: Education, training
Address: All Hallows School, Cranmore Hall, East Cranmore, Shepton Mallet, Somerset, BA4 4SF
Trustees: Ms Andrea Le Guevel, Mr Ralph Bell, Mrs Tracey Cotterell, Mrs Melanie Gillian Eyles, Dr Justin Weir, Mr James Alexandroff, Mr Nicholas David Gallop, Mr Michael Benedict Drummond Smith, Mr Bart Wielenga
Income: £3,742,253 [2016]; £3,611,622 [2015]; £3,963,362 [2014]; £4,029,858 [2013]; £3,808,505 [2012]

All Hallows Healthcare Trust Ltd
Registered: 26 Jun 2008 *Employees:* 296 *Volunteers:* 55
Tel: 01986 892728 *Website:* all-hallows.org.uk
Activities: The advancement of health or saving of lives; disability
Address: Station Road, Ditchingham, Bungay, Suffolk, NR35 2QL
Trustees: Sister Sheila Margaret Day, Mr Richard Musgrave, Dr Helen Jean Tucker, Mrs Maureen Davies, Mr John Chapmam, Mrs Suzanne Helen Jones
Income: £5,019,902 [2017]; £4,938,202 [2016]; £5,262,035 [2015]; £5,367,887 [2014]; £5,166,656 [2013]

All Nations Christian College Limited
Registered: 9 May 1972 *Employees:* 30 *Volunteers:* 15
Tel: 01920 443542 *Website:* allnations.ac.uk
Activities: Education, training; religious activities
Address: All Nations Christian College, Easneye, Ware, Herts, SG12 8LX
Trustees: Mr James Douglas Thornton, Mrs Melanie Fitton, Mr David Parry, Mr Danny John, Ms Katherine McLeish, Ms Alison Esther Grieve, Mr Peter Michael Oyugi, Mrs Judith Hanson-Taylor, Mrs Caroline Jane Louise Sanderson, Dr Harvey Collins Kwiyani
Income: £1,580,863 [2017]; £2,009,633 [2016]; £1,377,811 [2015]; £1,220,165 [2014]; £1,317,492 [2013]

All Nations
Registered: 21 Jul 2004 *Employees:* 9 *Volunteers:* 150
Tel: 029 2052 2838 *Website:* allnationschurch.org.uk
Activities: General charitable purposes; education, training; advancement of health or saving of lives; prevention or relief of poverty; overseas aid, famine relief; accommodation, housing; religious activities; other charitable purposes
Address: All Nations Church, All Nations Centre, Sachville Avenue, Cardiff, CF14 3NY
Trustees: Mr Andrew Guy, Dr Roger Aubrey, Mr Malcolm Clemo, Mr Terence Erlenbach
Income: £1,456,083 [2017]; £1,374,684 [2016]; £1,250,458 [2015]; £1,137,210 [2014]; £1,235,091 [2013]

Dame Allan's Schools
Registered: 9 Feb 2001 *Employees:* 174 *Volunteers:* 6
Tel: 0191 274 5910 *Website:* dameallans.co.uk
Activities: Education, training
Address: Dame Allan's Schools, Fowberry Crescent, Newcastle upon Tyne, NE4 9YJ
Trustees: Mrs Margaret Nicholson, Mr T Gray, Professor Eric Cross, Professor Ruth Plummer, Dr P V Paes, Mrs C Bell, Mr Brian Adcock, Mr Michael Davison, Mrs Deborah Cunningham, Professor Ruth Gregory, Mr Ian John Belsham, Mr C Bolland
Income: £10,415,356 [2017]; £9,903,823 [2016]; £8,868,411 [2015]; £8,320,665 [2014]; £8,193,010 [2013]

Allchurches Trust Limited
Registered: 3 May 1972
Tel: 01452 873184 *Website:* allchurches.co.uk
Activities: General charitable purposes; education, training; disability; religious activities; environment, conservation, heritage; economic, community development, employment
Address: Beaufort House, Brunswick Road, Gloucester, GL1 1JZ
Trustees: Archdeacon Annette Cooper, Mr Christopher Smith, Sir Laurence Henry Magnus Bt MA, Mr Timothy Carroll, Sir Philip Mawer, Ms Denise Pamela Wilson, Mr Michael Arlington BSc Hon, Mr Steven Charles Hudson
Income: £33,730,000 [2016]; £21,661,000 [2015]; £25,012,000 [2014]; £5,406,000 [2013]; £5,334,000 [2012]

The Allen & Overy Foundation
Registered: 9 Sep 2013
Tel: 020 3088 0000
Activities: General charitable purposes; education, training; prevention or relief of poverty; overseas aid, famine relief; economic, community development, employment; human rights, religious or racial harmony, equality or diversity; other charitable purposes
Address: One Bishops Square, London, E1 6AD
Trustees: Mark Mansell, Mrs Jane Finlayson-Brown, Mr Philip Mansfield, Mr Christopher Mainwaring-Taylor, Mr Andrew Roger Wedderburn-Day, Ms Jane Eleanor Bardo Townsend, Annelies Van Der Pauw
Income: £1,551,582 [2017]; £810,978 [2016]; £269,904 [2015]; £1,053,835 [2014]

The H B Allen Charitable Trust
Registered: 21 Nov 1989
Tel: 023 9263 2406 *Website:* hballenct.org.uk
Activities: General charitable purposes
Address: Homefield, Chidden Holt, Hambledon, Waterlooville, Hants, PO7 4TG
Trustees: Mr Peter Benthall Shone, Miss Helen Laura Ratcliffe
Income: £1,709,174 [2016]; £1,645,860 [2015]; £1,484,131 [2014]; £1,438,805 [2013]; £1,401,810 [2012]

James Allen's Girls' School
Registered: 7 Jul 2008 *Employees:* 295
Tel: 020 8299 8423 *Website:* jags.org.uk
Activities: Education, training
Address: James Allens Girls School, 144 East Dulwich Grove, London, SE22 8TE
Trustees: Dame Erica Pienaar, Frances Read, Ms Helen Nixseaman, Mrs Alison Elizabeth Fleming, Mr Simon Smith, Mr Nicolas Wood, Mrs Geraldine McAndrew, Mrs Elizabeth Jane Onslow, Mr David Miller, Dr Jane Marshall, Dr Rema Wasan
Income: £21,144,468 [2016]; £20,895,517 [2015]; £18,927,461 [2014]; £21,205,888 [2013]; £21,607,530 [2012]

Alleyn Court Educational Trust
Registered: 16 Feb 1993 *Employees:* 75
Tel: 01245 455400
Activities: Education, training
Address: 75 Springfield Road, Chelmsford, Essex, CM2 6JB
Trustees: Mr John Warren Theodore Wilcox, Mrs Sarah Nicole Drummond, Mr Richard Mark Green, Ms Shameem Nabi, Mr George William Denys Wilcox, Mr William Denys Anthony Wilcox, Mr Christopher Douglas Francis Mills, Mrs Nieves Vara Gonzalez, Dr Judith Mervyn Collis
Income: £2,861,105 [2017]; £3,012 [2016]; £2,538 [2015]; £2,662 [2014]; £2,670 [2013]

Alleyn's School
Registered: 27 May 2015 *Employees:* 258 *Volunteers:* 2
Tel: 020 7404 0606 *Website:* alleyns.org.uk
Activities: Education, training
Address: Goodman Derrick LLP, 10 St Bride Street, London, EC4A 4AD
Trustees: Mrs Laura Malkin, Mr Mark John Bishop, Richard Pinckard, Elizabeth Bowen-Rayner, Madeleine Campbell, Miss Tania Margaret Tribius, Ms Jennifer Anne Scott, Mr Kevin John Douglas, Iain Pulley, Mr Iain Barbour, Jonathan Lilly, Peter Yetzes, Miss Michelle Camilla Terry
Income: £26,240,000 [2017]

Alliance Family Foundation Limited
Registered: 28 May 1969
Activities: General charitable purposes; education, training; advancement of health or saving of lives; prevention or relief of poverty; religious activities; arts, culture, heritage, science
Address: Spencer House, 27 St James's Place, London, SW1A 1NR
Trustees: Lord David Alliance CBE, Graham Alliance, Sara Esterkin, Joshua Jacob Moshe Alliance
Income: £3,692,885 [2017]; £700,231 [2016]; £713,230 [2015]; £701,754 [2014]; £674,840 [2013]

Alliance Francaise de Londres Limited
Registered: 18 Apr 2006 *Employees:* 20
Tel: 020 7224 1908 *Website:* alliancefrancaise.london
Activities: Education, training; arts, culture, heritage, science
Address: Alliance Francaise, 6 Porter Street, London, W1U 6DD
Trustees: Mr Richard Michael Fairbairn, Dr Carole Gilling-Smith, Dr Chrystel Hug, Mr Gordon Smith
Income: £1,095,121 [2016]; £1,044,781 [2015]; £1,039,598 [2014]; £1,063,496 [2013]; £1,181,022 [2012]

Alliance Learning Ltd
Registered: 16 Dec 2002 *Employees:* 73 *Volunteers:* 1
Tel: 01204 677812 *Website:* alliancelearning.com
Activities: Education, training
Address: The Hurst Building, Horwich Loco Estate, Chorley New Road, Horwich, Bolton, Lancs, BL6 5UE
Trustees: Alex Kitchen, Mr Paul Taylor, Mrs Gabrielle MacDonald, Mr Benjamin Miller, Diana Morton, Mrs Margaret Lowe, Mr John Smith, Dr Kondal Reddy Kandadi
Income: £2,958,511 [2017]; £2,827,059 [2016]; £2,696,836 [2015]; £2,628,628 [2014]; £2,428,143 [2013]

Almeida Theatre Company Limited
Registered: 8 Jun 1981 *Employees:* 86
Tel: 020 7288 4921 *Website:* almeida.co.uk
Activities: Education, training; arts, culture, heritage, science
Address: Almeida Theatre, Almeida Street, London, N1 1TA
Trustees: Ms Sian Hansen, Mr Jonathan Church, Mr Axel Burrough, Ms Lucy Perman, Ms Caroline Cracknell, Mr Luke Johnson, Mr Rick Gildea, Mr John Cassy, Ms Tanya Seghatchian
Income: £6,512,223 [2017]; £5,950,191 [2016]; £5,357,275 [2015]; £4,950,216 [2014]; £4,275,842 [2013]

The Alnwick Garden Trust
Registered: 16 Jan 2003 *Employees:* 133 *Volunteers:* 75
Tel: 01665 511350 *Website:* alnwickgarden.com
Activities: General charitable purposes; education, training; advancement of health or saving of lives; disability; arts, culture, heritage, science; economic, community development, employment; other charitable purposes
Address: The Alnwick Garden, Denwick Lane, Alnwick, Northumberland, NE66 1YU
Trustees: Mr Jonathan Blackie, Mr Richard Hutton, Mr Ken McMeikan, Jane Northumberland, Ms Louise Halbert
Income: £4,701,680 [2017]; £4,660,884 [2016]; £4,382,486 [2015]; £4,354,635 [2014]; £5,513,950 [2013]

Alpha International
Registered: 18 Apr 2001 *Employees:* 108 *Volunteers:* 100
Tel: 0845 644 7533 *Website:* alpha.org
Activities: Education, training; religious activities; other charitable purposes
Address: Holy Trinity Brompton, Brompton Road, London, SW7 1JA
Trustees: Reverend Nicky Gumbel, Miss Tricia Neill, Mr John MacKay, Dato Seok Hong Yeoh, Mr David Gardner, Mr Al Gordon, Ms Jody Jonsson, Rt Revd Sandy Millar, Mr David Alexander Segel, Mr Chris Sadler, Mrs Rebecca Stewart, Mr Michael Timmis, Mr Bernard Mensah
Income: £9,278,220 [2016]; £10,388,616 [2015]; £9,084,912 [2014]; £9,229,314 [2013]; £8,251,102 [2012]

Alpha Preparatory School, Ltd
Registered: 17 Feb 1965 *Employees:* 26
Tel: 020 8427 1471 *Website:* alpha.harrow.sch.uk
Activities: Education, training
Address: 19-21 Hindes Road, Harrow, Middlesex, HA1 1SH
Trustees: Mr Ian Michael Nunn, Mrs Dipti Sodha, Dr Afrosa Ahmed, Mr Andrew Sims, Mr Hemant Desai, Mrs Karen Brookes, Mrs Reena Patel
Income: £1,560,412 [2017]; £1,586,465 [2016]; £1,452,248 [2015]; £1,381,256 [2014]; £1,395,522 [2013]

Alt Valley Community Trust Limited
Registered: 16 Feb 1988 *Employees:* 50 *Volunteers:* 9
Tel: 0151 546 4168 *Website:* altvalley.co.uk
Activities: Education, training; arts, culture, heritage, science; amateur sport; economic, community development, employment
Address: The Communiversity, Altcross House, Altcross Road, Liverpool, L11 0BS
Trustees: Ms Alma Margaret Mason, Mr Anthony Jennings, Mrs Lesley Baugh, Mrs Catherine Edwards, Mr Anthony Rimmer, Mr Gerry Brennan, Mr Joseph Donnelly, Mrs Lynne Lacey, Dr Brian McDonough
Income: £2,343,821 [2016]; £1,975,142 [2015]; £2,186,473 [2014]; £1,977,559 [2013]; £1,425,192 [2012]

The Alternative Animal Sanctuary
Registered: 22 Sep 2005 *Employees:* 1
Tel: 07818 406619 *Website:* alternativesanctuary.co.uk
Activities: Animals
Address: Chapelry Farm, Langrick Road, New York, Lincoln, LN4 4XH
Trustees: Mrs Edith Lloyd, Mr Nigel Scott Boutwood, Rachael Williams, Ms Tamara Lloyd, Mrs Deborah Dance
Income: £1,288,776 [2016]; £1,219,653 [2015]; £1,169,972 [2014]; £1,219,510 [2013]

Alternative Futures Group Limited
Registered: 21 Feb 1992 *Employees:* 1,969
Tel: 0151 489 5501 *Website:* alternativefuturesgroup.org.uk
Activities: The advancement of health or saving of lives; disability; accommodation, housing
Address: Alternative Futures Group, Unit 16 Lion Court, Kings Drive, Prescot, Merseyside, L34 1BN
Trustees: Mrs Chris Hannah, Mr Daniel Chaffer, Mr Michael Parkinson, Mr Iain Bell, Ms Jane McDonald, Mr Andrew Lomas, Mr Michael Clarke, Mr Jonathan Lloyd, Ms Janet Wilkinson, Ms Linda Whalley
Income: £59,157,000 [2017]; £60,020,438 [2016]; £58,164,831 [2015]; £56,283,260 [2014]; £55,064,526 [2013]

Alternative Theatre Company Limited
Registered: 23 Sep 1975 *Employees:* 27
Tel: 020 8743 3584 *Website:* bushtheatre.co.uk
Activities: Arts, culture, heritage, science
Address: H & F Asian Association, Shepherds Bush Library, 7 Uxbridge Road, London, W12 8LJ
Trustees: Mr Matthew Byam Shaw, Ms Grace Chan, Mr Simon Johnson, Ms Nike Jonah, Madani Younis, Mr Mark Dakin, Mr Stephen Greenhalgh, Ms Isabella Macpherson, Mrs Giancarla Alen-Buckley, Ms Khalfi Kareem, Mr Simon Dowson-Collins, Ms Kathryn Marten
Income: £4,244,878 [2017]; £2,625,842 [2016]; £1,800,225 [2015]; £2,566,387 [2014]; £1,838,974 [2013]

Alton Convent School Charity
Registered: 24 Sep 1998 *Employees:* 142
Tel: 01420 82070 *Website:* altonconvent.org.uk
Activities: Education, training
Address: Alton Convent School, Anstey Lane, Alton, Hants, GU34 2NG
Trustees: Sister Anne-Marie Marot, Sister Helen Samuel, Sister Margaret Evelyn Garman, Sister Cecilia Jackson, Sister Sylvette Orge
Income: £5,512,592 [2016]; £5,559,616 [2015]; £5,379,785 [2014]; £5,201,654 [2013]; £4,938,438 [2012]

Alzheimer's Research UK
Registered: 19 Aug 1999 *Employees:* 107 *Volunteers:* 1,783
Tel: 01223 824581 *Website:* alzheimersresearchuk.org
Activities: General charitable purposes; advancement of health or saving of lives
Address: Alzheimers Research UK, Unit 3-4, 3 Riverside, Granta Park, Great Abington, Cambridge, CB21 6AD
Trustees: Mrs Shirley Cramer, Prof Rob Howard, Mr David Mayhew CBE, Mr Nicholas Antill, Mrs Caroline Van Den Brul, Dr Ruth McKernan, Dr Rupert Evenett, Professor James William Fawcett, Mr Michael Cooper, Christopher Carter, Mr Giles Dennison
Income: £30,456,941 [2017]; £22,014,026 [2016]; £17,751,837 [2015]; £14,232,552 [2014]; £11,037,304 [2013]

Alzheimer's Society
Registered: 23 Apr 1987 *Employees:* 2,586 *Volunteers:* 6,124
Tel: 020 7423 5136 *Website:* alzheimers.org.uk
Activities: Education, training; advancement of health or saving of lives; disability
Address: Alzheimers Society, 43-44 Crutched Friars, London, EC3N 2AE
Trustees: Professor Gordon Keith Wilcock, Sir John Christopher Powell, Dr Emyr Gordon Roberts, Margaret Joy Allen, Mr David William Kelham, Ms Alison Harrison, Dr Bernard Herdan CB, Ms Sarah Weir OBE, Manish Shah, Jennifer Ann Owen, Mr Stephen Guy Hill, Duncan Jones
Income: £103,596,000 [2017]; £97,949,000 [2016]; £90,574,000 [2015]; £84,437,000 [2014]; £70,771,000 [2013]

Alzheimer's and Dementia Support Services
Registered: 30 Jul 1993 *Employees:* 69 *Volunteers:* 36
Tel: 01474 533990 *Website:* alz-dem.org.uk
Activities: General charitable purposes; education, training; advancement of health or saving of lives; disability; prevention or relief of poverty; arts, culture, heritage, science
Address: Alzheimers & Dementia Support Services, Deneholme House, Dene Holm Road, Northfleet, Kent, DA11 8JY
Trustees: Mr Tony Searles, Ms Paulette Lewis, Mr Alan Spencer, Mrs Abiodun Ademoyero, Mr Justin Bateman, Dr Lynfa Price, Mr Richard Graham, Miss Karen Du Rocher
Income: £1,232,811 [2017]; £1,173,377 [2016]; £911,725 [2015]; £656,403 [2014]; £592,499 [2013]

Alzheimers Support
Registered: 27 Jul 1995 *Employees:* 91 *Volunteers:* 120
Tel: 01225 776481 *Website:* alzheimerswiltshire.org.uk
Activities: The advancement of health or saving of lives; prevention or relief of poverty
Address: Alzheimers Support, 1 Park Road, Trowbridge, Wilts, BA14 8AQ
Trustees: Miss Janet Dore, Mr Harry Theobald, Mrs Rosie Westacott, Mrs Carolyn King, Ms Alison Middleton, Mr Micheal Weston
Income: £1,162,504 [2017]; £1,238,563 [2016]; £1,034,646 [2015]; £969,622 [2014]; £796,966 [2013]

Amabrill Ltd
Registered: 14 Jan 2000 *Volunteers:* 3
Tel: 020 8455 6785
Activities: General charitable purposes; education, training; prevention or relief of poverty; religious activities
Address: 1 Golders Manor Drive, London, NW11 9HU
Trustees: Mr C Lerner, Mr Israel Grossnass, Mrs Frances Rosalind Lerner, Mr Irving Marc Lerner
Income: £5,362,944 [2017]; £2,733,150 [2016]; £2,624,532 [2015]; £2,636,788 [2014]; £2,636,341 [2013]

Aman Foundation UK

Registered: 23 Dec 2015 *Employees:* 1 *Volunteers:* 2
Tel: 020 3540 1515 *Website:* amanfoundationuk.org.uk
Activities: General charitable purposes; education, training; advancement of health or saving of lives; prevention or relief of poverty; amateur sport; economic, community development, employment
Address: 1 Grafton Street, London, W1S 4FE
Trustees: Fayeeza Naqvi, Mr Sivendran Vettivetpillai MBA, Mr Pervez Akhtar, Dr Saadia Quraishy, Mrs Nisha Pillai, Mr Mikael Zoghbi
Income: £2,771,520 [2017]; £816,168 [2016]

Amana Trust

Registered: 13 Aug 2002 *Employees:* 111 *Volunteers:* 25
Tel: 01708 380301 *Website:* amanatrust.org.uk
Activities: Education, training; religious activities; other charitable purposes
Address: Bower House, Orange Tree Hill, Havering-Atte-Bower, Romford, Essex, RM4 1PB
Trustees: Joseph Davis, Paul Cooke, Mr Curtis James Kennard
Income: £4,647,056 [2016]; £2,895,919 [2015]; £2,303,559 [2014]; £3,655,527 [2013]; £3,931,906 [2012]

Amanat Charity Trust

Registered: 7 Nov 1990 *Employees:* 51 *Volunteers:* 100
Tel: 01204 383732 *Website:* uwt.org
Activities: General charitable purposes; education, training; advancement of health or saving of lives; prevention or relief of poverty; overseas aid, famine relief; accommodation, housing
Address: Amanat Charity Trust, 578-600 St Helens Road, Bolton, Lancs, BL3 3SJ
Trustees: Idris Atcha, Zakir Patel, Mr Iqbal Rawat, Mohammad Idrees, Mohammed Ahmed Seedat
Income: £30,230,349 [2016]; £24,913,797 [2015]; £27,287,003 [2014]; £18,487,318 [2013]; £16,154,895 [2012]

The Amar International Charitable Foundation

Registered: 22 Jun 1995 *Employees:* 65 *Volunteers:* 8
Tel: 020 7799 2217 *Website:* amarfoundation.org
Activities: Education, training; advancement of health or saving of lives; prevention or relief of poverty; overseas aid, famine relief; economic, community development, employment; human rights, religious or racial harmony, equality or diversity; other charitable purposes
Address: Foundation, 14th Floor, Amar International Charitable, 3 Albert Embankment, London, SE1 7SP
Trustees: Dr Theodore Zeldin, Mr Damon Parker, Canon Dr Edmund Newell, Ms Sharlene Wells Hawkes, Mr David James Kerr, Baroness Nicholson of Winterbourne, Dr Mohammed Hayder Hassan, Mr Mohammed Ali Charchafchi, Mr Alistair Llewellyn John Redfern, Michael Boardman
Income: £5,745,549 [2016]; £6,417,852 [2015]; £2,846,282 [2014]; £2,665,881 [2013]; £6,268,861 [2012]

The Amber Foundation

Registered: 13 Dec 1995 *Employees:* 59 *Volunteers:* 2
Tel: 01769 582024 *Website:* amberweb.org
Activities: Education, training; prevention or relief of poverty; accommodation, housing
Address: The Amber Foundation, Ashley Court, Chawleigh, Chulmleigh, Devon, EX18 7EX
Trustees: Mr Bartholomew Evan Eric Smith, The Rt Hon Sir Arthur Nicholas Winston Soames MP, Mr Richard John Oldfield, Mrs Penelope Mary Marland, Mrs Lucy Morris, Mr Stephen Charles Lyall
Income: £2,277,240 [2017]; £2,160,330 [2016]; £2,147,711 [2015]; £2,014,935 [2014]; £3,152,751 [2013]

Ambition School Leadership Trust

Registered: 18 Apr 2012 *Employees:* 197
Tel: 020 3828 2466 *Website:* ambitionschoolleadership.org.uk
Activities: Education, training
Address: 65 Kingsway, London, WC2B 6TD
Trustees: Jo Owen, Mr Jonathan Simons, Mrs Celia Berenguer, Sir Nick Weller, Mr Nicolas M Turner, Sally Morgan, Mrs Amanda Timberg, Richard Harpham, Ms Sonia Priya Sodha, Ms Rebecca Ann Vian Boomer-Clark
Income: £17,028,496 [2017]; £9,170,160 [2016]; £8,991,200 [2015]; £6,772,294 [2014]; £5,004,454 [2013]

Ambitious About Autism

Registered: 2 Jul 1997 *Employees:* 337 *Volunteers:* 14
Tel: 020 8815 5444 *Website:* ambitiousaboutautism.org.uk
Activities: Education, training; disability
Address: Pears National Centre for Autism, Woodside Avenue, London, N10 3JA
Trustees: Ms Elizabeth Stanton, Mr John Constantine, Mrs Philippa Stobbs, Mr Micheael Fiddy, Mrs Koral Anderson, Mr Jonathan Andrews, Mr Martyn Craddock, Mr Neil Goulden, Mr Paul Disley-Tindell, Mrs Lesley Longstone, Mrs Charlotte Warner
Income: £23,209,000 [2017]; £10,789,000 [2016]; £9,739,000 [2015]; £10,000,419 [2014]; £8,597,000 [2013]

The American Museum in Britain

Registered: 25 Nov 2004 *Employees:* 34 *Volunteers:* 140
Tel: 01225 460503 *Website:* americanmuseum.org
Activities: General charitable purposes; education, training; arts, culture, heritage, science; environment, conservation, heritage
Address: American Museum in Britain, Claverton Manor, Claverton, Bath, BA2 7BD
Trustees: Mr Richard Bernays, Mr Delton Harrison Jr, Mrs Stanley Deforest Scott, Dr Richard Wendorf, Mrs B Bovender, Dr J Ribel, Mr G Thomas, Mr Mark Haranzo, Mr Alfred Vinton, Mr William John Tyne, Ms Carol Morris, Mr H S Lynn Jr, Lady C Manning, Mr E Bayntun-Coward
Income: £1,144,099 [2016]; £1,050,279 [2015]; £1,212,777 [2014]; £1,037,959 [2013]; £967,068 [2012]

The American School in London Educational Trust Ltd
Registered: 23 Sep 1964 *Employees:* 344 *Volunteers:* 170
Tel: 020 7449 1235 *Website:* asl.org
Activities: Education, training
Address: The American School in London, 1 Waverley Place,
London, NW8 0NP
Trustees: Mr Bill Roedy, Caroline Mitchell Clark, Mrs Julie Skattum,
Mrs Priya Hiranandani Vandrevala, Mr Ivan Gazidis, Ms Elaine
Proctor-Bonbright, Mrs Erin Roth, Mr David Abrams, Mrs Cynthia
Bake, Mr Liad Meidar, Stacey Towfighi, Mrs Erin Jennifer Crawford,
Mr Daniel Hajjar, Mr Luca Bassi, Mr Ramez Sousou, William
Tucker, Ms Donna Lancia, Mrs Sherine Magar, Mr David Novak,
Mrs Alison Lemaire, Mr Nikos Stathopoulos, Mr Christopher Finn,
Ms Rebecca Manuel, Mr Christopher Whitman, Ms Virginia Keener,
Ms Robin Appleby, Ms Stephanie Schueppert
Income: £44,199,000 [2017]; £41,308,000 [2016]; £41,665,501
[2015]; £38,736,536 [2014]; £36,505,071 [2013]

The American School in London Foundation (UK) Limited
Registered: 5 Apr 2001
Tel: 020 7449 1200
Activities: Education, training
Address: The American School in London, 1 Waverley Place,
London, NW8 0NP
Trustees: Mr David Stillman, Mrs Mary Farnsworth Marsh, Barry
Sabloff
Income: £5,644,000 [2017]; £5,174,000 [2016]; £7,376,904 [2015];
£5,095,987 [2014]; £4,435,033 [2013]

Amesbury School Trust Limited
Registered: 27 Apr 1971 *Employees:* 85
Tel: 01428 604322 *Website:* amesburyschool.co.uk
Activities: Education, training
Address: Amesbury School, Hazel Grove, Hindhead, Surrey,
GU26 6BL
Trustees: Simon Miller, Mr Tarquin Henderson, Mrs Deborah
Livsey, Mr Robert Ward, Dr Susan Cooper, Mr Mark Milliken-Smith,
Christopher Bennie, Mr Alan Thomas, Mrs Justine Lago, Mr Mark
Whitby, Mr Ben Charles, Mr Omeed Starmer
Income: £4,000,710 [2016]; £3,607,119 [2015]; £3,318,142 [2014];
£3,073,889 [2013]; £2,915,657 [2012]

Amicus Trust
Registered: 11 Feb 1975 *Employees:* 43
Tel: 01234 334600 *Website:* amicustrust.org
Activities: Accommodation, housing
Address: Amicus Trust, 31a Prebend Street, Bedford, MK40 1QN
Trustees: Mrs Miranda Smythe, Mr Graham West, Ms Jane Owen,
Mr Julian Martin Hogarth Armitage, Mr John Sackett, Mr John
David Owen
Income: £1,907,989 [2017]; £1,464,277 [2016]; £1,222,681 [2015];
£1,171,067 [2014]; £1,102,877 [2013]

Amnesty International Charity Limited
Registered: 17 Apr 1986
Tel: 020 7413 5500 *Website:* amnesty.org
Activities: Education, training; human rights, religious or racial
harmony, equality or diversity; other charitable purposes
Address: Amnesty International, Peter Benenson House,
1 Easton Street, London, WC1X 0DW
Trustees: Mr Melvin Coleman, Ms Susan Wallcraft, Ms Rosie
Chapman, Mr Timothy Stuart Guy
Income: £1,236,000 [2016]; £4,987,000 [2015]; £451,000 [2014];
£365,000 [2013]; £3,775,000 [2012]

Amnesty International UK Section Charitable Trust
Registered: 4 Jan 1996 *Employees:* 36 *Volunteers:* 400
Tel: 020 7033 1784 *Website:* amnesty.org.uk
Activities: Human rights, religious or racial harmony, equality or
diversity
Address: Amnesty International, 17-25 New Inn Yard, London,
EC2A 3EA
Trustees: Ms Livia Aliberti, Mr Gareth Davies, Mr Meredith
Coombs, Ms Amie Jayne Ibrahimi Brown, Mr Nicolas Alexander
Patrick, Ms Emma France, Mr Thomas Hedley, Ms Ruth Breddal,
Mr Nicholas Mark Vogelpoel
Income: £16,565,000 [2016]; £14,333,000 [2015]; £16,213,000
[2014]; £14,041,000 [2013]; £13,938,000 [2012]

The Ampersand Foundation
Registered: 10 May 2016 *Employees:* 1
Tel: 01332 742777 *Website:* theampersandfoundation.com
Activities: Education, training; arts, culture, heritage, science
Address: 2 Riverside Chambers, Full Street, Derby, DE1 3AF
Trustees: Mr Simon Leo Conway, Mr John Alexander Kirkland,
Mr Thiago Arruda De Carvalho, Mr Alastair David Sooke
Income: £1,505,065 [2017]

Amphibian and Reptile Conservation Trust
Registered: 16 Jun 2009 *Employees:* 29 *Volunteers:* 250
Tel: 01202 391319 *Website:* arc-trust.org
Activities: Education, training; animals; environment, conservation,
heritage
Address: The Herpetological Conservation Trust, 655a
Christchurch Road, Bournemouth, BH1 4AP
Trustees: Mr Jonathan Webster, Professor Trevor John Clark
Beebee, Dr Roger Mitchell, Mr Robert Jehle, Mr Jeremy Larick
Bruce, Mrs Philippa Marion Perry OBE, Howard Inns, Mrs Jan
Clemons BSc, Professor Richard Griffiths
Income: £4,669,506 [2017]; £1,222,339 [2016]; £2,734,968 [2015];
£1,223,594 [2014]; £1,145,440 [2013]

Ampleforth Abbey
Registered: 24 Sep 1993 *Employees:* 520 *Volunteers:* 78
Tel: 01439 766710 *Website:* ampleforth.org.uk
Activities: Education, training; religious activities
Address: Ampleforth Abbey, York, YO62 4EN
Trustees: The Ampleforth Abbey Trustees
Income: £24,713,000 [2016]; £26,164,000 [2015]; £25,629,000
[2014]; £25,400,000 [2013]; £26,082,000 [2012]

Amref Health Africa
Registered: 27 Aug 1970 *Employees:* 14 *Volunteers:* 3
Tel: 020 7269 5520 *Website:* amrefuk.org
Activities: Education, training; advancement of health or saving of
lives; disability; prevention or relief of poverty; overseas aid, famine
relief; economic, community development, employment; human
rights, religious or racial harmony, equality or diversity
Address: Lower Ground Floor, 15-18 White Lion Street, London,
N1 9PD
Trustees: Ms Susan Hunt, Mrs Amanda Caine, Dr Nigel Lighfoot,
Mr Alistair Smith, Mr Mark Richard Chambers
Income: £4,424,240 [2017]; £5,610,432 [2016]; £5,695,704 [2015];
£4,366,951 [2014]; £4,458,117 [2013]

Ana Leaf Foundation
Registered: 11 Dec 2009
Activities: General charitable purposes; education, training; advancement of health or saving of lives; disability; arts, culture, heritage, science; amateur sport; other charitable purposes
Address: P O Box 155, Jersey, JE4 5NS
Trustees: Mrs Amanda Catherine Simmons, Hayley De Putron
Income: £2,002,594 [2016]; £1,601 [2015]; £2,776 [2014]; £2,505,131 [2013]; £5,927 [2012]

Anatomical Society
Registered: 6 Nov 1984 *Employees:* 1
Tel: 020 7468 1223 *Website:* anatsoc.org.uk
Activities: Education, training; advancement of health or saving of lives; arts, culture, heritage, science
Address: Royal Veterinary College, 4 Royal College Street, London, NW1 0TU
Trustees: Dr Lopa Leach, Professor Stefan Przyborski, Dr Claire Smith, Professor Thomas Clive Lee, Professor Zoltan Molnar, Professor Colin Douglas Ockleford, Dr Fabio Quondamatteo, Dr Adam Michael Taylor, Dr Iain Keenan, Dr Grenham Ireland, Professor Simon Parson, Dr Gabrielle Maria Finn, Dr Imelda McGonnell, Professor Kieran McDermott, Dr Siobhan Loughna, Dr Abigail Tucker, Mr Joy Balta, Dr Gavin Clowry
Income: £1,210,051 [2016]; £1,127,090 [2015]; £1,019,448 [2014]; £1,105,373 [2013]; £1,106,363 [2012]

Anawim - Women Working Together
Registered: 22 Dec 2014 *Employees:* 34 *Volunteers:* 35
Tel: 0121 440 5296 *Website:* anawim.co.uk
Activities: General charitable purposes; education, training; prevention or relief of poverty; accommodation, housing; economic, community development, employment
Address: 228 Mary Street, Balsall Heath, Birmingham, B12 9RJ
Trustees: Sister Jenny Coyne, Sr Josephine Collier, Mrs Susan Hanley, Paul Williams, Andrew Quinn, Ruth Drapkin JP, Mrs Janet Hemlin
Income: £1,761,719 [2017]; £1,928,194 [2016]

Anchor Trust
Registered: 22 Jan 1996 *Employees:* 7,169 *Volunteers:* 150
Tel: 020 7759 7249 *Website:* anchor.org.uk
Activities: The advancement of health or saving of lives; disability; accommodation, housing
Address: The Anchor Trust, Suites A & B, 3rd Floor, The Heals Building, 22-24 Torrington Place, London, WC1E 7HJ
Trustees: Mark Allan, Pamela Chesters CBE, Richard Jones CBE, Mr Stephen Jack, Alun Griffiths, Mr Richard Petty
Income: £329,387,000 [2017]; £367,327,000 [2016]; £269,817,000 [2015]; £268,310,000 [2014]; £274,974,000 [2013]

Andover and District Mencap
Registered: 16 Sep 1994 *Employees:* 134 *Volunteers:* 30
Tel: 01264 321840 *Website:* andovermencap.org
Activities: Disability; accommodation, housing
Address: The Wellington Centre, Winchester Road, Andover, Hants, SP10 2EG
Trustees: Mr David Anthony Atkins BEM, Mr Martyn Bullock, Mr Jamie Turner, Mr Colin Woods, Mrs Ann Woods, Mr Philip Woods, Mrs Elizabeth Austin
Income: £2,264,433 [2017]; £2,473,392 [2016]; £1,953,977 [2015]; £1,977,155 [2014]; £1,958,587 [2013]

Andrews Charitable Trust
Registered: 6 Aug 1965 *Employees:* 2 *Volunteers:* 2
Tel: 0117 946 1834 *Website:* andrewscharitabletrust.org.uk
Activities: Education, training; advancement of health or saving of lives; disability; prevention or relief of poverty; overseas aid, famine relief; accommodation, housing; religious activities; environment, conservation, heritage; economic, community development, employment; human rights, religious or racial harmony, equality or diversity; other charitable purposes
Address: The Clockhouse, Bath Hill, Keynsham, Bristol, BS31 1HL
Trustees: Mr David Westgate, Ms Helen Battrick, Mr Alastair Page, Mr Chris Chapman, Ms Alison Kelly, Mr Jon Charlesworth, Mr Nicholas Wright, Mr Paul Heal, Ms Elizabeth Hughes, Ms Ami Davis, Ms Ruth Knagg
Income: £2,051,600 [2016]; £646,378 [2015]; £617,856 [2014]; £599,945 [2013]; £459,783 [2012]

The Angel Foundation
Registered: 23 Feb 2000 *Employees:* 62
Tel: 01752 765765 *Website:* god.tv
Activities: General charitable purposes; education, training; prevention or relief of poverty; overseas aid, famine relief; religious activities
Address: 27 Burrington Way, Plymouth, PL5 3LR
Trustees: Mr Christopher John Cole, Mr Ward Simpson, Dr Graham Dacre, Mr Stephen Wright Beik, Mr Rafael Simpson, Mr David Wright
Income: £5,555,530 [2017]; £7,005,164 [2016]; £9,268,408 [2015]; £8,979,621 [2014]; £8,215,857 [2013]

Anglia Care Trust
Registered: 14 Jun 1989 *Employees:* 67 *Volunteers:* 120
Tel: 01473 622888 *Website:* angliacaretrust.org.uk
Activities: General charitable purposes; education, training; advancement of health or saving of lives; prevention or relief of poverty; accommodation, housing; economic, community development, employment; other charitable purposes
Address: 8 The Square, Martlesham Heath, Ipswich, Suffolk, IP5 3SL
Trustees: Mr Colin Reid, Mr Colin Shiers, Mrs Ann Bryant, Ms Rachael Wyartt, Roy Wisdon, Graham Walker, Mr Alexander Lloyd, Richard Trotter
Income: £2,351,969 [2017]; £2,080,971 [2016]; £2,311,565 [2015]; £2,175,773 [2014]; £1,478,962 [2013]

Anglia Region of The Guide Association
Registered: 16 Oct 1979 *Employees:* 31 *Volunteers:* 17,000
Tel: 01603 737357 *Website:* girlguidinganglia.org.uk
Activities: Education, training
Address: Girlguiding Anglia, Anglia Region Office, 7 Great Hautbois Road, Coltishall, Norwich, NR12 7JN
Trustees: Mrs Tracy Foster, Mrs Debbie Docherty, Mrs Julie Richards, Miss Nicola Gardner, Mrs Helen Pope, Ms Sandra Richardson, Mrs Angela Peel, Mrs Julia Winstanley, Mrs Andrea Oughton, Mrs Maxine Jones, Mrs Sue Howe
Income: £1,514,087 [2016]; £1,559,774 [2015]; £1,721,909 [2014]; £1,325,426 [2013]; £1,369,054 [2012]

Anglia Ruskin Students' Union
Registered: 15 Aug 2012 *Employees:* 34 *Volunteers:* 3,100
Tel: 01223 460008 *Website:* angliastudent.com
Activities: Education, training
Address: East Road, Cambridge, CB1 1PT
Trustees: Mr James Nevile Disney Barlow, Miss Melanie Digney, Mr Richard Halderthay, Jamie Smith, Eliza Torres, Miss Helena Schofield, Mrs Janice Argo MacLean, Mr Kirran Khan, Ms Tanya Curry, Ms Laura Douds, Miss Johanna Korhonen, Ms Lusungu Muwowo
Income: £2,040,331 [2017]; £2,034,993 [2016]; £1,956,949 [2015]; £1,920,978 [2014]; £1,784,246 [2013]

Anglican Consultative Council
Registered: 5 Aug 2010 *Employees:* 22
Tel: 020 7313 3901 *Website:* aco.org
Activities: Education, training; overseas aid, famine relief; religious activities
Address: Anglican Consultative Council, St Andrews House, 16 Tavistock Crescent, London, W11 1AP
Trustees: Lord Archbishop of Canterbury Justin Portal Welby, The Most Revd Dr Richard Clarke, The Rt Revd Eraste Bigirimana, The Most Revd Dr Thabo Makgoba, The Most Revd Philip Freier, The Right Revd Joel Waweru Mwangi, Mr Jeroham Melendez, Ms Margaret Anne Swinson, The Most Revd Dr Paul Kwong, Ms Louisa Mojela, The Most Revd and The Hon Dr John Holder, Mr Alistair Dinnie, Rev Nigel Lewellyn Pope, Rt Revd Jane Alexander
Income: £2,386,499 [2016]; £2,367,694 [2015]; £2,145,632 [2014]; £2,282,576 [2013]; £2,119,194 [2012]

Anglo American Group Foundation
Registered: 18 Oct 2005
Tel: 020 7968 8888 *Website:* angloamericangroupfoundation.org
Activities: General charitable purposes; education, training; advancement of health or saving of lives; disability; prevention or relief of poverty; accommodation, housing; environment, conservation, heritage; economic, community development, employment; human rights, religious or racial harmony, equality or diversity
Address: Anglo American PLC, Anglo American House, 20 Carlton House Terrace, London, SW1Y 5AN
Trustees: Mrs Angela Bromfield, Mr Jonathan Samuel, Mr Duncan Wanblad
Income: £2,298,451 [2016]; £1,203,120 [2015]; £1,230,317 [2014]; £1,449,895 [2013]; £1,999,105 [2012]

Anglo Australian Christian & Charitable Fund
Registered: 2 Apr 2007 *Employees:* 2
Tel: 020 7490 7766
Activities: Education, training; religious activities
Address: Lubbock Fine, Paternoster House, 65 St Pauls Churchyard, London, EC4M 8AB
Trustees: Mr John Kapend Tshiyamb, Ms Carine Martinez, Mr Peter William Jamieson, Mr Willy Schaper-Kotter, Angelo De Lubio Feril
Income: £12,680,999 [2017]; £1,859,188 [2016]; £2,524,087 [2015]; £122,378 [2014]; £356,217 [2013]

The Anglo-American Charity Limited
Registered: 29 Jan 2004
Tel: 01438 820577 *Website:* anglo-americancharity.org
Activities: General charitable purposes
Address: Priors Holt, Bibbs Hall Lane, Ayot St Lawrence, Welwyn, Herts, AL6 9BY
Trustees: Mr Jeffrey Leland Hedges, Mr Stuart Evan Horwich
Income: £1,993,081 [2016]; £1,592,243 [2015]; £2,411,667 [2014]; £714,674 [2013]; £666,680 [2012]

Anheddau Cyf
Registered: 6 Nov 1989 *Employees:* 197
Tel: 01248 675910 *Website:* anheddau.co.uk
Activities: Disability
Address: Anheddau Cyf, Unit 6 Llys Britannia, Ffordd Y Parc, Parc Menai, Bangor, Gwynedd, LL57 4BN
Trustees: Mr Brian Jones, Mr Jonathan Walsh, Gwylan Williams, Richard Barker, Mr John David Williams
Income: £4,982,728 [2017]; £4,839,235 [2016]; £4,940,443 [2015]; £4,795,865 [2014]; £4,881,982 [2013]

Animal Health Trust
Registered: 24 Apr 1966 *Employees:* 270 *Volunteers:* 20
Tel: 01638 751000 *Website:* aht.org.uk
Activities: Education, training; animals
Address: Animal Health Trust, Lanwades Park, Kentford, Newmarket, Suffolk, CB8 7UU
Trustees: The Lord Kirkham CVO, Mr Peter Harvey Locke BVSc MRCVS, Professor Tony Minson BSc PhD, Mr Ronnie Irving BCom CA, Mr David R Ellis BVetMed DEO FRCVS, Professor David BA Silk MD FRCP, Mrs Rachel Flynn, Mr Noel Gerard Byrne, Sir John Spurling KCVO OBE, HRH The Princess Royal KG KT GCVO QSO, Mr Steve Shore, Mr Jeff Whalley, Professor Christopher J Gaskell BVSc PhD DVR MRCVS, Mr Humphrey Salwey CBE TD DL, Professor Kevin Thomas Morley, Mr John Gildersleeve
Income: £15,748,000 [2016]; £17,038,000 [2015]; £14,169,000 [2014]; £13,321,000 [2013]; £11,746,000 [2012]

Animals Asia Foundation
Registered: 5 Jun 2001 *Employees:* 16 *Volunteers:* 160
Tel: 01752 224424 *Website:* animalsasia.org
Activities: Education, training; animals; environment, conservation, heritage
Address: Office 17, Mary Seacole Road, The Millfields, Plymouth, PL1 3JY
Trustees: Mr Boris Chiao, Mr John Simpson Warham, Ms Jill Robinson MBE
Income: £3,672,401 [2016]; £2,313,781 [2015]; £1,842,184 [2014]; £1,358,129 [2013]; £1,137,959 [2012]

Animals in Distress (Torbay and Westcountry)
Registered: 16 Aug 2004 *Employees:* 64 *Volunteers:* 248
Tel: 01803 812121 *Website:* animalsindistress.uk.com
Activities: Animals
Address: Biltor, Edgelands Lane, Ipplepen, Newton Abbot, Devon, TQ12 5UF
Trustees: Miss Robina Brand, Mr Peter Walmsley, Ms Amy Cross, Mrs Patricia Tucker, Mr Gordon Gooding, Mrs Geraldine Laura Dix, Mr David John Turner, Mrs Alison Truscott
Income: £1,278,106 [2016]; £1,297,538 [2015]; £3,364,478 [2014]; £1,374,524 [2013]; £1,156,190 [2012]

Anjuman-E-Badri (Birmingham)
Registered: 29 Mar 2000
Tel: 0121 440 6727
Activities: General charitable purposes; education, training; prevention or relief of poverty; religious activities; amateur sport; human rights, religious or racial harmony, equality or diversity
Address: 10 Court Road, Balsall Heath, Birmingham, B12 9LQ
Trustees: Mulla Fakhruddin Alibhai, Mulla Mohammed Husain Karimjee, Dr Mulla Turab Maimoon, Mr Fazle Abbas Hassanali, Ibnemadyan B H Hamiduddins, Mulla Zulficar Hassanali, Mulla Shabir Hirani, Mr Nurudin Abdulhussein
Income: £1,030,304 [2016]; £1,232,397 [2015]; £537,664 [2014]; £669,551 [2013]; £890,514 [2012]

Anjuman-E-Burhani (London)
Registered: 14 Dec 1999 *Employees:* 18 *Volunteers:* 2
Tel: 020 8841 5623 *Website:* londonjamaat.com
Activities: General charitable purposes; education, training; religious activities
Address: House No 5, Dar-Ul-Emarat, Mohammedi Park, Rowdell Road, Northolt Industrial Park, Northolt, Middlesex, UB5 6AG
Trustees: Dr Idris Bhaisaheb Zainuddin, Shaikh Yunus Abdulqadir, Shk Hamza Jivanji, Shaikh Shabbir Inayathusein, Zainulabideen Bhaisaheb Shujaee
Income: £1,555,840 [2016]; £1,632,446 [2015]; £1,799,331 [2014]; £1,605,122 [2013]; £1,962,170 [2012]

Ansbury
Registered: 11 Feb 2015 *Employees:* 72 *Volunteers:* 1
Tel: 01202 677557 *Website:* ansbury.co.uk
Activities: Education, training
Address: Ansbury, 3 Kingland Road, Poole, Dorset, BH15 1SH
Trustees: Mr Thomas Arthur James Grainger, Mr Peter John Caldwell, Mr Eric Michael McDonnell, Dr Tina Barton, Mrs Kay Maxine Williams, Mr Gareth Simon Griffiths
Income: £1,962,967 [2017]; £2,288,859 [2016]

Anti-Slavery International
Registered: 13 Sep 1995 *Employees:* 24
Tel: 020 7501 8920 *Website:* antislavery.org
Activities: General charitable purposes; education, training; overseas aid, famine relief; economic, community development, employment; human rights, religious or racial harmony, equality or diversity
Address: Anti-Slavery International, Unit 4, The Stableyard, Broomgrove Road, London, SW9 9TL
Trustees: Ms Lucy Claridge, Ms Tanya Ann English, Karen O'Connor, Mr Nicholas Griffin, Mrs Sarah Rachael Harrington Hemens, Malcolm John, Mr Thomas Edward Fyans, Ms Frances Morris-Jones, Katy Dent, Miss Jennifer Marie Harding
Income: £1,894,632 [2017]; £1,967,760 [2016]; £2,356,602 [2015]; £1,723,829 [2014]; £2,561,851 [2013]

The Antiquarian Horological Society
Registered: 8 Apr 1970 *Employees:* 2
Tel: 01580 200155 *Website:* ahsoc.org
Activities: Education, training; arts, culture, heritage, science; environment, conservation, heritage
Address: Antiquarian Horological Society, New House, High Street, Ticehurst, Wadhurst, E Sussex, TN5 7AL
Trustees: Mr Alan Treherne, Mr Ted Powell, David Rooney, Rory McEvoy, James Stratton, Mr David Robert Thompson, Jonathan Betts, James Nye, Mr Richard Stenning
Income: £1,789,143 [2017]; £144,676 [2016]; £117,053 [2015]; £120,818 [2014]; £164,930 [2013]

The Anvil Trust Limited
Registered: 16 Mar 1994 *Employees:* 53
Website: anvilarts.org.uk
Activities: Arts, culture, heritage, science
Address: Anvil Trust Offices, Churchill Way, Basingstoke, Hants, RG21 7QR
Trustees: David Whelton, Mr David Chatten-Smith, Mr Steven Hayward, Mrs Marilyn Jane Tucker, Ms Sara Michelle Catley, Andrew Finney, Dr Alei Duan, Mrs Laura Bryony Bell, Miss Abigail Helen Bowden
Income: £4,640,638 [2017]; £4,998,374 [2016]; £4,846,598 [2015]; £4,730,979 [2014]; £5,128,444 [2013]

Apasen
Registered: 18 May 2006 *Employees:* 226 *Volunteers:* 6
Tel: 020 7001 2266 *Website:* apasen.org.uk
Activities: Disability
Address: Apasenth, 30 Copenhagen Place, London, E14 7FF
Trustees: Mr Amir Hussain, Mrs Shoriful Nessa, Ms Momota Begum, Mr Tobaris Ali, Mr Syed Gulab Ali
Income: £4,887,983 [2017]; £3,836,981 [2016]; £3,673,179 [2015]; £3,249,351 [2014]; £2,695,904 [2013]

The Apax Foundation
Registered: 27 Jan 2006
Tel: 020 7872 6300
Activities: General charitable purposes; education, training; advancement of health or saving of lives; disability; prevention or relief of poverty; overseas aid, famine relief; accommodation, housing; religious activities; arts, culture, heritage, science; amateur sport; economic, community development, employment; human rights, religious or racial harmony, equality or diversity; other charitable purposes
Address: 33 Jermyn Street, London, SW1Y 6DN
Trustees: Sir Ronald Cohen, Dr Peter Englander, Mr Simon Cresswell, Mr Shashank Singh, Mr Jason Wright, Mr David Marks, Mr John F Megrue Jr, Mr Mitch Truwit, Mr Rohan Haldea
Income: £1,787,309 [2017]; £3,916,180 [2016]; £852,397 [2015]; £566,979 [2014]; £1,494,218 [2013]

Apostleship of the Sea
Registered: 1 Jun 1998 *Employees:* 27 *Volunteers:* 100
Tel: 020 7901 1931 *Website:* apostleshipofthesea.org.uk
Activities: General charitable purposes; advancement of health or saving of lives; religious activities; human rights, religious or racial harmony, equality or diversity; other charitable purposes
Address: Catholic Bishops Conference of England & Wales, General Secretariat, 39 Eccleston Square, London, SW1V 1BX
Trustees: Mr Juvenal Shiundu MSc BSc (Hons), Captain Kevin William Doyle, Mrs Louise Carter, Mgr Richard Madders, Mrs Helen Brennan, Rev Paul James Mason, Rev Dr Stephen Morgan MTh BA, Dr Marcus Jones, Mr James Brennan, Rev Stephen Robson, Mr Robert Ashdown
Income: £1,810,937 [2016]; £1,350,671 [2015]; £1,430,244 [2014]; £1,233,872 [2013]; £1,151,159 [2012]

The Apostolic Church
Registered: 1 May 1961 *Employees:* 71 *Volunteers:* 300
Tel: 020 7587 1802 *Website:* apostolic-church.org
Activities: The prevention or relief of poverty; religious activities
Address: The Apostolic Church, Head Office, Suite 105 & 110 Crystal House, New Bedford Road, Luton, Beds, LU1 1HS
Trustees: Rev Eric Parker, Rev Paul Howells, Rev Tim Jack, Rev Simon Taylor, Rev Phelim Doherty, Rev Ivan Parker, Rev Adeoye Abiodun
Income: £5,911,222 [2017]; £5,877,054 [2016]; £5,570,863 [2015]; £5,292,320 [2014]; £5,206,683 [2013]

Approach Supporting Your Life Your Way
Registered: 1 Mar 2013 *Employees:* 58 *Volunteers:* 45
Tel: 01782 214999 *Website:* approachstaffordshire.co.uk
Activities: Education, training; disability
Address: Approach Supporting Older Minds, Cauldon Chambers, 10 Stoke Road, Stoke on Trent, Staffs, ST4 2DP
Trustees: Mr Brian Tomkins, Dr Edward Francis Slade, Mrs Joan Cecelia Gratty, Mrs Carole Godwin, Mr Clive James Paddison, Mrs Jayne Wemyss, Mrs Miriam Darbyshire, Mr Paul Dobson
Income: £1,000,437 [2017]; £965,652 [2016]; £949,787 [2015]; £856,045 [2014]

The Apuldram Centre
Registered: 12 Feb 1990 *Employees:* 52 *Volunteers:* 55
Tel: 01243 783370 *Website:* apuldram.org
Activities: Education, training; disability; accommodation, housing
Address: The Apuldram Centre, Common Farm, Appledram Lane South, Chichester, W Sussex, PO20 7PE
Trustees: Mr George Seth, Mr Oliver Howard James, Mr Paul Anthony Reed, Mr Alan Nicholl, Mr Martin David Clack, Mrs Susan Margaret Saunders, Mr Andrew Christopher William Buckland, Mrs Lesley Claire Burford
Income: £1,161,660 [2017]; £1,137,130 [2016]; £1,024,394 [2015]; £981,936 [2014]; £1,318,242 [2013]

Aquaculture Stewardship Council
Registered: 9 Jan 2013 *Employees:* 5
Website: asc-aqua.org
Activities: Education, training; environment, conservation, heritage
Address: 27 Old Gloucester Street, London, WC1N 3AX
Trustees: Mr Petter Arnesen, Mrs Caroline Tippett, Dr Scott Edward Nicols, Mr Alastair Dingwall, Dr Peter Alan Cook, Miss Meghan Jeans, Miss Ling Cao, Mr Jose Villalon
Income: £3,628,719 [2016]; £1,479,459 [2015]; £236,490 [2014]; £387,460 [2013]

Aquaid Lifeline Fund
Registered: 12 May 2000
Tel: 01223 276710
Activities: General charitable purposes; education, training; prevention or relief of poverty; overseas aid, famine relief; environment, conservation, heritage
Address: 24 Thornton Way, Girton, Cambridge, CB3 0NJ
Trustees: Mr John Rees Searle, Mr Philip Hadridge, Mrs Christine Kimmitt, Mrs Josie Charter
Income: £1,066,589 [2016]; £877,441 [2015]; £840,392 [2014]; £731,855 [2013]; £698,136 [2012]

Aquarius Action Projects
Registered: 24 Sep 1992 *Employees:* 163 *Volunteers:* 66
Tel: 0121 622 8181 *Website:* aquarius.org.uk
Activities: Education, training; advancement of health or saving of lives; disability
Address: Aquarius, 236 Bristol Road, Birmingham, B5 7SL
Trustees: Derek Caren, John Mole, Maris Stratulis, Albert Fletcher, Faisal Mahmood, David Carrington
Income: £5,486,072 [2017]; £5,206,949 [2016]; £7,639,194 [2015]; £7,261,671 [2014]; £6,894,911 [2013]

Aquaterra Leisure
Registered: 14 Oct 1970 *Employees:* 51 *Volunteers:* 5
Tel: 020 3474 0608 *Website:* aquaterra.org
Activities: Education, training; advancement of health or saving of lives; disability; prevention or relief of poverty; arts, culture, heritage, science; amateur sport
Address: Suite 1.40, 1st Floor, Millbank Tower, 21-24 Millbank, London, SW1P 4QP
Trustees: Mr Neil Best, Mr Paul James St Hilaire, Ms Catrin Eluned Hughes, Ms Pamela Henry
Income: £1,643,000 [2017]; £2,577,000 [2016]; £5,788,113 [2015]; £15,419,000 [2014]; £15,023,000 [2013]

Arab World Ministries
Registered: 8 Nov 1996 *Employees:* 16 *Volunteers:* 12
Tel: 01509 239525 *Website:* awm-pioneers.org
Activities: Religious activities
Address: AWM, 28a Belton Road West, Loughborough, Leics, LE11 5TR
Trustees: Rev Dr I D Farley, Mr M S Hyde, Alex Mateer, Miss Naomi Lamont, Mr Richard Cromie, Dr S E Brown, Mark Billage, Miss Elizabeth Maggs, Mr Karl Butler
Income: £3,022,653 [2016]; £2,200,709 [2015]; £1,937,762 [2014]; £1,877,635 [2013]; £1,968,992 [2012]

The Arboricultural Association
Registered: 28 Nov 2000 *Employees:* 11 *Volunteers:* 10
Tel: 01242 522152 *Website:* trees.org.uk
Activities: Education, training; environment, conservation, heritage
Address: Malthouse, Standish, Stonehouse, Glos, GL10 3DL
Trustees: Mr Keith Sacre, Mr Laurence Vine-Chatterton, Mr Simon Holmes, Mr Jaime John Joseph Bray, Mr Alastair Durkin, Navin Sehmi, Mr Michael Sankus, Mr Jonathan Cocking, Mr Robin Jackson, Mr Ged Collins, Mr Ian Richard Murat
Income: £1,189,554 [2016]; £1,189,554 [2015]; £1,114,206 [2014]; £970,421 [2013]; £799,355 [2012]

Arch (North Staffs) Limited
Registered: 31 Mar 1989 *Employees:* 138 *Volunteers:* 41
Tel: 01782 744533 *Website:* archnorthstaffs.org.uk
Activities: Education, training; prevention or relief of poverty; accommodation, housing; economic, community development, employment
Address: Staffordshire Housing Association, 308 London Road, Stoke on Trent, Staffs, ST4 5AB
Trustees: Susan Shardlow, Miss Valarie Bourne, Mr John Arthur Yates
Income: £4,034,880 [2017]; £4,870,013 [2016]; £4,816,003 [2015]; £4,683,613 [2014]; £4,009,362 [2013]

Arch Initiatives
Registered: 23 Aug 1993 *Employees:* 181 *Volunteers:* 19
Tel: 01633 811950 *Website:* archfutures.com
Activities: General charitable purposes; education, training; advancement of health or saving of lives; economic, community development, employment
Address: 1 Resolven House, St Mellons Business Park, Fortran Road, St Mellons, Cardiff, CF3 0EY
Trustees: Mr David Antebi, Mrs Pamela Frances Rutter, Mr Stephen Davison
Income: £6,525,745 [2017]; £4,231,205 [2016]; £6,151,447 [2015]; £6,304,894 [2014]; £6,456,879 [2013]

Archange Lebrun Trust Limited
Registered: 9 Dec 2002
Tel: 01666 510832
Activities: General charitable purposes; education, training; advancement of health or saving of lives; prevention or relief of poverty; overseas aid, famine relief; accommodation, housing; religious activities; economic, community development, employment
Address: The White House, School Hill, Brinkworth, Chippenham, Wilts, SN15 5AX
Trustees: Sr Pat Trussell, Sister Margaret O'Reilly, Sister Winifred Anne Burke, Sr Helen Randles, Sister Caroline Njah Bongnavti, Sister Margaret Teresa Finn, Sister Rebecca Sepepka, Sister Theresa Horvath, Sister Paula Catherine Coelho, Sister Anselma Ilsa Jofre
Income: £2,182,000 [2016]; £1,936,000 [2015]; £661,649 [2014]; £407,000 [2013]; £405,000 [2012]

The Archbishops' Council
Registered: 25 Mar 1999 *Employees:* 106
Tel: 020 7898 1000 *Website:* churchofengland.org
Activities: Education, training; prevention or relief of poverty; religious activities; environment, conservation, heritage; economic, community development, employment
Address: Church House, Great Smith Street, London, SW1P 3AZ
Trustees: Mr John Spence, The Ven Cherry Vann, Rt Rev Stephen Conway, Mr Adrian Greenwood, Canon Mark Russell, Revd Canon Simon Butler, Rev Rosalyn Murphy, Ms Loretta Minghella, The Most Revd and Rt Hon Justin Welby, Revd Dr Ian Paul, Rev Martin Seeley, Canon Elizabeth Paver, Mr Mark Sheard, The Most Revd and Rt Hon John Tucker Mugabi Sentamu, Ms Mary Chapman, Rev Sarah Schofield, Canon Dr James Harrison, Ms Rebecca Swinson, Mr Matthew Frost
Income: £85,077,000 [2016]; £86,278,000 [2015]; £72,604,000 [2014]; £73,254,000 [2013]; £71,156,000 [2012]

L'Arche
Registered: 24 Jul 1972 *Employees:* 389 *Volunteers:* 240
Tel: 01535 656186 *Website:* larche.org.uk
Activities: Education, training; disability; overseas aid, famine relief; accommodation, housing
Address: 10 Briggate, Silsden, Keighley, W Yorks, BD20 9JT
Trustees: Kathleen O'Gorman, Mr Peter James Whalley, Marie Roberts, Dr Carole Glasson, Peter Harrison, Ben Moorhead, Mr Stewart Milne, Mrs Bernadette Elizabeth Ann Rijnenberg, Miss Catherine Baines, Mr John O'Brien, Dr David George Race BSc PGCE PhD, Mr Nick Boyle, Joan Blows, Mr Stephen Grice, Mrs Susan Margaret Williams, Isobel Gray
Income: £11,280,380 [2017]; £9,912,821 [2016]; £9,432,708 [2015]; £8,669,250 [2014]; £9,049,008 [2013]

Architects Benevolent Society
Registered: 21 Feb 1973 *Employees:* 7 *Volunteers:* 19
Tel: 020 7580 2823 *Website:* absnet.org.uk
Activities: The prevention or relief of poverty; accommodation, housing
Address: Architects Benevolent Society, 43 Portland Place, London, W1B 1QH
Trustees: Freni Shroff, Stella Saunders, Bill Evans, John Assael, Chris Goodall, Janet Dunsmore, Anthony Clerici, Karen Rogers, Mr Angus Kerr, Mr Nigel John Thorne, Mr John Lindsay Moakes, Kenneth Bingham RIBA FRSA, Ronnie McDaniel, Dr Geoffrey Purves, Lelia Dunlea-Jones, Hugh Woodeson, Mr Thomas M Young, Mrs Lucy Mori, Mr Mark Grzegorczyk, Mr Richard Brindley, Mrs Kathleen Barbara Thurman
Income: £1,403,454 [2016]; £1,073,634 [2015]; £1,444,859 [2014]; £1,316,320 [2013]; £1,010,720 [2012]

The Architectural Association (Incorporated)
Registered: 9 Sep 1963 *Employees:* 261
Website: aaschool.ac.uk
Activities: Education, training; arts, culture, heritage, science
Address: 36 Bedford Square, London, WC1B 3ES
Trustees: Ms Joanna Louise Chambers, Dr Mary Bishop, Professor David Martin Porter, Ms Elsie Margaret Akua Owusu, Mr David Gibson, Ms Samantha Isobel Hardingham, Mr Joel Newman, Ms Victoria Thornton, Mr Dan Marks, Mr Nicholas Viner, Ms Catherine Du Toit, Professor Mohammad Dastbaz, Timothy O'Hare
Income: £17,558,655 [2017]; £17,702,670 [2016]; £16,561,140 [2015]; £15,040,370 [2014]; £15,386,216 [2013]

The Architectural Heritage Fund
Registered: 29 Jan 1974 *Employees:* 5
Tel: 020 7925 0199 *Website:* ahfund.org.uk
Activities: Environment, conservation, heritage
Address: 3 Spital Yard, Spital Square, London, E1 6AQ
Trustees: Mr John Duggan, Ms Myra Barnes, Mrs Liz Peace, Ms Suzanne Snowden, Mr Adebayo Alao, Ms Eleanor McAllister, Ms Kate Dickson, Mr Richard Keen, Mr David Hunter, Mrs Susan Brown, Ms Karen Latimer
Income: £1,890,978 [2017]; £903,424 [2016]; £865,913 [2015]; £1,026,787 [2014]; £919,512 [2013]

Arcola Theatre Production Company
Registered: 16 Mar 2005 *Employees:* 35 *Volunteers:* 100
Tel: 020 7503 1645 *Website:* arcolatheatre.com
Activities: Education, training; arts, culture, heritage, science
Address: Arcola Theatre, 24 Ashwin Street, London, E8 3DL
Trustees: Mr Jack Shepherd, Lynne Alice McKenzie, Mr Abdulla Tercanli, Mehmet Ergen, Mr Gabriel Gbadamosi
Income: £1,336,681 [2017]; £1,123,900 [2016]; £904,010 [2015]; £1,084,934 [2014]; £3,509,845 [2013]

Ardingly College Limited
Registered: 8 Jul 1999 *Employees:* 402 *Volunteers:* 19
Tel: 01444 893020 *Website:* ardingly.com
Activities: Education, training; religious activities
Address: Ardingly College, College Road, Ardingly, Haywards Heath, W Sussex, RH17 6SQ
Trustees: Mr Graham Turner, Mr Jim Sloane, Mr Peter Nigel Bryan, Mr Douglas Johnson-Poensgen, Mr Guy Dixon, Mr Simon Kay, Mrs Elizabeth Hewer, Ms Katherine Sweeney, Professor Helen Smith, The Earl of Limerick Edmund Limerick, Mrs Sian Champkin, Mr Nicholas Walker, Ms Louise Lindsay, Mr Mark Beach, Mrs Mary Ireland, Mr Robert Brown
Income: £20,634,465 [2017]; £19,112,175 [2016]; £23,769,924 [2015]; £18,006,549 [2014]; £17,056,137 [2013]

Area 51 Education
Registered: 22 Dec 2010 *Employees:* 47 *Volunteers:* 2
Tel: 020 8881 7739 *Website:* area51ed.org.uk
Activities: Education, training; disability; economic, community development, employment
Address: 1 Mallard Place, Coburg Road, London, N22 6TS
Trustees: Dr Matthew Griffiths, Mr David Robert Stansell, Mr Adrian Charles Day, Ms Suzanne Elizabeth Foster
Income: £1,872,093 [2016]; £1,233,692 [2015]; £1,076,386 [2014]; £1,208,021 [2013]

The Arisaig Partners Foundation
Registered: 13 Jan 2004
Activities: General charitable purposes; education, training; advancement of health or saving of lives; prevention or relief of poverty; accommodation, housing; economic, community development, employment
Address: 11 Jurong Lake Link, #08-43, Singapore
Trustees: Ms Rebecca Jane Lewis, Mr Chee Seng Chua, Mr Hugo William James Robinson
Income: £2,698,302 [2016]; £1,002,439 [2015]; £1,684,754 [2014]; £626,462 [2013]; £565,933 [2012]

Ark UK Programmes
Registered: 9 Sep 2010 *Employees:* 28
Tel: 020 3116 0800 *Website:* arkonline.org
Activities: Education, training
Address: Absolute Return for Kids, 65 Kingsway, London, WC2B 6TD
Trustees: Mr Paul Fraser Dunning, Ms Lucy Heller, Mr Stanley Fink
Income: £2,226,083 [2016]; £9,043,000 [2015]; £6,107,000 [2014]; £3,355,000 [2013]

The Helen Arkell Dyslexia Centre
Registered: 1 Oct 1997 *Employees:* 22
Tel: 01252 792400 *Website:* helenarkell.org.uk
Activities: Education, training; disability
Address: Helen Arkell Dyslexia Centre, Arkell Lane, Frensham, Farnham, Surrey, GU10 3BL
Trustees: Gary Lawson, Ms Jilly Steventon, Mr Thomas Arkell, Gary Hay, Paul Cowell, Ms Elaine Allen, Tim Harrison, Sue Shoveller
Income: £1,320,025 [2017]; £1,139,654 [2016]; £1,136,886 [2015]; £1,097,058 [2014]; £1,074,994 [2013]

The Arkwright Society Limited
Registered: 1 Apr 1985 *Employees:* 34 *Volunteers:* 102
Tel: 01629 824297 *Website:* arkwrightsociety.org.uk
Activities: Education, training; environment, conservation, heritage
Address: Sir Richard Arkwright's Mill, Cromford Mill, Mill Lane, Cromford, Matlock, Derbys, DE4 3RQ
Trustees: Mr Julian Arthur Burgess, Mr David Henry Williams, Mr Greg Pickup, Mr Geoffrey Duncan Lewins, Mr Timothy Rogers, Dr Sarah Rawlinson, Mr Michael Atkinson
Income: £1,507,828 [2017]; £2,644,749 [2016]; £2,300,887 [2015]; £2,821,513 [2014]; £878,492 [2013]

Arlington Futures
Registered: 13 May 2003
Website: arlington.org.uk
Activities: General charitable purposes; education, training; advancement of health or saving of lives; prevention or relief of poverty; arts, culture, heritage, science; economic, community development, employment; recreation
Address: 16 Egremont Road, London, SE27 0BH
Trustees: John Gregory, Mr Paul Rickard
Income: £1,292,000 [2017]; £1,393,000 [2016]; £93,000 [2015]; £145,000 [2014]; £97,000 [2013]

Armed Forces Education Trust
Registered: 16 Jun 2016 *Employees:* 1 *Volunteers:* 1
Website: armedforceseducation.org
Activities: Education, training
Address: P O Box 684, Farnham, Surrey, GU9 1LP
Trustees: Mr Alan Behagg, Mrs Anne Goymer, Mrs Jenny Lycett, Mrs Maria Clohessy, Mr Merrick Willis, Mrs Janet Alison Melson
Income: £13,380,581 [2017]

The John Armitage Charitable Trust
Registered: 3 Mar 2000
Activities: Education, training; advancement of health or saving of lives; disability; prevention or relief of poverty; religious activities; arts, culture, heritage, science; economic, community development, employment; other charitable purposes
Address: c/o Sampson West, Mitre House, 12-14 Mitre House, London, EC3A 5BU
Trustees: Mr William Francklin, Mrs Catherine Mary Armitage, Mr J C Armitage, Mrs Celina Francklin
Income: £2,069,734 [2017]; £2,299,375 [2016]; £1,347,179 [2015]; £1,759,743 [2014]; £1,555,147 [2013]

The Army Cadet Force Association
Registered: 24 Sep 1962 *Employees:* 59 *Volunteers:* 8,500
Tel: 020 7426 8370 *Website:* armycadets.com
Activities: General charitable purposes; education, training; amateur sport; environment, conservation, heritage; economic, community development, employment
Address: Army Cadet Force Association, Holderness House, 51-61 Clifton Street, London, EC2A 4DW
Trustees: Mr Ruadhri Andrew Duncan, Lt Gen Andrew John Noble Graham CB CBE, Colonel Evan John Mytton, Mr Alan John Goodwin, Major General David McDowall CBE, Colonel Maurice Victor Warnock, Ms Agata Zukowska, Colonel Russell Edmond Stafford-Tolley, Lieutenant Colonel Michael Anthony Rushworth Shallow, Colonel David Ian Fuller OBE NMN DL, Colonel Hilary Williams, Colonel Andrew Hugh Cassidy, Colonel Christopher Tearney, Colonel Anthony Ian Denison OBE, Lieutenant Colonel Wendy Ann Adams, Major Joanna Susan Brocklehurst, Mrs Emily Anne Lincoln-Gordon
Income: £5,624,766 [2017]; £8,434,414 [2016]; £3,741,525 [2015]; £4,351,366 [2014]; £6,204,709 [2013]

The Army Central Fund
Registered: 11 Jan 1966 *Employees:* 1
Tel: 01980 615905
Activities: General charitable purposes; disability; accommodation, housing; amateur sport; armed forces, emergency service efficiency
Address: Army Central Fund, Trenchard Lines, Upavon, Pewsey, Wilts, SN9 6BE
Trustees: Guy Davies, Brig Hj Robertson QVRM TD, Brig Nc Allison, WO1 Army Sm Gj Haughton, Brian Wheelwright, Brig Andrew Sturrock, Maj Gen Ibl Jones, Brig Cmb Coles
Income: £2,848,726 [2017]; £2,758,497 [2016]; £2,720,317 [2015]; £2,929,420 [2014]; £2,667,174 [2013]

The Army Dependants' Trust
Registered: 22 Sep 1997 *Employees:* 2
Tel: 01980 615734 *Website:* army.mod.uk
Activities: The prevention or relief of poverty; armed forces, emergency service efficiency
Address: The Army Dependants Trust, Trenchard Lines, Upavon, Pewsey, Wilts, SN9 6BE
Trustees: Mr Martin Rutledge CB OBE, Mr Ivan Jones, Christopher Coles, Michael Sykes, Mr Newton Astbury, Martyn Gamble, Mrs Sara Wall-Baade, Mr Brian Alvin
Income: £1,855,920 [2016]; £1,831,847 [2015]; £1,781,981 [2014]; £1,758,129 [2013]; £1,713,838 [2012]

Army Families Federation
Registered: 22 Feb 1985 *Employees:* 33 *Volunteers:* 43
Tel: 01264 382325 *Website:* aff.org.uk
Activities: General charitable purposes; education, training; advancement of health or saving of lives; disability; accommodation, housing; economic, community development, employment; armed forces, emergency service efficiency; human rights, religious or racial harmony, equality or diversity; recreation; other charitable purposes
Address: AFF, Floor 1, Zone 6, Ramillies Building, Monxton Road, Marlborough Lines, Andover, Hants, SP11 8HJ
Trustees: Mr Robin Eccles, Mrs Julie Vere-Whiting, Mrs Catharine Moss, Father Stephen Sharkey, Mrs Julia Warren, Mrs Fiona Ellison
Income: £1,226,291 [2017]; £997,141 [2016]; £1,121,906 [2015]; £1,139,693 [2014]; £915,201 [2013]

The Army Museums Ogilby Trust
Registered: 27 Feb 1967 *Employees:* 1
Tel: 01722 332188 *Website:* armymuseums.org.uk
Activities: Education, training; arts, culture, heritage, science; environment, conservation, heritage; other charitable purposes
Address: 58 The Close, Salisbury, Wilts, SP1 2EX
Trustees: Colonel Stephen Henwood TD, Lieutenant General Sir Philip Trousdell KBE CB, Ms Diane Lees, Brigadier Allan Mallinson, Major General David McDowall CBE, Mr Timothy Parkes, Major General David Burden CB CVO CBE, Brigadier Charles Grant OBE, Marc Overton, Mr James Codrington, Mrs Victoria Wallace, Victoria Schofield
Income: £7,091,960 [2017]; £1,646,696 [2016]; £1,433,476 [2015]; £1,009,185 [2014]; £785,510 [2013]

Army Rugby Union Trust
Registered: 26 Sep 2012 *Employees:* 5 *Volunteers:* 21
Tel: 01252 787080 *Website:* armyrugbyunion.org.uk
Activities: General charitable purposes; amateur sport; armed forces, emergency service efficiency
Address: Army Sport Control Board, MacKenzie Building, Fox Lines, Queens Avenue, Aldershot, Hants, GU11 2LB
Trustees: Paddy Allison, Brenda Hobday, Sandy Fitzpatrick, Mr Andrew David Leach, Mr Clive Rattenbury, William Bramble, James Cook, Jason Kennedy, Mr David John Rutherford, Ms Charlotte Maxwell
Income: £1,383,799 [2017]; £1,481,388 [2016]; £1,151,561 [2015]; £1,977,174 [2014]

Yvonne Arnaud Theatre Management Limited
Registered: 21 Jun 1965 *Employees:* 33
Tel: 01483 440077 *Website:* yvonne-arnaud.co.uk
Activities: Education, training; arts, culture, heritage, science
Address: Yvonne Arnaud Theatre, Millbrook, Guildford, Surrey, GU1 3UX
Trustees: Ms Patricia Grayburn MBE DL, Mr Andrew French, Mr Stephen Bampfylde MA, Mr Julian Bird, Mr Roger Black MBE, Mr Jules Diccon Porter, Mr Peter Gordon, Mr Matt Furniss, Dr Michael Martin Clark JP, Jennifer Powell, Mr Nicholas Acomb, Mr Tony Phillips, Mr Peter Wilkins, Mr Paul Spooner, Mr Michael More Molyneux
Income: £4,010,459 [2017]; £4,225,154 [2016]; £4,049,500 [2015]; £3,266,187 [2014]; £3,581,124 [2013]

Yvonne Arnaud Theatre Trust
Registered: 19 Sep 1961 *Employees:* 36
Tel: 01483 440077 *Website:* yvonne-arnaud.co.uk
Activities: Arts, culture, heritage, science
Address: Yvonne Arnaud Theatre, Millbrook, Guildford, Surrey, GU1 3UX
Trustees: Ms Patricia Grayburn MBE DL, Mr Andrew French, Mr Stephen Bampfylde MA, Mr Julian Bird, Mr Roger Black MBE, Mr Julian Diccon Porter, Mr Peter Gordon, Mr Matt Furniss, Dr Michael Martin Clark JP, Jennifer Powell, Mr Nicholas Acomb, Mr Tony Phillips, Mr Peter Wilkins, Mr Paul Spooner, Mr Michael More Molyneux
Income: £3,888,887 [2017]; £3,556,814 [2016]; £3,542,667 [2015]; £3,485,838 [2014]; £3,880,414 [2013]

The Arnold Foundation for Rugby School
Registered: 6 Feb 2003 *Employees:* 5 *Volunteers:* 8
Tel: 01788 556260 *Website:* thearnoldfoundation.net
Activities: Education, training
Address: Rugby School Bursary, 10 Little Church Street, Rugby, Warwicks, CV21 3AW
Trustees: Mrs Lucinda J Holmes, Mr Peter Green, Mr Barry O'Brien, Mr Gareth Lloyd-Jones
Income: £1,676,499 [2017]; £967,760 [2016]; £1,634,141 [2015]; £1,476,988 [2014]; £1,274,095 [2013]

Arnold House School Ltd
Registered: 12 Oct 1966 *Employees:* 57 *Volunteers:* 1
Tel: 020 7266 6984 *Website:* arnoldhouse.co.uk
Activities: General charitable purposes; education, training; other charitable purposes
Address: Arnold House School, 1-3 Loudoun Road, London, NW8 0LH
Trustees: Mr Patrick Sibley Jan Derham, Dr Michele Badenoch, Mr Anastassis Fafalios, Ms Sarah Harrison, Mr Daniel Widdicombe, Mrs Claudia Mary Seton Douglass, Mr Barry O'Brien, Revd Dr Anders Bergquist, Mr John Prosser, Mrs Clarrie Elizabeth Wallis, Mr Mark Beard
Income: £5,152,172 [2016]; £5,170,575 [2015]; £4,961,069 [2014]; £4,784,285 [2013]; £4,553,903 [2012]

Arnolfini Gallery Limited
Registered: 20 Jun 1966 *Employees:* 53 *Volunteers:* 132
Tel: 0117 917 2300 *Website:* arnolfini.org.uk
Activities: Education, training; arts, culture, heritage, science
Address: Arnolfini Gallery Ltd, Narrow Quay, Bristol, BS1 4QA
Trustees: Mr James McAuliffe, Anna Southall, Ms Leonie Olivia Helene Parkin, Mr Gary Ian Sangster, Mr Jeremy Lewison, Mr Iain Canning, Ms Emmeline Rose Rodman, Ms Lucy Samantha Christabel Tutton
Income: £2,120,872 [2017]; £2,085,632 [2016]; £2,285,938 [2015]; £2,223,690 [2014]; £1,977,713 [2013]

The Arsenal Foundation
Registered: 30 Jan 2012
Tel: 020 7704 4406
Activities: General charitable purposes; education, training; advancement of health or saving of lives; prevention or relief of poverty; recreation
Address: Highbury House, 75 Drayton Park, London, N5 1BU
Trustees: David Miles, Kenneth Friar, Svenja Geissmar, Alan Sefton, Ivan Gazidis, Mr Andrew Jolly
Income: £1,908,139 [2017]; £872,214 [2016]; £857,350 [2015]; £761,193 [2014]; £2,071,049 [2013]

The Art Academy
Registered: 7 Jan 2000 *Employees:* 12 *Volunteers:* 2
Tel: 020 7407 6969 *Website:* artacademy.org.uk
Activities: Education, training; arts, culture, heritage, science
Address: Mermaid Court, 165a Borough High Street, London, SE1 1HR
Trustees: Mr Daniel John Howell Wright, Mr Stroud Cornock, Mr Paul Harris, Mrs Melanie Ruth Gerlis, Mr Paul Richard Kullich, Mr Mark William Tattersall, Mrs Jenna Caroline Litter, Mr Damian Fennell
Income: £1,678,526 [2017]; £1,586,538 [2016]; £1,306,363 [2015]; £868,220 [2014]; £690,315 [2013]

Art Services Grants Limited
Registered: 26 Mar 1974 *Employees:* 25
Tel: 020 8525 4330 *Website:* spacestudios.org.uk
Activities: Education, training; arts, culture, heritage, science
Address: Art Services Grants Ltd Space, 129-131 Mare Street, London, E8 3RH
Trustees: Mr Christopher Currell, Mr David Cotterrell, Mr Philip Clark, Miss Mary Evans, Ms Selina Mason, Mr Frank Boyd, Miss Maureen Paley
Income: £4,179,635 [2017]; £3,799,985 [2016]; £3,827,225 [2015]; £3,882,082 [2014]; £4,070,497 [2013]

The Artangel Trust
Registered: 30 Mar 1986 *Employees:* 11
Tel: 020 7713 1400 *Website:* artangel.org.uk
Activities: General charitable purposes; arts, culture, heritage, science
Address: 31 Eyre Street, Hill, London, EC1R 5EW
Trustees: Mr Brian Boylan, Miss Hannah Barry, Mr Oliver Haarmann, Mrs Stephanie Camu, Mr John William Hay, Kaveh Sheibani, Ms Kamila Shamsie, Mrs Ayelet Elstein, Mr Roger Hiorns
Income: £1,793,881 [2017]; £1,690,041 [2016]; £1,627,110 [2015]; £1,311,532 [2014]; £1,754,184 [2013]

Arthritis Care
Registered: 22 Sep 1962 *Employees:* 98 *Volunteers:* 8,200
Tel: 020 7307 2719 *Website:* arthritisresearchuk.org
Activities: Education, training; advancement of health or saving of lives; disability
Address: Arthritis Research UK, Saffron House, London, EC1N 8TS
Trustees: Mr Ian Walters, Dr Rodger Martin McMillan, Mr John Charles Nicholls, Mr Peter John Anscombe, Ms Karin Hogsander, Mrs Clare Louise Reid
Income: £5,287,000 [2016]; £4,669,000 [2015]; £4,472,000 [2014]; £5,932,000 [2013]; £5,353,000 [2012]

Arthritis Research UK
Registered: 22 Sep 1962 *Employees:* 199 *Volunteers:* 406
Tel: 0300 790 0400 *Website:* arthritisresearchuk.org
Activities: The advancement of health or saving of lives
Address: Arthritis Research UK, Copeman House, St Marys Court, St Marys Gate, Chesterfield, Derbys, S41 7TD
Trustees: Dr Ian Walters, Professor David Isenberg, Sylvie Jackson, Professor Jonathan Cohen, Ms Karin Hogsander, Mr Alex Hesz, Professor Martijn Pieter Marie Steultjens, Mr Peter John Anscombe, Mr Phillip Henry Gray, Mr Tom Hayhoe, Dr Rodger Martin McMillan, Ms Juliette Maria Scott, Professor Sarah Elizabeth Lamb
Income: £28,877,000 [2017]; £36,677,000 [2016]; £39,871,000 [2015]; £36,009,000 [2014]; £25,981,000 [2013]

Artichoke Trust
Registered: 13 Jan 2006 *Employees:* 18 *Volunteers:* 400
Tel: 020 7650 7611 *Website:* artichoke.uk.com
Activities: Education, training; arts, culture, heritage, science
Address: Artichoke, Toynbee Studios, 28 Commercial Street, London, E1 6AB
Trustees: Mr Peter Freeman, Mrs Ghislaine Kenyon, Ms Stephanie Flanders, Richard Kitson, Ms Janice Evelyn Boud, Ms Ruth Hogarth, Mr Tim Marlow, Mr Allan Cook, Mr Felix Gillies Creasey, Ms Helen Marriage, Ms Sarah Coop, Mr Dalwardin Babu OBE, Mr David Charles Micklem, Ms Judith Chan, Mr Ivo Dawnay, Mr Nii Sackey, Tailah-Rae Hudson
Income: £3,197,939 [2017]; £4,735,508 [2016]; £1,225,940 [2015]; £2,492,529 [2014]; £2,217,282 [2013]

Article 19
Registered: 7 Jan 1987 *Employees:* 82
Tel: 020 7324 2500 *Website:* article19.org
Activities: Education, training; human rights, religious or racial harmony, equality or diversity
Address: Article 19, Freeword Centre, 60 Farringdon Road, London, EC1R 3GA
Trustees: Ms Malak Poppovic, Mr Nigel Saxby-Soffe, Ms Tamar Anna Ghosh, Paddy Coulter, Mr Jacob Jiel Akol, Mr Frank Ledwidge, Ms Galina Arapova, Mr Evan Harris, Mr Arturo Franco, Jennifer Robinson, Ms Gayathry Venkiteswaran
Income: £6,005,309 [2016]; £4,356,196 [2015]; £4,005,835 [2014]; £4,000,000 [2013]; £3,075,044 [2012]

Artists Studio Company
Registered: 16 Mar 1995 *Employees:* 10
Tel: 020 7274 7474 *Website:* ascstudios.co.uk
Activities: Education, training; prevention or relief of poverty; arts, culture, heritage, science
Address: Artist Studio Company, The Chaplin Centre, Taplow House, Thurlow Street, London, SE17 2DG
Trustees: Norman Flack, John Hammond, Ms Carolyn Upson, Mr John Cassidy
Income: £1,609,093 [2016]; £1,802,961 [2015]; £2,346,302 [2014]; £1,748,839 [2013]; £1,542,394 [2012]

The Arts Council of England
Registered: 19 Apr 1994 *Employees:* 488
Tel: 0845 300 6200 *Website:* artscouncil.org.uk
Activities: Arts, culture, heritage, science
Address: 21 Bloomsbury Street, London, WC1B 3HF
Trustees: Mr Nicholas Andrew Serota, Ms Kathryn Charlotte Louise Willard, Mr David Paul Roberts, Veronica Wadley, Dr Maria Balshaw, Ms Elizabeth Murdoch, Mr Daudi George Mpanga, Mr Sukhbinder Singh Johal, Ms Tessa Sarah Ross, Rosemary Squire, Ms Veronica Tanya Marie Brown, Mr David Joseph, Mr Andrew James Millar
Income: £724,215,000 [2017]; £732,814,000 [2016]; £724,844,000 [2015]; £694,686,000 [2014]; £746,425,000 [2013]

The Arts Depot Trust Limited
Registered: 30 Nov 2000 *Employees:* 36 *Volunteers:* 11
Tel: 020 8369 5461 *Website:* artsdepot.co.uk
Activities: Education, training; arts, culture, heritage, science
Address: 5 Nether Street, London, N12 0GA
Trustees: Cllr Lisa Rutter, Mrs Jeanette Burnett, Nick Pelmont, Mr Mark Foster Ball, Mrs Liz McCarthy, Mr Mustafa Kemal Sahin, Andrew Hurst, Tony Shepherd, Mr David Londstaff, Mrs Rolanda Gail Hyams, Councillor John Hart, Mrs Emma Bier
Income: £2,035,649 [2017]; £1,941,817 [2016]; £1,899,776 [2015]; £1,814,468 [2014]; £1,459,643 [2013]

The Arts Educational Schools
Registered: 13 Feb 1962 *Employees:* 153
Tel: 020 8987 6666 *Website:* artsed.co.uk
Activities: Education, training; arts, culture, heritage, science
Address: 14 Bath Road, Chiswick, London, W4 1LY
Trustees: Ms Clare Miranda Ferguson, Mr Mark Burch, Mrs Sandra Cahill, Mrs Jacqueline Brunjes, Mr Brenlen Jinkens, Mrs Kathryn Norton-Smith, Mr Norman Bragg, Mr Mike Morris, Mrs Diana Maine, Ms Ann Cottis, Mr Guy Neil Mullin-Henderson, Mr Robert Mathieson, Mrs Emma Cherniavsky
Income: £7,870,802 [2016]; £7,391,952 [2015]; £8,188,320 [2014]; £8,506,256 [2013]; £6,059,460 [2012]

Artsadmin
Registered: 2 Mar 1995 *Employees:* 34
Tel: 020 7247 5102 *Website:* artsadmin.co.uk
Activities: Arts, culture, heritage, science
Address: Artsadmin, Toynbee Studios, 28 Commercial Street, London, E1 6AB
Trustees: Ms Alison Ritchie, Charles Garrad, Mr Jeremy Smeeth, Miss Feimatta Conteh, Mr Joost Frankeen, Ms Lois Keidan, Mhora Samuel, Ms Stella Mary Hall, Miss Freya Murray
Income: £2,247,223 [2017]; £2,200,208 [2016]; £2,918,186 [2015]; £1,472,793 [2014]; £1,358,382 [2013]

Artswork Limited
Registered: 6 Oct 1988 *Employees:* 24
Tel: 023 8033 2491 *Website:* artswork.org.uk
Activities: Education, training; arts, culture, heritage, science
Address: 1st Floor, Latimer House, 5-7 Cumberland Place, Southampton, SO15 2BH
Trustees: Ms Hilary Pamela Durman, Mr Richard Bryan Hall, Mrs Fiona Parkinson, Miss Emma Dyer, Professor Helen Rae Simons ACSS, Ms Sabita Kumari Dass, Mrs Norinne Betjemann
Income: £2,100,798 [2017]; £2,223,949 [2016]; £2,320,318 [2015]; £2,579,279 [2014]; £2,008,577 [2013]

Arundel Castle Trustees Limited
Registered: 27 Sep 1976 *Employees:* 106
Tel: 01903 882173 *Website:* arundelcastle.org
Activities: Education, training; arts, culture, heritage, science; environment, conservation, heritage
Address: Arundel Castle, High Street, Arundel, W Sussex, BN18 9AB
Trustees: Dr John Martin Robinson, The Duke of Norfolk, Mr Nicholas Richard Powell, Charles Fraser, The Duchess of Norfolk Georgina Susan FI, Mr Hugh Coghill
Income: £3,554,787 [2016]; £3,379,932 [2015]; £3,097,657 [2014]; £2,842,133 [2013]; £2,755,872 [2012]

Arundel and Brighton Diocesan Trust
Registered: 11 Jul 1967 *Employees:* 595 *Volunteers:* 4,000
Tel: 01273 859705 *Website:* dabnet.org
Activities: Education, training; religious activities
Address: Bishops House, The Upper Drive, Hove, E Sussex, BN3 6NB
Trustees: Mr Thomas William Allen, Mr Edward Bartram Totman, Mrs Bernadette Anne Brittain, Rt Rev Charles Phillip Richard Moth, Rev Kieron O'Brien, Rev Jonathan Michael How, Rev Michael Charles Thoms, Mr Anthony Campbell OBE KSG, Rev Jonathan Martin, Caroline Walsh
Income: £25,559,000 [2016]; £25,718,000 [2015]; £23,735,000 [2014]; £25,273,000 [2013]; £23,395,000 [2012]

The Arvon Foundation
Registered: 28 Mar 1973 *Employees:* 37 *Volunteers:* 6
Tel: 020 7324 2554 *Website:* arvon.org
Activities: Education, training; arts, culture, heritage, science
Address: Free Word Centre, 60 Farringdon Road, London, EC1R 3GA
Trustees: Daljit Nagra, Jonathan Teckman, Meriel Schindler, Neil Russell Harris, Nicholas Makoha, Lee Bilson, Dr Judith Abbott, Jeremy Treglown, Andrew Wimble, Mandy Teresa De Waal, Ashley Holloway
Income: £2,228,725 [2016]; £1,837,813 [2015]; £2,123,820 [2014]; £2,914,959 [2013]; £1,828,862 [2012]

Ascentis
Registered: 16 Apr 2009 *Employees:* 120
Tel: 01524 845046 *Website:* ascentis.co.uk
Activities: Education, training
Address: Office 4, Lancaster Business Park, Mannin Way, Caton Road, Lancaster, LA1 3SW
Trustees: Mr Stephen Carlisle, Mr Anthony Turjansky, Mrs Alison Bolton, Ruth Tomlinson, Mr Philip Charles Wilkinson, Robin Newton-Syms, Ms Rosemarie Davies, Joanne Afrin-Black
Income: £4,125,749 [2017]; £3,979,407 [2016]; £3,132,723 [2015]; £3,286,419 [2014]; £3,835,212 [2013]

The Asda Foundation
Registered: 31 May 2008
Tel: 0113 243 5435 *Website:* asdafoundation.org
Activities: General charitable purposes; education, training; advancement of health or saving of lives; disability; prevention or relief of poverty; religious activities; amateur sport
Address: Corporate Affairs, Asda House, Great Wilson Street, Leeds, LS11 5AD
Trustees: Mr Gerald Ernest Oppenheim, Mrs Ann Marie Rocks, Mrs Alison Seabrook, Mr Jason Martin, Mr John Giles Cookman, Ms Carolyn Heaney, Mrs Jane Earnshaw, Andrew Murray
Income: £7,702,112 [2016]; £8,231,526 [2015]; £8,770,496 [2014]; £8,574,248 [2013]; £6,483,980 [2012]

Asda Tickled Pink
Registered: 15 Aug 2013
Tel: 0113 826 2253
Activities: General charitable purposes; education, training; advancement of health or saving of lives
Address: Asda House, Southbank, Great Wilson Street, Leeds, LS11 5AD
Trustees: Mr Russell Craig, Mrs Samia Alqadhi, Mrs Ellen Fogden, Baroness Delyth Morgan, Mrs Maxine Green
Income: £3,245,313 [2016]; £5,137,419 [2015]; £3,522,554 [2014]; £5,000 [2013]

The Asfari Foundation
Registered: 10 Nov 2006 *Employees:* 7
Tel: 020 7372 3889 *Website:* asfarifoundation.org.uk
Activities: General charitable purposes; education, training; advancement of health or saving of lives; prevention or relief of poverty; overseas aid, famine relief; arts, culture, heritage, science; economic, community development, employment; human rights, religious or racial harmony, equality or diversity; other charitable purposes
Address: The Asfari Foundation, Unit A, 1-3 Canfield Place, London, NW6 3BT
Trustees: Mrs Sawsan Asfari, Mr Ayman Asfari, Mr John Ferguson, Mr Adeeb Asfari, Mrs Rasha Elmasry, Dr Marwan Muasher
Income: £5,080,103 [2016]; £3,426,403 [2015]; £2,710,820 [2014]; £4,448,961 [2013]; £12,803,790 [2012]

Ashburnham Christian Trust
Registered: 15 Jan 1963 *Employees:* 31 *Volunteers:* 25
Tel: 01424 892244 *Website:* ashburnham.org.uk
Activities: Education, training; religious activities
Address: Ashburnham Place, Ashburnham, Battle, E Sussex, TN33 9NF
Trustees: Mr Roger Hayden Mitchell, Dr Marijke Hoek, Dr John Cormode, Mrs Fiona Alexandra Margaret Oommen, Rev Ray Michael Djan, Mrs Jillian Kathryn Huntley
Income: £1,926,604 [2017]; £1,850,718 [2016]; £1,576,280 [2015]; £1,612,705 [2014]; £1,713,490 [2013]

Ashden Sustainable Solutions, Better Lives
Registered: 4 Jun 2004 *Employees:* 31
Tel: 020 7410 0330 *Website:* ashden.org
Activities: Education, training; advancement of health or saving of lives; prevention or relief of poverty; environment, conservation, heritage; economic, community development, employment
Address: The Peak, 5 Wilton Road, London, SW1V 1AP
Trustees: Mr David Wayland Blood, Hon Mark Sainsbury, Mr Adam Edward Brett, Mr Paul Gustav Josef Alexander Simon, Mr Nick Mabey, Miss Emma Susanne Colenbrander, Mr Jonathon Espie Porritt, Mrs Sarah Butler Sloss, Mr Michael Matthew Keating, Ms Diana Lisa Carney, Ms Caroline Holtum
Income: £2,215,673 [2017]; £1,922,316 [2016]; £1,725,275 [2015]; £1,526,335 [2014]; £1,548,012 [2013]

The Ashden Trust
Registered: 12 Jan 1990 *Employees:* 15
Tel: 020 7410 0330 *Website:* sfct.org.uk
Activities: Education, training; prevention or relief of poverty; overseas aid, famine relief; accommodation, housing; arts, culture, heritage, science; environment, conservation, heritage; economic, community development, employment
Address: Sainsbury Family Charitable Trusts, The Peak, 5 Wilton Road, London, SW1V 1AP
Trustees: Miss Judith Susan Portrait OBE, Sarah Butler-Sloss, Mr Robert Butler-Sloss
Income: £1,244,085 [2017]; £1,135,154 [2016]; £1,489,739 [2015]; £1,105,129 [2014]; £986,295 [2013]

Ashdown Medway Accommodation Trust
Registered: 26 Aug 2005 *Employees:* 67
Tel: 0800 698 1000 *Website:* amatuk.org
Activities: Accommodation, housing
Address: 10 Chelmar Road, Chatham, Kent, ME4 4PB
Trustees: Miss Emma Paterson, Mr David Bloomfield, Ms Andrea McNally, Mr George Crozer, Mr Christopher Doyle
Income: £4,415,646 [2017]; £4,525,668 [2016]; £4,471,319 [2015]; £4,327,826 [2014]; £4,171,755 [2013]

Ashfold School Trust Limited
Registered: 6 Jan 1977 *Employees:* 70
Tel: 01844 238237 *Website:* ashfoldschool.co.uk
Activities: Education, training
Address: Dorton House, Dorton, Aylesbury, Bucks, HP18 9NG
Trustees: Dr Anthony Wallersteiner, Mr Hugh Taylor, Mr Timothy Bailey, Mrs Catrin Weston, Ms Tracey Alison Wood, Mr Andrew Reekes, Mr Michael Tuckey, Mrs Angela Jillian Sanderson, Mr Jonathan Harker Newman, Mrs Margaret Myfanwy Hope
Income: £3,732,769 [2017]; £3,593,648 [2016]; £3,582,634 [2015]; £3,494,864 [2014]; £3,120,643 [2013]

Ashford Leisure Trust Limited
Registered: 12 Sep 2007 *Employees:* 78
Tel: 01233 667123
Activities: Education, training; amateur sport
Address: Stour Leisure Centre, Station Approach, Ashford, Kent, TN23 1ET
Trustees: Mr Brendan Morrissey, Charles Vavasour, Mr David Hill, Mrs Linda Doods
Income: £2,722,466 [2017]; £2,887,443 [2016]; £2,863,148 [2015]; £2,767,495 [2014]; £2,500,375 [2013]

Ashgate Hospicecare
Registered: 14 Sep 1988 *Employees:* 283 *Volunteers:* 723
Tel: 01246 568801 *Website:* ashgatehospicecare.org.uk
Activities: The advancement of health or saving of lives
Address: Ashgate Hospice, Ashgate Road, Chesterfield, Derbys, S42 7JD
Trustees: Mr Terry Gilby, Mrs Jean Elizabeth Horton, Dr Steve Bradder, Dr Roger Start, Mr Daniel Ratchford, Mrs Karen Lockwood, Mr Andrew Archibald, David Reynolds, Ian Ford, Mr Andrew Dukelow, Mrs Penelope Brooks, Mr Malcolm Pope, Mr Ian Snow
Income: £9,984,583 [2017]; £8,571,179 [2016]; £7,632,279 [2015]; £6,885,215 [2014]; £6,337,736 [2013]

Ashiana Network
Registered: 29 Nov 1994 *Employees:* 12 *Volunteers:* 8
Tel: 020 8539 0427 *Website:* ashiana.org.uk
Activities: The prevention or relief of poverty; accommodation, housing
Address: Suite 204, Oceanair House, 740-760 High Road, Leytonstone, London, E11 3AW
Trustees: Ms Sabina Mahmood, Ms Shivangi Medhi, Mrs Rashmi Nigam, Ms Jayne Paxton, Ms Urmi Mala Medhi, Mrs Anjum Shaheen Bashir, Ms Sonal Thaper
Income: £1,296,446 [2017]; £1,201,342 [2016]; £1,169,148 [2015]; £1,151,532 [2014]; £602,057 [2013]

The Ashley Foundation
Registered: 5 Jul 1997 *Employees:* 32 *Volunteers:* 10
Tel: 01253 297200 *Website:* tafblackpool.org
Activities: Accommodation, housing
Address: Ashley Foundation, 81-83 Abingdon Street, Blackpool, Lancs, FY1 1PP
Trustees: Mr Neville Bramhall, Mr David Kam, Mr Ashley Samuel Dribben, Mr Ronald Bell, Mrs Wendy Anne Swift
Income: £1,790,403 [2017]; £1,595,295 [2016]; £1,678,278 [2015]; £1,594,190 [2014]; £1,680,334 [2013]

The Ashmolean Museum Endowment Trust
Registered: 8 Dec 2013
Tel: 020 3375 7138
Activities: Arts, culture, heritage, science
Address: Farrer & Co, 65-66 Lincoln's Inn Fields, London, WC2A 3LH
Trustees: Sir Martin Smith, Lord Sainsbury of Preston Candover KG, Mr Bernard Taylor, Professor Louise Richardson
Income: £1,860,346 [2017]; £10 [2015]

Ashoka UK

Registered: 10 Mar 2006 *Employees:* 11 *Volunteers:* 14
Website: uk.ashoka.org
Activities: General charitable purposes; education, training; advancement of health or saving of lives; disability; prevention or relief of poverty; overseas aid, famine relief; environment, conservation, heritage; economic, community development, employment
Address: Ashoka UK, 15 Old Ford Road, London, E2 9PJ
Trustees: Ms Konstanze Maria Bernadette Frischen, Mrs Fabienne Serfaty, Ms Shauneen Lambe, Mr Edward Fidoe, Mr Mark Cheng
Income: £1,074,487 [2016]; £511,001 [2015]; £1,031,523 [2014]; £615,445 [2013]; £151,151 [2012]

Ashorne Hill Management College

Registered: 27 Jan 1967 *Employees:* 71
Tel: 01926 488000 *Website:* ashornehill.co.uk
Activities: Education, training
Address: Ashorne Hill College, Ashorne Hill, Leamington Spa, Warwicks, CV33 9QW
Trustees: Mr John Carson, Mr Alastair Stuart Aitken, Mr Adrian Mardell, Mr Graham Thompsett, Mrs Gillian Smillie, Mr Ian Harnett, Mr Chris Elliott, Mr Robert Seacombe
Income: £5,223,419 [2017]; £4,570,693 [2016]; £3,901,959 [2015]; £4,436,861 [2014]; £3,581,539 [2012]

The Ashridge (Bonar Law Memorial) Trust

Registered: 13 Nov 1962 *Employees:* 362
Tel: 01442 841426 *Website:* ashridge.org.uk
Activities: Education, training; environment, conservation, heritage
Address: Ashridge Executive Education, Ashridge, Berkhamsted, Herts, HP4 1NS
Trustees: Ashridge Ct Ltd
Income: £34,314,000 [2016]; £54,941,000 [2015]; £34,771,000 [2014]; £35,256,000 [2013]; £32,738,000 [2012]

Ashville College

Registered: 31 Dec 1964 *Employees:* 310
Tel: 01423 566358 *Website:* ashville.co.uk
Activities: Education, training
Address: Ashville College, Green Lane, Harrogate, N Yorks, HG2 9JP
Trustees: Ashville College Trustee Limited
Income: £12,290,256 [2017]; £11,689,003 [2016]; £11,498,223 [2015]; £10,074,464 [2014]; £9,835,956 [2013]

Asia House

Registered: 2 Dec 1998 *Employees:* 22 *Volunteers:* 10
Tel: 020 7307 5461 *Website:* asiahouse.org
Activities: General charitable purposes; education, training; arts, culture, heritage, science; recreation
Address: 63 New Cavendish Street, London, W1G 7LP
Trustees: Deborah Swallow, The Hon Mr Apurv Bagri, Mrs Sung Joo Kim, Mr Victor Chu, Mr Martin William Dewhurst, Mr Albert George Hector Ellis, Vasuki Shastry, Ann Almeida, Nicholas Butler, Ms Beth McKillop, Mr Stephen Ball, Sir Sherard Cowper-Coles KCMG LVO, Mr Timothy Fassam, Lord Steven Keith Green, Mr Thomas David Helsby, Ms Anne Ruth Herkes
Income: £1,831,677 [2016]; £2,047,812 [2015]; £1,704,516 [2014]; £1,620,736 [2013]; £1,379,711 [2012]

The Aspinall Foundation

Registered: 27 Apr 1984 *Employees:* 48
Tel: 020 3889 7550 *Website:* aspinallfoundation.org
Activities: Education, training; animals; environment, conservation, heritage
Address: LJ Partnership, 9 Clifford Street, London, W1S 2FT
Trustees: James Osborne, Mr Zac Goldsmith, Mr Robin Birley, Mr Charles Peter Nigel Filmer, Damian Aspinall, Mr Benjamin James Goldsmith
Income: £2,786,000 [2016]; £2,713,000 [2015]; £2,744,000 [2014]; £4,098,000 [2013]; £3,340,000 [2012]

Aspire (Association for Spinal Injury Research Rehabilitation and Reintegration)

Registered: 30 Apr 1999 *Employees:* 100 *Volunteers:* 50
Tel: 020 8954 5759 *Website:* aspire.org.uk
Activities: General charitable purposes; education, training; advancement of health or saving of lives; disability; accommodation, housing; amateur sport
Address: Aspire National Training Centre, Wood Lane, Stanmore, Middlesex, HA7 4AP
Trustees: Mrs Fiona Jerreat, Mr Luke Hamill, Dr Saroj Patel, Mr David Holden, Mr Andrew Chaplin, Mr Reg Coote, Mr David Anthony Edwards, Dr Angela Gall, Mr Edward Pattinson, Dr Frederick Riach Ironside Middleton, Mr Jonny Jacobs
Income: £3,945,183 [2017]; £3,593,326 [2016]; £3,291,816 [2015]; £2,796,824 [2014]; £4,552,226 [2013]

Aspire Living Limited

Registered: 16 Aug 1993 *Employees:* 167 *Volunteers:* 10
Tel: 0300 303 1280 *Website:* aspirehereford.org.uk
Activities: Education, training; disability; accommodation, housing; economic, community development, employment; recreation
Address: The West House, Alpha Court, Swingbridge Road, Grantham, Lincs, NG31 7XT
Trustees: Mr Bryan Casbourne MBE, Mrs Rosemary Jane Hunt, Mr Roger Whalley, Mr Eli Heathfield, Catherine Chima-Okereke, Charles Almond, Mr Kenneth Jollans, Karen Boyce Dawson, Kathryn Downton
Income: £4,359,300 [2017]; £2,941,006 [2016]; £3,126,371 [2015]; £2,136,787 [2014]; £2,233,764 [2013]

Aspire Sports and Cultural Trust

Registered: 22 Sep 2008 *Employees:* 82
Tel: 01452 396601 *Website:* aspiretrust.org.uk
Activities: Arts, culture, heritage, science; amateur sport
Address: GL1 Leisure Centre, Bruton Way, Gloucester, GL1 1DT
Trustees: Mrs M White, Mr Neil Cameron, Mr Sanjai Desai, Mr Clive Walford, Mr Andrew George Pain, Mr Neil Hampson, Mrs Caroline Corbett
Income: £3,618,295 [2017]; £3,772,130 [2016]; £4,203,743 [2015]; £3,818,247 [2014]; £3,916,466 [2013]

Aspire Sussex Limited

Registered: 23 Oct 2012 *Employees:* 261 *Volunteers:* 50
Tel: 01444 810729 *Website:* aspiresussex.org.uk
Activities: Education, training; advancement of health or saving of lives; economic, community development, employment; recreation
Address: Oakmeeds Adult Education, Adult Education Department, Marle Place, Leylands Road, Burgess Hill, W Sussex, RH15 8HZ
Trustees: Ms Caroline Pickup, Ms Robyn Kohler, Mr David Smith, Dr Norman Boyland, Mr John Burke, Dr Lyn Glanz
Income: £3,859,056 [2017]; £3,904,157 [2016]; £3,988,235 [2015]; £4,418,633 [2014]; £4,739,855 [2013]

Assemblies of God Incorporated
Registered: 27 Jan 1994 *Employees:* 38 *Volunteers:* 115
Tel: 01777 817663 *Website:* aog.org.uk
Activities: Education, training; overseas aid, famine relief; religious activities
Address: National Ministry Centre, Retford Road, Mattersey, Doncaster, S Yorks, DN10 5HD
Trustees: Mr Grayson Edward Jones, Mr Alan Leslie Hewitt, Mr Ian Watson, Rev Stuart Guy Mayho, Mr Ian Williams, Pastor Mark Andrew Wiltshire, Mr Aran Richardson
Income: £2,878,367 [2017]; £2,327,495 [2016]; £2,789,000 [2015]; £3,288,000 [2014]; £2,961,000 [2013]

Assemblies of God Property Trust
Registered: 13 Mar 1967 *Employees:* 32
Tel: 0115 921 7263
Activities: Religious activities
Address: Ruddington Fields Business Park, Mere Way, Ruddington, Nottingham, NG11 6JS
Trustees: Rev David Ernest Shearman, Robert J Hyde, Mr Kristian Paul Thorpe, Mr Remy Anekwe, Rev Angela Butcher, Mr Tim Bedward-Jones, Rev Brian Niblock
Income: £2,341,000 [2016]; £2,135,000 [2015]; £2,209,000 [2014]; £2,320,000 [2013]; £2,119,000 [2012]

Asser Bishvil Foundation
Registered: 9 Dec 2005 *Employees:* 1
Activities: General charitable purposes; education, training; prevention or relief of poverty; religious activities
Address: 2 New Hall Road, Salford, M7 4EL
Trustees: Mr D Orzel, Mr Chaim Simche Ehrentreu, Mrs S Orzel
Income: £9,656,906 [2017]; £7,394,492 [2016]; £8,671,710 [2015]; £6,926,877 [2014]; £6,496,010 [2013]

The Associated Board of The Royal Schools of Music
Registered: 23 Jul 1985 *Employees:* 157 *Volunteers:* 301
Tel: 020 7467 8223 *Website:* abrsm.org
Activities: Education, training; arts, culture, heritage, science
Address: Associated Board of The Royal Schools of Music, 4 London Wall Place, London, EC2Y 5AU
Trustees: Colette Bowe, Alan Smith, Mr Kevin Porter, Linda Merrick, David Roper, Mr Douglas Frank Gardner, Mr Jeremy Wilfrid Heap, Prof Colin Lawson, Professor Jonathan Freeman-Attwood BMus, Ms Judith Barber, John Gallacher, Robin Downie, Mr Jeffrey Neil Sharkey, Mr Damian Mark Alan Wisniewski
Income: £49,168,000 [2017]; £44,138,000 [2016]; £44,448,000 [2015]; £42,898,000 [2014]; £44,149,000 [2013]

Association for Cultural Advancement Through Visual Art Limited
Registered: 29 Mar 1984 *Employees:* 11 *Volunteers:* 446
Tel: 020 8960 5015 *Website:* acava.org
Activities: Education, training; advancement of health or saving of lives; disability; prevention or relief of poverty; arts, culture, heritage, science; economic, community development, employment
Address: Acava Ltd, 54 Blechynden Street, London, W10 6RJ
Trustees: Ms Caroline Jenkinson, Gavin Turk, Lorraine McGuinness, Jefford Horrigan, Colin Prescod, Mr Stephen Charles Caine, Karen Lee, David Powell
Income: £1,595,755 [2017]; £1,686,719 [2016]; £1,629,693 [2015]; £1,601,092 [2014]; £1,456,134 [2013]

The Association for Cultural Exchange Limited
Registered: 8 Apr 1980 *Employees:* 23 *Volunteers:* 2
Tel: 01223 849004 *Website:* acefoundation.org.uk
Activities: Education, training; arts, culture, heritage, science; environment, conservation, heritage; economic, community development, employment
Address: Stapleford Granary, Bury Road, Stapleford, Cambridge, CB22 5BP
Trustees: Dr Roland Randall, Mr Richard Burge, Professor Ann Barrett OBE, Ms Sally Hickling MSocSci
Income: £5,698,052 [2016]; £5,888,904 [2015]; £5,567,175 [2014]; £5,671,514 [2013]; £4,800,825 [2012]

The Association for Perioperative Practice
Registered: 20 Mar 2007 *Employees:* 14 *Volunteers:* 26
Tel: 01423 881300 *Website:* afpp.org.uk
Activities: The advancement of health or saving of lives
Address: 42 Freemans Way, Harrogate, N Yorks, HG3 1DH
Trustees: Mr Adrian Jones, Mrs Julie Peirce-Jones, Mrs Angela Cobbold, Tracey Williams, Mr John Dade
Income: £1,287,933 [2017]; £1,133,337 [2016]; £1,121,790 [2015]; £991,061 [2014]; £1,137,878 [2013]

The Association for Real Change
Registered: 12 Nov 1982 *Employees:* 23 *Volunteers:* 6
Tel: 01246 555043 *Website:* arcuk.org.uk
Activities: Education, training; disability; human rights, religious or racial harmony, equality or diversity; other charitable purposes
Address: ARC, 10a Marsden Street, Chesterfield, Derbys, S40 1JY
Trustees: Ms Anthea Jane Sully, Mr Gary Thompson, Mrs Kate Allen, Mr Graeme Fitzsimmons, Mr John Stephen Crawford, Agnes Philomena Lunny, Christopher Dowell-Bennett, Mr Peter Jung, Mr Philip John Morris
Income: £1,895,896 [2017]; £1,832,801 [2016]; £1,924,073 [2015]; £2,042,220 [2014]; £2,493,500 [2013]

The Association for Science Education
Registered: 7 Jan 1964 *Employees:* 23 *Volunteers:* 300
Tel: 01707 283000 *Website:* ase.org.uk
Activities: Education, training
Address: Association for Science Education, College Lane, Hatfield, Herts, AL10 9AA
Trustees: Ms Maggie Hannon, Mr Pete Robinson CSciTeach, Ali Redmore, Ms Margaret Fleming, Mrs Chris Colclough CSciTeach, Mrs Mary Whitehouse, Richard Needham, Ms Helen Roberts, Mr Roger McCune OBE
Income: £1,151,532 [2017]; £1,204,825 [2016]; £1,196,034 [2015]; £1,263,460 [2014]; £1,533,035 [2013]

The Association of Accounting Technicians
Registered: 15 Nov 1995 *Employees:* 249
Tel: 020 7397 3052 *Website:* aat.org.uk
Activities: Education, training
Address: 140 Aldersgate Street, London, EC1A 4HY
Trustees: David Walker, Mark Nelson, Mark McBride, Lee Maidment, Paul Rowlands, Tim Nicholls, June Anderson, Christina Earls, Helen Geatches, Susan Taylor, John Thornton, Heather Hill, Jane Cuthbertson, Allan Ramsay, Jane Towers, Nicky Fisher, Mr David Frederick, Carole Turner, Sarah Cox, Vernon Anderson, Rita Patel, Anne-Marie Townsend, Kevin Bragg, David Quigg, Marta Phillips
Income: £28,974,629 [2016]; £27,109,593 [2015]; £25,701,597 [2014]; £25,391,086 [2013]; £23,657,918 [2012]

The Association of British Members of The Sovereign Military Hospitaller Order of St. John of Jerusalem of Rhodes and Of Malta
Registered: 4 May 2004 *Employees:* 1 *Volunteers:* 800
Tel: 020 7286 1414 *Website:* orderofmalta.org.uk
Activities: The advancement of health or saving of lives; disability; prevention or relief of poverty; overseas aid, famine relief; religious activities
Address: 13 Deodar Road, London, SW15 2NP
Trustees: Mr Michael Jeremy Hodges, Mr Richard Fitzalan Howard, Lady Celestria Magdalen Mary Hales, Mr Richard John Berkley-Matthews, Mr Robert Morrisson Atwater, Mr Nicolas Graf Reuttner von Weyl-Mynett, Miss Louise Noble, Mr Donald Edward Wood, Rt Hon Lady Patricia Mary Talbot of Malahide, Mr James Robert Pavey, Mr Ian Charles Damien Scott, Mrs Anna Katherine Cox, Mr Paul St John Letman, Dr Gerard Robertson
Income: £4,031,281 [2016]; £3,334,341 [2015]; £500,989 [2014]; £678,177 [2013]; £641,208 [2012]

Association of Charitable Foundations
Registered: 10 Aug 2004 *Employees:* 12
Tel: 020 7255 4494 *Website:* acf.org.uk
Activities: General charitable purposes
Address: Acorn House, 314-320 Gray's Inn Road, London, WC1X 8DP
Trustees: Ms Paula Kahn, Ms Amanda Jordan, Andrew Stafford, Ms Sara Longmuir, Ms Sheila Jane Malley, Dr Joanne Louise Knight, Mr Anthony Tomei, Jane Streather, Mr Gary Beharrell, Mr Andrew Barnett, Tim Wilson, Mr James David Wragg, Mr Kenneth Ferguson, Ms Muna Munzer Wehbe
Income: £1,165,978 [2016]; £1,160,701 [2015]; £1,051,905 [2014]; £853,908 [2013]; £999,000 [2012]

Association of Chief Executives of Voluntary Organisations - ACEVO
Registered: 7 Jun 2006 *Employees:* 17
Tel: 020 7014 4600 *Website:* acevo.org.uk
Activities: General charitable purposes; education, training
Address: ACEVO, 8 Regents Wharf, All Saints Street, London, N1 9RL
Trustees: Mr Paul Farmer, Mr Othman Moqbel, Ms Jill Halford, Mr Kulbinder Kang, Mr Jehangir Malik, Mrs Menai Owen-Jones, Mrs Clare White, Mr David Smith, Vicky Browning, Mr Joe Irvin, Ms Katherine Welch, Ms Sue Tibballs, Ms Ruth Marks
Income: £1,123,341 [2017]; £1,289,132 [2016]; £1,775,269 [2015]; £1,925,270 [2014]; £1,998,956 [2013]

The Association of Coloproctology of Great Britain and Ireland
Registered: 22 Feb 2007 *Employees:* 4
Website: acpgbi.org.uk
Activities: Education, training; advancement of health or saving of lives
Address: Royal College of Surgeons of England, 35-43 Lincoln's Inn Fields, London, WC2A 3PE
Trustees: Prof James Hill, Ruth Margaret Fox MA LLB, Mr Jonathan Peter Bell, Professor Robert James Campbell Steele, Judith Anne Brodie, Mr Nigel Andrew Scott, Mr John Graham Williams FRCS MCh BSc, Mr Peter Sagar, Mr Timothy Cook, Mr Paul John Finan Professor
Income: £1,203,802 [2016]; £702,462 [2015]; £641,517 [2014]; £862,942 [2013]; £862,709 [2012]

Association of Commonwealth Universities
Registered: 5 Mar 1963 *Employees:* 110
Tel: 020 7380 6715 *Website:* acu.ac.uk
Activities: Education, training
Address: Woburn House, 20-24 Tavistock Square, London, WC1H 9HF
Trustees: Professor Nirmala Rao, Dr Amit Chakma, Professor Janette Barbara Thomas, Professor Paul Boyle, Mr Hargurdeep S Saini, Engr Ahmed Farooq Bazai, Professor Dhanjay Jhurry, Professor Willem J S De Villiers, Professor Abel Idowu Olayinka, Professor Colin Riordan, Professor Nigel Martin Healey, Professor Idris A Rai, Professor Ranbir Singh, Professor Stuart Edward Corbridge, Professor Gamini Senanayake, Professor Gabriel Ayum Teye, Professor Mehraj Uddin Mir
Income: £9,463,000 [2017]; £9,334,000 [2016]; £8,251,000 [2015]; £6,428,000 [2014]; £5,937,000 [2013]

The Association of Dental Implantology Limited
Registered: 14 Nov 1988 *Employees:* 4 *Volunteers:* 30
Tel: 020 8487 5555 *Website:* adi.org.uk
Activities: Education, training; advancement of health or saving of lives
Address: 20 Hill Rise, Richmond, Surrey, TW10 6UA
Trustees: Dr Craig Parker, Dr Stephen Jones, Dr Irene Amrore, Mr William Schaeffer, Dr Zaki Kanaan, Dr Pynadath George, Mr Hussam Elassar, Professor Nikolaos Donos, Mr Guy Edward Charles Laffan, Dr Abid Faqir, Dr Derek Bingham, Mr Giorgios Margaritis, Ms Eimear Keenan, Mr Amit Patel, Miss Julia Wilson, Mr Ashley Rowland Byrne, Dr Paul Shenfine
Income: £1,055,644 [2017]; £537,722 [2016]; £1,014,408 [2015]; £666,996 [2014]; £1,144,995 [2013]

The Association of Graduate Careers Advisory Services
Registered: 8 Dec 1999 *Employees:* 16 *Volunteers:* 200
Tel: 0114 251 5771 *Website:* agcas.org.uk
Activities: Education, training
Address: Association of Graduate Careers, R8D Riverside Building, Sheafbank Business Park, Prospect Road, Sheffield, S2 3EN
Trustees: Mr David Anthony Winter, Ms Shelagh Green, Sue Bennett, Liz Wilkinson, Mrs Naomi Oosman-Watts, Dr Nalayini Pushpam Thambar, Bob Gilworth, Mark Stow, Terry Dray, Mrs Helen Penelope Smith, Mr Paul Gratrick
Income: £1,385,230 [2017]; £1,350,390 [2016]; £1,226,216 [2015]; £1,423,096 [2014]; £1,206,133 [2013]

The Association of Jewish Refugees (AJR)
Registered: 23 Nov 2012 *Employees:* 51 *Volunteers:* 300
Tel: 020 8385 3070 *Website:* ajr.org.uk
Activities: General charitable purposes; education, training; prevention or relief of poverty
Address: Association of Jewish Refugees, Winston House, 2 Dollis Park, Finchley, London, N3 1HF
Trustees: Mr Andrew Charles Kaufman, Mrs Joanna Frances Millan, Mr David Rothenberg, Mrs Philippa Strauss, Sir Erich Reich, Mr Frank Harding, Mr Anthony John Spiro, Mrs Eleanor Angel, Mrs Gabrrielle Glassman
Income: £3,036,583 [2016]; £2,546,084 [2015]; £3,650,835 [2014]; £12,035,423 [2013]

The Association of Masters in Business Administration
Registered: 15 May 1969 *Employees:* 26
Tel: 020 7246 2686 *Website:* mbaworld.com
Activities: Education, training
Address: 25 Hosier Lane, London, EC1A 9LQ
Trustees: Professor Andrew Raymond Lock, Mr Bodo Bernd Schlegelmilch, Mr Timothy Arthur Randall, Ms Saba Shaukat, Mr Steven Leendert Van De Velde, Mr Christopher John Parkinson, Mr Saibal Chattopadhyay, Mr Peter Mozier, Mr Gary Narunsky
Income: £2,807,921 [2016]; £2,864,335 [2015]; £2,897,042 [2014]; £2,601,228 [2013]; £2,992,258 [2012]

The Association of Taxation Technicians
Registered: 2 Jul 1990 *Employees:* 70 *Volunteers:* 80
Tel: 020 7340 0580 *Website:* att.org.uk
Activities: Education, training; other charitable purposes
Address: Association of Taxation Technicians, Artillery House, 11-19 Artillery Row, London, SW1P 1RT
Trustees: Miss Yvette Elizabeth Nunn, Mr Ralph Steven Pettengell, Mrs Tanya Jane Wadeson, Mrs Tracy-Ann Jackson, Mrs Katharine Sarah Lindley, Mr Julian William Millinchamp, Mrs Hayley Claire Perkin, Ms Kay Pauline Aylott, Mrs Jacqueline Lesley Hall, Mr David Iain Bird, Mrs Nancy Jane Cruickshanks, Mrs Natalie Anne Miller, Mr Jeremy Coker, Mr Michael David Steed, Mr Graham David Batty, Mr Richard Mark Todd, Mr Steven Martin Holden, Mr David Bradshaw, Mr Richard Freeman, Mr Jonathan Stride, Mrs Senga Prior
Income: £2,615,631 [2016]; £2,385,313 [2015]; £2,233,000 [2014]; £2,022,345 [2013]; £1,903,999 [2012]

Association of Voluntary Organisations in Wrexham
Registered: 8 Feb 1995 *Employees:* 53 *Volunteers:* 40
Tel: 01978 312556 *Website:* avow.org
Activities: General charitable purposes; education, training; advancement of health or saving of lives; disability; prevention or relief of poverty; amateur sport; economic, community development, employment; recreation
Address: Ty Avow, 21 Egerton Street, Wrexham, LL11 1ND
Trustees: Mr John Leece Jones, Mrs Rosemarie Williams, Mr Stephen Perkins, Rev James Gareth Aylward, Mr Mervyn Robert Dean, Mrs Paticia Mary Walker, Mrs Barbara Fox Roxburgh, Miss Moira Jones, Mrs Kathleen Joyce M'caw, Mr Frederick Stephen Evans, Mrs Wanjiku Elizabeth Mbugua, Mr David Thompson
Income: £1,223,298 [2017]; £1,071,488 [2016]; £1,086,566 [2015]; £1,003,262 [2014]; £1,628,662 [2013]

Asthma UK
Registered: 2 Nov 1989 *Employees:* 85 *Volunteers:* 315
Tel: 0300 222 5800 *Website:* asthma.org.uk
Activities: The advancement of health or saving of lives
Address: Asthma UK, 18 Mansell Street, London, E1 8AA
Trustees: Mrs Jane Elizabeth Tozer, Mr John Channon Tucker, Mrs Mary Dolores Leadbeater, Ms Kate Clarke, Dr Paul Hodgkin, Mr Jean-Francois Bessiron, Professor Ian Hall, Dr Robert Wilson, Mr Martin John Sinclair, Mr George Rupert Anson, Professor Sir Lewis Ritchie OBE, Mr James Bowes
Income: £7,920,000 [2017]; £8,737,000 [2016]; £7,933,000 [2015]; £9,290,000 [2014]; £7,601,000 [2013]

Aston - Mansfield
Registered: 21 Nov 1963 *Employees:* 47 *Volunteers:* 60
Tel: 020 3740 8100 *Website:* aston-mansfield.org.uk
Activities: Education, training; prevention or relief of poverty; accommodation, housing; arts, culture, heritage, science; economic, community development, employment
Address: Durning Hall, Earlham Grove, London, E7 9AB
Trustees: The Venerable Elwin Cockett, Rev Paul Edward Regan, Mr Noor Choudhary, Mr Alex Patrick Minford, Ms Chloe May Halpin, Mr Chris Keen, Ms Gail Sheridan, Mr Sammy Shummo, Mr Mahendra Savjani
Income: £1,462,409 [2017]; £1,323,109 [2016]; £1,226,725 [2015]; £1,226,490 [2014]; £1,291,193 [2013]

Aston Student Village
Registered: 25 Jul 2003 *Employees:* 2
Tel: 0121 204 5351
Activities: Education, training; accommodation, housing
Address: Aston Student Village, Harriet Martineau Building, Aston Street, Birmingham, B4 7UP
Trustees: Mr Thomas Button, Mr Mark Gwynfor George Davies, Mr John Walter, Mr Philip Extance, Mr Peter McCormack, Mr Martyn Everett
Income: £26,178,738 [2016]; £16,677,501 [2014]; £11,206,256 [2013]; £10,623,653 [2012]

Aston Students' Union
Registered: 17 May 2013 *Employees:* 45 *Volunteers:* 1,230
Tel: 0121 204 4855 *Website:* astonsu.com
Activities: Education, training; amateur sport; recreation
Address: Aston University, Aston Students Guild, 60 Aston Street, Birmingham, B4 7ES
Trustees: Miss Sophie Davies, Mrs Gill Clark, Mr John Rogerson Bailey, Ms Amna Anteeq, Alice Coombes, Mrs Sandra Benbow, Mr Colin Shaw, Miss Reema Quessou, Samantha Searle, Mrs Sunita Goddard-Patel
Income: £2,581,962 [2017]; £2,063,270 [2016]; £1,961,763 [2015]; £1,387,941 [2014]

At Home in the Community Limited
Registered: 3 May 1990 *Employees:* 88
Website: athome.uk.net
Activities: Disability; accommodation, housing; religious activities
Address: Livability, 6 Mitre Passage, London, SE10 0ER
Trustees: Mr David Webber, Mrs Elizabeth Mell
Income: £1,133,725 [2017]; £1,197,780 [2016]; £1,632,561 [2015]; £2,049,261 [2014]; £1,959,196 [2013]

Ataxia UK
Registered: 27 Feb 2004 *Employees:* 11 *Volunteers:* 112
Tel: 020 7582 1444 *Website:* ataxia.org.uk
Activities: Education, training; advancement of health or saving of lives; disability
Address: 12 Broadbent Close, London, N6 5JW
Trustees: Dr Barry Hunt, Ms Alison Love, Mr Richard Brown, Dr Harriet Bonney, Mr John Abbott, Mr Philip Griffiths, Mr Howard Marshall, Mr Russell Brown, Mr Andrew Downie, Ms Grace Kay, Dr Tony Kaye, Mr Graham Fryatt
Income: £1,239,813 [2017]; £1,040,352 [2016]; £1,304,636 [2015]; £964,789 [2014]; £988,915 [2013]

Ategi Limited
Registered: 29 Sep 1999 *Employees:* 62
Tel: 01443 484400 *Website:* ategi.org.uk
Activities: Disability
Address: Flynn House, Cardiff Road, Rhydyfelin, Pontypridd, Rhondda Cynon Taf, CF37 5HP
Trustees: Mrs Jill Rosemary Davies, Mrs Diana Fentiman, Mr Owen Glynne Jones, Dr Howell Edwards, Mrs Pauline Roberts, Mr Stephen Philip Garland
Income: £3,455,733 [2017]; £3,333,192 [2016]; £2,776,356 [2015]; £3,801,774 [2014]; £4,943,383 [2013]

Atma Vignani Dada Bhagwan Foundation
Registered: 24 Apr 2003 *Volunteers:* 80
Tel: 020 8427 3374 *Website:* uk.dadabhagwan.org
Activities: General charitable purposes; education, training; advancement of health or saving of lives; disability; prevention or relief of poverty; overseas aid, famine relief; accommodation, housing; religious activities; arts, culture, heritage, science; environment, conservation, heritage
Address: 75 Anglesmede Crescent, Pinner, Middlesex, HA5 5ST
Trustees: Mr Chandrakant M Mistry, Mrs Hansa B Patel, Mr Rameshbhai Bhulabhai Patel, Mr Pranai Jitendra Karia, Dr Dilip S Patel, Dr Shobhna S Patel, Mr Prajay Vindodrai Shah
Income: £1,113,817 [2017]; £829,889 [2016]; £500,779 [2015]; £304,082 [2014]; £404,643 [2013]

The Auckland Castle Trust
Registered: 2 Mar 2012 *Employees:* 76 *Volunteers:* 282
Website: aucklandcastle.org.uk
Activities: General charitable purposes; education, training; prevention or relief of poverty; arts, culture, heritage, science; environment, conservation, heritage; economic, community development, employment; recreation
Address: 10 Waverley Road, St Albans, Herts, AL3 5PA
Trustees: Lady Riddell, Jonathan Ruffer, Dr Malcolm Austin Rogers CBE, Lady Nicholson, Mr Nicholas Timothy Turner, Jane Dean
Income: £22,255,274 [2017]; £17,634,351 [2016]; £10,729,959 [2015]; £3,377,428 [2014]; £11,115,702 [2013]

Audacious Church
Registered: 15 May 2009 *Employees:* 44 *Volunteers:* 400
Tel: 0161 830 7000 *Website:* audaciouschurch.com
Activities: General charitable purposes; education, training; prevention or relief of poverty; religious activities
Address: Trinity Way, Manchester, M3 7BB
Trustees: Mr Glyn Barrett, Mr Stuart Andrew Keir, Mrs Rachel Ray, Mr Jonathan Bracegirdle, Mr Neil Smith, Mr David John McPhail
Income: £2,638,891 [2017]; £1,942,400 [2016]; £1,841,803 [2015]; £1,440,850 [2014]; £1,378,628 [2013]

The Audience Agency
Registered: 29 Nov 2012 *Employees:* 43 *Volunteers:* 15
Tel: 0161 234 2956 *Website:* theaudienceagency.org
Activities: General charitable purposes; education, training; arts, culture, heritage, science
Address: The Audience Agency, Green Fish Resource Centre, 46-50 Oldham Street, Manchester, M4 1LE
Trustees: Mr Timothy Richard Hornsby, Mr Alan Rivett, Ms Geraldine Alice Collinge, Dr Benjamin Alexander Walmsley, Mr Roger Tomlinson, Mr Steven John Parker, Mr Roshan Singh Sidhu
Income: £2,271,331 [2017]; £2,532,177 [2016]; £3,364,694 [2015]; £2,132,988 [2014]

Augustinians of The Assumption
Registered: 18 Aug 2011
Tel: 01689 827505 *Website:* assumptionist.org.uk
Activities: Education, training; prevention or relief of poverty; religious activities
Address: Wilkins Kennedy, Greytown House, 221-227 High Street, Orpington, Kent, BR6 0NZ
Trustees: Rev William O'Dell, Rev Richard Andrew Joseph O'Brien, Rev Vincent Cabanac, Rev Michael Francis Lambert, Rev Didier Remiot, Mr Ghislain Lafont
Income: £1,144,010 [2016]; £765,578 [2015]; £10,998,156 [2014]; £211,719 [2013]; £4,308,921 [2012]

Aurora Options
Registered: 17 Aug 1988 *Employees:* 106
Tel: 020 8469 8103 *Website:* auroraoptions.org.uk
Activities: General charitable purposes; advancement of health or saving of lives; disability; accommodation, housing
Address: Unit 3 California Building, Deals Gateway, London, SE13 7SB
Trustees: Mr Jeremy Tosswell, Mr Mark Edward Ballantine, Isabelle Terrisson, Ms Jean Young
Income: £4,062,301 [2017]; £3,487,515 [2016]; £3,154,383 [2015]; £2,931,017 [2014]; £2,744,171 [2013]

The Aurum Charitable Trust
Registered: 16 Oct 2007
Tel: 0345 304 2424
Activities: General charitable purposes
Address: 6th Floor, Trustee Department, Trinity Quay 2, Avon Street, Bristol, BS2 0PT
Trustees: Mrs Elizabeth Jack, Coutts & Co, Mr Roderick Daniel Jack
Income: £1,015,486 [2017]; £495,890 [2016]; £332,674 [2015]; £244,277 [2014]; £193,269 [2013]

Austin Friars
Registered: 3 Apr 1985 *Employees:* 93
Tel: 01896 757746 *Website:* austinfriars.co.uk
Activities: Education, training
Address: 13 Barr Road, Galashiels, Selkirkshire, TD1 3HX
Trustees: Rev Peter Tiplady, Mr Stephen Joseph Bolger, Fr Ian Wilson, Stephen Graham, John Little, Mrs Joanne Graham, Mrs Bavidge, Mr Neil Elsender, Mr Michael Higginbottom, Mrs Susan Claire Dymond
Income: £4,855,921 [2017]; £4,906,785 [2016]; £4,654,915 [2015]; £4,202,245 [2014]; £4,205,391 [2013]

Autism Anglia
Registered: 31 Jul 1997 *Employees:* 296 *Volunteers:* 45
Tel: 01206 577678 *Website:* autism-anglia.org.uk
Activities: Education, training; disability; accommodation, housing
Address: Autism Anglia, Century House, North Station Road, Colchester, Essex, CO1 1RE
Trustees: Mr Andrew Charles Edwin Beevers, Mr David George Burrage MA, Mrs Janet Barker, Mrs Angela Eley, Mr Stephen Jonathan Pittuck, Mr James McElhinnery, Mrs Judith Winward, Mrs Corinna Cranch
Income: £10,492,977 [2016]; £10,273,000 [2015]; £10,129,000 [2014]; £9,854,000 [2013]; £9,601,000 [2012]

Autism East Midlands
Registered: 19 Sep 1986 *Employees:* 405 *Volunteers:* 11
Tel: 01909 506678 *Website:* autismeastmidlands.org.uk
Activities: General charitable purposes; education, training; disability
Address: Unit 31 Crags Industrial Estate, Morven Street, Creswell, Worksop, Notts, S80 4AJ
Trustees: Mr Keith Roy Doble, Mr Matthew James, Mr Terence Raymond Ousley, Mr Philip Dixon, Dr Elizabeth Marder, Mr Nicholas Bryan Chamberlain, Mr George James Smith
Income: £11,426,153 [2017]; £11,976,081 [2016]; £12,095,496 [2015]; £11,956,233 [2014]; £11,512,654 [2013]

Autism Hampshire
Registered: 30 Nov 1983 *Employees:* 200 *Volunteers:* 5
Tel: 01489 880881 *Website:* autismhampshire.org.uk
Activities: Education, training; disability; accommodation, housing; other charitable purposes
Address: Autism Hampshire, 1634 Parkway, Whiteley, Fareham, Hants, PO15 7AH
Trustees: Mr Graham Shields, Mr Ivan White, Mr James Robson, Ms Jane Louise Fish, Mrs Pauline Quan Arrow, Mr Andrew Edmonds, Mr Jonathan Hardie, Mrs Jayne Turnbull
Income: £5,056,696 [2017]; £5,035,520 [2016]; £5,473,600 [2015]; £5,225,149 [2014]; £5,514,740 [2013]

Autism Initiatives (UK)
Registered: 27 Mar 1990 *Employees:* 2,102 *Volunteers:* 10
Tel: 0151 330 9500 *Website:* autisminitiatives.org
Activities: General charitable purposes; education, training; disability; accommodation, housing
Address: Mrs Janice Howard, Sefton House, Bridle Road, Bootle, Merseyside, L30 4XR
Trustees: Mr Brian Edward Williams, Rose Buttery, Mr John McCarthy, Mrs Elizabeth Veronica Slater BA BSc Hons, Mrs Sian Elizabeth Hiscock, Mrs Carys Owen
Income: £47,558,000 [2017]; £44,616,000 [2016]; £42,541,000 [2015]; £45,066,000 [2014]; £43,809,000 [2013]

Autism Plus Limited
Registered: 10 Mar 1987 *Employees:* 350 *Volunteers:* 56
Tel: 0114 384 0284 *Website:* autismplus.org
Activities: Education, training; disability; accommodation, housing; economic, community development, employment
Address: Autism Plus Ltd, Exchange Brewery, 2 Bridge Street, Sheffield, S3 8NS
Trustees: Cllr Peter Price MBE, Mr Peter John Briggs, Mr Charles Lindsay, Mr Stephen Fletcher, Mr Ian Oldroyd, Mrs Valerie Lindsay, Ms Andrea Scott-Jones, Ms Joan Kennedy
Income: £8,984,025 [2017]; £9,021,457 [2016]; £8,927,906 [2015]; £8,627,516 [2014]; £9,230,409 [2013]

Autism Research Trust
Registered: 6 Jul 2010
Website: autismresearchtrust.org
Activities: The advancement of health or saving of lives
Address: Wrigleys Solicitors LLP, 17-21 Cookridge Street, Leeds, LS2 3AG
Trustees: Dr Lewis Owens, Mr Robert Leeming, Robert Verwaaijen, Mr Andrew James Buisson, Professor Simon Baron-Cohen, Mr Andrew Blyth Swann, Miss Catherine Lucy Hawking, Dr Jonathan Tobin
Income: £1,002,450 [2017]; £838,003 [2016]; £182,924 [2015]; £301,337 [2014]; £311,247 [2013]

Autism Sussex Limited
Registered: 14 Feb 1996 *Employees:* 224 *Volunteers:* 170
Tel: 01892 822168 *Website:* autismsussex.org.uk
Activities: Disability; accommodation, housing
Address: Pepenbury, Cornford Lane, Tunbridge Wells, Kent, TN2 4QU
Trustees: Gillian Marcus, Waseem Ali
Income: £5,372,785 [2017]; £5,756,200 [2016]; £5,569,099 [2015]; £5,489,758 [2014]; £5,361,379 [2013]

Autism Together
Registered: 30 Jan 1992 *Employees:* 936 *Volunteers:* 20
Tel: 0151 334 7510 *Website:* autismtogether.co.uk
Activities: Education, training; disability; accommodation, housing
Address: Autism Together, Unit C, Oak House, 6 Tebay Road, Bromborough, Merseyside, CH62 3PA
Trustees: Professor Hilary Dobson, John Kennedy, Mr Stephen Ashton, Mr Andrew Derek Davies, Mrs Carole Anne Forrester Battersby, Mr Anthony Cragg, Mrs Catherine Louise Ames, Mr John Callcott, Mr Michael Gerard Fortune, Mr Edward Behan, Mr Iain Nicholson Cadman
Income: £20,138,000 [2017]; £19,137,000 [2016]; £18,205,503 [2015]; £15,775,520 [2014]; £13,479,944 [2013]

Autism Wessex
Registered: 7 Nov 1990 *Employees:* 454 *Volunteers:* 79
Tel: 01202 483360 *Website:* autismwessex.org.uk
Activities: Education, training; disability; accommodation, housing
Address: Autism Wessex, Bargates Court, 22 Bargates, Christchurch, Dorset, BH23 1QL
Trustees: Mr Arnold Christopher Page, Mrs Mary Claire Boyd, Mr Bob Gilbertson, Martin James, Fiona Fox, Mr Jonathan Beebee, Mrs Joan Dampney, Mr Paul McGee, Adrian Trevett, Malcolm Farrell, Mike Leese, Gabriella Crouch
Income: £11,420,562 [2017]; £11,663,850 [2016]; £12,191,360 [2015]; £10,752,488 [2014]; £9,589,570 [2013]

Autism at Kingwood
Registered: 3 Nov 1994 *Employees:* 194
Tel: 0118 931 0143 *Website:* kingwood.org.uk
Activities: Disability
Address: 2 Chalfont Court, Chalfont Way, Lower Earley, Reading, Berks, RG6 5SY
Trustees: Mrs Sandra Meadows, Mr Chris White, Mrs Rebecca Vickers, Lady Sonia Hornby, Mr David Swann
Income: £5,038,477 [2017]; £4,744,573 [2016]; £4,567,768 [2015]; £4,316,007 [2014]; £4,211,227 [2013]

Autism.West Midlands
Registered: 13 Jan 1986 *Employees:* 267 *Volunteers:* 24
Tel: 0121 450 7582 *Website:* autismwestmidlands.org.uk
Activities: Education, training; disability; accommodation, housing; economic, community development, employment
Address: Autism West Midlands, 14-17 George Road, Edgbaston, Birmingham, B15 1NU
Trustees: Dr Ashok Roy, Justine Morton, Dr Glenys Jones, Ms Joy Taylor, Gurdip Singh, John Drozd, Mr Philip Jordan, Mr Ian Fellows
Income: £6,391,000 [2017]; £6,294,000 [2016]; £6,436,000 [2015]; £6,704,000 [2014]; £6,575,000 [2013]

Autistica
Registered: 20 Dec 2004 *Employees:* 15 *Volunteers:* 200
Website: autistica.org.uk
Activities: Education, training; advancement of health or saving of lives; disability
Address: St Saviour's House, 39-41 Union Street, London, SE1 1SD
Trustees: Mr Edward Chandler, Mr James Lowe, Mr Jeff Saul, John Carey, Ms Gillian Ackers, Dr Sarah Caddick, Professor Eric Taylor, Mr Michael James Earl, Vincent Smith
Income: £3,593,349 [2017]; £705,131 [2016]; £1,085,973 [2014]; £871,081 [2013]; £1,057,984 [2012]

Autograph ABP
Registered: 26 Jan 2009 *Employees:* 9 *Volunteers:* 3
Tel: 020 7729 9200 *Website:* autograph-abp.co.uk
Activities: Arts, culture, heritage, science
Address: Autograph ABP, 1 Rivington Place, London, EC2A 3BA
Trustees: Rupert Christopher Grey, Mr Mark Anthony Sealy, Ms Claire Victoria Antrobus, Ms Mitra Tabrizian, John Ellis, Anne Williams, Mr Guy Nicholson, Roger Malbert, Mr Anthony James Stevenson, Mr John Lionel Dyer, Mr Ronald Henocq, Mr Iqbal Wahhab, Mr Eric Davis Collins, Carol Tulloch, Gary Younge
Income: £1,291,462 [2017]; £1,304,342 [2016]; £699,819 [2015]; £466,978 [2014]; £501,848 [2013]

Avalon School Educational Trust
Registered: 15 Aug 2001 *Employees:* 39 *Volunteers:* 7
Tel: 0151 625 6993 *Website:* avalon-school.co.uk
Activities: Education, training
Address: Dr C M T Kidd, 27 Caldy Road, Wirral, Merseyside, CH48 2HE
Trustees: Dr Catherine Mary Theresa Kidd, Miss Julie Elizabeth Yardley, Mr Philip Neil Shread, Mrs Heather Jean Probert, Mrs Patricia Johnson
Income: £1,034,821 [2017]; £1,040,320 [2016]; £1,003,974 [2015]; £905,877 [2014]; £878,186 [2013]

Avante Care and Support Limited
Registered: 1 May 1991 *Employees:* 1,309 *Volunteers:* 14
Tel: 01795 597400 *Website:* avantecare.org.uk
Activities: Education, training; advancement of health or saving of lives; disability; prevention or relief of poverty; accommodation, housing; other charitable purposes
Address: De Gelsey House, 1 Jubilee Way, Faversham, Kent, ME13 8GD
Trustees: Mr Robert Perkins, Mrs Gillian Anne Gibb, Mrs Sandra Hendry, Mr Vinod Khanna Kumar, Mr Anthony James Godden, Mr Mark John Hosea, Mr Peter Smallridge, Ms Michelle Gardener, Mr Giles Craven, Mr Peter Richard Horn, Mrs Jacqueline Churchward-Cardiff
Income: £23,887,041 [2017]; £27,940,275 [2016]; £29,882,239 [2015]; £29,975,946 [2014]; £29,933,851 [2013]

Avenue House Estate Trust
Registered: 24 Sep 2002 *Employees:* 15 *Volunteers:* 65
Tel: 020 8346 7814 *Website:* stephenshouseandgardens.com
Activities: General charitable purposes; education, training; amateur sport; environment, conservation, heritage; recreation
Address: 17 East End Road, London, N3 3QE
Trustees: Mr John Lancaster, Mr Khalid Ghani, Mrs Alison Dean, Mr Philip Rubenstein, Mr Michael Conradi, Mr Julian Blackett Thornton Trevelyan, Mrs Alessandra Alonso
Income: £1,780,790 [2017]; £972,885 [2016]; £610,656 [2015]; £575,427 [2014]; £309,667 [2013]

Avenues East
Registered: 13 Mar 1997 *Employees:* 282 *Volunteers:* 44
Tel: 020 3535 0500 *Website:* avenuesgroup.org.uk
Activities: General charitable purposes; advancement of health or saving of lives; disability; amateur sport; other charitable purposes
Address: River House, 1 Maidstone Road, Sidcup, Kent, DA14 5TA
Trustees: Steve James, Peter Snelling, Mr Jeffrey Gritzman, Mr Martin Owen, Howard Pugh, Mrs Caroline Tuohy, Mr Mark Pittaway
Income: £4,909,000 [2017]; £5,164,443 [2016]; £4,146,815 [2015]; £4,133,003 [2014]; £4,951,242 [2013]

Avenues London
Registered: 3 Jul 2009 *Employees:* 258
Tel: 020 3535 0500 *Website:* avenuesgroup.org.uk
Activities: General charitable purposes; advancement of health or saving of lives; disability
Address: The Avenues Trust, River House, 1 Maidstone Road, Sidcup, Kent, DA14 5TA
Trustees: Mr Steve James, Mrs Carol Beaby-Williams, Ms Cathryn Law, Peter Snelling, Georgia Jerram, Ms Evlynne Gilvarry
Income: £9,064,000 [2017]; £8,677,847 [2016]; £8,301,377 [2015]; £8,267,008 [2014]; £6,452,181 [2013]

Avenues South East
Registered: 28 Feb 2000 *Employees:* 415
Tel: 020 3535 0500 *Website:* avenuesgroup.org.uk
Activities: General charitable purposes; advancement of health or saving of lives; disability
Address: The Avenues Trust, River House, 1 Maidstone Road, Sidcup, Kent, DA14 5TA
Trustees: Mr Steve James, Paul Wood, Bruce Calderwood, Mr Paul Newton, Mr Peter Snelling, Mrs Clare Graham, Miss Rebecca Clutterbuck, Miss Daria Kuznetsova
Income: £15,231,000 [2017]; £14,508,804 [2016]; £13,963,212 [2015]; £14,022,637 [2014]; £15,619,720 [2013]

The Avenues Trust Group
Registered: 9 Jul 2009 *Employees:* 1,783 *Volunteers:* 44
Tel: 020 3535 0500 *Website:* avenuesgroup.org.uk
Activities: General charitable purposes; education, training; advancement of health or saving of lives; disability
Address: The Avenues Trust, River House, 1 Maidstone Road, Sidcup, Kent, DA14 5TA
Trustees: Steve James, Peter Snelling, Terry Rich, Ms Evlynne Gilvarry, Janet Coltman, Mrs Nicola Ford, Jo Land, Mr Alistair Oag, Bruce Calderwood, Mrs Helen John, Mr Jeffrey Gritzman
Income: £45,653,000 [2017]; £28,618,159 [2016]; £26,989,220 [2015]; £27,081,416 [2014]; £27,245,115 [2013]

Avocet Trust
Registered: 9 Oct 1991 *Employees:* 277
Tel: 01482 329226 *Website:* avocettrust.co.uk
Activities: Disability
Address: Avocet Trust, Clarence House, 60-62 Clarence Street, Hull, HU9 1DN
Trustees: Mr Andrew Tearle, Mr Christopher Brown, Miss Florence Cartwright, Sue Baker, Mrs Lesley Cartwright
Income: £6,238,363 [2017]; £6,172,326 [2016]; £6,105,696 [2015]; £5,800,666 [2014]; £5,663,849 [2013]

Avon Autistic Foundation Limited
Registered: 1 Mar 1984 *Employees:* 24
Tel: 0117 938 0155 *Website:* avon-autistic.demon.co.uk
Activities: Disability; accommodation, housing
Address: Avon Autistic Foundation Centre, Ann Coleman Centre, Ridingleaze, Bristol, BS11 0QE
Trustees: Mr John Joseph Coleman, Mrs Ann Yvonne Coleman, Ms Justine Stoffel, Dr Peter Clark
Income: £1,020,541 [2017]; £1,028,134 [2016]; £983,154 [2015]; £997,108 [2014]; £1,006,998 [2013]

Avon Wildlife Trust
Registered: 10 Jul 1980 *Employees:* 40 *Volunteers:* 800
Tel: 0117 917 7270 *Website:* avonwildlifetrust.org.uk
Activities: Education, training; environment, conservation, heritage
Address: Avon Wildlife Trust, 32 Jacobs Wells Road, Bristol, BS8 1DR
Trustees: Mr Malcolm Shepherd, Professor Jane Memmott, Katharine Finn, Ms Lorna Fox, Zac Nicholson, Mr Christopher Curling, Mr Martin Brasher, Mr Nigel Morrison, Miss Madeleine Bartlett, Mike Harris
Income: £2,148,802 [2017]; £2,258,296 [2016]; £2,181,034 [2015]; £2,384,024 [2014]; £1,936,386 [2013]

Awen Cultural Trust
Registered: 4 May 2016 *Employees:* 157 *Volunteers:* 20
Tel: 01656 754825 *Website:* awen-wales.com
Activities: Education, training; arts, culture, heritage, science
Address: Bryngarw House, Brynmenyn, Bridgend, CF32 8UU
Trustees: Mr Alan Richard John Morgan, Mr Jefferson Houseman Tildesley, Mr Leighton Thomas, Mr Martyne David John Jones, Mr Peter David Lees, Ms Yvonne Clare Murphy, Mrs Claire Marshall, Mr John Richard McCarthy, Mrs Margaret Ann Griffith, Mr Paul David Roberts, Mr William Joseph Campion
Income: £4,830,768 [2017]

Aysgarth School Trust Limited
Registered: 31 Mar 1967 *Employees:* 68
Tel: 01677 450182 *Website:* aysgarthschool.com
Activities: Education, training
Address: Aysgarth School Trust Ltd, Aysgarth School, Newton-le-Willows, Bedale, N Yorks, DL8 1TF
Trustees: Mr David Faber, Mr Robert Brooksbank, Mr William Roe, Mrs Sarah Guthe, Mrs Melissa Bowring, Mrs Rebecca Jane Falkingham, Mr Petern John Stuart Thompson, Mr James Hawkins, Hon William Kay-Shuttleworth, Mr James Luke Bourne-Arton, Mr Mark Wallace, Mr Bennet Hoskyns-Abrahall, Mr Christopher York, Justin Nolan
Income: £3,820,555 [2017]; £3,561,590 [2016]; £3,585,367 [2015]; £3,301,765 [2014]; £3,187,024 [2013]

Azhar Academy
Registered: 23 May 2000 *Employees:* 66 *Volunteers:* 60
Tel: 020 8534 5959 *Website:* azharacademy.org
Activities: Education, training; religious activities
Address: Azhar Academy, 235a Romford Road, London, E7 9HL
Trustees: Mr Ismail Gangat, Mr Ismail Amla, Mr Faisal Bobat
Income: £1,973,979 [2016]; £1,175,243 [2015]; £1,096,205 [2014]; £1,020,115 [2013]; £883,535 [2012]

Azure Charitable Enterprises
Registered: 13 Oct 1982 *Employees:* 230
Tel: 01670 733966 *Website:* azure-charitable.co.uk
Activities: Education, training; disability; accommodation, housing; economic, community development, employment
Address: Kielder Avenue, Cramlington, Northumberland, NE23 8JT
Trustees: Mr Alan Edward Kilburn OBE, Mr Geoffrey William Robson, Mrs Marie Wood, Mr Graham Barnard, Mrs Christine Suzanne Litchfield, Mrs Isabelle Trewhitt Turnbull, Mr Eric Morgan, Mr Ronald Ian Watson, Isobel Hindle, Mr Ian Alastair Keddie
Income: £7,808,037 [2017]; £7,424,872 [2016]; £7,334,726 [2015]; £7,411,465 [2014]; £7,792,483 [2013]

B A S School Limited
Registered: 4 Feb 1964 *Employees:* 123
Tel: 01424 776806 *Website:* battleabbeyschool.com
Activities: Education, training
Address: Battle Abbey School, High Street, Battle, E Sussex, TN33 0AD
Trustees: Doctor Guy Baker, Mr Jeremy Simon Eliker Harrison, Mr Malcolm Christopher Melville, Mrs Fiona Breeze, Rev George Pitcher, Mr John Matthew Leonard Kingwell, Mr Ian Mercer CBE, Mrs Alison Clare Martin, Mrs Janet Elizabeth Dunn, Mr Stephen Rumsey, Mr Patrick William Eastman Hart, Mrs Elizabeth Capper Fidock
Income: £5,752,151 [2017]; £5,666,745 [2016]; £5,811,152 [2015]; £4,848,402 [2014]; £4,567,974 [2013]

B. O. Education Limited
Registered: 28 May 2004 *Employees:* 30 *Volunteers:* 12
Tel: 07850 172886
Activities: Education, training
Address: 97 Maidenhead Road, Windsor, Berks, SL4 5EY
Trustees: Miss Rosemary Bailey, Mr Matt Stoddart, Mr Robert Lazzaro
Income: £1,434,020 [2015]; £1,677,106 [2014]; £1,574,606 [2013]; £1,992,552 [2012]

B.T.D.A. Limited
Registered: 23 Dec 1998 *Employees:* 15
Tel: 0116 262 2279 *Website:* btda.org.uk
Activities: Education, training; arts, culture, heritage, science
Address: Garden Street, Leicester, LE1 3UA
Trustees: Mrs Helen Mence, Mrs Jane Carver, Mr Maurice Taylor, Mr Michael Colin O'Gleby, Ms Rosie Carpenter, Mr Neil Allen, Mr Peter Cooper, Ann Oliver, Mr David Ramsden
Income: £1,058,332 [2017]; £967,046 [2016]; £933,413 [2015]; £896,244 [2014]; £811,624 [2013]

BASIS (Registration) Limited
Registered: 12 Aug 1999 *Employees:* 23
Tel: 01335 340851 *Website:* basis-reg.com
Activities: Education, training
Address: BASIS (Registration) Ltd, St Monicas House, 37-39 Windmill Lane, Ashbourne, Derbys, DE6 1EY
Trustees: Dr Susannah Bolton, Mr Christopher Edwin Clarke, Mr Geoff Dodgson, Mr David Cairns, Mr Patrick Mitton, Mrs Sabra Everett, Mr Christopher Sprigg, Mr Andrew Richardson, Mrs Steph Melrose, Prof John Moverley OBE, Mr Peter Taylor, Mrs Margaret May, Ms Sarah Mukherjee, Mr Stephen Jacob, Mr Charles Wright
Income: £1,445,796 [2016]; £1,315,150 [2015]; £1,177,262 [2014]; £1,161,462 [2013]; £1,132,195 [2012]

The BASW Trust

Registered: 22 Feb 1988
Tel: 0121 622 8416 *Website:* basw.co.uk
Activities: Education, training; prevention or relief of poverty
Address: BASW, Wellesley House, 37 Waterloo Street, Birmingham, B2 5PP
Trustees: Ms Fran Fuller, Guy Leonard Shennan, Andrew Colin Reid, Stuart Alun Warrender, David Thomson, Hilary Margaret Tompsett, Jonathan Peter Dudley, Patrick Jude Morgan, Nick Lovell, The British Association of Social Workers
Income: £1,299,192 [2016]; £1,092,733 [2015]; £1,021,944 [2014]; £951,840 [2013]; £882,004 [2012]

BBC Children in Need

Registered: 1 Sep 1989 *Employees:* 136 *Volunteers:* 250
Tel: 0345 609 0015 *Website:* bbc.co.uk
Activities: General charitable purposes; education, training; disability; prevention or relief of poverty
Address: Ground Floor, Bridge House, Media City UK, Salford, M50 2BH
Trustees: Mr Phil Hodkinson, Peter McBride, Anne Bulford, Luke Mayhew, Mrs Gillian Veronica Sheldon, Joanna Berry, Charlotte Moore, Ms Stevie Spring, Mr Bob Shennan, Mrs Donalda MacKinnon, Matthew James Baker
Income: £67,718,000 [2017]; £64,829,000 [2016]; £56,046,000 [2015]; £55,564,000 [2014]; £47,494,000 [2013]

BBC Media Action (India) Limited

Registered: 22 Nov 2007 *Employees:* 102
Tel: 07753 302850 *Website:* bbcmediaaction.org
Activities: Education, training; advancement of health or saving of lives; prevention or relief of poverty; overseas aid, famine relief
Address: BBC Media Action, Ibex House, 42-47 Minories, London, EC3N 1DY
Trustees: Alison Woodhams, Mr Richard Dawkins
Income: £3,965,735 [2017]; £3,716,579 [2016]; £3,233,942 [2015]; £5,030,177 [2014]; £5,933,666 [2013]

BBC Media Action

Registered: 23 Jun 1999 *Employees:* 838
Tel: 020 3614 4272 *Website:* bbcmediaaction.org
Activities: Education, training; advancement of health or saving of lives; prevention or relief of poverty; overseas aid, famine relief
Address: British Broadcasting Corporation, Broadcasting House, Portland Place, London, W1A 1AA
Trustees: Alison Woodhams, Professor Keith Paul William James McAdam, Ms Zeinab Badawi, Mr Richard William Dawkins, Mr Shubhranshu Choudhary, Mr Gavin Alexander Mann, Mr Martin Dinham, Ms Francesca Mary Unsworth, Mr Michael James Wooldridge, Mr Nicholas James Pickles, Ms Sophia Swithern
Income: £44,151,000 [2017]; £45,278,000 [2016]; £47,435,000 [2015]; £40,381,000 [2014]; £39,977,000 [2013]

BCNO Limited

Registered: 26 May 1964 *Employees:* 65 *Volunteers:* 1
Tel: 020 7435 6464 *Website:* bcom.ac.uk
Activities: Education, training; advancement of health or saving of lives
Address: BCOM, Lief House, Finchley Road, London, NW3 5HR
Trustees: Mr John Newell, Mr Kurt Jager, Howard Kidd, Dr Roger Heathcote, Dr Alexander Charles Sautelle, Dr Miles Gaythwaite, Miss Deborah Hayes, Mr Mark Morgan, Mr Manoj Mehta, Ms Penny Christie, Mrs Kathy O'Callaghan Brown, Dr Kerstin Jane Rolfe, Ms Theodora Ogwesi, Mr Simeon Milton
Income: £1,815,391 [2017]; £1,697,926 [2016]; £1,587,808 [2015]; £1,301,289 [2014]; £1,431,356 [2013]

BF Adventure

Registered: 7 Oct 1998 *Employees:* 16 *Volunteers:* 65
Tel: 01326 340912 *Website:* bfadventure.org
Activities: Education, training; disability; amateur sport; environment, conservation, heritage
Address: Goodygrane Activity Centre, Halvasso, Longdowns, Penryn, Cornwall, TR10 9BX
Trustees: Mr John Hugh Murrell, Mr Paul Harman, Mr Laurence Osborne, Mrs Deborah Gillian Osborne, Mr David Wingham, Mr Robert Michael Padbury, Mr Kim Conchie, Ms Hilary Jane Beechey, Mr John Henry Maples, Mrs Antoinette Ellen Theresa Wilcox-Mclean
Income: £1,289,773 [2017]; £637,352 [2016]; £547,044 [2015]; £534,119 [2014]; £522,177 [2013]

BFCVDFF Limited

Registered: 17 Nov 2010
Tel: 020 7759 1999 *Website:* britishfashioncouncil.com
Activities: Arts, culture, heritage, science; economic, community development, employment
Address: British Fashion Council, Somerset House, South Wing, Strand, London, WC2R 1LA
Trustees: Ms Alexandra Shulman, Mrs Caroline Rush, Mr Christopher Inman, Mr Stephen Quinn
Income: £1,061,448 [2017]; £676,882 [2016]; £409,308 [2015]; £287,407 [2014]; £675,461 [2013]

BFI Trust

Registered: 18 Mar 2011
Tel: 020 7957 4751
Activities: Education, training; arts, culture, heritage, science
Address: British Film Institute, 21 Stephen Street, London, W1T 1LN
Trustees: Caroline Michel, Eric Fellner CBE, Mr Peter Foy, Mr Trevor Mawby, Ms Shami Chakrabarti, Mr David Kustow, Amanda Nevill
Income: £1,800,693 [2017]; £2,284,462 [2016]; £1,619,656 [2015]; £1,548,243 [2014]; £9,098,312 [2013]

BH Live

Registered: 7 Oct 2010 *Employees:* 1,608
Tel: 01202 055522 *Website:* bhlive.org.uk
Activities: Arts, culture, heritage, science; amateur sport; recreation
Address: Bournemouth International Centre, Exeter Road, Bournemouth, BH2 5BH
Trustees: Philip Dewhurst, Mr Sean Aita, Mrs Lyn Glass, Mr Michael Wright, Cllr Robert Chapman, Mr Paul Collins, Mr Robert Boulton, Mr Martin Kimberley, Ms Sandra Graham, Mr Peter Gunn, Cllr Andrew Mason Morgan, Mr Philip Anthony Gowers
Income: £29,139,918 [2017]; £27,425,969 [2016]; £23,757,282 [2015]; £20,270,804 [2014]; £17,228,790 [2013]

BHA for Equality

Registered: 7 Mar 2000 *Employees:* 34 *Volunteers:* 34
Tel: 0845 450 4247 *Website:* thebha.org.uk
Activities: Education, training; advancement of health or saving of lives; prevention or relief of poverty; other charitable purposes
Address: Democracy House, 609 Stretford Road, Manchester, M16 0QA
Trustees: Mr Richard Turvey, Ms Francesca Tackie, Mr Michael Naraynsingh, Mr Crispen Samson Sachikonye, Dr Kamie Chakib Kitmitto, Mrs Safina Nadeem, Mrs Anna Victoria Tebay, Dr Bethan Harries
Income: £1,001,012 [2017]; £1,087,326 [2016]; £1,639,660 [2015]; £1,726,052 [2014]; £2,052,334 [2013]

BHT Early Education and Training
Registered: 28 Feb 2008 *Employees:* 95
Website: surestartbht.org.uk
Activities: General charitable purposes; education, training; advancement of health or saving of lives; prevention or relief of poverty; economic, community development, employment
Address: BHT Early Education and Training, The Barn, 16 Teasdale Street, off Wakefield Road, Bradford, BD4 7QJ
Trustees: Mr Yashvant Chhiba, Ms Jayne Eastwood, Miss Victoria Louise Wadsworth, Mrs Katherine Spivey, Mr Dewi Williams, Mrs Glynis Maria Pedder, Mr Ian Christopher Pickup
Income: £1,624,688 [2017]; £2,153,543 [2016]; £2,094,183 [2015]; £2,256,123 [2014]; £2,013,076 [2013]

BJU International
Registered: 27 Apr 1984 *Employees:* 10
Tel: 020 7706 0177 *Website:* bjui.org
Activities: Education, training; advancement of health or saving of lives
Address: 3 Junction Mews, London, W2 1PN
Trustees: Prof Freddie Hamdy, Dr David Malouf, Mr Ruaraidh MacDonagh, Mr Anthony Koupparis, Dr David Winkle, Mr Krishna Sethia, Mr Alan McNeill, Joanne Cresswell, Dr Patricia Zondervan
Income: £1,079,779 [2016]; £909,643 [2015]; £890,612 [2014]; £840,498 [2013]; £716,595 [2012]

BRAC UK
Registered: 20 Jul 2006 *Employees:* 10 *Volunteers:* 3
Tel: 020 3434 3071 *Website:* bracuk.net
Activities: Education, training; advancement of health or saving of lives; prevention or relief of poverty; overseas aid, famine relief; economic, community development, employment; human rights, religious or racial harmony, equality or diversity
Address: 19 Wootton Street, Southwark, London, SE1 8TG
Trustees: Mr Robert John Emlyn Evans, Ms Simone Sultana, Jane Cooper, Alex Manu, Ms Kate Kuper, Peter Nicholas
Income: £3,027,845 [2016]; £1,296,270 [2015]; £1,189,356 [2014]; £609,710 [2013]; £577,894 [2012]

BRE Trust
Registered: 24 May 2002 *Employees:* 643
Tel: 01923 664477 *Website:* bretrust.org.uk
Activities: Education, training; environment, conservation, heritage
Address: Bucknalls Lane, Watford, Herts, WD25 9NH
Trustees: James Wates, Sir Kenneth Knight CBE, Regius Professor of Computer Scienc Nicholas Robert Jennings, Mr P Lobban OBE, Mrs Francesca Anne Howard Berriman, Mr Ashley Paul Pocock
Income: £46,747,000 [2017]; £47,830,000 [2016]; £45,992,000 [2015]; £45,238,000 [2014]; £44,487,000 [2013]

BRS Education Limited
Registered: 6 May 2015 *Employees:* 50
Tel: 01638 665103 *Website:* brs.org.uk
Activities: Education, training
Address: The British Racing School, 11 Newmarket Road, Newmarket, Suffolk, CB8 7NU
Trustees: Ms Lydia Hislop, Mr Alan King, Mr Andrew Merriam, Mr James Given, Mr Mark Pendlington, Mr Stephen Jonathan Leslie Johnson, Mr John Maxse, Mr Simon Eliot, Ms Emma Lavelle, Mr Martin Mitchell, Mr Justin John Wyndham Wadham
Income: £4,943,665 [2017]

BS3 Community Development
Registered: 9 Oct 1990 *Employees:* 27 *Volunteers:* 9
Tel: 0117 902 8198 *Website:* bs3community.org.uk
Activities: General charitable purposes; education, training; advancement of health or saving of lives; arts, culture, heritage, science; environment, conservation, heritage; economic, community development, employment; recreation; other charitable purposes
Address: 10 East Road, Street, Somerset, BA16 0DB
Trustees: Mr Matthew Symonds, Mr Peter Duncan Bird, Mrs Jill Walsh, Ms Catherine Hector, Mr Mark Coates, Ms Jenny Alice Brown, Mrs Celia Phipps, Mr Malcolm Brammar, Ms Zoe Rice
Income: £1,231,122 [2017]; £1,078,544 [2016]; £1,014,820 [2015]; £1,045,749 [2014]; £957,371 [2013]

BT Benevolent Fund
Registered: 1 Apr 1963 *Employees:* 5
Tel: 0845 602 9714 *Website:* benevolent.bt.com
Activities: The prevention or relief of poverty
Address: 41 Minster Street, Reading, Berks, RG1 2JB
Trustees: Mr John Holme, Mr Kevin Charlesworth, Mr Robert Leonard Jones, Matt Rogers, Mrs Jane Shipway, Mr Tom Keeney, Mr Clive Selley
Income: £1,035,064 [2016]; £1,032,122 [2015]; £1,280,587 [2014]; £975,509 [2013]; £908,246 [2012]

BW Foundation
Registered: 9 Nov 2007 *Employees:* 2 *Volunteers:* 5
Tel: 020 8863 8672 *Website:* thesalaamcentre.com
Activities: General charitable purposes; education, training; advancement of health or saving of lives; disability; prevention or relief of poverty; religious activities; amateur sport
Address: 14 Holmdene Avenue, Harrow, Middlesex, HA2 6HR
Trustees: Dr Nizar Merali, Mrs Sabira Kanji, Mr Mukhtar Manji, Mr Mohamed-Iqbal Asaria, Mr Murtaza Versi
Income: £1,827,008 [2017]; £3,983,195 [2016]; £1,396,778 [2015]; £1,192,282 [2014]; £1,102,029 [2013]

Babington House School Ltd
Registered: 24 Jul 1963 *Employees:* 91
Tel: 01689 829938 *Website:* babingtonhouse.com
Activities: Education, training
Address: Waldens Manor, Waldens Road, Orpington, Kent, BR5 4EU
Trustees: Mr Christopher Lloyd Turner, Mr Gavin McKay, Mr Steven Thompson, Mrs Hayley Porter-Aslet, Mrs Pauline Bresnik-Snasdell, Nicola Howard, Mr Aditya Gupta, Mr William Magill
Income: £4,321,999 [2017]; £4,328,537 [2016]; £3,453,140 [2015]; £2,950,118 [2014]; £2,890,751 [2013]

The Babraham Institute
Registered: 20 Mar 1996 *Employees:* 369
Tel: 01223 496207 *Website:* babraham.ac.uk
Activities: Education, training; advancement of health or saving of lives
Address: The Babraham Institute, Babraham Hall, Babraham, Cambridge, CB22 3AT
Trustees: Professor Clive Page, Dr Lynne Christine Gailey, Professor David Kipling, Prof Anne C Ferguson Smith, Prof Nicolas Jones, Mr Graham Peter Allen, Mr Anthony Clare, Dr Paul Johnson, Professor Peter Rigby, Professor Doreen Anne Cantrell, Mr Geoffrey Ernest Braham
Income: £40,901,000 [2017]; £38,001,000 [2016]; £44,213,000 [2015]; £44,450,000 [2014]; £40,290,000 [2013]

The Bacit Foundation
Registered: 3 Oct 2012 *Volunteers:* 1
Tel: 020 7968 6460 *Website:* synconaltd.com
Activities: General charitable purposes; advancement of health or saving of lives
Address: 91 Gower Street, London, WC1E 6AB
Trustees: Mr Martin Nicholas Caleb Thomas, Mr Thomas Alexander Gavin Henderson, Mrs Catherine Scivier, Mr Rupert Christian Rigbye Adams
Income: £3,533,765 [2017]; £2,646,975 [2016]; £2,509,638 [2015]; £1,593,867 [2014]; £492,829 [2013]

The Back-Up Trust
Registered: 30 Oct 1998 *Employees:* 34 *Volunteers:* 400
Tel: 020 8875 1805 *Website:* backuptrust.org.uk
Activities: Education, training; disability; amateur sport
Address: 4 Knightley Walk, London, SW18 1GZ
Trustees: Ms Anne Luttman-Johnson, Richard Paul Westlake Smith, Mr David Fraser, Ms Claire Pimm, Martine Petetin, Ms Helen Cooke, Ms Becky Hill, Clair Turnbull, Mrs Jo Wright, Mr Crispin Longden, Mr Ben Sneesby
Income: £1,603,708 [2017]; £1,622,511 [2016]; £1,358,786 [2015]; £1,328,587 [2014]; £1,165,580 [2013]

Backstage Trust
Registered: 14 Feb 2012
Tel: 020 7072 4498
Activities: General charitable purposes
Address: North House, 27 Great Peter Street, London, SW1P 3LN
Trustees: Lady Susie Sainsbury, Mr David Wood, Mr Dominic Flynn
Income: £3,497,561 [2017]; £1,697,169 [2016]; £4,456,161 [2015]; £4,180,764 [2014]; £4,544,126 [2013]

The Douglas Bader Foundation
Registered: 16 Nov 1988 *Employees:* 3 *Volunteers:* 8
Tel: 020 8748 8884 *Website:* douglasbaderfoundation.com
Activities: Disability
Address: 14 Raynham Road, London, W6 0HY
Trustees: Mr Justin Cadbury, Mr Jackson, Mr Stewart Riddick, Mr Robert Clive Pascall
Income: £1,058,116 [2016]; £346,877 [2015]; £274,434 [2014]; £317,216 [2013]; £327,267 [2012]

Bader International Study Centre
Registered: 24 Aug 1993 *Employees:* 90
Tel: 01323 834444 *Website:* queensu.ca
Activities: Education, training; arts, culture, heritage, science; environment, conservation, heritage; economic, community development, employment; human rights, religious or racial harmony, equality or diversity
Address: International Study Centre, Herstmonceux Castle, Herstmonceux, Hailsham, E Sussex, BN27 1RN
Trustees: Mr Joshua Purvis, Mr Andrew Michael Boggs, Mr Benoit-Antoine Bacon, Ms Karen Iona Fountain, Mr James Knowles
Income: £4,958,773 [2017]; £4,471,036 [2016]; £4,909,932 [2015]; £4,965,857 [2014]; £5,469,865 [2013]

Badminton School Limited
Registered: 11 Jul 1966 *Employees:* 215 *Volunteers:* 13
Tel: 0117 905 5200 *Website:* badmintonschool.co.uk
Activities: Education, training
Address: Badminton School, Westbury Road, Westbury on Trym, Bristol, BS9 3BA
Trustees: Alison Allden, Mrs Sibella Laing, Mrs Amanda Claire Webb, Mr Justin Chippendale, Mrs Sheila Bailey, Mr Justin Lewis, Mrs Sarah Mumford, Ms Heather Wheelhouse, Bill Ray, Dr Joyshri Sarangi, Mrs Victoria Stace, Mr Andrew Couper, Mrs Lynda Thomas
Income: £9,287,909 [2016]; £9,089,463 [2015]; £8,814,927 [2014]; £8,586,989 [2013]; £8,587,234 [2012]

The Badur Foundation
Registered: 15 Jun 2011 *Employees:* 3
Tel: 020 7317 5385 *Website:* badurfoundation.org
Activities: General charitable purposes; education, training; prevention or relief of poverty; arts, culture, heritage, science; environment, conservation, heritage; human rights, religious or racial harmony, equality or diversity
Address: 4th Floor, Marble Arch House, 66 Seymour Street, London, W1H 5BT
Trustees: Mr Daniel Hallgarten, Ms Judit Durst, Csaba Barta, Mr Zsombor Barta
Income: £1,031,490 [2017]; £35,701 [2016]; £1,025,427 [2015]; £1,714,279 [2014]; £617,828 [2013]

Leo Baeck College
Registered: 22 Sep 1962 *Employees:* 12 *Volunteers:* 2
Tel: 020 8349 5723 *Website:* lbc.ac.uk
Activities: Education, training; religious activities
Address: The Manor House, 80 East End Road, London, N3 2SY
Trustees: Rabbi Michael Hilton, Mr Simon Benscher, Rabbi Danny Rich, Rabbi Aaron Goldstein, Mr Geoffrey James Marx, Mr David Hockman, Mrs Hannah Jacobs, Mr Michael Anthony Frankl, Rabbi Thomas Salamon
Income: £1,034,968 [2016]; £901,113 [2015]; £1,029,712 [2014]; £1,096,382 [2013]; £1,139,707 [2012]

The Baily Thomas Charitable Fund
Registered: 7 May 1971
Tel: 01582 439205 *Website:* bailythomas.org.uk
Activities: General charitable purposes; disability
Address: TMF Global Services (UK) Ltd, 400 Capability Green, Luton, Beds, LU1 3AE
Trustees: Mr Kenneth Robert Young, Professor Anne Farmer, Mr Jonathan Snow, Mrs Suzanne Jane Marriott, Professor Sally-Ann Cooper
Income: £1,833,528 [2016]; £1,805,064 [2015]; £1,968,766 [2014]; £1,788,504 [2013]; £1,770,848 [2012]

The Bais Rochel Dsatmar Charitable Trust
Registered: 8 Jan 1981 *Employees:* 177 *Volunteers:* 12
Tel: 020 8800 9060
Activities: Education, training; religious activities
Address: 51-57 Amhurst Park, London, N16 5DL
Trustees: Mr Jacob Frankel, Mr Jacob Ostreicher, Mr J I Low, Mr Victor Langberg
Income: £2,172,379 [2016]; £2,112,158 [2015]; £2,170,771 [2014]; £1,620,245 [2013]; £1,242,273 [2012]

Baker Dearing Educational Trust
Registered: 9 Nov 2010 *Employees:* 6
Tel: 020 7960 1555 *Website:* utcolleges.org
Activities: Education, training; economic, community development, employment
Address: 4 Millbank, London, SW1P 3JA
Trustees: Sir Kevin Satchwell, Lord Baker, Dr Theresa Simpkin, Sir Michael Tomlinson, Lord Andrew Adonis, Professor The Lord Sushantha Kumar Bhattacharyya
Income: £1,672,202 [2016]; £1,323,474 [2015]; £1,260,997 [2014]; £1,362,044 [2013]; £950,259 [2012]

The C Alma Baker Trust
Registered: 24 Apr 2006 *Employees:* 11
Tel: 01480 411331 *Website:* calmabakertrust.co.uk
Activities: General charitable purposes; education, training; arts, culture, heritage, science; animals; environment, conservation, heritage; economic, community development, employment; other charitable purposes
Address: 20 Hartford Road, Huntingdon, Cambs, PE29 3QH
Trustees: Mr Charles Robin Boyes, Edward Valletta, Mr Simon Fred Boyton Taylor, Mr David Heneage Wynne-Finch
Income: £2,223,766 [2017]; £1,384,222 [2016]; £1,246,236 [2015]; £1,346,376 [2014]; £703,334 [2013]

Bakewell and Eyam Community Transport
Registered: 23 Sep 1995 *Employees:* 68 *Volunteers:* 100
Tel: 01629 641920 *Website:* bect.org.uk
Activities: Education, training; disability
Address: Unit 4 Longstone Business Park, Great Longstone, Bakewell, Derbys, DE45 1TD
Trustees: Mrs Judith Anne Twigg, Mr David William Monks, Mrs Ann Pamela Kenworthy, Mrs Barbara Elizabeth Ely, Mr Bill Kirkland, Mr Christopher John Webster, Mr Christopher John Plant
Income: £1,038,930 [2017]; £1,122,666 [2016]; £724,138 [2015]; £586,641 [2014]; £560,758 [2013]

Teresa Ball International Solidarity Fund
Registered: 2 May 2000
Tel: 00-353-1-424 0426
Activities: General charitable purposes; education, training; prevention or relief of poverty; overseas aid, famine relief; religious activities
Address: Loreto International House, 25 Rathfarnham Wood, Rathfarnham, Dublin 14
Trustees: Noelle Corscadden, Judith Nekesa, Brenda Eagan, Patricia Grant, Bernadette Boland, Igora Pinto, Macarena F De Bodadilla, Ita Moynihan, Anita Braganza, Geraldine McAleer
Income: £2,994,481 [2017]; £85,068 [2016]; £61,877 [2015]; £510,387 [2014]; £456,483 [2013]

Ballard School Limited
Registered: 13 Dec 1962 *Employees:* 98 *Volunteers:* 44
Tel: 01425 626900 *Website:* ballardschool.co.uk
Activities: Education, training
Address: Ballard School, Fernhill Lane, New Milton, Hants, BH25 5SU
Trustees: Mr Christopher Kean FCA, Mr Peter Robert Goodfellow, Rev Martin Poole, Mrs Anne Patricia Watson-Lee, Mrs Jane Mary Tudor, Mrs Susan Rogers, Mrs Wendy Margaret Roberts, Mrs Merrielle Billington, Mrs Fiona Elizabeth Morgan, Dr Emma Louise Halliwell, Mr Andrew William Stembridge
Income: £5,077,192 [2017]; £5,054,088 [2016]; £5,010,917 [2015]; £4,799,133 [2014]; £4,607,900 [2013]

Ballet Rambert Limited
Registered: 3 Sep 1985 *Employees:* 49 *Volunteers:* 29
Website: rambert.org.uk
Activities: Education, training; arts, culture, heritage, science; other charitable purposes
Address: Rambert, 99 Upper Ground, London, SE1 9PP
Trustees: Mr William Arthur McKee CBE, Dr Ali Joy, Ms Anu Giri, Mr Andrew Hill, Mr Graham Sheffield CBE, Mr Ray Oudkerk, Mr Jeremy Alun-Jones, Mr Howard Panter, Ms Jill Kowal MSc, Ms Chiara Chabanne, Dr Eleanor O'Keefe, Emma Lancaster
Income: £3,939,257 [2017]; £3,361,812 [2016]; £3,630,468 [2015]; £3,384,550 [2014]; £3,192,480 [2013]

BalletBoyz Ltd
Registered: 5 Sep 2001 *Employees:* 7 *Volunteers:* 6
Tel: 020 8549 8814 *Website:* balletboyz.com
Activities: Arts, culture, heritage, science
Address: BalletBoyz Ltd, 52a Canbury Park Road, Kingston upon Thames, Surrey, KT2 6JX
Trustees: Dame Vivien Duffield, Lady Kate Gavron, Mr Thomas William Hope, Anne Heal, Ms Mary Anne Cordeiro, Mr Michael Timothy Waldman, Miss Phoebe Elizabeth Reith, Adrianus Hendrikus Maria Van Schie
Income: £1,733,827 [2017]; £1,161,566 [2016]; £1,198,787 [2015]; £799,511 [2014]; £1,159,428 [2013]

The Ballinger Charitable Trust
Registered: 29 Nov 2007 *Employees:* 1
Tel: 0191 488 0520 *Website:* ballingercharitabletrust.org.uk
Activities: General charitable purposes
Address: P O Box 166, Ponteland, Newcastle upon Tyne, NE20 2BL
Trustees: Mrs Diana Susan Ballinger, Mr Andrew John Ballinger, Mr John Flynn, Ms Nicola Jane Crowther
Income: £3,218,774 [2016]; £3,108,915 [2015]; £3,119,226 [2014]; £2,815,003 [2013]; £2,796,609 [2012]

Baltic Flour Mills Visual Arts Trust
Registered: 24 Jun 1999 *Employees:* 82 *Volunteers:* 17
Tel: 0191 490 4970 *Website:* balticmill.com
Activities: Education, training; arts, culture, heritage, science
Address: Baltic Centre for Contemporary Art, South Shore Road, Gateshead, Tyne & Wear, NE8 3BA
Trustees: Mick Henry, Mrs Michaela Dawn Martin, Councillor Catherine Donovan, Darren Richardson, Manohari Saravanamuttu, Graham Thrower, Sara Bryson, Tina Gharavi, Mr Peter Buchan, Louise Hunter, Charlotte Sexton, Joanna Feeley, Louise Wilson, Ms Kirsty Lang
Income: £4,786,024 [2017]; £4,846,243 [2016]; £4,785,749 [2015]; £4,598,110 [2014]; £4,622,781 [2013]

Helen Bamber Foundation
Registered: 7 Nov 2012 *Employees:* 20 *Volunteers:* 80
Website: helenbamber.org
Activities: General charitable purposes; advancement of health or saving of lives; prevention or relief of poverty; human rights, religious or racial harmony, equality or diversity
Address: 60 Effingham Road, London, N8 0AB
Trustees: Ms Caroline Moorehead, Mrs Patricia Ann Pank, Mr Tom McLaughlan, Sir Nicolas Bratza, Mr Hugh Richardson, Ms Charlotte Seymour-Smith, Ms Rebecca Hirst, Dr Ian Watt
Income: £1,068,816 [2016]; £1,041,682 [2015]; £647,229 [2014]; £1,679,452 [2013]

Bancroft's School

Registered: 10 Mar 1998 *Employees:* 223 *Volunteers:* 15
Tel: 020 8505 4826 *Website:* bancrofts.org
Activities: Education, training
Address: Bancrofts School, 611-627 High Road, Woodford Green, Essex, IG8 0RF
Trustees: Professor Peter Kopelman Professor, Dr Peter Campbell David Southern MA PhD, Mrs Saheeda Siddiqui, Professor Philip Ogden, Ms Bernadette Sarah Conroy, Mr Ed Sautter, Mr Michael John Stark, Dr Anne Veronica Philp, Mr Raymond Gooding IEng ACIBSE, Mr James Michael Rose, Mr Rej Bhumbra, Mr Richard Williamson
Income: £15,777,778 [2016]; £15,006,257 [2015]; £13,952,500 [2014]; £14,018,310 [2013]; £17,717,646 [2012]

The Band Trust

Registered: 30 May 1980 *Employees:* 1
Tel: 020 7702 4243 *Website:* bandtrust.co.uk
Activities: General charitable purposes; education, training; advancement of health or saving of lives; disability; accommodation, housing; arts, culture, heritage, science; environment, conservation, heritage; armed forces, emergency service efficiency
Address: The Band Trust, BM Box 2144, London, WC1N 3XX
Trustees: Mr Richard John Spencer Mason, The Hon Mrs Nicholas Wallop MBE, Ms Victoria Urania Sophia Wallop, Mr Bartholomew Guy Peerless, The Hon Nicholas Valoynes Bermingham Wallop
Income: £1,041,996 [2017]; £956,174 [2016]; £823,849 [2015]; £1,024,886 [2014]; £822,563 [2013]

Bangor Diocesan Board of Finance Bwrdd Cyllid Esgobaeth Bangor

Registered: 10 Jun 1999 *Employees:* 10
Tel: 01248 354999 *Website:* bangor.churchinwales.org.uk
Activities: Religious activities
Address: Diocesan Centre, Cathedral Close, Bangor, Gwynedd, LL57 1RL
Trustees: The Rev'd Andrew Jones, The Rt Revd Andrew John, Mrs Jennifer Mary Evans, Mrs Eleanor Wenda Owen, Mrs Pamela Jean Odam, Ven Michael Frederick West, Rev Richard Stanton Wood, Rev Tracy Jane Jones, Mrs Sandra Dreen Ward, The Very Revd Kathy Louise Jones
Income: £3,179,188 [2016]; £2,952,829 [2015]; £3,194,416 [2014]; £3,016,233 [2013]; £2,955,551 [2012]

Bangor Students' Union

Registered: 10 Sep 2012 *Employees:* 25 *Volunteers:* 850
Website: undebbangor.com
Activities: Education, training
Address: 9 Glantraeth, Bangor, Gwynedd, LL57 1HQ
Trustees: Miss Joanna Candlish, Ms Helen Marchant, Mr Thomas Daniel Jones, Miss Ruth Ellen Plant, Mr Tatenda Shonhiwa, Mr Paul Ashley, Mr Dominic Passfield, Mr Paul John Sturges, Mr James Francis Williams
Income: £1,297,876 [2017]; £1,204,753 [2016]; £1,097,786 [2015]; £1,070,995 [2014]; £1,070,371 [2013]

Bangor University

Registered: 21 Apr 2011 *Employees:* 1,812 *Volunteers:* 114
Tel: 01248 382776 *Website:* bangor.ac.uk
Activities: Education, training
Address: Bangor University, College Road, Bangor, Gwynedd, LL57 2DG
Trustees: Professor Huw Gareth Ffowc Roberts, Professor Thomas Gerald Hunter, Professor John Hughes PhD FBCS, Mr David Williams, Dr Karen Jones, Ms Ellen Parry Williams, Dr Gillian Davies, Dr Griffith Wynn Jones, Mrs Alison Lea-Wilson, Professor Jo Rycroft-Malone, Sir Paul Lambert, Miss Ruth Ellen Plant, Mrs Marian Wyn Jones, Professor Oliver Turnbull, Professor Paul Spencer, Dr Peter John Priddle Higson, Professor Carol Tully, Mrs Stephanie Barbaresi, Professor Graham Upton, Dr Olwen Elizabeth Williams, Professor Andrew Edwards, Dr Loretta Murphy, Mr Marc Proudlove Jones, Miss Mirain Llwyd Roberts
Income: £143,380,000 [2017]; £143,442,000 [2016]; £142,671,000 [2015]; £138,930,000 [2014]; £135,361,000 [2013]

The Banner of Truth Trust

Registered: 25 Feb 1965 *Employees:* 12
Tel: 0131 337 7310 *Website:* banneroftruth.co.uk
Activities: Religious activities
Address: The Grey House, 3 Murrayfield Road, Edinburgh, EH12 6EL
Trustees: Reverend Iain Hamish Murray, Rev Mark Gardiner Johnston, Dr Sinclair B Ferguson, Rev Edward Donnelly, Rev Jeffrey Kingswood, Rev Ian Hamilton, Mr Thomas Earl Richwine, Mr Robert Strivens, Dr Donald John MacLean
Income: £1,808,901 [2017]; £1,431,512 [2016]; £1,275,783 [2015]; £867,559 [2014]; £1,008,667 [2013]

The Baptist Missionary Society

Registered: 3 May 1966 *Employees:* 171 *Volunteers:* 1,003
Tel: 01235 517604 *Website:* bmsworldmission.org
Activities: The prevention or relief of poverty; overseas aid, famine relief; religious activities
Address: B M S World Mission, P O Box 49, Didcot, Oxon, OX11 8XA
Trustees: Rev David Emanuel Ellis, Rev John Robert Western, Mrs Maureen Russell, Mr Robert Gerald Ashurst, Mr Peter James Maycock, Dr Kang-San Tan, Rev Simeon Thomas Baker, Rev Maureen Catherine Hider, Rev Lindsay Caplen, John Slater, Dr Marion Carson, Ms Lynn Cadman
Income: £7,598,552 [2016]; £8,606,824 [2015]; £7,237,603 [2014]; £6,737,503 [2013]; £6,767,141 [2012]

The Baptist Union of Great Britain

Registered: 16 Sep 2008 *Employees:* 39
Tel: 01235 517743 *Website:* baptist.org.uk
Activities: Religious activities
Address: The Baptist Union of Great Britain, P O Box 44, Didcot, Oxon, OX11 8RT
Trustees: Phil Jump, Rev Barbara Carpenter, Rev Joe Kapolyo, Rich Webb, Mrs Christina Jane Carter, Mr John Levick, Mrs Marion Fiddes, Rev Lynn Margaret Green BA MSt, Mrs Linda Hopkins, Andrew D Cowley
Income: £9,120,000 [2017]; £9,528,599 [2016]; £8,626,943 [2015]; £9,223,000 [2014]; £8,255,474 [2013]

The Henry Barber Trust
Registered: 2 Jun 1987 *Employees:* 1
Tel: 0121 471 1016
Activities: Education, training; arts, culture, heritage, science
Address: Barber Institute of Fine Arts, University of Birmingham, Edgbaston, Birmingham, B15 2TS
Trustees: Mr Joseph Bates FCA DChA, Major M C Burman TD, Mr Stephen Maddock OBE MA, Professor Sir David Eastwood, Mr Hugh Carslake, Canon Professor Michael Clarke, Professor Christopher Brown CBE, Ms Charlotte Higgins
Income: £2,147,511 [2017]; £1,957,199 [2016]; £2,754,317 [2015]; £2,093,668 [2014]; £4,687,433 [2013]

The Barbican Centre Trust Limited
Registered: 7 May 1986
Tel: 020 7382 6018 *Website:* barbican.org.uk
Activities: Education, training; arts, culture, heritage, science
Address: Barbican Centre, Silk Street, London, EC2Y 8DS
Trustees: Mr Richard Bernstein, Mr Alasdair Nisbet, Mr John Porter, Professor Henrietta Moore, Sir Michael Roger Gifford, Mr Steven Tredget, Dr Geraldine Susan Brodie, Sir Nicholas Kenyon CBE, Mrs Emma Victoria Kane, Dr Giles Shilson, Mr Torsten Thiele, Mr John Christopher Murray, Ms Kendall Langford
Income: £1,135,950 [2017]; £1,328,092 [2016]; £1,131,591 [2015]; £1,068,428 [2014]; £1,142,140 [2013]

Barca - Leeds
Registered: 4 Sep 1995 *Employees:* 138 *Volunteers:* 36
Tel: 0113 255 9582 *Website:* barca-leeds.org
Activities: General charitable purposes; education, training; advancement of health or saving of lives; prevention or relief of poverty; amateur sport; economic, community development, employment
Address: Manor House, 259 Upper Town Street, Bramley, Leeds, LS13 3JT
Trustees: Mr John Battle, Mrs Caroline Ann Johnstone, Mr Darren Hill, Miss Sophie Michelena, Dr Douglas Martin, Mr Robert Stubbs, Mr Stewart Paul Firth, Mrs Anna Middlemiss, Mr David Foxton
Income: £3,259,315 [2017]; £2,860,023 [2016]; £2,836,126 [2015]; £2,177,958 [2014]; £1,786,679 [2013]

The Baring Foundation
Registered: 31 Jul 1969 *Employees:* 5
Tel: 020 7767 1348 *Website:* baringfoundation.org.uk
Activities: General charitable purposes
Address: 8-10 Moorgate, London, EC2R 6DA
Trustees: David Elliott, Ms Lucy Manuela De Groot, Mrs Katherine Garrett-Cox, Ms Janet Morrison, Ms Alison Evans, Ms Poonam Joshi, Ms Victoria Amedume, Mr James Edward Thomas Moubray Jenkins, Dr Robert Dean Joseph Berkeley, Myles Wickstead, Ms Shauneen Lambe, Mr Andrew Hind, Ms Marie Rita Staunton, Mr Francois Louis Andre Matarasso, Mrs Emma Victoria Badman
Income: £1,636,185 [2016]; £869,786 [2015]; £1,592,970 [2014]; £2,165,831 [2013]; £2,165,832 [2012]

Lady Barn House School Limited
Registered: 6 Dec 1994 *Employees:* 77
Tel: 0161 428 2912 *Website:* ladybarnhouse.org
Activities: Education, training; amateur sport
Address: Lady Barn House School, Schools Hill, Cheadle, Cheshire, SK8 1JE
Trustees: Mr Ernest Barry Pollitt, Mr Peter John Ward, Mrs Joanna Berry, Mr Roger Hart, Mrs Julie Flynn, Gordon Falconer, Mr Fadi Kabbani, Mr Bruce Murray, Mrs Lisa Clift
Income: £3,976,958 [2017]; £3,739,933 [2016]; £3,387,280 [2015]; £3,249,140 [2014]; £3,166,945 [2013]

Barnabas Aid International
Registered: 27 Feb 2014 *Employees:* 30
Tel: 01672 564938
Activities: Education, training; advancement of health or saving of lives; prevention or relief of poverty; overseas aid, famine relief; accommodation, housing; religious activities; economic, community development; employment; human rights, religious or racial harmony, equality or diversity
Address: The Old Rectory, River Street, Pewsey, Wilts, SN9 5DB
Trustees: Mrs Rosemary Sookhdeo, Rev Ian McNaughton, Rt Rev Julian Dobbs, Mr Paul Mursalin, Rev Dr Vinay Samuel, Miss Caroline Julia Chenevix Kerslake, Rev Albrecht Bernhard Hauser, Mr Colin Johnston, Mr Ernest Pak Woh Poon, Rev Michael Hewat
Income: £15,923,340 [2017]; £17,598,403 [2016]; £23,286,748 [2015]

Barnabas Fund
Registered: 12 Jul 2002 *Employees:* 16 *Volunteers:* 353
Tel: 024 7623 1923 *Website:* barnabasfund.org
Activities: Education, training; advancement of health or saving of lives; prevention or relief of poverty; overseas aid, famine relief; accommodation, housing; religious activities; economic, community development, employment; human rights, religious or racial harmony, equality or diversity
Address: Barnabas Fund, 9-10 Priory Row, Coventry, Warwicks, CV1 5EX
Trustees: Lord Simon Reading, Rt Rev Julian Dobbs, Rev Dr Vinay Samuel, Mrs Rosemary Sookhdeo, Rev Albrecht Bernhard Hauser, Rev I McNaughton, Miss Caroline Kerslake
Income: £14,039,126 [2017]; £13,633,061 [2016]; £14,585,140 [2015]; £13,218,858 [2014]; £11,960,827 [2013]

Barnard Castle School
Registered: 6 Aug 2008 *Employees:* 198 *Volunteers:* 4
Tel: 01833 690222 *Website:* barnardcastleschool.org.uk
Activities: Education, training
Address: Barnard Castle School, Newgate, Barnard Castle, Co Durham, DL12 8UN
Trustees: Mr Don Starr, Dr Neil Thorpe, Mrs Ruth Dent JP, Mr Alan Fielder, Mr George M Richardson Councillor, Mr Peter Mothersill, Mrs Clare Newnam, Mr John Harvey Hunter, Mrs Donna Vinsome, Mr Clive Dennis, Mrs Catherine Sunley, Mr David Osborne, Mr Peter Hodges, Mrs Karen Pratt, Dr Jonathan Elphick, Mr Ian Martin Allison, Mr Robert Iain Moffat
Income: £9,165,946 [2016]; £8,822,469 [2015]; £8,843,312 [2014]; £8,436,187 [2013]; £8,615,012 [2012]

Barnardo's
Registered: 18 Jan 1963 *Employees:* 8,199 *Volunteers:* 20,000
Tel: 020 8498 7469 *Website:* barnardos.org.uk
Activities: Education, training; disability; prevention or relief of poverty
Address: Barnardos, Head Office, Tanners Lane, Barkingside, Ilford, Essex, IG6 1QG
Trustees: Lady Amanda Ellingworth, Mr John Bartlett, Ms Wendy Becker, Mr Neil Braithwaite, Ms Zoe Harris, Mr Dennis Hone, Mike Nicholson, Mr Darra Singh, Mr Stephen Michael Goldman, Mr Hugh Burkitt, Ms Alexis Jane Cleveland, Mr Colin James Walsh, Ms Jennifer Achiro, Mrs Sheikh Mansura Tal-At Mannings
Income: £312,847,000 [2017]; £298,660,000 [2016]; £295,052,000 [2015]; £285,774,000 [2014]; £258,112,000 [2013]

Barnet Carers Centre
Registered: 13 Aug 1996 *Employees:* 70 *Volunteers:* 55
Tel: 020 8343 9698 *Website:* barnetcarers.org
Activities: The advancement of health or saving of lives; disability; prevention or relief of poverty; other charitable purposes
Address: Barnet Carers Centre, Global House, 303 Ballards Lane, London, N12 8NP
Trustees: Ms Anne Hutton, Mrs Illa Pattni, Oliver Stanley, Mr Jonathan Supran, Mr Yusuf Gulamhusein, Mrs Jenny Rachel Manson, Mr Roger Bailey
Income: £1,215,932 [2017]; £1,339,753 [2016]; £1,142,861 [2015]; £1,171,765 [2014]; £1,128,628 [2013]

Barnet Education Arts Trust
Registered: 13 Dec 2012 *Employees:* 38 *Volunteers:* 35
Tel: 020 3209 7966 *Website:* beatrust.org.uk
Activities: Education, training; arts, culture, heritage, science
Address: Dollis Junior School, Pursley Road, London, NW7 2BU
Trustees: Mr Philip Charles Elgar, Mr Colin Brian Dowland, Mrs Florence Armstrong, Mr Tim Clark, Mr Peter Sydney White, Mrs Mary Musker, Mr Martin Joseph Baker, Mr Geoffrey A Thompson, Ms Jacqueline Boyle
Income: £2,023,891 [2017]; £1,938,862 [2016]; £1,853,448 [2015]; £1,986,865 [2014]

Barnet Mencap
Registered: 19 Nov 2001 *Employees:* 55 *Volunteers:* 17
Website: barnetmencap.org.uk
Activities: General charitable purposes; education, training; disability; prevention or relief of poverty; accommodation, housing; arts, culture, heritage, science; amateur sport
Address: 186 Sherrards Way, Barnet, Herts, EN5 2BS
Trustees: Mrs Sally Wickenden, Ms Sheila Oliver, Mr Michael Wiffen, Mr Andrew Waite, Mrs Meg Kirk, Miss Cristina Sarb
Income: £1,399,591 [2017]; £1,380,274 [2016]; £1,264,585 [2015]; £1,173,372 [2014]; £1,101,669 [2013]

Barnsley Community Build
Registered: 31 Jul 2001 *Employees:* 41 *Volunteers:* 30
Tel: 01226 786780 *Website:* barnsleycommunitybuild.com
Activities: Education, training; prevention or relief of poverty; economic, community development, employment
Address: 189 Sheffield Road, Barnsley, S Yorks, S70 4DE
Trustees: Mr Joseph William Hayward, John Clark, Mr Melvyn Lunn FCA MCMI AIBC CertCIH, Mrs Sylvia Ann Nixon, Mr John Bolan, Mrs Lorraine Heden
Income: £1,065,105 [2016]; £770,780 [2015]; £624,324 [2014]; £512,022 [2013]

Barnsley Hospice Appeal
Registered: 11 Oct 1988 *Employees:* 114 *Volunteers:* 380
Tel: 01226 244244 *Website:* barnsleyhospice.org.uk
Activities: General charitable purposes; education, training; advancement of health or saving of lives
Address: 104-106 Church Street, Gawber, Barnsley, S Yorks, S75 2RL
Trustees: Mr Frank Carter, Mr Raymond Knowles, Mr John David Pitt, Mr David White, Mrs Alison Salt, Mr David Hibbitt, Mrs Carole Ann Gibbard, Mr Simon James Eyre-Wood, Mr Alan Higgins
Income: £3,670,778 [2017]; £4,439,183 [2016]; £4,091,163 [2015]; £4,124,855 [2014]; £3,932,933 [2013]

Barnsley Premier Leisure
Registered: 22 Jul 1999 *Employees:* 253
Website: bpl.org.uk
Activities: Amateur sport; recreation
Address: Barnsley Premier Leisure, Metrodome Leisure Complex, Queens Road, Barnsley, S Yorks, S71 1AN
Trustees: Mr Alan Methley, Mr Ian Taylor, Miss Valerie Mills, Mr Andrew Skiffington, Mr Andrew Ainsworth, Mrs Janet Campbell-Smith, Mr Richard Owen Jones, Mr Barrie Betton, Mrs Denise Pozorski, Cllr Robert Frost, Mr Barry James Dolan, Mr Benjamin McFeely
Income: £14,856,060 [2017]; £15,653,435 [2016]; £12,060,969 [2015]; £11,295,340 [2014]; £10,750,226 [2013]

Barnwood Trust
Registered: 27 Jul 2015 *Employees:* 34 *Volunteers:* 70
Tel: 01452 614429 *Website:* barnwoodtrust.org
Activities: The advancement of health or saving of lives; disability
Address: Chief Executive, Barnwood House Trust, Ullenwood Manor Farm, Ullenwood, Cheltenham, Glos, GL53 9QT
Trustees: Mr James Davidson, Mrs Annabella Scott, Mr Michael North, Dr Jean Waters, Mr Shaun David Parson, Mr Edward Playne, Mrs Sally Pullen, Lucy Floyer-Aclan, Professor Ciair Chilvers, Ms Suzanne Beech, Ms Rachel Jane Robinson, Benjamin Preece-Smith
Income: £3,703,490 [2016]

Barod Project
Registered: 14 Dec 1972 *Employees:* 169 *Volunteers:* 30
Tel: 01792 472002 *Website:* barod.cymru
Activities: Education, training; advancement of health or saving of lives
Address: 73-74 Mansel Street, Swansea, SA1 5TR
Trustees: Miss Sylvia Scarf, Ms Joan Winifred Brown, Mr Steffan Reed, Mr Luke Clark, Mr William George David Smith, Mrs Linda Hodgson, Mrs Clare Strowbridge
Income: £6,234,959 [2017]; £6,200,222 [2016]; £2,698,651 [2015]; £2,727,668 [2014]; £2,680,295 [2013]

Bernhard Baron Cottage Homes
Registered: 6 Aug 1998 *Employees:* 62 *Volunteers:* 14
Tel: 01323 483613 *Website:* bbch.co.uk
Activities: Accommodation, housing; other charitable purposes
Address: Lewes Road, Polegate, E Sussex, BN26 5HB
Trustees: Peter Appleton, Jean Stock, Kim Ashcroft, John Thurley, David Hitchin, Trish Sear, Sue Hallett, Kathy Gibbs
Income: £1,700,000 [2017]; £1,723,499 [2016]; £1,576,107 [2015]; £1,502,995 [2014]; £1,581,419 [2013]

Baron Davenport's Charity
Registered: 18 Dec 1963 *Employees:* 3
Tel: 0121 236 8004 *Website:* barondavenportscharity.org
Activities: General charitable purposes
Address: Baron Davenports Charity, 5-7 Temple Row West, Birmingham, B2 5NY
Trustees: William Colacicchi, Mr Martin Easton, Peter Horton, Ashvin Pimpalnerkar, Sue Ayres, Lisa Bryan, Alec Jones, Victoria Milligan
Income: £1,054,878 [2017]; £1,387,455 [2016]; £1,213,162 [2015]; £1,315,657 [2014]; £1,246,009 [2013]

The Barrow Cadbury Trust
Registered: 20 Jul 2006 *Employees:* 11
Tel: 020 7632 9075 *Website:* barrowcadbury.org.uk
Activities: General charitable purposes; prevention or relief of poverty; economic, community development, employment; human rights, religious or racial harmony, equality or diversity; other charitable purposes
Address: Barrow Cadbury Trust, 6 Kean Street, London, WC2B 4AS
Trustees: Erica R Cadbury, Nicola J Cadbury, Tamsin Rupprecheter, Mr John Serle, Ms Binita Mehta, Anna C Southall, Ms Catherina Anna Pharoah, Harry Serle, Steven Skakel, Ms Esther Rose Mary McConnell
Income: £2,950,000 [2017]; £3,048,000 [2016]; £2,599,000 [2015]; £2,791,000 [2014]; £3,012,000 [2013]

Barrow and Districts Society for the Blind Limited
Registered: 28 Dec 1995 *Employees:* 58 *Volunteers:* 27
Tel: 01229 820698 *Website:* barrowblindsociety.org.uk
Activities: General charitable purposes; disability; accommodation, housing
Address: Barrow & Districts Society for The Blind, 67-69 Cavendish Street, Barrow in Furness, Cumbria, LA14 1QD
Trustees: Mr Alan Swinburne Todd FCIB, Mr Craig Michael Anderson, Mrs Wilhelmina Johanna Robinson, Mr Adrian Treharne, Mrs Norma Margaret Reynolds, Mr Graham Postlethwaite, Mr David John Cannell, Mrs Rachael Baxter, Mrs Anne Patricia Fleming, Mrs Tracy Culley-Brown
Income: £1,176,183 [2016]; £1,105,933 [2015]; £1,051,776 [2014]; £1,232,016 [2013]; £1,099,563 [2012]

Barrowmore Limited
Registered: 11 Jan 2007 *Employees:* 22 *Volunteers:* 246
Tel: 01829 740391 *Website:* barrowmore.co.uk
Activities: Education, training; disability; accommodation, housing
Address: Barnhouse Lane, Great Barrow, Chester, CH3 7JA
Trustees: Mr John Heber Donnison Heath, Dr Mr Neil Fergusson, Mr Nigel Andrew Eckersley FRICS, Mr Andrew Wright Morrison, Mr Richard Short, Mrs Anne Mary Davies
Income: £1,185,142 [2016]; £1,223,884 [2015]; £1,355,926 [2014]; £1,233,147 [2013]; £1,252,065 [2012]

Barts and The London Charity and Related Charities
Registered: 20 Feb 1997 *Employees:* 27 *Volunteers:* 3
Tel: 020 7618 1717 *Website:* bartscharity.org.uk
Activities: The advancement of health or saving of lives
Address: Barts Charity, Red Lion Buildings, 12 Cock Lane, London, EC1A 9BU
Trustees: Mr Nicholas John Anstee, Professor John Shepherd, Professor John Monson, Mr Paul Rawlinson, Mr Andrew Bruce, Mr Thomas Round, Mr Robert Stephen O'Brien, Mr William Jonathan Medlicott, Professor Ian Sanderson, Ms Sally Flanagan, Mr Ian Peters, Mr Vijay Bharadia
Income: £17,375,000 [2017]; £14,046,000 [2016]; £8,882,000 [2015]; £12,563,000 [2014]; £12,613,000 [2013]

BasicNeeds
Registered: 29 Feb 2000 *Employees:* 23 *Volunteers:* 2
Tel: 01926 330101 *Website:* basicneeds.org
Activities: Disability; prevention or relief of poverty
Address: Basic Needs, 158a Parade, Leamington Spa, Warwicks, CV32 4AE
Trustees: Basicneeds Trustee Limited
Income: £1,040,081 [2016]; £1,609,132 [2015]; £1,296,285 [2014]; £1,973,394 [2013]; £2,106,825 [2012]

Basildon Women's Aid
Registered: 16 Apr 1980 *Employees:* 26 *Volunteers:* 20
Tel: 01268 729707 *Website:* changingpathways.org
Activities: Education, training; accommodation, housing; other charitable purposes
Address: Basildon Womens Aid, P O Box 51, Basildon, Essex, SS14 0ND
Trustees: Mrs Ann Wiseall, Ms Suzanne Jane Tilling, Mrs S Davis, Mrs Janet Deeney
Income: £1,464,220 [2017]; £1,370,285 [2016]; £955,267 [2015]; £1,056,746 [2014]; £993,956 [2013]

Basingstoke Community Churches
Registered: 9 Jan 1998 *Employees:* 47 *Volunteers:* 50
Tel: 01256 316005 *Website:* bccnet.org.uk
Activities: Education, training; prevention or relief of poverty; overseas aid, famine relief; religious activities
Address: 22 Lymington Close, Basingstoke, Hants, RG22 4XL
Trustees: Mr Jonathan Smith, Mr Colin Grant, Mr Philip Wraight, Mr David Robotham, Mike Poulton, Andy Taylor, Mr Benjamin Stuart John Oliver
Income: £1,249,880 [2017]; £1,441,984 [2016]; £1,472,064 [2015]; £1,668,947 [2014]; £1,410,236 [2013]

Basingstoke Gymnastics Club
Registered: 17 Nov 1995 *Employees:* 58 *Volunteers:* 40
Tel: 01256 850170 *Website:* basingstokegym.co.uk
Activities: Amateur sport; economic, community development, employment
Address: 3 Bournefield, Sherborne St John, Basingstoke, Hants, RG24 9JB
Trustees: Mr Paul Temple, Mr Stephen Hough, Mr Gregg Dennis, Mrs Sara Preston, Mr Kevin White, Mr Vicent Bartlett, Mrs Rachel Kitson
Income: £1,047,058 [2017]; £960,487 [2016]; £821,151 [2015]; £890,661 [2014]; £794,314 [2013]

Basingstoke and Deane Community Leisure Trust
Registered: 29 Mar 2006 *Employees:* 179
Tel: 01256 472343 *Website:* basingstokeleisure.com
Activities: Amateur sport
Address: Basingstoke Aquadrome, Basingsoke Leisure Park, Worting Road, Basingstoke, Hants, RG22 6PG
Trustees: Mr Ian Walkom, Ms Toni Shaw, Mr Andrew Finn, Richard Eldridge, Ms Hazel Tilbury, Cllr Colin David Regan, Steven Swatton, Wendy Judge
Income: £3,819,827 [2017]; £3,742,748 [2016]; £3,562,600 [2015]; £3,535,100 [2014]; £3,550,508 [2013]

The Basingstoke and District Sports Trust Limited
Registered: 2 Jul 1965 *Employees:* 185
Tel: 01256 302212 *Website:* mybst.org
Activities: General charitable purposes; education, training; advancement of health or saving of lives; amateur sport; recreation
Address: Basingstoke Sports Centre, Porchester Square, Basingstoke, Hants, RG21 7LE
Trustees: Cllr Dan Putty, Mr Mark Austin Clancy, Mr Visko Matich, Mr Thomas Preston Millar, Miss Jackie Isgar, Dr Robert Walker, Mrs Elke Jackson, Mr Martyn William Richard Frost, Mrs Lynda Pickering, Mr Chris Welton, Mrs Viviene Whiteaker
Income: £3,604,977 [2017]; £3,327,155 [2016]; £2,513,386 [2015]; £2,448,596 [2014]; £2,587,607 [2013]

Basingview Trust Limited
Registered: 2 Aug 2011
Activities: Religious activities
Address: 17 Craven Walk, London, N16 6BS
Trustees: Mr Chaim Benedikt, Mr Simon Benedikt, Mrs Reitzy Reichman
Income: £1,324,343 [2017]; £2,373,415 [2016]; £701 [2015]; £1,133,975 [2014]; £399,831 [2013]

The Bat Conservation Trust
Registered: 29 Jun 1992 *Employees:* 35 *Volunteers:* 3,000
Tel: 020 7820 7171 *Website:* bats.org.uk
Activities: Education, training; animals; environment, conservation, heritage
Address: 5th Floor, The Bat Conservation Trust, Quadrant House, 250 Kennington Lane, London, SW11 5RD
Trustees: Mr Rupert Lancaster, Steve Parker, Sarah Escott, Mr Steve Markham, Professor Robert Vaughan Upex, Mr Roger Mortlock, David Gibbons, Mr Thomas James Andrews, Dr Kirsty Park, Mr Robert Geoffrey Cornes, Dr Abigail Entwistle
Income: £1,584,049 [2017]; £1,312,436 [2016]; £2,873,958 [2015]; £1,249,160 [2014]; £1,252,808 [2013]

Bath Festivals
Registered: 6 Jun 1989 *Employees:* 23 *Volunteers:* 2,000
Website: bathfestivals.org.uk
Activities: Education, training; arts, culture, heritage, science
Address: Bath Festivals, 9-10 The Colonnades, Bath, BA1 1SN
Trustees: Mr John David Cullum, Mr Richard Turner, Lady Evelyn Strasburger, Mr Stephen Taylor, Mr James Drummond, Mr Will Gregory, Mr Kevin Brown, Ms Celia Mead, Mr David Bates, Councillor Christopher Ormsby Pearce, Mr Peter Medlock
Income: £1,062,082 [2017]; £1,203,723 [2016]; £1,031,017 [2015]; £1,281,114 [2014]; £1,309,052 [2013]

The Bath Preservation Trust Ltd
Registered: 7 May 1962 *Employees:* 42 *Volunteers:* 175
Tel: 01225 338727 *Website:* bath-preservation-trust.org.uk
Activities: Education, training; arts, culture, heritage, science; environment, conservation, heritage
Address: 1 Royal Crescent, Bath, BA1 2LR
Trustees: Ms Diane Aderyn, Mr Robert Hellard, Mr Mark Wilson Jones, Ms Kristin Doern, Ms Sally Price, Peta Hall, Mr Thomas Sheppard, Ms Celia Mead, Ms Alison Streatfeild-James, Mr Thomas Warwick Marshall, Mr Colin Johnston, Bruce Haines
Income: £1,006,154 [2017]; £1,064,883 [2016]; £1,090,214 [2015]; £1,635,380 [2014]; £1,211,473 [2013]

Bath Spa University Students' Union
Registered: 16 Nov 2010 *Employees:* 49 *Volunteers:* 611
Tel: 01225 876264 *Website:* bathspasu.co.uk
Activities: Education, training; arts, culture, heritage, science; amateur sport; recreation
Address: Bath Spa University College, Newton Park, Newton St Loe, Bath, BA2 9BN
Trustees: Mr Graham Briscoe, Mr Michael Roy, Miss Rebecca Bishop, Miss Hannah Megan Evans, Mr Liam MacAuley, Mr Ryan Michael Lucas, Meghann McKeague, Mr Edward Stevens, Mrs Margaret Anne Thomas, Miss Alisha Burrell, Miss Louise Maria Thacker, Mr Joe David Simmonds, Mr Danny Jake Whitebread, Ms Ekta Mahajan
Income: £1,031,834 [2017]; £1,840,546 [2016]; £1,626,023 [2015]; £1,133,965 [2014]; £1,188,407 [2013]

The Bath and Wells Diocesan Board of Finance
Registered: 5 Oct 1966 *Employees:* 55 *Volunteers:* 175
Tel: 01749 670777 *Website:* bathandwells.org.uk
Activities: Education, training; accommodation, housing; religious activities
Address: The Old Deanery, Wells, Somerset, BA5 2UG
Trustees: The Revd Canon Roger Driver, The Ven Dr Adrian Youings, Mr Michael Tedstone, Mr Harry Musselwhite, Rev Diana Greenfield, The Right Revd Ruth Worsley, The Rt Rev Peter Hancock, Mr Stephen Grimshaw, Mrs Katherine Cannell, Mr Timothy Hind, Rev Jane Haslam, The Ven Simon Hill, The Very Revd Dr John Harverd Davies, Mrs Mary Masters, Ms Christina Baron, Rev Caroline Ralph, Rev Bruce Faulkner, Rev Simon Robinson, Mr Christopher Jenkins, Mrs Sally Bult, Mr Robert Norman, Rev Sally Buddle, The Ven Anne Gell
Income: £13,774,000 [2016]; £13,714,000 [2015]; £12,951,000 [2014]; £12,978,000 [2013]; £12,101,000 [2012]

The Batsford Foundation
Registered: 26 Feb 2002 *Employees:* 18 *Volunteers:* 1
Tel: 01452 831815 *Website:* batsarb.co.uk
Activities: Education, training; environment, conservation, heritage
Address: Harts Barn Farm, Monmouth Road, Longhope, Glos, GL17 0QD
Trustees: Mr Christopher Fleming, Hon Ian Wills, Mr Nicholas Dunn, Sir James Chichester Bt, Mr Tony David Russell, Mr Nicholas Williams-Ellis
Income: £1,378,705 [2017]; £1,238,400 [2016]; £1,079,275 [2015]; £913,386 [2014]; £833,799 [2013]

Michael Batt Charitable Trust
Registered: 19 Sep 1994 *Employees:* 47
Tel: 01752 206666 *Website:* rushymead.co.uk
Activities: The advancement of health or saving of lives; accommodation, housing
Address: 8 Philip Close, Plymouth, PL9 8QZ
Trustees: Mr Donald George Sainsbury, Mr Michael John Leslie Batt, Mr Alan David Forrester, Mr Alistair Bruce Mackie
Income: £1,089,798 [2017]; £1,054,447 [2016]; £1,221,140 [2015]; £790,148 [2013]; £796,660 [2012]

Battersea Arts Centre
Registered: 31 Jul 1981 *Employees:* 79 *Volunteers:* 174
Website: bac.org.uk
Activities: General charitable purposes; education, training; arts, culture, heritage, science
Address: Battersea Arts Centre, Lavender Hill, London, SW11 5TN
Trustees: Councillor Paul Ellis, Sheila Allen, Mr Bruce Thompson, Ms Sarah Elizabeth Hall, Sunita Pandya, Mr Patrick Harrison, Ms Fiona MacTaggart, Mr Jonathan Linton Callaway, Elizabeth Griffith, Michael Day, Finbarr Whooley
Income: £6,448,916 [2017]; £10,060,997 [2016]; £5,811,356 [2015]; £4,638,845 [2014]; £4,921,583 [2013]

Battersea Dogs' and Cats' Home
Registered: 22 Sep 1962 *Employees:* 420 *Volunteers:* 1,399
Tel: 020 7627 9000 *Website:* battersea.org.uk
Activities: Animals
Address: Battersea Dogs & Cats Home, 4 Battersea Park Road, London, SW8 4AA
Trustees: Mr Bradley Viner, Dr Matthew Pead, Miss Anne Montgomery, Mr David Turner, Ms Kari Daniels, Mr Alan Martin, Mr Brian Dunk, Ms Amanda Burton, Mr Patrick Aylmer, Ms Lydia Lee-Crossett, Ms Sophie Andrews, Ms Cassie Newman
Income: £41,323,547 [2016]; £36,716,707 [2015]; £33,566,315 [2014]; £22,749,852 [2013]; £19,231,134 [2012]

Battersea Methodist Mission
Registered: 4 Jun 2009 *Employees:* 2
Tel: 020 7207 6663 *Website:* batterseamission.info
Activities: Religious activities; other charitable purposes
Address: 20-22 York Road, London, SW11 3QA
Trustees: Mrs Doreen Ann Wright, Mrs Dora Bannerman, Mr George Atease, Annick Gneba, Mrs Buaku, Mrs Gertrude Boakye, Rev Grocott, Doris Blavo
Income: £1,700,456 [2016]; £327,714 [2015]; £414,314 [2014]; £148,918 [2013]; £238,653 [2012]

The Battersea Power Station Foundation
Registered: 10 Apr 2015 *Employees:* 2
Website: bpsfoundation.org.uk
Activities: General charitable purposes
Address: The Battersea Power Station Foundat, 7 Circus Road West, Battersea Power Station, London, SW11 8EZ
Trustees: Marquess of Salisbury Robert Michael James Gascoyne Cecil, Dato'Sri Amrin Bin Awaluddin, Right Honourable Lord Strathclyde
Income: £1,514,500 [2016]; £224,500 [2015]

The Battle of Britain Memorial Trust
Registered: 19 Jun 1990 *Employees:* 7 *Volunteers:* 37
Tel: 01732 870809 *Website:* battleofbritainmemorial.org
Activities: Education, training; environment, conservation, heritage
Address: P O Box 337, 5 Evergreen Close, West Malling, Kent, ME6 9AA
Trustees: Mr Richard Hugh Hunting BEng MBA, Mr Bernard Hyde, Mr Roland George Parry, Mrs Geraldine Allinson, Mr Robin Green, Al Pinner, Andy Simpson, Mr Nicholas Lawn, Mrs Deborah Burns, Air Chief Marshal Sir Michael James Graydon GCB CBE FRAeS, Patrick Tootal, Lady Violet Aitken, The Hon Rory Aitken, Air Cdre Jerry Witts DSO, David Rosier, Wing Commander Sophy Gardner MBE, Ven Ray Pentland
Income: £1,210,392 [2016]; £1,511,622 [2015]; £1,075,269 [2014]; £2,384,350 [2013]; £1,036,999 [2012]

Batus General Fund
Registered: 3 Jun 2010
Activities: Armed forces, emergency service efficiency
Address: HQ Batus, BFPO 14
Trustees: Col J Landon MBE
Income: £1,132,568 [2017]; £966,207 [2016]; £1,240,005 [2015]; £925,130 [2014]; £353,974 [2013]

Bauer Radio's Cash for Kids Charities
Registered: 19 Dec 2007 *Employees:* 31 *Volunteers:* 100
Tel: 01642 675788 *Website:* cashforkids.uk.com
Activities: General charitable purposes; disability; prevention or relief of poverty
Address: Hampdon House, Unit 3 Falcon Court, Preston Farm, Stockton on Tees, Cleveland, TS18 3TS
Trustees: Mrs Sally Fiona Aitchison MBE, Mr Mark James Mahaffy, Owen Ryan, Mr Martin Ball, Mr Sean Patrick Marley, Danny Simpson
Income: £15,699,876 [2016]; £13,636,627 [2015]; £12,009,362 [2014]; £9,769,920 [2013]; £7,663,135 [2012]

Bawso Ltd
Registered: 1 Feb 2001 *Employees:* 90 *Volunteers:* 60
Tel: 029 2064 4633 *Website:* bawso.org.uk
Activities: Education, training; accommodation, housing; human rights, religious or racial harmony, equality or diversity
Address: Clarence House, Clarence Road, Cardiff Bay, CF10 5FB
Trustees: Mrs Chetna Sinha, Ms Sujatha Thaladi, Mrs Jennifer Fletcher, Ms Rachel McDonald, Ms Barbara Street, Mrs Sheila Hendrickson Brown, Mrs Tahmina Khan, Mrs Selina Moyo, Miss Raidah Alam, Ms Anne Phillimore, Dr Mohammed Hassan, Mrs Sonia Khoury
Income: £2,993,080 [2017]; £2,942,418 [2016]; £3,211,182 [2015]; £2,940,353 [2014]; £2,549,883 [2013]

Baxendale
Registered: 16 Jan 1963 *Employees:* 51 *Volunteers:* 15
Tel: 020 8882 0494 *Website:* baxendalecare.org.uk
Activities: Accommodation, housing
Address: 109 Derwent Road, London, N13 4QA
Trustees: Mr Ray Ellis, Mr Bruce Roderick Maunder Taylor, Mr Brian Lloyd Charles, Mr Colin Liversidge, Mr Peter Smith, Mr Peter Burd, Mr Antony Jacobson, Mrs Jose Elaine Cronin, Mrs Claire Bannister, Mr Andy Henderson, Mrs Marilyn Testar, Mr Marco Tassi
Income: £2,033,454 [2017]; £2,137,659 [2016]; £1,971,055 [2015]; £1,847,277 [2014]; £1,859,379 [2013]

Bayis Sheli Ltd
Registered: 6 Apr 2006 *Employees:* 16
Tel: 020 8732 8031 *Website:* bayissheli.org.uk
Activities: Disability; accommodation, housing
Address: c/o New Burlington House, 1075 Finchley Road, London, NW11 0PU
Trustees: Mrs Cheryl Gluck, Mr Jacob Sorotzkin, Mr Moses Hirschler, Mrs Leah Stern, Mr Alexander Strom, Rabbi Alan Kimche
Income: £1,185,262 [2017]; £313,153 [2016]; £607,702 [2015]; £148,286 [2014]; £312,925 [2013]

Beachborough School Trust Limited
Registered: 11 Apr 1963 *Employees:* 118
Tel: 01280 700071 *Website:* beachborough.com
Activities: Education, training
Address: Beachborough School, Westbury Manor, Westbury, Brackley, Northants, NN13 5LB
Trustees: Mrs Sarah Anne Willis, Mr Paul William Sanderson, Mr Nicholas Mullineux, Mrs Joanne Askham, Mr Benjamin Wood, Mr Andrew George Bentley, Mr Jean-Marc Hodgkin, Mrs R Donaldson, Mrs Elizabeth Wilson, Mrs Susan Barrett, Mrs Georgina Eilbeck
Income: £4,906,089 [2017]; £4,657,769 [2016]; £4,251,357 [2015]; £3,958,012 [2014]; £3,689,243 [2013]

Beacon Centre for the Blind
Registered: 6 Mar 1964 *Employees:* 78 *Volunteers:* 270
Website: beaconvision.org
Activities: General charitable purposes; education, training; advancement of health or saving of lives; disability; arts, culture, heritage, science; amateur sport; economic, community development, employment; recreation; other charitable purposes
Address: 9 Sandford Rise, Wolverhampton, W Midlands, WV6 9JQ
Trustees: Mr Michael John Beardsmore, Mr Richard Ennis, Ms Pauline Heffernan, Jan Burns, Mr Colin Banks, Mrs Sue Rawlings, Mr Nick Price, Ms Carolyn Stokes
Income: £2,717,434 [2017]; £2,427,668 [2016]; £2,540,168 [2015]; £2,465,602 [2014]; £2,180,776 [2013]

The Beacon Educational Trust Limited
Registered: 10 Nov 1972 *Employees:* 124
Tel: 01494 736176 *Website:* beaconschool.co.uk
Activities: Education, training
Address: The Beacon School, 15 Amersham Road, Chesham Bois, Amersham, Bucks, HP6 5PF
Trustees: Mrs Joanna Ruth Pardon, Mr Michael Francis, Mr Andrew Thompson, Mrs Deborah Ann McGregor, Mrs Ziona Arcari, Mrs Stephanie Horrocks, Mrs Rosalind Josephine Garrett-Bowes, Mr David Hollander, Mr Andrew Reynolds, Mr Crispin Tomlinson, Mr Simon James Allcock, Mrs Philippa Jane Kirkbride, Mr Michael Bond, Mr Justin David Robert Hardman
Income: £7,764,888 [2017]; £7,363,102 [2016]; £6,737,570 [2015]; £6,216,695 [2014]; £5,839,263 [2013]

Beaconsfield Educational Trust Ltd
Registered: 16 Jul 1962 *Employees:* 72 *Volunteers:* 27
Tel: 01494 685402 *Website:* davenies.co.uk
Activities: Education, training
Address: Davenies Boys Preparatory School, 73 Station Road, Beaconsfield, Bucks, HP9 1AA
Trustees: Mr Stephen Nokes, Mrs Karie Janse Van Vuuren, Mr A Gregg S Davies, Mr Christopher Michael Hilditch, Mr Neil Gallagher, Mrs Antonia Dalmahoy, Mr Nicholas Edwards, Mr Michael Reyner, Mr Thomas Jenkin, Mrs Siobhan Lowrey, Mrs Susan Clifford, Mr Jamie Shuttle
Income: £4,874,026 [2017]; £4,931,708 [2016]; £4,616,872 [2015]; £4,290,055 [2014]; £4,110,310 [2013]

Beamish Museum
Registered: 17 Jan 2008 *Employees:* 412 *Volunteers:* 500
Tel: 0191 370 4000 *Website:* beamish.org.uk
Activities: Education, training; arts, culture, heritage, science; environment, conservation, heritage
Address: Regional Resource Centre, Beamish, Stanley, Co Durham, DH9 0RG
Trustees: Mr John Robinson, Ms Angela Douglas, Mrs Sarah Stewart, Mr David Stoker, Mr John Pennie, Mrs Marie Nixon, Mr Mike Barker, Mr John-Paul Stephenson, Mr Alan Ashburner, Mr Richard Alderson Bell, Mr Ossie Johnson, Councillour John Kelly, Mrs Sarah Salter, Ms Gillian Miller, Mrs Nancy Elizabeth Maxwell
Income: £12,233,000 [2017]; £10,353,000 [2016]; £32,897,000 [2015]; £7,718,000 [2014]; £6,704,000 [2013]

Sam Beare Hospice
Registered: 19 Jul 2006 *Employees:* 78 *Volunteers:* 800
Tel: 01483 881750 *Website:* wsbhospices.co.uk
Activities: The advancement of health or saving of lives
Address: Woking Hospice, 5 Hill View Road, Woking, Surrey, GU22 7HW
Trustees: Mr Rhodney Hayden Bray Lofting, Mr David Andrew Perry, Mr Timothy Andrew Stokes, Mr Marc Leslie Riggs, Mr Peter Lovibond, Ms Sian Wicks, Mr Jon Richard Jagger, Mr Simon John Geoffrey Oxley, Mrs Susan Mary Jones, Dr Christopher John Douglas Dunstan, Mr Piers Meadows, Mr Peter Goodyear, Mr Roy Anthony Jarvis, Mr Richard Michael Roberts
Income: £2,158,000 [2017]; £4,390,000 [2016]; £2,640,212 [2015]; £2,883,667 [2014]; £2,838,536 [2013]

Beating Bowel Cancer
Registered: 25 Jul 1997 *Employees:* 34 *Volunteers:* 527
Tel: 0845 071 9300 *Website:* beatingbowelcancer.org
Activities: The advancement of health or saving of lives
Address: 2nd Floor, Harlequin House, 7 High Street, Teddington, Middlesex, TW11 8EE
Trustees: Mr Patrick Figgis, Ms Lorraine Elizabeth Lander, Mauro Mattiuzzo
Income: £1,679,119 [2017]; £2,010,434 [2016]; £2,343,424 [2015]; £1,513,331 [2014]; £1,139,019 [2013]

The Beatrice Laing Trust
Registered: 4 Feb 1965
Tel: 020 8238 8890 *Website:* laingfamilytrusts.org.uk
Activities: General charitable purposes; education, training; disability; prevention or relief of poverty; overseas aid, famine relief; accommodation, housing; religious activities
Address: 33 Bunns Lane, London, NW7 2DX
Trustees: Mr Christopher Maurice Laing OBE DL, Mr David Eric Laing, Mrs Paula Joan Stephanie Blacker, Sir Martin Laing, Mr Charles William David Laing, Mrs Alex Gregory
Income: £2,622,798 [2017]; £2,611,620 [2016]; £2,443,637 [2015]; £2,553,397 [2014]; £2,259,330 [2013]

Beaudesert Park School Trust Limited
Registered: 3 Dec 1968 *Employees:* 152
Tel: 01453 837292 *Website:* beaudesert.gloucs.sch.uk
Activities: Education, training; arts, culture, heritage, science; amateur sport
Address: Beaudesert Park School Trust Ltd, Minchinhampton, Stroud, Glos, GL6 9AF
Trustees: Mrs Alexandra Mary Melvin, Mr Mark Christopher Spring-Rice Pyper, Mrs Christine Lough, Mr Marcus Campbell, Lady Ros Ford, Mrs Claire Kay, Mr Mark Christopher Fawcett, Mr Thomas Daniel Ahearne, Mr Guy Robertson Muir, Mr Roger Mather, Mr James Cope, Mr Jonathan Nettleton
Income: £6,408,409 [2017]; £5,870,621 [2016]; £5,802,683 [2015]; £5,299,512 [2014]; £4,755,285 [2013]

Beauland Limited
Registered: 18 May 1981
Activities: General charitable purposes; education, training; advancement of health or saving of lives; disability; prevention or relief of poverty; religious activities
Address: 32 Stanley Road, Salford, M7 4ES
Trustees: Mr Henry Neumann, Mr Maurice Neumann, Mrs Esther Henry, Mrs Miriam Friedlander, Mrs Hannah Roseman, Mr Pinchas Neumann, Mr Neumann, Mrs Janet Bleier, Mrs Rebecca Delange
Income: £1,572,822 [2017]; £656,262 [2016]; £1,502,022 [2015]; £803,486 [2014]; £458,582 [2013]

Beaumond House Community Hospice
Registered: 1 Sep 1993 *Employees:* 58 *Volunteers:* 188
Tel: 01636 640321 *Website:* beaumondhouse.co.uk
Activities: The advancement of health or saving of lives
Address: Newark & District Hospice Aid, Beaumond House, 32 London Road, Newark, Notts, NG24 1TW
Trustees: Mr Nicholas Porter, Ms Judith Amanda De La Motte, Mr John William Marshall, Mr David Andrew Tomkinson, Dr Della Frances Bulpitt Money, Mr Ian Phillips FCA, Dr Julie Anne Barker, Miss Joanna Mary Parlby, Miss Emma Louise Holden
Income: £1,038,623 [2017]; £932,358 [2016]; £760,564 [2015]; £1,100,224 [2014]; £1,151,147 [2013]

The Becht Family Charitable Trust
Registered: 7 Nov 2006
Tel: 0151 236 6666
Activities: General charitable purposes; education, training; advancement of health or saving of lives; disability; prevention or relief of poverty; overseas aid, famine relief; accommodation, housing; religious activities; arts, culture, heritage, science; amateur sport; animals; environment, conservation, heritage; economic, community development, employment; human rights, religious or racial harmony, equality or diversity; recreation; other charitable purposes
Address: 4th Floor, Rathbone Trust Company Limited, Port of Liverpool Building, Pier Head, Liverpool, L3 1NW
Trustees: Mr Lambertus Jonannes Hermanus Becht, Rathbone Trust Company Limited, Mrs Ann Marie Becht
Income: £5,303,222 [2016]; £4,463,686 [2015]; £5,300,876 [2014]; £4,485,933 [2013]; £4,048,748 [2012]

Bedales School
Registered: 11 Aug 1966 Employees: 252
Tel: 01730 711561 Website: bedales.org.uk
Activities: Education, training
Address: Bedales School, Church Road, Steep, Petersfield, Hants, GU32 2DG
Trustees: Radm Richard John Lippiett, Mr Nicholas Vetch, Mr Charles Basil Lucas Watson, Mr Owen Jonathan, Dr Anna Julia Keay, Mr Felix Grey, Mrs Avril Florence Hardie, Mr Matthew Rice BA, Mrs Joanna Pamela Michele Johnson, Mr Timothy Wise, Professor Geoffrey Christopher Ward, Mrs Clare Louise Bradbury
Income: £18,097,361 [2017]; £17,921,099 [2016]; £18,304,407 [2015]; £17,283,432 [2014]; £16,622,862 [2013]

Bede House Association
Registered: 30 Jul 1962 Employees: 38 Volunteers: 58
Tel: 020 7237 3881 Website: bedehouse.org.uk
Activities: General charitable purposes; education, training; disability; prevention or relief of poverty; amateur sport; economic, community development, employment; recreation
Address: 351 Southwark Park Road, London, SE16 2JW
Trustees: Ms Caroline Knight, Ms Katrina Ramsey, Ms Charlotte Cook, Ms Catherine McGrath, Mr John Christian William Kent, Ms Wendy Cookson, Ms Julie Cotton, Mr Paul Lindsay, Ms Jamaria Kong, Ms Nitu Panesar, Mr Martyn Lee Hickson
Income: £1,258,076 [2017]; £1,185,577 [2016]; £1,201,568 [2015]; £1,112,061 [2014]; £1,100,196 [2013]

Bedford Hospital NHS Trust Charitable Fund
Registered: 28 Feb 1997
Tel: 01234 792641 Website: bedfordhospital.org.uk
Activities: The advancement of health or saving of lives
Address: Bedford Hospital NHS Trust, South Wing, Kempston Road, Bedford, MK42 9DJ
Trustees: Bedford Hospital NHS Trust
Income: £1,248,000 [2017]; £268,000 [2016]; £166,000 [2015]; £344,000 [2014]; £211,000 [2013]

Bedfordshire Rural Communities Charity
Registered: 24 Mar 1997 Employees: 49 Volunteers: 100
Tel: 01234 834931 Website: bedsrcc.org.uk
Activities: General charitable purposes; education, training; disability; prevention or relief of poverty; accommodation, housing; arts, culture, heritage, science; environment, conservation, heritage; economic, community development, employment; recreation
Address: The Old School, Southill Road, Cardington, Bedford, MK44 3SX
Trustees: Mr Stephen Holroyd, Mrs June Mary Barnes, Miss Paula Grayson, Mr Brian George Prickett, Mr Tim Hill, Mr John Wheeler, Mr Eric Masih, Mr Barry Stanley George, Mr Ian James Kelly, Mrs Ann Lovesey, Dr Timothy John Hedges, Mr John Hilbert Lewis, Dr John Stewart May, Mr Ian Riches
Income: £1,654,851 [2017]; £1,579,834 [2016]; £1,372,305 [2015]; £1,712,136 [2014]; £1,518,982 [2013]

Bedfordshire and Luton Community Foundation
Registered: 9 May 2001 Employees: 3 Volunteers: 6
Tel: 01767 600725 Website: blcf.org.uk
Activities: General charitable purposes; education, training; advancement of health or saving of lives; disability; prevention or relief of poverty; arts, culture, heritage, science; amateur sport; environment, conservation, heritage; economic, community development, employment
Address: 20 Purcell Place, Sullivan Court, Biggleswade, Beds, SG18 8SX
Trustees: Dr Wendi Momen, Mr Keith Rawlings, Mrs Julia Siegler, Geoff Lambert, Mrs Pauline Stewart, Steve Leverton
Income: £1,599,352 [2017]; £1,574,974 [2016]; £1,631,264 [2015]; £1,227,180 [2014]; £506,864 [2013]

Bedstone Educational Trust Limited
Registered: 9 Oct 1962 Employees: 93
Tel: 01547 530303
Activities: Education, training
Address: Bedstone College, Bucknell, Salop, SY7 0BG
Trustees: David John Owens, Lt Col Terence Lowry, Mrs Yvonne Sandra Thomas, Mr James Smith, Mrs Susan Phillips, Mr J Jones, Group Captain Jonathan Peter Spencer Fynes, Mr Bruce Meldrum, Mrs Megan Janet Lawton, Mr Stephen John Stringer
Income: £5,534,288 [2017]; £2,752,603 [2016]; £2,762,418 [2015]; £2,540,038 [2014]; £2,652,801 [2013]

Beechwood Cancer Care Centre
Registered: 14 Nov 1991 Employees: 25 Volunteers: 240
Tel: 0161 476 0384 Website: beechwoodcancercare.co.uk
Activities: The advancement of health or saving of lives
Address: Beechwood Cancer Care Centre, Chelford Grove, Stockport, Cheshire, SK3 8LS
Trustees: Mrs Marjorie Whyte, Mrs Jacqueline Collins, Mr Reuben Fidler Fielding, Mr John Stevenson, Mr Graham Neil Timperley, Mr Ian Kelvin Cook, Dr Satish Chander Mehta MBE, Mr Anthony Wilson, Ms Sandra Sinclair, David Cheetham, Mr Paul Antony Harrison, Mrs Danila Armstrong
Income: £1,040,930 [2017]; £1,060,327 [2016]; £966,282 [2015]; £1,039,478 [2014]; £902,659 [2013]

Beechwood Education Trust

Registered: 20 Sep 1997 *Employees:* 24 *Volunteers:* 30
Tel: 01223 400190 *Website:* cambridge.focus-school.com
Activities: Education, training
Address: Focus School - Cambridge Campus, Shelford Bottom, Cambridge, CB22 3BF
Trustees: Mr Paul Hetherington, Mr Peter John Marsh, Mr Roger Nunn, Mr Richard Smith, Mr Cedric Fentiman, Mr Matthew Anderson, Mr Philip Anderson
Income: £1,730,966 [2016]; £1,316,742 [2015]; £1,128,071 [2014]; £988,799 [2013]; £962,278 [2012]

Beechwood Park School Limited

Registered: 16 Nov 1964 *Employees:* 158 *Volunteers:* 50
Tel: 01582 840333 *Website:* beechwoodpark.herts.sch.uk
Activities: Education, training
Address: Beechwood Park School, Beechwood Park, Markyate, St Albans, Herts, AL3 8AW
Trustees: Mr Michael William Spinney, Mr Desmond Mark Quigley, Mr James Simon Hodgson, Mr Jonathan William James Gillespie, Dr Russell Mardon Viner, Mrs Clare Elizabeth Cutler, Mrs Katharine Elizabeth Swaine, Mr Scott Wallace Black, Mr Gary John Freer, Mrs Linda Christine Roberts, Dr Richard James Maloney, Mr Gavin Eric Mairs, Mrs Rosalind Kate Hardy, Mr Mark William Hammond, Mr Simon James Thompson
Income: £6,594,846 [2016]; £6,224,412 [2015]; £6,101,238 [2014]; £5,776,637 [2013]; £5,774,287 [2012]

Beenstock Home Management Co. Ltd

Registered: 28 Jun 2001 *Employees:* 59 *Volunteers:* 10
Tel: 0161 792 1515
Activities: General charitable purposes; education, training; advancement of health or saving of lives; disability; prevention or relief of poverty; accommodation, housing; religious activities; arts, culture, heritage, science
Address: The Beenstock Home, 19-21 Northumberland Street, Salford, M7 4RP
Trustees: Mr Hoseas Aviedor Friedlander, Mrs Navah Kestenbaum, Mr Mordecai Halpern
Income: £1,440,953 [2017]; £998,678 [2016]; £932,263 [2015]; £939,859 [2014]; £784,422 [2013]

Beeston Hall School Trust Limited

Registered: 28 Sep 1967 *Employees:* 56
Tel: 01263 837324 *Website:* beestonhall.co.uk
Activities: Education, training
Address: Beeston Hall School Trust Ltd, West Runton, Norfolk, NR27 9NQ
Trustees: Mr Graham Able, Earl of Leicester, Mr Geoff Webster, Dr Pamela Ripley, Miss Sophie Carter, Mrs Jenny Little, Mr Gary Phillips, Mr James Pallister, Mrs Henrietta Lindsell, Mr David Brown
Income: £2,061,627 [2017]; £2,010,340 [2016]; £2,151,916 [2015]; £2,505,257 [2014]; £2,664,862 [2013]

Beis Aharon Trust Ltd

Registered: 13 Apr 1992
Activities: Education, training; religious activities
Address: 86 Darenth Road, London, N16 6ED
Trustees: Mr Yossel Lipschitz, Mr Mordechai Bard, Mr Aharon Hoffman
Income: £1,086,496 [2017]; £1,552,912 [2016]; £1,202,054 [2015]; £1,496,568 [2014]; £1,718,984 [2013]

Beis Chaye Rochel (The Gateshead Jewish Academy) Limited

Registered: 9 Jan 2004 *Employees:* 33
Tel: 0191 477 6450
Activities: Education, training
Address: 3 Oxford Terrace, Gateshead, Tyne & Wear, NE8 1RQ
Trustees: Dr Martin Terry Cope, Mr Yehoshua Yaakov Lobenstein, Mr Avram M Guttentag
Income: £1,333,650 [2017]; £989,743 [2016]; £935,350 [2015]; £986,855 [2014]; £716,679 [2013]

Beis Chinuch Lebonos Limited

Registered: 28 Sep 1995 *Employees:* 193
Tel: 020 8802 4591
Activities: Education, training
Address: Beis Chinuch Lebonos Girls School, Woodberry Down Centre, Woodberry Down, London, N4 2SH
Trustees: Mrs Spitzer, Mr Abraham Schechter, Mr Neil Spitzer, Mr Chanoch Henoch Teitelbaum
Income: £2,746,574 [2016]; £2,593,250 [2015]; £2,189,402 [2014]; £1,502,255 [2013]; £1,117,786 [2012]

The Beis Malka Trust

Registered: 10 May 1982 *Employees:* 189 *Volunteers:* 24
Tel: 020 8806 3336
Activities: Education, training
Address: 93 Alkham Road, London, N16 6XD
Trustees: Mr Aron Grossman, Mr Benzion Hopfstatter, Mr Avrohom Simcha Taub, Mr Jehuda Bleichfeld
Income: £1,581,409 [2017]; £1,372,033 [2016]; £1,382,845 [2015]; £1,076,165 [2014]; £721,087 [2013]

Beis Soroh Schenierer Seminary

Registered: 17 Jan 1992 *Employees:* 26
Tel: 0161 792 7770
Activities: Education, training; arts, culture, heritage, science; amateur sport; environment, conservation, heritage; economic, community development, employment
Address: 472-474 Bury New Road, Salford, M7 4NU
Trustees: Mr Modche Halperm, Mr Jacob Eckstein, Mr Dov Olsberg
Income: £1,463,090 [2016]; £1,288,931 [2015]; £1,209,228 [2014]; £1,246,705 [2013]; £1,290,481 [2012]

Beis Yaakov Primary School Foundation

Registered: 13 Aug 2008 *Employees:* 79
Tel: 020 8905 9590
Activities: Education, training
Address: 373 Edgware Road, London, NW9 6NQ
Trustees: Mr Benjamin Eliezer Perl MBE, Mr Mark Vorhand, Mr Sylvain Klein, Mr Andrew Selwyn Cohen
Income: £1,716,876 [2017]; £1,525,454 [2016]; £1,547,692 [2015]; £1,768,772 [2014]; £1,292,393 [2013]

Beit Halochem UK

Registered: 19 Apr 2012 *Employees:* 2 *Volunteers:* 20
Tel: 020 8458 2455 *Website:* bhuk.org
Activities: The advancement of health or saving of lives; disability
Address: 7 Golders Park Close, London, NW11 7QR
Trustees: Honourable Andrew Daniel Wolfson, Mr Daniel Naftalin, Mrs Orly Wolfson, Mrs Susan Kahn, Mr Nathaniel Meyohas
Income: £2,898,010 [2017]; £1,064,815 [2016]; £7,522,447 [2015]; £778,576 [2014]; £518,419 [2013]

The Beit Trust
Registered: 6 Jul 1964 *Employees:* 7 *Volunteers:* 15
Tel: 01483 772575 *Website:* beittrust.org.uk
Activities: General charitable purposes; education, training; advancement of health or saving of lives; disability; prevention or relief of poverty; overseas aid, famine relief; accommodation, housing; arts, culture, heritage, science; animals; environment, conservation, heritage; economic, community development, employment
Address: The Beit Trust, Beit House, Grove Road, Woking, Surrey, GU21 5JB
Trustees: Mr Jonty Driver, Professor Chris Lavy, Mr Alex Duncan, Sir Alan Munro, Sir Kieran Prendergast
Income: £2,871,296 [2016]; £2,780,369 [2015]; £2,666,961 [2014]; £2,451,103 [2013]; £2,188,914 [2012]

Belgrade Theatre Trust (Coventry) Limited
Registered: 30 Aug 1963 *Employees:* 83 *Volunteers:* 18
Tel: 024 7684 6720 *Website:* belgrade.co.uk
Activities: Arts, culture, heritage, science
Address: Belgrade Theatre, Corporation Street, Coventry, Warwicks, CV1 1GS
Trustees: Tony Skipper, Ms Joanna Reid, Mr Stewart Fergusson, Mr Geoffrey Brooke-Taylor, Mr Tim Mayer, Mr Hamish Glen, Ms Sheila Anne Bates, Mr Alan Pollock, Mr Paul Carvell, Mr Nathaniel Dodzo
Income: £6,018,431 [2017]; £5,996,239 [2016]; £5,041,547 [2015]; £5,199,145 [2014]; £4,943,876 [2013]

The Bell Concord Educational Trust Ltd
Registered: 18 Jan 1983 *Employees:* 232
Tel: 01694 731631 *Website:* concordcollegeuk.com
Activities: Education, training
Address: Concord College, Acton Burnell Hall, Acton Burnell, Shrewsbury, Salop, SY5 7PF
Trustees: Andrew Curtis, Mr Nicholas John Blackbourn, Mr Richard Dyson FCA, Ms Jean Krasocki, Mr David Peck, Mrs Ruth Margaret Mannell, Dr Iain Melvin Bride, Mr Brian Robert Yates, Mr Robin Durham, Mr Peter Ruben, Dr A M Fricker, Mr Peter Yong
Income: £19,710,000 [2017]; £16,971,826 [2016]; £15,952,455 [2015]; £14,191,545 [2014]; £13,172,879 [2013]

The Bell Educational Trust Limited
Registered: 1 Mar 1973 *Employees:* 215 *Volunteers:* 2
Tel: 01223 275501 *Website:* bell-foundation.org.uk
Activities: Education, training
Address: The Bell Educational Trust Ltd, Hillscross, Red Cross Lane, Cambridge, CB2 0QX
Trustees: Mr Reshard Auladin, Mr Andrew Fellows, Mr Nicholas John Tellwright, Mr Geoff Spink, Mr Mike Milanovic, Ms Elizabeth Jan King, Ms Sarah Squire, Mr Russell Prior, Mr Anthony Tomei, Mr John Gandy, Ms Pooja Sharma
Income: £14,397,000 [2016]; £14,833,000 [2015]; £17,513,000 [2014]; £19,168,000 [2013]; £20,950,000 [2012]

Bell House Dulwich
Registered: 5 Jun 2014 *Volunteers:* 20
Website: bellhouse.co.uk
Activities: General charitable purposes; education, training; environment, conservation, heritage
Address: 27 College Road, London, SE21 7BG
Trustees: Mr Angus Thomas Hanton, Mr Peter Alexander Hanton, Mr David Ryan Havryn Evans
Income: £9,010,792 [2016]; £182,829 [2015]; £277,430 [2014]

AG Bell International
Registered: 28 Nov 2007 *Employees:* 4
Tel: 020 7842 2000 *Website:* clave.org.uk
Activities: Education, training; disability
Address: Rawlinson & Hunter, 6 New Street Square, London, EC4A 3AQ
Trustees: Mr Simon Brooks, Ms Meredith K Sugar, Mr Don Goldberg, Mrs Carmen Burguera Arienza, Mr Ted Meyer
Income: £2,226,935 [2016]; £86,735 [2015]; £1,294,410 [2014]; £72,593 [2013]; £1,928,678 [2012]

Bellview Charitable Trust
Registered: 22 Dec 1995
Tel: 020 8455 6789
Activities: General charitable purposes; education, training; advancement of health or saving of lives; prevention or relief of poverty; religious activities
Address: 52 Knightland Road, London, E5 9HS
Trustees: Mr Jacob Friedman, Mr Cheskel Landau, Mrs Raechel Friedman
Income: £2,606,402 [2017]; £1,975,540 [2016]; £421,110 [2015]; £1,355,366 [2014]; £528,312 [2012]

Belmont School (Feldemore) Educational Trust Limited
Registered: 28 Nov 1966 *Employees:* 47 *Volunteers:* 10
Tel: 07867 526970 *Website:* belmont-school.org
Activities: Education, training
Address: The Oaks, Horsham Road, Mid Holmwood, Dorking, Surrey, RH5 4ER
Trustees: Mr Nicholas Butcher, Mrs Haidee Jane Priday, Mr James Alexander Turnbull, Mr Andrew John Baker, Mrs Taryn Elizabeth Timperlake, Mr Jeremy Sheldon, Mrs Tania Botting, Mr Andrew Goss, Dr Sarah MacKenzie Ross
Income: £2,529,866 [2017]; £2,471,624 [2016]; £2,418,643 [2015]; £2,239,234 [2014]; £1,982,236 [2013]

Belmont-Birklands School Trust Limited
Registered: 22 Oct 1969 *Employees:* 45
Website: belmontgrosvenor.co.uk
Activities: Education, training
Address: Belmont Grosvenor School, Swarcliffe, Birstwith, Harrogate, N Yorks, HG3 2JG
Trustees: Mrs Frances Trowell, Dr Belinda Whitehead, Mrs Victoria Grafton, Mr Geoffrey William Lowde, Mr Gordon Milne, Mr Timothy Waring, Ms Kathryn Emma Standen
Income: £1,670,614 [2016]; £1,556,027 [2015]; £1,778,170 [2014]; £1,611,662 [2013]; £1,338,637 [2012]

Belper Leisure Centre Limited
Registered: 6 Apr 2009 *Employees:* 69
Tel: 01773 825285 *Website:* belperleisurecentre.co.uk
Activities: Education, training; advancement of health or saving of lives; amateur sport
Address: Belper Leisure Centre Limited, Kilbourne Road, Belper, Derbys, DE56 1RZ
Trustees: Mr Adrian Evans, Mr Bernard Murphy, Councillor John Owen, Mrs Joyce Sanders, Mr Stuart Andrew Holliday
Income: £1,275,000 [2017]; £1,366,000 [2016]; £1,357,000 [2015]; £1,178,000 [2014]; £1,188,000 [2013]

The Belsize Square Synagogue

Registered: 1 Dec 2011 *Employees:* 13 *Volunteers:* 20
Tel: 07876 340059 *Website:* synagogue.org.uk
Activities: Education, training; religious activities
Address: Belsize Square Synagogue, 51 Belsize Square, London, NW3 4HX
Trustees: Mr James Strauss, Mr Frederick Allan Lehmann, Mr Nicholas Philip Viner, Mr John Matthew Abramson, Mr John Alfred George Alexander, Mr Keith Mark Conway, Mr Adam Howard Hurst, Mrs Annette Marion Nathan, Mrs Elizabeth Flora Nisbet, Mr Richard Gerard Pollins, Mrs Dilys Kim Tausz, Dr Claire Susan Walford, Mr Francis Joseph, Mr Simon Bernard Cutner, Mrs Jacqueline Ann Alexander, Mr David Michael Pollins, Mrs Michelle Ann Wayne, Paul Burger, Mr Michael Horowitz, Mr Steven Bruck, Mrs Suzanne Zwiah Goldstein, Dr Jocelyn Asher Simon Brookes, Mrs Patricia Hirschovits, Mr Adam David Nathan, Mrs Marion Ruth Nathan, Mr Robert Walter Simon Nothman, Mr Samuel Paul Sanders, Mr Justyn Jacob Trenner, Mr Anthony Stadlen, Mr Adam David Davis, Mrs Lea Dalia Lichfield, Mr Joseph Samuel Hacker, Mrs Sarah Dorabella Percival
Income: £1,194,220 [2016]; £995,872 [2015]; £842,614 [2014]; £987,364 [2013]; £5,320,024 [2012]

Belvedere Trust

Registered: 20 Dec 1999
Activities: General charitable purposes; education, training; advancement of health or saving of lives; disability; prevention or relief of poverty; arts, culture, heritage, science; environment, conservation, heritage; recreation
Address: The Belvedere, 2 Back Lane, London, NW3 1HL
Trustees: John Cracknell, Miss Pamela Klaber, Mr James Roditi, Mr Lawrence Hene, John Clive Viscount Mackintosh of Halifax
Income: £3,101,131 [2017]; £709,417 [2016]; £61,198 [2015]; £145,452 [2014]; £330,177 [2013]

Ben - Motor and Allied Trades Benevolent Fund

Registered: 2 Nov 1987 *Employees:* 404 *Volunteers:* 30
Tel: 01344 298150 *Website:* ben.org.uk
Activities: Education, training; advancement of health or saving of lives; disability; prevention or relief of poverty; accommodation, housing; economic, community development, employment; recreation; other charitable purposes
Address: Lynwood Court, Lynwood Village, Rise Road, Ascot, Berks, SL5 0FG
Trustees: Mr Robin Shaw, Michael Anthony Breitheam Judge, Robin Arthur John Woolcock, Mr Daksh Gupta, Mrs Lesley Upham, Mr Richard Jeffcoat, Mr Timothy Victor Holmes, Graeme John Potts, Mr Brian Philip Back, Mr Jeremy Hicks, Mr Steven Garry Nash, Mr Gerald Lee
Income: £26,331,000 [2017]; £32,288,000 [2016]; £13,461,620 [2015]; £13,445,013 [2014]; £12,886,200 [2013]

Bendrigg Trust

Registered: 15 Feb 1979 *Employees:* 22 *Volunteers:* 170
Tel: 01539 723766 *Website:* bendrigg.org.uk
Activities: Education, training; disability; amateur sport
Address: Bendrigg Trust, Bendrigg Lodge, Old Hutton, Kendal, Cumbria, LA8 0NR
Trustees: Mr Tom Hibbert, Mr John Holmes, Simon Drummond-Hay, Mrs Alyson Groom, Miss Rachael Hodgson, Mrs Anne Fleck, Mr Timothy Lowe, Don Harding, Mr Giles Wingate-Saul, Mrs Judy Rayner, Mr Brian McDonough
Income: £1,666,546 [2016]; £944,844 [2015]; £864,554 [2014]; £729,931 [2013]; £753,958 [2012]

The Benenden Hospital Trust

Registered: 20 Nov 1997 *Employees:* 269
Tel: 01580 240540 *Website:* benendenhospital.org.uk
Activities: The advancement of health or saving of lives
Address: Wheelwrights House, The Street, Benenden, Cranbrook, Kent, TN17 4DJ
Trustees: Mr Roy Mawford, Mr Deryck Lewis, Mr Alan Pilgrim, Mrs Louise Fowler, Mrs Gwenda Binks, Mr John Jackson, Mr Robert Andrews
Income: £32,005,582 [2016]; £28,841,000 [2015]; £26,903,000 [2014]; £28,745,000 [2013]; £23,022,000 [2012]

Benenden School (Kent) Limited

Registered: 7 Feb 1963 *Employees:* 361
Tel: 01580 240651 *Website:* benenden.kent.sch.uk
Activities: Education, training
Address: Benenden School (Kent) Ltd, Cranbrook Road, Benenden, Cranbrook, Kent, TN17 4AA
Trustees: Mr Jonathan Vezey Strong, Dr Fiona Cornish, Mr Paul Simpkin, Mrs Joanna Farah Birkett, Jaa McParland, Mrs Anne Elizabeth McNab, Ms Laurette Gallagher, Mr Ss Smart, Dr Rupert Evenett, Mrs Wm Carey, Ms Alison Jane Clarke, GS Pugh, Professor Liba Chaia Taub, Mr Christopher George
Income: £20,760,000 [2017]; £20,115,000 [2016]; £22,088,000 [2015]; £18,285,000 [2014]; £18,313,000 [2013]

The Benenden School Trust

Registered: 25 Apr 1983
Tel: 01580 240651 *Website:* benenden.kent.sch.uk
Activities: Education, training
Address: Benenden School, Benenden, Cranbrook, Kent, TN17 4AA
Trustees: Mrs C C Brooke, Mrs Deborah Buffini, Datin Kwl Chew, Mrs R J Hyslop, Mr Jr Metherell, Mrs C Tomazos, Mrs Sma Everist, Mrs Avc Hillier, Mr Cmc Preston, Mr Pe Flintoff, Mrs V L Hyman, Mrs Sa Price, Mr A Tomazos, Mr Adrian Cassidy
Income: £1,290,383 [2016]; £1,133,546 [2015]; £566,496 [2014]; £1,015,120 [2013]; £1,862,591 [2012]

Benesco Charity Limited

Registered: 18 Feb 1970
Activities: General charitable purposes
Address: Benesco Charity Ltd, 8-10 Hallam Street, London, W1W 6NS
Trustees: Mr Jonathan Ragol-Levy, Lord David Wolfson, Honourable Andrew Daniel Wolfson, Mr David Wolfson
Income: £7,450,791 [2017]; £7,517,310 [2016]; £8,173,873 [2015]; £8,547,082 [2014]; £8,252,344 [2013]

The Benevolent Fund of The Institution of Mechanical Engineers

Registered: 14 Dec 1962 *Employees:* 3 *Volunteers:* 54
Tel: 020 7304 6883 *Website:* imeche.org
Activities: The prevention or relief of poverty
Address: Institution of Mechanical Engineers, 1 Birdcage Walk, London, SW1H 9JJ
Trustees: Ms Anne Woodbridge, Mr Michael Greenwood, Ms Christine Clark, Ms Sarah Jane Templey, Ms Nicole Rinaldi, Mr Chris Taylor, Mr Dennis Wilcock, Mr Chirantan Shukla, Mr Brian Cooke, Mr Christian Thomas Young, Mr Bruce Dagley, Mr John Cornforth
Income: £1,295,514 [2016]; £1,335,277 [2015]; £1,223,468 [2014]; £1,414,722 [2013]; £796,027 [2012]

The Benjamin Foundation
Registered: 10 Jul 2008 *Employees:* 228 *Volunteers:* 60
Tel: 01603 615670 *Website:* benjaminfoundation.co.uk
Activities: General charitable purposes; education, training; disability; accommodation, housing; economic, community development, employment; recreation
Address: 23-27 St Andrews Street, Norwich, NR2 4TP
Trustees: Mr Philip Burton, Mr Julian Wright, Ms Catriona Sheret, Mr Simon Woodbridge, Mr Stephen Ede
Income: £5,773,802 [2017]; £5,553,107 [2016]; £5,276,123 [2015]; £4,748,885 [2014]; £3,450,776 [2013]

Benslow Music Trust
Registered: 22 Mar 1963 *Employees:* 35 *Volunteers:* 12
Tel: 01462 459446 *Website:* benslowmusic.org
Activities: Education, training; arts, culture, heritage, science
Address: Benslow Music, Benslow Lane, Hitchin, Herts, SG4 9RB
Trustees: Mr Peter Warwick Neville, Mrs Catherine Mary Steel, Mr Anthony Aston, Mr Selva Kumar, Mr Richard Dickins, Mr Andrew Jan Daniel Baruch, Mr Michael Taylor, Ms Ann Conchie, Mr John Herbert Witchell, Mr Tim Gillott, Mrs Norma King, Mr Roy Simpson
Income: £1,181,480 [2016]; £1,108,611 [2015]; £976,898 [2014]; £898,071 [2013]; £921,225 [2012]

The Bentley Priory Battle of Britain Trust
Registered: 12 Jul 2006 *Employees:* 5 *Volunteers:* 72
Tel: 01494 882628 *Website:* bentleypriorymuseum.org.uk
Activities: General charitable purposes; education, training; arts, culture, heritage, science; environment, conservation, heritage; armed forces, emergency service efficiency; other charitable purposes
Address: Wendleberie, Moor Common, Lane End, High Wycombe, Bucks, HP14 3HS
Trustees: Mrs Erica Ferguson, Wg Cdr Leslie Robert Powell, Air Marshal Cliff Spink, Ms Sangita Unadkat, Mr David Cuttill, Ms Karen Barker, Ms Bridgette Jones, Mr John Williams, Ms Melissa John, Ms Natasha Brown, Ms Derna Grundon, Air Vice-Marshal Clive Bairsto, Mr David Julian Ashton
Income: £1,205,267 [2016]; £352,656 [2015]; £287,519 [2014]; £862,370 [2013]; £420,670 [2012]

The Berkeley Charitable Foundation
Registered: 26 Jun 2013 *Employees:* 5 *Volunteers:* 1,456
Tel: 01932 584551 *Website:* berkeleyfoundation.org.uk
Activities: General charitable purposes; education, training; advancement of health or saving of lives; prevention or relief of poverty; accommodation, housing; environment, conservation, heritage; economic, community development, employment
Address: The Berkeley Group PLC, Berkeley House, 19 Portsmouth Road, Cobham, Surrey, KT11 1JG
Trustees: Mr Anthony William Pidgley CBE, Ms Wendy Joan Pritchard, Mr Robert Charles Grenville Perrins, Mrs Elaine Anne Driver
Income: £2,723,621 [2017]; £1,760,059 [2016]; £1,355,802 [2015]; £3,294,954 [2014]

Berkhampstead School (Cheltenham) Trust Limited
Registered: 26 Mar 1974 *Employees:* 80 *Volunteers:* 2
Tel: 01242 523263 *Website:* berkhampsteadschool.co.uk
Activities: Education, training; recreation
Address: Berkhampstead School, Pittville Circus Road, Cheltenham, Glos, GL52 2QA
Trustees: Mr Nigel Hosken, Mrs Julie Wand, Mr Adam Lewis Kirkham Lillywhite, Mrs Catherine Jane Kent, Miss Judie Hodsdon, Ms Charlotte Oosthuizen, Mrs Jo Simons, Mr Nicholas Arthur Folland, Mr Richard Green, Mr Nicholas Southwell, Mrs Susan Ellen Williams
Income: £2,939,288 [2016]; £2,629,731 [2015]; £2,485,540 [2014]; £2,051,924 [2013]

Berkhamsted Schools Group
Registered: 15 Nov 1962 *Employees:* 536
Tel: 01442 358005 *Website:* berkhamstedschool.org
Activities: Education, training
Address: Berkhamsted Schools Group, Central Office, 6 Chesham Road, Berkhamsted, Herts, HP4 3AA
Trustees: Mr Christopher Nicholls, Mr Stuart Rolland, Mr Gavin Laws, Dr Mark A Fenton, Miss Anne Fahy, Mr Andrew John Wilcock, Professor Sarah-Jayne Blakemore, Mrs Emma Jeffrey, Mrs Samantha Tidey, Mrs Sandra Turner, Mr David J Atkins, Mr Neil Twogood, Ms Sarah Ann Shields, Mr Jonathan David Williams
Income: £31,916,000 [2017]; £29,769,000 [2016]; £28,898,000 [2015]; £26,669,300 [2014]; £25,974,000 [2013]

Berkshire Community Foundation
Registered: 3 Jan 2014 *Employees:* 7 *Volunteers:* 7
Tel: 0118 930 3021 *Website:* berkshirecf.org
Activities: General charitable purposes; education, training; advancement of health or saving of lives; disability; prevention or relief of poverty; accommodation, housing; amateur sport; economic, community development, employment
Address: Green Park Reading, 100 Longwater Avenue, Reading, Berks, RG2 6GP
Trustees: Jane Wates, Mr Nick Burrows, Margaret Haines, Ms Jesal Dhokia BA Hons, Mr Gary Flather OBE QC, Debra Allcocktyler, Mr Sean Taylor, Mr David Oram, Mr Chris Dodson OBE DL, Mr Alexander Barfield, Kathryn Wiley, Stephen Howard
Income: £1,478,547 [2017]; £1,034,116 [2016]; £698,188 [2015]

Berkshire Health Charitable Fund and Other Related Charities
Registered: 9 Oct 1995
Tel: 01344 415808 *Website:* berkshirehealthcare.nhs.uk
Activities: General charitable purposes; education, training; advancement of health or saving of lives; disability; amateur sport; other charitable purposes
Address: Berkshire Healthcare NHS Foundation Trust, Fitzwilliam House, Skimpedhill Lane, Bracknell, Berks, RG12 1BQ
Trustees: Mr Julian Mark Emms, Mr Alex Gild, Mr Mark Lejman, Mrs Beverley Searle, Mr Christopher Fisher, Ms Nighat Mehmuda Mian, Mr Martin Earwicker, Mr Mark Day, Mr David Townsend, Mrs Helen MacKenzie, Mrs Ruth Lysons, Dr Minocher Irani, Dr David Buckle, Berkshire Healthcare NHS Foundation Trust
Income: £1,568,000 [2017]; £121,000 [2016]; £167,000 [2015]; £61,000 [2014]; £80,000 [2013]

Berkshire Women's Aid
Registered: 8 Nov 1995 *Employees:* 42 *Volunteers:* 3
Tel: 0118 950 0182 *Website:* berkshirewomensaid.org.uk
Activities: Accommodation, housing
Address: P O Box 413, Reading, Berks, RG1 8XL
Trustees: Mrs Jan Cooper, Mrs Margaret Rice-Jones, Kathryn Baddeley, Fiona Jones, Mrs Diana Hunt, Penny Spinks, Hannah Gail Langford, Nicolette Barton
Income: £1,192,752 [2017]; £1,143,543 [2016]; £1,273,098 [2015]; £1,159,577 [2014]; £1,041,103 [2013]

The Berkshire Young Musicians Trust
Registered: 11 Nov 1982 *Employees:* 117 *Volunteers:* 40
Tel: 0118 901 2370 *Website:* berkshiremaestros.org.uk
Activities: Education, training; arts, culture, heritage, science
Address: Berkshire Maestros Stoneham Court, 100 Cockney Hill, Tilehurst, Reading, Berks, RG30 4EZ
Trustees: Mr Andrew C Menzies, Mr Andrew Martin Jackson, Ms Irene Neill, Mr Robert Roscoe, Mrs Caroline Helen Hyde, Mr Nick Hobdell, Mr Robert Foster, Ms Carol Jackson-Doerge, Cllr Gerry Cark, Mr Colin Gordon Robinson, Mrs Mary K Stock, Mr Michael Harris, Mr John Gregory Sehringer, Mrs Charlotte Wilson, Mr James Manwaring, Mrs Marian Livingstone, Dr Garetth Bernard
Income: £4,911,801 [2016]; £4,294,355 [2015]; £4,177,270 [2014]; £4,093,880 [2013]; £4,220,242 [2012]

Berkshire, Buckinghamshire and Oxfordshire Wildlife Trust
Registered: 22 Feb 1962 *Employees:* 108 *Volunteers:* 1,400
Tel: 01865 775476 *Website:* bbowt.org.uk
Activities: Education, training; environment, conservation, heritage
Address: Berks Bucks & Oxon Wildlife Trust, The Lodge, 1 Armstrong Road, Littlemore, Oxford, OX4 4XT
Trustees: Mr Andrew Noel, Sir Paul Hayter KCB LVO, Ms Joanna Simons, Mr Chris Burgess, Mrs Frances Brindle, James Gillies, Mr Timothy Walter John Lowth, Mr John Pulsinelli, Ms Barbara Muston, Mrs Jane Cotton, Mr Ian Davidson
Income: £6,050,000 [2017]; £5,446,353 [2016]; £5,435,763 [2015]; £5,630,417 [2014]; £4,576,264 [2013]

Bespoke Supportive Tenancies Ltd
Registered: 22 Jul 2011 *Employees:* 23
Tel: 0845 833 8885 *Website:* bestha.co.uk
Activities: Accommodation, housing
Address: Bespoke Supportive Tenancies, Head Office, 2A Sentinel House, Albert Street, Eccles, Manchester, M30 0NJ
Trustees: Mr David Gerard Poppitt, Mr Andrew Douglas Bailey, Peter Howitt, Mr Hugh McCaw, Ms Marjorie Tutte
Income: £9,287,839 [2017]; £7,690,175 [2016]; £4,590,768 [2015]; £2,944,763 [2014]; £1,247,351 [2013]

Betel of Britain
Registered: 6 Jul 2000 *Employees:* 7 *Volunteers:* 17
Tel: 01564 822356 *Website:* betel.uk
Activities: Accommodation, housing; religious activities
Address: Windmill House, Weatheroak Hill, Alvechurch, Birmingham, B48 7EA
Trustees: Mr Elliott Tepper, Mr Billy Glover, Mr Kent Martin, Mrs Mary Alice Martin
Income: £5,087,537 [2016]; £5,738,250 [2015]; £5,045,410 [2014]; £4,492,287 [2013]; £3,809,989 [2012]

Beth Jacob Grammar School for Girls Limited
Registered: 19 Jul 1966 *Employees:* 50
Tel: 020 7836 1555
Activities: Education, training; religious activities
Address: 158-162 Shaftesbury Avenue, London, WC2H 8HR
Trustees: Mr Benzion Schalom Eliezer Freshwater, Mr Jacob Ellinson, Mr D Davis
Income: £2,147,615 [2017]; £2,613,194 [2016]; £1,846,858 [2015]; £1,843,756 [2014]; £1,811,415 [2013]

Beth Shalom Limited
Registered: 1 Aug 1979 *Employees:* 35 *Volunteers:* 18
Tel: 01623 836627 *Website:* nationalholocaustcentre.net
Activities: Education, training; human rights, religious or racial harmony, equality or diversity
Address: Beth-Shalom, Laxton, Newark, Notts, NG22 0PA
Trustees: Dame Helen Hyde DBE, Mr David Lipman, Mr Henry Grunwald OBE QC, Mr Scott Saunders, Ms Kay Andrews, Mr Matthew Robert Mellor, The Very Revd Dr John Robert Hall, Dr James Michael Smith CBE, Mr Howard Raingold, Mr John Petrie, Ms Hazel Dickinson, Mr Marc Neill Cave
Income: £1,728,111 [2016]; £1,790,817 [2015]; £1,270,546 [2014]; £925,069 [2013]; £937,229 [2012]

Bethany Care Trust
Registered: 23 Jan 1989 *Employees:* 48 *Volunteers:* 20
Tel: 0118 970 1710 *Website:* bethanycaretrust.org.uk
Activities: The advancement of health or saving of lives; accommodation, housing
Address: 17A Pamber Heath Road, Pamber Heath, Tadley, Hants, RG26 3TH
Trustees: Mr Harold Arthur Hatt, Mr Victor Michael, Scott Lindsay Dunn, Mr Jason Miller, Mr Philip Benjamin Singleton, Matthew David Bishop, Mr Reginald Garfield Albert Carnall
Income: £1,156,373 [2016]; £1,077,030 [2015]; £1,110,651 [2014]; £981,928 [2013]; £926,236 [2012]

Bethany Homestead
Registered: 11 Feb 2015 *Employees:* 84 *Volunteers:* 25
Tel: 01604 713171
Activities: General charitable purposes; advancement of health or saving of lives; prevention or relief of poverty; accommodation, housing; religious activities
Address: Bethany Homestead, Kingsley Road, Northampton, NN2 7BP
Trustees: Mr A A Foster, Mr F T G Bird, Mrs J E Stapleton, Mrs J H Wiggins, Mr R J Hardwick, Mr M P Buckby, Mr J D Payne, Mr V W Griffiths, Mrs D M Avery, Mr J W Stirling, Mr M R K Gibson, Rev A W Avery, Mr R Adams, Mr I D Brown, Mrs J M Letts, Mr J A Heard
Income: £1,463,141 [2017]

Bethany School
Registered: 14 Nov 1962 *Employees:* 108
Tel: 01580 211273 *Website:* bethanyschool.org.uk
Activities: Education, training
Address: Bethany School Ltd, Curtisden Green, Goudhurst, Cranbrook, Kent, TN17 1LB
Trustees: Mr Roger Collingwood Clark, Mr David Boniface, Mrs Wendy Sarah Kent, Mr Jonathan Mark Fenn, Mr Roger John Stubbs, Peter Askew, Ms Lindsay Roberts, Doctor Robert Hangartner, Mr Robert John Pilbeam, Mr Mark Lewis Hammerton, Mr Nigel Philip Kimber, Mr Andrew Cunningham, Michael Clark, Mr Kevin Sunnucks
Income: £6,945,887 [2016]; £6,772,138 [2015]; £6,588,753 [2014]; £6,467,221 [2013]

Bethphage
Registered: 4 May 1995 Employees: 277 Volunteers: 1
Tel: 01743 272880 Website: bethphage.co.uk
Activities: Disability; economic, community development, employment
Address: 8 Longbow Close, Harlescott Lane, Shrewsbury, Salop, SY1 3GZ
Trustees: Mrs Irena Sobolewska, Ruth Houghton, Ms Carol Mau, Mr Derek Lum, Anthony Aston
Income: £5,587,887 [2017]; £4,565,590 [2016]; £4,192,271 [2015]; £4,205,739 [2014]; £4,106,196 [2013]

Bethshan Sheltered Housing Association
Registered: 12 Sep 1997 Employees: 52 Volunteers: 32
Tel: 01686 610070 Website: bethshan.org.uk
Activities: The advancement of health or saving of lives; accommodation, housing
Address: Bethshan, Heol Treowen, Newtown, Powys, SY16 1JA
Trustees: Mr John David Smith, Mr Leslie Allen, Rev Simon Curgenven, Mr Michael Allport, Mrs Heather Yvonne Wenban, Rev Alan Leslie Hewitt, Roy Tappin, Rev Denise Curgenven, Mr Eddie Coomber
Income: £1,588,727 [2017]; £1,635,427 [2016]; £1,536,156 [2015]; £1,596,071 [2014]; £1,511,016 [2013]

Betsi Cadwaladr University Health Board Charity and Other Related Charities
Registered: 12 Nov 2010 Volunteers: 40
Tel: 01978 727013 Website: awyrlas.org.uk
Activities: Education, training; advancement of health or saving of lives; disability; arts, culture, heritage, science
Address: Ysbyty Gwynedd, Penrhosgarnedd, Bangor, Gwynedd, LL57 2PW
Trustees: Betsi Cadwaladr University Local Health Board
Income: £2,555,000 [2017]; £3,300,000 [2016]; £2,436,000 [2015]; £3,092,000 [2014]; £2,123,000 [2013]

Beva Limited
Registered: 29 Oct 2010 Employees: 11 Volunteers: 120
Tel: 01638 723550 Website: beva.org.uk
Activities: General charitable purposes; education, training; advancement of health or saving of lives; animals
Address: Beva Mulberry House, 31 Market Street, Fordham, Ely, Cambs, CB7 5LQ
Trustees: Mr Roland Owers, Mark Bowen, Mr Jonathan Pycock, Ms Lucy Grieve, Mr James Wood, Ms Victoria Nicholls, Dr Timothy Mair, Ms Renate Weller
Income: £1,738,253 [2016]; £1,821,441 [2015]; £1,719,628 [2014]; £1,677,843 [2013]; £2,204,205 [2012]

The Bevern Trust
Registered: 29 Apr 2004 Employees: 64 Volunteers: 20
Tel: 01273 400752 Website: beverntrust.org
Activities: Education, training; advancement of health or saving of lives; disability; accommodation, housing; economic, community development, employment
Address: The Bevern Trust, Bevern View, The Willows, Barcombe, Lewes, E Sussex, BN8 5FJ
Trustees: Dr Peter Frost, Benetta Adamson, Mrs Christine Patricia Howard, Mrs Sandra Elizabeth Schueler, Steve Brentnall, Mr Nicholas Houston, Dr Hazel Louise Fell
Income: £1,443,823 [2017]; £1,349,902 [2016]; £1,354,020 [2015]; £1,369,264 [2014]; £1,345,198 [2013]

BeyondAutism
Registered: 26 Sep 2000 Employees: 118 Volunteers: 24
Tel: 020 3031 9705 Website: beyondautism.org.uk
Activities: Education, training; disability
Address: BeyondAutism, 48 North Side Wandsworth Common, London, SW18 2SL
Trustees: Karen Sorab, Mrs Joanna Catherine Boait, Mrs Maeve Bromwich, Mrs Rozelyn Bristowe, Mr Patrick Riley, Andrew Lusk, Mr Kenneth Glover
Income: £4,984,553 [2016]; £3,828,247 [2015]; £3,116,276 [2014]; £2,556,561 [2013]; £1,784,720 [2012]

Bhaarat Welfare Trust
Registered: 18 Oct 1999 Employees: 8
Tel: 0116 266 7050 Website: indiaaid.com
Activities: General charitable purposes; education, training; advancement of health or saving of lives; disability; prevention or relief of poverty; overseas aid, famine relief; accommodation, housing; religious activities; animals; environment, conservation, heritage; economic, community development, employment; other charitable purposes
Address: 55 Loughborough Road, Leicester, LE4 5LJ
Trustees: Mrs Diptiben Bharat Mistry, Mrs Anar Bakrania, Miss Jesbir Kaur Uppal, Mr Punitkumar K Madhwani
Income: £1,081,300 [2017]; £1,198,957 [2016]; £1,392,075 [2015]; £1,218,099 [2014]; £1,454,376 [2013]

Biala Synagogue Trust
Registered: 1 Oct 1998 Employees: 1 Volunteers: 1
Tel: 020 8800 5603
Activities: General charitable purposes; education, training; prevention or relief of poverty; religious activities
Address: 14 Gilda Crescent, London, N16 6JP
Trustees: Rabbi Leone Rabinowitz, Mr Moshe Freund, Mrs Miriam Rabinowitz
Income: £3,475,074 [2017]; £2,102,766 [2016]; £1,195,702 [2015]; £419,218 [2014]; £136,781 [2013]

Bible Churchmen's Missionary Trust Limited
Registered: 19 Nov 2015 Employees: 96
Tel: 020 8691 6111 Website: crosslinks.org
Activities: Education, training; religious activities
Address: Crosslinks, 251 Lewisham Way, London, SE4 1XF
Trustees: Mr Nicholas Winther, Miss Alexandra Weston, Rev Leslie Jesudason, Mrs Sue Bennett, Rev Alastair Donaldson, Mrs Alison Miller, Rev Stephen Boon, Rev Neil Barber, Rev Trevor Cleland, Mrs Catherine Banting, Rev John Hamilton, Mr John Hall, Rev Tim Houghton
Income: £3,764,037 [2016]

Bible Reading Fellowship
Registered: 1 Feb 1965 Employees: 37 Volunteers: 154
Tel: 01865 319700 Website: brf.org.uk
Activities: Education, training; religious activities
Address: BRF, 15 The Chambers, Vineyard, Abingdon, Oxon, OX14 3FE
Trustees: Revd Colin John Matthews, Dr Christina Baxter CBE, Mrs Janian Green, Mr Paul Cox, Mrs Jane Melinda Agg, The Right Revd Colin William Fletcher OBE, Mr Alistair Edward Moncur Booth, Mr Peter Lloyd, Rev Sarah Elizabeth Hayes
Income: £2,291,898 [2017]; £2,433,661 [2016]; £1,982,937 [2015]; £2,043,725 [2014]; £1,814,366 [2013]

Bible and Gospel Trust
Registered: 17 Jun 2005 *Employees:* 31 *Volunteers:* 299
Tel: 020 8391 8822 *Website:* christiandoctrineandgospelpublishing.org
Activities: Religious activities
Address: Bible & Gospel Trust, Chelwood House, Cox Lane, Chessington, Surrey, KT9 1DN
Trustees: Mr B G Reiner, Mr W Hathorn, Mr K N Dunlop, Mr G J Stacey, Mr G R Olsson, Mr M J Walker, Mr C V Anderson, Mr S Whiley, Mr D F Druckenmiller
Income: £5,359,921 [2017]; £3,958,529 [2016]; £4,224,349 [2015]; £5,767,341 [2014]; £5,031,045 [2013]

Biblica Europe Ministries Trust
Registered: 29 Oct 1963 *Employees:* 8
Tel: 028 9073 5875 *Website:* biblicaeurope.com
Activities: General charitable purposes; religious activities
Address: The Mount Business Centre Ltd, 2 Woodstock Link, Belfast, BT6 8DD
Trustees: Ms Elaine Duncan, Mr Gareth Wilson Russell, Rev Kenneth Raymond Good, Mrs Lindsey Holley, Mr Nigel Pope, Mr Stephen Cave, Mr Damon Harding
Income: £1,101,330 [2017]; £896,432 [2016]; £1,032,348 [2015]; £996,917 [2014]; £1,043,994 [2013]

Bickley Park School Ltd
Registered: 7 Feb 1963 *Employees:* 74
Tel: 020 8467 2195 *Website:* bickleyparkschool.co.uk
Activities: Education, training
Address: Bickley Park School, 24 Page Heath Lane, Bromley, Kent, BR1 2DS
Trustees: Mr John Sheridan Tiley, Mrs Jane Margaret Carpenter, Bruce Grindlay, Mr Ian William Sturgess, Ms Angela Margaret Drew, Mrs Philippa Claire Almond, Tim Haynes, Mandeep Hansra, Ms Karen Diane Perry, Ms Geraldine Hazel Nuijens
Income: £4,206,098 [2017]; £4,008,226 [2016]; £3,420,317 [2015]; £3,190,366 [2014]; £3,309,672 [2013]

Bid Services
Registered: 23 Feb 1996 *Employees:* 112 *Volunteers:* 79
Tel: 0121 246 6100 *Website:* bid.org.uk
Activities: Education, training; disability; economic, community development, employment
Address: Bid Services, Deaf Cultural Centre, Ladywood Road, Birmingham, B16 8SZ
Trustees: Mr Christopher Richard Daniels, Mr Michael John Reynolds, Ms Sandeep Kaur, Mrs Gail Jacqueline Conway, Mr Mark Hillier, Mr Michael Price
Income: £4,450,234 [2017]; £5,100,065 [2016]; £5,121,712 [2015]; £5,811,752 [2014]; £5,405,995 [2013]

The Big C Appeal Limited
Registered: 6 Feb 1981 *Employees:* 58 *Volunteers:* 330
Tel: 01603 619900 *Website:* big-c.co.uk
Activities: The advancement of health or saving of lives
Address: Centrum, Norwich Research Park, Colney Lane, Norwich, NR4 7UG
Trustees: Mrs Marilyn Martin, Mr David Douglas Moar, Mr Jonathan Andrew Humphreys, Mr Philip Norton, Mr Alan Sidney Stephens, Mr Tristan Mark Laurence, Mr Peter James Lamble, Mrs Carolyn Sexton, Dr Jennifer Wimperis, Mrs Natasha Michelle Rennolds, Mr Edward Hare, Mr Simon Geoffrey Crocker, Ms Rebecca Louise Cooper, Professor Dylan Richard Warrilow Edwards
Income: £2,931,133 [2017]; £2,757,811 [2016]; £2,467,856 [2015]; £2,738,507 [2014]; £1,599,390 [2013]

Big Change Charitable Trust
Registered: 23 Dec 2011 *Employees:* 5
Tel: 020 3126 3971 *Website:* big-change.org
Activities: General charitable purposes; education, training; advancement of health or saving of lives; disability; prevention or relief of poverty; overseas aid, famine relief; amateur sport; economic, community development, employment; recreation
Address: Hanover House, 14 Hanover Square, London, W1S 1HP
Trustees: Mr Alistair McGregor, Mr Philip Nevin, Mr David William Scott, Beatrice York, Miss Holly Branson, Mr Sam Richardson, Mr Richard Perry, Benjamin Hay
Income: £3,087,562 [2016]; £501,621 [2015]; £1,460,636 [2014]; £201,396 [2013]; £555,147 [2012]

The Big Church Day Out
Registered: 11 Feb 2009 *Employees:* 9 *Volunteers:* 350
Tel: 01903 786890 *Website:* bigchurchdayout.com
Activities: General charitable purposes; religious activities; arts, culture, heritage, science; human rights, religious or racial harmony, equality or diversity; recreation
Address: P O Box 3340, Littlehampton, W Sussex, BN16 9FP
Trustees: Mr Michael Andrea, Mr Richard Goring, Leigh Hills
Income: £2,758,850 [2017]; £1,611,325 [2016]; £1,423,391 [2015]; £1,276,355 [2014]; £1,070,795 [2013]

The Big Give Trust
Registered: 23 Jun 2010 *Employees:* 6
Website: thebiggive.org.uk
Activities: General charitable purposes
Address: Dragon Court, 27-29 Macklin Street, London, WC2B 5LX
Trustees: Mr Richard Reed, Mr James Reed, Mrs Alexandra Chapman, Sir Alec Edward Reed CBE, Mr Martin Warnes
Income: £2,294,866 [2017]; £800,857 [2016]; £878,026 [2015]; £870,671 [2014]; £224,564 [2013]

The Big Issue Foundation
Registered: 13 Sep 1995 *Employees:* 20 *Volunteers:* 50
Tel: 020 7526 3298 *Website:* bigissue.org.uk
Activities: General charitable purposes; education, training; prevention or relief of poverty; accommodation, housing
Address: 3rd Floor, The Big Issue Foundation, 113-115 Fonthill Road, London, N4 3HH
Trustees: Jonathan Lachman, Mrs Alison Newman, Ms Giselle Ryan, Mr Mark Dempster, Peter Mills, Mr Patrick Foster, Mrs Parveen Bird, Mr Harry McAdoo, Ms Juliette Charmaine Foster, Mr Steven Robert Shirley
Income: £1,042,513 [2017]; £985,125 [2016]; £1,005,070 [2015]; £953,798 [2014]; £922,040 [2013]

Big Life Centres
Registered: 13 May 1997 *Employees:* 79 *Volunteers:* 218
Website: thebiglifegroup.com
Activities: General charitable purposes; education, training; advancement of health or saving of lives; economic, community development, employment
Address: Big Life Group, Kath Locke Community Centre, 123 Moss Lane East, Manchester, M15 5DD
Trustees: Ms Fay Selvan, Mrs Edna Robinson, Mr Mark James Fitzgibbon
Income: £3,943,485 [2017]; £4,618,261 [2016]; £3,962,795 [2015]; £1,483,902 [2014]; £1,253,684 [2013]

Big Local Trust
Registered: 15 Feb 2012 *Employees:* 13
Tel: 020 3588 0566 *Website:* localtrust.org.uk
Activities: Economic, community development, employment
Address: CAN Mezzanine, 7-14 Great Dover Street, London, SE1 4YR
Trustees: Local Trust
Income: £5,900,792 [2017]; £6,624,933 [2016]; £6,347,282 [2015]; £5,317,400 [2014]; £216,353,701 [2013]

Bikur Cholim Limited
Registered: 30 Mar 2001 *Employees:* 168 *Volunteers:* 328
Tel: 020 8800 7575 *Website:* bikurcholim.co.uk
Activities: The advancement of health or saving of lives; disability; prevention or relief of poverty
Address: Ground Floor, 2A Northfield Road, London, N16 5RN
Trustees: Mr Jacob Moishe Grosskopf, Mr Aron Oberlander, Mr Robert Grussgott, Mr Schloime Rand
Income: £2,444,836 [2017]; £2,116,569 [2016]; £2,066,969 [2015]; £2,414,256 [2014]; £2,254,010 [2013]

Bikur Cholim and Gemiluth Chesed Trust
Registered: 22 Jan 1982
Tel: 0161 792 2520
Activities: General charitable purposes; education, training; prevention or relief of poverty; religious activities
Address: 46 Broom Lane, Salford, M7 4FJ
Trustees: D Halberstadt Esq, Mrs Yocheved Brysh, Mrs Bertha Halberstadt, Mrs Deborah Rhein
Income: £2,176,904 [2017]; £1,756,614 [2016]; £1,975,729 [2015]; £1,493,869 [2014]; £1,485,904 [2013]

Bilton Grange Trust Limited
Registered: 9 Jan 1963 *Employees:* 105
Tel: 01788 810217 *Website:* biltongrange.co.uk
Activities: Education, training
Address: Bilton Grange School, Rugby Road, Dunchurch, Rugby, Warwicks, CV22 6QU
Trustees: Mr Charles Barwell OBE, Mr Peter Waine, David Fawcus, Mrs Jane Green-Armytage, Dr Richard James Maloney, Anup Sodhi, Mrs Faith Matthews, Mr William Assheton, Mr Terence Kyle, Mr Nicholas Sellars, Mrs Marilyn Nicholls, Dr Julie Anne Potter
Income: £5,066,585 [2017]; £9,309,551 [2016]; £5,384,880 [2015]; £4,957,252 [2014]; £4,656,930 [2013]

The Biochemical Society
Registered: 18 Oct 1967 *Employees:* 39
Tel: 020 7685 2427 *Website:* biochemistry.org
Activities: Education, training; advancement of health or saving of lives; arts, culture, heritage, science
Address: Biochemical Society, Charles Darwin House, 12 Roger Street, London, WC1N 2JU
Trustees: Professor Sir Charles Peter Downes, Professor Anne Dell, Professor Nicola Gray, Dr Helen Watson, Dr Malcolm Peter Weir, Dr Joanne Edwards, Dr Dominika Teresa Gruszka, Professor Richard Reece, Professor Robert Beynon, Professor Stefan Roberts, Dr David Pye, Professor Michelle Joanne West, Dr Martin Richard Pool, Professor Frank Sargent
Income: £4,669,000 [2016]; £5,042,534 [2015]; £5,470,551 [2014]; £6,046,695 [2013]; £2,643,486 [2012]

Bioregional Development Group
Registered: 18 Oct 1994 *Employees:* 25
Tel: 020 8404 4880 *Website:* bioregional.com
Activities: Education, training; environment, conservation, heritage
Address: 24 Helios Road, Wallington, Surrey, SM6 7BZ
Trustees: Paul Leonard Wickham, Mr John Hoadly, Kenneth Charles Glendinning, Joanna Claire Walton, Hilary Jennings, Theresa Zoe Arden, Sarah Louise Redshaw, Jonathan Griffin
Income: £1,298,618 [2017]; £1,353,655 [2016]; £1,439,318 [2015]; £1,920,877 [2014]; £1,959,132 [2013]

Bipolar UK Ltd
Registered: 10 Feb 1986 *Employees:* 25 *Volunteers:* 400
Website: bipolaruk.org
Activities: Education, training; advancement of health or saving of lives; disability
Address: Bipolar UK, 11 Belgrave Road, London, SW1V 1RB
Trustees: Mr William Courage, Mrs Hilary Samson-Barry, Ms Tamasin Little, Ms Mohini Morris, Mr Bill Walden-Jones, Ms Maggie Gibbons, Professor Allan Young, Mrs Clare Dolman, Mr Ashley Toft, Mrs Sarita Dent, Mr Jeremy Clark
Income: £1,164,485 [2017]; £773,091 [2016]; £772,224 [2015]; £1,065,081 [2014]; £738,728 [2013]

Birchfield Educational Trust Limited
Registered: 1 Jun 1962 *Employees:* 41 *Volunteers:* 15
Tel: 01902 393003 *Website:* birchfieldschool.co.uk
Activities: Education, training
Address: Regent House, Bath Avenue, Wolverhampton, W Midlands, WV1 4EG
Trustees: Mrs Tracy Katrina Carver, Mrs Lynne Statham, Mr Adam Frankling, Mr Paul Henry Reynolds, Mrs Alison Pass, Mr Martin Humphreys, Mr Stewart Legge, Mr Philip Cotter, Mr Matthew Parkes
Income: £1,498,843 [2016]; £1,467,614 [2015]; £1,536,072 [2014]; £1,501,649 [2013]; £1,461,404 [2012]

The Doreen Bird Foundation
Registered: 12 Feb 1999 *Employees:* 80
Tel: 020 8269 6865 *Website:* birdcollege.co.uk
Activities: Education, training
Address: The Doreen Bird Trust, The Birbeck Centre, Birbeck Road, Sidcup, Kent, DA14 4DE
Trustees: Mrs Shirley Coen, Geoff Pine, Mr David George Hayes, Mr Nitil Patel, Luis De Abreu, Mr Jonathan Paul Emery, Ms Sally Joy Atkins
Income: £4,897,618 [2016]; £4,191,816 [2015]; £3,964,357 [2014]; £3,574,304 [2013]

Birdlife International
Registered: 19 Nov 1994 *Employees:* 196 *Volunteers:* 15
Tel: 01223 277318 *Website:* birdlife.org
Activities: Animals; environment, conservation, heritage; economic, community development, employment
Address: Birdlife International, David Attenborough Building, Pembroke Street, Cambridge, CB2 3QZ
Trustees: Mr Alfred Johannes Maria Wouters, Dr Michael John Clarke, Mr Khaled Zand Irani, Ms Yvonne Altagacia Arias, Dr Shawn Kaihekulani Yamauchi Lum, Mr Idrissa Zeba, Mr Paul Sullivan, Dr Jaqueline Maria Goerk De Carvalho Macedo, Dr Braulio Ferreira De Souza Dias, Dr Philippe Raust, Mr Achilles Brunnel Byaruhanga, Mr Nicholas John Prentice, Professor Sarath Kotagama, Mr Assad Serhal, Miss Nada Tosheva, Mr Imad Al Atrash, Mr Simon Rye, Dr Gergo Denes Halmos
Income: £16,021,184 [2016]; £13,699,935 [2015]; £13,867,219 [2014]; £16,412,142 [2013]; £12,347,155 [2012]

Birkdale School

Registered: 19 Mar 1993 *Employees:* 168
Tel: 0114 266 8400 *Website:* birkdaleschool.org.uk
Activities: Education, training
Address: Birkdale School, 4 Oakholme Road, Sheffield, S10 3DH
Trustees: Mrs Angela Mary Rees BEd MA FRSA, Paul Houghton, Mrs Kathryn Walker MA, Mr Graham Richard Dunn, Mr Andrew McKenzie Smith LLB, Mrs Sarah Catherine Turner, Professor Jeremy Francis Dawson, The Revd Canon Christopher Mark Burke LLB MA, Mr James Adrian Viner MA MBA DipM MCIM, Dr Roger Richardson BSc PhD, Mr James Oliver RICS, Mrs Elizabeth Ann Hetherington, Mr Matthew Oliver Dennis
Income: £8,322,048 [2017]; £8,253,059 [2016]; £8,016,238 [2015]; £7,739,390 [2014]; £7,595,343 [2013]

Birkenhead School Foundation Trust

Registered: 14 Mar 1998
Tel: 0151 652 2435 *Website:* birkenheadschool.co.uk
Activities: Education, training
Address: The Lodge, 58 Beresford Road, Prenton, Birkenhead, Merseyside, CH43 2JD
Trustees: Mrs Lorraine Antonia Carrol Dodd BA Hons Chartered FCSI FRSA, Mr Edward Nicholas Rice FRICS MCIA, Mr M R Feeny LLB, Harry Fitzherbert, Mrs Kirsten Pankhurst, Mr A J Cross, Dr J K Moore FRCA MBA, Mr P R Vicars, Mr M R Cashin
Income: £1,035,233 [2016]; £150,039 [2015]; £112,757 [2014]; £180,573 [2013]; £182,362 [2012]

Birkenhead School

Registered: 14 Aug 2002 *Employees:* 147 *Volunteers:* 30
Tel: 0151 652 2435 *Website:* birkenheadschool.co.uk
Activities: Education, training
Address: 58 Beresford Road, Prenton, Birkenhead, Merseyside, CH43 2JD
Trustees: Mr Alasdair David Coates, Mr A F Watson FCA, Mr I G Boumphrey, Mr E N Rice FRICS, Dr J K Moore FRCA MBA, Mr David Pottinger, Mr W D C Rushworth BA, Mr A J Cross LLB, Mrs L A C Dodd BA Hons FSI FRSA, Mrs Judith Greensmith CBE DL, Mr M R Cashin MA
Income: £8,261,666 [2016]; £7,776,742 [2015]; £7,534,814 [2014]; £7,385,553 [2013]; £7,245,171 [2012]

Birkenhead Young Men's Christian Association

Registered: 15 Oct 1990 *Employees:* 30 *Volunteers:* 14
Tel: 0151 650 1015 *Website:* birkenheadymca.com
Activities: Education, training; advancement of health or saving of lives; prevention or relief of poverty; accommodation, housing; amateur sport; environment, conservation, heritage; economic, community development, employment; human rights, religious or racial harmony, equality or diversity; other charitable purposes
Address: 56 Whetstone Lane, Birkenhead, Merseyside, CH41 2TJ
Trustees: Mr Guiseppe Roberto, Mr Vincent John Hessey, Mr Allan Wayne Batty, Miss Alison Lousie Dean, Mrs Susan Nicholas, Mr Richard Jeremy Leslie, Mr Michael Andrew Huston, Mr Eric David Decorte
Income: £1,447,749 [2017]; £1,236,460 [2016]; £1,222,270 [2015]; £1,215,377 [2014]; £1,258,112 [2013]

Birmingham Association for Mental Health

Registered: 16 Aug 1991 *Employees:* 143 *Volunteers:* 4,487
Tel: 0121 608 8001 *Website:* birminghammind.org
Activities: The advancement of health or saving of lives; accommodation, housing
Address: 17 Graham Street, Birmingham, B1 3JR
Trustees: Revd Canon Frank Longbottom, Baljeet Ghataora, Mr Brendan Geary, Emeritus Professor Ann Davis, Miss Sharon Willis, Ms Diana Markman, Mark Alan Shakespeare, Mr Joseph Robert Piggott, Lorna Scully, Dr Ian McPherson, Mr Kyle Raffo
Income: £5,704,081 [2017]; £5,265,541 [2016]; £5,140,767 [2015]; £5,329,170 [2014]; £5,406,100 [2013]

The Birmingham Botanical and Horticultural Society Limited

Registered: 18 Feb 1963 *Employees:* 22 *Volunteers:* 54
Tel: 0121 454 1860 *Website:* birminghambotanicalgardens.org.uk
Activities: General charitable purposes; education, training; arts, culture, heritage, science; animals; environment, conservation, heritage; recreation
Address: Birmingham Botanical Gardens, Westbourne Road, Edgbaston, Birmingham, B15 3TR
Trustees: Mr John Ronald Taylor, Mr Desmond Bermingham, Mr Martyn Liberson, Mr Amit Sharma, Mr Darren Share, Mr Vic Aspland, Dr Barry Leadbeater, Mr Peter White, Harjinder Singh Kang, Mrs Christine Barve
Income: £1,348,228 [2017]; £1,210,673 [2016]; £1,182,204 [2015]; £1,156,200 [2014]; £1,044,864 [2013]

Birmingham Citizens Advice Bureau Service Ltd

Registered: 15 Dec 1987 *Employees:* 44 *Volunteers:* 50
Tel: 0121 236 5700 *Website:* bcabs.org.uk
Activities: Economic, community development, employment; other charitable purposes
Address: Citizens Advice Bureau, Gazette Buildings, 168 Corporation Street, Birmingham, B4 6TF
Trustees: Mrs Jill Lambert BSc MA FCLIP, Andrew Leigh, Councillor Victoria Elizabeth Quinn, Mr Stephen Andrew Morrison, Mr Paul Robin Southon, Abisola Latunji-Cockbill, Mr Neil Warner, Linden Thomas, Mr Gareth Raymond Moore, Ms Elizabeth Ann Alvey, Sunny Vashisht
Income: £1,678,029 [2017]; £2,054,327 [2016]; £2,123,719 [2015]; £2,288,506 [2014]; £2,454,554 [2013]

Birmingham City Mission

Registered: 27 Nov 1995 *Employees:* 36 *Volunteers:* 400
Tel: 0121 766 6603 *Website:* birminghamcitymission.co.uk
Activities: General charitable purposes; prevention or relief of poverty; religious activities; other charitable purposes
Address: The Clock Tower, 2 Langdon Street, Birmingham, B9 4BP
Trustees: Mr Owen George Nicholds, Mrs Ruth Miriam Mountford, Rev Stuart Conway Carter, Andrew Noble, Mr Anthony Ball MBE ACIS, Mr Simon David Loescher, Mr Roger Chapman, Mr David John Clark
Income: £1,063,675 [2017]; £1,005,966 [2016]; £835,361 [2015]; £1,139,747 [2014]; £803,525 [2013]

Birmingham City Students' Union
Registered: 12 Jul 2011 *Employees:* 58 *Volunteers:* 707
Tel: 0121 331 6806 *Website:* bcusu.com
Activities: General charitable purposes; religious activities; arts, culture, heritage, science; amateur sport; environment, conservation, heritage; economic, community development, employment
Address: The Union Building, Franchise Street, Perry Barr, Birmingham, B42 2SU
Trustees: Mr Michael Andrew Hill, Mr Edward Cook, Lucky Uddin, Mr Luke Christopher Shorrick Luke Shorrick, Mrs Lorraine Westwood, Mr Jaspreet Singh, Vicki Glynn, Natalie Chan
Income: £3,536,748 [2016]; £2,911,899 [2015]; £2,607,933 [2014]; £2,533,072 [2013]

The Birmingham Diocesan Board of Finance
Registered: 13 Sep 1966 *Employees:* 71
Tel: 0121 426 0414 *Website:* cofebirmingham.com
Activities: General charitable purposes; religious activities
Address: 1 Colmore Row, Birmingham, B3 2BJ
Trustees: David Urquhart, Rev Matthew Ivan Rhodes, Mr Philip Nunnerley BA (Hons) FCIB, Rev Anne Hollinghurst, Revd Martin Woodard Stephenson, The Revd Priscilla Audrey White, Rev Madhu Smitha Prasadam, The Revd Nigel Traynor, Mrs Gillian Gould, Rev Catherine Anne Grylls, Rev Christopher Hobbs, Mr Geoffrey Suttleworth, Rev Richard John Walker Hill, The Ven Hayward Osborne, Mr Stephen Fraser, Mr Julian Phillips, Rev Simon Heathfield, Mr Steven Skakel, Mr Michael Hastilow, Mr Trevor Lewis, Rev Claire Turner, Mrs Deirdre Moll, Rev Douglas Machiridza, Ms Tariro Matsveru, Rev Julian Francis
Income: £11,493,000 [2016]; £11,809,000 [2015]; £10,501,000 [2014]; £9,770,000 [2013]; £9,623,000 [2012]

Birmingham Diocesan Trust
Registered: 14 Oct 1966 *Employees:* 134 *Volunteers:* 11,700
Tel: 0121 230 6216 *Website:* birminghamdiocese.org.uk
Activities: Religious activities
Address: 3rd Floor, Treasurer's Dept, Cathedral House, St Chad's Queensway, Birmingham, B4 6EU
Trustees: Rev Jonathan Veasey, Rev Bernard Longley, Rev David McGough, Ms H Bardy, Rev Robert Byrne, Mr C Loughran, Rev William Kenney, Rev Timothy Menezes, David Palmer, Sister T Browne, Mr Matthew Weaver LLB Hons, Birmingham Roman Catholic Diocesan Trustees Registered
Income: £22,009,000 [2016]; £21,921,000 [2015]; £20,282,000 [2014]; £22,476,000 [2013]; £23,623,000 [2012]

The Birmingham Dogs Home
Registered: 25 Jun 1964 *Employees:* 47
Website: birminghamdogshome.org.uk
Activities: General charitable purposes; education, training; animals
Address: 19 Blacksmiths Lane, Hockley Heath, Solihull, W Midlands, B94 6QP
Trustees: Mr Rgh Crofts, Ms Fern Hordern, Mr David Johnson, Mrs CH Taylor, Mr John Wheatley, Mrs Claire Powell, Mr D S Ellis, Mr Richard Temple-Cox CBE, Mr Peter Barnett, Mrs Gill Wilyman, Mr Richard John Venner
Income: £2,624,091 [2016]; £3,320,742 [2015]; £2,314,467 [2014]; £2,292,750 [2013]; £2,007,835 [2012]

Birmingham Education Partnership Limited
Registered: 23 Feb 2016 *Employees:* 9
Tel: 0121 285 0924 *Website:* bep.education
Activities: Education, training
Address: 106 Arden Road, Acocks Green, Birmingham, B27 6AG
Trustees: Mr Timothy John Boyes, Mr Heath Jon Monk, Mrs Patricia Mary Smart, Ms Deborah Susan James, Mr James Frank Howse, Mr Andrew Hodge, Ms Estelle Morris, Mr Nick Scully, Mrs Michelle Anne Gay, Mr Mushtaq Ahmed-Khan
Income: £2,562,250 [2017]

Birmingham Hippodrome Theatre Trust Limited
Registered: 17 Nov 1980 *Employees:* 156 *Volunteers:* 50
Tel: 0121 689 3054 *Website:* birminghamhippodrome.com
Activities: Education, training; arts, culture, heritage, science
Address: 116 Quinton Road, Birmingham, B17 0QA
Trustees: The Bishop of Birmingham, Mr Vidar Paul Hjardeng, Mr Andrew John Hogarth, Mr Martin Frank Richard Guest, Professor David Jonathan Roberts, Ms Imandeep Kaur, Mr Glenn Howells, Mr Mark Smith, Mr Michael Laverty, Mrs Ann Miles Henderson Tonks, Mrs Harjinder Millington
Income: £27,772,000 [2017]; £24,803,000 [2016]; £23,321,000 [2015]; £31,563,000 [2014]; £23,793,000 [2013]

Birmingham Industrial Therapy Association Limited
Registered: 21 Sep 1965 *Employees:* 49 *Volunteers:* 23
Tel: 07921 802165 *Website:* betterpathways.org.uk
Activities: Disability
Address: 17 Leopold Avenue, Birmingham, B20 1ER
Trustees: Mr Peter Townley, Dermot McGovern, Dr William Calthorpe, Mr Michael Smith, Miss Ranjit Nall, Leslie Alexander Latchman, Mr Simon Lawrence, Miss Laura Charles, Dr Jagvir Singh Purewal, Mr Martin John Commander
Income: £1,530,203 [2017]; £1,399,231 [2016]; £1,524,154 [2015]; £1,523,514 [2014]; £1,723,725 [2013]

Birmingham Jewish Community Care
Registered: 12 Dec 1962 *Employees:* 91 *Volunteers:* 12
Tel: 0121 459 3819 *Website:* bhamjcc.co.uk
Activities: General charitable purposes; advancement of health or saving of lives; disability; prevention or relief of poverty; religious activities
Address: Bill Steiner Suite, 1 River Brook Drive, Birmingham, B30 2SH
Trustees: Mr Richard Henry Jaffa, Mrs Karen Georgevic, Mr Martin Brostoff, Mr Barry Henley, Ms Lynne Myers, Mrs Erica Barnett
Income: £2,070,959 [2016]; £1,979,480 [2015]; £2,164,810 [2014]; £2,200,973 [2013]; £2,050,067 [2012]

Birmingham Methodist Circuit

Registered: 23 Nov 2009 *Employees:* 32
Tel: 0121 472 1060 *Website:* birminghammethodistcircuit.org.uk
Activities: Religious activities
Address: Selly Oak Methodist Church, Langleys Road, Birmingham, B29 6HT
Trustees: Mrs Jean Sandra Jenkinson, Mike Fisher, Rev Dr Neil Johnson, Tony Malcolm, Mr Philip Osborn, Rev Donald Sampson, Rev Alison Mary Geary, Mrs Margaret Elizabeth Heath, Sue Mitchell, Ms Christine Graham, Mrs Helen Woodall, Lis Helliar, Mr Clive Sweet, Mrs Judith Wingate, Judith Kirby, Peter Astardjian, Miss Rhyllis Fiona Green, Mrs Jennifer Margaret Fisher, Rev Deborah Humphries, Mrs Sandra Gilbert, Mrs Ermine Kathleen Mitchell, Mrs Diane Mary Webb, Rev Samuel Uwimana, Mr C Yorke, Mrs Margaret Ann Joan Murphy, Rev Stanley Webb, Mr Keith Dennis, Mr Brian Dickens, Lorna Babb, Mr Mark Firmstone, Ms Maureen Knight, Ms Margery Benson, Gill Day, Mr Anthony Richard Cooper, Ms Janice Martin, Ms Joy Wadsworth, Mr Alan Wildbur, Miss Jo Powell, Jackie Farmer, Mr Keith Lovell, Libby Stretton, Mr Malcolm James, Mr Joseph James Herbert, Rev Caroline Hague, Rev Karen Webber, Caroline Gordon, Jane Taylor, Syble Morgan, Tina Brooker, Mrs A Lockyer, Mavis Gordon, Roger O'Hare, Mrs P Wallace, Andrew Morris, Mr Roger Boult, Rev Ken Howcroft, Rev David Meachem, Mr Andrew John Coldrick, Mrs Jenny Cockroft, Julian Bache, Ruth Yorke, Rev Alison Richards, Ms Norma Maynard, Mr Alan Bennett, Mr John Lycett, Mr Ian Crockford, Mr Philip Salmon, Mr Tony Ludlow, Kath Collman, Ms Patricia Stait, Mrs Pauline Astardjian, Rev Vincent Jambawo, Rev Farai Mapamula, Ponita Evans, Mrs Christine Burr, Ms Irene Rees, Mr Richard Burr, Sissy Wong, Mr Peter James Thomas, Mr Ian Smith, Mrs Gillian Judith Rose Wilkins, Malcolm Hamilton, Mr Stuart Aldridge, Mrs Dorothy Fitton, Hazel Abbott, Chris Parker, Graham MacKenzie, Annette Sampson, Mr Peter Woodall, Dr Mosese Dakunivosa, Bill Russell, Mr Michael Charles Fitz Horswell, Mrs Ping Ting Chen, Rev David Alford, Mrs Ann Denise Prentice, Rev Nicholas William Jones, Miss Valerie Elizabeth Combe, Mrs Linda Loo, Mr Richard Laurence Stretton, Maureen Foxall, Mr Raymond Glenn, Mr Oluremi Ayotunde Olatunbosun, Rev Gary Peter Hall, Brian Noake, Caroline Parkes, Jenni Kitson, Mr Peter Bethell, Mr Derek Gordon, Rev Vicki Atkinson, Mr Keith Harley Jenkinson, Deacon Josephine Mary Flute, Ms Jane Lee, Mr Danny Dorsett, Mr James Arthur Brookes, Ms Jean Williams, Ms Sylvia Emery, Mr Neilson Williams, Mr Joe Glasford, Ms Mary Farr, Mrs Janet Thomas, Mr Joe Pogson, Jenny Yeung, Sue Ball, Carol Morgan, Liz Lyons, William Yuen, Ms Gill Holmes, Bev Prater, John Cliff, Mrs Y Swain, Daphne Gray, Lorna Neale, Pat Rowley, Rachel Frank, Mr Peter Wayne, Laura Enonchong, Mr Adam Lloyd, Helen Greaves, Clive Prentice, Christine Tedstone, Ms Jeanne Thompson, Ms Pansie McKenzie, Dr Richard Atkinson, Mr Richard Kirby, Mr Paul Spence, Valerie Edden, Mrs Mal Glenn, Mr Peter Simpkin, Bright Aboagye Obeng, Rev Cleopas Sibanda, Susan Ford, Helen Xue, Mr Mike Cox, Ms Kath Ralph, Susan Bates
Income: £2,453,292 [2016]; £1,411,681 [2015]; £1,440,417 [2014]; £1,201,608 [2013]; £1,709,247 [2012]

Birmingham Multi-Care Support Services Ltd

Registered: 26 Sep 1989 *Employees:* 89
Tel: 0121 472 8220 *Website:* birmingham-multicare.org
Activities: Disability
Address: Birmingham Multi-Care, Prospect Hall, 12 College Walk, Birmingham, B29 6LE
Trustees: Neil Yorke, Mr David Browne, Susan Durrant
Income: £1,025,345 [2017]; £1,097,505 [2016]; £1,083,218 [2015]; £1,045,359 [2014]; £986,087 [2013]

Birmingham Museums Trust

Registered: 25 Apr 2012 *Employees:* 239 *Volunteers:* 900
Tel: 0121 202 2294 *Website:* birminghammuseums.org.uk
Activities: Education, training; arts, culture, heritage, science
Address: Birmingham Museum & Art Gallery, Chamberlain Square, Birmingham, B3 3DH
Trustees: Mr David John Lewis, Mrs Deborah De Haes, Professor Ian Grosvenor, Councillor Randal Brew, Councillor Muhammad Afzal, Miss Jan Teo, Mr Mohammed Rahman
Income: £10,900,000 [2017]; £12,875,000 [2016]; £10,301,000 [2015]; £12,918,000 [2014]; £9,444,000 [2013]

Birmingham Rathbone Society

Registered: 13 Jun 1985 *Employees:* 44 *Volunteers:* 14
Tel: 0121 449 1011 *Website:* rathbone.co.uk
Activities: Education, training; disability; accommodation, housing; economic, community development, employment; other charitable purposes
Address: Birmingham Rathbone Society, Morcom House, Ledsam Street, Birmingham, B16 8DN
Trustees: Dr Alastair Rae, Mr Dhiren Katwa, Ms Dalvinder Atwal, Mr James Larner, Mr Dominic Bradley
Income: £1,664,540 [2017]; £1,635,176 [2016]; £1,585,666 [2015]; £1,736,507 [2014]; £2,426,086 [2013]

Birmingham Repertory Theatre Limited

Registered: 4 Jun 1963 *Employees:* 147 *Volunteers:* 135
Tel: 0121 245 2041 *Website:* birmingham-rep.co.uk
Activities: Education, training; arts, culture, heritage, science
Address: Birmingham Repertory Theatre, Broad Street, Birmingham, B1 2EP
Trustees: Mr Gary William Sambrook, Mr Paul Phedon, Ms Johanne Mica Clifton, Mr Gregory John Lowton, Miss Amerah Saleh, Ms Lorna Laidlaw, Miss Grace Smith, Dr Angela Maxwell, Mrs Narinder Kalir Kooner, Mr Guy Richard Hemington, Professor Lionel Michael Whitby, Professor David Jonathan Shaw, Mrs Elizabeth James
Income: £11,210,000 [2017]; £10,745,000 [2016]; £8,434,467 [2015]; £7,012,093 [2014]; £5,407,644 [2013]

Birmingham Royal Ballet

Registered: 28 Feb 1997 *Employees:* 184 *Volunteers:* 7
Tel: 0121 245 3525 *Website:* brb.org.uk
Activities: Arts, culture, heritage, science
Address: Birmingham Royal Ballet, Thorp Street, Birmingham, B5 4AU
Trustees: Mrs Susan Harrison, Mr Charles Dixon Glanville, Mr Ross MacGibbon, Mr Ian Squires, Ms Deborah Jacqueline Spence, Ms Hemma Patel, Professor Michael Clarke, Dame Jennifer Abramsky, Mr Desmond Hughes, Mr Michael John Elliott, Mr Anthpny Michael Vincent Coombs
Income: £13,827,845 [2017]; £13,976,394 [2016]; £15,429,632 [2015]; £12,812,187 [2014]; £13,408,656 [2013]

The Birmingham Settlement

Registered: 21 Mar 1986 *Employees:* 37 *Volunteers:* 120
Tel: 0121 250 0777 *Website:* birminghamsettlement.org.uk
Activities: General charitable purposes; education, training; advancement of health or saving of lives; prevention or relief of poverty; economic, community development, employment
Address: Birmingham Settlement, 359-361 Witton Road, Aston, Birmingham, B6 6NS
Trustees: Professor Kenneth Maurice Spencer, Councillor John Leslie Barton Cotton, Ms Manisha Sharma, Mr Bruce Michael Thomson, Mrs Christine Carol Doolan, Dr Mervyn Jayakody, Dr Peter Brooks
Income: £1,271,908 [2017]; £1,306,497 [2016]; £1,387,665 [2015]; £1,622,006 [2014]; £1,868,393 [2013]

Birmingham Sport and Physical Activity Trust

Registered: 3 Jan 2014 *Employees:* 15 *Volunteers:* 150
Tel: 0121 296 5190 *Website:* sportbirmingham.org
Activities: General charitable purposes; education, training; advancement of health or saving of lives; disability; prevention or relief of poverty; arts, culture, heritage, science; amateur sport; economic, community development, employment; human rights, religious or racial harmony, equality or diversity; recreation
Address: 11th Floor, Sport Birmingham, Cobalt Square, 83-85 Hagley Road, Birmingham, B16 8QG
Trustees: Mrs Urvasi Naidoo, Mr Matthew Lloyd, Mr Lincoln Everett Moses, Mr Pritesh Vrajlal Pattni, Miss Merran Rose Sewell, Mr Michael David Osborne, Mr James William McLaughlin, Mr Paul John Faulkner, Mr Peter James Llewelyn Griffiths, Mr Stephen Paul Baker, Mr Keith Andrew Fraser, Mrs Jodie Cook
Income: £1,267,833 [2017]; £1,162,783 [2016]; £1,252,086 [2015]

Birmingham Voluntary Service Council

Registered: 28 Feb 1964 *Employees:* 55 *Volunteers:* 6
Tel: 0121 678 8802 *Website:* bvsc.org
Activities: General charitable purposes; education, training; advancement of health or saving of lives; disability; prevention or relief of poverty; arts, culture, heritage, science; environment, conservation, heritage; economic, community development, employment
Address: BVSC, 138 Digbeth, Birmingham, B5 6DR
Trustees: Mohammed Al-Rahim, Mr Guy Hordern, Beryl Brown, Ms Lisa Martinali, Mr Amrick Singh Ubhi, Mr Makhdoom Chishti, Mr Jonathan Driffill, Dr Peter Rookes, Mr Ricky Joseph, Mr Desmond Workman, Ms Gina Ciotaki, Mr Matthew Joseph Forsyth
Income: £4,093,426 [2017]; £4,014,368 [2016]; £3,134,425 [2015]; £1,871,908 [2014]; £1,922,192 [2013]

Birmingham Women's and Children's Hospital Charity

Registered: 12 Mar 2015 *Employees:* 3
Tel: 0300 323 1100 *Website:* bch.org.uk
Activities: The advancement of health or saving of lives
Address: 102 Colmore Row, Birmingham, B3 3AG
Trustees: Dame Christine Braddock, Mr Paul Faulkner, Miss Christina Michalos, Mr Keith Jecks, Mr Neil Edginton, Mr Matt Ferguson, Dr Peter Weller, Prof Jonathan Tritter, Mr Rob Nagra, Mr Jeremy Roper, Mr Tim Atack, Miss Ruth Lester
Income: £6,964,000 [2017]; £6,714,000 [2016]

Birmingham Young Men's Christian Association (Incorporated)

Registered: 19 May 1965 *Employees:* 105 *Volunteers:* 21
Tel: 0121 478 4244 *Website:* birminghamymca.co.uk
Activities: General charitable purposes; education, training; prevention or relief of poverty; accommodation, housing; religious activities; arts, culture, heritage, science; amateur sport; economic, community development, employment; recreation
Address: YMCA, Will Steel House, 109 Grosvenor Road, Aston, Birmingham, B6 7LZ
Trustees: Mr Arkle Leslie Bell, Rev Paul Nash, Mr Paul Harris, Mrs Oenca Rona Fontaine, Ms Diane Donaldson, Mr Michael Hew, Mr Mark Bruckshaw, Mr Samuel David Wyatt, Mr Nigel Reynolds
Income: £4,221,246 [2017]; £3,665,423 [2016]; £3,779,300 [2015]; £3,214,195 [2014]; £3,347,261 [2013]

Birmingham and Solihull Women's Aid

Registered: 12 Feb 1999 *Employees:* 118 *Volunteers:* 50
Tel: 0121 685 8687 *Website:* bswaid.org
Activities: Education, training; prevention or relief of poverty; accommodation, housing
Address: Birmingham Womens Aid, Ryland House, 44-48 Bristol Street, Birmingham, B5 7AA
Trustees: Erica Barnett, Ms Yvonne Palmer, Ms Julia Mary Lowndes, Ms Patricia McCabe, Dr Caroline Bradbury-Jones, Ms Joanne Lynn Williams, Ms Kerry Anne Bolister, Ms Sian McClure, Ms Mary Anne Fox, Ms Carol Herity, Mrs Abda Bibi Khan
Income: £4,809,397 [2017]; £4,799,324 [2016]; £4,630,626 [2015]; £3,579,366 [2014]; £3,541,029 [2013]

Birtenshaw

Registered: 4 Jul 2002 *Employees:* 278 *Volunteers:* 1
Tel: 01204 304230 *Website:* birtenshaw.org.uk
Activities: Education, training; advancement of health or saving of lives; disability; accommodation, housing; amateur sport
Address: Darwen Road, Bromley Cross, Bolton, Lancs, BL7 9AB
Trustees: Mr Glenn Tomison, Mr Ryan Armitage, Mrs Deborah Joanne Sidebottom, Mr James Pilkington, Mr Michael John Walmsley, Ms Kathryn Brown
Income: £8,410,596 [2017]; £6,819,914 [2016]; £5,530,458 [2015]; £3,791,032 [2014]; £3,057,192 [2013]

Bishop Challoner School

Registered: 25 Sep 2013 *Employees:* 73
Activities: Education, training
Address: c/o Bishop Challoner School, 228 Bromley Road, Shortlands, Bromley, Kent, BR2 0BS
Trustees: Mr Philip Cartin, Mrs Margaret Bernadine Brocklehurst, Mr Michael Vernon Cronin, Rev Stephen Gerard Wymer, Mrs Susannah Mary Watchorn, Mr Dean Lake FCA, Ms Susanne Gabriela Owen, Mr Christopher Antony Panas, Mrs Patricia Mary Colling, Mr Philip Walter Huggett, Ms Maria Anne Noone
Income: £3,084,280 [2017]; £3,234,994 [2016]; £3,111,425 [2015]; £2,550,012 [2014]

Bishop Grosseteste University

Registered: 26 Jan 1965 *Employees:* 304
Tel: 01522 583786 *Website:* bishopg.ac.uk
Activities: Education, training
Address: Bishop Grosseteste University, Longdales Road, Lincoln, LN1 3DY
Trustees: Mr Robert Vernon Walder, Mr Stephen Lawrence, Dr Kevin Brown, Dr Tony Hill, Rev Sally Myers, Rev Canon Professor Peter Neil, Air Vice-Marshal Gavin MacKay, Mr Alan Stacey, Rt Rev Dr Nigel Peyton, Rev David Dadswell, Mr Richard Hallsworth, Mrs Angela Crowe, Mr David Babb, Dr Stephen Critchley, Professor David Head, Mr Gareth Hughes, Mrs Jackie Croft, Dr Sacha Mason
Income: £22,113,286 [2017]; £20,435,916 [2016]; £20,102,154 [2015]; £17,232,704 [2014]; £17,688,409 [2013]

The Bishopsgate Foundation

Registered: 5 Mar 2002 *Employees:* 44
Tel: 020 7392 9251 *Website:* bishopsgate.org.uk
Activities: General charitable purposes; education, training; prevention or relief of poverty; arts, culture, heritage, science
Address: Bishopsgate Institute, 230 Bishopsgate, London, EC2M 4QH
Trustees: The Venerable Luke Miller, Ms Kathryn Martindale, Ms Liz Gibbons, Ms Joanne Bradshaw, Mr Christopher Patrick Eason Cook, Dr Aoife Monks, Mr Jonathan Clatworthy
Income: £2,245,508 [2017]; £2,179,724 [2016]; £2,049,478 [2015]; £2,272,761 [2014]; £2,294,787 [2013]

Bishopsgate School Limited

Registered: 14 Feb 1997 *Employees:* 71 *Volunteers:* 30
Website: bishopsgate-school.co.uk
Activities: Education, training
Address: Bishopsgate School, Bishopsgate Road, Englefield Green, Egham, Surrey, TW20 0YJ
Trustees: Mr Nicholas Derrick Jamison, Mr David Andrew Henderson-Williams, Mr Jonathan Carroll, Mrs Vanessa Cresswell, Mr Marc David Fisher, Mr Simon Sydenham, Mrs Barbara Breedon, Mrs Shirley Madeleine Winson, Mrs Linda Susan Buchanan, Mr Timothy Eddis, Mr Elio Leoni-Sceti, Mr Christiian Marriott, Mrs Claire Robertson, Mr Dudley Mills
Income: £4,088,873 [2017]; £4,375,807 [2016]; £4,235,691 [2015]; £4,235,421 [2014]; £4,110,504 [2013]

Bison in the Community

Registered: 11 Oct 2012 *Employees:* 70 *Volunteers:* 40
Tel: 01256 355266
Activities: General charitable purposes; education, training; disability; amateur sport; economic, community development, employment
Address: Basingstoke Ice Rink, West Ham Leisure Park, Worting Road, Basingstoke, Hants, RG22 6PG
Trustees: Mr Darren Green, Mr Heath Rhodes, Mr Tim Fife, Mr Dominic McDermott
Income: £2,122,020 [2016]; £2,027,986 [2015]; £1,958,000 [2014]; £617,355 [2013]

The Biswas Foundation

Registered: 9 Dec 2008
Tel: 0113 268 4162
Activities: Education, training; advancement of health or saving of lives; prevention or relief of poverty; arts, culture, heritage, science; environment, conservation, heritage
Address: 20 Sandmoor Drive, Leeds, LS17 7DG
Trustees: Dr Nalinarsha Biswas, Anu Biswas, Partha Biswas
Income: £2,111,406 [2016]; £1,346,334 [2015]; £6,571,934 [2014]; £624,198 [2013]; £156,277 [2012]

The John Black Charitable Foundation

Registered: 18 Aug 2011 *Employees:* 3
Tel: 020 7734 0424
Activities: The advancement of health or saving of lives; other charitable purposes
Address: 24 Old Burlington Street, London, W1S 3AW
Trustees: Mr Stephen Conway, Mr David Taglight
Income: £16,936,554 [2017]; £19,135,200 [2016]; £10,691,447 [2015]; £14,868,381 [2014]; £16,473,835 [2013]

The Black Country Living Museum Trust

Registered: 10 Oct 1975 *Employees:* 123 *Volunteers:* 242
Tel: 0121 557 9643 *Website:* bclm.com
Activities: Education, training; arts, culture, heritage, science; environment, conservation, heritage; recreation
Address: Black Country Museum, Tipton Road, Dudley, W Midlands, DY1 4SQ
Trustees: Mr Andrew Stewart Fry, Dr Malcolm Dick, Mr Lowell Williams, Mrs Nicola Harding, Mr Nicholas Loveland, Mr Patrick Harley Councillor, Mrs Parminder Dosanjh, Mike Williams, Mr Paul Belford, Fiona Toye, Mrs Christine Perks, Mr Jonathan Badyal, Mr Duncan Peter Bedhall
Income: £6,188,002 [2016]; £6,174,648 [2015]; £4,622,543 [2014]; £4,045,779 [2013]; £4,149,919 [2012]

Black Country Women's Aid

Registered: 28 Jan 1994 *Employees:* 94 *Volunteers:* 5
Tel: 0121 553 0090 *Website:* blackcountrywomensaid.co.uk
Activities: General charitable purposes; education, training; prevention or relief of poverty; accommodation, housing
Address: 21A Landchard House, Victoria Street, West Bromwich, W Midlands, B70 8HY
Trustees: Ms Karen Dowman, Bozena Benton, Mrs Patricia Ann Martin, Mrs Janet Ayliffe, Mrs Melvena Morton, Mrs Iris Boucher
Income: £3,389,196 [2017]; £2,480,692 [2016]; £1,885,560 [2015]; £1,604,450 [2014]; £1,440,874 [2013]

The Black Stork Charity

Registered: 16 May 2011 *Employees:* 6
Tel: 020 7312 6105 *Website:* thednrc.org.uk
Activities: The advancement of health or saving of lives; disability
Address: Grosvenor, 70 Grosvenor Street, London, W1K 3JP
Trustees: Mr Robin Shedden Broadhurst, Jane Sandars, Sir Robert Keith O'Nions, Mr Peter Lawrence Doyle, Ms Katherine Jean Philp, Mr David Richardson
Income: £45,661,664 [2016]; £53,884,314 [2015]; £12,513,659 [2014]; £4,589,495 [2013]; £800,030 [2012]

Blackburn Diocesan Board of Education

Registered: 22 Apr 1993 *Employees:* 26 *Volunteers:* 20
Tel: 01254 503404 *Website:* bdeducation.org.uk
Activities: Education, training; religious activities
Address: Blackburn Diocesan Board of Education, Clayton House, Walker Office Park, Guide, Blackburn, BB1 2QE
Trustees: Mr Jonathan Mark Phair Hewitt, Miss Jo Snape, Revered Philip Venables, Mrs Carolyn Johnson, Mr Tim Cox, Mr Richard Jones, Mrs Ruth Elizabeth Radford, Canon Andrew Holliday, Venerable Mark Ireland, Mrs Natalie Cox, Ven Michael Everitt, Mr Gerald Burrows
Income: £1,282,000 [2016]; £1,483,000 [2015]; £1,264,000 [2014]; £1,284,000 [2013]; £1,361,000 [2012]

The Blackburn Diocesan Board of Finance Limited
Registered: 25 May 1966 *Employees:* 63 *Volunteers:* 104
Tel: 01254 503070 *Website:* blackburn.anglican.org
Activities: Religious activities
Address: Diocesan Offices, Clayton House, Walker Office Park, Guide, Blackburn, BB1 2QE
Trustees: Very Revd Peter Howell-Jones, Ven Michael Everitt, Mr Nicholas Aves, Mr John Dell, Mr Timothy Cox, Rev Peter Lillicrap, Mr Gerald Burrows, Mr David Wilkinson, Mr Robert Collins, Ms Jacqueline Stamper, Rt Revd Philip North, Ven Mark Ireland, The Reverend Canon Doctor Simon Cox, Mr Peter Jelley, Revd Canon Andrew Holliday, Rev Canon Andrew Sage, Prof Richard Geoffrey Carter, Dr Awena Elizabeth Carter, Rev Richard Marshall, Rev Nancy Goodrich, Mr Colin Scott, Rt Revd Julian Henderson, Mr Michael Chew
Income: £12,354,000 [2016]; £12,202,000 [2015]; £11,376,000 [2014]; £11,169,000 [2013]; £10,678,000 [2012]

Blackburn Rovers Community Trust
Registered: 4 Dec 2006 *Employees:* 27 *Volunteers:* 30
Tel: 01254 296136 *Website:* brfctrust.co.uk
Activities: General charitable purposes; education, training; advancement of health or saving of lives; disability; amateur sport; economic, community development, employment
Address: Blackburn Rovers Community Trust, Ewood Park, Blackburn, Lancs, BB2 2BZ
Trustees: Mr George Robert Root, Mr Michael Anthony Cheston, Ms Maureen Bateson, Mr Ian Silvester, Mrs Lynsey Talbot, Mr Philip Staurt Watson
Income: £1,128,992 [2016]; £869,624 [2015]; £721,299 [2014]; £638,981 [2013]; £660,351 [2012]

Blackburn Youth Zone
Registered: 13 May 2010 *Employees:* 69 *Volunteers:* 45
Tel: 01254 292000 *Website:* blackburnyz.org
Activities: Education, training; disability; arts, culture, heritage, science; amateur sport; economic, community development, employment
Address: Blackburn Youth Zone, Jubilee Street, Blackburn, BB1 1EP
Trustees: Mr Ilyas Munshi, Adam Bromley, Mr David John Gorton, Right Honourable John Whitaker Straw, Mr Andrew Harold Graham, Mrs Lynn Jepson, Ms Kathryn Ann Morley
Income: £1,254,341 [2017]; £1,174,400 [2016]; £1,364,449 [2015]; £1,355,745 [2014]; £1,129,111 [2013]

Blackburne House
Registered: 15 Apr 1992 *Employees:* 54 *Volunteers:* 4
Tel: 0151 709 4356 *Website:* blackburnehouse.co.uk
Activities: General charitable purposes; education, training; other charitable purposes
Address: Blackburne House Group, Blackburne Place, Liverpool, L8 7PE
Trustees: Ms Elizabeth Cross, Ms Annette Hennessy, Ms Maureen Kathleen Mellor, Ms Therese Patten, Ms Sally-Anne Watkiss, Ms Lorna Rogers
Income: £1,513,151 [2017]; £958,635 [2016]; £956,082 [2015]; £908,909 [2014]; £1,258,132 [2013]

Blackfriars Settlement
Registered: 22 Sep 1962 *Employees:* 40 *Volunteers:* 300
Tel: 020 7269 6334 *Website:* blackfriars-settlement.org.uk
Activities: General charitable purposes; education, training; advancement of health or saving of lives; disability; prevention or relief of poverty; economic, community development, employment
Address: Blackfriars Settlement, 1 Rushworth Street, London, SE1 0RB
Trustees: Mr Brian Chandler, Mr Andrew Michael Peck, Ms Alexine Horsup, Miss Emma Victoria Wyatt, Dr Heather Heathfield, Ms Beatriz Montoya Blanco, Baroness Wheeler of Blackfriars, Ms Kim Duong, Mrs Frances Clare Bates, Mr Graham Keith Collins, Ms Jessica Northend, Ms Nadine Cartner
Income: £1,091,216 [2017]; £1,307,754 [2016]; £1,268,726 [2015]; £990,180 [2014]; £976,265 [2013]

The Blackheath Conservatoire of Music and The Arts Ltd
Registered: 27 Nov 1998 *Employees:* 8 *Volunteers:* 1
Tel: 020 8852 0234 *Website:* conservatoire.org.uk
Activities: Education, training; arts, culture, heritage, science
Address: Blackheath Conservatoire of Music & The Arts, 19-21 Lee Road, London, SE3 9RQ
Trustees: Ms Clare Cornwell, Ms Jane Burton, Ms Theano Sakkas, Mr Michael John O'Byrne, Ms Nichole Herbert
Income: £1,124,738 [2016]; £985,720 [2015]; £881,832 [2014]; £972,058 [2013]; £833,388 [2012]

The Blackheath Halls
Registered: 22 Dec 1983 *Employees:* 13
Website: blackheathhalls.com
Activities: General charitable purposes; education, training; arts, culture, heritage, science; environment, conservation, heritage
Address: Trinity Laban, King Charles Court, Old Royal Naval College, King William Walk, London, SE10 9JF
Trustees: Prof Anthony Bowne, Ms Francesca Robinson, Mr Peter Hearn, Mr Jonathan Peel, Dame Joan Ruddock, Barry Douglas
Income: £1,254,120 [2017]; £967,034 [2016]; £787,363 [2015]; £888,324 [2014]; £990,050 [2013]

Blackheath Preparatory School
Registered: 22 Nov 1966 *Employees:* 90
Tel: 020 8858 0692 *Website:* blackheathprepschool.com
Activities: Education, training
Address: Blackheath Preparatory School, 4 St Germans Place, Blackheath, London, SE3 0NJ
Trustees: Mrs Helen Christine Wisher, Dr Colin Niven, Gillian Ducharme, Mrs Claire Michele Wright, Mr Hugh George Stallard, Ms Sarah Jane Phipps, Simon Parton
Income: £4,722,974 [2017]; £4,462,579 [2016]; £4,312,633 [2015]; £4,087,414 [2014]; £3,846,527 [2013]

Blackpool Carers Centre Limited
Registered: 5 Jun 2006 *Employees:* 30 *Volunteers:* 145
Tel: 01253 393748 *Website:* blackpoolcarers.org
Activities: General charitable purposes; education, training; advancement of health or saving of lives; disability; prevention or relief of poverty; other charitable purposes
Address: Beaverbrooks House, 147 Newton Drive, Blackpool, Lancs, FY3 8LZ
Trustees: Mr James Carney, Miss Barbara Cummings, Miss Alison Gilmore, Mrs Sarah Lambert, Mrs Linda Endicott, Mr Anthony Ward, Mr Paul Jebb
Income: £1,400,711 [2017]; £865,135 [2016]; £731,257 [2015]; £619,350 [2014]; £576,704 [2013]

Blackpool FC Community Trust
Registered: 24 Feb 2009 *Employees:* 39 *Volunteers:* 35
Tel: 01253 404204 *Website:* blackpoolfccommunitytrust.co.uk
Activities: Education, training; disability; amateur sport; economic, community development, employment
Address: 509 Lytham Road, Blackpool, Lancs, FY4 1TE
Trustees: Ms Wendy Swift, Mrs Michaela Redfearn, Mr Christopher Lickiss, Rev Michael Ward, Mrs Paula Davies
Income: £1,002,999 [2016]; £707,398 [2015]; £532,891 [2014]; £502,243 [2013]; £621,357 [2012]

The Blackpool Fylde and Wyre Society for the Blind
Registered: 20 Mar 1992 *Employees:* 46 *Volunteers:* 238
Tel: 01253 362688 *Website:* nvision-nw.co.uk
Activities: Disability; accommodation, housing; other charitable purposes
Address: Princess Alexandra Home for the Blind, Bosworth Place, Blackpool, Lancs, FY4 1SH
Trustees: Mrs Joy Killip, Mrs Margaret Gough, Mrs Pat Lord, Miss Michelle Stevenson, Mr Joseph Nathan Bannister, Mr Neville Preston, Mr Clive Hirst, Mrs Barbara Whalley, Mr Alistair Humpreys, Mrs Beverley Jayne Garrity
Income: £1,402,017 [2017]; £1,307,738 [2016]; £1,366,857 [2015]; £1,715,773 [2014]; £1,354,164 [2013]

Blackpool Grand Theatre (Arts and Entertainments) Limited
Registered: 18 Jun 1993 *Employees:* 49
Tel: 01253 743300 *Website:* blackpoolgrand.co.uk
Activities: Education, training; arts, culture, heritage, science
Address: West Lodge, The Downs, Poulton-le-Fylde, Lancs, FY6 7EG
Trustees: Mr Anthony Paul Stone, Mr Anthony Depledge, Mr Michael Phillip Dickson, Susan M K Walker, Mr Glenn Bryan Mascord, Mr Philip Welsh, Ms Karen Ann Ross, Mr Stephen Crocker, Mr David William Parry, Mr Lindsay Campbell
Income: £3,451,685 [2017]; £3,947,881 [2016]; £2,980,148 [2015]; £2,963,943 [2014]; £2,813,651 [2013]

The Blagrave Trust
Registered: 19 Oct 2015 *Employees:* 2
Tel: 020 7399 0370 *Website:* blagravetrust.org
Activities: General charitable purposes
Address: The Blagrave Trust, c/o Rathbone Trust Company Ltd, 8 Finsbury Circus, London, EC2M 7AZ
Trustees: Julian Whately, Diana Leat, Ms Clare Cannock, Linda Epstein, Timothy Jackson-Stops, Sir Paul Neave Bt, Tasneem Alom
Income: £36,812,995 [2016]

The Tony Blair Faith Foundation
Registered: 18 Mar 2008 *Employees:* 39
Tel: 020 7242 2022 *Website:* tonyblairfaithfoundation.org
Activities: General charitable purposes; education, training
Address: Farrer & Co, 65-66 Lincoln's Inn Fields, London, WC2A 3LH
Trustees: Mr J Sinclair, Sir Michael Barber
Income: £4,440,000 [2017]; £4,067,000 [2015]; £2,971,000 [2014]; £1,618,000 [2013]; £1,639,000 [2012]

The Cherie Blair Foundation for Women
Registered: 8 Sep 2008 *Employees:* 28 *Volunteers:* 9
Tel: 020 7724 3109 *Website:* cherieblairfoundation.org
Activities: Education, training; prevention or relief of poverty; economic, community development, employment; other charitable purposes
Address: P O Box 60519, London, W2 7JU
Trustees: Mr Christopher John Lane, Lesley Robinson, Ms Jessica Learmond-Criqui, Mr Rajesh Agrawal
Income: £2,759,370 [2016]; £3,302,460 [2015]; £3,017,789 [2014]; £2,171,590 [2013]; £1,818,151 [2012]

The Tony Blair Governance Initiative
Registered: 3 Nov 2009 *Employees:* 60
Website: africagovernance.org
Activities: Education, training; advancement of health or saving of lives; prevention or relief of poverty; economic, community development, employment
Address: 16 Minerva Lodge, Sweyn Place, London, SE3 0EZ
Trustees: Mr Stephen Richard Lewin, Rt Hon Mp Hilary Armstrong, Elizabeth Ann Lloyd, 'tunde Olanrewaju
Income: £6,712,000 [2017]; £5,685,000 [2015]; £5,362,000 [2014]; £4,793,000 [2013]; £3,486,000 [2012]

William Blake House Northants
Registered: 23 Nov 2001 *Employees:* 29 *Volunteers:* 9
Tel: 01327 860906 *Website:* williamblakehouse.org
Activities: Education, training; advancement of health or saving of lives; disability; accommodation, housing
Address: 2 High Street, Blakesley, Towcester, Northants, NN12 8RE
Trustees: Major David Michael Crouch, Mrs Christine Rose Scott, Ms Puffin Pocock, Mrs Philippa Jenner
Income: £1,662,000 [2017]; £1,404,202 [2016]; £1,391,909 [2015]; £1,352,208 [2014]; £1,254,802 [2013]

Bleakholt Animal Sanctuary
Registered: 20 Jul 2005 *Employees:* 40 *Volunteers:* 36
Tel: 01706 822577 *Website:* bleakholt.org
Activities: Animals
Address: Bleakholt Animal Sanctuary, Bleakholt Farm, Bury Old Road, Ramsbottom, Bury, Lancs, BL0 0RX
Trustees: Mrs Denise Corrigan, Dr Muriel Bird, Ms Victoria Appleton, Mrs Jill Caldwell, Mrs Dorothy Walsh, Andrea Wiggans, Miss Julie Mahon
Income: £1,033,235 [2016]; £1,680,841 [2015]; £1,314,046 [2014]; £1,204,420 [2013]; £693,685 [2012]

Blenheim CDP
Registered: 18 Mar 1986 *Employees:* 240 *Volunteers:* 40
Tel: 020 7582 2200 *Website:* blenheimcdp.org.uk
Activities: Education, training; advancement of health or saving of lives; prevention or relief of poverty; economic, community development, employment
Address: Blenheim CDP, Central Office, Cantilever Court, 212 Wandsworth Road, London, SW8 2JU
Trustees: Mr Eric John Feltin, Mr Adam Shutkever, Mr Alex Boyt, Mr David Rice, Mr Tom Breen, Ms Gillian Susan Budd
Income: £9,202,481 [2017]; £10,153,677 [2016]; £9,738,569 [2015]; £10,416,644 [2014]; £10,603,345 [2013]

Blenheim Palace Heritage Foundation
Registered: 22 Mar 2016 *Employees:* 322
Tel: 01993 810500
Activities: Arts, culture, heritage, science; environment, conservation, heritage
Address: Estate Office, Blenheim Palace Grounds, Woodstock, Oxon, OX20 1PS
Trustees: Mr Alexander Pepys Muir, Lord Edward Spencer-Churchill, Mr Christopher Jonathan James Groves, Dominic Hare
Income: £8,535,684 [2017]

Bletchley Park Trust Limited
Registered: 10 Jul 1992 *Employees:* 93 *Volunteers:* 285
Tel: 01908 640404 *Website:* bletchleypark.org.uk
Activities: Education, training; arts, culture, heritage, science; environment, conservation, heritage
Address: Bletchley Park, Sherwood Drive, Bletchley, Milton Keynes, Bucks, MK3 6EB
Trustees: Ms Elizabeth Bushell, Mr Oliver Brookshaw, Mrs Hilary McGowan, Mr Michael Smith, Mr Alan Whelan, Mr Jonathan Martin Card, Mr Charles MacDonald, Professor Elisabeth Kabler, Sir Roger Carr, Mr John Brookes, Sir John Scarlett, Mr Duncan Philips, Sir John Dermot Turing, Mr Michael Sarna, Professor Andrew Martin, Mr Adam Singer, Miss Natalie Black, Mr Robert Hannigan
Income: £6,849,138 [2016]; £6,191,461 [2015]; £7,044,328 [2014]; £6,727,191 [2013]; £3,837,438 [2012]

Blind Children UK
Registered: 4 Jan 1996
Tel: 0118 983 8772 *Website:* blindchildrenuk.org
Activities: Disability
Address: Guide Dogs for the Blind Association, Hillfields, Reading Road, Burghfield Common, Reading, Berks, RG7 3YG
Trustees: Ms Clare Elizabeth Black, Dr Michael Nussbaum
Income: £4,908,000 [2016]; £11,220,000 [2015]; £1,924,000 [2014]; £787,000 [2013]; £1,053,669 [2012]

Blind Veterans UK
Registered: 16 Nov 1962 *Employees:* 446 *Volunteers:* 600
Tel: 020 7616 7919 *Website:* blindveterans.org.uk
Activities: Education, training; advancement of health or saving of lives; disability; accommodation, housing; amateur sport
Address: Blind Veterans UK, 12-14 Harcourt Street, London, W1H 4HD
Trustees: David Turner, Mr Kerry Levins, Mr Paul Palmer, Mr Ty Platten, James Leavesley, Mr Barry Coupe, Ms Liz Hunt, Mr Minoo Sahni Court, Mr David Buckley, Guy Davies, Air Vice Marshall Paul Luker CB OBE AFC DL, Ms Sarah-Lucie Watson, Rear Admiral Malcom Cree CBE MA, Mr Colin Williamson, Lieutenant General M W Poffley OBE, Ms Nicola Pulford, Mr Neeleah Heredia
Income: £28,613,000 [2017]; £27,820,000 [2016]; £27,167,000 [2015]; £26,753,000 [2014]; £24,202,000 [2013]

Bliss -The National Charity for The Newborn
Registered: 20 May 1991 *Employees:* 46 *Volunteers:* 182
Tel: 020 7378 4750 *Website:* bliss.org.uk
Activities: The advancement of health or saving of lives
Address: 212 Boundaries Road, London, SW12 8HF
Trustees: Ms Sarah Mullen, Mrs Elizabeth Gray, Verity Baldry, Mr Martyn Boyd, Ms Helen Louise Manley ACA, Mr John Robert Calder BSc, Miss Amy Eleanor Overend, Ms Sarah Woolnough, Philippa Sanderson, Ms Caroline Farrar, Mr Alan Edwards, Mr Jason Dominic Simon Parker ACA, Ms Mala Shah-Coulon
Income: £2,140,953 [2017]; £2,661,112 [2016]; £2,968,402 [2015]; £2,805,260 [2014]; £2,436,231 [2013]

Bloodwise
Registered: 27 Nov 1962 *Employees:* 98 *Volunteers:* 2,000
Tel: 020 7504 2200 *Website:* bloodwise.org.uk
Activities: The advancement of health or saving of lives
Address: Bloodwise, 39-40 Eagle Street, London, WC1R 4TH
Trustees: Professor Frances Balkwill, Mr John Reeve, Mr Jeremy Bird, Mr Michael Prescott, Ms Jane Margaret Stevens, Dr Sonali Thakrar, Mrs Maria Clarke, Mr Charles Metcalfe, Mr Simon Guild, Mr Glen Lucken, Mr Steven Prescott-Jones, Mrs Julia Whittaker
Income: £15,971,000 [2017]; £16,850,000 [2016]; £20,588,000 [2015]; £21,656,000 [2014]; £20,353,000 [2013]

The Bloom Foundation
Registered: 17 Mar 2016 *Employees:* 1
Activities: General charitable purposes
Address: The Bloom Foundation, 34-36 Jamestown Road, London, NW1 7BY
Trustees: Mrs Linda Bloom, Mrs Marcelle Lester, Mr Anthony Bloom, Mr Marc Sugarman, Mr Adam Stephen Franks, Mr Philip Jonathan Saunders
Income: £6,321,853 [2017]

Bloxham School Limited
Registered: 12 Jul 1999 *Employees:* 235
Tel: 01295 724302 *Website:* bloxhamschool.com
Activities: Education, training
Address: Bloxham School, Banbury Road, Bloxham, Banbury, Oxon, OX15 4PE
Trustees: Fiona Turner, Miles Hedges, Rob Loades, John Spratt, Mr Simon Wood, Mr Andrew John Nott, Mrs Hermione Harper, Martin Ward, Mr Ian Davenport, Geraint Jones, Charles Mann, Lis Lewis-Jones, Ms Carol Shaw, Mr Paul Clayson, Mrs Miranda E Hopkins
Income: £9,603,563 [2016]; £9,387,235 [2015]; £9,571,079 [2014]; £9,777,250 [2013]; £9,189,059 [2012]

The Blue Coat School Birmingham Limited
Registered: 31 May 2013 *Employees:* 143
Website: thebluecoatschool.com
Activities: Education, training
Address: 43 Georgian Way, Kidderminster, Worcs, DY10 2AQ
Trustees: Very Rev Matt Thompson, Mr William Guy Shubra Hordern, Mr Martin John Cotter, Mr Martin Hamilton Dyke, Mr Stephen Michael Raine, Mr Mike Abraham, Mrs Anita Poole, Mr Bernard Hugh Singleton, Dr Elizabeth Napier Rees, Mrs Karan Diedre Gilmore, Ms Michele Kitto, Rev Nick Tucker, Mrs Emma Cook, Mrs Persis Thomas
Income: £6,274,034 [2016]; £6,251,355 [2015]; £5,932,025 [2014]

Blue Cross
Registered: 8 Feb 1965 *Employees:* 637 *Volunteers:* 4,299
Tel: 0300 777 1897 *Website:* bluecross.org.uk
Activities: Education, training; animals
Address: Blue Cross, Shilton Road, Burford, Oxon, OX18 4PF
Trustees: Mr Tim Hutton, The Hon Henrietta Roper-Curzon, Ms Victoria Clare Hemming, Colonel Neil Smith, Mr Jeremy Ross Stewart, Catherine Ann Brown, Ms Nico Lutkins, Mr Zair Berry FCA, Ms Amy Clarke, Mr Timothy Henry Ralph Porter, Mr Stephen Paul Swift, Ms Deirdre Walker, Mr Clive Everest
Income: £35,294,000 [2016]; £34,158,000 [2015]; £33,368,000 [2014]; £29,493,000 [2013]; £30,979,000 [2012]

Blue Marine Foundation
Registered: 30 Jul 2010 *Employees:* 7
Website: bluemarinefoundation.com
Activities: Education, training; animals; environment, conservation, heritage; economic, community development, employment
Address: Somerset House, Strand, London, WC2R 1LA
Trustees: George Duffield, Chris Gorell Barnes, Dr Arlo Brady, Mr Tom Appleby, Mrs Sofia Blount, Callum Roberts, Mr Mark Rose, Lord John Deben, Mr Craig Davies
Income: £2,024,158 [2017]; £2,140,344 [2016]; £1,957,378 [2015]; £1,869,843 [2014]; £1,814,822 [2013]

Blue Sky Development and Regeneration
Registered: 14 Mar 2007 *Employees:* 15
Tel: 01895 839844 *Website:* blueskydevelopment.co.uk
Activities: Education, training
Address: Colne Valley Park Centre, Denham Court Drive, Denham, Uxbridge, Middlesex, UB9 5PG
Trustees: Ben Houghton, Mr David Riddle, Miss Merlin Gaston, Mike Trace, Mr Ron Sheldon, Andrew Wylie, David Bernstein, Buzz Hornett
Income: £1,950,061 [2017]; £2,009,996 [2016]; £2,378,958 [2015]; £1,648,040 [2014]; £1,681,994 [2013]

Blue Ventures Conservation
Registered: 7 Aug 2003 *Employees:* 130
Website: blueventures.org
Activities: Education, training; advancement of health or saving of lives; prevention or relief of poverty; animals; environment, conservation, heritage; economic, community development, employment
Address: Blue Ventures, Omnibus Business Centre, 39-41 North Road, London, N7 9DP
Trustees: Mr Oliver Gregson, Mr Abbas Hasan, Ms Anna Sorrel Kydd, Mr Tristram Lewis, Miss Frances Humber, Mr Robert Michael MacLay, Mr Jonathan Katz, Mr John Morrison Wareham, Dr Dominic Nelson Hoar, Mr Gavin Starks, Mrs Vola Parker, Mrs Mairi Fairley
Income: £3,006,982 [2017]; £2,237,554 [2016]; £1,900,114 [2015]; £933,591 [2014]; £923,285 [2013]

The Bluebell Railway Trust
Registered: 30 Aug 1985 *Volunteers:* 63
Tel: 01825 720800 *Website:* bluebell-railway.co.uk
Activities: Education, training; arts, culture, heritage, science; environment, conservation, heritage
Address: Bluebell Railway Ltd, Sheffield Park Station, Sheffield Park, Uckfield, E Sussex, TN22 3QL
Trustees: Mr Lionel Joseph Bee, Mr Roy John Watts, Mr Vernon Frederick Neil Blackburn, Mr Terrence Cyril Cole, Mr William James Brophy
Income: £1,229,429 [2016]; £1,469,989 [2015]; £1,081,751 [2014]; £505,896 [2013]; £1,489,506 [2012]

Bluebell Wood Children's Hospice
Registered: 10 Aug 1999 *Employees:* 164 *Volunteers:* 646
Tel: 01909 517360 *Website:* bluebellwood.org
Activities: Education, training; advancement of health or saving of lives; disability
Address: Bluebell Wood Childrens Hospice, Cramfit Road, North Anston, Sheffield, S25 4AJ
Trustees: Mrs Elizabeth Anne Fowlie, Mr Jon Lister, Mrs Patricia Seymour, Mr Richard Christopher Worth, Mrs Rosemary Downs, Mr Keith Metcalf, Mr Scott Paul Green, Ms Bethan Atkinson
Income: £4,102,000 [2017]; £5,146,000 [2016]; £4,061,000 [2015]; £3,907,000 [2014]; £3,596,492 [2013]

Bluecoat Sports
Registered: 26 Feb 2003 *Employees:* 36
Tel: 01403 246631 *Website:* bluecoatsports.co.uk
Activities: Education, training; advancement of health or saving of lives; amateur sport
Address: The Counting House, Christs Hospital, Horsham, W Sussex, RH13 0YP
Trustees: Mr Roger Paul Eades, Mr James MacLean, Mr Keith Willder MBE, Mr Patrick Dearsley
Income: £1,919,692 [2017]; £1,807,684 [2016]; £1,780,211 [2015]; £1,534,929 [2014]; £1,385,691 [2013]

The Bluecoat
Registered: 24 Nov 1988 *Employees:* 61 *Volunteers:* 105
Tel: 0151 702 5324 *Website:* thebluecoat.org.uk
Activities: Arts, culture, heritage, science
Address: Bluecoat, School Lane, Liverpool, L1 3BX
Trustees: Dr Emmanuel Matan, Ms Amy De Joia, Mr Robert Corbett, Kelly Salvoni, Mr Peter Mearns, Mr Cyril Powell, Mr Daniel Stinson, Edward Berg
Income: £1,946,743 [2017]; £1,724,910 [2016]; £1,716,522 [2015]; £1,737,452 [2014]; £1,640,153 [2013]

Blundell's School
Registered: 26 Jun 2000 *Employees:* 247 *Volunteers:* 4
Website: blundells.org
Activities: Education, training
Address: 4 Fairway, Tiverton, Devon, EX16 4NF
Trustees: Mr Nigel Arnold, Mr Nicholas John Cryer, Mr Peter Johnson MA FRSA, Mr James Macpherson, Rev Richard Leonard Maudsley, Mr Nigel Hall, Ian Robert George Thomas, Dr Sarah Ansell, Rt Rev Nicholas Howard Paul McKinnel, Mr Cedric Marsden Clapp, Mrs Jessica Mary Anne Mannix, Mr Barnabas John Hurst-Bannister, Dr Mark Elliott Wood, Martha MacNeice, Mr Randall Thane
Income: £13,695,000 [2016]; £12,844,000 [2015]; £12,169,000 [2014]; £11,350,000 [2013]; £11,477,000 [2012]

Blyth Star Enterprises Limited
Registered: 30 Oct 1987 *Employees:* 53 *Volunteers:* 15
Tel: 01670 338500 *Website:* blythstar.org.uk
Activities: Education, training; advancement of health or saving of lives; disability; accommodation, housing
Address: The Old Chandlery, 30 Ridley Street, Blyth, Northumberland, NE24 3AG
Trustees: Mr Stephen Gibson, Mrs Terri Rendell, Mrs Sharon Herron, Mr Tim Chrisp, Mr Bill McHugh
Income: £1,521,003 [2017]; £1,364,214 [2016]; £1,361,129 [2015]; £1,116,889 [2014]; £1,115,399 [2013]

Blyth Valley Disabled Forum Limited
Registered: 6 Aug 1999 *Employees:* 68 *Volunteers:* 18
Tel: 01670 360927 *Website:* bvdfhomecare.co.uk
Activities: General charitable purposes; disability; amateur sport
Address: Blyth Valley Disabled Forum Ltd, 20 Stanley Street, Blyth, Northumberland, NE24 2BU
Trustees: Mr John Gunn, Mrs Edna Charlton, Mr David Hopper, Mr John Clough, Mr Simpson Crawford, Mrs Kathleen Wilson, Mr A Hall, Mr Mike McAllister
Income: £1,337,617 [2017]; £1,384,072 [2016]; £1,377,069 [2015]; £1,321,448 [2014]; £1,335,052 [2013]

Bnos Yisroel School Manchester
Registered: 30 Jun 2011 *Employees:* 100 *Volunteers:* 25
Tel: 0161 792 3896
Activities: Education, training; religious activities
Address: Bnos Yisroel School, Leicester Road, Salford, M7 4DA
Trustees: Mr Adler, Mr Abittan
Income: £1,736,866 [2016]; £1,629,759 [2015]; £1,456,831 [2014];
£1,292,978 [2013]; £1,305,985 [2012]

Bnos Zion D'Bobov Limited
Registered: 24 May 2011 *Employees:* 55 *Volunteers:* 5
Tel: 020 8802 9947
Activities: Education, training
Address: 62 Rostrevor Avenue, London, N15 6LP
Trustees: Mr Moshe Brinner, Mr Zvi Elimelech Vorst, Mr Chaskel
Lipschitz
Income: £1,507,074 [2017]; £812,563 [2016]; £797,140 [2015];
£287,407 [2014]; £204,218 [2013]

Boarbank Hall Convalescent Home, Grange-Over-Sands
Registered: 2 Jun 1964 *Employees:* 71 *Volunteers:* 14
Tel: 015395 32288 *Website:* boarbankhall.org.uk
Activities: The advancement of health or saving of lives; religious
activities
Address: Convent of Our Lady of Lourdes, Allithwaite,
Grange-Over-Sands, Cumbria, LA11 7NH
Trustees: Sister Elizabeth Mary, Sister Eileen Anne Pollard
Income: £1,523,011 [2017]; £1,620,207 [2016]; £1,389,567 [2015];
£1,370,094 [2014]; £1,228,108 [2013]

Board of Deputies Charitable Foundation
Registered: 18 Sep 1996 *Employees:* 13
Tel: 020 7543 5400 *Website:* bod.org.uk
Activities: General charitable purposes; education, training;
prevention or relief of poverty; religious activities; environment,
conservation, heritage; economic, community development,
employment
Address: Board of Deputies, 1 Torriano Mews, London, NW5 2RZ
Trustees: Mr Jonathan Arkush, Dr Sheila Gewolb, Ms Marie Van
Der Zyl, Mr Stuart MacDonald, Mr Richard Verber
Income: £1,235,183 [2016]; £1,166,995 [2015]; £4,820,154 [2014];
£1,167,273 [2013]; £1,172,831 [2012]

Bobath Childrens Therapy Centre Wales
Registered: 3 Apr 1992 *Employees:* 41 *Volunteers:* 130
Tel: 029 2052 2600 *Website:* bobathwales.org
Activities: The advancement of health or saving of lives; disability
Address: 19 Park Road, Whitchurch, Cardiff, CF14 7BP
Trustees: Mrs Caroline Cooksley, Mr Frank Holmes, Mr Steve
Jones, Mr Ieuan Coombes, Mrs Marie Wood, Dr Cathy White,
Mr Paul Harrison Lubas, Ms Christine Barber, Mr Martin Gush
Income: £1,232,075 [2017]; £1,226,354 [2016]; £1,262,088 [2015];
£1,213,191 [2014]; £1,045,325 [2013]

**Bochasanwasi Shri Akshar Purushottam Swaminarayan
Sanstha**
Registered: 26 Jul 2011 *Employees:* 25 *Volunteers:* 1,000
Tel: 020 8965 2651 *Website:* londonmandir.baps.org
Activities: Religious activities
Address: Baps Shri Swaminarayan Mandir,
105-119 Brentfield Road, London, NW10 8LD
Trustees: Mr Dinesh Patel, Mr Harshad Patel, Mr Sanjay Kara,
Mr Jitu Patel, Mr Anup Vyas
Income: £10,137,863 [2016]; £11,311,252 [2015]; £7,831,957
[2014]; £7,226,441 [2013]; £7,426,719 [2012]

Body and Soul
Registered: 10 Jan 1997 *Employees:* 21 *Volunteers:* 250
Tel: 020 7923 6880 *Website:* bodyandsoulcharity.org
Activities: Education, training; advancement of health or saving of
lives; other charitable purposes
Address: St Ives House, 99-119 Rosebery Avenue, London,
EC1R 4RE
Trustees: Professor Maurice Biriotti, Ms Rachel Stevenson,
Mr Munya Chidakwa, Ms Sara Carter, Mr Chris Naylor, Mr Alex
Lifschutz, Ms Deborah Bee, Miss Marjorie Agwang, Ms Jane
Dutton
Income: £1,283,791 [2016]; £1,239,673 [2015]; £1,293,746 [2014];
£1,264,735 [2013]; £1,051,496 [2012]

Bollington Health & Leisure
Registered: 21 Mar 2013 *Employees:* 75 *Volunteers:* 60
Tel: 01625 574908 *Website:* bollingtonleisure.co.uk
Activities: Education, training; advancement of health or saving of
lives; disability; amateur sport; recreation
Address: Lower Brook Farm, Smithy Lane, Rainow, Macclesfield,
Cheshire, SK10 5UP
Trustees: Dr John A Murdoch, Mr Peter David Tunwell, Mr David
Spencer Broadhurst, Mr Christopher James Thompson, Mr Steven
Lee Hurst, Mr Richard Anthony Mason, Mr Stephen William Spinks,
Dr John David King, Dr Deborah Ann Maxwell
Income: £1,145,433 [2017]; £950,730 [2016]; £947,423 [2015];
£1,165,367 [2014]

**The Bologna Center of The Johns Hopkins University
Charitable Trust**
Registered: 27 Aug 1991
Tel: 020 7502 2813
Activities: Education, training
Address: 19 Norcott Road, London, N16 7EJ
Trustees: Mr Charles Anson, Mr Alex Ruck Keene, Naneen
Hunter-Neubohn, Ms Geraldine Kelly
Income: £5,005,361 [2017]; £20,987 [2016]; £318,756 [2015];
£781,696 [2014]; £453,978 [2013]

Bolton Community Leisure
Registered: 8 Dec 2006 *Employees:* 207
Tel: 01204 331608
Activities: Amateur sport
Address: Bolton Metropolitan Borough Council, Town Hall, Victoria
Square, Bolton, Lancs, BL1 1RU
Trustees: Mr John Byrne, Bob Atkinson, Mr Inayat Omaraji,
Dr Margaret Anne Talbot, Mr John Kirk Shepley, Mr David
Singleton, Mrs Anne Florence Bain, Mrs Sara Louise Sharrock
Income: £5,866,032 [2016]; £5,966,788 [2015]; £5,847,584 [2014];
£6,113,750 [2013]; £6,130,228 [2012]

Bolton Hospice
Registered: 8 Apr 1987 *Employees:* 94 *Volunteers:* 800
Tel: 01204 663066 *Website:* boltonhospice.org
Activities: The advancement of health or saving of lives
Address: Bolton Hospice, Queens Park Street, Bolton, Lancs,
BL1 4QT
Trustees: Mr Andrew Philip Morgan, Mrs Judith Bromley, Mrs Grace
Hopps, Mr John Kirk, Dr Robert Alan Hunt, Mr Patrick Anthony
Lydon, Dr Geoffrey McLardy, Mr Adrian Crook
Income: £5,262,878 [2017]; £4,781,204 [2016]; £4,892,763 [2015];
£3,962,077 [2014]; £3,296,911 [2013]

Bolton Lads and Girls Club Limited
Registered: 7 Dec 1995 *Employees:* 95 *Volunteers:* 223
Tel: 01204 540100 *Website:* blgc.co.uk
Activities: General charitable purposes; education, training; disability; arts, culture, heritage, science; amateur sport; economic, community development, employment; recreation
Address: Bolton Lads & Girls Club, 18 Spa Road, Bolton, Lancs, BL1 4AG
Trustees: Mr Peter Vinden, Prof George Holmes, Ms Debbie Sabini, Mr David Rowland Jones, Dave Singleton, Brandon Pilling, Mr Stuart Peter Stead
Income: £2,945,736 [2017]; £4,215,266 [2016]; £2,732,640 [2015]; £2,809,597 [2014]; £2,892,246 [2013]

Bolton Middlebrook Leisure Trust
Registered: 18 Jun 2001 *Employees:* 57
Tel: 01204 488100 *Website:* boltonarena.com
Activities: Education, training; amateur sport
Address: Bolton Arena, Arena Approach, Horwich, Bolton, Lancs, BL6 6LB
Trustees: Mr John Byrne, Mr Michael McBrien, Mr Kevin Peter McKeon, Professor George Edward Thomas Holmes, Mr Bill Charnley, Mr Richard Hurst, Mr Anthony John Turner, Mr Ibrahim Ismail, Dr Wirinder Bhatiani, Mr Anthony Emerson Jones
Income: £2,372,553 [2017]; £2,331,382 [2016]; £2,370,563 [2015]; £2,346,008 [2014]; £2,232,814 [2013]

Bolton NHS Charitable Fund
Registered: 8 Nov 1995
Tel: 01204 390048 *Website:* boltonft.nhs.uk
Activities: General charitable purposes
Address: The Royal Bolton Hospital, Minerva Road, Farnworth, Bolton, Lancs, BL4 0JR
Trustees: Bolton NHS Foundation Trust
Income: £1,105,000 [2017]; £629,000 [2016]; £369,000 [2015]; £179,000 [2014]; £813,000 [2013]

Bolton School
Registered: 3 Aug 2005 *Employees:* 454
Tel: 01204 840201 *Website:* boltonschool.org.uk
Activities: Education, training
Address: Bolton School, Boys Division, Chorley New Road, Bolton, Lancs, BL1 4PA
Trustees: Roger Gould, Mr Michael Griffiths, Ms Karen Wendy Diggle, Mr Charles Cowling, Miss Amanda Valentine, Mr David Niaz Mohyuddin, Mr Ian Riley, Mrs Manjeet Hundle, Mr Robert Seton Ogilvie, Mr Anthony Oldershaw, Mrs Sheila Fisher, Mr Eric Fairweather, Mrs Caroline Topham, Mrs Louise Relph, Mr Andrew Palmer, Mrs Helen Critchlow, Mr George Apsion
Income: £28,780,000 [2016]; £28,326,000 [2015]; £27,112,000 [2014]; £26,311,000 [2013]

Bolton Wise Limited
Registered: 17 Feb 1999 *Employees:* 63 *Volunteers:* 37
Tel: 01204 393081 *Website:* mojotrust.co.uk
Activities: General charitable purposes; education, training; prevention or relief of poverty; environment, conservation, heritage; economic, community development, employment; other charitable purposes
Address: The Quest Centre, Brownlow Way, Bolton, Lancs, BL3 3UB
Trustees: Mr David John Bagley, Mr Martin McLoughlin, Mrs Elizabeth Anne Ward, Mr Jay Patel, Mr Ian Alker, Mr Geoffrey Higginbottom, Mr Andrew Richard Taylor BSc DMS, Mrs Gillian Davies, Mrs Eileen Helen Scott
Income: £1,360,707 [2014]; £1,808,017 [2013]

Bolton Young Persons Housing Scheme
Registered: 3 Oct 1997 *Employees:* 43 *Volunteers:* 5
Tel: 01204 520183 *Website:* byphs.org.uk
Activities: Accommodation, housing
Address: Trinity House, Breightmet Street, Bolton, Lancs, BL2 1BR
Trustees: Catherine Patricia Burns, Ms Maura Jackson, Mr Chris Stevens, Dr Steve Sharples, Ms Resma Patel, Mr David Black, Ms Amy Lythgoe, Ms Jane Dibnah, Mr Paul Justin Pritchard
Income: £1,841,828 [2017]; £1,646,929 [2016]; £1,280,695 [2015]; £1,190,839 [2014]; £479,530 [2013]

The Linda and Gordon Bonnyman Charitable Trust
Registered: 3 Apr 2008
Tel: 01732 450744
Activities: General charitable purposes
Address: Ely Grange, Frant, Tunbridge Wells, Kent, TN3 9DY
Trustees: Mr James Gordon Bonnyman, Mr James Wallace Taylor Bonnyman, Linda Bonnyman
Income: £1,878,405 [2017]; £2,318 [2016]; £1,840 [2015]; £8,468 [2014]; £1,002,280 [2013]

Book Aid International
Registered: 4 Jul 1966 *Employees:* 21 *Volunteers:* 13
Tel: 020 7733 3577 *Website:* bookaid.org
Activities: Education, training; overseas aid, famine relief
Address: Book Aid International, 39-41 Coldharbour Lane, London, SE5 9NR
Trustees: Mr Nicholas Allen, Rosie Glazebrook, Mr Robert Sulley, Mr Charly Nobbs, Ed Bowers, Lord Paul Boateng, Ms Pam Dix, Mr Jonathan Hugh Macintosh
Income: £15,460,412 [2016]; £14,164,444 [2015]; £12,056,937 [2014]; £8,258,566 [2013]; £9,569,431 [2012]

The Book Trade Charity
Registered: 18 Feb 2009 *Employees:* 5 *Volunteers:* 6
Tel: 01923 263128 *Website:* btbs.org
Activities: General charitable purposes; education, training; advancement of health or saving of lives; prevention or relief of poverty; accommodation, housing
Address: The Foyle Centre, The Retreat, Kings Langley, Herts, WD4 8LT
Trustees: Ms Gemma Woodward, Fraser Tanner, Mr David Neale, Mr David Graham, Ms Ann Veronica Woodhall, Ms Isobel Dixon, Ms Elise Burns, Miss Emily-Jane Taylor
Income: £3,777,287 [2016]; £1,577,805 [2015]; £543,134 [2014]; £508,042 [2013]; £450,852 [2012]

BookTrust
Registered: 1 Jul 1963 *Employees:* 66
Tel: 020 7801 8800 *Website:* booktrust.org.uk
Activities: Education, training; arts, culture, heritage, science
Address: G8 Battersea Studios, 80 Silverthorne Road, Battersea, London, SW8 3HE
Trustees: Ms Claire Malcolm, Mr Derek Wyatt, Ms Nicola Briggs, Mr Peter Roche, Ms Eleanor Shawcross Wolfson, Mr John Coughlan, Ms Fiona Collins, Ms Meredith Niles, Mr Hugh Shanks, Ms Hsin Loke, Ms Harpal Dhillon
Income: £9,212,017 [2017]; £9,396,835 [2016]; £9,763,329 [2015]; £9,835,558 [2014]; £9,017,153 [2013]

Booker Prize Foundation
Registered: 11 Jan 2002
Tel: 020 7253 1008 *Website:* themanbookerprize.com
Activities: Arts, culture, heritage, science
Address: 28 St James's Walk, London, EC1R 0AP
Trustees: Mr Christopher Thomas Pearce, James Naughtie, Professor Louise Richardson, Baroness Helena Kennedy QC, Bidisha Shonarkoli Mamata, Ben Okri
Income: £1,529,783 [2016]; £1,652,750 [2015]; £1,403,819 [2014]; £1,367,928 [2013]; £1,546,940 [2012]

The John Booth Charitable Foundation
Registered: 7 Jan 2009
Tel: 020 7486 2201
Activities: General charitable purposes; education, training; religious activities; arts, culture, heritage, science; environment, conservation, heritage; other charitable purposes
Address: Flat 8, St Pauls Court, 56 Manchester Street, London, W1U 3AF
Trustees: Mr John David Sebastian Booth, Mr Tm Ashley, The Rt Revd Dr Mc Warner
Income: £1,554,311 [2017]; £1,362,755 [2016]; £884,527 [2015]; £1,164,726 [2014]; £523,739 [2013]

The Booth Charities
Registered: 24 Nov 1963 *Employees:* 5
Tel: 01606 334309
Activities: General charitable purposes; education, training; advancement of health or saving of lives; disability; prevention or relief of poverty; religious activities; amateur sport
Address: Butcher & Barlow LLP, 3 Royal Mews, Gadbrook Park, Rudheath, Northwich, Cheshire, CW9 7UD
Trustees: Mr John Christensen Willis, Mr David John Tully, Mr Richard Peter Kershaw, Mr William Thomas Whittle, Mr Alan Graham Dewhurst, Mrs Barbara Griffin, Mr Philip Charles Okell, Mr Roger Jeremy Weston, Mr Richard Fildes, Mr Jonathan Shelmerdine
Income: £1,014,000 [2017]; £1,014,000 [2016]; £941,000 [2015]; £962,000 [2014]; £964,000 [2013]

Bootham School
Registered: 26 Oct 1983 *Employees:* 169
Tel: 01904 654395 *Website:* boothamschool.com
Activities: Education, training
Address: Bootham School, 51 Bootham, York, YO30 7BU
Trustees: David Leslie Stanton, Stephen Frederick Sayers, Malcolm Sterratt, Sharon Hodgson, Alexander Raubitschek, David Benedict Pearcy, Peter David Wickham, Nigel Christopher Lindley, Robert Barton, Heather Woolley, Donald Andrew Purves, Catherine Limb, Richard John Vesey, Nicholas Burton
Income: £11,497,761 [2017]; £11,363,729 [2016]; £11,585,952 [2015]; £10,264,866 [2014]; £10,240,195 [2013]

Bootstrap Company (Blackburn) Limited
Registered: 10 Jan 1990 *Employees:* 101 *Volunteers:* 2
Tel: 01254 680367 *Website:* bootstrap.org.uk
Activities: Education, training; economic, community development, employment
Address: Bootstrap Enterprises, 35 Railway Road, Blackburn, BB1 1EZ
Trustees: Mr Ebrahim Kassim Bassa, Jamie Groves, Wendy Humphreys, Mr Stephen Anthony Bolton
Income: £2,588,925 [2017]; £3,449,624 [2016]; £3,933,420 [2015]; £4,129,527 [2014]; £2,954,522 [2013]

Bootstrap Company Limited
Registered: 28 Apr 1978 *Employees:* 14
Website: bootstrapcompany.co.uk
Activities: General charitable purposes; education, training; prevention or relief of poverty; arts, culture, heritage, science; environment, conservation, heritage; economic, community development, employment
Address: Bootstrap Co, 18-22 Ashwin Street, London, E8 3DL
Trustees: Mr Phil King, Ms Sarah Cary, Dr Ross Mitchell, Mr Alexander Tamburov, Mr Tomi Nummela, Ms Clarisse Simonek, Jordan Bookman
Income: £1,807,901 [2017]; £1,703,167 [2016]; £1,574,874 [2015]; £1,223,275 [2014]; £1,002,078 [2013]

The Boparan Charitable Trust
Registered: 4 Jun 2009 *Employees:* 2 *Volunteers:* 20
Tel: 0121 214 9364 *Website:* theboparancharitabletrust.com
Activities: General charitable purposes; advancement of health or saving of lives; disability; prevention or relief of poverty; other charitable purposes
Address: 2nd Floor, 9 Colmore Row, Birmingham, B3 2BJ
Trustees: Sir Keith MacDonald Porter, Mrs Baljinder Boparan, Mr Antonio Boparan
Income: £1,076,473 [2016]; £1,019,000 [2015]; £1,089,255 [2014]; £1,080,748 [2013]; £854,450 [2012]

The Border Consortium
Registered: 13 May 2005 *Employees:* 69
Website: theborderconsortium.org
Activities: Overseas aid, famine relief; economic, community development, employment
Address: 12/5 Convent Road, Bangrak, Bangkok, 10500
Trustees: Ms Alexis Chapman, Mr Leon De Riedmatten, Mr James Thomson, Ms Leslie Wilson, Mr Eivind Archer, Mr Rajan Khosla
Income: £13,599,500 [2017]; £12,705,383 [2016]; £15,625,374 [2015]; £17,295,191 [2014]; £21,502,759 [2013]

Borletti-Buitoni Trust
Registered: 20 May 2016 *Employees:* 1
Tel: 020 8993 0100 *Website:* bbtrust.com
Activities: Education, training; arts, culture, heritage, science
Address: Flat 1, 4 Highlands Avenue, London, W3 6ET
Trustees: Dr David Landau, Mr Paul Cutts, Mitsuko Uchida, Mrs Ilaria Borletti Buitoni
Income: £5,046,804 [2017]

The Born Free Foundation
Registered: 7 Aug 1998 *Employees:* 66 *Volunteers:* 4
Tel: 01403 240170 *Website:* bornfree.org.uk
Activities: Education, training; animals; environment, conservation, heritage
Address: Broadlands Business Campus, Langhurstwood Road, Horsham, W Sussex, RH12 4QP
Trustees: Anne Wignall, Ms Virginia McKenna, Mr Michael Drake, Mr Adam David Batty, Mrs Susan Olsen, Kate Snowdon, Ms Jenny Seagrove, Mr Michael Reyner, Mr Peter Ellis, Dr Graeme Young, Liz Tinlin
Income: £4,341,533 [2017]; £6,606,586 [2016]; £3,784,558 [2015]; £3,761,783 [2014]; £2,705,048 [2013]

The Borne Foundation
Registered: 13 May 2016 *Employees:* 3
Tel: 020 3315 3184 *Website:* borne.org.uk
Activities: The advancement of health or saving of lives
Address: Room H3.32, Academic Department of Obstetrics & Gynecology, Chelsea & Westminster Hospital, 369 Fulham Road, London, SW10 9NH
Trustees: Mr Francesco Vanni D'Archirafi, Professor Thomas Thornton MacDonald, Mr Nicholas Richard Hurrell, Mr Julian Mylchreest, Mrs Charlotte Moffat, Mrs Henriette Mary Pye
Income: £1,353,353 [2017]

Borough Market (Southwark)
Registered: 6 Aug 1999 *Employees:* 28
Tel: 020 7407 1002 *Website:* boroughmarket.org.uk
Activities: Education, training; advancement of health or saving of lives; environment, conservation, heritage; economic, community development, employment; other charitable purposes
Address: 8 Southwark Street, London, SE1 1TL
Trustees: Miss Claire Pritchard, Ms Julia Tybura, Mr David Lyon, Mr Adrian Bunnis, Mr Matthew Flood, Mr Donald Hyslop, Mr Drew Cullen, Dr Bengu Said, Ms Ann Ball, Mr Sean Ramsden
Income: £4,932,574 [2017]; £6,230,907 [2016]; £4,110,975 [2015]; £3,637,309 [2014]; £3,421,053 [2013]

Borough of Havant Sport and Leisure Trust
Registered: 24 Feb 1997 *Employees:* 222
Website: horizonlc.com
Activities: Education, training; amateur sport; recreation
Address: Havant Leisure Centre, Civic Centre Road, Havant, Hants, PO9 2AY
Trustees: Mr Peter Cyril Crane, Mr William John Ball, Mr Keith John Teesdale, Mr David Eric Symonds, Maggie Hoare, Ms Ruth Butler, Mr Christopher William Scott, Mr Philip Jones, Mr Geoffrey Arthur Lawton, Mr Mel Smith, Mr Jason Crouch
Income: £6,138,080 [2017]; £5,681,015 [2016]; £4,772,640 [2015]; £4,066,274 [2014]; £4,093,860 [2013]

The Borrow Foundation
Registered: 22 Jan 1997 *Employees:* 10
Website: borrowfoundation.org
Activities: The advancement of health or saving of lives
Address: Padnell Grange, Padnell Road, Waterlooville, Hants, PO8 8ED
Trustees: Mr John Trefor Price Roberts, Professor Andrew John Rugg-Gunn, Professor Christina Stecksen-Blicks, Mr Nigel Frederick Borrow, Mr Nigel Thomas
Income: £1,359,207 [2017]; £1,334,552 [2016]; £1,302,833 [2015]; £1,233,192 [2014]; £1,289,560 [2013]

The Bosco Centre
Registered: 30 Jun 2014 *Employees:* 25 *Volunteers:* 1
Tel: 020 7064 4985 *Website:* boscocentre.ac.uk
Activities: General charitable purposes; education, training; prevention or relief of poverty; accommodation, housing; recreation
Address: Bosco Centre, 281 Jamaica Road, London, SE16 4RS
Trustees: Sister Norma Kirkby, Annabel Clarkson, Prim Campbell, Barry Crawley, Mr Matthew Farrell BSc, Miss Valerie Stapleton
Income: £1,037,709 [2017]; £6,895,358 [2016]

Bosence Farm Community Limited
Registered: 28 Aug 2001 *Employees:* 79 *Volunteers:* 16
Tel: 01736 851292 *Website:* bosencefarm.com
Activities: The advancement of health or saving of lives; accommodation, housing
Address: 69 Bosence Road, Townshend, Hayle, Cornwall, TR27 6AN
Trustees: Gail Hunt, Mr Anthony Woodhams, Mrs Mary Winifred Vyvyan, Mr Clive Harrold, Dr Malcolm Rosser Jones, Mr Martin Jonathan Nixon
Income: £1,274,326 [2017]; £1,821,750 [2016]; £1,234,117 [2015]; £1,109,372 [2014]; £1,114,699 [2013]

Botanic Gardens Conservation International
Registered: 1 Aug 2003 *Employees:* 17 *Volunteers:* 10
Tel: 020 8332 5953 *Website:* bgci.org
Activities: Environment, conservation, heritage
Address: Botanic Gardens Conservation International, 199 Kew Road, Richmond, Surrey, TW9 3BW
Trustees: Sir Ghillean Prance, Mrs Beth Rothschild, Dr Peter Wyse Jackson, Dr Kathleen Sylvia McKinnon, Mr Stuart Jerome Clenaghan, Dr Gerard Thomas Donnelly, HRH Princess Basma Fatima Bent Ali Bin Nayef, Mr Martin Gibson, Professor Stephen Blackmore, Dr Charlotte Anne Grezo, Ms Anna Quenby, Mr Mark Webb, Mr Michael Todd Murphy
Income: £1,443,656 [2017]; £2,982,438 [2016]; £1,080,883 [2015]; £1,276,858 [2014]; £1,125,224 [2013]

Bounce Back Foundation
Registered: 17 Oct 2011 *Employees:* 13
Tel: 020 7735 1256 *Website:* bouncebackproject.com
Activities: Education, training; economic, community development, employment; other charitable purposes
Address: Pop Brixton, Unit L05, 49 Brixton Station Road, Brixton, London, SW9 8PQ
Trustees: Mr Charles Appleton, Mrs Francesca Joy Findlater, Mr Mark John Essex, Mr Iqbal Wahhab, Mr Antony Theodorou
Income: £1,272,706 [2017]; £935,317 [2016]; £885,472 [2015]; £491,048 [2014]; £156,647 [2013]

Bourneheights Limited
Registered: 9 Feb 1988
Tel: 020 8809 7398
Activities: The prevention or relief of poverty; religious activities
Address: Flat 10, Palm Court, Queen Elizabeths Walk, London, N16 5XA
Trustees: Mr Chaskel Rand, Erno Berger, Mr Schloime Rand, Esther Rand, Mr Yechiel Chersky
Income: £1,064,215 [2016]; £1,378,141 [2015]; £1,340,574 [2014]; £1,478,108 [2013]; £1,269,812 [2012]

The Bournemouth Healthcare Trust
Registered: 29 Jan 2008 *Employees:* 4
Website: bournemouthprivateclinic.co.uk
Activities: The advancement of health or saving of lives
Address: 13 Cannon Hill Gardens, Wimborne, Dorset, BH21 2TA
Trustees: Mr Anthony Spotswood, Mr Pete Papworth
Income: £2,234,663 [2017]; £3,157,364 [2016]; £4,138,498 [2015]; £3,826,297 [2014]; £3,673,466 [2013]

Bournemouth Symphony Orchestra
Registered: 24 Jul 1962 *Employees:* 82 *Volunteers:* 15
Tel: 01202 644716 *Website:* bsolive.com
Activities: Education, training; arts, culture, heritage, science; other charitable purposes
Address: Bournemouth Symphony Orchestra, 2 Seldown Lane, Poole, Dorset, BH15 1UF
Trustees: Mr Roger Preston, Mr Stephen Martin Edge, Mr Larry Arvid Dillner, Ms Mary O'Sullivan, Ms Annette D'Abreo, Mr Terence David O'Rourke, Professor Stuart Bartholomew, Miss Mary Jane Drabble, Mr Nicholas Ashley-Cooper
Income: £6,463,941 [2017]; £6,312,958 [2016]; £6,326,423 [2015]; £5,751,650 [2014]; £5,490,443 [2013]

Bournemouth War Memorial Homes
Registered: 9 Jun 2015 *Employees:* 4
Tel: 01202 302881 *Website:* bwmh.org.uk
Activities: Accommodation, housing
Address: 15 Woodsford Green, Castle Lane West, Bournemouth, BH8 9TP
Trustees: Mr Gordon Andrew Long, Mr Ricardo Dominic Cobelli, Mr Mark John Powell, Mr Peter Matthews, Eliezer John Kennar, Miss Sophie Burgess-Kennar
Income: £4,450,313 [2016]

Bournemouth Young Men's Christian Association
Registered: 22 Dec 1999 *Employees:* 88 *Volunteers:* 50
Tel: 01202 254880 *Website:* ymcabournemouth.org.uk
Activities: General charitable purposes; education, training; disability; prevention or relief of poverty; accommodation, housing; religious activities; arts, culture, heritage, science; amateur sport; recreation
Address: Bournemouth YMCA, Delta House, 56 Westover Road, Bournemouth, BH1 2BS
Trustees: Mr Simon Marsh, Rev Ian Terry, Mrs Lynn Dorcas Chisadza, Mr Richard Frank Elms, Mr David Williams, Mr Eamon Bundred, Mr Colin Hartland, Mrs Samantha Oak
Income: £4,957,000 [2016]; £4,268,000 [2015]; £4,771,000 [2014]; £4,795,000 [2013]; £3,218,000 [2012]

Bournville Village Trust
Registered: 3 Sep 1963 *Employees:* 278 *Volunteers:* 150
Tel: 0300 333 6540 *Website:* bvt.org.uk
Activities: Disability; prevention or relief of poverty; accommodation, housing; environment, conservation, heritage; economic, community development, employment
Address: Bournville Village Trust, 350 Bournville Lane, Birmingham, B30 1QY
Trustees: Roger Victor John Cadbury, Mr Adrian Allen FCA, Mr David Cockcroft, Mr Nigel Cadbury, Professor Philip John Lumley, Professor John Nolan, Mr Duncan James Cadbury MSc, Mr Roger Wilson BA ACA, Mrs Alison McKittrick, Councillor Peter Griffiths, Ms Caroline Cadbury
Income: £30,139,000 [2016]; £27,145,000 [2015]; £27,337,000 [2014]; £25,804,000 [2013]; £22,696,000 [2012]

Bow Arts Trust
Registered: 6 Jun 1995 *Employees:* 19 *Volunteers:* 120
Tel: 020 8980 7774 *Website:* bowarts.org
Activities: General charitable purposes; education, training; accommodation, housing; arts, culture, heritage, science; economic, community development, employment
Address: 183 Bow Road, London, E3 2SJ
Trustees: Mr Martyn Coles, Mr Rajen Madan, Mrs Michele Jean Faull, Mr Monuhar Ullah, Mr Habib Motani, Mrs Catherine Phillippa Smith, Ms Elizabeth Marshall, Mrs Sarah Elson, Mr Nicholas William Smales, Mr Brian David Smith, Ms Claire Swift
Income: £1,974,524 [2017]; £1,843,659 [2016]; £1,750,795 [2015]; £1,829,968 [2014]; £1,572,433 [2013]

Bowdon Preparatory School
Registered: 9 Jun 2011 *Employees:* 60
Tel: 0161 928 0678 *Website:* bowdonprep.org.uk
Activities: Education, training
Address: Ashley Road, Altrincham, Cheshire, WA14 2LT
Trustees: Mrs Marysia Bocquet, Mr Mark Haywood, Mrs Gillian Healey, Mr Ian Pinnington, Mrs Catriona Ashurst, Mr John Stevenson, Mrs Clare Withey, Dr Tessa Myatt, Mrs Susan Rylands
Income: £2,443,754 [2017]; £2,224,190 [2016]; £2,057,174 [2015]; £2,001,053 [2014]; £1,839,208 [2013]

Bowel Cancer UK
Registered: 17 Aug 1998 *Employees:* 31 *Volunteers:* 120
Tel: 020 7940 1765 *Website:* bowelcanceruk.org.uk
Activities: General charitable purposes; education, training; advancement of health or saving of lives
Address: Bowel Cancer UK Ltd, 140-148 Borough High Street, London, SE1 1LB
Trustees: Dr Diana Tait, Ms Deborah Mechaneck, Dr John Schofield, Mr Stephen Fenwick, Ms Kym Lang, Mr John Stebbing, Mrs Angela Wiles, Mrs Nita Ares, Mr Richard James Anderson, Mr Peter Robert Beverley, Dr Katharine Brown, Mr Patrick Figgis, Mr Joe Higgins, Mrs Lorraine Lander, Mr Mauro Mattiuzzo
Income: £2,307,222 [2016]; £2,013,684 [2015]; £1,729,104 [2014]; £1,608,378 [2013]; £1,527,491 [2012]

The Bowes Museum
Registered: 1 Mar 2000 *Employees:* 65 *Volunteers:* 90
Tel: 01833 690606 *Website:* thebowesmuseum.org.uk
Activities: General charitable purposes; education, training; arts, culture, heritage, science; environment, conservation, heritage
Address: The Bowes Museum, Newgate, Barnard Castle, Co Durham, DL12 8NP
Trustees: Mr Adrian Jenkins, Sir Mark Wrightson, Mr Peter Mottershill, Mr Mark Blackett Ord, Mrs Caroline Peacock, Ms Tracie Smith, Ms Susan Palmer OBE
Income: £4,530,058 [2017]; £5,802,784 [2016]; £2,551,394 [2015]; £3,812,566 [2014]; £3,848,926 [2013]

The Bowland Charitable Trust
Registered: 20 Jun 1985
Tel: 01254 688051
Activities: Education, training; religious activities; arts, culture, heritage, science; amateur sport; environment, conservation, heritage; human rights, religious or racial harmony, equality or diversity; recreation; other charitable purposes
Address: Bowland House, Philips Road, Blackburn, Lancs, BB1 5NA
Trustees: Mr Tony Cann CBE DL Hon LLD, Mrs Carole Fahy, Mr Hugh David Turner
Income: £1,089,908 [2016]; £52,385 [2015]; £519,703 [2014]; £365,714 [2013]; £373,835 [2012]

Bowles Rocks Trust Limited
Registered: 14 Aug 1964 *Employees:* 34
Tel: 01892 665665 *Website:* bowles.rocks
Activities: Education, training; amateur sport; recreation
Address: Bowles Centre, Sand Hill Lane, Eridge Green, Tunbridge Wells, Kent, TN3 9LW
Trustees: Mr Andrew Richard Blundell, Mr Martin Tomlinson, Mr David Charles Unwin QC, Mrs Frances Helen Ogden, Mr M J Darbyshire, Mr Martyn Styles, Mr Alan Gardner, Miss Catherine Gallagher
Income: £1,309,969 [2017]; £1,430,367 [2016]; £1,333,455 [2015]; £1,298,132 [2014]; £1,264,220 [2013]

Bows and Arrows
Registered: 7 Apr 2009 *Employees:* 87 *Volunteers:* 4
Tel: 01473 240304 *Website:* bowsandarrowsgroup.co.uk
Activities: Education, training; economic, community development, employment
Address: Wig Wam, Whitton Sports Community Centre, Whitton Church Lane, Ipswich, Suffolk, IP1 6LW
Trustees: Mr Roger Fern, Mrs Nicola Ann Rout, Mr Stuart Clive Greenacre, Miss Natasha Bedford, Ms Sarah Coombs, Mr Oliver Southgate, Mr James Roberts, Mrs Caroline Elizabeth Atkins, Ms Vanessa Rawlings, Mrs Hannah Cotton
Income: £1,341,245 [2017]; £1,221,142 [2016]; £892,035 [2015]; £760,236 [2014]; £565,209 [2013]

Box Hill School Trust Limited
Registered: 13 Mar 1963 *Employees:* 125 *Volunteers:* 1
Tel: 01372 385040 *Website:* boxhillschool.com
Activities: Education, training
Address: Box Hill School, London Road, Mickleham, Dorking, Surrey, RH5 6EA
Trustees: Mr Terry Knight, Mr John Banfield, Mr P M G Voller, Mr J W Chalker, Mrs Monica Pengilley, Mrs Della Kristin Fallon, Mr Trevor Johnson, Mrs D Malcolm-Green, Mrs K von Wedel, Mr J Harman, Mr James Angus Evans, Mrs Annabel Jane R Agace, Mr Christopher Townsend, Mr John Towers
Income: £9,408,500 [2017]; £9,374,031 [2016]; £8,924,101 [2015]; £9,298,509 [2014]; £8,435,523 [2013]

G & K Boyes Charitable Trust
Registered: 11 Mar 2016
Tel: 01892 506292
Activities: General charitable purposes; education, training; advancement of health or saving of lives; arts, culture, heritage, science; environment, conservation, heritage
Address: Cripps Harries Hall LLP, Number 22, Mount Ephraim, Tunbridge Wells, Kent, TN4 8AS
Trustees: Mr R A Henderson QC, Mr Mark Cannon-Brookes, Mrs A Dalmahoy, Cripps Trust Corporation Limited
Income: £1,253,025 [2017]

The Boys' Brigade
Registered: 27 Feb 1964 *Employees:* 57 *Volunteers:* 12,367
Website: boys-brigade.org.uk
Activities: Education, training
Address: Felden Lodge, Felden, Hemel Hempstead, Herts, HP3 0BL
Trustees: Mr Michael Elliott, Mr Raymond Leslie Buttimer, Mr Lindsay Stein, Mr Colin Clifton Smith, The Reverend The Lord Griffiths of Burry Port, Mr Stuart John Rankin, Ms Rachael Mary Knowles, Mr Paul Malcolm Haggan, Mr Philip McKinley, Mr Clifford Bygrave, Miss Sharon Heather Mackey, Mr David Hugh Sneddon, Mr Alistair Stewart Burrow, Mr Lee Scott Hiorns, Mr David John Love, Mr David John Aubrey QC, Mr Noel Clingan
Income: £2,636,705 [2017]; £3,013,658 [2016]; £3,476,768 [2015]; £3,178,340 [2014]; £3,072,763 [2013]

Bradford Trident Limited
Registered: 11 Jan 2005 *Employees:* 48 *Volunteers:* 148
Tel: 01274 768062 *Website:* bradfordtrident.co.uk
Activities: General charitable purposes; education, training; advancement of health or saving of lives; prevention or relief of poverty; arts, culture, heritage, science; amateur sport; economic, community development, employment; recreation; other charitable purposes
Address: Park Lane Centre, Park Lane, Bradford, BD5 0LN
Trustees: Mrs Sarah Hinton, Mr Taj Salam, Mr Mohammed Saeed Afsar, Mr Imran Younis, Mr Sadaqat Ali Khan, Ms Hawarun Hussain, Mr Yaqoob Ayoob, Miss Fareeda Mir, Mr Shahzada Meer, Mr Habib Rehman Afsar, Mr Talat Sajawal, Ms Nasreen Khan, Mr Balaal Hussian Khan, Ramen Haire
Income: £4,698,011 [2017]; £3,630,317 [2016]; £1,431,666 [2015]; £1,198,912 [2014]; £932,304 [2013]

Bradford Women's Aid
Registered: 10 Sep 2003 *Employees:* 37 *Volunteers:* 8
Tel: 01274 668049 *Website:* bradfordwomensaid.org
Activities: General charitable purposes; education, training; prevention or relief of poverty; accommodation, housing
Address: Bradford Womens Aid, P O Box 1102, Bradford, BD1 9NG
Trustees: Ms Rashmi Sudhir, Ms Tracy Ellis, Ms Zoe Duffy, Ms Michelle Blum, Ms Melanie Broadbent
Income: £1,173,643 [2017]; £984,338 [2016]; £655,028 [2015]; £657,444 [2014]; £482,069 [2013]

The Bradgate Park and Swithland Wood Charity
Registered: 30 Jul 1963 *Employees:* 56 *Volunteers:* 100
Tel: 0116 236 2713 *Website:* bradgatepark.org
Activities: Education, training; environment, conservation, heritage; recreation
Address: Estate Office, Deer Barn Buildings, Bradgate Park, Newtown Linford, Leicester, LE6 0HE
Trustees: Mr Peter Osborne, Mr David Lindley, Cllr Adam Clarke, Ms Deborah Taylor, Mrs Manjula Sood MBE, Colonel Robert Martin, Mrs Christine Radford, Mr Stewart Leslie Alcock, Mr John Leach, Mr Andy Beer
Income: £1,707,530 [2017]; £1,523,180 [2016]; £1,354,284 [2015]; £1,333,920 [2014]; £1,064,865 [2013]

The Bradley Family Charitable Foundation
Registered: 28 Jan 2016
Activities: General charitable purposes
Address: Stoneway, Stafford Road, Penkridge, Stafford, ST19 5AX
Trustees: Mrs Suzanne Evelyn Beatty, Miss Eleanor Elizabeth Bradley, Mr Keith Bradley, Mrs Irene Joyce Bradley
Income: £1,597,552 [2017]

Bradnet

Registered: 3 Nov 2005 *Employees:* 30 *Volunteers:* 12
Tel: 01274 224444 *Website:* bradnet.org.uk
Activities: General charitable purposes; education, training; advancement of health or saving of lives; disability; prevention or relief of poverty; amateur sport; economic, community development, employment
Address: Bradnet, Guardian House, 22 Manor Row, Bradford, BD1 4QU
Trustees: Mr Imtiaz Naqvi, Ms Farhat Yasin, Mr Matloob Hussain, Ms Gazala Iqbal
Income: £1,200,361 [2017]; £1,670,469 [2016]; £1,755,861 [2015]; £1,701,724 [2014]; £1,616,443 [2013]

Brahma Kumaris World Spiritual University (UK)

Registered: 25 Sep 1975 *Volunteers:* 287
Tel: 020 8955 1910 *Website:* brahmakumaris.org
Activities: The prevention or relief of poverty; religious activities
Address: 65-69 Pound Lane, London, NW10 2HH
Trustees: Mr Govind Vaswani, Mr Girish Wadhwani, Mr Sanjay Tulsidas, Mr Ratan Thadani, Mr Mahesh Patel
Income: £2,093,272 [2016]; £2,416,385 [2015]; £2,820,899 [2014]; £1,571,997 [2013]; £1,752,846 [2012]

Brain Research Trust

Registered: 24 Aug 2010 *Employees:* 9
Tel: 020 7404 9982 *Website:* brainresearchuk.org.uk
Activities: The advancement of health or saving of lives
Address: First Floor, The Dutch House, 307-308 High Holborn, London, WC1V 7LL
Trustees: Mr Jonathan Kropman, Professor Doug Turnbull, Dr Allister Wilson, Professor John Pickard, Mr Jim Gollan
Income: £1,998,000 [2017]; £2,610,000 [2016]; £2,152,000 [2015]; £1,872,000 [2014]; £1,651,000 [2013]

The Brain Tumour Charity

Registered: 5 Dec 2012 *Employees:* 80 *Volunteers:* 432
Tel: 01252 749990 *Website:* thebraintumourcharity.org
Activities: Education, training; advancement of health or saving of lives; disability
Address: 61-65 Victoria Road, Farnborough, Hants, GU14 7PA
Trustees: Mr Jack Morris CBE, Mrs Angela Deacon, Mr Graham Norton, Mrs Berendina Jill Norton, Mr Tim Burchell, Mr Neil Dickson MBE, Sir Martin James Narey, Dr Justine McIlroy, Dr Alan Palmer, Mr Andrew Foote, Mr Robert Posner, Mr Graham Lindsay, Mrs Angela Dickson MBE, Ms Phillipa Grace Murray, Mr Simon Hay, Mr Robert Edward Ritchie
Income: £8,600,686 [2017]; £10,272,063 [2016]; £7,158,946 [2015]; £5,137,952 [2014]; £4,933,807 [2013]

Brain Tumour Research

Registered: 20 Aug 2013 *Employees:* 30 *Volunteers:* 20
Tel: 01908 867200 *Website:* braintumourresearch.org
Activities: The advancement of health or saving of lives
Address: Suite 3, Shenley Pavilions, Chalkdell Drive, Shenley Wood, Milton Keynes, Bucks, MK5 6LB
Trustees: Mr Robert Hughes, Mr Jeremy Aron, Mr Stuart McKay, Mr Sandy Saunders, Dr Margaret Stockham Turner, Ms Wendy Fulcher, Mr Stephen John Painter, Mr Nigel Boutwood, Mr Gerard Kelly, Mrs Jessica Ranft
Income: £3,594,251 [2017]; £2,878,888 [2016]; £2,240,258 [2015]; £1,429,609 [2014]

The Brain and Spine Foundation

Registered: 11 Jul 2003 *Employees:* 12 *Volunteers:* 267
Tel: 020 7793 5900 *Website:* brainandspine.org.uk
Activities: Education, training; advancement of health or saving of lives; disability
Address: LG01, Lincoln House, Kennington Park, 1-3 Brixton Road, London, SW9 6DE
Trustees: Mr Clive Holland, Mr James Lamont, Mr Ian Basden-Smith, Mr Alistair Jh Watkins, Mr Mark Luce, Mr Colin Cosgrove, Mr Peter Hamlyn, Mr Eric Roux, Mr Christopher Welch, Mrs Joanne Garnham-Parks, Mrs Elizabeth Printer
Income: £1,089,385 [2017]; £643,732 [2016]; £877,482 [2015]; £621,945 [2014]; £631,759 [2013]

The Brainwave Centre Limited

Registered: 8 Jan 1999 *Employees:* 73 *Volunteers:* 360
Tel: 01278 429089 *Website:* brainwave.org.uk
Activities: The advancement of health or saving of lives; disability
Address: The Brainwave Centre, Huntworth, Bridgwater, Somerset, TA6 6LQ
Trustees: Mr Richard Adams, Mr David Martin Jackson, Mr Michael Giblin FCII, Mrs Caryn Musker, Mr Philip Austin, Mr Graham Blower, Mr Barrie Crow, Mrs Emma Jane Larcombe
Income: £2,823,608 [2017]; £2,948,142 [2016]; £2,871,858 [2015]; £2,944,611 [2014]; £2,768,131 [2013]

Brake

Registered: 31 Jul 2002 *Employees:* 23 *Volunteers:* 650
Tel: 01484 559909 *Website:* brake.org.uk
Activities: Education, training
Address: P O Box 548, Huddersfield, W Yorks, HD1 2XZ
Trustees: Mr Kris Gledhill, Mrs Deborah Johnson, Mr Richard William Cuerden, Prof Tim J Coats, Mr Steven McIntosh, Mr Christopher Linsell
Income: £1,302,197 [2016]; £1,338,296 [2015]; £1,259,892 [2014]; £1,158,599 [2013]; £1,075,754 [2012]

The Liz and Terry Bramall Foundation

Registered: 23 Nov 2007
Tel: 01423 566666
Activities: Education, training; advancement of health or saving of lives; disability; prevention or relief of poverty; accommodation, housing; religious activities; arts, culture, heritage, science; environment, conservation, heritage; economic, community development, employment
Address: c/o Raworths LLP, Eton House, 89 Station Parade, Harrogate, N Yorks, HG1 1HF
Trustees: Dr Terence George Bramall, Mrs Suzannah Clare Allard, Mrs Rachel Shirley Tunnicliffe, Mrs Elizabeth Bramall, Mrs Rebecca Helen Bletcher, Mr Anthony Richard Sharp
Income: £2,084,831 [2017]; £2,073,280 [2016]; £2,001,040 [2015]; £2,094,283 [2014]; £2,223,736 [2013]

Brambletye School Trust Limited

Registered: 19 Aug 1970 *Employees:* 81
Tel: 01342 321004 *Website:* brambletye.co.uk
Activities: Education, training
Address: Brambletye School, Lewes Road, East Grinstead, W Sussex, RH19 3PD
Trustees: Mr Philip James Lough, Mr Mark John Lascelles, Mr Simon Neville Ardens Leefe, Mrs Samantha Anna Price, Mr Lorne Alexander Armstrong, Mr Thomas Andrew Charles Nicholas Dawson, Mrs Jennifer Jean Donegan, Mrs Diana Lesley Walker, Mr Nicholas John Perry, Mrs Catherine Jane Atkin, Mr Miles Richard Marten, Mr Christopher James Beazley
Income: £4,213,974 [2017]; £4,103,214 [2016]; £3,973,640 [2015]; £3,971,775 [2014]; £3,810,100 [2013]

Brandon Centre for Counselling and Psychotherapy for Young People
Registered: 8 Oct 1984 *Employees:* 59 *Volunteers:* 2
Tel: 020 7267 4792 *Website:* brandoncentre.org.uk
Activities: The advancement of health or saving of lives
Address: Brandon Centre, 26 Prince of Wales Road, London, NW5 3LG
Trustees: Mrs Olivia Hannah Tatton-Brown, Mr Basil Tyson, Ms Dolores Maria Currie, Ms Yemi Oloyede, Dr Anna Catherine Higgitt, Dr Danielle Elizabeth Mercey, Professor Richard Julian Taffler, Ms Brenda Sutherland
Income: £1,663,666 [2017]; £1,663,422 [2016]; £1,729,340 [2015]; £1,663,363 [2014]; £1,600,615 [2013]

The Brandon Trust
Registered: 17 May 1989 *Employees:* 1,545 *Volunteers:* 484
Tel: 0117 907 7200 *Website:* brandontrust.org
Activities: The advancement of health or saving of lives; disability; accommodation, housing
Address: The Brandon Trust, Olympus House, Britannia Road, Patchway, Bristol, BS34 5TA
Trustees: Ms Bonnie Dean, Mr Gerald Davies, Mr Martin Mohan, Mr Christopher Mahood, Mr Guy Stenson, Mr John Adams, Mr Clive Pugh, Ms Heather Sandilands, Mrs Helen Marsden
Income: £50,669,790 [2017]; £46,627,545 [2016]; £44,889,778 [2015]; £47,484,637 [2014]; £48,776,590 [2013]

Bransby Horses
Registered: 20 May 1999 *Employees:* 99 *Volunteers:* 37
Tel: 01427 788464 *Website:* bransbyhorses.co.uk
Activities: General charitable purposes; education, training; animals
Address: Bransby Horses, Bransby, Lincoln, LN1 2PH
Trustees: Mrs Carole Nora Fisher, Elizabeth Anne Dawson, Susan Dolan, Miss Kathryn McFee, Steve Mitchell, Heather Elston, Miss Joanne Ticehurst, Mr Richard Charles Pope
Income: £4,333,974 [2016]; £5,035,165 [2015]; £4,120,133 [2014]; £3,723,025 [2013]; £4,426,383 [2012]

Branwood School Trust Limited
Registered: 17 Apr 1984 *Employees:* 33 *Volunteers:* 2
Website: branwoodschool.co.uk
Activities: Education, training
Address: Branwood Preparatory School, Stafford Road, Eccles, Manchester, M30 9HN
Trustees: Mr Terence Stanley Cramant, Mr Daniel Mark Taylor, Mr Mark Foster, Mr Mark Nicholas Fletcher, Mrs Joanne Eva Wilcox
Income: £1,013,187 [2017]; £986,656 [2016]; £986,652 [2015]; £911,022 [2014]; £952,495 [2013]

Brathay Trust
Registered: 24 May 1993 *Employees:* 109 *Volunteers:* 259
Tel: 015394 33041 *Website:* brathay.org.uk
Activities: Education, training; economic, community development, employment
Address: Brathay Hall Trust, Brathay Hall, Clappersgate, Ambleside, Cumbria, LA22 0HP
Trustees: Mr Howard Cooper, Ms Diane Millward, Mr Charles Cowling, Mrs Joanna Coleman, Ms Bethia Jane McNeil, Mr Neil Braithwaite, Mrs Michelle Skeer, Mr Marc Andrew Pate, Ms Katharine McIntyre, Mr Paul Johnson
Income: £5,128,000 [2017]; £5,266,000 [2016]; £5,238,000 [2015]; £4,702,000 [2014]; £4,685,000 [2013]

The Braunstone Foundation
Registered: 29 Dec 2010 *Employees:* 37 *Volunteers:* 70
Tel: 0116 279 5007 *Website:* b-inspired.org.uk
Activities: Education, training; advancement of health or saving of lives; prevention or relief of poverty; amateur sport; economic, community development, employment
Address: Business Box, 3 Oswin Road, Leicester, LE3 1HR
Trustees: Mrs Gwen Abraham MBE, Pauline Hurd, Mr Henry Thompson, Mrs Elaine Halford, Mr Michael Cooke, Rev Keith Magee, Mr Keith Beaumont
Income: £1,123,367 [2017]; £1,083,873 [2016]; £1,226,979 [2015]; £1,316,762 [2014]; £1,094,689 [2013]

Breadline Africa
Registered: 17 May 1999 *Employees:* 2
Tel: 01473 259048 *Website:* breadlineafrica.org
Activities: General charitable purposes; prevention or relief of poverty; overseas aid, famine relief
Address: 29 Lower Brook Street, Ipswich, Suffolk, IP4 1AQ
Trustees: Mr Anthony Michael Smyth, Mrs Philippa Jane Smyth, Mr Benedict Elwes, Mr Alex Chisholm, Professor Eric Atmore, Mrs Mariella Norman, Mr Hendrik Struik, Mrs Louise Seligman, Sir Robert Dunbar, Mrs Philippa Wallis, Mr Henk Kleizen, Mr Peter Attard Montalto, Dr Stephen Lalor
Income: £1,007,383 [2017]; £1,003,933 [2016]; £1,124,046 [2015]; £1,044,675 [2014]; £1,144,201 [2013]

The Breadsticks Foundation
Registered: 6 Aug 2008
Tel: 020 7288 0667 *Website:* breadsticksfoundation.org
Activities: Education, training; advancement of health or saving of lives
Address: 35 Canonbury Square, London, N1 2AN
Trustees: Ms Beatrix Mary Payne, Ms Beatrice Roberts, Ms Alison Bukhari, Dr Paul Dean Ballantyne, Mr Trevor Philip Macy, Dr Kirsty Le Doare
Income: £1,310,967 [2017]; £1,000,186 [2016]; £1,013,533 [2015]; £3,146 [2014]; £2,251,368 [2013]

Break
Registered: 6 May 1983 *Employees:* 279 *Volunteers:* 900
Tel: 01603 670100 *Website:* break-charity.org
Activities: Other charitable purposes
Address: Break, Schofield House, 1 Spar Road, Norwich, NR6 6BX
Trustees: Emeritus Professor June Thoburn, Mr Trevor Brown, Dr Maureen Catherine Gardiner, Mr Johnnie Sam, Mr Frank Shippam, Mr Adam Nicholls, Mrs Sally Martin, Mr Simon Fowler, Mr Alastair Peter Kennedy Roy, Mr Geoff Gildersleeve, Ms Anne Ovens, Mrs Anne Joyce
Income: £10,766,000 [2017]; £11,364,000 [2016]; £10,037,966 [2015]; £10,543,096 [2014]; £9,604,298 [2013]

Breakthrough (Deaf-Hearing Integration)
Registered: 25 Jan 1999 *Employees:* 18 *Volunteers:* 18
Tel: 020 3940 2202 *Website:* deafplus.org
Activities: General charitable purposes; education, training; disability; prevention or relief of poverty
Address: Deafplus, Trinity Centre, Key Close, Whitechapel, London, E1 4HG
Trustees: Mr David Paul Connolly, Mr Kevin Powell, Miss Angela Walker, Mr David Packham, Mrs Sheila Gibson, Thomas Adam Lichy
Income: £1,035,648 [2017]; £960,066 [2016]; £807,679 [2015]; £628,920 [2014]; £625,962 [2013]

Breast Cancer Care
Registered: 25 Feb 1993 *Employees:* 215 *Volunteers:* 4,300
Tel: 020 7960 3416 *Website:* breastcancercare.org.uk
Activities: The advancement of health or saving of lives
Address: Breast Cancer Care, Chester House, 1-3 Brixton Road, London, SW9 6DE
Trustees: Ms Emma Burns, Dr Alison Louise Jones, Ms Marion Lewis, Ms Jill Thompson, Ms Sonia Beverley Gayle, Ms Jill Pask, Mr Nick Morris, Mr Mark Astaire, Ms Barbara Ellen Brown, Ms Candice Nichol
Income: £16,899,000 [2017]; £17,036,000 [2016]; £16,575,000 [2015]; £15,353,000 [2014]; £13,359,000 [2013]

Breast Cancer Haven
Registered: 9 Apr 1997 *Employees:* 55 *Volunteers:* 100
Tel: 020 7384 0048 *Website:* breastcancerhaven.org.uk
Activities: The advancement of health or saving of lives
Address: Breast Cancer Haven, Effie Road, London, SW6 1TB
Trustees: Lord Rockley, Professor Dudley Sinnett, Mr Peter Bell, Miss Tania Adib, Mr Alastair King, Mr Christopher Whitworth, Ms Dorinda Hickey, Prof Ian Edward Smith
Income: £2,790,014 [2017]; £4,911,103 [2016]; £2,750,940 [2015]; £2,633,756 [2014]; £2,366,402 [2013]

Breast Cancer Now
Registered: 18 Feb 2015 *Employees:* 156 *Volunteers:* 400
Tel: 0333 207 0300 *Website:* breastcancernow.org
Activities: General charitable purposes; education, training; advancement of health or saving of lives; disability
Address: 5th Floor, Ibex House, 42-47 Minories, London, EC3N 1DY
Trustees: Mrs Johnson, Lynne Berry, Mrs Pascale Marie Alvanitakis-Guely, Mrs Susan Gallone, Mr Christopher Copeland, Professor Powles, Professor Adrian Llewellyn Harris BSc MBChB MA DPhil FRCP FAcadMedSci, Ms Simons, Mrs Ann Pickering
Income: £28,318,000 [2017]; £27,616,000 [2016]

Breckenbrough School Limited
Registered: 11 Jan 2008 *Employees:* 60 *Volunteers:* 3
Tel: 01845 587238 *Website:* breckenbrough.org.uk
Activities: Education, training; advancement of health or saving of lives
Address: Breckenbrough School, Breckenbrough, Thirsk, N Yorks, YO7 4EN
Trustees: Mr Graham Ralph, Mrs Alison Mary Clarke, Mrs Ruth McTighe, John Ling, Mrs Judith Campbell
Income: £3,303,464 [2016]; £3,088,222 [2015]; £2,922,231 [2014]; £2,986,628 [2013]; £2,796,080 [2012]

The Brendoncare Foundation
Registered: 19 Mar 1984 *Employees:* 685 *Volunteers:* 500
Tel: 01962 857098 *Website:* brendoncare.org.uk
Activities: The advancement of health or saving of lives; accommodation, housing
Address: The Brendoncare Foundation, The Old Malthouse, Victoria Road, Winchester, Hants, SO23 7DU
Trustees: Joe MacHale, Mr Nicholas Capon, Dr David Paul Stern, Dr Helen Roberts, Fay Gillott, Ms Lynne Lockyer, Mark Pullen, Dr Jackie Bridges, David Parfitt
Income: £20,448,000 [2017]; £19,795,000 [2016]; £19,210,000 [2015]; £18,104,000 [2014]; £17,520,000 [2013]

The Brenley Trust
Registered: 7 Mar 2013
Tel: 01372 841801
Activities: General charitable purposes; education, training; advancement of health or saving of lives; prevention or relief of poverty; overseas aid, famine relief
Address: 17 Princes Drive, Oxshott, Leatherhead, Surrey, KT22 0UL
Trustees: Mr Patrick Riley, Mr Robbert Zoet, Mrs Marie-Louise Brenninkmeyer
Income: £10,141,818 [2017]; £577,012 [2016]; £1,055,067 [2015]; £307,226 [2014]

Brent Citizens Advice Bureaux
Registered: 6 Oct 1995 *Employees:* 20 *Volunteers:* 114
Tel: 020 8438 1213 *Website:* citizensadvicebrent.org.uk
Activities: General charitable purposes; education, training; disability; prevention or relief of poverty; accommodation, housing
Address: Brent Citizens Advice Bureau, 270-272 High Road, London, NW10 2EY
Trustees: Mrs Mabel Sumner, Mr David Askwith, Mr Mohamoud Ibrahim, Mr Victor Rae-Reeves, Ms Louisa Martin, Ms Linda Lam, Ms Iris Brown, Mr Yoola Buko, Mr David Brodie, Mr John Julius Bash, Ms Marie Whyte
Income: £1,133,625 [2017]; £1,250,658 [2016]; £1,104,368 [2015]; £987,345 [2014]; £1,001,358 [2013]

Brent Community Transport
Registered: 21 Aug 1980 *Employees:* 34 *Volunteers:* 4
Tel: 020 3114 7022 *Website:* brentct.org.uk
Activities: General charitable purposes; education, training; disability; prevention or relief of poverty; economic, community development, employment; other charitable purposes
Address: Office 301, 10 Courtenay Road, East Lane Business Park, Wembley, Middlesex, HA9 7ND
Trustees: Ms Hazel Jane Sheppard, Mr Moses, Mrs Jacqueline Oliver, Mr Raymond Douglas Starr, Mr Roger Maurice Simmons
Income: £1,503,312 [2017]; £1,469,707 [2016]; £1,407,565 [2015]; £1,324,909 [2014]; £1,164,415 [2013]

Brent Mind (Association for Mental Health)
Registered: 27 May 1992 *Employees:* 20 *Volunteers:* 7
Tel: 020 7259 8100 *Website:* brentmind.org.uk
Activities: General charitable purposes; education, training; advancement of health or saving of lives; disability; prevention or relief of poverty; accommodation, housing; amateur sport; other charitable purposes
Address: Brent Mind, Design Works, Park Parade, London, NW10 4HT
Trustees: Mr Thomas Fitzgerald, Mr Jonathan Anthony Lawlor, Mr Ross O'Brien
Income: £1,154,415 [2017]; £1,397,813 [2016]; £1,387,570 [2015]; £1,421,475 [2014]; £1,711,045 [2013]

Brent, Wandsworth and Westminster Mind
Registered: 11 Oct 1985 *Employees:* 103 *Volunteers:* 60
Tel: 020 7259 8100 *Website:* bwwmind.org.uk
Activities: The advancement of health or saving of lives; disability; accommodation, housing
Address: Hopkinson House, 6 Osbert Street, London, SW1P 2QU
Trustees: Mr Julian Seidman, Ms Sue Williamson, Dr Momotaj Islam, Miss Jessica Laura Garbett, Ms Maureen Campbell, Mr Thomas James Fitzgerald, Mr Jonathan Anthony Lawlor, Dr Gail Alexandra Wingham, Miss Rosalind Frances Elizabeth Farrer, Mr Gavin McCabe, Mr Ross O'Brien
Income: £2,772,305 [2017]; £3,824,738 [2016]; £2,326,238 [2015]; £2,166,549 [2014]; £2,063,619 [2013]

Brentford FC Community Sports Trust

Registered: 20 Jan 2006 *Employees:* 68 *Volunteers:* 17
Tel: 020 8326 7030 *Website:* brentfordfccst.com
Activities: Education, training; advancement of health or saving of lives; disability; arts, culture, heritage, science; amateur sport; economic, community development, employment; recreation
Address: Brentford FC Community Sports Trust, 37 Half Acre, Brentford, Middlesex, TW8 8BH
Trustees: Mr Brian Robert Burgess, Mr Ian Dobie, Mr Christopher John Gammon, Mr Karl Adrian Reynolds, Mr John Lawrence Cudmore, Ms Eileen De Souza, Mr Donald Gilbert Kerr, Mrs Anita Ralli
Income: £1,773,663 [2017]; £1,521,657 [2016]; £1,464,624 [2015]; £1,245,909 [2014]; £1,447,298 [2013]

Brentry and Henbury Childrens Centre Limited

Registered: 24 Mar 2005 *Employees:* 52 *Volunteers:* 15
Tel: 0117 959 3800 *Website:* bhchildrenscentre.org.uk
Activities: Education, training
Address: BHCC, Brentry Lane, Brentry, Bristol, BS10 6RG
Trustees: Ms Gill Frost, Mrs Helen Rowe, Mrs Stephanie Pritchett, Ms Gail Hunter, Mr Paul Matthews, Ms Janet Horton, Mrs Monica Turnbull, Mrs Debra James, Mrs Melanie Murphy, Ms Amy Bodey, Mr David John Hinnigan, Ms Sarah Matthews
Income: £1,435,416 [2017]; £1,268,727 [2016]; £1,366,401 [2015]; £1,464,117 [2014]; £1,505,776 [2013]

Brentwood Leisure Trust

Registered: 16 Jun 2004 *Employees:* 45 *Volunteers:* 12
Tel: 01277 251151 *Website:* brentwood-centre.co.uk
Activities: The advancement of health or saving of lives; amateur sport
Address: The Brentwood Centre, Doddinghurst Road, Pilgrims Hatch, Brentwood, Essex, CM15 9NN
Trustees: Mr John Kerslake, Mr Mark Peter Reed, Mr David Johnston, David Morphew, Mr Philip Cadman, Mrs Louise Rowlands, Tina Davis
Income: £2,478,251 [2017]; £2,263,639 [2016]; £2,198,669 [2015]; £2,186,850 [2014]; £2,362,888 [2013]

Brentwood Roman Catholic Diocesan Trust

Registered: 23 Apr 1964 *Employees:* 212 *Volunteers:* 4,500
Tel: 01277 265280 *Website:* dioceseofbrentwood.net
Activities: Religious activities
Address: Cathedral House, Ingrave Road, Brentwood, Essex, CM15 8AT
Trustees: The Brentwood Roman Catholic Diocese Trustee
Income: £12,586,599 [2017]; £12,355,880 [2016]; £12,535,371 [2015]; £13,262,015 [2014]; £11,537,097 [2013]

Brentwood School CIO

Registered: 30 Aug 2013 *Employees:* 288
Tel: 01277 243251 *Website:* brentwoodschool.co.uk
Activities: Education, training
Address: Brentwood School, Middleton Hall Lane, Brentwood, Essex, CM15 8AS
Trustees: Sir Michael Snyder DSC FCA FRSA, Mr Michael Bolton BA MBE, Mrs Jenny Jones BA ARCM, Mr Paul Beresford FNAEA MARLA, Dr Christopher Tout MA PhD, Mr James Tumbridge CC MCIArb LLB, Lord Flight MA MBA, Ms Rosemary Martin MEd NPQH, The Venerable David Lowman BD AKC, Mr Robert McLintock MSc DMS DipEd, Mr David Elms MA FCA FCSI, Lord Black of Brentwood MA MCIPR FRSA, Professor Bruce Evans BSc PhD, Mr John May MA LLB, Miss Alison Chapman ACMA, Mrs Amanda Hardy
Income: £27,179,859 [2017]; £25,867,155 [2016]

Bridewell Royal Hospital

Registered: 23 Aug 1966 *Employees:* 263 *Volunteers:* 20
Tel: 01428 686798 *Website:* kesw.org
Activities: Education, training
Address: Ponds End Cottage, Ponds Lane, Albury, Guildford, Surrey, GU5 9DQ
Trustees: Mr Robert Angus Jack Stovold, Mr Michael Chadwick ACA CTA1, Councillor Carole Agnes Cockburn, Alderman Alastair John Naisbitt King, Mr Ian Christopher Norman Seaton, Mrs Elizabeth Caroline Cairncross, Mr Richard Ernest Tulloch Bennett, Mr Guy William Heason-Rockingham, Dr Alasdair Douglas Pinkerton, Mrs Justine Siobhan Voisin, Mrs Jane Neville, Deputy Richard David Regan, Alderman Peter Kenneth Estlin, Mr Antony John William Hudson, Mr David John Drysdale Allen, Alderman Sir David Hugh Wootton, Mr Benjimin George Burgher, Alderman Timothy Russell Hailes, The Venerable Stuart Alexander Beake, Mr Stephen Howard Ravenscroft, Mrs Caroline Haines
Income: £19,506,000 [2017]; £13,191,000 [2016]; £13,966,000 [2015]; £10,652,000 [2014]; £9,847,000 [2013]

Bridge 86 Limited

Registered: 7 Nov 1989 *Employees:* 50
Tel: 020 8298 8677 *Website:* bridgesupport.org
Activities: General charitable purposes; education, training; advancement of health or saving of lives; disability; accommodation, housing; economic, community development, employment; other charitable purposes
Address: Deepdene House, 30 Bellegrove Road, Welling, Kent, DA16 3PY
Trustees: Mr John Wilkes, Mr Haydn Gott, George Wilkinson, David Baldock, Debbie Okutubo, Al Beck, Dr Ahilan Nithiananthan, Ms Elaine Rassaby, Mrs Josephine Parnham, Mr Beez Fedia, Ms Sarah Boundy, Ms Amanda Hall
Income: £3,030,673 [2017]; £3,128,324 [2016]; £2,441,274 [2015]; £1,412,557 [2014]; £1,076,013 [2013]

Bridge Care Limited

Registered: 30 May 1988 *Employees:* 39 *Volunteers:* 24
Tel: 01225 338448 *Website:* bridgecare.org.uk
Activities: Disability; accommodation, housing
Address: 4 Beaufort West, Bath, BA1 6QB
Trustees: Mr Geoffrey Weekes, Mrs Tilly Jessie Wood, John Todman, Dr Paul Johnathan Booth, Mr Ross Evans, Mrs Shirley Furze, Graham Barber, Mr Nicholas Andrew Coates
Income: £1,431,425 [2017]; £1,309,090 [2016]; £1,411,654 [2015]; £1,255,759 [2014]; £1,280,852 [2013]

Bridge Estate

Registered: 13 Nov 1963
Tel: 0115 876 3649 *Website:* gossweb.nottinghamcity.gov.uk
Activities: Economic, community development, employment
Address: Nottingham City Council, Loxley House, Station Street, Nottingham, NG2 3NG
Trustees: Councillors of Nottingham City Council
Income: £2,277,916 [2017]; £2,278,178 [2016]; £2,037,709 [2015]; £1,999,947 [2014]; £1,996,586 [2013]

Bridge House Estates
Registered: 24 Mar 1994 *Employees:* 108
Tel: 020 7332 1382 *Website:* citybridgetrust.org.uk
Activities: Education, training; advancement of health or saving of lives; disability; prevention or relief of poverty; accommodation, housing; arts, culture, heritage, science; environment, conservation, heritage; economic, community development, employment; other charitable purposes
Address: City Solicitor's Department, City of London Corporation, P O Box 270, London, EC2P 2EJ
Trustees: The Mayor and Commonalty and Citizens of The City of London
Income: £34,100,000 [2017]; £31,400,000 [2016]; £92,600,000 [2015]; £40,900,000 [2014]; £43,200,000 [2013]

The Bridge Project
Registered: 17 Apr 1986 *Employees:* 77 *Volunteers:* 54
Tel: 01274 723863 *Website:* thebridgeproject.org.uk
Activities: Education, training; advancement of health or saving of lives
Address: The Bridge Project, 29-37 Salem Street, Bradford, BD1 4QH
Trustees: Mr Moh Mistry, Mr Peter Sleigh, Ms Marisa Lloyd, Ms Melva Burton, Dr Andrew Clayton-Stead, Mr Ralph Berry
Income: £3,252,255 [2017]; £3,567,212 [2016]; £3,230,884 [2015]; £2,767,156 [2014]; £2,647,810 [2013]

Bridge To The Future
Registered: 28 Aug 2013 *Volunteers:* 3
Tel: 020 7969 5500
Activities: Education, training
Address: 10 Queen Street Place, London, EC4R 1AG
Trustees: Mr Guglielmo Verdirame, Dr Emma Kathrine Widdis, Sir Michael David Jackson, Ms Fleur Meijs, Fraulein Jutta von Falkenhausen, Mr Andrea Mangoni, Mr Ewald Engelen
Income: £2,903,178 [2017]; £1,640,152 [2016]; £222,997 [2015]; £2,103,110 [2014]

Bridgend Association of Voluntary Organisations
Registered: 23 Mar 2012 *Employees:* 18 *Volunteers:* 40
Tel: 01656 810400 *Website:* bavo.org.uk
Activities: General charitable purposes; education, training; economic, community development, employment; other charitable purposes
Address: Bridgend Association of Voluntary Organisations, 112-113 Commercial Street, Maesteg, Bridgend, CF34 9DL
Trustees: M Davies, Stephen Curry, M Major MBE, C Owen, Mr Les Jones
Income: £1,033,314 [2017]; £1,169,089 [2016]; £1,192,149 [2015]; £1,222,542 [2014]; £1,215,677 [2013]

The Bridget Espinosa Memorial Trust
Registered: 12 Jul 1990 *Employees:* 37
Activities: General charitable purposes; education, training
Address: c/o Lester Aldridge LLP, 1 King Street, London, EC2V 8AU
Trustees: Eect Team, Ms Yvette Rathbone
Income: £4,272,452 [2016]; £4,273,091 [2015]; £3,633,913 [2014]; £3,396,930 [2013]; £3,183,806 [2012]

Bridgewater School
Registered: 19 Aug 2004 *Employees:* 69 *Volunteers:* 2
Tel: 0161 794 1463 *Website:* bridgewater-school.co.uk
Activities: Education, training
Address: Bridgewater School, Worsley Road, Worsley, Manchester, M28 2WQ
Trustees: Mr Christopher Edmund Haighton, Mrs Lisa Jayne Tyson, Mr Scott Alan Brenchley, Mrs Kirstie Simpson, Mr Craig Cheetham, Mrs Amanda Dagg, Mr Martin Christopher Moss, Mrs Jane Jones, Mrs Kathryn Mort, Mr Nicholas Robin Beesley, Mr Michael Gatenby
Income: £3,372,800 [2016]; £3,052,230 [2015]; £2,972,802 [2014]; £3,151,973 [2013]; £3,445,382 [2012]

Bridgewood Trust Limited
Registered: 16 Nov 1988 *Employees:* 163 *Volunteers:* 4
Tel: 01484 667866 *Website:* bridgewoodtrust.co.uk
Activities: Education, training; disability; accommodation, housing
Address: Bridgewood Trust Ltd, St Pauls House, Armitage Bridge, Huddersfield, W Yorks, HD4 7NR
Trustees: Mr John Leslie Turner, Mr Malcolm Tagg, Mrs Rowena Edwards, Mrs Jane Ireland, Mr Malcolm Riley, Mr Robert Wray, Mrs Linda Roberts
Income: £4,751,652 [2017]; £4,580,300 [2016]; £4,529,911 [2015]; £4,818,752 [2014]; £4,842,024 [2013]

Bridgwater Young Men's Christian Association
Registered: 7 Jul 1999 *Employees:* 121 *Volunteers:* 48
Tel: 01278 422511 *Website:* bridgwaterymca.org
Activities: General charitable purposes; education, training; accommodation, housing; religious activities; amateur sport; economic, community development, employment
Address: YMCA, George Williams House, Friarn Avenue, Bridgwater, Somerset, TA6 3RF
Trustees: Mr Arthur Herbert Leigh, Mr John Ennals, Patricia Collins, Mr Alistair Matthews, Mr David Cockcroft, Mr Jon Clarey, Jason Hobday, Mr David Eccles
Income: £3,758,636 [2017]; £2,811,774 [2016]; £2,556,278 [2015]; £2,059,622 [2014]; £1,907,746 [2013]

Bridport and West Dorset Sports Trust Limited
Registered: 14 Aug 1975 *Employees:* 87
Tel: 01308 427464 *Website:* bridportleisure.com
Activities: Amateur sport
Address: Bridport Leisure Centre, Skilling Hill Road, Bridport, Dorset, DT6 5LN
Trustees: Mr Alec Bailey MA FCA, Malcolm Heaver, Susanna Newall, Allan Staerck, Mr John Wright, John MacKenzie, Dr George Skellern, Peter Brook, Mrs Margery Hookings, Mr Christopher Baker
Income: £1,437,629 [2017]; £1,365,526 [2016]; £1,559,222 [2015]; £1,357,370 [2014]; £1,366,841 [2013]

Brighton & Sussex University Hospitals NHS Trust Charitable Fund
Registered: 20 Nov 1995 *Employees:* 2
Tel: 01273 696955
Activities: Education, training; advancement of health or saving of lives
Address: BSUH NHS Trust, Eastern Road, Brighton, BN2 5BE
Trustees: Brighton and Sussex University Hospitals NHS Trust
Income: £2,325,518 [2017]; £3,643,374 [2016]; £2,078,198 [2015]; £2,411,372 [2014]; £2,373,104 [2013]

Brighton College

Registered: 18 Mar 1963 Employees: 665
Tel: 01273 704200 Website: brightoncollege.net
Activities: Education, training
Address: Eastern Road, Brighton, BN2 0AL
Trustees: Mr Geoff Miller MBE FCIB, Mr Andrew John Symonds FRICS MCIArb, Miss Nicola Leach MBA JP, Mr Adam Pettitt, Mr Peter Jackson, Mrs Martina Asmar LLB, Ms Elizabeth Louise Weeks, Mr Miles Templeman, Mr Andrew Thomas Cayley CMG QC, Mr Robert James Hannington FRICS FSA FIABCI BSc, Mr Neville Abraham CBE BSc, Mr Robert John Stuart Weir FCA BA, Mr Philip Charles Ward, Rt Hon Francis Maude MP, Mrs Joan Deslandes, Mr Richard Thomas Ricci, Christopher Snell, Lord John Mogg KCMG, Mr Nicholas Alexander Pink FSA FSC
Income: £47,944,392 [2017]; £49,091,964 [2016]; £44,459,417 [2015]; £41,018,338 [2014]; £35,190,830 [2013]

Brighton Dome and Festival Ltd

Registered: 17 Oct 1966 Employees: 98 Volunteers: 73
Tel: 01273 260814 Website: brightondome.org
Activities: Arts, culture, heritage, science
Address: 12A Pavilion Buildings, Castle Square, Brighton, BN1 1EE
Trustees: Mr Simon Fanshawe, Mr Timothy Aspinall, Mrs Polly Toynbee, Mr David Jordan CBE, Prof David Gann, Councillor Carol Ann Theobald, Mr Adrian Leonard Morris, Mr Donald Clark, Mr Alan McCarthy, Professor Julian Crampton, Mr Nelson Fernadez, Mr Danny Homan, Mr Christopher George Martin, Mrs Lucy Alexandra Davies
Income: £8,354,175 [2017]; £8,211,106 [2016]; £7,098,449 [2015]; £7,265,173 [2014]; £7,913,929 [2013]

Brighton Housing Trust

Registered: 8 Jul 1982 Employees: 210 Volunteers: 91
Tel: 01273 645400 Website: bht.org.uk
Activities: The prevention or relief of poverty; accommodation, housing
Address: Brighton Housing Trust, 144 London Road, Brighton, BN1 4PH
Trustees: Sarah Butler, Peter Freeman, Hugh Burnett, Kelvin MacDonald, Bill Randall, Kirsty Coates, Mr Ian Millar, Roger Hinton Roger Hinton, Joan Mortimer, Melanie Davis, Leona Daniel, Ailsa Suttie
Income: £12,903,196 [2017]; £13,126,052 [2016]; £13,279,654 [2015]; £13,093,687 [2014]; £12,548,911 [2013]

Brighton YMCA

Registered: 22 Feb 1989 Employees: 102
Tel: 01273 220900 Website: brightonymca.co.uk
Activities: Accommodation, housing
Address: Steine House, 55 Old Steine, Brighton, BN1 1NX
Trustees: Mr Brian Allan Lucas, Mr Peter John Field, Ms Sarah Jane Johnston-Ellis, Mrs Susan Louise Trimingham, Mr David William Hancock, Mr Joao Pedro Bocas, Mr Peter Claud Jukes
Income: £3,929,122 [2017]; £3,851,755 [2016]; £3,467,917 [2015]; £2,860,656 [2014]; £2,791,338 [2013]

Brighton and Hove Seaside Community Homes Limited

Registered: 4 Jan 2010 Employees: 5
Tel: 01273 732061 Website: seaside-homes.org.uk
Activities: Accommodation, housing
Address: Unit F, Hove Technology Centre, St Josephs Close, Hove, E Sussex, BN3 7ES
Trustees: Mrs Mary Bridget Mears, Roy Crowhurst, Ms Susannah Jane McClintock, Mr David Gibson, Vivien Joan Woodcock-Downey, Mr Baboucarr Mbye Sohna, Mr Christopher Moquet, Mr Kevin Allen
Income: £3,950,127 [2017]; £3,615,515 [2016]; £3,394,903 [2015]; £2,710,852 [2014]; £1,409,471 [2013]

The Brilliant Club

Registered: 20 Jun 2012 Employees: 56
Tel: 020 7939 1948 Website: thebrilliantclub.org
Activities: Education, training
Address: The Brilliant Club, 66 Hammersmith Road, London, W14 8UD
Trustees: Dame Susan John, Mr James Turner, Mr Matthew Hood, John Timothy, Professor Ella Ritchie, Mr Ben Williams, Mr Russell Hobby, Jo Saxton
Income: £5,130,037 [2017]; £3,865,464 [2016]; £2,235,504 [2015]; £1,021,642 [2014]; £459,406 [2013]

Bristol Aero Collection Trust

Registered: 24 Apr 1992 Employees: 12 Volunteers: 140
Tel: 0117 931 5315 Website: aerospacebristol.org
Activities: Education, training; environment, conservation, heritage
Address: Hangar 16s, Hayes Way, Patchway, Bristol, BS34 5BZ
Trustees: Group Captain John Duncan Heron OBE, Mr Iain Gray, Mr Jonathan Edwards, Mr Lloyd Charles Burnell, Mr Andrew Duncan Mc Callam Gregg, Mr Roger Smart, Mr David James Perry, Mr Peter Richard Coombs, Ms Kate Anthony Wilkinson, Mr Howard Mason, Mr Christopher James Ware, Mr Paul Craig
Income: £1,911,640 [2017]; £11,789,996 [2016]; £4,250,998 [2015]; £913,283 [2014]; £22,356 [2013]

Bristol Charities

Registered: 20 Apr 2005 Employees: 19 Volunteers: 2
Tel: 0117 930 0301 Website: bristolcharities.org.uk
Activities: General charitable purposes
Address: Bristol Charities, 17 St Augustines Parade, Bristol, BS1 4UL
Trustees: Miss Laura Claydon LLB, Mrs Harriet Bosnell, Mr Paul Staples, Dr Ros Kennedy MB BS MRCP MRCGP DCH, Ms Michelle Meredith, Mr Nolan Ellis Webber, Mr John Webster, Mr Anthony Beauchamp Harris MSc FCA, Mr Richard Gore LLB, Mr Jonathan O'Shea, Dr Shaheen Shahzadi Chaudhry
Income: £3,819,606 [2017]; £1,673,707 [2016]; £2,921,715 [2015]; £1,486,934 [2014]; £1,600,693 [2013]

The Bristol Clifton and West of England Zoological Society Limited

Registered: 20 Jul 2004 Employees: 194 Volunteers: 241
Tel: 0117 428 5301
Activities: Education, training; animals; environment, conservation, heritage
Address: Bristol Zoo Gardens, Clifton, Bristol, BS8 3HA
Trustees: Mr Malcolm Broad, Mr Paul Kearney, Mrs Claire Ladkin, Mr David Richard Esam, Ms Victoria Ash, Professor Richard David Pancost, Mrs Charlotte Mary Moar, Mr Christopher Arthur Booy OBE, Mr Mathew Laws, Professor Steven Neill, Jo Price
Income: £11,608,000 [2017]; £10,231,000 [2016]; £9,555,000 [2015]; £8,943,000 [2014]; £8,528,000 [2013]

The Bristol Diocesan Board of Finance Limited
Registered: 23 Nov 1966 *Employees:* 47 *Volunteers:* 131
Tel: 0117 906 0100 *Website:* bristol.anglican.org
Activities: Religious activities
Address: First Floor, Diocese of Bristol, Hillside House, 1500 Parkway North, Newbrick Road, Stoke Gifford, Bristol, BS34 8YU
Trustees: Mr Andrew Lucas, Canon Nicholas Orman, Canon Peter Robottom, The Rev Canon Mat Ineson, Mr Edward Buchan, The Rev Kat Campion-Spall, Mr Bruce Finnamore, The Ven Christine Froude Archdeacon of Malmesbury, The Rt Rev Dr Lee Rayfield Bishop of Swindon, Professor David Clarke, The Rev Canon Raymond Adams, The Very Rev Dr David Hoyle Dean of Bristol, Canon David Froude
Income: £8,290,000 [2016]; £8,834,000 [2015]; £7,763,000 [2014]; £7,636,000 [2013]; £7,653,000 [2012]

Bristol Drugs Project Limited
Registered: 14 May 1985 *Employees:* 121 *Volunteers:* 84
Tel: 0117 987 6006 *Website:* bdp.org.uk
Activities: The advancement of health or saving of lives; prevention or relief of poverty; other charitable purposes
Address: Bristol Drugs Project, 11 Brunswick Square, Bristol, BS2 8PE
Trustees: Mr Ian Sherwood, Mr Paul Osterley, Mr Michael David Lea, Jonathan Davis, Mrs Jane Caroline Oakland, Dr Tom Smyth, Mr John Prior, Mr John Ross Long, Mr Keith Henry Francis Aston, Dr Rosalind Penelope Kennedy, Rozzy Amos
Income: £4,879,351 [2017]; £5,147,428 [2016]; £4,992,216 [2015]; £4,617,808 [2014]; £4,017,991 [2013]

Bristol Grammar School
Registered: 17 Jun 2004 *Employees:* 287
Tel: 0117 973 6006 *Website:* bristolgrammarschool.co.uk
Activities: Education, training
Address: Bristol Grammar School, University Road, Bristol, BS8 1SR
Trustees: Mrs Andrea Arlidge, Mrs Barbara Bates, Dr Julie Knox BSc PhD, Mrs Jane O'Gallagher MBChB MRCP FRCPCH FHEA, Ms Maria Crayton, Mr David Shelton, Mr David Pester, Mr Patrick Meehan, Prof Cedric Nishahthan Canagarajah, Mrs Candida Jill Gil, Mr Alan Barr LLB, Mr Romesh Vaitilingam BA MBE, Mr Nigel Pickersgill BSc FCA, Mr Mark Robert Wilson, Dr Dominique Thompson, Prof Julie Selwyn, Mr John Sisman, Mr Justin Babak Vafadari, Ms Kate Redshaw
Income: £17,125,618 [2017]; £15,493,179 [2016]; £15,193,942 [2015]; £14,337,497 [2014]; £13,746,314 [2013]

Bristol Islamic Schools Trust
Registered: 29 Jun 1998 *Employees:* 39 *Volunteers:* 10
Tel: 0117 929 1661 *Website:* bist.org.uk
Activities: Education, training; religious activities; arts, culture, heritage, science; amateur sport
Address: 27 Baileys Mead Road, Stapleton, Bristol, BS16 1AE
Trustees: Mr Warren Barrett, Dr Ghassan Nounu Phd Bsc (Hons) Milthe, Abdul Wahab, Mr Tahir Mahmood, Zaynab Qazi, Mrs Parveen Mahmood, Mr Nisar Ahmed, Razwan Akbar, Mukhtar Ahmad Younis, Tariq Khan, Mr Abdus Salaam Chowdhury
Income: £1,080,741 [2016]; £1,015,592 [2015]; £960,831 [2014]; £964,956 [2013]

Bristol Music Trust
Registered: 28 Mar 2011 *Employees:* 196 *Volunteers:* 8
Tel: 0117 922 3686 *Website:* colstonhall.org
Activities: General charitable purposes; education, training; arts, culture, heritage, science
Address: Colston Hall, Colston Street, Bristol, BS1 5AR
Trustees: Mr Andrew Nisbet, Miss Sonia Mills, Ms Martino Lois Burgess, Mr Paul Fordham, Sir Brian McMaster, Ms Estella Tincknell, Ms Marie Nixon, Mr Henry Kenyon, Miss Michele Balfe, Mr James Wetz, Mr Simon Chapman
Income: £7,625,404 [2017]; £7,362,313 [2016]; £6,552,682 [2015]; £5,651,664 [2014]; £4,155,582 [2013]

Bristol Old Vic Theatre School Limited
Registered: 30 Jan 1990 *Employees:* 32 *Volunteers:* 10
Tel: 0117 980 9256 *Website:* oldvic.ac.uk
Activities: Education, training
Address: 1-2 Downside Road, Clifton, Bristol, BS8 4XF
Trustees: Mr David John Marsh, Mr Michael Henry, Ms Lucy Bowden, Ms Ruth Ann Foreman, Ms Morag Ann Massey, Mr John Sunil Das, Mrs Vanessa Hope Wingate Stevenson, Mr David Halton, Mr Martin John Boddy, Mr Guy Winearls Stobart, Mr Edwyn Jon Wilson, Priscilla Macquire-Samson
Income: £2,858,827 [2017]; £3,126,883 [2016]; £2,772,994 [2015]; £2,827,921 [2014]; £2,830,210 [2013]

Bristol Old Vic and Theatre Royal Trust Limited
Registered: 4 Oct 1963 *Employees:* 114 *Volunteers:* 2
Tel: 0117 317 8655 *Website:* bristololdvic.org.uk
Activities: Arts, culture, heritage, science; environment, conservation, heritage
Address: Bristol Old Vic Trust Ltd, Theatre Royal, King Street, Bristol, BS1 4ED
Trustees: Denis Burn, Oliver Rawlins, Gareth Edwards, Mr Mark Geoffrey Sullivan, Stephen Allpress, Mr Mark Dakin, Ms Chinoyerem Odimba, Paul Morrell OBE, Mr Michael David Lea, Mrs Claire Michelle Hiscott, Dame Liz Forgan DBE, Ms Helen Wilde, Ms Estella Jane Tincknell
Income: £7,224,114 [2017]; £6,505,936 [2016]; £5,219,240 [2015]; £5,924,599 [2014]; £6,069,234 [2013]

Bristol Sheltered Accommodation & Support Limited
Registered: 22 Jun 2010 *Employees:* 3 *Volunteers:* 15
Tel: 0117 971 3613
Activities: The prevention or relief of poverty; accommodation, housing
Address: Wick House, 191 Wick Road, Bristol, BS4 4HW
Trustees: Mr Ian MacDonald, Mr Philip Geoffrey Barnett, Mr Reginald Ison, Mr Philippe Clark, Ms Noelle Holland, Mr Richard Cook
Income: £1,095,972 [2017]; £915,392 [2016]; £1,218,498 [2015]; £983,701 [2014]; £1,024,976 [2013]

Bristol and South Gloucestershire Circuit of The Methodist Church
Registered: 27 Dec 2012 *Employees:* 23
Tel: 0117 951 8822 *Website:* bsgc.org.uk
Activities: Religious activities
Address: Horfield Methodist Church, Churchways Avenue, Bristol, BS7 8SN
Trustees: Knight-Mary, Janet George, Wood Bob, Peter Jones, Holmes-Cherry, Hatton Peter, Wallace Robert, Barley-Richard, Bellamy Beryl, David Alderman, Stephen Newell, Adam Biddlestone, Michael Culshaw, Moon-Penny, Osmond-Ann, North Dottie, Calvin Roberts, Allen Hosking, Anne Beattie, Caroline Slinn, Charles Redman, Christopher Sledge, David Phillips, Diane Bailey, Elaine Hopper, Freda Haddrell, Helen Doggart, Janet Hawkins, Jean Keel, Jennifer McLaren, Joy Harris, Julie Mann, Laurence Garner, Harnell Margaret, Mary Hurlstone, Michael Vardy, Monica Ricketts, Richard Ascott, Ruth Berridge, Shirley Blanning, Tracey Phillips, Valerie Astill, Workman-Keith, Jane Stacey, Sutton-Clive, Reed-Melainie, Redgers-Valerie, Williams Valerie, Brazier-Pete, Albury Matt, Lowe Bryan, Elaine Gibson, Clive Farnham, Rosalie Doyle, David Faulkner, Vicky Davies, Jong Sin Lee, Ken Ladd, Joy Harris, Margaret Johnston, Lansdown Tim, Parry Eurfron, Ireland John, John Seward, Richard Sharples, Rev Patrick David Stonehewer, Taylor Ann, Young Nigel, Mandy Briggs, Langley Emma, Roberts Pamela, Bishop-Barry, David Bertram, Gillard-Angela, Pearl Luxon, Andrew Orton, New Emma, Andrew Eaves, Mr Barry Brown, Caroline Carter, Christine Varney, Dave Chandler, David King, Edith Ridsdale, Elizabeth Davies, Gordon Hicks, Ian Street, Janette Vardy, Jean Pickering, John Creech, Joy Yeoman, Keith Cornell, Mrs Margaret Spooner, Mary Eaves, Mary Barrington, Michael Stapleton, Pauline Harris, Rosalind Sledge, Sarah James, Sue Rooke, Trevor Watkins, Wendy Priddle, White-Philip, Christopher Spencer, Manners-June, Middleton-Keith, Phillimore-Patricia, Strode Kathryn, Sleath Colin, Mr Aylwyn Powell, Sue Rooke, Roy Howard, Janet Browning, Ann Street, Gwyneth Dean, Jenny McGrath, Doreen Stears, Jenny Cornell, Erica Geldart, Corinne Brown
Income: £1,342,968 [2016]; £1,832,448 [2015]; £1,061,838 [2014]; £1,085,737 [2013]

Britain Yearly Meeting of The Religious Society of Friends (Quakers)
Registered: 20 Jan 2009 *Employees:* 135 *Volunteers:* 1,000
Tel: 020 7663 1161 *Website:* quaker.org.uk
Activities: General charitable purposes; education, training; prevention or relief of poverty; religious activities; other charitable purposes
Address: Religious Society of Friends, Friends House, 173-177 Euston Road, London, NW1 2BJ
Trustees: Frances Voelcker, Graham Torr, James Eddington, Peter Ullathorne, Roy Love, Alastair Reid, Steve Pullan, Alison Breadon, Hazel Shellens, David Olver, Nick Eyre, Chris Willmore, Ingrid Greenhow, Sarah Donaldson, Caroline Nursey
Income: £10,902,000 [2016]; £10,900,000 [2015]; £11,336,000 [2014]; £12,063,000 [2013]; £10,918,000 [2012]

The Britford Bridge Trust
Registered: 19 Jan 2015
Activities: General charitable purposes
Address: Brodies House, 31-33 Union Grove, Aberdeen, AB10 6SD
Trustees: Mr Adrian Frost, Brodies & Co (Trustees) Limited, Dr Margaret Jane MacDougall
Income: £5,764,913 [2017]; £9,279,942 [2016]

The British Academy for The Promotion of Historical Philosophical and Philological Studies
Registered: 25 Nov 1965 *Employees:* 57
Tel: 020 7969 5200 *Website:* britac.ac.uk
Activities: Education, training; arts, culture, heritage, science; environment, conservation, heritage; other charitable purposes
Address: British Academy, 10 Carlton House Terrace, London, SW1Y 5AH
Trustees: Professor Genevra Richardson CBE FBA, Professor David Abulafia FBA, Professor Julian Birkinshaw FBA, Professor Sarah Worthington FBA QC, Professor Ash Amin CBE FBA, Professor Dominic Abrams FBA, Professor John Baines FBA, Professor Julia Barrow FBA, Professor Maxine Berg FBA, Professor Michael Keating FBA FRSE ACSS, Professor Anne Phillips FBA, Professor Eleanor Dickey FBA, Professor Stella Bruzzi FBA, Professor Sir David Cannadine PBA, Professor Nicholas Sims-Williams FBA, Professor Alan Bowman FBA, Professor Bencie Woll FBA, Professor Mary Morgan FBA, Professor Sally Shuttleworth FBA, Professor Roger Kain CBE FBA, Professor Glynis Jones FBA, Professor Marianne Elliott OBE FBA, Revd Professor Diarmaid MacCulloch KT FBA, Professor John Scott CBE FBA, Professor Christine Bell FBA
Income: £39,539,475 [2017]; £36,223,527 [2016]; £33,085,882 [2015]; £31,665,115 [2014]; £31,275,157 [2013]

The British Academy of Film and Television Arts
Registered: 15 Oct 1963 *Employees:* 142
Tel: 020 7734 0022 *Website:* bafta.org
Activities: Education, training; arts, culture, heritage, science
Address: 195 Piccadilly, London, W1J 9LN
Trustees: John Smith, Ms Anne Morrison, Ms Jane Lush, Marc Samuelson, Nick Button-Bown, Hannah Wyatt, Paul Morrell, Ms Philippa Harris, Sara Putt, Krishnendu Majumdar, Alison Jane Thompson
Income: £13,960,000 [2016]; £13,982,000 [2015]; £12,840,000 [2014]; £12,025,000 [2013]; £11,318,000 [2012]

The British Allergy Foundation
Registered: 17 Oct 2002 *Employees:* 25 *Volunteers:* 450
Tel: 01322 470337 *Website:* allergyuk.org
Activities: Education, training; advancement of health or saving of lives
Address: Allergy UK, Planwell House, 35 Edgington Way, Sidcup, Kent, DA14 5BH
Trustees: Professor Syed Hasan Arshad, Mrs Sarah Stoneham, Mr Brian Edward Hewitt, Mr James Redding, Ms Lynne Pritchard, Dr Adam T Fox, Mr Roy M Dudley-Southern, Mr Malcolm Christopher Elliott
Income: £1,475,813 [2017]; £1,394,549 [2016]; £1,264,959 [2015]; £1,485,117 [2014]; £1,142,395 [2013]

British American Drama Academy
Registered: 15 May 1985 *Employees:* 7
Website: bada.org.uk
Activities: Education, training
Address: 14-15 Gloucester Gate, London, NW1 4HG
Trustees: Mr Marcus Boyle, Ms Diane Gelon, Ms Maggie Whitlum-Cooper, Ms Louise Jeanne Chantal
Income: £2,281,260 [2017]; £2,344,781 [2016]; £2,242,548 [2015]; £2,070,694 [2014]; £2,481,770 [2013]

The British Asian Trust
Registered: 5 Jan 2009 *Employees:* 18 *Volunteers:* 1
Website: britishasiantrust.org
Activities: The prevention or relief of poverty; environment, conservation, heritage; economic, community development, employment
Address: Clarence House, St James's, London, SW1A 1BA
Trustees: Mrs Fayeeza Naqvi, Mr Christopher Mathias, Mr Nihal Arthanayake, Mrs Shalni Arora, Mr Asif Rangoonwala, Mr Manoj Badale, Mr Salman Mahdi, Mr Sonny Takhar
Income: £6,296,279 [2017]; £2,297,281 [2016]; £1,779,348 [2015]; £1,761,787 [2014]; £1,371,053 [2013]

British Association for Behavioural and Cognitive Psychotherapies
Registered: 23 Jul 2003 *Employees:* 29 *Volunteers:* 190
Website: babcp.com
Activities: Education, training; advancement of health or saving of lives
Address: British Association of Behavioural & Cognitive Psychotherapies, Imperial House, 79-81 Hornby Street, Bury, Lancs, BL9 5BN
Trustees: Dr Christopher Williams, Mr Gerard Martin McErlane, Ms Brenda Davis, Mr Allan Brownrigg, Dr Gillian Todd Miller, Professor Robert John Newell, Professor Kate Davidson, Mr Steve Flatt, Mr Yaa Nath, Mr Thomas Reeves
Income: £1,393,194 [2017]; £1,553,162 [2016]; £1,497,294 [2015]; £1,406,206 [2014]; £1,228,149 [2013]

British Association for Counselling and Psychotherapy
Registered: 15 Feb 1988 *Employees:* 104 *Volunteers:* 101
Tel: 01455 883336 *Website:* bacp.co.uk
Activities: Education, training; advancement of health or saving of lives
Address: British Association for Counselling, 15 St Johns Business Park, Lutterworth, Leics, LE17 4HB
Trustees: Prof Sophie Grace Chappell, Mrs Mhairi Jane Thurston, Rev Edwin William Carden, Miss Myira Khan, Mr Andrew Kinder, Dr Caryl Helen Sibbett, Dr Andrew Ronald Reeves, Mrs Vanessa Stirum, Ms Natalie Fiona Bailey, Ms Una Cavanagh
Income: £8,587,937 [2017]; £8,205,369 [2016]; £7,827,901 [2015]; £7,814,563 [2014]; £6,955,616 [2013]

British Association for The Advancement of Science
Registered: 27 Mar 1963 *Employees:* 31 *Volunteers:* 1,337
Tel: 0870 770 7101 *Website:* britishscienceassociation.org
Activities: Education, training; arts, culture, heritage, science; economic, community development, employment
Address: The British Association for The Advancement of Science, Wellcome Wolfson Building, 165 Queen's Gate, London, SW7 5HD
Trustees: Professor Brian Ratcliffe, Dr Sarah Main, Suzanne Gage, Steven Hill, Matthew Robert Locke, Mr Stephen Nuttall, David Willetts, Valerie Marshall, Ms Louise Archer, Emily Dawson, Mrs Lana Hampicke, Mr Colin Wilkinson
Income: £3,019,381 [2016]; £2,652,526 [2015]; £2,908,598 [2014]; £3,109,453 [2013]; £3,838,060 [2012]

British Association of Dermatologists
Registered: 25 Sep 1973 *Employees:* 33
Tel: 020 7383 0266 *Website:* bad.org.uk
Activities: Education, training; advancement of health or saving of lives
Address: 4 Fitzroy Square, London, W1T 5HQ
Trustees: Dr D J Eedy, Dr Anshoo Sahota, Dr Jenny Hughes, Dr Ruth Murphy, Dr Daron Carl Seukeran, Dr Wanda Sonia Robles, Dr Karen Gibbon, Dr Anna Chapman, Dr Colin Morton, Dr Julia Margaret Stainforth, Dr Irshad Zaki, Dr William Porter, Dr Nick Levell, Dr Tanya Ownsworth Bleiker, Dr Mark Richard Griffiths, Professor Alexander Vincent Anstey, Dr Robert Martin Graham, Dr Paul Farrant, Dr Richard Azurdia, Dr David Alderdice, Dr Vincent Li, Dr Graham Johnston, Dr Michelle Oakford
Income: £4,300,529 [2016]; £3,683,840 [2015]; £3,607,256 [2014]; £3,962,431 [2013]; £4,043,481 [2012]

The British Association of Plastic Reconstructive and Aesthetic Surgeons
Registered: 28 Oct 1991 *Employees:* 7 *Volunteers:* 125
Tel: 020 7831 5161 *Website:* bapras.org.uk
Activities: General charitable purposes; education, training; advancement of health or saving of lives
Address: BAPRAS, Royal College of Surgeons of England, 35-43 Lincoln's Inn Fields, London, WC2A 3PE
Trustees: Mr Simon Eccles, Miss Barbara Jemec, Mr Nicholas James, Mr Asit Khandwala, Mr David Ward, Mr Robert Ian Stewart Winterton, Mr Peter Dziewulski, Mr John Stephen Sinclair, Mr Richard Cole, Ms Ruth Waters, Mr Derek John Gordon, Mr Mark Henley, Mr Marc Swan, Mr Ashutosh Kotwal, Mr David McGill, Mr Ian Christopher Josty, Mr Joe O'Donoghue, Ms Monica Fawzy, Miss Reena Agarwal
Income: £1,110,959 [2016]; £1,165,264 [2015]; £1,470,683 [2014]; £1,163,566 [2013]; £1,121,292 [2012]

The British Association of Urological Surgeons Limited
Registered: 4 Dec 2008 *Employees:* 8
Tel: 020 7869 6950 *Website:* baus.org.uk
Activities: Education, training; advancement of health or saving of lives
Address: BAUS, 35-43 Lincoln's Inn Fields, London, WC2A 3PE
Trustees: Mr Ian Pearce, Mr Kenneth Mark Anson, Mr Damian Capel Hanbury, Mr Oliver James Wiseman, Mr Nicholas Andrew Watkin, Mr Kieran J O'Flynn, Mr Duncan John Summerton, Mrs Suzie Venn, Mr Paul Anthony Jones
Income: £1,566,062 [2016]; £2,945,833 [2015]; £1,676,585 [2014]; £1,773,814 [2013]; £1,619,836 [2012]

The British Cardiovascular Society
Registered: 7 Aug 2002 *Employees:* 13 *Volunteers:* 500
Tel: 020 7383 3887 *Website:* bcs.com
Activities: Education, training; advancement of health or saving of lives
Address: 9 Fitzroy Square, London, W1T 5HW
Trustees: Mr John Carrier, Dr David Michael Walker, Mr Nigel Turner, Dr Sarah Clarke, Mr Russell Smith, Professor John Greenwood, Professor Nick Linker, Mr Graham Meek, Professor Peter Weissberg, Dr Andrew Wragg, Malcolm Bell
Income: £2,381,084 [2016]; £2,542,264 [2015]; £2,521,957 [2014]; £2,261,625 [2013]; £2,279,431 [2012]

The British Computer Society

Registered: 10 Dec 1985 *Employees:* 273 *Volunteers:* 1,100
Tel: 01793 417417 *Website:* bcs.org.uk
Activities: Education, training; disability
Address: The Chartered Institute for IT, First Floor, BCS, Block D, North Star House, North Star Avenue, Swindon, Wilts, SN2 1FA
Trustees: Michael Cooper FBCS, Professor James Davenport FBCS CITP, Paul Martynenko FBCS, Gillian Arnold MBCS, Mr Chris Rees FBCS CITP, Helen Fletcher CEng MBCS CITP, Eur Ing Alaistair Revell CEng MBCS CITP, Michael Grant FBCS, Professor Tom Crick CEng CSci FBCS, Rebecca George OBE FBCS CITP, Eur Ing Professor Margaret Ross MBE CEng CSci HonFBCS CITP, Dr James Daniel McCafferty FBCS CITP, Stephen Pattison FBCS, Rubi Kaur FBCS CITP, Dr Indranil Nath FBCS CITP, Dr Ben Booth FBCS CITP
Income: £38,586,000 [2016]; £35,165,000 [2015]; £27,137,000 [2014]; £21,299,000 [2013]; £20,246,000 [2012]

The British Council

Registered: 3 Jan 1963 *Employees:* 10,596 *Volunteers:* 5
Website: britishcouncil.org
Activities: Education, training; overseas aid, famine relief; arts, culture, heritage, science; other charitable purposes
Address: The British Council, 10 Spring Gardens, London, SW1A 2BN
Trustees: Mr Christopher Rodrigues CBE, Professor Janet Beer, Ros Marshall, Rohan Gunatillake, Kirsty Lang, Deborah Bronnert CMG, Mr William Roe CBE, Mr Kevin John Havelock, Mr James Cronin, Baroness Usha Prashar CBE, Gareth Bullock, Tom Thomson OBE, Sir David Verey CBE, Oliver Laird, Mrs Yasmin Diamond CB
Income: £1,076,893,479 [2017]; £979,638,979 [2016]; £972,877,000 [2015]; £864,289,000 [2014]; £781,289,000 [2013]

British Deaf Association

Registered: 18 Jan 1994 *Employees:* 46 *Volunteers:* 10
Tel: 020 7697 4140 *Website:* bda.org.uk
Activities: Education, training; disability; human rights, religious or racial harmony, equality or diversity
Address: Second Floor, 356 Holloway Road, London, N7 6PA
Trustees: Ms Agnes Dyab, Mr Ashley Robert Kendall, Mr Robert Edward James Adam, Miss Abigail Gorman, Mrs Teresa Padden-Duncan, Ms Sarah Lawrence, Mrs Sylvia Olive Simmonds, Miss Alexandra Dury, Miss Dawn Marshall
Income: £1,668,932 [2017]; £1,932,183 [2016]; £1,545,774 [2015]; £1,555,007 [2014]; £1,208,974 [2013]

British Dental Association Trust Fund

Registered: 28 Sep 1965 *Employees:* 6 *Volunteers:* 6
Tel: 020 7563 4150 *Website:* bda.org
Activities: General charitable purposes; education, training; environment, conservation, heritage
Address: 73 Wickham Way, Beckenham, Kent, BR3 3AH
Trustees: Dr Peter Ward, Dr Philip Stanley Duff Henderson, Mr Paul David Blaylock, Dr Alison Ruth Lockyer, Dr Jason Martin Stokes, Mr Nigel Jones, Mr Richard David Shilling, Mr Michael Colin Armstrong, Dr Rasikkumar Arjan Rajshi Ladwa, Mr Timothy Harker, Dr Edward John Crouch
Income: £1,463,649 [2017]; £910,748 [2016]; £857,066 [2015]; £553,405 [2014]; £685,518 [2013]

The British Diabetic Association

Registered: 7 Jun 1967 *Employees:* 399 *Volunteers:* 7,000
Tel: 0345 123 2399 *Website:* diabetes.org.uk
Activities: Education, training; advancement of health or saving of lives
Address: Wells Lawrence House, 126 Back Church Lane, London, E1 1FH
Trustees: Sir Peter Dixon, Mr Julian Baust, Professor Rhys Williams, Mr Gareth Hoskin, Professor Wasim Hanif, Mr Robin Swindell, Ms Rosie Cunningham Thomas, Mr Noah Franklin, Dr Robert Young, Ms Helen McCallum, Mrs Janice Watson, Sir Harry Burns, Mr Ian King, Dr Wendy Thomson
Income: £36,474,000 [2016]; £37,028,000 [2015]; £41,808,000 [2014]; £38,840,000 [2013]; £27,834,000 [2012]

British Dressage

Registered: 15 Jan 2014 *Employees:* 38 *Volunteers:* 2,797
Tel: 024 7669 8843 *Website:* britishdressage.co.uk
Activities: Education, training; amateur sport; animals; recreation
Address: Meriden Business Park, Copse Drive, Meriden, W Midlands, CV5 9RG
Trustees: Mrs Julie Frizzell, Mrs Penelope Linda Denise Pollard, Mr Paul Hayler, Mr Peter Storr, Mr David John Trott, Dr Thomasina Mary Cowie, Mrs Claire Elaine Moir
Income: £4,337,363 [2016]; £4,222,189 [2015]; £3,744,056 [2014]

The British Dyslexia Association

Registered: 4 Feb 1985 *Employees:* 21 *Volunteers:* 20
Tel: 0333 405 4555 *Website:* bdadyslexia.org.uk
Activities: General charitable purposes; education, training; disability; economic, community development, employment
Address: The British Dyslexia Association, Unit 6a Bracknell Beeches, Old Bracknell Lane West, Bracknell, Berks, RG12 7BW
Trustees: Mr Richard John Phillips, Mrs Carolyn Fay Dutton, Mr John Levell, Mr Mark Edward Sherin, Patrick Elliot, Jeffrey Hughes, Mrs Liane Cockram, Mr William Plant, Pamela Tomalin, Michael Johnson, Mrs Lesley Anne Hill, Mr David George Philip Williams, Gillian Audley
Income: £1,861,562 [2017]; £1,838,750 [2016]; £2,270,645 [2015]; £2,466,697 [2014]; £1,819,900 [2013]

The British Ecological Society

Registered: 28 Jan 1981 *Employees:* 21 *Volunteers:* 53
Tel: 020 7685 2500 *Website:* britishecologicalsociety.org
Activities: Education, training; environment, conservation, heritage
Address: British Ecological Society, Charles Darwin House, 12 Roger Street, London, WC1N 2JU
Trustees: Dr Peter Arthur Thomas, Professor Rosemary Susan Hails, Dr Juliet Anne Vickery, Professor Richard David Bardgett, Professor Jane Hill, Dr Zoe Davies, Dr Nina Hautekeete, Dr Cristina Camargo Banks Leite, Dr Alison Jane Birkett, Dr William Daniel Gosling, Dr Thomas Harold George Ezard, Professor Helen Elizabeth Roy, Professor Susan Hartley, Dr Adam Vanbergen, Dr Peter Brotherton, Professor David James Hodgson
Income: £3,918,000 [2016]; £3,595,000 [2015]; £3,356,983 [2014]; £4,007,858 [2013]; £3,273,102 [2012]

The British Editorial Society of Bone and Joint Surgery

Registered: 22 Sep 1962 *Employees:* 18
Tel: 020 7782 0010 *Website:* boneandjoint.org.uk
Activities: Education, training
Address: The British Editorial Society of Bone & Joint Surgery, 22 Buckingham Street, London, WC2N 6ET
Trustees: Mr Martin Bircher, Mr Fergal Patrick Monsell, Mr Ananda Mohan Nanu, Mr Timothy Wilton, Ms Deborah Margaret Eastwood
Income: £2,574,817 [2016]; £2,503,762 [2015]; £2,373,431 [2014]; £2,598,816 [2013]; £2,389,204 [2012]

British Emunah Fund
Registered: 27 May 1963 *Employees:* 6 *Volunteers:* 60
Tel: 020 8203 6066 *Website:* emunah.org.uk
Activities: The prevention or relief of poverty; overseas aid, famine relief
Address: Shield House, Harmony Way, Hendon, London, NW4 2BZ
Trustees: Mr Laurence Paul Markham, Mrs Michelle Hirschfield, Mrs Camille Compton, Mrs Rochelle Selby, Lady Elaine Sacks
Income: £1,077,921 [2016]; £1,117,707 [2015]; £1,645,798 [2014]; £942,821 [2013]; £1,070,006 [2012]

British Epilepsy Association
Registered: 5 Aug 1964 *Employees:* 60 *Volunteers:* 300
Tel: 0113 210 8800 *Website:* epilepsy.org.uk
Activities: Education, training; advancement of health or saving of lives; disability
Address: New Anstey House, Gate Way Drive, Yeadon, Leeds, LS19 7XY
Trustees: Mrs Diane Jennifer Hockley, Mrs Janet Adrienne Follett, Mr Richard John Chapman, Mr Ian Walker, Mrs Jayne Burton, Ms Jane Elizabeth Riley, Mr Stephen Timewell, Ms Ellie Wilmshurst, Mrs Beryl Sharlot, Mr Michael John Harnor MEd MSc, Mrs June Eleanor Massey, Mr Gavin John Marsh Barlow, Dr Peter Clough, Dr James Irvine Morrow, Mr James Sheward, Mr Matthew Jelfs
Income: £3,758,239 [2016]; £2,955,941 [2015]; £2,533,665 [2014]; £2,381,501 [2013]; £3,067,607 [2012]

British Exploring Society
Registered: 5 Dec 1989 *Employees:* 13 *Volunteers:* 93
Tel: 020 7591 3141 *Website:* britishexploring.org
Activities: Education, training; advancement of health or saving of lives; arts, culture, heritage, science; amateur sport; environment, conservation, heritage
Address: British Exploring Society, c/o Royal Geographical Society, 1 Kensington Gore, London, SW7 2AR
Trustees: Ms Susan Redshaw, Ms Deidre Sorensen, Ms Jane Park-Weir, Mr Michael Blakey, John Frederick Hartz, Carolyn Margaret Young, Mr Douglas Robert David Oppenheim, Mr Rupert Eastwood, Ms Joanna Wolstenholme, David John William Bailey, Patrick Maria Emiel Van Daele
Income: £1,517,966 [2017]; £1,308,253 [2016]; £993,501 [2015]; £1,130,052 [2014]; £994,406 [2013]

British Eye Research Foundation
Registered: 26 Sep 2005 *Employees:* 19 *Volunteers:* 80
Tel: 020 7264 3905 *Website:* fightforsight.org.uk
Activities: General charitable purposes; education, training; advancement of health or saving of lives; disability; economic, community development, employment
Address: Fight for Sight, 18 Mansell Street, London, E1 8AA
Trustees: Mr Alistair Rae, Mrs Jennifer Mary Williams, Mrs Ginny Greenwood, Prof David Spalton, Mr Roy Quinlan, Prof Maria Francesca Cordeiro, Professor Jonathan Charles Grant, Mr Steven Blackman, Mr Nigel Pantling, Mrs Louisa Vincent, Mrs Fiona Hathorn, Barbara Jane Merry, Mr Thomas Bjorn, Mr Simon Craddock, Ms Alina Kessel
Income: £3,792,000 [2017]; £4,524,000 [2016]; £4,011,000 [2015]; £3,243,000 [2014]; £3,765,000 [2013]

The British Film Institute
Registered: 7 Sep 1983 *Employees:* 487
Tel: 020 7957 4751 *Website:* bfi.org.uk
Activities: Education, training; arts, culture, heritage, science
Address: British Film Institute, 21 Stephen Street, London, W1T 1LN
Trustees: Jonathan Ross, Josh Berger, Lisbeth Savill, Pat Butler, Pete Czernin, Oona King, Matthew Justice, Tom Hooper, J Timothy Richards, Andrea Wong
Income: £95,724,000 [2017]; £100,144,000 [2016]; £99,380,000 [2015]; £93,484,000 [2014]; £109,965,000 [2013]

British Friends of Ezrat Yisrael Kiryat Sefer
Registered: 15 Jul 2010
Tel: 0161 792 1230
Activities: General charitable purposes; prevention or relief of poverty; overseas aid, famine relief
Address: 66 Wellington Street East, Salford, M7 4DW
Trustees: Mr David Neuwirth, Mr Refoel Halpern, Mr Nissim Hassan
Income: £4,118,650 [2017]; £3,142,600 [2016]; £5,202,231 [2015]; £5,613,675 [2014]; £4,842,000 [2013]

British Friends of Igud Hakolelim B'yerushalayim
Registered: 26 Apr 2005 *Volunteers:* 6
Tel: 020 8731 0777
Activities: The advancement of health or saving of lives; disability; prevention or relief of poverty; religious activities
Address: 15 Alba Gardens, London, NW11 9NS
Trustees: Mr Julian Bamberger, Abigail Bamberger, Joel Aaron Rabinowitz
Income: £1,795,262 [2017]; £932,294 [2016]; £681,267 [2015]; £762,632 [2014]; £701,833 [2013]

British Friends of The Art Museums of Israel
Registered: 19 Jan 1967 *Employees:* 3 *Volunteers:* 48
Tel: 020 3463 8715 *Website:* bfami.org
Activities: Arts, culture, heritage, science
Address: Floor 33, Euston Tower, 286 Euston Road, London, NW1 3DP
Trustees: Mr Edward Lee, Mrs Janice Atkin, Mr Poju Zabludowicz, The Hon Mrs Marion Naggar, Mrs Wendy Fisher, Ms Giorgina Djanogly
Income: £1,362,745 [2017]; £1,542,358 [2016]; £1,037,076 [2015]; £1,242,161 [2014]; £9,064,549 [2013]

The British Friends of The Bar-Ilan University
Registered: 22 Jul 1964 *Employees:* 2
Tel: 020 7486 7394 *Website:* bfbiu.org
Activities: General charitable purposes; education, training; advancement of health or saving of lives; religious activities
Address: Second Floor, 28 Portland Place, London, W1B 1LY
Trustees: Mr Romie Tager QC, Mr David Gradel
Income: £1,555,407 [2016]; £1,164,454 [2015]; £523,949 [2014]; £597,930 [2013]; £512,341 [2012]

British Friends of The Bible Lands Museum, Jerusalem
Registered: 14 May 1997
Tel: 020 3036 7000
Activities: Education, training
Address: 16 Great Queen Street, London, WC2B 5DG
Trustees: Mr Richard Kaufman, Ms Amanda Weis, Mr Avishay Noam, Mrs Batya Borowski, Ms Jessica Eve Waller, Mr Zvi Nixon
Income: £1,118,859 [2017]; £1,139,378 [2016]; £1,751,628 [2015]; £1,868,629 [2014]; £1,612,167 [2013]

British Friends of The Hebrew University of Jerusalem

Registered: 21 Nov 2007 *Employees:* 6 *Volunteers:* 1
Tel: 020 8349 5757 *Website:* bfhu.org
Activities: General charitable purposes; education, training; advancement of health or saving of lives; arts, culture, heritage, science; animals
Address: Supreme House, 300 Regents Park Road, London, N3 2JX
Trustees: Mr Isaac Kaye, Mr Joseph Smouha QC, Mr Jonathan Marks, Mrs Jenny Arwas MBE, Mr Simon Tobelem, Mrs Denise Joseph, Mr Graham Edwards, Alan Philipp, Mr Anthony Page, Mr David Mark Wernick
Income: £6,583,934 [2016]; £5,695,176 [2015]; £6,900,295 [2014]; £7,457,217 [2013]; £6,467,179 [2012]

British Friends of the Rabbi Meir Baal Haness Charity (Kollel Shomrei Hachomos)

Registered: 21 Oct 1983 *Employees:* 1
Activities: General charitable purposes; prevention or relief of poverty
Address: 88 Queen Elizabeths Walk, London, N16 5UQ
Trustees: Mr Joseph Schischa, Mr Jakob Frankel, Mr Jehodah Baumgarten
Income: £1,539,346 [2017]; £1,262,817 [2016]; £1,635,649 [2015]; £980,721 [2014]; £1,286,008 [2013]

British Gas Energy Trust

Registered: 7 Oct 2004
Tel: 01733 421021 *Website:* britishgasenergytrust.org.uk
Activities: General charitable purposes; education, training; prevention or relief of poverty
Address: 3rd Floor, Trinity Court, Trinity Street, Peterborough, PE1 1DA
Trustees: Ms Imelda Redmond, Ms Daksha Piparia, Mr Peter Smith, Mr Andrew Brown, Mr Colin Trend, Mr Steven McClenaghan
Income: £12,719,275 [2017]; £24,822,228 [2016]; £12,366,326 [2014]; £18,175,810 [2013]; £12,765,432 [2012]

The British Geriatrics Society

Registered: 23 Jan 1975 *Employees:* 11 *Volunteers:* 1
Tel: 020 7608 1369 *Website:* bgs.org.uk
Activities: Education, training; advancement of health or saving of lives
Address: British Geriatrics Society, Marjory Warren House, 31 St John's Square, London, EC1M 4DN
Trustees: Dr Eileen Burns, Dr Christine McAlpine, Prof Tahir Masud, Dr Jonathan Hewitt, Dr Mark Roberts, Dr Stephen Lim, Mrs Caroline MacInnes, Ms Susan Went, Clifford Kilgore, Dr Tun Aung, Dr Owen David, Dr Frazer Anderson
Income: £1,461,868 [2017]; £1,438,550 [2016]; £1,310,986 [2015]; £1,393,376 [2014]; £832,988 [2013]

British HIV Association

Registered: 24 Jun 1996
Tel: 020 8369 5390 *Website:* bhiva.org
Activities: Education, training; advancement of health or saving of lives
Address: Mediscript Ltd, Unit 1 Mountview Court, 310 Friern Barnet Lane, London, N20 0LD
Trustees: Prof Brian Gazzard, Dr Yvonne Gilleece, Dr R Kulasegaram, Dr Stephen Taylor, Dr Iain Reeves, Prof Lucy Dorrell, Professor Brian Angus, Dr Laura Waters, Dr Gabriel Schembri, Dr Nicola Mackie, Professor Clifford Leen, Prof Chloe Orkin, Dr Duncan Churchill, Professor Caroline Sabin, Dr Mas Chaponda, Dr Ann Sullivan, Dr David Chadwick, Mr Paul Clift, Dr Fiona Burns
Income: £1,248,049 [2016]; £1,337,875 [2015]; £1,812,812 [2014]; £1,301,234 [2013]; £1,242,976 [2012]

British Heart Foundation

Registered: 26 Mar 1963 *Employees:* 3,641 *Volunteers:* 20,400
Website: bhf.org.uk
Activities: The advancement of health or saving of lives
Address: British Heart Foundation, Greater London House, 180 Hampstead Road, London, NW1 7AW
Trustees: Professor Liam Smeeth, Professor John Iredale, Professor Dame Anna Dominiczak, Professor David Lomas, Mr Iain MacKay, Professor Sussan Nourshargh, Lord Andrew Feldman, Mr Andrew Balfour, Dr Robert Easton, Mr Peter Phippen, Professor Sir Kent Woods, Dr Doug Gurr, Mrs Daryl Fielding
Income: £310,500,000 [2017]; £301,500,000 [2016]; £288,200,000 [2015]; £275,100,000 [2014]; £263,607,000 [2013]

British Home and Hospital for Incurables

Registered: 7 May 1964 *Employees:* 110 *Volunteers:* 34
Tel: 020 8670 8261 *Website:* britishhome.org.uk
Activities: The advancement of health or saving of lives; disability
Address: Crown Lane, Streatham, London, SW16 3JB
Trustees: David Green, Mr Dennis Vine FRICS, James Mill, Ms Alison Hughes RN HSM Cert, Mr Kenneth Dunn, Mrs Patricia Collinson RN DipNur (Lond) RNT, Mrs Kay Sonneborn BA Hons, Mrs Rowenna Hughes GradDip MCSP SRP, Mr Derek Prentice, Ms Eleanor Brown
Income: £3,565,318 [2017]; £5,331,583 [2016]; £4,328,383 [2015]; £4,156,573 [2014]; £4,365,282 [2013]

The British Horse Society

Registered: 22 Sep 1962 *Employees:* 108 *Volunteers:* 1,400
Tel: 024 7684 0522 *Website:* bhs.org.uk
Activities: Education, training; amateur sport; animals
Address: The British Horse Society, Abbey Park, Stareton, Kenilworth, Warwicks, CV8 2XZ
Trustees: Mrs Eva-Lotta von der Heyde, Mrs Diane Dorothy Tranter, Mrs Loraine Young, Ms Jane Amanda Domhill, Mr Kenneth Charles Law, Mr David Barclay Sheerin, Mrs Kirsty Louise Handel, Martin Clemmey, Miss Samantha Jayne York
Income: £10,291,480 [2016]; £10,425,665 [2015]; £9,581,419 [2014]; £9,901,689 [2013]; £8,351,914 [2012]

British Humanist Association
Registered: 17 Jan 1983 *Employees:* 19 *Volunteers:* 270
Tel: 020 7324 3066 *Website:* humanism.org.uk
Activities: Education, training; human rights, religious or racial harmony, equality or diversity; other charitable purposes
Address: Humanists UK, 39 Moreland Street, London, EC1V 8BB
Trustees: Mr David John Frederick Pollock, Mr Alexander Williams, Mr Blaise Egan, Tamar Ghosh, Tom Copley, Mr Jeremy Rodell, Mr Imtiaz Shams, Mr Ewan Main, Ms Naomi Phillips, Alom Shaha, Mr Guy Otten, Professor John C Adams, Ms Amy Walden, Ms Jennifer Bartle
Income: £1,643,329 [2016]; £1,703,344 [2015]; £1,879,050 [2014]; £1,126,899 [2013]; £1,087,395 [2012]

The British Institute of Florence
Registered: 22 Nov 1984 *Employees:* 38
Website: britishinstitute.it
Activities: Education, training; arts, culture, heritage, science
Address: Director and Legal Representative, The British Institute of Florence, Palazzo Lanfredini, Lungarno Guicciardini 9, Firenze, Italy, 50125
Trustees: Mrs Moira MacFarlane, The Hon Lady Roberts CVO, Dottoressa Beatrice Bargagli Stoffi, Architetto Agnese Mazzei, Rettore Luigi Dei, Mrs Sarah Percy-Davis, Mr James Stewart, Signore Diego Di San Giuliano, Mr Paul Sellers, Maria Grazia Antoci, Ms Jill Morris CMG, Mr Christopher N R Prentice CMG
Income: £1,758,000 [2017]; £1,610,000 [2016]; £1,313,254 [2015]; £1,462,000 [2014]; £1,497,000 [2013]

The British Institute of Innkeeping
Registered: 11 Feb 1982 *Employees:* 33
Website: bii.org
Activities: Education, training
Address: Infor House, 1 Lakeside Road, Farnborough, Hants, GU14 6XP
Trustees: Mr Richard Philip Slade CBII, Mr Nigel Herbert Williams, Mr Ian Holt, Mr Ludovick Halik, Mr Gregory John Mangham, Mr Stephen John Williams, Mr Anthony Pender, Mr Michael Connell, Mr Philip Stephen Davison, Ms Joanne Graham
Income: £4,519,909 [2016]; £4,444,607 [2015]; £4,090,013 [2014]; £4,112,803 [2013]; £4,219,266 [2012]

The British Institute of International and Comparative Law
Registered: 22 Sep 1962 *Employees:* 28 *Volunteers:* 49
Tel: 020 7862 5151 *Website:* biicl.org
Activities: General charitable purposes; education, training; environment, conservation, heritage; human rights, religious or racial harmony, equality or diversity; other charitable purposes
Address: British Institute of International & Comparative Law, Charles Clore House, 17 Russell Square, London, WC1B 5JP
Trustees: Professor Catherine Mary Elizabeth O'Regan, Ms Andrea Jane Coomber, Mr Andrew Mark Whittaker, Mr Philip Haberman, Mr Alan Nigel Parr, Professor Oladapo Akande, Mrs Sonja Judith Clara Branch, Mr Constantine Partasides QC, Mr Keith Andrew Ruddock, Sir David Lloyd Jones, Professor John Stephen Bell, Mr Iain MacLeod, Lord Robert Reed, Ms Diana Paulette Wallis, Ms Ingrid Ann Simler
Income: £2,159,039 [2016]; £2,135,175 [2015]; £1,794,825 [2014]; £1,668,901 [2013]; £1,502,109 [2012]

The British Institute of Learning Disabilities
Registered: 2 Apr 1993 *Employees:* 15
Tel: 0121 415 6962 *Website:* bild.org.uk
Activities: Education, training; disability
Address: Birmingham Research Park, 97 Vincent Drive, Edgbaston, Birmingham, B15 2SQ
Trustees: Dr Ashok Roy, Mr Frederick Augustus Mumford, Mr Alan Jefferson, Mrs Tina Cooper, Professor Nigel Beail, Dr Colin Dale, Miss Sally Helen Lapsley
Income: £1,424,247 [2017]; £979,197 [2016]; £900,152 [2015]; £1,306,050 [2014]; £1,238,066 [2013]

The British Institute of Non-Destructive Testing
Registered: 3 Mar 1970 *Employees:* 42 *Volunteers:* 200
Tel: 01604 438300 *Website:* bindt.org
Activities: Education, training
Address: Midsummer House, Riverside Way, Bedford Road, Northampton, NN1 5NX
Trustees: Mr Roger Francis Lyon, Mrs Evelyn Gail Long, Mr Stephen John Lavender, Ms Caroline Bull, Mr Joseph McLean Buckley, Mr Dean Whittle, Mr Richard Leslie Watson, Dr Colin Robert Brett, Dr Keith Newton, Dr John Michael Farley, Mr Richard John Day, Dr Martin Christopher Lugg, Mr Ian Cooper, Professor Katherine Joanne Kirk, Sir John William Trelawny, Dr Robert Alan Smith Ceng Finstndt, Mr Colin Forrester, Ronald Nisbet, Gary Elliott, Dr Iain Baillie, Mr Philip Mark Edwards, Mr Andrew Darren Ward, Prof Anthony David Hope, Mr John Peter Hansen, Mr Douglas Wylie, Mr Andrew Mark Dowell, Mr Steven Greenfield, Mr Paul Fidgeon, Mr James John Needham
Income: £2,604,559 [2016]; £2,742,349 [2015]; £2,688,469 [2014]; £2,489,137 [2013]; £1,987,413 [2012]

The British Institute of Radiology
Registered: 30 Oct 1963 *Employees:* 22 *Volunteers:* 315
Tel: 020 3668 2220 *Website:* bir.org.uk
Activities: Education, training; advancement of health or saving of lives
Address: The British Institute of Radiology, 48-50 St John Street, London, EC1M 4DG
Trustees: Ms Jane Phillips-Hughes, Peter Harrison, Rebecca Rafiyah Findlay, Andrew Craig, Mr Jonathan Alexander Cole, Ms Maryann Louise Hardy, Dr Alexandra Joy Stewart, Andrew Rogers, Leighton Chipperfield, Nicholas Woznitza, Nick Screaton, Ms Sharon Drake, Dr Sridhar Redla
Income: £1,608,611 [2017]; £1,671,610 [2016]; £1,493,612 [2015]; £1,307,715 [2014]; £5,273,000 [2013]

The British Isles Province of The Congregation of Sisters of Charity of Jesus and Mary
Registered: 31 Jan 1967 *Employees:* 57 *Volunteers:* 4
Tel: 020 8695 7492
Activities: The advancement of health or saving of lives; disability; prevention or relief of poverty; overseas aid, famine relief; religious activities
Address: 1st Floor, Church House, 61 College Road, Bromley, Kent, BR1 3QG
Trustees: Sister Joan Yates, Sister Mary Ellen O'Brien, Sister Philomena Enright, Sister Ann Devine, Sister Patricia Josephine Callaghan, Sister Elizabeth Roche, Sister Deborah Anne Windle
Income: £1,905,123 [2016]; £1,958,752 [2015]; £1,939,370 [2014]; £2,061,833 [2013]; £1,977,613 [2012]

British Journal of Anaesthesia
Registered: 4 Dec 2007 *Employees:* 14
Tel: 0113 206 0788 *Website:* bja.oxfordjournals.org
Activities: Education, training; advancement of health or saving of lives
Address: Institute of Molecular Medicine, Level 7, Clinical Sciences Building, St James's University Hospital, Beckett Street, Leeds, LS9 7TF
Trustees: Professor David John Rowbotham, Professor Philip Hopkins, Prof David George Lambert, Professor Nigel Robert Webster, Dr Simon Howell, Dr Liam Joseph Brennan
Income: £2,351,397 [2016]; £2,358,689 [2015]; £2,265,338 [2014]; £2,332,035 [2013]; £2,313,196 [2012]

The British Kidney Patient Association
Registered: 4 Nov 1975 *Employees:* 23 *Volunteers:* 25
Tel: 01420 541424 *Website:* britishkidney-pa.co.uk
Activities: General charitable purposes; advancement of health or saving of lives; disability; prevention or relief of poverty; accommodation, housing; other charitable purposes
Address: British Kidney Patient Association, 3 The Windmills, St Marys Close, Alton, Hants, GU34 1EF
Trustees: Andrew Chapman, Mrs Marcelle De Sousa MBE FRCN MA RGN RSCN, Professor Lesley Rees MD FRCPCH, Professor Donal O'Donoghue BSc MBChB FRCP, Ingrid Rachelle Gubbay, Miss Lisa Burnapp RN MA, Ms Kate Shipton, Sir Jonathan Michael, Mr Matthew Richard Patey, Sarah Hillary
Income: £1,873,646 [2016]; £1,391,705 [2015]; £1,437,735 [2014]; £1,794,599 [2013]; £1,667,726 [2012]

British Limbless Ex-Service Men's Association (Blesma)
Registered: 19 Dec 2000 *Employees:* 34 *Volunteers:* 240
Tel: 020 8548 3512 *Website:* blesma.org
Activities: General charitable purposes; advancement of health or saving of lives; disability; accommodation, housing
Address: British Limbless Ex-Service Mens Association, 185-187 High Road, Romford, Essex, RM6 6NA
Trustees: Mr Andrew Kenneth Mudd BEM, Mr Philip Monkhouse, Mr Anthony Harris, Mrs Rebecca Charlotte Maciejewska, Mr Robert John Watts, Miss Alison Laura Grant, Mr Colin Rouse, Mr Charles Bishop, Mr William Lloyd Dixon, Mr Mark Nicholas Pillans, General Sir Adrian J Bradshaw KCB OBE
Income: £9,496,641 [2017]; £6,662,561 [2016]; £5,777,211 [2015]; £4,683,435 [2014]; £4,823,268 [2013]

The British Limousin Cattle Society Limited
Registered: 4 Nov 1971 *Employees:* 5
Tel: 024 7669 6500 *Website:* limousin.co.uk
Activities: Animals
Address: British Limousin Cattle Society Ltd, Concorde House, 24 Warwick New Road, Leamington Spa, Warwicks, CV32 5JG
Trustees: Mr Peter Charles Kirton, Mr Stephen David Illingworth, Mr Michael Cursiter, Mr Derek Frew, Mr John Gary Swindlehurst, Mr Guy Maxwell Green, Mr Karl Suddes, Mr Martin Irvine, Mrs Mary Goodridge-Reynolds, Jamie Cooper, Mr John Phillips, Dr Delana B Davies, Mr Harry Parker, Mr Henry Savage, Mr Henry Brian Lear
Income: £1,049,180 [2016]; £955,577 [2015]; £959,084 [2014]; £959,289 [2013]; £936,813 [2012]

British Lung Foundation
Registered: 11 Dec 1984 *Employees:* 86 *Volunteers:* 2,400
Tel: 020 7688 5555 *Website:* blf.org.uk
Activities: The advancement of health or saving of lives; disability
Address: British Lung Foundation, Lung Foundation House, 73-75 Goswell Road, London, EC1V 7ER
Trustees: Prof Stephen Spiro BSc MD FRCP, Mr Ralph Mitchell Bernard CBE, Mr Richard James Pettit, Stephen Holgate, Dr Francis Gilchrist, Miss Emily Jane Bushby, Mrs Teresa Burgoyne, Baroness Tessa Blackstone, Mr John Martin Graham, David Gill, Mr Graham Peter Colbert, Dr Isabel Divanna, Mr John Philip Loots
Income: £7,507,000 [2017]; £7,000,000 [2016]; £6,646,852 [2015]; £6,103,961 [2014]; £6,130,571 [2013]

British Motor Industry Heritage Trust
Registered: 15 May 1983 *Employees:* 68 *Volunteers:* 78
Tel: 01926 645123 *Website:* britishmotormuseum.co.uk
Activities: Education, training; arts, culture, heritage, science; environment, conservation, heritage
Address: British Motor Industry Heritage Trust, British Motor Museum, Banbury Road, Gaydon, Warwick, CV35 0BJ
Trustees: Mr Kevin Timms, Mrs Julie Tew, Ms Fiona Pargeter, Mr Stephen Cropley, Ms Naomi Jane Bishop, Mr Jeffrey Colin Coope, Mr John Sterling Edwards, Mr Joel Nicholas Kordan
Income: £6,781,696 [2016]; £8,773,223 [2015]; £6,708,356 [2014]; £4,793,038 [2013]; £4,616,029 [2012]

The British Museum Friends
Registered: 9 Apr 2001 *Employees:* 13 *Volunteers:* 19
Tel: 020 7323 8619 *Website:* britishmuseum.org
Activities: Education, training; arts, culture, heritage, science
Address: British Museum, Great Russell Street, London, WC1B 3DG
Trustees: Professor Amartya Sen, Mr Mark Andrew Pears, Baroness Wheatcroft of Blackheath, Sir Richard Lambert, Sir Paul Ruddock, Miss Patricia Cumper, Mr John Micklethwait, Ms Ahdaf Souef, Lord James Sassoon, Mr Grayson Perry, Ms Muriel Gray, Lord Turner of Ecchinswell, Ms Clarissa Mary Farr, Mr Nigel Boardman, Sir Paul Nurse, Professor Nicola Lacey, Dr Clive Gamble, Mr Gavin Patterson, Ms Cheryl Carolus, Mr Deryck Maughan, Dr Nemat Shafik, Mrs Elizabeth Pauline Lucy Corley
Income: £5,155,682 [2017]; £4,922,239 [2016]; £4,935,639 [2015]; £4,859,860 [2014]; £2,826,049 [2013]

The British Museum Trust Limited
Registered: 21 Mar 2011
Tel: 020 7323 8621
Activities: Arts, culture, heritage, science
Address: British Museum, Great Russell Street, London, WC1B 3DG
Trustees: Lord Powell of Bayswater, Jack Ryan, Professor Barrington Windsor Cunliffe Sir, Mr David Ronald Norgrove
Income: £12,008,697 [2017]; £13,503,179 [2016]; £12,020,883 [2015]; £18,291,058 [2014]; £37,963,209 [2013]

The British Music Experience
Registered: 8 Sep 2008
Tel: 020 7224 1992 *Website:* britishmusicexperience.com
Activities: Education, training; arts, culture, heritage, science
Address: 3rd Floor, 113 Great Portland Street, London, W1W 6QQ
Trustees: Mr Simon Weil, Mr Keith Harris, Mr Kevin McManus, Mr Harvey Goldsmith CBE, Sir Mark Philip Featherstone-Witty
Income: £2,713,885 [2017]; £230,663 [2015]; £3,772,000 [2014]; £1,286,691 [2012]

British Muslim Heritage Centre

Registered: 20 Jun 2005 *Employees:* 7 *Volunteers:* 10
Tel: 0161 881 8062 *Website:* bmhc.org.uk
Activities: General charitable purposes; education, training; religious activities; arts, culture, heritage, science; amateur sport; environment, conservation, heritage; economic, community development, employment; recreation
Address: College Road, Whalley Range, Manchester, M16 8BP
Trustees: Mr Dilaver Valli, Naeem-Ul Hassan, Dr Abdullah Muhammad Al-Majid, Mr Farroukh Zaheer FCCA, Dr Adel Al-Falah, Dr Abdullah Al-Matouq, Mr Abdulkadir Abdulrahim Kawooya, Mr Sadiqbasha Thameembasha, Dr Ahmad Al Dubayan, Nasar Mahood, Dr Hamad Abdullah Al-Majed, Dr Mohammed Sarumi, Mr Mohammed Afzal Khan, Mr Mohammed Salim Al-Astewani, Dr Gaith Mubarak Al-Kuwari, Mrs Saima Alvi, Whaid Ahmed
Income: £1,511,835 [2017]; £660,341 [2016]; £678,956 [2015]; £911,481 [2014]; £640,699 [2013]

The British Nutrition Foundation

Registered: 7 Mar 1967 *Employees:* 17
Tel: 020 7557 7930 *Website:* nutrition.org.uk
Activities: Education, training; advancement of health or saving of lives
Address: British Nutrition Foundation, 3rd Floor, New Derwent House, 69-73 Theobalds Road, London, WC1X 8TA
Trustees: Professor Martin Jeremy Wiseman, Dr Richard Charles Pendrous, Mr David Webster, Professor John Cummings Mathers, Professor Christine Williams OBE PhD FSB RNutr FFAFN, Mr David Gregory, Miss Gill Fine, Mr Ian Christopher Metcalfe Rayson, Mr Graeme Findlay, Professor Gary Frost
Income: £1,457,722 [2017]; £1,491,501 [2016]; £1,532,486 [2015]; £1,585,327 [2014]; £1,496,699 [2013]

The British Occupational Hygiene Society

Registered: 11 Jan 2013 *Employees:* 20 *Volunteers:* 40
Tel: 01332 298101 *Website:* bohs.org
Activities: General charitable purposes; education, training; advancement of health or saving of lives
Address: British Occupational Hygiene Society, Unit 5-6 Melbourne Business Court, Pride Park, Derby, DE24 8LZ
Trustees: John Dobbie, Mr Alexander George Wilson, Mrs Karen Bufton, Mrs Marian Molloy, Mr Douglas Collin, Mr Kelvin Williams, Mr Neil Grace, Ms Kate Jones, Mrs Helen Maria Pearson, Mr Neil Pickering, Mrs Amanda Parker, Mr Jonathan Grant
Income: £1,459,974 [2017]; £1,303,140 [2016]; £1,631,912 [2015]; £1,226,418 [2014]; £1,230,701 [2013]

British Olympic Foundation

Registered: 20 Dec 2007 *Volunteers:* 1
Tel: 020 7842 5700 *Website:* getset.co.uk
Activities: Education, training; advancement of health or saving of lives; arts, culture, heritage, science; amateur sport
Address: 60 Charlotte Street, London, W1T 2NU
Trustees: Mr Richard Leman, Dr Neil William Norman Townshend
Income: £1,844,833 [2016]; £1,983,239 [2015]; £1,739,740 [2014]; £2,162,534 [2013]; £901,458 [2012]

The British Orthodontic Society

Registered: 22 Jan 1999 *Employees:* 4 *Volunteers:* 50
Tel: 020 7353 8680 *Website:* bos.org.uk
Activities: Education, training; advancement of health or saving of lives
Address: The British Orthodontic Society, 12 Bridewell Place, London, EC4V 6AP
Trustees: Dr David Manger, Dr Richard George, Dr Guy Deeming, Dr Andrew Dibiase, Dr Susan Moore, Dr Richard Jones, Dr Philip Benson, Professor Jonathan Sandler, Dr Joseph Noar
Income: £1,355,777 [2016]; £878,165 [2015]; £1,435,544 [2014]; £1,392,383 [2013]; £1,327,415 [2012]

British Orthopaedic Association

Registered: 19 Dec 1997 *Employees:* 19
Tel: 020 7405 6507 *Website:* boa.ac.uk
Activities: General charitable purposes; education, training; advancement of health or saving of lives; disability
Address: 35-43 Lincolns Inn Fields, London, WC2A 3PE
Trustees: Mr Mark Bowditch, Mr Stephen Bendall, Mr Ian Winson, Mr Lee Breakwell, Mr Ananda Nanu, Professor Simon Donell, Mr Michael Reed, Mr John Skinner, Mr Simon Hodkinson, Mr Robert Handley, Professor Philip Turner, Mr Donald McBride, Tim Wilton, Mr David Clark, Mr Andrew Robinson, Mrs Karen Daly, Miss Deborah Eastwood, Mr Richard Parkinson
Income: £3,230,326 [2016]; £3,289,967 [2015]; £2,302,217 [2014]; £2,973,076 [2013]; £2,798,338 [2012]

British Overseas NGOs for Development (Bond)

Registered: 25 Mar 1998 *Employees:* 35
Tel: 020 7837 8344 *Website:* bond.org.uk
Activities: Overseas aid, famine relief
Address: Bond, Regent's Wharf, 8 All Saints Street, London, N1 9RL
Trustees: Mr Gibril Faal, Ms Sally Copley, Ms Jessica Woodroffe, Mr Martin Paul Smith Lomas, Dr Husna Parvin, Ms Tania Songini, Ms Eleanor Harrison, Ms Caroline Mary Nursey, Mr Nicholas Hartley, Ms Catherine David
Income: £3,311,982 [2017]; £2,806,304 [2016]; £3,349,348 [2015]; £2,975,062 [2014]; £2,233,521 [2013]

The British Paralympic Association

Registered: 8 Nov 1989 *Employees:* 29 *Volunteers:* 118
Tel: 020 7842 5789 *Website:* paralympics.org.uk
Activities: Amateur sport
Address: The British Olympic Association, 60 Charlotte Street, London, W1T 2NU
Trustees: David Philip Clarke, Mr Geoffrey Newton, Mr Gregory Martin Nugent, Davida Mary Paterson, Mr David Hadfield, Mrs Emma Louise Boggis, James Forbes Dunlop, Nick Anthony Webborn
Income: £9,048,030 [2017]; £3,954,855 [2016]; £3,402,617 [2015]; £3,007,820 [2014]; £6,080,797 [2013]

British Pharmacological Society
Registered: 20 Dec 1993 *Employees:* 18 *Volunteers:* 325
Tel: 020 7239 0171 *Website:* bps.ac.uk
Activities: Education, training; advancement of health or saving of lives
Address: British Pharmacological Society Ltd, 16 Angel Gate, London, EC1V 2PT
Trustees: Professor Sir Munir Pirmohamed, Professor Robin Plevin, Mr Aidan Seeley, Dr Malcolm Skingle, Dr Rachel Marie Quinn, Professor Ian McFadzean, Professor Susan Clare Stanford, Professor Stephen Hill, Mr Charles Gloor, Dr Emma Morrison, Professor Jane Mitchell
Income: £3,716,676 [2016]; £4,196,902 [2015]; £3,478,009 [2014]; £3,352,484 [2013]; £3,512,566 [2012]

British Plumbing Employers Council (Training) Limited
Registered: 16 Jul 1992 *Employees:* 21
Tel: 0845 644 6558 *Website:* bpec.org.uk
Activities: Education, training; economic, community development, employment
Address: 2 Mallard Way, Pride Park, Derby, DE24 8GX
Trustees: Mr Graham Peter Beevers, Mr George Norman Thomson, Mr Preston Fleming, Mr David Mark Antrobus, Mr Raymond Leslie
Income: £1,300,814 [2016]; £1,448,861 [2015]; £1,487,515 [2014]; £1,546,142 [2013]; £1,456,552 [2012]

British Pregnancy Advisory Service
Registered: 25 Apr 1984 *Employees:* 682
Tel: 0870 365 5050 *Website:* bpas.org
Activities: The advancement of health or saving of lives
Address: British Pregnancy Advisory Service, 20 Timothys Bridge Road, Stratford Enterprise Park, Stratford upon Avon, Warwicks, CV37 9BF
Trustees: Mr John Collier, Professor Cathy Warwick, Dr David Dickson, Dr Anna Glasier, Mr Sanjay Shah, Dr Clare Gerada, Professor Sally Sheldon, Anne Shevas, Ms Amanda Callaghan, Professor Calliope Christina Samoulla Farsides
Income: £29,376,000 [2017]; £29,079,000 [2016]; £28,440,000 [2015]; £28,200,000 [2014]; £27,069,000 [2013]

The British Province of The Unitas Fratrum (Moravian Church)
Registered: 18 Jan 1967 *Employees:* 225
Tel: 020 8883 3409 *Website:* moravian.org.uk
Activities: Education, training; overseas aid, famine relief; accommodation, housing; religious activities
Address: Moravian Church House, 5 7 Muswell Hill, London, N10 3TJ
Trustees: Rev Robert Hopcroft, Mrs Zoe Marie-May Taylor, Mrs Gillian Taylor, Miss Roberta Margaret Ann Hoey
Income: £10,506,361 [2016]; £10,231,961 [2015]; £10,773,397 [2014]; £10,691,708 [2013]

The British Psychoanalytical Society (incorporating The Institute of Psychoanalysis)
Registered: 22 Nov 1962 *Employees:* 24 *Volunteers:* 200
Tel: 020 7563 5018 *Website:* psychoanalysis.org.uk
Activities: Education, training; advancement of health or saving of lives
Address: 112a Shirland Road, London, W9 2EQ
Trustees: Dr Margot Waddell, Mr David Millar, Dr David Taylor, Ms Megan Virtue, Dr Kate Pugh, Dr Duncan McLean, Ms Veronica Gore, Dr Edgard Sanchez Bernal, Ms Julia Fabricius, Mrs Susan Lawrence, Mr David William Riley, Prof Catalina Bronstein, Dr Sara Flanders, Dr Brian O'Neill, Ms Elizabeth Coates Thummel
Income: £1,966,087 [2016]; £2,081,037 [2015]; £1,857,144 [2014]; £1,878,626 [2013]; £1,664,669 [2012]

The British Psychological Society
Registered: 18 Jul 1962 *Employees:* 99 *Volunteers:* 1,500
Tel: 0116 254 9568 *Website:* bps.org.uk
Activities: Other charitable purposes
Address: British Psychological Society, St Andrews House, 48 Princess Road East, Leicester, LE1 7DR
Trustees: Dr Mark John Forshaw, Professor Jill Diane Wilkinson, Dr Carole Ann Allan, Professor Daryl Brian O'Connor, Dr Helen Clare Nicholas, Professor Kathryn Susan Bullen, Professor Raymond John Miller, Mr Christopher David Lynch, Ms Nicola Karen Gale, Ms Alison Clarke
Income: £12,684,000 [2016]; £12,747,000 [2015]; £12,790,000 [2014]; £12,238,000 [2013]; £11,865,000 [2012]

British Psychotherapy Foundation
Registered: 13 Feb 2013 *Employees:* 13 *Volunteers:* 9
Tel: 020 8452 9823 *Website:* britishpsychotherapyfoundation.org.uk
Activities: Education, training; advancement of health or saving of lives
Address: British Psychotherapy Foundation, 37 Mapesbury Road, London, NW2 4HJ
Trustees: Ms Mary Rose Miranda Feuchtwang, Ms Joanna Lee, Nigel Duerdoth, Hansjorg Messner, Dr Jo-Anne Carlyle, Mr Julian Lousada, Ferelyth Watt, Ms Jean Carr
Income: £1,098,979 [2017]; £1,100,461 [2016]; £1,174,006 [2015]; £1,214,086 [2014]

British Record Industry Trust
Registered: 27 Sep 1990
Tel: 020 7803 1300 *Website:* brittrust.co.uk
Activities: Education, training; arts, culture, heritage, science
Address: BPI, Riverside Building, County Hall, Westminster Bridge Road, London, SE1 7JA
Trustees: John Deacon, Andy Cleary, Rob Dickins, Mr David Kassner, Mr Korda Marshall, Mr William Rowe, Mrs Margaret Crowe OBE, Mr Simon Paul Thomas Presswell, Mr Gerald Vincent Doherty, Mr Max Hole, John Craig, Jonathan Morrish, Tony Wadsworth, Mr Geoff Taylor, David Sharpe, Mr David Peter Munns, Ms Angela Claire Mary Watts, Ms Melanie Fox, Mrs Rita Broe, Mr Henry Semmence
Income: £1,691,523 [2016]; £1,826,717 [2015]; £1,555,449 [2014]; £976,565 [2013]; £1,227,360 [2012]

The British Red Cross Society
Registered: 21 Mar 1963 *Employees:* 3,502 *Volunteers:* 20,598
Tel: 020 7877 7558 *Website:* redcross.org.uk
Activities: General charitable purposes; education, training; advancement of health or saving of lives; disability; prevention or relief of poverty; overseas aid, famine relief
Address: British Red Cross Society, 44 Moorfields, London, EC2Y 9AL
Trustees: Professor Geeta Nargund, Mr Paul Taylor, Dr Daniel Sedgewick, Mrs Gill Moffat, Mr John Dauth AO LVO, Mr David Bernstein CBE, Mr Lewis Iwu, Ms Hilary Douglas, Mr Keith Shipman, Mr Robert Dewar, Ms Liz Hazell, Mrs Fionnuala Cook OBE, Ms Deborah El-Sayed
Income: £251,700,000 [2016]; £275,100,000 [2015]; £261,800,000 [2014]; £228,400,000 [2013]; £200,100,000 [2012]

British Refugee Council
Registered: 2 Oct 1992 *Employees:* 128 *Volunteers:* 300
Tel: 020 7346 6714 *Website:* refugeecouncil.org.uk
Activities: General charitable purposes; education, training; economic, community development, employment; human rights, religious or racial harmony, equality or diversity
Address: British Refugee Council, Gredley House, 1-11 Broadway, London, E15 4BQ
Trustees: Ms Clare Emily Paterson, Mr Andrew Halper, Mr Salah Mohamed, Lord Kerr of Kinlochard, Ms Lyndall Norma Stein, Gerry Power, Mr Nick Whitaker, Mr Vaughan Jones, Mr Aneil Kumar Jhumat, Ms Rachael Marion Orr, Ms Anne Elizabeth McLoughlin, Dr Zaeem Haq
Income: £9,457,000 [2017]; £6,308,000 [2016]; £4,608,000 [2015]; £8,104,000 [2014]; £8,304,000 [2013]

British Safety Council
Registered: 29 Apr 2003 *Employees:* 107
Tel: 020 8741 1231 *Website:* britsafe.org
Activities: General charitable purposes; education, training
Address: British Safety Council, 70 Chancellors Road, London, W6 9RS
Trustees: Mr John McNamara, Mrs Lynda Armstrong, Mr Ian Jefferson, Mr Mark Hardy, Mr Philip White, Ms Ibironke Adeagbo, Mr John Pearce, Mr Paul Cottam, Mr Adrian Wild
Income: £9,107,624 [2016]; £8,798,569 [2015]; £7,933,022 [2014]; £7,788,556 [2013]; £8,622,089 [2012]

The British School at Athens
Registered: 22 Sep 1962 *Employees:* 23 *Volunteers:* 1
Tel: 020 7969 5315 *Website:* bsa.ac.uk
Activities: Education, training; arts, culture, heritage, science
Address: 27 Horton Road, London, E8 1DP
Trustees: Polly Low, Ian Jenkins, Dr Carol Bell, Professor Robin Osborne, Zosia Archibald, Cyprian Broodbank, Dr Joe Skinner, Mr Paul Smee, Robin Hunt, Sir Adam Ridley, Sir Michael Llewellyn Smith KCVO CMG, Archie Dunn, David Holton, Roddy Beaton, Yannis Galanakis, Dr Matthew Skuse, Anna Moles
Income: £1,633,467 [2017]; £1,310,397 [2016]; £1,471,409 [2015]; £1,408,967 [2014]; £1,870,387 [2013]

The British School at Rome
Registered: 26 Mar 1963 *Employees:* 30
Tel: 020 7969 5202 *Website:* bsr.ac.uk
Activities: Education, training; arts, culture, heritage, science; environment, conservation, heritage
Address: British School at Rome, 10 Carlton House Terrace, London, SW1Y 5AH
Trustees: Ms Eliza Bonham Carter, Mr Alan Gibbins, Vivien Lovell, Ian Hodgson, Mrs Robin Hambro, Professor Robert Gordon, Eric Parry, Professor Rosamond McKitterick, Colin James Blackmore, Mr Christopher Prentice, Mr Mark Getty, Professor Simon Keay
Income: £2,273,000 [2017]; £2,534,000 [2016]; £2,177,000 [2015]; £2,534,000 [2014]; £3,610,000 [2013]

The British School of Alexandria
Registered: 4 Dec 2001 *Employees:* 150
Website: bsalex.net
Activities: Education, training
Address: The British School, Alexandria, Mahmous Abou Ela Street, Kafr Abdou, Alexandria, Egypt
Trustees: Mr Wael Mansour, Mr Paul Walton, Mr Magdy El Garf
Income: £3,769,923 [2017]; £2,625,528 [2016]; £2,744,504 [2015]; £2,321,130 [2014]; £1,956,912 [2013]

British Sign Language Broadcasting Trust
Registered: 3 Jan 2012 *Employees:* 5
Tel: 07540 564228 *Website:* bslzone.co.uk
Activities: Arts, culture, heritage, science
Address: BSLBT, c/o Knox Cropper, 153-155 London Road, Hemel Hempstead, Herts, HP3 9SQ
Trustees: Ms Rubbena Aurangzeb-Tariq, Ms Ruth Griffiths, James Harvey, Mr John Wilson, Ms Marianne Matthews, Lynn Cutress, Mr Paul Johnston, Ms Jill Hipson, Ms Kerry Kent
Income: £1,663,755 [2016]; £1,274,053 [2015]; £1,146,511 [2014]; £1,089,192 [2013]; £1,095,773 [2012]

The British Skin Foundation
Registered: 16 Feb 1973 *Employees:* 5
Tel: 020 7391 6341 *Website:* britishskinfoundation.org.uk
Activities: Education, training; advancement of health or saving of lives
Address: 4 Fitzroy Square, London, W1T 5HQ
Trustees: Professor Chris Bunker, Dr Susan Mayou, Dr Robert Sarkany, Mrs Esra Erkal-Paler, Dr Bav Shergill, Professor Eugene Healy, Mrs Bernice McCabe, Dr Tamara Griffiths, Mr Hugo Drayton, Professor David Gawkrodger, Mr Roger Balson, Dr Nicholas Levell
Income: £1,141,799 [2016]; £945,361 [2015]; £1,002,767 [2014]; £1,232,423 [2013]; £1,098,767 [2012]

British Small Animal Veterinary Association
Registered: 1 Sep 1993 *Employees:* 37 *Volunteers:* 274
Tel: 01452 726717 *Website:* bsava.com
Activities: Education, training; animals
Address: Woodrow House, 1 Telford Way, Waterwells Business Park, Quedgeley, Gloucester, GL2 2AB
Trustees: Mrs Susan Paterson MA VetMB DVD DipEVDC MPhil MRCVS, Mrs Patricia Colville NVMS MRCVS, Mr Philip John Lhermette BSc CBiol MsB BVetMed MRCVS, Dr Krista Arnold DrMed Vet, Dr Rachel Dean, Mr Graeme Eckford, Dr Susan Dawson BVMS PhD MRCVS, David Godfrey BVetMed CertSAD CertSAM DipABVP, Dr Tim Williams MA VetMB PhD MRCVS, Ms Joanne Douglas BVMS, Mrs Louise Smith BVSc CertSAM, Mr Derek Attride, Mr Charles Gorman BVSc MRCVS, Mrs Caroline Queen MRCVS, Mr Jim Hughes, Professor Ian Ramsey, Mr Ross Allan BVMS MRCVS, Mr Michael Davies BVetMed CertVR CertSAO FRCVS, Mrs Susan MacAldowie, Mr Sheldon Middleton MA VetMB MRCVS, Mr John Chitty BVetMed CertZooMed CBiol MLBiol, Mrs Ellen Harmer MA VetMB MRCVS, Miss Sophie Adamantos BVSc CertVA DACVECC FHEA MRCVS, Mrs Helen Claire O'Kelly BVSc MRCVS, Mrs Pascale Collins DVM CertVR, Mr Andrew Iveson Bvsc Certsas, Mrs Gillian Alford, Mrs Branwen Davis BVMS MRCVS, Mrs Louise O'Hare BVSc MRCVS, Miss Esther Bijsmans, Mrs Madonna Livingstone
Income: £5,895,637 [2016]; £5,751,465 [2015]; £5,875,599 [2014]; £5,705,874 [2013]; £5,877,664 [2012]

British Society for Antimicrobial Chemotherapy
Registered: 25 Jul 2002 *Employees:* 12
Tel: 0121 236 1988 *Website:* bsac.org.uk
Activities: Education, training; advancement of health or saving of lives
Address: 53 Regent Place, Hockley, Birmingham, B1 3NJ
Trustees: Ms Carole Fry, Philip Howard, Professor Dilip Nathwani, Professor Kate Gould, Professor William Hope, Dr Sanjay Patel, Dr Enrique Castro-Sanchez, Dr Michael Allen, Dr Oliver Van Hecke, Dr Gavin Barlow, Dr Helena Parsons, Mr Mark Gilchrist, Dr Paul Frederick Long, Dr Susan Hopkins, Dr Timothy Walsh, Dr Jonathan Sandoe, Mrs Enas Newire, Dr Christopher Longshaw
Income: £2,200,228 [2016]; £1,975,559 [2015]; £1,719,175 [2014]; £2,021,789 [2013]; £1,510,823 [2012]

The British Society for Haematology
Registered: 7 Nov 1991 *Employees:* 7 *Volunteers:* 120
Tel: 020 7713 0990 *Website:* b-s-h.org.uk
Activities: Education, training; advancement of health or saving of lives
Address: BSH, 100 White Lion Street, London, N1 9PF
Trustees: Ms Eugenie Susannah Randall, Mr Trevor William Jones, Professor Claire Nicola Harrison, Professor David John Roberts, Dr Anne Naomi Parker, Dr Nazir Ahmad, Professor Cheng Hock Toh, Dr Josh Wright, Dr James Seale, Professor Adele Kay Fielding, Professor Simon Rule
Income: £1,901,533 [2016]; £1,775,710 [2015]; £1,605,453 [2014]; £1,464,530 [2013]; £1,519,572 [2012]

British Society of Gastroenterology
Registered: 24 Sep 2012 *Employees:* 10 *Volunteers:* 175
Website: bsg.org.uk
Activities: Education, training; advancement of health or saving of lives
Address: British Society of Gastroenterology, 3 St Andrews Place, London, NW1 4LB
Trustees: Professor Charles Baden-Fuller, Dr Stephen Hughes, Dr Duncan Loft MD FRCP, Professor Christopher Probert, Mr Nicholas Hoile, Dr Jayne Eaden, Mr Christopher Bromfield, Mr Richard Lanyon, Dr Cathryn Edwards, Professor Martin Lombard, Mrs Stella Dutton, Professor Colin Rees
Income: £2,907,138 [2016]; £4,229,726 [2015]; £2,958,259 [2014]; £2,739,272 [2013]

British Society for Immunology
Registered: 12 Jan 1995 *Employees:* 12 *Volunteers:* 178
Website: immunology.org
Activities: Education, training; advancement of health or saving of lives
Address: The British Society for Immunology, 34 Red Lion Square, London, WC1R 4SG
Trustees: Mr Edward Chandler, Professor Allan Mowat, Professor Anne Cooke, Dr Sofia Grigoriadou, Dr Edith Hessel, Fiona Culley, Dr Calum Cunningham Harris, Dr Peter Openshaw, Mr Paul Harding, Dr Sheena Cruickshank, Mr Matthias Eberl, Mr Robert Davies, Dr Simon Milling
Income: £2,046,871 [2017]; £1,436,182 [2016]; £1,772,992 [2015]; £1,799,058 [2014]; £1,447,897 [2013]

The British Sociological Association
Registered: 7 Apr 2000 *Employees:* 13 *Volunteers:* 440
Tel: 0191 383 0839 *Website:* britsoc.co.uk
Activities: Education, training
Address: British Sociological Association, Palatine House, Belmont Business Park, Durham, DH1 1TW
Trustees: Professor Eileen Green, Professor Nasar Meer, Professor John David Horne, Professor Alan Warde, Dr Aaron Winter, Professor Stephanie Jackson, Professor Rosaline Barbour, Dr John Bone, Professor Linda McKie, Professor David Inglis, Dr Lisa McKenzie, Professor Janice McLaughlin
Income: £1,428,513 [2016]; £1,220,546 [2015]; £1,419,276 [2014]; £1,246,366 [2013]; £1,096,611 [2012]

British Society for Rheumatology
Registered: 31 Dec 1997 *Employees:* 26 *Volunteers:* 178
Tel: 020 7842 0900 *Website:* rheumatology.org.uk
Activities: Education, training; advancement of health or saving of lives
Address: British Society for Rheumatology, 18-20 Bride Lane, London, EC4Y 8EE
Trustees: Mr Paul Stennett, Dr Jill Firth, Dr Elizabeth Price, Dr Lesley Kay, Ms Louise Redmond, Dr Zunaid Karim, Dr Elizabeth Reilly, Dr Kathryn Bailey, Dr Elaine Dennison, Dr Chetan Mukhtyar, Dr Kauschik Chaudhuri, Dr Caroline Flurey, Dr Gary MacFarlane
Income: £3,803,685 [2016]; £7,054,441 [2015]; £3,134,332 [2014]; £3,081,551 [2013]; £2,968,411 [2012]

The British Sports Trust
Registered: 9 Jan 2003 *Employees:* 34
Tel: 01908 689180 *Website:* sportsleaders.org
Activities: Education, training; amateur sport; recreation
Address: British Sports Trust, 23-25 Linford Forum, Rockingham Drive, Linford Wood, Milton Keynes, Bucks, MK14 6LY
Trustees: Ms Maria Turnbull-Kemp, Mr Duncan Mark Lewis, Mr Dominic Goggins, Ms Lara Lill, Mr Richard Ramsey, David Joseph Cove, Mrs Jill Lanning, Mr Shaun Dowling, Ms Judith Norrington, Mrs Charlotte Graham-Cumming
Income: £2,148,909 [2017]; £2,725,106 [2016]; £3,416,381 [2015]; £3,445,730 [2014]; £4,045,371 [2013]

The British Society for Surgery of The Hand
Registered: 22 Aug 1975 *Employees:* 7 *Volunteers:* 46
Tel: 020 7831 5162 *Website:* bssh.ac.uk
Activities: General charitable purposes; education, training; advancement of health or saving of lives
Address: British Society for Surgery of The Hand, 35-43 Lincoln's Inn Fields, London, WC2A 3PE
Trustees: Mr Alastair Platt, Mr David Warwick, Professor Grey Giddins, Mr Michael Waldram, Mr Dean Boyce, Mr David Shewring, Mr Chye Yew Ng, Mr Wee L Lam, Mrs Susan Margaret Fullilove, Mr David P Newington, Mr Donald Sammut, Mr Nicholas Downing, Mr Jonathan Hobby, Mr Ian McNab, Mr Zaf Naqui
Income: £1,087,576 [2017]; £929,521 [2016]; £900,115 [2015]; £936,471 [2014]; £831,578 [2013]

The British Thoracic Society
Registered: 25 Aug 1982 *Employees:* 12 *Volunteers:* 230
Tel: 020 7831 8778 *Website:* brit-thoracic.org.uk
Activities: Education, training; advancement of health or saving of lives
Address: 17 Doughty Street, London, WC1N 2PL
Trustees: Dr Martin Allen, Dr Gisli Jenkins, Dr Paul Walker, Dr Justine Hadcroft, Dr John Park, Dr Luke Howard, Mrs Alice Vawter Joy, Dr Lisa Davies, Professor Mark Elliott, Dr Jonathan Bennett, Professor Mark Woodhead, Dr Justin Pepperell, Dr Jennifer Quint, Dr Graeme Wilson
Income: £2,504,115 [2017]; £2,388,158 [2016]; £2,514,645 [2015]; £2,153,919 [2014]; £2,136,037 [2013]

The British Trust for Ornithology
Registered: 23 Mar 1964 *Employees:* 116 *Volunteers:* 50,000
Tel: 01842 750050 *Website:* bto.org
Activities: Environment, conservation, heritage
Address: British Trust for Ornithology, The Nunnery, Thetford, Norfolk, IP24 2PU
Trustees: Dr David Parker, Lt Col Roger Dickey, Dr Debby Reynolds, Ms Frances Hurst, Mr Andrew Henderson, Professor Stuart Bearhop, Mr David Jardine, Mr Ian Packer, Mr Chris Packham, Professor Jenny Gill, Nicholas Sherwin, Dr Fiona Barclay, Mr Chris Mills, Mrs Jean Spencer, Dr Ian Bainbridge, Stephen Hunter
Income: £6,461,812 [2017]; £5,825,216 [2016]; £5,419,059 [2015]; £6,323,768 [2014]; £5,045,600 [2013]

British Union Conference of Seventh-Day Adventists
Registered: 10 Feb 1995 *Employees:* 142 *Volunteers:* 9,100
Tel: 01923 672251 *Website:* adventist.uk
Activities: General charitable purposes; education, training; advancement of health or saving of lives; religious activities
Address: British Union Conference, Stanborough Park, Watford, Herts, WD25 9JZ
Trustees: Mr Earl Jude Ramharacksingh, Pastor John Surridge, Mr Mfakazi Ndebele, Mr Clement Morgan, Pastor Audrey Andersson, Mr William Joseph Donaldson, Mrs Lorraine Kay Dixon, Mr Nenad Jepuranovic, Pastor Dan Gheorghe Serb, Mr Paul King, Miss Elisabeth Sanguesa, Pastor Emanuel Bran, Mr Malcolm James Martin, Mrs Emily Ranita Tebbs-Ogutu, Pastor George Kwame Kumi, Pastor Dejan Stojkovic, Pastor Kirk Thomas, Dr Emmanuel Osei, Pastor Raafat Kamal, Pastor Ian Walter Wellington Sweeney, Pastor Julian Gavin Hibbert, Pastor Paul David Tompkins, Pastor Steve Anthony Thomas, Miss Annette Hutchinson, Dr John Denys Baildam, Mr Hugh David Santineer, Dr John Christopher Walton, Mrs Alison Awuku, Pastor Maureen Patsy Rock, Miss Crystal Knight, Shelley Prince, Pastor Richard Sebastian Jackson, Miss Abigail Hazel, Mr Matthew Herel
Income: £13,292,710 [2016]; £12,818,915 [2015]; £12,529,883 [2014]; £12,677,827 [2013]; £12,292,894 [2012]

British Universities and Colleges Sport Limited
Registered: 24 Nov 2008 *Employees:* 35 *Volunteers:* 1,500
Tel: 020 7633 5080 *Website:* bucs.org.uk
Activities: Education, training; amateur sport
Address: British Universities & Colleges Sport, 20-24 Kings Bench Street, London, SE1 0QX
Trustees: Professor Sir Ian Diamond, Steve Egan, Mr Matthew Nicholson, Miss Lil Roe, Mr Benedict Robert Kirwan Moorhead, Zena Wooldridge, Ms Vicky Foster-Lloyds, Mr Andrew Westlake
Income: £3,871,082 [2017]; £3,934,478 [2016]; £3,574,345 [2015]; £3,290,033 [2014]; £3,100,646 [2013]

British Wireless for the Blind Fund
Registered: 19 Nov 1999 *Employees:* 16 *Volunteers:* 51
Tel: 01622 754757 *Website:* blind.org.uk
Activities: Disability
Address: 10 Albion Place, Maidstone, Kent, ME14 5DZ
Trustees: Mr Daniel Smith, Mr Michael Wood, Mr Mark Anthony Noble, Mrs Margaret Rona Grainger, Mr Jason Charles Dominic Mowe, Mr Paul Easton, Mr Thomas Everest
Income: £1,939,687 [2016]; £1,379,274 [2015]; £1,197,841 [2014]; £1,431,024 [2013]; £1,158,763 [2012]

British Youth for Christ
Registered: 4 Feb 1972 *Employees:* 47 *Volunteers:* 31
Tel: 0121 502 9620 *Website:* yfc.co.uk
Activities: Education, training; prevention or relief of poverty; religious activities; arts, culture, heritage, science; amateur sport
Address: Youth for Christ, Unit D2, Coombswood Way, Halesowen, W Midlands, B62 8BH
Trustees: Mrs Pauline Joyce, Mrs Debbie Mitchell, Mr Ken Wright, Mr Timothy Wills, Mr Martin Bull, Mrs Jacqueline Ann Fowler, Mr Rakesh Kaul, Rev David Stillman, Mr Richard Child, Mr James Vardy, Mr Carl Lee, Ms Adedamola Adewunmi, Mrs Susan Joanna Godden
Income: £1,589,039 [2017]; £1,961,470 [2016]; £1,896,644 [2015]; £2,047,295 [2014]; £1,895,741 [2013]

The British and Foreign Bible Society
Registered: 1 Jun 1964 *Employees:* 130 *Volunteers:* 15,438
Tel: 01793 418100 *Website:* biblesociety.org.uk
Activities: Religious activities
Address: Stonehill Green, Westlea, Swindon, Wilts, SN5 7DG
Trustees: Mr Arfon Jones, Mrs Christina Rees, Dr Bunmi Olayisade, Mr Paul Chandler, Mr James Featherby, Mr Paul Bosson, Colonel Richard Sandy, Mrs Catherine Pepinster, Mrs Sue Heatherington, Mr Alan Eccles, Mr Ian Dighe, Professor Paul Williams
Income: £19,537,000 [2017]; £18,146,000 [2016]; £19,746,000 [2015]; £18,774,000 [2014]; £16,379,000 [2013]

Britten Sinfonia Ltd
Registered: 2 May 1985 *Employees:* 13 *Volunteers:* 6
Tel: 01223 300795 *Website:* brittensinfonia.com
Activities: Education, training; arts, culture, heritage, science; recreation
Address: 13 Sturton Street, Cambridge, CB1 2SN
Trustees: Dr Mary Archer, Mr Hamish Forsyth, Dr Andrew Harter, Mrs Margaret Mair, Mr Jerome Paul Booth Dr, Mr Bill Thompson
Income: £1,697,360 [2017]; £1,626,534 [2016]; £1,843,496 [2015]; £1,772,946 [2014]; £1,500,630 [2013]

The Britten-Pears Foundation
Registered: 11 Nov 1986 *Employees:* 17 *Volunteers:* 39
Tel: 01728 451700 *Website:* brittenpears.org
Activities: Education, training; arts, culture, heritage, science; environment, conservation, heritage
Address: Britten-Pears Foundation, The Red House, Golf Lane, Aldeburgh, Suffolk, IP15 5PZ
Trustees: Dr Colin Matthews, Sir Vernon James Ellis, Ms Janis Elizabeth Susskind, Mrs Penelope Chloe Heath, Mr Oliver Max Rivers, Sir Christopher Kingston Howes KCVO CB, Professor Christopher Francis Higgins, Mrs Caroline Brazier, Ms Jane Scott Hay, Mrs Angela Mallinson
Income: £1,522,264 [2016]; £1,440,072 [2015]; £2,169,955 [2014]; £3,500,703 [2013]; £2,215,791 [2012]

Broadening Choices for Older People
Registered: 31 Mar 1999 *Employees:* 181
Tel: 0121 459 7670 *Website:* bcop.org.uk
Activities: Education, training; accommodation, housing
Address: Broadening Choices, 7-8 Imperial Court, 12 Sovereign Road, Kings Norton, Birmingham, B30 3FH
Trustees: Ms Kathryn Halliday, Mr Stephen Long, Mr Brian Toner, Dr Nicola Bradbury, Mr Adrian Jones, Mr Neville William Topping, Dr Caroline Cooban, John Bennett, Gillian Maidens
Income: £7,094,358 [2017]; £6,719,994 [2016]; £7,200,073 [2015]; £7,062,277 [2014]; £6,702,454 [2013]

Broadreach House
Registered: 15 Jul 1982 Employees: 97
Tel: 01752 797101 Website: broadreach-house.org.uk
Activities: General charitable purposes; education, training; other charitable purposes
Address: Broadreach House, Rehabilitation Centre, 465 Tavistock Road, Plymouth, PL6 7HE
Trustees: Mr Raymond Hayes, Mr John Joseph Kiddey, Mr Timothy Michael Jones, Mr Craig Marshall, Mrs Christina Saunders Gavin, Mr James Buller Kitson, Mr Christopher Loftus, Dr Peter Urwin, Mrs Georgina Dormer, Dr Charlotte Massey
Income: £2,647,363 [2017]; £2,555,233 [2016]; £2,508,739 [2015]; £2,560,786 [2014]; £2,595,373 [2013]

Broadway Lodge Limited
Registered: 7 Apr 1975 Employees: 84 Volunteers: 6
Tel: 01934 818016 Website: broadwaylodge.org.uk
Activities: The advancement of health or saving of lives
Address: Broadway Lodge, 37 Totterdown Lane, Weston-Super-Mare, Somerset, BS24 9NN
Trustees: Mr Richard Dennis Flack, Mr Philip Gay, Mr Keith Leslie Burns, Mr Simeon Jon Barnes, Mr Christopher Jelf
Income: £2,392,777 [2017]; £3,207,870 [2016]; £3,344,253 [2015]; £3,123,763 [2014]; £2,686,299 [2013]

Penny Brohn Cancer Care
Registered: 30 Jun 1982 Employees: 62 Volunteers: 187
Tel: 01275 370100 Website: pennybrohn.org.uk
Activities: The advancement of health or saving of lives
Address: Penny Brohn UK, Chapel Pill Lane, Pill, Bristol, BS20 0HH
Trustees: Miss Francesca Barnes, Mrs Carol Sapsed, Mr Alexander Hamilton-Baily, Mr Stephen Jonathan Rosser, Mrs Rebecca Granger, Mrs Katherine Groombridge, Rev Dr Victor Barley, Mrs Felicity Ann Biggart, Mr Kenneth David Guy, Mr Mohammed Habedat Saddiq, Mrs Jacqueline Tania Graves, Mrs Charlotte White
Income: £4,045,105 [2016]; £2,459,994 [2015]; £2,275,000 [2014]; £2,169,000 [2013]; £2,497,000 [2012]

The Bromley By Bow Centre
Registered: 26 Oct 1994 Employees: 124 Volunteers: 60
Tel: 020 8709 9717 Website: bbbc.org.uk
Activities: General charitable purposes; education, training; advancement of health or saving of lives; disability; prevention or relief of poverty; arts, culture, heritage, science; amateur sport; environment, conservation, heritage; economic, community development, employment; human rights, religious or racial harmony, equality or diversity
Address: Bromley by Bow Centre, St Leonards Street, London, E3 3BT
Trustees: Marcia Maximin, Mr Chris Wilson, Ms Sarah Burton, Mr Simon Bevan, Ms Sophie Timson, David Smeed, Rachael Saunders, Prof Ajit Lalvani, Dr Savitha Pushparajah, Penny Shimmin, Mr Michael Gould, Mr Monjur Ali, Peter Thorne
Income: £4,373,000 [2017]; £4,108,000 [2016]; £3,665,000 [2015]; £3,343,000 [2014]; £2,835,000 [2013]

Bromley Mencap
Registered: 26 Jan 1989 Employees: 22 Volunteers: 82
Tel: 020 8466 0790 Website: bromleymencap.org.uk
Activities: Disability
Address: Bromley Mencap, Rutland House, 44 Masons Hill, Bromley, Kent, BR2 9JG
Trustees: Julie Spencer, Mrs Branwen Austyn-Jones, Mr Paul Nash, Mr Geoffrey Colin Gostt, Mrs Marion Gwyneth Moore, Mrs Ann Kean, Mr Michael Deves, Mr Paul Williams, Mr Peter Prentice
Income: £1,000,333 [2017]; £821,854 [2016]; £842,739 [2015]; £719,323 [2014]; £752,177 [2013]

Bromley Y
Registered: 25 Feb 1987 Employees: 32 Volunteers: 6
Tel: 020 3770 8848 Website: bromley-y.org.uk
Activities: Education, training; advancement of health or saving of lives
Address: Bromley Y, 17 Ethelbert Road, Bromley, Kent, BR1 1JA
Trustees: Mr Adrian Hollands, Mrs Kathy Morris, Dr Stuart Robertson, Ms Catherine Kane, Judge Anthony Gore, Alderman Ernest Noad, Dr Alan Beattie
Income: £1,051,860 [2017]; £876,296 [2016]; £543,655 [2015]; £494,223 [2014]; £472,843 [2013]

Bromley Youth Music Trust
Registered: 20 Jan 1994 Employees: 73 Volunteers: 88
Tel: 020 8467 1566 Website: bymt.co.uk
Activities: Education, training; arts, culture, heritage, science
Address: Bromley Youth Music Trust, Bromley Youth Music Centre, Southborough Lane, Bromley, Kent, BR2 8AA
Trustees: Mr Adrian Hollands, Mr Ernest Dennis Barkway, Mrs Sue Polydorou, Mr Richard Ernest Lane, Mr Leonard Edmund Blomstrand
Income: £1,690,138 [2017]; £1,678,808 [2016]; £1,627,582 [2015]; £1,622,285 [2014]; £1,688,173 [2013]

Bromley and Croydon Women's Aid
Registered: 9 Feb 1998 Employees: 13 Volunteers: 25
Tel: 020 8313 9303 Website: bcwa.org.uk
Activities: General charitable purposes; accommodation, housing
Address: 2 Oakfield Road, Penge, London, SE20 8QT
Trustees: Ms Jane Ward, Ms Julie Marian Foster, Ms Wendy Gordon, Mrs Paula Hills, Ms Jillian May, Ms Rosa Brennan, Mrs Nasima Ansary
Income: £1,101,869 [2017]; £806,554 [2016]; £754,631 [2015]; £799,519 [2014]; £888,588 [2013]

Bromley, Lewisham & Greenwich Mind Ltd
Registered: 20 Oct 2000 Employees: 96 Volunteers: 141
Tel: 01689 603574 Website: blmind.org.uk
Activities: Education, training; advancement of health or saving of lives; disability
Address: Anchor House, 5 Station Road, Orpington, Kent, BR6 0RZ
Trustees: Linda Jane Gabriel, Peter Cardell, Mr Peter Edmundson, Mrs Rebecca Jarvis, Mrs Lydia Lee, Mrs Paula Morrison, Mr Mike Ricketts, Margaret Jean Cunningham, Mr Stuart Robertson, Mr Donald Burford, Mrs Katherine Palley
Income: £3,891,455 [2017]; £3,431,213 [2016]; £3,128,336 [2015]; £2,837,252 [2014]; £2,480,394 [2013]

Bromsgrove Arts Centre Trust
Registered: 8 Jul 2008 *Employees:* 21 *Volunteers:* 76
Tel: 01527 572730 *Website:* artrix.co.uk
Activities: Education, training; arts, culture, heritage, science
Address: The Artrix, School Drive, Bromsgrove, Worcs, B60 1AX
Trustees: Mrs June Maud Lily Amott Griffiths, Christopher Bovey, Mrs Wiff Maton, Mrs Donna Farrugia, Samantha Preece, Ms Nicki Williams, Dorothy Wilson, Caroline Spencer, Chris Everall, Nicola Sharp, Charlotte Swain
Income: £1,031,673 [2017]; £996,786 [2016]; £974,204 [2015]; £907,908 [2014]; £862,550 [2013]

Bromsgrove District Housing Trust Limited
Registered: 23 Sep 2005 *Employees:* 131 *Volunteers:* 10
Tel: 01527 557557 *Website:* bdht.co.uk
Activities: The prevention or relief of poverty; accommodation, housing
Address: Buntsford Court, Buntsford Gate, Bromsgrove, Worcs, B60 3DJ
Trustees: Mr Barry Thompson, Ms Vikki Holloway, Ms Rachel Ward, Mary Miller, Ms Emma Windsor, Mr Peter Worthington, Mr Adam Wagner, Mr Barrie Payne, Ms Kathryn Coulson
Income: £22,797,000 [2017]; £19,861,000 [2016]; £18,253,000 [2015]; £16,927,000 [2014]; £16,073,000 [2013]

Bromsgrove School
Registered: 24 Jul 2003 *Employees:* 642 *Volunteers:* 15
Tel: 01527 579679 *Website:* bromsgrove-school.co.uk
Activities: Education, training
Address: Bromsgrove School, Worcester Road, Bromsgrove, Worcs, B61 7DU
Trustees: Mr Paul West, Mr R Brookes, Mr Nicholas Venning Mr Nicholas Venning, Mr Michael John Luckman, Mrs Jenny Loynton, Mrs Deborah Waltier, Mrs Anne Cleary, Mr G P J Strong, Mr Rupert Douglas Lane, Mr David Walters, Dr Clare Maria Lidbury, Mr James William Roden, Mr Charles Cameron, Mr Ian Stringer
Income: £37,860,642 [2017]; £29,717,120 [2016]; £30,886,401 [2015]; £29,154,224 [2014]; £27,932,098 [2013]

The Bronte Society
Registered: 21 Aug 1964 *Employees:* 38 *Volunteers:* 25
Website: bronte.org.uk
Activities: Education, training; arts, culture, heritage, science; environment, conservation, heritage
Address: Bronte Parsonage Museum, Church Street, Haworth, Keighley, W Yorks, BD22 8DR
Trustees: Sir James Aykroyd Bart, Miss Susan Aykroyd, Mrs Patricia Gurney, Mr John Derek Thirlwell, Mrs Michelle Rogers, Rev Peter Mayo-Smith, Mrs Anne Simpson, Mrs Catherine Rayner, Mr David Broadley
Income: £1,101,969 [2016]; £1,640,570 [2015]; £864,124 [2014]; £783,796 [2013]

The Brook Trust
Registered: 10 Apr 2008
Website: brooktrust.org
Activities: General charitable purposes; education, training; arts, culture, heritage, science; other charitable purposes
Address: The Brook Trust, P O Box 161, Cranbrook, Kent, TN17 9BL
Trustees: Tim Bull, Mrs Elinor Cleghorn, Ms Rosalind Riley
Income: £1,975,988 [2017]; £535,815 [2016]; £81,683 [2015]; £123,158 [2014]; £413,414 [2013]

Brook Young People
Registered: 20 Jun 1990 *Employees:* 416 *Volunteers:* 144
Tel: 0151 207 8238 *Website:* brook.org.uk
Activities: Education, training; advancement of health or saving of lives
Address: Brook, 81 London Road, Liverpool, L3 8JA
Trustees: Timothy Tod, Leon Ward, Chris Martin, Joanna Walker, Alice Birch, Scott Bennett, Jo Youle, Duy Hoang, Karim Mohamed
Income: £11,261,264 [2017]; £12,158,347 [2016]; £13,840,625 [2015]; £14,315,746 [2014]; £986,978 [2013]

The Brooke Hospital for Animals
Registered: 23 Mar 2001 *Employees:* 191 *Volunteers:* 3
Website: thebrooke.org
Activities: Education, training; animals
Address: The Brooke Hospital for Animals, 41-45 Blackfriars Road, London, SE1 8NZ
Trustees: Major General Sir Evelyn John Webb-Carter, Mr Ian Kerr, Paul Elphick, Mr Richard Michael Britten-Long, Dr Belinda Bennet, Professor Cheikh Ly, Ms Gaynor Miller, Jane Holderness-Roddam, Mr Michael Seton, Mr Anantkumar Pethraj Shah, Dr Graeme Cooke, Ms Sarah Arnold, Mr John Edward Otiene Rege
Income: £19,517,525 [2017]; £16,591,523 [2016]; £17,420,801 [2015]; £17,730,533 [2014]; £15,804,555 [2013]

Brooklands Museum Trust Limited
Registered: 28 Apr 1987 *Employees:* 55 *Volunteers:* 800
Tel: 01483 767183 *Website:* brooklandsmuseum.com
Activities: Environment, conservation, heritage
Address: Lindisfarne, Heath Road, Woking, Surrey, GU21 4DT
Trustees: Sir Gerald Acher CBE LVO, Mr Stewart John, Mr Michael Bannister, Mr Randolph Jr Sesson, Miss Georgina Wood, Mr Frederick Bryan Smart, Mr Timothy Richard Needell, Mrs Penelope Anne Tessa Timson, Mr Andrew Neil Mallery, Mrs Marilyn Scott
Income: £6,634,429 [2016]; £4,390,728 [2015]; £3,204,837 [2014]; £2,735,359 [2013]; £2,294,865 [2012]

Brookvale
Registered: 7 Oct 1963 *Employees:* 84
Tel: 0161 653 1767
Activities: The advancement of health or saving of lives
Address: Brookvale Home, Simister Lane, Prestwich, Manchester, M25 2SF
Trustees: Mr Stuart Gold, Mr Sidney Larah, Mr Carl Richmond, Mr Daniel Savage, Mr Stephen Pollock
Income: £3,129,657 [2016]; £3,116,447 [2015]; £3,228,826 [2014]; £3,255,577 [2013]; £3,071,792 [2012]

Broom Foundation
Registered: 3 Jan 2001 *Employees:* 6 *Volunteers:* 1
Activities: General charitable purposes; education, training; prevention or relief of poverty; religious activities
Address: 31 Broom Lane, Salford, M7 4EQ
Trustees: Mr David Neuwirth, Mr Benjamin Leitner, Mr Abraham Vogiel
Income: £2,812,085 [2017]; £2,143,742 [2016]; £2,111,146 [2015]; £1,881,086 [2014]; £1,583,671 [2013]

The Broomgrove Trust
Registered: 9 Dec 1983 *Employees:* 83 *Volunteers:* 3
Tel: 0114 266 1311 *Website:* broomgrove-trust.co.uk
Activities: The advancement of health or saving of lives; accommodation, housing
Address: The Broomgrove Trust Nursing Home, 30 Broomgrove Road, Sheffield, S10 2LR
Trustees: Dr Alan Anderson, Mrs Janet Cooper, Mrs Susan Franklin, Mr Michael Nicholas Pestereff, Mr Peter Hartland, Mr David Wilson
Income: £1,690,907 [2017]; £1,576,329 [2016]; £1,493,377 [2015]; £1,333,704 [2014]; £1,230,687 [2013]

Broughton House - Home for Ex-Service Men and Women
Registered: 7 Jan 2014 *Employees:* 68 *Volunteers:* 20
Tel: 0161 740 2737 *Website:* broughtonhouse.com
Activities: Disability; accommodation, housing
Address: Broughton House, Home for Ex-Service Men and Women, Park Lane, Salford, M7 4JD
Trustees: Brigadier T O'Brien, Lieutenant Colonel S Dixon, Colonel P Loynes, Air Vice Marshal Dr Jon Lamonte DL RAF, Mr Ken Bishop, Mrs E Conn OBE JP DL BA, Professor Sir Netar Mallick, Mr G Almond, Mrs Rebecca Rennison, Colonel P Harrison
Income: £1,537,530 [2017]; £1,659,611 [2016]; £5,515,450 [2015]

The Marcia and Andrew Brown Charitable Trust
Registered: 12 May 2004
Tel: 0161 455 6780
Activities: General charitable purposes
Address: c/o Miss S Chamberlain, P O Box 500, 2 Hardman Street, Manchester, M60 2AT
Trustees: Mr Andrew Brown MBE, Mrs Marcia Brown
Income: £1,219,667 [2017]; £13,520 [2016]; £33,253 [2015]; £8,811 [2014]; £12,000 [2013]

Brunelcare
Registered: 5 Mar 1962 *Employees:* 1,194 *Volunteers:* 71
Tel: 0117 914 4208 *Website:* brunelcare.org.uk
Activities: The advancement of health or saving of lives; disability; accommodation, housing
Address: Brunelcare Offices, Saffron Gardens, Prospect Place, Bristol, BS5 9FF
Trustees: Mr Richard Woolley, Mr S Thorpe, Mr S Boardman, Mr R Glover, Mrs Clare Crawford, Ms Deborah Evans, Mrs Barbara Hardy, Mrs Karen Taylor, Mr R Gaunt, Dr M Morse, Mr C Haynes, Mrs Julie Steed, Ms Maggie Hehir, Mrs Gill McLeod, Mr Kevni Fairman
Income: £33,012,000 [2017]; £33,201,000 [2016]; £31,321,000 [2015]; £27,057,000 [2014]; £24,090,000 [2013]

Bruton School for Girls
Registered: 15 Mar 2001 *Employees:* 83 *Volunteers:* 13
Tel: 01749 814430 *Website:* brutonschool.co.uk
Activities: General charitable purposes; education, training; accommodation, housing; religious activities; arts, culture, heritage, science; amateur sport
Address: Bruton School for Girls, Sunny Hill, Bruton, Somerset, BA10 0NT
Trustees: Mrs Christine Anne Davidson BA, Captain Lewis William Leonard Chelton RN, Mr Nicholas David Jefferis, Mr Michael Streatfeild, Miss Elizabeth Webbe LLB TEP, Mr Nigel Brian Noble, Mrs Lisa Anne Anderson, Mr David Hindley JP, Mr David Henry Cary Batten, Mrs Gillean Jean Hylson-Smith, Mr Hugh Llewelyn Davies BA CMG, Mrs Diana Wood, Mrs Elisabeth Alison Balfour, Mr Andrew Lane
Income: £3,966,740 [2017]; £3,841,905 [2016]; £4,086,224 [2015]; £4,115,362 [2014]; £4,498,709 [2013]

Bryanston School Incorporated
Registered: 18 Apr 1963 *Employees:* 528 *Volunteers:* 5
Tel: 01258 452411 *Website:* bryanston.co.uk
Activities: Education, training
Address: Bryanston School, Bryanston, Blandford Forum, Dorset, DT11 0PX
Trustees: Mr Sebastian Orby Conran, Mr Julian Greenhill MA, Mr Simon Bowes, Mrs Victoria McDonaugh MA DL, Mr Anthony Richard Poulton, Mr David Mark Trick, Dr Katherine Maire-Anne Fleming, Miss Mabel Ellen McKeown, Mr Christopher George Martin, Mr Bahman Irvani MA FCA, Mr Mark Laurence, Mrs Susan Foulser, Dr Hannah Pharaoh, Mrs Natalie Bickford, Rev Lucinda Jane Holt, Mr John Andrew Francis Fortescue, Mrs Louise Marcelle Victoria Soden, Mr Benedict Peter Broad
Income: £23,214,895 [2017]; £23,130,767 [2016]; £21,810,388 [2015]; £21,314,305 [2014]; £20,452,990 [2013]

Buckfast Abbey Trust (Held ICW The Religious Community of Benedictine Monks Established at St Marys Abbey Buckfast, Devon)
Registered: 6 Feb 1964 *Employees:* 120
Tel: 01364 645590 *Website:* buckfast.org.uk
Activities: Religious activities
Address: Buckfast Abbey Trust, Buckfast Abbey, Buckfast, Buckfastleigh, Devon, TQ11 0EE
Trustees: Very Rev Gavin Francis Straw OSB, Right Rev Martin Shipperlee OSB, Rev Vincent Gabriel Arnold OSB, Right Rev Stephen Ortiger, Right Reverend Dom David Roger Charlesworth OSB
Income: £10,356,827 [2016]; £8,840,421 [2015]; £7,931,045 [2014]; £8,026,901 [2013]; £7,997,998 [2012]

Buckinghamshire Healthcare NHS Trust Charitable Fund
Registered: 21 Feb 1996
Tel: 01494 734783 *Website:* buckshealthcare.nhs.uk
Activities: General charitable purposes; advancement of health or saving of lives
Address: South Buckinghamshire Hospitals NHS Trust, Amersham Hospital, Whielden Street, Amersham, Bucks, HP7 0JD
Trustees: Buckinghamshire Healthcare NHS Trust
Income: £2,848,000 [2017]; £1,260,000 [2016]; £761,000 [2015]; £1,428,000 [2014]; £2,854,000 [2013]

Buckinghamshire Learning Trust
Registered: 7 Mar 2013 *Employees:* 277
Website: learningtrust.net
Activities: Education, training; economic, community development, employment
Address: Buckinghamshire Learning Trust, King George V House, King George V Road, Amersham, Bucks, HP6 4BA
Trustees: Mr Alan Sherwell, Ms Sue Imbriano, Mrs Amanda Picillo, Mr Irfan Arif, Mr Marcus Pickover, Mr Roger Everson, Ms Nicola Jane Cook
Income: £12,803,503 [2017]; £12,873,593 [2016]; £14,542,318 [2015]; £15,814,434 [2014]

Bucks Students' Union
Registered: 28 Nov 2011 *Employees:* 42
Tel: 01494 601600 *Website:* bucksstudentsunion.org
Activities: Education, training
Address: Bucks Students' Union, Bucks New University, Queen Alexandra Road, High Wycombe, Bucks, HP11 2JZ
Trustees: Brian Tranter, Thomas Mitchell, Ben Parmar, Jimi Adeyinkia, Emily Nurden, Charlie Cotton, Nigel Copperwheat, Linsey Taylor, Lauren O'Shea, Jaylen Burrows, Emilee Platts
Income: £2,392,819 [2017]; £2,616,676 [2016]; £2,763,791 [2015]; £2,683,909 [2014]; £2,200,262 [2013]

Buglife The Invertebrate Conservation Trust
Registered: 30 May 2002 *Employees:* 23 *Volunteers:* 1,700
Tel: 01733 201210 *Website:* buglife.org.uk
Activities: Education, training; environment, conservation, heritage
Address: Buglife, Bug House, Ham Lane, Orton Waterville, Peterborough, PE2 5UU
Trustees: Mr Angus McCullough, Mr Mark Felton, Dr Stewart Clarke, Miss Rachel Hooper, Mr Hien Luong, Dr Scot Mathieson, Mr Richard Forster, Mrs Julie Smith
Income: £1,572,352 [2016]; £1,131,340 [2015]; £1,175,817 [2014]; £1,198,753 [2013]; £1,639,571 [2012]

Build Africa
Registered: 8 Jan 1988 *Employees:* 20 *Volunteers:* 1
Tel: 01892 519619 *Website:* build-africa.org
Activities: Education, training; prevention or relief of poverty; overseas aid, famine relief; economic, community development, employment
Address: 14th Floor, The Tower, 11 York Road, London, SE1 7NX
Trustees: Mr Michael Alan Noyes, Mr Chandra Apoorva, Richard Brown, Mr Andrew White, Mr Jeff Van Der Eems, Gabriele Cipparrone
Income: £2,565,195 [2016]; £3,307,939 [2015]; £3,129,485 [2014]; £2,694,672 [2013]; £2,783,519 [2012]

Build It International
Registered: 1 Sep 2006 *Employees:* 23 *Volunteers:* 17
Tel: 01743 246317 *Website:* builditinternational.org
Activities: Education, training; prevention or relief of poverty; overseas aid, famine relief; accommodation, housing; economic, community development, employment
Address: Build It International, The Pump House, Coton Hill, Shrewsbury, Salop, SY1 2DP
Trustees: Mr Andrew William Sentance, Mrs Liz Mayhew, Mr Rueben Lifuka, Ms Lauren Miller, Mr Ronald Gilbert Fleming, Mr John Lloyd Nutt, Mr Graham Wickenden, Ms Abigail Gammie
Income: £1,023,493 [2016]; £938,517 [2015]; £1,010,433 [2014]; £941,656 [2013]; £1,081,652 [2012]

Building Crafts College
Registered: 3 Feb 1964 *Employees:* 47
Tel: 020 7588 7001 *Website:* thebcc.ac.uk
Activities: Education, training
Address: Carpenters' Hall, 1 Throgmorton Avenue, London, EC2N 2JJ
Trustees: The Worshipful Company of Carpenters
Income: £2,984,043 [2017]; £2,696,432 [2016]; £2,794,494 [2015]; £2,667,659 [2014]; £2,562,506 [2013]

The Built Environment Trust
Registered: 4 Sep 2015 *Employees:* 15
Tel: 020 7692 6210
Activities: Education, training; environment, conservation, heritage
Address: The Building Centre, 26 Store Street, London, WC1E 7BT
Trustees: Mr Antony Mark Oliver, Mr Klaus Bode BSc Hons FRIBA, Dr James Michael Bradburne, Mr Richard William Hill FCCA, Mr Digby Flower, Ms Katayoun Ghahremani
Income: £3,313,758 [2017]; £3,927,925 [2016]

The Bulldog Trust Limited
Registered: 5 Mar 2008 *Employees:* 15 *Volunteers:* 120
Tel: 020 7240 6044 *Website:* bulldogtrust.org
Activities: General charitable purposes; arts, culture, heritage, science
Address: The Bulldog Trust Ltd, 2 Temple Place, London, WC2R 3BD
Trustees: Mr Brian Andrew Smouha, Mr Hamish McPherson, Mr Charles Jackson, Charles Hoare, Alex Williams
Income: £1,319,084 [2017]; £1,180,671 [2016]; £1,491,003 [2015]; £1,169,503 [2014]; £741,580 [2013]

Bumblebee Conservation Trust
Registered: 31 Jul 2006 *Employees:* 19 *Volunteers:* 500
Tel: 023 8064 2060 *Website:* bumblebeeconservation.org
Activities: Animals; environment, conservation, heritage
Address: Parkway House, Business Centre, Eastleigh Works, Campbell Road, Eastleigh, Hants, SO50 5AD
Trustees: Mr Nicholas Mann, Mr Les Moore, Professor Peter Hollingsworth, Mr Phill Jennison, Ms Victoria Louise Wilkins, Nigel Ajax-Lewis, Mr John Sanders, Mr Stuart Roberts, Dr Lena Bayer-Wilfert
Income: £1,099,801 [2017]; £784,206 [2016]; £607,843 [2015]; £669,129 [2014]; £496,570 [2013]

The Burberry Foundation
Registered: 5 Nov 2013
Website: burberryfoundation.org
Activities: General charitable purposes
Address: Burberry Ltd, Horseferry House, Horseferry Road, London, SW1P 2AW
Trustees: Christopher The Lord Holmes of Richmond, Mr Marco Gobbetti, Ms Leanne Wood
Income: £1,359,230 [2017]; £2,768,996 [2016]; £6,730,507 [2015]

The Burdett Trust for Nursing
Registered: 19 Dec 2001
Tel: 020 7399 0102 *Website:* btfn.org.uk
Activities: General charitable purposes; education, training; advancement of health or saving of lives; disability; prevention or relief of poverty; overseas aid, famine relief; accommodation, housing
Address: Rathbone Trust Company Limited, 8 Finsbury Circus, London, EC2M 7AZ
Trustees: Mr Alan Gibbs, Mr Andrew Everard Martin Smith, Dame Eileen Sills, Mr Evy Piers George Hambro, Mr Andrew Christopher Gibbs, Dame Christine Beasley, Mr David Sines CBE, Mr William John Gordon, Dr Michael Gormley
Income: £1,316,727 [2016]; £1,398,632 [2015]; £1,484,530 [2014]; £1,606,330 [2013]; £1,403,670 [2012]

Burgess Autistic Trust
Registered: 7 Mar 1991 *Employees:* 83
Tel: 01622 722400 *Website:* burgessautistictrust.org.uk
Activities: Education, training; advancement of health or saving of lives; disability; accommodation, housing
Address: mcch, One Hermitage Court, Hermitage Lane, Maidstone, Kent, ME16 9NT
Trustees: Mr Philip John Sayer, Dr Maria Metaxia Callias, Mr Cedric Charles Burke
Income: £1,815,267 [2017]; £2,034,883 [2016]; £1,888,125 [2015]; £1,864,888 [2014]; £1,918,939 [2013]

Burgess Hill School for Girls Company
Registered: 18 Dec 1962 *Employees:* 125
Tel: 01444 241050 *Website:* burgesshill-school.com
Activities: Education, training
Address: Burgess Hill School, Keymer Road, Burgess Hill, W Sussex, RH15 0EG
Trustees: Mr Christopher Armitage, Mr James Tasker, Dr Paul Michael Marshall, Dr Alison Smith, Dr Peter Carter, Mrs Rachel Kay, Mrs Jill Wilson, Mr Stuart James Condie, Mr Jeremy Reffin, Mr Stephen Charles King, Mrs Hilary Simpson, Mrs Isabella Keighley
Income: £6,823,969 [2017]; £6,833,299 [2016]; £6,662,353 [2015]; £6,956,572 [2014]; £8,166,057 [2013]

Burghley House Preservation Trust Limited
Registered: 12 May 1969 *Employees:* 103
Tel: 01780 752075 *Website:* burghley.co.uk
Activities: Environment, conservation, heritage
Address: Burghley Estate Office, 61 High Street, St Martins, Stamford, Lincs, PE9 2LQ
Trustees: Mr Andrew James Feilden, Mr Edward Harley, Mr Brian Turnbull Julius Stevens, Mr William Oswald, Sir John Nutting QC, Mr Jonathon Chenevix-Trench, Sir Giles Henry Charles Floyd Bt, Mr Edward Leigh-Pemberton, Mr Edward George Clive, Mr William Parente, Mr Stuart Richmond-Watson, Mrs Jane Tufnell
Income: £10,008,416 [2017]; £9,371,490 [2016]; £7,951,152 [2015]; £7,575,858 [2014]; £7,332,805 [2013]

Burnie's Foundation
Registered: 1 Jul 2016 *Volunteers:* 1
Tel: 020 7250 7000 *Website:* burniesfoundation.com
Activities: Animals
Address: 45 Britton Street, London, EC1M 5NA
Trustees: Kenneth Tonkin, Mr Richard Thoburn, Bethann Sells
Income: £1,263,320 [2017]

Burnley Leisure
Registered: 10 Sep 2014 *Employees:* 143 *Volunteers:* 170
Tel: 01282 477166 *Website:* burnleyleisure.co.uk
Activities: Recreation
Address: St Peters Centre, Church Street, Burnley, Lancs, BB11 2DL
Trustees: Mr Terry Hephrun, Mr Anthony Preston, Dr Susan Rosemary Minten, Mrs Joanne Baldwin, Mr Asif Raja, Dr Walter Duncan Park, Miss Michelle Grimes, Mr Mark Heaton, Mrs Donna Livesey, Mr Tony Harrison
Income: £4,066,356 [2017]; £3,581,909 [2016]; £3,636,703 [2015]

Burnley Pendle and Rossendale Council for Voluntary Service
Registered: 16 May 1997 *Employees:* 22 *Volunteers:* 80
Tel: 01282 433740 *Website:* bprcvs.co.uk
Activities: General charitable purposes; education, training; advancement of health or saving of lives; disability; prevention or relief of poverty; environment, conservation, heritage; economic, community development, employment; human rights, religious or racial harmony, equality or diversity; recreation; other charitable purposes
Address: The CVS Centre, 62-64 Yorkshire Street, Burnley, Lancs, BB11 3BT
Trustees: Mr Peter Kenyon, Mr Howard Eccles, Mr Walter Duncan Park MBE, Mrs Katthleen Susan Marjorie Hughes, Mrs Susan Biggs, Ms Barbara Ashworth, Mrs Jacqueline Isle Oakes, Mr Francis Leo Wren, Mrs Margaret Ann Lishman, Mr Mohammed Aslam, Miss Jacquie Devlin, Ms Irene Burton, Miss Lian Pate
Income: £1,373,599 [2017]; £955,077 [2016]; £792,840 [2015]; £1,001,691 [2014]; £1,116,974 [2013]

Burton Albion Community Trust
Registered: 18 Jul 2011 *Employees:* 47 *Volunteers:* 25
Tel: 01283 565938
Activities: General charitable purposes; education, training; amateur sport; recreation
Address: Burton Albion Football Club, Pirelli Stadium, Princess Way, Burton on Trent, Staffs, DE13 0AR
Trustees: Mr David Michael Mellor, Mr Clarence Bennie Robinson, Mr John Jackson, Mr Phil Pusey, Mrs Barbara Richardson, Miss Fleur Elizabeth Robinson, Mr Robert Trevor Haywood, Mr Christopher Wood, Dr Deborah Taylor
Income: £1,105,353 [2017]; £958,576 [2016]; £736,193 [2015]; £560,911 [2014]; £319,245 [2013]

Burton upon Trent and District YMCA
Registered: 14 Oct 1999 *Employees:* 40 *Volunteers:* 81
Tel: 01283 538802 *Website:* burtonymca.org
Activities: General charitable purposes; prevention or relief of poverty; accommodation, housing; religious activities
Address: Northside House, Northside Business Park, Hawkins Lane, Burton on Trent, Staffs, DE14 1DB
Trustees: Mrs Jill Penelope Lanham, Miss Sherrie Rowlands, Simon Thacker, Ms Alison Johnson, Mr Robert Joseph Magill, Miss Lynn Chapman, Mr Michael Edward Costelloe, Mr John Deeley, Ms Angela Christine Bailey
Income: £1,459,295 [2016]; £1,538,189 [2015]; £1,604,810 [2014]; £1,439,661 [2013]; £1,407,077 [2012]

Bury Grammar Schools Charity
Registered: 29 Mar 1966 *Employees:* 204 *Volunteers:* 3
Tel: 0161 764 4442
Activities: Education, training
Address: Bury Grammar Schools, Farraday House, Bridge Road, Bury, Lancs, BL9 0HG
Trustees: The Bury Grammar Schools Trustee Limited
Income: £12,619,000 [2017]; £13,194,000 [2016]; £12,938,000 [2015]; £13,109,000 [2014]; £13,428,000 [2013]

Bury Hospice
Registered: 13 Jul 2010 *Employees:* 45 *Volunteers:* 350
Tel: 0161 725 9800 *Website:* buryhospice.org.uk
Activities: The advancement of health or saving of lives
Address: Bury Hospice, Rochdale Old Road, Bury, Lancs, BL9 7RG
Trustees: Professor Eileen Fairhurst, Mr Graham Yardley, Ms Noreen Ann Kershaw, Ms Ruth Moyra Robinson, Dr Gillian Rink, Mr Simon John Attwell, The Rev'd Canon Peter Leslie Holliday, Mr Paul Horrocks, Ms Donna Maria McNicoll
Income: £2,097,060 [2017]; £2,175,725 [2016]; £2,425,219 [2015]; £2,291,723 [2014]; £2,859,483 [2013]

Bury Manor School Trust Limited (Dorset House School)
Registered: 26 Oct 1966 *Employees:* 45 *Volunteers:* 12
Tel: 01798 831456 *Website:* dorsethouseschool.com
Activities: Education, training
Address: Dorset House School, The Manor, Church Lane, Bury, Pulborough, W Sussex, RH20 1PB
Trustees: Richard Agutter, Mrs Hilary Dugdale, Mr Paul Wilson, Mr Nigel Parsons, Ms Helen Charmain Davies, Mr Dominic Mott, Willy Hockin, Mr John Barclay, Mr Michael Higham, Mrs Amanda Meyrick, Mr Ben Figgis
Income: £1,999,984 [2017]; £1,791,187 [2016]; £1,724,063 [2015]; £1,703,356 [2014]; £1,584,864 [2013]

Bury Metropolitan Arts Association
Registered: 10 Aug 1989 *Employees:* 11 *Volunteers:* 100
Tel: 0161 761 7107 *Website:* themet.biz
Activities: Arts, culture, heritage, science
Address: The Met, Market Street, Bury, Lancs, BL9 0BW
Trustees: Mr John Peter Costello, Ms Esther Ferry-Kennington, Mr Martin Gizzie, Ms Victoria Robinson, Mr Thomas Philip Besford, Kelvin Barlow, Mr David Nuttall, Ms Shefali Talukdar, Miss Karen Elizabeth Dyson
Income: £3,793,331 [2017]; £1,721,586 [2016]; £1,047,361 [2015]; £811,805 [2014]; £755,105 [2013]

Bury St Edmunds Heritage Trust
Registered: 3 May 2007
Tel: 01284 704435 *Website:* buryguildhallexperience.org.uk
Activities: Education, training; arts, culture, heritage, science; environment, conservation, heritage; economic, community development, employment
Address: 79 Whting Street, Bury St Edmunds, Suffolk, IP33 1NX
Trustees: Mr Simon Francis Pott, Mr Henry Reginald Saltmarsh, Mr Christopher James Evan Spicer, Mrs Jo Ellen Grzyb, Mr Robert Jeremy Lamb, Mr Richard Combes MRICS, Mr Martin Lightfoot, Mr Stefan Robert Morgan Oliver, Mrs Sarah Anne Green, Mr Richard Mitson Evans, Mr Robert Duane Carr
Income: £1,099,056 [2016]; £175,471 [2015]; £21,459 [2014]; £93,132 [2013]; £12,876 [2012]

Bury St Edmunds Theatre Management Limited
Registered: 15 Jun 1965 *Employees:* 44 *Volunteers:* 90
Website: theatreroyal.org
Activities: Education, training; arts, culture, heritage, science; environment, conservation, heritage
Address: Theatre Royal, 5 Westgate Street, Bury St Edmunds, Suffolk, IP33 1QR
Trustees: Mr Alan Michael Brown, Elizabeth Michie, Mr Keith Michael Turner, Mr Michael Redmond, Mr Roger Quince, Mrs Penelope Deborah Ann Croft, Ms Sara Whybrew, Mr Alistair Wayne
Income: £1,749,033 [2017]; £1,621,191 [2016]; £1,968,060 [2015]; £1,866,095 [2014]; £1,433,651 [2013]

Business Disability Forum
Registered: 9 Mar 1993 *Employees:* 31
Tel: 020 7403 3020 *Website:* businessdisabilityforum.org.uk
Activities: General charitable purposes; education, training; disability; economic, community development, employment; human rights, religious or racial harmony, equality or diversity
Address: Business Disability Forum, Nutmeg House, 60 Gainsford Street, London, SE1 2NY
Trustees: Graham Bann, Mr Warren Buckley, Mr Stephen James Trevor Miller, Dr Hari Sundaresan, Miss Paulette Cohen, Mr Jonathan Varley Millidge, Mrs Rachel Ann Gray
Income: £2,111,351 [2017]; £2,210,397 [2016]; £2,352,985 [2015]; £2,198,368 [2014]; £2,117,797 [2013]

Business Education Partnership (UK) Ltd
Registered: 2 Aug 1995 *Employees:* 50
Tel: 0845 273 2226 *Website:* bepgroup.net
Activities: Education, training; economic, community development, employment
Address: 10 Bridge Close, Romford, Essex, RM7 0AU
Trustees: Mr Keith Byford, Mr Robin Turbefield, Mr Steve Wilks
Income: £1,212,352 [2017]; £1,245,833 [2016]; £1,369,157 [2015]; £1,920,719 [2014]; £1,737,288 [2013]

Business Launchpad
Registered: 15 Jul 1988 *Employees:* 16 *Volunteers:* 7
Tel: 020 8516 7700 *Website:* businesslaunchpad.org.uk
Activities: Education, training
Address: 19 Muirdown Road, East Sheen, London, SW14 8JX
Trustees: Mrs Judith Roscoe, Mr William Sceats, Ms Yvonne Nelson, Mr Jonathan Stuart Gill, Mr William Hoyle, Mr David Adam Gordon, Miss Amma Mensah, Mr Emmet Byrne
Income: £1,011,342 [2017]; £1,010,576 [2016]; £930,275 [2015]; £769,302 [2014]; £732,691 [2013]

Business and Human Rights Resource Centre
Registered: 24 Mar 2003 *Employees:* 16 *Volunteers:* 32
Tel: 020 7636 7774 *Website:* business-humanrights.org
Activities: Education, training
Address: 2-8 Scrutton Street, London, EC2A 4RT
Trustees: Ms Seema Joshi, Mr Chris Jochnick, Ms Ashwini Sukthankar, Mr Michael Joseph Hirschhorn, Mr Cesar Rodriguez, Dr Mila Rosenthal, Ms Kathleen Parsons, Ms Tanya McVeigh Peterson, Ms Heather Maureen Grady, Ms Kirsty Fiona Jenkinson, Ms Anne Travers, Ms Komala Ramachandra
Income: £1,586,801 [2017]; £1,657,436 [2016]; £991,960 [2015]; £1,337,418 [2014]; £907,180 [2013]

Business in the Community
Registered: 28 Sep 1987 *Employees:* 310
Tel: 020 7566 8650 *Website:* bitc.org.uk
Activities: General charitable purposes
Address: Business in the Community, 137 Shepherdess Walk, London, N1 7RQ
Trustees: Mr John Neill CBE, Mr Francesco Vanni D'Archirafi, Mrs Christine Mary Hodgson, Mr Steven Holliday, Vivian Hunt, Roy Adair, Ms Claudine Blamey, Mr Duncan Andrew Tait, Stephen Hughes, Mr Jeremy Darroch, Mr John Williams, Mr Phil Hodkinson, Mr Christopher Hyman, Richard Hutton, Chris Satterthwaite, Jeremy Pocklington, Mr Adrian Christopher Joseph, Keith Weed, Mike Still
Income: £26,315,582 [2017]; £29,552,073 [2016]; £30,672,000 [2015]; £31,324,000 [2014]; £28,470,000 [2013]

Bute House Preparatory School for Girls Limited
Registered: 3 Feb 1964 *Employees:* 63 *Volunteers:* 2
Tel: 07767 675539 *Website:* butehouse.co.uk
Activities: Education, training
Address: Luxemburg Gardens, London, W6 7EA
Trustees: Mrs Susan Bailes, Mr Chris Jones, Mr Tom Clementi, Mrs Polly Mary Ruth McAndrew, Sneha Kooros, Mr Jonathan Paul Beckitt, Mr Simon W J Wathen, Miss Katharine Jane Scott Kerr, Mrs Alice Mary Rose Thomson, Mrs Jane Ann Aughwane, Mr Mark Perry, Dr Michelle Sherman
Income: £4,811,668 [2016]; £4,438,005 [2015]; £4,225,011 [2014]; £4,149,173 [2013]; £4,092,913 [2012]

Butterfly Conservation
Registered: 7 Mar 1968 *Employees:* 73 *Volunteers:* 15,000
Tel: 01929 400209 *Website:* butterfly-conservation.org
Activities: Environment, conservation, heritage
Address: Butterfly Conservation, Manor Yard, Shaggs, East Lulworth, Wareham, Dorset, BH20 5QP
Trustees: Mr David William Hanson, Dr James Asher, Mr Andrew Brown, Mr Michael Johnston, Dr Susan Foden, Mrs Kathryn Dawson, Mr Ilija Vukomanovic, Mr Michael Dean, Mr Roger Dobbs, Ms Karen Goldie-Morrison, Mrs Sue Smith, Mr Nigel Symington, Dr Andy Barker, Mr Chris Winnick
Income: £3,691,959 [2017]; £3,723,958 [2016]; £3,732,526 [2015]; £3,542,201 [2014]; £3,066,423 [2013]

Butterwick Limited
Registered: 7 Mar 1995 *Employees:* 129 *Volunteers:* 590
Website: butterwick.org.uk
Activities: The advancement of health or saving of lives
Address: Butterwick Hospice, Middlefield Road, Stockton on Tees, Cleveland, TS19 8XN
Trustees: Judith Hunter, Mrs Beverley Susan Blakey, Dr David Carr, Mrs Carol Mary Lancaster, Mr John Paul Bury, Mr Paul Langdon, Dr Neil George Reynolds, Dr Bruce Irving McClain
Income: £4,967,091 [2017]; £3,994,747 [2016]; £4,386,868 [2015]; £4,270,955 [2014]; £3,884,898 [2013]

Buttle UK
Registered: 30 Jul 1965 *Employees:* 21 *Volunteers:* 8
Tel: 020 7828 7311 *Website:* buttleuk.org
Activities: Education, training; prevention or relief of poverty
Address: Buttle UK, 15 Greycoat Place, London, SW1P 1SB
Trustees: Mr David Buttle, Mrs Caroline Gipps, Mr Trevor Reaney, Mr Leo Wong, Mr Mike Seaton, Mr Peter Orlov, Mr Damian Ettinger, Mr Antony Chapman, Ms Rosemary Norris, Mrs Jillian Dinsmore, Mrs Thomasina Findlay
Income: £4,574,000 [2017]; £4,274,000 [2016]; £4,288,000 [2015]; £4,299,000 [2014]; £4,603,000 [2013]

Buxton Arts Festival Limited
Registered: 20 Dec 1978 *Employees:* 7 *Volunteers:* 45
Tel: 01298 70395 *Website:* buxtonfestival.co.uk
Activities: Education, training; arts, culture, heritage, science
Address: 3 The Square, Buxton, Derbys, SK17 6AZ
Trustees: Mr Stuart Lester, Dame Sandra Burslem DL, Mrs Felicity Goodey CBE DL, Mr John Jesky, Mr Mark Sutherland, Ms Emily Gottlieb, Mrs Louise Potter DL, Mr Rod Dubrow-Marshall Professor, Mr Chris Fry, Mr Julian Glover
Income: £1,605,001 [2017]; £1,347,700 [2016]; £1,300,957 [2015]; £1,262,566 [2014]; £1,317,166 [2013]

C P S Preston Ltd
Registered: 3 Sep 1963 *Employees:* 56
Tel: 01772 735958 *Website:* stpiusx.co.uk
Activities: Education, training
Address: 35 Greenfield Way, Ingol, Preston, Lancs, PR2 3GE
Trustees: Mr Paul Clegg, Mr David Mark Hurst, Mrs Angela Morris, Mrs Ursula Walton, Mrs Sylvia Ann Fingleton, Mr Tim Bashall
Income: £1,744,377 [2016]; £1,815,396 [2015]; £1,705,650 [2014]; £1,691,850 [2013]; £1,730,386 [2012]

C.A.B. Cornwall
Registered: 24 Feb 2003 *Employees:* 45 *Volunteers:* 150
Tel: 01579 212025 *Website:* citizensadvicecornwall.org.uk
Activities: Education, training; prevention or relief of poverty; other charitable purposes
Address: Pitt Farm, Looe, Cornwall, PL13 2NB
Trustees: Mrs Susan Swift, Mr Michael John Cooper, Mr John Baker, Mr Paul Charlesworth
Income: £1,092,256 [2017]; £840,917 [2016]; £840,917 [2015]; £966,821 [2014]; £1,439,954 [2013]

CACDP
Registered: 22 Sep 1998 *Employees:* 23
Tel: 0191 383 1155 *Website:* signature.org.uk
Activities: Education, training; disability
Address: Mersey House, CACDP T/A Signature, Unit 8 Mersey House, Mandale Park, Belmont Industrial Estate, Durham, DH1 1TH
Trustees: Mr Craig Andrew Crowley MBE, Jonathan Farnhill, Liz Duncan, Mr Alan Blunt, Mr Ian Walton, Philida Schellekens, Paul Keen, Mr John Walker
Income: £1,884,904 [2016]; £1,705,036 [2015]; £1,884,242 [2014]; £1,793,034 [2013]; £1,808,266 [2012]

CAIS Limited
Registered: 12 Jul 1994 *Employees:* 161 *Volunteers:* 117
Tel: 01492 863007 *Website:* cais.co.uk
Activities: Education, training; advancement of health or saving of lives; prevention or relief of poverty; accommodation, housing; armed forces, emergency service efficiency
Address: CAIS, 12 Trinity Square, Llandudno, Conwy, LL30 2RA
Trustees: Miss Lucille Margaret Hughes, Doctor Dafydd Alun Jones MDB, Dr Avril Wayte, Mr Simon Paul Green, Carys Lloyd Roberts, Mr Robert Cledwyn Williams, Dr Dyfrig Ap Dafydd, Mr Geoffrey Simpson, Mr Brian Smith, Christopher James Prew
Income: £7,103,895 [2017]; £7,193,270 [2016]; £6,014,019 [2015]; £5,940,911 [2014]; £4,880,517 [2013]

CAN Mezzanine
Registered: 25 Feb 2009 *Employees:* 7
Tel: 020 3096 7659 *Website:* can-online.org.uk
Activities: General charitable purposes; education, training; economic, community development, employment
Address: 105 Marguerite Drive, Leigh on Sea, Essex, SS9 1NN
Trustees: Mrs Helen Taylor-Thompson, Alisitair Fraser, Mr Robin Pauley, Mr Clive Robert Dove-Dixon
Income: £3,893,389 [2017]; £3,029,889 [2016]; £2,064,689 [2015]; £1,813,972 [2014]; £1,691,860 [2013]

CAPITB Trust
Registered: 6 Sep 1990 *Employees:* 26
Tel: 07836 350012 *Website:* capitbgrants.com
Activities: Education, training; economic, community development, employment
Address: CapitB PLC, P O Box 91, Brighouse, W Yorks, HD6 2WB
Trustees: Michael Williams, Mr John Wilson, Mr Alan Cannon Jones, Robert Bright, Mrs Anne Carvell
Income: £2,116,149 [2017]; £1,930,416 [2016]; £2,309,338 [2015]; £2,069,581 [2014]; £1,886,684 [2013]

CASE Training Services
Registered: 20 Dec 1995 *Employees:* 29 *Volunteers:* 9
Tel: 01482 320200 *Website:* casetraininghull.co.uk
Activities: Education, training; disability; economic, community development, employment
Address: CASE Training Services, 60 Charles Street, Hull, HU2 8DQ
Trustees: Mr Terry Rust, Mr Mark John Cooke, Ms Anita Dawn Bielby
Income: £1,406,428 [2016]; £1,536,469 [2015]; £1,228,883 [2014]; £1,299,421 [2013]; £1,950,538 [2012]

CASP

Registered: 23 Feb 1988 *Employees:* 24
Tel: 01223 760700 *Website:* casp.cam.ac.uk
Activities: Education, training
Address: CASP, West Building, 181a Huntingdon Road, Cambridge, CB3 0DH
Trustees: Dr Peter Friend MA PhD, Dr D M D James, Professor John Marshall, Dr Sally Anne Gibson FGS, Dr Martin John Whiteley, Dr Philip Hirst, Dr J R Parker, Mr Clive Anthony Graham Pickton, Dr Gary Nichols, Dr Andrew Buckley, Dr Bruce K Levell
Income: £1,982,599 [2017]; £2,447,608 [2016]; £2,051,407 [2015]; £2,715,248 [2014]; £3,606,058 [2013]

CAYSH

Registered: 14 Oct 1993 *Employees:* 90 *Volunteers:* 2
Tel: 020 8683 5131 *Website:* caysh.org
Activities: Accommodation, housing; other charitable purposes
Address: CAYSH, 2 Whitgift Street, Croydon, Surrey, CR0 1FL
Trustees: Angela Clarke, Hannah Northern, Bob Cook, Alexandra Warren, Leonie Rose, Mick Williams, Fiona Claridge, Mr Bhavesh Padhiar
Income: £4,241,267 [2017]; £4,677,634 [2016]; £5,550,587 [2015]; £4,082,193 [2014]; £3,487,547 [2013]

CCCU UK

Registered: 12 Mar 2001 *Employees:* 17
Tel: 01865 559900 *Website:* scio-uk.org
Activities: Education, training
Address: 30 St Giles, Oxford, OX1 3LE
Trustees: Mr Charles Pollard, Mr Keith Graybill, Mrs Shirley Hoogstra, Mr James Hume Barnes III
Income: £2,456,840 [2017]; £2,193,590 [2016]; £1,652,120 [2015]; £1,557,878 [2014]; £1,373,069 [2013]

CDP Worldwide

Registered: 15 Jan 2008 *Employees:* 153 *Volunteers:* 42
Website: cdp.net
Activities: Environment, conservation, heritage
Address: Level 3, 71 Queen Victoria Street, London, EC4V 4AY
Trustees: Mr Jeremy Smith, Mr Alan Brown, Mr Martin Randal Wise, Jane Ambachtsheer, Rachel Kyte, Sonia Medina-Gomez, Mukundan Ramakrishnan, Katherine Garrett-Cox, Mr Takejiro Sueyoshi, Mr Jeremy Burke, Stephen Chow, Christine Loh, Annise Parker
Income: £14,900,000 [2017]; £9,100,000 [2016]; £8,404,568 [2015]; £6,093,398 [2014]; £5,741,812 [2013]

The CH Foundation (UK)

Registered: 17 Mar 2014
Activities: Education, training; advancement of health or saving of lives; prevention or relief of poverty; overseas aid, famine relief; economic, community development, employment; human rights, religious or racial harmony, equality or diversity
Address: 7 Clifford Street, London, W1S 2FT
Trustees: Mr Matthew John King, Sir Christopher Hohn
Income: £4,030,600 [2017]; £445,445 [2016]; £1,774,900 [2015]

CHK Charities Limited

Registered: 22 Nov 1995
Tel: 020 3207 7041 *Website:* chkcharities.co.uk
Activities: General charitable purposes
Address: 5th Floor, SG Kleinwort Hambros Trust Company, 8 St James's Square, London, SW1Y 4JU
Trustees: Mrs Charlotte Susanna Heber Percy, Mrs Katharine Sophie Loyd, Mr Rupert Prest, Mr Edward Peake, Miss Pandorra Morris, Mrs Joanna Alice Serena Prest, Mrs Lucy Henrietta Morris, Mrs Susanna Peake, Mrs Diana Acland
Income: £3,276,034 [2017]; £3,134,752 [2016]; £2,873,896 [2015]; £2,784,325 [2014]; £2,806,035 [2013]

CHUF

Registered: 11 Mar 2015 *Employees:* 5 *Volunteers:* 60
Tel: 0191 281 3166 *Website:* chuf.org.uk
Activities: Education, training; advancement of health or saving of lives; disability; accommodation, housing
Address: Gatehouse, Fleming Business Centre, Burdon Terrace, Newcastle upon Tyne, NE2 3AE
Trustees: Mr Arthur Campbell, Ms Joanne Moore, Mrs Christine Wood, Mr David Crossland, Mr Ivan Hollingsworth, Sarah Fitzpatrick, Professor Samir Gupta, Mr David Charlton
Income: £1,335,056 [2017]; £2,160,484 [2016]

CISV International Limited

Registered: 13 Jan 1999 *Employees:* 12
Tel: 0191 232 4998 *Website:* cisv.org
Activities: Education, training; arts, culture, heritage, science
Address: CISV International Ltd, Mea House, Ellison Place, Newcastle upon Tyne, NE1 8XS
Trustees: Mr Daniel Edelshaim, Ms Einav Dinur, Mr Calixto Mateo Hanel, Mr Vinh Velhelm Prag, Maarin Cabato, Ms Madhuri Parikh, Ms Anne-Caroline Paquet, Mr Gustavo Enrique Cuellar Rodriguez, Emmanuel Keates
Income: £2,488,467 [2016]; £2,040,764 [2015]; £1,842,225 [2014]; £1,839,771 [2013]; £936,425 [2012]

CITB

Registered: 31 Aug 1972 *Employees:* 1,426 *Volunteers:* 100
Website: citb.co.uk
Activities: Education, training
Address: National Construction College, Bircham Newton, King's Lynn, Norfolk, PE31 6RH
Trustees: Diana Garnham, David Harris, Maria Pilfold, Maureen Douglas, Karen Jones
Income: £310,570,000 [2016]; £298,319,000 [2015]; £263,964,000 [2014]; £273,659,000 [2013]; £245,605,000 [2012]

CLC International (UK)

Registered: 16 Dec 1992 *Employees:* 63 *Volunteers:* 100
Tel: 01244 520000 *Website:* clc.org.uk
Activities: Religious activities
Address: CLC International (UK), 5 Glendale Avenue, Sandycroft, Flintshire, CH5 2QP
Trustees: Viv Whitton, Bob Clark, John Watkins, Mrs Lynette Brooks, William MacKenzie, Gary Chamberlin, Mrs Esther Dowey, Mr John Lewis
Income: £5,797,491 [2017]; £5,015,875 [2016]; £4,869,377 [2015]; £4,405,368 [2014]; £4,429,025 [2013]

CLIC Sargent Cancer Care for Children
Registered: 17 Dec 2004 *Employees:* 545 *Volunteers:* 2,000
Tel: 020 8752 2878 *Website:* clicsargent.org.uk
Activities: The advancement of health or saving of lives; accommodation, housing
Address: Horatio House, 77-85 Fulham Palace Road, London, W6 8JA
Trustees: Ms Jane Stephanie Burt, Mr Ian Robert Lusk Gibson, Mr Graham Clarke, Mr Peter Hollins, Dr Julia Chisholm, Mr Jason Loo, Rachel Hollis, Mr Michael William Carter, Mr Keith Exford, Mr Dominic Grainger, Mr Peter Houghton, Mr Stephen George, Anna Hancock, Harry Howard
Income: £27,490,713 [2017]; £24,872,000 [2016]; £25,036,000 [2015]; £25,485,000 [2014]; £22,261,000 [2013]

CMSS
Registered: 12 Jan 1979 *Employees:* 33 *Volunteers:* 1
Tel: 020 8866 3711 *Website:* cmss.org.uk
Activities: Education, training; disability; amateur sport; economic, community development, employment
Address: CMSS, Wiltshire Lane, Northwood Hills, Pinner, Middlesex, HA5 2NB
Trustees: Mr Edmond Smart, Miss Angela Barnes, Mrs Isobel Chalcraft, Mrs H K Haston, Mr Patrick Brendan O'Sullivan, Mrs Christine Pauline Carse, Mr Leslie Michael Hardy, Mrs Juliet Burton
Income: £1,143,579 [2017]; £1,168,849 [2016]; £1,235,944 [2015]; £1,276,994 [2014]; £1,246,167 [2013]

CMZ Ltd
Registered: 6 Aug 2001
Tel: 020 8801 6038
Activities: General charitable purposes; education, training; advancement of health or saving of lives; disability; prevention or relief of poverty; overseas aid, famine relief; religious activities
Address: 206 High Road, London, N15 4NP
Trustees: Mr P Schneebalg, Mr Ephraim Gottesfeld, S Steinmetz
Income: £3,237,072 [2017]; £3,001,852 [2016]; £2,663,697 [2015]; £1,542,059 [2014]; £1,254,781 [2013]

CPA Studios
Registered: 7 Jan 2011 *Employees:* 13
Tel: 01708 766007 *Website:* cpastudios.co.uk
Activities: Education, training; arts, culture, heritage, science
Address: CPA Studios, The Studios, 219b North Street, Romford, Essex, RM1 4QA
Trustees: Keith Taylor, Mr Dan Micahael Moran, Mrs Jacqueline Parry
Income: £1,170,076 [2016]; £1,106,107 [2015]; £1,065,487 [2014]; £721,355 [2013]; £736,834 [2012]

CPotential Trust
Registered: 16 Jun 2008 *Employees:* 37 *Volunteers:* 20
Tel: 020 8444 7242 *Website:* cplondon.org.uk
Activities: Education, training; advancement of health or saving of lives; disability; amateur sport
Address: The Peter Rigby Trust, 143 Coppetts Road, London, N10 1JP
Trustees: Mr John Henry Martin, Ms Catharine Seddon, Mr Christopher John Gilbert, Mr Anthony Dowle, Mrs Marion Sheila Grimm, Mrs Barbara Smith, Mr Noel Gibb
Income: £1,221,878 [2016]; £1,687,640 [2015]; £1,493,480 [2014]; £1,344,821 [2013]; £1,132,513 [2012]

CTVC Limited
Registered: 14 Aug 1978 *Employees:* 25
Tel: 020 7378 3229 *Website:* ctvc.co.uk
Activities: Education, training; religious activities; other charitable purposes
Address: McBeath House, 310 Goswell Road, London, EC1V 7LW
Trustees: Joey Newton, Mr Andrew Edward Cowen MRICS, Rev Martin Allison Booth MA, Mr Duncan Charles Frearson, Mr Daniel Simon, Mr Graeme King MA CA, Mr Nicholas Buxton, Ms Lindsay Clay
Income: £2,673,000 [2017]; £5,714,000 [2016]; £2,984,000 [2015]; £2,608,000 [2014]; £7,670,000 [2013]

CVQO Ltd
Registered: 12 Jul 2006 *Employees:* 58 *Volunteers:* 8,000
Tel: 01276 601717 *Website:* cvqo.org
Activities: Education, training
Address: C V Q O Ltd, 3 Archipelago, Lyon Way, Frimley, Camberley, Surrey, GU16 7ER
Trustees: The Lord Lingfield DL, Mr Keith Ian Baldwin, Mr Martin Doel, Mrs Olga Bottomley, Mr Paul Luker, Mr John Dowty
Income: £4,639,445 [2017]; £4,392,005 [2016]; £4,757,824 [2015]; £4,711,949 [2014]; £4,048,849 [2013]

CWR
Registered: 10 Jun 1986 *Employees:* 65 *Volunteers:* 15
Tel: 01252 784700 *Website:* cwr.org.uk
Activities: Education, training; religious activities
Address: Waverley Abbey House, Waverley Lane, Farnham, Surrey, GU9 8EP
Trustees: Mr Graham Sopp, Mr Stephen Apted, Mr Sean Gubb, Mr Stephen Bradley, Mr Mervyn Thomas, Canon Derek Holbird
Income: £3,620,206 [2017]; £3,503,915 [2016]; £3,403,868 [2015]; £2,042,669 [2014]; £3,398,885 [2013]

CXK Limited
Registered: 4 Sep 2007 *Employees:* 175 *Volunteers:* 7
Tel: 01233 224266 *Website:* cxk.org
Activities: Education, training; economic, community development, employment
Address: Tufton House, Tufton Street, Ashford, Kent, TN23 1QN
Trustees: Mr Graham Briscoe, Mr Richard Edward Fedorcio, Suzanne O'Brien, Miss Charlotte Marie Walshe, Mr Robert Christian Robinson, Mr Alexander Graeme Dykes, Mr Barry Gordon Wilding, Mrs Kelly Amber Freeman, Catherine Mary Beare, Ms Pauline Smith, Mrs Sonette Andrea Schwartz, Mrs Rosemary Margaret Gould, Mr Dominic John Hilleand, Mr William Vernon
Income: £12,428,665 [2017]; £11,641,668 [2016]; £7,607,072 [2015]; £11,490,816 [2014]; £10,412,699 [2013]

The Edward Cadbury Charitable Trust
Registered: 4 Feb 2015 *Employees:* 1
Tel: 0121 472 1838 *Website:* edwardcadburytrust.org.uk
Activities: General charitable purposes
Address: Rokesley, Bristol Road, Selly Oak, Birmingham, B29 6QF
Trustees: Mr Andrew Stephen Littleboy, Mr Nigel Robin Cadbury, Dr William James Edward Southall, Mr Charles Robert Gillett, Mr Robert Hugh Stewart Marriott
Income: £1,018,710 [2017]; £977,762 [2016]

The Cadogan Charity
Registered: 7 Jun 1966
Tel: 020 7730 4567
Activities: The advancement of health or saving of lives; disability; accommodation, housing; animals
Address: 10 Duke of York Square, London, SW3 4LY
Trustees: Lady Anna Thomson, Countess Cadogan, The Hon William Cadogan, Rt Hon The Earl Cadogan, Viscount Chelsea
Income: £2,238,285 [2017]; £2,967,898 [2016]; £2,573,140 [2015]; £2,305,797 [2014]; £2,348,899 [2013]

Cae Post Limited
Registered: 6 Nov 2000 *Employees:* 22 *Volunteers:* 24
Tel: 01938 590454 *Website:* caepost.co.uk
Activities: Education, training; prevention or relief of poverty; environment, conservation, heritage
Address: Deep Cutting House, Pool Quay, Welshpool, Powys, SY21 9LL
Trustees: Mrs Gillian Mary Foulkes, John Harrington, Mrs Jacqueline Airlie Hawcroft, Susan Morley
Income: £1,223,451 [2017]; £1,181,746 [2016]; £1,123,787 [2015]; £1,087,495 [2014]; £1,039,619 [2013]

Caerphilly County Borough Citizens Advice Bureau
Registered: 8 Dec 2000 *Employees:* 103 *Volunteers:* 72
Tel: 01443 878050 *Website:* citizensadvicecbg.org.uk
Activities: Education, training; prevention or relief of poverty
Address: Citizens Advice Bureau, 41b Hanbury Road, Bargoed, Caerphilly, CF81 8QU
Trustees: Mr Tudor Davies, Mr Steven John Skivens, Mrs Angela Jones, Ms Shannon Robinson, Mr Glyn Jones, Mr Mostyn Wilfred Davies, Mr Gordon Pankhurst, Mr Hugh Jones, Mr Colin Mann, Mrs Julia Rose
Income: £3,197,154 [2017]; £2,225,201 [2016]; £1,783,463 [2015]; £1,199,188 [2014]; £1,225,028 [2013]

Caia Park Partnership Limited
Registered: 11 Nov 1998 *Employees:* 85 *Volunteers:* 40
Website: caiapark.org.uk
Activities: General charitable purposes; education, training; advancement of health or saving of lives; disability; prevention or relief of poverty; accommodation, housing; arts, culture, heritage, science; amateur sport; environment, conservation, heritage; economic, community development, employment
Address: Caia Park Partnership, Prince Charles Road, Caia Park, Wrexham, LL13 8TH
Trustees: Mrs Avril Ann Wright, Cllr Malcolm Christopher King, Calum Davies, Mr Francis John Hardman, Mr Lee Richardson, Professor Chris Fortune
Income: £1,491,572 [2017]; £1,520,575 [2016]; £1,130,850 [2015]; £1,054,268 [2014]; £941,890 [2013]

Calan DVS
Registered: 22 Feb 2012 *Employees:* 71
Tel: 01792 326800 *Website:* calandvs.org.uk
Activities: Education, training; advancement of health or saving of lives; prevention or relief of poverty; accommodation, housing; human rights, religious or racial harmony, equality or diversity
Address: Unit 24 Llan Coed House, Darcy Business Park, Llandarcy, Neath, SA10 6FG
Trustees: Mrs Sally Anne Shepherd, Mr Gwilym Huw Roberts, Ms Rhiannon Elizabeth Beaumont-Wood, Mrs Victoria Adele Pedicini
Income: £2,423,175 [2017]; £2,273,347 [2016]; £1,281,028 [2015]; £892,133 [2014]; £808,348 [2013]

Caldecott Foundation Limited
Registered: 21 Nov 1963 *Employees:* 157
Tel: 01303 815678 *Website:* caldecottfoundation.co.uk
Activities: Education, training; accommodation, housing
Address: Caldecott House, Smeeth, Ashford, Kent, TN25 6SP
Trustees: Mr John Fletcher, Mr Colin Green, Mr Jeremy Burke, Ms Ebony Hughes, Mr Michael Ross Buchanan, Mr Michael Lauerman, Mr Charles Lister, Mr Jerome Flechais
Income: £6,223,821 [2017]; £6,651,607 [2016]; £6,057,378 [2015]; £5,846,401 [2014]; £7,381,674 [2013]

Caldicott Trust Limited
Registered: 8 Jul 1969 *Employees:* 144 *Volunteers:* 30
Tel: 01753 649300 *Website:* caldicott.com
Activities: General charitable purposes; education, training
Address: Crown Lane, Farnham Royal, Slough, Bucks, SL2 3SL
Trustees: Mr George Marsh, Mr Andrew Metcalfe, Mr Christopher Rogers, Mrs Elisabeth Hungin, Mrs Beverley Hampshire, Mrs Anita Cranmer, Mr Malcolm Swift, Mr John Moule, Mr Manbhinder Rana, Mrs Victoria Peel
Income: £6,174,103 [2017]; £6,038,322 [2016]; £5,434,876 [2015]; £5,393,169 [2014]; £4,994,715 [2013]

Calibre Audio Library
Registered: 18 Mar 1983 *Employees:* 43 *Volunteers:* 182
Tel: 01296 432339 *Website:* calibre.org.uk
Activities: General charitable purposes; disability
Address: Calibre Audio Library, New Road, Weston Turville, Aylesbury, Bucks, HP22 5XQ
Trustees: Mr David Stephens, Mr Ian Yeoman, Revd Canon Andrew Meynell, Mr Richard Balkwill, Ms Sarah Frost, Mrs Anne Bolton, Mr Peter Gurney, Mrs Diana Le Clercq, Mr David Lillycrop, Mrs Rachel Gatley
Income: £1,177,807 [2017]; £1,174,739 [2016]; £1,788,346 [2015]; £1,321,670 [2014]; £1,183,774 [2013]

Calico Enterprise Limited
Registered: 1 Aug 2008 *Employees:* 157 *Volunteers:* 19
Tel: 0800 169 2407 *Website:* calico.org.uk
Activities: General charitable purposes; education, training; advancement of health or saving of lives; disability; prevention or relief of poverty; accommodation, housing; arts, culture, heritage, science; economic, community development, employment
Address: Calico Homes Ltd, Centenary Court, Croft Street, Burnley, Lancs, BB11 2ED
Trustees: Mr Stephen Aggett, Ms Georgina Nolan, Ms Shameem-Ara Khan, Ms Collette King, Mr Matthew Callcott, Ms Vina Mistry
Income: £4,469,654 [2017]; £4,371,000 [2016]; £4,247,000 [2015]; £2,974,000 [2014]; £2,991,000 [2013]

Calico Homes Limited
Registered: 8 May 2013 *Employees:* 215 *Volunteers:* 9
Tel: 0800 169 2407 *Website:* calico.org.uk
Activities: The prevention or relief of poverty; accommodation, housing; economic, community development, employment
Address: Calico Homes Ltd, Centenary Court, Croft Street, Burnley, Lancs, BB11 2ED
Trustees: Ms Karen Ainsworth, Andy Mullen, John Inglesfield, Ms Nickie Hallard, Mr Stewart Shaw, Mrs Christina MacKinnon Yates, Gemma Dyson, Peter Bevington, Mr Adam Greenhalgh
Income: £23,502,000 [2017]; £23,604,000 [2016]; £21,232,000 [2015]; £20,988,000 [2014]

The Calleva Foundation
Registered: 7 Jan 2000
Activities: Education, training; advancement of health or saving of lives; disability; overseas aid, famine relief; arts, culture, heritage, science; animals; environment, conservation, heritage
Address: The Calleva Foundation, P O Box 22554, London, W8 5GN
Trustees: Mrs Caroline Butt, Mr Stephen Butt
Income: £3,751,001 [2016]; £2,875,000 [2015]; £4,000 [2014]; £3,750,000 [2013]; £1,093,750 [2012]

The Cambrian Education Trust
Registered: 9 Apr 2003 *Employees:* 17 *Volunteers:* 120
Tel: 01743 457967 *Website:* newtown.focus-school.com
Activities: Education, training; disability
Address: The Chestnuts, Cruckton, Shrewsbury, Salop, SY5 8PW
Trustees: Robert Blackledge, Mr Nicholas Wallach, Mr Robert Hawgood, Mr Neville Simpson, Mr Timothy Carron, Mr Edward John Blackledge, Mr Peter Simpson
Income: £1,264,739 [2016]; £1,092,741 [2015]; £940,718 [2014]; £962,442 [2013]; £719,522 [2012]

The Cambridge Arts Theatre Trust Limited
Registered: 4 Jun 1998 *Employees:* 57 *Volunteers:* 59
Website: cambridgeartstheatre.com
Activities: General charitable purposes; education, training; disability; arts, culture, heritage, science
Address: The Cambridge Arts Theatre Trust Ltd, 6 St Edwards Passage, Cambridge, CB2 3PJ
Trustees: Sir Richard Dearlove, Mr Adam Glinsman, Mr Ian Mather, Ms Lily Bacon, Mr John Rodgers, Ms Griselda Yorke, Ms Amanda Jane Farnsworth, Mr Jeffrey Iliffe, Mr Andrew Swarbrick, Dr Keith Carne, Mr Shaun Grady, Mr David Rapley, Mr Lee Dean, Mr Rupert Christiansen
Income: £4,631,882 [2017]; £4,454,535 [2016]; £4,349,352 [2015]; £4,937,494 [2014]; £4,365,995 [2013]

Cambridge Centre for Sixth Form Studies
Registered: 19 Jan 2001 *Employees:* 69 *Volunteers:* 5
Tel: 01223 359952 *Website:* ccss.co.uk
Activities: Education, training; arts, culture, heritage, science; amateur sport
Address: 39 Grantchester Street, Cambridge, CB3 9HZ
Trustees: Mr Mark Slater, Tricia Pritchard, Mrs Katherine Julie Herbert, Mr Graeme Lockhart, Mr Randall White, Ms Lesley Ferney
Income: £5,430,231 [2016]; £5,688,857 [2015]; £5,400,969 [2014]; £5,419,318 [2013]; £5,082,832 [2012]

Cambridge Community Church
Registered: 13 Nov 2009 *Employees:* 23 *Volunteers:* 250
Tel: 01223 844415 *Website:* thec3.uk
Activities: Education, training; prevention or relief of poverty; overseas aid, famine relief; accommodation, housing; religious activities; human rights, religious or racial harmony, equality or diversity
Address: C3 Centre, 2 Brooks Road, Cambridge, CB1 3HR
Trustees: Steven Campbell, Mr Kevin Anthony McIntyre MBA, Mr Peter John Goodliffe, Howard Kettel, Mrs Alison Seekings
Income: £2,286,203 [2016]; £1,674,258 [2015]; £1,254,164 [2014]; £1,159,405 [2013]; £1,099,999 [2012]

The Cambridge Crystallographic Data Centre
Registered: 15 Dec 1988 *Employees:* 66
Tel: 01223 336408 *Website:* ccdc.cam.ac.uk
Activities: The advancement of health or saving of lives
Address: Cambridge Crystallographic Data Centre, 12 Union Road, Cambridge, CB2 1EZ
Trustees: Professor John Pyle, Professor Paul Raithby, Dr John Paul Overington, Ms Judith Currano, Dr Christoph Martin Stahl, Dr David Martinsen
Income: £5,258,749 [2016]; £4,980,731 [2015]; £4,436,915 [2014]; £4,737,787 [2013]; £3,912,667 [2012]

Cambridge House and Talbot
Registered: 20 Feb 1973 *Employees:* 57 *Volunteers:* 59
Tel: 020 7358 7000 *Website:* ch1889.org
Activities: General charitable purposes; education, training; disability; prevention or relief of poverty; arts, culture, heritage, science
Address: Cambridge House, 1 Addington Square, London, SE5 0HF
Trustees: Shveta Shah, Miss Nicola Frances Mellor, Fran Sanderson, Andy Carr, Ms Clarisse Simonek, Ms Lorna Alexandra Stabler, Ms Clarissa Anne Sara Lyons, Mr David Coleman, Dan Metcalfe, Julie Myers, Peter Jenkins, Mr Simon David Latham, Mr David Arthur Goode, Ms Stephanie Ellen Tidball
Income: £1,751,396 [2017]; £1,682,158 [2016]; £1,374,073 [2015]; £1,448,964 [2014]; £1,694,453 [2013]

Cambridge Live
Registered: 11 Dec 2014 *Employees:* 67 *Volunteers:* 100
Tel: 01223 791791 *Website:* cambridgelivetrust.co.uk
Activities: Education, training; arts, culture, heritage, science; recreation
Address: 3 Parsons Court, Wheeler Street, Cambridge, CB2 3QE
Trustees: Mr Mark Boon, Mr Jeremy Newton, Mrs Judith Elliott, Ms Sian Reid, Katy Astley, Miss Sara Sayer, Ms Sara Garnham, Mr Brian Howard Whitehead, Professor Lester Lloyd-Reason, Mr Jeremy Benstead
Income: £5,663,000 [2017]; £5,147,000 [2016]

The Cambridge Malaysian Education and Development Trust
Registered: 12 Jul 2010 *Employees:* 2
Tel: 01223 748738
Activities: Education, training; environment, conservation, heritage; economic, community development, employment
Address: Trinity College, Cambridge, CB2 1TQ
Trustees: Mr Jeremy Carver CBE, Tun Ahmad Sarji Bin Abdul Hamid, Prof Lord Hunt of Chesterton, The Hon Dato'Sri Mohamed Najib Bin Tun Abdul Razak, Dato'Henry Barlow, Dato'Thomas Lee
Income: £3,462,499 [2017]; £416,324 [2016]; £780,944 [2015]; £11,809 [2014]; £3,007,623 [2013]

The Cambridge Mosque Trust
Registered: 18 Dec 2015
Tel: 01223 871187 *Website:* cambridgemosqueproject.org
Activities: General charitable purposes; education, training; religious activities
Address: 32 London Road, Harston, Cambridge, CB22 7QH
Trustees: Mr Timothy John Winter, Prof Aziz Akgul, Dr Ersin Arioglu, Dr Ibrahim Kalin, Shahida Rehman, Mr Sohail Bhatti, Mr Burhanettin Aktas, Professor Halife Keskin, Ms Zeynep Coskun
Income: £11,979,104 [2016]

Cambridge Science Centre
Registered: 13 Mar 2012 *Employees:* 31 *Volunteers:* 33
Tel: 01223 967965 *Website:* cambridgesciencecentre.org
Activities: Education, training
Address: Unit 5 Sawston Trade Estate, London Road, Sawston, Cambridge, CB22 4SB
Trustees: John Short, Chris Lennard, Andrea Brand, Mrs Amanda Hazell East, David Cleevely, Elizabeth Crilly, Dr Darrin Disley
Income: £1,016,757 [2016]; £694,334 [2015]; £495,745 [2014]; £530,841 [2013]

Cambridge Sports Hall Trust Limited
Registered: 3 Jul 1970 *Employees:* 22
Tel: 01223 462226 *Website:* kelseykerridge.co.uk
Activities: Amateur sport
Address: Kelsey Kerridge Sports Hall, Queen Anne Terrace, Cambridge, CB1 1NA
Trustees: Paul Kerridge, Kambiz Amiri, Silvana Dean, Mr Raymond Boyce, Mr John Powley, Mr Anthony Lomax Johnson, Mr Miguel Roman, Kevin Devine, Mr Lee Phanco Phanco
Income: £1,181,898 [2017]; £1,198,869 [2016]; £1,140,066 [2015]; £1,180,260 [2014]; £1,110,010 [2013]

Cambridge Tutors Educational Trust Limited
Registered: 23 Aug 1973 *Employees:* 47
Tel: 020 8688 5284 *Website:* ctc.ac.uk
Activities: Education, training
Address: Cambridge Tutors Educational Trust Ltd, Water Tower Hill, Croydon, Surrey, CR0 5SX
Trustees: Dr Christopher Drew, Mrs Vatchala Sundaraparipooranan, Mr Sampathkumar Mallaya, Mr Karthikeyan Nagaraj, Senthil Kumar Jayachandran, Mrs Revathi Ramesh, Mrs Judith Patterson, Mrs Komathy Sampathkumar, Mr Veerakumar Krishnasamy, Ms Ashwini Sampathkumar, Mr Palanisamy Ramesh, Mr Vasudevan Ravi Shankar
Income: £3,937,304 [2016]; £3,981,303 [2015]; £3,891,428 [2014]; £3,732,738 [2013]; £3,845,375 [2012]

Cambridge in America (UK) Limited
Registered: 24 Mar 2009
Tel: 020 7502 2813
Activities: General charitable purposes; education, training; religious activities; amateur sport
Address: 19 Norcott Road, London, N16 7EJ
Trustees: Mr Robert Daniell Sansom, Ms Ruth Maria Whaley, Mr William Hall Janeway, Dr Adrian Vivian Weller
Income: £8,004,754 [2016]; £2,104,913 [2015]; £1,963,536 [2014]; £150,447 [2013]

Cambridgeshire Community Foundation
Registered: 21 Apr 2004 *Employees:* 7 *Volunteers:* 18
Tel: 01223 410535 *Website:* cambscf.org.uk
Activities: General charitable purposes; education, training; advancement of health or saving of lives; disability; prevention or relief of poverty; accommodation, housing; arts, culture, heritage, science; amateur sport; environment, conservation, heritage; economic, community development, employment
Address: Cambridgeshire Community Fundation, Hangar One, The Airport, Newmarket Road, Cambridge, CB5 8TG
Trustees: Mr Iain Crighton, Sam Weller, Catherine Stewart, Mr Simon Humphrey, Mr Stuart Thompson, Miss Claire Davis, Ms Caroline Jane Stenner, Mrs Linda Sinclair, Philip Woolner, Ms Alison Griffiths, Dr Joanna Slota-Newson
Income: £2,010,896 [2017]; £2,023,611 [2016]; £2,546,376 [2015]; £1,657,836 [2014]; £1,754,295 [2013]

Camden Arts Centre
Registered: 14 Nov 1997 *Employees:* 19 *Volunteers:* 119
Tel: 020 7472 5500 *Website:* camdenartscentre.org
Activities: Education, training; arts, culture, heritage, science
Address: Camden Arts Centre, Arkwright Road, London, NW3 6DG
Trustees: Ms Eliza Bonham Carter, Mr Alexandre Da Cunha, Mr Benjamin Rawlingson Plant, Ms Karen Sanig, Ms Merissa Marr, Ms Heather Johnson, Mr Guy Halamish, Ms Anne Hardy, Mr Porus Jungalwalla, Mr James Earl Fobert
Income: £2,098,015 [2017]; £1,714,350 [2016]; £1,615,483 [2015]; £1,532,966 [2014]; £1,470,566 [2013]

Camden Citizens Advice Bureaux Service Limited
Registered: 12 Jun 1985 *Employees:* 38 *Volunteers:* 180
Tel: 020 7383 9108 *Website:* camdencabservice.org.uk
Activities: General charitable purposes; prevention or relief of poverty; economic, community development, employment
Address: 88-91 Troutbeck, Albany Street, London, NW1 4EJ
Trustees: Dr Christina Townsend, Mr David Atkinson, Mr Clive Richardson, Mr Andi Dollia, Ms Orla Keady, Ms Helen MacFarlane
Income: £1,310,082 [2017]; £1,523,120 [2016]; £1,650,608 [2015]; £1,629,792 [2014]; £1,696,456 [2013]

Camden Garden Centre Charitable Trust
Registered: 26 May 1987 *Employees:* 41
Tel: 020 8348 5766 *Website:* cgctrust.org.uk
Activities: Education, training
Address: 106 Highgate Hill, Highgate, London, N6 5HE
Trustees: John Sewell Faulder, Ms Elizabeth Millar, Mrs Susan Crisp, Jim Hodgson, Mr David Granger Ure
Income: £1,687,201 [2017]; £1,508,764 [2016]; £1,428,440 [2015]; £1,342,461 [2014]; £1,315,736 [2013]

Camden School Foundation of Frances Mary Buss
Registered: 30 Jan 1970
Tel: 020 7485 3414 *Website:* camdengirls.camden.sch.uk
Activities: General charitable purposes; education, training
Address: Camden School for Girls, Sandall Road, London, NW5 2DB
Trustees: Ms Penelope Jean Barbara Wild, Ms Angela Margaret Mason, Mr John Atmore, Ms Matilda Blyth, Ms Lekha Klouda, Ms Janet Pope, Ms Diamond Ashiagbor
Income: £1,380,952 [2017]; £1,543,478 [2016]; £878,634 [2015]; £209,660 [2014]; £151,863 [2013]

The Camden Society
Registered: 4 Mar 1995 *Employees:* 372 *Volunteers:* 55
Tel: 020 7485 8177 *Website:* thecamdensociety.co.uk
Activities: General charitable purposes; education, training; advancement of health or saving of lives; disability; prevention or relief of poverty; accommodation, housing; arts, culture, heritage, science; amateur sport; economic, community development, employment; human rights, religious or racial harmony, equality or diversity
Address: The Camden Society, 60 Holmes Road, London, NW5 3AQ
Trustees: Mrs Bridget Gardiner, Ms Alice Etherington, Mr Simon Conway, Mr Martin Pilkington, Ms Edith Mueller, Jean Taylor, Ms Alex Kieffer, Mrs Claire Byrne, Ms Ruth Ormsby, Mr Bill Carter
Income: £10,341,040 [2017]; £9,915,833 [2016]; £10,974,105 [2015]; £11,781,652 [2014]; £11,218,909 [2013]

The Camelia Botnar Foundation

Registered: 28 Feb 1979 *Employees:* 77
Tel: 01403 864556 *Website:* cameliabotnar.com
Activities: Education, training
Address: Camelia Botnar Foundation, Burnt House Lane, Cowfold, Horsham, W Sussex, RH13 8DQ
Trustees: Mr Jamie Dann, Mr Graham Charles Booth, Mr John Desmond Appleton, Mrs Stephanie Ann Burford Pugh
Income: £2,934,026 [2016]; £3,082,605 [2015]; £3,032,199 [2014]; £3,379,106 [2013]; £3,007,001 [2012]

Camfed International

Registered: 26 Nov 1993 *Employees:* 273
Website: camfed.org
Activities: General charitable purposes; education, training; advancement of health or saving of lives; disability; prevention or relief of poverty; overseas aid, famine relief; economic, community development, employment; other charitable purposes
Address: St Giles Court, 24 Castle Street, Cambridge, CB3 0AJ
Trustees: Dr Robert Sansom, Dr Valerie Caton, Mr Nick Swift, Mrs Ann Lesley Cotton, Ms Miranda Theresa Claire Curtis, Grace Owen, Ms Rosemary O'Mahony
Income: £29,577,988 [2016]; £27,157,844 [2015]; £31,160,961 [2014]; £31,271,111 [2013]; £16,756,683 [2012]

M J Camp Charitable Foundation

Registered: 19 Mar 2001 *Employees:* 7
Tel: 023 9246 4276
Activities: Animals; environment, conservation, heritage; economic, community development, employment
Address: 50 Lysander Way, Waterlooville, Hants, PO7 8LH
Trustees: Mr Richard Michael Hampton Weekes, Miss Ann Rogers
Income: £15,476,785 [2016]; £300,000 [2015]; £8,750 [2014]; £9,778 [2013]; £9,000 [2012]

Camp Simcha

Registered: 9 Mar 1995 *Employees:* 16 *Volunteers:* 500
Tel: 020 8202 9297 *Website:* campsimcha.org.uk
Activities: The advancement of health or saving of lives; disability
Address: The House, 12 Queens Road, London, NW4 2TH
Trustees: Philip Goodman, Mr Sol Meyer, Mrs Allison Swift-Kanter, Mr Anthony Herman Stimler, Mrs Tanya Sima Persey, Mr Jeremy Philip Herman, Mr Julian David Taylor, Rabbi Simcha Scholar, Mrs Aviva Ruth Steinberg, Mrs Alison Fine, Mr Stephen Malcolm Davis, Mr Harold Gittelmon
Income: £1,568,731 [2016]; £2,580,970 [2015]; £1,364,011 [2014]; £1,935,425 [2013]; £690,118 [2012]

Campaign Against Living Miserably

Registered: 28 Jul 2005 *Employees:* 12 *Volunteers:* 300
Tel: 020 3697 9331 *Website:* thecalmzone.net
Activities: Education, training; advancement of health or saving of lives
Address: P O Box 68766, Southwark, London, SE1P 4JZ
Trustees: Mr George Henry Smart, Ms Aimee Luther, Mr Marcus Harry Chapman, Mrs Kathy Chalmers, Mr Richard Baskind, Mr Alexander Scott, Robert Kingdom, Mr James Richard Scroggs, Mr Philip Portal
Income: £1,564,759 [2017]; £1,267,117 [2016]; £647,454 [2015]; £634,227 [2014]; £560,939 [2013]

Campaign To Protect Rural England

Registered: 7 Dec 2001 *Employees:* 39 *Volunteers:* 15
Tel: 020 7981 2805 *Website:* cpre.org.uk
Activities: Environment, conservation, heritage
Address: Campaign to Protect Rural England, Europoint House, 5-11 Lavington Street, London, SE1 0NZ
Trustees: Mrs Margaret Clark, Ms Christine Drury, Dr Richard Simmons, Mr Steven Anderson, Mr Andrew Thomas Joseph Topley, Mr David Robin Bibby Thompson CBE DL, Mr Mike Benner, Mrs Su Sayer, Ms Lucie Jessica Hammond, Ms Corinne Margaret Pluchino
Income: £3,403,946 [2017]; £6,623,635 [2016]; £3,666,122 [2015]; £4,034,738 [2014]; £4,172,230 [2013]

The Campden Charities Trustee

Registered: 29 Jun 2004 *Employees:* 13
Tel: 020 7243 0551 *Website:* campdencharities.org.uk
Activities: Education, training; prevention or relief of poverty
Address: The Campden Charities Studio 3, 27a Pembridge Villas, London, W11 3EP
Trustees: Rev Gillean Craig, Ms Frances Manthos, Richard Brian Walker-Arnott, Sam Berwick, Dr Christopher Calman, Mr Robert Atkinson, Mr Timothy Harvey-Samuel, Mr Daniel Hawkins, Ms Susan Valerie Lockhart, Dr Christopher Olga Davis, Mr Terry Jeff Myers, Mr David Banks, Ms Marta Rodkina, Ms Julie Anne Mills, Mr Robert Orr-Ewing, Charles Manners
Income: £3,654,368 [2017]; £3,374,616 [2016]; £2,945,806 [2015]; £2,969,744 [2014]; £3,083,089 [2013]

Camphill Communities East Anglia

Registered: 12 Aug 1987 *Employees:* 31 *Volunteers:* 5
Tel: 01263 860305 *Website:* thornagehall.co.uk
Activities: Education, training; disability; accommodation, housing
Address: Camphill Community, Thornage Hall, Thornage, Holt, Norfolk, NR25 7QH
Trustees: Mrs Cynthia Hart, Lt Col John Francis Brooks Sharples OBE, Mr Thomas Michael Fitzalan-Howard, Mr Michael Pollitt, Mr Edward Joseph Hare, Mrs Anna Simpson, Ms Patricia Anne McIntosh, Ms Mary Marchant
Income: £1,500,769 [2017]; £1,401,104 [2016]; £1,318,445 [2015]; £1,187,404 [2014]; £1,062,470 [2013]

Camphill Devon Community Limited

Registered: 5 Jul 1979 *Employees:* 59 *Volunteers:* 4
Website: camphilldevon.org.uk
Activities: Disability
Address: Hapstead Village, Buckfastleigh, Devon, TQ11 0JN
Trustees: David Kemp-Gee, Mr John Hitchins, Tom King, Jo Woodcock, Diana White, Polly Elliott, Fiona McPhail, Steve Monk
Income: £1,760,077 [2017]; £1,722,369 [2016]; £1,605,587 [2015]; £1,556,894 [2014]; £1,336,558 [2013]

Camphill Milton Keynes Communities Limited

Registered: 27 Nov 1981 *Employees:* 35 *Volunteers:* 30
Tel: 01908 235000 *Website:* camphillmk.co.uk
Activities: Education, training; disability; accommodation, housing
Address: Camphill Milton Keynes Communities, Japonica Lane, Willen Park, Milton Keynes, Bucks, MK15 9JY
Trustees: Mr Martin Lightfoot, Mr Michael Robert St John Luxford, Mr Roger Dowthwaite, Mr John Peter Dixon, Mr Jeremy Cooper, Mrs Rachel Livermore
Income: £1,923,116 [2017]; £1,859,815 [2016]; £1,822,357 [2015]; £1,902,519 [2014]; £2,070,441 [2013]

The Camphill Village Trust Limited
Registered: 17 Jan 1964 *Employees:* 573 *Volunteers:* 20
Tel: 01653 228888 *Website:* cvt.org.uk
Activities: Education, training; advancement of health or saving of lives; disability; accommodation, housing
Address: The Camphill Village Trust, The Kingfisher Offices, 9 Saville Street, Malton, N Yorks, YO17 7LL
Trustees: Mr Christopher Cook, Mr Stephen Godwin, Mr Jeremy Rupert Young, Mrs Karen Walker, Mr Timothy John Michael Bishop, Miss Lindsey Marie Wishart, Ms Felicity Anne Chadwick-Histed, Mr Brian Martin Walsh, Mrs Jean Hendeson
Income: £21,028,000 [2017]; £20,515,000 [2016]; £19,673,000 [2015]; £20,344,000 [2014]; £25,085,000 [2013]

Canal & River Trust
Registered: 4 Apr 2012 *Employees:* 1,689 *Volunteers:* 9,282
Tel: 0113 281 6816 *Website:* canalrivertrust.org.uk
Activities: Education, training; arts, culture, heritage, science; environment, conservation, heritage; economic, community development, employment; recreation; other charitable purposes
Address: Canal & River Trust, Station House, 500 Elder Gate, Milton Keynes, Bucks, MK9 1BB
Trustees: Frances Done, Mr Joseph Benjamin Gordon, Susan Wilkinson, Mr Allan Leslie Leighton, Janet Hogben, Sir Christopher Kelly, Dame Jenny Abramsky, Mr Manish Jayantilal Chande, Mr Nigel Annett, Mr Tim Reeve
Income: £202,900,000 [2017]; £189,700,000 [2016]; £193,300,000 [2015]; £164,600,000 [2014]; £150,400,000 [2013]

Canbury School Limited
Registered: 24 Jul 1990 *Employees:* 25
Tel: 020 8549 8622 *Website:* canburyschool.co.uk
Activities: Education, training
Address: Canbury School, Kingston Hill, Kingston upon Thames, Surrey, KT2 7LN
Trustees: Mark Cook, John Powell, Dr Sarah McIntyre, Amanda Beck, Ms Mary Denise Harknett, Mr Charles Soden-Bird
Income: £1,177,812 [2017]; £988,906 [2016]; £1,090,561 [2015]; £1,021,103 [2014]; £1,155,893 [2013]

Cancer Research UK
Registered: 23 Nov 2001 *Employees:* 3,909 *Volunteers:* 40,000
Website: cancerresearchuk.org
Activities: Education, training; advancement of health or saving of lives
Address: Cancer Research UK, Angel Building, 407 St John Street, London, EC1V 4AD
Trustees: Wendy Becker, Mr Andrew William Palmer FCA, Dr Adrian Crellin MA FRCR FRCP, Professor Stephen Holgate CBE FMedSci, Professor Sir Bruce Ponder, Professor Dame Amanda Fisher, Ms Catherine Brown, Professor Sir Leszek Borysiewicz FRS FMedSci FRCP, Mr David Lindsell, Mrs Carolyn Jane Bradley, Mr Peter Alan Chambre, Professor Sir Michael Richards CBE MD FRCP
Income: £679,281,449 [2017]; £635,145,358 [2016]; £634,808,043 [2015]; £665,410,600 [2014]; £536,557,309 [2013]

Cancer Research Wales
Registered: 23 May 2016 *Employees:* 23 *Volunteers:* 250
Tel: 029 2031 6976 *Website:* cancerresearchwales.co.uk
Activities: The advancement of health or saving of lives
Address: Velindre Hospital, Velindre Road, Whitchurch, Cardiff, CF14 2TL
Trustees: Professor John Lake Moore, Mr Ian Sharp, Mrs Gillian Owens, Mr Simon Williams, Mr Gavin Moore, Mr Peter Weber, Mr Christopher Gaffney
Income: £3,630,274 [2017]

Cancercare (North Lancashire & South Cumbria)
Registered: 12 Jul 2007 *Employees:* 23 *Volunteers:* 134
Tel: 01524 381820 *Website:* cancercare.org.uk
Activities: General charitable purposes; advancement of health or saving of lives
Address: Cancer Care, Slynedales, Slyne Road, Lancaster, LA2 6ST
Trustees: Dr David Elliott, Mr Gary Rycroft, Dr John David Eaton, Mr Andrew Birchall, Mrs Fiona Weir, Mrs Elizabeth Anne Mayo, Mr Robert Webb, Mrs Mary Holland, Professor Anthony Gattrell, Professor Gillian Baynes, Mr Neil Townsend, Mr Shane Tickell
Income: £1,175,740 [2017]; £1,007,527 [2016]; £1,236,265 [2015]; £1,003,623 [2014]; £880,168 [2013]

The Candlelighters Trust
Registered: 17 Mar 1995 *Employees:* 16 *Volunteers:* 50
Website: candlelighters.org.uk
Activities: General charitable purposes; education, training; advancement of health or saving of lives
Address: 7 Redwood Grove, Yeadon, Leeds, LS19 7JW
Trustees: Doctor Edward Michael Richards, Dr Martin Elliott, The Honorableyorke Joseph Eaton, Mr Roger John Stocker, Mrs Patricia Thompson, Mr Gary Whitelam, Mr Stephen Charles Redman, Mr Keith Anthony Hardcastle, Mrs Susan Mariea Patterson
Income: £1,722,839 [2017]; £1,550,088 [2016]; £1,408,965 [2015]; £1,403,816 [2014]; £1,193,548 [2013]

Canford School Limited
Registered: 27 Jul 1964 *Employees:* 466 *Volunteers:* 177
Tel: 01202 847514 *Website:* canford.com
Activities: Education, training
Address: Canford School, Canford Magna, Wimborne, Dorset, BH21 3AD
Trustees: Rev John Harold Simmons, Mr James David Winn Stileman, Rear Admiral Sir Jeremy De Halpert, Mr John McGibbon, Miss Annabel Thomas, Mr Richard Nicholl, Mr Michael Jeffries DipArch RIBA FICE FRSA, Mr Nicholas Henniker Holloway, Mr Adam Bransom Richards, Mr David Levin, Mr Barry Coupe, Mr Robert Daubeney, Mr Matthew Keats, Ms Annette Anthony, Mr Michael Andrew Walshe BA, Mr Stephen Hedley Le Bas, Dr Philippa Dickins, Dr Georgina Anne Fozard
Income: £19,896,038 [2017]; £19,329,156 [2016]; £19,895,494 [2015]; £18,192,947 [2014]; £17,662,503 [2013]

Canine Partners for Independence
Registered: 17 Jul 1990 *Employees:* 71 *Volunteers:* 600
Tel: 01730 716003 *Website:* caninepartners.org.uk
Activities: Disability
Address: Canine Partners, Mill Lane, Heyshott, Midhurst, W Sussex, GU29 0ED
Trustees: Nicky Pendleton, Lady Suzetta Rankin, Mark Richardson, Claire Graham, Dr Clive Elwood, Jon Flint, Simon Clare, Stephen Fletcher, David Filmer, Jackie Staunton, Amanda Farren, Caroline Hoare
Income: £3,451,392 [2017]; £3,668,060 [2016]; £3,772,762 [2015]; £3,383,346 [2014]; £3,083,431 [2013]

Canolfan Uwchefrydiau Cymreig A Cheltaidd (Centre for Advanced Welsh and Celtic Studies) Cyfyngedig
Registered: 1 Oct 2015
Tel: 01970 636543 *Website:* wales.ac.uk
Activities: Education, training; arts, culture, heritage, science
Address: Canolfan Uwchefrydiau Cymreig a Cheltaidd Prifysgol Cymru, University of Wales Centre for Advanced Welsh and Celtic Studies, Aberystwyth, Ceredigion, SY23 3HH
Trustees: Professor Meurig Wynn Thomas, Mr Justin Albert, Dr Lynn Williams, Dr Ann Rhys, Mr Arwel Ellis Owen
Income: £1,616,000 [2017]

Canterbury Archaeological Trust Limited
Registered: 9 Nov 1979 *Employees:* 50 *Volunteers:* 25
Tel: 01227 462062 *Website:* canterburytrust.co.uk
Activities: Education, training; environment, conservation, heritage
Address: 92A Broad Street, Canterbury, Kent, CT1 2LU
Trustees: Professor Christopher Lloyd Bounds, Dr David Shaw, Mr Peter Thomas Goddard Hobbs, Miss Joanna Jones, Mr Richard Geoffrey Eales, Mr Martin George Pratt, Mr Nicholas James Watts, Brigadier Martin John Meardon, Dr Elizabeth Clare Edwards BA PhD, Mr Andrew John Corby, Miss Christine Lynn Waterman, Mr Robert Thomas Shine, Ms Melanie Jane Nye
Income: £1,917,895 [2017]; £2,058,876 [2016]; £1,075,393 [2015]; £1,587,145 [2014]; £1,200,470 [2013]

Canterbury Cathedral Trust Fund
Registered: 22 Dec 2005 *Employees:* 4 *Volunteers:* 2
Tel: 01227 865307 *Website:* canterbury-cathedral.org
Activities: Education, training; religious activities; arts, culture, heritage, science; environment, conservation, heritage; economic, community development, employment
Address: 8 The Precincts, Canterbury, Kent, CT1 2EE
Trustees: Rt Hon Sir Hugh Michael Robertson, Viscount De L'isle, Mrs Amanda Cottrell, Mr Benedict Robert Kirwan Moorhead, Mr Paul Barrett, Mr Hugo Mark Fenwick, Mr James Loudon, The Very Reverend Dr Robert Andrew Willis, Mr Richard John Oldfield, The Revd Canon Nicholas Charles Papadopulos, Mr Richard Henry Basden Holme
Income: £4,018,437 [2017]; £4,982,633 [2016]; £2,269,941 [2015]; £2,490,748 [2014]; £1,452,340 [2013]

Canterbury Christ Church University
Registered: 20 Jun 2003 *Employees:* 1,660
Website: canterbury.ac.uk
Activities: Education, training
Address: Rochester House, St Georges Place, Canterbury, Kent, CT1 1UT
Trustees: Rev Trevor Willmott, Mrs Pamela Jones, Mr Christopher Calcutt, Robert Stevenson, Professor Rama Thirunamachandran, Sir Ian Johnston, Ms Concepta Bernadette Nolan, Dr Alison Christine Eyden, Mrs Judith Anne Sally Harding, Quentin Roper, Mr Frank Martin, Ms Deborah Upton, Ms Judith Armitt, Mr Krum Tashev, Ms Meradin Peachey, Mr Philip John Fletcher, Mr Julian Philip Faber
Income: £135,054,000 [2017]; £134,833,000 [2016]; £126,399,000 [2015]; £122,095,755 [2014]; £122,970,000 [2013]

Canterbury Diocesan Board of Finance
Registered: 2 Nov 1966 *Employees:* 199
Website: canterburydiocese.org
Activities: Religious activities
Address: Diocesan Hosue, Lady Woottons Green, Canterbury, Kent, CT1 1NQ
Trustees: Lord Archbishop of Canterbury Justin Portal Welby, Rev Timothy Wilson, Rt Rev Trevor Willmott, Mr Ray Harris, Mr Philip Frederick Stephenson Sibbald, Mrs Amanda Cottrell, Rev Canon Andrew William Sewell, Rev Stephen Lillicrap, Miss Miriam Oliver, The Very Reverend Dr Robert Andrew Willis, Mrs Caroline Spencer, The Venerable Philip Roy Down, Mr Phillip Bromwich, Rev Andrew James Bawtree, Rev Anthony Everett, Mrs Ann Foat, The Venerable Stephen Ronald Taylor MBE, Venerable Joanne Kelly-Moore
Income: £10,146,000 [2016]; £10,637,000 [2015]; £11,324,000 [2014]; £9,616,000 [2013]; £11,967,130 [2012]

Canterbury Oast Trust
Registered: 25 Apr 1985 *Employees:* 177 *Volunteers:* 145
Tel: 01233 861493 *Website:* c-o-t.org.uk
Activities: Disability
Address: Highlands Farm, Woodchurch, Ashford, Kent, TN26 3RJ
Trustees: Mr Robert Perkins, Mr Peter Ergis, Mr Russell Ian Walters, Mr Peter Edward Pearson-Wood, Mr Kenneth James Hesketh, Elizabeth Emson, Mr Martin Read Lovegrove, Mr Chris Showell, Trevor Pearce, Ms Michaela Louise Tweedley
Income: £6,076,149 [2017]; £6,194,044 [2016]; £5,878,989 [2015]; £5,741,999 [2014]; £5,613,531 [2013]

The Capernwray Missionary Fellowship of Torchbearers
Registered: 31 Dec 1998 *Employees:* 31 *Volunteers:* 31
Tel: 01524 733908 *Website:* capernwray.org.uk
Activities: Education, training; religious activities
Address: Capernwray Hall, Capernwray, Carnforth, Lancs, LA6 1AG
Trustees: Mr Peter Maiden, Mr Neil Wrigley, Miss Angela Louise Mills, Mr Brian Sweeney, Mr Alexander Mark Thomas, Mr Michael Thompson, Mrs Rebecca Silver
Income: £1,903,845 [2017]; £2,142,953 [2016]; £2,040,700 [2015]; £2,261,438 [2014]; £2,331,896 [2013]

Cardboard Citizens
Registered: 29 Nov 1994 *Employees:* 19 *Volunteers:* 39
Tel: 020 7377 8948 *Website:* cardboardcitizens.org.uk
Activities: Education, training; arts, culture, heritage, science; other charitable purposes
Address: 77A Greenfield Road, London, E1 1EJ
Trustees: Ms Prue Skene, Mr Chris Jullings, Ms Diana Choyleva, Ms Sacha Milroy, Mr Riad Akbur, Ms Julie Hudson, Ms Linden Ife, Mr Andrew Pattison, Jon Opie
Income: £1,220,758 [2017]; £1,160,250 [2016]; £925,011 [2015]; £942,428 [2014]; £702,821 [2013]

Cardiac Risk in the Young
Registered: 18 Nov 1995 *Employees:* 81 *Volunteers:* 85
Tel: 01737 363222 *Website:* c-r-y.org.uk
Activities: The advancement of health or saving of lives
Address: 1140b The Axis Centre, Cleeve Road, Leatherhead, Surrey, KT22 7RD
Trustees: Dr Timothy Bowker, Dr Anthea Tilzey, Ms Louise Brooker-Carey, Mr Paul Quarterman, Mr Hugh Mulcahey, Mr Peter O'Donnell, Ms Rebecca Trewinnard
Income: £3,364,109 [2017]; £3,546,305 [2016]; £3,140,248 [2015]; £3,079,513 [2014]; £2,593,592 [2013]

Cardiff City FC Community Foundation
Registered: 6 Mar 2009 *Employees:* 34 *Volunteers:* 75
Tel: 029 2023 1212 *Website:* cardiffcityfcfoundation.org.uk
Activities: Education, training; disability; prevention or relief of poverty; amateur sport
Address: Cardiff City FC Foundation, The Pod, Capital Retail Park, Leckwith Road, Canton, Cardiff, CF11 8EG
Trustees: Mr Christopher David Hatcher, Ms Rachel Victoria Lewis, Mr Leighton Andrews, Mr Veh Ken Choo, Mr Steven Borley, Ms Shashikala Mansfield, Ms Melanie Anne Hamer, Ms Kayley Rachel Griffiths
Income: £1,430,491 [2017]; £1,699,614 [2016]; £1,774,454 [2015]; £1,649,340 [2014]; £1,143,904 [2013]

Cardiff Educational Endowment Trust
Registered: 19 Mar 2008 *Employees:* 110
Tel: 0191 230 8391
Activities: Education, training
Address: Womble Bond Dickinson (UK) LLP, St Anns Wharf, 112 Quayside, Newcastle upon Tyne, NE1 3DX
Trustees: Miss Tubasum Munawar, Mr Niaz Ali Khan
Income: £10,260,881 [2016]; £9,932,212 [2015]; £7,535,734 [2014]; £4,430,310 [2013]

Cardiff Met Students' Union
Registered: 18 Sep 2012 *Employees:* 45
Website: cardiffmetsu.co.uk
Activities: Education, training; amateur sport; economic, community development, employment; recreation
Address: Cardiff Met Cyncoed Campus, Cyncoed Road, Cardiff, CF23 6XD
Trustees: Mr Michael Wayne Davies, Mr Ieaun Gardiner, Miss Alexandra Kate Smith, Ms Jade Staniforth, Mr William George Fuller, Miss Keira Leigh Davies, Mr Mark Angel Fabro Tagara
Income: £2,647,248 [2017]; £2,394,315 [2016]; £2,360,827 [2015]; £2,215,322 [2014]; £2,043,944 [2013]

Cardiff Metropolitan University
Registered: 10 Mar 2011 *Employees:* 1,312
Tel: 029 2041 6072 *Website:* cardiffmet.ac.uk
Activities: Education, training; advancement of health or saving of lives; accommodation, housing; arts, culture, heritage, science; amateur sport; economic, community development, employment
Address: Llandaff Campus, Western Avenue, Cardiff, CF5 2YB
Trustees: Jo Berry, Barbara Wilding, Mr Gareth Hardacre, Ms Suzanne Hay, Ms Nicola Amery, Katy Chamberlain, Gareth Davies, Mr William George Fuller, Claire Morgan, Dr Christopher Ben Turner, Mr Saleem Kidwai, Professor Kelechi Nnoaham, Frank Holmes, Mr Graeme Howes Yorston, Dr Stephen Jackson, Mr Mohammed Umar Hussain, Mrs Sian Goodson, Mr Ieaun Gardiner, Professor Cara Carmichael Aitchison, Dr Malcom James
Income: £99,871,000 [2017]; £98,260,000 [2016]; £101,128,000 [2015]; £87,158,000 [2014]; £80,948,000 [2013]

Cardiff Mind Ltd
Registered: 6 May 1993 *Employees:* 40 *Volunteers:* 58
Tel: 029 2040 2040 *Website:* cardiffmind.org
Activities: Education, training; advancement of health or saving of lives; disability; accommodation, housing; economic, community development, employment
Address: 166 Newport Road, Cardiff, CF24 1DL
Trustees: Mrs Julie Ann Dawson, Mr Jonathan Cole, Mr Lee Lanciotti, Ms Isobel Birden, Mr Nixon Charles Thomas, Mr Bryan Williams, Mr Philip Edwards, Mr Mark Lowther
Income: £1,079,890 [2017]; £1,112,311 [2016]; £1,112,311 [2015]; £1,109,448 [2014]; £1,068,218 [2013]

Cardiff Roman Catholic Archdiocesan Trust
Registered: 12 May 1965 *Employees:* 42 *Volunteers:* 2,000
Tel: 029 2037 4148 *Website:* rcadc.org
Activities: Religious activities
Address: The Archdiocese of Cardiff, Archbishop's House, 41-43 Cathedral Road, Cardiff, CF11 9HD
Trustees: Rev George Stack, Rev Joseph Boardman, Rev Peter Gwilym Collins, Mr John Lawrence Antoniazzi FCA, Mr Michael Prior
Income: £6,643,849 [2017]; £5,462,362 [2016]; £5,986,764 [2015]; £4,959,000 [2014]; £5,211,000 [2013]

Cardiff Third Sector Council (C3SC)
Registered: 13 Mar 1998 *Employees:* 38 *Volunteers:* 60
Tel: 029 2048 5722 *Website:* c3sc.org.uk
Activities: Economic, community development, employment
Address: Cardiff Third Sector Council, Baltic House, Mount Stuart Square, Cardiff, CF10 5FH
Trustees: Ms Jan Walsh, Mr Terry Price, Althea Collymore, Martin Warren, Mrs Judith John
Income: £1,588,579 [2017]; £1,732,129 [2016]; £1,441,303 [2015]; £1,483,047 [2014]; £822,926 [2013]

Cardiff University Students' Union
Registered: 29 Jul 2010 *Employees:* 886 *Volunteers:* 1,390
Tel: 029 2078 1404 *Website:* cardiffstudents.com
Activities: Education, training; amateur sport
Address: University Union, Park Place, Cardiff, CF10 3QN
Trustees: Gethin Lewis, Denise Rich, Hollie Cooke, Lilly Ryan Harper, Tom Kelly, Kirsty Hepburn, Nick Fox, Richard Roberts CBE, Bethan Walsh, Alex Williams, Emma Mattin, Lamorna Hooker, Jake Smith, Fadhila Al Dhahouri
Income: £8,638,471 [2017]; £7,930,880 [2016]; £3,501,076 [2015]; £1,876,506 [2014]; £1,906,872 [2013]

Cardiff University
Registered: 13 Jul 2010 *Employees:* 5,598
Tel: 029 2087 4888 *Website:* cardiff.ac.uk
Activities: Education, training; advancement of health or saving of lives
Address: Cardiff University, Friary House, Greyfriars Road, Cardiff, CF10 3AE
Trustees: Rev Canon Gareth Powell, Dr Carol Bell, Professor Colin Riordan, Len Richards, Professor Karen Holford, Mr Robert Preece, Ms Linda Phillips, Dr Steven Luke, Ms Nicola Richards, Mrs Jan Juillerat, Dr Janet Wademan, Ms Fadhila Al-Dhahouri, Andy Skyrme, Judge Ray Singh, Professor Nora De Leeuw, Mr Alastair Gibbons, Professor Stuart Palmer, Mr Raj Aggarwal, Mr David Simpson, Professor A Coffey, Professor George Boyne, Ms Hollie Cooke, Professor Paul Milbourne, Mr Robert Lewis-Watkin, Mr Paul Baston
Income: £505,123,000 [2017]; £511,753,000 [2016]; £482,592,000 [2015]; £455,731,000 [2014]; £435,734,000 [2013]

Cardiff Women's Aid
Registered: 20 Mar 1987 *Employees:* 35 *Volunteers:* 10
Tel: 029 2046 0566 *Website:* cardiffwomensaid.org.uk
Activities: General charitable purposes; accommodation, housing
Address: Cardiff Womens Aid, 16 Moira Terrace, Cardiff, CF24 0EJ
Trustees: Mr Paul Bevan, Mrs Samantha Taylor, Rachel Minto, Deborah Perkin, The Ven Peggy Jackson, Margherita Carucci
Income: £1,173,068 [2017]; £1,207,499 [2016]; £1,198,601 [2015]; £1,348,840 [2014]; £1,429,606 [2013]

Cardiff YMCA (1910) Trust
Registered: 2 Oct 2015 *Employees:* 1
Tel: 07980 772397
Activities: General charitable purposes; education, training; prevention or relief of poverty; accommodation, housing; economic, community development, employment
Address: YMCA, The Walk, Roath, Cardiff, CF24 3AG
Trustees: Mr Roger Coombs, Mr John Littlechild MBE JP, Mr Michael Hales, Dr Lesley Pugsley, Ms Margaret Salisbury, Mr Gareth Ashfield
Income: £4,261,166 [2017]

Cardiff and Vale Citizens Advice Bureau
Registered: 12 Nov 2001 *Employees:* 55
Tel: 01446 704999 *Website:* cacv.org.uk
Activities: General charitable purposes; education, training; advancement of health or saving of lives; prevention or relief of poverty
Address: 119 Broad Street, Barry, Vale of Glamorgan, CF62 7TZ
Trustees: Mr Peter Leech, Mr Simon Berg, Mr Roy Edwards, Mr Stephen Davis, Mrs Denise Goode, Mr Christopher Graham, Mr Robert Lynn, Mr David Browne, Mr Neil O'Toole, Mr Peter Trott
Income: £1,738,339 [2017]; £1,635,856 [2016]; £1,526,639 [2015]; £1,079,858 [2014]; £986,730 [2013]

Cardiff and Vale University Local Health Board General Purpose Charity
Registered: 2 Jul 1996 *Employees:* 3
Website: cardiffandvaleuhbcharity.org
Activities: General charitable purposes; education, training; advancement of health or saving of lives; disability; other charitable purposes
Address: Postgraduate Centre, Whitchurch Hospital, Park Road, Whitchurch, Cardiff, CF14 7XB
Trustees: Cardiff and Vale University Local Health Board
Income: £1,605,678 [2017]; £1,171,874 [2016]; £1,433,230 [2015]; £1,499,000 [2014]; £1,680,001 [2013]

Cardinal Hume Centre
Registered: 28 Feb 2002 *Employees:* 53 *Volunteers:* 107
Website: cardinalhumecentre.org.uk
Activities: General charitable purposes; education, training; advancement of health or saving of lives; prevention or relief of poverty; accommodation, housing; economic, community development, employment
Address: The Cardinal Hume Centre, 3-7 Arneway Street, London, SW1P 2BG
Trustees: Ms Heather Petch, Mrs Caitlin Kennedy, Mr Patrick John Milner, Ms Philippa Greenslade, Mr Andrew Rose, Ms Philomena Egan, Mr Terry Philpot, Dr Robert Henry Arnott, Miss Amelia Fitzalan-Howard, Bishop Nicholas Gilbert Erskine Hudson, Mr William Van Klaveren
Income: £2,857,000 [2017]; £2,678,000 [2016]; £2,690,000 [2015]; £2,428,000 [2014]; £2,267,000 [2013]

Care & Repair Cardiff and The Vale
Registered: 9 Jun 2015 *Employees:* 26
Tel: 029 2047 3337
Activities: Other charitable purposes
Address: Tolven Court, Dowlais Road, Cardiff, CF24 5LQ
Trustees: Mr Jason Mark Wroe, Mrs Debra Anne Rosser, Ms Margaret Berry, Mr Michael Cuddy, Mr Julian Loach, Ms Sarah Prescott
Income: £1,567,768 [2017]; £1,053,586 [2016]

Care & Repair Cymru 2015
Registered: 14 Sep 2015 *Employees:* 12
Tel: 029 2010 7580 *Website:* careandrepair.org.uk
Activities: General charitable purposes; education, training
Address: First Floor, Care & Repair Cymru 2015 Ltd, Mariners House, Trident Court, East Moors Road, Cardiff, CF24 5TD
Trustees: Mrs Rachel Rowlands, Mr John Lord, Sarah Willey, Ms Denise Amelia Hines-Johnson, Mrs Elizabeth Warwick, Ms Maggie Berry, Mr Victor Wynne Williams, Ms Jocelyn Ann Davies, Mr Rhodri Huw Conway Davies, Mrs Clare Patricia Strowbridge
Income: £1,308,430 [2017]; £771,637 [2016]

Care (Christian Action Research and Education)
Registered: 18 Dec 1997 *Employees:* 23 *Volunteers:* 15
Tel: 020 7233 0455 *Website:* care.org.uk
Activities: General charitable purposes; education, training; religious activities; other charitable purposes
Address: CARE, 53 Romney Street, Westminster, London, SW1P 3RF
Trustees: Mr John O'Brien, The Reverend Pjs Perkin, Reverend Ruth Ann Cannings, Mr Lynn Green, Mrs Barbara Pashley, Mr Gareth Wilson Russell
Income: £2,109,940 [2017]; £2,384,857 [2016]; £1,996,855 [2015]; £2,093,305 [2014]; £2,127,211 [2013]

Care 4 All (North East Lincolnshire) Ltd
Registered: 6 Mar 2012 *Employees:* 79 *Volunteers:* 5
Tel: 07857 347844 *Website:* care4all.org.uk
Activities: General charitable purposes; prevention or relief of poverty; economic, community development, employment
Address: Grant Thorold Library, Durban Road, Grimsby, N E Lincs, DN32 8BX
Trustees: Ms Annie Darby, Mrs Natalie Cresswell, Mr Nigel Vernon Sheriden, Mr David Hilditch, Mr Gregory Paul Bacon
Income: £1,049,868 [2017]; £2,149,566 [2016]; £2,771,889 [2015]; £2,710,173 [2014]; £245,261 [2013]

Care After Combat
Registered: 25 Nov 2014 *Employees:* 13 *Volunteers:* 49
Tel: 0300 343 0255 *Website:* careaftercombat.org
Activities: Armed forces, emergency service efficiency
Address: Troon House, 4400 Parkway, Solent Business Park, Whitely, Hants, PO15 7JF
Trustees: Cdr Stephen Anderson RN, David Rogers, Bill Bones, Chris Davis, Mr Gary Stanley Cryer
Income: £1,322,251 [2016]; £252,156 [2015]

Care England
Registered: 16 Feb 1987 *Employees:* 8
Tel: 0845 057 7677 *Website:* careengland.org.uk
Activities: The advancement of health or saving of lives; disability
Address: 2nd Floor, Monmouth House, 40 Artillery Lane, London, E1 7LS
Trustees: Mr John Ransford, Tim Hammond, Mr Avnish Goyal, Mr Daniel Casson, Vishal Shah, Mark Wilson, Mrs Jane Ashcroft CBE, Dr Peter Calveley
Income: £1,071,332 [2017]; £1,031,086 [2016]; £959,414 [2015]; £833,603 [2014]; £702,358 [2013]

The Care Forum
Registered: 15 Mar 1996 Employees: 43 Volunteers: 150
Tel: 0117 965 4444 Website: thecareforum.org
Activities: General charitable purposes; advancement of health or saving of lives; disability; economic, community development, employment; other charitable purposes
Address: The Vassall Centre, Gill Avenue, Fishponds, Bristol, BS16 2QQ
Trustees: Therese Gillespie, Robin Butcher, Jenny Allen, Sandra Elmer, David Cottam, Gordon Podmore, Martin Dear, Rod Mayall
Income: £1,836,685 [2017]; £1,854,038 [2016]; £1,592,886 [2015]; £1,553,146 [2014]; £936,382 [2013]

Care International UK
Registered: 23 Aug 1985 Employees: 146 Volunteers: 7
Website: careinternational.org.uk
Activities: The advancement of health or saving of lives; prevention or relief of poverty; overseas aid, famine relief; human rights, religious or racial harmony, equality or diversity
Address: Care International UK, Camelford House, 87-90 Albert Embankment, London, SE1 7TP
Trustees: Mr Nigel Chapman CMG, Mr Oliver Henry James Stocken, Mr William Macpherson, Mr Michael Andrew Dyson, Ms Marian Rose, Ms Federica Sambiase, Mr Francis John Plowden, Ms Nadine Nohr, Mr Edward Sidney Cover Bickham, Mrs Carolyn Sarah Clarke, Mr Campbell Robb, Dr Yusaf Samiullah OBE
Income: £93,414,000 [2017]; £78,172,000 [2016]; £51,739,000 [2015]; £48,270,000 [2014]; £39,184,000 [2013]

Care South
Registered: 12 Oct 1992 Employees: 1,252 Volunteers: 25
Tel: 01202 712400 Website: care-south.co.uk
Activities: The advancement of health or saving of lives; accommodation, housing; other charitable purposes
Address: 39 Commercial Road, Poole, Dorset, BH14 0HU
Trustees: Mrs Felicity Ann Irwin DL, Mr Christopher Kean FCA, Mr Richard John Groom MBE, Dr Richard Day, Mr Paul Richard Causton, Mrs Lindsay Ann Ansell, Mrs Jane Stichbury CBE QPM DL, Mr Charles Hunter, Mr James Webster, Mr Richard Dyson, Mrs Stephanie Barnett
Income: £41,022,000 [2017]; £39,116,000 [2016]; £37,723,000 [2015]; £36,158,000 [2014]; £37,076,000 [2013]

Care for Children
Registered: 29 Oct 1998 Employees: 25 Volunteers: 10
Tel: 01603 627814 Website: careforchildren.com
Activities: Education, training; advancement of health or saving of lives; disability; prevention or relief of poverty; accommodation, housing
Address: Care for Children, 3 The Close, Norwich, NR1 4DH
Trustees: Mr Nicholas Chance CVO, Robert Glover, Mr Edward Amies, Dr Ian Milligan, Mr David Devenish, Mr Lorne Armstrong, Mr Jonathan Humphrey Campbell Scott, Mr Keith Hilton, Mrs Susan Johns, Mr Michael Bonehill, Mr Mark Stolkin
Income: £1,573,174 [2016]; £1,560,888 [2015]; £1,579,827 [2014]; £1,005,182 [2013]; £976,335 [2012]

Care for The Family
Registered: 17 Dec 1997 Employees: 61 Volunteers: 600
Website: careforthefamily.org.uk
Activities: General charitable purposes; education, training
Address: Care for The Family, Garth House, Leon Avenue, Taffs Well, Cardiff, CF15 7RG
Trustees: Mr John O'Brien, Paul Francis, Mr Norman Adams, Yolanda Ibbett
Income: £3,759,061 [2016]; £3,617,866 [2015]; £3,290,378 [2014]; £3,379,919 [2013]; £3,239,225 [2012]

Care for Veterans
Registered: 6 Nov 1998 Employees: 134 Volunteers: 25
Tel: 01903 213458 Website: qahh.org.uk
Activities: The advancement of health or saving of lives; disability; accommodation, housing
Address: Queen Alexandra Hospital Home, Boundary Road, Worthing, W Sussex, BN11 4LJ
Trustees: Mrs Jillian Annis, Dr Paul Hughes, Mrs Ruth Taylor, Captain Christopher Pile, Colonel John Robert Charles Saville, Mr Michael Anthony Walker, Commodore James Fanshawe, Mr Alan Martin Andrew Price, Commander David Habershon
Income: £4,786,078 [2016]; £4,177,149 [2015]; £4,339,661 [2014]; £4,514,355 [2013]; £3,701,884 [2012]

Career Connect
Registered: 1 Apr 2011 Employees: 371
Tel: 0151 600 7700 Website: careerconnect.org.uk
Activities: Education, training; economic, community development, employment
Address: Career Connect, 7th Floor, Walker House, Exchange House, Liverpool, L2 3YL
Trustees: Mr Nigel Edmund Bellamy, Kathleen Wyke, Mrs Deborah Shackleton, Mrs Christine Bennett, Mr Kieran Gordon, Mr Martin McEwan, Mrs Lorraine Dodd, Miss Ameena Ahmed
Income: £15,033,494 [2017]; £13,260,582 [2016]; £11,675,965 [2015]; £16,982,727 [2014]; £17,443,207 [2013]

The Careers Research and Advisory Centre (C R A C) Limited
Registered: 5 Mar 1965 Employees: 14
Tel: 01223 448501 Website: crac.org.uk
Activities: General charitable purposes; education, training
Address: 22 Signet Court, Swanns Road, Cambridge, CB5 8LA
Trustees: Professor John Wood, Mr Inderjit Seehra, Dr Mary Philips, Prof David Gani, Drs Astrid Wissenburg
Income: £1,357,262 [2017]; £1,129,984 [2016]; £1,989,376 [2015]; £2,418,539 [2014]; £3,281,056 [2013]

Carer Support Wiltshire
Registered: 3 Jul 2002 Employees: 31 Volunteers: 67
Tel: 01380 871690 Website: carersupportwiltshire.co.uk
Activities: General charitable purposes; education, training
Address: Carer Support Wiltshire, Independent Living Centre, St Georges Road, Semington, Trowbridge, Wilts, BA14 6JQ
Trustees: Mr Derek Hayes, Miss Laraine Marriot, Mr Arthur Douglas Minett, Mrs Janet Louise Surr, Mr Gerard Montgomery, Mrs Elizabeth Ruscoe Brown, Miss Ruth Martindale, Mr Malcolm Seymour, Mr Christopher Philip Meier, Mrs Jennifer Jane Mason, Dr Edward Toby Williams
Income: £1,276,003 [2017]; £1,373,377 [2016]; £1,260,279 [2015]; £1,032,154 [2014]; £1,154,712 [2013]

The Carers Centre (Bristol and South Gloucestershire)
Registered: 5 Jul 1997 *Employees:* 57 *Volunteers:* 137
Tel: 0117 939 2562 *Website:* carerssupportcentre.org.uk
Activities: General charitable purposes
Address: The Carers Support Centre, The Vassall Centre, Gill Avenue, Bristol, BS16 2QQ
Trustees: Ms Wendy Gregory, Mr Stuart Barnes, Mrs Louise Janis Manley Winn, Mrs Mary Winifred Whittington, Mrs Deborah Jane Means, Heather Thomas, Mr Andrew James Bell, Mr Bryan Daly
Income: £1,267,774 [2017]; £1,203,874 [2016]; £1,115,867 [2015]; £1,200,279 [2014]; £1,136,788 [2013]

Carers Federation Ltd
Registered: 17 Nov 1995 *Employees:* 63 *Volunteers:* 30
Tel: 0115 962 9311 *Website:* carersfederation.co.uk
Activities: General charitable purposes
Address: 1 Beech Avenue, New Basford, Nottingham, NG7 7LJ
Trustees: Mrs Usha Gadhia, Dr C J Berry, Mrs P J Cargill, Mr Alan Meadows, Mrs C G Thomas, Mrs Katherine Moore
Income: £1,662,156 [2017]; £2,271,886 [2016]; £2,827,658 [2015]; £3,042,367 [2014]; £6,204,353 [2013]

Carers First
Registered: 7 Mar 2001 *Employees:* 118 *Volunteers:* 70
Tel: 0300 303 1555 *Website:* carersfirst.org.uk
Activities: General charitable purposes; education, training; advancement of health or saving of lives; disability; prevention or relief of poverty; economic, community development, employment; human rights, religious or racial harmony, equality or diversity; recreation; other charitable purposes
Address: Michael Gill Building, Tolgate Lane, Strood, Kent, ME2 4TG
Trustees: Mr William Roger Daniels, Mr Ronald Martin, Mrs Iris Sell, Mr John Hunter Purdie, Ms Julie Flower, Bill Swann, Ms Mary Spillane, Ms Shirley Briggs, Susan Ilott, Mr Colin Raymond Russell, Ruth Rankine, Mr Peter Davis, Mr Robert Dennis
Income: £3,088,542 [2017]; £2,753,850 [2016]; £1,750,343 [2015]; £1,873,204 [2014]; £1,175,568 [2013]

Carers Gloucestershire
Registered: 21 Jul 2005 *Employees:* 36 *Volunteers:* 101
Tel: 01452 386283 *Website:* carersgloucestershire.org.uk
Activities: General charitable purposes; education, training; advancement of health or saving of lives; disability; prevention or relief of poverty; other charitable purposes
Address: Messenger House, 33-35 St Michaels Square, Gloucester, GL1 1HX
Trustees: Mr Simon Probert, Mrs Diana Billingham, Mr David Newcombe, Dr Christabel Makanjuola, Mr David Hilton, Dr Martin Freeman, Mrs Heather Beer
Income: £2,004,152 [2017]; £2,226,172 [2016]; £2,118,277 [2015]; £1,579,406 [2014]; £1,205,058 [2013]

Carers Leeds
Registered: 17 Oct 1996 *Employees:* 39 *Volunteers:* 50
Tel: 0113 246 8338 *Website:* carersleeds.org.uk
Activities: General charitable purposes; education, training; advancement of health or saving of lives; disability; prevention or relief of poverty
Address: Carers Leeds, 6-8 The Headrow, Leeds, LS1 6PT
Trustees: Mr Andrew Bottomley, Paul Ball, Mr Charlie Foote, Miss Daxa Manharlal Patel, Andrew Rawnsley, Ms Samantha Campbell, Miss Tanzeela Samad
Income: £1,501,737 [2017]; £1,380,732 [2016]; £1,488,912 [2015]; £786,454 [2014]; £687,327 [2013]

Carers Support West Sussex
Registered: 28 Mar 2008 *Employees:* 90 *Volunteers:* 60
Tel: 01293 220000 *Website:* carerssupport.org.uk
Activities: Education, training; advancement of health or saving of lives; disability; prevention or relief of poverty; economic, community development, employment
Address: Carers Support Service, The Orchard, 1-2 Gleneagles Court, Brighton Road, Crawley, Surrey, RH10 6AD
Trustees: Mrs Susan Knight, Mrs Sandra Burns, Mrs Yvette Elkana, Mr Alan Botterill, Mrs Sally Booker, Mr Neal Young, Mr Philip Michael Lansberry, Mr John Williamson, Paul Isaacs, Mr Peter Phillips, Ms Jane Green
Income: £2,717,426 [2017]; £2,311,884 [2016]; £1,975,352 [2015]; £1,988,697 [2014]; £534,737 [2013]

Carers Trust Bucks and Milton Keynes
Registered: 12 Nov 2004 *Employees:* 39 *Volunteers:* 98
Tel: 01296 392711 *Website:* carersbucks.org
Activities: General charitable purposes; education, training; advancement of health or saving of lives; disability
Address: Carers Bucks, Ardenham Court, Oxford Road, Aylesbury, Bucks, HP19 8HT
Trustees: Mr Mike Rowlands, Mrs Sheila Christine Syratt, Mrs Margaret Aston, Mr Stewart George, Ms Sarah Broadhurst, Mrs Audrey Coles, Dr Leslie Davies, Mr John Maitland, Ms Hanne Bogues
Income: £1,301,131 [2017]; £1,332,896 [2016]; £1,081,302 [2015]; £984,290 [2014]; £934,344 [2013]

Carers Trust Heart of England
Registered: 23 Jul 1996 *Employees:* 160 *Volunteers:* 36
Tel: 0116 279 6980 *Website:* carerstrusthofe.org.uk
Activities: Education, training; advancement of health or saving of lives; disability
Address: 3 Rectory Lane, Kibworth, Leicester, LE8 0NW
Trustees: Rosemarie June Tonkinson, Mrs Vivien Kershaw, Mr Gian Singh Seehra, Ms Jean Erica Jackson, Mrs Davinder Athwal JP, Mrs Rita Mary Evans, Mrs Janet Jones-Legg MBE, Mr Victor Keene, Ms Marcia Jarrett, Mr Dhiran Vagdia, Mr John Stephen Payne, Mr Abid Khan, Mr Garth Murphy, Ram Lakha OBE
Income: £3,048,948 [2017]; £3,117,348 [2016]; £2,525,359 [2015]; £2,639,274 [2014]; £2,816,676 [2013]

Carers Trust Mid Yorkshire
Registered: 28 Apr 1998 *Employees:* 111 *Volunteers:* 2
Tel: 01484 513671 *Website:* crossroadscareinmidyorkshire.org.uk
Activities: The advancement of health or saving of lives
Address: 3 Rose Mount, Birkby, Huddersfield, W Yorks, HD2 2BU
Trustees: Ron Etherington, Mr David Anthony Iredale, Mr Melvyn Baker, Mrs Hilary Anne Thompson, Mr Roger Mark Brook Nicholson, Mrs Maureen Hepworth, Richard Clampett, Mr John Edward Emms, Mr John Francis Holmes, Mr Kenneth Ronald Burnett, Miss Natalie Jayne Tarbatt
Income: £1,731,299 [2017]; £1,630,629 [2016]; £1,685,073 [2015]; £1,727,835 [2014]; £1,542,205 [2013]

Carers Trust South East Wales
Registered: 4 Apr 2008 *Employees:* 71 *Volunteers:* 21
Tel: 01495 769996 *Website:* ctsew.org.uk
Activities: The advancement of health or saving of lives; disability; other charitable purposes
Address: County Hospital, Griffithstown, Pontypool, Monmouthshire, NP4 5YA
Trustees: Mr Richard Bevan, Mr Alan Wintle, Steven Harford, Mrs Susan Mary Mansell, Mrs Sylvia Eileen Mason, Mr Robert Poore, Mrs Sylvia Jean Jones, David Kenny, Mr Stephen Williams, Ms Margaret Street, Mrs Sharon Harford, Ms Gillian Dentus
Income: £1,035,623 [2017]; £1,151,298 [2016]; £1,241,375 [2015]; £1,339,377 [2014]; £1,328,680 [2013]

Carers Trust Thames
Registered: 31 Jan 2002 *Employees:* 90 *Volunteers:* 19
Tel: 01494 873723 *Website:* carerstrustthames.org.uk
Activities: The advancement of health or saving of lives; disability
Address: 1 Garners End, Chalfont St Peter, Gerrards Cross, Bucks, SL9 0HE
Trustees: Mr David Eoin McCullagh, Stephen Sharples, Mr Ijaz Iqbal, Mr Michael Burleigh, Mr Barry Kermisch, Ms Pauline Irons, Mr Stephen Otter, Mr Anthony Bull, Ms Sunita Kundan
Income: £2,352,803 [2017]; £2,378,319 [2016]; £2,073,727 [2015]; £1,808,558 [2014]; £1,801,254 [2013]

Carers Trust
Registered: 21 Dec 2011 *Employees:* 92
Website: carers.org
Activities: The advancement of health or saving of lives; disability; prevention or relief of poverty
Address: 32-36 Loman Street, London, SE1 0EH
Trustees: Mr Tim Poole, Mark Currie, Ms Veronica Stonor, William McCormick, Mr Gareth Howells, Patrick Healy, Stuart Taylor, Lynne Powrie, Mr John Nigel Major McLean OBE
Income: £5,443,875 [2017]; £7,877,300 [2016]; £5,963,747 [2015]; £11,369,241 [2014]; £8,828,012 [2013]

Carers UK
Registered: 7 Feb 1966 *Employees:* 53 *Volunteers:* 500
Tel: 020 7378 4945 *Website:* carersuk.org
Activities: General charitable purposes
Address: Carers UK, 20 Great Dover Street, London, SE1 4LX
Trustees: Mr David Grayson, Mrs Paramjit Oberoi, Mr Kevin Daly, Ms Martha Wiseman, Dr Rosie Tope, Eleanor Bradley, Tim Anfilogoff, Canon Geoffrey Almond, Mr Terry Bryan, Mr Andrew Crawford Hensman, Ms Paula Marie Bryan, Siva Shan, Virginia Ann Pulbrook, Ms Lesley Bryce
Income: £4,962,123 [2017]; £2,969,143 [2016]; £3,484,667 [2015]; £3,281,595 [2014]; £4,292,034 [2013]

Carers in Bedfordshire
Registered: 14 Apr 2010 *Employees:* 28 *Volunteers:* 122
Tel: 0300 111 1919 *Website:* carersinbeds.org.uk
Activities: Education, training; advancement of health or saving of lives; disability; other charitable purposes
Address: Suite K, Sandland Court, Pilgrim Centre, Brickhill Drive, Bedford, MK41 7PZ
Trustees: Mrs Monica Cooper, Mr Barry Wootton, Michael Frampton, Mr Graham Mills, Mr Keith Charles Lee, Win Douglas, Jim Rose, Ms Emma Wilkinson, Mr Stephen Melville Peacey, Mrs Sue Janet Lowe
Income: £1,125,976 [2017]; £1,105,495 [2016]; £1,554,209 [2015]; £1,210,636 [2014]; £1,100,998 [2013]

Carers in Hertfordshire
Registered: 12 Mar 2001 *Employees:* 62 *Volunteers:* 225
Tel: 01992 586969 *Website:* carersinherts.org.uk
Activities: General charitable purposes
Address: Carers, 119 Fore Street, Hertford, SG14 1AX
Trustees: Christopher Watts, Santo Mann, Michael Ormerod, Mark Montgomery, Janice Guerra, Andrew Mills, Albert Binns, Miroslava Budin-Jones
Income: £3,140,406 [2017]; £1,604,390 [2016]; £1,364,098 [2015]; £1,329,360 [2014]; £1,315,184 [2013]

The Carers' Resource
Registered: 19 Sep 1995 *Employees:* 140 *Volunteers:* 205
Tel: 01423 500555 *Website:* carersresource.org
Activities: General charitable purposes; education, training; advancement of health or saving of lives; disability; prevention or relief of poverty; economic, community development, employment
Address: Carers' Resource, 11 North Park Road, Harrogate, N Yorks, HG1 5PD
Trustees: Mr David William Harbourne, Mrs Julia Lister, Mr Andrew Colin Makey, Mrs Stephanie Lawrence, Mr Robert Smith, Ms Elizabeth Ann Jones, Martyn Richards, Mrs Sarah Shaw
Income: £2,613,027 [2017]; £2,350,230 [2016]; £2,208,983 [2015]; £2,027,307 [2014]; £1,557,758 [2013]

Carers' Support - Canterbury,Dover & Thanet
Registered: 15 Jul 2010 *Employees:* 29 *Volunteers:* 11
Tel: 01304 364637 *Website:* carers-supportcdt.org.uk
Activities: Education, training; advancement of health or saving of lives; disability; prevention or relief of poverty
Address: Carer Support Canterbury Dover & Thanet, 80 Middle Street, Deal, Kent, CT14 6HL
Trustees: Mr Paul Curd, Miss Sarah Tait, Mrs Julie Marie Barker, Mr Gordon Viggers, Ms Janet Freer, Ms Sue Mott
Income: £1,137,890 [2017]; £938,445 [2016]; £769,797 [2015]; £937,537 [2014]; £318,838 [2013]

Caring for Communities and People Ltd
Registered: 10 Jan 1995 *Employees:* 101 *Volunteers:* 160
Tel: 01242 228800 *Website:* ccp.org.uk
Activities: General charitable purposes; education, training; prevention or relief of poverty; accommodation, housing; economic, community development, employment; human rights, religious or racial harmony, equality or diversity; recreation; other charitable purposes
Address: Wolseley House, Oriel Road, Cheltenham, Glos, GL50 1TH
Trustees: Mr Michael Richardson Ratcliffe, Mr Andrew Piggott, Mr Tadeusz Czapski, Mr Ian James Salter, Mrs Barbara Driver
Income: £3,244,530 [2017]; £3,031,197 [2016]; £2,705,419 [2015]; £2,603,103 [2014]; £2,562,648 [2013]

Caring for Life
Registered: 12 Aug 1987 *Employees:* 84 *Volunteers:* 120
Tel: 0113 230 3600 *Website:* caringforlife.co.uk
Activities: Disability; prevention or relief of poverty; accommodation, housing; religious activities; environment, conservation, heritage
Address: Crag House Farm, Cookridge, Leeds, LS16 7NH
Trustees: Pastor William Ernest Bygroves, Mr Graham Sharkey, Dr Jonathan William Birnie, Mrs Pamela Bronwen Young, Mrs Patricia Clegg, Mrs Florence Hendriksz
Income: £3,652,961 [2017]; £3,919,552 [2016]; £3,876,107 [2015]; £3,490,405 [2014]; £4,046,852 [2013]

Caritas - Anchor House

Registered: 22 Jun 2012 *Employees:* 46 *Volunteers:* 93
Tel: 020 7476 6062 *Website:* caritasanchorhouse.org.uk
Activities: Education, training; prevention or relief of poverty; accommodation, housing; economic, community development, employment
Address: 81 Barking Road, London, E16 4HB
Trustees: Mr Michael Jeremy Hodges, Bob Townsend, Mr Charles Ralph Abel Smith, Father Dominic Howarth, Teresa-Ann Hughes, Mr Simon Andrew Dalton Hall
Income: £2,967,175 [2017]; £2,392,579 [2016]; £4,191,012 [2015]

Caritas Care Limited

Registered: 8 Feb 1982 *Employees:* 189 *Volunteers:* 88
Tel: 07710 984481 *Website:* caritascare.org.uk
Activities: General charitable purposes; education, training; disability; prevention or relief of poverty; accommodation, housing; economic, community development, employment
Address: 92 Lynton Road, Southport, Merseyside, PR8 3AP
Trustees: Miss Mary Frances Leavy, Miss Jane Robinson, Mr Peter Buckley, Mrs Anne-Marie Morgan, Mrs Ellen Flood, Mr Paul Desborough, Christine Sutherland, Mr Graham Victor Blower, Ms Catherine Emma Parkinson, Mr Richard Stowe
Income: £7,448,883 [2017]; £7,119,097 [2016]; £6,175,256 [2015]; £4,989,102 [2014]; £4,711,100 [2013]

Caritas Diocese of Salford

Registered: 10 Sep 2008 *Employees:* 88 *Volunteers:* 450
Tel: 0161 817 2250 *Website:* caritassalford.org.uk
Activities: General charitable purposes; prevention or relief of poverty; religious activities; other charitable purposes
Address: Cathedral Centre, 3 Ford Street, Salford, M3 6DP
Trustees: Mr Anthony Murray, Mr Edward Nally, Right Reverend John Arnold, Miss Lorraine Leonard, Rev Mgr Thomas Mulheran, Fr David Glover, Canon Alan Denneny
Income: £2,843,225 [2017]; £2,767,544 [2016]; £2,182,954 [2015]; £2,107,188 [2014]; £3,737,453 [2013]

Carleton House Preparatory School Limited

Registered: 7 Jul 1976 *Employees:* 33
Website: carletonhouse.co.uk
Activities: Education, training
Address: 145 Menlove Avenue, Liverpool, L18 3EE
Trustees: Mr Thomas Manning, Mr Andrew Leong, Mrs Michelle Christian, Mrs Ann McGann, Mrs Elaien Czarnecki, Mrs Sarah Louise Fletcher, Mrs Ondrea Hayes, Mrs Jessica Leong, Mr Peter William Megann, Mr David John Fletcher, Ms Sarah Jane Swanson, Mr Gareth Hilton Beck
Income: £1,311,785 [2016]; £1,250,487 [2015]; £1,155,130 [2014]; £1,105,351 [2013]; £994,762 [2012]

Carlisle Diocesan Board of Finance

Registered: 1 May 1967 *Employees:* 62 *Volunteers:* 186
Tel: 01768 807761 *Website:* carlislediocese.org.uk
Activities: Religious activities
Address: Carlilse Diocesan Board of Finance, Church House, 19-24 Friargate, Penrith, Cumbria, CA11 7XR
Trustees: The Rt Rev James William Scobie Newcome, Rev Martin Philip Jayne, The Venerable Richard Pratt, Andrew Towner, Jim Johnson, The Venerable Vernon Ross, The Venerable Lee Stuart Townend, Mr David Dickinson, Mrs Gillian Ruth Troughton
Income: £8,335,346 [2016]; £9,077,354 [2015]; £9,362,358 [2014]; £8,723,979 [2013]; £8,920,679 [2012]

Carlisle Mencap Limited

Registered: 14 Jul 2006 *Employees:* 101 *Volunteers:* 40
Tel: 01228 674393 *Website:* carlislemencap.co.uk
Activities: The advancement of health or saving of lives; disability
Address: Carlisle Mencap Limited, 6 Brunswick Street, Carlisle, Cumbria, CA1 1PN
Trustees: Mrs Christine Bowditch, Miss Elizabeth Harkness, Mrs Georgina Ternent, Mr Nigel Steel, Mrs Joan Nicholson, Mr Neil Braiden, Miss Samantha McBean, Mr Steven Bowditch, Mrs Corrine Estelle Roberts Thompson, Mr Peter Edward Hindle, Mrs Tess Hart, Mr Peter Bradbrook, Mrs Irene Roberts Green
Income: £1,518,609 [2016]; £1,410,608 [2015]; £1,285,972 [2014]; £1,371,775 [2013]; £1,358,267 [2012]

Carmel Ministries International

Registered: 4 Oct 2002 *Employees:* 29 *Volunteers:* 205
Tel: 0117 977 5533 *Website:* carmelcitychurch.org
Activities: Education, training; prevention or relief of poverty; religious activities; other charitable purposes
Address: 817a Bath Road, Brislington, Bristol, BS4 5NL
Trustees: Gerri Di Somma, Wayne Skinner, John Quintanilla
Income: £1,091,480 [2016]; £1,140,324 [2015]; £1,115,273 [2014]; £991,519 [2013]; £811,094 [2012]

The Carmelite Charitable Trust

Registered: 17 Mar 1997 *Employees:* 10
Tel: 020 3114 2107 *Website:* carmelite.org
Activities: Religious activities
Address: The Carmelite Charitable Trust, Churchill House, Suite 320-321, 120 Bunns Lane, Mill Hill, London, NW7 2AS
Trustees: Rev Patrick O'Keeffe, Rev Brendan Grady, Rev Michael Cox, Rev Kevin Alban, Rev Patrick Fitzgerald-Lombard
Income: £4,218,573 [2016]; £2,276,928 [2015]; £1,205,431 [2014]; £1,260,695 [2013]; £1,314,470 [2012]

Carn Brea Leisure Centre Trust

Registered: 26 Jan 2000 *Employees:* 46
Tel: 01209 714766 *Website:* carnbrealeisurecentre.co.uk
Activities: The advancement of health or saving of lives; amateur sport; recreation
Address: Carn Brea Leisure Centre, Station Road, Pool, Redruth, Cornwall, TR15 3QS
Trustees: Mr Nick Lake, Mr Colin Rowe, Mr Mark Smith, Ms Clare Salmon, Mr David Price, Mr Bob Woods, Mr Malcolm Moyle, Mr Christopher Hunter, Mr Richard Beeching
Income: £1,579,413 [2017]; £1,451,696 [2016]; £1,450,333 [2015]; £1,419,560 [2014]; £1,411,807 [2013]

The Carningli Trust

Registered: 14 Jan 1988 *Employees:* 43
Tel: 07960 733257
Activities: Disability; accommodation, housing
Address: Panteg, St Clears, Carmarthen, SA33 4JR
Trustees: Mrs Margaret Cule, Mr William Cyril Phillips, Audrey Hancock, Timothy Fletcher, Mr John Hancock, Helen Kay Coram, Val Arnall
Income: £1,047,269 [2016]; £909,340 [2015]; £947,381 [2014]; £917,511 [2013]; £988,242 [2012]

Carnival Village Trust
Registered: 15 Aug 2008 *Employees:* 22
Tel: 020 7221 9700 *Website:* carnivalvillage.org.uk
Activities: Arts, culture, heritage, science
Address: The Tabernacle, 34-35 Powis Square, London, W11 2AY
Trustees: Mr Ansel Wong, Mr Alan Edwards, Ms Imani Walker-Douglas, Mr Ian Comfort, Ms Mary Genis
Income: £1,470,874 [2016]; £1,402,984 [2015]; £1,387,223 [2014]; £1,575,258 [2013]

The Carpenters Company Charitable Trust
Registered: 2 Feb 1979
Tel: 020 7588 7001 *Website:* carpentersco.com
Activities: General charitable purposes; education, training
Address: Carpenters' Hall, 1 Throgmorton Avenue, London, EC2N 2JJ
Trustees: Guy Morton-Smith, Michael Mathews, Peter Luton, Martin Samuel
Income: £1,502,701 [2017]; £1,484,451 [2016]; £1,099,496 [2015]; £1,101,071 [2014]; £1,064,609 [2013]

Cartref Limited
Registered: 21 Apr 2006 *Employees:* 141 *Volunteers:* 3
Tel: 029 2075 3123 *Website:* cartref.org
Activities: General charitable purposes; accommodation, housing
Address: Cartref, 88-90 Lake Road East, Cardiff, CF23 5NP
Trustees: Mr Steven Wynne Lloyd James, Mrs Margaret Heulwen Ashcroft, Mrs Joan Arwyn Collinge, Mrs Elizabeth Green
Income: £2,424,876 [2017]; £2,501,902 [2016]; £2,357,738 [2015]; £2,462,725 [2014]; £2,361,851 [2013]

Cartref NI Limited
Registered: 8 Sep 1998 *Employees:* 103
Tel: 01745 584527 *Website:* cartrefni.com
Activities: Disability
Address: Goleufan, 27 Chester Street, St Asaph, Denbighshire, LL17 0RE
Trustees: Tricia Bochenski, Mrs Mabel Russell, Susan Taylor, Mrs Helen Jane Brown, Ms Alison Brebner, Mr Mark Ian Roberts, Ms Joanne Elizabeth Norris
Income: £2,381,064 [2017]; £2,036,824 [2016]; £2,031,887 [2015]; £1,951,951 [2014]; £1,945,950 [2013]

Cartrefi Cymru Co-operative Limited
Registered: 30 Nov 1989 *Employees:* 828
Tel: 029 2064 2270 *Website:* cartreficymru.org
Activities: Education, training; disability; accommodation, housing; economic, community development, employment
Address: 5 Coopers Yard, Curran Road, Cardiff, CF10 5NB
Trustees: Mr Grant Duncan, Martin O'Neill, Mrs Ruth Dineen, Ms Heather Tyrell, Peter Higson, Mr Roger McMahon, Mr Ian Derrick
Income: £22,690,000 [2017]; £20,855,000 [2016]; £21,599,000 [2015]; £21,370,000 [2014]; £19,927,000 [2013]

The Case Centre Limited
Registered: 12 Aug 1974 *Employees:* 23
Tel: 01234 756405 *Website:* thecasecentre.org
Activities: Education, training
Address: The Case Centre Ltd, Cranfield University, Wharley End, Cranfield, Bedford, MK43 0JR
Trustees: Professor John Lister Thompson, Dr Josep Valor Sabatier, Mr Richard Jolly, Mr Jamie Rundle, Professor Rosa Chun, Professor Mark Fenton-O'Creevy, Professor Rachida Justo, Professor Thomas Burgi, Professor Douglas Webber, Professor Anand Narasimhan, Associate Professor Martin Kupp, Professor Ruth Bender, Professor Sahasranam Hariharan
Income: £2,721,902 [2017]; £2,467,205 [2016]; £2,576,806 [2015]; £2,747,636 [2014]; £2,684,107 [2013]

Sir John Cass's Foundation
Registered: 3 Feb 1965 *Employees:* 8
Tel: 020 7480 5884 *Website:* sirjohncassfoundation.com
Activities: Education, training
Address: Sir John Cass's Foundation, 31 Jewry Street, London, EC3N 2EY
Trustees: Kevin Everett Dsc Ostj Cc Deputy, Graham B Forbes, Helen Meixner, Prof Michael Thorne, The Reverend Trevor Critchlow, Mrs Jennifer Mary Moseley, HH Brian Barker CBE QC, Mr John Hall, David Hogben, Rev Laura Jane Jorgensen, Mr Paul David Bloomfield, Ms Sophie Anne Fernandes
Income: £6,847,988 [2017]; £5,510,307 [2016]; £6,200,399 [2015]; £6,171,294 [2014]; £6,124,025 [2013]

Castel Froma Neuro Care Limited
Registered: 1 Dec 2003 *Employees:* 177 *Volunteers:* 5
Tel: 01926 427216 *Website:* castelfroma.org.uk
Activities: The advancement of health or saving of lives; disability
Address: Royal Midland Counties Home, Castel Froma, 93 Lillington Road, Leamington Spa, Warwicks, CV32 6LL
Trustees: Mr Stephen John Nicklin, Mr David Leigh-Hunt, Mr John Atkins, Graham Murrell, Mr John Evison, Mrs Lesley Mary Holiday
Income: £7,093,809 [2017]; £6,127,025 [2016]; £5,269,395 [2015]; £5,706,510 [2014]; £5,066,938 [2013]

Castle Court School Educational Trust Limited
Registered: 22 Apr 1974 *Employees:* 118
Tel: 01202 694438 *Website:* castlecourt.com
Activities: Education, training
Address: Castle Court School, Knoll Lane, Corfe Mullen, Wimborne, Dorset, BH21 3RF
Trustees: Mr Neil Andrew Cullum, Mrs Catherine Noelle Jack, Mrs Patricia Knott, Ms Danielle Grady, Mr Jonathan Morley, Mr Timothy Peter Creswell Stone, Mr David William Nevile Aston, Mr John MacDiarmid, Robin Lweis
Income: £4,116,851 [2017]; £3,875,271 [2016]; £3,549,658 [2015]; £3,219,752 [2014]; £3,015,869 [2013]

Roy Castle Lung Cancer Foundation
Registered: 31 May 1995 *Employees:* 143 *Volunteers:* 511
Tel: 0333 323 7200 *Website:* roycastle.org
Activities: The advancement of health or saving of lives
Address: Roy Castle Centre, Enterprise Way, Wavertree Technology Park, Liverpool, L13 1FB
Trustees: Mr Jim Couton, Mr David Samuel Maples, Mr Peter Rainey, Mr Tony Coombs, Prof Joanne Cranwell, Mrs Alison Lobb, Professor Ray Donnelly FRCSEd, Mr Euan Imrie, Mr David Gilligan, Mr Andrew Martin Grange, Mr Max Steinburg
Income: £4,795,618 [2016]; £5,643,993 [2015]; £5,381,986 [2014]; £4,679,833 [2013]; £4,953,840 [2012]

Castle Supported Living Limited
Registered: 23 Oct 1992 *Employees:* 58
Tel: 01200 429990 *Website:* castlesupportedliving.com
Activities: Disability; accommodation, housing
Address: Castle Supported Living Ltd, 43a Moor Lane, Clitheroe, Lancs, BB7 1BE
Trustees: Mr Graham Jones, Mrs Pauline Howarth, Mr Peter Hopwood, Mr Gerald Michael Haworth, Mr Alan Clarke BEM, Mrs Lisa Parrot
Income: £1,067,994 [2017]; £1,029,523 [2016]; £1,046,539 [2015]; £987,203 [2014]; £972,889 [2013]

The Cat and Rabbit Rescue Centre
Registered: 25 Mar 1992 *Employees:* 27 *Volunteers:* 100
Tel: 01243 641409 *Website:* crrc.co.uk
Activities: Education, training; animals
Address: Holborow Lodge, Chalder Lane, Sidlesham, Chichester, W Sussex, PO20 7RJ
Trustees: Mr Nigel Charles Oddy, Miss Monique Yvonne Turk, Ms Judy Saxon, Helen Sinclair MBE, Mr Martin John Gomez, Miss Sarah Jane Oddy, Miss Janet Laws
Income: £1,388,488 [2017]; £615,338 [2016]; £694,263 [2015]; £681,441 [2014]; £490,979 [2013]

Catalyst Stockton on Tees Limited
Registered: 8 Nov 2000 *Employees:* 12 *Volunteers:* 4
Tel: 01642 733906 *Website:* catalyststockton.org
Activities: General charitable purposes
Address: Catalyst, 27 Yarm Road, Stockton on Tees, Cleveland, TS18 3NJ
Trustees: Ms Lesley Cooke, Mr Steven Iianson Nelson, Mrs Clara Jane Fawcett, Mr William Williams, Mr Guru Naidoo, Mr Oliver Mack, Mr Christopher David Marshall
Income: £1,059,269 [2017]; £413,428 [2016]; £561,209 [2015]; £479,488 [2014]; £421,239 [2013]

Catalyst Support
Registered: 9 Jun 1999 *Employees:* 58 *Volunteers:* 88
Tel: 01428 682901 *Website:* catalystsupport.org.uk
Activities: The advancement of health or saving of lives
Address: Falloden, Gasden Copse, Witley, Godalming, Surrey, GU8 5QD
Trustees: Mrs Elizabeth Grant, Mrs Susan Bowen, Mrs Katherine Mills, Ms Kirsty Collier, Mr Warren Rockett, Mr Peter Wallis, Mr Keith Deane, Dr Jane Winstone
Income: £2,148,872 [2017]; £1,937,764 [2016]; £1,907,136 [2015]; £1,655,868 [2014]; £870,551 [2013]

Catch 22 Charity Limited
Registered: 19 May 2008 *Employees:* 1,340 *Volunteers:* 314
Tel: 020 7336 4851 *Website:* catch-22.org.uk
Activities: Education, training; prevention or relief of poverty; accommodation, housing; economic, community development, employment; other charitable purposes
Address: Catch22 Charity Ltd, 27 Pear Tree Street, London, EC1V 3AG
Trustees: Mr Paul Barrington Williams, Mr Jim McKenna, Ms Tove Okunniwa, Ms Elaine Bailey, Mr Kieron Boyle, Mr Carl Cramer, Mr Ben Cooper, Mr Michael John Adamson, Mr John Stanley Marlor, Ms Honor Wilson-Fletcher, Ms Pauline Campbell, Mr Danny Rayne Kruger, Mr Sean Thomas Williams
Income: £46,818,000 [2016]; £89,747,000 [2015]; £54,917,000 [2014]; £53,399,000 [2013]; £48,327,000 [2012]

Caterham School Limited
Registered: 17 May 2005 *Employees:* 399 *Volunteers:* 38
Website: caterhamschool.co.uk
Activities: Education, training
Address: Caterham School, Harestone Valley Road, Caterham, Surrey, CR3 6YA
Trustees: Mr Jeremy Joiner, Mr David Charlesworth, Mr J Edward K Smith, Mrs Tracey Frances Eldridge Hinmers, Mr Mark Smith, Mr Ian Edwards, Mrs Suzi Whittle, The Reverend N Furley-Smith, Dr Stephen Richard Critchley, Mr Anthony Peter Wilson
Income: £19,012,000 [2016]; £17,925,000 [2015]; £17,246,000 [2014]; £16,906,000 [2013]; £15,812,000 [2012]

The Cathedral School (Llandaff) Limited
Registered: 29 Apr 2004 *Employees:* 140 *Volunteers:* 50
Tel: 029 2083 8503 *Website:* cathedral-school.co.uk
Activities: Education, training; amateur sport
Address: Cathedral School, Cardiff Road, Llandaff, Cardiff, CF5 2YH
Trustees: Mr Peter Lacey, Frank Holmes, Mrs Fiona Curteis, Mrs Jane Newley BA CertEd MA, Mrs Kathryn Bates, Professor Roger Mansfield, Mr Gilbert Lloyd FCA, Mr Robin Havard BSc Econ (Hons), Mr Jeremy Charles Rawlins
Income: £8,369,906 [2017]; £7,817,457 [2016]; £7,273,898 [2015]; £6,961,978 [2014]; £6,233,057 [2013]

The Catherine Cookson Charitable Trust
Registered: 17 Feb 1977
Tel: 0191 488 7459
Activities: General charitable purposes; education, training; advancement of health or saving of lives; disability; religious activities; arts, culture, heritage, science; animals; environment, conservation, heritage
Address: Thomas Magnay & Co, 8 St Marys Green, Whickham, Newcastle upon Tyne, NE16 4DN
Trustees: Mr Peter Magnay, Mr Hugo Marshall, Mr Daniel Edward Sallows, Mr David Stuart Spencer Hawkins, Mr Jack Ravenscroft
Income: £1,144,667 [2017]; £1,153,957 [2016]; £1,094,706 [2015]; £1,159,145 [2014]; £1,115,141 [2013]

Catholic Agency for Overseas Development
Registered: 9 Feb 2015 *Employees:* 460 *Volunteers:* 6,000
Tel: 020 7095 5579 *Website:* cafod.org.uk
Activities: General charitable purposes; education, training; advancement of health or saving of lives; disability; prevention or relief of poverty; overseas aid, famine relief; accommodation, housing; religious activities; economic, community development, employment; human rights, religious or racial harmony, equality or diversity
Address: CAFOD, Romero House, 55 Westminster Bridge Road, London, SE1 7JB
Trustees: Mary Ney, John Darley, Dominic Jermey, Bishop John Arnold, Megan Russell, Dr John Guy, Mr Christopher Perry, Bishop Patrick McKinney, Fr Jim O'Keefe, Margaret Mwaniki, Catherine Newman, Ms Mary Ward, Professor Karen Kilby
Income: £50,115,000 [2017]; £53,097,000 [2016]

Catholic Blind Institute
Registered: 16 Mar 2004 *Employees:* 193 *Volunteers:* 12
Tel: 0151 230 5097 *Website:* catholicblindinstitute.org
Activities: Education, training; disability; prevention or relief of poverty; accommodation, housing; other charitable purposes
Address: St Vincents Lodge, Yew Tree Lane, Liverpool, L12 9HL
Trustees: Terry Bates, Mr Paul Edward Robbins, Mrs Elizabeth Anne Jones, Sister Theresa Tighe, Mr Stephen Winstanley, Mrs Emma Victoria Lockwood, Dr Mary Felicity Knight, Mr Martin Gerard O'Rourke, Ms Anne Reading, Sian Snelling, Mr Brian Thomas Gibbs
Income: £5,528,041 [2017]; £5,061,798 [2016]; £5,005,199 [2015]; £4,707,066 [2014]; £4,442,813 [2013]

Catholic Care (Diocese of Leeds)
Registered: 23 Sep 1982 *Employees:* 140 *Volunteers:* 24
Tel: 0113 388 5400 *Website:* catholic-care.org.uk
Activities: General charitable purposes; advancement of health or saving of lives; disability; prevention or relief of poverty; accommodation, housing; economic, community development, employment
Address: 11 North Grange Road, Headingley, Leeds, LS6 2BR
Trustees: Mgr Peter Rosser, Rev Dr Joseph Cortis, Right Reverend Marcus Stock, Mrs Maureen Fletcher, Mgr Donal Lucey, Mr Timothy Parr, Mrs Susan Rix
Income: £3,520,465 [2017]; £3,768,987 [2016]; £3,644,274 [2015]; £3,633,074 [2014]; £3,939,993 [2013]

The Catholic Children's Society (Westminster)
Registered: 24 Sep 1963 *Employees:* 74 *Volunteers:* 15
Tel: 020 8969 5305 *Website:* cathchild.org.uk
Activities: General charitable purposes
Address: Catholic Childrens Society, 73 St Charles Square, London, W10 6EJ
Trustees: Mr John Gibbs, Mr Anthonyjames Michael O'Halloran, Pamela Singh, Monsignor Phelin Christopher Rowland, Mrs Maureen Roe, Ms Frances Ellen McCarthy, Mr John Michael O'Donnell, Dr Anne Burnage
Income: £2,583,453 [2017]; £2,482,936 [2016]; £2,051,168 [2015]; £2,393,117 [2014]; £2,239,672 [2013]

Catholic Marriage Care Limited
Registered: 22 Mar 1963 *Employees:* 16 *Volunteers:* 700
Tel: 0115 993 4255 *Website:* marriagecare.org.uk
Activities: Education, training; advancement of health or saving of lives
Address: Huntingdon House, 278-290 Huntingdon Street, Nottingham, NG1 3LY
Trustees: Mr Nigel Dorning, Mrs Deirdre Peden, Rev Mehall Lowry, Mrs Glenda Spencer, Dr Clare Watkins, Mr Anthony Brian Christopher Dollard, Mrs Margaret Morley, Mrs Shelia Mary Don
Income: £1,603,950 [2017]; £1,659,879 [2016]; £1,726,750 [2015]; £1,711,255 [2014]; £1,615,610 [2013]

Catholic Trust for England and Wales
Registered: 12 May 2003 *Employees:* 59
Tel: 020 7901 4808 *Website:* catholicchurch.org.uk
Activities: General charitable purposes; religious activities
Address: 39 Eccleston Square, London, SW1V 1BX
Trustees: Mr John Gibbs, Rt Rev Mgr Peter Brignall, Mr Edward Nally, Mr Michael Prior, Mr Nigel Newton, Mr Austin Richard King, Mr Kees Kempenaar, Dr James Whiston, Mrs Kathleen Smith, Rev John Nelson, Mr Edward Poyser, Dr Elizabeth Walmsley, Rev David Roberts
Income: £6,049,966 [2016]; £12,264,111 [2015]; £4,914,782 [2014]; £4,640,573 [2013]; £4,163,061 [2012]

Cats Protection
Registered: 22 Sep 1962 *Employees:* 678 *Volunteers:* 9,800
Tel: 0870 770 8649 *Website:* cats.org.uk
Activities: Animals
Address: Cats Protection, National Cat Centre, Chelwood Gate, Haywards Heath, W Sussex, RH17 7TT
Trustees: Cats Protection Trustee Limited
Income: £55,546,000 [2016]; £55,862,000 [2015]; £45,713,000 [2014]; £43,983,000 [2013]; £36,978,000 [2012]

Caudwell Children
Registered: 9 Mar 2000 *Employees:* 54 *Volunteers:* 750
Tel: 01782 600607 *Website:* caudwellchildren.com
Activities: The advancement of health or saving of lives; disability; prevention or relief of poverty
Address: Minton Hollins Building, Shelton Old Road, Stoke on Trent, Staffs, ST4 7RY
Trustees: Mr Craig Bennett, Dr John Alexander, Mrs Ramona Mehta, Ms Louise Margaret Morris, Mr Karl Roger Bamford, Mr Paul Clark, Mrs Jacqueline Griffiths
Income: £13,822,914 [2016]; £7,765,788 [2015]; £6,257,954 [2014]; £5,336,554 [2013]; £5,519,409 [2012]

The Cavendish School Charitable Trust Limited
Registered: 17 Nov 1970 *Employees:* 55 *Volunteers:* 40
Tel: 020 7482 9203 *Website:* cavendishschool.co.uk
Activities: Education, training
Address: The Cavendish School, 31 Inverness Street, London, NW1 7HB
Trustees: Mrs Mary Robey, Mrs Elizabeth Blain, Mrs Kathrin Hake, Ms Nicola Rushton, Mr Mark Alexander Chiverton, Mrs Alice Gotto, Mr Donald Kehoe, Mr Anthony Poole, Mr Paul Rothwell, Ms Helen Berry, Mr Daniel Matthews
Income: £3,445,176 [2017]; £3,421,653 [2016]; £3,333,425 [2015]; £2,979,936 [2014]; £2,749,891 [2013]

The Caxton Foundation
Registered: 22 Jun 2011 *Employees:* 9
Tel: 020 7808 1172 *Website:* caxtonfoundation.org.uk
Activities: Education, training; disability; prevention or relief of poverty
Address: The Caxton Foundation, Alliance House, 12 Caxton Street, London, SW1H 0QS
Trustees: Caxton Trustee Limited
Income: £1,932,513 [2017]; £2,533,070 [2016]; £2,267,204 [2015]; £1,525,535 [2014]; £1,495,358 [2013]

The Caxton Trust
Registered: 13 Nov 1998 *Employees:* 14
Tel: 01842 752297 *Website:* catchup.org
Activities: Education, training
Address: Keystone Innovation Centre, Croxton Road, Thetford, Norfolk, IP24 1JD
Trustees: Mrs Gay Drysdale, Ingrid Lunt Professor, Mr Jocelyn Atholl Stuart-Grumbar, Mr Alan Warner, Mrs Sioned Bowen, Mr Patrick Crawford, Vanessa Emmett, Mr Matthew Spence Roeser
Income: £1,584,776 [2016]; £1,283,655 [2015]; £753,600 [2014]; £1,370,744 [2013]; £1,060,648 [2012]

Cedars Castle Hill

Registered: 7 Mar 2000 *Employees:* 120 *Volunteers:* 2
Tel: 01747 854699 *Website:* cedarscastlehill.co.uk
Activities: The advancement of health or saving of lives
Address: Castle Hill House, Bimport, Shaftesbury, Dorset, SP7 8AX
Trustees: Mrs Sara Delano Jacson, Mr Michael Gregory Golberg, Mrs Elizabeth Westall, Dr Suzanne Daddy, Mr Michael Hall, Dr Geoffrey William Tapper, Mr Michael Ambrose Pattison, Mrs Penelope Hobbs, Mr Richard Keenlyside, Mrs Ruth Blacklock
Income: £2,267,490 [2017]; £2,247,207 [2016]; £2,151,644 [2015]; £2,161,316 [2014]; £2,099,392 [2013]

Celtic Leisure

Registered: 31 Mar 2015 *Employees:* 269 *Volunteers:* 5
Tel: 01639 640080 *Website:* celticleisure.org
Activities: The advancement of health or saving of lives; arts, culture, heritage, science; recreation
Address: Pontardawe Leisure Centre, Ynysderw Road, Pontardawe, Swansea, SA8 4EG
Trustees: Mr Harold Worth, Mr Christopher John Jones, Mr Leigh Andrew John Dineen, Mrs Philomena Lucy Fowler, Ms Hannah Stockham, Mr Andrew Davies, Mr Ieuan Michael Jones, Mr Michael Alfred Stephen Bendyk, Mr Jeremy Anthony Stephens, Mr Graham Jones
Income: £6,120,366 [2017]; £5,316,603 [2016]

The Central British Fund for World Jewish Relief

Registered: 18 Jul 1985 *Employees:* 37 *Volunteers:* 15
Tel: 020 8736 1250 *Website:* worldjewishrelief.org
Activities: General charitable purposes; education, training; advancement of health or saving of lives; disability; prevention or relief of poverty; overseas aid, famine relief; economic, community development, employment
Address: World Jewish Relief, 54 Crewys Road, London, NW2 2AD
Trustees: Ms Katerina Gould, Mr Adam Leigh, Ms Deborah Gundle, Mr Richard Frank, Ms Lucie Graham, Ms Natalie Patricia Tydeman, Ms Suzanne Kantor, Mr Philip Alan Bunt, Mr James Strauss, Ms Carolyn Ruth Bogush, Mrs Susannah Kintish, Mr Daniel Robert Rosenfield, Mr Zac Goodman, Mr David Semaya
Income: £6,290,822 [2017]; £5,972,396 [2016]; £5,360,942 [2015]; £7,162,200 [2014]; £7,213,831 [2013]

The Central England Area Quaker Meeting Charities

Registered: 14 Oct 1966 *Employees:* 45 *Volunteers:* 35
Tel: 0121 236 2644 *Website:* centralenglandquakers.org.uk
Activities: General charitable purposes; education, training; religious activities; environment, conservation, heritage
Address: 40 Bull Street, Birmingham, B4 6AF
Trustees: Robert Morris, Patricia Bradbury, Judith Jenner, Sue Thompson, Miriam Branson, John Kimberley, Mr Peter Brittain, Gill Coffin, Anthony Pegler, Roger Chapman, Anne Austin, Jill Stow, Rhiannon Grant
Income: £1,589,540 [2016]; £1,484,825 [2015]; £1,429,411 [2014]; £1,368,281 [2013]; £1,420,231 [2012]

Central England Law Centre Limited

Registered: 3 Jul 2001 *Employees:* 53 *Volunteers:* 60
Website: centralenglandlc.org.uk
Activities: The prevention or relief of poverty
Address: Oakwood House, St Patricks Road Entrance, Coventry, Warwicks, CV1 2HL
Trustees: Mr Keith Wilding, Professor Harinder Bahra, Mrs Celia Christie, Professor Jean McHale, Ms June Jeffrey, Councillor David Stuart Welsh, Mr Graham Moffat
Income: £2,133,636 [2017]; £1,777,398 [2016]; £1,608,968 [2015]; £1,285,137 [2014]; £1,285,137 [2013]

The Central Foundation Schools of London

Registered: 6 Apr 1964 *Employees:* 2
Tel: 020 7017 3022
Activities: Education, training
Address: 55 Skeena Hill, London, SW18 5PW
Trustees: Mr Clive Arding FRICS, Mr Nigel John Fletcher, Mr J E Cruse, Ms Mary Moore, Mr Robert Howard, Mr Shahid Malik, Mr Keith Bottomley, Mr Francis Sumner HonFCGI, The Rev The Lord Leslie John Griffiths, Mr Stephen Mark Brown, Mr Barrington Gooden, Mr Chris Gurney, Ms Dilnaz Khambata
Income: £2,199,000 [2017]; £2,289,000 [2016]; £9,610,000 [2015]; £1,786,000 [2014]; £2,333,000 [2013]

Central G H Trust

Registered: 4 Sep 2008 *Volunteers:* 7
Activities: General charitable purposes; religious activities; other charitable purposes
Address: Noble House, Eaton Road, Hemel Hempstead Industrial Estate, Hemel Hempstead, Herts, HP2 7UB
Trustees: Mr Philip James Hutchinson, Mr Colin Paul Barnes, Mr Oliver Muckle Whiley, Mr Laurie Roy Pollard
Income: £2,079,097 [2016]; £1,759,243 [2015]; £28,968,105 [2014]; £1,109,860 [2013]; £1,157,884 [2012]

Central Lancashire Age Concern Ltd

Registered: 26 Jun 2009 *Employees:* 126 *Volunteers:* 364
Tel: 01772 552850 *Website:* 55plus.org.uk
Activities: General charitable purposes; education, training; prevention or relief of poverty; amateur sport; recreation
Address: Central Lancashire Age Concern, Arkwright House, Stoneygate, Preston, Lancs, PR1 3XT
Trustees: Mr Philip Hughes, Mr Pratap Parmar, Mr Tony Readett, Ms Sylvia Williams, Mrs Audrey Knowles, Mrs Ann Gaskell, Mrs Teresa Maria Whittaker, Mrs Eve Carter
Income: £2,929,484 [2017]; £2,611,299 [2016]; £2,600,209 [2015]; £2,569,169 [2014]; £2,348,615 [2013]

Central School of Ballet Charitable Trust Limited

Registered: 15 Sep 1982 *Employees:* 69
Tel: 020 7837 6332 *Website:* centralschoolofballet.co.uk
Activities: Education, training; arts, culture, heritage, science
Address: Central School of Ballet, 10 Herbal Hill, London, EC1R 5EG
Trustees: Mrs Carole Gable, Virginia Brooke, Mr Jonathan Paul Wood, Mr David Gray, Mr Simon Sporborg, Mr Stephen Kane, Mr Tamas Wood, Mr Tim Parsonson, Ms Susan Scott-Parker, Mr Andrew Tuckey, Mr Ralph Bernard CBE, Mrs Wendy Pallot, Mr Simon Cole, Mrs Charlotte Shonberg, Ms Pim Baxter
Income: £3,232,258 [2017]; £2,535,342 [2016]; £2,399,160 [2015]; £2,245,542 [2014]; £2,084,817 [2013]

The Central Young Men's Christian Association

Registered: 3 Dec 1963 *Employees:* 373 *Volunteers:* 200
Tel: 020 7343 1844 *Website:* ymca.co.uk
Activities: Education, training; advancement of health or saving of lives; amateur sport
Address: Central YMCA, 112 Great Russell Street, London, WC1B 3NQ
Trustees: Mr Mark Bjornsen Andrews, Ms Philippa Campbell, Charlotte Elizabeth Dickens, Mrs Susan Morton, Mrs Janice Lloyd, Mrs Anne-Marie Smith, Mr Anthony Griffiths, Mrs Colleen Lorraine Harris, Mr Kern Roberts, Mr Alan Paul Smith, Mr Glenn Dunn
Income: £20,808,000 [2017]; £16,948,000 [2016]; £19,821,000 [2015]; £13,125,000 [2014]; £9,404,000 [2013]

Central and East Northamptonshire Citizens Advice Bureau
Registered: 8 Apr 2013 *Employees:* 36 *Volunteers:* 118
Tel: 01604 235080 *Website:* cencab.org.uk
Activities: General charitable purposes; prevention or relief of poverty
Address: Citizens Advice Bureau, 7-8 Mercers Row, Northampton, NN1 2QL
Trustees: Mr Clive Ireson, Mr Ahsan Khan, Ms Susan Barbara Hills, Carrick Ferguson
Income: £1,027,264 [2017]; £694,768 [2016]; £620,150 [2015]; £474,899 [2014]

Central and South Sussex Citizens Advice Bureau
Registered: 7 Nov 2006 *Employees:* 45 *Volunteers:* 50
Tel: 01903 252699 *Website:* cassca.org.uk
Activities: General charitable purposes; education, training; disability; prevention or relief of poverty; economic, community development, employment; human rights, religious or racial harmony, equality or diversity
Address: c/o Chris Smith, Citizens Advice, Town Hall, Chapel Road, Worthing, W Sussex, BN11 1HA
Trustees: Mrs Evelyn Gladys Lucy Wylde, Mr Andrew N Brock, Ms Sarah Trowbridge, Mrs Susan McMillan, Dr Irene Campbell, Mr Michael Terence Link, Mrs Francesca Arcidiaco, Nick Clay
Income: £1,211,743 [2017]; £1,466,161 [2016]; £1,489,136 [2015]; £1,665,636 [2014]; £1,489,399 [2013]

Centre 404
Registered: 17 Aug 1988 *Employees:* 175 *Volunteers:* 129
Tel: 020 7607 8762 *Website:* centre404.org.uk
Activities: General charitable purposes; disability; accommodation, housing
Address: Centre 404, 404 Camden Road, London, N7 0SJ
Trustees: Mrs Jean Willson, Mr Phillip Heycock, Mr Copeland Ingram, Mr Derek Weist, Miss Susan Pearson, Miss Tara Willson, Mr Paul Formosa, Miss Samantha Dunne
Income: £4,571,558 [2017]; £4,605,994 [2016]; £4,168,020 [2015]; £3,122,354 [2014]; £2,932,543 [2013]

Centre Ministries
Registered: 28 Aug 1962 *Employees:* 82 *Volunteers:* 15
Tel: 07719 757457 *Website:* centreministries.org
Activities: Education, training; religious activities
Address: 88 Ballyward Road, Ballyward, Castlewellan, Co Down, BT31 9PS
Trustees: Mr John Rosser, Mrs Jeanmary Rosser, Mr Philip George McElroy, Mr David Kelso, Mr Joel Longbone, Andrew Boulter, Ms Susan McKellen, Mr Michael Matthews, Mrs Cheri Kelso
Income: £1,219,782 [2017]; £1,194,246 [2016]; £1,138,659 [2015]; £1,071,615 [2014]; £1,142,275 [2013]

Centre for Ageing Better Limited
Registered: 3 Mar 2015 *Employees:* 18
Tel: 020 3829 0113 *Website:* ageing-better.org.uk
Activities: The advancement of health or saving of lives; prevention or relief of poverty; other charitable purposes
Address: Level 3, Angel Building, 407 St John Street, London, EC1V 4AD
Trustees: Miss Michele Louise Acton, Lord Geoffrey Filkin, Mr Mark Hesketh, Mrs Margaret Dangoor, Ms Cathy Garner, Cheryl Coppell, Ms Helena Herklots, Professor Nicholas Barron Mays, Dame Lin Homer, Mr Benjamin Page
Income: £1,291,751 [2017]; £1,746,144 [2016]

Centre for Ageing Better Trust
Registered: 26 Jan 2015 *Employees:* 18
Tel: 020 3829 0113 *Website:* ageing-better.org.uk
Activities: The advancement of health or saving of lives; prevention or relief of poverty; other charitable purposes
Address: Level 3, Angel Building, 407 St John's Street, London, EC1V 4AD
Trustees: Centre For Ageing Better Limited
Income: £1,089,751 [2017]; £50,784,649 [2016]

Centre for Alternative Technology Charity Limited
Registered: 2 Mar 1973 *Employees:* 55 *Volunteers:* 19
Tel: 01654 705951 *Website:* cat.org.uk
Activities: Education, training; environment, conservation, heritage
Address: Centre for Alternative Technology, Llwyngwern Quarry, Pantperthog, Machynlleth, Powys, SY20 9AZ
Trustees: Dr Stephanie Sanderson, Mrs Clare Jane Cherry, Mr Andrew Campbell Menzies, Mr Roger Denis Thomas, Mr Michael Austin Taylor, Dr Rosetta Margaret Plummer, Mr Karl Nicholas Wills
Income: £2,887,042 [2017]; £3,023,670 [2016]; £3,151,967 [2015]; £3,009,116 [2014]; £2,500,840 [2013]

Centre for Cities
Registered: 27 Jun 2007 *Employees:* 18
Tel: 020 7803 4300 *Website:* centreforcities.org
Activities: Education, training
Address: 2nd Floor, 9 Holyrood, London, SE1 2EL
Trustees: Mr Nigel Hugill, Sir Alan Geoffrey Wilson, Mr Greg Clark, Mr Martin Reeves, Mrs Nicola Jane Yates, Mr Stephen John Ashworth, Mr Tom Riordan, Mr Alexander Charles Plant, Ms Rosemary Feenan
Income: £1,298,658 [2016]; £1,439,114 [2015]; £2,000,837 [2014]; £1,241,649 [2013]; £1,059,883 [2012]

Centre for Counselling and Psychotherapy Education Trust
Registered: 27 Jun 1996 *Employees:* 8
Tel: 020 7266 3006 *Website:* ccpe.org.uk
Activities: Education, training
Address: Beauchamp Lodge, 2 Warwick Crescent, London, W2 6NE
Trustees: Dr Nigel Ian Hamilton, Mr Charles Flower, Mr Martin Roehrs, Mrs Louise Trowbridge
Income: £1,051,071 [2017]; £1,120,679 [2016]; £1,248,193 [2015]; £1,137,805 [2014]; £991,011 [2013]

The Centre for Economic Policy Research
Registered: 20 Jun 1983 *Employees:* 18
Tel: 020 7183 8801 *Website:* cepr.org
Activities: Education, training; economic, community development, employment
Address: Centre for Economic Policy Research, 33 Great Sutton Street, London, EC1V 0DX
Trustees: Prof Sir Charles Richard Bean, Professor David Miles, Ms Diane Coyle OBE, Mr Vittorio Umberto Grilli, Jean-Pierre Danthine, Professor Patrick Honohan, Mrs Bronwyn Curtis, Ms Lucrezia Reichlin, Mr Anthony Venables, Mr Andrew McIntyre, Mr John Fingleton
Income: £4,333,763 [2017]; £5,030,741 [2016]; £4,295,174 [2015]; £4,380,090 [2014]; £3,179,298 [2013]

Centre for Effective Altruism

Registered: 20 Nov 2012 *Employees:* 15 *Volunteers:* 36
Tel: 01865 241188 *Website:* centreforeffectivealtruism.org
Activities: General charitable purposes; education, training; advancement of health or saving of lives; prevention or relief of poverty; overseas aid, famine relief; animals; economic, community development, employment; human rights, religious or racial harmony, equality or diversity
Address: Centre for Effective Altruism, Suite 2, Littlegate House, 16-17 St Ebbes Street, Oxford, OX1 1PT
Trustees: Toby Ord, William MacAskill, Mr Nick Beckstead
Income: £4,019,637 [2017]; £3,507,482 [2016]; £719,358 [2015]; £482,639 [2014]; £226,282 [2013]

Centre for Effective Dispute Resolution Limited

Registered: 24 Jan 1997 *Employees:* 47
Tel: 020 7536 6000 *Website:* cedr.com
Activities: Education, training; economic, community development, employment
Address: International Dispute Resolution Centre, 70 Fleet Street, London, EC4Y 1EU
Trustees: Karl Mackie, Mr Neil Goodrum, Ms Tracey Fox, Mr Adrian Mecz, Ms Joanna Day, Ms Catherine Dixon, Ms Sheila Bates, Mr Alan Jacobs, Ms Felicity Steadman, Ms Joanna Page
Income: £5,015,000 [2017]; £4,992,000 [2016]; £5,720,000 [2015]; £5,841,000 [2014]; £5,497,000 [2013]

Centre for Engineering and Manufacturing Excellence

Registered: 30 Dec 2009 *Employees:* 23
Tel: 020 8596 5193 *Website:* ceme.co.uk
Activities: Education, training; prevention or relief of poverty; economic, community development, employment
Address: Marsh Way, Rainham, Essex, RM13 8EU
Trustees: Mr Bill Williams, Mr Martin Broadhurst, Mr Harjeet Sadheura, Mr Geoffrey Simon Richman, Miss Rachel Hadley, Dr Keyvan Djamarani, Mrs Judith Armitt, Mr Mike Peter Caine, Mr Wijay Pitumpe
Income: £3,708,291 [2017]; £3,633,006 [2016]; £6,183,946 [2015]; £5,811,707 [2014]; £4,018,807 [2013]

The Centre for Literacy in Primary Education

Registered: 28 Jun 2002 *Employees:* 16
Tel: 020 7401 3382 *Website:* clpe.co.uk
Activities: Education, training
Address: Centre for Literacy in Primary Education, Webber Street, London, SE1 8QW
Trustees: Ms Elaine Yvonne McQuade, Ms Nicola Parker, Mr Justin Shinebourne, Ms Antonia Byatt, Ms Beverley Greathead, Ms Cecilia Weiler, Miss Ali Mawle, Ms Jacqueline Gillan, Ms Catherine Rose, Mr Charlie Meredith, Mr Ronald Woods, Ms Caroline Pidgeon
Income: £1,250,382 [2016]; £1,238,693 [2015]; £1,302,458 [2014]; £1,191,604 [2013]; £1,207,410 [2012]

Centre for London

Registered: 27 Mar 2013 *Employees:* 13
Tel: 020 3757 5555 *Website:* centreforlondon.org
Activities: Education, training; prevention or relief of poverty; economic, community development, employment
Address: Unit 1, 32-33 Hatton Garden, London, EC1N 8DL
Trustees: Mr Andrew Travers, Prof Michael Arthur, Mr Tim Collerton, Liz Peace, Mr David Slater, Mr Mark John Boleat, Ms Rosie Bess Ferguson, Ms Sonal Shah, Mr Benjamin Charles Page, Mr Paul King
Income: £1,079,328 [2016]; £965,486 [2015]; £845,315 [2014]; £377,465 [2013]

Centre for Mental Health

Registered: 15 Mar 2002 *Employees:* 19
Tel: 020 7717 1558 *Website:* centreformentalhealth.org.uk
Activities: The advancement of health or saving of lives; disability
Address: Ms Agnieszka Dajczer, Southbank Technopark, Unit 2D21, 90 London Road, London, SE1 6LN
Trustees: Lady Edwina Grosvenor, Lady Elizabeth Vallance JP, Dr Ian Gordon McPherson, Sir Andrew Dillon, Lord Keith Bradley of Withington, Professor Susan Bailey, Mr Richard Fass FCA, Mr Michael John Morley
Income: £1,655,374 [2017]; £1,701,971 [2016]; £1,771,260 [2015]; £1,944,382 [2014]; £1,741,116 [2013]

Centre for Sustainable Energy

Registered: 8 Mar 1988 *Employees:* 41 *Volunteers:* 25
Tel: 0117 934 1400 *Website:* cse.org.uk
Activities: General charitable purposes; education, training; prevention or relief of poverty; environment, conservation, heritage; economic, community development, employment
Address: St James Court, St James Parade, Bristol, BS1 3LH
Trustees: Mr Peter Capener MBE, Prof Catherine Hilary Claire Mitchell, Mrs Anne Obey, Mr Peter Ellis, Mr Andrew Darnton, Bill Hull, Dr Andrew Douglas Garrard CBE, Mr Christopher Vernon, Ms Ariane Crampton, Mrs Kaye Welfare, Dr Brenda Mary Boardman MBE FInstE
Income: £1,902,749 [2017]; £1,907,936 [2016]; £2,176,502 [2015]; £2,277,235 [2014]; £2,145,855 [2013]

Centre of Life Church International

Registered: 9 Nov 1999 *Employees:* 19 *Volunteers:* 100
Tel: 020 8327 9060
Activities: General charitable purposes; education, training; prevention or relief of poverty; overseas aid, famine relief; religious activities
Address: Mail Boxes Etc, 336 Kennington Lane, London, SE11 5HY
Trustees: Dr Ramson Mumba
Income: £1,715,424 [2014]; £1,778,896 [2013]; £2,513,855 [2012]

Centrepoint Soho

Registered: 16 Aug 1985 *Employees:* 380 *Volunteers:* 556
Tel: 0845 466 3400 *Website:* centrepoint.org.uk
Activities: Education, training; advancement of health or saving of lives; accommodation, housing
Address: Centrepoint, Central House, 25 Camperdown Street, London, E1 8DZ
Trustees: Mr Robert Kerse, Ms Clare Montagu, Mr Jonathan Milward, Mr Michael Westcott, Ms Sally Scriminger, Mr Alan Wardle, Mr Symon Elliott, Mr Ian Holborn
Income: £32,586,000 [2017]; £27,295,000 [2016]; £21,777,000 [2015]; £20,565,000 [2014]; £19,110,000 [2013]

Cerebra - for Brain Injured Children and Young People

Registered: 17 Dec 2001 *Employees:* 104
Tel: 01267 244200 *Website:* cerebra.org.uk
Activities: Disability
Address: 2nd Floor, Cerebra, Lyric Building, King Street, Carmarthen, SA31 1BD
Trustees: Mr Michael Imperato, Mr Richard Peter Lumley, Dr Imogen Morgan, Mr Roland John Gooding OBE, Mr Jan Crosby, Professor David Rose, Mr David John Beattie, Dr Rim Al-Samsam, Ms Sonia Howe, Ms Sian Taylor
Income: £3,452,480 [2016]; £3,863,012 [2015]; £4,015,820 [2014]; £4,099,814 [2013]; £4,206,770 [2012]

The Certified Accountants Educational Trust
Registered: 4 Jan 1973
Tel: 0141 534 4045 *Website:* accaglobal.com
Activities: General charitable purposes; education, training
Address: A C C A, 110 Queen Street, Glasgow, G1 3BX
Trustees: Certified Accountants Educational Trustees Ltd
Income: £6,746,999 [2017]; £6,551,078 [2016]; £7,180,000 [2015];
£8,211,000 [2014]; £8,002,000 [2013]

The Chabad Jewish Community of Central London
Registered: 12 Mar 2012 *Employees:* 25
Tel: 07585 920195
Activities: Education, training; prevention or relief of poverty;
religious activities
Address: 10-11 Grosvenor Place, London, SW1X 7HH
Trustees: Mr Gerald Mimoun, Mr Robert Rackind, Dr Mark Gordon
Glaser
Income: £1,291,962 [2017]; £1,170,770 [2016]; £949,879 [2015];
£676,868 [2014]; £390,887 [2013]

Chabad Lubavitch UK
Registered: 24 Feb 1964 *Employees:* 289 *Volunteers:* 1,000
Tel: 020 8800 0022 *Website:* chabad.org.uk
Activities: Education, training; religious activities
Address: Lubavitch Foundation, 107-115 Stamford Hill, London,
N16 5RP
Trustees: Lubavitch (UK) Limited
Income: £9,598,284 [2015]; £8,749,623 [2014]; £7,508,202 [2013];
£7,954,618 [2012]

Chafyn Grove School
Registered: 3 Jul 2007 *Employees:* 111
Tel: 01722 323114 *Website:* chafyngrove.co.uk
Activities: Education, training
Address: Chafyn Grove School, 33 Bourne Avenue, Salisbury,
Wilts, SP1 1LR
Trustees: Mr D Fowler-Watt, Brigadier Mark Elcomb OBE, Mr John
Perry, Mr Mark Mortimer, Mr Mark Edward Curwen Wordsworth
MRICS, Mr Michael Roy David Roller, Mrs Helen Ruth Lello,
Mrs Annie Parnell, Mr Thomas Frederick Clay ACIB MBA,
Dr Philippa Swayne, Miss Penelope Sari Kirk BEd, Rev Dr Stella
Margaret Wood BA MA DPhil, Mr Nicholas Reginald Maurice Jones
Income: £3,911,266 [2016]; £4,063,818 [2015]; £4,112,946 [2014];
£4,095,933 [2013]; £3,997,203 [2012]

Chai-Lifeline Cancer Care
Registered: 14 Jan 2000 *Employees:* 23 *Volunteers:* 125
Tel: 020 8202 2211 *Website:* chaicancercare.org
Activities: General charitable purposes; education, training;
advancement of health or saving of lives
Address: 144-146 Great North Way, London, NW4 1EH
Trustees: Mrs Louise Hager, Mr Philip David Weinstein, Lord David
Young of Graffam, Dr Adrian Tookman, Lady Kalms, Mrs Susan
Lesley Shipman, Mr Jonathan Andrew Hodes, Mr Richard
Lawrence Segal
Income: £3,068,662 [2017]; £3,366,745 [2016]; £3,032,323 [2015];
£2,729,664 [2014]; £2,184,911 [2013]

Chaigeley Educational Foundation
Registered: 28 Jan 1997 *Employees:* 59
Tel: 01925 752357 *Website:* chaigeley.org.uk
Activities: Education, training
Address: 3 Lincoln Close, Woolston, Warrington, Cheshire,
WA1 4LU
Trustees: Mrs Judith Lukey BSc CertEd JP, Mr Christopher
Haines Bsc (Hons) Alcmeme, Mr Micheal Hennessey BSc PGCE,
Mrs Kay Bohm, Jillyann Atherton, Mrs Ethel Yates, Mr Eric Silk,
Professor Frank O'Gorman BA (Hons) PhD, Will Howell, Mrs Celia
Staunton BDS, Mr Stephen Robert Boothroyd
Income: £2,109,850 [2017]; £1,606,871 [2016]; £2,107,664 [2015];
£1,507,696 [2014]; £1,613,534 [2013]

Chailey Heritage Foundation
Registered: 4 Jun 1999 *Employees:* 393 *Volunteers:* 160
Tel: 01825 724444 *Website:* chf.org.uk
Activities: Education, training; accommodation, housing
Address: Chailey Heritage School, Haywards Heath Road, North
Chailey, Lewes, E Sussex, BN8 4EF
Trustees: Mr Christopher Stanley Jones, Mr Mark Francis Creamer,
Mr William Thomas Cornelius Shelford, Mr David Stoner Crowther,
Mrs Lucinda Baker, Mrs Helen Florence Britton, Mrs Jane Rosalind
Roberts, Mrs Verena Elizabeth Anne Hanbury DL, Mr Michael
Atkinson, Mr Robin Meyer, Dr Elizabeth Mary Green, Mrs Jennifer
Mary Clark
Income: £11,063,000 [2017]; £9,357,000 [2016]; £7,319,000
[2015]; £7,048,000 [2014]; £6,536,000 [2013]

Chain of Hope
Registered: 30 Jun 2000 *Employees:* 15 *Volunteers:* 356
Tel: 020 7351 1978 *Website:* chainofhope.org
Activities: Education, training; advancement of health or saving of
lives; overseas aid, famine relief
Address: Chain of Hope, South Parade, London, SW3 6NP
Trustees: Professor Sir Magdi Yacoub FRS, Professor De Leval,
Mr Victor Tc Tsang, Mr Jonathan Danos, Dr Gavin Wright, Dr Alan
Gordon Magee, Miss Joanna McDwyer
Income: £4,826,504 [2017]; £4,046,855 [2016]; £5,125,616 [2015];
£3,639,488 [2013]; £2,498,311 [2012]

Chalfords Limited
Registered: 24 Jun 1983
Tel: 020 8455 6075
Activities: Education, training; advancement of health or saving of
lives; prevention or relief of poverty; religious activities
Address: New Burlington House, 1075 Finchley Road, London,
NW11 0PU
Trustees: Mr Irwin Leo Weiler, Ms Paula Weiler, Miss Riki Weiler,
Miss Daniella Rosenthal, Mr M Weiler, Mr Nicky Rosenthal,
Ms Monica Frances Rosenthal, Miss Talia Rosenthal, Mr A Weiler
Income: £3,826,483 [2016]; £3,247,559 [2015]; £3,139,742 [2014];
£2,822,552 [2013]; £4,328,224 [2012]

The Chalk Cliff Trust
Registered: 18 Nov 2010
Website: chalkclifftrust.org
Activities: Disability; prevention or relief of poverty; overseas
aid, famine relief; arts, culture, heritage, science; environment,
conservation, heritage; economic, community development,
employment
Address: 18 Keere Street, Lewes, E Sussex, BN7 1TY
Trustees: Ms Justine Margaret Senior, Mr Robert Norman Senior,
Ms Sarah Frances Hunter, Ms Rachel Laura Hunter Senior
Income: £3,014,565 [2017]; £2,975,316 [2016]; £343,886 [2015];
£250,063 [2014]; £102,050 [2013]

The Challenge Network
Registered: 21 Apr 2009 *Employees:* 5,870 *Volunteers:* 876
Website: the-challenge.org
Activities: Education, training
Address: The Challenge Network, Mezzanine Floor, Elizabeth House, 39 York Road, London, SE1 7NQ
Trustees: Mr Colin Smith OBE, Mr Richard Wilson, Ms Michelle Cummins, Mrs Jennifer Ann Zaremba Nee Ashmore, Mr Paul Armstrong, Mr Dan Guthrie, Mr Martin Doel OBE, Mrs Christine Carole Ann Davies CBE
Income: £65,792,000 [2016]; £52,956,000 [2015]; £37,647,000 [2014]; £27,279,156 [2013]; £16,433,279 [2012]

Challenge Partners
Registered: 9 Oct 2012 *Employees:* 17
Tel: 020 7803 4977 *Website:* challengepartners.org
Activities: Education, training
Address: 15th Floor, Tower Building, 11 York Road, London, SE1 7NX
Trustees: Nick Pasricha, Dame Yasmin Bevan DBE, Mr Arwel Jones, Mrs Maxine Low, Dr Kate Chhatwal, Mr Jonathan Andrew Coles, Mr Christopher John Davison, Mr Gary Handforth, Dame Vicki Paterson OBE
Income: £2,696,352 [2017]; £1,970,260 [2016]; £2,147,043 [2015]; £2,152,065 [2014]; £2,366,069 [2013]

The Chamber Orchestra of Europe
Registered: 3 Nov 1981 *Employees:* 5
Tel: 020 7070 3212 *Website:* coeurope.org
Activities: Arts, culture, heritage, science
Address: North House, 27 Great Peter Street, London, SW1P 3LN
Trustees: James Judd, Michael Hoare, Peter Readman
Income: £2,554,461 [2016]; £2,323,755 [2015]; £2,558,857 [2014]; £2,190,128 [2013]; £2,684,326 [2012]

Chance (UK) Ltd
Registered: 5 Jun 1995 *Employees:* 18 *Volunteers:* 160
Tel: 020 7281 5858 *Website:* chanceuk.com
Activities: Education, training; economic, community development, employment
Address: Chance UK, Unit S1-S2, 89-93 Fonthill Road, London, N4 3JH
Trustees: Mr Peter James Stanford, Mr Daniel Houldsworth, Mr Richard James Gordon, Mr Hugh Osborn Thornbery, Mr Andrew George Davidson, Ms Ruth Helen Puttick, Ms Hilary Marion Ruth Reynolds, Ms Janet Lilian Mokades, Mr Debashish Dey, Ms Charlotte Reichwald
Income: £1,056,479 [2017]; £1,245,353 [2016]; £1,150,870 [2015]; £1,150,183 [2014]; £937,421 [2013]

Chance To Shine Foundation Ltd
Registered: 31 Mar 2008 *Employees:* 18 *Volunteers:* 25
Tel: 020 7735 2881 *Website:* chancetoshine.org
Activities: Education, training; disability; amateur sport; economic, community development, employment; recreation
Address: Chance To Shine Foundation, The Laker Stand, The Kia Oval, London, SE11 5SW
Trustees: Mr Caspar Rock, Mr Martin Darlow, Mr Garri Jones, Mr Douglas Peter McAllister, Mr Anshu Jain, Mrs Alison Oliver, Sir John Savill, Mr Donald Brydon, Charlotte Edwards, Sir Daniel Grian Alexander, Mrs Sophie O'Connor, Mr William Lawes
Income: £5,084,000 [2016]; £5,390,000 [2015]; £5,600,000 [2014]; £4,227,000 [2013]; £4,855,000 [2012]

Chance for Childhood
Registered: 11 Aug 1992 *Employees:* 10 *Volunteers:* 2
Tel: 01483 203250 *Website:* chanceforchildhood.org
Activities: Education, training; prevention or relief of poverty; overseas aid, famine relief; accommodation, housing; human rights, religious or racial harmony, equality or diversity
Address: Westmead House, Westmead, Farnborough, Hants, GU14 7LP
Trustees: Mr Dominic White, Mr Anthony William Wellby, Ms Brenda Killen, Ms Claire Hoffman-Mcconnell, Mr Sandip Shah, Mr Mirco Manlio Giacomo Adelchi Bardella
Income: £1,604,544 [2016]; £809,664 [2015]; £621,948 [2014]; £588,842 [2013]; £461,572 [2012]

The Change Foundation
Registered: 27 Apr 1995 *Employees:* 28 *Volunteers:* 1
Tel: 020 8669 2177 *Website:* thechangefoundation.org.uk
Activities: Education, training; disability; amateur sport; economic, community development, employment
Address: The Cricket Centre, Plough Lane, Wallington, Surrey, SM6 8JQ
Trustees: Mr Charles Vallance, Mr Charles Bretton, Mr Harry Lewis, Mrs Angela Gayle Murphy, Ms Asha Haji, Mr Alex Clode, Dr Kafui Tay, Miss Victoria Louise Lowe, Mr Stephen Richard Wootten, Mrs Catriona Helen Webster
Income: £1,101,122 [2017]; £767,062 [2016]; £1,160,945 [2015]; £1,180,172 [2014]; £1,068,348 [2013]

Change, Grow, Live
Registered: 10 Feb 2000 *Employees:* 2,527 *Volunteers:* 1,800
Tel: 01273 677019 *Website:* changegrowlive.org
Activities: Education, training; advancement of health or saving of lives; prevention or relief of poverty; accommodation, housing
Address: 3rd Floor, Northwest Suite, Tower Point, 44 North Road, Brighton, BN1 1YR
Trustees: Mr Nicholas Ernest Burstin, Mrs Gillian Parker, Dr Andreas Raffel, Mr Wilfred Bardsley, Ms Jean Margaret Daintith, Mrs Rachel Findlay, Mike Pringle, Mr John Howard Harris, Mrs Hilary Jackson, Mr Stuart Russell McMinnies, Mrs Sheena Nadine Marie Asthana
Income: £155,970,000 [2017]; £158,326,000 [2016]; £141,267,000 [2015]; £116,815,000 [2014]; £99,817,000 [2013]

Changes Health & Wellbeing
Registered: 6 Dec 2011 *Employees:* 60 *Volunteers:* 100
Tel: 01782 845660 *Website:* changes.org.uk
Activities: Education, training; advancement of health or saving of lives; disability; economic, community development, employment; recreation
Address: Changes Wellbeing Centre, Victoria Court, Booth Street, Stoke on Trent, Staffs, ST4 4AL
Trustees: Ernest John Irons, Kath Hancock, Mr D Tunstall, Miss Alison Ratcliffe, Clair Davis, Mrs Catherine Roberts, Mr B Butler, Mr Desmond Wootton
Income: £1,642,721 [2017]; £1,810,092 [2016]; £1,730,520 [2015]; £1,683,266 [2014]; £1,201,802 [2013]

Changing Faces
Registered: 18 May 1992 *Employees:* 40 *Volunteers:* 400
Tel: 0345 450 0275 *Website:* changingfaces.org.uk
Activities: Education, training; advancement of health or saving of lives; disability
Address: The Squire Centre, 33-37 University Street, London, WC1E 6JN
Trustees: Mr Christopher Walker, Mr Mark Landon, Susan Harrison, Ms Nicola Sawford, Tony Cline, Victoria Hunt, Mr Pieter Folmer, Paul Thomas, Mr David Rough, Richard Castle, Mr David Clayton
Income: £1,792,784 [2017]; £1,848,028 [2016]; £1,647,965 [2015]; £1,432,513 [2014]; £1,714,830 [2013]

Changing Lives Housing Trust
Registered: 10 Mar 2010 *Employees:* 7 *Volunteers:* 5
Website: changingliveshousingtrust.org
Activities: Accommodation, housing
Address: 16 Ownsted Hill, New Addington, Croydon, Surrey, CR0 0JQ
Trustees: Ms Danielle Tumler, Mr Osahon Andrew Okungbowa, Miss Patricia Songhurst
Income: £1,378,656 [2017]; £1,169,821 [2016]; £1,126,592 [2015]; £1,129,381 [2014]; £814,772 [2013]

Changing Lives in Cheshire
Registered: 24 Jan 2011 *Employees:* 29 *Volunteers:* 150
Website: clic-changinglives.org.uk
Activities: Education, training; disability; prevention or relief of poverty; environment, conservation, heritage; economic, community development, employment
Address: Unit 12, Bridge Building, Road Two, Winsford Industrial Estate, Winsford, Cheshire, CW7 3QL
Trustees: Graeme Sherman, Heidi Dilliway-Nickson, Sue Benyon, Gordon Dunn
Income: £1,007,687 [2016]; £898,934 [2015]; £873,991 [2014]; £751,221 [2013]; £356,415 [2012]

Channing House Incorporated, Highgate
Registered: 15 Oct 1964 *Employees:* 133 *Volunteers:* 25
Tel: 020 8340 2719 *Website:* channing.co.uk
Activities: Education, training
Address: Channing School, Highgate Hill, London, N6 5HF
Trustees: Miss Delva Patman FRICS ACIArb FRSA, Rev Daniel Costley, Mr John Alexander, Mr Andrew Appleyard, Mr William Spears, Dr Ingrid Wassenaar, Mr Gilberto Algar-Faria, Dr Helen Stringer, Ms Cindy Leslie, Mrs Julia Burns, Dr Ruth Williams, Ms Brigid Rentoul, Dr Amanda Sutton, Mr Chris Underhill, Ms Aileen Thomas, Ms Lisa Cristie
Income: £15,924,600 [2017]; £14,260,000 [2016]; £13,286,046 [2015]; £10,570,966 [2014]; £9,668,808 [2013]

Chapter (Cardiff) Limited
Registered: 17 May 1971 *Employees:* 113 *Volunteers:* 115
Tel: 029 2030 4400 *Website:* chapter.org
Activities: Education, training; arts, culture, heritage, science
Address: Chapter, Market Road, Canton, Cardiff, CF5 1QE
Trustees: Ms Elin Wyn, Mr Alun Gwynne Jones, Ms Romy Johnson, Ms Yvonne Clare Murphy, Mr Aled Singleton, Ms Cerys Furlong, Mr Laurence Kahn, Professor Steven John Blandford, Mr Enrico Carpanini, Ms Villida Catryn Jennet Ramasut, Mr Robert Andrews, Ms Emma Celeste Fass Del Torto, Mr Benedict Malcolm Borthwick
Income: £4,294,779 [2017]; £4,373,280 [2016]; £4,217,362 [2015]; £4,157,363 [2014]; £3,339,900 [2013]

Chapter 1 Charity Ltd
Registered: 11 Dec 1985 *Employees:* 225
Website: chapter1.org.uk
Activities: Accommodation, housing
Address: 2 Exton Street, London, SE1 8UE
Trustees: Mr Richard Alistair Heron, Mrs Jennifer Laurent-Smart, Mr Nigel Graham Parrington, Rich Blake-Lobb, Mr Andrew Taylor, Commissioner John Matear
Income: £18,551,000 [2016]; £17,639,000 [2015]; £16,392,000 [2014]; £13,970,000 [2013]

Chapter of The Order of The Holy Paraclete
Registered: 15 Apr 1976 *Employees:* 67
Tel: 01947 602079 *Website:* ohpwhitby.org
Activities: General charitable purposes; education, training; advancement of health or saving of lives; religious activities
Address: Chapter of The Order of The Holy Paraclete, St Hilda's Priory, Sneaton Castle, Whitby, N Yorks, YO21 3QN
Trustees: Sister Heather Francis Crane OHP, Sister Jocelyn OHP, Sister Carol Clee, Sister Louisa Ann McCabe, Sister Dorothy Maureen Dean OHP, Sister Janet Elizabeth Davey, Sister Janette Faulkner
Income: £1,434,056 [2017]; £1,448,654 [2016]; £1,713,904 [2015]; £1,300,012 [2014]; £1,483,341 [2013]

The Charis Trust
Registered: 2 Mar 2011 *Volunteers:* 2
Tel: 01245 222874
Activities: General charitable purposes; education, training; advancement of health or saving of lives; disability; prevention or relief of poverty; overseas aid, famine relief; accommodation, housing; religious activities
Address: 2 Hay Green, Danbury, Chelmsford, Essex, CM3 4NU
Trustees: Andrew Green, Mr Andrew Barker, Jonathan Harris, Jane Green, Mr Richard John Green
Income: £1,650,457 [2017]; £1,349,250 [2016]; £1,079,960 [2015]; £1,972,142 [2014]; £1,383,230 [2013]

The Charitable Trusts for University Hospitals Bristol
Registered: 20 Jun 1996 *Employees:* 18 *Volunteers:* 530
Tel: 0117 370 0483 *Website:* aboveandbeyond.org.uk
Activities: The advancement of health or saving of lives
Address: Above and Beyond, The Abbots House, Blackfriars, Bristol, BS1 2NZ
Trustees: Sue Jamison, Mr Peter Scott, Mrs Jane Dean MBA, Mr Lee Aston, Mr Drummond Forbes, Mr James Robert Fox, Dr Christopher Monk, Mr Steve Bluff
Income: £4,732,000 [2017]; £3,280,000 [2016]; £4,636,000 [2015]; £3,686,000 [2014]; £3,414,000 [2013]

Charitable Trusts of The Congregation of Franciscan Missionaries of The Divine Motherhood
Registered: 13 Mar 1964 *Employees:* 44
Tel: 01483 425775 *Website:* fmdminternational.co.uk
Activities: Education, training; advancement of health or saving of lives; disability; prevention or relief of poverty; overseas aid, famine relief; religious activities
Address: Ladywell Convent, Ashstead Lane, Godalming, Surrey, GU7 1ST
Trustees: Sister Jane Bertelsen, Sister Shirley Aeria, Sister Helena McEvilly, Sister Claudia Lee, Sister Helen Doyle, Sister Monica Weedon
Income: £4,653,328 [2016]; £5,257,146 [2015]; £7,574,044 [2014]; £4,553,229 [2013]; £4,475,174 [2012]

Charities Administered ICW The Honourable Society of the Middle Temple
Registered: 25 Nov 1964
Tel: 020 7427 4800
Activities: Education, training
Address: Ashley Building, Middle Temple Lane, London, EC4Y 9BT
Trustees: Miss Diana Cotton QC, Mrs Marilynne Morgan CB, Sir Richard Arnold, Mr William Rodney Stewart Smith
Income: £1,081,000 [2016]; £1,231,000 [2015]; £1,220,000 [2014]; £1,226,000 [2013]; £1,407,000 [2012]

The Charities Aid Foundation
Registered: 1 Jan 1974 *Employees:* 532 *Volunteers:* 35
Tel: 0300 012 3088 *Website:* cafonline.org
Activities: General charitable purposes
Address: Charities Aid Foundation, 25 Kings Hill Avenue, Kings Hill, West Malling, Kent, ME19 4TA
Trustees: Mr James Henry Leigh-Pemberton, Mr Peter Kellner, Mr Robin Bruce Barlow Creswell, Mr Matthew Sean Hammerstein, Miss Tiina Lee, Ms Susannah Storey, Mr Dominic Casserley, Ms Saphieh Ashtiany, Ms Janet Pope, Mr Roger Perkin, Dr Julie Katharine Maxton, Ms Carole Machell
Income: £604,747,000 [2017]; £503,327,000 [2016]; £466,932,000 [2015]; £418,213,000 [2014]; £384,747,000 [2013]

Charities ICW The Spanish and Portuguese Jews Synagogue
Registered: 22 Sep 1967 *Employees:* 33 *Volunteers:* 3
Tel: 020 7289 2573 *Website:* sephardi.org.uk
Activities: Education, training; prevention or relief of poverty; religious activities
Address: Spanish & Portuguese Synagogue, 2 Ashworth Road, Maida Vale, London, W9 1JY
Trustees: Mr David Ereira, Mr Alan Mendoza, Mr Richard Sassoon, Mr Anthony Tricot, Mrs Caroline Jackson-Levy, Mr Sabah Zubaida, Mr Rony Sabah, Mrs Kristine Musikant, Mr Mark Salem
Income: £2,537,042 [2017]; £2,110,860 [2016]; £1,731,417 [2015]; £1,656,341 [2014]; £1,797,617 [2013]

Charities Trust
Registered: 2 Jul 1987 *Employees:* 31
Tel: 0151 286 5129 *Website:* charitiestrust.org.uk
Activities: General charitable purposes
Address: Charities Trust, 22 Century Building, Tower Street, Brunswick Business Park, Liverpool, L3 4BJ
Trustees: Mr Graham John Morris, Mr John Jones, Mr Leslie John Thomas, Mr Mark Hogarth, Mrs Elizabeth Perry, Mr Mark John Blakeman
Income: £42,043,807 [2017]; £19,727,040 [2016]; £29,362,741 [2015]; £18,680,332 [2014]; £2,747,222 [2013]

Charitworth Limited
Registered: 26 Apr 1983
Activities: The prevention or relief of poverty; religious activities
Address: New Burlington House, 1075 Finchley Road, London, NW11 0PU
Trustees: Mr Samuel Jacob Halpern, Mr David Halpern, Mr Sidney Halpern, Mrs Relly Halpern
Income: £1,513,855 [2017]; £1,141,812 [2016]; £1,001,751 [2015]; £897,940 [2014]; £982,444 [2013]

Charity Assets Trust
Registered: 29 Feb 2012
Tel: 020 7963 8139 *Website:* ruffer.co.uk
Activities: Other charitable purposes
Address: Ruffer LLP, 80 Victoria Street, London, SW1E 5JL
Trustees: BNY Mellon (International) Limited
Income: £1,586,000 [2017]; £1,291,000 [2016]; £1,050,000 [2015]; £908,000 [2014]; £458,000 [2013]

The Charity Finance Group
Registered: 25 Apr 1996 *Employees:* 22 *Volunteers:* 235
Tel: 0845 345 3192 *Website:* cfg.org.uk
Activities: Education, training
Address: CFG, 15-18 White Lion Street, London, N1 9PG
Trustees: Ms Kerry Shea, Miss Samantha Anne Husband, Mr John Tranter, Ms Brigid Janssen, Mrs Arati Patel, Mr Simon David William Hopkins, Ms Nicola Jane Deeson, Mr Gary John Forster, Liz Fosbury
Income: £1,871,464 [2017]; £2,013,140 [2016]; £1,806,454 [2015]; £1,689,612 [2014]; £1,556,144 [2013]

Charity Projects
Registered: 18 Apr 1984 *Employees:* 295 *Volunteers:* 2
Tel: 020 7820 2222 *Website:* comicrelief.com
Activities: General charitable purposes; prevention or relief of poverty; overseas aid, famine relief
Address: 89 Albert Embankment, London, SE1 7TP
Trustees: Mr Michael Harris, Dr Dhananjayan Sriskandarajah, Mr Timothy Davie, Mr Harry Cayton OBE, Mrs Diana Barran MBE, Miss Suzi Aplin, Mr Tom Shropshire, Alex Reid, Mr Colin Howes, Mr Richard Curtis CBE, Ms Theo Sowa, Ms Tessy Ojo, Ms Tristia Clarke, Saul Klein, Charlotte Moore, Dr Sue Black
Income: £104,718,000 [2017]; £92,221,000 [2016]; £106,158,000 [2015]; £84,424,000 [2014]; £114,166,636 [2013]

Charity Right
Registered: 12 Oct 2015 *Employees:* 6 *Volunteers:* 10
Tel: 01274 400389 *Website:* charityright.org.uk
Activities: The prevention or relief of poverty; overseas aid, famine relief
Address: Oakwood Court, City Road, Bradford, BD8 8JY
Trustees: Mr Azim Ul-Hasan Kidwai, Mr Azhar Khan, Mr Fraz Butt, Dr Jaafar El-Murad
Income: £1,204,742 [2016]

Charity for Roman Catholic Purposes Administered in Connection with the Congregation of Our Lady of The Missions
Registered: 18 Jul 1968 *Employees:* 41
Tel: 020 8863 6717 *Website:* rndm.org
Activities: Education, training; advancement of health or saving of lives; overseas aid, famine relief; religious activities
Address: 108 Spencer Road, Harrow, Middlesex, HA3 7AR
Trustees: Sister Anne Cleary, Sister Margaret Trower Ward Murphy, Sister Margaret Anne McMahon, Sister Rosemary Harbinson, Sister Mary B Toner, Sister Brigid Mary Quinn, Sister Catherine Patricia Corrigan
Income: £1,476,735 [2016]; £1,221,727 [2015]; £1,358,232 [2014]; £1,447,488 [2013]; £1,327,541 [2012]

141

Charity for Roman Catholic Purposes Administered in Connection with the Congregation of The Franciscan Missionary Sisters (Littlehampton)
Registered: 20 Mar 1964 *Employees:* 76
Tel: 020 7566 4000 *Website:* franciscan.co.uk
Activities: The advancement of health or saving of lives; religious activities
Address: Kingston Smith & Partners LLP, Devonshire House, 60 Goswell Road, London, EC1M 7AD
Trustees: Sister Brenda Clare Bowers, Sister Ann McLaughlin, Susan Rudkin, Sister Clare Bernadette Knowles, Sister Elizabeth Morris
Income: £1,653,507 [2017]; £1,713,316 [2016]; £1,607,631 [2015]; £1,520,744 [2014]; £1,474,291 [2013]

Charity for Roman Catholic Purposes Administered in Connection with the English Province of The Community of The Religious of Jesus and Mary
Registered: 18 May 1966 *Employees:* 110
Tel: 01394 282386
Activities: Education, training; religious activities
Address: 63 Orwell Road, Felixstowe, Suffolk, IP11 7PP
Trustees: Sister Helen Mary Haigh, Sister Joan Hunter, Sister Patricia Ann Donovan, Sister Gerarda Lawler, Sister Brenda Kilbride, Rev John Mervyn Williams, Sister Maria Del Carmen Aymar Ducet
Income: £5,619,362 [2016]; £5,855,219 [2015]; £5,660,688 [2014]; £5,649,339 [2013]

Charity for Roman Catholic and Other Charitable Purposes Administered in Connexion with the Society of The Holy Child Jesus
Registered: 18 May 1966 *Employees:* 76
Tel: 01865 517852 *Website:* shcj.org
Activities: General charitable purposes; education, training; prevention or relief of poverty; overseas aid, famine relief; religious activities
Address: The Cherwell Centre, 14-16 Norham Gardens, Oxford, OX2 6QB
Trustees: Sister Maria Dinnendahl, Sister Marguerite Bouteloup, Sister Anne Stewart, Sister Jean Newbold, Sister Catriona McPhail, Cornelia Connelly Trustees Inc, Sister Geraldine MacCarthy, Sister Angela O'Connor, Sister Carmel Murtagh, Sister Jenny Bullen, Sister Celestina Oyidu Okwori
Income: £7,441,640 [2016]; £10,344,771 [2015]; £3,293,931 [2014]; £2,991,253 [2013]

Charity for St Joseph's Missionary Society (British Region)
Registered: 26 Jul 1963 *Employees:* 26 *Volunteers:* 2,093
Tel: 0191 383 0351 *Website:* millhillmissionaries.com
Activities: Education, training; prevention or relief of poverty; religious activities
Address: Office of The Regional Bursar, 17 Tenter Terrace, Durham, DH1 4RD
Trustees: Rev Paul Mooney, Bro Eddie Slawinski, Rev Stephen Botto, Rev Dermot Byrne
Income: £2,765,412 [2016]; £2,898,149 [2015]; £2,687,246 [2014]; £2,595,631 [2013]; £3,730,084 [2012]

Charity for St Joseph's Missionary Society (Generalate)
Registered: 17 Sep 2012 *Employees:* 3 *Volunteers:* 1
Tel: 01628 777211 *Website:* millhillmissionaries.com
Activities: General charitable purposes; education, training; prevention or relief of poverty; religious activities; human rights, religious or racial harmony, equality or diversity
Address: Mill Hill Missionaries, P O Box 3608, Maidenhead, Berks, SL6 7UX
Trustees: Bro Jos Boerkamp, Rev Desmond McGillicuddy, Rev Andrew Mukulu MHM, Rev Michael Corcoran, Rev Jimmy Adolacion Lindero MHM
Income: £3,369,487 [2016]; £2,604,350 [2015]; £3,098,510 [2014]; £2,364,851 [2013]

The Charity of The Order of The Marist Sisters Province of England
Registered: 27 May 1963 *Employees:* 156
Tel: 020 8949 1355
Activities: General charitable purposes; education, training; overseas aid, famine relief; religious activities
Address: 55 Thetford Road, New Malden, Surrey, KT3 5DP
Trustees: Sister Patricia Whelan, Sister Angelina McNamara, Sister Helena Coskeran, Sister Anne Ord, Sister Mary Gaffney, Sister Philomena Clyne, Sister Teresa Moran
Income: £7,805,515 [2017]; £7,915,517 [2016]; £7,992,117 [2015]; £7,705,700 [2014]; £7,667,610 [2013]

The Charity of The Roman Union of The Order of St Ursula
Registered: 26 Nov 1965 *Employees:* 22
Tel: 020 8305 0095 *Website:* ursulines.co.uk
Activities: General charitable purposes; education, training; religious activities
Address: Ursuline Community, 66 Crooms Hill, Greenwich, London, SE10 8HG
Trustees: Sister Kathleen Colmer OSU, Sister Felicity Young, Sister Marilyn Ashpole, Sister Maureen Moloney OSU, Sister Patricia Traveller
Income: £4,173,296 [2017]; £1,748,882 [2016]; £1,726,816 [2015]; £1,878,625 [2014]; £1,714,155 [2013]

The Charity of The Sisters of Christ
Registered: 11 Sep 1986 *Employees:* 15
Tel: 020 8543 0594
Activities: Religious activities
Address: Norlands, Mayfield Road, London, SW19 3NF
Trustees: Sister May Magenis, Sister Joyce Bone, Sister Margaret McCormick, Sister Ita Conlan, Sister Guenolee Le Jollec
Income: £2,346,786 [2016]; £404,905 [2015]; £426,166 [2014]; £435,823 [2013]; £435,752 [2012]

The Charles Dunstone Charitable Trust
Registered: 30 Mar 2001
Activities: General charitable purposes
Address: H W Fisher & Co, Acre House, 11-15 William Road, London, NW1 3ER
Trustees: Denis Dunstone, Mr John Edwin Gordon, Mr Adrian Bott, Mr Robert Clarkson
Income: £3,322,058 [2017]; £249,141 [2016]; £1,641,369 [2015]; £229,872 [2014]; £3,265,671 [2013]

The Charles Kalms, Henry Ronson Immanuel College

Registered: 19 Apr 1990 *Employees:* 157 *Volunteers:* 10
Tel: 020 8950 0604 *Website:* immanuelcollege.co.uk
Activities: Education, training
Address: Immanuel College, 87-91 Elstree Road, Bushey, Herts, WD23 4EB
Trustees: Mrs Annette Koslover, Mrs Lynda Dullop, Professor Anthony Warrens, Mr Edward Misrahi, Mr Eliezer Zobin, Mr Henry Clinton-Davis, Dr Daphna Atar, Mr Neal Menashe, Mr Keith Barnett, Mrs Ruth Hoyland, Mrs Michelle Sint, Mrs Lucy Marks, Mrs Erica Marks, Mrs Valerie Helen Eppel, Mrs Hannah Boyden
Income: £12,249,046 [2017]; £10,576,923 [2016]; £8,519,123 [2015]; £8,199,565 [2014]; £8,530,981 [2013]

The Charles Wolfson Charitable Trust

Registered: 8 Jan 1965
Tel: 020 7079 2506
Activities: General charitable purposes
Address: Charles Wolfson Charitable Trust, 8-10 Hallam Street, London, W1W 6NS
Trustees: Lord Simon Adam Wolfson, Honourable Andrew Daniel Wolfson, Dr Sara Levene, Lord David Wolfson
Income: £5,405,062 [2017]; £6,316,647 [2016]; £7,226,246 [2015]; £5,022,263 [2014]; £5,065,278 [2013]

The Charleston Trust (Bloomsbury in Sussex)

Registered: 17 Dec 2004 *Employees:* 30 *Volunteers:* 111
Tel: 01323 815165 *Website:* charleston.org.uk
Activities: General charitable purposes; education, training; arts, culture, heritage, science; environment, conservation, heritage
Address: Charleston, Firle, Lewes, E Sussex, BN8 6LL
Trustees: Mr David Pickard, Mrs Marion Gibbs CBE, Mr Mark Burch, Mr Simon Martin, Mr Jolyon Lawrence Brewis, Mrs Virginia Nicholson, Ms Anne Morrison, Professor Michael Farthing, Ms Pippa Harris
Income: £3,993,334 [2016]; £2,617,229 [2015]; £1,399,644 [2014]; £1,224,234 [2013]; £1,023,659 [2012]

Charlotte House School Limited

Registered: 27 Sep 1967 *Employees:* 24 *Volunteers:* 6
Tel: 01923 772101 *Website:* charlottehouseprepschool.co.uk
Activities: Education, training
Address: 88 The Drive, Rickmansworth, Herts, WD3 4DU
Trustees: Adam Hatfield, Mrs Sarah Starr BA Hons, Mr Paul McGlone, Mr David Kyrill Baker, Mrs Judith Margaret Parr, Mr Robert Frank Kay, Catriona Smith, Mrs Diana Margaret Phillipa Wilson, Mrs Helen Davison
Income: £1,410,195 [2017]; £1,412,450 [2016]; £1,360,870 [2015]; £1,217,138 [2014]; £1,047,619 [2013]

Charlton Triangle Homes Limited

Registered: 10 Mar 1999 *Employees:* 15
Tel: 020 8319 9262 *Website:* charltontriangle.org.uk
Activities: Accommodation, housing; economic, community development, employment
Address: Charlton Triangle Homes, 9-10 Cedar Court, Fairlawn, London, SE7 7JL
Trustees: Councillor Allan MacCarthy, Mr Aeron Allen, Mr Shafiq Ahmed, Ms Lisa Benge, Mrs Ambreen Hisbani, Mrs Claudia Hamilton, Mr Norman Adams, Mr Richard Stevens, Mr Aseem Kumar, Ms Gillian Dorren, Mrs Averil Lekau
Income: £6,465,000 [2017]; £6,308,000 [2016]; £5,897,000 [2015]; £5,580,000 [2014]; £5,337,000 [2013]

Charnwood 20:20

Registered: 29 Aug 2007 *Employees:* 32 *Volunteers:* 300
Tel: 01509 236144 *Website:* twentytwenty.org.uk
Activities: Education, training; economic, community development, employment
Address: The Schofield Centre, Greenclose Lane, Loughborough, Leics, LE11 5AS
Trustees: Ms Sarah Webster, Mr Yiannis Koursis, Mr Ian Lewis, Ms Sarah Tomlinson
Income: £1,242,831 [2017]; £1,229,239 [2016]; £861,922 [2015]; £618,007 [2014]; £538,039 [2013]

Chartered Accountants' Benevolent Association

Registered: 24 Nov 2006 *Employees:* 38 *Volunteers:* 49
Tel: 01788 556366 *Website:* caba.org.uk
Activities: General charitable purposes; education, training; advancement of health or saving of lives; disability; prevention or relief of poverty; accommodation, housing; other charitable purposes
Address: Chartered Accountants' Benevolent Association, 8 Mitchell Court, Castle Mound Way, Rugby, Warwicks, CV23 0UY
Trustees: Ms Heather Lamont, Mr Robin Fieth BA Hons FCA, Mrs Liz Hazell, Mr Kaaeed Mamujee, Mary Hardy, Mr Colin Williams, Ms Susan Field, Mr Kenneth Coppock, Mrs Caitriona Flynn, Mrs Helen Morris, Mr David Leafe
Income: £2,730,927 [2016]; £3,510,000 [2015]; £4,879,100 [2014]; £4,166,900 [2013]; £1,974,100 [2012]

The Chartered Association of Business Schools

Registered: 27 Jul 2015 *Employees:* 9
Tel: 020 7236 7678 *Website:* charteredabs.org
Activities: Education, training
Address: 3rd Floor, 40 Queen Street, London, EC4R 1DD
Trustees: Professor Baback Yazdani, Ms Donna Whitehead, Professor Angus Wallace Laing, Professor Veronica Hope Hailey, Professor Julia Clarke, Professor Heather Kathleen McLaughlin, Professor Simon Charles Collinson, Professor Zoe Jane Radnor, Mr Jerry William Forrester, Professor Frances Bowen, Professor David Richard Oglethorpe
Income: £1,486,066 [2017]; £1,315,446 [2016]

The Chartered Institute for Securities and Investment

Registered: 11 Nov 2009 *Employees:* 155
Website: cisi.org
Activities: Education, training
Address: 20 Fenchurch Street, London, EC3M 3BY
Trustees: Mr Alan Stuart Ramsay, Mr Richard Anthony Charnock, Richard Wastcoat, Mr David Arthur Kane, Miss Fionnuala Mary Carvill, Mrs Rebecca Taylor, Mr Andrew Thomas Karl Westenberger FCA, Mr Daniel John Corrigan, Mr Gary Teper, Mr Nicholas Roger Swales, Mr Clive John Shelton, Mr Alan Colin Drake Yarrow, Ms Philippa Foster Back, Martin Sean Watkins, Mrs Claire Michelle Perryman, Miss Debbie Elizabeth Clarke, Mr Ravikumar Puranam, Miss Joanna Ruth Place
Income: £14,356,401 [2017]; £14,426,118 [2016]; £13,274,530 [2015]; £12,589,730 [2014]; £11,777,101 [2013]

The Chartered Institute of Arbitrators
Registered: 19 Jul 1990 *Employees:* 61 *Volunteers:* 155
Website: ciarb.org
Activities: Education, training
Address: Chartered Institute of Arbitrators, 12-14 Bloomsbury Square, London, WC1A 2LP
Trustees: Christopher Ojo, Axel Reeg, Anthony Houghton SC, Jonathan Wood, Ms Marion Smith QC, Arran Dowling Hussey, Ann Ryan Robertson, Peter Rees QC, Richard Morris, Michael Tonkin, Mr Anthony Louis Marks, John Wakefield
Income: £7,037,058 [2016]; £7,119,456 [2015]; £6,333,602 [2014]; £5,645,313 [2013]; £5,460,850 [2012]

The Chartered Institute of Building
Registered: 25 Sep 1980 *Employees:* 121
Tel: 01344 630732 *Website:* ciob.org.uk
Activities: Education, training; economic, community development, employment
Address: The Chartered Institute of Building, Novell House, 1 Arlington Square, Downshire Way, Bracknell, Berks, RG12 1WA
Trustees: Prof Charles Egbu, Mr Nigel Croxford FCIOB, Mr Raymond Ford, Mr Christopher Soffe, Mr Stephen Lines, Mr Ivan McCarthy, Mr Timothy Barrett, Mr David Philp, Mr Gavin Maxwell-Hart FCIOB, Mr Michael Smith, Mrs Rebecca Thompson, Ms Christine Gausden, Mrs Virginia Borkoski, Mr Richard Sapcote, Mr Stephen Nitman
Income: £11,056,000 [2016]; £10,237,000 [2015]; £12,120,000 [2014]; £10,415,000 [2013]; £8,623,000 [2012]

Chartered Institute of Credit Management
Registered: 17 Jul 2015 *Employees:* 41
Tel: 01780 722912 *Website:* cicm.com
Activities: Education, training; other charitable purposes
Address: CICM, The Water Mill, Station Road, South Luffenham, Oakham, Rutland, LE15 8NB
Trustees: Mr Glen Stewart Bullivant FCICM, David Thornley FCICM, Mr Peter James Whitmore, Larry Coltman FCICM, Laurie Beagle FCICM
Income: £2,990,091 [2016]

Chartered Institute of Environmental Health
Registered: 1 Nov 1984 *Employees:* 108 *Volunteers:* 300
Tel: 020 7928 6006 *Website:* cieh.org
Activities: Education, training; environment, conservation, heritage
Address: 10 Beningfield Drive, St Albans, Herts, AL2 1UJ
Trustees: Mr Nicholas James Pahl, Ms Joanne Wyatt, Mr Kevin David Gould, Mr Graeme Kenneth Mitchell, Mr Jonathan Hayes, Mrs Dawn Michelle Welham, Mr Steven Cooper BA (Hons) MSc FCIEH, Mr Siraj Choudhury, Ms Terenja Humphries, Mr Timothy Jasper Aplin Nichols, Mr Mike Paul Owen
Income: £8,403,000 [2016]; £12,008,000 [2015]; £11,934,000 [2014]; £11,489,000 [2013]; £11,588,000 [2012]

The Chartered Institute of Housing
Registered: 9 Aug 1965 *Employees:* 110
Tel: 024 7685 1770 *Website:* cih.org
Activities: Education, training; accommodation, housing; economic, community development, employment; other charitable purposes
Address: Chartered Institute of Housing, Octavia House, Westwood Way, Westwood Business Park, Coventry, Warwicks, CV4 8JP
Trustees: Hiten Patel, Anne Chapman, Geraldine Howley, Keith Anderson, Elaine Elkington, Robert Grundy, Gordon Perry, Julie Fadden
Income: £9,333,000 [2016]; £10,154,000 [2015]; £11,230,000 [2014]; £11,259,000 [2013]; £11,774,000 [2012]

Chartered Institute of Library and Information Professionals
Registered: 5 May 1964 *Employees:* 49 *Volunteers:* 300
Tel: 020 7255 0512 *Website:* cilip.org.uk
Activities: Education, training; arts, culture, heritage, science; economic, community development, employment
Address: Cilip, 7 Ridgmount Street, London, WC1E 7AE
Trustees: Martyn Wade, Caroline Brazier, David Byrne, Gary Birkenhead, Caroline Carruthers, Chloe Menown, Alison Wheeler, Mike Hosking, Karen McFarlane, John Trevor-Allen, Jo Webb, Leon Bolton
Income: £4,738,350 [2016]; £4,562,547 [2015]; £4,714,342 [2014]; £4,722,938 [2013]; £4,811,550 [2012]

The Chartered Institute of Logistics and Transport in the UK
Registered: 17 Oct 1991 *Employees:* 71 *Volunteers:* 500
Tel: 01536 740147 *Website:* ciltuk.org.uk
Activities: Education, training
Address: CILT, Earlstrees Court, Earlstrees Industrial Estate, Corby, Northants, NN17 4AX
Trustees: Mr Geoffrey Howard Catterick, Mrs Margaret Everson, Mr David Pugh, Mr Martijn Gilbert, Ms Emma Ross, Mr Christopher John Marrow, Mr Christopher Hutchinson, Professor Richard Wilding, Ms Jane Green, Mr Nicholas Philip Richardson, Helen Gallimore, Mr Peter Karran, Mr John Carr, Mr Paul Hunter
Income: £4,443,000 [2017]; £4,682,000 [2016]; £4,701,000 [2015]; £4,519,000 [2014]; £5,533,000 [2013]

Chartered Institute of Personnel and Development
Registered: 10 Mar 2000 *Employees:* 364 *Volunteers:* 1,000
Tel: 020 8612 6700 *Website:* cipd.co.uk
Activities: General charitable purposes; education, training; economic, community development, employment
Address: Chartered Institute of Personnel & Development, 151 The Broadway, London, SW19 1JQ
Trustees: Mrs Louise Fisher, Ms Tanith Dodge, Ms Anna Kyprianou, Mr Alan Price, Ms Yetunde Hofmann, Ms Helen Pitcher, Professor Cary Cooper, Mr Peter Cheese, Mr Neil Morrison, Ms Anne Sharp, Mr Shakil Butt, Mr Jonathan Ferrar
Income: £40,042,000 [2017]; £40,028,000 [2016]; £41,225,000 [2015]; £45,849,000 [2014]; £43,955,000 [2013]

The Chartered Institute of Procurement and Supply
Registered: 5 Mar 1993 *Employees:* 140
Tel: 01780 761504 *Website:* cips.org
Activities: Education, training
Address: The Chartered Institute of Procurement & Supply, Easton House, Easton on the Hill, Stamford, Lincs, PE9 3NZ
Trustees: Mr Bill Crothers FCIPS, Ms Nikki Bell FCIPS, Ms Michelle Wang FCIPS, Mr Grahame Ball FCIPS, Ms Alison Barto FCIPS, Ms Fiona Revell FCIPS, Mr Guy Strafford FCIPS, Ms Sue Moffatt FCIPS, Mr Tim Richardson FCIPS, Ms Fabienne Lesbros FCIPS, Ms Sara Omer FCIPS
Income: £27,696,000 [2016]; £24,142,165 [2015]; £22,961,000 [2014]; £21,553,000 [2013]; £20,708,000 [2012]

The Chartered Institute of Public Finance and Accountancy
Registered: 13 Apr 1964 *Employees:* 275 *Volunteers:* 912
Tel: 020 7543 5600 *Website:* cipfa.org
Activities: Education, training
Address: CIPFA, 77 Mansell Street, London, E1 8AN
Trustees: Mr Andrew Burns CPFA, Mrs Sarah Howard CPFA, Mrs Carolyn Williamson CPFA, Mr Brian Roberts CPFA, Mr Peter Kane CPFA, Mr Andy Hardy CPFA
Income: £23,623,000 [2016]; £27,139,000 [2015]; £36,297,000 [2014]; £26,081,000 [2013]; £25,514,000 [2012]

The Chartered Institute of Taxation

Registered: 19 May 1994 *Employees:* 80 *Volunteers:* 700
Tel: 020 7340 0555 *Website:* tax.org.uk
Activities: Education, training; other charitable purposes
Address: Chartered Institute of Taxation, Artillery House, 11-19 Artillery Row, London, SW1P 1RT
Trustees: Mr Jonathan Leonard Endacott, Dr Andrew Neville Hubbard, Mr Paul Stephen Aplin, Ms Emma Jane Mary Chamberlain, Mr William John Ignatius Dodwell, Mr Keith Michael Gordon, Mr Gary James Ashford, Mr Christopher John Lallemand, Mr Raymond McCann, Mr Ian Edward Hayes, Mr Michael John Thexton, Mr Glyn William Fullelove, Mr Alexander Kenneth Garden, Mrs Mary Cicely Florence Monfries, Mrs Claire Hooper, Tracy Ann Easman, Mr Keith Edward Bell, Mr Ian Duncan Menzies-Conacher, Mr John Edward Barnett, Mr Christopher Malcolm Brydone, Mrs Catherine Anne Fairpo, Ms Susan Mary Ball, Mr Daniel Fletcher Lyons, Mr John David Preston, Mr John Henry Voyez, Mrs Moira Grace Kelly, Ms Amanda Jane Pearson, Mrs Jennifer Theresa Rimmer, Mr Peter Cyril Rayney, Mr Jonathan Charles Riley, Mrs Nichola Anne Ross Martin
Income: £7,541,372 [2016]; £7,491,601 [2015]; £7,261,855 [2014]; £6,811,421 [2013]; £6,415,359 [2012]

The Chartered Institution of Building Services Engineers

Registered: 19 Nov 1979 *Employees:* 60 *Volunteers:* 2,000
Tel: 020 8675 5211 *Website:* cibse.org
Activities: Education, training; environment, conservation, heritage
Address: CIBSE, 222 Balham High Road, London, SW12 9BS
Trustees: Mr Stephen Lisk FSLL, Mr John Field MCIBSE, Mr Ashley Bateson CEng FCIBSE, Mr Paddy Roger Thomas Conaghan, Mr Adrian Catchpole CEng FCIBSE, Mr Kevin Mitchell CEng MCIBSE, Mr Peter Yiu Sun Wong, Mr Stuart John Macpherson CEng FCIBSE, Ms Susan Angela Hone-Brookes, Professor Lynne Barbara Jack, Dr Kevin Kelly CEng FCIBSE FSLL
Income: £6,990,660 [2016]; £6,731,661 [2015]; £6,427,178 [2014]; £6,076,918 [2013]; £5,863,357 [2012]

Chartered Institution of Civil Engineering Surveyors

Registered: 2 Sep 2009 *Employees:* 10 *Volunteers:* 150
Tel: 0161 972 3100 *Website:* cices.org
Activities: Education, training
Address: Chartered Ices, Dominion House, Sibson Road, Sale, Cheshire, M33 7PP
Trustees: Mr Michael Sutton, Howard Klein, Mr Mark Andrew Hudson, Mr Ian Bush FCInstCES, Mr Robert Cowan MCInstCES, John Battersby, Richard Maltby, Bert Palmer, Mr Andrew Turner MCInstCES, Mr Chris Birchall, Mr John Bacon FInstCES, Mr Ivan Warnes FCInstCES, Mr Alan Barrow FCInstCES, Mr Henry Bell MCInstCES, David Loosemore, Peter Randall, Mr Mark Shaw FCInstCES
Income: £1,017,405 [2017]; £952,665 [2016]; £967,158 [2015]; £872,864 [2014]; £859,583 [2013]

The Chartered Institution of Highways and Transportation

Registered: 15 Jul 2010 *Employees:* 23 *Volunteers:* 750
Tel: 020 7336 1555 *Website:* ciht.org.uk
Activities: General charitable purposes; education, training; economic, community development, employment
Address: 119 Britannia Walk, London, N1 7JE
Trustees: Mr Steve Rowsell BSc CEng MICE MCIPS MCIHT, Mr Andreas Markides BSc MSc CEng FCIHT MICE, Ms Deborah Sims BSc Hons MSc CEng FCIHT HonMSoRSA, Mr Martin Tugwell BSc CEng MICE FCIHT, Russell Bennett BEng MBA CEng MICE MCMI FCIHT, Mr Glenn Lyons BEng TPP MCIHT PhD MTPS, Ms Ginny Clarke BSc CEng MICE FCIHT OBE, Mr Spencer Palmer BEng CEng FCIHT, Mr Matthew Lugg OBE BEng CEng MICE DMS MCIHT, Mr Peter Brown BSc MSc Eng DIC CEng FCIHT, Mr Gordon Baker BSc CEng FCIHT MIOD CDir, Ms Dana Barbara Skelley OBE BEng MBA CEng MICE MCMI FCIHT
Income: £2,592,129 [2016]; £2,557,424 [2015]; £2,341,252 [2014]; £2,222,529 [2013]; £2,041,475 [2012]

Chartered Institution of Wastes Management

Registered: 6 Mar 2002 *Employees:* 49 *Volunteers:* 400
Tel: 01604 620426 *Website:* ciwm.co.uk
Activities: General charitable purposes; education, training; arts, culture, heritage, science; environment, conservation, heritage
Address: 7-9 St Peter's Gardens, Marefair, Northampton, NN1 1SX
Trustees: Mr John Ferguson OBE, Mr Terrence March, Dr Margaret Bates, Mr Stephen J Didsbury, Mr Malcolm J Sharp, Mr Trevor J Nicoll, Mr David Wilson, Dr Anna Willetts, Mr Michael Ellis, Mr Charles Devine, Mr Stephen Corne, Mr Tony Law, Mr Gareth David Morton, Mrs Judith Harper, Ms Rebecca Colley, Mr Enda Kiernan, Dr Colin F Clark, Mr Dan A P Cooke, Ms Jennifer Watts, Mr John Downer, Dr Adam Read, Dr Stephen Wise, Mr Toddy Cuthbert, Mr Michael Dunn, Mr Robert Little
Income: £6,180,710 [2016]; £2,927,549 [2015]; £3,401,790 [2014]; £2,761,975 [2013]; £2,689,065 [2012]

The Chartered Institution of Water and Environmental Management

Registered: 19 Jan 1995 *Employees:* 20 *Volunteers:* 200
Tel: 020 7831 3110 *Website:* ciwem.org
Activities: Education, training; environment, conservation, heritage
Address: CIWEM, 106-109 Saffron Hill, London, EC1N 8QS
Trustees: Jim Oatridge, Mr Chris Bosher, Mr Rafid Alkhaddar Professor, Mr Bruce Keith, Mr Richard Edward Laikin, Mr Paul Seeley, Ms Stephanie Campbell, Mr David McHugh, Mr David Wickens, Dr Norman Lowe OBE, James Lamb, Mrs Angela Caroline Gray, Mr John Alexander Rowley, Mrs Nicola Jane Roach, Professor Roger Falconer
Income: £2,535,877 [2016]; £2,487,872 [2015]; £3,306,631 [2014]; £2,357,109 [2013]; £2,296,929 [2012]

Chartered Management Institute

Registered: 11 Mar 2002 *Employees:* 152 *Volunteers:* 180
Tel: 01536 207491 *Website:* managers.org.uk
Activities: Education, training
Address: Chartered Management Institute, Management House, Cottingham Road, Corby, Northants, NN17 1TT
Trustees: Mr Patrick Dunne CCMI, Mrs Valerie Dias CCMI, Mr Mike Clasper CBE CCMI, Mr Richard Thomas CMgr FCMI, Ms Liz White, Ms Heather Melville CCMI, Professor Baback Yazdani, Mrs Ann Francke CMgr CCMI, Mr Bruce Carnegie-Brown CCMI, Dr Marcella Monaghan CMgr MCMI, Mr Peter Marchbank, Ms Liz Hoskin CMgr FCMI
Income: £13,253,000 [2017]; £12,725,000 [2016]; £11,680,000 [2015]; £11,033,000 [2014]; £11,268,000 [2013]

The Chartered Quality Institute
Registered: 5 Nov 1969 *Employees:* 51 *Volunteers:* 75
Tel: 020 7245 8521 *Website:* quality.org
Activities: Education, training; economic, community development, employment
Address: 2nd Floor, North Chancery Exchange, 10 Furnival Street, London, EC4A 1AB
Trustees: Mr David Straker, Mr Andy Pitt, Mrs Louise Kavanagh, Ms Roxann Dawson, Ms Amanda Susan McKay, Mr Ian Mitchell, Mr Richard Allan, Mr Mike Turner
Income: £5,316,000 [2016]; £5,573,000 [2015]; £5,061,000 [2014]; £5,557,000 [2013]; £5,154,000 [2012]

Chartered Surveyors Training Trust
Registered: 11 Jun 1987 *Employees:* 9
Tel: 01273 708755 *Website:* cstt.org.uk
Activities: Education, training
Address: Oaklawn, Burnhams Road, Bookham, Leatherhead, Surrey, KT23 3BB
Trustees: William Hill, Ms Antonia Belcher BSc (Hons) FRICS, Dr Wendy Finlay BSc PhD, Mr Kevin Arnold BSc (Hons) MRICS, Mr Ashley Wheaton BA
Income: £1,799,783 [2017]; £1,114,138 [2016]; £508,927 [2015]; £399,069 [2014]; £338,683 [2013]

Charterhouse Club
Registered: 18 Sep 1995 *Employees:* 105
Website: charterhouseclub.co.uk
Activities: Education, training; amateur sport
Address: Charterhouse School, Brooke Hall, Charterhouse, Godalming, Surrey, GU7 2DX
Trustees: Mr James Bovill, Margaret Roser, Mr Hereward Taylor, Mrs Nicola Edge, Mr David Armitage MBE
Income: £1,323,486 [2017]; £1,340,827 [2016]; £1,243,402 [2015]; £1,219,140 [2014]; £1,225,996 [2013]

Charterhouse School
Registered: 6 Mar 1964 *Employees:* 455
Tel: 01483 291602 *Website:* charterhouse.org.uk
Activities: Education, training
Address: Charterhouse, Hurtmore Road, Godalming, Surrey, GU7 2DF
Trustees: Dr Ralph Townsend MA DPhil, Prof Michael Collins MA DPhil, Mr David Royds, Mrs Clare Curran, Professor Vince Clive Emery PhD FSB, Mr Julian Ide, Mr Edward Durell Barnes, Mr Charles Oulton, The Very Revd Dianna Gwilliams BA MA, Peter Norris, Mr Dale F Jennings MA DipArch RIBA, Mr James Bovill, Mr Andrew Reid MA MBA FCA, Mr David Macey, Ms Camilla Baldwin
Income: £31,140,000 [2017]; £29,558,000 [2016]; £28,168,000 [2015]; £27,797,000 [2014]; £26,996,000 [2013]

The Chaseley Trust
Registered: 13 Feb 2002 *Employees:* 140 *Volunteers:* 4
Website: chaseley.org.uk
Activities: The advancement of health or saving of lives; disability
Address: The Chaseley Trust, South Cliff, Eastbourne, E Sussex, BN20 7JH
Trustees: Mr Patrick Salmon, Mr Jeremy James Quinton Howes LLB, Tracey May, Mr Richard Bugler, Mr Roger Geoffrey Musson
Income: £4,456,121 [2016]; £2,888,009 [2015]; £3,524,243 [2014]; £3,944,325 [2013]; £5,125,635 [2012]

The Chatham Historic Dockyard Trust
Registered: 10 Jul 1985 *Employees:* 142 *Volunteers:* 306
Tel: 01892 852645 *Website:* thedockyard.co.uk
Activities: Education, training; environment, conservation, heritage
Address: Old Milk Lodge, Church Road, Rotherfield, Crowborough, E Sussex, TN6 3LA
Trustees: Mr Rodney Brian Chambers, Mr Paul David Hudson, Councillor David John Carr, Mrs Sandra Marie Matthews-Marsh, Sir Trevor Alan Soar, Miss Sarah Elizabeth Roots, Mr Pommy Sarwal, Sir Ian Charles Franklin Andrews, Mrs Laura Cicely Alison Nesfield, Mr Murray Hallam, Mr William Anthony Corbett
Income: £6,327,688 [2017]; £6,501,052 [2016]; £12,876,758 [2015]; £6,737,237 [2014]; £5,807,382 [2013]

Chatham Maritime Trust
Registered: 30 May 1996 *Employees:* 7
Tel: 01634 891888 *Website:* cmtrust.co.uk
Activities: Environment, conservation, heritage; other charitable purposes
Address: East Wing, Ground Floor, The Observatory, Brunel, Dock Road, Chatham Maritime, Kent, ME4 4AF
Trustees: Mr Adrian Horwood, Mr Steve Harriott, Mr Anthony Sutton, Ms Kelly Tolhurst, Mr Vince Maple, Mr Habib Tejan, Mr David Taylor, Mr Vic Towell, Mr Andrew Mackness, Mrs Deborah Sims, Mr Bob Russell, Peter Haigh
Income: £2,650,463 [2017]; £1,532,901 [2016]; £1,414,991 [2015]; £1,439,837 [2014]; £1,653,911 [2013]

Chatsworth House Trust
Registered: 6 Mar 1981 *Employees:* 150 *Volunteers:* 175
Tel: 01246 565300 *Website:* chatsworth.org
Activities: Arts, culture, heritage, science; environment, conservation, heritage
Address: Chatsworth House Trust, The Estate Office, Edensor, Bakewell, Derbys, DE45 1PJ
Trustees: Mr Edward Roland Haslewood Perks, Mr Henry Mark Wyndham, The Duke of Devonshire, Mr Guy Monson, Mr John David Sebastian Booth, The Hon Mrs C Chetwood, The Duchess of Devonshire, Mr Mark William Fane
Income: £13,203,000 [2017]; £13,639,000 [2016]; £11,735,460 [2014]; £10,858,696 [2013]; £10,715,923 [2012]

Cheadle Hulme School
Registered: 13 Aug 1999 *Employees:* 277 *Volunteers:* 15
Tel: 0161 488 3330 *Website:* cheadlehulmeschool.co.uk
Activities: Education, training
Address: Cheadle Hulme School, Claremont Road, Cheadle Hulme, Cheadle, Cheshire, SK8 6EF
Trustees: Dr David Noel Riley, Mr Peter John Driver, Mrs Catherine Jane Boyd, Mr Michael Birchall, Mr Martin Gavin Tyley, Mr Michael James Bolinbroke, Mrs Joanne Squire, Mr Philip Robert Johnson, Mr Chris Roberts, Mrs Kay Marie Marshall, Ms Joanne Elizabeth Birkett
Income: £14,827,000 [2017]; £14,964,000 [2016]; £13,942,000 [2015]; £14,531,000 [2014]; £12,685,000 [2013]

Cheam School Educational Trust
Registered: 22 Oct 1984 *Employees:* 165
Tel: 01635 267800 *Website:* cheamschool.co.uk
Activities: Education, training
Address: Cheam School, Newbury Road, Headley, Thatcham, Berks, RG19 8LD
Trustees: Mrs Sarah Scrope, Mrs Wendy Batchelor, Mr Richard Marsh, Mr Richard William Graham Hornsby, Mrs Antonia May, Mrs Emma Dawson, Mr Denis Tinsley, Mr Richard Haydon Moore, Mr Jonathan Leigh, Mr Brian Reid, Mr Nick Adams
Income: £7,475,634 [2017]; £7,343,661 [2016]; £7,442,594 [2015]; £7,195,839 [2014]; £6,861,256 [2013]

Chelmer Housing Partnership Limited
Registered: 19 Sep 2012 *Employees:* 266 *Volunteers:* 29
Tel: 0300 555 0500 *Website:* chp.org.uk
Activities: Education, training; advancement of health or saving of lives; disability; prevention or relief of poverty; accommodation, housing
Address: Myriad House, 23 Springfield Lyons Approach, Springfield, Chelmsford, Essex, CM2 5LB
Trustees: Mr Keith John Andrew, Rosemary Braithwaite, Mrs Joanna Wanmer, Mr Peter John Cogan, Mr Stephen George Bennett, Ms Nicola Sawford, Mr Robin John Tebbutt, Mr Neil Ian Fisher, Mr Marc Noaro
Income: £62,627,000 [2017]; £51,340,000 [2016]; £47,868,000 [2015]; £42,876,000 [2014]; £42,103,000 [2013]

The Chelmsford Diocesan Board of Finance
Registered: 13 Oct 1966 *Employees:* 139 *Volunteers:* 450
Tel: 01245 294426 *Website:* chelmsford.anglican.org
Activities: Religious activities
Address: 53 New Street, Chelmsford, Essex, CM1 1AT
Trustees: The Ven Michael John Lodge, The Ven Annette Cooper, Miss Mary Moore, The Ven Elizabeth Snowden, Canon Jillian Sarah Leonard, The Ven Dr John Perumbalath, Rev Louise Williams, The Rt Revd Stephen Cottrell, Mr Frank Hawkins, Mr Richard Ford Freeman, Miss Vevet Deer, Mr Percy Lomax, Mr Peter Morriss, Rt Revd Roger Morris, Canon Dean Gillespie, Canon Roger James Ennals, The Ven Vanessa Anne Herrick, The Ven Elwin Cockett, Mr Robert Hammond, Mr Roger Shilling, The Very Revd Nicholas Henshall, Rev Marie Segal, Mrs Mary Durlacher, The Revd Canon David Philip Ritchie, Canon John Winterbotham, Mr Ronald Mc Lernon, Mrs Christine Horton, Rt Revd Peter Hill, Mrs Isabel Adcock
Income: £23,859,000 [2016]; £23,905,000 [2015]; £22,836,000 [2014]; £21,647,000 [2013]; £20,937,000 [2012]

Chelsea FC Foundation
Registered: 19 May 2009 *Employees:* 85 *Volunteers:* 113
Tel: 020 7957 8221 *Website:* chelseafc.com
Activities: Education, training; disability; prevention or relief of poverty; amateur sport
Address: Chelsea Football Club, Stamford Bridge, Fulham Road, London, SW6 1HS
Trustees: Hugh Michael Robertson, Mr Piara Powar, Emma Hayes, Mr Bruce Michael Buck, Mr John Richard Devine, Mr Paul Ramos
Income: £6,493,857 [2017]; £6,796,355 [2016]; £6,502,891 [2015]; £5,430,248 [2014]; £4,682,831 [2013]

The Chelsea Physic Garden Company
Registered: 2 Mar 1983 *Employees:* 21 *Volunteers:* 102
Tel: 020 7352 5646 *Website:* chelseaphysicgarden.co.uk
Activities: Education, training; arts, culture, heritage, science; environment, conservation, heritage
Address: Chelsea Physic Garden, 66 Royal Hospital Road, London, SW3 4HS
Trustees: Mrs Sukie Hemming, Mr Colin Chisholm, Lady Arabella Lennox-Boyd, Mrs Sarah Speller, Mr Quoc Nghi Nguyen, Mr Paul Gray, Patricia Lankester, Mrs Anna Jobson, Mr Michael Prideaux, Mr Michael McGonigle, Mrs Cathy Arnold, Mr Tony Kirkham
Income: £1,501,081 [2016]; £1,416,799 [2015]; £1,369,565 [2014]; £1,157,230 [2013]; £1,019,283 [2012]

Cheltenham College and Cheltenham College Preparatory School
Registered: 10 Jun 1965 *Employees:* 555 *Volunteers:* 7
Tel: 01242 705573 *Website:* cheltenhamcollege.org
Activities: Education, training
Address: Cheltenham College, Bath Road, Cheltenham, Glos, GL53 7LD
Trustees: Mr Michael Wynne, Mrs Ruth Lewis, Dr Paul Wingfield, Mrs Kate Hickey, Mr Robin Badham-Thornhill, Mr Laurence Humphries-Davies, Mrs Emma Goldsmith, Mrs Gillian Ellwood, Mr Bill Straker-Nesbit, Mr Tim Smith BSc FRICS, Mr Hugh Monro, Dr Geraldine Valori, Mr Christopher Cooper, Mr Mark Chicken, Rev Canon Keith Wilkinson
Income: £25,664,000 [2017]; £25,005,000 [2016]; £24,011,000 [2015]; £24,426,000 [2014]; £21,273,000 [2013]

Cheltenham Festivals
Registered: 16 Mar 1967 *Employees:* 58 *Volunteers:* 460
Tel: 01242 537275 *Website:* cheltenhamfestivals.com
Activities: Education, training; arts, culture, heritage, science
Address: Cheltenham Festivals, 109-111 Bath Road, Cheltenham, Glos, GL53 7LS
Trustees: Mr Lewis Carnie, Professor Averil MacDonald, Mrs Susan Catherine Blanchfield, Ms Caroline Hutton, Ms Vivienne Parry, Mr Edward Gillespie, Mr Dominic Collier, Mrs Diane Rebeca Wendy Hill, Mr Peter Howarth
Income: £5,574,578 [2016]; £5,548,359 [2015]; £5,489,842 [2014]; £5,442,903 [2013]; £4,887,251 [2012]

Cheltenham Ladies College
Registered: 13 Jul 1966 *Employees:* 638
Tel: 01242 690445 *Website:* cheltladiescollege.org
Activities: Education, training
Address: Cheltenham Ladies College, Bayshill Road, Cheltenham, Glos, GL50 3EP
Trustees: Mrs Mary Henderson, Ms Sally Boyle, Ms Libby Bassett, Mrs Louise Terry, Mr David Pittaway QC, Dr Valerie Udale, Mrs Su-Mei Thompson, Mrs Fiona Weldin, Jonathan Briant, Mrs Louise Williamson, Mr Gerard Evans, Mr Robert Leechman, Mrs Dilys Williams, Mrs Katie Robyns, Mr Kevin Senior, Mrs Jane Clare Moulder, Miss Sara Michele Putt, Mr Roger Michael Denny
Income: £30,749,000 [2017]; £32,168,000 [2016]; £27,265,000 [2015]; £25,598,000 [2014]; £23,956,000 [2013]

The Cheltenham Trust
Registered: 18 Sep 2014 *Employees:* 210 *Volunteers:* 151
Tel: 01242 387499 *Website:* cheltenhamtrust.org.uk
Activities: Arts, culture, heritage, science; recreation
Address: The Wilson Art Gallery & Museum, Clarence Street, Cheltenham, Glos, GL50 3JT
Trustees: Ms Maxine Melling, Colin Hayes, Jacqui Grange, Peter Harkness, Mr Louis Leslie Alexander Eperjesi, Laura Brooks, Ms Jaki Meeking-Davis, Mr Karl Hobley, Duncan Smith, Judith Hodson, Mr Ian Renton, Ms Sian Morgan, Mr Paul Owen
Income: £5,904,524 [2017]; £5,768,867 [2016]; £2,955,080 [2015]

Cheltenham YMCA
Registered: 22 Mar 2000 *Employees:* 40 *Volunteers:* 12
Tel: 01242 524024 *Website:* cheltenhamymca.com
Activities: Education, training; accommodation, housing; amateur sport
Address: Cheltenham YMCA, 6 Vittoria Walk, Cheltenham, Glos, GL50 1TP
Trustees: Mr Benjamin Anthony Spencer Reed, Mr Peter Robert Worsley, Mrs Francesca Jane Tolond, Mr Michael Denzil Ede, Mr Hugh John Oliver Harries, Mr Stephen Andrew Jordan, Mr David Shoesmith, Mr Michael William Eric Horne
Income: £1,495,914 [2017]; £1,172,598 [2016]; £796,891 [2015]; £1,108,274 [2014]; £707,444 [2013]

Cherry Trees
Registered: 8 Nov 1988 *Employees:* 47 *Volunteers:* 60
Tel: 01428 683411 *Website:* cherry-trees.co.uk
Activities: Disability
Address: 5 Rose Cottages, Culmer Lane, Wormley, Godalming, Surrey, GU8 5SR
Trustees: Mrs Ann Taylor CBE, Mr Adrian James Thompson, Mr Simon Runton, Mrs Deborah Anne Powlesland, Mr Mark Rowland Clement, Dr Catherine Anne McMullan, Mr Michael Evans, Mr Peter William Regan, Mrs Caroline Anne Black
Income: £1,363,318 [2017]; £1,243,189 [2016]; £974,870 [2015]; £1,009,299 [2014]; £1,004,917 [2013]

Chescombe Trust Limited
Registered: 11 Mar 1991 *Employees:* 47 *Volunteers:* 1
Tel: 0117 969 6024 *Website:* chescombetrust.co.uk
Activities: Disability
Address: Chescombe, 168 Gloucester Road, Patchway, Bristol, S Glos, BS34 5BG
Trustees: Mr David Jones, Mr Aidan John Christopher Healy, Mr Dominic Anderson, Ms Sheila Margaret Henderson, Ms Donna Tremayne
Income: £1,229,437 [2017]; £1,210,812 [2016]; £1,195,477 [2015]; £1,398,354 [2014]; £967,727 [2013]

Chesham Preparatory School Trust Limited
Registered: 27 Sep 1967 *Employees:* 75 *Volunteers:* 75
Tel: 01494 782619 *Website:* cheshamprep.co.uk
Activities: Education, training
Address: Chesham Preparatory School, Orchard Leigh, Chesham, Bucks, HP5 3QF
Trustees: Mr Andrew Jordan, Mr Michael Patrick Hurd, Mrs Nicola Shepherd, Mr William Turner, Dr Rajashi Banerjee, Mr Paul Johnson, Mr Nicholas Baker, Mrs Ann Marie McNaney, Mrs Susan Peck, Mrs Catherine Almond
Income: £4,986,503 [2017]; £4,866,555 [2016]; £4,611,937 [2015]; £4,350,739 [2014]; £4,918,848 [2013]

Cheshire Agricultural Society CIO
Registered: 17 Apr 2013 *Employees:* 4 *Volunteers:* 400
Tel: 01565 650200 *Website:* cheshirecountyshow.org.uk
Activities: Education, training; animals; environment, conservation, heritage
Address
Trustees: Mrs Edwina Oldham, Mr Paul Janvier, Mr Richard Hague, Mr Mark Walton, Mr John Williamson, Mr Michael Daley, Mr Alan Greenway, Mr Alan Kay, Mr Tony Rimmer, Mr William Robert Turner, Mr David Williams, Mr Michael R Richardson, Mr Alan Ford, Mrs Karol Bailey, Mr Ken Oliver, Mr Steven Blakeman, Mr Roger Thomason, Mr John Anthony Garnett, Mrs Mary Leake, Mr Richard Ford, Mr Anthony Millington, Mr Dennis Parton, Mr Whitlow Peter, Mr Stephen Wharfe, Mr Graham Richardson, Mr Alan Sproston, Mr Richard Fryer, Ms Janice Wood, Mrs Margerey Hall, Mr Alan Walker, Mr John Edward Ball, Mr William Edward Massey, Mrs Christine Judith Bailey, Mr Alan R Hough, Mr Victor Croxson, Mr Robert A Davenport, Mr James Hague, Mr David Leech, Mr Paul Tanner, Mr Andrew K Wallace, Mr Stuart Ernest Yarwood, Mrs Christine Newton, Mr John Bell, Mrs Margaret Hollinshead, Mr William Horton, Mrs Christine Newton, Mr John Gate, Mr John Norbury, Mr Tom Earl, Ms Louise Young, Mr John Tickle, Rev Jane Parry, Mr Richard Johnson, Mr Keith Thomas, Mr Andrew Sutton, Mrs Carole Ford, Mr Andrew Garnett, Mr Steve Wilkinson, Mr Peter Robinson
Income: £1,050,057 [2016]; £1,068,262 [2015]; £977,465 [2014]

Cheshire Centre for Independent Living
Registered: 24 Apr 2002 *Employees:* 60 *Volunteers:* 3
Tel: 01606 331853 *Website:* cheshirecil.org
Activities: Disability
Address: Sension House, Denton Drive, Northwich, Cheshire, CW9 7LU
Trustees: Mr Simon Holden, Mr Andrew Johnston, Richard Lewis, Miss Amy Shemilt, Miss Georgina Wray, Sonja Jonas
Income: £2,143,018 [2017]; £1,664,921 [2016]; £1,508,876 [2015]; £1,537,831 [2014]; £1,259,676 [2013]

Cheshire Deaf Society
Registered: 12 Oct 1977 *Employees:* 46 *Volunteers:* 20
Tel: 0333 220 5050 *Website:* dsnonline.co.uk
Activities: General charitable purposes; education, training; advancement of health or saving of lives; disability; accommodation, housing; human rights, religious or racial harmony, equality or diversity; recreation
Address: Deafness Support Network, 144 London Road, Northwich, Cheshire, CW9 5HH
Trustees: Mr Peter Morley, Professor Thomas Christopher Gibbons, Mr John Pane, Mr Dan Birtles, Mrs Janet Huntington, Mr David Scott, Mr David Pane, Mr Liam Glennon
Income: £2,096,610 [2017]; £2,250,775 [2016]; £2,232,888 [2015]; £2,270,646 [2014]; £2,414,666 [2013]

Leonard Cheshire Disability
Registered: 10 Jul 1985 *Employees:* 4,448 *Volunteers:* 3,000
Tel: 020 3242 0200 *Website:* leonardcheshire.org
Activities: Disability
Address: 66 South Lambeth Road, London, SW8 1RL
Trustees: Mrs Victoria Grace Chittenden, Mr Vidar Hjardeng, Mrs Catriona Rayner, Mr Richard Brooman, Mr Justin Tydeman, Ms Anubha Shrivastava, Dr Colin Hunter, Sally Davis, Sir Martin Davidson, Mr Alastair Hignell, Dr Elizabeth Haywood, Mr Ranald Mair
Income: £161,339,000 [2017]; £159,117,000 [2016]; £162,241,000 [2015]; £154,559,000 [2014]; £159,922,000 [2013]

The Cheshire Residential Homes Trust
Registered: 19 Jan 1965 *Employees:* 57 *Volunteers:* 20
Tel: 01244 323178 *Website:* cheshire-residential-care-homes.org.uk
Activities: Accommodation, housing
Address: 2 Makepeace Close, Vicars Cross, Chester, CH3 5LU
Trustees: Mrs Anne Jennifer Marsh, Mrs Valerie Godfrey JP, Mrs Suzanne Cook, Mrs Patricia Joan Speechly, Mrs Gillian Mary Rushworth, Mrs Janice Tetlow, Mrs Margaret Offer, Mrs Julia Jackson, Mrs Candice Lynn Reeves, Mrs Anthea Lesley Brough, Mrs Diana Shirley Tudor-Evans, Mrs Sheena Stallard
Income: £1,981,109 [2017]; £2,161,893 [2016]; £2,087,124 [2015]; £2,279,787 [2014]; £2,239,355 [2013]

The Cheshire Wildlife Trust Limited
Registered: 20 Feb 1963 *Employees:* 34 *Volunteers:* 1,000
Tel: 01948 820728 *Website:* cheshirewildlifetrust.co.uk
Activities: Education, training; environment, conservation, heritage
Address: Bickley Hall Farm, Bickley Wood, Malpas, Cheshire, SY14 8EF
Trustees: Mr Frank Kerkham, Mr Philip Cheek, Mr Chris Koral, Professor Robert Hunter Marrs, Mr Peter Rushton, Mr Bill Stothart, Mrs H M Carey, Dr Neil Friswell, Mr Gerald George Coates, Ms Caroline Jones, Mr Mike Packer, Ms Sue Steer
Income: £2,015,128 [2017]; £1,829,941 [2016]; £1,864,718 [2015]; £2,010,460 [2014]; £1,773,042 [2013]

Chess in Schools and Communities
Registered: 4 Dec 2009 *Employees:* 5 *Volunteers:* 12
Website: chessinschools.co.uk
Activities: Education, training; environment, conservation, heritage
Address: 44 Baker Street, London, W1U 7RT
Trustees: Mr Andrew Philip Farthing, Mr Ian Iceton, Mr William Watson, Ms Katharine Walsh, Mr Stephen Meyler, Mrs Alison Sharp
Income: £1,704,510 [2016]; £1,549,802 [2015]; £1,533,908 [2014]; £937,335 [2013]; £784,176 [2012]

The Chester Diocesan Board of Finance
Registered: 16 Sep 1966 *Employees:* 45 *Volunteers:* 250
Tel: 01928 718834 *Website:* chester.anglican.org
Activities: Religious activities
Address: Chester Diocesan Board of Finance, 5500 Daresbury Park, Daresbury, Warrington, Cheshire, WA4 4GE
Trustees: Revd Simon Gales, David Felix, Mr Victor John Legg, Ven Ian Bishop, Dr Graham Campbell, Mr John Freeman, Rev Lynn Boyle, Ven Dr Michael Gilbertson, Revd Elizabeth Jane Holden Lane, Rev Dr David James Page, Mr David Anthony Marriott, Rev Andrew Quentin Greenhough, Rev Alison Fulford, Mr John Scrivener, Rev Simon Drew, Rt Revd Dr Peter Forster, Bishop Keith Sinclair, Revd Dr Rob Munro, Revd Canon Elaine Chegwin Hall, Mr Ian Roberts, Canon Dr John Philip Mason, Canon Elizabeth Renshaw MBE, Miss Fiona Goode, Revd Michael Ian Anthony Smith, Dr Alan Dowen, Rev Michael Laurence Ridley, Mr Ian Scott-Dunn, Rev Carrol Seddon, Mrs Jenny Kidd
Income: £14,915,000 [2016]; £16,063,000 [2015]; £16,999,000 [2014]; £14,161,000 [2013]; £13,660,000 [2012]

Chester Performing Arts Centre Limited
Registered: 28 Sep 2007 *Employees:* 16 *Volunteers:* 130
Tel: 01244 409113 *Website:* chesterperforms.com
Activities: Education, training; arts, culture, heritage, science; economic, community development, employment
Address: Storyhouse, Hunter Street, Chester, CH1 2AR
Trustees: Katrina Kerr, Mr Geoffrey Andrew Clifton, Professor Allan Arthur Owens, Ms Susie Stubbs, Mr Peter Mearns, Ms Susan Leech, Mr Richard Beacham, Jane Hyndman
Income: £2,447,190 [2017]; £1,998,671 [2016]; £1,360,593 [2015]; £1,162,357 [2014]; £887,203 [2013]

Chester Students' Union
Registered: 19 Oct 2012 *Employees:* 71 *Volunteers:* 90
Tel: 01244 511483 *Website:* chestersu.com
Activities: Education, training
Address: Parkgate Road, Chester, CH1 4BJ
Trustees: Dr Gavin Jeffrey Eyres, Mr James Christopher Brown, Mr Jamie Ian Christon, Miss Sabrina Lauren de Sa, Mr Ethan Jack Wade, Mr Alessandro Salemme, Miss Cherelle Louise Mitchell, Miss Eleanor Sarah Stevens
Income: £1,455,329 [2016]; £1,458,260 [2015]; £1,324,974 [2014]; £1,240,199 [2013]

Chesterfield and District Society for People with a Learning Disability
Registered: 3 Dec 1997 *Employees:* 80 *Volunteers:* 7
Tel: 01246 231256
Activities: General charitable purposes; disability
Address: Ability, Ash Lodge, 73 Old Road, Chesterfield, Derbys, S40 2RA
Trustees: Mr David Ernest Fuller, Ms Karen Bingham, Mr Thomas David Holmes, Ms Davina Bradley, Mr Paul Brown, Mr Andrew Oakley
Income: £2,286,540 [2017]; £1,881,278 [2016]; £1,618,116 [2015]; £1,414,511 [2014]; £1,190,531 [2013]

Chetham's Hospital School and Library
Registered: 21 Sep 1964 *Employees:* 289 *Volunteers:* 13
Tel: 0161 838 7212 *Website:* chethams.com
Activities: Education, training; arts, culture, heritage, science; environment, conservation, heritage
Address: Chethams School of Music, Long Millgate, Manchester, M3 1SB
Trustees: Mr Paul Lee, Mr Philip Ramsbottom, Carolyn Baxendale, Dr Stella Butler JP, The Rt Hon The Earl of Derby DL, Mr David Hill, Mr John Early, Mrs Susan Marks, Mr Alan Torevell, Mr Jeffrey Wainwright, Mr Harry Ross, Ms Pauline Newman, Councillor Joan Davies, Professor Edward Gregson, Mr Kevin Jaquiss, Professor Joseph Bergin D Litt FBA, Dame Alexandra Burslem DBE, The Very Rev Rogers Govender, Mr Simon Webb, Mr Michael Oglesby, Mr Malcolm Edge, Professor Hannah Barker, Ms Amanda Corcoran, Canon Philip Barratt, Dr Bernadette Brennan
Income: £15,676,781 [2016]; £11,273,323 [2015]; £10,583,899 [2014]; £9,670,205 [2013]; £11,599,183 [2012]

Chevras Mo'oz Ladol
Registered: 4 Dec 1986 *Employees:* 1
Tel: 020 8802 7862
Activities: General charitable purposes; advancement of health or saving of lives; prevention or relief of poverty
Address: 34 Heathland Road, London, N16 5LZ
Trustees: Mr Abraham Barchorin, Mr Yitzchuk Menachem Sternlicht, Mr Jehuda Baumgarten
Income: £5,823,258 [2017]; £5,427,829 [2016]; £3,953,757 [2015]; £2,903,627 [2014]; £2,434,175 [2013]

Chevras Tsedokoh Limited
Registered: 26 Sep 1996
Activities: General charitable purposes; education, training; prevention or relief of poverty; religious activities; other charitable purposes
Address: New Burlington House, 1075 Finchley Road, London, NW11 0PU
Trustees: Mr Michael Saberski, Mr Joshua Sternlicht, Mr Abraham Klein, Mrs Sarah Padwa
Income: £2,270,609 [2016]; £3,459,948 [2015]; £3,859,261 [2014]; £3,983,337 [2013]; £3,959,301 [2012]

The Chichester Diocesan Fund and Board of Finance (Incorporated)
Registered: 22 Jul 1965 *Employees:* 57 *Volunteers:* 71
Tel: 01273 421021 *Website:* chichester.anglican.org
Activities: General charitable purposes; education, training; religious activities
Address: Church House, 211 New Church Road, Hove, E Sussex, BN3 4ED
Trustees: The Venerable Douglas H McKittrick, Mrs Sara Stonor, The Reverend Dr Andrew Manson-Brailsford, The Venerable Martin Lloyd Williams, Mrs Valerie Burgess, The Revd Canon Julia Peaty, The Revd Nick Cornell, The Revd Luke Irvine-Capel, The Right Revd Richard Jackson, The Revd Lisa Helen Barnett, The Venerable Edward Dowler, The Very Revd Stephen John Waine, The Revd John Eldridge, Mr Philip Bowden, The Right Revd Dr Martin Warner, Mr John Head, Mrs Mary Nagel, Mr Guy Leonard, The Right Revd Mark Sowerby, Revd Canon Ann Elizabeth Waizeneker, The Reverend Canon Mark Gilbert, Mr Jacob Vince, Dr Graham D Parr, The Venerable Fiona Windsor, Mrs Lesley Lynn, Mr Martin Cruttenden
Income: £18,448,137 [2016]; £18,881,328 [2015]; £17,376,829 [2014]; £18,107,170 [2013]; £16,757,426 [2012]

Chichester Festival Theatre
Registered: 24 Sep 2001 *Employees:* 155 *Volunteers:* 136
Tel: 01243 784437 *Website:* cft.org.uk
Activities: Education, training; arts, culture, heritage, science
Address: Chichester Festival Theatre, Oaklands Park, Chichester, W Sussex, PO19 6AP
Trustees: Mr Alan Brodie, Ms Christina Webster, Sir William Castell, Mr Michael John McCart, Mr Nigel Brice Bennett, Ms Jill Rosemary Green, Mrs Susan Jane Wells, Stephanie Street, Rear Admiral Richard John Lippiett CB CBE, Mrs Denise Lesley Anne Patterson, Mrs Shelagh Jane Legrave, Ms Odile Lesley Griffith, Mr Harold Nsamba Matovu QC, Mr Nicholas Paul Backhouse, Mrs Patricia Mary Tull
Income: £17,165,300 [2017]; £14,668,463 [2016]; £17,017,524 [2015]; £20,874,400 [2014]; £15,587,322 [2013]

The Chicken Shed Theatre Trust
Registered: 29 Jun 1992 *Employees:* 116 *Volunteers:* 250
Tel: 020 8216 2712 *Website:* chickenshed.org.uk
Activities: General charitable purposes; education, training; disability; arts, culture, heritage, science
Address: 290 Chase Side, Southgate, London, N14 4PE
Trustees: Sir Trevor Nunn CBE, Dame Judi Dench CH DBE, Lady Jane Antonia Frances Rayne Lacey, Josh Berger, Mr Nicholas James Campsie, Mr Anthony David Gibbon, Jonathan Sigmund Shalit, Mrs Christine Hansine Mason Berger, Natasha Rayne, Mr Matthew Saul Rose, Mr Pete Constanti
Income: £3,783,145 [2017]; £3,947,429 [2016]; £3,808,898 [2015]; £3,856,508 [2014]; £3,041,684 [2013]

The Chief Fire Officers' Association
Registered: 19 Feb 1999 *Employees:* 19
Website: nationalfirechiefs.org.uk
Activities: Other charitable purposes
Address: West Midlands Fire Service Headquarters, 99 Vauxhall Road, Birmingham, B7 4HW
Trustees: Mr John Roberts, Ms Teresa Budworth, Mr Alexander Gary Thompson, Ms Danielle Amara Cotton, Mr Roger Simon Thomas, Ms Amy Catherine Webb, Mr Simon David Furlong, Mr Christopher Noel Kenny, Mr David McGown
Income: £2,483,608 [2017]; £7,275,896 [2016]; £12,761,570 [2015]; £8,401,380 [2014]; £8,787,674 [2013]

Chigwell School
Registered: 5 Jul 2006 *Employees:* 173 *Volunteers:* 56
Tel: 020 8501 5700 *Website:* chigwell-school.org
Activities: Education, training
Address: 27 Monkhams Avenue, Woodford Green, Essex, IG8 0HA
Trustees: Dr Graham Dixon, Mr John Frederick Christopher Cullis MBE BA MSc, Mr Robin Howard MA, Mr Nicholas Antony Garnish BSc MBA MCMI, Mrs Purnima Sen, Mr Andrew Howat, Mrs Jennifer Gwinn, Mrs Isobel Peck BA, Susie Aliker, Mr David Morriss, Rev Christopher Mark Davies BA, Mr Martin James Higgins, Rev Benjamin William King, Mrs Emma Brett ACA, Ms Melody Jones
Income: £13,765,957 [2017]; £13,584,000 [2016]; £12,404,000 [2015]; £11,946,000 [2014]; £10,602,000 [2013]

Child Action Northwest
Registered: 4 Oct 1963 *Employees:* 81 *Volunteers:* 18
Tel: 01254 244700 *Website:* canw.org.uk
Activities: General charitable purposes; education, training; disability; accommodation, housing; amateur sport; economic, community development, employment; other charitable purposes
Address: The Homestead, Whalley Road, Wilpshire, Blackburn, Lancs, BB1 9LL
Trustees: Mr Peter Griffin, Mr Gordon Fairweather, Mr John Drury, Miss Ann Ainsworth, Mr Jonathan Comyn-Platt, Mr Robert Dickinson, Mr Trevor Marklew, Mr John Townend, Mr Joseph Slater, Mr Martin Roche, Michelle Mayman, Mrs Jenny Hetherington
Income: £4,252,632 [2017]; £4,381,471 [2016]; £4,815,236 [2015]; £4,478,708 [2014]; £4,179,294 [2013]

The Child Beale Trust
Registered: 9 Jul 1964 *Employees:* 22 *Volunteers:* 24
Tel: 0118 976 7484 *Website:* bealepark.co.uk
Activities: Education, training; animals; environment, conservation, heritage; economic, community development, employment
Address: Beale Park, Lower Basildon, Reading, Berks, RG8 9NW
Trustees: Mr David Carr, Ms Michelle Carvell, Mr Nicholas White, Mr Robert Hutton
Income: £1,456,617 [2016]; £1,174,173 [2015]; £1,021,490 [2014]; £1,088,948 [2013]; £995,587 [2012]

Child Bereavement UK
Registered: 25 Aug 1994 *Employees:* 72 *Volunteers:* 200
Tel: 01494 568900 *Website:* childbereavement.org.uk
Activities: Education, training; other charitable purposes
Address: Clare Charity Centre, Wycombe Road, Saunderton, Bucks, HP14 4BF
Trustees: Rt Hon Lord Ryder, Nicola Gilham, Mr John Heathcoat-Amory, Mrs Julia Aline Samuel, Will Campion, Kristen Eshak Weldon
Income: £2,903,078 [2017]; £3,390,552 [2016]; £2,997,090 [2015]; £1,697,084 [2014]; £1,705,776 [2013]

Child Brain Injury Trust

Registered: 17 Mar 2006 *Employees:* 23 *Volunteers:* 5
Tel: 01869 341075 *Website:* childbraininjurytrust.org.uk
Activities: Education, training; advancement of health or saving of lives; disability
Address: Unit 1 The Great Barn, Baynards Green Farm, Bicester, Oxon, OX27 7SG
Trustees: Mr Robert Thomas, Ms Katie Byard, Ms Inez Brown, Mr Stephen O'Neill, Mr Terry Burt, Mr Andrew Caudell, Mrs Sarah Louise Mackie, Mr Christopher Owen
Income: £1,010,907 [2017]; £932,163 [2016]; £817,386 [2015]; £782,896 [2014]; £819,461 [2013]

Dr. Vivian Child Charitable Trust

Registered: 30 Sep 1999
Tel: 020 7248 4400
Activities: General charitable purposes
Address: Brewin Dolphin Securities Ltd, 12 Smithfield Street, London, EC1A 9BD
Trustees: Rupert David Tyler, Miss Miranda Emma Thompson-Schwab
Income: £1,849,367 [2017]; £5,035 [2016]; £5,054 [2015]; £5,511 [2014]; £5,503 [2013]

Child Dynamix

Registered: 24 May 2005 *Employees:* 84 *Volunteers:* 50
Tel: 01482 221425 *Website:* childdynamix.co.uk
Activities: Education, training; advancement of health or saving of lives; economic, community development, employment
Address: 95 Preston Road, Hull, HU9 3QB
Trustees: Miss Janet Boyd, Mr Brian Bradley, Ms Priyankari Perera, Ms Helen Schofield, Mr George Coyle, Mr Peter Duffield, Mrs Catherine Bishop, Mr Rory Clarke, Mr Kenneth Sturdy
Income: £1,661,761 [2017]; £1,713,072 [2016]; £1,801,594 [2015]; £1,526,984 [2014]; £1,337,501 [2013]

Child Light Limited

Registered: 29 Jun 1994 *Employees:* 41 *Volunteers:* 100
Tel: 01223 350615 *Website:* childlight.org
Activities: Education, training; religious activities
Address: 19 Brookside, Cambridge, CB2 1JE
Trustees: Mrs Susan MacAulay, Mr David Edward Charles Alderson, Mrs Rebecca Elisabeth Ashley Stone, Mrs Beryl Ann Loe, Mr R C Maculay, Mr Ian McCulloch Dunn, Mr Mark Joseph Stone, Mr Tom Amies
Income: £1,642,610 [2017]; £1,507,918 [2016]; £1,248,418 [2015]; £1,083,551 [2014]; £901,824 [2013]

Child Poverty Action Group

Registered: 24 Jul 1986 *Employees:* 47 *Volunteers:* 2
Tel: 020 7837 7979 *Website:* cpag.org.uk
Activities: The prevention or relief of poverty
Address: Child Poverty Action Group, 30 Micawber Street, London, N1 7TB
Trustees: Mr Mark O'Kelly, Mr Alan Buckle, Mr Alan Thackrey, Mr Tony Orhnial, Ms Fiona Forsyth, Professor Jonathan Bradshaw, Kim Catcheside, Ms Gaynor Humphrys, Diane Sechi, Prof Alan Marsh
Income: £3,071,805 [2017]; £3,047,329 [2016]; £3,092,338 [2015]; £4,785,815 [2014]; £2,574,000 [2013]

Childcare and Business Consultancy Services

Registered: 30 Nov 2000 *Employees:* 60
Tel: 020 7738 1958 *Website:* cbcservices.org.uk
Activities: Education, training
Address: Katherine Low Settlement, 108 Battersea High Street, London, SW11 3HP
Trustees: Mrs Carol Thurgood, Mrs Cathy Edwards, Mrs Carol Yala Hutchinson, Mr Graeme Stephen, Mrs Pauline Robinson, Mrs Sandra Margaret Gould, Mr Huw Jenkins, Mr Robert Parker
Income: £1,643,504 [2017]; £1,209,474 [2016]; £1,221,764 [2015]; £802,027 [2014]; £725,672 [2013]

Childhope (UK)

Registered: 20 Dec 1989 *Employees:* 12 *Volunteers:* 5
Tel: 020 7065 0950 *Website:* childhope.org.uk
Activities: Education, training; advancement of health or saving of lives; disability; prevention or relief of poverty; economic, community development, employment; human rights, religious or racial harmony, equality or diversity
Address: 6th Floor, Development House, 56-64 Leonard Street, London, EC2A 4LT
Trustees: Mr Charles Middleton, Ms Karen Kroger, Ms Kay Twine, Mr David Harding, Ms Laverne Antrobus, Ms Elizabeth Towl
Income: £3,014,627 [2016]; £3,386,100 [2015]; £2,400,976 [2014]; £3,053,798 [2013]; £1,877,344 [2012]

Childline

Registered: 8 Aug 1991 *Volunteers:* 1,400
Tel: 020 3772 9153 *Website:* childline.org.uk
Activities: General charitable purposes
Address: NSPCC, National Centre, 42 Curtain Road, London, EC2A 3NH
Trustees: Mr Mark Wood, Phillip Noyes, Peter Watt, David Roberts, Peter Wanless
Income: £1,303,625 [2017]; £916,000 [2016]; £984,000 [2015]; £962,000 [2014]; £1,194,000 [2013]

Childreach International

Registered: 20 Oct 2009 *Employees:* 22 *Volunteers:* 450
Website: childreach.org.uk
Activities: Education, training; advancement of health or saving of lives; prevention or relief of poverty; environment, conservation, heritage; economic, community development, employment
Address: 46A Rte de Luxemborg, Lorentzweiler, Luxembourg, 7372
Trustees: Jimena Paratcha, Mr Ross Milfort Kemp, Miss Angela Jane Windle, Mr Patrick Anthony Gill, Dr David Lawrence Durkee, Richard Anthony Bryars, Ms Annemarie Elsom
Income: £2,203,205 [2016]; £2,191,038 [2015]; £2,143,736 [2014]; £2,806,912 [2013]; £4,429,898 [2012]

Children & The Arts

Registered: 13 May 2004 *Employees:* 10
Tel: 020 3326 2230 *Website:* childrenandarts.org.uk
Activities: Education, training; arts, culture, heritage, science
Address: Oxford House, Derbyshire Street, Bethnal Green, London, E2 6HG
Trustees: Mr Alan Kelsey, Marth Genieser, Mr Hussam Otaibi, Ms Ruth Warder, Mr Michael Needley, Ms Francesca Hegyi, Robin Alexander, Ms Despoulla Violaris, Mr James Wilcox
Income: £1,249,152 [2017]; £933,141 [2016]; £1,078,917 [2015]; £1,225,075 [2014]; £2,099,328 [2013]

Children North East
Registered: 7 Oct 1963 Employees: 52 Volunteers: 91
Tel: 0191 256 2444 Website: children-ne.org.uk
Activities: General charitable purposes; education, training; advancement of health or saving of lives; disability; prevention or relief of poverty; other charitable purposes
Address: Children North East, 89 Denhill Park, Newcastle upon Tyne, NE15 6QE
Trustees: Hazel Jones-Lee, Debbie McCordall, Judy Stone, Ms Glenda Devlin, Ian Railton, Gemma Lockyer-Turnbull, Stephen Robinson, Mrs Lucy Kendall
Income: £1,917,892 [2017]; £1,696,467 [2016]; £1,986,044 [2015]; £1,964,964 [2014]; £1,788,974 [2013]

Children and Families Limited
Registered: 20 Jul 2006 Employees: 81 Volunteers: 97
Tel: 01795 667070 Website: children-families.org
Activities: General charitable purposes; education, training; advancement of health or saving of lives; prevention or relief of poverty; economic, community development, employment
Address: Children and Families Limited, Seashells, Rose Street, Sheerness, Kent, ME12 1AW
Trustees: Mr John Charles Bromiley, Mr David John Buckett, Mr Garry John Ratcliffe, Mrs Christine White, Mrs Lauren Anning
Income: £1,437,099 [2017]; £1,489,130 [2016]; £1,766,206 [2015]; £1,374,764 [2014]; £1,131,260 [2013]

Children in Crisis
Registered: 30 Apr 1993 Employees: 18 Volunteers: 3
Tel: 020 7627 1040 Website: childrenincrisis.org
Activities: Education, training; prevention or relief of poverty; overseas aid, famine relief
Address: 206-208 Stewarts Road, London, SW8 4UB
Trustees: Mrs Frances Prenn, Mr John Paul Axon, Mr Ron Friend, Mr Sebastain Ling, Mr Bastien Hibon, Dr Anthony Wallersteiner, Lady Caroline Julia Dalmeny, Ms Julia Streets, Mrs Neela Jane Stansfield
Income: £2,261,637 [2017]; £2,626,404 [2016]; £3,080,335 [2015]; £2,156,555 [2014]; £2,353,453 [2013]

Children in Wales-Plant Yng Nghymru
Registered: 28 Apr 1993 Employees: 32
Tel: 029 2034 2434 Website: childreninwales.org.uk
Activities: General charitable purposes; education, training; advancement of health or saving of lives; disability; prevention or relief of poverty
Address: 1 Maes-Yr-Awel, Radyr, Cardiff, CF15 8AN
Trustees: Mr Michael Stanhope Shooter, Mrs Hannah Williams, Dr David Williams, Mrs Kara Williams, Dr Sarah Jane Jones, Mrs Sarah Helen Crawley, Mrs Diane Susan Daniel, Professor Jonathan Bryn Scourfield, Ann Shabbaz, Jane Newby, David Egan, Nia John
Income: £1,592,049 [2017]; £1,144,432 [2016]; £1,157,518 [2015]; £1,127,969 [2014]; £1,372,114 [2013]

Children on the Edge
Registered: 9 Jan 2004 Employees: 7 Volunteers: 60
Tel: 01243 538530 Website: childrenontheedge.org
Activities: General charitable purposes; education, training; advancement of health or saving of lives; disability; prevention or relief of poverty; overseas aid, famine relief; economic, community development, employment; human rights, religious or racial harmony, equality or diversity; recreation
Address: Children on the Edge, 5 The Victoria, 25 St Pancras, Chichester, W Sussex, PO19 7LT
Trustees: Mr Paul Suter, Mr Stuart Gallimore, Mr Alan Finch, Mr Colin Buchanan, Mr Andrew Rush, Mrs Helen Pattinson
Income: £1,146,819 [2017]; £871,667 [2016]; £811,877 [2015]; £567,617 [2014]; £739,017 [2013]

Children with Cancer UK
Registered: 18 Jan 2005 Employees: 36 Volunteers: 5
Tel: 020 7404 0808 Website: childrenwithcancer.org.uk
Activities: General charitable purposes; education, training; advancement of health or saving of lives; disability; environment, conservation, heritage
Address: Children with Cancer UK, 51 Great Ormond Street, London, WC1N 3JQ
Trustees: Mr Edward O'Gorman, Mrs Sandra Mileham, Linda Robson, Mr Alasdair Philips
Income: £16,524,416 [2016]; £17,544,264 [2015]; £12,832,718 [2014]; £12,084,788 [2013]; £11,920,467 [2012]

The Children's Adventure Farm Trust Ltd
Registered: 30 Jul 1991 Employees: 18 Volunteers: 300
Website: caft.co.uk
Activities: The advancement of health or saving of lives; disability; prevention or relief of poverty
Address: 18 Lisson Grove, Hale, Altrincham, Cheshire, WA15 9AE
Trustees: Mr Nicholas Peter Montague, Mr Michael Bulcock FCA
Income: £1,046,007 [2016]; £970,858 [2015]; £1,080,781 [2014]; £1,069,200 [2013]; £1,036,963 [2012]

The Children's Cancer and Leukaemia Group
Registered: 13 Apr 1983 Employees: 10
Tel: 0116 252 5858 Website: cclg.org.uk
Activities: Education, training; advancement of health or saving of lives
Address: CCLG, Clinical Sciences Building, University of Leicester, Leicester Royal Infirmary, Leicester, LE2 7LX
Trustees: Rachel Wilcox, Lorenzo Moruzzi, Dr Daniel John Saunders, Mrs G Routledge, Mr David Oxnam
Income: £1,858,536 [2016]; £819,407 [2015]; £589,686 [2014]; £487,037 [2013]; £647,876 [2012]

Children's Discovery Centre East London
Registered: 9 Jul 1998 Employees: 47 Volunteers: 71
Tel: 020 8536 5555 Website: discover.org.uk
Activities: Education, training; arts, culture, heritage, science; environment, conservation, heritage; economic, community development, employment; recreation
Address: 383-387 High Road, Stratford, London, E15 4QZ
Trustees: Mr Andrew John Murray, Mr Stephen Crampton-Hayward, Mr Martin Clarke, Mr Paul Black, Mr Paul Jackson, Miss Michelle Ann Wright, Ms Katy Beale, Ms Tamsin Ace, Gemma Allen
Income: £1,639,828 [2017]; £1,868,732 [2016]; £1,579,384 [2015]; £1,310,527 [2014]; £1,346,296 [2013]

The Children's Family Trust
Registered: 22 Sep 1962 *Employees:* 44
Tel: 01527 574446 *Website:* thecft.org.uk
Activities: The prevention or relief of poverty
Address: Hanbury Court, Unit 16 Harris Business Park, Stoke Prior, Bromsgrove, Worcs, B60 4DJ
Trustees: Canon John Glover DL, Mr Nicholas Anthony Harrison, Dr Valerie Wigfall, Mrs Margaret Hine, Miss Alecia Forrest-Oliver, Mrs Sylvia Pinner, Mr Dale Williams
Income: £5,829,657 [2016]; £5,433,551 [2015]; £5,118,476 [2014]; £3,859,550 [2013]; £3,576,219 [2012]

The Children's Food Trust
Registered: 27 Apr 2007 *Employees:* 66
Website: childrensfoodtrust.org.uk
Activities: Education, training; economic, community development, employment
Address: 3 Alcott Place, Sheffield, Winwick, Warrington, Cheshire, WA2 8XN
Trustees: Mr William Higham, Mr Christopher Jones, Ms Caroline Margaret Price, Mr Adam Starkey, Mr Jonathan Townsend, Miss Meg Longworth
Income: £5,573,000 [2016]; £7,834,000 [2015]; £5,811,000 [2014]; £4,239,000 [2013]; £7,772,000 [2012]

Children's Hospice South West
Registered: 28 Jun 1991 *Employees:* 249 *Volunteers:* 770
Tel: 01271 325270 *Website:* chsw.org.uk
Activities: The advancement of health or saving of lives
Address: Little Bridge House, Redlands Road, Fremington, Barnstaple, Devon, EX31 2PZ
Trustees: Dr Simon Langton-Hewer FRCP, Gerry Sones, Karen Rogers, Mrs Beverley Horler, Mr Damian Whittard, Mrs Patricia Morris, Mr Stephen Hindley CBE DL, Mr David Mark Turner, Liz Redfern CBE, Mrs Katharine Stanton, Mrs Nicola Mason, Dr Hazel Curtis
Income: £12,708,206 [2017]; £12,160,713 [2016]; £16,951,355 [2015]; £11,842,989 [2013]; £11,718,198 [2012]

The Children's Hospital Charity
Registered: 23 Mar 1976 *Employees:* 16 *Volunteers:* 20
Tel: 0114 271 7203 *Website:* tchc.org.uk
Activities: The advancement of health or saving of lives
Address: Western Bank, Sheffield, S10 2TH
Trustees: Mr Paul Firth, Dr Julie MacDonald, Professor David Barnett, Mrs Sally Shearer, Professor Nic Bishop, Mr John Warner, Mrs Sarah Jones MBA
Income: £3,486,908 [2017]; £3,482,018 [2016]; £2,639,678 [2015]; £2,533,842 [2014]; £1,572,611 [2013]

The Children's House School
Registered: 15 Mar 2006 *Employees:* 42
Tel: 020 7354 2113 *Website:* childrenshouseschool.co.uk
Activities: Education, training
Address: The Children's House School, 77 Elmore Street, London, N1 3AQ
Trustees: Mrs Jane MacLean, Mrs Dawn Marie Brindle, Miss Marina Wyatt, Mr Andrew Taggart, Ms Danielle Anouk Dufey, Mrs Ruth Kermisch
Income: £1,773,222 [2016]; £1,592,584 [2015]; £1,498,019 [2014]; £1,415,440 [2013]; £1,347,225 [2012]

The Children's Investment Fund Foundation (UK)
Registered: 12 Mar 2002 *Employees:* 80
Website: ciff.org
Activities: General charitable purposes; education, training; advancement of health or saving of lives; overseas aid, famine relief; environment, conservation, heritage; other charitable purposes
Address: 7 Clifford Street, London, W1S 2FT
Trustees: Sir Christopher Hohn, Mr Benjamin Goldsmith, Masroor Siddiqui, Ms Jamie Cooper, Graeme Sweeney
Income: £412,318,816 [2016]; £158,667,954 [2015]; £114,595,830 [2014]; £99,871,418 [2013]; £101,232,000 [2012]

Children's Links
Registered: 17 Aug 1998 *Employees:* 167 *Volunteers:* 27
Tel: 01507 528300 *Website:* childrenslinks.org.uk
Activities: Education, training; advancement of health or saving of lives; disability; prevention or relief of poverty; arts, culture, heritage, science; amateur sport; environment, conservation, heritage; economic, community development, employment; human rights, religious or racial harmony, equality or diversity; recreation
Address: Suite 1 & 4 Gymphlex Buildings, Boston Road, Horncastle, Lincs, LN9 6HU
Trustees: Mrs Thomasin Nicholds, Miss Rachel Croft, Mr Alistair John Wright, Mr Tony Maione, Kate Truscott
Income: £3,423,000 [2017]; £2,767,000 [2016]; £4,259,000 [2015]; £4,169,000 [2014]; £3,585,000 [2013]

Children's Scrapstore
Registered: 28 Feb 1992 *Employees:* 20 *Volunteers:* 5
Tel: 0117 304 1788 *Website:* childrensscrapstore.co.uk
Activities: General charitable purposes; education, training; arts, culture, heritage, science; environment, conservation, heritage; economic, community development, employment
Address: The Childrens Scrapstore, Scrapstore House, 21 Sevier Street, Bristol, BS2 9LB
Trustees: Caroline Jane Casswell, Emma Jane Collier, Mrs Margaret Cousins, Ms Venetia Shah-Dyan, Mr Peter Richard Simpson
Income: £1,056,686 [2017]; £1,206,172 [2016]; £1,182,556 [2015]; £1,055,550 [2014]; £1,034,461 [2013]

The Children's Trust
Registered: 18 Oct 1983 *Employees:* 522 *Volunteers:* 680
Tel: 01737 365005 *Website:* thechildrenstrust.org.uk
Activities: Education, training; advancement of health or saving of lives; disability
Address: The Childrens Trust, Tadworth Court, Tadworth, Surrey, KT20 5RU
Trustees: Mr Toby Jonathan Mullins, Mr Christopher Tracey, Miss Imelda Charles-Edwards, Mrs Sarah Baker, Mr Roger Adrian Legate OBE, Mr Tim John Davies, Mr Nigel Keith Lethbridge Scott, Mr Michael Gercke, Mr Duncan Ingram, Mr Nicolas Grant, Ms Caroline Chang, Anne Walker
Income: £23,219,000 [2017]; £26,853,000 [2016]; £25,472,000 [2015]; £25,774,000 [2014]; £22,703,000 [2013]

The Childwick Trust
Registered: 9 Jan 2013 *Employees:* 3
Tel: 01727 844666 *Website:* childwicktrust.org
Activities: General charitable purposes; education, training; advancement of health or saving of lives; disability
Address: 9 Childwick Green, Childwickbury, St Albans, Herts, AL3 6JJ
Trustees: Mrs Clare Maurice, Mr Peter David Anwyl-Harris, Dr Alan Stranders, Mr Mark Philip Farmar, Mr John Wood, Mr Michael John Alexander Fiddes
Income: £2,206,498 [2017]; £2,257,168 [2016]; £2,050,881 [2015]; £79,978,556 [2014]

Chiltern College
Registered: 22 Sep 1962 *Employees:* 73
Tel: 0118 947 1847 *Website:* chilternntc.com
Activities: Education, training; other charitable purposes
Address: The Chiltern College, 18 Peppard Road, Caversham, Reading, Berks, RG4 8JZ
Trustees: Mr Jonathan Brian Gater, Mrs Sally Taylor, Mrs Alison Lindley, Mr Mazin Sharif, Mrs Diane Sandell, Mrs Carol Kelly, Mrs Karen Hillier
Income: £2,272,995 [2016]; £2,439,040 [2015]; £2,426,339 [2014]; £2,353,132 [2013]; £2,336,831 [2012]

Chiltern Student Villages Limited
Registered: 5 Jun 2008
Tel: 020 7385 9300
Activities: Education, training; accommodation, housing
Address: Chiltern Student Villages, Direct Control Ltd, Marvic House, Bishops Road, London, SW6 7AD
Trustees: Mr William Mitchell Brown, Mr Alexander Evelyn Giles Ward, Mr Jared Barclay Fox, Mr Timothy Middleton
Income: £1,029,490 [2017]; £1,525,083 [2016]; £1,495,550 [2015]; £1,424,066 [2014]; £1,364,209 [2013]

China Dialogue Trust
Registered: 6 Aug 2008 *Employees:* 8 *Volunteers:* 8
Tel: 020 7324 4767 *Website:* chinadialogue.net
Activities: Education, training
Address: Suite 306, The Grayston Centre, 28 Charles Square, London, N1 6HT
Trustees: Mr David Thomas Burke, Miss Elizabeth Wright, Ms Malini Mehra, Mr Jonathan Fenby, Mrs Jeanne-Marie Gescher, Mr Charles Parton, Ms Susan Hitch, Mr Tangwyn Morgan Copsey, Mr Stephen Christopher Ben Tinton, Mr Peter John Roussel Luff, Professor Kerry Brown
Income: £1,060,387 [2016]; £962,125 [2015]; £871,313 [2014]; £640,562 [2013]; £384,230 [2012]

China Fleet Trust
Registered: 12 May 2010 *Employees:* 215
Tel: 01752 854630 *Website:* china-fleet.co.uk
Activities: Armed forces, emergency service efficiency
Address: China Fleet Country Club Ltd, North Pill, Saltash, Cornwall, PL12 6LJ
Trustees: Ian Douglas, Rob Baldry, Michael Wood, Christopher David Green, Mr Trevor Mark Smith MBE, Mr Robert Edward Lowe, Mr Alastair Keith Camp, Simon Hill, Sarah Adkins, Richard Smith, David Halliday, Mrs Laura Hodgson
Income: £4,617,146 [2017]; £4,415,651 [2016]; £4,333,627 [2015]; £344,032 [2014]; £328,000 [2013]

Chinese Church in London
Registered: 11 Jan 2005 *Employees:* 18 *Volunteers:* 150
Tel: 020 7602 9092 *Website:* ccil.org.uk
Activities: General charitable purposes; religious activities
Address: 69-71 Brook Green, London, W6 7BE
Trustees: Allan Kwok, Mr Vincent Lim, Tommy Wong, Mr David Yat Tong Lee, Mrs Wing Tsee Alice Szeto, Rev Teck Sin Lau, Oliver Tang, Rev John Hung, Mr Peng Chiew Wong, Mrs Susana Tung Chu Chung Wong
Income: £1,271,151 [2016]; £1,224,783 [2015]; £1,133,668 [2014]; £1,157,333 [2013]; £1,119,226 [2012]

The Chinese Overseas Christian Mission
Registered: 12 May 2010 *Employees:* 30 *Volunteers:* 19
Tel: 01908 234100 *Website:* cocm.org.uk
Activities: Education, training; religious activities
Address: Chinese Overseas Christian Mission, 2 Padstow Avenue, Fishermead, Milton Keynes, Bucks, MK6 2ES
Trustees: Mr David Russell Wells, Mr James Lo, Rev Siew Huat Ong
Income: £1,340,634 [2016]; £1,170,384 [2015]; £1,132,208 [2014]; £1,140,406 [2013]; £3,460,604 [2012]

Chinthurst School Educational Trust Limited
Registered: 24 Jun 1976 *Employees:* 35
Tel: 01737 812011 *Website:* chinthurstschool.co.uk
Activities: Education, training
Address: 52 Tadworth Street, Tadworth, Surrey, KT20 5QZ
Trustees: Mr Alan James Walker, Mr Marc Benton, Mrs Maxine Hulme, Mr David Robert Huntley Adams, Miss Lisa Page
Income: £1,409,702 [2017]; £1,422,800 [2016]; £915,559 [2015]; £1,209,135 [2014]; £2,226,421 [2013]

The Chipping Norton Theatre Limited
Registered: 23 Sep 1974 *Employees:* 14 *Volunteers:* 5
Tel: 01608 649101 *Website:* chippingnortontheatre.com
Activities: Education, training; arts, culture, heritage, science
Address: Chipping Norton Theatre Ltd, 2 Spring Street, Chipping Norton, Oxon, OX7 5NL
Trustees: Mrs Glenna Chadwick, Mrs Camilla Peake, Mr John Hole, Ms Susannah Sheppard, Mr Kean Grive, Mr Richard Stephen Greaves, Ms Lisa Whordley-Hughes, Ms Alice Jane Brander, Mr Andrew Villars, Mr Tim Sumner
Income: £1,160,526 [2017]; £1,108,320 [2016]; £996,821 [2015]; £1,091,956 [2014]; £1,149,055 [2013]

Choice Support
Registered: 11 Dec 1987 *Employees:* 1,333 *Volunteers:* 30
Tel: 020 7261 4100 *Website:* choicesupport.org.uk
Activities: Disability
Address: Choice Support, 100 Westminster Bridge Road, London, SE1 7XA
Trustees: Mr Paul McGee, Mr Ian Bell, Mrs Kate Wood, Mr Oliver Arthur Seymour Mills, Mr Colin George Mills, Ms Linda Frampton, Mrs Anne Chapman, Mr Chris Dorey, Mr Peter Vincence Hasler
Income: £36,435,605 [2017]; £36,118,653 [2016]; £35,290,106 [2015]; £34,838,516 [2014]; £33,970,530 [2013]

Choices (formerly known as North Kent Women's Aid) Limited
Registered: 9 Sep 2008 *Employees:* 53 *Volunteers:* 4
Tel: 01322 280686 *Website:* choicesdaservice.org.uk
Activities: General charitable purposes; education, training; accommodation, housing
Address: 40 Chastilian Road, Dartford, Kent, DA1 3JJ
Trustees: Mrs Valerie Boswell, Mr Michael Bourne, Mr Steve Fox, Mrs Isobel Kesby, Emma Siers, Mr Derek Wager, Mrs Kelly Farewell
Income: £1,507,324 [2017]; £1,386,498 [2016]; £1,310,518 [2015]; £1,087,765 [2014]; £872,139 [2013]

Sir Roger Cholmeley's School at Highgate
Registered: 24 Aug 1965 *Employees:* 466
Tel: 020 8347 3567 *Website:* highgateschool.org.uk
Activities: Education, training
Address: Highgate School, North Road, London, N6 4AY
Trustees: Bob Rothenberg MBE BA FCA CTA MAE, Mr Paul Edward Marshall BSc MRICS, Mr John Claughton MA, Professor Brian Ritchie Davidson MD FRCS MB ChB MD FRCPS FRCSE, Mr Aly Patel MA MBA, Mr Paul Rothwell MA, Mr Kumar Panja BA LLDip, Dr Kate Jolowicz Little MB BS BSc, Mr Jeremy Dennis Randall BSc, Miss Rachel Langdale QC LLB MPhil, Mr Michael Danson MA, Rev Anthony Graham Buckley, Mrs Jemima Coleman MA LLDip, Mrs Gillian Elizabeth Aitken Ma Solicitor
Income: £33,829,005 [2017]; £30,640,151 [2016]; £28,801,955 [2015]; £26,658,938 [2014]; £38,762,986 [2013]

Chorley Youth Zone
Registered: 24 May 2016 *Employees:* 2
Tel: 01204 362128 *Website:* inspireyouthzone.org
Activities: Education, training; advancement of health or saving of lives; disability; arts, culture, heritage, science; amateur sport; recreation
Address: Onside Youth Zones, Atria, Spa Road, Bolton, Lancs, BL1 4AG
Trustees: James Carter, Jamie Carson, Matthew Currie, Stacey Turner, Christopher Sinnott, Gwynne Furlong, Andrew Turner, Mr Stephen Hitchen, Neale Spear Graham, Howard Antony Turner
Income: £1,371,487 [2017]

Christ Church Oxford United Clubs
Registered: 29 Mar 1984 *Employees:* 28
Tel: 020 7582 0080 *Website:* ovalhouse.com
Activities: Education, training; prevention or relief of poverty; arts, culture, heritage, science
Address: 52-54 Kennington Oval, London, SE11 5SW
Trustees: Mr Michael Bright, Martin Humphries, Ms Esther Leeves, Mr Mat Fraser, Mr John Arthur Spall, Mr Oladipo Agboluaje, Mr Robin Priest, Ms Elizabeth Rasskazova
Income: £1,138,432 [2017]; £1,271,551 [2016]; £1,029,957 [2015]; £1,146,820 [2014]; £1,057,423 [2013]

Christ Church Students' Union
Registered: 28 Jun 2011 *Employees:* 15
Tel: 01227 782117 *Website:* ccsu.co.uk
Activities: General charitable purposes; education, training; amateur sport; recreation
Address: St Georges Halls of Residence, St Georges Place, Canterbury, Kent, CT1 1UT
Trustees: Mr Hugh Lanning, Mr John Dieter Adams, Mr Nicholas Beard, Mr Krum Ivailov Tashev, Mr Conor Michael Dobbs, Professor Helen James, Miss Faizah Zaheri Azad Chuta, Mr Jordan Howard, Mr Jopseph Cooper, Miss Vanessa Yaa Dansoah Adofo
Income: £1,193,646 [2017]; £1,241,438 [2016]; £1,231,970 [2015]; £1,291,474 [2014]; £1,452,012 [2013]

Christ College, Brecon
Registered: 22 Jul 1964 *Employees:* 156
Tel: 01874 615440 *Website:* christcollegebrecon.com
Activities: Education, training; accommodation, housing; amateur sport
Address: Christ College, Brecon, Powys, LD3 8AF
Trustees: Mr Michael Hargest Gittins, Mrs Jane Mary James, Venerable Alan Neil Jevons, Mr A Whittall, Sir Evan Paul Silk, Professor Michael Charles Radcliffe Davies, Mrs Ann Bowen Mathias, Mr Clive Idris Dytor, Mrs Megan Watkins, The Honourable Mrs Elizabeth Shan Josephine Legge-Bourke DCVO, Mrs Susan Gwyer-Roberts, The Right Reverend John D E Davies Lord Bishop of Swansea and Brecon, Mr Haydn Warman, Mr David Edward James, Mrs Helen Clare Molyneux, Mr Andrew L P Lewis, Judge Milwyn Jarman
Income: £7,826,873 [2017]; £7,380,826 [2016]; £6,498,000 [2015]; £7,769,000 [2014]; £7,866,000 [2013]

Christ Embassy
Registered: 19 Nov 1996 *Employees:* 26 *Volunteers:* 2,778
Tel: 020 8594 5424 *Website:* christembassy.org
Activities: Education, training; overseas aid, famine relief; religious activities
Address: 45 Thames Reach, Barking, Essex, IG11 0HQ
Trustees: Mr Ikemefuna Oluwarotimi Nwankpele, Mrs Ann Ugonwa Enoyoze, Mr Akindamola Folahakin Paul Abolade, Mrs Tolulope Moradeke Osuntubo, Mr Olatoye Kudehinbu, Gabriel Adesina
Income: £4,681,905 [2015]; £14,055,229 [2014]; £14,055,229 [2013]; £16,720,094 [2012]

Christ Faith Tabernacle International
Registered: 31 Aug 2004 *Employees:* 4 *Volunteers:* 250
Tel: 020 7635 0447 *Website:* cftchurches.org
Activities: Religious activities
Address: Bethesda Buildng, 56-62 New Cross Road, London, SE14 5BD
Trustees: Tayo Bilewu, Sydney Ahamefula, Theo Adisa, Alfred Williams
Income: £1,702,763 [2017]; £1,574,621 [2016]; £1,515,917 [2015]; £1,443,082 [2014]; £1,504,483 [2013]

Christ for All Nations (U.K.)
Registered: 28 Aug 1987 *Employees:* 15 *Volunteers:* 5
Tel: 0121 602 2000 *Website:* cfan.org.uk
Activities: Overseas aid, famine relief; religious activities
Address: Christ for All Nations, Highway House, 250 Coombs Road, Halesowen, W Midlands, B62 8AA
Trustees: Dr Anthony Stone, Mr Petrus Van Den Berg, Mr Russell Benson, Mr Ian Gordon Pettie, Mr Daniel Kolenda, Mr Steven Uppal
Income: £2,090,557 [2016]; £2,082,315 [2015]; £1,330,232 [2014]; £1,279,318 [2013]; £1,728,244 [2012]

Christ's College Cambridge in the University of Cambridge First Founded By King Henry VI of England and After His Death
Registered: 18 Aug 2010 *Employees:* 120
Tel: 01223 334900 *Website:* christs.cam.ac.uk
Activities: Education, training
Address: St Andrew's Street, Cambridge, CB2 3BU
Trustees: Dr Julia Shvets, Dr Robert Edward Hunt, Dr Caroline Vout, Professor Ian Malcolm Leslie FREng, Professor Theresa Mary Marteau, Professor Jane Stapleton, Professor Gabor Betegh, Dr Elena Punskaya, Professor John Michael Edwardson, Mr David John Ball, Professor Nicholas J A Gay, Dr Helen Pfeifer, Dr Ori Ziv Shmuel Beck
Income: £12,675,774 [2017]; £11,583,562 [2016]; £10,147,185 [2015]; £9,792,990 [2014]; £9,389,900 [2013]

Christ's Hospital Foundation
Registered: 9 Apr 1964 *Employees:* 369 *Volunteers:* 7
Tel: 01403 247405 *Website:* christs-hospital.org.uk
Activities: Education, training; amateur sport
Address: The Counting House, Christs Hospital, Horsham,
W Sussex, RH13 0YP
Trustees: Christ's Hospital
Income: £39,768,000 [2017]; £37,114,000 [2016]; £22,993,005
[2015]; £22,100,848 [2014]; £18,719,524 [2013]

Christ's Hospital
Registered: 16 Jul 2007 *Employees:* 316
Tel: 01403 27405 *Website:* christs-hospital.org.uk
Activities: Education, training
Address: The Avenue, Christ's Hospital, Horsham, W Sussex,
RH13 0LJ
Trustees: Mr Christopher John Steane, Mr James Simon
Edward Arnell, Mr Andrew Gordon, Professor Michael Mainelli,
Air Vice-Marshal Robert Judson, Mr Guy Perricone, Mr Jan
Tadeusz Dewalden, Mr Robert Wallace Muir, Miss Delva Patman
FRICS ACIArb FRSA, Mr Dominic Fry, Ms Marianne Bernadette
Fredericks, Mr James MacLean, Mr Thomas Garnier, Mr Nicholas
Atkinson, Lord Mountevans
Income: £24,890,000 [2017]; £26,696,000 [2016]; £24,779,000
[2015]; £28,591,000 [2014]; £26,417,000 [2013]

Christadelphian Bible Mission
Registered: 5 May 1993 *Volunteers:* 500
Tel: 01656 880485 *Website:* cbm.org.uk
Activities: Overseas aid, famine relief; religious activities
Address: Vinyamar, Craig-Yr-Eos Avenue, Ogmore by Sea,
Bridgend, CF32 0PF
Trustees: Mr Michael Harry Green, Mr Stephen Robert Sykes,
Mr Steven Anthony Jefferies, Mark Basten, Mr Jonathan Mathias,
Jeremy Morgan, Mr Mark Sheppard, Mr Robert William Fox, Marc
Bilton, Mr Peter Desmond Hale, Mr Dafydd Jenkins
Income: £1,590,822 [2016]; £820,804 [2015]; £991,235 [2014];
£2,190,729 [2013]; £1,144,759 [2012]

Christadelphian Care Homes
Registered: 28 Aug 1963 *Employees:* 317 *Volunteers:* 100
Tel: 0121 764 3548 *Website:* cch-uk.com
Activities: Disability; accommodation, housing
Address: Christadelphian Care Homes, 17 Sherbourne Road,
Acocks Green, Birmingham, B27 6AD
Trustees: Mr John Mark Buckler, Mrs Lorraine Dray, Mr Roger
Griffiths, Mr Michael Dawson-Bowman, Mrs Rosemary Joan
Hanson, Mr Geoff Purkis, Mr Jonathan Edwards, Mr Alan Sutton,
Mrs Anna Clarke, Dr David Hanley
Income: £11,134,272 [2017]; £10,913,293 [2016]; £9,383,285
[2015]; £9,205,297 [2014]; £10,269,138 [2013]

Christadelphian Meal A Day Fund
Registered: 18 Dec 2009 *Volunteers:* 20
Website: meal-a-day.org
Activities: Education, training; advancement of health or saving
of lives; disability; prevention or relief of poverty; overseas aid,
famine relief; accommodation, housing; economic, community
development, employment
Address: Bittons Barn, Beech Trees Lane, Ipplepen, Newton Abbot,
Devon, TQ12 5TW
Trustees: Mrs Melanie Ford, Mr Neil David Brighouse, Mr Paul
Lucas, Mrs Marian Dawes, Mr Trevor Routledge, Mr Phillip
Lawrence, Mrs Esther Hemmings, Mr Gordon Dawes, Mrs Rebekah
Louise Brighouse, Mrs Elizabeth Lucas, Mr Martyn East, Mr Luke
Whitehorn, Mrs Catherine Elizabeth Lawrence, Mr Jeremy Dale
Income: £1,127,796 [2016]; £671,377 [2015]; £964,784 [2014];
£742,321 [2013]; £800,987 [2012]

Christchurch London
Registered: 7 Nov 2005 *Employees:* 18 *Volunteers:* 425
Tel: 020 7384 6486 *Website:* christchurchlondon.org
Activities: The prevention or relief of poverty; religious activities
Address: Christchurch London, Matrix Studio Complex, 91a
Peterborough Road, London, SW6 3BU
Trustees: Mr David William Arthur Stroud, Mr Ross Bull, Rosanna
Gibbs, Emily Ribeiro, Mr Samuel Kay, Joseph Mukungu, Mark
Goodchild
Income: £1,572,022 [2017]; £1,813,641 [2016]; £1,354,100 [2015];
£1,326,617 [2014]; £743,699 [2013]

Christian Aid
Registered: 13 Sep 2004 *Employees:* 931 *Volunteers:* 490
Tel: 020 7620 4444 *Website:* christianaid.org.uk
Activities: General charitable purposes; education, training;
advancement of health or saving of lives; prevention or relief of
poverty; overseas aid, famine relief
Address: Christian Aid, 35-41 Lower Marsh, London, SE1 7RL
Trustees: Dr Rowan Douglas Williams PC FBA FRSL FLSW, Wilton
Powell, Bala Gnanapragasam, Mrs Margaret Anne Swinson, Paul
Spray, Alan McDonald, Mervyn McCullagh, Pippa Greenslade,
Helene Bradley-Ritt, Jennifer Cormack, Rt Revd John Davies,
Alexis Chapman, Thomas Hinton, Trevor Williams, Victoria
Hardman, Valerie Traore, Hazel Baird, Mukami McCrum
Income: £97,030,000 [2017]; £106,976,000 [2016]; £99,912,000
[2015]; £103,604,000 [2014]; £95,445,000 [2013]

Christian Blind Mission (United Kingdom) Limited
Registered: 19 Sep 1996 *Employees:* 26 *Volunteers:* 10
Tel: 01223 484731 *Website:* cbmuk.org.uk
Activities: Education, training; advancement of health or saving of
lives; disability; prevention or relief of poverty; overseas aid, famine
relief; religious activities; economic, community development,
employment; human rights, religious or racial harmony, equality or
diversity
Address: Vision House, 7-8 Oakington Business Park, Dry
Drayton Road, Oakington, Cambridge, CB24 3DQ
Trustees: Edwin Godfrey, Dr Adrian Dennis Hopkins, Ms Rachel
Mai Jones, Mrs Janine Mary King, Mary Bishop, Pam Gosal,
Mr Richard Maxwell Teare, Dr Kristin Van Zwieten, Mrs Jan Flawn
CBE, Dr Chinwe Osuchukwu, James Raynor
Income: £7,508,696 [2017]; £6,020,029 [2016]; £7,078,257 [2015];
£6,309,528 [2014]; £5,405,405 [2013]

Christian Broadcasting Network (UK)
Registered: 21 Jan 2004 *Employees:* 30 *Volunteers:* 7
Tel: 0300 561 0700 *Website:* cbneurope.com
Activities: General charitable purposes; education, training; prevention or relief of poverty; overseas aid, famine relief; religious activities; human rights, religious or racial harmony, equality or diversity
Address: Mr M Dijkens, P O Box 700, Hereford, HR1 9EW
Trustees: Mr Peter Darg, Mrs Sandra Marie Smith, Mr Kim Mitchell
Income: £1,320,739 [2017]; £1,244,685 [2016]; £1,040,359 [2015]; £986,993 [2014]; £920,186 [2013]

Christian Care Homes
Registered: 5 Jul 1988 *Employees:* 105 *Volunteers:* 10
Tel: 01375 673104 *Website:* christiancarehomes.org
Activities: General charitable purposes; education, training; advancement of health or saving of lives; disability; prevention or relief of poverty; overseas aid, famine relief; accommodation, housing; religious activities; economic, community development, employment; recreation
Address: Christian Care Homes, Oak House, 103 Corringham Road, Stanford-le-Hope, Essex, SS17 0BA
Trustees: Mrs Kathleen Bienvenu, Mrs Helga Fonfara, Mr Edward William Prior, Mrs Victoria Louise Evripidou, Mrs Glenys Jane Maria Prentice, Mrs Diane Clare Prior, Mrs Sarah Aimee Newbury
Income: £2,530,791 [2017]; £2,248,807 [2016]; £2,181,920 [2015]; £2,034,881 [2014]; £1,585,097 [2013]

The Christian Conference Trust
Registered: 5 Jul 1996 *Employees:* 149
Tel: 0300 111 4444 *Website:* cct.org.uk
Activities: Religious activities
Address: The Hayes Conference Centre, Swanwick, Alfreton, Derbys, DE55 1AU
Trustees: Peter Brierley, Mrs Amanda Allchorn, Mr Keith Lander, Mr David Evans, Rev Howard Michael Page, Michael Kinton, Mrs Melanie Finch, Mr Michael Quantick
Income: £6,303,282 [2016]; £6,458,067 [2015]; £6,018,526 [2014]; £6,100,884 [2013]; £5,842,748 [2012]

Christian Education Movement
Registered: 12 Jun 2001 *Employees:* 16 *Volunteers:* 34
Tel: 0121 458 3313 *Website:* shop.christianeducation.org.uk
Activities: Education, training; religious activities
Address: 5-6 Imperial Court, 12 Sovereign Road, Birmingham, B30 3FH
Trustees: Mrs Sarah Lane Cawte, Mr Philip Leivers, Mrs Julie Grove, Mrs Jane Chipperton, Mr Daniel Hugill, Francis Loftus, Mr Norman Richardson, Mrs Susan Morag Leslie, Mrs Carole Gallant
Income: £2,020,907 [2016]; £1,229,231 [2015]; £1,052,034 [2014]; £949,874 [2013]; £804,448 [2012]

The Christian Institute
Registered: 16 Oct 1991 *Employees:* 46 *Volunteers:* 62
Tel: 0191 281 5664 *Website:* christian.org.uk
Activities: Religious activities
Address: The Christian Institute, 4 Park Road, Gosforth Business Park, Newcastle upon Tyne, NE12 8DG
Trustees: Mr John Burn OBE, Rev George Curry, Richard Turnbull, Mr Geoffrey Fox, Rev Rupert Bentley Taylor, Rev Dr William J U Philip, Rev David Holloway, Mr Trevor Ernest James, Mr Rod Badams, Dr Philip Robinson, Rev James Leggett, Kenneth Nelson
Income: £2,830,908 [2016]; £2,596,539 [2015]; £2,621,008 [2014]; £2,439,897 [2013]; £2,794,297 [2012]

Christian Life Ministries
Registered: 6 Jun 2007 *Employees:* 21 *Volunteers:* 238
Tel: 024 7622 6698 *Website:* clmchurch.co.uk
Activities: Education, training; prevention or relief of poverty; overseas aid, famine relief; religious activities; other charitable purposes
Address: Christian Life Ministries, Parkside, Coventry, Warwicks, CV1 2HG
Trustees: Rev David Bolton, Mr Matthew Davis, James Ombudo, Rev Martin Storey, Dr Matthew Baines, Miss Olivett Ihama
Income: £1,039,130 [2016]; £859,903 [2015]; £809,664 [2014]; £624,280 [2013]; £562,447 [2012]

Christian Medical Fellowship
Registered: 16 Sep 2009 *Employees:* 24 *Volunteers:* 400
Tel: 020 7234 9660 *Website:* cmf.org.uk
Activities: Education, training; advancement of health or saving of lives; religious activities
Address: Christian Medical Fellowship, 6 Marshalsea Road, London, SE1 1HL
Trustees: Dr Ken Toop, Dr Jonathan Fisher, Dr Kevin Vaughan, Dr Maggy Spence, Dr Alice Gerth, Miss Rebecca Holly Horton, Mr Philip Taylor, Mr John Scriven, Dr Johnson Samuel, Professor Sam Leinster, Dr Matthew Davis, Mrs Angela Ruth Ryan
Income: £1,329,874 [2016]; £1,317,732 [2015]; £1,347,206 [2014]; £1,321,935 [2013]; £1,210,374 [2012]

Christian Publishing and Outreach
Registered: 13 May 1963 *Employees:* 40
Tel: 01903 263354 *Website:* cpo.org.uk
Activities: General charitable purposes; religious activities
Address: Christian Publishing & Outreach, Garcia Estate, Canterbury Road, Worthing, W Sussex, BN13 1BW
Trustees: Terence Russoff, Rev Graham Jefferson, Tim Hunt, Alan Hare, Carola Breuning, Mike Elms
Income: £3,501,190 [2017]; £3,335,317 [2016]; £2,356,717 [2015]; £2,463,205 [2014]; £2,756,104 [2013]

Christian Schools Limited
Registered: 23 Jul 1964 *Employees:* 87
Tel: 0151 426 4333 *Website:* towercollege.com
Activities: Education, training; prevention or relief of poverty; overseas aid, famine relief; religious activities
Address: Tower College, Mill Lane, Rainhill, Prescot, Merseyside, L35 6NE
Trustees: Mr Daniel Oxley, Mr Hardy, Mr Charles Craig Calvert, Mr David Williams, Mrs Margaret Condliffe, Mrs Taylor, Mr Andrew John Orr Wilcockson
Income: £3,093,859 [2016]; £2,980,610 [2015]; £3,013,981 [2014]; £3,196,630 [2013]; £3,096,993 [2012]

Christian Solidarity International
Registered: 27 Jan 1981 *Employees:* 39 *Volunteers:* 4
Tel: 020 8329 0027 *Website:* csw.org.uk
Activities: General charitable purposes; education, training; prevention or relief of poverty; other charitable purposes
Address: 46-50 Coombe Road, New Malden, Surrey, KT3 4QF
Trustees: Mrs Sarah Snyder, Mr Hector Ian MacKenzie MA DipEd AIST, Mr David Reeves Taylor, Mr Simon Francis Benjamin George, Mike Gibbons, Dr Claire Upton, Miss Anne-Marie Msichili, Mr Franklin St Clair Melville Evans, Mrs Anne Audrey Coles, Mr Nigel James Grinyer, Peter Bibawy, Dr David Carl Landrum, Michael Gowen
Income: £2,204,158 [2016]; £1,873,279 [2015]; £2,113,766 [2014]; £1,853,483 [2013]; £1,813,352 [2012]

The Christian Trust
Registered: 30 Sep 1994 *Employees:* 84 *Volunteers:* 500
Website: ellel.org
Activities: Education, training; advancement of health or saving of lives; religious activities
Address: Ellel Ministries, Ellel Grange, Bay Horse, Lancaster, LA2 0HN
Trustees: Mr David Malcolm Cross, Mr Peter James Horrobin, Mr Roger Pook, Mrs Fiona Gillian Horrobin, Mr Andrew James Taylor
Income: £3,019,280 [2016]; £3,062,035 [2015]; £3,200,915 [2014]; £3,633,384 [2013]; £3,998,211 [2012]

Christian Vision
Registered: 6 Jan 1994 *Employees:* 251
Tel: 01675 435500 *Website:* cvglobal.co
Activities: Education, training; advancement of health or saving of lives; prevention or relief of poverty; religious activities
Address: The Pavilion, Coleshill Manor Office Campus, South Drive, Coleshill, Birmingham, B46 1DL
Trustees: Mr Ian Paul Baker, Lord Edmiston, Nick Cuthbert, Lady Edmiston
Income: £43,929,201 [2016]; £39,521,002 [2015]; £38,321,265 [2014]; £23,904,388 [2013]; £20,440,311 [2012]

Christian Witness To Israel
Registered: 7 May 1976 *Employees:* 22
Website: cwi.org.uk
Activities: General charitable purposes; religious activities
Address: 1 Oasis Park, Stanton Harcourt Road, Eynsham, Witney, Oxon, OX29 4TP
Trustees: Mr R Haffenden, Rev S R Cunnah, Rev J Watterson, Rev David McPherson, Dr Jane Harpur, Rev Alex Cowie, Mr Paul Morris
Income: £1,864,479 [2017]; £1,094,146 [2016]; £1,141,169 [2015]; £1,286,488 [2014]; £1,288,234 [2013]

Christians Against Poverty
Registered: 25 Apr 2003 *Employees:* 306 *Volunteers:* 400
Tel: 01274 760818 *Website:* capuk.org
Activities: Education, training; prevention or relief of poverty; religious activities
Address: Christians Against Poverty, Jubilee Mill, 30 North Street, Bradford, BD1 4EW
Trustees: Matthew Frost, Mr Andrew Parker, Mrs Joy Glayla Blundell, Roger Hattam, Ms Jane Kathleen Elizabeth Pleace, Mr Timothy Morfin, Ms Chine McDonald, Mrs Lisa Pearce, Simon Gates
Income: £11,313,000 [2016]; £9,525,000 [2015]; £9,454,765 [2014]; £8,290,272 [2013]; £7,426,221 [2012]

Christians in Sport
Registered: 14 May 2001 *Employees:* 29 *Volunteers:* 600
Tel: 01869 255635 *Website:* christiansinsport.org.uk
Activities: Education, training; prevention or relief of poverty; religious activities; amateur sport
Address: Frampton House, Unit D1, Telford Road, Bicester, Oxon, OX26 4LD
Trustees: Mr Chad Lion-Cachet, Rt Revd Tony Porter, Rev Peter Nicholas, Mrs Sarah Kathleen Creedy, Mr Kenneth MacRitchie
Income: £1,855,678 [2017]; £1,634,944 [2016]; £1,650,234 [2015]; £1,491,214 [2014]; £1,185,460 [2013]

The Christie Charitable Fund
Registered: 11 Mar 1996 *Employees:* 32 *Volunteers:* 206
Tel: 0161 446 3704 *Website:* christies.org
Activities: Education, training; advancement of health or saving of lives
Address: The Christie NHS Foundation Trust, 550 Wilmslow Road, Manchester, M20 4BX
Trustees: The Christie NHS Foundation Trust
Income: £14,482,000 [2017]; £15,901,000 [2016]; £13,350,000 [2015]; £14,841,000 [2014]; £13,217,000 [2013]

Chrysalis (Cumbria) Ltd
Registered: 14 Sep 2006 *Employees:* 70 *Volunteers:* 7
Tel: 016973 44751 *Website:* chrysalis-cumbria.co.uk
Activities: General charitable purposes; education, training; disability; prevention or relief of poverty; economic, community development, employment; recreation
Address: Chrysalis, Leaside, Longthwaite Road, Wigton, Cumbria, CA7 9JR
Trustees: Mr Joseph Raymond Fearon, Mrs Joan Teasdale, Ms Judith Lesley Whittam, Mrs Barbara Helen Earl, Mrs Gilda Wells, Mrs Catherynn Dunstan, Mrs Margaret Alice Drury
Income: £1,040,901 [2017]; £985,326 [2016]; £1,003,795 [2015]; £876,240 [2014]; £812,143 [2013]

The Church Army
Registered: 23 Apr 1963 *Employees:* 164 *Volunteers:* 1,000
Tel: 0300 123 2113 *Website:* churcharmy.org.uk
Activities: Education, training; prevention or relief of poverty; accommodation, housing; religious activities
Address: Church Army, Wilson Carlile Centre, 50 Cavendish Street, Sheffield, S3 7RZ
Trustees: Christine Corteen, Ms Joanna Cox, Rt Rev Stephen Cottrell, Captain Robert Barker CA, Ven Dr John Applegate, John Whitfield, Mr Alan Aberbethy Rt Rev, Sister Karen Webb, Mr Mark Russell, Joanna Penberthy, Captain Graham Nunn CA, Mr Stephen Eccleston, Judith Davis, Samuel Follett, Robert Gillies
Income: £6,086,000 [2017]; £6,937,000 [2016]; £6,162,000 [2015]; £6,791,000 [2014]; £5,692,000 [2013]

Church Burgesses Trust
Registered: 14 Aug 1964
Tel: 0114 267 5594 *Website:* sheffieldchurchburgesses.org.uk
Activities: General charitable purposes; religious activities
Address: Wrigleys Solicitors LLP, Fountain Precinct, Balm Green, Sheffield, S1 2JA
Trustees: Mr Peter Lee, Mr Michael R Woffenden, Mr D Stanley, Mr Ian G Walker, Mr David Henry Quinney, Dr Julie Banham, Mr Nicholas James Anthony Hutton, Mr D F Booker, Rverend Sap Hunter, Professor Peter Francis Ainsworth, Mrs B R Hickman, Mrs S Bain
Income: £1,729,279 [2016]; £2,133,959 [2015]; £2,088,494 [2014]; £2,091,656 [2013]; £2,257,230 [2012]

Church Commissioners for England

Registered: 27 Jan 2011 *Employees:* 66
Tel: 020 7898 1785 *Website:* cofe.anglican.org
Activities: Religious activities
Address: Church House, Great Smith Street, London, SW1P 3AZ
Trustees: The Reverend Stephen Trott, Ms Suzanne Avery, Rt Revd Christine Hardman, Dr Eve Poole, Dean of Gloucester, Mr Gavin Oldham, Mrs April Alexander, Rev Christopher Smith, The Dean of Wakefield, Bishop of Manchester, Mr Mark Woolley, Ms Poppy Allonby, Mr Alan Smith, Mr Duncan Owen, The Archbishop of York, Rt Revd David Urquhart, Lord Richard Best, Jeremy Clack, The Reverend Bob Baker, Mr Jacob Vince, Canon Peter Bruinvels, Ms Loretta Minghella, The Most Revd and Rt Hon Justin Welby, Bishop of Chichester, Mr Graham Oldroyd, Second Church Estates Commissioner, Mr William Featherby QC
Income: £167,327,468 [2017]; £154,700,000 [2016]; £148,000,000 [2015]; £140,400,000 [2014]; £139,700,000 [2013]

Church Communities UK

Registered: 13 Nov 1963 *Volunteers:* 375
Tel: 01580 883300 *Website:* churchcommunities.org.uk
Activities: General charitable purposes; education, training; prevention or relief of poverty; religious activities
Address: Darvell, Brightling Road, Robertsbridge, E Sussex, TN32 5DR
Trustees: Jorg Simon Barth, Joseph Enoch Hine, Lawrence Maendel, Elna Fischli, Gregory John Winter, Bernard Hibbs, Lael Page
Income: £24,010,992 [2017]; £24,131,564 [2016]; £22,954,847 [2015]; £20,823,450 [2014]; £16,269,051 [2013]

Church Extension Association (Incorporated)

Registered: 12 Jul 1963 *Employees:* 15 *Volunteers:* 50
Website: sistersofthechurch.org.uk
Activities: Education, training; prevention or relief of poverty; religious activities
Address: St Michaels Convent, Vicarage Way, Gerrards Cross, Bucks, SL9 8AT
Trustees: Sr Aileen Taylor CSC, Sister Susan McCarten CSC, Sr Elizabeth Claire Brogden CSC, Sr Hilda Mary CSC, Sister Ruth White CSC, Sr Catherine Margaret Heybourn CSC, Sister Anita Cook CSC, Sr Susan Jane Hird CSC, Sister Teresa
Income: £9,504,300 [2016]; £509,299 [2015]; £409,640 [2014]; £467,696 [2013]; £533,915 [2012]

Church Mission Society

Registered: 16 Sep 2009 *Employees:* 180 *Volunteers:* 25
Tel: 01865 787400 *Website:* churchmissionsociety.org
Activities: Education, training; advancement of health or saving of lives; prevention or relief of poverty; overseas aid, famine relief; religious activities; environment, conservation, heritage; economic, community development, employment
Address: Church Mission Society, Watlington Road, Cowley, Oxford, OX4 6BZ
Trustees: Mr Peter Robin Hyatt, The Revd Ian Wallace, Mr Craig Hampton, Prof Salim Munayer, Mr Anthony Bargioni, Lonah Cheptoo Hebditch, Dr Ian Bromilow, Dr Kevin McKemey, Rev Canon Andrew Bowerman, Mrs Naomi Aidoo, Dr Jane Shaw, Mr Charles Clayton, Mr Beauman Chong, Mr John Stansfeld
Income: £7,471,000 [2017]; £8,182,000 [2016]; £7,318,000 [2015]; £7,809,000 [2014]; £8,042,000 [2013]

Church Pastoral Aid Society

Registered: 13 Feb 1992 *Employees:* 27 *Volunteers:* 3,287
Tel: 0300 123 0780 *Website:* cpas.org.uk
Activities: Religious activities
Address: Unit 3 Sovereign Court One, Sir William Lyons Road, University of Warwick Science Park, Coventry, Warwicks, CV4 7EZ
Trustees: Mrs Jennifer Elizabeth Bray, Miss Deborah Buggs, Rod Street, The Rev Paul Peterson, Rev Andy Piggott, The Rev Tamsin Merchant, Mrs Sarah Gough ACA, Mrs Penelope Jane Jefferis, Rev Simon Chesters
Income: £3,354,435 [2017]; £3,080,848 [2016]; £3,140,000 [2015]; £3,210,000 [2014]; £3,677,000 [2013]

Church Urban Fund

Registered: 18 Sep 1987 *Employees:* 49 *Volunteers:* 9
Tel: 020 7898 1647 *Website:* cuf.org.uk
Activities: General charitable purposes; prevention or relief of poverty
Address: Church House, 27 Great Smith Street, London, SW1P 3AZ
Trustees: Mr Andrew Dorton, Mr Patrick Coldstream, Mr Derek Twine CBE, Mr Andrew Barnett, Mr Brian Carroll, Mrs Paula Miriam Nelson, Revd Canon Denise Poole BSc, Alison Grieve, Canon Paul Hackwood, Mr Philip John Fletcher, Mr John Graham Iles
Income: £5,605,000 [2016]; £4,432,000 [2015]; £4,190,000 [2014]; £4,157,000 [2013]; £4,540,000 [2012]

Church of England Central Services

Registered: 31 Dec 2013 *Employees:* 144
Tel: 020 7898 1795 *Website:* churchofengland.org
Activities: Religious activities; economic, community development, employment
Address: Church House, Great Smith Street, London, SW1P 3AZ
Trustees: Mr John Spence, Mr Jonathan Spencer, Mr Andreas Whittam Smith
Income: £12,356,000 [2016]; £11,992,000 [2015]; £7,179,000 [2014]

Church of England Children's Society

Registered: 7 May 1964 *Employees:* 916 *Volunteers:* 12,500
Website: childrenssociety.org.uk
Activities: General charitable purposes; education, training; economic, community development, employment
Address: Edward Rudolf House, Margery Street, London, WC1X 0JL
Trustees: Mr Adrian Bagg, Mr David Ramsden, Mrs Cindy Rampersaud, Mr Martin Woodroofe, Mrs Dianne Smith, Mr Jim Clifford, Mrs Nasima Patel, Mr Chris Gillies, Miss Jessica Katherine Lee, Mr Ken Caldwell, Mr Wesley Cuell, Ms Janet Legrand, The Rt Revd Elizabeth Lane
Income: £41,614,000 [2017]; £43,829,000 [2016]; £48,453,000 [2015]; £49,613,000 [2014]; £46,294,000 [2013]

The Church of England Pensions Board
Registered: 2 Sep 1964 *Employees:* 217
Tel: 020 7898 1000 *Website:* cepb.org.uk
Activities: The prevention or relief of poverty; accommodation, housing
Address: C of E, Pensions Board, 29 Great Smith Street, London, SW1P 3PS
Trustees: Mr William Trevor Seddon, Mr Ian Clark MA, Canon Sandra Newton, Mr Ian Boothroyd, Mr Jeremy Clack, Rev David Stanton, Mr Roger Mountford, Mrs Nicolete Fisher, Mrs Maggie Rodger, The Rt Revd Atl Wilson, Mr Alan Keith Fletcher, Rev Peter Ould, Dr Jonathan Spencer, Rev Nigel Bourne, Fr Paul Benfield, Mr Roger Boulton, Mr Richard Hubbard, Mrs Emma Osbourne
Income: £28,437,000 [2016]; £26,884,000 [2015]; £23,925,000 [2014]; £22,819,000 [2013]; £20,400,000 [2012]

Church of England Soldiers', Sailors' & Airmen's Clubs
Registered: 2 Jul 1963 *Employees:* 59
Tel: 023 9282 9319 *Website:* cessaha.co.uk
Activities: Accommodation, housing; armed forces, emergency service efficiency
Address: CESSAC, 1 Shakespeare Terrace, 126 High Street, Portsmouth, PO1 2RH
Trustees: Commander Stephen Carter Royal Navy, Mr Andrew Cobb, Rear Admiral Al Rymer, Mrs Amanda Rodgers BSc FCA, Commander Tony Mizen Royal Navy, Air Commodore David Hamilton-Rump, Colonel Charles Ackroyd TD RD DL
Income: £1,755,605 [2017]; £1,783,415 [2016]; £1,593,521 [2015]; £1,656,352 [2014]; £1,833,850 [2013]

Church of God of Prophecy Trust
Registered: 5 Oct 1983 *Employees:* 44 *Volunteers:* 1,000
Tel: 0121 358 2231 *Website:* cogop.org.uk
Activities: Education, training; prevention or relief of poverty; overseas aid, famine relief; religious activities; economic, community development, employment; other charitable purposes
Address: Church of God of Prophecy, 6 Beacon Court, Birmingham Road, Great Barr, Birmingham, B43 6NN
Trustees: Rev Bernard Morris, Bishop Jefferson Atherley, Rev Raymond Veira, Rev Errol Williams, Mrs Nathalie Gibson Wilson, Reverend Lenford Rowe, Bishop Delroy Hall, Rev Paul Stewart, Ms Jacqueline Ferguson, Bishop Tedroy Powell, Bishop Alfred Reid, Bishop Theophilus McCalla, Mrs Joyce Fletcher, Mrs Deborah Clarke, Mr Henroy Samuel Green, Mrs Audrey Taylor, Mr Vernon Samuels, Rev Daisy Bailey, Mr Delaney Brown, Bishop Paul McCalla
Income: £3,956,761 [2017]; £3,850,236 [2016]; £4,351,604 [2015]; £3,838,009 [2014]; £3,838,009 [2013]

The Church of Jesus Christ of Latter-Day Saints (Great Britain)
Registered: 12 Jul 1965 *Employees:* 237 *Volunteers:* 62,000
Tel: 07932 105317 *Website:* ldschurch.org.uk
Activities: Religious activities
Address: Samuels Law, Charleston House, 12 Rumford Place, Liverpool, L3 9DQ
Trustees: Mr Brian Cordray, Mr Luis Paulo Teixeira Dos Santos, Mr Matthew Bruce Robertson
Income: £39,072,000 [2016]; £72,954,000 [2015]; £44,065,000 [2014]; £48,345,000 [2013]; £52,486,000 [2012]

The Church of Pentecost - UK
Registered: 7 May 2008 *Employees:* 60 *Volunteers:* 1,584
Tel: 020 8590 5823 *Website:* copuk.org
Activities: Education, training; advancement of health or saving of lives; prevention or relief of poverty; overseas aid, famine relief; religious activities
Address: 746 Green Lane, Dagenham, Essex, RM8 1YX
Trustees: Elder Kwaku Joe Adomako, Rev George Kwaku Korankye, Rev Kwame Twumasi Appiah, Rev Emmanuel Danso, Rev Osei Owusu Afriyie, Rev James Kofi Sam, Mr Alex Appenteng Boateng
Income: £5,911,171 [2016]; £5,775,682 [2015]; £6,107,605 [2014]; £5,334,008 [2013]; £4,532,582 [2012]

The Church of The Holy Ghost Crowthorne Trust
Registered: 17 Jan 2014 *Employees:* 59 *Volunteers:* 2
Tel: 01344 762637 *Website:* olps.co.uk
Activities: Education, training
Address: 66 Upper Broadmoor Road, Crowthorne, Berks, RG45 7DF
Trustees: Mr Michael Norman Halpin, Mrs Yvonne Nicholls, Mrs Sharon Whitehouse-Faux, Mrs Karen Osment, Mr John Darnell
Income: £1,575,644 [2016]; £1,467,583 [2015]; £1,340,835 [2014]

Churches Child Protection Advisory Service
Registered: 8 Oct 1991 *Employees:* 36 *Volunteers:* 200
Tel: 0845 120 4550 *Website:* ccpas.co.uk
Activities: General charitable purposes; education, training; disability
Address: Rosedale, College Road, Hextable, Swanley, Kent, BR8 7LT
Trustees: Mr David Frederick Pearson, Mrs Ferzanna Riley, Mrs Bridget Noel Robb, Mr James Foy, Mrs Jane Dowdell, Mr Andrew Charles Pierce
Income: £1,691,549 [2017]; £1,724,174 [2016]; £1,543,329 [2015]; £1,325,175 [2014]; £1,106,584 [2013]

Churches Conservation Trust
Registered: 27 Jun 1969 *Employees:* 64 *Volunteers:* 1,914
Tel: 0845 303 2760 *Website:* visitchurches.org.uk
Activities: Arts, culture, heritage, science; environment, conservation, heritage
Address: Society Building, 8 All Saints Street, London, N1 9RL
Trustees: Mr Edward Harley, Rev Duncan Dormor, Lady Lucy French, Ms Elizabeth Claire McHatty, Mr Graham William Donaldson, Mr Simon David Jenkins, Mr Peter Michael Ainsworth, Ms Liz Peace, Ms Susan Linda Wilkinson, Ms Carol Pyrah
Income: £9,184,283 [2017]; £11,148,260 [2016]; £12,900,191 [2015]; £8,464,743 [2014]; £5,873,565 [2013]

Churches Conservation
Registered: 26 Feb 2013 *Volunteers:* 3
Tel: 020 7841 0403
Activities: Arts, culture, heritage, science; environment, conservation, heritage; economic, community development, employment
Address: Society Building, 8 All Saints Street, London, N1 9RL
Trustees: Adrian Clark, Jane Weeks, Mr Graham William Donaldson, Anne Vick, Mr Alec Paul Forshaw
Income: £1,075,863 [2017]; £2,379,081 [2016]; £2,959,139 [2015]; £1,541,623 [2014]

Churchill College in the University of Cambridge
Registered: 13 Aug 2010 *Employees:* 264
Website: chu.cam.ac.uk
Activities: Education, training
Address: Churchill College, Cambridge, CB3 0DS
Trustees: Dr Ian Barry Kingston, Dr Jeremy Toner, Dr Katherine Stott, Mrs Stephanie Cook, Professor Dame Athene Donald, Mr David Spaxman, Dr Seb Savory, Mrs Tamsin James, Ms Malavika Nair, Mr Marcel Hedman, Professor Alison Finch, Mr Richard Partington, Professor Kenneth Siddle, Dr Pieter Van Houten, Dr Lisa Jardine-Wright, Mr Barry Phipps, Dr Mark Holmes, Mr Ashley Brice, Mr Jack Hodkinson
Income: £20,039,000 [2017]; £20,493,000 [2016]; £19,268,156 [2015]; £18,623,000 [2014]; £17,787,335 [2013]

The Cinnamon Network
Registered: 8 May 2014
Website: cinnamonnetwork.co.uk
Activities: Education, training; economic, community development, employment; other charitable purposes
Address: c/o Andy Nash Accounting & Consultancy Ltd, The Maltings, Cardiff, CF24 5EA
Trustees: Mr David Westlake, Mr Martin Warner, Dr Shola Adeaga, Mr Jonathan Lloyd, Mr Paul Morrish, Mrs Kiera Phyo, Bishop Wayne Malcolm
Income: £1,092,071 [2017]; £903,814 [2016]; £506,851 [2015]

The Cinnamon Trust
Registered: 5 Mar 2010 *Employees:* 67 *Volunteers:* 12,923
Tel: 01736 757900 *Website:* cinnamon.org.uk
Activities: The advancement of health or saving of lives; animals
Address: Cinnamon Trust, 10 Market Square, Hayle, Cornwall, TR27 4HE
Trustees: Mr John Dale, Mr Dale Band, Mrs Averil Regina Jarvis, Mrs Patricia Atkins
Income: £6,348,744 [2017]; £5,803,041 [2016]; £4,586,068 [2015]; £3,833,470 [2014]; £3,771,797 [2013]

Cintre
Registered: 4 Jul 1980 *Employees:* 47
Tel: 0117 923 7129 *Website:* cintre.org
Activities: Education, training; disability; accommodation, housing; other charitable purposes
Address: 2nd Floor, Shore House, 68 Westbury Hill, Westbury-on-Trym, Bristol, BS9 3AA
Trustees: Mr Robert Barker, Mr Thomas Richardson, Mr Philip Harris, Mrs Lesley Farrall, Mr Robert Moore, Mrs Alison Webber, Mr Peter Clayton, Mrs Susan Margaret Elstob
Income: £1,273,654 [2017]; £1,271,811 [2016]; £1,179,324 [2015]; £1,159,041 [2014]; £1,004,028 [2013]

Circadian Trust
Registered: 27 Sep 2005 *Employees:* 274 *Volunteers:* 19
Tel: 01454 279927 *Website:* circadiantrust.org
Activities: Amateur sport
Address: Bradley Stoke Leisure Centre, Fiddlers Wood Lane, Bradley Stoke, Bristol, BS32 9BS
Trustees: Jonathan Charles Edwards, Mr Robert David Wimbush, Mrs Susan Timbrell, Mr Ross Parker, Mr Patrick Van Beek, Mr Neil McKen, Mr Adrian Dawe, Mrs Katherine Morris, Mr Derek Segger, Ms Gary Leadbeater, Mr Anthony Davis, Mr Peter Tuodolo
Income: £12,078,976 [2017]; £11,394,532 [2016]; £11,081,210 [2015]; £10,861,718 [2014]; £10,148,086 [2013]

Circle Care and Support
Registered: 30 Dec 2004 *Employees:* 296 *Volunteers:* 220
Tel: 020 3784 3726 *Website:* centragroup.org.uk
Activities: General charitable purposes
Address: Circle Care and Support Limited, Level 6, 6 More London Place, Tooley Street, London, SE1 2DA
Trustees: Mr Simon Fowler, Miss Ishaitu Kamara, Mr Andrew Hughes, Mrs Susan Holmes, Mr Frank Pycroft, Ms Joanna David
Income: £15,530,000 [2017]; £16,323,000 [2016]; £16,993,000 [2015]; £19,369,000 [2014]; £19,416,000 [2013]

Circles Network
Registered: 24 Jan 1995 *Employees:* 79 *Volunteers:* 100
Tel: 01788 816671 *Website:* circlesnetwork.org.uk
Activities: Education, training; disability; economic, community development, employment; other charitable purposes
Address: The Penthouse, Coventry Road, Cawston, Rugby, Warwicks, CV23 9JP
Trustees: Mr Andrew Martin Adrian Cater, Ms Andrea Florence McTeare, Mr James Inglis, Mr Amiya Kagalwala, Dr Susan Mary Pringle BSc PhD, Mr James John Peard McNeile, Mr Tony McTeare, Mr James Hirons
Income: £1,456,407 [2017]; £1,255,228 [2016]; £1,258,453 [2015]; £1,299,118 [2014]; £1,311,053 [2013]

Citizens Advice Bradford & Airedale and Bradford Law Centre
Registered: 21 Feb 2003 *Employees:* 68 *Volunteers:* 80
Tel: 01274 758030
Activities: Education, training; prevention or relief of poverty
Address: Citizens Advice Bradford & Airedale, 31 Manor Row, Bradford, W Yorks, BD1 4PS
Trustees: Mr John Prestage, Amanda Steele, Mr Shakil Azam, Ms Melanie June Mitchley, Mr Mark Hadfield, Mr Robin Walker Lister, Ms Peggy Alexander, Mrs Pam Essler, Ross Stinton, Mr David Fearnside, Mr Ashok Nair, Mr Andrew Charles Northage, Mr Nigel Charles Rowlands
Income: £2,003,442 [2017]; £2,177,041 [2016]; £1,866,326 [2015]; £1,522,887 [2014]; £1,336,982 [2013]

Citizens Advice Bureaux (Salford)
Registered: 11 May 1989 *Employees:* 35 *Volunteers:* 90
Website: salfordcab.org.uk
Activities: General charitable purposes
Address: Langworthy Cornerstone, 451 Liverpool Street, Salford, M6 5QQ
Trustees: Mrs Barbara Griffin, Peter Sutcliffe, Cllr Bernard Lea, Mr Eric Stelfox, Miss Natalie Whitehouse, Mr Malcolm Davies, Jane McGarry, Mr David Wolfson, Mrs Susan Lightup
Income: £1,020,817 [2017]; £1,118,767 [2016]; £1,150,785 [2015]; £1,189,325 [2014]; £1,590,639 [2013]

Citizens Advice Cheshire West
Registered: 3 Mar 2009 *Employees:* 37 *Volunteers:* 124
Tel: 01606 815262 *Website:* cwcab.org.uk
Activities: General charitable purposes; prevention or relief of poverty
Address: Citizens Advice Bureau, Meadow Court, Meadow Street, Northwich, Cheshire, CW9 5FP
Trustees: Mr Geoffrey Hope-Terry, Mr Max Herberg Griffiths, Mr Christopher Thomas Tomkinson, Mrs Helen Anne Armstrong, Mr Michael Joseph Snape, Mrs Gillian Linda Conway
Income: £1,201,876 [2017]; £1,559,916 [2016]; £1,241,281 [2015]; £1,298,017 [2014]; £1,416,784 [2013]

Citizens Advice County Durham

Registered: 26 Apr 2013 *Employees:* 68 *Volunteers:* 410
Tel: 0191 372 6702 *Website:* citizensadvicecd.org.uk
Activities: General charitable purposes; prevention or relief of poverty; human rights, religious or racial harmony, equality or diversity; other charitable purposes
Address: Armstrong House, Abbeywoods Business Park, Pity Me, Durham, DH1 5GH
Trustees: Ms Brenda Davidson, Mrs Kamila Coulson-Patel, Mr Alan Keith Roxbrough, Mr Michael Smith, Mr John Scollen, Colin McPherson, Councillor Angela Surtees, Mr Patrick Stephen Conway, Mr David Hall, Mr Anthony John Pensom, Mrs Alison Collins, John Taylor, Mrs Angela Cheek
Income: £2,460,490 [2017]; £2,166,357 [2016]; £2,543,826 [2015]; £1,977,077 [2014]

Citizens Advice Gateshead

Registered: 4 May 1993 *Employees:* 90 *Volunteers:* 60
Tel: 0191 478 5100 *Website:* citizensadvicegateshead.org.uk
Activities: General charitable purposes; education, training; advancement of health or saving of lives; prevention or relief of poverty; economic, community development, employment; other charitable purposes
Address: 4 Latton Close, Southfield Gardens, Cramlington, Northumberland, NE23 7XP
Trustees: Ms Maureen Kesteven Vice Chair, Ms Meg Dodd, Mr William John Smith Treasurer, Miss Catherine Ann Robson, Mrs Michelle Brannen, Mrs Sonya Dickie, Mrs Cathleen Watson, Mr Mike Nott, Mr Ian Logan, Mr Barry Taylor, Mr Stuart Phillipson Bell, Mr Anthony Robert McDonald
Income: £1,999,108 [2017]; £1,640,226 [2016]; £1,512,675 [2015]; £1,239,505 [2014]; £1,419,319 [2013]

Citizens Advice Leicestershire

Registered: 22 Mar 2010 *Employees:* 55 *Volunteers:* 230
Tel: 07949 126123 *Website:* leicscab.org.uk
Activities: General charitable purposes
Address: Clarence House, 46 Humberstone Gate, Leicester, LE1 3PJ
Trustees: Mr Timothy Ennis Render, Mr Malcolm Flaherty, Mr John Walters, Narendra Waghela, Mr Peter Symonds, Mrs Mumtaz Kynaston-Pearson, Ms Ann Elizabeth Melville, Mr Victor Goodman, Geoff Cook, Mrs Rita Rathod, Mrs Marie-Anne MacKenzie
Income: £1,495,995 [2017]; £1,720,495 [2016]; £1,572,681 [2015]; £1,799,447 [2014]; £1,166,622 [2013]

Citizens Advice Manchester Ltd

Registered: 30 Mar 1992 *Employees:* 75 *Volunteers:* 54
Tel: 0161 672 0526 *Website:* citizensadvicemanchester.org.uk
Activities: The prevention or relief of poverty
Address: Citizens Advice Manchester Ltd, Albert House, 17 Bloom Street, Manchester, M1 3HZ
Trustees: Mr Karl Tonks, Ms Karen Clarke, Miss Holly Markin, Dr Fiona McNair, Mrs Beverly D'Alessio, Mr Martin Singer, Mr Michael Kay, Mrs Aarti Gupta, Miss Nicola Sansom
Income: £2,930,015 [2017]; £3,439,344 [2016]; £2,865,144 [2015]; £2,900,059 [2014]; £3,385,627 [2013]

Citizens Advice Merton and Lambeth

Registered: 4 May 1995 *Employees:* 37 *Volunteers:* 105
Tel: 020 8288 0449 *Website:* caml.org.uk
Activities: General charitable purposes; education, training; disability; prevention or relief of poverty; other charitable purposes
Address: Citizens Advice Merton & Lambeth, 326 London Road, Mitcham, Surrey, CR4 3ND
Trustees: Shirley Ashby, Emma Cross, Caroline Taylor, Crystal Todd, Mike Wisgard, Jac Nunns, Alan Webster
Income: £1,232,096 [2017]; £1,603,327 [2016]; £1,291,432 [2015]; £845,176 [2014]; £828,378 [2013]

Citizens Advice Shropshire

Registered: 26 Feb 2001 *Employees:* 25 *Volunteers:* 69
Tel: 01743 284178 *Website:* cabshropshire.org.uk
Activities: The prevention or relief of poverty
Address: Fletcher House, 15 College Hill, Shrewsbury, Salop, SY1 1LY
Trustees: Mrs Claire Ann Cartlidge, Mr Keir Hirst, Mr Tony Hinkley, Penelope Cooper, Mr Christopher Boote, Mrs Linda Ann Binns, Mr Alan Taylor, Mr Paul Langton, Mr Andrew Howitt, Mr Nathan Hinks
Income: £1,080,185 [2017]; £1,106,131 [2016]; £936,616 [2015]; £761,309 [2014]; £1,052,264 [2013]

The Citizens Foundation (UK)

Registered: 6 Aug 2001 *Employees:* 2 *Volunteers:* 15
Tel: 020 3585 3011 *Website:* tcf-uk.org
Activities: Education, training; advancement of health or saving of lives; prevention or relief of poverty
Address: The Citizens Foundation (UK), 48 Charlotte Street, London, W1T 2NS
Trustees: Mr Tariq Hussain, Atif Ali, Mr Imtiaz Dossa, Mr Bilal Raja
Income: £1,710,920 [2016]; £1,123,380 [2015]; £1,003,892 [2014]; £1,265,452 [2013]; £1,068,501 [2012]

Citizens UK Charity

Registered: 14 Dec 2004 *Employees:* 69 *Volunteers:* 15,000
Website: citizensuk.org
Activities: Education, training; advancement of health or saving of lives; prevention or relief of poverty; economic, community development, employment; human rights, religious or racial harmony, equality or diversity
Address: 136 Cavell Street, London, E1 2JA
Trustees: Bishop of Stepney, Mr Farooq Salman Murad, Ms Sheila Bamber, Ms Meriel Barclay, Mrs Kaneez Shaid, Nabeel Al-Azami, Rosamund McCarthy, Jonathan Dunnett Clark, Mr Ranjit Sondhi, Paul Regan, Dr Steve Mowle, Mrs Noeleen Cohen, Rt Hon John Dominic Battle, Mr Nicholas Thomas, Mr David Edward Canham
Income: £4,942,816 [2017]; £3,578,998 [2016]; £2,388,070 [2015]; £1,095,924 [2014]; £954,566 [2013]

The Citizenship Foundation

Registered: 11 Apr 1989 *Employees:* 20 *Volunteers:* 150
Tel: 020 7566 4141 *Website:* citizenshipfoundation.org.uk
Activities: Education, training
Address: Universal House, 88-94 Wentworth Street, Aldgate, London, E1 7SA
Trustees: Professor David Miles, Mr Nicholas Johnson, Dr Emma Jane Watchorn, Mr Brian Walton, Mr Jason Arthur, Mr Martin Bostock, Mrs Laura Hamm, Ms Farzana Banu, Mrs Cecile Agbo-Bloua, Mr James Cathcart
Income: £1,114,510 [2017]; £1,292,642 [2016]; £1,146,209 [2015]; £1,206,323 [2014]; £1,405,840 [2013]

City Catering Southampton
Registered: 6 Mar 2015 *Employees:* 256
Tel: 023 8083 3108
Activities: Education, training; advancement of health or saving of lives
Address: 2nd Floor, Latimer House, 5-7 Cumberland Place, Southampton, SO15 2BH
Trustees: Mr Howells Jonathan, Miss Jennifer Karen Dagwell, Ms Lisa Church, Mrs Hayley Hammick, Miss Kathryn Bevan-Mackie, Rachel Hall
Income: £4,914,507 [2017]; £5,051,374 [2016]

City College Nottingham
Registered: 10 Nov 1993 *Employees:* 62 *Volunteers:* 8
Tel: 0115 910 1455 *Website:* citycollegenottingham.com
Activities: Education, training
Address: Nottingham Training & Enterprise CE, Carlton Road, Nottingham, NG3 2NR
Trustees: Ron Bell, Mr Jawaid Khalil, L Aslam, Mr Amrik Singh Sanghera, Mr Aurangzeb Khan, Mr Mohammed Mahruf, Mr Rashid Mohammad, Mrs Halima Gulzar Khalid
Income: £1,664,502 [2017]; £1,438,118 [2016]; £2,023,639 [2015]; £1,469,467 [2014]; £1,155,548 [2013]

City Gateway Limited
Registered: 25 Nov 1999 *Employees:* 122 *Volunteers:* 11
Tel: 020 3727 6310 *Website:* citygateway.org.uk
Activities: General charitable purposes; education, training; economic, community development, employment
Address: 32 Mastmaker Court, Mastmaker Road, London, E14 9UB
Trustees: Mr Deepak Mahtani, Ms Wei-Lynn Lum, Mr James Bishop, Mr Sean Greathead, Kate Monkhouse, Mr Edward Boyd, Mr David Pain, Mrs Rachel Duncombe-Anderson, Mr Alex Harris, Mr Nathan Oley, Mr Kenney Imafidon
Income: £2,607,043 [2017]; £7,543,902 [2016]; £7,608,285 [2015]; £8,037,401 [2014]; £5,726,722 [2013]

City Hearts (UK)
Registered: 5 Jul 2005 *Employees:* 87 *Volunteers:* 44
Tel: 0114 213 2065 *Website:* hopecitychurch.tv
Activities: General charitable purposes; education, training; advancement of health or saving of lives; prevention or relief of poverty; accommodation, housing; economic, community development, employment
Address: Hope City Church, The Megacentre, Bernard Road, Sheffield, S2 5BQ
Trustees: Mr Karl Downes, Mrs Leah Langizya Chilengwe, Dr Ngozi Patricia Anumba, Rev Jenny Gilpin
Income: £2,690,087 [2017]; £1,633,340 [2016]; £944,741 [2015]; £552,945 [2014]; £535,282 [2013]

The City Hospice Trust Limited
Registered: 30 Jun 1993 *Employees:* 28 *Volunteers:* 310
Website: cityhospice.org.uk
Activities: The advancement of health or saving of lives
Address: Ty Hosbis, Whitchurch Hospital, Park Road, Whitchurch, Cardiff, CF14 7BF
Trustees: Dr Elinor Kapp, Stephen Harries, Mrs Veronica Marshall, Mr John Lord, Dr Diana Evans, Mr Andrew Burns, Ms Helen Miller, Mrs Sandra Miles, Mr John Dwight, Mr David Lloyd
Income: £1,494,547 [2017]; £1,239,786 [2016]; £1,166,650 [2015]; £1,380,513 [2014]; £1,164,007 [2013]

City Hospitals Sunderland NHS Foundation Trust Charitable Funds
Registered: 27 Jan 1996
Tel: 0191 565 6256 *Website:* chscharity.com
Activities: The advancement of health or saving of lives
Address: Financial Services, The Childrens Centre, Durham Road, Sunderland, Tyne & Wear, SR3 4AD
Trustees: City Hospitals Sunderland NHS Foundation Trust
Income: £1,000,098 [2017]; £583,464 [2016]; £775,984 [2015]; £469,751 [2014]; £735,642 [2013]

The City Literary Institute
Registered: 1 Mar 1990 *Employees:* 290
Tel: 020 7492 2605 *Website:* citylit.ac.uk
Activities: Education, training
Address: Mrs Katrina O'Sullivan, Keeley House, 1-10 Keeley Street, London, WC2B 4BA
Trustees: Ms Annita Bennett, Mr Rajiv Parkash, Mark Malcomson, Mrs Penelope Allen, Ms Paula Smith, Ms Wendy Moss, Mr Michael Simmonds, Miss Sophie Neary, Sandy Pfeifer, Keith Moffitt, Jane Cooper, Dame Moira Gibb, Mr Jon Gamble, Dr Joseph Cullen, Mr Timothy Bolderson
Income: £17,943,000 [2017]; £16,906,000 [2016]; £17,630,000 [2015]; £17,800 [2014]; £17,728,000 [2013]

City South Manchester Housing Trust Limited
Registered: 8 Apr 2008 *Employees:* 364 *Volunteers:* 50
Tel: 0161 274 2140 *Website:* onemanchester.co.uk
Activities: Accommodation, housing; economic, community development, employment
Address: City South Manchester Housing Trust, Lovell House, Archway 6, Hulme, Manchester, M15 5RN
Trustees: Mr Stephen Arthur Kinsey, Ms Alison Gordon, Mr Nadim Ahmad, Emily Rowles, Angela Robinson, Mr David Dennehy, Graham Aitken, Stephen Mole, Mr John James Hughes, Dr Slawomir Pawlik
Income: £20,306,000 [2017]; £22,058,000 [2016]; £20,215,000 [2015]; £28,394,000 [2014]; £22,402,000 [2013]

City YMCA, London
Registered: 19 Mar 1996 *Employees:* 26 *Volunteers:* 46
Tel: 020 7549 0475 *Website:* cityymca.org
Activities: Education, training; accommodation, housing; amateur sport
Address: The Drum, 167, Whitecross Street, London, EC1Y 8JT
Trustees: Claudia Webbe, Mark Poulding-Wright, Gary Morley, Josefine Ahlstrom, Daniel Gerring, Patsy Mills, Robert James Thompson, Hanny Tirta, Mr Marek Wiluszynski, Mark Henshaw
Income: £2,780,396 [2017]; £2,723,923 [2016]; £1,876,892 [2015]; £1,980,716 [2014]; £2,365,556 [2013]

City Year UK
Registered: 25 Aug 2009 *Employees:* 65 *Volunteers:* 179
Website: cityyear.org.uk
Activities: Education, training
Address: 58-62 White Lion Street, London, N1 9PP
Trustees: Filippo Cardini, Mr James Balfanz, Mrs Pauline Maddison, Jonathan Beebe, Mr Patrick Flaherty, Mrs Caroline Clark, Mrs Annmaura Connolly, Ms Aliza Blachman-O'Keeffe, Mr Charles Geffen, Baroness Janet Royall
Income: £3,836,809 [2017]; £4,187,238 [2016]; £3,411,708 [2015]; £3,067,819 [2014]; £2,286,304 [2013]

City and Guilds of London Art School Limited
Registered: 17 Nov 2011 *Employees:* 88
Tel: 020 7091 1680 *Website:* cityandguildsartschool.ac.uk
Activities: Education, training; arts, culture, heritage, science
Address: 124 Kennington Park Road, London, SE11 4DJ
Trustees: Jonathan Marsden, Mr Laurence Benson, Mr Tim Statham, Mr Mark Cazalet, Mr Alister Warman, Mr Andrew Sich, Mr James Roundell, Mr William Andrew Allen, Mr Martin Hatfull, Robert Holland-Martin, Brendan Finucane QC, Mr Russell Martin, John Taylor, Ms Marjorie Angela Althorpe-Guyton, Ms Anne Beckwith-Smith, Ms Jane Margaret Rapley, Dr Caroline Campbell
Income: £2,331,141 [2017]; £2,476,201 [2016]; £2,422,048 [2015]; £2,194,722 [2014]; £2,015,033 [2013]

City and Guilds of London Art School Property Trust
Registered: 4 Dec 1970
Tel: 020 7735 2306
Activities: Education, training; arts, culture, heritage, science; environment, conservation, heritage
Address: City & Guilds of London Art School, 118-124 Kennington Park Road, London, SE11 4DJ
Trustees: Brendan Finucane QC, Mr William Parente, Mr Aidan Crawshaw, Mr John Taylor MBE, Mrs Janey Elliott
Income: £1,063,659 [2016]; £796,849 [2015]; £630,000 [2014]; £540,000 [2013]; £1,646,713 [2012]

The City and Guilds of London Institute
Registered: 25 May 1965 *Employees:* 1,257
Tel: 020 7294 3444 *Website:* cityandguilds.com
Activities: Education, training
Address: 1 Giltspur Street, London, EC1A 9DD
Trustees: Dr Ann Geraldine, Professor Alison Halstead, Sir John Armitt, Mr Andy Smyth, Ms Ann Brown, Mr Andy Marchant, Mr David Illingworth, Dr Tim Strickland, Mr Peter McKee, Mr Kevin Baughan, Mr Chris Fenton
Income: £137,371,289 [2016]; £141,051,218 [2015]; £129,853,369 [2014]; £113,935,072 [2013]; £117,887,692 [2012]

City of Birmingham Symphony Orchestra
Registered: 4 May 1977 *Employees:* 104 *Volunteers:* 356
Tel: 0121 616 6535 *Website:* cbso.co.uk
Activities: Arts, culture, heritage, science
Address: CBSO, Berkley Street, Birmingham, B1 2LF
Trustees: Sir Albert Bore, Mr David Gregory, John Osborn, Mrs Lucy Kate Williams, Mr Anthony Alfred Peter Davis, Ms Jane Fielding, Cllr Randal Anthony Maddock Brew, Mr David Lovell Burbidge, Mr Patrick Verwer, Mr Joe Godwin, Mr Graham Sibley, Mr David Andrew Roper
Income: £9,006,000 [2017]; £8,634,324 [2016]; £9,935,354 [2015]; £10,002,943 [2014]; £8,512,735 [2013]

City of Liverpool Young Men's Christian Association (Inc)
Registered: 1 Oct 1964 *Employees:* 82
Tel: 0151 600 3530 *Website:* liverpoolymca.org.uk
Activities: General charitable purposes; education, training; advancement of health or saving of lives; accommodation, housing; religious activities; amateur sport
Address: YMCA, 15 Leeds Street, Liverpool, L3 6HU
Trustees: Phil Shackell, Ms Winnie Lawlor, Simon Abrams, Robert Spowart, Dalite Lucy, Mr Ian Johnson, Miss Mary Compton Rickett, Jayne Price, Edward Naylor, Ms Louise Douglas
Income: £3,683,919 [2017]; £2,839,675 [2016]; £2,550,877 [2015]; £2,184,681 [2014]; £1,553,763 [2013]

The City of London Charities Pool
Registered: 25 May 1993
Tel: 020 7332 1334
Activities: General charitable purposes
Address: Corporation of London, P O Box 270, London, EC2P 2EJ
Trustees: The City of London Corporation
Income: £1,021,998 [2017]; £1,263,249 [2016]; £1,984,476 [2015]; £1,457,712 [2014]; £4,292,922 [2013]

City of London Sinfonia Limited
Registered: 5 Apr 1983 *Employees:* 12
Tel: 020 7621 2800 *Website:* cls.co.uk
Activities: Education, training; arts, culture, heritage, science
Address: 4th Floor, Piano House, 9 Brighton Terrace, London, SW9 8DJ
Trustees: Mr Colin Senior, Mr John Singer, Ms Teruko Iwanaga OBE, Countess Sarah Thun-Hohenstein, Marshall of The Royal Air Force The Lord Stirrup KG GBC AFC, Mrs Patricia Millett, Mr Michael Waggett, Mr Richard Spiegelberg, Mrs Sally Davis, Mr Alan William Morgan, Ms Joanna Livesey, Mr William David John Spurgin
Income: £1,494,110 [2017]; £1,555,625 [2016]; £1,402,455 [2015]; £1,611,383 [2014]; £1,329,064 [2013]

The City of Sheffield Theatre Trust
Registered: 18 Oct 2007
Tel: 0114 249 6000 *Website:* sheffieldtheatres.co.uk
Activities: Arts, culture, heritage, science
Address: 55 Norfolk Street, Sheffield, S1 1DA
Trustees: Mr Neil Andrew MacDonald, Ms Claire Pender, Mrs Surriya Falconer, Mrs Julie Kenny, Ms Carol Evelyn Pickering, Mr John Steven Cowling, Mr Giles Dominic Searby, Ms Jackie Labbe
Income: £6,774,912 [2017]; £6,409,941 [2016]; £5,746,200 [2015]; £4,792,973 [2014]; £4,436 [2013]

The Civil Service Benevolent Fund
Registered: 14 Jul 2010 *Employees:* 86 *Volunteers:* 225
Tel: 0800 056 2424 *Website:* foryoubyyou.org.uk
Activities: The advancement of health or saving of lives; disability; prevention or relief of poverty
Address: Civil Service Benevolent Fund, Fund House, 5 Anne Boleyns Walk, Sutton, Surrey, SM3 8DY
Trustees: Mr Mark Addison CB, Ms Janet Mary Aiston CB, Mr Barry Burton, Ms Susan Owen CB, Miss Deborah Loudon, Selvin Brown MBE, Mrs Vivienne Dews, Mr Kevin Sadler CBE, Mr Jonathan Russell CB, Miss Wendy Proctor, Maria Clohessy
Income: £6,983,000 [2016]; £7,824,000 [2015]; £8,788,000 [2014]; £8,218,000 [2013]; £8,169,000 [2012]

Clacton Family Trust Limited
Registered: 11 May 1999 *Employees:* 147
Tel: 01255 425913 *Website:* clactonfamilytrust.com
Activities: Disability; accommodation, housing
Address: 2 Burrows Close, Clacton on Sea, Essex, CO16 8EG
Trustees: Mr Colin Davey Hawkins, Mrs Colleen Patricia Johnson, Mr P Carratt, Mr David Harris, Mr Malcolm Thomas Chapman, Mrs J Martin
Income: £4,690,323 [2017]; £4,331,141 [2016]; £5,000,916 [2015]; £4,422,880 [2014]; £3,544,179 [2013]

Claire House

Registered: 2 Sep 1991 *Employees:* 238 *Volunteers:* 910
Tel: 0151 343 0883 *Website:* clairehouse.org.uk
Activities: The advancement of health or saving of lives; disability
Address: Claire House, Childrens Hospice, Clatterbridge Road, Wirral, Merseyside, CH63 4JD
Trustees: Mr Alan Rice, Briar Stewart, Mr John Anthony Gittens, Miss Valerie Ann Lawton, Mrs Helen Watson, Dr Eileen Baildham, Mr Mark William Thomas
Income: £7,696,237 [2017]; £6,700,743 [2016]; £6,703,317 [2015]; £6,592,997 [2014]; £5,723,390 [2013]

Clare College Cambridge

Registered: 17 Aug 2010 *Employees:* 233
Tel: 01223 333221 *Website:* clare.cam.ac.uk
Activities: Education, training
Address: Clare College, Trinity Lane, Cambridge, CB2 1TL
Trustees: Prof William Anthony Harris, Dr Jacqueline Anne Tasioulas, Dr Maciej Dunajski, Professor Anna Philpott, Lord Anthony Stephen Grabiner QC, Dr Alan David Chambers, Prof Jonathan Michael Goodman, Dr Heike Laman, Prof Simon Colin Franklin, Rev James Douglas Thomas Hawkey, Professor Philip Michael Allmendinger, Professor John Stanley Gibson, Mr Paul Charles Warren, Dr Jason Carroll, Dr Adria De Gispert Ramis, Dr Thomas Schindler, Prof Neil Howard Andrews, Dr Flavio Martin Obedman Toxvaerd
Income: £14,097,000 [2017]; £13,346,000 [2016]; £16,104,900 [2015]; £15,883,830 [2014]; £14,861,394 [2013]

Clare Hall in the University of Cambridge

Registered: 13 Aug 2010 *Employees:* 30
Tel: 01223 332360 *Website:* clarehall.cam.ac.uk
Activities: Education, training
Address: Clare Hall, Herschel Road, Cambridge, CB3 9AL
Trustees: Professor David Ibbetson, Ian Farnan, Prof Charles Alan Short, Hasok Chang, Dr Iain Stewart Black, Tim Coorens, Mr Stephen Bourne, Dr Anthony Street, Elizabeth Rowe, Ian Strachan, Lucia Tantardini, Sara Krum
Income: £3,556,314 [2017]; £3,438,277 [2016]; £3,310,568 [2015]; £3,057,348 [2014]; £2,741,639 [2013]

The Claremont Fan Court Foundation Limited

Registered: 10 Feb 1978 *Employees:* 201 *Volunteers:* 80
Tel: 01372 473601 *Website:* claremont-school.co.uk
Activities: Education, training
Address: Claremont Fan Court School, Claremont Drive, Esher, Surrey, KT10 9LY
Trustees: Mr Gordon Hunt, Mr Nigel Beavor, Mrs Angela Christine Bishop, Mr Stephen Eggins, Mr Andrew Sutherland, Mrs Jennifer Frances Long, Mrs Patricia Rickard, Dr Gerald Smart, Mr Julian Gall, Mr Jeremy Batchelor, Mrs Catherine Jackson
Income: £12,280,883 [2017]; £11,843,121 [2016]; £10,783,012 [2015]; £10,300,723 [2014]; £9,651,684 [2013]

Clarendon Trust Limited

Registered: 5 Jun 1998 *Employees:* 39 *Volunteers:* 800
Tel: 01273 840884 *Website:* weareemmanuel.com
Activities: The prevention or relief of poverty; religious activities; other charitable purposes
Address: 21-23 Clarendon Villas, Hove, E Sussex, BN3 3RE
Trustees: Mr Neville Derek Jones, Mr Stephen John Horne, Mr Ian Bailey, Mr Kenneth William Stevens, Mrs Kate Ball, Peter Jarvis, Mrs Helen Evans, Mr James Foreman, Mr Mxolisi Sibanda
Income: £3,077,068 [2016]; £3,478,248 [2015]; £2,224,282 [2014]; £2,430,372 [2013]

Clarets in the Community Limited

Registered: 19 Feb 2014 *Employees:* 49 *Volunteers:* 50
Tel: 01282 704716 *Website:* burnleyfccommunity.org
Activities: General charitable purposes; education, training; disability; amateur sport; economic, community development, employment; recreation
Address: Burnley Football & Athletic Co Ltd, Turf Moor, Harry Potts Way, Burnley, Lancs, BB10 4BX
Trustees: Mrs Alison Rushton, Mr Brian Thomas Nelson, Mr Lukman Patel, Mr David Michael Lawson, Mr Philip Alan Stuart Wilson, Mr Richard Herbert John Sutton, Mr Barry Kilby, Mrs Angela Noreen Allen
Income: £1,689,334 [2017]; £924,184 [2016]; £665,226 [2015]

Claridge House

Registered: 17 May 2016 *Employees:* 6 *Volunteers:* 4
Tel: 020 8852 6735 *Website:* claridgehousequaker.org.uk
Activities: Education, training; advancement of health or saving of lives; disability
Address: 78 Courtlands Avenue, London, SE12 8JA
Trustees: Cherry Simpkin, Frances Crampton, Anthony Franklin, Mrs Charlotte Ros Standish, Ms Jane Elizabeth Short, Mr William David Hugh Gardiner, Rachel Chancellor, Mr Francis Reginald Standish, Mr Paul Michael Grey, Ms Sarah Louise Robins-Hobden
Income: £1,339,455 [2017]

Clarion Futures

Registered: 22 Mar 2010 *Employees:* 64
Activities: Education, training; prevention or relief of poverty; accommodation, housing; economic, community development, employment
Address: Clarion Housing Group Limited, Level 6, 6 More London Place, Tooley Street, London, SE1 2DA
Trustees: Mr Peter Fortune, Mrs Lisa Gamble, Sue Killen, Bob Dinwiddy, Dr Usha Sundaram
Income: £5,250,000 [2017]; £4,794,000 [2016]; £4,660,000 [2015]; £5,209,000 [2014]; £4,909,000 [2013]

Clarity - Employment for Blind People

Registered: 13 May 1963 *Employees:* 109 *Volunteers:* 17
Tel: 020 3078 8950 *Website:* clarityefbp.org
Activities: Education, training; disability; accommodation, housing; economic, community development, employment
Address: Unit 7 Jubilee Avenue, Highams Park, London, E4 9JD
Trustees: Mrs Judith Mary Mellor, Mr Alessio Balduini, Mrs Anja Batista Sonksen, Mr Clive Howard Jackson, Mr John Kelvin Sharman, Mr Edmund Lawrence Peacock, Mrs Hester Louise Fielding Fairhurst
Income: £2,770,486 [2017]; £2,606,633 [2016]; £2,915,311 [2015]; £2,930,279 [2014]; £3,088,722 [2013]

The Roger and Sarah Bancroft Clark Charitable Trust

Registered: 15 Nov 1962
Activities: General charitable purposes
Address: Box 1, 40 High Street, Street, Somerset, BA16 0EQ
Trustees: Mrs Alice Clark, Caroline Gould, Mr Robert Baldwin Robertson, Mr Martin Lovell, Priscilla Goldby
Income: £2,931,781 [2016]; £563,277 [2015]; £354,438 [2014]; £327,612 [2013]; £302,114 [2012]

Classquote Limited
Registered: 28 Apr 2000 *Employees:* 1
Activities: Education, training; prevention or relief of poverty; religious activities; other charitable purposes
Address: 80A Darenth Road, London, N16 6ED
Trustees: Mr Shulem Berger, Mr G Berger, Mrs S Stein, Mrs Dinah Berger, Mrs S Grunzweig
Income: £1,055,543 [2017]; £608,920 [2016]; £479,094 [2015]; £432,435 [2014]; £669,958 [2013]

Clatterbridge Cancer Charity
Registered: 3 Jan 1996 *Volunteers:* 80
Tel: 0151 482 7680 *Website:* clatterbridgecc.org.uk
Activities: The advancement of health or saving of lives
Address: Clatterbridge Centre for Oncology, Clatterbridge Road, Bebington, Wirral, Merseyside, CH63 4JY
Trustees: Clatterbridge Cancer Centre NHS Foundation Trust
Income: £2,202,000 [2017]; £2,058,000 [2016]; £1,587,000 [2015]; £1,472,000 [2014]; £1,366,000 [2013]

Clayesmore School
Registered: 5 Apr 1963 *Employees:* 300 *Volunteers:* 30
Tel: 01747 813130 *Website:* clayesmore.com
Activities: Education, training; amateur sport
Address: Clayesmore School, Iwerne Minster, Blandford Forum, Dorset, DT11 8LL
Trustees: Mr Paul Dallyn, Mr David Malcolm Green, Rosie Stiven, Mr Andrew Beaton, Mr Tim Ingram, John Andrews, Maj Gen John Stokoe, Mr David Haywood, Mrs Frances Clair Deeming, Mr Stephen Richard Symonds
Income: £13,921,980 [2016]; £13,533,554 [2015]; £13,235,785 [2014]; £12,702,865 [2013]; £11,829,066 [2012]

Clean Break Theatre Company
Registered: 24 Feb 1993 *Employees:* 26 *Volunteers:* 47
Tel: 020 7482 8600 *Website:* cleanbreak.org.uk
Activities: Education, training; arts, culture, heritage, science
Address: 2 Patshull Road, London, NW5 2LB
Trustees: Ms Deborah Coles, Ms Susan Royce, Ms Alice Millest, Ms Doreen Foster, Ms Tanya Tracey, Despina Tsatsas, Ms Lucy Kirkwood, Ms Kim Evans, Ms Suzanne Bell, Miss Sabba Akhtar
Income: £1,144,590 [2017]; £1,121,466 [2016]; £1,050,515 [2015]; £1,012,154 [2014]; £887,632 [2013]

Cleveland Youth Association
Registered: 23 Jul 1987 *Employees:* 33 *Volunteers:* 6
Tel: 01642 282222 *Website:* shapetraining.co.uk
Activities: Education, training
Address: Cleveland Youth Association, Richard Crosthwaite Centre, Sotherby Road, Middlesbrough, Cleveland, TS3 8BT
Trustees: Mr Brian Whitfield, Rev Rachel Harrison, Mrs Karen Deen, Mr Brian Downie, Mr John Probert, Mr Martin Foster
Income: £1,036,122 [2017]; £1,122,895 [2016]; £1,028,867 [2015]; £1,065,451 [2014]; £1,086,266 [2013]

ClientEarth
Registered: 26 Mar 1996 *Employees:* 83 *Volunteers:* 12
Tel: 020 7749 5970 *Website:* clientearth.org
Activities: Environment, conservation, heritage; human rights, religious or racial harmony, equality or diversity
Address: The Hothouse, 274 Richmond Road, London, E8 3QW
Trustees: Sir Martin Smith, The Honorable Emily Young, Ms Christina Robert, Mrs Fabienne Serfaty, Mr Howard John Covington, Mr Georg Stratenwerth, Daniel Greenberg, Mrs Sarah Butler-Sloss, Mr Stephen Hockman QC, Mr Brian Eno, Ms Frances Beinecke, Mr Philippe Marie Joseph Maurice Joubert, Winsome McIntosh, Bwb Secretarial Ltd
Income: £7,311,514 [2016]; £6,653,500 [2015]; £4,745,573 [2014]; £4,046,138 [2013]; £3,276,402 [2012]

Cliff College
Registered: 27 Feb 1967 *Employees:* 27 *Volunteers:* 2
Tel: 01246 584200 *Website:* cliffcollege.ac.uk
Activities: Education, training; religious activities
Address: Cliff College, Calver, Hope Valley, Derbys, S32 3XG
Trustees: Rev Roger Walton, Rev Alistair Sharp, Mrs Joan Ryan, Mr Matthew Lee, Rev Ashley Cooper, Rev Rachel Deigh, Mr Stephen Holliday, Mr Ashley France
Income: £1,723,690 [2017]; £2,125,053 [2016]; £2,911,391 [2015]; £2,038,635 [2014]; £1,642,789 [2013]

Clifton College
Registered: 19 Mar 1964 *Employees:* 458 *Volunteers:* 3
Website: cliftoncollege.com
Activities: Education, training
Address: 13 Pennant Place, Portishead, Bristol, BS20 7AA
Trustees: John Cottrell, Alison Streatfeild-James, Jonathan Glassberg, Stuart Smith, Teresa Fisk, Chris Trembath, Richard Cartwright, Fiona Purcell, Mr James Womersley, Brigadier Richard Morris, Peter McCarthy, Hugh Harper, Lyn Harradine, Nick Tolchard, Sir Hector Sants, Julian Hemming, Mr Mark Eldridge, Mrs Alison Eynon
Income: £28,254,000 [2017]; £28,042,000 [2016]; £28,150,000 [2015]; £27,151,000 [2014]; £26,515,000 [2013]

Clifton High School
Registered: 26 Feb 1964 *Employees:* 128
Tel: 0117 973 3853 *Website:* cliftonhigh.bristol.sch.uk
Activities: Education, training
Address: Clifton High School, College Road, Clifton, Bristol, BS8 3JD
Trustees: Miss Lise Anne Seager, Mrs Hilary Vaughan BEng CEng MICE, Mr David Marval B Arch DipArch RIBA, Ms Katie Lee, Mr Richard Whitburn, Mr James Caddy, Mrs Jane Morrision
Income: £6,684,000 [2016]; £5,460,000 [2015]; £5,225,000 [2014]; £5,546,000 [2013]

Clifton Suspension Bridge Trust
Registered: 7 May 1962 *Employees:* 25 *Volunteers:* 20
Tel: 01242 234421
Activities: General charitable purposes
Address: Clerk To The Trustees, Clifton Suspension Bridge, Leigh Woods, Bristol, BS8 3PA
Trustees: Mr Chris Arthur Booy, Councillor Charles Cave, Professor Colin Taylor, Mrs Valerie Harland, Mr John Benson, Ms Margaret Cooke MS, Mr Steven David Walker, Mr William Mather, Mrs Ann Metherall, Mr Ian Jenkins, Mr Steve Denton
Income: £2,609,986 [2016]; £2,349,208 [2015]; £2,311,185 [2014]; £2,336,987 [2013]; £1,772,831 [2012]

Climate Bonds Initiative
Registered: 31 Oct 2013 *Employees:* 12
Tel: 07525 068331 *Website:* climatebonds.net
Activities: Environment, conservation, heritage
Address: 72 Muswell Hill Place, London, N10 3RR
Trustees: Mr Bryan Martell, Mr Karl Joseph Mallon, Professor Cynthia Williams, Mr Nicholas Gavin Silver
Income: £1,435,138 [2016]; £461,691 [2015]; £307,722 [2014]

The Climate Change Organisation
Registered: 26 Mar 2004 *Employees:* 53 *Volunteers:* 4
Tel: 020 7960 2990 *Website:* theclimategroup.org
Activities: Education, training; environment, conservation, heritage; economic, community development, employment
Address: 106 Derwent Avenue, Barnet, Herts, EN4 8LZ
Trustees: Viki Cooke, Miss Joan MacNaughton, Richard Gledhill, Mr Abyd Karmali, Victoria Keilthy, Zoe Ashcroft, Dominic Waughray, Mr Greg Barker, Mike Rann
Income: £4,830,524 [2017]; £4,842,713 [2016]; £4,523,053 [2015]; £3,746,579 [2014]; £5,723,654 [2013]

Climate Parliament
Registered: 11 Jan 2005 *Employees:* 6
Tel: 01273 239144 *Website:* climateparl.net
Activities: Education, training; advancement of health or saving of lives; prevention or relief of poverty; environment, conservation, heritage
Address: 21 The Cliff, Brighton, BN2 5RF
Trustees: Caroline Lucas MP, Mr Keith Taylor MEP, Mrs Sirpa Pietikainen MEP
Income: £1,050,972 [2016]; £1,045,013 [2015]; £1,271,768 [2014]; £1,052,391 [2013]; £663,352 [2012]

The Clink Charity
Registered: 1 Mar 2010 *Employees:* 41 *Volunteers:* 26
Tel: 020 7147 6749 *Website:* theclinkcharity.org
Activities: Education, training; economic, community development, employment
Address: The Clink Charity, Highdown Prison, Highdown, Highdown Lane, Sutton, Surrey, SM2 5PJ
Trustees: Mr Kevin David McGrath, Sir William Atkinson, Mr Timothy Wates, Lady Edwina Louise Grosvenor, Mr Finlay Thomas Kennedy Scott, Ms Rosemary Anne Davidson
Income: £2,341,329 [2016]; £2,070,014 [2015]; £1,512,953 [2014]; £1,268,263 [2013]; £366,972 [2012]

Clinks
Registered: 5 Mar 1999 *Employees:* 24 *Volunteers:* 1
Tel: 020 7383 0966 *Website:* clinks.org
Activities: Economic, community development, employment
Address: Clinks, Tavis House, 1-6 Tavistock Square, London, WC1H 9NA
Trustees: Ms Norma Hoyte, Nicola Mary Silverleaf, Rachael Byrne, Jessica Mary Southgate, Ms Liz Calderbank, Dame Anne Elizabeth Owers, Mr Steve Rawlins, Helen Attewell, Alison Frater, Christopher Stacey
Income: £1,208,317 [2017]; £1,378,864 [2016]; £1,505,118 [2015]; £1,635,056 [2014]; £2,065,049 [2013]

The Clockmakers' Charity
Registered: 14 Mar 1978 *Volunteers:* 40
Tel: 020 7998 8120 *Website:* clockmakers.org
Activities: General charitable purposes; education, training; arts, culture, heritage, science
Address: Worshipful Company of Clockmakers, 1 Throgmorton Avenue, London, EC2N 2BY
Trustees: Clockmakers' Company
Income: £1,821,513 [2017]; £44,448 [2016]; £89,252 [2015]; £59,871 [2014]; £208,558 [2013]

The Clocktower Foundation
Registered: 20 Jan 2015
Tel: 07768 508279
Activities: General charitable purposes; advancement of health or saving of lives; armed forces, emergency service efficiency; other charitable purposes
Address: No 1, St Martins-le-Grand, London, EC1A 4NP
Trustees: Lord Anthony Rockley, Mr James Patrick Eyre, Mr David Juster, Mr Andrew John Slater
Income: £5,864,652 [2016]; £2,941,755 [2015]

The Clore Duffield Foundation
Registered: 9 Jan 2001 *Employees:* 2
Tel: 020 7351 6061 *Website:* cloreduffield.org.uk
Activities: General charitable purposes; education, training; advancement of health or saving of lives; disability; prevention or relief of poverty; overseas aid, famine relief; arts, culture, heritage, science; environment, conservation, heritage
Address: The Clore Duffield Foundation, Unit 3 Chelsea Manor Studios, Flood Street, London, SW3 5SR
Trustees: Mr David Terence Digby Harrel LLB, Mr Richard John Oldfield, Melanie Clore, Dame Vivien Duffield DBE, Mr James Paul Harding, Mr Jeremy Vaughan Sandelson
Income: £1,750,157 [2016]; £260,484 [2015]; £275,197 [2014]; £659,977 [2013]; £14,050,397 [2012]

The Clore Leadership Programme
Registered: 30 Jul 2004 *Employees:* 8
Tel: 020 7420 9419 *Website:* cloreleadership.org
Activities: Education, training; arts, culture, heritage, science
Address: Clore Leadership Programme, South Building, Somerset House, The Strand, London, WC2R 1LA
Trustees: Dame Vivien Duffield, Mr David Terence Digby Harrel LLB, Mr Roland Francis Kester Keating, Sandy Nairne, Professor John Michael Holden, Professor Wayne McGregor, Nichola Johnson, Mr Stephen Alexander Page, Dr Maria Jane Balshaw, Mr David Kershaw
Income: £1,676,017 [2017]; £1,500,573 [2016]; £1,674,685 [2015]; £1,814,672 [2014]; £1,887,584 [2013]

The Clore Social Leadership Programme
Registered: 5 Jul 2010 *Employees:* 12
Tel: 020 7812 3770 *Website:* cloresocialleadership.org.uk
Activities: Education, training
Address: Clore Social Leadership Programme, Kings Place, 90 York Way, London, N1 9AG
Trustees: Anna Southall, Charles Good, Julie Mellor, Tina Alexandrou, Vyla Rollins, Mr David Terence Digby Harrel LLB, Arabella Duffield, Dominic Houlder, Mark Fisher
Income: £1,078,326 [2016]; £865,552 [2015]; £1,242,389 [2014]; £1,056,120 [2013]; £1,056,274 [2012]

The Clothworkers' Foundation
Registered: 26 Jul 1977
Tel: 020 7623 7041 *Website:* clothworkers.co.uk
Activities: General charitable purposes
Address: The Clothworkers Co, Clothworkers Hall, Dunster Court, London, EC3R 7AH
Trustees: Miss Anne Luttman-Johnson, Mr Michael William Jarvis FCA, Mr Melville Haggard, Mr Andrew Blessley, Mr John Wake, Mr Nicholas Horne, Dr Carolyn Joan Boulter BSc MA PhD JP, Hanif Virji, Mrs Joanna Louise Sayer Dodd, Mr Alexander Nelson, Dr Lucy Rawson, Mr John Coombe-Tennant
Income: £6,823,832 [2016]; £6,012,907 [2015]; £5,773,812 [2014]; £34,200,234 [2013]; £4,863,077 [2012]

Charity of Richard Cloudesley
Registered: 22 Sep 1962 *Employees:* 4
Tel: 020 7697 4094 *Website:* cloudesley.org.uk
Activities: The advancement of health or saving of lives; disability; prevention or relief of poverty; religious activities
Address: Richard Cloudesley's Charity, Office 1.1, Resource for London, 356 Holloway Road, London, N7 6PA
Trustees: Richard Cloudesley Trustee Limited
Income: £1,386,109 [2017]; £1,415,630 [2016]; £1,430,473 [2015]; £1,552,167 [2014]; £1,425,215 [2013]

Cloverleaf Advocacy 2000 Ltd
Registered: 20 May 2003 *Employees:* 165 *Volunteers:* 61
Tel: 01924 438438 *Website:* cloverleaf-advocacy.co.uk
Activities: The advancement of health or saving of lives; disability
Address: 1st Floor, 9 Wellington Road, Dewsbury, W Yorks, WF13 1HF
Trustees: Mrs Sarah Mitchell, Mr Nicholas Eugene Whittingham, Mr Jason Paul Anthony Hiscock, Mr Mark Chamberlain, Mr Iain Alasdair Hill, Mr David Marshall, Mr Christopher Sutherland, Mrs Dorothy Hardwick, Mr Rory Deighton, Mrs Jane Wilson
Income: £3,865,151 [2017]; £2,937,223 [2016]; £2,367,006 [2015]; £1,798,725 [2014]; £1,497,863 [2013]

Club Doncaster Community Sports & Education Foundation
Registered: 7 Feb 2008 *Employees:* 49 *Volunteers:* 20
Website: doncasterroversfoundation.co.uk
Activities: Education, training; disability; prevention or relief of poverty; arts, culture, heritage, science; amateur sport; economic, community development, employment
Address: Keepmoat Stadium, Stadium Way, Doncaster, S Yorks, DN4 5JW
Trustees: Mr Gavin Paul Samuel Baldwin, Mr Nigel Brewster BA (Hons) 2:1, Dr Rupert Suckling, Mrs Linda Patricia Tully, Mr John Arthur Wallbank, Mr James Robert Lord, Mr Allan Stewart, Mrs Natalie Louise Shaw
Income: £1,630,547 [2017]; £1,282,278 [2016]; £1,274,202 [2015]; £919,168 [2014]; £748,971 [2013]

Club Peloton
Registered: 9 Jan 2008 *Employees:* 4
Tel: 07958 443129 *Website:* clubpeloton.org
Activities: General charitable purposes
Address: Coram, 41 Brunswick Square, London, WC1N 1AZ
Trustees: Mr Steve Whyman, Ms Jennifer Ross, Mr Paul Simon Burke, Ms Sarah Elizabeth Cary, Mr Nick Searl, Mr Dominic Sebastian Millar, Mr Barry Alexander Fowler
Income: £1,761,538 [2017]; £1,290,345 [2016]; £950,877 [2015]; £783,503 [2014]; £566,252 [2013]

Clybiau Plant Cymru Kids Clubs
Registered: 1 Aug 2002 *Employees:* 32 *Volunteers:* 16
Tel: 029 2021 5048 *Website:* clybiauplantcymru.org
Activities: General charitable purposes; education, training; advancement of health or saving of lives; economic, community development, employment
Address: 37 Lionel Road, Canton, Cardiff, CF5 1HN
Trustees: Amy Baugh, Clare Macomish, Leanne Evans, Miss Louise Touhig, Brigid Lee, Mr Jason Roberts-Jones, Mr Christopher Hiddins
Income: £1,187,319 [2017]; £1,165,850 [2016]; £1,407,633 [2015]; £1,527,918 [2014]; £1,713,911 [2013]

Clydpride Limited
Registered: 10 Nov 1986 *Employees:* 3
Activities: Education, training; prevention or relief of poverty; overseas aid, famine relief; religious activities
Address: Rayner Essex, Entrance D, Tavistock House South, Tavistock Square, London, WC1H 9LG
Trustees: Mr A Faust, Mr L Faust, Mr M H Linton
Income: £2,876,782 [2016]; £3,279,397 [2015]; £4,209,265 [2014]; £2,687,177 [2013]; £4,893,768 [2012]

The Co-Mission Churches Trust
Registered: 19 Jan 2011 *Employees:* 42 *Volunteers:* 100
Tel: 020 8543 4411 *Website:* co-mission.org
Activities: The prevention or relief of poverty; religious activities
Address: The Factory, 577 Kingston Road, London, SW20 8SA
Trustees: Mr Gordon William Reid, Mr Mark Lewis Vernon, Mr Robert Turner, Philip David Cooper, Mr John Marland, Mr Gregor James Ferguson
Income: £3,533,266 [2017]; £3,192,862 [2016]; £2,557,299 [2015]; £2,406,369 [2014]; £2,221,548 [2013]

The Co-operative College
Registered: 6 Nov 2014 *Employees:* 25
Website: co-op.ac.uk
Activities: Education, training
Address: The Co-operative College, Holyoake House, Hanover Street, Manchester, M60 0AS
Trustees: Prof Hazel Johnson, Ms Alison Lamond, Mr John Chillcott, John Boyle, Mrs Emma Robinson, Mr Jon Nott, Mr Nigel Todd, Mrs Pamela Maxwell, Sophie Stewart
Income: £1,003,647 [2017]; £5,492,423 [2016]

Co-operative Community Investment Foundation
Registered: 18 Jul 2002 *Employees:* 4
Tel: 0843 751 9251 *Website:* coop.co.uk
Activities: General charitable purposes; education, training; prevention or relief of poverty; economic, community development, employment
Address: 9th Floor, 1 Angel Square, Manchester, M60 0AG
Trustees: Ms Sheila Jane Malley, Mr Martin Rogers, Jamie Ward-Smith, Saleem Chowdhery, Mr Daniel Crowe, Mr Andy Phelps
Income: £1,541,462 [2016]; £1,171,869 [2015]; £1,065,763 [2014]; £3,389,678 [2013]; £4,112,953 [2012]

The Coal Industry Social Welfare Organisation 2014
Registered: 26 Jan 2015 *Employees:* 103
Website: ciswo.org
Activities: Education, training; advancement of health or saving of lives; prevention or relief of poverty
Address: Coal Industry Social Welfare Organisation, The Old Rectory, Rectory Drive, Whiston, Rotherham, S Yorks, S60 4JG
Trustees: Mr Wayne Thomas, Mr Jonathan Leslie Hattersley, Mrs Christine Kaye, Mr Jeffrey Wood, Canon Robert Cooper, Mr Gary Smith, Mr Colin Ambler, Mr John Humble, Mrs Carole Langrick, Mr Terence Leslie Fox, Patrick Carragher
Income: £3,322,252 [2016]; £4,266,689 [2015]

The Coal Industry Social Welfare Organisation
Registered: 4 Dec 1992 *Employees:* 103
Tel: 01709 728115 *Website:* ciswo.org.uk
Activities: General charitable purposes; advancement of health or saving of lives; disability; prevention or relief of poverty; amateur sport; economic, community development, employment
Address: Coal Industry Social Welfare Organisation, The Old Rectory, Rectory Drive, Whiston, Rotherham, S Yorks, S60 4JG
Trustees: The Coal Industry Social Welfare Organisation 2014
Income: £3,277,832 [2016]; £4,184,710 [2015]; £4,111,171 [2014]; £3,094,363 [2013]; £3,353,561 [2012]

The Coalfields Regeneration Trust
Registered: 30 Mar 1999 *Employees:* 30
Tel: 01226 272810 *Website:* coalfields-regen.org.uk
Activities: Education, training; advancement of health or saving of lives; prevention or relief of poverty; amateur sport; economic, community development, employment
Address: The Coalfields Regeneration Trust, 1 Waterside Park, Valley Way, Wombwell, Barnsley, S Yorks, S73 0BB
Trustees: Mr Wayne Thomas, Mr Nicholas Wilson, Mrs Dawn Davies, Mr Terence O'Neill, Mr Nicky Stubbs, Mrs Sylvia Wileman, Mr Peter McNestry, Mr Michael Clapham, Mr Robert Young, Ms Trudie McGuinness
Income: £4,284,000 [2017]; £4,390,000 [2016]; £13,929,000 [2015]; £15,188,000 [2014]; £11,923,000 [2013]

Coastal West Sussex Mind
Registered: 24 Feb 2014 *Employees:* 60 *Volunteers:* 12
Tel: 01903 277000 *Website:* coastalwestsussexmind.org
Activities: Disability; other charitable purposes
Address: The Gateway, 8-10 Durrington Lane, Worthing, W Sussex, BN13 2QG
Trustees: Mr Neville James Pressley, Mr Andrew Kean, Mr Robert John Smytherman, Dr Alison Mary Langley, Mr Daniel William Bird, Jack Redfern, Buddhi Vinitharatne, Mrs Sally Lefroy, Mr David Brian Hughes, Dr Anthony Edward Woolgar, Mr David Marten, Susan Hawker
Income: £1,140,256 [2017]; £1,046,829 [2016]; £985,602 [2015]

Coastline Housing Limited
Registered: 17 Dec 1997 *Employees:* 249 *Volunteers:* 20
Tel: 01209 200125 *Website:* coastlinehousing.co.uk
Activities: Disability; accommodation, housing
Address: Coastline Housing Ltd, 4 Barncoose Gateway Park, Barncoose, Redruth, Cornwall, TR15 3RQ
Trustees: Mr Philip Bearne, Mrs Helen Riley-Humfrey, Mr Peter Robert Stephens, Mrs Susan Roberts, Mr Deepak Chandra, Mr John Newey, Mrs Sylvia Dudley, Mr Derek Law MBE, Mr Ian Leslie Cowley, Mr John Waldron, Mr Allister Young
Income: £26,612,000 [2017]; £25,477,000 [2016]; £21,684,000 [2015]; £21,983,000 [2014]; £20,438,000 [2013]

Cobalt Health
Registered: 26 Feb 2002 *Employees:* 84 *Volunteers:* 150
Tel: 01242 535906 *Website:* cobalthealth.co.uk
Activities: Education, training; advancement of health or saving of lives
Address: Cobalt Unit Appeal Fund, Linton House Clinic, Thirlestaine Road, Cheltenham, Glos, GL53 7AS
Trustees: Mr John Henry Parker, Professor Ann Barrett, Mr Neil Holbrook, Dr Mark Callaway, Dr Susan Owen, Mr Robert Derry-Evans, Dr Peter Thomas Warry
Income: £9,839,733 [2017]; £8,770,198 [2016]; £8,200,792 [2015]; £7,892,752 [2014]; £6,423,514 [2013]

Cobham Hall
Registered: 13 Nov 1961 *Employees:* 92
Tel: 01474 825903 *Website:* cobhamhall.com
Activities: Education, training
Address: Cobham Hall, Cobham, Gravesend, Kent, DA12 3BL
Trustees: Mr Colin Sykes, John Dick, Mr Marc Frost, Dr Katrina O'Neill-Byrne, Mrs Lynn Ellis, Martin Pennell, Mrs Sarah McRitchie, Mr Graham Francis Smith
Income: £3,826,095 [2017]; £3,914,878 [2016]; £4,131,676 [2015]; £4,282,006 [2014]; £4,594,850 [2013]

The Cochrane Collaboration
Registered: 26 Apr 1995 *Employees:* 65 *Volunteers:* 2,844
Tel: 020 7183 7503 *Website:* cochrane.org
Activities: The advancement of health or saving of lives
Address: St Albans House, 57-59 Haymarket, London, SW1Y 4QX
Trustees: Dr Martin James Burton, Dr Joerg Johannes Meerpohl, Ms Marguerite Koster, Ms Nancy Santesso, Mr Gerald Gartlehner, Ms Raewyn Megan Lamb, Ms Tracey Elizabeth Howe, Professor Cynthia Margaret Farquhar, Ms Catherine Marshall, Prof Janet Elizabeth Clarkson, Mr Peter Gotzsche, Mr David Hammerstein, Ms Maria Gladys Faba Beaumont
Income: £6,805,399 [2016]; £5,433,071 [2015]; £4,558,815 [2014]; £4,022,746 [2013]; £3,027,492 [2012]

Cockpit Arts
Registered: 2 Dec 1993 *Employees:* 9
Website: cockpitarts.com
Activities: Education, training; arts, culture, heritage, science
Address: 8 Albert Road, Twickenham, Middlesex, TW1 4HU
Trustees: Michael O'Neil Bedward, Ms Jane Kuria, Ms Sarah Myerscough, Ms Jane Adam, Mr Benjamin O'Neill, Mr Bill Amberg, Ms Jill Humphrey, Mr Cornelius Medvei, Mr David Moore, Mr Stephen Fletcher, Samuel Fry
Income: £1,019,334 [2017]; £952,252 [2016]; £919,678 [2015]; £925,335 [2014]; £891,167 [2013]

Coeliac UK
Registered: 20 Jul 1995 *Employees:* 39 *Volunteers:* 1,218
Tel: 01494 796128 *Website:* coeliac.org.uk
Activities: The advancement of health or saving of lives
Address: 3rd Floor, The Chief Executive, Apollo Centre, Desborough Road, High Wycombe, Bucks, HP11 2QW
Trustees: Les O'Dea, Professor David Surendran Sanders, Professor Alan Christopher Perkins, Mrs Claire Andrews, Ray Bremner, Ms Maureen Agnes Burnside, Dr Dai Lloyd, Mr Mike Elliott, Mr James Chappell, Mrs Margaret Morgan, Mr Robert Keith Trice
Income: £3,842,633 [2016]; £3,631,067 [2015]; £3,044,939 [2014]; £2,912,371 [2013]; £2,720,937 [2012]

Cokethorpe Educational Trust Limited
Registered: 20 Feb 1964   *Employees:* 207   *Volunteers:* 6
Tel: 01993 892327   *Website:* cokethorpe.org.uk
Activities: Education, training
Address: Cokethorpe School, Witney, Oxon, OX29 7PU
Trustees: Mrs S A Landon, Mr Robert Francois Jonckheer, Mrs Wendy Elizabeth Hart, Mr Mark Robert Booty, Mrs Rita Gunn, Dr Wai Wing Lau, Bishop Colin William Fletcher, Ms Geraldine McAndrew, Mr Philip Graham Riman, Mr Alan James Bark, Mr Paul Arthur Lindon Tolley, Mr John Peter Bennett
Income: £11,134,056 [2017]; £10,875,695 [2016]; £10,389,096 [2015]; £9,768,042 [2014]; £9,546,784 [2013]

Colchester League of Hospital and Community Friends Limited
Registered: 10 Nov 2008   *Employees:* 26   *Volunteers:* 120
Tel: 01206 286643   *Website:* clhf.co.uk
Activities: The advancement of health or saving of lives
Address: Colchester League of Hospital & Community Friend, Colchester Primary Care Centre, Turner Road, Colchester, Essex, CO4 5JR
Trustees: Mrs Carol Hirons, Mr Peter Pushman, Dr Helen Porter, Mr David Everiss, Mr John Bradley, Mr Peter Alfred Mockford, Mrs Joan Orme, Mr Francis Jordan
Income: £1,164,690 [2017]; £1,114,292 [2016]; £1,097,850 [2015]; £1,070,450 [2014]; £1,039,934 [2013]

Colchester Mercury Theatre Limited
Registered: 3 Jan 1964   *Employees:* 74   *Volunteers:* 5
Tel: 01206 577006   *Website:* mercurytheatre.co.uk
Activities: Arts, culture, heritage, science
Address: Mercury Theatre Co, Mercury Theatre, Balkerne Gate, Colchester, Essex, CO1 1PT
Trustees: Mr Bryan Campbell Johnston, Miss Jennifer Mary Skingsley, Mr Simon David Fisher, Ms Hassina Khan, Rob West, Mr David Addington, Ms Anita Thornberry, Ms Deborah Sawyerr, Mr Matthew Swan, Ms Kathleen Jane Hamilton, Linda Barton, Mr Patrick Sandford, Ms Samantha Blackwell-Heard
Income: £3,720,769 [2017]; £4,276,679 [2016]; £3,469,464 [2015]; £3,107,003 [2014]; £2,646,638 [2013]

Coleg Ceredigion
Registered: 12 Nov 2013   *Employees:* 127   *Volunteers:* 10
Website: ceredigion.ac.uk
Activities: Education, training
Address: Dobbin Walls, Kilgetty Lane, Stepaside, Arberth, Pembrokeshire, SA67 8JL
Trustees: Mr Geraint Roberts, Mr Barry William James Liles, Mrs Maria Stedman, Mrs Dilys Sandra Frances Isaac
Income: £5,644,000 [2017]; £4,940,159 [2016]; £5,401,039 [2015]; £5,766,133 [2014]

Coleg Elidyr Camphill Communities
Registered: 9 Jan 1976   *Employees:* 134   *Volunteers:* 35
Tel: 01550 760447   *Website:* colegelidyr.com
Activities: Education, training; disability; accommodation, housing
Address: Coleg Elidyr, Rhandirmwyn, Llandovery, Carmarthenshire, SA20 0NL
Trustees: Leigh Bradley, Mr Colin MacIntyre, Mr Robert Macey, Vicky Davies, Mr Wyn Llewellyn, Ms Jane Ann Hamilton
Income: £4,094,489 [2017]; £3,961,959 [2016]; £3,384,262 [2015]; £2,793,389 [2014]; £2,617,722 [2013]

Coleg Llanymddyfri
Registered: 28 Nov 2012   *Employees:* 104
Tel: 01550 723000   *Website:* llandoverycollege.com
Activities: Education, training; religious activities; arts, culture, heritage, science
Address: Llandovery College, Llandovery, Carmarthenshire, SA20 0EE
Trustees: Mr William Hopkin Joseph, Mr Jonathan Thomas Gravell, Mr David Rowland Rees-Evans, Mrs Ruth Elisabeth Williams
Income: £4,045,108 [2016]; £4,711,288 [2015]; £3,819,931 [2014]; £3,676,835 [2013]

Coleg Sir Gar
Registered: 20 Jun 2013   *Employees:* 504   *Volunteers:* 10
Tel: 01554 748536   *Website:* colegsirgar.ac.uk
Activities: Education, training
Address: Dobbin Walls, Kilgetty Lane, Stepaside, Arberth, Pembrokeshire, SA67 8JL
Trustees: Paul Jones, Mr Barry William James Liles, Mrs Rosemary Pritchard, Mr William Hywel Davies, Mr Delwyn Jones, Mr Huw Davies, Mr Joseph Toft, Mr Geraint Roberts, Mr Hywel Morgan Jones, Ms Maria Stedman, Mr John Edge, Mrs Janet Morgan, Mr Michael Evans, Ms Marion Phillips
Income: £30,971,000 [2017]; £30,350,000 [2016]; £31,320,000 [2015]; £33,158,000 [2014]

Colfe's School
Registered: 24 May 2005   *Employees:* 310
Tel: 020 8463 8112   *Website:* colfes.com
Activities: Education, training
Address: Colfes School, Horn Park Lane, London, SE12 8AW
Trustees: Mr Ian Anthony Russell MBE, Miss Serena Cheng, Mr Matthew Pellereau, Dr Angela Brueggemann, Mr Mark Graham Williams, Dr Dilkush Robert Ephrem Abayasekara, Mr Daniel George Coulson, Mr Timothy Norman Bramham Lister, Mr John Guyatt, Mr Andrew Brian Strong, Mrs Belinda Canham, Mr Sean Williams, Mr David Sheppard, Mrs Julie Anne Bradley, Mr Stuart Russell Fuller
Income: £15,430,000 [2016]; £14,263,000 [2015]; £13,447,000 [2014]; £12,874,000 [2013]; £12,926,000 [2012]

Collage Arts
Registered: 13 Aug 2013   *Employees:* 15
Tel: 020 8365 7500   *Website:* collage-arts.org
Activities: Education, training; arts, culture, heritage, science; economic, community development, employment
Address: Collage Arts, The Chocolate Factory, 5 Clarendon Road, Wood Green, London, N22 6XJ
Trustees: Mr Alan Richardson, Philip Sherman, Yousaf Ali Khan, Vasanthi Hirani, Emily Byron, Ms Yana Stajno
Income: £1,845,820 [2016]; £2,026,986 [2015]; £2,471,390 [2014]

College Francais Bilingue de Londres Ltd
Registered: 2 Nov 1993   *Employees:* 70   *Volunteers:* 12
Tel: 020 7993 7402   *Website:* cfbl.org.uk
Activities: Education, training
Address: College Francais Bilingue de Londres, 87 Holmes Road, London, NW5 3AX
Trustees: Mr Remi Bourrette, Mr Dimitri Hovine, Ms Karine Berron, Mr Thibaut Guy Eissautier, Benjamin Vedrenne-Cloquet, Gaelle Picardet, Mr Stuart Young, Mr Benoit Michel Remy Marie Belhomme, Mr Thomas Gilles Lefevre, Ms Veronique Brigitte Jeanne Aubert Bell, Dorothee Lepine
Income: £6,784,722 [2016]; £6,327,494 [2015]; £5,999,319 [2014]; £5,482,161 [2013]; £5,140,846 [2012]

The College of All Souls of The Faithful Departed, of Oxford
Registered: 15 Sep 2010 *Employees:* 122 *Volunteers:* 2
Tel: 01865 279379 *Website:* asc.ox.ac.uk
Activities: Education, training; religious activities
Address: High Street, Oxford, OX1 4AL
Trustees: Professor Hugh Collins FBA, Professor Sir John Vickers FBA, Professor Simon Green, Professor Neil Kenny FBA, Professor Timothy Besley CBE, Professor Suzanne Aigrain, Mr Fraser Campbell, The Very Revd Dr John Drury, Sir Launcelot Henderson, Professor John Nicholas Peregrine Horden, Sir Noel Malcolm FBA, Dr George Molyneaux, Lord David Pannick QC, Dr Daniel Rothschild, Dr Andrew Scott, Professor Cecilia Trifogli, Dr Benjamin Wardhaugh, Professor Andrew Burrows FBA QC, Professor Cecile Fabre FBA, Dr Frederick Wilmot-Smith, Mr George Woudhuysen, Dr Clare Bucknell, Dr Arthur Asseraf, Dr Claudio Sopranzetti, Dr Marius Ostrowski, Dr Peter-Daniel Szanto, Miss Tess Little, Dr Justine Firnhaber-Baker, Dr Philipp Nothaft, Professor Peter Wilson, Dr Erik Panzer, Professor Catriona Seth, Ms Claire Hall, Professor Diwakar Acharya, Professor Lucia Helen Zedner, Dr Alex Mullen, Mr Anthony Gottlieb, Dr Matthew Mandelkern, Dr Jasmine Nirody, Mr David Addison, Professor Efstathios Kalyvas, Professor Mark Armstrong FBA, Professor Ian Loader FRSA, Dr Sarah Beaver, Mr Edward Mortimer CMG, Professor Beata Javorcik, Professor Colin Burrow, Professor Vincent Paul Crawford FBA, Professor David Gellner, Professor Cecilia Heyes FBA, Professor Colin Kidd FBA, Professor Angela McLean FRS, Professor Deborah Jayne Oxley, Rt Hon Dr John Redwood, Dr Katherine Rundell, Mr Thomas Seaman, Lord William Arthur Waldegrave of North Hill, Professor Andrew Wilson, Professor Ruth Harris, Professor John Gardner, Professor Kevin O'Rourke FBA, Professor Ian Rumfitt, Professor Stephen Anthony Smith, Professor Susanne Bobzien, Dr Tessa Baker, Professor Catherine Redgwell, Professor Paul Fendley, Mr Max David Noble Harris, Professor Francis Brown, Professor Catherine Morgan, Dr Dmitri Levitin, Mr Andrew Wynn Owen, Professor Wolfgang Ernst, Mr Hasan Dindjer, Professor Julia Mary Howard Smith, Miss Katherine Backler, Ms Sarah Bufkin, Dr Lisa Lodwick, Dr Ross Anderson, Dr Srikanth Toppaladoddi, Mr Fitzroy Morrissey
Income: £12,168,000 [2017]; £15,089,000 [2016]; £11,097,076 [2015]; £9,153,000 [2014]; £8,946,000 [2013]

College of Corpus Christi and Of The Blessed Virgin Mary in the University of Cambridge
Registered: 12 Aug 2010 *Employees:* 163
Tel: 01223 338000 *Website:* corpus.cam.ac.uk
Activities: Education, training; religious activities
Address: Corpus Christi College, Cambridge, CB2 1RH
Trustees: Dr David Andrew Sneath, Ms Elizabeth Winter, Mr Stuart Laing MA, Dr Shruti Kapila, Dr Philip Bearcroft, Doctor Keith Seffen, Dr Marina Frasca-Spada, Professor Christopher Kelly, Ms Sarah Tamsin Cain, Dr David Greaves, Dr Patrick Zutshi, Dr Michael Sutherland, Dr Emma Spary, Professor Paul Hewett, Dr Judy Hirst, Dr Pontus Rendahl, Dr Andrew Milne, Dr Ben Samuel Pilgrim, Dr Aaron Rapport, Dr Vickie Braithwaite, Dr John David Rhodes, Dr Fumiya Iida, Dr Felicity Hill, Dr Ioan Stefanovici, Dr Felix Grey, Ms Harriet Soper, Professor Nigel Edward Simmonds, Professor Ian David Abrahams, Dr Christopher Brookes, Dr Barak Kushner, Professor Simon Godsill, Professor Mark Warner, Professor Christopher Howe, Dr James Warren, Dr Hugh Robinson, Professor Pietro Cicuta, Dr Emma Wilson, Mrs Susan Ainger-Brown, Dr John Carr, Dr Jonathan Edward Morgan, Professor Alison Smith, Dr Ewan St John Smith, Dr Sarah Elizabeth Bohndiek, Mr Tim Harvey-Samuel, Dr Andrew Paul Davison, Dr Alexis Joannides, Ms Anastasia Kisil, Dr Rune Damgaard, Dr Rhiannon Harries, Dr Sam Behjati, Dr Anastasia Artemyev Berg, Dr Melle Kromhout
Income: £9,938,154 [2017]; £10,157,218 [2016]; £12,633,616 [2015]; £11,687,671 [2014]; £11,191,923 [2013]

The College of Optometrists
Registered: 29 Jan 1997 *Employees:* 45 *Volunteers:* 31
Tel: 020 7766 4390 *Website:* college-optometrists.org
Activities: Education, training; advancement of health or saving of lives; environment, conservation, heritage
Address: The College of Optometrists, 41-42 Craven Street, London, WC2N 5NG
Trustees: Rob Hogan, Mr Andrew John Kitchen, Dr Edward Mallen, Miss Rasmeet Chadha, Kiki Soteri, Dr Gillian Rudduck, Dr Leon Davies, Dr Mary-Ann Sherratt, Mr John Thompson, Mr Colin Davidson, Dr Aleksandra Mankowska, Dr Parth Shah
Income: £6,882,706 [2017]; £6,839,233 [2016]; £6,627,963 [2015]; £6,505,428 [2014]; £6,324,005 [2013]

The College of Osteopaths
Registered: 16 Dec 1998 *Employees:* 41
Website: collegeofosteopaths.ac.uk
Activities: Education, training; advancement of health or saving of lives
Address: College of Osteopaths, 13 Furzehill Road, Borehamwood, Herts, WD6 2DG
Trustees: Mr Paul Grant, Ms Caroline Weber, Mr Roger Rogers, Mr Nigel Fawcett, Mr Desmond Henley, Dr Brian Isbell, Mrs Bernice Kaufman, Mr Mike Stubbs
Income: £1,060,244 [2016]; £1,025,329 [2015]; £889,256 [2014]; £619,751 [2013]

The College of Radiographers
Registered: 9 Dec 1976 *Employees:* 18
Tel: 020 7740 7200 *Website:* sor.org
Activities: Education, training; advancement of health or saving of lives
Address: 207 Providence Square, Mill Street, London, SE1 2EW
Trustees: Mr Ian Wolstencroft CPFA, Mr Derek Adrian-Harris, Ms Alison Vinall MSc BSc Hons, Mrs Karen Smith MSc DCRT, Mr Gareth Thomas MSc BSc Hons FHEA, Mrs Sue Barbara Webb BSc Hons, Mr Christopher Kalinka DCR(R) DRI, Mrs Sheila Hassan DCRT, Mrs Sandra Anne Mathers MSc, Mr Charles McCaffrey, Mr Steven Herring BSc Hons PGD, Ms Julie Jones, Dr Stephen Griffith Davies, Mrs Gill Marian Hodges DCRT
Income: £2,598,847 [2016]; £2,489,598 [2015]; £2,204,154 [2014]; £2,323,716 [2013]; £2,290,507 [2012]

The College of Saint Mary of Winchester in Oxford, Commonly Called New College
Registered: 4 Jul 2011 *Employees:* 309
Tel: 01865 279555 *Website:* new.ox.ac.uk
Activities: Education, training
Address: New College, Holywell Street, Oxford, OX1 3BN
Trustees: David Palfreyman, Timothy Williamson, Alain Townsend, Masud Husain, Susan Bright, Ruth Harris, Marcus Du Sautoy, Elizabeth Frazer, Mark Griffith, Dieter Helm, Karen Leeder, David Limebeer, John McGrady, Robert Parker, William Poole, Mari Sako, Rosalind Temple, Christiane Timmel, Andrew Wathen, Martin Williams, Dori Kimel, Laura Marcus, Erica Longfellow, Joseph Conlon, Fait Paolo, Professor Frances Kirwan, Dr Grant Churchill, Mr Giles Spackman, Professor Andrew Meadows, Professor Mark Stokes, Miles Young, Jonathan Black, Catriona Kelly, Michael Burden, Dr Alexander Morrison, Rene Banares-Alcantara, Eugene Flynn, David Gavaghan, Volker Halbach, Miles Hewstone, Jane Lightfoot, Richard Mash, Stephen Mulhall, David Parrott, Oliver Pybus, Adrianne Slyz, Caroline Thomas, Anthony Venables, Richard Whittington, Andrei Zorin, George Ratcliffe, Mark Curtis, Hannah Sullivan, Andrea Vedaldi, Steven Balbus, Dr Robert Easton, Dr Ashleigh Griffin, Mr Robert Quinney, Dr Andrew Counter
Income: £21,353,000 [2017]; £15,982,000 [2016]; £12,659,000 [2015]; £11,798,000 [2014]; £12,254,000 [2013]

College of St Barnabas

Registered: 2 May 1962 *Employees:* 38 *Volunteers:* 8
Tel: 01342 870260 *Website:* st-barnabas.org.uk
Activities: The advancement of health or saving of lives; accommodation, housing; religious activities
Address: Blackberry Lane, Lingfield, Surrey, RH7 6NJ
Trustees: Mrs Vivien Hepworth, Dr Joyce Ingrid Sethi, Rev Graham Paddick, Keith Luckhoo, Sir Paul Britton, Mr David Michael John Jessup, Mr Anthony Proctor, Mrs Shiona Monfries RGN HV RNT, Mr John R Cope, Tony Shillingford, Mr Martyn Douglas Williams
Income: £1,926,000 [2016]; £1,917,190 [2015]; £1,970,640 [2014]; £1,754,720 [2013]; £1,596,261 [2012]

The College of St Mary Magdalen in the University of Oxford

Registered: 27 May 2011 *Employees:* 185
Tel: 01865 276020 *Website:* magd.ox.ac.uk
Activities: Education, training; religious activities; arts, culture, heritage, science; environment, conservation, heritage
Address: Magdalen College, High Street, Oxford, OX1 4AU
Trustees: Mr Rory Maw, Prof Arzhang Ardavan, Mr Mark Blandford-Baker, Prof Felix Budelmann, Prof Robert Douglas-Fairhurst, Prof Liam Dolan, Dr Juan-Carlos Conde, Prof Alison Etheridge, Prof Toby Garfitt, Prof Stephen Goodwin, Prof Katharine Grevling, Prof Simon Horobin, Prof Stuart MacKenzie, Dr Alfonso Moreno, Dr Thomas Norman, Prof Quentin Sattentau, Prof Roger Smith, Prof Peter Sullivan, Prof Andrew Weller, Prof Zhong You, Dr Alexy Karenowska, Prof Robin Cleveland, Dr John Scholar, Dr Farhan Nizami, Prof Jane Gingrich, Prof Lucy Bowes, Prof Jeremias Prassl, Prof Roderick Bagshaw, The Revd Prof Rob Gilbert, Prof Jan Kristensen, Prof Christian Leitmeir, The Revd Dr Jonathan Arnold, Dr Rory McCarthy, Dr Katy Wells, Dr Thomas Prince, Dr Alexander Hetherington, Dr Elisabeth Bolorinos Allard, Mr Mark Williams, Prof Giles Barr, Prof Martin Bridson, Dr Jennifer Castle, Prof Tim Donohoe, Prof Constantin Coussios, Prof Sir David Clary, Prof Kevin Foster, Prof Christopher Garland, Prof John Gregg, Prof Adrian Hill, Prof Daniel Kroening, Prof Laurie Maguire, Prof John Nightingale, Dr Mark Pobjoy, Prof Andrew Smith, Prof Nicholas Stargardt, Prof Andrew Turberfield, Prof Harvey Whitehouse, Prof Ofra Magidor, Prof David Clark, Prof Marilyn Booth, Mr Sean Rainey, Prof Laura Fortunato, Prof Julien Berestycki, Prof Sian Pooley, Prof Gero Miesenboeck, Dr Reidar Due, Prof Clare Harris, Prof Paul Elbourne, Prof Rahul Santhanam, Dr Antone Martinho, Dr Giovanni Varelli, Dr Daniel Robinson, Dr Avi Lifschitz, Prof Simon Gilson
Income: £20,751,000 [2017]; £18,224,000 [2016]; £15,998,000 [2015]; £15,888,000 [2014]; £16,171,000 [2013]

The College of St Mary Magdalene in the University of Cambridge

Registered: 18 Aug 2010 *Employees:* 154
Tel: 01223 332100 *Website:* magd.cam.ac.uk
Activities: Education, training
Address: Magdalene College, Cambridge, CB3 0AG
Trustees: Dr Ari Ercole, Dr Hughes Azerad, Dr Cecilia Brassett, Dr Rowan Burnstein, Professor Howard Chase, Dr Antje Du Bois-Pedain, Dr Allegre Hadida, Dr Jane Hughes, Dr Stuart Martin, Dr Kanaklata Patel, Dr Gareth Pearce, Dr Marcus Waithe, Professor Saul Dubow, Dr Richard Roebuck, Dr Amira Bennison, Dr Emily So, Dr Rowan Williams, Dr Walid Khaled, Dr Tijmen Euser, Mr Nicholas Widdows, Dr Stephen John Eglen, Dr Nicholas Roger Carroll, Mr Steven John Morris, Professor Holger Babinsky, Dr Brendan Burchell, Professor Michael Carpenter, Dr Timothy Coombs, Professor Paul Dupree, Dr Timothy Harper, Dr Neil Jones, Ms Silke Mentchen, Dr John Patterson, Dr Thomas Spencer, Dr Carl Watkins, Dr Simon Stoddart, Mrs Corinne Lloyd, Dr Luke Skinner, Dr Alex Thom, Dr John Munns, Dr Alex Spectre, Dr Elizabeth Howell, Dr Sergio Bacallado, Dr Finbarr Livesey
Income: £11,813,104 [2017]; £11,053,689 [2016]; £9,919,178 [2015]; £8,849,050 [2014]; £8,897,746 [2013]

The College of St Peter Le Bailey in the University of Oxford

Registered: 29 Jul 2011 *Employees:* 138
Tel: 01865 278879 *Website:* spc.ox.ac.uk
Activities: Education, training
Address: St Peters College, New Inn Hall Street, Oxford, OX1 2DL
Trustees: Professor Cyrus Cooper, Professor Balazs Szendroi, Professor Michael Bonsall, Professor Hanneke Grootenboer, Dr Timothy Mawson, Dr Geoffrey Nicholls, Dr Ricardo Miguel Santos Soares De Oliveira, Professor Dariusz Wojcik, Dr Roger Allen, Dr Peter Kail, Dr Hartmut Mayer, Professor Peter Taylor MA PhD FRCP, Professor Sondra Hausner, Professor Danny Dorling, Dr Ines Moreno De Barreda, Professor Stephen Baxter, Dr Marc Macias-Fauria, Professor Charles Monroe, Dr Joanna Neilly, Mr James Mungo Murray Graham, Dr Massimo Antonini, Dr Huw Dorkins FRCP FRCPath, Professor Nicholas Lakin, Professor Mark Moloney, Dr Robert Hamilton Pitkethly, Professor Abigail Williams, Dr Claire Williams, Professor Christopher John Foot, Mr Mark Damazer CBE, Dr Dorota Leczykiewicz, Professor Thomas Adcock, Dr Daron Burrows, Professor Phillip Rothwell, Dr Nicolas James Tosca, Dr Marina MacKay, Dr Stephen Tuffnell, Professor Lionel Mason
Income: £9,086,000 [2017]; £7,431,000 [2016]; £8,456,000 [2015]; £12,764,000 [2014]; £6,623,000 [2013]

The College of The Holy and Undivided Trinity in the University of Oxford of The Foundation of Sir Thomas Pope

Registered: 12 Sep 2011 *Employees:* 110
Tel: 01865 279897 *Website:* trinity.ox.ac.uk
Activities: Education, training; religious activities; environment, conservation, heritage; recreation
Address: Trinity College, Broad Street, Oxford, OX1 3BH
Trustees: Bryan Ward-Perkins, Professor Martin Maiden, Dr Stefano-Maria Evangelista, Professor Kim Nasmyth, Dr Jan Czernuszka, Dr James Robert McDougall, Professor Justin Wark, Reverend Emma Percy, Dr Keith Buckler, Professor Craig Clunas, Professor Marta Kwiatkowska, Dr Steve Sheard, Dr Anil Gomes, Miss Gail Trimble, Dr Maria Del Pilar Blanco, Dr Andrea Ferrero, Mrs Susan Broers, Professor Christopher Butler, Dr Alexander Kentikelenis, Mr Luke Rostill, Professor Pepper Culpepper, Mr Peter McCulloch, Dr Kantik Ghosh, Dame Hilary Boulding, Professor Valerie Worth, Dr Stephen Fisher, Professor Peter Read, Dr Johannes Zachhuber, Professor Frances Ashcroft, Dr Nicholas Barber, Professor Alexander Korsunsky, Professor Louis Mahadevan, Professor Paul Fairchild, Professor Francis Barr, Dr Michael Moody, Dr Susan Perkin, Professor Charlotte Williams, Dr Ian Hewitt, Dr Julia Langbein, Dr Melanie Rupflin, Dr Pranav Singh, Professor Janet Breckenridge Pierrehumbert
Income: £8,055,000 [2017]; £8,797,000 [2016]; £9,042,000 [2015]; £8,459,000 [2014]; £9,565,000 [2013]

The College of The Lady Frances Sidney Sussex in the University of Cambridge

Registered: 25 Aug 2010 *Employees:* 158
Tel: 01223 338827 *Website:* sid.cam.ac.uk
Activities: Education, training
Address: Old Barn Farm, 1 Meadow Road, Great Gransden, Sandy, Beds, SG19 3BD
Trustees: Mr Massimo Beber, Dr Colin Roberts, Dr Berry Groisman, Professor Kenneth Armstrong, Professor Rodolphe Sepulchre, Dr Mette Eilstrup-Sangiovanni, Dr Paulina Sliwa, Mr Noah Froud, Mrs Sarah Bonnett, Mr Nathan Victor Jay, Dr Bernhard Fulda, Professor Richard Penty, Dr Jillaine Seymour, Professor Gary Lloyd Gerstle, Dr Michael Ramage, Dr Steven Lee, Dr Tom Lambert, Mr Jono Faber, Mr Jack Thompson
Income: £13,717,000 [2017]; £9,557,000 [2016]; £8,775,524 [2015]; £8,987,103 [2014]; £8,406,834 [2013]

The College or Hall of Valence Mary Commonly Pembroke College in the University of Cambridge

Registered: 13 Aug 2010 *Employees:* 254
Tel: 01223 338118 *Website:* pem.cam.ac.uk
Activities: Education, training
Address: Pembroke College, Cambridge, CB2 1RF
Trustees: Dr Hildegard Diemberger, Prof Kenneth George Campbell Smith, Dr Samuel Barrett, Professor Sylvia Huot, Dr Caroline Burt, Dr Renaud Gagne, Prof Colin Lizieri, Rev James Gardom, Dr Katrin Ettenhuber, Mr Matthew Mellor, Prof Ashok Venkitaraman, Dr Alexander William Tucker, Prof Jan Maciejowski, Prof Michael Payne, Prof Jonathan Philip Parry, Dr Donald Robertson, Dr Torsten Meissner, Professor Christopher Young, Prof Nigel Cooper, Dr Demosthenes Tambakis, Prof John Bell, Dr Andrea Ferrari, Dr Vikram Deshpande, Dr Maria Abreu, Professor Christoph Loch, Professor Randall Johnson, Ms Chloe Nahum-Claudel, Dr Stephen John, Dr Andrew Cates, Dr Maximilian Sternberg, Dr Paul Cavill, Dr Thomas Micklem, Dr Iza Hussain, Dr Giovanni Rosso, Ms Emily Jones, Rebecca Lammle, Dr Sertac Sehlikoglu Karakas, Dr Richard Webb, Ms Alice Corr, Prof Stephen O'Rahilly, Professor C P Melville, Chris Smith, Dr John Durrell, Dr Mina Gorji, Dr Alex Houen, Dr David Huggins, Dr Alexei Shadrin, Dr Sarah Nouwen, Dr Gabor Csanyi, Dr Simon Learmount, Prof Nick Davies, Prof Norman Andrew Fleck, Professor Allan Trevor, Dr Mark Roderick Wormald, Dr Loraine Gelsthorpe, Prof Robin James Milroy Franklin, Mr Nicholas John McBride, Dr Lauren Kassell, Dr Nilanjana Datta, Dr Tim Bussey, Dr Rosalind Blakesley, Dr Silvana Cardoso, Dr Paul Warde, Dr Krzysztof Kazimierz Koziol, Professor Clare Grey FRS, Dr Warren Galloway, Dr Henning Grunwald, Dr Sanne Cottaar, Dr Ambrogio Camozzi Pistosa, Dr Timothy Thomas Weil, Dr Waseem Yaqoob, Dr Mark Wyatt, Dr Hannah Mumby, Dr Guillaume Hennequin, Christoper Ness, Dr Daniela Passolt, Dr Anil Madhavapeddy
Income: £15,926,000 [2017]; £49,171,000 [2016]; £14,334,000 [2015]; £17,514,903 [2014]; £14,965,848 [2013]

Colleges Wales / Colegau Cymru

Registered: 16 Jan 1997 *Employees:* 12
Website: collegeswales.ac.uk
Activities: Education, training
Address: College Wales, Unit 7, Cae Gwyrdd, Tongwynlais, Cardiff, CF15 7AB
Trustees: Mr Paul Croke, Mrs Sharron Lusher, Mr John Clutton, Mr Dafydd Evans, Mr Iestyn Morris
Income: £1,643,567 [2017]; £1,484,793 [2016]; £1,975,556 [2015]; £1,654,689 [2014]; £1,627,390 [2013]

The Collegiate Charitable Foundation

Registered: 17 Jul 1992
Website: queenethelburgas.edu
Activities: General charitable purposes; education, training
Address: The Undercroft Offices, Thorpe Underwood Estate, Thorpe Underwood, Ouseburn, York, YO26 9SS
Trustees: Mr Francis David Martin, Miss Amy Martin, Mr Christopher Hall
Income: £13,886,491 [2016]; £7,051,641 [2015]; £6,167,290 [2014]; £5,761,697 [2013]; £5,667,233 [2012]

Jeremy Coller Foundation

Registered: 14 Oct 2015 *Employees:* 3
Tel: 020 7631 8500 *Website:* jeremycollerfoundation.org
Activities: General charitable purposes
Address: Park House, 116 Park Street, London, W1K 6AF
Trustees: Mr Peter Hutton, Mr Jeremy Joseph Coller, Mr Brian Markeson
Income: £3,502,557 [2017]

The Canon Collins Educational and Legal Assistance Trust

Registered: 11 Feb 2004 *Employees:* 6
Website: canoncollins.org.uk
Activities: Education, training; prevention or relief of poverty; overseas aid, famine relief; economic, community development, employment
Address: Canon Collins Trust, The Foundry, 17 Oval Way, London, SE11 5RR
Trustees: Dr Maano Ramutsindela, Beacon Mbiba, Mr John Daniel Battersby, Mr Lawson Naidoo, Mr David Holberton, Dr Mpalive Msiska, Kai Easton, Dr Maano Ramutsindela, Ms Pfungwa Nyamukachi, Ms Emily Hayter
Income: £1,112,539 [2016]; £1,004,867 [2015]; £1,296,533 [2014]; £1,319,741 [2013]; £1,093,886 [2012]

Colston's School

Registered: 25 Feb 2000 *Employees:* 127 *Volunteers:* 2
Tel: 0117 965 3376 *Website:* colstons.bristol.sch.uk
Activities: Education, training
Address: Colstons Collegiate School, Bell Hill, Bristol, BS16 1BJ
Trustees: Mr Charles James Hastings Lucas, Mr David John Mace, Dr Annela Mary Seddon, Mr Martin John Hughes, Mrs Anne Burrell, Mrs Bryn Allpress, Mr Tony Kenny, Mr Timothy Stuart Ross, Mr Ian Hugh Alexander Gunn, Mr Nicholas Paul Baker, Professor Joseph Peter McGeehan, Mrs Caroline Jane Duckworth, Mrs Jane Worthington
Income: £7,663,691 [2017]; £7,713,867 [2016]; £7,504,783 [2015]; £7,444,088 [2014]; £7,754,799 [2013]

Combat Stress

Registered: 22 Sep 1962 *Employees:* 335 *Volunteers:* 53
Tel: 01372 587100 *Website:* combatstress.org.uk
Activities: The advancement of health or saving of lives
Address: Combat Stress, Tyrwhitt House, Oaklawn Road, Leatherhead, Surrey, KT22 0BX
Trustees: Professor Simon Charles Wessely MD FRCP, Lieutenant General Andrew John Noble Graham, Mrs Jennifer Margaret Green, Mrs Mary Molesworth-St Aubyn DL, Mr Christian Melville, Mr Michael Morrissey, Mrs Sally Goldthorpe, Colonel Michael Robert Lorne Ward, Dr Suzy Walton, Professor Timothy Evans, Mr Peter Allen, Mr Jan Sobieraj, Mr Calvin Man, Mr Mark Izatt
Income: £15,709,000 [2017]; £13,043,000 [2016]; £14,961,000 [2015]; £17,385,000 [2014]; £15,567,000 [2013]

Comet Charities Ltd

Registered: 9 Jun 2003
Tel: 020 8810 4321
Activities: Education, training; religious activities
Address: 63 Cranbourne Gardens, London, NW11 0JB
Trustees: Mr Michael Lisser
Income: £1,430,508 [2017]; £1,132,316 [2016]; £1,117,295 [2015]; £996,186 [2014]; £993,289 [2013]

Commission Apostolic Trust Ltd

Registered: 3 Dec 2012 *Employees:* 10 *Volunteers:* 750
Tel: 01202 299628 *Website:* commission-together.org
Activities: General charitable purposes; education, training; advancement of health or saving of lives; prevention or relief of poverty; overseas aid, famine relief; accommodation, housing; religious activities; economic, community development, employment; human rights, religious or racial harmony, equality or diversity
Address: The Citygate Centre, 138a Holdenhurst Road, Bournemouth, BH8 8AS
Trustees: Mr James Stuart Salway, Mr Sean Desmond Theunissen, Mr Philip Morton, Mr Gary Antony Wood, Mr Miles Bartholomew Jarvis, Ms Kara Newman
Income: £1,469,816 [2016]; £1,068,628 [2015]; £1,038,495 [2014]; £805,689 [2013]

The Common Purpose Charitable Trust

Registered: 1 Jul 1993 *Employees:* 60
Tel: 020 7608 8100 *Website:* commonpurpose.org
Activities: Education, training
Address: Monmouth House, 38-40 Artillery Lane, London, E1 7LS
Trustees: Mr Richard Denis Paul Charkin, Mr Mark Linder, Robert Frank Care, Eamonn John Boylan, Mr Jonathan Edward Donner, Mr Riaz Ali Sha, Gordon Merrylees, David Grace, Liz Bromley, Peter Kulloi, Albert Tucker, Mrs Letitia Corinna Andrewartha, Simon Russell, Mr Shuvo Saha, Ms Vandana Saxena Poria, Mr David Robinson, Janis Sanders
Income: £5,010,652 [2017]; £4,740,733 [2016]; £5,080,178 [2015]; £4,534,184 [2014]; £4,225,542 [2013]

Commonwealth Parliamentary Association (United Kingdom Branch)

Registered: 19 Dec 2002 *Employees:* 28 *Volunteers:* 5
Tel: 020 7219 5373 *Website:* uk-cpa.org
Activities: Education, training; economic, community development, employment
Address: Westminster Hall, Houses of Parliament, London, SW1A 0AA
Trustees: Lord Navnit Dholakia, Rt Hon Baroness D'Souza, Dr Roberta Blackman Woods MP, Mr Andrew Richard Rosindell MP, Richard Peregrine Liddell-Grainger MP, Mr Ian Richard Paisley MP, Rt Hon Maria Miller, Nusrat Ghani, Ian Murray, Nigel Evans, Professor Lord Ian McColl of Dulwich CBE, Mrs Madeleine Moon MP, Baroness Jean Ann Corston, Rt Honourable David George Hanson MP, Rt Hon Lord Foulkes of Cumnock, Ms Valerie Vaz MP, Baroness Berridge, Keith Vaz, James Duddridge
Income: £2,328,527 [2017]; £1,962,721 [2016]; £1,875,420 [2015]; £1,832,115 [2014]; £1,496,467 [2013]

Commonwealth Parliamentary Association

Registered: 22 Oct 1971 *Employees:* 14
Tel: 020 7799 1460 *Website:* cpahq.org
Activities: General charitable purposes; education, training; other charitable purposes
Address: 7 Millbank, London, SW1P 3JA
Trustees: Rt Hon Sir Alan Haselhurst MP, Dr Shirin Sharmin Chaudhury MP, Hon Derek Thomas MLC, Mr Lim Biow Chuan MP, Hon Kezia Purick MLA, Mr Nafoitoa Keti, Hon Emilia Monjowa Lifaka MP, Mdm Alexandra Mendes MP, Hon Don Harwin MLC, Hon Russell Wortley MLC, Hon Bernard Songa Sibalatani, Hon Lazarous Chungu Bwalya, Ms Jo-Anne Dobson, Hon Senator Christine Kangaloo, Hon Shri Kavinder Gupta, Datuk Seri Dr Ronald Kiandee, Hon Muturi Zeno, Hon Vicki Dunne MLA, Hon Themba Msibi MP, Hon Niki Rattle MP, Hon Mian Tariq Mehmood MP, Mr Paul Forster-Bell MP, Mr Akbar Khan, Rt Hon Umar Buba Jibril MP, Dr Sitasaran Sharma MLA, Hon Imran Ahmad MP, Hon Dato'Noraini Ahmad MP, Rt Hon Rebecca Kadaga Speaker of Parliament, Hon Dr Fehmida Mirza, Hon Jackson Lafferty, Hon Anthony Michael Perkins, Hon Datuk Wira Haji Othman Muhamad, Hon Robin Swann, Hon Shri Feroze Varun Gandi
Income: £2,712,083 [2016]; £2,726,156 [2015]; £2,649,522 [2014]; £2,704,787 [2013]; £2,757,409 [2012]

Commonwork Trust

Registered: 3 Mar 2015 *Employees:* 22 *Volunteers:* 55
Tel: 01865 511748 *Website:* boreplace.org
Activities: General charitable purposes; education, training; advancement of health or saving of lives; environment, conservation, heritage; economic, community development, employment; human rights, religious or racial harmony, equality or diversity; recreation
Address: 6 Woodstock Close, Oxford, OX2 8DB
Trustees: Mr Nigel Edward Wates, Mr Richard John Hallett, Dr Linda Davies, Mr William Graham Waterfield
Income: £1,322,638 [2017]; £1,068,446 [2016]

Communities First Wessex

Registered: 30 May 2012 *Employees:* 91 *Volunteers:* 60
Tel: 023 9241 5556 *Website:* cfirst.org.uk
Activities: General charitable purposes; education, training; advancement of health or saving of lives; disability; prevention or relief of poverty; economic, community development, employment
Address: Langstone Technology Park, 2b Langstone Road, Havant, Hants, PO9 1SA
Trustees: Jennifer Owens, Trevor Lewis, Mr Beverley Jones, Mrs Susan Anne Bailey, Mr Denis Gibson, Mr John Evans, William Stevens, Margaret Woodhead, Dr Stephen Irving
Income: £2,319,981 [2017]; £2,356,306 [2016]; £1,069,264 [2015]; £974,666 [2014]; £768,307 [2013]

Community & Voluntary Support Conwy

Registered: 26 Mar 2013 *Employees:* 24 *Volunteers:* 7
Tel: 01492 534091 *Website:* cvsc.org.uk
Activities: General charitable purposes; education, training; advancement of health or saving of lives; disability; prevention or relief of poverty
Address: 8 Rivieres Avenue, Colwyn Bay, Conwy, LL29 7DP
Trustees: Gwyneth Mary Trinder, Mrs Christine Humphreys, Mrs Susan Carol Davies, Joanna Tann, Mrs Maggie Kelly, Councillor Mike Priestley, Mrs Sharon Jones
Income: £1,434,923 [2017]; £1,707,265 [2016]; £775,378 [2015]; £735,468 [2014]

Community Action Isle of Wight
Registered: 31 Jul 1997 *Employees:* 57 *Volunteers:* 65
Tel: 01983 524058 *Website:* communityactioniw.org.uk
Activities: General charitable purposes; disability; prevention or relief of poverty; environment, conservation, heritage; economic, community development, employment
Address: The Riverside Centre, The Quay, Newport, PO30 2QR
Trustees: Mr Richard Priest, Dr Brian John Coles Hinton MA Oxon PhD MCLIP MBE, Ms Emma Corina, Mr Raymond John Harrington-Vail, Mr Mark O'Sullivan, Mrs Tracy June Ringer, Mr Paddy Noctor FRSA, Mr Adrian Axford, Mrs Jacqueline Louise Casey, Mr Louis Frederick Brand, Mrs Joy Cleighton Hills, Mrs Charmain Arniger
Income: £1,475,199 [2017]; £1,591,597 [2016]; £1,858,075 [2015]; £1,830,620 [2014]; £1,508,807 [2013]

Community Action Suffolk
Registered: 15 Jan 2013 *Employees:* 56 *Volunteers:* 725
Tel: 01473 345400 *Website:* communityactionsuffolk.org.uk
Activities: General charitable purposes; education, training; economic, community development, employment
Address: Brightspace, 160 Hadleigh Road, Ipswich, Suffolk, IP2 0HH
Trustees: Mrs Helen Greengrass, Mr John Shaw, Mrs Julie Crudgington, Mr Christopher Betson, Baroness Rosalind Scott, Mr Graham Watson, Mr Stephen Javes, Dame Linda Homer, Mr Ben Matthews
Income: £1,929,704 [2017]; £2,125,477 [2016]; £2,169,424 [2015]; £2,685,312 [2014]

Community Advice and Law Service Ltd
Registered: 28 Jun 2001 *Employees:* 27 *Volunteers:* 3
Tel: 0116 242 1120 *Website:* leicestermoneyadvice.co.uk
Activities: The prevention or relief of poverty
Address: First Floor, Epic House, Charles Street, Leicester, LE1 3SH
Trustees: Mr Jim Munton, Mr Stephen Henry Lock, Adam Markillie-Mallinson, Mr Christopher John Smith, Mrs Kirsty Elizabeth Neale
Income: £3,482,778 [2017]; £3,628,078 [2016]; £2,927,566 [2015]; £2,759,087 [2014]; £2,539,815 [2013]

Community Care Trust (South West) Limited
Registered: 29 Jan 1992 *Employees:* 84 *Volunteers:* 20
Tel: 01392 255428 *Website:* communitycaretrust.com
Activities: The advancement of health or saving of lives; disability; accommodation, housing
Address: Beaufort House, 51 New North Road, Exeter, Devon, EX4 4EP
Trustees: Mr David Vaughan Hodgetts, Mr Mark Rusbrooke Forbes Taylor, Mr Imran Beider, Mr Peter McCann
Income: £2,184,708 [2017]; £2,304,886 [2016]; £2,479,599 [2015]; £2,332,024 [2014]; £2,147,523 [2013]

Community Childcare Centres
Registered: 7 Jun 2001 *Employees:* 101 *Volunteers:* 2
Website: growingplaces.org.uk
Activities: Education, training
Address: Growing Places @ Mill Hill, Mill Road, Waterlooville, Hants, PO7 7DB
Trustees: Mrs Emma Jervis, Mr Matthew Goodwin, Sue Cleaveley, Mrs Jacqueline Warren, Simon Tout, Mrs Katherine Bradbury
Income: £1,627,735 [2017]; £1,499,973 [2016]; £1,520,721 [2015]; £1,489,237 [2014]; £1,464,158 [2013]

Community Drug and Alcohol Recovery Services
Registered: 16 Nov 1993 *Employees:* 47 *Volunteers:* 32
Tel: 020 8417 1960 *Website:* cdars.org.uk
Activities: Education, training; advancement of health or saving of lives; disability; accommodation, housing; economic, community development, employment; other charitable purposes
Address: 296a Kingston Road, Wimbeldon Chase, London, SW20 8LX
Trustees: Mr David Knight, Mrs Anna Whitfield, Mr Laurence Mascarenhas, Dr Sharif Zarif, Ms Victoria Dalby, Mrs Jenny Rowley, Mr Mark Ingram, Miss Gemma Shaw, Ms Kerryn Wotton
Income: £1,645,931 [2017]; £1,804,729 [2016]; £1,329,814 [2015]; £1,283,093 [2014]; £984,911 [2013]

Community Equality Disability Action
Registered: 14 Mar 2003 *Employees:* 97 *Volunteers:* 22
Tel: 01392 360645 *Website:* cedaonline.org.uk
Activities: Education, training; disability
Address: CEDA, The Clare Milne Centre, Emperor Way, Exeter Business Park, Exeter, EX1 3QS
Trustees: Steve Keable, Mrs Rosemary Davison, Ms Helena Holt, Mr Bernard Hughes, Mr Trevor Smale, Michael Rick Banfield, Mrs Amy Laver, Mrs Leila Joanne Walsh, Mr Mark Picken
Income: £1,132,883 [2017]; £1,125,634 [2016]; £998,042 [2015]; £994,473 [2014]; £871,058 [2013]

Community Family Care
Registered: 13 Dec 2012 *Employees:* 19
Tel: 01452 849301 *Website:* communityfamilycare.co.uk
Activities: Education, training; prevention or relief of poverty
Address: 52 Mendip Road, Bristol, BS3 4NY
Trustees: Mrs Joanna Margaret Jansen, Mrs Elaine Haines, Mrs Jennifer Ann Dwight, Mrs Mariana Straton, Charles Wade, Dr Derek John Conaty
Income: £2,205,066 [2017]; £1,956,991 [2016]; £1,929,057 [2015]; £1,883,184 [2014]

Community First
Registered: 30 Nov 1983 *Employees:* 42 *Volunteers:* 50
Tel: 01380 732803 *Website:* communityfirst.org.uk
Activities: General charitable purposes; education, training; economic, community development, employment
Address: Unit C2, Beacon Business Centre, Hopton Road, Devizes, Wilts, SN10 2EY
Trustees: Mr Piers Farquhar Dibben, Mr James Moody, Mr Edward William Heard, Mr Anthony Henry Pooley, Mr Steven Boocock, Dr Martin Hamer, Brian Clake, Ms Jane Irene Rowell, Mr Peter Stanley Duke
Income: £1,623,124 [2017]; £1,984,219 [2016]; £2,302,689 [2015]; £2,303,448 [2014]; £2,690,454 [2013]

Community Forest Trust
Registered: 2 Dec 1998 *Employees:* 17 *Volunteers:* 500
Tel: 0161 872 1660 *Website:* cf-trust.org
Activities: General charitable purposes; education, training; advancement of health or saving of lives; disability; environment, conservation, heritage; economic, community development, employment
Address: Community Forests North West Ltd, 6 Kansas Avenue, Salford, M50 2GL
Trustees: Mr Martin Peter Boyett, Mrs Selma Carson, Mr Stephen Connor, Professor David Paul Shaw, Mrs Hilary Ruth Hampton, Prof Alan Simson, Mr Derek Antrobus, Prof John Moverley, Mr Iain Martin Taylor, Mrs Joanne Harrison, Mrs Christine Beyga, Mrs Victoria Merton
Income: £1,656,587 [2017]; £1,328,132 [2016]; £1,568,455 [2015]; £1,854,329 [2014]; £2,085,571 [2013]

Community Foster Care
Registered: 15 Dec 2000 *Employees:* 16
Tel: 01452 849301 *Website:* communityfostercare.co.uk
Activities: Education, training; economic, community development, employment
Address: 52 Mendip Road, Bristol, BS3 4NY
Trustees: Joanna Jansen, Mrs Elaine Haines, Mrs Jennifer Ann Dwight, Ms Mariana Straton, Charles Wade, Dr Derek John Conaty
Income: £2,147,024 [2017]; £1,907,897 [2016]; £1,871,099 [2015]; £1,858,246 [2014]; £1,677,549 [2013]

Community Foundation Serving Tyne & Wear and Northumberland
Registered: 1 Aug 1988 *Employees:* 22 *Volunteers:* 30
Tel: 0191 222 0945 *Website:* communityfoundation.org.uk
Activities: General charitable purposes
Address: Community Foundation, Philanthropy House, Gosforth, Newcastle upon Tyne, NE3 1DD
Trustees: Ms Lucy Winskell OBE DL, Alastair Conn, Mrs Fiona Cruickshank OBE, Mr Geoffrey Mark Hodgson, Ms Sharon Lesley Spurling, Mr Andrew Haigh, Mr Paul Neil Farquhar, Anna Blackett, Ms Jane Robinson, Mr Patrick Martin Melia, Ms Sally Anne Young, Mr Neil Warwick, Mr Jonathan Stuart Mallen-Beadle
Income: £10,148,027 [2017]; £8,874,166 [2016]; £8,664,065 [2015]; £4,692,538 [2014]; £4,846,350 [2013]

Community Foundation for Calderdale
Registered: 30 Apr 1991 *Employees:* 13 *Volunteers:* 2
Tel: 01422 349700 *Website:* cffc.co.uk
Activities: General charitable purposes
Address: First Floor, The 1855 Building, Discovery Road, Halifax, W Yorks, HX1 2NG
Trustees: Mrs Brenda Hodgson, Ms Alison Haskins, Mr Lee Kenny, Mrs Liz Bavidge, Mr Russell Galley, Mr Shabir Hussain, Mr Wim Batist, Mr Stuart Vincent Rumney, Mr Christopher Harris
Income: £1,097,270 [2017]; £3,772,223 [2016]; £663,021 [2015]; £801,402 [2014]; £1,381,719 [2013]

Community Foundation for Leeds
Registered: 7 Apr 2003 *Employees:* 13 *Volunteers:* 31
Tel: 0113 242 2426 *Website:* leedscf.org.uk
Activities: General charitable purposes
Address: First Floor, 51a St Paul's Street, Leeds, LS1 2TE
Trustees: Helen Thomson, Mr George Charles Nicholas Lane Fox, Mr Jonathan Morgan, Mr Michael Anthony Jackson, Mrs Roohi Sultana Collins, Craig Burton, Mrs Pat McGeever, Ms Rachel Louise Hannan, Mr John Patrick McGhee, Mr Nathan Lane, Mr Mark Emerton, Ms Lorraine Anne Hallam
Income: £4,194,000 [2017]; £4,811,000 [2016]; £3,650,000 [2015]; £2,794,000 [2014]; £3,560,939 [2013]

The Community Foundation for Staffordshire
Registered: 16 Apr 2002 *Employees:* 4 *Volunteers:* 1
Tel: 01785 339543 *Website:* staffsfoundation.org.uk
Activities: General charitable purposes; education, training; advancement of health or saving of lives; prevention or relief of poverty; other charitable purposes
Address: Communications House, University Court, Staffordshire Technology Park, Stafford, ST18 0ES
Trustees: Mr Terry Walsh, Mrs Helen Rosalind Dart, Mr Christopher John Spruce, Mr Prakash Samani, Mr Simon John Mason Price, Ms Adele Cope, Mr Roger Andrew Lewis, Ms Charlotte Anne Almond, Dr Teeranlall Ramgopal, Mrs Jean Marjorie Gibson, Mr Jonathan Andrew
Income: £1,446,104 [2017]; £1,824,894 [2016]; £1,167,750 [2015]; £827,493 [2014]; £749,079 [2013]

Community Foundation for Surrey
Registered: 7 Oct 2005 *Employees:* 7 *Volunteers:* 116
Tel: 01483 478092 *Website:* cfsurrey.org.uk
Activities: General charitable purposes; education, training; advancement of health or saving of lives; disability; prevention or relief of poverty; accommodation, housing; arts, culture, heritage, science; amateur sport; animals; environment, conservation, heritage; economic, community development, employment; human rights, religious or racial harmony, equality or diversity; recreation
Address: c/o Guildford Borough Council, Millmead House, Millmead, Guildford, Surrey, GU2 4BB
Trustees: Mr Graham Williams, Mr David Frank, Mr Richard Whittington, Mr Graham Healy, Mr Peter Cluff, Mrs Bridget Biddell, Mr Simon Whalley, Mrs Julie Llewelyn, Mr Nigel Gillott
Income: £1,449,700 [2017]; £1,451,391 [2016]; £975,317 [2015]; £1,116,347 [2014]; £836,459 [2013]

The Community Foundation for Wiltshire & Swindon
Registered: 7 Mar 2008 *Employees:* 10 *Volunteers:* 38
Tel: 01380 729284 *Website:* wiltshirecf.org.uk
Activities: General charitable purposes; education, training; disability; prevention or relief of poverty; accommodation, housing; economic, community development, employment
Address: Ground Floor, The Community Foundation for Wiltsh, Sandcliff House, 21 Northgate Street, Devizes, Wilts, SN10 1JT
Trustees: Mrs Helen Judith Birchenough, Dame Elizabeth Louise Neville, Mrs Denise Angela Bentley, Mr Jason Henry Stuart Dalley, Mr William Wyldbore-Smith, Mrs Susan Webber, Mr James Paul Phipps, Mr Christopher John Bertram Bromfield, Mr John David Adams, Mrs Alison Jane Radevsky, Mrs Gibbons Emma, Steve Wall, Mr Andy Tait
Income: £1,517,440 [2017]; £1,403,903 [2016]; £1,058,065 [2015]; £1,156,756 [2014]; £6,752,922 [2013]

The Community Foundation in Wales
Registered: 15 Mar 1999 *Employees:* 8 *Volunteers:* 40
Website: cfiw.org.uk
Activities: General charitable purposes; education, training; prevention or relief of poverty; arts, culture, heritage, science; environment, conservation, heritage; recreation
Address: Community Foundation in Wales, 24 St Andrews Crescent, Cardiff, CF10 3DD
Trustees: Mrs Kathryn Morris, Mrs Sheila Maxwell, Alun Evans, Mr Geraint Keith Jewson, Mrs Joy Iris Kent, Ms Lulu Ann Burridge, Mr Lloyd Fitzhugh OBE DL JP, Nigel Annett, Mrs Tanwen Grover
Income: £3,053,069 [2017]; £3,905,061 [2016]; £2,801,892 [2015]; £2,699,581 [2014]; £2,858,235 [2013]

Community Foundations for Lancashire and Merseyside
Registered: 26 Mar 1998 *Employees:* 13 *Volunteers:* 1
Tel: 0151 232 2420 *Website:* cfmerseyside.org.uk
Activities: General charitable purposes
Address: Community Foundation for Merseyside, 43 Hanover Street, Liverpool, L1 3DN
Trustees: Mr Arthur Roberts, Mr Chris Bliss, Ms Amanda Jane Meachin, Mr Miles Dunnett, Mr Andrew Myers, Carole Barbara Murphy, Mr William David Waring, Mr Colin Charles Wardale
Income: £3,127,420 [2017]; £2,932,789 [2016]; £6,459,230 [2015]; £2,199,030 [2014]; £2,451,717 [2013]

Community Housing Cymru
Registered: 12 Mar 2009 *Employees:* 20
Tel: 029 2067 4817 *Website:* chcymru.org.uk
Activities: Education, training; prevention or relief of poverty; accommodation, housing
Address: Community Housing Cymru, 2 Ocean Way, Cardiff, CF24 5HF
Trustees: Ms Deborah Anne Green, Mr Walis George, Mr Scott Sanders, Steve Higginson, Matt Brown, Mr Paul Roberts, Chris O'Meara, Paula Kennedy, Mr Andrew Bowden
Income: £1,765,137 [2017]; £2,039,586 [2016]; £2,326,142 [2015]; £2,077,831 [2014]; £1,733,980 [2013]

Community Housing and Therapy
Registered: 9 Sep 1994 *Employees:* 36 *Volunteers:* 10
Tel: 020 7381 5888 *Website:* cht.org.uk
Activities: Education, training; advancement of health or saving of lives; disability; accommodation, housing; other charitable purposes
Address: Community Housing & Therapy, Suite 5-6, Unit 24 Coda Studios, 189 Munster Road, London, SW6 6AW
Trustees: George Bush, Mr Robert Dowler, Mrs Tora Pickup, Dr Rex Haigh, Mr Dominic Lowe
Income: £3,147,134 [2017]; £2,163,942 [2016]; £2,525,380 [2015]; £2,947,952 [2014]; £2,246,460 [2013]

Community Integrated Care
Registered: 22 Mar 1988 *Employees:* 5,610
Tel: 0151 420 3637 *Website:* c-i-c.co.uk
Activities: The advancement of health or saving of lives; disability; accommodation, housing
Address: Community Integrated Care, 2 Old Market Court, Miners Way, Widnes, Cheshire, WA8 7SP
Trustees: Professor Dame Joan Stringer, Mr David Dennis McIntosh, Professor Heather Tierney-Moore, Mr Peter Pritchard, Mr Brian James Logan, Mr Nigel Fraser Lemmon, Mr Simon Martin Learoyd, Mr Peter Hay OBE, Mr Philip Jonathan Smyth, Mr Stuart William Joseph Lorimer, Ms Maria Juana Da Cunha, Mrs Teresa Esther Fenech, Lady Fiona Kathryne Lady MacGregor of MacGregor
Income: £114,909,000 [2017]; £107,003,000 [2016]; £104,352,000 [2015]; £99,743,000 [2014]; £93,988,000 [2013]

Community Law Service (Northampton and County)
Registered: 20 Mar 2009 *Employees:* 38 *Volunteers:* 5
Tel: 01604 621038 *Website:* communitylawservice.org.uk
Activities: The prevention or relief of poverty
Address: Community Law Service, Hazelwood Business House, 49-53 Hazelwood Road, Northampton, NN1 1LG
Trustees: Mrs Sally Beardsworth, Mrs Morcea Walker MBE, Ms Oladapo Sulaimon, Alan Maskell, Mr Ian Pears, Mrs Alison Symmers
Income: £1,195,754 [2017]; £1,258,929 [2016]; £1,295,487 [2015]; £1,305,972 [2014]; £1,438,055 [2013]

Community Leisure Services Partnership
Registered: 6 Feb 2015 *Employees:* 76
Website: clsp.org.uk
Activities: Education, training; advancement of health or saving of lives; recreation
Address: 43 Stickle Down, Deepcut, Camberley, Surrey, GU16 6GB
Trustees: Mr Justin Beavis, Mr Howard Braband, Mr Tim Richardson
Income: £1,657,625 [2017]; £1,343,222 [2016]

Community Links (Northern) Limited
Registered: 15 Feb 1984 *Employees:* 216 *Volunteers:* 12
Tel: 0113 273 9660 *Website:* commlinks.co.uk
Activities: Education, training; advancement of health or saving of lives; disability; accommodation, housing
Address: Community Links Ltd, 3 Limewood Way, Seacroft, Leeds, LS14 1AB
Trustees: Mr Damian Pocknell, Mrs Fawzia Mir, Ms Cielo Cartwright, Ms Anne Worrall-Davies, Mr David Maxwell Strachan, Mr Karl Milner, Mr Tobi Akintokun
Income: £9,216,865 [2017]; £9,014,710 [2016]; £8,692,225 [2015]; £7,436,322 [2014]; £7,129,214 [2013]

Community Links Trust Limited
Registered: 12 Mar 1993 *Employees:* 152 *Volunteers:* 556
Tel: 020 7473 2270 *Website:* community-links.org
Activities: Education, training; economic, community development, employment
Address: Community Links, 105 Barking Road, London, E16 4HQ
Trustees: Mr Alan Lazarus, Stephen Adam Wyler, Ms Gillian Susan Budd, Mr Christopher Wright, Mr Babu Bhattacherjee, Ms Radhika Bynon, Mr Javid Canteenwala
Income: £4,613,276 [2016]; £6,763,588 [2015]; £8,963,413 [2014]; £7,832,786 [2013]; £7,685,525 [2012]

Community Lives Consortium
Registered: 18 May 2015 *Employees:* 790
Tel: 01792 646640 *Website:* communitylives.co.uk
Activities: General charitable purposes; education, training; disability
Address: Community Lives Consortium, 24 Walter Road, Swansea, SA1 5NN
Trustees: Mr Christopher Edwards, Mrs Janice Margaret Connick-Evans, Mrs Patricia Ann Speakman, Mrs Wendy Doreen Evans, Ms Sarah Davies, Mr Cliff Alden, Mrs Nicola Joan Ann Roberts, Mr Stuart Haydn Harper, Mr Gareth Bickerton
Income: £15,845,967 [2017]; £17,177,389 [2016]

Community Southwark
Registered: 13 Sep 2004 *Employees:* 25 *Volunteers:* 15
Tel: 020 7358 7020 *Website:* communitysouthwark.org
Activities: General charitable purposes
Address: 1 Addington Square, London, SE5 0HF
Trustees: Ms Karin Woodley, Ms Khosi Manaka, Mr Matthew Guest, Ms Ruth Driscoll, Mrs Margaret Anderson, Mr Michael Bukola, Jacky Bourke-White, Mark Parker, Mrs Nicola Howard
Income: £1,262,288 [2017]; £1,302,970 [2016]; £1,092,180 [2015]; £1,258,121 [2014]; £572,412 [2013]

Community Sports Arts and Leisure Trust
Registered: 1 Apr 2011 *Employees:* 240
Tel: 01903 770365 *Website:* c-salt.org.uk
Activities: General charitable purposes; education, training; arts, culture, heritage, science; amateur sport
Address: 27 East Drive, Angmering, Littlehampton, W Sussex, BN16 4JH
Trustees: Mr Peter Spooner, Hilary Simon, Mr David Scott
Income: £14,034,212 [2016]; £12,186,151 [2015]; £8,912,151 [2014]; £5,786,951 [2013]; £953,165 [2012]

Community Transport Association UK
Registered: 15 Mar 1991 *Employees:* 19
Tel: 0161 351 1475 *Website:* ctauk.org
Activities: Education, training; disability; economic, community development, employment
Address: Community Transport Association UK Ltd, 12 Hilton Street, Manchester, M1 1JF
Trustees: Peter Hardy, Ms Rachel Milne, Susan Evans, Joe Hannett, Chris Kutesko, Mr Paul Applebe, Ms Joanne Foxall, Mr Lawrence Wilson, Mr Patrick McEldowney
Income: £3,202,299 [2017]; £1,258,363 [2016]; £1,196,681 [2015]; £1,153,026 [2014]; £1,263,972 [2013]

Community Transport for Town and County
Registered: 10 Jan 1997 *Employees:* 42 *Volunteers:* 50
Tel: 01773 746652 *Website:* ct4tc.org.uk
Activities: Other charitable purposes
Address: Community Transport, 272 Derby Road, Marehay, Ripley, Derbys, DE5 8JN
Trustees: Mrs Winifred Ann Galloway, Patrick Lindley Dawson, Mr Richard Booth, Mr Michael Francis Usherwood, Mr John Godfrey Beswarick, Mr Peter R Binks JP, Mrs Annette Elizabeth Bentley, Mr Michael William Bishop
Income: £1,511,055 [2017]; £1,528,202 [2016]; £1,566,125 [2015]; £1,499,261 [2014]; £1,482,257 [2013]

Community Transport
Registered: 7 Apr 1966 *Employees:* 76 *Volunteers:* 72
Tel: 07912 388185 *Website:* communitytransport.org
Activities: Education, training; advancement of health or saving of lives; disability; prevention or relief of poverty; accommodation, housing; economic, community development, employment; human rights, religious or racial harmony, equality or diversity; recreation
Address: 2nd Floor, Parkview House, Woodvale Office Park, Woodvale Road, Brighouse, W Yorks, HD6 4AB
Trustees: Mrs Akilah Akinola, Mrs Teri Stephenson, Miss Helen Marie Keenan, Mr Barry John Yeomans, Mr Ian David Kerr, Miss Corinne Elizabeth Taylor
Income: £2,972,566 [2017]; £2,877,710 [2016]; £2,965,699 [2015]; £3,137,280 [2014]; £3,498,842 [2013]

Community Ventures (Middlesbrough) Ltd
Registered: 31 May 1990 *Employees:* 51
Tel: 01642 230314 *Website:* cvl.org.uk
Activities: Education, training; prevention or relief of poverty; economic, community development, employment; other charitable purposes
Address: Community Ventures Ltd, 101 The Greenway, Middlesbrough, Cleveland, TS3 9PA
Trustees: Mr Simon Pearson, Mr Mike Milen, Mr David Judge, Mrs Stella Mary Spencer
Income: £1,058,259 [2017]; £1,215,491 [2016]; £1,257,407 [2015]; £1,399,385 [2014]; £1,252,342 [2013]

Community of St Mary at The Cross
Registered: 22 Sep 1962 *Volunteers:* 1
Tel: 020 7841 6360 *Website:* edgwareabbey.org.uk
Activities: The advancement of health or saving of lives; disability; prevention or relief of poverty; religious activities
Address: Invicta House, 108-114 Golden Lane, London, EC1Y 0TL
Trustees: Rev Paul Michael Reece, Reverend Mother Abbess Mary Therese Zelent OSB, Mrs Gisela Lotte Daniels, Mr John Stephen Ringguth, Sister Barbara Johnson OSB, Rev Peter William Wheatley, Mrs Denise Patricia Cooper
Income: £1,954,587 [2017]; £1,819,509 [2016]; £1,652,631 [2015]; £1,552,975 [2014]; £1,562,907 [2013]

The Community of The Resurrection
Registered: 21 Oct 1964 *Employees:* 37 *Volunteers:* 9
Tel: 01924 494318 *Website:* mirfield.org.uk
Activities: Education, training; religious activities
Address: Community of The Resurrection, Stocks Bank Road, Mirfield, W Yorks, WF14 0BN
Trustees: Fr George Guiver, Br Philip David John Nichols, Fr John Gribben, Fr Oswin Gartside, Fr Thomas Seville
Income: £1,619,000 [2017]; £1,792,000 [2016]; £6,852,794 [2015]; £1,569,611 [2014]; £1,826,490 [2013]

Community360
Registered: 21 Jun 2002 *Employees:* 39 *Volunteers:* 400
Tel: 01206 505250 *Website:* commnity360.org.uk
Activities: General charitable purposes; education, training; economic, community development, employment
Address: Winsley's House, High Street, Colchester, Essex, CO1 1UG
Trustees: David Evans, Mr Leslie Robert Nicoll, Mr Leslie Hugh Davis, Beverley Jones, Mr Stephen Shoesmith, Mr Mark Galloway, Mr Chris Jullings, Mr Graham Derek Lewis, Mrs Catherine Mary Cussell, Mr James Stocker, Ms Diane Drury
Income: £1,003,714 [2017]; £1,038,503 [2016]; £1,101,217 [2015]; £1,014,295 [2014]; £550,314 [2013]

Commutual
Registered: 17 Jul 2013 *Employees:* 30 *Volunteers:* 2
Tel: 0151 235 2402 *Website:* commutual.org.uk
Activities: Education, training; advancement of health or saving of lives; recreation
Address: Liverpool Mutual Homes, The Observatory, 1 Old Haymarket, Liverpool, L1 6RA
Trustees: Peter Morton, Colleen Deanna Martin, Mrs Angela Forshaw, Mrs Elaine Stewart, Mr Peter Brennan, Mr Phillip Garrigan, Mrs Stephanie Donaldson
Income: £2,641,000 [2017]; £568,726 [2016]; £611,452 [2015]; £401,220 [2014]

Compaid Trust
Registered: 29 Aug 1997 *Employees:* 49 *Volunteers:* 40
Tel: 01892 833664 *Website:* compaid.org.uk
Activities: General charitable purposes; education, training; disability; arts, culture, heritage, science; economic, community development, employment
Address: Compaid Trust, Unit 1 Eastlands Estate, Maidstone Road, Paddock Wood, Tonbridge, Kent, TN12 6BU
Trustees: Mr Trevor William Watkins, Mr Emmanuel Berard, Mr John Leonard Ashelford, Mrs Kathy Melling, Mr Paul Sheppard, Mr John Turner, Mr John Osmond, Mrs Sairah Merchant-Crawley, Mrs Fiona Jane Condron
Income: £1,038,402 [2017]; £978,095 [2016]; £676,795 [2015]; £677,935 [2014]; £618,460 [2013]

The Company of Biologists Limited
Registered: 27 Jun 1979 *Employees:* 47
Tel: 01223 632851 *Website:* biologists.com
Activities: Education, training; advancement of health or saving of lives; arts, culture, heritage, science; environment, conservation, heritage
Address: Bidder Building, Station Road, Histon, Cambridge, CB24 9LF
Trustees: Prof Julian Francis Burke, Prof Daniel St Johnston, Dr James Briscoe, Prof Clare Isacke, Professor Alan Martin Wilson BSc BVMS PhD MRCVS, Prof Simon Maddrell, Prof Jane Alison Langdale, Mr Alastair Downie, Prof Peter W J Rigby FRS, Prof Matthew Freeman FRS, Professor Andrew Cossins, Dr Bruce Sean Munro, Dr Kate Gillian Storey, Prof Sarah J Bray, Prof Goran Nilsson, Prof Laura Marie Machesky, Professor Paresh Vyas
Income: £7,448,131 [2016]; £6,740,843 [2015]; £6,671,960 [2014]; £6,477,387 [2013]; £6,166,619 [2012]

Compass - Services To Tackle Problem Drug Use
Registered: 25 Nov 1986 *Employees:* 165 *Volunteers:* 12
Tel: 01904 636374 *Website:* compass-uk.org
Activities: Education, training; advancement of health or saving of lives; prevention or relief of poverty
Address: Floor 2, Kensington House, Westiminster Place, York Business Park, Nether Poppleton, York, YO26 6RW
Trustees: Claire Wesley, Claire Wood, Mr Alan John Begg, Robert Brodie Clark, Rachel Victoria Bundock, Ms Amanda Jane Hughes, Mr David Webster, Ann Josephine Biddle, Mark Edward Roberts, Mr Peter Webster
Income: £7,408,823 [2017]; £7,592,411 [2016]; £7,444,119 [2015]; £8,925,803 [2014]; £9,818,741 [2013]

Compass Disability Services
Registered: 11 Sep 2003 *Employees:* 48 *Volunteers:* 50
Tel: 0844 984 2828 *Website:* compassdisability.org.uk
Activities: Disability; other charitable purposes
Address: Unit 11-12 Belvedere Trading Estate, Taunton, Somerset, TA1 1BH
Trustees: Mark Oldershaw, Mrs Pauline Tilley, Tracey Oldershaw, Mr Frank Raymond Hulbert, Dr Michael Hope, Mrs Valerie Palmer, Mrs Denise Mary Hole, Mrs Ceri-Ann Taylor, Mrs Alison Louise Hart
Income: £1,292,566 [2017]; £1,256,162 [2016]; £1,307,127 [2015]; £1,050,949 [2014]; £506,310 [2013]

Compassion UK Christian Child Development
Registered: 27 Aug 1999 *Employees:* 98 *Volunteers:* 1,700
Tel: 01932 836490 *Website:* compassionuk.org
Activities: The prevention or relief of poverty
Address: Compassion UK, Bridge House, 43 High Street, Weybridge, Surrey, KT13 8BB
Trustees: Mr Kenneth Morgan, Mrs Cathryn Clarke, Mr Jonathan Keith Toohey, Mr Graham Williams, Mrs Yetunde Yewande Hofmann
Income: £39,944,000 [2017]; £39,006,069 [2016]; £36,483,379 [2015]; £32,181,711 [2014]; £28,365,051 [2013]

Compassion in World Farming
Registered: 16 Dec 2002 *Employees:* 90 *Volunteers:* 4
Tel: 01483 521950 *Website:* ciwf.org
Activities: Education, training; animals
Address: Compassion in World Farming, River Court, Mill Lane, Godalming, Surrey, GU7 1EZ
Trustees: Mr Jeremy Hayward, Mr Teddy Bourne, Mrs Valerie James, Mr David Madden, Joyce D'Silva, Rev Prof Michael Jonathan Reiss, Mrs Sarah Petrini, Mrs Rosemary Marshall, Mr Mahi Klosterhalfen
Income: £8,055,852 [2017]; £7,526,967 [2016]; £6,232,151 [2015]; £6,377,541 [2014]; £5,853,696 [2013]

The Complete Works Limited
Registered: 21 Jun 2000 *Employees:* 49
Tel: 020 7377 0280 *Website:* tcw.org.uk
Activities: General charitable purposes; education, training; arts, culture, heritage, science; economic, community development, employment
Address: 38 Commercial Street, London, E1 6LP
Trustees: Fiona Stratford, Ms Margaret Josephine Pitfield, Mrs Mary Theresa Daunt, Miss Brigid Jackson-Dooley, Ms Susan Clark, Mrs Kay Elizabeth Turner
Income: £3,480,633 [2017]; £2,514,999 [2016]; £1,759,177 [2015]; £1,268,105 [2014]; £1,035,295 [2013]

Compton Care Group Limited
Registered: 12 Mar 1982 *Employees:* 285 *Volunteers:* 895
Tel: 0300 323 0250 *Website:* comptoncare.org.uk
Activities: Education, training; advancement of health or saving of lives
Address: Compton Care Group Ltd, Compton Hall, 4 Compton Road West, Wolverhampton, W Midlands, WV3 9DH
Trustees: Mr R J Bailey, Dr Janet Anderson, Mr Gary Burke, Mr James McKinnon, Mrs S Ray, Mr John Harris, Professor Rosemary Keeton
Income: £9,299,218 [2017]; £9,702,708 [2016]; £9,797,768 [2015]; £8,830,836 [2014]; £8,528,608 [2013]

Compton Verney House Trust
Registered: 1 Feb 1994 *Employees:* 76 *Volunteers:* 68
Tel: 01926 645500 *Website:* comptonverney.org.uk
Activities: Arts, culture, heritage, science
Address: Dr Steven Parissien, Compton Verney House, Compton Verney, Warwick, CV35 9HZ
Trustees: Mrs Janatha Stubbs, Rita McLean, Mr Christopher Carter, Ms Sarah Carthew, Dr Oliver Cox, Mr Paul Smith, Hon Kirsten Suenson-Taylor, Mr Loyd Grossman, Mrs Janet Smith, Will Hanrahan, Dr Howard Jones, Mr Peter Wilson
Income: £5,187,298 [2016]; £5,322,856 [2015]; £3,618,697 [2014]; £3,025,114 [2013]; £2,410,787 [2012]

ComputerAid International
Registered: 22 Apr 1998 *Employees:* 11 *Volunteers:* 20
Tel: 020 8361 5540 *Website:* computeraid.org
Activities: Education, training; prevention or relief of poverty; environment, conservation, heritage; economic, community development, employment
Address: 1E Mentmore Terrace, London, E8 3DQ
Trustees: Mr Daniel Dearlove, Mr Nils Barton Wager, Mr Riessen Hill, Miriam Mukasa, Mr Stephane Manuel Reissfelder, Ms Annie Minter
Income: £1,263,668 [2017]; £1,269,744 [2016]; £1,234,720 [2015]; £1,873,060 [2014]; £1,538,932 [2013]

Concern Worldwide (UK)

Registered: 28 May 2002 *Employees:* 70 *Volunteers:* 60
Tel: 020 7801 1850 *Website:* concern.net
Activities: The prevention or relief of poverty; overseas aid, famine relief
Address: Ms Rose Caldwell, 13-14 Calico House, Plantation Wharf, York Road, London, SW11 3TN
Trustees: Ms Zamila Bunglawala, Samuel Sims, Ms Jemima Jewell, Peggy Iona Esther Walters, Bernadette Ann Sexton, Donald Workman, Ms Linda Horgan, Mr Anthony Foster, Mr Rob McGrigor, Mr James Shaw-Hamilton, Dr Diane Chilangwa Farmer, Anthony Emmanuel McCusker, Gary Rice
Income: £26,498,915 [2016]; £31,636,364 [2015]; £23,511,552 [2014]; £17,839,839 [2013]; £14,618,608 [2012]

Conciliation Resources

Registered: 17 May 1996 *Employees:* 47 *Volunteers:* 6
Tel: 020 7359 7728 *Website:* c-r.org
Activities: Education, training; overseas aid, famine relief; other charitable purposes
Address: 112a Upton Park Road, London, E7 8LB
Trustees: Mr Peter Price, Mrs Diana Frances Good, Dr Avila Kilmurray, Ms Michelle Davis, Mr Carey Cavanaugh, Dr Catherine Anne Hayward, Mr Andrew Michael Peck, Dame Rosalind Mary Marsden, Ms Michelle Parlevliet, Mr Marc Van Bellinghen, Ms Catherine Mary Fearon
Income: £4,655,383 [2016]; £5,750,156 [2015]; £4,329,331 [2014]; £5,947,199 [2013]; £5,262,991 [2012]

Concordia (UK) Limited

Registered: 4 May 1964 *Employees:* 16 *Volunteers:* 107
Tel: 01273 422293 *Website:* concordia.org.uk
Activities: Education, training; environment, conservation, heritage; economic, community development, employment
Address: Concordia, 19 North Street, Portslade, Brighton, BN41 1DH
Trustees: Yvonne Petroushka Richards, Mr John Frederick Rodley, Mr Mark Robinson, Ventseslav Tsochev, Mr Stuart Piccaver, Mrs Christine Isabel Snell, Mrs Sue Wellman, Mr Jeremy Ogden, Mr Timothy Firmston
Income: £1,014,711 [2016]; £1,009,430 [2015]; £1,045,975 [2014]; £1,573,585 [2013]; £1,463,503 [2012]

Concordis International Trust

Registered: 1 Sep 2004 *Employees:* 23 *Volunteers:* 10
Tel: 07801 418615 *Website:* concordis.international
Activities: The prevention or relief of poverty; overseas aid, famine relief; other charitable purposes
Address: Concordis International, IDRC, 70 Fleet Street, London, EC4Y 1EU
Trustees: Mr Michael Gercke, William Lee Hallam Mills, Miss Victoria Sloan, Ms Anne Lloyd Williams, Mr Edward Granville Lionel Moore, Robyn Patricia O'Reilly, Mr Gareth John Siddorn, Mr James Dalby
Income: £1,080,604 [2016]; £1,625,415 [2015]; £1,598,079 [2014]; £965,200 [2013]; £915,510 [2012]

Congregation of Jesus Charitable Trust

Registered: 29 Mar 1988 *Employees:* 21 *Volunteers:* 21
Tel: 01904 464923
Activities: General charitable purposes; education, training; religious activities
Address: Congregation of Jesus, Charitable Trust, 17-19 Blossom Street, York, YO24 1AQ
Trustees: Congregation of Jesus Trustee
Income: £2,883,204 [2017]; £1,661,656 [2016]; £1,560,819 [2015]; £4,661,543 [2014]; £9,387,790 [2013]

The Congregation of La Sainte Union des Sacres Coeurs (Anglo-Hibernian Province)

Registered: 6 Aug 1965 *Employees:* 26
Tel: 020 8695 7492
Activities: General charitable purposes; education, training; advancement of health or saving of lives; prevention or relief of poverty; religious activities
Address: 1st Floor, Church House, 61 College Road, Bromley, Kent, BR1 3QG
Trustees: Sister Margaret O'Reilly, Sister Patricia Trussell, Sister Elisabetta MacCariello, Sister Margaret McCarthy, Sister Eileen Daly, Sister Helen Randles, Sister Rosaleen Egan, Sister Michele Totman
Income: £3,513,095 [2017]; £2,374,725 [2016]; £1,932,850 [2015]; £2,122,699 [2014]; £1,945,275 [2013]

The Congregation of Marie Auxiliatrice CIO

Registered: 8 Jan 2016 *Volunteers:* 9
Tel: 020 8695 7492
Activities: General charitable purposes; education, training; advancement of health or saving of lives; prevention or relief of poverty; religious activities
Address: First Floor, Church House, 61 College Road, Bromley, Kent, BR1 3QG
Trustees: Sister Mary Frawley, Sister Elizabeth O'Brien, Sister Kinuko Asahiro, Sister Marjorie Daly, Sister Eileen Cartin, Sister Kazuko Ogawa, Sister Marie Louise Youteu, Sister Mary O'Dea
Income: £7,888,030 [2016]

Congregation of Servants of Mary (London)

Registered: 3 Jan 1967 *Employees:* 37 *Volunteers:* 30
Tel: 020 8809 5674 *Website:* servitesistersinternational.org
Activities: General charitable purposes; education, training; advancement of health or saving of lives; prevention or relief of poverty; overseas aid, famine relief; religious activities
Address: St Mary's Convent, 90 Suffolk Road, London, N15 5RH
Trustees: Sister Michelle Reilly, Sister Francis Farrell, Sr Rachel O'Riordan OSM, Sr Joyce Mary Fryer
Income: £1,264,225 [2016]; £1,150,601 [2015]; £2,038,186 [2014]; £1,122,347 [2013]; £1,166,295 [2012]

Congregation of Sisters of Our Lady of Sion or Order of Our Lady of Sion

Registered: 19 Jul 1966 *Employees:* 4
Tel: 0121 426 6679 *Website:* sistersofourladyofsion.org
Activities: General charitable purposes; education, training; advancement of health or saving of lives; prevention or relief of poverty; overseas aid, famine relief; religious activities; human rights, religious or racial harmony, equality or diversity
Address: 49 St Peters Road, Harborne, Birmingham, B17 0AU
Trustees: Sister Michaela Fisher, Sr Brenda Dorrian, Sister Brenda McCole NDS, Sister Anne Lee
Income: £1,015,483 [2016]; £1,042,850 [2015]; £1,473,371 [2014]; £1,070,479 [2013]; £1,092,554 [2012]

Congregation of The Brothers of Charity

Registered: 8 May 1964 *Employees:* 1,092 *Volunteers:* 89
Tel: 01257 266311 *Website:* brothersofcharity.org.uk
Activities: Education, training; advancement of health or saving of lives; disability; overseas aid, famine relief; accommodation, housing; religious activities; economic, community development, employment
Address: Lisieux Hall, Dawson Lane, Whittle-le-Woods, Chorley, Lancs, PR6 7DX
Trustees: Brother Denis Kerins, Augustine Thomas (Otherwise Alfred Hassett, Brother Noel Corcoran, Brother John O'Shea, Patrick Joseph Killoran
Income: £22,783,367 [2017]; £22,302,407 [2016]; £21,233,504 [2015]; £20,952,852 [2014]; £21,380,494 [2013]

The Congregation of The Daughters of The Cross of Liege

Registered: 16 Mar 1998 *Employees:* 1,048 *Volunteers:* 1,118
Tel: 020 7565 5800 *Website:* daughtersofthecross.org.uk
Activities: General charitable purposes; education, training; advancement of health or saving of lives; disability; prevention or relief of poverty; religious activities
Address: The Provincialate, 29 Tite Street, London, SW3 4JX
Trustees: Sister Mary Agnes, Sister Annette Clemence, Sister Anne Kelly, Sister Veronica Hagen, Sister Patricia Ainsworth, Sr Mary Geraldine
Income: £37,289,000 [2017]; £36,088,000 [2016]; £47,329,000 [2015]; £65,353,000 [2014]; £67,032,000 [2013]

Congregation of The Daughters of The Holy Ghost (English Province)

Registered: 20 Jan 1965 *Employees:* 23
Tel: 020 8695 7492
Activities: Education, training; advancement of health or saving of lives; prevention or relief of poverty; religious activities
Address: 1st Floor, Church House, 61 College Road, Bromley, Kent, BR1 3QG
Trustees: Sister Ita Carmel Durnin, Sister Mary Bond, Sister Eileen Mary Gorman, Sister Anne Morris
Income: £1,257,711 [2016]; £919,997 [2015]; £947,971 [2014]; £972,262 [2013]; £1,053,666 [2012]

The Congregation of The Daughters of Wisdom

Registered: 4 Jun 1964 *Employees:* 22 *Volunteers:* 1
Tel: 01794 830206 *Website:* daughtersofwisdom.org.uk
Activities: General charitable purposes; education, training; advancement of health or saving of lives; prevention or relief of poverty; religious activities
Address: Provincial Administration, Wisdom House, Romsey, Hants, SO51 8EL
Trustees: Sr Patricia Reilly, Sr Margaret Morris, Sr Maureen Seddon, Sr Clare McCaffrey
Income: £1,196,246 [2016]; £1,128,404 [2015]; £1,519,217 [2014]; £1,413,017 [2013]; £1,479,986 [2012]

The Congregation of The Dominican Sisters of Malta

Registered: 13 Feb 1969 *Employees:* 16
Tel: 01256 762394 *Website:* maryfieldhook.fsnet.co.uk
Activities: Overseas aid, famine relief; accommodation, housing; religious activities
Address: Mayfield Convent, London Road, Hook, Hants, RG27 9LA
Trustees: Sister Mary Attard, Sister Filomenia Grima, Maria Dolores Schembri, Sister Mary Anne Cardona, Sister Maria Dolores Gauci, Sister Theresa Sciortino
Income: £1,331,092 [2017]; £1,048,139 [2016]; £890,815 [2015]; £714,823 [2014]; £579,176 [2013]

The Congregation of The Holy Spirit and The Immaculate Heart of Mary (British Province)

Registered: 30 Dec 1963 *Employees:* 19 *Volunteers:* 120
Tel: 01244 344048 *Website:* spiritans.co.uk
Activities: Education, training; prevention or relief of poverty; overseas aid, famine relief; religious activities; economic, community development, employment; human rights, religious or racial harmony, equality or diversity
Address: 60 Hoole Road, Chester, CH2 3NL
Trustees: Rev Kenneth Okoli, Rev Terry Donnelly CSSp, Rev James McHamungu CSSp, Rev John Kitchen CSSp, Rev Thomas Willberforce CSSp
Income: £1,519,407 [2016]; £1,411,507 [2015]; £1,192,529 [2014]; £1,304,328 [2013]; £989,361 [2012]

The Congregation of The Little Sisters of The Poor - English Province

Registered: 13 May 1964 *Employees:* 734 *Volunteers:* 252
Tel: 020 7735 0788
Activities: The advancement of health or saving of lives; prevention or relief of poverty; religious activities
Address: St Peters Residence, 2A Meadow Road, South Lambeth, London, SW8 1QH
Trustees: The Congregation of The Little Sisters of The Poor Trustee Company
Income: £17,285,131 [2016]; £16,431,641 [2015]; £15,089,451 [2014]; £15,622,520 [2013]; £15,123,450 [2012]

Congregation of The Missionary Oblates of The Most Holy and Immaculate Virgin Mary (Oblates of Mary Immaculate)

Registered: 1 Mar 1964 *Employees:* 18 *Volunteers:* 320
Tel: 0151 236 1494 *Website:* oblates.co.uk
Activities: The prevention or relief of poverty; religious activities; other charitable purposes
Address: Castle Chambers, 43 Castle Street, Liverpool, L2 9SH
Trustees: Rev Raymond Warren OMI, Rev Martin Moran OMI, Rev William Griffin OMI, Rev Oliver Barry OMI, Rev Lorcan O Reilly OMI, Oblates of Mary Immaculate Trustees Registered
Income: £1,417,736 [2016]; £1,601,610 [2015]; £1,081,651 [2014]; £1,105,210 [2013]; £946,186 [2012]

The Congregation of The Sisters of Nazareth Charitable Trust

Registered: 3 Sep 1965 *Employees:* 141 *Volunteers:* 100
Website: sistersofnazareth.com
Activities: The advancement of health or saving of lives; prevention or relief of poverty; accommodation, housing; religious activities
Address: Nazareth House, 162 East End Road, London, N2 0RU
Trustees: Sister Anna Maria Doolan, Sister Madeleine Merriman, Sr Teresa Bernadett Fallon
Income: £6,485,026 [2017]; £5,604,730 [2016]; £5,888,202 [2015]; £5,995,681 [2014]; £11,809,960 [2013]

Congregation of The Sisters of Nazareth Generalate

Registered: 9 Nov 2010 *Employees:* 5
Tel: 020 8600 6840 *Website:* sistersofnazareth.com
Activities: General charitable purposes; education, training; accommodation, housing; religious activities
Address: 169-175 Hammersmith Road, London, W6 8DB
Trustees: Mary Anne Monaghan aka Sister Mary, Kathleen Marie Hoye aka Sister Rose, Anne Bernadette Walsh aka Sister Teresa, Catherine Higgins aka Sister Catherine, Brenda McCall aka Sister Brenda
Income: £2,296,469 [2017]; £1,240,627 [2016]; £1,224,707 [2015]; £1,053,707 [2014]; £3,171,721 [2013]

Congregation of The Sisters of Saint Anne
Registered: 22 Apr 1964 *Employees:* 45 *Volunteers:* 10
Tel: 020 3441 1657 *Website:* sistersofstannewimbledon.org.uk
Activities: The advancement of health or saving of lives; disability; prevention or relief of poverty; religious activities
Address: 14 Lansdowne Road, London, SW20 8AN
Trustees: Sister Emmanuel Hannigan SSA, Sister Jennifer Brown, Sister Patricia Heller SSA
Income: £1,397,120 [2017]; £1,412,669 [2016]; £1,325,959 [2015]; £1,252,828 [2014]; £2,142,606 [2013]

Congregation of The Sisters of Saint Martha
Registered: 1 Apr 1964 *Employees:* 47
Tel: 01707 645901
Activities: Education, training; accommodation, housing; religious activities
Address: 1A The Avenue, Potters Bar, Herts, EN6 1EG
Trustees: Sister Cecile Archer, Sister Teresa Roseingrave, Sister Christina O'Dwyer
Income: £3,510,809 [2016]; £3,121,848 [2015]; £3,335,079 [2014]; £3,317,121 [2013]; £3,150,821 [2012]

Congregation of The Ursulines of Jesus
Registered: 25 Mar 1965 *Employees:* 32 *Volunteers:* 46
Tel: 020 8442 8800 *Website:* ursulinesjesus.org
Activities: Education, training; advancement of health or saving of lives; prevention or relief of poverty; overseas aid, famine relief; religious activities
Address: Flat 14 Kimpton Court, 2 Murrain Road, London, N4 2BN
Trustees: Sister Hilary Brown, Sister Catherine Ryan, Sister Eileen Ryan, Sister Mary McLoughney, Sister Anna Lee, Sister Nora Mary Ryan
Income: £1,162,321 [2016]; £1,105,230 [2015]; £1,147,042 [2014]; £1,222,486 [2013]; £1,331,437 [2012]

Congregational Federation
Registered: 8 Nov 1972 *Employees:* 40 *Volunteers:* 50
Tel: 0115 911 1460 *Website:* congregational.org.uk
Activities: Religious activities
Address: 8 Castle Gate, Nottingham, NG1 7AS
Trustees: Rev Susan Ann Wade, Mr Peter Butler, Rev C L Gillham, Mr Paul Anthony Davis, Mrs Elizabeth Bentham, Miss Marion Kerr, Mr Angus MacLeod, Mr Eric Peter Fenwick, Rev John Bentham, Miss Reiltin Hart, Rev Martin Spain, Mrs Margaret Morris, Rev Sandra Turner, Rev Jill Stephens, Rev May Kane Logan, Mrs Hillary Biggin, Mr Trevor Robert Wilson, Miss Margaret McEwen Carbarns McGuinness, Mr George Crossley
Income: £1,088,079 [2016]; £1,855,299 [2015]; £1,653,762 [2014]; £1,797,604 [2013]; £2,261,205 [2012]

Connection Oxford
Registered: 10 Oct 1995 *Employees:* 123 *Volunteers:* 70
Tel: 01865 711267 *Website:* connectionsupport.org.uk
Activities: General charitable purposes; prevention or relief of poverty
Address: First Floor, 213 Barns Road, Cowley, Oxford, OX4 3UT
Trustees: Mrs Jennifer Margaret Berill, Mr David Waters, Mrs Sally McEvoy, Mr Owen Webb, Mrs Jane Louise Allen, Ms Suzanne Jeanne Brain, Mrs Jacquie Hardman
Income: £3,530,539 [2017]; £2,885,010 [2016]; £2,354,253 [2015]; £2,347,149 [2014]; £2,058,968 [2013]

The Connection at St Martin-in-the-Fields
Registered: 12 Nov 1999 *Employees:* 84 *Volunteers:* 500
Tel: 020 7766 5544 *Website:* connection-at-stmartins.org.uk
Activities: General charitable purposes; education, training; advancement of health or saving of lives; prevention or relief of poverty; accommodation, housing; arts, culture, heritage, science; economic, community development, employment
Address: The Connection at St Martins, 12 Adelaide Street, London, WC2N 4HW
Trustees: Mr Rod Beadles, Mr Jeffrey Alan Claxton, Philippa Langton, Octavia Williams, Ms Lucy McNulty, Mr Ian James Watson, Revd Dr Samuel Wells, Bally Sappal, Mr Tim Jones
Income: £4,573,247 [2017]; £4,489,401 [2016]; £4,175,149 [2015]; £4,260,096 [2014]; £4,172,964 [2013]

Connexions Buckinghamshire
Registered: 20 Oct 2009 *Employees:* 42 *Volunteers:* 14
Tel: 0118 402 7170 *Website:* connexionsbucks.org.uk
Activities: Education, training; disability; economic, community development, employment
Address: Adviza Partnership, Ocean House, The Ring, Bracknell, Berks, RG12 1AX
Trustees: Mr James Edward Simmons, Mrs Laura Coughtrie, Mr Nigel Sims, Ms Tracey Lawrence, Ms Alison Muggridge, Mrs Katharine Mary Horler, Kath Dunn, Mrs Susan Gale, Miss Lucy Champion, Alison Woodiwiss
Income: £1,426,248 [2017]; £2,950,037 [2016]; £2,742,302 [2015]; £3,110,147 [2014]; £3,029,819 [2013]

Kathleen and Michael Connolly Foundation (UK) Limited
Registered: 19 Apr 2005 *Employees:* 20
Tel: 01525 872014 *Website:* connollyfoundation.co.uk
Activities: Education, training; prevention or relief of poverty; accommodation, housing
Address: Manor Farm Court, Lower Sundon, Luton, Beds, LU3 3NZ
Trustees: Mrs Vanessa Susan Connolly, Andrew Sutherland Rowe, Mr Shyam Sunder Ashoka, Michael Andrew Callanan, Mr Nigel Kevin Croft
Income: £15,599,256 [2017]; £18,324,234 [2016]; £2,096,877 [2015]; £16,354,727 [2014]; £190,523 [2013]

Conservation Education & Research Trust
Registered: 4 Nov 2002 *Employees:* 42 *Volunteers:* 10
Tel: 01865 318811 *Website:* earthwatch.org
Activities: Education, training; environment, conservation, heritage
Address: Earth Watch, Mayfield House, 256 Banbury Road, Oxford, OX2 7DE
Trustees: Ms Superna Khosla, Mrs Judith Mosely, Mr Nicholas Dobson, Dr Jack James Matthews, Miss Dorothee D'Herde, Mr Iain Michael Coucher, Mr Adam John Powell, Dr Mark Collins, Mr Lucian John Hudson, Mrs Lisa King, Mr Geoffrey Lane, Mr Dax Lovegrove, Dr Edmund Peter Green
Income: £5,251,906 [2016]; £6,371,377 [2015]; £7,411,469 [2014]; £6,781,503 [2013]; £6,861,556 [2012]

The Conservation Volunteers
Registered: 14 May 1970 *Employees:* 285 *Volunteers:* 11,000
Tel: 01302 388853 *Website:* tcv.org.uk
Activities: General charitable purposes; education, training; environment, conservation, heritage; economic, community development, employment
Address: TCV, Sedum House, Mallard Way, Doncaster, S Yorks, DN4 8DB
Trustees: Mr Roger Kitson Perkin, Julie Royce, Richard Stiff, Mr John Anthony Mallalieu, Mr Michael Kellet, Tony Burton CBE, Professor Anthony Derek Howell Crook CBE, Simon Rennie MBE, Ms Jane Stevenson
Income: £10,717,000 [2017]; £12,697,000 [2016]; £16,743,000 [2015]; £21,967,000 [2014]; £21,590,000 [2013]

The Conservatoire for Dance and Drama
Registered: 27 Jan 2003 *Employees:* 10
Tel: 020 7387 5101 *Website:* cdd.ac.uk
Activities: Education, training; arts, culture, heritage, science
Address: Conservatoire for Dance & Drama, Tavistock House, Tavistock Square, London, WC1H 9JJ
Trustees: Mr Clive MacDonald, Mr James Smith CBE, Prof Margaret Jean Woodall BA Hons PhD, Mrs Emily Fletcher, Mr Tamas Wood, Dr Roderick Edward Clayton, Professor David John Halton, Miss Sophie Stone, Mr Jason Clarke, Mr Matthew Allan Slater, Mr Peter Edmund Dunleavy, Mr Richard Cooper MA, The Hon Julian Roskill, Ms Rosemary Boot, Ms Alison Morris MA FCA, Mr Roger Miles, Mr Piers Daniel Butler, Mr Robert Jude, Mr Matthew David Nathaniel Lloyd, Mr Derek Alan Hicks, Ms Alexandra Kate Piro
Income: £20,271,000 [2017]; £20,084,000 [2016]; £18,833,000 [2015]; £18,057,000 [2014]; £16,633,000 [2013]

The Constable Educational Trust Limited
Registered: 4 Mar 1998 *Employees:* 33
Tel: 020 7286 5909 *Website:* moatschool.org.uk
Activities: Education, training
Address: The Moat School, Bishops Avenue, London, SW6 6EG
Trustees: Mr David Moed, Miss Fiona Colquhoun, Mr Colin O'Dell-Athill, Mrs Gill Moed, Mr Simon Goldhill, Mr Faris Aranki, Mr Christopher Scott
Income: £2,007,113 [2017]; £1,956,353 [2016]; £2,127,107 [2015]; £2,191,181 [2014]; £2,091,650 [2013]

The Constance Travis Charitable Trust
Registered: 2 Jul 1986
Activities: General charitable purposes
Address: 86 Drayton Gardens, London, SW10 9SB
Trustees: Mr Ernest Raymond Anthony Travis, Mr Matthew James Travis, Mrs Peta Jane Travis
Income: £18,652,050 [2016]; £2,120,511 [2015]; £2,716,570 [2014]; £1,571,852 [2013]; £1,340,705 [2012]

Construction Industry Relief, Assistance and Support for The Homeless and Hospices Limited
Registered: 27 Mar 1996 *Employees:* 6 *Volunteers:* 50
Tel: 020 8742 0717 *Website:* crash.org.uk
Activities: The prevention or relief of poverty; accommodation, housing
Address: Crash The Gatehouse, 2 Devonhurst Place, Heathfield Terrace, London, W4 4JD
Trustees: Mr Alan Brookes, Mr Jonathan Lasey Turk, Mr Kevin Corbett, Mr Ian James Bolster, Mr Francois Morrow, Mr Michael Chaldecott, Mr Anthony Giddings, Ms Fiona Duncombe, Mr Alastair Thomas Graham Bell
Income: £1,173,505 [2017]; £993,578 [2016]; £914,830 [2015]; £979,559 [2014]; £699,170 [2013]

Construction Industry Trust for Youth
Registered: 24 Oct 2002 *Employees:* 23 *Volunteers:* 230
Tel: 020 7467 9540 *Website:* constructionyouth.org.uk
Activities: Education, training; economic, community development, employment
Address: The Building Centre, 26 Store Street, London, WC1E 7BT
Trustees: Mr Richard Laudy, Jane Nelson, Mr Terry Spraggett, Mark Southwell, Mr Mathew Baxter, Mr Assad Maqbool, Mr Andy Wates, Mr John Abbott, Mr Steve Brewer, Mr Willam Rufus Charles Meredith, Ms Victoria Brambini
Income: £1,435,686 [2016]; £1,437,120 [2015]; £1,614,821 [2014]; £1,454,380 [2013]; £1,197,733 [2012]

The Construction Sector Transparency Initiative
Registered: 31 May 2013
Tel: 020 3206 0488 *Website:* constructiontransparency.org
Activities: Education, training; advancement of health or saving of lives; prevention or relief of poverty; overseas aid, famine relief; economic, community development, employment
Address: c/o EAP, Woolgate Exchange, 25 Basinghall Street, London, EC2V 5HA
Trustees: Mr Christiaan Poortman, Mr Vincent Lazatin, Alredo Cantero Callejas, Mr Petter Mervyn Matthews, Mr George Ofori, Mr Frank Kehlenbach
Income: £1,402,280 [2016]; £843,056 [2015]; £211,860 [2014]

Consumers International
Registered: 2 Jan 2008 *Employees:* 27
Tel: 020 7226 6663 *Website:* consumersinternational.org
Activities: Education, training; environment, conservation, heritage; economic, community development, employment; other charitable purposes
Address: 24 Highbury Crescent, London, N5 1RX
Trustees: Mr Marimuthu Nadason, Ms Anja Philip, Mr Alan Kirkland, Ms Maria Jose Troya, Mr Ivo Frans Mechels, Mr Bart Robert Combee, Ms Fung Han Wong, Ms Marta Tellado, Ms Rosemary Siyachitma
Income: £3,149,355 [2016]; £2,529,707 [2015]; £2,748,034 [2014]; £2,508,657 [2013]; £2,397,834 [2012]

Consumers' Association
Registered: 2 Feb 1987 *Employees:* 751
Tel: 020 7770 7000 *Website:* which.co.uk
Activities: Education, training
Address: Consumers Association Ltd, 2 Marylebone Road, London, NW1 4DF
Trustees: Ms Sharon Margaret Grant OBE, Ms Anna Walker, Mr Brian Douglas Yates, Mr Peter Shears, Mr Jonathan Nicholas Thompson, Mrs Shirley Bailey-Wood, Ms Caroline Mary Baker, Mr Roger John Pittock, Mr Timothy David Gardam, Ms Jennifer Oscroft, Mrs Sharon Helen Darcy, Mr Donald Grant, Dr Melanie Jayne Fuller
Income: £101,147,000 [2017]; £101,230,000 [2016]; £102,831,000 [2015]; £94,729,000 [2014]; £86,576,000 [2013]

Contact A Family
Registered: 20 Jun 1982 *Employees:* 122 *Volunteers:* 84
Tel: 020 7608 8700 *Website:* contact.org.uk
Activities: The advancement of health or saving of lives; disability
Address: Contact A Family, 209-211 City Road, London, EC1V 1JN
Trustees: Mr Christopher David Carr, Ms Sue Hurrell, Ms Liz North, Ms Kelly Evans, Mr Gary Lapthorn, Mr Brian O'Hagan, Mr Kevin Hutchens, Mr Andrew Clapham, Ms Nakita Singh, Mr David Duly
Income: £4,661,873 [2017]; £5,115,842 [2016]; £6,308,809 [2015]; £5,189,276 [2014]; £5,227,231 [2013]

Contact The Elderly Limited
Registered: 29 Feb 2012 *Employees:* 39 *Volunteers:* 10,412
Tel: 020 7240 0630 *Website:* contact-the-elderly.org.uk
Activities: The advancement of health or saving of lives; economic, community development, employment
Address: 2 Grosvenor Gardens, London, SW1W 0DH
Trustees: Christian Grobel, Sarah Reed, Mrs Claire Emma Gooch, Ms Sally-Anne Wilkinson, Sir John Humphrey De Trafford, Mr William David Iain Barney, Mr Philip Kelvin, Mr Alan Stewart Gilfillan
Income: £1,812,027 [2017]; £1,325,957 [2016]; £1,016,017 [2015]; £884,325 [2014]; £1,586,676 [2013]

The Contemporary Art Society
Registered: 22 Sep 1962 *Employees:* 16
Tel: 020 7017 8400 *Website:* contemporaryartsociety.org
Activities: Education, training; arts, culture, heritage, science
Address: Contemporary Art Society, 59 Central Street, London, EC1V 3AF
Trustees: Mr Christopher Jonas, Ms Antje Geczy, Mrs Sarah Elson, Cathy Wills, Mrs Valeria Napoleone, Mr Richard Punt, Dr Sabri Challah, Ms Anna Yang, Mr Edwin Wulfsohn, Mr Tommaso Corvi-Mora, Mr Keith Morris, Mr Michael Bradley, Mr Simon Davenport, The Lady Beatrice Lupton, Mrs Emma Goltz, Ms Nicola Blake
Income: £1,314,755 [2017]; £1,115,453 [2016]; £1,338,973 [2015]; £1,524,591 [2014]; £1,373,466 [2013]

Contemporary Dance Trust Limited
Registered: 19 Dec 1966 *Employees:* 119
Tel: 020 7121 1031 *Website:* theplace.org.uk
Activities: Education, training; arts, culture, heritage, science; other charitable purposes
Address: Contemporary Dance Trust, The Place, 17 Dukes Road, London, WC1H 9PY
Trustees: Mr Robert Cohan CBE, Mr David Nightingale, Mr Douglas Campbell, Jane Alexander, Mr John Godfrey, Mr Christopher Charles Rowland, Mrs Dawn Paine, Ms Catherine Rosalind Marston, Miss Janet Eager MBE, Mr Stephen Browning, Mr John Gillespie Stewart, Mrs Sharon Monica Watson, Mr Tom Lynch, Ms Catherine Ward, Miss Amelia Ideh, Mr Derek Hicks
Income: £9,059,601 [2017]; £6,684,824 [2016]; £6,998,056 [2015]; £7,196,253 [2014]; £6,543,628 [2013]

The Conversation Trust (UK) Limited
Registered: 27 Mar 2013 *Employees:* 21 *Volunteers:* 4
Tel: 0117 929 0425 *Website:* theconversation.com
Activities: Education, training; arts, culture, heritage, science
Address: 8 Queens Parade, Bristol, BS1 5XJ
Trustees: Mr Nicholas John Eldred, Professor Colin Bryan Riordan, Mr Michael Burke, Mr Ziyad Marar, Mr Adrian Neil Monck, Dr Joanna Newman MBE, Lady Caroline Thomson, Professor Sir Paul Curran, Professor Alice May Roberts
Income: £1,218,631 [2017]; £938,075 [2016]; £839,418 [2015]; £688,602 [2014]

Cool Earth Action
Registered: 15 Feb 2007 *Employees:* 18 *Volunteers:* 5
Tel: 01326 567200 *Website:* coolearth.org
Activities: Education, training; prevention or relief of poverty; environment, conservation, heritage; economic, community development, employment
Address: 27 Old Gloucester Street, London, WC1N 3AX
Trustees: Rt Hon Frank Field MP, Mr Mark Ellingham, Mr Johan Eliasch, Baroness Jenkin of Kennington
Income: £1,671,616 [2017]; £1,556,392 [2016]; £1,321,339 [2015]; £1,176,485 [2014]; £1,421,730 [2013]

Cope Childrens Trust
Registered: 4 Sep 1992 *Employees:* 176 *Volunteers:* 366
Tel: 01509 638000 *Website:* rainbows.co.uk
Activities: The advancement of health or saving of lives; disability
Address: Rainbows Childrens Hospice, Lark Rise, Loughborough, Leics, LE11 2HS
Trustees: Mr Chandrakant Kataria, Mrs Alison Jane Breadon, Mr Paul Stothard, Mrs Joanne Sarah Brunner, Dr Jane Williams, Sue Dryden, Mr Vipal Karavadra, Mrs Vijay Sharma, Mr Richard Whall, Mrs Anne-Maria Olphert, Mrs Diane Sandra Postle, Richard Bishop, Dr Chris Hewitt, Mr Matthew William Rooney
Income: £5,802,269 [2017]; £5,531,392 [2016]; £5,350,981 [2015]; £5,022,771 [2014]; £4,904,381 [2013]

Kenneth Copeland Ministries
Registered: 4 Jul 1983 *Employees:* 24 *Volunteers:* 20
Tel: 01225 787310 *Website:* kcm.org.uk
Activities: Religious activities
Address: Kenneth Copeland Ministries, P O Box 15, Bath, BA1 3XN
Trustees: Mr Barry Tubbs, Miss Leona Boateng, Mr Alex Ashton, Rev Philip Anthony Sheard, Mr Robert Howells
Income: £2,139,663 [2016]; £2,083,599 [2015]; £2,220,596 [2014]; £2,176,248 [2013]; £2,640,456 [2012]

CoppaFeel
Registered: 28 Oct 2009 *Employees:* 9 *Volunteers:* 200
Website: coppafeel.org
Activities: General charitable purposes; advancement of health or saving of lives
Address: CoppaFeel!, 1st Floor, 1-4 Pope Street, London, SE1 3PR
Trustees: Mrs Kate Lee, Mr Simon Finnis, Mrs Alice May Purkiss, Mr Stephen Stretton, Mr James Alexander Clews, Mr Michael ATTI
Income: £1,877,314 [2016]; £1,040,794 [2015]; £1,242,274 [2014]; £474,801 [2013]; £479,567 [2012]

The Copsewood Education Trust
Registered: 15 Jun 1995 *Employees:* 29 *Volunteers:* 75
Tel: 024 7668 0680
Activities: Education, training
Address: Focus School Atherstone Campus, Long Street, Atherstone, Warwicks, CV9 1AE
Trustees: Mr James Alan Clarke, Mr Bradley Gilliland, Mr Garth Stephen Bushnell, Kevin Porter, Mr John Derrick Gates, Mr Derek Shedden, Mr Jerry Douglass
Income: £3,058,882 [2016]; £1,597,001 [2015]; £1,448,976 [2014]; £1,545,032 [2013]; £1,074,309 [2012]

Copthorne School Trust Limited
Registered: 24 Feb 1976 *Employees:* 69
Tel: 01342 712311 *Website:* copthorneprep.co.uk
Activities: Education, training
Address: Copthorne School Trust, Effingham Lane, Copthorne, Crawley, Surrey, RH10 3HR
Trustees: Mr James Abdool, Dr Richard Haworth, Mr Alain Kerneis, Mrs Angela Higgs, Mrs Heather Jane Beeby, Mr Robin Skeete Workman, Mrs Kathryn Bell, Mr Rohit Nathaniel, Mrs Hasmita Kerai, Mrs Aileen Baker
Income: £3,717,296 [2017]; £3,571,763 [2016]; £3,496,768 [2015]; £3,461,711 [2014]; £3,413,100 [2013]

Coquet Trust

Registered: 4 Oct 2007 *Employees:* 177
Tel: 0191 285 9270 *Website:* coquettrust.co.uk
Activities: Disability
Address: Coquet Trust, 23 Lansdowne Terrace, Newcastle upon Tyne, NE3 1HP
Trustees: Mrs Janet Bewick, Mrs Susan Welsh, Ian Gale, Dr Paul Smith, Mr David Rowland
Income: £4,992,060 [2017]; £4,881,314 [2016]; £4,611,810 [2015]; £4,618,392 [2014]; £4,758,463 [2013]

Coram Cambridgeshire Adoption Limited

Registered: 7 Jan 2015 *Employees:* 42
Tel: 0300 123 1093 *Website:* coramcambridgeshireadoption.org.uk
Activities: Other charitable purposes
Address: Coram Cambridgeshire Adoption, 2nd Floor, Lincoln House, The Paddocks Business Centre, Cherry Hinton Road, Cambridge, CB1 8DH
Trustees: Dr Carol Homden, Mr Ade Adetosoye, Mr Adrian Loades, John Gregg, Celia Dawson, Mr Mourougavelou Singaravelou, Ms Mary Austin
Income: £1,847,521 [2017]; £1,729,505 [2016]

Coram Children's Legal Centre Limited

Registered: 12 Nov 1980 *Employees:* 57 *Volunteers:* 9
Tel: 01206 714650 *Website:* childrenslegalcentre.com
Activities: General charitable purposes; education, training
Address: Coram Childrens Legal Centre, Century House, North Station Road, Colchester, Essex, CO1 1RE
Trustees: Dr Carol Homden, Mr John Nordon, Mr Robert Aitken, Ms Kerry Smith, Ms Alison Lowton, Mr Jonathan Portes, Vicky Ling, Chris Brown
Income: £3,780,887 [2017]; £3,187,430 [2016]; £2,532,584 [2015]; £2,179,283 [2014]; £1,889,374 [2013]

Thomas Coram Foundation for Children (formerly Foundling Hospital)

Registered: 20 Oct 1966 *Employees:* 387 *Volunteers:* 36
Tel: 020 7520 0300 *Website:* coram.org.uk
Activities: General charitable purposes; education, training; prevention or relief of poverty; accommodation, housing; arts, culture, heritage, science; economic, community development, employment
Address: Coram, 41 Brunswick Square, London, WC1N 1AZ
Trustees: Sir David Bell, Lord Simon Russell of Liverpool, Mr Yogesh Chauhan, Ms Celia Dawson, Mr Anthony Gamble, Mr Robert Aitken, Mr Geoff Berridge, Dr Pui-Ling Li, Ms Judith Trowell, Mr Paul Curran, Mr Jonathan Portes, Mr William Gore, Mr Ade Adetosoye, Ms Jenny Coles
Income: £9,433,364 [2017]; £18,345,459 [2016]; £16,650,550 [2015]; £12,817,632 [2014]; £7,722,520 [2013]

Coram Voice (formerly Voice for The Child in Care)

Registered: 10 May 1995 *Employees:* 53 *Volunteers:* 88
Tel: 020 7520 0305 *Website:* coramvoice.org.uk
Activities: Other charitable purposes
Address: Coram Voice, Gregory House, Coram Community Campus, 49 Mecklenburgh Square, London, WC1N 2QA
Trustees: Ms Rosemary Mayes, Mr Simon Greenhalgh, Ms Jenny Coles, Ms Pui-Ling Li, Mr Roger Black, Mr Timothy Sharp, Mr Kevin Venosi, Mr Jonny Hoyle
Income: £1,750,341 [2017]; £1,895,798 [2016]; £2,048,772 [2015]; £1,994,412 [2014]; £2,108,079 [2013]

Coram's Fields and The Harmsworth Memorial Playground

Registered: 17 Jan 1963 *Employees:* 34 *Volunteers:* 146
Tel: 020 3384 2201 *Website:* coramsfields.org
Activities: Amateur sport; recreation
Address: Corams Fields, 93 Guilford Street, London, WC1N 1DN
Trustees: Coram's Fields Company Trustee Limited
Income: £1,530,557 [2017]; £1,610,979 [2016]; £1,607,846 [2015]; £1,594,990 [2014]; £1,181,357 [2013]

Cord Global

Registered: 24 Jul 1998 *Employees:* 86 *Volunteers:* 5
Tel: 024 7708 7777 *Website:* cord.org.uk
Activities: Education, training; prevention or relief of poverty; overseas aid, famine relief
Address: Floor 9, Eaton House, 1 Eaton Road, Coventry, Warwicks, CV1 2FJ
Trustees: Ms Helen Elizabeth Jackson, Mr Peter Davis, Mrs Helen Brownstone, Mr Stephen Lawrence Chard Hucklesby, Ms Abigail Knowles, Mr Ravi Gidoomal
Income: £2,612,340 [2016]; £3,418,987 [2015]; £3,360,742 [2014]; £3,547,608 [2013]; £3,357,373 [2012]

The Corn Exchange (Newbury) Trust

Registered: 4 May 2000 *Employees:* 44 *Volunteers:* 128
Tel: 01635 582666 *Website:* cornexchangenew.com
Activities: Education, training; arts, culture, heritage, science; recreation
Address: Corn Exchange, Market Place, Newbury, Berks, RG14 5BD
Trustees: Lord George Reginald Oliver Carnarvon, Mr Jeff Beck, Robert Holland, Mr Ian Vickerage, Ms Michelle Di Gioia, Christina Pepper
Income: £2,286,000 [2017]; £1,982,600 [2016]; £1,927,800 [2015]; £1,502,300 [2014]; £1,481,900 [2013]

Cornell University Foundation (UK) Limited

Registered: 24 Sep 2012
Tel: 020 7502 2813
Activities: Education, training
Address: 19 Norcott Road, London, N16 7EJ
Trustees: Dominic Collier, Mrs Tracy Cary, Richard Ely
Income: £1,040,441 [2017]; £199,751 [2016]; £60,212 [2015]; £79,722 [2014]; £139,545 [2013]

Cornerstone Evangelical Church

Registered: 12 Mar 2009 *Employees:* 14 *Volunteers:* 347
Tel: 0115 958 8711 *Website:* cornerstonechurch.org.uk
Activities: Education, training; advancement of health or saving of lives; overseas aid, famine relief; religious activities
Address: 228-230 Castle Boulevard, Nottingham, NG7 1FP
Trustees: Mr Colin West Webster, Mr Peter John Brown, Mr Paul Couchman, Mr John Mark Russell, Mr Simon Lister, Mr Richard Colin Lewis, Mr Jonathan Farquhar Gribbin, Mr William John Rettie, Mr Jonathan Graham, Mr Mark Collins
Income: £1,005,869 [2016]; £919,312 [2015]; £988,997 [2014]; £951,851 [2013]; £1,163,916 [2012]

Cornwall Air Ambulance Trust
Registered: 15 Dec 2009 *Employees:* 28 *Volunteers:* 250
Tel: 01637 889926 *Website:* cornwallairambulancetrust.org
Activities: The advancement of health or saving of lives
Address: Cornwall Air Ambulance Trust, Trevithick Downs, Newquay, Cornwall, TR8 4DY
Trustees: Ellen Winser, Dr Nicholas Clark, Mrs Sarah Pryce, Henry Orchard, Mr Ian Brackenbury, Mr Christopher Pomfret, Mr Robert Richard Cowie, Barbara Ann Sharples
Income: £4,503,932 [2016]; £4,675,841 [2015]; £3,820,303 [2014]; £3,182,954 [2013]; £3,374,716 [2012]

Cornwall Care Limited
Registered: 5 Mar 1996 *Employees:* 737
Tel: 01872 261787 *Website:* cornwallcare.com
Activities: Education, training; advancement of health or saving of lives; disability; accommodation, housing
Address: Cornwall Care Home, Glenthorne Court, Truro Business Park, Threemilestone, Truro, Cornwall, TR4 9NY
Trustees: Mr John Acornley, Ms Thelma Olive Sorensen, Dr Anthony Felton, Mr Philip Rees, Mr Michael Beadel, Mr Colin Champion Nicholls, Mrs Geraldine Lavery
Income: £32,163,000 [2016]; £28,537,000 [2015]; £27,514,000 [2014]; £25,956,000 [2013]; £25,162,000 [2012]

Cornwall Community Development Limited
Registered: 16 Jul 2001 *Employees:* 50 *Volunteers:* 45
Tel: 01872 223678 *Website:* cornwallrcc.org.uk
Activities: Education, training; prevention or relief of poverty; arts, culture, heritage, science; environment, conservation, heritage; economic, community development, employment
Address: Cornwall Rural Community Charity, 2 Princes Street, Truro, Cornwall, TR1 2ES
Trustees: Mr Philip John Willoughby, Mr Paul Parkin, Mr Neil Graham Robertson, Mrs Sandra Tregidgo, Ms Karen Jane Jackson, Councillor Hilary Anne Frank, Mrs Susan Mary Guard, Mr Alan Geoffrey Shepherd, Councillor Loic Joachim Rich, Mrs Kate McCavana, Mrs Karlene Grace Stokes, Lady Marian Kathleen Berkeley
Income: £2,268,269 [2017]; £1,604,869 [2016]; £1,377,311 [2015]; £1,609,386 [2014]; £1,737,025 [2013]

Cornwall Community Foundation
Registered: 10 Oct 2003 *Employees:* 6 *Volunteers:* 80
Tel: 01566 779333 *Website:* cornwallfoundation.com
Activities: General charitable purposes; education, training; advancement of health or saving of lives; disability; prevention or relief of poverty; accommodation, housing; arts, culture, heritage, science; amateur sport; environment, conservation, heritage; economic, community development, employment
Address: Suite 1, Sheers Barton Barns, Lawhitton, Launceston, Cornwall, PL15 9NJ
Trustees: Mrs Deborah Hinton OBE, Mrs Jane Margaret Hartley DL, Mr James Williams DL, Mr John Ede MBE, Mr Timothy Smith, Mr Toby Ashworth, Mr Stamford Galsworthy, Mrs Emma Mantle, The Hon Evelyn Boscawen DL, Mr Thomas Van Oss, Miss Daphne Skinnard DL, Mr Ian Taylor, Mrs Nicola Marquis, Mr Jonathan Cunliffe, Mr Kim Conchie
Income: £1,218,340 [2016]; £769,246 [2015]; £1,968,640 [2014]; £1,116,378 [2013]; £838,131 [2012]

Cornwall Food Foundation
Registered: 22 May 2007 *Employees:* 72 *Volunteers:* 4
Tel: 01637 861000 *Website:* cornwallfoodfoundation.org
Activities: Education, training; prevention or relief of poverty; economic, community development, employment
Address: On The Beach, Watergate Bay, Newquay, Cornwall, TR8 4AA
Trustees: Mr Malcolm Ellis Bell, Ms Judith Anne Blakeburn, Mr Raoul Humphreys, Lindsey Victoria Hall, Ms Catherine Mead
Income: £3,119,893 [2017]; £3,326,557 [2016]; £3,258,531 [2015]; £433,308 [2014]; £3,052,226 [2013]

Cornwall Hospice Care Limited
Registered: 2 Mar 2006 *Employees:* 283 *Volunteers:* 980
Tel: 01726 65711 *Website:* cornwallhospicecare.co.uk
Activities: The advancement of health or saving of lives
Address: Mount Edgcumbe Hospice, Porthpean Road, St Austell, Cornwall, PL26 6AB
Trustees: Dr Mary Elizabeth Turfitt, Mr Alistair James Whyte, Mr Alan Brownscombe, Mr David Renwick, Mrs Mary Alison Anson, Mrs Lesley Jane Ross, Mrs Lesley Ann Clarke, Dr Steve Hawkins, Dr Colin John Philip, Dr John Nicholas Barnes
Income: £9,259,703 [2017]; £9,461,542 [2016]; £7,500,125 [2015]; £8,002,406 [2014]; £7,470,655 [2013]

Cornwall Music Service Trust
Registered: 15 Dec 2014 *Employees:* 116
Tel: 01872 246043 *Website:* cornwallmusicservicetrust.org
Activities: Education, training; advancement of health or saving of lives; disability; arts, culture, heritage, science; recreation
Address: Cornwall Music Service Trust, Truro School, Trennick Lane, Truro, Cornwall, TR1 1TH
Trustees: David William Fryer, Alan Thomas Lane Retallack, Paul Kneebone, William Walker, Mrs Jowanna Conboye, Andrew Samler Gordon-Brown, Judith Margaret Bailey, Rebecca Mary Jane Thomas, Mr James Sargent, Bethany Lois Wade
Income: £1,429,239 [2017]; £1,318,258 [2016]; £829,063 [2015]

Cornwall Old People's Housing Society
Registered: 18 Aug 1998 *Employees:* 57 *Volunteers:* 33
Tel: 01872 572275 *Website:* perranbayhome.co.uk
Activities: Accommodation, housing
Address: St Pirans Road, Perranporth, Truro, Cornwall, TR6 0BH
Trustees: Mr John Rabey, Steve Burstow, Mrs Rosemary Ann Anderson, Mrs Olive Joyce Johns, Mr Andrew Nicholas Bown, Mrs Jacqueline Lenz, Mr Kenneth Claude Yeo, Mrs Alison Catherine Smith, Mrs Mary Jocelyn Mallett
Income: £1,260,793 [2016]; £1,230,667 [2015]; £1,077,157 [2014]; £909,413 [2013]; £932,935 [2012]

The Cornwall Trust for Nature Conservation Limited
Registered: 20 Feb 1963 *Employees:* 62 *Volunteers:* 2,000
Tel: 01872 273939 *Website:* cornwallwildlifetrust.org.uk
Activities: Education, training; animals; environment, conservation, heritage; economic, community development, employment
Address: Cornwall Wildlife Trust, Five Acres, Allet, Truro, Cornwall, TR4 9DJ
Trustees: Mrs Jean Bertha Smith, Mrs Caroline Jane Vulliamy, Ms Elizabeth Frances Tregenza, Mr Mark Nicholson BSc MPhil, Mr Daniel Eva BSc, John Gowenlock, Stephen Warman, Ian Pye, Frank Howie, Mr Frederick Anthony Currie, Ms Gillian Mary Saunders, Paul Coyne, David Leslie Thomas Esq, Dr Jan Pentreath, Mr Steve Crummay FInstLM, Mr Charles Vivian David, Mr Philip John McVey, Dr Nicholas Tregenza, Gordon Fuller, Dee Reeves, Mrs Christine Horsely
Income: £3,635,296 [2017]; £2,842,444 [2016]; £2,866,301 [2015]; £2,344,989 [2014]; £2,497,592 [2013]

The Corporation of Oundle School
Registered: 23 Mar 1965 *Employees:* 513 *Volunteers:* 40
Tel: 01832 273434 *Website:* oundleschool.org.uk
Activities: Education, training
Address: Oundle School, Bursars Office, Church Street, Oundle, Peterborough, PE8 4EE
Trustees: The Governing Body of Oundle School
Income: £38,648,000 [2017]; £40,400,000 [2016]; £37,812,000 [2015]; £35,132,000 [2014]; £34,117,000 [2013]

The Corporation of St Lawrence College
Registered: 13 Jun 1967 *Employees:* 253 *Volunteers:* 12
Tel: 01843 587666 *Website:* slcuk.com
Activities: Education, training
Address: College Road, Ramsgate, Kent, CT11 7AE
Trustees: Rev Gordon Lenham Warren, Mr John Guyatt MA, Mr Nick Marchant, Mr David Taylor Maoxon PGCE FRSA, Mr Tim Townsend, Mrs Julia Marilyn Challender BEd MA, Rev Stephen Rae PG Dip BA Hons, Dr John Neden, Mr Michael John Bolton, Mrs Alison Burgess TCNFF ACP, Mrs Gillian Page, Mr Jonathan Tapp BSc, Mr James Stewart Laslett BA Hons FCMA, Mr Graham Carter FRICS FCABE, Mr Guy Sanderson
Income: £10,925,906 [2017]; £10,123,485 [2016]; £9,192,180 [2015]; £8,397,170 [2014]; £7,832,837 [2013]

The Corporation of The Church House
Registered: 23 Jan 1963 *Employees:* 36
Tel: 020 7898 1310 *Website:* churchhouse.org.uk
Activities: Religious activities
Address: Corporation of The Church House, 27 Great Smith Street, London, SW1P 3AZ
Trustees: Andrew Penny, Canon Dr Christina Baxter CBE, David Kemp, Chris Smith CBE, David Barnett, The Venerable Norman Russell, Anne Toms, Canon Lucy Docherty
Income: £5,780,409 [2016]; £5,567,762 [2015]; £6,705,871 [2014]; £6,506,707 [2013]; £6,590,015 [2012]

The Corporation of The Hall of Arts and Sciences
Registered: 18 Dec 1967 *Employees:* 274
Tel: 020 7959 0505 *Website:* royalalberthall.com
Activities: Education, training; arts, culture, heritage, science; environment, conservation, heritage
Address: Royal Albert Hall, Kensington Gore, London, SW7 2AP
Trustees: Mr Gerald Bowden TD MA FRICS, Mr Mark Schnebli, Mr Jon Moynihan OBE MA MSc SM, Mr Leon Baroukh MA CFA, Mrs Lin Craig JP, Mr James Max, Mr Anthony Ratcliffe FRICS FRSA, Mr Robert Lipson, Professor James Stirling CBE FRS FCGI, Mr Stephen Brandon, Ms Lauren Ekon, Mr Stuart Corbyn FRICS, Sir Michael Dixon KBE BSc ARCS DPhil DSC FCGI, Mr John Cooper, Mr Richard Waterbury MA, Dr Monica Bloch PhD, Mr Michael Jackson MA FCA, Mr Ian McCulloch, Mr Peter B M Lim FCA MBA, Mr Stuart William Newey, Ms Lucinda Case, Mr Porter Kevin
Income: £32,616,000 [2016]; £31,067,000 [2015]; £27,583,000 [2014]; £25,933,000 [2013]; £22,853,000 [2012]

The Corporation of Trinity House of Deptford Strond
Registered: 23 Nov 1966 *Employees:* 19
Tel: 020 7481 6914 *Website:* trinityhouse.co.uk
Activities: Education, training; prevention or relief of poverty; accommodation, housing; environment, conservation, heritage; other charitable purposes
Address: Trinity House, Tower Hill, London, EC3N 4DH
Trustees: Captain Nigel Palmer OBE MNM, Cdre William Walworth CBE, Rear Admiral David Snelson CB FNI, Captain Stephen Gobbi JP MA LLB, Mr Malcolm Glaister, Captain Ian McNaught MNM, Captain Roger Barker FNI, Captain Nigel Hope RD RNR, Mr Richard Sadler, Commodore Robert Dorey RFA
Income: £9,403,000 [2017]; £8,841,000 [2016]; £8,598,000 [2015]; £8,056,000 [2014]; £7,998,000 [2013]

Corpus Christi College
Registered: 8 Sep 2011 *Employees:* 106
Tel: 01865 276700 *Website:* ccc.ox.ac.uk
Activities: Education, training
Address: Corpus Christi College, Merton Street, Oxford, OX1 4JF
Trustees: Dr Nigel Bowles, Mr John Harrison, Dr Nicole Grobert, Dr Mark Whittow, Dr John Watts, Professor Tobias Reinhardt, Dr Robin Murphy, Dr Neil McLynn, Revd Canon Dr Judith Maltby, Dr Michael Benjamin Johnston, Professor Stephen Harrison, Dr John Elsner, Professor Richard Cornall, Dr Paul Dellar, Dr Colin Akerman, Dr Andrew Fowler, Professor Constanze Magdalene Guthenke, Mr Steven Charles Cowley, Dr Matthew Niall Dyson, Dr Anna Marmodoro, Professor Alastair Buchan, Dr Mark Wormald, Mr Nicholas Thorn, Dr Pawel Sweitach, Professor Peter Nellist, Dr Helen Moore, Prof Colin McDiarmid, Professor Hans Kraus, Professor Peter John Hore, Dr Elizabeth Fisher, Professor Giovanni Capoccia, Professor Ursula Coope, Professor Martin Davies, Professor Mark Sansom, Mr Andrew William Rolfe, Dr Jefferson Alan McMahan, Dr James Alexander Duffy, Dr David James Russell
Income: £7,363,000 [2017]; £6,389,000 [2016]; £10,430,000 [2015]; £7,496,000 [2014]; £5,888,000 [2013]

Cosgarne Hall Ltd.
Registered: 1 Sep 2009 *Employees:* 9 *Volunteers:* 20
Tel: 01726 61979 *Website:* cosgarnehall.org
Activities: Accommodation, housing
Address: 81 Truro Road, St Austell, Cornwall, PL25 5JQ
Trustees: Mr Gareth Bray, Mr Roger Varney, Mr Tim Styles, Dr Clare Taylor, Mr Clive Stephens, Mr Hugh Hedderly, Mrs Janet Irene Varney, Mr William John Horton
Income: £1,118,202 [2017]; £1,063,322 [2016]; £847,651 [2015]; £729,741 [2014]; £728,978 [2013]

Cosmetic Toiletry and Perfumery Foundation
Registered: 20 Jan 1994 *Employees:* 17 *Volunteers:* 2,600
Tel: 01372 747500 *Website:* lgfb.co.uk
Activities: The advancement of health or saving of lives
Address: Look Good Feel Better, 32 West Hill, Epsom, Surrey, KT19 8JD
Trustees: Mr Per Ake Neuman, Mr Ian Jepson, Mrs Deborah Lewis, Mr Kenneth Green, Mrs Deborah Rix, Mr Peter Jeffrey Godden, Ms Alison Crawford, Geoffrey Percy, Justin Musgrove, Susan Taylor, Mrs Ruth Newton Jones, Mr David Allan, Mrs Catherine McMahon, Ms Deborah Ann Hunter, Mr Ian Marshall, Anna Bartle, Sara Stern
Income: £1,927,282 [2016]; £1,750,184 [2015]; £1,096,292 [2014]; £609,615 [2013]; £566,817 [2012]

The Costa Foundation
Registered: 23 May 2012
Website: costafoundation.com
Activities: Education, training; advancement of health or saving of lives; prevention or relief of poverty; overseas aid, famine relief; environment, conservation, heritage; economic, community development, employment
Address: The Costa Foundation, Whitbread Court, Porz Avenue, Houghton Hall Park, Houghton Regis, Beds, LU5 5XE
Trustees: Mr Clive Jonathan Bentley, Mrs Elizabeth Ann Perry, Mr Timothy Brett Johnson, Mr Kieran James Cooke, Ms Victoria Moorhouse, Mr Russell William Fairhurst, Clair Louise Preston, Mrs Kay Brunton, Mrs Katherine Joanna Seljeflot
Income: £1,988,241 [2017]; £2,099,171 [2016]; £1,804,383 [2015]; £1,569,948 [2014]; £1,340,650 [2013]

The Cote Charity
Registered: 7 Nov 1968 *Employees:* 48 *Volunteers:* 28
Tel: 0117 973 8058 *Website:* cotecharity.co.uk
Activities: Accommodation, housing
Address: The Old Court House, Church Street, Nailsworth, Stroud, Glos, GL6 0BP
Trustees: Smv Trustee Company Limited
Income: £1,756,263 [2016]; £1,556,943 [2015]; £1,464,693 [2014]; £1,309,368 [2013]; £1,289,568 [2012]

Cothill Trust
Registered: 1 Oct 1969 *Employees:* 449 *Volunteers:* 25
Tel: 01865 390030 *Website:* cothilltrust.org
Activities: Education, training
Address: Cothill House, Cothill, Abingdon, Oxon, OX13 6JL
Trustees: Mr Peter Morrison Cook, Mr Justin Marking, Mr Etienne Bottari, Mrs Kararine Pryce, Dr Ralph Townsend MA DPhil, Ms Denise Le Gal, Mr David Miles
Income: £22,166,000 [2017]; £22,453,000 [2016]; £17,937,000 [2015]; £17,658,935 [2014]; £19,094,610 [2013]

Cotswold Archaeology Ltd
Registered: 24 Jan 1991 *Employees:* 183 *Volunteers:* 25
Tel: 01285 771022 *Website:* cotswoldarchaeology.co.uk
Activities: Education, training; arts, culture, heritage, science; environment, conservation, heritage
Address: Building 11, Kemble Enterprise Park, Kemble, Cirencester, Glos, GL7 6BQ
Trustees: Professor Timothy Darvill OBE, Vikki Fenner, Keith Winmill, Sue Parsons, Mr Richard Courtenay Lord, Alan Chater, Paul Cullen, Bob Bewley
Income: £9,221,711 [2017]; £9,126,533 [2016]; £7,047,962 [2015]; £5,797,650 [2014]; £5,192,734 [2013]

Council for Advancement and Support of Education (Europe)
Registered: 9 Dec 1994 *Employees:* 21 *Volunteers:* 600
Tel: 020 7448 9940 *Website:* case.org
Activities: Education, training
Address: 3rd Floor, Paxton House, 30 Artillery Lane, London, E1 7LS
Trustees: Mr Stephen Large, Miss Claire Brown, Anton Muscatelli, Liesl Elder, James Harris, Mr Serhii Sych, Mr Lee Fertig, Mr Colin McCallum, Mr Xavier Michel, Mr Michael Lavery, Ms Sue Cunningham, Emma Jones, Dr Jean Van Sinderen-Law, Salima Virji
Income: £2,218,786 [2017]; £2,242,523 [2016]; £2,104,484 [2015]; £1,759,557 [2014]; £1,640,543 [2013]

Council for At-Risk Academics
Registered: 22 Sep 1962 *Employees:* 9 *Volunteers:* 17
Tel: 020 7021 0882 *Website:* cara.ngo
Activities: Education, training; prevention or relief of poverty; human rights, religious or racial harmony, equality or diversity
Address: Council for Assisting Refugee Academics, South Bank Technopark, 90 London Road, London, SE1 6LN
Trustees: Mrs Anne Lonsdale CBE, Professor Michael Worton, Professor Paul Weindling, Prof Alan J McCarthy, Professor John Joseph Naughton, Mr Stephan Roman, Mr Nigel Petrie, Ms Tabitha Nice, The Revd Canon Dr Nicholas Sagovsky, Professor Sir Deian Hopkin, Mr David Ure, Dr Joanna Frances Newman MBE, Mr Jonathan Mark Hammond, Ms Lilia Jolibois, Professor Penelope Gardner-Chloros, Ms Nicola Dandridge CBE
Income: £1,518,427 [2016]; £1,085,067 [2015]; £579,697 [2014]; £637,979 [2013]; £684,703 [2012]

The Council for Industry and Higher Education
Registered: 18 Dec 1997 *Employees:* 20
Tel: 020 7383 7667 *Website:* ncub.co.uk
Activities: General charitable purposes; education, training; economic, community development, employment
Address: The Council for Industry & Higher Education, 11 Tiger House, Burton Street, London, WC1H 9BY
Trustees: Professor Julia Clare Buckingham, Professor Sir Keith Burnett, Professor Richard Parker, Sam Laidlaw, Professor Julie Elspeth Lydon, Sir Roger Bone, Professor David Phoenix, Mr Phil Smith, Mr David Willetts
Income: £2,210,961 [2017]; £2,766,580 [2016]; £2,294,891 [2015]; £1,656,457 [2014]; £1,261,227 [2013]

Council for World Mission (UK)
Registered: 5 Jun 2003 *Employees:* 2
Tel: 020 7551 7777 *Website:* cwmission.org
Activities: Education, training; religious activities; environment, conservation, heritage; economic, community development, employment
Address: 10 Queen Street Place, London, EC4R 1BE
Trustees: Rev Jeffrey Williams, Dr Elizabeth John Zachariah, Mrs Rose Althea Wedderburn, Rev Mukondeleli Edward Ramulondi, Mrs Jennifer Joy Flett, Prof Victor Wan Chi Hsu Dr
Income: £4,129,303 [2016]; £15,135,272 [2015]; £5,469,345 [2014]; £5,029,752 [2013]; £4,429,753 [2012]

The Council of European Jamaats

Registered: 20 Feb 2003 *Employees:* 4 *Volunteers:* 150
Tel: 020 8696 5200 *Website:* coej.org
Activities: General charitable purposes; education, training; advancement of health or saving of lives; disability; prevention or relief of poverty; religious activities; arts, culture, heritage, science; amateur sport; economic, community development, employment; other charitable purposes
Address: Unit 101, 1st Floor, Metroline House, 118-122 College Road, Harrow, Middlesex, HA1 1BQ
Trustees: Mr Husein Jiwa, Mr Murtaza Gulamhusein, Syed Mohammed Naqvi, Mr Mehdi Najafi, Munir Datoo, Mr Razahusein Rahim, Mr Kassam Jaffer, Mr Jamil Bandali, Dr Rizwan Alidina, Mr Arif Hiridjee, Ms Sajeda Canani, Mr Salim Rehmatullah, Mr Qassim Mawjee, Mr Mohammadali Shigari, Mr Barkat Rajani, Mr Fayyaz Haji, Altaf Daya, Kamran Shah, Mr Salim Hamir, Dr Akber Mohamedali, Mrs Waheeda Rahim, Mr Rasool Bhamani, Mr Mazaher Remtulla, Mr Hussein-Ali Rahemtulla, Miss Esmat Jeraj, Mr Gulamraza Datoo, Mr Murtaza Bharwani, Mr Mazaheer Rajwani, Mr Abbasali Merali, Mr Azad Hedaraly, Mr Azim Jetha, Mr Mussadique Ladak, Mr Imran Ali Kassam, Mukhtarali Hirani, Muzaffer Sultanali Rashid
Income: £2,179,966 [2016]; £2,050,826 [2015]; £1,909,798 [2014]; £1,405,059 [2013]; £1,839,395 [2012]

The Council of Milton Abbey School Ltd

Registered: 18 Apr 1963 *Employees:* 143
Tel: 01258 880484 *Website:* miltonabbey.co.uk
Activities: Education, training
Address: Blandford Forum, Dorset, DT11 0BZ
Trustees: Mrs Jenifer Harley Simm, Charles Mitchell-Innes, Ms Katharine Butler, Mr Matthew Damian Lloyd Noyce MCSI, Mr Luke James Rake, Patrick McGrath, Colonel Oliver John Harben Chamberlain, Mr Ian Geoffrey Bromilow, Mr Neil Stephen Boulton
Income: £7,338,765 [2016]; £6,823,768 [2015]; £6,672,011 [2014]; £6,051,473 [2013]; £6,410,715 [2012]

The Council of The Inns of Court

Registered: 5 Feb 2014 *Employees:* 10 *Volunteers:* 70
Tel: 020 7822 0760 *Website:* coic.org.uk
Activities: Education, training; other charitable purposes
Address: The Council of Inns of Court, 9 Gray's Inn Square, London, WC1R 5JD
Trustees: Dr David Southern, Duncan Matthews QC, Mr Guy Perricone, Mr Desmond Browne, Mr Gregory John Dorey CVO, Brigadier Anthony Duncan Harking, Mr Peter Lodder QC, Ms Mary Kerr, Ms Helen Davies
Income: £1,339,732 [2016]; £1,271,781 [2015]; £1,057,380 [2014]

The Counselling Foundation

Registered: 30 Oct 1992 *Employees:* 29
Tel: 01727 868585 *Website:* counsellingfoundation.org
Activities: Education, training; advancement of health or saving of lives
Address: 1 College Yard, Lower Dagnall Street, St Albans, Herts, AL3 4PA
Trustees: Mr Martyn Hutchinson Taylor, Mr Philip Needham FCCA MBA, Ms Mandy MacQueen, Mr Julian Christopher Gell, Mrs Francine Godrich
Income: £1,538,994 [2017]; £1,073,842 [2016]; £869,101 [2015]; £979,314 [2014]; £831,028 [2013]

Countess Mountbatten Hospice Charity Limited

Registered: 25 Mar 2008 *Employees:* 13 *Volunteers:* 175
Tel: 023 8047 5313 *Website:* cmhcharity.org.uk
Activities: Education, training; advancement of health or saving of lives; disability
Address: Moorgreen Hospital, Botley Road, West End, Southampton, SO30 3JB
Trustees: Mrs Sue Hill, Mr Peter Pitcher, Mr Andrew Black, Mrs Ita Kelly, Gillian Owton
Income: £2,117,954 [2017]; £1,135,557 [2016]; £1,242,058 [2015]; £1,081,787 [2014]; £807,775 [2013]

Country Holidays for Inner City Kids

Registered: 31 May 2000 *Employees:* 42 *Volunteers:* 641
Tel: 01822 811020 *Website:* chicks.org.uk
Activities: Education, training; amateur sport
Address: Chicks, Moorland Retreat, Brentor, Tavistock, Devon, PL19 0LX
Trustees: Mrs Marion Ruth Luckhurst, Mr Robin Patrick Barlow, Mr Mark Francis Duddridge, Mr Stephen David Brearley, Mr Andrew Christopher Ryde, Mr Kenneth William George Cherrett, Mrs Gillian Parker, Mrs Morag Christine McLintock, Mr Stephen Paul Williams
Income: £1,462,483 [2016]; £1,730,433 [2015]; £2,971,801 [2014]; £1,195,186 [2013]; £1,130,141 [2012]

Countryside Restoration Trust

Registered: 26 May 2011 *Employees:* 11 *Volunteers:* 59
Tel: 01223 262999 *Website:* countrysiderestorationtrust.com
Activities: Education, training; environment, conservation, heritage
Address: Birds Farm, Haslingfield Road, Barton, Cambridge, CB23 7AG
Trustees: Robin Page, Mr Zac Goldsmith, Nicholas Watts, Mr Chris Knights, Mrs Annabelle Evans
Income: £2,222,586 [2017]; £2,653,312 [2016]; £1,262,944 [2015]; £3,128,849 [2014]; £631,002 [2013]

County Air Ambulance Trust

Registered: 24 Jul 1996 *Employees:* 11
Tel: 01922 618058 *Website:* countyairambulancetrust.co.uk
Activities: The advancement of health or saving of lives
Address: County Air Ambulance Trust, P O Box 999, Walsall, W Midlands, WS2 7YX
Trustees: Mr Hugh Bernard Meynell MBE, Mr Richard Anthony Spencer Everard DL, Dr Shaukat Ali, Margaret Jane Bishop, Mr Paul Joseph Harris, Mr John Lewis Jones DL, Michael Henriques, Mrs Angela Brinton DSTJ DL
Income: £7,865,801 [2016]; £7,321,715 [2015]; £5,875,013 [2014]; £4,011,474 [2013]; £2,537,917 [2012]

County Durham Community Foundation

Registered: 29 Jun 1995 *Employees:* 12 *Volunteers:* 75
Tel: 0191 378 6345 *Website:* cdcf.org.uk
Activities: General charitable purposes
Address: 36 Beechwood Road, Eaglescliffe, Stockton on Tees, Cleveland, TS16 0AE
Trustees: Mr Dennis Morgan, Dr Nigel Martin, Mr Arthur Raymond, Michele Armstrong, Prof Ray Hudson, Ms Lesley Anne Fairclough, Mr Stephen Hall, Mrs Carolyn Roberts, Mr Colin Fyfe, Paul Chandler, Mr Duncan Barrie, Mr James Fenwick, Mr Peter Cook, Mrs Annie Dolphin
Income: £3,779,677 [2017]; £4,937,583 [2016]; £5,187,742 [2015]; £4,919,749 [2014]; £3,766,205 [2013]

Court Based Personal Support
Registered: 26 Feb 2002 *Employees:* 36 *Volunteers:* 733
Tel: 020 7947 7705 *Website:* thepsu.org.uk
Activities: Other charitable purposes
Address: Royal Courts of Justice, Strand, London, WC2A 2LL
Trustees: Honourable Mrs Angela Felicity Camber, Mr Greville Simon Waterman, Kirit Naik, Mr Peter Michael Handcock, Ms Elisabeth Sian Davies, Prof David Wilkin, Mr Lucas Wilson, Peter Crisp, Ms Caroline May Field, Ms Elisabeth May Long
Income: £1,325,923 [2017]; £1,068,969 [2016]; £941,618 [2015]; £548,223 [2014]; £446,866 [2013]

The Courtauld Institute of Art Fund
Registered: 17 Jan 1984
Tel: 020 3751 0523
Activities: Education, training; arts, culture, heritage, science; environment, conservation, heritage
Address: Courtauld Institute of Art, Somerset House, Strand, London, WC2R 0RN
Trustees: Dr Deborah Swallow, Professor Antony Eastmond, Robert Thorpe
Income: £2,306,566 [2017]; £1,560,140 [2016]; £1,907,586 [2015]; £1,819,070 [2014]; £806,845 [2013]

The Courtyard Trust
Registered: 30 Jan 1998 *Employees:* 60 *Volunteers:* 170
Tel: 01432 346502 *Website:* courtyard.org.uk
Activities: Arts, culture, heritage, science
Address: The Barn, Cobhall Court, Allensmore, Hereford, HR2 9BG
Trustees: Dr Ian Peter Hine, Mr Roger Morgan, Ms Polly Ernest, Mr Michael Sharp, Mr Richard Heatly, Mr Chris Green, Mr Tom McEwen
Income: £2,924,541 [2017]; £2,708,134 [2016]; £2,744,648 [2015]; £2,924,059 [2014]; £2,519,460 [2013]

Coutts Charitable Foundation
Registered: 12 Feb 2013 *Volunteers:* 3
Tel: 020 7753 1000 *Website:* coutts.com
Activities: The prevention or relief of poverty
Address: Coutts, 440 Strand, London, WC2R 0QS
Trustees: Ms Lenka Setkova, Dr Linda Yueh, Ms Leslie Gent, Ms Alison Marie Rose-Slade, Mr Peter Gordon Flavel, Sir Christopher Geidt, Lord Waldegrave of North Hill, Mr Ali Hassan Hammad, Mr Thomas Joylon Kenrick, Ms Camilla Stowell
Income: £1,056,074 [2017]; £1,156,874 [2016]; £2,672,682 [2015]; £642,216 [2014]

Coventry & Warwickshire YMCA
Registered: 4 Nov 2003 *Employees:* 18 *Volunteers:* 41
Tel: 0121 478 4344 *Website:* ymca-cw.org.uk
Activities: General charitable purposes; education, training; accommodation, housing; amateur sport; economic, community development, employment
Address: YMCA, Endeavour Court, 20 Chelmarsh, Coventry, Warwicks, CV6 3LB
Trustees: Anne Linsey, Anne Woodley, David McKernan, Bill Parkinson, Jon Grant, Rebecca Fahy
Income: £1,258,562 [2017]; £1,151,859 [2016]; £1,128,140 [2015]; £1,044,578 [2014]; £977,129 [2013]

Coventry Citizens Advice
Registered: 2 Oct 1990 *Employees:* 67 *Volunteers:* 97
Tel: 024 7625 2001 *Website:* coventrycab.org.uk
Activities: General charitable purposes
Address: Kirby House, Little Park Street, Coventry, Warwicks, CV1 2JZ
Trustees: Mr Harold Hall, Mrs Susan Wyllie, Ms Carol Williams, Mr Timothy George Miller, Ms Catherine Anne Stephens, Mr David Lloyd, Mr Simon Brake, Councillor Abbott, Mr Leon Taylor, Rachel Dixon
Income: £3,075,138 [2017]; £3,557,660 [2016]; £2,784,834 [2015]; £2,205,675 [2014]; £1,748,564 [2013]

Coventry Cyrenians Limited
Registered: 31 May 1973 *Employees:* 23 *Volunteers:* 118
Tel: 024 7622 8099 *Website:* coventrycyrenians.co.uk
Activities: Accommodation, housing
Address: Oakwood House, Cheylesmore, Coventry, Warwicks, CV1 2HL
Trustees: Mr David Oliver, Rachel Hayward, Mr Richard Stephen Hadley, Ms Sally Ann Eason, Dr Yesret Bi
Income: £1,296,841 [2017]; £1,338,771 [2016]; £1,487,617 [2015]; £2,300,222 [2014]; £2,217,377 [2013]

The Coventry Diocesan Board of Finance Ltd
Registered: 14 Nov 1966 *Employees:* 35 *Volunteers:* 85
Tel: 024 7652 1200 *Website:* dioceseofcoventry.org
Activities: Religious activities
Address: Diocesan Offices, 1 Hill Top, Coventry, Warwicks, CV1 5AB
Trustees: Mr Peter C Rogers, Canon Ian E Francis, Revd Canon Barbara Clutton, Ven Sue Field, Mr David G Wigman, The Rt Revd Dr Christopher J Cocksworth, Mrs Felicity Hawke, The Revd Dr Jill Tucker, Very Revd John Witcombe, Revd Barry Jackson, Revd Stella Bailey, Mr Timothy Day-Pollard, Miss Helen Perryman, The Ven Morris Rodham, The Revd Canon Dr David Stone, The Rt Revd John R A Stroyan, Mr Christopher H Baker, Rev Charlotte Gale, Mrs Helen Simmonds, Revd Elaine Scrivens, Dr Yvonne Warren, Rev Andrew March, Revd Kate Massey, Mrs Karen Armbrister, Rev Nicholas Leggett
Income: £9,711,064 [2016]; £9,520,000 [2015]; £7,703,000 [2014]; £7,939,000 [2013]; £7,817,000 [2012]

The Coventry Refugee and Migrant Centre
Registered: 17 Jan 2002 *Employees:* 37 *Volunteers:* 86
Tel: 024 7652 7103 *Website:* covrefugee.org
Activities: General charitable purposes; education, training; advancement of health or saving of lives; prevention or relief of poverty; accommodation, housing; economic, community development, employment; human rights, religious or racial harmony, equality or diversity; other charitable purposes
Address: Norton House, Bird Street, Coventry, Warwicks, CV1 5FX
Trustees: Tim Brooke, Mr Timothy Godwin, Mr Tia Chuba AO, Dr Randhir Auluck, Mr Timothy James Mayer, Mr Tariq Khan, Dr David Knibb, Mrs Ravinder Kaur, Mr Thomas Fisher, Mr Furrukh Aslam, Mr Rupinder Singh
Income: £1,329,709 [2017]; £1,187,085 [2016]; £1,001,918 [2015]; £939,979 [2014]; £928,018 [2013]

Coventry School Foundation
Registered: 4 Dec 1975 *Employees:* 436
Tel: 024 7627 1301 *Website:* coventryschoolfoundation.org
Activities: Education, training
Address: Unit I, Kings Chambers, Queens Road, Coventry, Warwicks, CV1 3EH
Trustees: Coventry School Trustee Limited
Income: £20,854,901 [2017]; £20,244,217 [2016]; £19,979,666 [2015]; £19,375,349 [2014]; £18,949,000 [2013]

Coventry Sports Foundation
Registered: 28 Jun 1988 *Employees:* 248
Tel: 024 7685 6956 *Website:* covsf.com
Activities: Amateur sport
Address: XCEL Leisure Centre, Mitchell Avenue, Canley, Coventry, Warwicks, CV4 8DY
Trustees: Mr John Alistair Reid McIntosh, Mrs Rosemary Ruddick, Earl of Aylesford
Income: £4,665,175 [2017]; £4,681,709 [2016]; £4,127,898 [2015]; £3,494,628 [2014]; £3,332,476 [2013]

Coventry Sports Trust Ltd
Registered: 16 Jul 2002 *Employees:* 135
Tel: 024 7625 2522 *Website:* coventrysports.co.uk
Activities: General charitable purposes; education, training; advancement of health or saving of lives; disability; prevention or relief of poverty; arts, culture, heritage, science; amateur sport; economic, community development, employment
Address: c/o Coventry Sports Trust Ltd, Fairfax Street, Coventry, Warwicks, CV1 5RY
Trustees: Mr Alan Michael Shaw, Mr David Long, Mr Michael Anthony Breitheamh Judge, Mr Trevor Pepper
Income: £3,252,923 [2017]; £3,227,844 [2016]; £3,663,055 [2015]; £3,827,833 [2014]; £4,069,850 [2013]

Coventry University Students' Union Limited
Registered: 22 Dec 2010 *Employees:* 83
Tel: 024 7765 5211 *Website:* cusu.org
Activities: Education, training; recreation
Address: Coventry University Students' Union, The Hub, 4 Jordan Well, Coventry, Warwicks, CV1 5QT
Trustees: Mrs Baljit Dhadda, Dr Valerie Marie Cox, Mr Adebanjo Adedoyinsola, Miss Nyaknno Aniefiok Moses, Mr Scott Edward Staniland, Miss Laura Zickaite, Pat Noon, Mr Chidiebere Francis Ahanonu, Mr Tochukwu Ajare, Miss Burmun Shem Demisa, Mr Clinton Wilson
Income: £1,997,805 [2017]; £1,676,761 [2016]; £1,659,590 [2015]; £1,639,971 [2014]; £1,849,423 [2013]

Coventry and Warwickshire Mind
Registered: 1 Aug 1991 *Employees:* 139 *Volunteers:* 180
Website: cwmind.org.uk
Activities: Education, training; advancement of health or saving of lives; disability; accommodation, housing
Address: Coventry Mind, Wellington Gardens, Coventry, Warwicks, CV1 3BT
Trustees: Mr Darshan Dhilon, Ms Gill Bausor, Mr Malcolm Woodford, Ms Carol Testot, David Ruff, Mr Terence Donald Plant, Mrs Gail Jones ALCM, Mr Harry Anthony Wallace Jess, Mrs Patricia Allen, Mr Gary Montgomery, Ms Hannah Priest
Income: £4,748,390 [2017]; £4,358,432 [2016]; £3,864,459 [2015]; £4,015,275 [2014]; £3,972,201 [2013]

Coworth-Flexlands School Limited
Registered: 2 May 1973 *Employees:* 33 *Volunteers:* 1
Tel: 01276 855707 *Website:* coworthflexlands.co.uk
Activities: Education, training
Address: Mrs Margaret Kelly, Coworth-Flexlands School, Valley End, Chobham, Woking, Surrey, GU24 8TE
Trustees: Mrs Catherine Gray, Ms Elise Bailey, Mr Steve Russell, Mr Michael Thomas, Mr Paul Underwood, Mrs Helen Simpson, Mr Gordon Hague, Mrs Jenny Irvine, Emma Litwin, Mrs Nicole Basra, Mr Simon Thomson Aird
Income: £1,572,107 [2016]; £1,385,220 [2015]; £1,354,738 [2014]; £1,330,851 [2013]; £1,335,525 [2012]

The Hilary Craft Charitable Foundation Limited
Registered: 9 Sep 2011 *Employees:* 1 *Volunteers:* 12
Tel: 0161 280 4000 *Website:* aacancer.org
Activities: The advancement of health or saving of lives
Address: 2-3 Regency Chambers, Jubilee Way, Bury, Lancs, BL9 0JW
Trustees: Jonathan Craft, Percy Beckley, Mrs Michaela Mary Rees Jones, Maurice Craft, Mrs Hilary Craft FRSA, Mr Laurence Joel Frederic Tarlo
Income: £2,804,596 [2016]; £1,404,930 [2015]; £1,258,057 [2014]; £1,424,109 [2013]; £334,683 [2012]

Crafts Council
Registered: 19 Sep 1980 *Employees:* 42 *Volunteers:* 19
Tel: 020 7806 2500 *Website:* craftscouncil.org.uk
Activities: Arts, culture, heritage, science
Address: 44A Pentonville Road, London, N1 9BY
Trustees: Professor Bruce Brown, Anthony Lilley, Ms Brigid Rentoul, Mr Michael Eden, Mrs Jo Bloxham, Mr Andrew Marshall, Clare Twomey, Professor Geoffrey Crossick, Ms Beverley Rider, Dr Zoe Laughlin, Mr Matt Durran, Ms Maria Amidu
Income: £4,279,395 [2017]; £4,038,820 [2016]; £3,680,401 [2015]; £3,514,000 [2014]; £3,496,000 [2013]

Cranford House School Trust Limited
Registered: 10 Sep 1980 *Employees:* 110 *Volunteers:* 10
Tel: 01491 651218 *Website:* cranfordhouse.net
Activities: Education, training
Address: Cranford House School, Moulsford, Wallingford, Oxon, OX10 9HT
Trustees: Mrs Natalie Scott-Ely, Dr Robert Fisher, Mrs Alison Gray, Mr Peter Thomas, Lucy Kilroy, Mr Paul Tollet, Mr Jim Clarke, Mrs Amanda Page
Income: £5,614,119 [2017]; £5,337,455 [2016]; £5,086,964 [2015]; £5,166,142 [2014]; £5,113,498 [2013]

Cranleigh School
Registered: 4 Aug 1998 *Employees:* 308
Tel: 01483 273666 *Website:* cranleigh.org
Activities: Education, training
Address: Cranleigh School, Horseshoe Lane, Cranleigh, Surrey, GU6 8QQ
Trustees: Mr Oliver Alexander Radford Weiss, Mrs Elizabeth Stanton, Monica Fisher, Mrs Melanie Williamson, Alison Lye, Nick Sweet, Rick Johnson, David Williams, Simon Whitehouse, David Westcott, Patrick Going, Mr Adrian James Lajtha, Dr Rosalind Margaret Chesser, Mark Foster, Peter Wells, Jonathan Knight, Sam Watkinson, Sarah Bayliss, Michael Cathcart, Jenny Brown, Sanjaya Gunapala
Income: £25,895,000 [2017]; £24,967,000 [2016]; £23,778,000 [2015]; £22,391,000 [2014]; £20,829,000 [2013]

Cranmore School
Registered: 28 Oct 2010 *Employees:* 80
Tel: 01483 280348 *Website:* cranmoreprep.co.uk
Activities: Education, training; religious activities
Address: Cranmore School, Epsom Road, West Horsley, Surrey, KT24 6AT
Trustees: Mr Michael John Glidden Henderson, Mrs Anne Marie Fort, Mr Michael Edward Agius, Mr Jimmy William Pressley, Mr Edmund Anthony Edmund, Dr Catherine-Anne McMullan, Mr Brendan Alistair Cook, Mr Andrew James Leale, Mr Michael Gerald Patrick David Scoltock, Mrs Nina Katrin Brenninkmeijer
Income: £6,024,258 [2017]; £5,608,813 [2016]; £5,389,252 [2015]; £4,906,492 [2014]; £4,884,867 [2013]

Cransley Hospice Trust
Registered: 28 Feb 2013 *Employees:* 10 *Volunteers:* 100
Tel: 01536 452423 *Website:* cransleyhospice.org.uk
Activities: The advancement of health or saving of lives
Address: Cransley Hospice Trust, St Marys Hospital, 77 London Road, Kettering, Northants, NN15 7PW
Trustees: Mr Richard John Aveling, Ms Maureen Elizabeth Gaskell, Mr Andrew Attfield, Mr Christopher Turner, Rev Dr John Simon Smith, Mrs Laura Lee Allanson, Mr Daniel Freeland
Income: £1,557,992 [2017]; £1,100,063 [2016]; £878,000 [2015]; £709,274 [2014]

Cransley School Limited
Registered: 22 Nov 1977 *Employees:* 50
Tel: 07805 748620 *Website:* cransleyschool.org.uk
Activities: Education, training
Address: 38 Petersham Drive, Appleton, Warrington, Cheshire, WA4 5QF
Trustees: Mr Martin Lloyd, Mr Neil Mobsby, Mrs Margaret Denton, Mrs Gail Pearson, Mr John Michael, Mr Stephen Geoffrey Hine, Mr Martin Bailey, Mr Kristian Hansen, Mrs Alison Riley, Mr John Spencer
Income: £1,664,761 [2016]; £1,459,944 [2015]; £1,461,801 [2014]; £1,548,736 [2013]; £1,545,694 [2012]

Cranstoun
Registered: 26 Mar 1997 *Employees:* 247 *Volunteers:* 147
Tel: 020 8335 1830 *Website:* cranstoun.org
Activities: The advancement of health or saving of lives
Address: Thames Mews, Portsmouth Road, Esher, Surrey, KT10 9AD
Trustees: Mr Cees Goos, Katharine Patel, Mr Wayne Haywood, Ms Charlotte Bunyan, Ms Linda Moir, Mrs Faith Jenner, Mr Richard James Charles Drury Pertwee, Dr Franklin Apfel
Income: £19,560,000 [2017]; £15,708,000 [2016]; £10,974,000 [2015]; £11,103,000 [2014]; £12,014,000 [2013]

Crawley Open House
Registered: 9 Sep 1995 *Employees:* 31 *Volunteers:* 50
Tel: 01293 521191 *Website:* crawleyopenhouse.co.uk
Activities: Accommodation, housing
Address: Riverside House, Three Bridges, Crawley, W Sussex, RH10 1TN
Trustees: Mr Richard David Burrett, Mr John Higgins, Mr Michael Bolton, Mr James Abdool, Mrs Lesley Anne Copus, Mrs Susan Edith Miles, Mr Stephen Joyce, Mr Nigel Boxall, Clare Hiley, Mr Harlyn James Collins
Income: £1,191,262 [2017]; £985,334 [2016]; £913,572 [2015]; £920,271 [2014]; £948,988 [2013]

The Elizabeth Creak Charitable Trust
Registered: 30 Mar 1983
Tel: 01564 773951
Activities: Education, training
Address: 27 Widney Road, Knowle, Solihull, W Midlands, B93 9DX
Trustees: John Hulse, Mr Nicholas Quilter Abell, Mr Johnathan Paul May
Income: £1,273,227 [2017]; £1,258,538 [2016]; £24,484,487 [2015]; £2,192 [2014]; £1,695 [2013]

Create London
Registered: 22 Feb 2012 *Employees:* 10 *Volunteers:* 24
Tel: 020 7382 7284 *Website:* createlondon.org
Activities: Education, training; arts, culture, heritage, science; economic, community development, employment
Address: Create, Barbican Centre, Silk Street, London, EC2Y 8DS
Trustees: Ms Denise Jones, Ms Andrea Sullivan, Guy Nicholson, Mr Tony Elliott, Mr Darren Rodwell, Ms Lesley Morphy, Ms Bernice Vanier, John Studzinski, Mr Matthew Slotover, Mr Henry Ritchotte, Mr Ahsan Khan, Ms Karina McTeague, Mr David Bailey
Income: £1,021,436 [2017]; £1,286,062 [2016]; £844,099 [2015]; £1,288,656 [2014]; £1,810,557 [2013]

The Creative Foundation
Registered: 28 Jul 2004 *Employees:* 20 *Volunteers:* 100
Website: creativefoundation.org.uk
Activities: General charitable purposes; education, training; prevention or relief of poverty; accommodation, housing; arts, culture, heritage, science; environment, conservation, heritage; economic, community development, employment; recreation
Address: Quarterhouse, Mill Bay, Folkestone, Kent, Folkestone, Kent, CT20 1BN
Trustees: Timothy Llewellyn, Dr Stephen Deuchar, Mr Trevor Minter OBE DL, Mr Paul Hudson, Alastair Upton, Miss Rachel Higham, Mr Roger De Haan, Mr Grahame Ward, William Radnor, Lady Alison De Haan, Mr Andrew Ironside
Income: £2,470,197 [2016]; £3,179,538 [2015]; £3,934,231 [2014]; £4,989,788 [2013]; £2,407,515 [2012]

Creative Kernow Limited
Registered: 8 May 1986 *Employees:* 15 *Volunteers:* 200
Tel: 01209 313200 *Website:* krowji.org.uk
Activities: Education, training; arts, culture, heritage, science; amateur sport; environment, conservation, heritage; economic, community development, employment; recreation
Address: Mr Ross Williams, Krowji, West Park, Redruth, Cornwall, TR15 3AJ
Trustees: Mr Roff Rayner, Dinah Louise Graffy, Kim Conchie, Ms Eleanor Jubb, Mr John Alfred Pulford, Mr Ross Duncan Pascoe, Mr Simon Harvey, Rosanna Elliott
Income: £1,287,631 [2017]; £1,107,890 [2016]; £953,376 [2015]; £817,463 [2014]; £652,292 [2013]

Creative Skillset - Sector Skills Council Limited
Registered: 23 Nov 1992 *Employees:* 39
Website: creativeskillset.org
Activities: Education, training; arts, culture, heritage, science
Address: 94 Euston Street, London, NW1 2HA
Trustees: Ms Mary Teresa Rainey, Mr Alexander Hope, Mr Richard Johnston, Mr Ivan Dunleavy, Mr Mark Raymond Linsey, Mrs Arabella Clare McCabe, Mr Stephen Page, Mr Iain Alastair Robertson Smith, Ms Dinah Caine, Mr John Woodward, Ms Helen Louise Grainger, Mrs Samantha Gail Jukes-Adams
Income: £12,442,270 [2017]; £25,382,551 [2016]; £28,245,753 [2015]; £28,574,320 [2014]; £14,236,031 [2013]

Creative Youth Network
Registered: 16 Nov 1973 *Employees:* 70 *Volunteers:* 42
Tel: 0117 947 7948 *Website:* creativeyouthnetwork.org.uk
Activities: General charitable purposes; education, training; arts, culture, heritage, science; economic, community development, employment
Address: 20 Old School House, The Kingswood Estate, Britannia Road, Kingswood, Bristol, BS15 8DB
Trustees: Mrs Margaret Lily Curtis, Mr Mike Lea, Ms Joanna Grant, Ms Lynne Elvins, Mr Raj Kakar-Clayton, Mr Deepraj Singh, Mr Julian Davis, Mr Bob Durie, Mr Nicholas Holder, Robyn Sandilands, Robert Nye, Ms Kirsty Swan
Income: £1,908,392 [2016]; £2,184,547 [2015]; £2,303,151 [2014]; £1,869,975 [2013]; £4,026,210 [2012]

Creative and Cultural Industries Limited
Registered: 22 Sep 2004 *Employees:* 12
Tel: 020 3668 5753 *Website:* ccskills.org.uk
Activities: Education, training; arts, culture, heritage, science; economic, community development, employment
Address: Creative & Cultural Skills, The Backstage Centre, High House, Production Park, off Purfleet Bypass, Purfleet, Essex, RM19 1AS
Trustees: Ms Roisin McDonough, Mr Oliver Llywelyn Morris, Mr Kim Bromley Derry, Mrs Carol Ann Harvey-Barnes, Miss Alexandra Porter-Smith, Mr David Anderson, Mr Paul Robert Latham, Ms Clare Margaret Hawkins, Ms Vithleem Paraskevi Nikolaidou, Ms Yvonne Kelly
Income: £2,179,994 [2017]; £4,423,720 [2016]; £6,289,692 [2015]; £7,958,109 [2014]; £4,923,849 [2013]

Credit Suisse EMEA Foundation
Registered: 28 Jan 2008
Activities: General charitable purposes
Address: Credit Suisse, 1 Cabot Square, London, E14 4QJ
Trustees: Mr Stefano Toffolo BA ACA, Mr Russell Chambers, Mr Nicholas John Wilcock, Mr Colin Hely-Hutchinson, Mrs Marisa Drew, Mr Angus Kidd, Ms Natalia Nicolaidis, Mr Patrick Martin Flaherty, Ms Michelle Rebecca Mendelsson, Mr Markus Lammer, Mr Mark Ellis, Mr Marc Pereira-Mendoza, Mr Guy Varney
Income: £1,800,395 [2016]; £1,705,616 [2015]; £1,828,090 [2014]; £1,946,122 [2013]; £2,173,237 [2012]

The Credit Union Foundation
Registered: 24 Feb 2003
Tel: 0161 819 6997 *Website:* creditunionfoundation.org.uk
Activities: Education, training; prevention or relief of poverty; economic, community development, employment
Address: c/o Abcul, Holyoake House, Hanover Street, Manchester, M60 0AS
Trustees: Alan Robson, Gren Bingham, Mrs Annette Elizabeth Thomas, Mr Denis Greenall, Mr David Martin, Mr Daniel Michael Denning, Mrs Karen Bennett, Mrs Carol Strand
Income: £1,088,208 [2017]; £1,009,539 [2016]; £1,308,785 [2015]; £16,178 [2014]; £16,125 [2013]

The Cremation Society of Great Britain
Registered: 6 Jun 1963 *Employees:* 63
Tel: 01622 688292 *Website:* cremation.org.uk
Activities: Education, training; environment, conservation, heritage
Address: 1st Floor, Brecon House, 16/16a Albion Place, Maidstone, Kent, ME14 5DZ
Trustees: Mr Harvey Thomas, Revd Dr Peter Creffield Jupp, Mr Colin Francis Rickman, Mrs Barbara Ruth Kehoe, Mr Andrew Mallalieu, Professor Geoffrey Frederick Woodroffe, Professor Hilary Joyce Grainger, Dr Ian Robert Dungavell, Dr Heather Ann Conway, Lord Rupert Charles De Mauley
Income: £6,160,091 [2017]; £5,559,874 [2016]; £5,354,407 [2015]; £5,041,976 [2014]; £4,744,692 [2013]

Crescent Purchasing Limited
Registered: 7 Jul 2009 *Employees:* 22
Tel: 0161 974 0952 *Website:* thecpc.ac.uk
Activities: Education, training
Address: 22 Wensley Road, Salford, M7 3QJ
Trustees: Mr David Neil Pullein, Mr Robert Kilcoyne, Mr Graham Francis, Mr Lawrence Jenkins, Mr Peter Brewer, Mr Noel Cassidy, Mr Andrew John Comyn, Ms Joanne Christine Bentley
Income: £1,833,531 [2017]; £1,854,135 [2016]; £1,701,425 [2015]; £1,959,160 [2014]; £1,652,643 [2013]

The Crescent School Trust
Registered: 21 Aug 2007 *Employees:* 24 *Volunteers:* 3
Tel: 01788 521595 *Website:* crescentschool.co.uk
Activities: Education, training
Address: Crescent School, Bawnmore Road, Rugby, Warwicks, CV22 7QH
Trustees: Mrs Pat Lines, Mr John Shackleton, Paul Leonard, Mr Craig Calder, Mr Tony Darby, Mr Graham Mark William Cleverley, Mrs Victoria Pomfrett, Ms Linda Geraldine Horton, Mr Maurice Monteith, Mr Nigel Gove, Mr Derek Henry Holmes, Mrs Lisa Bell
Income: £1,269,006 [2016]; £1,244,805 [2015]; £1,280,885 [2014]; £1,261,518 [2013]; £1,195,371 [2012]

The Creswell Heritage Trust
Registered: 19 Jun 1989 *Employees:* 30 *Volunteers:* 30
Tel: 01909 720378 *Website:* creswell-crags.org.uk
Activities: Education, training; arts, culture, heritage, science; environment, conservation, heritage
Address: Creswell Crags Museum, Crags Road, Welbeck, Whitwell, Worksop, Notts, S80 3LH
Trustees: Doctor Christopher Eric Terrell-Nield, Mrs Rita Turner, Councillor John Elliott Cottee, Dr Timothy Caulton, Mr David Atkinson, Mr John Roberts, Cllr Duncan McGregor, Councillor Barry Lewis, Mr Thomas Ian Munro, Mr Kevin Lee Kuykendall, Mrs Alice Grice
Income: £1,113,878 [2017]; £1,240,683 [2016]; £1,071,568 [2015]; £844,967 [2014]; £873,206 [2013]

Crewe YMCA Limited
Registered: 21 Dec 1993 *Employees:* 32 *Volunteers:* 8
Website: creweymca.com
Activities: Education, training; accommodation, housing; religious activities
Address: YMCA, 189 Gresty Road, Crewe, Cheshire, CW2 6EL
Trustees: Miss Sharon Richards, Mrs Amanda Boffey, Bernard Clarke, Mr Mike Ridley, Mrs Cath Rugen
Income: £1,422,089 [2017]; £1,430,935 [2016]; £1,363,537 [2015]; £1,186,052 [2014]; £1,021,523 [2013]

The Francis Crick Institute Limited
Registered: 26 Jan 2011 *Employees:* 1,260 *Volunteers:* 7
Tel: 020 7611 2242 *Website:* crick.ac.uk
Activities: Education, training; advancement of health or saving of lives; arts, culture, heritage, science
Address: 215 Euston Road, London, NW1 2BF
Trustees: Lord Edmund John Phillip Browne, Rt Hon Lord David Willetts, Harpal Kumar, Mr Philip Edward Yea, Professor Doreen Cantrell, Ms Kate Bingham, Professor Sir Robert Ian Lechler, Dr Jeremy Farrar, Professor Margaret Dallman, Professor David Lomas
Income: £160,609,000 [2017]; £148,636,000 [2016]; £9,355,987 [2015]; £3,271,572 [2014]; £3,376,426 [2013]

Crimestoppers Trust
Registered: 22 Mar 2005 *Employees:* 108 *Volunteers:* 370
Tel: 020 8835 3700 *Website:* crimestoppers-uk.org
Activities: Economic, community development, employment
Address: P O Box 324, Wallington, Surrey, SM6 6BG
Trustees: Ms Angela Elizabeth Entwistle, Mr Zameer Mohammed Choudrey, Lord Michael Ashcroft KCMG, Mr Robert Scott CBE, Mr Nick Ross, Mr Bill Griffiths CBE BEM QPM, Mr Peter Clarke CVO OBE QPM, Mick Laurie, Mr Robert Stephen Rubin, Dr David Hammond FCA, Mr Richard Gamble FCA, Sir Ronnie Flanagan GBE MA, Sir Paul Stephenson, Mrs Ceris Mary Gardner, Mr Vivian Robinson
Income: £5,008,846 [2017]; £4,594,412 [2016]; £4,946,661 [2015]; £5,416,144 [2014]; £4,796,696 [2013]

Cripplegate Foundation
Registered: 22 Sep 1962 *Employees:* 9
Tel: 020 7288 6940 *Website:* cripplegate.org
Activities: General charitable purposes; prevention or relief of poverty
Address: 13 Elliott's Place, London, N1 8HX
Trustees: Cripplegate Foundation Ltd
Income: £2,190,665 [2017]; £2,278,259 [2016]; £2,248,899 [2015]; £2,543,264 [2014]; £2,255,672 [2013]

Crisis UK
Registered: 19 Oct 2000 *Employees:* 529 *Volunteers:* 11,000
Website: crisis.org.uk
Activities: Education, training; prevention or relief of poverty; accommodation, housing; economic, community development, employment
Address: 66 Commercial Street, London, E1 6LT
Trustees: Mr Martin Cheeseman OBE, Mr Steven Holliday, Mr Peter Redfern, Ms Caroline Lee-Davey, Mrs Ann McIvor, Ms Julia Goldsworthy, Mr Jason Warriner, Mr Richard Murley, Ms Emma Foulds, Terrie Alafat, Mr Damien Eric Marie Joseph Regent, Ms Geetha Rabindrakumar
Income: £35,208,000 [2017]; £29,500,000 [2016]; £25,746,000 [2015]; £23,532,000 [2014]; £22,194,000 [2013]

The Criterion Theatre Trust
Registered: 22 Oct 1992 *Employees:* 35
Tel: 020 7839 8811 *Website:* criterion-theatre.com
Activities: General charitable purposes; arts, culture, heritage, science
Address: Criterion Theatre, 2 Jermyn Street, London, SW1Y 4XA
Trustees: Mr Alan Banes, Robert Bourne, Ms Sally Greene, Ms Joyce Hytner, Mr Stephen Fry, Mr Peter Clayton
Income: £2,773,226 [2016]; £1,667,055 [2015]; £1,695,112 [2014]; £1,703,045 [2013]; £1,650,323 [2012]

Croft Care Trust
Registered: 31 Jul 1990 *Employees:* 74
Website: croftcaretrust.co.uk
Activities: Disability
Address: Croft Care Trust, The Croft, Hawcoat Lane, Barrow in Furness, Cumbria, LA14 4HE
Trustees: Mr Phillip John Heath, Mrs Margaret Hilda Pippard, Mrs Brenda Pearce, Mrs Avis Margaret Edmondson, Mr Simon John Edmondson, Mrs Hayley Lisa Edmondson
Income: £1,647,367 [2017]; £1,518,219 [2016]; £1,472,622 [2015]; £1,446,871 [2014]; £1,389,191 [2013]

Crohn's and Colitis UK
Registered: 6 Dec 2006 *Employees:* 51 *Volunteers:* 738
Tel: 01727 830038 *Website:* crohnsandcolitis.org.uk
Activities: General charitable purposes; advancement of health or saving of lives; disability
Address: Ground Floor, 45 Grosvenor Road, St Albans, Herts, AL1 3AW
Trustees: Mrs Deborah Hodges, Sarah Denselow, Mrs Susan Cherrie, Miss Azmina Verjee, Mr Thomas Reddy, Ms Amanda Quincey, Mr Alan Thackrey, Miss Caroline Silke, Dr Gillian Holdsworth, Mr Derek McEwan, Mr Graham Bell, Ms Justine Woolf
Income: £4,978,196 [2016]; £4,227,745 [2015]; £3,708,711 [2014]; £3,346,555 [2013]; £3,633,854 [2012]

Crosfields School
Registered: 1 Oct 1962 *Employees:* 155 *Volunteers:* 30
Tel: 0118 986 2535 *Website:* crosfields.com
Activities: Education, training
Address: Crosfields School, Shinfield Road, Shinfield, Reading, Berks, RG2 9BL
Trustees: Mr Hugh Fitzwilliams, Mr Peter Reid Lloyd, Mr Jonathan Mark Coles, Mr Charles Stuart Bradfield, Mr Greg Davies, Mr John Fisher, Mr Nigel Williams, Sally Jayne Bonner, Mr Michael John Hatch, Ms Clare Louise Furneaux, Mr Robert Graham Sutherland, Dr Vin Grantham Doctor, Mrs Carolyn Brown, Mrs Rekha Kapoor, Mr Nicholas John Habgood, Mrs Shashi Sachdeva
Income: £6,599,381 [2017]; £6,248,452 [2016]; £6,134,764 [2015]; £5,824,832 [2014]; £5,622,562 [2013]

Cross Keys Homes Limited
Registered: 2 Jul 2004 *Employees:* 246 *Volunteers:* 89
Tel: 01733 385001 *Website:* crosskeyshomes.co.uk
Activities: General charitable purposes; education, training; advancement of health or saving of lives; disability; prevention or relief of poverty; accommodation, housing; environment, conservation, heritage; economic, community development, employment; human rights, religious or racial harmony, equality or diversity
Address: Cross Keys Homes, Shrewsbury Avenue, Peterborough, PE2 7BZ
Trustees: Mr Donald James Bell, Ms Suzanne O'Brien, Ms Elizabeth Ellen Bisset, Diane Lamb, Sam Smith, Mr Carl Larter, Ms Claire Higgins, Ms Rachel Louise Blakemore, Mr Andrew Robert Orrey
Income: £65,434,000 [2017]; £61,031,000 [2016]; £52,277,000 [2015]; £48,661,028 [2014]; £45,463,238 [2013]

The Crossrail Art Foundation
Registered: 21 Nov 2014
Tel: 020 3197 5461
Activities: Arts, culture, heritage, science
Address: Crossrail Ltd, 25 Canada Square, London, E14 5LQ
Trustees: Sir Michael John Snyder, Sir Mark John Boleat, Sir Terence Keith Morgan CBE, Mr Jeremy Paul Mayhew, Mr Michael John Cassidy CBE, Mr Christopher Michael Sexton
Income: £4,355,952 [2016]; £704,438 [2015]

Crossroads Care Central & East Gloucestershire Limited
Registered: 26 Aug 2005 *Employees:* 60
Tel: 01452 302542 *Website:* crossroadscandeg.org.uk
Activities: The advancement of health or saving of lives; disability
Address: Crossroads Care Central & East Glos, Unit 4 St James Court, 285 Barton Street, Gloucester, GL1 4JE
Trustees: Mrs Elizabeth Anne Keen, Mr David Godding, Mrs Elaine Pearson-Scott, Mr Peter John Elliott, Mr Paul Holmes, Mrs Sheila Joan Reynolds
Income: £1,025,627 [2017]; £902,455 [2016]; £1,039,610 [2015]; £843,817 [2014]; £846,515 [2013]

Crossroads Care Cheshire, Manchester & Merseyside Limited
Registered: 28 Apr 1999 *Employees:* 258 *Volunteers:* 116
Tel: 01260 292850 *Website:* carerstrust4all.org.uk
Activities: The advancement of health or saving of lives; disability
Address: Overton House, West Street, Congleton, Cheshire, CW12 1JY
Trustees: Mr John Taylor, Mrs Adrienne Jane Fox, Mr Derek James Smith, Mr Geoffrey David Bull, Ms Jane Natasha Snow, Mr Christopher Burgess, Mr Michael James, Mrs Margaret Crichton, Mr Timothy Vincent Horton
Income: £3,942,667 [2017]; £3,769,678 [2016]; £4,386,394 [2015]; £3,667,053 [2014]; £1,708,109 [2013]

Crossroads Care Kent
Registered: 10 Feb 1999 *Employees:* 207 *Volunteers:* 198
Tel: 01227 743708 *Website:* carerskm.org
Activities: Disability
Address: Crossroads Care Kent, 16 Reculver Road, Beltinge, Herne Bay, Kent, CT6 6LE
Trustees: Mr Hugh Stirk, Mrs Deborah Frances Ward, Mrs Lynne Tindle, Mr Denis Linfoot, Mr Christopher Parkinson, Mrs Susan Victoria Cliffe, Mrs Patricia Hughes, Mr Sean Taggart, Mrs Lesley Lee
Income: £3,773,775 [2017]; £3,923,767 [2016]; £1,835,323 [2015]; £1,503,263 [2014]; £1,252,250 [2013]

Crossroads Care North West
Registered: 23 Mar 2004 *Employees:* 115
Tel: 01744 613001 *Website:* crossroadscarenorthwest.org.uk
Activities: The advancement of health or saving of lives; disability
Address: Unit 10 Waterside Court, St Helens, Merseyside, WA9 1UA
Trustees: Mrs Elizabeth Jane Dearden, Mr Peter Richard Cahill, Mrs Joyce Wilcock, Mr Anthony Narayanan, Mr Joseph Gordon Spencer, Mrs Christine Mather, Mr Arthur Gore, Ms Jacqueline Richards
Income: £1,828,273 [2017]; £1,737,287 [2016]; £1,702,244 [2015]; £1,875,641 [2014]; £1,610,385 [2013]

Crossroads Care South Central Ltd
Registered: 17 Dec 2008 *Employees:* 66 *Volunteers:* 5
Tel: 01903 790270 *Website:* crossroadscare-sc.org
Activities: The advancement of health or saving of lives; disability
Address: Tele Cottage, Horsemere Green Lane, Climping, Littlehampton, W Sussex, BN17 5QZ
Trustees: Mr David Michael Parker, Ms Alison Marshall, Mrs Louise Myles, Mrs Hannah Robins, Mrs Caroline Severne
Income: £1,245,503 [2017]; £1,311,520 [2016]; £1,265,177 [2015]; £1,168,282 [2014]; £1,223,999 [2013]

Crossroads Care Staffordshire Limited
Registered: 14 Sep 1994 *Employees:* 93
Activities: Education, training; advancement of health or saving of lives; disability; economic, community development, employment
Address: Clive Villas, 22 Cemetery Road, Stoke on Trent, Staffs, ST4 2DL
Trustees: Mrs Ann Flevill, Mrs Rita Ann Godwin, Mrs Anthea Bourne, Mr Richard John Whitehouse, Mr Richard Thomas Lamb, Mr Ian Douglas MacGregor Milne, Susan Mary Brookes
Income: £2,127,054 [2016]; £1,800,417 [2015]; £2,115,174 [2014]; £2,160,373 [2013]; £1,874,297 [2012]

Crossroads Sir Gar Limited
Registered: 22 Nov 2007 *Employees:* 122
Tel: 01267 220046 *Website:* carmarthenshirecarers.org.uk
Activities: Disability
Address: Suite 11, 2nd Floor, Crossroads Care Sir Gar, Ty Myrddin Old Station Road, Carmarthen, SA31 1LP
Trustees: Mrs Janet Knott, Mrs Ann Hopkins, Mrs Helen Nicholls, Mrs Jennifer Thomas, Mrs Pamela Jean Edmunds, Mrs Sylvia Evans, Mrs Liz Poulson, Mrs Anne Grimes
Income: £2,083,137 [2017]; £1,942,902 [2016]; £1,871,183 [2015]; £1,714,922 [2014]; £1,566,578 [2013]

Crossroads Together Ltd.
Registered: 23 Dec 1996 *Employees:* 126 *Volunteers:* 40
Tel: 01204 365025 *Website:* gmcarerstrust.co.uk
Activities: Disability
Address: The Thicketford Centre, Thicketford Road, Bolton, Lancs, BL2 2LW
Trustees: Mrs Barbara Bleeker, Mrs Diana Ward, Mr Robert Morris Jones, Mr David Peter Best, Mr Joseph Blaney, Mr Chris Jeffries, Miss Emily Allen
Income: £1,889,447 [2017]; £1,790,353 [2016]; £1,877,369 [2015]; £1,777,653 [2014]; £1,641,349 [2013]

Crossroads in Hertfordshire (North and Northeast) Caring for Carers
Registered: 20 Nov 2007 *Employees:* 154 *Volunteers:* 52
Tel: 01462 427011 *Website:* crossroadshn.org.uk
Activities: The advancement of health or saving of lives; disability
Address: Suite 5, Intech House, Wilbury Way, Hitchin, Herts, SG4 0TW
Trustees: Mrs Melanie Chammings, Mrs Jeannette Thomas, Mrs Vivien Jane Kerr, Mr Robert Fee, Mr John Daffern, Mr Justin Jewitt, Mr Peter Duffy, Mr Fraser Hill
Income: £2,172,398 [2017]; £2,139,238 [2016]; £1,682,094 [2015]; £1,430,896 [2014]; £1,158,235 [2013]

Crossways Community
Registered: 8 Jan 1992 *Employees:* 39
Tel: 01892 540843 *Website:* crosswayscommunity.co.uk
Activities: Education, training; advancement of health or saving of lives; disability; accommodation, housing; religious activities
Address: Crossways Community, Administration Building, 8 Culverden Park Road, Tunbridge Wells, Kent, TN4 9QX
Trustees: Mrs Mary Tuckwell, Dr James Thallon, Dr Michael Lawes, Mr John David Handley, Ms Eleanor Grey, Mrs Nicola Janet Goozee, Mr James Christopher Maher, Mrs Sabrina Lippell, Mr Boris Skulczuk
Income: £1,263,910 [2017]; £1,112,030 [2016]; £1,044,401 [2015]; £1,004,539 [2014]; £976,942 [2013]

The Croydon Almshouse Charities
Registered: 7 May 1962 *Employees:* 12 *Volunteers:* 1
Tel: 020 8688 2649 *Website:* croydonalmshousecharities.org.uk
Activities: The prevention or relief of poverty; accommodation, housing; other charitable purposes
Address: Croydon Almshouse Charities, Elis David Almshouses, Duppas Hill Terrace, Croydon, Surrey, CR0 4BT
Trustees: The Croydon Almshouse Charities Trustee Company Limited
Income: £1,237,626 [2016]; £957,207 [2015]; £1,024,577 [2014]; £1,049,177 [2013]; £847,518 [2012]

Croydon Voluntary Action
Registered: 17 Jan 1997 *Employees:* 18 *Volunteers:* 201
Tel: 020 8653 7060 *Website:* cvalive.org.uk
Activities: General charitable purposes; education, training; disability; prevention or relief of poverty; economic, community development, employment
Address: 82 London Road, Croydon, Surrey, CR0 2TB
Trustees: Mr Terry Roberts, Mr Ashok Kumar, Mr Isaac Edwards, Miss Carole Elaine Parnell, Mike Mulvey, Mr Ken Coelo, Mrs Ghazala Mirza, Mr Brian Stapleton, Mr Guy Pile-Grey, Mary MacCauley, Mr Javell Nelson
Income: £1,490,525 [2017]; £1,428,377 [2016]; £1,641,152 [2015]; £1,705,471 [2014]; £2,127,599 [2013]

The Crusaders' Union
Registered: 6 Dec 2011 *Employees:* 31 *Volunteers:* 450
Website: urbansaints.org
Activities: Religious activities
Address: Urban Saints, Kestin House, 45 Crescent Road, Luton, Beds, LU2 0AH
Trustees: Mr Anthony Obayori, Mr Brendan Bromley, Mrs Cara Wightman, Miss Sharon Evelyn Prior, Mr Stephen Dengate, Dr Avice Hall, Miss Jackie Smith, Mr Jeffrey Malloy Russell, Miss Sarah Elizabeth Palmer-Felgate
Income: £3,201,103 [2016]; £3,039,883 [2015]; £2,791,800 [2014]; £2,682,020 [2013]; £2,960,746 [2012]

Cruse Bereavement Care
Registered: 22 Sep 1962 *Employees:* 93 *Volunteers:* 4,904
Tel: 020 8939 9541 *Website:* cruse.org.uk
Activities: Education, training; advancement of health or saving of lives
Address: Unit 0.1, One Victoria Villas, Richmond, Surrey, TW9 2GW
Trustees: Mr Paul Butler, Mr Colin Ross Robertson, Ms Helen Causley, Dr Christine Challacombe, Ms Nilufar Anwar, Miss Pamela Rutter, Ms Poppy Elizabeth Maxwell Mardall, Mr Michael John Whitehouse, Ms Letizia Perna, Miss Jane Ann Cryer
Income: £4,871,356 [2017]; £4,795,238 [2016]; £5,222,125 [2015]; £4,674,930 [2014]; £4,442,362 [2013]

Culford School
Registered: 28 Apr 1965 *Employees:* 267 *Volunteers:* 2
Tel: 020 7935 3723 *Website:* culford.co.uk
Activities: Education, training; religious activities
Address: Methodist Church House, 25 Marylebone Road, London, NW1 5JR
Trustees: Culford School Trustee Company Limited, Methodist Independent Schools Trust
Income: £12,332,390 [2016]; £11,400,610 [2015]; £11,091,858 [2014]; £11,433,609 [2013]

Cullum Family Trust
Registered: 29 Nov 2006 *Employees:* 3
Activities: General charitable purposes
Address: Wealden Hall, Parkfield, Sevenoaks, Kent, TN15 0HX
Trustees: Mrs Ann Cullum, Peter Cullum, Ms Claire Louise Cullum, Mr Simon Timothy Cullum
Income: £1,408,685 [2017]; £1,168,371 [2016]; £1,628,292 [2015]; £1,341,819 [2014]; £4,060,386 [2013]

Culture Coventry
Registered: 16 Jul 2013 *Employees:* 80 *Volunteers:* 80
Website: culturecoventry.com
Activities: General charitable purposes; education, training; arts, culture, heritage, science; environment, conservation, heritage; recreation; other charitable purposes
Address: c/o Theherbert Art Gallery & Museum, Jordan Well, Coventry, Warwicks, CV1 5QP
Trustees: Cllr Ram Lakha, Mr Alfred George Pare, Mr Richard Andrew Shaw, Councillor Abbott, Cllr Tim Sawdon, Mr Manny Coulon, Mrs Becky Cund, Mr Joseph Warden Elliott, Mr Keith Railton, Cllr John McNicholas, Mr Roger Terrence Arthur Medwell, Cller Tony Skipper, Dr Geoff Willcocks
Income: £4,359,000 [2017]; £6,688,000 [2016]; £9,885,000 [2015]; £3,262,000 [2014]

Culture Warrington
Registered: 12 Mar 2013 *Employees:* 63 *Volunteers:* 123
Tel: 01925 624992
Activities: General charitable purposes; education, training; arts, culture, heritage, science; amateur sport; environment, conservation, heritage; economic, community development, employment; recreation; other charitable purposes
Address: Culture Warrington, The Pyramid, Palmyra Square South, Warrington, Cheshire, WA1 1BL
Trustees: Mrs Maureen Banner, Ms Dorothy Lynda Moore, Mr Alessandro Bucci, Mrs Hannah Chellaswamy, Mr Michael Thomas Corfield, Mrs Alexandra Appleton-Mitchell, Mrs Emma Louise Hutchinson, Mr Stephen James Rayner
Income: £2,574,523 [2017]; £2,639,586 [2016]; £2,428,677 [2015]; £2,547,574 [2014]

Cumberland Lodge
Registered: 22 Mar 2005 *Employees:* 73 *Volunteers:* 2
Tel: 01784 432316 *Website:* cumberlandlodge.ac.uk
Activities: Education, training
Address: Cumberland Lodge, The Great Park, Windsor, Berks, SL4 2HP
Trustees: Mr Charles Anson, Sir Stephen Wall, Ms Salley Vickers MA, Baroness Ruby McGregor-Smith, Mr Simon Marshall Pearce, Ms Jane Furniss, Ms Gwenda Lynne Berry OBE, Prof Malcom David Evans OBE, Mr Paul Hampden Smith, Baroness Jill Pitkeathly OBE
Income: £2,870,997 [2017]; £2,758,126 [2016]; £2,792,061 [2015]; £2,555,432 [2014]; £2,465,592 [2013]

Cumberland and Westmorland Convalescent Institution

Registered: 8 Oct 1963 *Employees:* 69 *Volunteers:* 4
Tel: 016973 31493 *Website:* sillothnursinghome.co.uk
Activities: The advancement of health or saving of lives
Address: Silloth Nursing And Residential Care Home, Convalescent Home, Silloth, Wigton, Cumbria, CA7 4JH
Trustees: Rev Bryan Rothwell, Mr Lawrence Marshall, Mrs Constance Anderson, Mrs Jill Martin, Mr Timothy Henry Cartmell, Robert Killen, Ms Joanna Jeeves, Mrs Jean Roberta Day, Mr I W Brown FCA, Mr Graham Wilkinson, Mr David John Dalton Arter, Mr Robert Mark Wharton, Mrs Zoe Anne Coulthard, Dr Rodney Marshall Jones, Mrs Jean Hodgson Fearon
Income: £1,258,775 [2017]; £1,171,070 [2016]; £1,103,096 [2015]; £1,079,141 [2014]; £1,040,355 [2013]

Cumbria Community Foundation

Registered: 15 Apr 1999 *Employees:* 17 *Volunteers:* 3
Tel: 01900 825760 *Website:* cumbriafoundation.org
Activities: General charitable purposes; education, training; advancement of health or saving of lives; disability; prevention or relief of poverty; religious activities; arts, culture, heritage, science; amateur sport; environment, conservation, heritage; economic, community development, employment
Address: Cumbria Community Foundation, Dovenby Hall, Dovenby, Cockermouth, Cumbria, CA13 0PN
Trustees: Mr R A Roberts, Mr T Cartmell, Mr Nicholas Coulson, Mrs J E Humphries, Mrs V Young, Mr Jim Johnson, Mr S Cockayne, Mr A B Keen, Mrs Katherine Anne Fairclough, Mrs Alison Johnston, Mr J F Whittle, Dr A Naylor MBE, Mr W Slavin, Mrs C Tomlinson, Mrs C A Giel, Mr A Burbridge, Mr Mike Starkie, Mr D Beeby, Ms Susan Coulson
Income: £3,182,258 [2017]; £11,815,174 [2016]; £2,580,633 [2015]; £3,388,142 [2014]; £2,790,045 [2013]

Cumbria Theatre Trust

Registered: 16 Sep 1985 *Employees:* 53 *Volunteers:* 241
Tel: 017687 72282 *Website:* theatrebythelake.com
Activities: Education, training; arts, culture, heritage, science
Address: Theatre-by-the-Lake, Lake Road, Keswick, Cumbria, CA12 5DJ
Trustees: Mrs Vicky Robinson, Mr Godfrey Charles Owen, Mr Martin Pugmire, Mr Ian Hill, Ms Janet Isabel Farebrother, Mr Graham Lamont, Mr Douglas Frank Cook BA DipEd, Geoffrey Hall, Dr James Cox OBE
Income: £3,282,605 [2017]; £3,559,413 [2016]; £3,295,268 [2015]; £3,428,727 [2014]; £3,256,350 [2013]

Cumbria Wildlife Trust Ltd

Registered: 4 Jun 1963 *Employees:* 39 *Volunteers:* 1,218
Tel: 01539 816300 *Website:* cumbriawildlifetrust.org.uk
Activities: Environment, conservation, heritage
Address: Cumbria Wildlife Trust, Plumgarths, Crook Road, Kendal, Cumbria, LA8 8LX
Trustees: Judith Wallen, Dr Peter Howard Woodhead, Mrs Jane Carson, Lady Cressida Inglewood, Dr Ann Margaret Lackie, Mr John Malcolm Farmer, Mrs Julie Anne Barrett, Mr John Handley, Graham Hooley, Miss Emily Sarah Coates
Income: £2,470,674 [2017]; £3,672,247 [2016]; £2,385,647 [2015]; £2,311,699 [2014]; £3,211,508 [2013]

Cumnor House School Trust

Registered: 17 Aug 1989 *Employees:* 93
Tel: 01825 792003 *Website:* cumnor.co.uk
Activities: Education, training
Address: Cumnor House School, London Road, Danehill, Haywards Heath, W Sussex, RH17 7HT
Trustees: Mr N Parkhouse, Mr Niall Fitzgerald, Mrs Sarah Jelly, Mrs Harriet Bastide, Mr James Bannon, Mr Mark Johnson, Mr Dominic Keenan, Mr Peter John Martin Roberts, Mr Nigel Welby, Mrs Shauna Bevan, Dr Olivia Hatrick, Mr Rob Boardman, Ms Christine O'Connell, Ms Nicola Collins
Income: £6,351,552 [2017]; £6,061,821 [2016]; £6,056,395 [2015]; £5,788,526 [2014]; £5,270,217 [2013]

Cundall Manor Limited

Registered: 19 Apr 1973 *Employees:* 91 *Volunteers:* 5
Tel: 01423 360911 *Website:* cundallmanor.org.uk
Activities: Education, training
Address: 18 Borrowdale Drive, York, YO30 5SX
Trustees: Mr Dennis Richards, Mrs Joyce Tinkler, Mr David John Lister, Ms Lindsay Austin, Mr David Willis, Mr Charles Foulds, Sir Thomas Ingilby, Mr Jonathan Charles Deacon Turner, Mr Simon James Kayll, Mr Ralph Zoing, Mrs Rachel Powell
Income: £4,472,349 [2016]; £4,202,187 [2015]; £4,152,263 [2014]; £3,971,342 [2013]; £3,991,235 [2012]

The Cunmont Charitable Trust

Registered: 2 Mar 2016
Tel: 020 7491 8811
Activities: General charitable purposes
Address: 12 Stanhope Gate, London, W1K 1AW
Trustees: Mr Alexander James Callander, Tc Trustco Limited, Mrs Rhona Callander
Income: £2,929,368 [2017]

Cure Leukaemia

Registered: 20 Oct 2003 *Employees:* 5 *Volunteers:* 20
Tel: 0121 511 2233 *Website:* cureleukaemia.co.uk
Activities: The advancement of health or saving of lives
Address: Silks Solicitors, 27 Birmingham Street, Oldbury, W Midlands, B69 4DY
Trustees: Professor Charles Frank Craddock, Mike Shaw, Paul Faulkner, Gregory Lowson, Guy Pratt, Graham Silk, Mr Ian Allen, Glynn Purnell, Richard Turnbull
Income: £2,222,720 [2017]; £1,485,956 [2016]; £1,620,749 [2015]; £762,310 [2014]; £863,474 [2013]

The Cure Parkinson's Trust

Registered: 25 Oct 2005 *Employees:* 14 *Volunteers:* 6
Tel: 020 7929 7656 *Website:* cureparkinsons.org.uk
Activities: General charitable purposes; education, training; advancement of health or saving of lives
Address: 5 Jupiter House, Calleva Park, Aldermaston, Reading, Berks, RG7 8NN
Trustees: Mr David Edward Murray, Mr Peter Berners-Price, Mrs Jennifer Dicken, Dame Barbara Logan Hay DCMG LVO MBE, Dr Peter Fletcher, Mr David Ashford Jones, Lady Shelagh Nichols, Mr Richard Cawdron, Dr Kenneth Mulvany, Mr Robert William Iain MacDonald, Mr Charles Ralph, Ms Kerry Anne Rock
Income: £2,026,924 [2016]; £2,056,069 [2015]; £1,652,921 [2014]; £1,421,669 [2013]; £1,309,875 [2012]

Marie Curie
Registered: 22 Sep 1962 Employees: 4,274 Volunteers: 9,600
Tel: 020 7599 7121 Website: mariecurie.org.uk
Activities: The advancement of health or saving of lives
Address: 89 Albert Embankment, London, SE1 7TP
Trustees: Professor Peter Rigby, Miss Linda Urquhart, Dame Barbara Monroe, Mr Manvinder Singh Banga, Dr Rachel Elizabeth Mary Burman, Mr Richard David Flint, Mr Charles William John Compton, Ms Ruth Holt, Mr Timothy Breedon, Ms Helen Weir, Professor Declan Walsh, Ms Patricia Lesley Lee, Mr Steve Carson, Mr Chris Martin
Income: £159,122,000 [2017]; £156,222,000 [2016]; £155,880,000 [2015]; £154,805,000 [2014]; £148,952,000 [2013]

Curious Minds
Registered: 6 Aug 2009 Employees: 20
Tel: 01772 827001 Website: curiousminds.org.uk
Activities: Education, training; arts, culture, heritage, science
Address: 23-27 Guild Hall, Preston, Lancs, PR1 1HR
Trustees: Ms Virginia Tandy OBE, Mr Mehboob Mohmed Bobat, Mr Peter Douglas Stevens, Mrs Ruth Raban, Mr Ivan Wadeson, Ms Debra King, Mrs Abigail Ledger-Lomas, Mrs Karen Crowshaw
Income: £1,658,204 [2017]; £1,537,653 [2016]; £1,668,311 [2015]; £980,993 [2014]; £1,735,592 [2013]

Customs House Trust Limited
Registered: 8 Feb 1994 Employees: 57 Volunteers: 12
Tel: 0191 454 5450 Website: customshouse.co.uk
Activities: Education, training; arts, culture, heritage, science
Address: The Customs House, Theatre & Restaurant, Mill Dam, South Shields, Tyne & Wear, NE33 1ES
Trustees: Mr Graeme Thompson, Mr Yusef Abdullah, Simon Mitchell, Carol Cooke, Mr Martin Wray, Miss Jayden Blacklock, Ms Vivienne Wiggins, Mrs Shuley Alam MS, Grahame Wright, David Cottam, Ms Claire Simmons, Ms Stephanie Finnon, Mr Darren Hymers
Income: £2,592,446 [2017]; £2,525,180 [2016]; £2,582,093 [2015]; £2,026,333 [2014]; £1,976,814 [2013]

Cwmni Cynnal
Registered: 28 Oct 1997 Employees: 31
Tel: 01286 677686 Website: cynnal.co.uk
Activities: Education, training
Address: Penrallt, Caernarfon, Gwynedd, LL55 1BN
Trustees: Mr Arwyn Williams, Mr Richard Meirion Jones, Mr Ieuan Williams, Ms Annwen Daniels, Mr Garem Jackson, Mr Gerallt Andrew Jones, Mr Huw Emyr Williams, Mr Tudur O Williams, Mr Gareth Thomas, Mr Iwan Wyn Taylor, Mr Dafydd Roberts
Income: £2,347,928 [2017]; £2,735,138 [2016]; £3,013,112 [2015]; £3,428,509 [2014]; £5,766,073 [2013]

Cwmni Urdd Gobaith Cymru (Corfforedig) / The Welsh League of Youth (Incorporated)
Registered: 4 Mar 1997 Employees: 276 Volunteers: 10,000
Tel: 01678 541010 Website: urdd.cymru
Activities: Education, training; arts, culture, heritage, science; other charitable purposes
Address: Urdd Gobaith Cymru, Gwersyll Glan Llyn, Llanuwchllyn, Bala, Merionethshire, LL23 7ST
Trustees: Mr Bob Roberts, Mr Aled Walters, Tudur Dylan Jones, W Dyfrig Davies, Andrea Parri, Mr Gwyn Morris, Ms Margaret Rhiannon Lewis, Mr Sion Edwards, Rheon Tomos, Carol Davies, Mr Dilwyn Price, Meriel Parry
Income: £10,021,162 [2017]; £9,591,094 [2016]; £9,714,551 [2015]; £9,764,379 [2014]; £10,705,313 [2013]

Cyclists' Touring Club
Registered: 7 Jun 2012 Employees: 43 Volunteers: 4,500
Tel: 01483 238304 Website: cyclinguk.org
Activities: Education, training; advancement of health or saving of lives; disability; amateur sport; environment, conservation, heritage; recreation
Address: Cycling UK, Parklands, Railton Road, Guildford, Surrey, GU2 9JX
Trustees: Jim Brown, Dr Julian Huppert, Dan Howard, Kristian Gregory, Mr Jonathan Naughton, Dr Janet Atherton, Martyn Bolt, Welna Bowden, Ms Jaki Lowe, Mr Ian McCabe, Mr Ian Wescombe, Rachel Kirkwood
Income: £5,418,879 [2016]; £6,278,501 [2015]; £5,550,156 [2014]; £5,326,933 [2013]

Cyfannol Women's Aid
Registered: 21 Apr 1995 Employees: 36 Volunteers: 15
Tel: 01495 742052 Website: cyfannol.org.uk
Activities: General charitable purposes; education, training; advancement of health or saving of lives; prevention or relief of poverty; accommodation, housing
Address: Torfaen Women's Aid, 3 Town Bridge Buildings, Park Road, Pontypool, Gwent, NP4 6JE
Trustees: Mrs Denise Pearce, Mr Merion Huw Watkins, Ms Debra Winney, Ms Katrina Eira Rigby, Mrs Karen Turner, Miss Kay Perrott, Mrs Nicola Jo Bowen
Income: £1,115,682 [2017]; £1,095,342 [2016]; £607,574 [2015]; £628,466 [2014]; £586,008 [2013]

Cyfle Building Skills Limited
Registered: 18 Nov 2016 Employees: 120
Tel: 01554 748181 Website: cyflebuilding.co.uk
Activities: Education, training
Address: Swwrsal, Dyffryn Road, Ammanford Campus, Ammanford, Carmarthenshire, SA18 3TA
Trustees: Mr Anthony Rhys Thomas, Mr William James Davies, Mr Kenneth Hartley Pearson, Mr Owain Jones, Mr William Gareth John, Mr Kevin Mark Gravell
Income: £1,315,097 [2017]

Cymdeithas Caer Las
Registered: 16 Dec 1975 Employees: 83 Volunteers: 7
Tel: 01792 646071 Website: caerlas.org
Activities: Education, training; prevention or relief of poverty; accommodation, housing; economic, community development, employment
Address: Cymdeithas Caer Las, The Customs House, Cambrian Place, Swansea, SA1 1RG
Trustees: Ms Alison Saunders, Mr Mike Vigar, Mr Howard Davies, Ms Carol Ann Prangle, Joy Williams
Income: £3,196,143 [2017]; £3,264,684 [2016]; £2,428,732 [2015]; £2,166,050 [2014]; £2,096,233 [2013]

Cymdeithas Gofal The Care Society
Registered: 9 Sep 2011 Employees: 42 Volunteers: 6
Website: caresociety.org.uk
Activities: Education, training; prevention or relief of poverty; accommodation, housing
Address: 21 Terrace Road, Aberystwyth, Ceredigion, SY23 1NP
Trustees: Mr Tony Kitchen, Mr Stephen Cripps, Mr Charles Alexander Symons, Mr John Rees, Tai Ceredigion, Mr Robert Gray, Mr Anthony Hearn, Mr Peter Saunders, Miss Catherine Shaw
Income: £1,165,584 [2017]; £1,238,408 [2016]; £1,172,061 [2015]; £1,032,736 [2014]; £1,279,846 [2013]

Cymryd Rhan
Registered: 6 Jan 1986 *Employees:* 134
Tel: 01597 828050 *Website:* cymryd-rhan.org.uk
Activities: Education, training; disability; prevention or relief of poverty; accommodation, housing
Address: Wellfield House, Temple Street, Llandrindod Wells, Powys, LD1 5HG
Trustees: Miss Julie Ann Davies, Mr Christopher Hay, Ms Friederike von Duecker-Wollensack, Miss Sarah Williams, Mr Kevin Hughes, Ms Susan Williams, Mr Tomos Glyn Turner, Mrs Birgit Walter, Ms Hayley Sian Fisk
Income: £2,071,271 [2017]; £2,322,235 [2016]; £2,945,922 [2015]; £3,155,302 [2014]; £3,043,071 [2013]

Cymunedau'n Ymlaen Mon Communities Forward
Registered: 9 Aug 2012 *Employees:* 28 *Volunteers:* 50
Tel: 01407 762004 *Website:* moncf.co.uk
Activities: The prevention or relief of poverty; economic, community development, employment
Address: Mon CF, 63 Market Street, Holyhead, Gwynedd, LL65 1UN
Trustees: Mrs Ann Kennedy, Mr Keith Thomas, John Tyrell Jones, John Lee, Mr Peter Davies OBE, Mr James Neil Lee MBE, Mrs Susan Fiona Williams, Dr William Roberts, Mr John Egryn Lewis
Income: £1,298,877 [2017]; £1,119,421 [2016]; £1,053,746 [2015]; £1,110,172 [2014]; £223,461 [2013]

Cyngor Celfyddydau Cymru
Registered: 2 Mar 1994 *Employees:* 88
Tel: 029 2044 1301 *Website:* arts.wales
Activities: Arts, culture, heritage, science
Address: The Arts Council of Wales, Bute Place, Cardiff, CF10 5AL
Trustees: Ms Marian Wyn Jones BA Hons, Dr Phillip George, Mr John C Williams BA (Oxon), Melanie Hawthorne, Mr Dafydd Gwyn Rhys, Iwan Bala, Dr Rachel O'Riordan, Mr Alan Watkin, Richard Turner, Mr Michael Griffiths OBE, Andrew Miller, Mr Andrew Robert Eagle, Kate Eden
Income: £49,864,000 [2017]; £53,698,000 [2016]; £52,784,000 [2015]; £52,553,000 [2014]; £56,601,000 [2013]

Cyngor Llyfrau Cymru-Welsh Books Council
Registered: 10 Jun 1976 *Employees:* 45
Tel: 01970 624151 *Website:* wbc.org.uk
Activities: General charitable purposes; education, training; arts, culture, heritage, science
Address: Cyngor Llyfrau Cymru, Castell Brychan, Aberystwyth, Ceredigion, SY23 2JB
Trustees: Yr Athro M Wynn Thomas, Mr Gwydion Hughes, Mr Dafydd John Pritchard, Lynda G Williams, Marian Delyth, Huw Thomas, Mrs Susan Jenkins, Meilyr Rowlands, Lorna Herbert Egan, Robat Arwyn, Yr Athro Jane Aaron, Mr Richard Bellinger, Mrs Kathryn Parry, B Towyn Evans, Chris Macey, Y Cynghorydd David W M Rees, Rona Aldrich, Hugh Jones, David R Daniels, Lyn Lewis Dafis, Bethan Gwanas, Linda Tomos, Cathryn Charnell-White, Mr Alun P Thomas, Mr Gareth Griffiths
Income: £6,707,598 [2017]; £6,713,407 [2016]; £6,934,804 [2015]; £7,938,293 [2014]; £7,591,814 [2013]

The Cyrenians Ltd
Registered: 19 Jul 1971 *Employees:* 347 *Volunteers:* 450
Tel: 0191 273 8891 *Website:* changing-lives.org.uk
Activities: General charitable purposes; prevention or relief of poverty; accommodation, housing
Address: Changing Lives (The Cyrenians Ltd), Dukesway, Team Valley Trading Estate, Gateshead, Tyne & Wear, NE11 0LF
Trustees: Maggie Pavlou, Baroness Hilary Jane Armstrong, Mr Dean Fielding, Mrs Lesley Telford, Mrs Geraldine Kay, Mr James Ramsbotham, Ms Fiona Wharton, Mr Steve Guyon, Mr Peter Brown
Income: £17,047,445 [2017]; £14,160,755 [2016]; £15,207,520 [2015]; £12,326,000 [2014]; £8,304,901 [2013]

Cystic Fibrosis Trust
Registered: 21 Jan 2000 *Employees:* 111 *Volunteers:* 619
Tel: 020 3795 1504 *Website:* cysticfibrosis.org.uk
Activities: The advancement of health or saving of lives; disability
Address: Cystic Fibrosis Trust, 1 Aldgate, London, EC3N 1RE
Trustees: Mr George Jenkins OBE, Mr Peter Norris, Dr Andrew Jones, Ms Hannah Begbie, Mr Michael Winehouse, Mr Ryan Tohill, Mrs Caroline Cartellieri-Karlsen, Mr David Turner QC, Mr Sean Collins, Miss Louise King, Ms Ffyona Dawber, Professor Rosalind Smyth
Income: £13,182,000 [2017]; £11,386,000 [2016]; £12,113,000 [2015]; £10,806,000 [2014]; £9,726,000 [2013]

D T F Limited
Registered: 3 Mar 1980
Tel: 020 8202 1066
Activities: General charitable purposes; prevention or relief of poverty; religious activities
Address: c/o Sutherland House, 70-78 West Hendon Broadway, London, NW9 7BT
Trustees: Mr David Tannen, Mr Jonathan Mark Miller
Income: £2,036,742 [2017]; £2,509,456 [2016]; £2,106,930 [2015]; £1,886,552 [2014]; £1,573,799 [2013]

D&AD
Registered: 4 Mar 1968 *Employees:* 71
Tel: 020 7840 1111 *Website:* dandad.org
Activities: Education, training; arts, culture, heritage, science
Address: 64 Cheshire Street, London, E2 6EH
Trustees: Ms Harriet Devoy, Mrs Nicola Bullard, Ms Alexandra Taylor, Mr Graham Shearsby, Mr Stephen Spence, Mr Vranakis Steve, Ms Lucy Anne Ronayne, Mr Bruno Maag, Ms Katherina Tudball, Mrs Katharine Stanners
Income: £7,366,545 [2017]; £6,768,231 [2016]; £5,063,718 [2015]; £5,063,718 [2014]; £4,882,193 [2013]

The D'Oyly Carte Charitable Trust
Registered: 8 Dec 2005
Tel: 01285 841900 *Website:* doylycartecharitabletrust.org
Activities: General charitable purposes; education, training; advancement of health or saving of lives; arts, culture, heritage, science; environment, conservation, heritage
Address: The D'Oyly Carte Charitable Trust, 6 Trull Farm Builidngs, Trull, Tetbury, Glos, GL8 8SQ
Trustees: Mrs Francesca Radcliffe, Jeremy Leigh Pemberton CBE DL, Dr Michael O'Brien, Mr Andrew Jackson, Mr Henry Freeland RIBA BArch, Mrs Julia Lesley Sibley MBE, Mr Andrew Bowring Wimble
Income: £1,482,677 [2017]; £1,303,690 [2016]; £1,557,171 [2015]; £1,361,483 [2014]; £1,264,950 [2013]

The D-Day Revisited Society
Registered: 20 May 2009 *Volunteers:* 12
Tel: 01244 531765 *Website:* d-dayrevisited.co.uk
Activities: General charitable purposes; education, training; environment, conservation, heritage; other charitable purposes
Address: The Armoury Building, Hawarden Airfield, Flint Road, Chester, CH4 0GZ
Trustees: Miss Victoria Phipps, Mr Fabian Faversham-Pullen, Mr Jonathan Harry Phipps
Income: £1,214,474 [2016]; £413,461 [2015]; £131,232 [2014]; £60,640 [2013]; £49,350 [2012]

DDRC Healthcare
Registered: 14 Mar 1980 *Employees:* 26
Tel: 01752 209999 *Website:* ddrc.org
Activities: Education, training; advancement of health or saving of lives
Address: Diving Diseases Research Centre, Hyperbaric Medical Centre, 8 Research Way, Derriford, Plymouth, PL6 8BU
Trustees: Mr Thomas Gavin Anthony, Mr Shaun Walbridge, Mr Keith Walker, Mr Tony Pearce, Mr Ian Berry, Mr Brian Clargo, Mr Raymond Sparrow, Mr Craig McLaren
Income: £2,036,201 [2017]; £1,998,624 [2016]; £2,055,403 [2015]; £2,125,747 [2014]; £2,126,961 [2013]

DEBRA
Registered: 9 Feb 2001 *Employees:* 360 *Volunteers:* 1,067
Tel: 01344 771961 *Website:* debra.org.uk
Activities: The advancement of health or saving of lives; disability
Address: DEBRA, Unit 13, Wellington Business Park, Dukes Ride, Crowthorne, Berks, RG45 6LS
Trustees: Mr Graham Marsden, Dr James Hinchcliffe, Mr Michael William Jaega, Mrs Joanne Merchant, Mr Andrew Grist, Mrs Vivien Mary Mundy, Ms Simone Bunting, Mr James Francis Irvine, Mr Simon Cuzner, Mr Timothy David Powell, Mr David Wilkinson, Mrs Rebecca Lucy Edwards
Income: £14,136,343 [2016]; £12,501,485 [2015]; £11,881,473 [2014]; £11,359,613 [2013]; £11,044,405 [2012]

DENS Limited
Registered: 24 Apr 2003 *Employees:* 37 *Volunteers:* 100
Tel: 01442 262274 *Website:* dens.org.uk
Activities: Education, training; prevention or relief of poverty; accommodation, housing
Address: 1 Queensway, Hemel Hempstead, Herts, HP1 1HT
Trustees: Eric Pillinger, Mr Ian Tottman, Mr Malcolm Lindo, Gail Albert, Mr Martin Russell Warner, Mr Ian Hilary Laidlaw-Dickson OBE, Michael J W Morgan, Miss Melanie Jane Eckert
Income: £1,775,080 [2017]; £1,725,324 [2016]; £1,096,777 [2015]; £1,033,839 [2014]; £859,875 [2013]

DFN Charitable Foundation
Registered: 24 Feb 2014 *Volunteers:* 1
Tel: 07503 292716 *Website:* dfnfoundation.org
Activities: General charitable purposes; education, training; advancement of health or saving of lives; disability; environment, conservation, heritage
Address: DFN Charitable Foundation, 10 Norwich Street, London, EC4A 1BD
Trustees: Mr David Forbes-Nixon, Mr Simon Nicholas Konsta, Mr James Dickson, Mr Eric William Low OBE
Income: £4,755,131 [2016]; £8,284,374 [2015]; £8,023,622 [2014]

The DHL UK Foundation
Registered: 22 Jul 1988 *Employees:* 5 *Volunteers:* 1,250
Tel: 01285 841914 *Website:* dhlukfoundation.org
Activities: General charitable purposes; education, training; prevention or relief of poverty
Address: Ocean House, The Ring, Bracknell, Berks, RG12 1AN
Trustees: Mr Christopher Berkeley Stephens, Mr Ralf Durrwang, Miss Julie Sandra Bentley, Mr John Martin Nestor, Mr Ian Wilson, Tim Slater, Ms Barbara Storch, Mr Perry Watts, Nicola Craig, Mr Christopher Berkeley Stephens
Income: £1,135,185 [2017]; £1,878,927 [2016]; £2,451,752 [2015]; £2,031,757 [2014]; £1,713,861 [2013]

DKMS Foundation
Registered: 5 Dec 2012 *Employees:* 37 *Volunteers:* 75
Tel: 020 8747 5620 *Website:* dkms.org.uk
Activities: The advancement of health or saving of lives
Address: DKMS Bone Marrow Donor Centre, Ashburnham House, Castle Row, Horticultural Place, London, W4 4JQ
Trustees: Benedict Abel, Dr Alexander Schmidt, Stephan Schumacher, Mr Sirko Geist
Income: £5,265,831 [2016]; £3,620,983 [2015]; £3,339,604 [2014]; £1,205,755 [2013]

DM Thomas Foundation for Young People
Registered: 21 Dec 2000 *Employees:* 6 *Volunteers:* 400
Tel: 020 7605 7733 *Website:* dmthomasfoundation.org
Activities: General charitable purposes; education, training; advancement of health or saving of lives; disability; prevention or relief of poverty; overseas aid, famine relief; accommodation, housing; amateur sport; economic, community development, employment
Address: DM Thomas Foundation, 179-199 Holland Park Avenue, London, W11 4UL
Trustees: Mr Ramesh Dewan, Mr Christopher John Ring, Mr William Differ, Dame Maureen Thomas DBE, Mr Simon Vincent, Mr Paul Farrow
Income: £2,014,661 [2017]; £1,548,891 [2016]; £1,505,168 [2015]; £2,184,587 [2014]; £2,588,670 [2013]

Dacorum Council for Voluntary Service
Registered: 28 Oct 1983 *Employees:* 19 *Volunteers:* 130
Tel: 01442 253935 *Website:* communityactiondacorum.org.uk
Activities: General charitable purposes; education, training; economic, community development, employment
Address: FAO Mr Mark Mitchell, Dacorum CVS, 48 High Street, Hemel Hempstead, Herts, HP1 3AF
Trustees: Mr Douglas Eric Root, Mrs Glenda Ferneyhough, Cllr Richard Roberts, Ms Pushpa Kulabowila, Mr Christopher John Dove, Mr Roger Martin Taylor, Mr Colin Gage, Mr Ian Hilary Laidlaw-Dickson, Mrs Tina Howard, Mr John Birnie
Income: £1,712,154 [2017]; £1,668,114 [2016]; £1,739,887 [2015]; £1,707,859 [2014]; £1,589,196 [2013]

Dacorum Sports Trust
Registered: 27 May 2004 *Employees:* 385 *Volunteers:* 10
Tel: 01442 952251 *Website:* sportspace.co.uk
Activities: Amateur sport
Address: Dacorum Sports Trust, XC, Jarman Park, Hemel Hempstead, Herts, HP2 4JS
Trustees: Mr Brian David Bickel, Mr Mark Carpenter, Mrs Elaine Craig Emptage, Mr Ian Charles Grant, Ms Paula Batten, Ms Janine Dealey, Mr Brian James Malyon, Mr Matthew William Armstrong, Mr Ian Phipps, Martin Wood, Mr Stephen Day
Income: £8,408,025 [2017]; £8,101,476 [2016]; £8,366,084 [2015]; £8,335,116 [2014]; £8,190,404 [2013]

Roald Dahl's Marvellous Children's Charity
Registered: 11 Aug 2010 *Employees:* 9 *Volunteers:* 10
Tel: 01494 917690 *Website:* roalddahlcharity.org
Activities: Education, training; advancement of health or saving of lives; disability; prevention or relief of poverty
Address: Roald Dahl's Children's Charity, Montague House, 23 Woodside Road, Amersham, Bucks, HP6 6AA
Trustees: Mr Martin Andrew Forrest Goodwin, Mr Graham Faulkner, Dr Husain Khaki, Ms Michelle Johnson, Mrs Virginia Louise Myer, Mr Donald Sturrock, Mr Niels Kirk, Mr Alex Hyde-Parker
Income: £1,543,634 [2017]; £940,259 [2016]; £827,949 [2015]; £868,730 [2014]; £706,778 [2013]

The Daiglen School Trust Limited
Registered: 18 Mar 1977 *Employees:* 34
Tel: 020 8989 0077 *Website:* daiglenschool.co.uk
Activities: Education, training
Address: Essex House, 7-8 The Shrubberies, George Lane, South Woodford, London, E18 1BD
Trustees: Mrs Susan Barnes, Mrs Christine Doughty, Mrs Susan Rosemary Stride, Mrs Andrea Dowling, Mr Philip Degen, Mr Nick White, Mrs Valerie Lynch
Income: £1,387,604 [2017]; £1,368,764 [2016]; £1,391,932 [2015]; £1,311,592 [2014]; £1,221,154 [2013]

Dair House School Trust Limited
Registered: 10 Feb 1976 *Employees:* 29
Tel: 01753 643964 *Website:* dairhouse.co.uk
Activities: Education, training
Address: Dair House School, Beaconsfield Road, Farnham Royal, Slough, SL2 3BY
Trustees: Mrs Jane Elizabeth Masih, Mrs Victoria Jane McNally, Mrs Maralynn Virginia Velasco-Mills, Mr Sudheer Sharma, Mr Paul McNally, Mrs Anne Terese King, Mr Michael Grant Hibbert, Mr John Frederick Thomas
Income: £1,316,519 [2017]; £1,228,083 [2016]; £1,187,494 [2015]; £1,083,576 [2014]; £1,005,026 [2013]

Daisy Chain Project Teesside
Registered: 1 Jun 2005 *Employees:* 75 *Volunteers:* 208
Tel: 01642 531248 *Website:* daisychainproject.co.uk
Activities: Disability; amateur sport; animals; economic, community development, employment
Address: Daisy Chain, Calf Fallow Lane, Stockton on Tees, Cleveland, TS20 1PF
Trustees: Mr Ian Parker, Mr Jonathan Dicken, Ian Kinnery, Mrs Elaine McLaine-Wood, Mr James Dale, Dr Edwin Pugh MBE, Lesley Clode, Mrs Leanne Boyd-Smith
Income: £1,906,033 [2017]; £1,948,062 [2016]; £1,489,780 [2015]; £1,077,779 [2014]; £692,030 [2013]

Dalaid
Registered: 2 Oct 1997
Tel: 020 8455 5059
Activities: General charitable purposes; education, training; prevention or relief of poverty; religious activities
Address: 22 Wentworth Road, London, NW11 0RP
Trustees: Mr Maurice Levenson, Mr Aron Baruch Balkin, Mr Uri Meir Roberg
Income: £1,154,111 [2017]; £1,146,787 [2016]; £863,477 [2015]; £808,986 [2014]; £821,701 [2013]

Dallaglio Rugbyworks
Registered: 25 Jun 2009 *Employees:* 13 *Volunteers:* 3
Tel: 01789 204185 *Website:* dallagliofoundation.com
Activities: General charitable purposes; education, training; amateur sport; economic, community development, employment
Address: Barclays Bank Chambers, Bridge Street, Stratford upon Avon, Warwicks, CV37 6AH
Trustees: Mr Lawrence Bruno Nero Dallaglio, Ms Jacqueline Stevenson, William Carey-Evans, Mr Andrew Timothy Cook, Jeff Dodds, Matthew Key, Charles Taylor
Income: £1,500,381 [2017]; £2,602,954 [2016]; £2,569,241 [2015]; £1,736,709 [2014]; £3,564,230 [2013]

Dance 4 Limited
Registered: 27 Nov 1992 *Employees:* 13 *Volunteers:* 31
Tel: 0115 924 2016 *Website:* dance4.co.uk
Activities: Arts, culture, heritage, science
Address: 2 Dakeyne Street, Nottingham, NG3 2AR
Trustees: Mr Peter Thornton, Professor Vida Midgelow, Mr Peter Shenton, Betsy Gregory, Mr Jaivant Patel, Ms Joanne Belton, Ms Amanda Schofield, Mrs Barbara Sargent, Mr Richard Woods
Income: £1,002,646 [2017]; £1,441,408 [2016]; £1,085,270 [2015]; £1,078,945 [2014]; £935,896 [2013]

Dance Consortium Limited
Registered: 23 Jun 2009
Tel: 0121 689 3054 *Website:* danceconsortium.com
Activities: Education, training; arts, culture, heritage, science
Address: 116 Quinton Road, Birmingham, B17 0QA
Trustees: Mr Philip Bernays, Alistair Spalding, Mr Adam Renton, Ms Fiona Allan, Mr John Stalker, Mr Simon Stokes, Mr Michael David Ockwell
Income: £1,895,953 [2017]; £1,274,795 [2016]; £1,326,336 [2015]; £812,997 [2014]; £1,257,601 [2013]

Dance East
Registered: 11 Dec 1997 *Employees:* 23 *Volunteers:* 23
Tel: 01473 295230 *Website:* danceeast.co.uk
Activities: Education, training; advancement of health or saving of lives; arts, culture, heritage, science; amateur sport; economic, community development, employment; recreation
Address: Jerwood Dancehouse, Foundry Lane, Ipswich, Suffolk, IP4 1DW
Trustees: Lizzie Fargher, Mrs Fleur Derbyshire-Fox, Mr Robert Gough, Mr Richard Wallace Pye, Ms Ann Mary Wixley, Mr Richard John Chaplin, Mr Anthony Hilton, Mr Daden Henry Edward Hunt, Mr Gary Christopher Avis
Income: £2,261,486 [2017]; £1,939,644 [2016]; £1,960,449 [2015]; £1,770,781 [2014]; £2,444,830 [2013]

Dance North
Registered: 19 Apr 1990 *Employees:* 80
Tel: 0191 261 0505 *Website:* dancecity.co.uk
Activities: Education, training; arts, culture, heritage, science
Address: Temple Street, Newcastle upon Tyne, NE1 4BR
Trustees: Mr Jeffrey Martin Dean, Mr Frank Wilson, Mr Michael Cockburn, Ms Ann Isabel Cooper, Mrs Kay Wilson, Mrs Roshan Israni, Mr Andrew Hammond Bairstow, Mr Timothy George Rubidge, Ms Lesley Anne Callaghan, Mr Alistair Mitchell Robson, Mrs Carol Wood
Income: £1,825,782 [2017]; £2,019,273 [2016]; £1,604,900 [2015]; £1,231,549 [2014]; £1,470,859 [2013]

The Dancexchange Limited
Registered: 29 Mar 1995 *Employees:* 17 *Volunteers:* 63
Tel: 0121 667 6730 *Website:* dancexchange.org.uk
Activities: Arts, culture, heritage, science
Address: Birmingham Hippodrome, Thorp Street, Birmingham, B5 4TB
Trustees: Mr Malcolm Kenneth McGivan, Ms Carnette Richardson-Jacquet, Mr John Alexander Houlden, Monique Morgan, Michael Hibbs, Mr Peter McHugh, Alexandra Claughton, Kevin Singh
Income: £1,723,528 [2017]; £1,392,545 [2016]; £1,578,880 [2015]; £1,435,772 [2014]; £2,075,826 [2013]

Danish Young Women's Christian Association in London
Registered: 19 Oct 1966 *Employees:* 6 *Volunteers:* 65
Tel: 020 7435 7232 *Website:* kfuk.co.uk
Activities: General charitable purposes; education, training; accommodation, housing; religious activities; arts, culture, heritage, science
Address: 43 Maresfield Gardens, Hampstead, London, NW3 5TF
Trustees: Mrs Anne Raill, Mr Egon Christiansen, Mrs Margit Christensen, Mr Rolf Dohm, Mrs Filippa Bjorg Connor, Mr Peter Niebuhr, Mrs Birte Trautmann, Mrs Karen Maibom, Miss Marie Moller, Mr Steen Rosenfalck, Ms Nina Juel Bigbie
Income: £1,068,973 [2017]; £493,527 [2016]; £439,147 [2015]; £368,475 [2014]; £409,715 [2013]

Darlington Association on Disability
Registered: 11 Sep 2008 *Employees:* 66 *Volunteers:* 80
Tel: 01325 489999 *Website:* darlingtondisability.org
Activities: General charitable purposes; education, training; disability; prevention or relief of poverty; economic, community development, employment; human rights, religious or racial harmony, equality or diversity; recreation; other charitable purposes
Address: Darlington Association on Disability, 1P Enterprise House, Valley Street, Darlington, Co Durham, DL1 1GY
Trustees: Mr Colin Light, Ms Carol Bogg, Mr Paul Edwards, Mrs Theresa Moss-Carbert, Gordon Pybus, Mr Joe Hutchinson, Miss Samantha Taylor
Income: £1,077,126 [2017]; £978,477 [2016]; £1,177,359 [2015]; £1,096,203 [2014]; £993,336 [2013]

Darlington and District Hospice Movement
Registered: 23 Jan 1987 *Employees:* 131 *Volunteers:* 357
Tel: 01325 254321 *Website:* darlingtonhospice.org.uk
Activities: Disability
Address: St Teresa's Hospice, The Woodlands, 91 Woodland Road, Darlington, Co Durham, DL3 7UA
Trustees: Mrs Anne Foster, Mr Nicholas Charles Tristram Millen OBE, Mr Richard Hepworth, Dr Helen McLeish, Tony Luckett, Mrs Mary Lovell, Dr Harry Byrne, Mr Steve Rose, Mrs Sasha Warr
Income: £2,968,516 [2017]; £2,816,269 [2016]; £2,664,160 [2015]; £2,863,385 [2014]; £2,731,785 [2013]

The Dartington Hall Trust
Registered: 21 Jul 1980 *Employees:* 222 *Volunteers:* 279
Tel: 01803 847002 *Website:* dartington.org
Activities: General charitable purposes; education, training; arts, culture, heritage, science; environment, conservation, heritage; economic, community development, employment; other charitable purposes
Address: The Dartington Hall Trust, The Elmhirst Centre, Dartington Hall, Totnes, Devon, TQ9 6EL
Trustees: Dame Josephine Williams DBE BA DL, Julia Unwin CBE, Dr Gregory Edward Parston, Mr Timothy Jones, Mrs Sangeeta Elizabeth Singh-Watson, Emma Stenning, Mr Robert Sexton, Andrew Ward, Mrs Sylvie Pierce, Nigel Topping
Income: £13,301,000 [2017]; £12,587,000 [2016]; £12,813,000 [2015]; £12,030,000 [2014]; £12,140,000 [2013]

Dartmoor Zoological Society
Registered: 2 Sep 2014 *Employees:* 58 *Volunteers:* 100
Tel: 01752 837645 *Website:* dartmoorzoo.org.uk
Activities: Education, training; animals; environment, conservation, heritage
Address: Dartmoor Zoological Park, Sparkwell, Plymouth, PL7 5DG
Trustees: Mr Benjamin David James, Mr Simon Almond, Mr Benjamin Mee, James Ross
Income: £1,277,522 [2016]; £1,188,887 [2015]

The E Hayes Dashwood of Aston Rowant House Oxfordshire Foundation
Registered: 24 Jan 1966 *Employees:* 1
Tel: 020 8445 0965 *Website:* hayesdashwood.org.uk
Activities: Disability
Address: Munros, 1341 High Road, London, N20 9HR
Trustees: Captain Alun Ryle RN Rtd, Captain Colin Stewart, Vice Admiral Sir Tom Blackburn, Commodore Annette Picton, Commodore Bill Walworth CBE RFA, Major General Bryan Dutton CB CBE, Air Commodore Iain McCoubrey, Colonel Christopher Pickup LVO OBE, Lieutenant Colonel Nicholas Tuck
Income: £1,064,971 [2016]; £1,227,959 [2015]; £1,141,754 [2014]; £928,615 [2013]; £1,020,771 [2012]

The Daughters of Charity of St Vincent de Paul
Registered: 9 Sep 1964 *Employees:* 320 *Volunteers:* 30
Tel: 020 8959 2257 *Website:* daughtersofcharity.org.uk
Activities: The advancement of health or saving of lives; disability; prevention or relief of poverty; overseas aid, famine relief; religious activities
Address: Provincial House, The Ridgeway, London, NW7 1RE
Trustees: Sister Ellen Flynn, Sister Margaret Bannerton, Sister Mary Theresa Bain, Sister Kathleen Fox, Sister Kathleen Harte, Sister Kathleen Kennedy, Sister Theresa Tighe
Income: £8,744,306 [2016]; £9,622,358 [2015]; £11,963,913 [2014]; £12,467,425 [2013]; £10,621,820 [2012]

The Daughters of Charity of St. Vincent de Paul Services
Registered: 16 Oct 2012 *Employees:* 383
Tel: 020 8906 3777
Activities: General charitable purposes; religious activities
Address: Provincial House, The Ridgeway, London, NW7 1RE
Trustees: Mrs Leona Roche, Sister Ellen Teresa Flynn, Sister Kathleen Kennedy, Sister Theresa Tighe, Rev Paul Roche, Sister Margaret Bannerton, Sister Mai O'Connor, Mr John Drury, Sister Moira Theresa Bain, Sister Kathleen Fox
Income: £6,687,627 [2017]; £7,538,044 [2016]; £936,649 [2015]; £2,334,943 [2014]

The Daughters of Divine Charity (Swaffham, Norfolk)
Registered: 24 Nov 1964 *Employees:* 36 *Volunteers:* 6
Tel: 01760 724577 *Website:* sacredheartschool.co.uk
Activities: Education, training; religious activities
Address: The Convent of The Sacred Heart, Mangate Street, Swaffham, Norfolk, PE37 7QW
Trustees: Sister Catherine, Sister Thomas More, Sister Francis, Sister Jacinta
Income: £1,205,117 [2016]; £1,053,601 [2015]; £966,616 [2014]; £997,949 [2013]; £1,116,761 [2012]

Daughters of Mary and Joseph Congregation Fund CIO
Registered: 8 Sep 2015 *Volunteers:* 2
Website: daughtersofmaryandjoseph.org
Activities: General charitable purposes; education, training; religious activities
Address: The Regional House, Daughters of Mary & Joseph, Layhams Road, West Wickham, Kent, BR4 9QJ
Trustees: Mr Phillip Joseph Jukes, Mr Ronald James Huggett, Sister Helen Catherine Lane, Sister Annette Lawrence, Sister Hedwig Birakwate, Sister Marie Claire Nakayiza
Income: £6,017,615 [2016]

Dauntsey's School
Registered: 31 Jul 2006 *Employees:* 340
Tel: 01380 814616 *Website:* dauntseys.org
Activities: Education, training
Address: Dauntseys School, High Street, West Lavington, Devizes, Wilts, SN10 4HE
Trustees: Angus Macpherson, Brigadier Peregrine Rawlins, Mr Ralph Mitchell Bernard CBE, Mrs Lucy Walsh Waring, Air Chief Marshal Sir Richard Johns GCB KCVO CBE, Mr Bill Scarborough, Mr Charles Henry De Neufville Lucas, Mr Nicholas John Spencer Fisk, Mrs Veryan Peta Nield, Mrs Sameera Rachel Broadhead, Mr Richard Handover, Mr Philip Lough, Mr Michael Liversidge, Venerable Alan Paul Jeans, Dr Rachel Quarrell, Mr Ian David Parker, Mrs Sandra Eugene Stewart Duncan Gamble, Mr Nicholas Blethyn Elliott, Mr David William Goodhew
Income: £18,217,418 [2017]; £18,039,009 [2016]; £17,043,085 [2015]; £16,301,854 [2014]; £15,803,125 [2013]

The Davidson Family Charitable Trust
Registered: 5 Nov 1971
Tel: 020 7224 1030
Activities: General charitable purposes; education, training; advancement of health or saving of lives; disability; prevention or relief of poverty; overseas aid, famine relief; religious activities; arts, culture, heritage, science; environment, conservation, heritage; human rights, religious or racial harmony, equality or diversity; other charitable purposes
Address: 58 Queen Anne Street, London, W1G 8HW
Trustees: Mr Gerald Abraham Davidson, Ms Maxine Yvette Davidson
Income: £1,125,173 [2017]; £937,850 [2016]; £750,135 [2015]; £937,668 [2014]; £1,125,100 [2013]

The Davis Foundation
Registered: 22 Jul 2013
Tel: 020 7389 9504
Activities: General charitable purposes; education, training; arts, culture, heritage, science; human rights, religious or racial harmony, equality or diversity
Address: 3 Beechworth Close, London, NW3 7UT
Trustees: Mr Michael Lawrence Davis, Ms Sarah Davis, Mrs Barbara Davis
Income: £1,514,195 [2017]; £11,865 [2016]; £1,781,940 [2015]; £7,005,000 [2014]

Dawat-E-Hadiyah Trust (United Kingdom)
Registered: 2 Jul 1986 *Employees:* 21
Tel: 020 8839 0750
Activities: General charitable purposes; education, training; advancement of health or saving of lives; disability; prevention or relief of poverty; overseas aid, famine relief; accommodation, housing; religious activities; arts, culture, heritage, science; amateur sport; animals; environment, conservation, heritage; economic, community development, employment
Address: 6 Mohammedi Park Complex, Rowdell Road, Northolt, Middlesex, UB5 6AG
Trustees: The 53rd Dai Al-Mutlaq His Holiness Syedna Mufaddal Saifuddin
Income: £8,273,126 [2016]; £6,560,883 [2015]; £6,091,235 [2014]; £6,191,298 [2013]; £8,419,395 [2012]

Dawat-E-Islami UK
Registered: 21 Jun 2005 *Employees:* 275 *Volunteers:* 240
Tel: 07976 234274 *Website:* dawateislamiuk.net
Activities: Education, training; prevention or relief of poverty; overseas aid, famine relief; religious activities
Address: 14 Richard Burch Street, Bury, Lancs, BL9 6DU
Trustees: Mr Khalid Nazir Mirza, Waseem Nazir, Mr Basharat Mohammed, Mr Mohammad Jamil, Hasan Ali Safdar
Income: £6,785,518 [2017]; £5,133,414 [2016]; £6,856,313 [2015]; £3,533,609 [2014]; £3,521,555 [2013]

Dawatul Islam UK and Eire
Registered: 26 Apr 1984 *Employees:* 50 *Volunteers:* 600
Tel: 020 7790 5166 *Website:* dawatul-islam.org.uk
Activities: General charitable purposes; education, training; prevention or relief of poverty; religious activities
Address: Darul Ummah, 56 Bigland Street, London, E1 2ND
Trustees: Burhan Uddin, Hasan Mueenuddin, Mr Khalilur Rahman, Faizul Islam, Abu Sayeed, Dr Abul Kalam Azad, Mrs Shahin Akther Rosey Mustafa, Mr Muhammad Abdur Rahman, Mr Farid Ahmed Reza, Mr A K Moudood Hasan, Mr Shabbir Ahmad Kawsar, H M Shafiqur Rahman, Marfath Ali, Nur Baksh, Dr Abdus Salam Abdus Salam, Mrs Mafruha Khatoon, Mr Abdul Mukit
Income: £1,040,109 [2017]; £1,178,241 [2016]; £1,163,850 [2015]; £1,219,084 [2014]; £1,124,239 [2013]

Dawliffe Hall Educational Foundation
Registered: 12 Nov 1979 *Employees:* 43 *Volunteers:* 344
Website: dhef.org.uk
Activities: Education, training; prevention or relief of poverty; overseas aid, famine relief; accommodation, housing; arts, culture, heritage, science; amateur sport; economic, community development, employment
Address: 4 Canterbury Road, Oxford, OX2 6LU
Trustees: Ms Ann C Bennett, Miss Ana Ferrer-B, Mrs Marta Sauri Lopez, Miss Caroline Sanderson, Gill Duval
Income: £1,802,880 [2016]; £1,780,813 [2015]; £1,918,798 [2014]; £2,027,079 [2013]; £2,266,304 [2012]

Daybreak Family Group Conferences
Registered: 30 Sep 1999 *Employees:* 22 *Volunteers:* 30
Tel: 023 8069 6644 *Website:* daybreakfgc.org.uk
Activities: Education, training; other charitable purposes
Address: West Lodge, Nobs Crook, Leylands Farm, Colden Common, Winchester, Hants, SO21 1TH
Trustees: Mr Max Bullough, Mr Geoffrey James Millard, Mr Vic Stenning, Mr Sohail Husain, Ms Claire Ryan
Income: £1,318,599 [2017]; £1,582,761 [2016]; £1,182,999 [2015]; £982,823 [2014]; £842,843 [2013]

De La Warr Pavilion Charitable Trust
Registered: 7 Nov 1997 *Employees:* 120 *Volunteers:* 28
Tel: 01424 229126 *Website:* dlwp.com
Activities: Education, training; arts, culture, heritage, science; environment, conservation, heritage
Address: De La Warr Pavilion, Marina, Bexhill on Sea, E Sussex, TN40 1DP
Trustees: Mr Ainsley Gill, Mr Stephen Williams, Mr Julian Bird, Mrs Judith West, Ms Jo Townshend, Ms Kate Adams, Mr Brian Kentfield, Mr Sean Albuquerque, Mr Amerjit Chohan, The Hon Lord Gregory Barker, Ms Sally-Ann Hart, Mr Lawrence Zeegan
Income: £2,849,534 [2017]; £3,044,666 [2016]; £2,552,760 [2015]; £2,457,481 [2014]; £2,242,768 [2013]

De Montfort University Students' Union Limited
Registered: 26 Oct 2010 *Employees:* 56 *Volunteers:* 1,500
Website: demontfortstudents.com
Activities: General charitable purposes; education, training; accommodation, housing; arts, culture, heritage, science; amateur sport; economic, community development, employment; human rights, religious or racial harmony, equality or diversity; recreation
Address: First Floor, Campus Centre Building, Mill Lane, Leicester, LE2 7DR
Trustees: Mr James Gardner, Mr Robert Paul Gofton, Mr Michael Kenneth David Clarke, Mr Carl King, Miss Holly Percival, Jessica Okwuonu, Daniel Czyzak, Mrs Danielle Amanda Gillett, Mr Ahtesham Mahmood, Mr Quinn Carter Franklin, Miss Keshana Davidson, Mollie Footitt, Derrick Mensah, Miss Laura Toher-Hindle
Income: £1,989,614 [2017]; £2,308,859 [2016]; £2,339,529 [2015]; £2,134,403 [2014]; £2,105,369 [2013]

Deafblind UK
Registered: 2 Mar 1990 *Employees:* 160 *Volunteers:* 272
Tel: 01733 358100 *Website:* deafblind.org.uk
Activities: General charitable purposes; education, training; advancement of health or saving of lives; disability; accommodation, housing
Address: Deafblind UK, Cygnet Road, Cygnet Park, Hampton, Peterborough, PE7 8FD
Trustees: Mr Asif Hussain, Ms Judie Martin-Jones, Ms Ruth Bridgeman, Mr Robert Jan Michiel Nolan, Mr John Greenhalgh, Mr Steve Wilson, Mr John Churcher
Income: £2,969,660 [2017]; £3,100,964 [2016]; £3,650,646 [2015]; £3,304,262 [2014]; £3,332,332 [2013]

Deafway
Registered: 31 Dec 2001 *Employees:* 70 *Volunteers:* 1
Tel: 01772 796461 *Website:* deafway.org.uk
Activities: Education, training; advancement of health or saving of lives; disability; prevention or relief of poverty; overseas aid, famine relief; accommodation, housing; arts, culture, heritage, science; amateur sport; environment, conservation, heritage; economic, community development, employment; human rights, religious or racial harmony, equality or diversity; recreation
Address: Deafway, Brockholes Brow, Preston, Lancs, PR1 5BB
Trustees: Mr Hadyn Gigg MBE, Mrs Hilda Frances Bentley, Mrs Claire Philomena Mingay, Mr Leonard Hodson, Mr John Ward, Mrs Elaine Colette Ridley, Mr Brian Stanley Donelly
Income: £2,076,891 [2017]; £1,982,676 [2016]; £2,083,631 [2015]; £1,992,996 [2014]; £1,916,415 [2013]

The Dean Close Foundation
Registered: 31 May 2001 *Employees:* 430 *Volunteers:* 17
Tel: 01242 258086 *Website:* deanclose.org.uk
Activities: Education, training
Address: Dean Close School, Shelburne Road, Cheltenham, Glos, GL51 6HE
Trustees: Rev Richard Coombs BSc MA, Mr Michael John Cartwright, Mrs Kathryn Ann Carden, Mrs Helen Stephanie Linford Daltry, Mrs Karen Riding, Mrs Sara Louise Hirst, Mr Richard Stuart Harman MA, Mr Charles Stephen Summers Drew MA, Mr Ian Andrew Duffin, Mr Matthew Paul Smith
Income: £21,448,697 [2016]; £18,288,784 [2015]; £16,637,424 [2014]; £16,012,394 [2013]

The Dean and Chapter of The Cathedral Church of Christ in Oxford of The Foundation of King Henry VIII
Registered: 17 Aug 2011 *Employees:* 415
Tel: 01865 276177 *Website:* chch.ox.ac.uk
Activities: Education, training; religious activities; arts, culture, heritage, science; environment, conservation, heritage
Address: Christ Church, St Aldates, Oxford, OX1 1DP
Trustees: Dr Stephen Darlington DMus FRCO, The Revd Canon Professor Martyn Percy, Professor Stefan Neubauer, The Revd Canon Edmund Newey, Professor Roger Davies, Ms Pauline Linieres-Hartley, Professor John Cartwright, Dr Anna Clark, Associate Professor Jason Davis, Associate Professor David Hine, Dr Belinda Jack, Associate Professor Lindsay Judson, Associate Professor Kevin McGerty, Associate Professor Sarah Mortimer, Professor Sarah Rowland-Jones, Mr Karl Sternberg, Associate Professor Richard Wade-Martins, Associate Professor Jennifer Yee, Associate Professor Richard Rutherford, Associate Professor Ian Watson, Mr James Lawrie, Associate Professor Peter McDonald, Professor Sir John Bell, Associate Professor Simon Dadson, Associate Professor Simon Newstead, Associate Professor Kayla King, Professor Jan Joosten, Dr Kalina Manova, Professor Alexander Kuo, Dr Alexander Vasudevan, Dr Yarin Gal, Professor Sir Timothy John Berners-Lee, Dr Per-Gunnar Martinsson, Dr James Allison, Professor Jonathan Cross, The Venerable Martin Gorick, Associate Professor Dirk Obbink, Associate Professor Mishtooni Bose, Professor Sarah Rosamund Irvine Foot, Professor Gregory Hutchinson, Canon Professor Nigel Biggar, Associate Professor Stephanie Cragg MA DPhil, Associate Professor Mark Edwards, Professor Sam Howison, Associate Professor Geraldine Johnson, Associate Professor Axel Kuhn, Dr Dominic Moran, Associate Professor Brian Parkinson, Associate Professor Joseph Schear, Associate Professor Emanuela Tandello-Cooper, Professor Guy Wilkinson, Associate Professor Brian Young, Professor Dirk Aarts, Associate Professor Edward Keene, Associate Professor Malcolm McCulloch, Associate Professor Edwin Simpson, Ms Liesl Elder, Professor Graham Ward, Dr Anna Camilleri, Professor Richard Barker, Professor Carol Harrison, Dr Katherine Lebow, Professor Mihaela Van Der Schaar, Dr David Alonso, Professor Petr Sedlacek, Dr Hayley Hooper, Professor Simon Hiscock
Income: £31,229,000 [2017]; £18,813,000 [2016]; £18,317,000 [2015]; £18,219,000 [2014]; £18,152,000 [2013]

Debate Mate Schools Limited
Registered: 15 Oct 2007 *Employees:* 16
Tel: 020 7922 8008 *Website:* debatemate.com
Activities: Education, training
Address: CAN Mezzanine, 32-36 Loman Street, Southwark, London, SE1 0EH
Trustees: Fiona Ann Edwards-Stuart, Mrs Britt Lintner, Ms Debra Judith Sara Thompson, Mr David John Haysey, Mr Rushabh Ranavat, Ms Sara Kate Geater, Mr Daniel Trotter
Income: £1,422,822 [2016]; £1,095,410 [2015]; £1,315,337 [2014]; £754,527 [2013]; £578,842 [2012]

Debenhams Foundation

Registered: 13 Jun 2012
Website: debenhamsplc.com
Activities: The advancement of health or saving of lives; prevention or relief of poverty
Address: Debenhams PLC, 10 Brock Street, London, NW1 3FG
Trustees: Mr Keith Markham, Mrs Sally Hyndman, Ms Patricia Valda Skinner
Income: £1,774,100 [2017]; £2,042,765 [2016]; £1,676,859 [2015]; £1,543,245 [2014]; £673,227 [2013]

Deeper Christian Life Ministry

Registered: 4 Dec 2012 *Employees:* 16 *Volunteers:* 50
Tel: 020 7223 6838 *Website:* dclmuk.org
Activities: General charitable purposes; education, training; prevention or relief of poverty; religious activities; economic, community development, employment
Address: 58 St John's Hill, Clapham Junction, London, SW11 1AD
Trustees: Mrs Mary Abike Okenwa, Mrs Monisola Moriyike Akinsanya, Pastor Paul Akowe, Mrs Esther Folashade Aduke Kumuyi, Dr William Folorunso Kumuyi
Income: £2,927,780 [2016]; £2,477,052 [2015]; £2,466,413 [2014]; £2,078,298 [2013]

Deeside House Educational Trust Limited

Registered: 13 Jun 1977 *Employees:* 105
Tel: 01244 332077 *Website:* abbeygatecollege.co.uk
Activities: Education, training
Address: Saighton Grange, Saighton, Chester, CH3 6EN
Trustees: Mr Andrew Frederick Grime, Mrs Felicity Ann Taylor, Mr Christopher John Swallow, Mrs Anna Marie Tiplady, Mrs Michelle Elizabeth Ellis, Mr Ian Peter Dutton, Mr Richard Andrew Flood, Canon Jeremy Neil James Christopher Dussek, Mr Brian Michael Dawson, Mr William Giles Osmond, Dr Simon Timothy Stanley, Miss Emma Alleyn Bunting, Mrs Joanne Marie Lucy
Income: £5,696,554 [2017]; £5,382,000 [2016]; £5,234,000 [2015]; £5,340,000 [2014]; £5,136,000 [2013]

Delapage Limited

Registered: 14 Jul 1978 *Employees:* 3
Activities: General charitable purposes; education, training; advancement of health or saving of lives; prevention or relief of poverty; religious activities
Address: The Ridgeway, London, NW11 8TB
Trustees: Mr Richard Kaufman, Mr David Goldberg, Mr Michael Ian Frenkel, Mr Allan Charles Becker, Mr Chagai Kahn
Income: £10,590,718 [2017]; £7,001,891 [2016]; £12,387,707 [2015]; £15,712,000 [2014]; £16,151,000 [2013]

Delphside Ltd

Registered: 15 Nov 1991 *Employees:* 58
Tel: 0151 431 0330 *Website:* avondale.org.uk
Activities: The advancement of health or saving of lives
Address: Avondale Mental Healthcare Centre, 11 Sandstone Drive, Whiston, Prescot, Merseyside, L35 7LS
Trustees: Mr Paul Harrison, Mr Stephen Atherton, Mr William Henry Devling, Mrs Joy Moore, Mr Victor Welsh, Mr Kenneth John Sanderson, Mr Christopher Andrew McNamara, Dr John Richard Ashcroft
Income: £1,817,452 [2017]; £1,940,618 [2016]; £1,896,779 [2015]; £1,767,803 [2014]; £1,647,762 [2013]

Delta-North Consett Limited

Registered: 11 Feb 1998 *Employees:* 43 *Volunteers:* 12
Tel: 01207 502680 *Website:* consettymca.org
Activities: Education, training; advancement of health or saving of lives; amateur sport; economic, community development, employment
Address: YMCA, Parliament Street, Consett, Co Durham, DH8 5DH
Trustees: Mr Derek Farthing, Mr Roy Reginald Tyerman, Rev Peter Sinclair, Mr Keith Gill, Mr Phillip Curran, Rev Valerie Shedden, Mr Alan Gallagher, Mrs Barbara Salkeld, Mr Alexander Watson, Miss Amanda Scott
Income: £1,459,101 [2017]; £1,286,958 [2016]; £1,190,634 [2015]; £1,400,891 [2014]; £1,035,448 [2013]

Demelza House Childrens Hospice

Registered: 21 Jul 1994 *Employees:* 276 *Volunteers:* 983
Website: demelza.org.uk
Activities: The advancement of health or saving of lives; disability
Address: Demelza Children's Hospice, Rook Lane, Bobbing, Sittingbourne, Kent, ME9 8DZ
Trustees: Mrs Rachel Sarah Phillips OBE DL, Dr Charles Unter, Mr Paul Richards, Mrs Rhiannedd Brooke, Ms Kate Mary Stephens, Mr Darren Charles Anstee, Mr Gerard Collins, Ms Bridget Skelton, Professor John Frederick Price, Mrs Eva Jolly, Mrs Susan Lowson
Income: £15,648,427 [2017]; £9,762,788 [2015]; £10,498,295 [2014]; £9,654,149 [2013]; £8,932,111 [2012]

Dementia Care

Registered: 3 Apr 1995 *Employees:* 130 *Volunteers:* 10
Tel: 0191 217 1323 *Website:* dementiacare.org.uk
Activities: Education, training; advancement of health or saving of lives; disability; prevention or relief of poverty; accommodation, housing
Address: Dementia Care Partnership, The Bradbury Centre, Darrell Street, Brunswick Village, Newcastle upon Tyne, NE13 7DS
Trustees: Mr Tim Chrisp, Mrs Jan Smith, Mike Nicholds, Paul Bell, Mr Martyn Ladds, Clare Abley, Mr John Lee, Mr Paul Taylor, Mr Steve Heminsley, Mr Ken Payne, Russell Ward, Moira Livingston
Income: £2,720,179 [2017]; £2,520,862 [2016]; £2,723,318 [2015]; £2,868,313 [2014]; £2,823,869 [2013]

Dementia Concern

Registered: 21 Oct 1992 *Employees:* 65 *Volunteers:* 25
Tel: 020 8568 4448 *Website:* dementiaconcern.co.uk
Activities: The advancement of health or saving of lives; disability; prevention or relief of poverty
Address: Dementia Concern, 223 Windmill Road, London, W5 4DJ
Trustees: Mrs Margaret Need, Mr Pierre Thomas, Mrs Elizabeth Rosemary Brown, Mrs Patricia Porter, Mrs Lillemor Christina McDerment, Mrs Julia Clements-Elliott, Kathryn Burns, Mrs Ann Billimoria, Ms Diane Jacqueline George
Income: £1,128,537 [2017]; £927,781 [2016]; £1,083,406 [2015]; £930,054 [2014]; £899,726 [2013]

Dementia UK

Registered: 12 Jul 1994 *Employees:* 66 *Volunteers:* 32
Tel: 020 7697 4160 *Website:* dementiauk.org
Activities: Education, training; advancement of health or saving of lives; disability
Address: Resource for London, 356 Holloway Road, London, N7 6PA
Trustees: Prof Hilary McCallion, Mr Merrick Charles Willis, Lady Barbara Judge, Mr Steven Clarke, Professor David Croisdale-Appleby, Mr Robert Orr, Ms Karen Patrick, Mr Stephen Jamieson
Income: £5,430,887 [2017]; £4,243,087 [2016]; £3,254,784 [2015]; £2,732,767 [2014]; £2,549,442 [2013]

Demos Limited
Registered: 11 Nov 1994 *Employees:* 18
Tel: 020 7367 4200 *Website:* demos.co.uk
Activities: Education, training
Address: Lloyd's Wharf, 2-3 Mill Street, London, SE1 2BD
Trustees: Nicholas Claydon, Mr Damian Leeson, Mr Ian Corfield, Neil Sherlock, Matt Nixon, Ms Alessandra Buonfino
Income: £1,183,425 [2016]; £969,023 [2015]; £1,221,456 [2014]; £1,222,672 [2013]; £1,473,499 [2012]

Denise Coates Foundation
Registered: 26 Sep 2012
Tel: 0845 600 0365
Activities: General charitable purposes; education, training; advancement of health or saving of lives; disability; prevention or relief of poverty; arts, culture, heritage, science; amateur sport; environment, conservation, heritage; economic, community development, employment; recreation
Address: Denise Coates Foundation, c/o RSM Tenon, Festival Way, Festival Park, Stoke on Trent, Staffs, ST1 5BB
Trustees: Ms Denise Coates, Mr Peter Coates, Mr James Edward White, Mr John Fitzgerald Coates, Mr Simon John Adlington, Mr Simon Hugh Galletley
Income: £1,586,556 [2017]; £21,529,786 [2016]; £11,135,150 [2015]; £105,500,000 [2014]; £1,155,000 [2013]

Denstone College Limited
Registered: 11 Mar 2004 *Employees:* 210 *Volunteers:* 15
Tel: 01889 594325 *Website:* denstonecollege.org
Activities: Education, training
Address: Denstone College, Denstone, Uttoxeter, Staffs, ST14 5HN
Trustees: Mr Andrew Coley, Mr Kevin Threlfall, Mr Barrie William Hinton MBA FCIPD MCIM, Mrs Jane Dickson BSc OT, Mr Malcolm F Coffin MA, Mrs Emma Jane Evans BA, Professor Nigel Thomas Ratcliffe BPharm PhD DMS FRPharmS CIBiol, Mr Simon Cash, Mr Christopher John Lewis, Mr David Thomas Brown ACA, Mrs Barbara Anne McNally-Young, Mrs Emily Louisa Bell MA, Mr Donald John Wilkinson MA MLitt FRSA
Income: £9,264,906 [2016]; £9,346,911 [2015]; £8,944,071 [2014]; £8,396,664 [2013]; £8,171,071 [2012]

Denville Hall 2012
Registered: 14 Sep 2012 *Employees:* 65
Tel: 01923 825843 *Website:* denvillehall.org.uk
Activities: The advancement of health or saving of lives; disability; accommodation, housing
Address: Denville Hall, 62 Ducks Hill Road, Northwood, Middlesex, HA6 2SB
Trustees: Joanna David, Geraldine James OBE, Derek Lamden, Hemlata Bountra, Mr Richard Langley Berry, Lalla Ward, Louisa Rix
Income: £2,450,444 [2017]; £2,434,885 [2016]; £2,095,156 [2015]; £2,125,362 [2014]; £963,488 [2013]

Depaul International
Registered: 21 Dec 2004 *Employees:* 776 *Volunteers:* 684
Tel: 020 3948 9872 *Website:* int.depaulcharity.org
Activities: General charitable purposes; education, training; advancement of health or saving of lives; prevention or relief of poverty; overseas aid, famine relief; accommodation, housing; economic, community development, employment
Address: Depaul International, St Vincent's Centre, Carlisle Place, London, SW1P 1NL
Trustees: Adrian Abel, John Darley, Ms Louise Casey, Father Vitaliy Novak, Kathryn Gerhardt, Sister Margaret Barrett DC, Ms Heidi Kruitwagen, Ms Patricia Jones, Mr Patrick Mark Silvester Litton, Rev Dennis Holtschneider
Income: £27,856,000 [2016]; £25,203,000 [2015]; £23,338,000 [2014]; £18,480,000 [2013]; £16,928,000 [2012]

Depaul UK
Registered: 14 Nov 1989 *Employees:* 227 *Volunteers:* 411
Tel: 020 7939 1220 *Website:* depaulcharity.org
Activities: Education, training; prevention or relief of poverty; accommodation, housing; amateur sport; economic, community development, employment
Address: Depaul UK, Sherborne House, 34 Decima Street, London, SE1 4QQ
Trustees: Rt Revd Mark Bryant, Suzanne McCarthy, Mr Peter Reynolds, Will Arnold-Baker, Katherine Hazel Porter, Mrs Helen O'Shea, Sister Mary Timmons, Rev Paul Roche, Michael Derek Jones, Michael Wells
Income: £12,444,000 [2016]; £11,314,000 [2015]; £9,445,000 [2014]; £7,044,634 [2013]; £6,354,494 [2012]

Derby County Community Trust
Registered: 8 Apr 2008 *Employees:* 59 *Volunteers:* 100
Tel: 01332 416140 *Website:* derbycountycommunitytrust.com
Activities: Education, training; advancement of health or saving of lives; disability; prevention or relief of poverty; amateur sport; economic, community development, employment
Address: Derby County Community Trust, 14 Pride Point Drive, Pride Park, Derby, DE24 8XB
Trustees: Ms Carol Ann Hart, Mr Edward Grant Pilkington, Mr Steve Hall, Mr Stephen Anthony Pearce, Mr Phillip Ellis, Mrs Tracy Harrison, Mr Peter Robert Sterling, Mr Leon Taylor, Ms Keeley Brown, Mrs Sharon Sewell, Mr Nick Britten
Income: £1,871,771 [2017]; £1,577,844 [2016]; £1,508,832 [2015]; £1,401,582 [2014]; £949,599 [2013]

The Derby Diocesan Board of Finance Limited
Registered: 17 Oct 1966 *Employees:* 40
Tel: 01332 388650 *Website:* derby.anglican.org
Activities: Religious activities
Address: The Derby Diocesan Board of Finance Ltd, Church House, Full Street, Derby, DE1 3DR
Trustees: The Rt Revd Dr A Redfern, Very Revd Dr Stephen Hance, Ven Carol Ann Coslett, Revd Dr Jason Ward, Mr M J Titterton, Revd Peter Davey, Canon Christine McMullen, Mr Peter Vincent, Revd Colin Pearson, Revd Jonathan Page, The Venerable Dr C Cunliffe, Mark Broomhead, John Gascoyne, Mr J Cooper, Mr Brian Parker, Mr Peter Collard, Madalaine Thomas-Goddard, Rt Revd Janet Elizabeth McFarlane, Christine Holmes-Elener, Hannah Grivell
Income: £11,030,281 [2016]; £9,509,760 [2015]; £8,568,471 [2014]; £8,604,829 [2013]; £5,775,905 [2012]

Derby Grammar School Trust Limited

Registered: 25 Nov 1992 *Employees:* 73
Tel: 01332 523331 *Website:* derbygrammar.org
Activities: Education, training
Address: Derby Grammar School, Rykneld Road, Littleover, Derby, DE23 4BX
Trustees: Mrs Elizabeth Anne Atkinson, Mr Simon Richardson, Mr Timothy George Wilson
Income: £3,313,191 [2017]; £3,088,556 [2016]; £3,023,535 [2015]; £2,977,530 [2014]; £3,045,877 [2013]

Derby High School Trust

Registered: 13 Jan 1992 *Employees:* 142
Website: derbyhigh.derby.sch.uk
Activities: Education, training
Address: Derby High School Trust Ltd, Hillsway, Littleover, Derby, DE23 3DT
Trustees: Mr Michael Hall, Mrs Rosemary Jane Hughes, Ms Hilary Barton, Veronica J Churchhouse, Mr Daniel Gerrard Clarkson, Mr Paul Rowley, Sarah Sandle, Dr Richard Jonathan Faleiro, Mrs Rosemary Williams, Mr Terry Ousley, Mrs Jane Paula Louise Bullivant, Rev Alicia Dring, Jack Atwal, Glenn Jones
Income: £6,344,078 [2017]; £5,891,931 [2016]; £5,298,110 [2015]; £5,306,975 [2014]; £5,278,478 [2013]

Derby Hospitals Charitable Trust

Registered: 11 Apr 1997 *Employees:* 8
Tel: 01332 785731 *Website:* derbyhospitalscharity.org.uk
Activities: Education, training; advancement of health or saving of lives; disability
Address: Royal Derby Hospital, Uttoxeter Road, Derby, DE22 3NE
Trustees: Derby Hospitals NHS Foundation Trust
Income: £2,261,000 [2017]; £2,124,000 [2016]; £3,798,000 [2015]; £2,050,000 [2014]; £1,539,000 [2013]

Derby Museums

Registered: 12 Nov 2012 *Employees:* 70 *Volunteers:* 914
Tel: 01332 641901 *Website:* derbymuseums.org
Activities: Arts, culture, heritage, science
Address: Derby Museums, Museum & Art Gallery, The Strand, Derby, DE1 1BS
Trustees: Mr Maxwell Arnold John Bradley Craven, Mr David Richard Ling, Mr Peter Howard Smith, Mrs Elizabeth Jane Fothergill, Professor Keith Andrew John McLay, Mrs Linda Joyce Sullivan, Miss Daisy Giuliano, Mr Charles Samuel Hanson, Alan Leslie Grimadell, Mrs Patricia Mary Coleman, Mr Raymond Harry Freeman, Mr Roger Merchant, Carrie McComb, Mrs Heather Broughton, Councillor Lucy Helen Care, Mrs Joanna West
Income: £2,810,431 [2017]; £2,094,983 [2016]; £2,255,630 [2015]; £2,062,644 [2014]

Derby Quad Limited

Registered: 24 Jul 2006 *Employees:* 53 *Volunteers:* 26
Tel: 01332 285444 *Website:* derbyquad.co.uk
Activities: Education, training; arts, culture, heritage, science
Address: Derby Quad Limited, Market Place, Derby, DE1 3AS
Trustees: Elizabeth Fothergill, Mr Nino John Simone, Charlotte Sexton, Mr Richard Mark Gerver, Judith Lamie, Ruth Dolby, Luke Earle, Jack Williams, Marsha O'Sullivan, Mr Gareth Singleton, Miss Beatrice Udeh, Mrs Camila Elizabeth Brown, Rebecca Goldsmith, Keith Donald, Sarah Loates
Income: £2,515,107 [2017]; £2,789,840 [2016]; £2,505,261 [2015]; £2,564,699 [2014]; £2,837,163 [2013]

Derbyshire Carers Association

Registered: 10 Jun 1997 *Employees:* 28 *Volunteers:* 25
Tel: 01773 833833 *Website:* derbyshirecarers.co.uk
Activities: Other charitable purposes
Address: 3 Park Road, Ripley, Derbys, DE5 3EF
Trustees: Ms Vicky Lyn Davison, Mr Keith Ian Gill, Mr Anthony Rowland Brookes, Dr Nohaid Ilyas, Mr Paul Edwin Lobley, Mrs Marilyn Hambly, Mr Guy Willetts, Mr Waldemar Julius Budzynski
Income: £1,133,012 [2017]; £999,779 [2016]; £1,227,548 [2015]; £1,127,947 [2014]; £1,005,895 [2013]

Derbyshire Districts Citizens Advice Bureau

Registered: 28 Oct 2002 *Employees:* 41 *Volunteers:* 203
Tel: 01629 832365 *Website:* ddcab.org.uk
Activities: General charitable purposes; education, training; advancement of health or saving of lives; disability; prevention or relief of poverty; accommodation, housing; economic, community development, employment; human rights, religious or racial harmony, equality or diversity
Address: DDCAB, Town Hall, Bank Road, Matlock, Derbys, DE4 3NN
Trustees: Carol Hart, Celia Cox, George Nicholson, Mr John Whitfield, Mr John Barker, Mr Anthony McIlveen, Elaine Michel, Alan Cox, Mr Andrew Powell, Mrs Jennifer Walker, Mr Digby Bown, Mrs Susan Campbell, Mrs Alexandra Newton
Income: £1,446,053 [2017]; £1,661,337 [2016]; £1,402,159 [2015]; £1,236,477 [2014]; £825,656 [2013]

The Derbyshire Environmental Trust Limited

Registered: 18 Aug 2006
Activities: Environment, conservation, heritage; economic, community development, employment
Address: Derbyshire Envrionmental Trust, County Hall, Matlock, Derbys, DE4 3AG
Trustees: Mr Barry Richard Joyce, Mr Ian James Leslie Cotter, Mr Anthony Vivian King, Mr Tony Richard Palmer, Mr Peter Francis Jones, Mr Eric Ashburner, Miss Jane Elizabeth Proctor, Ms Anna Badcock
Income: £1,274,685 [2016]; £1,207,771 [2015]; £1,894,251 [2014]; £1,570,835 [2013]; £1,682,213 [2012]

Derbyshire Wildlife Trust Limited

Registered: 31 Jan 1964 *Employees:* 46 *Volunteers:* 500
Tel: 01773 881188 *Website:* derbyshirewildlifetrust.org.uk
Activities: Environment, conservation, heritage
Address: Derbyshire Wildlife Trust, Sandy Hill, Main Street, Middleton, Matlock, Derbys, DE4 4LR
Trustees: Professor Paul Thomas Lynch, Dr Susan Jean Mayer, Daniel Cutts, Mrs Sarah Louise Lewis, Mr Nigel Peter Huish, Mr Peter John Bradbury, Anthony David Maurice Hams, Dr Huw Alun Edwards, Mr Charles Frederick Pickering, Jayn Sterland
Income: £1,757,000 [2017]; £1,940,000 [2016]; £1,574,304 [2015]; £1,368,260 [2014]; £2,077,659 [2013]

Derian House Childrens Hospice

Registered: 23 Oct 1991 *Employees:* 93 *Volunteers:* 94
Website: derianhouse.co.uk
Activities: The advancement of health or saving of lives; disability
Address: Derian House, Childrens Hospice, Chancery Road, Chorley, Lancs, PR7 1DH
Trustees: Mr Edward Hugh McClorry, Mrs Gretta Starks, Mrs Karen Swindley, Dr Ruth Christine O'Connor, Mr Mark Harris, Miss Helen Rotheram
Income: £3,658,916 [2016]; £4,258,689 [2015]; £3,561,273 [2014]; £3,473,514 [2013]; £4,225,921 [2012]

Derwen College
Registered: 7 Aug 2013 Employees: 373 Volunteers: 9
Tel: 01691 661234 Website: derwen.ac.uk
Activities: Education, training; disability; accommodation, housing
Address: Derwen College, Whittington Road, Gobowen, Oswestry, Salop, SY11 3JA
Trustees: Lord Lloyd Kenyon, Mr Andrew Hinchliff, Miss Irene Gull, Mr Michael Cowan, Mr Robert Macey, Mr John Morten, Mrs Kathleen Kimber, Mr David Paul Evison, Mr Peter Jones, Mr Jamie Ward, Councillor Paul Milner, Mrs Helen Owens
Income: £10,741,646 [2016]; £10,392,909 [2015]; £11,063,997 [2014]

Derwen Cymru Limited
Registered: 15 Feb 2001 Employees: 44
Tel: 01633 233802 Website: derwencymru.co.uk
Activities: Accommodation, housing
Address: Seren Group, Exchange House, The Old Post Office, High Street, Newport, NP20 1AA
Trustees: Pauline Card, Mr John Bader, Mr Glyn Jarvis, Mr John Evans, Ms Christine Rees, Mr William Langsford, Mr Roger Hoad, Mr Bill Gallagher, Ms Mary Edwards
Income: £5,679,000 [2017]; £5,856,000 [2016]; £5,193,000 [2015]; £2,244,000 [2014]; £1,981,000 [2013]

Derwent Rural Counselling Service
Registered: 1 Jul 2008 Employees: 27
Tel: 01629 812710 Website: drcs.org.uk
Activities: The advancement of health or saving of lives
Address: Newholme Hospital, Baslow Road, Bakewell, Derbys, DE45 1AD
Trustees: Professor Jack Yarwood, Mr Mark Serby, Miss Abby Jodi Worsnip, Mrs Nicola Jayne Adams, Mrs Lindsay Jane Sayers
Income: £1,359,570 [2017]; £887,274 [2016]; £723,854 [2015]; £401,448 [2014]; £115,886 [2013]

Derwentside Hospice Care Foundation
Registered: 12 Jul 1988 Employees: 86 Volunteers: 110
Tel: 01207 529224 Website: willow-burn.co.uk
Activities: The advancement of health or saving of lives
Address: Willow Burn Hospice, Maiden Law Hospital, Lanchester, Co Durham, DH7 0QN
Trustees: Mark Davies, Nigel Cook, Mrs Anne Britton, Paul Jackson, Mr Mark McArdle, Mrs Anita Burdon
Income: £1,741,667 [2017]; £1,109,150 [2016]; £1,120,996 [2015]; £2,043,566 [2014]; £1,240,872 [2013]

Design Council
Registered: 13 Oct 1976 Employees: 48
Website: designcouncil.org.uk
Activities: General charitable purposes; education, training; advancement of health or saving of lives; disability; prevention or relief of poverty; accommodation, housing; arts, culture, heritage, science; environment, conservation, heritage; economic, community development, employment; armed forces, emergency service efficiency; recreation; other charitable purposes
Address: Angel Building, 407 St John Street, London, EC1V 4AB
Trustees: Mr Sandeep Dwesar, Ms Annika Small, Mr Kieron Boyle, Mr Steve Pearce, Mr Tim Stonor, Mr Dale Harrow, Ms Pam Alexander, Professor Anne Boddington, Mr Terry Tyrrell, Mr Martin Darbyshire, Dr Andrew Mackintosh
Income: £9,670,947 [2017]; £7,062,532 [2016]; £7,928,000 [2015]; £6,312,000 [2014]; £8,855,000 [2013]

The Design Museum
Registered: 10 Jan 1989 Employees: 101 Volunteers: 77
Tel: 07896 358405 Website: designmuseum.org
Activities: Education, training; arts, culture, heritage, science
Address: 224-238 Kensington High Street, London, W8 6AG
Trustees: Professor Sir Christopher Frayling FCSD FRSA FRIBA, Mr Sebastian Orby Conran, Sir John Kevin Hegarty, Mr Rolf Sachs, Lady Jillian Rosemary Ritblat, Mr Julian Andrew Vogel, Mr Hugh Gerrard Devlin, Mr Asif Khan, Mr Nicholas James Douglas Bull, Sir Terence Orby Conran, Luqman Arnold, Ms Anya Hindmarch MBE, Mr Johannes P Huth, Mr Charles Rifkind, Mr Zdenek Bakala
Income: £12,939,609 [2017]; £13,847,581 [2016]; £8,016,122 [2015]; £24,972,954 [2014]; £10,185,704 [2013]

The Design and Technology Association
Registered: 8 May 1997 Employees: 16
Tel: 01789 473907 Website: data.org.uk
Activities: Education, training
Address: 16 Wellesbourne House, Walton Road, Wellesbourne, Warwicks, CV35 9JB
Trustees: Mr Christopher Lamb, Mr Mark Peter Williams, Mrs Lesley Morris, Professor Kay Stables, Miss Alison Hardy, Mr Jason Robert Simeon FCIPD FLPI, Ms Nicola Ralston, Mr Andrew Churchill, Mr Andrew Midgley, Mrs Jane Admans-Palmer, Miss Rebecca Topps, Mr Paul David Calver, Ms Llinos Jonathan, Dr Andrew Norwood
Income: £1,008,976 [2016]; £1,038,403 [2015]; £1,280,528 [2014]; £780,252 [2013]; £1,321,883 [2012]

Designability Charity Limited
Registered: 11 Jul 1968 Employees: 21 Volunteers: 3
Tel: 01225 824103 Website: designability.org.uk
Activities: The advancement of health or saving of lives; disability
Address: 7A Cockhill, Trowbridge, Wilts, BA14 9BG
Trustees: Professor Anthony William Miles, Professor Paul Olomolaiye, Mr Steve Tanner, Mr Gordon Richardson, Mr John Bishop, Mr Gavin Alexander Maggs, Professor Mark Arthur Tooley, Mr Mark Humphriss, Professor Ben James Hicks, Dr Elizabeth Anne White, Prof Christos Vasilakis, Ms Libby Gawith
Income: £1,952,924 [2017]; £1,034,064 [2016]; £842,621 [2015]; £781,064 [2014]; £835,707 [2013]

Developing Health and Independence
Registered: 10 Nov 1999 Employees: 143 Volunteers: 110
Website: dhi-online.org.uk
Activities: The prevention or relief of poverty; accommodation, housing; other charitable purposes
Address: Developing Health & Independence, 15a-16 Milsom Street, Bath, BA1 1DE
Trustees: Mr David Peter Guy, Ms Sarah Davies, David Ollendorff, Mr William Shaw, Katharine Hegarty, Sarah Talbot-Williams
Income: £4,516,758 [2017]; £4,758,557 [2016]; £5,188,998 [2015]; £4,661,159 [2014]; £3,844,646 [2013]

Developing Initiatives for Support in the Community Limited

Registered: 5 Nov 1984 *Employees:* 546 *Volunteers:* 74
Tel: 01325 731160 *Website:* disc-vol.org.uk
Activities: Education, training; disability; accommodation, housing; economic, community development, employment; other charitable purposes
Address: Developing Initiatives for Support, Sapphire House, IES Centre, Horndale Avenue, Aycliffe Business Park, Newton Aycliffe, Co Durham, DL5 6DS
Trustees: Mr Michael William Treasure, Mr Christopher Ranulph George Matthews-M, Mr Ian Dewhirst, Mrs Joyce Drummond-Hill, Mr James Black, Ms Vivienne Jane Holmes, Professor Roger Smith, Mr Craig Alistair Peterson
Income: £26,188,168 [2017]; £24,191,201 [2016]; £18,225,707 [2015]; £16,212,669 [2014]; £17,334,940 [2013]

Development Through Challenge

Registered: 24 May 1988 *Employees:* 34
Tel: 020 8980 0289 *Website:* mileendwall.org.uk
Activities: Education, training; amateur sport
Address: Mile End Climbing Wall, Haverfield Road, Bow, London, E3 5BE
Trustees: Salim Hafejee, Matthew Teague, Mrs Brenda Lorraine Taggart, Mr Martin Soulsby, Hiiren Joshi, Mr Damian Jaques, Mr Kevin Murphy, Mr Tim Nash
Income: £1,119,305 [2016]; £1,005,110 [2015]; £1,026,208 [2014]; £876,538 [2013]; £757,688 [2012]

Alexander Devine Children's Cancer Trust

Registered: 25 Apr 2007 *Employees:* 12 *Volunteers:* 150
Tel: 0845 055 8276 *Website:* alexanderdevine.org
Activities: The advancement of health or saving of lives
Address: 122 Tinkers Lane, Windsor, Berks, SL4 4LP
Trustees: Mrs Fiona Christine Devine, Dr Andrew Webster Boon, Mr Fraser Guy Silvey, Mr John Devine MBA BA Hons CMgr MCMI, Mrs Helen Johnson
Income: £2,039,869 [2017]; £2,386,259 [2016]; £1,831,473 [2015]; £1,185,171 [2014]; £798,161 [2013]

Devon Air Ambulance Trust

Registered: 29 Oct 1999 *Employees:* 75 *Volunteers:* 518
Tel: 01392 466666 *Website:* daat.org
Activities: The advancement of health or saving of lives
Address: Unit 5 Sandpiper Court, Harrington Lane, Exeter, EX4 8NS
Trustees: Mr Mark Russell Williams, Mr Stephen James Tyrrell, Ms Rachel Margaret Short, Mr Anthony John Hudson, Mr Barry Cole, Mr Richard David Plunkett, Mr Anthony Robert Noon, Mrs Margaret Davies
Income: £8,167,000 [2016]; £6,865,000 [2015]; £6,235,000 [2014]; £6,315,000 [2013]; £5,412,000 [2012]

Devon Community Foundation

Registered: 9 Sep 1996 *Employees:* 10 *Volunteers:* 70
Tel: 01884 235887 *Website:* devoncf.com
Activities: General charitable purposes; education, training; advancement of health or saving of lives; disability; prevention or relief of poverty; accommodation, housing; arts, culture, heritage, science; amateur sport; economic, community development, employment; armed forces, emergency service efficiency; human rights, religious or racial harmony, equality or diversity
Address: The Factory, Leat Street, Tiverton, Devon, EX16 5LL
Trustees: Mr Steve Hindley CBE, Mr Nigel Arnold, Mrs Christine Helen Allison, Rt Reverend Robert Atwell Bishop of Exeter, Mr Peter Holden, Mr Stewart Wallis, Ms Caroline Marks, Mr James Maxwell Griffiths Cross, Mrs Caroline Harlow, Mr Edward Burnand, Mrs Sally Wace, Mr Jeremy Colson
Income: £1,134,948 [2017]; £679,565 [2016]; £1,812,176 [2015]; £1,385,419 [2014]; £1,149,468 [2013]

Devon County Agricultural Association

Registered: 25 Oct 1985 *Employees:* 17 *Volunteers:* 300
Tel: 01392 446000 *Website:* devoncountyshow.co.uk
Activities: Education, training; arts, culture, heritage, science; amateur sport; animals; environment, conservation, heritage; recreation
Address: Westpoint, Clyst St Mary, Exeter, Devon, EX5 1DJ
Trustees: Mr Nigel Lindsay-Fynn, Mr M W Huxtable, David E Parish, Mr B Drake, Mr E A Darke, Mr J A T Hodge, Mr M H Batting, Mr P F J Force, Mr Richard Harvey, Mr T K Larcombe, Mrs V F Gundry, Mrs N Lindsay-Fynn, Sir John Cave Bt DL, Mr David Verney, Mrs Judith Mary Kauntze, Mr John Lee, Mr N A Maxwell-Lawford DL OBE, Major Ranulf Courtauld Rayner, Mr Jas Brasier, Mr Graham Cheriton, Mrs Deborah Custance-Baker, The Hon Mrs Mej D'Erlanger, Mrs Janet Mary Flinn, Mr Aj Hutchinson, Mr Ben Michael Moore, Mr Alan Henry Palmer, Mr Andrew Henry Richards, Mr Da Scoble, Mr Bernard Tom Stamp, Brig Rs Tailyour, Mr Rd Thomas, Mr Wa Uglow, Mr Ben Wadsworth, Mrs Gt Phillips, Mrs Am Woollard, Mr Mark Joseph Weekes, Mr Andrew Gray, Mrs Jacqueline Stamp, Mr Ian Parish, Mrs Elizabeth Roper, Mr Michael Dymond, Mrs Mary Quicke MBE, Mr Peter Endacott, Mr Peter Reed, Mrs Carol Plumstead, Mr Lewis Banfield, Mr David Perriment, Mr Philip Wolfgang, Mr Peter Dunning, Gordon Trump, Mr A E Cook, Mr C C Morgan, Mr H G Dart, Mr J W May, Mr N G Gilbert JP, Mr P W S Brockman, Mr T E Broom, Mr Thomas Leslie Hammett, Mrs J Kingdon, Sir I Amory Bt DL, Sir Simon Day, Mr M H Retallick, Sir Richard Peek Bt, Mr Henry Robert Parkin, Mr Richard Coley, Mr Pj Broom, Mr Gh Bush CB, Mr Jr Cummings, Mr WJ Daw, Mr Re Ellis, Mr Ja Haddy, Mr Jl Maunder JP DL, Mr Rm Northcott, Mrs Ja Penny, Mr Jcn Robinson, Mr Jp Short, Mr Str Stevens, Mr Lj Taverner, Mr Gh Tully, Mr Frederick John Verney, Mr Christopher Wise, Michael Townsend, Mr Paul Kingdon, Mr Nicholas Davey, Mr Neil Parish MP, Mr David Darke, Mr Peter Owen-Pawson, Mr Nicholas Burrington, Mrs Sarah Hammett, Mr Steven Philip Hodder, Mr Ralph Rayner, Mr Hugo Swire MP, Mrs Maunder Felicity Sarah, Mr Paul Coates, Mr Tim Russ
Income: £2,289,309 [2016]; £2,275,729 [2015]; £2,042,956 [2014]; £2,338,648 [2013]; £2,351,172 [2012]

Devon Wildlife Trust
Registered: 3 Jan 1963 *Employees:* 82 *Volunteers:* 1,500
Tel: 01392 279244 *Website:* devonwildlifetrust.org
Activities: Education, training; environment, conservation, heritage
Address: Cricklepit Mill, Commercial Road, Exeter, Devon, EX2 4AB
Trustees: Mr Andrew Charles John Cooper, Mr John Whetman, Ms Gail McKenzie, Mr Charles Edward Dixon, Miss Suzanne Goodfellow, Dr Michael Edward Moser, Commodore Andrew Paul Burns OBE, Mrs Gaynor Dorothy Castle, Professor Victoria Denise Pope, Mr Nigel Wilfred Rendle, Mr Geoffrey Wallace Hearnden, Mr Francis Vernon Clarke, Mr Trevor James Smale, Mr Richard Clack, Mr Barry Perkins Henwood, Miss Rebecca Anna Broad, Mrs Helen Nathanson
Income: £4,290,203 [2017]; £3,930,806 [2016]; £3,759,619 [2015]; £3,781,365 [2014]; £4,434,404 [2013]

Devon and Cornwall Autistic Community Trust
Registered: 30 Sep 1993 *Employees:* 468
Tel: 01326 371000 *Website:* spectrumasd.org
Activities: Education, training; advancement of health or saving of lives; disability; accommodation, housing; economic, community development, employment
Address: Sterling Court, Truro Hill, Penryn, Cornwall, TR10 8DB
Trustees: Mr Trevor Charles Grose, Mrs Barbara Moore, Mr Donald Harvey, Mrs Yvonne Marie Nelson, Mr Nicholas Simon Tostdevine, Mr Julian Giles Pykett, Mr Lionel Roger James
Income: £10,867,459 [2017]; £10,888,051 [2016]; £11,083,680 [2015]; £11,312,071 [2014]; £10,140,787 [2013]

Devon and Exeter Spastics Society
Registered: 15 May 1991 *Employees:* 62 *Volunteers:* 36
Tel: 01392 468333 *Website:* vranchhouse.org
Activities: Education, training; advancement of health or saving of lives; disability
Address: Devon & Exeter Spastics Society, Vranch House, Pinhoe Road, Exeter, EX4 8AD
Trustees: Mr Anthony Griffin, Mrs Constance Ann Ballman, Mrs Jill Morgan, Mr Clive Rendle, Miss Penelope Anne Hale, Mrs Julia Chantal Tolman-May, Mrs Catherine Tailford, Mr Sidney Torlot, Mrs Sheila Mathieson, Mr Andrew Philip Barge, Mr Douglas Barnes, Mr William Richards
Income: £1,908,325 [2017]; £1,743,047 [2016]; £1,630,594 [2015]; £1,631,559 [2014]; £1,620,685 [2013]

Devonport and Western Counties Association for Promoting The General Welfare of the Blind
Registered: 13 Apr 1962 *Employees:* 85
Tel: 01752 771710 *Website:* torrhome.org.uk
Activities: General charitable purposes; advancement of health or saving of lives; disability; accommodation, housing
Address: Torr Home for the Blind, The Drive, Plymouth, PL3 5SY
Trustees: Mr Neil Major, Mr John Roberts, Mr John Martin Modley, Mrs Susan Elizabeth Stidever, Mrs Elizabeth Bosworth
Income: £2,695,739 [2016]; £2,347,113 [2015]; £2,146,765 [2014]; £2,127,477 [2013]; £1,703,261 [2012]

Dewis Centre for Independent Living
Registered: 26 Jun 2003 *Employees:* 53 *Volunteers:* 3
Tel: 01443 827930 *Website:* dewiscil.org.uk
Activities: Disability
Address: Amber House, Upper Boat Business Park, Pontypridd, Mid Glamorgan, CF37 5BP
Trustees: Mrs Mairwen Jones, Paul Flower, Miss Lynda Jenkins, Mr Michael Williams, Mrs Elizabeth Ardden Guha, Mrs Julie Thomas, Mrs Dot Davey, Mrs Julie Haycox, Mr William Terence Evans, Mrs Helen Ruth Leigh
Income: £1,226,469 [2017]; £1,333,469 [2016]; £1,056,957 [2015]; £741,954 [2014]; £818,154 [2013]

Dhammakaya International Society of The United Kingdom
Registered: 26 May 2004 *Employees:* 12 *Volunteers:* 50
Tel: 07901 750915 *Website:* dhammakaya.org.uk
Activities: General charitable purposes; education, training; religious activities
Address: 2 Brushfield Way, Knaphill, Woking, Surrey, GU21 2TG
Trustees: Mr Paul Joseph Trafford, Phra Nicholas Thanissaro, Phra Sonthaya Wandee, Phra Pichit Choompolpaisal, Mr Theanchai Chitvicheankul, Phra Wairot Treenet, Phra Veera Vingvorn
Income: £1,290,029 [2016]; £1,108,222 [2015]; £1,134,558 [2014]; £2,529,279 [2013]; £320,864 [2012]

Diabetes Research & Wellness Foundation
Registered: 21 Jul 1998 *Employees:* 8 *Volunteers:* 24
Tel: 023 9263 7808 *Website:* drwf.org.uk
Activities: The advancement of health or saving of lives; other charitable purposes
Address: DRWF, Office 010 & 012, Northney Marina, Hayling Island, Hants, PO11 0NH
Trustees: Mrs Valerie Hussey, Mr John Alahouzos Jnr, Mrs Rae-Marie Lawson, Mr Jeffrey Harab, Mr Michael Gretschel
Income: £5,123,885 [2016]; £4,217,993 [2015]; £4,033,567 [2014]; £5,445,921 [2013]; £4,859,368 [2012]

Diagrama Foundation-Psychosocial Intervention
Registered: 12 Mar 2009 *Employees:* 143
Tel: 01634 545000 *Website:* diagramafoundation.org.uk
Activities: Education, training; advancement of health or saving of lives; disability; overseas aid, famine relief; economic, community development, employment
Address: 5th Floor, Anchorage House, High Street, Chatham, Kent, ME4 4LE
Trustees: Mr Francisco Legaz Cervantes, Ms Maureen Walby, Ms Elisa Moraga Sarrion
Income: £5,642,992 [2017]; £5,379,811 [2016]; £1,963,659 [2015]; £1,130,021 [2014]; £1,353,476 [2013]

Diana Award
Registered: 18 Dec 2006 *Employees:* 18 *Volunteers:* 6,000
Tel: 020 7628 7499 *Website:* diana-award.org.uk
Activities: General charitable purposes; education, training; economic, community development, employment; other charitable purposes
Address: The Diana Award, 120 Moorgate, London, EC2M 6UR
Trustees: Mr Wayne Bulpitt, Mr Michael Abiodun Olatokun, Mrs Kate Hardcastle, Mr Martin George Pilgrim, Miss Emily Murrell, Mr Peter Avis
Income: £1,054,465 [2017]; £943,442 [2016]; £734,571 [2015]; £722,431 [2014]; £412,360 [2013]

The Dickens House and The Dickens House Fund

Registered: 6 Feb 1963 *Employees:* 17 *Volunteers:* 100
Website: dickensmuseum.com
Activities: Education, training; arts, culture, heritage, science
Address: Charles Dickens Museum, 48 Doughty Street, London, WC1N 2LX
Trustees: The Charles Dickens Museum Limited
Income: £1,044,603 [2017]; £1,411,360 [2015]; £793,088 [2014]; £953,104 [2013]; £2,363,768 [2012]

Digartref Cyf

Registered: 22 Jul 1999 *Employees:* 41 *Volunteers:* 15
Tel: 01407 761653 *Website:* digartrefynysmon.co.uk
Activities: Education, training; accommodation, housing
Address: Digartref Cyf, Unit 1-5 Holyhead Enterprise, Workshops, Kingsland Road, Holyhead, Anglesey, LL65 2HY
Trustees: Mr Dafydd Jones, Mrs Marilyn Blackburn, Mrs Barbara Hughes, Mr Keith Alan Griffiths, Mr Stephen Richard Jones, Mrs Julia Morgan, Mr Graham Walker
Income: £1,099,078 [2017]; £1,081,214 [2016]; £1,140,517 [2015]; £1,122,947 [2014]; £793,202 [2013]

The Diocese in Europe Board of Finance

Registered: 7 Dec 1966 *Employees:* 12 *Volunteers:* 1
Tel: 020 7898 1155 *Website:* europe.anglican.org
Activities: Religious activities
Address: Diocese in Europe, 14 Tufton Street, London, SW1P 3QZ
Trustees: The Right Reverend Dr David Hamid, Rev Canon Simon James Tyndall, Mr Michael Hart, Rev David Waller, Venerable Colin Williams, Revd Canon Geoffrey Johnston, Mr David Coulston, The Rt Revd Dr Robert Innes, Ven Vickie Sims, Rev Canon Deborah Mary Rollins Flach, Rev Canon Philip Ian Mounstephen, Mr Paul Tillbrook, Mrs Thelma Ann Turner, Mr David Bean, The Revd Canon Simon Henry Martin Godfrey, Mr David John Gowan CMG, Mr Nigel Rowley, Ven Colin Henry Williams, The Very Reverend Dr John Paddock, Mrs Mary Talbot, Rev Anne Lowen, Rev Tuomas Makipaa, Ven Dr Paul Vrolijk, Rev Dr Frank Michael Hegedus, Rev Richard Bromley, Mrs Joan Berry, Mrs Miranda Kopetzky, Mr David White
Income: £1,005,697 [2016]; £955,094 [2015]; £921,571 [2014]; £962,191 [2013]; £791,879 [2012]

Diocese of Hexham and Newcastle

Registered: 18 Aug 2011 *Employees:* 165 *Volunteers:* 8,000
Tel: 0191 243 3300 *Website:* rcdhn.org.uk
Activities: Education, training; prevention or relief of poverty; overseas aid, famine relief; religious activities; human rights, religious or racial harmony, equality or diversity
Address: St Cuthbert's House, West Road, Newcastle upon Tyne, NE15 7PY
Trustees: Rev Seamus Cunningham, Rev Peter Leighton, Rev Simon Lerche, Rev Jeffrey John Dodds, Mr Rory Deane, Mr Matthew Boyle, Rev Martin Stempczyk, Mrs Maureen Anne Bates, Rev Colm Martin Hayden, Rev Ian David Hoskins, Mr Thomas Harrison
Income: £11,644,748 [2017]; £12,224,185 [2016]; £22,192,172 [2015]; £21,916,870 [2014]; £21,170,141 [2013]

Direct Help & Advice Ltd.

Registered: 8 Jan 1999 *Employees:* 31 *Volunteers:* 21
Tel: 01332 287850 *Website:* dhadvice.org
Activities: General charitable purposes; education, training; prevention or relief of poverty; economic, community development, employment
Address: c/o Mrs Jean Seaman, Direct Help & Advice, Phoenix Street, Derby, DE1 2ER
Trustees: Mr Alan Cartwright, Mr Paul Phillips, Ms Jean E Douglas, Miss Rachel Susan Morris, Mr John Scruton, Mrs Jean Seaman, Mr Andrew Knighton, Mr Andrew William Deighton, Mr Gavin Freeman
Income: £1,095,407 [2017]; £989,064 [2016]; £1,171,444 [2015]; £1,133,506 [2014]; £1,422,979 [2013]

The Directory of Social Change

Registered: 8 Dec 1988 *Employees:* 40 *Volunteers:* 4
Tel: 020 7697 4036 *Website:* dsc.org.uk
Activities: Education, training
Address: Directory of Social Change, 352 Holloway Road, London, N7 6PA
Trustees: Caron Bradshaw, Alistair Mortimer, Mrs Phyllida Valentine Alice Perrett, Ms Emily Hughes, Mr Andrew Edward Garnett, Lesley Thornley, William Butler, Dr Andrew Purkis
Income: £2,493,541 [2016]; £2,360,737 [2015]; £2,506,075 [2014]; £2,500,724 [2013]; £2,392,801 [2012]

The Disabilities Trust

Registered: 23 Jan 1989 *Employees:* 1,813 *Volunteers:* 1
Tel: 01444 239123 *Website:* thedtgroup.org
Activities: Education, training; disability; accommodation, housing
Address: The Disabilities Trust, 32 Market Place, The Martlets, Burgess Hill, W Sussex, RH15 9NP
Trustees: Dr Paula Bernadette Dobrowolski, Mr Stephen William Howell, Ms Sara Livadeas, Mrs Eileen Christina Jackman, Mrs Christine Yorath, Mr Mark Keith Rowe, Mr Roger Anthony Hoyle, Mr Michael Green, Dr Caroline Susan Drugan, Mr Christopher Philipsborn
Income: £57,093,000 [2017]; £60,901,357 [2016]; £56,002,533 [2015]; £50,676,021 [2014]; £46,519,895 [2013]

Disability Action Yorkshire

Registered: 22 Feb 1995 *Employees:* 38 *Volunteers:* 5
Tel: 01423 855410 *Website:* disabilityactionyorkshire.org.uk
Activities: Education, training; disability; accommodation, housing
Address: Unit 14a, Disability Action Yorkshire, 14 Hornbeam Park Oval, Harrogate, N Yorks, HG2 8RB
Trustees: Mr Howard Marshall, Mr Noel Moriarty, Mr Neil Revely, Mr Andrew Christopher Glen, Mrs Susan Elizabeth Grace Dr, Mr Michael Barry Patterson, Mr Andrew Newton, Mrs Alison Craggs
Income: £1,159,262 [2017]; £1,130,318 [2016]; £1,304,202 [2015]; £1,428,546 [2014]; £1,494,232 [2013]

Disability Challengers

Registered: 19 Dec 2002 *Employees:* 444 *Volunteers:* 117
Tel: 01483 579390 *Website:* disability-challengers.org
Activities: Disability; recreation
Address: Holly Lea, The Avenue, Grayshott, Hindhead, Surrey, GU26 6LA
Trustees: Mrs Sally Marie Dewar, Mr Graham Seddon, Mrs Gail Victoria Bedding, Mr Richard Andrew Rose, Miss Rachel Bartholomeusz, Mr Phil Heasman, Mr Robert Pickles, Mrs Ann Christine Baty, Mr David Robert Clinton, Mrs Elizabeth Jorden, Anele Griessel, Dr Mike Walker
Income: £3,165,475 [2016]; £2,873,941 [2015]; £2,742,201 [2014]; £3,345,148 [2013]; £2,328,157 [2012]

Disability Direct
Registered: 13 Mar 2000 *Employees:* 59 *Volunteers:* 30
Tel: 01332 404040 *Website:* disabilitydirect.com
Activities: The advancement of health or saving of lives; disability; prevention or relief of poverty; economic, community development, employment; human rights, religious or racial harmony, equality or diversity
Address: Disability Direct, 20 Royal Scot Road, Pride Park, Derby, DE24 8AJ
Trustees: Mr Robin Wood, Mr Steve Rigby, Miss Emma Renshaw, Mr George Coppen, Mr David Moss, Mr Michael Watts, Jonathan Smale
Income: £1,280,067 [2017]; £1,233,264 [2016]; £1,177,543 [2015]; £1,218,916 [2014]; £1,325,460 [2013]

The Disability Resource Centre
Registered: 27 Oct 1994 *Employees:* 57 *Volunteers:* 15
Tel: 01582 470900 *Website:* drcbeds.org.uk
Activities: Education, training; advancement of health or saving of lives; disability; prevention or relief of poverty
Address: The Disability Resource Centre, Unit 1A Humphrys Road, Woodside Estate, Dunstable, Beds, LU5 4TP
Trustees: Jill Pick, Miss Nadia Sara Deadman, Mr Andrew Giles Holcroft Buckley, Ms Sandra Brown, Mr Francis Gordon John Beck, Mrs Catherine Anne Ross, Mr Terence Brian Garthwaite, Dr Kay Taylor, Mrs Baerbel Dennis, Mr Robert Graham
Income: £1,807,685 [2017]; £1,975,752 [2016]; £1,986,889 [2015]; £1,782,739 [2014]; £1,595,987 [2013]

Disability Rights UK
Registered: 26 Oct 2010 *Employees:* 25 *Volunteers:* 32
Tel: 020 7250 8190 *Website:* disabilityrightsuk.org
Activities: Education, training; disability; prevention or relief of poverty; amateur sport; economic, community development, employment; human rights, religious or racial harmony, equality or diversity
Address: CAN Mezzanine, 49-51 East Road, London, N1 6AH
Trustees: Mr Ian Charles Loynes, Professor Michael Bromwich PhD, Mr Kush Kanodia, Martin Stevens, Ms Sophie Colchester Maziere, Ms Lucy Aliband, Martin Smith, Mr Roger Berry, Rob Trent, Daniel Holt, Frances Noel Hasler, Ms Jacqueline Winstanley
Income: £1,949,353 [2017]; £1,646,138 [2016]; £3,154,606 [2015]; £1,696,936 [2014]; £2,300,475 [2013]

Disabled Living
Registered: 7 Oct 1963 *Employees:* 23 *Volunteers:* 50
Tel: 0161 607 8200 *Website:* disabledliving.co.uk
Activities: General charitable purposes; education, training; disability; economic, community development, employment
Address: Burrows House, 10 Priestley Road, Wardley Industrial Estate, Worsley, Manchester, M28 2LY
Trustees: Mr Alan Norton, Mr Philip John Downs MBE, Mr Dean Styger, Mrs Sandra Mary Barrett, Paula Brown, Frederick Booth, Gerry Yeung, Gary Owen
Income: £1,186,853 [2017]; £1,386,521 [2016]; £1,079,368 [2015]; £1,216,489 [2014]; £963,330 [2013]

Disablement Association of Barking and Dagenham
Registered: 14 Jul 1993 *Employees:* 145 *Volunteers:* 15
Tel: 020 8592 8603 *Website:* dabd.org.uk
Activities: Education, training; disability; prevention or relief of poverty; economic, community development, employment; other charitable purposes
Address: DABD (UK), Pembroke Gardens, Dagenham, Essex, RM10 7YP
Trustees: Ms Emma Adams, Mr Keith Robert Mottram, Mr Adekunle Akande Trustee, Mr Peter Snell, Miss Raksha Patel Trustee
Income: £2,982,032 [2017]; £3,088,499 [2016]; £3,176,261 [2015]; £2,962,405 [2014]; £2,962,405 [2013]

Disasters Emergency Committee
Registered: 4 Jun 1997 *Employees:* 19 *Volunteers:* 35
Tel: 020 7255 9101 *Website:* dec.org.uk
Activities: Overseas aid, famine relief
Address: 43 Chalton Street, London, NW1 1DU
Trustees: Mr Charles Geoffrey Stewart-Smith, Mr Mark Ian Goldring, Mr Andrew James Green, Ms Clare Thompson, Ms Rose Caldwell, Mr Clive Jones CBE, Mr Laurie Lee, Baroness Helene Valerie Hayman, Mr Christopher Roles, Mr Nigel Harris, Ms Sue Clare Inglish, Mr Chris Bain, Mr Michael John Adamson, Mr Girish Menon, Mr Kevin Watkins, Ms Tanya Barron, Mr Richard Graham Tait, Mr Kenneth Phimister Burnett, Mr Timothy Pilkington, Amanda Khozi Mukwashi, Mr Nasereldin Ahmed Haghamed
Income: £54,053,000 [2017]; £57,570,000 [2016]; £40,658,000 [2015]; £70,028,000 [2014]; £6,384,000 [2013]

The Ditcham Park School Charity Association
Registered: 12 Aug 1982 *Employees:* 55 *Volunteers:* 10
Tel: 01730 825659 *Website:* ditchampark.com
Activities: Education, training
Address: Ditcham Park School Charity Association, Ditcham, Petersfield, Hants, GU31 5RN
Trustees: Sandy Dale, Mrs Mary Downes, Mrs Catherine Tyrrell, Mrs Peggy Field, Mr Steven Howarth Howarth, Mr Christopher Pickett, Mr Douglas Taylor, Mr Gethin Hughes, Mrs Sally Barber, Mrs Rebecca Parrett
Income: £4,244,661 [2016]; £4,078,312 [2015]; £4,002,375 [2014]; £3,838,700 [2013]; £3,715,237 [2012]

Diverse Abilities Plus Ltd.
Registered: 30 Apr 1981 *Employees:* 422 *Volunteers:* 122
Tel: 01202 718266 *Website:* diverseabilities.org.uk
Activities: Education, training; disability; accommodation, housing
Address: Diverse Abilities Plus, Unit C, Acorn Business Park, Ling Road, Poole, Dorset, BH12 4NZ
Trustees: Mr Martin Davies, Mr John Peter, Mr John Smith, Mr Richard Bavister, Mr Gary Leedale Knight, Mr Andrew Jeremy Harrop, Mr John Kennar, Mr Nigel Still, Mr Geoff Ridgway
Income: £6,767,628 [2017]; £6,151,382 [2016]; £6,175,151 [2015]; £5,851,450 [2014]; £5,150,774 [2013]

Diverse Excellence Cymru
Registered: 31 May 2011 *Employees:* 58 *Volunteers:* 10
Tel: 029 2036 8888 *Website:* diversecymru.org.uk
Activities: General charitable purposes; education, training; disability; prevention or relief of poverty; economic, community development, employment
Address: 307-315 Cowbridge Road East, Cardiff, CF5 1JD
Trustees: Donna Sibanda, Joel Williams, Mr Abyd Quinn Aziz, Ms Sarah Evans, Ms June Francois, Mervyn Harris, Angela Toby, Ms Rebecca Ballard, Ms Helen Susannah Dodoo
Income: £1,699,925 [2017]; £1,471,444 [2016]; £1,326,340 [2015]; £1,209,392 [2014]; £845,343 [2013]

The Divine Healing Mission
Registered: 1 Jul 1963 *Employees:* 20 *Volunteers:* 5
Tel: 01424 446488 *Website:* crowhursthealing.org.uk
Activities: Religious activities
Address: Sellens French, 93 Bohemia Road, St Leonards on Sea, E Sussex, TN37 6RJ
Trustees: Mr James Ian Douglas-Beveridge, Mr Paul Raynor, Mr Nigel John Thonger, Ms Vivien Lorely Drakes, Rev Denis Richard Smith
Income: £1,198,069 [2017]; £498,445 [2016]; £497,957 [2015]; £471,599 [2014]; £532,793 [2013]

Doctors of the World UK
Registered: 13 Jan 1998 *Employees:* 18 *Volunteers:* 212
Tel: 020 7167 5789 *Website:* doctorsoftheworld.org.uk
Activities: General charitable purposes; advancement of health or saving of lives; overseas aid, famine relief; other charitable purposes
Address: Doctors of the World UK, 1 Canada Square, London, E14 5AA
Trustees: Dr Peter Gough, Mr Tim Dudderidge, Dr Lisa Harrod-Rothwell, Ms Jill Whitehouse, Mr Serge Lipski, Dr Hannah Theodorou
Income: £3,136,246 [2016]; £8,119,803 [2015]; £7,036,156 [2014]; £3,291,080 [2013]; £1,021,700 [2012]

Dodderhill School
Registered: 1 Feb 1967 *Employees:* 62 *Volunteers:* 2
Tel: 01905 778290 *Website:* dodderhill.co.uk
Activities: Education, training
Address: Dodderhill School, Crutch Lane, Elmbridge, Droitwich, Worcs, WR9 0BE
Trustees: Mrs Janet Elizabeth Lowe, Mrs Wendy Pearl Haines, Mr John Michael Allchin, Mrs Alison Hines, Mr Martin Jordan Adams, Mrs Mary Jane Cross, Mrs Katherine Mary Wormington, Mr Alvin David Robinson, Mr Jonathan Ricketts, Rev Laura Jane Handy, Dr Sarah Bowater
Income: £2,072,969 [2017]; £2,094,464 [2016]; £1,912,556 [2015]; £1,865,186 [2014]; £1,950,331 [2013]

Dogs Trust Worldwide
Registered: 15 Jun 2016
Tel: 020 7837 0006 *Website:* dogstrustworldwide.com
Activities: Education, training; animals
Address: Clarissa Baldwin House, 17 Wakley Street, London, EC1V 7RQ
Trustees: Mr Philip Giles Daubeny, Miss Joanne Howard, Mr Graeme Robertson, Mr Stephen Paget Langton, Mr Phil White
Income: £3,668,379 [2017]; £102,039 [2016]

Dogs Trust
Registered: 7 Jun 1963 *Employees:* 1,110 *Volunteers:* 2,877
Tel: 020 7837 0006 *Website:* dogstrust.org.uk
Activities: Education, training; animals
Address: 17 Wakley Street, London, EC1V 7RQ
Trustees: Dogs Trust Trustee Ltd
Income: £106,446,000 [2017]; £98,395,000 [2016]; £89,894,000 [2015]; £84,743,000 [2014]; £76,560,000 [2013]

Dogs for Good
Registered: 16 Jul 2002 *Employees:* 64 *Volunteers:* 447
Tel: 01295 252600 *Website:* dogsforgood.org
Activities: Education, training; disability; animals
Address: The Frances Hay Centre, Blacklocks Hill, Banbury, Oxon, OX17 2BS
Trustees: Mr John Keith Starley, Mr John Sewell-Rutter, Mr John Michael Farrell, Mr Ross Tiffin, Ms Patricia Gilliam Thompson, Ms Ginette Ruth Bryant
Income: £4,232,040 [2017]; £3,053,092 [2016]; £3,239,191 [2015]; £2,482,387 [2014]; £2,850,934 [2013]

The Dohnavur Fellowship Corporation
Registered: 8 Apr 1964 *Employees:* 1
Website: thedohnavurfellowship.org
Activities: Education, training; advancement of health or saving of lives; disability; prevention or relief of poverty; overseas aid, famine relief; accommodation, housing; religious activities
Address: 80 Windmill Road, Brentford, Middlesex, TW8 0QH
Trustees: Rev Tarie Carlyon, Dr Rosie Saunders, Mr Ralph Manning, Suzanne Wavre, Dr Jacky Woolcock, Mrs Stella Gill, Miss Pauline Anderson
Income: £1,153,762 [2017]; £195,511 [2016]; £241,841 [2015]; £218,060 [2014]; £194,284 [2013]

Dollond Charitable Trust
Registered: 13 Jan 1986
Activities: General charitable purposes; education, training; advancement of health or saving of lives; disability; prevention or relief of poverty; religious activities
Address: 3rd Floor, Hathaway House, Popes Drive, Finchley, London, N3 1QF
Trustees: Mr Adrian Dollond, Mr Brian Dollond, Mrs Melissa Ruth Dollond, Mr Jeffrey Milston, Mrs Rina Dollond
Income: £1,502,236 [2017]; £3,180,740 [2016]; £1,345,536 [2015]; £1,828,524 [2014]; £1,078,384 [2013]

Dolphin School Trust
Registered: 16 Dec 2011 *Employees:* 49
Tel: 020 8543 4421 *Website:* dolphinschool.org.uk
Activities: General charitable purposes; education, training; religious activities
Address: Kwsr & Co, 136 Merton High Street, London, SW19 1BA
Trustees: Anthony Buckley, Dr Esther Chew, Mr Gordon Corera, Mr Paul Lufkin, Mrs Emma Keeling, Mr Matthew Goldschmeid, Mrs Petronella Van Der Vliet, Mrs Jo Watling
Income: £2,996,211 [2017]; £2,875,389 [2016]; £2,701,901 [2015]; £2,432,512 [2014]; £2,055,091 [2013]

The Dolphin Square Charitable Foundation
Registered: 17 Jun 2005 *Employees:* 12
Website: dolphinliving.com
Activities: Accommodation, housing
Address: Dolphin Square Charitable Foundation, 11 Belgrave Road, London, SW1V 1RB
Trustees: The Dolphin Square Charitable Trustee
Income: £19,009,242 [2017]; £3,258,742 [2016]; £10,909,515 [2015]; £31,788,210 [2014]; £3,366,032 [2013]

Domestic Violence Intervention Project
Registered: 20 Nov 2000 *Employees:* 40 *Volunteers:* 10
Tel: 020 7928 4620 *Website:* dvip.org
Activities: Other charitable purposes
Address: 65 Aspenlea Road, London, W6 8LH
Trustees: Mr Andrew Cottrell, Ms Ellen Storrar, Ms Ruth Fenby Taylor, Ms Karen Bailey
Income: £1,843,501 [2017]; £2,020,513 [2016]; £1,779,487 [2015]; £1,652,747 [2014]; £1,363,503 [2013]

Dominican Sisters (Third Order) Congregation of Newcastle Natal (Established at Bushey Heath, Herts)
Registered: 28 Apr 1964 *Employees:* 2
Tel: 020 8950 6065 *Website:* dominicansisters.co.uk
Activities: General charitable purposes; education, training; prevention or relief of poverty; religious activities; economic, community development, employment; other charitable purposes
Address: Rosary Priory Convent, 93 Elstree Road, Bushey Heath, Bushey, Herts, WD23 4EE
Trustees: St Rose of Lima Association Ltd
Income: £2,202,522 [2016]; £4,428,000 [2015]; £12,218,873 [2014]; £9,155,331 [2013]; £9,534,217 [2012]

Donating Charity Limited
Registered: 12 May 1966
Tel: 020 8455 0100
Activities: General charitable purposes; education, training; advancement of health or saving of lives; disability; prevention or relief of poverty; religious activities
Address: 121 Princes Park Avenue, London, NW11 0JS
Trustees: Mr Jeffrey Cooper, Mr Jacob Schimmel
Income: £1,507,710 [2017]; £1,310,811 [2016]; £1,096,527 [2015]; £1,010,581 [2014]; £1,173,251 [2013]

Doncaster Culture and Leisure Trust
Registered: 28 Apr 2004 *Employees:* 556
Tel: 01302 370777 *Website:* dclt.co.uk
Activities: General charitable purposes; education, training; advancement of health or saving of lives; amateur sport; economic, community development, employment
Address: The Dome, Doncaster Leisure Park, Bawtry Road, Doncaster, S Yorks, DN4 7PD
Trustees: Mr Peter Gleadhall, Andrew Russell Burden Esq, Mr Richard Byrne, Mr Marek Gutowski, Doncaster Council, Bobbie Roberts, Trevor Jones Esq, Mr Garry John Aylott, Miss Rebecca Leam
Income: £11,097,613 [2017]; £11,460,287 [2016]; £10,834,244 [2015]; £10,523,250 [2014]; £10,094,871 [2013]

Doncaster Deaf Trust
Registered: 15 Aug 2001 *Employees:* 248 *Volunteers:* 5
Tel: 01302 386750 *Website:* ddt-deaf.co.uk
Activities: Education, training; disability
Address: Doncaster Deaf Trust, Leger Way, Doncaster, S Yorks, DN2 6AY
Trustees: Bobbie Roberts, Mr Richard John Hazell, Mr John Edwin Hope, Mr Chris Mangle
Income: £8,013,000 [2017]; £7,543,000 [2016]; £7,119,000 [2015]; £6,700,000 [2014]; £6,170,000 [2013]

Doncaster Performance Venue Limited
Registered: 3 Aug 2012 *Volunteers:* 3
Tel: 0310 230 3950 *Website:* castindoncaster.com
Activities: Arts, culture, heritage, science; recreation
Address: Cast, Waterdale, Doncaster, S Yorks, DN1 3BU
Trustees: Mr Andy Carver, Marg Hunt, Mr Richard Byrne, Bobbie Roberts, Mrs Maureen Sydney, Mr Andrew Burden, Bill Mordue, Mr Kevin Spence, Mrs Joan Beck, Mr David Oldroyd, Mr Daniel Fell
Income: £1,937,145 [2017]; £1,972,284 [2016]; £1,941,642 [2015]; £1,964,807 [2014]; £232,203 [2013]

Doncaster Refurnish
Registered: 28 Feb 2007 *Employees:* 53 *Volunteers:* 71
Tel: 01302 337606 *Website:* refurnish.co.uk
Activities: Education, training; prevention or relief of poverty; environment, conservation, heritage; economic, community development, employment
Address: 19 Ivanhoe Way, Doncaster, S Yorks, DN5 8EA
Trustees: The Venerable Robert Aidan Fitzharris, Councillor Eva Theresa Hughes, Mr James McLaughlin, Mr Glen Barry Barnes, Mrs Jayne Evans, Mr David Middlemass
Income: £1,297,239 [2016]; £11,166,012 [2015]; £995,830 [2014]; £877,724 [2013]; £951,142 [2012]

Doncaster Rotherham and District Motor Trades
Registered: 10 Feb 1987 *Employees:* 31
Tel: 01302 832831 *Website:* doncastergta.co.uk
Activities: Education, training
Address: Doncaster Motor Trades, Unit 1 Meadowview Industrial Estate, Rands Lane, Armthorpe, Doncaster, S Yorks, DN3 3DY
Trustees: Mr Michael David Wainwright, Mr Geoffrey Michael Thompson FIMI CEng, Mr Andy Stockham, Mr Geoffrey Charles Harmer, Mr Peter Coggon, Mr Malcolm Stead
Income: £1,686,952 [2017]; £1,762,965 [2016]; £1,903,015 [2015]; £1,799,204 [2014]; £1,919,265 [2013]

Donisthorpe Hall
Registered: 28 Sep 1999 *Employees:* 215 *Volunteers:* 10
Tel: 0113 218 5186 *Website:* donisthorpehall.org
Activities: The advancement of health or saving of lives; accommodation, housing
Address: Donisthorpe Hall, Shadwell Lane, Leeds, LS17 6AW
Trustees: Mr Andrew Brown MBE, Dr Robert Jeremy Ross, Mrs Sue Cawthray, Mr Howard Sidney Cohen, Mr Ashley Robert Cohen
Income: £9,138,941 [2016]; £6,629,630 [2014]; £6,369,539 [2013]; £5,578,690 [2012]

The Donkey Sanctuary
Registered: 26 Mar 1973 *Employees:* 702 *Volunteers:* 547
Tel: 01395 578222 *Website:* thedonkeysanctuary.org.uk
Activities: Education, training; disability; animals
Address: Donkey Sanctuary, Slade House Farm, Sidmouth, Devon, EX10 0NU
Trustees: The Donkey Sanctuary Trustee Ltd
Income: £38,343,000 [2016]; £35,058,000 [2015]; £32,435,000 [2014]; £30,722,000 [2013]; £32,221,000 [2012]

Donmar Warehouse Projects Limited

Registered: 6 May 1982 *Employees:* 39 *Volunteers:* 9
Website: donmarwarehouse.com
Activities: Arts, culture, heritage, science
Address: 3 Dryden Street, London, WC2E 9NA
Trustees: Mr Peter Williams, Mr Ed Richards, Mrs Diane Henry Lepart, The Lord Browne of Madingley Edmund John Phillip Browne, David Kosse, Susan Boster, Josie Rourke, Mr Roger Wingate, Mr David Parkhill, Mr Simon Meadon, Lady Hannah Lowy Mitchell, William Eccleshare, Kate Pakenham
Income: £8,174,603 [2017]; £6,591,894 [2016]; £6,018,027 [2015]; £6,419,068 [2014]; £5,785,005 [2013]

The Donna Louise Trust

Registered: 20 May 1999 *Employees:* 98 *Volunteers:* 200
Website: donnalouisetrust.org
Activities: The advancement of health or saving of lives; disability
Address: The Donna Louise Trust, 1 Grace Road, Stoke on Trent, Staffs, ST4 8FN
Trustees: James Stuart Rushton, Mrs Karen Jane Gladman, Mr Jonathon May, Mr David Gladman, Mrs Helen Louise Inwood, Mrs Susan Cheryl Read, Miss Lynne Ingram, Ms Valerie Ann Wood, Mrs Amanda Elisabeth Harrison
Income: £3,268,440 [2017]; £3,350,632 [2016]; £2,729,334 [2015]; £2,850,337 [2014]; £2,301,226 [2013]

Donnington Hospital

Registered: 29 Aug 1963 *Employees:* 7
Tel: 01635 35255 *Website:* donningtonhospital.com
Activities: The prevention or relief of poverty; accommodation, housing
Address: James Cowper LLP, Mill House, Overbridge Square, Hambridge Lane, Newbury, Berks, RG14 5UX
Trustees: Dr Paul Edgar Bryant, Mr Piers Hartley Russell, Mr Rupert Francis Hartley Russell, Rev Marion Wood, Mr Guy Ropner, Dr Belinda Jane Bruce Gardner, Mr Robin Derek Hartley Russell, Mrs Marina Bronwen Lund, Rev William Hunter Smart
Income: £1,043,004 [2016]; £1,019,707 [2015]; £925,223 [2014]; £849,009 [2013]; £709,049 [2012]

Donnington House Care Home Limited

Registered: 11 Jul 2003 *Employees:* 65
Tel: 01243 783883 *Website:* donningtonhouse.co.uk
Activities: Accommodation, housing
Address: 12 Birdham Road, Chichester, W Sussex, PO19 8TE
Trustees: Mr John Hugh Shipstone Shippam JP DL, Mrs Valerie Barbara Bevis, Mr Richard Doman, Dr Greg Tamlyn, Mrs Anna Hutchings, Jill Evershed Martin, Mrs Anne Elizabeth Bareham, Mr Tony Hembling, Mrs Catherine Angel
Income: £1,377,659 [2017]; £1,233,993 [2016]; £1,155,222 [2015]; £1,088,901 [2014]; £1,042,142 [2013]

Dontchev Foundation

Registered: 16 Apr 2004
Tel: 020 7318 1180
Activities: Education, training
Address: Tulloch & Co, 4 Hill Street, London, W1J 5NE
Trustees: Mr Anthony Smith CBE, Mr Sasho Georguiev Dontchev, Mr Iavor Veselinov Manoilov, Mr Plamen Donchev
Income: £5,331,204 [2016]; £30,547,371 [2013]; £57,215 [2012]

Doorstep of Hull

Registered: 8 Jan 1987 *Employees:* 20
Tel: 01482 345006 *Website:* doorstep.org.uk
Activities: Accommodation, housing
Address: Doorstep, 151 Fairfax Avenue, Hull, HU5 4QZ
Trustees: Bill Stevens, Mr Dave Elliott
Income: £1,856,951 [2017]; £1,856,013 [2016]; £1,799,645 [2015]; £2,127,739 [2014]; £2,081,471 [2013]

The Dorothy House Foundation Limited

Registered: 14 Jun 1978 *Employees:* 260 *Volunteers:* 1,100
Tel: 01225 722988 *Website:* dorothyhouse.org.uk
Activities: Education, training; advancement of health or saving of lives
Address: Dorothy House, Hospice Care, Winsley, Bradford on Avon, Wilts, BA15 2LE
Trustees: Mrs Diane Hall, Mrs Kate Tompkins, Mr Ian Lafferty, Mr Tim Stacey, Mr David Cavaliero, Charlotte Parkin, Ms Francesca Thompson, Mr John Waldron, Rev Josette Crane, Ms Christine Davis, Mr Brian Mansfield, Mr Warren Reid, Dr Simon Burrell, Dr Mark Hunt
Income: £12,959,738 [2017]; £11,072,811 [2016]; £10,782,371 [2015]; £10,376,919 [2014]; £8,386,158 [2013]

Dorset Advocacy

Registered: 18 Feb 2003 *Employees:* 39 *Volunteers:* 65
Tel: 01305 251033 *Website:* dorsetadvocacy.co.uk
Activities: Disability
Address: Unit 13-15 Jubilee Court, Paceycombe Way, Poundbury, Dorchester, DT1 3AE
Trustees: John Smith, Mrs Barbara O'Brien, Mrs Frances Stevens, Mr Richard Timothy Wills, Graham Willetts, Mr Christopher Kippax, Ms Susan Jane Oliver
Income: £1,037,335 [2017]; £988,452 [2016]; £720,378 [2015]; £668,253 [2014]; £457,213 [2013]

The Dorset Natural History and Archaeological Society

Registered: 14 May 1997 *Employees:* 19 *Volunteers:* 200
Tel: 01305 756821 *Website:* dorsetcountymuseum.org
Activities: General charitable purposes; education, training; arts, culture, heritage, science; environment, conservation, heritage
Address: Dorset County Museum, 66 High West Street, Dorchester, DT1 1XA
Trustees: Mr Jeremy James Richard Pope, Mr Maxwell Graham Hebditch, Mrs Jill Margaret Minchin, Dr Jonathan Murden, Mr Peter Foster, Mrs Sarah Welton, Dr Andrew James Fleet, Mr John Hilton, Dr Clare Elizabeth Randall, Professor John Patrick Vaughan, Mr David John Norris
Income: £1,052,812 [2017]; £921,996 [2016]; £539,256 [2015]; £472,298 [2014]; £763,307 [2013]

Dorset Wildlife Trust

Registered: 7 Jul 1961 *Employees:* 59 *Volunteers:* 3,659
Tel: 01305 264620 *Website:* dorsetwildlifetrust.org.uk
Activities: General charitable purposes; education, training; environment, conservation, heritage
Address: Dorset Wildlife Trust, Brooklands Farm, Forston, Dorchester, DT2 7AA
Trustees: Jim White, Mr John Gaye, Mrs Jo Davies MBE, Professor Jeremy Ambler Thomas OBE, Mr Kelvyn Derrick, Mr Giles Pugh, Mr John Roland Raymond, Tony Bates, Prof Nigel Webb, Anne Wheatcroft, Mr Alick Simmons, Mark Kibblewhite
Income: £3,301,000 [2017]; £3,704,235 [2016]; £4,038,987 [2015]; £4,800,662 [2014]; £4,732,741 [2013]

The Dorset and Somerset Air Ambulance Charity
Registered: 20 Dec 1999 *Employees:* 13 *Volunteers:* 123
Tel: 01823 669604 *Website:* dsairambulance.co.uk
Activities: The advancement of health or saving of lives
Address: Landacre House, Castle Road, Chelston Business Park, Wellington, Somerset, TA21 9JQ
Trustees: Dr Gillian Bryce, Mr Richard Kennedy, Mr Michael Gallagher, Mrs Anna Phillips, Miss Hannah Nobbs, Mr Michael Laver, Mrs Glenys Taylor, Mr Richard Popper, Mr David Senior AFC JP
Income: £7,615,257 [2017]; £7,489,752 [2016]; £7,128,764 [2015]; £6,431,345 [2014]; £4,834,506 [2013]

Doteveryone
Registered: 24 Apr 2012 *Employees:* 8
Tel: 020 7257 9397 *Website:* doteveryone.org.uk
Activities: General charitable purposes; education, training; economic, community development, employment
Address: New Wing, Somerset House, Strand, London, WC2R 1LA
Trustees: Martha Lane Fox, Tom Wright, Richard A Lackmann, Diana Harding, Ms Sabrina Clarke
Income: £1,949,955 [2017]; £1,522,957 [2016]; £1,277,233 [2015]; £1,393,939 [2014]; £1,059,731 [2013]

Double Impact Services
Registered: 17 Jan 2011 *Employees:* 53 *Volunteers:* 40
Tel: 0115 824 0366 *Website:* doubleimpact.org.uk
Activities: Education, training; advancement of health or saving of lives; economic, community development, employment; other charitable purposes
Address: Double Impact Services Ltd, 22-24 Friar Lane, Nottingham, NG1 6DQ
Trustees: David Newmarch, Will Wakefield, Mr Paul Pearson, Mr Steve Little, Dr Ira Unell, Mrs Karen Glover, Ms Sandra Moya Scott
Income: £1,305,932 [2017]; £1,307,091 [2016]; £1,462,561 [2015]; £1,773,783 [2014]; £1,204,328 [2013]

The Henry Doubleday Research Association
Registered: 8 Jan 1988 *Employees:* 53 *Volunteers:* 800
Tel: 024 7630 3517 *Website:* gardenorganic.org.uk
Activities: Education, training; environment, conservation, heritage
Address: Garden Organic, Ryton Organic Gardens, Wolston Lane, Ryton on Dunsmore, Coventry, Warwicks, CV8 3LG
Trustees: Miss Elaine Margaret Shaw, Ms Judith Wayne, Mrs Naomi L'estrange, Mr Steve Howell, Mr Kevin James Wissett-Warner, Ms Amanda Jane Sandford, Dr Margaret Lynn Eyre, Ms Philippa Lyons MS, Mr Andrew Collins, Mr Adam Alexander, Mrs Marjan Bartlett-Freriks
Income: £2,599,654 [2016]; £2,710,356 [2015]; £2,795,744 [2014]; £2,900,377 [2013]; £2,560,539 [2012]

Douglas Macmillan Hospice
Registered: 18 Sep 1998 *Employees:* 390 *Volunteers:* 974
Tel: 01782 344300 *Website:* dmhospice.org.uk
Activities: The advancement of health or saving of lives
Address: Douglas Macmillan Hospice, Barlaston Road, Stoke on Trent, Staffs, ST3 3NZ
Trustees: Mr David Platt, Mrs Jessica Neyt, Mr Andrew Gordon Millward, Mr Kerry Brown, Dr Jane Sissons, Mr Daryl Harvey, Mrs S P Evans, Dr Edward Francis Slade, Ms Patricia Margaret Rathbone, Ms Laura Jean Rowley, Mrs Joanne Miller
Income: £10,613,634 [2017]; £11,347,745 [2016]; £11,577,173 [2015]; £10,666,020 [2014]; £10,788,195 [2013]

Dove House Hospice Limited
Registered: 18 Sep 1980 *Employees:* 244 *Volunteers:* 1,200
Tel: 01482 784343 *Website:* dovehouse.org.uk
Activities: Education, training; advancement of health or saving of lives; disability
Address: Dove House Hospice, Chamberlain Road, Hull, HU8 8DH
Trustees: Mr Philip Harry Daniels, Mr Anthony Bernard Rowland, Dr Rajarshi Roy, Mr James Doyle, Mr Francis John Grove Dunning, Mrs Helen Marshall, Mr David Smith, Mrs Janet Weatherill, Mrs Penelope Joan Stephenson, Mrs Margaret Butt, Mr Daniel Robert Harman Dr
Income: £6,998,884 [2017]; £6,848,219 [2016]; £7,433,501 [2015]; £7,284,882 [2014]; £6,786,486 [2013]

Dover College
Registered: 23 Jun 1964 *Employees:* 132 *Volunteers:* 20
Tel: 01304 244551 *Website:* dovercollege.org.uk
Activities: Education, training
Address: Dover College, Crescent House, Effingham Crescent, Dover, CT17 9RH
Trustees: Michael Goodridge, Rt Revd Trevor Willmott, James Ryeland, Mr James Gatehouse, Ms Karen Rogers, Mr Nathan Harris, Mr Michael Rutherford, Paul Brown, Mr Richard Foxwell, Claire Scholfield-Myers, Adam Walliker, Michael Dakers, Tony Lancaster, Mr Sunil Devalia, Mr Graham Conlon, Mr David Rolls, Mr Jonathan Hodge, Mr Paul Tapsell, Mr John Sinclair, Deborah Gispan, Dominic Spencer
Income: £5,220,504 [2017]; £5,128,720 [2016]; £4,638,569 [2015]; £4,907,006 [2014]; £5,109,728 [2013]

The Dover Counselling Centre
Registered: 20 Feb 1989 *Employees:* 10 *Volunteers:* 1
Tel: 01304 204123 *Website:* dovercc.org.uk
Activities: General charitable purposes; education, training
Address: Dover Counselling Centre, 9 St James Street, Dover, CT16 1QD
Trustees: Ms Penelope Svoronos Brown, Mrs Nita Elizabeth Grace Hodgkinson, Dr David Nigel Reeve Foley, Dr William Trevor Moses, Ms Sally Anne Spicer
Income: £1,500,693 [2016]; £1,149,575 [2015]; £928,283 [2014]; £491,212 [2013]; £264,203 [2012]

Dover Sholem Community Trust
Registered: 29 Oct 2010
Tel: 020 8800 6599
Activities: Education, training; disability; prevention or relief of poverty
Address: 122 Kyverdale Road, London, N16 6PR
Trustees: Mr Haim Dov Francoz, Mr Mordechai Jaakov Wind, Mr Shlomo Fink
Income: £1,482,545 [2017]; £947,279 [2016]; £723,025 [2015]; £637,200 [2014]; £99,983 [2013]

Downe House Foundation
Registered: 18 Nov 2014
Tel: 01635 200286 *Website:* downehouse.net
Activities: Education, training
Address: Downe House School, Downe House, Hermitage Road, Cold Ash, Thatcham, Berks, RG18 9JJ
Trustees: Nicholas Michael Hornby, James Anthony Christopher Hanbury, Philippa Blane Armitage, Fru Hazlitt, Nigel Alec Fenn
Income: £1,325,000 [2016]; £1,403,000 [2015]

Downe House School
Registered: 5 Nov 1992 *Employees:* 276
Tel: 01635 200286 *Website:* downehouse.net
Activities: Education, training
Address: Downe House School, Downe House, Hermitage Road, Cold Ash, Thatcham, Berks, RG18 9JJ
Trustees: Mr Mark Ridley, Ms Anne Frances Hazlitt, Mrs Joanna Grant Peterkin, Dr Christopher O'Kane, Mr Christopher Radford, Ms Veryan Jane Exelby, Mr Simon Creedy-Smith, Mr Matthew Kirk, Mrs Fiona Holmes, Mr Nicholas Hornby, Lady Caroline Cunningham, Mr Joseph Smith
Income: £20,509,000 [2017]; £20,824,000 [2016]; £20,416,000 [2015]; £19,212,000 [2014]; £17,870,000 [2013]

Downing College in the University of Cambridge
Registered: 12 Aug 2010 *Employees:* 185
Website: dow.cam.ac.uk
Activities: Education, training
Address: Downing College, Cambridge, CB2 1DQ
Trustees: Dr Susan Elizabeth Lintott, Dr Zoe Helen Barber, Dr Michael Trevor Bravo, Prof Nicholas Coleman, Prof David John Feldman, Prof Christopher Allim Haniff, Prof Adam Noel Ledgeway, Dr Paul Christopher Millett, Dr Natalia Mora-Sitja, Dr Catherine Lynette Phillips, Prof Ian Gareth Roberts, Dr Jay Theodore Stock, Prof Graham John Virgo, Dr Guy Barnett Williams, Dr Marta Morgado Correia, Dr Alicia Hinarejos Parga, Dr Tim Burton, Dr Kamran Yunus, Professor Geoffrey Grimmett, Dr Brendan Plant, Dr Harriet Groom, Dr Andrew Holding, Dr Priyanka Joshi, Dr Zoe Kourtzi, Prof William Mark Adams, Dr Paul Derek Barker, Prof Trevor William Clyne, Dr Sophia Demoulini, Miss Amy Catherine Goymour, Dr Ian James, Dr Jie Li, Dr Amy Louise Milton, Dr William O'Neill, Dr David Robert Pratt, Dr Brigitte Steger, Dr Marcus Tomalin, Prof David John Wales, Dr Liping Xu, The Revd Dr Keith Eyeons, Dr Robert Harle, Dr Ewan Jones, Dr Sarah Kennedy, Dr John Richer, Dr Monica Moreno Figueroa, Dr Ruth Ellen Nisbet, Dr Edward Cavanagh, Dr Michael Crisp, Dr Nick Rawlinson
Income: £11,563,045 [2017]; £13,904,357 [2016]; £10,668,874 [2015]; £10,156,000 [2014]; £9,885,000 [2013]

The Downs School (Charlton House) Limited
Registered: 6 Dec 1972 *Employees:* 95 *Volunteers:* 10
Tel: 01275 852008 *Website:* thedownsschool.co.uk
Activities: Education, training
Address: The Downs School, Charlton Drive, Wraxall, Bristol, BS48 1PF
Trustees: Mr Alastair Matthew James Currie, Mrs Rachel Thornton, Mrs Nicola Anne Huggett, Lady Emma Burgh, Mrs Rebecca Tear, Mr James Alistair Isaacs, Mr Stephen Holliday, Mr Mark Anthony Newman, Mr Jason Collard, Mr Barnaby Northover, Mr Charles Rupert Guy Biggin, Mr Mark Burchfield
Income: £3,819,184 [2016]; £3,695,117 [2015]; £3,412,531 [2014]; £3,099,032 [2013]; £3,009,962 [2012]

Downs Syndrome Association
Registered: 21 Mar 1997 *Employees:* 43 *Volunteers:* 200
Tel: 0845 230 0372 *Website:* downs-syndrome.org.uk
Activities: Education, training; disability
Address: Downs Syndrome Association, The Langdon Down Centre, 2A Langdon Park, Teddington, Middlesex, TW11 9PS
Trustees: Mrs Sarah Leggat, Dr John Gerard Coghlan, Mrs Georgie Hill, Mr Trevor Pearcy, Ms Anya Souza, Mr Ertan Taner, Mr Robert Stirling, Mr Darren Warkcup
Income: £2,186,863 [2017]; £2,442,418 [2016]; £2,288,691 [2015]; £2,278,831 [2014]; £1,839,653 [2013]

The Downs, Malvern College Prep School
Registered: 20 Aug 2007 *Employees:* 70
Website: thedowns.malcol.org
Activities: Education, training
Address: Malvern College, College Road, Malvern, Worcs, WR14 3DF
Trustees: Mr Kenneth Madden, Mr Carey A P Leonard, Mrs Sarah Caroline Guy, Mr Darren Morris, Mrs Charlotte Elizabeth Elgar, Mr Syd Hill, Mr Iain MacIntyre MacLeod, Mr Stuart King, Mr Christopher Le Bas
Income: £3,075,993 [2016]; £2,575,769 [2015]; £2,206,159 [2014]; £2,177,728 [2013]

Downside Abbey General Trust
Registered: 9 Sep 2014 *Employees:* 181 *Volunteers:* 1
Tel: 01761 235125 *Website:* downside.co.uk
Activities: General charitable purposes; education, training; religious activities; arts, culture, heritage, science
Address: Downside Abbey, Stratton on the Fosse, Radstock, Somerset, BA3 4RH
Trustees: Dom James Hood, Dom Leo Maidlow Davis, Rev John Barrett, Dom Anselm Brumwell, Rev Thomas John Holt OSB
Income: £10,488,022 [2017]; £27,515,230 [2016]

Downside Up Limited
Registered: 22 Mar 2012 *Employees:* 72
Website: downssideup.com
Activities: The advancement of health or saving of lives; disability; overseas aid, famine relief
Address: 14a, 3rd Parkovaya Street, Moscow, 105043, Russia
Trustees: Ms Veronique Garrett, Mr Jeremy Barnes, Mr Richard David Henry Brindle, Mr Kirill Gromov, Mr Marlen Manasov, Anna Portugalova, Irina Menshenina, Mr Martin Thomas
Income: £1,346,560 [2017]; £1,244,776 [2016]; £1,037,173 [2015]; £437,965 [2014]; £1,084,246 [2013]

The Dr Hadwen Trust
Registered: 17 Apr 2012 *Employees:* 13 *Volunteers:* 50
Tel: 01462 436819 *Website:* animalfreeresearchuk.org
Activities: Education, training; advancement of health or saving of lives
Address: Dr Hadwen Trust for Humane Research, Suite 8 Portmill House, Portmill Lane, Hitchin, Herts, SG5 1DJ
Trustees: Dr Christopher Byatt MB FRCP PGME, Miss Natalie Barbosa, Miss Fern Clark, Claire Cunniffe, Dr Amanda Ellison, Ms Laura-Jane Sheridan
Income: £1,115,697 [2017]; £822,767 [2016]; £1,269,268 [2015]; £531,959 [2014]

Dr Kershaw's Hospice
Registered: 16 Sep 2004 *Employees:* 58 *Volunteers:* 350
Tel: 01457 829462 *Website:* drkershawshospice.org.uk
Activities: The advancement of health or saving of lives
Address: 37A Huddersfield Road, Delph, Oldham, Lancs, OL3 5EG
Trustees: Alan Moran, Gordon Russell, Mirriam Lawton, Sally Ann Deaville, Paul Henry Vincent, Dr Paul Cook, Anne Sykes, Susan Ann Briscall, Jonathan Richard Lipton, Ms Lindsay McCluskie
Income: £2,903,001 [2017]; £2,686,642 [2016]; £2,997,560 [2015]; £2,166,721 [2014]; £2,437,398 [2013]

Dragon School Trust Limited
Registered: 2 Jan 1964 *Employees:* 354
Tel: 01865 315403 *Website:* dragonschool.org
Activities: Education, training
Address: Dragon School, Bardwell Road, Oxford, OX2 6SS
Trustees: Mr W G Touche, Mrs Mary Breen, Mr Christopher Ian Montague Jones, Mrs L J Holmes, Mr G P Candy, Professor Angela McLean, Mr S Chambers, Mr Nigel Portwood, Mrs Sarah Jane Kerr-Dineen, Mrs G H Wilson, Professor Roger William Ainsworth, Lady Stringer, Mr W A Webb, Mr Nigel Leslie Helliwell, Mr Nathan Millard, Mrs Ariane Chantal Cowley, Ms Caroline Underwood, Mr Edmund Graham Ralph King
Income: £18,209,000 [2017]; £18,261,000 [2016]; £18,507,000 [2015]; £17,757,000 [2014]; £17,025,000 [2013]

Drapers Charitable Fund
Registered: 14 Feb 1967 *Employees:* 2
Tel: 020 7588 5001 *Website:* thedrapers.co.uk
Activities: General charitable purposes
Address: The Drapers Company, Drapers Hall, Throgmorton Avenue, London, EC2N 2DQ
Trustees: The Drapers Company
Income: £2,461,025 [2017]; £8,276,721 [2016]; £2,462,835 [2015]; £2,046,178 [2014]; £1,739,247 [2013]

The Drapers' Almshouse Charity
Registered: 22 Sep 1962 *Employees:* 4
Tel: 020 7588 5001 *Website:* thedrapers.co.uk
Activities: Accommodation, housing
Address: The Drapers Company, Drapers Hall, Throgmorton Avenue, London, EC2N 2DQ
Trustees: The Drapers' Company
Income: £1,439,693 [2017]; £1,460,404 [2016]; £1,452,530 [2015]; £1,351,589 [2014]; £1,332,988 [2013]

The Drapers' Charities Pooling Scheme
Registered: 4 Apr 1997 *Employees:* 2
Tel: 020 7588 5001 *Website:* thedrapers.co.uk
Activities: General charitable purposes
Address: The Drapers Company, Drapers Hall, Throgmorton Avenue, London, EC2N 2DQ
Trustees: The Drapers' Company
Income: £4,494,663 [2017]; £4,036,334 [2016]; £3,240,292 [2015]; £3,847,372 [2014]; £3,028,051 [2013]

Dreamflight
Registered: 19 Dec 2006 *Employees:* 5 *Volunteers:* 200
Tel: 01494 722733 *Website:* dreamflight.org
Activities: Disability; recreation
Address: 15 Chiltern Court, Asheridge Road, Chesham, Bucks, HP5 2PX
Trustees: Dr Simon Bailey, Ms Patricia Mary Pearce, Mrs Catherine Sarah Turner, Mr Robert Bass, Mr David Gawn, Ms Gaylene Jennefer Kendall
Income: £1,018,435 [2017]; £1,060,313 [2016]; £1,058,168 [2015]; £1,112,231 [2014]; £796,956 [2013]

Dreams Come True Charity
Registered: 18 Oct 1988 *Employees:* 16 *Volunteers:* 450
Tel: 01428 726330 *Website:* dreamscometrue.uk.com
Activities: The advancement of health or saving of lives; disability; recreation; other charitable purposes
Address: Exchange House, 33 Station Road, Liphook, Hants, GU30 7DW
Trustees: Andrew Challis, Linda Gibson, Miranda Abraham-Thwaites, Annabelle Vaughan, Mrs Rachel Louise Humphrey, Julia Margo, David Weeks, Pam Cryer, Miranda McArthur, Mr Patrick Leoni Sceti
Income: £1,669,786 [2017]; £1,254,568 [2016]; £1,436,976 [2015]; £1,104,674 [2014]; £1,000,869 [2013]

The Drinkaware Trust
Registered: 13 Nov 2002 *Employees:* 20
Tel: 020 7766 9900 *Website:* drinkaware.co.uk
Activities: General charitable purposes; education, training; advancement of health or saving of lives
Address: Third Floor, (Room 519), Salisbury House, London Wall, London, EC2M 5QQ
Trustees: Dr Timothy Edward Hanson Walker, Ms Victoria Nobles, Mr Kate Elizabeth Morris, Mr David Ward, Sir Leigh Lewis, Mrs Penelope Newman, Dr Paul David Nelson, Dr Christopher John Spencer Jones
Income: £5,387,003 [2016]; £5,297,036 [2015]; £5,748,735 [2014]; £5,169,340 [2013]; £5,109,222 [2012]

Drive
Registered: 11 Jun 1990 *Employees:* 497 *Volunteers:* 5
Tel: 01443 845289 *Website:* driveltd.org.uk
Activities: Disability; economic, community development, employment
Address: Drive, Unit 8, Cefn Coed, Nantgarw, Cardiff, CF15 7QQ
Trustees: Ms Katrina Kurowski, Mr John Minkes, Ms Janet Sheldon, Mr Hugh Irwin, Mr Karmeno Gauci, Mr Dan O'Grady, Mr Geoff Lake, Ms Jean Gregson, Mrs Jenny Jones, Mr Anthony Isingrini, Ms Margot Hopwood
Income: £13,505,626 [2017]; £12,132,906 [2016]; £11,403,989 [2015]; £11,370,010 [2014]; £11,326,831 [2013]

Driving Mobility
Registered: 17 Dec 1987 *Employees:* 1
Tel: 01872 672520 *Website:* drivingmobility.org.uk
Activities: Disability
Address: 2 Princes Street, Truro, Cornwall, TR1 2ES
Trustees: Ms Ann Frye OBE, Mr Colin Robert Barnett, Mr Gary Jones, Ms Yvette Bateman, Dr Tashfeen Chaudhry, Ms Sandra Hoggins, Ms Michelle Giles, Ms Sarah Vines, Mr David Blythe, Ms Julie Chatburn
Income: £1,623,075 [2017]; £161,172 [2016]; £1,325,753 [2015]; £150,590 [2014]; £213,909 [2013]

The Drug Safety Research Trust
Registered: 12 Aug 1986 *Employees:* 34
Tel: 023 8040 8600 *Website:* dsru.org
Activities: Education, training; advancement of health or saving of lives
Address: Drug Safety Research Unit, Bursledon Hall, Blundell Lane, Bursledon, Southampton, SO31 1AA
Trustees: Professor Alan John Camm QHP BSc MD FRCP FESC FACC FAHA FCGC, Professor Martin Patterson Vessey CBE Fr, Professor Kenneth Ross Paterson, Professor Stephen Holgate MD DSC FRCP FRCPE CBiol, Professor David Hamilton Lawson CBE DSC, Professor Allan Hunter Young MB ChB MPhil PhD FRCPC FRCPsych
Income: £2,300,251 [2016]; £3,930,646 [2015]; £4,533,010 [2014]; £3,172,993 [2013]; £3,182,013 [2012]

Druglink Limited
Registered: 10 Oct 1986 *Employees:* 45 *Volunteers:* 8
Tel: 01923 260727 *Website:* druglink.co.uk
Activities: Education, training; advancement of health or saving of lives; prevention or relief of poverty; accommodation, housing
Address: Trefoil, Red Lion Lane, Hemel Hempstead, Herts, HP3 9TE
Trustees: Mr Geoffrey Rose, Rosemary Farmer, Mr Padraig Dowd, Mr Ray Knowles, Mrs Fiona Guest, Mr David Swarbrick, Mr Kevin Cohen
Income: £1,838,772 [2017]; £1,671,530 [2016]; £1,295,958 [2015]; £1,582,341 [2014]; £1,415,165 [2013]

The Duchenne Research Fund
Registered: 3 May 2007 *Employees:* 2
Tel: 020 8200 0985 *Website:* duchenne.org.uk
Activities: The advancement of health or saving of lives
Address: The Duchenne Research Fund, Symal House, Edgware Road, London, NW9 0HU
Trustees: Mr Simon Kanter, Mr Jeremy Shebson, Daniel Baum, Dr Sarah Shelley
Income: £1,370,532 [2016]; £274,278 [2015]; £109,644 [2014]; £974,175 [2013]; £119,031 [2012]

Duchenne UK
Registered: 2 May 2012 *Employees:* 3
Tel: 07929 623123 *Website:* duchenneuk.org
Activities: Education, training; advancement of health or saving of lives
Address: 11 Bedford Road, London, W4 1JD
Trustees: Mr Andrew Nebel, Harriet Moynihan, Mr Deepak Nambisan, Mrs Maria Hassard, Mrs Cecilia Crossley, Nick Crossley, Mrs Hannah Becker
Income: £2,356,582 [2017]; £1,199,339 [2016]; £964,031 [2015]; £975,759 [2014]; £482,176 [2013]

Duchesne Trust
Registered: 9 Jan 1984
Tel: 020 8741 4688 *Website:* societysacredheart.org.uk
Activities: Religious activities
Address: 9 Bute Gardens, London, W6 7DR
Trustees: Sister Bernadette Porter, Marie Jeanne Elonga, Isabelle Lagneau, Barbara Dawson, Monica Ballesteros
Income: £3,493,358 [2016]; £3,427,000 [2015]; £3,294,000 [2014]; £8,814,000 [2013]; £28,754,000 [2012]

The Dudley Council for Voluntary Service
Registered: 21 Jul 1986 *Employees:* 32 *Volunteers:* 35
Tel: 01384 573381 *Website:* dudleycvs.org.uk
Activities: General charitable purposes
Address: Mr Andy Gray, Dudley Council for Voluntary Service, 7 Albion Street, Brierley Hill, W Midlands, DY5 3EE
Trustees: Miss Anne Elizabeth Adams, Mr Michael Victor Abrahams, Jane Helen Clarke, Mr James Thompson Keys, Mrs Alison Jane Sayer, Mr Derek Liddington, Mrs Christine Szygowski, Mr Graham Martin Jones, Mrs Mary Elizabeth Jane Turner, Mrs Sally Ann Huband, Miss Asima Khalid, Mr Christopher Richard Campbell, Ms Rachael Taylor
Income: £1,595,780 [2017]; £1,250,973 [2016]; £1,263,016 [2015]; £1,663,355 [2014]; £744,539 [2013]

Dudley District Citizens Advice Bureaux
Registered: 31 May 1989 *Employees:* 39 *Volunteers:* 66
Tel: 01384 811629 *Website:* citizensadvicedudley.org
Activities: The prevention or relief of poverty
Address: Holloway Chambers, 28 Priory Street, Dudley, W Midlands, DY1 1HA
Trustees: Mr Mark Jones, Mrs Sarah Dugan, Cllr Timothy Crumpton, Mr Mark Darren Parsons, Mr Stephen Handscomb, Ms Sue Cooper
Income: £1,323,213 [2017]; £1,268,553 [2016]; £1,282,923 [2015]; £1,179,501 [2014]; £1,116,034 [2013]

Dudley Lodge
Registered: 15 Nov 1999 *Employees:* 87 *Volunteers:* 4
Tel: 024 7650 2800 *Website:* dudleylodge.co.uk
Activities: Education, training
Address: Dudley Lodge, 143 Warwick Road, Coventry, Warwicks, CV3 6AT
Trustees: Mr Paul Tudor, Mr David Spafford, Dr Serena Janet Calder, Mrs Margaret Elizabeth Egrot, Julie Sullivan, Mr William Frank Smith, Miss Jennifer Hailey, Mr Raza Ullah, Mark Crook
Income: £3,145,679 [2017]; £2,976,152 [2016]; £2,704,510 [2015]; £2,348,361 [2014]; £2,100,617 [2013]

Dudley and West Midlands Zoological Society Limited
Registered: 7 Feb 1978 *Employees:* 80 *Volunteers:* 2
Tel: 01384 215310 *Website:* dudleyzoo.org.uk
Activities: Education, training; animals; environment, conservation, heritage; recreation
Address: Dudley Zoological Gardens, Castle Hill, Dudley, W Midlands, DY1 4QF
Trustees: Mr David Sparks, Mr Peter Silver, Ms Kim Fuller, Mr Philip James Tart, Miss Justine Webb, Mr Steven Keith Vincent, Mr Michael Evans, Mr David Ian Anthony Vickers, Mr Philip Ian Loveday, Mr Stephen Paul Woollard, Mr Andrew James Taylor
Income: £4,672,503 [2016]; £4,234,265 [2015]; £4,790,887 [2014]; £4,385,726 [2013]; £3,053,060 [2012]

The Duke of Edinburgh's Award
Registered: 18 Nov 1998 *Employees:* 204
Tel: 01753 727410 *Website:* dofe.org
Activities: Education, training
Address: The Duke of Edinburghs Award, Gulliver House, Madeira Walk, Windsor, Berks, SL4 1EU
Trustees: The Lord Kirkham CVO, Ruth Anderson, Mr Malcolm Offord, Mel Ewell, Mr John Uzoma Ekwugha Amaechi OBE, HRH The Earl of Wessex, Patricia Tehan, Baroness Grey-Thompson DBE, Mr Julian Hough
Income: £19,256,000 [2017]; £13,921,000 [2016]; £11,523,000 [2015]; £10,715,000 [2014]; £9,661,000 [2013]

The Duke of Edinburgh's International Award Foundation
Registered: 16 Nov 1998 *Employees:* 46 *Volunteers:* 20
Tel: 020 7222 4242 *Website:* intaward.org
Activities: Education, training
Address: RCS, Award House, 7-11 St Matthew Street, London, SW1P 2JT
Trustees: HRH The Earl of Wessex, The Rt Hon The Lord Paul Boateng, Mr Paul Christian Bell, Ms Muna Issa, Mr Rock Chen, Mr Andrew Smith, Mr Garth Weston, Mr Adebayo Olawale Edun, Dr Howard Williamson
Income: £4,592,000 [2017]; £3,737,000 [2016]; £4,620,000 [2015]; £3,463,000 [2014]; £3,430,000 [2013]

Duke of Kent School
Registered: 1 Sep 1997 *Employees:* 76
Tel: 01483 277313 *Website:* dukeofkentschool.org.uk
Activities: Education, training
Address: Peaslake Road, Ewhurst, Cranleigh, Surrey, GU6 7NS
Trustees: Mr Douglas Maclan Jack, Mr Stephen Dallyn, Mrs Penelope May McKenna, Mr Alexander Rupert William Balls, Mr Graham Oliver, Mr Richard Brocksom, Mrs Jennifer Susan Cropper
Income: £4,042,982 [2016]; £3,310,516 [2015]; £3,256,378 [2014]; £2,827,660 [2013]; £2,751,690 [2012]

The Duke's Playhouse Limited
Registered: 4 Apr 1973 *Employees:* 29 *Volunteers:* 175
Tel: 01524 598517 *Website:* dukes-lancaster.org
Activities: Education, training; arts, culture, heritage, science
Address: The Dukes, Moor Lane, Lancaster, LA1 1QE
Trustees: Mr Neil James Townsend, Dr Alan John Hatton-Yeo, John Chell, Jane Booker, Mrs Julie Karen Gardner, Ms Carolyn Jane Reynolds, Miss Maya Anneke Elsie Dibley
Income: £2,067,174 [2017]; £1,925,488 [2016]; £1,722,143 [2015]; £1,738,831 [2014]; £1,465,163 [2013]

The Dulverton Trust
Registered: 21 Mar 2012 *Employees:* 3
Website: dulverton.org
Activities: General charitable purposes; education, training; prevention or relief of poverty; environment, conservation, heritage
Address: Dulverton Trust, 5 St James's Place, London, SW1A 1NP
Trustees: Mr Christopher Aubrey Hamilton Wills, The Lord Dulverton, Dame Mary Richardson, The Rt Hon The Earl of Grey Gowrie PC FRSL, The Lord Hemphill, Dr Catherine Wills, Mr Tara Douglas-Home, Mr Richard Andrew Fitzalan Howard, Sir Malcolm Rifkind, Mr Robert Anthony Hamilton Wills
Income: £5,100,416 [2017]; £3,780,713 [2016]; £3,649,871 [2015]; £3,539,384 [2014]; £3,209,443 [2013]

Dulwich College
Registered: 5 Dec 2012 *Employees:* 442 *Volunteers:* 500
Tel: 020 8299 9306 *Website:* dulwich.org.uk
Activities: Education, training
Address: Dulwich College, Dulwich Common, London, SE21 7LD
Trustees: Mr David John Parfitt, Sir Brian Geoffrey Bender KCB, Mr Graham Norman Charles Ward CBE, Mr Surojit Ghosh, Mrs Jayne Margaret Hill, Ms Victoria Caroline Flind, Mr Timothy J Pethybridge, Mr Peter Thompson RD MBBS FRCS, Professor Richard John Parish Professor, Mr Richard John Foster, Dr Irene Bishop CBE, The Rt Hon Peter John Robert Riddell CBE, Dr Andreas Kottering BSc MSc DPhil
Income: £44,765,391 [2017]; £40,321,380 [2016]; £39,541,959 [2015]; £35,526,161 [2014]; £35,483,191 [2013]

The Dulwich Estate
Registered: 18 Aug 1966 *Employees:* 26
Tel: 020 8299 1000 *Website:* thedulwichestate.org.uk
Activities: Education, training; environment, conservation, heritage
Address: The Old College, Gallery Road, London, SE21 7AE
Trustees: Mr Roger Westbrook MA CMG, Mr John Edward Cruse BSc Hons, Mr Richard Pinckard BSc Econ FCA, Mrs Catherine Jeffrey MA MA, Mr Russell Vaizey MA FCA, Dr Irene Bishop CBE BEd MA LLD, Ms Sarah Helen Slater BSc Hons MRICS, Mrs Nicola Caroline Meredith BA Hons FCCA, Mrs Patricia Anne Cox LLB, Mr Martin Bagley BA Hons, Mr Simon Anthony Taylor FRICS, Dr Andreas Hermann Koettering DPhil MSc BSc Econ, Mr Peter Alan Yetzes BA JP, Mr David Russell Miller MA FCSI
Income: £10,597,835 [2017]; £9,786,811 [2016]; £9,824,020 [2015]; £9,970,920 [2014]; £9,489,463 [2013]

Dulwich Preparatory Schools Trust
Registered: 7 Feb 1996 *Employees:* 341
Tel: 020 8766 5523 *Website:* dulwichpreplondon.org
Activities: Education, training
Address: 42 Alleyn Park, Dulwich, London, SE21 7AA
Trustees: Mrs Celia Randell, Mr Richard Maidment, Mr Joe Steel, Mr Michael Tiplady, Mr David Nelson, Mr Michael Ashley, Mrs Kate Nash
Income: £20,996,146 [2017]; £19,772,955 [2016]; £18,868,043 [2015]; £18,245,395 [2014]; £17,514,698 [2013]

Dumpton School
Registered: 7 Nov 1968 *Employees:* 98 *Volunteers:* 6
Tel: 01202 883818 *Website:* dumpton.com
Activities: Education, training
Address: Dumpton School, Deans Grove House, Wimborne, Dorset, BH21 7AF
Trustees: Mr Ben Davies, Mrs Catherine Ann Waterman, Mr Charles John Jarrold, Mr Mark Richard Timberlake, Mr Hugh Dean Cocke, Mrs Camilla Joyce Culley, Mr Nicholas Alexander Hopwood, Dr Torlief Rene Skule, Mrs Edrys Margaret Barkham, Mrs Nicola Louise Hunter
Income: £3,869,300 [2017]; £3,702,418 [2016]; £3,684,137 [2015]; £3,660,309 [2014]; £3,441,792 [2013]

The Dunhill Medical Trust
Registered: 11 Feb 2011 *Employees:* 4 *Volunteers:* 13
Tel: 020 7403 3299 *Website:* dunhillmedical.org.uk
Activities: The advancement of health or saving of lives; disability; accommodation, housing
Address: Fifth Floor, 6 New Bridge Street, London, EC4V 6AB
Trustees: Mrs Kay Glendinning, Professor James McEwen, Mrs Helen Davies, Ms Claire Keatinge, Mr James Lorigan, Professor Thomas Kirkwood CBE, Mr John Ransford CBE, Professor Peter Lansley, Professor Alison Jean Petch, Professor Deborah Dunn-Walters, Mr Keith Shepherd
Income: £3,936,920 [2017]; £3,406,882 [2016]; £3,342,189 [2015]; £3,165,498 [2014]; £3,852,102 [2013]

Durand Education Trust
Registered: 15 Jun 2010
Tel: 020 7735 8348 *Website:* durandeducation.org
Activities: General charitable purposes; education, training
Address: Durand Primary School, Hackford Road, London, SW9 0RD
Trustees: Mr David George Buckley, Mr John Wentworth, Mr Mark Adrian McLaughlin
Income: £1,185,718 [2016]; £578,515 [2015]; £567,111 [2014]; £496,441 [2013]; £366,525 [2012]

Durham Aged Mineworkers' Homes Association
Registered: 19 Sep 1963 Employees: 42
Tel: 0191 388 1111 Website: damha.org.uk
Activities: Accommodation, housing
Address: Durham Aged Mineworkers Homes Association, P O Box 31, Chester-le-Street, Co Durham, DH3 3YH
Trustees: Mr Cyril Smith, Mr Paul Stradling, Mrs Barbara Christie, Mrs Una Mack, Mr Derek Gray, Mr John Ball, Mr Gordon Parkin, Mr Stephen Fergus, Mrs Lesley Ann Armstrong, Mrs Shiela McIntyre, Mr Raymond Gibson, Paul Hewitson
Income: £9,233,000 [2017]; £8,689,458 [2016]; £7,892,780 [2015]; £7,490,796 [2014]; £7,232,000 [2013]

Durham County Carers Support
Registered: 24 Apr 1998 Employees: 38 Volunteers: 60
Tel: 0300 005 1213 Website: dccarers.org
Activities: Education, training; advancement of health or saving of lives; disability; prevention or relief of poverty
Address: Enterprise House, Enterprise City, Meadowfield Avenue, Spennymoor, Co Durham, DL16 6JF
Trustees: Mrs Anne Stobbs, Mrs Audrey Vasey, Mrs Susan Sumpton, Mr John Dannell, Cllr Arthur Ronald Passfield, Mr Ray Mumford, Mrs Elizabeth Whiting, Mrs Janet Potts
Income: £1,320,413 [2017]; £1,288,739 [2016]; £1,325,621 [2015]; £1,252,162 [2014]; £1,595,179 [2013]

The Durham Diocesan Board of Finance
Registered: 16 Aug 1966 Employees: 30 Volunteers: 117
Tel: 01388 604515 Website: durham.anglican.org
Activities: Education, training; religious activities
Address: Durham Diocesan Board of Finance, Cuthbert House, Stonebridge, Durham, DH1 3RY
Trustees: Mr Wyrley-Birch, Rt Revd Mark Bryant, Venerable Ian Jagger, Rev Sheila Jane Bamber, Mrs F Stenlake, Dr James Herbert Harrison, Mr Frank Andrew Rogers, Mr David Robert Tomlinson, Mr Barrie Kirton, Mr Michael Banks, Mrs Hylda Hopper, Venerable Stuart Bain, Revd Dr Norman Shave, Venerable N Barker, Dr Richard Goudie, Dr Colin Price, Ms Margaret Louise Vaughan, Right Revd Paul Butler, Mr Stephen Pickering, Revd David Brooke
Income: £9,699,646 [2017]; £10,659,960 [2016]; £11,428,421 [2015]; £9,820,025 [2014]; £10,223,838 [2013]

Durham High School for Girls
Registered: 10 Jul 2007 Employees: 106 Volunteers: 30
Tel: 0191 384 3226 Website: dhsfg.org.uk
Activities: Education, training
Address: Durham High School for Girls, Farewell Hall, South Road, Durham, DH1 3TB
Trustees: Mr Alan Ribchester MBE, Mr Kenneth Delanoy, Dr Michael Gilmore, Miss Linda Clark, Mr Andrew Michael Lake, Mr Ian Meston, Dr Mohammed Azfar Hyder, Mrs Elisa Joanne Berry, Mrs Morag Cummings, Mr Stephen Cheffings, Miss Marie Green, Mr Richard Metcalfe, Dr Christine Joy English, Mrs Patricia Walker, Mrs Katherine Gertrude Barker, Rev Joanne Logan
Income: £4,764,018 [2017]; £4,567,277 [2016]; £4,584,185 [2015]; £4,803,706 [2014]; £4,809,565 [2013]

Durham School
Registered: 5 Jul 1993 Employees: 118 Volunteers: 39
Tel: 0191 386 4783 Website: durhamschool.co.uk
Activities: Education, training
Address: Durham School, Durham, DH1 4SZ
Trustees: Mr Alasdair MacConachie OBE DL, Ms Sharon Eleanor Langridge, Maura Regan, Mr Robert William Ribchester, Mr Simon Patrick Joseph Dobson, Ritchie Salkeld, Dr Jacquelyn Marie Robson, Revd Canon Dr David Kennedy, Mrs Margaret Coates, Mr Geoffrey Mark Hodgson, Mr Neil Turner, Ms Jennifer Lynn Kirkley, Ms Joanne Cowie
Income: £7,840,891 [2017]; £7,805,767 [2016]; £7,614,749 [2015]; £7,725,569 [2014]; £7,497,232 [2013]

Durham Students' Union
Registered: 11 Jan 2012 Employees: 32
Website: durhamsu.com
Activities: General charitable purposes; education, training; advancement of health or saving of lives; disability; arts, culture, heritage, science; economic, community development, employment; recreation
Address: Durham Students Union, Dunelm House, New Elvet, Durham, DH1 3AN
Trustees: Mr Martin Parker, Mrs Louise Shillinglaw, David Evans, Miss Megan Croll, Miss Sabrina Seel, Mr Ted Coward, Mr James Creer, Mr Anthony Baker Chairperson, Mr Oliver Collling, Charles Walker, Miss Beth Watling, Miss Rosa Tallack, Mr Joshua Barker
Income: £2,272,606 [2017]; £2,052,449 [2016]; £2,152,827 [2015]; £1,923,619 [2014]; £1,944,196 [2013]

Durham Wildlife Trust
Registered: 14 Jun 1972 Employees: 30 Volunteers: 300
Tel: 0191 584 3112 Website: durhamwt.co.uk
Activities: Environment, conservation, heritage
Address: Rainton Meadows, Chilton Moor, Houghton-le-Spring, Co Durham, DH4 6PU
Trustees: Mr Robert Kirton-Darling, Mr Malcolm Shorney, Mr Christopher Gorman, Mr David Duell, Mrs Sarah Lister, Mr Michael Coates, Mr Christopher Smith, Dr Steven Gater, Mr Alan Holden, Mrs Janice Baker, Mr Peter Bell, Mr Ian Thomas
Income: £1,417,470 [2017]; £1,250,012 [2016]; £1,175,105 [2015]; £1,137,922 [2014]; £1,040,056 [2013]

Durlston Court School Trust Limited
Registered: 7 Mar 1973 Employees: 94 Volunteers: 25
Tel: 01425 626234 Website: durlstoncourt.co.uk
Activities: Education, training
Address: Durlston Court School, 52 Becton Lane, Barton on Sea, New Milton, Hants, BH25 7AQ
Trustees: Mrs Nicola James, Mr Martin Cooke, Mr Colin Lewis, Dr James Hickey, Mrs Angela Joan Bolam, Mr Chandra Ashfield, Mr David Thompson, Mr Peter John Hardy, Mrs Lesley Anne Allen, Mr Richard Maurice Porter
Income: £2,939,978 [2017]; £3,022,500 [2016]; £2,908,092 [2015]; £2,880,029 [2014]; £2,830,613 [2013]

Durrell Wildlife Conservation Trust - UK
Registered: 14 Dec 2007
Tel: 01534 860060 *Website:* durrell.org
Activities: Education, training; overseas aid, famine relief; animals; environment, conservation, heritage; economic, community development, employment
Address: Durrell Wildlife Conservation Trust, Les Augres Manor, Trinity, Jersey
Trustees: Mr I Lazarus, Mr S Dickson, Ms Kerry Lawrence, Mrs K Gordon, Mr J Persad, Mr John Miskelly
Income: £1,833,000 [2016]; £2,706,000 [2015]; £746,000 [2014]; £1,092,000 [2013]; £1,726,000 [2012]

Durston House School Educational Trust Limited
Registered: 18 Jun 1986 *Employees:* 74
Tel: 020 8991 6430 *Website:* durstonhouse.org
Activities: Education, training
Address: Durston House School, 12-14 Castlebar Road, London, W5 2DR
Trustees: Dr Patrick Magill, Mrs Susan Margaret Hay, Mr Stephen Andrew Armstrong, Professor Mark Bailey, Mr David Arthur Alexander, Mr Patrick Allan Harrington, Mr Colin Xavier Castelino, Mrs Rosamund Mary Reece, Mr James Allen, Mr David Glynne Henshall, Miss Harvinder Kaur, Mr Kevin John Mahoney, Ms Ann Collier
Income: £5,556,096 [2017]; £5,486,357 [2016]; £5,251,245 [2015]; £5,070,542 [2014]; £5,084,125 [2013]

Dyslexia Institute Limited
Registered: 12 Dec 1974 *Employees:* 127 *Volunteers:* 10
Tel: 01784 222300 *Website:* dyslexiaaction.org.uk
Activities: General charitable purposes; education, training; disability; other charitable purposes
Address: Dyslexia Action, 10 High Street, Egham, Surrey, TW20 9EA
Trustees: Ms Paula Whittle, Mr James Matthews, Mr Aktar Somalya, Mrs Judy Baker, Mr Andy Gregson, Mr Paul Webb
Income: £6,432,000 [2015]; £8,836,000 [2014]; £7,728,000 [2013]; £7,826,000 [2012]

The James Dyson Foundation
Registered: 29 Sep 2003
Tel: 01666 828416 *Website:* jamesdysonfoundation.com
Activities: General charitable purposes; education, training; advancement of health or saving of lives; religious activities
Address: Dyson Ltd, Tetbury Hill, Malmesbury, Wilts, SN16 0RP
Trustees: Sir James Dyson CBE, Ms Valerie West, Lady Deirdre Dyson, Dr Fenella Anne Dyson
Income: £9,856,326 [2016]; £5,503,345 [2015]; £9,113,657 [2014]; £1,109,813 [2013]; £175,243 [2012]

E B M Charitable Trust
Registered: 7 Sep 1982
Tel: 020 7334 9191
Activities: General charitable purposes; advancement of health or saving of lives; disability; prevention or relief of poverty; amateur sport; animals; environment, conservation, heritage; economic, community development, employment
Address: Moore Stephens, 150 Aldersgate Street, London, EC1A 4AB
Trustees: Mr Richard Moore, Mr Stephen Marcroft Hogg, Mrs Lucy Forsyth, Mr Michael MacFadyen DL, Francis Moore
Income: £1,281,303 [2017]; £1,345,180 [2016]; £1,238,570 [2015]; £1,249,195 [2014]; £1,272,009 [2013]

E D P Drug & Alcohol Services
Registered: 21 Aug 1987 *Employees:* 198 *Volunteers:* 35
Tel: 01392 666710 *Website:* edp.org.uk
Activities: General charitable purposes; education, training; advancement of health or saving of lives; economic, community development, employment
Address: EDP, Renslade House, Bonhay Road, Exeter, EX4 3AY
Trustees: Mr Anthony Stephen Woodward, Mr Rick Weeks, Mr Ian MacQueen, Janet Bilbie, Mr Tim Goodwin, Mr James Richard Andrew Hutchinson, Mr Morgen Lewis Witzel, Mr Charles Holme, Amy Webb, Mr Paul Taylor
Income: £6,541,500 [2017]; £6,535,500 [2016]; £6,172,000 [2015]; £4,683,900 [2014]; £3,834,900 [2013]

The E P A Cephalosporin Fund
Registered: 3 Sep 1970
Tel: 01865 275573
Activities: Education, training; advancement of health or saving of lives
Address: University of Oxford, Sir William Dunn School of Pathology, South Parks Road, Oxford, OX1 3RE
Trustees: Professor Jeffrey Errington FRS, Professor Tony Green, Professor Penny Handford, Sir John Walker FRS, Professor Neil Barclay, Professor Philip Anton Van Der Merwe
Income: £3,966,796 [2017]; £2,499,075 [2016]; £2,320,580 [2015]; £1,649,936 [2014]; £1,725,592 [2013]

ECFR
Registered: 24 Aug 2011 *Employees:* 52
Tel: 020 7227 6860 *Website:* ecfr.eu
Activities: Education, training
Address: 4th Floor, ECFR, Tennyson House, 159-165 Great Portland Street, London, W1W 5PA
Trustees: Mabel Van Oranje, Professor Javier Solana, Ms Lykke Friis, Mr Carl Bildt, Ms Sylvie Kauffmann, Mr Andrzej Olechowski, Mr Ivan Krastev, Ms Emma Bonino, Norbert Roettgen, Mr Ian Clarkson, Ms Helle Thorning-Schmidt, Mr Andrew Puddephatt
Income: £6,285,584 [2016]; £5,339,129 [2015]; £5,457,728 [2014]; £5,427,729 [2013]; £4,712,354 [2012]

ECI Schools
Registered: 13 Dec 2012 *Employees:* 7
Tel: 020 7824 7040 *Website:* ecis.org
Activities: Education, training
Address: Fourth Floor, 146 Buckingham Palace Road, London, SW1W 9TR
Trustees: Dr Christiane Sorenson, Arnie Bieber, Ms Anuradha Monga, Ms Nicola Helen Crush, Sheena Nabholz, Janecke Aarnaes, Mr Christopher Charleson, Marta Medved Krajnovic, Jane Elizabeth Thompson
Income: £1,901,184 [2016]; £1,826,555 [2015]; £1,913,822 [2014]; £2,478,338 [2013]

EDF Energy Trust
Registered: 16 Sep 2003
Tel: 01733 421021 *Website:* edfenergytrust.org.uk
Activities: General charitable purposes; education, training; prevention or relief of poverty
Address: 3rd Floor, Trinity Court, Trinity Street, Peterborough, PE1 1DA
Trustees: Ms Denice Fennell MBE, Mr David Hawkes, Mr Tim Cole, Mr Vic Szewczyk
Income: £1,465,946 [2016]; £7,761,654 [2015]; £2,859,093 [2014]; £3,015,533 [2013]; £2,095,843 [2012]

EMH Care and Support Limited
Registered: 29 Jan 1991 *Employees:* 579 *Volunteers:* 4
Tel: 01530 276000 *Website:* enable-group.org.uk
Activities: Education, training; advancement of health or saving of lives; disability; accommodation, housing
Address: East Midlands Housing Group, Memorial House, Whitwick Business Park, Stenson Road, Coalville, Leics, LE67 4JP
Trustees: Ms Vandna Gohil, Ms Patricia McCabe, Mr James Leslie Holden, Mr Timothy John Brown
Income: £15,257,629 [2017]; £13,516,240 [2016]; £14,348,052 [2015]; £15,132,610 [2014]; £14,427,069 [2013]

EMIH Limited
Registered: 11 Jan 1999 *Employees:* 158 *Volunteers:* 32
Tel: 01482 381094 *Website:* thedeep.co.uk
Activities: Education, training; arts, culture, heritage, science; animals; environment, conservation, heritage; economic, community development, employment; recreation
Address: The Deep, Tower Street, Hull, HU1 4DP
Trustees: Professor Graham Chesters, Tony Hunt, Trevor Boanas, Alan Kirkman, Mr John Parkes CBE, Mr David Gemmell, Sue Lockwood, Prof Philip Leigh
Income: £6,887,510 [2017]; £6,746,628 [2016]; £7,297,957 [2015]; £5,699,094 [2014]; £5,492,999 [2013]

EMLC
Registered: 14 Jan 2004 *Employees:* 20
Tel: 01234 880130 *Website:* emlc.co.uk
Activities: Education, training
Address: Bridge House, Bridge Street, Olney, Bucks, MK46 4AB
Trustees: Rob Briscoe, Andy Chew, Richard Moyse, Jackie Adams, Cathryn Henry
Income: £2,543,235 [2017]; £2,638,153 [2016]; £2,926,051 [2015]; £1,906,829 [2014]; £1,848,828 [2013]

ESCP Europe - Business School
Registered: 15 Nov 1985 *Employees:* 94
Tel: 020 7443 8820 *Website:* escpeurope.eu
Activities: Education, training
Address: ESCP Europe Business School, 527 Finchley Road, London, NW3 7BG
Trustees: Anthony Travis, Mr Laurent Feniou, Mr Franck Bournois, Mr Laurence Milsted, Mrs Valerie Henriot, Mrs Joelle Lellouche, Mr Jean-Paul Vermes, Dr Rodney Eastwood PhD BSc, Mr Yves Portelli, Mr Didier Kling, Mr Patrick Martinez
Income: £7,955,971 [2016]; £7,804,197 [2015]; £8,024,637 [2014]; £7,738,978 [2013]; £6,035,473 [2012]

The EY Foundation
Registered: 21 May 2014 *Employees:* 29 *Volunteers:* 2,186
Tel: 020 7951 3133 *Website:* ey.com
Activities: General charitable purposes
Address: Ernst & Young LLP, 1 More London Place, London, SE1 2AF
Trustees: Mr Patrick Dunne, Mr Nigel Halkes, Mr David Gittleson, Mr Mark William Harold Harvey, Mrs Brenda Trenowden, Miss Terri Lau, Mr Peter Ian Wallace, Ms Deborah O'Hanlon, Mr Daniel John Richards, Evelyn Cole, Miss Rebecca Robins
Income: £2,375,947 [2017]; £2,613,358 [2016]; £2,413,778 [2015]

Ealing Community Transport
Registered: 1 Apr 2010 *Employees:* 200 *Volunteers:* 134
Tel: 020 8813 3210 *Website:* ectcharity.co.uk
Activities: Education, training; disability; prevention or relief of poverty; economic, community development, employment
Address: Greenford Depot, Greenford Road, Greenford, Middlesex, UB6 9AP
Trustees: Rev John Willmington, Tim West, Mr Paul Creasey, Sonia Krishna, Mr Patrick O'Keeffe
Income: £5,390,900 [2017]; £4,815,924 [2016]; £4,366,534 [2015]; £4,562,155 [2014]; £6,962,468 [2013]

Ealing Educational Resources Trust
Registered: 21 Aug 1996 *Volunteers:* 20
Tel: 01491 824710
Activities: Education, training
Address: Old Woodlands House, Bakers Lane, Brightwell-Cum-Sotwell, Wallingford, Oxon, OX10 0PU
Trustees: Mr Charles Andrew White, Mr Cyril David Parsons, Mr Stuart Hill, Mr Stuart Barnes, Mr Henry Bruce Robertson, Mr Charles James Ker
Income: £1,216,472 [2016]; £244,481 [2015]; £121,045 [2014]; £1,244,192 [2013]

Ealing Mencap
Registered: 2 Apr 1996 *Employees:* 52 *Volunteers:* 12
Tel: 020 8566 9575 *Website:* ealingmencap.org.uk
Activities: Education, training; disability
Address: Enterprise Lodge, Stockdove Way, Perivale, Greenford, Middlesex, UB6 8TJ
Trustees: George Alfred Venus, Mr Thomas James Roy Willis, Jayesh Pankania, Mr David Russ Widdowson, Mr Stephen Paul Penfold
Income: £2,245,760 [2017]; £2,223,554 [2016]; £2,098,019 [2015]; £1,806,652 [2014]; £1,550,930 [2013]

Earl Mountbatten Hospice
Registered: 1 Jul 1994 *Employees:* 175 *Volunteers:* 600
Tel: 01983 535333 *Website:* iwhospice.org
Activities: The advancement of health or saving of lives
Address: Earl Mountbatten Hospice, Halberry Lane, Newport, PO30 2ER
Trustees: Mrs Carol Lorraine Alstrom, Mrs Anne Axford, Ms Susan Maureen Price, Mr Nitin Pradhan, Mrs Rosamond Poncia, Mr Philip Shears, Mrs Sara Jane Weech, Mr Edward Nicholson, Mr John Martin Trotter, Mr Alan Comer, Mrs Josephine Smith
Income: £7,034,455 [2017]; £6,159,576 [2016]; £5,337,703 [2015]; £7,023,832 [2014]; £6,206,499 [2013]

The Earl of Northampton's Charity
Registered: 9 Feb 1967 *Volunteers:* 78
Tel: 020 7726 4991 *Website:* mercers.co.uk
Activities: The prevention or relief of poverty; accommodation, housing
Address: The Mercers' Company, Becket House, 36 Old Jewry, London, EC2R 8DD
Trustees: The Mercers Company
Income: £1,026,000 [2017]; £963,000 [2016]; £940,000 [2015]; £914,000 [2014]; £796,000 [2013]

The Earley Charity
Registered: 4 Jul 1968 Employees: 47 Volunteers: 14
Tel: 0118 975 5663 Website: earleycharity.org.uk
Activities: General charitable purposes; education, training; disability; prevention or relief of poverty; arts, culture, heritage, science; amateur sport; environment, conservation, heritage; economic, community development, employment; recreation
Address: The Earley Charity, The Liberty of Earley House, Strand Way, Lower Earley, Reading, Berks, RG6 4EA
Trustees: Mr Robert Edward Ames, Mrs Miryam Eastwell BA, Dr Deborah Jenkins, Dr David Christopher Sutton, Mr Philip Reginald Hooper, Mrs Mary Waite
Income: £1,075,636 [2016]; £1,211,704 [2015]; £1,172,423 [2014]; £1,133,777 [2013]; £1,167,239 [2012]

Earlham Institute
Registered: 7 Jun 2010 Employees: 122
Tel: 01603 450861 Website: earlham.ac.uk
Activities: Education, training; advancement of health or saving of lives; arts, culture, heritage, science; animals; environment, conservation, heritage; economic, community development, employment
Address: Norwich Research Park, Colney, Norwich, NR4 7UZ
Trustees: Mr Terence John Gould, Professor Veronica Van Heyningen, Mrs Andrea Finegan, Jean Beggs, Professor Robbie Waugh, Professor Dame Janet Maureen Thornton, Dr Alasdair MacNab, Professor Edward Louis
Income: £13,602,000 [2017]; £14,921,000 [2016]; £15,396,000 [2015]; £9,871,000 [2014]; £18,167,000 [2013]

Early Intervention Foundation
Registered: 26 Jun 2013 Employees: 18
Tel: 020 3542 2481 Website: eif.org.uk
Activities: Education, training; advancement of health or saving of lives; prevention or relief of poverty; economic, community development, employment
Address: Early Intervention Foundation, 10 Salamanca Place, London, SE1 7HB
Trustees: Martin Pilgrim, Honor Rhodes OBE, Christine Davies CBE, David Simmonds, Clare Tickell DBE, Ryan Shorthouse, Jean Gross CBE, Ray Shostak CBE, Jake Hayman, Ben Lucas
Income: £2,327,767 [2017]; £1,582,074 [2016]; £1,276,450 [2015]; £1,042,611 [2014]

Earth Trust
Registered: 16 Dec 2002 Employees: 29 Volunteers: 583
Tel: 01865 407792 Website: earthtrust.org.uk
Activities: Education, training; environment, conservation, heritage
Address: Earth Trust, Little Wittenham, Abingdon, Oxon, OX14 4QZ
Trustees: Mr Julian Sayers, Ms Lynda Atkins, Dr Mary Barkham, Dr Ian Davidson, Mr Andrew James Duff, Mr Graham Shaw, Mr Richard Wrigley, Mr Christopher Phillips
Income: £1,274,428 [2017]; £994,554 [2016]; £1,107,830 [2015]; £1,245,732 [2014]; £1,133,531 [2013]

East Anglia Roman Catholic Diocesan Trust
Registered: 7 Jan 1980 Employees: 63 Volunteers: 200
Tel: 01508 492540 Website: rcdea.org.uk
Activities: Education, training; prevention or relief of poverty; overseas aid, famine relief; religious activities
Address: 21 Upgate, Poringland, Norwich, NR14 7SH
Trustees: Mgr Peter Leeming, Mgr Philip Bernard Shryane, Mr Peter Ledger, Rev Nicholas Greef, Bishop Alan Stephen Hopes, Mgr Tony Rogers, Mrs Moira Goldstaub, Mrs Marie Roberts, Rev David Bagstaff
Income: £6,744,086 [2016]; £6,329,957 [2015]; £5,585,640 [2014]; £5,790,744 [2013]; £9,720,838 [2012]

East Anglia's Children's Hospices
Registered: 24 Apr 1998 Employees: 281 Volunteers: 1,042
Tel: 01223 205188 Website: each.org.uk
Activities: Education, training; advancement of health or saving of lives
Address: East Anglias Childrens Hospice, 42 High Street, Milton, Cambridge, CB24 6DF
Trustees: Mrs Sheila Jean Childerhouse, Dr Virginia Warren, Mr John Pickering, Mr Paul Green, Mr Robert Michael Dawson, Mrs Judith Eve Ingram, Lily Bacon, Mr Roger Cobley, Mrs Tracy Caroline Cottis, Dr Donald McElhinney, Mr William Arthur Self, Mrs Ann Monks, Brad McLean, Mrs Emma Sophia Deterding
Income: £12,292,695 [2017]; £10,943,467 [2016]; £10,545,812 [2015]; £9,973,677 [2014]; £9,029,726 [2013]

East Anglian Air Ambulance
Registered: 30 Nov 2000 Employees: 71 Volunteers: 300
Tel: 01603 270356 Website: eaaa.org.uk
Activities: The advancement of health or saving of lives
Address: East Anglian Air Ambulance, Hangar E, Gambling Close, Norwich, NR6 6EG
Trustees: Mr Nigel Savory FCA DL, Mr Thomas Franey Wells, Mrs Penelope Walkinshaw DL, Major General Sir William Cubitt KCVO CBE, Rt Hon The Earl of Iveagh DL, Mrs Stephanie Bourne, Mr Duncan Astill, Mr Roger Holden
Income: £12,815,652 [2017]; £10,773,951 [2016]; £9,315,571 [2015]; £8,298,041 [2014]; £7,153,224 [2013]

East Bedlington Community Centre
Registered: 20 Feb 2013 Employees: 2 Volunteers: 6
Tel: 01670 828808
Activities: General charitable purposes; education, training; arts, culture, heritage, science; amateur sport; economic, community development, employment; recreation
Address: East Bedlington Community Centre, 16-17 Station Street, Bedlington, Northumberland, NE22 7JN
Trustees: Ms Jennifer Anne Tindale, Mr Ronald James Thornton, Mr Anthony MacDonald, Mr Andrew Allman, Mr Ronald Straughan, Mr Ian Yarrow, Mrs Irene Walker, Mr David Douglas Johnson
Income: £1,236,239 [2017]; £28,721 [2016]; £22,011 [2015]; £27,826 [2014]; £13,909 [2013]

East Cheshire Hospice
Registered: 25 Apr 1984 Employees: 83 Volunteers: 600
Tel: 01625 610364 Website: eastcheshirehospice.org.uk
Activities: The advancement of health or saving of lives
Address: East Cheshire Hospice, Millbank Drive, Macclesfield, Cheshire, SK10 3DR
Trustees: Mr Stephen William Spinks, Mr Paul Morrissey, Mrs Jane Stephens, Mr Alastair Kennedy, Mr Robert Barrow, Dr Jonathan Beck, Dr Alan Wills, Mrs Annamarie Challinor, Dr Louise Hastings, Jim Lovett
Income: £4,345,121 [2017]; £4,112,104 [2016]; £3,772,663 [2015]; £3,565,627 [2014]; £3,405,275 [2013]

East Cheshire Housing Consortium Limited
Registered: 18 Feb 1991 Employees: 51
Tel: 01625 500166 Website: echc.org.uk
Activities: Accommodation, housing
Address: The Courtyard, Catherine Street, Macclesfield, Cheshire, SK11 6ET
Trustees: Mr Arthur Dicken, Mr Barrie Hardern, Mr Max Hartley, Mr Jonathan Paul Wigmore, Mr James Bisset, Mrs Sarah Horne, Mr Stephen Shaughnessy
Income: £2,351,908 [2017]; £2,285,910 [2016]; £2,042,417 [2015]; £1,898,177 [2014]; £1,945,296 [2013]

East Cleveland M S Home

Registered: 23 Sep 1987 *Employees:* 42
Tel: 01642 480660 *Website:* anncharltonlodge-redcar.co.uk
Activities: The advancement of health or saving of lives; disability
Address: The Ann Charlton Lodge, Edenhall Grove, Redcar, Cleveland, TS10 4PR
Trustees: Mr Clive Victor Greenley, Mrs Susan Jackson-Wilson, Mrs Rose Hewitt, Mrs Nicola Idle, Mr Peter Wilson, Mrs Nicola Louise Tizard, Mr Malcolm Thompson
Income: £1,094,068 [2017]; £1,002,900 [2016]; £1,003,809 [2015]; £991,438 [2014]; £911,573 [2013]

East End Citizens' Advice Bureaux

Registered: 30 Aug 2000 *Employees:* 41 *Volunteers:* 200
Tel: 020 8525 6374 *Website:* eastendcab.org.uk
Activities: The prevention or relief of poverty
Address: 300 Mare Street, London, E8 1HE
Trustees: Mr James Robert Ludlam MBE JP, Mr David Ross, Mr Edward Jonathan Fry, Mr Nick Allen, Ms Sharmin Takin, Mr Stephen Anthony Vaudrey, Mr Jeremy Shapiro, Mrs Hazel Claire Capper, Miss Bridget Young, Ms Caroline Selman
Income: £1,879,016 [2017]; £1,774,327 [2016]; £1,457,819 [2015]; £1,215,758 [2014]; £1,282,108 [2013]

East End Community Foundation

Registered: 21 Jun 2012 *Employees:* 9 *Volunteers:* 100
Tel: 020 7345 4444 *Website:* eastendcf.org
Activities: General charitable purposes; education, training; prevention or relief of poverty; economic, community development, employment
Address: Jack Dash House, 2 Lawn House, Close, London, E14 9YQ
Trustees: Sister Christine Frost, Mr Howard Dawber, Ms Zena Cooke, Mr Praveen Joynathsing, Mr Sahidur Rahman, Ms Gabrielle Harrington, Ms Katherine Webster, Cllr Guy Nicholson, Rick Watson
Income: £1,526,836 [2017]; £2,447,272 [2016]; £1,188,643 [2015]; £2,603,227 [2014]; £15,416,856 [2013]

East End Homes Limited

Registered: 18 Jan 2005 *Employees:* 111
Tel: 07966 299660 *Website:* eastendhomes.net
Activities: Accommodation, housing
Address: 15 Mulberry Avenue, Adel, Leeds, LS16 8LL
Trustees: Kevin Moore, Mr Les Eldon, Ms Maureen McEleney, Miss Helen Goody, Carol Hinvest, Jahangir Mannan, Motin Uz-Zaman, Mr John Hedley Kettlewell, Mrs Margaret Frances Higgins, Cllr John Pierce, Mrs Susan Patricia Blunden, Kevin Whittle
Income: £26,067,000 [2017]; £36,921,000 [2016]; £25,189,000 [2015]; £21,880,000 [2014]; £18,126,000 [2013]

East Kent Mencap

Registered: 24 Apr 1964 *Employees:* 96 *Volunteers:* 32
Tel: 01843 224482 *Website:* eastkentmencap.co.uk
Activities: General charitable purposes; education, training; advancement of health or saving of lives; disability; accommodation, housing; arts, culture, heritage, science; amateur sport; economic, community development, employment; recreation
Address: East Kent Mencap, 132 Northdown Road, Margate, Kent, CT9 2RB
Trustees: Mr Keith Smith, Mrs Lynda Holding, Mrs Angela Stuart, Miss Amy Rutland, Mr Paul Pinder, Mrs Doreen Leach, Ms Claire Goldfinch, Miss Sarah Hammond, Mrs Audrey Emmett, Mrs Mandy Rackley
Income: £2,115,264 [2017]; £1,838,465 [2016]; £1,684,666 [2015]; £1,853,134 [2014]; £1,537,369 [2013]

East Lancashire Deaf Society Limited

Registered: 7 Sep 2000 *Employees:* 54 *Volunteers:* 59
Tel: 01254 844550 *Website:* elds.org.uk
Activities: General charitable purposes; disability
Address: 8 Heaton Street, Blackburn, Lancs, BB2 2EF
Trustees: Doug Alker, Paul Winterhalter, Mark Heaton, Mr Shanker Nath Waghray
Income: £1,563,701 [2017]; £1,619,883 [2016]; £1,354,090 [2015]; £1,225,119 [2014]; £1,151,838 [2013]

The East Lancashire Hospice

Registered: 24 May 1999 *Employees:* 108 *Volunteers:* 258
Tel: 01200 447480 *Website:* eastlancshospice.org.uk
Activities: The advancement of health or saving of lives
Address: East Lancashire Hospice, Park Lee Road, Blackburn, BB2 3NY
Trustees: Mrs Anne Rachel Pallister, Mrs Gill Leacy, Mr Thomas Kennedy, Mr Graham Parr JP, Mr Richard John Sutlieff, Councillor Yusuf Jan-Virmani, Mr Ian McGregor Willock, Mr David McDonough
Income: £3,777,926 [2017]; £4,056,443 [2016]; £4,134,749 [2015]; £3,336,832 [2014]; £3,392,768 [2013]

The East Lancashire Masonic Charity

Registered: 30 Jan 1964 *Employees:* 25
Tel: 0161 796 5493 *Website:* elmc.co.uk
Activities: Education, training; prevention or relief of poverty; accommodation, housing
Address: 9 Conway Avenue, Whitefield, Manchester, M45 7AZ
Trustees: Mark Davis, Mr Derek Nelson Thornhill, Philip Price, Jonathan Selwyn Brownson, Mr Steven Barton, Mr Michael Boden, William Waite, Brian Joseph Carter, Sir David Trippier, Robert Simon Curtis Mitchell, Mr Chad Anthony Northcott, Mr Kenneth Davies MBE
Income: £1,295,974 [2016]; £2,203,143 [2015]; £1,510,432 [2014]; £1,921,687 [2013]; £1,756,696 [2012]

East Lancashire Railway Holdings Company Limited

Registered: 17 Dec 2004 *Employees:* 49 *Volunteers:* 750
Tel: 0161 764 6955 *Website:* eastlancsrailway.org.uk
Activities: General charitable purposes; education, training; environment, conservation, heritage; economic, community development, employment
Address: 22 Victoria Street, Haslingden, Rossendale, Lancs, BB4 5DL
Trustees: Colin Jones, Richard Law, Mr Roland Hatton, Malcolm Kirkwood, Bill Beveridge, Mr David Stephen Layland, Mr Alex Walker, Mr David Alan Wright, Peter Duncan, Philip Bailey, Andrew Hardman, Brian Sutcliffe, John Tate, Mr Alan Lee, Mr David Robert Bulman
Income: £3,868,217 [2016]; £3,258,004 [2015]; £2,668,936 [2014]; £2,253,300 [2013]; £2,218,073 [2012]

East Lindsey Information Technology Centre

Registered: 29 Aug 1984 *Employees:* 50
Tel: 01507 601122 *Website:* firstcollegelincs.co.uk
Activities: Education, training
Address: Milford Court, Warwick Road, Fairfield Industrial Estate, Louth, Lincs, LN11 0YB
Trustees: Mr Haydn Biddle, Mr Paul McCooey, Mrs Helen Angela Matthews, Mr Louis Harman, Mr Stephen Russell Kirk, Miss Aleksandra Tusien, Mr William Fitzaden-Gray
Income: £1,886,410 [2017]; £1,833,171 [2016]; £2,224,627 [2015]; £1,947,114 [2014]; £1,874,373 [2013]

East London Advanced Technology Training
Registered: 3 Mar 1989 *Employees:* 43 *Volunteers:* 45
Tel: 020 7275 6758 *Website:* elatt.org.uk
Activities: Education, training
Address: Elatt, 260-264 Kingsland Road, London, E8 4DG
Trustees: Miss Natalie Stockmann, Cathy Walsh, Ms Sarah
Stimson, Lesley Ashman, Mr Baron Armah-Kwantreng, Mr Mark
Bethell, Julie Feest
Income: £1,813,824 [2017]; £1,683,125 [2016]; £1,981,915 [2015];
£1,808,976 [2014]; £1,857,806 [2013]

East London Business Alliance
Registered: 3 Jan 2008 *Employees:* 92 *Volunteers:* 12,731
Tel: 020 7068 6960 *Website:* elba-1.org.uk
Activities: Education, training; advancement of health or saving of
lives; prevention or relief of poverty; arts, culture, heritage, science;
amateur sport; environment, conservation, heritage; economic,
community development, employment
Address: East London Business Alliance, 5 Greenwich View Place,
London, E14 9NN
Trustees: Mr Christopher Ian Watson, Ms Marie Gabriel, Miss Jenny
Baskerville, Ms Payal Vasudeva, Ms Eileen Taylor, Ms Terry
Waldron, Miss Lisa Hollins, Mr Arthur Rakowski
Income: £3,869,711 [2017]; £4,014,796 [2016]; £3,019,440 [2015];
£2,997,434 [2014]; £4,033,225 [2013]

East London Mosque Trust
Registered: 5 Feb 2008 *Employees:* 141 *Volunteers:* 150
Tel: 020 7650 3003 *Website:* eastlondonmosque.org.uk
Activities: General charitable purposes; education, training;
religious activities; economic, community development,
employment; human rights, religious or racial harmony, equality or
diversity
Address: East London Mosque Trust Ltd, 82-92 Whitechapel Road,
London, E1 1JQ
Trustees: Mr Ayub Khan, Mr Muhammad Habibur Rahman,
Dr Muhammad Abdul Bari MBE, Dr Abdul Hayee Murshad,
Dr Mahera Ruby, Mr Mohammed Abdur Rahim Kamaly, Mrs Sayeda
Anzumara Begum, Mr Aman Ali, Mr Muhammad Siddique,
Mr Shafiur Rahman, Mr Sirajul Islam, Mrs Rahela Choudhury,
Mr Mohammad Abdul Malik, Mr Sirajul Islam, Mr Mazhar Baqaullah
Khan
Income: £3,698,348 [2017]; £3,641,762 [2016]; £3,680,875 [2015];
£3,369,518 [2014]; £3,386,652 [2013]

The East Malling Trust
Registered: 9 Mar 2010 *Employees:* 19
Tel: 01732 221952 *Website:* eastmallingtrust.org
Activities: Other charitable purposes
Address: Bradbourne House, New Road, East Malling, West
Malling, Kent, ME19 6DZ
Trustees: Dr Oliver Peter Doubleday, Professor John Mumford,
Ms Allis Beasley, Mrs Marion Regan, Mr Kevin Attwood,
Dr Jonathan Knight
Income: £2,061,176 [2017]; £6,314,233 [2016]; £6,894,226 [2015];
£6,772,380 [2014]; £5,539,111 [2013]

East Midlands Christian Fellowships
Registered: 9 May 2000 *Employees:* 46 *Volunteers:* 450
Tel: 01332 332044 *Website:* emcf.net
Activities: Education, training; prevention or relief of poverty;
overseas aid, famine relief; religious activities
Address: East Midlands Christian Fellowships, The Riverside
Centre, Riverside Road, Pride Park, Derby, DE24 8HY
Trustees: Mr Mark Nigel Mumford, Mr Emrys Llewelyn Ashmore
Jones, Ms Claire Louise Tapping, Mr Jonathan David Huw Bearn,
Mr Anthony Carnall Turner, Mr Benjamin Rook, Mr Andrew Steven
Townsend, Mr Martin Andrew Frost
Income: £1,343,104 [2017]; £1,264,167 [2016]; £1,214,899 [2015];
£1,347,157 [2014]; £941,615 [2013]

East Midlands Crossroads-Caring for Carers
Registered: 22 Dec 1995 *Employees:* 352 *Volunteers:* 72
Tel: 0115 962 8920 *Website:* carerstrustem.org
Activities: The advancement of health or saving of lives; disability
Address: 19 Pelham Road, Nottingham, NG5 1AP
Trustees: Mr Richard James Thomas, Mrs Anne Roberts, Mr Ian
Turnbull, Mrs Emily Convery, Mrs Christine Alexander, Mr Nick
Stringfellow, Dr David Tek Yung Liu
Income: £6,397,394 [2017]; £5,921,891 [2016]; £5,385,821 [2015];
£4,899,603 [2014]; £4,369,401 [2013]

East Northamptonshire Cultural Trust
Registered: 5 May 2005 *Employees:* 67 *Volunteers:* 28
Tel: 01933 350324 *Website:* aspirationswellbeing.org.uk
Activities: General charitable purposes; education, training;
advancement of health or saving of lives; disability; arts, culture,
heritage, science; amateur sport; environment, conservation,
heritage
Address: Pemberton Centre, H E Bates Way, Rushden, Northants,
NN10 9YP
Trustees: Mr James MacWilliam, Ms Fiona Higginbotham, Mr Phillip
Henry Grace, Mr Terence Bowen, Mr Ralph Allen
Income: £2,639,568 [2016]; £2,505,641 [2015]; £2,121,321 [2014];
£2,121,706 [2013]

East Street Arts
Registered: 14 Sep 1999 *Employees:* 22 *Volunteers:* 15
Tel: 0113 248 0040 *Website:* eaststreetarts.org.uk
Activities: Education, training; arts, culture, heritage, science
Address: Patrick Studios, St Marys Lane, Leeds, LS9 7EH
Trustees: Ms Gillian Holding, Mr Jeremy Wilson, Mr Jonathan
Wilson, Mr Nicholas Dyson, Mr Alan Dunn, Miss Helen Macrow,
Ms Julia Skelton, Mrs Kristal Ireland, Ms Deidre Reid
Income: £1,616,441 [2017]; £1,370,415 [2016]; £1,158,981 [2015];
£999,158 [2014]; £830,378 [2013]

East Surrey Rural Transport Partnership
Registered: 29 Nov 2007 *Employees:* 60 *Volunteers:* 5
Tel: 01883 732877 *Website:* eastsurreyrtp.org.uk
Activities: Education, training; disability; prevention or relief of
poverty
Address: Tandridge District Council, Council Offices, 8 Station
Road East, Oxted, Surrey, RH8 0BT
Trustees: Mrs Wendy Cope, Mr Andrew Emerson, Mrs Lynne
Martin, Mr Alan James Carter, Mr John Lyndon Phillips, Mr Timothy
Ward
Income: £1,513,108 [2017]; £1,577,221 [2016]; £1,369,639 [2015];
£1,327,980 [2014]; £1,103,115 [2013]

East and North Hertfordshire NHS Trust Charitable Fund
Registered: 27 Feb 1996 *Volunteers:* 300
Tel: 01438 314333 *Website:* enhherts-tr.nhs.uk
Activities: The advancement of health or saving of lives
Address: East and North Herts NHS Trust, Management Suite, Lister Hospital, Coreys Mill Lane, Stevenage, Herts, SG1 4AB
Trustees: East & North Herts NHS Trust
Income: £1,877,338 [2017]; £939,788 [2016]; £710,250 [2015]; £758,219 [2014]; £916,049 [2013]

East and West Looe Harbour and Bridge Charities
Registered: 7 Jun 1985 *Employees:* 10
Tel: 01503 262839 *Website:* looeharbour.com
Activities: General charitable purposes
Address: Looe Harbour Commissioners, The Quay, East Looe, Looe, Cornwall, PL13 1DX
Trustees: Mr Armand Jean Toms, Mr Melvyn Toms, Mr David Bond, Mr David Peat, Mr Jasper Graham-Jones, Mr Joseph Bussell, Mr Michael Hugh Soady, Mr Paul James Greenwood, Mr Michael Darlington, Dr Kathy Lang
Income: £1,029,369 [2017]; £838,594 [2016]; £1,233,126 [2015]; £870,055 [2014]; £973,026 [2013]

East of England Agricultural Society
Registered: 21 Dec 1981 *Employees:* 40 *Volunteers:* 750
Tel: 01733 234451 *Website:* eastofengland.org.uk
Activities: Education, training; environment, conservation, heritage
Address: East of England Agricultural Society, East of England Showground, Oundle Road, Alwalton, Peterborough, PE2 6XE
Trustees: Mr Robert William Dalgliesh FRICS FAAV, Martin Redfearn, Mr James Robert Parrish, Mr Geoffrey Dodgson, Benjamin Mark John Harris, Mr John Stuart Greer Paton JP, Nigel Rome, Mr Andrew Riddington, Mr Charles Reynolds, Mr Thomas Benjamin White Beazley
Income: £3,790,552 [2016]; £4,099,300 [2015]; £3,474,407 [2014]; £3,492,626 [2013]; £4,697,940 [2012]

Eastbourne College (Incorporated)
Registered: 26 Feb 1964 *Employees:* 412 *Volunteers:* 95
Tel: 01323 452300 *Website:* eastbourne-college.co.uk
Activities: Education, training
Address: Eastbourne College, Marlborough House, Old Wish Road, Eastbourne, E Sussex, BN21 4JY
Trustees: Mr George Marsh, Mr Philip Broadley MA FCA FRSA, Mr Andrew Robinson, Dr Robert McNeilly, Mrs Melanie Richards, Mr Colin Davies, Mr Darren Lindsey Meek, Mrs Amanda Claire Coxen, Mrs Helen Jane Toole, Mr Alexander James Gore Brown, Ms Julie Ann Wheeldon, Mr Charles Martin Peter Bush, Mrs Victoria Jane Henley, Mr Tom Richardson FRICS, Mr John Ryley BA AMP, Mrs Nicola Eckert, Mr Jonathan Watmough, Mrs Claire Locher, Mr Richard Vivian Davidson-Houston, Mr Nicholas James Philip Elliott, Ms Cherine Radwan
Income: £21,650,000 [2017]; £23,010,000 [2016]; £21,327,000 [2015]; £21,336,000 [2014]; £19,759,000 [2013]

Eastbourne and District Mencap Limited
Registered: 2 Sep 2008 *Employees:* 101 *Volunteers:* 9
Tel: 01323 722034 *Website:* eastbournemencap.org.uk
Activities: Disability
Address: 113 Pevensey Road, Eastbourne, E Sussex, BN22 8AD
Trustees: Mr David James Long, Mr Stephen Wibberley, Mr Piers Lott, Ms Justine White, Mr Christopher Mark Mizen, Mrs Linda Fennell, Ms Nikola Trimmer
Income: £2,008,957 [2016]; £1,821,137 [2015]; £1,919,567 [2014]; £1,990,945 [2013]

Eastbrook Education Trust
Registered: 6 Aug 1996 *Employees:* 34 *Volunteers:* 150
Activities: Education, training
Address: Goldcliffe, Church Lane, Whittington, Worcester, WR5 2RQ
Trustees: Mr Douglas Pomeroy, Mr Nigel Freeman, Mr Guy Knappett, Mr Barrie Freeman, Mr Andrew Trigwell, Mr Clive Haughton, Mr Gavin Tomkins
Income: £2,635,382 [2016]; £2,029,709 [2015]; £1,706,910 [2014]; £1,526,075 [2013]

Eastlands Homes Partnership Limited
Registered: 23 Sep 2004 *Employees:* 364 *Volunteers:* 50
Tel: 0161 274 2140 *Website:* onemanchester.co.uk
Activities: Disability; prevention or relief of poverty; accommodation, housing; economic, community development, employment
Address: Eastlands Homes, Lovell House, Archway 6, Hulme, Manchester, M15 5RN
Trustees: Mr Stephen Arthur Kinsey, David Dennehy, Graham Aitken, Mr John James Hughes, Dr Slawomir Pawlik, Sara Todd, Alison Gordon, Stephen Mole, Angela Robinson
Income: £37,625,000 [2017]; £37,282,000 [2016]; £33,209,000 [2015]; £40,620,000 [2014]; £40,264,000 [2013]

Eating Disorders Association
Registered: 7 Apr 1989 *Employees:* 41 *Volunteers:* 1,064
Tel: 01603 753305 *Website:* beateatingdisorders.org.uk
Activities: Education, training; advancement of health or saving of lives
Address: Beat (Eating Disorders Association), 1 Chalk Hill House, 19 Rosary Road, Norwich, NR1 1SZ
Trustees: Mr Neil Roskilly, Ms Anne-Marie Winton, Ms Melanie Smith, Mr Mike Cooke, Ms Valerie Jolliffe, Professor Hubert Lacey, Mr Richard Davis, Ms Jo Bennett
Income: £1,409,131 [2017]; £1,126,047 [2016]; £2,599,249 [2015]; £3,656,864 [2014]; £1,267,442 [2013]

Echoes of Service
Registered: 5 Aug 1965 *Employees:* 12
Tel: 01225 310893 *Website:* echoes.org.uk
Activities: The advancement of health or saving of lives; prevention or relief of poverty; overseas aid, famine relief; religious activities
Address: 124 Wells Road, Bath, BA2 3AH
Trustees: Dr John Henry Burness, Mr Eric Joseph Noble, Mr John Aitken, Mr Alan William Park, Mr Paul Young, Mr Benjamin Graham Scholefield, Mr James Crawford Crooks
Income: £4,333,565 [2016]; £5,384,325 [2015]; £5,866,843 [2014]; £5,007,113 [2013]; £4,981,337 [2012]

Eckling Grange Limited
Registered: 3 Dec 1967 *Employees:* 97 *Volunteers:* 18
Tel: 01362 820568 *Website:* ecklinggrange.org.uk
Activities: Accommodation, housing; religious activities
Address: The Old Farmhouse, Red Hall Lane, Southburgh, Thetford, Norfolk, IP25 7TG
Trustees: Mr David Hedley John Goddard, Mr David Cleveland, Mrs Fiona Mary Winser, Mr Graham Pickhaver, Philip Goddard, Mrs Thelma Johnson, Mrs Heather Havers
Income: £1,995,435 [2017]; £1,918,281 [2016]; £1,902,318 [2015]; £1,823,492 [2014]; £1,742,552 [2013]

Ecole Francaise de Londres Jacques Prevert Ltd
Registered: 25 Aug 1977 *Employees:* 30
Tel: 020 7602 6871 *Website:* ecoleprevert.org.uk
Activities: Education, training
Address: 59 Brook Green, London, W6 7BE
Trustees: Mr Didier Faure, Mr David Michael Peter Height, Mr Maxime Jean Pierre Jacqz, Mrs Nicole Semaan, Mrs Samantha Hardaway, Mr Stephane Redon, Mrs Emmanuelle Noyer, Mr Andrew Harvey, Mrs Marianne Megarbane, Mrs Catherine Michele Gaillard-Bourde, Mrs Mwenenge Monique
Income: £1,650,278 [2016]; £1,546,901 [2015]; £1,481,200 [2014]; £1,405,425 [2013]; £1,374,965 [2012]

Ecole Jeannine Manuel UK
Registered: 23 Sep 2014 *Employees:* 55
Tel: 020 3829 5970 *Website:* ecolejeanninemanuel.org.uk
Activities: Education, training
Address: Ecole Jeannine Manuel UK, 43-45 Bedford Square, London, WC1B 3DN
Trustees: Mr Bernard Marc Andre Manuel, Mrs Elisabeth Renee Jeanne Zeboulon, Shirley Ann Burchill, Mr Adrien Jean Marie Breart De Boisanger, Mr Claude Amar, Nicholas Charles Bunch, Georgina Elizabeth Van Welie
Income: £5,664,579 [2017]; £4,626,096 [2016]; £5,096,893 [2015]

The Eden Trust
Registered: 22 Jul 2002 *Employees:* 467 *Volunteers:* 111
Tel: 01726 811900 *Website:* edenproject.com
Activities: Education, training; arts, culture, heritage, science; environment, conservation, heritage; economic, community development, employment
Address: Eden Project, Bodelva, Par, Cornwall, PL24 2SG
Trustees: Mr Edward Benthall, Mr Jonathan Drori, Mr Richard Harry Reid, Dame Georgina Mace, Dr Adam Beaumont, Mr Geoffrey Austin, Sir Ralph Ferrers Alexander Vyvyan, Ms Lucy Blaise Parker, Penny Parker, Mr Kevin Havelock
Income: £27,707,000 [2017]; £25,653,000 [2016]; £23,666,913 [2015]; £23,265,275 [2014]; £27,938,003 [2013]

Eden Valley Hospice, Carlisle
Registered: 26 Feb 1992 *Employees:* 124 *Volunteers:* 487
Tel: 01228 810801 *Website:* evhospice.org.uk
Activities: The advancement of health or saving of lives
Address: Eden Valley Hospice, Durdar Road, Carlisle, CA2 4SD
Trustees: Mr James Porter, Chris Fell, Dr Carol Lesley Harvey, Mr Malcolm Iredale, Miss Karen Aitchison Jones, Ms Christine Margaret Weaving, Mr William John Priddle, Mr Andrew John Setters, Mrs Isabel Bowles, Mrs Racheal Bagshaw, Ms Hilary Ann Wade
Income: £3,655,837 [2016]; £3,331,738 [2015]; £3,653,501 [2014]; £3,546,492 [2013]; £3,011,441 [2012]

The Edgbaston High School for Girls
Registered: 4 Aug 1975 *Employees:* 212
Tel: 0121 454 5831 *Website:* edgbastonhigh.co.uk
Activities: Education, training
Address: Edgbaston High School for Girls, Westbourne Road, Edgbaston, Birmingham, B15 3TS
Trustees: Mrs Corinne Fatah, Mr Jeremy Payne, Dr Jane Valerie Leadbetter, Mrs Helen Jane Arnold, Mrs Vanessa Nicholls, Mrs Julia Ann Helen Tozer, Professor Lord Bhattacharyya, Mrs Sally Annaliese England Kerr, Mrs Anne Howarth, Mr Gordon Scott, Mrs Sarah Anne Shirley-Priest, Mr Iain Griffiths
Income: £9,829,012 [2017]; £9,425,236 [2016]; £9,107,879 [2015]; £8,560,529 [2014]; £8,315,834 [2013]

Edge Grove School Trust Ltd
Registered: 19 May 1969 *Employees:* 99 *Volunteers:* 1
Tel: 01923 855724 *Website:* edgegrove.com
Activities: Education, training
Address: Edge Grove, Aldenham, Watford, Herts, WD25 8NL
Trustees: Mr Andrew James Robson, Mr Ian Stewart Elliott, Mr Paul Ashley Kendall, Mr Charles Edward Lilley, Ms Amanda Jane Godfrey, Dr Susan Barbara Whiting, Mr David Anthony Ellis Williams, Mrs Samantha O'Sullivan, Mrs Jean Grant Scott, Mr Trefor Wilmot Llewellyn, Mr Christopher Howard John Clayden, Mr Jeremy Laurence Stevens, Professor Jill Elizabeth Maddison, Mrs Frances Margaret Raphael King, Dr Lucy Ann Johnson
Income: £6,251,687 [2017]; £5,783,537 [2016]; £5,383,717 [2015]; £4,554,209 [2014]; £4,139,359 [2013]

Edge Hill Students' Union Limited
Registered: 12 Sep 2011 *Employees:* 33
Tel: 01695 657301 *Website:* edgehillsu.org.uk
Activities: General charitable purposes
Address: Edge Hill University, St Helens Road, Ormskirk, Lancs, L39 4QP
Trustees: Miss Shannon-Rose McKenna, Joanne Caldwell, Miss Christina Donovan, Mr Daniel Bocharnikov, Mr Callum Johnston, Mr Colin Dyas, Mr Luke Myer, Mr Ben Whittle, Mr Richard Raymond
Income: £1,445,932 [2016]; £1,439,804 [2015]; £1,287,127 [2014]; £600,660 [2013]

Edge Hotel School Limited
Registered: 5 Dec 2014 *Employees:* 16 *Volunteers:* 1
Tel: 01206 872858 *Website:* edgehotelschool.ac.uk
Activities: Education, training; economic, community development, employment
Address: Constable Building, Wivenhoe Park, Colchester, Essex, CO4 3SQ
Trustees: Mr Richard Barnard, Mr Neil Roland Bates, Mrs Jane Mary Samuels, Mr David Tournay, Mr Craig Thatcher, Mr Daniel Pecorelli, Mr Owen Bryn Morris, Mr Peter Albert Jones, Mr Martin Bojam
Income: £1,014,179 [2017]; £1,068,570 [2016]

Edgeborough Educational Trust Limited
Registered: 11 Aug 1966 *Employees:* 100
Tel: 01252 792495 *Website:* edgeborough.co.uk
Activities: Education, training
Address: 84 Frensham Road, Frensham, Farnham, Surrey, GU10 3AH
Trustees: Mrs Patricia Fulker, Mr Lee Kent Walton, Mr Jeremy McIlroy, Mr Michael Walton, Dr Andrea Saxel, Mrs Melanie Feisbush, Mrs Sian Proudlock, Mr Roderick Ernest Dadak, Ms Colette Moscati, Mr Neeraj Kapur, Mr Daniel Thornburn
Income: £3,667,365 [2016]; £3,569,244 [2015]; £3,602,687 [2014]; £3,617,964 [2013]; £3,658,226 [2012]

The Edgware and District Reform Synagogue
Registered: 26 May 1994 *Employees:* 68 *Volunteers:* 275
Website: edrs.org.uk
Activities: General charitable purposes; education, training; religious activities
Address: Edgware & Hendon Reform Synagogue, Stonegrove, Edgware, Middlesex, HA8 8AB
Trustees: Mr Howard Moss, Mrs Janet Brand, Mr Bradley Trainis, Mr Neil Flash, Mr Robert Brand, Mrs Sandra Lerman, Mr Andrew Woolstone, Ms Amy Lerman, Mr Colin Wagner, Ms Helen Feller, Mr Stephen Garfinkel, Mr Jeremy Harrod, Mrs Jo Sigalov, Mr Michael Weber, Mr Michael Casale, Mr Joseph Nathan, Mrs Lisa Bard, Mr Philip Rose, Mrs Jo Weber
Income: £1,441,622 [2016]; £1,369,296 [2015]; £1,334,713 [2014]; £1,307,695 [2013]; £1,306,036 [2012]

Edhi International Foundation UK
Registered: 26 Nov 1992 *Employees:* 24
Tel: 020 7723 2050 *Website:* edhi.uk.org
Activities: General charitable purposes; education, training; advancement of health or saving of lives; disability; prevention or relief of poverty; overseas aid, famine relief; religious activities; animals; economic, community development, employment
Address: 316 Edgware Road, London, W2 1DY
Trustees: Mrs Kubra Edhi, Mrs Bilquis Edhi, Mr Faisal Edhi, Mrs Feroza Aka
Income: £7,828,410 [2016]; £7,323,638 [2015]; £5,827,722 [2014]; £6,171,602 [2013]; £5,588,892 [2012]

The Edmund Trust
Registered: 4 Jan 1994 *Employees:* 163
Tel: 01223 883130 *Website:* edmundtrust.org.uk
Activities: Education, training; disability; accommodation, housing
Address: Lancaster House, Capper Road, Waterbeach, Cambridge, CB25 9LY
Trustees: Mrs Tandy Harrison, Mr Greer Harbinson, Mr Nicholas John Tiley, Dr Derek William Ford, Mr Anthony John Day, Mrs Lynette Jenkins
Income: £5,091,854 [2017]; £3,939,962 [2016]; £3,563,273 [2015]; £2,986,099 [2014]; £2,759,969 [2013]

Education & Employers Taskforce
Registered: 27 Jul 2009 *Employees:* 22 *Volunteers:* 35,265
Tel: 020 7566 4893 *Website:* educationandemployers.org
Activities: Education, training
Address: Education and Employers Taskforce, Quantum House, 22-24 Red Lion Court, London, EC4A 3EB
Trustees: Mr Peter Dart, Mr David Cruickshank, Kenneth Roderick Bristow, Professor Sir Steve Smith, Margaret Elaine West, Dame Joan McVittie, Mr Will Butler-Adams, Mr Robert James Kenneth Peston, Mrs Jennifer Taylor
Income: £1,584,447 [2017]; £955,677 [2016]; £1,551,230 [2015]; £1,455,495 [2014]; £727,841 [2013]

Education Development Trust
Registered: 20 Feb 1976 *Employees:* 1,104
Tel: 0118 902 1216 *Website:* educationdevelopmenttrust.com
Activities: Education, training
Address: Education Development Trust, Highbridge House, 16-18 Duke Street, Reading, Berks, RG1 4RU
Trustees: Mr Charles Philip Graf CBE, Ms Alison MacLeod, Mr Stuart Laing, Mr Philip Wood, Mrs Christine Bridget Gilbert, Dr Timothy Walsh, Dr Peter Rawlinson, Ms Sue Hunt, Mr David Gordon Hawker
Income: £68,020,000 [2017]; £68,845,000 [2016]; £84,982,000 [2015]; £125,719,000 [2014]; £197,340,000 [2013]

The Education Endowment Foundation
Registered: 25 May 2011 *Employees:* 17
Tel: 020 7802 1676 *Website:* educationendowmentfoundation.org.uk
Activities: Education, training
Address: Education Endowment Foundation, 9th Floor, Millbank Tower, 21-24 Millbank, London, SW1P 4QP
Trustees: Mr Peter Oliver Gershon, Mr Louis Goodman Elson, Dr Lee Elliot Major, Mr Johannes Huth, Mr David Hall, Sir Peter Lampl, Mr Nat Sloane
Income: £5,333,867 [2017]; £10,024,774 [2016]; £6,147,031 [2015]; £7,820,311 [2014]; £15,768,583 [2013]

Education Policy Institute
Registered: 19 Feb 2004 *Employees:* 14
Tel: 020 7340 1165 *Website:* epi.org
Activities: General charitable purposes; education, training; advancement of health or saving of lives
Address: Centre for Reform, 6th Floor, 27 Queen Annes Gate, London, SW1H 9BU
Trustees: Sir Paul Roderick Clucas Marshall, Baroness Sally Morgan, Sir Michael Norman Wilshaw, Dr Kitty Stewart, Mr Charles David William Brand
Income: £1,079,200 [2017]; £1,157,014 [2016]; £667,650 [2015]; £673,394 [2014]; £627,347 [2013]

Education Support Partnership
Registered: 27 Apr 2015 *Employees:* 21
Tel: 020 7697 2750 *Website:* educationsupportpartnership.org.uk
Activities: Education, training; advancement of health or saving of lives; prevention or relief of poverty
Address: Education Support Partnership, 40a Drayton Park, London, N5 1EW
Trustees: Julie Davis, Mrs Lynne Tweed, Edward Sallis, Dr Jean Kelly, Mr Kevin Bartle, Ms Gwendolyn Jane Williams, Professor Christopher Day, Mr Darren Franklin, Jeremy Reynolds, Mr Harry James, Mr Rodney Ruffle
Income: £3,362,491 [2017]; £3,302,078 [2016]

Education and Services for People with Autism Limited
Registered: 25 May 1994 *Employees:* 541
Tel: 0191 516 5080 *Website:* espa.org.uk
Activities: Education, training; disability; accommodation, housing
Address: 2A Hylton Park Road, Sunderland, Tyne & Wear, SR5 3HD
Trustees: Malcolm Hooper, Paul Shattock OBE, Rita Jordan, Thomas Berney, Philip Moxon, Stephanie Robinson, Graeme Young
Income: £13,750,718 [2017]; £12,748,991 [2016]; £13,074,669 [2015]; £12,743,331 [2014]; £13,219,359 [2013]

The Education and Training Foundation
Registered: 19 Sep 2013 *Employees:* 45
Tel: 020 3740 8280 *Website:* etfoundation.co.uk
Activities: Education, training; economic, community development, employment
Address: Education & Training Foundation, 157-197 Buckingham Palace Road, London, SW1W 9SP
Trustees: Ms Sally Dicketts CBE, Mr Stephen Roy Freer, Dr Nigel Leigh OBE, Ms Lindsay Margaret Hayward-Smith, Dr Sue Pember OBE, Mr Daniel Williams, Mr Donald Hayes MBE, Mr Mark Steven White OBE DL, Ms Florence Orban, Mr Paul Mullins OBE, Mr Michael Ord, Mr Zayn Azam
Income: £32,192,000 [2017]; £28,221,000 [2016]; £27,853,066 [2015]; £15,094,220 [2014]

The Education and Training Trust of The Chartered Insurance Institute
Registered: 14 May 1993
Tel: 020 7417 4432
Activities: Education, training
Address: Chartered Insurance Institute, 20 Aldermanbury, London, EC2V 7HY
Trustees: Mr Stephen Ross, Ms Inga Beale, Ms Paula Williams, Mr Jonathan Clark, John Moore, Mr Alan Greville Clamp, Mr Simon White
Income: £6,106,000 [2016]; £6,845,000 [2015]; £7,073,000 [2014]; £9,656,000 [2013]

Education for Health
Registered: 22 Aug 1995 *Employees:* 38 *Volunteers:* 10
Tel: 01926 493313 *Website:* educationforhealth.org
Activities: Education, training; advancement of health or saving of lives
Address: Education for Health, The Athenaeum, 10 Church Street, Warwick, CV34 4AB
Trustees: Mr Robert William Hardy Strange, Mr Gary Parkinson, Dr Robert Martin Angus, Dr Jonathan Shapiro, Professor Ursula Gallagher
Income: £2,133,454 [2016]; £2,204,892 [2015]; £1,969,665 [2014]; £1,908,693 [2013]; £1,687,224 [2012]

Eduserv
Registered: 18 Feb 2000 *Employees:* 144
Tel: 0117 313 8446 *Website:* eduserv.org.uk
Activities: General charitable purposes
Address: Eduserv, 4 Portwall Lane, Bristol, BS1 6NB
Trustees: Mr Simon Jones, Mr Antony Martin Mather, Ms Jillian Moore, Ms Kate Ross, Mr Jonny Bourne, Mr Nevil Durrant, Mr Philip French, Mr Ceri Stephen Oliver Carlill, Jude Sheeran, Ms Joanne Stimpson, Mr David Owen
Income: £15,027,200 [2017]; £15,505,959 [2016]; £14,499,493 [2015]; £11,705,216 [2014]; £10,528,986 [2013]

Effective Intervention
Registered: 17 Oct 2005 *Employees:* 206
Tel: 07834 044609 *Website:* effint.org
Activities: Education, training; advancement of health or saving of lives; prevention or relief of poverty; overseas aid, famine relief; economic, community development, employment
Address: 5 Park Place Villas, London, W2 1SP
Trustees: Dr Peter David Boone, Professor Brigitte Evelyne Granville, Ms Amy Jo Boone
Income: £3,033,738 [2016]; £957,105 [2015]; £779,202 [2014]; £2,666,088 [2013]; £1,669,426 [2012]

Eglwys Bresbyteraidd Cymru - The Presbyterian Church of Wales
Registered: 7 Oct 2009 *Employees:* 112 *Volunteers:* 2,276
Tel: 029 2062 7465 *Website:* ebcpcw.org.uk
Activities: Education, training; religious activities
Address: Tabernacle Chapel, 81 Merthyr Road, Whitchurch, Cardiff, CF14 1DD
Trustees: Rev Robert Owen Roberts, Rev John Robert Bebb, Rev Brian Huw Jones, Rev John Paul Morgan, Rev Marcus Wyn Robinson, Mr Idris Owen Hughes, Mr Clifford Charles Williams, Mr Brian Lopez, Dr Wyn Rhys Morris
Income: £4,274,000 [2016]; £4,768,000 [2015]; £4,199,000 [2014]; £5,728,000 [2013]; £4,903,000 [2012]

The Egmont Trust
Registered: 21 Feb 2005 *Employees:* 4
Tel: 029 2078 6434 *Website:* egmonttrust.org
Activities: Education, training; advancement of health or saving of lives; prevention or relief of poverty; overseas aid, famine relief
Address: Temple Court, Cathedral Road, Cardiff, CF11 9HA
Trustees: Jeremy Michael Owen Evans, Mr Rory Stephen Powe, Mr Stuart Frank Powers, Clare Victoria Evans, Alison Mayne
Income: £1,345,811 [2016]; £1,623,679 [2015]; £834,351 [2014]; £564,695 [2013]; £850,141 [2012]

The Eikon Charity
Registered: 22 Apr 2005 *Employees:* 32 *Volunteers:* 50
Tel: 01932 347434 *Website:* eikon.org.uk
Activities: Education, training; amateur sport
Address: Eikon, Selsdon Road, New Haw, Addlestone, Surrey, KT15 3HP
Trustees: Mr Nigel David Blair, Mr Richard Folland, Ms Jane Hounsome, Mr Kevin Young, Sue McCauley, Mr Julian Lomas, Mrs Jenny Griffiths, Emma Wilson, Mr Nigel Goddard
Income: £1,257,016 [2017]; £585,489 [2016]; £937,718 [2015]; £614,951 [2014]; £410,838 [2013]

Eisteddfod Genedlaethol Cymru
Registered: 29 Jan 2014 *Employees:* 18 *Volunteers:* 1,000
Tel: 0845 409 0300 *Website:* eisteddfod.cymru
Activities: General charitable purposes; education, training; religious activities; arts, culture, heritage, science; amateur sport; environment, conservation, heritage; economic, community development, employment; recreation
Address: Eisteddfod Genedlaethol Cymru, 40 Parc Ty Glas, Llanishen, Cardiff, CF14 5DU
Trustees: Eric Davies, Dafydd Roberts, Eifion Lloyd Jones, Llyr Roberts, Stuart Cole, Gethin Thomas, Heledd Bebb, Gwerfyl Pierce Jones, Dyfrig Roberts, Christine James, Selwyn J Evans, Richard Davies, Elin Haf Gruffydd Jones
Income: £4,981,000 [2016]; £4,300,000 [2015]

Elam Ministries
Registered: 27 Aug 2003 *Employees:* 33 *Volunteers:* 9
Website: elam.com
Activities: Education, training; prevention or relief of poverty; overseas aid, famine relief; religious activities; arts, culture, heritage, science; human rights, religious or racial harmony, equality or diversity
Address: Grenville, Grenville Road, Shackleford, Godalming, Surrey, GU8 6AX
Trustees: Mr R Roshanzamir, Mr S Yeghnazar, Mrs Alexia Kuhn, Mr Kuniyal Kandi Devaraj, Dr John Anthony Sargent, Mrs Linaria Yeghnazar, Mr David Ara Yeghnazar, Mr Roland Worton
Income: £1,954,819 [2016]; £2,487,141 [2015]; £2,727,156 [2014]; £2,962,486 [2013]; £3,243,954 [2012]

The Elders Foundation
Registered: 29 Oct 2009 *Employees:* 12
Tel: 020 7013 4641 *Website:* theelders.org
Activities: General charitable purposes; education, training; advancement of health or saving of lives; prevention or relief of poverty; environment, conservation, heritage; economic, community development, employment; human rights, religious or racial harmony, equality or diversity
Address: Lyric House, 149 Hammersmith Road, London, W14 0QL
Trustees: President Mary Therese Robinson, Mr Kofi Atta Annan, Gro Brundtland, President Ernest Zedillo, Mr Ricardo Lagos, President Martti Ahtisaari, Mr Lakhdar Brahimi, Mrs Graca Machel, Ms Hina Jilani, Ban Ki-Moon
Income: £2,381,000 [2016]; £4,128,000 [2015]; £3,247,000 [2014]; £5,179,679 [2013]; £3,579,017 [2012]

The Electrical Industries Charity Limited
Registered: 24 Jun 1992 *Employees:* 10 *Volunteers:* 146
Tel: 020 3696 1710 *Website:* electricalcharity.org
Activities: General charitable purposes; disability; prevention or relief of poverty
Address: 36 Tanner Street, London, SE1 3LD
Trustees: Mrs Pauline Cooke, Mr Stuart MacKenzie, Mr Paul Loke, Mrs Margaret Fitzsimons, Mr David Gardiner, Mr Stewart Gregory, Ms Catherine Connolly, Mr Steve Bratt, Mr Ian Lawson, Chris Hutchinson
Income: £1,824,000 [2017]; £1,776,000 [2016]; £1,702,000 [2015]; £1,588,000 [2014]; £1,664,000 [2013]

The Electrical Safety Council
Registered: 1 Mar 1973 *Employees:* 20 *Volunteers:* 1
Tel: 020 3463 5110 *Website:* electricalsafetyfirst.org.uk
Activities: Education, training; advancement of health or saving of lives; other charitable purposes
Address: 45 Great Guildford Street, London, SE1 0ES
Trustees: Mr Bryndley Fraser Walker, Mr David Patrick Dossett, Alison Parkes, Anne Ferguson, Andy Chaplin, Samy Bounoua, Adam Williams, Mr Charles John Tanswell, Mr Newell Mc Guiness, Paul Canning, Nick Ratty, Simon Ashmore, Paul Hide
Income: £4,524,000 [2017]; £4,003,000 [2016]; £10,754,000 [2015]; £11,217,000 [2014]; £35,521,000 [2013]

Elephant Family
Registered: 18 Apr 2002 *Employees:* 14
Tel: 020 7251 5099 *Website:* elephant-family.org
Activities: Education, training; animals; environment, conservation, heritage; economic, community development, employment
Address: 1A Redchurch Street, London, E2 7DJ
Trustees: Mr David Alexander, Mr Patrick Mark, Mrs Belinda Stewart-Cox, Mr Sam Singh, Mrs Ruth Ganesh, Ms Sonya Timms, Feh Tarty, Mr Howard Mason, Mr Nigel Miller, Mr Ramani Ganesh
Income: £2,681,112 [2016]; £1,418,878 [2015]; £1,361,856 [2014]; £1,524,514 [2013]; £1,002,073 [2012]

Eleven Arches
Registered: 29 Oct 2014 *Employees:* 15 *Volunteers:* 1,010
Tel: 01388 439803 *Website:* elevenarches.org
Activities: Education, training; arts, culture, heritage, science; economic, community development, employment
Address: Eleven Arches, Flatts Farm, Toronto, Bishop Auckland, Co Durham, DL14 7SF
Trustees: Mr Jonathan Garnier Ruffer, Rev Dennis Tindall, Mr Nicholas Timothy Turner, Mr Louis Greig, Mrs Stefa Janita Lenc McManners
Income: £10,637,450 [2016]; £12,154,782 [2015]

Elim Foursquare Gospel Alliance
Registered: 20 Feb 1967 *Employees:* 1,944 *Volunteers:* 10,000
Tel: 0345 302 6750 *Website:* elim.org.uk
Activities: General charitable purposes; education, training; advancement of health or saving of lives; disability; prevention or relief of poverty; overseas aid, famine relief; accommodation, housing; religious activities; economic, community development, employment; recreation; other charitable purposes
Address: Elim International Centre, de Walden Road, West Malvern, Malvern, Worcs, WR14 4DF
Trustees: Rev Mr Colin Walter Dye BD, Rev Gordon Howard Neale, Rev Stuart Blount, Rev Christopher Paul Cartwright, Rev James Jeffrey Glass, The Elim Trust Corporation, Rev D Campbell, Rev Kevin Malcolm Peat, Rev Mark Pugh, Rev Duncan James Clark, Rev Simon Foster
Income: £66,291,442 [2016]; £65,334,229 [2015]; £68,270,617 [2014]; £66,519,130 [2013]; £62,292,265 [2012]

Gerald Palmer Eling Trust Company
Registered: 24 Nov 2003 *Employees:* 4
Tel: 01635 200268
Activities: General charitable purposes; advancement of health or saving of lives; prevention or relief of poverty; accommodation, housing; religious activities; environment, conservation, heritage
Address: Eling Estate Office, Wellhouse, Hermitage, Thatcham, Berks, RG18 9UF
Trustees: Mr Robin Shedden Broadhurst, Mr Desmond Roger Wingate Harrison, Mr Kenneth Robert McDiarmid, Mr James William Gardiner
Income: £1,612,107 [2017]; £1,597,690 [2016]; £1,435,282 [2015]; £1,324,122 [2014]; £1,317,486 [2013]

The T. S. Eliot Foundation
Registered: 7 Nov 2014 *Employees:* 3
Tel: 01908 674484
Activities: Education, training; arts, culture, heritage, science
Address: Keens Shay Keens MK LLP, Sovereign Court, 230 Upper Fifth Street, Milton Keynes, Bucks, MK9 2HR
Trustees: Mrs Clare Reihill, Philip Durrance, Jackie Bodley
Income: £2,393,380 [2017]; £10,623,419 [2016]

Elite Supported Employment Agency Limited
Registered: 21 Sep 1995 *Employees:* 50
Tel: 01443 226664 *Website:* elitesupportedemployment.co.uk
Activities: Education, training
Address: 8 Magden Park, Green Meadow, Llantrisant, Rhondda Cynon Taf, CF72 8XT
Trustees: Mr Andrew Hole, Mr Richard Jones, Mrs Vanessa Bowkett, Mr Geoffrey Wood, Miss Beth Thomas, Mr Joe Powell
Income: £1,319,581 [2017]; £832,476 [2016]; £895,089 [2015]; £1,166,467 [2014]; £1,210,929 [2013]

The Marian Elizabeth Trust
Registered: 5 May 2016
Tel: 01536 560394
Activities: General charitable purposes; advancement of health or saving of lives; disability
Address: The Enterprise Centre, Priors Hall, Corby, Northants, NN17 5EU
Trustees: Mr Robert Rowley LLB, Mr Michael John Edwards BA, Mrs Maureen Edwards, Ms Rosemary Alexandra Edwards BA
Income: £3,505,000 [2017]

Ellenor

Registered: 9 Nov 2007 *Employees:* 169 *Volunteers:* 600
Tel: 01322 221315 *Website:* ellenor.org
Activities: Education, training; advancement of health or saving of lives
Address: Ellenor Lions Hospices, Ellenor Centre, St Ronans View, Dartford, Kent, DA1 1AE
Trustees: Ann Barnes, Mr Maurice Anthony Tutty, Ms Catherine Jane Rossiter, Bryan Harris, Kerry-Jane Packman, Mr Andrew Roger Wedderburn-Day, Mrs Mary Saunders, Dr Vasu, Mrs Nancy Cogswell, Jan Stanton, Glynis Rogers
Income: £6,852,775 [2017]; £6,434,423 [2016]; £6,216,241 [2015]; £7,087,362 [2014]; £5,789,002 [2013]

John Ellerman Foundation

Registered: 29 Nov 1971 *Employees:* 5
Tel: 020 7930 8566 *Website:* ellerman.org.uk
Activities: General charitable purposes
Address: The Moorgate Trust Fund, Suite 10, Aria House, 23 Craven Street, London, WC2N 5NS
Trustees: Lady Sarah Riddell, Dr Brian Hurwitz, Mr Hugh Raven, Mr Gary Steinberg, Mr Keith Anthony Shepherd, Mr Peter Kyle, Mr Tufyal Choudhury, Ms Annika Small, Ms Geraldine Blake
Income: £4,100,000 [2017]; £3,931,000 [2016]; £3,692,000 [2015]; £2,312,000 [2014]; £1,951,000 [2013]

Ellesmere College Limited

Registered: 5 Apr 2004 *Employees:* 245
Tel: 01691 626509 *Website:* ellesmere.com
Activities: Education, training
Address: Ellesmere College, Ellesmere, Salop, SY12 9AB
Trustees: Mr Mark James Rylands The Right Reverend, Ms Jane Tomkinson, Mr Charles Lillis, Mrs Margaret Ann Denton CertEd, Mrs Jane Makie Trowbridge LLP JP, Mr John Stuart Hopkins, Mr Richard Alan Kelsey Hoppins, Miss Siobhan Connor, Mr Michael Donald Thomas Sampson
Income: £9,957,608 [2017]; £10,357,035 [2016]; £10,175,245 [2015]; £10,752,268 [2014]; £9,374,064 [2013]

Ellingham Employment Services

Registered: 6 May 1992 *Employees:* 65 *Volunteers:* 5
Tel: 020 8926 3931 *Website:* ellingham.org.uk
Activities: Education, training; disability; economic, community development, employment
Address: 5 Ellingham Road, London, E15 2AU
Trustees: Mr Peter John Barry Le Rasle, Mrs Saira Hussain, Mrs Fatima Vawda, Mrs Margaret Evelyn Willett, Mrs Beryl Streader MBE
Income: £1,329,995 [2016]; £1,358,574 [2015]; £1,414,947 [2014]; £1,387,486 [2013]; £1,348,270 [2012]

The Elm Foundation Ltd

Registered: 10 Jan 1992 *Employees:* 55 *Volunteers:* 20
Tel: 01246 238248 *Website:* ddvsas.org.uk
Activities: Accommodation, housing
Address: 6 Fairfield Road, Chesterfield, Derbys, S40 4TP
Trustees: Mr Carl Griffiths, Ms Mary McElvaney, Ms Deborah Jayne Marlow, Ms Jill Ryalls, Ms Jill Gregory, Miss Keeley Fletcher, Mr Mohammad Idriss, Mr Gerard Cahill
Income: £1,274,519 [2017]; £1,467,971 [2016]; £1,246,633 [2015]; £1,153,537 [2014]; £1,163,227 [2013]

Elmhurst Ballet School

Registered: 19 Aug 1994 *Employees:* 85 *Volunteers:* 10
Tel: 0121 472 6655 *Website:* elmhurstdance.co.uk
Activities: Education, training; arts, culture, heritage, science
Address: Ms Diana Wardle, Elmhurst School for Dance, 249 Bristol Road, Birmingham, B5 7UH
Trustees: Mr Roger Burman CBE BSc LLD DL, Mr Roy Shields, Miss Sarah Evans, Mr Tim Abbotts, Prof Matthew Wyon, Sue Butler, Dr John Bryson, Mr James Harris, Lynn Wallis, Mr Richard Ash, Ms Alison Matthews, Ms Pearl Chesterman
Income: £4,939,602 [2016]; £4,259,754 [2015]; £4,227,733 [2014]; £4,166,029 [2013]; £4,214,305 [2012]

The Elmhurst Foundation

Registered: 14 Sep 2015 *Employees:* 90
Tel: 01242 285895 *Website:* elmhurstfoundation.org
Activities: General charitable purposes; education, training; advancement of health or saving of lives; environment, conservation, heritage; economic, community development, employment; other charitable purposes
Address: 37 St George's Road, Cheltenham, Glos, GL50 3DU
Trustees: Miss Helen Louise Aylward-Smith, Mr Simon William Waterfield, Mr David James Cox
Income: £3,403,871 [2017]; £5,000 [2016]

The Elms (Colwall) Limited

Registered: 4 Nov 1965 *Employees:* 72
Tel: 01684 540344
Activities: Education, training
Address: The Elms School, Colwall Green, Malvern, Worcs, WR13 6EF
Trustees: The Reverend Prebendary The Revd Carl Attwood, Mr Nat Hone, Mrs Diana Holloway, Mrs Tamsin Clive, Lady Susanna McFarlane, Mr Charles William Milne, Mrs Jane Helen Sale, Mr Andrew Guy Wynn, Dr Valerie Beynon Payne, Mr Ian Falconer, Mr Patrick Bailey, Mrs Lucy Chenevix-Trench, Mr Tobias William Stubbs, Mr Philip Thomas
Income: £2,883,734 [2017]; £3,190,601 [2016]; £2,951,955 [2015]; £2,940,467 [2014]; £2,719,051 [2013]

Elrahma Charity Trust

Registered: 6 Oct 1993 *Employees:* 6
Tel: 020 3026 3397 *Website:* elrahma.org.uk
Activities: General charitable purposes; education, training; prevention or relief of poverty; overseas aid, famine relief
Address: Suite 201, Stanmore Business & Innovation Centre, Stanmore Place, Howard Road, London, HA7 1BT
Trustees: Mr O Megerisi, Mr Abubaker Megerisi, Mr Otman Megerisi, Mr Ali Abubaker Megerisi, Mr Patrick Daniels, Mr Hazem Megerisi, Mr Mohamed Megerisi, Mr Tarek Megerisi
Income: £1,211,470 [2016]; £1,189,617 [2015]; £1,452,388 [2014]; £1,169,723 [2013]; £1,237,430 [2012]

Elstree School Limited

Registered: 21 Jul 1961 *Employees:* 76 *Volunteers:* 1
Tel: 0118 971 2911 *Website:* elstreeschool.org.uk
Activities: Education, training
Address: 46 Okebourne Park, Swindon, Wilts, SN3 6AH
Trustees: Mrs Emma Elizabeth Ann McKendrick, Mr Mark Randall, Mr Niall Murphy, Mr Richard Waller, Mrs Elizabeth Jill Spacman Boggis, Mr Sydney Hill, Mr James Sunley, Mrs Emma Louise Duncan McGrath, Rev Rupert Shelley, Mrs Jane Lyons, Mr Gavin Owston, Mr Jonathan Alexander Justin Vincent
Income: £4,652,704 [2016]; £4,922,461 [2015]; £4,227,023 [2014]; £3,815,775 [2013]; £4,966,113 [2012]

Eltham College

Registered: 10 Oct 1996 *Employees:* 206 *Volunteers:* 30
Tel: 020 8857 7360 *Website:* eltham-college.org.uk
Activities: Education, training
Address: Eltham College, Grove Park Road, London, SE9 4QF
Trustees: Rev Richard Blyth, Mr Brian William O'Donoghue, Mrs Prupence Ann Corp BA, Mrs Anne Edwards, Mr Simon Robert Charlick, Mrs Isabelle Wort, Mr Robert Arthur Elliot Davey, Mr Timothy Wilson, Mr Lee David Jagger, Mrs Rosemary Ann Morgan, Mr Martin Fosten, Mr Nigel Betts, Mr Andrew Frederick John Neden, Mr Christopher John Ring, Mr William Oram, Mr Stephen Wells, Mr Graham Dransfield
Income: £13,509,277 [2016]; £12,683,873 [2015]; £11,692,564 [2014]; £11,294,540 [2013]; £11,219,638 [2012]

Ely Cathedral Trust

Registered: 24 Nov 1972
Tel: 01353 660321 *Website:* cathedral.ely.anglican.org
Activities: General charitable purposes; religious activities; environment, conservation, heritage
Address: The Chapter House, The College, Ely, Cambs, CB7 4DL
Trustees: Mr Richard Paul Slogrove, Canon Jessica Martin, The Very Reverend Mark Bonney, Mrs Jane Lewin-Smith, Mr Charles Rawlinson, Mr Tom Michael Curtis Green, Canon Paul Evans, Mr Ian Pattinson
Income: £1,185,678 [2016]; £688,446 [2015]; £543,874 [2014]; £383,925 [2013]; £454,606 [2012]

The Ely Diocesan Board of Finance

Registered: 3 Nov 1965 *Employees:* 36
Website: elydiocese.org
Activities: Religious activities
Address: Ely Diocesan Offices, Bishop Woodford House, Barton Road, Ely, Cambs, CB7 4DX
Trustees: The Rt Revd Stephen Conway Bishop of Ely, Mark Bonney, Mr Stephen Edgar Tooke, Rev Fiona Elizabeth Gordon Brampton, Brian Atling, Mrs Janet Perrett, Ven Dr Alex Hughes, Mr Donald Arthur Ashmore, Mr Timothy Burgess, Robert Needle, Andrew Chrich, Martin MacFarlane, Bishop David, Simon Talbott, Dr Arvan Pritchard, Hugh McCurdy, Mr Simon Kershaw, Rev Jason Taylor, Nicholas Moir, Peter Maxwell, Mr Tim Walters, Wendy Thomson, Carol Nicholas-Letch
Income: £10,078,000 [2016]; £9,162,000 [2015]; £9,137,000 [2014]; £8,821,000 [2013]; £8,037,000 [2012]

Embrace The Middle East

Registered: 30 Jun 1999 *Employees:* 64 *Volunteers:* 95
Tel: 01494 897950 *Website:* embraceme.org
Activities: Education, training; advancement of health or saving of lives; disability; prevention or relief of poverty; overseas aid, famine relief; religious activities; economic, community development, employment; other charitable purposes
Address: Embrace The Middle East, 24 London Road West, Amersham, Bucks, HP7 0EZ
Trustees: Mr Stephen Philip Dengate, Rev Canon Anthony Ball, Ms Madeleine Davies, Ms Mary Smith, Dr Kathryn Ann Kraft, Ms Alana Jane Harris, Mr Tanas Alqassis, Ms Mariam Tadros, John Neate, Mrs Christine Ann Clayton, Gareth David Williams
Income: £5,990,789 [2016]; £3,707,528 [2015]; £3,823,648 [2014]; £3,475,517 [2013]; £4,216,922 [2012]

The Embroiderers' Guild

Registered: 8 May 1964 *Employees:* 6 *Volunteers:* 1,019
Website: embroiderersguild.com
Activities: Education, training; arts, culture, heritage, science; environment, conservation, heritage
Address: Bucks County Museum, Church Street, Aylesbury, Bucks, HP20 2QP
Trustees: Anthea Godfrey, Elizabeth Rutt, Elizabeth Smith, Kirsty Whitlock, Penny Hill, Mrs Muriel Campbell, Linda M Danielis, Amanda Smith, Alex Messenger, Lesley Jones
Income: £1,535,922 [2016]; £1,669,793 [2015]; £1,630,307 [2014]; £1,517,371 [2013]; £1,589,475 [2012]

The Emerald Foundation

Registered: 8 Dec 2008
Tel: 01274 777700 *Website:* emeraldfoundation.org.uk
Activities: Arts, culture, heritage, science; amateur sport; animals
Address: The Emerald Group, Howard House, Dowley Gap Business Park, Dowley Gap Lane, Bingley, W Yorks, BD16 1WA
Trustees: Dr Keith Howard, Mr Timothy Harvey Ratcliffe, Miss Melissa Fojt, Mr Peter George Meredith, Mrs Karen Noelle Fojt
Income: £1,500,000 [2016]; £1,500,000 [2015]; £1,250,000 [2014]; £1,115,000 [2013]; £1,000,000 [2012]

Emergency Nutrition Network

Registered: 7 Jul 2006 *Employees:* 11
Tel: 01865 324996 *Website:* ennonline.net
Activities: Education, training; advancement of health or saving of lives; overseas aid, famine relief
Address: 32 Leopold Street, Oxford, OX4 1TW
Trustees: Mrs Marie McGrath, Mr Nigel Milway, Ms Victoria Lack, Dr Bruce Laurence, Mr Jeremy Shoham, Anna Taylor
Income: £1,225,956 [2017]; £907,046 [2016]; £650,675 [2015]; £505,257 [2014]; £1,092,036 [2013]

The Emerson College Trust Limited

Registered: 24 Oct 1967 *Employees:* 14
Tel: 01342 822238 *Website:* emerson.org.uk
Activities: Education, training; environment, conservation, heritage
Address: Emerson College, Forest Row, E Sussex, RH18 5JX
Trustees: Dr James Dyson, Ms Charlene Collison Briault, Ms Paulamaria Blaxland-De Lange, Diane Hume, Rev Thomas Oliver Ravets, Mr George Perry
Income: £1,229,969 [2017]; £686,048 [2016]; £1,028,483 [2015]; £971,380 [2014]; £633,505 [2013]

Emmanuel Bristol

Registered: 21 Dec 2010 *Employees:* 9 *Volunteers:* 350
Tel: 0117 930 4950 *Website:* emmanuelbristol.org.uk
Activities: Religious activities
Address: 35 Walsingham Road, Bristol, BS6 5BU
Trustees: Nicholas Brand, Andrew Paterson, Paul Stacey, Tim Colyer, Mr David Barton, David Rice, Christa Moll, Jack Butler
Income: £1,878,506 [2017]; £449,590 [2016]; £440,835 [2015]; £388,118 [2014]; £298,418 [2013]

The Emmanuel Community Charitable Trust Limited
Registered: 28 Jun 1994
Tel: 020 7240 5821
Activities: Religious activities
Address: Sovereign House, 212-224 Shaftesbury Avenue, London, WC2H 8HQ
Trustees: Mr Kevin Custis, Mr Laurent Landete, Mr Benoit Laplaize, Mr Philippe Jacques Marie Fayet, Mr Markus Trautmansdorff
Income: £9,798,746 [2016]; £7,635,804 [2015]; £7,879,765 [2014]; £946,251 [2013]; £1,311,783 [2012]

Emmanuel Evangelical Church
Registered: 4 Dec 2013 *Employees:* 19 *Volunteers:* 344
Tel: 020 7654 5649 *Website:* emmanuelchurch.org.uk
Activities: Education, training; overseas aid, famine relief; religious activities
Address: Emmanuel Centre, 9-23 Marsham Street, London, SW1P 3DW
Trustees: Mr Peter Yee Kong Loo, Andrew Teng Han Tan, Mrs Naomi Poo Phar, Ms Temitope Teniola, Miss Lorna Mary Thomson, Andy Tham, Mr Chiang Joo Lim
Income: £1,415,139 [2016]; £1,507,194 [2015]

Emmaus Cambridge
Registered: 18 Sep 1997 *Employees:* 15 *Volunteers:* 18
Tel: 01223 863657 *Website:* emmauscambridge.org
Activities: The prevention or relief of poverty; accommodation, housing; economic, community development, employment
Address: Emmaus Cambridge, Green End, Landbeach, Cambridge, CB25 9FD
Trustees: Mrs Hazel Smith, Matthew Last, Mr Stephen Boughton, Mr John Dawson, Mrs Carol Margaret Dasgupta, Mr Stephen Cook, Dr Andrew Cornish
Income: £1,190,051 [2016]; £1,045,455 [2015]; £923,649 [2014]; £837,265 [2013]; £838,530 [2012]

Emmaus Gloucestershire
Registered: 16 Jan 1998 *Employees:* 20 *Volunteers:* 33
Tel: 07788 404522 *Website:* emmaus.org.uk
Activities: Accommodation, housing; economic, community development, employment
Address: Emmaus Gloucestershire, Chequers Road Workshop, Chequers Road, Gloucester, GL4 6PN
Trustees: Mr Michael John Heap, Ms Andrea Creedon, Mr Richard Williams, Mr Clive Thomas, Ms Alison Beddoes, Mr Michael Hudson, Mrs Helen Wolfson, Mr Laurent Bovier, Mr Neil Mantle
Income: £1,068,832 [2017]; £1,080,252 [2016]; £1,113,847 [2015]; £896,132 [2014]; £899,909 [2013]

Emmaus South Lambeth Community
Registered: 19 May 1998 *Employees:* 26 *Volunteers:* 40
Website: emmaus.org.uk
Activities: Education, training; prevention or relief of poverty; accommodation, housing; economic, community development, employment
Address: 9 Knight's Hill, West Norwood, London, SE27 0HY
Trustees: Mr Jonathan Pallas, Catherine Emma Zahra, Mr Graham John Beattie, Mrs Protima Sikdar-Wood, Mr Robert Lee, Mr Ian Kevin Duffy, Mrs Claire Burton, Miss Sian Nicholson, Miss Saffron Clackson, Mr Jamie Palmer
Income: £1,339,727 [2017]; £1,102,816 [2016]; £985,117 [2015]; £856,137 [2014]; £644,656 [2013]

Emmaus St Albans
Registered: 3 Feb 1999 *Employees:* 13 *Volunteers:* 28
Tel: 01438 832451 *Website:* emmaus.org.uk
Activities: Accommodation, housing; economic, community development, employment
Address: 2 Brownfield Way, Wheathampstead, St Albans, Herts, AL4 8LL
Trustees: Mr Keith Neill Tolladay, Mr Ivan Marshall, Mrs Heather Margaret Hurford, Mr Jonathan Landau, Mrs Rosemary Susan Fraser, Mr Christopher Patrick Newton-Smith, Mr Richard Anthony Exact
Income: £1,103,643 [2017]; £1,107,971 [2016]; £1,116,338 [2015]; £845,970 [2014]; £762,266 [2013]

Emmaus Turvey
Registered: 31 Oct 2000 *Employees:* 15 *Volunteers:* 33
Tel: 01234 720123 *Website:* emmausvillagecarlton.org.uk
Activities: Accommodation, housing
Address: 36 High Street, Harrold, Bedford, MK43 7DQ
Trustees: Mr James Stewart, Mr Stephen Christopher Taylor Arnold MA MRTPI MRICS, Mr John Graham Moore, Mrs Lucia Jane Smith, Mr Colin Stephen Bramall, Mrs Primrose Pearl Hudson, Mr Alistair Edward Tusting, Dr Maria Fordham
Income: £1,270,595 [2017]; £1,059,797 [2016]; £1,027,296 [2015]; £1,085,869 [2014]; £1,061,697 [2013]

Emmaus U.K.
Registered: 18 Sep 1997 *Employees:* 26
Tel: 0300 303 7555 *Website:* emmaus.org.uk
Activities: The prevention or relief of poverty; economic, community development, employment
Address: 302 Scott House, The Custard Factory, Gibb Street, Digbeth, Birmingham, B9 4AA
Trustees: Mr Frank McMahon, Mr Keith Jeffrey, Miss Geraldine Tsakirakis, Mr John Nicholas Clarke, Mr Richard Wallace, Ms Monica Wallace, Ms Kelly Thompson, Mr David Cooper, Mr Anthony Harry Ferrier, Mrs Susan Brooksbank-Taylor, Miss Ruby Dickens, Ms Pauline Curl
Income: £1,939,065 [2017]; £1,903,545 [2016]; £3,761,613 [2015]; £2,576,551 [2014]; £1,856,021 [2013]

Employers Network for Equality and Inclusion
Registered: 5 Jan 2004 *Employees:* 15
Tel: 020 7922 7790 *Website:* enei.org.uk
Activities: General charitable purposes; education, training; prevention or relief of poverty; economic, community development, employment
Address: 32-36 Loman Street, London, SE1 0EH
Trustees: Mr Trevor Phillips, Mr Harry Gaskell, Mr Barry Mordsley, Mr Jonathan Crookall, Ms Claudine Adeyemi, Heather Jackson, Mr Jonathan Rees, Mr Daniel Mortimer, Ms Sarah Churchman, Ms Janine McDowell
Income: £1,378,874 [2017]; £1,301,386 [2016]; £1,026,089 [2015]; £669,306 [2014]; £518,285 [2013]

Empower - The Emerging Markets Foundation Limited
Registered: 23 Apr 2007 *Employees:* 3
Website: empowerweb.org
Activities: Education, training; prevention or relief of poverty; economic, community development, employment
Address: Empower, c/o Finisterre Capital, 10 New Burlington Street, London, W1S 3BE
Trustees: Mr Bradley James Wickens, Mrs Marta Cabrera, Mr Rafael Biosse-Duplan, Mr Jeremy Llewelyn, Ms Parvoleta Shtereva, Mrs Aditi Thorat, Mr Xavier Corin Mick, Mr Kunal Shah, Mr Fernando Ortega, Mr Peter Tolhurst, Mr Stephen Charles Jefferies, Mr Jonathan Andrew Bagot Bayliss, Mrs Helene Williamson, Mr Ozan Tarman, Mr Francisco Fernandez De Ybarra, Mr Marc Christopher Balston, Ms Pontso Mafethe, Mr Eric Levine, Mr Marcin Wiszniewski, Mr Pierre-Yves Bareau, Mr Michael Lekan, Mrs Angela Labombarda
Income: £2,876,153 [2017]; £1,447,879 [2016]; £1,773,089 [2015]; £2,859,751 [2014]; £1,348,771 [2013]

Empower Global
Registered: 26 Sep 1996 *Employees:* 24 *Volunteers:* 600
Tel: 01483 455244 *Website:* family-church.org.uk
Activities: General charitable purposes; education, training; prevention or relief of poverty; overseas aid, famine relief; religious activities
Address: First Floor, Family Church, Weyford House, 21-22 Woodbridge Meadows, Guildford, Surrey, GU1 1BA
Trustees: Mr Wayne Martin Keeping, Mr Simon Smith, Mr Derek Smith, Mr Mark Donald Charles Ward
Income: £1,084,730 [2017]; £1,054,033 [2016]; £1,140,023 [2015]; £1,049,952 [2014]; £774,225 [2013]

Empowering People Inspiring Communities Limited
Registered: 2 Apr 2007 *Employees:* 18
Tel: 01782 252575 *Website:* epichousing.co.uk
Activities: The prevention or relief of poverty; accommodation, housing; economic, community development, employment; other charitable purposes
Address: Empowering People Inspiring Communities Limited, 131-141 Ubberley Road, Bentilee, Stoke on Trent, Staffs, ST2 0EF
Trustees: Mr Andrew Stone, Mr Alexander Fury, Mr Darshan Singh Matharoo, Mrs Dawn Harries, Mr Peter Turner, Mr John Gething, Miss Kirsty Holmes, Mr Stephen Funnell, Mr Peter Lunio
Income: £3,926,277 [2017]; £3,747,013 [2016]; £3,494,011 [2015]; £3,302,371 [2014]; £3,204,577 [2013]

Emuno Educational Centre Limited
Registered: 11 Jun 1965 *Volunteers:* 3
Tel: 020 8802 9496
Activities: Education, training; advancement of health or saving of lives; prevention or relief of poverty; religious activities
Address: 11 Egerton Road, London, N16 6UE
Trustees: Mr Israel Yechiel Chersky, Mr Aron Kahn, Mr David Stobiecki
Income: £4,159,724 [2017]; £2,442,400 [2016]; £1,346,735 [2015]; £972,924 [2014]; £1,033,741 [2013]

The Ena Makin Educational Trust
Registered: 31 Mar 1966 *Employees:* 55 *Volunteers:* 1
Tel: 01732 453039 *Website:* granvilleschool.org
Activities: Education, training
Address: The Granville School, 2 Bradbourne Park Road, Sevenoaks, Kent, TN13 3LJ
Trustees: Mrs Elizabeth Sindall, Mr Rowland Constantine, Mrs Jane Holland, Mrs Charlotte Kramer, Mr Paul Sheldon, Mr Jonathan Sorrell, Mr Mark Kibblewhite, Mrs Charlotte Glanville
Income: £2,452,230 [2016]; £2,379,030 [2015]; £2,173,338 [2014]; £2,137,231 [2013]; £2,020,589 [2012]

Encompass (Dorset)
Registered: 8 Aug 1991 *Employees:* 188
Tel: 01305 267483 *Website:* encompassdorset.co.uk
Activities: The advancement of health or saving of lives; disability; accommodation, housing
Address: Grove House, Millers Close, Dorchester, DT1 1SS
Trustees: Rev Nigel Tooth, Mrs Patricia Elizabeth Mitchell, Mr Christopher John Kennedy, Mr David Corbin, Ms Norma Lee, Mr Grant Usmar
Income: £6,770,000 [2017]; £6,717,000 [2016]; £6,903,000 [2015]; £7,353,000 [2014]; £7,010,000 [2013]

The End of Life Partnership Limited
Registered: 15 Dec 1998 *Employees:* 21 *Volunteers:* 2
Tel: 01270 758120 *Website:* eolp.org.uk
Activities: Education, training; advancement of health or saving of lives
Address: Winterley Grange, Unit 8 Wheelock Heath Business, Court, Alsager Road, Winterley, Sandbach, Cheshire, CW11 4RQ
Trustees: Mr Geoffrey Briggs, Ms Kathy James, Mr James Michie MacDonald, Mrs Tracy Lynne Paine, Mr Burhanudin Zavery, Mrs Anita Christine Miller, Ms Rachael Lewis, Mrs Kate Joanna Handel, Ms Jayne Hartley
Income: £1,104,126 [2017]; £1,177,467 [2016]; £1,039,673 [2015]; £933,138 [2014]; £623,745 [2012]

Energise Me
Registered: 16 Feb 2016 *Employees:* 13 *Volunteers:* 392
Tel: 01962 676165 *Website:* energiseme.org
Activities: General charitable purposes; education, training; advancement of health or saving of lives; recreation; other charitable purposes
Address: Third Floor, Cromwell House, 15 Andover Road, Winchester, Hants, SO23 7BT
Trustees: Andrew Gibson, Jonathan Monkcom, Dawn Tilley, Jan Halliday, Selina Russell, Claire Beasley, Lucy Mediratta
Income: £2,669,234 [2017]

Energy 4 Impact
Registered: 11 May 2007 *Employees:* 98
Website: energy4impact.org
Activities: General charitable purposes; prevention or relief of poverty; environment, conservation, heritage; economic, community development, employment
Address: Energy 4 Impact, 34-36 Gray's Inn Road, London, WC1X 8HR
Trustees: Mr Anthony Charles Marsh, Mrs Richenda Van Leeuwen, Ms Sheila Oparaocha, Ms Dianne Rudo
Income: £4,027,502 [2017]; £3,722,246 [2016]; £3,258,506 [2015]; £4,739,644 [2014]; £3,238,802 [2013]

Energy Institute
Registered: 10 Jun 2003 *Employees:* 67 *Volunteers:* 1,632
Tel: 020 7467 7100 *Website:* energyinst.org
Activities: Education, training; arts, culture, heritage, science; environment, conservation, heritage
Address: Energy Institute, 61 New Cavendish Street, London, W1G 7AR
Trustees: Bernie Bulkin FEI, Malcolm Brinded CBE FEI, Christopher Boocock CEng FEI, Nicola Murphy, Jim Skea FEI, Jaz Rabadia MBE FEI, Andy Hadland, Dr Ceri Powell FEI, Alastair Robertson CEng MEI, Dr Ibilola Amao FEI, Vivienne Cox CBE FEI, Joanne Wade FEI, Boma Douglas CEng MEI, Mike Parker CBE FEI, Belinda Mindell FEI, Carl Hughes FEI, Paul Smith FEI, Emily Spearman CEng MEI, James MacRae FEI, Steve Holliday FEI, John Currie CEng FEI
Income: £7,136,000 [2016]; £6,877,000 [2015]; £7,419,000 [2014]; £7,036,000 [2013]; £6,098,000 [2012]

Engineering Construction Industry Training Board
Registered: 4 Sep 1972 *Employees:* 77
Tel: 01923 402124 *Website:* ecitb.org.uk
Activities: Education, training
Address: Blue Court, 1 Church Lane, Kings Langley, Herts, WD4 8JP
Trustees: Mike Hockey, Martyn Fletcher, Mrs Tracey Shelley, Mr Chris Claypole, Mrs Lynda Armstrong, Mr Philip Whitehurst, Mr David Boath, Ms Dawn James
Income: £37,035,000 [2016]; £39,371,374 [2015]; £32,239,169 [2014]; £29,035,656 [2013]; £27,580,971 [2012]

The Engineering Council
Registered: 26 Jan 1983 *Employees:* 26 *Volunteers:* 100
Tel: 020 3206 0500 *Website:* engc.org.uk
Activities: Economic, community development, employment
Address: 5th Floor, Woolgate Exchange, 25 Basinghall Street, London, EC2V 5HA
Trustees: Prof John Chudley Ceng Fimarest, Mr Simon Vaitkevicius, Miss Carolyn Griffiths CEng FIMechE FREng, Mr Douglas Moray Alexander, Col Martin Court CEng FIMechE, Mr Robin Philip Smith CEng FIMechE, Mr George Adams CEng FCIBSE, Mr Christopher Boyle BComm, William Hewlitt Eur Ing, Prof Christopher Atkins CEng FRAeS, Ms Michelle Richmond CEng FIET, Mr Paul Excell CEng FBCS MIET, Mr Tom Ridgman CEng FIRT, Prof Jonathan Seville FREng FIChemE, Mrs Jane Cannon MBE CEng FIET, Prof Roger Plank CEng FIStructE MICE, Col George Marsh Td Dl Ceng Dba Fice Finstre, Professor Kevin Jones CEng CITP CSci FBCS FIET, Eur Ing Dr Graham Woodrow CEng FIMMM, Dr Scott Steedman CBE CEng FICE Finstre FREng, Mr Stephen Catte Ieng Honsoe Honfiplante, Mr Terrance William Fuller CEng MICE MCIWEM
Income: £3,037,106 [2016]; £2,897,315 [2015]; £2,953,551 [2014]; £2,875,843 [2013]; £2,898,050 [2012]

The Engineering Development Trust
Registered: 7 Mar 2014 *Employees:* 116 *Volunteers:* 150
Tel: 01707 871504 *Website:* etrust.org.uk
Activities: Education, training
Address: Weltech Centre, Ridgeway, Welwyn Garden City, Herts, AL7 2AA
Trustees: Dr Rebecca Bowden, Mr Nicholas Buckland OBE, Dr Frances Saunders, Mr Philip Charles Pickering, Alison Hodge, Samantha Bulkeley, Peter Chivers, William McGawley, Mr Jim Davison, Dr Nike Folayan, Tracy Fennell, Mr Gareth Hedicker, Simon Humphrey
Income: £4,348,300 [2016]; £4,347,500 [2015]

The Engineering and Technology Board
Registered: 6 Dec 2001 *Employees:* 41 *Volunteers:* 1,991
Tel: 020 3206 0405 *Website:* engineeringuk.com
Activities: Education, training; arts, culture, heritage, science; economic, community development, employment
Address: 5th Floor, Engineeringuk, Woolgate Exchange, 25 Basinghall Street, London, EC2V 5HA
Trustees: Prof Christopher John Atkin, Mr Nigel Fine, Mr Nicholas Guy Baveystock, Ms Elaine Roberts, Dr Toby StJohn King, Mr Victor Manuel Chavez, Dr Hayaatun Sillem, Mrs Jacqueline Ferguson, Mr Malcolm Arthur Brinded, Mr Stephen Tetlow MBE, Ms Elizabeth Kathleen Meyrick, Prof Sarah Katherine Spurgeon, Mr Robin Gisby, Ms Miranda Abigail Appleton, Ms Rachel Clare Stringer
Income: £9,906,000 [2017]; £9,890,000 [2016]; £9,119,000 [2015]; £9,050,000 [2014]; £8,556,000 [2013]

England and Wales Cricket Trust
Registered: 16 Dec 2005
Activities: Education, training; amateur sport; recreation
Address: England and Wales Cricket Trust, Lord's Cricket Ground, St Johns Wood, London, NW8 8QZ
Trustees: Mr C D Fearnley, Mr Ian Nicholas Lovett, Mr Tom William Harrison, Rear Admiral Roger Charles Moylan-Jones, Ebony-Jewel Rainford-Brent, Mr Scott Smith
Income: £2,986,828 [2017]; £5,107,264 [2016]; £35,308,318 [2015]; £14,297,930 [2014]; £4,459,573 [2013]

The English Benedictine Order of Oulton Abbey Near Stone, Staffs
Registered: 5 Nov 1963 *Employees:* 62 *Volunteers:* 6
Tel: 01785 812049
Activities: General charitable purposes; religious activities
Address: 358 Sandon Road, Stoke on Trent, Staffs, ST3 7EB
Trustees: The Right Reverend Dom Walter Geoffrey Scott OSB, Dame Benedicta OSB, The Rev Dom Thomas Regan, Right Reverend Dom David Roger Charlesworth OSB, The Right Reverend David McGough
Income: £1,159,399 [2017]; £982,747 [2016]; £1,014,729 [2015]; £860,251 [2014]; £800,688 [2013]

The English Concert
Registered: 28 Sep 1976 *Employees:* 3
Tel: 020 7227 7000 *Website:* englishconcert.co.uk
Activities: Education, training; arts, culture, heritage, science
Address: Bircham Dyson Bell, 50 Broadway, London, SW1H 0BL
Trustees: Mr Robin Paul Binks, Mr Simon Weil, Mrs Nicola Anne Oppenheimer, Dr Richard James Arthur Golding, Nigel Martyn Carrington, Kimiko Shimoda, Mr George Barnett Burnett, Mr Alan Gemes, Professor Sir Curtis Price, Mr John Reeve FCA CBIM, Simon Jennings, Mr Joseph Smouha QC, Dr Vivienne Alexandra Monk, Mr Hugh James Tilney, Dr Alan Stuart Harley
Income: £1,393,710 [2017]; £792,387 [2016]; £1,103,575 [2015]; £1,094,022 [2014]; £937,014 [2013]

The English Dominican Congregation (Stone) Charitable Fund
Registered: 12 Aug 1976 *Employees:* 183 *Volunteers:* 15
Tel: 01785 813552 *Website:* stonedominicans.org.uk
Activities: General charitable purposes; education, training; advancement of health or saving of lives; disability; religious activities
Address: St Dominics Convent, 21 Station Road, Stone, Staffs, ST15 8EN
Trustees: Sister Mary Pauline Burling, Sister Angela Mary Leydon, Sister Ann Catherine Swailes, Sister Mary Teresa Billington, Sister Jane Ann Alves
Income: £5,936,416 [2017]; £5,494,694 [2016]; £5,290,408 [2015]; £5,265,005 [2014]; £7,362,054 [2013]

English Federation of Disability Sport
Registered: 20 Apr 1999 *Employees:* 25 *Volunteers:* 450
Tel: 01509 227750 *Website:* activityalliance.org.uk
Activities: Disability; amateur sport
Address: EFDS, Sportpark, Loughborough University, 3 Oakwood Drive, Loughborough, Leics, LE11 3QF
Trustees: Dr Phil Friend, Ms Janet Inman, Mr Ken Black, Mr Rob Belbin, Mr James Daly, Ms Kate Brentley, Ms Tracey McCillen, Mr Charles Reed, Ms Fran Williamson, Ms Genny Cotroneo, Ms Maria Palmer
Income: £2,600,112 [2017]; £1,944,154 [2016]; £1,666,090 [2015]; £1,551,768 [2014]; £2,192,611 [2013]

English Folk Dance and Song Society
Registered: 16 Sep 1963 *Employees:* 23 *Volunteers:* 10
Tel: 020 7485 2206 *Website:* efdss.org
Activities: Education, training; arts, culture, heritage, science; amateur sport; environment, conservation, heritage
Address: The English Folk Dance & Song Society, Cecil Sharp House, 2 Regents Park Road, London, NW1 7AY
Trustees: Mick Gallagher, Jim Moray, Mike Heaney, Mr Andrew Stephen Wooles, Fi Fraser, Ed Fishwick, Alistair Anderson, Mr Alan Davey, Ms Lorna Jane Aizlewood
Income: £1,630,573 [2017]; £1,634,357 [2016]; £1,400,862 [2015]; £1,738,990 [2014]; £1,226,504 [2013]

The English Heritage Trust
Registered: 10 Feb 2011 *Employees:* 1,109 *Volunteers:* 2,700
Tel: 020 7973 3464 *Website:* english-heritage.org.uk
Activities: Education, training; arts, culture, heritage, science; environment, conservation, heritage
Address: 6th Floor, English Heritage, 100 Wood Street, London, EC2V 7AN
Trustees: Mr Charles Gurassa, Mrs Victoria Barnsley, Mr James Douglas Robert Twining, Vice Admiral Sir Timothy James Hamilton Laurence KCVO CB ADC, Professor Ronald Edmund Hutton, Mrs Sukie Mary Hemming, Sir Laurence Henry Philip Magnus, Mr Ian McCaig, Mrs Kate Belinda James-Weed, Mr Alex Balfour, Ms Sarah Elizabeth Staniforth CBE CBE, Mr Ian Malcolm Reading
Income: £102,995,000 [2017]; £95,411,000 [2016]; £81,367,448 [2015]; £1,475,660 [2014]; £3,405,951 [2013]

The English Language Centre Limited
Registered: 2 Mar 1981 *Employees:* 62
Tel: 01273 721771 *Website:* elc-brighton.co.uk
Activities: Education, training
Address: 33 Palmeira Mansions, Hove, E Sussex, BN3 2GB
Trustees: Mr Richard A Stewart, Mr John Robert Rudd, Mrs Katherine Wells, Mr Graham White, Mr Duncan Quibell, Mr Michael West, Mr Peter Orpen, Ms Vanessa Hall-Smith
Income: £2,519,053 [2016]; £3,015,318 [2015]; £3,361,235 [2014]; £2,879,966 [2013]; £2,766,623 [2012]

English National Ballet School Limited
Registered: 13 Dec 1988 *Employees:* 18
Tel: 020 7376 7076 *Website:* enbschool.org.uk
Activities: Education, training; arts, culture, heritage, science
Address: 6 Hillary Drive, Isleworth, Middlesex, TW7 7EG
Trustees: Steve Sacks, Miss Alfreda Thorogood, Mrs Tanya Rose Simpson, Mrs Caroline Anne Levy, Mr James Adam Richard Mee, Ms Margaret Morris, Mr Zachary Jason Lewy, Ms Dara Ann Pizzuti, Ralph Coates, Mrs Dianna Alexandra Burgess
Income: £1,783,599 [2017]; £2,041,908 [2016]; £1,978,214 [2015]; £1,925,158 [2014]; £1,851,802 [2013]

English National Ballet
Registered: 21 Feb 1963 *Employees:* 218
Tel: 020 7590 2926 *Website:* ballet.org.uk
Activities: Arts, culture, heritage, science
Address: English National Ballet Ltd, Markova House, 39 Jay Mews, London, SW7 2ES
Trustees: Caroline Thomson, Mr Justin Bickle, Mr Stephen Sacks, Tanya Rose, Mr Grenville Turner, Mr Zachary Lewy, Ms Valerie Gooding, Sir Norman Rosenthal, Lord Andrew Adonis, Ms Susan Boster, Ms Sian Westerman, Mr Christopher Francis Irving Saul
Income: £18,175,060 [2017]; £15,282,000 [2016]; £15,690,000 [2015]; £13,368,012 [2014]; £13,812,342 [2013]

English National Opera
Registered: 4 Nov 1968 *Employees:* 344 *Volunteers:* 36
Tel: 020 7845 9252 *Website:* eno.org
Activities: General charitable purposes; education, training; arts, culture, heritage, science
Address: London Coliseum, St Martins Lane, London, WC2R 4ES
Trustees: Lord Jonathan Sumption, Mr Nicholas Allan, Ms Catherine May, Mr Nick Addyman, Ms Louise Felicity Jeffreys, Ms Patricia Dimond, Mrs Patricia Early White, Dr Henry Brunjes, Mr Stuart Anthony Whitworth-Jones, Mr Huw John Van Steenis, Mr Philip Edgar-Jones
Income: £49,061,000 [2017]; £40,277,000 [2016]; £37,738,000 [2015]; £36,967,000 [2014]; £40,066,000 [2013]

The English Province of The Congregation of Our Lady of Charity of The Good Shepherd CIO
Registered: 10 Sep 2015 *Employees:* 35
Tel: 020 8383 6014
Activities: General charitable purposes; education, training; prevention or relief of poverty; overseas aid, famine relief; religious activities
Address: The Brentano Suite, 915 High Road, London, N12 8QJ
Trustees: Sister Rosemary Kean, Sister Anne Furlong, Sr Charlotte Ann Cassidy, Sr Matilda Sinead Collier, Sr Anne Josephine Carr
Income: £32,320,749 [2017]

The English Province of The Institute of Franciscan Missionaries of Mary
Registered: 12 Dec 1966 *Employees:* 48 *Volunteers:* 33
Tel: 020 8748 4077 *Website:* fmmii.org
Activities: The prevention or relief of poverty; religious activities
Address: 5 Vaughan Avenue, London, W6 0XS
Trustees: Sr Mary Fitzpatrick, Sister Lillian Hunt, Sr Alberta Forson, Sr Marie Therese Chambers, Sister Helen Fennell, Vincenza Catania
Income: £2,429,231 [2016]; £2,833,243 [2015]; £2,635,390 [2014]; £2,518,591 [2013]; £2,401,440 [2012]

The English Province of The Order of Preachers
Registered: 18 Feb 1964 *Employees:* 21 *Volunteers:* 234
Tel: 01865 288231 *Website:* english.op.org
Activities: Education, training; religious activities
Address: Blackfriars Priory, St Giles, Oxford, OX1 3LY
Trustees: Fr John Farrell OP, Rev Robindra Ganeri OP, The Dominican Council Trustee Corporation, Fr Richard Ounsworth OP, Rev Simon Gaine OP
Income: £3,326,944 [2016]; £3,018,113 [2015]; £2,765,677 [2014]; £3,572,363 [2013]; £2,560,314 [2012]

The English Province of The Order of The Daughters of Mary and Joseph (otherwise known as the Ladies of Mary)
Registered: 7 Feb 1964 *Employees:* 30 *Volunteers:* 2
Tel: 020 8695 7492 *Website:* daughtersofmaryandjoseph.org
Activities: General charitable purposes; education, training; advancement of health or saving of lives; disability; prevention or relief of poverty; overseas aid, famine relief; accommodation, housing; religious activities
Address: 1st Floor, Church House, 61 College Road, Bromley, Kent, BR1 3QG
Trustees: Sister Sheila Josephine Moloney, Sister Margaret Elaine Eason, Sister Nora Florence Murray, Sister Felice Anne Bowker Wright, Sister Paula Spark, Sister Sheila Barrett
Income: £1,901,002 [2016]; £2,817,079 [2015]; £1,796,632 [2014]; £1,623,807 [2013]; £1,746,701 [2012]

The English Province of The Sisters of Saint Joseph of Annecy
Registered: 20 Mar 1964 *Employees:* 64 *Volunteers:* 55
Tel: 01633 245077 *Website:* sistersofstjoseph.org.uk
Activities: The advancement of health or saving of lives; prevention or relief of poverty; religious activities
Address: 173 Chepstow Road, Newport, NP19 8GH
Trustees: Sister Alice O'Dwyer, Sister Breda Gainey, Sister Marianne Donnelly, Sister Teresa Kolb, Sister Dorothy Butler, Sister Margaret Fox
Income: £2,001,035 [2016]; £1,749,850 [2015]; £5,552,729 [2014]; £9,504,713 [2013]; £10,545,664 [2012]

The English Region of The Sisters of Charity of St Jeanne Antide
Registered: 1 Jan 1967 *Employees:* 3
Tel: 020 8695 7492
Activities: General charitable purposes; education, training; advancement of health or saving of lives; prevention or relief of poverty; overseas aid, famine relief; accommodation, housing; religious activities; economic, community development, employment
Address: 1st Floor, Church House, 61 College Road, Bromley, Kent, BR1 3QG
Trustees: Sister Margaret Hunston, Sister Elizabeth Hannon, Brother Michael Newman OH
Income: £1,244,242 [2016]; £211,332 [2015]; £255,140 [2014]; £245,535 [2013]; £227,743 [2012]

The English Sangha Trust Limited
Registered: 4 May 1965 *Employees:* 1 *Volunteers:* 30
Tel: 01442 842455 *Website:* amaravati.org
Activities: Religious activities
Address: Amaravati Buddhist Monastery, St Margarets, Great Gaddesden, Hemel Hempstead, Herts, HP1 3BZ
Trustees: Mr John Peters Stevens, Mr Nicholas Carroll, Mrs Penelope Wakefield-Pearce, Mr Sudanta Abeyakoon, Ms Caroline Leinster, Kazuko Kawamura
Income: £1,413,617 [2017]; £686,109 [2016]; £1,339,350 [2015]; £845,632 [2014]; £942,681 [2013]

The English Schools' Football Association
Registered: 25 Jun 1963 *Employees:* 17 *Volunteers:* 4,000
Tel: 01785 785970 *Website:* esfa.co.uk
Activities: Education, training; amateur sport
Address: 4 Parker Court, Staffordshire Technology Park, Stafford, ST18 0WP
Trustees: Mr Michael John Coyne, Mr Stuart Inger, Mr David Anthony Woollaston
Income: £2,370,111 [2017]; £1,171,543 [2015]; £1,220,244 [2014]; £1,054,745 [2013]; £1,004,350 [2012]

English Speaking Board (International) Limited
Registered: 23 Dec 1976 *Employees:* 23
Tel: 01695 573439 *Website:* esbuk.org
Activities: Education, training
Address: 9 Hattersley Court, Burscough Road, Ormskirk, Lancs, L39 2AY
Trustees: Mrs Avril Newman, Mr Quentin Mark Oliver, Ms Merriel Halsall-Williams, Ms Stephanie Walsh, Mr Richard Ellis, Mrs Pippa Quarrell, Mr Ian Grant Kelly
Income: £1,697,044 [2017]; £1,361,123 [2016]; £1,367,256 [2015]; £1,291,491 [2014]; £784,672 [2013]

The English Stage Company Limited
Registered: 5 Nov 1963 *Employees:* 125
Tel: 020 7565 5050 *Website:* royalcourttheatre.com
Activities: Arts, culture, heritage, science
Address: Royal Court Theatre, Sloane Square, London, SW1W 8AS
Trustees: Ms Joyce Hytner, Ms Jennette Arnold, Mr James Richard Midgley, Stephen Jeffreys, Dr Stewart Wood, Mrs Emma Marsh, Mr Roger Michell, Mr Anthony Charles Burton, Graham Devlin, Ms Judy Elizabeth Daish, Ms Anita Scott, Sir David Green KCMG, Mr Mehdi Yahya
Income: £7,947,317 [2017]; £7,503,690 [2016]; £8,054,273 [2015]; £6,007,281 [2014]; £7,264,280 [2013]

English Touring Opera Limited
Registered: 12 Feb 1980 *Employees:* 13 *Volunteers:* 69
Tel: 020 7833 2555 *Website:* englishtouringopera.org.uk
Activities: Education, training; disability; arts, culture, heritage, science; economic, community development, employment; recreation; other charitable purposes
Address: English Touring Opera, 3rd Floor, 50 Britton Street, London, EC1M 5UP
Trustees: Ms Judith Jane Ackrill, Mrs Ursula Margaret Owen, Mr David Burke, Mr William Bush, Mr Daniel Sandelson, Mr Richard Salter, Mrs Jane Beverley Davies, Joseph Christos Karaviotis, Ms Sarah Botchway, Mr Mark Peter Beddy, Mr David Lasserson, Ms Sinead O'Neill, Ms Laura Liede
Income: £3,355,265 [2017]; £4,074,482 [2016]; £2,833,606 [2015]; £2,967,742 [2014]; £2,568,021 [2013]

English Touring Theatre Limited
Registered: 1 Feb 1993 *Employees:* 8
Website: ett.org.uk
Activities: General charitable purposes; education, training; arts, culture, heritage, science
Address: English Touring Theatre Ltd, 25 Short Street, London, SE1 8LJ
Trustees: Dame Jennifer Gita Abramsky CBE DBE, Mr Paul David Corrigan CBE, Robert Christian Delamere, Tara Wilkinson, Mr Paapa Essiedu, Mr Michael Hatchwell, Dan Bates, Michael Benedict McCabe, Alastair Keir, Mrs Olivia Highland
Income: £2,722,884 [2017]; £1,739,179 [2016]; £2,559,492 [2015]; £2,136,574 [2014]; £1,467,486 [2013]

English UK Limited
Registered: 1 Apr 2005 *Employees:* 18
Tel: 020 7608 7960 *Website:* englishuk.com
Activities: Education, training
Address: 219 St John Street, London, EC1V 4LY
Trustees: Mr Simon James Cleaver, Mr Stephen John Phillips, Mr Nigel Paul Paramor, Mrs Sarah Jane Etchells, Mr Jose Brinkmann, Mrs Shoko Doherty, Ms Jane Elizabeth Dancaster, Mr Stephen Abarrow, Mr Richard Andrew Fraser Simpson, Mr Mark Richard Rendell, Mr Fraser Davis, Mrs Ella Tyler
Income: £2,357,188 [2016]; £2,019,660 [2015]; £1,954,194 [2014]; £881,879 [2013]; £871,162 [2012]

English- Speaking Union of The Commonwealth
Registered: 29 Mar 1977 *Employees:* 48
Tel: 020 7529 1550 *Website:* esu.org
Activities: Education, training; arts, culture, heritage, science
Address: Dartmouth House, 37 Charles Street, London, W1J 5ED
Trustees: Mr Roderick Chamberlain, Professor James Raven, Mr Derek Morgan, Miss Natasha Dyer, Lady Susan Inkin, Miss Anikka Weersinghe, Ms April Heard, Dr Anthony Wood, The Rt Hon Paul Boateng, Mr Jonathan Sobczyk, Mr David Shaw, Mr Andrew Hay, Mr Alex Just, Ms Barbara Firth, Ms Ellen Punter, Mr James Scruby
Income: £3,580,392 [2017]; £3,873,889 [2016]; £3,691,607 [2015]; £3,576,165 [2014]; £3,761,066 [2013]

Enham Trust
Registered: 16 Apr 1963 *Employees:* 337 *Volunteers:* 195
Tel: 01264 345800 *Website:* enham.org.uk
Activities: Disability; accommodation, housing; economic, community development, employment
Address: Enham Trust, Enham Place, Enham Alamein, Andover, Hants, SP11 6JS
Trustees: Professor Khalid Aziz, Ms Elizabeth Margaret Wallace, Mr Neil Palmer, Mrs Judith Gillow, Mr Stuart Robert Lindsay, Mrs Clare Mary Scheckter, Mr Robert Simon Childs, Mr Matthew Samuel-Camps, Mr David Michael Brent
Income: £12,404,000 [2017]; £12,151,000 [2016]; £11,520,107 [2015]; £10,708,491 [2014]; £10,192,578 [2013]

Enhanceable
Registered: 28 Mar 1996 *Employees:* 50 *Volunteers:* 31
Tel: 020 8546 7350 *Website:* enhanceable.org
Activities: Education, training; disability; accommodation, housing
Address: Enhanceable, 13 Geneva Road, Kingston upon Thames, Surrey, KT1 2TW
Trustees: Ms Gail Alison MacIver, Mr Nick Ainley, Mr Mark Martin, Mr Brian Garcia, Mr Byron Turner, Mr Michael Kemsley, Mr Michael Anthony Parker, Ms Hannah Piper
Income: £1,837,239 [2017]; £1,660,674 [2016]; £1,340,362 [2015]; £1,117,099 [2014]; £1,036,799 [2013]

Enthuse Charitable Trust
Registered: 27 Nov 2008
Tel: 01904 328381 *Website:* stem.org.uk
Activities: Education, training
Address: University of York, Heslington, York, YO10 5DD
Trustees: Mr Ian Kevin Duffy, Dr Hilary Janet Leevers, The Hon Rosie Bailey, Mrs Allie Denholm, Ms Katherine Mathieson, Mrs Riffat Wall
Income: £2,719,926 [2017]; £2,638,866 [2016]; £2,459,709 [2015]; £2,139,811 [2014]; £3,321,699 [2013]

Entindale Limited
Registered: 7 Jun 1979
Tel: 020 8458 9266
Activities: General charitable purposes; education, training; prevention or relief of poverty; religious activities
Address: 8 Highfield Gardens, London, NW11 9HB
Trustees: Mr Joseph Pearlman, Mrs Barbara Lilian Bridgeman, Mr Allan Charles Becker
Income: £2,465,647 [2017]; £1,993,793 [2016]; £2,984,562 [2015]; £2,010,798 [2014]; £2,140,145 [2013]

Environmental Justice Foundation Charitable Trust
Registered: 20 Aug 2001 *Employees:* 29 *Volunteers:* 30
Tel: 020 7837 1242 *Website:* ejfoundation.org
Activities: General charitable purposes; education, training; prevention or relief of poverty; environment, conservation, heritage; human rights, religious or racial harmony, equality or diversity; other charitable purposes
Address: EJFCT, 1 Amwell Street, London, EC1R 1UL
Trustees: Steve McIvor, Andrew Kalman, Deirdre Anne Burley, Rachel Inman
Income: £2,268,743 [2016]; £1,728,054 [2015]; £1,323,675 [2014]; £693,362 [2013]; £834,370 [2012]

Eothen Homes Limited
Registered: 29 Apr 1963 *Employees:* 157 *Volunteers:* 13
Tel: 0191 281 9100 *Website:* eothenhomes.org.uk
Activities: Accommodation, housing
Address: 1 Osborne Road, Jesmond, Newcastle upon Tyne, NE2 2AA
Trustees: Dr Andrew David Shepherd, Mr Ian David Thomson, Ms Louise Marsh, Mr Alexander Lindsay McIlhinney, Ms Maureen Erny, Dr Sameh Mishreki
Income: £4,210,870 [2017]; £3,339,686 [2016]; £3,164,405 [2015]; £2,901,116 [2014]; £2,885,873 [2013]

Epilepsy Research UK
Registered: 30 Oct 2003 *Employees:* 5 *Volunteers:* 20
Tel: 020 8747 5024 *Website:* epilepsyresearch.org.uk
Activities: The advancement of health or saving of lives
Address: Epilepsy Research UK, Chiswick Town Hall, Heathfierld Terrace, London, W4 4JN
Trustees: Mr Barrie Simon Akin, Mr H Salmon, Mr John Hirst, Dr Yvonne Hart, Miss Judith Mary Spencer-Gregson, Professor Mark Ian Rees, Mary Gavigan, Mr Simon Harry Lanyon, Mr David William Donald Cameron MP, Professor Matthew Charles Walker, Dr Graeme Sills, Bruno Frenguelli, Professor Mark Richardson
Income: £1,402,998 [2017]; £1,236,209 [2016]; £1,378,430 [2015]; £1,153,133 [2014]; £1,141,339 [2013]

Epping Forest
Registered: 24 Mar 1964 *Employees:* 81 *Volunteers:* 400
Tel: 020 7332 3519
Activities: Amateur sport
Address: Corporation of London, P O Box 270, London, EC2P 2EJ
Trustees: The Mayor & Commonality & Citizens of The City of London
Income: £6,199,946 [2017]; £5,959,567 [2016]; £7,537,006 [2015]; £7,213,869 [2014]; £7,010,713 [2013]

The Equal Rights Trust
Registered: 15 Mar 2006 *Employees:* 9
Tel: 020 7610 2786 *Website:* equalrightstrust.org
Activities: General charitable purposes; education, training; prevention or relief of poverty
Address: The Equal Rights Trust, Acorn House, 314-320 Gray's Inn Road, London, WC1X 8DP
Trustees: Mr Robert Andrew Niven, Mr Andrew Charles Danby Bloch, Lord Justice Stephen Sedley, Ms Virginia Mantouvalou, Ms Ferdous Ara Begum, Miss Evelyn Collins, Ms Saphie Ashtiany, Ms Catherine Mary Elizabeth O'Regan, Ms Helen Mountfield, Mr Luc Victor Emmanuel Tyart De Borms, Ms Quinn Parker McKew, Mr Robin Allen
Income: £1,490,522 [2017]; £1,401,618 [2016]; £1,674,633 [2015]; £1,461,545 [2014]; £1,480,489 [2013]

Equality Challenge Unit
Registered: 31 May 2006 *Employees:* 34
Tel: 020 7438 1010 *Website:* ecu.ac.uk
Activities: Education, training; disability; economic, community development, employment
Address: 7th Floor, Queens House, 55-56 Lincoln's Inn Fields, London, WC2A 3LJ
Trustees: Prof Mary Stuart, Patrick Johnson, Prof Geoff Layer, Prof Nigel Seaton, Ms Donna Michelle Rowe-Merriman, Ms Alison Coralie Cross, Prof Stuart John Croft, Dr Chantal Davies, Prof Jane Norman, Prof Anthony William Forster, Prof Hilary Margaret Lappi-Scott
Income: £2,522,689 [2017]; £2,827,095 [2016]; £2,624,443 [2015]; £1,902,949 [2014]; £1,770,909 [2013]

Equinox Care
Registered: 21 May 1987 *Employees:* 88 *Volunteers:* 1
Tel: 020 3668 9270 *Website:* equinoxcare.org.uk
Activities: General charitable purposes; advancement of health or saving of lives; disability; prevention or relief of poverty; accommodation, housing
Address: Unit 1 Waterloo Gardens, Milner Square, London, N1 1TY
Trustees: Mr Adam Thwaites, Ms Deborah Ruth Rozansky, Dr Helen Carter, Mr Jonathan Robert Jesty
Income: £6,256,000 [2017]; £5,851,000 [2016]; £5,845,000 [2015]; £6,237,162 [2014]; £6,836,990 [2013]

Eritrea and The Horn of Africa Relief Ethar
Registered: 17 Jul 2006 *Employees:* 4 *Volunteers:* 32
Tel: 0121 309 0230 *Website:* etharrelief.org
Activities: General charitable purposes; education, training; advancement of health or saving of lives; disability; prevention or relief of poverty; overseas aid, famine relief; accommodation, housing; religious activities; arts, culture, heritage, science; amateur sport; economic, community development, employment
Address: 467 Coventry Road, Small Heath, Birmingham, B10 0TJ
Trustees: Mr Idriss Sayed, Mr Abdurahman Saleh Mahmud, Mr Abdulkadir A Naib, Mr Mohammed Bakhitt, Mr Abdelsalam Mohamed Ali, Hanan Basher
Income: £1,493,118 [2017]; £1,239,970 [2016]; £538,809 [2015]; £497,051 [2014]; £421,850 [2013]

Essential Christian
Registered: 28 Nov 2008 *Employees:* 41 *Volunteers:* 1,200
Tel: 01825 769111 *Website:* essentialchristian.org
Activities: Education, training; religious activities
Address: 14 Horsted Square, Bellbrook Industrial Estate, Uckfield, E Sussex, TN22 1QG
Trustees: The Rt Revd Pete Broadbent, Mr Geoffrey James Booker, Miss Elaine Duncan, Ms Tania Bright, Mr Peter Timothy Martin, Mr David Dorricott, Rev Roger Sutton, Rev Gavin Calver
Income: £4,819,854 [2016]; £4,736,915 [2015]; £3,833,153 [2014]; £4,627,629 [2013]; £5,205,030 [2012]

Essential Drug and Alcohol Services
Registered: 20 Jun 1990 *Employees:* 47 *Volunteers:* 16
Tel: 01202 743279 *Website:* edasuk.org
Activities: Education, training; advancement of health or saving of lives
Address: 54A Ashley Road, Poole, Dorset, BH14 9BN
Trustees: Mr Edward Taylor, Lyn Clarke, Mrs Doreen May Exon, Mrs Jacqueline Westmaas, Dr Linda Cartwright, Mr Marc Del Llano LLB, Mrs Sheila Smith, Diane Evans, Dr Dylan Phillips
Income: £1,239,323 [2017]; £1,307,728 [2016]; £1,385,519 [2015]; £1,404,019 [2014]; £1,337,049 [2013]

Essex & Herts Air Ambulance Trust
Registered: 12 Apr 2005 *Employees:* 46 *Volunteers:* 285
Tel: 0345 241 7690 *Website:* ehaat.uk.com
Activities: The advancement of health or saving of lives
Address: Essex & Herts Air Ambulance Trust, The Business Centre, Airfield, Earls Colne, Colchester, Essex, CO6 2NS
Trustees: Dr Ramzi Freij, Mr Philip Caborn, Mr Darren Hayward, Mr Roy John Marfleet, Mr Jonathan Charles Gosselin Trower, Mrs Clare Juliet Dobie, Mrs Anni Ridsdill Smith, Clive Gilham
Income: £12,450,330 [2017]; £13,248,000 [2016]; £9,985,000 [2015]; £8,482,000 [2014]; £6,023,000 [2013]

Essex Blind Charity
Registered: 13 May 2004 *Employees:* 65 *Volunteers:* 50
Tel: 01255 673654 *Website:* essexblind.co.uk
Activities: Disability; accommodation, housing
Address: Read House, 23 The Esplanade, Frinton on Sea, Essex, CO13 9AU
Trustees: Mr Brian Beveridge, Mrs Dorothy Aristides, Mrs S Mann, Mr Allan Richard Mabert, Mr Richard William Marshall, Mr Fitzpatrick FRICS, Mr G Waterer, Mr Robert Lionel Jackson, Mr Ronald Horace Stanley Coe
Income: £1,254,763 [2017]; £2,165,673 [2016]; £1,326,117 [2015]; £1,130,653 [2014]; £1,144,841 [2013]

Essex Boys and Girls Clubs
Registered: 21 Sep 2015 *Employees:* 38 *Volunteers:* 200
Tel: 01245 264783 *Website:* essexboysandgirlsclubs.org
Activities: General charitable purposes; education, training; amateur sport; recreation
Address: Harway House, Meadowside, Rectory Lane, Chelmsford, Essex, CM1 1RQ
Trustees: Mike Dyer, J P Douglas-Hughes, Mr Darren Goodey, Mr Peter Drummond, Mr Graham Middleton FCA, Mr Stephen Kavanagh, Mr David Springett, Mr Michael O'Brien
Income: £1,926,668 [2016]

Essex Coalition of Disabled People
Registered: 21 Mar 2002 *Employees:* 31 *Volunteers:* 1
Tel: 01245 392306 *Website:* ecdp.org.uk
Activities: Education, training; disability
Address: Essex Coalition of Disabled People, 1 Russell Way,
Chelmsford, Essex, CM1 3AA
Trustees: Ann Nutt, Tony Cox, Mrs Patricia Gaudin, Steve Carey,
Mr Brian Goodwin
Income: £1,451,494 [2017]; £1,527,069 [2016]; £1,598,930 [2015];
£1,467,754 [2014]; £1,222,428 [2013]

Essex Community Foundation
Registered: 16 Jan 1996 *Employees:* 9 *Volunteers:* 4
Tel: 01245 355947 *Website:* essexcommunityfoundation.org.uk
Activities: General charitable purposes; education, training;
advancement of health or saving of lives; disability; prevention or
relief of poverty; accommodation, housing; arts, culture, heritage,
science; amateur sport; environment, conservation, heritage;
economic, community development, employment; other charitable
purposes
Address: 121 New London Road, Chelmsford, Essex, CM2 0QT
Trustees: Mr Simon Andrew Dalton Hall MBE, Mr Owen Richards,
Mr Jonathan Minter, Mrs Rosemary Turner, Mr Charles Nicholas
Cryer, Mrs Etholle Matthews, Mr Russell Edey, Ms Joanna
Katherine Wells, Mr Peter Martin, Ms Kate Barker, Mr Lee Blissett,
Mrs Clare Jocelyn Ball, Ms Claire Read, Mr Nicholas Kenneth
Alston, Mrs Sandra Pennington Hollis
Income: £2,253,317 [2017]; £4,567,715 [2016]; £4,562,542 [2015];
£4,143,270 [2014]; £5,946,117 [2013]

Essex County Scout Council
Registered: 10 Aug 1966 *Employees:* 5 *Volunteers:* 5,973
Tel: 01268 743008 *Website:* essexscouts.org.uk
Activities: General charitable purposes; education, training;
religious activities; amateur sport; environment, conservation,
heritage; economic, community development, employment; other
charitable purposes
Address: 143 Bull Lane, Rayleigh, Essex, SS6 8NU
Trustees: Ann Nutt, Mr Paul Walker, Mr Robert Edward Lyon,
Mr Peter William Murray, Mr Robert Andrew Bye, Mr Alastair
MacLachlan, Mr Stuart Ian Gibson, Mr James Robert Bryan
Freake, Mr Paul Stennett, Mr Christopher Peter Dear, Mrs Sarah
Griffiths, Mr Martin Thomas Falder, Mrs Elizabeth Rose Smith,
Mr Kevyn Joseph Connelly, Miss Allana Megan Hannah Bailey
Income: £2,449,824 [2017]; £655,543 [2016]; £444,748 [2015];
£515,388 [2014]; £968,743 [2013]

Essex Wildlife Trust Limited
Registered: 22 Sep 1962 *Employees:* 110 *Volunteers:* 2,000
Tel: 01621 841573 *Website:* essexwt.org.uk
Activities: Education, training; animals; environment, conservation,
heritage; recreation
Address: Essex Wildlife Trust, Joan Elliot Visitor Centre, Abbotts
Hall Farm, Maldon Road, Great Wigborough, Colchester, Essex,
CO5 7RZ
Trustees: Mr Stewart Goshawk, Bob Holmes, Mrs Rachel Anne
Steward, Mr Will Akast, Mrs Keeley Ann Hazelhurst, Mr Geoffrey
Mark Duffield, Mr Malcolm John Hardy, Ms Penelope Anne
Johnson, Mrs Linda Wenlock, Mr David Anthony Holt, Miss Fiona
Wilson, Phil Ormond, Mr Charles Andrew Joynson
Income: £7,971,574 [2016]; £9,454,374 [2015]; £6,478,806 [2014];
£5,978,478 [2013]; £6,062,400 [2012]

Eric and Salome Estorick Foundation
Registered: 16 Jun 1995 *Employees:* 8 *Volunteers:* 90
Tel: 020 7704 9522 *Website:* estorickcollection.com
Activities: Arts, culture, heritage, science
Address: 39A Canonbury Square, London, N1 2AN
Trustees: Mr Gavin Douglas Henderson, Mr Michael Jacob
Estorick, Ms Vanessa Hall-Smith, Mrs Maria De Peverella Luschi,
Dr Martin Phillip Owen, Ms Isobel Nacha Estorick, Mr Alexander
Romain Estorick, Mr Christopher Kenneth Green Professor,
Mrs Patricia Susan Bond
Income: £5,500,582 [2017]; £356,974 [2016]; £372,199 [2015];
£298,302 [2014]; £454,890 [2013]

Ethiopiaid
Registered: 8 Nov 1989 *Employees:* 4 *Volunteers:* 2
Tel: 01225 476385 *Website:* ethiopiaid.org.uk
Activities: Education, training; advancement of health or saving of
lives; disability; prevention or relief of poverty; overseas aid, famine
relief; accommodation, housing; arts, culture, heritage, science;
economic, community development, employment
Address: Ethiopiaid, Upper Borough Court, Upper Borough Walls,
Bath, BA1 1RG
Trustees: Mrs Alex Chapman, Ms Alex Fenn, Edith Prak, Mrs Helen
Horn, Mrs Sally Louise Grimsdale, Mr Michael Charles Norman,
Nicola Reed
Income: £2,572,426 [2016]; £2,494,912 [2015]; £2,855,644 [2014];
£2,515,109 [2013]; £2,712,254 [2012]

The Ethiopian Christian Fellowship (UK)
Registered: 21 Sep 2015 *Employees:* 5 *Volunteers:* 300
Website: ecfcuk.org
Activities: Education, training; prevention or relief of poverty;
religious activities
Address: 80 Waverley Road, London, SE25 4HU
Trustees: Dr Getachew Zergaw Tiruneh, Mr Seyoum Alemayehu
Haileselassie, Mrs Luam Kidane, Mr Abebe Shiferaw, Mr Cherinet
Kefelegn Metaferia, Mr Abraham Seyoum-Zerfue, Mrs Zerfinesh
Abegaz
Income: £2,354,707 [2017]

The Ethnic Minority Foundation
Registered: 12 Aug 1999 *Employees:* 51
Website: emfoundation.org.uk
Activities: General charitable purposes; education, training;
advancement of health or saving of lives; disability; prevention or
relief of poverty; overseas aid, famine relief; arts, culture, heritage,
science; economic, community development, employment; human
rights, religious or racial harmony, equality or diversity; recreation;
other charitable purposes
Address: Ethnic Minority Foundation, Boardman House,
64 Broadway, Stratford, London, E15 1NT
Trustees: Mr Sunil Purohit, Mr Surinder Singh Syan, Mr Anil Kumar
Bhanot
Income: £2,139,370 [2016]; £2,523,915 [2015]; £1,978,250 [2014];
£2,452,113 [2013]; £1,033,474 [2012]

Eton End School Trust (Datchet) Limited
Registered: 19 Oct 1962 *Employees:* 49
Tel: 01753 541075 *Website:* etonend.org
Activities: Education, training
Address: 35 Eton Road, Datchet, Slough, SL3 9AX
Trustees: Mr Geoffrey Arthur Brian Hill, Mr James Lawther Fullerton Clark, Mrs Jeanette Elizabeth Lange, Mr John Allan Boothroyd, Mrs Dorothee Fowkes, Mrs Angela Wood-Dow, Mr Geoffrey Hilton Croasdale, Mrs Nicola Jane Brewster, Mr James William Frederic Stanforth
Income: £1,939,816 [2016]; £2,266,186 [2015]; £2,236,277 [2014]; £1,737,627 [2013]

Eureka The National Children's Museum
Registered: 8 Oct 1985 *Employees:* 76 *Volunteers:* 15
Tel: 01422 330069 *Website:* eureka.org.uk
Activities: Education, training; arts, culture, heritage, science; recreation
Address: Discovery Road, Halifax, W Yorks, HX1 2NE
Trustees: Leigh-Anne Stradeski, Mrs Alison Hope, Mr Alan John Aubrey, Mrs Diane Carole Watson, Mrs Jane Sheridan Rice-Bowen, Mrs Jin Craven, Fiona Hesselden, Peter Smart, Professor Elizabeth Ann Wood
Income: £3,517,194 [2016]; £3,247,175 [2015]; £3,296,691 [2014]; £3,267,656 [2013]; £4,826,489 [2012]

Euro Charity Trust
Registered: 4 Oct 1996 *Employees:* 1 *Volunteers:* 1
Activities: Education, training; advancement of health or saving of lives; prevention or relief of poverty
Address: 20 Brickfield Road, Yardley, Birmingham, B25 8HE
Trustees: Nasir Awan, Mr Abdul Majid Alimahomed, Mr Abdul S Malik
Income: £5,804,513 [2016]; £5,816,625 [2015]; £4,905,580 [2014]; £2,131,239 [2013]; £2,870,957 [2012]

Eurocentres UK
Registered: 8 Feb 1982 *Employees:* 112
Tel: 020 7783 3563 *Website:* eurocentres.com
Activities: Education, training
Address: Bircham Dyson Bell, 50 Broadway, London, SW1H 0BL
Trustees: Mr Guy Wyndham Vincent, Mr Thomas John Phillips
Income: £8,693,040 [2016]; £10,078,320 [2015]; £10,298,267 [2014]; £9,658,334 [2013]; £9,787,977 [2012]

The European Association for Cardio-Thoracic Surgery
Registered: 8 Feb 2011 *Employees:* 9
Tel: 01753 832166 *Website:* eacts.org
Activities: Education, training; advancement of health or saving of lives
Address: Eacts, Eacts House, Madeira Walk, Windsor, Berks, SL4 1EU
Trustees: Friedhelm Beyersdorf, Ruggero De Paulis, Peter Bjorn Licht, David Aaron Fullerton, Mark Hazekamp, Dr Domenico Pagano, Dr Giuseppe Cardillo, Dr Thomas Walther, Volkmar Falk, Pala Babu Rajesh, Joaquim Miguel Sennfelt De Sousa Uva, Marian Zembala, Emre Belli, Dr Miia Liisa Lehtinen, Dr David Pacini
Income: £6,120,413 [2017]; £5,034,373 [2016]; £4,977,101 [2015]; £5,055,348 [2014]; £4,910,420 [2013]

European Christian Mission (Britain)
Registered: 27 Nov 1996 *Employees:* 4 *Volunteers:* 4
Tel: 01604 497603 *Website:* ecmbritain.org
Activities: Religious activities
Address: Unit F34-35, Moulton Park Business Centre, Redhouse Road, Moulton Park, Northampton, NN3 6AQ
Trustees: Mr Simon Loveless, Mr Colyn Robinson, Mrs Joanne Appleton, Mr Richard Lawson, Esther Ross, Mr Michael Robert McMaster, Mr Don Gyton, Mr Tim Herbert, Mrs Simone Formolo-Lockyer, Stephen Thompson
Income: £1,111,173 [2016]; £1,028,551 [2015]; £980,389 [2014]; £863,066 [2013]; £1,005,087 [2012]

European College of Business and Management
Registered: 1 Dec 1994 *Employees:* 18
Tel: 020 7749 5930 *Website:* eurocollege.org.uk
Activities: Education, training
Address: European College of Business And, Management, 69-71 Great Eastern Street, London, EC2A 3HU
Trustees: Dr Ulrich Hoppe, Ms Ina Redemann, Mr William John Vivian Whitehead
Income: £1,750,020 [2017]; £1,590,334 [2016]; £1,714,885 [2015]; £1,764,523 [2014]; £1,557,176 [2013]

European Orthodontic Society
Registered: 23 Dec 2002 *Employees:* 2
Tel: 020 7637 0367 *Website:* eoseurope.org
Activities: Education, training; advancement of health or saving of lives; disability
Address: Flat 20, 49 Hallam Street, London, W1W 6JN
Trustees: Professor Fraser McDonald, Dr Ewa Czochrowska, Professor Christos Katsaros, Professor Olivier Albert Sorel, Professor Barbel Kahl-Nieke, Dr Christodoulos Laspos, Dr Ivo Marek, Professor Andreu Puigdollers, Professor Susan Cunningham, Professor Jan Huggare, Dr Dirk Bister, Dr Julian O'Neill, Professor Guy Arthur De Pauw, Professor Vaska Vandevska-Radunovic, Professor Pertti Pirttiniemi, Dr Demetrios Halazonetis
Income: £1,429,144 [2016]; £1,354,443 [2015]; £1,391,084 [2014]; £1,409,611 [2013]; £1,517,720 [2012]

European Renal Association-European Dialysis and Transplant Association
Registered: 14 Jan 1997 *Employees:* 13 *Volunteers:* 100
Website: era-edta.org
Activities: Education, training; advancement of health or saving of lives
Address: 150 Aldersgate Street, London, EC1A 4AB
Trustees: Prof Ivan Rychlik Secretary-Treasurer, Prof Denis Fouque Editor-In Chief of NDT, Prof Jolanta Malyszko Ordinary Council Member, Prof Ziad Massy Chairman of The Registry, Prof Goce Spasovski Ordinary Council Member, Prof Peter Blankestijn Ordinary Council Member, Prof Annette Bruchfeld Ordinary Council Member, Prof Markus Ketteler Chairperson of The Administrative Offices, Prof Mustafa Arici Ordinary Council Member, Prof Danilo Fliser Ordinary Council Member, Prof Giovambattista Capasso Ordinary Council Member, Prof Carmine Zoccali President, Prof Dimitrios Goumenos Ordinary Council Member
Income: £7,200,111 [2016]; £5,402,670 [2015]; £5,685,713 [2014]; £5,353,542 [2013]; £5,644,720 [2012]

European Social Network
Registered: 15 Feb 2000 *Employees:* 11
Tel: 01273 739039 *Website:* esn-eu.org
Activities: General charitable purposes
Address: Victoria House, 125 Queens Road, Brighton, BN1 3WB
Trustees: Mr Christian Fillet, Mr Harri Jokiranta, Mr Carlos Santos Guerrero, Mr Miran Kerin, Mrs Kate Bogh, Mr John Graham Owen
Income: £1,241,902 [2016]; £1,112,640 [2015]; £1,172,796 [2014]; £1,062,252 [2013]; £1,003,290 [2012]

European Society for Paediatric Endocrinology
Registered: 28 Jan 2008
Website: eurospe.org
Activities: Education, training; advancement of health or saving of lives
Address: Bioscientifica Limited, Starling House, 1600 Bristol Parkway North, Bristol, BS34 8YU
Trustees: Professor Peter Ellis Clayton, Professor Mehul Tulsidas Dattani, Professor Syed Faisal Ahmed, Professor Rasa Verkauskiene, Professor Anita Hokken-Koelega, Professor George Chrousos, Dr Annette Grueters-Kieslich, Professor Evangelia Charmandari
Income: £3,228,525 [2016]; £3,140,528 [2015]; £2,981,843 [2014]; £803,737 [2013]; £1,299,154 [2012]

European Society for Sexual Medicine
Registered: 7 Jun 2005
Website: essm.org
Activities: Education, training; advancement of health or saving of lives
Address: RSM, 5th Floor, Central Square, 29 Wellington Street, Leeds, LS1 4DL
Trustees: Yacov Reisman, Mr Lior Lowenstein, Dr Francois Giuliano
Income: £1,209,407 [2016]; £1,029,892 [2015]; £1,522,828 [2014]; £525,795 [2013]; £2,665,245 [2012]

European Society for Vascular Surgery
Registered: 9 Sep 2002 *Employees:* 12
Website: esvs.org
Activities: Education, training; advancement of health or saving of lives
Address: 18 Saxon Way, Romsey, Hants, SO51 5PT
Trustees: Dr Arkadiusz Jawien, Professor Tina Cohnert, Professor Sebastian Debus, Dr Patrick Peeters, Professor Fabien Thaveau, Dr Zoltan Szeberin, Professor Clark Zeebregts, Professor Piotr Gutowski, Dr Ivan Marjanovic, Professor Secundino Llagostera, Professor Jean-Marc Corpataux, Professor Philippe Kolh, Dr Mauro Garguilo, Dr Valeriy Arakelyan, Jurg Schmidli, Dr Tankut Akay, Dr Barbara Rantner, Dr Jesper Lautsen, Professor Athanasios Giannoukos, Mr Martin Donohoe, Dr Elin Hanna Laxdal, Professor Armando Mansilha, Dr Tomas Dulka, Dr Anders Wanhainen, Dr Hubert Stepak, Professor Frank Vermassen, Dr Thomas Holzenbein, Dr Harri Hakovirta
Income: £1,377,395 [2016]; £1,270,787 [2015]; £1,021,074 [2014]; £1,235,973 [2013]; £1,351,118 [2012]

European Society of Cataract and Refractive Surgeons Limited
Registered: 2 Dec 1997
Tel: 00-353-1-209 1100 *Website:* escrs.org
Activities: Education, training; advancement of health or saving of lives
Address: Temple House, Temple Road, Blackrock, Co Dublin
Trustees: Emanuel Rosen FRCS, Mr Paul Rosen, Mr Ulf Stenevi, Mr Rudy Nuijts
Income: £11,244,832 [2016]; £3,063,652 [2015]; £2,648,346 [2014]; £2,863,762 [2013]; £2,497,192 [2012]

European Society of Endocrinology
Registered: 7 Apr 2008 *Employees:* 1
Tel: 01454 642247 *Website:* ese-hormones.org
Activities: Education, training; advancement of health or saving of lives
Address: ESE Office, c/o Bioscientifica, Euro House, 22 Apex Court, Woodlands, Bradley Stoke, Bristol, BS32 4JT
Trustees: Professor Marta Korbonits, Professor Manuela Simoni, Professor Susan Webb, Professor Jerome Bertherat, Professor Beata Kos-Kudla, Professor Andrea Giustina, Professor Bulent Yildiz, Professor Aart Jan Van Der Lely, Dr Camilla Schalin-Jantti, Professor Felix Beuschlein
Income: £2,907,698 [2016]; £2,532,819 [2015]; £2,989,136 [2014]; £3,452,578 [2013]; £4,184,746 [2012]

European Society of Thoracic Surgeons
Registered: 3 Dec 2002 *Employees:* 1
Tel: 01392 430671 *Website:* ests.org
Activities: Education, training; advancement of health or saving of lives
Address: European Society of Thoracic Surgeons, P O Box 159, Exeter, Devon, EX2 5SH
Trustees: Kostas Papagiannopoulos, Professor Jaroslaw Kuzdzal, Dr Alessandro Brunelli
Income: £1,426,353 [2017]; £1,314,293 [2015]; £1,177,833 [2014]; £977,560 [2013]; £960,970 [2012]

Eurovision Mission To Europe
Registered: 27 Oct 2008 *Employees:* 7
Tel: 01924 453693 *Website:* eurovision.org.uk
Activities: Education, training; prevention or relief of poverty; religious activities
Address: Eurovision Mission To Europe, 41 Healds Road, Dewsbury, W Yorks, WF13 4HU
Trustees: Mr Leonard Holihan, Mr Eric Charles Woodward, Rachel Parkhouse, Rev Cyril Joseph Curtis, Dr Richard Colin Parkhouse, Rev Michael Wieteska
Income: £2,177,451 [2016]; £2,158,234 [2015]; £1,967,624 [2014]; £2,194,163 [2013]; £3,609,604 [2012]

The Evangelical Alliance
Registered: 5 Nov 1962 *Employees:* 47 *Volunteers:* 17
Tel: 020 7520 3830 *Website:* eauk.org
Activities: Education, training; religious activities; human rights, religious or racial harmony, equality or diversity
Address: 176 Copenhagen Street, London, N1 0ST
Trustees: Tani Omideyi, John Glass, Mr Julian Richards, Rev Dr David Hilborn, Ruth Walker, Rachel Phillips, Mr Peter Jeffrey, Pastor Steve Uppal, Rev John Coyne, Stephen Cave, Tracy Cotterell, Miss Ruth Awogbade
Income: £2,467,059 [2017]; £2,345,250 [2016]; £2,370,937 [2015]; £2,312,702 [2014]; £2,635,329 [2013]

The Evangelical Fellowship of Congregational Churches Trust Corporation Limited
Registered: 27 Jan 2009
Tel: 01482 860324 *Website:* efcc.org.uk
Activities: Religious activities
Address: E F C C Ltd, P O Box 34, Beverley, E Yorks, HU17 0YY
Trustees: Rev Gwynne Evans, Mr Philip James Williams, Rev John Brown, Mr Kevin Ivor Davies, Mr Robert William Nielson, Rev Bill Calder, Mr Gilbert Stephenson, Rev Matthew Lloyd Rees
Income: £1,407,535 [2016]; £97,277 [2015]; £131,840 [2014]; £553,071 [2013]; £53,156 [2012]

Mary Ann Evans Hospice
Registered: 16 Oct 1992 *Employees:* 59 *Volunteers:* 401
Tel: 024 7686 5466 *Website:* maryannevans.org.uk
Activities: The advancement of health or saving of lives
Address: Mary Ann Evans Hospice, George Eliot Hospital Site, Nuneaton, Warwicks, CV10 7QL
Trustees: Mrs Maureen Hawkins, Dr Peter Dermot Joseph Handslip, Mrs Hazel Davidson, Philip Robson, Mr Christopher John Bartup, Mrs Heather Norgrove, Mr John Clifford Barrett, Josie Town, Anne Booth, Sally Dibb
Income: £1,410,120 [2016]; £1,292,087 [2015]; £1,901,418 [2014]; £1,437,313 [2013]; £1,071,252 [2012]

Eversfield Preparatory School Trust Limited
Registered: 4 Feb 1965 *Employees:* 72
Tel: 0121 705 0354 *Website:* eversfield.co.uk
Activities: Education, training
Address: Warwick Road, Solihull, W Midlands, B91 1AT
Trustees: Mr Valentine James Harvey, Dr Timothy John Brain OBE QPM, Mr Barry Cross, Mrs Christine Elizabeth Skouby, John Clifford Barratt Shaw, Mr Derek Paul Adamson, Mrs Carol Burke, Mr M Eyles
Income: £3,094,169 [2017]; £2,910,610 [2016]; £2,766,639 [2015]; £2,626,737 [2014]; £2,488,984 [2013]

Everton in the Community
Registered: 10 Sep 2003 *Employees:* 72 *Volunteers:* 142
Website: evertonfc.com
Activities: Education, training; advancement of health or saving of lives; disability; prevention or relief of poverty; amateur sport; economic, community development, employment
Address: Everton Football Club, Goodison Road, Liverpool, L4 4EL
Trustees: Charles Mills, Mr Richard Kenyon, Mrs Michelle Kirk, Mrs Denise Barrett-Baxendale, Mr Alan McTavish, Sir John Francis Jones
Income: £4,385,340 [2017]; £3,062,059 [2016]; £2,715,151 [2015]; £2,166,033 [2014]; £1,829,147 [2013]

Everybody Sport & Recreation
Registered: 10 Mar 2014 *Employees:* 534 *Volunteers:* 33
Tel: 01625 383968 *Website:* everybody.org.uk
Activities: Education, training; advancement of health or saving of lives; arts, culture, heritage, science; recreation
Address: Holmes Chapel Community Centre, Station Road, Holmes Chapel, Crewe, Cheshire, CW4 8AA
Trustees: Mr Colin Chaytors, Mr Richard Middlebrook, Mr Andrew Michael James Kolker, Mr Martin Christopher Hardy, Ms Zoe Davidson, Mr Steven Percy, Mr Philip Jackson Bland MBE, Mr Andrew James Farr, Mrs Christine Gibbons, Mr Harry Korkov, Mrs Helen Gowin
Income: £14,821,232 [2017]; £13,634,670 [2016]; £12,630,995 [2015]

Everychild
Registered: 20 Dec 2001 *Employees:* 18
Website: familyforeverychild.org
Activities: General charitable purposes
Address: Family for Every Child, 23 Austin Friars, London, EC2N 2QP
Trustees: Mr Trevor Robert Pearcy, Mrs Amanda Griffith, Mr Ian Hanham
Income: £5,752,000 [2016]; £4,913,000 [2015]; £8,256,000 [2014]; £7,184,000 [2013]; £8,692,000 [2012]

Everyday Church
Registered: 7 Jan 2013 *Employees:* 34 *Volunteers:* 75
Tel: 020 8947 1859 *Website:* everyday.org.uk
Activities: Education, training; prevention or relief of poverty; religious activities
Address: Everyday Church, 30 Queens Road, London, SW19 8LR
Trustees: Kevin Andrew Richards, Mr Andrew Philip Moore, Mr Adam John Featherstone, Mr Lucas John Palmer
Income: £1,531,280 [2016]; £1,740,753 [2015]; £1,127,225 [2014]; £6,368,742 [2013]

Everyday Language Solutions
Registered: 10 Apr 2002 *Employees:* 11
Tel: 01642 603203 *Website:* everydaylanguagesolutions.co.uk
Activities: Education, training; prevention or relief of poverty; economic, community development, employment
Address: Carbury House, Concorde Way, Preston Farm, Stockton on Tees, Cleveland, TS18 3TB
Trustees: Mrs Suzanne Fletcher, Mr Michael Turnbull, Mr Jeff Lupton, Bill Overin, Mr Ian Hellawell
Income: £1,190,016 [2017]; £1,079,371 [2016]; £991,129 [2015]; £928,837 [2014]; £765,738 [2013]

Eveson Charitable Trust
Registered: 26 Jan 1994 *Employees:* 2
Tel: 01452 501352
Activities: The advancement of health or saving of lives; disability; accommodation, housing; other charitable purposes
Address: The Eveson Charitable Trust, 45 Park Road, Gloucester, GL1 1LP
Trustees: Mr David Philip Pearson OBE FCA, Louise Woodhead, Richard Mainwaring FCA, Vivien Cockerill, The Bishop of Hereford, Mr Martin Davies, Bill Wiggin MP, Judith Millward FCA, Tamsin Clive
Income: £1,644,637 [2017]; £1,425,441 [2016]; £1,259,286 [2015]; £1,260,413 [2014]; £1,417,268 [2013]

The Evolution Education Trust
Registered: 17 Aug 2010
Tel: 020 3207 7238
Activities: Education, training
Address: 8 St James Square, London, SW1Y 4JU
Trustees: Dr Jonathan Milner, Mr James Milner, Mr Michael Magnay
Income: £1,784,652 [2017]; £99,488 [2016]; £7,482,427 [2015]; £2,928,601 [2014]; £966,736 [2013]

Evolve Housing + Support
Registered: 19 Aug 2003 *Employees:* 184 *Volunteers:* 44
Tel: 020 7101 9960 *Website:* evolvehousing.org.uk
Activities: General charitable purposes; education, training; advancement of health or saving of lives; disability; prevention or relief of poverty; accommodation, housing; economic, community development, employment
Address: Marco Polo House, 3-5 Lansdowne Road, Croydon, Surrey, CR9 1LL
Trustees: Ms Rebecca Pritchard, Ms Philippa Thomas, Ms Visakha Sri Chandrasekera, Ms Isabel Sanchez, Mr Simon McGrath, Mr Andrew Lowe, Ms Karen Cooper, Mr David Shrimpton, Ms Diana Coman
Income: £10,499,125 [2017]; £10,372,632 [2016]; £9,394,520 [2015]; £8,538,158 [2014]; £8,259,177 [2013]

Ewell Castle School
Registered: 13 Feb 1963 *Employees:* 93
Tel: 020 8393 1413 *Website:* ewellcastle.co.uk
Activities: Education, training
Address: Ewell Castle School, Church Street, Ewell, Epsom, Surrey, KT17 2AW
Trustees: Mrs Jennifer Gay Moran, Mr David Michael Tucker, Mrs Doreen Parker, Mr Colin Alfred Griffith, Mr Nigel Geoffrey David Bird, Mr Anthony John Evans, Mr Sean Sullivan, Mr Antony Peter Shawyer
Income: £6,600,893 [2016]; £6,138,235 [2015]; £5,867,077 [2014]; £5,751,642 [2013]; £5,820,557 [2012]

Exbury Gardens Limited
Registered: 24 Apr 1989 *Employees:* 41 *Volunteers:* 17
Tel: 023 8089 7181 *Website:* exbury.co.uk
Activities: Education, training; arts, culture, heritage, science; environment, conservation, heritage; recreation; other charitable purposes
Address: Blacklands Farm, Exbury, Southampton, SO45 1AJ
Trustees: Sir Ghillean Prance, Miss Charlotte De Rothschild, Mr Marcus Agius, Mr Hugh Eric Allen Johnson, Mrs Caroline De Rothschild, Mr Lionel De Rothschild, Miss Marie-Louise Agius
Income: £1,127,244 [2017]; £1,050,926 [2016]; £1,048,705 [2015]; £1,610,680 [2014]; £1,119,291 [2013]

Exceed Worldwide
Registered: 2 Feb 1994 *Employees:* 129
Tel: 028 9266 7704 *Website:* exceed-worldwide.org
Activities: Education, training; advancement of health or saving of lives; disability; economic, community development, employment
Address: The Cambodia Trust, Wycombe Road, Saunderton, High Wycombe, Bucks, HP14 4BF
Trustees: Ed McBriar, Dr John Robert Fisk, John Orr, Mr Craig Martin, Dr Niamh O'Rourke, Daniel Blocka, Dr Vuthy Chhoeurn, Dr Debra Darosa, Mr Reynaldo Rey-Matius Doctor
Income: £4,799,870 [2017]; £3,388,488 [2016]; £3,208,436 [2015]; £3,952,164 [2014]; £5,695,020 [2013]

Excellent Development Limited
Registered: 4 Nov 2002 *Employees:* 13 *Volunteers:* 1
Website: excellent.org.uk
Activities: The prevention or relief of poverty; overseas aid, famine relief; environment, conservation, heritage; economic, community development, employment
Address: Excellent Development, Unit 1.17, The Foundry, 17 Oval Way, London, SE11 5RR
Trustees: Mr Nigel Reader, Miss Alison Bell, Mrs Barbara Busby, Ms Pamela Gilder, Mr Mark Murphy, Mr David Richard Jordan Jordan, Mr Alexander Day, Mr Bandish Suresh Dharamshi Gudka
Income: £1,143,573 [2017]; £1,533,637 [2016]; £1,291,076 [2015]; £1,158,259 [2014]; £1,177,316 [2013]

Exeter Cathedral School
Registered: 28 Mar 2013 *Employees:* 70 *Volunteers:* 3
Tel: 01392 255321 *Website:* exetercs.org
Activities: Education, training; accommodation, housing; religious activities
Address: Exeter Cathedral School, The Chantry, Palace Gate, Exeter, EX1 1HX
Trustees: Mr John Christopher Crowley, Mr Jonathan Lee Draper, Mrs Ann Margaret Barwood, Mr Neil Richard Pockett, Mr Richard Roger Biggs, Rev Ian Charles Morter, Mr Derek John Phillips, Mr Jeremy Mark Sugden, Dr Pamela Booker
Income: £2,557,952 [2016]; £2,886,308 [2015]; £1,574 [2014]

Exeter City Community Trust
Registered: 14 Nov 2007 *Employees:* 59 *Volunteers:* 25
Tel: 01392 411243 *Website:* exetercityfitc.co.uk
Activities: Education, training; disability; amateur sport; recreation
Address: Exeter City AFC Ltd, St James Park, Stadium Way, Exeter, EX4 6PX
Trustees: Mr Martin John Weiler, Mr Julian Tagg, Mr Christopher Gill, Mrs Catherine Hill, Mr David Compton Coard, Mr Robert Bosworth, Mr Graham John Cridland, Ms Jemma Anne Hodgkins
Income: £1,127,601 [2017]; £774,832 [2016]; £589,266 [2015]; £414,239 [2014]; £350,550 [2013]

Exeter Community Initiatives
Registered: 30 Sep 1993 *Employees:* 45 *Volunteers:* 108
Tel: 01392 205800 *Website:* eci.org.uk
Activities: Education, training; prevention or relief of poverty; economic, community development, employment
Address: 148-149 Fore Street, Exeter, Devon, EX4 3AN
Trustees: Mrs Ruth Saltmarsh, Mrs Heather Margaret Morgan, Mr Tim Goodwin, Mr Christopher Neale, Mr Terry Makewell, Mrs Pat Cusa, Mr John Barrett, Mr David Walters, Mr Richard James Clack
Income: £1,048,098 [2017]; £1,092,408 [2016]; £1,001,666 [2015]; £905,104 [2014]; £922,034 [2013]

The Exeter Diocesan Board of Finance
Registered: 13 Feb 1967 *Employees:* 51 *Volunteers:* 6
Tel: 01392 272686 *Website:* exeter.anglican.org
Activities: Religious activities
Address: Exeter Diocesan Board of Finance, The Old Deanery, The Cloisters, Cathedral Close, Exeter, EX1 1HS
Trustees: Mr Bruce Beacham, The Reverend Michael Partridge, Right Reverend Nicholas McKinnel, Mr Graham Lea, The Venerable Christopher Futcher, Mrs Sandra Andrews, Mrs Wendy Meredith, The Venerable Douglas Dettmer, The Reverend Guy Chave-Cox, The Right Reverend Robert Atwell, Mrs Annie Penelope Jefferies, Mr Giles Richard Frampton, The Very Reverend Jonathan Desmond Francis Greener, The Reverend Will Hazlewood, Mrs Marguerite Shapland, The Venerable Ian Chandler, Mrs Anne Foreman, The Right Reverend Dame Sarah Elisabeth Mullally, Mr Julian Payne, Mr Stephen Macey, The Venerable Mark Butchers, The Reverend Jeremy Charles Trew
Income: £14,586,261 [2016]; £14,389,434 [2015]; £13,903,083 [2014]; £13,927,023 [2013]; £13,494,939 [2012]

Exeter Northcott Theatre Company
Registered: 12 Apr 2013 *Employees:* 47 *Volunteers:* 86
Tel: 01392 722412 *Website:* exeternorthcott.co.uk
Activities: Arts, culture, heritage, science
Address: Northcott Theatre, Stocker Road, Exeter, EX4 4QB
Trustees: Professor Andrew James Thorpe, Lady Lucy Studholme, Mr Andrew Duncan Hay, Mr Jacob Blackburn, Mr Ian Hugh McWalter, Mrs Sara Jane Papworth, Ms Gillian Taylor, Prof Mark Andrew Goodwin, Mr Giuseppe Vicinanza
Income: £2,308,516 [2017]; £2,004,740 [2016]; £1,764,878 [2015]; £1,546,438 [2014]

Exeter Phoenix Ltd
Registered: 6 Sep 1984 *Employees:* 28 *Volunteers:* 48
Tel: 01392 667057 *Website:* exeterphoenix.org.uk
Activities: Arts, culture, heritage, science
Address: Bradninch Place, Gandy Street, Exeter, Devon, EX4 3LS
Trustees: Mr A Sands, Dr Claire Goldstraw, Mr Howard Noye, Mr Daniel Coxon, Mr D Phillips, Mr Oliver Pearson, Mr Andrew James Dean, Ms Amber Carnell
Income: £1,486,926 [2017]; £1,670,189 [2016]; £1,302,351 [2015]; £1,402,355 [2014]; £1,297,427 [2013]

Exeter Royal Academy for Deaf Education
Registered: 16 Jun 2008 *Employees:* 202 *Volunteers:* 10
Tel: 01392 267023 *Website:* exeterdeafacademy.ac.uk
Activities: Education, training; disability
Address: Exeter Deaf Academy, 50 Topsham Road, Exeter, EX2 4NF
Trustees: Mr Peter Burroughs, Dr Janet Harvey, Mr John Peter Alistair Dewhirst, Mr Charles Hampton II, Mr Rhodri Giles Davey, Mr Stephen Ritson King
Income: £7,208,840 [2016]; £7,034,291 [2015]; £6,120,390 [2014]; £6,078,327 [2013]; £6,698,063 [2012]

Exeter School
Registered: 23 Jul 2002 *Employees:* 171 *Volunteers:* 38
Tel: 01392 258723 *Website:* exeterschool.org.uk
Activities: Education, training
Address: Exeter School, Victoria Park Road, Exeter, EX2 4NS
Trustees: Mr Andrew Charles Woodley King, Mr Adrian Burbanks, Professor Anthony Francis Watkinson, Mrs Gillian Ann Hodgetts, Mr Kevin Andrew Cheney, Councillor Graham John Prowse, Brigadier Stephen Philip Hodder, Mr Richard Elliott May, Mr James Dominic Gaisford, Dr Martin Grossel, Mrs Helen Clark, Dr Sara Smart, Mrs Ruth Marie Brook, Miss Rowan Clare Edbrooke, Mr Paul Bernard Fisher, Mrs Alison Catherine Annetta O'Connor
Income: £10,828,871 [2017]; £10,497,711 [2016]; £11,842,015 [2015]; £9,740,394 [2014]; £9,284,827 [2013]

The Exilarch's Foundation
Registered: 12 Jul 1978
Tel: 020 7399 0850
Activities: General charitable purposes
Address: Exilarch's Foundation, 4 Carlos Place, London, W1K 3AW
Trustees: Mr David Alan Ezra Dangoor, Mr Robert Daniel Saul Dangoor, Mr Elie Basil Victor Dangoor, Mr Michael Arthur Jonathan Dangoor
Income: £5,442,077 [2016]; £5,921,632 [2015]; £5,435,370 [2014]; £5,408,809 [2013]; £4,810,223 [2012]

Exmoor Calvert Trust
Registered: 12 Nov 1991 *Employees:* 42 *Volunteers:* 19
Tel: 01598 763221 *Website:* calvert-trust.org.uk
Activities: Education, training; disability; accommodation, housing; amateur sport; environment, conservation, heritage
Address: Wistlandpound, Kentisbury, Barnstaple, Devon, EX31 4SJ
Trustees: Mr Jeremy Richard Holtom MRICS FAAV AC Arb, The Countess of Arran, Mr Christopher James Gregson MA, Lady Gass JP, Jim French, Mr Michael Ford, Will Vandersteen, Mr Paul Bannerman Patriedes, Doctor Thomas Leslie Bigge RD MA MB BChir DObst RGOG, Reverend David Cooper, Lady Jennifer Acland, Ms Susan May, Mrs Teresa Turner, Sir David Scott, Mr Philip Henry Sampson
Income: £1,407,891 [2016]; £1,388,879 [2015]; £1,486,485 [2014]; £1,331,837 [2013]; £1,607,860 [2012]

Expect Ltd
Registered: 15 Mar 1989 *Employees:* 151 *Volunteers:* 1
Tel: 0151 284 0025 *Website:* expect-excellence.org
Activities: Education, training; disability; economic, community development, employment
Address: Expect Ltd, 151 Stanley Road, Bootle, Merseyside, L20 3DL
Trustees: Mrs Mandy MacDonald, Mrs Janet Hardman, Mr David Egan, Mr Anthony Gilmore
Income: £3,140,198 [2016]; £3,180,464 [2015]; £2,947,475 [2014]; £3,068,987 [2013]; £2,951,927 [2012]

Expectations (UK)
Registered: 19 Jun 2013 *Employees:* 79
Activities: Disability; prevention or relief of poverty; accommodation, housing
Address: 146 Hagley Road, Edgbaston, Birmingham, B16 9NX
Trustees: Ms Yvonne Breen, Mr Joshua Hadley, Mr Marc Blanchette
Income: £3,313,060 [2015]; £1,709,457 [2014]

Extonglen Limited
Registered: 26 Jan 1983
Tel: 020 8731 0777
Activities: Education, training; prevention or relief of poverty; religious activities
Address: New Burlington House, 1075 Finchley Road, London, NW11 0PU
Trustees: Mr Isaac Katzenberg, Mrs C Levine, Mr Meir Levine
Income: £1,303,142 [2016]; £1,145,316 [2015]; £906,477 [2014]; £853,290 [2013]; £829,852 [2012]

The Extracare Charitable Trust
Registered: 31 May 1988 *Employees:* 1,679 *Volunteers:* 2,800
Tel: 024 7650 6011 *Website:* extracare.org.uk
Activities: The advancement of health or saving of lives; accommodation, housing
Address: 7 Harry Weston Road, Binley Business Park, Binley, Coventry, Warwicks, CV3 2SN
Trustees: Martin Shreeve, Judith Mortimer Sykes, Martin Leppard, Kathryn Sallah, Ms Rebekah Eden, Paul Jennings, Ruth Hyndman, Michael Higgs, David Martin, Mrs Mary Julia Martin
Income: £82,624,000 [2017]; £82,624,000 [2016]; £56,638,000 [2015]; £68,901,000 [2014]; £58,466,000 [2013]

The Grace Eyre Foundation
Registered: 23 Apr 1993 *Employees:* 110 *Volunteers:* 64
Tel: 01273 201900 *Website:* grace-eyre.org
Activities: Education, training; disability; accommodation, housing; arts, culture, heritage, science; amateur sport
Address: The Grace Eyre Foundation, 36 Montefiore Road, Hove, E Sussex, BN3 6EP
Trustees: Mr Ben Wood, Mr Peter Nigel Boorman, Mr Mark Sebastian Hendriks, Ms Tracy Rosalind Cullen, Ms Helen Odeniyi, Mr Russell Drayton, Ms Gillian Kinsey Marston
Income: £5,794,273 [2017]; £5,912,972 [2016]; £5,209,940 [2015]; £5,020,840 [2014]; £3,930,142 [2013]

Ezer V' Hatzalah Ltd
Registered: 5 Dec 2006 *Employees:* 5 *Volunteers:* 5
Activities: Education, training; prevention or relief of poverty; overseas aid, famine relief; religious activities
Address: 52 East Bank, London, N16 5PZ
Trustees: Mr Pincus Mann, Mr Samuel Lew, Mr Maurice Freund
Income: £14,856,568 [2016]; £9,559,885 [2015]; £8,224,926 [2014]; £7,084,860 [2013]; £5,632,649 [2012]

FARA Foundation

Registered: 16 Dec 2010 *Employees:* 263 *Volunteers:* 1,024
Tel: 020 8973 0910 *Website:* faracharity.org
Activities: Education, training; advancement of health or saving of lives; disability; prevention or relief of poverty; accommodation, housing; economic, community development, employment; human rights, religious or racial harmony, equality or diversity
Address: 51 High Street, Walsingham, Norfolk, NR22 6BZ
Trustees: Mr Donald Morton, Mrs Jane Rose Nicholson, Ms Siobhan Geraldine Cross, Richard Chalk, Mr Michael William Nicholson, Mrs Lucinda Jane Dawson, Ms Mary-Jo Hill
Income: £9,599,624 [2016]; £8,922,370 [2015]; £8,560,139 [2014]; £8,061,885 [2013]; £7,498,075 [2012]

FAW Football in the Community Limited

Registered: 2 Sep 1996 *Employees:* 44 *Volunteers:* 16,000
Tel: 01633 282911 *Website:* welshfootballtrust.org.uk
Activities: Education, training; amateur sport
Address: Dragon Parc, NTL Football Development Centre, Newport International Sports Village, Newport, NP19 4RA
Trustees: Chris Hatcher, Laura McAllister, Mr Timothy Goodson, Miss Kelly Davies, Mr Christopher Whitley, Mr Robert Paton, Mr Mark Adams, Mr Dai Alun Jones, Mr Peter Arthur Lee, Mr Michael Curson, Mr Timothy Hartley, Mr Trefor Lloyd Hughes, Mr William Lloyd Williams, Mr Neil Dymock
Income: £3,709,960 [2017]; £3,303,989 [2016]; £1,872,397 [2015]; £3,118,739 [2014]; £2,991,251 [2013]

FIA Foundation

Registered: 28 Sep 2001 *Employees:* 14
Tel: 020 7930 3882 *Website:* fiafoundation.org
Activities: General charitable purposes; education, training; advancement of health or saving of lives; amateur sport; environment, conservation, heritage; economic, community development, employment
Address: 60 Trafalgar Square, London, WC2N 5DS
Trustees: Mr Alan Gow, Mr Miquel Nadal, Mr Nicholas Wesson Craw, Graham Stoker, Ms Marilena Amoni, Lord George Robertson of Port Ellen, Mr Jose Abed, Dkfm Werner Kraus, Mr Jean Todt, Mr Martin Angle, Earl Jarrett, Brian Gibbons, Mr Takayoshi Yashiro, Gus Lagman, Mr Kenneth Woodier
Income: £7,802,238 [2016]; £7,735,128 [2015]; £7,486,398 [2014]; £7,432,559 [2013]; £7,353,782 [2012]

The FIEC (Legacy) Charity

Registered: 17 Dec 1971 *Employees:* 15 *Volunteers:* 50
Tel: 01858 434540 *Website:* fiec.org.uk
Activities: Religious activities
Address: 39 The Point, Market Harborough, Leics, LE16 7QU
Trustees: Bill James, Pastor Spencer Shaw, Rev Mark Lawrence BSc, Rev Michael Lewis Teutsch, Mike Kendall, Paul Mallard, Pastor Alan McKnight, Julian Hardyman, Dr Gregory Strain, Mr Jonathan Bond, Peter Walkingshaw, Ian Jones
Income: £1,101,612 [2016]; £1,011,956 [2015]; £1,036,976 [2014]; £731,517 [2013]

The Factory Youth Zone (Manchester) Limited

Registered: 1 Mar 2010 *Employees:* 66 *Volunteers:* 101
Website: thefactoryyz.org
Activities: Education, training; disability; arts, culture, heritage, science; amateur sport; economic, community development, employment
Address: Crown Farm, Frog Lane, Pickmere, Knutsford, Cheshire, WA16 0LL
Trustees: Mrs Katharine Jane Vokes, Mr James Edward Smith, Ms Heather Crosby, Sandra Patricia Collins, Helen Elizabeth Taylor, Mr Will Lewis, Mr Michael O'Connor, Mr Peter Henry, Miss Elizabeth Ann Peters, Mr Christopher Anthony Davis, Mr Francis James Shephard
Income: £1,168,209 [2017]; £1,253,700 [2016]; £1,078,649 [2015]; £1,065,464 [2014]; £941,346 [2013]

The Faculty of Pharmaceutical Medicine of The Royal Colleges of Physicians of The United Kingdom

Registered: 15 Jul 2009 *Employees:* 8
Tel: 020 3696 9040 *Website:* fpm.org.uk
Activities: Education, training; advancement of health or saving of lives
Address: Faculty of Pharmaceutical Medicine, 19 Angel Gate, 326a City Road, London, EC1V 2PT
Trustees: Professor Timothy Evans, Prof Alan Boyd, Dr Chris Worth, Dr Thomas Morris, Prof John Posner, Dr Cheryl Key, Dr David Jefferys, Mr William Payne, Professor Matthew Walters, Dr Isla MacKenzie, Dr Stuart Dollow, Prof Timothy Higenbottam, Dr Lalitha Mahadavan, Prof Alan Cribb
Income: £1,298,092 [2016]; £1,246,294 [2015]; £1,415,634 [2014]; £935,133 [2013]; £771,261 [2012]

Faculty of Public Health of The Royal Colleges of Physicians of The United Kingdom

Registered: 18 Apr 1972 *Employees:* 23 *Volunteers:* 496
Tel: 020 7935 0243 *Website:* fph.org.uk
Activities: Education, training; advancement of health or saving of lives
Address: Faculty of Public Health, 4 St Andrews Place, London, NW1 4LB
Trustees: Dr Toks Sangowawa, Dr David Williams, Ms Susan Lloyd, Dr John Duncan Middleton, Dr Julie Parkes, Dr Suzanna Mathew, Professor Selena Felicity Gray, Professor Jane Dacre, Dr Julie Cavanagh, Dr Ellis Friedman, Dr Dympna Edwards, Mrs Angela Treacy Jones, Mrs Margaret Rae, Dr Harald Roderick Rutter, Professor Simon Capewell Professor, Professor Sue Atkinson CBE MB BChir BSc MA FFPH, Dr Emilia Mihaela Crighton, Dr Brendan Mason, Dr Farhang Tahzib, Professor Patrick Joseph Saunders, Dr Neil Frederick Squires, Dr Judith Mary Hooper, Dr Adrian Philip Mairs, Professor Christopher John Packham, Mrs Alison Jane Challenger, Mrs Claire Jane Beynon, Dr Joanne Broadbent Rachel
Income: £2,027,026 [2016]; £1,838,683 [2015]; £1,682,926 [2014]; £1,628,037 [2013]; £1,585,901 [2012]

Faculty of Sexual and Reproductive Healthcare of The Royal College of Obstetricians and Gynaecologists

Registered: 16 Apr 1993 *Employees:* 17 *Volunteers:* 300
Tel: 020 7724 5524 *Website:* fsrh.org
Activities: Education, training; advancement of health or saving of lives
Address: FSRH, RCOG, 27 Sussex Place, London, NW1 4RG
Trustees: Dr Paula Baraitser, Dr Jennifer Anne Heathcote, Dr Helen Munro, Dr Emmert Roberts, Ms Roopa Aitken, Dr Diana Jane Ashton Mansour, Dr Asha Kasliwal, Dr Katherine Ann Guthrie, Mr Avtar Thamia, Mr Martyn Booth
Income: £2,271,243 [2016]; £2,407,429 [2015]; £2,164,036 [2014]; £1,905,723 [2013]; £2,068,623 [2012]

Fair Play (Workforce) Limited
Registered: 11 Jan 2001 *Employees:* 77
Tel: 029 2047 8900 *Website:* chwaraeteg.com
Activities: General charitable purposes; education, training; prevention or relief of poverty; economic, community development, employment; human rights, religious or racial harmony, equality or diversity
Address: Anchor Court, Keen Road, Cardiff, CF24 5JW
Trustees: Mr Jeffrey John Andrews, Mrs Carol Bogue-Lloyd, Ms Catherine Thomas, Dr Anita Mary Shaw, Ms Alison Thorne, Ms Sandra Busby, Mr David Wyn Pritchard, Mrs Susan Margaret Lane, Ms Rachael Cunningham, Mr Christopher James Warner
Income: £3,539,728 [2017]; £2,815,496 [2016]; £2,373,873 [2015]; £2,849,092 [2014]; £2,934,529 [2013]

Fair Ways Foundation
Registered: 8 Jan 2015 *Employees:* 268
Tel: 023 8023 0400 *Website:* fairways.co
Activities: Education, training; accommodation, housing
Address: Fairways Care UK Ltd, Fairways House, Alpha Business Park, Mount Pleasant Road, Southampton, SO14 0QB
Trustees: Ian Davies, Ms Anne Segall, Mr David Pilgrim, Mr Alexander Burnfield, Mr Adrian Fry
Income: £11,168,042 [2017]; £9,834,309 [2016]; £2,443,921 [2015]

Esmee Fairbairn Foundation
Registered: 7 Jun 1961 *Employees:* 27
Tel: 020 7812 3700 *Website:* esmeefairbairn.org.uk
Activities: General charitable purposes; education, training; disability; prevention or relief of poverty; accommodation, housing; arts, culture, heritage, science; environment, conservation, heritage; economic, community development, employment; human rights, religious or racial harmony, equality or diversity
Address: Esmee Fairbairn Foundation, Kings Place, 90 York Way, London, N1 9AG
Trustees: Kate Lampard, Mr James Hughes-Hallett, John Fairbairn, Joe Docherty, Eleanor Updale, Professor David Hill, Tom Chandos, Mrs Beatrice Hollond, Sir Jonathan Phillips, Stella Manzie CBE, Mr Edward Bonham Carter
Income: £5,344,000 [2016]; £4,954,000 [2015]; £6,570,000 [2014]; £8,948,000 [2013]; £11,952,000 [2012]

Fairfield (Croydon) Limited
Registered: 24 Sep 1993 *Employees:* 149 *Volunteers:* 95
Website: fairfield.co.uk
Activities: Arts, culture, heritage, science
Address: 366a Brighton Road, South Croydon, Surrey, CR2 6AL
Trustees: Mr Mohammad Aslam, Ms Kate Vennell, Mrs Fiona Satiro, Mr Richard Plant, Mr Vivian Davies, Mr Anthony Blin Stoyle
Income: £6,490,141 [2015]; £6,719,493 [2014]; £6,808,596 [2013]

Fairfield Farm Trust
Registered: 18 Jul 1977 *Employees:* 73 *Volunteers:* 6
Tel: 01225 767839 *Website:* fairfieldopportunityfarm.ac.uk
Activities: General charitable purposes; education, training; disability; economic, community development, employment
Address: 9 Ravenscroft Gardens, Trowbridge, Wilts, BA14 7JU
Trustees: Mrs Alison Mary Irving, Ms Emma-Jane Dalley, Ms Amanda Joy Callard, Mr Alan Best, Mrs Patricia Teague, Mrs Anne Marie Pelling, Mr Martin Cooper, Miss Julie Ann Cathcart
Income: £3,317,199 [2017]; £2,031,690 [2016]; £2,240,933 [2015]; £2,749,521 [2014]; £2,045,460 [2013]

Fairfield Residential Home
Registered: 13 Jun 2006 *Employees:* 28
Tel: 01865 558413 *Website:* fairfieldhome.co.uk
Activities: Accommodation, housing
Address: Fairfield, 115 Banbury Road, Oxford, OX2 6LA
Trustees: Mr John Cole, Mrs Heather Bliss, Mr Kevin Minns, Mr Charles Benedict Gardner, Dr Sally Hope, Ms Wendy Ann Robinson, Mr Adrian O'Hickey, Mrs Clare Irene Balme, Dr Charles Andrew Chivers
Income: £7,822,187 [2016]; £892,680 [2015]; £880,338 [2014]; £832,493 [2013]; £750,328 [2012]

Fairley House School
Registered: 2 Jan 1981 *Employees:* 85
Tel: 020 7630 3765 *Website:* fairleyhouse.org.uk
Activities: Education, training
Address: Fairley House School, 30 Causton Street, London, SW1P 4AU
Trustees: Ms Sarah Hamilton-Fairley, Mr Jonathan Brough, Mr Adam Constable QC, Mr Jolyon Luke, Mr Thomas Morrell, Ms Veronica Bidwell, Mr Paul Barnaby, Mrs Amanda Leach, Mrs Fiona Dixon
Income: £6,182,078 [2016]; £5,647,480 [2015]; £5,776,829 [2014]; £5,516,914 [2013]; £4,617,672 [2012]

The Fairlight Charitable Company
Registered: 12 Mar 2015 *Employees:* 25
Tel: 01344 874681
Activities: General charitable purposes; education, training; religious activities
Address: Fairlight, The Avenue, Ascot, Berks, SL5 7LY
Trustees: Sister Rosemary Kean, Anne Furlong, Charlotte Cassidy, Miss Matilda Sinead Collier, Anne Josephine Carr
Income: £1,127,471 [2017]; £21,557,809 [2016]

Fairshare Educational Foundation
Registered: 14 Dec 2006 *Employees:* 31
Tel: 020 7403 7800 *Website:* shareaction.org
Activities: General charitable purposes; education, training; prevention or relief of poverty; environment, conservation, heritage
Address: 16 Crucifix Lane, London, SE1 3JW
Trustees: Ms Jane Cooper, Mr Paul Dickinson, Mick McAteer, Mr Robert Ryan, Mr Stephen Davis, Mr Jonathan Clarke, Ms Emma Howard Boyd, Ms Lisa Warren
Income: £1,217,433 [2017]; £1,031,043 [2016]; £652,680 [2015]; £542,696 [2014]; £371,390 [2013]

Fairstead House School Trust Ltd
Registered: 9 Nov 1978 *Employees:* 50
Tel: 01638 662318 *Website:* fairsteadhouse.co.uk
Activities: Education, training
Address: Fairstead House School, Fordham Road, Newmarket, Suffolk, CB8 7AA
Trustees: Mr Ian Peter Radford, Dr Patrick Michael Round, Mr Jonathan David Edge, Mr Nicholas Jay, Mrs Elaine Lunn, Mrs Anna Marie Hall, Mrs Amanda Helen Childs
Income: £1,163,955 [2017]; £989,554 [2016]; £905,916 [2015]; £921,125 [2014]; £1,023,180 [2013]

The Fairtrade Foundation
Registered: 3 Feb 1995 *Employees:* 118 *Volunteers:* 65
Tel: 020 7405 5942 *Website:* fairtrade.org.uk
Activities: The prevention or relief of poverty; overseas aid, famine relief; economic, community development, employment
Address: 5.7 The Loom, Gowers Walk, London, E1 8PY
Trustees: Ms Alison Marshall, Mr Barney Tallack, Bob Doherty, Ms Jane Frost, Mr Paul Farthing, Mrs Brenda Achieng, Ms Rebecca Rowland, Mr Michael Jary, Mr Paul Thompson, Ms Elizabeth Sideris, Mr Didier Dallemagne
Income: £11,755,000 [2016]; £11,347,000 [2015]; £11,617,000 [2014]; £11,782,000 [2013]; £11,727,000 [2012]

Faith in Families
Registered: 27 Dec 1962 *Employees:* 27 *Volunteers:* 100
Website: faithinfamilies.org
Activities: General charitable purposes; education, training
Address: 2 Windermere Close, Gamston, Nottingham, NG2 6PQ
Trustees: Mr John Charles Gerard Bale FIPS, Mr Edward Hayes, Mr Patrick Adie, Mrs Joy Padmore, Margaret Staples, Mr Derek Huett, Mr Sanjeev Kumar
Income: £1,063,483 [2017]; £1,524,914 [2016]; £1,351,714 [2015]; £1,133,831 [2014]; £964,864 [2013]

Faithful Companions of Jesus
Registered: 2 Feb 1965 *Employees:* 32
Tel: 020 8232 9570 *Website:* fcjsisters.org
Activities: General charitable purposes; education, training; prevention or relief of poverty; overseas aid, famine relief; religious activities
Address: Gumley House Convent, 251 Twickenham Road, Isleworth, Middlesex, TW7 6DN
Trustees: Sister Mary C Sykes, Sister Katherine M Walsh, Sister Mary T Fitzpatrick, Sister Patricia M Binchy, Sister Barbara J Brown-Graham
Income: £10,025,698 [2016]; £2,797,318 [2015]; £2,903,230 [2014]; £3,245,196 [2013]; £3,657,892 [2012]

Lilian Faithfull Homes
Registered: 4 Jan 2008 *Employees:* 257
Tel: 01242 500414 *Website:* lilianfaithfull.co.uk
Activities: Accommodation, housing
Address: Ground Floor West, Festival House, Jessop Avenue, Cheltenham, Glos, GL50 3SH
Trustees: Canon David Nye BD MA, Mrs Julia Manning, Mrs Janet Elizabeth Ballinger, Mrs Eleanor Morag Sinclair Fox, Gareth Parry, Mr Alan Bishop, Mr Timothy P Griffin, Mr Richard Lyons, Miss Gill Pyatt, Jane Woodley, Mr Christopher John Dickenson
Income: £8,553,762 [2016]; £7,585,011 [2015]; £7,878,386 [2014]; £7,418,577 [2013]; £6,350,541 [2012]

Falcon Support Services E.M Ltd
Registered: 6 Apr 2004 *Employees:* 37 *Volunteers:* 10
Tel: 01509 268699 *Website:* falconsupportservices.org.uk
Activities: Accommodation, housing
Address: The Falcon Centre, 29 Pinfold Gate, Loughborough, Leics, LE11 1BE
Trustees: Mr Andrew Lawrence Cereseto, Dr Jane Ann Gray, Mr Benjamin Thomas Woolley, Dr Peter Mark Cannon, Mr Peter Dadswell, Mr William Robert Sharp
Income: £1,162,694 [2017]; £1,012,174 [2016]; £905,312 [2015]; £769,220 [2014]; £509,211 [2013]

Falmouth & Exeter Students' Union
Registered: 11 Jan 2012 *Employees:* 23 *Volunteers:* 236
Tel: 01326 259455 *Website:* fxu.org.uk
Activities: General charitable purposes; education, training; recreation
Address: Penryn Campus, Treliever Road, Penryn, Cornwall, TR10 9FE
Trustees: Mr Andrew Lugger, Miss Alexa Webster, Mr Tom Murray-Richards, Mr Andrew Harbert, Miss Wajeeha Sheik, Miss Amanda Chetwynd-Cowieson, Mr Chris Slesser, Mr Paul Kenneth Thomas Northmore, Miss Line Cecile Unumb Vangen
Income: £1,199,271 [2017]; £1,160,899 [2016]; £1,149,071 [2015]; £878,656 [2014]; £867,380 [2013]

Families Health and Well-Being Consortium
Registered: 11 Dec 2012 *Employees:* 4
Tel: 07717 530621 *Website:* fhwb.org.uk
Activities: General charitable purposes; education, training; advancement of health or saving of lives; disability; prevention or relief of poverty; accommodation, housing; amateur sport; economic, community development, employment; recreation
Address: FHWB Consortium, Unit 21 Business Development Centre, Eanam Wharf, Blackburn, BB1 5BL
Trustees: Ms Amanda Barrass, Mr David Edmundson, Mrs Vicky Shepherd, Mr Adrian Ruary Leather, Ms Sarah Swindley, Ms Susan Cotton, Ms Jacqui Chatwood, Mr Kevin Paul McGee
Income: £1,407,180 [2017]; £631,595 [2016]; £419,797 [2015]; £204,888 [2014]

Families for Children Trust
Registered: 25 Jul 2002 *Employees:* 48 *Volunteers:* 30
Tel: 01364 645480 *Website:* familiesforchildren.org.uk
Activities: General charitable purposes; prevention or relief of poverty; religious activities
Address: Families for Children, Higher Mill, Buckfast, Buckfastleigh, Devon, TQ11 0EE
Trustees: Mr Terence William Connor, Mr David Alan Howell, Ms Tina Cook, Mrs Charmian O'Kelly, Mrs Susan Phyllis Lucas, Lay Canon Ann Margaret Barwood BEM, Mr Nicholas Allan, Mr Roger Lake, Mr Hamish Adam, Rev Bruce Duncan MBE
Income: £1,662,970 [2016]; £1,785,285 [2015]; £1,556,902 [2014]; £1,717,694 [2013]; £1,114,466 [2012]

Family Action
Registered: 13 Nov 1972 *Employees:* 703 *Volunteers:* 583
Tel: 020 7241 7601 *Website:* family-action.org.uk
Activities: General charitable purposes; prevention or relief of poverty
Address: Family Action, 24 Angel Gate, London, EC1V 2PT
Trustees: Mr George Alastair Dunnett, Ms Aida Cable, Pim Piers, Mr Paul John Hayes, Mr Robert Wilfred Tapsfield, Ms Dez Holmes, Mr Ian Hargrave, Mr Sean O'Callaghan, Ms Mary Fulton, Siobhan Boylan, Ms Sophy Doyle, Mr Philip Andrew Bowkley, Mr Philippe Broadhead
Income: £21,930,000 [2017]; £21,466,000 [2016]; £22,124,000 [2015]; £20,219,000 [2014]; £18,486,000 [2013]

Family Care Trust
Registered: 15 Mar 1995 Employees: 58 Volunteers: 1
Website: familycaretrust.co.uk
Activities: Education, training; advancement of health or saving of lives; disability
Address: 119 Anglian Way, Coventry, Warwicks, CV3 1PE
Trustees: Mrs Catherine Llewellyn, Mr Paul Hughes, Mr David Gamble, Mr Roger James Look, Mr David Edwards, Mr Richard Purser, Mr Iain Dempster Morgan
Income: £1,739,989 [2017]; £2,008,353 [2016]; £2,281,459 [2015]; £2,392,412 [2014]; £2,417,153 [2013]

Family Care
Registered: 6 Sep 1982 Employees: 39 Volunteers: 18
Tel: 0115 960 3010 Website: familycare-nottingham.org.uk
Activities: General charitable purposes; education, training
Address: 28 Magdala Road, Nottingham, NG3 5DF
Trustees: Dr Richard John Turner, Professor Harriet Ward, Ms Nasima Haq, Mrs Margaret Bell, Ms Patricia O'Brien, Mr Nicholas Andrew Harding BEd JP, Mr Denis Tully, Mr Christopher John Blainey, Ms Angela Bright, Mr Tony William Mellor
Income: £1,431,222 [2017]; £1,274,675 [2016]; £1,242,654 [2015]; £1,230,792 [2014]; £1,148,836 [2013]

The Family Federation for World Peace and Unification
Registered: 14 Jul 1974 Employees: 9 Volunteers: 35
Tel: 020 7723 0721 Website: ffwpu.org.uk
Activities: General charitable purposes; education, training; religious activities; human rights, religious or racial harmony, equality or diversity; other charitable purposes
Address: The Family Federation for World Peace, FFWPU, 43 Lancaster Gate, London, W2 3NA
Trustees: Mr Edward Hartley, Andrew Johnson, Mr Terence Sweeney, Mrs Gillian Schroder, Mr Timothy P Read, Joanna Hartl
Income: £1,377,486 [2016]; £1,429,903 [2015]; £1,098,038 [2014]; £1,110,849 [2013]; £1,153,922 [2012]

The Family Fund Trust for Families with Severely Disabled Children
Registered: 19 Mar 1996 Employees: 93
Tel: 0844 974 4099 Website: familyfund.org.uk
Activities: Disability
Address: The Family Fund Unit 4, Alpha Court, Monks Cross Drive, Huntington, York, YO32 9WN
Trustees: Mr Gordon Quintin Anderson, Mr David Lewis, Mr Geoffrey Cyril Linnell, Miss Tara Marie Palmer, Mrs Lucy Anne Williams, Mr James Richard Turton, Mr Ian Black, Mr David Michael Braybrook, Mr John Grant MacRae, Mr Neil Robert Scott, Ms Mary Ann Bishop, Kate Fleck
Income: £35,279,000 [2017]; £36,964,000 [2016]; £37,990,000 [2015]; £36,964,000 [2014]; £35,566,000 [2013]

The Family Holiday Association
Registered: 25 Oct 1988 Employees: 12
Tel: 020 3117 0650 Website: familyholidayassociation.org.uk
Activities: The advancement of health or saving of lives; prevention or relief of poverty
Address: Family Holiday Association, 3 Gainsford Street, London, SE1 2NE
Trustees: Mr Keith Graham, Mr David Burling, Mr John Montague Appleby, Ms Julia Mary Ridgway, Mr Mark Saxon, Ms Alison Rice, Mr Jonathan Willoughby Scott, Ms Joelle Leader, Ms Philippa Harris
Income: £1,336,416 [2017]; £1,563,833 [2016]; £1,362,858 [2015]; £1,540,940 [2014]; £1,238,014 [2013]

Family Links (Educational Programmes)
Registered: 22 May 1997 Employees: 24
Tel: 01865 401800 Website: familylinks.org.uk
Activities: Education, training; advancement of health or saving of lives; economic, community development, employment
Address: Units 2 & 3, Fenchurch Court, Bobby Fryer Close, Cowley, Oxford, OX4 6ZN
Trustees: Mrs Rosalind Jeannette Portman, Avril McIntyre, Sarah Hargreaves, Ms Shaila Yasheen Khan, Ms Debbie Cowley, Mrs Vanessa Iris Emmett, Mr Geoffrey McDonald
Income: £1,280,642 [2017]; £2,110,115 [2016]; £1,575,113 [2015]; £1,439,577 [2014]; £1,209,650 [2013]

Family Lives
Registered: 8 Oct 1999 Employees: 163 Volunteers: 407
Tel: 020 7553 3080 Website: familylives.org.uk
Activities: Education, training
Address: Family Lives, 15-17 The Broadway, Hatfield, Herts, AL9 5HZ
Trustees: Ms Soona Vahid, Dr John Coleman, Ms Anastasia De Waal, Mr Warwick Jones, Ms Amanda Holt, Suzie Hayman, Mr Andrew Montgomery, Mr Stuart Bayliss, Ms Neena Rupani
Income: £2,983,000 [2017]; £3,465,000 [2016]; £4,984,000 [2015]; £4,182,000 [2014]; £3,616,000 [2013]

Family Planning Association
Registered: 22 Dec 1966 Employees: 18
Website: fpa.org.uk
Activities: General charitable purposes; education, training
Address: 23-28 Penn Street, London, N1 5DL
Trustees: Mr David Harris, Mr Jem Stein, Miss Ellie Munro, Ms Zoe Stewart, Ms Anthea Morris, Dr Brian Scott, Ms Marta Garcia Abadia, Mr Matthew Williams, Ms Helena Dollimore, Ms Gillian Holmes
Income: £1,390,342 [2017]; £1,344,472 [2016]; £1,780,850 [2015]; £1,814,573 [2014]; £2,035,595 [2013]

Family Society
Registered: 9 Apr 2009 Employees: 27 Volunteers: 178
Tel: 020 7769 6741 Website: adoptionfocus.org.uk
Activities: General charitable purposes; education, training; advancement of health or saving of lives; prevention or relief of poverty
Address: McCarthy Denning Ltd, Albert Buildings, 49 Queen Victoria Street, London, EC4N 4SA
Trustees: Mr Kevin Patrick Caffrey, Mr John Barley, Ms Janet Foster, Mr David Lewis, Mr Benjamin James, Mrs Mary Jones, Mr Anthony George Lawton OBE
Income: £1,393,706 [2017]; £947,655 [2016]; £1,232,886 [2015]; £989,517 [2014]; £746,904 [2013]

Family Support Centre [Kings Lynn]
Registered: 2 Oct 1996 Employees: 62 Volunteers: 2
Tel: 01553 816905 Website: mrbeesfscentre.co.uk
Activities: Education, training; prevention or relief of poverty
Address: St Augustines Healthy Living Centre, Columbia Way, King's Lynn, Norfolk, PE30 2LB
Trustees: Mrs J Nowrung, Richard High, Mrs Kathryn Ann Ray Le Serve, Dr Dennis Antony Christopher Barter, Mrs Lesley Louise Hartley
Income: £1,002,577 [2017]; £1,109,202 [2016]; £975,834 [2015]; £954,527 [2014]; £989,640 [2013]

Family and Childcare Trust
Registered: 16 Sep 1999 Employees: 26 Volunteers: 400
Website: familyandchildcaretrust.org
Activities: Education, training; prevention or relief of poverty; economic, community development, employment
Address: Family & Childcare Trust, 73-81 Southwark Bridge Road, London, SE1 0NQ
Trustees: Mr David Ian White, Mr Chris Pond, Ms Sarah-Jane Butler, Mr Martin Pilgrim, Ken Hogg, Ms Rebecca Asher
Income: £1,029,145 [2017]; £960,792 [2016]; £1,366,620 [2015]; £1,322,177 [2014]; £2,049,626 [2013]

Family for Every Child
Registered: 4 Oct 2012 Employees: 28
Website: familyforeverychild.org
Activities: Overseas aid, famine relief; economic, community development, employment; human rights, religious or racial harmony, equality or diversity
Address: Family for Every Child, 23 Austin Friars, London, EC2N 2QP
Trustees: Mr Ian Hanham, Ms Rita Panicker Pinto, Mr Chaste Uwihoreye, Mrs Jane Dekker Brimacombe, Yared Entonios Degefu, Isabel Maria Crowley, Mr Trevor Pearcy, Mr James Kofi Annan, Ms Omattie Madray, Estella Maria Duque Cuesta, Liudmila Sorokina
Income: £5,688,342 [2017]; £2,546,730 [2016]; £2,208,422 [2015]; £876,539 [2014]; £35,966 [2013]

Fareshare
Registered: 14 Oct 2003 Employees: 97 Volunteers: 150
Tel: 020 7394 2466 Website: fareshare.org.uk
Activities: General charitable purposes; education, training; advancement of health or saving of lives; prevention or relief of poverty; environment, conservation, heritage; economic, community development, employment
Address: Fareshare Ltd, Unit 7 Deptford Trading Estate, Blackhorse Road, London, SE8 5HY
Trustees: Mr William Garnett, Ms Kathryn Sowerby, Mr Vincent Craig, Mr Peter Freedman, Mr John Hinton, Mrs Helen Sisson, Mr Stephen Robinson, Mr John Bason, Ms Lucy Danger, Mrs Paola Bergamaschi Broyd, Mr Steven Jackson OBE DL
Income: £5,446,000 [2017]; £5,166,138 [2016]; £2,993,353 [2015]; £2,610,376 [2014]; £2,385,446 [2013]

Farleigh Hospice
Registered: 5 May 1982 Employees: 257 Volunteers: 783
Tel: 01245 457300 Website: farleighhospice.org
Activities: The advancement of health or saving of lives
Address: Farleigh Hospice, North Court Road, Broomfield, Chelmsford, Essex, CM1 7FH
Trustees: Dr Elizabeth Madge Towers, Mr John Chelchowski MBE, Mrs Hilary Mary Bebb, Mr Andrew Gordon Balfour, Mrs Joanna Pittman, Mr Keith Spiller, Mrs Suzanne Riches, Mr Jeffrey Slater, Mrs Emma Louise Wraight, Mrs Lesley Baliga, Dr Andrew David Blainey, Mr Patrick Forsyth, Mr Richard Shail
Income: £12,280,000 [2017]; £10,706,000 [2016]; £9,120,812 [2015]; £8,401,564 [2014]; £6,586,456 [2013]

Farleigh School Trust Limited
Registered: 14 Jul 2014 Employees: 195
Tel: 01264 710766 Website: farleighschool.com
Activities: Education, training; religious activities; economic, community development, employment
Address: Farleigh School, Red Rice, Andover, Hants, SP11 7PW
Trustees: Mrs Charlotte Cunningham, Mrs Bettina Betton, Mr Keith Abel, Mr Tim Syder, Mrs Jane Elizabeth Vyvyan, Mr Charles Ingram Evans, Fr Oswald McBride, Mr Gavin Hamilton, Mr Simon Henderson, Mrs Anna Dixon-Green, Mrs Sarah Raffray, Mrs Emma Elisabeth Jane Todd
Income: £8,358,943 [2017]; £7,989,639 [2016]; £7,592,587 [2015]

Farlington School Trust Limited
Registered: 22 Mar 1966 Employees: 107 Volunteers: 5
Tel: 01403 254967 Website: farlingtonschool.net
Activities: Education, training
Address: Farlington School, Guildford Road, Broadbridge Heath, Horsham, W Sussex, RH12 3PN
Trustees: Mrs Sue Mitchell, Ms Jenny Butler, Alex Bubb, Mrs Bernie Hoare, Bruce Phillips, Mr Andrew Thomas, Mrs Valerie Simpson, Mrs Sarah Riley, Mrs Dianna Fletcher
Income: £4,189,694 [2016]; £5,079,540 [2015]; £5,032,989 [2014]; £5,093,053 [2013]

Farm Africa Limited
Registered: 2 Aug 1985 Employees: 236 Volunteers: 150
Website: farmafrica.org
Activities: The prevention or relief of poverty; overseas aid, famine relief
Address: Farm Africa, Bastion House, 140 London Wall, London, EC2Y 5DN
Trustees: Mr Jan Bonde Nielsen, Mr John Shaw, Professor Jonathan Kydd, Mr Charles Reed, Mr Colin Brereton, Ms Serena Brown, Mr Tim Smith, Mr Carey Ngini, Mr Richard MacDonald, Ms Judith Batchelar, Mr John Young, Mr John Reizenstein, Laketch Mikael, Ms Minette Batters
Income: £17,900,000 [2016]; £12,145,000 [2015]; £13,784,000 [2014]; £12,822,000 [2013]; £11,055,000 [2012]

Farming and Wildlife Advisory Group South West Ltd
Registered: 23 Feb 2012 Employees: 27 Volunteers: 12
Tel: 01823 660684 Website: fwagsw.org.uk
Activities: Education, training; environment, conservation, heritage
Address: Hawkridge House, Summerfield Way, Chelston Business Park, Wellington, Somerset, TA21 8YA
Trustees: Richard Appleton, Mr Robert Jackson, Mrs Aloysia Daros, Miss Sarah Jane Bird, Mr Andrew Brian Hosford, Mrs Caroline Fowle
Income: £1,091,694 [2017]; £977,006 [2016]; £951,848 [2015]; £883,675 [2014]; £1,122,574 [2013]

Farmland Reserve UK Limited
Registered: 14 Mar 1978 Volunteers: 4
Tel: 020 7880 4379
Activities: The prevention or relief of poverty; overseas aid, famine relief; religious activities
Address: Devonshires, Salisbury House, 30 Finsbury Circus, London, EC2M 7DT
Trustees: Mr Don M Sleight, Mr Benjamin Michael Conway, Mr Todd Nelson Jones
Income: £5,324,000 [2016]; £5,328,000 [2015]; £6,993,000 [2014]; £21,764,000 [2013]; £26,156,000 [2012]

Farms for City Children Limited
Registered: 6 Nov 1974 *Employees:* 69 *Volunteers:* 70
Tel: 01392 276381 *Website:* farmsforcitychildren.org
Activities: Education, training; arts, culture, heritage, science; environment, conservation, heritage
Address: Farms for City Children, 17 St Davids Hill, Exeter, EX4 3RG
Trustees: Mrs Clare Morpurgo MBE, Mr Michael Andrew Bridge Morpurgo MBE, Ms Frances Harris, Mr Charles Andrew Huntington-Whiteley, Mr Perkin Evans, Mr Richard John Ash, Mr Anthony Gibson OBE, Mrs Elizabeth Owens, Mr Simon Gregory, Miss Alison Mawle, Mr Justin Albert, Mr Peter Michael Pantlin
Income: £1,318,504 [2016]; £1,270,758 [2015]; £1,260,238 [2014]; £1,228,818 [2013]; £1,263,347 [2012]

The Farnborough Hill Trust
Registered: 15 Jul 1994 *Employees:* 136 *Volunteers:* 1
Tel: 01252 529800 *Website:* farnborough-hill.org.uk
Activities: Education, training
Address: Farnborough Hill School, 312 Farnborough Road, Farnborough, Hants, GU14 8AT
Trustees: Mrs Janet Windeatt, Mr Timothy James Flesher, Mrs Gillian Rivers, Mrs Ann Berry, Mrs Julie Lynn Micklethwaite, Mr Mark Bernard, Mrs Claire Elizabeth Hamilton, Mrs Margaret Welford, Dr Cathryn Chadwick, Mr Gerard McCormack, Mr Anthony Grace, Mr Christopher Fowler-Tutt
Income: £7,681,442 [2017]; £7,389,718 [2016]; £7,318,664 [2015]; £6,955,456 [2014]; £6,818,568 [2013]

Farney Close School Ltd
Registered: 10 Mar 1967 *Employees:* 69
Tel: 01444 881811 *Website:* farneyclose.co.uk
Activities: Education, training
Address: Farney Close School Ltd, Bolney Court, Crossways, Bolney, Haywards Heath, W Sussex, RH17 5RD
Trustees: Mr Martin Gibrill, Mrs Jenny Bowry, Shelagh Urwin, Ms Carole Johns, Miss Sheila Mary Burt, Mrs Sue Deane, Mrs Clarissa Barry
Income: £3,078,916 [2017]; £3,174,831 [2016]; £3,246,989 [2015]; £3,581,858 [2014]; £3,166,649 [2013]

Farnham Maltings Association Limited
Registered: 13 Jan 1970 *Employees:* 35 *Volunteers:* 117
Website: farnhammaltings.com
Activities: Education, training; arts, culture, heritage, science; environment, conservation, heritage; other charitable purposes
Address: 51 Riverdale, Wrecclesham, Farnham, Surrey, GU10 4PJ
Trustees: Mrs Lisa Jane Hennessey, Ms Rebecca Anne Skeels, Mr Colin Andrew McWhirter, Mr Michael Joseph Cooper, Ms Marina Norris, Mr Simon Marlborough Lunn, Mrs Christina Isabella Victoria Hughes, Ms Catherine Elizabeth Hammond, Mr Emma Catherine Haigh, Ms Francesca Clare Miller, Mr Matthew Jonathan Wilkie
Income: £2,860,730 [2017]; £3,092,867 [2016]; £2,738,199 [2015]; £2,601,851 [2014]; £2,059,046 [2013]

Farringtons School
Registered: 29 Nov 1966 *Employees:* 166 *Volunteers:* 6
Website: farringtons.org.uk
Activities: Education, training; religious activities
Address: Methodist Church House, 25 Marylebone Road, London, NW1 5JR
Trustees: Farringtons School Trustee Company Limited, Methodist Independent Schools Trust
Income: £8,958,402 [2016]; £8,941,659 [2015]; £8,348,427 [2014]; £7,665,245 [2013]; £7,325,993 [2012]

Fashion Retail Academy
Registered: 7 Jun 2007 *Employees:* 58
Tel: 020 7307 2345 *Website:* fashionretailacademy.ac.uk
Activities: Education, training
Address: The Fashion Retail Academy, 7-15 Gresse Street, London, W1T 1QL
Trustees: Mrs Kim Longman, Mr Martin Gibson, Mr David St John Shepherd, Mr David Stanley Kaye, Mr Stephen Reid, Ms Elaine Susan Smith, Mrs Elizabeth Rouse, Mr Jonathan Richens, Ms Caryn Ann Swart, Mr David Wamlsey, Mr Lee Lucas, Ms Heather Pickard
Income: £7,198,000 [2017]; £7,320,000 [2016]; £5,706,000 [2015]; £5,888,000 [2014]; £5,652,000 [2013]

Fassnidge Memorial Trust
Registered: 21 Jan 1963
Tel: 01895 830700
Activities: General charitable purposes; education, training; disability; prevention or relief of poverty; recreation; other charitable purposes
Address: Old Bank Chambers, 32 Station Parade, Denham, Uxbridge, Middlesex, UB9 5ET
Trustees: Mr Andrew Retter, Mr Richard Walker, Mr Peter Ryerson, Cllr George Cooper, Mr Tony Burles, Cllr Susan O'Brien, Mr David Herriott, Mr Peter Allan Curling, Mr David Yarrow, Cllr Judith Cooper, Mr John Morgan
Income: £1,642,991 [2017]; £64,389 [2016]; £61,686 [2015]; £55,175 [2014]; £61,058 [2013]

Father Hudson's Society
Registered: 15 Sep 1982 *Employees:* 270 *Volunteers:* 116
Tel: 01675 434000 *Website:* fatherhudsons.org.uk
Activities: General charitable purposes; disability; prevention or relief of poverty; accommodation, housing; religious activities
Address: Father Hudsons Society, St Georges House, Gerards Way, Coleshill, Birmingham, B46 3FG
Trustees: Mr Anthony Ernest John Newton Broom, Sister Gillian Mary Murphy, Mr Kevin Patrick Caffrey, Mrs Anne Veronica Plummer, Ms Jessica Nash, Gail Brown, Mrs Julia Angela Fitzsimons, Mr Neil Joseph Handel, Mr Brian Peter Basford, Mr Peter Anthony William Deeley, Rev Michael Darren Gamble, Mr Rodney Kane, Mr John Barley, Rev Kevin Michael Kavanagh, Ms Mary Elizabeth Fionnuala Hegarty
Income: £6,342,621 [2017]; £6,238,233 [2016]; £6,167,378 [2015]; £10,525,139 [2014]; £5,773,682 [2013]

Fauna & Flora International
Registered: 13 May 1992 *Employees:* 341 *Volunteers:* 10
Tel: 01223 571000 *Website:* fauna-flora.org
Activities: Animals; environment, conservation, heritage; economic, community development, employment
Address: Governance & Risk Manager, Fauna & Flora International, The David Attenborough Building, Pembroke Street, Cambridge, CB2 3QZ
Trustees: Prof Nigel Leader Williams, Dr Sandra Knapp, Stephen Georgiadis, Dr Charlotte Grezo, Mr Edward Van Cutsem, Andrew Joy, Annette Lanjouw, Mr David Gibson, Mr John Prier Wotton, Mr Andrew Francis Sykes, Paul Baldwin, Dr Bhaskar Vira, Gareth Rhys Williams, Diana Van De Kamp, Richard Plackett, Dr Michael Maunder
Income: £15,782,969 [2016]; £20,729,083 [2015]; £15,801,237 [2014]; £16,410,011 [2013]; £18,285,608 [2012]

Feba Radio

Registered: 17 Feb 1969   *Employees:* 14
Tel: 01903 237281   *Website:* feba.org.uk
Activities: Education, training; advancement of health or saving of lives; prevention or relief of poverty; religious activities; economic, community development, employment
Address: FEBA Radio, Skywaves House, Ivy Arch Road, Worthing, W Sussex, BN14 8BX
Trustees: Rev Melanie Gayl Commandeur, Mr Rod Street, Miss Joanna Ruth Malton, Mr Brian Nicholas Henry, Mr Andrew Conrad Platts, Mr Francis A Gray, Mr George Richard Gilbert, Mrs Camilla Symes
Income: £1,641,280 [2016]; £1,503,450 [2015]; £1,651,432 [2014]; £2,133,727 [2013]; £3,298,335 [2012]

The February Foundation

Registered: 23 Feb 2006   *Employees:* 1
Tel: 01379 388200   *Website:* thefebruaryfoundation.org
Activities: General charitable purposes
Address: Spring Cottage, Church Street, Stradbroke, Eye, Suffolk, IP21 5HT
Trustees: Mr James Hubert Carleton, Mr Mark Raymond Clarke
Income: £12,275,570 [2017]; £9,380,964 [2016]; £12,530,052 [2015]; £16,438,161 [2014]; £13,010,158 [2013]

The Federation of British Artists

Registered: 6 Jul 1961   *Employees:* 18   *Volunteers:* 140
Tel: 020 7930 6844   *Website:* mallgalleries.org.uk
Activities: Arts, culture, heritage, science
Address: Federation of British Artists, 17 Carlton House Terrace, London, SW1Y 5BD
Trustees: John Walton, Susan Wolff, Mr Jonathan Glasspool, Mr Nicholas St John Rosse, Mr Peter Wileman, Mr Alan Power, Mr David Brammeld, Cheryl Culver, Mrs Rosa Sepple, Mr Marc Winer, Mr Toby Ward, Mr Nik Pollard, Mr Jonathan French
Income: £1,707,374 [2016]; £1,614,329 [2015]; £1,529,644 [2014]; £1,565,062 [2013]; £1,647,248 [2012]

The Federation of Disability Sport Wales Limited

Registered: 15 Nov 2011   *Employees:* 14   *Volunteers:* 7,303
Tel: 029 2033 4923   *Website:* disabilitysportwales.com
Activities: General charitable purposes; education, training; advancement of health or saving of lives; disability; amateur sport; recreation
Address: FDSW, Welsh Institute of Sport, Sophia Gardens, Cardiff, CF11 9SW
Trustees: Mr Richard Jones, Mr Neil Ashbridge, Ryan Jones, James Lusted, Mrs Jane Coia, Ian Stone, Liz Johnson, Andrew Thomas
Income: £1,325,551 [2017]; £1,333,756 [2016]; £1,353,886 [2015]; £1,202,194 [2014]; £1,190,685 [2013]

The Federation of European Biochemical Societies

Registered: 7 Nov 2012   *Employees:* 6
Tel: 01223 311010   *Website:* febs.org
Activities: Education, training; advancement of health or saving of lives; arts, culture, heritage, science
Address: 98 Regent Street, Cambridge, CB2 1DP
Trustees: Professor Laszlo Fesus, Professor Miguel Angel De La Rosa, Professor Beata Vertessy, Professor Vaclav Paces, Professor Emmanouil Fragkoulis, Professor Alain Krol, Dr Irene Diaz Moreno, Professor Gul Akdogan Guner, Professor Cecilia Arraiano, Professor Frank Michelangeli, Professor Nazmi Ozer, Professor Jerka Dumic, Joel Sussman
Income: £6,297,793 [2016]; £10,740,730 [2015]; £5,464,904 [2014]; £28,056,717 [2013]

The Federation of European Microbiological Societies

Registered: 26 Oct 1998   *Employees:* 9
Tel: 07976 261099   *Website:* fems-microbiology.org
Activities: Education, training; advancement of health or saving of lives; arts, culture, heritage, science; environment, conservation, heritage; economic, community development, employment
Address: Moneypenny House, Western Gateway, Wrexham, LL13 7ZB
Trustees: Dr Vaso Taleski, Dr Bauke Oudega, Dr Jozef Anne, Professor Patrik Michel Bavoil, Dr Stefano Donadio, Dr Colin Harwood, Dr Hilary Lappin-Scott, Professor Andriy Sibirny
Income: £2,473,904 [2016]; £2,201,896 [2015]; £1,332,300 [2014]; £1,392,713 [2013]; £1,303,493 [2012]

The Federation of Groundwork Trusts

Registered: 15 Apr 1985   *Employees:* 34   *Volunteers:* 74
Tel: 0121 236 8565   *Website:* groundwork.org.uk
Activities: Education, training; environment, conservation, heritage; economic, community development, employment
Address: Lockside, 5 Scotland Street, Birmingham, B1 2RR
Trustees: Mr Stuart Baker, Mrs Jenny Bradley, Mrs Catherine Joanna Culverhouse, Mr Mike Master, Mr Geoff Howsego, Mr Graham Michael Hartley, Mrs Wendy Golland, Miss June Campbell, Mr Brynley John Davies, Mr Ian Brown, Mr Alan Smith, Mr John Richard Bland
Income: £34,389,680 [2017]; £5,091,335 [2016]; £11,544,919 [2015]; £19,402,466 [2014]; £35,343,824 [2013]

Federation of Jewish Services

Registered: 4 Dec 2006   *Employees:* 375   *Volunteers:* 380
Tel: 0161 772 4936   *Website:* thefed.org.uk
Activities: The advancement of health or saving of lives; disability; prevention or relief of poverty; accommodation, housing; religious activities
Address: The Heathlands Village, Heathlands Drive, Prestwich, Manchester, M25 9SB
Trustees: Mr David Howard Eventhall, Mr Michael Ernest Sciama, Mr Mark Isaac Adlestone OBE DL, Mr Howard David Joseph, Mr Leslie Kay, Ms Deborah Rachael Hamburger, Mr Bernard Yaffe, Mrs Julie Vanessa Besbrode
Income: £8,880,409 [2017]; £8,938,644 [2016]; £11,438,417 [2015]; £8,641,400 [2013]; £9,950,907 [2012]

The Federation of London Youth Clubs

Registered: 20 Nov 1962   *Employees:* 135
Website: londonyouth.org.uk
Activities: Education, training; arts, culture, heritage, science; amateur sport; environment, conservation, heritage
Address: London Youth, 47-49 Pitfield Street, London, N1 6DA
Trustees: Mr Guy Bryce Davison, Mr Stuart Andrew Thomson, Mr Julian Beare, Ms Louise Rodgers, Mr Simon Andrew Turek, Susan Asprey Price, David Miller, Mr John Norman, Mr Keith Ward, Mr Nathaniel Joseph Edward Defriend, Miss Charline Zephoria King, Mr Edward Philip Hay
Income: £11,739,868 [2017]; £6,951,689 [2016]; £8,109,358 [2015]; £6,621,799 [2014]; £4,884,501 [2013]

Federation of Synagogues
Registered: 2 Nov 1968 *Employees:* 73 *Volunteers:* 100
Tel: 020 8202 2263 *Website:* federation.org.uk
Activities: Religious activities
Address: Federation of Synagogues, 65 Watford Way, London, NW4 3AQ
Trustees: Mr Dov Black, Mr Andrew Cohen, Mr Steven Gertner, Mr Jacob Weg, Mr Leon Newmark, Mr Adam Jacobs, Mr Moshe Winegarten
Income: £12,615,113 [2016]; £4,799,878 [2015]; £4,637,233 [2014]; £3,085,459 [2013]; £3,654,366 [2012]

Feed The Hungry, UK
Registered: 8 Feb 2006 *Employees:* 5 *Volunteers:* 12
Tel: 01455 618455 *Website:* feedthehungry.org.uk
Activities: General charitable purposes; education, training; prevention or relief of poverty; overseas aid, famine relief; religious activities
Address: Suite 1, Rooms B & C, 1 Castle Street, Hinckley, Leics, LE10 1DA
Trustees: Mrs Sandra Godley, Rev Gary James Weston, Mr Jaimie Oliver Garande, Mrs Sarah Tarisai Garande, Mr Nigel John Roberts, Mr Andrew James Richardson, Mr Stefan Radelich
Income: £2,272,383 [2016]; £1,221,050 [2015]; £380,322 [2014]; £147,759 [2013]; £83,693 [2012]

Fegans
Registered: 19 Sep 1963 *Employees:* 87 *Volunteers:* 23
Tel: 01892 538288 *Website:* fegans.org.uk
Activities: Education, training; advancement of health or saving of lives; disability; religious activities
Address: 160 St James Road, Tunbridge Wells, Kent, TN1 2HE
Trustees: Mrs Judith Margaret Spence, Mrs Helen Veronica Dobbin, Mrs Zoe Beth Smith, Mrs Sharon Buchanan, Mrs Alison Clare Collins, Mr Andrew Colbran
Income: £1,058,312 [2017]; £1,308,617 [2016]; £1,039,488 [2015]; £706,925 [2014]; £563,377 [2013]

Mary Feilding Guild
Registered: 22 Sep 1962 *Employees:* 30 *Volunteers:* 10
Tel: 020 8340 3915 *Website:* maryfeildingguild.co.uk
Activities: General charitable purposes; accommodation, housing
Address: Mary Fielding Guild, Truscott House, 103-107 North Hill, London, N6 4DP
Trustees: Derek John, Anne Keen, Helen Davies, Peter Robson, Linda Rose, Jeremy Hill
Income: £1,688,739 [2017]; £1,757,341 [2016]; £1,691,655 [2015]; £1,610,289 [2014]; £1,509,495 [2013]

The Fellowship of St Nicholas
Registered: 22 Sep 1962 *Employees:* 85 *Volunteers:* 105
Tel: 01424 423683 *Website:* fsncharity.co.uk
Activities: Education, training; prevention or relief of poverty
Address: St Nicholas Centre, 66 London Road, St Leonards on Sea, E Sussex, TN37 6AS
Trustees: Mr Peter Carcas, Mrs Sandra Garner, Mrs Janet Wyatt, Ms Jocelyn Tilbrook, Mr Gary Marriott, Rev Martin Harper, Miss Alison Bissett, Mr David Froude, Mr Michael Peter Blandy, Mr Richard Cuff
Income: £1,572,131 [2017]; £1,523,731 [2016]; £1,589,285 [2015]; £1,283,355 [2014]; £1,063,705 [2013]

The Fellowship of The School of Economic Science
Registered: 9 Mar 1964 *Employees:* 98 *Volunteers:* 500
Tel: 020 7034 4000 *Website:* schooleconomicscience.org
Activities: Education, training
Address: School of Economic Science, 11-13 Mandeville Place, London, W1U 3AJ
Trustees: Mr Hugh Venables, Mr Andrew Purves, Mrs Ann Hithersay, Mr William Brook, Mr Edward Saunders, Mr Stephen Silver, Mr Ian Mason, Mr Richard Glover, Mrs Sue Young, Mr Clive Meek, Mrs Anthea Douglas
Income: £5,594,000 [2016]; £5,235,000 [2015]; £4,156,000 [2014]; £4,251,700 [2013]; £6,757,300 [2012]

Felsted School
Registered: 10 Apr 1964 *Employees:* 363 *Volunteers:* 62
Tel: 01371 822621 *Website:* felsted.org
Activities: Education, training
Address: Felsted School, Felsted, Dunmow, Essex, CM6 3LL
Trustees: Felsted School Trustee Ltd
Income: £23,149,155 [2017]; £22,923,024 [2016]; £21,462,837 [2015]; £24,739,795 [2014]; £20,096,984 [2013]

Feltonfleet School Trust Limited
Registered: 7 Sep 1967 *Employees:* 89
Website: feltonfleet.co.uk
Activities: Education, training
Address: Feltonfleet School Trust Ltd, Byfleet Road, Cobham, Surrey, KT11 1DR
Trustees: Mrs Mary Jenner MBE, Mr Giles Douglas Ashbee, Mrs Hilary Humphry-Baker, Mrs Deborah Burgess, Mrs Rosaleen Bishop, Mr Graeme Owton, Mrs Tina Harvey, Mr Richard Murray Bray, Mr Michael George Sadler, Mr Paul Howard, Mr David Barry, Mrs Caroline St Gallay
Income: £6,111,380 [2017]; £6,041,826 [2016]; £5,952,290 [2015]; £5,623,922 [2014]; £5,406,637 [2013]

The Ferne Animal Sanctuary
Registered: 11 Nov 2015 *Employees:* 50 *Volunteers:* 140
Tel: 01460 65214 *Website:* ferneanimalsanctuary.org
Activities: Animals
Address: Ferne Animal Sanctuary, Wambrook, Chard, Somerset, TA20 3DH
Trustees: Ms Nanette Jane Wale, Ms Margaret Ann Bradshaw, Mr David Cook, Ms Bernadette Anne Steadman, Ms Sarah Gillian Dowell, Mr Graham Higgins
Income: £1,379,436 [2017]

Ferring Country Centre Limited
Registered: 29 Jul 1987 *Employees:* 25 *Volunteers:* 73
Tel: 01903 245078 *Website:* ferringcountrycentre.org
Activities: Disability
Address: Ferring Country Centre, Rife Way, Ferring, Worthing, W Sussex, BN12 5JZ
Trustees: Mr Andrew Dales, Mr Peter Benjamin Vos, Mrs Jane Cole, Mr Robert Rogers, Dr Barbara Anne Cook, Ms Linda Mary Clark
Income: £1,219,751 [2016]; £1,262,321 [2015]; £1,159,300 [2014]; £1,088,647 [2013]; £1,015,299 [2012]

The Ferry Project
Registered: 7 May 1999 *Employees:* 34 *Volunteers:* 88
Website: ferryproject.org.uk
Activities: Education, training; prevention or relief of poverty; accommodation, housing; economic, community development, employment; other charitable purposes
Address: Luminus Group, Brook House, Ouse Walk, Huntingdon, Cambs, PE29 3QW
Trustees: Mike Forrest, Mr Patrick Johnstone, Mrs Anne Davies
Income: £1,230,384 [2017]; £1,077,589 [2016]; £2,096,915 [2015]; £1,158,303 [2014]; £1,047,025 [2013]

Festival of Life
Registered: 26 Feb 2002 *Employees:* 9 *Volunteers:* 1,000
Tel: 020 8438 8285 *Website:* festivaloflife.org.uk
Activities: General charitable purposes; prevention or relief of poverty; religious activities
Address: 112 Brent Terrace, London, NW2 1LT
Trustees: Dr Sola Oludoyi, Mr Kola Bamigbade, Agu Irukwu
Income: £1,817,232 [2016]; £2,255,636 [2015]; £1,741,424 [2014]; £1,842,941 [2013]; £1,524,150 [2012]

The Fetal Medicine Foundation
Registered: 28 Apr 1994 *Employees:* 35
Tel: 020 7034 3070 *Website:* fetalmedicine.com
Activities: The advancement of health or saving of lives
Address: 137 Harley Street, London, W1G 6BF
Trustees: Mr Bruce Alexander Noble, Mr Jonathan Anthony Hyett, Mr Paul Jacobs, Professor Kypros Nicolaides, Miss Magita Khalouha, Dr Ranjit S Akolekar
Income: £7,055,602 [2017]; £6,362,399 [2016]; £5,035,894 [2015]; £5,055,737 [2014]; £4,290,967 [2013]

The Ffestiniog and Welsh Highland Railways Trust (Ymddiriedolaeth Rheilffyrdd Ffestiniog ac Eryri)
Registered: 3 Mar 1966 *Employees:* 89 *Volunteers:* 1,000
Tel: 01245 222920
Activities: Environment, conservation, heritage
Address: Valldemosa, Cherry Garden Lane, Danbury, Chelmsford, Essex, CM3 4QP
Trustees: Mr Richard Broyd OBE, Dr Dewi Wyn Roberts MBE, Dr D R Gwyn, Dr John Denys Charles Antice Prideaux CBE, Mr Mark Leonard Smith
Income: £8,342,746 [2016]; £8,043,085 [2015]; £8,251,066 [2014]; £7,813,991 [2013]; £8,003,054 [2012]

The Fidelity UK Foundation
Registered: 12 Aug 1988
Tel: 01732 777364 *Website:* fidelityukfoundation.org
Activities: Education, training; advancement of health or saving of lives; disability; prevention or relief of poverty; arts, culture, heritage, science; environment, conservation, heritage; economic, community development, employment
Address: Oakhill House, 130 Tonbridge Road, Hildenborough, Tonbridge, Kent, TN11 9DZ
Trustees: Mr Anthony Bolton, Mr Richard Millar, Ms Sally Walden, Dr Malcolm Austin Rogers CBE FSA, Mr Barry Bateman, John Owen CMG MBE, Ms Abigail Johnson, Mrs Elizabeth Bishop Johnson
Income: £7,534,482 [2016]; £5,193,261 [2015]; £6,866,884 [2014]; £5,787,053 [2013]; £6,670,397 [2012]

The Field Lane Foundation
Registered: 22 Sep 1962 *Employees:* 136
Tel: 020 7748 0303 *Website:* fieldlane.org.uk
Activities: The advancement of health or saving of lives; disability; prevention or relief of poverty; accommodation, housing
Address: Victoria Charity Centre, 11 Belgrave Road, London, SW1V 1RB
Trustees: Mr Timothy Hornsby, Ms Katherine Margaret Jane Andrews, Mr Keith Grehan, Ms Fiona Crispin-Jennings, Mr Francis Otho Moore, Ms Alexandra Mary MacDonald, Dr Sharleene Bibbings
Income: £4,594,002 [2017]; £4,457,161 [2016]; £4,088,296 [2015]; £4,431,601 [2014]; £5,024,274 [2013]

Field Studies Council
Registered: 12 Sep 1963 *Employees:* 475 *Volunteers:* 20
Tel: 01743 852100 *Website:* field-studies-council.org
Activities: Education, training; environment, conservation, heritage
Address: Field Studies Council, Preston Montford, Shrewsbury, Salop, SY4 1HW
Trustees: Prof Timothy Burt MA PhD DSC FRGS, Rob Cooke, Ms Jenifer White, Isabel Glasgow, Prof Des Thompson, Mrs Angela Bailey, Gill Miller, Mr Chris Lane, Kim Adams, Peter Anderson, Bill Rogers, Professor Tom Hutchinson BSc PhD, Mr Geoffrey Herbert Brown FCCA, Andy Simpson, Professor Peter Higgins, Dr Nicholas Howden MEng FRGS, Dr Caroline Bucklow, Mr John Thomson BA MSc FRSA, Tara Duncan, Paul Airey, Karen Kerr, Professor Robert Marrs, Ms Kim Somerville, Mr Jeff Sissons
Income: £17,795,408 [2016]; £17,389,975 [2015]; £17,339,813 [2014]; £18,225,517 [2013]; £14,632,867 [2012]

The Fifth Trust
Registered: 5 Jul 2010 *Employees:* 34 *Volunteers:* 16
Tel: 01732 457594 *Website:* fifthtrust.co.uk
Activities: General charitable purposes; education, training; disability
Address: 7 Middlings Rise, Sevenoaks, Kent, TN13 2NS
Trustees: Mr Stephen Charles Whittle, Mrs Eve Salomon, Mr Michael Donnelly, Mrs Anita Robson, Mr Jonathan Worrall, Mrs Anne Sayle, Mr John Noble Lennox Morrison, Mrs Jean Margaret Lines, Mr Andrew McKenzie Miller, Mr Neil Hope, Lesley Marchant, Susan Borthwick, Mrs Rebecca Lisney
Income: £1,253,232 [2017]; £1,170,900 [2016]; £1,051,953 [2015]; £986,207 [2014]; £736,272 [2013]

Fight for Peace International
Registered: 27 Aug 2010 *Employees:* 6
Tel: 020 7474 0054 *Website:* fightforpeace.net
Activities: Education, training; amateur sport; economic, community development, employment
Address: Fight for Peace, Community Centre, Woodman Street, London, E16 2LS
Trustees: Ms Anne-Marie Piper, Mr Sam Clarke, Mr Renato Lulia Jacob, Ms Andrea Felizitas Mathilde Sinclair, Alex Le Vey, Mr Warren Bramley
Income: £1,151,228 [2016]; £933,603 [2015]; £2,257,974 [2014]; £868,606 [2013]; £605,229 [2012]

Film London

Registered: 14 Oct 2015 *Employees:* 45 *Volunteers:* 24
Tel: 020 7613 7676 *Website:* filmlondon.org.uk
Activities: General charitable purposes; education, training; arts, culture, heritage, science; environment, conservation, heritage; economic, community development, employment
Address: The Arts Building, Morris Place, London, N4 3JG
Trustees: Mr Kevin Price, Ms Elizabeth Meek, Ms Angela Jain, Mr Ian George, Mr Andrea Lissoni, Mr Jeremy Simon Vernon, Ms Amanda Parker, Mr Daniel Battsek, Ms Isabel Begg, Mr Andrew Payne, Ms Anna Elizabeth Higgs, Mr Robin Urquhart Young, Mr Iain Alastair Robertson Smith, Mr Tyrone Walker-Hebborn, Mr Allon Joshua Reich
Income: £5,833,005 [2017]

Film Nation UK

Registered: 1 Oct 2013 *Employees:* 100
Tel: 0330 313 7600 *Website:* intofilm.org
Activities: Education, training; arts, culture, heritage, science
Address: 31 Islington Green, London, N1 8DU
Trustees: Mr Eric Fellner CBE, Baroness Beeban Kidron, Mr Alan Gregory Bushell, Mr Patrick Bradley, Colin Needham, Kate Lee, Ms Barbara Dana Broccoli, Mr Alasdair MacDonald, Heather Victoria Rabatts DBE, Mr Mark Jonathan Devereux, Mr Duncan Clark, Lisa A Bryer
Income: £7,758,521 [2017]; £7,769,952 [2016]; £8,454,751 [2015]

The Film and Television Charity

Registered: 25 Sep 2003 *Employees:* 74 *Volunteers:* 8
Tel: 020 7437 6567 *Website:* ctbf.co.uk
Activities: General charitable purposes; education, training; prevention or relief of poverty; accommodation, housing
Address: The Cinema & Television Benevolent Fund, 22 Golden Square, London, W1F 9AD
Trustees: Mr Trevor Green, Mr Gavin Hamilton-Deeley, Mr Andrew Wilson-Mouasher, Ms Deborah Rozansky, John Pike, Mr Cameron Saunders
Income: £3,181,000 [2017]; £3,944,000 [2016]; £3,264,000 [2015]; £3,522,000 [2014]; £3,555,000 [2013]

The Finchley Charities

Registered: 2 Aug 1982 *Employees:* 13
Tel: 020 8349 9167 *Website:* thefinchleycharities.org
Activities: The prevention or relief of poverty; accommodation, housing
Address: 41A Wilmot Close, London, N2 8HP
Trustees: Mr Colin Rogers, The Rev Philip Davison, Mr Andrew Galatopolous, Mr Martin O'Donnell, Miss Elizabeth Davies, Mr Graham Old, Mr Mahmood Syed FCA, Mr Ian Anderson, Mr Brian Coleman, Mr Christopher John Huckstep, Cllr Daniel Thomas, Mr Roger Chapman, Ms Toni Louise Morgan
Income: £1,436,080 [2016]; £1,338,104 [2015]; £1,386,591 [2014]; £1,251,205 [2013]; £1,174,590 [2012]

Finchley Reform Synagogue

Registered: 20 Aug 2010 *Employees:* 18 *Volunteers:* 128
Tel: 020 8446 3244 *Website:* frsonline.org
Activities: General charitable purposes; religious activities
Address: Finchley Reform Synagogue, 101 Fallow Court Avenue, London, N12 0BE
Trustees: Mrs Candice Gubbay, Robert Humphreys, Mr Michael Salida, Mr Avi David Marco, Mr Robert Stitcher, Miss Leah Jacobs, Mr Roger Barden, Ms Sara Gina Bensusan, Mr Matthew Stratton, Mr Benedict Noah, Mrs Gillian Yentis, Ms Jenny Nuni
Income: £1,103,293 [2016]; £1,131,242 [2015]; £1,005,692 [2014]; £1,016,538 [2013]; £971,322 [2012]

Find A Future

Registered: 18 Jan 1991 *Employees:* 39 *Volunteers:* 485
Tel: 020 3740 8233 *Website:* worldskillsuk.org
Activities: Education, training
Address: Floor Four, 157-197 Buckingham Palace Road, London, SW1W 9SP
Trustees: Mrs Carole Stott, Mr Mark Richard Dawe, Mr Barry Liles, Mrs Marion Plant, Ms Marie-Therese McGivern, Mrs Dawn Childs, Mr Pablo Lloyd, Mr Peter Woodhouse, Mrs Angela Joyce, Mr Stewart Segal, Mr Paul Little
Income: £10,253,185 [2017]; £10,847,373 [2016]; £14,961,313 [2015]; £13,839,030 [2014]; £10,638,014 [2013]

Elizabeth Finn Care

Registered: 4 Apr 1963 *Employees:* 775 *Volunteers:* 241
Tel: 020 8834 9200 *Website:* turn2us.org.uk
Activities: The prevention or relief of poverty
Address: Hythe House, 200 Shepherds Bush Road, London, W6 7NL
Trustees: Ms Catherine Hamp, Mr Richard Anthony Carter, Mr Neeraj Kapur, Mrs Christine Lenihan, Ms Jan Leightley, Mr Steven Andrew Hunter, Mr Mark Guymer, Mr Henry Richard Francis Elphick, Ms Sally O'Sullivan, Mr Richard Midmer, Dr Olivia Curno
Income: £30,397,000 [2017]; £29,161,000 [2016]; £28,846,000 [2015]; £26,611,000 [2014]; £26,434,161 [2013]

Finton House Educational Trust

Registered: 6 May 1987 *Employees:* 80
Tel: 020 8682 0921 *Website:* fintonhouse.org.uk
Activities: Education, training
Address: Finton House, Educational Trust, 171 Trinity Road, London, SW17 7HL
Trustees: Myles Pink, Mrs Frances Brown, Matthew John Hancox, Mrs Annabelle Elliott, Clare King, Nicholas Addyman, Ravi Ruparel, Mr Benjamin Freeman, Mark Chilton, Robin Chatwin, Ian Michael Priest, Sally Hobbs, Thomas Frost, Rhys Alexander-James Johnston, Victoria Andrews, Elizabeth Buckley
Income: £4,999,568 [2017]; £4,916,615 [2016]; £4,558,650 [2015]; £4,406,484 [2014]; £4,245,069 [2013]

Fircroft College Trust

Registered: 20 May 1980 *Employees:* 33
Tel: 0121 472 0116 *Website:* fircroft.ac.uk
Activities: Education, training
Address: Fircroft College, 1018 Bristol Road, Selly Oak, Birmingham, B29 6LH
Trustees: Mr Tom Pettitt, Dr Cheryl Turner, Mr Paul Caulfield, Mr Declan Vaughan, Ms Melanie Lenehan, Miss Martha Heasman, Mr Jonathon Darling, Ms Roanne Finch, Mr Martyn Keagle, Ms Birgit Kehrer, Mr Ahmad Makhdoom Chishti, Ms Lesley Lucas, Mr David Corns, Miss Neena Chauhan, Mrs Kirsty Woolls, Rev Jennifer Mullis, Ms Rosanna Griffiths
Income: £2,172,310 [2017]; £1,965,182 [2016]; £2,005,533 [2015]; £1,909,460 [2014]; £1,692,365 [2013]

Fire Fighters Charity
Registered: 12 Aug 2002 *Employees:* 196 *Volunteers:* 1,500
Tel: 01256 366566 *Website:* firefighterscharity.org.uk
Activities: General charitable purposes; education, training; advancement of health or saving of lives; disability; prevention or relief of poverty; accommodation, housing
Address: The Fire Fighters Charity, Belvedere, Basing View, Basingstoke, Hants, RG21 4HG
Trustees: Mr Howard Robinson, Mr Harvey Grenville, Mr Peter Davies, Mr Andrew Best, Mr Chris Wilson, Mrs Lynn Mirley, Mr David Brown, Dr Rowena Hill, Mr Paul Maurice Fuller, Mr Andrew Lynch, Ms Jane Nicklin, Mr Roddy MacLeod, Mr Andrew Hickmott, Mr Thomas Capeling, Mr Andrew Perry
Income: £8,129,788 [2017]; £8,065,396 [2016]; £8,816,047 [2015]; £8,278,858 [2014]; £7,952,529 [2013]

First Light South West Ltd
Registered: 6 Feb 2002 *Employees:* 55 *Volunteers:* 13
Tel: 01752 220400 *Website:* firstlight.org.uk
Activities: General charitable purposes; education, training; advancement of health or saving of lives; prevention or relief of poverty; accommodation, housing
Address: Twelves Co, Metropolitan House, 37 Craigie Drive, Plymouth, PL1 3JB
Trustees: Mr Ashley Smith, Mr Alastair Cuthbert, Mrs Vikki Martin, Mrs Jo Stones, Miss Rachael Bice, Mr Paul Mullin, Mrs Naomi Sutton, Mrs Alison Chitty
Income: £1,136,289 [2017]; £1,136,754 [2016]; £1,069,265 [2015]; £874,596 [2014]; £494,368 [2013]

First Rung Ltd
Registered: 19 Jun 1989 *Employees:* 39
Tel: 020 8803 4764 *Website:* firstrung.org.uk
Activities: Education, training
Address: 197-207 High Street, Ponders End, Enfield, Middlesex, EN3 4DZ
Trustees: Mr Michael Freyd, Michael Johns, Mrs Hilary Robinson, Mr Michael David Kutner, Mr Nigel Hathway, Mr Frank Longsworth, Mrs Suzanne Leila Ralton, Mr David John Taylor
Income: £1,430,774 [2017]; £1,356,877 [2016]; £1,403,089 [2015]; £1,439,156 [2014]; £1,592,266 [2013]

First Step Trust
Registered: 27 Oct 1999 *Employees:* 31 *Volunteers:* 412
Tel: 020 8855 7386 *Website:* firststeptrust.org.uk
Activities: General charitable purposes; education, training; disability; prevention or relief of poverty; economic, community development, employment
Address: Unit 9 Kingside Business Park, Ruston Road, London, SE18 5BX
Trustees: Ms Carol Hodson, Ms Teresa Sally Newcombe, Miss Amanda Jane Okill, Ms Carole Furnivall
Income: £1,606,616 [2017]; £1,780,899 [2016]; £1,924,484 [2015]; £2,123,528 [2014]; £2,226,158 [2013]

First Steps (Bath)
Registered: 10 Jul 1992 *Employees:* 43 *Volunteers:* 2
Tel: 01225 444791 *Website:* firststepsbath.org.uk
Activities: Education, training; prevention or relief of poverty; economic, community development, employment
Address: First Steps, Woodhouse Road, Bath, BA2 1SY
Trustees: Ms Isobel Michael, Ms Sue Pendle, Mr Kenneth Littlewood, Mr Robert Douglas Brown, Mrs Sarah Chikhani, Mr Thomas Williams, Mrs Valerie Wheeler, Mr Mike Turner, Meg North, Jane Millar OBE, Dr Janet Rose
Income: £1,366,866 [2017]; £1,271,135 [2016]; £1,300,347 [2015]; £1,245,409 [2014]; £1,270,173 [2013]

Firstsite Limited
Registered: 21 Jan 1994 *Employees:* 46 *Volunteers:* 64
Tel: 01206 577067 *Website:* firstsite.uk.net
Activities: Arts, culture, heritage, science
Address: Firstsite, Lewis Gardens, Colchester, Essex, CO1 1JH
Trustees: Mr Tim Young, Mr Mark Durham, Mr Roger Hirst, Mr Ranil Perera, Ms Julia Obasa, Mr Richard Polom, Mr Atul Shah, Mrs Jayne Roena Knowles, Mr Guy Armitage, Mr Martin Blackburn, Ms Charlotte Winter
Income: £1,586,733 [2017]; £2,199,564 [2016]; £2,115,714 [2015]; £1,790,171 [2014]; £1,835,132 [2013]

Fitzroy Support
Registered: 20 May 1992 *Employees:* 1,160 *Volunteers:* 34
Tel: 01730 711111 *Website:* fitzroy.org
Activities: General charitable purposes; disability
Address: Fitzroy, Fitzroy House, 8 Hylton Road, Petersfield, Hants, GU32 3JY
Trustees: Mr Ian White, Mr Michael Fitzroy, Mr Andy Lee, Mr David Evans, Ms Lucy Chaudhuri, Derrick McCourt, Mr Paul Wood, Mr Simon Mollett, Mrs Julia Le Blan, Mr Neil Matthewman, Ms Lucy Hovey, Andrew Gore, Mr Matthew Moth
Income: £27,351,438 [2017]; £26,700,674 [2016]; £23,272,554 [2015]; £22,352,413 [2014]; £22,715,206 [2013]

Fitzwilliam College in the University of Cambridge
Registered: 16 Aug 2010 *Employees:* 169 *Volunteers:* 3
Tel: 01223 332067 *Website:* fitz.cam.ac.uk
Activities: Education, training
Address: Fitzwilliam College, Storeys Way, Cambridge, CB3 0DG
Trustees: Prof David Anthony Cardwell, Prof Dominic Keown, Professor Martin Millett, Dr Subha Mukherji, Prof Nicola Padfield, Dr Rosemary Horrox, Dr Kenneth Walter Platts, Prof Epaminondas Mastorakos, Dr Rachel Deborah Camina, Dr Dilkush Robert Ophrem Abayasekara, Dr Andrew Wheatley, Dr Sara Owen, Dr Peter Jason Rentfrow, Dr Simon Gathercole, Dr Jonathan Michael Cullen, Dr Christos Genakos, Professor Nigel Kenneth Harry Slater, Dr Anna Maria Watson, Dr Matthew Wingate, Dr Andrew Jardine, Dr Stephen Sawiak, Dr Julia Guarneri, Dr Emma Lees, Prof Ianthi Tsimpli, Dr Daria Frank, Prof Michael Kenny, Dr Cora Uhlemann, Dr Rogier Kievit, Mr Francis Knights, Dr Louise Hanson, Mr Richard Hooley, Prof Michael Potter, Dr David Cole, Dr John Leigh, Prof Robin Langley, Prof David Anthony Coomes, Dr Alexei Kovalev, Prof James Elliott, Dr Kourosh Saeb-Parsy, Dr Angela Tavernor, Dr Paul Antony Chirico, Mr Andrew Powell, Dr Susan Larsen, Dr Gabriel Glickman, Dr James Keltie Aitken, Prof Bhaskar Vira, Dr Holly Corianda Canuto, Dr Kasia Jane Boddy, Dr Hero Chalmers, Dr Andreas Televantos, Dr Nicola Jones, Dr Enrico Ryunosuke Crema, Dr Richard Powell, Dr Yeonsook Heo, Mr David Winters, Dr Erik Gjesfjeld
Income: £10,752,184 [2017]; £11,512,000 [2016]; £9,611,121 [2015]; £9,458,279 [2014]; £9,015,063 [2013]

The Fitzwilliam Wentworth Amenity Trust
Registered: 31 May 1979 *Employees:* 3
Tel: 01226 742041 *Website:* wentworthestate.co.uk
Activities: Education, training; accommodation, housing; arts, culture, heritage, science; environment, conservation, heritage; recreation
Address: Fitzwilliam (Wentworth) Estates, 27 Clayfields Lane, Wentworth, Rotherham, S Yorks, S62 7TD
Trustees: Earl of Scarbrough, Sir Philip Naylor-Leyland, The Right Hon Ralph Foljambe, Lady Isabella Naylor-Leyland, Mr Jr Archdale
Income: £1,581,330 [2017]; £1,556,135 [2016]; £1,505,374 [2015]; £1,546,386 [2014]; £1,446,796 [2013]

The Five Lamps Organisation
Registered: 15 Dec 1989 *Employees:* 48 *Volunteers:* 14
Tel: 01642 608316 *Website:* fivelamps.org.uk
Activities: General charitable purposes; education, training; prevention or relief of poverty; accommodation, housing; economic, community development, employment
Address: Five Lamps Centre, Eldon Street, Thornaby, Stockton on Tees, Cleveland, TS17 7DJ
Trustees: Mr Ian Wright, Mrs Patricia Chambers, Mr Michael Poole, Mrs Vivienne Holmes, Mr Trevor Watson
Income: £2,976,462 [2017]; £3,196,592 [2016]; £4,401,132 [2015]; £3,607,243 [2014]; £2,262,640 [2013]

The Five Towns Plus Hospice Fund Limited
Registered: 3 Apr 1984 *Employees:* 136 *Volunteers:* 300
Tel: 01977 708868 *Website:* pwh.org.uk
Activities: The advancement of health or saving of lives
Address: Prince of Wales Hospice, Halfpenny Lane, Pontefract, W Yorks, WF8 4BG
Trustees: Mrs Ann Gleed MBE, Mr Brynton Stewart Parkes, Mr Stephen Rigby, Dr Ruth Roche, Mr Gordon Tollefson, Mr Dominic Hayes, Mr Adam Charles Wearing, Mrs Susan Jane Beddow
Income: £3,539,719 [2017]; £3,772,416 [2016]; £3,435,801 [2015]; £3,421,225 [2014]; £3,344,421 [2013]

The Fleet Air Arm Museum CLG Limited
Registered: 21 Jul 2011 *Volunteers:* 20
Tel: 023 9272 7582 *Website:* fleetairarm.com
Activities: Education, training; arts, culture, heritage, science; environment, conservation, heritage
Address: Defence Mail Centre, Stoney Lane, HM Naval Base, Portsmouth, PO1 3NH
Trustees: Jerry Stanford, Jeanne Spinks, Commodore Jon Pentreath, Ray Hatton, Rear Admiral Thomas Cunningham
Income: £1,047,557 [2017]; £2,348,439 [2016]; £2,393,797 [2015]; £2,454,822 [2014]; £2,312,717 [2013]

The Fleet Air Arm Museum
Registered: 12 Dec 1966 *Volunteers:* 20
Tel: 023 9272 7562 *Website:* fleetairarm.com
Activities: General charitable purposes; education, training; arts, culture, heritage, science; amateur sport; environment, conservation, heritage; economic, community development, employment
Address: NMRN, HM Naval Base PP66, Portsmouth, PO1 3NH
Trustees: National Museum of The Royal Navy
Income: £9,177,172 [2017]

Fleet Baptist Church
Registered: 9 Dec 2015 *Employees:* 4 *Volunteers:* 80
Tel: 01252 812590 *Website:* fleetbaptist.org.uk
Activities: Education, training; religious activities
Address: Fleet Baptist Church, 115 Clarence Road, Fleet, Hants, GU51 3RS
Trustees: Rev Christopher Bird, Mrs Alison Verrall, Mr Martin Lewis, Mr Hein Marais, Sue Rinaldi
Income: £1,258,410 [2016]

The Florida State University International Programs Association UK
Registered: 6 Jan 1993 *Employees:* 36
Tel: 020 7813 3223 *Website:* fsu.edu
Activities: Education, training
Address: 99 Great Russell Street, London, WC1B 3LA
Trustees: Fsu Europe Trustees Ltd, Fsu Florida Trustees Ltd
Income: £3,627,887 [2017]; £2,771,944 [2016]; £2,999,251 [2015]; £2,883,795 [2014]; £2,635,673 [2013]

Floris Books Trust Limited
Registered: 24 Jul 1989 *Employees:* 12
Tel: 0131 337 2372 *Website:* florisbooks.co.uk
Activities: Religious activities
Address: Floris Books Trust Ltd, 2A Robertson Avenue, Edinburgh, EH11 1PZ
Trustees: Rev Michael Jones, Tom Ravetz, Rev Paul Kyffin Newton, Mr Robert Michael Miller, Lesley Taylor
Income: £1,473,796 [2016]; £1,361,813 [2015]; £1,278,268 [2014]; £1,178,902 [2013]; £995,649 [2012]

The Focolare Trust
Registered: 11 Dec 1979 *Employees:* 3 *Volunteers:* 1,000
Tel: 01707 376780 *Website:* focolare.org
Activities: General charitable purposes; education, training; prevention or relief of poverty; overseas aid, famine relief; religious activities
Address: 39 Lemsford Village, Lemsford, Welwyn Garden City, Herts, AL8 7TR
Trustees: Miss Marie-Christine Fournier, Miss Patricia Whitney, Miss Elisa Zuin, Miss Paola Grazia, Elizabeth Taite
Income: £1,208,510 [2017]; £1,618,407 [2016]; £1,013,641 [2015]; £765,917 [2014]; £1,346,680 [2013]

Focus Birmingham
Registered: 13 Nov 1997 *Employees:* 142 *Volunteers:* 50
Tel: 0121 478 5200 *Website:* focusbirmingham.org.uk
Activities: Education, training; advancement of health or saving of lives; disability; accommodation, housing
Address: Focus, 48-62 Woodville Road, Harborne, Birmingham, B17 9AT
Trustees: Mr Mukesh Murria, Dr Marie Tsaloumas, Mrs Valerie Griffiths, Dr Richard Hindle, Ms Jean McDougall, Mr John Cade, Mr Christopher Gascoigne, Ms Victoria Smith, Ms Jo Dufty
Income: £3,400,473 [2017]; £3,314,303 [2016]; £3,125,386 [2015]; £3,438,766 [2014]; £3,668,741 [2013]

Focus Learning Trust
Registered: 29 Sep 2003 *Employees:* 21 *Volunteers:* 400
Tel: 0330 055 5600
Activities: Education, training
Address: Exchange Place, Poseidon Way, Warwick, CV34 6BY
Trustees: Mr Russell Charles Freeman, Mr Jonathan Marcus Lyons, Mr Bruce James
Income: £34,617,633 [2016]; £32,945,160 [2015]; £31,972,714 [2014]; £30,921,233 [2013]; £22,416,154 [2012]

Folkestone Sports Centre Trust Limited
Registered: 2 May 1973 *Employees:* 46
Tel: 01303 850222 *Website:* folkestonesportscentre.co.uk
Activities: Amateur sport
Address: Folkestone & District Sports Cen, Radnor Park Avenue, Folkestone, Kent, CT19 5HX
Trustees: Mr Glyn Hibbert, Mrs Allison Mackie, Mr Len Mayatt, Mr Robert Stearn, Mrs Lynne Smith, Mr Peter Gardner, Mr Derek Timmins, Mr Anthony White
Income: £1,547,513 [2017]; £1,640,729 [2016]; £1,527,281 [2015]; £1,589,978 [2014]; £1,749,592 [2013]

The Football Foundation
Registered: 9 Feb 2000 *Employees:* 55
Tel: 0345 345 4555 *Website:* footballfoundation.org.uk
Activities: General charitable purposes; education, training; advancement of health or saving of lives; disability; amateur sport; economic, community development, employment
Address: The Football Foundation, Whittington House, 19-30 Alfred Place, London, WC1E 7EA
Trustees: Mr Richard Craig Scudamore, Mr Peter McCormick OBE, Mr Gary Andrew Hoffman, Mrs Rona Chester, Mr Roger Francis Burden, Mr Richard George Caborn, Mr Martin Glenn
Income: £68,399,000 [2017]; £32,083,024 [2016]; £32,687,646 [2015]; £31,396,884 [2014]; £33,877,774 [2013]

The Football League (Community) Limited
Registered: 13 Nov 2009 *Employees:* 34
Tel: 0844 826 3108 *Website:* efltrust.com
Activities: General charitable purposes; education, training; advancement of health or saving of lives; disability; amateur sport; economic, community development, employment; other charitable purposes
Address: Football League Ltd, 5B Edward VII Quay, Navigation Way, Ashton on Ribble, Preston, Lancs, PR2 2YF
Trustees: Mr Gordon Taylor, Mr Donald Kerr, Ms Katie Reed, Mr Andrew Godfery Williamson OBE, Mr John Nixon, Ms Charlotte Hill, Mr Nicholas Perchard, Kelly Simmons
Income: £18,066,805 [2017]; £17,898,442 [2016]; £17,190,505 [2015]; £13,536,562 [2014]; £8,940,291 [2013]

Force Cancer Charity
Registered: 3 Mar 2011 *Employees:* 31 *Volunteers:* 135
Tel: 01392 406164 *Website:* forcecancercharity.co.uk
Activities: Education, training; advancement of health or saving of lives
Address: Corner House, Barrack Road, Exeter, EX2 5DW
Trustees: Mr Felix Medland, Mr Jeremy Roberts, Mrs Ruth Mary Boobier, Mr Morley Andrew Sage, Dr Joan Mary Cooper, Dr Sally Kidner, Mr John Renninson, Mr Nigel Acheson, Mr David Reginald Cantle, Dr Anne Hong, Dr Jennifer Louise Forrest, Mrs Louise Victoria Mayor
Income: £1,469,240 [2017]; £1,067,030 [2016]; £1,311,953 [2015]; £1,367,562 [2014]; £1,257,787 [2013]

Forces Support Limited
Registered: 18 Jun 2014 *Employees:* 78 *Volunteers:* 203
Tel: 01562 74279 *Website:* forcessupport.org.uk
Activities: General charitable purposes; armed forces, emergency service efficiency
Address: Forces Support CIC, 62-63 Worcester Street, Kidderminster, Worcs, DY10 1EL
Trustees: Mr Ronald Spurs, Mr David Simspon, Mrs Claire Locke, Mr Robert Barton, Mrs Grace Mathews, Mr Roger Booth
Income: £3,350,046 [2017]; £2,666,923 [2016]; £1,200,129 [2015]

Fordham University UK Charitable Trust
Registered: 24 Aug 1994 *Employees:* 4
Tel: 020 7937 5023 *Website:* fordham.edu
Activities: Education, training
Address: Fordham University London Centre, 23 Kensington Square, London, W8 5HQ
Trustees: Fordham University (Usa) UK Programs Ltd
Income: £1,161,197 [2017]; £939,563 [2016]; £970,763 [2015]; £685,747 [2014]; £669,155 [2013]

Foresight North East Lincolnshire Ltd
Registered: 19 Dec 2002 *Employees:* 37 *Volunteers:* 150
Tel: 01472 269666 *Website:* foresight-nelincs.co.uk
Activities: General charitable purposes; education, training; advancement of health or saving of lives; disability; accommodation, housing; arts, culture, heritage, science; amateur sport; recreation; other charitable purposes
Address: 60 Newmarket Street, Grimsby, S Humbers, DN32 7SF
Trustees: Mrs Mandy Bentham, Mr Kevin Arthur Fuller, Ms Janet Lea, Mr Paul Ashley Tofton, Mr Peter Barry Blendell, Mr Mansoor Gul, Mr Micheal James Inkson, Mr Anthony Newton Jewitt, Mr William John Maynell King, Miss Annabel Baxter, Ms Marie Tupman, Mr Christopher Foyster
Income: £1,311,617 [2017]; £1,658,225 [2016]; £1,726,067 [2015]; £1,539,587 [2014]; £1,587,910 [2013]

Forest Peoples Programme
Registered: 24 Aug 2000 *Employees:* 28 *Volunteers:* 2
Tel: 01386 840183 *Website:* forestpeoples.org
Activities: Education, training; environment, conservation, heritage; human rights, religious or racial harmony, equality or diversity
Address: Three Gables, High Street, Chipping Campden, Glos, GL55 6AG
Trustees: Paul Wolvekamp, Mr Barnaby Tallack, Silas Siakor, Martua Sirait, Johan Frijns, Mr Michel Pimbert, Rev Seamus Finn, Kate Geary, Ms Sarah Morrison
Income: £5,372,246 [2017]; £4,871,475 [2016]; £4,098,875 [2015]; £3,799,878 [2014]; £3,203,311 [2013]

Forest School, Essex
Registered: 28 Aug 1964 *Employees:* 215
Tel: 020 8520 1744 *Website:* forest.org.uk
Activities: Education, training; amateur sport
Address: Forest School, College Place, London, E17 3PY
Trustees: Mr Geoffrey Stephen Green, Mrs Glynis Jenkinson, Mrs Penny Oates, Mr David Thomas Monti Wilson, Mr Martin Robinson, Venerable Elwin Wesley Cockett, Judge Willam Kennedy, Mrs Jane Davies, Mr William Fuller
Income: £20,852,975 [2016]; £19,632,612 [2015]; £18,293,774 [2014]; £18,555,089 [2013]

The Forest Trust
Registered: 18 May 2006 *Employees:* 260
Tel: 023 8011 1220 *Website:* tft-earth.org
Activities: Education, training; prevention or relief of poverty; environment, conservation, heritage; economic, community development, employment
Address: The Forest Trust Ltd, The Clock House, Mansbridge Road, West End, Southampton, SO18 3HW
Trustees: Mr Brent Foster Wilkinson, Mr Michel Troussier, Mr Eric Jean Bouchet, Mr Andrew James Hewett, Mr David Roth, Ms Saskia Ozinga Luutsche
Income: £14,963,477 [2016]; £10,569,505 [2015]; £8,692,012 [2014]; £7,025,979 [2013]; £5,634,519 [2012]

Forest Young Men's Christian Association of East London
Registered: 26 Jun 1990 *Employees:* 94 *Volunteers:* 24
Tel: 020 8509 4600 *Website:* ymcalsw.org.uk
Activities: General charitable purposes; education, training; prevention or relief of poverty; accommodation, housing; religious activities; arts, culture, heritage, science; amateur sport; animals; economic, community development, employment
Address: 642 Forest Road, Walthamstow, London, E17 3EF
Trustees: Mr Ken Youngman, Mr Howard Dawson, Mrs Louise Hedges, Mrs Katherine Morrissey, Mr Andrew John Palmer
Income: £6,120,018 [2017]; £6,210,078 [2016]; £5,499,388 [2015]; £5,707,125 [2014]; £5,595,350 [2013]

Forest of Dean Crossroads Caring for Carers
Registered: 31 May 2001 *Employees:* 136 *Volunteers:* 5
Tel: 01594 823414 *Website:* crossroadsfd.org.uk
Activities: The advancement of health or saving of lives; disability
Address: St Annals House, Belle Vue Road, Cinderford, Glos, GL14 2AB
Trustees: Dr Jonathan Chambers, Mr Clive Dunning, Mrs Jackie Huck, Mr Hugh Aldridge, Mrs Carole Mercer, Mrs Kim Booth, Mr Tim Poole, Mr Chris Creswick, Mrs Brenda Barwell, Mr Bob Boulter, Mr Andrew Morgan-Watts, Mr Pat Williams
Income: £2,035,458 [2017]; £1,891,818 [2016]; £1,833,645 [2015]; £1,765,312 [2014]; £1,563,725 [2013]

The Forest of Marston Vale Trust
Registered: 22 Apr 1998 *Employees:* 52 *Volunteers:* 111
Tel: 01234 762601 *Website:* marstonvale.org
Activities: Environment, conservation, heritage
Address: Mr Nicholas John Webb, The Forest Centre, Station Road, Marston Moretaine, Bedford, MK43 0PR
Trustees: Mr Robert Wallace, Mr Gordon Johnston, Mr John Christopher Thelwall, Mr Gareth Richard Ellis, Mr Craig Austin, Mr Peter John Faulkner ACMA, Miss Debra Jane Hassall, Rod Calvert OBE, Mr Norman Bryan Costin, Miss Sally Williams
Income: £1,336,730 [2017]; £1,558,115 [2016]; £1,680,072 [2015]; £1,896,672 [2014]; £1,466,073 [2013]

Forever Manchester
Registered: 22 Feb 1993 *Employees:* 16 *Volunteers:* 50
Tel: 0161 214 0940 *Website:* forevermanchester.com
Activities: General charitable purposes; education, training; advancement of health or saving of lives; disability; prevention or relief of poverty; overseas aid, famine relief; accommodation, housing; arts, culture, heritage, science; amateur sport; animals; environment, conservation, heritage; economic, community development, employment; recreation; other charitable purposes
Address: 2nd Floor, Forever Manchester, 8 Hewitt Street, Manchester, M15 4GB
Trustees: Mr Michael Warner, Mrs Sandra Lindsay, Mrs Louise Marshall, Mr Philip Richard Hogben, Mr Alan Owen Mackin, Ms Samantha Jane Booth
Income: £2,511,296 [2017]; £3,219,945 [2016]; £1,763,274 [2015]; £3,061,038 [2014]; £3,793,353 [2013]

The Forget Me Not Children's Hospice
Registered: 15 Jul 2005 *Employees:* 91 *Volunteers:* 356
Tel: 01484 411040 *Website:* forgetmenotchild.co.uk
Activities: The advancement of health or saving of lives; disability; accommodation, housing
Address: Forget Me Not Hospice, Russell House, Fell Greave Road, Huddersfield, W Yorks, HD2 1NH
Trustees: Dr Gillian Sharpe, Mr Pritpal Singh Pooni, Ms Stacey Louise Hunter, Sarah Fothergill, Mrs Rosalind Edwards, Dr David Birkenhead, Rachael Heenan, Mr Jason Sharpe, Ms Kathryn Winterburn
Income: £3,521,971 [2017]; £3,256,836 [2016]; £3,152,792 [2015]; £2,848,932 [2014]; £1,999,867 [2013]

Formby Pool Trust
Registered: 9 Oct 2003 *Employees:* 65 *Volunteers:* 10
Tel: 01704 874434 *Website:* formbypool.co.uk
Activities: Recreation
Address: 3A Barkfield Lane, Formby, Liverpool, L37 3JW
Trustees: David Vaughan Pugh, Mr David Wilson, Mr Andrew Walker, Ms Kerry Davies, Dr Dympna Edwards, Cllr Catherine Mary Page, Mr Rod Dawson, Ms Sharon Crean
Income: £1,284,940 [2017]; £1,551,121 [2016]; £1,521,684 [2015]; £1,439,664 [2014]; £1,345,194 [2013]

Formission Ltd
Registered: 22 Nov 1996 *Employees:* 26 *Volunteers:* 1
Website: formission.org.uk
Activities: Education, training; religious activities
Address: 31 George Road, Alvechurch, Birmingham, B48 7PB
Trustees: Mr David L Fittro, Mr Roy Alan Baylis, Mrs Diane Lincoln, Iain MacRobert, Mrs Tammy Aho
Income: £1,167,342 [2017]; £1,286,009 [2016]; £893,421 [2015]; £963,950 [2014]; £822,051 [2013]

Forres Sandle Manor Educational Trust Limited
Registered: 29 Apr 1982 *Employees:* 84 *Volunteers:* 10
Tel: 01425 653181 *Website:* fsmschool.com
Activities: Education, training
Address: Forres Sandle Manor, Fordingbridge, Hants, SP6 1NS
Trustees: Carol Evans, Sarah Thomas, Colonel Peter Williams, Peter Tait, John Wallis, Ben Arnold, Mark Jenkins, Peter Rolph
Income: £3,625,917 [2017]; £3,285,011 [2016]; £3,568,680 [2015]; £3,523,024 [2014]; £3,767,322 [2013]

Fortunatus Housing Solutions
Registered: 12 Oct 2011 *Employees:* 25 *Volunteers:* 20
Tel: 01925 575601 *Website:* fortunatushousing.co.uk
Activities: The advancement of health or saving of lives; disability; prevention or relief of poverty; accommodation, housing
Address: Fortunatus Housing Solutions, Unit 9 Colville Court, Winwick Quay, Warrington, Cheshire, WA2 8QT
Trustees: Mr Ian Douglas Theobold, Mrs Susan Ellison, Mrs Sara Pimblett, Mrs Catherine Nicholson, Jeanne Dentith
Income: £2,176,033 [2017]; £2,007,920 [2016]; £1,860,039 [2015]; £1,772,338 [2014]; £1,659,828 [2013]

The Fortune Centre of Riding Therapy
Registered: 31 Mar 1995 *Employees:* 95 *Volunteers:* 79
Tel: 01425 673297 *Website:* fortunecentre.org
Activities: Education, training; disability
Address: The Fortune Centre of Riding Therap, Avon Tyrrell, Bransgore, Christchurch, Dorset, BH23 8EE
Trustees: Mrs Alison Frances Moore-Gwyn, Mr Andrew Jonathon Thomson, Lord Manners, Lady Swayne, Mrs Virginia Newsom, Charles Foster
Income: £2,604,925 [2017]; £2,347,049 [2016]; £2,375,763 [2015]; £2,156,171 [2014]; £2,042,224 [2013]

The Diana Forty Memorial Trust
Registered: 16 Jan 1990
Tel: 01989 562226
Activities: General charitable purposes
Address: 28 Redwood Close, Ross on Wye, Herefords, HR9 5UD
Trustees: Mr Andrew Harston, Mrs Helena Mary Duckett, Mr Charles Stanley Reeve Tucker, Mr Christian Sweeting
Income: £8,595,065 [2017]; £179,449 [2016]; £11,945,598 [2015]; £10,999 [2014]; £53,000 [2013]

The Forum Trust Limited
Registered: 10 Mar 1999 *Employees:* 31 *Volunteers:* 81
Website: theforumnorwich.co.uk
Activities: Education, training; arts, culture, heritage, science; environment, conservation, heritage; economic, community development, employment; recreation
Address: The Forum Trust Ltd, The Forum, Millennium Plain, Norwich, NR2 1TF
Trustees: Ms Rachel Higgs, Caroline Jarrold, Mr Andrew Jonathan Barnes, Mr John Fry, Professor Sarah Elizabeth Barrow, Mr Stephen John Morphew, Mr Christopher Maw, Professor John Last, Mrs Susan Elizabeth Guest, Ms Corrienne Peasgood, Gail Harris
Income: £2,479,947 [2017]; £2,499,659 [2016]; £2,355,059 [2015]; £2,278,456 [2014]; £2,342,116 [2013]

The Forum for The Future
Registered: 31 Aug 1994 *Employees:* 83 *Volunteers:* 28
Website: forumforthefuture.org
Activities: Education, training; environment, conservation, heritage; economic, community development, employment
Address: Forum for The Future, 19-23 Ironmonger Row, London, EC1V 3QN
Trustees: Ms Sara Parkin, Mrs A Fiona Thompson, Ms Katharine Leila Levick, Mr Kelvyn Garth Derrick, Jonathan Porritt, Mr Keith Clarke, Ms Anita Tiessen, Mr Volker Beckers
Income: £5,193,278 [2016]; £4,981,466 [2015]; £4,541,690 [2014]; £4,483,380 [2013]; £4,790,587 [2012]

Forward Housing SW
Registered: 29 Nov 1999 *Employees:* 4
Tel: 0300 303 1280
Activities: Disability; accommodation, housing
Address: The West House, Alpha Court, Swingbridge Road, Grantham, Lincs, NG31 7XT
Trustees: David Wain, Mrs Karen Boyce-Dawson, Mr Sebastian Blagbrough, Mr Sean Christopher Brew, Mr Alan Francis Partridge, Mr Simon Conway, Bob Graham
Income: £3,031,751 [2017]; £350,529 [2016]; £120,826 [2015]; £350,189 [2014]; £167,692 [2013]

Forward Thinking
Registered: 29 Jul 2004 *Employees:* 7
Tel: 020 7292 5555 *Website:* forwardthinking.org
Activities: Education, training; human rights, religious or racial harmony, equality or diversity
Address: Forward Thinking, The Griffin Building, 83 Clerkenwell Road, corner Hatton Garden, London, EC1R 5AR
Trustees: Mr William Sieghart, Lord Hylton, Mr Michael Holland, Baroness Helena Kennedy, Mr Chris Donnelly, Mr Francis Campbell
Income: £1,089,840 [2017]; £654,850 [2016]; £320,970 [2015]; £529,276 [2014]; £653,555 [2013]

The Forward Trust
Registered: 29 Jan 1991 *Employees:* 360 *Volunteers:* 115
Tel: 020 3752 5560 *Website:* forwardtrust.org.uk
Activities: General charitable purposes; education, training; advancement of health or saving of lives; accommodation, housing; other charitable purposes
Address: 2nd Floor, The Foundry, 17-19 Oval Way, London, SE11 5RR
Trustees: The Hon David Bernstein, Isabelle Laurent, Major Ben Houghton, Mr John Mason, Mr Andrew Wylie, Rev John Wates OBE, Lady Gibbings, Ms Marsha Taylor, David E Riddle, Dame Benita Refson DBE
Income: £18,255,000 [2017]; £20,987,000 [2016]; £20,823,000 [2015]; £18,134,508 [2014]; £14,321,732 [2013]

Forward in Faith Ministry U.K.
Registered: 27 Sep 1995 *Employees:* 51 *Volunteers:* 250
Tel: 0121 557 6508 *Website:* fifmi.org
Activities: General charitable purposes; education, training; advancement of health or saving of lives; disability; religious activities; economic, community development, employment; other charitable purposes
Address: 58 Hainge Road, Tividale, Oldbury, W Midlands, B69 2PB
Trustees: Mr Ralph Mandisodza, Mr Maxwell Marimba, Mr Joshua Dean Kennedy Samasuwo, Mr Ronald Chinyamunzore Bevan, Mrs Juliet Thondhlana, Mr Thaddaeus Mike
Income: £4,117,640 [2017]; £2,988,267 [2016]; £2,549,287 [2015]; £3,208,866 [2014]; £2,241,896 [2013]

Foscote Court (Banbury) Trust Limited
Registered: 3 Mar 1977 *Employees:* 41
Tel: 01295 252281 *Website:* thefoscotehospital.co.uk
Activities: The advancement of health or saving of lives
Address: The Foscote Hospital, 2 Foscote Rise, Banbury, Oxon, OX16 9XP
Trustees: Mr David William Guilford Budd, Mr Christopher John Lewis, Mr Andrew John McHugh, Dr Simon Keith Chamberlain, Mr Anthony Peter Matthews
Income: £2,622,817 [2016]; £2,888,246 [2015]; £3,114,277 [2014]; £3,069,798 [2013]; £3,034,128 [2012]

Fosse Bank New School
Registered: 30 Mar 1995 *Employees:* 33
Tel: 01732 834212 *Website:* fossebankschool.co.uk
Activities: Education, training; amateur sport; economic, community development, employment
Address: Mountains, Noble Tree Road, Hildenborough, Tonbridge, Kent, TN11 8ND
Trustees: Mrs Jacqueline Doris Richards, Mr Miles Cavey, Mr Douglas Wanstall
Income: £1,055,810 [2017]; £917,869 [2016]; £867,612 [2015]; £993,901 [2014]; £1,011,114 [2013]

The Fostering Network
Registered: 11 Jul 1980 *Employees:* 80
Tel: 020 7620 6433 *Website:* fostering.net
Activities: General charitable purposes; education, training; prevention or relief of poverty
Address: The Fostering Network, 87 Blackfriars Road, London, SE1 8HA
Trustees: Mr Ian Dixon, Daisy James, Janet Smith, Mr Gregory Andrew De Smidt, Mrs Julie Ann Barclay-Clark, Susanna Daus, Mervyn Erskine, Mr Nigel Paul McCartney, Mr Gary David Pickles, Dr Lynn Ashburner
Income: £6,748,208 [2017]; £7,887,563 [2016]; £7,018,176 [2015]; £6,969,015 [2014]; £6,381,857 [2013]

The Foundation Trust Network
Registered: 28 Mar 2011 *Employees:* 36
Tel: 020 7304 6840 *Website:* nhsproviders.org
Activities: Education, training; advancement of health or saving of lives
Address: Institution of Mechanical Engineers, 1 Birdcage Walk, London, SW1H 9JJ
Trustees: Sir Graham Meldrum, Mr Jagtar Singh, Mr Thomas Joseph Cahill, Mr John Norman Anderson, Dame Gillian Margaret Morgan, Mr John James Lawlor, Mr Joseph Richard Harrison, Ms Patricia Miller, Hattie Llewelyn-Davies, Ms Susan Maria Brain England, Mr Colin Scales, Mrs Susan Davis, Mr Alan Foster, Mrs Tracy Ann Taylor, Ms Ingrid Barker, Mr William Hancock, Ms Paula Clark, Mr Nicholas Moberly, Mr Nicholas Marsden, Christine Outram, Ms Angela Yvette Hillery, Jayne Brown
Income: £4,344,242 [2017]; £4,448,408 [2016]; £4,233,599 [2015]; £3,309,690 [2014]; £3,414,594 [2013]

The Foundation and Friends of The Royal Botanic Gardens,Kew
Registered: 20 Sep 1990 *Employees:* 49
Website: kew.org
Activities: Environment, conservation, heritage
Address: Royal Botanic Gardens, The Herbarium, Kew Green, Richmond, Surrey, TW9 3AE
Trustees: Mr Marcus Agius, Ms Johanna Waterous CBE, Mr Ian Karet, Mr Charles Sherwood, Mr Jan Pethick
Income: £21,921,000 [2017]; £25,167,000 [2016]; £28,840,000 [2015]; £15,853,000 [2014]; £11,928,000 [2013]

The Foundation for Art and Creative Technology
Registered: 16 May 1990 *Employees:* 31 *Volunteers:* 120
Tel: 0151 707 4400 *Website:* fact.co.uk
Activities: Education, training; arts, culture, heritage, science
Address: Foundation for Art & Creative Technology, 88 Wood Street, Liverpool, L1 4DQ
Trustees: Ms Rachel Higham, Mr Mark Gorton, Mr Simon Sprince, Ms Karen O'Donnell, Mr Wayne Scholes, Ms Pat Connor, Ms Andrea Cooper, Ms Dinah Birch, Ms Caroline Davies, Mr Neil McConnon, Mr Emlyn Williams, Mr Joe Yates
Income: £1,884,301 [2017]; £1,990,428 [2016]; £2,167,683 [2015]; £2,373,946 [2014]; £2,168,443 [2013]

Foundation for Conductive Education
Registered: 10 Feb 1987 *Employees:* 31 *Volunteers:* 23
Tel: 0121 442 5556 *Website:* conductive-education.org.uk
Activities: Education, training; disability
Address: 62 Colebourne Road, Birmingham, B13 0EY
Trustees: Mr Anthony Coombs, Mr Keith Matthew Dudley, Cllr Martin Straker Welds, Mr Andrew Moss, Mr Ian Sharp, Mrs Sara Collett, Mrs Jayne Titchener, Les Lawrence, Mr Kevin Mattinson, Mr Graham Coombs, Mr Roger David Wood
Income: £1,080,255 [2017]; £1,079,058 [2016]; £1,088,482 [2015]; £1,049,190 [2014]; £1,052,909 [2013]

Foundation for Credit Counselling
Registered: 28 Jan 1993 *Employees:* 1,464
Tel: 0113 297 0121 *Website:* stepchange.org
Activities: The prevention or relief of poverty
Address: 11th Floor, Wade House, Merrion Centre, Leeds, LS2 8NG
Trustees: Sir Hector Sants, Sir Geoffrey Mulcahy, Sue Lewis, Dame Suzi Leather, Andy Hill, Monica Kalia, Chris Stern, David Coates, John Fingleton, The Right Honourable Alun Michael, Tim Frost
Income: £49,487,000 [2016]; £46,306,811 [2015]; £39,771,810 [2014]; £37,274,765 [2013]; £35,688,275 [2012]

Foundation for Environmental Education
Registered: 24 Jul 2012 *Employees:* 12
Tel: 01603 610911 *Website:* fee.global
Activities: Education, training; environment, conservation, heritage
Address: Leathes Prior, 74 The Close, Norwich, NR1 4DR
Trustees: Ms Diaz Colon Lourdes, Mrs Lesley Jones, Mrs Josepha Hendriksen, Mr Nikos Petrou, Mr Mohammed Amine Ahlafi, Ms Laura Hickey, Mr Ian Clive Humphreys, Mr Boris Susmak
Income: £1,922,838 [2016]; £1,531,963 [2015]; £1,511,093 [2014]; £2,067,252 [2013]

Foundation for Integrated Transport
Registered: 25 Mar 2014
Tel: 020 8693 2618
Activities: General charitable purposes; education, training; environment, conservation, heritage; economic, community development, employment
Address: 8 Gilkes Crescent, London, SE21 7BS
Trustees: Mr Michael Aslan Norton, Mr Alastair Hanton OBE, Dr Simon Norton, Mrs Jenny Raggett, Mr Roger French, Dr Lynn Elizabeth Sloman, Mr Stephen Francis Waley Joseph OBE, Mr Chris Crean
Income: £2,936,438 [2017]; £118,889 [2016]; £75,061 [2015]

The Foundation for Liver Research
Registered: 1 Mar 2010 *Employees:* 19
Tel: 020 7679 6510 *Website:* liver-research.org.uk
Activities: The advancement of health or saving of lives; other charitable purposes
Address: Institute of Hepatology, 69-75 Chenies Mews, London, WC1E 6HX
Trustees: Sir Jeremy Vernon Elwes KT CBE, Sir Graeme Davies, Sir Anthony Joliffe, Professor Alan McGregor, Col Hamon Massey, Mr Robert McClatchey
Income: £4,031,373 [2017]; £2,249,892 [2016]; £2,208,539 [2015]; £2,646,289 [2014]; £2,029,066 [2013]

The Foundation for Social Entrepreneurs

Registered: 1 Feb 2002 *Employees:* 70 *Volunteers:* 291
Tel: 020 7566 1100 *Website:* unltd.org.uk
Activities: Education, training; prevention or relief of poverty; economic, community development, employment
Address: Unlimited, 123 Whitecross Street, London, EC1Y 8JJ
Trustees: Mr Rajeeb Dey, Mr Martin Wyn Griffith, Mrs Susan Charteris, Mr Nicolas Farhi, Mr Nicholas Petford, Mr Krishna Vishnubhotla, Mr Tim Davies-Pugh, Norman Cumming, Ms Lynne Berry, Mr Stephen Bediako, Ms Elizabeth Sideris, Ms Rachel Barton, Mr James Lawson
Income: £5,616,900 [2017]; £6,069,638 [2016]; £12,854,579 [2015]; £12,200,141 [2014]; £10,443,845 [2013]

Foundation for The Parks and Reserves of Cote D'Ivoire (FPRCI-UK)

Registered: 7 Sep 2010 *Employees:* 2
Activities: Education, training; overseas aid, famine relief; animals; environment, conservation, heritage
Address: Bridge House, 4 Borough High Street, London, SE1 9QR
Trustees: Dr Francis Lauginie, Ms Martine Coffi Studer, Mrs Marie Linger Djira, Mr Bernard N'doumi, Mr Soungalo Jules Prosper Coulibaly, Mr Rene Bourgoin, Mr Yao Bernard Koffi, Professor Valentin N'douba, Mr Victor Jerome Nembelessini-Silue, Dr Ilka Herbinger
Income: £1,918,350 [2016]; £1,843,418 [2015]; £1,485,538 [2014]; £76,272 [2013]; £31,863 [2012]

Foundation for Women's Health Research and Development

Registered: 30 Aug 1985 *Employees:* 30 *Volunteers:* 12
Tel: 020 8960 4000 *Website:* forwarduk.org.uk
Activities: General charitable purposes; education, training; advancement of health or saving of lives
Address: Suite 4.7-4.8, Chandelier Building, 8 Scrubs Lane, London, NW10 6RB
Trustees: Ms Lisa Smith, Ms Muna Dol, Ms Zainab Nur, Ms Joy Fraser-Amosu, Dr Soheir Elneil, Mrs Sally Anne Matthews, Ms Priti Dave Sen MS, Ms Anna Nsubuga
Income: £1,569,381 [2017]; £1,270,779 [2016]; £1,015,200 [2015]; £1,347,225 [2014]; £779,528 [2013]

The Foundation of Edward Storey

Registered: 30 Apr 1962 *Employees:* 37 *Volunteers:* 5
Tel: 01223 364405 *Website:* edwardstorey.org.uk
Activities: The prevention or relief of poverty; accommodation, housing
Address: Storey's House, Mount Pleasant, Cambridge, CB3 0BZ
Trustees: Mrs Elizabeth Walser BSc PhD, Mrs J Womack, Mrs Nicky Blanning MA, Mrs Carol Lyon, Mrs Sue Young, Mr Richard John Smith JP, Mrs Patricia Gail Clyne CertEd, Dr Antony Warren
Income: £2,374,395 [2017]; £1,544,966 [2015]; £1,443,312 [2014]; £1,439,119 [2013]; £1,360,327 [2012]

The Foundation of Lady Katherine Leveson

Registered: 30 Mar 2012 *Employees:* 32 *Volunteers:* 8
Tel: 01564 772415 *Website:* leveson.org.uk
Activities: Education, training; advancement of health or saving of lives; accommodation, housing; religious activities
Address: Temple House, Fen End Road West, Temple Balsall, Knowle, Solihull, W Midlands, B93 0AN
Trustees: Mr Michael Fetherston-Dilke, Mrs Clare Sawdon JP, The Rt Hon Viscount Daventry, Mr Robert Meacham OBE, Mr Michael Adlington, Mrs Clare Diana Hopkinson, Councillor David Bell, Lord Aylesford, Mr William Matthew Stratford Dugdale, The Bishop of Birmingham, Mr Jonathan Evans OBE, Mrs Clare Diana Hopkinson
Income: £1,406,988 [2017]; £1,645,931 [2016]; £1,382,226 [2015]; £1,291,039 [2014]; £1,699,491 [2013]

Foundation of Light

Registered: 14 Nov 2001 *Employees:* 135 *Volunteers:* 45
Tel: 0191 551 5126 *Website:* foundationoflight.co.uk
Activities: General charitable purposes; education, training; advancement of health or saving of lives; disability; amateur sport; economic, community development, employment
Address: Centre of Light, Stadium of Light, Sunderland, Tyne & Wear, SR5 1SU
Trustees: Sir Peter Vardy, Mr Robert Sydney Murray CBE, Mr Steve Cram MBE, James Ramsbotham, Mr George Clarke, Sir Tim Rice, Kate Adie, Baroness Estelle Morris, Mr Paul David Collingwood MBE
Income: £4,181,865 [2016]; £4,832,828 [2015]; £4,591,494 [2014]; £3,514,367 [2013]; £2,879,306 [2012]

The Foundation of Sir John Percyvale in Macclesfield of 1502, Re-Founded By King Edward VI in 1552

Registered: 30 Jul 2010 *Employees:* 249
Tel: 01625 260010 *Website:* kingsmac.co.uk
Activities: Education, training
Address: Kings School, Cumberland Street, Macclesfield, Cheshire, SK10 1DA
Trustees: Mrs Jose Spinks, Mr Christopher Petty, Mr Ian Bradley, Dr John William Kennerley, Mr Michael Strutt, Mrs Hilda Gaddum, Mr Simon Barriskell, Mr Jonathan Paul Watkins, Ayesha Choudhury, Mr Paul Findlow, Mr Stephen Wright, Mr Robert Anthony Greenham, Mr John Richard Sugden, Ms Juliette White, Mr Chris King, Miss Margaret Longden, Dr Neil Hanley
Income: £15,215,000 [2017]; £13,307,000 [2016]; £12,655,000 [2015]; £12,355,483 [2014]; £12,707,532 [2013]

Foundation of the Society of Retina Specialists

Registered: 11 Mar 2011
Tel: 00-353-1-209 1100 *Website:* euretina.org
Activities: General charitable purposes; education, training; advancement of health or saving of lives
Address: Temple House, Temple Road, Blackrock, Co Dublin, Ireland
Trustees: Mr Sebastian Wolf, Mrs Anat Loewenstein, Mrs Ursula Schmidt-Erfurth, Prof Jose Garcia Arumi, Mr Alistair Laidlaw, Prof Morten Dornonville De La Cour, Dr Frank Holz, Prof Jan Van Meurs, Prof Francesco Bandello, Prof Stefan Seregard, Prof Ramin Tadayoni
Income: £3,753,467 [2016]; £1,190,786 [2015]; £1,234,592 [2014]; £955,200 [2013]; £624,103 [2012]

Foundation

Registered: 4 Sep 1984 *Employees:* 212 *Volunteers:* 58
Tel: 0113 303 0152 *Website:* foundationuk.org
Activities: Education, training; prevention or relief of poverty; accommodation, housing
Address: Foundation, Unit 8 Northwest Business Park, Servia Hill, Leeds, LS6 2QH
Trustees: David Powell, Claire Vilarrubi, Mrs Julia Anne Bates, Ms Patricia Anne Taylor, Mr Christopher John Welch, Philip Turnpenny, Mr Peter Harry Johnston, Mr Richard Brenden Parry, Mr Mark Ogilvie Simpson
Income: £11,387,000 [2017]; £12,352,000 [2016]; £14,331,000 [2015]; £14,407,000 [2014]; £13,523,000 [2013]

Founders for Good Ltd
Registered: 15 Jun 2015 *Employees:* 8 *Volunteers:* 6
Tel: 020 8064 0186 *Website:* founderspledge.com
Activities: General charitable purposes; education, training
Address: Block A Unit 402A, The Biscuit Factory, 100 Clements Road, London, SE16 4DG
Trustees: Mr Richard Reed, Mrs Dafna Ciechanover Bonas, Damian Kimmelman, Mr Alexandre Maurus Semboglu, Mr Jonathan Philip Pryce Goodwin, Mr Neil Hutchinson
Income: £1,685,072 [2017]; £1,467,292 [2016]

Founders4schools
Registered: 15 Jun 2015 *Employees:* 14 *Volunteers:* 500
Website: founders4schools.org.uk
Activities: General charitable purposes; education, training; economic, community development, employment
Address: Dixon Wilson, Chartered Accountants, 22 Chancery Lane, London, WC2A 1LS
Trustees: Peter Gotham, Ms Herdeep Dosanjh, Mr Marc Allera, Kirsten Bodley, Joanne Hannaford, Mrs Sherry Coutu, Mrs Jane Galvin, Mrs Melissa Di Donato, Josh Graff
Income: £1,201,240 [2017]; £188,934 [2015]

The Foundling Museum
Registered: 24 Aug 1998 *Employees:* 19 *Volunteers:* 230
Tel: 020 7841 3600 *Website:* foundlingmuseum.org.uk
Activities: Education, training; arts, culture, heritage, science; environment, conservation, heritage
Address: 40 Brunswick Square, London, WC1N 1AZ
Trustees: Mr Jeremy Deller, Dr Paul Zuckerman, Mr William Hornby Gore, Mr Robert Aitken, Ms Larissa Joy, Ms Judith Bollinger, Mr Lemn Sissay, Mr Ronald Gould, Ms Geraldine MacDonald, Ms Perdita Hunt, Mr Spencer Hyman, Mr Geoff Berridge, Ms Alison Cole, Ms Margaret Reynolds, Mr Christopher Cotton, Ms Anne Beckwith Smith
Income: £1,182,643 [2017]; £1,152,995 [2016]; £1,455,103 [2015]; £874,728 [2014]; £770,448 [2013]

Four Paws
Registered: 26 Feb 2007 *Employees:* 14 *Volunteers:* 5
Tel: 020 7922 7956 *Website:* four-paws.org.uk
Activities: Education, training; advancement of health or saving of lives; animals; environment, conservation, heritage
Address: Four Paws, 32-36 Loman Street, London, SE1 0EH
Trustees: Major General Peter Davies CB, Mr Josef Pfabigan, Mr Helmut Dungler
Income: £2,589,977 [2017]; £2,085,679 [2016]; £2,292,568 [2015]; £1,637,481 [2014]; £1,745,103 [2013]

Four Towns and Vale Link Community Transport
Registered: 2 Feb 2001 *Employees:* 41 *Volunteers:* 25
Tel: 01454 250500 *Website:* 4tv.org.uk
Activities: Education, training; disability; economic, community development, employment; recreation
Address: Crossbow House, 58 School Road, Frampton Cotterell, Bristol, BS36 2DA
Trustees: Mr Lewis Gray, Mrs Lucy Margaret Humfrey Hamid, Mr Dennis Rogers, Mr John Bernard Francis, Mr Brian Andrew Freeguard, Mr Mike Stutter, Mr Robert Charles Griffin, Mr Peter Llewellyn Nock
Income: £1,377,820 [2016]; £1,274,949 [2015]; £1,201,644 [2014]; £1,014,272 [2013]

The Foyle Foundation
Registered: 28 Jul 2000 *Employees:* 6
Tel: 020 7430 9119 *Website:* foylefoundation.org.uk
Activities: General charitable purposes; education, training; arts, culture, heritage, science
Address: Rugby Chambers, 2 Rugby Street, London, WC1N 3QU
Trustees: James Korner, Roy Amlot, Vikki Heywood, Mr Michael Gordon Smith, Sir Peter Duffell
Income: £2,777,329 [2016]; £2,686,278 [2015]; £2,572,752 [2014]; £3,015,445 [2013]; £3,420,799 [2012]

Framework Housing Association
Registered: 25 Feb 1997 *Employees:* 725 *Volunteers:* 350
Tel: 0115 841 7711 *Website:* frameworkha.org
Activities: Education, training; advancement of health or saving of lives; accommodation, housing; other charitable purposes
Address: Val Roberts House, 25 Gregory Boulevard, Nottingham, NG7 6NX
Trustees: Mrs Diane Diacon, Mrs Jane Geraghty, Mrs Diana Parrish, Mrs Rebecca Jane Rance, Mr Patrick Michael Mitchell, Mr Kanwaljit Singh, Mr Christopher Prentice, Ms Deborah Maitland, Mr Caris Aran Henry, Dr Vinay Shankar
Income: £35,182,000 [2017]; £31,248,000 [2016]; £28,679,000 [2015]; £27,762,000 [2014]; £26,024,000 [2013]

Frampton Park Baptist Church
Registered: 19 Feb 2013 *Employees:* 11 *Volunteers:* 80
Tel: 020 8985 0877 *Website:* framptonpark.org.uk
Activities: General charitable purposes; education, training; advancement of health or saving of lives; disability; prevention or relief of poverty; overseas aid, famine relief; religious activities; arts, culture, heritage, science; amateur sport; economic, community development, employment; human rights, religious or racial harmony, equality or diversity; recreation
Address: Frampton Park Baptist Church, Frampton Park Road, London, E9 7PQ
Trustees: Richard Bowman, Mr Torquil Allen, Mr Petrus Burin, Mrs Liliana Vaquerano, Mr Adekunle Adeyiga, Mrs Zenani Sibindi
Income: £1,322,182 [2016]; £156,837 [2015]; £129,576 [2014]; £204,784 [2013]

Francis House Family Trust
Registered: 5 Jul 1990 *Employees:* 81 *Volunteers:* 73
Tel: 0161 434 4118 *Website:* francishouse.org.uk
Activities: The advancement of health or saving of lives; disability
Address: Francis House, Family Trust, 390 Parrs Wood Road, East Didsbury, Manchester, M20 5NA
Trustees: Right Reverend Terence Brain Bishop Emeritus, Rev Mgr Thomas Mulheran, Mr Michael Redfearn, Dr Susan Kirk, Mr Charles Ledigo, Mr Martin Lochery, Mr Christopher Roberts, Mr Vijay Srivastava, Dr Susan Mary O'Halloran, Judith Amosi-Khodadad
Income: £4,155,764 [2017]; £4,170,713 [2016]; £3,819,304 [2015]; £4,372,444 [2014]; £4,094,896 [2013]

The Franciscan Missionaries of St. Joseph
Registered: 13 Apr 2010 *Employees:* 37
Website: fmsj.co.uk
Activities: General charitable purposes; religious activities
Address: St Joseph's Convent, 150 Greenleach Lane, Worsley, Manchester, M28 2TS
Trustees: Sister Maureen Theresa Murphy, Sister Joan Patricia O'Gorman, Sister Joan Kerley, Sister Teresa Sylvia Wild, Sister Anne Moore
Income: £1,340,116 [2016]; £1,404,342 [2015]; £1,166,733 [2014]; £1,086,150 [2013]; £987,944 [2012]

Anne Frank Trust UK
Registered: 19 Jun 1991 *Employees:* 28
Tel: 020 7284 5858 *Website:* annefrank.org.uk
Activities: Education, training; human rights, religious or racial harmony, equality or diversity
Address: Star House, 104-108 Grafton Road, Kentish Town, London, NW5 4BA
Trustees: Dame Helen Hyde, Mr Isaac Zachary Mockton, Mrs Frances White, Ms Fiona Brydon, Ms Joanna Myerson, Mr Daniel Mendoza, Ms Caroline Hoare, Mr Dominic Abrams, Mr Bernard Howard
Income: £1,259,798 [2017]; £1,331,621 [2016]; £1,228,493 [2015]; £1,221,345 [2014]; £1,206,281 [2013]

Frankgiving Limited
Registered: 12 Jun 1967
Tel: 020 8731 0777
Activities: General charitable purposes; education, training; religious activities
Address: New Burlington House, 1075 Finchley Road, London, NW11 0PU
Trustees: Mrs Zisi Frankel, Mr Winston Samuel Gilbert, Mr Leslie Frankel, Mr Laurence Allan Foux
Income: £1,954,226 [2017]; £1,989,268 [2016]; £1,781,270 [2015]; £1,945,330 [2014]; £1,707,660 [2013]

Frantic Theatre Company Ltd
Registered: 10 Apr 2006 *Employees:* 15
Tel: 020 7841 3115 *Website:* franticassembly.co.uk
Activities: Education, training; arts, culture, heritage, science
Address: Frantic Assembly, 31 Eyre Street Hill, London, EC1R 5EW
Trustees: Ms Sian Alexander, Miss Sally Noonan, Ms Julie Crofts, Mr Matthew Littleford
Income: £1,183,701 [2017]; £760,780 [2016]; £1,180,028 [2015]; £630,880 [2014]; £625,964 [2013]

The Free Grammar School of King Charles II at Bradford
Registered: 11 Jul 1966 *Employees:* 189 *Volunteers:* 200
Tel: 01274 553706 *Website:* bradfordgrammar.com
Activities: Education, training
Address: Bradford Grammar School, Keighley Road, Bradford, BD9 4JP
Trustees: Bradford Grammar School Trustee Ltd
Income: £13,796,997 [2017]; £14,694,071 [2016]; £13,330,199 [2015]; £13,231,516 [2014]; £12,391,767 [2013]

Free The Children UK
Registered: 28 Oct 2010 *Employees:* 38 *Volunteers:* 450
Tel: 020 8266 1616 *Website:* we.org
Activities: Education, training
Address: 14 Bowden Street, London, SE11 4DS
Trustees: Mr Neil Roskilly, Pauline Elizabeth Latham, Ms Meigan Terry, Mr Carlos Vitorino Pinto, Mr Craig Burkinshaw, Graham Edwin Moysey, Lord Rumi Verjee
Income: £3,306,363 [2017]; £4,202,816 [2016]; £3,413,782 [2015]; £2,377,400 [2014]; £1,245,985 [2013]

Free Word
Registered: 13 Feb 2009 *Employees:* 21
Tel: 020 7324 2570 *Website:* freewordcentre.com
Activities: General charitable purposes; education, training; arts, culture, heritage, science; human rights, religious or racial harmony, equality or diversity
Address: Free Word Centre, 60 Farringdon Road, London, EC1R 3GA
Trustees: Philip Tranter, Mrs Ursula Margaret Owen, Ms Sasha Havlicek, Paul Field, Ms Razia Iqbal, Isabel Hilton, Mr Paul Aggett, Mr Timothy David Duffy, Mr Ekow Eshun, Elif Safak
Income: £1,052,069 [2017]; £1,090,288 [2016]; £1,312,050 [2015]; £861,473 [2014]; £862,695 [2013]

Freedom Church Hereford
Registered: 1 Jun 2015 *Employees:* 27 *Volunteers:* 250
Tel: 01432 340830 *Website:* freedomchurch.cc
Activities: General charitable purposes; education, training; advancement of health or saving of lives; prevention or relief of poverty; religious activities; recreation
Address: Freedom Church, 161 Holme Lacy Road, Hereford, HR2 6DG
Trustees: Mr Andrew Rattenbury, Mrs Megan Alexandra Cooke, Mr Andrew Churcher
Income: £1,238,287 [2017]; £771,888 [2016]

Freedom Festival Arts Trust
Registered: 3 Sep 2014 *Employees:* 4 *Volunteers:* 119
Tel: 01482 214036 *Website:* freedomfestival.co.uk
Activities: Education, training; arts, culture, heritage, science
Address: Freedom Festival Arts Trust, First Floor, Wykeland House, Queen Street, Hull, HU1 1UU
Trustees: Graham Chesters, Kate Hainsworth, John Meehan, Karen Ann Ama Okra, Sarah Humphreys, Ms Samantha Madden, Neil Porteus, Andrew Balman, Jon Pwyell, T Geraghty, Ms Kate Denby, Mark Hodson
Income: £1,195,225 [2017]; £856,230 [2016]; £583,431 [2015]

Freedom Food Limited
Registered: 19 Dec 1996 *Employees:* 31
Website: freedomfood.co.uk
Activities: Animals
Address: Freedom Food Ltd, Wilberforce Way, Southwater, Horsham, W Sussex, RH13 9RS
Trustees: Mr Michael Tomlinson, Ms Jane Tredgett, Mr Thomas Vaughan, Mr William Hamilton, Miss Miriam Parker, Mr Paul Baxter, Mr Robert Hallam Bayliss, Mr David Campbell James Main
Income: £2,751,593 [2016]; £2,376,605 [2015]; £2,147,778 [2014]; £2,386,274 [2013]; £2,524,721 [2012]

Freeways
Registered: 4 Feb 1988 *Employees:* 231 *Volunteers:* 10
Tel: 01275 372109 *Website:* freeways.org.uk
Activities: Disability
Address: Freeways, Leigh Court Business Centre, Pill Road, Abbots Leigh, Bristol, BS8 3RA
Trustees: Mr Peter Laszlo, Dr Leila Cooke, Mrs Lal Heaton, Mr Franklin Morton, Mr Christopher Clement Britton
Income: £5,497,000 [2017]; £5,771,000 [2016]; £6,035,000 [2015]; £5,841,000 [2014]; £5,877,000 [2013]

The Fremantle Trust
Registered: 30 Oct 1992 *Employees:* 1,097 *Volunteers:* 90
Tel: 01296 393000 *Website:* fremantletrust.org
Activities: The advancement of health or saving of lives; disability
Address: The Fremantle Trust, Woodley House, 64-65 Rabans Close, Rabans Lane Industrial Area, Aylesbury, Bucks, HP19 8RS
Trustees: Cherry Aston, Sandy Hutchison, Nic Heald, Mr Andrew David Hall Forrest, Ms Sandra Laird, Elizabeth Firth, Ian Shepherd, Diane Kerwood, Mr Alan John Howard, Mr Stephen Wooler
Income: £49,440,000 [2017]; £48,684,000 [2016]; £43,744,000 [2015]; £39,877,000 [2014]; £39,450,000 [2013]

French Education Charitable Trust
Registered: 11 Sep 2013
Tel: 020 7871 3119
Activities: General charitable purposes; education, training
Address: 23 Cromwell Road, London, SW7 2EL
Trustees: Richard Fairbairn, Arnaud Vaissie, Jean-Pierre Mustier, Lorene Lemor
Income: £1,852,000 [2016]; £2,920,000 [2015]; £470,000 [2014]

Frensham Heights Educational Trust Limited
Registered: 15 Aug 1966 *Employees:* 128
Website: frensham.org
Activities: Education, training
Address: Frensham Heights School, Frensham Heights Road, Rowledge, Farnham, Surrey, GU10 4EA
Trustees: Mr Philip Ward, Mr Richard Lowther, Mrs Katy Poulsom, Mr Dan Eley, Mr Alan Brown, Dr Claire Fuller, Mr Angus Carlill, Mr Gerry Holden, Mrs Jackie Sullivan, Mr Martin Lupton, Mr Jeff Hynam, Mr William Bird, Mrs Margaret Coltman
Income: £9,163,000 [2017]; £8,872,000 [2016]; £8,904,000 [2015]; £8,126,000 [2014]; £8,043,765 [2013]

Freshfields Animal Rescue
Registered: 5 Feb 2015 *Employees:* 55 *Volunteers:* 150
Tel: 0151 931 1604 *Website:* freshfields.org.uk
Activities: Animals; environment, conservation, heritage
Address: Freshfields Animal Rescue Centre, East Lodge Farm, East Lane, Liverpool, L29 3EA
Trustees: Ms Helen Stanbury, Dina Nixon, Annette Armstrong, Pamela Jane Young, Clare Metcalfe, Doug Martin
Income: £1,225,494 [2016]; £1,131,553 [2015]

Freshwater Biological Association
Registered: 21 May 1963 *Employees:* 33 *Volunteers:* 3
Website: fba.org.uk
Activities: Education, training; arts, culture, heritage, science; environment, conservation, heritage
Address: The Freshwater Biological Association, The Ferry Landing, Far Sawrey, Ambleside, Cumbria, LA22 0LP
Trustees: Mr Ronald Alfred Wilson Middleton, Mr Geoffrey Bateman, Mr Alan Crowden, Dr Guy Woodward, Mr Richard Chadd, Prof Keith John Beven, Prof Ann-Louise Heathwaite
Income: £1,093,623 [2017]; £1,149,866 [2016]; £691,179 [2015]; £884,827 [2014]; £906,374 [2013]

The Anna Freud Centre
Registered: 23 Aug 1999 *Employees:* 157 *Volunteers:* 16
Tel: 020 7794 2313 *Website:* annafreud.org
Activities: Education, training; advancement of health or saving of lives
Address: 12 Maresfield Gardens, London, NW3 5SU
Trustees: Mr Daniel Peltz, Mr Dominic Shorthouse, Peter Oppenheimer, Professor John Cape, Ms Sally Cairns, The Hon Michael Samuel, Professor Linda Mayes MD, Ms Ruby Wax, Dr Moshe Kantor
Income: £16,747,436 [2016]; £9,376,828 [2015]; £7,640,019 [2014]; £6,444,182 [2013]; £5,280,965 [2012]

The Frewen Educational Trust Limited
Registered: 1 Apr 1968 *Employees:* 65 *Volunteers:* 5
Tel: 01797 253388 *Website:* frewencollege.co.uk
Activities: Education, training
Address: Frewen Educational Trust Ltd, Frewen College Brickwall, Rye Road, Northiam, Rye, E Sussex, TN31 6NL
Trustees: Mr Graham Peters, Mr John Stevenson, Mrs Anne Moore-Bick, Mrs Jo Slater, Mrs Victoria Mills, Mrs Jane Pennock, Mr Jonathan Watts, Mr Phillip Noel, Mr Graham Nash, Mrs Fiona Flint
Income: £2,831,087 [2017]; £2,839,348 [2016]; £2,703,091 [2015]; £2,630,108 [2014]; £2,368,875 [2013]

The Friars, Aylesford
Registered: 10 Mar 1998 *Employees:* 31 *Volunteers:* 50
Tel: 01622 717272 *Website:* thefriars.org.uk
Activities: Religious activities; arts, culture, heritage, science; environment, conservation, heritage; human rights, religious or racial harmony, equality or diversity
Address: The Friars, Aylesford Priory, Aylesford, Kent, ME20 7BX
Trustees: Mr Julian Filochowski, Rev Kevin John Alban, Rev Brendan Grady, Rev Patrick O'Keeffe, Rev Francis Kemsley
Income: £1,440,735 [2016]; £1,162,618 [2015]; £1,231,608 [2014]; £1,430,603 [2013]; £1,471,606 [2012]

The Friendly Almshouses
Registered: 22 Apr 2016 *Employees:* 4
Tel: 020 7274 7176 *Website:* friendlyalmshouses.org
Activities: The prevention or relief of poverty; accommodation, housing
Address: 167 Stockwell Park Road, London, SW9 0TL
Trustees: Kate Woollcombe, Felicity Stonehill, Ms Sally Anne Louise Blaksley, Mrs Hilary Caroline Parsons, Ms Julia Margaret Cattle, Grace Bailey
Income: £2,190,144 [2017]

Friends International Ministries
Registered: 8 Oct 2002 *Employees:* 59 *Volunteers:* 1,000
Tel: 01920 460006 *Website:* friendsinternational.uk
Activities: Religious activities
Address: All Nations Christian College, Easneye, Ware, Herts, SG12 8LX
Trustees: Mr Robert Mallet, Mr Stephen John Peters, Ms Jennifer Rosemary Brown, Mr Henry Tsz Fung Lu, Sara Priscilla Slater, Mrs Sarah Hinson, Mrs Stroma Beattie, Mr Jonathan Salkeld
Income: £2,051,806 [2017]; £1,489,908 [2016]; £1,455,232 [2015]; £1,424,529 [2014]; £1,348,158 [2013]

Friends Therapeutic Community Trust
Registered: 23 Jun 2008 *Employees:* 50
Tel: 01799 584359 *Website:* glebehouse.org.uk
Activities: Other charitable purposes
Address: Glebe House, Church Road, Shudy Camps, Cambridge, CB21 4QH
Trustees: Mr Peter Sorrell, Mrs Susan Mary Brock-Hollinshead, Ms Kathy Hindle, Ms Carole Thomas, Mr Paul Keith Hodgkin, Ms Elizabeth Roman, Mrs Zoe Greening, Mr Eckhard Prolingheuer, Mr Christopher Paul Henson
Income: £2,457,809 [2017]; £2,394,953 [2016]; £2,394,953 [2015]; £2,266,183 [2014]; £2,117,967 [2013]

Friends of Achiezer Arad
Registered: 4 Jul 1990
Tel: 020 8211 7958
Activities: General charitable purposes; education, training; advancement of health or saving of lives; disability; prevention or relief of poverty; overseas aid, famine relief; religious activities
Address: 70 Lingwood Road, London, E5 9BN
Trustees: Mrs Chavi Moskovitz, Mr Solomon Reich, Mr Israel Moskovitz
Income: £3,086,523 [2017]; £599,156 [2016]; £788,808 [2015]; £654,234 [2014]; £939,803 [2013]

Friends of Animals League
Registered: 27 Mar 2002 *Employees:* 30 *Volunteers:* 200
Tel: 01959 572386 *Website:* foalfarm.org.uk
Activities: Animals
Address: Friends of Animals League, Foal Farm, Jail Lane, Biggin Hill, Westerham, Kent, TN16 3AX
Trustees: Mr Charles Johnston, Mrs Carole Veron, Mr Paul Dewdney, Mr Stephen Carlton, Mr Royston Abernethy, Mr Ian Price, Mrs Elizabeth Alice Cordingley, Ms Lydia Buttinger, Mr Ross Miller
Income: £1,156,921 [2016]; £708,660 [2015]; £827,447 [2014]; £1,060,541 [2013]; £419,887 [2012]

Friends of Beis Chinuch Lebonos Trust
Registered: 1 Aug 2013
Tel: 020 8211 0327
Activities: Religious activities
Address: Flat 9, Davis Court, Saw Mill Way, London, N16 6AG
Trustees: Mrs Libby Hoffman, Mrs Esther Bard, Mrs Chana Lieber
Income: £3,764,774 [2017]; £4,309,311 [2016]; £4,289,973 [2015]; £3,249,964 [2014]

Friends of Beis Soroh Schneirer
Registered: 3 Sep 2013
Tel: 020 8211 0327
Activities: Religious activities
Address: Flat 9, Davis Court, Saw Mill Way, London, N16 6AG
Trustees: Mrs Rivka Adler, Mr Samuel Pappenheim, Mrs Esther Pappenheim
Income: £2,982,842 [2017]; £4,015,935 [2016]; £3,467,254 [2015]; £2,314,725 [2014]

Friends of Highgate Cemetery Trust
Registered: 1 Oct 1996 *Employees:* 13 *Volunteers:* 200
Tel: 020 8340 1834 *Website:* highgatecemetery.org
Activities: Environment, conservation, heritage
Address: Highgate Cemetery, Swains Lane, London, N6 6PJ
Trustees: Mrs Teresa Sladen, Mr Matthew Lewis, Mrs Lucy Lelliott, Mr Charles Essex, Doreen Susan Aislabie, Nicola Jane Jones, Mr Adam Cooke, Mr Howard Martin Adeney, April Cameron, Dr Pat Hardy, Evelyn Barbara Wilder, Katherine Ann Baldwin
Income: £1,453,354 [2017]; £1,852,457 [2016]; £1,148,204 [2015]; £1,181,777 [2014]; £1,027,223 [2013]

Friends of Mercaz Hatorah Belz Macnivka
Registered: 26 Sep 2008
Tel: 020 8806 6907
Activities: General charitable purposes; education, training; advancement of health or saving of lives; prevention or relief of poverty; religious activities
Address: 114 Kyverdale Road, London, N16 6PR
Trustees: Mr Elozer Yonah Brander, Mrs Gitel Krautwirt, Mr Menachem Liber
Income: £11,302,559 [2017]; £9,190,076 [2016]; £8,268,975 [2015]; £6,743,360 [2014]; £5,672,685 [2013]

Friends of Michael Sobell House
Registered: 1 Mar 2000 *Employees:* 47 *Volunteers:* 181
Website: michaelsobellhospice.co.uk
Activities: The advancement of health or saving of lives
Address: Michael Sobell Hospice Charity, Mount Vernon Hospital, Northwood, Middlesex, HA6 2RN
Trustees: Mr Jim Sutcliffe, Mrs Jean Seymour, Mr John Kenneth Edward Hensley, Ms Daksha Dodhia, Mrs Rosalind Williams, Mrs Rowena Dean, Satish Kanabar
Income: £1,406,065 [2017]; £1,837,274 [2016]; £1,595,675 [2015]; £1,270,530 [2014]; £1,307,837 [2013]

Friends of Mir
Registered: 12 Mar 1976
Tel: 020 8455 6760
Activities: Education, training
Address: 30 Gresham Gardens, London, NW11 8PB
Trustees: Mr Barry Yehudah Bodner, Mr Ronald Edward Hochhauser, Mr Michael Bordon
Income: £1,182,758 [2017]; £1,288,266 [2016]; £2,226,922 [2015]; £635,870 [2014]; £1,308,236 [2013]

The Friends of Ohr Someach
Registered: 30 Oct 1985 *Employees:* 58 *Volunteers:* 150
Tel: 020 8458 4588 *Website:* jle.org.uk
Activities: General charitable purposes; education, training; religious activities; other charitable purposes
Address: 68 Brookside Road, London, NW11 9NG
Trustees: Mr Ashley Cohen, Mr Sony Douer, Mr Daniel Lyons
Income: £3,035,441 [2016]; £2,731,367 [2015]; £2,853,473 [2014]; £2,867,315 [2013]; £2,104,593 [2012]

The Friends of The Bobover Yeshivah
Registered: 27 Apr 1965 *Employees:* 63 *Volunteers:* 25
Tel: 020 8809 0476
Activities: Education, training; prevention or relief of poverty; religious activities
Address: 87 Egerton Road, London, N16 6UE
Trustees: Mr Levi Rottenberg, Rabbi Ben Zion Blum, Mr Naftoli Wachsman
Income: £1,424,284 [2017]; £977,030 [2016]; £979,514 [2015]; £897,907 [2014]; £751,566 [2013]

Friends of The Eastbourne Hospital
Registered: 18 Dec 1963 *Employees:* 6 *Volunteers:* 80
Tel: 01323 438236 *Website:* esht.nhs.uk
Activities: The advancement of health or saving of lives
Address: Friends Office, Eastbourne DGH, Kings Drive, Eastbourne, E Sussex, BN21 2UD
Trustees: Mr Anthony Walmsley, Mrs Bozenca Phillips, Mr Hugh Parker, Mrs Sandy Boyce-Sharpe, Mrs Gill Woolley, Mrs Catherine Mary Lock, Mrs Masayo Crumbie, Mrs Ann Caffyn MBE, Mrs Carole Naylor, Dr Peter Nash, Mrs Rosemary Cameron, Mrs Trisha Hamblin, Mrs Gilda Denise Perry
Income: £1,397,166 [2017]; £1,039,192 [2016]; £1,224,756 [2015]; £836,574 [2014]; £1,225,671 [2013]

Friends of The Elderly
Registered: 26 Nov 1964 *Employees:* 915 *Volunteers:* 103
Tel: 020 7730 8263 *Website:* fote.org.uk
Activities: The advancement of health or saving of lives; prevention or relief of poverty; accommodation, housing
Address: 40-42 Ebury Street, London, SW1W 0LZ
Trustees: Mr Jonathan Passman, Viscount Terence Devonport, Mrs Joannie Andrews, Rikki Garcia, Mr Chris Maidment, Mr Kerry Rubie, Mr James Ross, Mr Jeremy Withers Green, Mr Rob Chapman, Ms Sharon Prosser
Income: £28,801,050 [2017]; £25,335,963 [2016]; £23,451,360 [2015]; £22,996,843 [2014]; £29,220,304 [2013]

Friends of The Lake District
Registered: 18 Nov 2003 *Employees:* 12 *Volunteers:* 350
Tel: 01539 720788 *Website:* friendsofthelakedistrict.org.uk
Activities: Environment, conservation, heritage
Address: Friends of The Lake District, Murley Moss Business Park, Oxenholme Road, Kendal, Cumbria, LA9 7SS
Trustees: Mr Martin Brimmer, Professor Jeremy Rowan Robinson, Mrs Judith Cooke, Mr Gareth John McKeever, Mr John Entwistle OBE, Mr John Campbell, Sarah Hodgson, Mr Philip Alexander Cropper
Income: £1,030,616 [2016]; £708,381 [2015]; £958,761 [2014]; £555,589 [2013]; £812,355 [2012]

Friends of The National Libraries
Registered: 22 Mar 1963 *Volunteers:* 1
Tel: 01491 598083 *Website:* friendsofnationallibraries.org.uk
Activities: Arts, culture, heritage, science
Address: P O Box 4291, Reading, Berks, RG8 9JA
Trustees: Mr Charles Sebag-Montefiore, Dr Richard Ovenden, Dr Christopher Francis Rivers De Hamel, Dr Frances Harris, Mr James Fergusson, Mr Mark Storey, Mr Felix De Marez Oyens, Prof Andrew Solomon, Ms Rachel Bond, Lord Egremont DL FRSL, Mr Stephen Clarke, Mr Geordie Greig, Mr Roland Keating, Dr John Scally, Mrs Joan Winterkorn, Ms Isobel Hunter, Ms Linda Tomos, Dr Jessica Gardner
Income: £1,324,401 [2016]; £802,689 [2015]; £259,954 [2014]; £179,645 [2013]; £199,345 [2012]

The Friends of The Royal Academy
Registered: 10 Mar 1977 *Volunteers:* 68
Tel: 020 7300 8017 *Website:* royalacademy.org.uk
Activities: Arts, culture, heritage, science
Address: Royal Academy of Arts, Burlington House, Piccadilly, London, W1J 0BD
Trustees: Professor Christopher Orr, Ms Nicola Bannister, Mr Benjamin Joseph, Mr Charles Saunarez Smith, Mr Oliver Rawlins, Verity Harding, Ms Diana Carney, Mr Clive Humby, Mr Gregory Sanderson, Rebecca Salter RA, Mr Richard Philipps
Income: £11,104,299 [2017]; £11,049,323 [2016]; £9,626,681 [2015]; £9,585,609 [2014]; £10,072,880 [2013]

Friends of The United Institutions of Arad
Registered: 29 Jun 1992
Tel: 020 8211 7958
Activities: General charitable purposes; education, training; advancement of health or saving of lives; prevention or relief of poverty; religious activities
Address: 70 Lingwood Road, London, E5 9BN
Trustees: Mr Israel Moskovitz, Mr David Stobiecki, Mr Mordechai Pesach
Income: £1,153,379 [2017]; £1,090,370 [2016]; £557,933 [2015]; £866,327 [2014]; £416,220 [2013]

The Friends of The V & A
Registered: 29 Sep 1976 *Employees:* 9 *Volunteers:* 88
Tel: 020 7942 2270 *Website:* vam.ac.uk
Activities: Education, training; arts, culture, heritage, science; environment, conservation, heritage; recreation
Address: Victoria & Albert Museum, Cromwell Road, South Kensington, London, SW7 2RL
Trustees: Mr Jeremy Strachan, Ms Tricia Bey, Mrs Elizabeth Hamilton MBE, Ms Emma Skinmore, Mr Kenneth Draper, Mr Phil Dowson, Mrs Janet Gough
Income: £3,368,633 [2017]; £3,674,784 [2016]; £2,576,063 [2015]; £2,239,373 [2014]; £1,777,693 [2013]

The Friends of The Wisdom Hospice Limited
Registered: 18 Jun 1982 *Employees:* 11 *Volunteers:* 50
Tel: 01634 831163 *Website:* fowh.org.uk
Activities: The advancement of health or saving of lives
Address: Friends of The Wisdom Hospice, High Bank, Rochester, Kent, ME1 2NU
Trustees: Mr Raymond Harris, Mrs Anne Kathleen Skinner, Mr James Douglas Wootten, Mr Robert Frederick Coleman, Mrs Jane Shirley, Victoria Kirby, Mrs Sylvia Fairbrace, Mrs Margaret Barker, Mrs Shirley Berry, Mr David Roy Turner, Barbara Long
Income: £1,158,594 [2017]; £1,028,250 [2016]; £884,259 [2015]; £769,150 [2014]; £685,345 [2013]

Friends of Westonbirt Arboretum
Registered: 4 Dec 1985 *Employees:* 7 *Volunteers:* 5
Tel: 0300 067 3300 *Website:* fowa.org.uk
Activities: Environment, conservation, heritage
Address: Westonbirt Arboretum, Westonbirt, Tetbury, Glos, GL8 8QS
Trustees: Dr Michael Howarth, Mr Malcolm Buchanan Potter, Mr Liam Gavin Grant, Mr Michael Mintram, Mrs Elizabeth Faye Weston, Miss Margaret Bernice Headen, Mr John Donald Kerr Hammond, Mrs Christine Lesley Burt, Mr Martyn Douglas Smith, Mr Matthew Ryan Ulyatt
Income: £1,168,122 [2016]; £1,594,866 [2015]; £1,585,827 [2014]; £1,381,878 [2013]; £1,668,294 [2012]

Friends of Wiznitz Limited

Registered: 22 Apr 1968 *Volunteers:* 2
Activities: Education, training; prevention or relief of poverty; religious activities
Address: 8 Jessam Avenue, London, E5 9DU
Trustees: Heinrich Feldman, Mr Ephraim Gottesfeld, Shulom Feldman
Income: £2,225,149 [2017]; £2,749,964 [2016]; £1,741,642 [2015]; £1,517,178 [2014]; £836,640 [2013]

Friends of the Earth Trust

Registered: 6 Jan 1981 *Employees:* 119 *Volunteers:* 80
Tel: 020 7566 1609 *Website:* foe.co.uk
Activities: Environment, conservation, heritage; other charitable purposes
Address: Friends of the Earth, 139 Clapham Road, London, SW9 0HP
Trustees: Mr Chris Church, Mr Tony Burton, Mr William Swan, Ms Afsheen Kabir Rashid, Mr Matt Wright, Ms Frances Butler, Ms Anne Schiffer, Ms Kate Hand, Mrs Dorothy Kay Polley
Income: £9,126,746 [2017]; £9,172,767 [2016]; £9,359,113 [2015]; £10,204,463 [2014]; £8,929,023 [2013]

Frimley Health Charity

Registered: 4 Oct 1995 *Volunteers:* 10
Tel: 01276 526242 *Website:* fphcharity.org
Activities: The advancement of health or saving of lives
Address: Frimley Health NHS Foundation Trust, Portsmouth Road, Frimley, Camberley, Surrey, GU16 7UJ
Trustees: Frimley Health NHS Foundation Trust
Income: £1,910,000 [2017]; £1,027,000 [2016]; £2,061,000 [2015]; £709,000 [2014]; £599,000 [2013]

The Froebelian School (Horsforth) Limited

Registered: 20 Jun 1969 *Employees:* 60 *Volunteers:* 20
Tel: 0113 258 3047 *Website:* froebelian.co.uk
Activities: Education, training
Address: The Froebelian School, Clarence Road, Horsforth, Leeds, LS18 4LB
Trustees: Mr Andrew Nicholas Carter, Mr Ravi Naru, Mrs Susan Woodroofe, Mrs Rosemary Jane James, Mrs Katrina Paget, Mrs Judith Ann Doherty, Mr Richard Mann Taylor, Mrs Robyn Richmond LLB, Mrs Helen Forshaw, Mr Alec Jason Kendrick, Mrs Belinda Peacock, Mr Kenneth Robert Beaty
Income: £1,957,899 [2017]; £1,731,444 [2016]; £1,434,263 [2015]; £1,401,792 [2014]; £1,428,384 [2013]

The Frontiers Charitable Trust

Registered: 29 Oct 1997 *Employees:* 30 *Volunteers:* 334
Tel: 01323 521125 *Website:* kingschurch.eu
Activities: Education, training; prevention or relief of poverty; religious activities; amateur sport
Address: Kings Centre, Unit 27 Edison Road, Eastbourne, E Sussex, BN23 6PT
Trustees: Mr Andrew Martin Phillips, Mr Neil Barnett, Mr Richard John Butler, Mr Paul Jeffery, Mr Andrew Berry, Mrs Sandra Mary Wootton
Income: £1,201,098 [2017]; £951,332 [2016]; £1,067,196 [2015]; £1,433,030 [2014]; £975,336 [2013]

Frontiers

Registered: 3 Jul 1992 *Employees:* 8 *Volunteers:* 2
Tel: 0303 333 5051 *Website:* frontiers.org.uk
Activities: General charitable purposes; education, training; advancement of health or saving of lives; overseas aid, famine relief; religious activities
Address: Frontiers, P O Box 1445, High Wycombe, Bucks, HP12 9BU
Trustees: Ian Linton, Ms Ruth Bridger, Mr Daniel Aanderud, Mr Andrew Dimmock, Mr Philip Neil MacInnes, Mr Keith Elmitt
Income: £1,573,511 [2016]; £1,341,036 [2015]; £1,466,794 [2014]; £1,169,825 [2013]; £1,216,081 [2012]

The Frontline Organisation

Registered: 19 Aug 2015 *Employees:* 86 *Volunteers:* 3
Tel: 020 3892 9082 *Website:* thefrontline.org.uk
Activities: Education, training; advancement of health or saving of lives; prevention or relief of poverty; other charitable purposes
Address: 1 Rosebery Avenue, London, EC1R 4SR
Trustees: Mr Paul Fraser Dunning, Mr Andrew James Elvin, Mr Oliver Gayle, Mrs Sukriti Prova Sen, Ms Clare Chamberlain, Ms Hilary Camilla Cavendish, Mr Michael Clark, Mr James Barrington Huw Darley, Baroness Sally Morgan, Ms Zena Cooke, Charlotte Lintern, Mr Jacob Rosenzweig
Income: £11,650,000 [2017]; £9,164,000 [2016]

Fulham Football Club Foundation

Registered: 11 Oct 2005 *Employees:* 85 *Volunteers:* 25
Tel: 0870 442 5432 *Website:* fulhamfc.com
Activities: Education, training; advancement of health or saving of lives; disability; amateur sport; economic, community development, employment
Address: Fulham Football Club, Training Ground, Motspur Park, New Malden, Surrey, KT3 6PT
Trustees: Mrs Stella Fry, Darren Preston, Mr Alistair Julian Mackintosh, Mr Udo Onwere, Mr Thomas Noel Barry, Mr Craig Morris, Mr Lee Manning
Income: £1,961,055 [2017]; £2,035,111 [2016]; £1,815,410 [2015]; £1,739,630 [2014]; £1,679,335 [2013]

Fulham Palace Trust

Registered: 27 Jan 2011 *Employees:* 22 *Volunteers:* 235
Tel: 020 7610 7161 *Website:* fulhampalace.org
Activities: Arts, culture, heritage, science; environment, conservation, heritage
Address: Fulham Palace Trust, Fulham Palace, Bishop's Avenue, London, SW6 6EA
Trustees: Mr Gordon Edington CBE, The Rev Joe Hawes, Mr Phil Emery, Ms Alison Lightbown, Mr Kevin Rogers, John King, Mariana Spater, Mr Thomas Hackett, Ms Caroline Needham, Ms Victoria Quinlan, Ms Fiona Crumley
Income: £1,873,219 [2017]; £1,542,055 [2016]; £1,316,654 [2015]; £1,546,642 [2014]; £1,167,871 [2013]

Fulmer Education Trust

Registered: 5 Nov 1997 *Employees:* 28 *Volunteers:* 100
Tel: 020 8571 8612
Activities: Education, training
Address: Sefton Park School, School Lane, Stoke Poges, Slough, SL2 4QA
Trustees: Barry Robertson, Mr Warren Burgess, Mr Luke Bedford, Mr Daniel Gillmore, Craig Gulley, Tristan Parsons, Mr Adrian Batts
Income: £1,944,894 [2016]; £1,847,045 [2015]; £1,501,790 [2014]; £1,473,258 [2013]; £1,772,496 [2012]

Fundacao Focus Assistencia Humanitaria Europa
Registered: 2 Apr 1996 *Employees:* 173 *Volunteers:* 27
Tel: 020 7590 5499 *Website:* akdn.org
Activities: General charitable purposes; prevention or relief of poverty
Address: The Ismaili Centre, 1 Cromwell Gardens, London, SW7 2SL
Trustees: Mr Naushad Jivraj, Mrs Sahinaz Nasser, Miss Raisa Hemani, Mr Faiz Mitha, Dr Martin Hermann Bartels, Mr Mounir Franck Nourmamode, Mr Sherali Lakhani, Dr Shahin Boghani, Mr Munir Karmali Ahmad
Income: £4,056,782 [2016]; £4,186,162 [2015]; £3,263,733 [2014]; £4,534,969 [2013]; £3,335,177 [2012]

Funding Fish
Registered: 30 Sep 2015 *Employees:* 1
Website: fundingfish.eu
Activities: Environment, conservation, heritage
Address: Byeways, New Road, Bathford, Somerset, BA1 7TR
Trustees: Dr Kristian Parker, Mr Aaron McLoughlin, Ms Stephanie Stares
Income: £1,132,161 [2016]

Furniture Resource Centre Limited
Registered: 17 Nov 1988 *Employees:* 78 *Volunteers:* 71
Tel: 0151 702 0572 *Website:* frcgroup.co.uk
Activities: General charitable purposes; education, training; prevention or relief of poverty; environment, conservation, heritage; economic, community development, employment
Address: Units 12-14 Atlantic Way, Brunswick Business Park, Liverpool, L3 4BE
Trustees: Mr Christopher John Watson, Mrs Lesley Dixon, Mr Jeremy Nicholls, Mr Nigel Peter Wilson, Mr Erik Bichard, Mr Jeff Vernon, Dr John Hines
Income: £5,937,722 [2017]; £6,494,417 [2016]; £7,084,207 [2015]; £5,353,301 [2014]; £3,147,929 [2013]

Fusion Housing Kirklees Ltd
Registered: 2 Apr 2013 *Employees:* 91 *Volunteers:* 2
Tel: 01484 425522 *Website:* fusionhousing.org.uk
Activities: General charitable purposes; education, training; prevention or relief of poverty; accommodation, housing; economic, community development, employment; other charitable purposes
Address: Fusion Housing, 11-17 Market Street, Huddersfield, W Yorks, HD1 2EH
Trustees: Mr Robert Andrew Riley, Mrs Carole Pattinson, Mr Dennis Hullock, Mr Clifford Joseph Lorenzelli, Mr Eric Cannell, Mr Michael Brooke Robinson, Mrs Moira Vangrove, Mr Daniel Patrick Moriarty, Mr Simon David Smith, Mr Niel Stewart
Income: £3,504,129 [2017]; £3,142,722 [2016]; £2,538,717 [2015]; £2,377,094 [2014]

Fusion Lifestyle
Registered: 20 Jan 2005 *Employees:* 3,468
Tel: 020 7740 7500 *Website:* fusion-lifestyle.com
Activities: Amateur sport; recreation
Address: Fusion Lifestyle, 4 Bickels Yard, 151-153 Bermondsey Street, London, SE1 3HA
Trustees: Mr Michael Nelson, Mr Stephen David Boughton, Ms Lorraine Zuleta, Mr Scot Parkhurst, Ms Charlotte Mary Cole, Mrs Bianca Ioannides
Income: £85,927,000 [2016]; £83,568,000 [2015]; £76,227,000 [2014]; £68,474,000 [2013]; £55,927,138 [2012]

Future First Alumni Limited
Registered: 23 Apr 2010 *Employees:* 30 *Volunteers:* 7,050
Website: futurefirst.org.uk
Activities: General charitable purposes; education, training
Address: Future First, First Floor, 66 Hammersmith Road, London, W14 8UD
Trustees: Lindsey McMurray, Robin Tombs, Ms Christine Gilbert, Michael Ter-Berg, Sally Nelson, Deji Davies
Income: £1,522,595 [2017]; £1,538,983 [2016]; £879,658 [2015]; £790,231 [2014]; £415,960 [2013]

Future Leaders Charitable Trust Limited
Registered: 15 Nov 2006 *Employees:* 81
Tel: 020 3828 2466 *Website:* ambitionschoolleadership.org.uk
Activities: General charitable purposes; education, training
Address: 65 Kingsway, London, WC2B 6TD
Trustees: Mr Jonathan Robert Owen, Baroness Sally Morgan, Mr Andrew Day, Mr Matthew Jones, Mr Brett Wigdortz, Mrs Susan Margaret Williamson, Amanda Timberg
Income: £7,824,496 [2016]; £8,047,955 [2015]; £5,773,994 [2014]; £5,817,754 [2013]; £6,873,036 [2012]

Futures Homescape Limited
Registered: 6 Sep 2004 *Employees:* 129 *Volunteers:* 11
Tel: 0845 094 8311 *Website:* futureshomescape.co.uk
Activities: Disability; prevention or relief of poverty; accommodation, housing; economic, community development, employment
Address: Amber Valley Housing, Asher House, Asher Lane Business Park, Asher Lane, Ripley, Derbys, DE5 3SW
Trustees: Mr Raymond Harding, David Leathley, Mrs Sheila Hyde, Tony Taylor, Mr Michael William Stevenson, Mr David Gary Brooks, Mr Stephen Matthew Hale, Philip Tooley, Ms Lindsey Claire Williams, Ms Sophia Mary Fitzhugh, Mr Timothy Ian Slater
Income: £30,748,000 [2017]; £29,866,000 [2016]; £29,255,000 [2015]; £27,377,000 [2014]; £25,709,000 [2013]

Futures Homeway Limited
Registered: 21 Sep 2007 *Employees:* 47 *Volunteers:* 11
Tel: 0845 094 8312 *Website:* futureshg.co.uk
Activities: Disability; prevention or relief of poverty; accommodation, housing; economic, community development, employment
Address: Daventry & District Housing Ltd, Asher House, Asher Lane Business Park, Ripley, Derbys, DE5 3SW
Trustees: Mr Raymond Harding, Sophie Fitzhugh, Mr Philip John Tooley, Tony Taylor, Mr Michael William Stevenson, Mr Timothy Ian Brooks, Steve Hale, David Leathley, Ms Lindsey Claire Williams, Mrs Sheila Ann Hyde, Mr David Gary Brooks
Income: £17,701,000 [2017]; £16,442,000 [2016]; £15,768,000 [2015]; £15,309,000 [2014]; £14,370,000 [2013]

Fylde Coast YMCA
Registered: 8 Mar 1999 *Employees:* 579 *Volunteers:* 60
Tel: 01253 893928 *Website:* fyldecoastymca.org
Activities: General charitable purposes; education, training; prevention or relief of poverty; accommodation, housing; arts, culture, heritage, science; amateur sport; economic, community development, employment; other charitable purposes
Address: YMCA, St Albans Road, Lytham St Annes, Lancs, FY8 1XD
Trustees: Mr Ian Paterson, Mrs Rona Blanchard, Mr Anthony Keenan, Mr Andrew Haworth, Mr Brian Nicholson, Mr Russell Dawson, Mr Richard Nulty
Income: £9,551,216 [2017]; £9,106,277 [2016]; £8,835,842 [2015]; £7,568,302 [2014]; £8,454,866 [2013]

Fylde Community Link Limited
Registered: 16 Mar 1995 *Employees:* 174
Tel: 01253 795648 *Website:* fyldecommunitylink.co.uk
Activities: Disability; accommodation, housing
Address: 19 Church Road, Lytham, Lytham St Annes, Lancs, FY8 5LH
Trustees: Mr Barry W Lees, Mr Michael J Grayston, Mr Kenneth Harries, Dave Melling, Barbara Crawford, Miss Lorraine Helene Lipman, Mrs Anne T Grayston, Mr W Reginald Atkins, Mr Jim Watt, Terry Wright, Miss Katharine Mary Wykes
Income: £4,357,294 [2017]; £3,886,824 [2016]; £3,582,382 [2015]; £3,563,956 [2014]; £3,546,930 [2013]

Fyling Hall School Trust Limited
Registered: 17 Aug 1978 *Employees:* 49
Tel: 01947 880353 *Website:* fylinghall.org
Activities: Education, training
Address: 36 The Green, Norton, Stockton on Tees, Cleveland, TS20 1DX
Trustees: Miss Brenda Easton, Mr Philip Burley, Mrs Helen Fox, Mrs Amy Rebecca Arnold, Ms Caroline Spencer, Mr Kenneth David James, Mr Michael Swales, Mr Michael Bayes, Mr John Robert Jeakins, Ms Rebecca Margaret Mansoor, Mrs Jacqueline Golland
Income: £1,719,000 [2017]; £1,746,000 [2016]; £1,744,000 [2015]; £2,008,000 [2014]; £2,014,000 [2013]

Fynvola Foundation
Registered: 14 Feb 2008 *Employees:* 44 *Volunteers:* 6
Tel: 01795 537592 *Website:* fynvola.org.uk
Activities: The advancement of health or saving of lives; disability; economic, community development, employment; other charitable purposes
Address: Lady Dane Farmhouse, Love Lane, Faversham, Kent, ME13 8BJ
Trustees: Mr T Mogridge, Mrs Sue Maddison, Mr Trevor Aldrich, Mrs Doreen Shaw, Mr Martin Paul Godden, Mr Michael Paul Taylor, Mrs Hermione Jennifer Gurney, Mr Nicholas O'Shea, Michael Moore, Mr Peter George Cox, Louise Kirsch-Mills
Income: £1,203,470 [2016]; £1,148,156 [2015]; £1,129,304 [2014]; £956,089 [2013]; £658,169 [2012]

GFA World
Registered: 7 Oct 1997 *Employees:* 4 *Volunteers:* 10
Tel: 0161 946 9484 *Website:* gfauk.org
Activities: Education, training; prevention or relief of poverty; overseas aid, famine relief; religious activities; human rights, religious or racial harmony, equality or diversity
Address: Gospel for Asia, 6 Harper Road, Sharston Industrial Area, Manchester, M22 4RG
Trustees: Mr Kadappilaril Yohannan Punnose, Mr Daniel Punnose, Rev Paul Robert Blackham, Mr Christopher Geoffrey Cobbold, Rev Brian Kirik, Mr Paul Jonathan Thomson, Rev Stephen Nichols
Income: £1,924,616 [2017]; £2,006,399 [2015]; £1,931,252 [2014]; £1,669,054 [2013]; £1,776,746 [2012]

GFS Community Enterprise
Registered: 3 Oct 2016
Tel: 0113 242 2426 *Website:* theoldfirestationgipton.org.uk
Activities: General charitable purposes; education, training; advancement of health or saving of lives; disability; prevention or relief of poverty; economic, community development, employment; recreation
Address: 51A St Pauls Street, Leeds, LS1 2TE
Trustees: Helen Thomson, Mr Jonathan Philip Joseph Wilson, Mr David Aubrey Jackson, Jonathan Morgan, Mr Michael Anthony Jackson
Income: £1,082,000 [2017]

GIA England
Registered: 9 Dec 2003 *Employees:* 10
Tel: 020 7813 4321 *Website:* gia.edu
Activities: Education, training
Address: GIA, 104 Great Russell Street, London, WC1B 3LA
Trustees: Mr Thomas Merril Moses, Mrs Beverly Hori Uydea, Mr David Tearle, Ms Susan Jacques
Income: £1,264,324 [2017]; £974,350 [2016]; £1,025,888 [2015]; £1,035,049 [2014]; £1,079,235 [2013]

GMDN Agency
Registered: 31 Oct 2013 *Employees:* 10
Tel: 01235 799759 *Website:* gmdnagency.org
Activities: The advancement of health or saving of lives
Address: Park House, Milton Park, Milton, Abingdon, Oxon, OX14 4RS
Trustees: Liz Krell, Mark Wasmuth, John Wilkinson, Janet Trunzo, Christina Mei Wen Tong
Income: £1,359,451 [2017]; £1,006,882 [2016]; £1,010,045 [2015]

Gables Farm Dogs and Cats Home
Registered: 15 Dec 2008 *Employees:* 26 *Volunteers:* 65
Tel: 01752 331602 *Website:* gablesfarm.org.uk
Activities: Animals
Address: Gables Farm Dogs & Cats Home, 204 Merafield Road, Plymouth, PL7 1UQ
Trustees: Mr John Carter, Mrs Christine Holland, Mr Anthony Harris, Mr Scott James Horner, Mr Nick Head, Mr Alan Richard Anstey, Mr Bernard Taylor
Income: £1,099,218 [2016]; £596,219 [2015]; £765,947 [2014]; £940,514 [2013]; £703,941 [2012]

Gabrieli
Registered: 10 May 2006 *Employees:* 3 *Volunteers:* 1
Tel: 020 7613 4404 *Website:* gabrieli.com
Activities: Education, training; arts, culture, heritage, science
Address: Wright & Co, 57 High Street, London, SE25 6EF
Trustees: Mr Paul Dominic McCreesh, Mr Michael Steven Abrahams, Mr Roger Le Tissier, Mr Alan Gemes, Mr Steve Allen, Ms Susie York Skinner, Ms Louise Soden
Income: £1,014,559 [2017]; £572,919 [2016]; £379,971 [2015]; £493,634 [2014]; £774,224 [2013]

Gaddum Centre
Registered: 30 Jan 1978 *Employees:* 66 *Volunteers:* 115
Tel: 0161 834 6069 *Website:* gaddumcentre.co.uk
Activities: General charitable purposes; education, training; advancement of health or saving of lives; disability; prevention or relief of poverty
Address: Gaddum Centre, Gaddum House, 6 Great Jackson Street, Manchester, M15 4AX
Trustees: Mr David Carmichael, Mr Mike Dyble, Mr David Ian Cockill, Dr Celia Hynes, Mr Don Bancroft FCA, Mr Roy Harding, Miss Jennifer Rachel Platt, Mrs Rowena Birch
Income: £1,928,047 [2017]; £1,774,116 [2016]; £1,393,236 [2015]; £1,467,647 [2014]; £1,470,607 [2013]

Gads Hill School
Registered: 29 Mar 1990 *Employees:* 96 *Volunteers:* 3
Tel: 01474 822366 *Website:* gadshill.org
Activities: Education, training
Address: Gads Hill House School, Gads Hill Place, Gravesend Road, Higham, Rochester, Kent, ME3 7PA
Trustees: Mr David George Craggs BSc MA FCollP FRSA, Mr John Myatt, Ms Karen White, Mr Tony Hughes, Mrs Annette Eggleton, Mr Oliver Basi, Mrs Rosnah Hassell, Miss Nicola Barker, Mr Stephen Thomas Martin, Mrs Kirsty Hillocks, Mrs Marion Dickens, Mr Graham Noble, Mr Chris Whittington, Rev Paul Kerr, Mr Michael Charles Adams, Dr Paul Hastwell, Mrs Sarah Bates
Income: £4,038,938 [2016]; £4,145,737 [2015]; £4,278,648 [2014]; £4,225,587 [2013]

The Galilee Foundation
Registered: 26 Apr 2007 *Employees:* 1
Tel: 020 7993 8355 *Website:* galileefoundation.org.uk
Activities: Education, training; prevention or relief of poverty; arts, culture, heritage, science
Address: The Old Music Hall, 106-108 Cowley Road, Oxford, OX4 1JE
Trustees: Mrs Sawsan Asfari, Mrs Leila Garadaghi, Mr Khalil Jahshan, Mr Abdulrahman Elshayyal, Dr Marwan Bishara, Mr Yousef Salah Bazian, Mr Eyad Mahameed
Income: £1,595,641 [2017]; £763,250 [2016]; £922,581 [2015]; £833,262 [2014]; £810,596 [2013]

Galloway's Society for the Blind
Registered: 7 Aug 1963 *Employees:* 43 *Volunteers:* 350
Tel: 01772 744148 *Website:* galloways.org.uk
Activities: Education, training; advancement of health or saving of lives; disability; accommodation, housing; amateur sport
Address: Howick House, Howick Park Avenue, Penwortham, Preston, Lancs, PR1 0LS
Trustees: Mr John Ward, Mr Simon Kenyon Booth, Mr Robert Jon Mills, Mrs Carole Holmes, Mr Anthony Kimpton, Mrs Dorothy Elizabeth Crean, Mr John Bretherton, Mr Peter Robert Metcalf MBE FCA DChA, Mr Peter Howard
Income: £1,213,741 [2017]; £1,225,945 [2016]; £906,164 [2015]; £896,991 [2014]; £864,709 [2013]

GamCare
Registered: 7 Jan 1997 *Employees:* 33 *Volunteers:* 6
Tel: 020 7801 7000 *Website:* gamcare.org.uk
Activities: Education, training; advancement of health or saving of lives
Address: GamCare, CAN Mezzanine, 49-51 East Road, London, N1 6AH
Trustees: Dr Emily Finch, Mr Simon Thomas, Mr John Brackenbury, Mr Jon Grant, Sir Ian Prosser, Ms Jill Britton, The Lord Sharman, John Hagan, Mr Dominic Harrison, Margot Daly, Mrs Anita Gundecha
Income: £4,541,970 [2017]; £4,048,608 [2016]; £3,992,545 [2015]; £3,297,425 [2014]; £3,082,863 [2013]

GambleAware
Registered: 24 Sep 2002 *Employees:* 7
Tel: 020 7287 1994 *Website:* about.gambleaware.org
Activities: Education, training; other charitable purposes
Address: 7 Henrietta Street, London, WC2E 8PS
Trustees: Mr Alan Jamieson, Mr Christopher Richard Pond, Patrick Sturgis, Mrs Brigid Simmonds, Miss Michelle Highman, Professor Anthony Stephen Kessel, Ms Saffron Cordery, Ms Annette Dale-Perera, Professor Sian Meryl Griffiths, Mr Henry Birch, Ms Kathryn Lampard
Income: £8,621,499 [2017]; £7,632,371 [2016]; £6,543,925 [2015]; £6,277,934 [2014]; £5,696,142 [2013]

The Game and Wildlife Conservation Trust
Registered: 11 Nov 2005 *Employees:* 127 *Volunteers:* 350
Tel: 01425 652381 *Website:* gwct.org.uk
Activities: Education, training; arts, culture, heritage, science; animals; environment, conservation, heritage
Address: Game & Wildlife Conservation Trust, Burgate Manor, Fordingbridge, Hants, SP6 1EF
Trustees: Mr Hugh Richard Oliver-Bellasis FRAgS, Mrs Rebecca Shelley, Dr Anthony John Hamilton, Mr James Duckworth-Chad, The Marquess of Downshire, Mr John Shields, Mr Andrew Salvesen, Mr Richard Henry Benyon, Mr Jonathan Nigel Wildgoose, Miss Emma Maude Weir, Mr Stephen Peter Morant, The Hon Philip Douglas Paul Astor, Mr Ian Sinclair Coghill BSc, Mr Richard Bronks, Mr David Mayhew, The Rt Hom James Paice MP, Mr David Flux, His Grace The Duke of Norfolk, Sir Max Hastings, Mr Simon Chantler, Mr David Nicholas Owen Williams OBE
Income: £7,662,798 [2016]; £7,191,978 [2015]; £7,465,015 [2014]; £7,090,465 [2013]; £6,717,301 [2012]

Gard'ner Memorial Limited
Registered: 23 Jul 1963 *Employees:* 146
Tel: 01252 792303 *Website:* morehouseschool.com
Activities: Education, training
Address: More House School, Moons Hill, Frensham, Farnham, Surrey, GU10 3AP
Trustees: Mr William Anthony Woellwarth, Mr John Bertram Stares, Dr Anthony Britten Gardner, Mr John Manning-Smith, Mr Sean Anthony Collins MA FCA, Mr Patrick Andrew Wilson, Mrs Pamela Edworthy, Mr Gary Michael Hay
Income: £8,056,193 [2017]; £7,761,342 [2016]; £7,400,565 [2015]; £7,328,084 [2014]; £7,176,545 [2013]

Garden Bridge Trust
Registered: 8 Jan 2014 *Employees:* 9
Tel: 020 7783 3537 *Website:* gardenbridge.london
Activities: General charitable purposes; education, training; advancement of health or saving of lives; arts, culture, heritage, science; environment, conservation, heritage; economic, community development, employment; recreation
Address: Bircham Dyson Bell, 50 Broadway, London, SW1H 0BL
Trustees: Paul Dring Morrell, Mervyn Davies, Mr Robert Suss, John Robert Heaps, Lucy Dimes, Mr Alastair Subba Row, Mr Andrew Simon Lowenthal, Roland Rudd, Miss Joanna Lamond Lumley, Julie May Carlyle, Stephen Fitzgerald
Income: £39,196,316 [2016]; £12,653,675 [2014]

The Garden Museum

Registered: 28 Aug 2001 *Employees:* 7 *Volunteers:* 20
Tel: 020 7401 8865 *Website:* gardenmuseum.org.uk
Activities: General charitable purposes; education, training; arts, culture, heritage, science; amateur sport; environment, conservation, heritage
Address: The Garden Museum, 5 Lambeth Palace Road, London, SE1 7LB
Trustees: Lady Tania Compton, Mr Colin Campbell-Preston, Mr Alan Titchmarsh MBE VMH DL, Lady Caroline Egremont, Mr Mark Fane, Marchioness of Normanby, Mr Barry Newton, Mrs Emma Keswick, Mr Peter Lewis-Crown, The Viscountess Claudia Rothermere, Mr Thomas Stuart-Smith, Lady Jill Riblat, Mr Bryan Sanderson CBE
Income: £3,367,149 [2017]; £2,386,159 [2016]; £1,803,292 [2015]; £1,011,131 [2014]; £1,185,493 [2013]

The Garden Tomb (Jerusalem) Association

Registered: 10 Oct 2011 *Employees:* 17 *Volunteers:* 27
Website: gardentomb.org
Activities: General charitable purposes; education, training; religious activities; other charitable purposes
Address: The Garden Tomb, P O Box 19462, Jerusalem, Israel 91193
Trustees: Mr Peter Houston, Rev Paul Weaver, Mr Paul Mayo, Steven King, Mrs Fiona Saunderson, Alison Ann Laing
Income: £1,722,033 [2016]; £1,389,229 [2015]; £1,382,487 [2014]; £1,422,504 [2013]

Gardeners' Royal Benevolent Society

Registered: 31 Dec 2013 *Employees:* 46 *Volunteers:* 377
Tel: 01372 384032 *Website:* perennial.org.uk
Activities: General charitable purposes; education, training; disability; prevention or relief of poverty; accommodation, housing; environment, conservation, heritage
Address: Perennial, 115-117 Kingston Road, Leatherhead, Surrey, KT22 7SU
Trustees: Dr Heather Barrett-Mold, Mr James Robinson, Ms Carol Paris, Ms Carole Baxter, Mrs Emma Tinker, Ms Cindy Peck, Mr Dougal Philip, Mr Neville Stein, Mr Mark Lane, Mr Steven Palmer, Mrs Maureen Hart
Income: £4,470,141 [2016]; £4,061,191 [2015]; £3,530,121 [2014]

Gardens of Peace Muslim Cemetery

Registered: 17 Jul 2013 *Employees:* 13 *Volunteers:* 10
Tel: 020 8554 5937 *Website:* gardens-of-peace.org.uk
Activities: Religious activities
Address: 77 Vaughan Gardens, Ilford, Essex, IG1 3PB
Trustees: Mr Farouk Ismail, Mr Mehboob Patel, Mr Maqbul Mubeen, Mr Gulam Nadat
Income: £3,197,904 [2016]; £2,660,707 [2015]; £4,446,648 [2014]

Gardners Lane and Oakwood Federation

Registered: 13 Jan 2014 *Employees:* 85 *Volunteers:* 26
Tel: 01242 515761
Activities: Education, training; recreation
Address: Gardners Lane Childrens Centre, Gardners Lane, Cheltenham, Glos, GL51 9JW
Trustees: Ms Claire Price, Mr Charles Welsh, Mrs Tracy Brown, Mr Michael Andrew North, Mr Cordell Ray, Mrs Julie Hunt
Income: £2,689,134 [2017]; £2,789,867 [2016]; £2,697,000 [2015]

Garfield Weston Foundation

Registered: 6 May 1964
Tel: 020 7399 6565 *Website:* garfieldweston.org
Activities: General charitable purposes
Address: Weston Centre, 10 Grosvenor Street, London, W1K 4QY
Trustees: Jana Khayat, Kate Hobhouse, Galen W G Weston, Sophia Mason, Guy H Weston, Camilla Dalglish, Eliza L Mitchell, George G Weston, Melissa Murdoch
Income: £65,939,000 [2017]; £62,150,000 [2016]; £56,611,000 [2015]; £51,790,000 [2014]; £44,249,000 [2013]

Garsington Opera Limited

Registered: 28 May 1991 *Employees:* 11 *Volunteers:* 40
Tel: 01865 368201 *Website:* garsingtonopera.org
Activities: Education, training; arts, culture, heritage, science
Address: The Old Garage, The Green, Great Milton, Oxford, OX44 7NP
Trustees: Mr John Duncan Drysdale, Mr David Suratgar, Mr Iain Francis MacKinnon, Mr Bernard Taylor, Ms Miranda Curtis, Mr Neil Gerald Alexander King, Miss Catherine Ingrams, Professor Jonathan Freeman-Attwood, Clementine Medina Marks
Income: £5,497,908 [2016]; £4,718,465 [2015]; £4,529,453 [2014]; £3,620,688 [2013]; £3,467,358 [2012]

The Garwood Foundation

Registered: 22 Feb 1977 *Employees:* 99 *Volunteers:* 20
Tel: 020 8681 0460 *Website:* garwoodfoundation.org.uk
Activities: Education, training; advancement of health or saving of lives; disability
Address: 1A Melville Avenue, South Croydon, Surrey, CR2 7HZ
Trustees: Mr John Newton, Mrs Jackie Sanders, Mr Richard Jeffries, Miss Elizabeth Rosemary Mitchell Thomas, Mr Robin Adams, Mr Frank Newton, Mr Ian Trumper, Miss Charlotte Anne Louise Cooper
Income: £2,617,780 [2017]; £2,596,678 [2016]; £2,408,159 [2015]; £2,457,783 [2014]; £2,517,065 [2013]

Gatehouse Educational Trust Limited

Registered: 13 May 1981 *Employees:* 66
Tel: 020 8709 5222 *Website:* gatehouseschool.co.uk
Activities: Education, training
Address: Gatehouse Educational Trust, Gatehouse School, Sewardstone Road, London, E2 9JG
Trustees: Rehana Arnold, Sam Everington, Mr Roger Newhall, Mrs Donna Graham, Miss Joanna Scott, Penny Goodman, Mrs Belinda Canham, Mr Ian Lyon Duncan, Mrs Carol Clark, Miss Jennifer Beck
Income: £4,354,600 [2017]; £3,936,532 [2016]; £3,665,346 [2015]; £3,602,594 [2014]; £3,156,926 [2013]

Gateshead Crossroads Caring for Carers

Registered: 23 Dec 1996 *Employees:* 59 *Volunteers:* 19
Website: carerstrusttw.org.uk
Activities: The advancement of health or saving of lives; disability; other charitable purposes
Address: Gateshead Crossroads Caring For Carers, The Old School, Smailes Lane, Highfield, Rowlands Gill, Tyne & Wear, NE39 2DB
Trustees: Geoff Eggleston, Allan Smith, Sue Pickering, Mrs Helen Briggs, Michael O'Hare, Garry Pointer, Vicki Taylor, Averil Hedley
Income: £1,510,859 [2017]; £1,469,449 [2016]; £1,450,648 [2015]; £1,444,549 [2014]; £1,388,365 [2013]

The Gateshead Jewish Nursery
Registered: 23 Mar 1981 *Employees:* 82
Tel: 0191 478 3723
Activities: Education, training; disability
Address: Gateshead Jewish Nursery School, Alexandra Road, Gateshead, Tyne & Wear, NE8 1RB
Trustees: Mrs Agnes Katz, Mrs R Hirsch
Income: £1,260,028 [2017]; £1,165,674 [2016]; £996,264 [2015]; £912,481 [2014]; £708,092 [2013]

Gateshead Jewish Primary School
Registered: 17 Nov 1965 *Employees:* 135
Tel: 0191 477 2154
Activities: Education, training
Address: Gateshead Jewish Primary School, 18-22 Gladstone Terrace, Gateshead, Tyne & Wear, NE8 4EA
Trustees: Dr Sidney Mortimer Rutenberg, Mr Yehoshua Grossberger
Income: £1,417,311 [2015]; £1,267,729 [2014]; £1,089,181 [2013]

Gateshead Talmudical College
Registered: 30 Jan 1967 *Employees:* 48
Tel: 0191 477 2616
Activities: Education, training
Address: Gateshead Talmudical College, 88 Windermere Street West, Gateshead, Tyne & Wear, NE8 1UB
Trustees: Rabbi A Gurwicz, Rabbi M Salomon, Rabbi C O Gurwicz
Income: £2,262,154 [2017]; £2,313,810 [2016]; £2,073,634 [2015]; £1,998,343 [2014]; £1,766,474 [2013]

Gateway Qualifications Limited
Registered: 18 May 2006 *Employees:* 29
Website: gatewayqualifications.org.uk
Activities: Education, training
Address: 3 Tollgate Business Park, Tollgate West, Stanway, Colchester, Essex, CO3 8AB
Trustees: Ms Anne Thompson, Mr Philip Thirkettle, Mr Richard Stock, Mrs Karen Spencer, Mr Graham Razey, Ms Melanie Jayne Nicholson, Mrs Alison Andreas, Ms Elizabeth Laycock, Mr Miles Norman Cole, Ms Lynsi Hayward-Smith, Mr Patrick Lloyd Edwards, Ms Maxine Smith, Mrs Alison Davies
Income: £2,128,587 [2017]; £2,072,427 [2016]; £2,004,724 [2015]; £1,944,655 [2014]; £2,175,768 [2013]

Gateways Educational Trust Limited
Registered: 9 Nov 1961 *Employees:* 70
Tel: 0113 288 6345 *Website:* gatewaysschool.co.uk
Activities: Education, training
Address: Gateways School, Harewood, Leeds, LS17 9LE
Trustees: Mrs Lillian Croston, Mr Roger Marsh BSc FCA MSPI, Doctor Rosemary Helen Taylor BEd MA PhD, The Rev Canon Anthony Francis Bundock, Mr Robert Barr, Mr Martin Shaw LLB, Professor Diane Shorrocks-Taylor BA MA PhD, Mr Richard Michael Webster, Professor David Hogg, Mr Jonathan Graham
Income: £3,729,605 [2017]; £3,716,020 [2016]; £3,536,559 [2015]; £3,477,550 [2014]; £3,533,354 [2013]

Gatsby Africa
Registered: 14 Jul 2016 *Employees:* 61
Tel: 020 7410 0330
Activities: The prevention or relief of poverty
Address: Sainsbury Family Charitable Trusts, 5 Wilton Road, London, SW1V 1AP
Trustees: Miss Judith Susan Portrait, Mr Joseph Christopher Burns
Income: £9,819,000 [2017]

The Gatsby Charitable Foundation
Registered: 5 Apr 1967 *Employees:* 2,319
Tel: 020 7410 0330 *Website:* gatsby.org.uk
Activities: General charitable purposes; education, training; advancement of health or saving of lives; disability; overseas aid, famine relief; arts, culture, heritage, science; economic, community development, employment
Address: The Peak, 5 Wilton Road, London, SW1V 1AP
Trustees: Miss Judith Susan Portrait, Mr Joseph Christopher Burns, Sir Andrew Thomas Cahn KCMG
Income: £69,941,000 [2017]; £56,733,000 [2016]; £76,155,000 [2015]; £64,065,000 [2014]; £15,357,000 [2013]

Gatsby Technical Education Projects
Registered: 20 Feb 1997 *Employees:* 12
Tel: 020 7410 0330 *Website:* gtep.co.uk
Activities: Education, training
Address: Sainsbury Family Charitable Trusts, The Peak, 5 Wilton Road, London, SW1V 1AP
Trustees: Miss Judith Susan Portrait, Mr Joseph Christopher Burns
Income: £1,533,039 [2017]; £1,244,398 [2016]; £1,495,453 [2015]; £1,422,290 [2014]; £1,334,423 [2013]

The Gaudio Family Foundation (UK) Limited
Registered: 3 Jun 2014
Tel: 020 7597 6427
Activities: General charitable purposes
Address: Withers Ltd, 16 Old Bailey, London, EC4M 7EG
Trustees: Mr Alfred Cavallaro, Mr Julius Gaudio, Mrs Belma Gaudio
Income: £4,162,442 [2016]; £5,303,852 [2015]

Gayhurst School Trust
Registered: 18 Mar 1988 *Employees:* 70 *Volunteers:* 13
Tel: 01753 882690 *Website:* gayhurstschool.co.uk
Activities: Education, training
Address: Gayhurst School, Bull Lane, Chalfont St Peter, Gerrards Cross, Bucks, SL9 8RJ
Trustees: Mrs Anne Hatton, Mr Howard Machin, Mr Richard Thompson, Mrs Sally Porter, Mr Alexander MacPhee, Mrs Frances Cunningham, Mrs Caroline Shorten Conn, Mr Charles Pugh, Mrs Caroline Robson, Mrs Angela Dusek
Income: £4,534,013 [2017]; £4,366,071 [2016]; £4,277,150 [2015]; £3,914,128 [2014]; £3,564,249 [2013]

Gedling Homes
Registered: 31 Oct 2008 *Employees:* 91
Tel: 0161 331 2000 *Website:* gedlinghomes.co.uk
Activities: General charitable purposes; prevention or relief of poverty; accommodation, housing
Address: Jigsaw Homes Group Limited, 249 Cavendish Street, Ashton under Lyne, Lancs, OL6 7AT
Trustees: Melvin Kenyon, Tim Ryan, Mrs Hilary Roberts, Mr John Clarke, Ms Michelle Rudkin, Mrs Emma Wilson
Income: £15,556,000 [2017]; £15,834,000 [2016]; £15,329,000 [2015]; £17,123,000 [2014]; £16,320,000 [2013]

The Geffrye Museum Trust
Registered: 13 Mar 1990 *Employees:* 44 *Volunteers:* 140
Tel: 020 7739 9893 *Website:* geffrye-museum.org.uk
Activities: Education, training; arts, culture, heritage, science; environment, conservation, heritage
Address: 136 Kingsland Road, London, E2 8EA
Trustees: Mr John Tomlins, Ms Marilyn Scott, Mr Douglas Gilmore, Mr Jeremy Edge, Mr Jeremy Newton, Ms Alexandra Robson, Mr Jonathan Newby, Ms Clare Gough, Ms Edwina Sassoon, Prof Abigail Williams, Dr Samir Shah, Mr Bernard Donaghue, Ms Cynthia Polemis, Mr John Forrester
Income: £2,727,653 [2017]; £2,649,833 [2016]; £2,629,357 [2015]; £2,746,939 [2014]; £2,958,535 [2013]

Gellideg Foundation Community Association
Registered: 14 Jul 2005 *Employees:* 25 *Volunteers:* 25
Tel: 01685 383929 *Website:* gellideg.net
Activities: General charitable purposes; education, training; advancement of health or saving of lives; prevention or relief of poverty; amateur sport; environment, conservation, heritage; economic, community development, employment
Address: 1-2, Heol Parc-y-Lan, Gellideg Estate, Merthyr Tydfil, CF48 1HB
Trustees: Mrs Maria Owen, Mrs Sharon Northall, Mr Dean Jenkins, Miss Anne-Marie Howe
Income: £3,674,622 [2017]; £932,368 [2016]; £1,257,163 [2015]; £972,006 [2014]; £300,820 [2013]

Gemach Ltd
Registered: 21 Aug 2003
Tel: 020 8202 2277
Activities: General charitable purposes; education, training; prevention or relief of poverty; religious activities
Address: 18 Lodge Road, London, NW4 4EF
Trustees: Mr Leib Levison, Mr Yitzchok Zvi Zeidel Levison, Mrs Yael Levison
Income: £1,830,307 [2017]; £1,142,535 [2016]; £1,426,389 [2015]; £964,100 [2014]; £829,208 [2013]

The Gemmological Association and Gem Testing Laboratory of Great Britain
Registered: 19 May 2005 *Employees:* 24
Tel: 020 7404 3334 *Website:* gem-a.com
Activities: Education, training; arts, culture, heritage, science
Address: 21 Ely Place, London, EC1N 6TD
Trustees: Mr Nigel Israel, Ms Kerry Honor Gregory, Dr John Mullen Ogden, Ms Kathryn Leigh Bonnano Patrizzi, Mr Phillip Sadler, Mr Paul F Greer, Ms Justine Linda Cardmody, Mr Christopher Patrick Smith, Ms Joanna Hardy
Income: £3,479,762 [2016]; £3,297,831 [2015]; £2,924,634 [2014]; £2,423,059 [2013]; £2,196,660 [2012]

The General Assembly of Unitarian and Free Christian Churches
Registered: 21 Feb 1967 *Employees:* 10 *Volunteers:* 100
Tel: 020 7240 2384 *Website:* unitarian.org.uk
Activities: Religious activities
Address: The General Assembly of Unitarian & Essex Hall, 1-6 Essex Street, London, WC2R 3HY
Trustees: Sir Philip Colfox, Rev Lynne Readett, Mr Peter Hanley, Ms Sheena McKinnon, Mrs Marion Baker, Rev Matthew Smith, Rev Rob Whiteman, Mrs Christina Smith
Income: £2,071,735 [2016]; £713,888 [2015]; £713,783 [2014]; £767,261 [2013]; £823,157 [2012]

The General Conference of The New Church
Registered: 11 Jul 1967 *Employees:* 34 *Volunteers:* 12
Tel: 01827 712370 *Website:* generalconference.org.uk
Activities: Education, training; religious activities
Address: Purley Chase Centre, Purley Chase Lane, Mancetter, Atherstone, Warwicks, CV9 2RQ
Trustees: Mr Michael Hindley BA, Ms J Zoe Brooks BA, Mr R H Cunningham, Mrs Rachel Turner, Mr David Haseler, Mrs Judith Wilson, Mrs Lara Nicholls
Income: £1,311,441 [2017]; £1,596,115 [2016]; £1,242,854 [2015]; £2,072,727 [2014]; £1,753,650 [2013]

General Federation of Trade Unions Educational Trust
Registered: 19 Apr 1971 *Employees:* 60
Tel: 01509 410859 *Website:* gftu.org.uk
Activities: Education, training; economic, community development, employment
Address: 84 Wood Lane, Quorn, Loughborough, Leics, LE12 8DB
Trustees: Mr Stephen Orchard, Ms Lynn Ambler, Mrs Bindu Paul, Sian Moore, Michael Sanders, Mr Dami Benbow, Ms Alana Dave, Mr John Smith, Nadine Rae
Income: £1,687,433 [2016]; £1,780,252 [2015]; £1,941,722 [2014]; £640,299 [2013]; £811,208 [2012]

General Medical Council
Registered: 9 Nov 2001 *Employees:* 1,115
Tel: 020 7189 5037 *Website:* gmc-uk.org
Activities: Education, training; advancement of health or saving of lives
Address: Regent's Place, 350 Euston Road, London, NW1 3JN
Trustees: Denise Platt, Deirdre Kelly, Dr Shree Datta, Helene Hayman, Mr Steven Robert Burnett, Professor Anthony Richard Harden, Professor Terence Stephenson, Suzi Leather, Christine Eames, Miss Amerdeep Somal, Professor Paul Knight
Income: £106,958,176 [2016]; £99,261,000 [2015]; £97,054,000 [2014]; £95,437,000 [2013]; £97,975,000 [2012]

General Optical Council
Registered: 12 Dec 2012 *Employees:* 62
Tel: 07502 400803 *Website:* optical.org
Activities: Education, training; advancement of health or saving of lives
Address: General Optical Council, 10 Old Bailey, London, EC4M 7NG
Trustees: Ms Selina Ullah, Mr Glenn Tomison, Ms Helen Elizabeth Tilley, Ms Clare Minchington, Mrs Sinead Burns, Ms Roshni Samra, Mr David Parkins, Mr Gareth Morgan Hadley, Dr Scott Mackie, Mrs Rosie Glazebrook, Dr Josie Forte, Mr Michael Galvin
Income: £8,113,113 [2017]; £7,564,502 [2016]; £12,794,085 [2015]; £6,286,333 [2014]

The General Service Board of Alcoholics Anonymous (Great Britain) Limited
Registered: 19 Mar 1969 *Employees:* 17
Tel: 01904 644026 *Website:* alcoholics-anonymous.org.uk
Activities: The advancement of health or saving of lives
Address: Alcoholics Anonymous, P O Box 1, York, YO1 7NJ
Trustees: Mr Roger Duncan Edgington, Mr Brian Stanley Jenkins, Miss Denise Claire Hartley, Mr Peter Sivewright, Sandi Aarvold, Patrick McGuire, Michael Power, Stephen Smith, Erik Abbott, Mr Peter Maurice Edward Fryer, Mr Nigel Robert Patience, Dr Mani Mehdikhani, Miss Amanda Jane Stocks, Clive Kilmartin, Jonathan Pope, Terri Semple, Maxine Wilson, Norman Brown
Income: £1,415,933 [2017]; £1,373,270 [2016]; £1,373,270 [2015]; £1,282,837 [2014]; £1,375,104 [2013]

Generate Opportunities Ltd
Registered: 14 May 1998 *Employees:* 64 *Volunteers:* 6
Tel: 020 9979 6333 *Website:* generate-uk.org
Activities: Education, training; advancement of health or saving of lives; disability; arts, culture, heritage, science; economic, community development, employment; recreation
Address: Generate, 73 Summerstown, London, SW17 0BQ
Trustees: Mr Donald McKerrow, Ms Grace Sylvester, Mr Damian Brady, Ms Judith Mellis, Mr Alastair David Bearne
Income: £1,208,072 [2017]; £1,179,413 [2016]; £1,296,187 [2015]; £1,246,376 [2014]; £1,343,690 [2013]

The Generation Foundation
Registered: 22 Feb 2006 *Employees:* 1
Website: genfound.org
Activities: General charitable purposes; education, training; advancement of health or saving of lives; prevention or relief of poverty; overseas aid, famine relief; accommodation, housing; arts, culture, heritage, science; environment, conservation, heritage; economic, community development, employment
Address: 20 Air Street, London, W1B 5AN
Trustees: Mr David Wayland Blood, Mr Peter Malcolm Harris, Mr Colin Le Duc, Mr Miguel Roger Nogales, Ms Tamara Jean Arnold, Mr Albert Arnold Gore, Mr Mark Ferguson, Mr Peter Sage Knight, Mr Michael John Ramsay
Income: £4,560,671 [2016]; £3,451,166 [2015]; £2,289,637 [2014]; £2,109,753 [2013]; £1,480,641 [2012]

Genesis America (UK) Limited
Registered: 22 Apr 2004
Tel: 020 7603 9237 *Website:* genesisfoundation.org.uk
Activities: General charitable purposes; arts, culture, heritage, science
Address: P O Box 72511, London, SW3 9DZ
Trustees: Ms Joy Browne, Mrg Vladmir Felzmann, Mr John Joseph Studzinski
Income: £2,029,057 [2016]; £1,837,534 [2015]; £2,969,842 [2014]; £1,234,384 [2013]; £1,093,156 [2012]

The Genesis Charitable Trust
Registered: 20 Aug 2012 *Employees:* 1 *Volunteers:* 4
Website: giml.co.uk
Activities: Education, training; prevention or relief of poverty; overseas aid, famine relief; economic, community development, employment
Address: 21 Grosvenor Place, London, SW1X 7HU
Trustees: Mr Martyn Ryan, Chris Ellyatt, Ms Karen Roydon, Mr Arindam Bhattacharjee
Income: £1,074,514 [2016]; £1,418,078 [2015]; £1,699,950 [2014]; £2,320,797 [2013]

Genesis Research Trust
Registered: 11 Sep 1985 *Employees:* 8 *Volunteers:* 10
Tel: 020 7594 9741 *Website:* genesisresearchtrust.com
Activities: Education, training; advancement of health or saving of lives
Address: Imperial College London, du Cane Road, London, W12 0NN
Trustees: Professor Stephen Franks, Mrs Linda Carol Loftus, Professor Phillip Bennett, Professor Catherine Williamson, Mr Anthony Rosenfelder, Lord Winston, Lord Parry Mitchell, Miss Angela Hodes
Income: £1,321,499 [2017]; £1,390,217 [2016]; £1,441,508 [2015]; £1,223,495 [2014]; £1,198,072 [2013]

Genesis Trust Bath
Registered: 17 Oct 2013 *Employees:* 15 *Volunteers:* 700
Tel: 01225 463549 *Website:* genesistrust.org.uk
Activities: Education, training; advancement of health or saving of lives; prevention or relief of poverty
Address: Genesis Trust, Old School House, South Parade, Bath, BA2 4AF
Trustees: Sir Peter Heywood, Mr Ian James McKay, Mrs Cherry Beath, Mr Alastiar Gibson, Mr Stephen Lillicrap, Mr James McPhee, Mrs Eutrice Horwood
Income: £1,125,761 [2017]; £467,029 [2016]; £268,962 [2015]; £182,527 [2014]

Genetic Alliance UK Ltd
Registered: 15 May 2006 *Employees:* 15 *Volunteers:* 105
Tel: 020 7831 0883 *Website:* geneticalliance.org.uk
Activities: General charitable purposes; education, training; advancement of health or saving of lives; disability
Address: Level 3, Barclay House, 37 Queen Square, London, WC1N 3BH
Trustees: Ms Susan Jane Millman, Dr Susan Walsh, Mr Christopher Goard, Mrs Elizabeth Porterfield, Miss Sara Johanne Hunt, Ms Gloria Jane Clark, Dr Rafael Yanez
Income: £1,048,394 [2017]; £861,043 [2016]; £836,292 [2015]; £767,037 [2014]; £721,041 [2013]

Genetic Disorders UK
Registered: 26 Apr 2011 *Employees:* 10 *Volunteers:* 10
Website: geneticdisordersuk.org
Activities: Education, training; advancement of health or saving of lives; disability
Address: Orchard House, 2 Atwood, Little Bookham, Leatherhead, Surrey, KT23 3BH
Trustees: Mr Eric Pillinger, Mr David Barlow, Mrs Harriet Hanna, Mrs Alina Garcia-Lapuerta, Jill Lucas
Income: £1,387,960 [2017]; £1,361,023 [2016]; £1,541,725 [2015]; £1,654,763 [2014]; £1,725,904 [2013]

Genome Research Limited
Registered: 21 May 1993 *Employees:* 1,075
Tel: 01223 834244 *Website:* sanger.ac.uk
Activities: Education, training; advancement of health or saving of lives
Address: The Sanger Centre, Wellcome Trust Genome Campus, Hinxton, Saffron Walden, Essex, CB10 1SA
Trustees: The Rt Hon Lord David Willetts, Dr Jeremy Farrar, Mr Timothy Livett, Professor Dame Kay Davies, Professor Rolf-Dieter Heuer
Income: £135,336,000 [2017]; £124,141,000 [2016]; £156,412,000 [2015]; £119,484,000 [2014]; £113,933,000 [2013]

The Geographical Association
Registered: 24 Mar 2010 *Employees:* 17 *Volunteers:* 250
Tel: 0114 296 0088 *Website:* geography.org.uk
Activities: Education, training
Address: The Geographical Association, 160 Solly Street, Sheffield, S1 4BF
Trustees: Mr Roderick Howard Maxwell Plews, Mrs Gillian Miller, Mr Nicholas John Lapthorn, Ms Mary Alice Biddulph, Miss Kathryn Stephenson, Mr Iain Leslie Palot, Mrs Susan Anne Holden, Dr Stephen Scoffham, Mr Bob Digby, Mr Alan David Marvell, Ms Lindsay West, Dr Tariq Jazeel, Dr Rosemary Julia Gillman, Dr Paula Richardson
Income: £1,145,237 [2017]; £1,269,711 [2016]; £1,252,018 [2015]; £1,275,012 [2014]; £1,164,710 [2013]

The Geological Society of London
Registered: 6 Feb 1963 *Employees:* 54
Website: geolsoc.org.uk
Activities: Education, training; arts, culture, heritage, science
Address: Geological Society of London, Burlington House, Piccadilly, London, W1J 0BG
Trustees: Mrs Margaret Patricia Henton, Dr Sheila Peacock, Dr Marie Edmonds, Dr Colin Peter North, Ms Lesley Dunlop, Mr Frederick Charles Brassington, Prof Christine Peirce, Mr Jason Craig Canning, Dr Robert David Larter, Mr Nicholas Reynolds, Mr John Murray Booth, Miss Jessica Therese Smith, Mr John Charles Scott Talbot, Mr Malcolm Archibald Halliday Brown, Miss Liv Sorcha Carroll, Mr Keith John Seymour, Mr Graham Paul Goffey, Dr Jennifer Mary McKinley, Dr Katherine Rebecca Royse, Dr Sarah Helen Gordon, Dr Naomi Jordan, Dr Alexander Charters Whittaker, Prof Nicholas William Rogers
Income: £5,750,171 [2016]; £5,497,823 [2015]; £5,217,086 [2014]; £5,470,030 [2013]; £4,776,049 [2012]

The George Edward Smart Homes
Registered: 11 Dec 1962 *Employees:* 64 *Volunteers:* 20
Tel: 01723 375709 *Website:* combe-hay.co.uk
Activities: Accommodation, housing
Address: George Edward Smart Homes, Combe Hay House, Stepney Drive, Scarborough, N Yorks, YO12 5DJ
Trustees: Mrs Marjorie Priestley, Mrs Rhien Cocker, Mr Graeme Hay FCA, Ms Jane Nickson, Dr Ian Glaves, Mr John Cobb, Miss Carol Gaynor Boyes, Mrs Elaine Heritage
Income: £1,556,581 [2016]; £1,482,508 [2015]; £1,442,537 [2014]; £1,372,037 [2013]; £1,426,558 [2012]

Georgetown University (USA) UK Initiatives Organisation
Registered: 23 Feb 2012 *Employees:* 3
Tel: 020 3077 5900 *Website:* ctls.georgetown.edu
Activities: Education, training
Address: Swan House, 37-39 High Holborn, London, WC1V 6AA
Trustees: Mr Edward Quinn, Mr David Rubenstein, Mr William Treanor
Income: £1,288,609 [2017]; £807,885 [2016]; £1,075,195 [2015]; £758,549 [2014]; £912,726 [2013]

German School Association Limited
Registered: 1 Jul 1974 *Employees:* 115
Tel: 020 8939 1844 *Website:* dslondon.org.uk
Activities: Education, training; arts, culture, heritage, science
Address: The German School, Douglas House, Petersham Road, Richmond, Surrey, TW10 7AH
Trustees: Mrs Lynda Funke, Mr Peter Kaestel, Mrs Beate Baethke, Mrs Nadine Schmid, Mr Colin Thomann, Mr Michael Frieser, Mrs Charlotte von der Goltz, Mr Jan Peter Weiland
Income: £9,302,887 [2017]; £14,287,677 [2016]; £8,448,890 [2015]; £7,817,474 [2014]; £7,298,464 [2013]

German Young Men's Christian Association in London
Registered: 21 Nov 1966 *Employees:* 53 *Volunteers:* 40
Tel: 020 7723 9276 *Website:* german-ymca.org.uk
Activities: General charitable purposes; education, training; overseas aid, famine relief; accommodation, housing; religious activities; arts, culture, heritage, science
Address: 35 Craven Terrace, London, W2 3EL
Trustees: Mr Peter Stokes, Ms Sally Yates, Mr John Peacham, Ms Nora Daur, Rev Georg Amann, Mr Dieter Losse, Ms Angela Fox, Mr Christian Daur, Mr Martin Tinsley, Phillip Mallinckrodt
Income: £2,140,368 [2016]; £2,281,470 [2015]; £2,107,860 [2014]; £2,107,046 [2013]; £533,093 [2012]

Get Kids Going
Registered: 16 Jul 1997 *Employees:* 4 *Volunteers:* 28
Tel: 020 7481 8110 *Website:* getkidsgoing.com
Activities: Disability; amateur sport
Address: Get Kids Going, 10 King Charles Terrace, Sovereign Close, London, E1W 3HL
Trustees: Lesley Tadgell-Foster, Phillip John Patrick Fordham, Mrs Patti Fordyce
Income: £1,131,976 [2017]; £1,192,397 [2016]; £1,173,917 [2015]; £1,159,938 [2014]; £1,532,321 [2013]

J Paul Getty Jr General Charitable Trust
Registered: 31 Jul 1985
Tel: 020 7262 1470
Activities: General charitable purposes; education, training; advancement of health or saving of lives; disability; prevention or relief of poverty; overseas aid, famine relief; arts, culture, heritage, science; amateur sport; environment, conservation, heritage; economic, community development, employment; human rights, religious or racial harmony, equality or diversity; other charitable purposes
Address: 4 Queensborough Studios, London, W2 3SQ
Trustees: Mr Christopher Purvis CBE, Mr Christopher Gibbs, Mr Vanni Treves, Lady Getty
Income: £1,884,547 [2017]; £12,580 [2016]; £32,382 [2015]; £60,880 [2014]; £185,233 [2013]

The Gevurath Ari Torah Academy Trust
Registered: 5 Jun 1991 *Volunteers:* 3
Tel: 020 8806 2666
Activities: Education, training; religious activities
Address: 18 Woodlands Close, London, NW11 9QP
Trustees: Rabbi Yaacov Chanoch Baddiel, Mr Chaim Lopian, Mr Alfred Hercz
Income: £3,177,063 [2017]; £2,247,770 [2016]; £1,754,265 [2015]; £1,421,485 [2014]; £2,381,365 [2013]

Gideons UK
Registered: 30 Apr 1963 *Employees:* 14 *Volunteers:* 4,992
Tel: 01455 554241 *Website:* gideons.org.uk
Activities: Religious activities
Address: The Gideons International, 24 George Street, Lutterworth, Leics, LE17 4EE
Trustees: Graham Beckett, Alan Lansdown, Graham Sparkes, Neil Bourne, Bill Thomas, Annabel Howes, Rhoda Bourne, Iain Gray, Rick Hillard, Handley Hammond, David Patterson, David Andrew, Andrew Knight, Philip Bunting, Catherine Erbetta, Chris Axelby, Ivan Johnston
Income: £3,322,835 [2016]; £4,234,363 [2015]; £4,431,208 [2014]; £3,009,436 [2013]; £3,012,621 [2012]

Giggleswick School
Registered: 2 Jun 2005 *Employees:* 236 *Volunteers:* 2
Website: giggleswick.org.uk
Activities: Education, training
Address: Giggleswick School, Giggleswick, Settle, N Yorks, BD24 0DE
Trustees: Mrs H J Hancock, Miss A L Hudson, Mr Andrew Mullins, Miss Sarah Fox BMus ARCM, Sir Gary Keith Verity, Mr Andrew Miles Jarman, Ms Phoebe Gabriella Lebrecht, Mr J L Ellacott, Mr R A P Brocklehurst, The Hon William Kay-Shuttleworth BA, Mrs Gillian Harper BA, Mr Mark Robert Corner MSc MBA, Mr Roderick Richard Waldie, Mr Ian Michael Cornelius
Income: £8,878,778 [2017]; £9,374,706 [2016]; £8,911,560 [2015]; £8,390,480 [2014]; £9,450,632 [2013]

Gilbert Deya Ministries
Registered: 3 Jan 1996 *Employees:* 9 *Volunteers:* 25
Tel: 020 8770 1034 *Website:* gilbertdeya.com
Activities: The prevention or relief of poverty; religious activities
Address: Flat 40 Kelson House, Stewart Street, Poplar, London, E14 3JQ
Trustees: Prince Russ Tennyson Taylor, Ms Hannah Ogunjinmi, Ms Marie Zambo, Ms Rosie Nkundwe Mwambene, Mrs Lucy Jalloh, Ms Gifty Larbi, Mr Sylvester Conteh
Income: £3,876,583 [2016]; £652,833 [2015]; £865,686 [2014]; £1,044,432 [2013]; £960,341 [2012]

Gilbert White & The Oates Collections
Registered: 3 Nov 2014 *Employees:* 25 *Volunteers:* 102
Tel: 01420 511275 *Website:* gilbertwhiteshouse.org.uk
Activities: Education, training; arts, culture, heritage, science; environment, conservation, heritage
Address: Gilbert Whites House & Gardens, High Street, Selborne, Alton, Hants, GU34 3JH
Trustees: Mr Adam Vere Balfour Broke OBE FCA, Ms Liz Try, Ms Nicole Penn-Symons, Prof Paul Rodhouse DSC, Mr Nicholas Edwin John Heasman, Mr Philip Clinton Geddes, Heather Lane, Mr Robin Erskine Greenwood, Dr Rosemary Irwin, Mr Christopher Noblett Carter DipLA CMLI, Ms Eleanor Louise Marsden, Mr John Stewart Liddle, Mark Patterson, Mr Andrew Highman
Income: £1,508,763 [2017]

Gillingham Football Club Community Trust
Registered: 23 Jul 2008 *Employees:* 65
Tel: 01634 350224 *Website:* gfccommunitytrust.org.uk
Activities: Education, training; disability; prevention or relief of poverty; amateur sport; economic, community development, employment; recreation
Address: 7 Meesons Close, Eastling, Faversham, Kent, ME13 0AW
Trustees: Mr Paul Damien Philip Scally, Mrs Marian Dunning, Mr Peter Robert Lloyd, Mr Graham Holmes, Mr Mark Atkins
Income: £1,005,784 [2016]; £475,937 [2015]; £200,240 [2014]; £168,678 [2013]; £173,618 [2012]

Gilmoor Benevolent Fund Limited
Registered: 22 Aug 2002
Tel: 020 8806 1066
Activities: General charitable purposes; education, training; advancement of health or saving of lives; prevention or relief of poverty; overseas aid, famine relief; accommodation, housing; religious activities; arts, culture, heritage, science; amateur sport; economic, community development, employment; recreation; other charitable purposes
Address: 15 Clapton Common, London, E5 9AA
Trustees: Mrs Beila Low, Mr Marcus Landau, Mr Elieser Low, Mr Joel Freund, Rabbi Leon Rabinowitz, Mr Oscar Low, Mr Dov Rabinowitz
Income: £4,552,281 [2017]; £7,172,875 [2016]; £12,161,460 [2015]; £5,752,648 [2014]; £5,800,819 [2013]

Gingerbread, The Charity for Single Parent Families
Registered: 20 May 1964 *Employees:* 60
Tel: 020 7428 5419 *Website:* gingerbread.org.uk
Activities: Education, training; prevention or relief of poverty; economic, community development, employment
Address: Flat 406, City View House, 463 Bethnal Green Road, London, E2 9QY
Trustees: Ms Wendy Scott, Ms Victoria Benson, Mr Derek Gannon, Mr Patrick Mears, Ms Joyce Materego, Mr Jeremy Simpson, Lily Caprani, George Coleman, Mr Jonathan Welfare, Jenny Robson, Ms Mary Lumetta, Mrs Frances Parry, Ms Charlotte Thorne, Mrs Alison Taylor, Mrs Wanda Wyporska
Income: £2,868,561 [2017]; £3,175,700 [2016]; £3,571,857 [2015]; £3,331,471 [2014]; £3,282,726 [2013]

Girl Effect
Registered: 4 Apr 2011 *Employees:* 93
Tel: 020 3778 0490 *Website:* girleffect.org
Activities: Education, training; advancement of health or saving of lives; prevention or relief of poverty; overseas aid, famine relief; economic, community development, employment
Address: Ingeni Building, 17 Broadwick Street, London, W1F 0DJ
Trustees: Mr Jacob Schimmel, Ms Hilary Krane, Ms Anne Marie Burgoyne, Ms Maria Solandros Eitel, Haven Ley, Mrs Trishla Jain
Income: £28,882,698 [2017]; £35,770,642 [2016]; £3,695,616 [2015]; £2,465,320 [2014]; £2,083,977 [2013]

Girls Not Brides: The Global Partnership To End Child Marriage
Registered: 17 Oct 2013 *Employees:* 23
Tel: 020 3725 5858 *Website:* girlsnotbrides.org
Activities: Education, training; advancement of health or saving of lives; prevention or relief of poverty; human rights, religious or racial harmony, equality or diversity
Address: Girls Not Brides, Unit 25.4 Coda Studios, 2nd Floor, 189 Munster Road, London, SW6 6AW
Trustees: Ms Tanuja Pandit, Mrs Mabel Van Oranje, Mr Nicholas Grono, Ms Theresa Shaver, Miss Clare Amanda Melford, Ms Ann Lesley Cotton
Income: £3,058,512 [2016]; £2,408,874 [2015]; £1,485,146 [2014]

Girls' Brigade Ministries
Registered: 30 Sep 2009 *Employees:* 21 *Volunteers:* 3,000
Tel: 01246 582322 *Website:* girlsb.org
Activities: Religious activities
Address: Cliff College, Calver, Hope Valley, Derbys, S32 3XG
Trustees: Miss Vivienne Aitchison, Dr Kenneth Poulter, Sarah Hamlyn, Mrs Liz Sarkodie, Mr Dennis Pethers, Mrs Barbara Darby, Mrs Amanda Allcorn
Income: £1,143,179 [2016]; £1,207,704 [2015]; £1,407,132 [2014]; £1,104,501 [2013]; £800,953 [2012]

The Girls' Day School Trust
Registered: 29 Sep 1995 *Employees:* 3,566 *Volunteers:* 185
Tel: 020 7393 6666 *Website:* gdst.net
Activities: Education, training
Address: Girls Day School Trust, 100 Rochester Row, London, SW1P 1JP
Trustees: Ms Julie Chakraverty, Ms Rita Dhut, Mrs Maria Gordon, Ms Kathryn Davis, Mr Peter Geoffrey Oliver, Professor Judith Simons, Mr Richard Harris, Mrs Helen Williams CB, Ms Juliet Humphries, Ms Mary Hockaday, Mrs Anne Victoria Tuck, Mr Fraser Montgomery
Income: £260,919,000 [2017]; £253,796,000 [2016]; £254,084,000 [2015]; £273,689,000 [2014]; £233,553,000 [2013]

Girls' Education Company Ltd

Registered: 2 Aug 1963 *Employees:* 303
Tel: 01494 445552 *Website:* wycombeabbey.com
Activities: Education, training; economic, community development, employment
Address: Wycombe Abbey School, Abbey Way, High Wycombe, Bucks, HP11 1PE
Trustees: Rt Revd Dr Alan Wilson Bishop of Buckingham, The Hon Mrs Justice Carr, Mr P P Sherrington, Dr Louise Fawcett, Mr Richard Winter, Mr Simon Henderson, Dr Margaret Jane MacDougall, Dr Caro Godlee, Lady Sassoon, Mr D P Lillycrop, Mrs Diana Rose, Mr Richard Ashby, Mr Jeremy Bailey, Mr Patrick Lewis, Mr Timothy Clarke
Income: £23,900,000 [2017]; £23,367,330 [2016]; £22,569,053 [2015]; £20,711,779 [2014]; £24,091,296 [2013]

Girton College

Registered: 18 Aug 2010 *Employees:* 195
Tel: 01223 338999 *Website:* girton.cam.ac.uk
Activities: Education, training; accommodation, housing; religious activities; arts, culture, heritage, science; amateur sport; environment, conservation, heritage
Address: Girton College, Cambridge, CB3 0JG
Trustees: Ms Deborah Lowther, Dr Alexandra Mary Fulton, Ms Karen Lee, Dr Hugh R Shercliff, James Riley, Ms Tess Skyrme, Dr Sebastian Leonard Dundas Falk, Mr Liam James O'Connor, Mr George Cowperthwaite, Dr Clive Lawson, Dr Carlo Acerini, Professor Matthew James Allen, Professor Christopher B J Ford, Professor Susan J Smith, Mr Yu Yang Fredrik Liu, Ms Molly Sugar Brown Hale, Dr Emma Jane Louise Weisblatt
Income: £9,015,000 [2017]; £8,196,000 [2016]; £8,979,000 [2015]; £13,264,000 [2014]; £10,862,000 [2013]

Girton Town Charity

Registered: 22 Jun 2009 *Employees:* 2
Tel: 01223 276008 *Website:* girtontowncharity.co.uk
Activities: General charitable purposes; prevention or relief of poverty; accommodation, housing
Address: 1 Fairway, Girton, Cambridge, CB3 0QF
Trustees: Dr Robin Hiley, Mrs Jennifer Knights, Mr Brian Pycock, Miss Patsy Smith, Mrs Pippa Temple, Mr Ray Gordon, Mrs Ann Bonnett, Mrs Yvonne Higgons
Income: £1,049,000 [2017]; £961,671 [2016]; £916,000 [2015]; £851,246 [2014]; £816,763 [2013]

Gisda Cyfyngedig / Arfon Young Single Homeless Group

Registered: 27 Feb 1998 *Employees:* 49 *Volunteers:* 14
Tel: 01286 671153 *Website:* gisda.co.uk
Activities: General charitable purposes; education, training; prevention or relief of poverty; accommodation, housing
Address: Gisda, 22-23 Y Maes, Caernarfon, Gwynedd, LL55 2NA
Trustees: Parch James Ronald Williams, Mr Dewi Jones, Ms Ffion Jon Williams, Mr Laurence Smith, Cyng Tudor Owen, Mrs Carys Thomas, Mr Dafydd Gruffydd
Income: £1,775,563 [2017]; £1,789,247 [2016]; £1,808,178 [2015]; £1,240,180 [2014]; £1,117,483 [2013]

Give It Forward Today

Registered: 14 Aug 2013 *Employees:* 11 *Volunteers:* 250
Tel: 020 8457 4429
Activities: General charitable purposes; prevention or relief of poverty; other charitable purposes
Address: 379 Hendon Way, London, NW4 3LP
Trustees: Rabbi Neil Zeev Schiff, Neil Blair, Mr Oliver Zachary White, Mr Shimon Gillis, Mr Howard A Jackson, Mrs Cindy Levy
Income: £1,091,927 [2016]; £860,462 [2015]; £1,120,529 [2014]

Glasallt Fawr - Camphill Centre

Registered: 17 Dec 2007 *Employees:* 57
Tel: 01550 776200 *Website:* glasallt-fawr.com
Activities: Education, training; advancement of health or saving of lives; disability
Address: Glasallt Fawr, Llangadog, Carmarthenshire, SA19 9AS
Trustees: Rev Ian Henry Aveson, Mr Giuseppe Villa, Catrin James, Mr Peter Cyril Rees, Caroline Boorer, Mr Michael David Wicksteed, Mr Huwel Morgan Manley, Mr Handel Lewis Davies, David Boorer
Income: £1,630,243 [2017]; £1,546,838 [2016]; £2,063,747 [2015]; £1,419,460 [2014]; £1,390,354 [2013]

R L Glasspool Charity Trust

Registered: 25 Jan 1963 *Employees:* 5
Website: glasspool.org.uk
Activities: The prevention or relief of poverty
Address: R L Glasspool Charity Trust, 182 Hoe Street, London, E17 4QH
Trustees: R L Glasspool Trustee Limited
Income: £1,999,962 [2017]; £1,929,965 [2016]; £1,841,322 [2015]; £1,737,910 [2014]; £1,697,671 [2013]

Glastonbury Abbey

Registered: 22 Apr 2009 *Employees:* 23 *Volunteers:* 50
Tel: 01458 836112 *Website:* glastonburyabbey.com
Activities: Education, training; religious activities; arts, culture, heritage, science; environment, conservation, heritage
Address: Glastonbury Abbey, Abbey Gatehouse, Magdalene Street, Glastonbury, Somerset, BA6 9EL
Trustees: Mrs Janice White, Mr Robert Francis Richards, Dr William Bloom, Mr John Brendon, Prof Roberta Gilchrist, Mr Harry Musselwhite Ba Fkc Barrister, Mr Martin Thomas, Mr Peter Saunders, Venerable Anne Elizabeth Gell, Rev D MacGeoch, Mr Stephen Bird, Mr Robert Jackson, Mrs Pauline Grace Dodds
Income: £1,147,700 [2016]; £978,357 [2015]; £1,586,623 [2014]; £1,171,252 [2013]; £879,138 [2012]

Glebe House (Charnwood) Limited

Registered: 18 Mar 1993 *Employees:* 49 *Volunteers:* 14
Tel: 01509 218096 *Website:* glebehouseproject.org.uk
Activities: Disability
Address: Glebe House (Charnwood) Ltd, Woodgate Chambers, 70 Woodgate, Loughborough, Leics, LE11 2TZ
Trustees: Mr Naveed Chiragh, Mr Bryan Higgins, Mr Geoffrey Hodgson, Ms Louisa Whait, Mrs Marie Moore, Dr Geetha Balasubramaniam, Mr David Frost
Income: £1,112,879 [2017]; £1,126,141 [2016]; £967,752 [2015]; £904,833 [2014]; £862,013 [2013]

Glebe House School Trust Ltd

Registered: 22 Mar 1993 *Employees:* 50
Tel: 01485 532809 *Website:* glebehouseschool.co.uk
Activities: Education, training
Address: Glebe House School, 2 Cromer Road, Hunstanton, Norfolk, PE36 6HW
Trustees: Lloyd Sandy, Mrs Sharon Bottomley, Mr Adam Poulter, Mr Nicholas Crane, Mr Nigel Flowers, Mr Paul Richard Searle, Mr Tim Hipperson, Mr Richard Chalk, Mr Geoff Wingrove
Income: £1,694,108 [2017]; £1,235,820 [2016]; £1,030,818 [2015]; £1,037,469 [2014]; £1,033,544 [2013]

Glen Carne

Registered: 28 Mar 2011 *Employees:* 5 *Volunteers:* 35
Tel: 01872 554141 *Website:* glencarne.org.uk
Activities: Education, training; accommodation, housing
Address: Glen Carne, Barkla Shop, St Agnes, Cornwall, TR5 0XN
Trustees: Robert Crozier, Mrs Paula Jean Dunkley, Mr Les Donnithorne, Michael Leafe, Ms Ruth Clarke
Income: £1,175,256 [2017]; £1,111,108 [2016]; £990,412 [2015]; £773,712 [2014]; £308,478 [2013]

Glendower School Trust Limited

Registered: 24 May 1971 *Employees:* 50
Tel: 020 7370 1927 *Website:* glendowerprep.org
Activities: Education, training
Address: 87 Queens Gate, London, SW7 5JX
Trustees: Mr Rupert Harrison, Mrs Susan Kumleben, Mr Franklin Morton, Mr Paul Vanni, Mr David Goodhew, Mr Zac Pinkham, Mr Gagik Apkarian, Mrs Sarah Martyrossian, Mr Michael Uva BA (Harvard) MSc (LSE) MBA (Harvard), Rev Paul Cowley, Mrs Blake Daffey, Miss Angela Rawlinson, Mrs Juliet Richards
Income: £4,386,162 [2017]; £4,332,524 [2016]; £4,167,990 [2015]; £3,696,493 [2014]; £3,558,373 [2013]

Global Action Plan

Registered: 20 Sep 1993 *Employees:* 30 *Volunteers:* 6
Tel: 020 7420 4444 *Website:* globalactionplan.org.uk
Activities: Education, training; advancement of health or saving of lives; environment, conservation, heritage; economic, community development, employment
Address: 9-13 Kean Street, London, WC2B 4AY
Trustees: Jeremy Oppenheim, Jonathan Katz, Murray Birt, Sue Welland, Ms Lisa Marie Poole, Tom Rippin, Andrew Cartland, Jeremy Cooper, Ellen Miles
Income: £2,273,211 [2017]; £2,596,346 [2016]; £2,563,812 [2015]; £1,785,991 [2014]; £1,600,713 [2013]

Global Alliance for Livestock Veterinary Medicines

Registered: 28 Jul 2006 *Employees:* 40
Tel: 0131 445 6109 *Website:* galvmed.org
Activities: General charitable purposes; prevention or relief of poverty; animals; economic, community development, employment; other charitable purposes
Address: GALVmed, Doherty Building, Pentlands Science Park, Bush Loan, Penicuik, Edinburgh, EH26 0PZ
Trustees: Prof Peter Wells, Dr Narayan Hegde, Mr Michael Julian Ince, Prof Olanrewaju Smith, Dr William Amanfu, Prof Funso Sonaiya, Dr Paul Van Aarle, Prof Mark Rweyemamu, Dr Carolin Schumacher
Income: £6,162,552 [2017]; £10,146,947 [2016]; £11,761,485 [2015]; £9,044,890 [2014]; £10,194,443 [2013]

Global Canopy Foundation

Registered: 29 Oct 2001 *Employees:* 17
Tel: 01865 724333 *Website:* globalcanopy.org
Activities: General charitable purposes; education, training; animals; environment, conservation, heritage
Address: 3 Frewin Chambers, Frewin Court, Oxford, OX1 3HZ
Trustees: Lindsay Bury, Mr Hylton Robert Murray-Philipson, Mr Edward Mott, Dr William Wint, Ms Fiona McKenzie, Ms Laura Ipacs
Income: £2,968,110 [2017]; £2,854,353 [2016]; £2,595,073 [2015]; £2,260,256 [2014]; £2,258,936 [2013]

Global Charities

Registered: 17 Apr 2002 *Employees:* 20 *Volunteers:* 108
Tel: 0345 606 0990 *Website:* thisisglobal.com
Activities: General charitable purposes; disability; prevention or relief of poverty
Address: Global Charities, 29-30 Leicester Square, London, WC2H 7LA
Trustees: Mr Jonathan Norbury, Mr John McGeough, Mr Michael Connole, Mrs Sarah Homer, Dr Justin Davis Smith CBE, Mr Gareth Andrewartha, Mrs Joanne Louise Kenrick, Ulrika Hogberg
Income: £6,743,443 [2017]; £3,248,064 [2016]; £3,853,790 [2015]; £4,200,565 [2014]; £3,900,156 [2013]

Global Dialogue

Registered: 19 Dec 2007 *Employees:* 9
Tel: 020 3752 5540 *Website:* global-dialogue.eu
Activities: General charitable purposes; human rights, religious or racial harmony, equality or diversity; other charitable purposes
Address: Global Dialogue, 17 Oval Way, London, SE11 5RR
Trustees: Mr Andrew Puddephatt, Ms Elizabeth Palmer, Lisa Hashemi, Ms Debbie Pippard, Mr Walter Veirs
Income: £1,692,642 [2017]; £1,442,029 [2016]; £959,259 [2015]; £901,930 [2014]; £1,055,423 [2013]

Global Giving UK

Registered: 18 Feb 2008 *Employees:* 7 *Volunteers:* 72
Tel: 020 3441 8782 *Website:* globalgiving.co.uk
Activities: General charitable purposes
Address: Globalgiving UK, 6 Great James Street, London, WC1N 3DA
Trustees: Ms Deirdre McGlashan, Ms Mari Kuraishi, Mr Shawn Aguiar, Dr Anthjony Paul House
Income: £2,001,481 [2016]; £1,223,698 [2015]; £980,500 [2014]; £794,879 [2013]; £1,479,665 [2012]

Global New Car Assessment Programme (Limited By Guarantee)

Registered: 9 May 2011 *Employees:* 3
Tel: 020 7930 3882 *Website:* globalncap.org
Activities: The advancement of health or saving of lives; environment, conservation, heritage
Address: 60 Trafalgar Square, London, WC2N 5DS
Trustees: Mr Guido M F Adriaenssens, Mr Lauchlan McIntosh, Dr Verona Lucinda Lee Beckles, Mr Nirav Dumaswala, Mr Max Rufus Mosley, Dr Adrian Keith Lund, Dr Anders Lie
Income: £2,989,842 [2016]; £2,857,218 [2015]; £1,298,345 [2014]; £1,150,145 [2013]; £655,278 [2012]

Global One 2015

Registered: 21 Aug 2014 *Employees:* 8 *Volunteers:* 16
Website: globalone.org.uk
Activities: General charitable purposes; education, training; advancement of health or saving of lives; prevention or relief of poverty; religious activities; environment, conservation, heritage; economic, community development, employment; human rights, religious or racial harmony, equality or diversity
Address: 4 Gateway Mews, Bounds Green, London, N11 2UT
Trustees: Mrs Zarina Osman, Mr Ganiyu Laniyan, Mrs Syeda Afreena Shappir, Mr Umar Faisal Ahmad, Mrs Maya Sukkari, Najmun Khan
Income: £1,005,108 [2017]; £594,811 [2016]; £314,220 [2015]

Global Partners (UK)
Registered: 12 Mar 1992 *Employees:* 22
Tel: 01293 786964 *Website:* globalpartnersinternational.com
Activities: Education, training; advancement of health or saving of lives; overseas aid, famine relief
Address: P O Box 493, GP, Horley, Surrey, RH6 6DY
Trustees: Mrs Margaret Thomas, Miss Adele Bronkhorst, Mr Grant Robbins, Mr Brent Mayfield
Income: £3,520,659 [2016]; £4,036,590 [2015]; £4,691,568 [2014]; £4,029,656 [2013]; £3,932,326 [2012]

The Gloucester Charities Trust
Registered: 2 Feb 1971 *Employees:* 119
Tel: 01452 500429 *Website:* gloucestercharitiestrust.co.uk
Activities: The advancement of health or saving of lives; disability; prevention or relief of poverty; accommodation, housing
Address: Gloucester Charities Trust, Century House, 100 London Road, Gloucester, GL1 3PL
Trustees: Dr Janet Cecilia Lugg, Mr Terence Leslie Haines, Mr Brian John Henry Large, Mr Martyn White, Jackie Matthews, Mr Lee Hensley, Mr Neil Hampson, Mr Stephen Ayland, Mr Martin Charles Collins, Mr Graham Locke, Mr Graham Howell, Mrs Gillian Payne, Mr Graham Limbrick, Mrs Pam Tracey, Ms Dawn Melvin, Chris Gabb, Mr William Hewer
Income: £4,158,588 [2016]; £3,790,677 [2015]; £3,907,718 [2014]; £3,772,496 [2013]; £3,536,540 [2012]

The Gloucester Diocesan Board of Finance
Registered: 3 Feb 1967 *Employees:* 40
Tel: 01452 410022 *Website:* gloucester.anglican.org
Activities: Religious activities
Address: Gloucester DBF, Church House, College Green, Gloucester, GL1 2LY
Trustees: Mr Colin Rank, Mr Henry James Griffin Russell, Rev Katrina Scott, Professor Jennifer Tann, Venerable Phil Andrew, Professor Patricia Broadfoot, Rev Craig Bishop, Venerable Jackie Searle, Mr Michael Storey, Mr Martin Kingston, Bishop Robert Springett, Mr Graham Smith, Rt Revd Rachel Treweek, Mr Anthony Robert McFarlane, The Very Revd Stephen Lake, Ms Anna Venables, Rev Nick Bromfield, Mrs Karen Czapiewski, Revd Canon Helen Mary Kirkman Sammon
Income: £13,328,000 [2016]; £9,818,000 [2015]; £15,121,000 [2014]; £13,440,000 [2013]; £11,513,000 [2012]

Gloucestershire Association of Secondary Headteachers Limited
Registered: 3 Jun 2013
Tel: 0845 077 9005
Activities: Education, training
Address: Gash Ltd, 13 Ullenwood Court, Ullenwood, Cheltenham, Glos, GL53 9QS
Trustees: Ms Chiquita Henson, Mr Gary Watson, Mrs Sarah Tufnell, Mr Robert Ford, Mr Colin Belford, Mr William Morgan, Mr Andrew Harris, Mr Russel Bryan Ellicott, Mr Matthew Morgan
Income: £1,042,552 [2017]; £1,156,425 [2016]; £1,543,721 [2015]; £1,291,361 [2014]

The Gloucestershire Care Partnership
Registered: 2 Mar 2005
Tel: 01234 791000
Activities: The advancement of health or saving of lives; disability; prevention or relief of poverty; accommodation, housing
Address: 25 Crosspaths, Harpenden, Herts, AL5 3HE
Trustees: Mr Ralph Harry Stephenson, Mr Kevin Bolt, Mr Daniel Hayes, Mrs Kerry Margaret Dearden, Mr Paul Gray, Ms Janet Boulter, Ms Julie Wittich
Income: £16,064,789 [2016]; £16,907,000 [2015]; £30,722,000 [2014]; £28,381,000 [2013]

Gloucestershire Engineering Training Limited
Registered: 21 Jun 1977 *Employees:* 49
Tel: 01452 423461 *Website:* get-trained.org
Activities: Education, training
Address: Barnwood Point, Corinimum Avenue, Barnwood, Gloucester, GL4 3HX
Trustees: Colonel Michael Elston Bennett, Mrs Jill Brearley, Mr Jude Christopher Basil Rodrigues, Mr Gwyn Jones, Mr Charles Rupert Guy Biggin, Mr Gary Anthony Miller
Income: £2,449,765 [2017]; £2,428,503 [2016]; £2,231,323 [2015]; £1,702,324 [2014]; £1,544,862 [2013]

The Gloucestershire Everyman Theatre Company Limited
Registered: 15 Jun 1964 *Employees:* 157
Tel: 01242 512515 *Website:* everymantheatre.org.uk
Activities: Education, training; arts, culture, heritage, science
Address: Everyman Theatre, 7-10 Regent Street, Cheltenham, Glos, GL50 1HQ
Trustees: Mr Chung Fai Kong, Mr Clive Raymond Thomas, Mr Jason Blackburn, John Workman, Mr Dudley Russell, Ms Zareen Ahmed, Roger James Nicholls, Mr Thornton Michael Dey, Ms Carol Elaine Clarke, Mr Guy Woodcock, Mr Robin Herford, Ms Jane Cantwell
Income: £4,817,140 [2017]; £4,656,576 [2016]; £5,354,665 [2015]; £3,980,684 [2014]; £4,088,654 [2013]

Gloucestershire Group Homes Limited
Registered: 30 Mar 1994 *Employees:* 36
Tel: 01453 835023 *Website:* ggh.org.uk
Activities: Disability
Address: Court Farm, Downend, Horsley, Stroud, Glos, GL6 0PF
Trustees: Mrs Jane Elizabeth Archer, Mr Adrian Finn, Mr Edward Anthony Cawston, Mr John Silverman
Income: £1,476,477 [2017]; £1,357,615 [2016]; £1,358,833 [2015]; £1,347,787 [2014]; £1,343,232 [2013]

Gloucestershire Hospitals NHS Foundation Trust General Charitable Fund
Registered: 20 Dec 1995 *Employees:* 3
Activities: The advancement of health or saving of lives
Address: Charitable Fund Office, Cheltenham General Hospital, Cheltenham, Glos, GL53 7AN
Trustees: Gloucestershire Hospitals NHS Foundation Trust
Income: £1,028,000 [2017]; £1,215,100 [2016]; £1,088,000 [2015]; £909,000 [2014]; £1,630,000 [2013]

Gloucestershire Rural Community Council
Registered: 3 Apr 1996 *Employees:* 34 *Volunteers:* 309
Tel: 01452 528491 *Website:* grcc.org.uk
Activities: General charitable purposes; education, training; economic, community development, employment
Address: Community House, 15 College Green, Gloucester, GL1 2LZ
Trustees: Mr Simon King, Mrs Carole Helen Topple, Mr Charles Coats, Mr Duncan McGaw, Mr Stephen Francis Wood, Mrs Kate Hull, Mrs Sally Ann Louise Lewis
Income: £1,172,764 [2017]; £1,166,033 [2016]; £1,261,403 [2015]; £1,206,529 [2014]; £1,140,204 [2013]

Gloucestershire Wildlife Trust
Registered: 28 Apr 1964 *Employees:* 47 *Volunteers:* 450
Tel: 01452 383333 *Website:* gloucestershirewildlifetrust.co.uk
Activities: Environment, conservation, heritage
Address: Conservation Centre, Reservoir Road, Gloucester, GL4 6SX
Trustees: Mr Francis Rundall, Ms Hazel Millar, Mr Mark Southgate, Dr Sally Catherine Byng, Ms Amy Coyte, Prof Anne Goodenough, Mr David Wyndham Jones, Michael Smart, Sir David Pepper, Mr Martin Charles Horwood, Mrs Susan Crawford, Mr Ian Boyd, Mr Anthony Edward Richardson, Ms Jane Furze
Income: £3,695,828 [2017]; £2,292,155 [2016]; £2,037,681 [2015]; £2,212,620 [2014]; £1,947,497 [2013]

Glyndebourne Productions Limited
Registered: 28 Jul 1965 *Employees:* 340 *Volunteers:* 5
Tel: 01273 812321 *Website:* glyndebourne.com
Activities: Arts, culture, heritage, science
Address: Glyndebourne Productions Ltd, The Opera House, New Road, Ringmer, Lewes, E Sussex, BN8 5UU
Trustees: Mr John Botts CBE, Mr Hamish Forsyth, Mr Jolyon Barker, Ms Alina Kessel, Mrs Louise Flind, Lord Me Davies of Abersoch, Mr Franck Petitgas
Income: £29,733,397 [2016]; £27,926,529 [2015]; £39,593,168 [2014]; £25,126,146 [2013]; £25,341,225 [2012]

Glyndwr University
Registered: 23 May 2011 *Employees:* 471
Tel: 01978 290666 *Website:* glyndwr.ac.uk
Activities: Education, training
Address: Plas Coch, Mold Road, Wrexham, LL11 2AW
Trustees: Mr Askar Sheibani, Mr Neil Ashbridge, Mrs Celia Jenkins, Mrs Gill Kreft, Mrs Judith Ann Owen, Mr Travis Davis, Mr Paul McGrady, Mr Paul Barlow, Mrs Laura Gough, Dr Colin Stuhlfelder, Professor Norman Sharp OBE, Mrs Maxine Penlington OBE, Professor Maria Hinfelaar, Professor Sandra Jowett, Mr David Subacchi, Mr Barrie Phillips-Jones, Mr Angus Hamill-Stewart, Mr Lee Robinson
Income: £35,716,000 [2017]; £39,453,000 [2016]; £42,395,000 [2015]; £48,795,000 [2014]; £43,884,000 [2013]

Gnanam Foundation
Registered: 9 Mar 2015
Tel: 020 7536 6450
Activities: General charitable purposes
Address: Walbrook Building, 195 Marsh Wall, London, E14 9SG
Trustees: Dr Anwara Ali, Mr Allirajah Subaskaran, Mr Mohammed Abdul Mabidul Malique, Mr Aiadurai Sivasamy Premananthan, Mr Christopher Donald Michael Tooley, Mr Farokh Engineer
Income: £1,232,114 [2016]; £728,006 [2015]

Go Run for Fun Foundation
Registered: 17 Mar 2014
Tel: 023 8028 7066 *Website:* gorunforfun.com
Activities: General charitable purposes; education, training; advancement of health or saving of lives
Address: 38 Hans Crescent, London, SW1X 0LZ
Trustees: Mr John Reece, Mr John Paul Mayock, Mr Leen Heemskerk
Income: £1,169,946 [2016]; £210,325 [2015]; £15,000 [2014]

Goal (International)
Registered: 22 Dec 2004 *Employees:* 26
Website: goal-uk.org
Activities: The advancement of health or saving of lives; prevention or relief of poverty; overseas aid, famine relief
Address: Goal (International), 1-10 Praed Mews, London, W2 1QY
Trustees: Mr Ross Niland, Shelley M Deane PhD, Mr Alex Hutton Mills, Mr Gerry Turley, Mrs Jane Tully
Income: £12,123,366 [2016]; £28,876,989 [2015]; £22,333,642 [2014]; £3,822,630 [2013]; £2,923,693 [2012]

The Godinton House Preservation Trust
Registered: 19 Mar 1991 *Employees:* 12 *Volunteers:* 32
Tel: 01233 632652 *Website:* godintonhouse.co.uk
Activities: Environment, conservation, heritage
Address: Godinton House, Godinton Lane, Ashford, Kent, TN23 3BP
Trustees: The Hon John David Leigh-Pemberton, Mrs Amanda Cottrell, The Rt Hon Damian Green, Mr Michael Francis Jennings, The Hon Wyndham George Plumptre, Mrs Gina Jennings
Income: £1,004,567 [2016]; £1,030,675 [2015]; £935,001 [2014]; £816,791 [2013]; £792,252 [2012]

Godolphin International Thoroughbred Leadership Programme Limited
Registered: 12 Feb 2004
Tel: 01638 730070 *Website:* godolphinflyingstart.com
Activities: Education, training
Address: Godolphin Management Co Ltd, The Main Office, Duchess Drive, Newmarket, Suffolk, CB8 9HE
Trustees: Mr Edmond Mahony, Mr Lewis Daniel Pride Jr, Mrs Lisa-Jane Graffard, Mr Joseph Martin Osborne, Mr Hugh Alastair Anderson
Income: £1,005,991 [2016]; £887,900 [2015]; £921,563 [2014]; £947,111 [2013]; £888,089 [2012]

The Godolphin School
Registered: 5 Jul 1963 *Employees:* 162
Tel: 01722 430522 *Website:* godolphin.org
Activities: Education, training
Address: Godolphin School, Milford Hill, Salisbury, Wilts, SP1 2RA
Trustees: The Godolphin School Trustee Limited
Income: £7,999,553 [2016]; £7,763,393 [2015]; £7,533,298 [2014]; £7,498,796 [2013]; £7,466,942 [2012]

Godolphin and Latymer School
Registered: 12 Oct 1966 *Employees:* 230
Tel: 020 8735 9595 *Website:* godolphinandlatymer.com
Activities: Education, training
Address: Godolphin and Latymer, Iffley Road, London, W6 0PG
Trustees: The Godolphin and Latymer School Foundation
Income: £17,080,667 [2017]; £16,487,614 [2016]; £15,334,800 [2015]; £14,309,047 [2014]; £14,038,375 [2013]

The Godstowe Preparatory School Company Limited
Registered: 2 Oct 1963 *Employees:* 121
Tel: 01494 429000 *Website:* godstowe.org
Activities: Education, training
Address: Godstowe Preparatory School, Shrubbery Road, High Wycombe, Bucks, HP13 6PR
Trustees: Mrs Janet Brent, Mr Thomas Bunbury, Mrs Kathryn Ann Allner, Mr Martin Ashworth, Mrs Nichola Amanda Caroline Annable, Mr M J Tebbot, Mrs Linda Anne Poore, Mrs Tara Leaver, Mrs Rachel Owen, Mr A Wilkinson
Income: £6,505,359 [2016]; £6,160,454 [2015]; £5,996,256 [2014]; £5,454,639 [2013]; £5,399,315 [2012]

Gofal Cymru
Registered: 9 Nov 1990 *Employees:* 317 *Volunteers:* 22
Tel: 01656 647722 *Website:* gofal.org.uk
Activities: Education, training; advancement of health or saving of lives; disability; prevention or relief of poverty; accommodation, housing; economic, community development, employment
Address: 2nd Floor, Derwen House, 2 Court Road, Bridgend, CF31 1BN
Trustees: Miss Deborah Green, Mr Stewart Greenwell, Mr Neil Mark Hapgood, Mr Huw David Davies, Mr Stewart John Davison, Mr David John Davies, Mr Christopher Jamie Dowson Loughran
Income: £7,343,264 [2017]; £6,699,255 [2016]; £6,295,813 [2015]; £4,517,158 [2014]; £4,285,910 [2013]

The Golden Bottle Trust
Registered: 6 Feb 1986
Tel: 020 7353 4522
Activities: General charitable purposes
Address: C Hoare & Co, 37 Fleet Street, London, EC4P 4DQ
Trustees: Messrs Hoare Trustees
Income: £2,798,777 [2016]; £1,665,934 [2015]; £1,470,128 [2014]; £1,343,063 [2013]; £1,543,031 [2012]

Golden Gates Housing Trust
Registered: 31 Aug 2010 *Employees:* 263
Tel: 01925 452452 *Website:* gght.org.uk
Activities: Education, training; advancement of health or saving of lives; disability; prevention or relief of poverty; accommodation, housing; amateur sport; environment, conservation, heritage; economic, community development, employment
Address: Bank Park House, Kendrick Street, Warrington, Cheshire, WA1 1UZ
Trustees: Mr Ian Duncan Clayton, Mr Duncan James Craig, Mr Philip Pemberton, Mr Robert Clive Young, Mrs Christine Fallon, Mr Robert Charles Hepworth, Mr Roy Alfred Smith, Mr John Owen Fulham, Mr Graham William Burgess, Mr Anthony Vincent Williams
Income: £39,520,000 [2017]; £42,245,000 [2016]; £40,387,720 [2015]; £36,888,469 [2014]; £36,069,436 [2013]

Golden Lane Housing Ltd
Registered: 18 Aug 1998 *Volunteers:* 47
Tel: 0300 003 7007 *Website:* glh.org.uk
Activities: Disability; accommodation, housing
Address: Golden Lane Housing, 123 Golden Lane, London, EC1Y 0RT
Trustees: Mr Stuart Kelly, Mr Christopher Barrett, Mrs Louise Li, Mr Manny Lewis, Simon Beddow, Mr Stephen Jack
Income: £14,830,748 [2017]; £13,286,218 [2016]; £12,053,387 [2015]; £11,515,765 [2014]; £9,520,550 [2013]

The Goldman Sachs Charitable Gift Fund (UK)
Registered: 19 Jul 2007
Tel: 020 7774 1000
Activities: General charitable purposes
Address: Goldman Sachs, Peterborough Court, 133 Fleet Street, London, EC4A 2BB
Trustees: Mr Mike Housden, Mr Robert James Katz, Mr Peter Matthew Fahey
Income: £1,524,203 [2017]; £1,031,257 [2016]; £1,890,231 [2015]; £602,529 [2014]; £1,665,255 [2013]

Goldman Sachs Gives (UK)
Registered: 6 May 2008
Tel: 020 7774 1000
Activities: General charitable purposes
Address: Goldman Sachs, Peterborough Court, 133 Fleet Street, London, EC4A 2BB
Trustees: Mr Mike Housden, Ms Jennifer Evans, Mr Peter Matthew Fahey, Mr Robert James Katz
Income: £23,201,944 [2017]; £24,560,494 [2016]; £23,210,503 [2015]; £23,286,425 [2014]; £19,102,090 [2013]

The Goldsmiths Centre
Registered: 17 Jul 2007 *Employees:* 15
Tel: 020 7606 7010 *Website:* goldsmiths-centre.org
Activities: Education, training; arts, culture, heritage, science; environment, conservation, heritage; economic, community development, employment
Address: The Goldsmiths' Company, Goldsmiths' Hall, 13 Foster Lane, London, EC2V 6BN
Trustees: Mr Tom Fattorini, Mr Edward Braham, Mr Richard Fox, Mrs Gaynor Rosemary Andrews, Mr Grant MacDonald, Michael Prideaux, Miss Arabella Claire Felicity Slinger, Mr Arthur Philip Andrew Drysdale
Income: £2,321,345 [2016]; £1,456,215 [2015]; £1,095,522 [2014]; £11,498,426 [2013]; £3,131,820 [2012]

Goldsmiths Students' Union
Registered: 10 Apr 2013 *Employees:* 72 *Volunteers:* 600
Tel: 020 7717 2511 *Website:* goldsmithssu.org
Activities: Education, training; amateur sport; recreation
Address: Goldsmiths Students' Union, Goldsmiths College, 8 Lewisham Way, London, SE14 6NW
Trustees: Weiyen Hung, Ms Theresa Mamakoh Kanneh, Miss Eva Crossan Jory, Mr Toby Peacock, Mr Joseph Tema, Mr Patrick Moule, Dr Andrea Gilroy, Ms Tara Mariwany, Ms Tiia Meuronen, Mr Joseph Leam, Ms Taylor McGraa
Income: £2,125,680 [2017]; £2,200,923 [2016]; £1,901,993 [2015]; £1,939,111 [2014]

The Golf Foundation
Registered: 7 Dec 1982 *Employees:* 16
Tel: 01992 449830 *Website:* golf-foundation.org
Activities: Education, training; amateur sport
Address: Ambition Broxbourne Business Centre, Pindar Road, Hoddesdon, Herts, EN11 0FJ
Trustees: Mr Nicholas Sladden, Mr Stephen Proctor, Ms Deborah Allmey, Ms Sally Frances Stewart, Mr Stephen Geoffrey Lewis, Mr Nicholas Pink, Evie Carter, Sir Robin Miller, Mrs Di Horsley, Mr Ian Armitage, Mr Nick Bragg FCA, Mr Kevin Graham Barker, Jeremy Tomlinson
Income: £1,945,118 [2017]; £2,470,904 [2015]; £1,697,218 [2014]; £1,617,400 [2013]; £1,740,876 [2012]

Gonville and Caius College in the University of Cambridge Founded in Honour of The Annunciation of The Blessed Mary The Virgin
Registered: 17 Aug 2010 *Employees:* 152 *Volunteers:* 2
Tel: 01223 332400 *Website:* cai.cam.ac.uk
Activities: Education, training
Address: Gonville & Caius College, Cambridge, CB2 1TA
Trustees: Professor Joseph Herbert, Dr David Secher, Professor Sir Alan Roy Fersht, Dr Gareth Conduit, Dr John Robson, Professor Roger Carpenter, Dr Geoffrey Webber, Professor John Dixon Mollon, Dr David Michael Holburn, Professor Dominic Wright, Dr James Fox, Prof Malcolm Smith, Professor Richard Smith
Income: £17,679,338 [2017]; £21,137,190 [2016]; £13,915,885 [2015]; £12,405,433 [2014]; £11,936,552 [2013]

Good Things Foundation
Registered: 19 Jan 2016 *Employees:* 52
Tel: 0114 349 1666 *Website:* goodthingsfoundation.org
Activities: Other charitable purposes
Address: First Floor, 1 East Parade, Sheffield, S1 2ET
Trustees: Mr Roy Alexander George Clare, Liz Williams, Ms Zoe Elise Breen, Mr Laurence Robert Piercy, Miss Samantha Taylor, William Perrin, Helen Milner, Mr Chad Paul Bond, Mr James Edward Speake, Ms Nicola Anne Wallace-Dean
Income: £5,859,991 [2017]; £6,261,537 [2016]

Goodenough College
Registered: 1 Jan 1961 *Employees:* 82
Tel: 020 7520 1522 *Website:* goodenough.ac.uk
Activities: Education, training; accommodation, housing; economic, community development, employment
Address: Goodenough College, London House, Mecklenburgh Square, London, WC1N 2AB
Trustees: The Honourable Philip John Remnant CBE, Fabian French, Mr Charles McGregor, Mr Graham Norman Charles Ward CBE, Mr Alexander John Dyke Acland, Mr David Charles Brooks Wilson, Mr Eric Frank Tracey, Mrs Fiona Kirk, Mr Andrew Brown, Mr Martin Juergen Schwab, Mr Hugh Barnabas Crossley, Mr James Alexander Douglas
Income: £12,149,000 [2017]; £10,922,000 [2016]; £9,193,000 [2015]; £7,552,000 [2014]; £8,483,308 [2013]

Goodheart Animal Sanctuaries
Registered: 30 Jul 2015 *Employees:* 1 *Volunteers:* 1
Website: goodheartanimalsanctuaries.com
Activities: Animals
Address: Nickless, Milson, Kidderminster, Worcs, DY14 0BE
Trustees: Mr David Andrew Walker, Mr James Lee Cross, Miss Dwynwen Jones
Income: £2,506,193 [2017]; £1,210,495 [2016]

The Goodman Foundation
Registered: 28 Apr 2003
Activities: General charitable purposes; education, training; advancement of health or saving of lives; disability; prevention or relief of poverty; overseas aid, famine relief; other charitable purposes
Address: c/o ABP, Unit 6290, Bishops Court, Solihull Parkway, Birmingham Business Park, Birmingham, B37 7YB
Trustees: Ms Catherine Goodman, Mr Philip Morgan, Mr Laurence Joseph Goodman
Income: £6,105,740 [2017]; £672,398 [2016]; £6,669,685 [2015]; £10,163,749 [2014]; £710,334 [2013]

Goodwin Development Trust
Registered: 11 Jul 2003 *Employees:* 167 *Volunteers:* 162
Tel: 01482 587550 *Website:* goodwintrust.org
Activities: General charitable purposes; education, training; disability; accommodation, housing; amateur sport; economic, community development, employment
Address: Goodwin Development Trust Ltd, Pod 5, The Octagon, Walker Street, Hull, HU3 2RA
Trustees: Mrs Sharon Igoe, Ms Altynay Guney, Mr Robin Watkin, Mr Saulius Orechovas, Mrs Ruth Bean, Ms Kellock Ainley, Ms Natalja Batare, Mrs Anna Heddle
Income: £5,100,000 [2017]; £4,353,000 [2016]; £6,818,000 [2015]; £6,334,000 [2014]; £5,520,000 [2013]

The Mike Gooley Trailfinders Charity
Registered: 9 Sep 1995
Tel: 020 7938 3143 *Website:* trailfinders.com
Activities: General charitable purposes; education, training; advancement of health or saving of lives; amateur sport; armed forces, emergency service efficiency
Address: 9 Abingdon Road, London, W8 6AH
Trustees: Mr Mark Bannister, Mr Michael David William Gooley, Mrs Fiona Kathleen Gooley, Mr Tristan Gooley, Ms Bernadette Mary Gooley
Income: £11,239,584 [2017]; £3,835,881 [2016]; £4,447,496 [2015]; £989,376 [2014]; £987,282 [2013]

The Gordon Foundation
Registered: 11 Sep 1963 *Employees:* 193
Tel: 01276 859704 *Website:* gordons.surrey.sch.uk
Activities: Education, training
Address: Gordons School, Bagshot Road, West End, Woking, Surrey, GU24 9PT
Trustees: Michael More-Molyneux, Mr David John Munro, Mr Paul Darius Talbot, Mrs Pamela Lea, Mr Richard Whittington, Mrs Lynn Bannister, Dr John Harnden Higgs, Mr William Eason, Major General John Russell-Jones, Sir Peter Anthony Wall, Mr Martin Barnes, Mr Charles Henry Whiffin, Mr Mark Ledlie Hawkesworth, Mr Peter Wynter Bee, Mr Alan McClafferty, Lord Lingfield, Mr Thomas Oliver Gordon, Mr Jay Edward Tamsitt, Ms Alison MacLennan, Mr Christopher Nicholas Lomas, Mrs Jane Valner, Ms Gabriella De Turris
Income: £10,573,901 [2016]; £10,434,609 [2015]; £10,814,715 [2014]; £11,749,711 [2013]; £6,209,714 [2012]

Gosfield School Limited
Registered: 29 Mar 1967 *Employees:* 79 *Volunteers:* 15
Tel: 01787 474040 *Website:* gosfieldschool.org.uk
Activities: Education, training
Address: Gosfield School Ltd, Halstead Road, Gosfield, Halstead, Essex, CO9 1PF
Trustees: Mr Peter Sakal, Mr Simon Lambert, Jon Corrall, Mr Guy Martyn, Mr Max Ford
Income: £2,905,942 [2016]; £2,796,939 [2015]; £2,511,826 [2014]; £2,216,799 [2013]; £2,150,681 [2012]

The Gosling Foundation Limited
Registered: 7 May 1985
Tel: 020 7495 5599
Activities: General charitable purposes; education, training; advancement of health or saving of lives; disability; prevention or relief of poverty; religious activities; arts, culture, heritage, science; amateur sport; armed forces, emergency service efficiency; other charitable purposes
Address: 21 Bryanston Street, London, W1H 7AB
Trustees: Hon Vice Admiral Sir Donald Gosling KCVO RNR, Hon Capt Adam Gosling RNR
Income: £5,386,362 [2017]; £4,787,719 [2016]; £4,448,071 [2015]; £4,452,146 [2014]; £4,449,000 [2013]

Gosling Sports Park
Registered: 28 Mar 1969 *Employees:* 140
Tel: 01438 238876
Activities: General charitable purposes; education, training; advancement of health or saving of lives; disability; amateur sport; recreation
Address: 26 Petworth Close, Stevenage, Herts, SG2 8UP
Trustees: Mr Ian Miller, Mr Steve Ryan, Mr Simon Carter, Mr Tim Davies, Mr Andrew Hoare, Mrs Stephanie Dunn
Income: £4,904,106 [2016]; £3,412,230 [2015]; £3,409,961 [2014]; £3,483,084 [2013]

Gospel Standard Bethesda Fund
Registered: 22 Sep 1962 *Employees:* 99 *Volunteers:* 30
Tel: 01582 460522
Activities: The advancement of health or saving of lives; accommodation, housing
Address: Gospel Standard Bethesda Fund, 12b Roundwood Lane, Harpenden, Herts, AL5 3BZ
Trustees: Mr Trevor Harold William Scott, Mr Henry Mercer, Samuel Benjamin Cottingham, Mr Mark Oliver Wiltshire, Mr Michael George Bailey, Mr Michael David Ridout, Mr Alan Rayner, Mr Andrew John Collins
Income: £1,656,381 [2016]; £1,397,387 [2015]; £1,513,282 [2014]; £2,086,322 [2013]

Governance Ministries
Registered: 5 Jan 1996 *Employees:* 26
Tel: 020 8208 5680
Activities: Religious activities
Address: Governance Ministries, 226 Church Road, Willesden, London, NW10 9NR
Trustees: Mr R A Fleming, Mr Nick Marsh, Mr S Mallison-Jones, Miss Margie Tuccillo
Income: £9,200,950 [2017]; £9,226,239 [2016]; £4,764,805 [2015]; £3,155,062 [2014]; £3,501,936 [2013]

Governors for Schools
Registered: 23 Nov 1999 *Employees:* 14
Tel: 020 7354 9805 *Website:* sgoss.org.uk
Activities: Education, training
Address: AGP, Sycamore House, Sutton Quays Business Park, Clifton Road, Sutton Weaver, Cheshire, WA7 3EH
Trustees: Mr Martin Lawrence MBE, Mr Ian Armitage, Ms Anne Lucy Punter, Mr Henry Nicholas Almroth Colthurst, Mr David Paul Rowsell, Ms Joanna Page, Mrs Linda Wilding
Income: £1,353,527 [2017]; £665,835 [2016]; £764,190 [2015]; £839,265 [2014]; £749,073 [2013]

Governors of The Charity for Relief of The Poor Widows and Children of Clergymen (Commonly Called Sons and Friends of The Clergy)
Registered: 24 Apr 1963 *Employees:* 7
Tel: 020 7799 3696 *Website:* sonsandfriends.org.uk
Activities: The advancement of health or saving of lives; prevention or relief of poverty
Address: 1 Dean Trench Street, Westminster, London, SW1P 3HB
Trustees: The Revd Canon Christopher Davies, Mr Jonathan Prichard, The Rt Revd Tim Thornton, The Venerable David Lowman, The Venerable Christine Allsopp, Mr Patrick Walker, The Revd Wendy Kennedy, The Revd Dr Jack Dunn, Mr Tom Hoffman, Mr Andrew Gillett, The Rt Revd David Rossdale, Ms Jill Sandham, Ms Alex Brougham, Lady Mawer, The Revd Canon Roxanne Hunte
Income: £4,177,820 [2016]; £3,388,714 [2015]; £4,024,288 [2014]; £3,708,457 [2013]; £3,794,338 [2012]

Grace Dieu Manor School
Registered: 31 Aug 2006 *Employees:* 57
Tel: 01633 672334 *Website:* gracedieu.com
Activities: General charitable purposes; education, training; religious activities
Address: 151 Cromwell Road, Newport, NP19 0HS
Trustees: Father Brian, Richard Gamble, Reverend Father, Mr Brian Nelson Kennedy, Rev Joseph O'Reilly, Father Philip, Father Chris, Mr Paul Raymond Francis Rudd, Mrs Mary Espinasse, Reverend Father Tom Thomas
Income: £2,578,451 [2016]; £2,598,574 [2015]; £2,758,872 [2014]; £2,812,683 [2013]; £2,728,120 [2012]

The Grace Trust
Registered: 9 Dec 1968 *Volunteers:* 120
Tel: 020 3301 3806 *Website:* thegracetrust.org.uk
Activities: General charitable purposes; education, training; advancement of health or saving of lives; disability; prevention or relief of poverty
Address: 22 Barton Road, Haslingfield, Cambridge, CB23 1LL
Trustees: Scribefort Limited, Aller Brook Limited
Income: £100,723,956 [2016]; £97,731,048 [2015]; £91,678,745 [2014]; £78,533,624 [2013]; £73,542,108 [2012]

Grace and Compassion Benedictines
Registered: 11 Jun 1996 *Employees:* 127
Tel: 020 8695 7492 *Website:* graceandcompassionbenedictines.org.uk
Activities: The prevention or relief of poverty; accommodation, housing; religious activities
Address: 1st Floor, Church House, 61 College Road, Bromley, Kent, BR1 3QG
Trustees: Sister Carmel Murtagh, Sister Thaya Moses, Sister Jaya Susai, Sister Kathryn Anne Yeeles, Sister Paula Tharasanthiras
Income: £4,667,961 [2016]; £6,429,919 [2015]; £4,217,831 [2014]; £4,874,358 [2013]; £3,652,972 [2012]

The Graeae Theatre Company Limited
Registered: 24 Apr 1982 *Employees:* 12 *Volunteers:* 1
Tel: 020 7613 6900 *Website:* graeae.org
Activities: Education, training; disability; arts, culture, heritage, science
Address: Bradbury Studios, 138 Kingsland Road, London, E2 8DY
Trustees: Ms Jacqui Adeniji-Williams, Ms Sarah Howard, Ms Samantha Tatlow, Alice Holland, James Watson-O'Neill, Selma Dimitrijevic, Mr Tim Powell, Mr Fraser Nicol, Sharon Marshall
Income: £1,185,868 [2017]; £1,219,267 [2016]; £1,065,311 [2015]; £1,096,251 [2014]; £977,961 [2013]

The Grammar School at Leeds
Registered: 27 Jul 1995 *Employees:* 402 *Volunteers:* 107
Tel: 0113 229 1552 *Website:* gsal.org.uk
Activities: Education, training
Address: Leeds Grammar School, Harrogate Road, Leeds, LS17 8GS
Trustees: Mrs Elizabeth Enid Bailey BChD LDS RCS, Ian Martin Lloyd Jones, Mr John Woodward, Mrs Deborah Kenny, Mr Jeremy Cross, Sir Stephen David Reid Brown KCVO, Mr Anthony John Walsh, Mrs Joanne Semple, Jacqueline Harper, Mr David Peter Anthony Gravells JP BA MBA, Dr Hilary Luscombe, Mr Richard Obank, Mrs Claire Vilarrubi, Mrs Charlene Lyons, Mrs Susan Anne Solyom, Mr Angus Matthew Martin, Professor Abigail Harrison Moore
Income: £25,809,145 [2017]; £26,040,000 [2016]; £24,847,000 [2015]; £24,097,000 [2014]; £23,514,000 [2013]

The Grammar School of King Edward VI at Stratford-upon-Avon
Registered: 24 Oct 1963 *Employees:* 19 *Volunteers:* 22
Tel: 07816 751738
Activities: Education, training
Address: The Hunting Lodge, Billesley Road, Stratford upon Avon, Warwicks, CV37 9RA
Trustees: Prof James Ronald Mulryne, Councillor Mike Brain, Mr Victor Matts, Mr Anthony Patrick Michael Bird, The Most Honourable The Marquess of Hertford, Mayor Councillor John Bicknell
Income: £1,511,501 [2017]; £1,582,630 [2016]; £850,490 [2015]; £637,437 [2014]; £646,042 [2013]

The Grand Charity
Registered: 18 Feb 1981
Tel: 020 3146 3304 *Website:* mcf.org.uk
Activities: General charitable purposes; advancement of health or saving of lives; disability; prevention or relief of poverty; overseas aid, famine relief
Address: The Grand Charity, Freemasons Hall, 60 Great Queen Street, London, WC2B 5AZ
Trustees: Masonic Charitable Foundation
Income: £3,781,000 [2017]; £14,957,700 [2016]; £19,591,400 [2015]; £13,660,100 [2013]; £15,834,800 [2012]

The Grand Lodge of Mark Master Masons' Fund of Benevolence
Registered: 4 Jul 1963 *Employees:* 2
Tel: 020 7747 1166 *Website:* markbenevolence.org.uk
Activities: General charitable purposes; prevention or relief of poverty
Address: Mark Masons Hall, 86 St James's Street, London, SW1A 1PL
Trustees: Peter Hawken, Dr John Lawson William Wright, Mr J Bell, Mr C M Wilson, Mr C D Radmore, Mr Alexander McLaren, Mr P H Rollin, Mr H K Emmerson, Mr S Fenton, Mr A Morris, Mr David Ashbolt, Dr Tapesh Pakrashi
Income: £2,507,835 [2017]; £2,024,352 [2016]; £1,656,775 [2015]; £1,200,149 [2014]; £1,156,732 [2013]

The Grand at Clitheroe Ltd
Registered: 31 Aug 2005 *Employees:* 30
Tel: 01200 421599 *Website:* thegrandvenue.org.uk
Activities: Education, training; prevention or relief of poverty; religious activities; arts, culture, heritage, science
Address: 18 York Street, Clitheroe, Lancs, BB7 2DL
Trustees: Dr John Edward Lancaster MBE, Mr Steven John Lancaster, Mr Chris Richardson, Mrs Rosemary Lancaster MBE, Anna Catherine Lancaster
Income: £1,513,805 [2017]; £1,048,513 [2016]; £971,593 [2015]; £1,230,457 [2014]; £1,355,414 [2013]

Grandparents Plus
Registered: 30 Sep 2002 *Employees:* 21 *Volunteers:* 65
Tel: 020 8981 8001 *Website:* grandparentsplus.org.uk
Activities: Education, training; other charitable purposes
Address: Grandparents Plus, 1 Addington Square, Camberwell, London, SE5 0HF
Trustees: Professor Ann Buchanan, Mrs Sally Rowe, Jayne Harrill, Mr Julian Arthur Young, Mr Stephen Sowden, Brian Edwards, Elaine Farmer Professor, Mr Hans Stocker
Income: £1,067,949 [2017]; £1,038,791 [2016]; £688,308 [2015]; £480,231 [2014]; £451,298 [2013]

The Grange Centre for People with Disabilities
Registered: 22 Sep 1962 *Employees:* 125 *Volunteers:* 107
Tel: 01372 452608 *Website:* grangecentre.org.uk
Activities: Education, training; disability; accommodation, housing
Address: Rectory Lane, Bookham, Leatherhead, Surrey, KT23 4DZ
Trustees: Mrs Anna Coss, Mrs Carol Riddington, Mr Denis Coulon, Mrs Karen Stevens, Mr Peter Grose, Mr John Pagella, Mr George Kalorkoti, Mrs Pamela Barrett, Mrs Linda Ferguson
Income: £4,099,290 [2017]; £4,108,786 [2016]; £3,550,656 [2015]; £3,405,986 [2014]; £3,346,952 [2013]

Grange Farm Centre
Registered: 15 Sep 1982
Tel: 01992 578642 *Website:* grangefarmcentre.co.uk
Activities: Education, training; amateur sport; recreation
Address: 181 High Street, Epping, Essex, CM16 4BQ
Trustees: Mr John Knapman, Mr Charles Barry Scrutton, Mr Trevor Neil Johnson, Mrs Margaret McEwen, Mr Pesh Kapasiawala, Mr Roger Neville, Mr Peter Benedict Minoletti, Mr Robert William Church, Mrs Mary Sartin
Income: £2,152,685 [2017]; £397,152 [2016]; £360,248 [2015]; £333,338 [2014]; £325,858 [2013]

The Grange Festival
Registered: 3 Mar 2016 *Employees:* 4 *Volunteers:* 50
Website: thegrangefestival.co.uk
Activities: General charitable purposes; education, training; arts, culture, heritage, science
Address: c/o The Grange Estate, Estate Office, Folly Hill Farm, Itchen Stoke, Alresford, Hants, SO24 9TF
Trustees: Mr Mark Baring, Mr Timothy Charles Parker, Mr Owen Jonathan, Mr Charles Anthony Haddon-Cave, Mr Daniel Mark Benton, Mr Malcolm John Le May, Mrs Rosamund Bernays, Mr Alan Fred Titchmarsh, Mrs Rebecca Ann Shelley, Mr Richard South Morse, Mr Samuel Donald Jackson
Income: £2,936,797 [2017]; £825,816 [2016]

Grange Park Opera

Registered: 11 Feb 1998 *Employees:* 12
Website: grangeparkopera.co.uk
Activities: Education, training; arts, culture, heritage, science
Address: Sutton Manor Farm, Bishop's Sutton Road, Alresford, Hants, SO24 0AA
Trustees: Vivien Duffield, David Davies, Mrs Joanna Barlow, Tony Bugg, Mr David Andrew Kershaw, Mr Keith Frederick Charles Weed, Mr Iain Burnside, Mr Simon Freakley, Mr Jeremy Farr, Mary Creswell, Ms Susan Butcher
Income: £3,923,381 [2016]; £4,339,690 [2015]; £3,187,650 [2014]; £3,253,629 [2013]; £3,411,930 [2012]

Grange Rose Hill School Limited

Registered: 21 May 1976 *Employees:* 62 *Volunteers:* 3
Tel: 01892 547010 *Website:* rosehillschool.co.uk
Activities: Education, training
Address: 13 Woodside Road, Tunbridge Wells, Kent, TN4 8QA
Trustees: Mr Alan Baker, Rev Giles Walter, Mr Charles Arthur, Mrs Lone Hockley, Mr Nick Green, Mr Crispin Symes, Mrs Susan Gates, Mr Michael Scott, Mrs Karen Bilney, Mrs Jane Scott, John Pearson
Income: £3,690,303 [2017]; £3,608,111 [2016]; £3,353,436 [2015]; £3,244,649 [2014]; £3,154,106 [2013]

The Grange School Hartford Limited

Registered: 22 Nov 1962 *Employees:* 258
Tel: 01606 74007 *Website:* grange.org.uk
Activities: Education, training
Address: Grange School, Bradburns Lane, Hartford, Northwich, Cheshire, CW8 1LU
Trustees: Mr Simon Batey, Mrs Ann Arthur, Mrs Karen Jones, Mrs Clare Briegal, Mrs Sarah Hudson, Mrs Catherine Stanton, Mrs Susan Dawson, David Akka, Mr Chris Oglesby, Mr Jurgen Stamer, Mr Nigel Parkinson, Mr Neil Brougham, Mrs Karen Williams, Mr Larry Fairclough, Mr Jeremy Walker Simpson
Income: £11,993,365 [2017]; £11,594,853 [2016]; £10,951,807 [2015]; £10,877,822 [2014]; £10,526,891 [2013]

GrantScape

Registered: 23 Feb 2004 *Employees:* 7 *Volunteers:* 145
Tel: 01908 247630 *Website:* grantscape.org.uk
Activities: General charitable purposes; education, training; arts, culture, heritage, science; environment, conservation, heritage; economic, community development, employment
Address: GrantScape, Unit E, Whitsundoles Farm, Broughton Road, Salford, MK17 8BU
Trustees: Mr Antony Paul Cox, Mr Michael Anthony Singh, Ms Philippa Mary Lyons, Mr Mohammed Saddiq, Mr Michael James Clarke, Mr John Stafford Mills
Income: £1,843,158 [2017]; £1,843,158 [2016]; £1,904,152 [2015]; £1,709,963 [2014]; £1,470,448 [2013]

The Great Britain Sasakawa Foundation

Registered: 9 Jan 1985 *Employees:* 3
Tel: 020 7436 9042 *Website:* gbsf.org.uk
Activities: Education, training; arts, culture, heritage, science
Address: Great Britain Sasakawa Foundation, Dilke House, 1 Malet Street, London, WC1E 7JN
Trustees: Mr Michael French, Ambassador Hiroakii Fujii, Professor David Cope, Ms Joanna Pitman, Professor Yoriko Kawaguchi, Professor Ryuichi Teshima, Sir John Boyd, The Earl of St Andrews, Mr Tatsuya Tanami, Professor Yuichi Hosoya, Professor Janet Hunter
Income: £1,177,834 [2016]; £1,165,075 [2015]; £1,198,242 [2014]; £762,178 [2013]; £1,173,592 [2012]

Great Britain Wheelchair Basketball Association

Registered: 25 Nov 2011 *Employees:* 22 *Volunteers:* 128
Tel: 01509 279900 *Website:* britishwheelchairbasketball.co.uk
Activities: Disability; amateur sport
Address: British Wheelchair Basketball, Sportpark, 3 Oakwood Drive, Loughborough, Leics, LE11 3QF
Trustees: Mr Paul Hudson, Michelle Leavesley, Joanne Simpson, Mr Daniel Johnson, Ms Jacqueline Scoins-Cass MBE, Mr Graham Arthur, Mrs Susan Peel, David Kingstone, Mr Jaspal Dhani, Mr Austin Kentebe, Mr Sam Whale
Income: £2,101,002 [2017]; £2,999,902 [2016]; £2,402,148 [2015]; £1,673,551 [2014]; £1,834,054 [2013]

Great Britain Wheelchair Rugby Limited

Registered: 9 Jun 2009 *Employees:* 11 *Volunteers:* 5
Tel: 020 8831 7645 *Website:* gbwr.org.uk
Activities: General charitable purposes; amateur sport
Address: Rugby Football Union, 200 Whitton Road, Twickenham, Middlesex, TW2 7BA
Trustees: Mr Richard Allcroft, Mr Andrew Flatt, Mr Simon Lefevre, Ms Margaret Moore, Suzy Christopher, Mr Kevin Michael Aitchison, Mr Michael Spence, Ms Mary Daunt, Mr David Pond
Income: £1,244,709 [2017]; £1,701,020 [2016]; £1,143,695 [2015]; £1,079,553 [2014]; £829,092 [2013]

Great Commission Ministries

Registered: 29 Jun 2010 *Employees:* 4 *Volunteers:* 9
Tel: 020 8591 7704 *Website:* gcmuk.org
Activities: General charitable purposes; education, training; prevention or relief of poverty; religious activities; arts, culture, heritage, science; economic, community development, employment; human rights, religious or racial harmony, equality or diversity; recreation
Address: 102 Longbridge Road, Barking, Essex, IG11 8SF
Trustees: Eva Sekyanzi, Ms Florence Nakayiza, George Muwonge, Mr Mathias Ndenzi, Nivile Southgate, Mr Mathew Mugisha
Income: £7,552,701 [2017]; £1,829,817 [2016]; £509,994 [2015]; £106,765 [2014]; £77,017 [2013]

The Great Dixter Charitable Trust

Registered: 15 Mar 2010 *Employees:* 36 *Volunteers:* 36
Tel: 01797 254048 *Website:* greatdixter.co.uk
Activities: Education, training; environment, conservation, heritage
Address: The Great Dixter Charitable Trust, Great Dixter House and Gardens, Northiam, Rye, E Sussex, TN31 6PH
Trustees: Mr J French, Mr Geoffrey Dyer, Mr Kemal Mehdi, Mr Thomas Cooper, Mr John Massey, Mrs Henrietta Norman, Mr Gyr King, Ms Rosie Atkins, Mr Keith Sangster, Mrs Phyllida Earle, Mr Charles Hind, Mrs Rosemary Alexander, Mrs Olivia Eller
Income: £1,745,269 [2017]; £1,372,399 [2016]; £1,265,488 [2015]; £1,292,535 [2014]; £1,578,472 [2013]

Great Hospital

Registered: 2 Aug 1968 *Employees:* 52 *Volunteers:* 2
Tel: 01603 622022 *Website:* greathospital.org.uk
Activities: Accommodation, housing
Address: Great Hospital, Bishopgate, Norwich, NR1 4EL
Trustees: Mrs Elizabeth Ann Crocker, Doctor James Shanklin Powell, Mr David Howard Buck, Mr David Marris, Mr John Walker, Dr Clare Singh, Mr Michael John Brookes, The Honourable Mrs Alexandra De Bunsen, Mrs Julie Anne James, Catherine Jeffries, Mr Jon Stanley, Mr James Banham
Income: £3,419,295 [2017]; £2,862,393 [2016]; £1,676,317 [2015]; £1,581,629 [2014]; £1,648,918 [2013]

The Great North Air Ambulance Service
Registered: 24 May 2002 *Employees:* 75 *Volunteers:* 42
Tel: 01325 487263 *Website:* greatnorthairambulance.co.uk
Activities: Education, training; advancement of health or saving of lives
Address: Great North Air Ambulance, Imperial Centre, Grange Road, Darlington, Co Durham, DL1 5NQ
Trustees: John Richard Devine Esq, Peter Neal, Mr James Harris, Mr James Kyle, Mr Stephen Groves, Mr Kyee Han, Mr Paul Turner, Mr Brian Jobling, Joan Trench, Ms Dawn Catherine Dunn
Income: £7,008,666 [2017]; £7,325,763 [2016]; £7,833,221 [2015]; £7,656,702 [2014]; £6,802,210 [2013]

Great Ormond Street Hospital Children's Charity
Registered: 19 Jan 2015 *Employees:* 241 *Volunteers:* 1,926
Tel: 020 3841 3188 *Website:* gosh.org
Activities: The advancement of health or saving of lives
Address: 4th Floor, 40 Bernard Street, London, WC1N 1LE
Trustees: Professor Stephen Holgate, Nicky Bishop, Mrs Margaret Ewing, Mr Mark Sartori, Jennifer Bethlehem, Mr Sandeep Katwala, Mr John Connolly, Mrs Kaela Fenn-Smith, Mrs Nina Bibby, Michael Marrinan
Income: £93,290,056 [2017]; £93,777,000 [2016]

Great Walstead Limited
Registered: 18 Sep 1963 *Employees:* 106 *Volunteers:* 23
Tel: 01444 483528 *Website:* greatwalstead.co.uk
Activities: Education, training
Address: Great Walstead School, East Mascalls Lane, Lindfield, Haywards Heath, W Sussex, RH16 2QL
Trustees: Mr Rowen Bainbridge, Mr Jeremy Taylor, Mr Matthew Richard Searle, Mrs Jane Crouch, Mr Richard Hopkins Arthur, Mr Alan Laurent, Rev Christopher David Sutton, Mr Stephen Ulph, Mrs Philippa Hoyle, Mrs Cathryn Ann Chandler Browne, Mr Paul Antony Thurston
Income: £5,680,356 [2017]; £5,312,735 [2016]; £4,875,883 [2015]; £4,646,967 [2014]; £4,364,108 [2013]

Great Western Air Ambulance Charity
Registered: 19 Oct 2007 *Employees:* 12 *Volunteers:* 100
Tel: 0303 444 4999 *Website:* greatwesternairambulance.com
Activities: General charitable purposes; advancement of health or saving of lives
Address: 3rd Floor, County Gates, Ashton Road, Bristol, BS3 2LH
Trustees: Jonathan Skeeles, Professor Jonathan Richard Benger, Mr John Houlden, Ms Karen Edgington, Mr Nigel Pickersgill, Caroline Ann Peters MBE, Mr Martyn William Drake
Income: £3,733,910 [2016]; £3,050,912 [2015]; £2,629,154 [2014]; £2,010,000 [2013]; £1,648,242 [2012]

Great Western Hospital NHS Foundation Trust Charitable Fund and Other Related Charities
Registered: 22 Nov 1995 *Employees:* 5
Tel: 01793 605597 *Website:* brighterfuturesgwh.nhs.uk
Activities: The advancement of health or saving of lives; disability
Address: Great Western Hospital, Commonhead Offices, Marlborough Road, Swindon, Wilts, SN3 6BB
Trustees: Great Western Hospitals NHS Foundation Trust
Income: £1,186,392 [2017]; £1,017,000 [2016]; £403,000 [2015]; £339,000 [2014]; £814,000 [2013]

Great Western Society Limited
Registered: 1 Feb 1977 *Employees:* 16 *Volunteers:* 300
Tel: 01235 817200 *Website:* didcotrailwaycentre.org.uk
Activities: Education, training; arts, culture, heritage, science; environment, conservation, heritage
Address: Great Western Society Ltd, Didcot Railway Centre, Station Road, Didcot, Oxon, OX11 7NJ
Trustees: Mr Charles Martin Thompson, Dr John O'Hagan, Mr Peter Anthony Rance, Marita Ann Middleton, Mr Adrian Jocelyn Knowles, Mr Roger William Orchard, Mr Anthony Richard Croucher, Mr Roger James Horwood, Michael Bodsworth, Mr Richard John Gregory Antliff, Mr Richard John Varley
Income: £1,314,545 [2017]; £1,104,304 [2016]; £1,462,753 [2015]; £1,421,073 [2014]; £1,590,223 [2013]

Great Yarmouth & Waveney Mind
Registered: 19 Dec 1996 *Employees:* 41
Tel: 01493 842129 *Website:* gywmind.org.uk
Activities: Education, training; disability; accommodation, housing
Address: 28-31 Deneside, Great Yarmouth, Norfolk, NR30 3AX
Trustees: Mrs Louise Jordan-Hall, Mrs Katherine Mary Gill, Mr Christopher Harry Rees, Mrs Jeanette Margaret McMullen, Mrs Christine Anne Walsh, Janice Warford, Mr Peter Boczko
Income: £1,156,768 [2017]; £818,886 [2016]; £559,203 [2015]; £536,009 [2014]; £762,322 [2013]

Great Yarmouth Community Trust
Registered: 3 Jan 2003 *Employees:* 120 *Volunteers:* 30
Tel: 01493 743000 *Website:* priorycentre.co.uk
Activities: General charitable purposes; education, training; advancement of health or saving of lives; disability; prevention or relief of poverty; arts, culture, heritage, science; amateur sport; environment, conservation, heritage; economic, community development, employment; other charitable purposes
Address: Calthorpe House, 8 Alexandra Road, Great Yarmouth, Norfolk, NR30 2HW
Trustees: Mr John Alfred Holmes, Councillor Robert Peck, Mrs Sarah Spall, Mr Stephen Doyle
Income: £2,485,338 [2017]; £3,004,562 [2016]; £2,455,787 [2015]; £3,021,979 [2014]; £2,361,961 [2013]

Greater London Fund for the Blind
Registered: 31 Mar 1999 *Employees:* 43 *Volunteers:* 200
Tel: 020 7620 2066 *Website:* glfb.org.uk
Activities: General charitable purposes
Address: Greater London Fund for the Blind, 11-12 Whitehorse Mews, 37 Westminster Bridge Road, London, SE1 7QD
Trustees: Mr Keith David Felton, Mr Peter Harris, Mr Rashmikant Navalchand Mehta, Mr Charles Stopford Colquhoun, Ms Anna Margaret Tylor, Ms Sharon Petrie, Mr Daniel Stuart-Smith, Mr James Matthews Xavier
Income: £2,092,991 [2017]; £2,553,294 [2016]; £2,733,658 [2015]; £2,542,793 [2014]; £2,433,388 [2013]

Greater Manchester Accessible Transport Limited
Registered: 17 Jan 1992 *Employees:* 193
Tel: 0161 244 1504 *Website:* ringandride.info
Activities: Disability; prevention or relief of poverty
Address: 20th Floor, Manchester One, 53 Portland Street, Manchester, M1 3LF
Trustees: Greater Manchester Combined Authority
Income: £5,374,456 [2017]; £5,718,884 [2016]; £6,373,655 [2015]; £7,132,843 [2014]; £6,883,654 [2013]

Greater Manchester Arts Centre Limited
Registered: 13 Feb 1984 *Employees:* 120 *Volunteers:* 201
Tel: 0161 228 7621 *Website:* homemcr.org
Activities: Education, training; arts, culture, heritage, science
Address: Greater Manchester Arts Centre Ltd, 2 Tony Wilson Place, Manchester, M15 4FN
Trustees: Mr Stephen Terence Sorrell, Ms Catharine Braithwaite, Miss Maria Bota, Cllr Bernard Stone, Mr Christopher Jeffries, Mr Jonathan Sidney Claypole-Smith, Mr Karl Jackson, Ms Susan Webster, Professor Pavel Buchler, Ms Alison Ross, Cllr Luthfur Rahman, Ms Josephine Oniyama
Income: £6,507,079 [2017]; £6,519,771 [2016]; £5,564,465 [2015]; £4,550,730 [2014]; £4,738,209 [2013]

Greater Manchester Centre for Voluntary Organisation
Registered: 10 Sep 1975 *Employees:* 36 *Volunteers:* 3
Tel: 0161 277 1005 *Website:* gmcvo.org.uk
Activities: Education, training; economic, community development, employment; human rights, religious or racial harmony, equality or diversity
Address: GMCVO, St Thomas Centre, Ardwick Green North, Manchester, M12 6FZ
Trustees: Mr Tom McGee, Mr Alex Fairweather, Miss Kathryn Cheetham, Mrs Atiha Chaudry, Ms Jane Hamilton, Mrs Dora Blake, Richard George Dyson, Mr Mark Lee, Miss Edna Boampong, Mrs Priti Butler, Mrs Patsy Hodson
Income: £4,964,690 [2017]; £3,778,357 [2016]; £2,585,871 [2015]; £1,622,536 [2014]; £1,501,759 [2013]

Greater Manchester Sports Partnership
Registered: 11 Nov 1996 *Employees:* 27 *Volunteers:* 500
Website: greatersport.co.uk
Activities: Education, training; amateur sport
Address: Greatersport, Wenlock Way Offices, Wenlock Way, Manchester, M12 5DH
Trustees: Mr Eamonn O'Rourke, Mrs Yvonne Harrison, Mr Richard Roe, Ms Carol Couse, William Daniel Blandamer, Mr Rob Young, Ms Paula Dunn, Mr Mal Brannigan
Income: £2,132,409 [2017]; £2,037,386 [2016]; £2,065,507 [2015]; £1,934,972 [2014]; £1,336,447 [2013]

Greater Nottingham Groundwork Trust
Registered: 3 Jul 1991 *Employees:* 43 *Volunteers:* 39
Tel: 0115 978 8212 *Website:* groundworkgreaternottingham.org.uk
Activities: Education, training; prevention or relief of poverty; arts, culture, heritage, science; amateur sport; environment, conservation, heritage; economic, community development, employment; recreation
Address: Unit A, Tennyson Hall, Forest Road West, Nottingham, NG7 4EP
Trustees: Mrs Wendy Golland, Councillor Ronald Hetherington, Councillor Sally Longford, Mr Michael Hill, Mrs Susan Margaret Clarson, Mr Jim Creamer, Mr Roscoe Fernandes, Mr Martin Plackett
Income: £3,348,143 [2017]; £2,482,775 [2016]; £1,734,284 [2015]; £1,512,494 [2014]; £1,900,961 [2013]

Greater Together
Registered: 27 Jul 2012 *Employees:* 1
Website: greatertogether.org.uk
Activities: General charitable purposes
Address: Greater Together, Richard House, 9 Winckley Square, Preston, Lancs, PR1 3HP
Trustees: Mr Andrew Darron, Claire Bennett, Mr Paul Ireland, Ed Saville, Deborah Terras, Paul Maher
Income: £1,393,426 [2017]; £1,416,154 [2016]; £1,579,763 [2015]; £483,968 [2014]; £493,980 [2013]

Greek and Greek Cypriot Community of Enfield
Registered: 5 Dec 2000 *Employees:* 59 *Volunteers:* 5
Tel: 020 8373 6299 *Website:* ggcce.org.uk
Activities: General charitable purposes; education, training; advancement of health or saving of lives; disability; prevention or relief of poverty; accommodation, housing; arts, culture, heritage, science; economic, community development, employment
Address: Flat 66, Swinson House, 24 Highview Gardens, London, N11 1SJ
Trustees: Mrs Rena Andreou, Stephanie Collins, Mrs Eleni Yannaki Pilavakis, Mr Markos Markou, Mr Soteris Soteriou
Income: £1,205,926 [2017]; £1,376,642 [2016]; £1,131,326 [2015]; £1,159,046 [2014]; £1,252,545 [2013]

The Green Alliance Trust
Registered: 29 Mar 1995 *Employees:* 25
Tel: 020 7233 7433 *Website:* green-alliance.org.uk
Activities: Environment, conservation, heritage
Address: Fourth Floor, The Green Alliance Trust, Victoria Charity Centre, 11 Belgrave Road, London, SW1V 1RB
Trustees: Mr David Baldock, Ben Caldecott, Professor Mariana Mazzucato, Rosemary Boot, Mr Paul Lambert, Fiona Reynolds, Graham Wynne, Ms Alison Austin, Dr Claire Craig
Income: £1,199,829 [2017]; £1,457,563 [2016]; £1,082,353 [2015]; £1,216,405 [2014]; £1,051,482 [2013]

Margaret Green Animal Rescue
Registered: 1 Jul 2016 *Employees:* 48 *Volunteers:* 220
Tel: 01929 480474 *Website:* margaretgreenanimalrescue.org.uk
Activities: Animals
Address: Margaret Green Animal Rescue, Animal Sanctuary, Church Knowle, Wareham, Dorset, BH20 5NQ
Trustees: Mr Mike Nathan, Mr Alan William Simons, Mr Timothy Payne, Lorraine Suchanek, Mr Matt Devereux, Mr Duane Walker
Income: £8,355,310 [2017]

The Kenneth & Susan Green Charitable Foundation
Registered: 14 May 2012
Tel: 01932 827060
Activities: General charitable purposes; education, training; advancement of health or saving of lives; disability; prevention or relief of poverty; overseas aid, famine relief; religious activities; arts, culture, heritage, science; environment, conservation, heritage; economic, community development, employment; armed forces, emergency service efficiency
Address: Kenneth Green Associates, Hill House, Monument Hill, Weybridge, Surrey, KT13 8RX
Trustees: Mr Kenneth Green, Mrs Susan Green, Mrs Charlotte Garlick, Mr Philip Stokes, Mrs Sarah Scragg
Income: £1,660,843 [2016]; £596,824 [2015]; £1,110,505 [2014]; £305,924 [2013]; £540,303 [2012]

Jerry Green Dog Rescue
Registered: 17 Dec 2013 *Employees:* 56 *Volunteers:* 95
Tel: 01652 653343 *Website:* jerrygreendogs.org.uk
Activities: Education, training; animals
Address: Jerry Green Dog Rescue, Wressle, Brigg, N Lincs, DN20 0BJ
Trustees: Kevin Peart, Andrew Robinson, Victoria Taylor, Lynn Hewison, Paul McCartan, Ian Cawsey, Jayne Chudley
Income: £1,198,781 [2016]; £885,233 [2015]; £14,925,020 [2014]

Green Lane Masjid and Community Centre
Registered: 10 Sep 2008 *Employees:* 52 *Volunteers:* 60
Tel: 0121 713 0080 *Website:* greenlanemasjid.org
Activities: General charitable purposes; education, training; prevention or relief of poverty; overseas aid, famine relief; religious activities; amateur sport; economic, community development, employment
Address: 20 Green Lane, Small Heath, Birmingham, B9 5DB
Trustees: Mr Mohammed Saeed, Mr Sajjad Akram, Mr Mohammed Nahim, Mr Alee Stevenson
Income: £2,657,626 [2016]; £1,810,917 [2015]; £2,237,990 [2014]; £1,048,183 [2013]; £1,603,319 [2012]

Green Pastures
Registered: 5 Nov 1987 *Employees:* 55 *Volunteers:* 6
Tel: 01295 279963 *Website:* greenpastures.uk.com
Activities: The advancement of health or saving of lives
Address: Green Pastures Nursing Home, Bath Road, Banbury, Oxon, OX16 0TT
Trustees: Stuart White, Rev Wendy Biddington, Dr Melanie Kay Patton, Mrs Jane Adkins, Mrs Margaret Clark, Mr Nicholas Rory Alexander Grant, Mr Trevor Grant
Income: £1,572,325 [2017]; £1,740,662 [2016]; £1,305,009 [2015]; £1,253,654 [2014]; £1,364,886 [2013]

Green Templeton College
Registered: 7 Jun 2011 *Employees:* 49
Tel: 01865 274773 *Website:* gtc.ox.ac.uk
Activities: Education, training
Address: Green Templeton College, 43 Woodstock Road, Oxford, OX2 6HG
Trustees: Mr David Cranston, Prof Keith Hawton, Ms Elizabeth Padmore, Prof Paul Wordsworth, Mr Ian Laing, Prof Mark Harrison, Prof Dame Valerie Beral, Dr Richard Cuthbertson, Professor Richard Gibbons, Professor Carolyn Hoyle, Dr David Levy, Prof Neil Mortensen, Dr Rebecca Surender, Prof Kathryn Wood, Professor James Worrell, Prof Sue Dopson, Prof Tim Morris, Dr Jonathan Reynolds, Dr Marc Thompson, Mr Paul Beerling, Dr Andrew White, Professor Mary Daly, Professor Sarah Darby, Mr Ron Emerson, Dr Michael Smets, Mr Stephen Kennedy, Sir Tom Shebbeare, Professor Stephen Tucker, Prof Sir Richard Peto, Dr Stuart Basten, Dr Kunal Basu, Prof Shoumo Bhattacharya, Prof Peter Friend, Miss Linda Hands, Dr Laurence Leaver, Dr Niall Moore, Dr Felix Reed-Tsochas, Prof Robert Walker, Prof Stephen Woolgar, Professor Elisabeth Hsu, Professor Paul Montgomery, Dr Rafael Ramirez, Dr Chris Sauer, Dr Xiaolan Fu, Professor Linda Scott, Professor Richard McManus, Professor Harry Daniels, Professor Denise Lievesley, Dr Susan James Relly, Dr Marella De Bruijn
Income: £6,101,000 [2016]; £5,083,000 [2015]; £6,247,000 [2014]; £5,984,000 [2013]

The Greenbank Project
Registered: 2 Jun 1983 *Employees:* 113 *Volunteers:* 7
Tel: 0151 733 7255 *Website:* greenbank.org.uk
Activities: Education, training; disability; amateur sport; economic, community development, employment; recreation
Address: Greenbank College Project, Greenbank Lane, Liverpool, L17 1AG
Trustees: Mr James Alan Hulme, Mr Alan Irving, Mr Timothy Hall, Mr Mark Swift, Miss Emma Elizabeth Hulme, Mr Stephen Connolly, Ms Susan Cunningham, Mr John Lennon, Sandra Hulme, Mrs Jean Stephens, Mr William Shortall, Miss Stefanie O'Connor, Mr Anthony Baines
Income: £4,312,560 [2017]; £3,350,304 [2016]; £3,458,102 [2015]; £2,739,604 [2014]; £2,333,592 [2013]

Greenbank School Limited
Registered: 21 Sep 1971 *Employees:* 47
Website: greenbank.stockport.sch.uk
Activities: Education, training
Address: Greenbank School, 64 Heathbank Road, Cheadle Hulme, Cheadle, Cheshire, SK8 6HU
Trustees: Jack Williams, Mrs Kimberley Jane Challah, Mrs Brenda Skelton, Mr Phil Enstone, Miss Rachel Jane Chadwick, Mrs Sarah Crossley, Mr Andrew John Galloway, Mr Ian Bryning, Mr Neal Somaia, Mr Terence Walsh, Mrs Amanda Berezai, Dr Caroline Johnson
Income: £2,061,504 [2017]; £2,002,270 [2016]; £1,927,959 [2015]; £1,772,406 [2014]; £1,737,473 [2013]

Greenbelt Festivals
Registered: 15 May 1984 *Employees:* 5 *Volunteers:* 920
Tel: 020 7329 0039 *Website:* greenbelt.org.uk
Activities: Education, training; prevention or relief of poverty; overseas aid, famine relief; religious activities; arts, culture, heritage, science
Address: Greenbelt Festivals, Floor 2, Church House, 86 Tavistock Place, London, WC1H 9RT
Trustees: Andrew Turner, Rhian Roberts, Andrew Griffiths, David Farrow, Becky Hall, Marika Rose, Mr Graham Wilson, Revd Kate Bottley, Ruth Mountford, Mrs Chine McDonald, Steve Baker, Mr Ben Solanky
Income: £1,368,568 [2016]; £1,334,205 [2015]; £1,736,735 [2014]; £1,845,614 [2013]; £1,913,367 [2012]

Greendown Trust
Registered: 8 Jan 1990 *Employees:* 32
Tel: 0113 268 1812 *Website:* greendowntrust.co.uk
Activities: Accommodation, housing
Address: Dyneley House, Allerton Hill, Chapel Allerton, Leeds, LS7 3QB
Trustees: Mrs Catherine Yvonne Allen, Mrs Pauline Agnes Beecroft, Mrs Lindsey Webster, Mrs Beverly Ann Jaques, Mr D Pickersgill, Christopher Jaques, Mr Rodney Phillips
Income: £1,133,427 [2016]; £949,073 [2015]; £898,983 [2014]; £928,281 [2013]

Greenfield Gospel Hall Trust
Registered: 27 Jan 2015 *Volunteers:* 50
Tel: 0117 906 1282
Activities: Religious activities; other charitable purposes
Address: 47 Hortham Lane, Almondsbury, Bristol, BS32 4JJ
Trustees: Mr Laurie Charles Huntley, Mr Charles Anton Leflaive, Mr John Davies, Mr Timothy George Smith, Mr Edward Henry Nunn
Income: £3,933,612 [2017]; £169,784 [2016]

Greenfield School
Registered: 4 Sep 1986 *Employees:* 50
Tel: 01483 772525 *Website:* greenfield.surrey.sch.uk
Activities: Education, training
Address: Greenfield School, Brooklyn Road, Woking, Surrey, GU22 7TP
Trustees: Mrs Janet Rosemary Day, Mr Nick Phillips, Rev Mark Wallace, Mrs Charlotte Anne Beckett, Mr Jon Wood, Mrs Kathryn Mary Tyson, Mr Mark Hoskins, John Attwater, Mr Howard Tuckett, Mrs Jill Denyer
Income: £2,454,858 [2017]; £2,515,625 [2016]; £2,390,860 [2015]; £2,151,719 [2014]; £2,047,765 [2013]

The Greenfields Centre Limited
Registered: 17 Jan 1990 *Employees:* 58
Tel: 0115 841 8440 *Website:* greenfieldschildcare.org.uk
Activities: Education, training; economic, community development, employment
Address: Greenfields, 139 Russell Road, Nottingham, NG7 6GX
Trustees: Judy Tate, Jackie Topham, Ms Rachel Naomi Crookston, Mrs Sally Roberts, Miss Debbie Clarke, Ms Jillian Hilary Burn
Income: £1,025,429 [2016]; £1,098,062 [2015]; £1,085,548 [2014]; £860,867 [2013]; £700,630 [2012]

Greenfields Educational Trust
Registered: 18 May 1983 *Employees:* 63 *Volunteers:* 15
Tel: 01342 822189 *Website:* greenfieldsschool.com
Activities: Education, training
Address: Greenfield School, Priory Road, Forest Row, E Sussex, RH18 5JD
Trustees: Mr Peter David Hodkin, Mr Redvers Alastair Lycett, Mrs Susanne Lesley Rush, Mrs Jennifer Ann Scarfe-Beckett, Mr Andrew Chalmers
Income: £1,535,133 [2016]; £1,392,310 [2015]; £1,348,248 [2014]; £1,186,033 [2013]; £1,164,888 [2012]

Greenham Trust Ltd
Registered: 9 Jun 1997 *Employees:* 22
Tel: 01635 817444 *Website:* greenhamtrust.com
Activities: General charitable purposes; education, training; advancement of health or saving of lives; disability; prevention or relief of poverty; accommodation, housing; arts, culture, heritage, science; amateur sport; environment, conservation, heritage; economic, community development, employment; recreation
Address: Liberty House, The Enterprise Centre, New Greenham Park, Newbury, Berks, RG19 6HW
Trustees: Sir Peter Michael CBE, Mr Graham Mather, Dr Paul Bryant, Mr Julian Cazalet, Ms Biddy Hayward, Mr David Bailey, Mr Malcolm Morris, Zoe Benyon, Mr Charles Brims, Ms Victoria Fishburn
Income: £8,288,430 [2017]; £8,409,197 [2016]; £8,329,034 [2015]; £6,992,948 [2014]; £6,727,020 [2013]

Greenhouse Sports Limited
Registered: 25 Jul 2003 *Employees:* 82 *Volunteers:* 79
Tel: 020 8576 6118 *Website:* greenhousesports.org
Activities: Education, training; disability; amateur sport
Address: 7-8 St Martins Place, London, WC2N 4JH
Trustees: Mr Michael De Giorgio, Mr Jeffrey Berman, Mrs Lynn Gadd, Mr Andrew Lowenthal, Mrs Penny Linnett, Mr Michael Sherwood, Mr Stephen Luke Ellis, Mr Nicholas Prempeh
Income: £6,646,695 [2017]; £7,285,708 [2016]; £11,417,797 [2015]; £4,949,182 [2014]; £3,539,777 [2013]

Greenpeace Environmental Trust
Registered: 22 Jun 1982
Website: greenpeace.org.uk
Activities: Environment, conservation, heritage
Address: Greenpeace UK, Canonbury Villas, London, N1 2PN
Trustees: Mr Colin Hines, Ms Deborah Tripley, George MacFarlane, Mr Steve Warshal, Mr Martyn Day, Mr Andrew McParland
Income: £5,781,932 [2017]; £4,716,657 [2016]; £6,287,078 [2015]; £5,311,262 [2014]; £3,574,396 [2013]

Greenpower Education Trust
Registered: 18 Jan 2010 *Employees:* 6 *Volunteers:* 662
Tel: 01243 552305 *Website:* greenpower.co.uk
Activities: Education, training; amateur sport; environment, conservation, heritage
Address: Green Power Education Trust, The Green Power Centre, Arundel Road, Fontwell, Arundel, W Sussex, BN18 0SD
Trustees: Mr Vaughan Richard Clarke, Mrs Lisa Russell, Mr Alex Badowski, Miss Natasha Sophie Vracas, Mr Stuart Daniel Morgan, Miss Deborah Jane Beale, Mr Mark Groves, Mr Christopher Baylis, Mrs Emma Louise Smith, Mr Daniel Claude Holme, Mr Marcus Hall
Income: £1,175,460 [2016]; £1,051,784 [2015]; £771,540 [2014]; £701,072 [2013]; £634,286 [2012]

The Greensand Trust
Registered: 17 Aug 1999 *Employees:* 43 *Volunteers:* 159
Tel: 01234 743591 *Website:* greensandtrust.org
Activities: Environment, conservation, heritage
Address: The Working Woodland Centre, Maulden Wood, West End, Haynes, Bedford, MK45 3UZ
Trustees: Mrs Gillian Sharp, Mr Steven Denison Smith, Mr Sonnie Brian Wing, Mr Peter Smith, Mrs Sally Ann Hunt
Income: £1,174,259 [2017]; £1,202,701 [2016]; £1,148,367 [2015]; £870,744 [2014]; £1,071,799 [2013]

Greensleeves Homes Trust
Registered: 3 Feb 1997 *Employees:* 1,009 *Volunteers:* 25
Tel: 020 7793 1122 *Website:* greensleeves.org.uk
Activities: Accommodation, housing
Address: Greensleeves Homes Trust, 54 Fenchurch Street, London, EC3M 3JY
Trustees: Mr Robert Strange OBE, Mr Christopher Shaw, Mrs Leila Kyle Harris-Ryberg, Mr Charles Richard Costella, Ms Kim Davies, Mr Desmond Kelly OBE, Ms Lakshmi Ramakrishnan, Ms Elizabeth Ann Marsh, Mrs Kathryn Gray, Ms Dallas Pounds
Income: £28,805,759 [2017]; £23,985,857 [2016]; £20,136,491 [2015]; £19,151,085 [2014]; £18,197,557 [2013]

Greenwich + Docklands Festivals
Registered: 1 Jun 1994 *Employees:* 5 *Volunteers:* 80
Tel: 020 8305 5022 *Website:* festival.org
Activities: Arts, culture, heritage, science
Address: Greenwich & Dockland Festivals, Old Royal Naval College, Pepys Building, 2 Cutty Sark Gardens, London, SE10 9LW
Trustees: Dr Margaret Sheehy, Mr Antony McBride, Mr Marcus Hughes, Mr Oliver Hughes, Cllr Amina Ali, Ms Fiona Hughes, Mr Geoffrey Pine, Mr Paul Hanrahan, Ms Deepa Shastri, Maxine Room, Ms Claire Gevaux
Income: £1,780,654 [2017]; £1,756,006 [2016]; £1,158,742 [2015]; £1,391,330 [2014]; £1,298,602 [2013]

The Greenwich Foundation for The Old Royal Naval College
Registered: 22 May 1997 *Employees:* 70 *Volunteers:* 131
Tel: 020 8269 4754 *Website:* ornc.org
Activities: Environment, conservation, heritage
Address: Greenwich Foundation for The Old, Royal Naval College, Foundation House, 2 Cutty Sark Gardens, London, SE10 9LW
Trustees: Rear Admiral Brian Perowne CB, Mr Rupert Evenett, Mr Peter David Kenneth Shanks, Mr John Barnes, Ms Rosemarie MacQueen, Mr Desmond Shawe-Taylor, Mr Tony Hales, Mrs Susan Wilkinson, Ms Jamaria Kong, Mr Andrew Clark
Income: £6,619,159 [2017]; £5,892,638 [2016]; £5,758,115 [2015]; £5,501,675 [2014]; £5,581,282 [2013]

Greenwich Steiner School Initiative
Registered: 14 Jun 1999 *Employees:* 35
Tel: 020 8317 6460 *Website:* greenwichsteinerschool.org.uk
Activities: Education, training
Address: Wellesley House, Duke of Wellington Avenue, Royal Arsenal, London, SE18 6SS
Trustees: Mr Andrew Kevin Green, Mr Panos George Ferendinos, Miss Samantha Williams, Mrs Nora Sorenson, Ms Lucy Beverley, Mr Panagiotis Seretis, Mr Alexander Graf
Income: £1,188,744 [2017]; £1,097,323 [2016]; £1,004,071 [2015]; £936,293 [2014]; £808,546 [2013]

The Greenwich Theatre Limited
Registered: 6 Mar 1967 *Employees:* 17 *Volunteers:* 20
Tel: 020 8858 4447 *Website:* greenwichtheatre.org.uk
Activities: Education, training; arts, culture, heritage, science
Address: Crooms Hill, Greenwich, London, SE10 8ES
Trustees: Mr Ian Arthur Brown, Mr Norman Adams, Mr Gerald Lidstone, Mrs Rita Shirley Beckwith, Mr Stephen Brain Councillor, Miss Lucy Cuthbertson
Income: £1,135,425 [2017]; £1,276,481 [2016]; £1,303,833 [2015]; £1,155,654 [2014]; £1,100,684 [2013]

Greenwich and Bexley Community Hospice Limited
Registered: 25 Feb 1993 *Employees:* 175 *Volunteers:* 485
Tel: 020 8312 2244 *Website:* communityhospice.org.uk
Activities: Education, training; advancement of health or saving of lives; disability; other charitable purposes
Address: Greenwich & Bexley Cottage Hospice, 185 Bostall Hill, London, SE2 0GB
Trustees: Mr Timothy Barnes, Mr Peter Sowden, Mr David Matheson, Mrs Julia Fuller, Mrs Paula Keats, Mrs Ruth Russell, Mr Gerald Peters, Dr David Robson
Income: £9,028,306 [2017]; £8,033,757 [2016]; £8,597,034 [2015]; £7,311,281 [2014]; £7,330,059 [2013]

The Gregg and St Winifred's Schools Trust
Registered: 25 Oct 2001 *Employees:* 130 *Volunteers:* 15
Tel: 023 8047 2133 *Website:* gregg.southampton.sch.uk
Activities: Education, training
Address: The Gregg School, Townhill Park House, Atlantic Park View, West End, Southampton, SO18 3RR
Trustees: Mr Vincent John Davies, Mr John William Watts, Mr Roger Douglas Hart, Dr Thomas David William Randell, Mrs Carolyn Anne Pulman, Mr Michael Leonard Pulman, Mrs Sheri Sellers, Mrs Joanna Louise Preston
Income: £4,293,758 [2017]; £3,998,409 [2016]; £4,083,471 [2015]; £3,996,557 [2014]; £4,002,105 [2013]

The Greggs Foundation
Registered: 16 Apr 1987 *Employees:* 7
Tel: 0191 212 7626 *Website:* greggsfoundation.org.uk
Activities: The prevention or relief of poverty; environment, conservation, heritage
Address: Greggs House, Quorum Business Park, Newcastle upon Tyne, NE12 8BU
Trustees: Andrew John Davison, Richard Hutton, Jane Irving, Roisin Currie, Kate Bradley, Fiona Nicholson, Lindsay Graham, Tony Rowson, Karen Wilkinson-Bell
Income: £3,003,105 [2016]; £2,573,659 [2015]; £1,999,216 [2014]; £1,833,649 [2013]; £1,699,531 [2012]

Gresham's School
Registered: 17 Aug 2004 *Employees:* 284
Tel: 01263 714500 *Website:* greshams.com
Activities: Education, training
Address: Gresham's School, Cromer Road, Holt, Norfolk, NR25 6EA
Trustees: Mr Graham Able, A Martin Smith, Sir James Dyson, Peter Mitchell, Mr James Fforde, Simon Gorton, Mr David Jones, Dr Susan Penelope-Ann Rubin, Mrs Rosamund Jane Walwyn, Mr James William Maunder Taylor, Stephen Oldfield, Edward Gould, Mr Michael Lee Johnson Goff, The Rt Revd Jonathan Meyrick, Mr James Morgan, Paul Marriage, Mrs Virginia Graham, Mr Alexander Edward De Capell Brooke, Mrs Anna Maria Dugdale
Income: £18,675,127 [2017]; £17,560,570 [2016]; £22,381,859 [2015]; £15,250,302 [2014]; £16,095,987 [2013]

Grey Coat Hospital Foundation
Registered: 11 Aug 1966 *Employees:* 205
Tel: 020 7828 3055 *Website:* westminstergreycoat.org
Activities: Education, training
Address: Grey Coat Hospital Foundation, 57 Palace Street, London, SW1E 5HJ
Trustees: The Very Reverend Dr John Hall, Mr John Nesbitt ARICS, Ms Annabel Wiscarson BSc, Mr Jonathon Noakes MA, Mrs Miranda Richards, Mr Bill Andrewes, Mrs Susan Lowson MSc RSCN RGN DMS, Miss Rachel Whittaker BSc MBE, Mrs Vicky Simmons BA
Income: £11,453,000 [2017]; £11,092,000 [2016]; £10,698,000 [2015]; £9,811,000 [2014]; £9,053,000 [2013]

Grey Gables
Registered: 9 Aug 1963 *Employees:* 52
Tel: 0121 706 1684
Activities: Accommodation, housing
Address: Grey Gables, 39 Fox Hollies Road, Acocks Green, Birmingham, B27 7TH
Trustees: Mrs Heather Jones, Ms Jennifer Irene Sinclair, Mr Alan Laurence Boyars
Income: £1,006,204 [2017]; £914,210 [2016]; £926,327 [2015]; £896,366 [2014]; £875,649 [2013]

Greyhound Trust
Registered: 3 Jul 1975 *Employees:* 10 *Volunteers:* 1,000
Tel: 020 8335 3016 *Website:* greyhoundtrust.org.uk
Activities: Animals
Address: Greyhound Trust, Wings, Peeks Brook Lane, Horley, Surrey, RH6 9SX
Trustees: Mrs Jacqueline Dunn, Mr John Haynes, Professor Steven Dean BVetMed MRCVS DVR, Mr Simon Gray, Mr Anthony Collins, Mr John Simpson, Mr Matthias Scanlon, Clive Feltham, Mr Nathan Evans
Income: £4,135,511 [2016]; £4,463,363 [2015]; £4,233,138 [2014]; £3,823,473 [2013]; £3,622,000 [2012]

Grimsby Cleethorpes and Humber Region YMCA

Registered: 11 Oct 1996 *Employees:* 47 *Volunteers:* 159
Tel: 01472 693388 *Website:* ymca-humber.com
Activities: General charitable purposes; education, training; accommodation, housing; religious activities; amateur sport; economic, community development, employment
Address: Peaks Lane Housing Project, Peaks Lane, Grimsby, N E Lincs, DN32 9ET
Trustees: Mr Paul Terence Gallant, Mr David Wooldridge, Mr Spencer Hunt, Mr Mark Jones, Ms Laura Lougher, Ms Julie Keen, Mr Niel Strawson, Mr Donald Fortune, Mr Stephen Gallaher, Ms Kerry Jo Lynn, Mr Clive Rounce
Income: £1,815,103 [2016]; £2,040,395 [2015]; £1,427,377 [2014]; £1,558,068 [2013]; £1,551,363 [2012]

Grimsthorpe and Drummond Castle Trust Limited

Registered: 12 Mar 1978 *Employees:* 48
Tel: 01778 591205 *Website:* grimsthorpe.co.uk
Activities: General charitable purposes; education, training; arts, culture, heritage, science; environment, conservation, heritage
Address: Estate Office, Grimsthorpe, Bourne, Lincs, PE10 0LY
Trustees: Sir John Lucas-Tooth, Sir Mark Jones, Mr Richard Calvocoressi CBE, Mr David Laird OBE JP DL, Mr Hugh Matheson, Baroness Willoughby De Eresby, Mr Sebastian Miller, Mr Francis John Fane Marmion Dymoke
Income: £12,707,909 [2017]; £2,765,412 [2016]; £2,270,747 [2015]; £2,270,747 [2014]; £2,034,608 [2013]

The Grocers' Charity

Registered: 17 Jul 1968 *Employees:* 1
Tel: 020 7606 3113 *Website:* grocershall.co.uk
Activities: General charitable purposes; education, training; advancement of health or saving of lives; disability; prevention or relief of poverty; religious activities; arts, culture, heritage, science; environment, conservation, heritage; economic, community development, employment
Address: Grocers' Hall, Princes Street, London, EC2R 8AD
Trustees: The Grocers' Trust Company Limited
Income: £1,261,176 [2017]; £1,093,371 [2016]; £1,075,436 [2015]; £561,550 [2014]; £950,672 [2013]

M and R Gross Charities Limited

Registered: 29 Mar 1967
Tel: 020 8731 0777
Activities: General charitable purposes; education, training; prevention or relief of poverty; religious activities
Address: New Burlington House, 1075 Finchley Road, London, NW11 0PU
Trustees: Mr Michael Saberski, Mrs Sarah Padwa, Mrs Rifka Gross, Mr Leonard Lerner
Income: £4,263,991 [2017]; £4,207,751 [2016]; £25,531,205 [2015]; £8,195,834 [2014]; £9,556,201 [2013]

Groundwork Cheshire Lancashire & Merseyside

Registered: 20 Feb 1984 *Employees:* 103 *Volunteers:* 50
Tel: 01942 821444 *Website:* groundwork.org.uk
Activities: Education, training; advancement of health or saving of lives; amateur sport; environment, conservation, heritage; economic, community development, employment
Address: 74-80 Hallgate, Wigan, Lancs, WN1 1HP
Trustees: Ms Pamela Stewart, Ms Tracy Fishwick, Mr Paul Roots, Mr Guy Parker, Mr Michael Warner, Mrs Sian Jay, Mr Todd Holden, Mr Andrew Upton
Income: £4,599,746 [2017]; £4,438,374 [2016]; £2,600,779 [2015]; £2,229,733 [2014]; £2,321,673 [2013]

Groundwork Creswell, Ashfield and Mansfield

Registered: 26 Sep 1991 *Employees:* 34 *Volunteers:* 65
Tel: 01246 570977 *Website:* groundwork-creswell.org.uk
Activities: Education, training; advancement of health or saving of lives; prevention or relief of poverty; accommodation, housing; arts, culture, heritage, science; amateur sport; environment, conservation, heritage; economic, community development, employment
Address: Lilac Cottage, Mill Lane, Normanton on Trent, Newark, Notts, NG23 6RW
Trustees: Mr Colin Ambler, Harold Glasby, Mr John Swift, Mr Stephen Parkin, Mr John Davidson, Mr David Phillips, Mr Jim Creamer, Mrs Denise Edwards, Rob Wadd, Mr Duncan McGregor, Mr Ian Extance, Mrs Mary Bond, Mr John Smart, Mr Anthony Palmer, Ms Tricia Williams, Mr Nev Haslam
Income: £1,408,303 [2017]; £2,349,061 [2016]; £2,391,166 [2015]; £2,883,871 [2014]; £2,609,256 [2013]

Groundwork East

Registered: 2 Dec 1985 *Employees:* 78 *Volunteers:* 50
Tel: 01707 260129 *Website:* groundwork.org.uk
Activities: Education, training; amateur sport; environment, conservation, heritage; economic, community development, employment
Address: Groundwork East, Mill Green, Hatfield, Herts, AL9 5PE
Trustees: Mr Derrick Alan Ashley, Mr John Ball, Mr Neville Reyner CBE DL, Mrs Rebecca Britton, Ms Carole Hegley, Mr Michael Hamilton MBE, Mr Michael Master, Mr John Barrington Chevallier Guild, Ms Julie Catherine Smith, Mr Ralph Sangster
Income: £2,663,381 [2017]; £2,528,002 [2016]; £2,412,578 [2015]; £2,162,535 [2014]; £2,192,962 [2013]

Groundwork London

Registered: 9 Oct 2007 *Employees:* 222 *Volunteers:* 9,766
Tel: 020 7922 1230 *Website:* groundwork.org.uk
Activities: Education, training; prevention or relief of poverty; arts, culture, heritage, science; amateur sport; environment, conservation, heritage; economic, community development, employment
Address: Groundwork, 18-21 Morley Street, London, SE1 7QZ
Trustees: Mr Peter Head, Ms Cate Newness-Smith, Alan Smith, Mr Daniel Davidson, Ms Marilyn Baxter, Councillor Susan Wise, Mr John Smith, Mr Graham Beal, Mr Philip Stokes, Mr Keith Taylor
Income: £15,365,476 [2017]; £11,313,255 [2016]; £10,213,613 [2015]; £10,436,027 [2014]; £11,752,512 [2013]

Groundwork Manchester Salford Stockport Tameside and Trafford

Registered: 16 Jun 2008 *Employees:* 34 *Volunteers:* 200
Tel: 0161 220 1000 *Website:* groundwork.org.uk
Activities: Education, training; environment, conservation, heritage; economic, community development, employment; armed forces, emergency service efficiency
Address: Trafford Ecology Park, Lake Road, Trafford Park, Manchester, M17 1TU
Trustees: Mr David Leyssens, Mr Anthony Edward Berry, Ms Anne Heath, Mr Paul Booth, Mrs Lisa Joanne Kean, Ms Jan McDonald, Mr Peter Charles Styche, Mr Keith Barnes, Cllr Alan Mitchell, Cllr Peter Taylor, Mr Stephen Morris
Income: £1,708,307 [2017]; £1,902,256 [2016]; £1,751,709 [2015]; £5,861,015 [2014]; £9,103,677 [2013]

Groundwork North East
Registered: 1 Mar 1993 *Employees:* 153 *Volunteers:* 120
Tel: 01388 662666 *Website:* groundwork.org.uk
Activities: Education, training; environment, conservation, heritage; economic, community development, employment
Address: Grosvenor House, 29 Market Place, Bishop Auckland, Co Durham, DL14 7NP
Trustees: Cllr Peter Brookes, Mr David Martin, Mr Ian Brown, Mr Darush Hossginzadgh Dodds, Mrs Barbara-Anne Johnson, Professor Graham Street, Mrs Diana Catherine Pearce, Mr Nicola Ann Gott, Mr John Edward Pritchard, Mr Thomas Justice
Income: £7,911,930 [2017]; £8,151,402 [2016]; £8,960,130 [2015]; £7,674,298 [2014]; £10,408,765 [2013]

Groundwork North Wales
Registered: 12 Sep 1991 *Employees:* 31 *Volunteers:* 41
Tel: 01978 757524 *Website:* groundworknorthwales.org.uk
Activities: General charitable purposes; education, training; environment, conservation, heritage; economic, community development, employment
Address: Groundwork Wrexham & Flintshire, 3-4 Plas Power Road, Tanyfron, Wrexham, Clwyd, LL11 5SZ
Trustees: Mr Malcolm Booker, Mr John Troth, Mrs Helen Elizabeth Wright, Dr Stan Moore, Mr Robert David Williams, Mrs Claire Powell, Lee Rawlinson, Mrs Sarah Overson
Income: £1,032,490 [2017]; £1,602,060 [2016]; £2,125,562 [2015]; £1,467,885 [2014]; £1,278,981 [2013]

Groundwork Northamptonshire
Registered: 15 May 2006 *Employees:* 23 *Volunteers:* 78
Tel: 01536 526453 *Website:* gwknorthants.org.uk
Activities: General charitable purposes; education, training; arts, culture, heritage, science; environment, conservation, heritage; economic, community development, employment; recreation
Address: The Business Exchange, Rockingham Road, Kettering, Northants, NN16 8JX
Trustees: Mr Anthony Haldane Robbs, Mr Andre Gonzalez De Savage, Ms Lynn Marie Stubbs, Mr John McGhee, Mrs Gillian Lesley Mercer, Mr Jonathan Nunn, Cllr Maggie Don
Income: £1,041,862 [2017]; £974,671 [2016]; £1,038,244 [2015]; £719,372 [2014]; £743,254 [2013]

Groundwork Oldham and Rochdale
Registered: 20 Feb 1984 *Employees:* 66 *Volunteers:* 200
Tel: 0161 624 1444 *Website:* groundwork.org.uk
Activities: General charitable purposes; education, training; prevention or relief of poverty; accommodation, housing; environment, conservation, heritage; economic, community development, employment; other charitable purposes
Address: Groundwork Oldham & Rochdale, The Groundwork Environment Centre, Shaw Road, Oldham, Lancs, OL1 4AW
Trustees: Councillor Howard Sykes, Councillor David Chadwick, Ms Lorna Bustard, Ms Susan Southworth, Tom Stannard, Mr Neil William Manning, Mr Ian Whittaker, Ms Carol Hopkins, Mr John Bland, Mr John Leslie Searle, Councillor June West, Dr Shaid Mushtaq
Income: £2,110,459 [2017]; £2,897,768 [2016]; £4,480,786 [2015]; £4,320,326 [2014]; £3,774,909 [2013]

Groundwork South Tyneside and Newcastle-upon-Tyne
Registered: 31 Jan 1992 *Employees:* 74 *Volunteers:* 198
Tel: 0191 428 1144 *Website:* groundwork-stan.org.uk
Activities: Education, training; environment, conservation, heritage; economic, community development, employment
Address: South Tyneside Groundwork Trust Ltd, The Eco Centre, Windmill Way, Hebburn, Tyne & Wear, NE31 1SR
Trustees: Mr Mark Charlton, Mr Jeffrey David Owen, Mrs Diana Catherine Pearce, Mr John Short, Dr Geoff O'Brien, Miss Danielle Turton, Derrick Robson, Mr Michael James Cuthbertson, Mr James Perry, Mr Andrew Whittaker, Mrs Catherine Donnelly
Income: £2,037,558 [2017]; £2,218,219 [2016]; £2,156,503 [2015]; £2,281,280 [2014]; £2,174,667 [2013]

Groundwork South Yorkshire
Registered: 21 Sep 2005 *Employees:* 25 *Volunteers:* 50
Tel: 0114 263 6420 *Website:* groundwork-sheffield.org.uk
Activities: Arts, culture, heritage, science; amateur sport; environment, conservation, heritage; economic, community development, employment
Address: Groundwork South Yorkshire, The Tingas Site, Siemens Close, Tinsley, Sheffield, S9 1UN
Trustees: Cllr Martin Lawton, Cllr Ian Auckland, Mr Stephen David Parks, Mr Antony David Nelson, Miss Stephanie Elaine Holmes-Fletcher, Ms Catherine Leanne Stokowska, Mr John Charles Lees, Mr Paul John Griffiths, Mr Michael John Rix
Income: £1,374,690 [2017]; £1,503,712 [2016]; £1,083,548 [2015]; £977,741 [2014]; £868,045 [2013]

Groundwork Wakefield Limited
Registered: 15 Feb 1988 *Employees:* 100 *Volunteers:* 40
Tel: 0113 468 0946 *Website:* groundwork.org.uk
Activities: General charitable purposes; education, training; prevention or relief of poverty; amateur sport; environment, conservation, heritage; economic, community development, employment
Address: Groundwork Leeds, Environment & Business Centre, Merlyn-Rees Avenue, Morley, Leeds, LS27 9SL
Trustees: Mr Peter Cooper, Cllr Jacqueline Williams, Cllr Elaine Blezard, Cllr R"Lund, Ms Jan Wilson, Cllr Monica Graham
Income: £1,713,831 [2017]; £3,725,171 [2016]; £6,348,004 [2015]; £4,537,554 [2014]; £3,640,601 [2013]

Groundwork Wales
Registered: 24 Mar 2003 *Employees:* 45 *Volunteers:* 30
Tel: 01495 222605 *Website:* groundwork.org.uk
Activities: Education, training; arts, culture, heritage, science; amateur sport; environment, conservation, heritage; economic, community development, employment
Address: 3 Ivor Street, Cwmcarn, Newport, NP11 7EG
Trustees: Mr Brynley John Davies, Jeff Greenidge, Mr Bivin Mathew, Ms Helen Northmore, Derek Havard, Mrs Natalie Reees
Income: £1,741,633 [2017]; £1,643,734 [2016]; £1,085,473 [2015]; £1,327,733 [2014]; £1,753,678 [2013]

Groundwork West Midlands
Registered: 27 Mar 2009 *Employees:* 57 *Volunteers:* 30
Tel: 01782 829900 *Website:* groundwork.org.uk
Activities: Environment, conservation, heritage; economic, community development, employment
Address: Groundwork Environment Centre, Albany Works, Moorland Road, Stoke on Trent, Staffs, ST6 1EB
Trustees: Miss June Campbell, Mr Ian Shepherd, Mr Mark Chambers, Mr Steve Woods, Dr Kuda Bondamakara, Mr Ian Priest, Mr Matthew Daniels, Ms Anne Cranston, Mr Jay Patel, Mr Ben Brittain, Mr Stephen Barras
Income: £1,834,392 [2017]; £2,033,663 [2016]; £3,009,764 [2015]; £3,637,149 [2014]; £4,551,612 [2013]

Rennie Grove Hospice Care
Registered: 11 Feb 2011 *Employees:* 151 *Volunteers:* 1,500
Tel: 01727 731006 *Website:* renniegrove.org
Activities: The advancement of health or saving of lives
Address: Grove House, Waverley Road, St Albans, Herts, AL3 5QX
Trustees: Eric Pillinger, Chris Inman, Professor Stephen Spiro, Mrs Jane Elizabeth MacLeod, Dr Lesley Baillie, Mr John Wroe, Pippa Nightingale, Mr Christopher Langford, Dr Sara-Lisa Gresham Cottam, Dr Alie Wainwright, Mr Guy Upward
Income: £7,823,307 [2017]; £7,778,342 [2016]; £7,155,936 [2015]; £6,994,008 [2014]; £6,212,089 [2013]

Guerrand Hermes Foundation for Peace
Registered: 1 Mar 2010 *Employees:* 3
Tel: 01273 555022 *Website:* ghfp.org
Activities: General charitable purposes; education, training; prevention or relief of poverty; arts, culture, heritage, science; environment, conservation, heritage; economic, community development, employment
Address: 199 Preston Road, Brighton, BN1 6SA
Trustees: Sharif Horthy, Dr Patrice Brodeur, Mr Muhammad Ridwan, Mrs Alexandra Asseily, Isni Astuti Horthy, Simon Xavier Calixte Guerrand-Hermes
Income: £1,301,467 [2016]; £24,973 [2015]; £5,609 [2014]; £347,402 [2013]; £600,216 [2012]

The Guide Association London and South East England Region
Registered: 9 Aug 1973 *Employees:* 15 *Volunteers:* 16,400
Tel: 020 8675 7572 *Website:* girlguidinglaser.org.uk
Activities: General charitable purposes; education, training; disability; religious activities; arts, culture, heritage, science; amateur sport; environment, conservation, heritage; economic, community development, employment
Address: 3 Jaggard Way, Wandsworth Common, London, SW12 8SG
Trustees: Miss Sally Christmas, Mrs Lesley Bailey, Mrs Lisa Mitchell, Mrs Alison Gregory, Ms Rachael Graham, Ms Jacqueline Martyr, Mrs Fiona Jackson, Ms Liz Smith, Miss Catherine Breen, Miss Lyndsay Dewar
Income: £1,116,385 [2016]; £1,183,417 [2015]; £1,372,007 [2014]; £1,044,377 [2013]; £933,059 [2012]

The Guide Association
Registered: 1 Jan 1961 *Employees:* 262 *Volunteers:* 100,000
Tel: 020 7834 6242 *Website:* girlguiding.org.uk
Activities: General charitable purposes; education, training; recreation
Address: 17-19 Buckingham Palace Road, London, SW1W 0PP
Trustees: Della Salway, Carole Graham, Maya Dibley, Jaki Booth, Margaret Mackie, Alex Farrow, Valerie Elliott, Amanda Medler, Su Hassall, Robert Cox, Helen Shreeve, Mrs Catherine Irwin
Income: £19,984,726 [2016]; £19,017,084 [2015]; £19,492,596 [2014]; £17,507,143 [2013]; £17,723,108 [2012]

The Guide Dogs for the Blind Association
Registered: 8 Nov 1962 *Employees:* 1,357 *Volunteers:* 16,251
Tel: 0118 983 8772 *Website:* guidedogs.org.uk
Activities: Disability
Address: Guide Dogs for the Blind Association, Hillfields, Reading Road, Burghfield Common, Reading, Berks, RG7 3YG
Trustees: James Hambro, Mike Nussbaum, Amanda Ariss, Patricia Stafford, John Wrighthouse, Ms Clare Elizabeth Black, Polly Williams, David Anderson, David Bagley, Michael Hughes
Income: £107,000,000 [2016]; £103,700,000 [2015]; £101,100,000 [2014]; £74,900,000 [2013]; £69,100,000 [2012]

Guideposts Trust Limited
Registered: 12 Jan 1977 *Employees:* 166 *Volunteers:* 242
Tel: 01993 772886 *Website:* guideposts.org.uk
Activities: Education, training; advancement of health or saving of lives; disability
Address: Guideposts Trust, Willowtree House, Two Rivers Industrial Estate, Station Lane, Witney, Oxon, OX28 4BH
Trustees: Dr Catherine Oppenheimer, Ms Lydia Hirst, Mr Andrew Clive Woodhead, Ms Diana Billingham, Mr Martin Gallagher, Major Peter John Mayne Smith, Mrs Ingrid Blades
Income: £9,098,953 [2017]; £9,750,874 [2016]; £10,854,494 [2015]; £10,389,644 [2014]; £10,642,541 [2013]

Guides Cymru
Registered: 11 Jan 1972 *Employees:* 35 *Volunteers:* 4,400
Tel: 01686 688652 *Website:* girlguidingcymru.org.uk
Activities: Education, training
Address: Girl Guiding Cymru, Broneirion, Llandinam, Powys, SY17 5DE
Trustees: Ms Sian Rees, Mrs Caroline Judith Harries, Ms Janet Horton, Mrs Karilyn Jayne Hancock, Miss Elizabeth Ann Bradley, Miss Megan Andrea Jones, Mrs Lesley Mathews, Mrs Helen Murdoch, Mrs Rebecca Elizabeth Ode
Income: £1,041,328 [2017]; £1,143,456 [2016]; £912,347 [2015]; £731,809 [2014]; £678,943 [2013]

Guild Care
Registered: 3 Mar 1995 *Employees:* 590 *Volunteers:* 300
Website: guildcare.org
Activities: General charitable purposes; advancement of health or saving of lives; disability; accommodation, housing; other charitable purposes
Address: Guild Care, Methold House, North Street, Worthing, W Sussex, BN11 1DU
Trustees: Mr Allan John Ritchie Reid, Mrs Astrid Jagfeldt, Mr Mark Davis, Mrs Caroline MacLeod, Mr Peter Graham Baker, Mr Reginald Percival Nowell, Mrs Antonia Hopkins, Mrs Eileen Houghton, Mr Guy Clinch, Ms Cynthia Lyons
Income: £14,385,499 [2017]; £14,129,570 [2016]; £9,997,188 [2015]; £9,850,807 [2014]; £9,692,244 [2013]

The Guild Estate Endowment
Registered: 29 Apr 1964 *Employees:* 1 *Volunteers:* 18
Tel: 01789 207111 *Website:* stratfordtowntrust.co.uk
Activities: General charitable purposes; education, training; advancement of health or saving of lives; disability; prevention or relief of poverty; accommodation, housing; religious activities; arts, culture, heritage, science; amateur sport; environment, conservation, heritage; armed forces, emergency service efficiency; human rights, religious or racial harmony, equality or diversity; recreation; other charitable purposes
Address: Chief Executive, Stratford upon Avon Town Trust, Civic Hall, 14 Rother Street, Stratford upon Avon, Warwicks, CV37 6LU
Trustees: The Stratford Upon Avon Town Trust
Income: £2,406,789 [2016]; £2,327,319 [2015]; £2,294,916 [2014]; £2,278,102 [2013]; £2,206,547 [2012]

Guildford Baptist Church
Registered: 27 Apr 2010 *Employees:* 12 *Volunteers:* 250
Tel: 01483 485444 *Website:* guildfordbaptist.org
Activities: Religious activities
Address: Station House, Connaught Road, Brookwood, Woking, Surrey, GU24 0ER
Trustees: Revd Dr Ian Stackhouse, Martin Brunet, Miss Elizabeth Hodkinson, Rev Tim Judson, Mr Lance Redman, Mr David White, Mr David Subadha
Income: £1,035,088 [2017]; £1,422,698 [2016]; £1,423,131 [2015]; £1,453,881 [2014]; £1,262,556 [2013]

Guildford City Swimming Club
Registered: 10 Sep 2012 *Employees:* 67 *Volunteers:* 100
Tel: 01932 866387 *Website:* guildfordcitysc.com
Activities: Education, training; advancement of health or saving of lives; disability; amateur sport; recreation
Address: Holly House, Goose Rye Road, Worplesdon, Guildford, Surrey, GU3 3RQ
Trustees: Professor Christina Rita Victor, Mike Hodgson, Mr Jonathan Richard Steele, Mr Steve Middleton, Jon Coxeter-Smith
Income: £1,042,131 [2017]; £987,970 [2016]; £913,846 [2015]; £903,715 [2014]

Guildford Diocesan Board of Finance
Registered: 29 Sep 1967 *Employees:* 53 *Volunteers:* 510
Tel: 01483 790300 *Website:* cofeguildford.org.uk
Activities: Religious activities
Address: Church House Guildford, 20 Alan Turing Road, Surrey Research Park, Guildford, Surrey, GU2 7YF
Trustees: Canon Peter Bruinvels, The Rt Revd Dr Jo Bailey Wells, Mr John Oliver Alpass, The Right Reverend Andrew John Watson, The Revd Cathy Blair, Mr Christopher Bevis, The Very Revd Canon Dianna Gwilliams, Mr Stephen Peter Roberts, The Reverend Dr Peter Harwood, Mr Keith Robert Malcouronne MA FCA CF, The Revd Phillip Johnson, Mr Nigel Lewis, Mr Adrian Vincent, Mrs Sarah Gillies, The Venerable Paul Bryer, The Revd Jane Vlach
Income: £14,509,000 [2016]; £13,129,000 [2015]; £12,970,000 [2014]; £12,084,000 [2013]; £11,825,000 [2012]

The Guildhall School Trust
Registered: 20 Sep 2000
Tel: 020 7382 7082 *Website:* gsmd.ac.uk
Activities: Education, training
Address: Barbican Centre for Arts &, Conferences, Silk Street, Barbican, London, EC2Y 8DS
Trustees: Mr David Graves, Mr Martin Moore, Ms Melissa Scott, Deputy John Bennett, Ms Lynne Williams, Mr Michael Hoffman, Mr Tim Pethybridge, Mr Ken Ollerton, Mr Richard Griffith-Jones
Income: £1,450,354 [2017]; £1,726,093 [2016]; £1,448,158 [2015]; £1,361,733 [2014]; £1,848,441 [2013]

The Gurkha Welfare Trust
Registered: 10 May 2004 *Employees:* 459 *Volunteers:* 70
Tel: 01722 323955 *Website:* gwt.org.uk
Activities: Education, training; advancement of health or saving of lives; prevention or relief of poverty; overseas aid, famine relief; accommodation, housing
Address: The Gurkha Welfare Trust, P O Box 2170, 22 Queen Street, Salisbury, Wilts, SP2 2EX
Trustees: Colonel D G Hayes CBE, Mr Frank Dufficy, Mr David Hitchcock OBE, Mr John Keeling MBBS FRCGP DRCOG, Colonel James Robinson, Major Krishnabahadur Gurung MVO MBE, Ms Cathy Turner, Lieutenant General Nick Pope CBE, Mr Jeremy Brade MBE, Brigadier Gerald Mark Strickland DSO MBE, Mr D P Clifford MVO, Major General Richard Wardlaw OBE, Major General Jon Cole OBE, Major General Angus Fay CB
Income: £19,711,000 [2017]; £20,361,000 [2016]; £26,243,000 [2015]; £14,940,000 [2014]; £12,804,000 [2013]

The Guru Nanak Nishkam Sewak Jatha (Birmingham) UK
Registered: 21 Feb 1979 *Volunteers:* 500
Tel: 0121 551 1125
Activities: General charitable purposes; education, training; prevention or relief of poverty; overseas aid, famine relief; religious activities; environment, conservation, heritage
Address: 1 St Caroline Close, West Bromwich, W Midlands, B70 6TT
Trustees: Mr Mohinder Singh, Mr Jaswinder Pal Singh Chandan, Mr Jarnail Singh Bhinder, Mr Sucha Singh, Mr Parminder Singh Jhutti
Income: £2,867,410 [2017]; £2,905,506 [2016]; £2,709,072 [2015]; £2,756,830 [2014]; £2,167,044 [2013]

Guy's and St Thomas' Charity
Registered: 4 Feb 2015 *Employees:* 25
Tel: 020 7089 4550 *Website:* gsttcharity.org.uk
Activities: Education, training; advancement of health or saving of lives; disability; accommodation, housing; arts, culture, heritage, science; environment, conservation, heritage
Address: Francis House, 9 King's Head Yard, London, SE1 1NA
Trustees: Helen Ruth Bailey, Professor David Colin-Thome, Ms Barbara Moorhouse, Sir Ronald Kerr, Mr Oluwole Kolade, Mrs Sally Tennant, Mr Tom Joy, Mr Duncan James Milne Selbie
Income: £27,103,000 [2017]; £19,442,000 [2016]

Gwasanaeth Ysgolion William Mathias Cyf
Registered: 20 May 2003 *Employees:* 71
Tel: 01248 675960 *Website:* cerdd.com
Activities: Education, training; arts, culture, heritage, science
Address: Gwasanaeth Ysgolion William Mathias, Uned 13b Llys Castan, Parc Menai, Bangor, Gwynedd, LL57 4FH
Trustees: Mrs Elinor Bennett Wigley, Mr William Roger Jones, Mr David Mervyn Roberts, Mr Sion Glyn Pritchard, Alun Llwyd, Dewi Owen Jones, Mrs Beti Rhys Roberts, Dr Catrin Elis Williams
Income: £1,034,381 [2017]; £1,015,319 [2016]; £1,442,729 [2015]; £1,495,087 [2014]; £1,465,854 [2013]

Gwent Association of Voluntary Organisations
Registered: 4 Apr 2006 *Employees:* 105
Tel: 01633 241550 *Website:* gavowales.org.uk
Activities: General charitable purposes; education, training; advancement of health or saving of lives; disability; prevention or relief of poverty; environment, conservation, heritage; economic, community development, employment; human rights, religious or racial harmony, equality or diversity; other charitable purposes
Address: Greenacres, Trallong, Brecon, Powys, LD3 8HN
Trustees: Mr Andrew Lewis, Mr John Williams, Mr Edward John Watts, Mr Doiran Jones, Christine Williams, Mr Gareth Howells, Brigadier Aitken CBE, Mr Robert Malcolm Dutt, Ms Christine Davy, Councillor Philip Edward Hourahine, Mrs Sharon May Rebecca Smith, Joyce Steven, Mr Laurance Clay, Mr Stuart Russell Clark, Mr Christopher Hawker
Income: £4,761,240 [2017]; £4,828,866 [2016]; £4,886,936 [2015]; £4,466,002 [2014]; £4,951,623 [2013]

Gynaecology Cancer Research Fund
Registered: 23 Apr 2002 *Employees:* 12 *Volunteers:* 40
Tel: 020 7605 0100 *Website:* eveappeal.org.uk
Activities: Education, training; advancement of health or saving of lives
Address: The Eve Appeal, 15b Berghem Mews, Blythe Road, London, W14 0HN
Trustees: Mr Angus MacLennan, Miss Adeola Olaitan, Mrs Melanie Richards, Ms Sidonie Kingsmill, Ms Jennifer Leonard, Mr Ian Ashley Drew, Ms Anne Margaret Watts CBE, Sally Bailey, Mr Alexander Fitzgibbons, Emma Gervasio, Mrs Anne Elizabeth Judith Bloomer, Mr Clive Watson
Income: £1,301,424 [2017]; £2,084,207 [2016]; £1,469,659 [2015]; £1,100,204 [2014]; £1,351,000 [2013]

The HALO Trust
Registered: 5 Feb 1991 *Employees:* 5,046
Tel: 01848 331100 *Website:* halotrust.org
Activities: The advancement of health or saving of lives; prevention or relief of poverty; overseas aid, famine relief
Address: Carronfoot, Carronbridge, Thornhill, Dumfries & Galloway, DG3 5BF
Trustees: Col Jane Davis OBE QVRM TD DL RGN, Mr Anthony William Bird, Mr Timothyjohn Edward Church FCA, Ms Alnimah Elbagir, Ms Anastasia Staten, Paddy Nicoll, Mr Rupert Edward Alexander Younger, Mr Anthony Patrick Mycroft Beeley, Mr Mark Jonathan Aedy
Income: £40,903,000 [2017]; £25,627,000 [2016]; £26,627,000 [2015]; £24,157,000 [2014]; £26,442,000 [2013]

HCPT (Hosanna House and Children's Pilgrimage Trust)
Registered: 9 Oct 1980 *Employees:* 25 *Volunteers:* 3,500
Tel: 01788 564646 *Website:* hcpt.org.uk
Activities: Disability; religious activities; other charitable purposes
Address: HCPT, Oakfield Park, 32 Bilton Road, Rugby, Warwicks, CV22 7HQ
Trustees: Miss Claire Shanks, Dr Anthony Brooks, Mr Andrew Clare, Ms Siobhan Kelly, Mrs Patricia Franklin, Mr Timothy Paul Righton, Mr Timothy James Madeley, Rev John Carroll, Capt Anthony McEwen, Mrs Bridget Hanlon, Mr Ian O'Brien, Rev Patrick Sherlock, Dr Emma Jane Derby, Ms Helen Mary Young
Income: £6,180,219 [2016]; £5,353,579 [2015]; £4,509,478 [2014]; £4,474,006 [2013]; £5,505,291 [2012]

HCT Group
Registered: 22 Mar 2002 *Employees:* 1,170 *Volunteers:* 15
Tel: 020 7608 8959 *Website:* hctgroup.org
Activities: General charitable purposes; education, training; advancement of health or saving of lives; disability; prevention or relief of poverty; economic, community development, employment
Address: First Floor, 141 Curtain Road, London, EC2A 3AR
Trustees: Mr Adam James Levitt, Ms Christine Hewitt, Mr Edward William Siegel, Ms Judith Ann Winter, Mr Antony David Ross, Ms Patricia Brennan, Sir John Vincent Cable, Mr Robert Peter Sewell
Income: £49,904,932 [2017]; £44,192,312 [2016]; £45,418,319 [2015]; £43,715,082 [2014]; £37,593,527 [2013]

HENRY
Registered: 7 Nov 2009 *Employees:* 29 *Volunteers:* 98
Tel: 01865 302973 *Website:* henry.org.uk
Activities: Education, training; advancement of health or saving of lives
Address: HENRY, 8 Elm Place, Old Witney Road, Eynsham, Oxon, OX29 4BD
Trustees: Mr Michael Blane, Ms Sylvia Jean Cheater, Ms Joanna Mary Dyson, Mr Adam Buckles, Ms Samantha Olsen, Mr Louis Otto Balsiger, Mr Tom Spencer, Dr Anne Elizabeth Lloyd, Ms Anne Coufopoulos, Mr Alexander Vlassopulos
Income: £1,464,883 [2017]; £923,579 [2016]; £880,392 [2015]; £623,707 [2014]; £593,473 [2013]

HF Trust Limited
Registered: 8 Sep 1971 *Employees:* 3,207 *Volunteers:* 335
Tel: 0117 906 1700 *Website:* hft.org.uk
Activities: General charitable purposes; disability; accommodation, housing
Address: H F Trust Limited, 5-6 Brook Office Park, Emersons Green, Bristol, BS16 7FL
Trustees: Mr Simon Mark Howard Llewellyn, Baroness Judith Anne Jolly, Professor Anthony Holland, Ms Ros Wells, Dr Rowena Jane Tye, Mr Simon Robert Jones, Ms Barbara McIntosh, Mr Martin Laurence Taylor, Ms Madeleine Mary Cowley, Mr Ian Cooper, Mr Werner Andrew White, Mrs Amanda Jane Bunce
Income: £78,257,000 [2017]; £75,064,000 [2016]; £73,556,000 [2015]; £98,817,000 [2014]; £48,369,000 [2013]

HMC (UK)
Registered: 25 May 2012 *Employees:* 189 *Volunteers:* 90
Tel: 0116 326 0165 *Website:* halalhmc.org
Activities: Education, training; religious activities
Address: Leicester Business Centre, 111 Ross Walk, Leicester, LE4 5HH
Trustees: Mr Imtiaz Mahetar, Mr Yaseen Khalifa, Mr Umar Sheikh
Income: £2,599,560 [2017]; £2,160,449 [2016]; £1,934,860 [2015]; £1,490,641 [2014]; £1,400,298 [2013]

Haberdashers' Aske's Charity
Registered: 17 Dec 1963 *Employees:* 481
Tel: 020 7246 9988 *Website:* haberdashers.co.uk
Activities: Education, training
Address: The Clerk, Haberdashers Hall, 18 West Smithfield, London, EC1A 9HQ
Trustees: Haberdashers' Aske's Elstree Schools Limited, The Corporation Bearing The Name or Style of Governors of The Possessions and Revenues of The Hospital at Hoxton of The Foundation of Robert Aske Esquire
Income: £44,552,000 [2016]; £42,356,000 [2015]; £39,615,000 [2014]; £36,916,000 [2013]; £34,975,000 [2012]

Haberdashers' Charities Investment Pool

Registered: 27 May 2003
Tel: 020 7246 9988 *Website:* haberdashers.co.uk
Activities: Other charitable purposes
Address: The Clerk, Haberdashers Hall, 18 West Smithfield, London, EC1A 9HQ
Trustees: The Haberdashers Company
Income: £3,385,000 [2017]; £2,305,000 [2016]; £2,208,000 [2015]; £2,277,000 [2014]; £1,812,000 [2013]

Alexis and Anne- Marie Habib Foundation

Registered: 4 Jan 2006 *Employees:* 1
Website: habibfoundation.org
Activities: General charitable purposes; education, training; prevention or relief of poverty
Address: c/o Spinnaker Capital Limited, 6 Grosvenor Street, London, W1K 4PZ
Trustees: Mr Alexis Habib, Dr Anne Marie Habib, Mr Jamil Baz
Income: £2,531,474 [2016]; £784,008 [2015]; £1,675,693 [2014]; £2,243,181 [2013]; £863,860 [2012]

Habitat for Humanity Great Britain

Registered: 25 Jan 1995 *Employees:* 18 *Volunteers:* 2
Tel: 01753 313539 *Website:* habitatforhumanity.org.uk
Activities: The prevention or relief of poverty; overseas aid, famine relief; accommodation, housing; religious activities; economic, community development, employment
Address: Habitat for Humanity Great Britain, 10 The Grove, Slough, SL1 1QP
Trustees: Mr Larry Sullivan, Mr Simon Thomas, Mr Gary von Lehmden, Mr Michael John Freshney, Mr Torre Holmes Nelson, Mr Ian Kenneth Whitehead, Susan Revell, Mr Gordon Holmes, Mr John Brian Clark
Income: £2,805,890 [2017]; £3,406,917 [2016]; £3,277,334 [2015]; £3,870,196 [2014]; £2,727,816 [2013]

Hackney Council for Voluntary Service

Registered: 27 May 1998 *Employees:* 40 *Volunteers:* 38
Tel: 020 7923 1962 *Website:* hcvs.org.uk
Activities: General charitable purposes; education, training; advancement of health or saving of lives; disability; prevention or relief of poverty; accommodation, housing; arts, culture, heritage, science; amateur sport; environment, conservation, heritage; economic, community development, employment; other charitable purposes
Address: The Adiaha Antigha Centre, 24-30 Dalston Lane, London, E8 3AZ
Trustees: Ms Caroline Nelson, Mr Charles Middleton, Ms Olatinuke Opoosun, Mr Jack Griffin, Ms Elisabeth Jasmin Hashemi, Daniel Francis, Benjamin Mak, Mr Timothy John Maurice Vaughan
Income: £3,843,372 [2017]; £3,266,705 [2016]; £1,725,017 [2015]; £1,527,347 [2014]; £1,104,378 [2013]

Hackney Empire Limited

Registered: 24 Apr 1997 *Employees:* 109
Tel: 020 8510 4500 *Website:* hackneyempire.co.uk
Activities: General charitable purposes; education, training; arts, culture, heritage, science
Address: Hackney Empire Theatre, 291 Mare Street, London, E8 1EJ
Trustees: Ms Jean Nicholson, Ms Jo Cottrell, Ms Caroline Yates, Mr Jay Sheth, Ms Franny Moyle, Mrs Delphine Brand, Mr Kingsley Afemikhe, Mr Chris Unitt
Income: £3,104,050 [2017]; £2,947,268 [2016]; £3,135,532 [2015]; £2,911,989 [2014]; £3,862,512 [2013]

Hackney Joint Estate Charity

Registered: 28 Nov 1963
Tel: 01285 841900
Activities: General charitable purposes
Address: 6 Trull Farm Buildings, Trull, Tetbury, Glos, GL8 8SQ
Trustees: Hackney Endowed Trustee Ltd
Income: £1,316,038 [2017]; £1,203,663 [2016]; £1,018,956 [2015]; £931,746 [2014]; £832,216 [2013]

Hadassah Medical Relief Association U.K.

Registered: 22 Sep 1994 *Employees:* 3 *Volunteers:* 5
Tel: 020 8202 2860 *Website:* hadassahuk.org
Activities: General charitable purposes; education, training; advancement of health or saving of lives; disability; overseas aid, famine relief
Address: Hadassah UK, 25 The Burroughs, Hendon, London, NW4 4AR
Trustees: Mrs Alberta Strage, Mrs Guilda Shamash, Mrs Carolyn Simons, Dr Linda Helene Greenwall, Ms Anita Lowenstein-Dent, Mr Anthony Metzer, Mr Martin Paisner CBE, Mr David Waterman, Mr Jean Jacque Roboh, Mr Victor Hoffbrand, Mr Clive Freedman
Income: £1,035,105 [2017]; £626,803 [2016]; £209,022 [2015]; £570,084 [2014]; £572,086 [2013]

The Haddad Foundation

Registered: 18 Nov 2015
Tel: 020 7597 6000
Activities: General charitable purposes; education, training; human rights, religious or racial harmony, equality or diversity
Address: Withers Ltd, 16 Old Bailey, London, EC4M 7EG
Trustees: Mrs Dulce Packard, Ms Daniela Barone Soares, Mrs Tania Haddad Nobre, Mr Claudio Luiz Da Silva Haddad, Mrs Rosalie Rahal Haddad
Income: £5,486,963 [2016]

The Hadley Trust

Registered: 13 Oct 1997 *Employees:* 2
Tel: 020 8447 4577
Activities: General charitable purposes; advancement of health or saving of lives; disability; prevention or relief of poverty; overseas aid, famine relief; economic, community development, employment; other charitable purposes
Address: Gladsmuir, Hadley Common, Barnet, Herts, EN5 5QE
Trustees: Mr Philip William Hulme, Mr Thomas William Hulme, Mrs Sophie Ann Swift, Mrs Janet Hulme, Mrs Katherine Elizabeth Prideaux
Income: £2,721,828 [2017]; £2,199,870 [2016]; £2,177,063 [2015]; £4,850,775 [2014]; £2,765,799 [2013]

Hadras Kodesh Trust

Registered: 15 Sep 2004 *Volunteers:* 2
Tel: 020 8880 8941
Activities: General charitable purposes; education, training; overseas aid, famine relief
Address: 52 East Bank, London, N16 5PZ
Trustees: Mr Pincus Mann, Mr Yoel Fisher
Income: £5,396,599 [2017]; £5,281,839 [2016]; £4,439,909 [2015]; £3,415,224 [2014]; £2,849,316 [2013]

The Haemophilia Society
Registered: 30 Nov 1983 *Employees:* 10 *Volunteers:* 200
Tel: 020 7939 0784 *Website:* haemophilia.org.uk
Activities: The advancement of health or saving of lives
Address: The Haemophilia Society, Wilcox House, 140-148 Borough High Street, London, SE1 1LB
Trustees: Mr Jamie O'Hara, Mr Andrew Martin, Mrs Elizabeth De Freitas, Mr Bartholomew Flynn, Mrs Sonia O'Hara, Mr Simon Mower, Mr Clive Smith, Mrs Lisa Bagley, Mrs Eileen Ross
Income: £1,176,886 [2017]; £645,339 [2016]; £668,777 [2015]; £786,113 [2014]; £874,983 [2013]

Hafal
Registered: 9 Sep 2002 *Employees:* 215 *Volunteers:* 65
Tel: 01792 816600 *Website:* hafal.org
Activities: Education, training; advancement of health or saving of lives; disability; accommodation, housing; economic, community development, employment
Address: Unit B3, Lakeside Technology Park, Swansea Enterprise Park, Swansea, SA7 9FE
Trustees: Mrs Helen Natasha Philpin, Mr Dilwyn Davies Voyle, Suzanne Duval, Mr John Barnes, Miss Mair Elliott, Mrs Ceinwen Rowlands, Dr Elin Mair Jones, Mrs Pauline Bett, Mr Gerald Cole, Mr Michael Connor Miles
Income: £5,459,306 [2017]; £5,030,161 [2016]; £5,014,046 [2015]; £5,205,735 [2014]; £5,127,630 [2013]

Haig Housing Trust
Registered: 18 Aug 2008 *Employees:* 40
Tel: 020 8685 5777 *Website:* haighousing.org.uk
Activities: Accommodation, housing; armed forces, emergency service efficiency
Address: Haig Housing Trust, Alban Dobson House, Green Lane, Morden, Surrey, SM4 5NS
Trustees: Major General John Stokoe CB CBE, Major General John Milne, Mr Neil Graham White, Mr David Gareth Williams, Luise Locke, Mrs Cathy Lester-Walker MBE, Group Captain Robert Kemp, Mr Stephen Michael Elliott, Dr Mark James Stewart Weir, Mr Andrew Bruce Weir
Income: £10,887,000 [2017]; £12,590,000 [2016]; £24,905,000 [2015]; £8,543,000 [2014]; £2,315,000 [2013]

Haileybury and Imperial Service College
Registered: 26 Feb 1964 *Employees:* 371
Tel: 01992 706216 *Website:* haileybury.com
Activities: Education, training
Address: The Bursary, Haileybury & Imperial Service, College, Hertford, SG13 7NU
Trustees: Mr Alan Pilgrim, Rev Dr Gerard G Moate, Mr Charles Sherwood, Ms Charlotte Avery, Dr Nigel Richardson MA PGCE PhD, Colonel C I Darnell, Mr Nicholas Gilbert BA, Mrs Catherine Rawlin BSc FCA MAE MCIArb, Mr Richard Madden MA Cantab ACA, Mr Stephen Roberts MA, Mrs Janet Gough OBE, Mr Gerard Ellison, Mr Stuart Westley, Venerable Luke Miller MA, Mr Stewart Urry LLB FCA, Mr Chris Lowe MA, Prof William Stopford Harvey BA MPhil PhD, Mrs Sarah Beazley MA PGCE, Mr Richard Munn MA Cantab, Mr Adrian Brown MA Cantab PGCE, Mrs Karen Graves BA LLM, Mrs Gail Ganney BSc MSc, Rev Jenny Fennell BSc PGCert BTh MTh
Income: £23,589,000 [2017]; £22,219,000 [2016]; £22,629,000 [2015]; £21,356,000 [2014]; £21,278,000 [2013]

Halas Homes
Registered: 18 Aug 1989 *Employees:* 82 *Volunteers:* 3
Tel: 0121 550 8778 *Website:* halashomes.co.uk
Activities: Disability; accommodation, housing
Address: Halas House, Wassell Road, Halesowen, W Midlands, B63 4JX
Trustees: Mr Robert Smith, Mrs Sandra Elizabeth Hampton, Mr John Brettle, Mr Stephen Charles Scriven, Mrs Susan Jones, Mrs Yvonne Davies, Mr Roger Smith, Mr Raymond Francis Eades, Mr Anthony John Billingham, Mrs Nadia Jane Billingham, Mrs Gillian Leno
Income: £1,563,601 [2016]; £1,439,900 [2015]; £1,454,126 [2014]; £1,430,988 [2013]; £1,360,596 [2012]

Halcrow Foundation
Registered: 9 Aug 2006
Tel: 01672 515740 *Website:* halcrowfoundation.org
Activities: General charitable purposes; education, training; prevention or relief of poverty; overseas aid, famine relief; economic, community development, employment
Address: 15 Davies Close, Marlborough, Wilts, SN8 1TW
Trustees: Mr David John Kerr, Mr Andrew John Yeoward, James Billinghurst, Mr Malcolm Francis Wallace, Miss Anna Laurelie Mann, Madhu Rajesh
Income: £1,026,183 [2016]; £4,225,358 [2015]; £6,590 [2014]; £8,126 [2013]; £209,590 [2012]

Halcyon London International School
Registered: 10 Dec 2012 *Employees:* 35
Tel: 020 7258 1169 *Website:* halcyonschool.com
Activities: Education, training
Address: 33 Seymour Place, London, W1H 5AP
Trustees: Ms Pamela Sears, Ms Julia Alden, Mr Achim Beck, Mrs Julie Matthaeus
Income: £3,198,069 [2017]; £2,272,144 [2016]; £1,599,698 [2015]; £895,218 [2014]; £308,091 [2013]

Halifax Opportunities Trust
Registered: 18 Apr 2001 *Employees:* 173 *Volunteers:* 60
Tel: 01422 399400 *Website:* regen.org.uk
Activities: Education, training; advancement of health or saving of lives; prevention or relief of poverty; environment, conservation, heritage; economic, community development, employment
Address: Hanson Lane Enterprise Centre Ltd, Hanson Lane, Halifax, W Yorks, HX1 5PG
Trustees: Pauline Nash, Ms Sally Elizabeth Morrell, Mr Shabir Hussain, Mrs Rizwana Rehman, Ms Asmat Ali, Jon Craven, Ms Helen Laura Wright, Rev Hilary J Barber, Mr Khalid Saeed, Mr Richard Hemblys, Mrs Ruksana Bostan, Cllr Dorothy Susan Foster, Jeanette Harkness
Income: £4,860,079 [2017]; £4,895,526 [2016]; £4,366,746 [2015]; £2,404,456 [2014]; £2,281,906 [2013]

The Hall School Charitable Trust
Registered: 11 Sep 1963 *Employees:* 134 *Volunteers:* 10
Website: hallschool.co.uk
Activities: Education, training
Address: The Hall School Charitable Trust, 23 Crossfield Road, London, NW3 4NU
Trustees: Mr Patrick Derham, Mr Anthony Fobel, Mr Ben Walford, Mr Simon Friend, Lord James Bethell, Professor Mark Bailey, Mr David Leigh, Mrs Diana Watkins, Mr Robert Palmer, Mr Nick Ritblat
Income: £8,157,866 [2016]; £7,718,437 [2015]; £7,234,018 [2014]; £6,884,525 [2013]; £6,715,504 [2012]

Michael Hall School
Registered: 24 Jul 1963 Employees: 121 Volunteers: 45
Website: michaelhall.co.uk
Activities: Education, training
Address: 15 The Pageant, South Street, Sherborne, Dorset, DT9 3LF
Trustees: Mr Andrew Scott, Ms Daphne Kitty Hagenbach, Mr Sean Salter-Rafferty, Mrs Heidi Hebrank, Mrs Vanessa King, Mr William Forward
Income: £4,186,170 [2017]; £4,076,685 [2016]; £3,893,940 [2015]; £4,000,623 [2014]; £4,157,766 [2013]

The Hall for Cornwall Trust
Registered: 16 Feb 1996 Employees: 105 Volunteers: 103
Tel: 01872 262465 Website: hallforcornwall.co.uk
Activities: Arts, culture, heritage, science
Address: Hall for Cornwall, Back Quay, Truro, Cornwall, TR1 2LL
Trustees: Dame Rosemary Anne Squire DBE, Miss Kathryn Elizabeth Ludlow, Mr Toby Parkins, Mr Christopher Charles Pomfret, Mr David John Pollard, Ms Susan Whitford, Mr Timothy Brooksbank, Mr Richard Williams
Income: £6,369,645 [2017]; £6,177,384 [2016]; £4,834,153 [2015]; £5,212,639 [2014]; £4,699,558 [2013]

Halle Concerts Society
Registered: 31 Oct 1963 Employees: 109 Volunteers: 140
Tel: 0161 237 7000 Website: halle.co.uk
Activities: Education, training; arts, culture, heritage, science
Address: Halle Orchestra, Bridgewater Hall, Great Bridgewater Street, Manchester, M1 5HA
Trustees: Mr David McKeith, Ms Azra Ali, Ms Theresa Noeleen Grant, Katrina Michel, Professor Linda Joyce Merrick, Alex Connock, Ms Christine Gaskell, Mr Brandon Leigh, Cliff Morris, Jon McLeod, His Honour John Andrew Phillips CBE, Tim Edge
Income: £9,279,000 [2017]; £8,434,000 [2016]; £9,166,000 [2015]; £7,922,000 [2014]; £9,461,000 [2013]

Hallfield School Trust
Registered: 12 Nov 1963 Employees: 127
Tel: 0121 454 1496 Website: hallfieldschool.co.uk
Activities: Education, training
Address: Hallfield School Trust, 48 Church Road, Edgbaston, Birmingham, B15 3SJ
Trustees: Mr Keith Uff, Mr Peter John Millward, Mrs Diane Price, Mr Gavin Mark Faber BA LL Dip Law, Mr Sukh Aulak, Mr Neil Price, Mr Timothy Venner, Mr Peter Mason Wall, Mrs Sheila Sherlock PGCE, Mr John Bernard Austin FRICS, Rev Julian Francis, Mrs Sharon Stotts, Mr Rupert Heathcote, Mr Deepak Ahuja
Income: £6,068,849 [2016]; £5,831,473 [2015]; £5,834,007 [2014]; £5,534,699 [2013]; £5,330,490 [2012]

Halliford School Limited
Registered: 23 Dec 1966 Employees: 71
Tel: 01932 234934 Website: hallifordschool.co.uk
Activities: Education, training
Address: Halliford School, Russell Road, Shepperton, Middlesex, TW17 9HX
Trustees: Mr Richard Parsons, Mrs Pamela Ann Horner, Mr Colin Stuart Squire, Mr Michael Anthony Crosby, Mr Nigel Jonathan Maud, Mr Alex Lenoel, Dr Millan Sachania, Mr Andrew Philip Bertram Hirst, Mr Peter Roberts, Mr Brian Thomas Harris, Mr Kenneth Harry Woodward, Mr Richard Davison, Mrs Norma Cook, Professor Jonathan Phillips, Mrs Kate Gulliver
Income: £6,231,794 [2017]; £5,847,792 [2016]; £5,904,794 [2015]; £5,895,171 [2014]; £5,663,835 [2013]

Halo Leisure Services Limited
Registered: 5 Apr 2002 Employees: 700 Volunteers: 48
Tel: 0845 241 0340 Website: haloleisure.org.uk
Activities: General charitable purposes; education, training; advancement of health or saving of lives; disability; prevention or relief of poverty; amateur sport; recreation
Address: Halo Leisure, Lion Yard, Broad Street, Leominster, Herefords, HR6 8BT
Trustees: Mr Richard Kirby CBE, Mr Stephen Leonard Brewster, Mr Nigel Sellar, Mrs Amelia Anne Cavaghan, Mr Kenneth Edward Bush, Mr Warren Hobden, Mr Bryan Sanderson White, Mr Alan Curless, Mr David Halpern, Mr Ronald John Wilkie, Mr Clive Richard Butler, Mrs Valerie Hill
Income: £14,032,056 [2016]; £12,089,000 [2015]; £12,585,255 [2014]; £12,639,578 [2013]; £6,848,069 [2012]

Halstead (Educational Trust) Limited
Registered: 16 Dec 1975 Employees: 42
Tel: 01483 772682 Website: halstead-school.org.uk
Activities: Education, training
Address: Halstead Preparatory School, Woodham Rise, Woking, Surrey, GU21 4EE
Trustees: Mr John Olsen, Mr Christopher Guy Betts, Mr Richard Roberts, Mrs Victoria Stanton, Mr Simon Hartley, Rev Peter James Harwood, Mrs Ann Marie Stewart, Mr David Burke, Mr Christopher Muller, Dr Jill Owen
Income: £2,570,230 [2017]; £2,559,016 [2016]; £2,462,868 [2015]; £2,368,182 [2014]; £2,208,530 [2013]

Halton Haven Hospice
Registered: 5 Apr 1990 Employees: 73 Volunteers: 100
Tel: 01928 719454 Website: haltonhavenhospice.co.uk
Activities: The advancement of health or saving of lives
Address: Barnfield Avenue, Murdishaw, Runcorn, Cheshire, WA7 6EP
Trustees: Mrs Judith Guthrie, Mr Neil James Townsend, Mr John Maddock, Mrs Teresa Mary Tierney, Dr Charles Philip Hallam, Mr William John Christopher Parlane, Mr Stephen Paul Hankinson, Mr Colin Marshall McKenzie, Michelle Wood
Income: £2,518,755 [2017]; £2,569,019 [2016]; £2,509,306 [2015]; £2,879,637 [2014]; £2,367,954 [2013]

Halton Tennis Centre
Registered: 3 Jul 2006 Employees: 6
Tel: 01296 425243 Website: haltontennis.co.uk
Activities: Education, training; disability; amateur sport; armed forces, emergency service efficiency; recreation; other charitable purposes
Address: Chestnut End, Halton, Aylesbury, Bucks, HP22 5PD
Trustees: Mr John Walker, Flt Lt Chris Evans, Mr Gerard David Groom, Mr Robert John Pain, Damian Gange, Mrs Gillian Roe, Mr Andrew Robert James Southam, Mr Chris Duffin
Income: £1,200,814 [2017]; £1,189,707 [2016]; £1,145,822 [2015]; £1,226,979 [2014]; £1,059,007 [2013]

Hamelin Trust
Registered: 7 Oct 1991 *Employees:* 160 *Volunteers:* 35
Tel: 01277 653889 *Website:* hamelintrust.org.uk
Activities: General charitable purposes; education, training; disability; accommodation, housing; environment, conservation, heritage; economic, community development, employment; recreation
Address: Hamelin Trust, Unit 19, Radford Crescent, Billericay, Essex, CM12 0DU
Trustees: Mrs Gwen Martin, Mrs Josephine Ellen Davies, Mr Adam Christian Sewell, Mr David Firth, Mr Mohammed Akram Ayyubi, Mr Jeremy Henry Gibson, Mr John Tweddell, Ms Jenny Hartland, Mr Terry John Gregson, Mr Scott William Barton, Dassos Alexandrou
Income: £3,697,317 [2017]; £3,403,197 [2016]; £3,346,320 [2015]; £3,209,873 [2014]; £3,433,596 [2013]

Hamilton Lodge (Brighton)
Registered: 30 Jan 1963 *Employees:* 108 *Volunteers:* 3
Tel: 01273 682362 *Website:* hamiltonlsc.co.uk
Activities: Education, training
Address: 48 Great College Street, Brighton, BN2 1HL
Trustees: Ms Charlotte Lucie Holtam, Mr David Sawyer, Mr Stephen William Kent, Mrs Susan Furdas, Mr Martin Charles Gransden Redshaw, Mr Paul Newbury, Mrs Sue Benton-Stace, Ms Gail Pilling
Income: £3,535,757 [2017]; £3,284,392 [2016]; £2,970,983 [2015]; £2,887,147 [2014]; £3,250,323 [2013]

Hamilton Lodge Trust Limited
Registered: 13 Nov 1962 *Employees:* 98
Tel: 01444 239123 *Website:* thedtgroup.org
Activities: Disability; accommodation, housing
Address: The Disabilities Trust, 32 Market Place, The Martlets, Burgess Hill, W Sussex, RH15 9NP
Trustees: Dr Paula Bernadette Dobrowolski, Mr Stephen William Howell, Mr Michael Green, Dr Caroline Susan Drugan, Mr Mark Keith Rowe, Mr Roger Anthony Hoyle, Mrs Eileen Christina Jackman
Income: £2,717,100 [2016]; £2,820,779 [2015]; £2,610,062 [2014]; £2,246,929 [2013]; £1,538,529 [2012]

William Rowan Hamilton Trust
Registered: 17 Jan 2013 *Employees:* 10
Tel: 01865 253980 *Website:* hamilton-trust.org.uk
Activities: General charitable purposes; education, training
Address: Hamilton Trust, 1A Howard Street, Oxford, OX4 3AY
Trustees: Mr Kenneth Brooks, Jane O'Regan, Michael O'Regan, James McMillan
Income: £1,068,353 [2016]; £1,209,256 [2015]; £2,716,208 [2014]; £10,000 [2013]

The Hamlet Centre Trust
Registered: 24 Oct 1990 *Employees:* 50 *Volunteers:* 40
Website: thehamletcharity.org.uk
Activities: Education, training; advancement of health or saving of lives; disability; arts, culture, heritage, science; amateur sport; recreation; other charitable purposes
Address: The Hamlet, 221 St Leonards Road, Norwich, NR1 4JN
Trustees: Irene MacDonald, Mrs Tania Davies, Mr Nicholas Hancox, Emma Randall, Mrs Jenny Mayne, Mr Stuart Marpole, Mrs Ann Way, Mr Gary Pearce
Income: £1,210,017 [2017]; £1,116,862 [2016]; £1,142,520 [2015]; £1,327,301 [2014]; £958,564 [2013]

Paul Hamlyn Foundation
Registered: 29 Mar 2004 *Employees:* 37
Tel: 020 7812 3300 *Website:* phf.org.uk
Activities: General charitable purposes; education, training; arts, culture, heritage, science; other charitable purposes
Address: Paul Hamlyn Foundation, 5-11 Leeke Street, London, WC1X 9HY
Trustees: Ms Claire Whitaker, Sir Anthony Michael Vaughan Salz, Mr James Lingwood, Mr Tom Wylie OBE, Charles Leadbeater, Lord Anthony William Hall CBE, Ms Jane Hamlyn, Mr Michael Hamlyn, Mr Tim Bunting, Janet McKenley-Simpson
Income: £19,409,654 [2017]; £19,776,474 [2016]; £16,323,000 [2015]; £17,936,011 [2014]; £16,225,000 [2013]

The Helen Hamlyn Trust
Registered: 31 Jan 2001 *Employees:* 6
Tel: 020 7351 7600
Activities: General charitable purposes; education, training; advancement of health or saving of lives; arts, culture, heritage, science; environment, conservation, heritage; other charitable purposes
Address: 129 Old Church Street, London, SW3 6EB
Trustees: Mr Stephen Richard Lewin, Mr Brendan Cahill, Dr Kate Gavron, Dr Shobita Punja, Dr Deborah Swallow, Mrs Margaret O'Rorke, Lady Hamlyn, Dame Alison Margaret Peacock
Income: £2,579,168 [2017]; £2,688,568 [2016]; £2,533,357 [2015]; £2,514,890 [2014]; £4,395,942 [2013]

Hammersmith United Charities
Registered: 16 Apr 1962 *Employees:* 7
Tel: 020 8741 4326 *Website:* hamunitedcharities.org.uk
Activities: General charitable purposes; education, training; disability; prevention or relief of poverty; accommodation, housing; economic, community development, employment; recreation
Address: Sycamore House, Sycamore Gardens, London, W6 0AS
Trustees: Hammersmith United Trustee Company
Income: £1,487,333 [2017]; £1,393,253 [2016]; £1,372,239 [2015]; £1,287,021 [2014]; £1,199,306 [2013]

Hammersmith and Fulham Association for Mental Health
Registered: 6 Apr 1989 *Employees:* 28 *Volunteers:* 100
Tel: 020 7471 0580 *Website:* hfmind.org.uk
Activities: Education, training; advancement of health or saving of lives; disability; arts, culture, heritage, science; economic, community development, employment
Address: 309 Lillie Road, London, SW6 7LL
Trustees: Mrs Melanie Carlebach, Ms Nicola Labuschagne, Miss Katherine Hattersley, Johnathan James, Jane Bullen, Professor Jonathan Timothy Newton, Claire Devine, Mr Raja Saggi
Income: £1,229,452 [2017]; £995,138 [2016]; £944,476 [2015]; £1,079,185 [2014]; £1,434,623 [2013]

Celia Hammond Animal Trust
Registered: 21 Feb 1986 *Employees:* 82
Tel: 01892 783820 *Website:* celiahammond.org
Activities: Animals
Address: Celia Hammond Animal Trust, High Street, Wadhurst, E Sussex, TN5 6AG
Trustees: Ms Celia Hammond, Ms Barbara Connolly, Miss Naomi Sheen
Income: £2,711,824 [2016]; £2,318,370 [2015]; £2,843,541 [2014]; £2,073,477 [2013]; £2,243,236 [2012]

The Hammond School Limited
Registered: 9 Jun 1993 *Employees:* 74 *Volunteers:* 1
Tel: 01244 305372 *Website:* thehammondschool.co.uk
Activities: Education, training
Address: Hammond School, Hoole Bank, Hoole Village, Chester, CH2 4ES
Trustees: Mrs Jo Sykes, Mr John McLintock FCA FCCA, Mrs Kathleen Mary Smith, Ms Carol Penny BA(Hons) ACMA, Ms Anna Sutton, Mr John Devoy
Income: £4,684,202 [2017]; £4,023,315 [2016]; £3,623,748 [2015]; £2,997,463 [2014]; £3,044,581 [2013]

Hampshire Advocacy Regional Group
Registered: 5 Jun 2008
Tel: 01256 332795 *Website:* hampshireadvocacy.org.uk
Activities: Education, training; advancement of health or saving of lives; disability; accommodation, housing; economic, community development, employment
Address: c/o Speakeasy Advocacy, 17 New Road, Basingstoke, Hants, RG21 7PR
Trustees: Miss Amanda Kent, Mrs Alison Louise Flack
Income: £1,241,959 [2017]; £295,753 [2016]; £433,465 [2015]; £471,993 [2014]; £633,682 [2013]

Hampshire Christian Education Trust
Registered: 1 Oct 2004 *Employees:* 31 *Volunteers:* 11
Tel: 023 8060 0986 *Website:* thekingsschool.eu
Activities: Education, training; prevention or relief of poverty; religious activities
Address: The Kings School, Lakesmere House, Allington Lane, Fair Oak, Eastleigh, Hants, SO50 7DB
Trustees: Mr Daryl Frederick Martin, Mr James Pavey, Mr Neil Osborne, Fred Kinchin, Mr Christopher Caws
Income: £1,319,349 [2017]; £1,313,321 [2016]; £1,286,223 [2015]; £1,382,615 [2014]; £1,462,634 [2013]

Hampshire County Scout Council
Registered: 16 Dec 1992 *Employees:* 13 *Volunteers:* 60
Tel: 023 8084 7847 *Website:* scouts-hants.org.uk
Activities: Education, training; amateur sport
Address: Hampshire County Scout Council, Ferny Crofts, Beaulieu Road, Beaulieu, Brockenhurst, Hants, SO42 7YQ
Trustees: Martyn Rose, Mr Paul Richard Hedges, Mr Russ Parke, Mr Kerie Wallace, Mr Martin Mackey, Mr Peter Marcus McDowell Impey, Mr Thomas Fisher, Mrs Jacqueline Noakes, Miss Joanne Nellie Day, Mrs Thelma Young, Mr Paul O'Beirne, Mr Peter Moody, Mr Leslie John Farrington, Mr Anthony Frank Gosden, Mrs Donna Kerrigan, Mr Andy Cullen, Mr Nigel Valette, Miss Emma Louise Hale
Income: £1,005,442 [2016]; £1,456,558 [2015]; £1,137,633 [2014]; £1,214,832 [2013]; £992,541 [2012]

Hampshire Cultural Trust
Registered: 16 Sep 2014 *Employees:* 214 *Volunteers:* 400
Tel: 01962 678140 *Website:* hampshireculturaltrust.org.uk
Activities: Arts, culture, heritage, science
Address: Hampshire Cultural Trust, Chilcomb House, Chilcomb Lane, Winchester, Hants, SO23 8RD
Trustees: Alan Lovell DL, Yinnon Ezra MBE MA FRSA, Ms Helen Jackson, Mr Douglas Andrew Connell, Mrs Tracy Osborn, Roy Perry, Mike Southgate, Ms Rachel Bebb, Mr Robert Boyle
Income: £7,489,740 [2017]; £6,734,435 [2016]; £3,453,380 [2015]

Hampshire Hospitals Charity
Registered: 13 Jan 1997
Tel: 01256 473202 *Website:* hampshirehospitals.nhs.uk
Activities: Education, training; advancement of health or saving of lives
Address: North Hampshire Hospital, Aldermaston Road, Basingstoke, Hants, RG24 9NA
Trustees: Hampshire Hospitals NHS Foundation Trust
Income: £1,352,524 [2017]; £661,917 [2016]; £581,209 [2015]; £918,522 [2014]; £663,898 [2013]

Hampshire and Isle of Wight Air Ambulance
Registered: 8 Oct 2004 *Employees:* 17 *Volunteers:* 157
Tel: 023 8074 3510 *Website:* hiowaa.org
Activities: The advancement of health or saving of lives
Address: 22 Oriana Way, Nursling, Southampton, SO16 0YU
Trustees: Robert Prescott, Mr Jonathan Moseley, Mrs Rachel Peppiatt, Mr Peter Taylor, Sir John Day, Mr Graham Hill, David Drew, Mrs Lisa Gagliani, Mrs Elizabeth Brown, Mr Andy Cheesewright, Dr Andy Eynon, Mrs Gwen Moulster
Income: £6,735,559 [2017]; £6,432,057 [2016]; £6,720,124 [2015]; £5,783,807 [2014]; £4,546,049 [2013]

Hampshire and Isle of Wight Wildlife Trust
Registered: 22 Dec 1961 *Employees:* 76 *Volunteers:* 1,400
Tel: 01489 774422 *Website:* hiwwt.org.uk
Activities: Education, training; environment, conservation, heritage
Address: Hampshire & Isle of Wight Wildlife Trust, Vicarage Lane, Curdridge, Southampton, SO32 2DP
Trustees: Mr Andrew Lee, Mr Christopher Langford, Mr Timothy Pinchen, Jane Page, Mr David Jordan, Lesley Chin, Oliver Cox, Ms Mary Parker, Christopher Collins, Dr Peter Vaughan, Professor Paul Tyler, Mr Malcolm John Sonnex, Mr Matthew Prescott, Dr Helen McCormack
Income: £4,189,290 [2017]; £3,792,678 [2016]; £4,306,563 [2015]; £4,160,447 [2014]; £4,637,332 [2013]

Hampshire and The Isle of Wight Community Foundation
Registered: 30 Oct 2003 *Employees:* 8
Tel: 01256 776101 *Website:* hiwcf.com
Activities: General charitable purposes; education, training; advancement of health or saving of lives; disability; prevention or relief of poverty; accommodation, housing; arts, culture, heritage, science; amateur sport; environment, conservation, heritage; economic, community development, employment; recreation; other charitable purposes
Address: Mr Jakes Ferguson, Dame Mary Fagan House, Chineham Court, Lutyens Close, Lychpit, Basingstoke, Hants, RG24 8AG
Trustees: Mr Hugh Mason, Mrs Jane Sandars, Ms Jo Ash, Mrs Rebecca Kennelly, Mr Richard John Norman Hibbert, Mrs Virginia Lovell, Mr James Kennedy, Mr Richard Prest, Mr Dan Putty, Mr Jonathan Corderoy Cheshire, Rev Jonathan Frost, Mr Jonathan Moseley, Mr Adrian Rutter, Councillor Andrew Ian Philip Joy
Income: £1,395,493 [2016]; £1,315,422 [2015]; £2,326,516 [2014]; £3,168,255 [2013]; £1,569,657 [2012]

The Matt Hampson Foundation
Registered: 13 Jan 2011 *Employees:* 6 *Volunteers:* 50
Tel: 0116 259 7618 *Website:* matthampsonfoundation.org
Activities: General charitable purposes; advancement of health or saving of lives; disability; amateur sport
Address: Halstead House Cottage, Oakham Road, Tilton on the Hill, Leicester, LE7 9DJ
Trustees: Judith Batchelar, Roy Jackson, Mr Graham Christopher Rowntree, Peter Harrison, Sir Clive Woodward, Julian Evans
Income: £1,659,715 [2017]; £957,823 [2016]; £943,662 [2015]; £836,792 [2014]; £517,264 [2013]

The Hampstead Garden Suburb Trust Limited
Registered: 23 Oct 1995 *Employees:* 14 *Volunteers:* 17
Tel: 020 8455 1066 *Website:* hgstrust.org
Activities: Arts, culture, heritage, science; environment, conservation, heritage
Address: 862 Finchley Road, London, NW11 6AB
Trustees: Mr Jonathan Ross, Ms Claire Calman, Mr Michael Peter Franklin, Ms Elspeth Margaret Clements, David White, Mr Richard Max Wiseman, Ms Alison Blom-Cooper, Mrs Jacqueline Barnett
Income: £1,514,660 [2017]; £1,505,966 [2016]; £1,498,144 [2015]; £1,666,127 [2014]; £1,023,385 [2013]

Hampstead Heath
Registered: 4 May 1990 *Employees:* 96 *Volunteers:* 2,998
Tel: 020 7332 3519
Activities: Amateur sport
Address: Corporation of London, P O Box 270, London, EC2P 2EJ
Trustees: The Mayor & Commonality & Citizens of The City of London
Income: £14,957,608 [2017]; £17,421,059 [2016]; £11,317,895 [2015]; £9,369,678 [2014]; £8,436,216 [2013]

Hampstead Theatre Limited
Registered: 27 Jun 1963 *Employees:* 89
Tel: 020 7449 4200 *Website:* hampsteadtheatre.com
Activities: Arts, culture, heritage, science
Address: Hampstead Theatre Ltd, Eton Avenue, London, NW3 3EU
Trustees: Mr Jeremy Vaughan Sandelson, Ms Meera Syal, Ms Susie Flora Boyt, Mrs Karen Melanie Paul, Katja Tangen, Adam Jones, Mr Daniel Jonathan Marks, Mr David Alan Tyler, Mr Simon Charles Parry-Wingfield, Mrs Gillian Budd, Mr James Harding, Ms Zeinab Badawi-Malik
Income: £5,775,038 [2017]; £5,572,012 [2016]; £5,251,035 [2015]; £4,614,525 [2014]; £4,437,440 [2013]

Hampton Fuel Allotment
Registered: 19 Nov 1962 *Employees:* 4
Tel: 020 8941 7866 *Website:* hfac.co.uk
Activities: General charitable purposes; prevention or relief of poverty
Address: Hampton Fuel Allotment Charity, 15 High Street, Hampton, Surrey, TW12 2SA
Trustees: Dr James Brockbank, Paula Williams, Richard Montgomery, Derek Terrington, Martin Duffy, Rev Ben Lovell, David Meggitt, Clive Beaumont, Hilary Hart, Victoria Reid, Martin Seymour, Mark Boyle
Income: £2,084,735 [2017]; £1,882,081 [2016]; £1,439,876 [2015]; £2,042,927 [2014]; £1,967,510 [2013]

Hampton School
Registered: 10 Jul 2007 *Employees:* 325 *Volunteers:* 2
Tel: 020 8979 0476 *Website:* hamptonschool.org.uk
Activities: Education, training
Address: Hampton School, Hanworth Road, Hampton, Surrey, TW12 3HD
Trustees: Mr John Perry BA, Mr Nigel Spooner Cert Arch, Mr Laurence Richard Llewellyn BSc (Hons) MBA FCMA FRSA, Rev Ben Lovell, Mr Robert Walker MA, Mr Stuart Alan Bull BSc ACA, Alice Yandle, Mrs Helen Lowe, Mr Andrew Hugh Munday QC, Mr Anthony John Roberts CBE BA FRSA, Mrs Christine Ruth Mercer, Mrs Marie-Louise Ellis, Mrs Mona Choueiri BA MBA, Richard Washington, Leslie Welch
Income: £25,027,407 [2016]; £23,040,536 [2015]; £21,461,921 [2014]; £20,206,000 [2013]; £19,244,883 [2012]

Hand in Hand International
Registered: 24 Apr 2006 *Employees:* 9 *Volunteers:* 15
Tel: 020 7514 5091 *Website:* hihinternational.org
Activities: Education, training; advancement of health or saving of lives; prevention or relief of poverty; overseas aid, famine relief; economic, community development, employment
Address: Caparo House, 101-103 Baker Street, London, W1U 6LN
Trustees: Dr Rita Rakus, Mr Percy Barnevik Honorary Chairman, Ms Paola Uggla, John Barrett, Mr Bruce Grant Chairman, Mr Lars Josefsson, Madhvi Chanrai, Stephanie Whittier
Income: £5,784,344 [2017]; £5,552,393 [2016]; £3,778,236 [2015]; £2,740,116 [2014]; £3,808,247 [2013]

Hand in Hand for Aid and Development
Registered: 13 Feb 2012 *Employees:* 371 *Volunteers:* 145
Tel: 07867 367251 *Website:* hihfad.org
Activities: General charitable purposes; education, training; advancement of health or saving of lives; prevention or relief of poverty; overseas aid, famine relief; accommodation, housing
Address: 30 Whinlatter Drive, West Bridgford, Nottingham, NG2 6QS
Trustees: Razan Sahloul, Fadi Al-Dairi, Omar Abdulgabbar, Faddy Sahloul, Nada Kordi, Bassim Alrahbi
Income: £9,920,670 [2016]; £10,355,810 [2015]; £7,337,492 [2014]; £2,508,413 [2013]; £472,163 [2012]

The Handel House Trust Limited
Registered: 14 Nov 1991 *Employees:* 8 *Volunteers:* 90
Tel: 020 7495 1685 *Website:* handelhouse.org
Activities: Education, training; arts, culture, heritage, science; environment, conservation, heritage
Address: 25 Brook Street, London, W1K 4HB
Trustees: Mr Simon Weil, Rob Dickins, Mr Austen Bruno Issard-Davies, Ms Victoria Rowland Broackes, Mr Robin Shedden Broadhurst, Mr Adrian Charles Frost, Mr Michael Howard Ridley, Mr William James Conner
Income: £1,426,809 [2017]; £1,864,005 [2016]; £1,261,309 [2015]; £884,605 [2014]; £698,298 [2013]

Handicap International UK
Registered: 22 Sep 2000 *Employees:* 17 *Volunteers:* 18
Tel: 0870 774 3737 *Website:* humanity-inclusion.org.uk
Activities: General charitable purposes; education, training; advancement of health or saving of lives; disability; prevention or relief of poverty; overseas aid, famine relief; economic, community development, employment; human rights, religious or racial harmony, equality or diversity
Address: 9 Rushworth Street, London, SE1 0RB
Trustees: Ms Joyce McNeill, Mr David Rouane, Ms Berangere Hassenforder, Ms Chloe Marshall, Richard Gordon Elliott, Mr Benjamin Cohen, Mr Nicolas Ponset, Mr Peter Burdin
Income: £6,190,748 [2016]; £10,402,565 [2015]; £7,810,774 [2014]; £3,522,818 [2013]; £1,333,907 [2012]

Handmaids of The Sacred Heart of Jesus (Regents Park, London, and Christchurch, Hants)
Registered: 8 Jul 1963 *Employees:* 37 *Volunteers:* 15
Tel: 020 7722 2756 *Website:* acilondon.org.uk
Activities: Education, training; overseas aid, famine relief; religious activities; human rights, religious or racial harmony, equality or diversity
Address: Handmaids of The Sacred Heart of Jesus, 25 St Edmunds Terrace, London, NW8 7PY
Trustees: Sister Sarah-Anne Kane, Sister Eileen O'Neill, Sister Noella Pereira, Sister Patricia Lynch, Sister Maria Vaz Pinto, Sister Marta Isabel Silva
Income: £3,076,611 [2016]; £3,016,432 [2015]; £2,790,258 [2014]; £2,651,999 [2013]; £2,904,097 [2012]

The Hands Up Foundation
Registered: 1 Apr 2014 *Employees:* 1 *Volunteers:* 2
Tel: 07894 985107 *Website:* handsupfoundation.org
Activities: General charitable purposes; advancement of health or saving of lives; overseas aid, famine relief
Address: 10A Whorlton Road, London, SE15 3PD
Trustees: George Butler, Louisa Barnett, Joe Roberts, Thierry Heathcoat Amory, Johnnie Barnett, Rose Lukas, Amanda Ogilvie, Nick Haslam
Income: £3,265,269 [2017]; £1,028,180 [2016]; £62,172 [2015]

The Hanford School Charitable Trust Limited
Registered: 1 Feb 1991 *Employees:* 60 *Volunteers:* 2
Tel: 01258 860219 *Website:* hanford.dorset.sch.uk
Activities: Education, training
Address: Hanford School, Child Okeford, Blandford Forum, Dorset, DT11 8HN
Trustees: Mrs Lucinda Jane Frances Sunnucks, Brigadier Alexander Potts, Mr Michael Steinmetz, Mrs Charlotte Watson, Mrs Catherine White, Mr Phillip Evitt, Mr Giles David Anderson, Mrs Sarah Jane Thomas, Mrs Amelia Brooks, Mr Christophe Stourton
Income: £2,010,893 [2016]; £1,858,211 [2015]; £1,930,761 [2014]; £2,067,015 [2013]; £2,045,630 [2012]

The Haramead Trust
Registered: 21 Jun 1995
Activities: The advancement of health or saving of lives; disability; prevention or relief of poverty; overseas aid, famine relief; accommodation, housing; religious activities
Address: Park House, Park Hill, Gaddesby, Leicester, LE7 4WH
Trustees: Mr David Leslie Tams, Mrs Winifred Mary Linnett, Mrs Victoria Louise Duddles, Mr Robert Henry Smith, Mr Simon Peter Astill, Dr Mary Bridget Hanlon
Income: £1,881,823 [2017]; £2,626,763 [2016]; £1,500,052 [2015]; £751,934 [2014]; £627,233 [2013]

The Harborne Parish Lands Charity
Registered: 21 May 1979 *Employees:* 11 *Volunteers:* 4
Tel: 0121 426 1600 *Website:* hplc.org.uk
Activities: The prevention or relief of poverty; accommodation, housing
Address: Harborne Parish Lands Charity, 109 Court Oak Road, Birmingham, B17 9AA
Trustees: Councillor Roger Horton, Mr Frank G Wayt, Geoff Hewitt, Mr David John Jeffery, Mr Vic Silvester, Mrs Rachel Silber, Mr Nigel Thompson, Mrs Buddhi Chetiyawardana, Ms Kerry Bolister, Bawa Dhallu
Income: £1,421,354 [2017]; £1,400,263 [2016]; £1,308,748 [2015]; £1,274,581 [2014]; £1,324,309 [2013]

The Harbour Centre (Plymouth)
Registered: 14 Feb 1986 *Employees:* 62
Website: harbour.org.uk
Activities: Education, training; advancement of health or saving of lives; accommodation, housing
Address: Harbour Drug & Alcohol Services, Hyde Park House, Mutley Plain, Plymouth, PL4 6LF
Trustees: Mrs Jillian Carroll, Mrs Amanda Clements, Mr Christopher Andrews, Dr Adrian Barton, Dr Anthony Murray, Mr Jeremy Michael Prichard, Mr Nigel Hugh Lyons LLB, Mr Morris Watts, Mr Mark Patterson, Mrs Jane Yeates
Income: £2,518,580 [2017]; £2,440,873 [2016]; £2,627,038 [2015]; £2,455,807 [2014]; £2,470,968 [2013]

The Harbour Foundation
Registered: 13 Dec 1972
Tel: 020 7456 8180
Activities: General charitable purposes; education, training; advancement of health or saving of lives; disability; prevention or relief of poverty; overseas aid, famine relief; religious activities; arts, culture, heritage, science; environment, conservation, heritage; economic, community development, employment; other charitable purposes
Address: 1 Red Place, London, W1K 6PL
Trustees: Mrs Susan Harbour, Mr Edmond Harbour, Harry Rich, Dr Daniel Harbour, Mr Gideon Harbour, Mr Richard Hermer QC
Income: £1,901,222 [2017]; £1,723,150 [2016]; £1,535,936 [2015]; £1,412,179 [2014]; £1,559,673 [2013]

Harbour Support Services
Registered: 4 Jun 2001 *Employees:* 150 *Volunteers:* 12
Tel: 01429 270110 *Website:* myharbour.org.uk
Activities: The prevention or relief of poverty; accommodation, housing; other charitable purposes
Address: Lesley Gibson, 15 Whitburn Street, Hartlepool, Cleveland, TS24 7QR
Trustees: Mrs Wendy Morris, Mrs Caroline Skerry, Ms Louise Hurst, Mrs Denise Rudkin, Mrs Victoria Duncan, Mrs Marilyn Davies, Ms Christine Mulgrew
Income: £3,731,937 [2017]; £3,337,182 [2016]; £2,713,009 [2015]; £2,286,783 [2014]; £2,077,892 [2013]

William Harding's Charity
Registered: 19 Oct 1978
Tel: 01296 318501 *Website:* whardingcharity.org.uk
Activities: General charitable purposes; education, training; prevention or relief of poverty; accommodation, housing; arts, culture, heritage, science; amateur sport; economic, community development, employment
Address: 14 Bourbon Street, Aylesbury, Bucks, HP20 2RS
Trustees: Mr Les Sheldon, Mrs Anne Brooker, Mr Roger Evans, Mrs Ranjula Takodra, Mrs Susan Hewitt, Mrs Freda Doris Roberts MBE, Mrs Penni Thorne, Mr William John Yendell Chapple, Mr Lennard Maurice Wakelam
Income: £1,007,422 [2016]; £1,005,542 [2015]; £784,514 [2014]; £887,083 [2013]; £834,239 [2012]

The Sir Alister Hardy Foundation for Ocean Science
Registered: 12 Dec 1990 *Employees:* 30
Tel: 01752 426415 *Website:* cprsurvey.org
Activities: Education, training; arts, culture, heritage, science; environment, conservation, heritage
Address: Sahfos, The Laboratory, Citadel Hill, The Hoe, Plymouth, PL1 2PB
Trustees: Mr Robert John Mills, Professor Philip Stephen Rainbow, Professor John Raven FRS, Professor Alison Smith, Professor Michael Whitaker, Professor Stuart Rogers, Professor Christopher Leslie John Frid, Dr Jennifer Sarah Ashworth, Professor Alistair Hetherington, Sir John Beddington CMG FRS, Professor Peter Holland FRS, Professor Rory Wilson
Income: £1,719,253 [2016]; £1,690,488 [2015]; £1,637,687 [2014]; £2,177,758 [2013]; £1,777,230 [2012]

Mary Hare
Registered: 1 Aug 1995 *Employees:* 215 *Volunteers:* 6
Tel: 01635 244229 *Website:* maryhare.org.uk
Activities: Education, training
Address: Mary Hare School, Arlington Manor, Snelsmore Common, Newbury, Berks, RG14 3BQ
Trustees: Mrs V Bragg, Mr David Barron, Mrs Rosemary Sanders-Rose, Mr Adrian McAlpine, Mrs Nicol Maria Thomas, Mr Peter Robert Gale, Mr Ryan Wayne Clement, Mr Andrew James Strivens, Miss Simone Goldberg, Mr Michael Granatt, Mr Ray Evans, Mr Jeremy Paul Sharpe, Mr James Podger, Mrs Ailsa Jane Emerson, Mrs Kirsten Mary Loyd, Miss Alexia Granatt
Income: £11,008,000 [2016]; £10,185,000 [2015]; £10,377,000 [2014]; £8,958,000 [2013]

Harewood House Trust Limited
Registered: 4 Jul 1986 *Employees:* 42 *Volunteers:* 232
Tel: 0113 218 1045 *Website:* harewood.org
Activities: Education, training; arts, culture, heritage, science; environment, conservation, heritage; recreation
Address: Estate Office, Harewood Yard, Harewood, Leeds, LS17 9LF
Trustees: Mr Charles Adam Laurie Sebag-Montefiore, David Lascelles Earl of Harewood, Sir Hugh Roberts, Mr Paul David Broomfield Dolan, Ms Iwona Blazwick OBE, Mr Jeremy Burton, Diane Lascelles Countess of Harewood, The Dowager Countess of Harewood, The Hon Emily Tsering Shard
Income: £1,904,695 [2016]; £5,993,942 [2015]; £4,367,551 [2014]; £2,560,279 [2013]; £1,993,189 [2012]

Haringey Advisory Group on Alcohol
Registered: 17 Apr 1996 *Employees:* 44 *Volunteers:* 14
Tel: 020 8800 6999 *Website:* haga.co.uk
Activities: The advancement of health or saving of lives; economic, community development, employment
Address: 177 Park Lane, London, N17 0HJ
Trustees: Mr Eric Appleby, Mrs Sue Baker, Dr John Foster, Mr James Foyle, Mr Timothy Nicholls, Ms Gillian Taylor
Income: £1,700,103 [2017]; £2,036,313 [2016]; £2,480,249 [2015]; £2,244,660 [2014]; £1,787,097 [2013]

Haringey Citizens Advice Bureaux
Registered: 27 Apr 1998 *Employees:* 22 *Volunteers:* 96
Tel: 020 3872 5840 *Website:* haringeycabx.org.uk
Activities: General charitable purposes; prevention or relief of poverty
Address: Haringey Citizens Advice Bureaux, 20e Waltheof Gardens, London, N17 7DN
Trustees: Mrs Gloria Saffrey-Powell, Mr Richard Warner, Rachel Williamson, Mrs Stephanie Jenna Pilling, Mr Sean O'Donovan, Mrs Lourdes Keever, Mr Andy Love, Ms Mridu Thanki
Income: £1,198,097 [2017]; £1,345,842 [2016]; £1,820,450 [2015]; £1,771,161 [2014]; £1,160,334 [2013]

The Harington Scheme Limited
Registered: 21 Feb 1980 *Employees:* 52 *Volunteers:* 26
Tel: 020 3457 7997 *Website:* harington.org.uk
Activities: Education, training; disability; economic, community development, employment
Address: The Harington Scheme, 55a Cholmeley Park, London, N6 5EH
Trustees: Mrs Leila Hodge, Joanna Sheehan, Mr Keith Roberts, Mr Anthony Baker, Mrs Rachel Allison, Ms Margaret Barth, Mrs Jennifer Horne-Roberts, Carol Burgess, Mr David Aitchison-Tait, Pauline Treen, Mr Adam Alvarez
Income: £1,410,763 [2017]; £1,119,149 [2016]; £1,156,790 [2015]; £1,030,342 [2014]; £808,804 [2013]

Harlaxton College
Registered: 7 Apr 2009 *Employees:* 108 *Volunteers:* 25
Tel: 01476 403012 *Website:* harlaxton.ac.uk
Activities: Education, training; environment, conservation, heritage
Address: Harlaxton College, Harlaxton Manor, Harlaxton, Grantham, Lincs, NG32 1AG
Trustees: Mr Robert Anthony Brownlow, Mrs Henrietta Joscelyne Chubb, Dr Thomas Allen Kazee
Income: £3,623,314 [2017]; £3,493,898 [2016]; £3,123,488 [2015]; £3,292,608 [2014]; £3,393,465 [2013]

The Harlington Area Schools Trust
Registered: 19 May 2009 *Employees:* 49
Tel: 01525 755100 *Website:* hast-education.co.uk
Activities: Education, training; disability
Address: Harlington Upper School, Goswell End Road, Harlington, Dunstable, Beds, LU5 6NX
Trustees: Mr Paul Dickens, Mr Anthony Frederick Wildman, Mrs Nicola Neal, Mr Owen Flack, Mr Timothy Peacock, Mr Anthony David Williams, Mr Richard Alfred Holland, Mr Ali Hadawi, Mr Alan Euinton, Mr Stephen John Alcock
Income: £1,630,611 [2017]; £1,551,020 [2016]; £1,422,143 [2015]; £1,235,920 [2014]; £6,194,754 [2013]

Harlington Hospice Association Limited

Registered: 9 Sep 2003 *Employees:* 42 *Volunteers:* 108
Tel: 020 8759 0453 *Website:* harlingtonhospice.org
Activities: The advancement of health or saving of lives
Address: Harlington Hospice Association, St Peters Way, Harlington, Hayes, Middlesex, UB3 5AB
Trustees: Mr John Martin McDonnell, Mr Sean Fitzpatrick, Mr Mick Edwards, Ms Catherine Hepplethwaite, Miss Margaret Roberts, Mr Brian Neighbour, Mrs Carol Coventry, Dr Elizabeth Horak
Income: £1,526,544 [2017]; £1,165,444 [2016]; £933,689 [2015]; £952,478 [2014]; £738,373 [2013]

The Harlow Health Centres Trust Limited

Registered: 8 Nov 1995 *Employees:* 1
Tel: 01279 453976 *Website:* hhct.org.uk
Activities: The advancement of health or saving of lives; accommodation, housing
Address: Latton Bush Centre, Southern Way, Harlow, Essex, CM18 7BL
Trustees: Mr Stanley Newens, Mr Derek Gordon Fenny, Mr Byron Jones, Mr Steve Lemay, Mrs Pamela Heeks, Ms Patrica Larkin, Ms Samantha Fancett
Income: £2,276,696 [2016]; £2,570,702 [2015]; £2,188,867 [2014]; £2,184,209 [2013]; £2,121,441 [2012]

Harlow and District Sports Trust

Registered: 30 Oct 1963 *Employees:* 39
Tel: 01279 621500 *Website:* harlowleisurezone.co.uk
Activities: Education, training; advancement of health or saving of lives; disability; arts, culture, heritage, science; amateur sport; economic, community development, employment; recreation
Address: Harlow Leisurezone, Second Avenue, Harlow, Essex, CM20 3DT
Trustees: Mr Derek Gordon Fenny, Mr David Charles Sharp, Mr Tony Graham Crisp, Mr Richard Little, Mrs Lucy Jane Lomas, Mr Charles Richard Cochrane, Mr Patrick Andrew Hay MA DMS, Mr John William Wright, Mr Robin Alton, Ms Gabriela Helena Horecka
Income: £4,936,541 [2017]; £4,351,177 [2016]; £4,298,527 [2015]; £3,445,878 [2014]; £3,370,428 [2013]

Harpenden Mencap

Registered: 22 Mar 1994 *Employees:* 57 *Volunteers:* 20
Tel: 01582 460055 *Website:* harpendenmencap.org.uk
Activities: Disability; accommodation, housing; economic, community development, employment
Address: 7 Moreton Place, Harpenden, Herts, AL5 2UF
Trustees: Dr Derek Oliver Bird, Freddie Gee, Julie Caseberry, Mrs Anne Hignell, Mr Patrick Fisher, Nick Latham
Income: £1,875,919 [2017]; £1,853,518 [2016]; £1,808,728 [2015]; £1,882,677 [2014]; £1,557,394 [2013]

The Harpur Trust

Registered: 15 Dec 1997 *Employees:* 1,092 *Volunteers:* 35
Tel: 01234 369500 *Website:* harpurtrust.org.uk
Activities: Education, training; prevention or relief of poverty; recreation
Address: The Harpur Trust, Princeton Court, The Pilgrim Centre, Brickhill Drive, Bedford, MK41 7PZ
Trustees: Mr David Wilson, Mr Philip Wedgwood Wallace, Mr William Andrew Justin Phillimore, Mr Mark Taylor, Professor Stephen Mayson, Sir Clive Loader, Mrs Sally Peck, Dr Anne Egan MA BM BCh MRCP FRCR, Mrs Rhian Castell, Mrs Shirley Jackson, Mrs Rose-Marie Wellington, Professor Rajkumar Roy, Mr Michael Womack, Mr Anthony Nutt, Mrs Susan Clark, Miss Tina Beddoes, Mr Hugh Murray Stewart, Professor Richard George Ratcliffe, Dr Jennifer Sauboorah Till, Councillor Randolph Charles, Mr Linbert Spencer, Councillor Luigi Reale, Ms Harriett Mather, Professor Rebecca Taylor
Income: £52,794,000 [2017]; £53,185,000 [2016]; £51,822,000 [2015]; £55,270,000 [2014]; £49,568,000 [2013]

Harris (Belmont) Charity

Registered: 5 Oct 2012 *Employees:* 16 *Volunteers:* 19
Tel: 01223 728222 *Website:* belmont-house.org
Activities: Arts, culture, heritage, science; environment, conservation, heritage
Address: Peters Elworthy & Moore, Salisbury House, 2-3 Salisbury Villas, Cambridge, CB1 2LA
Trustees: Mr Patrick Alexander Evans, Rt Hon Isabelle Jacqueline Laline Hay Countess of Erroll, Mr Alastair Mathewson, Mr Alisdair Nigel Scott, Lord Alastair Campbell Colgrain
Income: £1,331,773 [2017]; £1,331,680 [2016]; £1,310,190 [2015]; £1,323,516 [2014]

Peter Harrison Foundation

Registered: 15 Jul 1999 *Employees:* 3
Tel: 01737 228013 *Website:* peterharrisonfoundation.org
Activities: General charitable purposes; education, training; disability; amateur sport
Address: Foundation House, 42-48 London Road, Reigate, Surrey, RH2 9QQ
Trustees: Mrs Julia Caron Harrison-Lee, Peter Robert Harrison KGCN CBE, Mr Peter John Gorringe Lee DL, Mr Nicholas Peter Harrison
Income: £2,876,431 [2017]; £2,463,713 [2016]; £2,616,559 [2015]; £2,642,326 [2014]; £2,351,647 [2013]

Harrison Housing

Registered: 10 Dec 2003 *Employees:* 9 *Volunteers:* 7
Website: harrisonhousing.org.uk
Activities: Accommodation, housing
Address: Harrison Housing, 42-46 St James's Gardens, London, W11 4RQ
Trustees: Mrs Corinne Rose Knowles, Mr Neil Gerald Alexander King, Mr John Malpass, Mr Ian Morrison, Mr Paul Lautman, Mrs Margaret Regina Gunther, Mr Mark Le Fanu, Mr Hugh Stanley Keith Knowles, Ms Samantha Barber, Mr Robert Hicks
Income: £1,123,680 [2016]; £1,089,420 [2015]; £1,045,837 [2014]; £1,245,658 [2013]; £1,557,504 [2012]

Harrogate (White Rose) Theatre Trust Ltd
Registered: 3 May 1963 *Employees:* 26 *Volunteers:* 150
Tel: 01423 502710 *Website:* harrogatetheatre.co.uk
Activities: Arts, culture, heritage, science
Address: Harrogate (White Rose) Theatre Trust, 3 Garrick Buildings, Oxford Street, Harrogate, N Yorks, HG1 1QF
Trustees: Mr Jim Clark
Income: £3,237,489 [2017]; £3,637,608 [2016]; £3,109,548 [2015]; £2,803,033 [2014]; £3,031,284 [2013]

Harrogate District Hospice Care
Registered: 22 Jun 1987 *Employees:* 99 *Volunteers:* 640
Tel: 01423 878181 *Website:* saintmichaelshospice.org
Activities: Education, training; advancement of health or saving of lives
Address: Crimple House, Hornbeam Park Avenue, Harrogate, N Yorks, HG2 8QL
Trustees: Revd John Dobson, Ms Jean Macquarrie, Mrs Karen Jane Wheeldon, Mr John William Charlton, Sarah Hay, Mrs Lesley Rosemary Bers, Mr Mark Robinson, Mr Colin James Tweedie, Dr Claire Hall, Mrs Victoria Ashley
Income: £4,881,247 [2017]; £4,616,976 [2016]; £4,149,753 [2015]; £4,460,406 [2014]; £4,846,303 [2013]

Harrogate International Festival Limited
Registered: 28 Sep 1965 *Employees:* 9 *Volunteers:* 50
Tel: 01423 562303 *Website:* harrogateinternationalfestivals.com
Activities: Education, training; arts, culture, heritage, science
Address: 32 Cheltenahm Parade, Harrogate, N Yorks, HG1 1DB
Trustees: David Salter, Craig Ratcliffe, Kate Spencer, Susan Rumfitt, Mrs Fiona Armitage, Matthew Osbourne, Jennifer Harris, Sofia Cann
Income: £1,254,564 [2016]; £884,994 [2015]; £836,371 [2014]; £733,229 [2013]; £748,202 [2012]

Harrogate Ladies' College Limited
Registered: 1 Jul 1964 *Employees:* 181 *Volunteers:* 29
Tel: 01423 504543 *Website:* hlc.org.uk
Activities: Education, training
Address: Harrogate Ladies College, Clarence Drive, Harrogate, N Yorks, HG1 2QG
Trustees: Mrs Shirley Hooper, Dr Angela Fahy, Mrs Lesley Byrne, Mr John Skinner, Mrs Susan J Hundleby, Mrs Julia Roe, Mr Barry Huggett OBE, Mr Mark Gardiner, Miss Nicola Loudon, Mrs Patricia Jones, Mrs Rachel Tunnicliffe, Mrs Caroline Peasgood, Mrs Susan B Jackson, Mrs Jessica Crossley, Dame Francine Holroyd, Mrs Susan Clark, Mrs Susan Papworth
Income: £8,453,592 [2016]; £8,216,270 [2015]; £8,784,523 [2014]; £8,344,980 [2013]; £7,930,712 [2012]

The Harrow Development Trust
Registered: 28 Dec 1988 *Employees:* 6
Tel: 020 8872 8500 *Website:* harrowdevtrust.com
Activities: Education, training
Address: The Harrow Development Trust, 5a High Street, Harrow on the Hill, Middlesex, HA1 3HP
Trustees: Harriet Spencer Crawley, Mr Matthew Fosh, Mr Nikhil Hirdaramani, John Paul Batting, Mr Kevin Wb Gilbert, Mr Patrick Wong
Income: £8,335,513 [2017]; £16,092,698 [2016]; £8,043,464 [2015]; £11,900,535 [2014]; £5,889,269 [2013]

Harrow Mencap
Registered: 20 Oct 1986 *Employees:* 90 *Volunteers:* 100
Tel: 020 8869 8484 *Website:* harrowmencap.org.uk
Activities: General charitable purposes; education, training; disability; amateur sport; economic, community development, employment; other charitable purposes
Address: 3 Jardine House, Harrovian Business Village, Bessborough Road, Harrow, Middlesex, HA1 3EX
Trustees: Mr Paul Williams, Mr Peter CH Stones, Ms Hazel Paterson, Mr Rikesh Tailor, Mr Moiz Tayabali Daydali, Ms Marie-Louise Nolan, Mr David Mark House
Income: £2,163,336 [2017]; £1,873,387 [2016]; £1,497,338 [2015]; £1,204,870 [2014]; £1,058,549 [2013]

Hartcliffe and Withywood Ventures
Registered: 10 Jan 1986 *Employees:* 59 *Volunteers:* 12
Tel: 0117 978 1708 *Website:* hwv.org.uk
Activities: Education, training; prevention or relief of poverty; economic, community development, employment
Address: 79 Church Lane, Backwell, Bristol, BS48 3JL
Trustees: Ms Helen Holland, Christina Clements, Margaret Theresa Owens, Mr Justin Ricks, Ronald James Sheppard, Mrs Teresa Anstey, David Robert Portingale
Income: £1,178,340 [2017]; £1,197,165 [2016]; £1,222,075 [2015]; £1,248,166 [2014]; £1,370,842 [2013]

The Hartlepool Hospice Limited
Registered: 19 Dec 1980 *Employees:* 84 *Volunteers:* 211
Tel: 01429 855555 *Website:* alicehousehospice.co.uk
Activities: The advancement of health or saving of lives
Address: Alice House Hospice, Alice House, Wells Avenue, Hartlepool, Cleveland, TS24 9DA
Trustees: Lorna Jones, Mr Malcolm John Cairns, Dr Robin William Wylie Armstrong, Mr Sunil Thomas Chacko, Mr Clive Shotton, Mr Paul Jones-King, Mr Francis Matthew Gibbon, Mr Raymond Priestman, Joanne Regan, Mr James Frederick Ainslie, Mrs Annaliese Barber
Income: £3,204,561 [2017]; £3,012,976 [2016]; £3,200,537 [2015]; £2,722,815 [2014]; £2,607,663 [2013]

Hartlepool and East Durham Mind
Registered: 17 Sep 2008 *Employees:* 52 *Volunteers:* 20
Tel: 01429 269303 *Website:* hartlepoolmind.com
Activities: Education, training; advancement of health or saving of lives; amateur sport
Address: Mind, Crown Buildings, Raby Road, Hartlepool, Cleveland, TS24 8AS
Trustees: Mr Keith Bayley, Colin Thompson, Kathryn Hall, Julie Rudge, Susan Hales, Miss Jillian Best
Income: £1,516,984 [2017]; £1,275,138 [2016]; £1,138,744 [2015]; £957,474 [2014]; £727,471 [2013]

Harvard Global UK
Registered: 22 Apr 2015 *Employees:* 3
Activities: General charitable purposes; education, training; arts, culture, heritage, science; environment, conservation, heritage
Address: 83 Hill Street, Lexington, Ma 02421, USA
Trustees: Mr James Victor Baker, Ms Meredith Weenick, Mr Joseph Hugh O'Regan
Income: £2,676,648 [2017]; £9,500 [2016]

The William Harvey Research Foundation
Registered: 12 Mar 1990 Employees: 8
Website: whrf.org.uk
Activities: The advancement of health or saving of lives
Address: William Harvey Research Foundation, Charterhouse Square, London, EC1M 6BQ
Trustees: Mr Peter Marshall, Mr Jeremy Tigue, Professor Timothy Williams, Prof Steve Thornton, Mr Steven Andrew Ralph Bates, Dr Stephen Decherney, Mrs Lisbet Coulton, Dr John Gordon, Mr Gary McRae
Income: £2,075,740 [2017]; £1,700,952 [2016]; £1,582,202 [2015]; £833,157 [2014]; £783,393 [2013]

Harvey's Foundry Trust
Registered: 3 Feb 2006 Employees: 4 Volunteers: 50
Tel: 01736 757683 Website: harveysfoundrytrust.org.uk
Activities: General charitable purposes; education, training; environment, conservation, heritage; economic, community development, employment
Address: 17 Dowren House, Foundry Lane, Hayle, Cornwall, TR27 4HH
Trustees: Mr Brian Capper, John Pollard, Mr Kingsley John Thomas Rickard, Mr Marshall Hutchens, Mr Robb Lello, Bernadette Wills, Lawrence Butler, Barbara Bromley, Stella Runnalls Thomas, Mr Richard John Gyles Morton, Mr John Bennett, Mr Nicholas John Harvey, Mr John Richard Lloyd, Mr Christopher John Quick
Income: £1,902,532 [2017]; £359,718 [2016]; £294,319 [2015]; £186,720 [2014]; £169,217 [2013]

Harvington School Educational Trust Ltd
Registered: 24 Aug 1970 Employees: 29
Tel: 020 8997 1583 Website: harvingtonschool.com
Activities: Education, training
Address: Harvington Prep School, 20 Castlebar Road, London, W5 2DS
Trustees: Professor Alan Henry Puckridge Gillett, Mrs Anna Evans, Arthur Bray, Mr Manjeet Mudan
Income: £1,480,723 [2016]; £1,272,206 [2015]; £1,277,277 [2014]; £1,313,686 [2013]

Hasmonean High School Charitable Trust
Registered: 25 Feb 1998
Tel: 07974 151494 Website: hasmonean.co.uk
Activities: Education, training
Address: 17 Wykeham Road, London, NW4 2TB
Trustees: Mr Jonathan Feinmesser, Ms Jacqueline Rashbass, Mr Ari Joseph Bloom
Income: £3,617,340 [2016]; £3,727,452 [2015]; £2,417,539 [2014]; £2,568,863 [2013]; £2,866,973 [2012]

Hastings and St Leonards Foreshore Charitable Trust
Registered: 26 Aug 2004
Tel: 01424 451066 Website: hastings.gov.uk
Activities: General charitable purposes
Address: Hastings Town Hall, Queens Road, Hastings, E Sussex, TN34 1QR
Trustees: Hastings Borough Council
Income: £1,459,009 [2017]; £1,405,997 [2016]; £1,380,534 [2015]; £1,100,461 [2014]; £1,033,451 [2013]

Estate Charity of William Hatcliffe
Registered: 25 Feb 1964
Tel: 07887 777256
Activities: The prevention or relief of poverty
Address: St Margarets Visitor Centre, Brandram Road, Lewisham, London, SE13 5EA
Trustees: Andrew Blundy, Ray Brookes, Mr Geoffrey Coulson, Mr Gregory Kirby, Mrs Wyn Kirkman, Mr Richard Quibell, Mrs Gloria Phillips MBE, Mr Julian Watson, Rev Chris Moody, Mr Roger Hough, Rev Steve Hall, Mr Anthony Austin
Income: £1,676,891 [2017]; £1,613,938 [2016]; £1,508,653 [2015]; £1,343,584 [2014]; £1,140,669 [2013]

The Maurice Hatter Foundation
Registered: 24 Nov 1987
Activities: Education, training; advancement of health or saving of lives; disability; religious activities; environment, conservation, heritage; armed forces, emergency service efficiency; human rights, religious or racial harmony, equality or diversity
Address: 1 Bishops Wharf, Walnut Tree Close, Guildford, Surrey, GU1 4RA
Trustees: Mr Richard Hatter, Mr Piers Barclay, Mr Fausto Furlotti
Income: £3,252,345 [2017]; £2,884,440 [2016]; £3,339,810 [2015]; £2,905,268 [2014]; £1,462,012 [2013]

Hatzola Trust Limited
Registered: 3 Feb 2015 Volunteers: 20
Tel: 020 3603 4111 Website: hatzola.org
Activities: Education, training; advancement of health or saving of lives
Address: Office 4, Sir John & Lady Cohen CT, 1 Rookwood Road, Hackney, London, N16 6SD
Trustees: Mr Gabriel Schleider, Mr Moses Breuer, Mr Yisroel Kohn, Mr Jacob Sorotzkin, Dr Sholaum Springer
Income: £1,006,868 [2017]; £297,110 [2016]

The Havebury Housing Partnership
Registered: 17 May 2002 Employees: 172
Tel: 01284 722174 Website: havebury.com
Activities: Accommodation, housing; environment, conservation, heritage; economic, community development, employment
Address: The Havebury Housing Partnership, Havebury House, Western Way, Bury St Edmunds, Suffolk, IP33 3SP
Trustees: Mr Robert Everitt, Mr Ian Michael Mashiter, Mrs Helen Thomas, Miss Lucy Adams, Mr Donald John McKenzie, Mr Clive Leonard Gardner, Mr Michael Sheren
Income: £34,992,000 [2017]; £33,549,000 [2016]; £31,506,000 [2015]; £30,550,000 [2014]; £29,118,000 [2013]

Haven House Foundation
Registered: 16 Feb 1995 Employees: 63 Volunteers: 367
Tel: 020 8505 9944 Website: havenhouse.org.uk
Activities: Education, training; advancement of health or saving of lives; disability
Address: Whitehouse, High Road, Woodford Green, Essex, IG8 9LB
Trustees: Chas Hollwey, Frances Daley, David Bayton, Inge Linneman-Hussein, Mr Jonathan Harding, Daniel Fluskey, Michael Herst, Emma Devereux, Mr Mohamed Omer, Matt Barrett
Income: £3,404,332 [2017]; £3,074,627 [2016]; £3,906,973 [2015]; £2,959,398 [2014]; £2,284,541 [2013]

The Haven Wolverhampton
Registered: 3 Nov 1997 *Employees:* 47 *Volunteers:* 158
Tel: 01902 904677 *Website:* havenrefuge.org.uk
Activities: Education, training; advancement of health or saving of lives; prevention or relief of poverty; accommodation, housing; economic, community development, employment; other charitable purposes
Address: P O Box 105, 18 Waterloo Road, Wolverhampton, W Midlands, WV1 4BL
Trustees: Mr Harry Colin Brown, Mrs Kim Marie Benton, Mrs Alison Westwood, Ms Gillian Atkins, Mrs Katarina Fidler, Mrs Stephanie Harris, Ms Philippa Pringle, Mrs Andrea Spence-Ferguson, Mrs Carwen Wynnye-Howells, Ms Angela Morgan, Mr David James Taylor, Mrs Narinder Rehal
Income: £1,765,706 [2017]; £2,015,649 [2016]; £2,425,994 [2015]; £2,470,201 [2014]; £2,653,279 [2013]

Havencare (South West) Limited
Registered: 9 Sep 1988 *Employees:* 202
Tel: 01752 251476 *Website:* havencare.com
Activities: Disability
Address: 3 Pennance Parc, Lanner, Redruth, Cornwall, TR16 5TY
Trustees: Mr Stephen John Reynolds, Mrs Kathleen Cuthbert, Mr David William May
Income: £4,409,887 [2017]; £4,170,634 [2016]; £3,270,941 [2015]; £3,083,033 [2014]; £2,945,813 [2013]

Havens Christian Hospice
Registered: 2 Jun 1993 *Employees:* 276 *Volunteers:* 898
Tel: 01702 220350 *Website:* havenshospices.org.uk
Activities: Education, training; advancement of health or saving of lives; disability
Address: Fairhavens Christian Hospice, Stuart House, 47 Second Avenue, Westcliff on Sea, Essex, SS0 8HX
Trustees: Mr Richard Player, Mr Brian Gillard, Mr Roberto Decristofano, Mr Clive Pegler, Marion Roberts-Smith, Mr Reginald Ramm, Mr Brian Terry, Mrs Ruth Lynette Morris, Terry Harding, Mr Stewart Turner
Income: £10,085,000 [2017]; £10,348,000 [2016]; £10,204,000 [2015]; £11,740,000 [2014]; £8,654,000 [2013]

The Havering Theatre Trust Limited
Registered: 11 Sep 1967 *Employees:* 70 *Volunteers:* 36
Tel: 01708 462362 *Website:* queens-theatre.co.uk
Activities: Education, training; arts, culture, heritage, science; recreation
Address: Queens Theatre, Theatre House, Billet Lane, Hornchurch, Essex, RM11 1QT
Trustees: Councillor Gillian Ford, Claire Gevaux, Ms Julie Ann Parker, Mr Steve Moffitt, Mr Timothy Henry Walford-Fitzgerald, Councillor Patricia Rumble, Mr Damian White, Ms Asma Hussain, Ms Sara Thompson
Income: £3,503,856 [2017]; £3,113,128 [2016]; £3,377,652 [2015]; £3,208,173 [2014]; £3,272,892 [2013]

Hawk Conservancy Trust Limited
Registered: 6 Jun 2002 *Employees:* 42 *Volunteers:* 43
Tel: 01264 773850 *Website:* hawk-conservancy.org
Activities: Environment, conservation, heritage
Address: Hawk Conservancy Trust, Sarson Lane, Weyhill, Andover, Hants, SP11 8DY
Trustees: Dr Matthew Dryden-Director, Mr Nick Gent-Director, Mr Scott Jones-Director, Mr Adam Johnson-Director, Mr Denzil Sharp-Director, Mr Gary Wyles-Director
Income: £1,736,363 [2017]; £1,522,712 [2016]; £1,685,656 [2015]; £1,692,550 [2014]; £1,529,305 [2013]

Hawthorne Trust Limited
Registered: 2 Oct 1968 *Employees:* 26 *Volunteers:* 16
Tel: 01322 863116 *Website:* chartonmanor.org
Activities: Education, training; accommodation, housing; religious activities
Address: Hawthorne Trust Ltd, Charton Manor, Gorse Hill, Farningham, Dartford, Kent, DA4 0JT
Trustees: Mrs Margaret Chaplin, Mr James Weaver, Brian Blandford, Mrs Susan Thomas
Income: £1,014,509 [2016]; £1,311,994 [2015]; £2,470,054 [2014]; £960,081 [2013]; £1,301,766 [2012]

The Hawthorns Educational Trust Limited
Registered: 7 May 1970 *Employees:* 111
Tel: 01883 743048 *Website:* hawthorns.com
Activities: Education, training; amateur sport
Address: The Hawthorns School, Pendell Court, Pendell Road, Bletchingley, Redhill, Surrey, RH1 4QJ
Trustees: Mr John Baart, Mr Rob Buckingham, Mrs Susan Chrysanthou, Mr Mark Dockery, Mr Brad Dyer, Mr Jeremy Edwards, Mrs Zoe Creighton, Mr Robin Kirkland, Mrs Sylvia Hill, Mr Rob Davey, Mr Simon Daniell, Mr Dickon Searle
Income: £6,408,498 [2017]; £6,247,120 [2016]; £5,956,147 [2015]; £6,014,334 [2014]; £5,684,477 [2013]

Hayfran Trust
Registered: 2 Feb 1988 *Employees:* 48
Tel: 01672 569088 *Website:* st-francis.wilts.sch.uk
Activities: Education, training
Address: 9 High Street, Manton, Marlborough, Wilts, SN8 4HH
Trustees: Mr Philip Humphries-Cuff, Mr Mark Richard John Piper, Mrs Nicola Botterill, Dr Richard William Hook, Mrs Fabia Alyson Bromovsky, Mr Robin John Anthony White, Jane Stevens, Mr Benjamin Henry Miller
Income: £2,195,767 [2017]; £2,360,796 [2016]; £2,242,627 [2015]; £2,067,338 [2014]; £1,934,178 [2013]

The Haynes International Motor Museum
Registered: 10 Jul 1985 *Employees:* 50 *Volunteers:* 60
Tel: 01963 442782 *Website:* himm.co.uk
Activities: Education, training; environment, conservation, heritage
Address: Haynes International Motor Museum, Sparkford, Yeovil, Somerset, BA22 7LH
Trustees: Annette C Haynes, Mr N B Sanders, Mr H Mayes, Mr J H Haynes OBE, Mr Timothy Miles Marsh, Michael Penn
Income: £2,401,903 [2017]; £2,363,724 [2016]; £1,964,820 [2015]; £1,227,017 [2014]; £1,192,659 [2013]

The Charles Hayward Foundation
Registered: 14 Jan 2000 *Employees:* 4
Tel: 020 7370 7063 *Website:* charleshaywardfoundation.org.uk
Activities: General charitable purposes
Address: Hayward House, 45 Harrington Gardens, London, SW7 4JU
Trustees: Mrs Julia Mary Chamberlain, Mr Brian Douglas Insch, Mr Alexander James Heath, Mr Richard Griffith, Mrs Susan Jane Heath, Mr Nikolas Van Leuven QC, Ms Caroline Donald
Income: £1,375,349 [2016]; £1,349,248 [2015]; £1,357,974 [2014]; £1,391,002 [2013]; £1,484,312 [2012]

Hazelwood School
Registered: 17 Feb 1969 *Employees:* 160
Tel: 01883 733841 *Website:* hazelwoodschool.co.uk
Activities: Education, training
Address: Hazelwood School, Wolfs Hill, Oxted, Surrey, RH8 0QU
Trustees: Mrs Annabel Lark, Mr David Anthony Bersey Hughes, Mr John Attwater MA, Mr Bill Crothers, Mrs Alison Curson, Mrs Melanie Lewis, Mrs Emma Francis, Mrs Jayne Adams LLB, Josephine Naismith, Mr Tim Manly, Mr Guy Graham, Mr Alex Arterton, Mr John Bleakley, Mrs Alexia Bolton
Income: £6,916,774 [2017]; £6,697,244 [2016]; £6,595,592 [2015]; £5,803,313 [2014]; £5,084,427 [2013]

Hazrat Sultan Bahu Trust (UK)
Registered: 4 Oct 1985 *Employees:* 137 *Volunteers:* 20
Tel: 0121 440 4096 *Website:* bahutrust.org
Activities: General charitable purposes; education, training; prevention or relief of poverty; overseas aid, famine relief; religious activities; economic, community development, employment
Address: 17-21 Ombersley Road, Balsall Heath, Birmingham, B12 8UR
Trustees: Sultan Fiaz Ul Hassan, Latif Bhatti, Mr Mohammed Zain Sultan, Mr Mohammed Amar, Sultan Niaz Ul Hassan, Mr Muhammad Shafiq, Mr Ghulam Rasool
Income: £2,694,493 [2017]; £2,316,295 [2016]; £2,118,822 [2015]; £2,717,926 [2014]; £2,595,545 [2013]

Headington School Oxford Limited
Registered: 14 Jan 1966 *Employees:* 398 *Volunteers:* 23
Tel: 01865 759856 *Website:* headington.org
Activities: Education, training
Address: The Bursary, Headington School, Headington Road, Headington, Oxford, OX3 0BL
Trustees: Miss Margaret Rudland, Mrs Penelope Anne Lenon, Miss Bryony Crawford Moore, Lady Nancy Caroline Kenny, Rev Darren McFarland, Mrs Sallie Christina Ellen Salvidant, Dr Catherine Mary Ringham, Mr Christopher Ian Knowles Harris, Prof Katya Drummond, Mr Steven Charles Andres Harris BA ACA, Mr Reginald Stephen Shipperley, Dr Susan Mary Burge, Mrs Sandra Claire Phipkin, Mrs Carol Oster Warriner
Income: £20,915,221 [2017]; £20,344,587 [2016]; £18,786,869 [2015]; £18,724,183 [2014]; £17,130,676 [2013]

The Headley Trust
Registered: 20 Feb 1974 *Employees:* 17
Tel: 020 7410 0330 *Website:* sfct.org.uk
Activities: General charitable purposes; education, training; advancement of health or saving of lives; disability; prevention or relief of poverty; overseas aid, famine relief; arts, culture, heritage, science; environment, conservation, heritage; economic, community development, employment
Address: Sainsbury Family Charitable Trusts, The Peak, 5 Wilton Road, London, SW1V 1AP
Trustees: Lady Susan Sainsbury, Mr Timothy James Sainsbury OBE, Mrs Camilla Davan Sainsbury, Miss Judith Susan Portrait OBE, The Rt Hon Sir Timothy Sainsbury, Mrs Amanda McCrystal
Income: £2,343,000 [2017]; £2,292,000 [2016]; £3,621,000 [2015]; £2,235,000 [2014]; £4,971,000 [2013]

Headlong Theatre Limited
Registered: 5 Aug 1974 *Employees:* 9
Tel: 020 7633 2090 *Website:* headlong.co.uk
Activities: Arts, culture, heritage, science
Address: 17 Risborough Street, London, SE1 0HG
Trustees: Ms Donna Munday, Mr Robin Paxton, Ms Lesley Wan, Ms Nicky Jones, Ms Caroline Phillippa Donald, Mr Mark Trevor Phillips, Mr Prasanna Puwanarajah, Mr Richard Huntrods, Ms Maggie Whitlum
Income: £1,601,741 [2017]; £1,389,620 [2016]; £1,452,415 [2015]; £1,508,702 [2014]; £889,331 [2013]

Headway - The Brain Injury Association
Registered: 16 Sep 1993 *Employees:* 117 *Volunteers:* 1,000
Tel: 0115 924 0800 *Website:* headway.org.uk
Activities: Education, training; advancement of health or saving of lives; disability
Address: Bradbury House, 190 Bagnall Road, Old Basford, Nottingham, NG6 8SF
Trustees: Ms Julie Bridgewater, Mr Andrew Harding, Mr Allistair Renton, Dr June Gilchrist, Mr Brendan McKeever, Mr Colin Louis Shieff, Dr Andrew Douglas Tyerman, Mrs Evelyn Vincent, Pastor Abraham Lawrence, Dr Colin Reeves CBE, Mr Denzil Lush, Mr Andrew Kenneth Green MBE, Mrs Jane Elizabeth Hales, Mrs Jane Muriel Allberry CBE
Income: £5,321,761 [2016]; £4,251,394 [2015]; £3,686,458 [2014]; £3,393,216 [2013]; £3,192,451 [2012]

Headway Birmingham & Solihull
Registered: 26 Feb 1992 *Employees:* 65 *Volunteers:* 166
Tel: 0121 457 7541 *Website:* headway-bs.org.uk
Activities: Education, training; advancement of health or saving of lives; disability
Address: Headway Birmingham & Solihull, Leighton House, 20 Chapel Rise, Rednal, Birmingham, B45 9SN
Trustees: Mr Peter Edward Durham, Mr John Henry Barnes, Mr Richard Crispin Langton, Mrs Rachel May Kinning, Mr David Gordon Chater, Mrs Dilini Tanya De Silva, Mr Christopher John Roach
Income: £1,524,081 [2017]; £1,215,797 [2016]; £1,057,779 [2015]; £904,338 [2014]; £895,932 [2013]

Headway East London
Registered: 1 Dec 2000 *Employees:* 36 *Volunteers:* 80
Tel: 020 7749 7790 *Website:* headwayeastlondon.org
Activities: Disability
Address: Headway East London, 238 Kingsland Road, London, E2 8AX
Trustees: Mr Norman Keen, Ms Marilene Antoni, Ms Katharine Hibbert, Mrs Sarah Griggs, Mr Tom Hughes, Mr Daniel Smith, Mr John Burns Comninos, Miss Penny Wrout, Miss Julie Louise Woodward, Mr Steven John Groves, Mr Jeremy Stockdale
Income: £1,650,204 [2017]; £1,414,356 [2016]; £1,232,336 [2015]; £1,212,970 [2014]; £1,146,822 [2013]

Headway Shropshire
Registered: 29 Oct 2003 *Employees:* 66 *Volunteers:* 6
Tel: 01743 365271 *Website:* headwayshropshire.org.uk
Activities: Disability
Address: Headway Shropshire, Holsworth Park, Oxon Business Park, Bicton Heath, Shrewsbury, Salop, SY3 5HJ
Trustees: Mr John Mark Ankers, Mr Neil Lorimer, Mrs Clare Dalby, Mr Timothy Lunt, Sandy Ramsay, Mr Mark Anthony Gibson, Mrs Shirley Stewart, Mrs Gayle Elizabeth Kinsey
Income: £1,406,768 [2016]; £1,396,229 [2015]; £860,843 [2014]; £479,061 [2013]

Headway Suffolk Ltd

Registered: 4 May 1999 *Employees:* 82 *Volunteers:* 10
Tel: 01473 712225 *Website:* headwaysuffolk.org.uk
Activities: Education, training; advancement of health or saving of lives; disability; economic, community development, employment
Address: Ground Floor, Headway, Epsilon House, West Road, Ransomes Europark, Ipswich, Suffolk, IP3 9FJ
Trustees: Mrs Brenda Elizabeth Williams, Mr David Baker, Mr Humphry Michael Adair, Alan Moore, Mr Kevin Woolard, Mr Terence Dean Hunt, Allistair Renton, Tom Cook, Dr Owen Anthony Thurtle, Mrs Gail Joan Fogg-Elliot, Roy Dunnett
Income: £1,657,422 [2017]; £1,408,381 [2016]; £1,444,276 [2015]; £842,974 [2014]; £729,159 [2013]

Headway Worcestershire

Registered: 30 Jan 1990 *Employees:* 56 *Volunteers:* 30
Tel: 01905 729729 *Website:* headwayworcestershire.org.uk
Activities: Education, training; advancement of health or saving of lives; disability; accommodation, housing
Address: 3 Longleat Drive, Cheswick Green, Solihull, W Midlands, B90 4SN
Trustees: Ms Mary Gleaves, Ms Lyn Archer, Malcolm Scott, Mrs Rosemary Joan Grove, Mr Simon Marriott, Mr Keith Allen, Mrs Catherine Margaret Mansell, Mr Thomas Patrick Naughton
Income: £1,018,073 [2017]; £1,054,130 [2016]; £1,070,585 [2015]; £1,132,581 [2014]; £945,115 [2013]

The Health Foundation

Registered: 12 May 1983 *Employees:* 117 *Volunteers:* 4
Tel: 020 7257 8000 *Website:* health.org.uk
Activities: Education, training; advancement of health or saving of lives; other charitable purposes
Address: 90 Long Acre, London, WC2E 9RA
Trustees: Mrs Bridget McIntyre, Sir Hugh Taylor KCB, Ms Rosalind Louise Smyth, Sir David Dalton, Mr Eric Gregory, Dr Ruth Hussey CB OBE, Mr David Zahn, Mr Martyn Christopher Hole, Mrs Melloney Marina Caroline Poole, Ms Branwen Jeffreys, Ms Loraine Hawkins
Income: £14,939,000 [2016]; £15,512,000 [2015]; £17,209,000 [2014]; £14,405,000 [2013]; £15,126,000 [2012]

Health Limited

Registered: 6 Nov 1984 *Employees:* 570
Tel: 020 7840 3750 *Website:* healthpovertyaction.org
Activities: Education, training; advancement of health or saving of lives; disability; prevention or relief of poverty; overseas aid, famine relief; environment, conservation, heritage; economic, community development, employment
Address: Health Unlimited, 31-33 Bondway, London, SW8 1SJ
Trustees: Dr Emma Crewe, Dr Ruth Stern, Miss Nouria Brikci-Nigassi, Mr James Thornberry, Mrs Betty Ann Williams, Mrs Carolyn Ann Ramage, Mr Oliver Kemp, Mr Simon Wright, Dr Rory Honney, Mrs Sharon Louise Jackson, Dr Anna Graham
Income: £16,045,101 [2017]; £20,923,887 [2016]; £13,204,440 [2015]; £14,374,239 [2014]; £8,339,045 [2013]

Health for All (Leeds) Ltd

Registered: 14 Mar 1998 *Employees:* 81 *Volunteers:* 10
Tel: 0113 270 6903 *Website:* healthforall.org.uk
Activities: Education, training; advancement of health or saving of lives; disability; prevention or relief of poverty; economic, community development, employment
Address: Tenants Hall Enterprise Centre, Acre Close, Middleton, Leeds, LS10 4HX
Trustees: Mr Timothy Francis McSharry, Dr Rajgopalan Menon, Mrs Hannah Ruth Pearson, Mr Paul Truswell, Mr Timothy Eric Snell, Ms Susan Linda Brearley, Mr Martin Bartholomew, Mrs Lynn Bailey, Mrs Audrey Dickinson, Ms Maggie Dawkins, Mrs Ambia Khatun
Income: £2,205,108 [2017]; £2,252,895 [2016]; £2,137,447 [2015]; £2,176,781 [2014]; £2,257,402 [2013]

Healthcare Financial Management Association

Registered: 1 Jun 2006 *Employees:* 84 *Volunteers:* 110
Tel: 0117 929 4789 *Website:* hfma.org.uk
Activities: Education, training; advancement of health or saving of lives
Address: 6th Floor, Healthcare Financial Management Association, 1 Temple Way, Bristol, BS2 0BU
Trustees: Mrs Susan Jacques, Mrs Susan Lorimer, Mr Tony Whitfield, Mr Mark Orchard, Mr Christopher Michael Hurst, Mr Stephen Patrick McNally, Rosalind Franke, James Rimmer, Huw Thomas, Mr Andrew Hardy, Ms Shahana Khan, Mrs Susan Goldsmith, Keely Firth, Alex Gild, Bill Gregory
Income: £7,266,000 [2017]; £8,516,000 [2016]; £7,592,000 [2015]; £5,920,000 [2014]; £5,637,000 [2013]

Healthcare Infection Society

Registered: 8 Aug 2014 *Employees:* 4
Tel: 020 7713 0273 *Website:* his.org.uk
Activities: Education, training; advancement of health or saving of lives
Address: 162 King's Cross Road, London, WC1X 9DH
Trustees: Dr Chris Settle, Dr Jim Gray, Dr Peter Jenks, Dr David Enoch, Dr David Jenkins, Dr Richard Cunningham, Dr Gemma Wheldon, Professor Gary French, Dr Lisa Ridgway, Dr Manjula Meda, Dr Emma Boldock, Mrs Karren Staniforth, Ms Andrea Parsons
Income: £1,655,993 [2017]; £880,605 [2016]; £7,945,782 [2015]

The Healthcare Management Trust

Registered: 15 Nov 1985 *Employees:* 573 *Volunteers:* 9
Tel: 020 7222 1177 *Website:* hmt-uk.org
Activities: General charitable purposes; advancement of health or saving of lives
Address: Health Care Management Trust, 14 Queen Annes Gate, London, SW1H 9AA
Trustees: Mr Nick Stephens DL FCA, Mr Glen von Malachowski, Mr Mark Gerold, Lynne Roberts, Mr John Richard Quentin Folliott Vaughan, Mr Dylan Jones, Mr Nigel Draper
Income: £32,635,771 [2016]; £29,739,627 [2015]; £27,892,412 [2014]; £24,311,381 [2013]; £21,687,255 [2012]

Healthcare Quality Improvement Partnership

Registered: 4 Dec 2008 *Employees:* 27
Tel: 020 7997 7370 *Website:* hqip.org.uk
Activities: Education, training; advancement of health or saving of lives
Address: 6th Floor, HQIP, Tenter House, 45 Moorfields, London, EC2Y 9AE
Trustees: Mr Robert Johnstone, Dame Donna Kinnair, Ms Sarah Dunnett, Dr Sheila Marriott, Dr Victoria Tzortziou Brown, Professor Anne Marie Rafferty, Mr Alastair Henderson, Mr Philip Grimshaw Baker, Dr Linda Patterson
Income: £24,435,466 [2017]; £24,479,589 [2016]; £20,068,814 [2015]; £19,445,280 [2014]; £20,340,484 [2013]

Healthworks Newcastle

Registered: 25 Aug 1994 *Employees:* 76 *Volunteers:* 172
Tel: 0191 272 4244 *Website:* hwn.org.uk
Activities: General charitable purposes; education, training; advancement of health or saving of lives; prevention or relief of poverty; economic, community development; employment
Address: Health Resource Centre, Adelaide Terrace, Newcastle upon Tyne, NE4 8BE
Trustees: Professor Christopher Drinkwater, Mrs Rebecca McCready, Mr John Dawson MBE, Ms Diane Creighton, Mr Joel Hanoch Marks, Mr Kenneth Graham, Mr Mark Ions, Mr Michael Edward Turner, Professor Elizabeth Sarah Todd, Dr Patricia Anne Cresswell
Income: £1,389,445 [2017]; £1,540,291 [2016]; £1,589,490 [2015]; £1,506,681 [2014]; £1,355,447 [2013]

Hearing Dogs for Deaf People

Registered: 2 Jan 1986 *Employees:* 158 *Volunteers:* 2,155
Tel: 01844 348100 *Website:* hearingdogs.org.uk
Activities: Education, training; advancement of health or saving of lives; disability; animals
Address: Hearing Dogs for Deaf People, The Grange, Wycombe Road, Saunderton, Princes Risborough, Bucks, HP27 9NS
Trustees: Mr John Bower BVSc MRCVS, Air Vice-Marshal David Crwys-Williams CB, Doctor Bruce Fogle, Mr Kenneth William Keir, Mr Adrian Mark Horsley, Mr Andrew Peter Freeland, Ms Victoria Augusta Hunt, Mr Barry Downes, Jeremy Holmes, Professor Richard Ramsden, Mrs Faith Beatrice Clark, Dr Hilary Harris MB ChB FRCGP, Mrs Jenny Smith, Mr Gary Burchett, Dr Anne Victoria Harrison
Income: £8,730,662 [2017]; £7,503,395 [2016]; £8,433,583 [2015]; £8,332,956 [2014]; £6,651,309 [2013]

Heart Church

Registered: 8 Jun 2007 *Employees:* 24 *Volunteers:* 500
Tel: 0115 947 4038 *Website:* heartchurch.co.uk
Activities: Education, training; prevention or relief of poverty; overseas aid, famine relief; religious activities
Address: Christian Centre, 104-114 Talbot Street, Nottingham, NG1 5GL
Trustees: Mr Jim Clarke, Mr Nigel Charles Gale, Mr Malcolm Baxter, Mr Laurence Charles James-Davis, Mr Andrew Malcolm Dickin, Mr Guy Bowen, Miss Sally Abel, Mr Robert James Andrew Steel, Mrs Jayne Poppy Green
Income: £1,181,907 [2016]; £1,241,659 [2015]; £1,233,155 [2014]; £1,211,996 [2013]; £1,611,263 [2012]

The Heart Research Institute (UK)

Registered: 21 Nov 2006 *Employees:* 1
Website: hriuk.org
Activities: Education, training; advancement of health or saving of lives
Address: 7 Eliza Street, Newtown, NSW 2042, Australia
Trustees: Mr Antony William Pollitt, Dr Stephen Lindsay Hollings, Mr Alan Caton, Ms Kerry Ann Cunningham, Mr Adrian Phillips, Ms Elena Louise Pintado, Mr John Louis Batistich, Mr Stephen Bruce Moodey, Mr Sathiyaseelan Sappany
Income: £1,601,774 [2017]; £1,650,768 [2016]; £1,700,055 [2015]; £1,652,057 [2014]; £1,796,832 [2013]

Heart Research UK

Registered: 8 Mar 1995 *Employees:* 19 *Volunteers:* 20
Tel: 0113 234 7474 *Website:* heartresearch.org.uk
Activities: The advancement of health or saving of lives
Address: Heart Research UK, 12d Josephs Well, Hanover Walk, Leeds, LS3 1AB
Trustees: Mr Paul Rogerson, Mr Richard Colwyn Hemsley MA FCA, Dr David Frederick Dickinson MB ChB DCH, Mr Anthony David Knight, Dr Catherine Jane Dickinson, Mr Paul Wilson Smith, Mr Peter Braidley, Pierre Bouvet, Mr Keith Loudon, Mrs Christine Mortimer, Mr Kevin Gerard Watterson MB BS FRACS, Mr Antony Gregg Oxley, Mr Anthony Roger Kilner, Mr Richard John Brown, Mrs Julie Fenwick, Christopher Newman
Income: £2,975,653 [2016]; £1,674,148 [2015]; £1,852,516 [2014]; £1,916,423 [2013]; £1,820,614 [2012]

Heart of England Community Foundation

Registered: 20 Dec 2006 *Employees:* 12 *Volunteers:* 51
Tel: 024 7688 3260 *Website:* heartofenglandcf.co.uk
Activities: General charitable purposes
Address: c/o PSA Group, Torrington Avenue, Coventry, Warwicks, CV4 9AP
Trustees: Sir Nicholas Dominic Cadbury, Mrs Sally Elizabeth Carrick, Mr John Taylor, Mr Philip Gordon Ewing, Mr Philip Arthur Pemble, Mr Daniel Worthing, Mr Amrik Bhabra, Mr Christopher West, Mr Paul Belfield, Ms Lucie Byron, Ms Michelle Vincent, Jude Jennison
Income: £2,346,119 [2017]; £3,602,774 [2016]; £5,070,238 [2015]; £1,320,921 [2014]; £2,378,863 [2013]

The Heart of England Forest Ltd

Registered: 17 Apr 2003 *Employees:* 13 *Volunteers:* 656
Tel: 01789 491391 *Website:* heartofenglandforest.com
Activities: Education, training; environment, conservation, heritage
Address: Colletts Farm, Dorsington, Stratford upon Avon, Warwicks, CV37 8AU
Trustees: Mr Anthony Charles Burton, Mr Ian Geoffrey Harvey Leggett, Mr Anthony Steven Price, Mr Desmond Patrick Bermingham, Mr Jon Snow, Ms Alison Hunter, Ms Nicola Mary Corbishley
Income: £16,683,633 [2016]; £5,124,961 [2015]; £2,918,212 [2014]; £1,276,212 [2013]; £163,615 [2012]

Heart of England Mencap

Registered: 27 Jun 1994 *Employees:* 219 *Volunteers:* 10
Tel: 01789 298709 *Website:* heartofenglandmencap.org.uk
Activities: Disability; accommodation, housing
Address: Suite 1, Clifford Mill, Clifford Road, Clifford Chambers, Stratford upon Avon, Warwicks, CV37 8HW
Trustees: Wendy Strophair, Mrs Audrey Rose, Mrs Louise Frances Sandford, Mrs Margaret Glynne Harrison, Mr Robert Malcolm Pearce, Mrs Jane Christine Reed, Mr Glen von Malachowski, Mrs Julie Ann Baker, Ms Sally Victoria Wykeham Smith, Ms Fiona Pethick
Income: £4,644,127 [2017]; £4,229,182 [2016]; £3,252,820 [2015]; £3,049,693 [2014]; £2,927,333 [2013]

The Heart of Kent Hospice

Registered: 18 Jan 1988 *Employees:* 119 *Volunteers:* 538
Tel: 01622 792200 *Website:* hokh.co.uk
Activities: Education, training; advancement of health or saving of lives
Address: Chief Executive, Heart of Kent Hospice, Preston Hall, Royal British Legion Village, Aylesford, Kent, ME20 7PU
Trustees: Ms Elizabeth Howe, Mr Timothy Cathcart, Mr Sykes Roger, Gary Hodnett, James Barker-Mccardle, Lorna Potts, Mr George Hunter, Mrs Joanne Lindsay, Mrs Victoria Stoodley, Dr Antony Michael Dibble, Sandra Malone, Paula Wilkins, Helen Corbett, Mr Simon Richard Briscoe Langworthy
Income: £4,932,413 [2017]; £4,714,623 [2016]; £5,247,823 [2015]; £4,280,195 [2014]; £3,693,188 [2013]

The Hearth Foundation

Registered: 11 Feb 2016
Tel: 0116 240 2162
Activities: General charitable purposes
Address: Monkstone, Main Street, Mowsley, Lutterworth, Leics, LE17 6NU
Trustees: Chris Bosworth, Mrs J Bosworth, Dr S Bosworth, Mrs H E Bosworth, Michael Bosworth, Mrs V M Bosworth MEng MBA
Income: £2,584,012 [2017]

Heath Mount School Trust Ltd

Registered: 18 Aug 1970 *Employees:* 138 *Volunteers:* 10
Tel: 01920 830230 *Website:* heathmount.org
Activities: Education, training
Address: Heath Mount School, Woodhall Park, Watton at Stone, Hertford, SG14 3NG
Trustees: Ian Neale, Mrs Helen Rayfield, Edward Campbell Gray, Mrs Juliette Hodson, Mr Paul McKeown, Mrs Karen Ann Sallybanks, Gerry Wade, Richard Dent, Mr David De Boinville, Mr James Steel, Mr Martin Collier, Mr Alexander John Mitchell
Income: £6,409,421 [2016]; £5,762,420 [2015]; £5,530,542 [2014]; £5,330,844 [2013]; £5,004,877 [2012]

Thomas Heatherley Educational Trust

Registered: 24 Jan 1972 *Employees:* 23
Tel: 07786 846781 *Website:* heatherley.org
Activities: Education, training; arts, culture, heritage, science
Address: 75 Lots Road, London, SW10 0RN
Trustees: Dr Penelope Hunting, Mr Richard Sharp, Mr Stephen George Bryan Bartley, Mr Andrew Thompson, Ms Sophie Balhetchet, Mr Robin Hazlewood, Mr Harry MacAuslan, Colonel David Waddell, Ms Jane Gordon Clark, Mr Raymond Wilson
Income: £1,153,743 [2017]; £1,096,156 [2016]; £994,100 [2015]; £948,134 [2014]; £867,648 [2013]

Heathfield Educational Trust

Registered: 11 Aug 2003 *Employees:* 67
Tel: 01562 720629 *Website:* hkschool.org.uk
Activities: Education, training
Address: 27 Pinewoods Avenue, Hagley, Stourbridge, W Yorks, DY9 0JF
Trustees: Mr John Richard Painter, Mrs Sarah Burns, Mr Matthew Barnett, Mr Lee Nicholas, Mr Douglas Jackson, Mr Tim Bayliss, Mrs Jennifer Hine
Income: £2,317,658 [2017]; £1,799,445 [2016]; £1,997,470 [2015]; £2,110,252 [2014]; £2,163,809 [2013]

Heathfield School

Registered: 17 Oct 1963 *Employees:* 123
Tel: 01344 898303 *Website:* heathfieldschool.net
Activities: Education, training
Address: 63 Sheepfold Road, Guildford, Surrey, GU2 9TT
Trustees: Mr Robert Benedict Gregory, Mr Tom Cross Brown, Revd Canon Philip Ursell, Mr Peter William Guy Egerton-Smith, Mrs Rosemary Martin, Hon Frances Caroline Stanley, Mrs Sally Virginia Tulk Hart, Rev Jonathan Baker MA (Oxon) MPhil Dip Theol, Mrs Sally-Anne Barrett, Mr Robert Leslie Owen, Mr Richard Pilkington, Miss Charlotte Faber
Income: £7,038,297 [2017]; £7,494,531 [2016]; £7,287,158 [2015]; £6,638,086 [2014]; £6,678,469 [2013]

Heathrow School of Gymnastics & Dance Ltd

Registered: 26 Jul 2005 *Employees:* 37 *Volunteers:* 10
Tel: 020 8977 9772 *Website:* heathrowgymnastics.org.uk
Activities: Education, training; amateur sport
Address: Penningtons, 209-217 High Street, Hampton Hill, Hampton, Surrey, TW12 1NP
Trustees: Dr Timothy John Anstiss, Mrs Mihaela Zdrali, Mrs Maria McLoughlin
Income: £1,082,547 [2017]; £1,124,988 [2016]; £986,499 [2015]; £939,459 [2014]; £858,418 [2013]

The Heathside Charitable Trust

Registered: 16 Oct 1985
Tel: 020 7431 7739
Activities: General charitable purposes
Address: 32 Hampstead High Street, London, NW3 1QD
Trustees: Sir Harry Solomon, Geoffrey Jayson, Mr Daniel Mark Solomon, Mr Sam Jack Jacobs, Lady Judith Solomon, Mrs Louise Sara Jacobs, Ms Juliet Kate Solomon, James Jacobs
Income: £1,242,011 [2016]; £126,750 [2015]; £1,041,008 [2014]; £328,670 [2013]; £598,382 [2012]

Hebron Hall Limited

Registered: 11 Aug 1983 *Employees:* 48
Tel: 029 2051 5665 *Website:* hebronhall.org
Activities: General charitable purposes; accommodation, housing; religious activities; amateur sport
Address: Hebron Hall Christian Centre, Cross Common Road, Dinas Powys, Vale of Glamorgan, CF64 4YB
Trustees: Mr Alan Lansdown, Mr Julian Haines, Mr Timothy Paul Trotman, Mr Paul Young, Mr David Mark Rees
Income: £1,491,190 [2017]; £1,511,194 [2016]; £1,465,063 [2015]; £1,431,086 [2014]; £1,329,954 [2013]

Hedley Foundation Limited
Registered: 22 Oct 1971 *Employees:* 3
Tel: 020 7489 8076 *Website:* hedleyfoundation.org.uk
Activities: General charitable purposes
Address: The Hedley Foundation, Victoria House, 1-3 College Hill, London, EC4R 2RA
Trustees: Mr George Robin Straton Broke, Mrs Lorna B M Stuttaford, Mr Angus Edward Fanshawe, David William Byam-Cook, Major John Francis Meadows Rodwell, Mr Patrick Roy Holcroft, Lieutenant Colonel Andrew Charles Ford, Mr Charles Bennett
Income: £1,337,359 [2017]; £1,278,343 [2016]; £1,252,595 [2015]; £1,369,435 [2014]; £1,489,399 [2013]

The Percy Hedley Foundation
Registered: 16 Jan 1985 *Employees:* 863 *Volunteers:* 50
Tel: 0191 238 1333 *Website:* percyhedley.org.uk
Activities: Education, training; disability; accommodation, housing; amateur sport; other charitable purposes
Address: Percy Hedley School, Forest Hall, Newcastle upon Tyne, NE12 8YY
Trustees: Mr David Robson Arthur, Mr Jonathan Jowett, Dr Mary Gibson, Mr Raymond Johnstone, Mr Damon Kent, Ms Maxine Tennet, Ms Anne Woods, Ms Angela Curran, Ms Lisa Charles-Jones, Ms Susan Jopling, Mr Ajeet Chadda, Ms Angela Russell, Dr Nick Spencer
Income: £25,759,000 [2016]; £23,121,000 [2015]; £21,732,146 [2014]; £18,717,502 [2013]; £23,330,384 [2012]

Helen & Douglas House
Registered: 30 Mar 2001 *Employees:* 274 *Volunteers:* 873
Tel: 01865 794749 *Website:* helenanddouglas.org.uk
Activities: The advancement of health or saving of lives; disability
Address: Helen & Douglas House, 14a Magdalen Road, Oxford, OX4 1RW
Trustees: Professor Andrew Wilkinson, Mrs Elizabeth Drew, Mr Nicholas Wilkinson, Mr Colin Andrew Love, Sister Jean Raphael, Sir Stephen Bubb, Yvette Gayford, Katherine Boyce, Fleur Claire Perry, Mrs Catherine Chumbley
Income: £9,958,000 [2017]; £9,466,000 [2016]; £12,014,000 [2015]; £10,413,000 [2014]; £10,458,000 [2013]

Helen Rollason Heal Cancer Charity Limited
Registered: 9 Feb 1996 *Employees:* 25 *Volunteers:* 322
Tel: 01245 380719 *Website:* helenrollason.org.uk
Activities: The advancement of health or saving of lives
Address: Yvonne Stewart House, The Street, Hatfield Peverel, Chelmsford, Essex, CM3 2EH
Trustees: Ms Elaine Anne Oddie, Mrs Margaret McIlroy, Mr Terry Green, Mr Stephen Morley, Dave Rome, Mr David T Houghton BPharm MRPharmS, Miss Chantal Constable, Mr Graham Hart, Mr Andrew Thorpe-Apps
Income: £1,015,018 [2017]; £1,471,877 [2016]; £1,102,860 [2015]; £1,336,518 [2014]; £1,148,745 [2013]

Helena Partnerships Limited
Registered: 1 Dec 2004 *Employees:* 361
Tel: 01744 418135 *Website:* helenapartnerships.co.uk
Activities: The prevention or relief of poverty; accommodation, housing; economic, community development, employment
Address: Helena Partnerships Ltd, 4 Corporation Street, St Helens, Merseyside, WA9 1LD
Trustees: Mr Ian Duncan Clayton, Mr Roy Alfred Smith, Mr John Owen Fulham, Mr Duncan Craig, Mrs Christine Fallon, Mr Robert Charles Hepworth, Mr Philip Pemberton, Mr Robert Clive Young, Mr Graham William Burgess, Mr Anthony Vincent Williams
Income: £68,689,000 [2017]; £69,736,000 [2016]; £68,488,000 [2015]; £65,502,000 [2014]; £63,081,000 [2013]

Help The Needy Charitable Trust
Registered: 31 Dec 1996 *Employees:* 8 *Volunteers:* 5
Tel: 020 8838 0000 *Website:* helptheneedy.org.uk
Activities: General charitable purposes; education, training; advancement of health or saving of lives; disability; prevention or relief of poverty; overseas aid, famine relief; accommodation, housing
Address: Suite 303-501, Crown House, North Circular Road, London, NW10 7PN
Trustees: Mr Raad Salman, Ali Mare, Mr Mohamad Abdul Wahab Kasim
Income: £6,357,778 [2017]; £3,594,135 [2016]; £1,808,120 [2015]; £613,935 [2014]; £1,173,296 [2013]

Help and Care
Registered: 30 Apr 1996 *Employees:* 125 *Volunteers:* 45
Tel: 0300 111 3303 *Website:* helpandcare.org.uk
Activities: General charitable purposes; disability; prevention or relief of poverty
Address: Help & Care, 896 Christchurch Road, Bournemouth, BH7 6DL
Trustees: Mr Edward Taylor, Mr Roger Browning, Mr John Adrian Dawson, Mrs Ann Patricia Nicholson, Mrs Fiona Knight, Ms Sara Mousley, Mr Neil Bacon, Mr Terry Colin Hayden
Income: £3,180,920 [2017]; £2,943,629 [2016]; £2,884,143 [2015]; £3,097,637 [2014]; £2,412,045 [2013]

Help for Carers
Registered: 11 Oct 1993 *Employees:* 103 *Volunteers:* 40
Tel: 020 8648 9677 *Website:* helpforcarers.org.uk
Activities: The advancement of health or saving of lives; disability
Address: Mr Stefan Kuchar, Vestry Hall, London Road, Mitcham, Surrey, CR4 3ND
Trustees: Miss Andrea Ruddock-West, Mrs Sally Aitken-Davies, Dr Peter Roseveare, Mr Calum Benson, Mr Alex Ramamurthy, John Mays, Jane Norton, Dr John French, Mr Stephen Moore, Mr Paresh Raval
Income: £1,719,342 [2017]; £1,875,801 [2016]; £1,928,028 [2015]; £2,325,180 [2014]; £2,207,475 [2013]

Help for Heroes Recovery
Registered: 21 Jul 2011 *Employees:* 78 *Volunteers:* 59
Tel: 01725 514119 *Website:* helpforheroes.org.uk
Activities: Education, training; disability; other charitable purposes
Address: Help for Heroes, Unit 14 Parkers Close, Downton Business Centre, Salisbury, Wilts, SP5 3RB
Trustees: Philip Trousdell, Robert Watsham
Income: £6,710,308 [2016]; £11,550,000 [2015]; £8,509,000 [2014]; £3,203,000 [2013]; £2,628,000 [2012]

Help for Heroes

Registered: 20 Sep 2007 *Employees:* 380 *Volunteers:* 2,073
Tel: 01725 514119 *Website:* helpforheroes.org.uk
Activities: Education, training; advancement of health or saving of lives; disability; accommodation, housing; other charitable purposes
Address: Help for Heroes, Unit 14 Parkers Close, Downton Business Centre, Salisbury, Wilts, SP5 3RB
Trustees: Sir Robert Fry, Judge Jeff Blackett, Anthony Schofield, Mr Robert Thomas Watsham, Peter Norton, Mr Charles Michael Lake, Steve Harman, Roderick Dunn, Tom Wright, Professor Veronica Rosemary Hope Hailey, Sir Phillip Charles Cornwallis Trousdell
Income: £36,514,568 [2016]; £40,963,000 [2015]; £37,212,000 [2014]; £33,914,000 [2013]; £40,551,000 [2012]

Helpage International

Registered: 17 Nov 1983 *Employees:* 561 *Volunteers:* 4
Tel: 020 7148 7692 *Website:* helpage.org
Activities: Education, training; advancement of health or saving of lives; prevention or relief of poverty; overseas aid, famine relief; economic, community development, employment
Address: Age UK, Tavis House, 1-6 Tavistock Square, London, WC1H 9NA
Trustees: Mr David Causer, Ms Laura Machado, Arun Maira, Mrs Abla Mehio, Mrs Vappu Tuulikki Taipale, Mr John Gordon Kingston OBE, Mr Sola Mahoney, Mrs Ferdous Ara Begum, Mrs Robin Jane Talbert
Income: £26,979,000 [2017]; £30,232,000 [2016]; £29,114,000 [2015]; £26,400,000 [2014]; £26,658,000 [2013]

The Helping Foundation

Registered: 22 Jun 2004
Tel: 01617 40116
Activities: General charitable purposes; education, training; prevention or relief of poverty; religious activities
Address: Flat 1, Allanadale Court, Waterpark Road, Salford, M7 4JN
Trustees: Rabbi Aubrey Weis, Mr David Neuwirth, Mr Sir Weis, Mrs Rachel Weis, Mr Benny Stone
Income: £42,499,341 [2016]; £36,726,742 [2015]; £28,993,172 [2014]; £35,616,320 [2013]; £13,734,804 [2012]

Hendon Mosque & Islamic Centre

Registered: 26 Jul 1984 *Employees:* 15 *Volunteers:* 11
Tel: 020 8202 3236 *Website:* hendonmosque.org
Activities: General charitable purposes; education, training; prevention or relief of poverty; overseas aid, famine relief; religious activities
Address: Brent View Road, West Hendon, London, NW9 7EL
Trustees: Sayed Mushtaq Ahmed Rehman, Alimiya Faki, Sayed Maqbul Al-Hadad, Sayed Mohammed Kadri, Jahan Zeb, Sayed Abdulla Kadri, Jabar Nazir, Mr Abdul Alim Rehman, Aboo Mohammad Faki Ahmad Mehdi, Mushtaq Hasan Dhakam, Ahmed Ibrahim Herwitker, Sayed Mohidin Kadri, Sayed Shakil Ahmed, Abdul Alim Daroge, Atta-Ullah Roghey, Mr Sayed Ahmed Alhaddad
Income: £1,080,826 [2017]; £1,108,276 [2016]; £1,149,544 [2015]; £1,075,651 [2014]; £1,092,623 [2013]

The Henfrey Charitable Trust

Registered: 30 Apr 2015
Tel: 01669 620335
Activities: General charitable purposes
Address: Debdon Primrose Cottage, Rothbury, Morpeth, Northumberland, NE65 7QB
Trustees: Mr J P Radgick, Mr J S R Swanson, Mr A W Henfrey, Mary Jean Henfrey
Income: £1,255,715 [2016]; £21,500 [2015]

The Henley Festival Trust

Registered: 3 Jun 1987 *Employees:* 6
Website: henley-festival.co.uk
Activities: Arts, culture, heritage, science
Address: The River & Rowing Museum at Henley, Mill Meadows, Henley on Thames, Oxon, RG9 1BF
Trustees: Mr Jonathan Richard Barnard Hobbs, Mrs Rita Ann Clifton, Lord Stephen Carter of Barnes, Mr Mark Webber, Mr Mark Edward Smith, Anthony Mallin
Income: £2,455,939 [2016]; £2,322,570 [2015]; £1,985,111 [2014]; £2,205,433 [2013]; £312,548 [2012]

Henshaws Society for Blind People

Registered: 14 Apr 1980 *Employees:* 396 *Volunteers:* 226
Tel: 0161 786 3645 *Website:* henshaws.org.uk
Activities: Education, training; disability; accommodation, housing
Address: Henshaws Society for Blind People, 4a Washbrook House, Lancastrian Office Centre, Talbot Road, Stretford, Manchester, M32 0FP
Trustees: Henshaws Society For Blind People Trustee Ltd
Income: £9,544,000 [2016]; £9,176,000 [2015]; £9,054,000 [2014]; £9,801,000 [2013]; £14,361,000 [2012]

The Hepworth Wakefield

Registered: 17 Sep 2010 *Employees:* 78 *Volunteers:* 38
Tel: 01924 247203 *Website:* hepworthwakefield.org
Activities: Arts, culture, heritage, science
Address: The Hepworth Wakefield, Gallery Walk, Wakefield, W Yorks, WF1 5AW
Trustees: Dr Sophie Bowness, Ms Linda Harley, Mr David Roberts, Ms Jane Aine Mee, Ms Jane Elisabeth Madeley, Mrs Merran McCrae, Mr Peter Box, Mr David Liddiment, Ms Diane Howse, Mr Stuart Fletcher, Mr Neil Wenman
Income: £3,387,917 [2017]; £3,012,061 [2016]; £2,824,184 [2015]; £3,488,371 [2014]; £3,664,031 [2013]

The Hereford Cathedral Perpetual Trust

Registered: 30 Nov 1995 *Employees:* 3 *Volunteers:* 300
Tel: 01432 374261 *Website:* herefordcathedral.org
Activities: Education, training; religious activities; arts, culture, heritage, science; environment, conservation, heritage; other charitable purposes
Address: 5 College Cloisters, Cathedral Close, Hereford, HR1 2NG
Trustees: The Very Revd Michael Tavinor, Mr Rhoderick Swire, Mrs Domenica Margaret Anne Dunne, Mr Andrew Guy Wynn LVO, Mr Luke Purser
Income: £1,090,253 [2016]; £1,605,013 [2015]; £1,312,386 [2014]; £703,910 [2013]; £1,620,609 [2012]

Hereford Cathedral School

Registered: 18 Jun 1987 *Employees:* 142 *Volunteers:* 15
Website: herefordcs.com
Activities: Education, training
Address: Hereford Cathedral School, The Old Deanery, Cathedral Close, Hereford, HR1 2NG
Trustees: Mr Jonathan Richard Sheldon, Mr Stephen Robert Borthwick, Mr Andrew Terence Teale BSc, Mr William John Hanks, Mr Timothy Harold Keyes MA, Mr Jonathan Derek Preece, Mr Christopher David Hitchiner LLB ACIS, The Right Reverend Alistair James Magowan MTh, Mrs Lisa Catherine Glover BA, Rear Admiral Philip Lawrence Wilcocks CB DSC DL, Mrs Karen Schuldt Usher DL, Mrs Jacquelyne Deval-Reed
Income: £8,882,575 [2017]; £8,718,742 [2016]; £8,438,796 [2015]; £8,504,245 [2014]; £8,329,361 [2013]

The Hereford Diocesan Board of Finance

Registered: 18 Oct 1966 *Employees:* 38 *Volunteers:* 50
Tel: 01432 373300 *Website:* hereford.anglican.org
Activities: Education, training; prevention or relief of poverty; religious activities; arts, culture, heritage, science; environment, conservation, heritage; human rights, religious or racial harmony, equality or diversity; other charitable purposes
Address: Hereford Diocesan Board of Finance, Hereford Diocesan Board of Education, The Palace, Palace Yard, Hereford, HR4 9BL
Trustees: Mr Christopher John Whitmey, Rt Revd Richard Michael Cokayne Frith, The Venerable George Patrick Benson, Mrs Susan Lewis, Mr Andrew Mence, Mr Nat Hone, Mrs Janet Woodroffe, Mr Christopher Hugh Edwards Smith, Revd Constance Jane Rogers, Rt Revd Alistair Magowan, Mrs Rosemary Lording, Rev Linda Cronin, Mr Charles Hunter
Income: £6,805,334 [2017]; £6,463,972 [2016]; £5,799,931 [2015]; £5,907,000 [2014]; £5,885,187 [2013]

Herefordshire Group Training Association Limited

Registered: 26 Aug 1982 *Employees:* 43
Tel: 01432 377003 *Website:* hwgta.org
Activities: Education, training
Address: Herefordshire Group Training Association, Holmer Road, Hereford, HR4 9SX
Trustees: Mr Michael Robert Barker, Mr David Alan Goldsmith, Mrs Gail Deborah Gittoes, Miss Catherine Rowles, Mr Robert Paul Hunt, Mr Allen Robert Green, Mr Allen Merrick
Income: £2,541,167 [2016]; £2,366,955 [2015]; £2,380,658 [2014]; £2,202,737 [2013]; £2,137,405 [2012]

Herefordshire Housing Limited

Registered: 16 Sep 2004 *Employees:* 258 *Volunteers:* 12
Tel: 01432 384002 *Website:* hhl.org.uk
Activities: Disability; prevention or relief of poverty; accommodation, housing; economic, community development, employment
Address: Hereford Housing Association, Legion Way, Hereford, HR1 1LN
Trustees: Mr Michael Parkes, Ms Allison Taylor, Mr Michael Anthony McCarthy, Gill Jones, Peter Brown, Sonia Higgins, Mrs Ruth Cooke, Mr David Lincoln, James Williamson, Jake Berriman, Graham Biggs, Liz Walford
Income: £30,349,000 [2017]; £29,739,000 [2016]; £27,269,000 [2015]; £25,428,000 [2014]; £24,568,000 [2013]

Herefordshire Mind

Registered: 27 Feb 1989 *Employees:* 53 *Volunteers:* 12
Tel: 01432 372403 *Website:* herefordshire-mind.org.uk
Activities: Education, training; advancement of health or saving of lives; disability; accommodation, housing; amateur sport
Address: Herefordshire Mind, Heffeman House, 130-132 Widemarsh Street, Hereford, HR4 9HN
Trustees: Ms Cathi Shovlin, Hilary Baker, Mr Doug King, Mark Waller, Mrs Judith Faux, Mr Adrian Wilcox
Income: £1,058,960 [2017]; £1,112,427 [2016]; £1,123,384 [2015]; £1,213,091 [2014]; £1,454,506 [2013]

The Herefordshire Wildlife Trust Limited

Registered: 17 Jan 1964 *Employees:* 38 *Volunteers:* 273
Tel: 01432 356872 *Website:* wildlifetrust.org.uk
Activities: Environment, conservation, heritage; economic, community development, employment
Address: Herefordshire Wildlife Trust, Lower House Farm, Ledbury Road, Hereford, HR1 1UT
Trustees: Mr Brian Hurrell, Mrs Marie Clarke, Mr Peter Graham Garner, Mrs Sheila Spence, Mr James Hugh Marsden, Mr Peter James Ford, Mr Roger Beck, Mrs Natalie Buttriss, Ms Susannah Garland, Ms Elizabeth Overstall, Dr William Bullough
Income: £2,076,314 [2017]; £2,076,314 [2016]; £1,298,222 [2015]; £1,100,800 [2014]; £711,701 [2013]

Heritage Care Limited

Registered: 1 Apr 2010 *Employees:* 1,691 *Volunteers:* 30
Tel: 020 8502 3933 *Website:* heritagecare.co.uk
Activities: Disability; prevention or relief of poverty; accommodation, housing
Address: Heritage Care, Connaught House, 112-120 High Road, Loughton, Essex, IG10 4HJ
Trustees: Ms Jeanette Mitchell, Mr Simon William Paul Griffiths, Miss Margaret Mary Lally, Scott Thomas Haldane, Mr Nigel Owen Fletcher, Mr Selman Ansari, Ms Lorraine Reynolds, Mr John Peter Schuster, Mr Richard John Smallwood
Income: £39,693,000 [2017]; £38,581,000 [2016]; £37,803,000 [2015]; £37,517,000 [2014]; £36,729,000 [2013]

The Heritage Trust for The North West

Registered: 14 Dec 1978 *Employees:* 36 *Volunteers:* 500
Tel: 01282 877686 *Website:* htnw.co.uk
Activities: Environment, conservation, heritage
Address: Pendle Heritage Centre, 2 Colne Road, Barrowford, Nelson, Lancs, BB9 6JQ
Trustees: Mr Leslie George Coop, Mr Michael Bannister, Dr Kathryn Davies, John Turner, Mr Lawrence Edward Stanworth, Mr Mark Francis Whitlock Blundell, Ms Laurie Peake, Mr Anthony Preston
Income: £1,374,982 [2017]; £1,317,920 [2016]; £2,349,692 [2015]; £2,012,635 [2014]; £1,966,246 [2013]

Herne Hill Velodrome Trust

Registered: 31 Jan 2011 *Employees:* 2 *Volunteers:* 30
Website: hernehillvelodrome.com
Activities: Education, training; amateur sport
Address: 10 Brockley Hall Road, London, SE4 1RH
Trustees: Mr Nicholas Rusling, Mr Andrew John Cawdell, Mr Timothy Jonathan McInnes, Mr Christopher Cole, Mr Andrew David Smith, Mrs Sarah Hammond, Mr Richard Williams, Simon Price, Mr Martin Charles Young, Mr Len Delicaet, Dr Max Reuter, Mr Paul Richard Merrey
Income: £1,684,330 [2016]; £65,035 [2015]; £109,828 [2014]; £407,305 [2013]; £114,278 [2012]

Herries Educational Trust Limited
Registered: 29 Mar 2001 *Employees:* 25 *Volunteers:* 30
Tel: 01628 483350 *Website:* herries.org.uk
Activities: Education, training
Address: Herries School, Dean Lane, Cookham, Maidenhead, Berks, SL6 9BD
Trustees: Mr Chris Lenton, Mr Richard Buckeridge, Mrs Paula Lesley Prewett, Mrs Ann Elizabeth Bedford, Ms Helen Essa, Mr Michael Kells, Mr George Hugo Stinnes, Mrs Margaret Robinson, Mr Andrew Buchanan Yuille, Mrs Fiona Long, Mr Ian Johnson
Income: £1,017,051 [2017]; £1,003,665 [2016]; £831,686 [2015]; £744,552 [2014]; £640,096 [2013]

Hertford British Hospital Corporation, Paris
Registered: 15 Aug 1991 *Employees:* 23
Website: british-hospital.org
Activities: The advancement of health or saving of lives; disability
Address: 39 Quai d'Anjou, Paris, 75004
Trustees: Charles Wilson, Jane Maurin, Christopher Wicker, David Blanchard, Christopher Gilmore, Richard Seguin, Bridget Terrell, Daniel Roulston, Susan Cheyne, Ian Gosling, Michel De Fabiani, Peter Howard, Peter Terrell, Ian McDonald, Stephen Cowen, Mrs Alicia Suminski, Sandra Esquiva-Hesse, Julia Bache
Income: £4,185,671 [2016]; £3,690,280 [2015]; £3,927,583 [2014]; £4,144,679 [2013]; £4,096,678 [2012]

Hertfordshire Community Foundation
Registered: 10 Mar 2014 *Employees:* 8 *Volunteers:* 4
Tel: 01707 251351 *Website:* hertscf.org.uk
Activities: General charitable purposes; advancement of health or saving of lives; prevention or relief of poverty
Address: Hertfordshire Community Foundation, Foundation House, 2-4 Forum Place, Fiddlebridge Lane, Hatfield, Herts, AL10 0RN
Trustees: Mr John Donaldson Saner, Mr James Williams, Mr William Arthur Hobhouse, Mr Gerald Corbett, Mrs Josephine Connell, Mrs Jill Burridge, Mrs Margaret Turner, Mrs Penelope Williams, Mr John Palmer, Mr Henry Holland Hibbert, Mr Simon Tilley, Mr Terence Liam Francis Douris
Income: £1,161,605 [2017]; £1,034,120 [2016]

Hertfordshire County Scout Council
Registered: 1 Oct 1963 *Employees:* 47 *Volunteers:* 5,000
Tel: 01727 869724 *Website:* hertfordshirescouts.org.uk
Activities: Education, training
Address: 198 Beech Road, St Albans, Herts, AL3 5AX
Trustees: Mr Dave Pullen, Mr Stephen Lindsay, Mr Kevin O'Bryan, Mr Roger Sands, Mr Alexander Stephen Tomkins, Mr Mark Adrian Jefferson, Mr Nigel Reed, Mr Alexander Duncan Holmes, Mr Michael Shurety, Mr Frank William Monnington, Mr Christopher Searle, Mr David Roy Sturt, Mr Graham Woolley, Ms Elizabeth Jane Claire Walker, Miss Pippa Joanne Furey, Mr Geoffrey Declan Kavanagh
Income: £1,896,185 [2016]; £1,814,006 [2015]; £2,313,684 [2014]; £1,912,686 [2013]; £1,761,650 [2012]

The Hertfordshire and Middlesex Wildlife Trust Limited
Registered: 3 Jan 1965 *Employees:* 32 *Volunteers:* 494
Tel: 01727 858901 *Website:* hertswildlifetrust.org.uk
Activities: Environment, conservation, heritage
Address: Grebe House, St Michaels Street, St Albans, Herts, AL3 4SN
Trustees: Mr Peter Delaloye, Dr Agneta Burton PhD, Mr Paul Knutson, Clive Hinds, Andy Brown, Mrs Olivia Bertham, Mr Michael Master, Dr Veronica Edmonds-Brown PhD, Mr Andrew Woods, Sarah Kohl, Mr Keith Michael Cotton
Income: £2,106,000 [2017]; £1,786,000 [2016]; £1,823,000 [2015]; £1,556,000 [2014]; £1,903,583 [2013]

Herts Mind Network Ltd
Registered: 12 Dec 2005 *Employees:* 49 *Volunteers:* 120
Tel: 020 3727 3600 *Website:* hertsmindnetwork.org
Activities: Education, training; advancement of health or saving of lives; disability; prevention or relief of poverty; other charitable purposes
Address: 501 St Albans Road, Watford, Herts, WD24 7RZ
Trustees: Ms Fran Deschampsneufs, Ms Siobhan Nundram, Ms Erika Brown, Mr Omar Daniels, Mrs Janet Court, Mr Ian Kevin Pearce, Mr Mark Andrew Craigen, Mr Peter Goodman
Income: £1,754,357 [2016]; £1,616,779 [2015]; £1,473,111 [2014]; £1,381,558 [2013]; £1,190,703 [2012]

Herts Young Homeless Group
Registered: 11 May 1998 *Employees:* 43 *Volunteers:* 33
Tel: 0333 320 2384 *Website:* hyh.org.uk
Activities: Education, training; advancement of health or saving of lives; accommodation, housing
Address: 1st Floor, Gracemead House, Wood Avenue, Hatfield, Herts, AL10 8HX
Trustees: Mr Brian Littlechild, Mrs Kathleen Belinis, Mrs Susan Cumming, Mrs Sukhvinder Rai, Mrs Rebecca Victoria Sumner Smith, Mr Mathew Baxter, Dorothy Telfer, John Robinson, Mrs Anna Moore, Ms Debbie Bezalel, Mr Peter Mazzarese
Income: £1,698,948 [2017]; £1,703,759 [2016]; £1,613,136 [2015]; £1,752,010 [2014]; £1,741,787 [2013]

Hertsmere Leisure
Registered: 2 Sep 2002 *Employees:* 990 *Volunteers:* 100
Tel: 01727 744254 *Website:* hertsmereleisure.co.uk
Activities: General charitable purposes; arts, culture, heritage, science; amateur sport
Address: Hertsmere Leisure, Unit 8 Borderlake House, Riverside Industrial Estate, London Colney by Pass, London Colney, Herts, AL2 1HG
Trustees: Mr Michael Gibson, Mr Colin Warne, Mr Anthony Keating, Mrs Christine Ayrton, Mr Gavin Key, Mr Kevin O'Malley, Mrs Alison Sinclair, Mrs Miranda Fleur Barnett
Income: £20,089,265 [2017]; £20,225,413 [2016]; £18,887,811 [2015]; £18,152,764 [2014]; £16,951,744 [2013]

Hestercombe Gardens Trust Limited
Registered: 7 Jan 1997 *Employees:* 56 *Volunteers:* 135
Tel: 01823 413923 *Website:* hestercombe.com
Activities: Education, training; arts, culture, heritage, science; amateur sport; environment, conservation, heritage
Address: Hestercombe Gardens, Hestercombe, Cheddon Fitzpaine, Taunton, Somerset, TA2 8LG
Trustees: Ms Josephine Waley-Cohen, Mr Godfrey Davis, Councillor Marcia Hill, Mr Rupert Taylor, Miss Gemma Trudy Verdon, Ms Catherine O'Sullivan, Sir Andrew Burns, Mrs Jo Matthews, Dr Marion Harney, Ms Catherine Pease, Ms Annie Prebenson
Income: £1,883,442 [2016]; £1,667,835 [2015]; £1,420,586 [2014]; £3,696,779 [2013]; £1,362,560 [2012]

Hestia Housing and Support
Registered: 10 Jul 1986 *Employees:* 501 *Volunteers:* 257
Tel: 020 7378 3100 *Website:* hestia.org
Activities: General charitable purposes; education, training; accommodation, housing; economic, community development, employment; other charitable purposes
Address: Hestia Housing & Support, Maya House, 134-138 Borough High Street, London, SE1 1LB
Trustees: Mr David Jobbins, Mr Martin Cheeseman, Mr Anil Shenoy, Mr Alex Hyde-Smith, Mr Charles Fraser, Mr Malcolm Jenkin, Ms Vic Rayner
Income: £24,338,487 [2017]; £23,708,527 [2016]; £21,565,721 [2015]; £19,216,159 [2014]; £17,485,458 [2013]

Hethersett Old Hall School Limited
Registered: 31 Jan 1973 *Employees:* 74
Tel: 01603 810390 *Website:* hohs.co.uk
Activities: Education, training
Address: Hethersett Old Hall School, Norwich Road, Hethersett, Norwich, NR9 3DW
Trustees: Mr Robert Chalmers, Dr Calum Ross, Mrs Laura Mallett, Martin Matthews, Mr Peter Hazell
Income: £2,064,095 [2017]; £2,043,870 [2016]; £1,954,859 [2015]; £2,024,584 [2014]; £2,092,951 [2013]

The Hetton Charitable Trust
Registered: 29 Sep 2016
Tel: 020 7309 2222
Activities: General charitable purposes
Address: Jeffreys Henry LLP, 5-7 Cranwood Street, London, EC1V 9EE
Trustees: M Biber, S D Biber
Income: £4,056,388 [2017]

Hetton Home Care Services
Registered: 4 Nov 1998 *Employees:* 133
Tel: 01915 17479 *Website:* hettonhomecareservices.co.uk
Activities: The advancement of health or saving of lives
Address: Hetton Homecare Services, The Hetton Centre, Welfare Road, Hetton-le-Hole, Houghton-le-Spring, Co Durham, DH5 9NE
Trustees: Mrs Audrey Oliver, Mrs Kathleen Young, Mr George Davison, Mrs Elaine Davison, Mrs Dianne Storey, Mr Jim Thompson, Mrs Edna Sanderson, Mr Richard David Tate, Mrs Marilyn Barnfather, Mrs Joan Hall, Mrs Anne Thompson, Mr James Blackburn
Income: £1,783,352 [2017]; £1,567,978 [2016]; £1,385,844 [2015]; £1,414,610 [2014]; £1,346,618 [2013]

Heythrop College
Registered: 15 Sep 1971 *Employees:* 69 *Volunteers:* 2
Tel: 020 7795 4269 *Website:* heythrop.ac.uk
Activities: Education, training
Address: Heythrop College, 23 Kensington Square, London, W8 5HN
Trustees: Mr Michael Egan, Very Rev Damian Howard Sj, Rev Brendan Callaghan, Most Rev Kevin McDonald, Mr Jeremy Heap, Mrs Tamsin Eastwood, Rev Prof Michael Barnes, Mr Matthew Holland, Mr John Ward, Ms Shade Olutobi, Rev Edward Bermingham Sj, Mr John Darley, Dr Michael Kirwan, Rev Keith McMillan, Professor John Davies, Dr Edel Mahony, Mr Loughlin Hickey, Mr Anthony O'Mahony, Rev Professor John Morrill, Dr Edward Howells, Mr Henry Edwards-Xu, Rev John Moffat Sj
Income: £9,023,935 [2017]; £10,642,231 [2016]; £14,102,163 [2015]; £7,949,943 [2014]; £6,676,893 [2013]

High Hilden Limited
Registered: 26 Jan 2005 *Employees:* 31 *Volunteers:* 2
Tel: 01732 353070 *Website:* highhilden.co.uk
Activities: Education, training; accommodation, housing
Address: High Hilden Home, High Hilden Close, Tonbridge, Kent, TN10 3DB
Trustees: Mr Harry Pool, Mr Richard Roberts, Dr Juliet Roberts, Mr Tom Chaloner, Mrs Mary Cottle, Mr Charles Kinloch, Bill Wass
Income: £1,044,718 [2017]; £1,035,501 [2016]; £1,023,056 [2015]; £928,843 [2014]; £899,894 [2013]

High House Production Park Limited
Registered: 12 Jan 2012 *Volunteers:* 10
Tel: 07770 328292 *Website:* hhpp.org.uk
Activities: Education, training; arts, culture, heritage, science; economic, community development, employment
Address: 4 Selwyn Gardens, Cambridge, CB3 9AX
Trustees: Ms Pauline Ann Tambling, Mr Tunde Ojetola, Ms Suzanne Macpherson, Mr John Kent, Mr James Heaton, Mr Bj Chong, Alexander Charles Beard, Mr Andrew Swarbrick, Ms Clare Ruby, Ms Rosalind Johnson, Jonathan Nigel Vigurs Harvey
Income: £1,156,076 [2017]; £776,981 [2016]; £4,548,641 [2015]; £607,168 [2014]; £1,176,598 [2013]

High Peak Hospicecare
Registered: 10 Jan 1994 *Employees:* 27 *Volunteers:* 250
Tel: 01298 816990 *Website:* blythehousehospice.org.uk
Activities: The advancement of health or saving of lives
Address: Blythe House, Eccles Fold, Chapel-en-le-Frith, High Peak, Derbys, SK23 9TJ
Trustees: Dr Simon Hugh Cocksedge, Mr James Dunlop, Mr Bryan Colville McGee, Mr John William George Preece, Mr Timothy John Mourne, Dr Sean Fredrick King, Mr John Michael McNamara, Mrs Patricia Holland, Mrs Delia Butler, Mrs Lesley Middleton, Dr Michael Hardman, Dr Natalie Capper
Income: £1,185,000 [2017]; £1,127,000 [2016]; £1,172,443 [2015]; £989,639 [2014]; £910,737 [2013]

High Peak Theatre Trust Limited
Registered: 16 Mar 1978 *Employees:* 65 *Volunteers:* 180
Tel: 01298 72050 *Website:* buxtonoperahouse.org.uk
Activities: Education, training; arts, culture, heritage, science; environment, conservation, heritage
Address: 5 The Square, Buxton, Derbys, SK17 6XN
Trustees: The Lady Jasmine Nancy Cavendish, Mr John Scampion, Mr Colin Sykes, Mr Paul Rooney, Emily Thrane, Mrs Beverley Carter, Mrs Louise Telford Potter, Mrs Carol Anne Prowse, Mr John Silverwood
Income: £1,627,392 [2017]; £1,553,065 [2016]; £1,413,063 [2015]; £1,678,480 [2014]; £1,628,421 [2013]

Highclare School
Registered: 18 Apr 1973 *Employees:* 212
Tel: 0121 522 2018 *Website:* highclareschool.co.uk
Activities: General charitable purposes; education, training
Address: Studio 1, Basement, 87 Branston Street, Birmingham, B18 6BT
Trustees: Mrs Patricia Mayall, Mr Ian Hazel, Mrs Louise Elizabeth Flowith, Mrs Judith Hurst, Mr Keith Hopkinson, Mrs Stephanie Watson, Mr John Arthur Barrett, Mr John Brain, Mr Adrian Davison
Income: £6,670,689 [2017]; £6,586,414 [2016]; £6,422,812 [2015]; £6,131,815 [2014]; £5,989,366 [2013]

The Highcombe Edge Trust
Registered: 28 Sep 1999 *Volunteers:* 1
Tel: 0845 505 4444
Activities: Education, training; religious activities
Address: Somerville, Bridle Close, Grayshott, Hindhead, Surrey, GU26 6EA
Trustees: Mr Bob Critchley, Mr James Gavin Spencer, Mr Wayne Antony Lynes, Mr Brian Anderson, Mr Angus Dalrymple
Income: £1,208,351 [2017]; £1,787,722 [2016]; £1,270,699 [2015]; £634,800 [2014]; £243,438 [2013]

Higher Education Statistics Agency Ltd
Registered: 29 Jul 1994 *Employees:* 119
Tel: 01242 211116 *Website:* hesa.ac.uk
Activities: Education, training; economic, community development, employment
Address: 95 Promenade, Cheltenham, Glos, GL50 1HZ
Trustees: Professor Paul John Layzell, Professor Richard John Last, Professor Christopher Roy Husbands, Professor Mark Edmund Smith, Professor Andrea Mary Nolan OBE, Ms Roma Chappell, Mr Andrew McConnell OBE, Professor Julie Lydon OBE FLSW, Mr Iain Anthony Littlejohn, Dr Paul Michael Greatrix, Mr Paul Francis Clark
Income: £9,194,349 [2017]; £8,065,067 [2016]; £8,721,970 [2015]; £5,732,814 [2014]; £5,805,459 [2013]

Highfield Preparatory School Limited
Registered: 8 Jul 1966 *Employees:* 39 *Volunteers:* 6
Tel: 01628 624918 *Website:* highfieldprep.org
Activities: Education, training
Address: Highfield Prep School, West Road, Maidenhead, Berks, SL6 1PD
Trustees: Ms Dana Slade, Mr Wayne Bradley, Miss Helen Jackson, Miss Naomi Bartholomew, Mr Paul William Pickering, Mrs Caroline Emma Smith, Mrs Sarah Lee, Mr Peter Campbell, Mrs Martina Keyte, Mrs Claudia Munn, Mr Michael James O'Flaherty
Income: £1,348,275 [2016]; £1,469,805 [2015]; £1,430,470 [2014]; £1,258,085 [2013]

Highfield Priory School Limited
Registered: 9 May 1974 *Employees:* 64
Tel: 01772 690880 *Website:* highfieldpriory.co.uk
Activities: Education, training
Address: Whinney Cottage, Whinneyfield Lane, Woodplumpton, Preston, Lancs, PR4 0LL
Trustees: Mrs Melissa Conlon, Mr Mark Goodwin, Andrew Bradshaw, Mrs Nicola Mason, Mrs Eman Ahmed, Mrs Divia Patel-Smith, Mr John Robert Wood, Mr William Robert Garment, Mr Darren Whitman, Mrs Judith Nairn, Mr Benjamin Robert Hall
Income: £1,926,738 [2016]; £1,777,835 [2015]; £1,648,013 [2014]; £1,630,115 [2013]; £1,505,389 [2012]

Highgate Wood and Queens Park Kilburn
Registered: 26 Aug 1962 *Employees:* 18 *Volunteers:* 529
Tel: 020 7332 3519
Activities: Amateur sport
Address: Corporation of London, P O Box 270, London, EC2P 2EJ
Trustees: The Mayor & Commonality & Citizens of The City of London
Income: £1,401,374 [2017]; £1,418,450 [2016]; £1,332,850 [2015]; £1,420,693 [2014]; £1,344,403 [2013]

Hilden Oaks School Educational Trust Limited
Registered: 12 Oct 1965 *Employees:* 55 *Volunteers:* 15
Tel: 01732 353941 *Website:* hildenoaks.co.uk
Activities: Education, training
Address: 38 Dry Hill Park Road, Tonbridge, Kent, TN10 3BU
Trustees: Mrs Wendy Carey, Mrs Janet Whitaker, Mr Derick Walker, Mrs Linda Alexander, Mr William Mark Faure Walker, Mrs Emma Charlotte Pocock, Mrs Sarah Hall, Dr Ben Waugh, Mrs Susan Robertson, Mr Rick McHattie, Colin Swainson
Income: £2,021,201 [2017]; £1,956,651 [2016]; £1,889,607 [2015]; £1,684,507 [2014]; £1,575,719 [2013]

Hill Holt Wood
Registered: 3 Jul 2007 *Employees:* 37 *Volunteers:* 30
Tel: 07843 617218 *Website:* hillholtwood.com
Activities: Education, training; accommodation, housing; arts, culture, heritage, science; environment, conservation, heritage; economic, community development, employment
Address: 4 Barnby Crossing, Newark, Notts, NG24 2NG
Trustees: Mr Stephen Catney, Mr Andrew Turner, Mr Phil Considine, Mrs Sarah Clarke, Mr John Taylor, Mr Nicholas Jon Chambers, Canon Rev Alan Robson, Mrs Phyllida Perrett, Dr Katherine Roach
Income: £1,117,675 [2017]; £1,030,207 [2016]; £1,068,885 [2015]; £1,193,458 [2014]; £919,754 [2013]

Hill House School Limited
Registered: 11 Sep 1967 *Employees:* 130
Website: hillhouse.doncaster.sch.uk
Activities: Education, training
Address: 26 Millstream Close, Sprotbrough, Doncaster, S Yorks, DN5 7YA
Trustees: Mr Richard Anthony De Mulder, Mrs Maura Jacqueline Jameson, Mrs Valerie Cusworth, Mr Robert Paul Leggott, Mr Michael John Wilson-Maccormack, Dr Madeline Jane Fraser, Mr Robert Scott Colbear, Mr Russell John Fennell, Mr Neil Royston Ebden, Mr Jason Antony Lee Sprenger, Dr Antonia Cooper
Income: £6,843,184 [2017]; £6,609,126 [2016]; £6,182,208 [2015]; £5,663,667 [2014]; £5,184,670 [2013]

Hill Valley & Vale Children's Centres
Registered: 30 Apr 2012 *Employees:* 52 *Volunteers:* 50
Tel: 01453 549860 *Website:* hillvalleyandvale.org.uk
Activities: Education, training; advancement of health or saving of lives; prevention or relief of poverty
Address: Treetops Children's Centre, Dursley Primary School, Highfields, Glos, GL11 4NZ
Trustees: Mr John Richard Thompson, Mr William John Church, Ms Sally Margaret Poskett, Ms Julie Cigman, Ms Alexandra Elizabeth Llewellyn, Ms Jenni Wilson
Income: £1,601,855 [2016]; £1,542,798 [2015]; £1,553,843 [2014]; £1,000 [2013]

Hillingdon Community Trust

Registered: 27 Jun 2003 *Employees:* 2 *Volunteers:* 15
Tel: 020 8581 1676 *Website:* hillingdoncommunitytrust.org.uk
Activities: Education, training; arts, culture, heritage, science; amateur sport; environment, conservation, heritage; economic, community development, employment
Address: Barra Hall, Wood End Green Road, Hayes, Middlesex, UB3 2SA
Trustees: Miss Isabel King, Mr Keith Wallis, Mrs Carole Ann Jones, Mr Jasvir Jassal, Mr Jack Paul Taylor, Miss Balwinder Sokhi, Miss Freda Ritchie, Mr Dominic Gilham, Mr Stephen John Coventry, Mr Matthew Gorman, Mr Clive Andrew Gee, Mr Peter Fraz Money, Mr Shane Ryan, Paul John Lewis
Income: £1,027,150 [2017]; £1,031,755 [2016]; £1,031,755 [2015]; £1,042,351 [2014]; £1,057,103 [2013]

Hillsong Church London

Registered: 30 Jul 2007 *Employees:* 97 *Volunteers:* 2,000
Tel: 020 7384 9200 *Website:* hillsong.com
Activities: Religious activities
Address: Hillsong Church London, 425 New Kings Road, London, SW6 4RN
Trustees: Scott Wilson, Dr Rebecca Newton, Ed Simmons, Shaun Sinniah, Russ Dacre, George Aghajanian, Mr Jeffrey Lestz, Ray Newton, David Whitewood
Income: £17,605,867 [2016]; £14,843,214 [2015]; £12,997,094 [2014]; £11,650,973 [2013]; £10,620,366 [2012]

Benny Hinn Ministries Limited

Registered: 11 Sep 1997 *Employees:* 4
Tel: 020 7242 2022 *Website:* bennyhinn.org
Activities: Religious activities
Address: Farrer & Co, 65-66 Lincoln's Inn Fields, London, WC2A 3LH
Trustees: Mr Larry Sims, Mr Miles Woodlief, Mr Donald Price
Income: £1,651,513 [2016]; £1,118,588 [2015]; £1,114,262 [2014]; £1,567,404 [2013]; £2,101,888 [2012]

The Hinrichsen Foundation

Registered: 15 Dec 1976 *Employees:* 60
Website: hinrichsenfoundation.org.uk
Activities: Arts, culture, heritage, science
Address: 2-6 Baches Street, London, N1 6DN
Trustees: Keith Potter, Professor Stephen Walsh, Tabby Estell, Ms Eleanor Gussman, Dr Linda Hirst, Tim Berg, Ed McKeon, Mark Bromley
Income: £7,153,540 [2016]; £5,905,622 [2015]; £6,185,767 [2014]; £6,295,851 [2013]; £7,077,738 [2012]

The Hintze Family Charitable Foundation

Registered: 30 Jan 2004 *Employees:* 1
Tel: 020 7201 2444
Activities: Education, training; advancement of health or saving of lives; religious activities; arts, culture, heritage, science
Address: 4th Floor, One Strand, London, WC2N 5HR
Trustees: Sir Michael Peat, Mr Duncan Baxter, Sir Michael Hintze
Income: £9,936,306 [2016]; £4,883,611 [2015]; £6,907,950 [2014]; £1,167,387 [2013]; £5,922,290 [2012]

Hinxton Hall Limited

Registered: 20 Jul 1995
Website: hinxton.wellcome.ac.uk
Activities: Education, training
Address: The Wellcome Trust, 183-193 Euston Road, London, NW1 2BE
Trustees: Dr Martin Dougherty, Mrs Genevieve Kiff
Income: £22,768,000 [2017]; £30,933,000 [2016]; £49,831,000 [2015]; £28,704,000 [2014]; £25,710,000 [2013]

Hipperholme Grammar School Foundation

Registered: 10 Feb 1986 *Employees:* 63
Tel: 01422 202256 *Website:* hgsf.org.uk
Activities: General charitable purposes; education, training; amateur sport
Address: Hipperholme Grammar School, Bramley Lane, Halifax, W Yorks, HX3 8JE
Trustees: Mr Christopher David Redfearn BSc DMS MBI, Mrs Patricia Atkinson, Mr David James Smith, Ben Redfearn, Mrs Susan Jennifer Sutcliffe JP, Mr David Harrison, Canon James Allison
Income: £2,697,058 [2016]; £3,022,867 [2015]; £3,322,445 [2014]; £3,430,667 [2013]; £3,554,870 [2012]

Historic Royal Palaces

Registered: 25 Mar 1998 *Employees:* 985 *Volunteers:* 338
Tel: 020 3166 6610 *Website:* hrp.org.uk
Activities: Education, training; arts, culture, heritage, science; environment, conservation, heritage
Address: Historic Royal Palaces, Hampton Court Palace, East Molesey, Surrey, KT8 9AU
Trustees: Mr Jonathan Marsden CVO FSA, Ms Jane Kennedy, Ms Carole Souter CBE, Mr Bruce Carnegie-Brown, Mr Rupert Gavin, Mr Ajay Chowdhury, Professor Sir David Cannadine, General Sir Nicholas Houghton GCB CBE ADC Gen, Ms Louise Wilson FRSA, Sir Michael Stevens KCVO, Ms Zeinab Badawi, Ms Sue Wilkinson MBE
Income: £91,497,000 [2017]; £86,555,000 [2016]; £92,236,000 [2015]; £79,788,000 [2014]; £72,356,000 [2013]

History of Parliament Trust

Registered: 25 Oct 1966 *Employees:* 23
Tel: 020 7219 3285 *Website:* historyofparliamentonline.org
Activities: Education, training; arts, culture, heritage, science
Address: Telford House, 14 Tothill Street, London, SW1H 9NB
Trustees: Mr Gordon Marsden MP, Lord Rowlands, Professor The Lord Morgan FBA, Sir Graham Hart, Dr Philippa Tudor, Lord John Francis McFall, Lord Robert Lisvane, Professor The Lord Norton of Louth, Lord Clark of Windermere, Mr Lindsay Hoyle MP, Kwasi Kwarteng MP, Dr John Benger, Mrs Helen Jones
Income: £1,721,288 [2017]; £1,703,289 [2016]; £1,730,435 [2015]; £1,687,886 [2014]; £1,600,710 [2013]

The Hobson Charity Limited

Registered: 14 May 1985
Tel: 020 3880 6425
Activities: Education, training; advancement of health or saving of lives; prevention or relief of poverty; religious activities; arts, culture, heritage, science; amateur sport; animals; environment, conservation, heritage; armed forces, emergency service efficiency
Address: P O Box No 57691, London, NW7 0GR
Trustees: Deborah Hobson, Mrs J Richardson, Lady Hobson OBE
Income: £1,955,932 [2017]; £1,977,161 [2016]; £1,892,655 [2015]; £1,757,410 [2014]; £1,682,420 [2013]

The David Hockney Foundation (UK) Limited
Registered: 23 Dec 2008
Website: hockneyfoundation.org
Activities: General charitable purposes; arts, culture, heritage, science
Address: Hill House, 1 Little New Street, London, EC4A 3TR
Trustees: Mr David Hockney, Mr Gregory Preston Evans, Mrs Janine Hill, Mr Charles Dare Scheips, Ms Edith Devaney Jones
Income: £5,533,418 [2016]; £650,095 [2012]

The Jane Hodge Foundation
Registered: 29 Jan 1963 *Employees:* 1
Tel: 029 2078 7693 *Website:* hodgefoundation.org.uk
Activities: General charitable purposes
Address: One Central Square, Cardiff, CF10 1FS
Trustees: Ian Davies, Adrian Piper, Alun Bowen, Jonathan Hodge, Karen Hodge, Mrs Helen Molyneux
Income: £3,226,295 [2016]; £4,304,656 [2015]; £3,269,893 [2014]; £1,097,783 [2013]; £815,293 [2012]

Hoe Bridge School Limited
Registered: 12 Jan 1987 *Employees:* 91
Tel: 01483 227904 *Website:* hoebridgeschool.co.uk
Activities: Education, training
Address: Hoe Bridge School, 224 Old Woking Road, Woking, Surrey, GU22 8JE
Trustees: The Venerable Stuart Alexander Beake, Mrs Fiona Boulton, Mr Philip Walton, Mr Simon Brennan, Mrs Samantha Arnold, Mrs Susan Joy Lacey, Mr Ian Katte, Mr Robert William Ellis, Mr Giles Verity
Income: £5,792,770 [2017]; £5,556,881 [2016]; £5,376,436 [2015]; £5,279,689 [2014]; £4,771,259 [2013]

Hofesh Shechter Company Ltd
Registered: 22 Jun 2009 *Employees:* 23
Tel: 020 3701 7490 *Website:* hofesh.co.uk
Activities: General charitable purposes; education, training; arts, culture, heritage, science
Address: Somerset House, New Wing, London, WC2R 1LA
Trustees: Mr Andrew Charles Hillier QC, Gerard Lemos, Sarah Coop, Ms Theresa Beattie, Mr Jules Burns, Mr Jason Gonsalves
Income: £1,183,243 [2017]; £1,902,424 [2016]; £1,506,960 [2015]; £1,590,107 [2014]; £1,354,407 [2013]

Hoffmann Foundation for Autism
Registered: 20 Jan 1988 *Employees:* 107
Tel: 020 7269 6930 *Website:* hfa.org.uk
Activities: Disability; accommodation, housing
Address: 4 Gordon Avenue, Stanmore, Middlesex, HA7 3QD
Trustees: Mr Falak Yussouf, Mrs Ayesha Pathmanadan, Mr Qamar Hamid, Mrs Alison Watson, Mr Charles Kesser, Mr Alex Jarman, Mrs Floretta Lewis
Income: £3,187,049 [2017]; £2,591,772 [2016]; £2,712,920 [2015]; £2,753,385 [2014]; £2,364,284 [2013]

Quintin Hogg Trust
Registered: 10 Apr 1992
Website: quintinhoggtrust.org
Activities: General charitable purposes; accommodation, housing
Address: 66 Lincoln's Inn Fields, London, WC2A 3LH
Trustees: Quintin Hogg Trustee Company
Income: £4,707,079 [2017]; £4,462,313 [2016]; £4,250,353 [2015]; £2,591,100 [2014]; £2,519,479 [2013]

Holbeach and East Elloe Hospital Trust
Registered: 20 Apr 1989 *Employees:* 91 *Volunteers:* 4
Tel: 01775 820055 *Website:* holbeach-hospital.org.uk
Activities: The advancement of health or saving of lives
Address: 23 High Street, Donington, Spalding, Lincs, PE11 4TA
Trustees: Mr Christopher John Penney, Mrs Jean Ruck, Mrs Dorothy Jean Ellerbroek, Mr Andrew James Bines, Mr Michael James Brett, Lady Julia Aileen Taylor, Mr Alan John Inns, Mrs Eileen Ambrose, Mr Norman Frederick Adcock, Mrs Jean Garner
Income: £1,570,088 [2017]; £1,516,965 [2016]; £1,737,610 [2015]; £1,577,334 [2014]; £1,310,698 [2013]

The Francis Holland (Church of England) Schools Trust
Registered: 6 Nov 1962 *Employees:* 234
Website: francisholland.org
Activities: Education, training
Address: 35 Bourne Street, London, SW1W 8JA
Trustees: Mr Antony Romer Beevor, Mr Ian Ross McGregor Ramsay, Miss Charlotte Black, Mrs Alison Olivia Edelshain MA MBA MCIPD, Dr Helen Alexandra Spoudeas, Ms Maxine Louise Harrison, Lady Rachael Robathan, Mr George Charles Stead, Mr Gregory Bennett, Mrs Aimee O'Keeffe, Dr Claire Gwenlan, Miss Susan Anne Ross BSc FInstP, Mr James Bruce Hawkins, Ms Marie Winckler, Mrs Sumita Honey, Mr Dominic Myles Dowley, Professor Jonathan Parry, Ms Jennifer May Williams, Rev Michael Nicholas Roderick Bowie, Mr Anthony Leonard Rupert Fincham, Mr Michael Cuthbert, Mrs Novella De Renzo
Income: £20,165,000 [2017]; £18,376,000 [2016]; £16,095,000 [2015]; £14,679,000 [2014]; £14,520,791 [2013]

Holland House School
Registered: 27 May 1974 *Employees:* 30 *Volunteers:* 5
Tel: 020 8958 6979 *Website:* hollandhouse.org.uk
Activities: Education, training
Address: 1 Broadhurst Avenue, Edgware, Middlesex, HA8 8TP
Trustees: Mr Stephen Wilson, Mr Neel Shah, Mr Amit Shah, Mrs Olawafunso Adebola-Lawal, Mr Krishna Majeethia, Mr Gaon Hart, Mrs Irum Wahid
Income: £1,166,743 [2017]; £1,169,515 [2016]; £1,193,076 [2015]; £1,129,065 [2014]; £1,098,414 [2013]

The Lady Eleanor Holles School
Registered: 19 Jun 2009 *Employees:* 268 *Volunteers:* 5
Tel: 020 8979 1601 *Website:* lehs.org.uk
Activities: Education, training
Address: The Lady Eleanor Holles School, 102 Hanworth Road, Hampton, Surrey, TW12 3HF
Trustees: Ms Alison Meyric Hughes, Mr Neil Lewis, Mrs Wendy Jennifer Wildman, Mr Sandeep Kamat, Miss Charlotte Thomas, Mr David King, Mr Christopher Stokes, Dr Sophie McCormick, Mr Robert Milburn, Ms Cathy Millis, Mrs Catherine Thomas
Income: £17,249,122 [2017]; £17,306,164 [2016]; £15,921,189 [2015]; £14,967,887 [2014]; £14,112,969 [2013]

The Hollick Family Charitable Trust
Registered: 20 Jan 1997
Tel: 020 7632 1400
Activities: General charitable purposes; education, training; advancement of health or saving of lives; overseas aid, famine relief; accommodation, housing; arts, culture, heritage, science; amateur sport; economic, community development, employment
Address: David William Beech, Prager Metis LLP, 5a Bear Lane, Southwark, London, SE1 0UH
Trustees: Mrs Caroline Mary Kemp, Mr David Beech, Lady Sue Woodford Hollick OBE, The Honourable Georgina Louise Hollick, The Honourable Abigail Miranda Benoliel, Lord Clive Richard Hollick
Income: £2,973,169 [2017]; £1,331,671 [2016]; £290,977 [2015]; £658,127 [2014]; £449,794 [2013]

The Fred Hollows Foundation (UK)
Registered: 8 Feb 2011 *Employees:* 4
Tel: 020 7298 2340 *Website:* unitedkingdom.hollows.org
Activities: The advancement of health or saving of lives
Address: 12-15 Crawford Mews, York Street, London, W1H 1LX
Trustees: Mr Stephen Bell, Dr Richard Wormald, Ms Jennifer Anne Dunstan
Income: £3,888,389 [2016]; £2,196,930 [2015]; £1,201,964 [2014]; £294,070 [2013]; £358,329 [2012]

Hollybank Trust
Registered: 5 Jan 1995 *Employees:* 404 *Volunteers:* 275
Tel: 01924 490833 *Website:* hollybanktrust.com
Activities: Education, training; advancement of health or saving of lives; disability; accommodation, housing
Address: Hollybank Trust, Far Common Road, Mirfield, W Yorks, WF14 0DQ
Trustees: Hollybank Trustees Ltd
Income: £12,051,421 [2017]; £11,867,142 [2016]; £11,959,263 [2015]; £12,117,176 [2014]; £11,495,947 [2013]

Holme Grange Ltd
Registered: 29 Mar 1967 *Employees:* 100
Tel: 0118 978 1566 *Website:* holmegrange.org
Activities: Education, training
Address: Holme Grange School, Heathlands Road, Wokingham, Berks, RG40 3AL
Trustees: Mr Gerald William Priestman Barber, Mr David Macken, Mr Peter Brooks, Mr Miles Halliwell, Mrs Areti Bizior, Mr Charles Henry Paulyn Gillow, Mr Alan Finch, Mr John Ellis, Mrs Stephanie Rose, Mrs Delyth Lynch
Income: £5,389,624 [2017]; £4,479,306 [2016]; £3,927,243 [2015]; £3,604,864 [2014]; £3,155,864 [2013]

Dame Kelly Holmes Trust
Registered: 12 Mar 2009 *Employees:* 27 *Volunteers:* 10
Tel: 020 3167 1874 *Website:* damekellyholmestrust.org
Activities: Education, training; amateur sport; economic, community development, employment
Address: South Vaults, Green Park Station, 2-3 Westmoreland Station Road, Bath, BA1 1JB
Trustees: Mike Kelly, Nicky Roche, Ed Bracher, Mr Amerjit Chohan, Jeremy Pearce, Clare Hunt
Income: £3,204,969 [2017]; £3,656,922 [2016]; £3,114,815 [2015]; £2,883,309 [2014]; £1,864,425 [2013]

Holmewood House School
Registered: 1 Feb 1980 *Employees:* 117 *Volunteers:* 50
Tel: 01892 860038 *Website:* holmewoodhouse.co.uk
Activities: Education, training
Address: Holmewood House School, Barrow Lane, Langton Green, Tunbridge Wells, Kent, TN3 0EB
Trustees: Mrs Jill Milner, Mrs Susan Marshall, Mr Michael Kilgour, Mr Christopher Ray, Mr Nigel Hammond, Mr Mark Christopher Pettman, Mr Simon Philip Davies MA, Mr Timothy Hugh Penzer Haynes, Mr Andrew Colin Harfoot, Mrs Amanda Barnes, Mr Graham John Piper, Mr Jeremy John Thompson
Income: £7,137,065 [2016]; £7,247,492 [2015]; £7,349,112 [2014]; £7,007,144 [2013]; £6,435,950 [2012]

Holocaust Educational Trust
Registered: 10 Jul 2002 *Employees:* 25
Tel: 020 7222 6822 *Website:* het.org.uk
Activities: Education, training
Address: Holocaust Educational Trust, Bcm Box 7892, London, WC1N 3XX
Trustees: Mrs Alberta Strage, Mr Robert Stephen Rubin, Mr Ben Helfgott MBE, Richard Harrington, Ms Kirsty Jean McNeill, Mr Edward James Lewin, Mr Olivier Blechner, Mrs Hannah Lewis, Mr Martin Paisner CBE, Mr Paul Phillips, Mrs Helen Hyde, Mr Nigel Graham Layton, Mr Paul Philip Berlyn, Michael Karp, Ms Marilyn Ofer
Income: £3,951,562 [2017]; £3,578,583 [2016]; £3,513,596 [2015]; £3,622,079 [2014]; £3,148,609 [2013]

Holstein UK
Registered: 16 Dec 1998 *Employees:* 115
Tel: 01923 695315 *Website:* holstein-uk.org
Activities: General charitable purposes; education, training; animals; environment, conservation, heritage
Address: Holstein UK, Speir House, Stafford Park 1, Telford, TF3 3BD
Trustees: Mr John Cousar, Mr Andrew Dutton, Mrs Jane Targett, Mr Carl Smith, Mr Aled Rhys Jones, Mr Michael Smale, Mr Peter Prior, Mr Malcolm McLean, Mr Stephen Brough, Mr Edward Griffiths, Mr Iwan Rhys Morgan, Mr Andrew Birkle, Mr Mark Nutsford, Sandy Pirie, Mr David Jones
Income: £9,566,320 [2016]; £9,530,090 [2015]; £8,659,619 [2014]; £8,490,935 [2013]; £8,057,714 [2012]

Holy Trinity (Hull) Development Trust
Registered: 11 Apr 2014 *Employees:* 1
Tel: 07768 301707
Activities: Education, training; prevention or relief of poverty; religious activities; arts, culture, heritage, science
Address: Holy Trinity Parish Church, Market Place, Hull, HU1 1RR
Trustees: Mr Stephen Martin, Dr Neal Barnes, Mr John Robinson
Income: £1,159,829 [2017]; £881,745 [2016]; £812,921 [2015]

Home for Aged Jews (Liverpool and District)
Registered: 25 Mar 1963 *Employees:* 90
Tel: 0151 724 3260 *Website:* merseyside-jewish-community.org.uk
Activities: The advancement of health or saving of lives; disability; accommodation, housing; religious activities
Address: Stapeley Residential & Nursing Home, North Mossley Hill Road, Liverpool, L18 8BR
Trustees: Mr Philip Saul Ettinger, Mr Robert Joel Ettinger
Income: £2,514,993 [2017]; £1,747,772 [2016]; £1,672,911 [2015]; £1,488,206 [2014]; £1,412,625 [2013]

Home of Comfort for Invalids
Registered: 19 Feb 1962 *Employees:* 39
Tel: 023 9273 0063 *Website:* homeofcomfort.org.uk
Activities: The advancement of health or saving of lives; accommodation, housing
Address: The Home of Comfort Nursing Home, 17 Victoria Grove, Southsea, Hants, PO5 1NF
Trustees: Mr Fred Matthews, Mrs Sally Vida King, Rev Giles Evans-Harris, Mrs Susan Smy, Mrs Valerie Croughan, Mrs Deborah Bridger
Income: £1,239,725 [2017]; £1,252,024 [2016]; £1,130,667 [2015]; £1,096,815 [2014]; £1,043,257 [2013]

Home-Start Greenwich
Registered: 28 Jan 1994 *Employees:* 32 *Volunteers:* 63
Tel: 020 8317 4298 *Website:* homestartgreenwich.org.uk
Activities: General charitable purposes; education, training; advancement of health or saving of lives
Address: Oak House, 71 Barnfield Road, Plumstead, London, SE18 3UH
Trustees: Mrs Sheila Jones, Mrs Mary Hardcastle, Ms Lorraine Robinson, Mr Alan Fuller
Income: £2,652,607 [2016]; £1,059,532 [2015]; £93,701 [2014]; £181,279 [2013]; £191,395 [2012]

Home-Start Lincolnshire
Registered: 7 Apr 2008 *Employees:* 37 *Volunteers:* 243
Activities: General charitable purposes
Address: 19 Stewton Lane, Louth, Lincs, LN11 8SB
Trustees: Mr Patrick Fowler, Chris Johnson, Mr Alan Nesbitt, Mr Philip Sturman
Income: £1,334,220 [2017]; £723,499 [2016]; £255,696 [2015]; £246,735 [2014]; £247,514 [2013]

Home-Start UK
Registered: 4 Apr 2005 *Employees:* 33
Tel: 0116 464 5490 *Website:* home-start.org.uk
Activities: General charitable purposes; education, training; other charitable purposes
Address: Home-Start UK, The Crescent, King Street, Leicester, LE1 6RX
Trustees: Ms Felicity Clarkson, Karen Graham, Ms Anne Shevas, Ms Joanna Dennis, Ms Karen Foster, Ms Sue Bishop MS, Ms Margot Madin MS, Ms Elizabeth Hill-Smith, Mr Philip Sugarman
Income: £3,137,954 [2017]; £2,992,001 [2016]; £2,728,587 [2015]; £2,699,619 [2014]; £3,910,186 [2013]

Homefield College Limited
Registered: 29 Jun 2006 *Employees:* 124
Tel: 01509 583033 *Website:* homefieldcollege.ac.uk
Activities: Education, training; disability; accommodation, housing
Address: 42 St Marys Road, Sileby, Loughborough, Leics, LE12 7TL
Trustees: Mrs Jenny Pearce Married, Mr John Kershaw, Mr David Howard, Rosie Philpott, Mrs Isabel Wilson Married, Mr Warren Anthony Franics, Mrs Rosie Lowe, Mr John Perry Accountant, Susan Pesic Smith, Sarah Dornyei, Mr Tim Smith Married
Income: £4,207,585 [2017]; £3,622,720 [2016]; £3,512,396 [2015]; £3,535,715 [2014]; £3,276,255 [2013]

Homefield Preparatory School Trust Limited
Registered: 1 Mar 1967 *Employees:* 76
Tel: 020 8642 0965 *Website:* homefield.sutton.sch.uk
Activities: Education, training; religious activities; arts, culture, heritage, science; amateur sport
Address: Homefield Preparatory School, Western Road, Sutton, Surrey, SM1 2TE
Trustees: Mr Anthony Jeans BSc FCA, Dr Hervey Wilcox MA MSc LLM MBA MRCP MRCPath, Mr Paul Kavanagh LLB, Mr Andrew Lestrange, Mrs Jacqueline Whittingham, Mr David Hutchings, Mrs Marjorie Harris CertEd BEd MEd, Dr Inderpreet Dhingra BSc MBA PhD, Mr Joe Nutt BA MA PGCE, Dr Gillian Bamford, Mrs Margaret Gardiner, Mr Asif Ahmed
Income: £4,301,818 [2017]; £4,402,713 [2016]; £4,120,290 [2015]; £4,166,493 [2014]; £3,941,138 [2013]

Homeless Action Resource Project
Registered: 20 Jun 2003 *Employees:* 59 *Volunteers:* 60
Tel: 07876 405710 *Website:* harpsouthend.org.uk
Activities: Education, training; advancement of health or saving of lives; prevention or relief of poverty; accommodation, housing
Address: 9 Warwick Road, Southend on Sea, Essex, SS1 3BN
Trustees: Mrs Lilias Felton, Mr Richard Robert Hair, Mrs Yvonne Hazel Vickers, Mr Iain Campbell, Dr Haroon Aqeel Siddique, Mr Peter Nigel Thorn, Mrs Alexsandra Kaye, Debbie Stanton MS, Mr David Mark Rothman
Income: £3,458,602 [2017]; £1,990,865 [2016]; £2,307,515 [2015]; £3,647,533 [2014]; £1,579,281 [2013]

Homeless Link
Registered: 1 Nov 2001 *Employees:* 47
Tel: 020 7840 4430 *Website:* homeless.org.uk
Activities: General charitable purposes; education, training; prevention or relief of poverty; accommodation, housing
Address: 2nd Floor, Minories House, 2-5 Minories, London, EC3N 1BJ
Trustees: Mr Ian Watson, Mr Steven Benson, Fiona Humphrey, Ms Maura Jackson, Mr Harish Sumanlal Bhayani, Ms Amanda Dubarry, Mr Jeremy Swain, Mr Piers Feilden MBE, Jamie Whysall, Mr Michael Patrick Egan
Income: £4,436,492 [2017]; £4,110,787 [2016]; £4,047,654 [2015]; £7,726,661 [2014]; £11,496,917 [2013]

Homeless Oxfordshire Limited
Registered: 20 Oct 1987 *Employees:* 68 *Volunteers:* 115
Tel: 01865 304600 *Website:* oxhop.org.uk
Activities: The prevention or relief of poverty; accommodation, housing
Address: O'Hanlon House, Luther Street, Oxford, OX1 1UL
Trustees: Mr William Downing, Ms Gail Siddall, Ms Anne Clarke, Ms Isabelle Pitt, Ms Karen Simeons, Mr Robin Aitken, Mr Graham Robert Edward Beith
Income: £3,223,570 [2017]; £3,223,570 [2016]; £3,509,447 [2015]; £3,071,038 [2014]; £3,382,413 [2013]

Homerton College Cambridge
Registered: 16 Aug 2010 *Employees:* 217
Tel: 01223 747151 *Website:* homerton.cam.ac.uk
Activities: Education, training
Address: 5 Great Eastern Street, Cambridge, CB1 3AB
Trustees: Mr Matthew Moss, Dr Penelope Barton, Mr Stephen Watts, Professor Geoffrey Christopher Ward, Dr Louise Joy, Dr Michelle Oyen, Mr Paul Warwick, Professor Simone Hochgreb, Dr William Foster, Ms Deborah Griffin OBE, Dr Melanie Keene, Dr Andre Neves, Dr Timoleon Kipouros
Income: £14,829,046 [2017]; £12,697,685 [2016]; £12,476,502 [2015]; £12,088,469 [2014]; £10,635,290 [2013]

The Honeypot Children's Charity
Registered: 8 Jun 1992 *Employees:* 31 *Volunteers:* 60
Tel: 020 7602 2631 *Website:* honeypot.org.uk
Activities: General charitable purposes
Address: The Honeypot Charity, 19 Berghem Mews, Blythe Road, London, W14 0HN
Trustees: Mr Caspar MacDonald-Hall, Mr Laurie Oppenheim, Mrs Mary Davis, Mr Hugh Whitaker, Mr Verne Grinstead, Mr Mikhail Watford, Mr David Clark, Mr Paddy Grafton Green, Mr Michael Jolliffe, Mr Carl Leighton-Pope, Mr Michael Steele, Ms Natalie Rebeiz
Income: £1,590,008 [2017]; £1,778,071 [2016]; £1,181,888 [2015]; £911,978 [2014]; £921,312 [2013]

Honeywood House Nursing Home
Registered: 6 Aug 1963 *Employees:* 53
Tel: 01306 627389 *Website:* honeywoodhouse.co.uk
Activities: The advancement of health or saving of lives; disability
Address: Honeywood House, Nursing Home, Horsham Road, Rowhook, Horsham, W Sussex, RH12 3QD
Trustees: Mr David William Triggs, Paul Johnson, Miss Sandra Margaret White, Mrs Wilma Kathryn Trett
Income: £1,172,369 [2017]; £946,480 [2016]; £1,237,173 [2015]; £948,285 [2014]; £903,314 [2013]

Honourable Artillery Company
Registered: 22 Apr 1964 *Employees:* 25 *Volunteers:* 140
Website: hac.org.uk
Activities: Education, training; prevention or relief of poverty; arts, culture, heritage, science; amateur sport; animals; armed forces, emergency service efficiency
Address: Honourable Artillery Co, Finsbury Barracks, City Road, London, EC1Y 2BQ
Trustees: Major Charles Marment, Major John Longbottom MBE, Major Simon Briggs TD, Major James Leighton TD, Jhj Phipson Esq, Csgt N J Goode, James Brooke, Major General Simon Lalor CB TD, Lcpl Henry Michael Norman Campbell-Ricketts, Sir Richard Lawson Barrons, Mr Andrew G Wallis, Mr Thomas Holme Cardwell, Mr Timothy Lloyd Davies, Lt Geroid Patrick O'Connor, Major James Alexander Robinson, Lt Col Mark William Wood, Mr Edwin Seabrook, Major Patrick Marsland-Roberts TD, Sir James Pickthorn Bt, Major Rp Quain TD, Sgt H G Adams, Captain Roger Mark Huleatt-James TD, Mr William Benedict De Cusance Cussans, Captain Hugo Roland Jee, Csgt Melissa Jane Shepherd, Colonel The Honourable Mark Vincent MBE, Mr Alan Willis, Mr David Llewelyn Daniel, Mr William Hulbert Grove, Mrs Lenore Alison Dudman, Captain Hari Voyantis
Income: £5,742,000 [2016]; £4,574,000 [2015]; £4,384,000 [2014]; £3,825,000 [2013]; £3,973,000 [2012]

Honourable Society of Gray's Inn Trust Fund
Registered: 16 Oct 1992 *Employees:* 16 *Volunteers:* 209
Tel: 020 7458 7803 *Website:* graysinn.org.uk
Activities: Education, training; religious activities
Address: The Hon Society of Gray's Inn, Treasury Office, 8 South Square, Gray's Inn, London, WC1R 5ET
Trustees: The Rt Hon Sir David Kitchin, Helen Malcolm QC, Sarah Turvill, The Hon Hugo Keith QC
Income: £2,329,497 [2016]; £2,543,916 [2015]; £2,258,684 [2014]; £3,362,861 [2013]; £2,586,498 [2012]

Hope City Church
Registered: 21 Jun 2007 *Employees:* 142 *Volunteers:* 398
Tel: 0114 213 2065 *Website:* hopecitychurch.tv
Activities: Education, training; prevention or relief of poverty; overseas aid, famine relief; religious activities
Address: Hope City Church, The Megacentre, Bernard Road, Sheffield, S2 5BQ
Trustees: Mr Colin Davies, Mr Paul Benger, Mr Edward John Newton, Reverend David Gilpin, Mr Christopher Wyn Davies
Income: £4,952,734 [2017]; £3,725,629 [2016]; £2,823,295 [2015]; £2,265,408 [2014]; £2,287,984 [2013]

Hope Consultants International Ltd
Registered: 27 Feb 1998 *Employees:* 10 *Volunteers:* 18
Website: hopeconsultants.org
Activities: Education, training; religious activities
Address: P O Box 1502, High Wycombe, Bucks, HP11 9JA
Trustees: Mr Andrew Dimmock, Mr Robert Goldmann, Ms Zoe Jean Alexander, Dr Friedrich Leonhardt, Mr David Jagger, Mrs Annette Elder, Mr Trent Joshua Mills
Income: £1,003,256 [2016]; £1,082,547 [2015]; £853,033 [2014]; £1,798,994 [2013]; £1,039,636 [2012]

Hope House Children's Hospices
Registered: 12 Aug 1991 *Employees:* 243 *Volunteers:* 620
Tel: 01691 679679 *Website:* hopehouse.org.uk
Activities: The advancement of health or saving of lives; disability
Address: Hope House, Childrens Hospice, Nant Lane, Morda, Oswestry, Salop, SY10 9BX
Trustees: Mrs Barbara Jane Evans, Mr Philip Richard Inch, Mrs Meinir Wigley, Mrs Jacquelyn Ann Hughes, Mr Chris Hudson, Mr Russell Pentz, Mrs Janette Margaret Welch, Mr Gwyn Bartley LLB, Dr Jean Watt, Mr Stephen Henly, Dr David Sharp, Miss Claire Elizabeth Williams
Income: £7,739,805 [2016]; £7,811,495 [2015]; £7,671,617 [2014]; £7,591,734 [2013]; £6,470,276 [2012]

Hope Worldwide
Registered: 21 Apr 1995 *Employees:* 13 *Volunteers:* 700
Tel: 020 7713 7655 *Website:* hopeworldwide.org.uk
Activities: General charitable purposes; education, training; advancement of health or saving of lives; disability; prevention or relief of poverty; overseas aid, famine relief; accommodation, housing; amateur sport; economic, community development, employment
Address: 360 City Road, London, EC1V 2PY
Trustees: Mr David Kaner, Mr Richard Mobbs, Mr James Shoemark, John Partington, Ms Amanda Rigby, Mr Barry Edwards, Muriel Gutu, Iain Williams
Income: £1,008,352 [2017]; £1,052,384 [2016]; £1,411,150 [2015]; £1,205,628 [2013]; £1,144,535 [2012]

Hope and Homes for Children
Registered: 26 Nov 2001 *Employees:* 186 *Volunteers:* 10
Tel: 01722 790111 *Website:* hopeandhomes.org
Activities: The prevention or relief of poverty; overseas aid, famine relief
Address: East Clyffe Farm Barn, East Clyffe, Steeple Langford, Salisbury, Wilts, SP3 4LZ
Trustees: Ms Carol Haslam, Professor Andrew Bilson, Mr Mark Grinonneau, Mr Malcolm John Sweeting, Ms Anna Julien Segall, Mr Mark Andrew Shadrack, Mr Richard Cecil Greenhalgh, Mr Dean Williams, Mrs Victoria Jane Bruce, Mr Matthew Graham Banks, Mr Alexander James Matheou, Ms Camilla Ulfdotter Otto
Income: £9,511,899 [2016]; £7,787,830 [2015]; £7,850,501 [2014]; £7,833,452 [2013]; £6,185,941 [2012]

Hope for Children
Registered: 5 Oct 1994 *Employees:* 11 *Volunteers:* 100
Tel: 01442 234561 *Website:* hope4c.org
Activities: Education, training; disability; prevention or relief of poverty; overseas aid, famine relief; economic, community development, employment
Address: Hope for Children, 6 Progression Centre, Mark Road, Hemel Hempstead, Herts, HP2 7DW
Trustees: Miss Helen McMillan, Mr David Sherratt, Mr David Rose, Ms Amanda Neylon, Miss Georgina Irvine Robertson, Mr Neil Robertson, Mr Iain Smith, Ms Marianne Rowley
Income: £1,380,505 [2017]; £1,431,409 [2016]; £1,803,139 [2015]; £1,523,038 [2014]; £1,619,157 [2013]

Hope for Justice
Registered: 30 Sep 2008 *Employees:* 38 *Volunteers:* 272
Tel: 0300 008 8000 *Website:* hopeforjustice.org
Activities: General charitable purposes; education, training; prevention or relief of poverty; overseas aid, famine relief; human rights, religious or racial harmony, equality or diversity; other charitable purposes
Address: P O Box 5527, Manchester, M61 0QU
Trustees: Mr Martin Warner, Mr Gareth Henderson, Mr Peter Elson, Mrs Wendy Taylor, Mr Chris Dacre, Ms Natalie Herms, Mr Allan Gibson
Income: £1,849,246 [2017]; £1,445,153 [2016]; £1,436,666 [2015]; £990,328 [2014]; £595,946 [2013]

Hope for Tomorrow
Registered: 19 Nov 2002 *Employees:* 13 *Volunteers:* 50
Tel: 01666 505055 *Website:* hopefortomorrow.org.uk
Activities: General charitable purposes; advancement of health or saving of lives; disability
Address: Upton Lodge, Upton, Tetbury, Glos, GL8 8LP
Trustees: Sean Elyan, Mr Patrick Temple Barnard, Mr Andrew Michael Goodall, Mr Christopher John Daniels, Mrs Christine Angela Mills, Mr Paul William Tuck, Mrs Sophie Louise Jeal
Income: £1,152,460 [2017]; £1,184,805 [2016]; £1,515,838 [2015]; £1,015,254 [2014]; £726,332 [2013]

Hopscotch Asian Women's Centre
Registered: 28 Feb 2000 *Employees:* 66 *Volunteers:* 6
Tel: 020 7388 8198 *Website:* hopscotchawc.org.uk
Activities: Education, training; advancement of health or saving of lives; disability; prevention or relief of poverty; arts, culture, heritage, science; economic, community development, employment; human rights, religious or racial harmony, equality or diversity
Address: 50-52 Hampstead Road, London, NW1 2PY
Trustees: Sandra Machado, Ms Diya Mukarji, Miss Meenara Islam, Ms Morenike Ajayi, Ms Alison Jane Lowton, Karen Ng
Income: £1,160,407 [2017]; £1,335,465 [2016]; £1,223,822 [2015]; £1,040,826 [2014]; £724,394 [2013]

Horatio's Garden
Registered: 2 Apr 2013 *Employees:* 2 *Volunteers:* 81
Tel: 01722 781160 *Website:* horatiosgarden.org.uk
Activities: The advancement of health or saving of lives; disability
Address: 41A Vicarage Street, Warminster, Wilts, BA12 8JQ
Trustees: Ms Victoria Holton, Ms Bianca Roden, Ms Margaret Cameron, Mr Yan Swiderski, Ms Lisa Stratton, Dr David Chapple, Mr David Gregg, Dr Susan Chapple, Mrs Catherine Ogilvie Burns
Income: £1,171,954 [2017]; £1,242,830 [2016]; £299,941 [2015]; £292,880 [2014]

Horder Healthcare
Registered: 26 May 1995 *Employees:* 391 *Volunteers:* 57
Tel: 01892 665577 *Website:* horderhealthcare.co.uk
Activities: The advancement of health or saving of lives; disability
Address: Horder Healthcare, The Horder Centre, St Johns Road, Crowborough, E Sussex, TN6 1XP
Trustees: Mrs Sarah E Brown OBE, Dr Richard John Tyler, Mr Peter Alan Flamank FCA CPFA, Dr Catherine E D Bell, Mrs Rosemary Cunningham Thomas, Mr Peter Julius Soer, Dr Susan Jane Grieve, Mr Paul Christopher Allen BA FCA, Dr David William Yates, Mr Steven L Dance, Mrs Amanda Louise Parker, Mr John William Turner
Income: £31,638,000 [2017]; £29,969,000 [2016]; £24,889,822 [2015]; £23,187,353 [2014]; £23,708,022 [2013]

The Horizon Foundation
Registered: 27 Sep 2016 *Employees:* 1
Website: horizonfoundation.info
Activities: General charitable purposes; education, training
Address: 37 Chapelfield East, Norwich, NR2 1SF
Trustees: Patrick Smulders, Maury Shenk, Catherine Roe, Kirkland Newman-Smulders
Income: £1,338,183 [2017]

The Horniman Public Museum and Public Park Trust
Registered: 8 Feb 1990 *Employees:* 138 *Volunteers:* 281
Tel: 020 8699 1872 *Website:* horniman.ac.uk
Activities: Education, training; arts, culture, heritage, science; environment, conservation, heritage
Address: 100 London Road, London, SE23 3PQ
Trustees: Sarah Kemp, Ms Hilary Carty, Mrs Carole Souter, Geoffrey Crossick, Mr Nico Iacuzzi, Mrs Caroline Cole, Ms Clare Elizabeth Matterson, Ms Eve Salomon, Mr Surojit Ghosh, Mr Simon Hesketh
Income: £8,375,223 [2017]; £6,480,985 [2016]; £6,639,560 [2015]; £6,703,885 [2014]; £6,353,886 [2013]

Hornsby House Educational Trust
Registered: 31 Oct 1988 *Employees:* 83
Tel: 020 8675 4325 *Website:* hornsbyhouse.org.uk
Activities: Education, training
Address: Hornsby House School, Hearnville Road, London, SW12 8RS
Trustees: Michael Hornsby, Huw Davies, Mandy Brown, Mr Neil Newman, Miss Jennifer Alice Kathleen MacKay, Mrs Alison Theresa Siddiqui, Mrs Susan Lesley Pepper, Ms Corinne Aldridge, Andrew Skinnard, Mr David Smith
Income: £6,129,501 [2016]; £5,831,771 [2015]; £5,584,439 [2014]; £5,275,504 [2013]; £5,025,639 [2012]

Hornsey Y.M.C.A.
Registered: 7 Jan 2002 *Employees:* 66 *Volunteers:* 25
Tel: 020 8347 2543 *Website:* ymcahornsey.org.uk
Activities: General charitable purposes; education, training; religious activities; amateur sport
Address: 54 Grove Way, Wembley, Middlesex, HA9 6JT
Trustees: Michael Baker, Mr Maurice Cheng, Mr Paul Philippe Tredwell, Mrs Virginia Ward, Mr Andrew Redfearn, Mr Mark Richard Phillip Thompson
Income: £1,155,180 [2017]; £1,154,362 [2016]; £1,100,382 [2015]; £958,666 [2014]; £1,081,346 [2013]

Horris Hill Preparatory School Trust Limited
Registered: 8 Jan 1964 *Employees:* 60
Tel: 01635 30323 *Website:* horrishill.com
Activities: Education, training
Address: Horris Hill School, Newtown, Newbury, Berks, RG20 9DJ
Trustees: Mr Edward Garton Woods, Mr Michael Antony Grenier, Ms Marina Lund, Mr Richard Michael Curling, Mr Simon Leigh Hayes, Mrs Amanda Block, Mr Dominic Edward McCausland Armstrong, Mr Ralph Oliphant-Callum, Mr Alexander Frederick James Roe, Mr Alexander William Rainger Mitchell, Mr Simon Hedley Dalrymple, Mr Ian Fraser
Income: £3,107,226 [2016]; £2,989,338 [2015]; £2,720,248 [2014]; £2,771,817 [2013]; £2,661,584 [2012]

The Horse Trust
Registered: 29 Jun 1964 *Employees:* 31 *Volunteers:* 10
Tel: 01494 488960 *Website:* horsetrust.org.uk
Activities: Animals
Address: Speen Farm, Slad Lane, Speen, Princes Risborough, Bucks, HP27 0PP
Trustees: Professor Josh Slater Bvmes PhD MRCVS, Lord Rupert De Mauley TD, Professor Ian Mark Bowen, Professor Bruce McGorum, Mr David Cook, Professor Peter Clegg MRCVS, Ms Bronwen Jones, Mr Christopher James William Marriott, Mrs Milly Soames, Mr Rupert Hugh Maxwell Neal
Income: £2,846,469 [2016]; £2,994,937 [2015]; £2,252,106 [2014]; £2,786,971 [2013]; £2,401,261 [2012]

The John Horseman Trust
Registered: 15 Oct 1999
Activities: The prevention or relief of poverty; religious activities; environment, conservation, heritage
Address: 7 College Road, London, SE21 7BQ
Trustees: Mr John Richard Horseman, Mrs Moyra Claire Susan Horseman, Mr Andrew Charles Green
Income: £2,098,257 [2017]; £1,102,743 [2016]; £1,107,378 [2015]; £906,128 [2014]; £991,730 [2013]

Horseworld Trust
Registered: 11 Dec 2007 *Employees:* 32 *Volunteers:* 49
Tel: 01275 832425 *Website:* horseworld.org.uk
Activities: General charitable purposes; education, training; animals; environment, conservation, heritage
Address: Horseworld, The Delmar Hall, Staunton Lane, Bristol, BS14 0QL
Trustees: Mr Kerry Gwyther, Mr Ernest Richard Hemmings, Mr Andrew Dowden, Mrs Patricia Marianne Shand, Mrs Annette Katarina Newman, Mr John Newman, Mr Michael Neale, Mr Nigel Daniel, Mr Duncan John Ballard
Income: £1,412,040 [2016]; £1,060,501 [2015]; £1,323,822 [2014]; £1,174,539 [2013]; £1,059,552 [2012]

Hospice UK
Registered: 21 Oct 1992 *Employees:* 53 *Volunteers:* 2
Tel: 020 7520 8200 *Website:* hospiceuk.org
Activities: General charitable purposes; education, training
Address: Hospice UK, 34-44 Britannia Street, London, WC1X 9JG
Trustees: Ms Tina Lynn Swani, Mr Paul Francis Dyer, Mr Anthony James Collins, Mrs Christine Gibbons, John Stephen, Mrs Stephanie Louise Peters, The Rt Hon Lord Howard of Lympne CH QC, Ms Ann Smits, Mrs Catherine Janet Tompkins, Mr Stephen Roberts, Emma Reynolds
Income: £5,876,000 [2017]; £5,545,000 [2016]; £6,431,000 [2015]; £66,533,000 [2014]; £5,995,000 [2013]

Hospice at Home Carlisle and North Lakeland
Registered: 30 Jan 2003 *Employees:* 54 *Volunteers:* 200
Tel: 01768 210719 *Website:* hospiceathome.co.uk
Activities: The advancement of health or saving of lives
Address: Barras Lane, Dalston, Carlisle, Cumbria, CA5 7NY
Trustees: Mr Michael Kevin Clementson, Dr Alison Miles, Mr Michael Cousins, Mr Peter Lambert, Mrs Margaret Alice Drury, Mr Nicholas John Coulson, Mr John McLaren, Lady Elizabeth Mary Cecilia Leeming, Professor Shirley Reveley, Mr James Douglas Claxton
Income: £1,340,439 [2017]; £1,135,349 [2016]; £1,263,705 [2015]; £1,111,061 [2014]; £861,754 [2013]

Hospice at Home West Cumbria
Registered: 31 May 2001 *Employees:* 69 *Volunteers:* 200
Website: hospiceathomewestcumbria.org.uk
Activities: The advancement of health or saving of lives
Address: Upper Floor, Cumbria House, New Oxford Street, Workington, Cumbria, CA14 2NA
Trustees: Mr Richard Stout, Dr Robert Walker, Dr Margaret Jean Bober, Mr John Ernerst Knewstubb, Mr Steven Roy Bostock, Mr Dennis Lydon, Mrs Joanne Bowe
Income: £1,112,797 [2017]; £1,069,234 [2016]; £1,113,407 [2015]; £1,513,502 [2014]; £913,291 [2013]

Hospice in the Weald
Registered: 27 Jun 1980 *Employees:* 240 *Volunteers:* 1,200
Tel: 01892 520518 *Website:* hospiceintheweald.org.uk
Activities: Education, training; advancement of health or saving of lives; disability
Address: Hospice in the Weald, Maidstone Road, Pembury, Tunbridge Wells, Kent, TN2 4TA
Trustees: Ms Christine Freshwater, Mr Brian Dudley, Mr Simon Lee, Mr Tim Rolfe, Miss Susan Pinkney, Prof Julia Downing, Mr Michael J Wheatley, Ms Clare Wykes, Miss Joanna Felicity Ford, Dr Nicholas Eric Benson
Income: £9,916,973 [2017]; £8,631,318 [2016]; £8,638,724 [2015]; £7,944,590 [2014]; £7,532,633 [2013]

Hospice of Hope Romania Limited
Registered: 18 Sep 2001 *Employees:* 72 *Volunteers:* 343
Tel: 01959 525110 *Website:* hospicesofhope.co.uk
Activities: Education, training; advancement of health or saving of lives; overseas aid, famine relief
Address: 11 High Street, Otford, Sevenoaks, Kent, TN14 5PG
Trustees: Rev Anthony Redman, Dr Simon Pennell, Dr Jo Hockley, Mr Douglas Paterson, Dr Alison Sarah Landon, Mr Trevor Alan Snuggs, Mr Brian Davies, Mrs Marilyn Boggust, Mr Philip Batson
Income: £2,468,617 [2016]; £3,265,680 [2015]; £3,402,535 [2014]; £4,168,116 [2013]; £3,261,802 [2012]

Hospice of St Francis (Berkhamsted) Ltd
Registered: 30 Sep 1980 *Employees:* 137 *Volunteers:* 1,183
Tel: 01442 869550 *Website:* stfrancis.org.uk
Activities: Education, training; advancement of health or saving of lives
Address: Spring Garden Lane, off Shootersway, Northchurch, Berkhamsted, Herts, HP4 3GW
Trustees: Mrs Margaret Salmon, Mrs Susan Noble, Matthew Gorman, Ms Sarah Byrt, Mr Mark Hampton, Mr Nick Hanling, Mrs Alison Woodhams, Mr David Williams, Ms Julia Bolsom, Dr Berndine Tipple, Mr Timothy Curry, Mrs Tracy Jane Moores
Income: £6,207,000 [2017]; £6,561,003 [2016]; £5,847,000 [2015]; £6,533,000 [2014]; £6,232,000 [2013]

Hospice of St Mary of Furness

Registered: 14 Jul 1986 *Employees:* 84 *Volunteers:* 350
Website: stmaryshospice.org
Activities: The advancement of health or saving of lives
Address: 52 Lindale Road, Longridge, Preston, Lancs, PR3 3FT
Trustees: Mr Graham Arthur Jowett, Mr Richard Bird, Miss Lucy Cavendish, Miss Elise Higham, Mr Andrew Philip James, Mr Andrew Wrenn, Mrs Denise Hardy, Kay Gilbey, Mr Robert Dudley Clark, Mr Graham Servante, Dr Andrew Luksza, Mrs Kim Wilson
Income: £3,023,531 [2017]; £3,802,324 [2016]; £3,326,239 [2015]; £2,987,087 [2014]; £2,716,225 [2013]

Hospice of The Good Shepherd Ltd

Registered: 13 Sep 1984 *Employees:* 135 *Volunteers:* 370
Tel: 01244 851091 *Website:* hospiceofthegoodshepherd.com
Activities: The advancement of health or saving of lives
Address: Gordon Lane, Backford, Chester, CH2 4DG
Trustees: Mr Malcolm Booker, Mr Andrew Banks, Mrs Josephine Maria Nelligan, Mr W Benoy, Mr Robert James Mee, Mrs Justine Watkinson, Mr Alistair Taylor Jones, Dr Isabelle Hughes, Mrs Margaret Hopkins, Mr Stephen Britton, Dr Neil Fergusson
Income: £4,345,099 [2017]; £3,975,616 [2016]; £3,815,405 [2015]; £4,034,737 [2014]; £3,298,312 [2013]

Hospice of The Valleys

Registered: 7 Jul 1986 *Employees:* 46 *Volunteers:* 162
Tel: 01495 717277 *Website:* hospiceofthevalleys.org.uk
Activities: The advancement of health or saving of lives
Address: Hospice of The Valleys, Festival Drive, Ebbw Vale, Blaenau Gwent, NP23 8XF
Trustees: Mr Allan Frank Harris, Miss Susan Vida Kent, Dr Simon Ian Robert Noble, Rev Barry Robert Frances Roche, Robert James, Mr Alan Williams, Mr Kevan Leslie Lines, Mr Philip Robson, Mrs Sally Mirando
Income: £1,069,361 [2017]; £955,764 [2016]; £924,463 [2015]; £856,275 [2014]; £948,421 [2013]

Hospiscare

Registered: 22 Oct 1987 *Employees:* 269 *Volunteers:* 1,050
Tel: 01392 688000 *Website:* hospiscare.co.uk
Activities: The advancement of health or saving of lives
Address: Hospiscare, Dryden Road, Exeter, EX2 5JJ
Trustees: Mr Peter Brennan, Mrs Susan Sutherland, Geoffrey Pringle, Mrs Barbara Honor Sweeney, Mrs Cathy Durston, Dr Sarah Jane Jackson, Mr Ben Anthony Turner, Mrs Lesley Ann Murray, Geoffrey Bush, Dr John Coop, Mr Matthew Bryant, Mr Peter Serjeant, Mrs Jennifer Winslade
Income: £8,861,320 [2017]; £8,672,098 [2016]; £8,464,512 [2015]; £7,497,885 [2014]; £6,620,988 [2013]

The Hospital Saturday Fund

Registered: 31 Mar 2008 *Employees:* 75
Tel: 020 7202 1334 *Website:* hospitalsaturdayfund.org
Activities: The advancement of health or saving of lives
Address: The Hospital Saturday Fund, 24 Upper Ground, London, SE1 9PD
Trustees: Mr Paul Palmer, Mrs Jane Laidlaw Dalton, Mr David John Thomas, Mrs Margaret Rogers, Mr John Greenwood, Mr John Randel, Mr Mark Davies
Income: £30,850,204 [2017]; £28,022,689 [2016]; £25,484,524 [2015]; £25,730,247 [2014]; £25,307,557 [2013]

The Hospital of God at Greatham

Registered: 9 Apr 2008 *Employees:* 174 *Volunteers:* 3
Tel: 01429 870247 *Website:* hospitalofgod.org.uk
Activities: Disability; prevention or relief of poverty; accommodation, housing; religious activities
Address: The Estate Office, Greatham, Hartlepool, Cleveland, TS25 2HS
Trustees: Mr Peter Shields, Venerable Ian Jagger, Mr John De Martino, Mr Michael Poole, Ms Annette Nylund, The Ven Geoffrey Miller, Mike Taylerson, Colonel (Retd) Chris Dickinson QCVS, Mrs Philippa Sinclair, Mrs Margaret Bousfield
Income: £4,550,285 [2016]; £4,308,687 [2015]; £4,235,281 [2014]; £4,029,518 [2013]; £3,867,519 [2012]

Hospital of William Wyggeston and The Hospital Branch

Registered: 29 Mar 1963 *Employees:* 53
Tel: 0116 255 9174 *Website:* wyggestons.org.uk
Activities: Education, training; prevention or relief of poverty; accommodation, housing
Address: The Administration Office, Wyggestons Hospital, Hinckley Road, Leicester, LE3 0UX
Trustees: The Wyggeston's Hospital and Hospital Branch Trustee
Income: £2,125,990 [2016]; £2,096,583 [2015]; £2,016,728 [2014]; £1,746,466 [2013]; £1,753,812 [2012]

Hospitality Action

Registered: 8 Dec 2003 *Employees:* 11 *Volunteers:* 27
Tel: 020 3004 5511 *Website:* hospitalityaction.org.uk
Activities: General charitable purposes; education, training; prevention or relief of poverty
Address: 62 Britton Street, London, EC1M 5UY
Trustees: Mr William Baxter, Mr Jon Dee, Robert Walton, Mr Jonathan Raggett, Ian Sarson, Mr Ringo Francis, Tim Jones, Mr Simon Esner, Mr Andrew Guy, Mr Simon Dobson, Matt Johnson, Andrew Latham, Mr David Walker, Mr Jason Atherton, Ms Hazel Detsiny
Income: £1,569,384 [2016]; £1,563,971 [2015]; £1,349,576 [2014]; £1,143,212 [2013]; £1,137,746 [2012]

The Sir Joseph Hotung Charitable Settlement

Registered: 29 Sep 2000
Activities: Education, training; advancement of health or saving of lives; prevention or relief of poverty; arts, culture, heritage, science; human rights, religious or racial harmony, equality or diversity
Address: Penningtons Manches LLP, 125 Wood Street, London, EC2V 7AW
Trustees: Sir Joseph E Hotung, Sir Robert David Hugh Boyd, Professor Dame Jessica Mary Rawson, Mr Peter Henry Painton
Income: £3,029,980 [2017]; £1,568,233 [2016]; £1,490,359 [2015]; £1,058,754 [2014]; £766,834 [2013]

The Hounslow Arts Trust Ltd

Registered: 28 May 1974 *Employees:* 41
Tel: 020 8232 1015 *Website:* watermans.org.uk
Activities: Education, training; arts, culture, heritage, science
Address: Watermans, 40 High Street, Brentford, Middlesex, TW8 0DS
Trustees: Mr Duncan Smith, Ms Susan Marsh, Mr Graeme Baker, Mr Adam Jackson, Mr William David Evans, Karen Hinton-Platt, Ms Jacqueline Kormornick, Ajay Mehta, Ms Margaret Fawcett McNab, Ms Mary Dalton, Mr Jeffrey Lee Dawson, Mrs Paula Jayne Foulds, Myra Savin
Income: £1,722,069 [2017]; £1,630,231 [2016]; £1,588,934 [2015]; £1,180,523 [2014]; £1,081,063 [2013]

Hounslow Jamia Masjid and Islamic Centre
Registered: 9 Jan 1974 *Employees:* 33 *Volunteers:* 11
Tel: 020 8570 0938 *Website:* hounslowmasjid.co.uk
Activities: General charitable purposes; education, training; prevention or relief of poverty; overseas aid, famine relief; religious activities; economic, community development, employment
Address: 367 Wellington Road South, Hounslow, Middlesex, TW4 5HU
Trustees: Mr Mohammed Amin Chaudhry, Mr Shafiq Rehman, Mr Mohammad Rashad, Mr Mohammad Ajaib, Mr Qazi Saleem, Mr Wahid Hussain, Mr Chaudhry Abdul Majid, Mr Nadeem Akhtar, Mr Raja Jawaid Akhtar, Mr Raja Ghazanfar Ali, Mr Zubair Awan
Income: £1,289,284 [2017]; £1,235,186 [2016]; £1,162,339 [2015]; £1,103,960 [2014]; £987,014 [2013]

Hounslow Music Service
Registered: 26 Feb 2016 *Employees:* 66
Tel: 020 8583 2967 *Website:* houslowmusic.org.uk
Activities: Education, training; arts, culture, heritage, science; recreation
Address: Cast, Summit Centre, 4-6 School Road, Hounslow, Middlesex, TW3 1QZ
Trustees: Mr Charles Rupert Cautley Holderness, Oonagh Barry, Mrs Katherine Helen Bull, Mr Steven John Shotton
Income: £1,152,959 [2017]

The House of St Barnabas
Registered: 22 Sep 1962 *Employees:* 24 *Volunteers:* 50
Tel: 020 7437 1894 *Website:* hosb.org.uk
Activities: Education, training; prevention or relief of poverty; economic, community development, employment
Address: The House of St Barnabas, No 1 Greek Street, London, W1D 4NQ
Trustees: Mr Kevin Arnold, Mr Nigel Wright, Ms Frances Mary Mapstone, Mr Simon Close, Ms Jennifer Watson, Mr Warren Geoffrey Colquitt, Ms Esther Foreman, Ms Rachel Roxburgh
Income: £2,090,562 [2017]; £1,684,181 [2016]; £1,430,644 [2015]; £2,019,663 [2014]; £958,101 [2013]

The Housing Associations' Charitable Trust
Registered: 2 Apr 2003 *Employees:* 15
Tel: 020 7250 8500 *Website:* hact.org.uk
Activities: The prevention or relief of poverty; accommodation, housing; economic, community development, employment
Address: CAN Mezzanine, 49-51 East Road, London, N1 6AH
Trustees: Mr Babu Bhattacherjee, Ms Samantha Marie Hyde, Mrs Suzanne Rastrick, Mrs Jitinder Takhar, Mr John Wood, Mr Paul Jameson, Mr Gavin Cansfield, Mr Matthew Gardiner, Mrs Davida Johnson, Mr Boris Worrall, Mr Nick Atkin
Income: £1,064,230 [2017]; £1,107,381 [2016]; £1,666,465 [2015]; £1,166,043 [2014]; £1,111,290 [2013]

The Housing Link (2003)
Registered: 31 Jan 2003 *Employees:* 16
Tel: 0161 723 2040 *Website:* thehousinglink.org.uk
Activities: General charitable purposes; accommodation, housing
Address: 12 Mather Street, Radcliffe, Manchester, M26 4TL
Trustees: Mrs Sylvia Mason, Councillor Tony Cummings, Mike Priestley, Mr Wayne Campbell, Rebecca Heap, Mr Michael Chambers, Mr Anthony Isherwood
Income: £1,051,251 [2017]; £1,105,450 [2016]; £1,023,566 [2015]; £1,040,234 [2014]; £987,892 [2013]

Housing Pathways Trust
Registered: 2 Nov 1962
Tel: 020 8579 7411 *Website:* yourpathways.org.uk
Activities: General charitable purposes; prevention or relief of poverty; accommodation, housing; religious activities
Address: Housing Pathways, 33 Dean Court, London, W13 9YU
Trustees: Housing Pathways
Income: £1,247,136 [2017]; £1,371,210 [2016]; £1,557,382 [2015]; £1,040,778 [2014]; £988,612 [2013]

Housing Pathways
Registered: 4 Aug 2011 *Employees:* 10
Tel: 020 8579 7411 *Website:* yourpathways.org.uk
Activities: General charitable purposes; education, training; prevention or relief of poverty; accommodation, housing; economic, community development, employment
Address: Housing Pathways, 33 Dean Court, London, W13 9YU
Trustees: Mr Philip Young, Mr Stephen McNaughton, Mr Ross Tudor, Ms Katherine Yentumi, Mr Timothy Charles James Edwards, Ms Alice Maureen MacKenzie, Ms Janet Weekes
Income: £2,267,534 [2017]; £2,270,950 [2016]; £2,391,611 [2015]; £1,919,218 [2014]; £12,335,489 [2013]

Housing for Women
Registered: 8 Aug 1962 *Employees:* 58 *Volunteers:* 44
Tel: 020 7501 6120 *Website:* hfw.org.uk
Activities: The prevention or relief of poverty; accommodation, housing
Address: Housing for Women, Blue Star House, 234-240 Stockwell Road, London, SW9 9SP
Trustees: Mrs Caroline Donaldson, Safeena Allison, Dianne Hart, Ms Bernadtte O'Shea, Mr Mark Cooper, Ms Joanne Norris, Helen Webb, Ms Christine Pointer, Mr Christopher Worrall, Ms Anne Langton
Income: £8,174,704 [2016]; £7,431,553 [2015]; £6,805,514 [2014]; £6,300,547 [2013]; £5,749,449 [2012]

The Howard League for Penal Reform (incorporating The Howard Centre for Penology)
Registered: 18 May 1967 *Employees:* 20 *Volunteers:* 26
Tel: 020 7241 7891 *Website:* howardleague.org
Activities: General charitable purposes; education, training
Address: Howard League for Penal Reform, 1 Ardleigh Road, London, N1 4HS
Trustees: Professor Pamela Taylor, Ms Lucy Ann Scott-Moncrieff, Mr Gerald Marshall, Mr Eoin McLennan-Murray, Ms Elizabeth Morony, Samantha Kennedy, Ms Sally Lewis, Ms Danielle Vidal
Income: £1,070,386 [2017]; £1,102,864 [2016]; £916,067 [2015]; £1,459,145 [2014]; £1,471,832 [2013]

The Howe Green Educational Trust Limited
Registered: 10 Jul 1987 *Employees:* 40
Tel: 01279 501300 *Website:* howegreenhouseschool.co.uk
Activities: Education, training
Address: Howe Green House, Great Hallingbury, Bishop's Stortford, Herts, CM22 7UF
Trustees: Mr Paul Bashford, Elizabeth Lester, Ms Nicola Ann Barker-King, Mr Allan Stewart, Mr Robert Wood, Mr Simon Hutley, Mrs Amanda Cutlan-Smyth, Mrs Tanith Warwick-Watson, Mrs Alison White, Ms Hannah Petersen
Income: £1,560,691 [2016]; £1,497,022 [2015]; £1,537,476 [2014]; £1,510,259 [2013]

Howgill Family Centre

Registered: 12 Oct 1987 *Employees:* 58 *Volunteers:* 45
Tel: 01946 817900 *Website:* howgill-centre.co.uk
Activities: General charitable purposes; education, training; advancement of health or saving of lives; arts, culture, heritage, science; economic, community development, employment
Address: Howgill Family Centre, Birks Road, Cleator Moor, Cumbria, CA25 5HR
Trustees: Eric Holmes, Willie Slavin, Mr Geoffrey Toogood, Mrs Judith Mary Smith, Mr Ian Harvie, Neville Denson, Mrs Brenda Holden
Income: £1,296,265 [2017]; £1,340,618 [2016]; £1,457,807 [2015]; £1,515,468 [2014]; £1,440,309 [2013]

The Howletts Wild Animal Trust

Registered: 21 Nov 2003 *Employees:* 290 *Volunteers:* 68
Website: aspinallfoundation.org
Activities: General charitable purposes; education, training; animals; environment, conservation, heritage
Address: Howletts & Port Lympne Wild Animal Parks, Aldington Road, Lympne, Hythe, Kent, CT21 4PD
Trustees: Damian Aspinall, Miss Tansy Aspinall, Mr Amos Courage
Income: £12,429,617 [2016]; £10,703,487 [2015]; £11,673,385 [2014]; £10,883,507 [2013]; £10,714,413 [2012]

Hoylake Cottage

Registered: 18 Oct 1984 *Employees:* 130 *Volunteers:* 50
Tel: 0151 632 3381 *Website:* hoylakecottage.org.uk
Activities: The advancement of health or saving of lives; disability
Address: Hoylake Cottage, Birkenhead Road, Hoylake, Meols, Wirral, Merseyside, CH47 5AQ
Trustees: Stephen Heywood, Albert Mitchell, Mr James Southworth, Ann Boon, Mr Michael David Sutton, Mr Tony Twemlow, Mr Peter Wilcox, Mr Russell Oakden, Richard Holmes, Mrs Kathryn Rose Roberts
Income: £2,662,551 [2017]; £2,627,165 [2016]; £3,311,064 [2015]; £2,822,294 [2014]; £2,753,545 [2013]

Hubbub Foundation UK

Registered: 26 Sep 2014 *Employees:* 12 *Volunteers:* 130
Tel: 020 3701 7541 *Website:* hubbub.org.uk
Activities: Education, training; prevention or relief of poverty; environment, conservation, heritage; economic, community development, employment
Address: F60 First Floor, New Wing, Somerset House, Strand, London, WC2R 1LA
Trustees: Viki Cooke, Ms Catherine Brown, Ms Theresa Zoe Arden, Mr Simon Oswold, Mr Jonathan Katz, Mr Nicholas Flavelle Merriman, Mr James Stewart Murray, Mr Robert Leslie Gordon
Income: £1,480,921 [2016]; £629,400 [2015]

Huddersfield Christian Fellowship

Registered: 6 Dec 1983 *Employees:* 35 *Volunteers:* 300
Tel: 01484 514088 *Website:* huddersfieldchristianfellowship.com
Activities: Religious activities
Address: FAO Mr James Lewis, Cathedral House, St Thomas Road, Huddersfield, W Yorks, HD1 3LG
Trustees: Mr Stuart Gladstone, Mr James Norman Clarkson, Mr Jonathan Edward Skinner, Mr Jonathan Luke Nichols, Mr Colin James Campbell, Mr Adrian Smith, Mr James Adam Lewis, Mr Andrew James Goggins
Income: £1,788,183 [2017]; £2,056,060 [2016]; £1,886,931 [2015]; £2,064,328 [2014]; £1,798,149 [2013]

Huddersfield Community Trust

Registered: 31 Jan 2007 *Employees:* 66 *Volunteers:* 35
Tel: 01484 484172 *Website:* huddersfieldcommunitytrust.co.uk
Activities: Education, training; advancement of health or saving of lives; disability; prevention or relief of poverty; amateur sport; economic, community development, employment; recreation
Address: Huddersfield Community Trust, The Zone, off St Andrews Road, Huddersfield, W Yorks, HD1 6PT
Trustees: Mr Richard Leslie Thewlis, Mr Michael Farrar CBE, Mrs Tina Vink, Mr Jason Whitworth, Ms Helen Elizabeth Stevens, Ms Helen Laura Taylor
Income: £1,849,398 [2016]; £1,560,590 [2015]; £1,358,261 [2014]; £1,373,626 [2013]; £1,553,421 [2012]

The Hudson Foundation

Registered: 26 Jun 1980 *Employees:* 21
Tel: 01945 461456
Activities: General charitable purposes; accommodation, housing
Address: 1-3 York Row, Wisbech, Cambs, PE13 1EA
Trustees: David William Ball, Mr Stephen Henry Hutchinson, Mr Stephen Grounds Layton, Mr Edward Charles Newling
Income: £1,350,653 [2017]; £843,406 [2016]; £40,260 [2015]; £225,059 [2014]; £92,878 [2013]

Huggard

Registered: 28 Jun 1990 *Employees:* 48 *Volunteers:* 48
Tel: 029 2064 2000 *Website:* huggard.org.uk
Activities: Education, training; prevention or relief of poverty; accommodation, housing
Address: Huggard Centre, Huggard Buildings, Hansen Street, Cardiff, CF10 5DW
Trustees: Mr Stephen Thomas, Mr Ken Haines, Mr David Henry Shadbolt, Ms Janice Christine Hill, Mrs Andrina Rhiannon Matthewson, Mrs Diane Robbins, Mr David Williams
Income: £1,971,476 [2017]; £2,080,156 [2016]; £1,979,599 [2015]; £2,064,879 [2014]; £4,087,628 [2013]

The Frederick Hugh Trust

Registered: 10 Dec 2009 *Employees:* 16
Website: frederickhughhouse.com
Activities: Education, training; disability
Address: 45 Southsea Avenue, Leigh on Sea, Essex, SS9 2AX
Trustees: Mrs Anne Marie Carrie, Ms Amanda Rica Barclay, Mr William Brown
Income: £1,145,994 [2017]; £877,136 [2016]; £822,131 [2015]; £700,458 [2014]; £694,411 [2013]

E Ivor Hughes Educational Foundation

Registered: 10 Feb 1986 *Employees:* 34
Tel: 020 8427 8070
Activities: Education, training
Address: 1 Hamilton Road, Harrow, Middlesex, HA1 1SU
Trustees: Mr Andrew Olins, Mr Robert Brock, Mrs Lynn Denise Grimes, Mrs Andrea Aron, Mrs Penelope Ann Broadhurst, John Corcut
Income: £1,317,626 [2016]; £1,803,739 [2015]; £1,803,739 [2014]; £2,934,704 [2013]; £3,312,540 [2012]

Hughes Hall in the University of Cambridge

Registered: 13 Aug 2010 *Employees:* 51
Tel: 01223 334891 *Website:* hughes.cam.ac.uk
Activities: Education, training
Address: Hughes Hall, Wollaston Road, Cambridge, CB1 2EW
Trustees: Professor Ian Hodge, Dr Nigel Yandell, Dr Philip Johnston, Prof Mary Elizabeth Anne Buckley, Dr Bernard Devereux, Dr Nidhi Singal, Dr William Nuttall, Dr Elizabeth Swann, Dr Hilary Burton, Prof James Kaufman, Dr Ajith Parlikad, Dr Sara Hennessy, Dr Agnieszka Iwasiewicz-Wabnig, Prof Jonathan Powell, Dr Eugene Shwageraus, Dr Suzanne Turner, Dr Sonia Ilie, Dr Paul Tracey, Dr Martin Steinfeld, Dr Lydia Drumright, Dr Danika Hill, Dr Caroline Trotter, Dr Arne Jungwirth, Dr Lydia Drumright, Dr Mark Bale, Dr Jacob Stegenga, Dr Paula De Oliveira-Banca, Dr Stephen Axford, Dr Othman Cole, Dr Bart De Nijs, Dr Sarah Hoare, Dr Yury Korolev, Dr John Park, Dr Ricardo Sabates-Aysa, Prof Rupert Wegerif, Dr Anthony Freeling, Mrs Victoria Espley, Dr John Barker, Mr William Francis Charnley, Dr Jessica White, Dr Carole Anne Sargent, Prof Ming-Qing Du, Prof Michael Barrett, Dr Markus Gehring, Dr Alistair Lockhart, Dr Corinne Roughley, Dr Heather Blackmore, Dr Bianca Jupp, Dr Aisling Redmond, Dr Jeff Skopek, Dr Kishore Sengupta, Dr Peter Dudley, Mr Nick Gray, Dr Mark Bale, Dr Gishan Dissanaike, Dr Charles Pigott, Dr Andrew Mackintosh, Dr Clive Wells, Prof Gishan Dissanaike, Prof John Doorbar, Dr Miguel Fernando Gonzalez Zalba, Mr Mark Anderson, Dr Stephen Cave, Mr Martin Coleman, Prof Emanuele Giovannetti, Prof Bill Irish, Ms Lena Milosevic, Mr Tim Pilkington, Dr Andreas Stylianides, Dr Vanessa Wong
Income: £7,188,270 [2017]; £6,726,934 [2016]; £4,648,639 [2015]; £4,449,223 [2014]; £3,722,848 [2013]

Hughes Travel Trust

Registered: 13 Jun 1994 *Employees:* 5 *Volunteers:* 12
Tel: 020 8391 9740
Activities: Religious activities
Address: Hughes Travel Trust, Maxx House, Western Road, Bracknell, Berks, RG12 1QP
Trustees: Mr Arthur Lewis, Mr Philip C Aston, Mr Andrew Paterson, Mr Cyril David Parsons, Mr Andrew Turner
Income: £8,347,643 [2016]; £12,507,795 [2015]; £6,732,714 [2014]; £6,109,747 [2013]; £5,040,339 [2012]

Hull Community and Voluntary Services Ltd

Registered: 10 Oct 1983 *Employees:* 20 *Volunteers:* 62
Tel: 01482 324474 *Website:* hullcvs.org.uk
Activities: General charitable purposes; education, training; prevention or relief of poverty; economic, community development, employment
Address: Hull Community & Voluntary Services Ltd, 75 Beverley Road, Hull, HU3 1XL
Trustees: Mr Andrew Dorton, Rev Michael Hills, Mr Jonathan Slater, Ms Linda Tock, Ms Julie Robinson
Income: £2,000,806 [2017]; £2,443,483 [2016]; £2,491,439 [2015]; £849,073 [2014]; £540,052 [2013]

Hull Resettlement Project Limited

Registered: 30 Jan 1992 *Employees:* 24
Tel: 01482 585323
Activities: Accommodation, housing
Address: Hull Resettlement Project, 20 Bourne Street, Hull, HU2 8AE
Trustees: Mr Rob Batty, Rev Stephen Deas, Councillor Rilba Jones, Mr Ian Agius, Mrs Julia Lowery, Councillor Dean Kirk
Income: £1,231,521 [2017]; £1,186,769 [2016]; £944,807 [2015]; £923,558 [2014]; £888,690 [2013]

Hull Trinity House Charity

Registered: 9 Jan 1964 *Employees:* 32
Tel: 01482 324956 *Website:* trinityhousehull.org.uk
Activities: The prevention or relief of poverty; accommodation, housing
Address: Hull Trinity House Charity, Trinity House, Trinity House Lane, Hull, HU1 2JG
Trustees: Captain Brian Bradshaw Pearson, Captain John Dennis Coggin, Capt Philip Arthur Watts, Captain John Dennis Robinson, Captain David Henry Atkin, Captain John William Sutton, Captain Philip John Cowing, Captain Brian Morley Mitchell, Captain Michael Edward Taylor, Capt Stuart Leonard Gamble, Captain Cyril Bernard Middleton, Captain David Malcolm Shaw, Captain Raymond John Hancock, Captain John Tindall
Income: £1,765,750 [2017]; £1,780,085 [2016]; £1,787,748 [2015]; £1,607,283 [2014]; £1,801,817 [2013]

Hull Truck Theatre Company Limited

Registered: 24 Jun 1975 *Employees:* 54 *Volunteers:* 395
Tel: 01482 488230 *Website:* hulltruck.co.uk
Activities: Education, training; arts, culture, heritage, science
Address: Hull Truck Theatre, 50 Ferensway, Hull, HU2 8LB
Trustees: Mr Alan Dix, Ms Dawn Walton, Ms Jenni Grainger, Ms Helene O'Mullane Councillor, Mr Steve Gallant, Mrs Sophie Buckley, David W Gemmell, Mr David Hilton, Mr Alan Kirkman, Mr Paul Clay, Mr Anthony McReavy, Sharon Darley
Income: £2,573,472 [2017]; £1,954,180 [2016]; £2,141,475 [2015]; £2,075,548 [2014]; £2,858,139 [2013]

Hull University Union Limited

Registered: 21 Jun 2013 *Employees:* 80 *Volunteers:* 549
Tel: 01482 466255 *Website:* hullstudent.com
Activities: Education, training; arts, culture, heritage, science; amateur sport; recreation; other charitable purposes
Address: HUU University House, Cottingham Road, Hull, HU6 7RX
Trustees: Mr Stuart Ferguson, Andrew Paluszkiewicz, Mr Gaius Jonathan Powell, Miss Jennifer Watts, Miss Madeline Holden, Ms Rebekah Greaves, Ms Osaro Otobo, Mr Salman Anwar, Miss Kathryn Sharman, Mr Alan Bolchover
Income: £5,908,825 [2017]; £4,867,649 [2016]; £4,627,610 [2015]; £5,187,234 [2014]

Hull and East Riding Citizens Advice Bureau Ltd

Registered: 26 Oct 2004 *Employees:* 54 *Volunteers:* 129
Tel: 01482 328990 *Website:* hullandeastridingcab.org.uk
Activities: General charitable purposes; education, training; disability; prevention or relief of poverty; accommodation, housing
Address: The Wilson Centre, Alfred Gelder Street, Hull, HU1 2AG
Trustees: Mr Richard Primmer, Mrs Tracy-Jayne Wharvell, Mr Ryan Crellin, Ms Alex Holgate, Mr Bryan Jones, Mr David Bellenie, Mr Jim Doyle, Ms Judith Warnes
Income: £1,827,805 [2017]; £1,792,893 [2016]; £1,569,445 [2015]; £1,244,966 [2014]; £1,135,851 [2013]

Hull and East Yorkshire Medical Research Centre
Registered: 28 Jan 2003 *Employees:* 1
Tel: 01482 461909 *Website:* daisyappeal.org
Activities: Education, training; advancement of health or saving of lives
Address: The Daisy Appeal, Daisy Building, Castle Hill Hospital, Castle Road, Cottingham, E Yorks, HU16 5JQ
Trustees: Professor John Cleland, Prof N D Stafford, Mr Andrew Nigel Horncastle, Dr Assem Allam, Professor Peter Edward Dyer, Mr Michael Colin Auton, Miss Karen M Guest, Professor Michael John Lind, Mr T S E Boanas, Dr C A Rowland Hill, Mr Sydney Howey, Victoria Heuck, Mr John E Hartley, Mrs Lisa Bellsey
Income: £2,002,356 [2016]; £219,398 [2015]; £472,596 [2014]; £233,973 [2013]; £1,031,546 [2012]

Hull and East Yorkshire Mind
Registered: 9 Feb 2004 *Employees:* 52 *Volunteers:* 129
Tel: 01482 240200 *Website:* heymind.org.uk
Activities: Education, training; advancement of health or saving of lives; disability; accommodation, housing; arts, culture, heritage, science; amateur sport
Address: Wellington House, 108 Beverley Road, Hull, HU3 1YA
Trustees: Mr Alex Denholm, Mr Stephen Thomas Wakefield, Mr Mike Gill, Nathalie Louise Stewart, Mr David Richard Kitney, Mr Peter Christopher Wheatley, Mrs J Oraka, Mr Nick Smith, Mrs Vanessa Walker, Mr Peter Anthony Archer, Mrs Angela Catherine Mason
Income: £1,941,255 [2017]; £1,549,471 [2016]; £1,650,305 [2015]; £1,701,653 [2014]; £1,765,137 [2013]

Hulme Grammar Schools
Registered: 11 Aug 1966 *Employees:* 184
Tel: 0161 624 8442 *Website:* hulme-grammar.oldham.sch.uk
Activities: Education, training
Address: The Oldham Hulme Grammar Schools, Chamber Road, Oldham, Lancs, OL8 4BX
Trustees: Mr Stuart Illingworth, Mrs Valerie Stocker LLB, Mr Kevin Sanders, Mr Richard Brian Lobley ARICS, Mr Zahid Chauhan, Mr Ian Mills, Jack Williams, Mr Andrew Milnes BA FCA, Mr Vijay Srivastava LLB, Mrs Ann Richards, Mr Jeremy Sutcliffe BA MEd, Mr David Mark Meredith, John Greenwood
Income: £7,670,688 [2017]; £8,106,780 [2016]; £8,006,494 [2015]; £7,881,297 [2014]; £8,342,394 [2013]

Hulme Hall Educational Trust Limited
Registered: 16 Mar 1965 *Employees:* 65
Tel: 0161 485 3524 *Website:* hulmehallschool.org
Activities: Education, training
Address: Hulme Hall School, 75 Hulme Hall Road, Cheadle Hulme, Cheadle, Cheshire, SK8 6LA
Trustees: Mr Timothy Lowe, Mr Andrew Richard Stripe, Mr Paul Wise, Mr John Shackelton, Mr Eain Hodge, Mr Sean Adams, Mr Sam Moore
Income: £1,928,895 [2017]; £2,118,552 [2016]; £2,332,899 [2015]; £1,981,162 [2014]; £2,102,165 [2013]

Hult International Business School Ltd
Registered: 31 May 2002 *Employees:* 105
Tel: 020 7636 5667 *Website:* hult.edu
Activities: Education, training
Address: 35 Commercial Road, London, E1 1LD
Trustees: Mr David Lloyd Bennett, Mr Bo Anders Harald Schoug, Mr Fredrik Henriksson, Mr Ravindra Kirthi Goonesena, Mr Reina Ingemar Beltzer
Income: £32,048,744 [2016]; £28,885,553 [2015]; £22,310,465 [2014]; £20,472,347 [2013]; £15,030,260 [2012]

Human Aid UK
Registered: 17 Sep 2010 *Employees:* 7 *Volunteers:* 60
Tel: 020 7650 8922 *Website:* human-aid.org
Activities: General charitable purposes; education, training; advancement of health or saving of lives; prevention or relief of poverty; overseas aid, famine relief; accommodation, housing; arts, culture, heritage, science; economic, community development, employment; human rights, religious or racial harmony, equality or diversity
Address: East London Business Centre, 93-101 Greenfield Road, London, E1 1EJ
Trustees: Mr Mahmudur Rashid Khan, Mr Abdullah-Fahim Tozoful Miah
Income: £1,375,604 [2017]; £679,104 [2016]; £779,283 [2015]; £1,006,510 [2014]; £250,211 [2013]

Human Appeal
Registered: 21 Oct 2013 *Employees:* 104 *Volunteers:* 4,000
Tel: 0161 225 0225 *Website:* humanappeal.org.uk
Activities: General charitable purposes; education, training; advancement of health or saving of lives; prevention or relief of poverty; overseas aid, famine relief
Address: Human Appeal, 1 Cheadle Point, Carrs Road, Cheadle, Cheshire, SK8 2BL
Trustees: Dr Hussein Nagi, Mr Mohamad Hamed Ahmad Yousef, Mr Imad Zahidah, Mr Kamil Omoteso
Income: £36,493,079 [2016]; £30,551,733 [2015]; £21,227,051 [2014]

Human Capability Foundation
Registered: 15 Dec 2011
Tel: 07531 098972 *Website:* humancapabilityfoundation.com
Activities: General charitable purposes; education, training; advancement of health or saving of lives; prevention or relief of poverty; overseas aid, famine relief; environment, conservation, heritage; human rights, religious or racial harmony, equality or diversity
Address: Flat 49, Bishops Court, 76 Bishops Bridge Road, London, W2 6BE
Trustees: Mr Luke Pagarani BA 1st(Cam) Post Grad Cert in Maths, Mr Davinder Pagarani Ba 1st Philosophy & English, Miss Natasha Pagarani BMus 1st
Income: £1,464,628 [2016]; £500,000 [2015]; £1,616,616 [2014]; £560,000 [2013]; £1,330,092 [2012]

Human Care Foundation Worldwide
Registered: 15 Dec 2011 *Employees:* 4 *Volunteers:* 120
Tel: 020 7118 9596 *Website:* humancaresyria.org
Activities: General charitable purposes; education, training; advancement of health or saving of lives; prevention or relief of poverty; overseas aid, famine relief
Address: Suite 1A, 3rd Floor, Alperton House, Bridgewater Road, Wembley, Middlesex, HA0 1EH
Trustees: Hamza Alsibaai, Dr Ahmad Abdul-Rahman, Mr Hassan Walid
Income: £1,317,454 [2016]; £754,065 [2015]; £1,133,172 [2014]; £927,086 [2013]; £362,697 [2012]

Human Relief Foundation
Registered: 14 Oct 2008 *Employees:* 50 *Volunteers:* 100
Tel: 01274 392727 *Website:* hrf.org.uk
Activities: The prevention or relief of poverty; overseas aid, famine relief
Address: Human Relief Foundation, P O Box 194, Bradford, BD7 1YW
Trustees: Dr Haytham Al-Khaffaf, Dr Haitham Al-Rawi, Mr Bara Abdul-Salam, Mr Mohanned Rahman, Mr Suhail Sharief
Income: £5,650,169 [2016]; £4,089,641 [2015]; £3,838,824 [2014]; £3,952,093 [2013]; £4,277,435 [2012]

The Humane Society International (UK)
Registered: 11 Aug 2003 *Employees:* 7 *Volunteers:* 1
Tel: 020 3174 2185 *Website:* hsiuk.org
Activities: Animals; environment, conservation, heritage
Address: HSI UK, 5 Underwood Street, London, N1 7LY
Trustees: Mr Andrew Rowan, Mr Wayne Pacelle, Mr Tom Waite
Income: £1,745,654 [2016]; £2,541,070 [2015]; £1,092,258 [2014]; £1,254,893 [2013]; £1,102,374 [2012]

Humanitarian Leadership Academy
Registered: 11 May 2015 *Employees:* 26 *Volunteers:* 1
Tel: 020 3763 0381 *Website:* humanitarianleadershipacademy.org
Activities: General charitable purposes; education, training; advancement of health or saving of lives; prevention or relief of poverty; overseas aid, famine relief
Address: Humanitarian Leadership Academy, 1 St John's Lane, London, EC1M 4AR
Trustees: Mr Mark Ian Goldring CBE, Ms Fiona McBain, Mr Jeffrey Tarayao, Professor Funmi Olonisakin, Mrs Rebecca Marmot, Dr Ahmed Mushtaque Raza Chowdhury, Mrs Janti Soeripto, Dr Jemilah Mahmood, Ambassador Hesham Yousseff, Mr Richard George Winter
Income: £6,432,629 [2016]; £1,104,702 [2015]

Humber Learning Consortium
Registered: 1 May 2003 *Employees:* 25
Tel: 01482 327438 *Website:* hlc-vol.org
Activities: Education, training
Address: 63-71 Anlaby Road, Hull, HU3 2LL
Trustees: Clive Darnell, Mr Gavin Paul Betts, Mr Paul Nicholson, Kathryn Sowerby, Mrs Lynn Benton
Income: £5,157,961 [2017]; £4,949,821 [2016]; £5,906,694 [2015]; £1,903,930 [2014]; £3,791,983 [2013]

Humbercare Limited
Registered: 7 Dec 1989 *Employees:* 140 *Volunteers:* 96
Website: humbercare.co.uk
Activities: General charitable purposes; education, training; disability; prevention or relief of poverty; accommodation, housing
Address: Humbercare Ltd, Elan Lodge, 81 Beverley Road, Hull, HU3 1XR
Trustees: Mrs Georgina McArthur Ziae, Mr Paul Robinson, David Walker, Mrs Lesley Ann Alderson-Speight
Income: £4,738,689 [2017]; £3,590,271 [2016]; £2,040,298 [2015]; £1,689,503 [2014]; £1,640,314 [2013]

Humberside Engineering Training Association Limited
Registered: 31 May 1979 *Employees:* 70
Tel: 01482 826635 *Website:* heta.co.uk
Activities: Education, training; economic, community development, employment
Address: Humberside Engineering Training Association, Copenhagen Road, Hull, HU7 0XJ
Trustees: Mr Richard Mark Swain, Mr John Gerard Weir, Mr Robert Bryan Charles Ripley, Mr David Paul Sowden, Mr Ashley John Hepton, Dr Malcolm Tony Joslin, Mr Ian Christopher Palmer, Mr Timothy Mottershead, Mrs Louise Maloigne
Income: £6,027,766 [2017]; £5,631,928 [2016]; £5,235,569 [2015]; £5,165,532 [2014]; £5,204,983 [2013]

Humberside Offshore Training Association
Registered: 18 Feb 1988 *Employees:* 43
Tel: 01482 820567 *Website:* hota.org
Activities: Education, training
Address: Humberside Offshore Training Association Ltd, Malmo Road, Hull, HU7 0YF
Trustees: Miss Linda Ellis, Mr Michael James Gibbons, Mr Neil McCracken, Mr Mark Walter Hoddinott, Mr Ian James Livingston, Mr Mark Austin Ranson, Mr Andrew Martin Rhodes, Mrs Victoria Irene Jackson, Ian Richard Coates
Income: £2,234,702 [2016]; £2,135,266 [2015]; £2,592,722 [2014]; £2,473,318 [2013]; £2,505,276 [2012]

Humentum UK
Registered: 3 Jul 2000 *Employees:* 25
Tel: 01865 423818 *Website:* mango.org.uk
Activities: Education, training; prevention or relief of poverty; overseas aid, famine relief
Address: Mango, Chester House, 21-27 George Street, Oxford, OX1 2AY
Trustees: Mr Toby Porter, Tamara Lynn Ward-Dahl, Mrs Helen McEachern, Kim Schwartz
Income: £1,884,000 [2016]; £1,663,000 [2015]; £1,621,000 [2014]; £2,270,000 [2013]; £1,293,030 [2011]

The Hunslet Club
Registered: 29 May 2008 *Employees:* 50 *Volunteers:* 104
Tel: 0113 271 6489 *Website:* hunsletclub.org.uk
Activities: Education, training; amateur sport; economic, community development, employment
Address: Hunslet Club, Hillidge Road, Leeds, LS10 1BP
Trustees: Mr Andrew Geoffrey Beadnall, Mr Rupert Arnold, Eric Lumley, Mrs Rachel Roberts, Clifford Spracklen, Mr Peter Cyril Robert Lewis, Mr Tom Holliday, Mr Richard Shaw
Income: £1,463,521 [2016]; £1,420,939 [2015]; £1,390,539 [2014]; £1,226,703 [2013]; £1,323,116 [2012]

Huntingdon Mencap Society Limited
Registered: 5 Feb 2004 *Employees:* 39
Tel: 01480 450596
Activities: The advancement of health or saving of lives; disability
Address: Huntingdon Mencap Society, Stanley House, 11 Orchard Lane, Huntingdon, Cambs, PE29 3QT
Trustees: Mr Stephen Anthony Moss, Mrs Pauline Theresa Robson, Mrs Wendy Law, Mrs Anne Aldred, Miss Danielle Law
Income: £1,040,604 [2017]; £976,800 [2016]; £1,014,450 [2015]; £903,279 [2014]; £783,745 [2013]

Huntingtons Disease Association

Registered: 20 Mar 1987 *Employees:* 35 *Volunteers:* 2,000
Tel: 0151 331 5444 *Website:* hda.org.uk
Activities: Education, training; advancement of health or saving of lives; disability; prevention or relief of poverty
Address: Suite 24, The Liverpool Science Park, Innovation Centre 1, 131 Mount Pleasant, Liverpool, L3 5TF
Trustees: Mr Nicholas Heath, Matt Ellison, Dr George El-Nimr, Christine Clarke, Mrs Catherine Lyon, Dr Elizabeth Mary Howard, Andrew Bickerdike, Prof Hugh Rickards, Dr Alan Fryer, Mrs Sian Baker
Income: £1,531,987 [2017]; £1,677,940 [2016]; £1,390,133 [2015]; £1,393,939 [2014]; £1,779,438 [2013]

Huo Family Foundation (UK) Limited

Registered: 9 Dec 2009
Tel: 020 7597 6427
Activities: General charitable purposes; education, training; arts, culture, heritage, science
Address: Withers Ltd, 16 Old Bailey, London, EC4M 7EG
Trustees: Mr Yan Huo, Mr Philip J Michaels, Mrs Xue Fang, Mr Samuel Xun-Wei Lowe
Income: £35,876,540 [2016]; £12,887,242 [2015]; £5,682,028 [2014]; £3,494,534 [2013]; £6,099,068 [2012]

Hurdale Charity Limited

Registered: 6 Apr 1979
Activities: Education, training; advancement of health or saving of lives; religious activities
Address: 162 Osbaldeston Road, London, N16 6NJ
Trustees: Mr Abraham Oestreicher, Mr David Oestreicher, Mr Benjamin Oestreicher, Mr Jacob Oestreicher
Income: £1,735,986 [2017]; £1,511,461 [2016]; £1,321,929 [2015]; £1,192,266 [2014]; £1,171,539 [2013]

Hurstpierpoint College Limited

Registered: 12 Jul 1999 *Employees:* 377 *Volunteers:* 10
Tel: 01273 833636 *Website:* hppc.co.uk
Activities: Education, training
Address: Hurstpierpoint College, College Lane, Hurstpierpoint, Hassocks, W Sussex, BN6 9JS
Trustees: Anthony Jarvis, Robert Ebdon, Dr Sadhana Brydie, Paul Dillon-Robinson, George Rushton, Mrs Fran Hampton, Jonathan Chocqueel-Mangan, Professor Jonathan Bacon, John Taysom, Karen Mack, Kevin Powell, Lesley Corbett
Income: £22,743,000 [2017]; £21,881,000 [2016]; £20,675,000 [2015]; £20,246,000 [2014]; £19,019,000 [2013]

Hyelm

Registered: 27 Feb 1963 *Employees:* 7
Tel: 020 7336 9000 *Website:* hyelm.com
Activities: Accommodation, housing; amateur sport
Address: Hyelm, 43-51 New North Road, London, N1 6JB
Trustees: Mr Keith Scott Douglas, Mr Wayne Willis, Mrs Charlotte Zelia Paxton, Mr Joel Inbakumar, Mr Graham Briscoe, Ms Helen Taylor, Ms Joanne Clare Foster, Ms Ruth Goldfeather
Income: £1,337,151 [2017]; £1,359,912 [2016]; £24,150,610 [2015]; £2,117,186 [2014]; £2,270,028 [2013]

Hymers College

Registered: 15 Mar 1967 *Employees:* 188 *Volunteers:* 8
Tel: 01482 470224 *Website:* hymerscollege.co.uk
Activities: Education, training; other charitable purposes
Address: 83 Hymers Avenue, Hull, HU3 1LL
Trustees: Mrs Nicola Shipley, Mrs Glenda Greendale, Mr John Maybin Vivian Redman, John Robinson, Mr Martin C S Hall, Mr Dominic Anthony Gibbons, Kit Read, Professor Glenn Burgess, Mr John Ferdinand Connolly, Mrs Elizabeth Anne Maliakal, Mr Michael Roberts, Mr Peter Wildsmith, Mr Jamie Wheldon, Mr P Adrian B Beecroft, Mrs Tracey Carruthers, Dr Ashok Pathak, Mr William Hornby Gore, Mrs Gemma Victoria Vickerman, Dr Georgina Gateshill, Mr Jonathan Leafe
Income: £9,424,536 [2016]; £9,636,194 [2015]; £8,858,722 [2014]; £8,678,835 [2013]; £8,472,610 [2012]

Hymns Ancient and Modern Limited

Registered: 15 Sep 1975 *Employees:* 67
Tel: 01603 785908 *Website:* hymnsam.co.uk
Activities: Religious activities
Address: Hymns Ancient & Modern Ltd, 13a Hellesdon Park Road, Drayton High Road, Norwich, NR6 5DR
Trustees: Rt Rev S G Platten, Rev Paula Vennells, Rev Dr Simon Matthew Jones, Ms Sumita Honey, Mr Christopher Adams
Income: £7,328,886 [2017]; £7,551,002 [2016]; £7,321,323 [2015]; £7,376,934 [2014]; £7,147,778 [2013]

Hyndburn Leisure

Registered: 11 Feb 2002 *Employees:* 67 *Volunteers:* 40
Tel: 01254 380134 *Website:* hyndburnleisure.co.uk
Activities: Arts, culture, heritage, science; amateur sport; recreation
Address: Hyndburn Leisure, Town Hall, Blackburn Road, Accrington, Lancs, BB5 1LA
Trustees: Mr Peter Britcliffe, Mrs Irene Ryan, Mrs Anne Ellwood, Mr Ken Moss, Mr Patrick Swanney, Mr Brian Roberts, Mr Ciaran Wells, Mr Andrew O'Brien, Ms Marie Demaine, Mr Peter Baron
Income: £2,389,765 [2017]; £2,429,957 [2016]; £2,611,454 [2015]; £2,650,634 [2014]; £2,487,629 [2013]

Hyperlipidaemia Education & Atherosclerosis Research Trust UK

Registered: 27 Aug 1991 *Employees:* 10 *Volunteers:* 103
Tel: 01628 777046 *Website:* heartuk.org.uk
Activities: Education, training; advancement of health or saving of lives
Address: 7 North Road, Maidenhead, Berks, SL6 1PE
Trustees: Professor Elizabeth Hughes, Dr John Alan Rees, Ms Gaenor Howells, Dr Robert Cramb, Ms Joanne Bennett, Ms Tricia Kennerley, Mr Bryan Dobson, Andrew Greaves, Dr John Phillip David Reckless, Mr Stephen Boley, Dr Dermot Neely, Zoe Merchant, Mr Raymond Brunton Edwards, Dr Peter Green, Sandy Kerr
Income: £1,177,560 [2017]; £793,055 [2016]; £766,009 [2015]; £820,986 [2014]; £679,422 [2013]

Hywel DDA Health Charities

Registered: 28 Jun 2012
Tel: 01267 227675 *Website:* howis.wales.nhs.uk
Activities: Education, training; advancement of health or saving of lives
Address: Mrs Karen Miles, Ystwyth, Hafan Derwen, St David's Park, Jobswell Road, Carmarthen, SA31 3BB
Trustees: Hywel Dda University Local Health Board
Income: £1,427,379 [2017]; £947,873 [2016]; £1,030,530 [2015]; £852,307 [2014]; £1,086,644 [2013]

The I T F Seafarers Trust
Registered: 20 Feb 1981 *Employees:* 5
Tel: 020 7940 9305 *Website:* seafarerstrust.org
Activities: General charitable purposes; education, training; advancement of health or saving of lives; disability; prevention or relief of poverty; overseas aid, famine relief; accommodation, housing; amateur sport; economic, community development, employment; human rights, religious or racial harmony, equality or diversity; recreation
Address: International Transport Workers' Federation, 49-60 Borough Road, London, SE1 1DR
Trustees: Mr Brian Orrell, Mr Dave Heindel, Stephen Cotton, Mr Lars Lindgren, Mr Paddy Crumlin, Mr Abdulgani Serang, Ms Jacqueline Smith
Income: £5,200,255 [2016]; £1,861,147 [2015]; £11,696,520 [2014]; £7,721,407 [2013]; £1,602,032 [2012]

IBM United Kingdom Trust
Registered: 29 Oct 1984
Activities: General charitable purposes; education, training; advancement of health or saving of lives; disability; prevention or relief of poverty; overseas aid, famine relief; arts, culture, heritage, science; economic, community development, employment; armed forces, emergency service efficiency; human rights, religious or racial harmony, equality or diversity; other charitable purposes
Address: IBM United Kingdom Ltd, 76 Upper Ground, London, SE1 9PZ
Trustees: Professor Derek Bell, Naomi Hill, Mrs Anne Wolfe, Mr Andrew Gerrard Fitzgerald
Income: £1,011,000 [2016]; £938,000 [2015]; £2,874,000 [2014]; £1,891,000 [2013]; £2,824,000 [2012]

ICAEW Foundation
Registered: 28 Sep 1962 *Employees:* 15
Tel: 020 7920 8755 *Website:* icaew.com
Activities: General charitable purposes; education, training
Address: Chartered Accountants' Hall, 1 Moorgate Place, London, EC2R 6EA
Trustees: Chartered Accountants' Trustees Limited
Income: £1,496,577 [2016]; £1,962,688 [2015]; £1,961,274 [2014]; £2,204,237 [2013]; £2,058,736 [2012]

ICAN Charity
Registered: 9 May 1967 *Employees:* 191 *Volunteers:* 11
Tel: 020 7843 2545 *Website:* ican.org.uk
Activities: Education, training
Address: 31 Angel Gate, Goswell Road, London, EC1V 2PT
Trustees: Professor Vicky Joffe, Mrs Katharine Weston, Mr Charles Newman, Mrs Susan Patricia Gregory, Mr David Huw Davies, Mr Riccardo Basile, Mr Adrian Joseph Hosford, Mr Oliver Robert Hunter Bates, Mrs Jean Elizabeth Ogilvie Gross, Dr Judy Clegg, Mr Stuart Michael Shepley
Income: £7,793,000 [2017]; £8,417,000 [2016]; £9,123,000 [2015]; £9,358,000 [2014]; £8,956,000 [2013]

ICC Missions
Registered: 21 May 2002 *Employees:* 30 *Volunteers:* 1,294
Tel: 020 8505 9146 *Website:* iccmissions.org
Activities: The prevention or relief of poverty; religious activities
Address: Tower Bridge House, St Katherine's Way, London, E1W 1DD
Trustees: Mr Peter Frost, Mr Dwight Lawrence, Mr Michael Joseph Farrell, Mr Ian Tootill, Mr Andrew Agerbak, Mr Scott Walter Douglas Bryden
Income: £2,147,886 [2016]; £2,052,000 [2015]; £1,940,000 [2014]; £1,761,000 [2013]; £1,393,000 [2012]

ICE Benevolent Fund
Registered: 6 Nov 2008 *Employees:* 4 *Volunteers:* 63
Tel: 01444 417979 *Website:* icebenfund.com
Activities: Education, training; advancement of health or saving of lives; disability; prevention or relief of poverty; accommodation, housing
Address: 5 Mill Hill Close, Haywards Heath, W Sussex, RH16 1NY
Trustees: Mr William R Kemp MBE CEng FICE, Mr Colin Hillary CEng MICE, Mr Brian Waters MBE CEng FICE, Ms Yvonne Murphy CEng MICE, Mr Michael Chater CEng FICE, Mr Jon Sturgess CEng FICE, Mr Edwin J S Hiscocks CEng MICE, Mr David Orr CBE CEng FICE, Mr Andrew Scrimgeour EngTech TMICE, Mr Tom Barton CEng FICE, Mr David Porter CEng FICE, Mr Ian Gee CEng MICE
Income: £1,401,738 [2016]; £1,568,677 [2015]; £1,203,734 [2014]; £1,178,265 [2013]; £1,104,219 [2012]

IES London The London Centre of The Institute for The International Education of Students (Illinois) Limited
Registered: 16 Nov 1984 *Employees:* 37
Tel: 020 7299 4420
Activities: Education, training
Address: IES London, 5 Bloomsbury Place, London, WC1A 2QP
Trustees: Mr Geoffrey Bennett, Ms Kimberly Cameron, Mr William Hoye
Income: £4,955,480 [2017]; £4,518,593 [2016]; £1,982,049 [2015]; £4,343,729 [2014]; £3,779,145 [2013]

IHG Foundation (UK) Trust
Registered: 10 Dec 2015 *Volunteers:* 2
Tel: 020 7655 1780
Activities: Education, training; advancement of health or saving of lives; environment, conservation, heritage
Address: IHG Foundation, Broadwater Park, Denham, Bucks, UB9 5HR
Trustees: Ms Emily Kathryn Gibson, Nick Watson, Jennifer Laing, George Turner
Income: £2,048,431 [2016]

IM01 Limited
Registered: 19 Sep 2011 *Employees:* 11
Tel: 020 7148 0290 *Website:* inter-mediate.org
Activities: Human rights, religious or racial harmony, equality or diversity; other charitable purposes
Address: 3 Dean Trench Street, London, SW1P 3HB
Trustees: Lord Stevenson, Ms Lyse Doucet, Lady Jasmine Zerinini, Sir Sebastian John Lechmere Roberts, Michael Hatchard, Mr Eamonn McGrath
Income: £2,079,995 [2017]; £1,504,044 [2016]; £1,685,887 [2015]; £950,426 [2014]; £1,198,603 [2013]

IOL Educational Trust
Registered: 25 Jan 2002 *Employees:* 17
Tel: 020 7940 3100 *Website:* ciol.org.uk
Activities: Education, training
Address: IOL Educational Trust, Dunstan House, 14a St Cross Street, London, EC1N 8XA
Trustees: Mr Michael Cunningham, Mr George Zhang, Ms Bernadette Susan Holmes, Ms Karen Elizabeth Stokes, Mr Keith Moffitt, Prof Christopher John Pountain, Ms Helen Jean Laura Campbell, Mrs Anne Elizabeth Stevens
Income: £1,356,732 [2016]; £1,311,943 [2015]; £1,155,234 [2014]; £1,331,066 [2013]; £1,332,727 [2012]

IOM Communications Ltd
Registered: 3 Dec 1996
Tel: 020 7451 7300 *Website:* iom3.org
Activities: Education, training
Address: The Institute of Materials Minerals & Mining, 297 Euston Road, London, NW1 3AQ
Trustees: Dr BA Rickinson, Mr Jan Charles Hugh Lewis CEnv FIMMM, Mick May, Dr Stephen John Garwood, Mr Keith Shankland, Dr A T Cole, Prof Lindsay Greer, Dr Andrew John Tinker
Income: £2,171,908 [2016]; £2,162,568 [2015]; £3,393,710 [2014]; £3,910,059 [2013]; £4,355,113 [2012]

ISSA Foundation
Registered: 14 Mar 2016 *Employees:* 2 *Volunteers:* 10
Tel: 07590 275134
Activities: General charitable purposes
Address: Euro Garages Ltd, Haslingden Road, Blackburn, BB1 2EE
Trustees: Mr Mohsin Issa, Mr Zuber Issa
Income: £15,045,257 [2016]

ITEC North East Limited
Registered: 14 Oct 1987 *Employees:* 26
Tel: 01325 320052 *Website:* itecne.co.uk
Activities: Education, training; economic, community development, employment
Address: ITEC North East Limited, The Digital Factory, Durham Way South, Aycliffe Business Park, Newton Aycliffe, Co Durham, DL5 6XP
Trustees: Mr Geoffrey Brown, Mr Graham Wood, Mr Stephen William Bellwood, Mrs Tracy Ann Wilson
Income: £1,484,477 [2017]; £1,880,425 [2016]; £1,628,333 [2015]; £1,909,515 [2014]; £1,968,239 [2013]

IVCC
Registered: 5 Mar 2009 *Employees:* 14
Website: ivcc.com
Activities: The advancement of health or saving of lives; economic, community development, employment
Address: School of Tropical Medicine, Pembroke Place, Liverpool, L3 5QA
Trustees: Mr Jeremy Lefroy MP, Mr Fred Binka, Sir Mark Moody-Stuart, Prof Qiyong Liu, Mr Pascal Housset, Right Honourable Stephen O'Brien, Mr Anthony David Brandling-Bennett, Mr Martin James Peter Cooke, Ms Karmen Bennett, Mr Richard Walter Steketee
Income: £20,369,000 [2017]; £18,578,000 [2016]; £9,914,000 [2015]; £8,793,000 [2014]; £8,299,000 [2013]

Ibad-Ur-Rahman Trust
Registered: 24 May 1982 *Employees:* 20
Tel: 0161 740 3696 *Website:* thejamiamosque.org
Activities: General charitable purposes; education, training; prevention or relief of poverty; overseas aid, famine relief; religious activities; amateur sport; other charitable purposes
Address: 8 Boardman Road, Manchester, M8 4WJ
Trustees: Maulana Azmi, Ghulam Hassan, Dawood Fozdar, Mr Khadim Hussain, Mr Irfan Hanif
Income: £1,277,699 [2017]; £545,533 [2016]; £382,188 [2015]; £495,117 [2014]; £435,428 [2013]

Ibstock Place School
Registered: 20 Jan 2012 *Employees:* 158
Website: ibstockplaceschool.co.uk
Activities: Education, training
Address: Ibstock Place School, Clarence Lane, London, SW15 5PY
Trustees: Lt Col Robert Cartwright, Mr Richard Jackson, Mr Peter Walker, Mrs Susan Parsons, Mr Jeremy Allen, Mr Sean O'Brien, Mr Christopher Tanfield, His Hon Judge Fergus Mitchell
Income: £16,914,729 [2017]; £16,674,024 [2016]; £15,216,976 [2015]; £14,859,244 [2014]; £13,988,626 [2013]

The Iceland Foods Charitable Foundation
Registered: 3 Mar 1981
Tel: 01244 842885 *Website:* ifcf.org.uk
Activities: General charitable purposes
Address: Second Avenue, Deeside Industrial Park, Deeside, Flintshire, CH5 2NW
Trustees: Mr Tarsem Singh Dhaliwal, Mr Richard Malcolm Walker, Mr Malcolm Walker
Income: £6,798,817 [2017]; £3,342,960 [2016]; £1,310,940 [2015]; £2,219,166 [2014]; £142,653 [2013]

Ichthus Christian Fellowship
Registered: 12 Sep 2003 *Employees:* 14 *Volunteers:* 300
Tel: 020 8694 7171 *Website:* ichthus.org.uk
Activities: Education, training; prevention or relief of poverty; religious activities
Address: Ichthus Christian Fellowship, c/o Armstrong & Co, 4b Printing House Yard, Hackney Road, London, E2 7PR
Trustees: Dr Robert George, Mr D Pharoah, Mr James William Chapman CEng, Roger Forster, Faith Forster, Mr David Jules Steinegger
Income: £1,681,651 [2017]; £1,006,404 [2016]; £966,112 [2015]; £985,556 [2014]; £1,074,855 [2013]

If...
Registered: 27 Jan 2003
Website: ifcharity.org.uk
Activities: General charitable purposes; education, training; advancement of health or saving of lives; disability; prevention or relief of poverty; overseas aid, famine relief; environment, conservation, heritage; economic, community development, employment
Address: 32 Store Street, London, E15 1PU
Trustees: Mr Ismail Ginwalla, Mr Hachmi Bannani, Mr Ibrahim Sayam
Income: £1,634,237 [2016]; £427,403 [2015]; £3,031,085 [2014]; £300,000 [2013]; £396,724 [2012]

Iglesia ni Cristo (Church of Christ)
Registered: 3 Sep 1973 *Employees:* 40 *Volunteers:* 1,000
Tel: 01932 755422
Activities: General charitable purposes; religious activities
Address: Iglesia ni Cristo, 79 Staines Road West, Sunbury on Thames, Surrey, TW16 7AH
Trustees: Mr Gerry B Sison, Mr Eduardo V Manalo, Mr Ernesto V Suratos, Mr Radel G Cortez, Mr Harley Alcantara, Mr Allistair Cagnayo, Mr Vernon J Cunanan, Mr Bienvenido C Santiago, Mr Glicerio B Santos Jr, Mrs Dorothy Kristine M Orosa, Mr Philip Velasquez
Income: £6,248,113 [2016]; £4,646,386 [2015]; £5,532,483 [2014]; £5,643,942 [2013]; £9,093,502 [2012]

Ikon Gallery Limited
Registered: 31 Jul 1967 *Employees:* 23
Tel: 0121 248 0708 *Website:* ikon-gallery.org
Activities: Education, training; arts, culture, heritage, science
Address: Ikon Gallery, 1 Oozells Square, Birmingham, B1 2HS
Trustees: Mr John Claughton, Mr Oliver David Longmore, Mr Tristan Chatfield, Professor Helen Elisabeth Higson OBE, Ms Jenny Loynton, Ms Victoria Tester
Income: £1,407,400 [2017]; £2,136,513 [2016]; £1,523,371 [2015]; £1,699,315 [2014]; £2,314,930 [2013]

Illuminated River Foundation
Registered: 21 Jul 2016 *Employees:* 3
Tel: 020 3598 6317
Activities: Arts, culture, heritage, science
Address: J Rothschild Services Ltd, Windmill Hill, Silk Street, Waddesdon, Aylesbury, Bucks, HP18 0JZ
Trustees: Mr Neil Francis Jeremy Mendoza, Munira Mirza, The Hon Hannah Rothschild, Fabia Bromovsky
Income: £5,456,662 [2017]

Imagine Act and Succeed
Registered: 11 May 2011 *Employees:* 505
Tel: 01942 807009 *Website:* imagineactandsucceed.co.uk
Activities: Education, training; advancement of health or saving of lives; disability
Address: 110 Church Street, Leigh, Lancs, WN7 2DB
Trustees: Mr Paul Cassidy, Mr Steve Howard, Mr Martin Routledge, Mr Peter Rowlinson, Miss Katrina Waring, Mrs Beverley Latham
Income: £8,844,518 [2017]; £8,199,791 [2016]; £7,841,423 [2015]; £8,934,276 [2014]; £9,647,886 [2013]

Imagine Independence
Registered: 30 Mar 1992 *Employees:* 193 *Volunteers:* 105
Tel: 0151 709 2366 *Website:* imagineindependence.org.uk
Activities: General charitable purposes; education, training; advancement of health or saving of lives; disability; accommodation, housing
Address: Imagine Independence, 25 Hope Street, Liverpool, L1 9BQ
Trustees: Mr Irfon Clarke, Mrs Geraldine Poole, Ms Pauline Berry, Ms Jennifer Ann Chapman, Mr Charles Doyle, Mr Christopher Poole, Ms Aurora Martinez, Mr Nicholas Bram Kennon
Income: £6,981,426 [2017]; £7,021,965 [2016]; £6,136,584 [2015]; £6,193,611 [2014]; £6,137,437 [2013]

Imago Community
Registered: 2 Mar 2005 *Employees:* 58 *Volunteers:* 240
Tel: 01892 530330 *Website:* vawk.org.uk
Activities: General charitable purposes; education, training; advancement of health or saving of lives; disability; prevention or relief of poverty; economic, community development, employment; other charitable purposes
Address: 17-19 Monson Road, Tunbridge Wells, Kent, TN1 1LS
Trustees: Mr Paul Woodhouse, Mr David Oguntoye, Mr Edward Weeks, Mr John Andrew Cheesman, Mr Andrew Barrow, Bill Fearon, Mrs Danielle Swanson, Miss Elizabeth Rogula, Mrs Laura Ellis
Income: £1,918,556 [2017]; £2,057,766 [2016]; £1,849,410 [2015]; £1,918,833 [2014]; £1,424,203 [2013]

Impact Family Services
Registered: 20 Aug 1998 *Employees:* 51 *Volunteers:* 14
Tel: 0191 456 7577 *Website:* impactfs.co.uk
Activities: General charitable purposes
Address: 17 Beach Road, South Shields, Tyne & Wear, NE33 2QA
Trustees: Mr Keith Younghusband, Mr Steven Frederick Lincoln, Mrs Joan Heckels, Mr Ulrich Reichard
Income: £1,066,673 [2017]; £814,960 [2016]; £750,575 [2015]; £733,320 [2014]; £630,858 [2013]

Impact Foundation
Registered: 5 Feb 1985 *Employees:* 9 *Volunteers:* 24
Tel: 01444 457080 *Website:* impact.org.uk
Activities: General charitable purposes; education, training; advancement of health or saving of lives; disability; prevention or relief of poverty; overseas aid, famine relief; economic, community development, employment
Address: 151 Western Road, Haywards Heath, W Sussex, RH16 3LH
Trustees: Peter Webster, Lady Prance, Brenda Luck, David Walker, Jean Wilson, Mr David Jameson Evans FRCS FRCS(C), Claire Hicks, Mr Rob West, Ralph James D'Olier Hope, John Mowbray, John Scott, Nick Astbury, Vinit Shah, Mr Gordon Bennett, Dr Keith Barnard-Jones, Michael O'Connell
Income: £1,808,875 [2017]; £1,741,662 [2016]; £2,601,718 [2015]; £2,392,918 [2014]; £1,610,954 [2013]

Impact Giving UK Trust
Registered: 3 Jun 1987 *Employees:* 1
Tel: 01768 594082 *Website:* impactgiving.org.uk
Activities: Religious activities
Address: P O Box 220, Penrith, Cumbria, CA11 1BH
Trustees: Mr Stephen James Burt, Rev Darren Mayor, Mr Charles W Bethune, Mr Fraser Jeremy Clark
Income: £1,540,610 [2016]; £1,578,705 [2015]; £1,686,454 [2014]; £1,455,682 [2013]; £1,320,943 [2012]

Impact Initiatives
Registered: 30 Apr 1979 *Employees:* 55 *Volunteers:* 143
Tel: 01273 322940 *Website:* impact-initiatives.org.uk
Activities: General charitable purposes; advancement of health or saving of lives; disability; prevention or relief of poverty; accommodation, housing; economic, community development, employment
Address: 19 Queens Road, Brighton, BN1 3XA
Trustees: Mr Leo Jago, Mr Andrew Wealls, Mr Simon Knight DL FRICS, Ms Amanda Mortensen, Mr Neil Moscrop, Rabbi Charles Wallach, Mr Ronald Arthur Jenkins
Income: £2,410,115 [2017]; £2,325,127 [2016]; £2,259,835 [2015]; £2,239,385 [2014]; £1,836,711 [2013]

Imperial College Healthcare Charities
Registered: 1 Apr 2009 *Employees:* 18 *Volunteers:* 4
Tel: 020 3312 7840 *Website:* imperial.nhs.uk
Activities: The advancement of health or saving of lives; arts, culture, heritage, science
Address: Ground Floor, Imperial College Healthcare Charity, Clarence Memorial Wing, St Mary's Hospital, Praed Street, London, W2 1NY
Trustees: Mr Robert Creighton, Ms Valerie Jolliffe, Mr David Crundwell, Professor Hilary Thomas, Dr Mary O'Mahony
Income: £5,496,000 [2016]; £6,820,000 [2015]; £4,575,000 [2014]; £3,874,000 [2013]

Imperial College Trust
Registered: 14 Mar 1977
Tel: 020 7594 2892 *Website:* imperial.ac.uk
Activities: Education, training
Address: Imperial College Administration, Imperial College, London, SW7 2AZ
Trustees: Mr Anthony Bruce, Professor Desmond Geoffrey Johnston, Professor Richard Thompson, Professor Jackie De Belleroche, Mr Nigel Wheatley, Professor Anthony Kinloch
Income: £1,753,401 [2017]; £2,441,414 [2016]; £2,303,566 [2015]; £3,789,468 [2014]; £6,511,317 [2013]

Imperial College Union
Registered: 14 Mar 2013 *Employees:* 61 *Volunteers:* 3,158
Tel: 020 7594 8060 *Website:* imperialcollegeunion.org
Activities: Education, training; amateur sport; recreation
Address: Imperial College, Beit Hall, Prince Consort Road, London, SW7 2BB
Trustees: Mr Graham Parker, Dr Paul Beaumont, Mrs Jill Finney, Mr Finton O'Connor, Mr Matthew Blackett, Mr Thomas Waite, Mr Thomas Bacarese-Hamilton, Professor Dorothy Griffiths, Mrs Kate Owen, Miss Alexandra Compton, Mr Nicholas Burstow, Mr Owen Heaney, Mr Eric Suen
Income: £9,178,608 [2017]; £8,490,806 [2016]; £8,158,600 [2015]; £7,211,413 [2014]

Imperial Health Charity
Registered: 15 Mar 2016 *Employees:* 21 *Volunteers:* 150
Tel: 020 3857 9840 *Website:* imperialcharity.org.uk
Activities: The advancement of health or saving of lives; arts, culture, heritage, science
Address: Second Floor, 178-180 Edgware Road, London, W2 2DS
Trustees: Robert Creighton, Valerie Jolliffe, Mrs Caroline Lien, Michelle Dixon, Mr Nick Ross, Hilary Thomas, Julian Redhead, Dr Mary O'Mahony, David Crundwell
Income: £4,013,000 [2017]

Imperial Society of Teachers of Dancing
Registered: 6 Jan 1969 *Employees:* 62 *Volunteers:* 150
Tel: 020 7655 8867 *Website:* istd.org
Activities: Education, training; arts, culture, heritage, science; amateur sport
Address: Imperial Society of Teachers of Dancing, Imperial House, 22-26 Paul Street, London, EC2A 4QE
Trustees: Miss Chitra Sundaram, Mrs Kay Ball, Mr Simon Adkins, Ms Annabelle Louise Mannix, Ms Erin Sanchez, Ms Julie Tomkins, Mr Keith-Derrick Randolph, Ms Julie Earnshaw, Susan Harwood, Ms Karen King, Mrs Vivienne Saxton, Mrs Elisabeth Swan, Mr Sho Shibata, Mr Jeremy Kean, Mr Christopher Adrian Hawkins
Income: £6,727,844 [2016]; £6,550,272 [2015]; £6,298,388 [2014]; £5,939,731 [2013]; £6,031,111 [2012]

Impetus - The Private Equity Foundation
Registered: 3 Jun 2013 *Employees:* 35 *Volunteers:* 107
Tel: 020 3474 1000 *Website:* impetus-pef.org.uk
Activities: General charitable purposes; education, training; economic, community development, employment
Address: Impetus, 183 Eversholt Street, London, NW1 1BU
Trustees: Mr Louis Elson Finance Professional, Prof Becky Francis, Mr Marc Boughton, Mr Nikos Stathopoulos, Ms Lisa Stone, Mr Simon Turner, Ms Shani Zindel, Mr Craig Dearden-Phillips, Mr Lionel Assant, Hanneke Smits, Ms Caroline Louise Mason, Mr Patrick Healy, Mr Bill Benjamin
Income: £6,678,625 [2016]; £11,464,569 [2015]; £10,558,470 [2014]; £15,539,456 [2013]

Improving Lives Plymouth
Registered: 10 Dec 1997 *Employees:* 47 *Volunteers:* 85
Tel: 01752 201766 *Website:* improvinglivesplymouth.org.uk
Activities: General charitable purposes; advancement of health or saving of lives; disability
Address: Ernest English House, Buckwell Street, Plymouth, PL1 2DA
Trustees: Mr Michael John Lincoln, Mrs Katharine Lesley Bourke, Mrs Maggie Paine, Ms Elaine Latham, Mrs Stephanie Rogers, Mr Jeremy Prichard, Mr Chris Kemp
Income: £1,318,171 [2017]; £1,328,147 [2016]; £1,460,221 [2015]; £1,632,061 [2014]; £1,154,297 [2013]

In Kind Direct
Registered: 6 Feb 1996 *Employees:* 17 *Volunteers:* 2
Tel: 0300 302 0200 *Website:* inkinddirect.org
Activities: General charitable purposes
Address: In Kind Direct, 11-15 St Mary at Hill, London, EC3R 8EE
Trustees: Andrew Rubin, Ms Teresa Tideman, Ajay Kavan, Debra Allcock Tyler, Amar Abbas, Graham Burridge, Amanda MacKenzie, Michael Ross, Andrew Wright, Tom Moody, Graham Inglis, Tim Hinton
Income: £22,501,427 [2016]; £15,493,845 [2015]; £13,350,672 [2014]; £15,615,403 [2013]; £14,351,146 [2012]

Inaura
Registered: 22 May 2002 *Employees:* 52 *Volunteers:* 1
Tel: 01458 830434 *Website:* inaura.net
Activities: Education, training; disability; economic, community development, employment; human rights, religious or racial harmony, equality or diversity
Address: Manor Farm Cottage, Lower Godney, Wells, Somerset, BA5 1RZ
Trustees: Mr Andrew John Norton Warner, Dr Adam Abdelnoor CPsychol, Mrs Julia Gibb, Tessa Munt, Mr Nick Donnelly, Mr Norman James Tyson, Mr Emile Etheridge, Mrs Amanda Hannah
Income: £1,545,222 [2016]; £1,401,910 [2015]; £1,224,044 [2014]; £1,131,893 [2013]; £844,127 [2012]

Include
Registered: 17 Jul 1990 *Employees:* 76
Tel: 01959 578236 *Website:* catch-22.org.uk
Activities: Education, training
Address: Catch22, Rectory Lodge, High Street, Brasted, Westerham, Kent, TN16 1JF
Trustees: Mr Christopher Robert Wright, Ms Francesca Pollard
Income: £3,286,722 [2017]; £7,611,456 [2016]; £6,298,902 [2015]; £4,705,670 [2014]

The Incorporated Bishop's Stortford College Association
Registered: 22 Jul 1964 *Employees:* 306 *Volunteers:* 21
Tel: 01279 838671 *Website:* bishops-stortford-college.herts.sch.uk
Activities: Education, training
Address: 10 Maze Green Road, Bishop's Stortford, Herts, CM23 2PJ
Trustees: Dr Philip Hargrave, Mrs Irene Pearman, Mr Guy Baker, Mrs Linda Farrant, Mr Richard Harrison, Mr Peter Solway, Mrs Pauline Mullender, Sir Stephen Lander, Mr David Thomson, Ms Monica Goitiandia, Doug Alexander, Mr Andrew Conti, Mr Richard Wells
Income: £21,573,000 [2017]; £18,221,000 [2016]; £17,035,000 [2015]; £15,955,000 [2014]; £15,352,000 [2013]

The Incorporated Catholic Truth Society

Registered: 18 Jun 1963 *Employees:* 29 *Volunteers:* 500
Tel: 020 7640 0042 *Website:* ctsbooks.org
Activities: Education, training; religious activities; other charitable purposes
Address: The Incorporated Catholic Truth, 40-46 Harleyford Road, London, SE11 5AY
Trustees: Rt Revd Paul Hendricks, Mrs Carrie Ann Gates, Mr Peter Stephen Fisher, Mr Stephen John Boughton, Rev Dr Andrew Pinsent, Miss Jennie Burbury, Mr Luke Parsons QC, Dr William Peter O'Neil, Katherine Nash
Income: £1,852,367 [2016]; £1,912,563 [2015]; £1,952,036 [2014]; £1,873,717 [2013]; £3,020,220 [2012]

Incorporated Council of Law Reporting for England and Wales

Registered: 4 Mar 1967 *Employees:* 54
Tel: 020 7242 6471 *Website:* iclr.co.uk
Activities: Education, training; other charitable purposes
Address: ICLR, Megarry House, 119 Chancery Lane, London, WC2A 1PP
Trustees: Sir Patrick Elias, Mr Joseph Bernard Egan, Mr Timothy Hugh William Piper, Simon Gault, His Honour Judge David Hodge QC, Sir Peter Roth, Mr Timothy Christopher Dutton QC, Ms Sarah Thomas, The Right Honourable Jeremy Paul Wright QC MP, Kenneth Hamer, Mr James Michael Turner, Mr Richard Fleck CBE, Miss Carolyn Walton, Miss Margaret Ruth Bowron QC, Mrs Linda Karen Hadfield Lee, Sir Alastair Hubert Norris, Sir Mark George Turner, Mr Robert James Buckland QC MP, Mr Peter Joseph Susman QC, Mrs Sushila Abraham
Income: £4,846,608 [2016]; £4,930,305 [2015]; £4,875,717 [2014]; £4,275,129 [2013]; £5,890,674 [2012]

Independence Trust

Registered: 22 Nov 2000 *Employees:* 131 *Volunteers:* 20
Tel: 01588 676262 *Website:* independencetrust.co.uk
Activities: The advancement of health or saving of lives; economic, community development, employment
Address: Connexus Housing Limited, The Gateway, Auction Yard, Craven Arms, Salop, SY7 9BW
Trustees: Michael McCarthy, David Lincoln, Sonia Higgins, Paul O'Driscoll, James Williamson, Graham Biggs, Jake Berriman
Income: £2,589,879 [2017]; £2,729,467 [2016]; £2,047,583 [2015]; £1,734,797 [2014]; £3,316,326 [2013]

Independent Cinema Office

Registered: 14 Apr 2005 *Employees:* 14
Tel: 020 7636 7120 *Website:* independentcinemaoffice.org.uk
Activities: General charitable purposes; education, training; arts, culture, heritage, science
Address: Independent Cinema Office, Kenilworth House, 79-80 Margaret Street, London, W1W 8TA
Trustees: Julia Short, Mr Miles Kettley, Sudhar Bhuchar, Simon Ward, Dorothy Wilson, Mr Trevor Mawby, Susan Lovell
Income: £1,228,854 [2017]; £1,230,419 [2016]; £939,010 [2015]; £597,879 [2014]; £563,399 [2013]

Independent Domestic Abuse Services

Registered: 25 Feb 2004 *Employees:* 55 *Volunteers:* 20
Website: idas.org.uk
Activities: Education, training; accommodation, housing
Address: St Mary's Court, 39 Blossom Street, York, YO24 1AQ
Trustees: Mr James Cannon, Mrs Carol Butterill, Miss Claudia Francesca Gilham, Ms Francesca Haynes, Mr Nicholas John Long, Ms Susan Collins, Ms Jane Adam, Ms Jill Christine Heal Widgery, Ms Sarah Therese Opie, Mr Martin Walker
Income: £1,988,497 [2017]; £1,838,001 [2016]; £1,284,334 [2015]; £1,098,508 [2014]; £1,032,944 [2013]

The Independent Educational Association Limited

Registered: 8 Dec 1975 *Employees:* 195 *Volunteers:* 30
Tel: 020 7348 1700 *Website:* stjamesschools.co.uk
Activities: Education, training
Address: St James Schools, Earsby Street, London, W14 8SH
Trustees: Mr Hugh Venables, Mr John Story, Mr Aatif Hassan, Dr Fenella Willis, Mrs Jennie Buchanan, Mr Jeremy Sinclair, Mr George Cselko, Mr Jerome Webb, Mrs Koula Ansell, Mrs Miranda Munden
Income: £15,818,791 [2016]; £16,133,145 [2015]; £13,716,896 [2014]; £13,852,460 [2013]; £12,311,681 [2012]

Independent Housing UK Ltd

Registered: 5 Dec 2007 *Employees:* 9
Tel: 01625 877522 *Website:* ihl-uk.com
Activities: Accommodation, housing
Address: Europa House, Adlington Business Park, Adlington, Cheshire, SK12 1NL
Trustees: Guy Bosanko, Mr John Ward, Nigel Richmond
Income: £2,985,182 [2017]; £1,066,018 [2016]; £1,980,095 [2015]; £3,127,237 [2014]; £174,561 [2013]

Independent Lives (Disability)

Registered: 16 Sep 2013 *Employees:* 100 *Volunteers:* 10
Tel: 07423 432440 *Website:* independentlives.org
Activities: Education, training; disability; economic, community development, employment
Address: Southfield House, 11 Liverpool Gardens, Worthing, W Sussex, BN11 1RY
Trustees: Mr Malcolm Dennett, Miss Valerie Kiln-Barfoot, Miss Sue Lines, Mr David Andrew Hardman, Mr Irvine Caplan, Mrs Amanda Paine MBE, Mr Chandos David Green, Mr Simon David Wilson
Income: £2,103,778 [2016]; £2,189,641 [2015]; £2,035,249 [2014]

Independent Living Alternatives

Registered: 7 Nov 1989 *Employees:* 146 *Volunteers:* 8
Tel: 020 8369 6032 *Website:* ilanet.co.uk
Activities: Disability
Address: Rowlandson House, 289-293 Ballards Lane, London, N12 8NP
Trustees: Ms Michelle Daley, Mr Anthony Dates, Mr Gabriel Pepper, Ms Eleanor Chooi Wah Thoe Lisney, Ms Katherine Araniello, Mr Simon Walls, Miss Susa Elsegood
Income: £1,268,072 [2017]; £1,348,292 [2016]; £1,005,130 [2015]; £787,317 [2014]; £658,370 [2013]

Independent Options (North West)

Registered: 17 Jun 1993 *Employees:* 121 *Volunteers:* 18
Tel: 0161 456 6502 *Website:* independentoptions.org.uk
Activities: Disability
Address: 67 Chester Road, Hazel Grove, Stockport, Cheshire, SK7 5PE
Trustees: Mrs Pauline White, Mr Peter Milham, Mr Eric Richard Stelfox, Andrew Maunder, Mr James Grassick, Mr Sean Monaghan, Mr Paul Rose
Income: £3,521,993 [2017]; £3,426,969 [2016]; £3,516,453 [2015]; £3,091,349 [2014]; £2,954,191 [2013]

The Independent Schools Association

Registered: 23 Oct 2014 *Employees:* 13
Tel: 01799 523619 *Website:* isaschools.org.uk
Activities: Education, training
Address: ISA House, 5-7 Great Chesterford Court, Great Chesterford, Saffron Walden, Essex, CB10 1PF
Trustees: Mrs Angela Culley, Dr Sarah Jane Lockyer, Mrs Pauline Marie Wilson MBE, Mr Andrew Simon Hampton BA LTCL MEd NPQH, Mr James Thomas Wilding BA FRSA, Mrs Claire Rosanna Osborn, Mr Jeff Shaw, Mr Amjad Vaqar Ahmed, Mrs Pamela Susan Hutley, Mr Phil Soutar, Mrs Dionne Seagrove, Mr David Ward, Mr John Southworth, Mr David Preston, Mr John Robert Wood, Mr Paul Moss, Mr Alex James Gear, Mrs Deborah Ann Leek-Bailey OBE BA Hons PGCE NPQH FRSA, Mr Richard Michael Walden, Mr Matthew John Adshead, Mr Barry George Huggett, Mr Nilesh Motilal Manani, Mr Stephen McKernan, Miss Kaye Marilyn Lovejoy, Mrs Kishwar Ali, Mrs Tracey Wilson, Mrs Helen Chalmers
Income: £1,097,133 [2016]; £921,044 [2015]

The Independent Schools' Bursars Association

Registered: 30 Nov 2007 *Employees:* 8 *Volunteers:* 20
Tel: 01256 330369 *Website:* theisba.org.uk
Activities: Education, training
Address: Bluett House, Unit 11-12 Manor Farm, Cliddesden, Basingstoke, Hants, RG25 2JB
Trustees: Mr James William Doherty, Mr Norman Patterson, Mr Paul Flowerday, Mr Stephen Holliday, Mr John Pratten, Mr Guyon Ralphs, Mrs Maureen Elizabeth Adams, Mrs Eleanor Sharman, Mrs Alison Shakespeare, Mr Rodney Cook, Mrs Penelope Rudge, Mr John Robert Wynham Wilder
Income: £1,491,421 [2016]; £1,469,461 [2015]; £1,427,645 [2014]; £1,254,187 [2013]; £1,186,006 [2012]

Independent Training Services Limited

Registered: 23 Apr 2002 *Employees:* 67
Tel: 01226 295471 *Website:* ind-training.co.uk
Activities: Education, training; economic, community development, employment
Address: Independent Training Services, Park Road, Barnsley, S Yorks, S70 1YD
Trustees: Mr Michael Henry Mallinson, Mr John James Butt, Mr Alasdair John Parker, Ms Andrea Cook, Mr David Alan Peake, Mr Graham Charles Mustin, Mr Martin James Hornshaw
Income: £3,342,151 [2017]; £2,680,635 [2016]; £2,234,517 [2015]; £2,219,636 [2014]; £3,122,480 [2013]

The Indigo Trust

Registered: 10 Jun 1999 *Employees:* 13
Tel: 020 7410 0330 *Website:* sfct.org.uk
Activities: General charitable purposes; education, training; economic, community development, employment; other charitable purposes
Address: Sainsbury Family Charitable Trusts, The Peak, 5 Wilton Road, London, SW1V 1AP
Trustees: Mr Dominic Brendan Flynn, Mr William John Perrin, Miss Francesca Elizabeth Perrin
Income: £1,408,531 [2017]; £203,339 [2016]; £942,402 [2015]; £972,457 [2014]; £905,168 [2013]

Individual Care Services

Registered: 12 Feb 1992 *Employees:* 139
Tel: 01527 857280 *Website:* individualcare.org.uk
Activities: The advancement of health or saving of lives; disability; accommodation, housing
Address: 25 Alcester Road, Studley, Warwicks, B80 7LL
Trustees: Mr Gilbert Allan Smith, Mr Andrew Crompton, Mr David Hartley, Mr Andrew Crompton, Mrs Helle Charles, Mr Anthony Hyla Crompton, Victoria Crompton, Mrs Louisa Hartley, Mr Paul Ashmore
Income: £3,295,717 [2017]; £3,166,061 [2016]; £2,977,345 [2015]; £2,825,667 [2014]; £2,626,345 [2013]

Indochina Starfish Foundation

Registered: 20 Jul 2006 *Employees:* 97 *Volunteers:* 3
Tel: 01548 844698 *Website:* indochinastarfish.org
Activities: Education, training; advancement of health or saving of lives; prevention or relief of poverty
Address: The Pines, Main Road, Salcombe, Devon, TQ8 8JW
Trustees: Mr Martin Cubbon, Mr Paul Anthony Scott Markland, Mr Robert Gazzi, Mr Andrew Riddick, Ms Belinda Margaret Greer, Mr St John Andrew Flaherty, Mr Mark Ashall, Mr Leo Brogan, Martin Murray, Mr Patrick Healy, Mr Neil Llewelyn Cutler
Income: £1,133,123 [2017]; £805,903 [2016]; £1,101,649 [2015]; £886,450 [2014]; £347,509 [2013]

Infant Jesus Sisters (Nicolas Barre) Generalate CIO

Registered: 9 Nov 2015
Tel: 01403 262629 *Website:* infantjesussisters.org
Activities: General charitable purposes; education, training; advancement of health or saving of lives; disability; prevention or relief of poverty; overseas aid, famine relief; accommodation, housing; religious activities; environment, conservation, heritage; economic, community development, employment; human rights, religious or racial harmony, equality or diversity
Address: Flat 12, Delancey Court, Wimblehurst Road, Horsham, W Sussex, RH12 2DU
Trustees: Sister Alice Kilbride, Sister Maria Lau, Sister Noreen T McGrath, Sister Kimiko Matsumoto, Sister Marie Pitcher
Income: £10,963,443 [2016]

The Injured Jockeys Fund

Registered: 21 Dec 2004 *Employees:* 34 *Volunteers:* 30
Tel: 01638 662246 *Website:* ijf.org.uk
Activities: General charitable purposes; education, training; advancement of health or saving of lives; disability; prevention or relief of poverty; accommodation, housing; amateur sport
Address: Millfarm Stud, Mill Lane, Cowlinge, Newmarket, Suffolk, CB8 9HZ
Trustees: Mr Jonathan Powell, Mr Jeff Smith, Mr William Norris, Mrs Hazel Peplinski, Mrs Valda Burke, Mr Andrew Thornton, Mr John Brough Scott, Mr Guy Henderson, Mr Sam Waley Cohen, Mr Michael Caulfield MSc, Mr Michael Foy
Income: £5,847,662 [2017]; £5,267,469 [2016]; £6,702,448 [2015]; £5,654,489 [2014]; £3,161,490 [2013]

The Inland Waterways Association
Registered: 17 Dec 1962 *Employees:* 25 *Volunteers:* 2,000
Tel: 01494 783453 *Website:* waterways.org.uk
Activities: Education, training; arts, culture, heritage, science; amateur sport; environment, conservation, heritage; recreation
Address: Inland Waterways Association, Island House, Moor Road, Chesham, Bucks, HP5 1WA
Trustees: Miss Verna Hilary Smith, Mr Les Etheridge, Mr Peter Scott, Mr Christopher Walter Howes, Ms Gillian Smith, Helen Whitehouse, Mr Jonathan Mark Smith, Mr Michael Keith Palmer, Mr Paul Rodgers, Mr Raymond Carter, Mr Ivor Henry Caplan, Mr Paul Roland Strudwick, Mr Roger Holmes, Mr Richard John Christopher Barnes, Sir Robert Atkins
Income: £1,555,811 [2016]; £1,807,001 [2015]; £1,329,635 [2014]; £1,442,407 [2013]; £1,336,854 [2012]

Inner City Music Limited
Registered: 15 Apr 1985 *Employees:* 31
Tel: 0161 830 3895 *Website:* bandonthewall.org
Activities: Education, training; arts, culture, heritage, science; economic, community development, employment
Address: c/o Band on the Wall, 27 Swan Street, Northern Quarter, Manchester, M4 5JZ
Trustees: Mr Stephen Sorrell, Mr Gavin Sharp, Ms Karen Gabay, Mr Nick Reed, Mr Richard Jones, Mr David Kaye, Mr Howard Sharrock, Ms Lisa Ashurst, Mr Andy Booth, Mr Julian Curnuck
Income: £1,979,544 [2017]; £1,651,890 [2016]; £1,553,741 [2015]; £1,399,295 [2014]; £1,702,825 [2013]

John Innes Centre
Registered: 4 Oct 1976 *Employees:* 406
Tel: 01603 450000 *Website:* jic.ac.uk
Activities: Education, training; environment, conservation, heritage
Address: John Innes Institute, Colney Lane, Colney, Norwich, NR4 7UH
Trustees: Mr Stuart Holmes, Prof Ottoline Leyser, Dr Deborah Keith, Ms Jennifer Kristin Midura, Keith Norman, Mr Robert Maskell, Prof John Colin Murrell
Income: £40,506,163 [2017]; £37,916,000 [2016]; £46,339,000 [2015]; £40,321,000 [2014]; £34,614,000 [2013]

The Innocent Foundation
Registered: 11 Jun 2004 *Employees:* 2 *Volunteers:* 35
Tel: 020 3235 0352 *Website:* innocentfoundation.org
Activities: General charitable purposes; prevention or relief of poverty; overseas aid, famine relief; environment, conservation, heritage; economic, community development, employment
Address: The Innocent Foundation, 342 Ladbroke Grove, London, W10 5BU
Trustees: Mr Adam Balon, Mr Richard Reed, Mr Douglas Lamont, Mr Jon Wright, Ms Christina Archer, Ms Sarah-Jane Norman
Income: £1,003,864 [2017]; £1,018,459 [2016]; £1,009,296 [2015]; £1,011,088 [2014]; £2,056,356 [2013]

Innovate Trust Ltd
Registered: 14 Apr 1992 *Employees:* 863
Tel: 029 2038 2151 *Website:* innovate-trust.org.uk
Activities: Education, training; advancement of health or saving of lives; disability; accommodation, housing; amateur sport; environment, conservation, heritage; economic, community development, employment
Address: Innovate Trust, 433 Cowbridge Road East, Cardiff, CF5 1JH
Trustees: Mrs Charlotte Kletta, Mr Ben Lewis, Miss Jess Rumble, Mr Kevin O'Neill, Ms Georgina Powell, Mr David Pratt, Mr Cameron Dunlop, Ms Emma Board-Davies
Income: £19,120,095 [2017]; £16,684,158 [2016]; £13,594,107 [2015]; £11,211,198 [2014]; £7,804,364 [2013]

Inspiration Ministries UK
Registered: 4 May 2007
Website: ini.tv
Activities: Religious activities
Address: 3000 Worldreach Drive, Indian Land, SC 29707, USA
Trustees: Mr Charles David Cerullo, Mrs Barbara Joyce Cerullo, Mr Albert Wray Denson, Mr Douglas Peter Preudhomme, Mr Ramon Ardizzone
Income: £1,431,416 [2017]; £1,895,823 [2016]; £3,037,303 [2015]; £4,721,154 [2014]; £2,374,349 [2013]

Inspire Community Trust
Registered: 26 Jan 2005 *Employees:* 84 *Volunteers:* 10
Tel: 020 3045 5100 *Website:* inspirecommunitytrust.org
Activities: Disability
Address: 20 Whitehall Lane, Erith, Kent, DA8 2DH
Trustees: Ranjit Bhamra, Hugh Miller, Mr Roland Horace French, Anne Bramley, Vinod Kumar Khanna, Dr Peter Paul Catterall
Income: £3,012,526 [2017]; £3,201,585 [2016]; £3,047,736 [2015]; £3,230,465 [2014]; £3,230,465 [2013]

Institute for Employment Studies
Registered: 2 Apr 1969 *Employees:* 41
Tel: 01273 763423 *Website:* employment-studies.co.uk
Activities: Education, training; disability; economic, community development, employment
Address: City Gate, 185 Dyke Road, Hove, E Sussex, BN3 1TL
Trustees: Mr David Guest, Mr Geoffrey Podger, Mr Steve Barnett, Ms Nicola Smith, Sarah Cook, Ms Randeep Kaur Kular, Mr David Smith, Ms Sam Mercer, Mr John Russell Greatrex, Ms Kathleen Poole
Income: £3,067,336 [2017]; £2,916,804 [2016]; £3,116,793 [2015]; £3,375,384 [2014]; £3,860,605 [2013]

Institute for European Environmental Policy, London
Registered: 2 Mar 1990 *Employees:* 27 *Volunteers:* 6
Tel: 020 7799 2244 *Website:* ieep.eu
Activities: Education, training; environment, conservation, heritage; economic, community development, employment
Address: Floor 3, IEEP Offices, 11 Belgrave Road, London, SW1V 1RB
Trustees: Mr Derek Osborn CB, Mr Paul Meins, Mr Domingo Jimenez-Beltran, Dr Christian Hey, Dr Claudia Alexandra Soares, Sir John Harman FRSA Hon FICE FIWEM FIWM FSE DCL, Tricia Henton, Sir Graham Wynne, Mr Herman Johan Wolters
Income: £3,134,405 [2017]; £2,408,694 [2016]; £2,533,909 [2015]; £2,146,097 [2013]; £2,633,721 [2012]

The Institute for Fiscal Studies
Registered: 12 Jun 1969 *Employees:* 60
Tel: 020 7291 4800 *Website:* ifs.org.uk
Activities: Education, training; economic, community development, employment
Address: 7 Ridgmount Street, London, WC1E 7AE
Trustees: Mr John Francis Chown, Mr Ian Duncan Menzies-Conacher, Mr Christopher Davidson, Margaret Cole, Mr James Bell, Mr Michael Ridge, Prof Denise Anne Lievesley, Sir Gus O'Donnell, Professor David Miles, Mr Jonathan Athow, Mr Nicholas Timmins
Income: £7,617,608 [2016]; £7,586,220 [2015]; £7,408,750 [2014]; £6,720,685 [2013]; £6,027,508 [2012]

Institute for Government
Registered: 30 Apr 2008 *Employees:* 45
Tel: 020 7747 0400 *Website:* instituteforgovernment.org.uk
Activities: Education, training; other charitable purposes
Address: Institute for Government, 2 Carlton Gardens, London, SW1Y 5AA
Trustees: Dame Sandra Dawson, Sir Andrew Cahn, Lord Sainsbury of Turville, Lord David Alec Gwyn Roberts Simon, Rt Hon George Freeman, Mr Philip Rutnam, Sir Ian Michael Cheshire, Lord John Sharkey, Ms Miranda Theresa Claire Curtis, Sir Richard Lambert, Mr Liam Byrne MP, Baroness Valerie Amos
Income: £4,387,284 [2017]; £4,207,142 [2016]; £4,170,927 [2015]; £3,929,997 [2014]; £3,913,175 [2013]

Institute for Human Rights & Business Limited
Registered: 23 Sep 2009 *Employees:* 13
Tel: 01323 727389 *Website:* ihrb.org
Activities: The prevention or relief of poverty; economic, community development, employment; human rights, religious or racial harmony, equality or diversity
Address: Railview Lofts, 19c Commercial Road, Eastbourne, E Sussex, BN21 3XE
Trustees: Mr Christopher Marsden, Ms Lilian Rae Lindsay, Ms Deanna Louise Kemp, Mr Bjoern Edlund, Mr Mark Beaumont Taylor, Mr Ronald James David Popper
Income: £2,762,608 [2016]; £1,728,912 [2015]; £3,525,938 [2014]; £1,916,883 [2013]; £902,140 [2012]

The Institute for Optimum Nutrition
Registered: 22 Jul 1992 *Employees:* 34 *Volunteers:* 4
Website: ion.ac.uk
Activities: Education, training
Address: The Institute for Optimum Nutrition, Ambassador House, Paradise Road, Richmond, Surrey, TW9 1SQ
Trustees: Ms Dian Mills, Ms Susan Hillman, Mrs Rachel Hampson, Ms Jackie Lynch, Mrs Anita Wyles
Income: £1,737,540 [2017]; £1,545,084 [2016]; £1,337,480 [2015]; £1,345,226 [2014]; £1,016,262 [2013]

Institute for Public Policy Research
Registered: 26 Sep 1988 *Employees:* 51
Website: ippr.org
Activities: Education, training; other charitable purposes
Address: 3 Collins Street, London, SE3 0UG
Trustees: Dr Donald Peck, Sir John Christopher Powell, Lord Eatwell of Stratton St Margaret, Dr Margaret Aderin MBE, Ms Jess Search, Ms Caroline Daniel, David Pitt-Watson, Lord Hollick of Notting Hill, Ms Kathryn Parminter, Lord Andrew Adonis, Professor Mariana Mazzucato, Baroness Suttie
Income: £5,288,160 [2016]; £4,407,193 [2015]; £3,530,894 [2014]; £3,080,349 [2013]; £2,733,859 [2012]

Institute for Strategic Dialogue
Registered: 1 Apr 2011 *Employees:* 25 *Volunteers:* 3
Tel: 020 7493 9333 *Website:* strategicdialogue.org
Activities: General charitable purposes; education, training
Address: P O Box 7814, London, W1C 1YZ
Trustees: Mr Michael Lewis, Mr Stuart Fiertz, Mr John Kremer, Mr Mark Bergman, Mrs Carol Saper
Income: £1,449,273 [2016]; £3 [2015]; £36,889 [2014]; £115,769 [2013]

The Institute for War and Peace Reporting (IWPR)
Registered: 14 Oct 1993 *Employees:* 13
Tel: 020 7269 9564 *Website:* iwpr.net
Activities: Education, training
Address: Institute for War & Peace Reporting, 48 Gray's Inn Road, London, WC1X 8LT
Trustees: Sir David Bell, Mr Richard Caplan, Ms Christina Lamb, Mr Will Gardiner, Mr Zoran Pajic, Professor Stephen Jukes, Mr Christian Toksvig, Mr Michael S Immordino
Income: £4,710,779 [2016]; £4,680,619 [2015]; £5,097,663 [2014]; £3,265,148 [2013]; £1,778,354 [2012]

The Institute of Acoustics Limited
Registered: 19 Mar 1974 *Employees:* 8 *Volunteers:* 150
Tel: 01727 848195 *Website:* ioa.org.uk
Activities: Education, training
Address: The Institute of Acoustics, St Peters House, 45 Victoria Street, St Albans, Herts, AL1 3HZ
Trustees: Ms Pamela Lowery, Miss Jo Webb, Mr Peter Rogers, Mrs Hilary Notley, Dr Paul Lepper, Dr Martin Lester, Ms Vicky Stewart, Prof Barry Gibbs, Daniel Goodhand, Mr William Edward Egan, Dr Keith Holland, Mr Russell Richardson, Mr Daren Wallis, Miss Emma Shanks, Mr Graham Parry, Mr James Glasgow, Mr Richard Watson
Income: £1,047,490 [2016]; £1,035,921 [2015]; £981,126 [2014]; £870,853 [2013]; £1,019,844 [2012]

The Institute of Advanced Motorists Limited
Registered: 18 Nov 1966 *Employees:* 68 *Volunteers:* 4,200
Tel: 020 8996 9600 *Website:* iamroadsmart.com
Activities: Education, training
Address: IAM Roadsmart, 1 Albany Place, Hyde Way, Welwyn Garden City, Herts, AL7 3BT
Trustees: Dr Peter John Pashley Holden, Mr Kenneth William Keir, Mr Derek John McMullan, Dr Charles James Doyle, Mr Peter Graham Shaw, Professor Angus Wallace, Gina Bromage, Mrs Catherine Ann Lloyd, Mrs Elizabeth Marguerite Coyle-Camp, Ms Anna Marie McLaren
Income: £7,239,000 [2017]; £11,445,000 [2016]; £7,636,000 [2015]; £7,770,000 [2014]; £6,642,000 [2013]

Institute of Biomedical Science
Registered: 24 Dec 1970 *Employees:* 27 *Volunteers:* 840
Tel: 020 7713 0214 *Website:* ibms.org
Activities: Education, training
Address: Institute of Biomedical Science, 12 Coldbath Square, London, EC1R 5HL
Trustees: Mr Andrew Usher, Mr Daniel Smith, Mr James Gordon McNair, Mr David Eccleston, Mrs Debra Padgett, Mrs Sandra Phinbow, Mr Nigel Coles, Mr Colin Mudd, Mr Charles Houston, Mrs Jane Harrison-Williams, Ms Helen Archer, Mr Ian Sturdgess, Mr Robert Simpson, Dr Jane Needham, Ms Joyce Overfield, Mr Allan John Wilson, Mr Matthew William Smith, Mr Sean Conlan, Mr David Wells, Mrs Alison Geddis, Mrs Joanna Andrew
Income: £5,165,874 [2017]; £3,180,132 [2016]; £4,299,554 [2015]; £3,032,063 [2014]; £4,023,477 [2013]

The Institute of Brewing & Distilling
Registered: 14 Aug 1975 *Employees:* 12 *Volunteers:* 30
Tel: 020 7499 8144 *Website:* ibd.org.uk
Activities: Education, training
Address: 44A Curlew Street, Butler's Wharf, London, SE1 2ND
Trustees: Mr Kenneth Fairbrother, Dr Peter Channon, Mr J Kevin Mitchell, Prof Katherine Smart, Mr Nigel Fitch, Mr Colin S McCrorie, Prof Charles W Bamforth, Mr Tim Cooper
Income: £2,181,104 [2016]; £1,982,361 [2015]; £2,361,316 [2014]; £3,399,663 [2013]; £1,653,630 [2012]

Institute of Contemporary Arts Limited
Registered: 28 Nov 1969 *Employees:* 96 *Volunteers:* 6
Tel: 020 7930 0493 *Website:* ica.art
Activities: Education, training; arts, culture, heritage, science
Address: The Mall, London, SW1Y 5AH
Trustees: Mr Pesh Framjee, Mr Donald Ashton Moore, Ms Maria Sukkar, Ms Joanna Jadwiga Kirkpatrick, Vanessa Oliviera Carlos, Mr Wolfgang Tillmans, Miss Hadeel Ibrahim, Ms Sara Blonstein, Ms Prue O'Day, Christopher Robert Kirkland, Ms Charlotte Appleyard, Ms Dilyara Allakhverdova
Income: £4,164,027 [2017]; £4,059,558 [2016]; £3,674,582 [2015]; £3,187,590 [2014]; £4,165,689 [2013]

The Institute of Development Studies
Registered: 13 Jun 1966 *Employees:* 248
Tel: 01273 606261 *Website:* ids.ac.uk
Activities: Education, training; prevention or relief of poverty; human rights, religious or racial harmony, equality or diversity
Address: Institute of Development Studies, University of Sussex, Falmer, Brighton, BN1 9RE
Trustees: Dr Rajesh Tandon, Ms Nkoyo Toyo, Professor Jonathan Kydd, Professor Frances Stewart, Professor Adam Tickell, Dr Ali Cheema, Ms Emilie Wilson-Pike, Dr David O'Brien, Professor Melissa Leach, Mr Gareth Davies, Professor Mick Moore, Mr Michael Anderson, Professor Takyiwaa Manuh, Mr Kim Frost
Income: £23,071,000 [2017]; £22,555,000 [2016]; £20,575,000 [2015]; £21,671,000 [2014]; £20,567,000 [2013]

The Institute of Economic Affairs Limited
Registered: 25 Aug 1969 *Employees:* 22
Tel: 020 7799 8900 *Website:* iea.org.uk
Activities: Education, training
Address: 2 Lord North Street, London, SW1P 3LB
Trustees: Mr Michael Hintze, Mr Kevin Bell, Patrick Minford PhD, Mr Neil Record, Mr Bruno Prior, Professor Martin Ricketts, Mrs Linda Whetstone, Mr Robert Boyd, Dr Mark Pennington, Robin Edwards
Income: £1,913,000 [2016]; £1,693,000 [2015]; £1,922,000 [2014]; £1,527,000 [2013]; £1,059,000 [2012]

Institute of Export and International Trade (The)
Registered: 26 Mar 1976 *Employees:* 15
Tel: 01733 404400 *Website:* export.org.uk
Activities: Education, training
Address: Institute of Export, Export House, Minerva Business Park, Lynch Wood, Peterborough, PE2 6FT
Trustees: Ms Maria Helena Malinowska, Mr Marcel Hugo Landau, Mr David James Maisey, Mr Sean David Ramsden, Mr Terence Charles William Scuoler CBE MIEX, Mr Doug Fermie Fiex, Miss Nicola Jane Bolton, Mr Robert Stanford Keller, Mr Richard Smith-Morgan
Income: £1,076,210 [2016]; £1,058,102 [2015]; £842,261 [2014]; £712,034 [2013]; £592,956 [2012]

The Institute of Family Therapy
Registered: 5 Jul 1982 *Employees:* 18
Tel: 020 7391 9150 *Website:* ift.org.uk
Activities: Education, training; advancement of health or saving of lives; disability
Address: Stephenson Way, London, NW1 2HX
Trustees: Ms Kathleen Waters, Mr Alastair Pearson, Mr Alastair Gaskin, Miss Catherine Connolly, Ms Cynthia Creavalle, Mr Philip Dick
Income: £1,219,010 [2017]; £1,334,769 [2016]; £1,247,369 [2015]; £1,086,164 [2014]; £936,795 [2013]

Institute of Fundraising
Registered: 28 Feb 2000 *Employees:* 49 *Volunteers:* 670
Tel: 020 7840 1000 *Website:* institute-of-fundraising.org.uk
Activities: Education, training
Address: Charter House, 13-15 Carteret Street, London, SW1H 9DJ
Trustees: Irene Chambers, Danielle Atkinson, Giles Pegram CBE, Liz Tait, Helen Elliott, Isobel Michael, Kath Abrahams, Emily Drayson, Carol Akiwumi, Dominic Will, Amanda Bringans, Claire Rowney
Income: £5,375,957 [2017]; £4,929,155 [2016]; £4,664,581 [2015]; £4,682,826 [2014]; £4,534,936 [2013]

The Institute of Grocery Distribution
Registered: 26 Nov 1971 *Employees:* 140
Tel: 01923 857141 *Website:* igd.com
Activities: Education, training; other charitable purposes
Address: Institute of Grocery Distribution, Grange Lane, Letchmore Heath, Watford, Herts, WD25 8GD
Trustees: Ms Emma Louise Evison, Mr Philip Tenney, Ann Bell, Jill Ross, Mr Bradley Moore, Mr Christopher Paul Whitfield, Mr Mark Webster, Susan Barratt, Mr Andrew Clappen, Ian Morley, Mr David O'Flynn
Income: £16,184,840 [2016]; £15,549,257 [2015]; £14,244,453 [2014]; £13,090,240 [2013]; £11,705,701 [2012]

Institute of Integrated Systemic Therapy
Registered: 12 May 1983 *Employees:* 194
Tel: 020 7928 7388 *Website:* childhoodfirst.org.uk
Activities: Education, training
Address: 210 Borough High Street, London, SE1 1JX
Trustees: Mr Daniel Peltz, Mrs Patricia Phillips, Mr Sebastian Lyon, Mr John Harrison, Lady Jane Grabiner JP, Dr Samatha Deacon, Mr Scott Murdoch, Miss Elizabeth Szwed, Mr Keith Miller, Mr Simon Villette, Margaret Wilson, Mrs Sarah Scarratt, Mr Matthew Fletcher
Income: £9,530,240 [2017]; £8,327,873 [2016]; £7,488,336 [2015]; £7,731,141 [2014]; £7,206,828 [2013]

The Institute of Leadership and Management
Registered: 22 May 1968 *Employees:* 43
Tel: 01827 219752 *Website:* institutelm.com
Activities: Education, training
Address: The Institute of Leadership and Man, Pacific House, Relay Point, Wilnecote, Tamworth, Staffs, B77 5PA
Trustees: Mr Andrew Sharman, Ms Stella Chandler, Ms Annabel Graham, Mr John Gavin, Ms Karen Waite, Ms Joy Marie Lisa Maitland
Income: £9,250,000 [2016]; £10,360,000 [2015]; £10,310,000 [2014]; £9,397,000 [2013]; £9,220,000 [2012]

The Institute of Marine Engineering, Science and Technology

Registered: 22 Aug 1963 *Employees:* 35 *Volunteers:* 500
Tel: 020 7382 2658 *Website:* imarest.org
Activities: Education, training
Address: 1 Birdcage Walk, London, SW1H 9JJ
Trustees: Professor C G Hodge Freng Fimarest, Barry Brooks, Captain Matthew Bolton Ceng Cmareng Fimarest, Mr Philip Stanley Parvin, Dr A R Greig, Eur Ing Dr John Lawson Ceng Cmareng Fimarest, Alan Mills, Dr Andrew Tyler, Rear Adm Nigel Guild Cb Freng Ceng Cmareng Fimarest, Mr Richard Vie Ceng Cmareng Fimarest, Mr Martin Murphy Ceng Cmareng Fimarest, Dr R J Wakefield, Ms Sarah Dhanda, Rob Dorey, Dr Rachel Nicholls-Lee
Income: £2,855,206 [2016]; £2,699,676 [2015]; £3,259,913 [2014]; £3,365,585 [2013]; £3,333,976 [2012]

The Institute of Materials, Minerals & Mining

Registered: 12 Feb 1975 *Employees:* 57 *Volunteers:* 100
Tel: 020 7451 7300 *Website:* iom3.org
Activities: Education, training
Address: The Institute of Materials Minerals & Mining, 297 Euston Road, London, NW1 3AQ
Trustees: Dr Ken Ridal, Mr Barry Douglas Lye, Mr Samuel James Wood, Mr Stannas Leslie John Bellaby, Mr Keith Leonard Forsdyke, Mick May, Mr Keith Albert Harrison, Colin Hindle, Martin Cox, Dr Alan Keith Wood MIMMM, Mr A D Francis, Mrs Christine Blackmore, Professor Andrew Lennard Lewis FIMMM, Prof Ra Dorey, Dr Ds Rickerby, Dr Am McDermott, Mr Daniel Kells, Dr Andrew John Sturgeon, Mr Robert G Siddall, Mr David Ronald Evetts, Dr Siobhan Matthews, Dr Serena Michelle Best, Dr Philip John Erwin Bischler, Dr Mike Hicks, Chris Corti, Professor Jonathan Graham Peel Binner, John Wilcox, Mr A A Haggie, Dr Michael Raymond Clinch, Dr Kate Thornton Profgradimmm, Mr Julian John Aldridge MIMMM, Mr Michael Steeper, Mr John Park, Prof Mr Jolly, Mr Christopher Barry Waterhouse, Professor Zhongyun Fan
Income: £3,542,000 [2016]; £3,666,000 [2015]; £19,702,000 [2014]; £5,689,000 [2013]; £6,114,000 [2012]

The Institute of Mathematics and Its Applications

Registered: 1 Mar 1993 *Employees:* 16
Tel: 01702 354020 *Website:* ima.org.uk
Activities: Education, training
Address: The Institute of Mathematics and Its Applications, Catherine Richards House, 16 Nelson Street, Southend on Sea, Essex, SS1 1EF
Trustees: Professor Alistair David Fitt, Professor Neil Victor Challis, Dr Alan Stevens, Professor Dame Celia Hoyles DBE, Ms Noel-Ann Bradshaw, Dr Malcolm Benjamin Dias, Professor Elizabeth Mansfield, Professor Paulo Jorge Gomes Lisboa, Dr Jennifer Margaret Macey, Dr Zoe Frances Kelson, Professor Catherine Ann Hobbs, Mr Nathan John Turner, Dr Rachel Naomi Bearon, Doctor Charles William Evans, Professor Nigel Steele, Dr Nira Cyril Chamberlain, Mr Garrod John Musto, Professor Paul Alexander Glendinning, Professor Robert Sinclair MacKay FRS, Dr Danielle Bewsher, Professor Paul Glaister, Professor Christopher Mark Linton, Professor Christopher James William Breward, Mr Michael James Grove, Professor Richard Craster, Miss Wing Ka Karrie Liu
Income: £1,119,198 [2016]; £1,193,990 [2015]; £1,226,160 [2014]; £1,136,217 [2013]; £1,399,600 [2012]

Institute of Our Lady of Mercy

Registered: 30 Nov 1984 *Employees:* 399 *Volunteers:* 325
Tel: 0113 250 0253 *Website:* ourladyofmercy.org.uk
Activities: Education, training; advancement of health or saving of lives; disability; prevention or relief of poverty; overseas aid, famine relief; accommodation, housing; religious activities
Address: Institute of Our Lady of Mercy Convent of Mercy, Cemetery Road, Yeadon, Leeds, LS19 7UR
Trustees: Sister Anne Hewitt, Sister Sue Randall, Sister Joan Breen, Sister Norah Frances Cronin, Sister Barbara Jeffery, Sister Jean Frances Fitzpatrick
Income: £12,580,775 [2016]; £14,681,598 [2015]; £14,185,749 [2014]; £13,874,641 [2013]; £14,155,283 [2012]

Institute of Physics and Engineering in Medicine

Registered: 17 Jul 1995 *Employees:* 14 *Volunteers:* 400
Tel: 01904 610821 *Website:* ipem.ac.uk
Activities: Education, training; advancement of health or saving of lives; disability; arts, culture, heritage, science
Address: Institute of Physics & Engineering in Medicine, Fairmount House, 230 Tadcaster Road, York, YO24 1ES
Trustees: Professor Mark Arthur Tooley, Dr Christopher Callicott, Dr David Brettle, Miss Kimberley Jane Saint, Dr George Dempsey, Dr Richard Stephen Scott, Professor Panayiotis Kyriacou, Mr John Graham Turner, Mr Hugh Bernard Wilkins, Mr David Haydn Ellis, Ms Christine Usher, Mrs Alison Robinson Canham, Professor Paul Alan While, Professor Julie Anne Horrocks, Dr Balbir Singh Sanghera, Mr Mark Brian Knight, Miss Fiona Elizabeth Wall
Income: £1,321,930 [2016]; £1,335,898 [2015]; £1,423,673 [2014]; £1,493,193 [2013]; £1,371,553 [2012]

The Institute of Physics

Registered: 21 Mar 1986 *Employees:* 542 *Volunteers:* 1,900
Website: iop.org
Activities: General charitable purposes; education, training; arts, culture, heritage, science
Address: 76 Portland Place, London, W1B 1NT
Trustees: Mr Jonathan Flint CBE MBA BSc FREng FInstP, Professor Dame Julia Higgins DBE FRS CPhys HonFInstP FREng, Professor Angela Newing FInstP, Dr Lisa Jardine-Wright CPhys MInstP, Professor Sarah Thompson MBE CPhys FInstP, Deborah Phelps MInstP, Dr James McKenzie, Dr Becky Parker MBE CPhys HonFInstP, Dr Mark Telling CPhys FInstP, Professor Brian Fulton CPhys FInstP, Professor Julian Jones OBE FRSE CPhys FInstP, Mr Mark Wrigley MInstP, Dr Trevor Cross FInstP, Professor Kevin McGuigan FRSC FInstP, Mr Neil Thomson CPhys FInstP, Dr Carol Davenport CSciTeach CPhys MInstP, Professor Lesley Cohen, Dr June McCombie MBE CPhys FInstP FRAS FRSC, Professor Wendy Flavell CPhys FInstP, Professor Anne Tropper CPhys FInstP FOSA
Income: £67,448,000 [2016]; £56,861,000 [2015]; £55,040,000 [2014]; £63,053,000 [2013]; £53,149,000 [2012]

Institute of School Business Leadership

Registered: 12 Jun 2006 *Employees:* 13 *Volunteers:* 20
Website: isbl.org.uk
Activities: Education, training; economic, community development, employment
Address: 53 Butts, Coventry, Warwicks, CV1 3BH
Trustees: Mrs Alexandra Hunt, Mrs Tracey Anne Gray, Yvonne Maria Spencer, Marie Louise Hatswell, Ms Rachel Margaret Prince, Mr Gary Corban, Mr Matthew James Clements-Wheeler, Alison Jefferson, Matthew Burrell, Simon Oxenham, Mr Trevor Summerson, Dr Paul Armstrong
Income: £1,171,369 [2016]; £1,145,075 [2015]; £1,063,077 [2014]; £882,857 [2013]; £780,873 [2012]

Institute of The Blessed Virgin Mary Commonly Called The Sisters of Loreto
Registered: 12 Jan 1967 *Employees:* 69
Tel: 0161 227 0220
Activities: General charitable purposes; education, training; prevention or relief of poverty; overseas aid, famine relief; religious activities; economic, community development, employment; other charitable purposes
Address: 28 Hartley Road, Altrincham, Cheshire, WA14 4AY
Trustees: Sister Kathryn Mary Keigher, Sister Una Coogan, Sister Josette Zammit-Mangion, Sister Kathleen Myers, Sister Bernadette Boland
Income: £2,213,294 [2016]; £3,169,573 [2015]; £2,404,783 [2014]; £3,485,185 [2013]; £2,311,101 [2012]

Institute of The Religious of The Sacred Heart of Mary Immaculate Virgin
Registered: 7 Jan 1964 *Employees:* 22
Tel: 020 7969 5500
Activities: General charitable purposes; religious activities
Address: Haysmacintyre, 26 Red Lion Square, London, WC1R 4AG
Trustees: Sister Ellen O'Leary, Sister Rosemary Lenehan, Sister Bernadette McNamara, Sister Ursula Canavan, Sister Kathleen Buckley
Income: £1,391,718 [2016]; £2,091,853 [2015]; £2,837,219 [2014]; £1,451,282 [2013]; £1,619,297 [2012]

The Institution of Chemical Engineers
Registered: 23 Jan 1963 *Employees:* 93 *Volunteers:* 500
Tel: 01788 578214 *Website:* icheme.org
Activities: Education, training; environment, conservation, heritage
Address: Institution of Chemical Engineers, 165-189 Railway Terrace, Rugby, Warwicks, CV21 3HQ
Trustees: Mr William James Harper CEng FIChemE, Mr Kenneth John Rivers CEng FIChemE, Dr Jarmila Glassey CEng FIChemE, Mr John Martin McGagh CEng FIChemE, Professor Lynn F Gladden CEng FIChemE, Mrs Allyson Black CEng FIChemE, Professor D W York, Professor Colin Webb CEng CSci FIChemE, Mr Iain James Martin CEng FIChemE, Mr Paul Ronald Ellis CEng FIChemE, Professor Jonathan Peter Kyle Seville CEng FIChemE, Mr David Haydn Platts CEng FIChemE, Mrs Jane Victoria Atkinson CEng Eur Ing FIChemE, Dr Christina Phang CEng FIChemE
Income: £7,954,000 [2016]; £7,369,000 [2015]; £8,542,000 [2014]; £7,681,175 [2013]; £7,305,370 [2012]

The Institution of Civil Engineers
Registered: 4 Mar 1963 *Employees:* 319 *Volunteers:* 6,766
Website: ice.org.uk
Activities: Education, training
Address: Institution of Civil Engineers, 1 Great George Street, London, SW1P 3AA
Trustees: Prof Robert Mair, Mr Edward James McCann, Mr Kyle Jonathan Clough CEng CEnv FICE APMP, Mr Steven Balliston, Mrs Emer Marie Murnaghan, Mr Richard Ian Philip Burleigh CEng FICE, Ms Kate Lydia Cairns CEng FICE, Mr Geoffrey Ogden, Maj Gareth Walker, Ms Emily Bonner, Mr Gary Brian Cutts, Ms Rachel Susan Skinner, Mr Andrew William Lewis Wolstenholme OBE FREng BSc CEng, Mr David Leonard Goodliff CEng FICE, Professor Andrew George McNaughton FREng CEng FICE, Miss Nicola Robins GMICE, Mrs Teresa June Frost IEng FICE, Mr Edward Philip Bingham CEng FICE, Mr Patrick Wing Tung Chan CEng FICE, Mr Stephen James Dellow CEng FICE, Miss Zoe Henderson GMICE, Miss Emma Julia Kent CEng MICE, Mr David Caiden CEng FICE, Professor Timothy William Broyd BSc PhD FREng FICE FRSA, Mr Chai-Kwong Mak JP FICE, Mr Peter John Hallsworth, Mr David Norman Porter, Mr Ronald Thomas Hunter CEng MICE, Mr Richard Giffen, Dr Jane Smallman, Mr Jeffrey Ashurst, Ms Denise Ann Bower, Ms Yvonne Murphy, Mr Andrew Wyllie, Mr Norman Frederick Brent CEng FICE, Mr Damian John Kilburn CEng FICE, Ms Claire Louise Oliver CEng MICE, Miss Helen Julia Samuels CEng FICE, Mr John Robert Beck CEng FICE, Mrs Karen Ann Britton CEng FICE, Mr Matthew James Colton CEng FICE, Mr Mark James Downes CEng MICE, Mr Mark Esdaile Jamieson CEng FICE, Mr Stephen Lonsdale Larkin CEng MICE
Income: £30,778,000 [2016]; £33,240,000 [2015]; £31,283,000 [2014]; £31,360,000 [2013]; £28,774,000 [2012]

The Institution of Engineering and Technology Benevolent Fund
Registered: 22 Sep 1962 *Employees:* 9 *Volunteers:* 20
Tel: 020 7344 5719 *Website:* ietconnect.org
Activities: General charitable purposes; advancement of health or saving of lives; disability; prevention or relief of poverty
Address: IET Connect, Napier House, 24 High Holborn, London, WC1V 6AZ
Trustees: Mrs J Brownsword MEng MIET, Mr R M North CEng MIET, Dr S Hart MEng CEng FIET, Eur Ing Professor A L Dowd BSc PhD CEng FIET, Dr P B Connor, Mrs Albina Dorothy Giles CEng FIET, Mrs Jayne Kathryn Bryant FREng CEng FIET FWES, Mr J A Aust BSc ACGI CEng MIET, Mr A R Clarke BSc CEng MIET, Mr Richard Edmund Howden Spalding CEng FIET
Income: £1,225,931 [2017]; £1,967,548 [2016]; £2,139,296 [2015]; £1,190,366 [2014]; £1,169,145 [2013]

The Institution of Engineering and Technology
Registered: 6 Feb 1964 *Employees:* 584 *Volunteers:* 3,080
Tel: 020 7344 5415 *Website:* theiet.org
Activities: Education, training
Address: The Institution of Engineering And Technology, 2 Savoy Place, London, WC2R 0BL
Trustees: Professor Bob Cryan, Professor Alison Noble, Dr Simon Harrison, Mrs Virginia Hodge, Mr Nick Winser, Eur Ing Graeme Hobbs, Air Marshal Julian Young, Miss Sam Hubbard, Mr Mike Carr, Mrs Jayne Bryant, Professor Jeremy Watson, Dr Peter Bonfield, Eur Ing Tom Hlaing, Mr Andy Bevington, Professor Danielle George, Miss Alyssa Randall
Income: £58,453,000 [2016]; £54,299,000 [2015]; £51,689,000 [2014]; £57,596,000 [2013]

The Institution of Gas Engineers and Managers
Registered: 12 Dec 1963 *Employees:* 23 *Volunteers:* 422
Tel: 01509 678167 *Website:* igem.org.uk
Activities: Education, training
Address: IGEM, 28 High Street, Kegworth, Derby, DE74 2DA
Trustees: David Jones, Mr Andy Cummings, Mr Ben Clarke, Mrs Shelia Lauchlan, Mr Nicholas Blair, Mr Karl Miller, Antony Green, Martin Kee, Mr Paul Lawrence, Mrs Rosemary McAll, Mr Tommy Knott, Miss Helen Fitzgerald, Mr Gregg Dadson, Steven Edwards, Mr Glen Judge, Mr Paul Denniff, Mr Duncan Wong, Phil Jenkins, David Parkin, Martin Alderson, Miss Katie Higgins, Mr David Butler, Mr Andrew Middleton, Ms Philippa Wrenn, Mr Peter Amos
Income: £1,654,087 [2016]; £1,589,514 [2015]; £1,713,128 [2014]; £1,479,437 [2013]; £1,334,981 [2012]

The Institution of Mechanical Engineers
Registered: 29 Jul 1963 *Employees:* 199 *Volunteers:* 5,000
Website: imeche.org
Activities: Education, training; economic, community development, employment
Address: Institution of Mechanical Engineers, 1 Birdcage Walk, London, SW1H 9JJ
Trustees: Mr John Herbert Lowe, Dr Clive Hickman, Professor Alan Lau, Dr Patrick Finlay, Mr Phil Peel, Mrs Heather Ann Clarke, Mrs Salma Suleyman, Carolyn Jane Griffiths FREng CEng FIMechE, Mr Geoff Baker, Mr Robin Philip Smith BSc CEng FIMechE, Professor Stephen Beck, Mr Ian Raymond Joesbury, Mrs Helena Clare Rivers CEng FIMechE
Income: £21,941,000 [2016]; £26,172,000 [2015]; £24,525,000 [2014]; £21,127,000 [2013]; £17,078,000 [2012]

The Institution of Occupational Safety and Health
Registered: 1 Apr 2003 *Employees:* 182 *Volunteers:* 700
Website: iosh.co.uk
Activities: Education, training; advancement of health or saving of lives
Address: Institution of Occupational Safety & Health, The Grange, Highfield Drive, Wigston, Leics, LE18 1NN
Trustees: Mr Nicholas Martens, Mr Steve Fowler, Ms Jane McCloskey, Mr Tony Bough, Miss Rebecca Joyce, Mr Neal Walker, Ms Candy Perry, Mrs Maria Darby-Walker, Dr William Gunnyeon CBE, Dr Robert Cooling, Mr Kevin Furniss
Income: £13,042,000 [2017]; £13,259,000 [2016]; £11,890,000 [2015]; £11,417,000 [2014]; £10,726,000 [2013]

The Institution of Railway Signal Engineers
Registered: 6 Jun 1995 *Employees:* 7 *Volunteers:* 80
Tel: 020 7808 1180 *Website:* irse.org
Activities: Education, training
Address: 4th Floor, 1 Birdcage Walk, Westminster, London, SW1H 9JJ
Trustees: Mr Andrew Simmons, Mr Gary Simpson, Mr Peter Robert Symons, Dr Daniel Woodland, Mr Martin Ramzi Fenner, Mrs Lynsey Hunter, Mr Ryan Gould, Professor Yuji Hirao, Mr Andrew Knight, Ms Jane Elizabeth Power, Mr Bogdan Godziejewski, Ms Cassandra Kelly Gash, Mr Charles Page, Mr George Edward Clark, Dr Markus Montigel, Mr Robert Emory Burkhardt, Mr Firas Al-Tahan, Mr Ian Bridges, Mr Philip Wai Ming Wong, Mr Stephen Walter Boshier, Mr Peter Andrew Allan, Mr Pierre Damien Jourdain, Mr Paul McSharry, Dr Xiaolu Rao
Income: £1,018,007 [2016]; £1,085,350 [2015]; £1,015,683 [2014]; £926,627 [2013]; £1,051,623 [2012]

The Institution of Structural Engineers
Registered: 5 Mar 1964 *Employees:* 53 *Volunteers:* 450
Tel: 020 7235 4535 *Website:* istructe.org
Activities: Education, training; environment, conservation, heritage; economic, community development, employment
Address: 47-58 Bastwick Street, London, EC1V 3PS
Trustees: Dr Ronald Basil Watermeyer, Mr Simon Jeremy Pitchers, Mr Ian Firth, Mr Glenn Russell Bell, Mr Donald McQuillan, Mr David Furnival Knight, Ms Jane Anne Entwistle, Ms Faith Helen Wainwright, Mrs Victoria Claire Martin, Mr Joseph Anthony Kindregan, Mrs Elizabeth Maria Visser
Income: £6,615,707 [2016]; £6,473,200 [2015]; £6,151,300 [2014]; £10,965,638 [2013]; £5,602,660 [2012]

Instructus
Registered: 2 Dec 2011 *Employees:* 32
Website: instructus.org
Activities: Education, training
Address: Unit 3 Cherry Hall Road, North Kettering Business Park, Kettering, Northants, NN14 1UE
Trustees: Mr Nigel Hopkins, Ms Ann Clayton, Mrs Emma Rush, Mr Simon Mercer, Ms Judith Norrington, Richard Traish
Income: £2,870,871 [2017]; £2,672,385 [2016]; £1,477,972 [2015]; £1,939,528 [2014]; £3,611,148 [2013]

The Insurance Charities
Registered: 22 Sep 1962 *Employees:* 6 *Volunteers:* 82
Tel: 020 7606 3763 *Website:* theinsurancecharities.org.uk
Activities: General charitable purposes; prevention or relief of poverty
Address: 3rd Floor, 2 St Andrew's Hill, London, EC4V 5BY
Trustees: Professor David Bland, Ms Adrienne O'Sullivan, Mr John Greenway, Mr Graham Cave, Mr Richard Wood, Mr Kevin Wood, Mr Tony Alderman, Mrs Kirsten Watson, Mr Kenneth Muir Davidson, Mr Lindsay Williamson, Mr Peter Staddon
Income: £1,375,000 [2017]; £3,829,000 [2016]; £1,225,000 [2015]; £1,259,000 [2014]; £1,311,000 [2013]

Integrate (Preston and Chorley) Limited
Registered: 7 Mar 1991 *Employees:* 313 *Volunteers:* 22
Tel: 01772 730312 *Website:* integratepreston.org.uk
Activities: Disability
Address: Integrate Preston & Chorley Ltd, 112-116 Tulketh Brow, Ashton on Ribble, Preston, Lancs, PR2 2SJ
Trustees: John Terrence Dunn, Thomas Adam McLean, Nancy Homan, Mr Paul McKeown, Mrs Lynda Arkwright RMN UKP Registered Psychoanalytic, Mr Terence Keely, Maureen Jocelyn Robinson, Mr David George Naden, Mr John Michael Kay, Mrs Kathleen Mercer, Mr Mark Bleasdale
Income: £7,488,951 [2017]; £6,397,311 [2016]; £5,754,246 [2015]; £5,220,294 [2014]; £4,689,526 [2013]

Integrated Neurological Services
Registered: 15 Dec 2004 *Employees:* 28 *Volunteers:* 45
Tel: 020 8755 4000 *Website:* ins.org.uk
Activities: The advancement of health or saving of lives; disability
Address: 82 Hampton Road, Twickenham, Middlesex, TW2 5QS
Trustees: Mr Telfer Saywell, Mrs Susan Stevens, Sarah Coleby, Mrs Susan Patricia Jeffers, Mr Chris Williams, Dugald Millar, Mr Lewis Hyde Gray
Income: £1,398,210 [2017]; £1,334,686 [2016]; £1,512,257 [2015]; £977,239 [2014]; £553,470 [2013]

Intensive Care National Audit and Research Centre
Registered: 13 Jul 1994 *Employees:* 37
Tel: 020 7831 6878 *Website:* icnarc.org
Activities: Education, training; advancement of health or saving of lives
Address: ICNARC, Napier House, 24 High Holborn, London, WC1V 6AZ
Trustees: Prof N Black, Dr Simon Baudouin, Mr Tim Gould, Mr Robert Nicholls, Ms Carolyn Sulin Seet, Prof Dk Menon, Ms Lisa Hinton, Mr Gareth Sellors, Mr Paul Geoffrey Maddox
Income: £2,631,437 [2016]; £2,160,804 [2015]; £2,879,637 [2014]; £2,447,458 [2013]; £3,007,786 [2012]

The Intensive Care Society
Registered: 6 Jul 1994 *Employees:* 6
Tel: 020 7280 4350 *Website:* ics.ac.uk
Activities: Education, training; advancement of health or saving of lives
Address: Churchill House, 35 Red Lion Square, London, WC1R 4SG
Trustees: Dr Jeremy Groves, Dr Hugh Edward Montgomery, Dr Richard John Innes, Dr Jagtar Singh Pooni, Dr Jamie Strachan, Dr Tony Whitehouse, Miss Fiona Wallace, Mrs Andrea Berry, Dr G R Masterson, Mr Craig Ian Brown, Dr Ganesh Suntharalingam, Dr Stephen Thomas Webb, Ms Sarah Elizabeth Clarke, Dr Steve Mathieu, Dr Jeremy Bewley
Income: £1,304,783 [2016]; £1,315,662 [2015]; £1,196,209 [2014]; £1,329,799 [2013]; £1,281,812 [2012]

Inter-Varsity Press
Registered: 6 Sep 2004
Tel: 020 7590 3900
Activities: Religious activities
Address: Society for Promoting Christian Knowledge, 36 Causton Street, London, SW1P 4ST
Trustees: Mr James Catford, Dr Andrew Fergusson, The Society For Promoting Christian Knowledge, The Rt Revd John Pritchard, Mr Eric Thompson
Income: £1,592,069 [2017]; £3,218,159 [2016]; £4,427,503 [2015]; £3,643,275 [2014]; £3,238,129 [2013]

Interact Chelmsford Limited
Registered: 12 Aug 1995 *Employees:* 26 *Volunteers:* 200
Tel: 01245 608201 *Website:* interact.org.uk
Activities: Education, training; disability; economic, community development, employment; recreation
Address: Essex Disabled Peoples Association, Moulsham Mill, Parkway, Chelmsford, Essex, CM2 7PX
Trustees: David Peacock, Mr Chris Rigler, Mrs Jenny McLean, Mr John Tweddell, Mrs Debbie Knight
Income: £2,122,254 [2017]; £1,822,309 [2016]; £2,079,523 [2015]; £2,872,421 [2014]; £1,996,339 [2013]

Intercountry Adoption Centre
Registered: 9 Jan 1998 *Employees:* 34
Tel: 020 8449 2562 *Website:* icacentre.org.uk
Activities: Education, training; other charitable purposes
Address: Intercountry Adoption Centre, 22 Union Street, Barnet, Herts, EN5 4HZ
Trustees: Ms Katherine Lucy Samwell-Smith, Ms Frances Elizabeth Petterson, Ms Barbara Hudson, Ms Anastasia Kathleen Ansell, Ms Tabitha Elinor Jane Northrup
Income: £1,674,554 [2017]; £1,105,458 [2016]; £966,940 [2015]; £790,698 [2014]; £626,873 [2013]

International Agency for The Prevention of Blindness
Registered: 6 Nov 2003 *Employees:* 23
Website: iapb.org
Activities: Education, training; advancement of health or saving of lives; disability; prevention or relief of poverty
Address: London School of Hygiene & Tropical Medicine, Keppel Street, London, WC1E 7HT
Trustees: Dr Caroline Harper, Ms Kathy Spahn, Ms Debra Davis, Prof Serge Resnikoff, Mr Robert Francis McMullan, Dr Taraprasad Das, Prof Hugh Taylor, Dr Ahmed Trabelsi, Dr Tirtha Prasad Mishra, Dr Juan Carlos Aragon, Mr Rupert Roniger, Dr Aaron Thembinkosi Magava, Dr Francisco Guillermo Martinez, Ms Victoria Sheffield, Prof Haidong Zou, HRH Prince Abdullaziz Ahmad Abdulaziz, Professor Kovin Shunmugam Naidoo, Ms Amanda Davis, Mr Arnt Holte, Dr Janos Nemeth, Dr Neil Lawrence Murray, Dr Astrid Elizabeth Bonfield, Ms Jennifer Gersbeck, Mr Job Heintz, Dr Muhammad Babar Qureshi, Mr Kashinath Bhoosnurmath, Dr Scott Gordon Mundle, Dr Suzanne Gilbert, Chancellor Bob Corlew
Income: £8,198,557 [2016]; £6,457,293 [2015]; £6,435,602 [2014]; £8,621,072 [2013]; £14,267,271 [2012]

International Aid Trust
Registered: 16 May 2001 *Employees:* 26 *Volunteers:* 320
Tel: 01772 611000 *Website:* internationalaidtrust.org.uk
Activities: General charitable purposes; education, training; advancement of health or saving of lives; disability; prevention or relief of poverty; overseas aid, famine relief; accommodation, housing; religious activities; amateur sport; economic, community development, employment
Address: International Aid Trust, Unit 2-3 Longton Business Park, Station Road, Little Hoole, Preston, Lancs, PR4 5LE
Trustees: Mr Derrick Leach, Mr Alexander Robert Taylor, Mr Paul Mansfield Cook, Dr Colin Edward Crawforth PhD, Miss Julie Denise Rowlandson
Income: £1,018,646 [2016]; £1,123,262 [2015]; £5,856,787 [2014]; £5,796,896 [2013]; £4,407,591 [2012]

International Alert
Registered: 24 Sep 1987 *Employees:* 214 *Volunteers:* 27
Tel: 020 7627 6800 *Website:* international-alert.org
Activities: Education, training; prevention or relief of poverty; overseas aid, famine relief; environment, conservation, heritage; economic, community development, employment; human rights, religious or racial harmony, equality or diversity; other charitable purposes
Address: 346 Clapham Road, London, SW9 9AP
Trustees: Dr Dhananjayan Sriskandarajah, Mr Oliver Kemp, Mrs Carol Allen Storey, Mr Padma Jyoti, Dr Alaa Murabit, Ms Lisa Lynn Ross, Mr Christopher John Mullin, Mrs Gordana Duspara Moriarty, Mr Gregor Ninian Stewart, Ms Helena Puig Larrauri, Mr Christopher Deri
Income: £17,921,000 [2016]; £15,118,000 [2015]; £14,784,000 [2014]; £12,962,000 [2013]; £12,979,000 [2012]

International Animal Rescue
Registered: 8 Mar 2007 *Employees:* 12 *Volunteers:* 2
Website: internationalanimalrescue.org
Activities: Education, training; animals; environment, conservation, heritage
Address: Lime House, Regency Close, Uckfield, E Sussex, TN22 1DS
Trustees: Mr Paul Cassar, Miss Lisa Caroline Milella, Mr Peter George Bennett, Mr Alastair John Irons
Income: £2,989,582 [2016]; £2,567,287 [2015]; £2,075,109 [2014]; £1,631,807 [2013]; £2,395,500 [2012]

International Association of Teachers of English as a Foreign Language
Registered: 1 Mar 2002 *Employees:* 10 *Volunteers:* 100
Tel: 01795 591414 *Website:* iatefl.org
Activities: Education, training
Address: Unit 2-3 The Foundry Business Park, Seager Road, Faversham, Kent, ME13 7FD
Trustees: Mr Colin MacKenzie, Ms Margit Szesztay, Ms Ros Wright, Dr Harry Kuchah Kuchah, Dr Lou McLaughlin, Ms Mojca Belak, Mr Shaun Wilden, Ms Judith Eunice Mader
Income: £1,106,125 [2016]; £1,088,262 [2015]; £1,088,227 [2014]; £1,047,794 [2013]

International Baccalaureate Fund UK
Registered: 6 Jan 2009
Website: ibo.org
Activities: Education, training
Address: Mrs Liliane von Wyl, International Baccalaureate, Route des Morillons 15, CH-1218 Grand-Saconnex, Geneva, Switzerland
Trustees: Ms Carolyn Adams, Paula Wilcock, Siva Kumari, Mr Thaimur Changezi
Income: £1,480,229 [2017]; £1,807,133 [2016]; £1,170,031 [2014]; £1,205,880 [2013]; £403,587 [2012]

International Baccalaureate Organization (UK) Limited
Registered: 14 Oct 2008 *Employees:* 236
Website: ibo.org
Activities: Education, training
Address: Ms Liliane von Wyl, International Baccalaureate, Route des Morillons 15, CH-1218 Grand-Saconnex, Geneva, Switzerland
Trustees: Robert Sackville-West, Dr Siva Kumari, Ms Paula Margaret Wilcock, Andrew Bennett, Ms Sian Elizabeth Thornhill
Income: £18,382,300 [2017]; £36,566,800 [2016]; £18,821,600 [2014]; £19,351,500 [2013]; £23,009,000 [2012]

International Bible Students Association
Registered: 18 Nov 1964 *Volunteers:* 300
Tel: 020 8906 2211
Activities: Overseas aid, famine relief; religious activities
Address: Ibsa House, The Ridgeway, London, NW7 1RN
Trustees: Mr Paul Stuart Gillies, Karl W Snaith, Mr Jonathan Manley, Mr Stephen Papps, Mr Ivor Darby
Income: £29,591,385 [2017]; £43,009,677 [2016]; £38,919,770 [2015]; £28,326,223 [2014]; £18,987,169 [2013]

International Cat Care
Registered: 20 Dec 2006 *Employees:* 18
Tel: 01747 871872 *Website:* icatcare.org
Activities: Education, training; animals
Address: International Cat Care, Place Farm, Court Street, Tisbury, Salisbury, Wilts, SP3 6LW
Trustees: Mr Philip Sketchley, Professor Stuart Carmichael, Kevin Cope, Deborah Mary Webb, Mr Robert Ross Tiffin, Mr Alexander Campbell, Ms Martha Cannon, Helen Dennis, Ms Susan Badger
Income: £1,637,199 [2016]; £1,617,059 [2015]; £1,406,357 [2014]; £1,507,466 [2013]; £1,122,983 [2012]

International Centre for Life Trust
Registered: 5 Dec 1996 *Employees:* 161
Tel: 0191 243 8222 *Website:* life.org.uk
Activities: Education, training; advancement of health or saving of lives; arts, culture, heritage, science; other charitable purposes
Address: Management Suite, Times Square, Scotswood Road, Newcastle upon Tyne, NE1 4EP
Trustees: Lucy Winskell OBE DL, Dr Steven Gater, Clive Cookson, Fiona Cruickshank OBE, Mr Andrew Hodgson OBE, Professor Richard Davies, Alastair Balls CB DL, Linda Conlon MBE, Professor Patrick Hussey PhD, Professor Roy Sandbach OBE, Professor Joris Veltman, Councillor Stella Postlethwaite
Income: £7,095,750 [2017]; £7,403,252 [2016]; £7,307,587 [2015]; £6,045,149 [2014]; £4,860,125 [2013]

International Development Enterprises (UK)
Registered: 9 Jul 2001 *Employees:* 4
Tel: 020 3290 5510 *Website:* ideglobal.org
Activities: The prevention or relief of poverty; overseas aid, famine relief; economic, community development, employment
Address: Aldgate Tower, 2 Leman Street, London, E1 8FA
Trustees: Mr Robert Hill, Mrs Elizabeth Ellis, Mr Bradley McLean, Mr Timothy Prewitt, Ms Dora Panagides
Income: £4,598,504 [2016]; £3,938,348 [2015]; £2,275,621 [2014]; £2,592,453 [2013]; £2,324,918 [2012]

International Federation of Gynecology and Obstetrics
Registered: 14 Mar 2006 *Employees:* 24 *Volunteers:* 20
Website: figo.org
Activities: The advancement of health or saving of lives
Address: International Federation of Gynecology & Obstetrics, Unit 3 Waterloo Court, 10 Theed Street, London, SE1 8ST
Trustees: Professor Gian Carlo Di Renzo, Dr Seija Grenman, Dr Ralph Hale, Professor Chittaranjan Narahari Purandare, Dr Carlos Fuchtner, Dr Yirgu Gebrehiowot
Income: £7,381,456 [2016]; £5,288,355 [2015]; £3,230,609 [2014]; £2,256,449 [2013]; £6,496,032 [2012]

International Fellowship of Evangelical Students
Registered: 13 Jun 1966 *Employees:* 69 *Volunteers:* 30
Tel: 01865 263777 *Website:* ifesworld.org
Activities: Religious activities
Address: I F E S, Blue Boar House, 5 Blue Boar Street, Oxford, OX1 4EE
Trustees: Mr Christopher Collins, Mr Glenn Smith, Dr Nishan De Mel, Mrs Renee Gibson, Mr Vinicio Javier Zuquino Barrientos, Rev Samuel McCook, Mr Timothy Rudge, Mr Septi Bukula, Mr Michel Kenmogne, Ms Esther Phua, Mr David Edmund, Ms Valerie Goold, Mrs Mi Sook Lim, Rev Riad Kassis
Income: £5,855,206 [2016]; £5,086,725 [2015]; £4,540,139 [2014]; £4,533,572 [2013]; £3,772,831 [2012]

International Finance Facility for Immunisation Company
Registered: 18 Jul 2006
Tel: 020 7600 1200 *Website:* iffim.org
Activities: The advancement of health or saving of lives
Address: Trusec Limited, 2 Lamb's Passage, London, EC1Y 8BB
Trustees: Mr Marcus Fedder, Mr Cyrus Ardalan, Ms Doris Aida D Lourdes Herrera Pol, Mr Christopher Egerton-Warburton, Ms Fatimatou Zahra Diop, Mr Bertrand De Mazieres
Income: £23,235,077 [2016]; £3,855,694 [2015]; £2,458,818 [2014]; £3,102,627 [2013]; £4,579,760 [2012]

International Food Information Service (IFIS Publishing)
Registered: 17 Feb 1998 *Employees:* 14
Tel: 0118 988 3895 *Website:* ifis.org
Activities: Education, training
Address: Ifis Publishing, J2 The Granary, Bridge Farm, Reading Road, Arborfield, Reading, Berks, RG2 9HT
Trustees: Mrs Barbara Byrd Keenan, Mr David Hugh Duncan, Mr Predrag Pavlicic, Professor Colin Dennis, Mr Weibiao Zhou
Income: £2,063,462 [2017]; £1,994,530 [2016]; £2,623,319 [2015]; £1,867,409 [2014]; £1,804,873 [2013]

International Foundation for Aids To Navigation
Registered: 22 Feb 1963 *Employees:* 10
Website: menas.org
Activities: The advancement of health or saving of lives; environment, conservation, heritage
Address: Ifan, 8-9 Lovat Lane, London, EC3R 8DW
Trustees: Mr Hussain Sultan, Mr John Wilson Hughes, Mr Rob Brummer, John Evans, Conrad Blakey, Mr Guy Mason, Mr Yousuf Al Saqer, Mr Tomoyuki Koyama
Income: £8,148,428 [2016]; £5,107,470 [2015]; £10,222,022 [2014]; £12,283,447 [2013]; £10,346,707 [2012]

International Fund for Animal Welfare (IFAW)
Registered: 11 Aug 1993 *Employees:* 26 *Volunteers:* 6
Tel: 020 7587 6707 *Website:* ifaw.org
Activities: Education, training; animals; environment, conservation, heritage
Address: International Fund for Animal Welfare, Camelford House, 87-90 Albert Embankment, London, SE1 7UD
Trustees: Brian Hutchinson, Kathleen Savesky Buckley, Debobrata Mukherjee, Barbara Ungerman Birdsey, Susan Wallace, Catherine Lilly, Mr Robert Cushman Barber, Mr Daniel Thomas Lenyo, Margaret Kennedy, Graeme Robin Cottam, Thomas O'Neill, Joyce Carol Doria, Mark Beaudouin, Mr Gregory Mertz, Ms Virginia Alejandra Pollak
Income: £20,117,783 [2017]; £19,776,361 [2016]; £20,669,770 [2015]; £19,564,699 [2014]; £20,890,879 [2013]

International Glaucoma Association Limited
Registered: 20 Dec 1977 *Employees:* 13 *Volunteers:* 21
Tel: 01233 648164 *Website:* glaucoma-association.com
Activities: Education, training; advancement of health or saving of lives; disability
Address: Woodcote House, 15 Highpoint Business Village, Henwood, Ashford, Kent, TN24 8DH
Trustees: Mrs Mary E Shaw, Mr Julian J M Exeter, Mr Stephen Epstein, Mr Philip Bloom, Professor Anthony King, Dr Susan Parkins, Sheila Page, Yolanda Laybourne, Mr Raymond Spendiff, Mr Nicholas Strouthidis, Mr David Sanders
Income: £1,297,666 [2017]; £1,373,543 [2016]; £1,012,764 [2015]; £897,347 [2014]; £1,307,935 [2013]

International HIV/Aids Alliance
Registered: 8 Jul 1994 *Employees:* 131
Tel: 01273 718900 *Website:* aidsalliance.org
Activities: The advancement of health or saving of lives
Address: 1st and 2nd Floor, Preece House, 91-101 Davigdor Road, Hove, E Sussex, BN3 1RE
Trustees: Mr Martin Dinham, Mr Zhen Li, Angela Gomez Kopp, Ms Marika Fahlen, Kieran Daly, Ms Thoko Moyo, Miss Janet Tatenda Bhila, Mr Prasada Rao Jonnalagadda, Kevin Moody, Andrea Monica Marmolejo, Warren Buckingham III, Dr Christoph Benn, Ms Maya Mungra
Income: £20,412,051 [2016]; £27,880,413 [2015]; £29,631,608 [2014]; £24,310,918 [2013]; £23,582,740 [2012]

International Health Partners (UK) Limited
Registered: 12 Aug 2004 *Employees:* 10 *Volunteers:* 1
Tel: 020 3735 5489 *Website:* ihpuk.org
Activities: The advancement of health or saving of lives; overseas aid, famine relief
Address: Unit 402 Clerkenwell Workshops, 27-31 Clerkenwell Close, London, EC1R 0AT
Trustees: Helen Leighton, Professor Richard Barker, Mr Ian B L Walker, Mr Peter Ballard, Mr Glyn Williams, Mr Andrew Russell FCA, Mr Peter O'Driscoll, Dr Nigel Pearson, Mr Simon Howard
Income: £19,268,456 [2016]; £7,802,183 [2015]; £22,777,102 [2014]; £11,506,474 [2013]; £15,974,875 [2012]

International House Trust Limited
Registered: 12 Mar 1976 *Employees:* 290
Tel: 07785 228816 *Website:* ihlondon.com
Activities: Education, training
Address: 46 Hemingford Road, London, N1 1DB
Trustees: Mr Paul Lindsay Mason, Ms Gillian Murray, Mr Simon Anthony Greenall, Mr Gavin David Dudeney, Mr Ricard Alonso, Mr Fintan Somers, Dr Angela Dean, Ms Maggie Van Reenen, Mr Adrian Guilford Underhill, Ms Monica Green, Ms Elizabeth McGlynn
Income: £14,494,000 [2016]; £14,936,000 [2015]; £15,146,625 [2014]; £13,360,792 [2013]; £12,845,146 [2012]

International Institute for Environment and Development
Registered: 28 Apr 1989 *Employees:* 125
Tel: 020 3463 7399 *Website:* iied.org
Activities: Education, training; prevention or relief of poverty; overseas aid, famine relief; environment, conservation, heritage; economic, community development, employment; human rights, religious or racial harmony, equality or diversity
Address: 80-86 Gray's Inn Road, London, WC1H 8NX
Trustees: Ms Elizabeth Stephen, Mrs Filippa Norman Bergin, Ms Fatima Denton, Ms Tara Shine, Mrs Angela Mc Naught, Mr Michael Horgan, Ms Susan Parnell, Mr Lorenzo Jose Dr Rosenzweig, Ms Somsook Boonyabancha, Ms Rebeca Grynspan Mayufis, Mr Ahmed Galal, Mr David Aiken Elston, Mr Les Campbell
Income: £21,030,675 [2017]; £17,875,785 [2016]; £18,042,226 [2015]; £19,400,435 [2014]; £16,300,983 [2013]

The International Institute for Strategic Studies
Registered: 22 Sep 1962 *Employees:* 126
Tel: 020 7379 7676 *Website:* iiss.org
Activities: General charitable purposes; education, training; other charitable purposes
Address: Arundel House, 6 Temple Place, London, WC2R 2PG
Trustees: Professor Francois Heisbourg, Mr Thomas Seaman, Mr Jens Tholstrup, Dr Kurt Lauk, Chris Jones, Ms Catherine Roe, Ms Fleur Olive Lourens De Villiers, Mr William Emmott, Ms Sophie-Caroline De Margerie, Mr Matthew Symonds
Income: £17,772,783 [2017]; £17,471,109 [2016]; £14,926,674 [2015]; £16,108,000 [2014]; £16,020,000 [2013]

International Institute of Risk and Safety Management
Registered: 18 Jan 2005 *Employees:* 10 *Volunteers:* 10
Tel: 020 8741 9100 *Website:* iirsm.org
Activities: Education, training; advancement of health or saving of lives; other charitable purposes
Address: 77-85 Fulham Palace Road, Hammersmith, London, W6 8JA
Trustees: Dr Su Wang, Mr Andy Hawkes, Mr Clive Johnson, Mr Andrew Butt, Mrs Siobhan Donnelly, Mr Paul Simpson, Ms Anne Mallory
Income: £1,232,013 [2017]; £1,260,854 [2016]; £1,072,162 [2015]; £1,002,520 [2014]; £944,525 [2013]

International Justice Mission UK
Registered: 22 Aug 2003 Employees: 17 Volunteers: 7
Website: ijmuk.org
Activities: General charitable purposes; education, training; prevention or relief of poverty
Address: P O Box 12251, Witham, Essex, CM8 9BX
Trustees: Raj Parker, Miss Joanna Rice, Andrew Legg, Martin Greenslade, Mrs Melanie Lane, Mr Philip Andrew Langford
Income: £1,276,711 [2016]; £1,173,437 [2015]; £1,134,595 [2014]; £709,824 [2013]; £675,877 [2012]

International Learning Movement (Ilm)
Registered: 5 Mar 2004 Employees: 4 Volunteers: 4
Website: ilmuk.org
Activities: General charitable purposes; education, training; advancement of health or saving of lives; disability; prevention or relief of poverty; overseas aid, famine relief; accommodation, housing; economic, community development, employment; human rights, religious or racial harmony, equality or diversity; other charitable purposes
Address: 52 Tontine Street, Blackburn, Lancs, BB1 7ED
Trustees: Ms Joyce Bishop, Mrs Hamida Patel, Mr Nasir Ahmed, Mr Waqaar Aktar
Income: £1,545,504 [2017]; £1,209,748 [2016]; £491,311 [2015]; £588,454 [2014]; £188,256 [2013]

International Liberty Association
Registered: 23 Feb 2015 Volunteers: 29
Tel: 020 8452 3481
Activities: General charitable purposes; education, training; advancement of health or saving of lives; human rights, religious or racial harmony, equality or diversity
Address: Flat 22, Garden Court, 63 Holden Road, London, N12 7DG
Trustees: Ms Carolyn Sara Beckingham, Mrs Fatemeh Oliyaei, Mr Freidoon Seyedamady, Mr David Clifford Wood, Mr William Hughes, Mr Hoshang Dookani
Income: £4,283,327 [2017]; £2,989,347 [2016]

International Medical Corps (UK)
Registered: 19 Sep 2002 Employees: 29 Volunteers: 5
Tel: 020 3870 9992 Website: internationalmedicalcorps.org.uk
Activities: Education, training; advancement of health or saving of lives; disability; prevention or relief of poverty; overseas aid, famine relief; economic, community development, employment; other charitable purposes
Address: International Medical Corps UK, Scandinavian Centre, 161 Marsh Wall, Canary Wharf, London, E14 9SJ
Trustees: Mr Andrew Geczy, Mr Timothy Stewart Kirk, Ms Nancy Anne Aossey, Mr William Sundblad
Income: £123,658,942 [2017]; £109,008,883 [2016]; £98,344,749 [2015]; £66,603,656 [2014]; £50,581,155 [2013]

International NGO Safety Organisation
Registered: 8 Feb 2011 Employees: 650
Website: ngosafety.org
Activities: The prevention or relief of poverty; overseas aid, famine relief
Address: INSO, 10 Queen Street Place, London, EC4R 1BE
Trustees: Foluke Mogaji, Mr Mario Stephan, Sonia Di Mezza, Nicolas Lee, Chris Roberts, Emmanuel Rinck
Income: £13,519,942 [2017]; £8,848,914 [2016]; £5,660,083 [2015]; £3,501,515 [2014]; £3,014,534 [2013]

International Network for The Availability of Scientific Publications
Registered: 18 Oct 2004 Employees: 29
Tel: 01865 249909 Website: inasp.info
Activities: Education, training; overseas aid, famine relief
Address: INASP, 2-3 Cambridge Terrace, Oxford, OX1 1RR
Trustees: Mrs Anne Tutt, Mr Sohail Naqvi, Ms Felicity Jones, Mr John Young, Ms Liz Carlile, Dr Josephine Beall, Mr Omotade Aina
Income: £4,576,926 [2016]; £5,342,085 [2015]; £4,421,596 [2014]; £3,448,515 [2013]; £3,167,495 [2012]

International Non-Governmental Organisation Training and Research Centre
Registered: 27 Jan 1993 Employees: 24 Volunteers: 1
Tel: 01865 201852 Website: intrac.org
Activities: General charitable purposes; education, training; prevention or relief of poverty; overseas aid, famine relief; other charitable purposes
Address: Oxbridge, Old Fruiterers Yard, Osney Mead, Oxford, OX2 0ES
Trustees: Ms Carolyn Miller, Ms Sue Turrell, Mr Philip Edward Vernon, Dr Sheila Ochugboju, Tom Travers, George Gelber, Mr James Copestake, Ms Ana Filipa Fernandes
Income: £1,981,814 [2017]; £1,996,285 [2016]; £1,950,001 [2015]; £2,041,347 [2014]; £1,921,515 [2013]

International P.E.N.
Registered: 30 Nov 2006 Employees: 18 Volunteers: 8
Tel: 020 7405 0338 Website: pen-international.org
Activities: Education, training; arts, culture, heritage, science; economic, community development, employment; human rights, religious or racial harmony, equality or diversity
Address: International P E N, Brownlow House, 50-51 High Holborn, London, WC1V 6ER
Trustees: Mr Antonio Della Rocca, Mr Mohammed Sheriff, Margie Orford, Ms Jennifer Sibley Clement, Ms Ma Thida, Ms Iman Humaydan, Mr Jarrko Tontti, Mr Anders Heger, Dr Regula Venske, Ms Elisabeth Heister, Ms Katlin Kaldmaa
Income: £1,581,131 [2017]; £1,401,314 [2016]; £1,307,324 [2015]; £1,148,916 [2014]; £954,390 [2013]

International Planned Parenthood Federation
Registered: 8 Aug 1963 Employees: 358
Tel: 020 7939 8294 Website: ippf.org
Activities: Education, training; advancement of health or saving of lives; disability; overseas aid, famine relief; human rights, religious or racial harmony, equality or diversity
Address: IPPF, 4 Newhams Row, London, SE1 3UZ
Trustees: Dr Esther Vicente, Mr Bert Van Herk, Mr Kweku Osae Brenu, Mrs Safieh Shahriari Afshar, Mr Tawfeeq Naseeb, Ms Kristina Ljungros, Ms Jeanne Francoise Leckomba Loumeto Pombo, Mr Charles Kelly, Mr Napoleon Hernandez, Ms Deandra Walker, M M Muzibur Rahman, Ms Khadija Ghoussain Nader, Mrs Naomi Seboni, Mrs Diana Barco, Mr Mohammad Tarek Ghedira, Mrs Sujatha Natarajan, Ms Lene Stavngaard, Ms Dilnoza Shukurova, Ms Adama Dicko, Ms Helena O'Dwyer-Strang, Ms Atashendartini Habsjah, Mr Santiago Cosio, Ms Shambhavi Poudel, Ms Nadine Nabulsi
Income: £95,875,735 [2016]; £75,961,438 [2015]; £81,167,686 [2014]; £82,536,753 [2013]; £89,634,898 [2012]

International Psychoanalytical Association
Registered: 28 Sep 1998 *Employees:* 12 *Volunteers:* 12
Tel: 020 8446 8324 *Website:* ipa.world
Activities: Education, training; advancement of health or saving of lives
Address: 1 Winchester Road, Bromley, London, BR2 0PZ
Trustees: Dr William Glover, Mrs Alexandra Billinghurst, Mrs Ruth Axelrod Praes, Magister Jorge Bruce, Dr Jack Novick, Dr Andrew Brook, Ms Mira Erlich-Ginor, Dr Giovanni Foresti, Ms Beth Kalish, Dr Sergio Lewkowicz, Mr Alvaro Nin Novoa, Dr Jonathan Sklar, Dr Stefano Bolognini, Dr Giovanna Ambrosio, Dr Carlos Ernesto Barredo, Dr Nicolas De Coulon, Mrs Arlene Kramer Richards, Lic Luis Jorge Martin Cabre, Mr Abel Mario Fainstein, Mr Martin Gauthier, Dr Lewis Kirshner, Prof Peter Loewenberg, Mr Claudio Rossi, Dr Martin Teising
Income: £1,878,499 [2016]; £2,777,151 [2015]; £1,661,887 [2014]; £2,560,427 [2013]; £1,803,435 [2012]

International Rescue Committee, U.K
Registered: 20 Nov 1997 *Employees:* 64
Tel: 020 7692 2727 *Website:* rescue-uk.org
Activities: Education, training; advancement of health or saving of lives; prevention or relief of poverty; overseas aid, famine relief; economic, community development, employment
Address: 3 Bloomsbury Place, London, WC1A 2QL
Trustees: Mr George Biddle, Mr John Holmes, Mr Jake Ulrich, Dylan Pereira, Mr Ian Charles Barry, Ms Christina Ceelen, Mr William Winters, Mr Kemal Ahmed, Sir Michael Lockett, Mrs Iliane Ogilvie Thompson, Ms Lynette Lowndes, Ms Susan Gibson, Sir Hugh Bayley, Mr Ciaran Donnelly, Mr Francesco Garzarelli
Income: £142,618,000 [2017]; £146,336,000 [2016]; £124,222,000 [2015]; £109,512,000 [2014]; £83,631,000 [2013]

International Road Assessment Programme
Registered: 10 Feb 2011 *Employees:* 13
Tel: 07753 321190 *Website:* irap.org
Activities: Education, training; prevention or relief of poverty; economic, community development, employment
Address: 46 Queens Road, Aberdeen, AB15 4YE
Trustees: Mr Saul Peter Billingsley, Mr Miquel Nadal, Mr Ferdinand Emanuel Smith, Mr John Peter Kissinger, Mr Gary John Liddle
Income: £1,992,610 [2016]; £1,769,290 [2015]; £1,358,193 [2014]; £1,984,821 [2013]; £2,017,769 [2012]

The International Schools Theatre Association
Registered: 23 Oct 1995 *Employees:* 5
Tel: 01326 560398 *Website:* ista.co.uk
Activities: Education, training; arts, culture, heritage, science
Address: 3 Omega Offices, 14 Coinagehall Street, Helston, Cornwall, TR13 8EB
Trustees: Mr Iain Stirling, Ms Sherri Denise Sutton, Ms Emily Ross, Mrs Anne Drouet, Ms Jessica Alice Thorpe, Mr Alan Hayes, Mr Michael Bindon
Income: £1,261,923 [2017]; £1,159,350 [2016]; £1,043,009 [2015]; £1,015,886 [2014]; £829,694 [2013]

International Seafarers' Welfare and Assistance Network
Registered: 30 Mar 2004 *Employees:* 15
Tel: 0300 012 4279 *Website:* seafarerswelfare.org
Activities: Education, training; advancement of health or saving of lives; prevention or relief of poverty; amateur sport; economic, community development, employment
Address: ISWAN, Suffolk House, George Street, Croydon, Surrey, CR0 1PE
Trustees: Martin Foley, Captain Syed Mahmoodi, Dr Suresh Idnani, Soren Sorensen, Mr Andrew Winbow, Michael Pinto, Peter Swift, Mr Torbjorn Husby, Mr Per Gullestrup, Mr John Canias, Mrs Karin Orsel, Mr Deepak Shetty
Income: £1,030,654 [2017]; £764,319 [2016]; £479,943 [2015]; £665,212 [2014]; £520,925 [2013]

International Service Fellowship Trust
Registered: 7 May 1993 *Employees:* 79 *Volunteers:* 6
Tel: 01908 552700 *Website:* interserve.org.uk
Activities: Education, training; advancement of health or saving of lives; prevention or relief of poverty; overseas aid, famine relief; religious activities
Address: 5-6 Walker Avenue, Wolverton Mill, Milton Keynes, Bucks, MK12 5TW
Trustees: Mr Thomas Chacko, Mr Kevin Stewart Ashman, Mr Colin Sheppard, Mr Malcolm Kemp, Professor Mark Arthur Charles Pietroni, Mrs Ruth Downes, Rev Jane Methven Howitt, Mr Onkar Singh, Dr Sean Oliver-Dee, Rev John Peter Smuts, Mrs Jane Showell-Rogers, Dr Mark Laing, Mrs Patricia Ann McConkey
Income: £2,770,790 [2016]; £2,811,319 [2015]; £2,878,768 [2014]; £2,604,065 [2013]; £2,345,947 [2012]

International Society for Influenza and Other Respiratory Diseases
Registered: 16 Apr 2007
Tel: 020 8560 3850 *Website:* isirv.org
Activities: Education, training; advancement of health or saving of lives
Address: 54A Castle Road, Isleworth, Middlesex, TW7 6QS
Trustees: Mr John Michael Wood, Dr Lance Jennings, Dr Alan James Hay, Dr Stephen Mark Tompkins, Dr Benjamin John Cowling, Dr Cheryl Cohen, Dr Nancy Jane Cox, Professor Nelson Lee, Dr Hassan Zaraket, Eeva Broberg, Dr Barbara Rath, Professor John William McCauley, Dr Mario Augusto Melgar, Dr Jacqueline Katz, Dr Norio Sugaya, Professor Rebecca Cox, Dr Jean-Michel Heraud, Dr Maria Zambon, Professor Peter Openshaw, Dr Alan William Hampson, Professor Vernon Lee, Aeron Hurt, Gregory Gray, Prof Emmanuele Montomoli, Dr Jude Jayamaha, Dr Rodrigo Fasce Pineda
Income: £1,112,535 [2017]; £357,490 [2016]; £93,573 [2015]; £78,372 [2014]; £94,823 [2013]

International Society for Krishna Consciousness Bhaktivedanta Manor
Registered: 16 Jul 2014 *Employees:* 77 *Volunteers:* 1,500
Tel: 07429 416657 *Website:* bhaktivedantamanor.co.uk
Activities: General charitable purposes; education, training; advancement of health or saving of lives; prevention or relief of poverty; accommodation, housing; religious activities; arts, culture, heritage, science; animals; environment, conservation, heritage
Address: Iskcon Bhaktivedanta Manor, Dharam Marg, Hilfield Lane, Watford, Herts, WD25 8EZ
Trustees: His Grace Shailesh Patel, Mr Ramesh Hirji Rajpal Shah, Mr Dilip Kumar Patel, Yasoda Suta Das, Mr Sanjiv Kumar Agarwal, Mr William John Martin Fleming, Madhavi Dasi
Income: £4,142,777 [2016]

International Society for Krishna Consciousness Limited
Registered: 16 Oct 1969 *Employees:* 198 *Volunteers:* 2,500
Tel: 01923 856173 *Website:* iskconuk.com
Activities: Education, training; religious activities; arts, culture, heritage, science
Address: International Society for Krishna, Consciousness, 1 Watford Road, Radlett, Herts, WD7 8LA
Trustees: Mr Anthony Howchin, Mr Niresh Ranjan Dey, Mr Kamlesh Kumar Maheshwar Patel, Mr Paul Murphy, Mr Terry Michael Anderson
Income: £9,515,945 [2016]; £7,370,146 [2015]; £7,041,505 [2014]; £6,198,254 [2013]; £6,000,526 [2012]

International Society for Krishna Consciousness London
Registered: 19 Nov 2009 *Employees:* 38 *Volunteers:* 500
Tel: 020 7437 3662 *Website:* iskcon-london.org
Activities: Education, training; advancement of health or saving of lives; prevention or relief of poverty; religious activities; arts, culture, heritage, science; animals; environment, conservation, heritage; economic, community development, employment
Address: Radha Krishna Temple, 10 Soho Street, London, W1D 3DL
Trustees: Mr James Edwards, Martin Hayes, Mrs Bhavna Edwards, Mr Robert Gregory Marks
Income: £1,651,892 [2016]; £1,715,926 [2015]; £1,594,298 [2014]; £1,450,469 [2013]; £1,128,241 [2012]

The International Society of Ultrasound in Obstetrics and Gynecology
Registered: 22 Dec 1993 *Employees:* 18 *Volunteers:* 90
Tel: 020 7471 9955 *Website:* isuog.org
Activities: Education, training; advancement of health or saving of lives
Address: The International Society of Ultrasound in Obstetrics and Gynecology, 122 Freston Road, London, W10 6TR
Trustees: Professor Joshua Copel, Dr Alain Gagnon, Dr Christoph Andreas Brezinka, Antonia Testa, Mr Aris Papageorghiou, Professor George Yeo, Professor Jonathan Hyett, Dr Prashant Acharya, Dr Christoph Lees, Professor Thomas Bourne, Daniela Fischerova, Dr Andrew Choo Choon Ngu, Dr Caterina Bilardo, Nicholas Raine-Fenning, Dr Gustavo Malinger, Mr Laurent Salomon, Professor Dirk Timmerman, Professor Daniela Prayer, Professor Mauricio Herrera, Dr Antonia Testa, Dr Boris Alexander Tutscheck
Income: £2,925,509 [2016]; £2,087,818 [2015]; £3,201,404 [2014]; £2,255,637 [2013]; £2,463,943 [2012]

International Spinal Research Trust
Registered: 28 Feb 2013 *Employees:* 9 *Volunteers:* 75
Tel: 020 7653 8935 *Website:* spinal-research.org
Activities: The advancement of health or saving of lives
Address: International Spinal Research Trust, 80 Coleman Street, London, EC2R 5BJ
Trustees: Mr D Thomson, Miss E F Blois, Professor James Fawcett PhD FRCP, Mr J Hick, Mr D Allan, Miss S J Pelly, Mr Ian Curtis, Mr R Shelton
Income: £1,738,000 [2017]; £1,469,000 [2016]; £1,750,000 [2015]; £2,072,271 [2014]

International Students House
Registered: 11 Oct 1962 *Employees:* 82
Tel: 020 7631 8301 *Website:* ish.org.uk
Activities: Overseas aid, famine relief; accommodation, housing; amateur sport
Address: 1 Park Crescent, Regents Park, London, W1B 1SH
Trustees: Ms Tesse Akpeki, Mr Ian Barry, Mrs Ipek De Vilder, Mr Vikram Mathur, Ms Gillian Hammond, Mr Michael Hedley Carrier, Dr Geoffrey Malcolm Copland, Prof Ajit Lalvani, Mrs Julie Costley-White, Mr Russel Peters, Lord Nicholas Bourne
Income: £8,137,859 [2017]; £7,919,152 [2016]; £7,868,794 [2015]; £7,333,507 [2014]; £7,116,334 [2013]

International Water Association
Registered: 22 Jul 1999 *Employees:* 47
Tel: 020 7654 5505 *Website:* iwahq.org
Activities: Education, training; advancement of health or saving of lives; environment, conservation, heritage
Address: International Water Association Ltd, Alliance House, 12 Caxton Street, London, SW1H 0QS
Trustees: Mrs D Arras Diane, Mr Enrique Cabrea Rochera, Mr Hiroaki Furumai, Mr Thomas Michael Mollenkopf, Ms Norhayati Abdullah, Ms Helle Katrine Andersen, Dr Marie-Pierre Whaley, Dr Kalanithy Vairavamoorthy, Mr Helmut Kroiss, Mr Daniel Alfredo Nolasco, Mr Xiaojun Fan, Mr Sudhir Narasimha Murthy, Mr Silver Mugisha, Dr Joan Rose, Dr Hamanth Chotoo Kasan
Income: £8,309,912 [2016]; £6,519,266 [2015]; £8,510,013 [2014]; £6,155,043 [2013]; £7,645,984 [2012]

The International Youth Foundation
Registered: 1 Jan 1981 *Employees:* 5 *Volunteers:* 2
Tel: 020 7235 7671 *Website:* euyo.eu
Activities: Education, training; arts, culture, heritage, science
Address: 6A Pont Street, London, SW1X 9EL
Trustees: Sir John Tusa, Mrs Lesley King-Lewis, Martijn Sanders, Mr Ian Stoutzker OBE, Anthony Sargent
Income: £1,515,076 [2016]; £1,488,250 [2015]; £1,586,021 [2014]; £1,837,867 [2013]; £1,744,062 [2012]

International Youth Hostel Federation
Registered: 28 Nov 2006 *Employees:* 26
Tel: 01707 324170 *Website:* hihostels.com
Activities: Education, training; accommodation, housing; amateur sport; environment, conservation, heritage
Address: International Youth Hostel Federation, Gate House, Fretherne Road, Welwyn Garden City, Herts, AL8 6RD
Trustees: Mrs Angela Braasch-Eggert, Mr Eric Oetjen, Mr Sander Allegro, Mr Stephan Kurmann, Ms Milena Tevanovic, Mr Alex Zilkens, Mr Abdulla Al-Bikri, Mr Benoit Graisset-Recco, Mr Ramis Jose Pires Bedran
Income: £1,672,237 [2017]; £2,017,697 [2016]; £1,854,453 [2015]; £2,142,805 [2014]; £2,890,984 [2013]

Internet Watch Foundation
Registered: 5 Dec 2005 *Employees:* 31
Tel: 01223 203030 *Website:* iwf.org.uk
Activities: General charitable purposes
Address: Internet Watch Foundation, Discovery House, Chivers Way, Histon, Cambridge, CB24 9ZR
Trustees: Mr Jonathan Drori, Miss Becky Foreman, Mr John Parkinson, Dr Uta Kohl, Mrs Katherine O'Donovan, Ms Claire Bassett, Mr Andrew Puddephatt, Mrs Helen Dent, Mr Jonathan Lea, Miss Susan Pillar, Ms Jacqueline Mellor
Income: £2,887,298 [2017]; £2,885,356 [2016]; £2,272,805 [2015]; £1,753,761 [2014]; £1,473,392 [2013]

Internews Europe
Registered: 1 Aug 2012 *Employees:* 32 *Volunteers:* 2
Tel: 020 7566 3300 *Website:* internews.org
Activities: Education, training; advancement of health or saving of lives; prevention or relief of poverty; overseas aid, famine relief; environment, conservation, heritage; economic, community development, employment; human rights, religious or racial harmony, equality or diversity
Address: Internews Europe, 43-51 New North Road, London, N1 6LU
Trustees: Mr Mark Stephens, Mr Stephen Salyer, Mr Sachitt Chandaria, Mrs Daisy McAndrew, Secretary General Eva Kristina Henschen, Dr Saleyha Ahsan, Mr David Hoffman, Mr Yann Ghislain, Mr Matt Chanoff
Income: £6,598,638 [2016]; £3,877,967 [2015]; £3,455,293 [2014]; £3,198,119 [2013]

Intouni
Registered: 26 Mar 2007 *Employees:* 136 *Volunteers:* 2,229
Tel: 020 7243 0242 *Website:* intouniversity.org
Activities: Education, training
Address: Into University, Head Office, 95 Sirdar Road, London, W11 4EQ
Trustees: Mr Patrick Derham, Mr James Nicholas Lambert, Ms Sarah Havens, Sir Eric Thomas, Mr Christoph Henkel, Ms Sophia Anne Lewisohn, Ms Clare Richards, Mr Oliver Haarmann, Mr Steve Windsor, Mrs Nilufer von Bismarck
Income: £5,728,993 [2017]; £4,878,476 [2016]; £4,456,191 [2015]; £3,349,184 [2014]; £3,373,240 [2013]

The Invesco Cares Foundation
Registered: 6 Jun 1984 *Employees:* 1 *Volunteers:* 9
Activities: General charitable purposes
Address: Invesco Perpetual, Perpetual Park, Perpetual Park Drive, Henley on Thames, Oxon, RG9 1HH
Trustees: Mr Graeme Proudfoot, Clive Bouch, Mr Freddy Bruce
Income: £2,829,233 [2016]; £117,597 [2015]; £62,250 [2014]; £115,720 [2013]; £25,090 [2012]

Involve Northwest
Registered: 12 Jul 1996 *Employees:* 41
Tel: 0151 644 4500 *Website:* involvenorthwest.org.uk
Activities: General charitable purposes; education, training; prevention or relief of poverty; economic, community development, employment
Address: 334 New Chester Road, Birkenhead, Wirral, Merseyside, CH42 1LE
Trustees: Mr Graham Williamson, Mr John Callcott, Mr David Cheyne, Mr Greg Doran
Income: £1,616,399 [2017]; £1,742,977 [2016]; £1,202,366 [2015]; £1,132,665 [2014]; £1,285,153 [2013]

Ipswich Hospital NHS Trust Charitable Funds
Registered: 23 Aug 1995
Tel: 01473 704401 *Website:* ipswichhospital.nhs.uk
Activities: The advancement of health or saving of lives
Address: Ipswich Hospital NHS Trust, Heath Road, Ipswich, Suffolk, IP4 5PD
Trustees: The Ipswich Hospital NHS Trust
Income: £1,081,000 [2017]; £3,084,000 [2016]; £624,000 [2015]; £592,000 [2014]; £606,000 [2013]

Ipswich Housing Action Group Limited
Registered: 28 Jan 2005 *Employees:* 40 *Volunteers:* 15
Tel: 01473 213102 *Website:* ihag.co.uk
Activities: The prevention or relief of poverty; accommodation, housing
Address: 22-24 Carr Street, Ipswich, Suffolk, IP4 1EJ
Trustees: Mr William Hewlett, Mr John Grierson, Mr Jeremy Hennell James, Tracy Murphy, Mr Christopher McEwen, Mr Daniel Bristow, Ms Elaine Webb, Mrs Christine Anne Thorpe, Mr Thomas Jell
Income: £1,320,777 [2017]; £1,360,830 [2016]; £1,405,697 [2015]; £1,353,798 [2014]; £1,369,690 [2013]

Ipswich School
Registered: 6 Feb 1964 *Employees:* 335 *Volunteers:* 42
Tel: 01473 408300 *Website:* ipswich.school
Activities: Education, training
Address: Ipswich School, 25 Henley Road, Ipswich, Suffolk, IP1 3SG
Trustees: Mr Christopher Brown, Mr James St John Davey, Mr John William Poulter, Mrs Jane Crame, Mr Adrian Charles Seagers, Mr Nigel C Farthing, Dr Rosemary Elizabeth Gravell, Dr Orla Ann Goble, Mr Richard Philip Edgar Wilson, Dr Toby Alexander Howard Wilkinson, Mr Chris Joshua Oxborough, The Right Reverand Martin Seeley, Revd Dr GMW Cook, Mr Nigel Hugh Hamilton Smith, Mrs Elizabeth Garner, Mr Henry Eric Staunton, Edward Hyams, Mr William David Coe, Dr Richard Arthur Watts, Mr Mark Jason Taylor, Mr Terry George Baxter
Income: £15,408,396 [2016]; £14,619,114 [2015]; £13,099,137 [2014]; £13,026,164 [2013]; £12,848,666 [2012]

Ironbridge Gorge Museum Trust Limited
Registered: 15 Jan 1968 *Employees:* 227 *Volunteers:* 803
Tel: 01952 435900 *Website:* ironbridge.org.uk
Activities: Education, training; arts, culture, heritage, science; environment, conservation, heritage
Address: Ironbridge Gorge Museum Trust, Coach Road, Coalbrookdale, Telford, TF8 7DQ
Trustees: Mr Barrie Williams, Miss Gaye Blake Roberts, Mr Richard Clowes, Mr Terence John Lipscombe, Mr Rupert Kenyon-Slaney, Ms Karen MacKenzie, Mr Ray Hoof, Mr Hugh Trevor-Jones, Mr David John Roberts, Mr John Freeman, Mr Jonathan Kidson
Income: £6,295,267 [2016]; £5,701,180 [2015]; £5,621,440 [2014]; £6,084,034 [2013]; £5,570,375 [2012]

The Ironmongers Common Investment Fund
Registered: 4 Aug 1994
Tel: 020 7776 2311 *Website:* ironmongers.org
Activities: Other charitable purposes
Address: Ironmongers Hall, Barbican, London, EC2Y 8AA
Trustees: The Ironmongers' Trust Company
Income: £1,284,898 [2017]; £1,101,041 [2016]; £1,111,658 [2015]; £910,466 [2014]; £488,906 [2013]

Irshad Trust
Registered: 1 Jul 1996 *Employees:* 29
Tel: 07703 009435 *Website:* islamic-college.ac.uk
Activities: Education, training
Address: 133 High Road, London, NW10 2SW
Trustees: Dr Syed Naqi Hassan Kirmani, Mr Ali Akbar Heshmati Rafsanjani, Mr Isa Jahangir, Mr Mirza Mohammed Abbas Raza
Income: £1,009,946 [2016]; £912,607 [2015]; £1,051,457 [2014]; £592,179 [2013]; £1,825,375 [2012]

Isabel Hospice Limited
Registered: 30 May 1995 *Employees:* 181 *Volunteers:* 667
Tel: 01707 382502 *Website:* isabelhospice.org.uk
Activities: The advancement of health or saving of lives
Address: 61 Bridge Road East, Welwyn Garden City, Herts, AL7 1JR
Trustees: Keith Warnell, Mr John Morris, Mr William Mitchell, Dr Helen Glenister, Justyna Pyra, Deborah Curtis, Mrs Marlene Duke, Mr Kalyan Ray, Mr Rodney Leggetter, Mr Anthony Jackson, Sandra Reddy, Julie Quinn
Income: £7,095,000 [2017]; £6,357,000 [2016]; £7,163,000 [2015]; £5,741,000 [2014]; £6,478,000 [2013]

Isha Foundation
Registered: 13 Jun 2013 *Employees:* 1 *Volunteers:* 250
Tel: 07973 322750 *Website:* ishafoundation.org
Activities: Education, training
Address: 2 Empress Avenue, Ilford, Essex, IG1 3DD
Trustees: Mr Arun Patel, Mr Lawrence Clive Bloom, Mr Elie Khoury Zabbal
Income: £1,328,538 [2017]; £395,082 [2016]; £187,098 [2015]

Islamia Schools Limited
Registered: 25 Feb 2010 *Employees:* 57
Tel: 020 7372 2171 *Website:* islamiaschools.com
Activities: General charitable purposes; education, training
Address: 131b Salusbury Road, Kilburn, London, NW6 6RG
Trustees: Mrs Fawziah Islam, Muhammad Adamos, Mrs Hasana Islam, Mrs Aminah Islam
Income: £1,917,609 [2017]; £1,847,746 [2016]; £1,856,452 [2015]; £1,720,840 [2014]; £1,617,189 [2013]

Islamic Aid
Registered: 7 Dec 1999 *Employees:* 4 *Volunteers:* 25
Tel: 0300 111 3001 *Website:* islamicaid.com
Activities: The prevention or relief of poverty
Address: 29 Church Hill, London, E17 3AB
Trustees: Mr A Raje, Mr M Shabbir, S Iqbal Sajid, Dr M H Durrani, Mr M Hassan, Mrs R Gul, Dr M Alam
Income: £4,200,168 [2017]; £4,200,168 [2016]; £3,679,549 [2015]; £3,582,465 [2014]; £3,327,332 [2013]

Islamic Help
Registered: 13 Feb 2015 *Employees:* 60 *Volunteers:* 30
Tel: 0121 446 5682 *Website:* islamichelp.org.uk
Activities: Education, training; prevention or relief of poverty; overseas aid, famine relief; religious activities
Address: 19 Ombersley Road, Birmingham, B12 8UR
Trustees: Mr Rafaqat Hussain, Sultan Fiaz Ul Hassan, Mr Mohammad Masood Alam Khan, Sultan Niaz Ul Hassan
Income: £5,097,320 [2017]; £5,902,747 [2016]

Islamic Relief Worldwide
Registered: 6 Apr 1989 *Employees:* 419 *Volunteers:* 1,900
Tel: 0121 605 5555 *Website:* islamic-relief.com
Activities: General charitable purposes; education, training; advancement of health or saving of lives; prevention or relief of poverty; overseas aid, famine relief; economic, community development, employment; other charitable purposes
Address: 19 Rea Street South, Birmingham, B5 6LB
Trustees: Mr Adnan Saif, Mrs Lamia El Amri, Mr Abdul Rahman Bin Bidin, Mr Tahir Salie, Mr Almoutaz Tayara, Dr Mohamed Amr Attawia
Income: £110,395,914 [2016]; £105,576,484 [2015]; £99,142,152 [2014]; £82,814,292 [2013]; £100,368,169 [2012]

The Island Project
Registered: 2 May 2007 *Employees:* 55
Tel: 01675 442588 *Website:* theislandproject.co.uk
Activities: Education, training; disability
Address: Diddington Hall, Diddington Lane, Meriden, W Midlands, CV7 7HQ
Trustees: Mr Gordon Booth, Claire Bennett, Jacqui Walters-Hutton, Miss Lucy Doble
Income: £1,654,858 [2017]; £1,666,549 [2016]; £1,360,513 [2015]; £1,257,777 [2014]; £993,783 [2013]

The Isle of Wight Railway Company Limited
Registered: 13 Nov 1981 *Employees:* 30 *Volunteers:* 400
Tel: 01983 882204 *Website:* iwsteamrailway.co.uk
Activities: Education, training
Address: Isle of Wight Railway Co Ltd, The Railway Station, Station Road, Havenstreet, Ryde, Isle of Wight, PO33 4DS
Trustees: Mr John Suggett, Mr Peter James Conway, Mr Stephen Oates, Mr Simon Futcher, Iain Whitlam, Mr Steven Smart, Peter Keeling, Mr James Loe, Mr Stephen Castle, Mr Derek Bishop, Mr Stuart Duddy, Mr Peter Taylor, Nick Felton, Malcom Smith
Income: £1,861,254 [2016]; £1,804,859 [2015]; £1,828,692 [2014]; £1,592,529 [2013]; £1,822,724 [2012]

Islington Law Centre
Registered: 23 Nov 1977 *Employees:* 43 *Volunteers:* 200
Tel: 020 7288 7649 *Website:* islingtonlaw.org.uk
Activities: The prevention or relief of poverty; human rights, religious or racial harmony, equality or diversity
Address: Islington Law Centre, 38 Devonia Road, London, N1 8JH
Trustees: Mr Paul George Lowenberg, Ms Lindsay Edkins, Ms Susan Mary Lee, Ms Paula Punjwaria-Alessandro, Ms Marian Ellingworth, Mr Russell Austin Smith-Becker, Ms Jemima Joll, Mr Peter Mant, Ms Onika Adams, Mr Laurence David Ingram Mills, Mr Michael Collins
Income: £1,684,676 [2017]; £1,681,035 [2016]; £1,955,980 [2015]; £1,572,484 [2014]; £1,626,218 [2013]

Islington Play Association
Registered: 17 Apr 2001 *Employees:* 78 *Volunteers:* 107
Tel: 020 7607 9637 *Website:* islingtonplay.org.uk
Activities: General charitable purposes
Address: Paradise Park Childrens Centre, 164 MacKenzie Road, London, N7 8SE
Trustees: Mr Robin James Sinclair Taylor, Miss Laura John, Miss Eleanor Nichol, Mr Adeep Sethi, Mr Richard Stephens, Miss Melea Mapes, Ms Jane Deighton, Miss Manisha Kaur Kohli, Mrs Julie Edwina Lowe
Income: £1,456,789 [2017]; £1,461,953 [2016]; £1,393,961 [2015]; £1,484,201 [2014]; £918,832 [2013]

Itzchok Meyer Cymerman Trust Limited
Registered: 25 Jan 1973
Activities: General charitable purposes; education, training; advancement of health or saving of lives; prevention or relief of poverty; religious activities
Address: 497 Holloway Road, London, N7 6LE
Trustees: Mrs H F Bondi, Mrs Sara Heitner, Mr Ian Heitner, Mr Leonard Harry Bondi, Mrs S Cymerman, Mr Bernard Hoffman, Mr Michael David Cymerman, Mr Michel Richard Gehler
Income: £1,628,827 [2017]; £1,072,391 [2016]; £978,894 [2015]; £864,166 [2014]; £488,164 [2013]

Ivy Manchester Limited

Registered: 23 Feb 2010 *Employees:* 16 *Volunteers:* 400
Tel: 0161 434 5505 *Website:* ivychurch.org
Activities: Education, training; prevention or relief of poverty; overseas aid, famine relief; religious activities; amateur sport
Address: 97 Barlow Moor Road, Manchester, M20 2GP
Trustees: Reverend Anthony Delaney, Dr Adam Firth, Mrs Rebecca Mary Cheung, Robert Jackson, Dr Robert Michael Varnam, Mrs Sarah Small, Mr Andy Lee
Income: £1,253,840 [2017]; £1,155,626 [2016]; £930,461 [2015]; £888,685 [2014]; £803,490 [2013]

J J Charitable Trust

Registered: 17 Dec 1992 *Employees:* 16
Tel: 020 7410 0330 *Website:* sfct.org.uk
Activities: Education, training; advancement of health or saving of lives; disability; prevention or relief of poverty; overseas aid, famine relief; environment, conservation, heritage; economic, community development, employment
Address: Sainsbury Family Charitable Trusts, The Peak, 5 Wilton Road, London, SW1V 1AP
Trustees: Miss Judith Susan Portrait OBE, Mr Mark Leonard Sainsbury, Mr John Julian Sainsbury, Ms Lucy Guard
Income: £1,143,234 [2017]; £1,401,202 [2016]; £1,548,130 [2015]; £1,229,913 [2014]; £1,011,920 [2013]

JCD Foundation

Registered: 30 Jun 2016
Activities: General charitable purposes; education, training; advancement of health or saving of lives; disability; prevention or relief of poverty; overseas aid, famine relief; accommodation, housing; religious activities; animals; environment, conservation, heritage; economic, community development, employment; human rights, religious or racial harmony, equality or diversity
Address: Suite 137, 28a Church Road, Stanmore, Middlesex, HA7 4AW
Trustees: Chunilal Shah, Paras Dodhia, Jayaben Dodhia
Income: £1,776,102 [2016]

The JD Foundation

Registered: 13 May 2016
Tel: 0161 767 2626
Activities: General charitable purposes
Address: J D Sports Fashion, Edinburgh House, Hollins Brook Way, Bury, Lancs, BL9 8RR
Trustees: Mr Brian Small, Mrs Mawdsley Siobhan, Mr Nigel Keen, Mrs Julie Blomley, Mr Neil Greenhalgh, Mrs Traci Corrie
Income: £1,336,558 [2017]

The JGW Patterson Foundation

Registered: 8 Oct 2002
Tel: 0191 226 7878 *Website:* jgwpattersonfoundation.co.uk
Activities: The advancement of health or saving of lives
Address: Sintons, The Cube, Arngrove Court, Barrack Road, Newcastle upon Tyne, NE4 6DB
Trustees: Mr D R Gold, Mr Stephen Thomas Gilroy, Professor Timothy Edward Cawston, Professor Sir Alan William Craft MBBS MRCP MD FRCP FRCPCH FFPHM FAAP, Mr James Curry Dias
Income: £1,074,211 [2017]; £1,029,034 [2016]; £1,017,569 [2015]; £1,040,301 [2014]; £919,883 [2013]

The JMCMRJ Sorrell Foundation

Registered: 23 Apr 2007
Activities: General charitable purposes; education, training; advancement of health or saving of lives; prevention or relief of poverty; overseas aid, famine relief; religious activities; arts, culture, heritage, science; human rights, religious or racial harmony, equality or diversity; other charitable purposes
Address: 19 Wilton Row, London, SW1X 7NS
Trustees: Sir Martin Stuart Sorrell, Mr Robert Alexander Sorrell, Lady Cristiana Sorrell, Mr Mark Richard Antony Sorrell, Mr Jonathan Edward Hugh Sorrell
Income: £1,704,510 [2017]; £1,499,061 [2016]; £743,201 [2015]; £13,670,506 [2014]; £2,307,060 [2013]

JMWM Hussain Foundation

Registered: 4 Oct 2016
Tel: 07814 444213
Activities: General charitable purposes
Address: Nisiac House, 1 Cunningham Court, Lions Drive, Blackburn, Lancs, BB1 2QX
Trustees: Mr Jawid Hussain, Mr Mozam Hussain, Mr Majid Hussain, Mr Wajid Hussain
Income: £3,750,674 [2017]

JNF Charitable Trust

Registered: 20 Jun 1963 *Employees:* 19 *Volunteers:* 20
Tel: 020 8732 6124 *Website:* jnf.co.uk
Activities: General charitable purposes; education, training; advancement of health or saving of lives; disability; prevention or relief of poverty; accommodation, housing; religious activities; arts, culture, heritage, science; environment, conservation, heritage; economic, community development, employment; recreation
Address: JNF Charitable Trust, Mountcliff House, 154 Brent Street, London, NW4 2BF
Trustees: Mr Michael Sinclair, Mr Samuel Hayek, Ms Marilyn Waisman, Mr Guy Avshalom, Mr Howard Norman Wayne, Rabbi Alan Kimche, Mr Morris Mansoor, Mr Benjamin Eliezer Perl MBE, Mr Murray Lee, Mr Elan Gorji, Mr David Anthony Berens, Mr Gary Mond, Mr Daniel Seal, Mr Gideon Falter
Income: £12,417,000 [2016]; £14,389,000 [2015]; £13,431,000 [2014]; £13,855,000 [2013]; £17,537,000 [2012]

JRoots Limited

Registered: 22 Jun 2010 *Employees:* 3
Tel: 020 8457 2121 *Website:* jroots.org.uk
Activities: General charitable purposes; education, training; arts, culture, heritage, science; other charitable purposes
Address: 379 Hendon Way, London, NW4 3LP
Trustees: Mr Edward Michael Lee, Mr Philip Vecht, Neil Zeev Schiff, Mr D Goldberg
Income: £1,428,242 [2016]; £876,667 [2015]; £982,128 [2014]; £847,151 [2013]; £798,338 [2012]

JTL

Registered: 10 Apr 2000 *Employees:* 295
Tel: 01689 884104 *Website:* jtltraining.com
Activities: Education, training; economic, community development, employment
Address: Stafford House, 120-122 High Street, Orpington, Kent, BR6 0JS
Trustees: Mr Bernard McAulay, Mr John Allott, Paul McNaughton, Mr Christopher Victor Fenton, Mr Andrew Colin Eldred, Mr Geoffrey Russell, Mr Richard Jeremy Clarke, Mr William Cameron Spiers, Mr John Alexander Burrows, Mr Paul Bird, Mrs Tracey Elaine Shelley
Income: £32,996,775 [2017]; £25,113,564 [2016]; £24,363,134 [2015]; £20,002,297 [2014]; £17,435,388 [2013]

JW3 Development
Registered: 18 Mar 2014 *Employees:* 3
Tel: 020 7433 8962 *Website:* jw3development.org.uk
Activities: General charitable purposes
Address: 341-351 Finchley Road, London, NW3 6ET
Trustees: Mr Nicholas Viner, Mr Graham Harris, Mrs Denise Joseph
Income: £2,712,354 [2016]; £1,719,160 [2015]; £473,479 [2014]

JW3 Trust Limited
Registered: 22 Jan 2007 *Employees:* 75 *Volunteers:* 180
Tel: 020 7433 8968 *Website:* jw3.org.uk
Activities: General charitable purposes
Address: 341-351 Finchley Road, London, NW3 6ET
Trustees: Mr Michael Howard Goldstein, Ms Lisa Ronson, Lady Melanie Morris PhD, Mr Marc Nohr, Dame Vivien Duffield DBE, Mr Harry Black, Ms Claudia Rosencrantz, Mr Elliott Goldstein, Mr Neil Blair, Mr Nicholas Viner, Mr Lloyd Dorfman CBE, Mr Michael Marx, Mr Paul Viner, Ms Moira Benigson
Income: £4,491,272 [2016]; £5,877,288 [2015]; £4,077,420 [2014]; £32,473,464 [2013]; £14,949,750 [2012]

Jaamiatul Imaam Muhammad Zakaria Muhajir Madani
Registered: 29 Jun 1992 *Employees:* 64
Tel: 01274 882007
Activities: Education, training; religious activities
Address: Jamia-Tul-Imam Muhammad Zakaria, Thornton View Road, Clayton, Bradford, BD14 6JX
Trustees: Mr Shokat Dadhiwala, Mr Abdrur Rahim Limbada, Mr Mohmed Juned Desai, Mr Yusuf Kara, Ebrahim Hasan Sader, Mr Hassimbhai Hassanji Patel
Income: £1,062,321 [2016]; £1,059,542 [2015]; £918,432 [2014]; £967,501 [2013]; £809,387 [2012]

The Daphne Jackson Memorial Fellowships Trust
Registered: 15 Sep 2008 *Employees:* 5
Tel: 01483 689166 *Website:* daphnejackson.org
Activities: Education, training; economic, community development, employment
Address: University of Surrey, Guildford, Surrey, GU2 7XH
Trustees: Professor Edward Smith, Edith Sim, Teresa Anderson, Janet Purnell, Ms Susan Jayne Kay, Sue Angulatta, Rebecca Lingwood, Professor Graham James Davies, Dr Pia Ostergaard, Margaret Jack, Stephen Newstead, Ms Wendy Harle, Carole Lesley Thomas, Lesley Yellowlees, Hilary L-Scott, John Whitehead, Ms Amy McLaren
Income: £1,128,684 [2016]; £1,028,771 [2015]; £969,467 [2014]; £704,063 [2013]

The Henry Jackson Society
Registered: 18 Feb 2011 *Employees:* 18 *Volunteers:* 19
Tel: 020 7340 4520 *Website:* henryjacksonsociety.org
Activities: Education, training
Address: 26th Floor, Millbank Tower, Millbank, London, SW1P 4QP
Trustees: Mrs Gisela Gschaider Stuart, Dr Brendan Simms, Mr David Rasouly, Mr Stuart Lennard Caplan, Dr Alan Mendoza, Mr Adam Levin LLB
Income: £1,313,156 [2016]; £1,107,191 [2015]; £1,634,734 [2014]; £1,313,126 [2013]; £1,020,659 [2012]

Jackson's Lane
Registered: 21 May 2007 *Employees:* 26 *Volunteers:* 225
Website: jacksonslane.org.uk
Activities: General charitable purposes; education, training; disability; prevention or relief of poverty; arts, culture, heritage, science; economic, community development, employment; other charitable purposes
Address: Jacksons Lane, 269a Archway Road, London, N6 5AA
Trustees: Katherine Elizabeth Anderson, Adam Garfunkel, Richard Webber, Richard Smith-Bingham, Ms Melian Mansfield, Ms Leila Jones, Caroline McCarthy
Income: £1,318,309 [2017]; £1,096,175 [2016]; £1,034,383 [2015]; £964,379 [2014]; £855,842 [2013]

Jacobs Well Appeal
Registered: 20 Jul 1984 *Employees:* 5 *Volunteers:* 150
Website: jacobswellappeal.org
Activities: General charitable purposes; education, training; advancement of health or saving of lives; disability; prevention or relief of poverty; overseas aid, famine relief
Address: 11 The Croft, Beverley, E Yorks, HU17 7HT
Trustees: Dr Beryl Beynon OBE, Mr John Sutton, Dr Michael Lavine MB BS MRCS LRCP, Mr Michael Adams, Dr Alistair Robertson, Mrs Elizabeth Lyle, Mrs Margaret Hargreaves, Mrs Veronica Bemrose, Mr John Young OStJ TD BA(Educ) RGN RMN RNT, Mrs Betty Luciola, Dr Margaret Robertson
Income: £2,275,802 [2017]; £1,537,018 [2016]; £905,108 [2015]; £753,665 [2014]; £124,805 [2013]

Jaffray Care Society
Registered: 12 Feb 1991 *Employees:* 251
Tel: 0121 377 2420 *Website:* jaffraycare.com
Activities: Disability
Address: 39 Jaffray Crescent, Erdington, Birmingham, B24 8BE
Trustees: Dr Ashok Roy, Mr Chris Lees, Mr Mike Weir, Mr Gavin Cumberland, Mr Marcus Fellows, Ms Lee Hendon, Mr Martin McEachran
Income: £5,520,225 [2017]; £5,563,076 [2016]; £5,490,178 [2015]; £5,371,216 [2014]; £5,478,032 [2013]

Jah-Jireh Charity Homes
Registered: 23 Apr 1997 *Employees:* 231
Tel: 01772 633380 *Website:* jah-jireh.org
Activities: The advancement of health or saving of lives; disability; accommodation, housing; religious activities
Address: 317 Lytham Road, Warton, Preston, Lancs, PR4 1TE
Trustees: Mr Jeffrey Stacey, Frank Sartin, Eddie Delaney, Anthony Kendall, Mr Graham Cockshott, Mr Robin Telles, Charles Stringer, Russell Jones, Phil Cutting, Mr Jock Wigmore, Mr Charles Bland, Mr Richard Daniels
Income: £3,985,623 [2016]; £3,853,347 [2015]; £3,970,039 [2014]; £3,917,098 [2013]; £3,865,342 [2012]

John James Bristol Foundation
Registered: 10 Feb 1984 *Employees:* 4
Tel: 0117 923 9444 *Website:* johnjames.org.uk
Activities: General charitable purposes; education, training; advancement of health or saving of lives; disability; prevention or relief of poverty; accommodation, housing
Address: John James Bristol Foundation, 7 Clyde Road, Redland, Bristol, BS6 6RG
Trustees: Mr John Evans, Mrs Joan Johnson, Mr Andrew Jardine, Mr Andrew Webley, Mrs Nicola Parker, Mrs Elizabeth Chambers, Mr David Johnson, Mr Peter Goodwin, Dr John Haworth
Income: £2,338,636 [2017]; £2,169,019 [2016]; £2,089,022 [2015]; £2,289,833 [2014]; £1,642,935 [2013]

The Edward James Foundation Limited
Registered: 26 Sep 2008 *Employees:* 141 *Volunteers:* 100
Tel: 01243 818240 *Website:* westdean.org.uk
Activities: Education, training; arts, culture, heritage, science; environment, conservation, heritage
Address: The Edward James Foundation Limited, Estate Office, West Dean Park, Chichester, W Sussex, PO18 0QZ
Trustees: Lady Egremont, Professor Nigel Llewellyn PhD FSA, Mr David Seddon, Mr Francis Plowden, The Hon Peter Benson LVO MA FCA, Professor Paul O'Prey PhD, Mrs Caroline Griffith, Mr Martin Ashley
Income: £9,640,159 [2016]; £9,410,405 [2015]; £9,417,068 [2014]; £18,792,495 [2013]; £8,832,273 [2012]

Jami Mosque and Islamic Centre (Birmingham) Trustees Limited
Registered: 20 Nov 1990 *Employees:* 45 *Volunteers:* 45
Tel: 0121 772 6408 *Website:* jamimosque.org.uk
Activities: General charitable purposes; education, training; religious activities; amateur sport; other charitable purposes
Address: 523 Coventry Road, Small Heath, Birmingham, B10 0LL
Trustees: Mr Nurul Haque, Mr Farid Miah, Abdullah Mohammad Ismail, Mr Tofael Ahmed, Mr Shahdul Islam, Mr Nozmul Mohomed Hussain, Mr Abdus Salam Md Masum, Mohammed Babul Miah, Abu Tahir Md Mukarram Hasan, Mr Habibur Rahman, Mr Lutfur Rahman Belal, Mr Salim Khan, Mr Suhail Muhammad Abdur Rahim
Income: £1,097,770 [2017]; £860,261 [2016]; £808,874 [2015]; £989,675 [2014]; £1,042,590 [2013]

Jamie's Farm
Registered: 12 May 2009 *Employees:* 16 *Volunteers:* 150
Tel: 01225 743608 *Website:* jamiesfarm.org.uk
Activities: Education, training; advancement of health or saving of lives; animals; environment, conservation, heritage
Address: Hill House Farm, Ditteridge, Box, Corsham, Wilts, SN13 8QA
Trustees: Professor Peter Alexander Clegg, Dame Sally Coates, Mr Philip Percival, Roderick James, James Westhead, Sian Parry
Income: £2,746,391 [2017]; £3,329,077 [2016]; £1,048,973 [2015]; £778,805 [2014]; £1,078,605 [2013]

Jamiyat Tabligh-Ul-Islam
Registered: 6 Feb 2015 *Employees:* 40 *Volunteers:* 50
Tel: 01274 732959 *Website:* jamiyat.org
Activities: General charitable purposes; education, training; advancement of health or saving of lives; prevention or relief of poverty; overseas aid, famine relief; religious activities; economic, community development, employment; human rights, religious or racial harmony, equality or diversity
Address: 72 Duckworth Lane, Bradford, BD9 5HA
Trustees: Khadim Hussain, Mr Liaqat Hussain, Mr Zulfiqar Ali Karim, Mr Khalil Ur Rehman, Mr Mahroof Hussain
Income: £1,975,275 [2017]; £919,831 [2016]

The Japanese School Limited
Registered: 20 Jul 1976 *Employees:* 123
Tel: 07920 569295 *Website:* thejapaneseschool.ltd.uk
Activities: Education, training
Address: 17A Mayfield Road, London, W3 9HQ
Trustees: Mr Haruki Hayashi, Mr Kiyoshi Sunobe, Mr Junichi Ishikawa, Mr Ryuichi Hirokawa, Mr Hironobu Ishikawa, Mr Naoki Iizuka, Mr Minoru Shinohara, Mr Kazuo Abe, Mr Tokikazu Aoki, Mr Yusuke Otsuka, Mr Kunihiko Tanabe, Mr Takuji Nakai, Mr Masato Miyachi, Mr Naoya Iwashita, Mr Yoshitaka Ihokibe, Mr Ken Sasaki, Mr Hideki Uyama
Income: £2,061,368 [2016]; £2,049,746 [2015]; £2,158,858 [2014]; £2,156,990 [2013]; £2,098,815 [2012]

Caryl Jenner Productions Limited
Registered: 27 Jun 1963 *Employees:* 65
Website: unicorntheatre.com
Activities: Education, training; arts, culture, heritage, science
Address: Unicorn Theatre, 147 Tooley Street, London, SE1 2HZ
Trustees: Ms Henny Finch, Mr Colin Terence Maitland Simon, Mr John Langley, Ms Agnes Quashie
Income: £200,694,484 [2017]; £2,660,687 [2016]; £2,693,689 [2015]; £2,493,313 [2014]; £1,891,647 [2013]

The Jericho Foundation
Registered: 28 Apr 1994 *Employees:* 70 *Volunteers:* 8
Tel: 0121 647 1960 *Website:* jericho.org.uk
Activities: General charitable purposes; education, training; prevention or relief of poverty; economic, community development, employment
Address: Jericho Foundation, Jericho Building, 196-198 Edward Road, Balsall Heath, Birmingham, B12 9LX
Trustees: Ms Christine Traxson, Mr Martin Warner, Mr Karamat Iqbal, Mr Michael Thomas, Mr Michael Andrew Royal, Mr Graham Irving Cook
Income: £2,613,036 [2017]; £3,248,696 [2016]; £2,683,929 [2015]; £2,382,396 [2014]; £1,821,814 [2013]

The Jerusalem Foundation
Registered: 14 Apr 1969 *Employees:* 1
Tel: 020 7224 2528
Activities: Education, training; advancement of health or saving of lives; disability; prevention or relief of poverty; religious activities; arts, culture, heritage, science; amateur sport
Address: 20 Gloucester Place, London, W1U 8HA
Trustees: Jerusalem Foundation Trustees Limited
Income: £3,128,979 [2016]; £1,065,216 [2015]; £1,494,611 [2014]; £1,476,308 [2013]; £1,905,986 [2012]

The Jerusalem Trust
Registered: 13 Dec 1982 *Employees:* 11
Tel: 020 7410 0330 *Website:* sfct.org.uk
Activities: Education, training; overseas aid, famine relief; religious activities; arts, culture, heritage, science
Address: Sainsbury Family Charitable Trusts, The Peak, 5 Wilton Road, London, SW1V 1AP
Trustees: Lady Susan Sainsbury, Hartley Booth, Mrs Phillida Goad, Mr David Nathanael Beresford Wright, The Rt Hon Sir Timothy Sainsbury, Dr Peter Doimi De Frankopan, Mrs Melanie Townsend
Income: £3,049,000 [2017]; £2,822,000 [2016]; £4,317,000 [2015]; £3,590,000 [2014]; £3,885,000 [2013]

The Jerwood Charitable Foundation
Registered: 18 Feb 1999 *Employees:* 5
Tel: 020 7261 0279 *Website:* jerwoodcharitablefoundation.org
Activities: Arts, culture, heritage, science
Address: Jerwood Charitable Foundation, 171 Union Street, London, SE1 0LN
Trustees: Ms Katharine Goodison, Ms Juliane Wharton, Thomas De Sivrac Grieve, Ms Philippa Hogan-Hern, Ms Catrin Griffiths, Rupert David Tyler, Mr Timothy George Eyles, Lucy Amanda Ash, Ms Vanessa Engle
Income: £1,269,860 [2017]; £1,319,418 [2016]; £1,010,083 [2015]; £1,215,794 [2014]; £1,212,116 [2013]

The Jesmond Trust
Registered: 18 Sep 1975 *Employees:* 41 *Volunteers:* 500
Tel: 0191 212 7404 *Website:* church.org.uk
Activities: Religious activities
Address: Jesmond Parish Church, Eskdale Terrace, Newcastle upon Tyne, NE2 4DJ
Trustees: Rev David Holloway, Dr Joy Holloway, Mr Andrew Coulson, Rev Jonathan Pryke, Mr Bob Clifton, Will Tufton
Income: £1,687,638 [2017]; £2,231,766 [2016]; £2,153,293 [2015]; £2,099,299 [2014]; £2,260,726 [2013]

Jesus College Within The University and City of Oxford of Queen Elizabeth's Foundation
Registered: 11 Aug 2010 *Employees:* 132
Tel: 01865 279700 *Website:* jesus.ox.ac.uk
Activities: Education, training; religious activities; arts, culture, heritage, science; environment, conservation, heritage
Address: Jesus College, Turl Street, Oxford, OX1 3DW
Trustees: Prof Shankar Srinivas, Prof Patricia Daley, Prof Edward Anderson, Prof H Charles J Godfray, Dr Alexandra Lumbers, Assoc Prof Suzanne Aspden, Prof Patricia Mekia Clavin, Prof Katrin Kohl, Dr Armand D'Angour, Prof Mark Brouard, Dr James Oliver, Prof James Tilley, Dr Andreas Mogensen, Dr Richard Greyner, Dr Alexandra Gajda, Prof Kylie Vincent, Dr Malcolm John, Mr Paul Goffin, Mr David Stevenson, Prof Tim Coulson, Prof Stefan Dercon, Prof Paul Riley, Dr Benjamin Williams, Dr Miles Jackson, Dr Brittany Wellner James, Dr Anne Winifred Mullen, Prof Sir Nigel Shadbolt, Dr Peter Eso, Dr Caroline Warman, Prof Graham Taylor, Prof Andrew Dancer, Dr David Barron, Dr Marion Turner, Prof Paulina Kewes, Dr Stuart Gordon White, Dr Stephen John Magorrian, Dr Stephen Morris, Dr Simon Douglas, Dr Yulin Chen, Mr Ruedi Baumann, Dr Robin Evans, Mrs Rosalyn Green, Prof Georg Hollander, Prof Luca Enriques, Prof Raymond Pierrehumbert, Prof Donal Bradley, Mr Stuart Woodward, Prof Judith Rousseau, Dr Stanislas Zivny, Dr Ralf Wolfer
Income: £12,923,000 [2017]; £14,238,000 [2016]; £12,396,000 [2015]; £12,139,000 [2014]; £12,263,000 [2013]

Jesus College in the University of Cambridge
Registered: 12 Aug 2010 *Employees:* 227 *Volunteers:* 1
Tel: 01223 339339 *Website:* jesus.cam.ac.uk
Activities: Education, training
Address: Jesus College, Cambridge, CB5 8BL
Trustees: Dr Geoff Parks, Dr Stephen Siklos, Professor Sarah Colvin, Professor Cecilia Mascolo, Dr Gregory Conti, Dr Yaron Peleg, Dr Rebecca Reich, Professor Peter Williamson, Ms Taylor Saunders-Wood, Dr Hillary Taylor, Professor Ian Hugh White, Dr Richard Anthony, Professor Anna Vignoles, Rev Paul Dominiak, Dr Anne Ramsey Bowden, Dr Brechtje Post, Professor Timothy Wilkinson, Dr Jeremy Green, Miss Holly Scott, Mr Edward Parker-Humphreys
Income: £16,049,345 [2017]; £18,653,153 [2016]; £15,320,029 [2015]; £15,345,268 [2014]; £13,791,280 [2013]

Jesus House
Registered: 27 Sep 2001 *Employees:* 68 *Volunteers:* 650
Tel: 020 8438 8285 *Website:* jesushouse.org.uk
Activities: The prevention or relief of poverty; religious activities
Address: 112 Brent Terrace, London, NW2 1LT
Trustees: Mr Olubunmi Oluwasanmi Toyobo, Reverend Nims Obunge, Shola Adeaga, Mrs Alero Ayida-Otobo
Income: £4,940,587 [2016]; £5,162,247 [2015]; £5,259,533 [2014]; £5,242,090 [2013]; £4,856,076 [2012]

The Jewish Association for Mental Illness
Registered: 3 Jul 1991 *Employees:* 54 *Volunteers:* 130
Tel: 020 8458 2223 *Website:* jamiuk.org
Activities: Education, training; advancement of health or saving of lives; disability; accommodation, housing
Address: Jewish Association Mental Illness, Leila's House, 55 Christchurch Avenue, London, N12 0DG
Trustees: Bob Shemtob, Alan Lazarus, Debbie Fox, Jose Grayson, Raymond Ian Harris, Suzanne Joels, Mr Neil Taylor, Doug Krikler
Income: £2,491,354 [2017]; £2,919,046 [2016]; £1,822,862 [2015]; £2,189,332 [2014]; £1,075,584 [2013]

Jewish Blind & Physically Handicapped Society Limited
Registered: 12 Sep 1969 *Employees:* 49 *Volunteers:* 100
Tel: 020 8371 6611 *Website:* jbd.org
Activities: General charitable purposes; disability; accommodation, housing
Address: Frances & Dick, James Court, Langstone Way, London, NW7 1GT
Trustees: Mr Malcolm John Ozin, Mr John Michael Joseph, Mr Michael Jeremy Kurer, Mr Peter Howard Silverman, Mr Stuart Russell, Mr Lance Joseph, Mr Martin Mendoza, Stuart Simmons, Mr Ian David Green
Income: £3,708,984 [2016]; £3,535,956 [2015]; £3,387,708 [2014]; £2,954,478 [2013]; £3,468,261 [2012]

Jewish Care
Registered: 5 Dec 1989 *Employees:* 1,249 *Volunteers:* 3,000
Tel: 020 8922 2000 *Website:* jewishcare.org
Activities: Disability; prevention or relief of poverty; accommodation, housing
Address: Jewish Care, 221 Golders Green Road, London, NW11 9DQ
Trustees: Mr Steven David Lewis, Mr Michael Blake, Mr Stuart Roden, Mrs Linda Bogod, Mrs Nicola Loftus, Mr Michael Brodtman, Ms Rachel Anticoni, Mrs Gayle Klein, Mr Arnold Wagner OBE, Mrs Debra Fox, Mr Antony Grossman, Mr Simon Friend, Mr Douglas Krikler, Dr Dean Noimark, Lord Ian Livingston, Mr Matthew Weiner
Income: £56,089,000 [2017]; £52,707,000 [2016]; £50,976,000 [2015]; £54,041,000 [2014]; £45,265,000 [2013]

Jewish Child's Day
Registered: 28 Sep 1962 *Employees:* 7 *Volunteers:* 12
Tel: 020 8446 8804 *Website:* jcd.uk.com
Activities: Education, training; advancement of health or saving of lives; disability; prevention or relief of poverty
Address: Jewish Childs Day, First Floor, Elscot House, Arcadia Avenue, London, N3 2JU
Trustees: Mrs June Jacobs, Mr Stephen Moss, Mrs Frankie Epstein, Mr David Collins, Mrs Gaby Lazarus, Mr Charles Spungin, Mrs Joy Moss, Mrs Virginia Campus, Mrs Susie Olins, Mrs Amanda Ingram, Mrs Dee Lahane
Income: £1,221,981 [2017]; £1,240,081 [2016]; £1,238,557 [2015]; £905,709 [2014]; £1,130,433 [2013]

The Jewish Community Secondary School Trust
Registered: 19 Jan 2005
Tel: 07773 138968 *Website:* jcoss.org
Activities: General charitable purposes; education, training; disability; religious activities; amateur sport
Address: 6 Lullington Garth, London, N12 7AS
Trustees: Stephen David Moss CBE, Mr David Mark Kyte, Mr Jamie Robert Cassell, Mrs Nicole Julia Ronson Allalouf, Mr Mark David Freedman, Alfred Garfield FCA, Mr Jeremy Paul Kosky, Tamara Finkelstein, Mr Stephen Alan Clayman
Income: £2,162,588 [2017]; £1,420,146 [2016]; £1,322,045 [2015]; £915,841 [2014]; £1,635,320 [2013]

The Jewish Day Primary School
Registered: 5 Feb 1963 *Employees:* 123
Tel: 0161 773 6364
Activities: Education, training; religious activities; arts, culture, heritage, science
Address: Yesoidey Hatorah School, Bury New Road, Prestwich, Manchester, M25 0JW
Trustees: Mr Mordecai Halpern, Mr Sefton Yodaiken, Mr David Halpern
Income: £1,516,519 [2016]; £1,362,304 [2015]; £1,224,378 [2014]; £1,059,441 [2013]

Jewish Futures Trust Limited
Registered: 4 Mar 2013 *Employees:* 82 *Volunteers:* 300
Tel: 020 8457 4444 *Website:* jfutures.org
Activities: General charitable purposes; education, training; arts, culture, heritage, science; other charitable purposes
Address: 379 Hendon Way, London, NW4 3LP
Trustees: Mr David Samuel Hammelburger, Mr Edward Misrahi, Mr Steven James Neerkin, Mr Shlomo Farhi, Rabbi Neil Schiff
Income: £6,476,882 [2016]; £5,053,942 [2015]; £4,992,068 [2014]; £3,441,633 [2013]

Jewish Joint Burial Society
Registered: 25 Dec 1968 *Employees:* 6
Tel: 020 8989 5252 *Website:* jjbs.org.uk
Activities: Religious activities
Address: Jewish Joint Burial Society, 1 Victory Road, London, E11 1UL
Trustees: Mr David Leibling MA, Janet Posner, Mr Frank Godson, Mr Maurice Gold, Professor Reza Razavi, Mrs Clare Lubin, Mr Roger Woolf, Mr Ian Cave, Mr Peter Benjamin Vos, Mr Michael Berkson, Mr Keith Anthony Price, Mr Paul William Ian Hoffbrand, Mr Martin Denis Silverman, Jocelyn Alexis Shepherd, Ms Josie Estelle Knox, Mr Peter Daniel Kornhauser, Mr Jon Burden, Mr Stanley Keller, Mr Keith Feldman, Mr Mike Frankl, Mrs Barbara Grant, Mr David Jacobs, Mr Henry Fried, Mr Edward Kafka, Mrs Frances Niman, Dr Naomi Simmonds, Mr Stephen Maurice Fidler, Mr John David Sabel, Mr Steven Howard Wynne, Ms Eleanor Lorraine Bloom, Mrs Hilary June Roer
Income: £1,302,372 [2016]; £1,597,237 [2015]; £1,451,045 [2014]; £1,502,701 [2013]; £1,362,881 [2012]

Jewish Lads' and Girls' Brigade
Registered: 1 Jun 1983 *Employees:* 22 *Volunteers:* 300
Tel: 020 8989 8990 *Website:* jlgb.org
Activities: Education, training
Address: Camperdown, 3 Beechcroft Road, London, E18 1LA
Trustees: Mr Barry Clive Shine FCMA, Mr Richard Marshall, Mr Howard Freeman, Mrs Joanne Claire Rams, Ms Symmie Swil, Mr Norman Terret JP, Mr Adam Solomon Shelley, Mrs Ruth Helen Green, Mrs Ruth Dwight, Miss Jordana Price
Income: £1,189,249 [2017]; £1,204,418 [2016]; £1,152,135 [2015]; £914,637 [2014]; £887,685 [2013]

The Jewish Leadership Council
Registered: 14 Jul 2006 *Employees:* 28
Tel: 020 7242 9734 *Website:* thejlc.org
Activities: Education, training; religious activities; human rights, religious or racial harmony, equality or diversity; other charitable purposes
Address: Jewish Leadership Council, Shield House, Harmony Way, London, NW4 2BZ
Trustees: Mr Leo Noe, Mr Mark Morris, Mr Steven Lewis, Mrs Debra Fox, Mrs Marie Van De Zyl, Mr Gerald Ronson CBE, Mr William Benjamin, Mr Edward Misrahi, Mr Adrian Cohen
Income: £2,795,331 [2016]; £2,544,352 [2015]; £3,284,235 [2014]; £2,905,344 [2013]; £1,727,490 [2012]

The Jewish Museum London
Registered: 17 Mar 1992 *Employees:* 32 *Volunteers:* 110
Tel: 020 7284 7384 *Website:* jewishmuseum.org.uk
Activities: General charitable purposes; education, training; arts, culture, heritage, science; environment, conservation, heritage; human rights, religious or racial harmony, equality or diversity
Address: Jewish Museum, 129-131 Albert Street, London, NW1 7NB
Trustees: Lady Wendy Ann Levene, Mr Jonathan Gestetner, Mr Ronald Michael Harris, Rt Hon Lord Young of Graffham, Ms Emily King, Ms Julia Hobsbawm, Mr Richard Moshe Sopher, Mr Ronald Shelley, Mr Michael Lawrence Davis, Ms Rhian Harris, Ms Abigail Morris
Income: £2,647,677 [2017]; £2,468,705 [2016]; £1,857,661 [2015]; £1,423,033 [2014]; £952,373 [2013]

The Jewish Philanthropic Association for Israel and The Middle East
Registered: 23 Aug 1968
Tel: 020 7424 6400
Activities: General charitable purposes; education, training; advancement of health or saving of lives; prevention or relief of poverty
Address: 1 Torriano Mews, London, NW5 2RZ
Trustees: United Jewish Israel Appeal
Income: £1,136,000 [2017]; £243,000 [2016]; £364,000 [2015]; £253,000 [2014]; £570,000 [2013]

Jewish Secondary Schools Movement
Registered: 31 Dec 1963 *Employees:* 43
Tel: 020 8202 1066
Activities: Education, training
Address: Sutherland House, 70-78 West Hendon Broadway, London, NW9 7BT
Trustees: The Trustees of The J S S M (A Company Limited By Guarantee)
Income: £4,908,076 [2016]; £643,330 [2015]; £4,000,765 [2014]; £655,844 [2013]; £2,882,907 [2012]

Jewish Teachers' Training College
Registered: 25 Jan 1965 *Employees:* 34
Tel: 0191 477 2620
Activities: Education, training
Address: Jewish Teachers Training College, 50 Bewick Road, Gateshead, Tyne & Wear, NE8 4HB
Trustees: S Kohn, Rabbi J Grunfeld
Income: £2,110,684 [2017]; £1,825,867 [2016]; £1,829,861 [2015]; £1,748,047 [2014]; £1,773,478 [2013]

Jews' College
Registered: 28 Sep 2009 *Employees:* 10 *Volunteers:* 16
Tel: 020 8203 6427 *Website:* lsjs.ac.uk
Activities: Education, training; religious activities
Address: 11 Talbot Avenue, London, N2 0LS
Trustees: Mr Leon Nahon, Elliott Goldstein, Mr Gary Phillips, Mr Andrew Wolfson, Mr Alan Richard Bekhor, Samuel Alexander Rubin, Ms Josephine Giselle Rosenfelder, Mr Jason Michael Marantz, Ms Daniella Klein
Income: £1,139,700 [2017]; £1,214,392 [2016]; £1,240,577 [2015]; £1,157,474 [2014]; £1,530,975 [2013]

Jigsaw +
Registered: 23 Apr 2013 *Employees:* 28
Tel: 01483 273874 *Website:* jigsawplus.co.uk
Activities: Education, training; disability; accommodation, housing; economic, community development, employment
Address: Building 20, Dunsfold Park, Stovolds Hill, Cranleigh, Surrey, GU6 8TB
Trustees: Mr Simon Vincent, Ms Lynn Grant, Mr Graham Prothero
Income: £1,339,067 [2017]; £800,667 [2016]; £566,156 [2015]; £347,609 [2014]

The Jigsaw Trust
Registered: 13 May 1999 *Employees:* 107
Tel: 01483 273874 *Website:* jigsawschool.co.uk
Activities: Education, training; disability
Address: Building 21, Dunsfold Park, Stovolds Hill, Cranleigh, Surrey, GU6 8TB
Trustees: Mr Simon Vincent, Mr Graham Prothero, Mrs Claudia Krinks, Theo Barclay, Mrs Abigail Elisabeth Cox, Jillian Kiely, Mr Leo McHugh, Mrs Lynne Smith, Ms Aishnine Marie Benjamin, Mrs Mary Asante
Income: £3,477,468 [2017]; £3,386,106 [2016]; £3,301,896 [2015]; £3,072,749 [2014]; £2,727,012 [2013]

Jimmy's Cambridge
Registered: 18 Oct 1996 *Employees:* 30 *Volunteers:* 200
Tel: 01223 353161 *Website:* jimmyscambridge.org.uk
Activities: The prevention or relief of poverty; accommodation, housing
Address: Zion Baptist Church, East Road, Cambridge, CB1 1BD
Trustees: Jane Elizabeth Fardell Mann, Dr Fiona Blake, Mrs Kiran Kapur, Dr John Philip Stanton, Mrs Irena Jozefa Spence, John Durrant, Mr Geoff Mann, Mr David Silver, Mr John Christopher McHale, Mrs Wendy Alison Godfrey
Income: £1,415,174 [2017]; £1,312,096 [2016]; £1,273,165 [2015]; £1,519,247 [2014]; £1,024,374 [2012]

Jisc
Registered: 13 Nov 2012 *Employees:* 521
Tel: 020 3697 5802 *Website:* jisc.ac.uk
Activities: Education, training; disability
Address: One Castlepark, Tower Hill, Bristol, BS2 0JA
Trustees: Professor Philip Gummett, Professor Elizabeth Barnes, Professor Anne Elizabeth Trefethen, Dr Ken Thomson, Dr Paul Barrie Feldman, Miss Susan Bowen, Professor Paul Layzell, Professor Mark Smith, Professor David John Maguire, Professor Nigel Anthony Seaton, Mr Robin Ghurbhurun, Mr Robert Gerard McWilliam
Income: £132,967,000 [2017]; £130,895,000 [2016]; £137,877,000 [2015]; £161,011,000 [2014]; £163,718,000 [2013]

Jo's Cervical Cancer Trust
Registered: 18 Jan 2010 *Employees:* 18 *Volunteers:* 400
Tel: 020 3096 8100 *Website:* jostrust.org.uk
Activities: Education, training; advancement of health or saving of lives
Address: CAN Mezzanine, 7-14 Great Dover Street, London, SE1 4YR
Trustees: Dr Mina Desai, Lucy Maxwell, Tessa Bamford, Mr Hugh John Grootenhuis, Mrs Carol Louise Taylor, Thomas Ind, Rebecca McCreath, Clodagh Ward, Mrs Catherine Louise Newton, Dr Kevin Pollock
Income: £1,749,644 [2017]; £1,067,221 [2016]; £1,120,165 [2015]; £773,582 [2014]; £650,977 [2013]

The Elton John Aids Foundation
Registered: 12 Feb 1993 *Employees:* 10 *Volunteers:* 12
Tel: 020 7603 9996 *Website:* ejaf.org
Activities: The advancement of health or saving of lives; prevention or relief of poverty; overseas aid, famine relief
Address: 1 Blythe Road, London, W14 0HG
Trustees: Mrs Anne Aslett, Sir Elton Hercules John, Mr Evgeny Lebedev, Mr Scott Campbell, Dr Mark Richard Dybul, Mr David James Furnish, Mr Johnny Bergius, Mr Rafi Manoukian, Mr Graham William Norton, Mrs Tracy Blackwell
Income: £12,177,230 [2017]; £10,662,321 [2016]; £5,069,132 [2015]; £6,232,371 [2014]; £7,136,999 [2013]

The Johnson Trust Limited
Registered: 26 Jun 1980 *Employees:* 171 *Volunteers:* 3
Tel: 01798 867212 *Website:* seaford.org.uk
Activities: Education, training
Address: Seaford College, Lavington Park, Petworth, W Sussex, GU28 0NB
Trustees: Mr Richard Venables Kyrke, Mrs Elizabeth Lawrence, Mr Nic Karonias, Mr Hugh Phillips, Mr Robert Norton, Mr Jonathan Scrase, Mrs Susan Kowszun, Mrs Susan Sayer, Mr John Roderick Hall, Mr James Cooper, Mr Andrew Hayes
Income: £12,351,620 [2016]; £11,821,800 [2015]; £9,953,654 [2014]; £12,509,325 [2013]; £9,166,170 [2012]

William Jones's Schools Foundation
Registered: 12 Nov 1987 *Employees:* 530
Tel: 020 7246 9988 *Website:* haberdashers.co.uk
Activities: Education, training
Address: The Clerk, Haberdashers Hall, 18 West Smithfield, London, EC1A 9HQ
Trustees: Haberdashers' Monmouth Estates Limited, Haberdashers' Monmouth Schools Limited
Income: £22,229,000 [2016]; £22,411,000 [2015]; £21,535,000 [2014]; £20,388,000 [2013]; £19,667,000 [2012]

The Joseph Cox Charity
Registered: 1 Jun 1978 *Employees:* 38 *Volunteers:* 1
Tel: 0161 225 8504
Activities: General charitable purposes; prevention or relief of poverty
Address: Flat 60, Agnes Court, Wilmslow Road, Manchester, M14 6AJ
Trustees: Mr John Hubert Cox, Mr Paul Adam Cox, Mr Jonathan Mather, Mrs Helen Mary MacKenzie, Mr Andrew Morgan, Mr James Doyle
Income: £1,233,611 [2016]; £1,133,613 [2015]; £1,091,429 [2014]; £1,069,415 [2013]; £1,052,100 [2012]

The Joseph Rowntree Charitable Trust
Registered: 12 Feb 1963 *Employees:* 14
Tel: 01904 627810 *Website:* jrct.org.uk
Activities: General charitable purposes; religious activities; environment, conservation, heritage; human rights, religious or racial harmony, equality or diversity; other charitable purposes
Address: Joseph Rowntree Charitable Trust, The Garden House, Water End, York, YO30 6WQ
Trustees: Linda Batten, Susan Seymour, Imran Tyabi, Janet Slade, Hannah Torkington, Huw Davies, Margaret Bryan, Helen Carmichael, John Fitzgerald, Michael Eccles, Jenny Amery, David Newton
Income: £1,764,000 [2016]; £2,348,000 [2015]; £2,127,000 [2014]; £4,917,000 [2013]; £5,465,000 [2012]

The Joseph Rowntree Foundation
Registered: 15 Nov 1962 *Employees:* 673
Tel: 01904 629241 *Website:* jrf.org.uk
Activities: Disability; prevention or relief of poverty; accommodation, housing; economic, community development, employment
Address: Joseph Rowntree Foundation, The Homestead, 40 Water End, York, YO30 6WP
Trustees: Mrs Maureen Loffill, Professor Dianne Willcocks CBE DL, Ms Deborah Cadman OBE, Mrs Gillian Ashmore, Mr David Lunts, Mrs Carol Tannahill, Mr Graham Millar, Mr Steven Burkeman, Ms Saphieh Ashtiany, Mr William David Adams Haire, Mr Paul Jenkins OBE, Ms Helen Evans
Income: £6,934,000 [2016]; £5,749,000 [2015]; £9,434,000 [2014]; £8,747,000 [2013]; £8,189,000 [2012]

The Joseph Storehouse Trust
Registered: 20 Nov 2000 *Employees:* 3 *Volunteers:* 10
Tel: 01793 279111 *Website:* josephstorehouse.co.uk
Activities: General charitable purposes; education, training; advancement of health or saving of lives; disability; prevention or relief of poverty; overseas aid, famine relief; religious activities
Address: The Joseph Storehous Trust, Newport House, 19-21 Newport Street, Swindon, Wilts, SN1 3DX
Trustees: Mr Alistair Martin Scott, Mr Barry Segal, Mr Christopher Frank Stanley Cooke, Mr Colin Mouque, Mrs Batya Segal, Mr Roger Overton-Smith
Income: £1,838,184 [2016]; £2,061,532 [2015]; £1,860,681 [2014]; £1,346,471 [2013]; £1,203,603 [2012]

The Joshua Trust
Registered: 30 May 1968 *Employees:* 1
Activities: General charitable purposes; education, training; prevention or relief of poverty; religious activities
Address: 88 Edgware Way, Edgware, Middlesex, HA8 8JS
Trustees: Mr Robert Grussgott, Mr Chaim Landau, Mr Solomon Grusgott, Mr Moshe Rubin
Income: £1,557,352 [2016]; £1,144,030 [2014]; £737,682 [2013]; £682,990 [2012]

Jubilee Hall Trust Limited
Registered: 9 May 1977 *Employees:* 33
Website: jubileehalltrust.org
Activities: Amateur sport
Address: 30 The Piazza, Covent Garden, London, WC2E 8BE
Trustees: Janet Owen Cochrane, Cllr Linda Chung, Josephine Anne Weir, Ms Roslyn Fiona Perkins, Ms Diana Barrett, Mr John McQuillan, Mr John David Guy, Timothy Mitchell, Mr Allan Hill
Income: £2,023,961 [2017]; £1,996,639 [2016]; £2,077,404 [2015]; £2,041,767 [2014]; £2,176,604 [2013]

Jubilee House Care Trust Ltd
Registered: 27 Nov 1987 *Employees:* 49 *Volunteers:* 38
Tel: 01707 390107 *Website:* jubileehouse.com
Activities: Education, training; disability; accommodation, housing
Address: 1st Floor, St David's House, 11 Blenheim Court, Welwyn Garden City, Herts, AL7 1AD
Trustees: John Watson, Philip Brooks, Jon Banerjee, Philip Kelsey, James Yianni, Larry Shaw, Steve Stokes, Marie Scales, Mrs Jennifer Cooke
Income: £1,815,607 [2017]; £1,732,960 [2016]; £1,703,652 [2015]; £1,686,863 [2014]; £1,761,360 [2013]

Jubilee Sailing Trust (Tenacious) Limited
Registered: 20 Jul 2000 *Volunteers:* 100
Website: jst.org.uk
Activities: Disability; amateur sport
Address: La Huterie, La Longue Rue, St Martin, Jersey, JE3 6ED
Trustees: Mr Tom Fm Stewart, Mr James Crill
Income: £3,974,950 [2017]; £644,714 [2016]; £1,784,683 [2015]; £1,526,460 [2014]; £1,501,253 [2013]

Jubilee Sailing Trust Limited
Registered: 15 Jul 1983 *Employees:* 30 *Volunteers:* 180
Website: jst.org.uk
Activities: Disability; amateur sport
Address: La Huterie, La Longue Rue, St Martin, Jersey, JE3 6ED
Trustees: Tom Stewart, Mr James Crill
Income: £3,485,906 [2017]; £786,496 [2016]; £2,332,903 [2015]; £1,094,680 [2014]; £1,239,222 [2013]

The Jubilee Sailing Trust
Registered: 14 Jun 1979 *Employees:* 31 *Volunteers:* 300
Tel: 023 8044 9108 *Website:* jst.org.uk
Activities: Disability; amateur sport
Address: Jubilee Sailing Trust, 12 Hazel Road, Woolston, Southampton, SO19 7GA
Trustees: Niall Tarrell, Mr Martyn James Cuff, Mr James Crill, Mr Mark Rawson, Tom Stewart, Mr Kevin Curran, Mrs Emma Crabtree
Income: £4,355,936 [2017]; £2,779,792 [2016]; £3,522,745 [2015]; £3,812,760 [2014]; £2,934,829 [2013]

Julia's House Limited
Registered: 31 Dec 1997 *Employees:* 107 *Volunteers:* 475
Tel: 01202 644220 *Website:* juliashouse.org
Activities: General charitable purposes; advancement of health or saving of lives; disability
Address: Julia's House Limited, Barclays House, 1 Wimborne Road, Poole, Dorset, BH15 2BB
Trustees: Mr Brian Peter Hutchinson, Mr Vernon Michael Phillips, Ms Elizabeth Kay Labrow, Dr Simon Craigen Pennell, Mr Barrie Thomas, Ms Jacqui Scrace, Mr Peter Graham Wragg, Ms Lisa Karen Johnston, Mr Christopher Robert Twaits, Ms Susan Cianchetta, Warren Munson
Income: £6,633,798 [2016]; £7,270,881 [2015]; £5,670,725 [2014]; £4,494,697 [2013]

Julian Support Limited
Registered: 2 Feb 1998 *Employees:* 106
Tel: 01603 767718 *Website:* juliansupport.org
Activities: The advancement of health or saving of lives; disability; accommodation, housing
Address: Suite 2, 9 Norwich Business Park, Whiting Road, Norwich, NR4 6DJ
Trustees: Mr Mark Julian Taylor, Mr Brendan Bergin, Mr Anthony James Brice, Mr Paul Rao, Mrs Marilyn Evans, Mr Chris King, Pat Holman, Mr Clive Gardner, Dr Kate Nash
Income: £3,765,508 [2017]; £3,683,217 [2016]; £3,404,559 [2015]; £4,853,763 [2014]; £5,475,432 [2013]

Junction CDC Limited
Registered: 7 Feb 1991 *Employees:* 63
Tel: 01223 403477 *Website:* junction.co.uk
Activities: General charitable purposes; education, training; arts, culture, heritage, science
Address: Menagerie Theatre Company, Cambridge Junction, Clifton Way, Cambridge, CB1 7GX
Trustees: Mrs Helen Taylor, Ms Nicola Buckley, Mr Jonathon Payne, Mr Julius Edward Benedick Stobbs, Dr Merev Rosenfeld, Mr Michael John Keith Stone, Mrs Christine Doddington, Mr Godric Smith, Mr Richard Ian Arnold
Income: £2,480,790 [2017]; £2,234,827 [2016]; £2,347,405 [2015]; £2,130,536 [2014]; £2,299,190 [2013]

Just for Kids Law
Registered: 21 Nov 2007 *Employees:* 35 *Volunteers:* 65
Website: justforkidslaw.org
Activities: Education, training; prevention or relief of poverty; economic, community development, employment
Address: Just for Kids Law Ltd, Unit 4d, Leroy House, 436 Essex Road, London, N1 3QP
Trustees: Ms Carolyn Ann Regan, Mr Ronan McCrea, Mr Anthony David Landes, Kathryn Hollinsgworth, Amira Bhatt, Ms Brenda Campbell, Ms Jennie Fleming, Mr Peter George Gibbs, Helen Louise Lunt
Income: £1,287,759 [2017]; £789,529 [2016]; £763,449 [2015]; £556,661 [2014]; £332,810 [2013]

Justice & Care
Registered: 27 Jan 2010 *Employees:* 9
Website: justiceandcare.com
Activities: Other charitable purposes
Address: Suite 139, Mail Boxes Etc, Hill House, 210 Upper Richmond Road, London, SW15 6NP
Trustees: Mr James Thomas, Mr Jonathan Pugh-Smith, Ms Lauran Dale Bethell, Mr Jon Simpson
Income: £13,559,830 [2016]; £3,828,665 [2015]; £2,070,360 [2014]; £557,856 [2013]; £473,240 [2012]

Juvenile Diabetes Research Foundation Limited
Registered: 14 May 1987 *Employees:* 66 *Volunteers:* 600
Tel: 020 7713 2030 *Website:* jdrf.org.uk
Activities: The advancement of health or saving of lives; disability
Address: 17-18 Angel Gate, City Road, London, EC1V 2PT
Trustees: Mr Dominic Gerard Christian, Mr James Richard Nigel Cripps, Mrs Karen Judith Loumansky, David McTurk, Mr James Lurie, Ms Eleanor Mills, Mr Ian Schneider, Mrs Christina Croft
Income: £6,084,517 [2017]; £6,100,673 [2016]; £5,182,425 [2015]; £4,712,975 [2014]; £4,172,403 [2013]

KFC Foundation
Registered: 14 Sep 2015
Tel: 07837 093381
Activities: General charitable purposes
Address: KFC, Orion Gate, Guildford Road, Woking, Surrey, GU22 7NJ
Trustees: Mr Akram Khan, Mr William Huw James, Meg Farren, Mrs Paula Jane MacKenzie, Mr Neil Morrison
Income: £2,093,081 [2016]

KH Theatre Limited
Registered: 29 Apr 2015 *Employees:* 6
Tel: 020 7226 8561 *Website:* kingsheadtheatre.com
Activities: Education, training; arts, culture, heritage, science
Address: Kings Head Theatre, 115 Upper Street, London, N1 1QN
Trustees: Mrs Mary Lauder, Mr Richard Williamson, Ms Molly Waiting, Ms Amanda Moulson, Mr Tahmid Rahman Chowdhury, Mr Jesper Groenvold, Miss Heather Ruck, Mr James Arthur Richard Seabright, Ms Yasmin Hafesji
Income: £1,048,722 [2016]; £670,774 [2015]

KKL Charity Accounts
Registered: 23 Sep 2004 *Employees:* 2
Tel: 020 8732 6124 *Website:* smartgiving.org.uk
Activities: General charitable purposes
Address: JNF Charitable Trust, Mountcliff House, 154 Brent Street, London, NW4 2BF
Trustees: Mr Michael Sinclair, Mr Samuel Hayek, Mr Elan Gorji, Mr Benjamin Eliezer Perl MBE, Ms Marilyn Waisman, Mr Howard Norman Wayne
Income: £8,229,733 [2016]; £8,256,532 [2015]; £10,177,545 [2014]; £7,735,890 [2013]; £9,932,081 [2012]

KT Educational Charitable Trust
Registered: 18 Mar 2010
Tel: 020 7871 3119
Activities: General charitable purposes; education, training
Address: 23 Cromwell Road, London, SW7 2EL
Trustees: Richard Fairbairn, Arnaud Vaissie, Jean-Pierre Mustier, Lorene Lemor
Income: £1,535,000 [2016]; £1,643,000 [2015]; £2,654,000 [2014]; £2,283,000 [2013]; £1,602,000 [2012]

Kabbalah Centre
Registered: 10 Mar 2000 *Employees:* 40 *Volunteers:* 300
Tel: 020 7499 4974 *Website:* kabbalah.com
Activities: General charitable purposes; education, training; religious activities
Address: 12 Stratford Place, London, W1C 1BB
Trustees: Lady Homa Alliance, Mrs Gladys Obadiah, Mr Michael Berg, Mr Marcus Joel Weston, Rabbi Yarom Yardeni
Income: £5,769,262 [2016]; £5,716,417 [2015]; £7,213,699 [2014]; £6,236,922 [2013]; £6,685,138 [2012]

The Kadas Prize Foundation
Registered: 26 Jun 2014 *Employees:* 1
Tel: 020 7317 5385 *Website:* kadasprize.org
Activities: Education, training; arts, culture, heritage, science; economic, community development, employment
Address: Scandinavian House, 2-6 Cannon Street, London, EC4M 6YH
Trustees: Mr Peter Kadas, Mrs Tehseen Yunus Overy, Mr Daniel Hallgarten
Income: £1,195,460 [2017]; £100,025 [2016]

Kahal Chassidim Bobov
Registered: 27 Mar 1980 *Volunteers:* 3
Tel: 020 8880 8910
Activities: Education, training; prevention or relief of poverty; religious activities
Address: 87 Egerton Road, London, N16 6UE
Trustees: Mr Moshe Brinner, Mr Zushia Hochhauser, Mr L Stempel, Mr Abraham Schlaff
Income: £3,823,123 [2017]; £3,065,990 [2016]; £2,338,242 [2015]; £3,712,088 [2014]; £3,258,107 [2013]

Kairos Community Trust
Registered: 31 Jan 2007 *Employees:* 37 *Volunteers:* 21
Tel: 020 8677 7292 *Website:* kairoscommunity.org.uk
Activities: The advancement of health or saving of lives; accommodation, housing
Address: 235 Valley Road, London, SW16 2AF
Trustees: Mrs Hanora Antinette Morrin, Mr Robert James Dundas Finlay, Mr Gerald David St Clair'Barry, Mr Giles William Kirwan Beale, Ms Sarah Potter, Shawn McCarthy, Mr Paul Thomas Carter, Dr Jasper Christian Mordhorst
Income: £2,890,656 [2017]; £2,649,068 [2016]; £2,564,761 [2015]; £2,600,990 [2014]; £2,417,457 [2013]

Kaleidoscope Plus Group
Registered: 12 Mar 2003 *Employees:* 67 *Volunteers:* 100
Tel: 0121 565 5605 *Website:* kaleidoscopeplus.org.uk
Activities: Education, training; advancement of health or saving of lives; disability; accommodation, housing; economic, community development, employment
Address: First Floor, Sandwell Mind, Hawthorns House, Halfords Lane, West Bromwich, Smethwick, W Midlands, B66 1BB
Trustees: Ms Monica Shafaq, Clarke Carlisle, Mr Benjamin John Purkiss, Mr John Levy, Mr Mark Wood, Mrs Sharon Rowe, Mr Darren Moore
Income: £2,845,268 [2017]; £2,881,566 [2016]; £3,064,417 [2015]; £3,235,719 [2014]; £2,897,662 [2013]

Kaleidoscope Project
Registered: 30 Jun 2006 *Employees:* 405 *Volunteers:* 50
Tel: 01633 811950 *Website:* kaleidoscopeproject.org.uk
Activities: Education, training; advancement of health or saving of lives; accommodation, housing; arts, culture, heritage, science; economic, community development, employment
Address: 1 Resolven House, St Mellons Business Park, Fortran Road, St Mellons, Cardiff, CF3 0EY
Trustees: Mrs Pamela Francis Rutter, Ms Catherine Pepinster, Mr Stephen Davison, Mr Julian Mark Quentin Knight, Mrs Eleanor Jane Chima-Okereke, Mr Christopher Freegard, Susan Carol Dicken, Mr Kevin David Ward, Mr Daniel Leo Antebi, Mrs Lynda Jane Astell
Income: £12,134,740 [2017]; £6,855,603 [2016]; £4,973,281 [2015]; £5,475,619 [2014]; £5,735,350 [2013]

Kaleidoscope South Hams Limited
Registered: 20 Mar 2002 *Employees:* 103
Tel: 01548 288504 *Website:* kaleidoscope.org.uk
Activities: General charitable purposes; education, training; advancement of health or saving of lives; disability; prevention or relief of poverty; accommodation, housing; arts, culture, heritage, science; amateur sport; economic, community development, employment
Address: 16 Southville Gardens, Kingsbridge, Devon, TQ7 1LE
Trustees: Mr Graham Roberts, Mrs Lorraine Gwendoline Buckley, Mrs Julia Meany, Mr Jeffrey Adrian Buckley, Mrs Janice Jeffery
Income: £2,142,032 [2017]; £2,073,529 [2016]; £1,872,364 [2015]; £1,843,209 [2014]; £1,866,546 [2013]

The Karuna Trust
Registered: 5 Jun 1987 *Employees:* 25 *Volunteers:* 15
Tel: 020 7700 3434 *Website:* karuna.org
Activities: General charitable purposes; education, training; advancement of health or saving of lives; disability; prevention or relief of poverty; overseas aid, famine relief; religious activities; arts, culture, heritage, science; environment, conservation, heritage; economic, community development, employment; human rights, religious or racial harmony, equality or diversity
Address: The Karuna Trust, 72 Holloway Road, London, N7 8JG
Trustees: Mr Dominic Houlder, Mrs Ulla Elina Brown, Ms Zoe Stephenson, Mr Bill McGinley, Mr Pratap Rughani, Mr Nicolas Soames, Ms Amanda Seller
Income: £1,755,809 [2017]; £1,829,991 [2016]; £1,861,458 [2015]; £1,855,505 [2014]; £1,551,806 [2013]

Katharine House Hospice Trust
Registered: 26 Jun 1987 *Employees:* 128 *Volunteers:* 348
Tel: 01295 811866 *Website:* khh.org.uk
Activities: The advancement of health or saving of lives
Address: Aynho Road, Adderbury, Banbury, Oxon, OX17 3NL
Trustees: Mrs Heather Stewart, Dr Rolf Smith, Dr Jonathan Williams, Ms Carol Ann Shaw, Ms Dorothy Bean, Mr Richard Greaves, Mr Roger Worrall, Mr Anthony Lowe, Ms Geraldine Burke, Mr David Anthony Summersgill
Income: £3,785,677 [2017]; £3,602,855 [2016]; £3,647,012 [2015]; £3,343,060 [2014]; £3,149,152 [2013]

Katharine House Hospice
Registered: 8 Jun 1992 *Employees:* 276 *Volunteers:* 645
Tel: 01785 254645 *Website:* khhospice.org.uk
Activities: Education, training; advancement of health or saving of lives
Address: Katharine House Hospice, Weston Road, Stafford, ST16 3SB
Trustees: Mr David Malcolm Harding, Mr Barry John Baggott, Mr David Sandy, Mr Jean-Pierre Parsons, Dr Christopher John Secker, Mrs Karen Lesley Overmass, Ms Jennifer Woodyard, Lady Judith Clare Mitting, Terry Mingay, Mr Ian David Starkie, Mr Bernard Bester, Mrs Allison Jayne Cape
Income: £7,368,550 [2017]; £7,628,299 [2016]; £6,925,272 [2015]; £6,201,803 [2014]; £5,224,850 [2013]

The Kays Foundation
Registered: 21 Nov 2012
Tel: 020 7380 0080
Activities: General charitable purposes; education, training; disability; prevention or relief of poverty; overseas aid, famine relief; accommodation, housing; religious activities; environment, conservation, heritage; economic, community development, employment
Address: 173 Cleveland Street, London, W1T 6QR
Trustees: Mr Tom Kabuga, Mr Mitaj Nathwani, Mrs Sejal Kanani, Mr Mansukhlal Gudka, Mr Pankaj Nathwani
Income: £1,743,193 [2017]; £1,277,509 [2016]; £1,387,664 [2015]; £775,814 [2014]

Keble College in the University of Oxford
Registered: 27 Sep 2011 *Employees:* 124
Tel: 01865 272727 *Website:* keble.ox.ac.uk
Activities: Education, training
Address: Keble College, Parks Road, Oxford, OX1 3PG
Trustees: Professor Christopher Gosden, Sir Jonathan Phillips, Professor Paul Newman, Dr Lisa Maria Bendall, Professor Gui-Qiang Chen, Dr Edward Harcourt, Dr Dieter Jaksch, Dr Stephen Eric Kearsey, Dr Daniel McDermott, Dr Stephen Payne, Professor Stephen F Rayner, Dr Alasdair Peter Rogers, Dr Howard Smith, Professor Richard Washington, Dr Michael Norman Hawcroft, Professor Harry Laurence Anderson, Dr Sarah Apetrei, Dr Matthew Bevis, Dr Morgan Clarke, Professor Ulrike Gruneberg, Rev Nevsky Everett, Professor Nathan Eubank, Dr Kazbi Soonawalla, Professor Francois Caron, Mr Roger John Boden, Professor Sarah Whatmore, Dr Ian Wallace Archer, Professor Markus Bockmuehl, Professor Stephen Faulkner, Dr Thomas Franklin George Higham, Professor Timothy Jenkinson, Professor Viktor Mayer-Schonberger, Dr Anna-Maria Susheila Misra, Dr Diane Maree Purkiss, Professor Gesine Reinert, Dr Kevin Sheppard, Miss Jennifer Susan Tudge, Dr Simon Julian Bevan Butt, Professor Edwin Peel, Professor Ursula Coope, Dr James Goudkamp, Dr Stephen Cameron, Dr Nicola Gardini, Professor Andras Juhasz, Professor Jeremy William Tomlinson, Professor Fletcher Stephen, Dr Beth Greenhough, Professor Helen Mary Byrne
Income: £38,352,000 [2017]; £11,511,000 [2016]; £10,499,000 [2015]; £10,439,000 [2014]; £8,609,000 [2013]

Keble Preparatory School (1968) Ltd
Registered: 7 Jun 1968 *Employees:* 38
Tel: 020 8360 3359 *Website:* kebleprep.co.uk
Activities: Education, training
Address: Keble Preparatory School (1968) Ltd, Wades Hill, London, N21 1BG
Trustees: Mr John Reid Hetherington FCA, Mrs Rosalie Anne Davie, Mr Paul Anthony Ruocco, Mr Rohin Shah, Mr David Fotheringham, Sir John Bryany Bourn KCB, Mrs Christine Edmundson, Rev Jill Northam, Mr Christopher Reynolds, Mr David Tyme
Income: £3,160,616 [2016]; £2,906,622 [2015]; £2,760,642 [2014]; £2,631,965 [2013]; £2,546,191 [2012]

Keech Hospice Care
Registered: 15 Mar 1994 *Employees:* 262 *Volunteers:* 1,500
Tel: 01582 492339 *Website:* keech.org.uk
Activities: The advancement of health or saving of lives
Address: Great Bramingham Lane, Luton, Beds, LU3 3NT
Trustees: Bronwen Philpott, Mr Michael Hubbocks, Robert Ryall, Mr Sukhdeep Saini, Mrs Nicola Frances Bannister, Ms Patricia Ann Norman, Mrs Maria Collins, Ms Karen Proctor, Ms Angela Harkness, Mr Clive Edward Medlam, Mr Frances James Dalton, Mr Lee Robert Gazey
Income: £10,051,000 [2017]; £9,914,000 [2016]; £10,217,000 [2015]; £10,484,000 [2014]; £8,454,000 [2013]

Keele University Student Union
Registered: 10 Aug 2010 *Employees:* 127 *Volunteers:* 3,000
Tel: 01782 733700 *Website:* keelesu.com
Activities: Education, training
Address: Keele University Students' Union, Keele University, Keele, Newcastle-under-Lyme, Staffs, ST5 5BJ
Trustees: Ms Meghan Harrison, Mr Thomas Campbell, Mr Thomas Snape, Mrs Valerie Newman, Mr Jeffrey Wiltshire, Ms Aysha Panter, Mr Samuel Gibbons
Income: £4,679,126 [2017]; £4,535,679 [2016]; £4,085,665 [2015]; £4,111,951 [2014]; £4,014,742 [2013]

Keelman Homes Limited
Registered: 16 Dec 2009
Tel: 0191 433 5353
Activities: The prevention or relief of poverty
Address: Keelman Homes, Civic Centre, Regent Street, Gateshead, Tyne & Wear, NE8 1JN
Trustees: Mr Paul Foy, Mrs Anne Connolly, Linda Hitman, Mrs Joanne Carr, Mr Brian Kelly, Ms Leigh Kirton
Income: £1,359,000 [2017]; £1,335,000 [2016]; £679,000 [2015]; £841,000 [2014]; £754,034 [2013]

Keep Britain Tidy
Registered: 28 Sep 1998 *Employees:* 80 *Volunteers:* 2,000
Tel: 01942 612619 *Website:* keepbritaintidy.org
Activities: Education, training; environment, conservation, heritage; economic, community development, employment
Address: Keep Britain Tidy, Elizabeth House, Pottery Road, Wigan, Lancs, WN3 4EX
Trustees: Mr David Membrey, Ms Suzy Brain England OBE, Mrs Angela Smith-Morgan, Mr Alfred Hill, Ms Amanda Rendle, Mrs Philippa Anderson, Mr James Millar, Mrs Hillary Bauer, Mrs Sarah Lund
Income: £5,607,812 [2017]; £4,252,209 [2016]; £4,314,102 [2015]; £5,470,060 [2014]; £7,792,100 [2013]

Keep Wales Tidy
Registered: 16 Aug 2000 *Employees:* 55 *Volunteers:* 11,185
Tel: 029 2025 6767 *Website:* keepwalestidy.cymru
Activities: Environment, conservation, heritage
Address: Keep Wales Tidy Campaign, 33-35 Cathedral Road, Cardiff, CF11 9HB
Trustees: Mr David King, Mr Mathew Prosser, Mr Ceri Davies, Ms Mari Arthur, Miss Ruth Lovell, Mr Stephen Williams, Mr Edward Evans, Mr Philip Styles, Dr Michelle Webber, Mr Richard Mynott
Income: £2,230,967 [2017]; £2,845,169 [2016]; £3,291,855 [2015]; £2,322,556 [2014]; £2,423,662 [2013]

Kehal Charedim Trust
Registered: 10 Jul 2003
Activities: Religious activities
Address: 99 Kyverdale Road, London, N16 6PP
Trustees: Mr Samuel Berkovitz, Mr Israel Pinchas Karniol, Mr Martin Wosner, Mr David Margulies, Mr Nathan Benjamin Bindinger
Income: £1,378,315 [2017]; £1,098,097 [2016]; £522,080 [2015]; £84,658 [2014]; £46,251 [2013]

Kehal Yisroel D'Chasidei Gur
Registered: 28 Jun 2006 *Volunteers:* 2
Tel: 020 8809 5072
Activities: General charitable purposes; education, training; advancement of health or saving of lives; prevention or relief of poverty; religious activities
Address: 125 Craven Park Road, London, N15 6BP
Trustees: Mr Mordechai Pesach, Mr Joseph Margulies, Rabbi Abraham Zonszajn
Income: £1,601,412 [2016]; £1,212,046 [2015]; £1,102,865 [2014]; £1,015,242 [2013]; £1,054,834 [2012]

Keighley & Worth Valley Railway Preservation Society Limited
Registered: 13 Jul 2010 *Employees:* 12 *Volunteers:* 500
Tel: 01535 645214 *Website:* kwvr.co.uk
Activities: Education, training; environment, conservation, heritage; economic, community development, employment
Address: The Railway Station, Haworth, Keighley, W Yorks, BD22 8NJ
Trustees: Dr Matthew Stroh, Mr Michael Tarran, Mr John Duijsters, Mr William Black, Mr Robin Higgins, Mr Stephen Richard Harris, Mr Martin Andrew Shaw, Mr Philip Lawton, Mr John Hoyle, Mr Peter Eastham, Mr Robert Hustwick, Mr Christopher Smyth, Mr Robert Malcolm Ross Graham, Mrs Jacqueline Ann Warburton, Mr Philip Balmforth, Mr Nicholas Bennett
Income: £2,656,903 [2017]; £1,843,968 [2016]; £1,591,976 [2015]; £1,506,442 [2014]; £1,501,809 [2013]

The Kelmarsh Trust
Registered: 12 Sep 1986 *Employees:* 19 *Volunteers:* 40
Tel: 01604 686543 *Website:* kelmarsh.com
Activities: Education, training; environment, conservation, heritage
Address: Kelmarsh Hall, Main Road, Kelmarsh, Northampton, NN6 9LY
Trustees: Mr Charles Lovatt Greville-Heygate, Lady Anne Parsons, Robert Bargery, Lady Nutting, Mr Richard Flenley
Income: £1,551,045 [2017]; £1,270,763 [2016]; £1,252,601 [2015]; £1,095,450 [2014]; £1,171,239 [2013]

Kemp House Trust Ltd
Registered: 9 Mar 2012 *Employees:* 50 *Volunteers:* 348
Tel: 01562 756000 *Website:* kemphospice.org.uk
Activities: The advancement of health or saving of lives
Address: Kemp Hospice, 41 Mason Road, Kidderminster, Worcs, DY11 6AG
Trustees: Mr Christopher Kenneth Skinner, Mr Tim Gulliver, Mrs Alison Louise Field, Mr Shayne Winston Taylor, Mr Malcolm Westbury Plant, Ms Janet Anne Rowe
Income: £1,591,170 [2017]; £1,724,722 [2016]; £1,325,449 [2015]; £1,921,789 [2014]; £1,246,943 [2013]

The Kendal Brewery Arts Centre Trust Limited
Registered: 29 May 2001 *Employees:* 55 *Volunteers:* 100
Tel: 01539 722833 *Website:* breweryarts.co.uk
Activities: Education, training; arts, culture, heritage, science
Address: Brewery Arts Centre, Highgate, Kendal, Cumbria, LA9 4HE
Trustees: Richard Foster, Ms Jenny Kagan, Ms Claire Elizabeth Welburn, Ms Helen Mary Holmes, Mr Conrad Charles Francis Lynch, Mr Philip Lawrence Whitehurst, Christopher Thomas Stafford Batten, Mr Michael Jones, Ms Pauline Yarwood, Mr Terence Richard Clarke, Mr Antony John Preedy
Income: £3,006,813 [2017]; £3,093,294 [2016]; £3,005,680 [2015]; £3,165,890 [2014]; £3,267,675 [2013]

The Kenelm Youth Trust Limited
Registered: 10 Oct 2011 *Employees:* 39 *Volunteers:* 18
Tel: 01538 703224 *Website:* kenelmyouthtrust.org.uk
Activities: Education, training; religious activities
Address: Alton Castle, Castle Hill Road, Alton, Stoke on Trent, Staffs, ST10 4TT
Trustees: Mrs Janet Tibbits, Ms Helen Bardy, Mr Tommy Rowan, Mrs Catherine Clement, Rt Rev William Kenney, Mr John Benet Farrell, Ms Hannah Weaver, Miss Carmel Bridget Keane
Income: £1,730,695 [2016]; £72,389 [2015]; £47,986 [2014]; £12,802 [2013]

Kennedy Independent School Trust Limited
Registered: 23 Aug 1966 *Employees:* 74 *Volunteers:* 30
Tel: 01273 592681 *Website:* shorehamcollege.co.uk
Activities: Education, training
Address: Shoreham College, St Julians Lane, Shoreham-by-Sea, W Sussex, BN43 6YW
Trustees: Mr Peter Booth, Mrs Lorraine Wingrove, Mrs Ann Read, Mr Simon Barnett, Ms Karen Barry, Mr Peter Kent, Mr Sean Mills, Mr Ian Rudge, Mr John Kittow, Mr David Kelsey
Income: £4,659,128 [2017]; £4,072,556 [2016]; £4,078,465 [2015]; £3,875,866 [2014]; £4,079,686 [2013]

The Kennedy Trust for Rheumatology Research
Registered: 29 Jan 1970 *Employees:* 2
Tel: 020 8834 1562 *Website:* kennedytrust.org
Activities: The advancement of health or saving of lives
Address: The Kennedy Trust For Rheumatology Research, 26-28 Hammersmith Grove, London, W6 7BA
Trustees: Mrs Jennifer Johnson, Professor Sir Ravinder Maini, Mr Rodney Hornstein, Mr David Paterson, Mrs Margaret Frost, Professor Andrew Cope, Professor Hill Gaston, Dame Nicola Davies, James Davis, Sir Gregory Winter, Professor Stephen Holgate
Income: £37,282,000 [2016]; £28,401,000 [2015]; £37,022,000 [2014]; £29,435,000 [2013]; £88,618,000 [2012]

Kensington and Chelsea Citizens Advice Bureau Service
Registered: 30 Jul 1996 *Employees:* 24 *Volunteers:* 50
Tel: 020 8962 3481 *Website:* kensingtonandchelseacitizensadvice.org.uk
Activities: The prevention or relief of poverty
Address: Citizens Advice Kensington, 2 Acklam Road, London, W10 5QZ
Trustees: Mr Robert Freeman, Mr Anthony Keith Usher, Ms Shelina Thawer, Mr Bevan Powell, Mrs Helen Jane Bush, Ms Judith Schrut, Miss Marie-Therese Rossi, Mr Christopher David, Mr John Manuel Gago De Oliveira
Income: £1,154,960 [2017]; £1,236,001 [2016]; £1,431,903 [2015]; £1,265,419 [2014]; £1,301,218 [2013]

Kensington and Chelsea Social Council
Registered: 11 Jul 2001 *Employees:* 8
Tel: 020 7243 9800 *Website:* kcsc.org.uk
Activities: General charitable purposes; education, training; prevention or relief of poverty; economic, community development, employment; other charitable purposes
Address: London Lighthouse, 111-117 Lancaster Road, London, W11 1QT
Trustees: Mr Michael Ernest Bach, Mr Jamie Renton, Mr Mark Anfilogoff, Daisy Ryan, Kevin Masters, Judith Davey, Mr Stephen Duckworth, Ms Christine Bennett, Angela Wilson, Annie Redmile
Income: £1,177,654 [2017]; £615,142 [2016]; £527,415 [2015]; £842,022 [2014]; £729,462 [2013]

Kent Association for Spina Bifida and Hydrocephalus
Registered: 28 Mar 2008 *Employees:* 49 *Volunteers:* 16
Tel: 01474 536501 *Website:* kasbah.org.uk
Activities: General charitable purposes; education, training; advancement of health or saving of lives; disability; accommodation, housing
Address: 7 The Hive, Northfleet, Gravesend, Kent, DA11 9DE
Trustees: Mrs Ann Elizabeth Everett, Sarah Helsdon, Mr Philip Willmott, Mrs Christine Taylor, Mr Richard Chapman, Mr Trevor Sinclair, Mr Stephen Field, Jason Owen
Income: £1,244,968 [2017]; £1,162,674 [2016]; £928,320 [2015]; £824,756 [2014]; £664,939 [2013]

Kent Association for the Blind
Registered: 14 May 1997 *Employees:* 60 *Volunteers:* 700
Tel: 01622 691357 *Website:* kab.org.uk
Activities: General charitable purposes; education, training; advancement of health or saving of lives; disability
Address: Kent Association for the Blind, 72 College Road, Maidstone, Kent, ME15 6SJ
Trustees: Mr Malcolm Ketley, Mr John Daffarn, Mr James Burke, Mr Michael Benson, Mr Greg Munton, Mr Tim Harris, Mrs Jennifer Terry, Hazel Groves
Income: £2,394,003 [2017]; £2,325,629 [2016]; £2,355,538 [2015]; £2,246,258 [2014]; £2,497,964 [2013]

The Kent Autistic Trust
Registered: 11 Aug 1989 *Employees:* 211
Tel: 01634 405168 *Website:* kentautistic.com
Activities: Disability; accommodation, housing; other charitable purposes
Address: 14 High Street, Brompton, Gillingham, Kent, ME7 5AE
Trustees: Mr Philip White, Mr Andrew Warner, Ms Victoria Louise Sampson BSc Hons, Mrs Vanessa Kelsey Jansen, Nicola August, Veen Rama, Professor Georges Dussart, Mrs Helen Jones, Mr Gary Warner, Ms Laura Smith, Mr Rasheed Said, Mr Martin Connolly
Income: £6,552,962 [2017]; £6,391,850 [2016]; £6,024,190 [2015]; £5,667,472 [2014]; £5,509,093 [2013]

Kent College, Canterbury
Registered: 5 Feb 1964 *Employees:* 283 *Volunteers:* 5
Tel: 020 7935 3723 *Website:* kentcollege.com
Activities: Education, training; religious activities
Address: Methodist Church House, 25 Marylebone Road, London, NW1 5JR
Trustees: Kent College Canterbury Trustee Company Limited, Methodist Independent Schools Trust
Income: £13,114,114 [2016]; £12,486,347 [2015]; £10,951,575 [2014]; £10,355,488 [2013]; £10,091,930 [2012]

Kent College, Pembury
Registered: 5 Feb 1965 *Employees:* 221 *Volunteers:* 25
Tel: 020 7935 3723 *Website:* kent-college.co.uk
Activities: Education, training; religious activities
Address: Methodist Church House, 25 Marylebone Road, London, NW1 5JR
Trustees: Kent College Pembury Trustee Company Limited, Methodist Independent Schools Trust
Income: £10,764,385 [2016]; £10,395,288 [2015]; £10,379,683 [2014]; £10,274,473 [2013]; £9,840,106 [2012]

Kent Community Foundation
Registered: 5 Jan 2001 *Employees:* 9
Tel: 01303 814500 *Website:* kentcf.org.uk
Activities: General charitable purposes; education, training; advancement of health or saving of lives; disability; prevention or relief of poverty; accommodation, housing; religious activities; arts, culture, heritage, science; amateur sport; environment, conservation, heritage; economic, community development, employment; armed forces, emergency service efficiency; human rights, religious or racial harmony, equality or diversity; recreation; other charitable purposes
Address: Evegate Park Barn, Evegate, Ashford, Kent, TN25 6SX
Trustees: Mr Arthur Blair Gulland, Mr William Peter Williams, Tim Bull, Mrs Melissa Murdoch, Robert Sackville-West, Mrs Sarah Hohler, Ann West, Mrs Georgina Mary Warner, Hugo Fenwick, Dr Emilia Falcetti Boscawen
Income: £2,473,529 [2017]; £3,362,182 [2016]; £2,911,966 [2015]; £4,992,950 [2014]; £3,531,452 [2013]

Kent County Agricultural Society
Registered: 17 Dec 1990 *Employees:* 21 *Volunteers:* 250
Tel: 01622 633056 *Website:* kentshowground.co.uk
Activities: General charitable purposes; education, training; animals; environment, conservation, heritage; economic, community development, employment
Address: Kent County Show Ground, Detling Hill, Detling, Maidstone, Kent, ME14 3JF
Trustees: Mr Hugh John Edward Summerfield, Mr Mark James Lumsdon-Taylor, Mrs Mary Anthony, Mr Charles Stanley Tassell, Mr James Peter Forknall, Mr Richard Julian Barnes, Mr Thomas John Coultrip, Mrs Rosamund Phyllis Deirdre Day, Mr Kevin Attwood, Mr Timothy Daniel Lyle Cathcart, Mr Stuart Gibbons, Miss Gail Patricia Hickmott
Income: £2,645,580 [2017]; £2,458,671 [2016]; £2,160,845 [2015]; £2,854,004 [2014]; £1,910,469 [2013]

Kent Music
Registered: 29 Jul 2005 *Employees:* 59 *Volunteers:* 7
Tel: 01622 358415 *Website:* kent-music.com
Activities: Education, training
Address: 24 Turkey Court, Turkey Mill, Ashford Road, Maidstone, Kent, ME14 5PP
Trustees: Mrs Sarah Hohler, Mr Timothy Philip Leates, Mr James Wyndham Williams, Ms Liz Moran, Ms Joanne Winkler, Mrs Elizabeth Topiwala, Mr Paul Danielsen, Mr Geoff Miles, Dr Nicholas McKay, Mrs Francesca Christmas, Mr Robin Hammerton, Mr Geoffrey Lymer
Income: £3,218,167 [2017]; £3,300,944 [2016]; £5,068,665 [2015]; £3,183,419 [2014]; £3,519,013 [2013]

Kent Union
Registered: 29 Sep 2010 *Employees:* 376 *Volunteers:* 2,800
Tel: 01227 824250 *Website:* kentunion.co.uk
Activities: Education, training
Address: University of Kent at Canterbury, Mandela Building, Canterbury, Kent, CT2 7NW
Trustees: Ruth Wilkinson, Neil Thornburn, Charlie Bond, Abigail Harris, Aaron Thompson, Clara Lee, Peter Gingell, Jake Pitt, Stuart Lidbetter
Income: £11,999,586 [2017]; £11,168,279 [2016]; £11,400,479 [2015]; £11,617,816 [2014]; £10,646,697 [2013]

Kent Wildlife Trust
Registered: 9 Mar 1965 *Employees:* 76 *Volunteers:* 1,056
Tel: 01622 662012 *Website:* kentwildlifetrust.org.uk
Activities: Education, training; environment, conservation, heritage; economic, community development, employment
Address: Kent Wildlife Trust, Tyland Barn, Chatham Road, Sandling, Maidstone, Kent, ME14 3BD
Trustees: Dr Caroline Jessel, Mike O'Connor, Tim Simmons, Dr Chris West, Mr Martin Garwood, Mr Richard Joseph Kinzler, Mr Graham Hill, Mr Michael Bax, Mr Colin Peters, Mr Charles Tassell, Pauline Bateson, Mrs Victoria Golding, Ian Tittley, Mrs Charlotte Osborn-Forde, Mrs Andrea Byerley, Mr Clive Maxwell, Mr Nigel Steele
Income: £3,989,000 [2016]; £4,427,000 [2015]; £4,155,000 [2014]; £3,684,000 [2013]; £3,732,000 [2012]

The Kent and East Sussex Railway Company Limited
Registered: 19 May 1971 *Employees:* 30 *Volunteers:* 500
Website: kesr.org.uk
Activities: Education, training; environment, conservation, heritage
Address: Flat 6a Herbert Court Mansions, Earl's Court Square, London, SW5 9DH
Trustees: Mrs Carol Rosemary Mitchell, Mr Geoffrey Alan Crouch, Mr Philip Duncan Shaw, Mr Jamie Alexander Douglas, Mr David Jeffrey Hazeldine, Mr Brian Malcolm Janes, Mr Ian Campbell Legg, Mr Stuart Clifton Phillips, Paul Jessett, Mr Bryan Ronald Atkins
Income: £1,878,769 [2016]; £1,513,321 [2015]; £2,078,337 [2014]; £2,205,325 [2013]; £1,784,075 [2012]

Kent, Surrey & Sussex Air Ambulance Trust
Registered: 21 May 1993 *Employees:* 45 *Volunteers:* 232
Tel: 01622 833833 *Website:* kssairambulance.org.uk
Activities: The advancement of health or saving of lives
Address: Kent Air Ambulance Trust, Unit 14 Wheelbarrow Park Estate, Pattenden Lane, Marden, Tonbridge, Kent, TN12 9QJ
Trustees: Mr James Loudon, Patrick Stewart, Paul Barrett, Andrew Farrant, Michael Docherty, Barney Burgess, Mrs Wendy Simkins, Dr Helen Bowcock, Stuart Millar, Tim Oakes, Caitlin Blewett
Income: £12,426,673 [2017]; £14,204,835 [2016]; £10,693,358 [2015]; £9,275,126 [2014]; £8,793,249 [2013]

The Kentown Wizard Foundation
Registered: 13 Oct 2015 *Employees:* 1
Tel: 01253 446923
Activities: General charitable purposes
Address: Metro House Ltd, Unit 14-17 Metropolitan Business Park, Preston New Road, Blackpool, Lancs, FY3 9LT
Trustees: David Bamber, Mr Richard George Ingle, Kenneth Townsley, Kathryn Graham
Income: £57,191,953 [2017]

The Kenward Trust
Registered: 21 Mar 2012 *Employees:* 56 *Volunteers:* 15
Tel: 01622 814187 *Website:* kenwardtrust.org.uk
Activities: Education, training; advancement of health or saving of lives; disability; prevention or relief of poverty; accommodation, housing
Address: Kenward Trust, Head Office, Kenward Road, Yalding, Maidstone, Kent, ME18 6AH
Trustees: Dr Anthony Jones, Mr Peter Brook, Mrs Bridget Langstaff, Mr Jeremy Simon, Mr Paul Fletcher, Mr Roger Bedford, Mr Jean-Pierre Darque
Income: £1,529,767 [2017]; £1,648,588 [2016]; £1,743,931 [2015]; £1,907,951 [2014]; £1,913,393 [2013]

Kerem Schools
Registered: 6 Aug 1997 *Employees:* 59 *Volunteers:* 19
Tel: 020 8455 0909 *Website:* keremschool.co.uk
Activities: Education, training
Address: Kerem School, Norrice Lea, London, N2 0RE
Trustees: Mr Julian Taylor, Mr Asher David Miller, Mr David Wolfson QC
Income: £2,073,084 [2017]; £2,043,649 [2016]; £1,963,594 [2015]; £2,081,378 [2014]; £1,961,019 [2013]

Keren Association Limited
Registered: 15 Feb 1962
Activities: General charitable purposes
Address: 136 Clapton Common, London, E5 9AG
Trustees: Mrs S Englander, Mrs H Z Weiss, Mr Jacob Shea Englander, Mr S Z Englander, Mr E Englander, Mrs N Weiss, Mr Pinkus Naftola Englander
Income: £16,697,528 [2017]; £11,179,660 [2016]; £17,603,617 [2015]; £13,150,227 [2014]; £4,986,906 [2013]

Keren Chochmas Shloma Trust
Registered: 28 Aug 2013 *Volunteers:* 2
Tel: 020 8800 0827
Activities: Education, training; prevention or relief of poverty; religious activities
Address: 123 Castlewood Road, London, N15 6BD
Trustees: Mr Joel Herzog, Mr Mordechai Blumenberg, Mrs Miriam Schiff
Income: £1,771,979 [2016]; £1,410,441 [2015]; £1,532,437 [2014]

Keren Hatzolas Doros Alei Siach
Registered: 16 Dec 2013 *Volunteers:* 3
Tel: 020 8802 1886
Activities: Education, training; advancement of health or saving of lives; disability; religious activities
Address: 19 Castlewood Road, London, N16 6DL
Trustees: Mrs Esther Stobiecki, Mr Barouch Itzhak Perkal, Mr Meir Yerachmiel Glaser
Income: £4,478,433 [2017]; £3,668,490 [2016]; £930,549 [2015]

The Dorothy Kerin Trust
Registered: 13 Feb 2003 *Employees:* 165 *Volunteers:* 112
Tel: 01892 865971 *Website:* burrswood.org.uk
Activities: The advancement of health or saving of lives; disability; religious activities
Address: Burrswood Health & Wellbeing, Burrswood, Groombridge, Tunbridge Wells, Kent, TN3 9PY
Trustees: Mr Robin Graham Hepburn, Dr Andrew Taylor, Mr Anthony Castle Bennett, Rt Revd Brian Colin Castle, Mrs Sarah Davies, Mr Timothy Cripps
Income: £3,629,000 [2016]; £3,681,000 [2015]; £3,988,000 [2014]; £4,127,000 [2013]; £4,040,000 [2012]

Kerith Community Church
Registered: 16 Jun 2008 *Employees:* 18 *Volunteers:* 400
Tel: 01344 828861 *Website:* kerith.church
Activities: Education, training; prevention or relief of poverty; overseas aid, famine relief; accommodation, housing; religious activities; economic, community development, employment; human rights, religious or racial harmony, equality or diversity
Address: Kerith Community Church, Kerith Centre, Church Road, Bracknell, Berks, RG12 1EH
Trustees: Mr Jonathan Richard Davis, Mr Lincoln Olusola Osunkoya, Mr Jeff Whitton, Mrs Daniele Seidu, Mr Simon Latimer Benham, Mr Olusola Osinoiki, Mr Duncan Robert Gordon Klitgaard
Income: £1,527,365 [2016]; £1,333,236 [2015]; £1,573,117 [2014]; £1,660,430 [2013]; £1,348,568 [2012]

E and E Kernkraut Charities Limited
Registered: 17 Jul 1978
Tel: 020 8806 7947
Activities: Education, training; prevention or relief of poverty; religious activities
Address: The Knoll, Fountayne Road, London, N16 7EA
Trustees: Mr Eli Kernkraut, Mr Jacob Kernkraut, Mrs Esther Kernkraut, Mr Joseph Kernkraut
Income: £1,118,282 [2017]; £1,096,629 [2016]; £784,508 [2015]; £792,148 [2014]; £1,208,914 [2013]

The Kessler Foundation
Registered: 7 Dec 1984 *Employees:* 49
Website: kesslerfoundation.org
Activities: General charitable purposes; education, training; advancement of health or saving of lives; disability; prevention or relief of poverty; religious activities; arts, culture, heritage, science; amateur sport; environment, conservation, heritage
Address: Jewish Chronicle Newspaper Ltd, 25 Furnival Street, London, EC4A 1JT
Trustees: Mr Clive Wollman, Mrs Laura Joseph, Anthony Ian Grossman, Mrs Sarah Gumb
Income: £3,424,239 [2017]; £2,961,337 [2016]; £4,208,642 [2015]; £11,581,186 [2014]; £4,346,314 [2013]

The Keswick Convention Trust
Registered: 22 Nov 2000 *Employees:* 12 *Volunteers:* 635
Tel: 017687 80075 *Website:* keswickministries.org
Activities: Religious activities
Address: Rawnsley Centre, Main Street, Keswick, Cumbria, CA12 5NP
Trustees: Dr Tim Chester, Mrs Elizabeth McQuoid, Mr David Gascoigne, Revd Dr Matthew Sleeman, Mr Stephen Henry Adam, Mrs Anna Putt, Mr Jonathan Chatfield, Mr Derek Burnside, Rev Alasdair Paine, Mr Martin Salter, Mr Simon Hale, Mrs Clare Heath-Whyte
Income: £2,461,842 [2016]; £2,052,152 [2015]; £1,148,264 [2014]; £1,189,604 [2013]; £1,077,676 [2012]

Keswick Enterprises Holdings Charitable Trust
Registered: 23 Jun 2016
Tel: 01923 825436
Activities: Education, training; religious activities; environment, conservation, heritage
Address: 32 Frithwood Avenue, Northwood, Middlesex, HA6 3LU
Trustees: Mr John Anthony Harvey CBE, Mrs Joanna Ruth Svarovsky, Mrs Philippa Sarah Reid, Mrs Nicola Mary Sawday BA Hons
Income: £1,034,250 [2017]

Keswick Foundation Limited
Registered: 11 Sep 1979 *Employees:* 4
Tel: 020 7816 8100 *Website:* keswickfoundation.org.hk
Activities: Education, training; disability; economic, community development, employment
Address: Matheson & Co Ltd, Scottish Provident Building, 3 Lombard Street, London, EC3V 9AQ
Trustees: Mrs Clara Mary Weatherall, Mr Marcus Joytak Shaw, Mr Ivor Cosimo Jencks, Mr Sin Cheok Chiew, Mr Kin Ping Christophe Lee, Mrs Kathryn Mary Greenberg, Ms Deming Chen, Ms Christine Meng Sang Fang, Mrs Evelyn Lee Hough Parr, Mr Stephen Charles Li, Professor Woon Ki Angelina Yuen-Tsang, Mrs Stacey Anne Hildebrandt, Mrs Martha Keswick, Ms Lily Clare Jencks, Mrs Clare Jane Keswick, Professor Wing Sun Nelson Chow, Mr Benjamin William Keswick, Mrs Francine Wing Ting Fu Kwong, Mrs Alice Sophie Keswick
Income: £2,799,927 [2016]; £2,540,657 [2015]; £2,343,906 [2014]; £2,166,281 [2013]; £2,084,595 [2012]

Kew College
Registered: 5 Jan 1982 *Employees:* 54
Tel: 020 8940 2039 *Website:* kewcollege.com
Activities: Education, training
Address: 24-26 Cumberland Road, Kew, Richmond, Surrey, TW9 3HQ
Trustees: Mr Mark Roydon Allen Fenhalls, Mr Gerald Alexander Richard McGregor, Mrs Serena Alexander, Mr David Imrie, Mrs Susannah Ouseley, Miss Paula Vanninen, Ms Aylsa Geeson, Mrs Susan Bourne
Income: £3,275,109 [2017]; £3,064,176 [2016]; £2,924,917 [2015]; £2,715,518 [2014]; £2,623,443 [2013]

Kew Community Trust
Registered: 9 Jul 1984 *Employees:* 7 *Volunteers:* 15
Tel: 020 8948 8806 *Website:* kewcommunitytrust.org.uk
Activities: General charitable purposes
Address: 17 Ruskin Avenue, Richmond, Surrey, TW9 4DR
Trustees: Mrs Sally Durant, Dr Joanna Mary Stewart, Mrs Shahareen Hilmy, Mrs Lucinda Evans, Mr Richard Hannan, Mr Mark Boyle, Shiona Williams, Mrs Margaret Anne Marshall, Mrs Susan Stone, Mr Stephen Robinson, Mrs Tara Quick, Mrs Janet Chesterton, Mrs Rita Kamat
Income: £3,380,730 [2017]; £302,032 [2016]; £290,966 [2015]; £222,896 [2014]; £222,896 [2013]

Key House Project
Registered: 25 Jan 1989 *Employees:* 40 *Volunteers:* 2
Tel: 01535 211311 *Website:* keyhouse.co.uk
Activities: Education, training; prevention or relief of poverty; accommodation, housing
Address: Keyhouse, 130 North Street, Keighley, W Yorks, BD21 3AD
Trustees: Mr Zafar Ali JP, Mrs Josephine Nixon, Mr Andrew Gray, Mrs Shirley Sample, Mr Lionel Lockley, Ms Susan Elizabeth Evans
Income: £1,547,591 [2015]; £2,130,763 [2014]; £2,110,913 [2013]

Keychange Charity
Registered: 17 Mar 1997 Employees: 420 Volunteers: 40
Tel: 020 7633 0533 Website: keychangecare.org.uk
Activities: The advancement of health or saving of lives; prevention or relief of poverty; accommodation, housing; religious activities; other charitable purposes
Address: Keychange, 5 St Georges Mews, 43 Westminster Bridge Road, London, SE1 7JB
Trustees: Mr David John Hedley Goddard, Mr Roger Hugh Taylor FRICS, Mrs Imogen Taylor, Ms Joan Henshaw, Mrs Rosemary Joy Milner, Mr Charles Paul Murray Douglas, Mr Timothy Cotterall
Income: £8,188,391 [2017]; £7,711,767 [2016]; £8,580,190 [2015]; £7,753,384 [2014]; £7,156,310 [2013]

Keyring-Living Support Networks
Registered: 4 Apr 1996 Employees: 129 Volunteers: 48
Tel: 020 3119 0960 Website: keyring.org
Activities: Disability; prevention or relief of poverty; accommodation, housing; economic, community development, employment
Address: Key Ring Living Support Networks, Unit 21 St Olav's Court, City Business Centre, Lower Road, London, SE16 2XB
Trustees: Ms Lindsey Wishart, Mrs Jo Land, Mr Roberto Chiarotti, Ms Isabella Edwards, Mr Chris Bielby, Mr Andy Tonner, Ms Cassia Colling
Income: £4,311,000 [2017]; £4,680,000 [2016]; £4,539,254 [2015]; £4,258,642 [2014]; £3,956,891 [2013]

Keystone Accountability
Registered: 27 Apr 2007 Employees: 13
Tel: 020 3735 6367 Website: keystoneaccountability.org
Activities: Education, training; prevention or relief of poverty; overseas aid, famine relief; economic, community development, employment
Address: Keystone Accountability, Unit 121, 222 Kensal Road, London, W10 5BN
Trustees: Ms Emma Turner, Ms Alice Brown, Mr Jack Lange
Income: £1,463,208 [2017]; £699,882 [2016]; £723,828 [2015]; £471,166 [2014]; £336,468 [2013]

Keystone Education Trust
Registered: 8 Apr 2003 Employees: 19 Volunteers: 28
Tel: 01792 896693
Activities: Education, training
Address: 19 Home Farm Way, Penllergaer, Swansea, SA4 9HF
Trustees: Mr Richard Nunn, Mr David John Gardiner, Mr Clive Marsh, Mr Roy Mark Wells, Mr Nelson Bruce Ker, Mr Nigel Hill, Mr Edward Swanson
Income: £1,376,720 [2016]; £914,028 [2015]; £817,574 [2014]; £646,580 [2013]

Khalsa Aid
Registered: 18 Apr 2000 Employees: 4 Volunteers: 50
Website: khalsaaid.org
Activities: General charitable purposes; education, training; advancement of health or saving of lives; prevention or relief of poverty; overseas aid, famine relief; environment, conservation, heritage
Address: Suite 3, Big Yellow Offices, 111 Whitby Road, Slough, SL1 3DR
Trustees: Mr Pardeep Singh Manan, Mr Jaswinder Singh Bahra, Mr Inderveer Singh Hothi, Mr Jaspal Singh, Mr Paramjeet Sigh Saini, Mr Amarjit Singh Bansal
Income: £1,034,205 [2017]; £1,550,945 [2016]; £793,874 [2015]; £818,333 [2014]; £537,080 [2013]

G G S Khalsa College
Registered: 8 Mar 1999 Employees: 36 Volunteers: 5
Tel: 020 8559 9160 Website: ggskcollege.co.uk
Activities: General charitable purposes; education, training; religious activities; arts, culture, heritage, science; other charitable purposes
Address: Guru Gobind Singh Khalsa College, Roding Lane, Chigwell, Essex, IG7 6BQ
Trustees: Mr Sukhwant Singh Sidhu, Mr Baljinder Singh Gill, Mr Vijay Kumar Sennake Savan
Income: £2,013,453 [2016]; £1,704,841 [2015]; £1,586,097 [2014]; £1,414,436 [2013]; £1,357,408 [2012]

Khodorkovsky Foundation
Registered: 19 Nov 2004
Tel: 020 7318 1180
Activities: Education, training
Address: 4 Hill Street, London, W1J 5NE
Trustees: Mr Anthony Smith CBE, Mr Boris Georgievich Saltykov, Mr Anton Drel, Mr Alastair Robert Clifford Tulloch, Rupert Caldecott
Income: £5,356,214 [2016]; £2,770,000 [2015]; £3,249,026 [2014]; £5,131,787 [2013]; £3,184,314 [2012]

The Khoja Shia Ithnaasheri Muslim Community of London
Registered: 19 Dec 1983 Employees: 56 Volunteers: 400
Tel: 020 8954 6247 Website: hujjat.org
Activities: General charitable purposes; education, training; advancement of health or saving of lives; prevention or relief of poverty; overseas aid, famine relief; religious activities; arts, culture, heritage, science; amateur sport; environment, conservation, heritage; economic, community development, employment; human rights, religious or racial harmony, equality or diversity; recreation
Address: Islamic Centre, Wood Lane, Stanmore, Middlesex, HA7 4LQ
Trustees: Dr Munir M Datoo, Mr Musafir Kassamali Somani, Mr Altaf Daya, Mr Shams Kermalli, Mr Shaahid Hasan Jaffer, Dr Tauseef Mehrali, Mrs Sukaina Karim-Hussein, Mr Muhammad Salim Kassam, Mrs Marzia Jaffer, Mr Munir Chandoo, Mr Muzaffer Sultanali Rashid, Dr Sadik Merali, Mr Asim Nurmohamed, Mrs Farzana Karawalli
Income: £1,703,232 [2016]; £1,614,001 [2015]; £1,538,267 [2014]; £1,378,397 [2013]; £1,377,028 [2012]

Khoo Teck Puat UK Foundation
Registered: 8 Jul 2011
Tel: 020 7937 8000
Activities: Education, training; advancement of health or saving of lives; prevention or relief of poverty; arts, culture, heritage, science
Address: 2-24 Kensington High Street, London, W8 4PT
Trustees: Jennifer Carmichael, Ms Mavis Khoo Bee Geok, Ms Elizabeth Khoo, Neil Carmichael, Mr Eric Khoo Kim Hai
Income: £5,748,189 [2017]; £3,403,164 [2016]; £3,179,289 [2015]; £3,155,356 [2014]; £3,014,025 [2013]

Kidney Research UK
Registered: 24 Jul 1967 *Employees:* 50 *Volunteers:* 376
Tel: 0845 070 7601 *Website:* kidneyresearchuk.org
Activities: General charitable purposes; education, training; advancement of health or saving of lives
Address: Kidney Research UK, Nene Hall, Peterborough Business Park, Lynch Wood, Peterborough, PE2 6FZ
Trustees: Professor John Feehally, Mr Andrew Tripp, Dr Jill Norman, Mrs Anna-Maria Steel, Charles Tomson, Sunil Bhandari, Deirdre Jennings, Professor Jeremy Hughes, Professor Fiona Karet, Mr Iain Pearson, Mr David Prosser, Mrs Federica Pizzasegola, Tom Kelly, Julia Moross, Mr Adrian Akers, Dr Adnan Sharif
Income: £9,372,872 [2017]; £8,989,170 [2016]; £9,160,325 [2015]; £8,356,086 [2014]; £7,468,151 [2013]

Kids Out UK
Registered: 2 Jun 1999 *Employees:* 10 *Volunteers:* 12,490
Tel: 01525 385252 *Website:* kidsout.org.uk
Activities: General charitable purposes; disability; prevention or relief of poverty; amateur sport
Address: Kidsout UK Ltd, 14 Church Square, Leighton Buzzard, Beds, LU7 1AE
Trustees: Pamela Child, Ms Jayne Mee, Mr Alex Wilson, Mr Kevin Derek Green, Miss Amanda Elizabeth Wills, Miss Joan Cummins, Mr Robert Michael Burgess, Mr Steve Cartwright, Ms Fiona Rodford, Nicky Richmond, Mrs Helen Pitcher, Mr Bernard Buckley, Mr Stephen Gerald Glancey, Peter Blom, Andrew Griffin, Miss Caroline Marie Lawes, Ms Sue O'Brien, Mr James O'Hagan, Mr Simon Linares, Michael John Westcott
Income: £2,551,680 [2017]; £2,450,068 [2016]; £2,036,350 [2015]; £1,611,737 [2014]; £791,498 [2013]

Kids
Registered: 27 Jun 1978 *Employees:* 236 *Volunteers:* 444
Tel: 020 7359 3635 *Website:* kids.org.uk
Activities: General charitable purposes; education, training; disability
Address: Kids, 7-9 Elliotts Place, London, N1 8HX
Trustees: Mrs Teresa Culverwell, Mr Christopher Stefani, Mr Austin Erwin, Mrs Gabby Bertin, Kerry Anne Demora Crichlow, Mr Stephen James Unwin, Mr Steven Clarke, Christopher Stefani, Mr David De Paeztron, Mr Lindsay Thomas, Mr Richard Progel, Mr Benet Michael Peter Middleton, Ms Zoe Michelle Peden, Mr Christopher Charles Blackhurst, Samantha Clare Bowerman
Income: £10,468,714 [2017]; £10,730,442 [2016]; £11,034,488 [2015]; £10,369,021 [2014]; £10,562,599 [2013]

Kiln Theatre Limited
Registered: 15 Dec 1978 *Employees:* 20
Tel: 020 7372 6611 *Website:* kilntheatre.com
Activities: General charitable purposes; education, training; arts, culture, heritage, science
Address: 269 Kilburn High Road, London, NW6 7JR
Trustees: Jonathan Levy, Lady Simone Warner, Judy Lever, Fiona Calnan, Mrs Anneke Rachel Mendelsohn, Mr Philip Himberg, Mr Nicholas Bernard Basden, Nick Starr, Baz Bamigboye, Barbara Harrison, Kay Ellen Consolver, Jeremy Rodney Pines Lewison, Ms Sita McIntosh, Mr Barrie Alvin Tankel, Gilla Diana Harris
Income: £2,843,965 [2017]; £3,035,179 [2016]; £3,607,334 [2015]; £4,457,014 [2014]; £3,333,068 [2013]

Kimbolton School
Registered: 16 Jul 2003 *Employees:* 296 *Volunteers:* 104
Tel: 01480 860505 *Website:* kimbolton.cambs.sch.uk
Activities: Education, training
Address: Kimbolton School, Kimbolton, Huntingdon, Cambs, PE28 0EA
Trustees: Mr John Bridge OBE DL, Mr Simon Page BA Hons, Professor Fiona Broughton Pipkin, Lady Duberley DL, Cllr Jonathan Gray, Mr Peter Aylott MA MNI, Mr George Yeandle, Mrs Sarah Brereton, Mrs Debra Ann Hellett, Mr Charles Paull, Dr Thomas Hynes BA MA PLD, Mrs Katie Lancaster, Mrs Joanna Doyle, Mr Graham Peace, Bron Madson, Mr Peter J Farrar, Mrs Jo Rice, Mr Derek John Suckling
Income: £14,530,287 [2017]; £13,980,031 [2016]; £13,476,564 [2015]; £12,761,215 [2014]; £12,968,700 [2013]

The Kimmeridge Trust
Registered: 8 Nov 2004 *Employees:* 6 *Volunteers:* 20
Tel: 01929 270000 *Website:* kimmeridgetrust.org
Activities: Education, training; arts, culture, heritage, science; environment, conservation, heritage; recreation
Address: The Etches Collection Museum, Kimmeridge, Wareham, Dorset, BH20 5PE
Trustees: Mrs Helen Margaret Earwicker, Sir Michael Frederick Hobbs, Dr David Michael Martill, Sir Richard Peter Lambert, Mr Robert John Vearncombe, Mrs Elizabeth Anita Morgan, Professor John Edward Alan Marshall, Dr Andrew Racey, Dr Stephen Charles Earwicker, Mrs Carola Claire Campbell, Simon Conway Morris, Mr Richard Smith BA, Mr Chris Langham, Mr Richard Henry Bond, Dr Neil Langley Frewin, Ms Sarah Anne Brazier
Income: £1,951,417 [2016]; £1,713,080 [2015]; £638,227 [2014]; £81,139 [2013]; £22,882 [2012]

King Alfred School Society
Registered: 10 Dec 1965 *Employees:* 149
Tel: 020 8457 5203 *Website:* kingalfred.org.uk
Activities: Education, training
Address: King Alfred School, 149 North End Road, London, NW11 7HY
Trustees: Mrs Fiona Hackett, Mrs Areta Hautman, Mr Ian Laming, Mrs Annabel Cody, Sophie Ricard, Ms Christine Prowse, Polly Catriona Bennett, Alistair McConville, Sophie Silocchi, Mrs Kara Conti, Ms S A Phillips, Mr Philip Whale, Stacy Adam Eden, Mr Nick Friedlos, Samantha Jukes-Adams, Sandra Denicke-Polcher, John Nevin, Mrs Sheila Jaswon
Income: £11,517,549 [2017]; £10,936,169 [2016]; £10,157,605 [2015]; £9,530,720 [2014]; £8,984,638 [2013]

King David Schools (Manchester)
Registered: 8 Feb 1967 *Employees:* 88
Tel: 0161 832 8721
Activities: Education, training
Address: 6th Floor, Cardinal House, 20 St Marys Parsonage, Manchester, M3 2LG
Trustees: Kds Trustees Limited
Income: £2,304,330 [2016]; £2,158,157 [2015]; £2,016,871 [2014]; £2,280,752 [2013]

King Edward The Sixth Grammar School, Norwich
Registered: 25 May 1966 *Employees:* 233 *Volunteers:* 14
Tel: 01603 728432 *Website:* norwich-school.org.uk
Activities: Education, training
Address: Norwich School, 69-71a The Close, Norwich, NR1 4DD
Trustees: Mr Anthony Little, Mr James Chambers FCA, Alison Green, Tracy Yates, Anne Fry, Mr David W Talbot, Mr Alan Burdon-Cooper, Mr Terence J Gould MA, Dr Kay Yeoman, The Very Reverend Dr J Hedges, Mr Mark Scholfield, Jeremy Haselock, Ms Michelle Jarrold, Patrick Smith, Dr Diana Frances Wood MA MD FRCP, Professor J Last, Mr Christopher W Hoffman ACIB, Mr Iain Reid BSc MRICS, Dr Stephen Bamber, Mr Andrew Grant MA FRSA, Mr James Maurice Holme, Mrs Deirdre Annuncia Willmott
Income: £17,267,000 [2016]; £15,933,257 [2015]; £15,271,476 [2014]; £14,431,969 [2013]; £13,687,501 [2012]

King Edward VI School Southampton
Registered: 14 Aug 2001 *Employees:* 233
Tel: 023 8079 9208 *Website:* kes.hants.sch.uk
Activities: Education, training
Address: King Edward VI School, Wilton Road, Southampton, SO15 5UQ
Trustees: Dr Alan Thomas MA PhD, Mr Keith Wiseman MA, Mr Philip Brazier BSc FCIOB, Mr Benjamin William Richards, Councillor Roy Perry, Mr Alastair Reid, Mrs Sara Jane Mancey, Mrs Caryn Musker, Mrs Mary Chant, Mark Chaloner, Mrs Wendy Swinn, Mrs Harriet Victoria Langford Nicholson, Mr Brian Gay BA, Mr Michael Mayes MA MSc MBA MRICS, Dr Yvonne Binge MB ChB, Dr Roger Buchanan, Mr Alan Morgan, Mr John William James Mist, Miss Janet May, Mrs Jessica Wadsworth, Mr Ian Rudland, Mr Julian Gray, Dr Jane Mitchell
Income: £21,187,535 [2017]; £20,386,643 [2016]; £19,529,702 [2015]; £18,585,038 [2014]; £17,207,369 [2013]

King Edward VI's Grammar School (The Royal Grammar School) Guildford
Registered: 7 May 1963 *Employees:* 235
Tel: 01483 880604 *Website:* rgs-guildford.co.uk
Activities: Education, training
Address: Royal Grammar School, High Street, Guildford, Surrey, GU1 3BB
Trustees: The Royal Grammar School Guildford
Income: £22,477,815 [2017]; £20,430,517 [2016]; £19,453,526 [2015]; £18,790,043 [2014]; £16,648,596 [2013]

King Edward VII's Hospital Sister Agnes
Registered: 12 Nov 1962 *Employees:* 287
Tel: 020 7486 4411 *Website:* kingedwardvii.co.uk
Activities: The advancement of health or saving of lives
Address: Beaumont Street, London, W1G 6AA
Trustees: Mr Simon Weil, Charles Mackworth-Young, Lord Ajay Kakkar, Sir Michael Stevens, Mr David Badenoch, Mrs Alison Dean, Mr Robin Shedden Broadhurst, Sir Stuart Lipton, Lt General Sir William Rollo KCB CBE, Professor Justin Cobb, Mrs Virginia Lovell
Income: £36,436,000 [2017]; £23,008,000 [2016]; £21,929,000 [2015]; £27,650,000 [2014]; £20,169,000 [2013]

King Edward's School Bath
Registered: 22 Aug 2006 *Employees:* 270 *Volunteers:* 20
Tel: 01225 820320 *Website:* kesbath.com
Activities: Education, training
Address: King Edwards School, North Road, Bath, BA2 6HU
Trustees: David John Medlock, Professor Stephen Lillicrap, Mr Simon Coombe, Mr John Reid Bowman, Mrs Catherine Ann Colston, Prof Ann Millar, Prof Bernard John Morley, Mr Thomas Robert Boyce, Mr J Isherwood, Mrs Winifred Thomson, Mr Alan John Morsley, Mr Philip Gavin Cobb, Mr Richard Paul Stevens, Mr Paul Roper, Mr Danny Moar, Mrs Ginny Chalmers
Income: £12,812,056 [2016]; £11,825,793 [2015]; £11,081,758 [2014]; £10,807,488 [2013]

The King Edward's School Birmingham Trust
Registered: 21 May 2009 *Volunteers:* 12
Tel: 0121 415 6055 *Website:* trust.kes.org.uk
Activities: Education, training
Address: King Edwards School, Edgbaston Park Road, Edgbaston, Birmingham, B15 2UA
Trustees: Mr Stephen Campbell, Mr James Patrick Nicholas Martin, Mr Stuart Malcolm Southall, Dr Mark Fenton, Mr Richard Paul Maitland Thomson, Mr Adam Kendall
Income: £1,110,502 [2016]; £1,897,066 [2015]; £846,566 [2014]; £1,100,176 [2013]; £792,515 [2012]

The King Fahad Academy Limited
Registered: 27 Jan 1987 *Employees:* 135
Tel: 020 8743 0131 *Website:* thekfa.org.uk
Activities: Education, training
Address: King Fahad Academy, Bromyard Avenue, Acton, London, W3 7HD
Trustees: Prof Muhammed Abdel Haleem, HRH Prince Mohammed Bin Nawaf, Mr Abdul Aziz Alfaleh, Mr Abdullah Alshaghrood, Dr Ahmad Al-Dubayan, Dr Saud Al-Ammari, Dr Faisal Mohammad Almohanna Abaalkhail, Dr Abdulaziz Alwasil
Income: £6,074,933 [2016]; £10,976,999 [2015]; £498,870 [2014]; £2,965,615 [2013]; £6,368,967 [2012]

King George's Field, Mile End
Registered: 20 Oct 1999 *Employees:* 7 *Volunteers:* 1,000
Tel: 020 7364 5231
Activities: Amateur sport; environment, conservation, heritage
Address: London Borough of Tower Hamlets, Mulberry Place, 5 Clove Crescent, London, E14 2BG
Trustees: London Borough of Tower Hamlets
Income: £1,060,604 [2016]; £841,240 [2015]; £737,644 [2014]; £864,501 [2013]

The King Henry VIII Endowed Trust, Warwick
Registered: 28 Jan 1964
Tel: 01926 495533 *Website:* kinghenryviii.org.uk
Activities: General charitable purposes; education, training; advancement of health or saving of lives; disability; prevention or relief of poverty; religious activities; arts, culture, heritage, science; amateur sport; environment, conservation, heritage; recreation
Address: Clerk and Receiver, King Henry VIII Endowed Trust, 12 High Street, Warwick, CV34 4AP
Trustees: Mr Neil Thurley, Mr Stephen Copley, Miss Kathryn Parr, Mr Ian Furlong, Mr Michael Peachey, Mr Stephen John Jobburn, Mr Gerry Guest, Mr Rupert Griffiths, Mr John Edwards, Rev David Brown, Mrs Marie Ashe, Mrs Susan Grinnell
Income: £1,113,680 [2016]; £1,361,222 [2015]; £1,367,813 [2014]; £1,368,199 [2013]; £1,456,140 [2012]

King's Arms Project (Bedford)

Registered: 20 Jan 2011 *Employees:* 44 *Volunteers:* 77
Tel: 01234 350900 *Website:* kingsarmsproject.org
Activities: The prevention or relief of poverty; accommodation, housing; religious activities
Address: King's House, 245 Ampthill Road, Bedford, MK42 9AZ
Trustees: Roydon Loveley, Mr Paul Gregory Johnson, Mr Stephen James Wilson, Simon Holley, Kirstie Cook
Income: £1,368,819 [2017]; £1,084,618 [2016]; £845,488 [2015]; £774,029 [2014]; £749,328 [2013]

King's Arms Trust (Bedford)

Registered: 11 Oct 2006 *Employees:* 63 *Volunteers:* 440
Tel: 01234 838878 *Website:* kingsarms.org
Activities: Education, training; prevention or relief of poverty; overseas aid, famine relief; religious activities; economic, community development, employment
Address: King's Arms Trust, King's House, 245 Ampthill Road, Bedford, MK42 9AZ
Trustees: Roydon Loveley, Mr Mark Richard Vassall Adams, Mr Paul Gregory Johnson, Mr Paul Stanyard, Simon Holley
Income: £1,584,096 [2016]; £1,259,619 [2015]; £1,114,522 [2014]; £1,321,687 [2013]; £983,787 [2012]

King's Church Enfield

Registered: 10 Feb 1997 *Employees:* 19 *Volunteers:* 361
Tel: 020 8363 1324 *Website:* jubileechurchlondon.org
Activities: General charitable purposes; education, training; prevention or relief of poverty; overseas aid, famine relief; religious activities; other charitable purposes
Address: 2 Lumina Way, Enfield, Middlesex, EN1 1FS
Trustees: Tope Koleoso, David Pask, Mr Emmanuel Mensah, Vincent Santeng
Income: £2,167,943 [2017]; £2,102,356 [2016]; £1,701,949 [2015]; £1,205,000 [2014]; £1,054,189 [2013]

King's Church London

Registered: 28 Sep 2000 *Employees:* 23 *Volunteers:* 750
Tel: 020 3889 6819 *Website:* kingschurchlondon.org
Activities: General charitable purposes; education, training; prevention or relief of poverty; overseas aid, famine relief; accommodation, housing; religious activities
Address: Kings Church, 21 Meadowcourt Road, London, SE3 9DU
Trustees: Mr Stephen John Tibbert, Mr William Dalziel, Mr Osbert Morris Alexander Klass, Mr Simon Linley, Mr Odunayo Oyabayo
Income: £2,314,119 [2016]; £2,044,901 [2015]; £2,912,238 [2014]; £2,416,236 [2013]

King's Church in Greater Manchester

Registered: 20 Feb 2008 *Employees:* 26 *Volunteers:* 400
Tel: 0161 273 2168 *Website:* makingjesusfamous.org
Activities: Education, training; prevention or relief of poverty; accommodation, housing; religious activities
Address: Kings House, Sidney Street, Manchester, M1 7HB
Trustees: Gavin White, David Emmett, Simon Smith, Dami Fagade, Bamidele Adebisi, Melanie Harkness, Akin Ande
Income: £1,319,906 [2017]; £1,239,588 [2016]; £1,288,125 [2015]; £1,224,443 [2014]; £1,229,541 [2013]

King's College Hospital Charity

Registered: 16 Feb 2016 *Employees:* 5 *Volunteers:* 10
Tel: 020 3299 3365 *Website:* kchcharity.org.uk
Activities: The advancement of health or saving of lives
Address: Kings College Hospital, Denmark Hill, London, SE5 9RS
Trustees: Mr Timothy Hornsby, Mr Paul Newman, Mr Christopher Stooke, Dr Elizabeth Robertson, Hilary Sears, Mr John William Beck, Mrs Ali Parvin, Mr George King IV CFA, Professor Julia Wendon MB ChB MRCP FRCP FFICM
Income: £4,278,630 [2017]

King's College London Students' Union

Registered: 5 Jul 2010 *Employees:* 57 *Volunteers:* 830
Tel: 020 7848 1588 *Website:* kclsu.org
Activities: Education, training
Address: Kings College Union of Students, The Macadam Building, Surrey Street, London, WC2R 2NS
Trustees: Mrs Sonika Sidhu, Mr Uzair Patel, Mr Momin Saqib, Mrs Kate Wickes Bull, Miss Imaan Ashraf, Mr Nishan Nagarajan, Miss Larebb Butt, Mrs Leah Hurst, Mr Mahamed Abdullahi, Mr Yousef El-Tawil, Miss Tayyaba Rafiq, Miss Rahma Hussein, Mr Hannan Badar, Miss Shagun Gupta
Income: £6,418,064 [2017]; £5,769,881 [2016]; £5,356,863 [2015]; £5,078,376 [2014]; £5,094,798 [2013]

King's College School

Registered: 25 Mar 1963 *Employees:* 381
Website: kcs.org.uk
Activities: Education, training
Address: King's College School, Southside Common, London, SW19 4TT
Trustees: Mr Glen James, Mrs Susan Mary Bourne, Mr Duncan George Ingram, Prof Denise Lievesley CBE, Mr Patrick Stafford, Mrs Deborah Walls, Mr Robert Parker, Mr Ian Macmillan, Ms Julie Linda Robinson BA PGCE MEd, Mr Owen Carlstrand, Mr Guy Slimmon, Sir Robert Maurice Jay BA QC, Mr Matthew Sharp, Mrs Sally Hobbs, Lord Paul Clive Deighton, Mrs Stephanie Bennett, Mr Christopher Hale, Mrs Joyce Grace Sarpong BSc MBA
Income: £36,348,000 [2017]; £31,791,000 [2016]; £30,356,000 [2015]; £28,860,000 [2014]; £27,178,000 [2013]

The King's College of Our Lady and Saint Nicholas in Cambridge

Registered: 21 Dec 2010 *Employees:* 330 *Volunteers:* 14
Tel: 01223 331100 *Website:* kings.cam.ac.uk
Activities: Education, training; religious activities
Address: Kings College, Cambridge, CB2 1ST
Trustees: Dr John Barber, Dr James Laidlaw, Professor John Dunn, Prof Clement Mouhot, Mr James Trevithick, Ms Rebecca Love, Professor M Proctor, Rev Dr Stephen Cherry, Professor Ashley Moffett, Dr James Taylor, Dr Hanna Weibye, Mr Ben Abrams
Income: £24,052,802 [2017]; £21,186,471 [2016]; £24,737,183 [2015]; £19,907,417 [2014]; £20,372,458 [2013]

The King's Foundation

Registered: 12 Aug 2004 *Employees:* 164
Tel: 0114 263 2150 *Website:* kingsfoundation.org
Activities: Amateur sport; other charitable purposes
Address: Osborne House, 47 Snaithing Lane, Sheffield, S10 3LF
Trustees: Mr Geoff Thompson JP, Mr David Helliwell Taylor, Rachel Brown, Mr Barry Ninnes, Mrs Jane Fardon
Income: £2,578,885 [2016]; £2,407,075 [2015]; £2,237,177 [2014]; £2,220,735 [2013]; £2,210,218 [2012]

The King's Fund
Registered: 27 Nov 2008 *Employees:* 134
Tel: 020 7307 2400 *Website:* kingsfund.org.uk
Activities: Education, training; advancement of health or saving of lives; economic, community development, employment
Address: The Kings Fund, 11-13 Cavendish Square, London, W1G 0AN
Trustees: Sir Christopher Kelly KCB, Dr Jane Collins, Rt Hon Jacqui Smith, Dr Aseem Malhotra, Mr Dominic Dodd, Mr Paul Johnson, Strone Macpherson, Sir Jonathan Michael FRCP, Dame Ruth Carnall, Mr Simon Fraser
Income: £10,754,000 [2016]; £11,435,000 [2015]; £11,492,000 [2014]; £13,491,000 [2013]; £15,211,000 [2012]

The King's Hall and College of Brasenose in Oxford
Registered: 18 Aug 2011 *Employees:* 135 *Volunteers:* 9
Tel: 01865 277871 *Website:* bnc.ox.ac.uk
Activities: Education, training
Address: Brasenose College, Radcliffe Square, Oxford, OX1 4AJ
Trustees: Professor Nicholas Purcell, Rev Dr Dominic Keech, Mr Philip Parker, Dr Harvey Burd, Professor Ronald Daniel, Dr Sos Eltis, Prof Eamonn Gaffney, Prof David Groiser, Professor William James, Professor Paul Klenerman, Prof Owen Lewis, Dr Llewelyn Morgan, Dr David Popplewell, Prof William Swadling, Dr Christopher Timpson, Prof Mark Wilson, Dr Simon Smith, Prof Konstantin Ardakov, Dr Elias Dinas, Prof Conrad Nieduszynski, Prof Giovanni Zifarelli, Dr Elspeth Garman, Dr Anne Edwards, Dr Edward Bispham, Professor Richard Cooper, Professor Anne Davies, Prof Rui Ferreira Da Costa Esteves, Prof Abigail Green, Professor Guy Houlsby, Professor Jonathan Jones, Prof Thomas Krebs, Prof Christopher McKenna, Professor Simon Palfrey, Prof Jeremy Robertson, Prof Eric Thun, Prof Giles Wiggs, Dr Ferdinand Rauch, Dr Alan Strathern, Prof Rob Fender, Dr Liz Miller, Prof Andrea Ruggeri
Income: £11,092,000 [2017]; £12,070,000 [2016]; £10,038,000 [2015]; £8,855,000 [2014]; £8,032,000 [2013]

The King's School Development Trust
Registered: 15 Apr 1975
Tel: 01625 260010
Activities: Education, training
Address: Kings School, Cumberland Street, Macclesfield, Cheshire, SK10 1DA
Trustees: The King's School in Macclesfield
Income: £1,621,237 [2017]; £50,495 [2016]; £16,322 [2015]; £44,819 [2014]; £64,644 [2013]

The King's School Worcester
Registered: 27 Jun 2003 *Employees:* 364 *Volunteers:* 37
Tel: 01905 721721 *Website:* ksw.org.uk
Activities: Education, training
Address: Kings School, Hostel House, 5 College Green, Worcester, WR1 2LL
Trustees: Mr Jeremy Wynne Ruthven Goulding, Mr Hugh Carslake BA LLB, Prof Michael Clarke, Rev Michael Brierley, Prof John Vickerman PhD DSC FRSC, Mrs Jane Helen Jarvis, Mr Robert Mark Atkins MRICS, Mrs Carolyn Pike, Peter Atkinson, Mr Andrew Reekes, Douglas Dale, Mr David Laurence Green, Mr Paul Walker, Mrs Patricia Anne Preston, Mr Robert Sean McClatchey, Dr Leah Tether
Income: £17,486,000 [2017]; £17,442,000 [2016]; £16,858,012 [2015]; £16,596,204 [2014]; £15,377,444 [2013]

The King's School of The Cathedral Church of Canterbury
Registered: 4 Aug 1966 *Employees:* 620 *Volunteers:* 14
Tel: 01227 595720 *Website:* kings-school.co.uk
Activities: Education, training
Address: The Kings School, Bursars Office, 25 The Precincts, Canterbury, Kent, CT1 2ES
Trustees: The Revd Canon Clare Edwards, Mr Roger De Haan, Mr Nicholas Stephen Lyons, Mr Jonathan Tennant MRICS, Mr Robert Cyril Alan Bagley LLB, Mr Michael William Bax, Mr Tim Steel, Mrs Camila Swire, The Very Reverend Robert Willis, Mrs E McKendrick BA, Canon Christopher Irvine BTh MA PGCE, Dr Michael Sutherland, Mrs Carol Anne Evelegh DipCE Dip SPLD, Miss Frances Judd, The Revd Cannon Nicholas Papadopulos, Venerable Jo Kelly-Moore The
Income: £34,435,000 [2016]; £34,001,000 [2015]; £31,697,000 [2014]; £30,590,000 [2013]

King's School, Bruton
Registered: 16 Oct 1998 *Employees:* 305
Tel: 01749 814203 *Website:* kingsbruton.com
Activities: Education, training
Address: Kings School, Plox, Bruton, Somerset, BA10 0ED
Trustees: Prof Philip Duffus, Mr Robin Badham-Thornhill, Miss Helena Sampson, Lt General Anthony Malcolm Douglas Palmer, Mr Christopher Birrell, Mr Adam Clutterbuck, Mr Walter Jones, Mr Giles Pretor-Pinney, Mr Richard Case, Mr Edward Hobhouse, Mr Mark Fisher, Mrs Teresa Grace Jones, The Rev'd Canon Brain McConnell, Mr Julian Mant, Mr Peter Wells
Income: £14,718,737 [2017]; £13,886,592 [2016]; £13,275,515 [2015]; £12,989,808 [2014]; £12,493,681 [2013]

The King's School, Ely
Registered: 15 Nov 1989 *Employees:* 461 *Volunteers:* 14
Tel: 01353 660711 *Website:* kingsely.org
Activities: Education, training
Address: King's Ely, Barton Road, Ely, Cambs, CB7 4DB
Trustees: Mr Graham Frank Chase, Mr Philip John Simon Cantwell, Professor Michael Richard Edward Proctor FRS, Mr Richard Phillips, Mrs Anthea Jane Kenna MEd LRAM, Air Vice-Marshal Clive Arthur Bairsto, Mrs Isobel Philippa Newport-Mangell, Mr Mark Edward Myers, Dr Kathryn Jane Skoyles LLB LLM PhD, The Very Revd Mark Philip John Bonney, Mr Jeffrey Christopher Hayes, Canon David Pritchard, Mrs Amanda Hazell East, Sir James Edward Thornton Paice, Mr David John Day
Income: £16,789,835 [2017]; £16,382,292 [2016]; £16,562,079 [2015]; £15,376,865 [2014]; £14,737,094 [2013]

The King's School, Gloucester
Registered: 9 May 2000 *Employees:* 175 *Volunteers:* 10
Tel: 01452 337337 *Website:* thekingsschool.co.uk
Activities: Education, training; religious activities; arts, culture, heritage, science; amateur sport; other charitable purposes
Address: 18 St Patricks Court, Brockworth, Gloucester, GL3 4NT
Trustees: Canon Celia Stephana Margaret Thomson MA, Mr Robert Ingram, Mr Adrian Brett BSc (Hons) PSC MInstRE, Mr Mark Hurrell, Mrs Alyson Gillespie, Rev Nicola Mary Arthy Canon, Mrs Alice Reeve LLB, Mr Martin Watson, Mrs Susan Lewis, Mr Paul Francis Markey, Canon Richard Mitchell, Rev Stephen Lake, Mrs Gill Brook, Mr Philip Dancey, Mrs Elizabeth Sullivan, Mr Kurt Wyman, Mr Miles Dunkley
Income: £7,356,016 [2017]; £7,031,486 [2016]; £6,453,749 [2015]; £6,032,502 [2014]; £5,936,461 [2013]

King's School, Rochester

Registered: 22 Dec 2000 *Employees:* 252
Tel: 01634 888588 *Website:* kings-rochester.co.uk
Activities: Education, training; other charitable purposes
Address: Kings School Rochester, Satis House, Boley Hill, Rochester, Kent, ME1 1TE
Trustees: Mr Markham James Chesterfield, The Venerable Simon Burton-Jones, Rev Canon Philip John Hesketh, Mrs Rozanna Anne Rouse, Mrs Jane Patricia Glew, Mr Paul Leonard Rothwell, Mr Robert James Kennett, Mr Daniel Robert Graves, Mr Christopher Rayman Shepherd, Mr John Kenneth Daffarn, Mr John Richard Franklin, Mr Matthew John Rushton, Mr Bruce Andrew Bell, Miss Jacqueline Ann Shicluna, Rev Rachel Susan Philipps, Mrs Rosemary Ann Olley
Income: £9,236,041 [2016]; £8,817,856 [2015]; £8,544,403 [2014]; £7,930,304 [2013]; £7,600,208 [2012]

King's School

Registered: 25 Mar 1964 *Employees:* 170 *Volunteers:* 14
Tel: 01244 683534 *Website:* kingschester.co.uk
Activities: Education, training; amateur sport; recreation
Address: King's School, Wrexham Road, Chester, CH4 7QL
Trustees: Mr David Knowles Rowlands, Mrs Jo Clague, Prof John Hagan Pryce Bayley MA PhD FRS, Mr Richard Arnold, Mr Steve Docking BA, Mrs Janet Carr BA FCA, Mr Nick Wood, Mr Ian O'Doherty, Mr Graham Ramsbottom BSc MSc MRICS, Prof Jonathan Billowes MA DPhil FInstP, Mr W J Timpson, Mr David Monk MBChB FRCS, Mrs Ruth Ashford PhD FCIM FHEA BEd, Mrs Carol Anne Edwards
Income: £12,972,000 [2017]; £12,240,000 [2016]; £11,644,000 [2015]; £10,892,000 [2014]; £10,668,000 [2013]

King's Schools Taunton Ltd

Registered: 22 Apr 2004 *Employees:* 225 *Volunteers:* 50
Tel: 01823 328100 *Website:* kings-taunton.co.uk
Activities: Education, training
Address: Kings College, Mailroom, 20 Holway Avenue, Taunton, Somerset, TA1 3AR
Trustees: Chris Hirst, Dr Roger Mott, Reverend Prebendary Lynda Mary Barley, Mr John Houghton, Mrs Charis Cavaghan-Pack, Mr Melville Fitzgibbon Trimble, Mr Michael Featherstone, Mr Charles Clark MA MRICS FAAV, Mrs Linda Nash, Simon Carder, Mr Godfrey Davis FCA, Mrs Carolyn Cooper, Mrs Linda Clare Scott
Income: £13,129,765 [2016]; £15,067,590 [2015]; £12,158,457 [2014]; £11,910,963 [2013]; £11,823,489 [2012]

King/Cullimore Charitable Trust

Registered: 30 Mar 1999 *Employees:* 189
Activities: General charitable purposes; disability
Address: 52 Ledborough Lane, Beaconsfield, Bucks, HP9 2DF
Trustees: Mr Peter Anthony Cullimore, Mr Christopher John Gardner, Mr Richard Davies, Mr Alastair Graham McKechnie, Mrs Jill Noelle Pye
Income: £6,020,454 [2017]; £5,594,499 [2016]; £402,377 [2015]; £416,349 [2014]; £466,816 [2013]

Kingdom Education Limited

Registered: 4 Jun 1985 *Employees:* 39 *Volunteers:* 20
Tel: 01582 767566 *Website:* thekingsschool.com
Activities: Education, training
Address: Kingdom Education Limited, Elmfield, Ambrose Lane, Harpenden, Herts, AL5 4DU
Trustees: Mr D Crook, Mr Charles Hammond, Mr Jeremy Curtis, Mr Ashraf Farahat, Mr Robert Peter Smith
Income: £1,253,278 [2017]; £1,203,637 [2016]; £1,113,211 [2015]; £1,107,439 [2014]; £1,131,643 [2013]

Kingdom Faith Church

Registered: 14 Nov 1979 *Employees:* 39
Website: kingdomfaith.com
Activities: Religious activities
Address: 22 Wagtail Close, Horsham, W Sussex, RH12 5HL
Trustees: Rev Michael Keith Barling, Mr Jonathan Croft, Mr Bengt Wedemalm, Mr Jeremy Michael Blake, Mr Clive Urquhart, Simon Coles
Income: £1,592,965 [2016]; £1,846,146 [2015]; £1,711,506 [2014]; £2,937,046 [2013]; £1,895,619 [2012]

The Kingham Hill Trust

Registered: 16 Jul 1999 *Employees:* 213
Tel: 01787 376835 *Website:* kinghamhill.org
Activities: Education, training; religious activities
Address: 19 Ballingdon Street, Sudbury, Suffolk, CO10 2BT
Trustees: Justin Mote, Mrs Caroline Margaret Pellereau, John Richardson, Jeremy Anderson, Rev Robert Marsden, Nicholas Bewes, John Lewis, Simon Pilcher, Mr Kenji Michael Batchelor
Income: £9,948,122 [2017]; £9,976,244 [2016]; £9,682,519 [2015]; £12,177,854 [2014]; £8,572,440 [2013]

Kings Church Centre Norwich

Registered: 26 Oct 2000 *Employees:* 17 *Volunteers:* 250
Tel: 01603 765795 *Website:* kings-norwich.com
Activities: Religious activities
Address: Kings Community Church, The Kings Centre, King Street, Norwich, NR1 1PH
Trustees: Dr Jerome Pereira, Mr David Pull, Ms Alison Hopley, Mr Kevin Magee, Mr David Lees, Mr Kevin Vinson, Mr Ian Nelson FCA CLCA
Income: £1,002,423 [2017]; £1,015,362 [2016]; £1,040,224 [2015]; £969,313 [2014]; £959,956 [2013]

Kings Church International

Registered: 4 Aug 1994 *Employees:* 26 *Volunteers:* 254
Tel: 01753 832444 *Website:* kcionline.org
Activities: Education, training; prevention or relief of poverty; overseas aid, famine relief; religious activities
Address: King's House, 77a Frances Road, Windsor, Berks, SL4 3AQ
Trustees: Terry Beasley, Jim Treherne, Richard Kay, Christine Humphrey, Brenda Johnston
Income: £1,899,473 [2016]; £1,340,334 [2015]; £1,304,065 [2014]; £1,098,822 [2013]; £2,611,339 [2012]

Kings Community Church (Southampton)

Registered: 8 Jun 2007 *Employees:* 19 *Volunteers:* 500
Tel: 01489 784333 *Website:* kccsouthampton.org
Activities: Education, training; prevention or relief of poverty; overseas aid, famine relief; religious activities; economic, community development, employment
Address: Kings Community Church, Upper Northam Road, Hedge End, Southampton, SO30 4BZ
Trustees: Mr Maurice Sydney Redmill, Mr Ian Howard Chiddle, Mrs Bryre Catherine Butcher, Mr Richard David Hemming, Mrs Pauline Quan Arrow, Mr Martin Edward Fakley, Mrs Emma Louise Curtayne
Income: £1,393,000 [2017]; £1,359,000 [2016]; £1,420,700 [2015]; £1,058,900 [2014]; £896,000 [2013]

Kings House School Trust (Richmond) Limited

Registered: 31 Jul 1964 *Employees:* 114
Tel: 020 8940 1878 *Website:* kingshouseschool.org
Activities: Education, training
Address: 68 Kings Road, Richmond, Surrey, TW10 6ES
Trustees: Mr Graham Charles Corbishley, Mr Tom Delay, Mrs Kelly-Lu Lindberg, Dr Stephen Harrison, Mrs Catherine Urch, Mr Nicholas Collins, Mr Jeffrey Peter Van Der Eems, Mr John Julian Davison, Mr Michael Leonard Hobbs, Mr Kevin Knibbs, Mrs Jane Shalders, Ms Margaret Hunnaball, Mr David James Barbour, Mrs Christine Laverty, Mr Brian Richard Girvan, Mr James Wintringham Owen
Income: £7,033,834 [2017]; £6,820,821 [2016]; £6,662,199 [2015]; £5,967,212 [2014]; £5,805,862 [2013]

Kings Place Music Foundation

Registered: 27 Jan 2005 *Employees:* 58
Tel: 07980 769561 *Website:* kingsplace.co.uk
Activities: Education, training; arts, culture, heritage, science; recreation
Address: The Old Vicarage, Matfen, Newcastle upon Tyne, NE20 0RS
Trustees: Mr Peter John Millican, Ms Anna Frances Rowe, Mrs Anne Deborah Millican
Income: £4,502,489 [2017]; £4,145,867 [2016]; £4,107,425 [2015]; £3,475,932 [2014]; £3,209,452 [2013]

The Kings Theatre Trust Limited

Registered: 29 Aug 2001 *Employees:* 35 *Volunteers:* 119
Tel: 023 9285 2228 *Website:* kingsportsmouth.co.uk
Activities: Education, training; arts, culture, heritage, science; environment, conservation, heritage
Address: Kings Theatre, Albert Road, Southsea, Hants, PO5 2QJ
Trustees: Mr Ian Heggie Pratt, Councillor Hugh Laurence Mason, Bill Taylor, Jane Prescott, Mr David Terrence Gant, Mr Neill Matthew Young, Mr Paul Ian Woolf, Mr David James Henderson, Mr Ron Hasker, Mr Damon Repton, Dr Gareth James Morgan, Sue Love, Miss Clare Jane Brown, Cllr Linda Rae Symes, Mr Robert Andrew Charles Peck
Income: £1,488,694 [2017]; £1,275,221 [2016]; £1,376,269 [2015]; £1,244,302 [2014]; £1,226,710 [2013]

Kingsgate Community Church

Registered: 12 Oct 2004 *Employees:* 89 *Volunteers:* 1,100
Tel: 01733 311156 *Website:* kingsgateuk.com
Activities: Education, training; prevention or relief of poverty; religious activities
Address: 2 Staplee Way, Peterborough, PE1 4YT
Trustees: Dr David Andrew Smith, Mr Norman Paskin, Mr Simon Duncan Wilson, Mr William James Edwards, Mr Richard Johnson, Barry Featherstone
Income: £3,723,228 [2016]; £3,949,216 [2015]; £3,705,441 [2014]; £3,251,019 [2013]; £2,751,015 [2012]

Kingshott School Trust Limited

Registered: 7 Aug 1980 *Employees:* 78 *Volunteers:* 25
Tel: 01462 432009 *Website:* kingshottschool.co.uk
Activities: Education, training
Address: Kingshott School, Stevenage Road, Hitchin, Herts, SG4 7JX
Trustees: Mr Edmund Wright, David Keast, Mrs Sarah Hamilton, Mrs Lisa Chambers, James Bentall, Ms Lara Pechard, Mr Jonathan Marsh, Mr Martin Sudweeks, Mrs Louise Fitzpatrick, Mr Richard Midgley, Mrs Samantha Selkirk, Mr David Morgan
Income: £4,438,477 [2016]; £4,336,190 [2015]; £3,791,544 [2014]; £3,636,869 [2013]; £3,703,096 [2012]

Kingsley School, Bideford

Registered: 23 Nov 1965 *Employees:* 131 *Volunteers:* 29
Tel: 020 7935 3723 *Website:* kingsleyschoolbideford.co.uk
Activities: Education, training; religious activities
Address: Methodist Church House, 25 Marylebone Road, London, NW1 5JR
Trustees: Kingsley School Bideford Trustee Company Limited, Methodist Independent Schools Trust
Income: £4,691,373 [2016]; £4,411,220 [2015]; £4,470,280 [2014]; £4,484,520 [2013]; £4,494,671 [2012]

The Kingsley School

Registered: 9 Jul 1963 *Employees:* 78
Website: thekingsleyschool.com
Activities: Education, training
Address: Kingsley School, Beauchamp Avenue, Leamington Spa, Warwicks, CV32 5RD
Trustees: Mrs Maureen Patricia Hicks, Mr Andrew George Merriman Bye, Mr David William Cleary, Dame Yve Buckland, Mr Jason William Strain, Mrs Caroline Lesley Ellis, Nicholas Button, Mrs Julia Burns, Mrs Erica Smith, Mr Andrew William Maher, Mrs Caroline Maria Rigby
Income: £4,398,028 [2016]; £4,133,121 [2015]; £4,103,011 [2014]; £3,798,080 [2013]

Kingsmead School Hoylake Trust Ltd

Registered: 2 Feb 1967 *Employees:* 56 *Volunteers:* 3
Tel: 0151 632 3156 *Website:* kingsmeadschool.com
Activities: Education, training
Address: Kingsmead School, 6-12 Bertram Drive, Wirral, Merseyside, CH47 0LL
Trustees: Mrs Eleanor Davies MA CertEd, Mr Jonathan Mark Francis, Mr Timothy Turvey, Mrs Ann Renison, Mr Ian Murray Watts, Mr David Ian Renison, Mr Edward Hugh Bradby, Mrs Olivia Higgins, Mrs Anikphe Oyedeji, Mr Sunil Kumar
Income: £2,008,197 [2016]; £1,878,352 [2015]; £1,862,420 [2014]; £1,972,919 [2013]; £2,125,288 [2012]

Kingston Grammar School

Registered: 3 Dec 1999 *Employees:* 203
Tel: 020 8939 8823 *Website:* kgs.org.uk
Activities: Education, training
Address: Kingston Grammar School, 70 London Road, Kingston upon Thames, Surrey, KT2 6PY
Trustees: Mrs Diana Rose, Mr Edward Alexander Kershaw, Mr Duncan Paul David Combe, Mr Andrew David Evans, Mrs Lorraine Tanya Adam, Mrs Frances Claire Le Grys, Catherine Chevallier, Mr Nima Khandan-Nia, Mr Robin Wayland Brown, Mr Joseph Dermot Rice, Mr Robert George O'Dowd, Mrs Kerstin Sonnemann, Mr Mark Annesley, Mr Karim Alexander Nicholas Ian McLean, Professor Michael Dohler
Income: £16,930,000 [2017]; £14,241,000 [2016]; £13,680,000 [2015]; £12,979,000 [2014]; £12,401,000 [2013]

Kingston Theatre Trust
Registered: 29 Aug 1990 *Employees:* 63 *Volunteers:* 117
Tel: 020 8939 4062 *Website:* rosetheatrekingston.org
Activities: General charitable purposes; education, training; arts, culture, heritage, science; economic, community development, employment
Address: Rose Theatre, 24-26 High Street, Kingston upon Thames, Surrey, KT1 1HL
Trustees: Mr Robin Hutchinson, Mr Robert O'Dowd, Baroness Sally Hamwee, Mr David Tallis, Miss Ciara Morris, Councillor John Ayles, Mr William Price, Miss Molly Akins-Hanson, Mr Christopher Foy, Martyn Jones, Mr Luke Nunneley, Mrs Marit Mohn, Councillor Andrea Craig, Councillor Julie Pickering, Mr Jason Christopher Piper, Mr Sri Samir Bhamra
Income: £4,304,951 [2017]; £3,975,783 [2016]; £5,577,885 [2015]; £3,557,944 [2014]; £3,042,173 [2013]

Kingsway International Christian Centre
Registered: 16 Feb 2004 *Employees:* 59 *Volunteers:* 1,000
Tel: 020 8525 0000 *Website:* kicc.org.uk
Activities: General charitable purposes; religious activities
Address: KICC Prayer City, Buckmore Park, Maidstone Road, Chatham, Kent, ME5 9QG
Trustees: Mr Mayomi Anuwe, Charles Clarke, Rexford Sam, Muyiwa Banwo, Dr Olaniyi Opaleye, Toye Adedeji, Wyn Knuckles, Kemi Babatunde, Dr Timothy Abioye, Ms Peace Ani
Income: £11,153,588 [2017]; £8,002,926 [2016]; £7,787,205 [2015]; £8,086,260 [2014]; £9,542,172 [2013]

Kingswood House School Trust Limited
Registered: 3 Apr 1964 *Employees:* 62
Tel: 01737 843034
Activities: Education, training
Address: Willow Grange, The Street, Betchworth, Surrey, RH3 7DJ
Trustees: Mrs Jane Bourne, Dr Hywel Bowen-Perkins, Mr Keith Crombie, Linda Susan Culm, Mr Alan Matthews, Mr Christopher Conway Shipley, Mr Raymond Leslie Clarke, Mr Alistair Gibbon Law, Mr Robert Hugh Austen, Mr Roger Stephen Parkin, Judge GR Kent, Mr Rob Johnstone
Income: £2,317,101 [2016]; £2,132,714 [2015]; £1,979,552 [2014]; £1,971,824 [2013]; £1,874,210 [2012]

Kingswood School
Registered: 26 Oct 1962 *Employees:* 317
Tel: 01225 734300 *Website:* kingswood.bath.sch.uk
Activities: Education, training
Address: Kingswood School, Lansdown Road, Bath, BA1 5RG
Trustees: Kingswood School Trustee Ltd
Income: £17,001,515 [2017]; £16,109,898 [2016]; £15,088,569 [2015]; £14,677,422 [2014]; £13,285,865 [2013]

The Kirby Laing Foundation
Registered: 14 Jun 1972 *Employees:* 3
Tel: 020 8238 8890 *Website:* laingfamilytrusts.org.uk
Activities: General charitable purposes; education, training; advancement of health or saving of lives; disability; prevention or relief of poverty; overseas aid, famine relief; religious activities; arts, culture, heritage, science; environment, conservation, heritage
Address: 33 Bunns Lane, Mill Hill, London, NW7 2DX
Trustees: Simon Webley, Rev Charles Burch, Mr David Eric Laing, Dr Frederick Terence Wyndham Weller Lewis
Income: £2,252,407 [2016]; £2,085,960 [2015]; £1,849,251 [2014]; £1,856,408 [2013]; £1,850,817 [2012]

Kirkdale Industrial Training Services Limited
Registered: 18 May 1978 *Employees:* 30
Tel: 01484 711462 *Website:* kits-training.co.uk
Activities: Education, training
Address: Kirkdale Industrial Training SVCS, Kirkdale House, Armytage Road, Brighouse, W Yorks, HD6 1QF
Trustees: Mr Andrew Mark Denford, Mr Malcolm Proctor, Mr Alan Myers, Mr David Edwards, Miss Ingrid Rona Holdsworth, Mr William Dawson Currie, Mr Colin Athony Somers
Income: £2,126,310 [2017]; £2,121,821 [2016]; £2,038,044 [2015]; £1,818,738 [2014]; £1,666,445 [2013]

Kirkham Grammar School
Registered: 24 Apr 2008 *Employees:* 193 *Volunteers:* 14
Tel: 01772 684462 *Website:* kirkhamgrammarschool.co.uk
Activities: Education, training; arts, culture, heritage, science; amateur sport
Address: Kirkham Grammar School, Ribby Road, Kirkham, Preston, Lancs, PR4 2BH
Trustees: Dr James Barry Johnson, Mr John Kelsall, Mr John Borradaile, Mr Larry Fairclough, Mr Sean Wilkinson, Mr Alan Raymond Berry, Mrs Lorraine Wareing, Mrs Rosemary Cartwright, Mr Julian E S Kollard, Mrs Barbara Lund, District Judge Thomas Andrew Lewis Greensmith, Mr Paul Robert Anthony Ribchester
Income: £7,991,768 [2017]; £7,882,932 [2016]; £7,763,209 [2015]; £8,006,911 [2014]; £8,274,356 [2013]

Kirklees Active Leisure
Registered: 20 Mar 2002 *Employees:* 279
Tel: 01484 234146 *Website:* kalleisuretrust.org.uk
Activities: The advancement of health or saving of lives; amateur sport; recreation
Address: Kirklees Active Leisure, Stadium Way, Huddersfield, W Yorks, HD1 6PG
Trustees: Mr David Morby, Mr Satnam Singh Khela, Mr Mohan Singh Sokhal MBE JP, Ms Dawn Stephenson, Mr Adam Neil Fletcher, Mr Brian Charles Stahelin, Mr John Briggs, Mr William James Dodds, Mrs Melanie Brooke, Mr Derek Charles Thomson, Mrs Sinead Marie Sopala, Mr John Stephen Fletcher
Income: £15,852,553 [2017]; £15,873,013 [2016]; £14,155,950 [2015]; £13,432,266 [2014]; £12,606,320 [2013]

Kirklees Citizens Advice and Law Centre
Registered: 28 Sep 2001 *Employees:* 39 *Volunteers:* 48
Tel: 01924 868141 *Website:* advicekirklees.org.uk
Activities: General charitable purposes; education, training; prevention or relief of poverty
Address: Units 11-12 Empire House, Wakefield Old Road, Dewsbury, W Yorks, WF12 8DJ
Trustees: Mrs Judith Priestley, Mr Laurence James Campbell, Linda Summers, Mr Mark Robinson, Mr Adrian Cruden, Gulnaz Akhtar, Ms Joanna Gadsby
Income: £1,440,676 [2017]; £1,878,521 [2016]; £1,506,325 [2015]; £1,970,480 [2014]; £1,510,342 [2013]

Kirklees Music School
Registered: 26 Aug 1992 *Employees:* 90
Tel: 01484 426426 *Website:* kirkleesmusicschool.org.uk
Activities: Education, training
Address: 7-9 Beast Market, Huddersfield, W Yorks, HD1 1QF
Trustees: Councillor Andrew Charles Pinnock, Councillor Carole Ann Pattison, Mrs Beryl Elizabeth Smith, Mr David Blakeborough, Mrs Nina Simica Garforth, Mrs Barbara Ruth Jones, Councillor Hilary Richards
Income: £1,795,000 [2017]; £1,951,882 [2016]; £1,974,786 [2015]; £1,938,491 [2014]; £1,936,066 [2013]

Kirklees Theatre Trust
Registered: 13 Nov 1980 *Employees:* 59 *Volunteers:* 96
Tel: 01484 221459 *Website:* thelbt.org
Activities: Education, training; arts, culture, heritage, science
Address: 2nd Floor, Legal Services, Civic Centre 3, Huddersfield, W Yorks, HD1 2WZ
Trustees: Ms Val Javin, Cllr Carole Pattison, Mrs Laura Rawnsley, Miss Sue Underwood, Mr Michail Kagioglou, Cllr Karen Louise Allison, Mr Andrew Bird, Mrs Tracy Sheldon, Ms Marie Peacock, Mr David Charles Douglas Thompson aka Jack Thompson, Cllr Gemma Wilson, Ms Kate Elizabeth Edwards
Income: £1,637,734 [2017]; £1,711,882 [2016]; £1,246,313 [2015]; £967,390 [2014]; £1,276,227 [2013]

Kirkwood Hospice
Registered: 3 Aug 1982 *Employees:* 153 *Volunteers:* 795
Tel: 01484 557900 *Website:* kirkwoodhospice.co.uk
Activities: Education, training; advancement of health or saving of lives
Address: Kirkwood Hospice, 21 Albany Road, Dalton, Huddersfield, W Yorks, HD5 9UY
Trustees: John Denham, Mr Kenneth Dunning, David Harling, Mrs Jane Brady, Mrs Kathryn Susan Hinchliff, Susan Galvin, Miss Lorraine Annette Chapman, Mr Bernard Francis Ainsworth, Philip Sands, Mrs Caroline Black
Income: £6,949,461 [2017]; £7,083,361 [2016]; £5,588,417 [2015]; £5,970,455 [2014]; £5,866,758 [2013]

Kisharon
Registered: 27 Sep 1976 *Employees:* 160 *Volunteers:* 50
Tel: 020 3209 1170 *Website:* kisharon.org.uk
Activities: Education, training; disability; accommodation, housing
Address: Floor 1, 333 Edgware Road, London, NW9 6TD
Trustees: Mr Leo Noe, Mr Andrew David Loftus, Mr David Rasouly, Mrs Emma Nathalie Castleton, Mrs Joanne Greenaway, Mr Philip Goldberg, Mr Daniel Theodore Klein, Mr Irving Lerner, Mr Richard Levy, Mr Joseph Coogan
Income: £6,549,331 [2017]; £5,783,270 [2016]; £5,088,811 [2015]; £4,800,278 [2014]; £4,669,602 [2013]

The Ernest Kleinwort Charitable Trust
Registered: 16 Mar 1964
Tel: 020 3207 7337 *Website:* ekct.org.uk
Activities: General charitable purposes; disability; prevention or relief of poverty; environment, conservation, heritage
Address: 5th Floor, 8 St James's Square, London, SW1Y 4JU
Trustees: Miss Marina Rose Kleinwort, Mr Alexander Hamilton Kleinwort, Lord Chandos, Sg Kleinwort Hambros Trust Company (UK) Limited, Sir Richard Kleinwort, Rt Hon Edmund Christopher Earl of Limerick, Charlie Mayhew
Income: £1,500,112 [2017]; £1,774,857 [2016]; £1,889,818 [2015]; £1,761,550 [2014]; £1,543,702 [2013]

Kneehigh Theatre Trust Limited
Registered: 14 Sep 1984 *Employees:* 10 *Volunteers:* 30
Tel: 01872 267913 *Website:* kneehigh.co.uk
Activities: Arts, culture, heritage, science
Address: Kneehigh Theatre, 15 Walsingham Place, Truro, Cornwall, TR1 2RP
Trustees: Mrs Clare Morpurgo, Simon Williams, Teresa Gleadowe, Professor Alan George Livingston, Mr Peter Cox, Daphne Skinnard
Income: £2,001,857 [2017]; £1,781,913 [2016]; £1,498,239 [2015]; £1,919,297 [2014]; £1,234,241 [2013]

The Knightland Foundation
Registered: 27 Jul 2011
Tel: 020 8432 2014
Activities: General charitable purposes; education, training; prevention or relief of poverty; religious activities
Address: 52 Knightland Road, London, E5 9HS
Trustees: Mr Jacob Friedman, Mr Samuel Lew, Mr Uriel Sholom Kaplan
Income: £2,341,396 [2017]; £373,027 [2016]; £323,313 [2015]; £777,447 [2014]; £877,257 [2013]

Knighton House School Limited
Registered: 10 Jul 1963 *Employees:* 52 *Volunteers:* 4
Tel: 01258 450711 *Website:* knightonhouse.co.uk
Activities: Education, training
Address: Knighton House School, Durweston, Blandford Forum, Dorset, DT11 0PY
Trustees: Mrs Camilla Jane Elizabeth Masters, Mr Iain Gary Weatherby, Richard Storey Walker, Mrs Sarah Louise Ryder, Mr Paul Andrew Slight, Peter Hardy, Miss Sophie Boyle, Mr Julian Spencer Grazebrook
Income: £1,565,583 [2016]; £1,569,144 [2015]; £1,786,905 [2014]; £1,570,376 [2013]; £1,540,659 [2012]

The Sir James Knott Trust
Registered: 21 Dec 1990 *Employees:* 2
Tel: 0191 230 4016 *Website:* knott-trust.co.uk
Activities: General charitable purposes
Address: Sir James Knott Trust, 16-18 Hood Street, Newcastle upon Tyne, NE1 6JQ
Trustees: Ben Speke, John Cresswell, Oliver James, Fiona Sample
Income: £1,638,004 [2017]; £1,659,376 [2016]; £1,501,374 [2015]; £1,530,268 [2014]; £1,466,735 [2013]

Knowle West Media Centre
Registered: 10 Jun 2002 *Employees:* 26 *Volunteers:* 44
Tel: 0117 377 3161 *Website:* kwmc.org.uk
Activities: Education, training; disability; arts, culture, heritage, science; environment, conservation, heritage; economic, community development, employment
Address: Knowle West Media Centre, Leinster Avenue, Bristol, BS4 1NL
Trustees: Karron Chaplin, Mr Robert Thomas Fisher, Mr Edward Graham Boal, Mrs Iris Partridge, Ms Polly Alice Davis, Mark Baker, Mr Matthew Little, Mr Oliver Callaghan, Mrs Helen Frances Bream
Income: £1,080,489 [2017]; £1,036,515 [2016]; £1,045,320 [2015]; £976,866 [2014]; £699,244 [2013]

Knowsley Housing Trust
Registered: 7 May 2004 *Employees:* 108
Website: k-h-t.org
Activities: Accommodation, housing
Address: Knowsley Housing Trust, Lakeview, Kings Business Park, Kings Drive, Prescot, Merseyside, L34 1PJ
Trustees: Mr Nicholas Paul Gerrard, Mr Ian Foy, Ms Susan Giles, Ms Helen White, Mr Philip John Summers, Mr Paul Deehan
Income: £65,620,000 [2017]; £64,555,000 [2016]; £61,582,000 [2015]; £57,303,000 [2014]; £55,785,000 [2013]

Koinonia Christian Care
Registered: 9 Apr 2010 Employees: 57 Volunteers: 11
Tel: 01903 237764 Website: koinoniacare.org
Activities: The advancement of health or saving of lives; prevention or relief of poverty; accommodation, housing
Address: Koinonia Christian Care Home, 4 Winchester Road, Worthing, W Sussex, BN11 4DJ
Trustees: Mr Phillip Hudson, Mrs Sheila Berry, Mr Colin Carpenter, Mr Robin Turnbull, Miss Janet Bradley
Income: £1,334,361 [2017]; £1,267,291 [2016]; £1,169,868 [2015]; £914,767 [2014]; £1,211,571 [2013]

Kollel and Co Limited
Registered: 26 Aug 1999
Tel: 020 8806 1570
Activities: General charitable purposes; education, training; advancement of health or saving of lives; prevention or relief of poverty; religious activities; economic, community development, employment; other charitable purposes
Address: 7 Overlea Road, London, E5 9BG
Trustees: Mr Simon Low, Mrs Judith Weiss, Mrs Rachel Kalish
Income: £1,752,344 [2016]; £700,696 [2015]; £338,651 [2014]; £856,077 [2013]

Kolyom Trust Limited
Registered: 16 Nov 2005
Tel: 0161 740 5998
Activities: General charitable purposes; education, training; prevention or relief of poverty; religious activities
Address: 44 Stanley Road, Salford, M7 4HN
Trustees: Mr Leopold Zahn, Mr Isaac Bamberger, Mr Hyman Weiss
Income: £3,420,677 [2017]; £2,693,029 [2016]; £2,245,765 [2015]; £1,622,690 [2014]; £1,516,865 [2013]

Kosher Outlet Assistance Ltd
Registered: 13 Apr 2010 Employees: 18
Activities: General charitable purposes; prevention or relief of poverty
Address: Churchill House, 137 Brent Street, London, NW4 4DJ
Trustees: Mr J Perl, Mr Irving Marc Lerner, Mr J Cope, Mr D Fluss
Income: £6,333,215 [2017]; £4,920,139 [2016]; £4,800,226 [2015]; £3,973,509 [2014]; £4,160,119 [2013]

Krishnamurti Foundation Trust Ltd
Registered: 12 Mar 1973 Employees: 82 Volunteers: 3
Tel: 01962 793820 Website: kfoundation.org
Activities: Education, training
Address: Krishnamurti Foundation Trust Ltd, Brockwood Park, Brockwood, Bramdean, Alresford, Hants, SO24 0LQ
Trustees: Mr Derek Hook, Mr Gary Primrose, Mr Viswanatha Alluri, Mme Gisele Balleys, Mrs Wendy Smith, Mr Alistair Cavan Herron
Income: £1,898,038 [2017]; £2,082,060 [2016]; £2,272,927 [2015]; £2,103,901 [2014]; £2,064,936 [2013]

Krizevac Project
Registered: 28 Jul 2006 Employees: 7 Volunteers: 23
Tel: 01543 888494 Website: krizevac.org
Activities: General charitable purposes; education, training; prevention or relief of poverty; overseas aid, famine relief; arts, culture, heritage, science; economic, community development, employment
Address: Krizevac Project, Atlas Works, Paragon Road, Longton, Stoke on Trent, Staffs, ST3 1NR
Trustees: Mr Anthony Joseph Smith, Mr Vincent Kenneth Owen, Miss Josephine Mary Smith, Mr David Haworth
Income: £1,837,086 [2016]; £565,134 [2015]; £923,180 [2014]; £1,226,027 [2013]; £1,240,442 [2012]

Kusuma Trust UK
Registered: 28 Nov 2008 Employees: 5
Tel: 020 7420 0650 Website: kusumatrust.org
Activities: General charitable purposes; education, training; arts, culture, heritage, science; economic, community development, employment; other charitable purposes
Address: Kusuma Trust UK, 5th Floor, 55 New Oxford Street, London, WC1A 1BS
Trustees: Dr Soma Pujari, Mr Nitin Dass Jain, Anurag Dikshit
Income: £3,032,355 [2017]; £2,530,666 [2016]; £2,568,562 [2015]; £2,746,226 [2014]; £3,126,046 [2013]

The Kynge's College of Our Ladye of Eton Besyde Windesore
Registered: 18 Nov 2010 Employees: 983
Tel: 01753 370542 Website: etoncollege.com
Activities: Education, training
Address: The Bursary, Eton College, Windsor, Berks, SL4 6DJ
Trustees: Dr Andrew Gailey, Professor Michael Proctor, Mr Hamish Forsyth, Professor Kim Nasmyth, Dr Caroline Moore, Sir George Leggatt, Mr Thomas Seaman, Mr Mark Esiri, The Duchess of Wellington, Lord Waldegrave of North Hill, Dame Helena Morrissey, Sir Mark Lyall Grant
Income: £73,378,000 [2017]; £62,833,000 [2016]; £67,151,000 [2015]; £61,927,000 [2014]; £55,750,000 [2013]

The L G S General Charitable Trust
Registered: 1 Feb 1990
Tel: 0113 229 1552
Activities: General charitable purposes
Address: The Grammar School at Leeds, Harrogate Road, Leeds, LS17 8GS
Trustees: Peter Sparling LLB, Mrs Susan Woodroofe, Mrs Alice Margaret Marian Eaton ACA, Mr Stephen Kingston
Income: £4,413,774 [2017]; £3,501,823 [2016]; £3,854,028 [2015]; £3,503,631 [2014]; £2,476,466 [2013]

L.E.A.D. Academy Trust
Registered: 5 Aug 2013 Employees: 661
Tel: 07815 206278 Website: leadacademytrust.co.uk
Activities: Education, training
Address: Huntingdon Primary & Nursery School, Alfred Street Central, Nottingham, NG3 4AY
Trustees: Howard Dowell, Ms Diana Owen, Mr Peter Berry, Mr Mark Blois, Ms Deryn Harvey
Income: £21,750,000 [2016]; £25,276,000 [2015]; £28,878,000 [2014]

LGBT Foundation Ltd
Registered: 7 Aug 1998 *Employees:* 40 *Volunteers:* 140
Tel: 0345 330 3030 *Website:* lgbt.foundation
Activities: General charitable purposes; education, training; advancement of health or saving of lives; economic, community development, employment
Address: LGBT Foundation, 5 Richmond Street, Manchester, M1 3HF
Trustees: Mr Glyn Jenkins, Ms Catherine Denise Poulton, Olivia Butterworth, Sharmila Frances Kar, Ms Aderonke Apata, Mr Simon Mark Bracewell, Mr Lee Broadstock, Mr Smyth William Harper, Matthew Webber, Mr Charlie Jonathan Mallinson, Ms Anjalee Pawasker
Income: £2,096,378 [2017]; £1,935,731 [2016]; £1,884,762 [2015]; £2,034,091 [2014]; £1,937,450 [2013]

LHA London Ltd
Registered: 6 May 1998 *Employees:* 72 *Volunteers:* 297
Tel: 020 7834 1545 *Website:* lhalondon.com
Activities: The prevention or relief of poverty; accommodation, housing
Address: 11 Belgrave Road, London, SW1V 1RB
Trustees: Mrs Sue Johnson, Mrs Linda Holford, Mrs Alison Craze, Mr Alexander McTavish, Mrs Kay Buxton, Mr Giles Byford, Mrs June O'Sullivan, Mr David Malcolm Robertson, Miss Emma Elizabeth Beardmore, Miss Alexandra Jane Whiston-Dew, Mr Ian Mackie, Mrs Petra Green
Income: £14,270,372 [2016]; £13,021,680 [2015]; £11,534,255 [2014]; £11,227,971 [2013]; £10,825,605 [2012]

LHR Airport Communities Trust
Registered: 14 Oct 1996 *Volunteers:* 11
Tel: 07885 271257 *Website:* heathrowcommunityfund.com
Activities: Education, training; environment, conservation, heritage; economic, community development, employment
Address: Heathrow Communities Trust, Compass Centre, Nelson Road, Hounslow, Middlesex, TW6 2GW
Trustees: Alison Moore, Dr Prabhjot Bobby Basra, Mr Andrew Kerswill, Ms Carol Hui, Mr Darius Nasimi, Jason Holmes, Mr Michael Murphy, Mr Richard De Belder, Mr Chris Johnston, Ms Gennie Dearman
Income: £1,142,765 [2016]; £830,977 [2015]; £930,483 [2014]; £930,000 [2013]; £750,000 [2012]

LICC Limited
Registered: 13 Jan 1983 *Employees:* 16 *Volunteers:* 30
Tel: 020 7399 9555 *Website:* licc.org.uk
Activities: Education, training; religious activities; arts, culture, heritage, science
Address: St Peters Church, Vere Street, London, W1G 0DQ
Trustees: Mr John Charles Ibbett, Mr Paul Charles Valler, Ms Anna Marie Detert, Mr Paul Thomas Woolley, Miss Karen Ruth Brown, Miss Hester McCurdy, Rev Paul Gavin Williams, Mr Keith James Wlson
Income: £1,460,712 [2017]; £1,342,301 [2016]; £1,111,201 [2015]; £992,100 [2014]; £959,811 [2013]

LPW Limited
Registered: 3 Sep 2012
Tel: 020 8731 0777
Activities: General charitable purposes; prevention or relief of poverty; religious activities
Address: Cohen Arnold, New Burlington House, 1075 Finchley Road, London, NW11 0PU
Trustees: Mr Irwin Leo Weiler, Mrs Riki Greenberg, Miss Daniela Rosenthal, Mr Nicholas Nicky Rosenthal, Mrs Paula Weiler, Mr Alexander Weiler, Mrs Monica Frances Rosenthal, Mrs Talia Cohen
Income: £1,248,460 [2016]; £829,457 [2015]; £513,172 [2014]

La Scuola Italiana a Londra
Registered: 5 Jul 2007 *Employees:* 24 *Volunteers:* 5
Tel: 020 7603 5353 *Website:* scuolaitalianalondra.org
Activities: Education, training; arts, culture, heritage, science
Address: 154 Holland Park Avenue, London, W11 4UH
Trustees: Mr Alberto Pravettoni, Ms Ernestina Meloni, Raffaella Celia, Ms Michaela Rees-Jones, Mr Christian Iachini, Mrs Silvia Carrara De Sambuy, Mrs Francesca Nelson-Smith, Mr Domimic Pini, Mrs Silvia Jackson-Proes
Income: £1,360,023 [2017]; £1,326,305 [2016]; £1,161,584 [2015]; £848,695 [2014]; £477,151 [2013]

The Lady Fatemah (A.S.) Charitable Trust
Registered: 4 Nov 1998
Tel: 01494 762063 *Website:* ladyfatemahtrust.org
Activities: General charitable purposes; education, training; advancement of health or saving of lives; prevention or relief of poverty; overseas aid, famine relief; economic, community development, employment
Address: September Lodge, Village Way, Amersham, Bucks, HP7 9PU
Trustees: Mr Amirali G Karim, Dr Thuha Jabbar, Mrs Kanize Fatma A Karim, Ms Ahlam M El Hattab
Income: £1,459,224 [2016]; £2,224,828 [2015]; £1,571,760 [2014]; £1,615,086 [2013]

The Lady Nuffield Home
Registered: 6 Nov 1992 *Employees:* 26
Tel: 01865 888500 *Website:* ladynuffieldhome.co.uk
Activities: The advancement of health or saving of lives; accommodation, housing
Address: The Lady Elizabeth Nuffield Home, 165 Banbury Road, Oxford, OX2 7AW
Trustees: Mr John Donald, Mrs Jane Curran, Mr Mark Charter, Mrs Elizabeth Cheng, Dr Judith Mary Shakespeare, Mr Edward Pilling
Income: £1,200,530 [2016]; £1,141,924 [2015]; £1,042,754 [2014]; £985,936 [2013]

Lady Verdin Trust Limited
Registered: 16 Nov 1992 *Employees:* 118 *Volunteers:* 5
Tel: 01270 256700 *Website:* ladyverdintrust.org.uk
Activities: Education, training; disability; accommodation, housing; economic, community development, employment
Address: 196 Nantwich Road, Crewe, Cheshire, CW2 6BP
Trustees: Mrs Sarah Maguire, Mrs Roanne Elizabeth Crowther Foster, Mr Kenneth Oliver James, Mrs Lorraine Yearsley, Mr Gareth Roberts
Income: £3,458,706 [2017]; £2,941,976 [2016]; £2,911,718 [2015]; £2,722,682 [2014]; £2,434,495 [2013]

John Laing Charitable Trust
Registered: 24 Nov 1964 *Employees:* 6
Tel: 020 7901 3307 *Website:* laing.com
Activities: General charitable purposes; education, training; prevention or relief of poverty; accommodation, housing; economic, community development, employment
Address: 33 Bunns Lane, London, NW7 2DX
Trustees: Mr Christopher Maurice Laing OBE DL, Mrs Lynette Krige, Mr Benjamin Laing, Mr Daniel John Partridge, Sir Martin Laing, Mrs Alexandra Gregory, Mr Christopher Brian Waples, Mr Stewart Laing
Income: £2,263,000 [2016]; £1,996,000 [2015]; £1,910,000 [2014]; £1,810,000 [2013]; £1,935,000 [2012]

The Lake District Calvert Trust
Registered: 17 Mar 1976 *Employees:* 55 *Volunteers:* 50
Tel: 017687 72255 *Website:* calvert-trust.org.uk
Activities: Disability
Address: Lake District Calvert Trust Keswick, Underskiddaw, Keswick, Cumbria, CA12 4QD
Trustees: Mr James Walter Fryer-Spedding, Mr Robin Burgess OBE DL, Mr Giles Mounsey Heysham, Mrs Corinna Cartwright, Mr W Bell, Ms Susan Kellock, Mr Julian Handy, Mrs Christine Sheldon, Mrs Claire Hensman, Lord William Richard Fletcher Vane Ingle, Mr Stephen Nicol, Mrs Cherryl Fitzgerald, Mr Roger Cooke, Mr Mark Winfield, Mr Martin Mullin
Income: £2,022,050 [2016]; £1,549,170 [2015]; £1,494,977 [2014]; £1,501,882 [2013]; £1,516,704 [2012]

Lakeland Arts
Registered: 22 Jul 2013 *Employees:* 48 *Volunteers:* 150
Tel: 015394 48060 *Website:* lakelandarts.org.uk
Activities: Education, training; arts, culture, heritage, science; environment, conservation, heritage; economic, community development, employment; recreation
Address: Blackwell Arts & Crafts House, Newby Bridge Road, Windermere, Cumbria, LA23 3JT
Trustees: Mr Anthony Rickards Collinson, Mr Henry Charles Fraser Bowring, Miss Sara Louise Keegan, Mr Charles William Nepean Crewdson OBE, Mr Nicholas William Robert Thompson, Mrs Elizabeth Mary Rink, Mrs Susan Anne Crewe, Mrs Anthea Fiendley Case CBE, Ms Sarah Beatrice Dunning, Mr Martin John Ainscough, Mr Christopher Michael Clarke CBE FRSE, Professor Charles Edward Gere, Mr John Hudson
Income: £7,825,344 [2016]; £3,064,124 [2015]; £3,334,544 [2014]

Lakshmi-Narayana Trust
Registered: 11 Dec 1985 *Employees:* 19 *Volunteers:* 50
Tel: 020 8552 5082 *Website:* srimahalakshmitemple.net
Activities: General charitable purposes; education, training; overseas aid, famine relief; religious activities; arts, culture, heritage, science
Address: Lakshmi Narayana Trust, 241 High Street North, London, E12 6SJ
Trustees: Dr Radhakrishnan Venkatasamy, Mr Alwarsamy Rengamannar, Mr Sennakesavan Viajayakumar, Mr Krishnan Sreenivasan, Mr Subburam S Naidu, Mr Seetharaman Subbanaidu, Mr Kannan Rajan, Mr Sivarupan Karthigesu, Mr Thayalasamy Naidu Subbiahnaicker, Mr Sethuraman Seeni, Mr Navaneethakrishnan Raju, Ms Kumari Selliappan, Mr Alagirisamy Vn, Mr Ramakrishnan Mohanaprakas, Mr Thiyagarajan Jayaraman, Mr Markandu Sutharsanan
Income: £2,208,961 [2016]; £1,603,489 [2015]; £1,787,932 [2014]; £900,217 [2013]; £732,156 [2012]

Lambeth Elfrida Rathbone Society
Registered: 27 Mar 2003 *Employees:* 80 *Volunteers:* 13
Tel: 020 8670 4039 *Website:* rathbonesociety.org.uk
Activities: The advancement of health or saving of lives; disability; accommodation, housing
Address: 8 Chatsworth Way, London, SE27 9HR
Trustees: Mr Phillip Kerry, Ms Laura Walton, Ms Gail Emerson, Mrs Jaqueline Jefferson
Income: £1,490,148 [2017]; £1,667,644 [2016]; £1,656,447 [2015]; £1,475,292 [2014]; £1,287,155 [2013]

Lambeth and Southwark Mencap
Registered: 10 Aug 1995 *Employees:* 66 *Volunteers:* 40
Tel: 020 8655 7711 *Website:* lsmencap.org.uk
Activities: Disability
Address: Lambeth Mencap, 43 Knights Hill, London, SE27 0HS
Trustees: Paul Evans, Lolita Bartlett, Carol Britton, Margaret Brennan, Sabina Laher, Ben Thomas, Brian Stocker, Mary Wells, Dana Brown, Victor Willmott, Vicki Prout
Income: £2,005,720 [2017]; £2,017,890 [2016]; £2,139,309 [2015]; £2,145,433 [2014]; £2,151,310 [2013]

Lambrook School Trust Limited
Registered: 29 Mar 1967 *Employees:* 144 *Volunteers:* 40
Tel: 01344 882717 *Website:* lambrookschool.co.uk
Activities: Education, training
Address: Lambrook, Winkfield Row, Bracknell, Berks, RG42 6LU
Trustees: Mr Christopher Bromfield MA, Mrs Annabel Suva Nicoll, Mr Thomas Edward Winshaw Hawkins, Miss Annette Lisa Dobson, Mrs Hannah Katharine Lyman MSc, Mr Angus Neil, Mr Donald MacLeod FCA, Mr Tom Beardmore-Gray, Dr Alex Peterken BA MA EdD, Mrs Claire Hetherington, Mr Paddy Burrowes, Mr Benjamin Chukwuemeka
Income: £9,572,025 [2017]; £8,579,812 [2016]; £8,024,172 [2015]; £7,546,254 [2014]; £7,226,489 [2013]

Lamda Ltd
Registered: 3 Mar 1963 *Employees:* 173
Tel: 020 8834 0500 *Website:* lamda.org.uk
Activities: Education, training; arts, culture, heritage, science
Address: 155 Talgarth Road, London, W14 9DA
Trustees: Mr Robert Noble, Rt Hon Shaun Anthony Woodward, Mrs Patricia Ann Hodge, Miss Sarah Habberfield, Mrs Olga Basirov, Mr Mark Ralph Delano Cornell, Mr John Wynne Owen, Mr Philip Edward Carne, Mr Thomas Orlando Chandos, Mr Matt Applewhite, Professor Sir George Peter Scott, Mr Richard Johnston, Ms Joanne Margaret Hirst, Ms Helen Sarah Wright
Income: £13,498,285 [2017]; £12,488,399 [2016]; £13,202,890 [2015]; £9,183,874 [2014]; £8,676,761 [2013]

Lamport Hall Preservation Trust Limited
Registered: 27 Aug 1974 *Employees:* 8
Tel: 01604 686272 *Website:* lamporthall.co.uk
Activities: Education, training; environment, conservation, heritage
Address: Lamport Hall, Lamport, Northampton, NN6 9HD
Trustees: Mr Benedict Fenwick, Lady Gayle Robinson, Mr Willum Butterfield, Mr John Harris, Mrs Charlotte Brudenell, Mrs Libby Brayshaw, Mr Richard Isham, Mr Crispin Holborow, Mrs Rosemary Newman
Income: £1,132,282 [2017]; £1,178,811 [2016]; £1,044,282 [2015]; £1,040,949 [2014]; £674,835 [2013]

Lancashire Environmental Fund Limited
Registered: 1 Apr 1999 *Employees:* 3
Tel: 01772 317247 *Website:* lancsenvfund.org.uk
Activities: Environment, conservation, heritage
Address: Lancashire Environmental Fund, The Barn, Berkeley Drive, Bamber Bridge, Preston, Lancs, PR5 6BY
Trustees: Mr Albert Atkinson, Mr John Michael Drury, Mr Francis Patrick McGinty, Mr John Wilkinson
Income: £1,453,075 [2017]; £1,255,855 [2016]; £806,741 [2015]; £1,073,148 [2014]; £1,061,177 [2013]

The Lancashire Wildlife Trust
Registered: 9 Apr 1964 *Employees:* 103 *Volunteers:* 1,242
Tel: 01772 324129 *Website:* lancswt.org.uk
Activities: Education, training; environment, conservation, heritage
Address: The Barn, Berkeley Drive, Bamber Bridge, Preston, Lancs, PR5 6BY
Trustees: Mr Geoffrey Higginbottom, Mr Steve Garland, Mr Duncan James Craig, Mr Anthony Hatton, Dr Clive Harry Elphick, Hazel Ryan, Mr Andrew John Martin Berry, Julian Jackson, Mr Anthony Richard Thomas, Mr Andrew Diccon James Royce, Miss Jane Ashley Houldsworth, Mr John Drury, Stephen Niven, Mr Ronald Wade, Mr John Michael Wells, Ross Duggan
Income: £4,308,000 [2017]; £3,966,000 [2016]; £3,947,000 [2015]; £3,758,000 [2014]; £5,082,065 [2013]

Lancashire Women's Centres
Registered: 2 Dec 2003 *Employees:* 42 *Volunteers:* 190
Tel: 01254 871771 *Website:* womenscentre.org
Activities: General charitable purposes; education, training; prevention or relief of poverty; economic, community development, employment; other charitable purposes
Address: 21-23 Blackburn Road, Accrington, Lancs, BB5 1HF
Trustees: Mrs Susan Ramsdale, Mrs Catherine Alexandra Hanson, Mr M Barry Foley, Mrs Lynette Harwood, Mrs Angela Thornton
Income: £2,096,440 [2017]; £1,937,685 [2016]; £1,191,784 [2015]; £882,368 [2014]; £499,115 [2013]

Lancaster Foundation
Registered: 15 Dec 1997 *Employees:* 2 *Volunteers:* 30
Tel: 01200 444404
Activities: Overseas aid, famine relief; religious activities
Address: Lancaster Foundation, Text House, Bawdlands, Clitheroe, Lancs, BB7 2LA
Trustees: Dr John Edward Lancaster, Mrs Rosemary Lancaster, Mrs Julie Rose Broadhurst, Mr Steven John Lancaster
Income: £2,869,358 [2017]; £3,075,176 [2016]; £4,264,514 [2015]; £2,721,350 [2014]; £3,474,370 [2013]

Lancaster Roman Catholic Diocesan Trust
Registered: 19 May 1964 *Employees:* 112 *Volunteers:* 1,000
Tel: 01524 596059 *Website:* lancasterrcdiocese.org.uk
Activities: General charitable purposes; education, training; disability; prevention or relief of poverty; overseas aid, famine relief; accommodation, housing; religious activities
Address: The Pastoral Centre, Balmoral Road, Lancaster, LA1 3BT
Trustees: Mr Matthew Forrest, Mr Martin Callagher, Rev Cooper Dunstan, Rev Tim Sullivan, Mr Paul Briers, Miss Anne Lorraine Goddard, Rev Peter Hart, Ms Nikki Wisdom, Rev Harry Doyle, Sister Harriet Thomas, Rev Francis Ademola Olaseni, Rev Paul Swarbrick
Income: £9,967,378 [2017]; £8,969,452 [2016]; £9,889,427 [2015]; £9,627,718 [2014]; £8,358,000 [2013]

Lancaster Training Services Limited
Registered: 26 May 1981 *Employees:* 18
Tel: 01524 858326 *Website:* lantrain.co.uk
Activities: Education, training
Address: Lancaster Training Services Ltd, 5 Penrod Way, Heysham, Morecambe, Lancs, LA3 2UZ
Trustees: Mr Richard Warwick Little, Mr George Michael Sierpinski
Income: £1,099,922 [2017]; £1,056,396 [2016]; £1,054,796 [2015]; £1,059,966 [2014]; £1,031,008 [2013]

Lancing College Limited
Registered: 12 Jul 1999 *Employees:* 284
Website: lancingcollege.co.uk
Activities: Education, training
Address: Lancing College, Lancing, W Sussex, BN15 0RW
Trustees: Baroness Julia Cumberlege, Mr Richard Stapleton, Rev Jonathan Meyrick, Mrs Anne-Marie Edgell, Mrs Charlotte Elizabeth Houston, Mr Charles Frederick Dennis, Dr Harry Brunjes, Mr Martin Richard Slumbers BSc FCA, Mr Henry Clifford Ryder Lawson, Mr David Elliott Austin, Mr Timothy Hancock
Income: £19,700,415 [2016]; £19,379,725 [2015]; £17,367,478 [2014]; £16,444,811 [2013]; £15,843,288 [2012]

Lancing College Preparatory School at Worthing Limited
Registered: 31 Dec 2013 *Employees:* 27
Tel: 01798 821386 *Website:* lancingcollege.co.uk
Activities: Education, training
Address: Lancing College, Lancing, W Sussex, BN15 0RW
Trustees: Mrs Pauline Bulman, Mrs Anne-Marie Edgell, Dr Henry Otto Brunjes
Income: £1,016,903 [2016]; £775,876 [2015]; £584,882 [2014]

The Land Restoration Trust
Registered: 8 Oct 2010 *Employees:* 37 *Volunteers:* 550
Tel: 01925 852005 *Website:* thelandtrust.org.uk
Activities: Education, training; advancement of health or saving of lives; amateur sport; environment, conservation, heritage; economic, community development, employment
Address: 7 Birchwood One, Dewhurst Road, Birchwood, Warrington, Cheshire, WA3 7GB
Trustees: Mr Walter Menzies, Mr Jeffrey Moore, Jane Garrett, Mr Ian Piper, Mr William John Hiscocks, Anthony Bickmore, Patrick Aylmer, Ms Dinah Nichols, Mr Peter Alan Smith, Mr Simon Gregor MacGillivray, Janet Haddock-Fraser, Mrs Sarah Jane Whitney, Mr Tom Keevil
Income: £15,240,000 [2017]; £10,874,000 [2016]; £11,097,000 [2015]; £23,993,000 [2014]; £5,523,219 [2013]

Landaid Charitable Trust Limited
Registered: 24 Oct 1986 *Employees:* 10 *Volunteers:* 336
Website: landaid.org
Activities: General charitable purposes; education, training; prevention or relief of poverty; accommodation, housing; economic, community development, employment
Address: 5th Floor, St Albans House, 57-59 Haymarket, London, SW1Y 4QX
Trustees: Mr Robert John Bould, Ms Suzanne Avery, Mr David Taylor, Mr Timothy Andrew Roberts, Mr Alistair Elliott, Mr Scott Cameron Parsons, Mr Andrew Stephen Gulliford, Mr Michael Eric Slade, Mrs Elizabeth Ann Peace, Ms Lynette Lackey, Mr Mark Peter Reynolds, Mr David Erwin, Melanie Leech
Income: £2,229,769 [2017]; £1,794,820 [2016]; £1,726,828 [2015]; £1,781,529 [2014]; £1,368,532 [2013]

The Landmark Trust

Registered: 25 Aug 1965 *Employees:* 156 *Volunteers:* 90
Tel: 01628 825920 *Website:* landmarktrust.org.uk
Activities: Arts, culture, heritage, science; environment, conservation, heritage
Address: The Landmark Trust, Shottesbrooke Park, Broadmoor Road, White Waltham, Maidenhead, Berks, SL6 3SW
Trustees: The Landmark Trustee Company Limited
Income: £15,699,000 [2017]; £12,818,000 [2016]; £11,630,000 [2015]; £11,981,000 [2014]; £10,250,000 [2013]

Landmarks

Registered: 27 Jun 1995 *Employees:* 63
Tel: 01246 433788 *Website:* landmarks.ac.uk
Activities: Education, training; disability; animals; environment, conservation, heritage
Address: Littlemoor House, Littlemoor, Eckington, Sheffield, S21 4EF
Trustees: Mr John Spooner, Miss Kimberley Kirk, Mrs Sally Edwards, Mrs Susan Margaret Windle, Mr Paul Francis Battiste, Mrs Christine O'Neill
Income: £1,733,887 [2017]; £1,220,712 [2016]; £1,181,157 [2015]; £1,311,322 [2014]; £1,141,148 [2013]

The Landscape Institute

Registered: 20 Jan 1999 *Employees:* 21 *Volunteers:* 700
Tel: 020 7685 2645 *Website:* landscapeinstitute.org
Activities: Education, training; environment, conservation, heritage
Address: Landscape Institute, 2 Charles Darwin House, 107 Gray's Inn Road, London, WC1X 8TZ
Trustees: Mr Merrick Denton-Thompson FLI, Ms Helen Tranter FLI, Mr James Lord, Mr Charles Young MA MBA, Mr James Stuart Smyllie, Mr Adam White FLI, Ms Carolin Gohler CMLI, Dr Phyllis Starkey, Ms Michelle Bolger CMLI, Ms Kathryn Bailey CMLI MRTPI, Mr Marc Van Grieken FLI, Mr Niall Williams
Income: £2,528,899 [2017]; £2,274,587 [2016]; £1,922,880 [2015]; £1,802,906 [2014]; £1,675,870 [2013]

Langdon Community

Registered: 30 Apr 2001 *Employees:* 150 *Volunteers:* 52
Tel: 020 8731 2188 *Website:* langdonuk.org
Activities: Education, training; advancement of health or saving of lives; disability; accommodation, housing
Address: Camrose House, 2A Camrose Avenue, Edgware, Middlesex, HA8 6EG
Trustees: Mr Graham Rubin, Mr Nigel John Henry, Mr Nicky Sugarman
Income: £3,708,890 [2016]; £3,041,520 [2015]; £3,478,119 [2014]; £2,330,318 [2013]; £2,482,870 [2012]

The Langdon Foundation

Registered: 6 Jul 2011 *Employees:* 197 *Volunteers:* 54
Tel: 020 8731 2188 *Website:* langdonuk.org
Activities: Education, training; advancement of health or saving of lives; disability; accommodation, housing
Address: 2 Camrose Avenue, Edgware, Middlesex, HA8 6EG
Trustees: Mr Jonathan Joseph, Mr Nigel Henry, Mr Michael Blane, Mr Benjamin Mark Simon Kenneth Miller, Mr Jeremy Bolchover, Mr Sam Shaerf, Mrs Antonia Leila Mitchell, Mr Richard Davis
Income: £6,493,093 [2016]; £5,991,474 [2015]; £7,662,717 [2014]; £5,660,049 [2013]; £5,881,051 [2012]

Langdon Housing

Registered: 6 Jul 2011 *Employees:* 3
Tel: 020 8731 2188 *Website:* langdonuk.org
Activities: Accommodation, housing
Address: Camrose House, 2A Camrose Avenue, Edgware, Middlesex, HA8 6EG
Trustees: Mr Gary Silver, Mr Warren Phillip Rosenberg, Mr Stuart Levington, Mr Paul Joseph
Income: £1,167,148 [2016]; £1,146,787 [2015]; £1,310,718 [2014]; £916,893 [2013]; £820,225 [2012]

The Langham Partnership (UK and Ireland)

Registered: 28 May 2002 *Employees:* 25 *Volunteers:* 10
Tel: 07816 065518 *Website:* langham.org
Activities: Education, training; religious activities
Address: 14 East Block, Shaddon Mill, Shaddongate, Carlisle, CA2 5WD
Trustees: Mr David Turner, Mr Norman Fraser, Dr Mary Evans, Mrs Gillian Phillips, Mr Adelbert Jennings, Mr Steven MacKay, Mr John Thomas, Mr Stephen Osei-Mensah, Dr Ronald Clements, Mrs Judith Sawers, Mr Paul Cornelius
Income: £2,764,606 [2017]; £2,221,221 [2016]; £1,982,614 [2015]; £1,607,013 [2014]; £1,793,259 [2013]

Langley House Trust

Registered: 8 Mar 2012 *Employees:* 222 *Volunteers:* 106
Tel: 024 7658 7369 *Website:* langleyhousetrust.org
Activities: Education, training; accommodation, housing; religious activities; other charitable purposes
Address: Langley House Trust, P O Box 6364, 3 & 4 The Square, Manfield Avenue, Coventry, Warwicks, CV2 2QJ
Trustees: Mr Michael Maiden, Mr Piers Feilden, Mr Philip Hilton, Mr Robert Clarke, Mrs Ruth Williams, Mr Andrew Newell, Ms Denise Sanderson-Estcourt, Mr Malcolm Hayes, Mrs Sandra Keene, Amanda Coyle
Income: £12,000,000 [2017]; £12,067,668 [2016]; £10,983,026 [2015]; £10,161,390 [2014]; £9,006,037 [2013]

Langley School

Registered: 28 Sep 1962 *Employees:* 232 *Volunteers:* 2
Tel: 01508 522474 *Website:* langleyschool.co.uk
Activities: Education, training
Address: Langley School, Langley Park, Chedgrave, Norwich, NR14 6BJ
Trustees: Mr Anthony Harmer, Mrs Janet Timmins, Mr Geoffrey Barham, Mrs Sharon Turner, Mr John Miller, Lt Col Mark Nicholas MBE, Mr Graham Watson, Mr Stephen Brown, Mr Matthew Newnham, Mr Brett Burton, Dr Hannah Mary Nearney
Income: £9,561,129 [2016]; £8,800,897 [2015]; £8,463,080 [2014]; £8,617,976 [2013]; £8,330,454 [2012]

Langstone Society

Registered: 13 Jun 1986 *Employees:* 141
Tel: 01384 243665 *Website:* langstonesociety.org
Activities: Disability
Address: Langstone Society, 98-99 Dixons Green Road, Dudley, W Midlands, DY2 7DJ
Trustees: Jane Helen Clarke, Mr John Harris, Mr Nicholas Webb, Ms Jane Hatton, Mrs Dale Field, Mrs Ann Blackman, Mr M Sampson, Ms Anna Gillespie
Income: £2,734,371 [2017]; £2,400,375 [2016]; £2,261,312 [2015]; £2,254,514 [2014]; £2,244,165 [2013]

The Lankellychase Foundation
Registered: 12 Jan 2005 *Employees:* 12
Tel: 020 3747 9930 *Website:* lankellychase.org.uk
Activities: General charitable purposes
Address: Greenworks, Dog & Duck Yard, Princeton Street, London, WC1R 4BH
Trustees: Ms Marion Janner, Ms Hilary Berg, Mr Simon Tucker, Jacob Hayman, Mr Robin Tuddenham, Ms Morag Burnett, Ms Jane Millar, Mr Oliver Batchelor, Mr Darren Murinas, Mr Myron Kellner-Rogers
Income: £3,669,039 [2017]; £3,393,268 [2016]; £4,146,033 [2015]; £3,864,287 [2014]; £3,759,939 [2013]

The Lantern Community
Registered: 4 Jun 1999 *Employees:* 88 *Volunteers:* 11
Tel: 01425 460191 *Website:* lanterncommunity.org.uk
Activities: General charitable purposes; education, training; disability; accommodation, housing; arts, culture, heritage, science
Address: The Lantern Centre, Folly Farm Lane, Ringwood, Hants, BH24 2NN
Trustees: Mrs Maria Verhoeven, Miss Anna Iveson, Mr Alan Hollands, Mr Luigi Carnelli, Miss Elizabeth Bord, Mr Ian Humphries, Mrs Louise Tonkin, Mrs Loraine Morgan
Income: £2,834,155 [2017]; £1,630,591 [2016]; £2,415,148 [2015]; £9,059,542 [2014]; £190,218 [2013]

Lantra
Registered: 23 Jun 1993 *Employees:* 91 *Volunteers:* 120
Tel: 024 7669 6996 *Website:* lantra.co.uk
Activities: Education, training
Address: Lantra, Lantra House, Stoneleigh Park, Kenilworth, Warwicks, CV8 2LG
Trustees: Mr Richard Ian Clarke, Mr Nigel Titchen, Mr Richard Capewell, Mr Ian James Marshall, Mr Cyril Peter Rees, Mr Richard Longthorp OBE, Mr Stephen Vickers, Mrs Valerie Owen OBE, Mr Henry Ralph Graham, Dr Geoffrey William Mackey
Income: £5,425,229 [2017]; £5,221,710 [2016]; £6,030,528 [2015]; £7,236,557 [2014]; £7,699,351 [2013]

Larchcroft Education Trust
Registered: 27 Jul 1998 *Employees:* 32 *Volunteers:* 100
Tel: 01473 464975
Activities: Education, training
Address: Stoke by Nayland Campus, Sudbury Road, Stoke by Nayland, Colchester, Essex, CO6 4RW
Trustees: Mr Andrew Frank Bradshaw, Mr Ivan James Hopkins, Mr Dave Bowen, Mr James Hutchins, Mr Roger Murphy, Mr Michael Parsons, Mr Stephen Bradshaw
Income: £2,203,346 [2016]; £1,924,439 [2015]; £1,473,996 [2014]; £1,120,887 [2013]; £832,136 [2012]

Larkfield with Hill Park Autistic Trust Limited
Registered: 1 Oct 1962 *Employees:* 257 *Volunteers:* 55
Tel: 01892 822168 *Website:* pepenbury.info
Activities: Disability; accommodation, housing
Address: 16 Waldegrave Road, Bromley, Kent, BR1 2JP
Trustees: Ms Gillian Diane Marcus, Mrs Kirsty Zia Marshall, Ms Stephanie Jane Upton
Income: £7,085,842 [2017]; £7,167,803 [2016]; £6,846,666 [2015]; £6,743,450 [2014]; £6,238,523 [2013]

The Basil Larsen 1999 Charitable Trust
Registered: 28 Apr 2000
Activities: General charitable purposes
Address: High House, Highlands Road, Reigate, Surrey, RH2 0LA
Trustees: Bob Wightman, Mrs Maryjane Dixson Pugsley
Income: £1,366,293 [2017]; £19,845,601 [2016]; £35,153,047 [2015]; £6,250 [2014]; £6,250 [2013]

Latate Limited
Registered: 21 Mar 2002
Tel: 0191 490 0686
Activities: General charitable purposes; education, training; prevention or relief of poverty; religious activities
Address: 80 Bewick Road, Gateshead, Tyne & Wear, NE8 1RS
Trustees: Mrs Anna Schleider, Mr Shamai Schleider, Mr Harold Emanuel, Mrs Miriam Silver, Mr Yosef Schleider, Mr Louis Wittler
Income: £1,256,093 [2017]; £3,420,825 [2016]; £1,334,116 [2015]; £1,115,683 [2014]; £1,081,293 [2013]

Latch Welsh Children's Cancer Charity
Registered: 28 Nov 2003 *Volunteers:* 50
Tel: 01633 250077 *Website:* latchwales.org
Activities: General charitable purposes; advancement of health or saving of lives; disability; prevention or relief of poverty
Address: 54 Oakfield Road, Newport, NP20 4LP
Trustees: Mr Paul Wilkins, Mrs Sian Howell, James Rudolf, Mr John Milner, Mr Philip Reardon-Smith, Mr Ian Rogers, Mrs Emma Jane Hingston, Ms Sarah Lloyd, Ms Emma Wilkins, Mr Lyn Howell
Income: £1,902,915 [2016]; £868,628 [2015]; £679,549 [2014]; £1,049,003 [2013]; £683,643 [2012]

Latin Link
Registered: 12 May 1993 *Employees:* 36 *Volunteers:* 21
Website: latinlink.org.uk
Activities: Education, training; advancement of health or saving of lives; disability; prevention or relief of poverty; overseas aid, famine relief; religious activities; other charitable purposes
Address: Latin Link, 87 London Street, Reading, Berks, RG1 4QA
Trustees: Mr Roger Pearce, Margaret Morgan, Mr David Simpson, Mr James Butler, Mr Andrew Binmore, Mr Keith Farman, Mr Simon Huw Griffiths, Mrs Rachel Stone
Income: £2,007,791 [2017]; £2,097,983 [2016]; £2,271,455 [2015]; £2,560,542 [2014]; £2,177,454 [2013]

Lattitude Global Volunteering
Registered: 10 Feb 1977 *Employees:* 37 *Volunteers:* 620
Tel: 0118 956 2914 *Website:* lattitude.org.uk
Activities: Education, training; environment, conservation, heritage; economic, community development, employment
Address: 69B Elmstone Drive, Tilehurst, Reading, Berks, RG31 5NS
Trustees: Mr Charles Reynolds, Mr Nigel Cribb, Mr Simon Fisher, Mr Alejandro Vleming, Mr Ian Lee, Mr Pat Upson, Mr Benjamin Geoffrey White, Dr Harvey Smith, Mrs Joanne Rachel Burgon, Mr Stephen McCann
Income: £1,521,743 [2017]; £2,797,654 [2016]; £2,870,589 [2015]; £2,169,773 [2014]; £2,160,344 [2013]

The Latvian Welfare Trust

Registered: 21 Jun 2008 *Employees:* 109 *Volunteers:* 25
Tel: 01788 860599 *Website:* daugavasvanagi.co.uk
Activities: General charitable purposes; education, training; advancement of health or saving of lives; disability; prevention or relief of poverty; accommodation, housing; arts, culture, heritage, science; environment, conservation, heritage
Address: Latvian Welfare Fund, Catthorpe Manor, Lilbourne Road, Catthorpe, Lutterworth, Leics, LE17 6DF
Trustees: Mr Uldis Janis Revelins, Mrs Ilze Grickus, Ms Karoline Isabella East, Mr Miks Vizbulis, Mr Kriss Ligers, Mr Ivar Aivars Juris Sinka, Mr Rudolfs Sulcs, Mr Marcis Jansons
Income: £2,752,487 [2016]; £1,822,739 [2015]; £1,851,029 [2014]; £1,053,865 [2013]; £889,120 [2012]

Latymer Foundation at Hammersmith

Registered: 12 Nov 1963 *Employees:* 329
Tel: 0845 638 5960 *Website:* latymer-upper.org
Activities: Education, training
Address: Latymer Upper School, 237 King Street, London, W6 9LR
Trustees: Mrs Gubby Ayida, Mr James Priory, Mrs Annamarie Phelps, Mr Nicholas Jordan, Mrs Rosalind Sweeting, Mr Charles Wijeratna, Mr Mark Brewer, Revd Simon Downham, Mr Stephen Richard Hodges, Professor James Smith, Ms Tracey Scoffield, Miss Joanna Mackle, Mr Alex Plavsic, Mrs Chantal Free
Income: £30,322,635 [2017]; £26,229,106 [2016]; £24,218,488 [2015]; £26,002,582 [2014]; £26,890,387 [2013]

The Norman Laud Association

Registered: 31 Mar 2004 *Employees:* 52 *Volunteers:* 28
Tel: 0121 373 6860 *Website:* normanlaud.org.uk
Activities: General charitable purposes; disability; accommodation, housing; other charitable purposes
Address: The Norman Laud Association, Lime Grove House, Lime Grove, Sutton Coldfield, W Midlands, B73 5JN
Trustees: Mrs E A Mountford, Mrs Heather Legge, Mrs Saima Zulfiqar, Mrs Drina Marija Walters, Mr Neil Atkinson Insurance Broker, Mrs Rose Griffith, Mrs Linda Marie Brown
Income: £1,395,504 [2017]; £1,229,501 [2016]; £1,395,482 [2015]; £1,262,747 [2014]; £1,246,810 [2013]

Lauderdale House Trust

Registered: 7 Aug 1995
Tel: 020 7974 4172
Activities: General charitable purposes; education, training; arts, culture, heritage, science
Address: London Borough of Camden, 7th Floor, Town Hall, Argyle Street, London, WC1H 8EQ
Trustees: L B Camden
Income: £2,827,139 [2017]; £1,909,392 [2016]; £450,547 [2015]; £159,785 [2013]

Launchpad Reading

Registered: 2 Jun 1980 *Employees:* 47 *Volunteers:* 98
Tel: 0118 950 7656 *Website:* launchpadreading.org.uk
Activities: General charitable purposes; education, training; prevention or relief of poverty; accommodation, housing; economic, community development, employment; other charitable purposes
Address: Launchpad Reading, 1A Merchants Place, Reading, Berks, RG1 1DT
Trustees: Mr Matt Andrews, Mr William Montague, Mrs Helen Waring, Ms Hannah Powell, Mr Ian Haslam, Suzanne Stallard, Mr Roger Chester, Mr Sean Sutcliffe, Victoria Oakes, Mr Philip Jones
Income: £3,162,287 [2017]; £2,918,686 [2016]; £2,205,629 [2015]; £2,078,959 [2014]; £1,929,279 [2013]

Laureus Sport for Good Foundation

Registered: 19 Sep 2005 *Employees:* 9
Tel: 020 7514 2898 *Website:* laureus.com
Activities: General charitable purposes; amateur sport
Address: 460 Fulham Road, London, SW6 1BZ
Trustees: Mr Edwin Corley Moses, Baroness Tanni Grey-Thompson DBE, Mr Sean Brian Thomas Fitzpatrick, Dr Guy Restom Sanan, Mr Hugo Porta, Dr Jens Thiemer
Income: £2,825,181 [2016]; £2,865,050 [2015]; £4,224,713 [2014]; £2,477,308 [2013]; £2,466,386 [2012]

Lavant House School Educational Trust Limited

Registered: 12 Jan 1967 *Employees:* 36
Website: lavanthouse.org.uk
Activities: Education, training
Address: Portland Business & Financial Solutions Ltd, Eagle Point, Little Park Farm Road, Fareham, Hants, PO15 5TD
Trustees: Mr Aubrey Malcolm-Green, Mr Rollo Malcolm-Green CEng BSc, Ms Hilary Herson, Mrs Jennifer Buckley, Mr Christopher Maultby, Mrs L Butt, Mr John Pressdee, Mrs Marian Scott, Mrs Rosalynd Kamaryc, Mr Robert Carlysle, Mr Mark Sullivan
Income: £1,631,905 [2014]; £1,971,629 [2013]; £2,221,590 [2012]

The Law Family Charitable Foundation

Registered: 19 May 2011
Tel: 020 7947 4057
Activities: General charitable purposes
Address: 40 Berkeley Square, London, W1J 5AL
Trustees: Miss Carole Ann Elizabeth Cook, Ms Zoe Law, Mr Andrew Eric Law
Income: £28,777,342 [2017]; £16,314 [2016]; £19,889 [2015]; £23,754,734 [2014]; £1,425,660 [2013]

Lawes Agricultural Trust

Registered: 12 Mar 2014
Tel: 01582 938440 *Website:* rothamsted.ac.uk
Activities: Arts, culture, heritage, science
Address: Lawes Agricultural Trust, Rothamsted Research, West Common, Harpenden, Herts, AL5 2JQ
Trustees: Lord Cameron, Charles Godfray, Sir Peter Kendall, Mr Will Gemmill, Professor David Baulcombe, Dr Tina Barsby, Dr Graham Birch
Income: £1,465,277 [2017]; £2,001,947 [2016]; £1,129,079 [2015]

The Simon Mark Lazarus Foundation

Registered: 28 Nov 2002
Tel: 01707 876867
Activities: General charitable purposes; education, training; disability; overseas aid, famine relief; other charitable purposes
Address: 117 The Ridgeway, Northaw, Potters Bar, Herts, EN6 4BG
Trustees: Mr Michael Joseph Lazarus, Mrs Diana Elizabeth Lazarus, Mr David Michael Barbanel
Income: £1,339,486 [2016]; £29,779 [2015]; £68,830 [2014]; £21,375 [2013]; £17,162 [2012]

Le Platon Home, Guernsey
Registered: 2 May 1967 *Employees:* 35
Tel: 01481 722461 *Website:* leplaton.com
Activities: Accommodation, housing
Address: Le Platon Home, Clifton, St Peter Port, Guernsey, GY1 2PW
Trustees: Mr Bryan Mauger, Jurat Michael Tanguy, Dr Robert George Hanna, Miss Eileen Baird, Mr Drew Pollock
Income: £1,169,484 [2017]; £1,149,735 [2016]; £1,125,584 [2015]; £1,074,956 [2014]; £1,025,393 [2013]

Leaden Hall School Limited
Registered: 4 Oct 1963 *Employees:* 33 *Volunteers:* 3
Tel: 01722 439260 *Website:* leaden-hall.com
Activities: Education, training
Address: The Old Dairy, Lower Street, Harnham, Salisbury, Wilts, SP2 8HB
Trustees: Mr Trevor Austreng, Mrs Trudy Austreng BA (Hons), Mrs Georgina Louise Bateman, Mr Peter Anthony Edward Dix, Mrs Anne Huntley, Mrs Jennifer Claire Dwyer, Mrs Caroline Marking, Mr Alexander Edward Northcott, Mrs Christine Mary Cooper
Income: £1,559,978 [2015]; £1,589,440 [2014]; £1,656,517 [2013]

The Leaders of Worship and Preachers Homes
Registered: 2 Dec 2005 *Employees:* 82
Tel: 01702 342059 *Website:* lwphomes.org.uk
Activities: Accommodation, housing; religious activities
Address: 1 Winton Avenue, Westcliff on Sea, Essex, SS0 7QU
Trustees: Mr Philip Nuttall, Mr Graeme Garden, Miss Jenny Benfield, Rev Colin Braithwaite, Mr David Hudson, Mr John Draper, Mr John Hardy
Income: £2,520,482 [2017]; £2,707,699 [2016]; £2,692,741 [2015]; £2,522,431 [2014]; £2,515,215 [2013]

The Leadership Centre for Local Government
Registered: 18 Mar 2008 *Employees:* 6
Tel: 020 7187 7385 *Website:* leadershipcentre.org.uk
Activities: Education, training
Address: Leadership Centre, 76-86 Turnmill Street, London, EC1M 5LG
Trustees: Councillor Keith House, Mr David Lloyd, Councillor Richard Stay, Ms Helen Bailey, Mr Jan Sobieraj, Lord Peter Smith, Mr Kim Ryley, Ms Tamara Finkelstein
Income: £1,291,895 [2017]; £1,149,382 [2016]; £1,579,456 [2015]; £1,148,326 [2014]; £50,163 [2013]

The Leadership Foundation for Higher Education
Registered: 6 Feb 2004 *Employees:* 36
Tel: 020 3468 4810 *Website:* lfhe.ac.uk
Activities: Education, training
Address: The Leadership Foundation, Peer House, 8-14 Verulam Street, London, WC1X 8LZ
Trustees: Mrs Gillian Camm, Mr Colin Riordan, Mr David Llewellyn, Mr Geoffrey Dawson, Mr Nicholas Petford, Mr Craig Austin Mahoney, Sophie Bowen, Steve West, Ms Julie Lydon, Ms Janet Legrand, Mr Stephen Marston, Ms Wendy Alexander, Ms Rose Wangen Jones, Andy Chew
Income: £6,225,030 [2017]; £7,107,360 [2016]; £5,940,114 [2015]; £6,049,722 [2014]; £6,525,879 [2013]

The League Against Cruel Sports
Registered: 6 Jan 2003 *Employees:* 47 *Volunteers:* 60
Website: league.org.uk
Activities: General charitable purposes; education, training; animals; environment, conservation, heritage
Address: League Against Cruel Sports, New Sparling House, Holloway Hill, Godalming, Surrey, GU7 1QZ
Trustees: Mr P Anderson, Mr Chris Williamson, Professor Clive Nancarrow, Mr Andrew Charles Wood, Mr I Blake-Lawson, Ms Sally Louise Denbigh, Mr Alan Tapp, Ms Sarah Louise Miller
Income: £2,991,877 [2016]; £6,497,797 [2015]; £2,885,653 [2014]; £2,537,315 [2013]; £2,020,712 [2012]

League Football Education
Registered: 15 Jul 2004 *Employees:* 29
Tel: 0870 458 9250 *Website:* lfe.org.uk
Activities: Education, training
Address: League Football Education, 5B Edward VII Quay, Navigation Way, Ashton on Ribble, Preston, Lancs, PR2 2YF
Trustees: Mr Gordon Taylor BSc (Econ) Hon Dart Hon MA OBE, Mr Darren Wilson, Mr Andrew Godfrey Williamson, Mr Shaun Harvey
Income: £9,957,597 [2017]; £9,223,115 [2016]; £9,038,767 [2015]; £8,676,663 [2014]; £8,451,662 [2013]

The League of Friends of The Royal United Hospital
Registered: 21 Jun 1978 *Employees:* 14 *Volunteers:* 350
Tel: 01225 824046 *Website:* friends-of-the-ruh.co.uk
Activities: The advancement of health or saving of lives
Address: Royal United Hospital, Combe Park, Bath, BA1 3NG
Trustees: Mrs Madeline Baker, Jane Rymer, Mr Stan Barker, Pat Ost, Mr Graham Charles Hart
Income: £1,063,012 [2016]; £869,490 [2015]; £955,896 [2014]; £652,553 [2013]; £118,233 [2012]

Leap Confronting Conflict
Registered: 10 Nov 1998 *Employees:* 21 *Volunteers:* 55
Tel: 020 7561 3700 *Website:* leapcc.org.uk
Activities: Education, training; economic, community development, employment
Address: Leap Confronting Conflict, Unit 7, 5-7 Wells Terrace, London, N4 3JU
Trustees: Mr David Causer, Mr Matt Bell, Mr Derek Bardowell, Chantal Chang, Mr Aaron Jean-Baptiste, Rachel Sandby-Thomas, Teresa Clarke, Mr Peter Olawaye, Mr Mark Spelman, Miss Deborah O'Neill
Income: £1,423,886 [2016]; £1,204,693 [2015]; £1,007,150 [2014]; £993,343 [2013]; £968,288 [2012]

Learning Disability Wales - Anabledd Dysgu Cymru
Registered: 16 Jun 1997 *Employees:* 13 *Volunteers:* 1
Website: learningdisabilitywales.org.uk
Activities: Disability
Address: 36 Chapel Road, Abergavenny, Monmouthshire, NP7 7DP
Trustees: Ms Denise Inger, Mr Philip Madden, Mrs Jacqui Caldwell, Mr Stephen Barnard, Mr Stephen Cox, Miss Kathy Rivett, Mrs Amanda Evans, Miss Dawn Gullis
Income: £2,226,526 [2017]; £544,658 [2016]; £660,112 [2015]; £791,978 [2014]; £697,067 [2013]

Learning Foundation
Registered: 26 Apr 2001 *Employees:* 5 *Volunteers:* 5
Tel: 01344 636413 *Website:* learningfoundation.org.uk
Activities: Education, training
Address: Index House, St George's Lane, Ascot, Berks, SL5 7ET
Trustees: Diana Laurillard, Mr William Niel McLean, Mr David Doherty, Mr David Stuart Burrows, Mrs Jennifer Bailey, Mr Martin Sandford
Income: £1,614,402 [2017]; £1,882,286 [2016]; £1,984,779 [2015]; £1,761,185 [2014]; £1,505,885 [2013]

Learning Links (Southern) Limited
Registered: 17 Oct 2000 *Employees:* 34 *Volunteers:* 47
Tel: 023 9229 6460 *Website:* learninglinks.co.uk
Activities: Education, training; advancement of health or saving of lives; prevention or relief of poverty; economic, community development, employment
Address: Learning Links (Southern) Ltd, 3 St Georges Business Centre, St Georges Square, Portsmouth, PO1 3EY
Trustees: Mrs Linda Taylor, Bob Wardley, Mrs Christine Payne, Mrs Kirsten Walton, Mr John Brookes-Daniels, Mr Brian Davenport, Dr Kieron Vincent John Hatton
Income: £1,117,645 [2017]; £1,124,631 [2016]; £1,556,957 [2015]; £1,634,007 [2014]; £1,533,260 [2013]

The Learning Through Landscapes Trust
Registered: 23 Apr 1990 *Employees:* 21 *Volunteers:* 5
Tel: 01962 846497 *Website:* ltl.org.uk
Activities: General charitable purposes; education, training; advancement of health or saving of lives; arts, culture, heritage, science; environment, conservation, heritage; recreation
Address: Ground Floor, F Block, Clarendon House, Monarch Way, Winchester, Hants, SO22 5PW
Trustees: Mrs Usha Sahni OBE, Mr Mukund Patel, Mrs Deborah Jane Allmey, Miss Susan Humphries OBE MA, Mr David John Troake, Mr David Edward Coleman, Mr Mike Greenaway, Sir Robert Paul Reid, Mr David John Peniket, Mr Merrick Hugh Denton Thompson OBE, Professor Angela Anning, Mr Stefan Mark Jakobek, Mr David Stephen Cameron, Mrs Julie Ann Wilson
Income: £1,609,380 [2017]; £742,690 [2016]; £820,115 [2015]; £1,103,025 [2014]; £1,367,347 [2013]

Learning on Screen - The British Universities and Colleges Film and Video Council
Registered: 16 Jul 1969 *Employees:* 16
Tel: 020 7393 1500 *Website:* bufvc.ac.uk
Activities: Education, training
Address: Learning on Screen, 77 Wells Street, London, W1T 3QJ
Trustees: Mr James Alexander Bethel Bain, Mr Jon Shears, Ms Shona Cameron, Mr Nicholas Ralph Davy, Mr John Wyver, Prof Simon John Lancaster, Dr Damien Mansell, Professor John Ellis, Dr Chris Willmott, Sean Thornton, Ms Caroline Ogilvie, Mr Richard George McCracken, Mr Lee Patrick Clark, Ms Eleri Rhiannon Kyffin
Income: £1,341,432 [2017]; £1,481,914 [2016]; £1,412,487 [2015]; £2,073,275 [2014]; £1,977,024 [2013]

Leasowe Community Homes
Registered: 23 Nov 1998 *Employees:* 8
Tel: 0151 227 1001 *Website:* primagroup.org
Activities: Accommodation, housing; economic, community development, employment
Address: 8 Columbus Quay, Riverside Drive, Liverpool, L3 4DB
Trustees: Mr David Hugh McGaw, Ms Louise Carter, Mr Martin John Latham, Mr Philip Robert Wragg, Mr Andrew John Paling, Mrs Anita Leech, Ms Wendy Gooley, Mr Anthony Dunne, Mr Marcus Evans
Income: £4,624,000 [2017]; £4,724,000 [2016]; £4,567,231 [2015]; £4,432,000 [2014]; £5,603,000 [2013]

The Leathersellers' Company Charitable Fund
Registered: 12 Jul 1979 *Employees:* 2
Tel: 020 7330 1444 *Website:* leathersellers.co.uk
Activities: General charitable purposes; education, training; advancement of health or saving of lives; disability; prevention or relief of poverty; arts, culture, heritage, science; environment, conservation, heritage
Address: The Leathersellers Company, 7 St Helen's Place, London, EC3A 6AB
Trustees: Mr David Manuel Santa-Olalla, The Leathersellers Company
Income: £1,868,000 [2017]; £1,714,000 [2016]; £1,539,000 [2015]; £1,585,000 [2014]; £1,449,000 [2013]

Leazes Homes Limited
Registered: 20 Jan 2010
Tel: 0191 278 8718 *Website:* leazeshomes.org.uk
Activities: Education, training; prevention or relief of poverty; accommodation, housing
Address: Jubilee Court, Kenton Road, Newcastle upon Tyne, NE3 3BW
Trustees: Bill Midgley, Cameron Waddell, Mrs Dawn Marie Keightley, Mr Gerard Joseph Walsh, Veronica Dunn, Michael Reynolds, Mr Michael Thomas Brady, Mr William Thompson
Income: £4,292,000 [2017]; £3,583,000 [2016]; £2,409,000 [2015]; £1,906,000 [2014]; £1,523,000 [2013]

Lebara Foundation
Registered: 11 Feb 2008 *Employees:* 7
Tel: 07884 551868 *Website:* lebarafoundation.org
Activities: General charitable purposes; education, training; advancement of health or saving of lives; disability; prevention or relief of poverty; overseas aid, famine relief; accommodation, housing; environment, conservation, heritage; other charitable purposes
Address: Lebara Foundation, Russel House, 140 Highstreet, Edgware, Middlesex, HA8 7LW
Trustees: Mr Gobinath Kalarampatti, Sanju Leon, Mr Barry Rees, Robin Kandasamy, Arjun Saigal
Income: £1,298,007 [2015]; £1,943,597 [2014]; £3,501,815 [2013]; £759,742 [2012]

Lee Abbey Fellowship
Registered: 9 Oct 2002 *Employees:* 87 *Volunteers:* 80
Website: leeabbey.org.uk
Activities: Religious activities
Address: Lindisfarne, Landkey Road, Barnstaple, Devon, EX32 9BW
Trustees: Rev Dr Graham Robert Cappleman, Rev Selina Garner, Mr Mark Beedell, Mrs Jilia Laurel Claire Hocking, Mr Magnus Proctor, Rev Simon Charles Farrar, Mr Adrian Christopher Male, Rev David Charles Roland Widdows
Income: £2,426,446 [2017]; £2,191,441 [2016]; £2,465,318 [2015]; £2,042,502 [2014]; £2,113,740 [2013]

Lee Abbey International Students' Club
Registered: 31 Jul 1964 *Employees:* 29 *Volunteers:* 10
Website: leeabbeylondon.com
Activities: Accommodation, housing; religious activities
Address: Lindisfarne, Landkey Road, Barnstaple, Devon, EX32 9BW
Trustees: The Revd Canon Yemi Ladipo, Rev Dr Graham Robert Cappleman, Miss Emma Claire Holland, Ms Fiona Elizabeth Nouri, Prof Alexander Anthony Pepper, Revd Dr Lynda Brigid Taylor
Income: £1,132,124 [2017]; £881,171 [2016]; £1,551,584 [2015]; £1,500,040 [2014]; £1,514,770 [2013]

The Lee Abbey Movement
Registered: 9 Oct 2002 *Employees:* 121 *Volunteers:* 100
Website: leeabbey.org.uk
Activities: Religious activities
Address: Lindisfarne, Landkey Road, Barnstaple, Devon, EX32 9BW
Trustees: John Simmons, Margaret Anne Paul, Rev James Denniston, Mrs Susan Margaret Edmondson, Prof Alexander Anthony Pepper, Rev David Charles Roland Widdows, Rev Canon Yemi Ladipo, Mr Stephen Weatherley, Rev Dr Graham Robert Cappleman, Sister Susan Berry, Rev Lynda Brigid Taylor
Income: £3,627,601 [2017]; £3,237,972 [2016]; £4,129,589 [2015]; £3,678,740 [2014]; £234,096 [2013]

The Samuel Tak Lee Charitable Trust
Registered: 1 Jun 2015
Tel: 020 7580 5656
Activities: General charitable purposes; education, training
Address: c/o Langham Estate Management Ltd, London House, 9a Margaret Street, London, W1W 8RJ
Trustees: Stl Ptc UK Limited, Stl Ptc UK (No 2) Limited
Income: £2,500,175 [2017]; £25,410,445 [2016]

Leeds Autism Services
Registered: 13 Jul 1995 *Employees:* 91 *Volunteers:* 3
Tel: 0113 245 2645 *Website:* las.uk.net
Activities: Education, training; disability; accommodation, housing
Address: 16 Church Road, Armley, Leeds, LS12 1TZ
Trustees: Mr Geoffrey Bennett, Mrs Ruth Sheldrake, Mr Edward A Britton, Mr David Thomson, Mr Iain Cant, Mr Anthony Sheppard
Income: £2,335,297 [2017]; £2,244,962 [2016]; £2,020,541 [2015]; £1,859,262 [2014]; £1,721,289 [2013]

Leeds Beckett Students' Union
Registered: 10 Dec 2010 *Employees:* 40 *Volunteers:* 1,050
Tel: 0113 209 8400 *Website:* leedsbeckettsu.co.uk
Activities: Education, training
Address: Leeds Met Students' Union, B Block, Calverley Street, Leeds, LS1 3HE
Trustees: Carolyn Cooper-Black, James Starnes, Meg Robinson, Ro Sewell, Jack Harrison, Charles Hind, Sherry Iqbal, John Toon, Kelly-Anne Watson, Paul Hogg, Aidan Thatcher, Jo Gibson, Andrew Harrison
Income: £2,171,661 [2017]; £2,276,576 [2016]; £2,388,948 [2015]; £1,924,944 [2014]; £1,991,487 [2013]

Leeds Castle Foundation
Registered: 29 Oct 1974 *Employees:* 262 *Volunteers:* 25
Tel: 01622 765400 *Website:* leeds-castle.com
Activities: Education, training; advancement of health or saving of lives; arts, culture, heritage, science; amateur sport; animals; environment, conservation, heritage
Address: Leeds Castle, Broomfield, Maidstone, Kent, ME17 1PL
Trustees: The Honourable Mark Thomas Bridges, Mr Richard George Laing, Dr Anna Keay, Mr Jonathan Beale Neame, Mr Thomas Charles Wright, Mr Timothy Stevens OBE, Mr Niall Dickson, Mr Michael Covell, Laura C A Nesfield
Income: £10,851,000 [2017]; £10,324,000 [2016]; £9,733,060 [2015]; £8,977,098 [2014]; £8,453,358 [2013]

Leeds Citizens Advice Bureau
Registered: 16 Jun 1988 *Employees:* 44 *Volunteers:* 80
Tel: 0113 243 3339 *Website:* citizensadviceleeds.org.uk
Activities: General charitable purposes; education, training; prevention or relief of poverty
Address: Leeds Citizens Advice Bureau, Westminster Buildings, 31 New York Street, Leeds, LS2 7DT
Trustees: Dr Kenneth James Patterson, Mr Ian Lawson, Mrs Isobel Mills, Caroline MacKay, Rebecca Dearden, Mrs Alison Lowe, Mr Nigel John Turner, Mr Richard Balfe
Income: £2,110,360 [2017]; £2,194,741 [2016]; £2,276,362 [2015]; £1,715,639 [2014]; £1,773,876 [2013]

Leeds Diocesan Board of Finance
Registered: 20 Feb 2014 *Employees:* 97 *Volunteers:* 30
Tel: 0113 353 0272 *Website:* leeds.anglican.org
Activities: Education, training; religious activities; other charitable purposes
Address: 17-19 York Place, Leeds, LS1 2EX
Trustees: The Very Reverend John Richard Dobson, Mrs Ann Dorothea Nicholl, Rt Revd Dr Jonathan Robert Gibbs, Mr Andrew Alexander Maude, Major Geoffrey Berry, The Rt Revd Dr Toby Howarth, Mrs Kay Elizabeth Brown, Revd Canon Simon Charles Cowling, Mrs Anita Jane Wardman, The Rt Revd Dr Helen-Ann MacLeod Hartley, Simon Baldwin, The Rt Revd Nicholas Baines, Rt Revd Anthony Robinson, Rt Revd Paul Slater, Revd Canon Anthony Stuart Macpherson, Mrs Marilyn Banister, Rev Nigel Christopher James Wright, The Ven Dr Anne Frances Dawtry, Mrs Jane Catherine Evans
Income: £24,445,771 [2016]; £22,621,000 [2015]; £15,636,000 [2014]

Leeds Diocesan Trust
Registered: 12 Sep 1966 *Employees:* 152
Tel: 0113 261 8023 *Website:* dioceseofleeds.org.uk
Activities: Religious activities
Address: Diocese of Leeds Pastoral Centre, Hinsley Hall, 62 Headingley Lane, Leeds, LS6 2BX
Trustees: Diocese of Leeds Trustee
Income: £11,183,000 [2017]; £11,378,000 [2016]; £10,832,000 [2015]; £11,086,000 [2014]; £9,491,000 [2013]

Leeds Grand Theatre and Opera House Limited
Registered: 1 Jul 1970 *Employees:* 211 *Volunteers:* 93
Tel: 0113 297 7013 *Website:* leedsgrandtheatre.com
Activities: General charitable purposes; education, training; arts, culture, heritage, science; environment, conservation, heritage
Address: Julie Wainwright, Leeds Grand Theatre & Opera House, 46 New Briggate, Leeds, LS1 6NU
Trustees: Lucinda Yeadon, Mr Paul Andrew Scholey, Mr Neil Clephan, Dr Fiona Spiers, Mr Kris Brewster, Bob Gettings, Mr Gerald Thomas Harper, Cllr Peter Harrand, Mr Alan Trevor Gay
Income: £12,707,508 [2017]; £10,690,566 [2016]; £14,229,859 [2015]; £10,651,115 [2014]; £14,187,691 [2013]

The Leeds Groundwork Trust
Registered: 6 Nov 1986 *Employees:* 34 *Volunteers:* 30
Tel: 07545 926695 *Website:* groundwork.org.uk
Activities: Education, training; environment, conservation, heritage; economic, community development, employment
Address: Environment & Business Centre, Merlyn-Rees Avenue, Morley, Leeds, LS27 9SL
Trustees: Mr Geoffrey Driver, Councillor Gerald Wilkinson, Susan Bentley, Councillor Pauleen Grahame, Mr Trevor Lincoln, Ms Laura Strickland, Mr Stuart Kemp Baker, Mrs Ann Blackburn, Councillor Jane Dowson, Mr Nicholas Burr, Ms Rowena Hall
Income: £1,506,248 [2017]; £1,374,307 [2016]; £1,491,296 [2015]; £1,717,222 [2014]; £2,167,944 [2013]

Leeds Jewish Welfare Board
Registered: 4 Oct 1994 *Employees:* 148 *Volunteers:* 221
Tel: 0113 268 4211 *Website:* ljwb.co.uk
Activities: General charitable purposes; disability; prevention or relief of poverty; recreation
Address: 311 Stonegate Road, Leeds, LS17 6AZ
Trustees: Mr Russell John Manning, Mrs Nicola Ross, Matthew Lewis, Ms Helen Lewis, Mr Michael Sandpearl, Mr Jonathan Straight, Ms Joanne Mornin, Dr Victor Jeffrey Leslie
Income: £3,634,818 [2017]; £3,537,699 [2016]; £3,483,840 [2015]; £3,561,109 [2014]; £3,364,356 [2013]

Leeds Mencap
Registered: 29 Apr 2002 *Employees:* 72 *Volunteers:* 25
Tel: 0113 235 1331 *Website:* leedsmencap.org.uk
Activities: General charitable purposes; education, training; advancement of health or saving of lives; disability; accommodation, housing
Address: 20 Vinery Terrace, East End Park, Leeds, LS9 9LU
Trustees: Mr Martin Staniforth, Miss Danielle Brearley, Ms Emma Farrar, Mrs Ruth Hardill, Mr Chris Wilson, Sarah Louise Dobson, Mrs Alison Vanderwert, Mr Tom Metcalfe
Income: £1,228,969 [2017]; £2,571,138 [2016]; £867,770 [2015]; £675,844 [2014]; £665,300 [2013]

Leeds Mind
Registered: 29 Jan 1992 *Employees:* 89 *Volunteers:* 175
Tel: 0113 305 5800 *Website:* leedsmind.org.uk
Activities: Education, training; advancement of health or saving of lives; disability; prevention or relief of poverty; accommodation, housing; arts, culture, heritage, science; amateur sport; environment, conservation, heritage; economic, community development, employment; human rights, religious or racial harmony, equality or diversity; recreation; other charitable purposes
Address: Mind, 11 Clarence Road, Horsforth, Leeds, LS18 4LB
Trustees: Ms Bev Harrison, Mr Satvinder Mann, Mr David Gee, Ms Sarah Bronsdon, Ms Rebecca Hanson, Mr Paul Cunningham, Mrs Linda Grant, Mr Andy Graham, Mr Edward Bellamy
Income: £3,164,977 [2017]; £2,606,558 [2016]; £2,142,480 [2015]; £1,778,398 [2014]; £1,562,166 [2013]

Leeds Theatre Trust Limited
Registered: 26 Mar 1968 *Employees:* 176 *Volunteers:* 120
Website: wyp.org.uk
Activities: Education, training; arts, culture, heritage, science
Address: West Yorkshire Playhouse, Playhouse Square, Leeds, LS2 7UP
Trustees: Mr Kevin Harry Emsley LLB, Councillor Chris Townsley, Sir Rodney Brooke, Ms Claire Lowson, Mr Kenneth Reid, Mike Ellis, Mr Neil Adleman, Miss Sarah Friskney, Mr Alan Dix, Cllr Keith Wakefield, Sharon Watson, David Jones, Mr Simon Walker, Ali Rashid, Miss Susan Pitter, Michael Nabarro
Income: £8,762,746 [2017]; £9,106,484 [2016]; £7,656,132 [2015]; £7,329,514 [2014]; £5,751,889 [2013]

Leeds Trinity University
Registered: 17 Jul 2007 *Employees:* 427 *Volunteers:* 100
Tel: 0113 467 3940 *Website:* leedstrinity.ac.uk
Activities: Education, training
Address: Leeds Trinity University, Brownberrie Lane, Horsforth, Leeds, LS18 5HD
Trustees: Mr Paul Rogerson, Mr James Poskitt, Mr Ian Burrell, Mr Andy Gilliland, Mrs Justine Andrew, Mr Aidan Grills, Rt Rev Marcus Stock, Ms Liz Richards, Mr Charles Isherwood, Ms Roohi Collins, John Taylor, Ms Carolyn Lord, Professor Vivien Jones, Professor Margaret House, Mr Richard Marchant, Mrs Susan Rix, Mr Andrew Micklethwaite, Mr David Haslam, Mr Mark Brockbank
Income: £32,657,987 [2017]; £30,967,469 [2016]; £28,162,430 [2015]; £25,766,611 [2014]; £23,645,127 [2013]

Leeds University Union
Registered: 6 Jul 2010 *Employees:* 475 *Volunteers:* 2,000
Website: leedsuniversityunion.org.uk
Activities: Education, training
Address: Leeds University Union, P O Box 157, Leeds, LS1 1UH
Trustees: Mr Colin Ions, Mr Asad Ali, Mr Jack Rhys Palmer, Miss Natasha Mutch-Vidal, Miss Chloe Sparks, Mr Zaki Kaf Al-Ghazal, Mr Roland Maposa, Mr Andrew Digwood, Mr Richard Grindrod, Miss Sarah Fenton, Miss Jessica Bassett, Ms George Bissett, Miss Eyong Ebot-Arrey
Income: £10,607,354 [2017]; £10,116,849 [2016]; £10,304,622 [2015]; £10,390,845 [2014]; £10,093,737 [2013]

Leeds Women's Aid
Registered: 12 Nov 1991 *Employees:* 17 *Volunteers:* 5
Tel: 0113 246 0401 *Website:* leedswomensaid.org.uk
Activities: General charitable purposes; prevention or relief of poverty; accommodation, housing
Address: P O Box 826, Leeds, LS1 9PL
Trustees: Ms Anne-Marie Norman, Ms Marcia Clarke, Mrs Judith Mcara, Ms Nneka Ikeogu, Miss Suzie Bogle, Ms Tahira Rahman, Mrs Helen Womersley Doolan, Mrs Lorrain Whewell
Income: £1,242,640 [2017]; £1,090,758 [2016]; £905,962 [2015]; £869,585 [2014]; £811,998 [2013]

Leehurst Swan Limited
Registered: 4 Nov 1988 *Employees:* 46
Tel: 01722 424123 *Website:* leehurstswan.org.uk
Activities: Education, training
Address: 45 Windsor Road, Durrington, Salisbury, Wilts, SP4 8HG
Trustees: Mr Richard Thorp, Mrs Victoria Zissis, Mr Stephen James Spicer, Mr Ian McDonald, Mr Douglas James Gale, Mr Jonathan Paul Wansey, Guygu Riley, Mrs Penny Anne Joyce
Income: £2,797,794 [2016]; £2,646,523 [2015]; £2,819,854 [2014]; £2,956,779 [2013]; £2,851,987 [2012]

Leeway Domestic Violence and Abuse Services
Registered: 2 Feb 2000 *Employees:* 61 *Volunteers:* 30
Tel: 01603 623803 *Website:* leewaysupport.org
Activities: Accommodation, housing
Address: Leeway Womens Aid, P O Box Leeway, City Hall, St Peters Street, Norwich, NR2 1NH
Trustees: Mr Stephen Bernard Burke, Ms Anne Faulkner, Ms Emma Clare Corlett, Sarah Gibb, Ms Anne Elizabeth Brighton, Ms Joanne Kay Hollows, Mrs Karen Nethercott, Mrs Judy Leggett, Ms Vanessa Morton, Jane Jiggins, Francesca Easter, Miss Darryl Smith, Mr Matthew James Cotton, Miss Simone Elizabeth Dewell
Income: £1,619,222 [2017]; £1,196,992 [2016]; £1,069,683 [2015]; £1,355,504 [2014]; £1,466,042 [2013]

Legacy Leisure Limited
Registered: 12 Jun 2013 *Employees:* 1,981 *Volunteers:* 2
Tel: 07904 316633 *Website:* legacyleisure.co.uk
Activities: Amateur sport; recreation
Address: Legacy Leisure Limited, Attwood House, Perdiswell Park, Worcester, WR3 7NW
Trustees: Miss Eva Holmes, Mr Martin Neil Johnson, Miss Janette Mary Wood
Income: £30,219,843 [2016]; £21,853,046 [2015]; £4,382,919 [2014]; £1,841,807 [2013]

The Legal Education Foundation
Registered: 24 May 1976 *Employees:* 12
Tel: 020 3005 5692 *Website:* thelegaleducationfoundation.org
Activities: Education, training
Address: Suite 2, Ground Floor, River House, Broadford Park, Shalford, Guildford, Surrey, GU4 8EP
Trustees: Ms Jane Reeves, Mr Edward Nally, Mr Guy Beringer QC, Mr Jonathan Freeman, Mr Timothy Dutton QC, Mr Rupert Baron, Mr Mark Harding, Professor David Armstrong, Mr Roger Finbow, Ms Sally James, Ms Ailsa Beaton
Income: £3,969,000 [2017]; £3,849,000 [2016]; £3,782,000 [2015]; £1,591,000 [2014]; £149,412,000 [2013]

Legatum Institute Foundation
Registered: 8 Mar 2011 *Employees:* 31
Tel: 020 7148 5400 *Website:* li.com
Activities: Education, training; economic, community development, employment
Address: 11 Charles Street, Mayfair, London, W1J 5DW
Trustees: Mr Toby Baxendale, Mr Alan McCormick BA, Jane Marie Siebels, Mr Richard Briance, Mr Robert Vickers, Baroness Philippa Stroud
Income: £4,398,079 [2016]; £4,272,670 [2015]; £2,878,420 [2014]; £2,500 [2013]; £35,053 [2012]

Leicester Arts Centre Limited
Registered: 3 Feb 1989 *Employees:* 40 *Volunteers:* 10
Website: phoenix.org.uk
Activities: Education, training; advancement of health or saving of lives; arts, culture, heritage, science; economic, community development, employment; recreation
Address: Phoenix, Phoenix Square, 4 Midland Street, Leicester, LE1 1TG
Trustees: Ali Sinclair, Mr Azam Mamujee, Mr Kevin Lacey, Mrs Ruth Coalson, Mr Colin Geoffrey Sharpe, Mr Bennedict Carpenter, Bill Shelton, Mr Alan Tuckett, Suzanne Overton-Edwards, Mr Bill Haley, Mrs Lisa Jones, Prof Nigel Wright
Income: £2,024,149 [2017]; £2,066,720 [2016]; £2,085,200 [2015]; £1,471,632 [2014]; £1,234,049 [2013]

Leicester Cathedral Charitable Trust
Registered: 22 Jul 2013
Tel: 0116 261 5326 *Website:* leicester.anglican.org
Activities: Education, training; religious activities; arts, culture, heritage, science; environment, conservation, heritage
Address: St Martin's House, 7 Peacock Lane, Leicester, LE1 5PX
Trustees: Mrs Janet Cicely Arthur, Very Reverend David Robert Malvern Monteith, Mr Jonathan William Kerry
Income: £1,086,877 [2017]; £611,916 [2016]; £1,070,668 [2015]; £984,015 [2014]

Leicester Charity Organisation Society
Registered: 18 Nov 1999 *Employees:* 13 *Volunteers:* 30
Tel: 0116 222 2200 *Website:* charity-link.org
Activities: The prevention or relief of poverty
Address: 20A Millstone Lane, Leicester, LE1 5JN
Trustees: Mr Rod Hudson, Mr Anthony Henry Jarvis FCA, Ms Cheryl Pharoah, Professor Surinder Mohan Sharna DL, Clive Smith, Mr Christopher Thomas Saul, Mr Craig Ewan Shevas
Income: £1,064,709 [2017]; £1,269,026 [2016]; £1,468,215 [2015]; £1,253,764 [2014]; £753,593 [2013]

Leicester City Football Club Trust Limited
Registered: 31 Oct 2008 *Employees:* 21 *Volunteers:* 138
Website: lcfc.co.uk
Activities: General charitable purposes; education, training; advancement of health or saving of lives; disability; prevention or relief of poverty; amateur sport; economic, community development, employment; human rights, religious or racial harmony, equality or diversity; recreation
Address: Leicester City Football Club PLC, The King Power Stadium, Filbert Way, Leicester, LE2 7FL
Trustees: Mr John Andrew Folwell, Ms Susan Whelan, Mr John Byrne, Mr Arvind Michael Kapur, Mr Jonathan Robert Rudkin, Mr Andrew Beddow
Income: £1,038,613 [2017]; £693,410 [2016]; £876,474 [2015]; £450,864 [2014]; £450,864 [2013]

The Leicester Diocesan Board of Finance
Registered: 18 Oct 1966 *Employees:* 49
Tel: 0116 262 5326 *Website:* leicester.anglican.org
Activities: Accommodation, housing; religious activities
Address: 7 Peacock Lane, Leicester, LE1 5PZ
Trustees: Ven Timothy Richard Stratford, Mr David Beeson, Mr Stephen George Barney, The Reverend John Whittaker, Mrs Sheila Anne Newbury, Rt Revd Martyn James Snow, Mr Christopher John Sheldon, Mr Gary Brown, Mrs Madeleine Wang, Rev Anthony Robert Leighton, Rev Cynthia Margaret Hebden, Mr John Charles Frank Roberson, Rev Stephen Andrew Bailey, Ven Claire Wood, Mr Guy William Newbury, Canon David John Palmet
Income: £9,645,000 [2016]; £14,401,000 [2015]; £8,536,000 [2014]; £9,230,000 [2013]; £8,814,000 [2012]

Leicester Grammar School Trust
Registered: 17 Dec 1980 *Employees:* 237 *Volunteers:* 171
Tel: 0116 259 1900 *Website:* leicestergrammar.org.uk
Activities: Education, training
Address: London Road, Great Glen, Leicester, LE8 9FL
Trustees: Dr Deenesh Khoosal, Mr James Mark Saker, Mr Steven Gasztowicz QC, Mrs Julia Burns, Dr Sarah Margaret Dauncey, Nathan Imlach, Ms Amanda Georgina O'Donovan, Mr Keith John Julian, Michael John Holley Esq, Dr Susan Hadley, Mr Duncan Comrie Green, Mrs Elisabeth Michelle Bailey, Dr Laura Mongan-Cockcroft, The Very Revd David Monteith
Income: £15,157,224 [2017]; £15,189,618 [2016]; £13,770,096 [2015]; £13,402,467 [2014]; £12,840,298 [2013]

Leicester High School Charitable Trust Limited
Registered: 17 Jun 1975 *Employees:* 94
Tel: 0116 270 5338 *Website:* leicesterhigh.co.uk
Activities: Education, training
Address: Leicester High School for Girls, 454 London Road, Leicester, LE2 2PP
Trustees: Mark Dunkley, Mr Tim Leah, Rev Adrian Jones, Mr Jeremy Richard Tomlinson, Mrs Kay Mayes, Mrs Margaret Bowler, Mrs Mary Neilson, Mr John Albert Allen, Mrs Susan Siesage, Mr Michael Joannou
Income: £3,650,817 [2017]; £3,762,875 [2016]; £3,647,090 [2015]; £3,650,670 [2014]; £3,595,547 [2013]

Leicester Hospitals Charity
Registered: 15 Jul 1996 *Employees:* 9 *Volunteers:* 25
Tel: 0116 258 5788 *Website:* leicesterhospitalscharity.org.uk
Activities: General charitable purposes; education, training; advancement of health or saving of lives
Address: Leicester Royal Infirmary NHS Trust, Leicester Royal Infirmary, Infirmary Square, Leicester, LE1 5WW
Trustees: University Hospitals of Leicestershire NHS Trust
Income: £1,802,000 [2017]; £2,191,216 [2016]; £1,823,000 [2015]; £2,424,000 [2014]; £2,120,000 [2013]

Leicester Theatre Trust Limited
Registered: 11 Oct 1963 *Employees:* 98 *Volunteers:* 22
Tel: 0116 242 3591 *Website:* curveonline.co.uk
Activities: Education, training; arts, culture, heritage, science
Address: Curve, 60 Rutland Street, Leicester, LE1 1SB
Trustees: Mr Gautam Bodiwala, Ian Squires, Mr Piara Singh Clair, Mrs Donna Williams, Mike Dalzell, Shobna Gulati, Mrs Vivien Waterfield, Mr Anthony James Clare, Mr Gary Dixon, Mrs Nicola Paula Hurley, Emily Gamble
Income: £11,728,000 [2017]; £10,199,256 [2016]; £7,852,424 [2015]; £5,077,784 [2014]; £7,671,101 [2013]

Leicester YMCA
Registered: 30 Sep 1966 *Employees:* 57 *Volunteers:* 2
Tel: 0116 255 6507 *Website:* leicesterymca.co.uk
Activities: Education, training; accommodation, housing; arts, culture, heritage, science; amateur sport; economic, community development, employment
Address: Paul Brown, 7 East Street, Leicester, LE1 6EY
Trustees: Mr Ian David Pearce, Mr Chris Bolas, Mr Matthew Cooney, Ms Janet Mary Bliss, Ms Sharon Mitchell-Halliday, Ms Kathryn Hamylton, Mr Rob Brannen, Ms Emma Louise Brown, Mr Phil Hawkins, Ms Viv McKee
Income: £2,882,040 [2017]; £2,908,072 [2016]; £2,271,405 [2015]; £2,100,629 [2014]; £2,055,099 [2013]

Leicestershire & Rutland Organisation for The Relief of Suffering Limited
Registered: 30 Mar 1977 *Employees:* 344 *Volunteers:* 1,142
Tel: 0116 231 3771 *Website:* loros.co.uk
Activities: Education, training; advancement of health or saving of lives
Address: Loros Hospice, Groby Road, Leicester, LE3 9QE
Trustees: Mr Andrew Stant, Mr David Lindley, Dr Kathryn Oliver, Mrs Rani Mahal, Mrs Pauline Tagg, Mr Chris Greenwell, Tim Maxted, Mr Richard Louis Brucciani, Mrs Elizabeth Kitchen, Mr Michael Pearson, Mr Priyesh Patel, Dr Robin Graham-Brown, Dr Sian Cheverton, Dr Nik Kotecha
Income: £13,032,903 [2017]; £12,786,948 [2016]; £11,189,023 [2015]; £10,971,838 [2014]; £11,364,332 [2013]

Leicestershire Education Business Company Limited
Registered: 27 Jan 1993 *Employees:* 69
Tel: 0116 240 7000 *Website:* leics-ebc.org.uk
Activities: Education, training; economic, community development, employment
Address: 30 Frog Island, off North Bridge Place, Leicester, LE3 5AG
Trustees: Mr Dennis Raymond Kent, Dr Richard Moody, Mr Francis Lawlor, Mrs Arinder Bhullar, Mr Thomas Henry Nicholls, Mr Mark Esho, Miss Sandhya G Zavery, Mr Philip John Elliott, Mr Mark Colton
Income: £2,172,053 [2017]; £1,761,973 [2016]; £1,481,149 [2015]; £1,797,597 [2014]; £1,417,067 [2013]

Leicestershire Independent Educational Trust
Registered: 20 Oct 1983 *Employees:* 111 *Volunteers:* 2
Tel: 01455 292244 *Website:* dixie.org.uk
Activities: Education, training
Address: The Dixie Grammar School, Market Bosworth, Leics, CV13 0LE
Trustees: Mrs Catherine Emma Ellis, Rebecca Davies, Mr Andrew James Churchill, Mr Ian Andrew Smith, Ms Lisa Pittwood, Mrs Joan Mumby, Ms Jo Fenton Parkes, Dr Charles Kendall, Mr Mark Ashfield, Mr Tim Richardson
Income: £4,811,108 [2016]; £4,393,497 [2015]; £4,538,284 [2014]; £4,280,105 [2013]

Leicestershire and Rutland Wildlife Trust Limited
Registered: 30 Nov 1962 *Employees:* 37 *Volunteers:* 600
Tel: 0116 262 9968 *Website:* lrwt.org.uk
Activities: Environment, conservation, heritage
Address: The Old Mill, 9 Soar Lane, Leicester, LE3 5DE
Trustees: Linda Jones, Dr Anthony Biddle, Mr Andrew Moffat, Mr Andrew Cotton, Mr Peter Williams, Mr Bob Bearne, Mr Anthony Clarke, Ann Tomlinson, Miss Maggie Morland, Mr John Bleby, Mr Stuart Love, Dr Ian Selmes, Dr Ray Morris, Helen Nott
Income: £2,640,009 [2017]; £2,974,239 [2016]; £2,843,286 [2015]; £2,530,460 [2014]; £2,195,629 [2013]

Gerald Leigh Charitable Trust
Registered: 29 May 1974
Tel: 020 7491 4190
Activities: General charitable purposes
Address: 6 Arlington Street, London, SW1A 1RE
Trustees: Mrs Anna Leigh, Mr Robin Leigh
Income: £1,689,546 [2017]; £87,024 [2016]; £87,653 [2015]; £87,605 [2014]; £99,401 [2013]

Leighton Park Trust
Registered: 10 Sep 1962 *Employees:* 296 *Volunteers:* 8
Tel: 0118 987 9600 *Website:* leightonpark.com
Activities: Education, training
Address: Leighton Park School, Shinfield Road, Reading, Berks, RG2 7DE
Trustees: Edwina Mary Ellen Dean-Lewis, David Isherwood, Simon Hollands, Martin Lloyd, Christopher Houston, Mary Phipps, David Hickok, Caroline George, John Crosfield, Simon Clemison, Sally Jayne Bonner, Janet Digby, Bruce Johnson, Helen Johnson, Philip Griffin, Matthew James Winkless
Income: £11,977,794 [2017]; £11,522,181 [2016]; £12,343,145 [2015]; £11,532,684 [2014]; £10,865,351 [2013]

Lempriere Pringle 2015
Registered: 1 May 2015
Tel: 01642 647906
Activities: General charitable purposes
Address: 17 Ilderton Road, Stockton on Tees, Cleveland, TS18 2SR
Trustees: Mr Jonathan Garnier Ruffer, Mr Ashe Windham, Mr Nicholas Timothy Turner, Rev Matthew Hutton, Mrs Jane Ruffer, Ms Harriet Cecilia Ruffer
Income: £16,524,567 [2017]; £63,295,086 [2016]

Lench's Trust
Registered: 10 Feb 2012 *Employees:* 35 *Volunteers:* 1
Tel: 0121 426 0455 *Website:* lenchs-trust.co.uk
Activities: The advancement of health or saving of lives; prevention or relief of poverty; accommodation, housing; other charitable purposes
Address: William Lench Court, 80 Ridgacre Road, Quinton, Birmingham, B32 2AQ
Trustees: Timothy Cuthbertson, Anthony Guest, Sarah Davis, Mr Tim Sewell, Ms Rachel Titley, Mr Richard Sarjeant, Shihab Hossain, Mr Tom Storrow, Ms Ruth Evans
Income: £2,503,272 [2016]; £1,973,724 [2015]; £1,678,762 [2014]; £1,509,572 [2013]; £1,498,151 [2012]

Lepra
Registered: 4 Feb 1963 *Employees:* 591 *Volunteers:* 8
Tel: 01206 216700 *Website:* lepra.org.uk
Activities: Education, training; advancement of health or saving of lives; disability; prevention or relief of poverty; overseas aid, famine relief
Address: Lepra, 28 Middleborough, Colchester, Essex, CO1 1TG
Trustees: Dr Vijay Rukmini Rao, Professor Michael Adler CBE, Ms Anna Anderson, Mrs Nina Amin, Mr Sunil Thapar, Mr Michael McGrath, Mr Dinesh Dhamija, Professor Roderick Hay, Mr Julian Briant, Mr Charles Bland, Professor Diana Lockwood, Mr Sri Sharma, Ms Katie Bigmore
Income: £5,001,352 [2017]; £5,941,504 [2016]; £4,972,842 [2015]; £5,791,448 [2014]; £4,250,650 [2013]

The Leprosy Mission England, Wales, The Channel Islands and The Isle of Man
Registered: 10 Jan 1996 *Employees:* 35 *Volunteers:* 80
Tel: 01733 370505 *Website:* leprosymission.org.uk
Activities: Education, training; advancement of health or saving of lives; disability; prevention or relief of poverty; overseas aid, famine relief; accommodation, housing; religious activities; economic, community development, employment; human rights, religious or racial harmony, equality or diversity
Address: The Leprosy Mission, Goldhay Way, Orton Goldhay, Peterborough, PE2 5GZ
Trustees: Dr Beryl Dennis, Miss Catherine Benbow, Mr Timothy Brooks, Mrs Anne Christine Fendick, Mr Paul Craig, Mrs Diana White, Mr Jean Le Maistre, Mr Ralph Colin Turner, Mr Henry Michael Anstey, Mr Peter Watson, Dr Vanessa Halford, Mr Andrew Lancaster
Income: £7,728,234 [2016]; £8,301,758 [2015]; £6,385,609 [2014]; £6,573,211 [2013]; £6,131,425 [2012]

The Leprosy Mission International
Registered: 2 Jul 1999 *Employees:* 30 *Volunteers:* 1
Tel: 020 8326 6733 *Website:* leprosymission.org
Activities: Education, training; advancement of health or saving of lives; disability; prevention or relief of poverty; overseas aid, famine relief; accommodation, housing; economic, community development; employment
Address: The Leprosy Mission International, 80 Windmill Road, Brentford, Middlesex, TW8 0QH
Trustees: Mr Philip Putman, Dr Nalini Abraham, Mr Kenneth Martin, Pamela Packett, Mr Eric Chollet, Mr Colin Osborne, Rev Ashok Adhikari, Paul Emans, Shem Nuhu, Mrs Anne Ratliff
Income: £13,836,520 [2016]; £14,269,357 [2015]; £13,680,850 [2014]; £14,072,849 [2013]; £12,928,069 [2012]

The Leri Charitable Trust
Registered: 15 Apr 1999
Tel: 020 7691 4048
Activities: General charitable purposes; education, training; advancement of health or saving of lives; prevention or relief of poverty; overseas aid, famine relief; human rights, religious or racial harmony, equality or diversity
Address: Edwin Coe LLP, 2 Stone Buildings, London, WC2A 3TH
Trustees: Mr Leon Rosselson, Mrs Alison Lesley Caroline Broadberry, Mr Geoffrey Justin Hellings, Mrs Rina Rosselson, Ms Ruth Rosselson
Income: £16,101,467 [2017]; £597,447 [2016]; £106,560 [2015]; £728,112 [2014]; £726,857 [2013]

Lessons for Life Foundation
Registered: 15 Jan 2008 *Employees:* 12
Tel: 020 8483 6309 *Website:* lessonsforlifefoundation.org
Activities: Education, training; prevention or relief of poverty
Address: Griffin House, 161 Hammersmith Road, London, W6 8BS
Trustees: Mr Jeremy Evans, Mr Andrea Salvato, Mr Manuel Kohnstamm, Ms Suzanne Schoettger, Gary Heffernan, Mr James Sean Ryan, Mr Eric John Tveter, Mr John Clinton Porter, Marcel Van Den Berg
Income: £3,202,994 [2016]; £2,890,178 [2015]; £2,501,796 [2014]; £2,253,420 [2013]; £1,985,277 [2012]

The Leukaemia Care Society
Registered: 11 Sep 1969 *Employees:* 17 *Volunteers:* 44
Tel: 01905 755977 *Website:* leukaemiacare.org.uk
Activities: The advancement of health or saving of lives
Address: Leukaemia Care, One Birch Court, Blackpole East, Worcester, WR3 8SG
Trustees: Mr Christopher Matthews-Maxwell, Mr Douglas Moseley, Kris Griffin, Mr Albert Podesta, Mrs Wendy Davies, Manos Nikolousis
Income: £1,091,213 [2017]; £1,243,354 [2016]; £804,294 [2015]; £899,145 [2014]; £894,027 [2013]

Leverhulme Trade Charities Trust
Registered: 12 Nov 2014
Tel: 020 7042 9881 *Website:* leverhulme-trade.org.uk
Activities: General charitable purposes; education, training; prevention or relief of poverty
Address: The Leverhulme Trust, 1 Pemberton Row, London, EC4A 3BG
Trustees: Mr Niall Fitzgerald KBE, Mr Steve Williams, Professor Keith Gull, Mr Rudy Markham, Mr Doug Baillie, Ms Leena Nair, Mr Patrick J-P Cescau, Mr Paul Polman, Mr Clive Butler, Mr Christopher Saul, Amanda Sourry
Income: £2,850,000 [2017]; £2,468,000 [2016]; £2,111,000 [2015]

The Leverhulme Trust
Registered: 11 Nov 2014 *Employees:* 14
Tel: 020 7042 9881 *Website:* leverhulme.ac.uk
Activities: General charitable purposes; education, training
Address: The Leverhulme Trust, 1 Pemberton Row, London, EC4A 3BG
Trustees: Mr Niall Fitzgerald KBE, Mr Steve Williams, Keith Gull, Mr Rudy Markham, Mr Doug Baillie, Ms Leena Nair, Mr Patrick J-P Cescau, Mr Paul Polman, Mr Clive Butler, Mr Christopher Saul, Amanda Sourry
Income: £99,383,000 [2017]; £86,707,000 [2016]; £74,131,000 [2015]

Lewes Community Screen
Registered: 8 Feb 2013 *Employees:* 1
Tel: 01273 470620 *Website:* lewesdepot.org.uk
Activities: Education, training; arts, culture, heritage, science
Address: 18 Keere Street, Lewes, E Sussex, BN7 1TY
Trustees: Ms Sarah Frances Hunter, Mr John Letheren Kenward, Ms Jennifer Margaret Sibree Leeburn, Mr Robert Norman Senior, Mr Martin Charles Kay
Income: £1,802,978 [2017]; £2,528,165 [2016]; £2,500,000 [2015]; £2,918,765 [2014]

Lewes Old Grammar School Trust
Registered: 9 Sep 2015 *Employees:* 126
Tel: 01273 472634 *Website:* logs.uk.com
Activities: Education, training
Address: Lewes Old Grammar School, 140 High Street, Lewes, E Sussex, BN7 1XS
Trustees: Mr Michael Pierre Chartier, Mr Stephen Andrew Ogden, Mrs Janine Brooks, Mr Joseph Light, Mrs Rebecca Swindells, Mrs Frances Jane O'Halloran, Mr Alistair Harvey, Mr William Telford, Dr Cathy Watts, Mrs Amanda Clarke
Income: £6,573,517 [2017]; £9,709,579 [2016]

Leweston School Trust
Registered: 17 Sep 1986 *Employees:* 131
Website: leweston.co.uk
Activities: Education, training; religious activities
Address: Leweston School, Sherborne, Dorset, DT9 6EN
Trustees: Dr Nicholas Bathurst, Mr Christopher Fenton, Fr Richard Meyer, Mr Hugh Tatham, Ms Caroline Gill, Mr Charles Comyn, Mrs Sarah Gordon Wild, Lieutenant Colonel Ian Stanton JP, Mr Jim Massey
Income: £5,339,140 [2017]; £5,723,128 [2016]; £5,460,832 [2015]; £5,395,708 [2014]; £5,462,366 [2013]

The David Lewis Centre
Registered: 19 Sep 1990 *Employees:* 955
Tel: 01565 640000 *Website:* davidlewis.org.uk
Activities: Education, training; advancement of health or saving of lives; disability; accommodation, housing
Address: 55 Barnfield, Urmston, Manchester, M41 9EW
Trustees: Timothy Mann, Mr Geoff Loughlin, Mr Alastair Milne Imrie, Ms Marie Shahin, Mr Darren Karl Cornwall, Mrs Linda Feerick, Mr George Devlin, Ms Marie Elizabeth McLaughlin, Mr Stephen Devlin, Mrs Roisin Beressi, Mr Alistair Hollows
Income: £26,389,000 [2017]; £26,195,000 [2016]; £25,584,000 [2015]; £36,303,000 [2014]; £25,689,000 [2013]

Bernard Lewis Family Charitable Trust
Registered: 17 Jul 2008
Activities: General charitable purposes; education, training
Address: c/o The Giving Department, Sky Light City Tower, 50 Basinghall Street, London, EC2V 5DE
Trustees: Mr Clive Lewis, Mrs Caroline Jane Grainge, Mr Bernard Lewis, Mr Leonard Richard Lewis
Income: £3,357,337 [2016]; £2,064,180 [2015]; £1,562,604 [2014]; £1,583,920 [2013]; £1,583,127 [2012]

David & Ruth Lewis Family Charitable Trust
Registered: 24 Nov 1969
Tel: 020 8991 4502
Activities: General charitable purposes; education, training; advancement of health or saving of lives; disability; prevention or relief of poverty; overseas aid, famine relief; religious activities; animals; economic, community development, employment; other charitable purposes
Address: Chelsea House, West Gate, Ealing, London, W5 1DR
Trustees: Mr Julian Lewis, Mr Benjamin Lewis, Ms Rachel Lewis, Ms Deborah Lewis, Mr Simon Lewis
Income: £3,591,714 [2017]; £2,271,148 [2016]; £1,739,723 [2015]; £1,764,162 [2014]; £1,658,494 [2013]

Samuel Lewis Foundation
Registered: 6 May 1962
Website: shgroup.org.uk
Activities: Accommodation, housing
Address: Southern Housing Group, Fleet House, 59-61 Clerkenwell Road, London, EC1M 5LA
Trustees: Southern Housing Group Ltd
Income: £1,780,000 [2017]; £1,780,000 [2016]; £1,711,000 [2015]; £1,610,000 [2014]; £1,544,000 [2013]

The Lewis-Manning Trust
Registered: 23 Jul 2007 *Employees:* 60 *Volunteers:* 250
Tel: 01202 708470 *Website:* lewis-manning.co.uk
Activities: The advancement of health or saving of lives
Address: Lewis Manning Trust, 1 Crichel Mount Road, Lilliput, Poole, Dorset, BH14 8LT
Trustees: Mr Anthony Charles Roberts, Mr Steven Harris, Mr Geoffery Harold Walker, Mr Paul Crompton, Rev Elizabeth Jane Lloyd, Mr Jeremy Allin
Income: £2,297,670 [2017]; £3,563,395 [2016]; £1,922,348 [2015]; £1,684,257 [2014]; £2,474,624 [2013]

Lewisham Citizens Advice Bureaux Service Limited
Registered: 9 Apr 1999 *Employees:* 19 *Volunteers:* 66
Tel: 020 3893 4685 *Website:* citizensadvice.org.uk
Activities: General charitable purposes; education, training; advancement of health or saving of lives; prevention or relief of poverty; economic, community development, employment
Address: Lewisham Citizens Advice Bureau Service, Leemore Community Hub, Bonfield Road, Lewisham, London, SE13 5EU
Trustees: Mr Mark David Simons, Mr James Joseph Banks, Ms Barbara Limon, Ms Erika Moisl, Pamela Grieve Angell, Nigel Prout, Mr Iain McDiarmid, Ms Verena Hefti, Mr John Wray, Sophie Park
Income: £1,032,959 [2017]; £1,084,634 [2016]; £1,260,122 [2015]; £1,194,754 [2014]; £1,055,120 [2013]

Lewisham Nexus Service
Registered: 16 Mar 1994 *Employees:* 109
Tel: 020 8613 9965 *Website:* nexussupportservices.org
Activities: Disability
Address: 84-86 Rushey Green, London, SE6 4HW
Trustees: Mr Alastair William Mossman, Mr Paul Norman-Brown, Ms Susan Storrar, Mr Jonathan Richard Dutton, Mr Kay Mafuba
Income: £2,225,723 [2017]; £2,048,945 [2016]; £2,074,808 [2015]; £2,151,763 [2014]; £2,116,240 [2013]

The Leys and St Faith's Schools Foundation
Registered: 28 Sep 2011 *Employees:* 395 *Volunteers:* 50
Tel: 01223 508900 *Website:* theleys.net,www.stfaiths.co.uk
Activities: Education, training
Address: The Leys School, Fen Causeway, Cambridge, CB2 7AD
Trustees: Mr Peter Lacey, Mr David Unwin, Mr Stephen Michael Peak, Rev Julian Pursehouse, Mr Martin Beazor, Mr Mark Elliott, Mr Timothy Moore, Mr Rick Willmott, Mrs Judith Helen Elizabeth Bell, Mrs Elizabeth Anne Hooley, Mrs Wendy Nelson-Challen, Mrs Julia Louise Clarke, Ms Helena Margaret Renfrew-Knight, Mrs Stephanie Loft, Mrs Annabel Brunner, Mr Charles Kidman, Rev Thomas Oliver Buchanan, Rev Alison Elizabeth Walker, Mr Anthony Brenton, Mr Charles Hewitson, Mr Roger Webster, Dr Robin Walker, Mrs Patricia Mary Graves, Mr David Humphreys, Mr Christopher Ian Kirker, Mr Martin Brown, Mr Richard Mitchell, Mr Alexander Barrett
Income: £24,609,521 [2017]; £23,976,507 [2016]; £22,995,892 [2015]; £21,298,629 [2014]; £20,814,480 [2013]

Lhasa Limited
Registered: 18 Jan 1985 *Employees:* 123
Tel: 0113 394 6069 *Website:* lhasalimited.org
Activities: Education, training; advancement of health or saving of lives; animals; economic, community development, employment
Address: 2 Canal Wharf, Holbeck, Leeds, LS11 5PS
Trustees: Professor Valerie Jane Gillet, Dr Deborah Marion Richardson, Mr David Hollins, Mr Andrew Thomas Bowie, Dr Krista Dobo, Dr Richard John Brennan, Dr William Edward Lindup, Dr Susanne Glowienke, Ms Samantha Clark, Dr Camilla Kay Alexander-White, Dr James Harvey
Income: £8,376,000 [2016]; £7,501,000 [2015]; £6,496,378 [2014]; £6,397,320 [2013]; £5,561,467 [2012]

The Liberal Jewish Synagogue
Registered: 20 Nov 2014 *Employees:* 63 *Volunteers:* 100
Tel: 020 7286 5181 *Website:* ljs.org
Activities: Religious activities; human rights, religious or racial harmony, equality or diversity
Address: The Liberal Jewish Synagogue, 28 St Johns Wood Road, St Johns Wood, London, NW8 7HA
Trustees: Mrs Barbara Fidler, Mr Anthony Sefton, Mr Peter Frederick Loble, Josie Lane, Mr Steve Penn, Mr Steven Behr, Chris Godbold, Mr David Murray Davidson, Susan Head, Mr Bryan Clive Diamond, Ms Karen Newman, Mr Russell Delew, Mrs Isobel Davies-Benjamin, Sylvia Churba, Mrs Alexandra Weiss
Income: £1,605,438 [2016]; £8,409,580 [2015]

Liberal Judaism (ULPS)
Registered: 5 Mar 2013 *Employees:* 14 *Volunteers:* 80
Tel: 020 7631 9835 *Website:* liberaljudaism.org
Activities: Religious activities; human rights, religious or racial harmony, equality or diversity
Address: Liberal Judaism, The Montagu Centre, 21 Maple Street, London, W1T 4BE
Trustees: Amanda McFeeters, Jackie Richards, Mr Ed Herman, Ms Tamara Schmidt, Mr Robin Moss, Mrs Rosalind Clayton, Mr David Hockman, Simon Benscher, Ms Rosie Ward, Ms Amelia Viney, Graham Carpenter
Income: £1,607,296 [2016]; £1,615,183 [2015]; £1,600,162 [2014]; £1,490,263 [2013]

The Library and Museum Charitable Trust of The United Grand Lodge
Registered: 7 Oct 1996 *Employees:* 17
Tel: 020 7395 9257 *Website:* freemasonry.london.museum
Activities: Education, training; arts, culture, heritage, science; environment, conservation, heritage
Address: Library and Museum of Freemasonry, Freemasons Hall, 60 Great Queen Street, London, WC2B 5AZ
Trustees: Mr Geoffrey Bond, Mr Colin Frank Harris, Mr Robert Christopher Vaughan, Mr Anthony Charles Wilson, Mr Keith Ramsey Smith, Mr Stephen Richard Nigel Fenton, Dr Richard Andrew Berman, Mr Peter Geoffrey Lowndes, Mr Russell John Race, Mrs Philippa Jane Glanville, Mr Jeremy Michael Jayne Havard, Mr George Pipon Francis, Mr James Martin Long
Income: £1,883,892 [2017]; £1,682,342 [2016]; £1,617,590 [2015]; £1,745,816 [2014]; £1,677,155 [2013]

Libury Hall
Registered: 1 Jul 2013 *Employees:* 40 *Volunteers:* 1
Tel: 01920 438722
Activities: The advancement of health or saving of lives; disability; accommodation, housing
Address: Libury Hall, Great Munden, Ware, Herts, SG11 1JD
Trustees: Barry Bennett, Ms Marianne Marie Paule Mead, Brian Sykes
Income: £1,236,594 [2017]; £1,218,801 [2016]; £1,279,696 [2015]; £4,129,975 [2014]

The Licensed Trade Charity
Registered: 26 Feb 1964 *Employees:* 382 *Volunteers:* 48
Tel: 01344 884440 *Website:* licensedtradecharity.org.uk
Activities: General charitable purposes; education, training; advancement of health or saving of lives; disability; prevention or relief of poverty; accommodation, housing
Address: Heatherley, London Road, Ascot, Berks, SL5 8DR
Trustees: Mrs Anita Adams, Mr Jeff Booth, Mr Ian Inder, Mr William Boulter, Mr Peter Raynsford, Mr Jeremy Phillips, Mrs Tracy Bird, Michael Hill, Mrs A King, Mr Anthony Mears, Mrs Pauline Ross, Mr Patrick Duddy, Mr Paul Wigham, Mr Toby Brett, Mr Gerry Cleary
Income: £26,289,950 [2016]; £21,964,943 [2015]; £20,055,563 [2014]; £18,703,302 [2013]; £17,785,399 [2012]

Lichfield Cathedral School
Registered: 13 Aug 2010 *Employees:* 84 *Volunteers:* 6
Tel: 01543 306172 *Website:* lichfieldcathedralschool.com
Activities: Education, training; religious activities
Address: Lichfield Cathedral School, The Palace, The Close, Lichfield, Staffs, WS13 7LH
Trustees: Mrs Jennifer Mason, Diocesan Director of Education, Clive Rickart, Mrs Claire Tonks, Mrs Nicola Roy, Rev Andrew Michael Stead, The Very Rev Adrian Dorber, Mrs Kate Abbott, Ms Nina Dawes, Rev Pat Hawkins, Mr Robert Oakley
Income: £4,571,102 [2017]; £4,324,832 [2016]; £4,347,155 [2015]; £4,505,466 [2014]; £4,498,914 [2013]

The Lichfield Diocesan Board of Education
Registered: 1 Jan 1961 *Employees:* 13
Tel: 01543 306054 *Website:* lichfield.anglican.org
Activities: Education, training; religious activities
Address: St Marys House, The Close, Lichfield, Staffs, WS13 7LD
Trustees: Archdeacon of Stoke-Upon- Trent, The Revd Preb Michael Ralph Metcalf, Mr David John Morgan, Mr Michael Revell, Rev Alison Mary Morris, Mr David Swift, Rev Simon Alexander Douglas, Mrs Helen Frances Sinclair McKay, Mr Cyril George Randles, Rev John William Allan, Rt Rev Mark Rylands, Mr Robert John Heath, Miss Margaret Anne Everett
Income: £1,241,000 [2016]; £5,331,000 [2015]; £13,848,000 [2014]; £19,828,000 [2013]; £1,310,000 [2012]

The Lichfield Diocesan Board of Finance (Incorporated)
Registered: 27 Jan 2005 *Employees:* 100 *Volunteers:* 12
Tel: 01543 306030 *Website:* lichfield.anglican.org
Activities: Religious activities
Address: The Diocesan Secretary, St Marys House, The Close, Lichfield, Staffs, WS13 7LD
Trustees: Ven Matthew John Parker, Mrs Josephine Locke, The Rt Revd Michael Ipgrave, The Rt Rev Mark James Rylands, Rt Revd Clive Malcolm Gregory, Mr David Beswick, Mr Cyril George Randles, Rev John William Allan, Mr David Litchfield, The Ven Paul Thomas, Mrs Penelope Allen, Ven Simon Nicholas Hartland Baker, The Venerable Dr Susan Weller, Rev Julia Cody, Rev Canon Patricia Hawkins, The Very Rev Adrian Dorber, Mr William Charles Nicholls, Mr John Guthrie Clark, Mr Tug Wilson, Rt Revd Geoff Annas, Rev Martin Rutter, Mr Christopher Gill, Rev Philip John Cansdale, Lilas Rawling, Mr John Thomas Naylor, Mr Andrew Paul Charles, Alison Primrose, Mr Paul Graetz, Rev Preb Benjamin Whitmore
Income: £18,873,000 [2016]; £18,418,000 [2015]; £18,459,000 [2014]; £17,988,000 [2013]; £17,040,000 [2012]

Lichfield Garrick Theatre
Registered: 14 Jun 2012 *Employees:* 63 *Volunteers:* 44
Tel: 01543 412125 *Website:* lichfieldgarrick.com
Activities: Education, training; arts, culture, heritage, science
Address: The Lichfield Garrick Theatre, Castle Dyke, Lichfield, Staffs, WS13 6HR
Trustees: Mr Thomas Marshall, Mr James Leavesley, Mrs Deborah Frances Baker, Mr Andrew John Michael Geer, Mr Richard Anthony Barnes, Mr Paul Richards, Mrs Karen Marie Tracey, Mr Daniel Paul Gee
Income: £2,421,791 [2017]; £2,173,923 [2016]; £2,247,327 [2015]; £2,232,294 [2014]; £1,135,430 [2013]

Life 2009
Registered: 3 Mar 2009 *Employees:* 74 *Volunteers:* 372
Website: lifecharity.org.uk
Activities: General charitable purposes; education, training; advancement of health or saving of lives; prevention or relief of poverty; accommodation, housing
Address: 4 Jephson Court, Leamington Spa, Warwicks, CV31 3RZ
Trustees: Mr Matthew Paul Gibbs, Mr Edward Fawcett, Mrs Laura Jane Higgins, Mr Edward Neville Smith, Ms Charlotte Jane Kynaston, Mrs Eileen Maher, Mr Jonathan William Emlyn Wright, Mrs Annabel Jennifer Therese Osborn, Mr Philip John Campbell, Mr Andrew Thomas Plasom-Scott
Income: £3,086,506 [2017]; £3,568,957 [2016]; £3,558,221 [2015]; £3,498,892 [2014]; £3,382,800 [2013]

Life Church UK
Registered: 7 Mar 1989 *Employees:* 82 *Volunteers:* 825
Tel: 01274 307233 *Website:* lifechurchhome.com
Activities: Education, training; prevention or relief of poverty; religious activities
Address: Wapping Road, Bradford, BD3 0EQ
Trustees: Mr David Lupton, Mr Phil Manchester, Mrs Foluke Oshin, Jonathon Beale, Mr Matthew Walker
Income: £3,480,245 [2016]; £3,399,130 [2015]; £3,324,968 [2014]; £3,719,551 [2013]; £2,608,226 [2012]

Life Leisure Trust
Registered: 6 Nov 2014 *Employees:* 384 *Volunteers:* 211
Tel: 01495 355606 *Website:* aneurinleisure.org.uk
Activities: Education, training; arts, culture, heritage, science; recreation
Address: Regain Building, Mill Lane, Ebbw Vale, Blaenau Gwent, NP23 6GR
Trustees: Mrs Donna Hardman, Mr Lyn James Evans, Mr Wayne Hodgins, Ms Tania Frowen, Ms Claire Beynon, Mr Meirion Morgan, Mrs Sharon Howell, Mr Lee Parsons, Jennifer Ames, Mr Mark Langshaw
Income: £8,560,383 [2017]; £13,589,773 [2016]

Life Opportunities Trust
Registered: 24 Mar 1995 *Employees:* 118
Tel: 01923 299770 *Website:* lot-uk.org.uk
Activities: Disability; accommodation, housing
Address: The Office Suite, 96 The Crescent, Abbots Langley, Herts, WD5 0DS
Trustees: Mr Howard Kent, Mr Philip Mickleborough, Mrs Claire Stanley, Mr Wasim Ahmed, Mr Keith Rudd, Ms Caroline McCaffrey BA DipSW, Ms Edna Petzen
Income: £5,249,968 [2017]; £5,143,519 [2016]; £5,064,363 [2015]; £5,283,932 [2014]; £5,274,014 [2013]

Life Path Trust Limited
Registered: 29 Jul 1992 *Employees:* 269 *Volunteers:* 2
Tel: 024 7665 0530 *Website:* life-path.org.uk
Activities: Disability
Address: 511 Walsgrave Road, Coventry, Warwicks, CV2 4AG
Trustees: Mr John Higgins, Mr Keith Philip Chapman, Mr Phillip James Rusk, Mrs Jennifer Withey, Mrs Judith Ann Ryan, Dr John Herrick, Mr Robert Edward Hall, Mr Edward Lamb, Mr John Stuart Ellis
Income: £6,498,165 [2017]; £5,613,821 [2016]; £5,316,255 [2015]; £5,131,127 [2014]; £4,706,600 [2013]

LifeArc
Registered: 17 Nov 1992 *Employees:* 157
Tel: 020 7391 2777 *Website:* lifearc.org
Activities: The advancement of health or saving of lives
Address: Lynton House, 7-12 Tavistock Square, London, WC1H 9LT
Trustees: Dr Declan Mulkeen, Mrs Aisling Burnand, Dr Annette Doherty OBE BSc FRSC, Dr Sally Sutherland Burtles, Dr Leslie Hughes, Mr Daniel Morgan, Dr John Stageman, Mr Stephen Visscher, Mr Peter Keen, Dr Paul Mussenden, Dr Mike Romanos, Dr Jessica Mann
Income: £128,967,000 [2017]; £29,708,000 [2016]; £25,196,000 [2015]; £25,196,000 [2014]; £24,156,000 [2013]

Lifeline Community Projects
Registered: 22 Jan 2001 *Employees:* 61 *Volunteers:* 3
Tel: 020 8597 2900 *Website:* lifelineprojects.co.uk
Activities: General charitable purposes; education, training; advancement of health or saving of lives; prevention or relief of poverty; economic, community development, employment; human rights, religious or racial harmony, equality or diversity
Address: Lifeline House, 25 Neville Road, Dagenham, Essex, RM8 3QS
Trustees: Mr John William Singleton, Mr Philip Akerman, Miss Avril Martha McIntyre, Mr Neil Jaques
Income: £2,191,288 [2017]; £2,770,431 [2016]; £4,364,097 [2015]; £5,527,774 [2014]; £4,837,230 [2013]

Lifeline Project
Registered: 1 Nov 1984 *Employees:* 1,473 *Volunteers:* 150
Tel: 0161 834 7160 *Website:* lifeline.org.uk
Activities: Education, training; advancement of health or saving of lives
Address: Lifeline Ltd, 101-103 Oldham Street, Manchester, M4 1LW
Trustees: Ms Jocelyn Jean-Pierre, Mr Michael McCarron, Ms Susan Ramprogus, Mr Michael Atkinson, Davy Iredale, Ms Claire Evans, Mr Nigel De Noronha, Ms Michelle Howard
Income: £61,812,600 [2016]; £42,616,462 [2015]; £33,861,874 [2014]; £26,367,128 [2013]

Lifeworks Charity Limited
Registered: 29 Mar 1996 *Employees:* 96 *Volunteers:* 60
Tel: 01803 840744 *Website:* lifeworks-uk.org
Activities: Education, training; disability; accommodation, housing; recreation
Address: Blacklers, Park Road, Dartington Hall, Totnes, Devon, TQ9 6EQ
Trustees: Mr Paul Clarkson, Mr Frank Reed, Mr Michael John Boon, Mr Ian Thompson, Mr John O'Connell, Ms Moira Devlin
Income: £2,333,474 [2017]; £1,887,549 [2016]; £2,067,529 [2015]; £1,712,897 [2013]; £1,623,374 [2012]

The Lighthouse Chapel International
Registered: 28 Jul 2005 *Employees:* 6
Tel: 020 7277 7772
Activities: Religious activities
Address: The Lighthouse Chapel International, 2A Carden Road, London, SE15 3UD
Trustees: Mr Jude Baiden, Mr Edmund Ansa-Ansamoah, Mr Clement Amaning
Income: £1,374,765 [2016]; £674,455 [2015]; £520,598 [2014]; £532,327 [2013]; £458,928 [2012]

Lighthouse Construction Industry Charity
Registered: 25 Oct 2012 *Employees:* 5 *Volunteers:* 200
Tel: 0345 609 1956 *Website:* lighthouseclub.org
Activities: General charitable purposes; education, training; advancement of health or saving of lives; prevention or relief of poverty; economic, community development, employment
Address: 11 Northgate Street, Ipswich, Suffolk, IP1 3BX
Trustees: Mr Cormac MacCrann, Mr Robert Berrigan Smith, Mr Nazir Dewji, Miss Lyndsey Gallagher, Mr Michael McGee, Mr Martin B Roddy, Mr Eward George Naylor, Mr Thomas Fitzpatrick, Miss Ceire O Rourke
Income: £1,540,257 [2016]; £1,467,905 [2015]; £1,125,031 [2014]; £847,236 [2013]

Lighthouse Women's Aid Limited
Registered: 27 Apr 1998 *Employees:* 46 *Volunteers:* 30
Tel: 01473 220770 *Website:* lighthousewa.org.uk
Activities: Accommodation, housing; other charitable purposes
Address: Westgate House, Museum Street, Ipswich, Suffolk, IP1 1HQ
Trustees: Ms Cynthia Glinos, Mrs Judith Rose, Mrs Sandra Gage, Louise Thomas, Miss Rebecca Martin, Ms Sarah Harvey, Ms Catherine Bright, Margaret Parry, Mrs Sallyann Weston-Scales, Mrs Jane Bailey
Income: £1,171,947 [2017]; £1,089,667 [2016]; £906,206 [2015]; £855,858 [2014]; £843,939 [2013]

Lime Walk Gospel Hall Trust
Registered: 2 Jan 2015 *Volunteers:* 25
Tel: 01491 824710
Activities: Religious activities; other charitable purposes
Address: Old Woodlands House, Bakers Lane, Brightwell-Cum-Sotwell, Wallingford, Oxon, OX10 0PU
Trustees: Mr Andrew Greenfield, Mr Stuart Hill, Mr Mark John Hearn, Mr Bruce Robertson, Mr Stuart Robertson
Income: £1,519,082 [2017]; £187,212 [2016]; £143,702 [2015]

Limmud
Registered: 14 Nov 2000 *Employees:* 5 *Volunteers:* 550
Website: limmud.org
Activities: Education, training; religious activities; arts, culture, heritage, science
Address: Limmud, 1A Hall Street, London, N12 8DB
Trustees: Mr David Bilchitz, Ms Shoshana Bloom, Mr Robert Owen, Ms Miriam Edelman, Mr David Hoffman, Mr Shep Rosenman, Miss Shana Boltin
Income: £1,331,712 [2017]; £1,345,854 [2016]; £1,152,209 [2015]; £1,194,621 [2014]; £1,294,912 [2013]

Linacre College
Registered: 26 May 2011 *Employees:* 36
Tel: 01865 271650 *Website:* linacre.ox.ac.uk
Activities: Education, training; accommodation, housing
Address: Linacre College, St Cross Road, Oxford, OX1 3JA
Trustees: Nick Brown, Jocelyn Alexander, Hazel Assender, Simon Bailey, Richard Caplan, Sergei Dudarev, Matthew Gibney, Anne Keene, Nick La Thangue, Mark Pollard, Alison Reid, Subir Sarkar, Simon Travis, Cathy Ye, Alessandro Abate, John MacKay, Samar Khatiwala, Christopher Morton, Asma Mustafa, Cezar Ionescu, Heath Rose, Rebecca-Ann Burton, Jane Hoverd, Kimberly Schoemaker, James King, Laura Peers, Myles Allen, Dan Awrey, Victor Burlakov, Martin Castell, Elizabeth Ewart, Jim Hall, Angus Kirkland, Heather O'Donoghue, Gail Preston, Laura Rival, Alan Stein, Jonathan Whiteley, Colin Kleanthous, Jerry Tsai, Andrew Hector, Jenni Ingram, Silke Ackermann, Robert Iliffe, Man Yee Kan, Toby Nicholas Young, Laura Van Broekhoven, Ian Mills, Nehir Banaz, Isabel Al-Dhahir
Income: £4,730,000 [2017]; £3,581,000 [2016]; £3,330,000 [2015]; £3,111,000 [2014]; £4,874,000 [2013]

The Linbury Trust
Registered: 25 May 1983 *Employees:* 8
Tel: 020 7410 0330 *Website:* linburytrust.org.uk
Activities: General charitable purposes; education, training; advancement of health or saving of lives; overseas aid, famine relief; arts, culture, heritage, science; environment, conservation, heritage
Address: The Peak, 5 Wilton Road, London, SW1V 1AP
Trustees: Mr Richard Butler Adams, Mr James Philip Barnard, Lady Anya Sainsbury CBE, Lord Sainsbury of Preston Candover, Mrs Sarah Butler-Sloss, Mr John Julian Sainsbury, Sir Martin Jacomb, Hon Mark Sainsbury
Income: £6,172,000 [2017]; £6,242,000 [2016]; £8,133,000 [2015]; £8,784,000 [2014]; £6,954,000 [2013]

Lincoln College Oxford
Registered: 3 Dec 2010 *Employees:* 133
Tel: 01865 279800 *Website:* lincoln.ox.ac.uk
Activities: Education, training
Address: Lincoln College, Turl Street, Oxford, OX1 3DR
Trustees: Dr Jordan Raff, Dr Maria Stamatopoulou, Dr Radu Coldea, Dr Louise Durning, Mr Simon Gardner, Professor David Anthony Hills, Dr Edward Nye, Professor Roland Smith, Dr Michael Willis, Dr Mark Williams, Professor Henry Ruxton Woudhuysen, Dr Ioannis Vakonakis, Dr Timothy Michael, Professor Stefan Enchelmaier, Dr Aleksei Parakhonyak, Professor Cigdem Issever, Dr Paul Nicholas Stavrinou, Mr Alexis Radisoglou, Professor Pedro Carvalho, Professor Matthew Freeman, Dr Dominic Vella, Dr Roel Dullens, Dr Nigel Emptage, Dr Peregrine Gauci, Dr Peter McCullough, Professor Nicholas Proudfoot FRS, Dr David Vaux, Dr Daniela Omlor, Dr Qian Wang, Dr Philippe Trinh, Ms Susan Rosemary Harrison, Professor Catherine De Vries, Dr Barbara Havelkova, Dr Samuel Brewitt-Taylor, Mr Alex Dominic Spain, Dr Daniel McCann, Dr Lucy Wooding
Income: £13,028,000 [2017]; £13,370,000 [2016]; £12,732,000 [2015]; £14,009,000 [2014]; £13,100,192 [2013]

The Lincoln Diocesan Trust and Board of Finance Ltd
Registered: 14 Nov 1966 *Employees:* 79 *Volunteers:* 5,000
Tel: 01522 504050 *Website:* lincoln.anglican.org
Activities: Religious activities
Address: Edward King House, The Old Palace, Lincoln, LN2 1PU
Trustees: The Rt Revd Christopher Lowson, Canon Prof Muriel Robinson, Mr Nigel Bacon, Rev Nicholas James Watson Brown, Mr Douglas Horn, Mr Richard Hilton Clegg, Rev Elaine Turner, Mr Paul James Arnold, Rev Canon Christopher Howard Lilley, Miss Jane Powell, Mr Christopher James Clarke, Mr James Julius Christopher Birch, The Ven Dr Justine Allain Chapman, Mr James Milligan-Manby, Mr Alan Ronald Wilson, Mr David Thomas Wright
Income: £10,655,000 [2016]; £12,663,000 [2015]; £10,808,000 [2014]; £12,280,000 [2013]

Lincolnshire Agricultural Society
Registered: 23 Oct 1984 *Employees:* 23 *Volunteers:* 200
Tel: 01522 585527 *Website:* lincolnshireshowground.co.uk
Activities: Education, training; animals; environment, conservation, heritage
Address: Lincolnshire Agricultural Society, Lincolnshire Show Ground, Grange-de-Lings, Lincoln, LN2 2NA
Trustees: Mr Andrew Charles Read, Mrs Jane Hiles, Mr Robert Howard, Mr Andrew William Ward, Mr Andrew Lawrence Buckley, Mr David John Wallis, Mr Ian Harrup Walter, Mr Christopher Charles Rothery, Mr Steve Ward, Mr Nigel R Bottom, Mr Andrew Harding Price, Mr Greame Beattie
Income: £2,752,331 [2016]; £3,128,719 [2015]; £3,843,758 [2014]; £1,963,439 [2013]

Lincolnshire Bomber Command Memorial
Registered: 7 Oct 2011 *Volunteers:* 421
Tel: 01778 421420 *Website:* internationalbcc.co.uk
Activities: General charitable purposes
Address: International Bomber Command Centre, Canwick Avenue, Lincoln, LN4 2RF
Trustees: Mr Sidney C McFarlane, Air Vice-Marshal C J Luck, Mrs Camilla Carlbom-Flinn, Mr Richard Lake, Mrs Jenny Worth, Mr Stephen John Ellwood, Mr Charles Bishop
Income: £4,889,754 [2017]; £866,337 [2016]; £654,752 [2015]; £1,046,214 [2014]; £52,225 [2013]

Lincolnshire House Association
Registered: 17 Oct 1988 *Employees:* 83 *Volunteers:* 14
Tel: 01724 844168 *Website:* lincshouse.com
Activities: Education, training; disability; accommodation, housing
Address: Lincolnshire House Association, Brumby Wood Lane, Scunthorpe, N Lincs, DN17 1AF
Trustees: Mr Nicos Sofroniou, Mr Brendan George Taylor, Pauline Fiddler, Mr John David Beverley, Miss Gillian Smith, Mrs Wendy Liles, Mr Michael Burnett, Mrs Susan Kathleen Eynott, Mr Robert Charles Eynott, Mr Steven Warne, Ms Irene Victoria Crowther
Income: £1,765,336 [2017]; £1,664,118 [2016]; £1,524,958 [2015]; £1,459,557 [2014]; £1,423,635 [2013]

Lincolnshire Integrated Voluntary Emergency Service
Registered: 4 Jul 2003 *Employees:* 15 *Volunteers:* 966
Tel: 01507 525999 *Website:* lives.org.uk
Activities: General charitable purposes; education, training; advancement of health or saving of lives
Address: Lives Headquarters, Units 5-8 Birch Court, Boston Road Industrial Estate, Horncastle, Lincs, LN9 6SB
Trustees: Dr Derrick Alan Sagar BSc MB, Mrs Susan Cousland, Mr Timothy Downing, Mr Michael Adie, Mr Peter Carlsson, Dr Yvonne Owen
Income: £1,070,616 [2017]; £982,915 [2016]; £1,028,743 [2015]; £918,005 [2014]; £767,309 [2013]

Lincolnshire Sports Partnership
Registered: 17 Mar 2010 *Employees:* 20 *Volunteers:* 200
Tel: 01522 730325 *Website:* lincolnshiresport.com
Activities: Amateur sport
Address: Suite 4, Eco One, Highcliffe Farm, Ingham, Lincoln, LN1 2WE
Trustees: Mr Daniel James Ellmore, Professor Jayne Mitchell, Dr Rona MacKenzie-Batterbury, Mr William Leonard Taylor, Mrs Jaqueline Anita Allen, Mr Philip Edward Perry
Income: £1,171,128 [2017]; £1,102,033 [2016]; £1,013,121 [2015]; £1,070,255 [2014]; £1,315,566 [2013]

Lincolnshire Wildlife Trust
Registered: 4 Jul 1963 *Employees:* 61 *Volunteers:* 1,250
Tel: 01507 526667 *Website:* lincstrust.co.uk
Activities: Education, training; environment, conservation, heritage
Address: Lincolnshire Wildlife Trust, Banovallum House, Manor House Street, Horncastle, Lincs, LN9 5HF
Trustees: Mrs C E Harrison, Mr Tim Sands, Mr David Cohen, Mrs Beth Tyrrel, Janet Mellor, Peter Stapleton, Mrs Stephanie Round, Dr D A Sheppard, Mr Robert Oates, Mr Julian Purvis, Anita Quigley, Cliff Morrison, Mr Matthew Capper
Income: £2,812,266 [2017]; £2,615,438 [2016]; £3,124,075 [2015]; £3,601,377 [2014]; £2,774,951 [2013]

Lincolnshire Y.M.C.A. Ltd
Registered: 9 Jul 1965 *Employees:* 121 *Volunteers:* 79
Tel: 01522 508360 *Website:* lincsymca.co.uk
Activities: Education, training; advancement of health or saving of lives; prevention or relief of poverty; overseas aid, famine relief; accommodation, housing; religious activities; arts, culture, heritage, science; amateur sport; economic, community development, employment; recreation
Address: The Showroom, Tritton Road, Lincoln, LN6 7QY
Trustees: Mr Graham Bratby, Mr Edmund Walter Strengiel, Mr John Latham, Mr Richard Whittaker, Mr Richard Mair, Simon Smith, Mr Ian Sackree, Mr Christopher John Trigg, Mrs Margaret Botterill, Ms Beth Curtis, Mrs Dawn Barron, Rona MacKenzie
Income: £2,913,128 [2017]; £2,908,063 [2016]; £3,070,522 [2015]; £2,987,795 [2014]; £3,212,898 [2013]

The Lincolnshire and Nottinghamshire Air Ambulance Charitable Trust
Registered: 19 Feb 1993 *Employees:* 28 *Volunteers:* 400
Tel: 01522 548469 *Website:* ambucopter.org.uk
Activities: The advancement of health or saving of lives
Address: LNAACT House, Bentley Drive, Bracebridge Heath, Lincoln, LN4 2QW
Trustees: Dr Alan Sagar (Anaethetist), Mr Andrew John Pearce, Mr Jonty Pearson, Mr Graham Secker, Mrs Penny Would, Mr Paul Ronald Croft, Dr Robert Winter, Mr Jack O'Hern, Miss Lucie Briggs
Income: £4,263,797 [2017]; £5,482,411 [2016]; £4,369,854 [2015]; £3,910,949 [2014]; £3,622,191 [2013]

Lincs Inspire Limited
Registered: 7 Sep 2016 *Employees:* 735
Website: lincsinspire.com
Activities: Education, training; advancement of health or saving of lives; disability; arts, culture, heritage, science; amateur sport; recreation
Address: Bradley Football Development Centre, Bradley Road, Grimsby, N E Lincs, DN37 0AG
Trustees: Ms Michelle Lalor, Mr Terence Walker, Dr Sudip Bhaduri, Ms Sally Jack, Mr Malcolm Reginald Towle, Mr Alan Leslie Bird
Income: £8,408,410 [2017]

The Lind Trust
Registered: 4 Mar 1990
Tel: 01603 262626
Activities: General charitable purposes
Address: The Lind Trust, Drayton Hall, Hall Lane, Drayton, Norwich, NR8 6DP
Trustees: Mr Gavin Wilcock, Dr Graham Martin Dacre, Mr Samuel Edward Dacre, Mr Leslie Charles Brown, Mrs Julia May Dacre
Income: £1,368,635 [2017]; £1,507,834 [2016]; £699,098 [2015]; £2,015,032 [2014]; £2,625,116 [2013]

Lindfield Christian Care Home
Registered: 18 Sep 1989 *Employees:* 47 *Volunteers:* 60
Tel: 01444 482662 *Website:* lcchome.co.uk
Activities: The advancement of health or saving of lives; disability; accommodation, housing; religious activities
Address: Lindfield Christian Care Home, 40 Compton Road, Lindfield, Haywards Heath, W Sussex, RH16 2JZ
Trustees: Mr Jeremy Nurse, Mrs Celia Sykes, Mrs Susan Cowdy, Mr Michael Peter Odell, Mrs Jacqueline Lee, Mrs Kirsty Taylor, Dr Ian Johnson
Income: £1,454,910 [2016]; £1,379,527 [2015]; £1,318,412 [2014]; £1,286,496 [2013]; £1,258,921 [2012]

Lindley Educational Trust Limited
Registered: 20 Apr 1966 *Employees:* 23 *Volunteers:* 20
Tel: 01433 622082 *Website:* lindleyeducationaltrust.org
Activities: Education, training
Address: Hollowford Centre, Castleton, Hope Valley, Derbys, S33 8WB
Trustees: David Butterfield, Douglas Jones, John Price, Timothy Soar, Richard Hall, James Reynolds, David Henderson, Mrs Karen Lesley Jones
Income: £1,467,013 [2017]; £1,401,654 [2016]; £1,452,972 [2015]; £1,422,680 [2014]; £1,041,655 [2013]

Lindsey Lodge Limited
Registered: 22 May 1990 *Employees:* 133 *Volunteers:* 400
Tel: 01724 270835 *Website:* lindseylodgehospice.org.uk
Activities: The advancement of health or saving of lives
Address: Lindsey Lodge Hospice, Burringham Road, Scunthorpe, N Lincs, DN17 2AA
Trustees: Michael Boughton, Dr David Gordon Leitch, Mr Andrew Samuel Horwich, Mrs Karen Dunderdale, Paul Clark, Angela Lidgard, Mr Andrew Wignall
Income: £2,886,372 [2017]; £2,358,665 [2016]; £2,336,453 [2015]; £2,627,385 [2014]; £2,321,791 [2013]

Lingfield College
Registered: 13 Oct 1986 *Employees:* 148
Tel: 01444 892667 *Website:* lingfieldcollege.co.uk
Activities: Education, training
Address: Little Meadows, Ardingly Road, West Hoathly, East Grinstead, Surrey, RH19 4RD
Trustees: Mr Peter Trevor Samuels, Ms Clare Higgins, Mr Ian Rolfe, Mrs Susan Rutherford, Rev Nigel Hinton
Income: £11,233,513 [2017]; £10,487,119 [2016]; £9,890,194 [2015]; £8,867,896 [2014]; £8,211,097 [2013]

Link Community Development International
Registered: 17 Jul 1995 *Employees:* 8
Tel: 0131 225 3076 *Website:* lcdinternational.org
Activities: General charitable purposes; education, training; prevention or relief of poverty
Address: 4 Hunter Square, Edinburgh, EH1 1QW
Trustees: Gari Donn, Mr Mark Beaumont, Mr Alasdair Beaton, Mr Roger Cunningham, Ms Seonaid Crosby, Miss Elaine Graham, Professor Martyn Roebuck, Mr Christopher O'Brien, Mr Fergus Mackintosh, Mr Richard Santandreu
Income: £1,654,432 [2017]; £1,688,029 [2016]; £1,621,725 [2015]; £899,536 [2013]; £1,264,294 [2012]

The Link Day School Ltd
Registered: 14 Oct 1966 *Employees:* 68
Tel: 020 8688 5239 *Website:* thelinksecondaryschool.org.uk
Activities: Education, training
Address: 82-86 Croydon Road, Beddington, Croydon, Surrey, CR0 4PD
Trustees: Mr Peter Stocker, Dr Victoria Liebe Joffe, Mr Martin Norton, Mr Euan MacDonald
Income: £2,678,664 [2017]; £3,156,611 [2016]; £3,112,711 [2015]; £3,173,733 [2014]; £2,944,415 [2013]

Link-Ability
Registered: 2 Mar 1989 *Employees:* 186
Tel: 01257 241899 *Website:* linkability.org.uk
Activities: Disability
Address: Linkability, Conway House, Ackhurst Business Park, Foxhole Road, Chorley, Lancs, PR7 1NY
Trustees: Ms Rosemary Trustam, Mr Robert Crabtree, Mr Philip Entwistle, Mr John Holland, Mrs Alison Tupling, Mr David George Naden, Mr Paul Michael Jonas, Mr Duncan Mitchell, Kathryn Pattinson
Income: £3,182,226 [2017]; £2,631,389 [2016]; £2,665,145 [2015]; £2,569,088 [2014]; £2,573,615 [2013]

The Linkage Community Trust Limited
Registered: 9 Dec 1976 *Employees:* 627 *Volunteers:* 10
Tel: 01790 755056 *Website:* linkage.org.uk
Activities: Education, training; disability; accommodation, housing; economic, community development, employment
Address: Toynton Hall, Main Road, Toynton All Saints, Spilsby, Lincs, PE23 5AE
Trustees: Mr Reginald Roger Harfoot, Mr John Raymond Sutton John Raymond Sutton, Mrs Clare Jervis, Ashwin Kagdadia, Professor Stephen Brown, Mrs Stephanie Simpson, Mr Michael Oliver, Mr Anthony Bake, Mr Azad Najmaldin, Mr Mike Bell, Dr Jeremy Pearce
Income: £13,545,519 [2016]; £13,225,284 [2015]; £14,012,679 [2014]; £13,939,483 [2013]; £15,360,379 [2012]

Linking Environment and Farming
Registered: 12 Apr 1995 *Employees:* 14
Tel: 01926 419300 *Website:* leafuk.org
Activities: Environment, conservation, heritage
Address: 3 Barford Woods, Barford Road, Warwick, CV34 6SZ
Trustees: Mr Philip Graham Wynn, Mr Cedric William Porter, Mr Thomas Michael Curtis Green, Mr Richard Thomas Whitlock, Professor Christopher David Collins, Mrs Kathryn Mary Winrow, Mr Ian Pigott, Mr Ian Andrew Ashbridge, Mr Andrew Stanley Burgess, Philip Huxtable, Mrs Sara Caroline Eppel
Income: £1,038,119 [2017]; £1,109,918 [2016]; £969,859 [2015]; £1,098,522 [2014]; £909,066 [2013]

Links International Trust
Registered: 13 Jan 1986 *Employees:* 4 *Volunteers:* 10
Tel: 01903 778515 *Website:* linksinternational.org.uk
Activities: General charitable purposes; education, training; advancement of health or saving of lives; disability; prevention or relief of poverty; overseas aid, famine relief; religious activities; economic, community development, employment
Address: P O Box 198, Littlehampton, W Sussex, BN16 3UX
Trustees: Mr Matthew Bell, Mr Leigh Hills, Mrs Lina Read, Mrs Catherine Stewart, Dr Philip Moore, Mr Simeon Dendy, Mr Andrew King
Income: £1,333,991 [2016]; £1,178,668 [2015]; £1,157,933 [2014]; £1,015,357 [2013]; £981,591 [2012]

The Linnean Society of London
Registered: 4 Jun 1964 *Employees:* 18 *Volunteers:* 10
Tel: 020 7434 4479 *Website:* linnean.org
Activities: Education, training; environment, conservation, heritage
Address: Linnean Society of London, Burlington House, Piccadilly, London, W1J 0BF
Trustees: Ms Rosie Atkins FLS, Dr Rosie Trevelyan FLS, Dr Malcolm John Scoble BSc MPhil PhD DSC, Dr Paul Smith FLS, Professor Simon John Hiscock FLS, Dr Francis Brearley FLS, Miss Laura D'Arcy FLS, Professor Jeffrey Duckett FLS, Dr Zerina Johanson FLS, Dr Paul Jeremy James Bates FLS, Dr Christopher Michaels FLS, Professor Paul Martin Brakefield FLS, Professor Anthony Keith Campbell, Professor Mark Chase FRS FLS, Dr John Charles David FLS, Dr Michael Wilson FLS, Dr Maximilian Telford FLS, Mrs Deborah Wright FLS, Dr Michael Francis May FLS, Professor Juliet Ann Brodie FLS, Dr Maarten Christenhusz FLS, Professor Mark Richard David Seaward FLS
Income: £2,125,241 [2017]; £1,335,623 [2016]; £2,880,890 [2015]; £1,156,165 [2014]; £1,380,272 [2013]

The Linskill and North Tyneside Community Development Trust
Registered: 10 May 2007 *Employees:* 64 *Volunteers:* 26
Tel: 0191 257 8000 *Website:* linskill.org
Activities: General charitable purposes; education, training; prevention or relief of poverty; arts, culture, heritage, science; amateur sport; economic, community development, employment; recreation
Address: Linskill Centre, Linskill Terrace, North Shields, Tyne & Wear, NE30 2AY
Trustees: Mrs Jill Prendergast, Mrs Ellie Patience, Mr Walter Raymond Charlton, Mr Samuel McLoughlin, Mr Michael Wood, Mr Daniel John Entwisle, Mrs Georgina Cox
Income: £1,261,754 [2017]; £901,862 [2016]; £762,490 [2015]; £781,134 [2014]; £791,411 [2013]

The Lisieux Trust Limited
Registered: 13 Mar 2013 *Employees:* 78 *Volunteers:* 5
Tel: 0121 377 7071 *Website:* lisieuxtrust.org.uk
Activities: Education, training; disability; accommodation, housing; economic, community development, employment; human rights, religious or racial harmony, equality or diversity
Address: 184 Sutton New Road, Birmingham, B23 6QU
Trustees: Miss Elizabeth Fruer, Mr James Michael Downes, Mrs Sally Ann McHugh, Mr Gary Harris, Mr Kevin Richard Nagle, Miss Pauline Mary Lucas, Mr John Fazakerley, Miss Kathleen Corrigan
Income: £1,866,732 [2017]; £2,035,067 [2016]; £1,952,170 [2015]; £3,747,012 [2014]

Listening Books
Registered: 6 Jul 1972 Employees: 11 Volunteers: 27
Tel: 020 7407 9417 Website: listening-books.org.uk
Activities: General charitable purposes; disability
Address: Listening Books, 12 Lant Street, London, SE1 1QH
Trustees: Mr Christopher Sinclair-Stevenson, Ms Julia Eccleshare, Mr David Owen O'Neill, Mrs Gillie Howarth, Mrs Anne-Marie Williams, Mr Nicholas David Forster
Income: £1,185,565 [2017]; £969,498 [2016]; £641,057 [2015]; £1,243,072 [2014]; £921,778 [2013]

The Frank Litchfield General Charitable Trust
Registered: 27 Jun 1994
Tel: 01223 358012
Activities: General charitable purposes; advancement of health or saving of lives; disability; prevention or relief of poverty
Address: 12 de Freville Avenue, Cambridge, CB4 1HR
Trustees: Mr M T Womack, Mr Michael Hamilton, Mr David Malwell Chater
Income: £8,270,792 [2017]; £69,525 [2016]; £77,531 [2015]; £66,403 [2014]; £69,427 [2013]

The Little Angel Theatre
Registered: 11 Mar 1964 Employees: 15 Volunteers: 88
Tel: 020 3780 5980 Website: littleangeltheatre.com
Activities: Education, training; arts, culture, heritage, science
Address: Little Angel Theatre, 14 Dagmar Passage, London, N1 2DN
Trustees: Ms Fiona Phillips, Mr James Russell Bierman, Ms Catherine Louise Owen, Ms Melinda Rose Burton, Ms Rhian Harris, Mr Christopher Lowry, Ms Bailey Lock, Ms Emily O'Byrne
Income: £1,153,446 [2017]; £1,029,773 [2016]; £926,096 [2015]; £890,569 [2014]; £808,864 [2013]

Little Bookham Manor House School
Registered: 29 Aug 1962 Employees: 65 Volunteers: 1
Tel: 01372 459089 Website: manorhouseschool.org
Activities: Education, training
Address: Manor House School, Manor House Lane, Bookham, Leatherhead, Surrey, KT23 4EN
Trustees: Mr Jonathan Robert Compton, Mr Martin Stephen Ruscoe, Mrs G Sims-Brassett, Cp Heath-Taylor, Ms M Kieran, Mr Michael Robert Parkhouse, Mrs Marjorie Joy Richardson, Se Clare, Mr David Anthony Harris
Income: £3,783,527 [2017]; £3,720,200 [2016]; £3,845,387 [2015]; £3,984,701 [2014]; £3,841,201 [2013]

The Little Princess Trust
Registered: 6 Mar 2006 Employees: 8 Volunteers: 7
Tel: 01432 352359 Website: littleprincesses.org.uk
Activities: The advancement of health or saving of lives
Address: The Little Princess Trust, Broadway House, 32-35 Broad Street, Hereford, HR4 4AR
Trustees: Mrs Wendy Ann Tarplee-Morris, Mr Simon Tarplee, Mrs Tania Elizabeth Fitzgerald, Mr Robert Luigi Pizii, Mr Tim Lowe, Mr Tim Wheeler, Mr Philip Clive Brace
Income: £4,632,951 [2017]; £4,622,022 [2016]; £3,072,007 [2015]; £1,505,723 [2014]; £767,098 [2013]

The Little Way Association
Registered: 5 Aug 1964 Employees: 9 Volunteers: 8
Tel: 020 7622 0466 Website: littlewayassociation.com
Activities: The prevention or relief of poverty; overseas aid, famine relief; religious activities
Address: Sacred Heart House, 119 Cedars Road, London, SW4 0PR
Trustees: Peter John Beynon, Mrs Nan Katharine Waldron, Rev Daniel O'Riordan SDB, Mr Dennis Charlick
Income: £3,238,980 [2016]; £3,840,093 [2015]; £4,135,441 [2014]; £4,377,797 [2013]; £5,074,106 [2012]

Littlegarth School Limited
Registered: 11 Jun 1974 Employees: 65 Volunteers: 5
Tel: 01206 262332 Website: littlegarth.essex.sch.uk
Activities: Education, training
Address: Littlegarth School, Horkesley Park, Park Road, Nayland, Colchester, Essex, CO6 4JR
Trustees: Mr David Burden CB CVO CBE, Mrs Margaret Charlotte McKenna, Mr Geoffrey Post, Mrs Deborah Lisa Stanton, Mrs Catherine Clouston, Mr Charlie Erith, Mr James Henderson, Mrs Wai-Fung Thompson, Mr Arcot Maheshwar, Mr Michael Thomas McKaughan
Income: £3,123,732 [2017]; £2,991,494 [2016]; £2,791,497 [2015]; £2,725,601 [2014]; £2,642,559 [2013]

The Littlegate Trust
Registered: 25 May 2016
Tel: 01865 553226
Activities: Religious activities
Address: Keston, 37 Spring Road, Abingdon, Oxford, OX14 1AR
Trustees: Mr Alexander Marcham, Mr Simon Pillar, Mrs Elizabeth Mortimer, Mr Jack Pitman, Mr John Miller, Dr Stephen Willis, Rev Timothy Dossor
Income: £2,743,826 [2017]

Livability
Registered: 30 Oct 2006 Employees: 1,204 Volunteers: 179
Website: livability.org.uk
Activities: General charitable purposes; education, training; advancement of health or saving of lives; disability; prevention or relief of poverty; accommodation, housing; economic, community development, employment; recreation
Address: Livability, 6 Mitre Passage, London, SE10 0ER
Trustees: Nicola Tallett, Mrs Hannah Foster, Mr Andrew Wilson, Anne-Marie Costigan, Mr Craig Philbrick, Kate Clare, John Robinson, Mrs Caroline Armitage MA, Brian James, Mr Keith Hickey, Rev Agnita Oyawale, Mr David Bentley, Sally Chivers, Mr Angus Brown
Income: £50,334,000 [2017]; £37,836,000 [2016]; £44,423,000 [2015]; £40,776,000 [2014]; £40,332,000 [2013]

The Live Theatre Winchester Trust
Registered: 24 Aug 1999 Employees: 22 Volunteers: 192
Website: theatreroyalwinchester.co.uk
Activities: Education, training; arts, culture, heritage, science
Address: Theatre Royal, 22-23 Jewry Street, Winchester, Hants, SO23 8SB
Trustees: Mr Yinnon Ezra, Tamzin Sallis, Mr Anthony Arkwright, Sarah Drewery, Mr Stephen Gates, Mr David Hill, Mr Geoff Curran, Mr Paul Spencer, Sarah Wilson-White
Income: £1,723,886 [2017]; £1,568,230 [2016]; £1,736,576 [2015]; £1,476,306 [2014]; £1,253,533 [2013]

Liverpool Biennial of Contemporary Art Limited
Registered: 15 Feb 1999 *Employees:* 24 *Volunteers:* 108
Tel: 0151 709 7444 *Website:* biennial.com
Activities: General charitable purposes; education, training; arts, culture, heritage, science
Address: P O Box 1200, 55 Jordan Street, Liverpool, L69 1XB
Trustees: Mr Tony Wilson, Mr John Shield, Mr Paul Hyland, Ms Judith Nesbitt, Mr Chris Evans, Ms Anna Valle, Mr Jonathan Falkingham, Ms Kathleen Soriano, Mr Roland George Hill, Ms Sandeep Parmar, Ms May Calil
Income: £1,617,201 [2017]; £1,461,914 [2016]; £1,483,757 [2015]; £1,317,304 [2014]; £1,366,095 [2013]

Liverpool Charity and Voluntary Services
Registered: 11 Aug 1964 *Employees:* 30 *Volunteers:* 1
Tel: 0151 227 5177 *Website:* lcvs.org.uk
Activities: General charitable purposes
Address: 151 Dale Street, Liverpool, L2 2AH
Trustees: Mrs Heather Akehurst, Mr Andrew Whitehead, Mr John Price, Mr James Alexander Sloan, Mrs Dorcas Olanike Olatundun Akeju OBE, Mr Michael Salla, Mr Adeyinka Olushonde, Mr Michael Thomas, Mr Michael Frederick James, Mr Kenneth William Perry, Mrs Louise Ann Scholes
Income: £3,974,263 [2017]; £3,536,470 [2016]; £3,721,863 [2015]; £3,900,611 [2014]; £4,328,787 [2013]

Liverpool Citizens Advice Partnership
Registered: 6 Jul 1999 *Employees:* 18
Tel: 0151 733 8833 *Website:* liverpoolcap.org.uk
Activities: General charitable purposes
Address: L'pool Citizens Advice Partnership, 242 Picton Road, Wavertree, Liverpool, L15 4LP
Trustees: Mrs Gwenllian White, Mr Paul Jones, Mrs Robena Sarah Harrison, Mr Paul Wilkie, Mr Ian Hunter, Alison Gibbon, Mr Paul Radford, Mrs Carol Ann Walsh, Mr John Gibson
Income: £1,209,967 [2016]; £1,345,728 [2015]; £1,119,676 [2014]; £1,340,573 [2013]

The Liverpool Diocesan Board of Finance
Registered: 14 Nov 1966 *Employees:* 66
Tel: 0151 709 9722 *Website:* liverpool.anglican.org
Activities: Religious activities
Address: St James' House, 20 St James Road, Liverpool, L1 7BY
Trustees: Rt Rev Richard Blackburn, Mr David Greensmith, Mr David Burgess, Rev Crispin Alexander Pailing, Ven Roger Preece, Ven Pete Spiers, Mrs Angela Matthewson, Ven Mike McGurk, Mr Peter Russell Owen, Mr Michael Yate Pitts, Rev Hannah Lewis, Rev Mark Stanford, Ven Jennifer McKenzie, Mr Philip Stott, Mr Andrew John Orr Wilcockson
Income: £11,283,667 [2016]; £12,117,416 [2015]; £10,904,154 [2014]; £10,966,817 [2013]; £10,613,281 [2012]

Liverpool FC Foundation
Registered: 18 Mar 2003 *Employees:* 20 *Volunteers:* 35
Tel: 0151 907 9342 *Website:* foundation.liverpoolfc.com
Activities: General charitable purposes; education, training; amateur sport
Address: Liverpool FC Foundation, Anfield Road, Liverpool, L4 0TH
Trustees: Mr Gavin Crawford Laws, Mrs Linda Karen Pizutti, Professor Fiona Catherine Beveridge, Dr Simon Bowers, Mr Thomas Charles Wener, Mr William Hogan, Mrs Susan Black, Mr Peter Robert Moore
Income: £2,802,078 [2017]; £1,404,899 [2016]; £2,642,610 [2015]; £1,435,521 [2014]; £1,346,982 [2013]

Liverpool Guild of Students
Registered: 10 Aug 2010 *Employees:* 184 *Volunteers:* 2,013
Tel: 0151 794 6868 *Website:* liverpoolguild.org
Activities: Education, training; amateur sport
Address: University of Liverpool, Guild of Students, 160 Mount Pleasant, Liverpool, L3 5TR
Trustees: Ms Pamela Bell-Ashe, Ciaran Grafton-Clarke, Mr Sean Turner, Mr Obafemi Akinwale, Ed Moloney, Miles Tidman, Adam Dawkins, Ms Polly Thompson, Mr Ananda Mohan, Mrs Emma Gray Carter-Brown, Rory Hughes, Dominic Calleja
Income: £3,773,304 [2017]; £3,633,734 [2016]; £3,506,009 [2015]; £2,227,250 [2014]; £2,248,150 [2013]

Liverpool Hope University
Registered: 6 Feb 1997 *Employees:* 652
Tel: 0151 291 3233 *Website:* hope.ac.uk
Activities: Education, training; economic, community development, employment
Address: Liverpool Hope University College, Hope Park, Taggart Avenue, Liverpool, L16 9JD
Trustees: Professor Gerald John Pillay, Judge Graham Nash Wood, Mrs Diane Susan Shaw, Mr Charles Gerard Mills, Mr Michael John Gilbertson, Rt Rev Paul Bayes, Sr Mary Charles-Murray, Dr Simon Jeremy Hulme, Dr Sonja Tiernan, Mr Ultan Russell, Sr Maureen McKnight, Ms Jane Beever, Dr Arthur Naylor, Mrs Margaret Swinson, Mr John Douglas Norbury, Rev Peter Winn, Rev Sheryl Milanda Anderson, Dr John Michael Bennett, Fr Christopher McCoy, Ian Vandewalle, Mr Jack David Johnson, Rev Christopher Anthony Fallon, Cllr Jane Mary Sandford Corbett, Dr Winifred Joan McClelland
Income: £51,307,062 [2017]; £51,322,363 [2016]; £48,893,135 [2015]; £50,819,556 [2014]; £51,723,489 [2013]

The Liverpool Institute for Performing Arts
Registered: 18 Jan 1991 *Employees:* 135
Tel: 0151 330 3000 *Website:* lipa.ac.uk
Activities: Education, training; other charitable purposes
Address: Liverpool Institute for Performing, Mount Street, Liverpool, L1 9HF
Trustees: Roger Morris, Mr Ian Malcolm Jones, Mr Kenneth James Webster, Mr Geoffrey Goodwin, Mr Simon Jeffrey Fowler, Professor Frank Sanderson, Mrs Claire Workman, Mr John Reynolds, Ms Victoria Lucy Fea, Mrs Louise Joyce Ellman, Mr Mark Philip Featherstone-Witty, Mr Richard Young, Mr James Alexander Thomas Dow, Ms Isabel Begg, Mr Jonathon Ford, Mr Andrew Westwood, Ms Julie Margaret Cullen
Income: £10,259,510 [2017]; £10,839,092 [2016]; £10,464,692 [2015]; £10,183,448 [2014]; £9,720,946 [2013]

The Liverpool Merchants' Guild
Registered: 28 Feb 1963
Tel: 0151 703 1080 *Website:* liverpoolmerchantsguild.org.uk
Activities: The prevention or relief of poverty
Address: Moore Stephens, 110-114 Duke Street, Liverpool, L1 5AG
Trustees: Mr Roy Morris, Mr Sandy Timothy Chapple Gill, Mrs Gillian Ferrigno, Mr Andrew Morris, Mr Kenneth Head, Mrs Michele Ibbs, Mr Robert John Carter, Mr David Stern, Mrs Susan Newton, Mr Lawrence Downey, Mr Duncan Bailey
Income: £1,449,462 [2016]; £1,316,201 [2015]; £1,085,347 [2014]; £1,249,851 [2013]; £1,210,058 [2012]

Liverpool Roman Catholic Archdiocesan Trust
Registered: 23 Aug 1965 *Employees:* 422 *Volunteers:* 1,000
Tel: 0151 522 1020 *Website:* liverpoolcatholic.org.uk
Activities: Religious activities
Address: Liverpool Archdiocese, Centre for Evangelisation, Croxteth Drive, Liverpool, L17 1AA
Trustees: Rt Rev Vincent Malone, Rt Reverend Thomas Williams, Rev Michael O'Dowd, Miss Carol Chapman, Rev Philip Inch, Rev Canon Thomas Neylon, Rev Matthew Nunes, Mr John Cowdall, Rev Canon Anthony O'Brien, Most Rev Malcolm McMahon OP, Rev Sean Kirwin, Rev Godric Timney OSB, Rev Philip Gregory, Rev Stephen Maloney
Income: £32,400,052 [2016]; £35,743,743 [2015]; £37,816,635 [2014]; £39,579,633 [2013]; £41,728,110 [2012]

Liverpool School of Tropical Medicine
Registered: 11 Oct 1963 *Employees:* 508 *Volunteers:* 368
Tel: 0151 705 3167 *Website:* lstmed.ac.uk
Activities: Education, training; advancement of health or saving of lives; other charitable purposes
Address: Liverpool School of Tropical Medicine, Pembroke Place, Liverpool, L3 5QA
Trustees: Mr Jeremy Lefroy, Mr James H Ross, Mr Julian Lob-Levyt, Mr Nick Earlam, Ms Jennifer Amery, Ms Eileen Thornton, Ms Rebecca Nightingale, Professor Janet Hemingway, Mr Jonathan Schofield BA, Professor Stephen Andrew Ward, Mr Mark Allanson, Ms Susan Russell, Mr John O'Brien
Income: £111,496,000 [2017]; £78,358,000 [2016]; £73,066,000 [2015]; £65,390,000 [2014]; £59,994,000 [2013]

Liverpool Student Union
Registered: 5 Jul 2011 *Employees:* 132 *Volunteers:* 750
Tel: 0151 231 4900 *Website:* liverpoolsu.com
Activities: General charitable purposes; education, training; disability; accommodation, housing; arts, culture, heritage, science; amateur sport; environment, conservation, heritage; economic, community development, employment; human rights, religious or racial harmony, equality or diversity; recreation; other charitable purposes
Address: Liverpool Students' Union, John Foster Building, 98 Mount Pleasant, Liverpool, L3 5UZ
Trustees: Ms Wendi Bestman, Mark Hodgson, Ms Angelina Cliff, Ms Howisha Charlery, Mr Robert Morris, Jean McLean, Ms Rachael Smart, Mr Robert Johnson, Ms Yasmin Ibrahim
Income: £2,008,482 [2017]; £1,808,990 [2016]; £1,733,563 [2015]; £1,907,355 [2014]; £2,088,511 [2013]

Liverpool and Merseyside Theatres Trust Limited
Registered: 22 Jun 2000 *Employees:* 222
Website: everymanplayhouse.com
Activities: Arts, culture, heritage, science
Address: Liverpool & Merseyside Theatres Trust Ltd, The Everyman Theatre, 5-11 Hope Street, Liverpool, L1 9BH
Trustees: Ms Claire Dove, Ms Deborah Aydon, Mr David Morrissey, Mr Michael Mansfield, Ms Bren Hutchinson, Mr Peter Bennett-Jones, Mr Paul Corcoran, Ms Wendy Simon, Ms Gemma Redropp
Income: £5,409,000 [2017]; £6,027,865 [2016]; £7,722,529 [2015]; £14,153,815 [2014]; £9,121,054 [2013]

The Liversage Trust
Registered: 10 Jan 2014 *Employees:* 50
Tel: 01332 348199 *Website:* liversagetrust.org
Activities: General charitable purposes; advancement of health or saving of lives; prevention or relief of poverty; accommodation, housing
Address: The Liversage Trust, London Road, Derby, DE1 2QW
Trustees: Mr Roy Webb, Councillor Frank Harwood, Mr John Brittain, Mr Malcolm Allsop, Mr Michael Foote, Ms Susan Glithero, Mr Richard Docker, Mr Mike Carr, Councillor Shiraz Khan, Mrs Janet Till, Mr Leslie Allen, Ms Mary Streets, Revd Canon Paul Morris, Mr Timothy Benson, Mr Shaker Khaliq
Income: £2,219,002 [2017]; £2,175,615 [2016]; £2,020,396 [2015]

Living Coasts
Registered: 20 Aug 2003 *Employees:* 28 *Volunteers:* 41
Tel: 01803 697500 *Website:* livingcoasts.org.uk
Activities: Education, training; animals; environment, conservation, heritage; recreation
Address: Paignton Zoo, Totnes Road, Paignton, Devon, TQ4 7EU
Trustees: Mr Andrew Charles John Cooper, Mrs Sylvia Jo-Ann Greinig, Mr Richard William John Ford, Mrs Sarah Barr, Dr Judy Ravenscroft, Mr Richard Alexander Rowe, Dr Paul Robert Francis Chanin, Mr Stephen Kings, Mrs Rachael Hill BA, Peter Stevens, Mrs Beth Kathleen McLaughlin, Mr Mark Salmon
Income: £1,200,676 [2017]; £1,101,046 [2016]; £1,010,603 [2015]; £885,792 [2014]; £1,016,356 [2013]

Living Options Devon
Registered: 4 Mar 2004 *Employees:* 20 *Volunteers:* 175
Tel: 01392 459222 *Website:* livingoptions.org
Activities: Education, training; advancement of health or saving of lives; disability
Address: Ground Floor, Units 3-4 Cranmere Court, Lustleigh Close, Matford Business Park, Marsh Barton Trading Estate, Exeter, EX2 8PW
Trustees: Mr Andrew Philip Barge, Ms S P Fallon, Mr Patrick Healy, Mr Derek William Smithers, Mr Mark Saunders, Mr Peter Charles Swain OBE, Mr Brian Imeson, Mr Nevil Salisbury-Rood, Mrs Claudia Jean Ahnes Thorpe
Income: £1,493,281 [2017]; £1,577,834 [2016]; £1,504,326 [2015]; £1,173,641 [2014]; £1,740,906 [2013]

Living Streets (The Pedestrians Association)
Registered: 4 Mar 2005 *Employees:* 63
Tel: 020 7377 4904 *Website:* livingstreets.org.uk
Activities: Education, training; advancement of health or saving of lives; arts, culture, heritage, science; environment, conservation, heritage; economic, community development, employment
Address: 4th Floor, Universal House, 88-94 Wentworth Street, London, E1 7SA
Trustees: Mr Archie Robertson, Mr William Tyler-Greig, Ms Susan Claris, Mr Tom Rye, Ms Barbara Walshe, Mr Mohammed Mohsanali, Miss Averil Price, Mr Alexander Veitch, Ms Jo Field, Ms Fiona Walker, Ms Mollie Bickerstaff
Income: £5,611,388 [2017]; £5,079,871 [2016]; £5,733,386 [2015]; £4,129,281 [2014]; £3,476,827 [2013]

Llamau Limited

Registered: 25 Jul 1989 *Employees:* 266 *Volunteers:* 23
Tel: 029 2023 9585 *Website:* llamau.org.uk
Activities: General charitable purposes; education, training; prevention or relief of poverty; accommodation, housing; other charitable purposes
Address: Llamau Ltd, 23-25 Cathedral Road, Cardiff, CF11 9HA
Trustees: Mrs Carol Ravenscroft, Mrs Helen Cahill, Mr Daniel Lewis, Ms Sheila O'Brien, Mr Thomas Graham Breed, Dr Julie Highfield, Ms Angela Mary Gascoigne, Mr Peter Mackie, Mr David Blair, Mrs Wendy Richards, Mr Adrian Peters
Income: £10,297,922 [2017]; £11,373,308 [2016]; £10,865,840 [2015]; £9,980,210 [2014]; £8,914,091 [2013]

The Llandaff Diocesan Board of Finance

Registered: 20 May 1965 *Employees:* 13
Tel: 01656 868868 *Website:* llandaff.org.uk
Activities: Accommodation, housing; religious activities
Address: Llandaff Diocesan Board of Finan, The Court, Coychurch, Bridgend, CF35 5EH
Trustees: The Rt Revd June Osborne, Father Robert Emlyn Davies, Mr Geoffrey Ian Moses, Venerable Christopher Blake Walters Smith, Mr Evan Peter Umbleja, Mr Phillip Hopkins, Ms Anna Cory, Revd Andrew Meredith, The Venerable Frances Anne Jackson, Mr Adrian Gerald Parker, Mrs Deryn McAndrew, Mr Tony Davies, Rev Jonathan Ormrod, Mr Michael Anthony Lawley, Mrs Julia Lewis
Income: £6,425,450 [2016]; £6,310,382 [2015]; £6,438,529 [2014]; £6,540,348 [2013]; £7,553,065 [2012]

The Llangollen International Musical Eisteddfod Limited

Registered: 13 Oct 1975 *Employees:* 6 *Volunteers:* 800
Tel: 01978 862000 *Website:* international-eisteddfod.co.uk
Activities: Education, training; arts, culture, heritage, science; human rights, religious or racial harmony, equality or diversity
Address: Royal International Pavilion, Abbey Road, Llangollen, Denbighshire, LL20 8SW
Trustees: Mr Simon Robert Maurice Baynes, Mr Keith Potts, Mrs Jillian Sanders, Mrs Rhiannon Jedwell, Dr John Rhys Adams Davies, Mr Roy Jones MBE, Mr Ian Andrew Lebbon, Mr Nicolaus Stuart Jenkins, Morag Webb, Mr Paul Duncan Coleman, Claire Marie Brock
Income: £1,234,388 [2016]; £1,151,323 [2015]; £1,263,366 [2014]; £1,129,039 [2013]; £1,056,903 [2012]

Llanthony Secunda Priory Trust

Registered: 18 Jun 2007 *Employees:* 1 *Volunteers:* 30
Tel: 01453 844203 *Website:* llanthonysecunda.org
Activities: Education, training; arts, culture, heritage, science; environment, conservation, heritage
Address: 5 Gloucester Street, Wotton under Edge, Glos, GL12 7DN
Trustees: Jeremy Williamson, Mr Graham Howell, Mr Martyn White, Miss Elizabeth Griffiths, Miss Sarah Gilbert, Mr Ian Jackson Maxwell Patton, Sir Henry Elwes, Mr Philip John Staddon, Julie Finch, Mr Paul Toleman, Mr Ian Richard Stainburn, Mr Patrick Taylor
Income: £3,806,609 [2017]; £190,784 [2016]; £345,648 [2015]; £16,690 [2014]; £35,638 [2013]

Llenyddiaeth Cymru - Literature Wales

Registered: 23 Mar 2012 *Employees:* 22
Website: literaturewales.org
Activities: Education, training; arts, culture, heritage, science
Address: Literature Wales, Glyn Jones Centre, Wales Millennium Centre, Bute Place, Cardiff, CF10 5AL
Trustees: Ms Delyth Roberts, Mr John O'Shea, Mr William Ayot, Eric Ngalle Charles, Mr Owain Taylor-Shaw, Professor Radihka Mohanram, Mrs Elizabeth Margaret George, Ms Angharad Wynne Evans, Dr Katie Teresa North, Mr Jacob Dafydd Ellis, Ms Annie Finlayson, Mr Craig Austin
Income: £1,204,282 [2017]; £1,429,541 [2016]; £1,429,541 [2015]; £1,495,653 [2014]; £1,450,971 [2013]

The Lloyd Park Children's Charity

Registered: 17 Feb 2004 *Employees:* 92 *Volunteers:* 8
Tel: 020 8531 9522 *Website:* tlpcc.org.uk
Activities: Education, training; prevention or relief of poverty
Address: The Lloyd Park Centre, Winns Avenue, Lloyd Park, London, E17 5JW
Trustees: Mr Leonard Leslie, Ms Sandra Schembri, Mrs Anoushka Huntington-Bowles, Mr Paul Hugh Turnham Fraser, Ms Widiane Moussa, Mrs Pauleen Colligan-Genova, Ms Sarah Jessica Parsons, Mr James Wragg, Ms Vivienne Barrett, Mr Vairavar Iyampillai Sivagunam, Mrs Maria Fitzjohn, Ms Sarah Lloyd-Scott, Mr Max Jervis-Read, Ms Laura Bellotti
Income: £2,878,685 [2017]; £2,400,910 [2016]; £2,306,783 [2015]; £2,407,316 [2014]; £2,276,026 [2013]

Lloyd's Register Foundation

Registered: 20 Feb 2012 *Employees:* 7,489
Tel: 020 7423 2783 *Website:* lr.org
Activities: Education, training; advancement of health or saving of lives
Address: 71 Fenchurch Street, London, EC3M 4BS
Trustees: Mrs Carol Frances Sergeant, Thomas Thune Andersen, Mr Lambros Varnavides, Sir Brian Bender, Ron Henderson, Mrs Rosemary Martin
Income: £908,172,000 [2017]; £901,037,000 [2016]; £1,062,537,000 [2015]; £1,048,102,000 [2014]; £951,392,000 [2013]

Lloyd's Register International

Registered: 10 May 2013 *Employees:* 65
Website: lr.org
Activities: Education, training; advancement of health or saving of lives; arts, culture, heritage, science
Address: 71 Fenchurch Street, London, EC3M 4BS
Trustees: Mr Simon Nice, Miss Ashley Gerrard, Alan Williams
Income: £13,754,000 [2017]; £14,712,000 [2016]; £20,827,000 [2015]; £18,826,000 [2014]

Lloyds Bank Foundation for England & Wales

Registered: 13 May 1986 *Employees:* 28
Tel: 020 7378 4601 *Website:* lloydsbankfoundation.org.uk
Activities: General charitable purposes; education, training; advancement of health or saving of lives; disability; prevention or relief of poverty
Address: Pentagon House, 52-54 Southwark Street, London, SE1 1UN
Trustees: Paul Farmer, Mr James Garvey, Professor Patricia Broadfoot CBE, Rennie Fritchie, Ms Joanna Kate Harris, Dame Gillian Margaret Morgan, Dr Neil Rhys Wooding, Hilary Armstrong, Helen Edwards, Ms Catharine Lucy Cheetham, Ms Lesley Alison King-Lewis, Ms Sara Weller
Income: £13,835,000 [2016]; £13,826,000 [2015]; £13,920,000 [2014]; £26,758,000 [2013]; £26,693,000 [2012]

Local Information Unit Limited
Registered: 30 Mar 2006 *Employees:* 18
Tel: 020 7554 2800 *Website:* lgiu.org.uk
Activities: Education, training; other charitable purposes
Address: 3rd Floor, Local Government Information Unit, 251 Pentonville Road, Islington, London, N1 9NG
Trustees: Mrs Eunice Fay Campbell, Councillor Robert James Wheeler, Michael Payne, Christopher Saint, Kyle Robinson, Abdul Jabbar, Brian Robinson, Mr Mike Short, Cllr Neil Nerva
Income: £1,612,871 [2016]; £2,004,004 [2015]; £1,485,878 [2014]; £3,541,916 [2013]; £1,634,389 [2012]

Local Solutions
Registered: 17 May 1984 *Employees:* 1,027 *Volunteers:* 158
Tel: 0151 709 0990 *Website:* localsolutions.org.uk
Activities: Education, training; advancement of health or saving of lives; disability; prevention or relief of poverty; accommodation, housing; amateur sport; environment, conservation, heritage; economic, community development, employment; recreation
Address: Local Solutions, Mount Vernon Green, Hall Lane, Kensington, Liverpool, L7 8TF
Trustees: Jonathan Howard Henry Mounsey, Rev Crispin Pailing, Mr Nigel Stuart Lanceley, Mr Andrew James Cooke, Ms Katie Elizabeth Clubb, Mr Richard Maxwell White, Mr Robert Tudor Hooson Owen, Nina Patel, Ms Hazel Julie Snell
Income: £16,467,385 [2017]; £19,508,305 [2016]; £17,766,185 [2015]; £17,773,254 [2014]; £17,756,885 [2013]

Local Trust
Registered: 30 May 2012 *Employees:* 13
Tel: 020 3588 0565 *Website:* localtrust.org.uk
Activities: Economic, community development, employment
Address: CAN Mezzanine, 7-14 Great Dover Street, London, SE1 4YR
Trustees: Ms Alice Casey, Mr J K Sugrue, Ms Penelope Anne Shepherd, Dr John David Whitton, Mr Sahil Khan, Mr Bob Thust, Ms Nicola Pollock, Mr B Y M Lee, Mr Peter Ensell Mills, Mr David Warner, Ms Jeannette Ann Lichner, Mr Richard Wilson
Income: £5,908,285 [2017]; £7,219,239 [2016]; £6,347,282 [2015]; £5,317,400 [2014]; £19,403,156 [2013]

Localgiving Foundation
Registered: 29 Oct 2009 *Employees:* 17
Tel: 0300 111 2340 *Website:* localgivingfoundation.org
Activities: General charitable purposes; economic, community development, employment
Address: Unit 2, 189-190 Shoreditch High Street, London, E1 6HU
Trustees: Mr Tom Latchford, Miss Gillian Mead, Mr Tom Williamson
Income: £3,619,181 [2017]; £3,188,661 [2016]; £2,708,719 [2015]; £5,151,567 [2014]; £625,276 [2012]

Locality (UK)
Registered: 13 Apr 1994 *Employees:* 49
Tel: 0345 458 8336 *Website:* locality.org.uk
Activities: The prevention or relief of poverty; economic, community development, employment
Address: 33 Corsham Street, London, N1 6DR
Trustees: Ms Sona Mahtani, Steve Rundell, Mr Chandranesan Priyanath Thamotheram, Mr Dominic Ellison, Mr Steve Sayers, Ms Celia Richardson, Ms Karin Woodley, Mr Mark Law, Ms Laura Brodie, Ms Helen Quigley, Ms Andrea Mennell, Ms Maxine Ennis
Income: £4,561,000 [2017]; £8,514,000 [2016]; £12,159,000 [2015]; £10,843,000 [2014]; £8,454,000 [2013]

Lochinver House School
Registered: 12 Mar 2002 *Employees:* 95 *Volunteers:* 30
Tel: 01707 642560 *Website:* lochinverhouse.com
Activities: Education, training
Address: Lochinver House School, Heath Road, Potters Bar, Herts, EN6 1LW
Trustees: Mrs Jane Elizabeth Renshaw Oram, Mr William Moores, Mr Nicholas Gilbert, Mr Duncan Alexander Taylor, Mr James Le Couilliard, Dr Rami Atalla, Miss Olivia Jacobs, Mrs Amanda English, Mrs Christine Ann Smith, Mr Jonathan Gillespie, Mr Martin Collier, Miss Helen Philp
Income: £4,404,493 [2017]; £5,714,490 [2016]; £4,078,416 [2015]; £4,057,077 [2014]; £3,824,450 [2013]

The Locker Foundation
Registered: 1 Aug 1972
Tel: 020 8455 9280
Activities: General charitable purposes; advancement of health or saving of lives
Address: 9 Neville Drive, London, N2 0QS
Trustees: Mrs Susanna Segal, Mr Malcolm Brian Carter, Mr Irving Carter
Income: £1,075,902 [2017]; £1,189,535 [2016]; £696,212 [2015]; £689,283 [2014]; £993,058 [2013]

Lockers Park School Trust Limited
Registered: 2 Jan 1974 *Employees:* 52 *Volunteers:* 3
Tel: 01442 251712 *Website:* lockerspark.herts.sch.uk
Activities: Education, training
Address: Lockers Park School, Lockers Park Lane, Hemel Hempstead, Herts, HP1 1TL
Trustees: Mr Douglas Collins, Dr Justin Muston, Ms Deborah Dolce, Mr Christopher Tolman, Dr Susie Jordache, Mr Andrew Tivey, Mr Christopher Lister, Mr Oliver Abel-Smith
Income: £2,870,757 [2017]; £2,349,020 [2016]; £2,371,323 [2015]; £2,605,685 [2014]; £2,320,297 [2013]

The Loddon Foundation Ltd
Registered: 18 Dec 1989 *Employees:* 181
Tel: 01256 884600 *Website:* loddonschool.co.uk
Activities: Education, training; disability; overseas aid, famine relief
Address: The Loddon School, Wildmoor Lane, Sherfield on Loddon, Hook, Hants, RG27 0JD
Trustees: Mrs Marion Lesley Cornick, Mr Stephen Dobson, Mrs Jennifer Lewendon, Ms Jennifer Wright, Dr Robert William Lycett, Mrs Ruth Jones, Mike Lakin, Ms Chipo Foweraker, Mr Johnathan Beebee, Mr Steve Fussey, Mr Joy Wake
Income: £6,826,121 [2017]; £6,564,627 [2016]; £6,513,593 [2015]; £6,252,294 [2014]; £6,327,237 [2013]

The Lodge Trust CIO
Registered: 19 May 2015 *Employees:* 57 *Volunteers:* 18
Tel: 01572 767234 *Website:* lodgetrust.org.uk
Activities: Education, training; disability; accommodation, housing; religious activities
Address: The Lodge, Main Street, Market Overton, Oakham, Rutland, LE15 7PL
Trustees: Mr Richard Stevens, Mr M Kallow, Dr E J Hodges, Mrs Stacey Matthews, Mr D Donegani, Miss E Harrison, Dr J N I Dickson, Mr David John Kindred
Income: £1,823,178 [2017]

Loftus Charitable Trust
Registered: 5 Oct 1987
Tel: 020 7604 5900
Activities: Education, training; advancement of health or saving of lives; disability; prevention or relief of poverty; religious activities
Address: 55 Blandford Street, Marylebone, London, W1U 7HW
Trustees: Mr Andrew David Loftus, Mr Richard Ian Loftus, Mr Anthony Louis Loftus
Income: £6,654,743 [2017]; £1,837,850 [2016]; £1,331,250 [2015]; £862,500 [2014]; £248,750 [2013]

Lohana Charitable Foundation Ltd
Registered: 21 May 2015
Tel: 020 8498 0163
Activities: General charitable purposes; education, training; disability; prevention or relief of poverty; religious activities; arts, culture, heritage, science
Address: Hunter House, 109 Snakes Lane, Woodford Green, Essex, IG8 0DY
Trustees: Mr Pradip Dhamecha, Mr Narendra Thakrar, Mr Vinod Kotecha, Mr Manish Sangani Chartered Accountant, Mrs Pratibha Lakhani, Mr Mansukhlal Raichura, Mr Rameshchandra Kantaria, Mr Ajaykumar Gokani, Mr Yatin Dawada, Mr Bhavesh Radia, Mr Deenesh Thakerar, Mr Vimal Pau, Mr Amratlal Radia, Mr Jagdish Nagrecha, Mr Vinod Thakrar, Dr Rasiklal Kantaria, Mr Depak Dayalji Jatania
Income: £4,159,965 [2017]

The Lohana Mahajan (UK) Trust
Registered: 18 Aug 2004 *Employees:* 5 *Volunteers:* 25
Tel: 020 8902 8885 *Website:* jalaramjyotuk.com
Activities: Education, training; prevention or relief of poverty; religious activities; arts, culture, heritage, science; amateur sport
Address: c/o Wasp, Repton Avenue, Wembley, Middlesex, HA0 3DW
Trustees: Mr Dhiren Gadhia, Mr Mahendra Gokani, Mr Girish Mashru
Income: £1,156,884 [2016]; £181,082 [2015]; £153,079 [2014]; £122,922 [2013]; £110,204 [2012]

The Lolev Charitable Trust
Registered: 9 Dec 1982 *Volunteers:* 4
Tel: 020 8806 3457
Activities: The advancement of health or saving of lives; disability; prevention or relief of poverty; religious activities
Address: 14A Gilda Crescent, London, N16 6JP
Trustees: Mr Abraham Tager, Mr Michael Tager, Mrs Eve Tager
Income: £8,660,267 [2016]; £7,100,229 [2015]; £5,378,859 [2014]; £4,310,849 [2013]; £4,157,141 [2012]

London Board for Shechita
Registered: 19 Jun 1964 *Employees:* 31 *Volunteers:* 21
Tel: 020 8349 9160 *Website:* shechita.org
Activities: General charitable purposes; education, training; religious activities
Address: Elscot House, Arcadia Avenue, London, N3 2JU
Trustees: Isaac Levy Vice President, Mr Russell Kett, Incorporated Trustees of The London Board For Shechita, Mr Leo Winter Honorary Treasurer, Mr Benjamin Mire President
Income: £2,199,369 [2016]; £2,301,865 [2015]; £2,446,329 [2014]; £2,382,583 [2013]; £2,325,263 [2012]

The London Buddhist Centre
Registered: 20 Jun 1968 *Employees:* 28 *Volunteers:* 100
Tel: 020 8981 1225 *Website:* lbc.org.uk
Activities: Education, training; advancement of health or saving of lives; religious activities
Address: 51 Roman Road, London, E2 0HU
Trustees: Dr Paramabandhu Groves, Ms Srivati Skelton, Mr Paul Newman, Ms Erica Light, Ms Joanne Quirke, Mr Dishir Thakkar, Mr Jefferey Reeves, Ms Mary Healy, Mr Alban Leigh, Ms Sandra Turner
Income: £1,398,701 [2017]; £1,190,180 [2016]; £1,113,368 [2015]; £1,170,062 [2014]; £1,104,682 [2013]

London Business School Student Association
Registered: 28 Mar 2011
Tel: 020 7000 7024 *Website:* clubs.london.edu
Activities: Education, training
Address: London Business School, Sussex Place, London, NW1 4SA
Trustees: Mr Andre Luciano Moscoso, Mr Thomas Henry Ormsby Priestley, Ms Tsitsi Sophia Khuntsaria, Ms Grete Coco Karuso, Ms Kara Bloch, Ms Laure Kroely, Mr Josh Chakravarty, Mr Shirsesh Nath Bhaduri, Ms Richa Priyadarshee, Mr Fredy Afif, Ms Madeline Rejene Bloch, Ms Jenny Cheng, Mr Renato Teruo Yamasaki Akaishi
Income: £2,325,287 [2017]; £2,141,440 [2016]; £1,835,207 [2015]; £1,631,302 [2014]; £1,349,595 [2013]

The London Central Mosque (Algame) Fund
Registered: 3 May 1965 *Employees:* 40 *Volunteers:* 7
Tel: 020 7725 2151 *Website:* iccuk.org
Activities: General charitable purposes; education, training; advancement of health or saving of lives; prevention or relief of poverty; overseas aid, famine relief; religious activities; arts, culture, heritage, science; other charitable purposes
Address: Islamic Cultural Centre & London CE, Regents Lodge, 146 Park Road, London, NW8 7RG
Trustees: Dr Ahmed Al-Dubayan, Major General Aminuddin Ihsan Poksm Dsp Hj Abidin, Embassy of The Sultanate of Oman, Embassy of The State of Qatar, Embassy of Jordan, Embassy of The Kingdom of Malaysia, Embassy of The Syrian Arab Republic, Embassy of Bahrain, His Excellency Mr Khaled Al-Duwaisan, Royal Embassy of Saudi Arabia, High Commission For Islamic Republic of Pakistan, Embassy of The Arab Republic of Egypt, Embassy of Yemen, Embassy of The Kingdom of Morocco, Embassy of The United Arab Emirates
Income: £1,285,229 [2016]; £2,256,055 [2015]; £1,093,041 [2014]; £3,068,205 [2013]; £1,186,199 [2012]

London Central Young Men's Christian Association Limited
Registered: 30 Nov 1990
Tel: 020 7343 1844 *Website:* ymcafit.org.uk
Activities: Education, training; amateur sport
Address: Central YMCA, 112 Great Russell Street, London, WC1B 3NQ
Trustees: Mr Anthony Griffiths, Ms Philippa Campbell
Income: £4,396,128 [2017]; £3,342,382 [2016]; £3,630,980 [2015]; £3,187,656 [2014]; £3,066,135 [2013]

London Christian School Ltd
Registered: 22 Jan 2010 *Employees:* 26
Website: londonchristianschool.com
Activities: Education, training; religious activities
Address: 40 Tabard Street, London, SE1 4JU
Trustees: Sir Charles Hoare, Mr Samuel Wilde, Mr Timothy Catt, Mr Theo Jones, Miss Nicola Collett White, Chris Fishlock, Mrs Georgina Withane, Mr Joseph Ammoun, Mrs Natalie Trowbridge, Mr Dan Lewis
Income: £1,054,595 [2017]; £1,001,514 [2016]; £925,113 [2015]; £841,816 [2014]; £761,799 [2013]

The London City Mission
Registered: 1 Mar 1966 *Employees:* 182 *Volunteers:* 175
Tel: 020 7407 7585 *Website:* lcm.org.uk
Activities: General charitable purposes; prevention or relief of poverty; religious activities
Address: London City Mission, 175 Tower Bridge Road, London, SE1 2AH
Trustees: Mr Ian Nash, Mr Richard Westacott Godden, Mr Roger Evans, Mr Richard Montgomery, Mr Graham David Miller, Mr Richard Bulmer, Mr Nigel Parrington, Mark Dominic Harding, Carolyn Louise Ash, Dr Mosun Dorgu, Mrs Marcia Shields, Mr Ewen McAlpine, Mr Andrew Burkinshaw, Mr Bryan Duncan
Income: £9,628,093 [2016]; £8,068,365 [2015]; £12,789,434 [2014]; £9,054,874 [2013]; £6,225,023 [2012]

The London Community Foundation
Registered: 21 Mar 2002 *Employees:* 20 *Volunteers:* 1
Tel: 020 7326 2905 *Website:* londoncf.org.uk
Activities: General charitable purposes; education, training; advancement of health or saving of lives; disability; prevention or relief of poverty; accommodation, housing; arts, culture, heritage, science; amateur sport; environment, conservation, heritage; economic, community development, employment; other charitable purposes
Address: Unit 1.04, 9 Brighton Terrace, London, SW9 8DJ
Trustees: Mrs Gaynor Humphreys, Mr Sanjay Mazumder, Mr Martin Edgar Richards, Mr Nicholas Timothy John Reid, Miss Rosanna Manuela Machado, Mr William Rhys Moore, Mr Timothy Charles William Ingram, Mr Francis Salway, Mr Paul Gurney Cattermull
Income: £7,219,000 [2017]; £7,761,000 [2016]; £6,596,000 [2015]; £5,562,000 [2014]; £6,798,000 [2013]

London Cycling Campaign
Registered: 14 Aug 2006 *Employees:* 18 *Volunteers:* 200
Tel: 020 7234 9310 *Website:* lcc.org.uk
Activities: Education, training; advancement of health or saving of lives; environment, conservation, heritage; economic, community development, employment
Address: London Cycling Campaign, Unit 201 Metropolitan Wharf, 70 Wapping Wall, London, E1W 3SS
Trustees: Christian Wolmar, Dr Rachel Aldred, Tom Harrison, Simon Clark, Megan Sharkey, Ms Terry Patterson, Amy Foster, Mr James Heath, Chris Kenyon, Neil Webster
Income: £1,065,157 [2017]; £1,296,427 [2016]; £1,317,853 [2015]; £1,224,071 [2014]; £1,060,085 [2013]

London Cyrenians Housing Limited
Registered: 15 Apr 1975 *Employees:* 260 *Volunteers:* 3
Tel: 020 7938 2004 *Website:* londoncyrenians.org.uk
Activities: General charitable purposes; accommodation, housing
Address: Carlyle House, 235-237 Vauxhall Bridge Road, London, SW1V 1EJ
Trustees: Mr Stephen Bashorun, Miss Hannah Maxwell, Mrs Adine Kinchant Diggle, Mr Colin Makin, Dr Benjamin Lawrance Thomas, Mr Stephen Paul Chamberlain, Ms Chantal Diana Curtois Thompson, Dr Bhaskar Punukollu, Mr Michael Driver, Lucy Semmens, Mr Danny Cammiade
Income: £11,759,148 [2017]; £11,808,852 [2016]; £13,253,499 [2015]; £12,575,670 [2014]; £11,914,347 [2013]

The London Diocesan Board for Schools
Registered: 26 Jan 1967 *Employees:* 51
Tel: 020 7932 1165 *Website:* ldbs.co.uk
Activities: Education, training; religious activities
Address: London Diocesan Board for Schools, London Diocesan House, 36 Causton Street, London, SW1P 4AU
Trustees: Mr Simon Charles Villiers Surtees, The Venerable Luke Jonathan Miller, Rev Christopher Matthew Smith, Mr David Westlake Richards, Rev Desmond Banister, Mrs Carole Bevis-Smith, Rev Trevor Critchlow, Mrs Mary Embleton, Mrs Ianthe Priscilla McWilliams, Mr David Ackerman, Mr Mark Dunning, Mrs Mary Annannesta Findlow, Mrs Hannah Clemency Mason, Kate Henry, Rev Simon Atkinson, Mrs Helen Mary Morgan Edwards, Ms Sylvia Duthie, Rev Simon Peter John Clark, Mr Malcolm John Eady, Mr Roger Dean, Mrs Eliza Low, Mr Adrian Robert Barrett, Mr Richard Hugh Nicholson, Rev Stuart John King, Mrs Ann George, Mrs Judith Standing, Mrs Sonia George, Mr Richard Edmund Scott Walton, Mr Richard Bunce, Mr Andrew Paul Russell Garwood-Watkins
Income: £39,019,000 [2017]; £26,376,000 [2016]; £30,558,000 [2015]; £34,967,000 [2014]; £30,414,000 [2013]

The London Diocesan Fund
Registered: 18 Jul 1966 *Employees:* 84 *Volunteers:* 3
Tel: 020 7932 1000 *Website:* london.anglican.org
Activities: Religious activities
Address: Diocese of London, London Diocesan House, 36 Causton Street, London, SW1P 4AU
Trustees: Bishop of Stepney, Inigo Rodney Milman Woolf, Mr E D Roberts, Mr John Ronald Dolling, The Rev C J Amos, Mr D Hurst, Mr Clive Scowen, The Revd E Cargill Thompson, Mr James Normand, Archdeacon of Middlesex, Bishop of Fulham, Bishop of Islington, Mr M J Bithell, Ms Deborah Buggs, Mrs E M Barron, Mr Nigel Challis, Rev Judith Blackburn, Mr J Wilson, Archdeacon of Northolt, Dr Christopher Ward, Archdeacon of Hampstead, Mrs S Tett, The Revd S R Divall, Archdeacon of Hackney, Mr L Humby, Archdeacon of London, Rev Leslie Alan Moses, Mr Brian O'Donoghue, Bishop of Willesden, Mrs M D Roberts, Bishop of Kensington, Ms Josile Wenus Alexandra Munro, Mr Howard Arthur Evans, The Revd S M France, The Revd Canon Dr A J Joyce, The Revd C Smith, Mr David Richards, The Revd G Hunter, Mr J Thomas, Dr Phillip Rice, Associate Archdeacon of London, Mrs Anne Barrett, Very Reverend David Ison, Mrs Christina Sosanya, Bishop of Edmonton, Rev William John Rogers, The Rev A Foreshew-Cain, Ms A Casson, Miss A McLntyre, Mr Adam Benjamin Farlow
Income: £40,100,000 [2016]; £40,900,000 [2015]; £36,800,000 [2014]; £35,000,000 [2013]; £34,000,000 [2012]

The London Early Years Foundation

Registered: 31 Mar 1988 *Employees:* 554
Tel: 020 7834 8679 *Website:* leyf.org.uk
Activities: General charitable purposes
Address: London Early Years Foundation, 121 Marsham Street, London, SW1P 4LX
Trustees: Alethea Siow, Ms Helen Jenner, Latif Sayani, Michael Garstka, Sarah Wilson, Ms M Doogan, Caroline Tulloch, Ms Madeleine Clare Blackburn
Income: £18,336,086 [2017]; £14,814,489 [2016]; £12,311,471 [2015]; £10,568,992 [2014]; £9,037,329 [2013]

London Emergencies Trust

Registered: 28 Mar 2017 *Employees:* 3
Tel: 020 7255 4488
Activities: General charitable purposes; disability
Address: London Funders, Acorn House, 314-320 Gray's Inn Road, London, WC1X 8DP
Trustees: Clare Thomas, Carole Souter, Robin Allen, Thelma Stober, Bharat Mehta, Gerald Oppenheim, Ms Geeta Nargund
Income: £10,465,878 [2017]

London Film School Limited

Registered: 14 Nov 1975 *Employees:* 47
Tel: 020 7836 9642 *Website:* lfs.org.uk
Activities: Education, training; arts, culture, heritage, science; other charitable purposes
Address: London International Film School, 24 Shelton Street, London, WC2H 9UB
Trustees: Mr Graham John Easton, Ms Helen Patricia Dudley, Dan Chambers, Mr Kemal Akhtar, Mr Gisli Snaer, Mr Gregory Dyke, Mr Peter Armstrong, Professor Diana Green Davy CBE DL, Julie Parmenter
Income: £4,177,436 [2017]; £3,881,936 [2016]; £3,854,370 [2015]; £3,243,187 [2014]; £3,121,710 [2013]

London Grid for Learning Trust

Registered: 4 Feb 2002 *Employees:* 25
Tel: 020 8408 4455 *Website:* lgfl.net
Activities: Education, training
Address: CI Tower, St Georges Square, New Malden, Surrey, KT3 4TE
Trustees: Mr Paul Robinson, Mr Gary Hipple, Mr Nicholas Mitchell, Mr Sean Green, Ms Helen Warner, Ms Yvette Stanley
Income: £25,841,000 [2017]; £23,139,208 [2016]; £24,065,100 [2015]; £26,842,008 [2014]; £26,383,656 [2013]

London Higher

Registered: 26 Jun 2006 *Employees:* 21
Tel: 020 7391 0689 *Website:* londonhigher.ac.uk
Activities: Other charitable purposes
Address: London Higher, Tavistock House, Tavistock Square, London, WC1H 9JJ
Trustees: Professor Anthony Bowne, Dr Celia Caulcott, Professor John Raftery, Professor Deborah Gill, Mr Pat Loughrey, Professor Linda Drew, Professor Sir Adrian Smith FRS, Professor Paul O'Prey CBE, Professor David Maguire, Professor Peter John, Professor Paul Layzell
Income: £1,489,449 [2017]; £1,287,679 [2016]; £1,085,633 [2015]; £1,060,523 [2014]; £1,175,218 [2013]

The London Institute of Banking & Finance

Registered: 29 Jun 1987 *Employees:* 167
Tel: 01227 818635 *Website:* libf.ac.uk
Activities: Education, training
Address: London Institute of Banking & Finance, 4-9 Burgate Lane, Canterbury, Kent, CT1 2XJ
Trustees: Mr David Kennedy, Ms Amanda Francis, Alex Fraser, Mr Saajid Patel, Dr Jakob Pfaudler, Dr Maria Carapeto, Ms Shelley Doorey-Williams, Mr Ali Miraj, Professor Steven Haberman, Professor James Devlin, Mr Ian Stuart, Professor Damian Ward, Dr Thomas Huertas, Mr Harry Crossley, Ms Elona Gega, Ms Sakhila Mirza
Income: £14,073,000 [2017]; £13,996,000 [2016]; £13,671,000 [2015]; £15,048,000 [2014]; £13,099,000 [2013]

The London International Festival of Theatre Limited

Registered: 16 Feb 1983 *Employees:* 8 *Volunteers:* 60
Tel: 020 7968 6800 *Website:* liftfestival.com
Activities: Education, training; arts, culture, heritage, science
Address: Lift, Unit 19, Toynbee Studios, 28 Commercial Street, London, E1 6AB
Trustees: Bernard Donoghue Esq, Mr David Philip, Ms Aileen Walker, Ms Mitra Memarzia, Mr Simon London, Ms Hannah Azleb Pool, Mr Craig Hassall, Mr George Kessler, Mr Richard Huntington, Ms Helen Miranda Shute, Mr Alan James Strong
Income: £1,425,638 [2017]; £962,657 [2016]; £1,334,627 [2015]; £931,588 [2014]; £2,912,780 [2013]

The London Irish Centre

Registered: 16 Nov 2012 *Employees:* 19 *Volunteers:* 117
Tel: 020 7916 2222 *Website:* londonirishcentre.org
Activities: General charitable purposes; prevention or relief of poverty; religious activities; arts, culture, heritage, science; economic, community development, employment
Address: London Irish Centre, 52 Camden Square, London, NW1 9XB
Trustees: Ms Philomena Cullen, Ms Mary Kerrigan, Professor Mary Hickman, Mr Alex O'Cinneide, Ms Anna Doyle, Mr Michael O'Connor, Dermot Murphy, Ian McKim, Mr Nyall Stephen Jacobs, Mr Paddy Cowan, Ms Fiona Margaret Nolan, Mr Tom Goddard
Income: £1,004,783 [2017]; £1,240,697 [2016]; £990,421 [2015]; £1,084,427 [2014]

London Legal Support Trust

Registered: 4 Feb 2004 *Employees:* 5 *Volunteers:* 20
Tel: 020 7092 3972 *Website:* londonlegalsupporttrust.org.uk
Activities: General charitable purposes; prevention or relief of poverty
Address: London Legal Support Trust, National Pro Bono Centre, 49 Chancery Lane, London, WC2A 1JF
Trustees: Richard Dyton, Mr Peter John Gardner, Mr Steve Hynes, Mr Jeremy David Thomas, Ms Amanda Marguerite Illing, Mr Alistair Simon Woodland, Mr James Ian Harper, Mr Marc Norman Sosnow, Mr Graham Paul Huntley, Ms Joy Julien, Mrs Emma Turnbull, Mr Rodger Douglas Pressland, Ms Katharine Mary Pasfield
Income: £1,155,636 [2016]; £1,128,912 [2015]; £785,928 [2014]; £758,648 [2013]; £634,423 [2012]

The London Library
Registered: 8 Oct 1968 *Employees:* 62 *Volunteers:* 6
Tel: 020 7766 4713 *Website:* londonlibrary.co.uk
Activities: Education, training; arts, culture, heritage, science
Address: The London Library, 14 St James's Square, London, SW1Y 4LG
Trustees: Mr Philip Broadley, Miss Sophie Murray, Mr Philip Hook, Mr David Reade QC, Mr Anthony McGrath, Mr David Anthony Bisset Lough, Mr Giles Milton, Ms Isabelle Dupuy, Sir Howard Davies, Ms Sara Wheeler, Sir Andrew Popplewell, Mr Peter Stewart, Miss E B Herridge, Mr Will Harris, Mr Rick Stroud
Income: £4,077,447 [2017]; £3,468,953 [2016]; £3,581,153 [2015]; £4,241,142 [2014]; £4,415,173 [2013]

The London Marathon Charitable Trust Limited
Registered: 18 Jan 1982 *Employees:* 63 *Volunteers:* 8,000
Tel: 020 7902 0200 *Website:* lmct.org.uk
Activities: Amateur sport
Address: Marathon House, 190 Great Dover Street, London, SE1 4YB
Trustees: Mr John Eric Austin, Ms Dawn Austwick, Sir John Spurling KCVO OBE, Ms Rosie Chapman, Mr Charles Patterson Reed, Mr Alan Pascoe MBE, Ms Donna Fraser, Terry O'Neil, Sir Rodney Walker, Mr Simon Cooper, Mr Lee Mason, Mr Charles Maddock Johnston, Mr Robert Charles Rigby, Ms Clare Shepherd, Ms Gillian McKay
Income: £36,132,990 [2017]; £36,045,288 [2016]; £31,125,778 [2015]; £28,663,541 [2014]; £25,786,045 [2013]

The London Mathematical Society
Registered: 6 Nov 1967 *Employees:* 19
Tel: 020 7291 9979 *Website:* lms.ac.uk
Activities: Education, training
Address: London Mathematical Society, de Morgan House, 57-58 Russell Square, London, WC1B 4HS
Trustees: Professor Alexandre Borovik, Professor John Greenlees, Professor Robert Curtis, Professor Stephen Huggett, Dr Francis Clarke, Professor Iain Stewart, Professor Tara Brendle, Professor Sarah Zerbes, Professor Mark Chaplain, Professor Brita Nucinkis, Professor June Barrow-Green, Dr Anthony Gardiner, Professor John Hunton, Professor Catherine Hobbs, Professor Gwyneth Stallard, Professor David Evans, Dr Alina Vdovina, Dr Kevin Houston, Professor Andrew Dancer, Professor Emeritus Caroline Series
Income: £2,970,370 [2017]; £3,129,850 [2016]; £2,908,113 [2015]; £2,747,959 [2014]; £2,927,383 [2013]

London Oratory Charity
Registered: 17 Jun 1965 *Employees:* 15 *Volunteers:* 200
Website: bromptonoratory.co.uk
Activities: Religious activities; arts, culture, heritage, science; environment, conservation, heritage
Address: Brompton Oratory, Brompton Road, London, SW7 2RP
Trustees: Revd Ronald Creighton-Jobe, Rev Julian Peter Large, Rev Michael Lang, Rev George Bowen, Rev Rupert McHardy
Income: £1,698,302 [2016]; £1,151,588 [2015]; £1,811,445 [2014]; £1,404,605 [2013]; £1,723,038 [2012]

The London Orphan Asylum (Reed's School)
Registered: 7 May 1964 *Employees:* 158
Tel: 01932 868680 *Website:* reeds.surrey.sch.uk
Activities: Education, training
Address: Reeds School, Sandy Lane, Cobham, Surrey, KT11 2ES
Trustees: David Barnett, Mr John Simpson, Mr Ronald Stewart, Mrs Lucinda Napier FSI, Ms Bridget O'Brien-Twohig, Dr Alison McLean, Mr Martin Robinson, Mr Nigel Taunt, Mrs Mandy Donald, Mr David Richard Blomfield, Miss Karen Richardson, Mr Michael Wheeler BCom FCA, Mr Hugh Michael Priestley, Professor P J Sellin, Mr Steven Poole, Mrs Diana Mary Peacock, Mr Benn Shepherd, Mr James Fulton
Income: £15,708,000 [2017]; £15,006,000 [2016]; £14,495,000 [2015]; £14,837,000 [2014]; £13,007,000 [2013]

London Philharmonic Orchestra Limited
Registered: 12 Jan 1965 *Employees:* 35 *Volunteers:* 1
Tel: 020 7840 4200 *Website:* lpo.org.uk
Activities: Arts, culture, heritage, science
Address: London Philharmonic Orchestra Ltd, Camelford House, 87-90 Albert Embankment, London, SE1 7TP
Trustees: Mr Timothy Walker AM, Mr David Buckley, Roger Barron, Victoria Robey, Mr Neil Philip Westreich, Mr David Whitehouse, Henry Baldwin, Martin Hohmann, Mr Bruno De Kegel, Stewart McIlwham, Mr Gareth Newman, Dr Catherine Hogel, Mr Richard Brass, Mr Andrew Tusa, Al MacCuish, Ms Susanne Martens, Mr Pei Jee Ng
Income: £10,919,136 [2017]; £9,569,065 [2016]; £10,836,201 [2015]; £9,486,087 [2014]; £10,641,430 [2013]

The London Playing Fields Society
Registered: 18 Oct 1965 *Employees:* 27
Tel: 020 7323 0331 *Website:* lpff.org.uk
Activities: Education, training; advancement of health or saving of lives; amateur sport
Address: The London Playing Fields Foundation, 58 Bloomsbury Street, London, WC1B 3QT
Trustees: Mr Andy Sutch, Mr Colin Ainger, Mr Evan D R Stone QC, Ms Cara Turtington, Mr Anthony Ratcliffe FRICS FRSA, Ms Lucy McCrickard, Mr Dennis Hone, Mr Jack Miller, The Rt Hon The Earl Cadogan DL, Mrs Christine Double, Mrs Sally Hopper, Mr James William Murray Dalrymple, Ms Henrietta Martin-Fisher
Income: £1,426,700 [2017]; £1,683,340 [2016]; £1,283,123 [2015]; £1,278,637 [2014]; £1,925,735 [2013]

London School of Economics Students' Union
Registered: 26 Jul 2011 *Employees:* 246 *Volunteers:* 1,500
Tel: 020 7955 7158 *Website:* lsesu.com
Activities: Education, training; amateur sport; recreation
Address: Saw Swee Hock Centre, 1 Sheffield Street, London, WC2A 2AP
Trustees: Mr Zulum Elumogo, Mr Mahatir Pasha, Miss Eshoe Uwadiae, Miss Megan Beddoe, Miss Anjali Srinivas, Mr Rohan Sankhla, Mr Philip Ershov, Mr Daniel Cayford, Mr Peter Elliott, Miss Khadija Ahmed
Income: £7,357,951 [2017]; £6,637,542 [2016]; £6,245,217 [2015]; £5,721,403 [2014]; £3,380,675 [2013]

London School of Theology
Registered: 15 Jan 1964 *Employees:* 64
Tel: 01923 456000 *Website:* lst.ac.uk
Activities: Education, training; religious activities
Address: Green Lane, Northwood, Middlesex, HA6 2UW
Trustees: Prof Hugh Godfrey Maturin Williamson, Mr Paul Smith, Mr Steve Hughes, Rev Johnny Douglas, Mrs Margaret Doyle, Miss Elizabeth Hodkinson, Mr Malcolm Douglas Peckham, Mr Alex Irving, Rev Yemi Adedeji, Mr Ian Thompson
Income: £3,070,984 [2017]; £11,754,216 [2016]; £4,221,596 [2015]; £3,172,367 [2014]; £3,307,944 [2013]

London Skills for Growth Limited
Registered: 16 Jan 1984 *Employees:* 54
Tel: 020 8304 8527 *Website:* skillsforgrowth.org.uk
Activities: Education, training
Address: 19 Upland Road, Bexleyheath, Kent, DA7 4NR
Trustees: Sam Parrett, Mr Allan Carey, Mrs Mary Herbert, Mr David Eastgate, Ms Lucy Butler, Mr John Hunt
Income: £2,390,660 [2017]; £2,809,576 [2016]; £3,116,108 [2015]; £3,173,120 [2014]; £3,100,159 [2013]

London South Bank University Students' Union
Registered: 3 Sep 2014 *Employees:* 19 *Volunteers:* 1,159
Tel: 020 7815 6060 *Website:* lsbsu.org
Activities: General charitable purposes; education, training; amateur sport; recreation
Address: South Bank University, 103 Borough Road, London, SE1 0AA
Trustees: Mr Dean Casswell, Ms Nicola Allen, Mr Simon Little, Miss Samantha Robson, Mr Stevyn Kemp, Mr Joseph Anieke, Jennifer Diver, Sodiq Akinbade, Ms Katharine Colangelo, Ms Patrica Godwin, Mr Adnan Abdulhusein, Kate Wicklow
Income: £1,258,127 [2017]; £1,229,228 [2016]; £1,048,867 [2015]

London Sport
Registered: 8 Jan 2016 *Employees:* 50
Tel: 020 3848 4630 *Website:* londonsport.org
Activities: General charitable purposes; education, training; advancement of health or saving of lives; disability; amateur sport; recreation
Address: 4 Carisbrooke Close, Hornchurch, Essex, RM11 3QP
Trustees: Ms Joyce Ellen Ryan, Mr Richard Barker, Mr Kelvin Darren Charles Walker, Ms Kim Wright, Mr Shaun Richard Dawson, Mr Derek Michael Brewer, Dr Yvonne Doyle, Mr Doug Taylor, Ms Sadie Fiona Mason
Income: £5,706,950 [2017]

The London Symphony Orchestra Limited
Registered: 8 May 1964 *Employees:* 79 *Volunteers:* 27
Tel: 020 7382 1116 *Website:* lso.co.uk
Activities: Education, training; arts, culture, heritage, science
Address: Barbican Centre, Silk Street, London, EC2Y 8DS
Trustees: Mr Christopher John Moran, Mr Jonathan Moulds, Mr Gareth Davies, Mr Richard Hardie, Mr David Alberman, Mr Joost Bosdijk, Mr David Jackson, Ms Kathryn Alexandra McDowell, Mr Anthony Bloom, Dame Mary Marsh, Mr Matthew Gardner, Ms Clare Duckworth, Mr Niall Keatley
Income: £18,271,794 [2017]; £14,613,679 [2016]; £16,719,000 [2015]; £16,028,000 [2014]; £16,271,000 [2013]

London Transport Museum Limited
Registered: 7 Mar 2008 *Employees:* 95 *Volunteers:* 341
Tel: 020 7379 6344 *Website:* ltmuseum.co.uk
Activities: Education, training; arts, culture, heritage, science; environment, conservation, heritage
Address: London Transport Museum, 39 Wellington Street, London, WC2E 7BB
Trustees: Sam Mullins, Mr Andrew Philip Rothery, Mr David Howard Worthington, Sir Peter Gerard Hendy CBE, Mr Keith Ludeman, Hayaatun Sillem, Mrs Liz Alana Williams, Mr Philip Walter Swallow, Angela McConville, Mr Andrew Smith, Vernon Everitt, Ms Michelle Dix CBE, Mr Leon Daniels
Income: £16,359,000 [2017]; £15,599,000 [2016]; £15,095,000 [2015]; £15,492,000 [2014]; £14,661,000 [2013]

The London Wildlife Trust
Registered: 18 Jan 1982 *Employees:* 47 *Volunteers:* 1,005
Tel: 020 7261 0447 *Website:* wildlondon.org.uk
Activities: General charitable purposes; education, training; animals; environment, conservation, heritage
Address: Part First Floor, Dean Bradley House, 52 Horseferry Road, London, SW1P 2AF
Trustees: Ruth Chambers, Iona Joy, Stuart Wetherly, Helen Newman, Dr Melissa Glackin, Elaine Sullivan, Dianne Murphy, Richard Grimshaw, Dr John Tweddle, Rufus Radcliffe
Income: £3,126,000 [2017]; £3,195,050 [2016]; £2,734,052 [2015]; £2,605,491 [2014]; £3,141,162 [2013]

London Youth Games Limited
Registered: 16 Aug 1995 *Employees:* 10 *Volunteers:* 3,200
Tel: 01923 771977 *Website:* londonyouthgames.org
Activities: Amateur sport
Address: Cox Costello & Horne, Langwood House, 63-81 High Street, Rickmansworth, Herts, WD3 1EQ
Trustees: Cllr Joyce Ryan, Mr Marc Hope, Ms Karen Rothery, Mr Mark Campbell, Mr William Fraser, Cllr Christopher Hayes, Cllr Alan Till, Ms Jo Aitken, Mr Stephen Fitzgerald, Mr Martyn Worsley, Mr Stuart Burnside
Income: £1,341,624 [2017]; £1,114,866 [2016]; £1,021,628 [2015]; £1,033,194 [2014]; £1,260,505 [2013]

London Youth Rowing Ltd
Registered: 25 Feb 2008 *Employees:* 28 *Volunteers:* 120
Tel: 020 8223 7977 *Website:* londonyouthrowing.com
Activities: Education, training; disability; amateur sport; recreation
Address: Knowledge Dock Business Centre, 4 University Way, London, E16 2RD
Trustees: Mr John Desmond Kinsella, Mr Jonathan Grussing, Mr Samuel Sims, Mr Ian Edmondson, Mr James Downing, Mr David Browne, Krystyna Novak, Mr Alan Skewis
Income: £1,304,216 [2017]; £1,476,613 [2016]; £1,233,081 [2015]; £859,642 [2014]; £713,809 [2013]

London's Air Ambulance Limited
Registered: 16 Mar 1989 *Employees:* 41 *Volunteers:* 158
Tel: 020 3023 3300 *Website:* londonsairambulance.co.uk
Activities: The advancement of health or saving of lives
Address: 5th Floor, London Air Ambulance, 77 Mansell Street, London, E1 8AN
Trustees: Doctor Gareth Davies, Doctor David Lockey, Ms Samantha Walker, Mr Robert Gordon Neil Stewart Forsyth, Mr Adrian Walker, Mr Nicholas James Charrington, Mr Mark Vickers, William Michael Walden, Mr Edmund Paul Owen
Income: £9,193,909 [2017]; £10,731,732 [2016]; £8,082,060 [2015]; £4,802,180 [2014]; £4,092,039 [2013]

Longacre School
Registered: 18 Mar 2003 *Employees:* 51 *Volunteers:* 10
Tel: 01483 893225 *Website:* longacre.surrey.sch.uk
Activities: Education, training
Address: Hullbrook Lane, Shamley Green, Guildford, Surrey, GU5 0NQ
Trustees: Mr Jocelyn Monk, Mr Andrew Blurton, Mr Charles Henry Zorab, Mr Richard Herring, Dr Dominique Paul Daulton, Mrs Sheila Maxwell, Mrs Sue Brocksom, Mr Tim Pettit, Mrs Helen Jenkins, Mrs Deryle Whitehouse, Mrs Tracy Belinda Kirnig, Mr Simon David Moore
Income: £3,127,913 [2017]; £2,791,814 [2016]; £2,257,543 [2015]; £2,113,371 [2014]; £2,133,627 [2013]

Longborough Festival Opera
Registered: 2 Jul 2001 *Employees:* 6 *Volunteers:* 38
Website: lfo.org.uk
Activities: Education, training; arts, culture, heritage, science
Address: Linhay Barn, Hirons Hill, Little Rollright, Chipping Norton, Oxon, OX7 5QE
Trustees: Mrs E MB Graham, Mrs Lucy Le Fanu, Mrs Rosamund Bernays, Mr Denys Calder Firth, Mr Martin Graham, Mr Brian Muirhead, Mr Joseph Patrick Ralph Green
Income: £1,460,662 [2016]; £1,354,424 [2015]; £797,240 [2014]; £1,717,379 [2013]

Longfield Hospice Care
Registered: 29 Jan 1988 *Employees:* 134 *Volunteers:* 350
Tel: 01453 886868 *Website:* longfield.org.uk
Activities: Education, training; advancement of health or saving of lives
Address: Burleigh Lane, Minchinhampton, Glos, GL5 2PQ
Trustees: Mr Philip Parkinson, Ben Kushner, Dr Trevor John Bentley, Mr Neil Hampson, Mr Alan Kevin Simmons, Susan Reynolds, Dr Sarah Robinson, Dr Pam Swindell
Income: £3,421,418 [2017]; £2,940,679 [2016]; £4,013,833 [2015]; £2,618,435 [2014]; £2,606,179 [2013]

Longleigh Foundation
Registered: 2 Sep 2016
Tel: 0118 909 9266
Activities: General charitable purposes; education, training; advancement of health or saving of lives; disability; prevention or relief of poverty; accommodation, housing; environment, conservation, heritage; economic, community development, employment; recreation
Address: 100 Longwater Avenue, Green Park, Reading, Berks, RG2 6GP
Trustees: Mrs Elizabeth Jane Morris, Susan Terry, Anne Dokov, Stuart Shore, Mr Ron Williamson
Income: £1,467,356 [2017]

Longridge Towers School
Registered: 28 Feb 1983 *Employees:* 75 *Volunteers:* 4
Tel: 01289 307584 *Website:* lts.org.uk
Activities: Education, training
Address: Longridge Towers School, Berwick upon Tweed, Northumberland, TD15 2XQ
Trustees: Dr Emma Miller, Mrs Joanne Coats, Mr Adrian Bell, Mrs Christine Davies, Mr Thomas Bramald, Mrs Diane Dakers, Mr James Andrew Houston, Mr John Robertson, Mrs Jill McGregor, Rev Alastair Birkett, Mrs Alison Marshall
Income: £3,525,843 [2017]; £3,374,918 [2016]; £3,075,754 [2015]; £2,872,328 [2014]; £2,733,638 [2013]

Lonia Limited
Registered: 28 Apr 1981
Activities: General charitable purposes; education, training; disability; prevention or relief of poverty; overseas aid, famine relief; religious activities; economic, community development, employment
Address: c/o 8 Millfields Road, London, E5 0SB
Trustees: Mr Mathias Kraus, Mrs Miriam Kraus, Mr Moses Kennedy
Income: £2,520,581 [2017]; £1,744,323 [2016]; £1,938,968 [2015]; £3,372,547 [2014]; £2,863,172 [2013]

Henry Lonsdale Charitable Trust
Registered: 6 Jul 1979 *Employees:* 128
Tel: 01228 552222
Activities: Accommodation, housing
Address: Burnetts, 6 Victoria Place, Carlisle, CA1 1ES
Trustees: Mrs Christine Bowditch, Mr John Mallinson, Mrs Ann McKerrell, Ms Joanna Leith, Mrs Jessica Riddle, Mr John Bell, Mr Colin Stothard
Income: £2,159,878 [2017]; £1,978,850 [2016]; £1,879,232 [2015]; £1,765,894 [2014]; £1,718,850 [2013]

Lord Crewe's Charity
Registered: 20 Dec 2013 *Employees:* 1
Tel: 0191 384 7736 *Website:* lordcrewescharity.org.uk
Activities: Education, training; prevention or relief of poverty; religious activities
Address: The Miners' Hall, Durham, DH1 4BD
Trustees: The Venerable John Stuart Bain, Venerable Geoffrey Miller, Mr John Anderson, Mr James Fenwick, The Ven Ian Jagger, Professor Henry Ruxton Woudhuysen, Mr John Blackett-Ord
Income: £1,402,480 [2016]; £1,339,042 [2015]; £1,205,582 [2014]

The Lord Mayor's Appeal
Registered: 17 Sep 2012 *Employees:* 10
Tel: 020 7332 1320
Activities: Education, training; advancement of health or saving of lives; prevention or relief of poverty; arts, culture, heritage, science; environment, conservation, heritage
Address: Financial Services, Chamberlain's Department, Guildhall, London, EC2P 2EJ
Trustees: Dr Andrew Charles Parmley Alderman, Mr William Anthony Bowater Russell Alderman, Mr Vincent Thomas Keaveny Alderman, Ms Karina Ann Margarita Anastasia Robinson, Mr Peter Kenneth Estlin Alderman, Mr Timothy Russell Hailes JP, Mr Charles Edward Beck Bowman Alderman
Income: £1,828,967 [2016]; £3,432,317 [2015]; £2,751,088 [2014]; £1,885,751 [2013]

Lord Wandsworth College
Registered: 15 Aug 2011 *Employees:* 189 *Volunteers:* 4
Tel: 01256 862201 *Website:* lordwandsworth.org
Activities: Education, training
Address: Lord Wandsworth College, Long Sutton, Hook, Hants, RG29 1TB
Trustees: Mr Nicholas Clive Goulding, Mr Timothy Richard Prideaux, Mr David Walter Watts, Mr Robert Hannington, Mrs Lucinda Jane Fleming, Mrs Rachael Henshilwood, Mr Richard George Janaway, Mr Alasdair Kennedy, Mrs Caroline Cazenove, Mr Simon Clements, Mr Daniel Gowan, Mrs Karen Petty
Income: £14,815,101 [2017]; £12,475,777 [2016]; £12,408,750 [2015]; £11,894,227 [2014]; £11,512,524 [2013]

The Lord's Taverners
Registered: 20 Apr 1964 *Employees:* 31 *Volunteers:* 300
Tel: 020 7025 0000 *Website:* lordstaverners.org
Activities: Education, training; disability; amateur sport; economic, community development, employment
Address: 90 Chancery Lane, London, WC2A 1EU
Trustees: Mr David Collier OBE, Mrs Ruth Fitzsimons, Samantha Gladwell, Mr Ian Martin, Angela Rippon CBE, Richard White, John Taylor, Tim Graveney, Mr Alistair Subba Row, Suzy Christopher
Income: £6,301,655 [2017]; £5,932,907 [2016]; £6,719,282 [2015]; £5,461,186 [2014]; £5,701,041 [2013]

Lordswood Leisure Centre Limited
Registered: 22 Aug 2003 *Employees:* 37
Tel: 01634 682862 *Website:* lordswood-leisure.co.uk
Activities: The advancement of health or saving of lives; amateur sport
Address: Lordswood Leisure Centre, North Dane Way, Chatham, Kent, ME5 8YE
Trustees: Mr Michael George Rider, Mr Spencer John Grimwade, Mr Edward Turcan, Mr Simon Laurence Mannering, Mr Rodney William Hills, Mr Anthony Delaney, Miss Rachel Vanessa Attwood
Income: £1,115,578 [2016]; £1,006,250 [2015]; £939,486 [2014]; £918,836 [2013]

Lorenden School
Registered: 24 Aug 1995 *Employees:* 22 *Volunteers:* 1
Tel: 01795 590030 *Website:* lorenden.org
Activities: Education, training; amateur sport
Address: Painters Forstal, Faversham, Kent, ME13 0EN
Trustees: Mr David Charles Humphreys, Kent College Canterbury Trustee Company Limited
Income: £1,084,326 [2017]; £1,048,779 [2016]; £1,003,416 [2015]; £985,053 [2014]; £920,635 [2013]

Loughborough Schools Foundation
Registered: 28 Jul 2000 *Employees:* 612
Website: endowedschools.org
Activities: Education, training
Address: 3 Burton Walks, Loughborough, Leics, LE11 2DU
Trustees: Jennifer Lady Gretton, Mr Geoffrey Peter Fothergill BA FCIM, Mrs Mary Gershlick, Mrs Elizabeth Critchley, Mrs Phillippa Helen Mary O'Neill, Professor Alan Henry Dodson, Professor Robert John Allison BA PhD, Mr Anthony David Jones BA FCA, Sister Celine Leydon, Peter Middleton, Mrs Gillian Richards, Professor John Pliny Feather BLitt MA, Mr John Arthur Stone, Mr Peter M Jackson, Mrs Rowena Jane Elizabeth Limb, Mr Roger Harrison MA, Professor Julian Mark Ketley, Admiral Sir Trevor Alan Soar OBE, Mr Paul Simon Alexander, Paul Snelling
Income: £28,575,000 [2016]; £24,668,000 [2015]; £23,510,000 [2014]; £22,796,000 [2013]; £21,947,000 [2012]

Loughborough Students' Union
Registered: 30 Mar 2012 *Employees:* 214
Tel: 01509 635000 *Website:* lsu.co.uk
Activities: Education, training
Address: Loughborough Students Union, Ashby Road, Loughborough, Leics, LE11 3TT
Trustees: Mr John Palmer, Mr Doug Livingston, Miss Ashlea Prescott, Mr Sam Hanys, Miss Elliya Gemili, Mr Edward Radford, Mr Leo Yang, Richard Taylor, Mr Andrew James Doyle, Mr Hershil Patel, Mr George Etherington, Mr Dickens Ngoma, Mr Joey Scarf, Mr Rahul Mathasing
Income: £12,680,525 [2017]; £11,766,831 [2016]; £11,159,615 [2015]; £10,662,557 [2014]; £9,490,969 [2013]

Love Jesus Fund
Registered: 4 Dec 2014
Tel: 01737 768810
Activities: Religious activities
Address: 63 Ladbroke Road, Redhill, Surrey, RH1 1JU
Trustees: Mr Hugh Geoffrey Saunders, Mrs Patricia Maria McMenamin, Mr James Gerald McMenamin
Income: £1,399,523 [2017]; £259,986 [2016]

Low Cost Living Limited
Registered: 1 Sep 2008 *Employees:* 12
Tel: 020 8809 3569
Activities: The prevention or relief of poverty
Address: 4A Manor Road, London, N16 5SA
Trustees: Mr Sholem Gross, Mr Isaac Hochauser, Mr Moshe Lew
Income: £3,228,126 [2017]; £2,963,697 [2016]; £2,752,961 [2015]; £2,765,686 [2014]; £2,325,645 [2013]

The Lowry Centre Trust
Registered: 22 Mar 1996 *Employees:* 206 *Volunteers:* 280
Tel: 0161 876 2023 *Website:* thelowry.com
Activities: Education, training; arts, culture, heritage, science
Address: The Lowry Pier, 8 The Quays, Salford, M50 3AZ
Trustees: Councillor John Merry, Mr Michael Blackburn, Jane Frost, Councillor Bill Hinds, Adrian Vinken, Baroness Beverley June Hughes Privy Counsellor, Mr Nadav Kander, Rod Aldridge, Jim Taylor, Ian Currie, Mr Jeremy Glover, Mr Thomas Burns Russell, Baroness Jane Bonham-Carter
Income: £20,270,000 [2017]; £24,747,000 [2016]; £20,852,000 [2015]; £903,559 [2014]; £818,339 [2013]

The Loyola Preparatory School
Registered: 20 Feb 2001 *Employees:* 37 *Volunteers:* 1
Tel: 020 8506 9074 *Website:* loyola.essex.sch.uk
Activities: Education, training; religious activities; arts, culture, heritage, science; amateur sport; economic, community development, employment
Address: 60 Cuffley Hill, Goffs Oak, Waltham Cross, Herts, EN7 5EU
Trustees: Mr Michael Blundell, Fr John Joseph Harvey, Mr Dominic Savage, Mrs Anne Archibald, Mr David Maxim, Reverend Paul Abraham Ernest Fox, Mrs Patricia Alder
Income: £1,739,264 [2017]; £1,663,128 [2016]; £1,637,007 [2015]; £1,504,895 [2014]; £1,468,324 [2013]

Luckley House School Limited
Registered: 24 Jul 1962 *Employees:* 70
Tel: 0118 974 3201 *Website:* luckleyhouseschool.org
Activities: Education, training
Address: Luckley House School, Luckley Road, Wokingham, Berks, RG40 3EU
Trustees: Dr John Ledger, The Lady Jenny Farmer, Mr Bruce Gardiner, Mrs Claire Tao, Mrs L Moor, Mrs L Horrocks, Revd George Curry, Mr Michael Walker, Mr Andrew Imlay, Dr Verna Houghton, Mr D Kratt
Income: £3,714,684 [2017]; £3,732,701 [2016]; £6,225,933 [2015]; £5,717,588 [2014]; £3,833,809 [2013]

Lucton Pierrepoint School Educational Trust
Registered: 10 Oct 1986 *Employees:* 105
Tel: 01568 782000 *Website:* luctonschool.org
Activities: Education, training
Address: Queen Anne House, Lucton School, Lucton, Leominster, Herefords, HR6 9PN
Trustees: Mr Richard Tovey CertEd (Oxon), Simon Sherrey, Mrs Sarah Jane Eburn Handley, Mr Paul Maynard, Mr Patrick Armstrong, Mr Richard Michael Walden
Income: £4,523,105 [2017]; £4,171,171 [2016]; £4,192,095 [2015]; £3,804,804 [2014]; £3,466,691 [2013]

Lucy Cavendish College in the University of Cambridge
Registered: 7 Sep 2010 *Employees:* 80
Tel: 01223 332190 *Website:* lucy-cav.ac.uk
Activities: Education, training
Address: Lucy Cavendish College, Cambridge, CB3 0BU
Trustees: Dr Karen Ottewell, Dr Isobel Maddison, Dr Susan Jackson, Dr Jane Davies, Dr Sarah Gull, Dr Orsola Rath Spivack, Ms Lesley Thompson, Dr Sabine Bahn, Dr Shona Wilson, Dr Jennifer Louise Gibson, Dr Rumiana Vladimirova Yotova, Dr Annette Mahon, Dr Victoria Harvey, Dr Mary Augusta Brazelton, Dr Emma Howarth, Dr Kate Daniels, Ms Helen Louise Wain, Professor Ruth Cameron, Mrs Christine Houghton, Dr Jacqueline Brearley, Dr Jane Greatorex, Dr Henriette Hendriks, Dr Helen Louise Taylor, Ms Alison Vinnicombe, Dr Astrid Gall, Ms Jackie Ashley, Dr Eileen Mary Nugent, Dr Anne-Laura Van Harmelen, Dr Isabel Clare Huntington Clare, Ms Hanadi Jabado, Ms Joanna Kathleen Ryan, Dr Amber Ruigrok, Dr Marissa Quie
Income: £4,020,695 [2017]; £3,818,691 [2016]; £3,812,281 [2015]; £4,029,093 [2014]; £3,852,361 [2013]

The Lucy Faithfull Foundation
Registered: 20 Jul 1992 *Employees:* 48 *Volunteers:* 35
Tel: 01527 591922 *Website:* lucyfaithfull.org
Activities: Education, training; other charitable purposes
Address: The Lucy Faithfull Foundation, Bordesley Hall, The Holloway, Alvechurch, Birmingham, B48 7QA
Trustees: Dr Arnon Bentovim, Dr Michael Harris, Professor Derek Perkins, Ms Annie Shepperd, Dr Michael Robert Marett-Crosby, Mrs Susan Elizabeth Gubbins, Mr Paul West, Mr John Trotter, Proffessor Alec Spencer, Mrs Jane Leach, Mr David Aiden Lundholm
Income: £2,233,408 [2017]; £2,725,670 [2016]; £2,479,262 [2015]; £2,507,400 [2014]; £3,166,904 [2013]

Ludgrove School Trust Limited
Registered: 1 Sep 1972 *Employees:* 104 *Volunteers:* 10
Tel: 0118 978 9881 *Website:* ludgrove.net
Activities: Education, training
Address: Ludgrove Preparatory School, Ludgrove, Wokingham, Berks, RG40 3AB
Trustees: Mr Benedict John Holden, Mr Philip David Edey, Mr Rupert Michael Wiggin, Mr Paul Williams, Mr Michael Alexander Smyth-Osbourne, Mrs D'Arcy Donna Vigors, Mr Charles Langhorne Butterworth, Mr William Stewart Johnston, Mrs Emily Charlotte Chappell, Mr Guy Barker, Mr Richard Cormack, Mr Neil Brooks
Income: £5,486,018 [2017]; £5,422,005 [2016]; £4,974,546 [2015]; £5,028,821 [2014]; £4,699,207 [2013]

The Lullaby Trust
Registered: 1 Jan 1971 *Employees:* 31 *Volunteers:* 100
Tel: 020 7802 3205 *Website:* lullabytrust.org.uk
Activities: Education, training; advancement of health or saving of lives
Address: The Lullaby Trust (formerly FSID), 11 Belgrave Road, London, SW1V 1RB
Trustees: Ms Ethna Dillon, Mr Terrence George Hebden, Ms Gabrielle Osrin, Mr David Nicholas Marshall, Ms Kirsti Robertshaw, Mr Chris Cleaver, Mrs Rupal Kantaria, Doctor C E Daman Willems, Dr Stephen John Gould, Lavinia Postlethwaite, Ms Holly Butcher, Mr Justin Daniels, Dr Peter David Sidebotham
Income: £1,533,489 [2017]; £1,519,791 [2016]; £1,801,992 [2015]; £1,461,396 [2014]; £1,258,985 [2013]

Lumos Foundation
Registered: 21 Dec 2005 *Employees:* 78
Tel: 020 7253 6464 *Website:* wearelumos.org
Activities: Education, training; advancement of health or saving of lives; disability; prevention or relief of poverty; overseas aid, famine relief; accommodation, housing
Address: Peninsular House, 30-36 Monument Street, London, EC3R 8NB
Trustees: Miss Rita Dattani, Mr Sandy Loder, Mr Daniel Nicholas Cohen, Tanya Jeneme Motie, James Harding, Michelle Lee-Izu, Mr Neil Lyndon Marc Blair, Mr Robert Suss, Mr Mark Smith, Dianne Moore, Carol Copland
Income: £8,773,767 [2016]; £4,985,563 [2015]; £3,204,192 [2014]; £4,475,958 [2013]; £3,759,294 [2012]

Lupus UK
Registered: 29 Dec 1995 *Employees:* 7 *Volunteers:* 100
Tel: 01708 731251 *Website:* lupusuk.org.uk
Activities: The advancement of health or saving of lives; disability
Address: St James House, Eastern Road, Romford, Essex, RM1 3NH
Trustees: Mrs Yvonne Norton, Mrs Tina Stemp, Mrs Janet McComiskey, Mr Kevin Weston, Dr E Mellon, Mrs Jan Roberts, Mrs Karen Newby, Mr David Hopkins, Mrs Elaine Holland
Income: £1,074,479 [2016]; £920,747 [2015]; £917,115 [2014]; £940,315 [2013]; £1,036,972 [2012]

Luther King House Educational Trust
Registered: 12 Sep 2000 *Employees:* 35
Website: lutherkinghouse.org.uk
Activities: Education, training; religious activities
Address: Luther King House, Brighton Grove, Manchester, M14 5JP
Trustees: Rev Alexander Bradley, Rev Gerald Stanley Broadbent, Rev Keith Grant Jones, Margaret Swinson, Rev Dr Rosalind Selby, Rev Charles Nevin, Mrs Clare McBeath, Rev Fiona Thomas, Rev Simon Oxley, Revd Dr Andrew John Lunn
Income: £1,360,588 [2017]; £1,233,036 [2016]; £1,221,967 [2015]; £1,171,074 [2014]; £1,204,626 [2013]

Luton Cultural Services Trust
Registered: 27 Feb 2008 *Employees:* 175 *Volunteers:* 250
Website: lutonculture.com
Activities: Education, training; arts, culture, heritage, science
Address: Luton Cultural Services Trust, Luton Central Library, St Georges Square, Luton, Beds, LU1 2NG
Trustees: Mr David James Goodridge, Mr Andrew Strange, Mohammed Ahad, Nick Gibson, Mr Clive Borthwick, Mr Geoffrey John Mulgan
Income: £7,262,310 [2017]; £7,216,918 [2016]; £7,216,918 [2015]; £8,228,547 [2014]; £8,874,895 [2013]

The Luton and Dunstable Hospital Charitable Fund
Registered: 16 Oct 1996
Tel: 01582 718152 *Website:* ldh.nhs.uk
Activities: General charitable purposes; education, training; advancement of health or saving of lives
Address: 48 West Hill, Dunstable, Beds, LU6 3PW
Trustees: Luton & Dunstable Hospital NHS Foundation Trust
Income: £1,212,000 [2017]; £555,000 [2016]; £678,000 [2015]; £496,000 [2014]; £570,000 [2013]

Lycee International de Londres
Registered: 2 Mar 2015 *Employees:* 108
Tel: 020 3758 8571 *Website:* lyceeinternational.london
Activities: Education, training
Address: Lycee International de Londres, 54 Forty Lane, Wembley, Middlesex, HA9 9LY
Trustees: Arnaud Vaissie, Emma De Fontaubert, Laurent Bigorgne, Jennifer Banks Oughourlian, Mr Emmanuel Yann Simon Caradec, Bertrand Michaud, Jean-Christophe Gerard, Lionel Bouvard, Mrs Jane Anne Camblin
Income: £8,716,032 [2017]; £5,269,860 [2016]

Lymphoma Action
Registered: 2 Mar 1998 *Employees:* 30 *Volunteers:* 200
Tel: 01296 619428 *Website:* lymphoma-action.org.uk
Activities: Education, training; advancement of health or saving of lives; other charitable purposes
Address: Lymphoma Action, 3 Cromwell Court, New Street, Aylesbury, Bucks, HP20 2PB
Trustees: David Barnett, Mr Gordon Johns, Mrs June Cook, Mr Burton Paul, Mrs Tricia Cavell-Hill, Mr Mark Harrison, Mr Steve Dunn, Mrs Nicola King, Mr Jeremy Mark Harrington, Dr Cathy Burton
Income: £1,677,351 [2016]; £1,500,165 [2015]; £1,184,550 [2014]; £1,282,309 [2013]; £1,289,433 [2012]

Lyng Community Association
Registered: 31 Oct 2001 *Employees:* 4
Tel: 0121 525 5969 *Website:* lyng.org
Activities: General charitable purposes; prevention or relief of poverty; accommodation, housing; economic, community development, employment
Address: 3 Frank Fisher Way, West Bromwich, W Midlands, B70 7AW
Trustees: Ms Corilee Williams, Mr John Edwards, Mr Ian Keay, Mr Norman Hickson, Mrs Emma Neads, Mrs Wendy Bodenham, Miss Hannah Patrick, Mr Roger Clough, Mr Alan Moorhouse
Income: £1,091,072 [2017]; £1,060,639 [2016]; £988,249 [2015]; £931,536 [2014]; £867,106 [2013]

John Lyon's Charity
Registered: 16 Oct 1964 *Employees:* 9
Tel: 020 7259 1700 *Website:* jlc.london
Activities: Education, training; disability; prevention or relief of poverty; accommodation, housing; arts, culture, heritage, science; amateur sport; environment, conservation, heritage; economic, community development, employment; human rights, religious or racial harmony, equality or diversity; recreation
Address: Griffin Lodge, 45a Cadogan Gardens, London, SW3 2TB
Trustees: The Keepers & Governors of Possessions Revenues & Goods of Free Grammar School of John Lyon
Income: £7,886,000 [2017]; £8,427,000 [2016]; £7,993,000 [2015]; £7,246,000 [2014]; £6,755,000 [2013]

The Keepers and Governors of The Free Grammar School of John Lyon
Registered: 11 Jul 1966 *Employees:* 513
Tel: 020 7591 3333 *Website:* harrowschool.org.uk
Activities: Education, training; religious activities; arts, culture, heritage, science; amateur sport; environment, conservation, heritage
Address: Pemberton Greenish, 45 Cadogan Gardens, London, SW3 2AQ
Trustees: David Faber, Mr Mark Stroyan, Mr Richard Thomas George Winter BA FCA, Mr John P Batting MA FFA, The Hon Robert J Orr-Ewing, Admiral George M Zambellas DSC BSc FRAeS, Mr Charles Gerald Thoroton Stonehill MA, Mr Giles William Jeremy Goodfellow QC MA LLM, Angus Charles Goswell, David Eyton, Dr David James Payne MChem DPhil, Mr John H Dunston MA ACIL FRSA, Mrs Claire Marion Oulton MA PGCE, Mr Crispin Odey BA, Professor Graham Furniss PhD, Mr Matthew Kailey Fosh BA MSI, Susan Whiddington AB, Professor Paul Binski MA PhD FBA FSA, Dr Isis Abiodun Dove-Edwin BSc MDCM MRCP, Mrs Marina Spencer Brounger LLB, Mr Andrew Butler QC, Mr Adam David Hart LLB ACA FRSA, Mr James Philip John Glover BA
Income: £59,571,000 [2017]; £62,714,000 [2016]; £52,818,000 [2015]; £55,128,000 [2014]; £47,344,000 [2013]

Lyonsdown School Trust Ltd
Registered: 11 Jan 1974 *Employees:* 41
Tel: 020 8449 0225 *Website:* lyonsdownschool.co.uk
Activities: Education, training
Address: Lyonsdown School, 3 Richmond Road, New Barnet, Barnet, Herts, EN5 1SA
Trustees: Ms Andrea Morley, Mr Neil Cowie, Mrs Claire Osborn, Mr Lee Sigrist, Mr Simon Courtney, Ms Brenda Sheridan, Mr David Glass, Mr Alexis Andrea Kyriacou
Income: £1,893,859 [2017]; £1,839,380 [2016]; £1,708,446 [2015]; £1,815,160 [2014]; £1,732,492 [2013]

Lyric Theatre Hammersmith Limited
Registered: 10 Sep 1979 *Employees:* 84
Tel: 020 8741 6822 *Website:* lyric.co.uk
Activities: Arts, culture, heritage, science
Address: 139 Loder Road, Brighton, BN1 6PN
Trustees: Mrs Lisa Burger, Miss Janet Ellis, Belinda Donovan, Mr Kamran Mallick, Sue Fennimore, Sir William Atkinson, Mr Rajiv Parkash, Ashley Herman, Adam Peter Alexander Connell, Councillor Caroline Frances Needham
Income: £5,533,101 [2017]; £6,143,512 [2016]; £5,456,007 [2015]; £6,226,381 [2014]; £5,012,921 [2013]

M B Foundation (also known as Mossad Horav Moshe Aryeh Halevy)
Registered: 3 Mar 1965
Tel: 0161 787 7898
Activities: General charitable purposes; religious activities
Address: Fairways House, George Street, Prestwich, Manchester, M25 9WS
Trustees: Rabbi Wolf Kaufman, Rabbi Mordechai Bamberger
Income: £1,259,431 [2017]; £1,586,513 [2016]; £1,544,503 [2015]; £2,035,749 [2014]; £1,358,958 [2013]

M.G.S. Trust
Registered: 24 Oct 1966
Tel: 07814 611352
Activities: Education, training
Address: Manchester Grammar School, Old Hall Lane, Manchester, M13 0XT
Trustees: Mr James Herbert Tully, Mr Nigel John Richens, Mr Ian Thorpe, Mr William Lees-Jones, Mr Rowland Francis Warburton Flower
Income: £1,671,538 [2016]; £3,225,252 [2015]; £1,528,068 [2014]; £1,625,809 [2013]; £2,825,808 [2012]

MAC AIDS Fund
Registered: 11 May 2012
Tel: 0370 034 2545
Activities: Education, training; advancement of health or saving of lives
Address: Unit 3 Kites Croft Business Park, Warsash Road, Fareham, Hants, PO14 4FL
Trustees: Professor Jane Anderson, Ms Karen Sue Weiler, Ms Nancy Mahon
Income: £2,176,000 [2017]; £3,084,000 [2016]; £2,708,000 [2015]; £1,940,000 [2014]; £2,648,000 [2013]

MCCH
Registered: 1 Apr 2014 *Employees:* 1,356 *Volunteers:* 72
Tel: 01622 722410 *Website:* mcch.org.uk
Activities: General charitable purposes; education, training; advancement of health or saving of lives; disability; accommodation, housing; economic, community development, employment
Address: One Hermitage Court, Hermitage Lane, Maidstone, Kent, ME16 9NT
Trustees: Mr Paul McGee, Mr Colin Mills, Ms Anne Chapman, Mrs Kate Wood, Ms Lynda Frampton, Mr Ian Bell, Mr Oliver Mills, Mr Peter Hasler, Mr Chris Dorey
Income: £33,073,000 [2017]; £34,019,000 [2016]; £38,741,385 [2015]

MK Gallery
Registered: 10 Dec 1996 *Employees:* 20 *Volunteers:* 8
Tel: 01908 558321 *Website:* mkgallery.org
Activities: Education, training; arts, culture, heritage, science
Address: MK Gallery, 3 Theatre Walk, Milton Keynes, Bucks, MK9 3PX
Trustees: Cllr David Hopkins, Ms Jill Veronica Stansfield, Kirsty Anson, Neil Smith, Mr Charles Douglass Welch, Mr David John Chadwick Danskin, Mr David King, Mr Will Cousins, Mrs Elizabeth Patricia Gifford, Mr Peter Marland, Mr Mark Rayner, Mrs Sunita Yeomans, Mr Kevin Bowsher
Income: £2,029,156 [2017]; £2,233,964 [2016]; £1,154,866 [2015]; £1,301,213 [2014]; £1,054,206 [2013]

MQ: Transforming Mental Health
Registered: 19 Jan 2011 *Employees:* 23 *Volunteers:* 10
Tel: 0300 030 8100 *Website:* mqmentalhealth.org
Activities: Education, training; advancement of health or saving of lives; disability
Address: 6 Honduras Street, London, EC1Y 0TH
Trustees: Clare Matterson, Sir Philip Campbell, Professor Emily Holmes, Helen Munn, Shahzad Malik, John A Herrmann Jr, Ms Irene Tracey, Peter Jones, Shaun Horan, Chris Parsons, Arash Hejazi
Income: £6,341,449 [2017]; £6,111,220 [2016]; £234,897 [2015]; £100,160 [2014]; £250,466 [2013]

MV Balmoral Fund Limited
Registered: 15 Jan 2014 *Employees:* 6 *Volunteers:* 107
Tel: 01737 642305 *Website:* mvbalmoral.org.uk
Activities: Arts, culture, heritage, science
Address: 21 South Close Green, Merstham, Redhill, Surrey, RH1 3DU
Trustees: Mr Andrew James Jardine, Dr John Douglas Naysmith, Mr John Robert Thomas, Mr David Gwyn Bassett, Mr Henry Richard Adye Mills
Income: £1,771,567 [2016]; £812,943 [2015]

MYBNK
Registered: 21 Apr 2008 *Employees:* 22 *Volunteers:* 15
Website: mybnk.org
Activities: Education, training
Address: Unit 4 Huguenot Place, 17a Heneage Street, London, E1 5LN
Trustees: Ms Margaret Mary Louise Morrissey, Mr Karim Kefi, Ms Elisabetta Lapenna-Huda, Mr Gary Coyle, Mr Viral Kataria, Mr Michael Mompi, Ms Simona Paravani-Mellinghoff
Income: £1,100,619 [2016]; £1,064,510 [2015]; £959,508 [2014]; £928,997 [2013]; £683,604 [2012]

Ellen MacArthur Cancer Trust
Registered: 12 Mar 2003 *Employees:* 13 *Volunteers:* 187
Tel: 01983 297750 *Website:* ellenmacarthurcancertrust.org
Activities: Education, training; advancement of health or saving of lives; amateur sport
Address: East Cowes Marina, Britannia Way, East Cowes, Isle of Wight, PO32 6UB
Trustees: Mr Richard Butcher, Mr Christopher Micklethwaite, Ms Claire Amaladoss, Mr Joseph Burnie, Mr Martin Pluves, Dr David Hobin, Joanne Grindley, Dame Ellen Patricia MacArthur, Ms Sally Tami, Mr Peter Charles Grenville Cazalet
Income: £1,456,390 [2017]; £1,370,816 [2016]; £1,085,308 [2015]; £1,058,860 [2014]; £693,546 [2013]

Ellen MacArthur Foundation
Registered: 23 Jun 2009 *Employees:* 85
Tel: 01983 296463 *Website:* ellenmacarthurfoundation.org
Activities: Education, training; economic, community development, employment
Address: The Sail Loft, 42 Medina Road, Cowes, Isle of Wight, PO31 7BX
Trustees: Mr Philip Sellwood, Dame Ellen MacArthur, Mr Peter Morgan
Income: £8,694,235 [2017]; £9,814,284 [2016]; £3,803,045 [2015]; £2,761,229 [2014]; £2,166,056 [2013]

The MacDaibhidh Charitable Trust
Registered: 7 Sep 2016
Tel: 0141 428 3353
Activities: General charitable purposes
Address: c/o Brodies LLP, 110 Queen Street, Glasgow, G1 3BX
Trustees: Mr John Davidson, Brodies & Co (Trustees) Limited, Mrs Janet Alison Davidson
Income: £6,429,039 [2017]

The MacFarlane Trust

Registered: 22 Mar 1988
Tel: 020 7808 1172 *Website:* macfarlane.org.uk
Activities: The advancement of health or saving of lives; disability; prevention or relief of poverty
Address: The MacFarlane Trust, Alliance House, 12 Caxton Street, London, SW1H 0QS
Trustees: Mr Patrick Spellman, Ms Vanessa Martlew, Mr Jamie O'Hara, Mr Matt Gregory, Mr Alasdair Murray, Mr Paul Biddle
Income: £2,048,836 [2017]; £2,087,821 [2016]; £2,137,692 [2015]; £2,160,593 [2014]; £2,153,100 [2013]

MacIntyre Care

Registered: 23 Dec 1966 *Employees:* 2,059 *Volunteers:* 150
Tel: 01908 230100 *Website:* macintyrecharity.org
Activities: Education, training; disability; accommodation, housing
Address: MacIntyre Care, 602 South Seventh Street, Milton Keynes, Bucks, MK9 2JA
Trustees: Mr John Robert Lloyd Berriman, Mrs Rosemary Hart, Mrs Nikki Williams-Ellis, Rachel Taylor Rachel Taylor, Ruth Smyth, Dr Dragana Josifova, Mr Duncan Strachan, Mr Martin Zahra, Mr Neil MacMillian, Adam Goldstein, Pamela Meek
Income: £47,846,000 [2017]; £45,652,000 [2016]; £45,232,000 [2015]; £45,870,000 [2014]; £47,846,000 [2013]

Maccabi GB

Registered: 25 Jun 2003 *Employees:* 19 *Volunteers:* 250
Tel: 020 8457 2333 *Website:* maccabigb.org
Activities: Education, training; religious activities; amateur sport
Address: Maccabi GB, Shield House, Harmony Way, London, NW4 2BZ
Trustees: Mr David Pinnick, Mr Daniel James Rubin, James Lever, Mr Marc Jeremy Levy, Daniel Gordon
Income: £1,011,216 [2016]; £1,654,481 [2015]; £1,291,177 [2014]; £2,736,856 [2013]; £1,022,137 [2012]

The Machzikei Hadass Communities

Registered: 14 Aug 1964 *Employees:* 23
Tel: 0161 660 3492
Activities: General charitable purposes; prevention or relief of poverty; religious activities
Address: Enterprise House, 3 Middleton Road, Manchester, M8 5DT
Trustees: Mr A Reich, Mr Yehuda Aryeh Sanger, Mr Morris Brunner, Mr Yaakov Menachem Salomon
Income: £2,711,971 [2016]; £2,646,389 [2015]; £2,376,533 [2014]; £2,039,295 [2013]; £1,882,664 [2012]

Macmillan Cancer Support

Registered: 21 Jun 1989 *Employees:* 1,642 *Volunteers:* 20,000
Website: macmillan.org.uk
Activities: Education, training; advancement of health or saving of lives; prevention or relief of poverty
Address: Macmillan Cancer Support, 89 Albert Embankment, London, SE1 7UQ
Trustees: Ms Julia Palca, Mr Andrew Duff, Ms Una Noelle O'Brien, Mr Toby Strauss, Mr Feilim Mackle, Dr Jagjit Singh Ahluwalia, Professor Timothy Eisen, Ms Suki Thompson, Mr Richard Andrew Murley, Ms Jane Cummings, Mr Iain Charles Andrew Cornish, Ms Susan Carol Langley
Income: £247,441,000 [2016]; £230,211,000 [2015]; £218,430,000 [2014]; £189,709,000 [2013]; £155,688,000 [2012]

Macmillan Caring Locally

Registered: 10 Sep 1974 *Employees:* 42 *Volunteers:* 150
Tel: 01202 477628 *Website:* macmillanlocal.org
Activities: The advancement of health or saving of lives
Address: Christchurch Hospital, Fairmile Road, Christchurch, Dorset, BH23 2JX
Trustees: Mr Keith Lomas, Mrs Jean Kelleway, Mr Keith Thomas Wilkinson, Mr Michael Emsley, Mr Jonathan Harvey
Income: £3,163,372 [2017]; £2,367,178 [2016]; £2,225,661 [2015]; £2,004,435 [2014]; £1,887,625 [2013]

The Macular Disease Society

Registered: 10 Dec 1990 *Employees:* 49 *Volunteers:* 1,430
Website: macularsociety.org
Activities: The advancement of health or saving of lives; disability
Address: Crown Chambers, South Street, Andover, Hants, SP10 2BN
Trustees: Timothy Ffytche, Mr John Dunston, Mrs Margaret Packham, Mr Paul Ryb, Mr Toby Evans, Mr Stephen Stacey, Mrs Cecilia Bufton, Mrs Frances Luff, Mr Steven Kendall, Mr Alan Howell, Dr Lucy Howe, Mr Alan MacFarlane, Mr Marytn Long CBE, Mrs Alison Guthrie, Mr Richard Piller, Ms Anna Fletcher, Mr Wiilliam John Best
Income: £4,161,000 [2017]; £3,735,000 [2016]; £3,759,000 [2015]; £3,661,000 [2014]; £3,313,000 [2013]

Magdalen & Lasher Charity - Old Hastings House, Charitable Incorporated Organisation

Registered: 22 Oct 2014 *Employees:* 81 *Volunteers:* 10
Tel: 01424 452642 *Website:* oldhastingshouse.co.uk
Activities: The advancement of health or saving of lives; prevention or relief of poverty; other charitable purposes
Address: Old Hastings House, 132 High Street, Hastings, E Sussex, TN34 3ET
Trustees: Mr Gareth Bendon, Mr Keith Donaldson, Mrs Ann Wing, Mrs Jenny Blackburn, Mr Ian Steel, Cllr Andrew Patmore, Dr Patricia Lock, Mr Clive Galbraith, Mr Michael Foster, Mrs Susan Phillips, Mrs Dawn Poole, Mrs Susan Parsons, Cllr James Bacon, Fr Luke Irvine Capel
Income: £1,659,615 [2017]; £1,545,169 [2016]

The Magdalen College Development Trust

Registered: 9 Jul 1977
Tel: 01865 276105 *Website:* magd.ox.ac.uk
Activities: Education, training
Address: Magdalen College, High Street, Oxford, OX1 4AU
Trustees: Prof John Nightingale, Mr Mark Loveday, Prof Paul O'Brien CBE, Mr Anthony Todd, Dr Jan Hruska, Mr Paul Beckwith, Mr Simon Haslam, Lord Jay of Ewelme, Ms C A Berman, Mr Robert Peter Leechman, Prof Toby Garfitt, Ms Felicity Toube, Prof Sir David Charles Clary, Mr David Foxton, Mr James Cronin, Mrs E C Davies, Dr Barbara Domayne-Hayman, Mr Rory Maw, Mr Thomas Meakin
Income: £4,162,365 [2017]; £4,620,252 [2016]; £3,482,696 [2015]; £3,529,351 [2014]; £2,975,402 [2013]

Magdalen College School Oxford Limited
Registered: 13 Mar 1987 *Employees:* 261
Tel: 01865 242191 *Website:* mcsoxford.org
Activities: Education, training; religious activities; arts, culture, heritage, science; amateur sport
Address: Magdalen College School, Cowley Place, Oxford, OX4 1DZ
Trustees: Mr Timothy Peter Warren Edwards, Dr Nigel Richardson, Dr Catharine Alice Benson, Mr Charles Young, Dr Stuart Robert MacKenzie, Prof Constantin Coussios, Mr Paul Withers, Mr Benjamin Vessey, Mr Neil Record, Ms Penny Cameron Watt, Ms Judith Anne Lennox Longworth, Professor Daniel Heinrich Friedrich Kroening, Mr Adrian Dennis James, Ms Jan Phillips, Dr Richard Saldanha
Income: £16,252,525 [2017]; £17,257,414 [2016]; £16,753,605 [2015]; £13,964,531 [2014]; £12,805,834 [2013]

The Magdi Yacoub Institute
Registered: 3 Oct 2000 *Employees:* 9
Activities: Education, training; advancement of health or saving of lives
Address: Heart Science Centre, Hill End Road, Harefield, Uxbridge, Middlesex, UB9 6JH
Trustees: The Hon Anne Collins, Mr Asghar Khaghani, Dr Luis Alberto Tomatis, Dr Assem Allam, Alan Hargreaves, Lord Gowrie, Dr Rosemary Claire Radley Smith, Professor Yacoub, Professor Kim Fox, Doctor Magdy Ishak
Income: £1,546,021 [2017]; £876,197 [2016]; £1,496,113 [2015]; £1,201,807 [2014]; £1,448,429 [2013]

Magen David Adom UK
Registered: 23 Mar 2006 *Employees:* 7 *Volunteers:* 150
Website: mdauk.org
Activities: The advancement of health or saving of lives; overseas aid, famine relief
Address: Shield House, Harmony Way, off Victoria Road, Hendon, London, NW4 2BZ
Trustees: Mr Robin Ellison, Mr Nicholas Springer, Mr Russell Jacobs, Mr Adam Clyne, Mr Daniel Levy, Mr Nicholas Posnansky, Mr Marc Ian Franks, Mrs Lorraine Grossmith, Mr Toni Shasha, Mr James Ward, Dr David James Curtis, Mrs Patricia Abram, Mr Brian Kalms
Income: £4,534,708 [2016]; £5,702,190 [2015]; £5,662,067 [2014]; £6,970,307 [2013]; £3,769,087 [2012]

Magic Breakfast
Registered: 5 Mar 2004 *Employees:* 24
Tel: 020 7836 5434 *Website:* magicbreakfast.com
Activities: Education, training; advancement of health or saving of lives; prevention or relief of poverty
Address: 190 High Holborn, London, WC1V 7BH
Trustees: Ms Paula Smith, Ms Nicola Noble, Mr Stephen Bethel, Mr John McIvor, Ms Tamar Kasriel, Ms Alexandra Prentice, Mr David Reay
Income: £2,131,219 [2016]; £1,963,731 [2015]; £755,732 [2014]; £509,228 [2013]; £495,689 [2012]

Magna Trust
Registered: 8 Mar 1999 *Employees:* 75
Tel: 01709 723109 *Website:* visitmagna.co.uk
Activities: Education, training; arts, culture, heritage, science; environment, conservation, heritage; recreation
Address: Magna Science Adventure Centre, Sheffield Road, Rotherham, S Yorks, S60 1DX
Trustees: Mr Michael John Smith, Mr Michael Yarlett, Mr Brian Chapple, Mr Kevin Tomlinson
Income: £1,772,693 [2017]; £2,061,280 [2016]; £2,061,280 [2015]; £1,972,102 [2014]; £2,191,764 [2013]

Magna Vitae
Registered: 26 Jan 2015 *Employees:* 171 *Volunteers:* 42
Tel: 01507 613441 *Website:* magnavitae.org
Activities: Arts, culture, heritage, science; recreation
Address: Meridian Leisure Centre, Wood Lane, Louth, Lincs, LN11 8RS
Trustees: Mr Peter Helps, Mrs Pauline Watson, Mr Ashley Robert Lidgard, Mr Terence Charles Ball, Mr Jonathan Stones, Ms Hollie Wells, Mrs Doreen Stephenson, Mr Roger Edward Goldsmith, Mr Ian Robert Emmerson OBE, Mrs Sarah Dodds, Mrs Susan Lorraine Kitchen
Income: £7,433,130 [2017]; £8,525,362 [2016]

Magpas
Registered: 17 May 2007 *Employees:* 17 *Volunteers:* 150
Tel: 01480 371060 *Website:* magpas.org.uk
Activities: The advancement of health or saving of lives
Address: Magpas, Centenary House, St Marys Street, Huntingdon, Cambs, PE29 3PE
Trustees: Mr Mark John Broadbent, Nigel Brown OBE, Lorraine Ann Greasley, Anne Booth, Mr Paul Casciato, Mr Simon Standen, Dr Peter John Pashley Holden, Mr Christopher Dodd, Mr Thomas John Hampton Bennett, Loretto Leavy, Mr Hugh Robert Parnell
Income: £3,766,387 [2016]; £3,543,403 [2015]; £2,777,425 [2014]; £2,318,426 [2013]; £1,583,275 [2012]

Maharishi Foundation
Registered: 16 Oct 1975 *Employees:* 53 *Volunteers:* 40
Tel: 01342 825020 *Website:* uk.tm.org
Activities: Education, training
Address: 41 Park Crescent, Forest Row, E Sussex, RH18 5ED
Trustees: Mr Gwyndaf Evans, Mr Ajay Prakash Shrivastava, Mr William Graham Orr, Mr Keith Parker, Miss Jane Jemima Pitman, Mr David Clark Rae, Mr David Emrys Hughes
Income: £4,503,024 [2016]; £2,610,005 [2015]; £2,479,968 [2014]; £2,198,818 [2013]; £2,015,745 [2012]

Maharishi School Trust Limited
Registered: 17 Sep 1986 *Employees:* 33 *Volunteers:* 2
Tel: 01695 729912 *Website:* maharishischool.com
Activities: Education, training
Address: Maharishi School, Cobbs Brow Lane, Lathom, Ormskirk, Lancs, L40 6JJ
Trustees: Mr Gwyndaf Evans, Dr Ian Brian Birnbaum OBE, Mrs Ellen Freel, Mrs Lavinia Wilkinson, Mrs Paula Wynne, Mr Steven Panter, Mr Richard William Buswell, Lisa Walters, Mrs Mareanna Ingram, Mr Jonathon Gregory Phillips, Mrs Lisa Edwards, Mrs Jane Ann Smalley
Income: £1,299,715 [2016]; £1,222,474 [2015]; £1,074,216 [2014]; £843,049 [2013]; £1,604,078 [2012]

Mahdlo (Oldham Youth Zone)
Registered: 22 Feb 2010　*Employees:* 53　*Volunteers:* 91
Tel: 0161 624 0111　*Website:* mahdloyz.org
Activities: Education, training; disability; arts, culture, heritage, science; amateur sport
Address: Mahdlo, Egerton Street, Oldham, Lancs, OL1 3SE
Trustees: Mrs Janelle Meuth Barker, Mr William George Richard Lees-Jones, Mr Terence Flanangan, Mr John Ainley, Mr David Benstead, Mr Shadab Qumer, Mr Kashif Ashraf, Mr Timothy Robert Mitchell, Mr Lindsay Walsh, Ms Carol O'Hare, Mr David Richard Whaley
Income: £1,955,515 [2017]; £1,894,467 [2016]; £5,776,733 [2015]; £1,142,750 [2014]; £1,009,891 [2013]

Maidstone YMCA
Registered: 17 Jun 2005　*Employees:* 76　*Volunteers:* 50
Tel: 01622 749404　*Website:* maidstoneymca.org.uk
Activities: General charitable purposes; education, training; religious activities; amateur sport; economic, community development, employment; recreation
Address: Maidstone YMCA Sports Centre, Melrose Close, Cripple Street, Maidstone, Kent, ME15 6BD
Trustees: Mrs Valerie Wallis MBE, Michael Yates, Mr Derek John Mortimer, Mr John Andrew Collins, Miss Stephanie Joy Rose, Mr Bryan Price, David Thomas, Mrs Susan Watson, Mr Keith Anthony Mandy
Income: £1,006,410 [2017]; £1,079,989 [2016]; £888,143 [2015]; £843,733 [2014]; £789,966 [2013]

Maidwell Hall School
Registered: 11 Nov 1962　*Employees:* 50
Tel: 01604 233233　*Website:* maidwellhall.co.uk
Activities: Education, training
Address: Hewitsons, Elgin House, Billing Road, Northampton, NN1 5AU
Trustees: Dr Anthony Wallersteiner, Mr Richard Cunningham, Mr William Wyatt, Mr Karl Barrie Jenkins, Hector MacLennan, Mr David Frank Chaplin, Mrs Clare Macro, Claire Redmayne, Mrs Henrietta Wates
Income: £2,650,762 [2017]; £2,635,286 [2016]; £2,366,078 [2015]; £3,376,553 [2014]; £2,524,965 [2013]

The Makaton Charity
Registered: 25 Jun 2007　*Employees:* 12
Tel: 01276 606760　*Website:* makaton.org
Activities: General charitable purposes; education, training; disability
Address: The Makaton Charity, Westmead House, Farnborough, Hants, GU14 7LP
Trustees: Matthew Cock, Mr Michael Richard Barnett, Ms Juliet Claire Armstrong, Mrs Sue Sjuve, Mrs Lori Cunningham
Income: £1,047,612 [2017]; £1,184,410 [2016]; £1,080,312 [2015]; £1,096,057 [2014]; £1,256,940 [2013]

Make-a-Wish Foundation UK
Registered: 9 Dec 1986　*Employees:* 71　*Volunteers:* 588
Tel: 01276 405060　*Website:* make-a-wish.org.uk
Activities: The advancement of health or saving of lives
Address: 7th Floor, Thames Tower, Station Road, Reading, Berks, RG1 1LX
Trustees: Mr David Hockley, Mr Damian Thornton, Mrs Catherine Salter, Mr Per Harkjaer, Mr Brian Edward Robinson, Mr Ed Smith
Income: £7,031,367 [2016]; £9,934,741 [2015]; £7,439,474 [2014]; £6,400,442 [2013]; £6,294,834 [2012]

Making Space
Registered: 27 Jul 1982　*Employees:* 995　*Volunteers:* 1,245
Tel: 01925 581798　*Website:* makingspace.co.uk
Activities: General charitable purposes; education, training; advancement of health or saving of lives; disability; accommodation, housing
Address: Making Space, 46 Allen Street, Warrington, Cheshire, WA2 7JB
Trustees: Mr Ted McGuinness, Mr Brian Marshall, Mr Alan Richard Teague, Mrs Elaine Johnstone, Mr Neil Allen, Mrs Anne Josephine Broadhurst, Mr John Heritage
Income: £24,824,000 [2017]; £23,647,151 [2016]; £23,754,965 [2015]; £21,295,266 [2014]; £20,679,376 [2013]

Malaria Consortium
Registered: 1 Oct 2003　*Employees:* 395
Tel: 020 7549 0213　*Website:* malariaconsortium.org
Activities: Education, training; advancement of health or saving of lives; prevention or relief of poverty; overseas aid, famine relief
Address: Malaria Consortium, 56-64 Leonard Street, London, EC2A 4LT
Trustees: Professor Brian Greenwood, Dr Precious Lunga, Dr Joanna Schellenberg, Dr Simon Kay, Mr Canisius Anthony, Mrs Sarah Veilex, Mr Mark Clark, Baroness Shaista Sheehan, Professor Fred Binka, Dr Nermeen Varawalla, Mr Peter Potter-Lesage, Dr Neil Frederick Squires, Dr Allan Max Schapira, Mr Anthony Davy, Professor Marcel Tanner
Income: £55,031,000 [2017]; £40,853,000 [2016]; £58,298,000 [2015]; £54,534,699 [2014]; £31,222,204 [2013]

Malaria No More United Kingdom
Registered: 8 Oct 2008　*Employees:* 12　*Volunteers:* 5
Tel: 020 3752 5862　*Website:* malarianomore.org.uk
Activities: The advancement of health or saving of lives; overseas aid, famine relief
Address: The Foundry, 17 Oval Way, London, SE11 5RR
Trustees: Justine Margaret Frain, Dr Linda Yueh, Mr Philip Thomas, Dr Alaa Murabit, Mr Andrew Cook, Mr Paul Green, Mr Simon James Robert Bland
Income: £2,026,811 [2016]; £1,063,296 [2015]; £1,787,569 [2014]; £1,081,439 [2013]; £983,223 [2012]

Malawi Relief Fund UK
Registered: 11 Jun 2007　*Volunteers:* 30
Tel: 01254 675030　*Website:* malawirelief.org
Activities: General charitable purposes; education, training; advancement of health or saving of lives; prevention or relief of poverty; overseas aid, famine relief; religious activities; arts, culture, heritage, science; amateur sport; environment, conservation, heritage
Address: P O Box 620, Blackburn, BB2 9LR
Trustees: Mr Faruk Ibrahim Bharucha, Mr Yusuf Mahomed Mangera, Qari Ismail, Mr Ahmed Bobat, Mr Ismail Valli, Mr Zunaid A Saeed Chunara
Income: £1,185,989 [2016]; £591,829 [2015]; £402,747 [2014]; £318,231 [2013]; £293,152 [2012]

The Malden Trust Limited
Registered: 23 May 1963 *Employees:* 190
Tel: 01903 874705 *Website:* windlesham.com
Activities: Education, training; arts, culture, heritage, science; amateur sport
Address: Windlesham House School, London Road, Washington, Pulborough, W Sussex, RH20 4AY
Trustees: Mr John David Michael King, Mr Adam Richard Perry, Dr Joseph Spence, Mrs Amanda Jane Line, Mr Charles Anthony Ashton Goddard, Mr Nigel Roberts, Mr Ronald Neil Chisman, Mr Douglas Moody-Stuart, Ms Martina Asmar, Mr Niall Hamilton
Income: £8,816,096 [2017]; £8,999,762 [2016]; £8,467,411 [2015]; £7,688,080 [2014]; £7,180,236 [2013]

The Mall School Trust
Registered: 19 Aug 1986 *Employees:* 74
Tel: 020 8614 1084 *Website:* themallschool.org.uk
Activities: Education, training
Address: 185 Hampton Road, Twickenham, Middlesex, TW2 5NQ
Trustees: Mr Rupert Walker, Mrs Kanwaljeet Mahajan, Dr Charmian Smith, Mrs Tiana Collett, Dr Deborah Clark, Mr Owen Morris
Income: £3,942,006 [2017]; £4,141,350 [2016]; £4,134,151 [2015]; £3,942,079 [2014]; £3,436,429 [2013]

Maltman's Green School Trust Limited
Registered: 22 Mar 1967 *Employees:* 105 *Volunteers:* 34
Tel: 01753 883022 *Website:* maltmansgreen.com
Activities: Education, training
Address: Maltmans Green School, Maltmans Lane, Chalfont St Peter, Gerrards Cross, Bucks, SL9 8RR
Trustees: Mrs Carolyn Mary Bradley MA Cantab, Mrs Deborah Maria Starrs BA Hons Oxon, Mrs Joanna Bond BSc MRICS, Mrs Pauline Elizabeth Rhodes Bennett-Mills, Mrs Judith Rachel Lavery, Mr Howard Mann OBE FCIM, Mr Ian Cooksey, Mr David Ian Segall FCCA, Mr Robert George Simmons BA, Mrs Claire Elizabeth Gowers
Income: £5,515,594 [2017]; £5,386,544 [2016]; £5,308,492 [2015]; £5,053,685 [2014]; £4,893,317 [2013]

Malvern College
Registered: 1 Nov 1963 *Employees:* 416
Website: malcol.org
Activities: Education, training
Address: Malvern College, College Road, Malvern, Worcs, WR14 3DF
Trustees: Mr G E Jones MA, Mr Felix Francis BSc CPhys MInstP, Professor Kenneth Jackson Davey OBE, Mr Robin Kennedy Black, Mr Doug Robertson, Dr Nick Bampos, Dr Christophe Stoecker, Mr Andrew Trotman, Mr Jeremy Havard, Ms Christine Fairchild, Mr Nicholas Engert, Mrs Fiona Bridge, Mr Jim Foxall, Mrs Sue Raby-Smith, Mr Dominic Sandbrook, Mr Richard Thomas Henry Wilson, Miss Michele Edwards, Mr Peter Brough, Dr Angus Kennedy, Mr Peter J Cartwright, Mr Kenneth Madden, Mr Syd Hill, Mr William Burke, Professor Paul Jackson, Mr Tim Straker, Mr Carey Leonard, Miss Sue Duff, Mr Paul Nicholls, Dr Helen Wright
Income: £22,476,544 [2016]; £20,960,648 [2015]; £22,764,674 [2014]; £20,900,457 [2013]

Malvern Hills Conservators
Registered: 20 Nov 1984 *Employees:* 16 *Volunteers:* 60
Tel: 01684 892002 *Website:* malvernhills.org.uk
Activities: Environment, conservation, heritage
Address: Manor House, Grange Road, Malvern, Worcs, WR14 3EY
Trustees: Mr Simon Freeman, Mr Martin Cordey, Mr David Bryer, Mrs Helen Stace, Mr David Charles Baldwin, Mr David Hawkins, Mr Tom Yapp, Mrs Chris O'Donnell, Ms Sara Stewart, Mr Peter Forster, Mr Mick Davies, Mr James O'Donnell, Mr Roger Hall-Jones, Professor John Raine, Mr Chris Rouse, Ms Lucy Hodgson, Mr Peter J Watson, Mr Charles Penn, Ms Emma Holton, Mr David Street, Mr Angus Golightly, Mr Richard Bartholemew, Mr Stephen Braim, Mrs Caroline Bovey, Mr John Michael, Mrs Pamela Cumming, Mrs Gwyneth Rees, Miss Sarah Rouse
Income: £1,210,674 [2017]; £963,771 [2016]; £946,558 [2015]; £892,029 [2014]; £958,025 [2013]

Malvern St James Limited
Registered: 26 Mar 1963 *Employees:* 223 *Volunteers:* 2
Tel: 01684 892288 *Website:* malvernstjames.co.uk
Activities: Education, training
Address: Malvern St James's, 15 Avenue Road, Malvern, Worcs, WR14 3BA
Trustees: Mrs Anne Coles, Miss Elizabeth Mullenger BA CertEd FRSA, Mrs Carol Bawden, Mrs Gemma Bruce, Mr Mark Colin Groome BEd MA ICT, Miss Irene Monyo, Miss Christine Kelly, Mr Bill Ballard BSc FCA, Mr J G Bartholomew, Dr Shelagh Wynn, Mr William Richards, Mr Alistair James Lloyd Thomas GTTP, Mrs Alison Warne, Mr Robert John Pearce
Income: £11,084,636 [2016]; £10,398,677 [2015]; £9,539,436 [2014]; £8,511,736 [2013]; £8,436,969 [2012]

Malvern Theatres Trust Limited
Registered: 25 Mar 1965 *Employees:* 73 *Volunteers:* 180
Tel: 01684 580942 *Website:* malvern-theatres.co.uk
Activities: Education, training; arts, culture, heritage, science
Address: The Malvern Theatres, Grange Road, Malvern, Worcs, WR14 3HB
Trustees: Prof Tamar J Thompson OBE, Mr Leslie Douglas Kinmond, Mr David Chambers, Professor Judith C Elkin, Mr Simon Richard Marks, Mr Richard Hastilow-Smith
Income: £6,093,357 [2017]; £5,956,447 [2016]; £5,735,706 [2015]; £4,794,036 [2014]; £4,654,051 [2013]

The Malvernian Society Limited
Registered: 1 Nov 1963 *Employees:* 4
Tel: 01684 581517 *Website:* malverniansociety.org.uk
Activities: Education, training; accommodation, housing; arts, culture, heritage, science; amateur sport
Address: Malvern College, College Road, Malvern, Worcs, WR14 3DF
Trustees: The Rt Hon Sir Stephen Brown GBE, Mr Richard Thomas Henry Wilson, Mr Jeremy Michael Jayne Havard, Mr Anthony Richard Higgins, Mr James Peter Foxall, Mrs Caroline Louise Ferris, Miss Judith Mueller, Mr Jonathan Andrew Staniforth, Mr Antony Clark, Mr Stephen Charles Holroyd, Mr Nicholas Charles Stokes Engert, Miss Philippa Lambert, Mr Rupert James Harris, Mr Ben Walker
Income: £4,035,281 [2017]; £872,217 [2016]; £698,655 [2015]; £3,126,489 [2014]; £399,110 [2013]

Manchester Alliance for Community Care

Registered: 15 Feb 2012 *Employees:* 22 *Volunteers:* 5
Tel: 0161 834 9823 *Website:* macc.org.uk
Activities: General charitable purposes; advancement of health or saving of lives; human rights, religious or racial harmony, equality or diversity
Address: Macc, Swan Buildings, 20 Swan Street, Manchester, M4 5JW
Trustees: Rev Charles Kwaku-Odoi, Edward Dylan Cox, Ms Louise Yates, John Downes, Dr Julian Skyrme
Income: £1,181,080 [2017]; £860,282 [2016]; £823,692 [2015]; £995,442 [2014]; £994,913 [2013]

Manchester Camerata Limited

Registered: 8 Oct 1974 *Employees:* 9
Tel: 0161 226 8696 *Website:* manchestercamerata.com
Activities: Education, training; arts, culture, heritage, science
Address: 6th Floor, 2 Atherton Street, Manchester, M3 3GS
Trustees: Alistair Cox, Mr Michael Gerard Emmerich, Mr Stephen Dauncey, Mrs Susan Early, Mr Rudolph Anthony Kidd, Mrs Jane Elizabeth Delfino, Mr Neal Chamberlain, Mr Andrew Daniel Spinoza, Mrs Deborah McLauglin, Mr Joe Duddell, Ms Veronica Lucy Makinson
Income: £1,318,211 [2017]; £1,413,189 [2016]; £1,333,875 [2015]; £1,218,918 [2014]; £1,012,605 [2013]

Manchester Care and Repair

Registered: 9 May 2012 *Employees:* 33 *Volunteers:* 2
Tel: 0161 872 5500 *Website:* careandrepair-manchester.org.uk
Activities: General charitable purposes
Address: Unit 14 Empress Business Centre, 380 Chester Road, Manchester, M16 9EA
Trustees: Mr Philip Laker, Mrs Pamela Smith, Mr Steven William Jackson, Mr Muhammad Khalid Barkat, Ms Julie Savory, Ms Susan Dorothy Goldthorpe, Mrs Janine Owen, Ms Heather Margaret Lang
Income: £1,699,017 [2017]; £1,647,349 [2016]; £1,530,308 [2015]; £1,474,034 [2014]; £1,621,396 [2013]

Manchester Cathedral Development Trust

Registered: 13 Feb 1992
Tel: 0161 833 2220
Activities: Environment, conservation, heritage; economic, community development, employment; other charitable purposes
Address: Manchester Cathedral, Victoria Street, Manchester, M3 1SX
Trustees: Peter Wainwright, Mr Warren Smith, Canon Philip Norman Barratt, The Very Reverend Rogers Govender, Mr Philip Deakin, Canon David Andrew Holgate
Income: £1,224,345 [2016]; £1,345,396 [2015]; £197,905 [2014]; £235,086 [2013]; £294,669 [2012]

Manchester City F.C. City in the Community Foundation

Registered: 1 Dec 2010 *Employees:* 53 *Volunteers:* 62
Tel: 0161 438 7712 *Website:* mcfc.co.uk
Activities: General charitable purposes; education, training; advancement of health or saving of lives; disability; prevention or relief of poverty; amateur sport; recreation; other charitable purposes
Address: Etihad Stadium, Etihad Campus, Manchester, M11 3FF
Trustees: Mr Tom Glick, Mr Robert Kevin Ballantine, Thomas Pitchon, Kevin Parker, Mr Patrick Joseph Dominic Loftus, Ms Sara Maria Todd, Simon Cliff, Danny Wilson
Income: £2,686,799 [2017]; £1,627,423 [2016]; £1,604,160 [2015]; £1,319,595 [2014]; £1,370,364 [2013]

Manchester Diocesan Board of Finance

Registered: 26 Sep 1966 *Employees:* 47
Tel: 0161 828 1461 *Website:* manchester.anglican.org
Activities: Religious activities
Address: Diocesan Board of Finance, Church House, 90 Deansgate, Manchester, M3 2GH
Trustees: Rt Rev David Stuart Walker, Rev David Roy Penny, The Venerable Cherry Elizabeth Vann, Mrs Yvonne Muriel Mackereth, Ven David John Sharples, Mr Geoffrey Dent, Venerable Karen Belinda Lund, Rev Anne Joan Edwards, The Very Reverend Rogers Morgan Govender, Ms Hyacinth Elaine Lightbourne, Mr Philip John Bilson, Mr Phillip Steel Blinkhorn, Mr Richard Lewis, The Right Reverend Mark Davies, The Right Reverend Mark David Ashcroft, Mrs Barbara Ann Hodgson, Canon Barbara Christine Taylor, Mr Keith Lewis, Mrs Jane Ann Jones, The Reverend Canon Dr Christopher Andrew Bracegirdle, Mr Jeremy Robinson
Income: £14,048,000 [2016]; £14,259,000 [2015]; £14,284,000 [2014]; £13,764,000 [2013]; £14,006,000 [2012]

The Manchester Grammar School Foundation

Registered: 30 Mar 1966 *Employees:* 321 *Volunteers:* 26
Tel: 0161 224 7201 *Website:* mgs.org
Activities: Education, training
Address: Manchester Grammar School, Old Hall Lane, Manchester, M13 0XT
Trustees: The Manchester Grammar School Foundation Trustee Limited
Income: £21,179,597 [2017]; £20,220,065 [2016]; £19,665,484 [2015]; £19,809,725 [2014]; £18,151,678 [2013]

Manchester Great New & Central Synagogue

Registered: 16 Apr 2010 *Employees:* 5
Tel: 0161 740 3941 *Website:* stenecourt.com
Activities: Religious activities
Address: 48 Park Road, Prestwich, Manchester, M25 0FA
Trustees: Mr Barry Cohen, Mr Howard Gordon, Mr Mike Jacobs, Mr Jonathan Joseph Davies, Mr Michael Livshin
Income: £2,373,356 [2016]; £303,387 [2015]; £328,951 [2014]; £261,797 [2013]; £367,381 [2012]

Manchester High School for Girls

Registered: 10 Nov 2015 *Employees:* 133
Tel: 0161 224 0447 *Website:* manchesterhigh.co.uk
Activities: Education, training
Address: Manchester High School for Girls, Grangethorpe Road, Manchester, M14 6HS
Trustees: Mrs Marie Grant, Mrs Merlyn Vivienne Lowther, Mr Christopher John Saunders, Prof Robert William Munn, Dr Amar Ahmed, Mrs Susan Gillian Beales, Mr Andrew Bland, Mr Alan Clarke, Mrs Stephanie Klass, Mrs Susan Elizabeth Spence, Mr Kui Shum Yeung, Prof Rachel Faith Davies Cooper, Ms Laura Earnshaw, Mrs Victoria Kloss
Income: £10,346,395 [2017]

Manchester International Festival

Registered: 26 Apr 2006 *Employees:* 23
Tel: 0161 817 4510 *Website:* mif.co.uk
Activities: Arts, culture, heritage, science
Address: 11 Moreton Avenue, Stretford, Manchester, M32 8BP
Trustees: Sir Brian McMaster, Mr Richard Paver, Mr Jeremy Deller, Mr Peter Salmon, Mr Chris Oglesby, Cllr Luthfur Rahman, Professor Malcolm Press, Mr Charles Richard Bell, Sir Howard Bernstein, Mr Thomas Paul Richard Bloxham MBE, Ms Kulwinder Thiarai, Ms Cathryn Wright, Dr Maria Balshaw, Mr Lemn Sissay, Mr Alan John Bishop, Mr Jamil Khalil
Income: £2,858,738 [2016]; £8,077,545 [2015]; £3,106,273 [2014]; £8,240,045 [2013]; £3,345,949 [2012]

Manchester Islamic Educational Trust Ltd
Registered: 8 Feb 1999 *Employees:* 129
Tel: 0161 860 7575 *Website:* mietltd.org.uk
Activities: Education, training; religious activities
Address: Hartley Hall, Alexandra Road South, Manchester, M16 8NH
Trustees: Mr Salim Al-Astewani, Mr Abdulkadir Kawooya, Dr Haytham Al Khaffaf, Mr Farroukh Zaheer, Dr Hamad Al Majid, Mrs Farhat Javid, Mr Nasar Mahmood, Dr Abdullah Al Majid, Mr Imad Al-Salam, Dr Abdul Mohsen Al Saif, Mr Samer Salam, Mr Aman Sheikh
Income: £3,303,291 [2017]; £3,276,893 [2016]; £3,306,127 [2015]; £2,975,958 [2014]; £2,970,366 [2013]

The Manchester Metropolitan University Students' Union
Registered: 29 Jan 2015 *Employees:* 82 *Volunteers:* 3,299
Tel: 0161 247 6529 *Website:* theunionmmu.org
Activities: Education, training
Address: Manchester Metropolitan Students Union, 21 Higher Cambridge Street, Manchester, M15 6AD
Trustees: Mr Matthew Searle, Mr Alex Delap, Mr Luca Raimo, Miss Lily Smith, Mr James Coe, Mr Hussain El-Amin, Miss Amie Atkinson
Income: £4,879,187 [2017]; £4,817,442 [2016]; £4,242,702 [2015]

Manchester Mind
Registered: 11 Feb 2004 *Employees:* 60 *Volunteers:* 345
Tel: 0161 226 9907 *Website:* manchestermind.org
Activities: The advancement of health or saving of lives; disability; prevention or relief of poverty
Address: Zion Community Resource Centre, 339 Stretford Road, Hulme, Manchester, M15 4ZY
Trustees: Ms Joy Wales, Mr Nigel Doran, Ms Jamie Bytheway, Ms Emily Hughes, Dr Nicholas O'Donovan, Mrs Shanaz Essafi, Ms Susan Brown, Ms Esta Innes, Ms Ayse Ince, Ms Lynn McCracken, Mr Matt Smith, Mr James Clark
Income: £1,752,265 [2017]; £1,446,055 [2016]; £1,426,393 [2015]; £1,463,242 [2014]; £1,482,139 [2013]

Manchester Pride Limited
Registered: 6 Feb 2007 *Employees:* 5 *Volunteers:* 180
Tel: 0161 831 7700 *Website:* manchesterpride.com
Activities: General charitable purposes; education, training; arts, culture, heritage, science; amateur sport; environment, conservation, heritage; economic, community development, employment; human rights, religious or racial harmony, equality or diversity
Address: Suite 9c, Manchester One, 53 Portland Street, Manchester, M1 3LF
Trustees: Mr Robert James Hammond Malcomson, Miss Karen Richards, Mr Nicholas Curtis, Mr Paul Wheeler, Max Emmerson, Mr Stephen Crocker, Mrs Tracey Walsh, Miss Becki Scott, Mr Rajesh Joshi
Income: £1,601,385 [2016]; £1,657,882 [2015]; £1,348,314 [2014]; £1,058,285 [2013]; £991,656 [2012]

Manchester United Foundation
Registered: 9 Mar 2007 *Employees:* 57 *Volunteers:* 123
Tel: 0151 600 3079 *Website:* mufoundation.org
Activities: General charitable purposes; education, training; advancement of health or saving of lives; disability; overseas aid, famine relief; amateur sport; economic, community development, employment
Address: Horton House, Exchange Flags, Liverpool, L2 3YL
Trustees: Michael Edelson, Tarun Kapur, Eamonn Holmes OBE, Richard Arnold, Tom Bloxham MBE, David Maples, Virginia Buckley, John Arnold
Income: £3,888,468 [2017]; £3,334,195 [2016]; £4,145,536 [2015]; £2,771,220 [2014]; £3,760,839 [2013]

Manchester University NHS Foundation Trust Charity
Registered: 19 Sep 1995
Tel: 0161 276 4938 *Website:* cmftcharity.org.uk
Activities: General charitable purposes; education, training; advancement of health or saving of lives; religious activities
Address: Ground Floor, Wilmslow Park, K Block, 211 Hathersage Road, Manchester, M13 0JR
Trustees: Manchester University NHS Foundation Trust
Income: £4,634,000 [2017]; £4,634,000 [2016]; £5,439,000 [2015]; £4,813,000 [2014]; £3,777,196 [2013]

Manchester Young Lives Ltd
Registered: 23 Jul 1998 *Employees:* 55 *Volunteers:* 86
Tel: 0161 437 5923 *Website:* manchesteryounglives.org.uk
Activities: General charitable purposes; education, training
Address: The Addy Young, People's Centre, Woodhouse Lane, Manchester, M22 9TF
Trustees: Christine Zastawny, Jacqueline Wright, Mr Nicolas John Harney, Mr Shaun Wilcock, Miss Hollie Louise Walsh, Mr Christopher Duncan, Mr Jeff Mills, Rosemary Knox, Mr Hojol Uddn
Income: £1,217,257 [2017]; £1,218,081 [2016]; £1,092,594 [2015]; £1,176,572 [2014]; £1,678,064 [2013]

The Manchester Young Men's Christian Association (Incorporated)
Registered: 29 Dec 1966 *Employees:* 41 *Volunteers:* 25
Tel: 0161 837 3515 *Website:* ymcamanchester.org.uk
Activities: Education, training; advancement of health or saving of lives; amateur sport; recreation
Address: Manchester YMCA, Liverpool Road, Manchester, M3 4JR
Trustees: Mr John William Cooper, Mr John Sharples, Andrew Birtwistle, Carol O'Hare, Mr Graham Rothwell, Mr Derek Butterworth, Mrs Sylvia Hood, Mr Paul Hudders, Ray Mashiter
Income: £2,332,552 [2017]; £2,162,410 [2016]; £2,116,228 [2015]; £2,026,582 [2014]; £2,219,894 [2013]

The Manchester Young People's Theatre Limited
Registered: 31 Oct 1972 *Employees:* 38 *Volunteers:* 45
Website: contactmcr.com
Activities: Arts, culture, heritage, science; economic, community development, employment; recreation
Address: Contact Theatre, Devas Street, Manchester, M15 6JA
Trustees: Mr Bill Thomson, Mr Reece Williams, Ms Joanne Laura Beggs, Miss Afreena Islam, Mags Bradbury, Dr Kate Dorney, Mr Carl Jason Austin-Behan, Mr Patrick Johnson, Councillor Janet Emsley, Mr Steven James Lindsay, Ms Lucy Rachel Dusgate, Ms Gemma Gibb, Mr Andrew Chamberlain, Ms Sameem Ali
Income: £1,857,306 [2017]; £2,026,268 [2016]; £1,792,513 [2015]; £1,729,313 [2014]; £1,481,065 [2013]

Manchester and District Home for Lost Dogs Limited
Registered: 20 Dec 1990 *Employees:* 52 *Volunteers:* 211
Tel: 0161 205 7136 *Website:* dogshome.net
Activities: Animals
Address: Crofters House, Moss Brook Road, Harpurhey, Manchester, M9 5PG
Trustees: Mr Geoffrey Bridson, Mr Terence James Askew, Mrs Maureen Fletcher, Mr Clive Winterburn, Mrs Josephine Jackson, Mrs Jean Bridson, Mr Simon Stansfield
Income: £2,117,763 [2016]; £1,974,041 [2015]; £4,163,823 [2014]; £1,652,862 [2013]; £1,825,614 [2012]

Manchester and Warrington Area Quaker Meeting (Religious Society of Friends)
Registered: 26 Feb 2010 *Employees:* 19 *Volunteers:* 50
Tel: 0161 834 5797 *Website:* manchesterquakers.org.uk
Activities: General charitable purposes; education, training; prevention or relief of poverty; religious activities; human rights, religious or racial harmony, equality or diversity; other charitable purposes
Address: Friends Meeting House, 6 Mount Street, Manchester, M2 5NS
Trustees: Judith Lukey BSc JP, Hilary Tucker, Ben Lukey, Branwen McHugh, John Booth, Wendy Olsen, Roger Hensman, Lesley Wilson Thomson, Margaret Everitt, Michael Taylor, Richard Taylor
Income: £1,132,362 [2017]; £808,921 [2015]; £682,117 [2014]; £601,362 [2013]; £439,618 [2012]

Mancroft Advice Project (MAP)
Registered: 3 Feb 2005 *Employees:* 50 *Volunteers:* 12
Tel: 01603 766994 *Website:* map.uk.net
Activities: Education, training; advancement of health or saving of lives; disability; prevention or relief of poverty; arts, culture, heritage, science; economic, community development, employment; human rights, religious or racial harmony, equality or diversity
Address: The Risebrow Centre, Chantry Road, Norwich, NR2 1RF
Trustees: Susan Heathcote Gale, Tom Fry, Sarah Louise Thorp, Ms Kate Prout, Barbara Elizabeth Miller, Mr Craig Hooper, Stephen Paul Taylor, Mrs Caroline Billings
Income: £1,794,005 [2017]; £1,750,976 [2016]; £1,543,932 [2015]; £1,874,114 [2014]; £1,170,193 [2013]

Manor Gardens Welfare Trust Ltd
Registered: 24 Jun 1997 *Employees:* 32 *Volunteers:* 341
Tel: 020 7561 5263 *Website:* manorgardenscentre.org
Activities: General charitable purposes; education, training; advancement of health or saving of lives; disability; arts, culture, heritage, science; economic, community development, employment; other charitable purposes
Address: Manor Gardens Welfare Trust, 6-9 Manor Gardens, London, N7 6LA
Trustees: Mr Andrew Chaplin, Mrs Ann Jennings, Mrs Catherine Balston, Ms Jenita Rahman, Ms Clare McNeill, Mr Nicholas Tait, Ms Crystal Rolfe, Mrs Katie Greywood, Mr Allan Sutherland, Mrs Mary Gibson, Ms Inara Khan
Income: £1,104,139 [2017]; £1,117,926 [2016]; £1,175,034 [2015]; £1,102,412 [2014]; £999,723 [2013]

Manor Gospel Trust
Registered: 27 Jan 2015 *Volunteers:* 45
Activities: Religious activities; other charitable purposes
Address: 68 Craven Road, Chelsfield, Orpington, Kent, BR6 7RT
Trustees: Mr Garth Oliver Woodcock, Mr Lee Darren Hazell, Mr Anthony George Hazell, Mr Paul Adrian Brown, Mr Dean Ellis
Income: £3,609,000 [2017]; £404,054 [2016]

Manor Lodge School
Registered: 25 Aug 1995 *Employees:* 85 *Volunteers:* 21
Tel: 01707 642424 *Website:* manorlodgeschool.com
Activities: Education, training
Address: Manor Lodge School, Ridge Hill, Shenley, Radlett, Herts, WD7 9BG
Trustees: Mr Stephen Wilson, Mr Mark Cherry, Mrs Helen Gunasekera, Mr Andrew Williams, Mrs Trudy Capaldo, Mrs Sonia Coventry, Mr David Arnold, Mr Graham Black, Mrs Sarah Hollis, Ms Melody Jones, Dr Shahzad Malik
Income: £4,612,102 [2016]; £4,507,083 [2015]; £4,308,626 [2014]; £4,065,084 [2013]; £3,957,806 [2012]

The Manor Preparatory School Trust
Registered: 9 Mar 1990 *Employees:* 122 *Volunteers:* 36
Tel: 01235 858458 *Website:* manorprep.org
Activities: Education, training
Address: The Manor Preparatory School, Faringdon Road, Shippon, Abingdon, Oxon, OX13 6LN
Trustees: Mr Mark Charter, Mrs Janet Rimmer, Dr Lucy Maclaren, Mr Darren Jones, Ms Pauline Ivy Matchwick, Mrs Caroline Steinsberg, Mrs Sian Champkin, Mr Shaun Forrestal, Mrs Margaret Ruiseal, Mrs Susan Sowden
Income: £5,010,754 [2017]; £4,711,918 [2016]; £4,604,874 [2015]; £4,261,512 [2014]; £4,150,321 [2013]

Manor and Castle Development Trust Limited
Registered: 13 Mar 2008 *Employees:* 75 *Volunteers:* 364
Tel: 0114 227 0100 *Website:* manorandcastle.org.uk
Activities: General charitable purposes; education, training; advancement of health or saving of lives; disability; prevention or relief of poverty; accommodation, housing; arts, culture, heritage, science; amateur sport; environment, conservation, heritage; economic, community development, employment
Address: Manor & Castle Development Trust Ltd, Norfolk House, Stafford Lane, Sheffield, S2 5HR
Trustees: Mrs Ruth Dowling, Mr Keith Crawshaw, Mr Mike King, Mr Martin Lawton, Ms Masoba Kromah, Mr Ken Curran, Mrs Patricia Ann Midgley, Miss Yvonne Bramall, Ms Sarah Hopkinson
Income: £1,904,930 [2017]; £1,897,635 [2016]; £2,009,523 [2015]; £1,543,035 [2014]; £2,189,444 [2013]

The Manufacturing Institute
Registered: 22 Dec 1994 *Employees:* 14 *Volunteers:* 330
Website: manufacturinginstitute.co.uk
Activities: Education, training; economic, community development, employment; other charitable purposes
Address: The Manufacturing Institute, Lee House, 90 Great Bridgewater Street, Manchester, M1 5JW
Trustees: Mr Paul Anthony Simpson, Mrs Donna Elizabeth Edwards, Mr Mark Anthony Hughes
Income: £1,816,974 [2017]; £1,816,947 [2016]; £2,146,325 [2015]; £2,470,505 [2014]; £2,996,017 [2013]

MapAction
Registered: 14 Nov 2008 *Employees:* 12 *Volunteers:* 101
Tel: 01494 568899 *Website:* mapaction.org
Activities: Education, training; advancement of health or saving of lives; overseas aid, famine relief
Address: Clare Charity Centre, Wycombe Road, Saunderton, High Wycombe, Bucks, HP14 4BF
Trustees: Major General Roy Wood, Mr Alan Mills, Mrs Carolyn Twist, Barbara Bond, Nicholas Moody, Benjamin Parker, Mr Nigel Press, James Brown, Mr Peter Beaumont, Anne Frankland, Phillip Moore
Income: £1,097,155 [2017]; £575,586 [2016]; £1,333,225 [2015]; £581,255 [2014]; £595,658 [2013]

The Marcela Trust
Registered: 14 Jan 2009 *Employees:* 113
Tel: 01865 343802
Activities: General charitable purposes
Address: 4 Monks Close, Dorchester on Thames, Wallingford, Oxon, OX10 7JA
Trustees: Mrs Jeanette Franklin MBE, Mrs Dawn Pamela Rose, Mr Paul Hotham, Mr Brian Arthur Groves, Mr Mark Robert Spragg
Income: £5,968,958 [2017]; £4,750,000 [2016]; £2,043,500 [2014]; £500,000 [2013]

Marchant-Holliday School Limited
Registered: 31 Dec 1963 *Employees:* 55 *Volunteers:* 5
Tel: 01749 812407 *Website:* marchantholliday.co.uk
Activities: Education, training; advancement of health or saving of lives; disability; human rights, religious or racial harmony, equality or diversity
Address: 3 Brue Close, Bruton, Somerset, BA10 0HY
Trustees: Mr Michael Beaumont, Mr Simon David Miller, Mrs Lisa Jane Prior, Mr Simon William Thorrold Sixtus Jaggard, Mr Nicolas Lawrence Short, Emma Ramsay, Mr Stephen Murcer, Maj Michael Ralph Henry Liddicoat, Mrs Rachel Sarah Harris
Income: £2,077,054 [2017]; £2,150,399 [2016]; £2,165,275 [2015]; £1,963,421 [2014]; £1,607,006 [2013]

The Marchig Animal Welfare Trust
Registered: 26 Sep 1989
Tel: 01383 737084 *Website:* marchigtrust.org
Activities: Animals
Address: c/o Lindsays, Solicitors, Caledonian Exchange, 19a Canning Street, Edinburgh, EH3 8HE
Trustees: Mr Colin Moor MSI Dip, Dr Jerzy A Mlotkiewicz, Mr Les Ward, Mrs Janice McLoughlin
Income: £2,723,333 [2016]; £1,335,763 [2015]; £876,803 [2014]; £8,433,388 [2013]; £1,052,879 [2012]

The Mare and Foal Sanctuary
Registered: 11 May 2011 *Employees:* 117 *Volunteers:* 100
Tel: 01626 355969 *Website:* mareandfoal.org
Activities: Education, training; animals
Address: Honeysuckle Farm, Haccombe with Combe, Newton Abbot, Devon, TQ12 4SA
Trustees: Mr Nigel Brown, Mrs Donna Hallett, Miss Louise Sharpe, Mr James Fitzpatrick, Mr Robert Jonathan Lovell, Miss Alison Wallace, Miss Elizabeth Gaffer
Income: £4,403,549 [2016]; £4,391,407 [2015]; £3,986,681 [2014]; £4,215,217 [2013]; £4,513,776 [2012]

The Margaret Thatcher Scholarship Trust
Registered: 11 Nov 2013 *Employees:* 2
Tel: 01865 270600
Activities: Education, training
Address: Somerville College, Woodstock Road, Oxford, OX2 6HD
Trustees: Mrs Clara Freeman, Ms Joanna Mary Innes, Sir John Vickers, Dr Alice Marjorie Sheila Prochaska, Professor Stephen Robson Weatherill
Income: £1,836,883 [2017]; £3,631,907 [2016]; £2,538,422 [2015]; £335,000 [2014]

Marina Theatre Trust
Registered: 27 Sep 2012 *Employees:* 37 *Volunteers:* 35
Tel: 01502 533202 *Website:* marinatheatre.co.uk
Activities: Arts, culture, heritage, science
Address: Marina Theatre, The Marina, Lowestoft, Suffolk, NR32 1HH
Trustees: Janet Craig, Mrs Hazel Clover, Mr Mike Pinner, Mr Andrew John Gallant, Mr David Blyth, Mr Joseph Larter, Mr Norman Cullingford, Mr Paul Geoffrey Ashdown
Income: £1,736,707 [2017]; £1,656,089 [2016]; £1,529,516 [2015]; £1,532,603 [2014]; £2,068,783 [2013]

The Marine Biological Association of The United Kingdom
Registered: 21 Feb 2014 *Employees:* 56 *Volunteers:* 192
Tel: 01752 426484 *Website:* mba.ac.uk
Activities: General charitable purposes; education, training; arts, culture, heritage, science; environment, conservation, heritage
Address: Marine Biological Association, The Laboratory, Citadel Hill, Plymouth, PL1 2PB
Trustees: Mr Robert John Mills, Professor Philip Stephen Rainbow, Professor John Raven FRS, Professor Alison Smith, Professor Michael Whitaker, Professor Stuart Rogers, Professor Christopher Leslie John Frid, Dr Jennifer Sarah Ashworth, Professor Alistair Hetherington, Sir John Beddington CMG FRS, Professor Peter Holland FRS, Professor Rory Wilson
Income: £3,331,758 [2017]; £3,207,215 [2016]; £19,388,693 [2015]

Marine Conservation Society
Registered: 28 Aug 1991 *Employees:* 58 *Volunteers:* 835
Tel: 01989 566017 *Website:* mcsuk.org
Activities: Education, training; advancement of health or saving of lives; arts, culture, heritage, science; animals; environment, conservation, heritage; economic, community development, employment
Address: Overross House, Ross Park, Ross on Wye, Herefords, HR9 7US
Trustees: Miss Tara Ann Aldwin, Mr Giles Robertson, Professor David Glyn Kipling, Mr Leigh Sheridan Morris, Hugh Raven, Mr Stephen Anthony Gray, Mr James Hugh Marsden, Mr Alexander John Diebler Wilson
Income: £2,460,369 [2017]; £2,888,594 [2016]; £2,206,263 [2015]; £2,034,745 [2014]; £1,815,695 [2013]

The Marine Society and Sea Cadets
Registered: 25 Oct 1962 *Employees:* 181 *Volunteers:* 8,805
Tel: 020 7654 7000 *Website:* ms-sc.org
Activities: Education, training; other charitable purposes
Address: The Marine Society & Sea Cadets, 202 Lambeth Road, London, SE1 7JW
Trustees: Mr Robert Woods CBE, Captain Ian McNaught, Dr Louise Bennett, Ms Kathryn Stone OBE, Mr Alex Marsh, Commodore William Walworth OBE, Mr Tony Allen, Mr Simon Figgis, Andrew Bull, Jeremy Penn, Dr Sheila Fitzpatrick, Mr John May, Sir Alan Massey KCB CBE, Mr Alan Marsh, Ms Elizabeth Cassidy, Mr Andrew Davenall, Mr Nicholas Mason
Income: £16,548,000 [2017]; £16,309,000 [2016]; £16,676,000 [2015]; £15,293,000 [2014]; £14,421,000 [2013]

Marine Stewardship Council

Registered: 10 Dec 1997 *Employees:* 147 *Volunteers:* 8
Tel: 020 7246 8951 *Website:* msc.org
Activities: Environment, conservation, heritage
Address: Marine Stewardship Council, 1-3 Snow Hill, London, EC1A 2DH
Trustees: Dr Werner Kiene, Ms Lynne Hale, Mr Jean-Jacques Maguire, Mr Peter James Trott, Mr Felix Ratheb, Ms Christine Penney, Mr David Mureithi, Mr Eric Barratt, Mr Paul Stewart Uys, Mr James Leape, Professor Simon Jennings
Income: £19,942,284 [2017]; £15,272,126 [2016]; £14,040,951 [2015]; £14,400,018 [2014]; £15,415,429 [2013]

The Claude and Sofia Marion Foundation

Registered: 15 Dec 2006
Activities: General charitable purposes; education, training; advancement of health or saving of lives; prevention or relief of poverty; religious activities; arts, culture, heritage, science
Address: c/o Spinnaker Capital Limited, 6 Grosvenor Street, London, W1K 4DJ
Trustees: Mr Marcel Marion, Mr Pedro Miguel Duarte Rebelo De Sousa, Mrs Nicole Gerault
Income: £7,480,412 [2016]; £2,583,871 [2015]; £3,388,430 [2014]; £2,258,355 [2013]; £1,328,082 [2012]

Maritime + Engineering College North West

Registered: 18 Sep 1998 *Employees:* 38
Tel: 0151 227 3463 *Website:* mecnw.co.uk
Activities: Education, training
Address: Haines Watts, Pacific Chambers, 11-13 Victoria Street, Liverpool, L2 5QQ
Trustees: Cllr Phillip Leslie Davies, Jim Teasdale, Councillor Brian Kenny, Mr Ian Clinton Higby, Mr John Raymond Syvret, Mrs Lesley Ann Rennie
Income: £1,626,649 [2015]; £1,453,373 [2014]; £1,670,150 [2013]

The Maritime Educational Foundation

Registered: 17 Oct 2003
Tel: 020 7417 2840 *Website:* meftraining.org
Activities: Education, training
Address: Maritime Educational Foundation, 30 Park Street, London, SE1 9EQ
Trustees: Mark Dickinson, Stephen William Todd, Nigel Lehmann-Taylor, Ms Kathryn Neilson, Mr Mark Carden, Cliff Roberts, Mr Guy Platten, Mr Steven Gosling
Income: £1,501,058 [2016]; £2,234,779 [2015]; £2,017,978 [2014]; £1,970,427 [2013]; £2,311,216 [2012]

Marks Hall Estate

Registered: 17 Apr 1973 *Employees:* 28 *Volunteers:* 90
Tel: 01376 563116 *Website:* markshall.org.uk
Activities: Environment, conservation, heritage
Address: Marks Hall Estate, Marks Hall, Coggeshall, Colchester, Essex, CO6 1TG
Trustees: Mr Robert Arthur David Cowlin FRICS, Mr William Conner, Mr Peter Griffiths, Mr Michael John Lear, Professor James Raven, Mrs Meriel Barclay MA, Mrs Margaret Attwood
Income: £1,140,025 [2016]; £1,134,734 [2015]; £872,528 [2014]; £906,931 [2013]; £759,101 [2012]

Marlborough College Foundation

Registered: 10 Apr 1997
Tel: 01672 892390 *Website:* marlboroughcollege.org
Activities: Education, training
Address: Marlborough College, Marlborough, Wilts, SN8 1PA
Trustees: Mr John Manser, Mr W F Wyldbore-Smith, Mr Jonathan Leigh, Mr Christopher Bruce Dowling, Mr Richard John Hugo Fleck CBE, Mr Steven Bishop, Mr Timothy Martin-Jenkins, Mr Richard Pembroke
Income: £3,029,931 [2017]; £2,373,374 [2016]; £1,160,623 [2015]; £822,252 [2014]; £355,360 [2013]

Marlborough College

Registered: 8 Oct 1963 *Employees:* 690
Tel: 01672 892390 *Website:* marlboroughcollege.org
Activities: Education, training
Address: Marlborough College, Marlborough, Wilts, SN8 1PA
Trustees: Ms Sarah Hamilton-Fairley, Sir John Irving Bell, Rev Rachel Weir, Mr John Baker, Mr Christopher Pymont, Mr Bill Mills, Mr Peter Freeman, Ms Geeta Gopalan, Mr Jonathan Piers Worsley Coleman, The Right Reverend Nicholas Holtam, Lord Malloch-Brown, Dr Tracy Elisabeth Long, Mr Steven Bishop, Lieutenant General John Lorimer, Mrs Amanda Cooke, Rev Charlotte Bridget Melander Bannister-Parker
Income: £53,192,000 [2017]; £49,005,000 [2016]; £44,810,000 [2015]; £41,348,000 [2014]; £36,709,000 [2013]

Marlborough House School

Registered: 8 Sep 1965 *Employees:* 79
Website: marlboroughhouseschool.co.uk
Activities: Education, training
Address: Marlborough House School, High Street, Hawkhurst, Cranbrook, Kent, TN18 4PY
Trustees: Mr Simon Hodson, Mr Henry Somerset, Mr Peter Smallwood, Mrs Jenny Webb, Mr Simon Cloke, Mr Nigel Gerrard Taylor, Mrs Gillian Du Charme, Mr Arthur Reynolds, Mr Jonathan Watts, Mrs Amanda Petch, Hon Thomas Nigel MacLear Lawson, Mrs Sarah Reeves
Income: £4,118,177 [2016]; £3,923,667 [2015]; £3,933,222 [2014]; £4,001,301 [2013]; £3,839,264 [2012]

The J Van Mars Foundation

Registered: 27 Aug 2009
Tel: 0345 304 2424
Activities: General charitable purposes
Address: 6th Floor, Trustee Department, Trinity Quay 2, Avon Street, Bristol, BS2 0PT
Trustees: Mr Guy Rupert Berryman, Mr William Champion, Mr Paul Darren Makin, Mr Jonathan Mark Buckland, Mr Christopher Anthony John Martin, Coutts & Co
Income: £2,056,882 [2017]; £695,216 [2016]; £1,687,966 [2015]; £1,689,371 [2014]; £756,443 [2013]

The Marsh Christian Trust

Registered: 6 May 1982 *Employees:* 3 *Volunteers:* 10
Tel: 020 7233 3112 *Website:* marshchristiantrust.org
Activities: General charitable purposes; education, training; advancement of health or saving of lives; disability; arts, culture, heritage, science; animals; environment, conservation, heritage; economic, community development, employment
Address: 4 Matthew Parker Street, London, SW1H 9NP
Trustees: Mr Brian Peter Marsh OBE, Miss Antonia Marsh, Mr Charles Micklewright, Ms Natalie Claire Susannah Collings, Ms Camilla Kenyon, Mr Nicholas Carter
Income: £1,448,782 [2017]; £793,159 [2016]; £866,938 [2015]; £731,734 [2014]; £723,873 [2013]

Charity of John Marshall
Registered: 6 Oct 1962 Employees: 3
Tel: 020 7939 0720 Website: marshalls.org.uk
Activities: Education, training; religious activities
Address: Marshalls Charity, 66 Newcomen Street, London, SE1 1YT
Trustees: Antony Paul Guthrie, Mr Stephen Clark, Anthea Mary Nicholson, John Anthony Nicholas Heawood, Ms Surbhi Beatrice Malhotra-Trenkel BA, Miss Eleanor Jean Lang, Mr Alastair Michael Moss MA FRSA, Mr Colin Graham Bird FCA, William Duncan Eason, Georgina Mary Farquhar Isaac, Revd Jonathan Rust, Mrs Lesley Bosman, Mr Charles Ledsam, Mr Adrian MacKenzie Smallwood
Income: £1,273,918 [2017]; £1,355,539 [2016]; £1,195,376 [2015]; £1,074,586 [2014]; £1,071,530 [2013]

Martha Trust Hereford Limited
Registered: 1 Mar 1996 Employees: 120
Tel: 01432 279314 Website: marthatrusthereford.co.uk
Activities: Disability
Address: Hampton Green, Old Eign Hill, Hereford, HR1 1UB
Trustees: Mr R E L Smith, Mr Alastair Charles Stewart, Mr W Somers, Miss Susan Smith, Mrs Sarah Josephine Sharp-Smith, Lucinda Sharp Smith
Income: £3,732,933 [2017]; £3,284,884 [2016]; £3,262,749 [2015]; £3,318,133 [2014]; £3,197,386 [2013]

Martha Trust
Registered: 2 Feb 1998 Employees: 177 Volunteers: 33
Tel: 01304 615223 Website: marthatrust.org.uk
Activities: The advancement of health or saving of lives; disability
Address: Homemead Lane, Hacklinge, Deal, Kent, CT14 0PG
Trustees: Mr Humphrey Clarke, John Quin, Liz Acarnley, Roger Walton, Mrs Georgina Hovey, Amy Chapman, Mr Rob Sparkes
Income: £4,535,738 [2016]; £4,374,075 [2015]; £4,227,491 [2014]; £3,753,104 [2013]; £3,822,202 [2012]

The Katherine Martin Charitable Trust
Registered: 7 Dec 1970
Tel: 020 8788 0559
Activities: General charitable purposes
Address: Flat 16, Westpoint, 49 Putney Hill, London, SW15 6RU
Trustees: Air Vice-Marshal Martyn John Gardiner OBE, Mr Peter Bell, Mr John Paul Richards, Mr Stuart Robin Counsell, Miss Susan Hester Kay, Mrs Lesley Edmonds, John Leeson
Income: £43,704,000 [2017]; £52,652,000 [2016]; £455,506 [2014]; £415,625 [2013]; £374,105 [2012]

The Martin Foundation
Registered: 23 Jun 2005
Activities: General charitable purposes; education, training
Address: The Undercroft Offices, Thorpe Underwood Estate, Thorpe Underwood, Ouseburn, York, YO26 9SS
Trustees: Mr Martin Calvert, Mr Francis Martin, Miss Amy Martin
Income: £6,255,251 [2016]; £8,470,805 [2015]; £9,385,856 [2014]; £6,280,168 [2013]; £2,425,147 [2012]

Martin House
Registered: 28 Apr 1987 Employees: 181 Volunteers: 390
Tel: 01937 845045 Website: martinhouse.org.uk
Activities: The advancement of health or saving of lives; disability
Address: 5 Boston Mews, Boston Spa, Wetherby, W Yorks, LS23 6JE
Trustees: Mrs Jenny Wilkinson, Dr John Henry Livingston, Mr Michael Joseph Paul Millington, Mr Timothy Halstead, Miss Clair Challenor-Chadwick, Prof Barry Wright, Mr Tim Straughan, Dr Robert Anthony Smith, Mr Stephen A Plews, Zoe Donaldson, Mrs Jennifer Slee, Mrs Susan Barbara Rumbold, Mrs Rifhat Maiik
Income: £6,251,324 [2017]; £6,252,491 [2016]; £6,335,110 [2015]; £5,804,923 [2014]; £5,200,706 [2013]

The Martlets Hospice Limited
Registered: 7 Nov 1989 Employees: 288 Volunteers: 506
Tel: 01273 273400 Website: themartlets.org.uk
Activities: The advancement of health or saving of lives
Address: Martlets Hospice, Wayfield Avenue, Hove, E Sussex, BN3 7LW
Trustees: Dr Matthew Fletcher, Dr Duncan Stewart, Ms Christine Ann D'Cruz, Barry Egan, Dr Emily McWhirter, Andy Gillies, Mr Giles Ings, Mr Kevin Gerald Smyth, Dick Knight, Mrs Ann Norman, Mr Barry Hancock, Chris Thomas, Mrs Juliet Anne Smith
Income: £9,573,422 [2017]; £10,167,672 [2016]; £8,572,593 [2015]; £10,130,550 [2014]; £7,352,605 [2013]

Marwell Wildlife
Registered: 2 Mar 1978 Employees: 253 Volunteers: 140
Tel: 01962 777407 Website: marwell.org.uk
Activities: Education, training; animals; environment, conservation, heritage
Address: Marwell Wildlife, Owslebury, Winchester, Hants, SO21 1JH
Trustees: Mr Barry Watson, Dr Mark Stanley Price, David Stalker, Mrs Teresa Frost, Mr David Pape, Mr Richard Mark Charter, Dr Miranda Stevenson OBE, Mr Christopher Langford, Mrs Nicola Robinson, Pete Jakob, Mr Francis McCaffrey
Income: £11,164,279 [2016]; £9,961,540 [2015]; £9,643,216 [2014]; £9,042,420 [2013]; £8,194,967 [2012]

The Mary Rose Trust
Registered: 28 Mar 1979 Employees: 49 Volunteers: 117
Website: maryrose.org
Activities: Education, training; arts, culture, heritage, science; environment, conservation, heritage
Address: Mary Rose Trust, 1 College Road, HM Naval Base, Portsmouth, PO1 3LX
Trustees: Professor Sir Barry Cunliffe KB CBE FSA FBA, Mrs Sophia Mary Mason, Mr David Errol Prior Palmer CBE, Dr Robert Bewley, Dr Janet Elizabeth Owen, Mr Christopher Brandon, Mrs Helen Bonser-Wilton, Mr Rupert Grey, Mr Alan Lovell, Ms Caroline Dudley OBE, Dr David Starkey CBE, Mr Adam Humphryes, Professor Van Gore, Mr Peter Hudson
Income: £4,911,072 [2017]; £8,533,817 [2016]; £4,105,571 [2015]; £4,195,225 [2013]; £7,110,762 [2012]

The Mary Stevens Hospice

Registered: 2 Jun 1986 *Employees:* 182 *Volunteers:* 260
Tel: 01384 445410 *Website:* marystevenshospice.co.uk
Activities: Education, training; advancement of health or saving of lives; disability
Address: 221 Hagley Road, Oldswinford, Stourbridge, W Midlands, DY8 2JR
Trustees: Mr Peter Marsh, Ms Candy Cooley, Dr Jane Flint BSc MD FRCP, Councillor Julie Baines, Mr Robert Glaze, Councillor Angus Stuart Macpherson Lees, Mr Steve Waltho, Cliff Gammon, Mr John Turner, Mr Spencer Hodgson, Mr Nigel Dace
Income: £5,578,778 [2017]; £4,586,112 [2016]; £6,048,876 [2015]; £5,057,637 [2014]; £4,056,008 [2013]

Marymount International School

Registered: 2 Feb 2007 *Employees:* 96
Website: marymountlondon.com
Activities: Education, training; religious activities
Address: 35 Burghley Avenue, New Malden, Surrey, KT3 4SW
Trustees: Sister Mary Jo Martin, Ms Miriam Twaalfhoven, Mr Andre Brenninkmeijer, Sister Catherine Vincie, Mr Mark John Rigotti, Ms Cristina Serrano, Ms Noreen Doyle, Mrs Helena Reimnitz Zu Hohenlohe, Mr Francis Campbell, Miss Lorraine Ann Smiley, Mrs Julie Darwent
Income: £7,315,782 [2017]; £7,366,051 [2016]; £7,280,382 [2015]; £6,635,879 [2014]; £6,639,139 [2013]

Maryvale Institute

Registered: 14 Mar 1998 *Employees:* 20 *Volunteers:* 2
Tel: 0121 360 8118 *Website:* maryvale.ac.uk
Activities: Education, training; religious activities
Address: Maryvale Institute, Maryvale House, Old Oscott Hill, Birmingham, B44 9AG
Trustees: Archbishop Bernard Longley, Ms Elizabeth Slinn, James Quinn, Rev David Oakley, Rev Timothy Menezes, Rev David Palmer, Mr Simon Lee, Ms Sophia Pain
Income: £1,110,730 [2017]; £880,640 [2016]; £990,932 [2015]; £1,055,169 [2014]; £1,150,885 [2013]

Sir Josiah Mason's Almshouse Charity

Registered: 20 Jul 1962 *Employees:* 33
Tel: 0121 245 1001 *Website:* sjmt.org.uk
Activities: Accommodation, housing
Address: Mason Court, Hillborough Road, Birmingham, B27 6PF
Trustees: Cllr Kenneth Meeson, Mr Michael Harman Goodwin, Alison Crawley, Mrs Julie Houlder, Mr Philip Soule, Mike Smith, Mrs Annabel Ruth Anderson, Mrs Betty Foster, Councillor Gareth Moore, Mr Michael Baylis, Jonathan Pyke
Income: £1,771,717 [2017]; £1,751,923 [2016]; £1,752,623 [2015]; £1,632,376 [2014]; £1,585,379 [2013]

Masonic Charitable Foundation

Registered: 4 Dec 2015 *Employees:* 1,099 *Volunteers:* 240
Tel: 020 3146 3304 *Website:* mcf.org.uk
Activities: General charitable purposes; education, training; advancement of health or saving of lives; disability; prevention or relief of poverty; overseas aid, famine relief
Address: Freemasons Hall, 60 Great Queen Street, London, WC2B 5AZ
Trustees: Mr John Michael Codd JP, Mr John Boyington CBE, Dr Charles Assad Akle, Dr Michael Woodcock, Mr Antony David George Harvey BA (Hons) GCGI CertEd FCIPD, Mr Andrew George Wauchope, Mr Timothy David Dallas-Chapman, His Honour Judge Richard Michael Hone QC, Mr Howard Ian Sabin, Sir Paul Williams OBE CStJ DL, Mr Christopher Geoffrey John Head, Mr Howard Gerald Wilson, Mr David Charles Watson, Mr Andrew Campbell Ross OBE Ha MBA, Mr Christopher George White, Mr James Henry Newman, Mr Michael Richard Heenan, Mr John D'Olier Duckworth OBE DL, Mr Jean-Paul Da Costa, Mr John Edward Hornblow, Mr Charles Andrew Gregory Cunnington, Mr Adrian John Richardson Flook, Mr Nigel James Vaughan
Income: £67,008,000 [2017]

Masonic Samaritan Fund

Registered: 30 Jun 2009
Website: msfund.org.uk
Activities: The advancement of health or saving of lives; prevention or relief of poverty
Address: Masonic Charitable Foundation, Freemasons Hall, 60 Great Queen Street, London, WC2B 5AZ
Trustees: Mr James Henry Newman, Masonic Charitable Foundation
Income: £2,482,000 [2017]; £2,977,000 [2016]; £5,927,000 [2015]; £4,248,000 [2013]; £3,219,000 [2012]

Masorti Judaism

Registered: 16 Jan 2007 *Employees:* 16 *Volunteers:* 200
Tel: 020 8349 6658 *Website:* masorti.org.uk
Activities: Religious activities
Address: Masorti Judaism, Alexander House, 3 Shakespeare Road, London, N3 1XE
Trustees: Mr Laurence Harris, Mr James Richard Burns, Mr Simon Samuels, Mr Ben Russell, Miss Leonie Fleischmann, Mr Bruce Rigal, Shirley Fenster, Mr Paul Collin, Mrs Miriam Benchetrit
Income: £1,306,811 [2017]; £1,195,902 [2016]; £986,536 [2015]; £1,133,958 [2014]; £1,597,978 [2013]

Masschallenge

Registered: 31 Mar 2015 *Employees:* 13 *Volunteers:* 268
Website: masschallenge.org
Activities: Education, training; economic, community development, employment
Address: International House, 24 Holborn Viaduct, London, EC1A 2BN
Trustees: Mr John Warren Harthorne, Miss Alexandra Ritchie, Mr Simon Turek
Income: £1,036,127 [2016]; £1,337,041 [2015]

The Master (or Keeper) and Fellows of Peterhouse in the University of Cambridge
Registered: 12 Aug 2010 *Employees:* 182
Tel: 01223 338200 *Website:* pet.cam.ac.uk
Activities: Education, training
Address: Peterhouse, Cambridge, CB2 1RD
Trustees: Professor M Jones, Dr Robert Ross Russell, Dr James Carleton Paget, Rev Dr Stephen Hampton, Dr Christopher Lester, Prof Paul Midgley, Dr Magnus Ryan, Dr Christopher Tilmouth, Dr Alexander White, Dr Andras Zsak, Mr Ian Wright, Ms Bridget Kendall Master, Professor Connor, Dr Timothy Dickens, Dr Antara Haldar, Prof John Ernest Robb, Dr Nick Zair, Prof Brendan Simms, Prof Andrew Lever, Prof Simon Deakin, Professor Sophie Jackson, Mr Scott Mandelbrote, Prof Andrew Parker, Dr Solomos Solomou, Dr Jennifer Wallace, Prof Philip Woodland, Dr Saskia Murk Jansen, Prof Michael Moriarty, Dr Sophie Lunn-Rockliffe, Dr James Talbot, Professor Richard Holton, Dr Graham Christie, Dr Teng Long, Dr David Colin Eric Bulmer
Income: £13,089,000 [2017]; £12,393,000 [2016]; £10,850,000 [2015]; £10,388,000 [2014]; £10,455,000 [2013]

The Master Charitable Trust
Registered: 19 Jan 2011
Tel: 020 7353 4522
Activities: General charitable purposes; education, training; advancement of health or saving of lives; disability; prevention or relief of poverty; overseas aid, famine relief; religious activities; arts, culture, heritage, science; amateur sport; animals; environment, conservation, heritage; economic, community development, employment; armed forces, emergency service efficiency; human rights, religious or racial harmony, equality or diversity; recreation; other charitable purposes
Address: 37 Fleet Street, London, EC4P 4DQ
Trustees: Messrs Hoare Trustees
Income: £9,273,500 [2016]; £10,361,770 [2015]; £7,484,407 [2014]; £833,997 [2013]; £4,298,337 [2012]

The Master Fellows and Scholars of Emmanuel College in the University of Cambridge
Registered: 12 Aug 2010 *Employees:* 190
Website: emma.cam.ac.uk
Activities: Education, training
Address: Emmanuel College, St Andrews Street, Cambridge, CB2 3AP
Trustees: Professor Christopher John Burgoyne, Professor Nigel Peake, Dr Philip Mark Rust Howell, Dr Richard William Broadhurst, Dr Carolin Susan Crawford, Professor Mark John Francis Gales, Dame Fiona Reynolds, Dr Michael John Gross, Dr Robert Michael Henderson, Professor Barry Alexander Windeatt, Dr Alex Jeffrey, Dr Penelope Watson
Income: £17,877,531 [2017]; £16,756,027 [2016]; £16,182,768 [2015]; £13,834,483 [2014]; £12,452,030 [2013]

Master Fellows and Scholars of Pembroke College
Registered: 16 Aug 2010 *Employees:* 147
Website: pmb.ox.ac.uk
Activities: Education, training
Address: 27 Linton Road, Oxford, OX2 6UL
Trustees: Mr Roger Boning, Prof Guido Bonsaver, Prof Benjamin Davis, Prof Linda Flores, Prof Andre Furger, Prof Raphael Hauser, Prof Nicholas John Kruger, Dr Eamonn Molloy, Prof Jonathan Rees, Prof Helen Small, Rev Dr Andrew Teal, Prof Stephen Tuck, Prof Stephen Whitefield, Dr Timothy Farrant, Prof Ingmar Posner, Prof Min Chen PhD FBCS FEG, Mr Mike Wagstaff, Mr Jeremy Bennett, Mr Michael Peter Naworynsky, Prof Andrew James Baldwin, Prof Justin Rhys Jones, Professor Henrietta Katherine Harrison, Professor Damian Rossler, Ms Nancy Braithwaite, Mr Stephen Gosztony, Mr Nick Hawes, Dr Brian A'Hearn, Prof Owen Darbishire, Prof Ariel Ezrachi, Prof Mark Fricker, Prof Adrian Gregory, Mrs Beatrice Hollond, Prof Christopher Melchert, Prof Lynda Mugglestone, Prof Clive Siviour, Prof Jeremy Taylor, Prof Irene Tracey, Prof Theo Maarten Van Lint, Prof Rebecca Williams, Prof Sandra Fredman, Prof Hannah Elizabeth Smithson, Prof Nicolai Sinai, Prof Alfons Weber, Dame Lynne Janie Brindley DBE, Prof Tim James Woolings, Dr Peter Claus, Prof Andrew Philip McDowell Orchard, Prof Guy Kahane, Professor Anandi Mani, Professor Pramila Kishnan, Ms Alice Gosling
Income: £11,727,000 [2017]; £10,961,000 [2016]; £11,101,000 [2015]; £10,763,000 [2014]; £12,886,000 [2013]

The Master and Fellows of Darwin College in the University of Cambridge
Registered: 4 Apr 2011 *Employees:* 49
Tel: 01223 335660 *Website:* darwin.cam.ac.uk
Activities: Education, training
Address: Darwin College, Cambridge, CB3 9EU
Trustees: Professor Martin K Jones PhD, Professor Michael Edwin Akam, Mr John Dix, Professor Russell Cowburn PhD FRS, Professor Anne Ferguson-Smith PhD FMedSci, Professor C Mary R Fowler MA PhD FRAS FGS, Dr Duncan Needham PhD, Dr Sara Baker PhD
Income: £6,763,364 [2017]; £4,702,450 [2016]; £4,463,738 [2015]; £4,328,034 [2014]; £4,186,447 [2013]

The Master and Fellows of The College of The Great Hall of The University Commonly Called University College in the University of Oxford
Registered: 8 Apr 2011 *Employees:* 201 *Volunteers:* 43
Website: univ.ox.ac.uk
Activities: Education, training
Address: University College, High Street, Oxford, OX1 4BH
Trustees: Ivor Crewe, Ngaire Woods, Frank Arntzenius, Bill Child, Keith Dorrington, Nicholas Halmi, Gideon Henderson, Peter Howell, Peter Jezzard, Lisa Kallet, David Logan, Robin Nicholas, Bill Roscoe, Martin Smith, John Wheater, Oliver Zimmer, Dr Justin Benesch, Dr Polly Jones, Dr Nikolay Nikolov, Professor Mark Smith, Mrs Angela Unsworth MBE, Dr Lars Hansen, Dr Michael A Barnes, Dr Stephen Eliot Kelton Hansen, Professor Karen O'Brien, Dr Andrew Ian Grant, Dr Joseph Eliezer Salkie Moshenska, Thomas Povey, William Allan, Michael Benedikt, Steve Collins, Andrew Gregory, Jotun Hein, Catherine Holmes, Benjamin Jackson, Angus Johnston, Andrew Ker, Sophocles Mavroeidis, Catherine Pears, Trevor Sharp, Edman Tsang, Nicholas Yeung, Dr Clare Leaver, Dr Martin Galpin, Dr Karolina Milewicz, Mr Jacob Rowbottom, Professor Ter Haar Barend, Dr Andrew Bell, Mr William Akers Roth, Caroline Ej Terquem, Dr Ine Jacobs, Dr Sophie McGregor Smith, Dr Patrick Rebeschini
Income: £14,372,766 [2017]; £13,454,145 [2016]; £12,541,984 [2015]; £11,758,921 [2014]; £11,416,242 [2013]

The Master and Fellows of The College or Hall of Saint Catharine The Virgin in the University of Cambridge

Registered: 12 Aug 2010 *Employees:* 180
Tel: 01223 338329 *Website:* caths.cam.ac.uk
Activities: Education, training
Address: St Catharine's College, Cambridge, CB2 1RL
Trustees: Prof John Pyle, Dr Paul Hartle, Dr Robert Wardy, Prof Eilis Ferran, Dr Philip Oliver, Prof Christopher Clark, Dr Rose Melikan, Dr John Xuereb, Dr Katharine Dell, Dr Nora Berend, Dr Richard Dance, Dr Mark Elliott, Dr Abigail Brundin, Dr Matthew Mason, Dr David Bainbridge, Mr Simon Summers, Dr Edward Wickham, Dr Miranda Griffin, Dr Jeffrey Dalley, Dr Ivan Scales, Mr Peter Turner, Dr Fatima Santos, Professor Nicholas Morrell, Dr Jerome Anthony Neufeld, Dr Michael Hurley, Rev David Neaum, Dr Jessica Gwynne, Dr Mairi Kilkenny, Dr Charalampos Haris Psarris, Mr Michael Kitson, Professor Peter Tyler, Dr Patrick Palmer, Prof Johan Jacob Van De Ven, Dr Ian Willis, Dr Elia Kantaris, Dr Michael Sutcliffe, Dr Anthony Davenport, Dr Caroline Gonda, Dr David Aldridge, Dr Peter Wothers, Mrs Irena Borzym, Dr Sriya Iyer, Dr Sergei Taraskin, Dr Harald Wydra, Dr Hester Lees-Jeffries, Dr Gillian Clare Carr, Dr Richard Harrison, Mrs Deborah Loveluck, Prof William Sutherland, Dr Matthew De Jong, Dr Stuart Althorpe, Dr Stefan Marciniak, Dr Robert Smith, Dr Hazem Kandil, Dr Timothy Rogan, Dr Michael Amior, Dr Simon Taylor, Professor Sir Mark Welland
Income: £12,833,000 [2017]; £11,677,000 [2016]; £9,382,000 [2015]; £9,149,000 [2014]; £9,227,000 [2013]

The Master and Scholars of Balliol College in the University of Oxford

Registered: 28 Sep 2011 *Employees:* 150
Tel: 01865 277715 *Website:* balliol.ox.ac.uk
Activities: Education, training; religious activities
Address: Balliol College, Broad Street, Oxford, OX1 3BJ
Trustees: Dame Helen Ghosh, Mr Seamus Perry, Professor Robin Choudhury BA MA Oxf BM BCh DM Oxf FRCP, Mr Richard Collier, Professor Timothy Endicott, Dr James Forder, Professor Freddie Hamdy, Professor Frances Kirwan, Dr David Lucas, Dr Sophie Marnette, Dr Dominic O'Brien, Dr Sandra Paoli, Dr Sebastian Shimeld, Professor Lloyd Nicholas Trefethen, Dr Simon Skinner, Professor Christopher Minkowski, Dr Adrian Kelly, Professor James Christopher Belich, Professor Peter Tufano AB MBA PhD, Dr Martin Burton BM BCh, Dr Matthew Robinson MA DPhil, Dr Scot Peterson, Dr Edith Elkind, Dr Adam Smyth, Dr Rachel Quarrell, Dr Laura Miguelez-Cavero, Rev Bruce Kinsey, Dr David Clifton, Dr Adam Edward Philip Caulton, Dr Kaiserman Alexander, Dr Helen Gittos, Mr Richard Ovenden, Professor Brian Foster, Dr William Barford, Dr Martin Conway, Dr Robert Field, Professor Leslie Green, Professor Andrew Hurrell, Dr Grant Lamond, Professor Andre Lukas, Professor Thomas Melham, Professor Dermot O'Hare, Dr Armin Reichold, Dr Rosalind Thomas, Dr Nicola Trott, Dr Sudhir Hazareesingh, Professor Thomas Noe, Dr Lisa Jane Walker, Professor Manuela Zaccolo, Professor Stefano Zacchetti BA PhD, Dr Elena Lombardi MA PhD, Dr Jin-Chong Tan BSc MEng PhD, Dr Coralia Cartis, Dr Daniel Butt, Professor Charles Conn, Mr Richard Norman, Dr Derek Moulton, Dr Nadia Elizabeth Hilliard, Dr Miguel Ballester, Professor Philip Howard, Dr John-Paul Ghobrial
Income: £12,149,000 [2017]; £13,435,000 [2016]; £10,639,000 [2015]; £12,625,000 [2014]; £12,116,000 [2013]

Mathematics in Education and Industry

Registered: 29 Oct 1996 *Employees:* 198
Tel: 01225 776776 *Website:* mei.org.uk
Activities: Education, training
Address: Mathematics in Education & Industry, Monkton House, Epsom Square, White Horse Business Park, Trowbridge, Wilts, BA14 0XG
Trustees: Mr Richard Browne, Mr Martin John Reed, Mrs Jean Snook, Dr A Bainbridge, Jayne Mee, Mr Steven Labedz, Mr David Arthur Holland, Mr Peter Graham Bossom, Mr Gerald William Goodall, Mr Andrew Vernon Ramsay, Malcolm Grubb, Dr David Bedford
Income: £6,489,172 [2017]; £6,527,449 [2016]; £6,578,095 [2015]; £4,765,804 [2014]; £4,281,686 [2013]

The Matthew Project

Registered: 15 Feb 2008 *Employees:* 129 *Volunteers:* 11
Tel: 01603 626123 *Website:* matthewproject.org
Activities: Education, training; advancement of health or saving of lives; prevention or relief of poverty
Address: 4 Rookery Hill, Rockland St Mary, Norwich, NR14 7EW
Trustees: Mr Stephen Lock, Mr Andrew Warren, Christopher Paul Hoey, Lorie Lain Rogers, Richard Capper, Mr Greg Gibson, Margaret Wade
Income: £3,158,000 [2017]; £3,225,617 [2016]; £3,465,839 [2015]; £3,434,230 [2014]; £2,181,562 [2013]

Maudsley Charity

Registered: 17 May 1996 *Employees:* 13
Tel: 020 3228 6000 *Website:* maudsleycharity.org
Activities: The advancement of health or saving of lives
Address: Maudsley Charity Trust Headquarters, The Maudsley Hospital, Denmark Hill, London, SE5 8AZ
Trustees: Slam NHS Foundation Trust
Income: £5,469,000 [2017]; £4,738,000 [2016]; £4,857,000 [2015]; £3,966,000 [2014]; £6,055,000 [2013]

The Jessie May Trust

Registered: 5 Apr 2001 *Employees:* 17 *Volunteers:* 5
Tel: 0117 961 6840 *Website:* jessiemaytrust.org.uk
Activities: The advancement of health or saving of lives; disability
Address: 35 Old School House, Britannia Road, Kingswood, Bristol, BS15 8DB
Trustees: Dr Nicola Eaton, Dr Mary Gainsborough, Mrs Julie Kembrey, Ms Alison Pavier, Ms Shelley Crofts, Ms Carole Nicholls, Mr Roger Harper, Linda Parker, Dr Anna Graham, Ms Sarah Jane Merritt
Income: £1,296,785 [2017]; £1,035,102 [2016]; £805,387 [2015]; £761,947 [2014]; £618,464 [2013]

Mayday Trust

Registered: 23 Mar 1994 *Employees:* 56 *Volunteers:* 22
Tel: 01865 670028 *Website:* maydaytrust.org.uk
Activities: Education, training; advancement of health or saving of lives; disability; prevention or relief of poverty; accommodation, housing
Address: 10C Littlegate Street, Oxford, OX1 0QT
Trustees: Mr Brian Wheelwright, Mr Andrew David Meehan, Vincent Patrick Bowen, Jason Mollring, Keith Starling, Mr Stephen Thomas Brown, Andrew Peter Hudson, Julie McEver, Thomas Murtha
Income: £3,008,479 [2017]; £4,012,058 [2016]; £4,018,439 [2015]; £3,724,482 [2014]; £3,671,533 [2013]

Mayfair Charities Limited
Registered: 6 Mar 1968
Tel: 020 7836 1555
Activities: General charitable purposes; education, training; prevention or relief of poverty; religious activities
Address: Freshwater Group of Companies, Freshwater House, 158-162 Shaftesbury Avenue, London, WC2H 8HR
Trustees: Mr Benzion Schalom Eliezer Freshwater, Mr Richard Fischer, Mr D Davis, Mr Solomon Israel Freshwater
Income: £4,607,000 [2017]; £4,562,000 [2016]; £4,398,000 [2015]; £4,389,000 [2014]; £4,570,000 [2013]

Mayfield Fellowship
Registered: 30 May 1985 *Employees:* 43 *Volunteers:* 1
Website: mayfieldcourt.org
Activities: Disability
Address: 33 Gipsy Lane, Liverpool, L18 3HL
Trustees: Mr Laurence Myles Lee, Ms Deborah Slee, Marlene Downey, Derek Downey, Jacqueline Annette Speariett, Mr Christopher Speariett, Andrew Jackson
Income: £1,452,943 [2017]; £1,395,029 [2016]; £1,354,073 [2015]; £1,205,993 [2014]; £1,188,540 [2013]

Mayfield School Ltd
Registered: 29 Jun 1995 *Employees:* 194
Tel: 01435 874608 *Website:* mayfieldgirls.org
Activities: Education, training; religious activities
Address: Mayfield School, The Old Palace, High Street, Mayfield, E Sussex, TN20 6PH
Trustees: Sister Maria Dinnendahl, Dr Christopher Storr, Mrs Maureen Martin, Miss Julia Bowden, Mr Christopher John Buxton, Mrs Marion Diane McGovern, Marlane Mellor, Mrs Sara Hulbert-Powell, Lady Chantal Davies, Sister Paula Thomas, Mr Edward Walshe, Mrs Rhona Lewis, Mr Timothy Reid
Income: £9,506,966 [2017]; £8,804,769 [2016]; £8,937,912 [2015]; £8,326,110 [2014]; £8,474,981 [2013]

The Mayfield Trust
Registered: 28 Mar 1991 *Employees:* 121 *Volunteers:* 3
Tel: 01422 322552 *Website:* mayfield-trust.org.uk
Activities: Disability; accommodation, housing
Address: The Mayfield Trust, Horley Green Works, Horley Green Road, Halifax, W Yorks, HX3 6AS
Trustees: Val Sharp, Mrs Jennifer Crossland, Mrs Louise Shute, Mr Adam Milner
Income: £1,923,878 [2017]; £1,717,215 [2016]; £1,824,075 [2015]; £1,593,447 [2014]; £1,694,085 [2013]

The Mayflower Theatre Trust
Registered: 30 Jun 1986 *Employees:* 116 *Volunteers:* 13
Website: mayflower.org.uk
Activities: Education, training; arts, culture, heritage, science
Address: 22-26 Commercial Road, Southampton, SO15 1GE
Trustees: Mr Colin Lewis, Mr Robert Primmer BSc FRICS, Mr Mike Denis Smith, Mrs Paula Irena Claisse, Mr Shaun William Pantling, Mr Nicholas John Vaughan, Mr Malcolm Le Bas, Mr John Hannides, Ms Lindsey Noble
Income: £21,646,261 [2017]; £18,161,099 [2016]; £25,630,295 [2015]; £16,190,942 [2014]; £17,553,551 [2013]

Mayheights Limited
Registered: 25 Nov 2005
Tel: 020 8806 1234
Activities: General charitable purposes; prevention or relief of poverty; religious activities
Address: 36 Gilda Crescent, London, N16 6JP
Trustees: Mr Oscar Low, Mr Menashe Eichenstein, Mrs Rachel Low
Income: £7,783,684 [2017]; £2,711,581 [2016]; £1,837,211 [2015]; £2,563,091 [2014]; £818,787 [2013]

The Mayhew Home
Registered: 28 Sep 1999 *Employees:* 60 *Volunteers:* 200
Website: themayhew.org
Activities: General charitable purposes; education, training; advancement of health or saving of lives; animals
Address: Mayhew Animal Home, Trenmar Gardens, London, NW10 6BJ
Trustees: Mr Adam Halsey, Ms Svetlana Ignatieva, Mr Julian Carl Beynon, Ms Denise McFarland Cruickshanks, Sabahat Salahuddin, Mr John Matthews, Ms Corinna McShane, Mr Shailen Jasani, Miss Roisin Clare Williams
Income: £2,197,123 [2016]; £2,794,339 [2015]; £2,436,754 [2014]; £3,525,536 [2013]; £2,581,491 [2012]

The Maynard School
Registered: 18 Aug 2003 *Employees:* 109 *Volunteers:* 12
Website: maynard.co.uk
Activities: Education, training
Address: Maynard School, Denmark Road, Exeter, EX1 1SJ
Trustees: Lady Jan A Stanhope, Mr Nicholas Bruce-Jones, Ms Sarah Witheridge, Mrs Jane Chanot, Alan Gibbons, Mrs Wendy Dersley, Miss Christina Walton, Mr Christopher Gatherer, Miss Wendy Manfield, Mr Henry Luce, Mrs Lynn Turner, Mr James Ronald Dart, Mrs Caroline Pascoe, Mrs Cynthia Thompson, Miss Sara Randall Johnson
Income: £4,328,543 [2017]; £4,345,873 [2016]; £4,182,140 [2015]; £4,271,831 [2014]; £4,172,934 [2013]

The Mayor's Fund for London
Registered: 4 Jul 2008 *Employees:* 23
Tel: 020 7983 6544 *Website:* mayorsfundforlondon.org.uk
Activities: General charitable purposes; education, training; advancement of health or saving of lives; prevention or relief of poverty; amateur sport; economic, community development, employment
Address: Greater London Authority, City Hall, 110 The Queens Walk, London, SE1 2AA
Trustees: Harvey McGrath, Ian Livingstone, Mr Manmohan Varma, Mrs Jennifer Halpern Prince, Mrs Elena Baturina, Mr Timothy Roberts, Michelle Pinggera, Ms Melanie Grant, Mr Mehmet Dalman
Income: £2,128,147 [2016]; £3,572,603 [2015]; £2,712,156 [2014]; £2,115,278 [2013]; £2,179,909 [2012]

Mayville High School Limited
Registered: 26 Mar 1983 *Employees:* 107
Tel: 023 9273 4847 *Website:* mayvillehighschool.com
Activities: General charitable purposes; education, training
Address: 35-37 St Simons Road, Southsea, Hants, PO5 2PE
Trustees: Mr Clive Hartridge, Mr Mohamedtaki Mohamedall Jaffer, Mrs Jeanne Eames, Mrs Alison Susan Ellwood, Mr Michael Leonard Babcock, Mr Robin Philip Keeler, Ms Vanda Skonieczna, Mrs Susan Harden-Davies
Income: £4,325,324 [2017]; £4,259,685 [2016]; £3,886,034 [2015]; £3,611,912 [2014]; £3,539,836 [2013]

Ronald McDonald House Charities (UK)

Registered: 7 Sep 1989 *Employees:* 130 *Volunteers:* 4,029
Tel: 020 8700 7187 *Website:* rmhc.org.uk
Activities: The advancement of health or saving of lives; accommodation, housing
Address: Ronald McDonald House, Charities, 11-59 High Road, East Finchley, London, N2 8AW
Trustees: Penny Hurst, Mr Jeff Fergus, Dr Anu Ohrling, Sydney Hunsdale, Mr Henry William Trickey, Mr Jason Clark, Dr Simon Oakley Fradd, Mr Simon Robert Kirk, Mrs Afia Sirkhot, Michael Morgan, Mr Ron Mounsey
Income: £14,027,000 [2016]; £10,398,000 [2015]; £14,247,838 [2014]; £9,088,021 [2013]; £7,448,664 [2012]

The Rory McIlroy Foundation Limited

Registered: 20 May 2014 *Employees:* 1
Tel: 020 8104 1000
Activities: General charitable purposes; advancement of health or saving of lives; economic, community development, employment
Address: Arena Wealth, Chiswick Gate, 598-608 Chiswick High Road, London, W4 5RT
Trustees: Mr Philip James Barker, Mr James McIlroy, Dr Andrew David Crone, Mr Barry Funston, Mr Rory McIlroy
Income: £1,624,813 [2016]; £985,511 [2015]; £780,000 [2014]

The McPin Foundation

Registered: 20 Dec 2006 *Employees:* 17 *Volunteers:* 4
Tel: 020 7922 7877 *Website:* mcpin.org
Activities: General charitable purposes; education, training; advancement of health or saving of lives; disability; other charitable purposes
Address: The McPin Foundation, 32-36 Loman Street, London, SE1 0EH
Trustees: Dr Nicholas McNally, Ms Jo Loughran, Ms Emma Harding, Ms Amy Meadows, Mrs Liz Meek, Dr Alison Brabban
Income: £1,517,855 [2017]; £710,405 [2016]; £596,559 [2015]; £469,703 [2014]; £108,504 [2013]

Meadowhall Education Centre

Registered: 28 Jan 2003 *Employees:* 36
Tel: 0114 263 5600 *Website:* thesourceacademy.co.uk
Activities: Education, training; prevention or relief of poverty; amateur sport; economic, community development, employment
Address: The Source at Meadowhall, 300 Meadowhall Way, Sheffield, S9 1EA
Trustees: Mr John Mothersole, Darren Pearce, Tricia Smith, Mr Paul Woodcock, Mr David Tudor-Morgan
Income: £1,407,929 [2017]; £1,421,969 [2016]; £1,451,781 [2015]; £1,437,318 [2014]; £1,276,833 [2013]

Meath Epilepsy Charity

Registered: 22 Sep 1962 *Employees:* 171 *Volunteers:* 85
Tel: 01483 415095 *Website:* meath.org.uk
Activities: Disability; accommodation, housing
Address: The Meath Epilepsy Trust, Westbrook Road, Godalming, Surrey, GU7 2QH
Trustees: The Meath Trustee Company Limited
Income: £6,075,481 [2017]; £5,709,555 [2016]; £4,727,645 [2015]; £4,591,479 [2014]; £4,781,088 [2013]

The Medaille Trust Limited

Registered: 5 Feb 2007 *Employees:* 78 *Volunteers:* 12
Tel: 0161 817 2260 *Website:* medaille.co.uk
Activities: Education, training; advancement of health or saving of lives; accommodation, housing; other charitable purposes
Address: The Diocese of Salford, Cathedral Centre, 3 Ford Street, Salford, M3 6DP
Trustees: Terry Tennens, Patrick Edward John Patterson, Mr Folkert Van Galen, Sister Mary Louise Toner, Mr Luke De Pulford, Mr Simon Young, Sister Theresa Lenahan, Mrs Susan Thomas, Sister Henrietta Curran, Mrs Sharon Benningprince, Sister Anne
Income: £2,475,526 [2017]; £1,861,201 [2016]; £1,320,568 [2015]; £1,172,867 [2014]; £1,407,556 [2013]

Medair UK

Registered: 11 Jul 1996 *Employees:* 6 *Volunteers:* 2
Tel: 020 8772 0100 *Website:* medair.org
Activities: The prevention or relief of poverty; overseas aid, famine relief
Address: Medair UK, 345 Canterbury Court, 1-3 Brixton Road, London, SW9 6DE
Trustees: Ms Fiona Petit, Anna Stobart, Shelley Pigott, Mr Gregory Pasche, Mr James Eyre, Robert Schofield, Alex Starling
Income: £1,736,436 [2016]; £1,517,298 [2015]; £1,382,897 [2014]; £1,422,671 [2013]; £427,552 [2012]

Medecins Sans Frontieres (UK)

Registered: 29 Sep 1993 *Employees:* 181 *Volunteers:* 51
Website: msf.org.uk
Activities: Education, training; advancement of health or saving of lives; overseas aid, famine relief
Address: Medecins Sans Frontieres, 10 Furnival Street, London, EC4A 1AB
Trustees: Mr Dennis Kerr, Ms Heidi Quinn, Mr Javid Abdelmoneim, Ms Alyson Froud, Damien Regent, Ms Nicola McLean, Mr Colin Herrman, Dr Tejshri Harivallabh Shah, Dr Gabriel Fitzpatrick, Ms Emma Simpson, Mr Keith Longbone
Income: £54,118,000 [2016]; £46,003,000 [2015]; £44,095,000 [2014]; £35,986,000 [2013]; £23,892,000 [2012]

Medeshamstede Education Trust

Registered: 6 Oct 1998 *Employees:* 35 *Volunteers:* 140
Tel: 01760 336939 *Website:* brecklandparkschool.co.uk
Activities: Education, training
Address: Breckland Park School, Ecotech Centre, Turbine Way, Swaffham, Norfolk, PE37 7XD
Trustees: Mr Gordon Fentiman, Mr William Goodenough, Russell Evershed, Benjamin Evershed, Mr Stuart Gardner, Mr Jeremy Briston, Mr Kevin Dunham, Dane Lawrence
Income: £1,747,730 [2016]; £1,619,373 [2015]; £1,365,727 [2014]; £1,289,304 [2013]; £1,132,551 [2012]

Media Diversity

Registered: 29 Jun 2005 *Employees:* 5 *Volunteers:* 5
Tel: 020 7255 2473 *Website:* media-diversity.org
Activities: Education, training
Address: Media Diversity Institute, 11 Belgrave Road, London, SW1V 1RB
Trustees: Mr Andrew Julian Blake, Ms Joy Anita Francis, Mr Paresh Solanki, Ms Christina Pribichevich-Zoric
Income: £1,165,706 [2016]; £1,186,414 [2015]; £805,953 [2014]; £571,014 [2013]; £736,359 [2012]

Media Legal Defence Initiative
Registered: 24 Mar 2009 *Employees:* 7 *Volunteers:* 13
Tel: 020 3752 5555 *Website:* mediadefence.org
Activities: Human rights, religious or racial harmony, equality or diversity; other charitable purposes
Address: 19 Oval Way, London, SE11 5RR
Trustees: Ms Smita Shah, Mr Robert Jobbins, Ms Sarah Bull, Mr Joshua Castellino, Mr Matthew Richard Francis, Mr Leo Skyner, Mr Gary Born, Mr Korieh Duodu, Mr Olexiy Solohubenko
Income: £3,657,453 [2016]; £2,322,774 [2015]; £2,084,104 [2014]; £1,470,260 [2013]; £1,075,386 [2012]

The Media Trust
Registered: 12 Dec 1994 *Employees:* 35 *Volunteers:* 34
Tel: 020 7871 5600 *Website:* mediatrust.org
Activities: Education, training
Address: Fourth Floor, Block A, Centre House, Wood Lane, London, W12 7SB
Trustees: Mr Richard Eyre CBE, Mr Rupert Howell, Ms Sarah Andrea Davis, Shirley Watson, Mr Kamal Ahmed, Mr Andy Duncan, Mr Matthew John Brittin, Mr Jeremy Martin Buhlmann, Mr John Ryley
Income: £2,437,305 [2017]; £3,125,352 [2016]; £3,363,777 [2015]; £3,335,025 [2014]; £3,330,897 [2013]

The MedicAlert Foundation
Registered: 15 Sep 1995 *Employees:* 27
Tel: 01908 951045 *Website:* medicalert.org.uk
Activities: The advancement of health or saving of lives
Address: MedicAlert House, 327-329 Upper Fourth Street, Milton Keynes, Bucks, MK9 1EH
Trustees: Mr Benet Hiscock, Mr Tony Gadsby, Ms Winifred Chime, Mr Ian Henderson, Ms Caroline Sheridan, Mr Stephen Galliano, Ms Anne Gill, Mr Christopher Gee, Helen Newman
Income: £1,763,999 [2016]; £1,832,156 [2015]; £1,798,163 [2014]; £1,796,374 [2013]; £1,477,036 [2012]

Medical Aid for Palestinians
Registered: 29 Mar 1995 *Employees:* 57 *Volunteers:* 4
Tel: 020 7226 4114 *Website:* map-uk.org
Activities: Education, training; advancement of health or saving of lives; disability; prevention or relief of poverty; overseas aid, famine relief; economic, community development, employment
Address: Medical Aid for Palestine, 33a Islington Park Street, London, N1 1QB
Trustees: Ms Lina Nashef, Mr Graham Watt, Mr Johnny Rizq, Dr Phyllis Starkey, Mr Steven James, Mr Vincent Fean, Ms Nabila Ramdani, Mr Andrew Lumsdaine Karney CEng FIET, Mr Peter Coleridge, Ms Siham Bortcosh, Dr Ezzidin Gouta, Ms Jean Brown, Ms Sarah Eldon
Income: £5,430,000 [2017]; £4,861,000 [2016]; £8,298,000 [2015]; £3,104,727 [2014]; £3,325,908 [2013]

Medical Detection Dogs
Registered: 17 Jun 2008 *Employees:* 36 *Volunteers:* 569
Tel: 01296 655888 *Website:* medicaldetectiondogs.org.uk
Activities: The advancement of health or saving of lives; disability
Address: Medical Detection Dogs, 3 Millfield, Greenway Business Park, Winslow Road, Great Horwood, Milton Keynes, Bucks, MK17 0NP
Trustees: Mr Peter Mimpriss CVO, The Hon Mrs Elizabeth Duncan Smith, Dr Alan Rutherford Makepeace FRCR FRCS, Mr Andrew Keegan ACMA CGMA, Dr Victoria Hordern MBBS BSc MD FRCP
Income: £1,861,691 [2017]; £1,474,352 [2016]; £1,440,878 [2015]; £1,502,131 [2014]; £541,760 [2013]

Medical Foundation for The Care of Victims of Torture
Registered: 13 Sep 1990 *Employees:* 153 *Volunteers:* 169
Tel: 020 7697 7823 *Website:* freedomfromtorture.org
Activities: The advancement of health or saving of lives; human rights, religious or racial harmony, equality or diversity; other charitable purposes
Address: Medical Foundation, 111 Isledon Road, London, N7 7JW
Trustees: Ms Sonali Naik, Ms Susan Helena Berelowitz, Mr Serge Eric Yamou, Mr Raj Chada, Dr Rebecca Wright, Mrs Sarah Jane Taylor Peace, Mr Peter John Atfield, Ms Melanie Lizbeth Essex, Ms Gillian Fawcett, Dr Michael Alwyn Johnson, Mr Charles James Middleton, Dr Fiona Goudie
Income: £8,560,808 [2016]; £8,018,301 [2015]; £8,168,253 [2014]; £7,759,137 [2013]; £8,281,818 [2012]

Medical Mission International (UK)
Registered: 15 Aug 2003 *Employees:* 1
Tel: 020 8464 4612 *Website:* mminternational.org.uk
Activities: The advancement of health or saving of lives; prevention or relief of poverty; overseas aid, famine relief
Address: 34 High Street, Bromley, Kent, BR1 1EA
Trustees: Mr Joseph Lam, Lincoln L Poorman, Mrs Ruth Kendrick, Gerald F Poorman
Income: £5,147,040 [2016]; £3,383,295 [2015]; £3,202,032 [2014]; £3,551,135 [2013]; £2,795,776 [2012]

Medical Missionary News Fund
Registered: 16 Mar 1964 *Employees:* 3 *Volunteers:* 4
Tel: 01268 765266 *Website:* mmn.uk.com
Activities: Education, training; advancement of health or saving of lives; disability; prevention or relief of poverty; overseas aid, famine relief; accommodation, housing; religious activities
Address: Medical Missionary News, 1 Victory Close, Fulmar Way, Wickford, Essex, SS11 8YW
Trustees: Mr Wesley Emerson, Mr Travers Harpur, Mr Barry Hanley, Mr David Keith, Dr Christine Sansom, Miss Ruth Cushing, Peter Gill, Dr Raymond Allen, Mr Jason Freeman, Dr Tessa Bonnett
Income: £1,002,467 [2017]; £1,249,767 [2016]; £786,636 [2015]; £831,445 [2014]; £789,375 [2013]

Medical Research Foundation
Registered: 30 Sep 2010 *Employees:* 11
Tel: 020 7395 2268 *Website:* medicalresearchfoundation.org.uk
Activities: Education, training; advancement of health or saving of lives
Address: 2nd Floor, David Phillips Building, Polaris House, North Star Avenue, Swindon, Wilts, SN2 1FL
Trustees: Mr David Zahn, Mr Stephen Visscher CBE, Professor Bobbie Farsides, Mr Russell Delew, Professor Nicholas Lemoine, Professor Daniel Altmann, Mrs Susan Linda Wilkinson
Income: £4,481,993 [2017]; £2,654,000 [2016]; £5,230,000 [2015]; £2,589,000 [2014]; £2,589,000 [2013]

Medical Schools Council
Registered: 17 Jan 2014 *Employees:* 10
Tel: 020 7419 5494 *Website:* medschools.ac.uk
Activities: Education, training; advancement of health or saving of lives
Address: Medical Schools Council, Woburn House, 20-24 Tavistock Square, London, WC1H 9HD
Trustees: Dr Malcolm Reed, Professor Paul Michael Stewart, Dr Anna Dominiczak, Dr Steve Thornton, Dr John Peter Iredale, Dr Jenny Higham, Dr David Christopher Crossman, Dr John Atherton
Income: £1,093,540 [2017]; £994,000 [2016]; £1,350,792 [2015]; £2,961,218 [2014]

Medway Education Trust
Registered: 3 Dec 1997 *Employees:* 35 *Volunteers:* 6
Tel: 01622 699960 *Website:* lintonpark.focus-school.com
Activities: General charitable purposes; education, training
Address: Chapter Cottage, Dean Street, East Farleigh, Maidstone, Kent, ME15 0PU
Trustees: Clive Groombridge, James Bruce, Vincent Woodcock, Mr Kelvin Dupont, Shane Frost, Stuart Bell, Mr Simon Campbell, Peter Alexander, Steve Lyon, Dean Allen, Tim Dupont, Mr Jason Anderson, Mr Ross Worsley
Income: £2,033,404 [2016]; £2,113,655 [2015]; £2,167,460 [2014]; £1,789,393 [2013]; £1,810,215 [2012]

Medway League of Friends
Registered: 25 Feb 1965 *Employees:* 17 *Volunteers:* 110
Tel: 01634 830000 *Website:* medwayleagueoffriends.co.uk
Activities: The advancement of health or saving of lives
Address: Medway Hospital, Windmill Road, Gillingham, Kent, ME7 5NY
Trustees: John Spence, Mr Colin Silk, Mrs Janet Harsent, Mrs Marion Cogger, Mrs Christine Harvey, Mr Derek May, Mrs Eunice Norman, Mr Stephen Towsey
Income: £1,835,465 [2017]; £1,710,916 [2016]; £1,635,657 [2015]; £1,631,183 [2014]; £1,534,310 [2013]

Medway Youth Trust
Registered: 28 May 2008 *Employees:* 94 *Volunteers:* 40
Tel: 07500 895820 *Website:* themytrust.org
Activities: General charitable purposes; education, training; advancement of health or saving of lives; disability; prevention or relief of poverty; accommodation, housing; arts, culture, heritage, science; amateur sport; economic, community development, employment; recreation
Address: The Fort, Primrose Close, Chatham, Kent, ME4 6HZ
Trustees: Mr Robert John Marsh, Peter Martin, Ms Janet Stephens, Ms Carol Anne Stewart, Mr Eduardo Jackson, Ms Carole Hardy, Mr Michael Beckwith, Mrs Andrea Ashman, Miss Alice Finnegan, Ms Helen Robinson
Income: £2,681,841 [2017]; £2,712,511 [2016]; £2,751,954 [2015]; £2,187,791 [2014]; £1,972,809 [2013]

The Anthony and Elizabeth Mellows Charitable Settlement
Registered: 7 Nov 1980
Activities: The advancement of health or saving of lives; arts, culture, heritage, science
Address: Apartment 23, Clement House, 190 Strand, London, WC2R 1AB
Trustees: Mrs Elizabeth Mellows, Mr Graham Ogilvie
Income: £3,818,620 [2017]; £49,809 [2016]; £72,590 [2015]; £32,573 [2014]; £25,038 [2013]

The Melow Charitable Trust
Registered: 17 Apr 1978
Activities: General charitable purposes; education, training; advancement of health or saving of lives; prevention or relief of poverty; religious activities
Address: 21 Warwick Grove, London, E5 9HX
Trustees: Esther Weiser, Miriam Spitz
Income: £1,826,150 [2015]; £1,778,214 [2014]; £1,626,970 [2013]; £1,751,649 [2012]

Melton Mowbray Town Estate
Registered: 30 Aug 1963 *Employees:* 28
Tel: 01664 564559 *Website:* meltonmowbraytownestate.co.uk
Activities: General charitable purposes; amateur sport; economic, community development, employment
Address: Town Bailiffs Cottage, 2 Park Lane, Melton Mowbray, Leics, LE13 0PT
Trustees: Mr John Southerington, Mr Derek Fredrick Whitehouse MBE, Mr Peter Roffey DL, Mr Richard Sage, Mrs Dinah Hickling, Mrs Susan Bailey, Mr Eric Tindall, Mrs Adrienne Holland, Mr John Rudman, Mr Graham Bett, Mr Tim Webster, Mr Keith Hallam, Mr Ian Anthony Neale, Mr Ian Wilkinson
Income: £1,890,877 [2017]; £536,276 [2016]; £622,679 [2015]; £519,891 [2014]; £495,517 [2013]

Memhay Limited
Registered: 28 Jan 1999
Activities: General charitable purposes; education, training; prevention or relief of poverty; religious activities
Address: Haffner Hoff LLP, Parkgates, Bury New Road, Prestwich, Manchester, M25 0TL
Trustees: Mr Chaim Shimen Lebrecht, Mr Michael Yehuda Lebrecht, Mrs Susan Lebrecht
Income: £1,725,376 [2016]; £1,353,986 [2015]; £2,206,143 [2014]; £2,011,141 [2013]

Mencap in Kirklees
Registered: 25 Jan 1990 *Employees:* 124 *Volunteers:* 35
Tel: 01484 340811 *Website:* mencapinkirklees.org.uk
Activities: General charitable purposes; education, training; disability; accommodation, housing; human rights, religious or racial harmony, equality or diversity
Address: Mencap in Kirklees, Brunswick House, 33 East Street, Huddersfield, W Yorks, HD3 3ND
Trustees: Mrs Linda Wrigley, Mr Peter James Hutchinson, Mr Anthony Scott Horsfall, Mrs Jill Robson, Mr Dennis Roughsedge, Mr Brian Mettrick, Mrs Angela Bradshaw
Income: £3,073,453 [2017]; £2,775,903 [2016]; £2,633,946 [2015]; £2,505,908 [2014]; £2,453,587 [2013]

Mendip Young Mens Christian Association
Registered: 16 Mar 1999 *Employees:* 65 *Volunteers:* 40
Tel: 01749 679553 *Website:* mendipymca.org.uk
Activities: Education, training; accommodation, housing; amateur sport
Address: Mendip YMCA, The Old Glasshouse, South Street, Wells, Somerset, BA5 1SL
Trustees: Mr Robert Paul Taylor, Rev Christopher Hare, Mr Richard J A Oliver, Mr Piers Rose, Mr Stephen Harrison, Ms Frances Hale, Mrs Miriam Hare
Income: £1,901,465 [2017]; £1,431,539 [2016]; £1,505,389 [2015]; £1,349,279 [2014]; £913,117 [2013]

Menevia Diocesan Trust
Registered: 18 Nov 1965 *Employees:* 12 *Volunteers:* 252
Tel: 01792 659281 *Website:* menevia.org
Activities: Religious activities
Address: Diocese of Menevia, 27 Convent Street, Swansea, SA1 2BX
Trustees: Sister Angela, Right Reverend Bishop Thomas Mathew Burns, Rev Canon Michael Lewis BA VF, Rev Monsignor Joseph Cefai MA PhD VF VG, Mrs Karen Jones, Very Reverend Mgr Canon Brian Kinrade, Mr Adrian Murphy KSG JP, Mrs Helen Sinclair, Rev Michael Smith
Income: £2,474,956 [2017]; £2,239,239 [2016]; £2,921,839 [2015]; £2,605,753 [2014]; £2,345,117 [2013]

Meningitis Now
Registered: 9 Mar 1990 *Employees:* 54 *Volunteers:* 650
Tel: 01453 768000 *Website:* meningitisnow.org
Activities: General charitable purposes; education, training; advancement of health or saving of lives; disability; amateur sport
Address: Meningitis Now, Fern House, Bath Road, Stroud, Glos, GL5 3TJ
Trustees: Mr Alastair Irvine, Mr Stephen Gazard, Mr Andrew Fletcher, Mr Gary Price, Mr James Sutherland, Hannah Marsh, Mitchell Wolfe, Mrs Anna Freeman, Mr Craig Jones, Mr Roderick Adlington, Samantha Blackie
Income: £3,182,586 [2017]; £3,331,560 [2016]; £3,434,641 [2015]; £3,399,825 [2014]; £2,686,237 [2013]

Meningitis Research Foundation
Registered: 14 Mar 2002 *Employees:* 42 *Volunteers:* 250
Tel: 0333 405 6262 *Website:* meningitis.org
Activities: General charitable purposes; advancement of health or saving of lives; disability
Address: Newminster House, 27-29 Baldwin Street, Bristol, BS1 1LT
Trustees: Mr David Daniel Moed FCA, Professor George Griffin, Mr Mathew Gilbert, Mr Stephen Trump, Dr Nick Manson, Ms Deborah Ann Warman, Dr Brian Scott, Mr Martin Vaggers, Dr Jane Cope MBE, Prof Ray Borrow
Income: £2,944,689 [2017]; £2,334,715 [2016]; £2,322,518 [2015]; £2,589,861 [2014]; £2,581,403 [2013]

Menorah Foundation
Registered: 3 Mar 1995
Tel: 020 8203 4195
Activities: General charitable purposes; education, training; religious activities
Address: 13 Beaufort Gardens, London, NW4 3QN
Trustees: Mr Michael Wechsler, Mr Paul Kreditor, Mr Alan Perrin, Mr Stephen Goldberg, Mr Jeremy Kon, Mr Adrian Jacobs
Income: £1,479,320 [2016]; £615,160 [2015]; £927,177 [2014]; £608,915 [2013]; £780,054 [2012]

The Menorah Primary School
Registered: 22 Dec 1966 *Employees:* 51
Activities: Education, training
Address: 26 Woodlands Close, London, NW11 9QR
Trustees: Mr D Chontow, Mr Philip David Weinstein, Mr Ronald Hofbauer
Income: £1,483,387 [2017]; £1,111,858 [2016]; £1,132,795 [2015]; £1,258,881 [2014]; £1,197,741 [2013]

Mens Accommodation and Support
Registered: 7 Jun 2011 *Employees:* 14
Tel: 0151 548 8180 *Website:* mascommunityinterestcompany.webs.com
Activities: Education, training; advancement of health or saving of lives; prevention or relief of poverty; accommodation, housing; recreation
Address: 102 Belmont Road, Liverpool, L6 5BJ
Trustees: Peter Moores, Anne Moores
Income: £1,181,232 [2017]; £873,472 [2016]; £1,100,929 [2015]; £1,124,325 [2014]; £1,198,513 [2013]

Mental Health Concern
Registered: 22 Oct 1987 *Employees:* 605 *Volunteers:* 1
Tel: 0191 217 0377 *Website:* mentalhealthconcern.org
Activities: The advancement of health or saving of lives; disability; accommodation, housing
Address: Mental Health Concern, 34-38 Brenkley Way, Blezard Business Park, Seaton Burn, Newcastle upon Tyne, NE13 6DS
Trustees: Mr David Robson Arthur, Mrs Elizabeth Ann Robinson, Mrs Zena Jones, Mr Richard McEvoy, Ms Rosemary Granger, Mrs Angela Mary Walsh, Mr David Smith, Christine Brown
Income: £20,643,000 [2017]; £18,797,665 [2016]; £16,766,002 [2015]; £16,185,329 [2014]; £13,780,012 [2013]

The Mental Health Foundation
Registered: 16 Mar 1989 *Employees:* 69 *Volunteers:* 23
Tel: 020 7803 1136 *Website:* mentalhealth.org.uk
Activities: Education, training; advancement of health or saving of lives; disability
Address: Mr C Hughes, Colechurch House, 1 London Bridge Walk, London, SE1 2SX
Trustees: Mr Paul Hodgkinson, Mr Keith Leslie, Mr Peter Robert Byrne, Ms Jennifer Ellen Forrester-Paton, Dr Linda De Caestecker, Ms Jacqueline Maria Dyer MBE, Mr James O'Leary, Mrs Kyla Brand, Mr Neil Richard Caldicott, Miss Aisha Iqbal Sheikh-Anene, Professor Ann John
Income: £4,683,430 [2017]; £4,451,974 [2016]; £4,459,219 [2015]; £4,218,429 [2014]; £4,152,375 [2013]

Mental Health Matters
Registered: 9 Feb 1984 *Employees:* 271 *Volunteers:* 4
Tel: 0191 516 3500 *Website:* mhm.org.uk
Activities: General charitable purposes; disability; accommodation, housing; economic, community development, employment
Address: Mental Health Matters, Avalon House, St Catherines Court, Sunderland Enterprise Park, Sunderland, Tyne & Wear, SR5 3XJ
Trustees: Mrs Lynette Eastman, Mr Bruce Neville Howorth, Mr Andrew Britton, Mr David Brown, Dr Stirling Moorey, Mr David Corner, Ms Naomi Hankinson
Income: £10,380,943 [2017]; £8,604,402 [2016]; £11,138,765 [2015]; £11,384,347 [2014]; £13,610,827 [2013]

Mentor Foundation UK
Registered: 30 Nov 2005 *Employees:* 23 *Volunteers:* 27
Tel: 020 7553 9920 *Website:* mentoruk.org.uk
Activities: General charitable purposes; education, training; advancement of health or saving of lives
Address: CAN Mezzanine, 49-51 East Road, London, N1 6AH
Trustees: Ms Sim Scavazza, Ms Rachel Anne Lee, Mr Clive Standish, Mr Robert Haas, Mrs Antonia Kathryn De Gier, Mr Harry Robin Sumnall, Ms Kelly Allen
Income: £1,281,855 [2017]; £1,199,892 [2016]; £723,902 [2015]; £628,672 [2014]; £444,420 [2013]

Mercaz Torah Vechesed Limited
Registered: 25 Apr 2005
Tel: 020 8880 5366
Activities: Education, training; prevention or relief of poverty; religious activities
Address: 28 Braydon Road, London, N16 6QB
Trustees: Mr Joseph Ostreicher, Mordche David Rand
Income: £2,103,289 [2017]; £894,325 [2016]; £913,555 [2015]; £856,579 [2014]; £594,252 [2013]

The Brian Mercer Charitable Trust
Registered: 6 Aug 1999
Tel: 01254 686600 *Website:* brianmercercharitabletrust.org
Activities: The advancement of health or saving of lives; arts, culture, heritage, science
Address: Beever & Struthers, Central Buildings, Richmond Terrace, Blackburn, BB1 7AP
Trustees: Mrs Christine Jane Clancy, Mr Roger Peter Terence Duckworth, Mr Kenneth John Merrill, Mrs Mary Ann Edgar Turner Clitheroe
Income: £1,120,199 [2017]; £1,065,648 [2016]; £858,440 [2015]; £850,438 [2014]; £833,622 [2013]

The Mercers Charitable Foundation
Registered: 29 Apr 1983 *Volunteers:* 129
Tel: 020 7726 4991 *Website:* mercers.co.uk
Activities: General charitable purposes; education, training; religious activities; arts, culture, heritage, science; environment, conservation, heritage
Address: The Mercers' Company, Becket House, 36 Old Jewry, London, EC2R 8DD
Trustees: The Mercers' Company
Income: £4,901,000 [2017]; £5,188,000 [2016]; £8,979,000 [2015]; £7,813,000 [2014]; £4,483,000 [2013]

Merchant Taylors School
Registered: 31 Jul 1997 *Employees:* 355 *Volunteers:* 34
Tel: 01923 845513 *Website:* mtsn.org.uk
Activities: Education, training
Address: Merchant Taylors School, Sandy Lodge, Northwood, Middlesex, HA6 2HT
Trustees: Mr Christopher Peter Hare, Mr Andrew Moss, Mr Duncan Guy MacDonald Eggar, Mrs Lynda Barbara Gadd, Mr Robert Jan Temmink, Mr John Henry Sylvester Sichel, Mrs Sarah Angharad Morgan, Dr Graham Barrett, Sir Michael John Tomlinson, Mr Richard Brooman, Mrs Jane Redman, Mr Dipesh Jayantilal Shah, Mr Deepakkumar Velji Vajabhai Haria, Mr Jonathan Mark Cox, Mr Guy Beetham Maurice Henry Du Parc Braham, Mr Alan Eastwood
Income: £22,512,190 [2017]; £21,370,195 [2016]; £16,641,407 [2015]; £15,426,664 [2014]; £16,000,816 [2013]

Merchant Taylors' Educational Trust
Registered: 4 Sep 1967 *Employees:* 423
Tel: 020 7562 2320 *Website:* merchant-taylors.co.uk
Activities: Education, training
Address: Merchant Taylors, Merchants Taylors Hall, 30 Threadneedle Street, London, EC2R 8JB
Trustees: Mr Peter Howard Watkins, Mr John Aidan Joseph Price, Mr Christopher Peter Hare, Mr Johny Armstrong, Mr Peter Godfrey Magill
Income: £26,492,618 [2016]; £20,217,595 [2015]; £20,189,025 [2014]; £20,776,968 [2013]; £21,001,126 [2012]

The Merchant Taylors' Schools Crosby
Registered: 13 Aug 2008 *Employees:* 347 *Volunteers:* 14
Tel: 0151 949 9325 *Website:* merchanttaylors.com
Activities: Education, training
Address: 186 Liverpool Road, Crosby, Liverpool, L23 0QP
Trustees: Mrs Beverley Claire Bell LLB Hons FCILT FRSA, Mr John Cartwright, Mrs Lesley Martin-Wright, Mr Clive Robert Williams FCA FIMC, Miss Anna Gabriella Gervasoni, Mr David Yip, Mr Stephen Alan Wilkinson BA Hons FCA, Dr Jennifer Ann Fox MBChB Birm DRCOG MRCGP, Mr David Stephen Evans, Mr Charles Cowling, Mrs Kathryn Anne Crewe-Read
Income: £16,179,835 [2016]; £15,726,911 [2015]; £16,350,512 [2014]; £15,222,458 [2013]; £14,708,371 [2012]

Mercy Ministries UK
Registered: 20 Sep 2005 *Employees:* 28 *Volunteers:* 30
Tel: 01535 642042 *Website:* mercyuk.org
Activities: Education, training; advancement of health or saving of lives; prevention or relief of poverty; accommodation, housing; religious activities
Address: Cragg Royd, Lowertown, Oxenhope, Keighley, W Yorks, BD22 9JE
Trustees: Rev William Richard Van Der Hart, Mr Mark Pugh, Mrs Juliet Mayhew, Mrs Samantha Lea Coates, Mr Justin Cooper, Mr Robert Martin, Mrs Rachel Hughes
Income: £1,291,210 [2016]; £2,102,736 [2015]; £921,419 [2014]; £784,877 [2013]; £636,411 [2012]

Mercy Ships - U.K Ltd
Registered: 21 Feb 1996 *Employees:* 23
Website: mercyships.org.uk
Activities: Education, training; advancement of health or saving of lives; prevention or relief of poverty; economic, community development, employment
Address: The Lighthouse, Unit 12, Meadway Court, Rutherford Close, Stevenage, Herts, SG1 2EF
Trustees: Mr Andrew Kenneth Billington, Mr Paul Benjamin Ramsbottom, Mrs Ruth Guy, Mrs Ann Gloag, Donovan Palmer, Mrs Angharad Jane Milenkovic, Mr Henry Benwell Clarke, Dr Keith Thomson, Mr Peter Ewins, Mr Anthony Gordon Dunnett, Mr Mel Zuydam
Income: £5,790,410 [2017]; £5,672,341 [2016]; £4,984,552 [2015]; £6,480,530 [2014]; £4,595,772 [2013]

Mercy in Action
Registered: 19 Feb 2003 *Employees:* 76 *Volunteers:* 152
Tel: 01225 443600 *Website:* mercyinaction.org.uk
Activities: General charitable purposes; education, training; advancement of health or saving of lives; prevention or relief of poverty; overseas aid, famine relief; accommodation, housing; religious activities
Address: Jubilee Centre, Lower Bristol Road, Bath, BA2 9ES
Trustees: Mrs Allison Todd, Mrs Hilary Jane Law, Julie Sheard, Mr Tim Jones, Mrs Claire Scurr
Income: £1,582,680 [2016]; £1,449,297 [2015]; £1,338,782 [2014]; £1,241,700 [2013]; £1,117,574 [2012]

The Mereside Education Trust
Registered: 30 Oct 1996 *Employees:* 27 *Volunteers:* 45
Tel: 01270 527470
Activities: Education, training
Address: Pinfold Farm, Stock Lane, Wybunbury, Nantwich, Cheshire, CW5 7HF
Trustees: Mr K Devenish, Mr A Wells, Mr Lewis Justin Baldwin, Mr M Dunbar, Mr C Lewis, Mr J Hayward, Mr N Simpson, Mr Mark Chadwick, Mr M Hutchins, Mr V Wells
Income: £2,000,924 [2016]; £1,816,082 [2015]; £1,688,541 [2014]; £1,694,824 [2013]; £1,485,018 [2012]

Meriden Sports and Recreation Trust
Registered: 25 Nov 2015
Tel: 01676 522496 *Website:* meridensrt.org.uk
Activities: Amateur sport; recreation
Address: Hill Rise, Leys Lane, Meriden, Coventry, Warwicks, CV7 7LQ
Trustees: Howard Farrand, Gerry Russell, Iain Roxburgh, Ms Frances Lynch-Smith, Tessa Roxburgh, Damian Cassidy, Paul Blewitt
Income: £1,405,938 [2017]

Merlin MS Centre Ltd
Registered: 4 Sep 2002 *Employees:* 13 *Volunteers:* 65
Tel: 01726 885530 *Website:* merlinmscentre.org.uk
Activities: General charitable purposes; advancement of health or saving of lives; disability
Address: Merlin MS Centre, Hewas Water, St Austell, Cornwall, PL26 7JF
Trustees: Mr Simon Sherrard DL, Mr David Anthony Perks, Judge Christpher Harvey Clark, Mr Michael James, Mr Michael John Gifford, Mrs Sally-Jane Coode DL, Mr Stephen Bernard Lawrence, Dr Emma Campbell, Mr Michael John Ford, Mr Andrew Edmund James
Income: £1,224,890 [2016]; £1,072,496 [2015]; £412,178 [2014]; £361,781 [2013]; £297,278 [2012]

The Merlin Magic Wand Children's Charity
Registered: 15 May 2008 *Employees:* 5
Website: merlinsmagicwand.org
Activities: Disability; recreation
Address: Link House, 25 West Street, Poole, Dorset, BH15 1LD
Trustees: Merlin's Magic Wand Trustees Ltd
Income: £1,696,753 [2016]; £1,290,396 [2015]; £1,283,843 [2014]; £920,223 [2013]; £858,339 [2012]

Merseycare Transport Services Ltd
Registered: 30 Dec 2009 *Employees:* 85 *Volunteers:* 6
Tel: 0151 678 8467
Activities: Education, training; disability; prevention or relief of poverty
Address: Unit 12 Peninsula Business Park, Reeds Lane, Moreton, Wirral, Merseyside, CH46 1DW
Trustees: Mrs Jean Hickson, Mr Ben Mighall, Mrs Julie Chew BA Hons, Mr Paul James Wylde
Income: £2,173,784 [2017]; £1,471,942 [2016]; £1,657,132 [2015]; £1,695,381 [2014]; £1,542,838 [2013]

Merseyside Youth Association Limited
Registered: 10 Feb 1989 *Employees:* 81 *Volunteers:* 4
Tel: 0151 702 0700 *Website:* mya.org.uk
Activities: Education, training; disability; arts, culture, heritage, science; amateur sport; economic, community development, employment; recreation
Address: Merseyside Youth Association Ltd, Abney Building, 65-67 Hanover Street, Liverpool, L1 3DY
Trustees: Mr John Cadwaladr Lewys-Lloyd, Ms Debra Cooke, Mr Andrew Gibbons, Mr Nicholas Hugh Ellis, Mr David Richard Swaffield, Mr Richard Dears
Income: £3,420,999 [2017]; £2,885,962 [2016]; £3,273,972 [2015]; £2,403,398 [2014]; £1,617,702 [2013]

Merthyr Tydfil College Limited
Registered: 8 Feb 2011 *Employees:* 214
Tel: 01443 654171 *Website:* merthyr.ac.uk
Activities: Education, training
Address: University of South Wales, Treforest, Pontypridd, Rhondda Cynon Taf, CF37 1DL
Trustees: Dr John Graystone, Mrs Helene Mansfield, Mr John O'Shea, Katy Burns, Mr Gareth Chapman, Miss Lowri Braddock, Professor Julie Lydon, Mr Huw Williams, Mr Gareth Morgan, Mr Anthony Jenkins, Ms Rachel Moxey
Income: £13,988,000 [2017]; £13,816,000 [2016]; £14,137,000 [2015]; £15,097,000 [2014]; £10,888,000 [2013]

Merthyr Tydfil Institute for the Blind
Registered: 9 Jan 1992 *Employees:* 80 *Volunteers:* 1
Tel: 01685 370072 *Website:* mtib.co.uk
Activities: Education, training; disability; economic, community development, employment; other charitable purposes
Address: Merthyr Tydfil Inst for Blind, Unit 4 Triangle Business Park, Pentrebach, Merthyr Tydfil, CF48 4TQ
Trustees: Mr Tom Lewis, Mr Lyndon Thomas, Mr Ralph Cooper, Mr Alan Gunter, Mr Alan Bush, Mr Gareth Meredith, Mrs Lisa Victoria Mytton, Mr Jonathan Ellis
Income: £1,782,297 [2017]; £1,566,973 [2016]; £1,730,770 [2015]; £1,583,459 [2014]; £1,431,375 [2013]

Merthyr Tydfil Leisure Trust Limited
Registered: 18 Mar 2015 *Employees:* 101 *Volunteers:* 14
Tel: 01685 725253
Activities: General charitable purposes; education, training; advancement of health or saving of lives; disability; arts, culture, heritage, science; environment, conservation, heritage; economic, community development, employment; recreation
Address: Merthyr Tydfil Central Library, High Street, Merthyr Tydfil, CF47 8AF
Trustees: Mr Aled Gruffydd Jones, Dr Hefin Jones OBE, Mr Christopher Felton, Martin Veale, Mrs Hannah Louisa Kester, Mr Alan John Hope, Miss Janet Lydia Morgan, Mr Geraint Vaughan Thomas, Mr Delcan Sammon, Mrs Lanne Marie Jones
Income: £4,834,310 [2017]; £4,693,726 [2016]

Merton Music Foundation
Registered: 11 Sep 1991 *Employees:* 10
Tel: 020 8640 5446 *Website:* mmf.org.uk
Activities: Education, training; arts, culture, heritage, science
Address: c/o Harris Academy Morden, Lilleshall Road, Morden, Surrey, SM4 6DU
Trustees: Mr William Ian Newman, Mr Michael Collins, Mr Edward Andrew John Hickman, Mrs Rowena Louise Maybury, Mr Andrew Freeman, Mrs Doreen Ruth Hewitt, Ms Ana Sallavuard, Mr Clive Antony Grinyer, Mr Ian Bond
Income: £1,085,674 [2016]; £1,061,590 [2015]; £924,281 [2014]; £971,276 [2013]; £929,309 [2012]

The Message Enterprise Centre
Registered: 17 May 2012 *Employees:* 22 *Volunteers:* 50
Tel: 0161 946 2300 *Website:* themec.org.uk
Activities: Education, training; prevention or relief of poverty; religious activities; economic, community development, employment
Address: Message Enterprise Centre, 6 Harper Road, Sharston Industrial Area, Manchester, M22 4RG
Trustees: Mr Colin Hardicre, Mr Andrew Christoper Leakey, Mr Gordon Haynes, Rev Rober White, Mr Paul Nadin, Mr Jonathan Wainwright, David Moore
Income: £1,021,926 [2016]; £1,032,281 [2015]; £870,535 [2014]; £576,541 [2013]

The Message Trust
Registered: 6 Jul 2000 *Employees:* 90 *Volunteers:* 500
Tel: 0161 946 2300 *Website:* message.org.uk
Activities: Education, training; religious activities; arts, culture, heritage, science
Address: The Message Trust, Lancaster House, Harper Road, Sharston Industrial Area, Manchester, M22 4RG
Trustees: Mr Andrew Leakey, Mr Colin Hardicre, Mr Jonathan Wainwright, Mr David Moore, Rev Robert White, Mr Paul Nadin, Mr Gordon Haynes
Income: £4,729,571 [2016]; £4,374,329 [2015]; £3,613,577 [2014]; £3,504,478 [2013]; £3,377,926 [2012]

Metal Culture Limited

Registered: 29 Jun 2004 *Employees:* 16 *Volunteers:* 436
Tel: 01702 470700 *Website:* metalculture.com
Activities: Education, training; accommodation, housing; arts, culture, heritage, science
Address: Chalkwell Hall, Chalkwell Avenue, Southend on Sea, Westcliff on Sea, Essex, SS0 8NB
Trustees: Ms Jude Kelly OBE, Mr Nihal Arthanayake, Mr Ian Thompson, Ms Sally Elizabeth Tallant, Mr Paul Robert Morley, Sir Ian McKellen, Yasmin Alibhai-Brown, Ms Rachel Lichtenstein, Mark Blenkinsop
Income: £1,751,639 [2017]; £1,659,837 [2016]; £1,131,531 [2015]; £577,235 [2014]; £649,333 [2013]

The Metanoia Institute

Registered: 27 Oct 1995 *Employees:* 44 *Volunteers:* 138
Tel: 020 8832 3078 *Website:* metanoia.ac.uk
Activities: Education, training
Address: Metanoia Institute, 13 North Common Road, London, W5 2QB
Trustees: Mr Ronald Parker MB ChB FRCS, Jerry Arnott, Mr Dotun Olaleye, Mr Jeffrey White, Catriona MacKay, Dr Elizabeth Pearson
Income: £3,484,984 [2016]; £3,279,623 [2015]; £3,102,791 [2014]; £2,454,579 [2013]

Methodist Action (North West) Limited

Registered: 28 Jun 2010 *Employees:* 20 *Volunteers:* 80
Tel: 01772 751000 *Website:* methodistaction.co.uk
Activities: Education, training; advancement of health or saving of lives; disability; prevention or relief of poverty; accommodation, housing; economic, community development, employment
Address: Howick House, Howick Park Avenue, Penwortham, Preston, Lancs, PR1 0LS
Trustees: Mr James Mitchell Irving, Rev Kenneth George Walton, Mr Peter Lumsden, Mr Michael Hart, Mr John Kenvyn Wales, Mrs Amanda Latham, Mr Geoffrey Tyson
Income: £1,867,203 [2017]; £1,945,860 [2016]; £2,463,746 [2015]; £3,097,284 [2014]; £1,246,713 [2013]

Methodist Central Hall Westminster

Registered: 1 Feb 2010 *Employees:* 20 *Volunteers:* 10
Tel: 0118 977 1269 *Website:* church.methodist-central-hall.org.uk
Activities: Education, training; religious activities; arts, culture, heritage, science; economic, community development, employment
Address: 4 Purslane, Wokingham, Berks, RG40 2DD
Trustees: Mr Kojo Amoah-Arko, Revd Dr Martyn David Atkins, Mr Nevil Edwin Tomlinson, Rev Michaela Youngson, Ms Helen Tudor, Ms Grace Sangmuah, Mr Joseph Anoom LLB LLM PgDip Law, Revd Canon Graham Thompson, Rev Anthony Miles, Mr Ian Serjeant, Rev Jason Vinyard, David Morgan, Ms Genevieve Patnelli
Income: £7,468,537 [2016]; £6,977,352 [2015]; £7,002,602 [2014]; £4,577,755 [2013]; £5,407,958 [2012]

The Methodist Church - Chester and Stoke-on-Trent District

Registered: 21 Oct 2009 *Employees:* 9 *Volunteers:* 27
Tel: 01270 627774 *Website:* chestokemethodists.com
Activities: Religious activities
Address: Methodist District Centre, Bishops Wood, Nantwich, Cheshire, CW5 7QD
Trustees: Rev Patricia Ann Billsborrow BA Hons, Rev Ashley Cooper, Rev'd Peter Barber, Rev Susan Levitt, Mrs Valerie Ann Mayers, Rev Simon Christopher Sutcliffe BA MA, Rev Julie Herbert, Rev Derek James Balsdon, Mrs Sally Graham, Rev Andrew Stuart Farrington, Mr Brian Robert Barber, Mrs Heather Staniland, Mr Glenn Gerald Parkes, Mr Ian Christopher White LLB, Mr Stephen Edward Best, Rev Linda Jane Catlow, Mrs Barbara Alice Guile
Income: £1,025,426 [2017]; £1,063,004 [2016]; £1,271,867 [2015]; £1,124,073 [2014]; £1,106,740 [2013]

The Methodist Church in Great Britain
Registered: 20 Oct 2009 *Employees:* 431 *Volunteers:* 139
Tel: 020 7486 5502 *Website:* methodist.org.uk
Activities: Religious activities
Address: Methodist Church House, 25 Marylebone Road, London, NW1 5JR
Trustees: Rev Dr Sheryl Anderson, Rev David Frank Lavender, Mr Denis Beaumont, Rev Dr Christine Jones, Rev Anne E Brown BSc, Miss Audrey Ilderton, Mr David A Clitheroe, Dr John A Hargreaves, Rev D Paul C Smith, Revd Canon Gareth J Powell, Rev Dr Jane V Craske, Dr Margaret P Williams, Rev Dr Andrew Wood, Mr Martin Harker, Mr David H James, Mrs Nellie Showers, Mrs Christine Armstrong, Rev Peter Barber, Deacon Julie A Hudson, Mrs Sue Smith, Rev Terry C W Wright, Rev William E Davis, Rev Novette S Headley, Rev Caroline Wickens, Mrs Christine Holland, Rev Rachel E Parkinson, Deacon Ellie Griffin, Mrs Hazel D Miles, Rev Gill Newton, Ms Elizabeth Ovey, Rev Paul Martin, Rev John Hellyer, Mr Graham Kay, Rev Rosamund V Hollingsworth, Mr David C Humphreys, Mr Andrew Lowe, Mr Ronald A Jordan, Rev Dr David Easton, Revd Michaela Youngson, Mrs E Anne Offler, Rev Rodney Hill, Rev Elaine M Lindridge, Rev Paul H Davis, Mrs Caroline Stead, Dr Stephen Leah, Rev David Goodall, Rev Richard Hall, Rev David C Newlove, Rev M Ruth Parry, Mrs M Anne Haggarty, Mr R Arfon Williams, Rev Dr Jonathan Pye, Rev Catherine Dixon, Rev Tom Osborne, Rev David M Chapman, Rev Kathryn Flynn, Miss Sarah E Cave, Dr Anne E Hollows, Mr Steve Cooper, Ms M Frances Hopwood, Rev Faith Nyota, Deacon Josephine Critchley, Mr Sam E McBratney, Rev Naomi Kaiga, Deacon Lisa D Rathbone, Mrs Shelagh Morgan, Rev Dr Gareth J Edwards, Rev Sharon Lovelock, Rev Stephanie J Jenner, Rev Ian Howarth, Dr Geoffrey J Dickinson, Mrs Michele K Jones, Rev Ann M Anderson, Ms Jenny Jackson, Revd Tony Miles, Rev Graham M Edwards, Miss Margaret A Bowerman, Mrs Dorothy G North, Mrs Beatrice M Cloke, Rev Dr Jongikaya Zihle, Mrs Denise Tomlinson, Mr Frank L Watson, Mrs Katrin A Hackett, Rev Gail J Hunt, Mrs Roberta Lunt, Mrs Janet M Clark, Mr Matthew Collins, Deacon Tracey J Hume, Mrs Sue Brumpton, Ms Alison E Stacey-Chapman, Mrs Jenny Wai Hung Yeung, Rev Kerry W Tankard, Rev Lynita Conradie, Ms Rachel E Allison, Prof Peter D Howdle, Rev Eleanor G Jackson, Ms M Virtue Ryan, Rev Andy Fyall, Rev Julie Herbert, Rev Julia Skitt, Rev Lesley Dinham, Mrs Eileen Clarkson, Mr Mike Anderson, Miss Claudia S T Eleady-Cole, Mrs Jennie A Harris, Mrs Anna Malnutt, Mr Anthony Boateng, Rev Helen J Harrell, Mr Robert Lewin-Jones, Rev Dr Andrew J Lunn, Ms Nancy Aquaah, Ms Sian F A Davidson, Rev David P Martin, Rev Jennifer R Pathmarajah, Rev Eva Walker, Rev Canon Helen D Cameron, Mrs Libby Craggs, Ms Jasmine Dempsey, Miss Georgia Harrison, Mr John D Heard, Mr Thomas W Hunt, Ms Rachel J Lampard, Ms Emma J Mills, Mr Josh Orme, Rev Billy Slatter, Rev Dr John Stephens, Rev Leonora J Wassell, Mr Keith W Norman, Ms Whitney K Addow, Rev Karen A Beecham, Rev Ronald Bobb-Williams, Rev Carole A Chaplin, Ms Daphne Creasman, Deacon Flip Den Uil, Rev Simon C Edwards, Mr Christopher R Finbow, Mrs Laura Gallery, Rev Dr Laurence Graham, Rev Dr Mark A Jason, Mrs Pedzisai G Katsande, Miss Victoria Lawrence, Mrs Mary Ludlow, Mrs Susan Marshall-Jennings, Mr Michael May, Rev R Margaret K Mwailu, Dr Fergus O'Ferrall, Mr C Anthony Potts, Mrs Janice Ross, Mrs Marcia Y Tull, Dr Jean Ware, Rev E Adam Wells, Ms Jasmine F Yeboah, Miss Alison M Baalham, Mr David Storry Walton, Rev Dr Jane Leach, Rev Andrew Hollins, Mr Gerry Davis, Rev Graham Thompson, Rev Peter Hancock, Rev Colin A Smith, Rev Dr Stephen J Day, Rev Philip P Wagstaff, Rev Dr Daniel M Mwailu, Professor David Matthews, Rev Stephen J Radford Dip Theol, Rev Ashley R Cooper, Rev Dr Stephen D Wigley, Rev Mark F Pengelly, Mrs Wendy V Holt, Rev Stuart Earl, Deacon Eunice Attwood, Rev Jenny Dyer, Rev Daniel P Reed, Rev David M Butterworth, Mr David S Pendle, Rev Richard J Teal, Rev Bruce Thompson, Ms Helen E Woodall, Mr S Robert Peach, Rev Julian M Pursehouse, Rev Darren Garfield, Mr Ofori Mensah, Rev Jill Marsh, Rev Leslie M Newton, Rev Ruth M Gee, Rev Tim Swindell, Mrs Heather Staniland, Mr John M Troughton, Rev Philip James Jackson, Rev Steven Wild, Rev Loraine N Mellor, Mr Andrew R Owen, Rev Beverly Hollings, Mr Peter Smith, Mr Ralph Dransfield, Rev Dr Jonathan Gichaara, Mrs Heather Shipman, Rev Graham Horsley, Ms Julie Compton, Mrs Jean Hamilton, Rev Dr Barbara C Glasson, Deacon Karen McBride, Rev David W Hookins, Mrs Angela Marie Doyle, Mrs Catherine Roots, Rev Sally Ann Ratcliffe, Mrs Jacqueline Gaitley, Rev Susan Levitt, Mrs Shirley Crook, Rev Nicola Vidamour, Mrs Biddy Bishop, The Revd Dr David Hinchliffe BA MA, Mr David C Marsh, Miss Rebecca M

Methodist Homes
Registered: 4 Dec 2000 *Employees:* 6,007 *Volunteers:* 5,500
Tel: 01332 221805 *Website:* mha.org.uk
Activities: The advancement of health or saving of lives; accommodation, housing
Address: Methodist Homes, Epworth House, 3 Stuart Street, Derby, DE1 2EQ
Trustees: Mr Graham Smith, Mr Bala Gnanapragasam, Mr David Hall, Miss Moira Simpson, Mr Andrew Mason, Ms Hilary Cocker, Prof Malcolm Johnson, Mr Ian Ailles, Ms Vanella Jackson, Mr Andrew Cozens, Mr Norman Mann, Ms Debbie Aplin
Income: £207,089,000 [2017]; £191,468,000 [2016]; £179,826,000 [2015]; £196,500,000 [2014]; £179,697,000 [2013]

Methodist Independent Schools Trust
Registered: 8 Jul 2011 *Employees:* 2,349 *Volunteers:* 173
Tel: 020 7935 3723 *Website:* methodistschools.org.uk
Activities: General charitable purposes; education, training; religious activities
Address: Methodist Church House, 25 Marylebone Road, London, NW1 5JR
Trustees: Miss Margaret Faulkner, Revd Dr John Barrett, Rev Stephen Burgess, Mr Robert Cowie, Mrs Veronica Knight, Mrs Elaine Cleland, Mrs Lorna Cocking, Mr Keith Norman, Mrs Barbara Easton, Mr Michael Saltmarsh, Air Vice-Marshal Ret'd Steven Abbott
Income: £99,557,000 [2017]; £99,868,000 [2016]; £88,031,000 [2015]; £83,447,000 [2014]; £81,282,000 [2013]

The Methodist Relief and Development Fund
Registered: 17 Jun 1985 *Employees:* 20 *Volunteers:* 260
Tel: 020 7467 5145 *Website:* allwecan.org.uk
Activities: The prevention or relief of poverty; overseas aid, famine relief
Address: Methodist Church House, 25 Marylebone Road, London, NW1 5JR
Trustees: Caroline Blower, Louise Brooke-Smith, Andrew Dye, Richard Vautrey, Robert Mahoney, Carolyn Lawrence, Christy-Anna Briggs, Ria Delves, Claire Boxall, Diola Bijlhout, Christopher Lewis, Rev David Nixon
Income: £3,039,542 [2017]; £2,416,410 [2016]; £3,061,045 [2015]; £2,706,726 [2014]; £2,722,170 [2013]

The Metro Centre Ltd
Registered: 17 Jul 1998 *Employees:* 76 *Volunteers:* 40
Website: metrocharity.org.uk
Activities: General charitable purposes; education, training; advancement of health or saving of lives; prevention or relief of poverty; arts, culture, heritage, science; economic, community development, employment; human rights, religious or racial harmony, equality or diversity; recreation; other charitable purposes
Address: First Floor, Equitable House, 7 General Gordon Square, London, SE18 6FH
Trustees: Ms Alison White, Mr Richard Walton, Mr Adam Reeves, Ms Caroline Pillay, Mr David Burgess, Ms Dawn Brown, Mr Shaun Waller, Ms Gwen Bryan
Income: £3,207,754 [2017]; £3,242,372 [2016]; £2,519,496 [2015]; £2,437,247 [2014]; £2,179,469 [2013]

434

The Metropolitan Masonic Charity
Registered: 21 Jun 2000
Tel: 020 7539 2930
Activities: General charitable purposes
Address: 60 Great Queen Street, London, WC2B 5AZ
Trustees: Mr David James Thompson, Mr Augustus Rupert Patrick Anthony Ullstein QC, Mr Peter Alexander Christopher Jennings, Mr Quentin Charles Triscott Humberstone, Mr Marios Phillip Stylianides, Thomas Christoforos Toumazis MBE
Income: £1,154,792 [2017]; £1,793,475 [2016]; £753,681 [2015]; £562,049 [2014]; £855,243 [2013]

Metropolitan Police Benevolent Fund
Registered: 7 Aug 2008
Tel: 020 7161 1481   *Website:* met.police.uk
Activities: The advancement of health or saving of lives; prevention or relief of poverty
Address: Metropolitan Police Services, Charities Section, 9th Floor, Empress State Building, Lillie Road, London, SW6 1TR
Trustees: Mr Mark Nurthen, Mr Paul Deller, Mr Graham McNulty, Superintendent Simon Ovens, Mr Clive Knight, Mr Peter Stevenson
Income: £2,870,116 [2016]; £1,903,058 [2015]; £1,981,162 [2014]; £1,927,541 [2013]; £2,027,843 [2012]

Metropolitan Tabernacle
Registered: 13 Mar 2013   *Employees:* 17   *Volunteers:* 400
Tel: 020 7840 1963   *Website:* metropolitantabernacle.org
Activities: General charitable purposes; education, training; religious activities
Address: Metropolitan Tabernacle, Elephant & Castle, London, SE1 6SD
Trustees: Mr Christopher Charles Cooper, Mr David Linkens, Dr Peter Masters, Mr Andrew Charles William Owen, Mr Mark Augustus Whyte, Mr Olutunde Olajide Odumala, Mr Philip Wainwright, Mr Ibrahim Ag Mohamed, Mr Christopher Malcolm Laws, Dr Duncan Lloyd Andrew Wyncoll, Mr Ajibola Oyetola Oyenubi, Mr David Anthony Edgar Smith, Mr Michael Anthony Hunt, Mr Paul Charles Tunstell, Mr Robin James Dean Compston
Income: £1,430,244 [2016]; £1,528,650 [2015]; £1,317,321 [2014]; £1,503,764 [2013]

The Metropolitan and City Police Orphans Fund
Registered: 1 May 1964   *Employees:* 2
Tel: 020 8788 5140   *Website:* met-cityorphans.org.uk
Activities: General charitable purposes; education, training; disability; prevention or relief of poverty
Address: Metropolitan & City of London, Police Orphans Fun, 30 Hazlewell Road, London, SW15 6LH
Trustees: Mr Glen Smyth, Constable Andrea O'Donnell, Constable Samantha Richardson, Constable Debbie Davies, Mr David Lawes, Mr Mark Nurthen, Chief Superintendent Simon Ovens, Commander Neil Basu, Commander Richard John Martin, Mr Clive Knight, Mr Graham Gilbert
Income: £1,092,383 [2016]; £1,084,845 [2015]; £1,007,806 [2014]; £938,995 [2013]; £945,054 [2012]

Joyce Meyer Ministries
Registered: 17 Jul 2000   *Employees:* 14
Tel: 01753 834881   *Website:* joycemeyer.org
Activities: General charitable purposes; advancement of health or saving of lives; prevention or relief of poverty; overseas aid, famine relief; religious activities
Address: Joyce Meyer Ministries, 4-5 Windsor Business Centre, Vansittart Estate, Windsor, Berks, SL4 1SP
Trustees: Mrs Delanie Trusty, Mr Timothy Simon Jupp, Mr David Josiah Meyer, Mrs Rosemary Sambrook, Mr Kevin Sambrook
Income: £2,170,144 [2016]; £2,325,768 [2015]; £2,064,676 [2014]; £2,130,460 [2013]

Mezzanine 2 Limited
Registered: 15 Jul 2004   *Employees:* 6
Tel: 020 3096 7659   *Website:* can-online.org.uk
Activities: General charitable purposes; accommodation, housing; economic, community development, employment
Address: 105 Marguerite Drive, Leigh on Sea, Essex, SS9 1NN
Trustees: Mrs Helen Taylor-Thompson, Alistair Fraser, Mr Robin Pauley, Mr Clive Robert Dove-Dixon
Income: £1,235,844 [2017]; £1,250,754 [2016]; £1,329,945 [2015]; £1,302,531 [2014]; £1,290,471 [2013]

The Michael Bishop Foundation
Registered: 9 Oct 1987
Tel: 01530 564388
Activities: General charitable purposes; education, training; advancement of health or saving of lives; disability; arts, culture, heritage, science; amateur sport; human rights, religious or racial harmony, equality or diversity; other charitable purposes
Address: Staunton House, Ashby-de-La-Zouche, Leics, LE65 1RW
Trustees: Mr Grahame Nicholas Elliott CBE, Mr Martin Peter Ritchie, Baron Glendonbrook of Bowdon, Mr Timothy John Bye
Income: £3,174,658 [2017]; £3,159,927 [2016]; £4,092,796 [2015]; £741,792 [2014]; £547,306 [2013]

Micklefield School (Reigate) Limited
Registered: 2 Nov 1962   *Employees:* 46   *Volunteers:* 2
Tel: 01737 224212   *Website:* micklefieldschool.co.uk
Activities: Education, training
Address: Micklefield School, 10-12 Somers Road, Reigate, Surrey, RH2 9DU
Trustees: Mr Alexander Beaufort De Marigny Hunter, Mrs Rosalind Julia Rokison, Mrs Caroline Cartmell, Mrs Helen Skrine, Mr James Emmerton, Dr Taraneh Khalafpour, Dr Barry Cecil Hutt, Mrs Maggie Stansfield, Mrs Fiona Gent, Mr Roger Alan Richardson, Mr Justin Willoughby Geoffrey Makin, Mrs Johanna Maria Hamilton
Income: £2,804,656 [2017]; £2,777,076 [2016]; £2,693,014 [2015]; £2,615,720 [2014]; £2,366,645 [2013]

Microbiology Society
Registered: 18 May 1972   *Employees:* 37
Tel: 020 7685 2540   *Website:* microbiologysociety.org
Activities: Education, training; advancement of health or saving of lives; overseas aid, famine relief; arts, culture, heritage, science; environment, conservation, heritage
Address: Microbiology Society, Charles Darwin House, 12 Roger Street, London, WC1N 2JU
Trustees: Professor George Salmond, Professor Maggie Smith, Professor Neil Gow, Professor Stephen Oliver, Dr David Bhella, Professor Ian Roberts, Dr Tadhg O Croinin, Professor Mick Tuite, Professor Paul Kellam, Dr Pat Goodwin, Professor Nicola Stonehouse, Dr Helen Brown, Professor Jodi Lindsay, Dr John Morrissey, Professor Tracy Palmer
Income: £4,202,000 [2016]; £4,086,000 [2015]; £4,059,000 [2014]; £4,039,000 [2013]; £4,088,000 [2012]

Microloan Foundation
Registered: 11 Jun 2004 *Employees:* 161 *Volunteers:* 10
Tel: 020 8827 1688 *Website:* microloanfoundation.org.uk
Activities: The prevention or relief of poverty
Address: 1 Canal Court, 152-154 High Street, Brentford, London,
TW8 8JA
Trustees: Mr Robert Ian Jenkins, Miss Caroline Norma Beck,
Mr Daniel Christopher Witter, Mrs Lesley-Anne Alexander, Mr Alan
Penson, Ms Dina Shiloh, Mrs Sally Burton-Graham
Income: £2,005,564 [2016]; £2,208,324 [2015]; £2,031,805 [2014];
£1,831,351 [2013]; £1,433,761 [2012]

Mid Essex Hospitals NHS Trust Charitable Fund
Registered: 9 Aug 1995
Tel: 01245 514559 *Website:* meht.nhs.uk
Activities: The advancement of health or saving of lives
Address: Broomfiled Hospital, Chelmsford, Essex, CM1 7ET
Trustees: The Board of Directors of Mid Essex Hospitals N H S
Trust
Income: £1,375,000 [2017]; £1,106,000 [2016]; £480,000 [2015];
£341,000 [2014]; £589,000 [2013]

**Mid Warwickshire Society for Mentally Handicapped Children
and Adults**
Registered: 8 Sep 1994 *Employees:* 78 *Volunteers:* 1
Tel: 01788 890565 *Website:* wayaheaduk.org
Activities: Disability; accommodation, housing
Address: The Parlour, Manor Farm Barns, Brooks Close,
Willoughby, Rugby, Warwicks, CV23 8BY
Trustees: Mrs Gillian Williams, Mrs Karen Ralph, Mrs Sheila
Cunningham, Mrs Amelia Tankard, Mr Michael Porter, Mr Alan
Rhead, Mr Michael Powell-Brett
Income: £1,741,912 [2017]; £1,721,348 [2016]; £1,668,120 [2015];
£1,625,656 [2014]; £1,446,090 [2013]

Mid and North Essex Mind
Registered: 10 Sep 1997 *Employees:* 43 *Volunteers:* 20
Tel: 01206 764600 *Website:* mnessexmind.org
Activities: General charitable purposes; advancement of health or
saving of lives; disability
Address: Colchester Mind, 272a Mersea Road, Colchester, Essex,
CO2 8QZ
Trustees: Peter Cheng, Miss Louisa Brewster, Miss Lucy Taylor,
Mr Scott Barlow, Mr Peter Pushman, John Wood, Mrs Mary
Edwards, Mr Dominic Tyler-Lovett, Mrs Stephanie Shilton
Income: £1,365,355 [2017]; £1,423,313 [2016]; £1,155,675 [2015];
£1,543,269 [2014]; £1,701,371 [2013]

Mid-Hants Railway Preservation Society Limited
Registered: 25 May 1982 *Employees:* 35 *Volunteers:* 450
Website: watercressline.co.uk
Activities: Education, training; arts, culture, heritage, science;
environment, conservation, heritage; economic, community
development, employment; recreation
Address: Mid-Hants Railway Preservation Society, Alresford
Station, Station Road, Alresford, Hants, SO24 9JG
Trustees: Mrs Stephanie Claire Crowther, Mr Robert Latham,
Mr David Ford, Mr Liam Kenchenten, Dr John Trigg, Mr Derek
Robert Simmonds, Sue Clements, Mr Michael Charles Neep
Income: £3,170,238 [2017]; £3,194,509 [2016]; £3,191,246 [2015];
£2,979,520 [2014]; £2,924,449 [2013]

Middlesbrough Diocesan Trust
Registered: 21 Apr 1964 *Employees:* 24 *Volunteers:* 2,000
Tel: 01642 850505 *Website:* middlesbrough-diocese.org.uk
Activities: Education, training; religious activities; human rights,
religious or racial harmony, equality or diversity
Address: Diocese of Middlesbrough, 50a The Avenue,
Middlesbrough, Cleveland, TS5 6QT
Trustees: Diocese of Middlesbrough Trustee
Income: £6,158,002 [2016]; £6,464,385 [2015]; £5,562,778 [2014];
£6,507,025 [2013]; £7,710,799 [2012]

Middlesbrough Environment City Trust Limited
Registered: 19 Jun 1998 *Employees:* 35 *Volunteers:* 50
Tel: 01642 579820 *Website:* menvcity.org.uk
Activities: Education, training; advancement of health or saving of
lives; prevention or relief of poverty; environment, conservation,
heritage; economic, community development, employment
Address: Middlesbrough Environment City, Sandy Flatts Lane,
Acklam, Middlesbrough, Cleveland, TS5 7YN
Trustees: Mr Joe McMonagle, Mrs Valerie Cunningham, Mr Russell
Mills, Mr Martin Harvey, Mr Brian Glover, Mr Keith Lewis,
Mrs Samantha Jane Granger, Mrs Lynne Hammond, Dr Azrini
Wahidin, Mr Jeremy Garside, Cllr Julia Rostron, Cllr Nicky Walker,
Cllr Tracy Harvey, Mrs Janet Stevenson
Income: £1,133,051 [2017]; £1,117,003 [2016]; £1,136,214 [2015];
£1,279,011 [2014]; £916,663 [2013]

Middlesbrough Football Club Foundation
Registered: 25 Nov 1996 *Employees:* 56 *Volunteers:* 20
Tel: 01642 236844 *Website:* mfcfoundation.co.uk
Activities: Education, training; advancement of health or saving of
lives; disability; amateur sport; recreation
Address: The Gibson O'Neill Company Limited, Brignell Road,
Middlesbrough, Cleveland, TS2 1PS
Trustees: Mr Robin Bloom, Mr Neil Bausor, Mr Graham John
Redman, Mr Stewart Smith, Mrs Yasmin Akhtar Khan, Mr Peter
William Rowley, Mr Alan Bage, Mr John Baker, Mr Ray Mallon,
Ms Joanne Patricia Fryett
Income: £1,873,998 [2017]; £1,305,011 [2016]; £1,142,279 [2015];
£1,213,729 [2014]; £704,666 [2013]

Middlesbrough Voluntary Development Agency
Registered: 9 Oct 2002 *Employees:* 17 *Volunteers:* 2
Tel: 01642 249300 *Website:* mvda.info
Activities: General charitable purposes; education, training;
economic, community development, employment
Address: St Marys Centre, 82-90 Corporation Road,
Middlesbrough, Cleveland, TS1 2RW
Trustees: Mr John Martin Daniels, Mr Matthew Fowler, Ms Ailsa
Mary Adamson, Mrs Amanda Buck, Mrs Michelle Rose O'Rourke,
Mrs Nicola Harkin
Income: £1,000,400 [2017]; £422,828 [2016]; £318,414 [2015];
£974,201 [2014]; £933,527 [2013]

Middlesbrough and Stockton Mind Limited
Registered: 23 Feb 2007 *Employees:* 110 *Volunteers:* 84
Tel: 01642 257020 *Website:* middlesbroughandstocktonmind.org.uk
Activities: Education, training; advancement of health or saving of lives; disability; environment, conservation, heritage; economic, community development, employment
Address: The Mind Centre, 90-92 Lothian Road, Middlesbrough, Cleveland, TS4 2QX
Trustees: Mr David King, Mrs Ruth Hicks, Mrs Marian Ramsey, Mr Stuart Graham, Mrs Angie Papprill, Ms Jennifer Morris, Mr John Harrison, Mr Charlie Nettle, Mrs Susan Cash, Mrs Angela Halloway, Mrs Joanne Ramsay
Income: £3,760,999 [2017]; £3,115,396 [2016]; £2,586,384 [2015]; £1,064,789 [2014]; £902,213 [2013]

Middlesex University Students' Union
Registered: 7 Feb 2011 *Employees:* 46 *Volunteers:* 1,000
Tel: 020 8411 6450 *Website:* mdxsu.com
Activities: Education, training; amateur sport; economic, community development, employment
Address: Middlesex University, Hatchcroft Building, The Burroughs, Hendon, London, NW4 4BF
Trustees: Philip Pilkington, Mr Matthew Visconti, Mr Ben Edwards, Miss Rahma Ali, Mr Ben Morrison, Mr Joseph Cox, Miss Raquel Alexandra Oliviera Marques, Miss Erica Da Fonseca Ramos, Miss Summer White, Mrs Lynette Elaine Phillips
Income: £1,251,526 [2017]; £1,210,790 [2016]; £1,019,945 [2015]; £990,252 [2014]; £876,526 [2013]

Midland Group Training Services Limited
Registered: 9 Dec 1970 *Employees:* 42
Tel: 024 7663 0333 *Website:* mgts.co.uk
Activities: Education, training
Address: Midland Group Training Services Ltd, Gulson Road, Coventry, Warwicks, CV1 2JG
Trustees: Mr Bernard Desmond Hawkins, Mr Dennis Anthony Butler, Mr Anthony Keith Watson, Mr Paul Hone, Mr Giles Frederick Lawton, Mr Graham Henry Reynolds, Mr Andrew Churchill, Mr Kevan Robert Kane
Income: £4,539,109 [2017]; £3,615,806 [2016]; £3,142,066 [2015]; £3,011,792 [2014]; £2,445,337 [2013]

Midland Mencap
Registered: 16 Jan 1995 *Employees:* 279 *Volunteers:* 101
Tel: 0121 442 2944 *Website:* midlandmencap.org.uk
Activities: Disability; accommodation, housing
Address: 171 Alcester Road, Moseley, Birmingham, B13 8JR
Trustees: Doctor Robert Charles Young, Mrs Valerie Penney, Mrs Jennifer Cleminson, Mrs Helen Elwell, Miss Corin McGinley, Mr Martin Friel Gallagher, Mr Kuldip Gujral, Mr Nigel Smith, Mr Andrew Westwood
Income: £7,473,785 [2017]; £6,892,094 [2016]; £6,738,222 [2015]; £5,121,353 [2014]; £5,291,591 [2013]

Midlands Air Ambulance Charity
Registered: 27 Jul 2011 *Employees:* 39 *Volunteers:* 150
Tel: 0800 840 2040 *Website:* midlandsairambulance.com
Activities: The advancement of health or saving of lives; armed forces, emergency service efficiency
Address: Midlands Air Ambulance HQ, Hawthorn House, Dudley Road, Stourbridge, W Midlands, DY9 8BQ
Trustees: Mr Robin Richmond, Mr Brendan Connor, Mr Robert Fulton, Mr Nicholas Andrew Whale, Mr Roger Pemberton, Mr Ian Graves, Mr Timothy Rice, Mr Andrew Gordon Lennox
Income: £13,028,129 [2017]; £11,487,977 [2016]; £9,076,867 [2015]; £10,797,098 [2014]; £8,290,830 [2013]

Midlands Arts Centre
Registered: 9 May 1962 *Employees:* 201 *Volunteers:* 61
Tel: 0121 446 3200 *Website:* macbirmingham.co.uk
Activities: Education, training; arts, culture, heritage, science
Address: Midlands Arts Centre, Cannon Hill Park, Birmingham, B12 9QH
Trustees: Mary Martin, Emrys Jones, Mike Williams, Linda Saunders, Sue Scholes, Ms Stephanie Dale, Sharon Lea, Mr Owen Dutton, Jonnie Turpie, Greg Lowson, Councillor Martin Straker-Welds, Sara Meyer, Louise McCathie, Councillor Matt Bennett, Junaid Bhatti
Income: £4,820,708 [2017]; £4,708,705 [2016]; £4,401,690 [2015]; £4,480,697 [2014]; £4,023,104 [2013]

Midstream (West Lancs) Ltd
Registered: 20 Jun 1995 *Employees:* 45 *Volunteers:* 3
Tel: 01695 555316 *Website:* midstream.org.uk
Activities: Education, training; disability; environment, conservation, heritage; economic, community development, employment
Address: Midstream (West Lancs) Ltd, 2 Penrose Place, Skelmersdale, Lancs, WN8 9PR
Trustees: Mr Robert Johnstone, Peter Anthony Atherton, Mr John Richardson OBE
Income: £1,593,349 [2017]; £1,566,014 [2016]; £1,621,662 [2015]; £1,388,449 [2014]; £1,088,366 [2013]

Mifal Hachesed Vehatzedokoh
Registered: 13 Dec 2010
Tel: 020 8211 0327
Activities: Education, training; prevention or relief of poverty; religious activities
Address: Flat 9, Davis Court, Saw Mill Way, London, N16 6AG
Trustees: Mr Yshaya Sprung, Mr Neil Spitzer, Mrs Michelle Sprung
Income: £4,250,490 [2016]; £5,710,299 [2015]; £5,427,523 [2014]; £3,712,794 [2013]; £2,000,179 [2012]

Mifal Tzedoko V'chesed Limited
Registered: 14 Jul 2008
Tel: 020 8880 2430
Activities: Education, training; prevention or relief of poverty; religious activities
Address: 98 Lewis Gardens, London, N16 5PJ
Trustees: Mr David Ciment, Mr Avraham Rosen, Mr Aron Steinmetz
Income: £3,564,869 [2016]; £908,025 [2015]; £745,159 [2014]; £350,712 [2013]

The Mighty Creatives
Registered: 3 Apr 2009 *Employees:* 20
Tel: 0116 261 6834 *Website:* themightycreatives.com
Activities: Education, training; arts, culture, heritage, science; environment, conservation, heritage; economic, community development, employment; human rights, religious or racial harmony, equality or diversity
Address: LCB Depot, 31 Rutland Street, Leicester, LE1 1RE
Trustees: Mr Anthony John Butler, Mr Hassnain Ali Safdar, Ms Ina Nikonova-Lavda, Ms Kim Johnson, Ms Alison Halls Taylor, Ms Felicity Woolf, Miss Madeleine Grace Handy Smart, Ms Rachel Amery, Mr Edward Boott
Income: £1,314,596 [2017]; £1,356,127 [2016]; £1,438,498 [2015]; £1,475,036 [2014]; £1,416,612 [2013]

The Migraine Trust
Registered: 28 Jun 2000 *Employees:* 7 *Volunteers:* 8
Website: migrainetrust.org
Activities: Education, training; advancement of health or saving of lives
Address: 52-53 Russell Square, London, WC1B 4HP
Trustees: Professor Peter James Goadsby, Dr Fayyaz Ahmed, Dr Brendan Davies, Sir Denis O'Connor, Dr Shazia Afridi, Mrs Jennifer Mills, Mr Ian Watmore, Mr David Cubitt, Sir Nicholas Stadlen
Income: £1,020,619 [2017]; £838,157 [2016]; £734,746 [2015]; £504,017 [2014]; £567,341 [2013]

Migrant Helpline
Registered: 27 Sep 2001 *Employees:* 157 *Volunteers:* 5
Tel: 01304 218714 *Website:* migranthelpuk.org
Activities: General charitable purposes; education, training; prevention or relief of poverty; accommodation, housing; economic, community development, employment
Address: Charlton House, Dour Street, Dover, Kent, CT16 1AT
Trustees: Mr Denis Philip King, Mrs Lucy Bracken, Ms Jan Annan, Mr Jasper Hanebuth, Mr Mark Leigh, Mr Robert Phillips, Mr Martin Bunch, Mr Neil Everett, Mr David Noble
Income: £9,074,000 [2017]; £9,395,000 [2016]; £8,751,186 [2015]; £3,066,387 [2014]; £1,729,974 [2013]

Migrants Resource Centre
Registered: 21 May 1985 *Employees:* 24 *Volunteers:* 50
Tel: 020 7354 9631 *Website:* migrantsresourcecentre.org.uk
Activities: General charitable purposes; education, training; advancement of health or saving of lives; prevention or relief of poverty; economic, community development, employment; human rights, religious or racial harmony, equality or diversity
Address: Berol House, 25 Ashely Road, London, N17 9LJ
Trustees: Mr Vebi Kosumi, Ms Isabella Maria Coelho Pereira, Miss Susanna Tamimi, Sile Reynolds, Catherine Robinson, Mr Richard Priestman, Ms Doris Afreh
Income: £1,558,141 [2017]; £501,994 [2016]; £718,580 [2015]; £627,017 [2014]; £595,717 [2013]

Mildmay Mission Hospital
Registered: 22 Jul 1985 *Employees:* 68 *Volunteers:* 50
Website: mildmay.org
Activities: Education, training; advancement of health or saving of lives; overseas aid, famine relief
Address: 19 Tabernacle Gardens, London, E2 7DZ
Trustees: Rev John Stephen Richardson, Dr Rosalind Furlong, Mr James Duncan Bennett, Miss Christabel Kunda, Emma Buchan, Mr Barry Rowan, Mrs Carol Lesley Stone, The Prebendary Ronald Swann, Dr Diana Forrest, Andrew Warrilow, Ms Anna Turco
Income: £3,490,000 [2017]; £3,117,000 [2016]; £3,203,000 [2015]; £3,773,000 [2014]; £4,314,000 [2013]

Milestones Trust
Registered: 15 May 1986 *Employees:* 1,105 *Volunteers:* 53
Tel: 0117 970 9328 *Website:* milestonestrust.org.uk
Activities: Disability; accommodation, housing
Address: Milestones Trust, Unit 10-11 Eclipse Office Park, High Street, Staple Hill, Bristol, BS16 5EL
Trustees: Mr Robin Nash, Mr Ken Guy, Dr Lydia Margaret Henderson PhD FCMI, Jane Buswell, Mrs Samantha Griggs, Mrs Margaret Shovelton, Mrs Jill Broadhead, Mr Peter Collins, David Wilson, Mr Kim Peter Heath
Income: £28,477,867 [2017]; £28,938,037 [2016]; £28,117,318 [2015]; £27,527,262 [2014]; £27,464,893 [2013]

The Mill Hill School Foundation
Registered: 8 Oct 1997 *Employees:* 342
Tel: 020 8959 8131 *Website:* millhill.org.uk
Activities: Education, training
Address: Walker House, Millers Close, London, NW7 1AQ
Trustees: Mr Elliot Lipton MBA, Mrs Mangal Patel, Mrs Pamela Helen Wilkes, Mr Andrew Welch BA MA, Mr Andrew Millet BA MBA FCA, Professor Eric Alton MA MB BS MD FRCP FHEA FERS, Ms Sophie Law, Ms Sunena Stoneham LLB Hons LPC, Dr Amanda Craig, Ms Charlotte Avery, Mr David Dickinson DipQS MRICS, Mrs Stephanie Jones Miller, Mr Rudolf Eliott Lockhart MA, Mr Robin Burdell FCMA, Mr Jamie Hornshaw
Income: £25,692,000 [2016]; £23,166,000 [2015]; £22,751,000 [2014]; £21,795,000 [2013]; £20,895,000 [2012]

The Millby Foundation
Registered: 23 Mar 2011
Website: millbyfoundation.org
Activities: General charitable purposes
Address: 10 Cresswell Place, London, SW10 9RD
Trustees: Kevin Ho, Ms Stephanie Wong, Michelle Yue, Mrs Sarah Mitchell
Income: £2,052,683 [2016]; £508,717 [2015]; £729,262 [2014]; £324,971 [2013]; £134,957 [2012]

The Millennium Awards Trust
Registered: 31 Jan 2003
Tel: 020 7566 1100 *Website:* unltd.org.uk
Activities: Education, training; prevention or relief of poverty; economic, community development, employment
Address: UN Ltd, 123-127 Whitecross Street, London, EC1Y 8JG
Trustees: The Foundation For Social Entrepreneurs
Income: £4,464,041 [2017]; £4,120,533 [2016]; £4,897,633 [2015]; £3,329,862 [2014]; £3,294,945 [2013]

Millennium Point Trust
Registered: 26 Nov 1996 *Employees:* 19
Tel: 07495 901586 *Website:* millenniumpoint.org.uk
Activities: Education, training; economic, community development, employment
Address: Level 4, Millennium Point, Curzon Street, Birmingham, B4 7XG
Trustees: Mrs Helen Elizabeth Bates, Linda Saunders, Mr Paul Calvin Tilsley, Professor Melvyn Allen Lees, Mr David Wilkin, Mr Simon Manville Topman, Mr Saqib Bhatti, Councillor Karen Teresa McCarthy
Income: £7,272,000 [2017]; £6,876,000 [2016]; £5,634,000 [2015]; £5,507,000 [2014]; £5,779,000 [2013]

The Don Miller Charitable Trust CIO
Registered: 10 Jul 2015 *Employees:* 9 *Volunteers:* 3
Tel: 020 8508 5111
Activities: General charitable purposes; education, training; recreation
Address: The Cottage, adjacent to The Gardens of Hanbury, Pynest Green Lane, Waltham Abbey, Essex, EN9 3QL
Trustees: D Miller, C Mead, J Smith
Income: £2,626,415 [2016]

Millfield
Registered: 5 Nov 1963 *Employees:* 708 *Volunteers:* 4
Tel: 01458 444596 *Website:* millfieldschool.com
Activities: Education, training
Address: Millfield, Street, Somerset, BA16 0DY
Trustees: Mr Stephen John East, Mr David Simpson Williamson, Mr John Rennie Maudslay, Mr Timothy Malcolm Taylor, Mr William John Bushell, Mr Timothy Philip Griffiths, Mr Christopher Halliwell Hirst, Mr Richard John Exley, Dr Peter Marston Warner, Mr John Darcy Lever, Mr Marc Alfred Liston Simon, Mrs Anabel Sexton, Mrs Clare Cripps, Mr Roland Dacre Rudd, Mr Richard James Roger Clark, Mr Robert Patrick Thornton, Mr Andrew Stuart Jackson, Kate Griggs
Income: £49,278,000 [2016]; £48,477,000 [2015]; £46,723,000 [2014]; £45,900,000 [2013]; £43,439,000 [2012]

Millwall Community Trust
Registered: 4 Sep 2000 *Employees:* 45 *Volunteers:* 20
Tel: 020 7740 0503 *Website:* millwallcommunity.co.uk
Activities: Education, training; advancement of health or saving of lives; disability; amateur sport; economic, community development, employment; human rights, religious or racial harmony, equality or diversity
Address: The Den, Zampa Road, London, SE16 3LN
Trustees: Peter Walsh, Sir Simon Hughes, Mr Stephen Kavanagh, Rev Owen Beament MBE, Andy Ambler, Peter Garston
Income: £1,068,528 [2017]; £983,974 [2016]; £993,654 [2015]; £741,560 [2014]; £799,474 [2013]

The Clare Milne Trust
Registered: 26 Jan 2001
Tel: 01395 270418 *Website:* claremilnetrust.com
Activities: Disability
Address: Claypitts, Ladram Road, Otterton, Budleigh Salterton, Devon, EX9 7HT
Trustees: Margaret Rogers, Mr Nigel Urwin, Mrs Christine Kirk, Mr Robert Spencer
Income: £1,671,786 [2017]; £1,454,197 [2016]; £10,499,194 [2015]; £748,692 [2014]; £915,337 [2013]

Milton Keynes Christian Centre
Registered: 21 May 2007 *Employees:* 57 *Volunteers:* 520
Tel: 01908 670655 *Website:* mkcc.org.uk
Activities: Education, training; prevention or relief of poverty; overseas aid, famine relief; religious activities
Address: Christian Centre, Strudwick Drive, Oldbrook, Milton Keynes, Bucks, MK6 2TG
Trustees: Mr Mark Sherratt, Mr Billy Ritchie, Mr Bola Odunlami, Mr Peter Takacs, Mr Phil Verity, Mrs Fola Komolafe, Mr Andrew Kiff
Income: £2,016,193 [2016]; £1,926,356 [2015]; £2,113,429 [2014]; £1,670,983 [2013]; £1,366,795 [2012]

Milton Keynes Community Foundation Limited
Registered: 2 Dec 1986 *Employees:* 19
Tel: 01908 690276 *Website:* mkcommunityfoundation.co.uk
Activities: General charitable purposes; education, training; advancement of health or saving of lives; disability; prevention or relief of poverty; accommodation, housing; arts, culture, heritage, science; amateur sport; environment, conservation, heritage; economic, community development, employment
Address: Acorn House, 381 Midsummer Boulevard, Central Milton Keynes, Bucks, MK9 3HP
Trustees: Mrs Anna Francesca Skelton, Mr Richard Brown, Mrs Carole Diane Baume, Dr Alice Mary Maynard, Mr Keith Silverthorne, Mr Lawrence Revill, Mr Ben Stoneman, Mr Shaun Lee, Ms Kurshida Mirza, Mr Peter Duncan Selvey, Mr Steven Norrish, Mrs Kate Elizabeth Chadwick, Mrs Fola Komolafe, Mr Stephen Harris, Ms Melanie Beck, Mr Stephen Norrish, Ms Jill Heaton
Income: £2,993,740 [2017]; £3,009,468 [2016]; £3,534,157 [2015]; £9,068,282 [2014]; £2,478,859 [2013]

Milton Keynes Dons Football Club Sports & Education Trust
Registered: 18 Apr 2008 *Employees:* 30 *Volunteers:* 100
Tel: 01908 622888 *Website:* mkdonsset.com
Activities: Education, training; advancement of health or saving of lives; disability; arts, culture, heritage, science; amateur sport; economic, community development, employment; recreation
Address: Stadium M K, Stadium Way West, Milton Keynes, Bucks, MK1 1ST
Trustees: Mr Ian Leslie Zant-Boer, Mr Peter John Winkelman, Mr Kevin Wilson, Mr Ric Brackenbury, Janice Flawn, Julie Mills, Mr Simon Ingram, Mr John Cove, Mr Andy Dransfield, Mr Anthony Rickens, Vijay Champaklal Thakrar, Mr Michael Sheridan
Income: £1,292,710 [2017]; £1,342,358 [2016]; £1,403,143 [2015]; £1,421,171 [2014]; £1,330,530 [2013]

Milton Keynes Parks Trust Limited
Registered: 9 Jan 1992 *Employees:* 56 *Volunteers:* 200
Tel: 01908 233600 *Website:* theparkstrust.com
Activities: Environment, conservation, heritage
Address: Milton Keynes Parks Trust Ltd, 1300 Silbury Boulevard, Campbell Park, Milton Keynes, Bucks, MK9 4AD
Trustees: Mr Norman Miles, Mr Richard Forman, Ms Zoe Raven, Mr John Eaton, Gamiel Yafai, Mr Sam Crooks, Mrs Janice Flawn, Mrs Junita Fernandez, Mr Ian Russell, Mr Andrew Lawes, Mr Peter James Geary, Mr James Macmillan, Mrs Jean Nicholas, Mr Alexander Chapman, Dr Philip Wheeler, Mr Richard Pearce, Ms Clare Stacey
Income: £11,765,000 [2017]; £10,438,000 [2016]; £9,594,000 [2015]; £9,631,000 [2014]; £8,328,736 [2013]

Milton Keynes YMCA Limited
Registered: 8 Sep 2008 *Employees:* 22 *Volunteers:* 5
Tel: 01908 295600 *Website:* mkymca.com
Activities: General charitable purposes; education, training; accommodation, housing; arts, culture, heritage, science; amateur sport; economic, community development, employment
Address: YMCA, 63 North Seventh Street, Milton Keynes, Bucks, MK9 2DP
Trustees: Mr Preston Thomas Ayres, Mr Timothy Stone, Miss Magdalena Zamojska, Rev John Robertson, Mr Charles Newman, Mr Jas Bhamber, Mrs Julia Valentine, Dr Anthony James Holden, Mrs Cheryl Montgomery, Mrs Susan Payne, Mrs Julia Upton, Dr Vasco Fernandes
Income: £1,577,263 [2017]; £1,642,700 [2016]; £1,484,634 [2015]; £1,444,651 [2014]; £1,308,291 [2013]

The Minack Theatre Trust CIO
Registered: 27 Apr 2016 *Employees:* 50
Tel: 01297 489519 *Website:* minack.com
Activities: Education, training; arts, culture, heritage, science
Address: Greenway Cottage, Ryall, Bridport, Dorset, DT6 6EN
Trustees: Charles Sinclair, Mr Michael Anthony Conboye, Mr Jeremy Mark Sinclair, Mrs Elizabeth Romana Smith, Mr Michael John Iles
Income: £2,016,229 [2017]

Minchinhampton Centre for the Elderly Limited
Registered: 27 Nov 2000 *Employees:* 155 *Volunteers:* 6
Website: horsfallhouse.co.uk
Activities: The advancement of health or saving of lives
Address: Woodvale Cottage, Box, Stroud, Glos, GL6 9HW
Trustees: Mr Simon Moreland, Mr Christopher Paul Fisher, Mr Christopher Edward James Blackstone, Mr Christopher Price
Income: £3,136,751 [2016]; £2,844,672 [2015]; £2,733,740 [2014]; £2,572,948 [2013]; £2,380,511 [2012]

The Minchinhampton Centre for the Elderly
Registered: 20 Jul 1983 *Employees:* 155 *Volunteers:* 6
Tel: 01453 731227 *Website:* horsfallhouse.co.uk
Activities: The advancement of health or saving of lives; accommodation, housing
Address: Horsfall House, Windmill Road, Minchinhampton, Stroud, Glos, GL6 9EY
Trustees: Mr Gerald Ford, Mr Christopher Roderick James Marlow, Mr Anthony Pearson, Mr Arthur White, Nigel Parry, Mr Christopher Paul Fisher
Income: £3,219,952 [2016]; £3,554,322 [2015]; £2,872,428 [2014]; £2,768,061 [2013]; £2,772,571 [2012]

Mind (The National Association for Mental Health)
Registered: 20 Dec 1962 *Employees:* 564 *Volunteers:* 2,845
Tel: 020 8215 2262 *Website:* mind.org.uk
Activities: The advancement of health or saving of lives; disability
Address: Mind N A M H, Granta House, 15-19 Broadway, London, E15 4BQ
Trustees: Mr Ryan Campbell, Mr John Binns, Mr Ian Ruddock, Mr Emrys Elias, Ms Joanne Stella Maria Theodoulou, Ms Alexandra Naomi Jensen, Mr Steve Gilbert, Mrs Sarah Rae, Mr Richard Addy, Mrs Valerie Harrison, Mr Christer Eric Stoyell, Mr Peter David Rodgers, Mrs Anna Hughes, Mr Nick Stafford
Income: £41,329,000 [2017]; £39,903,000 [2016]; £37,062,000 [2015]; £33,655,000 [2014]; £29,074,000 [2013]

Mind BLMK
Registered: 18 Mar 1998 *Employees:* 56 *Volunteers:* 147
Tel: 0300 330 0648 *Website:* mind-blmk.org.uk
Activities: Education, training; advancement of health or saving of lives; disability; economic, community development, employment
Address: Mind BLMK, The Rufus Centre, Steppingley Road, Flitwick, Bedford, MK45 1AH
Trustees: Mrs Sandra Kay Fielding, Margaret Stockham, John Banks, James Culling, Mrs Melanie Brooks, Ms Helen Mundy, Steven Horner, Mrs Caroline Lewis
Income: £1,134,518 [2017]; £1,212,167 [2016]; £1,632,200 [2015]; £1,465,721 [2014]; £1,195,286 [2013]

Mind in Bexley Limited
Registered: 21 Jun 2005 *Employees:* 45 *Volunteers:* 40
Tel: 020 8303 5816 *Website:* mindinbexley.org.uk
Activities: The advancement of health or saving of lives; disability
Address: Milton House, 240a Broadway, Bexleyheath, Kent, DA6 8AS
Trustees: Councillor Ronald Horace French, Mr Martin Robinson, Dr Sally Browning, Fungai Gonhi, Dr Irene Guerrini, Dr Fazlur Rashid, Mrs Joan Scher, Susan Frame, Shasheen Westcombe
Income: £2,300,816 [2017]; £2,467,057 [2016]; £2,244,962 [2015]; £1,910,150 [2014]; £1,410,000 [2013]

Mind in Brighton & Hove
Registered: 9 Sep 1998 *Employees:* 35 *Volunteers:* 43
Tel: 01273 666950 *Website:* mindcharity.co.uk
Activities: Education, training; advancement of health or saving of lives; disability; human rights, religious or racial harmony, equality or diversity
Address: Mind, 51 New England Street, Brighton, BN1 4GQ
Trustees: Mr Alex James Simm, Mr Tony Newton, Mr Philip Pragnell, Howard Moore, Mr Andrew John Clinton, Ann Williams, Mrs Sara Candler, Deborah Fortescue
Income: £1,267,573 [2017]; £1,388,204 [2016]; £1,235,084 [2015]; £1,210,684 [2014]; £1,141,634 [2013]

Mind in Cambridgeshire Ltd
Registered: 25 Jan 1973 *Employees:* 63 *Volunteers:* 35
Tel: 01223 311320 *Website:* cpslmind.org.uk
Activities: Education, training; advancement of health or saving of lives; disability
Address: 100 Chesterton Road, Cambridge, CB4 1ER
Trustees: Mr Ian Cunningham, Mr Stuart Jessup, Mr Kevin Vanterpool, Dr Christopher Cooper, Ms Joanna Lucas, Ms Caroline Newman, Josh Jackson
Income: £1,513,807 [2017]; £1,142,836 [2016]; £868,697 [2015]; £810,849 [2014]; £800,057 [2013]

Mind in Croydon Ltd
Registered: 9 Feb 1999 *Employees:* 37 *Volunteers:* 130
Tel: 020 8668 2210 *Website:* mindincroydon.org.uk
Activities: The advancement of health or saving of lives; disability
Address: Mind in Croydon, 26 Pampisford Road, Purley, Surrey, CR8 2NE
Trustees: Mr Luege Minchella, Mrs Jo Leck, Mr David Martin Clark, Mr Tariq Salim, Ms Susie Pinchin, Anthony John Horton, Mr John Philip Pestell, Mr Aleck Graeme Thomson, Mr Benjamin Ellis
Income: £1,620,654 [2017]; £1,514,015 [2016]; £1,458,876 [2015]; £1,433,102 [2014]; £1,425,696 [2013]

Mind in Harrow
Registered: 16 Jan 1998 *Employees:* 23 *Volunteers:* 110
Tel: 020 8426 0929 *Website:* mindinharrow.org.uk
Activities: Education, training; advancement of health or saving of lives; disability; arts, culture, heritage, science; amateur sport; economic, community development, employment
Address: 132-134 College Road, Harrow, Middlesex, HA1 1BQ
Trustees: Mr Robin Hanau, Mr Mahesh Vaid, Ms Katharine McIntosh, Mr Ashok Gudka, Mr Hamza Don De Silva, Mr Ikhlaq Hussain, Mr Bhavesh Parmar, Prof Stephen Bach, Ms Jaishree Mistry, Mr Hansraj Shah, Dr Abdullahi Fido, Ms Sandrasagary Jayacodi, Ms Sonam Patel, Katherine Saminaden
Income: £1,047,098 [2017]; £1,034,764 [2016]; £868,788 [2015]; £652,066 [2014]; £706,569 [2013]

Mind in the City, Hackney and Waltham Forest Ltd
Registered: 9 Feb 1982 *Employees:* 83 *Volunteers:* 27
Tel: 020 8525 2312 *Website:* cityandhackneymind.org.uk
Activities: Education, training; advancement of health or saving of lives; disability; economic, community development, employment
Address: 8-10 Tudor Road, London, E9 7SN
Trustees: Ms Janis Grant, Mr Daniel Casson, Ms Carrie Deacon, Mr Jeremy Cohen, Mr Luke Jackson, Mr Thomas Newby, Mr Edmund Nkrumah, Mr Ade Afilaka, Hilary Potter, Mr Anunay Jha, Ms Mary Jones, Ms Lyssa Barber, Mr Nigel McKeverne
Income: £3,815,551 [2017]; £3,843,219 [2016]; £2,396,245 [2015]; £2,188,637 [2014]; £1,912,147 [2013]

The Mines Advisory Group
Registered: 24 Oct 2000 *Employees:* 2,819
Tel: 0161 236 4311 *Website:* maginternational.org
Activities: Education, training; disability; prevention or relief of poverty; environment, conservation, heritage; economic, community development, employment
Address: Suite 3a, South Central, 11 Peter Street, Manchester, M2 5QR
Trustees: Karen Brown, Ms Kathy Peach, Dr Tapera Knox Chitiyo, Mr Matthew Sherrington, Ms Jane Marriott, Mr Anthony Paul Collier, Mr Neil Turton, Mrs Diane Elizabeth Reid, Mr John Shinnick, Mr Bertrand Taithe, Mr Dominic Kendal-Ward, Christopher Kemp
Income: £46,879,000 [2017]; £36,577,000 [2016]; £31,932,613 [2015]; £33,907,726 [2014]; £33,204,588 [2013]

Minhaj-Ul-Quran International
Registered: 24 Mar 2004 *Employees:* 28 *Volunteers:* 28
Tel: 020 8257 1786 *Website:* minhajuk.org
Activities: General charitable purposes; education, training; prevention or relief of poverty; religious activities; arts, culture, heritage, science; economic, community development, employment; human rights, religious or racial harmony, equality or diversity
Address: 292-296 Romford Road, Forest Gate, London, E7 9HD
Trustees: Mr Dawood Hussain, Mr Shahid Mursaleen, Mr Rizwan Rehman, Muzaffar Ali, Mr Osman Ghani, Mr Muhammed Afzal
Income: £1,319,626 [2016]; £1,183,482 [2015]; £1,314,955 [2014]; £1,926,731 [2013]; £1,295,971 [2012]

Minhaj-Ul-Quran Welfare Foundation
Registered: 11 Dec 2000 *Employees:* 17 *Volunteers:* 36
Tel: 0300 303 0777 *Website:* minhajwelfare.org
Activities: General charitable purposes; education, training; advancement of health or saving of lives; prevention or relief of poverty; overseas aid, famine relief; religious activities; other charitable purposes
Address: Minhaj Welfare Foundation, 298 Romford Road, London, E7 9HD
Trustees: Mr Rehan Ahmed Raza, Mr Dawood Hussain, Mr Shahid Mursaleen, Mr Muhammed Qasim Rauf, Mohammad Naveed
Income: £2,303,673 [2017]; £2,135,826 [2016]; £1,768,171 [2015]; £1,402,939 [2014]; £1,309,109 [2013]

Minority Rights Group
Registered: 11 May 1981 *Employees:* 34 *Volunteers:* 20
Tel: 020 7422 4203 *Website:* minorityrights.org
Activities: Education, training; prevention or relief of poverty; human rights, religious or racial harmony, equality or diversity
Address: 54 Commercial Street, London, E1 6LT
Trustees: Mr William Edgar Foyle Samuel, Ms Meena Varma, Ms Mahdis Keshavarz, Mr Thomas Astor, Professor Joshua Castellino, Ms Gay McDougall, Prof Francoise Hampson, Dr Albert Kwokwo Barume, Mr Joe Frans, Mr Willy Munyoki Mutunga
Income: £2,266,224 [2016]; £3,221,380 [2015]; £2,767,569 [2014]; £2,340,408 [2013]; £2,153,528 [2012]

Minstead Trust
Registered: 27 Feb 1996 *Employees:* 100 *Volunteers:* 107
Tel: 023 8081 2297 *Website:* minsteadtrust.org.uk
Activities: Education, training; disability; accommodation, housing; economic, community development, employment
Address: Minstead Lodge, London Minstead, Minstead, Lyndhurst, Hants, SO43 7FT
Trustees: Mr R G Woolgar, Mrs Amanda Dixon, Mr Graham Keith Waters, Mr Zahid Nawaz, Josephine Grunwell, Robert Stirling, Professor David Ashley Clutterbuck, Mr Alistair James Duncan, Mrs Elizabeth Selby, Olivia McDonald
Income: £2,301,341 [2017]; £1,789,868 [2016]; £1,874,376 [2015]; £1,719,051 [2014]; £1,507,408 [2013]

The Minster Centre
Registered: 11 Nov 1994 *Employees:* 39 *Volunteers:* 88
Tel: 020 7644 6240 *Website:* minstercentre.co.uk
Activities: Education, training; other charitable purposes
Address: The Minster Centre, 20 Lonsdale Road, London, NW6 6RD
Trustees: Mr Christopher Brooks, Ms Norma Clayton, Ms Susanna Wright, Mr David Collins, Mr Nick Carley, Dr Tamar Posner, Mr Sean Titley, Mr Malcolm Couldridge, Ms Lynn Hanford-Day
Income: £1,203,221 [2016]; £1,000,796 [2015]; £995,797 [2014]; £1,197,403 [2013]; £1,207,777 [2012]

Mirus - Wales
Registered: 11 Feb 1986 *Employees:* 674 *Volunteers:* 11
Tel: 029 2023 6216 *Website:* mirus-wales.org.uk
Activities: General charitable purposes; education, training; advancement of health or saving of lives; disability; accommodation, housing
Address: Mirus-Wales, Unit 5 Cleeve House, Lambourne Crescent, Llanishen, Cardiff, CF14 5GP
Trustees: Mrs Pauline Young MBE, Mr Geraint James, Mr Michael Jorgensen, Mrs Deborah Bainbridge, Mr Ellis Williams, Mr Arthur Exton, Mr Matthew Exton, Mrs Clare Birt, Mr David Callow, Mr Bernard Gibson
Income: £14,444,514 [2017]; £14,980,399 [2016]; £16,072,588 [2015]; £15,150,706 [2014]; £15,541,772 [2013]

Mirza Sharif Ahmad Foundation
Registered: 12 Jul 2006 *Employees:* 4
Tel: 020 8544 7628 *Website:* msaf.org.uk
Activities: General charitable purposes; education, training; advancement of health or saving of lives; disability; prevention or relief of poverty; overseas aid, famine relief; accommodation, housing; religious activities; amateur sport; economic, community development, employment
Address: 22 Deer Park Road, London, SW19 3TL
Trustees: Mr Mirza Mahmood Ahmad, Mr Shajar Ahmad Farooqi, Mr Fateh Ahmad Khan Dahri, Dr Chaudhry Nasir Ahmad, Mr Zaheer Ahmed Choudhry
Income: £1,131,000 [2016]; £1,592,000 [2015]; £718,000 [2014]; £945,000 [2013]; £925,000 [2012]

Missing People Limited
Registered: 30 Apr 1993 *Employees:* 87 *Volunteers:* 166
Tel: 020 8392 4504 *Website:* missingpeople.org.uk
Activities: General charitable purposes; other charitable purposes
Address: Roebuck House, 284 Upper Richmond Road West, London, SW14 7JE
Trustees: Mr Caryl Edward Agard, Ms Jane Harwood, Mr Justin McLaren, Mr Craig Ling, Mr Paul Victor Boughton, Mrs Kate Adams, Ms Sarah Godwin, Ms Rachel Louise Eyre, Mr Samuel Kenneth Waterfall
Income: £3,097,979 [2017]; £2,814,961 [2016]; £2,409,405 [2015]; £2,225,157 [2014]; £2,510,911 [2013]

Missio
Registered: 9 Jul 1996 *Employees:* 20 *Volunteers:* 7,000
Tel: 020 7821 9755 *Website:* missio.org.uk
Activities: Education, training; advancement of health or saving of lives; disability; religious activities; economic, community development, employment; human rights, religious or racial harmony, equality or diversity; other charitable purposes
Address: Missio, 23 Eccleston Square, London, SW1V 1NU
Trustees: Right Reverend Declan Ronan Lang, Mr Eammon Doran, Mr Andrew Clarke, Ms Mary Reynolds, Mr Neil Twist, Mr Michael Kelly, Ms Caroline Mayhew
Income: £5,714,629 [2017]; £4,768,684 [2016]; £5,534,222 [2015]; £4,747,793 [2014]; £4,772,690 [2013]

Mission Aviation Fellowship International
Registered: 24 Sep 1996 *Employees:* 524
Tel: 01233 895524 *Website:* mafint.org
Activities: The prevention or relief of poverty; overseas aid, famine relief; religious activities; economic, community development, employment
Address: Operations Centre, Henwood, Ashford, Kent, TN24 8DH
Trustees: Ann Saunders, Mr A Ralph Gunn, Mr Leighton Pittendrigh-Smith, Mr William Watson, Mr John Barrington Quin, Peter Curtis, Jan Ivar Andresen, Mr Ndabaethethwa Mazabani
Income: £27,141,743 [2016]; £25,709,000 [2015]; £27,310,000 [2014]; £28,351,000 [2013]; £27,940,000 [2012]

Mission Aviation Fellowship UK
Registered: 25 Sep 1997 *Employees:* 88 *Volunteers:* 622
Tel: 01303 850950 *Website:* maf-uk.org
Activities: Education, training; advancement of health or saving of lives; prevention or relief of poverty; overseas aid, famine relief; religious activities; economic, community development, employment; human rights, religious or racial harmony, equality or diversity
Address: Mission Aviation Fellowship, Castle House, Castle Hill Avenue, Folkestone, Kent, CT20 2TQ
Trustees: Diana White, Mr Richard Jones, Mr David West, Max Gove, Steve Osei-Mensah, Mr Matthew Burton, Gareth Mitchell, Mr Ian Bromilow, Mrs Maeve Marnell, Mr Stephen Bentley CBE
Income: £13,314,000 [2017]; £13,002,000 [2016]; £13,638,000 [2015]; £12,201,000 [2014]; £12,050,000 [2013]

Mission Care
Registered: 27 Jun 1982 *Employees:* 305 *Volunteers:* 52
Tel: 0303 123 3201 *Website:* missioncare.org.uk
Activities: The advancement of health or saving of lives; disability; prevention or relief of poverty; overseas aid, famine relief; accommodation, housing; religious activities
Address: Mission Care, The Living Building, 3 Sherman Road, Bromley, Kent, BR1 3JH
Trustees: Mission Care Management Limited
Income: £10,969,489 [2017]; £11,085,962 [2016]; £10,110,215 [2015]; £10,393,786 [2014]; £10,167,392 [2013]

Mission Direct Limited
Registered: 26 Jan 2005 *Employees:* 7 *Volunteers:* 417
Tel: 01582 720056 *Website:* missiondirect.org
Activities: Education, training; prevention or relief of poverty; overseas aid, famine relief; accommodation, housing; religious activities; economic, community development, employment
Address: Mission Direct, 27 Bury Mead Road, Hitchin, Herts, SG5 1RT
Trustees: Tim Martindale, Dr Felicity Cooper, Mr Mark Vickers, Mr Peter Wright, Mr Paul Holbrook, Mr Peter Ian Richardson
Income: £1,645,427 [2017]; £1,690,698 [2016]; £1,686,348 [2015]; £1,731,841 [2014]; £1,853,809 [2013]

Mission Rabies Limited
Registered: 18 Jun 2015 *Employees:* 8
Tel: 01725 551123 *Website:* missionrabies.com
Activities: General charitable purposes; education, training; advancement of health or saving of lives; overseas aid, famine relief; animals
Address: 4 Castle Street, Cranborne, Wimborne, Dorset, BH21 5PZ
Trustees: Philip G Daubeny, Mr Ian Battersby BVSc DSAM DipECVIM CA MRCVS, Dr Rachel Foster MB ChB, Mrs Clarissa Baldwin OBE, Professor Michael Day BSc BVMS(Hons) PhD DSC DiplECVP FASM FRCPath FRCVS
Income: £1,155,546 [2016]; £757,645 [2015]

The Mission To Seafarers

Registered: 12 Apr 2008 *Employees:* 79 *Volunteers:* 440
Tel: 020 7246 2911 *Website:* missiontoseafarers.org
Activities: Religious activities; human rights, religious or racial harmony, equality or diversity; other charitable purposes
Address: The Missions To Seafarers, St Michael Paternoster Royal, College Hill, London, EC4R 2RL
Trustees: The Venerable Andrew Tremlett, The Revd Canon Christopher Mark Burke, David Moorhouse CBE, Capt Neale Rodrigues, Mrs Rosemary Ann Alexander, Miss Claire Elizabeth Sneddon, Mr Robert Thomas Ferris, Mr Thomas Boardley, Mr Stephen Paul Lyon, The Rt Revd Richard Frith, Mr Samuel Compton Swire, Mr David John Cockroft, Mr William MacLachlan, Mr Andrew Victor Winbow, Mr Mark Edwin Patterson
Income: £4,458,000 [2016]; £4,441,000 [2015]; £4,601,000 [2014]; £5,087,000 [2013]; £4,750,000 [2012]

Mission Without Borders

Registered: 26 Jan 1976 *Employees:* 4 *Volunteers:* 20
Tel: 020 7940 1370 *Website:* mwbuk.org
Activities: General charitable purposes; education, training; prevention or relief of poverty; overseas aid, famine relief; religious activities; economic, community development, employment
Address: Mission Without Borders, 175 Tower Bridge Road, London, SE1 2AG
Trustees: Mr Rudi Luthi, Rev Harry John Graham, Elizabeth Waldy, Adam Houghton, Mr Harald Hem
Income: £2,269,205 [2016]; £2,199,636 [2015]; £3,407,108 [2014]; £4,303,012 [2013]

Missionaries of Charity of Mother Teresa of Calcutta Trust

Registered: 3 Feb 1999 *Volunteers:* 112
Activities: General charitable purposes; education, training; advancement of health or saving of lives; disability; prevention or relief of poverty; overseas aid, famine relief; accommodation, housing; religious activities
Address: Missionaries of Charity, 177 Bravington Road, London, W9 3AR
Trustees: Sister M Prema MC, Sr M-P Chantal MC, Sr M Imelda MC, Sr M Anna MC, Sr M Piotra MC
Income: £1,826,386 [2016]; £2,009,994 [2015]; £1,265,626 [2014]; £1,069,889 [2013]; £1,569,403 [2012]

Mitcham Lane Baptist Church CIO

Registered: 19 May 2015 *Employees:* 4 *Volunteers:* 50
Tel: 020 8677 5376 *Website:* mlbc.org.uk
Activities: General charitable purposes; education, training; prevention or relief of poverty; overseas aid, famine relief; religious activities
Address: Mitcham Lane Baptist Church, 230 Mitcham Lane, London, SW16 6NT
Trustees: Mr Christopher James Buss, Mrs Valerie Jackson, Ms Dorett White, Mrs Dora Afrane, Ms Melanie Thomas, Mr Peter Taylor, Mrs Jennifer Elaine Buss, Mr David McLlroy, Rev Ian Hare
Income: £4,458,347 [2016]

The Mittal Foundation

Registered: 27 Mar 2012 *Volunteers:* 2
Tel: 020 7659 1033
Activities: General charitable purposes
Address: Mittal Investments, Floor 3, Berkeley Square House, Berkeley Square, London, W1J 6BU
Trustees: Mrs Usha Mittal, Mrs Vanisha Mittal Bhatia, Mrs Megha Mittal, Mr Aditya Mittal
Income: £11,000,000 [2016]; £11,000,000 [2015]; £1,113,031 [2014]; £4,897,452 [2013]; £506,250 [2012]

Modern Electric Tramways Limited

Registered: 28 Oct 2015 *Employees:* 33 *Volunteers:* 32
Tel: 01297 20375 *Website:* tram.co.uk
Activities: General charitable purposes; education, training; arts, culture, science, heritage; environment, conservation, heritage
Address: Seaton Tramway, Riverside Depot, Harbour Road, Seaton, Devon, EX12 2NQ
Trustees: Bruce Warnes, Roger Lane, Mark Horner, Mr David William Keay
Income: £2,020,551 [2016]

Modiano Charitable Trust

Registered: 9 Oct 1989
Tel: 020 7012 0000
Activities: General charitable purposes; education, training; advancement of health or saving of lives; disability; prevention or relief of poverty; religious activities; arts, culture, heritage, science
Address: Broad Street House, 55 Old Broad Street, London, EC2M 1RX
Trustees: Mr Laurence Modiano, Mr Michael Modiano
Income: £1,950,000 [2017]; £200,000 [2014]

Mohs Workplace Health Limited

Registered: 28 Apr 1964 *Employees:* 33
Website: mohs.co.uk
Activities: Education, training; advancement of health or saving of lives
Address: 19 Grange Park, Albrighton, Wolverhampton, W Midlands, WV7 3EN
Trustees: Mr David Lynham, Mr Laurence Lemming-Latham, Helen Hooper, Alan Boulton, Mr Martyn Jones, Mr Martyn Round, Dr Emma McCollum
Income: £2,064,080 [2017]; £1,832,834 [2016]; £1,829,875 [2015]; £1,765,205 [2014]; £1,635,701 [2013]

Moira House School Limited

Registered: 25 Jun 1963 *Employees:* 98 *Volunteers:* 8
Tel: 01323 644144 *Website:* moirahouse.co.uk
Activities: Education, training
Address: Moira House, Upper Carlisle Road, Eastbourne, E Sussex, BN20 7TE
Trustees: Dr Henry Olufemi Fajemirokun PhD, Mr P J Henshaw, Mr Andrew Pianca, Mrs Camilla Nightingale, Ms Anne-Marie Martin, Mrs Teresa Outhwaite, Ms Jenny Barnard-Langston JP, Mrs Vivien Smiley
Income: £4,019,686 [2016]; £4,529,864 [2015]; £4,762,143 [2014]; £4,653,225 [2013]; £4,646,622 [2012]

Mola Northampton

Registered: 6 Jan 2014 *Employees:* 89
Tel: 020 7410 2226 *Website:* mola.org.uk
Activities: Environment, conservation, heritage
Address: Museum of London Archaeology Service, 46 Eagle Wharf Road, London, N1 7ED
Trustees: Mr Alan Michael Hoffman, Drs Maria Helen Groen, Mr Eric Sorenson, Ms Taryn Jane Pearson Nixon
Income: £3,520,822 [2017]; £3,220,915 [2016]; £2,624,922 [2015]

The Monastery of St Francis Gorton Trust Ltd
Registered: 20 Mar 1997 *Employees:* 50 *Volunteers:* 25
Tel: 0161 223 3211 *Website:* themonastery.co.uk
Activities: Education, training; advancement of health or saving of lives; arts, culture, heritage, science; environment, conservation, heritage; economic, community development, employment; other charitable purposes
Address: The Monastery, 89 Gorton Lane, Manchester, M12 5WF
Trustees: Mr Paul Griffiths, Mr Piers Sturridge, Mr David Dickinson, Mr Jeremy Cole, Mrs Janet Louise Wallwork, Mr Tim Isherwood, Mr Ray Hanks, Mr David Oliver
Income: £3,189,990 [2017]; £2,115,392 [2016]; £1,583,030 [2015]; £1,561,278 [2014]; £1,367,786 [2013]

Monday Charitable Trust
Registered: 5 Mar 2008
Tel: 020 7783 3685
Activities: Accommodation, housing; environment, conservation, heritage; armed forces, emergency service efficiency
Address: Bircham Dyson Bell, 50 Broadway, London, SW1H 0BL
Trustees: Sarah Elizabeth Baxter, Mr Robert Reginald Lane, Mr Jonathan Brinsden, Mrs Elspeth Margaret Lorimer Lane
Income: £2,776,825 [2017]; £2,060,665 [2016]; £2,150,471 [2015]; £57,010,534 [2014]; £874,275 [2012]

Money Advice Trust
Registered: 18 Sep 2003 *Employees:* 190
Tel: 020 7653 9721 *Website:* moneyadvicetrust.org
Activities: Education, training; prevention or relief of poverty
Address: Money Advice Trust, 21 Garlick Hill, London, EC4V 2AU
Trustees: Ms Claire Whyley, Mr Merrick Willis, Mr Adam Sharples, Paul Smee, Ms Anna Bennett, Mr Simon Crine, Ms Sian Williams, Ms Gail Scott-Spicer, Mr Ade Keasey, Mr Lawrence Slade
Income: £9,015,029 [2016]; £8,792,725 [2015]; £8,952,950 [2014]; £9,476,479 [2013]; £9,683,652 [2012]

Money Advice and Community Support Service
Registered: 29 Mar 1995 *Employees:* 31 *Volunteers:* 8
Tel: 01273 664000 *Website:* moneyadviceplus.org.uk
Activities: The prevention or relief of poverty
Address: 24 Old Steine, Brighton, BN1 1EL
Trustees: Peter Hilditch, Mr Terry Mase, Mr Andrew Berry, Ms Nicola Myers, Mr Stewart Beamont, Mr Robert Phillips, Mr Djan Omer, Paul Heathorn, Mr Jonathan Hyman
Income: £1,112,923 [2017]; £954,260 [2016]; £974,879 [2015]; £957,074 [2014]; £591,861 [2013]

The Monkey Business Foundation Limited
Registered: 9 Nov 2012 *Employees:* 3
Tel: 01628 634791 *Website:* monkeybusinessfoundation.co.uk
Activities: Education, training; advancement of health or saving of lives; disability
Address: 30 Thurlby Way, Maidenhead, Berks, SL6 3YZ
Trustees: Mr Sufian Sadiq, Mr Paul Monk, Mr Robert George Dylan Willis, Mr Naynesh Desai, Mr Nigel Donald Morris, Mr Justin Matthew King
Income: £1,415,070 [2016]; £1,235,554 [2015]; £1,146,635 [2014]; £346,305 [2013]

Monkton Combe School
Registered: 29 Jul 1996 *Employees:* 354
Tel: 01225 721143 *Website:* monktoncombeschool.com
Activities: Education, training
Address: Monkton Combe School, Church Lane, Monkton Combe, Bath, BA2 7HG
Trustees: Prof Helen Langton, Melanie Townsend, Mark Womersley, Christopher Alexander, Julian Pringle, Rev Simon Barnes, David Rosser, Charles Fillingham, Rosie Coates, Jenny Perry, Ed Shaw, Stephen Young
Income: £14,308,445 [2017]; £15,479,659 [2016]; £14,037,018 [2015]; £14,198,721 [2014]; £13,138,535 [2013]

Monmouth Diocesan Board of Finance
Registered: 23 Jan 1998 *Employees:* 18 *Volunteers:* 50
Tel: 01633 267490 *Website:* churchinwales.org.uk
Activities: Religious activities
Address: Diocese of Monmouth, Diocesan Board of Finance, 64 Caerau Road, Newport, NP20 4HJ
Trustees: Miss Paulette Rosemary Brown, The Venerable Jonathan Simon Williams, Revd Canon Tim Clement, Sandy Blair, The Very Revd Lister Tonge, Mr Philip John Masters, The Venerable Ambrose Mason, Revd Canon Patricia Anne Golledge, Mrs Sarah Mulcahy, Mr Peter Lea, Rev Richard Pain BA, Mr C Wray, Rev Canon Soady, Mr Timothy Russen, Mr George Hughes, Rev Jeremy Harris, Rev Martyn Hywel Evans
Income: £3,550,024 [2016]; £4,097,821 [2015]; £3,838,154 [2014]; £3,803,617 [2013]; £3,744,479 [2012]

Maria Montessori Training Organisation
Registered: 8 Jan 1964 *Employees:* 43
Tel: 020 7435 3646 *Website:* mariamontessori.org
Activities: Education, training
Address: Montessori Maria Training Organisation, 26 Lyndhurst Gardens, London, NW3 5NW
Trustees: Mrs Hilla Patell, Mr Richard Partridge, Mrs Amanda Lake, Mrs Wendy Innes, Mr David Murphy, Mrs Nicola Forsyth, Mr Benedict Faccini, Mrs Farran Scott, Mrs Linda Webster, Dr Daleep Mukarji, Mrs Christine Laubin CJ
Income: £2,665,602 [2017]; £2,527,343 [2016]; £2,456,074 [2015]; £2,219,067 [2014]; £1,997,964 [2013]

The Monteverdi Choir and Orchestras Limited
Registered: 4 Nov 1976 *Employees:* 8
Tel: 020 7719 0120 *Website:* monteverdi.co.uk
Activities: Education, training; arts, culture, heritage, science
Address: Level 12, 20 Bank Street, Canary Wharf, London, E14 4AD
Trustees: Mr Michael Beverley, Mr Nicholas Snowman, Mr Antony Peattie, Ms Nicola Frances Elizabeth Ramsden, Ms Joanne Merry, Lady Deben, Sir John Eliot Gardiner, Mrs Virginia Fraser, Mr David Campbell Brierwood, Professor Emeritus John Fletcher Smyth, Mr David Best
Income: £3,198,571 [2016]; £2,325,292 [2015]; £1,891,875 [2014]; £1,819,815 [2013]; £1,876,816 [2012]

The Monument Trust

Registered: 15 Jul 1965 *Employees:* 15
Tel: 020 7410 0330
Activities: General charitable purposes; advancement of health or saving of lives; arts, culture, heritage, science; environment, conservation, heritage; economic, community development, employment
Address: The Peak, 5 Wilton Road, London, SW1V 1AP
Trustees: Ms Linda Heathcoat-Amory, Mr Charles Henry Cator, Mr Stewart Grimshaw, Mr Dominic Flynn
Income: £3,144,000 [2017]; £3,210,000 [2016]; £4,507,460 [2015]; £4,440,372 [2014]; £5,336,000 [2013]

Gordon Moody Association

Registered: 30 Jun 2008 *Employees:* 20 *Volunteers:* 4
Tel: 01384 241292 *Website:* gordonmoody.org.uk
Activities: Education, training; advancement of health or saving of lives; prevention or relief of poverty; accommodation, housing; other charitable purposes
Address: 43-47 Maughan Street, Dudley, W Midlands, DY1 2BA
Trustees: Ms Rekha Wadhwani, Ms Janine Elizabeth Edwards, Mr Mark McRae Otway, Mr Edward Wyatt, Dr John McAlaney, Mr Robert John Lemon, Mr John David Blake, Mrs Lindsey Jane Hayes, Mr Peter William Hannibal
Income: £1,116,044 [2017]; £1,069,409 [2016]; £909,308 [2015]; £855,267 [2014]; £834,810 [2013]

Mooji Foundation Ltd

Registered: 27 Sep 2011 *Employees:* 7 *Volunteers:* 256
Tel: 020 8678 6364 *Website:* moojifoundation.org
Activities: Religious activities
Address: 447 Staines Road West, Ashford, Surrey, TW15 2AB
Trustees: Martha Callejas, Ms Amrit Kaur, Ms Rhonda Lee Johnson, Ms Roma Paula Mascarenhas
Income: £1,879,722 [2016]; £1,496,053 [2015]; £890,122 [2014]; £635,129 [2013]; £697,373 [2012]

Moon Hall Schools Educational Trust

Registered: 30 May 1990 *Employees:* 66 *Volunteers:* 30
Tel: 01306 611939 *Website:* moonhallcollege.co.uk
Activities: Education, training; disability
Address: 10 Catlin Gardens, Godstone, Surrey, RH9 8NT
Trustees: Mr David Sherman Baker, Michael Fanya, Bruce Dean, Ms Amber Wilson, Mrs Joanna Clare Roche, Mr Neil Walker, Dr Barry Noel Edwards
Income: £3,104,826 [2016]; £2,871,448 [2015]; £2,662,168 [2014]; £2,365,866 [2013]; £2,510,157 [2012]

Moondance Foundation

Registered: 29 Nov 2010
Activities: General charitable purposes; environment, conservation, heritage; other charitable purposes
Address: 3 Assembly Square, Britannia Quay, Cardiff Bay, CF10 4AX
Trustees: Ms Louisa Scadden, Mrs Diane Briere De L'isle-Engelhardt, Mr Adrian Engelhardt, Ms Tara Briere De L'isle Engelhardt, Mr Henry Allan Engelhardt, Mr Damien Engelhardt, Ms Shanna Briere De L'isle Engelhardt
Income: £34,031,548 [2016]; £29,888,497 [2015]; £28,137,234 [2014]; £37,421,540 [2013]; £20,775,277 [2012]

Moor House School & College

Registered: 5 Nov 1968 *Employees:* 136
Website: moorhouseschool.co.uk
Activities: Education, training
Address: Moor House School, Mill Lane, Oxted, Surrey, RH8 9AQ
Trustees: Veronica Connery, Mr John Stanley Stevens, Mr Donald Hedley Payne, Mr Stuart James Dennison, Mrs Susan Jones, Ms Lisa Annette Harlow, Mr Andrew Dick, Mr Roger McCorriston, Mr David Francis Badman, Mr David J Taylor, Mrs Christine Combes
Income: £9,129,385 [2016]; £5,343,031 [2015]; £4,526,925 [2014]; £4,198,256 [2013]; £3,467,658 [2012]

Moor Park Charitable Trust Limited

Registered: 9 Sep 1981 *Employees:* 96
Tel: 01584 872342 *Website:* moorpark.org.uk
Activities: Education, training
Address: Moor Park Charitable Trust Ltd, Richards Castle, Ludlow, Salop, SY8 4DZ
Trustees: Mrs Karen Mary Brade, Mrs Emma Louise Taylor, Mr Michael John Tonks, Mr Paul Standen Avery, Mr Michael Verdin, Reverend Simon McGurk, Mr Julian Rogers-Coltman, Ms Andrea Marianne Jane Minton Beddoes, Mr Peter Gosling, Mrs Anna Mary Spreckley, Mr James David Davenport, Mrs Camilla Jane Bengough
Income: £3,405,786 [2017]; £3,229,457 [2016]; £3,304,261 [2015]; £3,210,360 [2014]; £3,421,886 [2013]

The Henry Moore Foundation

Registered: 15 Jun 1976 *Employees:* 58 *Volunteers:* 60
Tel: 01279 843333 *Website:* henry-moore.org
Activities: Education, training; arts, culture, heritage, science
Address: Henry Moore Foundation, Dane Tree House, Perry Green, Much Hadham, Herts, SG10 6EE
Trustees: Antony Griffiths, Nigel Carrington, Celia Clear, Anne Wagner, Mrs Pamela Raynor, Henry Channon, William Edgerley, Peter Wienand, Charles Asprey, Martin Barden
Income: £3,606,212 [2017]; £6,197,219 [2016]; £2,427,435 [2015]; £6,349,092 [2014]; £1,990,954 [2013]

Moorfields Eye Charity

Registered: 3 Mar 2011 *Employees:* 18
Tel: 020 7566 2565 *Website:* moorfieldseyecharity.org.uk
Activities: The advancement of health or saving of lives
Address: Kemp House, 152-160 City Road, London, EC1V 2NX
Trustees: Sir Thomas Boyd-Carpenter KBE, Dr Virginia Spence-Jones, Mr Andrew Ballheimer, Prof Ian Grierson, Mr Colin MacLean, Mr Mervyn Walker, Mr David Probert, Mr Robert John Jones, Sir Eric Jackson Thomas, Mr Declan Flanagan, Mr Anthony Briam, Dr Lee-Ann Coleman, Mr Noland Carter, Mrs Vicky Hastings, Ms Johanna Moss, Mr Michael Donald McCartney Izza
Income: £6,919,000 [2017]; £5,837,000 [2016]; £4,066,000 [2015]; £2,545,000 [2014]; £3,217,000 [2013]

Moorlands College

Registered: 13 May 2002 *Employees:* 34 *Volunteers:* 3
Tel: 01425 674500 *Website:* moorlands.ac.uk
Activities: Education, training; religious activities
Address: Moorlands College, Sopley, Christchurch, Dorset, BH23 7AT
Trustees: Mr Blair Crawford, Mr John Fowler, Mr John Hurley, Mr Steven May-Miller, Mrs Ruth Elizabeth Flanagan, Mr Keith Lawson Brown, Mr Donald Charles McQueen, Mrs Janice Tuck, Dr Jonathan James Loose, Mr Tim Goulding
Income: £2,052,753 [2017]; £2,224,862 [2016]; £3,082,618 [2015]; £1,981,644 [2014]; £2,203,390 [2013]

Moorlands School Ltd
Registered: 7 Jul 1965 Employees: 29 Volunteers: 4
Tel: 020 7935 3723 Website: moorlands-school.co.uk
Activities: Education, training
Address: Methodist Church House, 25 Marylebone Road, London, NW1 5JR
Trustees: Rev Peter Whittaker, Mrs Valerie Snowden, Mr Richard Hemsley, Mr Ronald Drake, Mrs Gill Wilson, Mr Francis McAleer, Prof Michael Manogue, Mr Stephen Burnhill, Rev Dr Roger Walton, Mr Alan Wintersgill, Dr Georgina Haslam, Mrs Pamela Essler, Ms Palwinder Kaur, Mr Ian Small, Rev Christopher Edmonson, Mr Charles Best
Income: £1,236,955 [2016]; £1,106,760 [2015]; £1,229,401 [2014]; £1,333,513 [2013]; £1,462,090 [2012]

Morden College
Registered: 11 Nov 1986 Employees: 184
Tel: 020 8463 8330 Website: mordencollege.org.uk
Activities: Accommodation, housing; religious activities; other charitable purposes
Address: Clerk's House, Morden College, 19 St Germans Place, Blackheath, London, SE3 0PW
Trustees: Sir David Brewer CMG CVO, Sir John Stuttard MA FCA, Alderman David Wootton, Alderman Peter Estlin, Sir Michael Oliver LLD DL, Alderman William Russell, Alderman Professor Michael Mainelli
Income: £11,921,000 [2017]; £11,203,000 [2016]; £10,857,000 [2015]; £11,533,000 [2014]; £10,765,000 [2013]

More House Trust Ltd
Registered: 11 Dec 1969 Employees: 42
Tel: 01462 338234 Website: morehouse.org.uk
Activities: Education, training
Address: More House School, 22-24 Pont Street, London, SW1X 0AA
Trustees: Mr Paul Ewings BA, Mr Kevin D Lake, Mr James Fyfe BA, Mrs Sue Shale BA FCA, Mrs Susan Sturrock BMus ARCM, Mr William Ralston-Saul
Income: £3,456,983 [2017]; £3,374,863 [2016]; £2,871,592 [2015]; £3,016,621 [2014]; £2,660,472 [2013]

Moreshet Hatorah Ltd
Registered: 14 Dec 1999 Employees: 67
Tel: 020 8800 6599
Activities: General charitable purposes; education, training
Address: 122 Kyverdale Road, London, N16 6PR
Trustees: Mr Ahron Klein, Mr Moses Moskowits, Mr Jehudan Baumgarten
Income: £6,744,135 [2017]; £6,193,796 [2016]; £3,865,476 [2015]; £4,267,727 [2014]; £3,893,373 [2013]

Moreton Hall Educational Trust Limited
Registered: 8 Oct 1964 Employees: 222
Tel: 01691 773671 Website: moretonhall.com
Activities: Education, training; other charitable purposes
Address: Moreton Hall School, Weston Rhyn, Oswestry, Salop, SY11 3EW
Trustees: Mr Stewart Brian Roberts, Mrs Katie Neilson, Mrs Susan Margaret Tunstall, Mrs Laura Virginia Yule, Mr Charles Norman Pursglove, Dr Melissa MacKay Grant, Dr Jeremy John Dixey, Doctor Lynne Veronica Boon, Mr Martyn Heath, Mrs Eithne Josephine Flynn, Mr Anthony Leonard Stockdale
Income: £9,013,147 [2016]; £9,164,562 [2015]; £8,705,309 [2014]; £8,694,355 [2013]; £8,598,575 [2012]

Moreton Hall School Trust Limited
Registered: 12 Sep 1980 Employees: 43 Volunteers: 5
Tel: 01284 753532 Website: moretonhallprep.org
Activities: Education, training; religious activities; arts, culture, heritage, science; amateur sport
Address: Mount Road, Bury St Edmunds, Suffolk, IP32 7BJ
Trustees: Paul Loft, Mr Neil Ronald Smith
Income: £1,121,036 [2016]; £1,150,973 [2015]; £1,160,405 [2014]; £1,088,113 [2012]

Morgan Stanley International Foundation
Registered: 20 Dec 1994
Website: morganstanley.com
Activities: Education, training; advancement of health or saving of lives; economic, community development, employment
Address: Morgan Stanley, 20 Bank Street, London, E14 4AD
Trustees: Ms Clare Woodman, Ms Maryann McMahon, Mr Fergus O'Sullivan, Mr Oliver Stuart, Mr Simon Evenson, Mr William Chalmers, Hanns Christoph Seibold, Mr Stephen Mavin, Ms Sue Watts, Jon Bendall, Ms Mandy Defilippo
Income: £1,867,698 [2016]; £1,662,580 [2015]; £1,359,539 [2014]; £1,341,573 [2013]; £1,688,186 [2012]

The Morley Agricultural Foundation
Registered: 23 Apr 2003 Employees: 3
Website: tmaf.co.uk
Activities: Education, training
Address: The Morley Agricultural Association, Morley Business Centre, Deopham Road, Morley St Botolph, Wymondham, Norfolk, NR18 9DF
Trustees: Mr Philip Edward Richardson, Mr John Sale Wallace, Mr Nicholas John Steed, Mr Robert John Salmon, Mrs Christine Elizabeth Alexandra Hill, Mr Michael John Whatmoor Gamble
Income: £1,512,875 [2016]; £1,477,177 [2015]; £1,516,948 [2014]; £1,545,812 [2013]; £1,245,093 [2012]

Morley College Limited
Registered: 8 Jul 1993 Employees: 475 Volunteers: 65
Tel: 020 7450 1848 Website: morleycollege.ac.uk
Activities: Education, training
Address: Morley College Ltd, 61 Westminster Bridge Road, London, SE1 7HT
Trustees: Mr Nicholas Roy Durston, Dr Steven Ketteridge, Mr Mash Seriki, Mr Peter Davies, Ms Pauline Egan, Mr Andrew Gower, Mr Martin Bamford, Ms Sharon Potter, Miss Justine Brian, Dr Stuart Edwards, Ms Marilyn McMenemy, Mx Mustafa Korel, Mr Victor Olowe, Dr Fiona Stephen, Mrs Sara Robertson-Jonas, Mr Luke Howson, Ms Heather Fry, Ms Heather Smith
Income: £10,377,000 [2017]; £10,052,000 [2016]; £10,329,000 [2015]; £9,481,000 [2014]; £9,145,000 [2013]

William Morris (Camphill) Community Limited
Registered: 5 Nov 1979 Employees: 50 Volunteers: 6
Tel: 020 8332 9950 Website: wmcc.ac.uk
Activities: Education, training; disability
Address: 5 Catherine Drive, Richmond, Surrey, TW9 2BX
Trustees: Mr Stephen Parker, Mr Adrian Rosser, Mr Graham Barton, Mrs Frances Allan
Income: £1,268,697 [2016]; £2,158,259 [2015]; £2,658,121 [2014]; £2,739,078 [2013]; £2,585,254 [2012]

Morris Cerullo World Evangelism
Registered: 20 Dec 1990 *Employees:* 9 *Volunteers:* 20
Tel: 01442 232432 *Website:* mcwe.co.uk
Activities: Religious activities
Address: Morris Cerullo, Unit 10 Sovereign Park, Cleveland Way, Hemel Hempstead Industrial Estate, Hemel Hempstead, Herts, HP2 7DA
Trustees: Mr Andrew Taylor, Reverend Greg Mauro, Mr Julian Richards, Mr Andreas Yiangou, Mr Lynn Hodge, Dr Morris Cerullo (President), Mrs Theresa Cerullo (Secretary), Mr Peter Graham Tod, Mrs Verona Powell
Income: £2,017,237 [2017]; £1,669,134 [2015]; £2,078,514 [2014]; £1,751,366 [2013]; £1,855,855 [2012]

The Morrisons Foundation
Registered: 29 Jan 2015 *Employees:* 1
Tel: 0845 611 5364 *Website:* morrisonsfoundation.co.uk
Activities: General charitable purposes
Address: Hilmore House, Gain Lane, Bradford, W Yorks, BD3 7DL
Trustees: Mr Charles Martyn Jones, Mr John Layfield Holden, Ms Kathryn Tunstall, Mr David Frazer John Scott, Mr Guy Hurlstone Mason, Mr Jonathan James Burke, Mrs Sharon Mawhinney, Mr Andrew James Clappen
Income: £9,162,394 [2017]; £4,097,241 [2016]

Morthyng Limited
Registered: 20 Sep 1990 *Employees:* 42
Tel: 01709 372900 *Website:* morthyng.co.uk
Activities: Education, training; prevention or relief of poverty; economic, community development, employment
Address: Morthyng Ltd, North Grove House, South Grove, Rotherham, S Yorks, S60 2AF
Trustees: Mr Alan Corbridge, Mr Peter Rodney Clements, Mr Jeremy Neal, Mr John Irving, Mr Paul Hudson, Mrs Janet Elizabeth Wheatley, Mrs Carole Haywood
Income: £2,544,176 [2017]; £2,651,217 [2016]; £2,525,578 [2015]; £2,284,253 [2014]; £2,975,608 [2013]

The Mortimer Society
Registered: 24 Sep 1983 *Employees:* 132
Tel: 01634 244689 *Website:* mortimersociety.org.uk
Activities: Disability
Address: Birling House, 91-93 High Street, Snodland, Kent, ME6 5AN
Trustees: Mrs Jacqueline Westwood, Dr Timothy Cantor, Mr David John Oliver, Mrs Yvonne Clarke, Mrs Jennifer Grimmett, Mr James Donald Miller
Income: £3,661,528 [2017]; £3,489,032 [2016]; £3,250,719 [2015]; £3,170,395 [2014]; £3,193,819 [2013]

The Dr Mortimer and Theresa Sackler Foundation
Registered: 1 Apr 2009
Tel: 020 7930 4944
Activities: General charitable purposes; education, training; advancement of health or saving of lives; overseas aid, famine relief; arts, culture, heritage, science; environment, conservation, heritage; armed forces, emergency service efficiency
Address: 9th Floor, New Zealand House, 80 Haymarket, London, SW1Y 4TQ
Trustees: Dame Theresa Sackler, Mrs I Sackler Lefcourt, Mrs Sophia Davina Sackler Dalrymple, Dr Kathe Anne Sackler, Mr Michael Daniel Sackler, Mr C B Mitchell, Ms Marissa Sackler, Mr Mortimer David Alfons Sackler, Mrs Samantha Sophia Sackler Hunt, Mr Anthony Collins
Income: £15,099,421 [2016]; £6,536,754 [2015]; £9,342,468 [2014]; £28,278,299 [2013]; £8,433,375 [2012]

Mosaic Clubhouse
Registered: 25 Sep 1998 *Employees:* 24 *Volunteers:* 4
Tel: 020 7924 9657 *Website:* mosaic-clubhouse.org
Activities: Education, training; disability; economic, community development, employment
Address: 65 Effra Road, Brixton, London, SW2 1BZ
Trustees: Mr Peter Cardell, Ms Philippa De Lacy, Mr Patrick John Gillespie, Ms Aneta Wodyczko, Mrs Mary Robertson, Mr Jordan Jarrett-Bryan, Mr Michael Paul Barrett, Dr Charlotte Augst, Ms Amy Galea, Ms Kate Jopling, Ms Lucy Hastings
Income: £1,064,404 [2017]; £984,238 [2016]; £900,174 [2015]; £806,665 [2014]; £579,826 [2013]

Mosaic: Shaping Disability Services
Registered: 21 Mar 1963 *Employees:* 60 *Volunteers:* 89
Website: mosaic1898.co.uk
Activities: Disability
Address: 21 Argyle Street, Nottingham, NG7 3JX
Trustees: Mr Glynn Paul Finney, Mr Steve Smith, Mr Warwick Best, Mr Bhavin Vijay Gohil, Deborah Ann Southwick, Smith Mary June, Mr Nic Ellis, Karen Joy Cane, Ms Lyndsey Marie Wickes, Ms Salma Banv Kaji, Janet Easingwood, Miss Lesley Anne Taylor
Income: £1,442,285 [2017]; £1,296,020 [2016]; £1,193,599 [2015]; £1,138,971 [2014]; £1,219,047 [2013]

The Most Venerable Order of The Hospital of St John of Jerusalem (The Order of St John)
Registered: 17 Sep 1964 *Employees:* 7 *Volunteers:* 11
Tel: 020 7251 3292 *Website:* stjohninternational.org
Activities: General charitable purposes; education, training; advancement of health or saving of lives; other charitable purposes
Address: The Order of St Johns, 3 Charterhouse Mews, London, EC1M 6BB
Trustees: Right Reverend Timothy John Stevens CBE, Dr Steven Evans Chancellor of The Priory in New Zealand, Mr Patrick Burgess, Mr Paul Philip Clarke, Sir Walter Hugh Malcolm Ross GCVO OBE, Mr Nicholas Woolf, Dr Teh Peng Hooi, Dr Lionel John Jarvis, Mr John Chomicki Baril Mah QC, Rev Gerard Cecil Sharp
Income: £1,120,636 [2016]; £1,009,592 [2015]; £1,049,416 [2014]; £864,822 [2013]; £1,428,313 [2012]

The Motability Tenth Anniversary Trust
Registered: 11 Apr 1989
Tel: 020 3375 7462
Activities: Disability
Address: Farrer & Co, 65-66 Lincoln's Inn Fields, London, WC2A 3LH
Trustees: Mr C Brearley CB DL, Mr Brian Addison Carte TD, Mr David Peter Pritchard, Sir Gerald Acher CBE LVO, Lord Jeffrey Maurice Sterling of Plaistow GCVO CBE
Income: £4,995,000 [2017]; £4,955,000 [2016]; £4,810,000 [2015]; £54,376,000 [2014]; £3,369,000 [2013]

Motability
Registered: 15 Jul 1988 *Employees:* 116
Tel: 01279 635999 *Website:* motability.org.uk
Activities: Disability
Address: Warwick House, Roydon Road, Harlow, Essex, CM19 5PX
Trustees: Sir Gerald Acher CBE LVO, Lord Sterling of Plaistow GCVO CBE, Mr P Spencer CBE, Mr Alan Dickinson, Barry Le Grys, Prof Av Stokes OBE, Mr R Bennison FCA, Mrs Joanna Lewis, Mr Ed Humpherson
Income: £53,325,000 [2017]; £67,133,000 [2016]; £181,970,000 [2015]; £29,527,000 [2014]; £28,893,000 [2013]

The Mothers' Union

Registered: 10 May 1965 *Employees:* 44 *Volunteers:* 61,000
Tel: 020 7222 5533 *Website:* mothersunion.org
Activities: The prevention or relief of poverty; overseas aid, famine relief; religious activities; economic, community development, employment
Address: The Mothers'union, 24 Tufton Street, London, SW1P 3RB
Trustees: Mrs Barbara Taylor, Mrs Lynne Tembey, Mrs Margaret Jones, Mrs Nicola Mary Sweatman, Mrs Jocelyn Hilary Wright, Mrs Helen Margaret Parry, Mrs Sheran Roxanna Harper, Frida Kazembe, Mrs Joyce Julius Kibaja, Mrs Jean Price, Margaret Edwards, Rev Katherine Irene Warrington, Mrs Phyllis Elizabeth Grothier, Mrs Pauline Jean McPherson Richardson, Mrs Jane Angela Tibbs, Mrs Maria Akrofi, Rev Elisabeth Fancourt Crossman
Income: £3,525,687 [2016]; £3,673,892 [2015]; £3,793,261 [2014]; £3,694,869 [2013]; £3,596,337 [2012]

Mothers2mothers (UK) Limited

Registered: 19 Jun 2007 *Employees:* 8 *Volunteers:* 30
Tel: 020 7589 8254 *Website:* m2m.org
Activities: General charitable purposes; education, training; advancement of health or saving of lives; prevention or relief of poverty; economic, community development, employment
Address: St Marks Studios, 14 Chillingworth Road, London, N7 8QJ
Trustees: Mr Carl Stewart, Dr Timothy Evans, Mrs Ngozi Nnenna Orji, Miss Stephanie Power, Mr Derek Lubner, Mrs Carolina Manhusen Schwab, Mrs Louise Palmer
Income: £1,758,683 [2016]; £2,032,932 [2015]; £672,564 [2014]; £561,767 [2013]; £320,690 [2012]

Motiv8 South

Registered: 8 Apr 1998 *Employees:* 41 *Volunteers:* 21
Tel: 023 9283 2727 *Website:* motiv8south.org.uk
Activities: Economic, community development, employment
Address: Chief Executive, Motiv8 South Ltd, 6 Queen Street, Portsmouth, PO1 3HL
Trustees: Professor Mark Button, Ms Valerie Hopkins, Mr Stephen James Dimon, Mrs Frances Portia Charles, Mr Mark Mitchell, Ms Lisa Marie Sigalet, Mr Julian Titmuss
Income: £1,318,333 [2017]; £1,393,753 [2016]; £1,651,528 [2015]; £1,384,699 [2014]; £1,271,680 [2013]

The Motivation Charitable Trust

Registered: 11 Feb 2000 *Employees:* 28 *Volunteers:* 5
Tel: 0117 966 0398 *Website:* motivation.org.uk
Activities: Education, training; advancement of health or saving of lives; disability; prevention or relief of poverty; overseas aid, famine relief; amateur sport; economic, community development, employment
Address: Motivation, Unit 2 Sheene Road, Bedminster, Bristol, BS3 4EG
Trustees: Prunella Bramwell-Davis MSDC FRCA, Mr Richard Hawkes, Mrs Jen Browning, Mr Scott Drysdale Roy, Mr Nigel Daniel
Income: £4,832,854 [2016]; £4,970,193 [2015]; £3,116,566 [2014]; £3,277,600 [2013]; £2,855,389 [2012]

Motor Neurone Disease Association

Registered: 14 May 1986 *Employees:* 170 *Volunteers:* 3,000
Website: mndassociation.org
Activities: Disability
Address: MNDA, 10-15 Notre Dame Mews, Northampton, NN1 2BG
Trustees: Ms Wendy Balmain, Mr Richard John Coleman, Ms Janis Ruth Parks, Miss Charlotte Jane Layton, Dr Nikhil Sharma, Mr Timothy Charles Kidd, Mrs Siobhan Rooney, Mrs Emma Adams, Mr Alun Owen, Dr Heather Jacqueline Louise Smith, Mrs Susan Edwards, Mr Steven Charles Parry-Hearn, Mrs Janet Warren, Mrs Lyndsay Ann Lonsborough, Katy Styles
Income: £16,683,000 [2016]; £25,278,000 [2015]; £16,756,000 [2014]; £13,270,000 [2013]; £12,715,265 [2012]

Moulsford Preparatory School Trust Limited

Registered: 4 Apr 1967 *Employees:* 84 *Volunteers:* 20
Tel: 01491 651438 *Website:* moulsford.com
Activities: Education, training
Address: Moulsford Preparatory School, Moulsford, Wallingford, Oxon, OX10 9HR
Trustees: Mr Thomas Garnier, Mr Edward Boddington, Mrs Gwyneth Mary Crane, Mr Justin Friend, Charlotte Miles-Kingston, Mr Richard Bussell, Mr Timothy Davis, Mrs Catherine Elaine Dreyer, Mr Richard Alexander Buchan Smith, Mr Hugh Osmond, Mr John Moule, Mrs Susan Morley, Mr Toby Phelps
Income: £5,146,912 [2017]; £4,709,346 [2016]; £4,616,907 [2015]; £4,330,887 [2014]; £4,057,899 [2013]

The Mount Camphill Community Limited

Registered: 13 Mar 1972 *Employees:* 51 *Volunteers:* 2
Tel: 01892 782505 *Website:* mountcamphill.org
Activities: Education, training; disability
Address: The Mount Camphill Community, Faircrouch Lane, Wadhurst, E Sussex, TN5 6PT
Trustees: Mr Alasdair Paterson, Mr Steve Briault, Mr Peter Bateson, Jo-Anne King, Virginia Ibbott, Mrs Brigitte Van Rooij
Income: £1,471,950 [2017]; £2,114,691 [2016]; £1,881,315 [2015]; £1,780,807 [2014]; £1,788,120 [2013]

The Mount Kelly Foundation

Registered: 29 Jul 1964 *Employees:* 188
Tel: 01822 813105 *Website:* mountkelly.com
Activities: Education, training; amateur sport
Address: Kelly College, Parkwood Road, Tavistock, Devon, PL19 0HZ
Trustees: Mount Kelly Foundation Governors
Income: £9,278,481 [2017]; £9,015,672 [2016]; £8,591,426 [2015]; £11,688,723 [2014]; £6,383,336 [2013]

The Mount School (York)

Registered: 26 Oct 1983 *Employees:* 129
Tel: 01904 667500 *Website:* mountschoolyork.co.uk
Activities: Education, training
Address: Dalton Terrace, York, YO24 4DD
Trustees: Mrs Joan Concannon, Mr Greg Willmott, Miss Linda Clark, Paul Stansfield, Mrs Mary Patricia Young, Miss Shoana MacKay, Ms Janet Dean, Miss Alice Unwin, Joanna Mahler, Mr Mike Anthony Porter, Ms Margaret Bryan, Dr Nicola Spence
Income: £4,861,343 [2016]; £4,755,667 [2015]; £5,659,576 [2014]; £4,458,744 [2013]; £4,170,831 [2012]

Mount St Mary's

Registered: 16 Feb 2007 *Employees:* 191
Tel: 01246 439301 *Website:* msmcollege.co.uk
Activities: Education, training; religious activities
Address: Mount St Mary's College, Spinkhill, Derbys, S21 3YL
Trustees: Father John Dominic Twist, Mrs Joan Marian Bolton, Fr Adrian Porter, Mr Ian Murphy, Professor Martial Staub, Mr James Phinn, Father Michael Beattie Sj, Dr Helen Phillips, Mrs Kerrie Spiby, Mr Mike O'Hara, Mr William George Shaw
Income: £6,339,642 [2017]; £5,995,387 [2016]; £5,500,925 [2015]; £6,326,072 [2014]; £6,894,741 [2013]

Mount Zion Christian Ministries International (Freedom Arena)

Registered: 15 Oct 2008 *Employees:* 9 *Volunteers:* 200
Tel: 020 8310 4747 *Website:* freedomarena.org.uk
Activities: Education, training; prevention or relief of poverty; religious activities
Address: 3 North Road, off White Hart Road, Plumstead, London, SE18 1BS
Trustees: Mr Lukuman Kolawole Olaniyan, Olanrewaju Joda, Mr Emmanuel Oluwaleke Oni, Mr Rotimi William Awopeju
Income: £1,264,321 [2017]; £1,185,765 [2016]; £1,215,975 [2015]; £1,414,650 [2014]; £1,519,455 [2013]

Mountain Rescue England and Wales

Registered: 11 Mar 1964 *Volunteers:* 19
Tel: 01633 254244 *Website:* mountain.rescue.org.uk
Activities: The advancement of health or saving of lives; other charitable purposes
Address: 12 Edward VII Avenue, Newport, NP20 4NF
Trustees: Penny Brockman, Mr Michael John France, Mr Philip Papard OBE, Mr Peter Dymond OBE, Mrs Shirley Priestley, Mr Steven David Wood
Income: £1,248,226 [2016]; £526,372 [2015]; £603,858 [2014]; £433,042 [2013]; £679,021 [2012]

Mountain Training Trust

Registered: 19 Aug 1997 *Employees:* 75 *Volunteers:* 8
Tel: 01690 720214 *Website:* pyb.co.uk
Activities: Education, training; amateur sport
Address: Mountain Training Trust, Plas Y Brenin, Capel Curig, Betws-y-Coed, Conwy, LL24 0ET
Trustees: Immacolata Pescatore, Mrs Stephanie Price, Mr David Faulconbridge, Mr Andrew Gareth Preece, Mrs Sarah Mogel, Mr Roger Ward, Mr Samuel Turnbull, Mr John Michael Atkinson, Mr Rodrick Andrew Findlay, Lisa O'Keefe
Income: £3,248,729 [2017]; £3,404,778 [2016]; £3,511,236 [2015]; £3,531,340 [2014]; £3,246,618 [2013]

Mountain of Fire and Miracles Ministries International

Registered: 30 Oct 2003 *Employees:* 31 *Volunteers:* 60
Tel: 020 8804 5577 *Website:* mountainoffire.org.uk
Activities: General charitable purposes; education, training; prevention or relief of poverty; religious activities
Address: 21 Queensway, Ponders End, Enfield, Middlesex, EN3 4SZ
Trustees: Mr Franklin Olugbemiga Oyegbesan, Mr Thomas Oke, Ms Patricia Blankson, Dr Daniel Olukoya
Income: £4,244,840 [2016]; £4,373,417 [2015]; £3,117,295 [2014]; £2,813,307 [2013]; £3,767,816 [2012]

Mountview Academy of Theatre Arts Limited

Registered: 15 Aug 1977 *Employees:* 121
Tel: 020 8881 2201 *Website:* mountview.org.uk
Activities: Education, training; arts, culture, heritage, science
Address: Mountview Academy of Theatre Arts, Kingfisher Place, Clarendon Road, London, N22 6XF
Trustees: Dame Colette Bowe, Mr Paul Roberts, Mr Vincent Wang, Mrs Victoria Heywood, Sir Brendan Barber, Mr Benjamin Rodger Sumner, Miss Indhu Rubasingham, Mr Patrick Spottiswoode, Mr Andrew Parker, Mr Mark Peter Williams, Mr Arian Mirzaali
Income: £5,412,580 [2016]; £5,268,005 [2015]; £5,288,733 [2014]; £4,747,084 [2013]; £4,524,213 [2012]

Movember Europe

Registered: 10 Sep 2010 *Employees:* 32
Website: movember.com
Activities: General charitable purposes; education, training; advancement of health or saving of lives
Address: 539 Rialto Avenue, Venice, California, USA
Trustees: Mr Paul Villanti, Ms Colleen Nelson, Mr Nicholas Charles Reece, Mr Simon William Traynor, Mr Andrew Gibbins, Mr John Hughes, Ms Katherine Howard, Ms Kellie Louise Johnston
Income: £10,108,984 [2017]; £9,988,233 [2016]; £12,003,613 [2015]; £20,547,036 [2014]; £27,104,901 [2013]

The Movement for Non-Mobile Children (Whizz-Kidz)

Registered: 17 Apr 1990 *Employees:* 106 *Volunteers:* 225
Website: whizz-kidz.org.uk
Activities: Education, training; disability
Address: 4th Floor, Whizz - Kidz, Portland House, Bressenden Place, London, SW1E 5BH
Trustees: Mr Adrian Michael Pitts, Mr Andrew Granger, Dr Charles Fairhurst, Mr Richard Verden, Mr Daniel Mathews, Mr David Edward Reid, Mr Robert Alastair Mathieson, Ms Pamela Garside, Mr Rahul Moodgal
Income: £7,047,000 [2017]; £7,836,000 [2016]; £7,931,000 [2015]; £6,372,000 [2014]; £7,457,000 [2013]

The Movement for Reform Judaism

Registered: 12 Jan 2011 *Employees:* 25
Tel: 020 8349 5723 *Website:* reformjudaism.org.uk
Activities: Religious activities
Address: Sternberg Centre, 80 East End Road, London, N3 2SY
Trustees: Mr Geoffrey Marx, Mr Paul Winter, Mrs Debbie Jacobs, Mrs Sue Pearlman, Ms Cathy Schindel Knowles, Mrs Alisa Gerrard, Mr Roger Benjamin Nagioff, Mr Paul Anthony Langsford, Mrs Brenda Dinsdale, Mr Jonathan Oppenheimer, Mrs Sherry Ashworth, Rabbi Joshua Benjamin Israel Levy, Sophie Lipton
Income: £3,534,996 [2016]; £3,429,508 [2015]; £3,611,069 [2014]; £3,686,618 [2013]; £3,559,081 [2012]

Mr Willats' Charity

Registered: 22 Sep 1962 *Employees:* 2
Tel: 01225 331499 *Website:* mrwillats.org
Activities: Religious activities
Address: P O Box 3883, Bath, BA1 0AQ
Trustees: Mr Willats' Corporate Trustee Limited
Income: £1,012,395 [2016]; £968,841 [2015]; £915,309 [2014]; £874,159 [2013]; £830,564 [2012]

The Muath Trust
Registered: 3 Nov 2003 *Employees:* 45 *Volunteers:* 20
Tel: 0121 753 0297 *Website:* muathtrust.org
Activities: General charitable purposes; education, training; prevention or relief of poverty; accommodation, housing; religious activities; arts, culture, heritage, science; economic, community development, employment; recreation
Address: The Muath Trust, The Bordesley Centre, Stratford Road, Camp Hill, Birmingham, B11 1AR
Trustees: Dr Ali Qirbee, Mr Adnan Saif, Mr Nageeb Mohamed Ali, Mrs Faten Yafai, Dr Dawood Abdulmalek Al-Hidabi, Mr Dirhem Abdo Saeed, Mr Jaffer Mansour Mohammed Al-Shamery
Income: £1,117,655 [2016]; £1,127,060 [2015]; £1,554,029 [2014]; £1,036,482 [2013]; £1,065,950 [2012]

The Mudchute Association
Registered: 28 Jul 1982 *Employees:* 46 *Volunteers:* 700
Tel: 020 7515 5901 *Website:* mudchute.org
Activities: General charitable purposes; education, training; disability; arts, culture, heritage, science; amateur sport; animals; environment, conservation, heritage; economic, community development, employment
Address: Pier Street, Isle of Dogs, London, E14 3HP
Trustees: Dr Michael Barraclough, Mr Justin Hesman Abbott, Mrs Lorraine Cavanagh OBE, Dr Justine Aw, Mr Klaus Bernhard Woeste, Ms Mary Gray, Raymond John Swindells, Mrs Kathleen McTasney, Mrs Margaret Rose Phillips, Mr Abs Haiyum, Mrs Lindsay Draffan, Mrs Carolyn Kirkwood
Income: £1,260,784 [2017]; £1,244,886 [2016]; £1,284,479 [2015]; £1,276,355 [2014]; £1,180,695 [2013]

Mudiad Meithrin
Registered: 8 Jun 1993 *Employees:* 257 *Volunteers:* 100
Tel: 01970 639639 *Website:* meithrin.co.uk
Activities: General charitable purposes; education, training
Address: Mudiad Meithrin, Boulevard St Briuec, Aberystwyth, Ceredigion, SY23 1PD
Trustees: Mr John Arthur Jones, Mrs Rhianwen Huws Roberts, Mr Geraint James, Mr Gruff Hughes, Mrs Mai Roberts, Mrs Rhiannon Lloyd, Mr Rhodri Llwyd Morgan
Income: £5,010,000 [2017]; £5,746,000 [2016]; £5,990,568 [2015]; £5,884,660 [2014]; £5,748,016 [2013]

The Mulberry Bush Organisation Ltd
Registered: 5 Jan 1966 *Employees:* 105
Tel: 01865 300202 *Website:* mulberrybush.org.uk
Activities: Education, training; other charitable purposes
Address: The Mulberry Bush Organisation Ltd, Abingdon Road, Standlake, Witney, Oxon, OX29 7RW
Trustees: Mr Richard Rollinson, Mr Michael Sarrington, Mr Mark Thomas, Mr Hugh Randall Pidgeon, Mr John Henry Whitwell, Mrs Margaret Dawn Eynon, Mr Barry Alexander Armstrong, Mrs Satvinder Sondhi
Income: £5,999,952 [2017]; £5,894,213 [2016]; £4,910,583 [2015]; £4,756,699 [2014]; £4,513,965 [2013]

The Mulberry Trust
Registered: 21 Nov 1991
Activities: General charitable purposes; education, training; advancement of health or saving of lives; disability; prevention or relief of poverty; overseas aid, famine relief; accommodation, housing; religious activities; arts, culture, heritage, science; amateur sport; animals; environment, conservation, heritage; economic, community development, employment; other charitable purposes
Address: P O Box 4781, Marlow, Bucks, SL7 9DZ
Trustees: Mr Robert James Frost, Mrs Anthea Rosalind Mirkowski, Mrs Elsie Margaret Frost, Mrs Helen Lorraine Fowler
Income: £2,095,854 [2017]; £185,947 [2016]; £224,209 [2015]; £237,442 [2014]; £281,406 [2013]

The George Muller Charitable Trust
Registered: 11 Dec 1997 *Employees:* 4 *Volunteers:* 10
Tel: 0117 924 5001 *Website:* mullers.org
Activities: Education, training; prevention or relief of poverty; overseas aid, famine relief; accommodation, housing; religious activities
Address: The George Muller Charitable Trust, Muller House, 7 Cotham Park, Bristol, BS6 6DA
Trustees: Quentin Elston, Tigist Grieve, Stewart North, Liz Small, Tony Davies, Ed Marsh, Derek Powell, Josh Kingston
Income: £2,462,060 [2017]; £2,558,304 [2016]; £1,862,256 [2015]; £1,775,934 [2014]; £2,468,945 [2013]

Multiple Sclerosis International Federation
Registered: 5 Aug 2004 *Employees:* 11 *Volunteers:* 1
Tel: 020 7620 1911 *Website:* msif.org
Activities: Education, training; advancement of health or saving of lives; disability; overseas aid, famine relief; human rights, religious or racial harmony, equality or diversity
Address: 3rd Floor, Skyline House, 200 Union Street, London, SE1 0LX
Trustees: Dr Mario Alberto Battaglia, Mr Weyman Johnson, Mrs Victoria Annis, Professor Mai Mohamed Helmy Sharawy, Mrs Maria Jose Wuille-Bille, Ms Michelle Mitchell, Ms Dimitra Kalogianni, Mr Graham McReynolds, Ms Magdalena Fac-Skhirtladze, Ms Anne Winslow, Prof Reinhard Hohlfeld, Prof Xavier Montalban, Marlies Jansen Landheer, Mr Viresh Oberoi, Mr Charles Van Der Straten Waillet, Mr Pedro Carrascal, Mr Alan Martin Stevens, Ms Cynthia Zagieboylo, Mr Daniel Larouche, Guillaume Courault, Ms Marie Vaillant, Mr Peter Galligan, Dr Matthew Miles, Mr Christian Bardenfleth, Ms Ana Torredemer, Mr Klaus Hom, Mr Hendrik Schmitt
Income: £1,690,382 [2016]; £1,839,290 [2015]; £1,650,865 [2014]; £1,507,090 [2013]; £1,393,509 [2012]

The Multiple Sclerosis Research and Relief Fund
Registered: 13 Jun 1969 *Employees:* 12 *Volunteers:* 7
Tel: 01670 505829 *Website:* ms-researchandrelief.org
Activities: The advancement of health or saving of lives; disability; arts, culture, heritage, science; amateur sport
Address: M S Research & Relief Fund, Benmar House, Choppington Road, Morpeth, Northumberland, NE61 2HX
Trustees: Mr Paul Dennis Atkinson, Mrs Margery Rose Tate, Mrs Barbara Ellis, Mrs Margaret Sharp, Mr Kevin Carr, Mr Peter Dawson
Income: £1,088,962 [2017]; £1,751,585 [2016]; £255,250 [2015]; £733,936 [2014]; £722,804 [2013]

Multiple Sclerosis Society

Registered: 2 Dec 2010 *Employees:* 303 *Volunteers:* 5,500
Website: mssociety.org.uk
Activities: General charitable purposes; education, training; advancement of health or saving of lives; disability
Address: 372 Edgware Road, London, NW2 6ND
Trustees: Mrs Sarah Schol, Mrs Christine Gibbons, Miss Ruth Hasnip, Mr John Grosvenor, Ms Karen Angela Penhorwood Jones, Jason Atkinson, Mr Dowshan Humzah, Mr Stuart Secker, Ms Esther Tamara Foreman, Mr Nicholas Paul Winser CBE FREng BSc CEng FIET, Mr Ceri Ivor Daniel Smith, Dr Anne Shinkwin, Ms Marion King
Income: £29,023,000 [2016]; £27,743,000 [2015]; £26,132,000 [2014]; £24,093,000 [2013]; £25,414,000 [2012]

Multiple Sclerosis Trust

Registered: 7 Sep 2001 *Employees:* 30 *Volunteers:* 100
Tel: 01462 476700 *Website:* mstrust.org.uk
Activities: Education, training; advancement of health or saving of lives; disability
Address: Multiple Sclerosis Trust, Spirella Building, Bridge Road, Letchworth Garden City, Herts, SG6 4ET
Trustees: Professor Dawn Langdon, Mr Paul Budd, Honourable Sarah Louise Joiner, Mr David Philpot, Ms Caitlin Sorrell, Professor Neil Scolding, Mr Nicholas Kavanagh, Mrs Laura Chapman, Ms Christine Singleton
Income: £2,360,991 [2017]; £3,328,944 [2016]; £3,212,293 [2015]; £4,246,423 [2014]; £3,408,425 [2013]

Multiple Sclerosis-UK Limited

Registered: 24 Feb 1994 *Employees:* 12 *Volunteers:* 62
Tel: 01206 226500 *Website:* ms-uk.org
Activities: Education, training; advancement of health or saving of lives; disability
Address: Multiple Sclerosis Resource Centre, Unsworth House, Hythe Quay, Colchester, Essex, CO2 8JF
Trustees: Mr Martin Hopkins, Mr Michael Herington, Mrs Claire Michelle Offord, Mr Matthew Peter Swan, Mrs Fiona Sakal, Mr Philip Startin, Mr Keith William Graham
Income: £1,011,508 [2016]; £757,158 [2015]; £691,045 [2014]; £631,536 [2013]; £740,539 [2012]

Multiple System Atrophy Trust

Registered: 27 Aug 2010 *Employees:* 9
Tel: 0333 323 4591 *Website:* msatrust.org.uk
Activities: The advancement of health or saving of lives
Address: Multiple System Atrophy Trust, 51 St Olav's Court, City Business Centre, Lower Road, London, SE16 2XB
Trustees: Hugh Matheson, Geoffrey Murray, Professor David Burn, Ms Amy Jean Couture, Mrs Linda Nicolaides, Carole Ferguson Walker, Alexander Loehnis, Prof Clare Juliet Fowler CBE FRCP, Ms Helen Craik, Professor Niall Patrick Quinn MA MD FRCP, Ms Roseanne Blaze
Income: £1,029,755 [2017]; £617,877 [2016]; £642,167 [2015]; £651,636 [2014]; £537,901 [2013]

Muntada Aid

Registered: 19 May 2014 *Employees:* 11 *Volunteers:* 200
Tel: 020 7471 8272 *Website:* muntadaaid.org
Activities: General charitable purposes; education, training; advancement of health or saving of lives; prevention or relief of poverty
Address: M W B Business Exchange, 26-28 Hammersmith Grove, London, W6 7BA
Trustees: Mr Hisham Bella, Mr Imran Asif, Mr Musaed Binajlan
Income: £1,438,564 [2016]; £990,439 [2015]

Muntham House School

Registered: 23 Jul 2004 *Employees:* 67
Tel: 07976 815804 *Website:* muntham.org.uk
Activities: Education, training
Address: Beechey Knowle, Borers Arms Road, Copthorne, Crawley, Surrey, RH10 3LU
Trustees: Mr Vernon Lewis Jennings, Mr Martin Fuller, Dr Alan Vallon, Mr John Knightley, Mr Robert Fryatt, Mr Andrew John Barnes, Mr Peter Francis Higgins, Dr B Jones, Mrs Eileen Vining Vose, Mrs Angela Luff, Mrs Karen Furse
Income: £3,447,775 [2017]; £3,358,055 [2016]; £3,611,725 [2015]; £3,283,612 [2014]; £3,139,201 [2013]

Murray Hall Community Trust

Registered: 16 Aug 1994 *Employees:* 123 *Volunteers:* 60
Tel: 01902 826513 *Website:* murrayhall.co.uk
Activities: General charitable purposes; education, training; advancement of health or saving of lives; disability; prevention or relief of poverty; economic, community development, employment
Address: Manjula Patel, The Bridge, St Marks Road, Tipton, W Midlands, DY4 0SL
Trustees: Mr John James Miller, Mrs Vicky Powell, Mr Christopher Patterson, Mr John Blewitt, Mr David Hill
Income: £4,049,268 [2017]; £4,456,586 [2016]; £4,716,914 [2015]; £5,029,917 [2014]; £4,228,218 [2013]

Muscular Dystrophy Group of Great Britain and Northern Ireland

Registered: 16 May 1962 *Employees:* 78 *Volunteers:* 500
Tel: 020 7803 4800 *Website:* musculardystrophyuk.org
Activities: Education, training; advancement of health or saving of lives; disability
Address: Muscular Dystrophy UK, 61a Great Suffolk Street, London, SE1 0BU
Trustees: Mr Robert Warner, Professor Michael Hanna, David Hastie, Dr Amy Jane McKnight, Mr Richard Price, Mr Charles Henry Scott, Mr Ian Gordon, Baroness Celia Thomas, Sheila Hawkins, Mr Marcus Brown, Mrs Louisa Alexandra Hill, Mr Andrew McCulloch Graham
Income: £7,675,000 [2017]; £8,340,000 [2016]; £6,112,000 [2015]; £6,660,000 [2014]; £4,544,000 [2013]

The Museum of Army Flying Limited

Registered: 20 Nov 1987 *Employees:* 35 *Volunteers:* 47
Tel: 01460 432982 *Website:* armyflying.com
Activities: Education, training; arts, culture, heritage, science; environment, conservation, heritage; armed forces, emergency service efficiency
Address: Museum of Army Flying Ltd, Middle Wallop, Stockbridge, Hants, SO20 8DY
Trustees: Mr Phillip John Webb, Mr Jonathon Nelson Deacon, Brigadier Colin Sibun, Caroline Hopkins, Colonel Alex Willman, Sir Gary Robert Coward KBE CB, Colonel Jonathan David Bryant, Mrs Christine Jennifer Leslie, WO1 Ben Rieper AAC
Income: £1,547,233 [2017]; £657,119 [2016]; £587,070 [2015]; £401,907 [2014]; £466,212 [2013]

Museum of Brands, Packaging and Advertising

Registered: 23 Aug 2002 *Employees:* 16 *Volunteers:* 79
Tel: 020 7908 0804 *Website:* museumofbrands.com
Activities: Education, training; arts, culture, heritage, science
Address: Manager, 1 Colville Mews, Lonsdale Road, London, W11 2AR
Trustees: Jeffrey Chew, Mr John Noble, Ms Sarah Ann Du Boscq De Beaumont, Ms Kate Frame
Income: £1,163,340 [2016]; £465,871 [2015]; £545,988 [2014]; £498,335 [2013]; £485,375 [2012]

Museum of London Archaeology
Registered: 30 Aug 2011 *Employees:* 288 *Volunteers:* 698
Tel: 020 7410 2200 *Website:* mola.org.uk
Activities: Environment, conservation, heritage
Address: Museum of London Archaeology Service, 46 Eagle Wharf Road, London, N1 7ED
Trustees: Alison Gowman, Mr Michael Hoffman, Mr Peter Stewart, Ms Joanna Averly, Mr William Arthur McKee, Drs Marleen Groen, Ms Sharon Ament, Mrs Rosamund Blomfield Smith
Income: £13,479,248 [2017]; £13,060,375 [2016]; £9,731,126 [2015]; £7,204,532 [2014]; £8,620,042 [2013]

Museum of London
Registered: 2 Dec 2010 *Employees:* 239 *Volunteers:* 285
Tel: 020 7814 5501 *Website:* museumoflondon.org.uk
Activities: Education, training; arts, culture, heritage, science
Address: Museum of London, 150 London Wall, London, EC2Y 5HN
Trustees: Alderman Alison Gowman, Professor Sir Richard Trainor KBE, Councillor Richard Watts, Vivienne Littlechild JP, John Scott JP, Clive Bannister, David Camp, Jorn Rausing, Sir Edward Lister, Simon Fanshawe OBE, Sonita Alleyne OBE, Rt Hon The Lord Boateng DL, Tom Hoffman, Sally Balcombe, David Wormsley, Evan Davis, Mr Paul Martinelli, Judith Pleasance CC
Income: £22,157,000 [2017]; £21,163,000 [2016]; £19,922,000 [2015]; £20,797,000 [2014]; £19,827,000 [2013]

Museum of Modern Art Limited
Registered: 5 Jun 1967 *Employees:* 26 *Volunteers:* 35
Tel: 01635 813804 *Website:* modernartoxford.org.uk
Activities: Arts, culture, heritage, science
Address: 73 Rectory Close, Newbury, Berks, RG14 6DD
Trustees: Mr Hussein Barma, Ms Heidi Baravalle, Ms Nicola Walton, Ms Anna Yang, Mr Andrew Verschoyle, Ms Tania Rotherwick, Mr Patrick Holmes, Dom Loehnis
Income: £1,887,082 [2017]; £2,027,649 [2016]; £1,858,687 [2015]; £1,392,543 [2014]; £1,815,644 [2013]

The Museums Association
Registered: 7 Nov 1962 *Employees:* 21
Tel: 020 7566 7800 *Website:* museumsassociation.org
Activities: Education, training; arts, culture, heritage, science; environment, conservation, heritage
Address: 42 Clerkenwell Close, London, EC1R 0AZ
Trustees: Mrs Heather Lees, Ms Margaret Mary Appleton Maggie, Mr Patrick Gilmore, Ms Heledd Fychan, Miss Gillian Findlay, Sue MacKay, Mr David Liddiment, Mr Iain Watson, Mr Alexander John Bird, Mrs Dhikshana Pering, Mr Simon Brown, Miss Rachael Ann Minott
Income: £2,371,449 [2017]; £2,263,187 [2016]; £2,052,208 [2015]; £1,939,174 [2014]; £3,354,094 [2013]

Mushkil Aasaan Limited
Registered: 11 May 2000 *Employees:* 154 *Volunteers:* 23
Tel: 020 8672 6581
Activities: General charitable purposes; advancement of health or saving of lives; disability; accommodation, housing; religious activities; economic, community development, employment; other charitable purposes
Address: Mushkil Aasaan, 220-222 Upper Tooting Road, London, SW17 7EW
Trustees: Mrs Anuara Begum Ali, Shaheen Adiba Farhat, Mrs Khalida Zafar Mehal, Shamim Lone
Income: £1,522,806 [2017]; £1,434,614 [2016]; £1,336,807 [2015]; £1,279,929 [2014]; £1,384,905 [2013]

Music in Hospitals and Care
Registered: 22 Dec 1995 *Employees:* 19 *Volunteers:* 68
Tel: 01932 260810 *Website:* mihc.org.uk
Activities: The advancement of health or saving of lives; disability; arts, culture, heritage, science
Address: Music in Hospitals & Care, Unit 40 Enterprise House, 44-46 Terrace Road, Walton on Thames, Surrey, KT12 2SD
Trustees: Dr Jeremy Huw Williams, Dr Alan Jacques, Mr Roger Luxmoore-Styles, Dr Andrew Robert Christie Kelso, Ms Fiona McIntosh, Lorimer William Peters MacKenzie, Mr John Middleton, Helen Ashley Taylor, Mr Peter Fairlie, Ms Sarah Mallock, Anne Murray O'Hagan, Sian Carter
Income: £1,527,842 [2017]; £1,257,029 [2016]; £1,052,021 [2015]; £1,408,008 [2014]; £968,763 [2013]

The Music in Secondary Schools Trust
Registered: 17 Apr 2013 *Employees:* 4
Tel: 07811 701875 *Website:* misst.org.uk
Activities: Education, training
Address: MiSST, 320 City Road, London, EC1V 2NZ
Trustees: Lady Madeleine Astrid Lloyd Webber, Mr Martin Bavinton, Mr Andrew Daniel Wolfson
Income: £1,164,649 [2017]; £998,478 [2016]; £718,717 [2015]; £316,848 [2014]

Musicians Benevolent Fund
Registered: 17 Oct 1963 *Employees:* 30 *Volunteers:* 34
Website: helpmusicians.org.uk
Activities: General charitable purposes
Address: Help Musicians UK, 7-11 Britannia Street, London, WC1X 9JS
Trustees: Mr Graham Edward Sheffield, Mrs Kathryn Langridge, Mrs Felicity Osmond, Mr Richard Wigley, Mr David Anthony Williams, Mr Sandeep Dwesar, Mr John Axon, Mr Alex Spofforth, Ms Suzi Williams, Mr Stephen Daltrey
Income: £5,504,000 [2016]; £4,781,000 [2015]; £5,056,000 [2014]; £4,117,000 [2013]; £4,317,000 [2012]

The Muslim Academic Trust
Registered: 13 Nov 1997 *Volunteers:* 10
Tel: 01223 871187
Activities: Education, training; religious activities
Address: 32 London Road, Harston, Cambridge, CB22 7QH
Trustees: Mr Sohail Bhatti, Mrs Nabila Winter, Mr Timothy Winter
Income: £1,308,229 [2015]; £275,128 [2014]; £146,804 [2013]; £164,618 [2012]

Muslim Charity Helping The Needy
Registered: 7 Dec 1999 *Employees:* 6
Tel: 01777 702555 *Website:* muslimcharity.org.uk
Activities: General charitable purposes; education, training; advancement of health or saving of lives; prevention or relief of poverty; overseas aid, famine relief; accommodation, housing; economic, community development, employment; other charitable purposes
Address: Eaton Hall, Retford, Notts, DN22 0PR
Trustees: Mr Bakhtyar Haider Pirzada, Mrs Ghulam Fatima, Mr Mohammed Yousaf, Mr Mohammad Imdad Hussain Pirzada, Mr Ali Qudar Raja
Income: £2,041,346 [2016]; £2,101,437 [2015]; £3,243,338 [2014]; £2,106,557 [2013]; £2,677,945 [2012]

Muslim Hands

Registered: 22 Jul 2004 *Employees:* 86 *Volunteers:* 120
Tel: 0115 911 7222 *Website:* muslimhands.org.uk
Activities: General charitable purposes; education, training; advancement of health or saving of lives; prevention or relief of poverty; overseas aid, famine relief; religious activities
Address: Muslim Hands, 148-164 Gregory Boulevard, Nottingham, NG7 5JE
Trustees: Mr Syed Lakhte Hassanain, Mr Mohammad Amin-Ul Hasanat Shah, Mr Sahibzada Ghulam Jeelani, Dr Musharaf Hussain, Mr Saffi Ullah, Mr Muhammad Arshad Jamil
Income: £15,797,759 [2016]; £14,442,632 [2015]; £14,762,543 [2014]; £14,212,504 [2013]; £13,230,574 [2012]

The Mustard Tree

Registered: 25 Mar 2010 *Employees:* 32 *Volunteers:* 150
Tel: 07912 289283 *Website:* mustardtree.org.uk
Activities: Education, training; prevention or relief of poverty; economic, community development, employment
Address: 436 Bolton Road, Bury, Lancs, BL8 2DA
Trustees: Mrs Bronwen Rapley, Paul Wenham, Professor Christopher Summerton, Mr Anthony Preston, Mr Simon Jonothan Downing, Vikas Shah, Mr James Kielty
Income: £1,230,347 [2017]; £1,030,659 [2016]; £1,065,781 [2015]; £686,652 [2014]; £730,961 [2013]

My Life Legacy

Registered: 27 Jun 2016 *Employees:* 25 *Volunteers:* 11
Tel: 01257 472900 *Website:* my-life.org.uk
Activities: Disability
Address: Thompson House, off Pepper Lane, Standish, Wigan, Lancs, WN6 0PP
Trustees: Mr Stephen Morris Jones, Mr Alan Bell, Mr Andrew William Keogh, Mrs Caroline Tomlinson, Mrs Amanda McDonough
Income: £1,259,666 [2017]

My Space Housing Solutions

Registered: 28 Nov 2012 *Employees:* 39
Tel: 01204 694154 *Website:* my-spacehousing.co.uk
Activities: Education, training; disability; accommodation, housing
Address: My Space Housing Solutions, Paragon Business Park, Chorley New Road, Horwich, Bolton, Lancs, BL6 6HG
Trustees: Mr Carl McCready, Mr Barry Campbell, Miss Denize Alston, Mr Andrew Goodson, Mr Peter Lynch
Income: £3,753,081 [2016]; £1,733,369 [2015]; £605,671 [2014]; £91,117 [2013]

MyTime Active

Registered: 3 Mar 2004 *Employees:* 1,149 *Volunteers:* 359
Tel: 020 8323 1775 *Website:* mytimeactive.co.uk
Activities: Education, training; advancement of health or saving of lives; arts, culture, heritage, science; amateur sport
Address: My Time Active, Linden House, 153-155 Masons Hill, Bromley, Kent, BR2 9HY
Trustees: Mr Adrian Hollands, Ms Isobel Gowan, Mr Robert John Evans, Mr Johnny Heald, Mr Andrew Muzzelle, Mr Mark David Oakley, Ms Christine Whatford CBE BA (Hons), Dr Val Lowman, Mr Michael Evans, Mrs Harvinder Minoo Sahni-Court
Income: £33,059,355 [2017]; £32,625,472 [2016]; £32,515,692 [2015]; £32,797,722 [2014]; £29,545,952 [2013]

Mylnhurst Limited

Registered: 10 Jul 1996 *Employees:* 66
Tel: 0114 236 1411 *Website:* mylnhurst.co.uk
Activities: Education, training; other charitable purposes
Address: Mylnhurst Lodge, Button Hill, Sheffield, S11 9HJ
Trustees: Mrs Anne Raftery, Mrs Catherine Thompson, Mrs Martina Bradshaw, Mr Jonathan Mark Saunders
Income: £1,656,871 [2016]; £1,543,080 [2015]; £1,479,963 [2014]; £1,387,200 [2013]; £1,313,053 [2012]

The Myton Hospices

Registered: 29 Apr 1985 *Employees:* 293 *Volunteers:* 878
Tel: 01926 492518 *Website:* mytonhospice.org
Activities: Education, training; advancement of health or saving of lives
Address: The Myton Hospices, Myton Lane, Warwick, CV34 6PX
Trustees: Mr Noel Hunter OBE, Mrs Nadiya Virani-Bland, Mr Graham Nicoll, Mr Paul Taylor, Dr Valerie Robson, Dr Ruth Girvan, Karl Demian, Mrs Margaret Morris, Mrs Suzannah Patchett, Mr Kelvin Beer-Jones
Income: £11,043,496 [2017]; £11,091,615 [2016]; £10,158,383 [2015]; £10,632,906 [2014]; £9,238,932 [2013]

N-Compass North West Limited

Registered: 26 Mar 2009 *Employees:* 107 *Volunteers:* 138
Tel: 0345 013 8208 *Website:* ncompassnorthwest.co.uk
Activities: General charitable purposes; education, training; advancement of health or saving of lives; disability; prevention or relief of poverty; economic, community development, employment
Address: 1 Edward VII Quay, Navigation Way, Ashton on Ribble, Preston, Lancs, PR2 2YF
Trustees: Mr David Lodge, Ms Catherine Scivier, Ms Diane Bellinger, Ms Imelda Hatton-Yeo, Mr Jonathan Church, Dr Mandy Patricia Dixon, Mr Jonathan Thomas, Mrs Barbara Aird, Mr Brian Watson, Ms Janet Walton, Ms Hannah Woodcock, Mr Ian Merrill
Income: £4,843,817 [2017]; £3,932,234 [2016]; £2,128,924 [2015]; £1,817,034 [2014]; £1,642,790 [2013]

NABS

Registered: 16 Jul 1998 *Employees:* 112
Tel: 020 7290 7070 *Website:* nabs.org.uk
Activities: General charitable purposes; education, training; advancement of health or saving of lives; disability; prevention or relief of poverty; accommodation, housing; economic, community development, employment
Address: NABS Ltd, 388 Oxford Street, London, W1C 1JT
Trustees: Ms Judith Salinson, Phillipa Hughes, Mr Simon Daglish, Mr Matthew Bush, Mr Andrew Harris, Mr Keith Fowler, Mr Charlie Rudd, Mr Naren Patel, Amanda Pitt, Mr Hamish Nicklin
Income: £4,915,455 [2016]; £4,390,030 [2015]; £4,857,637 [2014]; £4,259,054 [2013]; £4,094,909 [2012]

NCFE

Registered: 10 Mar 1994 *Employees:* 303
Tel: 0191 239 8008 *Website:* ncfe.org.uk
Activities: Education, training
Address: NCFE, Q6, Quorum Business Park, Benton Lane, Newcastle upon Tyne, NE12 8BT
Trustees: Mrs Deborah Jenkins, Mr Nigel Hudson, Mr David Wilson, Mrs Rosalino Anna Cuschieri, Ms Heather Ashton, Greg Michael Austin, Christopher Mark Victor
Income: £20,255,000 [2017]; £26,117,000 [2016]; £19,571,000 [2015]; £19,317,000 [2014]; £21,025,000 [2013]

NECA
Registered: 20 Jun 1985 *Employees:* 118 *Volunteers:* 19
Tel: 0191 414 6446 *Website:* neca.co.uk
Activities: Education, training; advancement of health or saving of lives; accommodation, housing
Address: NECA Headquarters, Derwent Point, Clasper Way, Swalwell, Newcastle upon Tyne, NE16 3BE
Trustees: Mr Norman Richardson, Mr David Gregory, Mr Ronald Ian Watson, Mr Barry Neil Speker OBE DL, Dr Peter Brian Moore
Income: £4,833,258 [2017]; £5,325,951 [2016]; £8,582,086 [2015]; £9,234,852 [2014]; £10,197,417 [2013]

NEPACS
Registered: 15 Aug 2001 *Employees:* 81 *Volunteers:* 200
Tel: 0191 332 3453 *Website:* nepacs.co.uk
Activities: Education, training; prevention or relief of poverty
Address: 20 Old Elvet, Durham, DH1 3HW
Trustees: Mr Donald MacKay, Mrs Sheila Seacroft, Mrs Ruth Elizabeth Getrude Cranfield, Mrs Margaret Stockdale, Mrs Sareth Ann Nainby-Luxmoore, Mrs Linda Norfolk Lovell, Russell Bruce, Mr Richard John Courtney Booth, Mr James Black, Mrs Kathleen Ogilvie, Mr Mark Weeding, Mr Clive Constance, Rev Kate Brooke, Mr David Abrahams, Mrs Margaret Smith
Income: £1,657,301 [2017]; £1,540,198 [2016]; £1,429,462 [2015]; £1,383,020 [2014]; £1,311,830 [2013]

NETA Training Trust
Registered: 3 Oct 1978 *Employees:* 41
Tel: 01642 865402 *Website:* neta.co.uk
Activities: Education, training
Address: Stockton Riverside College, Harvard Avenue, Thornaby, Stockton on Tees, Cleveland, TS17 6FB
Trustees: John Hornby, Mr Philip Cook, Mr Jeremy Faulkner, Mr Russell Warren McCallion, Mr Steven Cossins
Income: £2,388,529 [2017]; £3,793,894 [2016]; £3,903,421 [2015]; £4,618,159 [2014]; £3,826,362 [2013]

NEWCIS
Registered: 14 Jan 2015 *Employees:* 29 *Volunteers:* 99
Tel: 01352 752525 *Website:* carers.org
Activities: Education, training; advancement of health or saving of lives; disability; prevention or relief of poverty
Address: NEWCIS, 28-44 New Street, Mold, Flintshire, CH7 1NZ
Trustees: Mrs Lynne Hughes, Mr Colin Holstein, Mrs Gill Harrison, Mr Keith Corbett, Miss Emily Littlehales, Mrs Patricia Ann Carlin, Mrs Elizabeth Taylor, Mrs Ann Sharman Roberts, Mrs Angela Jones-Thomas, Mr David Paul Pennant-Williams
Income: £1,088,463 [2017]; £953,325 [2015]

The NGT Foundation
Registered: 30 Sep 1997
Tel: 020 7747 2801
Activities: Arts, culture, heritage, science
Address: The National Gallery, Trafalgar Square, London, WC2N 5DN
Trustees: Dr David Landau, Mr Michael Anthony Cowdy, The Hon Hannah Mary Rothschild, Mr Nicholas Baring CBE, Sir Stuart Anthony Lipton, Mrs Katrin Henkel
Income: £3,365,865 [2017]; £3,832,250 [2016]; £2,687,216 [2015]; £2,830,938 [2014]; £2,854,453 [2013]

The NHS Confederation
Registered: 30 Jan 2002 *Employees:* 207
Tel: 0113 306 3064 *Website:* nhsconfed.org
Activities: General charitable purposes; advancement of health or saving of lives; disability; prevention or relief of poverty; human rights, religious or racial harmony, equality or diversity; other charitable purposes
Address: Floor 15, Portland House, Bressenden Place, London, SW1E 5BH
Trustees: Mr Stephen James Dorrell, Sir Andrew Cash, Owen Williams, Mr Paul Jenkins, Mrs Bernadine Rees OBE, Dr Tony Stevens, Julia Hickey, Mr Prem Singh, Ruth Poole, Dr Graham Jackson, Mr James William Easton
Income: £16,922,618 [2017]; £19,190,211 [2016]; £20,631,999 [2015]; £22,448,340 [2014]; £22,583,817 [2013]

The NIA Project
Registered: 28 Apr 1994 *Employees:* 48 *Volunteers:* 25
Tel: 020 7683 1270 *Website:* niaendingviolence.org.uk
Activities: Accommodation, housing; other charitable purposes
Address: 436 Essex Road, London, N1 3QP
Trustees: Karen Ingala Smith, Grace Elena Banks, Oyinlola Okolosie, Mina Rai, Sophia Antoniazzi, Ruth Tweedale, Ms Amy Terry, Felicity Slater
Income: £2,096,802 [2017]; £1,486,507 [2016]; £1,338,933 [2015]; £1,427,902 [2014]; £510,205 [2013]

NIAB EMR
Registered: 5 Jan 2016 *Employees:* 74
Tel: 01223 342200 *Website:* niab.com
Activities: Education, training; arts, culture, heritage, science; environment, conservation, heritage; human rights, religious or racial harmony, equality or diversity; other charitable purposes
Address: Huntingdon Road, Cambridge, CB3 0LE
Trustees: Mr Peter Gregory, Dr Nigel Kerby, Ms Tina Barsby
Income: £5,879,000 [2017]

NIAB
Registered: 4 Sep 1997 *Employees:* 350
Tel: 01223 342304 *Website:* niab.com
Activities: Education, training; arts, culture, heritage, science; environment, conservation, heritage; other charitable purposes
Address: National Institute of Agricultural, Huntingdon Road, Cambridge, CB3 0LE
Trustees: Dr Tina Lorraine Barsby, Mr Robert Harle, Professor Alison Smith, Mrs Kathy Fidgeon, Dr Nigel Kerby, Dr Ian Puddephat, Mr Richard MacDonald, Mr Andrew Kuyk CBE, Mr James Godfrey, Dr Charles Lang, Mr Stephen Ellwood
Income: £25,044,000 [2017]; £19,192,000 [2016]; £16,685,000 [2015]; £15,121,000 [2014]; £13,726,000 [2013]

NLT Training Services Limited
Registered: 10 Sep 1980 *Employees:* 37
Tel: 01246 206520 *Website:* nlt-training.co.uk
Activities: Education, training
Address: Devonshire House, Station Road, Brimington, Chesterfield, Derbys, S43 1JU
Trustees: Mr Nicholas John Hilton Crowther, Mr Ben Dexter, Simon Oxspring, Mr Christopher William Cox, Mrs Nan Patricia Hanlon, Philip Catton, Mr Colin Cave
Income: £1,317,162 [2017]; £1,411,222 [2016]; £1,557,591 [2015]; £1,455,012 [2014]; £1,515,563 [2013]

NMRN Operations
Registered: 6 Sep 2016 *Employees:* 236 *Volunteers:* 250
Tel: 023 9272 7582 *Website:* nmrn.org.uk
Activities: Education, training; arts, culture, heritage, science; environment, conservation, heritage; armed forces, emergency service efficiency
Address: National Museum of The Royal Navy, HM Naval Base, Portsmouth, PO1 3NH
Trustees: Professor John Craven, Mr Michael Bedingfield, Mrs Jane Dean, Mr Richard Hatfield, Professor Dominic Tweddle, Ms Carol Marlow
Income: £22,477,516 [2017]

NMRN Services
Registered: 4 Mar 2014 *Employees:* 142
Tel: 023 9272 7582 *Website:* nmrn.org.uk
Activities: Education, training; arts, culture, heritage, science; environment, conservation, heritage; armed forces, emergency service efficiency
Address: National Museum of The Royal Navy, HM Naval Base, Portsmouth, PO1 3NH
Trustees: Mr John Rawlinson, Professor Dominic Tweddle, Captain John Rees, Mrs Sarah Dennis
Income: £1,302,107 [2017]; £1,802,479 [2016]; £1,505,081 [2015]

NOCN
Registered: 10 Mar 2000 *Employees:* 34
Tel: 0114 227 0500 *Website:* nocn.org.uk
Activities: Education, training
Address: The Quadrant, Parkway Business Centre, 99 Parkway Avenue, Sheffield, S9 4WG
Trustees: Mr Seb Schmoller, Mr John Fuller, Miss Kay Dickinson, Gareth Jones, Ms Corrina Hembury, Ms Kam Penglin, Mr Leckraz Boyjoonauth, Ms Alison Lamplough, Mr Peter Wallwork, Mr Anthony Saunders, Mr Graham McPhail, Mr Michael John Mason
Income: £2,931,144 [2017]; £2,549,908 [2016]; £2,790,435 [2015]; £2,964,912 [2014]; £2,601,722 [2013]

NPT (UK) Limited
Registered: 13 Aug 2013 *Employees:* 2
Tel: 0800 133 7540 *Website:* npt-uk.org
Activities: General charitable purposes
Address: Suite 1510, Citypoint, 1 Ropemaker Street, London, EC2Y 9HT
Trustees: Mr Charles Gordon Lubar, Ms Eileen Heisman, Mr Iain Peter Younger, Mrs Ceris Mary Gardner, Claire Fiona Brown
Income: £19,656,798 [2017]; £7,322,478 [2016]; £5,534,142 [2015]; £448,424 [2014]

NUS Students' Union Charitable Services
Registered: 1 Feb 2011 *Volunteers:* 120
Website: nusconnect.org.uk
Activities: General charitable purposes; education, training; environment, conservation, heritage
Address: NUS HQ, Macadam House, 275 Gray's Inn Road, London, WC1X 8QB
Trustees: Ms Dianne Gwenllian Nelmes, Mr Tom Vaughan, Mr Aidan Grills, Ms Jacqueline Anne Clements
Income: £4,517,030 [2017]; £4,202,765 [2016]; £4,141,208 [2015]; £3,922,299 [2014]; £2,409,652 [2013]

NWL Jewish Day School
Registered: 17 Mar 2016 *Employees:* 10
Tel: 020 8459 3378
Activities: Education, training
Address: North West London Jewish Day, Primary School, 180 Willesden Lane, London, NW6 7PP
Trustees: Mr Graham Morris, Mr Michael Weinstein, Mr David Fishel, Mr Charles Nicholas Lossos, Ms Sheila Taylor, Mr Abraham David Landy, Mr Arnold Kosiner, Mr Dayan Ivan Binstock
Income: £3,096,412 [2017]

NYU in London
Registered: 25 Feb 2000 *Employees:* 34
Tel: 020 7907 3200 *Website:* nyu.edu
Activities: Education, training
Address: NYU in London, 6 Bedford Square, London, WC1B 3RA
Trustees: Thorkild Juncker, Dr Linda Mills, Caroline Guen
Income: £14,249,860 [2016]; £12,201,126 [2015]; £10,800,409 [2014]; £11,016,528 [2013]; £9,466,164 [2012]

Nacro
Registered: 28 Aug 1964 *Employees:* 749 *Volunteers:* 70
Tel: 020 7902 5423 *Website:* nacro.org.uk
Activities: Education, training; accommodation, housing; economic, community development, employment
Address: N A C R O, 46 Loman Street, London, SE1 0EH
Trustees: Mr Nigel Chapman, Mr Robert Booker, Mr Darren Hughes, Ms Sarah Nelson-Smith, Mrs Brenda Shiels, Mrs Helen Willis, Mr Dominic McGonigal, Andrew Billany, Mr Ron Crank, Mrs Lynn Emslie, Mrs Jenni Douglas-Todd
Income: £46,940,000 [2017]; £52,587,000 [2016]; £41,812,000 [2015]; £46,587,000 [2014]; £47,465,000 [2013]

Naima JPS
Registered: 11 Apr 1984 *Employees:* 55
Tel: 020 7328 2802 *Website:* naimajps.org.uk
Activities: General charitable purposes; education, training; religious activities; other charitable purposes
Address: Naima JPS, 21 Andover Place, London, NW6 5ED
Trustees: Mr Robert Yentob, Mr Julian Levy, Mr Isaac Levy, Mrs Veronica Shamoon, Mr Isaac Levy, Rabbi Dr Abraham Levy OBE, Mrs Jennica Arazi, Mrs Sabine Howard, Mr Isaac Daniel Corre
Income: £2,501,507 [2016]; £3,183,611 [2015]; £2,577,909 [2014]; £2,172,598 [2013]; £1,872,556 [2012]

The Naked Heart Foundation
Registered: 16 Jan 2008 *Employees:* 4 *Volunteers:* 7
Website: nakedheart.org
Activities: Recreation
Address: Naked Heart Foundation, Bloomsbury House, 26 Bloomsbury Street, London, WC1B 3QJ
Trustees: Ms Natalie Vodyanova, Mr Francois Chateau, Mr Jamey Hargreaves, Miss Lucy Yeomans
Income: £5,003,613 [2016]; £1,294,319 [2015]; £811,512 [2014]; £2,112,121 [2013]; £3,574,427 [2012]

Nanaksar Thath Isher Darbar (Guru Nanak Sikh College)
Registered: 14 Sep 1993 *Employees:* 5 *Volunteers:* 6
Tel: 020 8561 5678 *Website:* gurunanaksikhacademy.org.uk
Activities: General charitable purposes; education, training; prevention or relief of poverty; religious activities
Address: Guru Nanak Sikh Academy, Springfield Road, Hayes, Middlesex, UB4 0LT
Trustees: Mr Amarjit Singh, Mr Sukhdev Singh Nahal, Baba Amar Singh, Mr Gursharan Singh
Income: £1,396,005 [2017]; £788,659 [2016]; £1,024,238 [2015]; £858,725 [2014]; £2,145,475 [2013]

Narconon Trust
Registered: 23 Nov 2005
Tel: 01342 325765
Activities: Education, training
Address: Hodkin & Co, 42-44 Copthorne Road, Felbridge, East Grinstead, Surrey, RH19 2NS
Trustees: Mr Massimo Angius, Mrs Heather Ann Muir, Mr Richard Edward Wilkins
Income: £1,454,142 [2016]; £56,588 [2015]; £1,431,704 [2014]; £798,434 [2013]

The Rosemarie Nathanson Charitable Trust
Registered: 30 Dec 2008
Tel: 020 3023 8200
Activities: Education, training; advancement of health or saving of lives; prevention or relief of poverty
Address: 7th Floor, South Block, 55 Baker Street, London, W1U 8EW
Trustees: Mr Hilton Nathanson, Mr David Bearman, Mrs Louise Nathanson
Income: £1,688,874 [2016]; £593,811 [2015]; £85,923 [2014]; £355,239 [2013]; £191,870 [2012]

National Animal Welfare Trust
Registered: 8 Feb 2002 *Employees:* 130 *Volunteers:* 500
Tel: 020 8950 0177 *Website:* nawt.org.uk
Activities: Education, training; animals
Address: National Animal Welfare Trust, Tylers Way, Watford, Herts, WD25 8WT
Trustees: Miss Diana Margaret Brown, Mr John Richard Pearce, Mr James Moore, Mrs Debbie Matthews, Mrs Lynley Griffiths, Ms Laura Magee, Miss Susan Jane Francombe, Miss Claire Elizabeth James, Mr Harvey Carruthers
Income: £3,511,348 [2017]; £4,016,821 [2016]; £3,881,529 [2015]; £2,171,599 [2014]; £2,414,025 [2013]

National Aquarium Limited
Registered: 11 Jul 2003
Tel: 01752 275207 *Website:* national-aquarium.co.uk
Activities: General charitable purposes; education, training; animals; environment, conservation, heritage
Address: National Marine Aquarium, Rope Walk, Plymouth, PL4 0LF
Trustees: Mr Paul Benjamin Cox, Dr Chapman, Mr R Maslin, Martin Attrill, Mr Timothy Paul Cresswell, Dr M White
Income: £1,474,963 [2017]; £1,505,278 [2016]; £1,508,958 [2015]; £1,519,771 [2014]; £1,466,484 [2013]

The National Army Museum
Registered: 10 Nov 1964 *Employees:* 67 *Volunteers:* 95
Tel: 020 7881 2401 *Website:* nam.ac.uk
Activities: Arts, culture, heritage, science; environment, conservation, heritage
Address: National Army Museum, Royal Hospital Road, Chelsea, London, SW3 4HT
Trustees: Mr Patrick Aylmer, The Rt Hon The Lord Archibald Gavin Hamilton PC, Mr Patrick Bradley, General Sir Alexander Richard David Shirreff KCB CBE, Mr Douglas Vernon Erskine Crum CBE, Mr William Alexander Wells, Ms Caroline Wyatt, Mr Keith Baldwin, Mrs Deborah Younger, Professor William Philpott, Lieutenant General Sir Barney William Benjamin Spunner KCB CBE, Miss Jessica Spungin
Income: £14,487,000 [2017]; £12,180,000 [2016]; £13,727,805 [2015]; £7,497,904 [2014]; £7,315,713 [2013]

National Art Collections Fund
Registered: 16 Oct 1962 *Employees:* 52 *Volunteers:* 550
Tel: 020 7225 4833 *Website:* artfund.org
Activities: Arts, culture, heritage, science
Address: 2 Granary Square, King's Cross, London, N1C 4BH
Trustees: Professor Antony Griffiths, Mr Michael Wilson, Mr James Lingwood, Chris Smith, Mrs Caroline Butler, Dame Liz Forgan, Ms Monisha Shah, Axel Ruger, Isaac Julien, Mr Jeremy Palmer, Mr Richard Calvocoressi CBE, Mrs Philippa Glanville OBE, Prof Chris Gosden, Professor Lisa Tickner, Mr Alastair Laing, Professor Richard Deacon, Professor Marcia Pointon
Income: £15,192,000 [2016]; £14,802,000 [2015]; £24,111,000 [2014]; £10,558,000 [2013]; £15,070,000 [2012]

The National Association for Special Educational Needs (Nasen)
Registered: 20 Dec 1991 *Employees:* 11 *Volunteers:* 100
Tel: 01827 311500 *Website:* nasen.org.uk
Activities: Education, training; disability
Address: Nasen, Unit 4-5, Amber Business Village, Amber Close, Tamworth, Staffs, B77 4RP
Trustees: Mr Christopher Paul Marshall, Mr John Alexander Griffiths, Mr Trevor Rodney Daniels, Ms Elaine Mary Colquhoun, Mrs Allison Clare Goddard, Mrs Bridget Bolwell, Mr Mark Jonathan Blois, Mr Stephen Bajdala-Brown, Mr David Ryan, Mrs Carolyn Eyre, Mr Richard Edwin Owen Carpenter, Dr Susan Elizabeth Soan, Mrs Helen Cooper
Income: £1,079,746 [2016]; £1,151,310 [2015]; £1,387,035 [2014]; £1,210,157 [2013]; £1,025,663 [2012]

National Association of Almshouses
Registered: 18 Sep 2003 *Employees:* 7 *Volunteers:* 4
Tel: 01344 452922 *Website:* almshouses.org
Activities: The prevention or relief of poverty; accommodation, housing
Address: Billingbear Lodge, Maidenhead Road, Wokingham, Berks, RG40 5RU
Trustees: John Broughton, Mr Alan Martin FCIH, Mr Richard Anthony Knipe LLB, Mrs Ellen Patricia Scouller, Mrs Elizabeth Fathi, Mr Richard Waite, Mr Rob Douglas, Mr Blair Gulland, Mr David James Dunbar MBE, Mr Robin Derek William Hartley Russell, Mrs Margaret Stewart, Dr Meryl Aldridge, Mr Adam Sedgwick, Mr Paul Stephen Mullis
Income: £1,378,881 [2017]; £786,310 [2016]; £782,608 [2015]; £759,062 [2014]; £826,335 [2013]

The National Association of Citizens Advice Bureaux
Registered: 21 Jan 1980 *Employees:* 729 *Volunteers:* 23,000
Tel: 0300 023 1231 *Website:* citizensadvice.org.uk
Activities: General charitable purposes; education, training; advancement of health or saving of lives; prevention or relief of poverty
Address: 200 Aldersgate Street, London, EC1A 4HD
Trustees: Mrs Barbara Shaw, Mr Mark Haysom, Mr John Woodman, Ms Fran Keen, Sir David Varney, Mr Andrew Stephenson, Mr Will Cavendish, Mrs Rolande Anderson, Mr Warren Buckley, Ms Lucy Inmonger, Mr Ashok Vaswani
Income: £99,110,000 [2017]; £108,610,000 [2016]; £88,242,000 [2015]; £77,217,000 [2014]; £77,553,000 [2013]

The National Association of Decorative and Fine Arts Societies
Registered: 11 Dec 2001 *Employees:* 18 *Volunteers:* 10,000
Tel: 020 7430 0730 *Website:* theartssociety.org
Activities: Education, training; arts, culture, heritage, science; environment, conservation, heritage
Address: Nadfas House, 8 Guilford Street, London, WC1N 1DA
Trustees: Mr Roger Duckworth, Mrs Hilary Alcock, Mrs Jacqueline Varley, Mrs Jillie Moss, Mr Ben Moorhead, Ms Caroline Houlden, Mrs Julia Charlton-Weedy, Mrs Alison Galvin-Wright, Mrs Julie Goldsmith, Mr Peter Kirrage, Mr John Parkinson, Ms Jennifer Harding-Edgar
Income: £2,090,842 [2016]; £2,350,880 [2015]; £2,093,114 [2014]; £2,132,271 [2013]; £1,878,558 [2012]

The National Autistic Society
Registered: 15 Aug 1975 *Employees:* 3,452 *Volunteers:* 2,000
Website: autism.org.uk
Activities: Education, training; disability; accommodation, housing
Address: National Autistic Society, 393-395 City Road, London, EC1V 1NG
Trustees: Mrs Pamela Reitemeier, Mr Krishnaswamy Murali, Ms Felicity Chadwick-Histed, Mr David Harbott, Professor Sylvia Johnson, Mr Stewart Rapley, Dr David Alan Reeves, Ms Roberta Doyle, Ms Amanda Forshaw, Dr Carol Homden, Dr Sophie Castell, Mr Stephen Davies, Ms Judy Berkowicz, Mr Michael Stanton, Ms Elisa Maria Rita Menardo
Income: £97,290,000 [2017]; £98,657,000 [2016]; £95,755,000 [2015]; £98,317,000 [2014]; £92,257,000 [2013]

The National Botanic Garden of Wales
Registered: 12 Apr 1994 *Employees:* 68 *Volunteers:* 250
Tel: 01558 667102 *Website:* gardenofwales.org.uk
Activities: Education, training; arts, culture, heritage, science; environment, conservation, heritage
Address: Middleton Hall, Llanarthne, Carmarthenshire, SA32 8HG
Trustees: Heather Stevens, Sir Roger Jones, Mr Timothy William Jones, Mrs Elisabeth Hannah Whittle, Mr Steffan Rhys Williams, Dr Michael Ian Woods, Mr Rhodri Glyn-Thomas, Mr Gary Davies, Mrs Julie James, Mr Robert Hylton Jolliffe, Mr Derek Anthony Howell, Councillor David Michael Jenkins, Mr Patrick O'Reilly, Ms Eluned Parrott, Dr Paul Philip Smith
Income: £2,898,000 [2017]; £3,309,000 [2016]; £3,488,000 [2015]; £3,037,000 [2014]; £3,063,000 [2013]

National Cancer Research Institute
Registered: 23 Feb 2015 *Employees:* 28 *Volunteers:* 60
Tel: 020 3469 8466 *Website:* ncri.org.uk
Activities: The advancement of health or saving of lives
Address: NCRI Secretariat, Angel Building, 407 St John Street, London, EC1V 4AD
Trustees: Baroness Delyth Morgan, Mr Alan Chant, Ms Mary Basterfield, Mrs Catherine Scivier, Helen Campbell, Mr Angus McNair
Income: £4,005,764 [2017]

National Centre for Circus Arts
Registered: 11 Feb 1991 *Employees:* 110
Tel: 020 7613 8233 *Website:* nationalcircus.org.uk
Activities: Education, training; arts, culture, heritage, science
Address: The Circus Space, Coronet Street, London, N1 6HD
Trustees: Mr Paul Steggall, Ms Lesley Ann Strachan, Mr David Chinn, Mr Bil Morris, Mr Tarun Nagpal, Mr Thomas Nowacki, Ms Kathryn Jane Cavelle, Mr Matthew Cooper, Ms Rebecca Sinclair, Ms Sue James, Mr Iain Stuart Martin, Mr Craig Calvert, Mr Matthew Lloyd, Ms Kate Anderson, Ms Kirsten Becker-Valero, Ms Fiona Ann Dent, Ms Jane Louise Crowther, Mr Mark Clarke, Ms Elizabeth Anne Lynch
Income: £2,526,620 [2017]; £2,801,972 [2016]; £2,789,210 [2015]; £2,801,644 [2014]; £2,631,349 [2013]

National Centre for Social Research
Registered: 26 Apr 2002 *Employees:* 258
Website: natcen.ac.uk
Activities: Education, training
Address: 35 Northampton Square, London, EC1V 0AX
Trustees: Professor Sir Robert George Burgess, Alan Botterill, Mrs Barbara Noble, Mr James Thickett, Miss Maureen Duffy, Professor Sue Heath, Mr Peter Richard David Havelock, Ms Jude England, Mr Stephen West, Dame Jilian Norma Matheson, Dr Walter James Cormack
Income: £33,108,712 [2017]; £30,015,981 [2016]; £32,948,498 [2015]; £34,171,468 [2014]; £41,565,649 [2013]

The National Centre for Young People with Epilepsy Charitable Trust
Registered: 24 Jul 1963 *Employees:* 630
Website: youngepilepsy.org.uk
Activities: Education, training; advancement of health or saving of lives; disability
Address: Young Epilepsy, St Piers Lane, Lingfield, Surrey, RH7 6PW
Trustees: Professor Helen Cross, Mr Nigel Kennedy, Ms Vivienne Dews, Mr Murray Orr, Ms Jane Ramsey, Mr John Stebbings, The National Centre For Young People With Epilepsy, Mr Ben Osborn, Dr Anita Devlin, Dr Julia Coop, Mr Keith Cameron, Mrs Lesley Steeds, Mr Steve Whittingham
Income: £25,510,000 [2017]; £27,692,000 [2016]; £29,199,000 [2015]; £27,501,000 [2014]; £27,372,000 [2013]

The National Childbirth Trust
Registered: 24 Apr 1989 *Employees:* 259 *Volunteers:* 5,689
Tel: 020 8752 2334 *Website:* nct.org.uk
Activities: Education, training; advancement of health or saving of lives
Address: 30 Euston Square, London, NW1 2FB
Trustees: Ms Marsha Daniel, Mr Richard Smothers, Ms Carey Ruth Oppenheim, Ms Stephanie Maurel, Mrs Elaine Sharon Lambe, Ms Caroline Flint, Mrs Jessica Figueras, Mr David James Shanks, Mrs Seana Catherine Talbot, Mrs Sarah Louise Brown
Income: £16,723,000 [2017]; £17,331,000 [2016]; £17,312,000 [2015]; £17,557,000 [2014]; £16,651,000 [2013]

National Children's Bureau
Registered: 12 Jun 1969 *Employees:* 98
Tel: 020 7843 6000 *Website:* ncb.org.uk
Activities: Education, training; advancement of health or saving of lives; disability; economic, community development, employment
Address: WeWork London Fields, 115 Mare Street, London, E8 4RU
Trustees: Mr Karl Podmore, Mr Kenneth Meeson, Mrs Elaine Simpson, Ms Anita Diane Tiessen, Ms Page Nyame-Satterthwaite, Ms Kiri Jolliffe, Dr Kiki Syrad, Miss Yvonne Campbell, Mr Terrence Collis, Ms Clare Laxton, Mr Edward Hannan, Ms Thivya Jeyashanker, Ms Elizabeth Railton, Mr Fergal Patrick McFerran, Mr Brendan Whittle
Income: £19,354,000 [2017]; £20,702,000 [2016]; £22,173,000 [2015]; £10,489,000 [2014]; £11,520,000 [2013]

National Children's Centre
Registered: 4 Nov 1983 *Employees:* 88 *Volunteers:* 268
Tel: 01484 519988 *Website:* yorkshirechildrenscentre.org.uk
Activities: General charitable purposes; education, training; advancement of health or saving of lives; prevention or relief of poverty; environment, conservation, heritage; economic, community development, employment; other charitable purposes
Address: National Childrens Centre, Brian Jackson House, 2 New North Parade, Huddersfield, W Yorks, HD1 5JP
Trustees: Dr Michael Sills, Mr Barry John Sheerman MP, Mrs Emma Louise Reed, Gillian Mary Peel Goodswen, Mr Mark Wild, Mrs Alda Flowers, Mr Philip Richard Longworth, Mr Roger Bryant, Mr Kevin Newson, Mrs Claire Sedgwick
Income: £2,105,874 [2017]; £1,957,614 [2016]; £1,815,514 [2015]; £1,869,656 [2014]; £1,730,156 [2013]

National Children's Orchestras of Great Britain
Registered: 9 Mar 1990 *Employees:* 11 *Volunteers:* 20
Tel: 01934 418855 *Website:* nco.org.uk
Activities: Education, training; arts, culture, heritage, science
Address: National Childrens Orchestra of Great Britain, 57 Buckingham Road, Weston-Super-Mare, Avon, BS24 9BG
Trustees: Mr Paul Charles Jackson, Charles Bligh, Clare Thompson, Mr Howard John Gough, Mrs Janet Baker, Mr Peter Harry Geoffrey Stark, Andrew Kemble, Howard Williams, Mr Edmond Charles Paul Fivet
Income: £1,423,254 [2016]; £1,608,067 [2015]; £1,384,963 [2014]; £1,443,791 [2013]; £1,242,966 [2012]

The National Churches Trust
Registered: 27 Jun 2007 *Employees:* 14 *Volunteers:* 2
Tel: 020 7227 1935 *Website:* nationalchurchestrust.org
Activities: Religious activities; environment, conservation, heritage
Address: 7 Tufton Street, London, SW1P 3QB
Trustees: Mr Alastair James Hunter, Dr Julie Patricia Banham, Mr John Richard Drew, Mr Luke March, Dr Stephen Sklaroff, Mr Richard Joseph Carr-Archer, Rev Lucy Winkett, Miss Jennifer Page, Sir Paul John James Britton, Mr Nicholas Warns
Income: £1,589,700 [2016]; £2,532,326 [2015]; £1,409,584 [2014]; £1,664,869 [2013]; £2,146,529 [2012]

The National Coaching Foundation
Registered: 6 Feb 1987 *Employees:* 133
Website: ukcoaching.org
Activities: Education, training; amateur sport; recreation
Address: Chelsea Close, off Amberley Way, Leeds, LS12 4HP
Trustees: Ms Gillian C Wilmot, Elizabeth Jane Broadbent, Mr Richard Thomas James Wheater, Mr Colin Eveold Rattigan, Mr Alastair Gilmartin Smith, Martha Rolle, Dr Rosemary Anne Leonard, Mr Wayne Anthony Allison
Income: £9,621,838 [2017]; £8,890,089 [2016]; £9,327,006 [2015]; £9,524,725 [2014]; £10,314,552 [2013]

National Coal Mining Museum for England Trust Ltd
Registered: 10 Apr 1986 *Employees:* 98 *Volunteers:* 35
Tel: 01924 848806 *Website:* ncm.org.uk
Activities: Education, training; arts, culture, heritage, science; environment, conservation, heritage
Address: National Coal Mining Museum for England, Caphouse Colliery, New Road, Overton, Hants, WF4 4RH
Trustees: Mr Nigel Pearce, Sir John Harman, Baroness Winifred Ann Taylor, Councillor Denise Jeffery, Mr John Philip Whyatt, The Rt Hon Kevin Barron MP, Mrs Julie Ann Kenny CBE DL, Mr Patrick Matthew Carragher MBE, Mr Trevor Shaw
Income: £3,293,521 [2017]; £3,523,355 [2016]; £3,454,541 [2015]; £3,516,629 [2014]; £3,822,445 [2013]

National Coastwatch Institution
Registered: 16 Jan 2015 *Volunteers:* 2,280
Tel: 07899 993500 *Website:* nci.org.uk
Activities: The advancement of health or saving of lives
Address: 1 Retyn Barns, Summercourt, Newquay, Cornwall, TR8 5DE
Trustees: David Littlemore, Blake Holt, Ian Whalley, Mr Mike Byrne, Tim Colquhoun, Lesley Suddes, Steve Ashby, Mr Jonathan Rothwell
Income: £1,577,175 [2016]

National College for Digital Skills
Registered: 29 Aug 2014 *Employees:* 6
Tel: 020 3105 0125 *Website:* adacollege.org.uk
Activities: Education, training
Address: Unit 2 Fountayne Business Centre, Broad Lane, London, N15 4AG
Trustees: Mr Mark Smith, Mr Tom Ilube, Mr Nicholas Wilcock, Mr Tom Fogden
Income: £5,925,505 [2017]; £1,578,679 [2016]; £715,000 [2015]

The National Communities Resource Centre Limited
Registered: 12 Nov 1991 *Employees:* 41 *Volunteers:* 4
Tel: 01244 300246 *Website:* traffordhall.com
Activities: Education, training
Address: Trafford Hall, Ince Lane, Wimbolds Trafford, Chester, CH2 4JP
Trustees: Mr Michael Arthur Hamilton, Professor Anne Power, Lord Richard George Rogers, Mrs Margaret Calista Jarret, Geoff Smith, Ms Mary Josephine White, Mr Richard John McCarthy, Miss Emily Clare Potter
Income: £1,080,781 [2017]; £948,619 [2016]; £1,000,784 [2015]; £831,442 [2014]; £1,240,687 [2013]

National Confidential Enquiry Into Patient Outcome and Death
Registered: 20 May 1999 *Employees:* 15
Tel: 020 7251 9060 *Website:* ncepod.org.uk
Activities: Education, training; advancement of health or saving of lives
Address: Ground Floor, Abbey House, 74-76 St John Street, London, EC1M 4DZ
Trustees: Professor Lesley Regan, Mrs Janice Barber, Professor Timothy James Hendra, Mr Ian Martin, David G Mason
Income: £1,628,715 [2017]; £1,719,440 [2016]; £1,252,070 [2015]; £1,108,703 [2014]; £969,607 [2013]

The National Council for Palliative Care
Registered: 5 Nov 1991 *Employees:* 16
Tel: 020 7697 1520 *Website:* hospiceuk.org
Activities: General charitable purposes; education, training; advancement of health or saving of lives; disability
Address: 4th Floor, Hospice House, 34-44 Britannia Street, London, WC1X 9JG
Trustees: Mr Gary Francis Rycroft, Mr John Bonser, Baroness Ilora Finlay, Mrs Jacqueline Ann Davis, Mr Michael John Hobday, Mr Arthur Mark Ruston Smith
Income: £1,444,230 [2017]; £1,667,818 [2016]; £1,401,668 [2015]; £1,390,408 [2014]; £1,613,426 [2013]

National Council for The Training of Journalists
Registered: 30 Sep 1993 *Employees:* 11 *Volunteers:* 249
Tel: 01799 544014 *Website:* nctj.com
Activities: Education, training
Address: New Granary, Station Road, Newport, Saffron Walden, Essex, CB11 3PL
Trustees: Mr Kim Thomas Fletcher, Ms Alison Jane Moore, Dr Colm Murphy, Mr Abu-Bakarr Bundu-Kamara, Mr Andrew Cairns, Mr Gavin Piers Allen, Mr Martin Wright, Mr Donald Martin, John Ryley, Mrs Laura Adams, Miss Rosalind Carol McKenzie, Mr Andrew Philip Martin, Mr Jeremy Clifford
Income: £1,125,239 [2017]; £1,134,017 [2016]; £1,161,243 [2015]; £1,025,624 [2014]; £1,022,545 [2013]

The National Council for Voluntary Organisations
Registered: 1 Jan 1964 *Employees:* 95
Tel: 020 7520 2538 *Website:* ncvo.org.uk
Activities: General charitable purposes
Address: National Council for Voluntary Organisations, Society Building, 8 Regents Wharf, All Saints Street, London, N1 9RL
Trustees: Ms Julie Bentley, Ms Vanessa Griffiths, Richard Leaman CB OBE, Mr Bruce Gordon, Ms Chris Freed, Mr Andy Cook, Mr Peter Kellner, Ms Jenny Field, Mr Christopher Wade, Sally Young, Ms Anne Heal
Income: £8,210,000 [2017]; £9,334,000 [2016]; £10,365,000 [2015]; £9,588,000 [2014]; £8,939,000 [2013]

National Council of Young Men's Christian Associations (Incorporated)
Registered: 24 Sep 1962 *Employees:* 308 *Volunteers:* 816
Tel: 01823 325860 *Website:* ymca.org.uk
Activities: Education, training; accommodation, housing; religious activities; other charitable purposes
Address: Lisieux Way, Taunton, Somerset, TA1 2LB
Trustees: Mr Graham Bratby, Mr Peter Charles Edward Calderbank, Mr Martin Houghton-Brown Chairperson, Mr Ian North, Mr Duncan George Ingram, Mr Paul Laffey, Ms Maxine Joan Green, Mr Reginald William Bailey, Ms Emma White, Mr Timothy James Fallon
Income: £19,888,000 [2017]; £24,209,000 [2016]; £21,579,000 [2015]; £24,132,000 [2014]; £22,641,000 [2013]

National Dance Company Wales
Registered: 8 Dec 1982 *Employees:* 27 *Volunteers:* 28
Tel: 029 2063 5606 *Website:* ndcwales.co.uk
Activities: Arts, culture, heritage, science
Address: Dance House, Wales Millennium Centre, Pierhead Street, Cardiff, CF10 4PH
Trustees: Tessa Shellens, Andrew Davies, Assis Carreiro, Gareth Powell, Helen Protheroe, Ms Julie Elizabeth Hobday, Emma Evans, Gary Thomas
Income: £1,042,357 [2017]; £982,380 [2016]; £1,001,359 [2015]; £1,044,607 [2014]; £1,158,418 [2013]

National Day Nurseries Association
Registered: 18 Nov 1999 *Employees:* 59 *Volunteers:* 75
Tel: 01484 407070 *Website:* ndna.org.uk
Activities: Education, training; economic, community development, employment
Address: National Day Nursery Association, Unit 6, Longbow Close, Bradley, Huddersfield, W Yorks, HD2 1GQ
Trustees: Mrs Sarah Carr, Mrs Karen Veitch, Mrs Penelope Vaughan-Pipe, Mr Christopher Robert Gray, Mrs Mary Ann Tee, Mrs Helen Claire Gration, Mr David Smyllie, Ms Sally Mayer, Ms Tina Jones, Ms Jane Elizabeth Haywood, Mrs Linda Maurice, Mrs Hazel Moody, Ms Courteney Ann Donaldson, Mr David Ambrose Poulsom, Mrs Elizabeth Ann McEwan, Miss Tracey Anne Storey
Income: £3,122,076 [2017]; £2,742,331 [2016]; £3,269,029 [2015]; £2,632,993 [2014]; £2,440,985 [2013]

The National Deaf Children's Society
Registered: 21 Jan 1993 *Employees:* 229 *Volunteers:* 700
Tel: 020 7014 1159 *Website:* ndcs.org.uk
Activities: Disability
Address: National Deaf Children's Society, Castle House, 37-45 Paul Street, London, EC2A 4LS
Trustees: Ms Lisa Jane Capper, Ms Sheila McKenzie, Mr Timothy Polack, Ms Jan Rutherford, Ms Jennie Rayson, Mr Gerard Featherstone, Jane Hill, Mrs Helen Selwood, Mrs Suzanne Rebecca Beese, Mr Dominic James Holton
Income: £22,525,000 [2017]; £23,516,000 [2016]; £22,762,000 [2015]; £21,472,000 [2014]; £22,069,233 [2013]

National Energy Action
Registered: 8 Nov 1984 *Employees:* 115
Tel: 0191 261 5677 *Website:* nea.org.uk
Activities: Education, training; prevention or relief of poverty; environment, conservation, heritage; economic, community development, employment
Address: National Energy Action, West One, Forth Banks, Newcastle upon Tyne, NE1 3PA
Trustees: Mrs Tessa Sayers, Mr James Kirby ACMA CGMA, Mr Derek Arthur Lickorish MBE, Professor Christopher Patrick Underwood, Mr Philip John Hudson, Mrs Helen Christine McLeod, Norrie Kerr, Mrs Alison Cole, Syed Ahmed, Mr Andrew Mavor Brown, Mr Noel Francis Rice, Mrs Jacqueline Gardner
Income: £27,853,956 [2017]; £13,163,130 [2016]; £10,061,441 [2015]; £10,779,255 [2014]; £19,973,279 [2013]

The National Energy Foundation
Registered: 23 Mar 1988 *Employees:* 26 *Volunteers:* 5
Tel: 01908 354543 *Website:* nef.org.uk
Activities: Education, training; prevention or relief of poverty; environment, conservation, heritage; economic, community development, employment
Address: The National Energy Foundation, Davy Avenue, Knowlhill, Milton Keynes, Bucks, MK5 8NG
Trustees: Stewart Fergusson, Ms Liz Reason, Mr Andrew Wordsworth, Matthew Rhodes, Chris Hall, Mr John Doggart, Liz Male, Peter Rickaby
Income: £1,499,243 [2017]; £1,379,008 [2016]; £1,124,372 [2015]; £958,232 [2014]; £1,340,431 [2013]

The National Examination Board in Occupational Safety and Health
Registered: 9 Apr 1992 *Employees:* 95
Tel: 0116 263 4727 *Website:* nebosh.org.uk
Activities: Education, training; advancement of health or saving of lives; environment, conservation, heritage; economic, community development, employment
Address: Nebosh, 5 Dominus Way, Meridian Business Park, Leicester, LE19 1QW
Trustees: Sir Bill Callaghan, Mr Leslie Philpott, Mrs Emma Roach, Mr David Morgan, Brenig Moore, Dr William Nixon, Mr Derrick Allen Farthing, Ms Antonina Sulkhova, Mr Darren Brunton, Professor Mariane Cavalli
Income: £8,630,211 [2017]; £9,097,691 [2016]; £9,055,658 [2015]; £8,555,930 [2014]; £7,462,466 [2013]

National Examining Board for Dental Nurses
Registered: 29 Nov 2005 *Employees:* 14
Tel: 01772 439993 *Website:* nebdn.org
Activities: Education, training
Address: First Floor, Quayside Court, Chain Caul Way, Ashton on Ribble, Preston, Lancs, PR2 2ZP
Trustees: Ms Lindsay Mitchell, Mr Philip Bunnell, Mrs Sarah Young, Thomas MacGregor, Dr Gill Jones, Mr James Ashworth-Holland, Mrs Marie Parker, Mrs Julia Frew, Professor Barry Mitchell, Julie Edmonds, Mrs Rebecca Cox
Income: £1,420,500 [2017]; £1,148,245 [2016]; £1,051,069 [2015]; £1,054,937 [2014]; £1,301,344 [2013]

The National Federation of Women's Institutes of England, Wales, Jersey, Guernsey and The Isle of Man
Registered: 27 Jul 1990 *Employees:* 89 *Volunteers:* 112
Tel: 020 7371 9300 *Website:* thewi.org.uk
Activities: Education, training; advancement of health or saving of lives; environment, conservation, heritage; economic, community development, employment
Address: N F W I, 104 New Kings Road, London, SW6 4LY
Trustees: Mrs Lydia Mair Stephens, Mrs Lynne Stubbings, Mrs Sarah Ann Kingman, Mrs Julia Mary Roberts, Mrs Mary Linda Clarke, Mrs Susan Wilson, Mrs Yvonne Eunice Price, Mrs Ann Margaret Jones, Miss Patricia Tulip, Mrs Catriona Elizabeth Adams, Mrs Jeryl Stone, Mrs Amanda Willday, Mrs Hilary Ruth Haworth
Income: £7,626,663 [2017]; £7,177,128 [2016]; £6,836,792 [2015]; £6,551,648 [2014]; £7,443,815 [2013]

The National Film and Television School
Registered: 17 Jul 1970 *Employees:* 102 *Volunteers:* 250
Tel: 01497 731330 *Website:* nfts.co.uk
Activities: Education, training; arts, culture, heritage, science
Address: National Film & Television School, Station Road, Beaconsfield, Bucks, HP9 1LG
Trustees: Patrick McKenna, Mr Steve William Mertz, Mr Thomas Matthew Betts, Mrs Naomi Climer, Mr Philip Robert Harrison, Mr Oliver Richard Hyatt MBE, Mr Balraj Samra, Miss Paidamoyo Mutonono, Mr Laurent Samama, Mr Andrew MacDonald, Mr Stephen David Louis, Mr Patrick Fuller, Mr Geoffrey Crossick, Mrs Susan Moffat, Mr Neil Andrew Forster, Mr Ian Lewis, Mr Tim Kyte, Mr Raja Adil Rehman, Miss Beth Willis
Income: £15,235,374 [2017]; £12,552,930 [2016]; £10,630,639 [2015]; £6,400,803 [2014]; £10,184,939 [2013]

The National Football Museum
Registered: 17 Nov 1995 *Employees:* 63 *Volunteers:* 83
Tel: 0161 870 9275 *Website:* nationalfootballmuseum.com
Activities: Education, training; arts, culture, heritage, science; amateur sport; environment, conservation, heritage
Address: Urbis, Cathedral Gardens, Manchester, M4 3BG
Trustees: Fayyaz Ahmed Ali, Ms Moira Stevenson, Mr Simon Barker, Mr Ian Penrose, Mr Luthfur Rahman, Mr Paul Mainds, Mr John Alan Farquharson, Mr Clive Memmott, Mrs Madeleine Joy Digby, Mr Steven Broomhead, Mr Nick Paske, Ms Sara Todd
Income: £3,297,129 [2017]; £3,256,197 [2016]; £3,275,578 [2015]; £3,274,840 [2014]; £2,678,531 [2013]

The National Forest Charitable Trust
Registered: 9 Feb 1999 *Employees:* 2
Tel: 01283 229494 *Website:* nationalforestcharitabletrust.co.uk
Activities: Education, training; environment, conservation, heritage; economic, community development, employment; recreation
Address: The Gatehouse, Bath Yard, Moira, Swadlincote, Derbys, DE12 6BA
Trustees: Mr Michael Ballantyne, Mr S H Woolfe, Mr Colin Jenkins, Peter Osbourne, Mr Christopher James Newton Frostwick, Mr Martin John Devereux Traynor, Dale Mortimer, Graham Smith, Andrew Bridge, Kathryn Preece, Joanne Guyl, Mr Thomas Spaul
Income: £1,396,681 [2016]; £1,411,657 [2015]; £1,354,919 [2014]; £1,080,078 [2013]; £1,027,013 [2012]

The National Forest Company
Registered: 15 Apr 2016 *Employees:* 23 *Volunteers:* 29
Tel: 01283 551211 *Website:* nationalforest.org
Activities: General charitable purposes; education, training; advancement of health or saving of lives; environment, conservation, heritage; economic, community development, employment; human rights, religious or racial harmony, equality or diversity; recreation
Address: The National Forest Co, Enterprise Glade, Bath Yard, Moira, Swadlincote, Derbys, DE12 6BA
Trustees: Dr Anthony John Ballance, Mr Arvind Michael Kapur, Sir William Ralph Worsley, Mrs Alison Blanche Field, Mr John Neil Everitt, Mr Christopher Peter Holmes, Mr Jack Richard Buckner, Mr Patrick David Harrop
Income: £3,109,468 [2017]

The National Foundation for Educational Research in England and Wales
Registered: 3 Nov 1965 *Employees:* 476
Tel: 01753 637168 *Website:* nfer.ac.uk
Activities: General charitable purposes; education, training
Address: National Foundation for Educational, The Mere, Upton Park, Slough, SL1 2DQ
Trustees: Mr Ian Bauckham, Ms Lorna Cocking, Mrs Susan Douglas, Mr Conor Ryan, Mr Nick Hillman, Mr Neil Hollister, Mr Melvyn Keen, Professor Michael Day, Mr Samuel MacDonald, Ms Hema Ghantiwala
Income: £17,753,000 [2017]; £15,498,000 [2016]; £11,888,000 [2015]; £11,309,000 [2014]; £11,160,000 [2013]

The National Foundation for Youth Music
Registered: 9 Apr 1999 *Employees:* 19
Website: youthmusic.org.uk
Activities: Education, training; arts, culture, heritage, science; amateur sport
Address: Youth Music, Suites 3-5 Swan Court, 9 Tanner Street, London, SE1 3LE
Trustees: Mr Richard Peel, Mr Timothy Berg, Mr Ademola Olutayo Adeluwoye, Mr Peter Low, Ms Rachel Nelken, Mr Clive Grant, Mr Rafi Eytan Gokay, Chris Price, Mrs Rachel Clare Lindley, Ms Yolanda Brown
Income: £10,253,082 [2017]; £10,196,103 [2016]; £10,561,437 [2015]; £9,973,009 [2014]; £10,199,518 [2013]

The National Fund
Registered: 26 May 1995
Tel: 01606 313280
Activities: General charitable purposes; economic, community development, employment
Address: Zedra Fiduciary Services (UK) Ltd, Osborne Court, Gadbrook Park, Rudheath, Northwich, Cheshire, CW9 7UE
Trustees: Zedra Fiduciary Services (UK) Limited
Income: £7,369,726 [2017]; £4,702,580 [2016]; £6,269,178 [2015]; £4,628,976 [2014]; £7,094,404 [2013]

The National Gallery Trust
Registered: 21 Jun 1988 *Employees:* 86
Tel: 020 7747 2801
Activities: Arts, culture, heritage, science
Address: The National Gallery, Trafalgar Square, London, WC2N 5DN
Trustees: Dr David Landau, The Hon Hannah Mary Rothschild, Kate Trevelyan, Mr Lance Batchelor, Mr Michael Anthony Cowdy, Lady Monck, Lady Stevenson DL, Mr Nicholas Ritblat
Income: £14,309,591 [2017]; £14,570,071 [2016]; £17,771,686 [2015]; £15,805,819 [2014]; £16,347,681 [2013]

The National Garden Scheme
Registered: 9 Jan 2006 *Employees:* 11 *Volunteers:* 370
Tel: 01483 211535 *Website:* ngs.org.uk
Activities: General charitable purposes
Address: The National Garden Scheme, 1 Courtyard Cottage, Hatchlands, East Clandon, Guildford, Surrey, GU4 7RT
Trustees: Mr Martin McMillan, Mrs Miranda Allhusen, Mrs Susan Phipps, Patrick Ramsay, Mr Colin Olle, Susan Copeland, Andrew Ratcliffe, Mrs Heather Skinner, Mrs Rosamund Davies, Mr Peter Clay, Mark Porter, Richard Thompson, Rupert Tyler
Income: £4,228,340 [2016]; £3,888,661 [2015]; £4,023,655 [2014]; £3,531,545 [2013]; £3,326,968 [2012]

National Governance Association
Registered: 1 Jul 1998 *Employees:* 25
Tel: 0121 237 3780 *Website:* nga.org.uk
Activities: Education, training
Address: National Governance Association, 36 Great Charles Street Queensway, Birmingham, B3 3JY
Trustees: Duncan Haworth, Mrs Margaret Mary Bull, Mrs Nicolette Joan Lamont, Dave Harries, Ms Katie Paxton-Doggett, Mr Gordon McDonald Anderson, Mr Mark Steven White, Mr Nigel Brent Fitzpatrick, Mr Ian Courtney, Mr Ian John Preston
Income: £1,695,118 [2017]; £1,142,324 [2016]; £999,149 [2015]; £760,431 [2014]; £531,819 [2013]

National Grocers Benevolent Fund
Registered: 10 Feb 2003 *Employees:* 23 *Volunteers:* 347
Tel: 01252 875925 *Website:* groceryaid.org.uk
Activities: General charitable purposes; education, training; prevention or relief of poverty
Address: Unit 2 Lakeside Business Park, Swan Lane, Sandhurst, Berks, GU47 9DN
Trustees: Mr Nigel Frederick Matthews OBE, Mr Bart Dalla Mura, Mr John Henry Black, Mr Mark Paul Smith, Mr Simon John Twigger, Ms Helen Mary Tucker, Mrs Lorraine Denise Hendle, Mr Zameer Mohammed Choudrey CBE, Mr David Charles Hudson, Mr Ruston Arthur Mark Smith, Mr John Munro Gordon, Mr Jason Charles Uttley, Mr Mark Richard Williamson, Mr David Clifford Wheeler
Income: £6,101,947 [2017]; £6,616,329 [2016]; £6,589,817 [2015]; £6,282,587 [2014]; £8,413,117 [2013]

National Health Service Retirement Fellowship
Registered: 9 Nov 1983 *Employees:* 5 *Volunteers:* 1,000
Tel: 01305 361317 *Website:* nhsrf.org.uk
Activities: General charitable purposes; education, training; advancement of health or saving of lives; prevention or relief of poverty; recreation
Address: 24 Stuart Road, Halesowen, W Midlands, B62 0ED
Trustees: Mr Mik Webb, Mrs Margaret Moffat, Chris Kitchin, Mr Paul Farenden, Ms Clare Panniker, Mr George Kempton, Mrs Audrey Harris, Mercedes Madden, Mrs Wendy Lindley, Mr Danny Mortimer, David Paterson
Income: £1,113,744 [2017]; £1,304,424 [2016]; £1,298,673 [2015]; £1,262,200 [2014]; £1,162,722 [2013]

National Heart and Lung Institute Foundation
Registered: 18 Jul 1995
Tel: 020 7351 8180 *Website:* nhlif.info
Activities: Education, training; advancement of health or saving of lives
Address: National Heart and Lung Institute Foundation, Guy Scadding Building, Dovehouse Street, London, SW3 6LY
Trustees: Professor Sir Malcolm Green, Dr Paul Oldershaw, Professor Kim Michael Reginald Fox, Mr Alexander Ludovic Lindsay, Professor Sian Elizabeth Harding, Richard Reid, Baroness Sally Morgan, Dr Michael Harding, Ms Magdalene Sarah Brereton
Income: £1,036,259 [2017]; £905,932 [2016]; £622,575 [2015]; £979,957 [2014]; £1,038,993 [2013]

The National Horseracing Museum
Registered: 19 Nov 1987 *Employees:* 36 *Volunteers:* 100
Tel: 01638 667314 *Website:* palacehousenewmarket.co.uk
Activities: Education, training; arts, culture, heritage, science; environment, conservation, heritage
Address: National Horse Racing Museum, National Heritage Centre, Palace Street, Newmarket, Suffolk, CB8 8EP
Trustees: Mr David Oldrey, Mr Derek William Lewis, Mr William Angus Gittus, Mr Timothy Cox, Mrs Sara Doon Cumani, Mr Peter Sinclair Jensen, Mr Ian Edward Barlow, Hon Frances Caroline Stanley, Mrs Patricia Thompson, Ms Rachel Dene Serena Hood, Mr Richard Lionel William Frisby, Mr Christopher William Courtenay Tregoning MA FCA, Mr Guy Martin James Morrison, Mrs Katherine Stewart, Ms Patricia Glyn Connor
Income: £1,926,352 [2016]; £856,789 [2015]; £893,130 [2014]; £599,957 [2013]; £563,480 [2012]

The National Hospital for Neurology and Neurosurgery Development Foundation
Registered: 25 Sep 1984 *Employees:* 6 *Volunteers:* 10
Tel: 020 7829 8724 *Website:* nationalbrainappeal.org
Activities: The advancement of health or saving of lives; disability
Address: Queen Square, London, WC1N 3BG
Trustees: Joanna David, Mr Edward Leyland Datnow, Mr Peter John Stone, Professor John Duncan, Mrs Herchel Maclear-Jordan, Mr Diarmid Ogilvy, Mr Michael Peter Powell, Mr Michael Gordon Smith, Professor Alan Thompson, Professor Michael Hanna, Mrs Elizabeth Kornat, Mrs Caroline Frances Church, Miss Joan Grieve
Income: £2,314,396 [2017]; £1,889,427 [2016]; £1,869,585 [2015]; £1,737,942 [2014]; £1,368,845 [2013]

The National Institute of Economic and Social Research
Registered: 27 Aug 1962 *Employees:* 36
Tel: 020 7222 7665 *Website:* niesr.ac.uk
Activities: Education, training; economic, community development, employment
Address: National Institute of Economic & Social Research, 2 Dean Trench Street, London, SW1P 3HE
Trustees: Charles Bean, Ms Diane Coyle, Mr Neville Manuel, Professor Lorna Unwin, Mr Keith Ashley Victor MacKrell, Mr Ralph Neil Gaskell, Dr John Llewellyn, Mr Sadeq Sayeed, Sir Alan Budd, Ms Tera Paulina Allas, Mr Stephen Daryl King, Mr Alexander Jesse Baker
Income: £2,721,084 [2017]; £3,068,048 [2016]; £2,829,726 [2015]; £3,070,560 [2014]; £2,884,726 [2013]

National Justice Museum
Registered: 16 Dec 1993 *Employees:* 49 *Volunteers:* 216
Tel: 0115 952 0555 *Website:* nationaljusticemuseum.org.uk
Activities: General charitable purposes; education, training; arts, culture, heritage, science; environment, conservation, heritage; economic, community development, employment
Address: Shire Hall, High Pavement, Nottingham, NG1 1HN
Trustees: Mrs Jennifer Spencer, Mr Paul Bowden, Mr Michael John Blair, Mr Martin Paul Mellor, Professor Janine Elizabeth Griffiths-Baker, Mr Michael Robert Mathews, His Honour Jonathan James Teare, Mrs Karin Harrison, His Honour Roger Graham Chapple
Income: £1,970,167 [2017]; £1,448,410 [2016]; £1,534,940 [2015]; £1,164,839 [2014]; £1,065,627 [2013]

The National League Trust
Registered: 24 Jan 2012 *Employees:* 1 *Volunteers:* 1
Tel: 0121 643 3143 *Website:* nationalleaguetrust.og.uk
Activities: Education, training; disability; amateur sport; economic, community development, employment; recreation
Address: The Football Conference Ltd, Waterloo House, 20 Waterloo Street, Birmingham, B2 5TB
Trustees: Mr Dennis Leman, Lord Richard Oliver Faulkner, Paul Fairclough, Mr Brian Russell Lee, Mr Nick Perchard
Income: £1,201,081 [2017]; £903,513 [2016]; £905,096 [2015]; £907,230 [2014]; £810,459 [2013]

National Learning and Work Institute
Registered: 2 May 1991 *Employees:* 57
Website: learningandwork.org.uk
Activities: Education, training
Address: National Learning & Work Institute, 21 de Montfort Street, Leicester, LE1 7GE
Trustees: Mr Nicholas Willoughby Stuart CB MA, Maggie Galliers, Arvind Michael Kapur, Jeremy Moore, Mike Langhorn, Mr Jeffrey Douglas Greenidge, Ms Haf Merrifield
Income: £5,727,000 [2017]; £5,458,000 [2016]; £6,195,000 [2015]; £9,828,000 [2014]; £11,976,000 [2013]

National Library of Wales
Registered: 21 Aug 1967 *Employees:* 223 *Volunteers:* 700
Tel: 01970 632923 *Website:* llgc.org.uk
Activities: Education, training; arts, culture, heritage, science; environment, conservation, heritage; economic, community development, employment
Address: National Library of Wales, Penglais, Aberystwyth, Ceredigion, SY23 3BU
Trustees: Mr Richard Houdmont, Mr David Hugh Thomas, Dr Elizabeth Siberry, Susan Davies, Y Cynghorydd Dyfrig Jones, Mr Gwilym Dyfri Jones, Mr Lee Yale-Helms, Lord Aberdare, Mr Iwan Davies, Mr Stephen Williams, Phil Cooper, Mr Rhodri Glyn Thomas, Ms Eleri Twynog Davies
Income: £12,255,000 [2017]; £13,450,776 [2016]; £18,506,527 [2015]; £16,704,000 [2014]; £14,729,000 [2013]

The National Literacy Trust
Registered: 3 Oct 2006 *Employees:* 48 *Volunteers:* 660
Tel: 020 7587 1842 *Website:* literacytrust.org.uk
Activities: Education, training; arts, culture, heritage, science; economic, community development, employment
Address: 1st Floor, National Literacy Trust, 68 South Lambeth Road, London, SW8 1RL
Trustees: Neil Sherlock, Frank Carter, Liz Robinson, Ben Fletcher, Luisa Edwards, Dame Julia Cleverdon, Joanna Trollope OBE, Joanna Prior, Lara White, Clare Wood
Income: £3,134,328 [2017]; £3,947,606 [2016]; £3,759,425 [2015]; £2,914,749 [2014]; £2,346,689 [2013]

National Marine Aquarium Limited
Registered: 1 Feb 1994 *Employees:* 95 *Volunteers:* 50
Tel: 01752 275207 *Website:* national-aquarium.co.uk
Activities: General charitable purposes; education, training; animals; environment, conservation, heritage
Address: National Marine Aquarium, Rope Walk, Plymouth, PL4 0LF
Trustees: Professor Wendy Purcell, Mr Mark Lomas, Mr K Lewins, Prof M Attrill, Mrs Philippa Clarke, Mr R Maslin
Income: £3,627,593 [2017]; £3,797,175 [2016]; £3,367,634 [2015]; £3,347,101 [2014]; £3,130,751 [2013]

National Maritime Museum Cornwall Trust
Registered: 2 Feb 1998 *Employees:* 30 *Volunteers:* 180
Tel: 01326 313388 *Website:* nmmc.co.uk
Activities: Education, training; arts, culture, heritage, science; environment, conservation, heritage
Address: Discovery Quay, Falmouth, Cornwall, TR11 3QY
Trustees: The Hon Evelyn Boscawen DL, Mr Anthony Josiah Pawlyn, Mr Simon Sherrard DL, Mr Simon James Staughton, Mr Christopher John Hunt, Jonathan Cunliffe, Ms Sara Victoria Pugh, Mr Peter Wilton Davies MBE, Mr Simon Charles Tregoning, Robert Holmes, Mr Brian Derrick Steward, Mr Peter Searle, Mr Sam Hugh D'Aquilar Hunt, Ms Tamsin Rebecca Mann
Income: £2,439,642 [2017]; £2,818,868 [2016]; £2,274,942 [2015]; £2,102,170 [2014]; £1,849,519 [2013]

The National Memorial Arboretum Company Limited
Registered: 9 Feb 1995 *Employees:* 44 *Volunteers:* 250
Website: thenma.org.uk
Activities: Education, training; environment, conservation, heritage
Address: Croxall Road, Alrewas, Staffs, DE13 7AR
Trustees: Major General Andrew Farquhar CBE, Mr Colin Kemp, Mr Gary John Ryan, Mr Jason Coward, Mr David Whimpenny
Income: £4,650,656 [2017]; £11,544,000 [2016]; £5,668,491 [2015]; £7,266,397 [2014]; £5,235,859 [2013]

The National Motor Museum Trust Limited
Registered: 17 Jan 2005 *Employees:* 20 *Volunteers:* 60
Tel: 01590 614650 *Website:* nationalmotormuseum.org.uk
Activities: Education, training; arts, culture, heritage, science; environment, conservation, heritage
Address: Beaulieu, Brockenhurst, Hants, SO42 7ZN
Trustees: Mr Christopher MacGowan, The Hon Mrs Mary Montagu-Scott, Mr Robert Stephen Taylor, Mr Michael David Timmins, Mrs Caroline Marcus, Mrs Helen Evenden, Lord Montagu, Mr Nicholas Berkeley Mason, Lord Strathcarron, Mr John Reed, Mr Andrew John Barratt
Income: £2,971,609 [2016]; £2,791,286 [2015]; £2,828,173 [2014]; £3,155,689 [2013]; £3,262,673 [2012]

The National Museum of Labour History
Registered: 20 Oct 1986 *Employees:* 30 *Volunteers:* 30
Tel: 0161 838 9190 *Website:* phm.org.uk
Activities: Education, training; arts, culture, heritage, science; environment, conservation, heritage
Address: 5 Beaumont Avenue, Horwich, Bolton, Lancs, BL6 7BQ
Trustees: Mr Bernard Donoghue, Mr Derek Antrobus, Ms Kay Carberry, Mr Russell Mark Gill, Mr Maziar Jamnejad, Mr Steven James Lindsay, Mr Paul Nowak, Ms Lucy Maria Powell, Mrs Alveena Malik, Mr Mike Pye, Dr Wayne Garvie, Mr Tom Jones, Mr Martin Alexander Carr, Baroness Jan Royall, Miss Beth Knowles, Lord John Steven Bassam, Mr John Hannett
Income: £1,263,842 [2017]; £1,291,295 [2016]; £1,401,903 [2015]; £1,295,837 [2014]; £1,240,056 [2013]

The National Museum of The Royal Navy
Registered: 14 Oct 2008 *Employees:* 315 *Volunteers:* 330
Tel: 023 9272 7582 *Website:* nmrn.org.uk
Activities: Education, training; arts, culture, heritage, science; environment, conservation, heritage; economic, community development, employment; other charitable purposes
Address: NMRN, HM Naval Base, Portsmouth, PO1 3NH
Trustees: Professor John Craven, Mr Richard Timothy Schadla-Hall, Mr John Brookes, Sir Jonathon Band, Dr Caroline Williams, Vice Admiral Sir Adrian Johns, Major General Jeffrey Sinclair Mason MBE, Mr Charles Wilson, Mr Michael Bedingfield, Councillor Donna Jones, Ms Kimberley Anne Reade Marshall, Mr Mike Gambazzi, Captain Daniel Conley OBE, Mr Gavin Whitter
Income: £19,873,323 [2017]; £19,927,149 [2016]; £18,094,350 [2015]; £22,146,148 [2014]; £15,327,683 [2013]

National Museum of Wales
Registered: 6 Aug 1963 *Employees:* 531 *Volunteers:* 747
Website: museumwales.ac.uk
Activities: Education, training; arts, culture, heritage, science; environment, conservation, heritage
Address: National Museum Wales, Cathays Park, Cardiff, CF10 3NP
Trustees: Keshav Singhal FRCS MCh, Mr Hywel Ceri Jones, Dr Carol Bell, Professor Anthony Atkins ScD FREng, Prof Robert Pickard, Baroness Kay Andrews, Ms Jessica Seaton, Dr Catherine Duigan, Ms Carys Howell, Dr Glenda Jones, Victoria Provis MBA, Ms Rachel Hughes, Mr Michael Prior, Mr Laurie Pavelin, Mr Hywel John
Income: £33,580,000 [2017]; £37,212,000 [2016]; £35,291,000 [2015]; £35,356,000 [2014]; £29,441,000 [2013]

National Operatic and Dramatic Association
Registered: 19 Dec 1967 *Employees:* 5 *Volunteers:* 185
Tel: 0121 244 6495 *Website:* noda.org.uk
Activities: Arts, culture, heritage, science
Address: 6 The Woodleys, Birmingham, B14 4AU
Trustees: Mrs Kay Rowan, Mr Michael Hastilow, Mr John Barnes, Ms Christine Hunter Hughes, Gordon Richardson, Mr Ian G Cox, Miss Nanette Lovell, Mrs Jacquie Stedman, Mr Nick Lawrence, Don McKay, Mr Robert Thomas Lumsden
Income: £1,101,210 [2017]; £591,274 [2015]; £583,371 [2014]; £537,581 [2013]; £560,037 [2012]

National Osteoporosis Society
Registered: 18 Mar 2004 *Employees:* 62 *Volunteers:* 521
Tel: 01761 473251 *Website:* nos.org.uk
Activities: Education, training; advancement of health or saving of lives; disability
Address: National Osteoporosis Society, Manor Farm, Skinners Hill, Camerton, Bath, BA2 0PJ
Trustees: Professor Juliet Compston, Mrs Frances Grigg, Dr Anne Louise Dolan, Mrs Rebecca Thompson, Dr Lynne Wigens, Mrs Carole Mary Walker, Mrs Catherine Janet Tompkins, Dr Neil Gittoes, Miss Caroline Trewhitt
Income: £4,841,209 [2016]; £4,801,457 [2015]; £4,921,634 [2014]; £3,369,471 [2013]; £3,469,416 [2012]

National Playing Fields Association
Registered: 13 Dec 1979 *Employees:* 17
Tel: 020 7427 2110 *Website:* fieldsintrust.org
Activities: Amateur sport; environment, conservation, heritage; economic, community development, employment
Address: Unit 2d Woodstock Studios, 36 Woodstock Grove, London, W12 8LE
Trustees: Mr Paul Garber, Mr Richard Schuster, Mr Tom Barber, Mr Graeme Le Saux, Mr Mark Campion, Ms Debbie Jevans CBE, Mrs Carlotta Calleri Zavanelli Newbury, Mr Jeremy Hammond, Dr Ann Heywood, Mr Tim Smith, Mr Brian Samson, Mr Tim Phillips CBE, Mr Mike Street OBE, Mr Brynmor Williams
Income: £1,290,000 [2016]; £688,000 [2015]; £1,874,000 [2014]; £1,992,588 [2013]; £3,943,676 [2012]

The National Rheumatoid Arthritis Society
Registered: 11 Mar 2010 *Employees:* 22 *Volunteers:* 200
Tel: 01628 823524 *Website:* nras.org.uk
Activities: General charitable purposes; education, training; advancement of health or saving of lives; disability
Address: The National Rheumatoid Arthritis Society, 4 The Switchback, Gardner Road, Maidenhead, Berks, SL6 7RJ
Trustees: Mr Stephen John Crowther, Simon Collins, Miss Kirsten Jane Fox, Gordon Taylor, Jennie Jones, Richard Boucher, Ellie Andrews, Zoe Ide
Income: £1,201,455 [2016]; £1,034,544 [2015]; £980,943 [2014]; £947,389 [2013]; £1,120,253 [2012]

National Rifle Association
Registered: 21 Mar 1963 *Employees:* 72 *Volunteers:* 155
Tel: 01483 798807 *Website:* nra.org.uk
Activities: Education, training; disability; amateur sport; other charitable purposes
Address: National Rifle Association, Bisley Camp, Brookwood, Woking, Surrey, GU24 0PB
Trustees: Mr Derek Lowe, Mr John G M Webster, Mr Gary Alexander, Mr James Harris, Mr David Lacey, David Evans, Mr Richard Bailie, Mr Barry Morgan, Mrs Alice Gran, Mr Reginald Roberts
Income: £5,982,619 [2017]; £5,731,182 [2016]; £5,478,663 [2015]; £5,267,814 [2014]; £5,067,176 [2013]

National Schizophrenia Fellowship
Registered: 31 Oct 1991 *Employees:* 999 *Volunteers:* 121
Tel: 020 7840 3101 *Website:* rethink.org
Activities: Disability
Address: Rethink, Camelford House, 87-90 Albert Embankment, London, SE1 7TP
Trustees: Mr Shaun Johnson, Ms Jane Elizabeth Watkinson, Mr Christopher David Lynch, Mr George Hook, Ms Katie Groom, Mrs Kathryn Tyson, Mrs Philippa Lowe, Ms Denise Porter, Dan Fletcher, Mrs Frances Jean Ashworth, Ms Aphra Tulip, Mr John Liver
Income: £33,717,000 [2017]; £37,005,034 [2016]; £39,095,224 [2015]; £48,475,000 [2014]; £50,930,814 [2013]

National Sheep Association
Registered: 5 Jul 1967 *Employees:* 13 *Volunteers:* 400
Tel: 01684 892661 *Website:* nationalsheep.org.uk
Activities: Education, training; animals; environment, conservation, heritage
Address National Sheep Association, The Sheep Centre, Blackmore Park Road, Malvern, Worcs, WR13 6PH
Trustees: Mr Llew Thomas, Mr Christopher James Lewis, Mr Bryan Griffiths, Mr David Gregory, Mr John Geldard, Mr Daniel Phipps, Mr Peter Delbridge, Timothy Ward, Andrew Barr, Mr Paul Wozencraft, Mr John Blaney, Mrs Aileen McFadzean, Mr Henry Dunn, Mr Peter Myles
Income: £1,211,226 [2016]; £1,302,945 [2015]; £1,508,740 [2014]; £1,278,477 [2013]; £985,925 [2012]

The National Small-Bore Rifle Association
Registered: 23 Apr 1964 *Employees:* 35 *Volunteers:* 72
Tel: 01483 485500 *Website:* nsra.co.uk
Activities: General charitable purposes; education, training; amateur sport
Address: Lord Roberts Centre, Bisley Camp, Brookwood, Woking, Surrey, GU24 0NP
Trustees: Mrs Jean Ann Coleman, Mr Charlie Blow, Mr John Oram Lloyd, Mr Michael John Chapman, Mr Rw Newman, Mr Richard Watchorn, Mr Ken Nash, Mr Edward William Kendall, Mr Robert Baker Loughridge, Mr Mj Arnstein
Income: £2,621,866 [2016]; £2,661,186 [2015]; £2,769,487 [2014]; £2,557,319 [2013]; £2,650,488 [2012]

The National Society (Church of England and Church in Wales) for The Promotion of Education
Registered: 26 Aug 1966 *Employees:* 12
Tel: 020 7898 1501 *Website:* churchofengland.org
Activities: Education, training
Address: The National Society, Church House, Great Smith Street, London, SW1P 3BL
Trustees: Priscilla Chadwick, Revd Jeremy Fletcher, Peter Ballard, Maurice Smith, Stephen Conway, Marion Plant, June Osborne, Susan Witts, Simon Lloyd, Peter Neil, Rosemary Lyon
Income: £1,919,437 [2016]; £4,011,320 [2015]; £1,086,355 [2014]; £1,224,230 [2013]; £1,216,825 [2012]

The National Society for Epilepsy
Registered: 22 Sep 1962 *Employees:* 391 *Volunteers:* 41
Tel: 01494 601300 *Website:* epilepsysociety.org.uk
Activities: Education, training; advancement of health or saving of lives; disability; accommodation, housing
Address: National Society for Epilepsy, Chalfont Centre, Chalfont St Peter, Gerrards Cross, Bucks, SL9 0RJ
Trustees: Mr Harold Keith Porter, Mr Ian Garlington, Ms Catherine Alcock, Mr Adrian Waddingham, Mr Christopher Blue, Dr James Hagan, Mr Joe Brice, Ms Deborah Wheeler, Mr John Barradell, Mr Michael Kirilloff, Dr Richard Roberts, Mr Peter James Goodfellow, Dr Ian Pike
Income: £17,056,000 [2017]; £16,992,000 [2016]; £16,515,000 [2015]; £19,884,000 [2014]; £16,837,000 [2013]

The National Society for The Prevention of Cruelty To Children

Registered: 1 Apr 1963 *Employees:* 1,732 *Volunteers:* 9,100
Tel: 020 3772 9153 *Website:* nspcc.org.uk
Activities: General charitable purposes; education, training
Address: NSPCC, National Centre, 42 Curtain Road, London, EC2A 3NH
Trustees: Dame Esther Rantzen DBE, John Worth, Ann Morrison, Lady Brenda McLaughlin CBE, Fiona Curteis, Dr Joanna Begent, Antonia Consett, Clement Brohier, James Bailey, Professor Tanya Byron, Mark Wood, Sir David Normington GCB, Tarek Khlat, Elizabeth Brash, Andrew Briggs
Income: £127,407,530 [2017]; £128,912,000 [2016]; £134,467,000 [2015]; £125,877,000 [2014]; £129,432,000 [2013]

National Space Centre

Registered: 10 Jan 2000 *Employees:* 166
Website: spacecentre.co.uk
Activities: Education, training
Address: 3 The Square, Glenfield, Leicester, LE3 8DQ
Trustees: Professor David John Southwood, Sir Martin Sweeting, Mr Nigel Paul Siesage, Mr Jeffrey Moore, Mr Gary Moss, Ms Karen Thomas, Ms Rebecca Anne Evernden, Mr Surinder Mohan Sharma, Mr Ted Cassidy, Mr Charles Bishop, Mr Arvind Michael Kapur, Prof Emma Bunce, Mr James Edward Fry
Income: £6,463,321 [2017]; £5,966,458 [2015]; £5,618,103 [2014]; £4,962,798 [2013]; £103,419 [2012]

National Spiritual Assembly of The Baha'is of The United Kingdom

Registered: 4 Jan 1967 *Employees:* 30 *Volunteers:* 1,000
Tel: 020 7584 2566 *Website:* bahai.org.uk
Activities: Education, training; religious activities; economic, community development, employment
Address: 27 Rutland Gate, London, SW7 1PD
Trustees: Dr Wendi Momen, Mr Darren Smith, Mr Patrick O'Mara, Mr Robert Matthew Weinberg, Mrs Vivien Craig, Hon Barnabas Leith, Fidelma Meehan, Dr Vafa Ram, Mr Olinga Tahzib
Income: £3,809,506 [2016]; £4,691,393 [2015]; £3,531,587 [2014]; £3,558,167 [2013]; £3,387,708 [2012]

National Star Foundation

Registered: 25 Nov 1963 *Employees:* 797 *Volunteers:* 20
Tel: 01242 534903 *Website:* nationalstar.org
Activities: Education, training; disability; accommodation, housing
Address: Ullenwood, Cheltenham, Glos, GL53 9QU
Trustees: Mr Shaun D E Parsons, Mr Brian Michael Chatfield MBA FCIPD, Mr Robert Russell Thompson, Mr Chas Howes, Mr Barry Seamons, Mr Paul Keith Styles BSc, Mr Timothy Cooper, Ben Higgins
Income: £20,891,172 [2016]; £21,030,214 [2015]; £20,081,976 [2014]; £15,425,737 [2013]

National Theatre of Wales

Registered: 9 Feb 2009 *Employees:* 24
Website: nationaltheatrewales.org
Activities: Education, training; arts, culture, heritage, science
Address: National Theatre Wales, 30 Castle Arcade, Cardiff, CF10 1BW
Trustees: Clive Jones, Ian Hargreaves, Miss Bethan Cousins, Richard Lynch, Mr Derry John Newman, Rachel Miller, Sian Ede, Mr Simon Pirotte, Clare Pillman, Mrs Rosaleen Moriarty-Simmonds, Bedwyr Elias Williams
Income: £3,337,012 [2017]; £2,330,929 [2016]; £2,758,233 [2015]; £2,174,756 [2014]; £2,509,394 [2013]

The National Trust for Places of Historic Interest or Natural Beauty

Registered: 5 Nov 1962 *Employees:* 6,548 *Volunteers:* 65,000
Tel: 01793 817400 *Website:* nationaltrust.org.uk
Activities: Environment, conservation, heritage
Address: National Trust, Kemble Drive, Swindon, Wilts, SN2 2NA
Trustees: Professor Carys Swanwick, Mrs Caroline Goodall, Mr Sandy Nairne CBE FSA, Mr David Eynon Smart, Mr David Fursdon, Mr Michael Day CVO, Ms Orna Nichionna, Mr Timothy Parker, Mr John Sell CBE DipCons(AA) AABC FRSA, Mr Nick Stace
Income: £591,742,000 [2017]; £522,165,000 [2016]; £494,108,000 [2015]; £460,298,000 [2014]; £456,926,000 [2013]

The National Youth Advocacy Service

Registered: 2 Jul 1992 *Employees:* 172 *Volunteers:* 154
Tel: 0151 649 8700 *Website:* nyas.net
Activities: General charitable purposes
Address: Units 1-3 Tower House, 1 Tower Road, Birkenhead, Merseyside, CH41 1FF
Trustees: Mr Robert Annesley Wright, Roy Jones, Mrs Judith Timms OBE, Mr Martyn James Best, HHJ Jeremy Hugh Chaloner Lea, Mr Michael Blackburn, Dr Eileen Anna Vizard, Mr Neil McCarthy, Mr Daniel Alexander Hanson, Barry Hulme
Income: £6,454,136 [2017]; £5,881,239 [2016]; £6,058,027 [2015]; £5,123,969 [2014]; £4,703,324 [2013]

The National Youth Agency

Registered: 29 Mar 1994 *Employees:* 48
Tel: 0116 242 7350 *Website:* nya.org.uk
Activities: Education, training
Address: National Youth Agency, Eastgate House, 19-23 Humberstone Road, Leicester, LE5 3GJ
Trustees: Mr Michael Robert Bracey, Mr Charles Mills, Mr Gabriel Buck, Mr Mark Norris, Mr Toby Ducker, Miss Yasmin Josephine Greenaway, Ms Helen Thomson, Cllr Ken Meeson, Ms Carol Anne Stone, Mrs Barbara Bradley, Miss Natalie Smith, Liz Hacket Pain
Income: £4,582,000 [2017]; £6,471,000 [2016]; £6,559,000 [2015]; £10,386,000 [2014]; £7,178,000 [2013]

National Youth Choirs of Great Britain

Registered: 23 Oct 1984 *Employees:* 9
Tel: 0191 383 7355 *Website:* nycgb.org.uk
Activities: Education, training
Address: The Rivergreen Centre, Aykley Heads, Durham, DH1 5TS
Trustees: David Aspinall, Mr Andrew Garth Pollard, Mr Anthony Garnett, Mr Nicholas Stephen Sears, Ms Rebecca Driver, Dr Christopher Higgins, Mr James Olley, Mr Nigel Peter Brookes, Patricia Keir
Income: £1,456,831 [2016]; £1,098,151 [2015]; £1,052,449 [2014]; £1,187,958 [2013]; £964,517 [2012]

The National Youth Orchestra of Great Britain

Registered: 4 Jan 1985 *Employees:* 16
Tel: 020 7759 1880 *Website:* nyo.org.uk
Activities: Education, training; arts, culture, heritage, science
Address: National Youth Orchestra, Somerset House, Strand, London, WC2R 1LA
Trustees: Mr Peter Jeremy Moorhouse, Ms Tatjana May, Mr Andrew Gambrell, Dame Liz Forgan DBE, Mr Mazdak Sanii, Ms Chi-Chi Nwanoku MBE, Mr Donagh Collins, Mr Christopher Luke Mayhew, Mr David Butcher, Miss Lyn Fletcher
Income: £2,080,235 [2016]; £1,658,517 [2015]; £2,087,329 [2014]; £2,909,245 [2013]; £1,386,482 [2012]

The National Youth Theatre of Great Britain
Registered: 13 Nov 1961 *Employees:* 12 *Volunteers:* 543
Tel: 020 3696 7055 *Website:* nyt.org.uk
Activities: Education, training; arts, culture, heritage, science
Address: National Youth Theatre, 101 Bayham Street, London, NW1 0AG
Trustees: Dr Simon Stockill, Ms Mary Fitzpatrick, Miss Janet Ellis, Mrs Tania Henrietta Black, Peter Jonathan Clayton, Mr Timothy Lloyd-Hughes, Alistair Summers, Mr Edward Henry Butler Vaizey, Eve Stewart, Ms Dawn Airey, Mr John Capps, Mr Simon Davies, Dr Prasanna Puwanarajah, Mr David Hockley, Katherine Mavor, Nicola Howson, Mr David Lindon Lammy
Income: £2,605,122 [2017]; £2,304,960 [2016]; £3,187,953 [2015]; £2,807,736 [2014]; £2,308,983 [2013]

National Zakat Foundation (NZF)
Registered: 6 Sep 2013 *Employees:* 19 *Volunteers:* 100
Tel: 0333 312 3123 *Website:* nzf.org.uk
Activities: The prevention or relief of poverty
Address: Zakat Centre, National Zakat Foundation, 41 Fieldgate Street, London, E1 1JU
Trustees: Ibrar Majid, Sultan Choudhury, Azim Kidwai, Mrs Sabah Gilani, Tariq Surty, Muhammed Taha Yesilhark
Income: £3,439,880 [2016]; £2,507,984 [2015]; £1,700,621 [2014]

National Zoological Society of Wales
Registered: 18 Jul 1983 *Employees:* 40 *Volunteers:* 50
Tel: 01492 532938 *Website:* welshmountainzoo.org
Activities: Education, training; arts, culture, heritage, science; animals; environment, conservation, heritage; recreation
Address: Mr Nicholas Lawrence Jackson MBE, Welsh Mountain Zoo, Old Highway, Colwyn Bay, Conwy, LL28 5UY
Trustees: Mr Paul Loveluck CBE, Dr Caroline Harcourt, Nigel Brown, Mr Henry Douglas Roberts, Mr Peter Gibson, Mr Terry Deakin, Mr Robert Jackson
Income: £1,688,308 [2016]; £1,601,685 [2015]; £1,587,440 [2014]; £1,453,582 [2013]; £1,118,791 [2012]

The Nationwide Foundation
Registered: 6 Nov 1997 *Employees:* 5
Tel: 01793 655113 *Website:* nationwidefoundation.org.uk
Activities: General charitable purposes; accommodation, housing; human rights, religious or racial harmony, equality or diversity
Address: Nationwide House, Pipers Way, Swindon, Wilts, SN38 2SN
Trustees: Mr Ian Williams, Mr Benedict Stimson, Mr John Taylor, Sarah Mitchell, Mrs Clara Govier, Mr Martin John Coppack, Juliet Clare Cockram, Ms Antonia Bance, Mr Tony Paul Prestedge, Mrs Sara Phillipa Bennison
Income: £2,641,746 [2017]; £1,672,512 [2016]; £990,753 [2015]; £726,567 [2014]; £852,138 [2013]

Natural Breaks Limited
Registered: 11 Aug 2016 *Employees:* 123
Tel: 0151 207 9120 *Website:* naturalbreaks.co.uk
Activities: The advancement of health or saving of lives; disability; recreation
Address: Natural Breaks Ltd, Millennium Resource Centre, Blenheim Street, Liverpool, L5 8UX
Trustees: Mr Joe Steen, Mr Kevin Lloyd, Ian Meyer, Mrs Julia Erskine, Mr Robert Itiokiet
Income: £2,490,679 [2017]

Natural Resource Charter Limited
Registered: 18 Oct 2011 *Employees:* 21
Tel: 07823 442954 *Website:* naturalresourcecharter.org
Activities: Education, training; environment, conservation, heritage; economic, community development, employment; other charitable purposes
Address: 1 Knightrider Court, London, EC4V 5BJ
Trustees: Mr Alan Detheridge, Mr Joseph Charles Bell, Mr Anthony James Venables, Mr Mark Henstridge
Income: £1,936,769 [2016]; £1,786,327 [2015]; £309,994 [2014]

The Nautical Institute
Registered: 8 Apr 1991 *Employees:* 37 *Volunteers:* 150
Tel: 020 7928 1351 *Website:* nautinst.org
Activities: Education, training; other charitable purposes
Address: Flat 1, Shaftesbury Court, Alderney Mews, London, SE1 4JR
Trustees: Captain Robbie Middleton FNI, Captain Michael K Barritt FNI, Mr Peter B Hinchliffe OBE FNI, Captain Jakub Szymanski FNI, Captain Trevor Bailey FNI, Mr Frank Coles MNI, Captain Zillur Rahman Bhuiyan FNI, Captain Ian Mathison FNI, Captain James Alphonus Robinson DSM FNI, Mr David Bendall MNI, Captain Nand Hiranandani FNI, Captain Duncan McC Telfer FNI, Captain Marc Nuytemans FNI, Captain John Prasad Menezes FNI, Captain Graham Cowling FNI
Income: £3,045,132 [2016]; £3,529,876 [2015]; £2,876,318 [2014]; £2,433,938 [2013]; £2,482,355 [2012]

Nautilus Welfare Fund
Registered: 4 Nov 1963 *Employees:* 81
Tel: 0151 639 8454 *Website:* nautiluswelfarefund.org
Activities: Disability; prevention or relief of poverty; accommodation, housing
Address: Numast, Nautilus House, Mariners Park, Wallasey, Merseyside, CH45 7PH
Trustees: Nautilus International Council
Income: £3,618,506 [2016]; £2,883,868 [2015]; £2,536,453 [2014]; £4,292,335 [2013]; £2,700,021 [2012]

The Navigators UK Limited
Registered: 27 Aug 2003 *Employees:* 5 *Volunteers:* 24
Tel: 023 8055 8800 *Website:* navigators.co.uk
Activities: Education, training; religious activities
Address: The Navigators UK, 54 The Avenue, Southampton, SO17 1XQ
Trustees: Professor Kevin David Glazebrook, Mrs Dawn Allison Brathwaite, Mr Stephen John Peters, Mr Simon Neville Wroe, Mrs Shelley Mulholland, Mr Martin William Osborn
Income: £1,669,190 [2017]; £1,628,713 [2016]; £1,538,086 [2015]; £1,650,942 [2014]; £1,584,758 [2013]

Nazarene Theological College
Registered: 6 Aug 1970 *Employees:* 22 *Volunteers:* 8
Tel: 0161 438 1926 *Website:* nazarene.ac.uk
Activities: Education, training; religious activities
Address: Nazarene Theological College, Dene Road, Didsbury, Manchester, M20 2GU
Trustees: Mr Christopher Ross, Mr Andrew Graystone, Mr Steven Leach, Mrs Mary Wood, Mr Ian Burleigh, Mr David Davies, Rev David Montgomery, Rev Karl Stanfield, Rev Lynn McLean Birkinshaw, Rev James Ritchie, Rev Nicole McConkey, Rev Nathan Payne
Income: £1,172,975 [2017]; £1,159,834 [2016]; £1,078,459 [2015]; £970,040 [2014]; £1,186,393 [2013]

Nazareth Care Charitable Trust

Registered: 6 Apr 2006 *Employees:* 1,095 *Volunteers:* 150
Tel: 020 8444 4427 *Website:* sistersofnazareth.com
Activities: The advancement of health or saving of lives; accommodation, housing; religious activities
Address: Larmenier Centre, 162 East End Road, London, N2 0RU
Trustees: Mr John Joseph Martin, Sister Sheila Collingborn, Sister Rose Ita Doody, Mr Paul Williams, Sister Teresa Fallon, Sister Anna Maria Doolan, Sister Madeleine Merriman
Income: £32,186,243 [2017]; £23,905,235 [2016]; £24,220,844 [2015]; £24,182,467 [2014]; £27,617,903 [2013]

The Near East Foundation UK

Registered: 27 Feb 2013 *Employees:* 2
Tel: 01225 480357 *Website:* neareast.org
Activities: Education, training; advancement of health or saving of lives; environment, conservation, heritage; economic, community development, employment
Address: 17 Burlington Street, Bath, BA1 2SB
Trustees: Mr Anthony Geraint Williams, Mr Robert Neil Palmer, Ms Linda Katherine Jacobs, Mr Anthony Ronald Williams, Mr Johnson Garrett
Income: £1,417,627 [2017]; £478,338 [2016]; £148,372 [2015]; £40,193 [2014]

Near Neighbours

Registered: 15 Jun 2011 *Employees:* 1 *Volunteers:* 10
Tel: 020 7898 1647 *Website:* near-neighbours.org.uk
Activities: The prevention or relief of poverty; economic, community development, employment; human rights, religious or racial harmony, equality or diversity; other charitable purposes
Address: Church House, 27 Great Smith Street, London, SW1P 3AZ
Trustees: Baroness Eaton DBE DL, Rt Revd Richard William Bryant Atkinson OBE, Rt Revd Mark Davies BA Hons, Mr Brian Dirck Carroll, The Rt Rev Dr Michael Ipgrave, Revd Canon Eve Pitts, Rev Canon Denise Poole BSc, The Rt Revd Dr Toby Howarth, Rev Sarah Schofield, Rev Mark Alban Poulson, Matthew Toby Nathan Girt, Mr Francis Thomas Davis
Income: £1,893,000 [2016]; £1,949,000 [2015]; £1,335,000 [2014]; £1,933,000 [2013]; £1,925,000 [2012]

Nectar Trust

Registered: 27 Mar 2012 *Employees:* 5
Tel: 020 7118 0505 *Website:* qcharity.org.uk
Activities: The prevention or relief of poverty; overseas aid, famine relief; economic, community development, employment
Address: 115 Park Street, London, W1K 7AP
Trustees: Mr Saleh Mohd F G Al-Marri, Mr Yousuf Ahmed Hassan Al-Hammadi, Mr Mohammed Abdulrahman Dabwan Saif
Income: £27,850,434 [2017]; £5,173,484 [2016]; £4,457,191 [2015]; £460,511 [2014]; £900 [2013]

Nekton Foundation

Registered: 14 Jul 2015 *Employees:* 4
Website: nektonmission.org
Activities: Education, training; environment, conservation, heritage
Address: 47 Lessar Avenue, London, SW4 9HW
Trustees: Mr Rupert Grey, Professor Alex David Rogers, Captain Paul Anthony Crowther, Ms Emily Victoria Penn, Mrs Juliet Catharine Burnett, Mr Nigel Winser, Mr Paul Andrew Jardine
Income: £3,418,715 [2016]; £310,000 [2015]

The Nelson Trust

Registered: 9 Jul 1996 *Employees:* 83 *Volunteers:* 43
Tel: 01453 885633 *Website:* nelsontrust.com
Activities: Education, training; advancement of health or saving of lives; accommodation, housing
Address: Port Lane, Brimscombe, Stroud, Glos, GL5 2QJ
Trustees: Ms Kamala Das, Dr Anne-Marie Marlow, Mrs Amanda Fadero, Mr Andrew Jardine, Mrs Naina Mandleker, Mr John Bensted, Mrs Ann Buxton, Mrs Claire Wynne Hughes, Mr Rhona MacDonald
Income: £5,228,208 [2017]; £3,095,243 [2016]; £2,862,740 [2015]; £2,517,866 [2014]; £2,985,590 [2013]

Nene Park Trust

Registered: 3 Feb 1989 *Employees:* 46 *Volunteers:* 60
Tel: 01733 234193 *Website:* neneparktrust.org.uk
Activities: Recreation
Address: Nene Park Trust, Ham Farm House, Ham Lane, Orton Waterville, Peterborough, PE2 5UU
Trustees: Mr Martin Chillcott, Mr Jonathan Marsden, Mr Simon Leatham, Cllr Graham Casey, Cllr June Stokes, Dr Colin Prosser, Professor Ian Hodge, Mr Mike Williams, Mr Thomas Bingham, Mrs Elizabeth Mugova, Dr Janice Allister
Income: £2,546,000 [2017]; £1,871,000 [2016]; £1,714,000 [2015]; £1,438,000 [2014]; £1,795,000 [2013]

Nene Valley Railway

Registered: 23 Feb 1972 *Employees:* 15 *Volunteers:* 325
Tel: 01780 784444 *Website:* nvr.org.uk
Activities: Education, training; arts, culture, heritage, science; environment, conservation, heritage
Address: Nene Valley Railway, Wansford Station, Old Great North Road, Stibbington, Peterborough, PE8 6LR
Trustees: Mr Alfred Martin Sixsmith, Mr Robert John Maskill, Mr David James O'Connell, Mr Paul Nigel Starbuck, Mr Philip Marshall, Mr Keith John Parkinson, Mrs Ambie Haydon, Mr Adrian Laurence Oates
Income: £1,550,735 [2017]; £1,160,093 [2016]; £1,223,506 [2015]; £1,143,899 [2014]; £1,156,550 [2013]

The Nesta Trust

Registered: 16 Nov 2011
Tel: 020 7438 2595 *Website:* nesta.org.uk
Activities: General charitable purposes; education, training; advancement of health or saving of lives; prevention or relief of poverty; arts, culture, heritage, science; environment, conservation, heritage; economic, community development, employment; other charitable purposes
Address: Nesta, 58 Victoria Embankment, London, EC4A 1DE
Trustees: Nesta
Income: £1,298,000 [2017]; £1,976,000 [2016]; £2,957,000 [2015]; £3,369,000 [2014]; £5,145,000 [2013]

Nesta

Registered: 30 Sep 2011 *Employees:* 173
Tel: 020 7438 2500 *Website:* nesta.org.uk
Activities: General charitable purposes; education, training; advancement of health or saving of lives; prevention or relief of poverty; arts, culture, heritage, science; environment, conservation, heritage; economic, community development, employment
Address: Nesta, 58 Victoria Embankment, London, EC4A 1DE
Trustees: Mr Simon Linnett, Mrs Natalie Tydeman, Ms Kim Shillinglaw, Ms Judy Gibbons, Mr Edward James Wray, Ms Moira Wallace, Sir John Gieve, Mr David Pitt-Watson, Mr Imran Khan, Kersten England, Piers Linney, Professor Anthony Lilley
Income: £24,908,000 [2017]; £14,492,000 [2016]; £15,641,000 [2015]; £15,974,000 [2014]; £12,681,000 [2013]

Netherhall Educational Association
Registered: 22 Apr 1965 *Employees:* 35 *Volunteers:* 46
Tel: 020 7794 9996 *Website:* nea.netherhall.org.uk
Activities: Education, training
Address: 18A Netherhall Gardens, London, NW3 5TH
Trustees: Mr Jack Valero, Dr Andrew James Curtis, Mr James Maurice Mirabal, Mr Andrew Tucker, Mr Andrew Hegarty, Mr Clifford George Cobb, Mr Xavier Bosch
Income: £4,107,366 [2016]; £3,468,053 [2015]; £3,251,772 [2014]; £3,330,744 [2013]; £3,195,178 [2012]

Netherthorpe and Upperthorpe Community Alliance
Registered: 19 Aug 1999 *Employees:* 69 *Volunteers:* 76
Tel: 0114 270 2041 *Website:* zestcommunity.co.uk
Activities: Education, training; advancement of health or saving of lives; disability; prevention or relief of poverty; amateur sport; economic, community development, employment
Address: Zest, 18 Upperthorpe, Sheffield, S6 3NA
Trustees: Mr Abdul Rahman Abdulrub, Helen Sims, Mr Toby James Netting, Mr Liton Ullah, Ms Jean Alison Grist, Mr David Thornett, Miss Kathryn Mudge, Mr Thomas Hunt, Mr Khalid Hadrami
Income: £1,182,837 [2017]; £1,221,038 [2016]; £1,429,373 [2015]; £1,508,316 [2014]; £1,828,421 [2013]

Network for Social Change Charitable Trust
Registered: 12 Jan 1987 *Volunteers:* 114
Tel: 01647 61106 *Website:* thenetworkforsocialchange.org.uk
Activities: General charitable purposes
Address: BM 2063, London, WC1N 3XX
Trustees: Chris Marks, Giles Wright, Marian Tucker, Imran Tyabji, Ms Carolyn Hayman, Jessica Paget
Income: £1,349,954 [2017]; £1,558,000 [2016]; £1,526,162 [2015]; £1,255,355 [2014]; £1,341,084 [2013]

Neuromuscular Centre
Registered: 9 Jul 1993 *Employees:* 21 *Volunteers:* 339
Tel: 01606 863464 *Website:* nmcentre.com
Activities: Education, training; advancement of health or saving of lives; disability
Address: Neuromuscular Centre, Woodford Lane West, Winsford, Cheshire, CW7 4EH
Trustees: Mr Edward James Sands, Ms Denise Coy, Dr Ros Quinlivan, Mrs Anne Craig MBE, Gareth Edwards, Miss Debbie Leather, Mr Stephen Clough, Mrs Susan McDowell
Income: £1,388,920 [2017]; £1,197,399 [2016]; £934,674 [2015]; £842,445 [2014]; £820,921 [2013]

The New Art Exchange Ltd
Registered: 30 Nov 2007 *Employees:* 30 *Volunteers:* 47
Tel: 0115 924 8630 *Website:* nae.org.uk
Activities: Education, training; arts, culture, heritage, science; environment, conservation, heritage
Address: 39-41 Gregory Boulevard, Hyson Green, Nottingham, NG7 6BE
Trustees: Mrs Jennifer Spencer, Mr Leslie McDonald, Mr Sardul Gill, Professor Christopher O'Brien, Mrs Lorna Holder, Mr Mohan Khera, Dr Lisa Mooney, Ms Tasleem Kauser Iqbal, Ms Reyahn King, Mrs Veronica Pickering
Income: £1,134,862 [2017]; £1,154,782 [2016]; £1,318,380 [2015]; £978,310 [2014]; £867,612 [2013]

The New Beacon Educational Trust Limited
Registered: 4 Aug 1970 *Employees:* 109
Website: newbeacon.org.uk
Activities: Education, training
Address: New Beacon School, Brittains Lane, Sevenoaks, Kent, TN13 2PB
Trustees: The Rev'd Lionel Kevis, James Thorne, Mr Robert Pearl, Marie-Louise Kinsler, Kathryn Tsang, Mr Andrew Hedger, Dr Nicki Perry, Miss Theresa Homewood, Mr Timothy Haynes, Mrs Katharine Long, Simon Hall, Michael Hill, Mr Thomas Patrick MacGregor
Income: £5,443,283 [2017]; £5,550,039 [2016]; £5,411,220 [2015]; £5,085,936 [2014]; £4,716,042 [2013]

New Charter Homes Limited
Registered: 16 Mar 2012 *Employees:* 60
Tel: 0161 331 2000 *Website:* newcharterhomes.co.uk
Activities: The prevention or relief of poverty; accommodation, housing; economic, community development, employment
Address: Jigsaw Homes Group Limited, 249 Cavendish Street, Ashton under Lyne, Lancs, OL6 7AT
Trustees: Mr Shoab Akhtar, Mr Vincent Paul Ricci, Mr Bruce Jassi, Ms Janet Mutch, Mr Andrew Peter Leah, Mr Warren Bray, Mr Michael Richmond
Income: £72,808,000 [2017]; £72,378,000 [2016]; £70,630,000 [2015]; £67,312,000 [2014]; £62,907,000 [2013]

New College Worcester
Registered: 14 Mar 2007 *Employees:* 135 *Volunteers:* 30
Tel: 01386 561901 *Website:* ncw.co.uk
Activities: Education, training
Address: 5 Fleury Close, Pershore, Worcs, WR10 3EJ
Trustees: Mr Brian Harrington, Mrs Diana Fulbrook, Mr Steven Tyler, Mr Rory Alan Cobb, Mrs Tracey Marie Smith, Mrs Karen Jane Holyoak, Mr Iain Paul, Mrs Sandra Bannister, Mrs Susan Ayres, Mr Aslam Tanvir, Miss Nicola Ross, Mr Robert Dredge
Income: £4,832,049 [2017]; £4,492,429 [2016]; £4,562,106 [2015]; £4,651,490 [2014]; £4,495,883 [2013]

New Community Network
Registered: 30 Nov 1998 *Employees:* 31 *Volunteers:* 520
Website: newcommunity.org.uk
Activities: Education, training; prevention or relief of poverty; accommodation, housing; religious activities; arts, culture, heritage, science; economic, community development, employment
Address: 39 Chapel Crescent, Southampton, SO19 8JU
Trustees: Mr William Kennedy, Mr Kevin Rayner, Mrs Theodora Ngozi Ugo, Mr Chan Raj Abraham, Mrs Shelly-Ann Frame, Mr Christopher Nigel David
Income: £1,146,937 [2017]; £1,148,649 [2016]; £1,128,388 [2015]; £1,070,423 [2014]; £1,215,448 [2013]

New Covenant Church
Registered: 30 Sep 1991 *Employees:* 28 *Volunteers:* 55
Tel: 020 7231 9817 *Website:* newcovenant.org.uk
Activities: Education, training; advancement of health or saving of lives; prevention or relief of poverty; religious activities
Address: 506-510 Old Kent Road, London, SE1 5BA
Trustees: Mrs Deborah Adesina, Mr Ayobami Olugbemiga Popoola, Tunde Aikomo, James Bamigboye, Kayode Adewumi
Income: £3,443,443 [2016]; £3,017,687 [2015]; £2,123,266 [2014]; £2,092,992 [2013]; £2,084,066 [2012]

New Directions (Rugby) Limited
Registered: 24 Oct 1991 *Employees:* 87 *Volunteers:* 20
Tel: 01788 573318 *Website:* newdirectionsrugby.org.uk
Activities: General charitable purposes; education, training; disability; accommodation, housing; recreation; other charitable purposes
Address: 27 Bilton Road, Rugby, Warwicks, CV22 7AN
Trustees: Mrs Wendy Back, Mrs Margaret Sedgley, Mr Stuart Bayley, Peter Jenkins, Mr Sukhraj Singh Barhey, Mr Philip John Hughes, Mr Martin Robert Orrill, Mrs Sophie Shaw, Mrs Julia Sanders, Diana Rayner, Jv Phillips
Income: £2,757,476 [2017]; £2,370,749 [2016]; £2,418,499 [2015]; £2,200,496 [2014]; £1,786,571 [2013]

New Economics Foundation
Registered: 10 May 1996 *Employees:* 59
Website: neweconomics.org
Activities: Education, training; economic, community development, employment
Address: Manor Farm, 165 Fitton Road, Wiggenhall St Germans, King's Lynn, Norfolk, PE34 3AY
Trustees: Mr Jules Peck, Tess Gill, Miss Mary Riddell, Rukaya Sarumi, Professor Jeremy Till, Mr Michael William Tuffrey, Ian Peter Christie, Ms Fiona Weir, Ms Rebecca Willis, Margaret Gardner, Gurnek Singh Bains, Professor Ciaran Driver
Income: £3,519,786 [2017]; £3,168,687 [2016]; £5,329,172 [2015]; £3,556,076 [2014]; £3,116,287 [2013]

The New Forest Agricultural Show Society
Registered: 9 Jan 1992 *Employees:* 7 *Volunteers:* 495
Tel: 01590 622400 *Website:* newforestshow.co.uk
Activities: Education, training; arts, culture, heritage, science; amateur sport; animals; environment, conservation, heritage
Address: New Forest Agricultural Show Society, The Showground, New Park, Lyndhurst Road, Brockenhurst, Hants, SO42 7QH
Trustees: Mr Christopher Gwyn-Evans, Mr Christopher Antony Whitlock, Hazel Long, Mr Martin Stewart, Mrs Alexandra Margaret Jennings, Mr Timothy Michael Dalton, Earl of Malmesbury, Mrs Kirsty Slocombe, Mr Michael Smales, Mr Aaron James Lawford
Income: £2,013,007 [2017]; £2,072,983 [2016]; £2,134,178 [2015]; £1,962,378 [2014]; £1,884,665 [2013]

New Forest Quaker Care Home
Registered: 5 Mar 2014 *Employees:* 39
Tel: 01425 617656 *Website:* quakerhouse.org.uk
Activities: Accommodation, housing; other charitable purposes
Address: Quaker House, 40-44 Barton Court Road, New Milton, Hants, BH25 6NR
Trustees: Ms Margaret Richens, Mr Chris Walker, David Collins, Ms Jeni Bremner, Dr Ingrid Eyers, Mr Anthony Fox, Mr Cyril Lanch, Mr Brian Dempster, Mr Stephen John Hinson, Mrs Ann Bond
Income: £1,093,377 [2016]; £1,102,991 [2015]; £1,043,281 [2014]

New Hackney Education Business Partnership Limited
Registered: 25 Aug 2005 *Employees:* 31 *Volunteers:* 1,607
Tel: 020 7275 6060 *Website:* inspire-ebp.org.uk
Activities: General charitable purposes; education, training; economic, community development, employment
Address: 34-38 Dalston Lane, London, E8 3AZ
Trustees: Patsy Francis, Mr Matthew Sparkes, Georgios Markakis, Ms Tracey Fletcher, Anton Francic, Jenny Wilkins, Ms Caroline King, Ms Helen Cooper Nee France, Mr Barnaby Neville Fitzgerald O'Kelly
Income: £1,220,261 [2017]; £1,167,549 [2016]; £1,267,521 [2015]; £1,410,456 [2014]; £1,350,152 [2013]

New Hall School Trust
Registered: 1 Jul 2005 *Employees:* 298 *Volunteers:* 66
Tel: 01245 467588 *Website:* newhallschool.co.uk
Activities: Education, training; religious activities; environment, conservation, heritage
Address: New Hall School, The Avenue, Boreham, Chelmsford, Essex, CM3 3HS
Trustees: Mr John Francis Aldridge, Mr John Westnedge, Mrs Rachel Marion Skells, Mrs Pauline Marie Wilson, Mr Robert Edwin Talbut, Mr Joseph Anthony Peake, Mrs Katherine Jeffrey, Mr Vincent Marley, Mr Malcolm John Day, Dr Miriam Edelsten, Ms Agnes Therese Williams, Mrs Janis Croom
Income: £21,417,552 [2017]; £20,688,110 [2016]; £19,107,408 [2015]; £19,489,341 [2014]; £16,528,217 [2013]

New Horizon Youth Centre
Registered: 20 Dec 1978 *Employees:* 42 *Volunteers:* 10
Tel: 020 7388 5560 *Website:* nhyouthcentre.org.uk
Activities: Education, training; advancement of health or saving of lives; accommodation, housing
Address: 68 Chalton Street, London, NW1 1JR
Trustees: Robert Barnes, Nick Hardwick, Hu Clarke, Mrs Samata Khatoon, Mrs Laura Jackson, Mrs Katherine Grant Hawthorne, Ms Paula McDonald, Ellie Roy, Ms Jennifer Stoker, Mr John Howard Williams, Mr Martin Stuart Remington Dibben
Income: £1,627,804 [2017]; £1,572,286 [2016]; £1,684,820 [2015]; £1,549,870 [2014]; £1,611,148 [2013]

New Israel Fund
Registered: 10 Jan 1997 *Employees:* 6 *Volunteers:* 50
Tel: 020 7724 2266 *Website:* newisraelfund.org.uk
Activities: General charitable purposes; education, training; advancement of health or saving of lives; disability; prevention or relief of poverty; overseas aid, famine relief; accommodation, housing; environment, conservation, heritage; economic, community development, employment; other charitable purposes
Address: New Israel Fund, Unit 2, Bedford Mews, London, N2 9DF
Trustees: Mr Martin Paisner CBE, Mr Lance Blackstone, Clive Sheldon QC, Ms Sarah Peters, Mr Noam Tamir, Ms Julie Blane Damelin, Mr Sam Grodzinski QC, Mrs Jane Grabiner, Sir Trevor Chinn CVO, Lord Beecham, Mr David Bernstein, Mr Paul Burger, John Cohen, Dr Eli Silber, Dr Juliet Stevens
Income: £2,006,063 [2016]; £1,576,779 [2015]; £1,521,442 [2014]; £1,652,607 [2013]; £1,279,167 [2012]

New Kadampa Tradition - International Kadampa Buddhist Union
Registered: 4 Nov 1992 *Employees:* 34 *Volunteers:* 250
Tel: 01229 588533 *Website:* kadampa.org
Activities: Education, training; religious activities
Address: Conishead Priory, Priory Road, Ulverston, Cumbria, LA12 9QQ
Trustees: Miss Heather Wright, Mr Henry Freyermueller Shefveland, Ms Jennifer Jane Andrews, Paul Boseley
Income: £4,367,319 [2016]; £3,549,135 [2015]; £2,632,507 [2014]; £4,004,043 [2013]; £3,003,727 [2012]

New Life Christian Centre (Croydon)
Registered: 19 Mar 2008 *Employees:* 26 *Volunteers:* 400
Tel: 020 8680 7671 *Website:* newlifecroydon.co.uk
Activities: Education, training; advancement of health or saving of lives; prevention or relief of poverty; religious activities
Address: New Life Christian Centre, 5 Cairo New Road, Croydon, Surrey, CR0 1XP
Trustees: Mr Neville Pinto, Mr Chima Amiaka, Mr Mark Andrew Rossell, Adetayo Aderemi, Mr Tony Sokan, Dr Olukunle Onabolu, Mr Jay Bhatt
Income: £1,195,991 [2017]; £1,218,282 [2016]; £1,109,436 [2015]; £1,223,085 [2014]; £1,339,477 [2013]

New Linx Housing Trust
Registered: 9 Mar 2006 *Employees:* 94
Tel: 0121 788 7535 *Website:* waterloo.org.uk
Activities: Accommodation, housing; other charitable purposes
Address: 1700 Solihull Parkway, Birmingham Business Park, Birmingham, B37 7YD
Trustees: Mr Jeffrey Sharnock, Prof Janet Russum Ford, Mr David John Pickering, Mr Dennis Sleath, Ms Jennifer Gertrude Wood, Waterloo Housing Group Ltd
Income: £42,061,000 [2017]; £39,360,000 [2016]; £38,209,000 [2015]; £34,092,000 [2014]; £32,656,000 [2013]

New Marston Limited
Registered: 2 Jul 2002
Tel: 0161 660 3492
Activities: General charitable purposes; education, training; prevention or relief of poverty; religious activities
Address: Enterprise House, 3 Middleton Road, Manchester, M8 5DT
Trustees: Mr David Neuwirth, Mr Refoel Halpern, Mr Jacob Adler, Mr Sir Weis
Income: £3,794,699 [2017]; £5,194,221 [2016]; £14,253,877 [2015]; £17,563,319 [2014]; £9,623,056 [2013]

New North London Synagogue
Registered: 18 Nov 2002 *Employees:* 21 *Volunteers:* 350
Tel: 020 8346 8560 *Website:* nnls-masorti.org.uk
Activities: General charitable purposes; education, training; religious activities
Address: 80 East End Road, Finchley, London, N3 2SY
Trustees: Mr Richard Gold, Ms Caroline Ruth Lessof, Mrs Tamara Isaacs, Ms Claire Mandel, Richard Edward Laikin, Mr David Michael Waksman, Mr Paul Simon Harris, Mrs Harriet Ruth Oppenheimer, Mr Martin Joseph Burstyn, Debra Virchis, Rabbi Jonathan Theodore Wittenberg, Mr Anthony Harry Bogod, Ms Abigail Levitt, Mrs Judith Williams, Mr Micah Jethro Gold, Mr Richard Michael Morris Stephens, Mr Jonathan Michael Polin, Mrs Danielle Rubin, Sarah Miller
Income: £1,706,380 [2016]; £1,664,183 [2015]; £1,597,920 [2014]; £1,544,263 [2013]; £1,563,785 [2012]

New Pathways Family Friendly Therapeutic Centre of Excellence
Registered: 1 Oct 2008 *Employees:* 77 *Volunteers:* 60
Tel: 01685 379310 *Website:* newpathways.org.uk
Activities: General charitable purposes; education, training; advancement of health or saving of lives; disability; economic, community development, employment
Address: Willow House, Lower Thomas Street, Merthyr Tydfil, CF47 0BY
Trustees: Ms Ruth Avril Davies, Mr Graeme Gibson, Mr David Pritchard, Mr Phillip Simon Jones, Ms Anna Slatter, Mrs Lynne Schofield, Alison Smith, Mrs Maria Julie Ann Jones
Income: £1,540,490 [2017]; £1,926,794 [2016]; £1,228,607 [2015]; £1,169,456 [2014]; £1,246,153 [2013]

New Philanthropy Capital
Registered: 27 Mar 2002 *Employees:* 41
Tel: 020 7620 4896 *Website:* thinknpc.org
Activities: General charitable purposes
Address: N P C, 185 Park Street, London, SE1 9BL
Trustees: Sir Harvey Andrew McGrath, Mr John Bertram Stares, Mr Richard Atterbury, Mr Simon Buckby, Peter Spencer William Wheeler, Ms Lucy De Groot CBE, Marcelle Speller
Income: £3,036,911 [2017]; £2,675,154 [2016]; £2,088,533 [2015]; £2,604,754 [2014]; £2,069,700 [2013]

The New Phytologist Trust
Registered: 4 Dec 2013 *Employees:* 8
Tel: 01970 625117 *Website:* newphytologist.org
Activities: Education, training; arts, culture, heritage, science; environment, conservation, heritage
Address: 15 Y Lanfa, Trefechan, Aberystwyth, Ceredigion, SY23 1AS
Trustees: Prof Alastair Hugh Fitter, Mr Richard James Norby, Prof Anne Elisabeth Osbourn, Prof Keith Lindsay, Professor Liam Dolan, Prof Alistair MacCulloch Hetherington, Prof Howard Thomas, Mr Alisair Robert MacBrair Campbell, Professor Maria Harrison, Mr Leslie Ross
Income: £1,001,505 [2016]; £1,011,071 [2015]; £2,689,789 [2014]

The New Rachmistrivke Synagogue Trust
Registered: 27 Nov 1995
Activities: Education, training; prevention or relief of poverty; religious activities
Address: 12 Portland Avenue, London, N16 6ET
Trustees: Mr Malcolm Stern, Mrs Rachel Margulies, Mr David Margulies
Income: £1,749,549 [2016]; £1,322,812 [2015]; £1,066,455 [2014]; £1,529,340 [2013]; £1,711,622 [2012]

The New Room/John Wesley's Chapel
Registered: 10 Sep 2010 *Employees:* 5 *Volunteers:* 70
Tel: 0117 926 4740 *Website:* newroombristol.org.uk
Activities: Religious activities
Address: The New Room, 36 The Horsefair, Bristol, BS1 3JE
Trustees: Ms Eleanor Jane Allin, Mr Stephen Williams, Mr Michael Rose, Rev Jonathan Pye, Mr Philip Carter, Mr Gary Best, Mr Robert Wood, Mr Stephen Duckworth, Mr Michael Culshaw, Mr John Hirst, Mrs Linda Jones, Rev Anthony Ward Jones, Mrs Aroona Smith MBE DL, Rev David Alderman, Mr Martin Hunt, Mrs Jenny Carpenter, Rev David Weeks, Mr Thomas David Bainbridge, Mr Peter Knowles, Rev Jonsing Lee, Mr Geoffrey Gollop OBE
Income: £2,412,729 [2016]; £336,101 [2015]; £241,000 [2014]; £221,928 [2013]; £195,526 [2012]

New Roots Limited
Registered: 31 May 1996 *Employees:* 23
Tel: 0121 429 3933 *Website:* newrootsltd.co.uk
Activities: Disability; prevention or relief of poverty; accommodation, housing
Address: 369 City Road, Edgbaston, Birmingham, B16 0EN
Trustees: June Mone, Esther Titchen, Andrew Howell, Mr John McQuay, Shaun McDonald
Income: £4,406,988 [2016]; £2,232,474 [2015]; £1,946,180 [2014]; £2,114,902 [2013]; £2,131,473 [2012]

New Schools Network
Registered: 14 Oct 2009 *Employees:* 29
Tel: 020 7952 8497 *Website:* newschoolsnetwork.org
Activities: Education, training; prevention or relief of poverty
Address: 8th Floor, Westminster Tower, 3 Albert Embankment, London, SE1 7SL
Trustees: Mr Laurence Justin Dowley, Sir Nicholas John Weller, Mr David Peter John Ross, Miss Katharine Birbalsingh, Mr Geoffrey Ronald Davies, Mr Barnaby John Lenon, Mr Andrew Eric Law, Mr Stephen Gregory Peter De Heinrich
Income: £2,482,053 [2017]; £1,334,455 [2016]; £1,721,967 [2015]; £1,898,255 [2014]; £1,546,411 [2013]

New Servol
Registered: 15 Sep 2008 *Employees:* 45 *Volunteers:* 2
Tel: 0121 454 3081 *Website:* servolct.org.uk
Activities: Education, training; advancement of health or saving of lives; prevention or relief of poverty; accommodation, housing
Address: 235-237 Dudley Road, Birmingham, B18 4EJ
Trustees: Ms Cyndi Colis, Mr George Branch Branch, Ms Marcia Jean Arnett, Ms Lorrette Harris, Ms Laura Claire Bugby
Income: £1,549,116 [2017]; £1,275,842 [2016]; £1,061,723 [2015]; £1,140,494 [2014]; £1,190,530 [2013]

New Testament Church of God
Registered: 2 Mar 1967 *Employees:* 132 *Volunteers:* 3,500
Website: ntcg.org.uk
Activities: Religious activities
Address: New Testament Church of God, 3 Cheyne Walk, Northampton, NN1 5PT
Trustees: Louis R McLeod, D A Webley, Rev Headley Gayle, Mr Spencer Anderson Rev, Rev Paul Thomas Rev, Rev Barrington Mullings, Donald Bolt, D Douglas, Rev Jonathan Jackson, Rev Claion Grandison Rev, Rev Donnovan Allen, Rev Brian Robinson
Income: £10,394,159 [2016]; £10,266,963 [2015]; £9,328,679 [2014]; £9,457,379 [2013]; £9,029,266 [2012]

The New Theatre Royal-Trustees (Portsmouth) Limited
Registered: 4 Oct 1976 *Employees:* 32 *Volunteers:* 13
Tel: 023 9264 9000 *Website:* newtheatreroyal.com
Activities: Education, training; arts, culture, heritage, science; economic, community development, employment; recreation
Address: 57 St Leonards Avenue, Hayling Island, Hants, PO11 9BN
Trustees: Mrs Drusilla Moody, Mr David Michael Penrose, Ms Susan Elizabeth Aistrope, Mr Timothy Nigel Herman, Councillor Neill Young, Mr Alexander Martin Wardle, Mr Scott Ramsay, Mr Colin Bradey, Mrs Krystyna Stefania Butwilowska, Mrs Judith Deborah Smyth, Ms Fiona Louise Baxter
Income: £1,113,289 [2017]; £1,338,695 [2016]; £1,988,973 [2015]; £1,483,536 [2014]; £1,009,725 [2013]

New Tribes Mission
Registered: 22 Feb 1980 *Volunteers:* 105
Tel: 01472 387700 *Website:* ntm.org.uk
Activities: Education, training; religious activities
Address: New Tribes Mission, Kenneth Campbell Road, North Cotes, Grimsby, N E Lincs, DN36 5XU
Trustees: Mr Frank Brearley, Mr Norman Robert McCready, Mr Stephen Bosley, Mr Matthew Cuthbert, Mr Stephen Jerrard
Income: £1,740,269 [2016]; £1,801,526 [2015]; £1,853,251 [2014]; £2,363,755 [2013]; £2,129,612 [2012]

The New Victoria Hospital Limited
Registered: 9 May 2011 *Employees:* 260
Tel: 020 8949 9644 *Website:* newvictoriahospital.co.uk
Activities: Education, training; advancement of health or saving of lives
Address: New Victoria Hospital, 184 Coombe Lane West, Kingston upon Thames, Surrey, KT2 7EG
Trustees: Mr Graham Arthur Ridgeway Ball, Mr Mark James Curtis, Ms Catriona Ann MacKay, John Hamblin, Mr Martin Anthony Matthews
Income: £15,157,000 [2017]; £14,874,000 [2016]; £14,772,000 [2015]; £14,279,000 [2014]; £14,151,000 [2013]

New Wine International
Registered: 16 Feb 2001 *Employees:* 16 *Volunteers:* 500
Tel: 020 8855 5888 *Website:* newwine.co.uk
Activities: General charitable purposes; education, training; prevention or relief of poverty; religious activities
Address: New Wine Church, Gateway House, John Wilson Street, London, SE18 6QQ
Trustees: Mr Babajide Olaleye, Mrs Adejoke Adeyemi, Mr Adekola Adewale Taiwo, Mr Philip Olusegun Adeyi
Income: £2,453,435 [2016]; £2,258,229 [2015]; £2,243,481 [2014]; £2,292,731 [2013]; £2,209,977 [2012]

New Wine Trust
Registered: 9 Jan 2001 *Employees:* 22 *Volunteers:* 4,000
Tel: 020 8567 6717 *Website:* new-wine.org
Activities: Religious activities
Address: New Wine Trust, 4a Ridley Avenue, London, W13 9XW
Trustees: Canon John Hughes, Mr Richard Antcliffe, Rev Ian Parkinson, Christina Fuller, Mr David Lynch, Rev John Coles, Mr Michael Royal, Mrs Elizabeth Anne Fell
Income: £4,173,395 [2016]; £3,923,233 [2015]; £4,009,112 [2014]; £4,571,673 [2013]; £4,500,241 [2012]

The New Wolsey Theatre Company Limited
Registered: 14 Aug 2000 *Employees:* 55 *Volunteers:* 123
Tel: 01473 295900 *Website:* wolseytheatre.co.uk
Activities: Arts, culture, heritage, science
Address: New Wolsey Theatre Co Ltd, Civic Drive, Ipswich, Suffolk, IP1 2AS
Trustees: Mr Adrian Grady, Mr Richard Lister, Miss Hannah Skeates, Mr David Hutchinson, Mr Andy Alexander Yacoub, Mr David Clements, Mr Christopher Waters, Miss Louise Rogers, Mrs Sarah Jane Collins, Ms Charlotte Gail Wormstone
Income: £4,813,883 [2017]; £4,138,891 [2016]; £3,075,905 [2015]; £3,289,482 [2014]; £3,454,985 [2013]

New World Mission Association UK
Registered: 22 Nov 2005 *Employees:* 29 *Volunteers:* 100
Tel: 020 7729 1514 *Website:* cclnewma.org
Activities: Education, training; prevention or relief of poverty; religious activities
Address: London City Mission Christian Centres, Nasmith Christian Centre, 14 Penn Street, London, N1 5DJ
Trustees: Mr David Ravelo, Mr Alejandro Torres, Mrs Nancy Miguel, Mr Jesus Ignacio Bedoya Martinez, Mr Alvaro Vinasco
Income: £1,132,482 [2016]; £1,148,075 [2015]; £1,341,059 [2014]; £1,354,512 [2013]

Newark Preparatory School Company Limited
Registered: 1 Apr 1963 *Employees:* 46 *Volunteers:* 14
Tel: 01636 704103 *Website:* highfieldsschool.co.uk
Activities: Education, training; arts, culture, heritage, science; amateur sport
Address: Rivermead, Trent Lane, South Clifton, Newark, Notts, NG23 7AE
Trustees: Mr David Ackroyd, Mr Will Staunton, Mrs Janet Marion Beaumont, Mr Jeffrey John Parr, Mrs Catherine Morrison, Mr Will Bicknell, Mrs Sarah Cameron, Mr James Robinson
Income: £1,335,077 [2016]; £844,339 [2015]; £825,689 [2014]; £890,865 [2013]; £884,831 [2012]

Newark and Nottinghamshire Agricultural Society
Registered: 19 Jul 1983 *Employees:* 81 *Volunteers:* 85
Tel: 01636 705796 *Website:* newarkshowground.com
Activities: General charitable purposes; environment, conservation, heritage; recreation
Address: Newark & Nottinghamshire Agricultural Society, The County Showground, Winthorpe, Newark, Notts, NG24 2NY
Trustees: Mr Bill Whysall, Bob Sheldon, Mr Charlie White, Mrs Gill Lewis, Mr Pete Croft, Mr Pip Hallam, Mr Roger James Jackson, Mr John Paul Brydon, Mr Clive Ian Applewhite, Mr David M Lambert, Mr Des Allen, Lady Helen Nall, Neil Clarke, Liz Lambert, Jenny Saint, Kate Thomas, Mr Frank Abbot Reynolds MBE, Mrs Angela Mary Hardstaff, Mrs Emma Jane Harriet Hawthorne, Mr Mike Sheldon, Mr Richard Alvey Sheldon, Mr Roger Edward Pykett, Mr Robin Hall FRICS FAAV, Mrs Rachel Gascoine FRICS, Mr Charles Lawrence, Mr Philip Guy Staniforth, Mr Roger Merryweather, Tony Aspbury, Nigel Crockford, David Rhodes, Tony Strawson, Mrs Carolyne Jane Cree
Income: £2,504,854 [2017]; £2,427,520 [2016]; £2,321,267 [2015]; £1,984,036 [2014]; £2,179,000 [2013]

Newbold College
Registered: 1 Feb 1996 *Employees:* 50
Tel: 01344 407402 *Website:* newbold.ac.uk
Activities: Education, training
Address: 5 Harmar Close, Wokingham, Berks, RG40 1SG
Trustees: Mr Berton Samuel, Dr Emmanuel Osei, Pastor Raafat Kamal, Pr Ian Walter Wellington Sweeney, Pr Djordje Trajkovski, Pr Kalervo Aromaki, Mr Carsten Waern, Rev Patrick Johnson, Mr Jaroslaw Dziegielewski, Mr David Nommik, Dr Jacqueline Claudette Comerasamy, Mr Robert Malcolm Pearce, Rev Drago Mojzes, Rev Rob De Raad, Mrs Isabel De Moraes, Mrs Sophia Nicholls, Dr Daniel Duda, Mr Styrkar Alvar Dramstad, Pastor Tamas Ocsai, Mrs Audrey Andersson, Mrs Ingalill Gimbler Berglund, Mr Nenad Jepuranovic, Dr John Baildam, Mr Ian Redfern, Pastor Thomas Muller, Ms Kathleen Suzelle Hanson, Rev Victor Marley, Rev Robert Sjolander, Rev Victor Hulbert
Income: £5,118,192 [2016]; £4,003,804 [2015]; £4,729,368 [2014]; £3,858,559 [2013]; £3,699,310 [2012]

Newbridge Preparatory School Limited
Registered: 2 Apr 1993 *Employees:* 47
Tel: 01902 751088 *Website:* newbridgeprepschool.org.uk
Activities: Education, training
Address: Newbridge Preparatory School, 51 Newbridge Crescent, Wolverhampton, W Midlands, WV6 0LH
Trustees: Mrs Helen Mary Hughes, Mr Guy Jonathan Birkett, Mrs Paula Margaret Timmins, John Hollingsworth, Mr Peter Neil Beech, Miss Kirpal Kaur Bhambra
Income: £1,130,547 [2017]; £1,003,183 [2016]; £1,064,037 [2015]; £958,166 [2014]; £925,633 [2013]

The Newbury Community Resource Centre Limited
Registered: 31 Aug 2000 *Employees:* 45 *Volunteers:* 865
Tel: 01635 43933 *Website:* n-c-r-c.org
Activities: Education, training; disability; prevention or relief of poverty; accommodation, housing; environment, conservation, heritage; economic, community development, employment
Address: Newbury Community Resource Centre, Unit F, Hambridge Road, Newbury, Berks, RG14 5SS
Trustees: Ms Sally-Ann Jay, Mrs Gillian Durrant, Mr Peter Hulme, Mrs Lesley Ann Reilly, Mrs Patricia Phipps, Mr John Samuel Austin, Mr Simon Hunt, John Unsworth
Income: £1,250,088 [2017]; £1,231,334 [2016]; £1,215,149 [2015]; £1,243,907 [2014]; £1,235,539 [2013]

The Newbury and District Agricultural Society
Registered: 21 Aug 1991 *Employees:* 5 *Volunteers:* 370
Tel: 01935 247111 *Website:* newburyshowground.co.uk
Activities: Education, training; animals; environment, conservation, heritage
Address: The Newbury & District Agricultural, Newbury Showground, Priors Court, Hermitage, Thatcham, Berks, RG18 9QZ
Trustees: Mr Christopher D'Olley, Mrs Eleanor Redmond, Mr Christopher Turner, Mr Jon Drew, Mrs Alison Brown, Mr Ian Wilson, Mr Adrian Scrope
Income: £1,483,756 [2016]; £1,319,553 [2015]; £1,270,576 [2014]; £1,230,678 [2013]; £1,213,795 [2012]

Newbury and Thatcham Hospital Building Trust
Registered: 21 Jan 1998
Tel: 0118 959 7222
Activities: The advancement of health or saving of lives
Address: Aquis House, 49-51 Blagrave Street, Reading, Berks, RG1 1PL
Trustees: Mr Peter Griffiths Gubb, Mr Julian James Ronald Parkes, Dr Keith Endersby, Shane Prater, Dr Robert Geoffrey Tayton, Sue Bishop, Paul Townsend, Victoria Hopgood
Income: £6,776,279 [2017]; £4,176,511 [2016]; £4,073,967 [2015]; £3,878,002 [2014]; £3,672,643 [2013]

The Newcastle Diocesan Board of Finance

Registered: 16 Jun 1966 *Employees:* 35
Tel: 0191 270 4130 *Website:* newcastle.anglican.org
Activities: Education, training; religious activities; environment, conservation, heritage
Address: Newcastle Diocesan Board of Finance, Church House, St Johns Terrace, North Shields, Tyne & Wear, NE29 6HS
Trustees: Revd Canon John Robert Sinclair, Mr Matthew William King, Venerable Geoffrey Miller, Canon Simon Robert Harper, Revd Christine Lilian Brown, Revd Canon Paul Malcolm Scott, Miss Isabella McDonald-Booth, Rt Revd Mark Simon Austin Tanner, Rev Rachel Wood, Dr John Christopher Appleby, Canon Susan Hart, The Venerable Peter John Alan Robinson, Canon Carol Wolstenholme OBE, Revd Dr Benjamin Huw Carter, Right Revd Christine Elizabeth Hardman, Mrs Elizabeth Anne Chadwick, Mrs Elizabeth Anne Kerry
Income: £7,318,824 [2016]; £7,692,552 [2015]; £7,531,641 [2014]; £7,029,324 [2013]; £6,679,639 [2012]

The Newcastle Preparatory School Trust Limited

Registered: 22 Sep 1964 *Employees:* 56 *Volunteers:* 8
Tel: 0191 281 1769 *Website:* newcastleprepschool.org.uk
Activities: Education, training
Address: Newcastle Preparatory School, 6 Eslington Road, Newcastle upon Tyne, NE2 4RH
Trustees: Mr R S Appleby, Ms Rachel Hudson, Mrs Sharmishta Chatterjee-Banerjee, Mrs Susan Blair, Mr Nigel Herdman, Mrs Patricia Kimmond Caine, Mr Richard Waterhouse
Income: £2,760,939 [2017]; £3,017,931 [2016]; £2,511,177 [2015]; £2,335,487 [2014]; £2,271,593 [2013]

Newcastle School for Boys

Registered: 10 Feb 1975 *Employees:* 70 *Volunteers:* 3
Tel: 0191 255 9300 *Website:* newcastleschool.co.uk
Activities: Education, training
Address: Newcastle School for Boys, 30 West Avenue, Gosforth, Newcastle upon Tyne, NE3 4ES
Trustees: Dr Neil Daniel Lloyd Jones, Mr Michael Gregory Austin, Mrs Claire King, Mr Timothy James Care, Mr Philip Douglas Parkinson
Income: £4,160,847 [2017]; £3,706,754 [2016]; £3,864,248 [2015]; £3,612,953 [2014]; £3,697,980 [2013]

Newcastle Theatre Royal Trust Limited

Registered: 14 Aug 1975 *Employees:* 297
Tel: 0191 244 2500 *Website:* theatre.royal.co.uk
Activities: Education, training; arts, culture, heritage, science; recreation
Address: Theatre Royal, 100 Grey Street, Newcastle upon Tyne, NE1 6BR
Trustees: Bill Midgley OBE, Mr Adam Fenwick, Mrs Julie Blackie, Mr John Paul Lee, Mr Raymond Mills, Mr Howard William Tait, Ms Sheila Mary Chapman MA, Mrs Joan Eileen Louw, Mr John Carver
Income: £16,011,703 [2017]; £11,478,073 [2016]; £12,442,502 [2015]; £9,839,969 [2014]; £11,073,777 [2013]

Newcastle United Foundation

Registered: 8 Jul 2008 *Employees:* 53 *Volunteers:* 50
Tel: 0191 201 8450 *Website:* nufoundation.org.uk
Activities: Education, training; advancement of health or saving of lives; disability; amateur sport
Address: Newcastle United Foundation, St James Park, Strawberry Place, Newcastle upon Tyne, NE1 4ST
Trustees: Mrs Claire Alexander, Mr Lee Charnley, Mr Graeme Mason, Mr Stephen Harper, Mr John Marshall, Mr Brian Thorpe, Ms Judith Doyle, Mr Michael Thompson
Income: £2,711,266 [2017]; £1,924,227 [2016]; £1,754,688 [2015]; £2,217,550 [2014]; £1,307,009 [2013]

Newcastle University Students' Union

Registered: 16 Sep 2010 *Employees:* 66 *Volunteers:* 5,731
Tel: 0191 239 3900 *Website:* nusu.co.uk
Activities: Education, training; amateur sport
Address: Newcastle University Students Union, University of Newcastle upon Tyne, Kings Walk, Newcastle upon Tyne, NE1 8QB
Trustees: Mr Peter Alexander Gibson, Mr Christopher Mark Simpson, Mr James William Sproston, Mr Rowan South, Mr George Reid, Mr Jonathan Alan Bennett, Mr Benjamin John Sadler, Miss Clara Pettitt, Miss Sarah Elizabeth Craggs, Miss Rebecca Bainbridge, Ms Carmen Huang, Mrs Gillian Salmon
Income: £3,795,000 [2017]; £4,007,000 [2016]; £4,064,000 [2015]; £3,457,000 [2014]; £3,327,000 [2013]

Newcastle upon Tyne Council for Voluntary Service

Registered: 15 Sep 2008 *Employees:* 42 *Volunteers:* 47
Tel: 0191 232 7445 *Website:* cvsnewcastle.org.uk
Activities: General charitable purposes; advancement of health or saving of lives; economic, community development, employment
Address: NCVS, Higham House, Higham Place, Newcastle upon Tyne, NE1 8AF
Trustees: Ruth Abrahams, Mr John Litherland, Mr Steven Nash, Katherine Israel, Mr Simon Peter Elliott, Gemma Dyer, Jamie Sadler, Anne Bonner, Mr Nitin Shukla, Mr Martin Stuart Horrocks, Mrs Joanne Patricia McKenna
Income: £1,328,981 [2017]; £1,214,876 [2016]; £1,448,778 [2015]; £1,250,613 [2014]; £998,337 [2013]

Newcastle upon Tyne Dog and Cat Shelter and Animal Sanctuary

Registered: 1 Apr 1964 *Employees:* 28 *Volunteers:* 25
Tel: 0191 215 0435 *Website:* dogandcatshelter.com
Activities: Animals
Address: Newcastle Dog & Cat Shelter & Animal Sanctuary, Benton North Farm, Benton Lane, Newcastle upon Tyne, NE12 8EH
Trustees: Mrs Jennifer Mary Simpson, Mr Adam Mitchell Harrison, Mr Timothy Fife, Andrea Wylie, Nick Manson, Suzanne Tracey Syson, Mrs Wendy Davison, Mr George Young, Mrs Tina Scrafton
Income: £1,270,043 [2017]; £808,431 [2016]; £784,771 [2015]; £670,755 [2014]; £1,074,852 [2013]

Newcastle upon Tyne Hospitals NHS Charity

Registered: 30 Jul 1996 *Employees:* 10 *Volunteers:* 3
Tel: 0191 256 6131 *Website:* newcastle-hospitals.org.uk
Activities: Education, training; advancement of health or saving of lives; disability
Address: Regent Point, Regent Farm Road, Newcastle upon Tyne, NE3 3HD
Trustees: Newcastle Upon Tyne Hospitals Foundation Trust
Income: £4,781,191 [2017]; £2,842,565 [2016]; £2,884,061 [2015]; £2,907,342 [2014]; £2,546,385 [2013]

The Newcastle upon Tyne Royal Grammar School

Registered: 31 May 2006 *Employees:* 228 *Volunteers:* 19
Tel: 0191 281 3940 *Website:* rgs.newcastle.sch.uk
Activities: Education, training
Address: Royal Grammar School, Eskdale Terrace, Newcastle upon Tyne, NE2 4DX
Trustees: Mr Paul Campbell, Councillor Trevor Thorne, Alan Fletcher, Prof Sophie Hambleton, Mrs Julie Drummond, Aarti Gupta, Mr Tony Murphy, Alex Lamb, Mr Ian Simpson, Isaac Evbuomwan, Mrs Catherine Murphy, Mr Robert Hugh Fell FRICS, Ms Tracey Elizabeth Bridget Hartley MRICS BSc MSc MBA, Professor Muzlifah Haniffa, Scarlett Milligan
Income: £16,899,197 [2017]; £16,077,720 [2016]; £15,265,976 [2015]; £14,760,764 [2014]; £14,449,627 [2013]

Newcastle-Under-Lyme School

Registered: 11 Jun 2008 *Employees:* 242
Tel: 01782 664605 *Website:* nuls.org.uk
Activities: Education, training
Address: Newcastle-under-Lyme School, Mount Pleasant, Newcastle-under-Lyme, Staffs, ST5 1DB
Trustees: Mrs Kathleen Miller, Mrs Elizabeth Gillow, Mr Graham Eric Neyt, Mrs Julie Grant BA, Mr Iain MacDonald LLB Dip LP MBA, Mr David Holland MA, Mr David Wallbank, Mr Matt Warren, Dr Shireen Edmends MBBS FRCA MMedSci, Ms Fiona Tordoff, Mr Andrew McGowan
Income: £9,552,882 [2017]; £9,082,560 [2016]; £8,857,650 [2015]; £8,288,710 [2014]; £8,461,081 [2013]

Newells School Trust Limited

Registered: 5 Jun 1969 *Employees:* 107 *Volunteers:* 12
Tel: 01444 400526 *Website:* handcrossparkschool.co.uk
Activities: Education, training
Address: Handcross Park School, London Road, Handcross, Haywards Heath, W Sussex, RH17 6HF
Trustees: Mr Geoff Miller MBE FCIB, Mrs Jo-Anne Riley, Mrs Wendy Challen, Mr Geoffrey Bush, Mrs Jane Hamblett-Jahn, Mr Martin Colyer, Mrs Shirley Harris, Mr Rishi Soni, Mr Miles Templeman
Income: £5,398,063 [2017]; £5,360,976 [2016]; £4,428,732 [2015]; £3,886,943 [2014]; £3,079,182 [2013]

Newground Together

Registered: 6 Jul 1990 *Employees:* 79 *Volunteers:* 50
Website: newground.co.uk
Activities: Education, training; environment, conservation, heritage; economic, community development, employment
Address: Newground, Bob Watts Building, Nova Scotia Wharf, Bolton Road, Blackburn, BB2 3GE
Trustees: Mr Laurence Loft, Mr John Townend, Mr Alan Cotton, Mr Malcolm Ivan Harrison, Mr Kevin Leith, Mr Graham Haworth, Mr James Hartley
Income: £5,784,258 [2017]; £6,284,983 [2016]; £5,738,004 [2015]; £4,684,143 [2014]; £3,559,706 [2013]

Newham Community Renewal Programme Limited

Registered: 5 Jun 1978 *Employees:* 49 *Volunteers:* 41
Tel: 020 8471 6954 *Website:* renewalprogramme.org.uk
Activities: General charitable purposes; education, training; disability; prevention or relief of poverty; accommodation, housing; amateur sport; economic, community development, employment
Address: 395 High Street North, London, E12 6PG
Trustees: Mr Jonathan Charles Griffiths, Mr Christopher Lindsey, Dr Martha Foley, Mr Peter Koczerzat, Mr Arnold Ridout, Mr Elis Matthews, Ms Agnieszka Schirm
Income: £1,473,960 [2017]; £1,745,641 [2016]; £2,016,484 [2015]; £2,286,331 [2014]; £2,933,992 [2013]

Newham Foundation

Registered: 8 Nov 2004
Tel: 020 8257 4000
Activities: Education, training
Address: Newham College of Further Education, East Ham Campus, High Street South, London, E6 6ER
Trustees: Paul Stephen, Ms Jane Moon, Ms Deborah Hindson
Income: £3,236,000 [2016]; £1,087,000 [2015]; £229,000 [2014]; £238,000 [2013]

Newham Music Trust

Registered: 23 Oct 1995 *Employees:* 64
Tel: 020 3598 6260 *Website:* newham-music.org.uk
Activities: Education, training; advancement of health or saving of lives; disability; arts, culture, heritage, science
Address: Unit 13 St Luke's Business Centre, 85 Tarling Road, Canning Town, London, E16 1HN
Trustees: Christine Bowden, Mr John Leslie Barber, Mrs Fiona Chesney Cullen, Mrs Elizabeth Ayofeji Oriakhi, Jean Lane, Mr Jonathan Andre Boux, Ms Martyne Alexandra Callender, Chris Brannick
Income: £1,088,031 [2017]; £1,095,649 [2016]; £1,164,686 [2015]; £1,000,664 [2014]; £1,111,761 [2013]

Newham Training and Education Centre

Registered: 20 Feb 1990 *Employees:* 158
Tel: 020 8519 5843 *Website:* newtec.ac.uk
Activities: Education, training
Address: Newham Training and Education Centr, 1 Mark Street, London, E15 4GY
Trustees: Ms Linda Jordan, Ms Marcia Samuels, Mrs Marzieh Chipperfield, Ms Elizabeth Laycock, Mrs Sheila Weeden, Ms Nadege Nakubuhizi
Income: £6,519,195 [2017]; £5,511,731 [2016]; £5,598,352 [2015]; £5,059,913 [2014]; £4,164,775 [2013]

Newland House School Trust Limited

Registered: 16 Jul 1973 *Employees:* 78
Website: newlandhouse.net
Activities: Education, training
Address: Newland House School, Waldegrave Park, Twickenham, Middlesex, TW1 4TQ
Trustees: Mr David Howard Ridgeon, Mrs Julia Louise Higgins, Mr Andrew Gumpert, Mr Matthew Duncan Battle, Mr Henry Kilpatrick Mann, Mrs Belinda Canham, Mr Richard Burden, Mr Adrian Warwick Hughes QC, Mr Henry Howard Cook, Mrs Dee Suzanne Masters
Income: £4,902,000 [2017]; £4,649,769 [2016]; £4,494,611 [2015]; £4,281,429 [2014]; £3,940,092 [2013]

Newman University

Registered: 6 Jul 2005 *Employees:* 319
Tel: 07736 678027 *Website:* newman.ac.uk
Activities: Education, training
Address: 50 Forest Road, Moseley, Birmingham, B13 9DH
Trustees: Archbishop Bernard Longley, Ms Deirdre Finucane, Mr Glen Alexander, Mr Jonathan Day, Mr Phillip Lennon, Mr John Westwood, Mr Richard Wallace, Dr Karen Graham, Mrs Gayle Ditchburn, Rev David Ernest Charles Evans, Professor Scott Davidson, Dr Mark Goodwin, Mr Stephen Kenny, Dr John Carlisle, Professor Femi Oyebode, Mr Colin Harris, Mr Nathan Ganley, Miss Elizabeth McGrath QC
Income: £24,451,477 [2017]; £23,960,656 [2016]; £21,596,873 [2015]; £20,876,784 [2014]; £20,310,238 [2013]

Newpier Charity Limited

Registered: 20 Mar 1986
Tel: 020 8802 4449
Activities: General charitable purposes; prevention or relief of poverty; religious activities
Address: 186 Lordship Road, London, N16 5ES
Trustees: Mr Charles Marguiles, Mrs Helen Knopfler, Mrs Rachel Marguiles
Income: £1,472,711 [2017]; £924,319 [2016]; £277,395 [2015]; £1,097,243 [2014]; £1,006,577 [2013]

Newport Live

Registered: 16 Jun 2015 *Employees:* 332 *Volunteers:* 200
Tel: 01633 656757 *Website:* newportlive.co.uk
Activities: Arts, culture, heritage, science; recreation
Address: Newport International Sport Village, Velodrome Way, Newport, NP19 4RB
Trustees: Mr Martin John Warren, Mr David Frank Graham, Mrs Joanna Hardman, Mr Kevin David Ward, Ms Stephanie Elizabeth Hazlehurst, Mr Michael John Butler, Mr John Anthony Standerline, Councillor Deborah Ann Wilcox, Mr John Roger Harrhy, Mr Thomas Anthony Dean Lewis, Mr Mark Jeffrey Denley Whitcutt
Income: £8,861,876 [2017]; £8,713,646 [2016]

Newport Mind

Registered: 27 Apr 1994 *Employees:* 30 *Volunteers:* 35
Tel: 01633 258741 *Website:* newportmind.org
Activities: General charitable purposes; education, training; advancement of health or saving of lives; disability; prevention or relief of poverty; accommodation, housing
Address: Newport Mind, 100-101 Commercial Street, Newport, NP20 1LU
Trustees: Mrs Annette Calnon, Ms Lynne Cooper, Mr Jonathan Jones, Mr Patrick Felkin, Ms Janice Foxley, Mr Jonathan Hughes, Mr Andrew Sutton
Income: £1,360,143 [2017]; £1,302,408 [2016]; £1,192,932 [2015]; £1,087,705 [2014]; £984,143 [2013]

The Newspaper Press Fund

Registered: 16 Nov 1962 *Employees:* 31 *Volunteers:* 17
Tel: 01306 887511 *Website:* journalistscharity.org.uk
Activities: General charitable purposes; prevention or relief of poverty; accommodation, housing
Address: Newspaper Press Fund, Dickens House, 35 Wathen Road, Dorking, Surrey, RH4 1JY
Trustees: Mr Stephen Somerville, Mr Michael Anthony Watson, Mr Robert James Gibson, Mr William John Gell Hagerty, Mr Ramsay John Angus Smith, Mr Raymond Massey, Mr Paul Jones, Mr Derek Inman, Mr Richard Savill, Ms Catherine Reid, Ms Gillian Ann James, Mr Nicholas Clement Jones, Mr William Newman, Mr Laurie Upshon, Mr Chris Boffey, Ms Anna Botting, Ms Susan Ryan, Mrs Jill Palmer, Mr Thomas Clarke, Mr John Crowley
Income: £2,190,000 [2016]; £1,855,000 [2015]; £1,677,000 [2014]; £1,589,000 [2013]; £1,591,000 [2012]

Newstraid Benevolent Fund

Registered: 16 Nov 2006 *Employees:* 8 *Volunteers:* 150
Tel: 01279 879569 *Website:* newstraid.org.uk
Activities: General charitable purposes; prevention or relief of poverty
Address: Suites 1 & 2, Thremhall Estate, Start Hill, Bishop's Stortford, Herts, CM22 7TD
Trustees: Mr David Holliday, Mr Thomas Melvyn Lewis, Mr Ronald William Rushbrook, Mr Neil Hilton Jagger, Mark Stephen Cassie, Mr Colin Fletcher, Mrs Ingrid Jones, Mr Michael David Mirams, Mr Richard John Webb, Mr John George Stranger, Mr Daniel Alexander Scott
Income: £2,146,350 [2016]; £2,057,187 [2015]; £2,182,363 [2014]; £1,820,386 [2013]; £2,077,723 [2012]

The Next Step Trust

Registered: 15 May 2006 *Employees:* 41 *Volunteers:* 4
Tel: 01422 330938 *Website:* thenextsteptrust.org.uk
Activities: Education, training; disability; amateur sport; economic, community development, employment
Address: Community Foundation for Calderdale, 162a King Cross Road, Halifax, W Yorks, HX1 3LN
Trustees: Mrs Christine Ann Naylor, Mr Jonathan Christopher Pearson, Mr John Mooney, Leigh-Anne Stradeski, Mrs Maureen Sneddon Cawthorn, Mr Andrew Peers
Income: £1,226,430 [2017]; £1,155,278 [2016]; £1,077,100 [2015]; £915,760 [2014]; £728,087 [2013]

Nexus Institute of Creative Arts

Registered: 29 Nov 2007 *Employees:* 14 *Volunteers:* 10
Tel: 024 7671 3209 *Website:* nexus-ica.co.uk
Activities: General charitable purposes; education, training; religious activities; arts, culture, heritage, science; economic, community development, employment
Address: Astoria House, 71 Albany Road, Coventry, Warwicks, CV5 6JR
Trustees: Mr Steve Smith, Mr Chris Edwards, Mr Matthew Ling, Mr David Bertram, Mrs Charlotte Maytum, Revd Jenette Jones
Income: £1,087,986 [2017]; £435,835 [2016]; £497,898 [2015]; £493,161 [2014]; £411,897 [2013]

The Florence Nightingale Foundation

Registered: 2 Jan 1967 *Employees:* 5
Tel: 020 7730 3030 *Website:* florence-nightingale-foundation.org.uk
Activities: Education, training; advancement of health or saving of lives
Address: The Florence Nightingale Foundation, Room AB.48, 11-13 Cavendish Square, London, W1G 0AN
Trustees: Rt Hon Lord Remnant, Dr Colin Reeves, Mr B Sanderson CBE, Mr Peter Siddall, Mrs Ann Keen, Captain Alison Hofman, Professor Dame Jill Linda MacLeod Clark, Mr Brian Wilson, Mrs Mary Spinks CBE, The Baroness Mary Watkins of Tavistock, Mr Martin Bradley, Mr Andrew Andrews MBE, Dr Edward Libbey, Mr David Hulf, Miss Theo Noel Smith
Income: £1,546,826 [2016]; £1,207,512 [2015]; £1,347,907 [2014]; £764,300 [2013]; £655,867 [2012]

Nightingale Hammerson

Registered: 22 Sep 1962 *Employees:* 373 *Volunteers:* 200
Tel: 020 8772 2355 *Website:* nightingalehammerson.org
Activities: Other charitable purposes
Address: Nightingale House, 105 Nightingale Lane, London, SW12 8NB
Trustees: Nightingale Hammerson Trustee Company Limited
Income: £15,586,000 [2016]; £15,635,000 [2015]; £19,372,000 [2014]; £18,823,000 [2013]; £15,044,000 [2012]

Florence Nightingale Hospice Charity
Registered: 5 Jun 2007 *Employees:* 23 *Volunteers:* 400
Tel: 01296 429975 *Website:* fnhospice.org.uk
Activities: Education, training; advancement of health or saving of lives; disability
Address: Florence Nightingale Hospice Charity, Walton Lodge, Walton Street, Aylesbury, Bucks, HP21 7QY
Trustees: Mr John Leggett, Miss Sarah Plumridge, Mr Michael Bennett, Mr Clive Gilbert, Mrs Jane Lillian Naismith, Mr Peter Cotton, Mr Noel John Ratcliffe, Mrs Ann Tomkins, Dr Alan Watt, Ms Jane Wilson, Mr Peter Lindley Bridgman BSc FRICS
Income: £1,906,187 [2017]; £1,868,340 [2016]; £1,775,956 [2015]; £1,681,899 [2014]; £1,599,116 [2013]

Nilkanth Estates
Registered: 3 Aug 2012 *Volunteers:* 100
Activities: Accommodation, housing; religious activities
Address: 105-119 Brentfield Road, Neasden, London, NW10 8LD
Trustees: Dr Mayank Shah, Kishorkant Bhattessa, Mr Sunilkumar Patel, Mr Jitu M Patel, Arvind Patel
Income: £7,654,803 [2016]; £3,429,921 [2015]; £730,531 [2014]; £47,353,912 [2013]

No Limits (South)
Registered: 10 Oct 2001 *Employees:* 105 *Volunteers:* 166
Tel: 023 8022 4224 *Website:* nolimitshelp.org.uk
Activities: Education, training; advancement of health or saving of lives; prevention or relief of poverty; accommodation, housing; economic, community development, employment; other charitable purposes
Address: 35 The Avenue, Southampton, SO17 1XN
Trustees: Mrs Sarah Anderson, Ms Anjelica Finnegan, Mr Stephen Taylor, Ms Carol Evans, Mr Thom Young, Pat James, Mr Simon Derrick, Mr Martin Roscoe, Ms Natalie Webb, Ms Maryam Minhas
Income: £3,189,981 [2017]; £2,409,984 [2016]; £1,852,911 [2015]; £1,818,561 [2014]; £1,492,768 [2013]

The Noah Enterprise (New Opportunities and Horizons)
Registered: 12 Dec 1996 *Employees:* 45 *Volunteers:* 300
Tel: 01582 417785 *Website:* noahenterprise.org
Activities: General charitable purposes; education, training; advancement of health or saving of lives; prevention or relief of poverty; economic, community development, employment
Address: 141 Park Street, Luton, Beds, LU1 3HG
Trustees: Dr P J Ward, Mr Stephen Guyon, Mr Tyrone Jack Spence, Lord McKenzie of Luton, Mr James Hannigan, Mr Anthony William Gray
Income: £1,407,672 [2017]; £1,418,523 [2016]; £1,441,013 [2015]; £1,186,790 [2014]; £943,622 [2013]

Noah's Ark - The Children's Hospice
Registered: 16 Jun 2000 *Employees:* 34 *Volunteers:* 220
Website: noahsarkhospice.org.uk
Activities: The advancement of health or saving of lives
Address: 3 Beauchamp Court, 10 Victors Way, Barnet, Herts, EN5 5TZ
Trustees: Mr Jeremy Isaacs, Mrs Mary O'Toole, Dr Heather MacKinnon, Mr David Michael Lazarus, Mr Nilesh Jethwa, Mr Adam Leigh, Mr Adam Levin, Mr David Mark Greenhalgh-Todd, Mr Jonathan Rose
Income: £2,832,090 [2016]; £2,027,248 [2015]; £2,312,165 [2014]; £2,378,188 [2013]; £1,600,309 [2012]

Noah's Ark Children's Hospital Charity
Registered: 11 May 1998 *Employees:* 7 *Volunteers:* 50
Website: noahsarkcharity.org
Activities: The advancement of health or saving of lives
Address: Upper Ground Floor, Noah's Ark, Children's Hospital for Wales, Heath Park, Cardiff, CF14 4XW
Trustees: Mr Edward Hayward, Mr Robert Lloyd-Griffiths, Ms Julie Ann Hayward, Dr Roger Verrier Jones, Mrs Aruna Abhyankar, Mr Lyndsay Hugh Doyle
Income: £1,088,325 [2016]; £1,095,737 [2015]; £1,863,586 [2014]; £1,356,467 [2013]; £1,306,429 [2012]

The Noam Primary School Limited
Registered: 28 Feb 2000 *Employees:* 34
Tel: 020 8203 4684 *Website:* noamprimary.org
Activities: General charitable purposes; education, training
Address: Elite House, The Broadway, West Hendon, London, NW9 7BP
Trustees: Mrs Tamara Weisz, Mr Richard Mark Denton, Dr Jeremy Rees
Income: £1,200,004 [2016]; £1,158,410 [2015]; £1,219,750 [2014]; £1,010,890 [2013]

Nofit State Community Circus Ltd
Registered: 25 Mar 2004 *Employees:* 20 *Volunteers:* 6
Tel: 029 2022 1330 *Website:* nofitstate.com
Activities: Education, training; arts, culture, heritage, science
Address: Four Elms, Four Elms Road, Cardiff, CF24 2NY
Trustees: Ms Hilary Garnham, Ms Louise Elizabeth Evans, Mr George William Fuller, Ms Manjula Karsan Bray, Ms Lisa Every, Ms Yvette Vaughn Jones, Ms Rachel Helena Walsh
Income: £2,133,643 [2017]; £2,190,460 [2016]; £2,170,174 [2015]; £2,625,921 [2014]; £1,922,527 [2013]

Anthony Nolan
Registered: 12 Jul 1990 *Employees:* 295 *Volunteers:* 1,017
Tel: 020 7284 8222 *Website:* anthonynolan.org
Activities: The advancement of health or saving of lives
Address: Anthony Nolan, 2-3 Heathgate Place, London, NW3 2NU
Trustees: Mr Lionel Morrow Cashin, Mr Brian Turner CBE, Mr Michael Altendorf, Dr James Kustow, Mr Simon Spyer, Ms Carol MacKinnon, Dr Chonnettia Jones, Mr Ian Stephen Krieger, Mrs Francis Joy Burke, Dr Ann Robinson, Mr Olivier Zucker, Mr Peter Frank Robinson, Mr Peter Aitken, Mr Martin John Hallam Laws
Income: £51,335,000 [2017]; £47,087,000 [2016]; £44,962,000 [2015]; £44,688,000 [2014]; £58,054,000 [2013]

Noor Trust
Registered: 27 Nov 2001 *Employees:* 37 *Volunteers:* 30
Tel: 020 8204 1167
Activities: Education, training; amateur sport
Address: Dr Isam Ajina, 4 Dalston Gardens, Stanmore, Middlesex, HA7 1BU
Trustees: Dr Isam Ajina, Mr Emad Dean Hilli, Dr Asaad Shallal, Dr Seyed Fazel Hosseini Milani
Income: £1,716,589 [2017]; £1,503,690 [2016]; £1,219,232 [2015]; £997,562 [2014]; £691,093 [2013]

The Norden Farm Centre Trust Limited
Registered: 13 Aug 1992 *Employees:* 46 *Volunteers:* 222
Tel: 01628 682557 *Website:* nordenfarm.org
Activities: Arts, culture, heritage, science
Address: Norden Farm Centre for The Arts, Altwood Road, Maidenhead, Berks, SL6 4PF
Trustees: Mr Clifford Derek Joseph, Mr Martin Wallace Kaye, Mr John Seymour, Mr Iain Alexander Donaldson, Mr Nick Winton, Mrs Norma Herdson, Ms Susan Flinders, Mr Roger Stock, Mr Clifford Perkins
Income: £1,034,558 [2017]; £1,057,608 [2016]; £1,101,284 [2015]; £947,635 [2014]; £909,474 [2013]

The Nordoff-Robbins Music Therapy Centre
Registered: 23 Sep 1980 *Employees:* 84 *Volunteers:* 75
Tel: 020 7267 4496 *Website:* nordoff-robbins.org.uk
Activities: Education, training; advancement of health or saving of lives; disability
Address: 2 Lissenden Gardens, London, NW5 1PQ
Trustees: Mr Mike Miller, Ms Jane Bryant, Mr Perry Crosthwaite, Mrs Caroline Buckley, Mr Ivan Rudd, Mr David Munns, Mr Howard Jones, Mr Neil Warnock, Ms Karen Ann Allchurch
Income: £5,666,966 [2017]; £5,284,035 [2016]; £5,306,315 [2015]; £4,753,075 [2014]; £4,089,365 [2013]

Norfolk Carers Support
Registered: 7 Feb 2014 *Employees:* 31 *Volunteers:* 4
Tel: 01603 219924 *Website:* norfolkfamilycarers.org
Activities: General charitable purposes; education, training; prevention or relief of poverty; economic, community development, employment
Address: Norfolk Family Carers, 1st Floor, 69-75 Thorpe Road, Norwich, NR1 1UA
Trustees: C J Deane, G M Hadman, Mr Jason Hodgkiss, Felicity Hartley, Mr Paul Kay, Mr Maximillian Applin
Income: £1,102,451 [2017]; £786,818 [2016]; £339,518 [2015]

Norfolk Coalition of Disabled People
Registered: 13 Dec 2000 *Employees:* 80 *Volunteers:* 93
Tel: 01508 491214 *Website:* equallives.org.uk
Activities: Disability
Address: 15-18 Manor Farm Barns, Fox Road, Framingham Pigot, Norwich, NR14 7PZ
Trustees: Mr Martin Symons, Miss Penny Holden, Mr Shaun McGarry, Miss Cathrine Meijer, Dr William Albert, Cathy Combs, Mr Kevin Collor, Mr Rick Cotton, Mr Dan Barrett, Mrs Kate Mary Wyatt, Mr Jonathon Moore, Mr Tom Shakespear, Mr Martin Fleming, Mr Thomas Fadden
Income: £2,066,311 [2017]; £2,248,269 [2016]; £2,640,732 [2015]; £2,960,075 [2014]; £3,152,864 [2013]

Norfolk Community Foundation
Registered: 10 Aug 2005 *Employees:* 10
Tel: 01603 623958 *Website:* norfolkfoundation.com
Activities: General charitable purposes; education, training; advancement of health or saving of lives; disability; prevention or relief of poverty; accommodation, housing; arts, culture, heritage, science; amateur sport; animals; environment, conservation, heritage; economic, community development, employment; human rights, religious or racial harmony, equality or diversity; recreation; other charitable purposes
Address: Norfolk Community Foundation, St James Mill, Whitefriars, Norwich, NR3 1TN
Trustees: Lady Kay Fisher, Peter Franzen, Mrs Virginia Edgecombe, Mr Stephen Graham Stafford Allen, Mr Timothy Seeley, Michael Gurney, Mrs Michelle Raper, Mr Henry Greville Cator, Mr Frank Eliel, Jo Pearson, Charles Iain H Mawson, Mrs Caroline McKenzie Money, Nick Pratt
Income: £4,012,000 [2016]; £2,711,000 [2015]; £2,385,945 [2014]; £5,403,534 [2013]; £5,404,224 [2012]

The Norfolk Hospice
Registered: 10 Jun 1997 *Employees:* 71 *Volunteers:* 333
Tel: 01485 601700 *Website:* norfolkhospice.org.uk
Activities: Education, training; advancement of health or saving of lives; disability; arts, culture, heritage, science; other charitable purposes
Address: Tapping House, Wheatfields, Hillington, King's Lynn, Norfolk, PE31 6BH
Trustees: Lady Margaret Ann Ponder, Rev Richard Collier, Dr Peter Coates, Mr Brian Winden Pinker, Mrs Patricia Broke, Mrs Elaine Mash, Mrs Felicity Ruth Lyons, Mr Robert Brindley Cocks
Income: £2,648,030 [2017]; £2,639,085 [2016]; £2,453,908 [2015]; £3,614,609 [2014]; £1,670,825 [2013]

Norfolk Wildlife Trust
Registered: 30 Oct 1963 *Employees:* 90 *Volunteers:* 1,403
Tel: 01603 625540 *Website:* norfolkwildlifetrust.org.uk
Activities: Education, training; animals; environment, conservation, heritage
Address: Bewick House, 22 Thorpe Road, Norwich, NR1 1RY
Trustees: Mrs Susan Roe, Mr David Thompson, Mr Garth Inman, Mr John Sharpe, Mrs Ann Roberts, Mr Jeff Price, Miss Alice Liddle, Mr Jon Humphreys, Mr Geoffrey Randall, Miss Heather Tyrrell, Mr Philip Norton, Mr Gregory Beeton, Mr Michael Toms
Income: £6,274,477 [2017]; £5,733,527 [2016]; £5,524,892 [2015]; £6,870,531 [2014]; £6,160,751 [2013]

The Norfolk and Norwich Association for the Blind
Registered: 9 Jan 1964 *Employees:* 83 *Volunteers:* 255
Tel: 01603 629558 *Website:* nnab.org.uk
Activities: Education, training; advancement of health or saving of lives; disability; accommodation, housing; arts, culture, heritage, science; amateur sport; recreation
Address: 21 Flordon Road, Newton Flotman, Norwich, NR15 1QX
Trustees: Mr Richard West, Mr Paul Bowerbank, Mr Richard Hanson, Mrs Amanda Lockett, Miss Emily Barnston, Mrs Karen Norton, Mrs Brenda Jones, Canon Simon Stokes, Mr Andrew Orves, Mrs Georgina Holloway, Mr Guy Gowing, Mr Tim Hirst, Mr David Harris
Income: £2,092,235 [2017]; £2,423,467 [2016]; £1,827,550 [2015]; £1,659,405 [2014]; £1,868,358 [2013]

Norfolk and Norwich Festival Trust
Registered: 16 Nov 2015 *Employees:* 27 *Volunteers:* 118
Tel: 01603 877753 *Website:* nnfestival.org.uk
Activities: Education, training; arts, culture, heritage, science
Address: Norwich & Norfolk Festival Ltd, Augustine Steward House, Tombland, Norwich, NR3 1HF
Trustees: Mr John Howkins, Ms Brenda Arthur, Jackie Higham, Mr Fred Corbett, Ms Anthea Fiendly Case, Dr Karyn Maier, Mrs Eva Pepper, Mr Andrew Jonathan Barnes, Ms Rachel Savage, Mr Mark Proctor, Mr Neil MacKinnon
Income: £2,414,317 [2016]

Norfolk and Norwich Scope Association
Registered: 20 Oct 1993 *Employees:* 77 *Volunteers:* 65
Website: nansa.org.uk
Activities: Disability
Address: 33 Woodcock Road, Norwich, NR3 3TT
Trustees: Mrs Gillian Doy, Mr Thomas Garrod, Ms Margaret Smith, Mrs Lesley Everett, Mr John Sorrell, Miss Charlene Ledgard
Income: £1,342,460 [2017]; £1,354,731 [2016]; £1,376,985 [2015]; £1,214,155 [2014]; £1,048,336 [2013]

Norfolk and Norwich University Hospitals NHS Foundation Trust Charitable Fund
Registered: 20 Jul 1995 *Volunteers:* 10
Tel: 01603 286286 *Website:* nnuh.nhs.uk
Activities: General charitable purposes; education, training; advancement of health or saving of lives; disability; prevention or relief of poverty; arts, culture, heritage, science
Address: Norfolk & Norwich University Hospital, Colney Lane, Norwich, NR4 7UY
Trustees: Norfolk and Norwich University Hospitals NHS Foundation Trust
Income: £1,978,016 [2017]; £2,303,392 [2016]; £1,269,945 [2015]; £1,588,450 [2014]; £1,459,513 [2013]

The Normandy Memorial Trust Ltd
Registered: 30 Aug 2016
Tel: 020 7828 0818 *Website:* normandymemorialtrust.org
Activities: Arts, culture, heritage, science
Address: 56 Warwick Square, London, SW1V 2AJ
Trustees: Lord Peter Ricketts, Sir Michael Rake, General Sir Peter Wall, Andrew Whitmarsh, Lord Robin Janvrin, Lord Richard Dannatt, Nicholas Witchell, David McDonough
Income: £20,150,468 [2017]

North Bristol NHS Trust Charitable Funds
Registered: 5 Jun 1996 *Employees:* 7
Tel: 0117 414 3767 *Website:* southmeadhospitalcharity.org.uk
Activities: Education, training; advancement of health or saving of lives; disability
Address: Southmead Hospital, Southmead Road, Bristol, BS10 5NB
Trustees: North Bristol NHS Trust
Income: £1,476,280 [2017]; £2,133,000 [2016]; £1,826,000 [2015]; £2,110,000 [2014]; £1,890,000 [2013]

North Cestrian Grammar School Limited
Registered: 14 Sep 1972 *Employees:* 47 *Volunteers:* 1
Tel: 0161 928 1856 *Website:* ncgs.co.uk
Activities: Education, training; amateur sport; other charitable purposes
Address: North Cestrian Grammar School, Dunham Road, Altrincham, Cheshire, WA14 4AJ
Trustees: John Humphrey Moss, Timothy Brown, John-Phillippe Glaskie, Mr Peter Chenery Dicker, Mr Christopher Smart, Mr Jason Johnathon Finley, Ian Parrott, Mrs Rosemary Smart, Mrs Sharon Forster, Mr Nicholas Bailey, Mr Nicholas John Evans
Income: £2,977,690 [2017]; £2,294,721 [2015]; £2,258,277 [2014]; £2,409,711 [2013]; £2,733,422 [2012]

North Country Leisure
Registered: 7 Apr 1999 *Employees:* 206
Tel: 01434 613200 *Website:* northcountryleisure.org.uk
Activities: Amateur sport
Address: North Country Leisure, NCL House, Hexham Business Park, Burn Lane, Hexham, Northumberland, NE46 3RU
Trustees: Mr Chris Roberts, Mr Roger Tames, Mr Jon Argent, Mr Chris Horner, Mr David Powlesland, Greenwich Leisure Limited
Income: £10,676,911 [2016]; £12,026,209 [2015]; £8,925,538 [2014]; £9,045,021 [2013]; £7,584,838 [2012]

North Devon Homes Limited
Registered: 27 Oct 2015 *Employees:* 104
Tel: 01271 312500 *Website:* ndh-ltd.co.uk
Activities: General charitable purposes; advancement of health or saving of lives; disability; prevention or relief of poverty; accommodation, housing; economic, community development, employment; human rights, religious or racial harmony, equality or diversity
Address: North Devon Homes Ltd, Westacott Road, Barnstaple, Devon, EX32 8TA
Trustees: Delyth Lloyd-Evans, Mr Robert Stronge, Mr Asad Mansur Butt, James Barrah, Sabina Goodman, Mrs Dawn Evelyn Ann Ash, Suzanne Ingman, Mr Scott John Murray, Debbie Hay, Mr Jonathan Paul Oldroyd
Income: £18,428,148 [2017]

North Devon Hospice
Registered: 22 Mar 1983 *Employees:* 189 *Volunteers:* 570
Tel: 01271 347244 *Website:* northdevonhospice.org.uk
Activities: The advancement of health or saving of lives
Address: Deer Park, Newport, Barnstaple, Devon, EX32 0HU
Trustees: Mr Michael Reginald Arthur Ford, Mrs Doreen Ivy Woodrow, Mrs Alison Carol Dyer, Sharon Bates, Dr Annabelle Tree, Mr Christopher Clapp, Mr Kevin Ronald Underwood, Mary Elizabeth Brooks, Kate Cox, Ms Zara Jane Svensson
Income: £4,727,205 [2017]; £5,824,846 [2016]; £5,922,806 [2015]; £4,774,639 [2014]; £4,591,501 [2013]

North East Autism Society
Registered: 11 Nov 1993 *Employees:* 586 *Volunteers:* 43
Tel: 0191 410 9974 *Website:* ne-as.org.uk
Activities: Education, training; disability
Address: Lumley Court, Drum Industrial Estate, Chester-le-Street, Co Durham, DH2 1AN
Trustees: Captain Donald Cottew Walker, Mrs Jillian Crumbie, Mr Malcolm Bainbridge, Dr Rakesh Chopra, Mr David Parker, Mr Gavin Bestford, Mr John O'Sullivan, Mr Kevin Patrick McAlister, Mr John Terence Hodgson
Income: £18,038,440 [2017]; £17,369,573 [2016]; £17,105,392 [2015]; £17,482,078 [2014]; £16,689,047 [2013]

North East Theatre Trust Limited
Registered: 25 Apr 1983 *Employees:* 27 *Volunteers:* 51
Tel: 0191 269 3497 *Website:* live.org.uk
Activities: Arts, culture, heritage, science
Address: Live Theatre, 27 Broad Chare, Newcastle upon Tyne, NE1 3DQ
Trustees: Ms Kathryn Lucy Hay Winskell, Mrs Susan Brown, Mr Jim Beirne, Mrs Michelle Frances Percy, Ms Susan Emmas, Mr Michael Francis Henry, Ms Susan Margaret Wilson, Professor Peter Michael Fidler, Mr Paul Callaghan, Mr James Rhys McKinnell
Income: £1,866,088 [2017]; £2,225,525 [2016]; £2,215,389 [2015]; £2,016,901 [2014]; £1,949,482 [2013]

North Eastern YWCA Trustees Ltd
Registered: 13 Dec 1965 *Employees:* 23
Tel: 0191 281 5466 *Website:* neywca.co.uk
Activities: Accommodation, housing
Address: Jesmond House, Clayton Road, Jesmond, Newcastle upon Tyne, NE2 1UJ
Trustees: Mr Roger Robert Darsley, Mrs Margaret Lee, Miss Victoria Gray, Mrs Janet Smith, Miss Caroline Mortlock, Ms Linda Hitman, Mr David Gibson, Mrs Linda Baird Adams
Income: £1,061,985 [2017]; £1,133,717 [2016]; £965,615 [2015]; £958,095 [2014]; £955,869 [2013]

North England Conference of Seventh-Day Adventists
Registered: 31 Mar 1995 *Employees:* 70 *Volunteers:* 10,600
Tel: 0115 960 6312 *Website:* necadventist.org.uk
Activities: General charitable purposes; education, training; advancement of health or saving of lives; prevention or relief of poverty; overseas aid, famine relief; religious activities; environment, conservation, heritage; human rights, religious or racial harmony, equality or diversity; recreation
Address: c/o North England Conference, 22 Zulla Road, Mapperley Park, Nottingham, NG3 5DB
Trustees: Mr Alan Hush, Pastor Michael Simpson, Mr Charles Bramble, Dr Andrew West, Mr Sureen Rayavarapu, Mrs Herlene Simon, Pastor Dan Majaducon, Mrs Rose Bull, Mr Horace Radcliff, Mr Fortune Mahlangu, Mr Richard Jackson, Mr Clive Palmer, Mr Michael Mudzamiri, Mrs Sheryl Lawrence, Pastor Samuel Appiah
Income: £8,496,356 [2016]; £8,730,365 [2015]; £7,813,504 [2014]; £7,700,132 [2013]; £7,493,834 [2012]

North Herts Hospice Care Association
Registered: 23 Sep 1986 *Employees:* 148 *Volunteers:* 500
Tel: 01462 67940 *Website:* ghhospice.co.uk
Activities: The advancement of health or saving of lives
Address: Garden House Hospice, Gillison Close, Letchworth Garden City, Herts, SG6 1QU
Trustees: Mr John Procter, Prof Ken Farrington, Sir Tim Wilson DL, Dr John Machen, Dawn Morrish, Mrs Rhona Seviour, Helen Dodd, Susan Greenbank, Mrs Janet Nevitt, Mr Roger Gochin, Mrs Eleanor Cooke JP, Mr Steve Mellish, Mr James David Silsby
Income: £4,772,012 [2017]; £3,820,364 [2016]; £3,785,805 [2015]; £3,629,216 [2014]; £3,445,156 [2013]

North Kent Mind
Registered: 18 May 2004 *Employees:* 49 *Volunteers:* 70
Tel: 01322 291380 *Website:* northkentmind.co.uk
Activities: The advancement of health or saving of lives; disability; accommodation, housing
Address: The Almshouses, 6-22 West Hill, Dartford, Kent, DA1 2EP
Trustees: Mr Donald Iain MacLeod, Mr Philip Matthews, Mrs Lyndsey Stukalov-Stone, Mr Oleg Stukalov-Stone, Mr Andrew Upstill, Mr James Aitchison, Mr Harley Clark, Mrs Diljeet Nota
Income: £1,842,195 [2017]; £1,422,332 [2016]; £1,149,982 [2015]; £965,781 [2014]; £505,281 [2013]

North Liverpool Regeneration Company Ltd
Registered: 1 Dec 1999 *Employees:* 6
Tel: 0151 207 4612 *Website:* nlrco.com
Activities: General charitable purposes; education, training; prevention or relief of poverty; arts, culture, heritage, science; economic, community development, employment
Address: 55 Garden Lane, Liverpool, L9 9DZ
Trustees: Mrs Pauline Connolly, Mr Scott McAllister, Mr John Nelson
Income: £1,500,150 [2016]; £1,167,904 [2015]; £3,629,753 [2014]; £1,524,769 [2013]; £1,238,369 [2012]

North London Asian Care
Registered: 14 Jul 2006 *Employees:* 107
Tel: 020 8888 0999 *Website:* northlondonasiancare.org
Activities: General charitable purposes; advancement of health or saving of lives
Address: 83-85 Bowes Road, Palmers Green, London, N13 4RU
Trustees: Mr Raman Tailor, Md Anwar Kabir Khan, Mrs Rina Choudhury, Mr Bharat Solanki, Mr Alok Agrawal
Income: £1,333,254 [2017]; £1,032,323 [2016]; £1,183,001 [2015]; £1,129,726 [2014]; £994,385 [2013]

North London Bikur Cholim Limited
Registered: 9 Mar 2001 *Employees:* 40
Tel: 020 8806 1844
Activities: The advancement of health or saving of lives; disability; prevention or relief of poverty
Address: 11 Ashtead Road, London, E5 9BJ
Trustees: Mrs Caroline Joseph, Mrs Rachel Alter, Mrs Judith Hager, Mrs Rachel Klien
Income: £1,294,376 [2016]; £1,155,553 [2015]; £1,046,150 [2014]; £934,404 [2013]; £767,103 [2012]

The North London Collegiate School
Registered: 17 Aug 2006 *Employees:* 314
Website: nlcs.org.uk
Activities: Education, training
Address: North London Collegiate School, Canons Drive, Edgware, Middlesex, HA8 7RJ
Trustees: Mrs Eileen Annabelle Raperport, Dr Adam Fox, Mr Steven Jaffe, Mr Peter Linthwaite, Mrs Elaine Davis, Mr John Herlihy MA Oxon, Mr Peter David Needleman, Dr Anton Emmanuel, Mrs Sophie Carter, Ms Julie Quinn, Mr Tim Suter MA, Mr Keith Breslauer, Mrs Sherin Aminossehe FRICS RIBA, Professor Brian Young
Income: £23,834,570 [2017]; £21,604,737 [2016]; £21,647,706 [2015]; £19,644,113 [2014]; £20,183,769 [2013]

The North London Conservatoire
Registered: 19 May 2015 *Employees:* 6
Tel: 020 8444 9435
Activities: Education, training; arts, culture, heritage, science; recreation
Address: 76 St James's Lane, London, N10 3RD
Trustees: Mr P West, Ms S Chamberlain, Mr Aiden G M Brindley LLB
Income: £1,123,422 [2016]

North London Hospice
Registered: 22 Oct 1982 *Employees:* 174 *Volunteers:* 750
Website: northlondonhospice.org
Activities: The advancement of health or saving of lives
Address: North London Hospice, 47 Woodside Avenue, London, N12 8TT
Trustees: Mr Geoffrey Stanley Hill FCA, Mrs Carol Miriam Holmes, Mrs Julia Rachel Brown, Mr Sanjay Kumar Bhaduri, Dr Judith Ann Tobin, Mr John Reid, Mr Simon Morris, Mr Gareth William Wilson, Ms Elisabeth Burgess Jones, Ms Lesley Ann Nash, Rev Lynn Davidson
Income: £8,315,354 [2017]; £10,398,987 [2016]; £9,405,373 [2015]; £8,754,092 [2014]; £7,006,960 [2013]

North Music Trust
Registered: 10 Jul 2001 *Employees:* 449 *Volunteers:* 23
Tel: 0191 443 4620 *Website:* sagegateshead.com
Activities: Education, training; arts, culture, heritage, science; recreation
Address: The Sage Gateshead, St Marys Square, Gateshead, Tyne & Wear, NE8 2JR
Trustees: Ms Hilary Patricia Florek, Mrs Anne Millman, Lord Falconer of Thoroton, Mr Alistair Miles Anderson, Sir Martin James Narey, Mr Subashis Das, Ms Jacinta Mary Scannell, Mr Roy James McEwan-Brown, Councillor Martin Gannon, Mr John Arthur Cuthbert, Mrs Margaret Fay, Mr Marcus Damon Robinson, Ms Susan Lois Underwood, Mr Young Herb Kim, Mrs Vidya Sarangapani
Income: £13,812,077 [2017]; £13,808,066 [2016]; £16,761,388 [2015]; £16,828,554 [2014]; £14,990,016 [2013]

North Notts Crossroads Caring for Carers
Registered: 19 Apr 2005 *Employees:* 88 *Volunteers:* 6
Tel: 01623 658535 *Website:* crossroadscarenorthnotts.com
Activities: Disability
Address: 1ntake Business Centre, Kirkland Avenue, Mansfield, Notts, NG18 5QP
Trustees: Mrs Susan Marriott, Mr Paul Alfred McDuell, Mrs Gillian Anne Dodd, Mr Philip Ronald Marsh, Mr David Rowley, Mr Neil Conieczny
Income: £1,311,725 [2017]; £1,641,430 [2016]; £1,807,120 [2015]; £1,873,740 [2014]; £1,783,002 [2013]

North Staffs Mind
Registered: 17 Nov 1988 *Employees:* 85 *Volunteers:* 65
Tel: 01782 262100 *Website:* nsmind.org.uk
Activities: The advancement of health or saving of lives; accommodation, housing
Address: 83 Marsh Street, Hanley, Stoke on Trent, Staffs, ST1 5HN
Trustees: Mrs Briege Cullinane BA Hons ATC, Ms Helen Barnes BA Hons CQSW PhD, Ms Anji Dyke, Miss Jenna Birchall, Mrs Amy Spruce, Mr David Cotton, Mr Neil James Dingley, Mrs Linda Jane Holt, Ms Claire Skelson, Mr Richard Gorton
Income: £1,813,332 [2017]; £1,859,556 [2016]; £1,722,454 [2015]; £1,575,991 [2014]; £1,226,339 [2013]

North Wales Wildlife Trust
Registered: 4 Feb 1964 *Employees:* 27 *Volunteers:* 331
Tel: 01248 351541 *Website:* northwaleswildlifetrust.org.uk
Activities: General charitable purposes; education, training; advancement of health or saving of lives; environment, conservation, heritage
Address: North Wales Wildlife Trust, Llys Garth, Garth Road, Bangor, Gwynedd, LL57 2RT
Trustees: Les Starling, Mr Charles James Robertson, Howard Davies, Ian Dunsire, Ms Susan Allen, Mr John Edward George Good, Roger Thomas, Ms Frankie Hobro, Simon Mills, Gillian Coates, Mrs Lyndell Ellen Williams, Stephem Palin
Income: £1,410,384 [2017]; £1,168,292 [2016]; £1,290,217 [2015]; £1,021,241 [2014]; £852,631 [2013]

North West Air Ambulance
Registered: 24 May 1999 *Employees:* 29 *Volunteers:* 202
Tel: 0151 547 7830 *Website:* nwaa.net
Activities: The advancement of health or saving of lives
Address: North West Air Ambulance, North Mersey Business Centre, Woodward Road, Liverpool, L33 7UY
Trustees: Ms Kim March, Mr Stewart Meehan, Dr Rachel Christine Hall, Mr Daniel Head, Mr Allan Jude, Mrs Dorothy Jane Marie Smith, Mr Simon John Williams
Income: £8,784,495 [2017]; £8,335,415 [2016]; £7,990,374 [2015]; £7,135,513 [2014]; £5,622,971 [2013]

North West Cancer Research (incorporating Clatterbridge Cancer Research CCR)
Registered: 8 Oct 1987 *Employees:* 10 *Volunteers:* 250
Tel: 0151 709 2919 *Website:* nwcr.org
Activities: The advancement of health or saving of lives
Address: North West Cancer Research, North West Cancer Research Centre, 200 London Road, Liverpool, L3 9TA
Trustees: Miss Catherine Jones, Mr Stephen Claus, Mrs Moira Jane Owen, Mrs Catherine Bond, Mr Philip Charles Robertshaw, Mr Steven Smith, Mr Nigel Stuart Lanceley, Ms Francis Margaret Leigh Street, Mr Mark Haig, Mrs Hilary Atherton, Prof David Ross Sibson
Income: £1,338,957 [2017]; £1,562,386 [2016]; £1,854,784 [2015]; £1,389,675 [2014]; £1,747,512 [2013]

The North West Police Benevolent Fund
Registered: 12 Mar 1974 *Employees:* 21
Tel: 01254 245571 *Website:* nwpbf.org
Activities: General charitable purposes; disability; prevention or relief of poverty
Address: St Michael's Lodge, Northcote Road, Langho, Lancs, BB6 8BG
Trustees: Mr David Anderton, Mrs Sandie Wilde, Ms Rachael Hanley, Mr Carl Cruger, Mr Paul Senior, Mr Stephen Rothwell, Mrs Deryn O'Connor, Mr David Sim, Mr Martin Plumber, Mr Craig Trow, Mr Edward Newton, Mr Derek Lloyd, Ms Jane Arrowsmith, Mrs Jacqueline Ann Smithies, Mr Ken Davies, Mr Mark Unsworth, Mr Peter Singleton, Mrs Kate Rowley, Mr Ian Taylor, Mr Andrew Rhodes, Mr Edward Thistlethwaite, Mr Simon Roberts, Mr Anthony Bradley, Mr Graham Houston, Mr David Lowe
Income: £1,207,744 [2016]; £1,617,921 [2015]; £2,009,774 [2014]; £2,055,336 [2013]; £1,895,283 [2012]

North West Training Council
Registered: 30 Sep 1970 *Employees:* 58
Tel: 0151 523 0808 *Website:* nwtc.co.uk
Activities: Education, training
Address: North West Training Council, Dunnings Bridge Road, Bootle, Merseyside, L30 6XT
Trustees: Mr Robert Leigh William Holme, Councillor Sir Ronald Watson CBE, Ms Jo Higgins, Mr Gordon Robert Hunter, Mr Roy Williams
Income: £2,749,305 [2017]; £2,330,594 [2016]; £2,348,298 [2015]; £3,861,910 [2014]; £3,861,910 [2013]

North Western Reform Synagogue
Registered: 21 Feb 1966 *Employees:* 35 *Volunteers:* 250
Tel: 020 8457 8788 *Website:* alyth.org.uk
Activities: General charitable purposes; education, training; religious activities
Address: North Western Reform Synagogue, Alyth Gardens, London, NW11 7EN
Trustees: Mr Michael Overlander, Mrs Caronne Graham, Mr Russell Baum, Mr David Brown, Mr Arieh Miller, Mrs Noeleen Cohen, Ms Nicole Feuchtwang, Mr Michael Simon, Mr Nicholas Minter-Green, Ms Julia Simmonds
Income: £1,733,533 [2016]; £1,788,315 [2015]; £1,657,278 [2014]; £1,632,653 [2013]; £1,354,524 [2012]

North York Moors Historical Railway Trust Limited
Registered: 14 Feb 1972 *Employees:* 130 *Volunteers:* 1,000
Website: nymr.co.uk
Activities: Education, training; environment, conservation, heritage
Address: 20 Pepys Way, Girton, Cambridge, CB3 0PA
Trustees: John Bruce, Jim Dedicoat, Simon Barraclough, Mr Philip Martin Benham, Andrew Bullivant, Alan Whitehouse, Jennifer Halmshaw, Mr Christopher Dickerson, Chris Cubitt, Murray Brown, Andrew John Scott, Dave Torbet, John Bailey, Dr Simon Brockington, Bernard Warr, Mr Colin Graham
Income: £7,202,377 [2017]; £6,757,614 [2016]; £8,482,971 [2014]; £6,395,116 [2013]; £5,450,316 [2012]

The North of England Horticultural Society
Registered: 29 Sep 1989 *Employees:* 7 *Volunteers:* 83
Tel: 01423 561049 *Website:* flowershow.org.uk
Activities: Education, training; arts, culture, heritage, science; recreation
Address: Regional Agricultural Centre, Great Yorkshire Showground, Railway Road, Harrogate, N Yorks, HG2 8NZ
Trustees: Mr Michael John I'anson, Mr David Beardall, Ms Josephine Mary Makin, Mrs Caroline Jane Bayliss, Mrs Christine Stewart, Mrs Dianne Kilburn, Mrs Sarah Anne Hopps, Mr David Barker, Mr Christopher Stephen Hattersley Smith, Mr Dennis Bryan Hutchinson, Mrs Margaret Ann Dabell, Mrs Pamela Anne Grant, Lady Penelope Lucy Mowbray, Mrs Susan Margaret Brown, Mr Rae Beckwith
Income: £1,467,757 [2016]; £1,843,302 [2015]; £183,155 [2014]; £214,827 [2013]

The North of England Zoological Society
Registered: 18 Jan 1967 *Employees:* 545 *Volunteers:* 140
Tel: 01244 650202 *Website:* chesterzoo.org
Activities: Education, training; animals; environment, conservation, heritage
Address: The North of England Zoological Society, Cedar House, Chester Zoo, Caughall Road, Upton, Chester, CH2 1LH
Trustees: Mr Tony Williams, Prof Peter Edward Wheeler, Mrs Rebecca Burke Sharples, Prof Stefan Buczacki, Mr Bruce Ursell, Mrs Sandra Donnelly, Professor Russell Newton, Mrs Catherine Buckley, Miss Angela Pinnington, Mr Malcolm Ardron, Prof Malcolm Bennett, Mr Richard Griffiths, Mr Simon Venables, Mr William Beale
Income: £42,052,000 [2016]; £35,626,000 [2015]; £29,767,000 [2014]; £28,161,000 [2013]; £25,626,000 [2012]

The Northam Care Trust
Registered: 31 Jul 2000 *Employees:* 84 *Volunteers:* 25
Tel: 01237 477238 *Website:* northamlodge.co.uk
Activities: Education, training; disability; accommodation, housing
Address: Rosehill, Heywood Road, Bideford, Devon, EX39 3PG
Trustees: Mr Roderick Mole, Dr Michael Cracknell, Mrs Carole Tudor, Mrs Susan Brown, Mr John Hare, Mr Timothy Malone, Mr James Corkery, Mr Chris Fulford, Mr Richard Ker, Mr Robin Stoneman
Income: £2,077,627 [2017]; £1,889,877 [2016]; £1,716,646 [2015]; £1,699,750 [2014]; £1,648,531 [2013]

Northampton Roman Catholic Diocesan Trust
Registered: 22 Apr 1969 *Employees:* 120 *Volunteers:* 1,000
Tel: 01604 712065 *Website:* northamptondiocese.org
Activities: Religious activities
Address: Bishops House, Marriott Street, Semilong, Northampton, NN2 6AW
Trustees: Rt Rev Bishop Peter Doyle, Mr Charles Whitehead, Mgr Kevin McGinnell, Mr John Peachey, Rev Anthony William Brennan, Monsignor Sean Healy, Rev Brendan Killeen, Mrs Margaret Mary Bull, Mrs Margaret Anne Harwood, The Northampton Roman Catholic Diocese Trustee
Income: £7,920,594 [2017]; £10,034,032 [2016]; £8,845,606 [2015]; £9,769,608 [2014]; £9,290,963 [2013]

The Northampton Theatres Trust Limited
Registered: 28 May 1999 *Employees:* 143 *Volunteers:* 116
Tel: 01604 655712 *Website:* royalandderngate.co.uk
Activities: Arts, culture, heritage, science
Address: Northampton Theatres Trust Ltd, 19-21 Guildhall Road, Northampton, NN1 1DP
Trustees: Mrs Victoria Miles, Mr Stephen Robert Edmonds, Mrs Heather Anne Smith, Mr Roger George Snowden Martin, Miss Jane Catherine Bloomer, Ms Frances Eleanor Holloway, Cllr Danielle Stone, Miss Clare Siobhan Slater, Mr Brandon Eldred, Miss Hannah Fay Miller, Mrs Kay Elizabeth Roberts, Miss Bernadette Angela Lally
Income: £9,827,081 [2017]; £8,704,440 [2016]; £8,271,023 [2015]; £8,724,761 [2014]; £7,643,874 [2013]

Northamptonshire Arts Management Trust
Registered: 16 Nov 2010 *Employees:* 186 *Volunteers:* 238
Tel: 01604 655712
Activities: Arts, culture, heritage, science
Address: Northamptonshire Arts Management Trust, c/o Royal & Derngate, 19-21 Guildhall Road, Northampton, NN1 1DP
Trustees: Mrs Morag Carmichael, Mr Stephen Robert Edmonds, Mrs Victoria Jane Miles, Mr Gary Robert Tate
Income: £11,047,068 [2017]; £9,661,688 [2016]; £9,143,470 [2015]; £9,565,491 [2014]; £8,450,293 [2013]

Northamptonshire Association for the Blind
Registered: 9 Apr 1962 *Employees:* 42 *Volunteers:* 328
Tel: 01604 719193 *Website:* nab.org.uk
Activities: Disability
Address: NAB Sight Centre, 37 Harborough Road, Kingsthorpe,
Northampton, NN2 7BB
Trustees: Mrs Christine Stewart, Mr Trevor George, Mr Christopher
Malpas, Mrs Susan Francis, Mr Tristan Francis Wallace McMullan,
Mr Laurence Henry Embury, Mr Hafiz Khandwala, Mrs Sarah
Bedding, Mrs Joy Fedden, Mr Edwin Slinn
Income: £2,051,982 [2017]; £1,075,048 [2016]; £1,242,564 [2015];
£2,402,727 [2014]; £1,083,055 [2013]

Northamptonshire Association of Youth Clubs
Registered: 2 Jul 1990 *Employees:* 212
Website: nayc.org
Activities: Education, training; religious activities; amateur sport
Address: Northamptonsire Association of Youth Clubs, Kings
Park Road, Moulton Park Industrial Estate, Northampton, NN3 6LL
Trustees: Mr John P Gilmour, Mr Tim Leese, Rev D Shearer,
Mrs Joan Tice DL, Rachel Mallows, Mr Peter Hales, David Laing,
Mr David Darby, Mrs Sylvia Susan Gilmour
Income: £5,253,680 [2017]; £5,890,650 [2016]; £5,437,531 [2015];
£4,557,060 [2014]; £4,136,565 [2013]

Northamptonshire Carers
Registered: 20 Mar 1997 *Employees:* 47 *Volunteers:* 70
Tel: 01933 677837 *Website:* northamptonshire-carers.org
Activities: General charitable purposes; education, training;
advancement of health or saving of lives; disability; prevention or
relief of poverty
Address: 123 Midland Road, Wellingborough, Northants, NN8 1LU
Trustees: Mrs Agnes Anne Goodman MBE DL, Mrs Elaine Yates,
Mr James Philip Douglas, Miss Nathalie Jane Scott, Mrs Pam
Byles, Miss Nanette Lovell, Mrs Sally Grace Bresnahan, Dr Peter
Inns, Miss Rachel Ann Hawkins, Mr Christopher Best
Income: £1,695,371 [2017]; £1,717,112 [2016]; £1,421,905 [2015];
£939,608 [2014]; £821,451 [2013]

Northamptonshire Community Foundation
Registered: 15 Nov 2002 *Employees:* 6 *Volunteers:* 10
Tel: 01604 230033 *Website:* ncf.uk.com
Activities: General charitable purposes; education, training;
advancement of health or saving of lives; disability; prevention or
relief of poverty; accommodation, housing; arts, culture, heritage,
science; amateur sport; environment, conservation, heritage;
economic, community development, employment; other charitable
purposes
Address: 18 Albion Place, Northampton, NN1 1UD
Trustees: Mr Paul Southworth, Mrs Sally Robinson, Mrs Deirdre
Morag Newham, Mr Paul Thomas Serge Parsons, Mr Hassan Raza
Shah, Mr Philip Lomas, Anne Burnett, Mr David Knight, Mr John
Griffiths-Elsden, Miss Dawn Icedell Thomas, Ms Joanna Rose
Gordon, Mrs Janine Jepson
Income: £1,515,941 [2017]; £1,130,380 [2016]; £1,456,152 [2015];
£1,430,869 [2014]; £1,310,803 [2013]

Northamptonshire Health Charitable Fund
Registered: 23 Feb 2016 *Employees:* 5 *Volunteers:* 15
Tel: 01604 545091 *Website:* nhcfgreenheart.co.uk
Activities: The advancement of health or saving of lives
Address: Northampton General Hospital, Northampton, NN1 5BD
Trustees: Mr Nicholas Anthony Norman Stuart Robertson,
Mrs Elizabeth Nicholls, Mr John Archard-Jones, Mr Andrew Phillip
Cockerill, Mrs Moira Ingham, Mr Sushel Kumar Ohri, Mrs Jane
Bradley, Mr John Keeble, Phil Zeidler
Income: £1,772,000 [2017]

**Northamptonshire Independent Grammar School Charity Trust
Limited**
Registered: 5 Aug 1988 *Employees:* 72 *Volunteers:* 2
Tel: 01604 880306 *Website:* ngs-school.com
Activities: Education, training
Address: Northamptonshire Grammar School, Pitsford Hall,
Moulton Road, Pitsford, Northampton, NN6 9AX
Trustees: Mr Mark Adams, Mr Andrew Ross, Mr James Jackson
Brown, Mrs Joan Harrop, Mr Stephen John Coleman, Mr Keith
William Mason, Mr James Andrew Hartshorne, The Reverend
Stephen Trott, Mrs Sherry Burditt, Alisdair Tait, Mr Andrew Kenneth
Johnstone Moodie, Dr Martin Stuart Gaskell, Peter Morton
Income: £4,290,370 [2017]; £3,489,649 [2016]; £4,065,112 [2015];
£2,891,336 [2014]; £3,057,609 [2013]

Northamptonshire Industrial Training Association Limited
Registered: 20 Jun 1978 *Employees:* 15
Tel: 01536 408188 *Website:* nital.co.uk
Activities: Education, training
Address: NITAL, 2230, Kettering Parkway, Kettering Venture Park,
Kettering, Northants, NN15 6XR
Trustees: Mr John Gardner, Mr David Knight, Mr Christopher
Long, Mr Paul Batson, Mr Robert Anthony Scott, Mr David Brodie,
Mr Peter Larkins, Mr Michael Anthony Clarke
Income: £1,637,655 [2017]; £1,938,691 [2016]; £1,938,691 [2015];
£1,407,808 [2014]; £1,188,515 [2013]

Northamptonshire Music and Performing Arts Trust
Registered: 26 Jan 2012 *Employees:* 133 *Volunteers:* 50
Tel: 01604 637117 *Website:* nmpat.co.uk
Activities: Education, training; arts, culture, heritage, science;
recreation
Address: 125-129 Kettering Road, Northampton, NN1 4AZ
Trustees: Mrs Joan Kirkbride, Mr Dudley Hughes, Clive Gresham,
Mr Iain Christopher Massey, Mrs Renuka Popat, Roger Griffiths,
Trevor Shipman
Income: £5,348,212 [2016]; £5,312,913 [2015]; £5,940,298 [2014];
£5,188,335 [2013]

Northbourne Park School Limited
Registered: 29 May 1980 *Employees:* 68 *Volunteers:* 2
Website: northbournepark.com
Activities: Education, training
Address: Northbourne Park School, Betteshanger, Deal, Kent,
CT14 0NW
Trustees: Mr Anthony Lucas, Mrs Stephanie Aiyagari,
Professor Benjamin Hutchinson, Miss Rebecca Jones, Ms Suzanne
Barter, Mr Henry James, Ms Mary Williamson, Mr James Outram,
Mrs Fiona Poole, Mrs Marian Jane Nairac, Mr Mark Keir
Income: £2,285,258 [2016]; £2,352,637 [2015]; £2,228,484 [2014];
£2,156,337 [2013]; £2,469,682 [2012]

Northease Manor School Ltd
Registered: 5 Dec 1972 *Employees:* 65
Tel: 01273 472915 *Website:* northease.co.uk
Activities: Education, training; arts, culture, heritage, science;
amateur sport
Address: Northease Manor School, Newhaven Road, Rodmell,
Lewes, E Sussex, BN7 3EY
Trustees: Mr D Roberts, Mr M Roberts, Mrs Clare Asher Gillies,
Mrs Sophie J Skinner, Mrs Julie Toben, Mr Mark Cummins,
Mrs Jean Melanie Rolfe
Income: £2,154,806 [2016]; £2,226,005 [2015]; £2,663,940 [2014];
£2,307,290 [2013]; £2,246,006 [2012]

Northern Ballet Limited
Registered: 27 Sep 1969 *Employees:* 120 *Volunteers:* 46
Tel: 0113 220 8000 *Website:* northernballet.com
Activities: Education, training; arts, culture, heritage, science
Address: Northern Ballet, 2 St Cecilia Street, Leeds, LS2 7PA
Trustees: Councillor John Procter, Mr Kevin O'Hare, Mrs Elizabeth Jackson, Mr Paul Smith, Miss Anita Rani, Sir David Wootton, Mr Daniel Evans, Mrs Carol Arrowsmith, James Taylor, Mrs Jane Gilbert Boot
Income: £9,240,588 [2017]; £8,301,750 [2016]; £7,691,921 [2015]; £7,455,514 [2014]; £7,171,128 [2013]

Northern Broadsides Theatre Company
Registered: 27 Jul 1999 *Employees:* 19
Tel: 01422 369704 *Website:* northern-broadsides.co.uk
Activities: Education, training; arts, culture, heritage, science
Address: 139 E Mill, Dean Clough Mills, Halifax, W Yorks, HX3 5AX
Trustees: Mr Roger Andrew Harvey, Frances Tighe, Mrs Gillian Margaret Johnson, Mrs Kathryn Anne Moreton-Deakin, Mrs Rachel Louise Harris
Income: £1,166,672 [2017]; £816,991 [2016]; £916,927 [2015]; £820,733 [2014]; £735,308 [2013]

The Northern College for Residential Adult Education Limited
Registered: 24 Feb 1978 *Employees:* 78
Tel: 01226 776005 *Website:* northern.ac.uk
Activities: Education, training; economic, community development, employment
Address: Northern College, Wentworth Castle, Lowe Lane, Stainborough, Barnsley, S Yorks, S75 3ET
Trustees: Mr Seb Schmoller, Mr Clive MacDonald, Mr John Albert Edwards, Professor Timothy John Thornton, Kate Fleming, Ms Elizabeth Stanley, Mrs Anne Laverack, Mr Jake Gibbins, Mr Kenneth Richardson, Frank Lord, Mr Robert Harrison, Ms Jill Westerman, Professor Michael Douglas Bramhall, Mrs Sarah Joyce Tyler, Mr Neil James
Income: £5,610,835 [2017]; £5,321,284 [2016]; £5,838,037 [2015]; £5,854,767 [2014]; £5,615,983 [2013]

Northern Land Trust
Registered: 6 Feb 2004
Activities: General charitable purposes
Address: First Floor, Winston House, 349 Regents Park Road, London, N3 1DH
Trustees: Nathan Teitelbaum, Mr Rafael Roitenbarg, Mr Baruch Mordechai Roitenbarg
Income: £2,303,635 [2017]; £5,777,422 [2016]; £180,198 [2015]; £69,137 [2013]; £472,704 [2012]

Northern Racing College
Registered: 8 Jul 1988 *Employees:* 35 *Volunteers:* 1
Tel: 01302 861000 *Website:* northernracingcollege.co.uk
Activities: Education, training
Address: Northern Racing College, The Stables, Great North Road, Rossington, Doncaster, S Yorks, DN11 0HN
Trustees: Mr Tim Lyle, Mr James Hetherton, Mr Richard McIllroy, Mr Christopher Mallinson, Mr Trevor Beaumont, Mr Oliver Greenall, Mr Howard Wright, Mr Tim Adams, Mr Jeff Ennis, Mrs Sarah Easterby, Mr Christopher Bell, Ms Susannah Cordelia Gill
Income: £2,167,468 [2017]; £1,829,994 [2016]; £2,039,732 [2015]; £1,926,757 [2014]; £1,702,129 [2013]

Northern Stage (Theatrical Productions) Limited
Registered: 28 Mar 1988 *Employees:* 94 *Volunteers:* 17
Tel: 0191 242 7200 *Website:* northernstage.co.uk
Activities: Arts, culture, heritage, science
Address: Barras Bridge, Newcastle upon Tyne, NE1 7RH
Trustees: Mr Simon Elliott, Mr Keith Proudfoot, Mr Jean-Pierre Van-Zyl, Ms Laura Collier, Mr Timothy Smith, Mr Charles Penn, Mr Vikas Kumar, Mrs Anne Bonner, Ms Johanna Darby, Mr Michael Knowles, Professor Julie Christina Sanders, Mrs Natalia Blagburn
Income: £3,432,031 [2017]; £3,075,192 [2016]; £2,850,238 [2015]; £2,543,212 [2014]; £2,740,378 [2013]

Northmoor Educational Trust
Registered: 24 Nov 1998 *Employees:* 26 *Volunteers:* 40
Tel: 01482 849563 *Website:* cottingham.focus-school.com
Activities: Education, training
Address: 107 Stockbridge Road, Elloughton, Brough, E Yorks, HU15 1HW
Trustees: Mr Dan Turner, Mr Craig Peter Haughton, Mr Dan Arnett, Mr Keith Ryan Wade, Mr Aaron Gilmore
Income: £1,294,027 [2016]; £1,284,151 [2015]; £943,461 [2014]; £972,769 [2013]; £844,644 [2012]

Northorpe Hall Child & Family Trust
Registered: 4 Apr 2011 *Employees:* 38 *Volunteers:* 25
Website: northorpehall.co.uk
Activities: The advancement of health or saving of lives
Address: Northorpe Hall Trust, 53 Northorpe Lane, Mirfield, W Yorks, WF14 0QL
Trustees: Mr Graeme Sunderland, Mark Feeny, Mrs Philippa Ghosh, Martin Purcell, Jo Brook, Colin Ward, Mr George William Beaumont
Income: £1,284,290 [2017]; £1,000,593 [2016]; £832,209 [2015]; £862,234 [2014]; £1,400,551 [2013]

Northpoint Wellbeing Limited
Registered: 9 Sep 1996 *Employees:* 79
Tel: 0113 245 0303 *Website:* northpoint.org.uk
Activities: General charitable purposes; education, training; advancement of health or saving of lives; economic, community development, employment
Address: Leeds Bridge House, Hunslet Road, Leeds, LS10 1JN
Trustees: Mrs Mary Day, Mrs Joanna Heywood, Mr Gregory Nolan, Brenda Etchells, Mr James Dunmore, Ms Elizabeth Carey, Mrs Donna Mary Wheelhouse
Income: £2,819,577 [2016]; £2,177,030 [2015]; £1,931,187 [2014]; £1,489,817 [2013]; £1,378,027 [2012]

Northumberland Aged Mineworkers' Homes Association
Registered: 2 Dec 1963 *Employees:* 8
Tel: 01670 853200
Activities: Accommodation, housing
Address: 7 Esther Court, Wansbeck Business Park, Ashington, Northumberland, NE63 8AP
Trustees: Mr Denis Murphy, Mr John Pease, Mr Michael John Scullion, Mr Ian Lavery
Income: £1,203,226 [2016]; £1,110,214 [2015]; £994,123 [2014]; £948,552 [2013]; £935,010 [2012]

Northumberland Wildlife Trust Limited
Registered: 15 Jan 1964 *Employees:* 54 *Volunteers:* 290
Website: nwt.org.uk
Activities: Environment, conservation, heritage
Address: Northumberland Wildlife Trust, The Garden House, St Nicholas Park, Jubilee Road, Gosforth, Newcastle upon Tyne, NE3 3XT
Trustees: Mr Ian Hamilton Armstrong, Mr Derek Coates, Mr James Graham Simpson Gill, Mrs Elaine Rigg, Mr I Jackson, Miss Rachel Martin, Dr Angus George Lunn, Ms Sandra King, Mr Anthony John Douglas Barber, Mr Nigel Porter, Mr Thomas Lloyd, Mrs Ailsa Katharine Hobson
Income: £2,545,287 [2017]; £2,729,962 [2016]; £2,469,314 [2015]; £2,760,953 [2014]; £2,124,389 [2013]

Northumbria Calvert Trust
Registered: 17 Dec 1981 *Employees:* 42 *Volunteers:* 45
Tel: 01434 250232 *Website:* calvert-trust.org.uk
Activities: Education, training; disability; amateur sport
Address: Calvert Trust Kielder, Kielder Water & Forest Park, Hexham, Northumberland, NE48 1BS
Trustees: Mr Edward Caverley Thornton Trevelyan, Mr Peter Robert Loyd, Dr Anna Charlton, Mr Peter Straker, Mr Charles Ranfurly Drax, Dr John Neville Bridge, Mr Chris Green, Ms Marion Schooler, Mr Mark Simon Priestley, Mr Roger Anderton
Income: £1,922,582 [2017]; £1,967,309 [2016]; £2,078,227 [2015]; £1,621,239 [2014]; £2,097,807 [2013]

The Northumbria Education Trust
Registered: 7 Jan 2004 *Employees:* 30 *Volunteers:* 120
Tel: 01904 663300
Activities: Education, training
Address: Focus School York Campus, Bishopthorpe Road, York, YO23 2GA
Trustees: Mr John Carruth, Mr Lee Armstrong, Mr Roger Edwards, Mr Neil Trevvett, Mr Keith Culmer, Mr Antony James, Mr Darren Anderson
Income: £1,575,982 [2016]; £1,747,466 [2015]; £631,329 [2014]; £608,037 [2013]

Northumbria Health Care National Health Service Trust Charity
Registered: 31 Oct 2000 *Volunteers:* 463
Tel: 0191 203 1501 *Website:* northumbria.nhs.uk
Activities: Education, training; advancement of health or saving of lives
Address: Finance Department, Unit 7-8, Silver Fox Way, Cobalt Business Park, Newcastle upon Tyne, NE27 0QJ
Trustees: Jim Mackey, Mr Paul Graham Dunn, Ann Stringer, Dr Jeremy Rushmer, Dr Peter Sanderson Dr Peter Sanderson, Mr Allan Hepple, Mr Malcolm Page, Alison Marshall, Birju Bartolli, Alan Richardson, Mr Martin Knowles, Mr David Chesser
Income: £1,655,000 [2017]; £1,447,000 [2016]; £1,474,000 [2015]; £1,428,000 [2014]; £1,568,000 [2013]

Northumbria Students' Union
Registered: 27 Sep 2010 *Employees:* 184 *Volunteers:* 5,000
Tel: 0191 227 4757 *Website:* mynsu.co.uk
Activities: General charitable purposes; arts, culture, heritage, science; amateur sport; environment, conservation, heritage; economic, community development, employment
Address: University of Northumbria at Newcastle, 2 Sandyford Road, Newcastle upon Tyne, NE1 8SB
Trustees: Mr Timothy Alexander Hill, Ms Kristy Deanne Weegram, Mr Ryan Sean Bush, Mr Simon Noble, Mr Andrew Quested Harvey, Ms Tally Kerr, Mr Karl Robert Robson
Income: £5,111,547 [2017]; £4,044,854 [2016]; £3,511,951 [2015]; £3,293,784 [2014]; £2,369,517 [2013]

Northumbrian Citizens Advice Bureau
Registered: 10 Feb 2014 *Employees:* 46 *Volunteers:* 139
Tel: 01670 853823 *Website:* citizensadvice.org.uk
Activities: General charitable purposes; education, training; prevention or relief of poverty
Address: Citizens Advice Bureau, 89 Station Road, Ashington, Northumberland, NE63 8RS
Trustees: Mr David Charles Sharp, John Woodman, Mr Gerald Martin Townshend, Mr Graham Antony Sargent, Mr Mark Donkin, Edward Aitchison, Mrs Lynn Collins
Income: £1,422,321 [2017]; £1,310,596 [2016]; £1,147,921 [2015]

The Northumbrian Educational Trust Limited
Registered: 12 Sep 1963 *Employees:* 63 *Volunteers:* 9
Website: westfield.newcastle.sch.uk
Activities: Education, training
Address: Westfield School, Oakfield Road, Newcastle upon Tyne, NE3 4HS
Trustees: Mrs Jane Keep, Dr Kathryn Manzo, Mr Lex Dowie, Mrs Liz Keightley, Mr Iain Greenshields, Mr Kris Bainbridge, Mr Ian Henderson, Mrs Isabel Smales
Income: £2,410,613 [2017]; £2,441,072 [2016]; £2,375,975 [2015]; £2,374,515 [2014]; £2,213,222 [2013]

Northwick Park Institute for Medical Research Limited
Registered: 29 Apr 2009 *Employees:* 24
Tel: 020 3958 0500 *Website:* npimr.org
Activities: The advancement of health or saving of lives
Address: NPIMR, Northwick Park Hospital, Watford Road, Harrow, Middlesex, HA1 3UJ
Trustees: Mr Bruce Mauleverer, Prof George Hamilton, Professor John Nicholls FRCS, Mrs Grace Margaret Tye, Mr Kirankumar Patel, Prof Barry Fuller, Mr Ranjit Baxi, Professor Robin Kennedy
Income: £4,407,485 [2017]; £3,775,147 [2016]; £4,455,765 [2015]; £2,713,898 [2014]; £2,741,233 [2013]

The Norwegian School in London Limited
Registered: 1 May 1981 *Employees:* 21
Tel: 020 8947 6617 *Website:* norwegianschool.org.uk
Activities: Education, training
Address: 28 Arterberry Road, London, SW20 8AH
Trustees: Mr Geir Johansen, Mrs Silje Johnsen, Ms Kaia Thune, Ms Linda Hetlelid, Mr Tor-Ivar Guttulsrod, Mr Anders Haerland
Income: £1,531,936 [2016]; £1,540,596 [2015]; £1,901,017 [2014]; £1,841,995 [2013]; £1,587,870 [2012]

Norwich City Community Sports Foundation
Registered: 28 Aug 2001 *Employees:* 79 *Volunteers:* 411
Tel: 01603 761122 *Website:* communitysportsfoundation.org.uk
Activities: General charitable purposes; education, training; advancement of health or saving of lives; disability; prevention or relief of poverty; amateur sport; economic, community development, employment; other charitable purposes
Address: Community Sports Foundation, Norwich City FC, Carrow Road, Norwich, NR1 1JE
Trustees: Mr Paul Knowles, Mr Gavin Drake, Mr Thomas Smith, Miss Genie Barham, Mr Mark Ronald Kerr, Mick Dennis, Mr Jake Humphrey, Steve Stone, Raffi Coverdale
Income: £4,591,659 [2016]; £4,109,641 [2015]; £3,354,828 [2014]; £2,366,428 [2013]; £1,798,496 [2012]

Norwich Consolidated Charities

Registered: 14 Nov 2002 *Employees:* 52
Tel: 01603 621023 *Website:* norwichcharitabletrusts.org.uk
Activities: The advancement of health or saving of lives; prevention or relief of poverty; accommodation, housing
Address: Norwich Charitable Trusts, 1 Woolgate Court, St Benedicts Street, Norwich, NR2 4AP
Trustees: David Fullman, Geoffrey Loades, Dr Iain Brooksby, Ms Heather Tyrrell, Mr Michael Flynn, Ms Christine Herries, Cllr Marion Frances Maxwell, Ms Brenda Ferris, Philip Blanchflower, Mrs Jeanne Southgate, Mr Peter Shields, Mrs Lesley Grahame, Cllr Karen Davis, Ms Elspeth Jones
Income: £2,031,631 [2017]; £2,007,926 [2016]; £1,933,449 [2015]; £1,890,885 [2014]; £1,937,684 [2013]

The Norwich Diocesan Board of Finance Limited

Registered: 11 Nov 1966 *Employees:* 47 *Volunteers:* 500
Tel: 01603 880853 *Website:* dioceseofnorwich.org
Activities: Education, training; religious activities
Address: Diocesan House, 109 Dereham Road, Easton, Norwich, NR9 5ES
Trustees: Rev Simon Stokes, Mr Ray Hollands, The Reverend Jeremy Gordon Sykes, Mr Robin Philip Back, The Revd Canon Sally Theakston, Mr Michael Gurney, Mr Julian Taylor, Mrs Susan Gail Martin, Mr William Eric Husselby, The Rt Reverend Graham James, The Venerable Steven James Betts, Angela Robson, Captain Anthony Mervyn Poulter OBE Royal Navy, Mrs Patricia Menaul, Ms Vivienne Clifford-Jackson, Rev Timothy Weston
Income: £13,027,000 [2016]; £12,327,000 [2015]; £11,202,000 [2014]; £10,875,000 [2013]; £10,643,000 [2012]

Norwich and Central Norfolk Mental Health Resources

Registered: 21 Mar 2007 *Employees:* 92 *Volunteers:* 30
Tel: 01603 432457 *Website:* norwichmind.org.uk
Activities: Education, training; advancement of health or saving of lives; disability
Address: 50 Sale Road, Norwich, NR7 9TP
Trustees: Mr John Robert Brierley, Mr Steven Bloomfield, Mr Keith Hedley Davis, Mr Stephen Bazire, Ms Sarah Hurren, Mr Kevin Edward Long, Mrs Holly Marshall, Mr John Allton Jones, Mr Nick Francis, Mr Richard Gorrod
Income: £3,079,052 [2017]; £2,959,864 [2016]; £1,954,666 [2015]; £1,548,790 [2014]; £1,527,269 [2013]

Norwood Ravenswood

Registered: 6 Nov 1996 *Employees:* 1,064 *Volunteers:* 623
Tel: 07730 283740 *Website:* norwood.org.uk
Activities: General charitable purposes; education, training; disability; accommodation, housing
Address: Norwood, Broadway House, 80-82 The Broadway, Stanmore, Middlesex, HA7 4HB
Trustees: Mrs Julia Chain, Mr Elliott Goldstein, Mr Mark Pollack, Mr Anthony Rabin, Mr Philip Lee Hertz, Ms Angela Hodes, Mrs Glynnis Joffe, Gary Sacks, Lady Elaine Sacks, Mr David Stanton, Mr Yonni Abramson, Mr David Smith, Ms Tamara Finkelstein, Mr Neville Kahn
Income: £31,534,000 [2017]; £33,292,000 [2016]; £35,828,000 [2015]; £36,046,000 [2014]; £33,753,000 [2013]

Norwood Schools Ltd

Registered: 26 Sep 1962 *Employees:* 1,029 *Volunteers:* 623
Tel: 07730 283740 *Website:* norwood.org.uk
Activities: Education, training; disability; accommodation, housing
Address: Norwood, Broadway House, 80-82 The Broadway, Stanmore, Middlesex, HA7 4HB
Trustees: Mr Neville Kahn, Mr David Smith, David Stanton
Income: £29,253,000 [2017]; £30,680,000 [2016]; £30,265,000 [2015]; £33,114,000 [2014]; £30,883,000 [2013]

The Not Forgotten Association (NFA)

Registered: 21 Jan 2013 *Employees:* 8 *Volunteers:* 11
Tel: 020 7730 0020 *Website:* nfassociation.org
Activities: Disability; prevention or relief of poverty; recreation
Address: 4th Floor, The Not Forgotten Association, 2 Grosvenor Gardens, London, SW1W 0DH
Trustees: Mr Paul Botterill, Mr David John Cowley, James Partridge, Jaqueline Gross, Lord Newall DL, Dr Catherine Mary Goble, Mr Barry Plummer, Mr Glenn Charles Hurstfield, Mr Mark Nicholls, Capt Jeremy Michael Archer MA, Commodore Peter John Tribe RN, Commodore Samuel James Scorer, Mr Mathew Tomlinson
Income: £1,006,271 [2017]; £1,094,301 [2016]; £1,082,329 [2015]; £1,244,707 [2014]

Notre Dame Preparatory School (Norwich) Limited

Registered: 8 Jul 1975 *Employees:* 40 *Volunteers:* 10
Tel: 01603 625593 *Website:* notredameprepschool.co.uk
Activities: Education, training
Address: Notre Dame Preparatory School, 147 Dereham Road, Norwich, NR2 3TA
Trustees: Mr Richard Bailey, Dr Andrew Eburne, Mr Kevin James Pearson, Canon David Brown Paul, Mrs Gillian Holland, Mrs Susan Deborah Clamp, Mr Swee Hong Chia, Mr Thomas William Bailey, Miss Anthea Ruth Spray
Income: £1,300,341 [2017]; £1,215,476 [2016]; £1,195,335 [2015]; £1,168,378 [2014]; £1,009,962 [2013]

Notre Dame School Cobham

Registered: 7 Aug 2000 *Employees:* 134 *Volunteers:* 5
Tel: 01932 869997 *Website:* notredame.co.uk
Activities: Education, training; religious activities
Address: Notre Dame Preparatory & Senior School, Burwood House, Convent Lane, Cobham, Surrey, KT11 1HA
Trustees: Sister Ernestine Velarde ODN, Sr Anne Gill ODN, Mrs Suzanne Ware, Mrs Wanda Nash, Sister Maria Nieves Escalada, Mrs Susan Bailes, Father Mervyn Williams SDB, Sister Maria Quinn ODN, Mr Gerald Russell, Mr Simon Frost
Income: £7,634,003 [2017]; £8,244,000 [2016]; £8,257,291 [2015]; £8,272,563 [2014]; £8,433,955 [2013]

Nottingham Community Transport Ltd

Registered: 15 Jul 1988 *Employees:* 97
Tel: 0115 985 6904 *Website:* ct4nottingham.co.uk
Activities: The advancement of health or saving of lives; disability; prevention or relief of poverty
Address: Sherwood Bus Garage, Mansfield Road, Sherwood, Nottingham, NG5 2JN
Trustees: Mr Dillon Stephen Mansbridge, Mr Brian Wooding, Mr Nirav Shah, Mr David Bingham, Mrs Joan Fisher, Mr Laurance Wright, Mrs Phillippa Spencer, Mr Richard Mynett, Mrs Pam Jarvis
Income: £3,544,416 [2017]; £3,318,881 [2016]; £2,412,555 [2015]; £1,239,635 [2014]; £768,966 [2013]

Nottingham Contemporary

Registered: 7 Nov 2006 *Employees:* 67 *Volunteers:* 10
Tel: 0115 948 9758 *Website:* nottinghamcontemporary.org
Activities: Education, training; arts, culture, heritage, science
Address: Nottingham Contemporary, Weekday Cross, Nottingham, NG1 2GB
Trustees: Ms Barbara Matthews, Mr Thomas Dane, Ann Priest, Mrs Claire Elizabeth Baxter, Dr Simon Baker, Mr Niruban Ratnam, Paul Roberts, Mr Nicholas Ebbs, Mr John Kirkland, Mrs Susan Elizabeth Greenaway, Mr Matthew Symonds, Miss Anthea Hamilton
Income: £2,188,682 [2017]; £2,418,977 [2016]; £1,968,679 [2015]; £2,020,149 [2014]; £1,898,600 [2013]

Nottingham Diocesan Sick and Retired Priests Fund

Registered: 13 Jun 1980 *Volunteers:* 30
Tel: 0115 953 9800
Activities: The advancement of health or saving of lives; prevention or relief of poverty
Address: NRCDT, Willson House, 25 Derby Road, Nottingham, NG1 5AW
Trustees: Nottingham Roman Catholic Diocesan Trustees
Income: £1,073,000 [2017]

Nottingham Forest Community Trust

Registered: 29 Dec 2010 *Employees:* 48 *Volunteers:* 28
Website: nottinghamforestcommunitytrust.co.uk
Activities: General charitable purposes; education, training; advancement of health or saving of lives; amateur sport; economic, community development, employment; armed forces, emergency service efficiency; human rights, religious or racial harmony, equality or diversity; recreation; other charitable purposes
Address: Nottingham Forest Football Club, Pavilion Road, West Bridgford, Nottingham, NG2 5FJ
Trustees: Mrs Oonagh Turnbull, Mr John Saunders, Mrs Karen Lesley Frankland, Mr Nicholas Randall QC, Mr Colin Morrell, Mr Tom Gribbin, Mr Michael Vincent Dugher
Income: £1,228,385 [2016]; £879,391 [2015]; £474,105 [2014]; £538,427 [2013]; £393,130 [2012]

Nottingham High School

Registered: 10 Jun 2004 *Employees:* 248 *Volunteers:* 10
Website: nottinghamhigh.co.uk
Activities: Education, training
Address: 1 Balmoral Road, Nottingham, NG1 4HX
Trustees: David William Wild, Tim Allen, Mr Peter Munro, Mr Mark Flanagan, Dr Sharmini Krishanand, The Lord Mayor of Nottingham, Mr Stephen Banks, Mr John Stephen Jackson, Dr Basheera Hanslo, Mrs Jacqueline Morris, Mr Christopher Robinson, The Lord Lieutenant, Mr S M Green, Mr Navdeep Sethi, Mrs Catherine Lucy Nolan, Mrs Philippa Kate McNamara, Mr Christopher Francis Doleman, Mr Russell Philip Meakin, Mr Syed Mohyuddin, Dr Gail Walton
Income: £15,804,000 [2017]; £14,432,000 [2016]; £13,728,000 [2015]; £13,432,000 [2014]; £13,002,897 [2013]

Nottingham Media Centre Limited

Registered: 17 Nov 1988 *Employees:* 76
Tel: 0115 850 7811 *Website:* broadway.org.uk
Activities: Education, training; arts, culture, heritage, science; economic, community development, employment
Address: 14-18 Broad Street, Nottingham, NG1 3AL
Trustees: Mr Laurence Eric Moran, Mr Fred Brookes, Ms Ann Carol Priest, Mr Richard Edwin Gerrard, Patricia Dorothy Silburn, Mr Marc Yves Denis Gaudart, Ms Sonia Long, Mr Michael Robert David Smith
Income: £2,747,002 [2017]; £2,952,050 [2016]; £3,420,370 [2015]; £2,735,503 [2014]; £2,410,876 [2013]

Nottingham Playhouse Trust Limited

Registered: 6 May 2005 *Employees:* 125 *Volunteers:* 15
Tel: 0115 873 6245 *Website:* nottinghamplayhouse.co.uk
Activities: Education, training; arts, culture, heritage, science; recreation; other charitable purposes
Address: Nottingham Playhouse Trust Ltd, Wellington Circus, Nottingham, NG1 5AF
Trustees: Mr Harvey Goodman, Mrs Sofia Nazar-Chadwick, Ms Michelle Vacciana, Caroline Shutter, Councillor Stephen Battlemuch, Councillor Catharine Arnold, Mr David Belbin, Mr Tim Challans, Paul Southby, Mr Andrew Batty
Income: £4,922,873 [2017]; £4,482,642 [2016]; £5,795,745 [2015]; £5,308,475 [2014]; £4,791,528 [2013]

Nottingham Roman Catholic Diocesan Trustees

Registered: 23 Feb 2010 *Employees:* 80 *Volunteers:* 1,070
Tel: 0115 953 9800
Activities: Education, training; religious activities
Address: NRCDT, Willson House, 25 Derby Road, Nottingham, NG1 5AW
Trustees: Rev Canon Eddy Jarosz, Rt Rev Patrick McKinney STL, Mr David Wilson, Rev Martin Hardy BA STL, Mr Edmund Whittaker, Rev Wheat Joseph, Rev M Moore, Mr Michael Thomas Abbott, Miss Katherine Mary Cohoon, Mr Christopher Sowman FCA, Rev Paul Chipchase
Income: £11,350,000 [2017]; £11,528,000 [2016]; £12,046,000 [2015]; £10,205,000 [2014]; £9,997,000 [2013]

Nottingham Trent Students' Union

Registered: 30 Oct 2013 *Employees:* 378
Tel: 0115 848 6200 *Website:* trentstudents.org
Activities: General charitable purposes; education, training; arts, culture, heritage, science; amateur sport; economic, community development, employment
Address: The Benenson Building, Clifton Campus, Clifton Lane, Nottingham, NG11 8NS
Trustees: Mr Mike Walmsley, Mr Paul Edward Bott, Mr Kieran Goncalves, Ms Martha Longdon, Miss Madeeha Kamall, Mr Ryan Aidat-Sarran, Mr Akil Hunte, Mr Roger Spells, Miss Jelena Matic, Mr Afonso Martins, Mr Lucas Swain-Britton, Mr Kieran Gething, Miss Isabel Gregson, Miss Georgina Makin
Income: £6,231,801 [2017]; £6,249,632 [2016]; £6,304,522 [2015]; £5,872,943 [2014]

Nottingham University Hospitals Charity

Registered: 2 Feb 2016 *Employees:* 15 *Volunteers:* 55
Tel: 0115 969 1169 *Website:* nottinghamhospitalscharity.org.uk
Activities: The advancement of health or saving of lives
Address: Nottingham University Hospitals Charity, Sherwood Building, Nottingham City Hospital, Nottingham, NG5 1PB
Trustees: Miss Carole Ayre, Professor Harish Vyas, Mr Laurence Coppel, Mr Roger Whittle, Mr William Colacicchi, Dr Jane Johnson, Mandie Sunderland, Mr Jonathan English
Income: £3,511,000 [2017]

Nottingham and District Citizens Advice Bureau

Registered: 7 Mar 1989 *Employees:* 39 *Volunteers:* 60
Tel: 0115 938 8088 *Website:* citizensadvicenottingham.org.uk
Activities: The prevention or relief of poverty
Address: 32-36 Carrington Street, Nottingham, NG1 7FG
Trustees: Mr John Frederick Mason, Pat Carmody, Mr Philip Leslie Slocombe, Mr Jamie Shrivastava, Mr Steven Colin Lawson Calvert, Sue Taylor, Richard Alan Hodge, Ms Yesmean Khalil, Mr Ashley Shuresh Fredericks
Income: £1,624,024 [2017]; £1,641,682 [2016]; £1,517,257 [2015]; £1,516,003 [2014]; £1,452,238 [2013]

The Nottinghamshire Hospice Limited

Registered: 11 Sep 1980 *Employees:* 127 *Volunteers:* 480
Tel: 0115 910 1008 *Website:* nottshospice.org
Activities: General charitable purposes; education, training; advancement of health or saving of lives; other charitable purposes
Address: 384 Woodborough Road, Nottingham, NG3 4JF
Trustees: Mr Bernard Brady, Mr Colin Peacock, Dr Douglas George Black, Mrs Tracy Madge, Mrs Jenifer Richmond, Mr David Robert Saunders, Mrs Joanne Sarah Brunner, Mrs Christine Anne Claydon-Butler, Mr Matthew John Youdale
Income: £2,968,472 [2017]; £2,707,283 [2016]; £2,832,855 [2015]; £3,259,501 [2014]; £2,752,934 [2013]

Nottinghamshire Miners Welfare Trust Fund Scheme

Registered: 20 Dec 1990
Tel: 01623 625767
Activities: General charitable purposes; education, training; advancement of health or saving of lives; disability; prevention or relief of poverty; arts, culture, heritage, science; amateur sport; environment, conservation, heritage
Address: Ciswo, Welfare Offices, Berry Hill Lane, Mansfield, Notts, NG18 4JR
Trustees: Mr Jeffrey Edward Wood, Mr Michael Francis Ball, Mr Longden, Mr Trevor Barker
Income: £1,275,531 [2016]; £133,713 [2015]; £121,073 [2014]; £123,913 [2013]; £116,848 [2012]

Nottinghamshire Wildlife Trust

Registered: 17 Mar 1964 *Employees:* 68 *Volunteers:* 700
Tel: 0115 958 8242 *Website:* nottinghamshirewildlife.org
Activities: Education, training; environment, conservation, heritage
Address: The Old Ragged School, Brook Street, Nottingham, NG1 1EA
Trustees: Mr Nick Parsons, Mr David Schwarz, Mr Robert Armitage, Mr Michael Spencer, Mr Gordon Paul Dyne, Mr Simon Benjamin Staples, Ms Katherine Wilson, Mr Timothy Hordern Farr, Mr Ian Johnston, Mr Colin Gibson, Mr Martin Willis, Mr William Francis Logan, Ms Cally Keetley, Mr Rodney David Jones
Income: £3,117,778 [2017]; £2,954,231 [2016]; £3,143,999 [2015]; £3,344,778 [2014]; £2,443,388 [2013]

Nottinghamshire Women's Aid Limited

Registered: 23 May 1983 *Employees:* 57 *Volunteers:* 22
Tel: 01909 533610 *Website:* nottswa.org
Activities: General charitable purposes; accommodation, housing; other charitable purposes
Address: The Farr Centre, Chapel Walk, Westgate, Worksop, Notts, S80 1LR
Trustees: Miss Annie Littlewood, Mrs Angela Margaret Pixsley, Patricia Henson, Miss Jacqueline Fennell, Mrs Anthea Jean Bloomer, Ms Ann Snowden, Ms Dawn Colborn
Income: £1,145,699 [2017]; £1,240,005 [2016]; £1,243,908 [2015]; £1,229,783 [2014]; £1,061,986 [2013]

Nottinghamshire YMCA

Registered: 16 Aug 1965 *Employees:* 183 *Volunteers:* 63
Tel: 0115 956 7600 *Website:* nottsymca.com
Activities: General charitable purposes; education, training; accommodation, housing; amateur sport; recreation
Address: Nottingham Voluntary Action Centre, 7 Mansfield Road, Nottingham, NG1 3FB
Trustees: Mr Michael McKeever, Miss Angela Euphrasia Lyons, Ms Angela Barbaro Robins, Mr David Hemming, Mr Paul Murphy, Ms Jackie Lymn Rose
Income: £6,387,716 [2017]; £6,131,740 [2016]; £5,552,011 [2015]; £4,442,358 [2014]; £3,919,852 [2013]

Notts County F.C. Community Programme

Registered: 8 May 2002 *Employees:* 48 *Volunteers:* 3
Tel: 0115 955 7215 *Website:* nottscountyfitc.org.uk
Activities: General charitable purposes; education, training; amateur sport
Address: Notts County Football Club, Meadow Lane, Nottingham, NG2 3HJ
Trustees: Mr Colin Slater MBE, Dr David Hindley, Ms Beryl Anne Rippon, Mr Richard Posner, Mr Kevin Bartlett, Ms Arwen Makin
Income: £1,258,387 [2016]; £1,583,703 [2015]; £957,372 [2014]; £768,718 [2013]; £801,216 [2012]

The Novak Djokovic Foundation (UK) Limited

Registered: 18 May 2012 *Employees:* 1
Tel: 020 8104 1000 *Website:* novakdjokovicfoundation.org
Activities: General charitable purposes; education, training; advancement of health or saving of lives; prevention or relief of poverty
Address: 3rd Floor, Chiswick Gate, 598-608 Chiswick High Road, London, W4 5RT
Trustees: Mr David Patrick Lumley, Mr Novak Djokovic, Mrs Jelena Djokovic
Income: £2,383,010 [2016]; £2,570,790 [2015]; £1,306,504 [2014]

Novalis Trust

Registered: 26 May 2004 *Employees:* 208
Tel: 01453 837551 *Website:* novalis-trust.org.uk
Activities: Education, training; disability
Address: 235 Westward Road, Ebley, Stroud, Glos, GL5 4SX
Trustees: Mr Gordon Cole, Christopher Graham Lee, Mr Matthew Bennett, Mrs Barbara Titmuss, Mr Ian Michael Davies, Mrs Christine Williams
Income: £9,185,816 [2017]; £8,665,189 [2016]; £8,907,568 [2015]; £9,033,129 [2014]; £8,381,658 [2013]

The Nuclear Institute

Registered: 7 Aug 2008 *Employees:* 7 *Volunteers:* 100
Tel: 020 3475 4701 *Website:* nuclearinst.com
Activities: Education, training
Address: CK International House, 1-6 Yarmouth Place, London, W1J 7BU
Trustees: Mr John Clarke Fnuci, Mr Mark George Lyons, Dr Fiona Elizabeth Rayment, Dr Rebecca Weston CPhys CEng FInstP, Neil Thomson, Dr Juliet Lucy Adams Long, Mr Alastair Laird, Rear Admiral Timothy Clive Chittenden, Mr Anindya Sen, Mr Clive Sherrif Smith, Mr John Lindsay Robertson, Ms Miranda Louise Kirschel, Ms Jacqueline Gritt
Income: £1,057,401 [2016]; £1,271,875 [2015]; £889,370 [2014]; £1,281,966 [2013]; £858,169 [2012]

Nuffield College in the University of Oxford
Registered: 16 Aug 2010 *Employees:* 132 *Volunteers:* 5
Tel: 01865 278500 *Website:* nuffield.ox.ac.uk
Activities: Education, training
Address: Nuffield College, New Road, Oxford, OX1 1NF
Trustees: Professor Stephen Broadberry, Sir Andrew Dilnot, Prof Nan Dirk De Graaf, Prof Geoffrey Evans, Prof Ian Jewitt, Prof Paul Klemperer, Prof Colin Mills, Prof Kevin Roberts, Dr Christiaan Monden, Professor Janne Jonsson, Dr Janina Dill, Prof Ian Anderson Crawford, Prof Melinda Mills, Prod Martin Ellison, Prof Ezequiel Gonzalez Ocantos, Dr Eleni Kechagia-Ovseiko, Professor Cecile Laborde, Professor Sir David F Hendry FBA, Dr Stephen Bond, Prof Raymond Duch, Prof Raymond Fitzpatrick, Prof Desmond King, Dr Margaret Meyer, Dr Bent Nielsen, Dr Gwendolyn Sasse, Dr Erzsebet Bukodi, Professor Duncan Snidal, Prof Benjamin William Ansell, Prof Francisco David Rueda, Prof Andy Eggers, Prof Richard Breen, Prof David Kirk, Mr Thomas Moore, Ms Ridhi Kashyap
Income: £11,392,000 [2017]; £10,224,000 [2016]; £8,494,000 [2015]; £8,051,000 [2014]; £7,648,000 [2013]

The Nuffield Foundation
Registered: 21 Oct 1966 *Employees:* 38
Tel: 020 7681 9610 *Website:* nuffieldfoundation.org
Activities: General charitable purposes; education, training; prevention or relief of poverty
Address: The Nuffield Foundation, 28 Bedford Square, London, WC1B 3JS
Trustees: Professor The Lord Krebs, Professor Sir David Rhind CBE FRS FBA, Dame Colette Bowe, Professor The Right Honourable Lord Justice Ernest Ryder, Sir Keith Burnett, Professor Terrie Moffitt PhD FBA FMedSci, Professor James Banks, Professor Anna Vignoles
Income: £7,343,000 [2016]; £6,637,000 [2015]; £6,438,000 [2014]; £17,232,000 [2013]; £4,933,000 [2012]

Nuffield Health
Registered: 22 Sep 1962 *Employees:* 13,672
Tel: 01372 426885 *Website:* nuffieldhealth.com
Activities: The advancement of health or saving of lives
Address: Nuffield Health, Epsom Gateway, 2 Ashley Avenue, Epsom, Surrey, KT18 5AL
Trustees: Mr Russell Stephen Mons Hardy, Guy McCracken, Dame Denise Mary Holt, Mr David William Lister, Dr Natalie-Jane Anne MacDonald, Ms Fiona Elizabeth Driscoll, Mrs Joanne Mary Shaw, Mr Martin Warwick Bryant, Mr Stephen Maslin
Income: £839,600,000 [2016]; £767,600,000 [2015]; £711,100,000 [2014]; £661,600,000 [2013]; £645,700,000 [2012]

The Nuffield Trust for Research and Policy Studies in Health Services
Registered: 2 Mar 1964 *Employees:* 41 *Volunteers:* 3
Tel: 020 7631 8450 *Website:* nuffieldtrust.org.uk
Activities: General charitable purposes; advancement of health or saving of lives
Address: The Nuffield Trust, 59 New Cavendish Street, London, W1G 7LP
Trustees: Dr Jocelyn Cornwell, Professor Timothy Evans, Mrs Kathryn Matthews, Mr Christian Van Stolk, Tara Donnelly, Michael Deegan, Mr Ian Krieger, Judge Julia Palca, Mr Andrew John McKeon, Rosemarie Benneyworth
Income: £2,922,000 [2016]; £3,244,000 [2015]; £2,958,000 [2014]; £3,272,000 [2013]; £2,685,000 [2012]

Nugent Care
Registered: 8 Aug 1963 *Employees:* 683 *Volunteers:* 201
Tel: 0151 261 2000 *Website:* wearenugent.org
Activities: General charitable purposes; education, training; disability; prevention or relief of poverty; accommodation, housing; religious activities
Address: 99 Edge Lane, Edge Hill, Liverpool, L7 2PE
Trustees: Mr Malcolm Boardman, Mr John-Paul Dennis, Nugent Care Trustees Incorporated, Father Michael Stephen Fitzsimons, Mrs Kathleen Batt
Income: £18,550,000 [2017]; £23,275,000 [2016]; £20,635,000 [2015]; £21,378,000 [2014]; £20,962,000 [2013]

Nuneaton & Bedworth Leisure Trust
Registered: 13 Jun 2005 *Employees:* 147
Tel: 024 7640 0560 *Website:* nbleisuretrust.org
Activities: General charitable purposes; education, training; advancement of health or saving of lives; amateur sport; recreation
Address: NB Leisure Trust, Heron House, Newdegate Street, Nuneaton, Warwicks, CV11 4EL
Trustees: Mrs Catherine Ann Hayes, Mr Pat Sowter, Mrs Emma Mitchell, Mrs Janet Stubbs, Mr John Alexander Dolman, Mrs Georgina June Waddingham
Income: £5,023,478 [2017]; £2,591,385 [2016]; £2,556,556 [2015]; £5,786,677 [2014]; £5,550,044 [2013]

Nursing and Midwifery Council
Registered: 27 Mar 2002 *Employees:* 681
Website: nmc.org.uk
Activities: Education, training; advancement of health or saving of lives
Address: NMC, 23 Portland Place, London, W1B 1PZ
Trustees: Mr Stephen Thornton, Ms Ruth Walker, Dr Anne Wright, Derek Pretty, Mrs Maura Devlin, Miss Marta Phillips, Sir Hugh Bayley, Mr Philip Graf CBE, Mr Robert Parry, Mrs Lorna Tinsley, Professor Karen Cox
Income: £86,155,000 [2017]; £80,265,000 [2016]; £73,204,000 [2015]; £65,193,000 [2014]; £73,355,000 [2013]

The Nurture Group Network Limited
Registered: 31 Aug 2006 *Employees:* 13
Tel: 020 3475 8980 *Website:* nurturegroups.org
Activities: Education, training
Address: The Nurture Group Network, 18a Victoria Park Square, Bethnal Green, London, E2 9PB
Trustees: Mr Mark John Turner, Ms Jacqueline Brooks, Dr Marianne Coleman, Ms Alison Betts, Mr Alan John Leaman, Mrs Kelly Amber Freeman, Mrs Susan Henderson OBE, Ms Nicola Jane Hannam, Ms Caley Amanda Eldred, Mr Michael Andrew Clifford
Income: £1,046,733 [2016]; £911,081 [2015]; £811,962 [2014]; £708,139 [2013]; £601,702 [2012]

Nutley Hall
Registered: 21 Mar 1966 *Employees:* 39
Tel: 01825 712696 *Website:* nutleyhall.org
Activities: Education, training; disability; accommodation, housing
Address: High Street, Nutley, Uckfield, E Sussex, TN22 3NJ
Trustees: Mr Piet Blok, Miss Margarete Albath, Mrs Helen Compson, Mr Guy Bridge, Mr Paul Bradford, Mr Hamish J Dow, Mr Ian Walker, Mr Raz Levy
Income: £1,457,257 [2017]; £1,413,960 [2016]; £1,356,395 [2015]; £1,371,028 [2014]; £1,322,220 [2013]

The Nutrition Society
Registered: 30 Sep 1976 *Employees:* 10 *Volunteers:* 200
Tel: 020 7605 6551 *Website:* nutritionsociety.org
Activities: Education, training; advancement of health or saving of lives; economic, community development, employment
Address: 28 High Street, Ipswich, Suffolk, IP1 3QJ
Trustees: Professor Harry John McArdle, Susan Bird, Paul Trayhurn, Prof Philip Calder, Professor Christopher Seal, Dr Alison Gallagher, Andrew Salter, Mrs Penelope Jane Hunking, Dr Frank Thies
Income: £1,273,370 [2016]; £1,329,404 [2015]; £1,398,704 [2014]; £1,314,858 [2013]; £1,106,910 [2012]

Paul O'Gorman Lifeline
Registered: 14 Feb 2005
Tel: 01243 535303 *Website:* lifelinegb.org
Activities: General charitable purposes; advancement of health or saving of lives; disability; overseas aid, famine relief
Address: Up Marden Farm, Up Marden, Chichester, W Sussex, PO18 9JR
Trustees: Mrs Valerie Seddon, Mr Jeremy Graham Seddon, Mrs Carolyn Damaris Finlay-Notman, Mr Rodney Guy Seddon
Income: £1,121,226 [2016]; £598,828 [2015]; £810,671 [2014]; £832,006 [2013]; £3,341,340 [2012]

O.F.M. Capuchin GB Charitable Trust
Registered: 5 Nov 1963 *Employees:* 13 *Volunteers:* 27
Tel: 01322 444960 *Website:* capgb.org
Activities: Religious activities
Address: Franciscan Friary, Carlton Road, Erith, Kent, DA8 1DN
Trustees: Brother James Boner OFM Cap, Brother Lucjan Zaniewski OFM Cap, Brother Martin Mikuskiewicz OFM Cap, Brother Charles Serignat OFM Cap, Brother Michael Hargan
Income: £1,541,028 [2016]; £1,157,085 [2015]; £1,174,035 [2014]; £1,169,849 [2013]; £1,329,789 [2012]

OM International Services (Carlisle) Ltd
Registered: 6 Jan 2006 *Employees:* 50 *Volunteers:* 4
Tel: 01228 615121
Activities: General charitable purposes; education, training; religious activities
Address: OM International, Unit B, Clifford Court, Cooper Way, Parkhouse, Carlisle, CA3 0JG
Trustees: Mr Julyan Lidstone, Mr Wei Leong Goh, Mr Dennis Wright, Mr Jon Seeley, Mr Paul Hynam, Mr Bert Van De Haar, Ms Mary Lederleitner, Mr Dale Rhoton, Albert Teh, Mr Grant Porter, Mr Kelvin Samwata, Ms Shura Facanha, Lawrence Tong, Ms Zenet Maramara
Income: £3,474,967 [2016]; £3,591,507 [2015]; £3,327,585 [2014]; £2,877,345 [2013]; £3,011,802 [2012]

OMF International (UK)
Registered: 7 May 2008 *Employees:* 16 *Volunteers:* 98
Tel: 01732 887299 *Website:* omf.org.uk
Activities: Education, training; advancement of health or saving of lives; prevention or relief of poverty; religious activities; economic, community development, employment
Address: Unit 6 Station Approach, Borough Green, Sevenoaks, Kent, TN15 8BG
Trustees: Mr John Thomas, Miss Stephanie Clare Biden, Rev Raymond John Porter, Dr Onesimus Annos Ngundu, Professor Paul Fleming, Mr Kevin Stewart Ashman, Mr Martin Jonathon Rutty, Mrs Susan Margaret Belstead, Dr Stroma Beattie, Mrs Gail Featherstone
Income: £7,415,174 [2016]; £6,873,227 [2015]; £6,482,317 [2014]; £6,110,703 [2013]; £7,772,620 [2012]

Oak Foundation
Registered: 19 Aug 2003
Tel: 01480 428724 *Website:* luminus.org.uk
Activities: Education, training; advancement of health or saving of lives; disability; prevention or relief of poverty; accommodation, housing; economic, community development, employment
Address: Luminus Group, Brook House, Ouse Walk, Huntingdon, Cambs, PE29 3QW
Trustees: Miss Elizabeth Ddamulira, Mr Mike Forrest, Rev Kevin Burdett, Luminus Group Ltd, Mrs Janet Boston, Mrs Roz Brench, Mrs Rita Mathews
Income: £8,797,000 [2017]; £6,331,000 [2016]; £5,374,000 [2015]; £3,708,000 [2014]; £3,867,000 [2013]

Oakdene Education Trust
Registered: 16 Jul 1996 *Employees:* 26
Tel: 01392 368409 *Website:* plymouth.focus-school.com
Activities: Education, training
Address: 40 Ringswell Avenue, Exeter, EX1 3EF
Trustees: Mr Reuben J Prisgrove, Mr Wayne Jenner, Mr Roger Hill, Mr Richard Scott, Jeff Keam, Mr Malcolm Wallis, Eddie Bell
Income: £1,374,516 [2016]; £1,339,522 [2015]; £1,108,598 [2014]; £1,000,642 [2013]; £1,013,711 [2012]

Oakfield (Easton Maudit) Limited
Registered: 11 Sep 1981 *Employees:* 46
Tel: 01933 664059 *Website:* oakfieldcommunity.org.uk
Activities: Disability
Address: 5A Mill Road, Bozeat, Wellingborough, Northants, NN29 7JY
Trustees: Mrs Marion Rebecca Woodall, Mr John David Payne, Mr Clive Anthony Reeder, Mr Stephen Thomas Partridge-Underwood, Mrs Brenda Jane Howard, Mrs Sophie White
Income: £1,070,198 [2016]; £1,171,213 [2015]; £1,048,501 [2014]; £1,075,727 [2013]; £874,697 [2012]

Oakham School
Registered: 28 Aug 2009 *Employees:* 409 *Volunteers:* 17
Tel: 01572 758600 *Website:* oakham.rutland.sch.uk
Activities: Education, training
Address: Oakham School, Chapel Close, Market Place, Oakham, Rutland, LE15 6DT
Trustees: The Rt Revd The Lord Bishop of Peterborough, Mr Stephen Howard Woolfe, Mr Martin George Wilson, Mr Anthony Little MA, Professor Neil T Gorman, Mrs Julia Grundy, Mrs Jane Lucas, Mrs Rashmi Patel, Professor Stewart Alan Petersen, Mrs Josephine Osborne, Mr Philip Douty, Mr Nicholas Jones BSc, Mr John Czarnota, Mrs Joan Gibson, Mr Richard Foulkes, Mr Hans Haefeli, Mr Mark Dorsett
Income: £27,500,000 [2017]; £26,540,000 [2016]; £25,410,000 [2015]; £25,980,000 [2014]; £22,823,000 [2013]

The Oakhaven Trust
Registered: 13 Nov 1989 *Employees:* 212 *Volunteers:* 453
Tel: 01590 677773 *Website:* oakhavenhospice.co.uk
Activities: The advancement of health or saving of lives
Address: Oakhaven Hospice, Lower Pennington Lane, Pennington, Lymington, Hants, SO41 8ZZ
Trustees: Dr Peter Hockey, Professor Paul Dodson, David Butler, Mel Kendal, Mr David Christopher Wansey, Mr Peter Dunford, Jeremy Caldwell, Adam Terpening, Debbie Ware, Mr Adrian Noel Bunston
Income: £3,720,092 [2017]; £4,714,152 [2016]; £4,037,581 [2015]; £3,892,063 [2014]; £3,219,064 [2013]

Oakhill Education Trust
Registered: 21 Jan 1998 Employees: 27 Volunteers: 50
Tel: 020 8647 8904
Activities: Education, training
Address: 101 Sandy Lane South, Wallington, Surrey, SM6 9NW
Trustees: Mr Kenneth Gardiner, Mr Damian Lynes, Mr Iain Cooper, Mr Daryl Stanley
Income: £2,801,577 [2016]; £1,585,003 [2015]; £1,369,649 [2014]; £1,310,104 [2013]; £1,202,586 [2012]

The Oakhyrst Grange Educational Trust at Caterham in the County of Surrey
Registered: 1 May 1974 Employees: 29
Website: oakhyrstgrangeschool.co.uk
Activities: Education, training
Address: 3 Benenden Close, Seaford, E Sussex, BN25 3PG
Trustees: Mr Paul Anthony Collis, Ms Louise Anne Rose, Mrs Brenda Davis
Income: £1,274,052 [2016]; £1,192,304 [2015]; £1,184,256 [2014]; £1,041,695 [2013]; £981,993 [2012]

The Oaklea Trust
Registered: 24 Apr 2002 Employees: 390 Volunteers: 19
Tel: 01539 735025 Website: oakleatrust.co.uk
Activities: Education, training; disability; accommodation, housing
Address: 48 Stramongate, Kendal, Cumbria, LA9 4BD
Trustees: Mr Andrew Blackman, Mr Kevin Jones, Miss Pamela Clark, Mr Paul William Bardsley, Mr Michael Anthony Bedworth, Ms Cate Grimes, Mrs Janet McMeekin
Income: £7,431,854 [2017]; £7,694,731 [2016]; £7,809,604 [2015]; £7,832,671 [2014]; £7,724,469 [2013]

Oakwood School
Registered: 22 Jul 2004 Employees: 50 Volunteers: 25
Tel: 01243 575209 Website: oakwoodschool.co.uk
Activities: Education, training; arts, culture, heritage, science; amateur sport; environment, conservation, heritage; recreation
Address: Oakwood School, Oakwood, Chichester, W Sussex, PO18 9AN
Trustees: Mrs Jennie Peel, Mr Derek Bowerman, Mrs Lynda Butt, Mrs Shirley Barnes, Mr Neville Lacey, Mr James Priory, Mr Richard Solly, Mr Richard Geffen, Mr Steven Parvin, Mr Richard Pailthorpe
Income: £2,642,110 [2017]; £2,428,083 [2016]; £2,292,510 [2015]; £2,315,165 [2014]; £2,217,499 [2013]

Oasis Aquila Housing
Registered: 11 Jan 2005 Employees: 78 Volunteers: 31
Tel: 0191 477 3535 Website: oasisaquilahousing.org
Activities: General charitable purposes; prevention or relief of poverty; accommodation, housing; religious activities
Address: 11 Walker Terrace, Gateshead, Tyne & Wear, NE8 1EB
Trustees: Dr Anna Caroline Wroe, Nicholas William Salisbury, Ms Kate Ginks, Bishop Mark Bryant, Mr Ian Elliott, Mr Chris Aldridge
Income: £2,484,114 [2017]; £2,465,129 [2016]; £2,617,919 [2015]; £2,700,467 [2014]; £1,053,858 [2013]

Oasis Care and Training Agency (OCTA)
Registered: 16 Feb 1996 Employees: 405 Volunteers: 14
Tel: 020 7639 6192 Website: oasiscareandtraining.org.uk
Activities: General charitable purposes; education, training; advancement of health or saving of lives; disability; prevention or relief of poverty; overseas aid, famine relief; amateur sport; economic, community development, employment
Address: 24-32 Murdock Street, London, SE15 1LW
Trustees: Mrs Sabah Ahmed Yusuf, Mr Musa Jama, Mr Guled Abdullahi, Mr Hussein Yousuf Abdullahi
Income: £7,808,561 [2017]; £6,904,764 [2016]; £5,421,324 [2015]; £4,491,335 [2014]; £3,960,538 [2013]

Oasis Charitable Trust
Registered: 24 Sep 1993 Employees: 4,945 Volunteers: 2,000
Tel: 020 7921 4200 Website: oasisuk.org
Activities: General charitable purposes; education, training; advancement of health or saving of lives; prevention or relief of poverty; accommodation, housing; religious activities; economic, community development, employment; human rights, religious or racial harmony, equality or diversity; recreation; other charitable purposes
Address: 1 Kennington Road, London, SE1 7QP
Trustees: Mr Graham Mungeam, David Bright, Janice Ann Smith, Mr Mark Francis McAllister, Andy Simmonds, Nicholas Salisbury, Mr Philip Warland
Income: £210,393,000 [2016]; £198,446,000 [2015]; £271,709,000 [2014]; £160,323,000 [2013]; £204,913,694 [2012]

Oasis Community Partnerships
Registered: 8 Oct 2015 Employees: 45 Volunteers: 400
Tel: 020 7921 4248
Activities: Education, training; advancement of health or saving of lives; prevention or relief of poverty; religious activities
Address: 1 Kennington Road, London, SE1 7QP
Trustees: Pauline Muir, Mr Peter John Brierley, Rebecca Claydon, Mr David Francis Bright, Andy Briers, Ruth Cox
Income: £1,266,587 [2016]

Oasis Domestic Abuse Service Ltd
Registered: 7 Oct 2008 Employees: 35 Volunteers: 65
Tel: 01843 269400 Website: oasisdaservice.org
Activities: Education, training; accommodation, housing; other charitable purposes
Address: P O Box 174, Margate, Kent, CT9 4GA
Trustees: Mr Colin John Chapman, Miss Kristel Bridget Moore, Mrs Margaret Stella Elliott, Esther Coren, Sheridan Morrison, Mr Derrick Downs, Rev Beatrice Musindi, Jacqueline Morris, Helen Jones
Income: £1,563,282 [2017]; £1,511,393 [2016]; £1,340,112 [2015]; £1,288,326 [2014]; £677,497 [2013]

The Oasis Partnership UK
Registered: 11 Apr 1996 Employees: 25 Volunteers: 80
Tel: 01494 898480 Website: oasispartnership.org
Activities: General charitable purposes; education, training; advancement of health or saving of lives; prevention or relief of poverty
Address: Oasis House, George Street, High Wycombe, Bucks, HP11 2RZ
Trustees: Mrs Stella Frances Haylett, Mr Wadell Ranzino Wilson JP, Mr Gary John Clayton, Mr Frank Hodge, Dr Robert Fieldsend, Mr David Shaw, Ms Simone Cadette
Income: £1,053,917 [2017]; £956,310 [2016]; £1,918,315 [2015]; £1,695,312 [2014]; £1,531,215 [2013]

Obstetrics Anaesthetists Association
Registered: 20 Sep 2005
Tel: 020 7631 8883 *Website:* oaa-anaes.ac.uk
Activities: Education, training; advancement of health or saving of lives
Address: Association of Anaesthetists of GB & Ireland, 21 Portland Place, London, W1B 1PY
Trustees: Dr Felicity Plaat, Dr Gary Stocks, Dr Matthew Wilson, Dr Roshan Anton Gabriel Fernando, Dr Sarah Armstrong, Dr Emma Evans, Dr Robin Russell, Dr Queenie Lo, Dr Nuala Lucas, Dr Kerry Litchfield, Dr Thierry Girard, Dr Christopher Elton, Dr Rupert Gauntlett, Dr James Bamber, Dr Marc Alice Frans Van De Velde
Income: £1,029,138 [2017]; £888,491 [2016]; £857,037 [2015]; £903,300 [2014]; £1,019,831 [2013]

Octagon Theatre Trust Limited
Registered: 3 Aug 1966 *Employees:* 99 *Volunteers:* 120
Tel: 01204 529407 *Website:* octagonbolton.co.uk
Activities: General charitable purposes; education, training; arts, culture, heritage, science; amateur sport; economic, community development, employment
Address: Octagon Theatre, Howell Croft South, Bolton, Lancs, BL1 1SB
Trustees: Councillor John Byrne, Councillor Madeline Murray, Ms Sophy Jacob, Mr Stephen Arnfield, Mr Stephen Morgan Parry, Mr Stephen Joseph McArdle, Mrs Kaye Alison Grogan, Mr William Henry Charles Webster, Councillor Linda Thomas, Mrs Claire Josephine Moreland, Ms Elizabeth Wilson, Ms Vivienne Lesley Jones, Councillor Ann-Marie Humphreys, Rosslyn Colderley, Ms Natalie Eva Wilson
Income: £3,042,762 [2017]; £2,689,549 [2016]; £2,453,931 [2015]; £2,831,033 [2014]; £2,163,913 [2013]

October Gallery Trust
Registered: 25 Feb 1986 *Employees:* 16 *Volunteers:* 17
Tel: 020 7242 7367 *Website:* octobergallery.co.uk
Activities: Education, training; arts, culture, heritage, science
Address: 24 Old Gloucester Street, London, WC1N 3AL
Trustees: Mrs Judy Ann Hawes, Mr John Allen, Peter Mayer, Ms Deborah Snyder, Ms Marie Harding, Mr Ian Goodfellow
Income: £1,076,884 [2016]; £1,144,274 [2015]; £540,437 [2014]; £1,305,444 [2013]; £1,169,832 [2012]

Odstock Charitable Trust
Registered: 8 May 2008 *Employees:* 2
Tel: 01722 412412
Activities: The advancement of health or saving of lives
Address: Alexandra House, St Johns Street, Salisbury, Wilts, SP1 2SB
Trustees: Mr Stephen Craig Kenneth Oxley, Mr Simon Richards, Mrs Sara Anne Willan, Mr Michael Andrew Hall
Income: £1,107,245 [2017]; £1,140,736 [2016]; £1,026,766 [2015]; £1,038,880 [2014]; £1,115,629 [2013]

Off Centre Limited
Registered: 9 Dec 1983 *Employees:* 17 *Volunteers:* 5
Tel: 020 8986 4016 *Website:* offcentre.org.uk
Activities: Education, training; advancement of health or saving of lives; prevention or relief of poverty
Address: Units 1-3, 68-82 Digby Road, London, E9 6HX
Trustees: Ms Imelda Redmond CBE, Mr Andrew Zimmerman, Mr Peter O'Callaghan, Dr Francesca Cleugh, Ms Rachel Pigott
Income: £1,968,257 [2017]; £583,165 [2016]; £634,245 [2015]; £506,614 [2014]; £486,482 [2013]

Off The Record (Bristol)
Registered: 1 Mar 2001 *Employees:* 43 *Volunteers:* 58
Tel: 0117 922 6747 *Website:* otrbristol.org.uk
Activities: Education, training; advancement of health or saving of lives; prevention or relief of poverty; accommodation, housing; economic, community development, employment; human rights, religious or racial harmony, equality or diversity
Address: 2 Horfield Road, St Michael's Hill, Bristol, BS2 8EA
Trustees: Mr Tony Whitlock, Dr Rachel Brown, Mrs Jean Sapeta, Mrs Amanda Bancroft, Ms Amanda John, Peter Hobbs, Mrs Patsy Hudson, Dr Jochen Binder-Dietrich, Karen Drake
Income: £1,643,755 [2017]; £1,221,989 [2016]; £648,218 [2015]; £394,702 [2014]; £314,879 [2013]

Off The Record Youth Counselling Croydon
Registered: 1 Dec 1995 *Employees:* 43 *Volunteers:* 28
Tel: 020 8251 0251 *Website:* talkofftherecord.org
Activities: General charitable purposes; advancement of health or saving of lives; human rights, religious or racial harmony, equality or diversity
Address: Off The Record Youth Counselling, 72 Queens Road, Croydon, Surrey, CR0 2PR
Trustees: Mr John Colin Denham, Ms Patricia Davies Nearn, Ms Sanghamitra Chakravarty, Mrs Roza Watson, Ms Arlene Clapham, Mr Clement Amankwah, Mrs Nousheen Hassan, Ms Jayne Oye Kumi
Income: £1,119,071 [2017]; £1,017,718 [2016]; £729,139 [2015]; £725,807 [2014]; £687,513 [2013]

The Office of The Independent Adjudicator for Higher Education
Registered: 11 Apr 2011 *Employees:* 72
Tel: 0118 959 9813 *Website:* oiahe.org.uk
Activities: Education, training
Address: Second Floor, Office of The Independent Adjudicator, Abbey Gate, 57-75 Kings Road, Reading, Berks, RG1 3AB
Trustees: Dr Simon Walford, Mr Richard Walters, Mr Mark Humphriss, Mrs Carey Haslam, Professor Geoffrey Elliott, Mr Andrew Lawrence Mack, Mr Amatey Doku, Mr William Callaway, Mrs Sophie Williams, Mr Gareth Lindop, Professor Alistair Fitt, Professor Paul Layzell, Mr Peter Forbes, Dame Suzi Leather, Ms Gillian Fleming, Mr Andrew Frank Chandler, Mr David Hall, Mr Jon Renyard, Dr Wendy Finlay, Mr Jonathan Nigel Rees
Income: £4,357,795 [2016]; £4,154,083 [2015]; £4,191,230 [2014]; £3,867,988 [2013]; £3,059,971 [2012]

The Officers' Association
Registered: 17 Apr 1964 *Employees:* 36 *Volunteers:* 736
Tel: 020 7808 4160 *Website:* officersassociation.org.uk
Activities: Education, training; prevention or relief of poverty; other charitable purposes
Address: The Officers' Association, Mountbarrow House, 6-20 Elizabeth Street, London, SW1W 9RB
Trustees: Major General Martin Rutledge CB OBE, Ms Deanne Thomas, Mr Richard Sankey, Air Vice-Marshal Steven Chisnall CB, Commander John Lea RN, Ryan Sinclair, Mr Alastair Singleton JP, Mr Jonathan Holdsworth, Mr Alex Spofforth, Mrs Diana Stephenson, Mr Ben Farrell MBE
Income: £3,250,000 [2017]; £3,414,000 [2016]; £3,326,670 [2015]; £3,038,000 [2014]; £3,138,000 [2013]

Oglesby Charitable Trust
Registered: 30 Sep 1993
Website: oglesbycharitabletrust.co.uk
Activities: Education, training; advancement of health or saving of lives; disability; prevention or relief of poverty; arts, culture, heritage, science; environment, conservation, heritage; economic, community development, employment
Address: Lowry House, 17 Marble Street, Manchester, M2 3AW
Trustees: Mrs Jean Oglesby, Mr Bob Kitson, Mrs Katharine Vokes, Mr Peter Renshaw, Mr Michael Oglesby, Mrs Jane Oglesby, Mr Chris Oglesby
Income: £1,051,963 [2016]; £5,676,539 [2015]; £6,382,366 [2014]; £1,285,940 [2013]; £1,023,959 [2012]

Oizer Charitable Trust
Registered: 24 Sep 1992
Tel: 0161 832 8721
Activities: General charitable purposes; education, training; advancement of health or saving of lives; disability; prevention or relief of poverty; overseas aid, famine relief; accommodation, housing; religious activities
Address: 6th Floor, Cardinal House, 20 St Marys Parsonage, Manchester, M3 2LG
Trustees: Mr Joshua Halpern, Cindy Halpern
Income: £1,171,707 [2017]; £664,404 [2016]; £1,168,399 [2015]; £462,927 [2014]; £1,080,651 [2013]

Old Buckenham Hall (Brettenham) Educational Trust Ltd
Registered: 10 Jun 1968 *Employees:* 91 *Volunteers:* 12
Tel: 01449 740252 *Website:* obh.co.uk
Activities: Education, training
Address: Old Buckenham Hall School, Brettenham, Ipswich, Suffolk, IP7 7PH
Trustees: Sarah Kerr-Dineen, Mr Nicholas Francis Bullen, Mr Duncan J M Liddell, Kate Pryke, Mrs Nicola Harrison, Louise Martin, Melissa Weller-Poley, Mrs Claire Crawshay, Mr Adam W G Dixon-Smith, Mr Nicholas Page, Mr Christopher John Minter, Innes MacAskill, Edward Mason, Ms Emma Watson
Income: £3,533,737 [2016]; £2,746,160 [2015]; £2,760,863 [2014]; £3,099,486 [2013]; £2,529,741 [2012]

The Old Dart Foundation
Registered: 29 Aug 2013 *Employees:* 1
Tel: 020 7842 2000 *Website:* olddartfoundation.org
Activities: General charitable purposes; education, training; advancement of health or saving of lives; disability; prevention or relief of poverty; accommodation, housing; economic, community development, employment
Address: Rawlinson & Hunter, 6 New Street Square, London, EC4A 3AQ
Trustees: Mr Charles Patrick Lutyens, Mrs Clare Elizabeth Loudon, Mrs Caroline Perry, Mr Archibald Geoffrey Loudon, Dr Katherine Mary O'Reilly, Mr Luis Jose Baertl
Income: £7,484,722 [2016]; £5,501,016 [2015]

Old Oak Housing Association Limited
Registered: 12 Oct 2000 *Employees:* 14
Tel: 020 8319 8870 *Website:* oldoakhousing.co.uk
Activities: Accommodation, housing
Address: Old Oak Housing Association, Old Oak House, 43-45 Erconwald Street, London, W12 0BP
Trustees: Councillor Wesley Harcourt, Councillor Elaine Chumnery, Mr Tony Hennessey, Ms Kathleen Francis, Mr Andrew Kimmance, Mrs Helena Peacock, Mr Mark Higton, Mrs Entisar Abdulraizig, Mrs Gracie Kutubu-Kamara, Ms Jill Collins
Income: £1,427,000 [2017]; £2,291,000 [2016]; £1,759,000 [2015]; £1,145,000 [2014]; £1,536,000 [2013]

The Old Vic Theatre Trust 2000
Registered: 25 Nov 1998 *Employees:* 181
Tel: 020 7902 7345 *Website:* oldvictheatre.com
Activities: Arts, culture, heritage, science
Address: Old Vic Theatre, 103 The Cut, London, SE1 8NB
Trustees: Mr Alan Banes, Robert Anthony Bourne, Mr Kevin David McGrath, Mr Anthony Horowitz, Nicholas James Clarry, Ms Julia Peyton-Jones, Sally Greene, Joyce Anita Hytner, Katherine Veronica Horton, Anthony David Gibbon, Ms Annie Pleshette Murphy, Ian Clifford Powell
Income: £12,290,567 [2016]; £15,707,971 [2015]; £12,477,029 [2014]; £13,916,180 [2013]; £13,373,890 [2012]

Old Vicarage School Trust
Registered: 26 Mar 1973 *Employees:* 42 *Volunteers:* 50
Website: oldvicarageschool.com
Activities: Education, training; overseas aid, famine relief
Address: Old Vicarage School, 48 Richmond Hill, Richmond upon Thames, Surrey, TW10 6QX
Trustees: Mr Guy Cowley, Dr Charlotte Bearcroft, Ms Claire Nightingale, Miss Mekhla Barua, Mrs Sally Yeadon, Sarah Brown, Mr Richard David Lewis, Mr Jerzy Krol, Mr Greg Caplan, Mr Simon Waldman, Christian Heidl, Suzanne Longstaff
Income: £2,778,852 [2017]; £2,662,890 [2016]; £2,529,415 [2015]; £2,390,943 [2014]; £2,270,006 [2013]

Henry Oldfield Trust
Registered: 2 Apr 2014
Tel: 01795 886385
Activities: General charitable purposes; prevention or relief of poverty; arts, culture, heritage, science; environment, conservation, heritage; economic, community development, employment
Address: Doddington Place, Church Lane, Doddington, Sittingbourne, Kent, ME9 0BB
Trustees: Mr Richard John Oldfield, Mrs Amicia Oldfield, Mr Edward Oldfield, Mrs Leonora Rose Philipps, Mr Christopher Oldfield
Income: £2,916,155 [2017]; £1,406,151 [2016]; £4,273,880 [2015]

The Oldham Coliseum Theatre Limited
Registered: 26 Jun 1979 *Employees:* 59 *Volunteers:* 54
Tel: 0161 785 7001 *Website:* coliseum.org.uk
Activities: Education, training; arts, culture, heritage, science
Address: Oldham Coliseum Theatre Ltd, Coliseum Theatre, Fairbottom Street, Oldham, Lancs, OL1 3SW
Trustees: Mr Kashif Ashraf, Mr Atul Patel, Peter Crowther, Councillor Bernard Sharp, Mrs Gail Richards, Ms Elaine McLean, Councillor Derek Heffernan, Mrs Sandy Hawkins, Ms Shirley Lundstram, Mr Michael Holt, Mrs Susan Wildman, David Gray, Mr Simon Whitehead, Mrs Lynne Sarah Farnell, Mr Jeremy Woodhouse, Cllr Barbara Brownridge, Mr Stephen Abell
Income: £2,479,974 [2017]; £2,429,572 [2016]; £2,229,724 [2015]; £2,178,202 [2014]; £2,159,338 [2013]

Jamie Oliver Food Foundation
Registered: 7 Nov 2002 *Employees:* 14
Website: jamieoliverfoodfoundation.org.uk
Activities: General charitable purposes; education, training; advancement of health or saving of lives; prevention or relief of poverty; economic, community development, employment
Address: 15 Westland Place, London, N1 7LP
Trustees: Eric Archambeau, Louise Holland, Dafna Bonas, Elizabeth Peyton-Jones
Income: £2,864,102 [2016]; £1,884,766 [2015]; £1,461,473 [2014]; £779,687 [2013]; £825,343 [2012]

One Awards
Registered: 13 Jul 2001 *Employees:* 56
Tel: 01642 311321 *Website:* oneawards.org.uk
Activities: Education, training; economic, community development, employment
Address: 18 The Grove, Marton in Cleveland, Middlesbrough, Cleveland, TS7 8AA
Trustees: Peter Stonell, Mrs Alaine McCartney, Lesley Griffin, Les Woodward, Michelle Elliott, Nigel Harrett, Nigel Hardy, Heloise Allan, Andrew McHale
Income: £1,157,458 [2017]; £1,069,666 [2016]; £1,296,764 [2015]; £1,451,098 [2014]; £1,850,551 [2013]

One Community Eastleigh
Registered: 14 Feb 1996 *Employees:* 94 *Volunteers:* 202
Tel: 023 8090 2400 *Website:* 1community.org.uk
Activities: General charitable purposes; education, training; advancement of health or saving of lives; disability; arts, culture, heritage, science; environment, conservation, heritage; economic, community development, employment
Address: Ms Jean Roberts-Jones, 16 Romsey Road, Eastleigh, Hants, SO50 9AL
Trustees: Sri Kandiah, Gareth Davies, Mrs Patricia Statham, Mr Peter Booker, David Wrighton, Mrs Janice Bassett, Mr Adrian Hughes, Dr Emma Hilton
Income: £1,470,109 [2017]; £1,508,824 [2016]; £1,419,948 [2015]; £1,356,463 [2014]; £1,440,980 [2013]

One Community Foundation Limited
Registered: 29 Mar 2010 *Employees:* 2 *Volunteers:* 4
Tel: 01484 468397 *Website:* one-community.org.uk
Activities: General charitable purposes
Address: c/o Chadwick Lawrence Solicitors, 13 Railway Street, Huddersfield, W Yorks, HD1 1JS
Trustees: Mrs Judith Ramsden Charlesworth, Sir John Harman, Mr Ian Brierley, Mr Jonathan Henry Thornton, Mr Jeremy Peter Garside, Mr Abdul Aslam, Mr Eric Firth, Mrs Joanne Woodhouse Bell
Income: £1,372,508 [2017]; £139,024 [2016]; £137,085 [2015]; £97,372 [2014]; £78,517 [2013]

One Dance UK
Registered: 10 Nov 1994 *Employees:* 18 *Volunteers:* 30
Tel: 020 7713 0730 *Website:* onedanceuk.org
Activities: General charitable purposes; education, training; arts, culture, heritage, science
Address: Ensign House, Battersea Reach, Juniper Drive, London, SW18 1TA
Trustees: Ms Susannah Catherine Simons, Ms Anu Giri, Mr David Jnr Watson, Mr Anthony Doran Bowne, Mrs Piali Ray, Mr Julian Flitter, Ms Susan Marjorie Wyatt, Miss Victoria Igbokwe, Mr Andrew Gerard Carrick
Income: £1,136,027 [2017]; £747,281 [2016]; £589,179 [2015]; £593,787 [2014]; £370,557 [2013]

The One Foundation
Registered: 13 Apr 2007 *Employees:* 2
Tel: 020 8334 6950 *Website:* onedifference.org
Activities: The advancement of health or saving of lives; prevention or relief of poverty; overseas aid, famine relief
Address: Steel House, 13-17 Princes Road, Richmond, Surrey, London, TW10 6DQ
Trustees: Mr Kenechukwu Umeasiegbu, Ms Karina Morawska, Mr Duncan Goose
Income: £1,373,123 [2016]; £1,282,863 [2015]; £1,282,863 [2014]; £641,612 [2013]; £1,831,318 [2012]

One Heart - Lev Echod
Registered: 19 May 2016
Tel: 020 8211 0327
Activities: The advancement of health or saving of lives
Address: Flat 9, Davis Court, Saw Mill Way, London, N16 6AG
Trustees: Mrs Michelle Sprung, Mrs Hannah Moskovitz, Mr Dov Krautwirt
Income: £3,791,061 [2017]

One Nation
Registered: 14 Mar 2014 *Employees:* 7 *Volunteers:* 10
Tel: 01924 856923 *Website:* onenationuk.org
Activities: General charitable purposes; education, training; advancement of health or saving of lives; prevention or relief of poverty; overseas aid, famine relief; accommodation, housing; religious activities
Address: 2A Oxford Street, Batley, W Yorks, WF17 7PZ
Trustees: Maqsood Motala, Nadeem Seedat, Mr Muhammad Luqmaan Vania
Income: £3,999,599 [2017]; £2,746,471 [2016]; £792,127 [2015]; £496,269 [2014]

One Plus One Marriage and Partnership Research
Registered: 13 Aug 2001 *Employees:* 19 *Volunteers:* 1
Tel: 020 3096 7871 *Website:* oneplusone.org.uk
Activities: Education, training
Address: CAN Mezzanine, 7-14 Great Dover Street, London, SE1 4YR
Trustees: Ms Erica De'ath OBE, Ms Ruth Kennedy, Ms Katharine Landells, Mr Axel Heitmueller, Liz Mills, Ms Emma Ries, Ms Josephine Richardson, Ms Sarah Healey
Income: £1,093,814 [2017]; £1,595,720 [2016]; £2,387,207 [2015]; £2,029,001 [2014]; £1,816,578 [2013]

One To One Children's Fund
Registered: 17 Apr 2001 *Employees:* 8 *Volunteers:* 1
Tel: 020 7317 7040 *Website:* onetoonechildrensfund.org
Activities: General charitable purposes; education, training; advancement of health or saving of lives; disability; prevention or relief of poverty; overseas aid, famine relief
Address: Hillsdown House, 32 Hampstead High Street, London, NW3 1QD
Trustees: Dr Jennifer Altschuler, Mr Lawrence Gould, Mr Russell Mishcon, Ms Lauren Jacobson, Mr David Thompson, Mr David Altschuler, Mr Gary Lubner, Ms Emma Bell, Mr Jonathan Penkin
Income: £1,124,072 [2017]; £989,804 [2016]; £980,126 [2015]; £1,140,486 [2014]; £768,716 [2013]

One Trust
Registered: 23 Nov 2015 *Employees:* 83 *Volunteers:* 3
Website: onetrust.co.uk
Activities: The advancement of health or saving of lives; disability; human rights, religious or racial harmony, equality or diversity; recreation
Address: Church Lane Day Centre, 21 Church Lane, London, SW17 9PW
Trustees: Mr William Robert Luigi Olmi, Mr Alistair Duncan Rush, Mr Robert Little, Mrs Melanie Robinson, Mr Ian Lewer, Mrs Catherine Parsons, Mr David Pyper, Mrs Diane Moore, Ms Sarah Alice Graham, Mr Jacobus Van Der Bent, Ms Massy Larizadeh
Income: £3,179,600 [2017]; £1,552,696 [2016]

One YMCA

Registered: 25 Feb 2004 *Employees:* 265 *Volunteers:* 200
Tel: 01923 353600 *Website:* oneymca.org
Activities: General charitable purposes; education, training; prevention or relief of poverty; accommodation, housing; religious activities; amateur sport; economic, community development, employment; recreation
Address: YMCA, Charter House, Charter Place, Watford, Herts, WD17 2RT
Trustees: Mr Andrew Newell, Ms Christine Neyndorff, Ms Jane Cotton, Ms Nicola Lucas, Mr John Ball, Mr Max Beddard, John Robinson, Mr Nicholas Mourant, Mr Benjamin Johnson, Ms Clare Hearnshaw, Mr Simon Boz
Income: £9,195,175 [2017]; £8,180,596 [2016]; £8,703,904 [2015]; £8,956,518 [2014]; £5,279,281 [2013]

One Young World Limited

Registered: 17 May 2012 *Employees:* 15 *Volunteers:* 6
Tel: 07584 473619 *Website:* oneyoungworld.com
Activities: General charitable purposes; education, training; prevention or relief of poverty; environment, conservation, heritage; economic, community development, employment; human rights, religious or racial harmony, equality or diversity
Address: Central London Law Centre, 14 Irving Street, London, WC2H 7AF
Trustees: Mr David Jones, Mr Jonathan Mitchell, Kate Robertson, Mr Elio Leoni Sceti
Income: £3,890,000 [2016]; £3,590,000 [2015]; £3,725,000 [2014]; £4,567,000 [2013]; £5,308,000 [2012]

Ongo Communities Limited

Registered: 4 Mar 2014 *Employees:* 23 *Volunteers:* 37
Tel: 01724 279900 *Website:* ongo.co.uk
Activities: General charitable purposes; education, training; advancement of health or saving of lives; prevention or relief of poverty; accommodation, housing; economic, community development, employment
Address: Ongo, Meridian House, Normanby Road, Scunthorpe, N Lincs, DN15 8QZ
Trustees: Mr James Trowsdale, Mr James McKellar Main, Mr Kevin Yorath, Mr Paul Elliott, Mr Nicholas Tharratt, Mrs Avril Bairstow
Income: £1,129,754 [2017]; £914,833 [2016]; £669,499 [2015]

The Onside Foundation

Registered: 30 May 2014
Tel: 01204 369297 *Website:* onsideyouthzones.org
Activities: General charitable purposes; education, training; advancement of health or saving of lives; disability; arts, culture, heritage, science; amateur sport; economic, community development, employment; recreation
Address: Atria, Spa Road, Bolton, Lancs, BL1 4AG
Trustees: Mr Ross Warburton, Mr Bill Ainscough, Mr Bill Holroyd, Nick Sleep
Income: £4,697,000 [2017]; £1,700,030 [2016]; £250,000 [2015]

Onside Independent Advocacy

Registered: 10 Feb 2004 *Employees:* 51 *Volunteers:* 146
Tel: 01905 27525 *Website:* onside-advocacy.org.uk
Activities: General charitable purposes; education, training; advancement of health or saving of lives; disability; economic, community development, employment; human rights, religious or racial harmony, equality or diversity
Address: Williamson House, 14 Charles Street, Worcester, WR1 2AQ
Trustees: Mrs Carol Anne Chapman, Mr John Douglas, Mrs Alison Frances Robinson, Mr Johnathan Hildred, Mrs Julia Adams, Mr Roger Colin Aldridge, Mr Richard Bartholomew
Income: £1,072,592 [2017]; £1,115,672 [2016]; £1,176,929 [2015]; £1,156,895 [2014]; £1,143,643 [2013]

Onside Youth Zones

Registered: 15 Sep 2008 *Employees:* 26
Tel: 01204 362128 *Website:* onsideyouthzones.org
Activities: Education, training; arts, culture, heritage, science; amateur sport; economic, community development, employment; recreation
Address: Onside Youth Zones, Atria, Spa Road, Bolton, Lancs, BL1 4AG
Trustees: Ross Warburton, Jim Smith, Daniel Hall, Nigel Richens, Mr John Charles Roberts, Bill Holroyd, Charles Mindenhall, John Marsh, Karen Griffiths, Nick Sleep
Income: £3,511,705 [2017]; £3,649,738 [2016]; £1,646,787 [2015]; £1,351,934 [2014]; £859,604 [2013]

Open Age

Registered: 23 Jan 2015 *Employees:* 34 *Volunteers:* 100
Tel: 020 8962 4141 *Website:* openage.org.uk
Activities: Education, training; advancement of health or saving of lives; economic, community development, employment; recreation
Address: 47 Avondale Rise, London, SE15 4AJ
Trustees: Jean Daintith, Jean Sheppard, Andrew Kelly, Allen Molesworth, Marie Kamara, Mrs Maggy Pigott CBE, Mr Michael Odwyer, Mrs Hilary Bowker, Rose Hayles, David Sinclair, Ms Marcia Blakenham, Garvin Brown, Mrs Anna Tully, Mrs Lesley Butler, Mr John Henwood
Income: £1,622,939 [2017]; £1,486,566 [2016]

Open Awards

Registered: 5 Apr 2006 *Employees:* 28
Tel: 0151 494 4358 *Website:* openawards.org.uk
Activities: Education, training
Address: Open Awards, 17 de Havilland Drive, Speke, Liverpool, L24 8RN
Trustees: Janet Trigg, Adel Ahmed, Ms Julie Frances Wilson, Nicola Mailey, Dr Gordon Laing, David Tilley, Mrs Karen Grant, Peter Taaffe, Mr Kieran Gordon, Mrs Claire Blanchard, Mr Philip Hunter, Gill Mason, Adrian Bevin
Income: £1,246,962 [2017]; £1,117,876 [2016]; £1,315,553 [2015]; £1,684,573 [2014]; £1,553,341 [2013]

Open College Network London Region

Registered: 10 Mar 1994 *Employees:* 22
Website: ocnlondon.org.uk
Activities: Education, training
Address: 15 Angel Gate, 326 City Road, London, EC1V 2SF
Trustees: Mr Nicholas Rampley, Mr John Martin Dishman, Mrs Nicola Anne Foster, Ms Kim Maria Caplin, Mr Mark Malcomson, Mr Peter Robin Wilson, Ms Lucy Ann Arnold, Mrs Julie Frances Farmer
Income: £1,218,946 [2016]; £1,396,297 [2015]; £1,528,533 [2014]; £1,910,666 [2013]; £1,838,166 [2012]

The Open College Network South East Region Limited
Registered: 1 Jun 2006 *Employees:* 24
Tel: 01227 811827 *Website:* laser-awards.org.uk
Activities: Education, training
Address: Laser Learning Awards, OCN South East Region Ltd, Canterbury Innovation Centre, University Road, Canterbury, Kent, CT2 7FG
Trustees: Mr David Nightingale, Mrs Lindsey Morgan, Ms Pamela Jill Lumsden, Mrs Sharon Phillips, Mr Malcolm Bell, Mr Paul Phillips, Ms Fiona Morey, Mr Stephen Batchelor
Income: £1,313,707 [2017]; £1,250,938 [2016]; £1,106,842 [2015]; £1,050,631 [2014]; £1,012,986 [2013]

Open College Network West Midlands
Registered: 21 Mar 2006 *Employees:* 31
Tel: 01902 624230 *Website:* opencollnet.org.co.uk
Activities: Education, training; economic, community development, employment
Address: Aldersley House, Overstrand, Pendeford Business Park, Wolverhampton, W Midlands, WV9 5HA
Trustees: Mrs Louise Catherine Marian Toner, Mr Christopher David Morecroft, Dr Marie Ann Stowell, Christine Vincent, Paris Clark-Roden, Mr Harvey Woolf, Norman John Wood, Professor Geoffrey Mark Layer, Linus Teku Fon
Income: £1,135,083 [2016]; £1,173,350 [2015]; £1,324,751 [2014]; £1,881,934 [2013]; £2,023,708 [2012]

Open College of The Arts
Registered: 13 May 1987 *Employees:* 17
Tel: 01252 892603 *Website:* uca.ac.uk
Activities: Education, training; arts, culture, heritage, science
Address: University for The Creative Arts, Falkner Road, Farnham, Surrey, GU9 7DS
Trustees: Professor Patricia Barbara Cullen, Professor Roni Brown, Carlos Sa, Ms Cathy Baxandall, Mr Alan Cooke, John Oliver
Income: £1,517,522 [2017]; £1,165,279 [2016]; £1,495,744 [2015]; £1,376,122 [2014]; £1,041,264 [2013]

Open Doors with Brother Andrew
Registered: 2 Sep 2008 *Employees:* 70 *Volunteers:* 250
Tel: 01993 777360 *Website:* opendoorsuk.org
Activities: General charitable purposes; education, training; prevention or relief of poverty; religious activities
Address: P O Box 6, Witney, Oxon, OX29 6WG
Trustees: Mr Matthew Adrian Frost, Mr Matthew George Barlow, Mr Robert John McIntyre, Mr Andrew Selley, Mrs Rachel Belshaw, Alan McDowell, Mrs Susan Tyme, Mr Jonathan Paul Bryson
Income: £11,758,414 [2016]; £11,788,082 [2015]; £10,146,687 [2014]; £7,865,922 [2013]; £6,605,729 [2012]

Open Road Visions
Registered: 20 Apr 1993 *Employees:* 100 *Volunteers:* 265
Website: openroad.org.uk
Activities: The advancement of health or saving of lives
Address: Open Road Visions, 12 North Hill, Colchester, Essex, CO1 1DZ
Trustees: Mr Martin Mears, Ms Yvonne Maria Larkin, Mr Nicholas Kenneth Alston, Mr Robert Smith, Mr Nigel South, Ms Melinda Setanoians
Income: £3,307,709 [2017]; £3,295,811 [2016]; £3,314,708 [2015]; £2,991,307 [2014]; £2,970,511 [2013]

The Open School Trust
Registered: 8 Nov 1989 *Employees:* 15
Tel: 01223 352024 *Website:* nec.ac.uk
Activities: Education, training
Address: 115c Milton Road, Cambridge, CB4 1XE
Trustees: Ros Morpeth, Mr Richard Dorrance, Mrs Rachel Alexandra Marshall, Professor Mary Cecilia Kellett, Tony Dodds, Corrinne Callaway, Mr Richard Edward Moore
Income: £1,073,170 [2017]; £1,079,598 [2016]; £1,044,833 [2015]; £1,092,242 [2014]; £998,838 [2013]

Open Society Foundation
Registered: 23 Jul 2004 *Employees:* 108
Tel: 020 7031 0223 *Website:* opensocietyfoundations.org
Activities: General charitable purposes; education, training; disability; prevention or relief of poverty; human rights, religious or racial harmony, equality or diversity; other charitable purposes
Address: Open Society Foundation, 7th Floor, Millbank Tower, 21-24 Millbank, London, SW1P 4QP
Trustees: Richard Fries, Mrs Wen Liao, Ms Gail Scovell, Dr William Newton-Smith, Mrs Vivien Stern, Mrs Mabel Van Oranje
Income: £15,097,093 [2016]; £17,067,983 [2015]; £13,233,981 [2014]; £14,347,074 [2013]; £15,293,961 [2012]

Open University Students Association
Registered: 12 Oct 2011 *Employees:* 26 *Volunteers:* 500
Tel: 01908 652026 *Website:* open.ac.uk
Activities: Education, training
Address: The Open University, P O Box 397, Walton Hall, Milton Keynes, Bucks, MK7 6BE
Trustees: Mr Andrew Hulme, Mrs Anna Jenkins, Mrs Nicola Simpson, Miss Melanie Philpott, Mr Peter Cowan, Mr Peter Bell, Mr Andrew Cooke, Mrs Mary Oparaocha
Income: £1,590,280 [2017]; £1,314,294 [2016]; £1,237,022 [2015]; £1,182,679 [2014]; £1,137,179 [2013]

Open Youth Trust
Registered: 24 Mar 2005 *Employees:* 53 *Volunteers:* 105
Tel: 01603 763111 *Website:* opennorwich.org.uk
Activities: General charitable purposes; education, training; advancement of health or saving of lives; disability; arts, culture, heritage, science; amateur sport; recreation
Address: Open Youth Trust, 20 Bank Plain, Norwich, NR2 4SF
Trustees: Mr Leslie Charles Brown, Mr Edward Savory, Mr Karl Sandall, Miss Emily Groves, Mrs Rachele Kelsall, Mr Russell Barclay Dacre, Mr Donald Stuart, Mr Michael Ni'man, Alex Marsden
Income: £1,456,752 [2017]; £1,503,588 [2016]; £1,402,203 [2015]; £1,315,834 [2014]; £1,094,305 [2013]

Opera Holland Park
Registered: 27 Feb 2003 *Employees:* 24 *Volunteers:* 100
Tel: 020 7361 3910 *Website:* operahollandpark.com
Activities: General charitable purposes; education, training; arts, culture, heritage, science; economic, community development, employment
Address: 37 Pembroke Road, London, W8 6PW
Trustees: Sir Trevor McDonald, Mr Anupam Ganguli, Mr Charles Dorsey MacKay, Mr Martin Kramer, Miss Fiona Christine Campbell, Ms Jessica Hepburn
Income: £7,574,946 [2016]; £483,136 [2015]; £521,444 [2014]; £566,986 [2013]; £570,029 [2012]

Opera North Limited
Registered: 31 Jul 1981 *Employees:* 207
Tel: 0113 223 3534 *Website:* operanorth.co.uk
Activities: Arts, culture, heritage, science
Address: The Grand Theatre, 46 New Briggate, Leeds, LS1 6NU
Trustees: Ed Anderson, Mr Richard Mantle, John Bywater, Martin Vander Weyer, Ms Rosie Millard, Irving Warnett, Peter Maniura, Cllr J Pryor, Paul Lee, Mr Clive Roland Lloyd, Ms Nicola Christine Brentnall MVO, Dr Nima Poovaya-Smith, Ms Liza Kellett, Mr Mark Armour, Paul Baverstock, Mrs Henrietta Jowitt
Income: £17,933,027 [2017]; £16,280,960 [2016]; £15,856,765 [2015]; £14,835,726 [2014]; £18,043,991 [2013]

Operation Mobilisation
Registered: 12 Feb 1992 *Employees:* 168 *Volunteers:* 20
Tel: 01691 773388 *Website:* uk.om.org
Activities: Education, training; prevention or relief of poverty; religious activities
Address: O M United Kingdom, The Quinta, Weston Rhyn, Oswestry, Salop, SY10 7LT
Trustees: David Skews, Mr David Ost, Dr Kathryn Myers, Dr Geffrey Meyer, Mr Paul John Lindsay, Rev Celia Apeagyei-Collins, Mike Young
Income: £10,325,725 [2016]; £11,545,719 [2015]; £10,266,412 [2014]; £9,957,748 [2013]; £10,274,536 [2012]

Operation Smile United Kingdom
Registered: 22 Mar 2002 *Employees:* 13 *Volunteers:* 250
Tel: 020 3475 5126 *Website:* operationsmile.org.uk
Activities: General charitable purposes; education, training; advancement of health or saving of lives; disability; prevention or relief of poverty; overseas aid, famine relief
Address: 10 The Broadway, Wimbledon, London, SW19 1RF
Trustees: Mr Phil McDonald, Dr Maria Ellen Moore, Ms Catherine Elizabeth De Maid, Dr William Preston Magee, Mr Christopher John Pinnington
Income: £3,452,428 [2017]; £2,342,297 [2016]; £1,780,890 [2015]; £1,550,781 [2014]; £1,496,092 [2013]

Operational Research Society Limited
Registered: 19 Jan 1968 *Employees:* 12 *Volunteers:* 500
Tel: 0121 233 9300 *Website:* theorsociety.com
Activities: Education, training
Address: 12 Edward Street, Birmingham, B1 2RX
Trustees: Prof Richard Eglese, Mr John Hopes, Dr Janet Williams, Dr Pavel Albores, Mr Alan Robinson, Ms Ruth Kaufman, Professor Sanja Petrovic, Ms Sayara Beg, Mr Jonathan Batson, Alistair Clark
Income: £1,303,899 [2016]; £1,864,655 [2015]; £1,142,875 [2014]; £1,071,747 [2013]; £1,032,550 [2012]

Opportunity International United Kingdom
Registered: 19 Jan 2005 *Employees:* 13 *Volunteers:* 5
Tel: 01865 725304 *Website:* opportunity.org.uk
Activities: Education, training; prevention or relief of poverty
Address: Opportunity International, 81 St Clements Street, Oxford, OX4 1AW
Trustees: Mr John Richard Ford, Edward Fox, Mrs Kristine Braden, Clifford Hampton, Mr Robert Andrew Goldspink, Ireti Samuel Ogbu
Income: £4,507,509 [2016]; £5,528,443 [2015]; £6,528,406 [2014]; £5,003,935 [2013]; £3,985,245 [2012]

Options for Life
Registered: 13 Oct 1997 *Employees:* 89 *Volunteers:* 7
Tel: 0121 544 6611 *Website:* optionsforlife.info
Activities: Disability
Address: Oak Green Lodge, Oak Green Way, Oldbury, W Midlands, B68 8LR
Trustees: Ms Debbie White, Ms Harriet Moat, Dr Kudakwashe Bondamakara, Mr Alan Daffern, Mr Nicholas Kirby
Income: £2,255,720 [2017]; £2,177,303 [2016]; £2,088,665 [2015]; £1,947,472 [2014]; £1,871,221 [2013]

Options for Supported Living
Registered: 24 Jun 1997 *Employees:* 308
Tel: 0151 236 0855 *Website:* options-empowers.org
Activities: Disability
Address: 1st Floor, St Nicholas House, Old Churchyard, Liverpool, L2 8TX
Trustees: Brian Thomas Simpson, Julia Erskine, Mr Ivor Paul Langley, Louise Patricia Barry, Miss Nicola Daley, Mr Kevin James Peacock
Income: £6,157,683 [2017]; £6,169,718 [2016]; £6,153,241 [2015]; £6,288,813 [2014]; £5,381,977 [2013]

Oral Health Foundation
Registered: 8 Nov 1971 *Employees:* 14
Tel: 01788 546365 *Website:* dentalhealth.org
Activities: The advancement of health or saving of lives
Address: Oral Health Foundation, Smile House, 2A East Union Street, Rugby, Warwicks, CV22 6AJ
Trustees: Elizabeth Kay, Nairn Wilson, Mhari Coxon, Ms Tracy Posner, David Mason, Steve Hardiman, Ms Janet Goodwin, Dr Ben Atkins, Ed Martin, Dr Chet Trivedy, Maureen Bennett
Income: £1,061,727 [2017]; £1,079,288 [2016]; £1,097,360 [2015]; £1,197,270 [2014]; £1,299,908 [2013]

Orange Tree Theatre Ltd
Registered: 24 Aug 1978 *Employees:* 38 *Volunteers:* 20
Tel: 020 8940 0141 *Website:* orangetreetheatre.co.uk
Activities: Education, training; arts, culture, heritage, science
Address: Orange Tree Theatre, 1 Clarence Street, Richmond, Surrey, TW9 2SA
Trustees: Mrs Kate Ellis, Ms Joanna Sunita Pandya, Mr Richard Humphreys, Mr David Hunt, Ms India Semper-Hughes, Mr Nigel Hall, Mr Duncan Tatton-Brown, Mrs Rosalind Sweeting, Ms Stephanie Ann Turner, Ms Carolyn Tracey Backhouse
Income: £1,988,275 [2017]; £1,538,533 [2016]; £2,167,369 [2015]; £1,579,190 [2014]; £1,525,057 [2013]

The Oratory Schools Association
Registered: 16 Feb 1972 *Employees:* 300
Tel: 01491 683600 *Website:* oratory.co.uk
Activities: Education, training; religious activities
Address: The Oratory School, Woodcote, Reading, Berks, RG8 0PJ
Trustees: Mr Michael Henry Roche Hasslacher, Mr Francis Fitzherbert Brockholes, Right Reverend Robert John Byrne, Mr Matthew William Stilwell, Rev John Saward, Mrs Christina B T Hill Williams, Mr Martin Berkley, Mr Nicholas Tanner, Mr Jamie Sehmer FCA, Mr Nicholas Robert Purnell, Mrs Mary Anne Cochrane, Professor Peter William Evans, Mr Barney Bettesworth, Mrs Margaret E Edwards, Colonel Craig Sutherland
Income: £13,888,569 [2016]; £13,565,409 [2015]; £13,450,689 [2014]; £13,487,717 [2013]; £13,005,500 [2012]

Orbis Charitable Trust

Registered: 17 Mar 1997 *Employees:* 29 *Volunteers:* 10
Tel: 020 7608 7280 *Website:* orbis.org.uk
Activities: Education, training; advancement of health or saving of lives; disability; prevention or relief of poverty
Address: Fourth Floor, Fergusson House, 124-128 City Road, London, EC1V 2NJ
Trustees: Ms Christine Tomkins, Mr Bruce Buck, Mr Peter Hickson, Major Gen Retd Charles Vyvyan, Mr Michael Boyd, Mr Nigel Young, Mrs Yvette Dunne, Catharina Waller, Mr Tony Cowles, Mr Robert Walters, Mr Larry Benjamin, Nicola Floyd, Sir Michael Arthur, Mr Christopher Braden, Mr Rob Pinchbeck, Patricia Moller
Income: £7,597,915 [2016]; £4,758,956 [2015]; £5,741,581 [2014]; £4,713,710 [2013]; £4,947,041 [2012]

Orchard Hill College

Registered: 6 Dec 2011 *Employees:* 259
Website: orchardhill.ac.uk
Activities: Education, training
Address: Orchard Hill College, Old Town Hall, Woodcote Road, Wallington, Surrey, SM6 0NB
Trustees: Dr Caroline Allen OBE, Mr Eamonn Gilbert, Mr Darren Coghlan, Dr David Watkins, Mr Rama Venchard, Mr Staynton Curtis Brown
Income: £13,685,126 [2017]; £12,482,894 [2016]; £40 [2014]; £3 [2013]

The Orchard Trust

Registered: 14 Mar 1989 *Employees:* 179 *Volunteers:* 14
Tel: 01594 861137 *Website:* orchard-trust.org.uk
Activities: Education, training; disability; accommodation, housing; animals; environment, conservation, heritage
Address: Valley Springs, Central Lydbrook, Lydbrook, Glos, GL17 9PP
Trustees: Mrs Susan Frances Henchley, Mr Robert Harry Morgan, Mr Nicholas Peter Budd, Ms Rachel Clare Adams, Mrs Rita Mary Dodsworth, Mrs Elaine Hewison, Mr Christopher David Nicholas Duckett, Mr Leon Brian Kaye, Mrs Judith Jane Morris Kaye, Mrs Katharine Helena Morley, Mrs Claire Eleanor Smart, Mr David John Pitts
Income: £3,336,447 [2017]; £3,180,347 [2016]; £3,129,249 [2015]; £3,080,256 [2014]; £2,810,705 [2013]

Orchard Vale Trust Limited

Registered: 4 Oct 1985 *Employees:* 70 *Volunteers:* 2
Tel: 01749 671706 *Website:* orchardvaletrust.org.uk
Activities: The advancement of health or saving of lives; disability
Address: East Court, Wookey, Wells, Somerset, BA5 1AR
Trustees: Peter Coulson, Liz Lumley Smith, Mr Tony Mullin, Dr Joanna Sudell, Ms Catherine Steele, Dr Christopher John Absolon, Mrs Hannah Allan, Mr Peter Crump, Mr Adrian Lumley Smith
Income: £1,828,310 [2017]; £1,813,837 [2016]; £1,858,414 [2015]; £1,729,550 [2014]; £1,831,744 [2013]

Orchestra of The Age of Enlightenment

Registered: 28 Oct 1986 *Employees:* 15
Tel: 020 7239 9370 *Website:* oae.co.uk
Activities: Education, training; arts, culture, heritage, science
Address: OAE, Kings Place, 90 York Way, London, N1 9AG
Trustees: Mr Martin Gregory Smith, Mr David Norman Marks, Mr Mark Stephen Williams, Mrs Imogen Patricia Charlton Overli, Miss Anna-Luise Buchberger, Miss Olivia Roberts, Mr Max Thomas Mandel, Ms Rebecca Jayne Miller, Ms Susannah Catherine Simons, Ms Katharina Spreckelsen, Mr Nigel Huw Jones, Crispin Woodhead, Mr Roger Montgomery, Mr Denys Calder Firth, Mr Steven John Devine
Income: £3,297,222 [2016]; £3,353,182 [2015]; £2,386,290 [2014]; £3,144,094 [2013]; £2,866,310 [2012]

Orchestras Live

Registered: 11 Dec 2006 *Employees:* 6 *Volunteers:* 6
Tel: 020 7520 1494 *Website:* orchestraslive.org.uk
Activities: General charitable purposes; education, training; arts, culture, heritage, science
Address: The Music Base, Kings Place, 90 York Way, London, N1 9AG
Trustees: Mark Bromley, Ellen Gallagher, Jane Williams, Rebecca Saunders, William Daniel Watson, Matthew Littlewood, Kevin Appleby, Neil Mathur, David Bray, Simone Willis, Catrin Griffiths
Income: £1,082,368 [2017]; £1,051,352 [2016]; £1,017,113 [2015]; £1,224,592 [2014]; £1,195,583 [2013]

The Order of Friars Minor

Registered: 21 Jan 1964
Tel: 020 8504 7540 *Website:* friar.org
Activities: The prevention or relief of poverty; religious activities
Address: Church of St Thomas of Canterbury, 557 High Road, Woodford Green, Essex, IG8 0RB
Trustees: Rev Edmund Highton OFM, Rev Antony Jukes, Rev Isidore Faloona OFM, Rev Patrick Lonsdale OFM, Rev Donal Walsh
Income: £1,069,879 [2016]; £958,727 [2015]; £959,436 [2014]; £1,139,414 [2013]; £887,023 [2012]

Order of Hermit Friars of St Augustine (Augustinian Order)

Registered: 20 Mar 1964 *Employees:* 7 *Volunteers:* 10
Tel: 020 8748 3788 *Website:* augustinians.org.uk
Activities: Religious activities
Address: St Augustines Catholic Church, 55 Fulham Palace Road, London, W6 8AU
Trustees: Rev Stefan Park, Rev Ian Wilson, Rev Barry Clifford, Rev Robert Marsh, Rev Gianni Notarianni
Income: £1,008,390 [2017]; £2,138,485 [2016]; £497,922 [2015]; £1,382,887 [2014]; £2,183,044 [2013]

The Order of St. Augustine of The Mercy of Jesus

Registered: 4 Nov 1963 *Employees:* 335
Tel: 01444 235874 *Website:* anh.org.uk
Activities: The advancement of health or saving of lives; disability; accommodation, housing; religious activities
Address: St Georges Retreat, P O Box 1, Burgess Hill, W Sussex, RH15 0SQ
Trustees: Sr Thomas, Sr Carmel, Sister Mary Cyprian, Sr Monica, Sister Miriam
Income: £27,417,304 [2016]; £10,843,931 [2015]; £12,226,413 [2014]; £13,579,507 [2013]; £13,548,019 [2012]

Order of The Sisters of St Joseph of The Apparition
Registered: 27 May 1963 *Employees:* 92
Tel: 0151 228 8849
Activities: General charitable purposes; advancement of health or saving of lives; disability; prevention or relief of poverty; overseas aid, famine relief; religious activities
Address: Sisters of St Joseph, Oakhill Park, Liverpool, L13 4BP
Trustees: Sister Janet Arrowsmith, The Incorporated Trustees of The Order of The Sisters of St Joseph of The Apparition
Income: £2,796,664 [2017]; £2,651,913 [2016]; £2,535,599 [2015]; £2,426,635 [2014]; £2,398,081 [2013]

The Orders of St John Care Trust
Registered: 28 Jul 1995 *Employees:* 3,566 *Volunteers:* 607
Tel: 01993 323232 *Website:* osjct.co.uk
Activities: Accommodation, housing
Address: The Orders of St John Care Trust, 1 des Roches Square, Witney, Oxon, OX28 4BE
Trustees: Mr Graham Stuart Hutton, Mr Don Wood CBE, Mrs Millie Wentworth-Stanley, Dr Ralph Stephenson, Prof Jill Manthorpe, Dr Anne De Bono, Mr Richard Fitzalan-Howard, Mrs Judith Kathleen Wright, Mrs Jill Hughes, Earl Robert Ferrers, Professor Claire Goodman
Income: £116,156,620 [2017]; £110,619,949 [2016]; £108,281,000 [2015]; £99,573,000 [2014]; £95,085,000 [2013]

Ordinary Life Project Association
Registered: 9 Jan 1987 *Employees:* 76
Tel: 01225 464759 *Website:* olpa.org.uk
Activities: Disability; accommodation, housing
Address: 14 Darlington Place, Bath, BA2 6BX
Trustees: Mr Raymond Eason Edwards, Mr Martin William Bransfield Lockley, Mrs Claire Gill, Adam Brill
Income: £2,151,392 [2017]; £2,094,331 [2016]; £2,130,422 [2015]; £2,076,770 [2014]; £2,155,979 [2013]

Ordinary Lifestyles
Registered: 30 Sep 1996 *Employees:* 80 *Volunteers:* 1
Tel: 07740 859555 *Website:* ordinary-lifestyles.org.uk
Activities: Disability
Address: 3rd Floor, Office 14, Ivy Mills Business Centre, Crown Street, Failsworth, Manchester, M35 9BG
Trustees: Ms Althea Margaret Dickinson, Mrs Jane White, Mrs Elayne Rushton, Ms Chelsea Williams, Ms Joyce Beard, Suzanne Harrison, Mr Sukhbir Singh
Income: £1,594,646 [2017]; £1,395,083 [2016]; £1,258,773 [2015]; £1,132,814 [2014]; £988,423 [2013]

The Organisation for New Music and Sound
Registered: 20 Jun 2008 *Employees:* 15
Tel: 020 7759 1800 *Website:* soundandmusic.org
Activities: Education, training; arts, culture, heritage, science; economic, community development, employment
Address: Somerset House, Strand, London, WC2R 1LA
Trustees: John Knell, Sasha Afanasieva, Jean-Baptiste Thiebaut, Jo Thomas, Dr Shirley Thompson, Edward Corn, Greg Davies, Ms Belinda Caroline Dee, Dennis Lee
Income: £1,041,719 [2017]; £1,062,809 [2016]; £1,176,716 [2015]; £1,103,206 [2014]; £825,358 [2013]

Orison Charitable Trust
Registered: 31 Jul 2003 *Employees:* 1 *Volunteers:* 1
Tel: 01923 842919 *Website:* orisonct.org
Activities: General charitable purposes; education, training; advancement of health or saving of lives; prevention or relief of poverty; overseas aid, famine relief; accommodation, housing; religious activities; environment, conservation, heritage; economic, community development, employment
Address: Orison Charitable Trust, P O Box 704, Harrow, Middlesex, HA2 7BB
Trustees: Mohamed Akhtar Jaffer, Shabbir Kassam, Musafir Kassamali Somani, Mustafa Mohsin Ali Mohamed
Income: £1,171,792 [2017]; £1,042,232 [2016]; £1,043,899 [2015]; £899,051 [2014]; £814,658 [2013]

Orley Farm School Trust
Registered: 11 Sep 1963 *Employees:* 108
Tel: 020 8869 7600 *Website:* orleyfarm.harrow.sch.uk
Activities: Education, training
Address: Orley Farm School, South Hill Avenue, Harrow, Middlesex, HA1 3NU
Trustees: Philippa Jackson, Mr Colin John Hayfield, Mr Dilip Navapurkar, Ms Kim Louise Brook-Hill, Mr Alan Smith, Dr Philip David Hills, Mr Anil Sofat, Mr James Bruce Hawkins, Mrs Samantha Charlotte Seth, Mrs Catherine Pain, Mr Michael John Andrews, Dr Mary Elizabeth Short, Mr Rajesh Mansukhlal Raithatha
Income: £7,141,179 [2017]; £6,836,577 [2016]; £6,545,494 [2015]; £6,225,606 [2014]; £6,187,683 [2013]

The Ormerod Home Trust Limited
Registered: 26 Feb 1973 *Employees:* 215 *Volunteers:* 4
Tel: 01253 723513 *Website:* ormerodtrust.org.uk
Activities: Education, training; disability; accommodation, housing
Address: The Ormerod Home Trust Ltd, 2 Headroomgate Road, Lytham St Annes, Lancs, FY8 3BD
Trustees: Mrs Freda Gwilliam CertEd, Mr Anthony John Christopher Winter, Councillor Angela Rosemary Jacques, Ms Leisa Marie Splaine LLB Hons, Mr Ian Douglas Everard, Mrs Katherine Angela White
Income: £5,328,341 [2017]; £5,136,543 [2016]; £4,511,743 [2015]; £4,072,908 [2014]; £3,812,972 [2013]

Ormiston Families
Registered: 11 Dec 1992 *Employees:* 251 *Volunteers:* 212
Tel: 01473 724517 *Website:* ormiston.org
Activities: Education, training; advancement of health or saving of lives; prevention or relief of poverty; human rights, religious or racial harmony, equality or diversity
Address: Ormiston Childrens Centre, 333 Felixstowe Road, Ipswich, Suffolk, IP3 9BU
Trustees: Mr Peter Murray, Mrs Julie Spence, Robert Parkinson, Brian Stewart OBE, Ms Catherine Jane McLaughlin, Mr James Earl Murray, Mr Stephen Thomas Bennett, Mrs Hannah Claire Catchpool, Rosemary Gutteridge, Mr Simon Walker
Income: £6,295,000 [2017]; £5,482,000 [2016]; £4,405,000 [2015]; £4,676,000 [2014]; £3,566,000 [2013]

Orphans in Need

Registered: 25 Nov 2011 *Employees:* 25 *Volunteers:* 50
Tel: 020 7100 8866 *Website:* orphansinneed.org
Activities: General charitable purposes; advancement of health or saving of lives; prevention or relief of poverty; overseas aid, famine relief; religious activities
Address: Orphans in Need, Windsor House, 10 Manchester Road, Bradford, BD5 0QH
Trustees: Mr Anish Musa, Mrs Valerie Scarll, Dr Shoukat Ali, Mr Ismail Vania, Mr Ellyot Vincent Doyle, Mr Asif Mohammad
Income: £7,909,414 [2017]; £7,571,176 [2016]; £8,965,601 [2015]; £4,353,572 [2014]; £2,968,662 [2013]

The Orpheus Centre Trust

Registered: 30 Jul 2004 *Employees:* 68 *Volunteers:* 85
Tel: 01883 744664 *Website:* orpheus.org.uk
Activities: Education, training; disability; accommodation, housing; arts, culture, heritage, science; economic, community development, employment
Address: The Orpheus Centre, North Park Lane, Godstone, Surrey, RH9 8ND
Trustees: Mr Richard Stilgoe, Dr Helen Mary Swain, Mr Antoun Edouard Elias, Mr Matthew Charles Truelove, Dr John Beer, Richard Groom, Mr Russell Geoffrey Barrow, Mr Neil White
Income: £2,936,373 [2017]; £2,803,964 [2016]; £2,659,287 [2015]; £2,127,057 [2014]; £2,115,138 [2013]

The Orr Mackintosh Foundation Limited

Registered: 5 Feb 1996 *Employees:* 4
Tel: 020 7930 3737 *Website:* sharegift.org
Activities: General charitable purposes
Address: 4th Floor, 67-68 Jermyn Street, London, SW1Y 6NY
Trustees: Mr Paul Geoffrey Killik, Mrs Susan Margaret Swabey, Mr John Liam Alexander Roundhill, Mr Alan George Scott
Income: £3,092,520 [2017]; £4,167,905 [2016]; £2,718,181 [2015]; £3,624,165 [2014]; £1,164,794 [2013]

Ort UK Foundation

Registered: 3 Aug 2004 *Employees:* 5 *Volunteers:* 10
Website: ortuk.org
Activities: Education, training; prevention or relief of poverty
Address: 11 Oakfields Road, London, NW11 0JA
Trustees: Mr David Woolf, Mr Mark Mishon, Mr Simon Alberga, Simon Aron, Mr Anthony Ivor Brittan, Mr Alastair Falk, Mr Ashley James Reeback, Mrs Roslyn Wagman, Ms Karen Myers, Mr Yorai Linenberg, Mr Anthony Daniel Silverman, Mr Yaron Tal
Income: £1,118,761 [2016]; £1,318,885 [2015]; £748,682 [2014]; £839,851 [2013]; £1,263,898 [2012]

Orwell Mencap

Registered: 8 Feb 2007 *Employees:* 137 *Volunteers:* 15
Tel: 01473 723888 *Website:* orwellmencap.co.uk
Activities: Disability
Address: Genesis Garden Furniture, 6 Wright Road, Ipswich, Suffolk, IP3 9JG
Trustees: Mr Anthony Baker, Ms Kay Parr, Mrs Michelle Bevan-Margetts, Mr Paul John Cowell, Mrs Jill Knell, Mr John Stevens, John Goodship
Income: £1,642,084 [2017]; £1,669,286 [2016]; £1,574,772 [2015]; £1,510,931 [2014]; £1,449,760 [2013]

Orwell Park School Educational Trust Ltd

Registered: 6 Nov 1967 *Employees:* 103 *Volunteers:* 2
Tel: 01473 659225 *Website:* orwellpark.co.uk
Activities: Education, training
Address: Orwell Park School, Nacton, Ipswich, Suffolk, IP10 0ER
Trustees: Mr James Davison, Mr Charles Bowen Farquharson, Mr Simon Marchant, Mrs Victoria Molony, Ms Finola Stack, Mr Jeremy Middle Tomlinson, Mr Stephen Clark, Mrs Melissa Halfhide, Mrs Kathryn Henry, Mrs Ancilla Shirley, Ms Alison Leyshon
Income: £4,836,775 [2017]; £4,606,135 [2016]; £4,356,984 [2015]; £3,872,969 [2014]; £3,672,331 [2013]

Oshwal Association of The UK

Registered: 6 Mar 1974 *Employees:* 10 *Volunteers:* 175
Tel: 01707 643838 *Website:* oshwal.org
Activities: Education, training; disability; prevention or relief of poverty; overseas aid, famine relief; religious activities; arts, culture, heritage, science; other charitable purposes
Address: Oshwal Centre, Coopers Lane Raod, Northaw, Potters Bar, Herts, EN6 5DG
Trustees: Mr Bhikhalal Velji Bidd, Mr Chiman Shah, Mrs Mradula B Shah, Mr Dhirajlal Devraj Shah, Mrs Varsha Dilip Shah, Mr Nikunj Prabhulal Shah, Mr Rajesh Jethalal Shah, Mrs Rekha Mahesh Shah, Ms Hina Rameshchandra Shah, Mr Rahul Malde, Mr Kishore Lalji Haria, Miss Hemini Rajnikant Shah, Mr Tushar Jayantilal Shah, Mr Ashok Mulchand Shah, Mr Aswin Babulal Shah, Mr Sudhir Meghji Shah, Mr Nilesh Bhagwanji Shah, Ms Nishma Ramesh Shah, Mr Aswin Jethlal Shah, Mr Paresh Raishi Shah, Mr Kunjal Haria, Mr Ashish Jayantilal Patani, Mr Laxmichand Devraj Shah, Miss Bhavni Amritlal Shah
Income: £5,231,614 [2016]; £2,567,058 [2015]; £2,936,456 [2014]; £2,185,617 [2013]; £2,390,726 [2012]

Osprey Quay Management Services Company Limited

Registered: 21 Apr 2016
Tel: 01925 852005 *Website:* thelandtrust.org.uk
Activities: Environment, conservation, heritage; other charitable purposes
Address: 7 Birchwood One, Dewhurst Road, Birchwood, Warrington, Cheshire, WA3 7GB
Trustees: Mr Paul Oberg, Mrs Helen Norris, Mr Euan Hall
Income: £1,342,127 [2017]

Osteopathic Education and Research Limited

Registered: 17 Oct 1974 *Employees:* 40
Tel: 07511 097707 *Website:* eso.ac.uk
Activities: General charitable purposes; education, training; advancement of health or saving of lives
Address: Crestwood, Loughborough Lane, Lyminge, Folkestone, Kent, CT18 8DG
Trustees: Mr John Barkworth, Graham N G Mason, Ms Audrey Baxter, Miss Caroline Louise Troy, Mr David Tasker, Mr Peter Ward, Mr Keith Robinson, Ms Sarah Wallace, Mr Graham Kenneth Jones, Mr Conor McDermott
Income: £2,538,468 [2016]; £2,541,800 [2015]; £2,727,922 [2014]; £2,607,294 [2013]; £2,611,193 [2012]

Oswestry School
Registered: 10 Mar 2000 Employees: 141
Tel: 01691 655711 Website: oswestryschool.org.uk
Activities: Education, training
Address: Oswestry School, Upper Brook Street, Oswestry, Salop,
SY11 2TL
Trustees: Miss Betty Gull, Mr Brian Welti, Mr Tim Moore-Bridger,
Mr Jonathan Edwards, Mrs Rachel Warner, Mr Christopher
Schofield, Mrs Andrea Jane Lee, Mr Peter Wilcox-Jones, Mr David
Paul Evison, Mr Jon Hancock, Mr Anthony Moss, Mr Edward
Bowen, Mr Jonathan Mark Wastling, Mr Howard Edward Jones
Income: £6,048,212 [2016]; £6,131,739 [2015]; £5,688,791 [2014];
£5,553,900 [2013]

The Oundle School Foundation
Registered: 26 May 1999
Tel: 01832 273434 Website: oundleschool.org.uk
Activities: Education, training
Address: Oundle School, Bursars Office, Church Street, Oundle,
Peterborough, PE8 4EE
Trustees: Martyn Hedley, Alex Scott-Barrett, Mr John Scott, William
Hiscocks, Clive Anderson, Mr Edward Campbell-Johnston
Income: £1,990,000 [2017]; £1,716,000 [2016]; £3,147,000 [2015];
£1,611,254 [2014]; £3,529,554 [2013]

Our Daily Bread Ministries Trust
Registered: 1 May 1987 Employees: 22 Volunteers: 25
Tel: 015395 64149 Website: ourdailybread.org
Activities: Religious activities
Address: Our Daily Bread Ministries, P O Box 1, Millhead,
Carnforth, Lancs, LA5 9ES
Trustees: Rev Paul Baxendale, Mr Richard William Dehaan Jr,
Mr Andrew Paul Plowman MA FIA, Mr David Mills
Income: £2,346,734 [2016]; £1,772,487 [2015]; £1,555,281 [2014];
£1,579,251 [2013]; £1,738,939 [2012]

Our Kids
Registered: 20 Apr 2005 Employees: 47 Volunteers: 5
Website: our-kids.org.uk
Activities: General charitable purposes; education, training;
prevention or relief of poverty; economic, community development,
employment
Address: 2B Mather Avenue, Prestwich, Manchester, M25 0LA
Trustees: Mrs Malka Steinberg, Mr Shlomo Alexander Marks,
Mrs Hanna Deborah Corn
Income: £4,284,142 [2016]; £3,797,783 [2015]; £2,934,966 [2014];
£2,243,486 [2013]; £95,460 [2012]

Our Lady of Fidelity Established at Upper Norwood, London
Registered: 10 May 1965 Employees: 61
Tel: 020 8670 6917 Website: ourladyoffidelity.org.uk
Activities: General charitable purposes; education, training;
prevention or relief of poverty; overseas aid, famine relief;
accommodation, housing; religious activities; environment,
conservation, heritage; other charitable purposes
Address: Virgo Fidelis Convent Senior School, 147 Central Hill,
London, SE19 1RS
Trustees: Sr Sandra Davey, Rev Joy Alappat, Sister Sophie Pepper,
Mr William Martin, Sr Josephine
Income: £1,775,760 [2016]; £2,068,315 [2015]; £2,016,139 [2014];
£4,784,293 [2013]; £2,105,601 [2012]

Our Lady of Sion School, Worthing
Registered: 29 Oct 2007 Employees: 86
Website: sionschool.org.uk
Activities: Education, training
Address: 33 First Avenue, Worthing, W Sussex, BN14 9NJ
Trustees: Sister Brenda McCole NDS, Mrs Katherine Henwood,
Mrs Patricia Akyol, Mr John Wiseman, Mrs Anna Ansted,
Professor David Read, Mr David Mark Spofforth, Sister Mary
Cannon, Sister Isabella Herd, Dr Anna Varughese, Mrs Angela
Tanner, Sister Anne Lee Sister
Income: £3,863,513 [2016]; £3,886,806 [2015]; £3,729,289 [2014];
£3,779,160 [2013]; £3,461,072 [2012]

Our Lady's Abingdon Trustees Limited
Registered: 31 Jul 2007 Employees: 122
Tel: 01235 524658 Website: olab.org.uk
Activities: Education, training
Address: Our Ladys Abingdon Senior School, Radley Road,
Abingdon, Oxon, OX14 3PS
Trustees: Mr John Francis Cunliffe, Mr T R Ayling, Mrs Helen
Ronaldson, Mrs Andrea Elizabeth Freeman, Mr Peter Brian
Williams, Dr Lesley Ann Bergmeier, Mr Edward Gerard Francis
McCabe, Mrs M Shinkwin, Rev James McGrath, Sister Penelope
Diane Roker, Mr Andrew Peter Hearn
Income: £6,518,295 [2017]; £6,394,805 [2016]; £5,957,589 [2015];
£6,116,830 [2014]; £5,817,585 [2013]

Outreach 3 Way
Registered: 21 Mar 1980 Employees: 221 Volunteers: 25
Tel: 0300 303 9001 Website: outreach3way.org
Activities: Disability
Address: Dimensions Group, 1430 Arlington Business Park,
Theale, Reading, Berks, RG7 4SA
Trustees: Mrs Helen Baker, Mr Calum Mercer, Ms Anne Barnard,
Ms Delyth Lloyd-Evans, Ms Supriya Suri Malik, Mr Kevin Lewis,
Ms Christine Cryne, Mr Gordon Lyle, Mr Nicholas Turner
Income: £5,874,000 [2017]; £5,484,000 [2016]; £5,250,000 [2015];
£5,191,000 [2014]; £5,183,000 [2013]

Outreach Community and Residential Services
Registered: 16 Apr 1981 Employees: 96
Tel: 0161 740 3456 Website: outreach.co.uk
Activities: Disability; accommodation, housing; religious activities;
other charitable purposes
Address: Outreach Community & Residential Services, Redbank
House, 4 St Chads Street, Manchester, M8 8QA
Trustees: Mr Ivor Silver, Mr Barry Fine, Dr Peter Elton
Income: £1,934,201 [2017]; £1,823,197 [2016]; £1,803,602 [2015];
£1,723,236 [2014]; £1,525,681 [2013]

The Outward Bound Trust
Registered: 17 Feb 2009 Employees: 308
Tel: 01931 740000 Website: outwardbound.org.uk
Activities: Education, training; economic, community development,
employment
Address: The Outward Bound Trust, Hackthorpe Hall, Hackthorpe,
Penrith, Cumbria, CA10 2HX
Trustees: Dr Nick Gair MBE, Mr Paul Voller, Mr Leo Houlding,
Mr Charles Philipps, Mr Colin Maund, Ms Caroline Sellar, Mr Guy
Williams, Ms Christine Walker, Mr Jonathan Lewis, HRH The Duke
of York, Mr Ian Roderick Gowrie-Smith, Mr Terence Mordaunt,
Dame Louise Makin, Mr Ian Ashman, Ms Philippa Kramer,
Mr Fasha Mahjoor, Mr Andrew Cartwright
Income: £15,631,325 [2017]; £16,814,529 [2016]; £15,649,852
[2015]; £13,488,495 [2014]; £12,278,617 [2013]

Outward Housing
Registered: 5 Dec 1988 *Employees:* 456 *Volunteers:* 400
Tel: 020 8980 7101 *Website:* outward.org.uk
Activities: Education, training; accommodation, housing; recreation
Address: 4 Daneland Walk, Hale Village, Tottenham Hale, London, N17 9FE
Trustees: Jackie Ballard, Ms Susan Shakespeare, Tim Miller, Joyce Saunds, Mr Edon Sojeva, George Barrow, Maria Grogan, Kathryn Briggs, Ms Shelley Joyce, Mr James O'Rourke
Income: £18,911,529 [2017]; £18,309,650 [2016]; £17,464,884 [2015]; £17,455,271 [2014]; £16,502,072 [2013]

Ovarian Cancer Action
Registered: 27 May 2005 *Employees:* 15 *Volunteers:* 5
Tel: 020 7380 1730 *Website:* ovarian.org.uk
Activities: The advancement of health or saving of lives
Address: Ovarian Cancer Action, 8-12 Camden High Street, London, NW1 0JH
Trustees: Mr Martin Paisner, Mrs Allyson Kaye, Jenny Knott, Mrs Nathalie Burdet, Professor Richard Hunt, Professor Sir Nicholas Wright, Ms Emma Scott, Mr Wayne Philips, Ms Jane Wolfson
Income: £2,072,195 [2017]; £1,785,527 [2016]; £1,684,829 [2015]; £1,241,211 [2014]; £2,334,827 [2013]

Over The Wall
Registered: 5 May 1999 *Employees:* 27 *Volunteers:* 641
Tel: 023 9247 7110 *Website:* otw.org.uk
Activities: Education, training; advancement of health or saving of lives; disability
Address: Langstone Technology Park, Langstone, Havant, Hants, PO9 1SA
Trustees: Mr Jonathan Goring, Mr Richard Chapman, Mrs Jocelyn Sharp, Dr Lara Lohr, Mr Paul Raeburn, Ms Catherine Doran, Andrew Richards, Mr Joseph Cronly, Mr Duncan King, Mr Graham Collins, Mrs Anne Stevens, Mr John Welsh, Mr Anthony Diamandakis, Neil McDonald
Income: £1,184,963 [2016]; £1,052,372 [2015]; £950,570 [2014]; £831,928 [2013]; £692,854 [2012]

Overgate Hospice
Registered: 3 Jun 1979 *Employees:* 105 *Volunteers:* 580
Tel: 01422 379151 *Website:* overgatehospice.org.uk
Activities: The advancement of health or saving of lives
Address: Overgate Hospice, 30 Hullen Edge Road, Elland, W Yorks, HX5 0QY
Trustees: Dr Anne Moncrieff, Mr Brian Craven, Mrs Jackie Murphy, Dr Sue Whishart, Mr Ian Firth, Miss Valerie Anne Steele, Miss Lucy Hodgson, Mrs Liz Dixon, Mrs Tanya Jackson
Income: £4,129,488 [2017]; £4,573,668 [2016]; £3,891,033 [2015]; £3,151,108 [2014]; £3,514,059 [2013]

The Overseas Development Institute
Registered: 24 Feb 1965 *Employees:* 260
Website: odi.org.uk
Activities: The prevention or relief of poverty; overseas aid, famine relief; environment, conservation, heritage; economic, community development, employment
Address: 203 Blackfriars Road, London, SE1 8NJ
Trustees: Mr Martin Tyler, Mr James Cameron, Mr Sam Sharpe, Ms Dianna Melrose, Mr Jeff Seabright, Ms Fiona Thompson, Ms Elizabeth Heneghan Ondaatje, Yves Daccord, Mr Shantayanan Devarajan
Income: £41,320,000 [2017]; £37,821,000 [2016]; £34,788,000 [2015]; £28,541,000 [2014]; £25,593,236 [2013]

The Ovo Charitable Foundation
Registered: 27 Feb 2014
Tel: 0800 599 9440 *Website:* ovoenergy.com
Activities: General charitable purposes; education, training; prevention or relief of poverty; accommodation, housing; environment, conservation, heritage; economic, community development, employment
Address: 1 Rivergate, Bristol, BS1 6ED
Trustees: Mr Samuel Kasumu, Mr Stephen James Fitzpatrick, Mr Matthew Owen
Income: £1,009,019 [2016]; £521,548 [2015]; £2,433 [2014]

Robert Owen Communities
Registered: 30 Jul 1986 *Employees:* 415 *Volunteers:* 5
Tel: 020 8246 5200 *Website:* unitedresponse.org.uk
Activities: Education, training; disability; accommodation, housing
Address: FAO Jerome Walls, Highland House, 165 The Broadway, Wimbledon, London, SW19 1NE
Trustees: Mr David Arthur Willis, Mrs Helen Margaret England, Mr Maurice Edward Rumbold
Income: £6,430,646 [2017]; £6,631,020 [2016]; £6,014,969 [2015]; £6,607,264 [2014]; £6,034,665 [2013]

Dame Alice Owen's Foundation
Registered: 3 Oct 1968
Tel: 020 7600 1801 *Website:* brewershall.co.uk
Activities: Education, training
Address: Brewers' Hall, Aldermanbury Square, London, EC2V 7HR
Trustees: The Brewers Company
Income: £3,287,551 [2016]; £3,241,128 [2015]; £3,017,279 [2014]; £4,024,419 [2013]; £2,651,537 [2012]

Oxfam
Registered: 7 Sep 1965 *Employees:* 4,986 *Volunteers:* 27,000
Tel: 0870 333 2444 *Website:* oxfam.org.uk
Activities: The prevention or relief of poverty; overseas aid, famine relief
Address: Oxfam, 2700 John Smith Drive, Oxford Business Park South, Oxford, OX4 2JY
Trustees: Ms Caroline Agnes Morgan Thomson, Ms Angela Cluff, Mr Stephen Mark Walton, Mr Kul Chandra Gautam, Ms Lois Alyson Jacobs, Mr Kenneth Mathieson Caldwell, Ms Katherine Mary Steward, Mr Gavin MacNeill Stewart, Mr Babatunde Taiwo Olanrewaju, Mr Mohammed Wakkas Khan, Ms Lydinyda Bunyi Nacpil, Mr Nicholas Drew Cheeseman
Income: £408,600,000 [2017]; £414,700,000 [2016]; £401,400,000 [2015]; £389,100,000 [2014]; £367,900,000 [2013]

Oxford Archaeology Limited
Registered: 27 Oct 1982 *Employees:* 267 *Volunteers:* 50
Tel: 01865 263800 *Website:* oxfordarchaeology.com
Activities: Education, training; arts, culture, heritage, science; environment, conservation, heritage
Address: Oxford Archaeology Ltd, Janus House, Osney Mead, Oxford, OX2 0ES
Trustees: Mr Richard Briant, Chris Gosden, Helena Hamerow, Mr Richard John Cruse, Ms Jan Wills, Professor John Barrett
Income: £11,519,831 [2017]; £11,829,477 [2016]; £11,613,157 [2015]; £10,064,241 [2014]; £9,391,360 [2013]

Oxford Brookes Students' Union
Registered: 8 Feb 2011 *Employees:* 37 *Volunteers:* 540
Tel: 01865 484757 *Website:* brookesunion.org.uk
Activities: Education, training; arts, culture, heritage, science; amateur sport
Address: Oxford Brookes Students' Union, John Henry Brookes Building, Headington Campus, Gipsy Lane, Headington, Oxford, OX3 0BP
Trustees: Miranda Markham, Sam Kamperis, Miss Diko Blackings, Miss Sharelle Holdsworth, Mr Laurence Drake, Mr Thomas Charles Andrew Smith, Mr Sam Cockle-Hearne, Ms Harriet Stella Ann Cherry, Mrs Wendy Hart
Income: £1,443,501 [2017]; £1,390,886 [2016]; £1,341,147 [2015]; £1,359,382 [2014]; £1,308,177 [2013]

Oxford Centre for Hebrew and Jewish Studies
Registered: 5 Jul 1973 *Employees:* 16
Website: ochjs.ac.uk
Activities: Education, training
Address: 2 Morrells Close, Didcot, Oxon, OX11 7DJ
Trustees: Mr Martin Paisner CBE, Mr Daniel Peltz, Mr George Richard Pinto, Lord Charles Ronald Llewelyn Guthrie, Lord Stanley Fink, Professor Edmund Martin Herzig, Mr Stuart Roden, Professor Hugh Williamson, Ms Anne Webber, Professor Abba Brechta Sapir Abulafia, Mr David J Lewis, Mr Charles Sebag-Montefiore, Professor Martin Goodman, Sir Bernard Rix, Mr Daniel Patterson, Mr David Joseph QC, Mr Marc Polonsky, Dr Laurent Mignon, Dr Sondra Leslie Hausner
Income: £1,085,985 [2017]; £1,438,387 [2016]; £2,659,202 [2015]; £1,532,127 [2014]; £2,253,191 [2013]

The Oxford Centre for Mission Studies
Registered: 17 Sep 1984 *Employees:* 11 *Volunteers:* 6
Tel: 01865 517730 *Website:* ocms.ac.uk
Activities: Education, training; religious activities; economic, community development, employment
Address: Church of St Phillip & St James's, Woodstock Road, Oxford, OX2 6HR
Trustees: Dr Makonen Getu, Dr Asamoah-Gyadu Johnson, Dr Stanley Douglas Birdsall, Mr Marcos Ami Sosmena, Mr Keith Malcouronne, Rev Samuel Cyuma, Dr Soo Ann Lee, Mr Nathan Andrews
Income: £1,257,995 [2017]; £1,319,447 [2016]; £1,243,371 [2015]; £1,154,117 [2014]; £1,163,226 [2013]

Oxford Diocesan Board of Education
Registered: 20 Jan 2010 *Employees:* 21
Tel: 01865 208208 *Website:* oxford.anglican.org
Activities: Education, training; religious activities
Address: Church House Oxford, Langford Lane, Kidlington, Oxon, OX5 1GF
Trustees: Mr Gordon Scott Anderson, The Revd Mary Ann Harwood, The Rt Revd Dr Steven John Lindsey Croft, Mr Kieran Patrick Salter, The Revd Timothy James Lincoln Harper, Mrs Carol Rose Worthington, Mrs Maureen Elizabeth Lomas, Mr Peter Norman, Mrs Sally-Anne Jarvis, The Right Revd Dr Alan Thomas Lawrence Wilson, The Revd Sarah Elizabeth Sharp, Mr Geoffrey Strutt, The Revd Darren William McFarland, The Revd Mark Bennet, Ms Joanna Moriarty, Mrs Kathy Winrow, Mrs Nicola Flower, Mrs Helen Jane Crolla
Income: £1,549,000 [2016]; £1,478,000 [2015]; £1,541,000 [2014]; £1,385,000 [2013]; £1,012,000 [2012]

The Oxford Diocesan Board of Finance
Registered: 20 Oct 1966 *Employees:* 67 *Volunteers:* 211
Tel: 01865 208200 *Website:* oxford.anglican.org
Activities: Religious activities
Address: Church House Oxford, Langford Lane, Kidlington, Oxon, OX5 1GF
Trustees: The Rt Revd Andrew Proud, Mrs Judith Scott, The Right Revd Colin William Fletcher, Mr Michael Brian Powell, Mrs Susan Elizabeth Scane, Revd Canon Adrian Mark Daffern, The Revd Canon Andrew Marsden, The Rt Revd Dr Steven John Lindsey Croft, The Venerable Guy Charles Elsmore, Mrs Julie Dziegiel, Rev Camilla Iris Walton, The Reverend Dr Graeme Fancourt, Mr John Pescott Smith, The Venerable Olivia Graham, Mr Andrew Fredrick John Glaze, Revd Canon Jeffrey James West, Mr Martin Frederick Chandler, Mr James Justin MacNamara, Revd Canon Susan Elizabeth Booys, The Venerable Martin Gorick, Revd Canon Rosemary Elizabeth Harper, The Very Revd Professor Martyn Percy, The Right Revd Dr Alan Thomas Lawrence Wilson, Mr Michael Hugh Waring, The Venerable Judy French, Dr Anna Thomas-Betts, The Reverend John Tattersall, Mr Graeme Henry Slocombe, Rev Darren William McFarland, Mr Simon Richards, Mr Henry Gibbon, Ms Jayne Ozanne, Mr Richard Gavin Merrylees
Income: £25,436,000 [2016]; £25,323,000 [2015]; £25,829,000 [2014]; £24,571,000 [2013]; £23,420,000 [2012]

Oxford Diocesan Council for Social Work Incorporated
Registered: 2 Sep 1982 *Employees:* 64 *Volunteers:* 30
Tel: 0118 402 1700 *Website:* pactcharity.org
Activities: The prevention or relief of poverty; accommodation, housing; economic, community development, employment
Address: 12 Waybrook Crescent, Reading, Berks, RG1 5RG
Trustees: Mrs Diana Hasting, Mrs Stephanie Gibbons, Mr James George Brown, Mr Philip John Sapwell, Mr Philip Greenwood, Rev Tim Edge, Mr Guy Davies, Mr Anthony William Poole King, Mrs Elizabeth McAuley
Income: £3,101,894 [2017]; £3,881,898 [2016]; £4,670,461 [2015]; £4,222,822 [2014]; £4,663,973 [2013]

Oxford Institute for Energy Studies
Registered: 13 Jan 1983 *Employees:* 12
Tel: 01865 311377 *Website:* oxfordenergy.org
Activities: Education, training
Address: Oxford Institute for Energy Studies, 57 Woodstock Road, Oxford, OX2 6FA
Trustees: Dr Abdullah Al-Kuwaiz, Dr Christopher Adam, Prince Abdulaziz Bin Salman Al Saud, Mr Laurence Whitehead, Professor Roger Goodman, Mr Masakazu Toyoda, Mr Michael Toll, Mr Anwar Al Maatoq, Mr Adrian Lajous, Professor Roger Ainsworth, Dr Anwar Ali Al-Mudhaf, Mr Abbas Ali Naqi, Mr Nader Sultan, Mr Steve Reynish, Mr Sigurd Nikolai Lyngo, Dr Ahmed Ali Attiga
Income: £1,238,940 [2016]; £1,490,941 [2015]; £1,626,369 [2014]; £1,523,132 [2013]; £1,493,591 [2012]

Oxford Philharmonic Orchestra Trust
Registered: 22 Dec 2000 *Employees:* 11 *Volunteers:* 15
Tel: 01865 987222 *Website:* oxfordphil.com
Activities: General charitable purposes; education, training; arts, culture, heritage, science
Address: 29A Teignmouth Road, London, NW2 4EB
Trustees: Desmond Cecil, Mr David Haenlein, Mr George Tsavliris, Professor Michael John Earl, Mr Raymond Blanc OBE, Sir Andrew Jonathan Bate, Dr Marios Papadopoulos MBE, Mr Peter Earl, Mrs Elena Ambrosiadou, Ms Saphieh Ashtiany, Mr James Blair Sherwood, Mr Geoffrey De Jager, Mr Aviad Meitar, Mr John Donald Read Fothergill
Income: £1,517,088 [2017]; £1,716,201 [2016]; £1,833,992 [2015]; £2,013,056 [2014]; £1,706,493 [2013]

The Oxford Playhouse Trust

Registered: 13 Jul 1989 *Employees:* 52 *Volunteers:* 101
Tel: 01865 305319 *Website:* oxfordplayhouse.com
Activities: Education, training; arts, culture, heritage, science
Address: The Oxford Playhouse Theatre, 11-12 Beaumont Street, Oxford, OX1 2LW
Trustees: Ms Sos Ann Eltis, Ms Saphie Ashtiany, Ms Liesl Elder, Elizabeth Paris, Ms Debbie Dance, Ms Sue Staunton, Moss Cooper, Mr Colin Mayer, Mr Alan Grafen, Andrew Parker, Miss Eleanor Rose Lloyd, Mr Paul Moore, Warwick Hampden-Woodfall
Income: £3,914,133 [2017]; £4,339,300 [2016]; £3,731,510 [2015]; £3,720,001 [2014]; £3,678,005 [2013]

Oxford Russia Fund

Registered: 11 Apr 2005 *Employees:* 3
Tel: 020 7318 1180 *Website:* oxfordrussiafund.org
Activities: Education, training
Address: Tulloch & Co, 4 Hill Street, London, W1J 5NE
Trustees: Anthony Smith, Boris Saltykov, Rupert Caldecott, Mr Alastair Tulloch, Lord Patten of Barnes, John Nightingale
Income: £2,407,052 [2016]; £2,445,742 [2015]; £3,112,897 [2014]; £4,506,725 [2013]; £3,770,147 [2012]

The Oxford School of Drama Trust

Registered: 3 Dec 1998 *Employees:* 7
Tel: 01993 812883 *Website:* oxforddrama.ac.uk
Activities: Education, training; arts, culture, heritage, science
Address: The Oxford School of Drama, Sansomes Farm Studios, Wootton, Woodstock, Oxon, OX20 1ER
Trustees: Mr Nicholas Allott, Mr Peter Wilson-Smith, Rick Scott, Miss Nina Raine, Mr David Etherington QC, Mrs Georgina Rowse, Diane Borger
Income: £1,014,389 [2016]; £945,207 [2015]; £900,939 [2014]; £859,892 [2013]; £824,190 [2012]

The Oxford Trust

Registered: 27 Nov 1985 *Employees:* 24 *Volunteers:* 25
Tel: 01865 810000 *Website:* scienceoxford.com
Activities: Education, training; economic, community development, employment
Address: The Oxford Trust, Oxford Centre for Innovation, New Road, Oxford, OX1 1BY
Trustees: Dr Paul Robert Brankin OBE, Ms Georgina Ferry, Professor William Siward James, Mrs Lynne Pebworth, Dr John Boyle, Professor Alistair David Fitt, Mr Jonathan Welfare, Professor Julia Alison Noble, Ms Megan Mai Morys, Mr Paul David Dean
Income: £1,731,062 [2017]; £1,283,318 [2016]; £1,360,251 [2015]; £1,416,560 [2014]; £1,308,990 [2013]

Oxford University Student Union

Registered: 3 Mar 2011 *Employees:* 19
Tel: 01865 288452 *Website:* oxfordsu.org
Activities: General charitable purposes; education, training; arts, culture, heritage, science; amateur sport
Address: 4 Worcester Street, Oxford, OX1 2BX
Trustees: Richard Jackson, Tom Flynn, Ms Marianne Oesterberg Melsen, Mr Thomas Charles Barringer, Catherine Frances Canning, Atticus Stonestrom, James Hunt, Miss Katy Haigh, Miss Farheen Ahmed, Kathryn Maddison Cole, Jack Colin Wands
Income: £1,120,417 [2017]; £1,106,094 [2016]; £1,097,852 [2015]; £1,002,308 [2014]; £795,716 [2013]

The Oxfordshire Care Partnership

Registered: 16 Jul 2001
Tel: 01234 791000
Activities: General charitable purposes; advancement of health or saving of lives; disability; prevention or relief of poverty; accommodation, housing
Address: 25 Crosspaths, Harpenden, Herts, AL5 3HE
Trustees: Mrs Millie Wentworth-Stanley, Mr Kevin Bolt, Mr Daniel Hayes, Mrs Kerry Margaret Dearden, Mr Paul Gray, Ms Janet Boulter, Ms Julie Wittich
Income: £20,358,984 [2016]; £20,534,000 [2015]; £19,179,000 [2014]; £19,808,000 [2013]

Oxfordshire Community Churches

Registered: 18 Jul 1996 *Employees:* 55 *Volunteers:* 600
Tel: 01865 297403 *Website:* occ.org.uk
Activities: Education, training; prevention or relief of poverty; overseas aid, famine relief; religious activities
Address: Oxfordshire Community Churches, The Kings Centre, Osney Mead, Oxford, OX2 0ES
Trustees: Dr Stephen Alan Jones, Mr Peter Nigel Charles Allen, Dr Daniel James Kirk, Mr Stephen Burchell Martin Young, Mr John Green, Dr Jansen Philip Jacob, Miss Grace Janyan Le, Mr Andrew John O'Connell
Income: £2,867,935 [2016]; £2,668,810 [2015]; £2,615,333 [2014]; £2,446,925 [2013]; £2,306,376 [2012]

Oxfordshire Community Foundation

Registered: 12 Apr 2013 *Employees:* 5 *Volunteers:* 35
Tel: 01608 238401 *Website:* oxfordshire.org
Activities: General charitable purposes; education, training; advancement of health or saving of lives; disability; prevention or relief of poverty; other charitable purposes
Address: Pound Cottage, Pound Hill, Charlbury, Chipping Norton, Oxon, OX7 3QN
Trustees: Mrs Glyn Benson, Mrs Anne Davies, Mr Nicholas Case, Mrs Laura Chapman, Mrs Katharine Fyson, Ms Jane Wates OBE, Mrs Amanda Phillips, Mr John Taylor, Mr Neil Preddy
Income: £1,416,160 [2017]; £1,212,751 [2016]; £1,330,349 [2015]; £90,610 [2014]

Oxfordshire Crossroads

Registered: 21 Aug 2009 *Employees:* 89 *Volunteers:* 1
Tel: 01865 260280 *Website:* oxfordshirecrossroads.org.uk
Activities: Disability
Address: Crossroads Centre, Marston Court, Harberton Mead, Marston, Oxford, OX3 0EA
Trustees: Dr Robin Foster, Mr Bruce William Hunt, Mrs Janice Evans, Ms Vivienne Davies RGN, Mr James Robert Bradshaw, Ms Melanie Ann Proudfoot
Income: £2,359,133 [2017]; £2,448,433 [2016]; £2,334,427 [2015]; £2,111,154 [2014]; £1,867,367 [2013]

Oxfordshire Mind

Registered: 27 Aug 1970 *Employees:* 111 *Volunteers:* 60
Tel: 01865 263730 *Website:* oxfordshiremind.org.uk
Activities: Education, training; advancement of health or saving of lives; accommodation, housing
Address: 2 Kings Meadow, Osney Mead, Oxford, OX2 0DP
Trustees: Mr John Copley, Ms Carolyn McKee, Mr Tony Talbot, Mr Nick Welch, Mr John Hall, Mr Nick Georgiou, Ms Katherine Nicholas, Mr Mike Farwell, Mr Andrew Reiss
Income: £3,474,161 [2017]; £3,395,124 [2016]; £3,315,240 [2015]; £4,236,368 [2014]; £2,965,010 [2013]

P F Charitable Trust

Registered: 10 Mar 1965
Tel: 020 3696 6721
Activities: General charitable purposes; education, training; advancement of health or saving of lives; disability; prevention or relief of poverty; overseas aid, famine relief; accommodation, housing; religious activities; arts, culture, heritage, science; amateur sport; animals; environment, conservation, heritage; economic, community development, employment; armed forces, emergency service efficiency; human rights, religious or racial harmony, equality or diversity; other charitable purposes
Address: The Secretary, PF Charitable Trust, c/o RF Trustee Co Limited, 15 Suffolk Street, London, SW1Y 4HG
Trustees: Mr Philip Fleming, Mr Rory David Fleming, Mr Robert Fleming, Mr Matthew Valentine Fleming
Income: £3,284,669 [2017]; £2,953,968 [2016]; £3,061,449 [2015]; £3,205,038 [2014]; £3,332,992 [2013]

PAC-UK Ltd

Registered: 25 Sep 1986 *Employees:* 43 *Volunteers:* 50
Tel: 01634 840066 *Website:* pac-uk.org
Activities: General charitable purposes; education, training
Address: The Post Adoption Centre, 5 Torriano Mews, London, NW5 2RZ
Trustees: Mr Ian Spafford, Ms Anna Boyle, Mr Jim Clifford, Mr Barry Morris, Mrs Paula Newson Smith
Income: £2,599,858 [2017]; £2,154,677 [2016]; £1,513,123 [2015]; £966,305 [2014]; £844,952 [2013]

PAS Housing Association

Registered: 10 Dec 2007 *Employees:* 22
Tel: 01202 306070 *Website:* pashousingassociation.co.uk
Activities: The prevention or relief of poverty; accommodation, housing
Address: PAS Ltd, Unit 9, Central Business Park, Southcote Road, Bournemouth, BH1 3SJ
Trustees: Ms Joy Malyon, Mrs Carol Nicklin, Mrs Fiona Carolyn Dixon, Miss Chloe Dixon
Income: £2,389,550 [2017]; £1,691,550 [2016]; £1,185,442 [2015]; £876,153 [2014]; £430,239 [2013]

PESGB

Registered: 17 Mar 2001 *Employees:* 9 *Volunteers:* 50
Tel: 020 7408 2000 *Website:* pesgb.org.uk
Activities: Education, training
Address: 7th Floor, Petroleum Exploration Society of GB, No 1 Croydon, 12-16 Addiscombe Road, Croydon, Surrey, CR0 0XT
Trustees: Mr Gavin Ward, Mr Nick Terrell, Nick Holgate, Nick Allan, Mr Henk Kombrink, Ms Alyson Harding, Ms Tracey Dancy, Andy Racey, Martin Durham, Ms Amanda Turner, Ms Ann Watkins, Mr Neil Frewin
Income: £1,220,646 [2016]; £1,159,678 [2015]; £2,414,401 [2014]; £1,398,326 [2013]; £2,163,121 [2012]

PHAB Limited

Registered: 27 Jan 1982 *Employees:* 8 *Volunteers:* 350
Tel: 020 8667 9443 *Website:* phab.org.uk
Activities: Education, training; disability; amateur sport; economic, community development, employment
Address: Summit House, Wandle Road, Croydon, Surrey, CR0 1DF
Trustees: Mr Geoffrey Chivers CTA FRPSL, Mrs Julia Gaye Giles MBE, Mr John Barrie William Corless, Mr Christopher Gilbert Sneath, Mr Philip Peel, Mrs Rosalind Probert, Phil Ford, Mr Nicholas John Maloney
Income: £1,143,420 [2017]; £914,541 [2016]; £1,090,333 [2015]; £938,135 [2014]; £1,001,727 [2013]

PLUS (Providence LINC United Services)

Registered: 17 Jan 1994 *Employees:* 93 *Volunteers:* 8
Tel: 020 8297 1250 *Website:* plus-services.org
Activities: Disability
Address: 6 Belmont Hill, Lewisham, London, SE13 5BD
Trustees: Mr David Ion Dannreuther, Ms Alison Hill, Ms Ester Janko Mulcahy, Ms Ambrita Shahani, Ms Sarah Clare Broad, Mr James Thomas Wallington, Mr John Burgess, Ms Burcu Borysik, Ms Julia Rogers
Income: £3,674,812 [2017]; £3,630,560 [2016]; £3,744,926 [2015]; £4,065,192 [2014]; £4,174,155 [2013]

POhWER

Registered: 25 Mar 1997 *Employees:* 336 *Volunteers:* 184
Tel: 0300 456 2370 *Website:* pohwer.net
Activities: The advancement of health or saving of lives; disability; prevention or relief of poverty; economic, community development, employment; other charitable purposes
Address: POhWER, Hertlands House, Primett Road, Stevenage, Herts, SG1 3EE
Trustees: Ms Aruna Patel, Mrs Bridget Flint, Richard Carter, Mr Sundera Moorthy Kumara-Moothy, Mr John Barzey, Mrs Sarifa Patel, Mr Leigh Peter Hutchings, Mr Geoffrey Stephen Gibbs, Mr Toby Cotton, Mr Waqas Chauhdry
Income: £11,120,393 [2017]; £10,027,629 [2016]; £9,359,247 [2015]; £8,611,996 [2014]; £9,819,164 [2013]

The PSP Association

Registered: 27 Apr 1994 *Employees:* 17 *Volunteers:* 170
Tel: 01327 322410 *Website:* pspassociation.org.uk
Activities: The advancement of health or saving of lives; disability
Address: 167 Watling Street West, Towcester, Northants, NN12 6BX
Trustees: Mr Simon Robert Bellingham Koe, Mr Thomas James Orchard, Mrs Antoinette Oglethorpe, Prof Colin Brian Blakemore, Ms Claire Perry, Mrs Shauna MacKenzie
Income: £1,188,291 [2017]; £1,467,293 [2016]; £1,131,699 [2015]; £1,215,058 [2014]; £1,190,126 [2013]

PSS (UK)

Registered: 14 Oct 1963 *Employees:* 382 *Volunteers:* 157
Tel: 0151 702 5540 *Website:* psspeople.com
Activities: General charitable purposes; education, training; disability; prevention or relief of poverty; accommodation, housing; economic, community development, employment
Address: PSS, 18-24 Seel Street, Liverpool, L1 4BE
Trustees: Geoffrey Manning, John Andrew Kellaway, Hilary Berg, Veronica Jackson, Mark Rathbone, Angela Jones, Samantha Proffitt, Julie Cooke
Income: £13,808,840 [2017]; £13,401,296 [2016]; £13,725,078 [2015]; £14,749,795 [2014]; £13,949,288 [2013]

The PWC Foundation

Registered: 4 Oct 2011
Tel: 07764 902846
Activities: General charitable purposes; education, training; advancement of health or saving of lives; environment, conservation, heritage; economic, community development, employment
Address: PricewaterhouseCoopers, 1 Embankment Place, London, WC2N 6RH
Trustees: Neil Sherlock, Mr David Raymond Adair, Ms Kalee Talvitie-Brown, Ms Emma Cox, Mr Kevin Ellis, Mr Zelf Hussain, Mr David Walters
Income: £1,831,754 [2017]; £1,601,327 [2016]; £1,436,628 [2015]; £1,190,157 [2014]; £1,026,916 [2013]

The Pace Centre Ltd
Registered: 18 May 1992 Employees: 91 Volunteers: 73
Tel: 01296 392739 Website: thepacecentre.org
Activities: Education, training; disability
Address: The Pace Centre, Philip Green House, Coventon Road, Aylesbury, Bucks, HP19 9JL
Trustees: Mr Michael Doyle, Mr Julian Lovelock, Mr Adrian Lan Pikett, Mr Dennis Foxton Craggs, Mr Clive John
Income: £2,536,902 [2016]; £2,956,311 [2015]; £3,797,883 [2014]; £4,573,911 [2013]; £3,168,790 [2012]

Paces Sheffield
Registered: 15 Jun 2004 Employees: 46 Volunteers: 2
Tel: 0114 284 4488 Website: pacessheffield.org.uk
Activities: Education, training; disability
Address: Paces Campus, Pack Horse Lane, Sheffield, S35 3HY
Trustees: Ann Menzies-Blythe, Walter Hirst, Kerri Wood, Janet Baker, Angela Sandhal
Income: £1,076,599 [2017]; £954,143 [2016]; £916,264 [2015]; £902,051 [2014]; £716,734 [2013]

Packwood Haugh School Limited
Registered: 2 Apr 1963 Employees: 76
Tel: 01939 260120 Website: packwood-haugh.co.uk
Activities: Education, training; other charitable purposes
Address: Packwood Haugh School, Ruyton Xi Towns, Shrewsbury, Salop, SY4 1HX
Trustees: Mr Richard Graham Tovey, Mr Mark Turner, Mr Jon Ollier, Mrs Sally Anne Rosser, Mr Robin Clifford Morris, Mr Richard Jebb Richard, Mr David Stacey, Mrs Liz Lewis, Mr Andrew Johnston, Mrs Antoinette Geraldine Mackeson-Sandbach, Dr Caron May Morton
Income: £3,466,192 [2016]; £3,487,209 [2015]; £3,644,323 [2014]; £3,728,297 [2013]; £4,008,211 [2012]

Pact Educational Trust Limited
Registered: 14 Mar 1996 Employees: 107 Volunteers: 4
Tel: 020 8668 8080 Website: pactschools.org.uk
Activities: Education, training
Address: The Cedars School, Coombe Road, Croydon, Surrey, CR0 5RD
Trustees: Dr Anthony Paul Gerard Newman Sanders, Mrs Jane Claire Phillips, Mrs Eleanor Sorel Leonard, Mr Philip James Leonard, Mr Mark Philip Selby Stables, Mr Peter Denis Millington, Mr Edward Allen Victor Thompson, Mrs Maria Louise Newman Sanders, Mr Alexander George Frans Maria Jonkheer Alting von Geusau, Mr Jose Antonio Clausell-Terol, Mr Xavier Bosch, Miss Sarah Margaret Cassidy
Income: £4,951,878 [2017]; £4,713,138 [2016]; £4,573,065 [2015]; £3,707,047 [2014]; £3,338,633 [2013]

Paddington Development Trust
Registered: 25 May 2000 Employees: 34 Volunteers: 90
Tel: 020 3214 3113 Website: pdt.org.uk
Activities: Education, training; prevention or relief of poverty; accommodation, housing; economic, community development, employment
Address: Mr Neil Johnston, 122 Great Western Studios, 65 Alfred Road, London, W2 5EU
Trustees: Mrs Virginia Ashton, Andy Watson, Miss Maryam Zonouzi BA Hons, Mrs Gillian Fitzhugh, Smita Bora, Hasna Kahlalech, Craig MacDonald, Dr William Mungo Jacob, Mrs Ines Marian Newman, Mr Ken Braithwaite, Lena Choudary, Saima Rana, Abigail Carter
Income: £2,108,077 [2017]; £1,431,800 [2016]; £2,243,274 [2015]; £2,080,659 [2014]; £1,852,314 [2013]

Padworth College Trust Limited
Registered: 12 Mar 1974 Employees: 40
Tel: 0118 983 2644 Website: padworth.com
Activities: Education, training; accommodation, housing
Address: Padworth College, Sopers Lane, Padworth, Reading, Berks, RG7 4NR
Trustees: Mr John West, Angus Cater, Mr Jonathan Rawes, Prof Colin Nicholas Jocelyn Mann, Mrs Tina Ann Elder, Mr John Hugh Miller, Mr Jeremy Robertson, Mrs Diedre Dyson, Mr David George Crawford
Income: £2,494,028 [2016]; £2,772,863 [2015]; £2,777,718 [2014]; £2,771,949 [2013]

James Paget University Hospitals Charitable Fund
Registered: 6 Nov 1995
Tel: 01493 453519 Website: jpaget.nhs.uk
Activities: The advancement of health or saving of lives
Address: James Paget Hospital, Lowestoft Road, Gorleston, Great Yarmouth, Norfolk, NR31 6LA
Trustees: James Paget University Hospitals NHS Foundation Trust
Income: £1,420,235 [2017]; £952,829 [2016]; £1,090,043 [2015]; £1,332,116 [2014]; £1,732,256 [2013]

Paines Plough Limited
Registered: 21 Jun 1974 Employees: 10
Tel: 020 7240 4533 Website: painesplough.com
Activities: Arts, culture, heritage, science
Address: 4th Floor, 43 Aldwych, London, WC2B 4DN
Trustees: Ms Caroline Denise Newling, Mrs Niove Rachel Janis Smith, Mr Christopher Millard, Ms Andrea Stark, Mr Matthew David Littleford, Mrs Kim Marie Grant, Cindy Polemis, Mrs Anne McMeehan, Mr Dennis Kelly, Miss Carolyn Louise Saunders
Income: £1,301,952 [2017]; £1,106,620 [2016]; £884,754 [2015]; £690,766 [2014]; £796,944 [2013]

Painshill Park Trust Limited
Registered: 8 Jul 1982 Employees: 22 Volunteers: 105
Tel: 01932 868113 Website: painshill.co.uk
Activities: Education, training; disability; arts, culture, heritage, science; environment, conservation, heritage
Address: Pains Hill Park, Portsmouth Road, Cobham, Surrey, KT11 1JE
Trustees: Dr David Charles Taylor, Mr Ian Godfrey Sampson JP, Sir Roger John Buckley, Mr Adrian Dear, Lady Alexander of Weedon, Mr Richard Philip Morley Reay Smith, Paul Tiller, Louise Russell
Income: £1,250,095 [2016]; £1,050,502 [2015]; £1,139,520 [2014]; £1,071,619 [2013]; £1,695,909 [2012]

The Palace Theatre Watford Limited
Registered: 19 Jul 1996 Employees: 70 Volunteers: 31
Tel: 01923 235455 Website: watfordpalacetheatre.co.uk
Activities: Education, training; arts, culture, heritage, science
Address: Watford Palace Theatre Ltd, 20 Clarendon Road, Watford, Herts, WD17 1JZ
Trustees: Mr George Derbyshire, Patrick Stoddart, Deborah Lincoln, Brett Spencer, Carol Lingwood, Mr John Pritchard, Mrs Jayne Trotman, Mr Alex Bottom, Mr John Hunt, Gary Townsend Vila, Georgina Rae, Anne Fenton, Mrs Binita Mehta-Parmar, Mr Mark Lawrence
Income: £2,413,924 [2017]; £2,421,878 [2016]; £3,048,330 [2015]; £2,618,181 [2014]; £2,474,232 [2013]

The Palace Trust
Registered: 11 Mar 2015 *Employees:* 25 *Volunteers:* 220
Tel: 01749 988111 *Website:* bishopspalace.org.uk
Activities: Education, training; religious activities; arts, culture, heritage, science; environment, conservation, heritage
Address: The Bishops Palace, Wells, Somerset, BA5 2PD
Trustees: Mr Nicholas Denison, Mr Michael Blandford, Dr Kevin Brown, Ms Ruth Gofton, The Very Revd Dr John Davies, Lady Elizabeth Acland Hood Gass, Ms Maureen Boylan, Mr Brian Roberts-Wray, Mr Peter Stickland, Prebendary Maureen Bollard, Rear Admiral David Wood, The Right Revd Peter Hancock, Mrs Nicola Nuttall, Mr Matthew Trimmer
Income: £1,269,953 [2016]; £947,440 [2015]

Palace for Life Foundation
Registered: 15 Sep 2008 *Employees:* 68 *Volunteers:* 30
Tel: 020 8768 6047 *Website:* cpfcfoundation.org
Activities: Education, training; advancement of health or saving of lives; disability; prevention or relief of poverty; amateur sport; economic, community development, employment
Address: Crystal Palace FC Foundation, Selhurst Park Stadium, Whitehorse Lane, London, SE25 6PU
Trustees: Ms Christine Double, Mr Kevin Day, Mrs Yama Otung, Mr Mark Osikoya, Mr Paul Clark, Mr Steve O'Connell, Mr Ed Warner, Ms Stephanie Fuller, Mr Neil McIntosh
Income: £1,700,688 [2017]; £1,138,808 [2016]; £1,116,726 [2015]; £830,172 [2014]; £562,342 [2013]

Palestine Association for Childrens Encouragement of Sports
Registered: 30 Nov 2006 *Employees:* 36
Tel: 020 7465 8000 *Website:* pacescharity.org
Activities: Education, training; advancement of health or saving of lives; amateur sport; environment, conservation, heritage
Address: c/o Sookias & Sookias, 6th Floor, Napier House, 24 High Holborn, London, WC1V 6AZ
Trustees: Mr Hani Abdul Muhsen Al Qattan, Mrs Nahed Ahmad Abusneneh, Mrs Helen Al Uzaizi, Dr Mamdouh Barakat, Mr Ghassan Nuqul
Income: £2,125,501 [2016]; £1,270,449 [2015]; £997,746 [2014]; £999,733 [2013]; £1,911,307 [2012]

Palestinians Relief and Development Fund
Registered: 11 Aug 1994 *Employees:* 53 *Volunteers:* 300
Tel: 020 8961 9993 *Website:* interpal.org
Activities: General charitable purposes; education, training; advancement of health or saving of lives; disability; prevention or relief of poverty; overseas aid, famine relief; accommodation, housing; religious activities; arts, culture, heritage, science; environment, conservation, heritage; economic, community development, employment; other charitable purposes
Address: P O Box 53389, London, NW10 6WT
Trustees: Mr Ghassan Faour, Mr Ismail Ginwalla, Mrs Shabana Pinjara, Mr Ibrahim Hewitt, Dr Essam Mustafa, Ms Saher Usmani
Income: £6,077,075 [2016]; £6,164,486 [2015]; £8,270,727 [2014]; £4,543,620 [2013]; £5,998,538 [2012]

Palfrey Community Association
Registered: 26 Sep 2003 *Employees:* 51 *Volunteers:* 20
Tel: 01922 649716 *Website:* palfreycommunity.co.uk
Activities: Education, training; advancement of health or saving of lives; arts, culture, heritage, science; amateur sport; economic, community development, employment; human rights, religious or racial harmony, equality or diversity
Address: Palfrey Community Association, Milton Street, Walsall, W Midlands, WS1 4LA
Trustees: Mr Mark Pulford, Mr Allah Ditta, Mr Mohammed Bari, Mr Thakorbhai D Patel, Debra Pace, Mr Vijay Mistry, Mrs Hajran Bashir, Mr Matloob Hussain, Mrs Hasina Nadat, Mr Aftab Nawaz, Mrs Tilat Noreen Ajmal, Mr Shaminm Ahmed, Mrs Jamila Madari
Income: £1,137,808 [2017]; £1,608,296 [2016]; £1,290,730 [2014]; £1,394,482 [2013]; £1,503,311 [2012]

Pallant House Gallery
Registered: 2 Mar 2004 *Employees:* 43 *Volunteers:* 250
Tel: 01243 774557 *Website:* pallant.org.uk
Activities: Education, training; arts, culture, heritage, science
Address: 9 North Pallant, Chichester, W Sussex, PO19 1TJ
Trustees: Mr John Booth, Mr Charles David Zelenka Martin, Mr Brendon Finucane QC, Mrs Jacqueline Russell, Ms Jane Weeks, Mr Harold Roger Wallis Mavity, Lady Nicholas Gordon Lennox, Ms Tania Slowe, Mr Edward Scott Greenhalgh, Ms Andrea Rose, Mrs Pamela Dignum, Mrs Elizabeth Davis
Income: £2,064,269 [2017]; £3,103,588 [2016]; £4,195,834 [2015]; £1,774,696 [2014]; £1,905,282 [2013]

Pallottine Missionary Sisters of The Catholic Apostolate
Registered: 26 Jun 1964 *Employees:* 47 *Volunteers:* 5
Tel: 01625 616459 *Website:* parkmountcarehome.co.uk
Activities: General charitable purposes; education, training; advancement of health or saving of lives; disability; prevention or relief of poverty; religious activities; human rights, religious or racial harmony, equality or diversity
Address: 52 Park Mount, Macclesfield, Cheshire, SK11 8NT
Trustees: Father John Joseph Martin, Mary McNulty Sister, Sister Leonie Rowan
Income: £1,403,959 [2017]; £1,344,567 [2016]; £1,429,933 [2015]; £1,192,930 [2014]; £1,072,368 [2013]

Eleanor Palmer Trust
Registered: 5 Nov 1963 *Employees:* 30
Tel: 020 8441 3222 *Website:* eleanorpalmertrust.org.uk
Activities: The prevention or relief of poverty; accommodation, housing
Address: Eleanor Palmer Trust, 106b Wood Street, Barnet, Herts, EN5 4BY
Trustees: Eleanor Palmer Trustee Limited
Income: £1,668,873 [2017]; £1,741,520 [2016]; £1,541,211 [2015]; £1,586,100 [2014]; £1,522,371 [2013]

Palmers Green High School Limited
Registered: 23 May 1963 *Employees:* 58 *Volunteers:* 1
Tel: 020 8886 1135 *Website:* pghs.co.uk
Activities: Education, training
Address: Palmers Green High School, 104 Hoppers Road, London, N21 3LJ
Trustees: Mr Dermot Gillespie Lewis, Ms Melanie Curtis, Mr John Kenneth Atkinson Chartered Surveyor, Mr Robert Keys, Mr Jeremy Piggott, Mrs Bronwen Goulding, Jeffrey Zinkin, Ms Anna Averkiou, Mrs Gay Sandra Kettle, Mrs Karen Tidmarsh, Miss Alexia Eliades
Income: £3,390,899 [2017]; £3,349,398 [2016]; £3,086,265 [2015]; £2,958,462 [2014]; £2,962,517 [2013]

Pancreatic Cancer Research Fund
Registered: 14 Jan 2014 *Employees:* 2 *Volunteers:* 15
Tel: 020 8360 1119 *Website:* pcrf.org.uk
Activities: The advancement of health or saving of lives; prevention or relief of poverty
Address: Pancreatic Cancer Research Fund, P O Box 47432, London, N21 1XP
Trustees: Mr Brian Raper, Mr Stephen Collen, Margaret Blanks, Mr Peter Blanks
Income: £2,365,668 [2016]; £2,008,931 [2015]; £1,549,680 [2014]

Pancreatic Cancer UK
Registered: 13 Jan 2006 *Employees:* 45 *Volunteers:* 6
Tel: 020 3780 5675 *Website:* pancreaticcancer.org.uk
Activities: The advancement of health or saving of lives
Address: Pancreatic Cancer UK, 6th Floor, Westminster Tower, 3 Albert Embankment, London, SE1 7SP
Trustees: Stephen Smith, Mr David Probert, Ms Carole Challen, Stuart Fletcher, Tim Allsop, Mr Simon Collins, Ms Lynne Walker, Daniel Benjamin, Claire Cardy
Income: £3,862,963 [2017]; £4,387,085 [2016]; £4,275,013 [2015]; £2,835,753 [2014]; £1,458,198 [2013]

Pangbourne College Limited
Registered: 20 Feb 1963 *Employees:* 115 *Volunteers:* 35
Tel: 0118 984 2101 *Website:* pangbourne.com
Activities: Education, training
Address: Pangbourne College, Pangbourne Hill, Pangbourne, Reading, Berks, RG8 8LA
Trustees: Mr Grant Macpherson, Rear Admiral Roger Lane-Nott, Mrs Charlotte Butterworth, Mrs Pamela Bale, Mrs Rebecca Tear, Mr Nicholas Wood, Rhidian Llewellyn, Mr Patrick Roberts, Dr Matilda Oppenheimer, Mr A Bond, Mr Roger Barklett, Mr Frank Slevin, Mrs Julie Digby, Mrs Helen Wright, Sally Rossiter
Income: £9,892,235 [2016]; £9,274,029 [2015]; £8,518,890 [2014]; £8,660,547 [2013]; £12,277,270 [2012]

The Pankhurst Trust (incorporating Manchester Women's Aid)
Registered: 24 Oct 2008 *Employees:* 43 *Volunteers:* 25
Tel: 0161 820 8414 *Website:* manchesterwomensaid.org
Activities: The prevention or relief of poverty; accommodation, housing; arts, culture, heritage, science; environment, conservation, heritage; other charitable purposes
Address: Pankhurst Centre, 60-62 Nelson Street, Manchester, M13 9WP
Trustees: Mrs Janet Pickering, Mrs Mary Watson, Ms Melanie Sharples, Louise Sutherland, Ms Sara Radcliffe, Ms Laura Fisher, Ms Emma Evans, Mrs Elizabeth Ann Jones, Mrs Yvonne Lauder, Mrs Sally Hobbs, Suzie Thompson, Ms Polly Simpson, Kate Stone, Ms Saleema Kauser
Income: £1,678,779 [2017]; £1,617,474 [2016]; £1,465,757 [2015]; £1,047,938 [2014]; £1,092,447 [2013]

Papplewick Educational Trust Limited
Registered: 4 Oct 1966 *Employees:* 66
Tel: 01344 636903 *Website:* papplewick.org.uk
Activities: Education, training
Address: New Lodge, Papplewick School, Windsor Road, Ascot, Berks, SL5 7LH
Trustees: The Venerable Norman Russell, Brigadier Alwin Hutchinson, Mr Simon Dieppe Walker, Mrs Elizabeth Hewer, Mr Andrew Try, Mr Tim Lord, John Frost, Andrew McGregor
Income: £5,263,204 [2017]; £4,755,678 [2016]; £4,317,841 [2015]; £4,939,189 [2014]; £4,268,215 [2013]

The Papworth Trust
Registered: 16 Apr 1963 *Employees:* 318 *Volunteers:* 178
Tel: 01480 357240 *Website:* papworth.org.uk
Activities: Education, training; disability; accommodation, housing
Address: Bernard Sunley Centre, Papworth Everard, Cambridge, CB23 3RG
Trustees: Mr Robert Hammond, Ms Debra Sorkin, Mr Peter Agar, Mr Andrew John Hirst, Mrs Vanessa Stanislas, Mr Patrick Hughes, Mr Richard Norton, Mr Wesley Cuell, Mr David Atkinson
Income: £16,940,800 [2017]; £22,396,000 [2016]; £22,087,000 [2015]; £22,411,000 [2014]; £19,867,000 [2013]

Papyrus Prevention of Young Suicide
Registered: 6 Aug 1998 *Employees:* 27 *Volunteers:* 244
Tel: 01925 572444 *Website:* papyrus-uk.org
Activities: Education, training; advancement of health or saving of lives
Address: Lineva House, 28-32 Milner Street, Warrington, Cheshire, WA5 1AD
Trustees: Mr Stephen Habgood, Don Hart, Lauren Williams, Mr Anthony James Harrison, Marie Stocks, Mr Harry John Hesketh Biggs-Davison, Ms Annessa Rebair, Dr Sangeeta Mahajan, Mrs Sarah Jane Fitchett
Income: £1,023,936 [2017]; £843,980 [2016]; £668,404 [2015]; £387,732 [2014]; £305,265 [2013]

The Parachute Regiment Charity
Registered: 5 Oct 2009 *Employees:* 8
Tel: 01206 817074 *Website:* supportourparas.org
Activities: General charitable purposes; armed forces, emergency service efficiency
Address: Merville Barracks, Post Room, Circular Road South, Colchester, Essex, CO2 7UT
Trustees: Major General Adrian Freer OBE, General Sir Mike Jackson GCB CBE DSO, Mr Bernard Cazenove TD, Lt Col Liam Cradden, Lt Col Duncan James Mann, Lt Col Langley Sharp, WO1 Kurt Johann Perzylo, Lt Col Andrew Wareing, Mr Austin Bendall, Brigadier Matthew Lowe MBE, Mr Giles Rackley Orpen-Smellie, Lt Gen Sir John Lorimer, Lt Col Geoffrey Hargreaves, Richard Moore, Fred Gray
Income: £1,560,171 [2016]; £2,763,094 [2015]; £976,402 [2014]; £531,753 [2013]; £687,818 [2012]

Parayhouse School
Registered: 21 Feb 2002 *Employees:* 31 *Volunteers:* 9
Tel: 020 8741 1400 *Website:* parayhouse.com
Activities: Education, training
Address: Parayhouse School, Hammersmith and Fulham College, Gliddon Road, London, W14 9BL
Trustees: Mr Nicholas Guy Greville Herrtage, Miss Rosanna Safell, Mr Steven Palmer Hussey, Mr Randall Peterson, Miss Anna Elizabeth Hextall
Income: £1,382,688 [2017]; £1,451,353 [2016]; £1,305,713 [2015]; £1,279,231 [2014]; £1,228,320 [2013]

Parchment Trust
Registered: 15 Jun 2000 *Employees:* 80 *Volunteers:* 14
Tel: 01424 755800 *Website:* parchment-trust.org.uk
Activities: Disability
Address: Ore Place Farm, The Ridge, Hastings, E Sussex, TN34 2RA
Trustees: Mrs Susan Jane Geater, Mrs Karen Theresa Walker, Ms Nina Margaret Siddall-Ward, Dr David Michael Walker, Mr John Anthony Hassell, Mr Andrew David Phillips
Income: £1,612,632 [2017]; £1,478,358 [2016]; £1,362,871 [2015]; £1,309,369 [2014]; £1,323,508 [2013]

The Parenting Project
Registered: 31 Jul 2008 *Employees:* 62 *Volunteers:* 30
Tel: 01789 490845 *Website:* parentingproject.org.uk
Activities: General charitable purposes; other charitable purposes
Address: 2 Holmwood Gardens, Formby, Liverpool, L37 1NH
Trustees: Jane Williams, Mr Adam William John Sherratt, Mrs Beverley Jane Ballinger, Mrs Hannah Emily Joy Alexander, Mrs Andrea Joyce Milton, Mr Ian Thompson, Mrs Rachel Helen Faulkner
Income: £1,106,141 [2017]; £1,115,436 [2016]; £881,563 [2015]; £573,729 [2014]; £623,027 [2013]

Parentkind
Registered: 7 Dec 1998 *Employees:* 25
Tel: 01732 375460 *Website:* pta.org.uk
Activities: Education, training
Address: 39 Shipbourne Road, Tonbridge, Kent, TN10 3DS
Trustees: Mrs Yvonne Wood, Mrs Doris Neville-Davies, Ms Pauline Doohan, Mr Steven Bannister, Mrs Jennifer Dyer, Joe Saxton, Mr Gary David Sims, Mrs Amanda Shepard
Income: £1,357,863 [2016]; £1,321,131 [2015]; £1,351,293 [2014]; £1,266,090 [2013]; £1,268,464 [2012]

Parham Park Limited
Registered: 12 Oct 1978 *Employees:* 102 *Volunteers:* 44
Tel: 020 7828 4091 *Website:* parhaminsussex.co.uk
Activities: Environment, conservation, heritage
Address: 33 Queen Anne Street, London, W1G 9HY
Trustees: Lady Emma Barnard, Mr Timothy Aidan John Knox, Mr Christopher John Schooling, Mrs Lynn Petts, Mr J V Naunton Davies, Mr Robert Todd Longstaffe-Gowan
Income: £1,323,867 [2016]; £1,052,407 [2015]; £905,901 [2014]; £1,011,856 [2013]; £1,043,392 [2012]

Parish Giving Scheme
Registered: 9 Apr 2014 *Employees:* 4
Tel: 01452 410022 *Website:* parishgivingscheme.org.uk
Activities: Religious activities; other charitable purposes
Address: Gloucester DBF, Church House, College Green, Gloucester, GL1 2LY
Trustees: Mr John Preston, Mr Benjamin Tudur Llywelyn Preece Smith BA ACA, Mr John Sherlock, Mr Adrian Beney, Mr Neil Williams, Ms Victoria James, Rev David Brooke, Ms Rebecca Evans
Income: £16,829,775 [2016]; £10,135,496 [2015]; £1,406,363 [2014]

Parity for Disability
Registered: 16 Sep 1998 *Employees:* 60 *Volunteers:* 108
Tel: 01252 375581 *Website:* parityfordisability.org.uk
Activities: Disability
Address: 93-94 Whetstone Road, Farnborough, Hants, GU14 9SX
Trustees: Mr Kelvin Smith, Mr John Owen Durrett JP, Mrs Aghdas Cullen, David Turnidge, Mr Christopher Porter, Mr Brian Frederick Blewett, Paul Roper, Barbara Hurst, Mr Martin Hassett
Income: £1,366,353 [2017]; £1,322,331 [2016]; £1,172,478 [2015]; £1,096,765 [2014]; £965,918 [2013]

Park Families Limited
Registered: 22 Jul 2004 *Employees:* 75 *Volunteers:* 14
Tel: 023 9242 4980 *Website:* parkfamilies.co.uk
Activities: Education, training; advancement of health or saving of lives; prevention or relief of poverty; amateur sport
Address: Sandleford Road, Leigh Park, Havant, Hants, PO9 4LR
Trustees: Reverend Jonathan George Piers Jeffery, Mrs Linda Hoole, Ms Faith Ponsonby, Mrs Sarah Lamburne, Ms Eliabeth Jane Cooper, Mrs Elizabeth Betty Jane Holdaway, Mr Clint David Thresher, Mrs Beryl Spencer Francis, Miss Sasha Lindsay-Pentoney
Income: £1,130,852 [2017]; £1,238,696 [2016]; £1,433,452 [2015]; £1,312,012 [2014]; £1,196,924 [2013]

The Park School (Yeovil) Limited
Registered: 29 Mar 1967 *Employees:* 42 *Volunteers:* 8
Tel: 01935 423514 *Website:* parkschool.com
Activities: Education, training
Address: The Park, Yeovil, Somerset, BA20 1DH
Trustees: Mr Roy Moody, Mr Keith Stevens, Mrs Diane Kershaw, Rev Ronald Charles John Richard Martin, Mrs Frances Wilson, Neil Baker, Mr Leslie Idris Whittle
Income: £1,730,283 [2016]; £1,748,097 [2015]; £1,905,859 [2014]; £1,767,621 [2013]; £1,878,467 [2012]

Park School for Girls (Ilford) Limited
Registered: 9 Oct 1975 *Employees:* 30 *Volunteers:* 10
Website: parkschool.org.uk
Activities: Education, training
Address: 20-22 Park Avenue, Ilford, Essex, IG1 4RS
Trustees: Mr Henry Smith, Mr Il Ahmed, Mrs Semina Beg, Sukhjit Singh Kondel, Mrs Kay Knight, Mrs Tammy Sher
Income: £1,465,277 [2017]; £1,483,948 [2016]; £1,532,718 [2015]; £1,366,453 [2014]; £1,298,096 [2013]

The Park Theatre
Registered: 2 Aug 2010 *Employees:* 39 *Volunteers:* 40
Tel: 020 7870 6876 *Website:* parktheatre.co.uk
Activities: Arts, culture, heritage, science
Address: Park Theatre, 11 Clifton Terrace, London, N4 3JP
Trustees: Mr Bharat Mehta, Mr Frank McLoughlin CBE, Mr Rufus Olins, Mr Robert Charles Anthony Hingley, Ms Joanne Marie Parker, Mr Andrew Cleland-Bogle, Mr Nigel Pantling, Mr Nicholas Henry Frankfort, Ms Victoria Mary Phillips, Ms Leah Schmidt, Ms Marcia Lord
Income: £1,279,000 [2017]; £1,354,323 [2016]; £2,108,293 [2015]; £1,033,309 [2014]; £554,975 [2013]

Parkhaven Trust
Registered: 19 Jul 1963 *Employees:* 187 *Volunteers:* 17
Tel: 0151 526 4133 *Website:* parkhaven.org.uk
Activities: General charitable purposes; education, training; disability; accommodation, housing
Address: Parkhaven Trust, Liverpool Road South, Liverpool, L31 8BR
Trustees: Mrs Hilary Torpey, Mr Charles Flynn, Mr Kevin Fairclough, Mrs Elizabeth Kitt, Mr Rory McDonnell, Dr Julie Williams
Income: £3,992,383 [2017]; £4,100,663 [2016]; £4,190,938 [2015]; £4,179,368 [2014]; £4,030,496 [2013]

Parkinson's Disease Society of The United Kingdom
Registered: 18 Mar 1969 *Employees:* 373 *Volunteers:* 3,978
Tel: 020 7963 1327 *Website:* parkinsons.org.uk
Activities: The advancement of health or saving of lives; disability
Address: Parkinson's UK, 215 Vauxhall Bridge Road, London, SW1V 1EJ
Trustees: Mrs Nadra Ahmed OBE DL, Mary Whyham, Mr Mark Goodridge, Freda Lewis, Paul Warner, Richard Raine, Tim Tamblyn, Miss Margaret Chamberlain, Mrs Anne Josephine MacColl Turpin, David John Burn
Income: £32,864,000 [2016]; £31,451,000 [2015]; £30,911,000 [2014]; £24,518,000 [2013]; £23,937,000 [2012]

Parks Options Limited
Registered: 5 Nov 1999 *Employees:* 91 *Volunteers:* 1
Tel: 0151 300 8420 *Website:* parksoptions.co.uk
Activities: Education, training; prevention or relief of poverty; economic, community development, employment
Address: Life Bank, 23 Quorn Street, Liverpool, L7 2QR
Trustees: Mr Richard Keenan, Mr Michael James Edwards, Mr Kenneth Newbold, Mr Steve McElroy, Mr Philip Moore
Income: £1,572,984 [2017]; £1,754,976 [2016]; £2,299,672 [2015]; £2,154,156 [2014]; £821,971 [2013]

Parkside School Trust
Registered: 9 Apr 1963 *Employees:* 82 *Volunteers:* 2
Tel: 01932 869975 *Website:* parkside-school.co.uk
Activities: Education, training
Address: Parkside School, 78-80 Stoke Road, Stoke D'Abernon, Cobham, Surrey, KT11 3PX
Trustees: Mr Roger MacDonald Morris MA FCA, Mr Robin Southwell, Mrs Pauline Stoffberg, Mrs Celia Gregory, Mr Michael Stevens, Mr Edward Kesterton, Miss Kerry Gallagher, Mr Peter Brooks, Mr Andrew Shilton, Mrs Monique Herne, Mr John Cahill, Mr Jonathan Wood
Income: £3,681,723 [2016]; £3,764,743 [2015]; £3,814,222 [2014]; £3,979,432 [2013]; £4,084,934 [2012]

Parkway Green Housing Trust
Registered: 2 Oct 2006 *Employees:* 160 *Volunteers:* 191
Tel: 0161 946 9552 *Website:* parkwaygreen.co.uk
Activities: General charitable purposes; education, training; prevention or relief of poverty; accommodation, housing; amateur sport; economic, community development, employment
Address: Wythenshawe House, 8 Poundswick Lane, Manchester, M22 9TA
Trustees: Mr Ian Hilton, Cllr Sarah Russell, Ms Bernadette Mary Heanue, Cllr Glynn Evans, Mrs Clare Flynn, Mr Robert William Cressey
Income: £25,021,000 [2017]; £25,458,000 [2016]; £25,383,000 [2015]; £23,712,000 [2014]; £27,230,000 [2013]

The Parochial Church Council of St Mary Abbots, Kensington
Registered: 21 Oct 2009 *Employees:* 15 *Volunteers:* 120
Tel: 020 7937 6032 *Website:* stmaryabbotschurch.org
Activities: Religious activities
Address: St Mary Abbots Centre, Vicarage Gate, London, W8 4HN
Trustees: Rev Gillean Craig, Canon Stephen Fielding, Eliza Low, Max Croft, Hannah Stewart, Mrs Sally Bessada, Mrs Emma Jane Porteous, Mrs Martina Sadovska, Mr Peter David Darrell, Rev Jonathan Niall Agnew MacNeaney, Mr Andrew Richard Giblin, Nigel Grieve, Pippa Currey, David Wilkinson, Mr James Elliott Dunford-Wood, David Peerless, Miss Laura Jane Sylvester, Anna McNally, Andrew Freestone, Otto Barrow, Mr Kiaron Whitehead
Income: £1,569,363 [2016]; £1,548,801 [2015]; £1,852,722 [2014]; £1,148,669 [2013]; £958,778 [2012]

The Parochial Church Council of The Ecclesiastical Parish of All Saints Woodford Wells
Registered: 12 Feb 2009 *Employees:* 23 *Volunteers:* 200
Tel: 020 8504 2084 *Website:* asww.org.uk
Activities: Religious activities
Address: 14 Harts Grove, Woodford Green, Essex, IG8 0BN
Trustees: Mrs Eunice Jean Sparks, Rev Paul Harcourt, Rev David Blackledge, Rev Simon Marshall, Mrs Sheila Oakes, Mrs Kathleen Edith Berry, Mr Frank Hawkins, Mrs Heather Housden, Miss Gillian Wendy Hampton, Mrs Sarah Ann Schroder, Rev Denis James Martin, Mrs Josephine Winifred Smith, Mr Martin John Williamson, Mr Kawku Agyei Akuffo-Akoto, Mr Bayo Dosunmu, Rev Gareth Roger Milroy Dicks BA, Mr Peter Dowsett, Mr Christopher Abbess MSc CStat, Mr Richard Moules, Mr Nicholas Clayton, Mr Huw Williams, Mr Bruce Stuart Fisher, Mrs Anne Marie Sachs, Mrs Melanie Anita Paterson, Dr Mary Eleanor Nunns, Mrs Karen Mary Watling, Miss Nicola Canning, Mr Simon Mark Richard Williams, Mrs Stella Margaret Redburn BEd ALCM, Mr Paul Victor Sherrington, Miss Joanne Elizabeth Cull
Income: £1,111,490 [2016]; £1,225,040 [2015]; £884,257 [2014]; £1,136,666 [2013]; £1,605,693 [2012]

The Parochial Church Council of The Ecclesiastical Parish of All Souls, Langham Place, London
Registered: 21 Nov 2009 *Employees:* 45 *Volunteers:* 1,400
Website: allsouls.org
Activities: Religious activities
Address: 2 All Souls Place, London, W1B 3DA
Trustees: Rev Hugh Palmer, Mr Mark O'Leary, Mr Robert Turner, Mr Michael James Hall, Ms Alison MacKenzie, Mr Martin Mills, Judge David Turner, Mary Hanson, Mr Jeremy Thomas, Mr Gordon Hockey, Mr Raymond Asfour, Mr Peter Hamm, Miss Patrizia Lee, Miss Henny Saunders, Ms Erna Smit, Mr Ross Hendry, Mrs Caroline Millar, Ms Jessica Turvey, Mr Victor Cumberbatch, Mary Currie, Mrs Sue Stamper-Iveson, Mr Paul Hawkins, Mr Paul Stamper-Iveson, Mr John Ellerton, Mr Steven Ho, Mr Richard Bagwell, Ms Louise Gibson, Mr John Grainger, Mr Masao Sinulingga, Mr James Brightwell, Mrs Gill Phillips, Mr Kevin Ashman, Mr James Huang, Mr David Rollason, Mr Michael Sharp, Mr Nicolai Stawinoga, Mr Brian Weaver, Mr Hibist Mesfin, Ms Rachel Wilson, Mr Kejeh Ndubuisi, Dr Jenny Gallagher
Income: £3,103,848 [2016]; £2,959,976 [2015]; £2,969,498 [2014]; £2,875,956 [2013]; £2,701,199 [2012]

The Parochial Church Council of The Ecclesiastical Parish of Bath Abbey with St James, Bath
Registered: 4 Feb 2010 *Employees:* 17 *Volunteers:* 250
Tel: 01225 422462 *Website:* bathabbey.org
Activities: Religious activities
Address: The Abbey Offices, 11a York Street, Bath, BA1 1NG
Trustees: Mr Derek Smith, Mr Barry Cooper, Mr Michael Hammer, Mr Andrew Bragg, Dr James Playfair MB BS MRCGP, Rev Claire Robson, Mr Timothy Westbrook, Mr Ivor Lloyd, Mr Peter Henry Campbell Jones, Mrs Margaret Roberts, Mrs Iris Shanahan, Mr Timothy Rutherford, Mr Tim Baldwin, Mrs Catherine Skinner, Miss Rhiannon Teather, Mr Jeremy Robin Key-Pugh, Mrs Mary Henderson, Revd Jane Mitchell, Mr David Grendon, Mr Ian Stratton, Prebendary Edward Mason, Mrs Elizabeth Westbrook, Mrs Pauline O'Hanlon, Mrs Rebecca Elizabeth Brett Seear-Day, Rev Evelyn Lee-Barber, Rev Steven Girling, Miss Ann Stainforth, Ms Jane Pleace, Mrs Patricia Shuttleworth
Income: £3,979,729 [2016]; £2,534,711 [2015]; £1,928,902 [2014]; £2,017,878 [2013]; £1,716,074 [2012]

The Parochial Church Council of The Ecclesiastical Parish of Brighton, St Peter
Registered: 28 Mar 2012 *Employees:* 31 *Volunteers:* 150
Tel: 01273 698182 *Website:* stpetersbrighton.org
Activities: Religious activities
Address: St Peters Church, York Place, Brighton, BN1 4GU
Trustees: Mrs Sarah Bellamy, Miss Hannah Turpin, Mrs Samantha Brewer, Mrs Camilla Foottit, Mr Ben Jacob, Mr Christopher Lomas, Mr Rohit Nathaniel, Mr Leslie Taylor, Mr Chris Willis, Rev Steve Burston, Mr Tom Holbird, Mr Steve Waring, Mrs Julia Jacob, Revd Archie Coates, Mr James Foottit, Rev Jonathan Gumbel, Mr David Jonnes, Mr Steve Luke, Mrs Sarah Nelson, Mrs Paula Turton, Rev Keir Laurence Shreeves, Miss Fiona Finch, Mr James Mullineux, Mr Robert Verheul
Income: £1,728,097 [2016]; £1,491,067 [2015]; £1,327,208 [2014]; £1,108,467 [2013]; £1,310,862 [2012]

The Parochial Church Council of The Ecclesiastical Parish of Emmanuel, South Croydon
Registered: 21 Nov 2009 *Employees:* 6 *Volunteers:* 200
Tel: 020 8688 6676 *Website:* emmanuelcroydon.org.uk
Activities: Religious activities
Address: Emmanuel Church, Normanton Road, South Croydon, Surrey, CR2 7AF
Trustees: Mr Eric John Thompson, Helen Calder, Mary Knight, Trevor Mapstone, Jan Wilson, Mrs Wendy Riches, Peter Burt, Mr Daniel Orazulume, Mrs Marlene Antoinette Rose-Marie Hinds, Rev Benjamin Jones, Peter Gowland, Ranil Perera, Alistair Hynd, David Lawton, Richard Mash, Peter Cox, Garry Winterburn, Mr Paul Gulliford, Mrs Alison Lawton, Rebecca Pickering, Mrs Esther Barradell, Mr Jeremy Sinclair
Income: £1,099,403 [2016]; £602,194 [2015]; £544,346 [2014]; £541,880 [2013]; £1,342,679 [2012]

The Parochial Church Council of The Ecclesiastical Parish of Fulwood Christ Church, Sheffield
Registered: 4 Feb 2010 *Employees:* 11 *Volunteers:* 250
Website: fulwoodchurch.co.uk
Activities: Religious activities
Address: Christ Church Fulwood, Canterbury Avenue, Sheffield, S10 3RT
Trustees: Paul Houghton, Jane Patterson, Paul Williams, Tim Cudmore, Ben Cooper, Pete Scamman, Jonathan Lockwood, James Hamilton, Tim Burkill, Tom Smiles, Abi Holyoak, Sally Hewson, Kate Gerrish, Sandy Priestley, Tom Cudmore, Miss Rebecca Stephens, Paul German, Roger Richardson, Mrs Cherette Morley, Bob Edmonds, Alan Butler, Catherine Cooper, Geoffrey Wilson, Ian Harris, Andy Flood, Stephi Dennis, Jon Ulley, Rachel Bhatia, Josef Korchinsky, Max Broadbent, Dr Heather Charlton MB ChB
Income: £1,623,694 [2017]; £2,057,338 [2016]; £1,195,442 [2015]; £1,190,515 [2014]; £1,170,996 [2013]

The Parochial Church Council of The Ecclesiastical Parish of Great Chesham
Registered: 6 May 2009 *Employees:* 10 *Volunteers:* 300
Tel: 01494 773713 *Website:* greatchesham.org.uk
Activities: Religious activities
Address: 239 Chartridge Lane, Chesham, Bucks, HP5 2SF
Trustees: Jacquie Hardman, Mr Michael Hardman FCA, Dr Tim Yates, Rev Simon Cansdale, Hilary Povey, Don Sanderson, Rev John Shepherd, Stephen Taylor, Tom Watts, Jenny Allison, Graham Green, Mr John Mayne, Geoffrey Tolcher, Mrs Linda Emery, Mr Rodney Leslie Newth BA FCA, Mr David Graham Dougans, Mrs Marjorie Ann Davies BMus AICC, Miss Sarah Janet Wyman, Simon Evans, Christopher Embleton-Smith, Mr George Norman Thackray, Margaret Gingell, Julie Dziegiel, Sarah Shelley, Stuart Stockdale, Rev Hilary Wilson, Sylvester Liyanage, Sara Barlow, Mr Nigel Edward-Few MInstF, Tim Allan, Mrs Lisbeth Cameron, Mrs E Foster BTh DipCOT, Prof Hazel Rymer CPhys FInstP FGS, Hilary Richardson, Mr Ian Hamilton
Income: £1,001,503 [2016]; £891,073 [2015]; £898,033 [2014]; £882,042 [2013]; £881,361 [2012]

The Parochial Church Council of The Ecclesiastical Parish of Greyfriars Reading
Registered: 1 May 2009 *Employees:* 106 *Volunteers:* 300
Tel: 0118 951 6712 *Website:* greyfriars.org.uk
Activities: Religious activities
Address: Greyfriars Church, Friar Street, Reading, Berks, RG1 1EH
Trustees: Dr John Ledger, Mr Chris Tinker, Philip Giddings, Mark Hinckley, Alfred Kolawole, Mrs Tanya Newell, Rev Joy Atkins, Mr Arfon Rees, Sarah Underwood, Charlotte Barker, Mrs Emma Bettes, Mr Simon Porter, Rev Sarah Jones, Mr Peter Douglas Spriggs, Anthony Wisdom, Katy Lyne, John Missenden, Mrs Ruth Hampton, Mrs Helen Tinker, Mrs Margaret Stone, Mr Ayo Akintoye, John Hudson, Rev David Walker, Mr Harvey Jessop, Mrs Gemma Thomas
Income: £2,900,513 [2016]; £2,336,872 [2015]; £2,371,012 [2014]; £1,875,885 [2013]; £1,556,558 [2012]

The Parochial Church Council of The Ecclesiastical Parish of Holy Trinity with Saint Paul Onslow Square and Saint Augustine South Kensington
Registered: 27 Jan 2010 *Employees:* 132 *Volunteers:* 1,875
Tel: 0845 644 7533 *Website:* htb.org
Activities: Religious activities
Address: Holy Trinity Brompton, Ennismore Gardens Mews, London, SW7 1JA
Trustees: Mr David M Orton, Mr Angus Christian Winther, The Hon David Charles Kay-Shuttleworth, Rev Nicholas Knyvett Lee, Rev Paul Cowley, Mrs Harriet Flanagan, Mr Pasquale Tartaglia, Professor Margaret Ellen Hodson MD MSc FRCP DA DipMedEd, Mr Erik Holten Castenskiold, Rev Andrew Emerton, Mr James Patrick Normand, Rev Sue Colman, Mr Calum Dyke, Rev Martyn Layzell, Mr Tom Orton, Mrs Eli Gardner, Mr Jamie Dundas, Rev William Van Der Hart, Mr Paul Ferguson, Rev Tom Jackson, Mrs Genevieve Mensah, Mr Will Taylor-Jackson, Mr Watson Alexander, Mr Jon Cha, Jeremy Basset, Steven Kang, Osagie Omokhodion, Nic Shearer, Rev Jamie Mulvaney, Ms Christina Abbott, Mr Jonathan Bacon, Mr Jens Hofmann, Mr Julian Parris, Mrs Busola Sodeinde, Mrs Melanie Stanton, Dr James Behrens, Mr David Berkeley Hurst, Mrs Gubby Ayida, Ms Marcia Da Costa, Rev Stephen Foster, Miss Julia Kathleen Mackworth, Paul G Crinion, Mr Ademola Adebajo, Mrs Emma Alexandra Keeling, Rev Toby John Barnaby Flint, Mr Andrew Edward Brydon, Rev Nicholas Glyn Paul Gumbel, Mrs Ceinwen Rees, Rev Sam Follett, Mr Mark Balcar, Major Thomas Archer-Burton, Mr Sam Pritchard, Matthew Withers, Rev Ed Hodges, Rev Pete Wynter, Miss Shelley Pigott, Mr Michael Wirth, Mrs Emma Watson, Ms Marie-Christine Nibagwire, Cecily Colahan, Jessica O-George, Sarah Ritchie, Hannah Branch, Rev Joel Sales, Mr Usman 'oz'Alashe, Mr Theodore Brun, Mr Reiner Krammer, Mr Matthew Passante, Mr John Soong, Mr Gus Kennedy
Income: £12,371,876 [2016]; £10,975,397 [2015]; £10,934,218 [2014]; £10,878,911 [2013]; £9,694,341 [2012]

The Parochial Church Council of The Ecclesiastical Parish of Holy Trinity, Cambridge
Registered: 23 Feb 2009 *Employees:* 11 *Volunteers:* 190
Tel: 01223 355397 *Website:* htcambridge.org.uk
Activities: General charitable purposes; education, training; religious activities
Address: Holy Trinity Church, Market Street, Cambridge, CB2 3NZ
Trustees: Michael Pollitt, Joanna Stonehouse, Mrs Karen Goldstone, Mrs Joanne George, Mr Keith Bennett, Blake Hansen, Mr Richard Meakin, Christopher Stanford-Beale, Rev Rupert Charkham, Mrs Elizabeth How, Mr Stephen Rymill, Mrs Tolulope Anifalaje, Mrs Sarah Butlin
Income: £1,734,832 [2016]; £1,450,945 [2015]; £981,117 [2014]; £821,391 [2013]; £554,996 [2012]

The Parochial Church Council of The Ecclesiastical Parish of Holy Trinity, Cheltenham
Registered: 23 Jun 2009 *Employees:* 20 *Volunteers:* 300
Tel: 01242 808947 *Website:* trinitycheltenham.com
Activities: Education, training; religious activities
Address: Holy Trinity Church, Trinty House, 100-102 Winchcombe Street, Cheltenham, Glos, GL52 2NW
Trustees: Rev Andrew Blyth, Mrs Helen Stott, Mrs Michelle Dearman, Mrs Jenny Harris, Mr James Mears, Mr Luke Briner, Mr David Lee, Mr Thomas Johnson, Mr Simon Firkins, Mr Peter Strachan, Mr Alexander Metcalfe, Mrs Joanna Daykin, Mr James De Courcy, Mrs Madeleine Stanimeros, Mr Mark Giles
Income: £1,076,106 [2017]; £1,040,451 [2016]; £1,316,600 [2015]; £1,376,403 [2014]; £1,285,305 [2013]

The Parochial Church Council of The Ecclesiastical Parish of Howell Hill with Burgh Heath
Registered: 24 Feb 2009 *Employees:* 29 *Volunteers:* 200
Tel: 020 8224 9838 *Website:* saintpauls.co.uk
Activities: Religious activities
Address: St Pauls Church Centre, 15 Northey Avenue, Sutton, Surrey, SM2 7HS
Trustees: Margaret Hobbs, Alistair Fraser, Vanessa Cope, Sheila Harris, Les King, John Woolley, Mr Mark Simon Goodman, Adam Hansen, Mr Neil Ambler, Mrs Hilary Latham, Simon Morrison, Mervyn Wolffsohn, Nick Lipscomb, Rev Martin Wainwright BEng BA, Miss Melissa Jane Wynn, Sue Wharton, Ruth Sharma, Sue Glanville, Rev Paul Dever, Simon Clark, Jan Ganney, Rob Baldry, Mrs Judith Sarah Parnall, Hannah Woolridge, David Wright
Income: £2,055,497 [2016]; £990,634 [2015]; £1,318,030 [2014]; £1,119,927 [2013]; £1,018,742 [2012]

The Parochial Church Council of The Ecclesiastical Parish of St Aldates, Oxford
Registered: 18 Aug 2009 *Employees:* 34 *Volunteers:* 500
Tel: 01865 254800 *Website:* staldates.org.uk
Activities: Religious activities
Address: 40 Pembroke Street, Oxford, OX1 1BP
Trustees: Mr Andrew James Davisson, Revd Charles Saint George Cleverly, Mr Chris Gillies, Mr John Tranter, Dr Damian Randell, Mrs Joanna Mitchell, Mr Mark Edward Withers, Miss Alison Chevassut, Mr Toby Benjamin Walker, Mrs Funmi Durodola, Ms Claire Helen Mortimer, Mr Richard Clive Hunter, Mrs Jennifer Rosemary Lee, Rev Mark Brickman, Miss Lorna Box, Miss Helen Erica Downey, Mrs Julie Michelle Turner, Rev Tim Bateman
Income: £1,660,987 [2016]; £1,723,728 [2015]; £1,475,777 [2014]; £1,358,391 [2013]; £1,248,964 [2012]

The Parochial Church Council of The Ecclesiastical Parish of St Barnabas Woodside Park
Registered: 28 Aug 2009 *Employees:* 16 *Volunteers:* 300
Tel: 020 8343 5774 *Website:* stbarnabas.co.uk
Activities: General charitable purposes; education, training; disability; prevention or relief of poverty; overseas aid, famine relief; religious activities; economic, community development, employment
Address: St Barnabas Church, Holden Road, London, N12 7DN
Trustees: Reverend Henry David Kendal, Miss Virginia Jane Knox MSc, Rev Michael Pavlou, Miss Margaret Elizabeth Peach, Miss Hannah Louise Parker, Mrs Elizabeth Boreham BA Hons, Mr Christopher Aslan Alexander, Mrs Rosamund Jane Hoare, Mr Jan Kovar, Miss Kristina Drew, Mr Peter Grant, Mrs Bridget Nunn-Harvey, Mrs Julia Connick, Miss Rinret Leks, Mr Alexander Fraser MacKay, Mr Colin Stuart Brookes, Mrs Helen Shannon, Mr David Jonathan Vincent, Mrs Sarah Restall, Mr Oluwatosin Coker, Mrs Alice Gavin Atashkar, Mrs Shirley Uloma Boateng, Mr Neil Nathaniel Richards, Mrs Wendy Chan, Mrs Megan Landry, Miss Emma Westbury, Mr Peter Troup, Mr Robert Bowman-Scott
Income: £2,273,576 [2016]; £1,899,650 [2015]; £1,286,809 [2014]; £1,020,856 [2013]; £1,045,756 [2012]

The Parochial Church Council of The Ecclesiastical Parish of St Ebbe with Holy Trinity and St Peter Le Bailey, Oxford
Registered: 2 Feb 2009 Employees: 38 Volunteers: 250
Website: stebbes.org.uk
Activities: Religious activities
Address: 1-2 Roger Bacon Lane, Oxford, OX1 1QE
Trustees: Miss Susan Elizabeth Berry, Mr Robert David Horner, Mr Simon Hamilton Neal, Ms Suzanne Wilson-Higgins, Mrs Penny Wearn, Miss Georgina Smallman, Dr Graham Peter Collins, Mr Richard Hugh Roger Mortimer, Mr Edward David Heywood-Lonsdale, Rev Vaughan Edward Roberts, Mr Jeffrey Jonathan Hunter, Mr Jonathan Charles Harwood Anelay, Mr Trevor Rayment, Julia E M Cameron, Dr Paul Nigel Taylor, Mr Alistair Cory, Dr Philip Wee Jin Goh, Mrs Anna Gittins
Income: £1,819,164 [2016]; £1,774,549 [2015]; £1,332,938 [2014]; £1,292,338 [2013]; £1,294,919 [2012]

The Parochial Church Council of The Ecclesiastical Parish of St Helen, Bishopsgate
Registered: 4 Sep 2009 Employees: 46 Volunteers: 350
Tel: 020 7283 2231 Website: st-helens.org.uk
Activities: Religious activities
Address: St Helens Church, Great St Helens, London, EC3A 6AT
Trustees: Revd W T Taylor, Mr Jeremy Anderson CBE, Mr Richard Andrews, Mr Simon Congdon, Dr Geoffrey Haire, Mr Andrew Ross, Rev Charles Skrine, Mr Andrew Wales, Mr Richard Peter Tett, Charlie Campbell, Jacqui Sondhi, Mr Luke William Swatman, Mr Joe Robert Livingstone Carr, Mr Charles Kasenene, Mr Michael Mantle Rev, Mr Julian Miles Pulman, Miss Lucy Brock, Mr David Vinton, Mrs Mickella Nikoi, Mr Geoff Silk, Mr Robert Keep, Miss Sarah Samantha Too, Mr Rory Anderson, Miss Deborah Buggs, Mrs Sarah Finch, Miss Kyla Malcolm, Mr Paul Simpkin, Mr Peter Swift, Mr Stephen Michael McGowan, Revd Dr Aneirin Glyn, Dr Yih-Choung Teh, Mr James Houghton, Mr Timothy David Webster, Mr Brian Hoyan Wong, Mr Yann Monclair, Miss Breckwoldt Natasha, Mr Mike Thorpe, Ms Hannah Tyler, Mr Tim Catt, Mr Stephen Harbage, Mr Tony Thomas, Miss Omegie Momoh
Income: £3,390,541 [2016]; £3,429,363 [2015]; £3,548,714 [2014]; £3,391,763 [2013]; £4,974,787 [2012]

The Parochial Church Council of The Ecclesiastical Parish of St James Gerrards Cross with St James Fulmer
Registered: 28 Apr 2009 Employees: 13 Volunteers: 500
Tel: 01753 883311 Website: saintjames.org.uk
Activities: Religious activities
Address: St James Church, Oxford Road, Gerrards Cross, Bucks, SL9 7DJ
Trustees: Reverend Meyrick Richard Legge Beebee, Mrs Francesca Hall-Drinkwater, Mr Richard John Lawrence, Mr Edwin Clark, Mr Martin Josten, Mr Ian John Mitton, Ms Jean Mary Meakin, Mrs Stephanie Jane Summerell, Mr Anthony Richard Bargioni, Mr Paul Walker, Mrs Laurianne Griffiths, Chris Lion, Mr David Kidner, Mr Steven Cooper, Rev Di Rolandson, Mr Geoffrey Marks, Mrs Jacqui Pannett, Mr Lawerence Tebboth, Keith Wilson, Mrs Jacky Hughes, Rev Martin Jonathan Williams BA Hons DipTheol, Mr Brian Lewin Weild, Mr David Michael Steel, Mr Keith Lucas, Mr Gordon James Scorer, Mr Andrew Robert Bell, Mr Samuel Jonathan Eastwood, Mr Roland White, Ben Topham, Mrs Yve Stewart, Mr David Mackie, Rev James Leach, Mrs Jill Roth, Mrs Jane Sheldon, Mr Cobus Van Der Walt
Income: £1,163,484 [2016]; £1,484,278 [2015]; £1,199,194 [2014]; £1,130,574 [2013]; £1,373,433 [2012]

The Parochial Church Council of The Ecclesiastical Parish of St James, Westminster
Registered: 1 Dec 2009 Employees: 21 Volunteers: 132
Tel: 020 7734 4511 Website: sjp.org.uk
Activities: Religious activities
Address: St James's Church, 197 Piccadilly, London, W1J 9LL
Trustees: Rev Lucy Clare Winkett, Mercedes Pavlicevic, Dr Wilson Wong, Mr Kevin Hipgrave, Rev Ivan Patricio Khovacs, Ms Nicola McKnight, Dr Lia Dong Shimada, Ms Elizabeth Edith Pearl Willis, Ms Evelyn Namutebi, Ms Carolyn Davies, Revd Lindsay Meader, Rev Hugh Valentine, Ms Deborah Colvin, Ms Rakshita Patel, Mr Trevor Lines, Mr Adolfo Sansolini, Ms Heather Williams, Ms Leah Hoskin, Mr Robert Duirs, Ms Natasha Imison
Income: £1,075,340 [2016]; £1,025,876 [2015]; £872,334 [2014]; £1,393,653 [2013]; £880,562 [2012]

The Parochial Church Council of The Ecclesiastical Parish of St Martin-in-the-Fields, London
Registered: 1 Feb 2010 Employees: 115 Volunteers: 150
Tel: 020 7766 1105 Website: stmartin-in-the-fields.org
Activities: General charitable purposes; education, training; overseas aid, famine relief; religious activities; arts, culture, heritage, science; environment, conservation, heritage; human rights, religious or racial harmony, equality or diversity
Address: 5 St Martin's Place, London, WC2N 4JH
Trustees: Mr Jim Sikorski, Mr Eugene Ling MSc BSc, Rev Richard Carter, Ms Susanne Wood, Mr Duncan James McCall QC, Mr Craig Alan Norman, Ms Kate Emily Hilton, Ms Catherine Mary Jackson, Mr Will Charnley, Mr Christopher Braganza, Rev Katherine Hedderly, Rev Paul Lau, Rev Samuel Martin Bailey Wells, Mr Harold Oriel Alby, Ms Kathryn Fleur Harris, Ms Bella Ikpasaja, Mr Ivan Ho Fung Yuen
Income: £5,418,541 [2016]; £5,354,850 [2015]; £5,060,596 [2014]; £5,056,531 [2013]; £4,429,904 [2012]

The Parochial Church Council of The Ecclesiastical Parish of St Mary Magdalene, Richmond with St Matthias and St John The Divine
Registered: 8 Jun 2009 Employees: 10 Volunteers: 150
Tel: 020 8605 3701 Website: richmondteamministry.org
Activities: Religious activities
Address: 8 Grena Road, Richmond, Surrey, TW9 1XS
Trustees: Martin Brecknell, Charles Stiller, Gillian Doling, David Shaw, Rev Alan Sykes, Susan Eastaugh, Judith Pearson, Rev Anne Crawford, Fiona Morgan, John Arthur, Alexandra Barr, Margot Gallie, Margaret Morrison, Jackie Harrison, Rev Neil Summers, Rev Wilma Roest, Mary Ricketts, Stephen Cockell, Geoff Bates, James Arnold, Alice Eastaugh, Cedric Lee
Income: £1,046,396 [2016]; £1,154,643 [2015]; £1,094,305 [2014]; £767,890 [2013]; £704,100 [2012]

The Parochial Church Council of The Ecclesiastical Parish of St Marylebone with Holy Trinity St Marylebone
Registered: 6 May 2009 Employees: 11 Volunteers: 50
Tel: 020 7677 3490 Website: stmarylebone.org
Activities: Religious activities
Address: 73 Pentonville Road, London, N1 9LP
Trustees: The Revd S J Evans, Mr D A Garnier, Mr R W Lloyd-Davies, Mrs J Sumpter, Ms A Murphy, Mr Graham P G Norton, Mrs Helen K H Hollingsworth, The Revd E C Thornley, Miss M E Queenan, Mr M E Onah, Mr A D Hine, Mrs B E Ormerod, Ms C Alexander, Mr P M Mwaniki, Miss K J Timperley, Mrs H H Guise, Mr Thomas F Moore
Income: £1,034,974 [2016]; £782,241 [2015]; £722,315 [2014]; £698,731 [2013]; £845,131 [2012]

The Parochial Church Council of The Ecclesiastical Parish of St Michael & All Angels, Summertown
Registered: 5 May 2009 *Volunteers:* 50
Tel: 01865 311762 *Website:* stmichaels-summertown.org.uk
Activities: Religious activities
Address: Summertown Church Hall, Portland Road, Oxford, OX2 7EZ
Trustees: Ann Stedman, Doreen Barrett, The Revd Gavin Knight, Jan Cook, Keith Lewis, David Smith, Irim Sarwar, Emma Wilkinson, Sarah Scheele, Richard Dodd, Nigel Hamilton, Sam Bickersteth, Ali McIntosh
Income: £1,224,214 [2017]; £235,927 [2016]; £227,963 [2015]; £178,648 [2014]; £162,698 [2013]

The Parochial Church Council of The Ecclesiastical Parish of St Nicholas, Sevenoaks
Registered: 21 Nov 2009 *Employees:* 15 *Volunteers:* 250
Tel: 01732 740340 *Website:* stnicholas-sevenoaks.org
Activities: Religious activities
Address: St Nicholas Church, Rectory Lane, Sevenoaks, Kent, TN13 1JA
Trustees: Rev Angus MacLeay, Brigadier Ian Dobbie, Mr John Collett, Mrs Jean Heather Surrey, Mr Stephen Wehrle, Mr Haydn Cooper, Mrs Chris Brindley, Mrs Alice Beckett, Mr Andrew Coates, Mr Ian Nash, Mr Peter Scott, Mrs Sarah MacKenzie, Mr David McIlroy, Mr Ben Stone, Mr Anthony Jennings, Mr Ian Leigh, Mr Chris Webb, Rev Gavin McGrath, Mr Henry Warde, Rev Tom Nash, Mr Justin Greig, Mrs Marion Russell, Mr Mark Walkington
Income: £1,168,935 [2017]; £1,212,222 [2016]; £1,235,405 [2015]; £1,209,796 [2014]; £1,138,732 [2013]

The Parochial Church Council of The Ecclesiastical Parish of St Paul, Hammersmith
Registered: 9 Jul 2009 *Employees:* 18 *Volunteers:* 315
Tel: 020 8746 5273 *Website:* sph.org
Activities: Religious activities
Address: St Pauls Church, Queen Caroline Street, Hammersmith, London, W6 9PJ
Trustees: Rev Simon Garrod Downham, Captain Robert John Read, Miss Rosemary Brown, Mr Francis Woods, Mr Alexander Starling, Associate Pastor Mark Ruoff, Mr Oliver Wright, Mrs Alyson Evans, Mr David Salisbury, Mrs Helen Madeline Parry, Revd Dr Vivian Ivor Thomas, Mr Francis Ellison, Miss Susan Hussey, Mr David Bell, Mrs Margaret Rogers, Mr Clive Thompson, Mr Max Harris, Mrs Judith Sara Thomas
Income: £1,189,212 [2016]; £1,276,286 [2015]; £1,342,633 [2014]; £1,409,968 [2013]; £1,357,336 [2012]

The Parochial Church Council of The Ecclesiastical Parish of St. Andrew and St. Mary Magdalene, Maidenhead
Registered: 19 Jan 2009 *Employees:* 8 *Volunteers:* 100
Tel: 01628 820146 *Website:* stmarysmaidenhead.org
Activities: Religious activities
Address: Manor House, New Road, Hurley, Maidenhead, Berks, SL6 5LN
Trustees: Rev Will Stileman, Rev Samuel Allberry, Mr Peter John Blackbeard, Mrs Kate Wheatley, Dr Richard David Brunt, Rob Hurley, Mrs Fiona West, Rev Neil Watkinson, Mr Neil James McDonald, Mrs Amy O'Donovan, Rev Jon Drake, Mr David Atallah, Mr Damian Eustace, Mrs Jill Palfrey, Rob Wingfield, Mr Robert Weeks, Rev Samuel Brewster, Mr Thomas Walton, Miss Tanja Ten Have, Mr Jonathan Harris, Mr Rhys Mitchell, Miss Katherine Elford, Mrs Rae Binning
Income: £1,916,996 [2017]; £689,155 [2016]; £908,193 [2015]; £686,639 [2014]; £595,380 [2013]

The Parochial Church Council of The Ecclesiastical Parish of Uxbridge
Registered: 30 Mar 2009 *Employees:* 9 *Volunteers:* 75
Tel: 01895 258766 *Website:* standrewsuxbridge.org
Activities: Religious activities
Address: St Margarets Church, Windsor Street, Uxbridge, Middlesex, UB8 1AB
Trustees: Ian MacDonald, Jackie Woodruff, Rosie Halford, Mrs Joanna Mason, Rev Cliff Bowman, Julie Churchyard, Ms Janet Kerr, Rev John Jenkins, Mr David Thomas, Rev Tim Atkins, Mrs Rosemary Jenkins, Mrs Ali Singleton, Mr Laurence Frankel, Mark Skinner, Sally Clargo, Mrs Suzan Valerie Leatherby, Rev June Hughman, Rev Andrew Sheard, Tina Rapson, Mrs Carol Connolly, Debbie Botes, Miss Angela Lewis, Mr Iain McKay, Mr Barry Hancock, Mrs Dianne Deeks
Income: £1,318,122 [2016]; £440,001 [2015]; £404,384 [2014]; £436,977 [2013]; £391,982 [2012]

The Parochial Church Council of The Ecclesiastical Parish of Wimbledon
Registered: 8 Feb 2010 *Employees:* 4
Website: stmaryswimbledon.org
Activities: General charitable purposes; religious activities
Address: 9 Woodspring Road, London, SW19 6PL
Trustees: John Bright, Mr William Frederick Charles Varlow, Mrs Wendy Judith Mila Ziegler, Mr Thomas Jonathan Hopkinson, Mr Neal Donald Harvey, Mrs Margaret Elizabeth Broad, Mrs Fiona Hills, Mrs Julia Poham, Mr David Jennings, Mr Graham John Crofts, Mrs Mary-Jane Taylor, Rev Clive Bruce Gardner, Mr Christopher Sidney Jolly, Rev Bruce Walter Rickards, Rev Helen Claire Orchard, Ms Pauls Thorvaldsen, Mr Mark Christopher Richard Leeson, Mrs Alison Neilson, Mr Cherles Esdale, Mr William Smith, Mrs Louise Mary Hebbourn
Income: £3,118,321 [2016]; £1,383,830 [2015]; £1,167,913 [2014]; £1,222,770 [2013]; £887,094 [2012]

The Parochial Church Council of The Ecclesiastical Parish of Woking Christ Church
Registered: 5 Jun 2009 *Employees:* 15 *Volunteers:* 202
Tel: 01483 740897 *Website:* christchurchwoking.org
Activities: Education, training; religious activities
Address: 1 Howards Close, Woking, Surrey, GU22 9AR
Trustees: Jon Cheney, Rev Phil Simpson, Rev Dr Peter James Harwood MB CLB MA, Mr Peter George Hall, Steve Roberts, David Fernandez, Andy Reid, Jan Tait, Rev Martin Stanley Smith, Mr Steve Morris, Nigel Anderson, Mrs Sarah Joyce Creen, Mrs Beryl Keeley, Jo Frank, Walter Coxon, Richard Edward Stone
Income: £1,330,493 [2016]; £1,020,015 [2015]; £1,047,284 [2014]; £1,108,599 [2013]; £949,326 [2012]

Partners of Prisoners and Families Support Group
Registered: 20 Jul 1995 *Employees:* 130 *Volunteers:* 55
Tel: 0161 702 1000 *Website:* partnersofprisoners.co.uk
Activities: The prevention or relief of poverty; accommodation, housing; economic, community development, employment
Address: Valentine House, 1079 Rochdale Road, Manchester, M9 8AJ
Trustees: Mr Gilmour Buchan Black, Ms Liz Norris, Mr Mark Hilditch, Mr Richard Rowley, Ms Sarah Beresford, Ms Heather Williams, Mr Richard Barnes
Income: £1,532,562 [2017]; £1,680,809 [2016]; £1,760,864 [2015]; £1,532,284 [2014]; £1,669,080 [2013]

Partnership for Growth
Registered: 26 May 1998 *Employees:* 18 *Volunteers:* 100
Tel: 01903 529333 *Website:* linktohope.co.uk
Activities: Education, training; prevention or relief of poverty; overseas aid, famine relief; accommodation, housing
Address: Links House, Park Road, Worthing, W Sussex, BN11 2AN
Trustees: Mrs Jan Susan Davey, Mr Patrick Woodward, Mr Timothy Weller, Mr John Lelliott
Income: £1,593,236 [2017]; £1,665,047 [2016]; £1,319,614 [2015]; £1,243,516 [2014]; £1,397,049 [2013]

Passage 2000
Registered: 9 Mar 2000 *Employees:* 101 *Volunteers:* 450
Tel: 020 7592 1855 *Website:* passage.org.uk
Activities: Education, training; prevention or relief of poverty; accommodation, housing
Address: The Passage, St Vincent's Centre, Carlisle Place, London, SW1P 1NL
Trustees: Mrg Vladmir Felzmann, Sister Eileen Glancy, Dr Iram Sattar, Ms Victoria Stephenson, Ms Roisin Murphy, Mr Michael John Kelly, Mr Christopher Williams, Mr Antonio Orlando, Mr Christopher Morris
Income: £4,254,654 [2017]; £5,536,669 [2016]; £13,283,470 [2015]; £11,416,574 [2014]; £4,692,803 [2013]

Pate's Grammar School Foundation
Registered: 19 Sep 1966 *Employees:* 68
Tel: 01242 522052
Activities: Education, training
Address: Mrs L J Cox, The Richard Pate School, Southern Road, Cheltenham, Glos, GL53 9RP
Trustees: Mr Christopher John Mourton, Mrs Eleanor Kirby, Mr John Clarke, Mr Guy Bradshaw, Mr Robert May, Mr David Graham Waters, Mr Richard James Comstive Wright, Mr John Harrison, Alderman Lloyd Marcus Surgenor, Mrs Judith Wynn, Mrs Lesley Sanchez, Mr Wallace Priestley Ascham
Income: £2,849,426 [2017]; £2,705,368 [2016]; £2,600,924 [2015]; £2,574,369 [2014]; £2,545,076 [2013]

The Pathological Society of Great Britain and Ireland
Registered: 3 Dec 2013 *Employees:* 3
Tel: 020 7347 5751 *Website:* pathsoc.org
Activities: Education, training
Address: The Pathological Society, 150 Minories, London, EC3N 1LS
Trustees: Dr Emyr Wyn Benbow, Dr Richard John Byers, Prof Mark Johan Arends, Dr Christopher Michael Bacon, Professor Graeme Ian Murray, Professor Heike Irmgard Grabsch, Professor Sara Ellen Coupland, Dr Anne Marie Quinn, Professor Adrienne Margaret Flanagan, Prof Ming-Qing Du, Prof Philip Quirke, Dr Emad Abd Elaziz Rakha, Dr Nicholas Paul West, Dr Aurelie Fabre, Prof Manuel Salto-Tellez, Dr Abhik Mukherjee
Income: £1,213,001 [2016]; £1,170,828 [2015]; £1,098,496 [2014]

Pathways To Independence Ltd
Registered: 25 Sep 1985 *Employees:* 27 *Volunteers:* 10
Tel: 01634 819649 *Website:* beyondhomelessness.org.uk
Activities: Education, training; prevention or relief of poverty; accommodation, housing; economic, community development, employment
Address: Pathways To Independence, 25 Victoria Street, Rochester, Kent, ME1 1XJ
Trustees: Mr James Gilbourne, Kelly Freeman, Sarah Louise Miller, Laura Elizabeth Anne Blake, Mr John Norley, Andrew Jon Vincent, Philippa Nancoo, Mr Timothy Licence
Income: £1,426,685 [2017]; £1,376,677 [2016]; £1,396,619 [2015]; £1,635,574 [2014]; £889,281 [2013]

Paul Foundation
Registered: 10 Jun 1991
Tel: 01451 844500
Activities: The advancement of health or saving of lives; disability; prevention or relief of poverty; overseas aid, famine relief
Address: Haycroft, Sherbourne, Cheltenham, Glos, GL54 3NB
Trustees: D Harvey, P R D Paul, N Michaelis
Income: £1,371,522 [2017]; £149,901 [2016]; £154,538 [2015]; £170,082 [2014]; £173,828 [2013]

The Paul Mellon Centre for Studies in British Art
Registered: 17 Nov 1970 *Employees:* 24
Tel: 020 7580 0311 *Website:* paul-mellon-centre.ac.uk
Activities: Education, training; arts, culture, heritage, science
Address: The Paul Mellon Centre, 16 Bedford Square, London, WC1B 3JA
Trustees: Dr Amy Meyers, Mr Benjamin Polak, Mr Peter Salovey, Mr Stephen C Murphy
Income: £4,919,990 [2017]; £4,486,261 [2016]; £6,096,404 [2015]; £3,925,713 [2014]; £3,167,031 [2013]

Pavilion Dance South West Limited
Registered: 11 Oct 2005 *Employees:* 22 *Volunteers:* 65
Website: pdsw.org.uk
Activities: Education, training; arts, culture, heritage, science
Address: 2 Bay View Road, Lyme Regis, Dorset, DT7 3AT
Trustees: Mr Stephen Godsall, Natasha Tobin, Sarah Trist, Mr Ebi Sosseh, Ms Dorcas Jacqueline Williams, Mandy Fitzmaurice, Mr Benjamin Peter Dunks, Susan Kay, Mr Toby Alexander Marden
Income: £1,068,014 [2017]; £1,071,260 [2016]; £1,088,277 [2015]; £1,028,046 [2014]; £897,631 [2013]

Paypal Giving Fund UK
Registered: 22 Jul 2005 *Employees:* 5
Website: paypalgivingfund.org.uk
Activities: General charitable purposes
Address: Whittaker House, Whittaker Avenue, Richmond, Surrey, TW9 1EH
Trustees: Mr Sean Milliken, Ms Alison Sagar, Ms Angela Cummings, Ms Eva Gustavsson, Mr Llewellyn Thomas, Ms Naomi Marek, Ms Julia Hutton-Potts, Amit Ghosh
Income: £7,594,474 [2017]; £5,213,545 [2016]; £5,949,454 [2015]; £4,530,071 [2014]; £4,222,716 [2013]

Peabody Community Foundation
Registered: 20 Aug 1976 *Employees:* 98 *Volunteers:* 1,112
Tel: 020 7021 4236 *Website:* trust-thamesmead.co.uk
Activities: General charitable purposes; prevention or relief of poverty; arts, culture, heritage, science; amateur sport; economic, community development, employment
Address: Peabody Trust, Minster Court, 45-47 Westminster Bridge Road, London, SE1 7JB
Trustees: Mr Keith Clancy, Ms Helen Edwards, Ms Deirdre Moss, Ms Janice Tucker, Mr Michael Cleaver, Ms Catherine O'Kelly
Income: £6,083,848 [2017]; £2,205,272 [2016]; £7,398,625 [2015]; £2,996,468 [2014]; £3,612,247 [2013]

George Peabody Donation Fund
Registered: 1 Jan 1961 *Employees:* 506 *Volunteers:* 519
Tel: 020 7021 4236 *Website:* peabody.org.uk
Activities: General charitable purposes; prevention or relief of poverty; accommodation, housing; economic, community development, employment
Address: Peabody Trust, Minster Court, 45-47 Westminster Bridge Road, London, SE1 7JB
Trustees: Peabody Trust (Charitable CBS Reg 7223)
Income: £131,254,000 [2017]; £252,670,000 [2016]; £158,190,000 [2015]; £149,204,000 [2014]; £123,146,000 [2013]

Peace Direct
Registered: 18 Mar 2008 *Employees:* 14 *Volunteers:* 11
Tel: 020 3422 5549 *Website:* peacedirect.org
Activities: Education, training; overseas aid, famine relief; economic, community development, employment; human rights, religious or racial harmony, equality or diversity; other charitable purposes
Address: 1st Floor, Peace Direct, 1 King Edward's Road, London, E9 7SF
Trustees: Mr David Ian Cutler, Ms Carol Hodson, Eleanor Harrison, Michael Ryder, Ms Niamh Neville, Dan Jones
Income: £1,821,399 [2016]; £1,821,682 [2015]; £879,305 [2014]; £1,077,810 [2013]; £889,018 [2012]

Peace Hospice Care
Registered: 21 May 1991 *Employees:* 131 *Volunteers:* 504
Tel: 01923 330330 *Website:* peacehospicecare.org.uk
Activities: Education, training; advancement of health or saving of lives; disability
Address: Peace Hospice, Peace Drive, Watford, Herts, WD17 3PH
Trustees: Mrs Belinda Chadwick, Mr David Ellis, Mr Patrick Brennan, Mr Jarmo Kesanto, Mrs Yolanda Woolf, Mr Alan Graham, Mrs Virginia Edwards, Mr Ragen Amin, Mr Terence Ritchie, Kate Locke
Income: £6,740,397 [2017]; £6,109,784 [2016]; £5,042,526 [2015]; £5,287,625 [2014]; £5,088,622 [2013]

Peaceful Change Initiative
Registered: 4 Aug 2015 *Employees:* 18
Tel: 07507 612645 *Website:* peacefulchange.org
Activities: Human rights, religious or racial harmony, equality or diversity
Address: 1st Floor, Peaceful Change Initiative, 25b Lloyd Baker Street, London, WC1X 9AT
Trustees: Mr Michael Holland, Mr James Freeman, Mr An Shihoff
Income: £3,451,841 [2017]; £1,869,256 [2016]

Peacehaven House
Registered: 2 Mar 1998 *Employees:* 50 *Volunteers:* 8
Tel: 01704 227030 *Website:* peacehavenhouse.com
Activities: General charitable purposes; advancement of health or saving of lives; prevention or relief of poverty; accommodation, housing
Address: Peacehaven House, 101 Roe Lane, Southport, Merseyside, PR9 7PD
Trustees: Mr Roger Ian Foulkes, Mrs Heather Sidebotham, Mrs Barbara Cox, Mr David Wood, Mr Charles Kirk Caton, Mrs Margaret Cotton, Mr David Wall, Mr Adrian P Shandley, Mr Douglas Edmundson
Income: £1,319,032 [2016]; £1,236,190 [2015]; £1,258,046 [2014]; £1,265,324 [2013]; £1,245,917 [2012]

The Pears Family Charitable Foundation
Registered: 4 Mar 1992 *Employees:* 11
Website: pearsfoundation.org.uk
Activities: General charitable purposes; education, training; advancement of health or saving of lives; disability; prevention or relief of poverty; overseas aid, famine relief; accommodation, housing; religious activities; arts, culture, heritage, science; environment, conservation, heritage; economic, community development, employment; armed forces, emergency service efficiency; human rights, religious or racial harmony, equality or diversity; other charitable purposes
Address: 2 Old Brewery Mews, London, NW3 1PZ
Trustees: Mr David Alan Pears, Mr Mark Andrew Pears, Sir Trevor Steven Pears
Income: £18,263,232 [2017]; £14,925,559 [2016]; £13,650,461 [2015]; £10,630,598 [2014]; £9,081,521 [2013]

Pembrokeshire Agricultural Society Limited
Registered: 17 Feb 2015 *Employees:* 8 *Volunteers:* 180
Tel: 01437 764331 *Website:* pembsshow.org
Activities: General charitable purposes
Address: Pembrokeshire Agricultural Society, County Showground, Withybush Road, Haverfordwest, Pembrokeshire, SA62 4BW
Trustees: Mr Roger James Mathias JP, Mr John Lewis, Mr Michael Stanley Davies, Mr Paul Bridgman Hnd Electrical Engineering, Mr William John Evans, Mr Adam Robert Thorne BSc Hons Rural Land Mngmt, Mr Malcolm Thomas John Lewis Mrac Mem of Royal Agri College, Mrs Nicola Elizabeth Owen FCCA, Mr Robert John James
Income: £1,109,596 [2016]; £932,172 [2015]

Pembrokeshire Association of Voluntary Services
Registered: 5 Jul 1997 *Employees:* 15
Tel: 01239 841288 *Website:* pavs.org.uk
Activities: General charitable purposes; education, training; disability; prevention or relief of poverty; economic, community development, employment
Address: Postgwyn, Boncath, Pembrokeshire, SA37 0JR
Trustees: Mrs Dilys Fletcher, Mr Bernie Scourfield, Mr Marc Tierney, Mr Gerard Davies, Mrs Barbara Ann Priest, Mr Alan Thomas, Mr John Gossage
Income: £1,103,041 [2017]; £798,251 [2016]; £1,141,222 [2015]; £1,110,719 [2014]; £1,023,037 [2013]

The Penderels Trust Limited
Registered: 26 Jan 1999 *Employees:* 179
Tel: 024 7651 1611 *Website:* penderelstrust.org.uk
Activities: Disability
Address: Resource House, 1A Brandon Lane, Coventry, Warwicks, CV3 3GU
Trustees: Mr Richard Harris, Mrs Monica Macheng, Yvonne Barnes, Mr John Finnie, Miss Yvonne Barnes
Income: £4,981,897 [2017]; £4,624,225 [2016]; £4,108,021 [2015]; £4,149,554 [2014]; £4,323,858 [2013]

Pendleside Hospice
Registered: 19 Dec 1988 *Employees:* 87 *Volunteers:* 450
Tel: 01282 440104 *Website:* pendleside.org.uk
Activities: The advancement of health or saving of lives
Address: Pendleside Hospice, Pendleside, Colne Road, Burnley, Lancs, BB10 2LW
Trustees: Mr David Brown, Miss Dianne Sarah Evans, Mrs Margaret Hynes, Mr Giles Scott Williams, Mr Roger Cornes, Mr David Robert Walker, Mrs Francesca Chapman, Mrs Mary Angela Brown
Income: £3,955,835 [2017]; £3,452,000 [2016]; £3,340,659 [2015]; £2,999,459 [2014]; £3,203,353 [2013]

The Pennies Foundation
Registered: 28 Jan 2008 Employees: 13 Volunteers: 3
Tel: 020 7600 9286 Website: pennies.org.uk
Activities: General charitable purposes; other charitable purposes
Address: Third Floor, 140 London Wall, London, EC2Y 5DN
Trustees: Graham Edwards, Mr Peter Nugent, Robert Leitao, Peter Ayliffe, Mr Julian Taylor, Penny Lovell, Ian Filby, Mark Anderson
Income: £4,228,680 [2017]; £2,986,074 [2016]; £3,270,945 [2015]; £2,783,681 [2014]; £2,032,566 [2013]

The Pennine Acute Hospitals Charity and Other Related Charities
Registered: 26 Oct 1995
Tel: 0161 921 4914 Website: pat.nhs.uk
Activities: The advancement of health or saving of lives
Address: North Manchester General Hospital, Delaunays Road, Manchester, M8 5RB
Trustees: Pennine Acute Hospitals NHS Trust
Income: £1,236,000 [2017]; £362,000 [2016]; £422,000 [2015]; £474,000 [2014]; £710,000 [2013]

Pennine Camphill Community
Registered: 16 Sep 1977 Employees: 23
Tel: 01924 255281 Website: pennine.org.uk
Activities: Education, training; advancement of health or saving of lives; disability; animals; economic, community development, employment
Address: Pennine Camphill Community, Wood Lane, Chapelthorpe, Wakefield, W Yorks, WF4 3JL
Trustees: Mr Austin McIntyre, Mr G Franklin, Mr Nicolas Dodd, Ms D Jenkins, Mrs Jane Barry
Income: £1,456,343 [2017]; £1,414,565 [2016]; £1,391,817 [2015]; £1,483,510 [2014]; £1,625,364 [2013]

Pennthorpe School Trust Limited
Registered: 14 Jun 1965 Employees: 70 Volunteers: 3
Tel: 01403 822391 Website: pennthorpe.com
Activities: Education, training
Address: Pennthorpe School, Church Street, Rudgwick, W Sussex, RH12 3HJ
Trustees: Mr Dominic Edginton, Mr Mark Lucas, Mr Richard Kelly, Mr Christopher Hibbs, Mr Timothy Manly, Mrs Ann Gilchrist, Rev Martin King, Mr Stephen Marshall-Taylor, Mr Stephen Browning
Income: £3,073,569 [2017]; £2,996,339 [2016]; £3,165,324 [2015]; £3,249,526 [2014]; £3,132,184 [2013]

Penny Appeal
Registered: 2 Mar 2009 Employees: 118 Volunteers: 103
Tel: 01924 231088 Website: pennyappeal.org
Activities: General charitable purposes; education, training; advancement of health or saving of lives; prevention or relief of poverty; overseas aid, famine relief
Address: Penny Appeal, Cross Street Chambers, Cross Street, Wakefield, W Yorks, WF1 3BW
Trustees: Mr Eric Robert Timmins, Mr Rizwan Khaliq, Mr Adeem Younis, Isha Begum
Income: £18,629,628 [2017]; £13,808,844 [2016]; £8,973,229 [2015]; £2,504,097 [2014]; £392,500 [2013]

Penrose Options
Registered: 28 Mar 2013 Employees: 146 Volunteers: 10
Tel: 020 3668 9270 Website: penrose.org.uk
Activities: General charitable purposes; education, training; advancement of health or saving of lives; prevention or relief of poverty; accommodation, housing
Address: Unit 1 Waterloo Gardens, Milner Square, London, N1 1TY
Trustees: Mrs Carol Stewart, Neil Moloney, Mr Craig Ian Brown
Income: £7,205,000 [2017]; £7,175,000 [2016]; £5,102,000 [2015]; £5,785,000 [2014]

Pentreath Limited
Registered: 25 Oct 1991 Employees: 52 Volunteers: 8
Tel: 01726 862727 Website: pentreath.co.uk
Activities: Education, training; advancement of health or saving of lives; disability; economic, community development, employment; human rights, religious or racial harmony, equality or diversity
Address: Glebe Farm, Narrow Lane, Summercourt, Newquay, Cornwall, TR8 5EE
Trustees: Mr Christopher Terence Hazell, Mr Julian Tyson, Mr Liam Mannall, Mr Jason Coad, Mr Mark Steer, Mr David McAuley, Chris Iremonger, Mrs Pamela Stansfield, Dr Gilda Nadine Davies
Income: £1,010,157 [2016]; £1,371,443 [2015]; £1,476,393 [2014]; £1,295,691 [2013]; £1,091,373 [2012]

People 1st
Registered: 6 Dec 1990 Employees: 56
Tel: 020 3074 1222 Website: people1st.co.uk
Activities: Education, training
Address: People 1st, Hospitality House, 11-59 High Road, London, N2 8AB
Trustees: Mr David Fairhurst, Mrs Natalie Bickford, Mr Geoffrey Charles Harrison, Ms Sara Louise Edwards, Ms Fiona Ryland, Charles Henry Prew, Mr John McEwan, Ms Liz Chandler, Therese Procter, Ms Lesley Flora Allan
Income: £4,272,000 [2017]; £4,002,000 [2016]; £5,346,000 [2015]; £9,510,000 [2014]; £9,538,000 [2013]

People Potential Possibilities
Registered: 24 Jul 1990 Employees: 605 Volunteers: 60
Tel: 07790 960139 Website: p3charity.com
Activities: General charitable purposes; education, training; advancement of health or saving of lives; accommodation, housing; economic, community development, employment
Address: Eagle House, Cotmanhay Road, Ilkeston, Derbys, DE7 8HU
Trustees: Mrs Dorothy Lane, Miss Dale Simon, Mr Adam Johnathan Patrick Hackett, Ms Carol Ann Carter, Mr John Spriggs-Taylor, Mrs Bobbie Rebecca Graham, Mr Mark Terry
Income: £19,130,773 [2017]; £18,973,231 [2016]; £14,816,055 [2015]; £13,018,841 [2014]; £9,776,460 [2013]

People for Animal Care Trust (PACT)
Registered: 4 Nov 2013 Employees: 77 Volunteers: 50
Tel: 01362 821306 Website: pactsanctuary.org
Activities: Education, training; disability; animals; environment, conservation, heritage
Address: Hefferlump House, River Farm, Woodrising, Norwich, NR9 4PJ
Trustees: Mrs Christine Rockingham, Miss Suzie Lay, Mrs Allison Grant, Miss Jannette Sammonds
Income: £1,450,799 [2017]; £1,177,712 [2016]; £1,021,723 [2015]

People for The Ethical Treatment of Animals (PETA) Foundation
Registered: 27 Jun 1996 *Employees:* 35 *Volunteers:* 100
Activities: Animals
Address: c/o Stone King LLP (Ref JRB), Boundary House, 91 Charterhouse Street, London, EC1M 6HR
Trustees: Ms Ingrid Newkirk, Mr Leslie Chappell, Ms Lene Lovich
Income: £4,572,284 [2017]; £3,823,920 [2016]; £3,161,382 [2015]; £3,306,139 [2014]; £2,587,145 [2013]

People in Action
Registered: 10 May 1990 *Employees:* 567
Tel: 024 7664 3776 *Website:* people-in-action.com
Activities: Disability; accommodation, housing; economic, community development, employment
Address: People in Action, White Lion Chambers, 44 High Street, Bedworth, Warwicks, CV12 8NY
Trustees: Mr Jeffrey William Hunt, Mrs Jean Seton, Mr Robert Darlaston, Mrs Susan Janet Morris, Mrs Rosemary Ann Frankel
Income: £9,966,413 [2017]; £10,292,878 [2016]; £11,132,029 [2015]; £10,383,178 [2014]; £9,795,482 [2013]

The People's Dispensary for Sick Animals
Registered: 22 Sep 1962 *Employees:* 1,593 *Volunteers:* 3,686
Tel: 01952 290999 *Website:* pdsa.org.uk
Activities: The prevention or relief of poverty; animals
Address: PDSA, Whitechapel Way, Priorslee, Telford, TF2 9PQ
Trustees: Mr Richard Clowes, Ms Catherine Dixon, Mr John Miller BSc MCIPD AFBPsS, Mrs Carole Pomfret MA ACA, Mrs Alison Tattersall, Mr Andrew Tinlin BEng DipMgt, Mr Noel Guilford BA FCA MSI, Ms Laurie Mayers BA MA, Mr John Smith FCA, Mrs Mary Margaret Reilly BA FCA FUCL, Professor Gary England
Income: £94,213,002 [2016]; £83,256,592 [2015]; £89,728,101 [2014]; £87,202,255 [2013]; £85,918,604 [2012]

People's Health Trust
Registered: 15 Aug 2008 *Employees:* 26
Tel: 020 7749 9119 *Website:* peopleshealthtrust.org.uk
Activities: The advancement of health or saving of lives
Address: People's Health Trust, 64 Great Eastern Street, London, EC2A 3QR
Trustees: Ms Barbara Simmonds, Mr Nigel Turner, Mr Alan Francis, Mr Paul Ballantyne, Mr Duncan Stephenson, Ms Sue Hawkett OBE, Dr Eva Elliott, Ms Sue Cohen, Prof Elizabeth Dowler
Income: £12,212,836 [2017]; £12,141,883 [2016]; £14,598,966 [2015]; £17,162,435 [2014]; £14,893,782 [2013]

People's Trust for Endangered Species
Registered: 17 Aug 1977 *Employees:* 16 *Volunteers:* 30,000
Tel: 020 7498 4533 *Website:* ptes.org
Activities: Animals; environment, conservation, heritage
Address: Peoples Trust for Endangered Specie, Studio 3 Cloisters House, Cloisters Business Centre, Battersea Park Road, London, SW8 4BG
Trustees: Ms Sylvia Kahn Freund, Ms Sheila Anderson, Dr Andrew Kitchener, Mr Martin Rowson, Dr Anthony Mitchell-Jones
Income: £1,097,455 [2016]; £1,118,642 [2015]; £1,076,275 [2014]; £1,295,107 [2013]; £1,066,272 [2012]

Pepperdine University (USA)
Registered: 13 Sep 1991 *Employees:* 16
Website: pepperdine.edu
Activities: Education, training
Address: Pepperdine University, 24255 Pacific Coast Highway, Malibu, California, USA, 90263
Trustees: Mr Richard Rawlence, Andrew K Benton, Thomas G Bost, Gary A Hanson, Charles J Pippin, Dr Charles F Hall
Income: £3,498,414 [2017]; £3,335,789 [2016]; £8,840,312 [2015]; £2,916,676 [2014]; £2,945,914 [2013]

Dina Perelman Trust Limited
Registered: 7 Sep 1977
Tel: 020 8809 2345
Activities: General charitable purposes; education, training; prevention or relief of poverty; religious activities
Address: 39 Overlea Road, London, E5 9BG
Trustees: Mr Asher Isiah Perelman, Mr Jonah Perelman, Mrs Sara Perelman
Income: £1,096,233 [2017]; £896,202 [2016]; £955,686 [2015]; £644,750 [2014]; £627,228 [2013]

Performances Birmingham Limited
Registered: 21 Mar 1996 *Employees:* 68
Tel: 0121 200 2000 *Website:* thsh.co.uk
Activities: Arts, culture, heritage, science
Address: Performances Birmingham Limited, Symphony Hall, 8 Centenary Square, Birmingham, B1 2EA
Trustees: Councillor Carl Joseph Rice, Mrs Mary Martin, Vidar Hjardeng, Mr Ian Myatt, Professor Michael Whitby, Mr Davinder Bansal, Ms Claire Evans, Ms Anita Bhalla, Ms Helen Bates, Mr Paul Faulkner, Mr James Tait, Mr Joel Blake, Councillor Ewan Forbes McKey
Income: £12,901,000 [2017]; £13,442,000 [2016]; £12,427,000 [2015]; £12,664,690 [2014]; £11,674,000 [2013]

The Performing Right Society Foundation
Registered: 23 May 2000 *Employees:* 8
Tel: 020 3741 4233 *Website:* prsfoundation.com
Activities: Arts, culture, heritage, science
Address: 2 Pancras Square, London, N1C 4AG
Trustees: Mr Simon Platz, Mr Royce Bell, Ms Vanessa Swann, Mr Richard King, Mr Mark Poole, Ms Hannah Kendall, Ms Susannah Catherine Simons, Mr Ameet Shah, Mr John Reid, Mr Julian Nott, Ms Caroline Norbury, Mr Chris Butler
Income: £3,818,218 [2016]; £3,227,741 [2015]; £2,021,704 [2014]; £2,249,912 [2013]; £2,089,999 [2012]

Sir William Perkins's Educational Foundation
Registered: 31 Jan 1962 *Employees:* 94 *Volunteers:* 66
Tel: 01932 574914 *Website:* swps.org.uk
Activities: Education, training
Address: Sir William Perkins School, Guildford Road, Chertsey, Surrey, KT16 9BN
Trustees: Sir William Perkins's School
Income: £9,592,234 [2016]; £8,963,002 [2015]; £8,174,637 [2014]; £8,182,536 [2013]; £7,525,504 [2012]

B E Perl Charitable Trust
Registered: 21 Sep 1981
Activities: General charitable purposes; prevention or relief of poverty
Address: Foframe House, 35-37 Brent Street, London, NW4 2EF
Trustees: Mr Benjamin Eliezer Perl MBE, Mrs Rachel Jeidel, Mrs Naomi Tsorotzkin, Mr Joseph Perl, Dr Shoshanna Perl, Mr J Perl
Income: £2,625,095 [2017]; £2,818,186 [2016]; £2,421,118 [2015]; £2,613,750 [2014]; £1,960,147 [2013]

Perrott Hill School Trust Limited
Registered: 30 Jan 1967 *Employees:* 58
Tel: 01460 72051 *Website:* perrotthill.com
Activities: Education, training
Address: Perrott Hill School, North Perrott, Crewkerne, Somerset, TA18 7SL
Trustees: Mr Keith Moore, John Bradbury, Mrs Kathryn Latham, Mrs Sarah Thomas, Mr Justin Lowe, Mrs Geraldine Bevis Kerton-Johnson, Mr Richard King, Mr Marcus Longbottom, Mr John Lever, Mrs Kate Frost
Income: £2,995,024 [2016]; £2,990,646 [2015]; £2,846,742 [2014]; £2,762,390 [2013]; £2,500,458 [2012]

The Perse School
Registered: 23 Aug 2007 *Employees:* 360 *Volunteers:* 33
Tel: 01223 403874 *Website:* perse.co.uk
Activities: Education, training
Address: The Perse School, Hills Road, Cambridge, CB2 8QF
Trustees: Mr Michael Philip Holmes Pooles QC LLB, Mr Brian Phillip Smith MA CPFA FCIHT, Dr Virginia Warren MA MD, Dr Elizabeth Mary Harper BA MA PhD, Dr Helen Bettinson MA PhD, Mr Stephen William Graves BSc MBA, Mr Robert Geoffrey Gardiner, Mr Stephen Cheveley Roberts MA, Mr Graeme John Proudfoot BA Oxon Jurisprudence, Mr Simon David Lebus MA, Mr Ian Geoffrey Galbraith, Sir David Wright GCMG LVO MA, Dr Anita Mary Bunyan BA PhD, Ms Caroline Jane Stenner LLB, Dr Louise Ann Merrett MA PhD, Mrs Diana Miller Shave MA MBACP, Dr Richard Colin St Helier Mason BSc MBBS MRCP MBA, Mrs Sian Louise Steele CTA, Mr William Mark Dawkins BA Cantab
Income: £24,921,000 [2017]; £23,804,000 [2016]; £22,466,000 [2015]; £21,028,000 [2014]; £19,624,000 [2013]

The Persula Foundation
Registered: 14 Feb 1995 *Employees:* 2
Tel: 020 7551 5343 *Website:* persula.com
Activities: General charitable purposes; disability; prevention or relief of poverty; accommodation, housing; arts, culture, heritage, science; animals; economic, community development, employment
Address: The Persula Foundation, Gallery Court, Hankey Place, London, SE1 4BB
Trustees: Mrs Hanna Oppenheim, Mr David Robinson, Mr Robert Rosenthal, Mr Julian Richer, Mrs Rosie Richer, Mr Jonathan Levy
Income: £1,402,967 [2017]; £1,313,969 [2016]; £1,056,082 [2015]; £881,961 [2014]; £759,956 [2013]

Perthyn
Registered: 25 May 1995 *Employees:* 754
Tel: 01792 311980 *Website:* perthyn.org.uk
Activities: Education, training; disability; accommodation, housing
Address: Vivian Court, Llys Felin Newydd, Swansea Enterprise Park, Swansea, SA7 9FG
Trustees: John Wood, Mr John Lord, Mrs Angela Gascoigne, Mr Andrew Thomas, Mr David William Lloyd, Mrs Dilys R Williams, Mrs Fay Letitcia Blakeley
Income: £16,864,623 [2017]; £17,024,265 [2016]; £17,114,978 [2015]; £16,689,013 [2014]; £17,894,308 [2013]

Pestalozzi International Village Trust
Registered: 8 Jul 2003 *Employees:* 28 *Volunteers:* 105
Tel: 01424 870444 *Website:* pestalozzi.org.uk
Activities: Education, training; prevention or relief of poverty; human rights, religious or racial harmony, equality or diversity
Address: Pestalozzi Village, Ladybird Lane, Sedlescombe, Battle, E Sussex, TN33 0UF
Trustees: Mr Richard Henry Morby Meade, Mr Abdul Nassir Farraj, Mr Satnam Singh, Professor Stuart Ian Laing, Ms Kendall Beaudry, Mr Peter John Paley Lynam
Income: £1,131,655 [2017]; £906,294 [2016]; £1,356,015 [2015]; £937,206 [2014]; £1,152,187 [2013]

Peta Limited
Registered: 13 Feb 1987 *Employees:* 63
Tel: 023 9253 8700 *Website:* peta.co.uk
Activities: Education, training
Address: 12 Davids Lane, Ringwood, Hants, BH24 2AW
Trustees: Mr Nicholas Paul Loader, Mr Kevin John Rough, Mr Simon Peter Escott, Mr Elliot John David Seymour, Mr Huw Frank Chapman, Mr Adrian Mark Waring, Mr Philip Andrew Deer, Mr Nicolas Vincenzo Iacobucci, Mrs Corinne France Lucienne Johns
Income: £3,376,565 [2017]; £3,496,910 [2016]; £3,394,740 [2015]; £4,903,800 [2014]; £3,457,907 [2013]

Petans Limited
Registered: 16 Nov 1984 *Employees:* 52
Tel: 01603 890870 *Website:* petans.co.uk
Activities: Education, training
Address: Petans Ltd, Imperial Way, Horsham St Faith, Norwich, NR10 3GJ
Trustees: John Best, Robin Burden, Mark Goodall, Stephen Rose
Income: £2,772,835 [2017]; £3,063,426 [2016]; £3,816,275 [2015]; £4,707,417 [2014]; £3,978,493 [2013]

The Jack Petchey Foundation
Registered: 4 Aug 1999 *Employees:* 16 *Volunteers:* 39
Tel: 020 8252 8000 *Website:* jackpetcheyfoundation.org.uk
Activities: General charitable purposes; education, training; advancement of health or saving of lives; disability; accommodation, housing; arts, culture, heritage, science; amateur sport; economic, community development, employment; other charitable purposes
Address: Ms Trudy Kilcullen, Dockmaster's House, 1 Hertsmere Road, London, E14 8JJ
Trustees: Jack Petchey Corporate Trustees Limited
Income: £7,517,383 [2016]; £7,155,239 [2015]; £7,034,444 [2014]; £7,242,279 [2013]; £5,647,217 [2012]

The Peterborough Diocesan Board of Finance
Registered: 14 Dec 1966 *Employees:* 188
Tel: 01733 887003 *Website:* peterborough-diocese.org.uk
Activities: Religious activities
Address: Diocesan Office, The Palace, Minster Precincts, Peterborough, PE1 1YB
Trustees: Dr Paul Buckingham, Rev George Rogers, Mr Norman Critchlow, The Revd Jane Elizabeth Baxter, The Revd David Randell, Bishop Donald Allister, Mr Neil Robertson, Rev Katrina Hutchins, Bishop John Holbrook, Archdeacon Richard Ormston, Rev Mark Lucas, Mrs Isobel Burbidge, Mr Andrew Kenneth Owst, Mr Michael John Truman, Mr Peter Burchell, Mr John Hindle, Mr Gerard Hoare, Ms Hilary Daniels, Hilary Creek, Mr Jeremy Orme, The Venerable Gordon Steele Archdeacon of Oakham, Mr Robert Purser, Mr Robert Baker, Mr Chris Haynes, Mrs Christine Hall
Income: £9,975,144 [2016]; £9,419,411 [2015]; £10,354,371 [2014]; £12,888,338 [2013]; £10,860,698 [2012]

The Peterborough School Limited
Registered: 11 Jul 1975 *Employees:* 150
Tel: 01733 355720 *Website:* thepeterboroughschool.co.uk
Activities: Education, training
Address: The Peterborough School, Thorpe Road, Peterborough, PE3 6AP
Trustees: Mrs Lydia Frisby, Professor Christopher Howe, Mr Peter Southern, Rev Ian Christopher Black, Mrs Jacqueline Thompson, Mr Paul Thomas Simmons, Mrs Pamela Jane Dalgliesh, Ms Lynne Ayres LLB, Mrs Elizabeth Payne, Mr Dickon Sandbach, Mrs Katie Caroline Hart, Mr Philip Hayes, Miss Helen Louise Milligan
Income: £6,245,499 [2017]; £5,921,870 [2016]; £5,844,336 [2015]; £5,181,242 [2014]; £4,713,763 [2013]

Peterborough Winter Sports Club
Registered: 24 Sep 2012 *Employees:* 90 *Volunteers:* 20
Tel: 01733 260222
Activities: Education, training; advancement of health or saving of lives; disability; amateur sport; economic, community development, employment
Address: Planet Ice Ltd, Ice Rink, 1 Mallard Road, Peterborough, PE3 8YN
Trustees: Mr Darren Green, Mr Heath Rhodes, Mr Tim Fife, Mr Dominic McDermott
Income: £3,554,732 [2016]; £2,848,267 [2015]; £962,757 [2014]; £76,294 [2013]

Petrus Community
Registered: 3 Mar 1981 *Employees:* 41 *Volunteers:* 80
Tel: 01706 345844 *Website:* petrus.org.uk
Activities: General charitable purposes; accommodation, housing
Address: Craig Lee House, 25 Church Lane, Rochdale, OL16 1NR
Trustees: Mrs Lynda Robinson, Mr Christopher Richard Blackwell, Mrs Jean Jenkins, Mrs Collette Banton, Mr Addie Giwa, Ms Anne Fleming, Mr Patrick Culkin, Mr Andrew Underdown, Dr Elvet Edward Smith, Dr Michael Birkett
Income: £2,058,032 [2017]; £1,892,176 [2016]; £1,485,519 [2015]; £1,419,409 [2014]; £1,307,094 [2013]

Petworth Cottage Nursing Home
Registered: 21 Oct 1996 *Employees:* 45 *Volunteers:* 40
Tel: 01798 342391
Activities: The advancement of health or saving of lives
Address: Wisteria House, Market Square, Petworth, W Sussex, GU28 0AJ
Trustees: Mr Andrew William Brooke Solicitor, Mr David Heath Mathieson Burrell, Dr Graham Lyons, Miss Samantha Elizabeth Spriggs, Dr Anthony John Smoker, Mr Thomas Robert William Longmore, Mr Christopher Richard Hubbard, Dr Simon Pett, Mr Timothy John Barrington
Income: £1,798,698 [2016]; £1,216,232 [2015]; £1,439,300 [2014]; £931,283 [2013]; £994,815 [2012]

The Pharo Foundation
Registered: 28 Jul 2011 *Employees:* 14
Tel: 020 7838 0266 *Website:* pharofoundation.org
Activities: Economic, community development, employment
Address: 3rd Floor, 154 Brompton Road, London, SW3 1HX
Trustees: Mr Guillaume Henri Andre Fonkenell, Mr Matthieu Baumgartner, Mr Christophe Beauvilain, Ms Gulden Kazandag, Ms Farah Jirdeh, Mr Papa Mbor Nicolas Sagna
Income: £1,474,292 [2016]; £4,089,897 [2015]; £3,317,765 [2014]; £3,128,597 [2013]; £4,047,007 [2012]

Phenomen Trust
Registered: 20 May 2015 *Employees:* 17
Tel: 07917 923060
Activities: General charitable purposes; education, training
Address: 100 Picadilly, London, W1J 7NH
Trustees: Mr Anthony Julius, Ms Susanne Marian, Mr Simon Shvarts, Ms Swietlana Dragajewa-Turowska
Income: £4,965,117 [2016]; £330,948 [2015]

Philadelphia Church of God
Registered: 9 Mar 1995 *Employees:* 18 *Volunteers:* 4
Tel: 01789 581900 *Website:* pcog.org
Activities: Religious activities
Address: Edstone Hall, Wootton Wawen, Henley in Arden, Warwicks, B95 6DD
Trustees: Mr Calvert Howard, Mr Andrew Locher, Mr Brent Nagtegaal, Mr Gerald Flurry, Mr Wayne Turgeon
Income: £1,016,343 [2015]; £418,199 [2014]; £351,081 [2013]; £319,852 [2012]

The Philadelphia Network Limited
Registered: 16 Mar 2010 *Employees:* 28 *Volunteers:* 230
Tel: 0114 241 9560 *Website:* ncsheffield.org
Activities: The prevention or relief of poverty; religious activities; other charitable purposes
Address: St Thomas Church, 6 Gilpin Street, Sheffield, S6 3BL
Trustees: Rev P Findley, Mr J S Wilson, Mr J Burch, Mrs Rachel Marshall, Dr A Adebajo, Mr Brian Gooch, Mrs Miriam Cates
Income: £1,204,082 [2016]; £1,499,607 [2015]; £1,895,462 [2014]; £1,499,276 [2013]; £1,440,837 [2012]

Philharmonia Ltd
Registered: 28 Nov 1966 *Employees:* 42 *Volunteers:* 1
Tel: 020 7921 3940 *Website:* philharmonia.co.uk
Activities: Education, training; arts, culture, heritage, science
Address: Philharmonia Ltd, 6 Chancel Street, London, SE1 0UX
Trustees: Rev John Wates, Mr Laurent Ben Slimane, Mr Robin
O'Neill, Ms Heidi Krutzen, Mr Rupert Harry Darbyshire, Mr Michael
Fuller, Ms Kira Doherty, Mr Christian Geldsetzer, Ms Victoria Irish,
Ms Carol Jennifer Hultmark
Income: £11,353,790 [2017]; £10,325,127 [2016]; £10,334,379
[2015]; £9,483,315 [2014]; £11,594,334 [2013]

The Reginald M Phillips Charitable Foundation
Registered: 8 Nov 1965
Tel: 0345 304 2424
Activities: Education, training; advancement of health or saving of
lives
Address: 6th Floor, Trinity Quay 2, Avon Street, Bristol, BS2 0PT
Trustees: Natwest Trust Services
Income: £7,424,468 [2017]; £400,264 [2016]; £216,449 [2015];
£217,956 [2014]; £220,418 [2013]

Philo Trust
Registered: 9 Dec 1982 *Employees:* 10 *Volunteers:* 6
Tel: 01923 287777 *Website:* philotrust.com
Activities: Education, training; religious activities
Address: Witton House, Lower Road, Chorleywood,
Rickmansworth, Herts, WD3 5LB
Trustees: Mrs Juanita Baker, Mr Terry Baker, Mr Adrian Bignell,
Mr Peter Wright, Mr Mike Carson, Mr Alex Stewart-Clark
Income: £1,415,234 [2017]; £797,863 [2016]; £755,012 [2015];
£712,769 [2014]; £620,563 [2013]

Phoenix House
Registered: 19 Jul 1982 *Employees:* 447 *Volunteers:* 178
Tel: 020 7234 9740 *Website:* phoenix-futures.org.uk
Activities: General charitable purposes; education, training;
advancement of health or saving of lives; accommodation, housing;
environment, conservation, heritage; economic, community
development, employment
Address: 68 Newington Causeway, London, SE1 6DF
Trustees: Ms Anne Hooper, Annie Bartlett, Dr Karim Dar, Sue
Ellenby, Emanuele Labovitch, Susan Kinnaird, Ian Watson,
Mr James Cook, Dr Michael Ewart, Iain McGourty, Dorothy Brown
Income: £21,095,000 [2017]; £25,171,000 [2016]; £28,253,000
[2015]; £27,571,000 [2014]; £23,180,246 [2013]

Phoenix Sports and Recreation (Rotherham)
Registered: 26 Apr 2016 *Employees:* 42
Tel: 01709 363788 *Website:* phoenixsportsrecreation.co.uk
Activities: The advancement of health or saving of lives;
arts, culture, heritage, science; amateur sport; environment,
conservation, heritage; recreation
Address: Phoenix Sports & Recreation Rotherham, Pavilion Lane,
Brinsworth, Rotherham, S Yorks, S60 5PA
Trustees: Mr Carl Roderic Brown, Mr Kenneth Dyson, Mr Michael
Windle, Mr Neil Watkins, Mr Roger Spenceley, Mr Justin Scott
Carpenter, Mr Martin Read, Mr Michael John Marsden, Mr Nicholas
Mark Evison
Income: £4,877,771 [2017]

The Photographers' Gallery Ltd
Registered: 9 Jun 1971 *Employees:* 41
Tel: 020 7087 9318 *Website:* thephotographersgallery.org.uk
Activities: General charitable purposes; education, training; arts,
culture, heritage, science
Address: The Photographers Gallery Ltd, 16 Ramillies Street,
London, W1F 7LW
Trustees: Mrs Myfanwy Barrett, Alex Hess, Matthew Stephenson,
Ms Melanie Manchot, Jonathan Shaw, Jananne Al-Ani
Income: £3,558,145 [2017]; £3,447,327 [2016]; £3,117,757 [2015];
£3,117,757 [2014]; £3,458,899 [2013]

Phyllis Tuckwell Memorial Hospice Ltd
Registered: 8 Sep 1972 *Employees:* 187 *Volunteers:* 1,025
Tel: 01252 729402 *Website:* pth.org.uk
Activities: Education, training; advancement of health or saving of
lives; disability
Address: Phyllis Tuckwell Memorial Hospice, Waverley Lane,
Farnham, Surrey, GU9 8BL
Trustees: Mr Michael Maher, Dr David Eyre-Brook, Mr Kenneth
Kent, Mrs Helen Franklin, Ms Rosy Anand, Ms Veronica Carter,
Mr Ian Trotter, Mrs Anne Whelan, Professor Michael Bailey,
Mr Kenneth Ratcliff
Income: £9,902,366 [2017]; £9,777,846 [2016]; £7,344,987 [2015];
£7,748,169 [2014]; £6,119,163 [2013]

The Physiological Society
Registered: 28 Sep 1962 *Employees:* 23 *Volunteers:* 100
Tel: 020 7269 5714 *Website:* physoc.org
Activities: Education, training; advancement of health or saving of
lives; accommodation, housing; arts, culture, heritage, science;
other charitable purposes
Address: The Physiological Society, Hodgkin Huxley House,
30 Farringdon Lane, London, EC1R 3AW
Trustees: Dr Rachel Tribe, Dr Susan Deuchars, Dr Philip
Aaronson, Professor Frank Sengpiel, Dr Holly Shiels, Federico
Formenti, Sarah Hall, Dr Elizabeth Sheader, Dr Lucy Donaldson,
Prof Deborah Baines, Prof David Eisner, Dr Guy Bewick,
Prof Graham McGeown, Bridget Lumb, Dr Stefan Trapp,
Dr Charlotte Haigh
Income: £4,205,000 [2016]; £3,815,757 [2015]; £3,985,138 [2014];
£4,313,276 [2013]; £4,178,000 [2012]

Picker Institute Europe
Registered: 21 Jul 2000 *Employees:* 53 *Volunteers:* 58
Tel: 01865 208100 *Website:* pickereurope.org
Activities: The advancement of health or saving of lives
Address: Picker Institute Europe, Buxton Court, 3 West Way,
Oxford, OX2 0JB
Trustees: Professor Wendy Reid, Mr Paul Blunden, Ms Elizabeth
Hampson, Mrs Sally Ann Sykes, Mrs Annie Laverty, Mr Stuart Bell,
Dr Ann Abraham, Ms Ronny Odegbami, Professor Aileen Clarke
Income: £4,599,000 [2017]; £4,933,000 [2016]; £4,962,000 [2015];
£4,651,595 [2014]; £4,548,390 [2013]

Pickering and Ferens Homes
Registered: 20 Oct 1992 *Employees:* 35 *Volunteers:* 1
Tel: 01482 223783 *Website:* pfh.org.uk
Activities: Accommodation, housing
Address: Pickering & Ferens Homes, Silvester House,
Silvester Street, Hull, HU1 3HA
Trustees: Councillor Peter Allen, Brian Godfrey Burley, Vanessa
Walker, Mr John Holliday, Councillor Gwen Lunn, Mr Paul Common,
Mrs Cheryl Walker, Tom Hogan, Mr Peter Stones, Mr Andy Gladwin,
Mr George Stewart, Mrs Lucie Bryan
Income: £7,673,374 [2017]; £7,577,042 [2016]; £6,886,818 [2015];
£6,734,623 [2014]; £6,637,638 [2013]

The Piece Hall Trust
Registered: 7 May 2014 *Employees:* 13
Tel: 01422 525203 *Website:* thepiecehall.co.uk
Activities: Education, training; arts, culture, heritage, science; environment, conservation, heritage; economic, community development, employment
Address: The Piece Hall, Blackledge, Halifax, W Yorks, HX1 1RE
Trustees: Mr Roger Marsh, Mr Clive Roland Lloyd, Mrs Rupinder Kaur Ashworth, Gavin Morton, Mrs Nicola Chance Thompson, Mr Roger Andrew Harvey OBE, Mr Stephen Baines, Mr Timothy John Swift, Roland Stross, Mrs Laura Jane Crawford
Income: £1,252,348 [2017]; £283,428 [2016]; £250,050 [2015]

Pilgrim Homes (formerly Aged Pilgrims' Friend Society)
Registered: 21 May 1965 *Employees:* 181 *Volunteers:* 250
Tel: 0300 303 1405 *Website:* pilgrimsfriend.org.uk
Activities: The advancement of health or saving of lives; prevention or relief of poverty; accommodation, housing; religious activities
Address: Pilgrims' Friend Society, 175 Tower Bridge Road, London, SE1 2AL
Trustees: APFS 1807
Income: £2,548,000 [2017]; £12,187,000 [2016]; £8,533,000 [2015]; £9,078,000 [2014]; £7,555,000 [2013]

The Pilgrim Trust
Registered: 22 Sep 1962 *Employees:* 3
Tel: 020 7834 6510 *Website:* thepilgrimtrust.org.uk
Activities: Arts, culture, heritage, science; environment, conservation, heritage; other charitable purposes
Address: 3rd Floor, Ebury Gate, 23 Lower Belgrave Street, London, SW1W 0NR
Trustees: Mr David Barrie, Professor Sir Colin Blakemore FMedSci FRS, Mr Michael Baughan, Ms Caroline Butler, Sarah Elizabeth Staniforth CBE, Lady Sarah Riddell LVO, Sir Mark Jones, Mr James Fergusson, Mr Simon Antrobus, Kevin Pakenham
Income: £1,846,313 [2016]; £1,773,254 [2015]; £1,627,359 [2014]; £1,886,604 [2013]; £1,625,647 [2012]

Pilgrims Hospices in East Kent
Registered: 28 Aug 1986 *Employees:* 351 *Volunteers:* 1,700
Tel: 01227 812601 *Website:* pilgrimshospices.org
Activities: Other charitable purposes
Address: 56 London Road, Canterbury, Kent, CT2 8JA
Trustees: Mr Richard Davis, Mr Simon Harvey Perks, Ms Stephanie Bates, Mr Terry Smith, Rt Rev Anthony Turnbull, Mrs Margo Laing, Mrs Karen Warden, Mr Philip Bradshaw, Dr Ronald McWilliams, Mr Grahame Connor, Professor Jennifer Billings, Miss Elizabeth Sharp, Mr Hereward Harrison, Mr Paul Williamson, Dr Ruth Wilsom
Income: £13,915,000 [2017]; £12,024,587 [2016]; £12,612,000 [2015]; £12,572,000 [2014]; £11,959,000 [2013]

Pilgrims' Friend Society
Registered: 16 May 1995 *Employees:* 460 *Volunteers:* 380
Tel: 0300 303 1405 *Website:* pilgrimsfriend.org.uk
Activities: The advancement of health or saving of lives; prevention or relief of poverty; accommodation, housing; religious activities
Address: Pilgrims' Friend Society, 175 Tower Bridge Road, London, SE1 2AL
Trustees: Mr Alan Richard Copeman, Mr Robin Barry Turnbull, Mr Andrew Symonds, Mr Thomas John Creedy, Mr Bryan Roger Jarvis, Mr Alan John Hare, Dr Judith Ann McLaren, Mrs Genefer Denise Espejo
Income: £5,749,000 [2017]; £6,133,000 [2016]; £4,096,580 [2015]; £1,283,517 [2014]; £1,297,584 [2013]

The Pilgrims' School
Registered: 10 Apr 2002 *Employees:* 94
Tel: 01962 857602 *Website:* thepilgrims-school.co.uk
Activities: Education, training; religious activities
Address: Pilgrims School, 3 The Close, Winchester, Hants, SO23 9LT
Trustees: Dr Helen Lesley Harvey, Mr Nicholas Wilks, Caspar Ridley, Dr James Webster, Mike Wilson, George Medd, Michael Wheeler, Dean Catherine Ogle, Mr Martin Bruce, Mrs Margaret Chin-Wolf, Rev Susan Marilyn Wallace, Dominic Luckett, Stuart Woodward
Income: £4,493,901 [2017]; £4,137,531 [2016]; £3,907,212 [2015]; £3,973,512 [2014]; £3,925,470 [2013]

The Guy Pilkington Memorial Home Limited
Registered: 26 Nov 1973 *Employees:* 191
Tel: 01744 746401 *Website:* fairfield.org.uk
Activities: Education, training; advancement of health or saving of lives; disability
Address: The Guy Pilkington Memorial Home, Crank Road, St Helens, Merseyside, WA11 7RS
Trustees: Mr John Watts, Mrs Carolyn Dodwell, Mr K Suraliwala, Mr G Hammond, Mr Len Marlow, Dr Colin Ince, Mr Cyril Barratt, Mrs R Floyd, Mr C Bridge
Income: £12,822,182 [2016]; £12,136,090 [2015]; £11,797,035 [2014]; £11,559,996 [2013]; £10,502,798 [2012]

The Cecil and Alan Pilkington Trust Fund
Registered: 8 Feb 1965 *Employees:* 76 *Volunteers:* 14
Tel: 01744 457902 *Website:* pilkingtonfamilytrust.com
Activities: General charitable purposes; prevention or relief of poverty
Address: Welfare Centre, Chalon Way, St Helens, Merseyside, WA10 1AU
Trustees: Pilkington Employees Trustee No 1 Ltd, Pilkington Employees Trustee No 2 Limited
Income: £3,810,266 [2017]; £3,742,604 [2016]; £3,560,718 [2015]; £3,707,969 [2014]; £3,384,091 [2013]

Pilotlight
Registered: 6 Dec 1996 *Employees:* 19 *Volunteers:* 447
Tel: 020 3440 9302 *Website:* pilotlight.org.uk
Activities: General charitable purposes; prevention or relief of poverty; economic, community development, employment
Address: c/o EPE Administration Limited, Audrey House, 16-20 Ely Place, London, EC1N 6SN
Trustees: Mr Graham Clempson, Mr Kevin Bone, Ms Christina Alexandrou, Mr Christopher James Connelly, Mr Jose Salas, Ms Andrea Felizitas Mathilde Sinclair, Mr Scott Greenhalgh, Ms Tulsi Naidu, Mr Gary Hale
Income: £1,149,145 [2017]; £1,224,792 [2016]; £954,450 [2015]; £1,183,806 [2014]; £1,326,599 [2013]

Pinewood School Ltd
Registered: 1 Nov 1962 *Employees:* 94 *Volunteers:* 1
Tel: 01793 784808 *Website:* pinewoodschool.co.uk
Activities: Education, training
Address: Pinewood School, Bourton, Swindon, Wilts, SN6 8HZ
Trustees: Mr Philip James Lough, Mr Nick Cleverley, Mr Robin Badham-Thornhill, Mr Guy Peter Woodroffe Foster, Mr Edward George Mawle, Mr Adrian Paul Ballard, Mrs Emma Ann Cripwell, Mr Richard Ian White, Mr David Fawcus, Mrs Helen Wilkes, Mr James Caldwell Campbell, Mr Julian Charles Birch, Mrs Catherine Ann Mary France, Mr Randal Timothy Brown, Mrs Rebecca Jane Dougall
Income: £6,192,416 [2017]; £6,068,484 [2016]; £5,824,475 [2015]; £5,783,564 [2014]; £5,292,842 [2013]

Pioneer Theatres Limited
Registered: 15 Apr 1964 *Employees:* 98 *Volunteers:* 20
Website: stratfordeast.com
Activities: Education, training; arts, culture, heritage, science
Address: Theatre Royal Stratford East, Gerry Raffles Square, London, E15 1BN
Trustees: Mr Mark Pritchard, Mr Paul O'Leary, Mr Derek Joseph, Ms Hazel Province, Ken Clark, Mr Andrew Cowan, Ms Deborah Mattinson, Ms Josephine Melville, Rt Hon Dame Margaret Hodge
Income: £3,778,262 [2017]; £3,608,031 [2016]; £3,113,662 [2015]; £3,263,362 [2014]; £3,281,022 [2013]

Pioneering Care Partnership
Registered: 2 Feb 1998 *Employees:* 75 *Volunteers:* 176
Tel: 01325 321234 *Website:* pcp.uk.net
Activities: Education, training; advancement of health or saving of lives; disability; economic, community development, employment; recreation
Address: Pioneering Care Centre, Carers Way, Newton Aycliffe, Co Durham, DL5 4SF
Trustees: Mr Brian Crawford Wilson, Ms Brenda Davidson, Melanie Fordham, Mr Barry Knevitt, Mrs Carol Briggs, Dr Marta Evans, Mrs Angela Dinsdale, Mrs Heather Brewster
Income: £2,907,084 [2017]; £2,654,968 [2016]; £2,620,232 [2015]; £2,281,951 [2014]; £1,490,676 [2013]

Pioneers UK Ministries
Registered: 29 Apr 1994 *Employees:* 54 *Volunteers:* 20
Website: pioneers-uk.org
Activities: Education, training; advancement of health or saving of lives; prevention or relief of poverty; overseas aid, famine relief; religious activities
Address: Bawtry Hall, South Parade, Bawtry, Doncaster, S Yorks, DN10 6JH
Trustees: Mr David Ware, Dr Julie Hickson, Mrs Kate Register, Dr C J Bignell, Mr David Maddock, Mr Peter Maddock, Steve Jenkins, Katy McConkey
Income: £1,303,011 [2016]; £1,066,587 [2015]; £1,206,997 [2014]; £1,086,434 [2013]; £949,527 [2012]

The Pious Society of The Daughters of St Paul
Registered: 6 Feb 1987 *Employees:* 22
Tel: 01753 577629 *Website:* paulineuk.org
Activities: Education, training; religious activities
Address: Middle Green, Slough, Berks, SL3 6BS
Trustees: Sister Mary Connell FSP, Sister Angela Grant FSP, Sister Gregoria Mignolli FSP, Sister Germana Santos FSP
Income: £3,078,319 [2016]; £1,208,026 [2015]; £1,247,584 [2014]; £1,338,241 [2013]; £1,530,328 [2012]

Pipers Corner School
Registered: 25 Oct 1962 *Employees:* 151 *Volunteers:* 10
Tel: 01494 719801 *Website:* piperscorner.co.uk
Activities: Education, training
Address: Pipers Corner School Ltd, Pipers Lane, Great Kingshill, High Wycombe, Bucks, HP15 6LP
Trustees: Lady Ann Redgrave, Professor Bryan Mogford, Mr Hugh Roberts, Mr Philip Wayne, Mr Adrian Cannon, Mrs Elizabeth Carrighan, Mr Marcus Harborne, Lady Allison, Rev Helen Elizabeth Peters, Ms Helen Morton, Mrs Janet Smith, Mrs Joan Ingram
Income: £9,569,057 [2017]; £9,506,920 [2016]; £8,685,162 [2015]; £8,244,723 [2014]; £7,873,357 [2013]

The Pirbright Institute
Registered: 25 Jul 1977 *Employees:* 321
Website: pirbright.ac.uk
Activities: Education, training
Address: 86 Meadow Close, Farmoor, Oxford, OX2 9NZ
Trustees: Professor Quintin McKellar CBE, Mr Mike Samuel, Professor John Stephenson, Dr Vanessa Mayatt, Mr Roger Louth, Dr Theo Kanellos, Professor David Rowlands, Sir Bertie Ross
Income: £34,495,000 [2017]; £39,368,000 [2016]; £63,732,000 [2015]; £61,553,000 [2014]; £82,994,000 [2013]

Place2Be
Registered: 12 Sep 1994 *Employees:* 404 *Volunteers:* 1,200
Website: place2be.org.uk
Activities: Education, training; advancement of health or saving of lives
Address: 175-179 St John Street, London, EC1V 4LW
Trustees: Mrs Benita Margaret Refson, Miss Elpha Mary Lecointe, Professor Eric Taylor, Mr William Russell, Mr Stephen Dorrell, Countess Louise Alice St Aldwyn, Mrs Sian Hill, Mr Simon MacKenzie-Smith, The Hon Robert Rayne, Professor Stephen Scott, Dr Robert Jezzard, Sir Charlie Mayfield, Mr Adrian Joseph Levy, Professor David Rose, Ms Elizabeth Greetham
Income: £13,791,000 [2017]; £14,823,000 [2016]; £11,839,000 [2015]; £9,277,000 [2014]; £7,384,000 [2013]

Plan International UK
Registered: 12 Aug 1978 *Employees:* 204 *Volunteers:* 37
Tel: 0300 777 9777 *Website:* plan-uk.org
Activities: Education, training; advancement of health or saving of lives; prevention or relief of poverty; overseas aid, famine relief; economic, community development, employment; human rights, religious or racial harmony, equality or diversity
Address: Plan International UK, 5-7 Cranwood Street, London, EC1V 9LH
Trustees: Lady Amanda Ellingworth, Professor Sir Ian Diamond, Mrs Meredith Niles, Ms Hanah Burgess, Ms Gillian Smith, Ms Olivia Beecham, Ms Jane French, Mr Richard Laing, Mr Spencer McHugh, Lara Oyesanya, Mr Richard Norman Street, Mr Adam Wood
Income: £64,262,000 [2017]; £70,160,000 [2016]; £80,442,000 [2015]; £63,170,000 [2014]; £52,949,000 [2013]

Plantlife International-The Wild Plant Conservation Charity
Registered: 3 Dec 1996 *Employees:* 44 *Volunteers:* 1,384
Tel: 01722 342738 *Website:* plantlife.org.uk
Activities: Environment, conservation, heritage
Address: Brewery House, 36 Milford Street, Salisbury, Wilts, SP1 2AP
Trustees: Mr Richard Benyon MP, Ms Ann Rowswell, Mr Simon Acland, Mr Robin Payne, Mrs Philippa Lyons, Dr Katherine Drayson, Mr Philip Mould OBE, Professor David Hill, Mrs Helen Priday, Dr Tim Stowe, Dr Rosetta Margaret Plummer, Mr Clive Aslet
Income: £3,250,355 [2017]; £2,805,902 [2016]; £2,974,957 [2015]; £2,472,298 [2014]; £1,906,272 [2013]

Play Adventures & Community Enrichment

Registered: 2 Oct 2012 *Employees:* 52
Tel: 020 7183 5120 *Website:* paceforall.com
Activities: Education, training; disability; prevention or relief of poverty; arts, culture, heritage, science; economic, community development, employment; recreation
Address: Fairfield Play Centre, Mary Terrace, London, NW1 7LR
Trustees: Miss Le Ho, Mr Colin Gale, Miss Jennifer Duncan, Mrs Teresa Bolton, Mr John Mann, Ms Kathleen Kadri, Mr Matthew Jennings
Income: £1,084,454 [2016]; £860,152 [2015]; £746,490 [2014]; £506,687 [2013]

The Pleasance Theatre Trust

Registered: 22 Nov 1995 *Employees:* 33
Tel: 020 8995 3041 *Website:* pleasance.co.uk
Activities: Arts, culture, heritage, science
Address: 28 Ellesmere Road, London, W4 4QH
Trustees: Mr Richard Michael House, Mr Piers Francis Torday, Mr David Johnson, Ms Letitia Graham, Jeremy Lucas, Mr Andrew Leigh, Alan Brown
Income: £2,619,500 [2016]; £2,504,682 [2015]; £2,275,270 [2014]; £2,226,177 [2013]; £2,308,636 [2012]

Plunkett Foundation

Registered: 7 Jan 1964 *Employees:* 14
Website: plunkett.co.uk
Activities: Education, training; economic, community development, employment
Address: The Quadrangle, Banbury Road, Woodstock, Oxon, OX20 1LH
Trustees: Mr David Arthur Dickman, Mrs Karen Lowthrop, Ms Jane Elizabetth Ryall, Mrs Margaret A Clark, Mrs Susan Jean Boer, Ms Helen Gillian Seymour, Dr Wilmoth Gibson, Mr Thomas Kee Scanlon, Mr Julian Alexander McGregor Ross, Mr Richard Anscombe
Income: £1,220,644 [2016]; £814,608 [2015]; £1,064,783 [2014]; £1,014,512 [2013]; £2,625,363 [2012]

Plymouth Age Concern

Registered: 30 Apr 1980 *Employees:* 101 *Volunteers:* 50
Tel: 01752 256020 *Website:* ageukplymouth.org.uk
Activities: The advancement of health or saving of lives; disability; prevention or relief of poverty
Address: Plymouth Age Concern, The William & Patricia Venton Centre, Astor Drive, Plymouth, PL4 9RD
Trustees: Linda Wheeler, Mrs Mary McClarey, Mr Benny Wright, Ms Naomi Hoare, Mrs Stuart Kegan, Mrs Susan Williams, Mrs Elizabeth Edwards-Smith, Mrs Andrea Wright, Mrs Donna Barnes
Income: £1,292,649 [2017]; £1,784,750 [2016]; £1,942,913 [2015]; £2,009,421 [2014]; £2,194,319 [2013]

Plymouth Argyle Football in the Community Trust

Registered: 31 Mar 2009 *Employees:* 96 *Volunteers:* 15
Tel: 01752 562561 *Website:* argylecommunitytrust.co.uk
Activities: Education, training; amateur sport
Address: Plymouth Argyle Football Co Ltd, Home Park, Plymouth, PL2 3DQ
Trustees: Mr Paul Baker, Mr Gordon Bennett, Mrs Cindy Dennerly, Mr John Morgan, Captain David Tall OBE, Mr Steven Brownlow, Mr Paul Berne
Income: £1,734,285 [2016]; £1,190,318 [2015]; £842,183 [2014]; £704,062 [2013]; £768,659 [2012]

Plymouth Citizens Advice Bureaux

Registered: 13 Apr 1992 *Employees:* 64 *Volunteers:* 31
Tel: 01752 507709 *Website:* plymouthcab.org.uk
Activities: General charitable purposes; education, training; prevention or relief of poverty
Address: Cobourg House, 32 Mayflower Street, Plymouth, PL1 1QX
Trustees: Mr David Morgan, Mr Luke Fisher, Mr Jon Abrahams, Ms Paula Ashworth, Paul Williams, Mr Thomas Cox
Income: £1,652,622 [2017]; £1,757,042 [2016]; £2,020,489 [2015]; £1,722,161 [2014]; £1,113,268 [2013]

Plymouth College and St Dunstan's Abbey Schools Charity

Registered: 19 Aug 2004 *Employees:* 240 *Volunteers:* 2
Tel: 01752 505107 *Website:* plymouthcollege.com
Activities: Education, training
Address: Plymouth College, Ford Park, Plymouth, PL4 6RN
Trustees: Mr Peter Harvey Lowson, Mr David Woodgate, Mrs Clare Hammond, Dr Penelope Atkinson, Dr Andrew Graham Williams, Mr Christopher Morton, Mrs Alison Mills, Mrs Samantha Coutinho, Professor David Huntley, Dr Sue Thorpe, Mrs Kelly Marie Davis, Mr Adrian Brett
Income: £9,032,605 [2017]; £8,908,739 [2016]; £9,504,755 [2015]; £9,957,317 [2014]; £9,057,874 [2013]

Plymouth Diocesan Trust

Registered: 19 Aug 1964 *Employees:* 152 *Volunteers:* 510
Tel: 01364 645383 *Website:* plymouth-diocese.org.uk
Activities: Education, training; prevention or relief of poverty; religious activities
Address: Diocese of Plymouth, St Boniface House, Ashburton, Newton Abbot, Devon, TQ13 7JL
Trustees: Plymouth Roman Catholic Diocesan Trustees Registered
Income: £6,838,000 [2017]; £8,102,000 [2016]; £7,584,000 [2015]; £6,888,000 [2014]; £7,552,000 [2013]

Plymouth Hospitals General Charity and Other Related Charities

Registered: 15 Aug 1995 *Employees:* 2 *Volunteers:* 100
Tel: 01752 437047 *Website:* plymouthhospitals.nhs.uk
Activities: The advancement of health or saving of lives
Address: Charitable Funds Accounting, Nu Building, Derriford Business Park, 1 Brest Road, Derriford, Plymouth, PL6 5YE
Trustees: Plymouth Hospitals NHS Trust
Income: £1,319,718 [2017]; £1,496,609 [2016]; £1,967,377 [2015]; £985,502 [2014]; £865,526 [2013]

Plymouth Marine Laboratory

Registered: 20 Mar 2002 *Employees:* 151 *Volunteers:* 3
Tel: 01752 633100 *Website:* pml.ac.uk
Activities: Education, training; arts, culture, heritage, science; environment, conservation, heritage
Address: Plymouth Marine Laboratory, Prospect Place, Plymouth, PL1 3DH
Trustees: Professor Ralph Rayner, The Baroness Watkins of Tavistock, Nick Buckland, Mrs Janice Timberlake, Mr Nigel John Godefroy, Sir James Burnell-Nugent KCB CBE, Professor Bess Ward, Mr Simon Sherrard, Professor Timothy Jickells
Income: £10,681,000 [2017]; £9,980,000 [2016]; £10,879,016 [2015]; £10,897,024 [2014]; £11,274,063 [2013]

Plymouth Society for Mentally Handicapped
Registered: 2 Jun 1967 *Employees:* 75 *Volunteers:* 50
Tel: 01752 773333 *Website:* plymouthhighburytrust.org.uk
Activities: Education, training; disability
Address: Plymouth Highbury Trust, 207 Outland Road, Plymouth, PL2 3PF
Trustees: Mrs Joey Warren, Mrs Rosemary Stoggall, Mrs Hilary Ann Harris, Mr David Behan, Mrs Wendy Elizabeth Brimmicombe, Mrs Janis Elizabeth Jones, Mr Peter Richards
Income: £1,503,380 [2017]; £1,354,481 [2016]; £1,237,408 [2015]; £1,273,032 [2014]; £1,172,727 [2013]

Plymouth Young Men's Christian Association - YMCA
Registered: 17 Dec 1997 *Employees:* 47 *Volunteers:* 14
Tel: 01752 201915 *Website:* ymcaplymouth.org.uk
Activities: General charitable purposes; education, training; advancement of health or saving of lives; disability; prevention or relief of poverty; religious activities; amateur sport; economic, community development, employment; recreation; other charitable purposes
Address: YMCA, Honicknowle Lane, Plymouth, PL5 3NG
Trustees: Mr David Watson, Mr Christopher William Goodman, Mr Micheal Reburn, Mr Tim Shobrook, Mr John Goad, Miss Rachel Steele, Ms Ashima Sawhney, Mr John Coates, Mrs Helen Jayne Meneilly, Mr Ernest Nicholas Edgcumbe, Mr David John Warwick Baylis
Income: £1,538,601 [2017]; £1,588,288 [2016]; £1,632,109 [2015]; £1,629,426 [2014]; £1,594,671 [2013]

The Pocklington School Foundation
Registered: 28 Feb 1969 *Employees:* 204 *Volunteers:* 8
Tel: 01759 321200 *Website:* pocklingtonschool.com
Activities: Education, training
Address: Pocklington School, West Green, Pocklington, York, YO42 2NJ
Trustees: Pocklington School Trustee Ltd
Income: £11,134,117 [2017]; £11,192,214 [2016]; £11,887,740 [2015]; £10,408,294 [2014]; £9,910,732 [2013]

Thomas Pocklington Trust
Registered: 10 Apr 2006 *Employees:* 102 *Volunteers:* 459
Tel: 020 8995 0880 *Website:* pocklington-trust.org.uk
Activities: Education, training; advancement of health or saving of lives; disability; accommodation, housing; economic, community development, employment
Address: Thomas Pocklington Trust, Tavistock House South, Tavistock Square, London, WC1H 9LG
Trustees: Mr Rodney Powell, Mr Mervyn Williamson, Mr Philip James Longworth, Ms Fadeia Hossian, Matt Wadsworth, Mrs Jenny Pearce, Mr Alastair Balfour Chapman BSc FRICS, Mr Graham Arthur Findlay, Mr John Anthony Thompson, Ms Marsha Chantol De Cordova
Income: £6,152,000 [2017]; £6,278,000 [2016]; £8,444,000 [2015]; £8,495,000 [2014]; £9,539,000 [2013]

The Poetry Society
Registered: 20 Jul 1964 *Employees:* 13 *Volunteers:* 18
Tel: 020 7420 9880 *Website:* poetrysociety.org.uk
Activities: Education, training; arts, culture, heritage, science
Address: 22 Betterton Street, London, WC2H 9BX
Trustees: Mr Neil Reeder, Mr Andrew Smardon, Ms Catriona White, Ms Sarah Ellis, Mr Christopher Anthony Beckett, Ms Emma Dai'an Wright, Mr Jesper Groenveld, Ms Elizabeth Crump, Ms Kathryn Gray, Ms Mairi Johnson, Mrs Sarah Louise Thompson
Income: £1,087,351 [2017]; £899,172 [2016]; £924,033 [2015]; £828,147 [2014]; £784,722 [2013]

Polam Hall Darlington Limited
Registered: 29 Jun 2010 *Employees:* 87 *Volunteers:* 5
Tel: 01325 463383 *Website:* polamhall.com
Activities: Education, training
Address: Polam Hall School, Grange Road, Darlington, Co Durham, DL1 5PA
Trustees: Dr Mary Matheson Carr, Nicholas Millar, Mrs Clare Louise Curran, Sarah Pelham, Mrs Mary Patricia Vere Atkins
Income: £4,450,299 [2015]; £3,026,102 [2014]; £3,450,604 [2013]; £6,671,828 [2012]

Polesworth Group Homes Limited
Registered: 18 Jun 1991 *Employees:* 108 *Volunteers:* 2
Tel: 01827 896124 *Website:* polesworthhomes.co.uk
Activities: Disability; accommodation, housing; recreation
Address: Mrs Clare Forbes, Laurel End, Laurel Avenue, Polesworth, Tamworth, Staffs, B78 1LT
Trustees: Dr Susan Ann Barratt, Mrs Gillian Ann Irons, Mr David Lockwood, Mr Walter George Wilkinson, David Price, Mrs Ann Wilson
Income: £2,916,596 [2017]; £2,753,383 [2016]; £2,635,786 [2015]; £2,747,857 [2014]; £2,711,462 [2013]

The Police Dependants' Trust Limited
Registered: 21 Mar 2013 *Employees:* 6 *Volunteers:* 9
Tel: 020 8941 6907 *Website:* pdtrust.org
Activities: The advancement of health or saving of lives; disability; prevention or relief of poverty
Address: Police Dependants, 3 Mount Mews, Hampton, Surrey, TW12 2SH
Trustees: Mr Mark Lindsay, Bernard Higgins, Mr Stuart Edward Purdy, Mr Gordon Crossan, Andrea MacDonald, Tim Packham, Simon Bray, Tim Jackson, Mr Christopher Greany, Mr Neil Fraser Massey, Mr Paul Griffiths
Income: £1,262,137 [2017]; £982,058 [2016]; £1,387,991 [2015]; £1,404,243 [2014]

Police Now
Registered: 26 Jul 2016 *Employees:* 23
Tel: 07715 663832 *Website:* policenow.org.uk
Activities: Education, training; armed forces, emergency service efficiency
Address: Albert House, 250-254 Old Street, London, EC1V 9DD
Trustees: Robert Rothenberg, Clare Davies, Mrs Judith Clegg, Mr Dominic Fry, Mr James Bowler, Miss Amelia Tanner, Helen Ball, James Darley, Mr Martin Coleman, Mr Ian Powell, Mr Simon Woolley
Income: £5,739,204 [2017]

The Police Rehabilitation Centre
Registered: 17 Apr 2012 *Employees:* 144
Tel: 01491 874499 *Website:* flinthouse.co.uk
Activities: Armed forces, emergency service efficiency
Address: The Police Rehabilitation Centre, Flint House, Reading Road, Goring, Reading, Berks, RG8 0LL
Trustees: Dr Rhys William Hamilton, David Ball, Mr Simon Bray, Mr Clive Robert Field, Ms Samantha Jayne Willetts, Mrs Jenny Abbott, Mark Nurthen, Mr Kenneth James Marsh MBE, Mr Graham Gilbert, Dr Peter Russell Sudbury, Mr Stephen Bozward, Mr Daniel Murphy
Income: £5,549,212 [2016]; £5,701,020 [2015]; £4,782,959 [2014]; £5,028,882 [2013]; £2,505,754 [2012]

The Police Treatment Centres
Registered: 25 May 2012 *Employees:* 150 *Volunteers:* 8
Tel: 01423 504448 *Website:* thepolicetreatmentcentres.org
Activities: The advancement of health or saving of lives; disability; armed forces, emergency service efficiency
Address: Northern Police Convalescent Home, St Andrews, Harlow Moor Road, Harrogate, N Yorks, HG2 0AD
Trustees: Mr Alan Lees, Mr Mark Davis, Martin Fotheringham, Mr Guy King, Mr Conor Moore, Mr Nigel Bathgate, Mr Ian Hopkins, Mr George Clarke, Ms Rachel Alison Barber, Ms Lisa Winward, Mrs Andrea MacDonald, Mr Martin Lally, Mr David Simpson, Mr Mark Lindsay, Mr Raymond Dutton, Craig Grandison, Mr Liam Kelly, Mr David Orford, Mr Darren Townsend, Mr Jeremy Andrew Harris, Mr John Skelton, Mr John Patrick Robins, Ms Paula Booth, Mr Grant McDowall, Mr Dan Patrick Murphy, Mr Jason Harwin
Income: £5,518,323 [2016]; £4,451,175 [2015]; £4,713,865 [2014]; £4,652,516 [2013]; £4,992,767 [2012]

Policy Exchange Limited
Registered: 3 Mar 2003 *Employees:* 26
Tel: 020 7340 2650 *Website:* policyexchange.org.uk
Activities: Education, training
Address: 6th Floor, Policy Exchange, 8-10 Great George Street, London, SW1P 3AE
Trustees: Mr Andrew Roberts, Mr Edward Lee, Mr Robert Rosenkranz, General Sir Peter Wall GCB CBE ADC Gen, Professor Greta Jones, Lord Feldman of Elstree, The Hon Alexander Downer AC, Mr George Robinson, Ms Candida Gertler, Mr Roger Orf, Ms Diana Berry, Ms Charlotte Metcalf, Mr Nigel Wright
Income: £2,567,901 [2016]; £2,380,566 [2015]; £3,968,050 [2014]; £2,519,915 [2013]; £3,224,162 [2012]

The Polish Catholic Mission
Registered: 31 May 2007 *Employees:* 6 *Volunteers:* 1,317
Tel: 020 7226 3439 *Website:* pcmew.org
Activities: General charitable purposes; education, training; prevention or relief of poverty; religious activities
Address: Polish Catholic Mission, 2-4 Devonia Road, London, N1 8JJ
Trustees: Rev Janusz Tworek, Rev Stefan Wylezek, Ms Anna Zimand, Mrs Maria Aleksandra Rejman, Mrs Nelly Langer, Rev Krzysztof Tyliszczak, Mr Zenon Handzel, Mr Zygmunt Green, Rev Rafal Jaroslawski, Rev Romuald Szczodrowski
Income: £5,596,575 [2016]; £5,902,390 [2015]; £5,402,188 [2014]; £5,221,113 [2013]; £4,690,144 [2012]

Polish Social and Cultural Association Limited
Registered: 23 Aug 1965 *Employees:* 17 *Volunteers:* 70
Tel: 020 8746 3798 *Website:* posk.org
Activities: Education, training; arts, culture, heritage, science
Address: Polish Social & Cultural Association Ltd, 238-246 King Street, London, W6 0RF
Trustees: Dr Olgierd Romuald Lalko, Mrs Krystyna Bell, Mr Andrzej Zakrzewski, Dr Leszek Bojanowski, Mrs Joanna Mludzinska, Mr Piotr Kaczmarski, Mr Pawel Pastuszek, Mr Andrzej Formaniak, Mr Robert Wisniowski, Mr Richard Wojciech Tobiasiewicz, Ms Miroslawa Wrona, Mr Jakub Krupa
Income: £1,019,747 [2016]; £1,188,835 [2015]; £1,109,198 [2014]; £967,218 [2013]; £2,221,437 [2012]

Polka Children's Theatre Limited
Registered: 2 Oct 1968 *Employees:* 37 *Volunteers:* 6
Tel: 020 8545 8323 *Website:* polkatheatre.com
Activities: Education, training; disability; arts, culture, heritage, science
Address: 240 The Broadway, Wimbledon, London, SW19 1SB
Trustees: Nigel Halkes, Bilal Hafeez, Vivienne Creevey, Despo Stevens, Jane Moorman, Rebecca Holt, Sarah King, Mairi Brewis, Iain McNicol, Katy Manuel, Ms Nicola Theron, Lotte Wakeham
Income: £2,096,043 [2017]; £2,265,537 [2016]; £2,214,950 [2015]; £1,812,218 [2014]; £1,869,342 [2013]

Pompey in the Community
Registered: 1 Oct 2008 *Employees:* 89 *Volunteers:* 100
Website: pompeyitc.org.uk
Activities: General charitable purposes; education, training; advancement of health or saving of lives; disability; prevention or relief of poverty; amateur sport
Address: 7 The Crest, Waterlooville, Hants, PO7 5DG
Trustees: Ms Alison Lee, Mr Melvin Stuart Hartley, Lucy Smith, Forhad Ahmed, Mr Stephen Dale Frampton, Ms Jacqueline Ita Petula Jones, Isabella Pearson, Christina Burgess
Income: £2,002,549 [2017]; £1,822,886 [2016]; £1,482,611 [2015]; £1,403,632 [2014]; £1,307,374 [2013]

The Pontesbury Project for People with Special Needs
Registered: 21 Apr 2008 *Employees:* 57
Tel: 01743 790074
Activities: Disability
Address: Meadow Brook, Little Minsterley, Pontesbury, Minsterley, Shrewsbury, Salop, SY5 0BP
Trustees: Dr Ian Cuthbert Bradley, Jane Cooke, Mrs Shirley Maureen Small, Mrs Susan Audrey Picken
Income: £2,064,501 [2017]; £1,994,130 [2016]; £1,950,783 [2015]; £1,910,449 [2014]; £1,945,844 [2013]

The Pony Club
Registered: 25 Oct 1995 *Employees:* 25 *Volunteers:* 10,000
Tel: 024 7669 8300 *Website:* pcuk.org
Activities: Education, training; amateur sport; animals
Address: The Pony Club, National Agricultural Centre, Stoneleigh Park, Kenilworth, Warwicks, CV8 2RW
Trustees: Mr Christopher Bromfield, Mr Martin Dalziel Wright, Mrs Lucinda Mary Rose, Miss Hannah Westropp, Mrs Elizabeth Lowry, Mrs Claire Hetherington, Mr Andrew William James, Mrs Sha Starr, Mrs Clare Mary Gabrielle Valori
Income: £13,388,383 [2016]; £12,734,265 [2015]; £13,040,537 [2014]; £12,093,122 [2013]; £12,083,150 [2012]

Poole Arts Trust Limited
Registered: 24 Aug 1978 *Employees:* 44 *Volunteers:* 40
Tel: 01202 280000 *Website:* lighthousepoole.co.uk
Activities: Arts, culture, heritage, science
Address: Lighthouse, 21 Kingland Road, Poole, Dorset, BH15 1UG
Trustees: Mr Ian Metcalfe, Mr Robert Reeve, Mrs Sally Crawford, Mrs Amanda Stainer, Mrs Rowena Julie Gaston, Mr Mark Powell, Mr Amir Sadeh, Mr Michael Jeffries, Mrs Nicola Jane Oliver
Income: £6,413,011 [2017]; £5,172,928 [2016]; £3,817,380 [2015]; £3,708,967 [2014]; £3,651,026 [2013]

Poole Hospital NHS Foundation Trust Charitable Fund
Registered: 23 Oct 1996 *Employees:* 3 *Volunteers:* 260
Tel: 01202 665511 *Website:* poole.nhs.uk
Activities: The advancement of health or saving of lives
Address: Poole Hospital NHS Foundation Trust, Longfleet Road, Poole, Dorset, BH15 2JB
Trustees: Mr Philip Ernest Green, Mr Nick Ziebland, Mrs Debbie Fleming, Dr Calum McArthur, Mr Mark Anthony Orchard, Ms Patricia Reid, Mr Angus Donald Graham Wood, Mr Paul Miller, Mr David Peter Walden, Mr Mark Ashley Mould, Mr Stephen George Mount, Mrs Caroline Marion Tapster, Mr Steven Erskine
Income: £8,594,460 [2017]; £6,697,569 [2016]; £942,041 [2015]; £1,157,086 [2014]; £987,346 [2013]

Poor Servants of The Mother of God
Registered: 3 Dec 1963 *Employees:* 474 *Volunteers:* 60
Tel: 020 8788 4351 *Website:* poorservants.com
Activities: General charitable purposes; education, training; advancement of health or saving of lives; disability; prevention or relief of poverty; overseas aid, famine relief; accommodation, housing; religious activities; economic, community development, employment; other charitable purposes
Address: Maryfield Convent, Mount Angelus Road, Roehampton, London, SW15 4JA
Trustees: Sister Margaret Herlihy, Sr Rosarii O'Connor, Sr Kathleen Coleman, Sr Margaret Cashman, Sr Anne Curran, Sr Meki Ngemu
Income: £15,867,926 [2017]; £17,860,431 [2016]; £15,269,316 [2015]; £14,643,127 [2014]; £14,593,432 [2013]

Porchlight
Registered: 26 Apr 1974 *Employees:* 193 *Volunteers:* 117
Tel: 01227 760078 *Website:* porchlight.org.uk
Activities: Education, training; prevention or relief of poverty; accommodation, housing
Address: Porchlight, 18-19 Watling Street, Canterbury, Kent, CT1 2UA
Trustees: Mrs Patricia Unwin, Dr Susan Hornibrook, Mr Bob Porter, Mr Howard Cohn, Mr Thomas Evans, Mrs Celia Glynn-Williams, Mr Colin Wright, Mr Dominic Deeson, Ms Hilary Edridge
Income: £8,679,980 [2017]; £6,098,052 [2016]; £6,371,927 [2015]; £6,053,939 [2014]; £5,735,087 [2013]

Port Regis School Ltd
Registered: 4 Sep 1963 *Employees:* 200 *Volunteers:* 10
Tel: 01747 857885 *Website:* portregis.com
Activities: Education, training
Address: Macstead, Shorts Green Lane, Motcombe, Shaftesbury, Dorset, SP7 9PA
Trustees: Mr Christopher John Holloway, Mrs Claire Felicity MacDonald, Mr Jeremy John Hamer, Mrs Judy Williamson, Mr Oliver Hawkins, Mr Gavin White, Lady Cathryn Mary Cayley, Mr James Stevenson, Mr Anthony Oswald Cumine, Mrs Fiona Elisabeth Loveridge, Mr Stephen Edlmann, Mr Craig Considine, Mr William Gething, Mr Mark Aichroth, Mr Hugh Cocke
Income: £6,028,743 [2016]; £6,277,771 [2015]; £6,581,232 [2014]; £6,973,568 [2013]; £6,978,531 [2012]

The Port Sunlight Village Trust
Registered: 17 Mar 1999 *Employees:* 48 *Volunteers:* 70
Tel: 0151 644 4800 *Website:* portsunlightvillage.com
Activities: Environment, conservation, heritage
Address: 23 King Georges Drive, Wirral, Merseyside, CH62 5DX
Trustees: Mr John Cocker, Mr Peter David De Figueiredo, Mr Stephen Connolly, Mr John Jones, Miss Emma Chaplin, Mr Rob Young
Income: £3,248,353 [2017]; £3,109,711 [2016]; £2,813,966 [2015]; £2,729,911 [2014]; £2,629,607 [2013]

Sir John Port's Charity
Registered: 30 May 2002 *Employees:* 572
Tel: 01283 559200 *Website:* repton.org.uk
Activities: Education, training
Address: The Bursar, Repton School, Willington Road, Repton, Derby, DE65 6FH
Trustees: Mr Robert John Richard Owen MA, Dr Katharine Julia Dell, Mr Roy Bates, Sir Henry John Michaelevery Bt, Professor Alistair Mitchell Buchan, Mr David Nigel Vardon Churton, Mr Matthew James Charles Needham LLB, Mr Edward Mark Shires, Mr Andrew Michael Bock, Mrs Dawn Patricia Ward, Mr Roger Anthony Litchfield ACMA, Mrs Anne Elisabeth Hill JP, Mr Martin Wimbush, Mr Ian Richard Davenport, Mr William Tucker, Ms Kathryn Elizabeth Stone, Mr Andrew James Churchill, Mr Timothy James Hannam, Mrs Daphne St Clair Cawthorne
Income: £24,733,222 [2016]; £23,728,215 [2015]; £22,211,865 [2014]; £21,379,687 [2013]; £21,094,717 [2012]

Portland College
Registered: 22 Mar 1963 *Employees:* 374 *Volunteers:* 50
Tel: 01623 499101 *Website:* portland.ac.uk
Activities: Education, training; disability
Address: 10 Bull Lane, Matlock, Derbys, DE4 5LX
Trustees: Mr Alan Earnshaw, Mr Thalej Vasishta, Mrs Harvinder Atwal, Mr Nicholas Edward Aspley, Mr Dean Harry Fathers, Mr James Aleander, Mr Timothy Stewart Richmond, Mr Shaun Walsh, Dr Dawn Elizabeth Green, Mr Peter Arthur Emerson
Income: £10,336,000 [2017]; £9,270,000 [2016]; £9,812,149 [2015]; £10,018,256 [2014]; £10,793,606 [2013]

The Portland Trust
Registered: 26 Oct 2004 *Employees:* 15
Tel: 020 7182 7782 *Website:* portlandtrust.org
Activities: General charitable purposes; education, training; advancement of health or saving of lives; prevention or relief of poverty; economic, community development, employment
Address: The Portland Trust, 25 Farringdon Street, London, EC4A 4AB
Trustees: Sir Harry Solomon, Sir Michael Lawrence Davis, Sir Ronald Cohen, Mrs Nicola Cobbold
Income: £1,637,380 [2016]; £1,595,135 [2015]; £1,907,814 [2014]; £1,850,782 [2013]; £1,509,652 [2012]

Portsmouth Cultural Trust
Registered: 12 Aug 2013 *Employees:* 117 *Volunteers:* 3
Tel: 023 9283 4158 *Website:* portsmouthguildhall.org.uk
Activities: Education, training; arts, culture, heritage, science; environment, conservation, heritage; economic, community development, employment; recreation
Address: The Guildhall, Guildhall Square, Portsmouth, PO1 2AB
Trustees: Mr Simon Frost, Mr Anthony Brown, Mrs Jacquie Shaw, Mrs Linda Symes, Mrs Clare Elizabeth Hardy, Mr Declan Murphy, Mr Chris Gilder, Mr Nicholas Leach, Mr Luke Stubbs, Mr Gregory John Perry
Income: £1,921,142 [2017]; £1,838,801 [2016]; £1,877,949 [2015]; £2,004,376 [2014]

Portsmouth Diocesan Board of Finance

Registered: 8 Sep 1966 *Employees:* 32 *Volunteers:* 45
Website: portsmouth.anglican.org
Activities: Education, training; religious activities
Address: Portsmouth Diocesan Board of Finance, Peninsular House, Wharf Road, Portsmouth, PO2 8HB
Trustees: Canon Dr Hugh Mason, The Ven Peter Sutton, Miss Irene Anne James, Canon Lucy Docherty, Mr Robert Solomon, Canon David Bennison, The Revd Michael Ian Duff, The Revd Paul Richard Armstead, Mr Stuart Forster, Canon Hilary Spurgeon, The Reverend Marcus Bagg, Mrs Louise Clay, The Revd Dr Paul Martin Chamberlain, Mr Keith Archibald Doyle, Mr William George Berry, Reverend Canon Robert Charles White, Bishop of Portsmouth, The Very Revd David Brindley, Canon John Gwynn, Canon Debbie Sutton, The Revd Ian Snares, The Ven Gavin Collins, Mr Geoffrey Barwick, The Revd Canon Graham Morris, Rev Will Hughes, Mr Norman Chapman, The Ven Dr Joanne Woolway Grenfell, The Revd Alison Kerr, Mrs Mary Anne Crittenden, Mrs Jenny Hollingsworth
Income: £10,340,771 [2016]; £7,536,284 [2015]; £7,243,909 [2014]; £7,212,221 [2013]; £7,688,682 [2012]

The Portsmouth Grammar School

Registered: 31 Jul 1997 *Employees:* 282 *Volunteers:* 20
Tel: 023 9236 4213 *Website:* pgs.org.uk
Activities: Education, training
Address: Portsmouth Grammar School, High Street, Portsmouth, PO1 2LN
Trustees: The Very Revd David Brindley BD MTh MPhil AKC, Mrs Margaret Scott BSc, Mr Neil Degge Latham Cbe Bsc Msc Ceng Mimeche, Mr Walter J B Cha BA, Mr Philp Parkinson, Commodore Jeremy Rigby, Dr Martin Grossel, Mrs Rachel Duff, Mr Howard William Gordon Tuckett, Mr Brian Stewart Larkman BSc, Mr Michael Robert Coffin, Rev Edmund Newey, Mr Barry Martin, Mrs Fiona Jane Boulton, His Honour Judge Peter Lodder, Mrs Kathy Lee Carol Bishop, Mrs Anne Stanford
Income: £20,789,697 [2016]; £19,926,025 [2015]; £18,817,239 [2014]; £18,817,141 [2013]; £17,811,036 [2012]

Portsmouth Hospitals Charity

Registered: 14 Jul 1995 *Employees:* 7 *Volunteers:* 30
Website: porthosp.nhs.uk
Activities: General charitable purposes; education, training; advancement of health or saving of lives
Address: Queen Alexandra Hospital, Southwick Hill Road, Cosham, Portsmouth, PO6 3LY
Trustees: Portsmouth Hospitals N H S Trust
Income: £1,108,260 [2017]; £949,000 [2016]; £832,397 [2015]; £1,180,000 [2014]; £832,402 [2013]

Portsmouth Naval Base Property Trust

Registered: 12 Dec 1985 *Employees:* 79 *Volunteers:* 100
Tel: 023 9282 0921 *Website:* pnbpropertytrust.org
Activities: Arts, culture, heritage, science; environment, conservation, heritage; economic, community development, employment
Address: 19 College Road, HM Naval Base, Portsmouth, PO1 3LJ
Trustees: Rear Admiral Neil Rankin CB, Mr Michael Ridley, Roger Ching, Cllr Lee Mason, Philip Marriott, Mrs Michal Cohen, David Butters, Robert Palmer
Income: £5,672,285 [2017]; £5,234,856 [2016]; £6,355,439 [2015]; £4,518,802 [2014]; £2,527,770 [2013]

Portsmouth Roman Catholic Diocesan Trust (Trust Property)

Registered: 2 Mar 1966 *Employees:* 273 *Volunteers:* 5,000
Website: portsmouthdiocese.org.uk
Activities: General charitable purposes; education, training; disability; prevention or relief of poverty; religious activities
Address: Diocesan Office, St Edmund House, Bishop Crispian Way, Portsmouth, PO1 3QA
Trustees: Canon Paul Townsend, Mr Alan Sendall, Rev James McGrath, Canon Michael Dennehy, Rev Simon Thomson, Mrs Susan Masser, Dr Anthony Murphy, Canon Dominic Golding, Rt Rev Philip Egan, Rev Mark Hogan, Mrs Alison Humphreys, Rev Gerard Dailly, Mr Martin McCloskey, Mr Michael Elks
Income: £14,526,470 [2016]; £14,194,769 [2015]; £14,835,725 [2014]; £14,897,327 [2013]; £16,141,234 [2012]

Portsmouth Royal Maritime Club

Registered: 4 Jan 1999 *Employees:* 87
Website: royalmaritimeclub.co.uk
Activities: Accommodation, housing; amateur sport; other charitable purposes
Address: Queen Street, Portsmouth, PO1 3HS
Trustees: Commodore David Andrew Harry McGregor SM, Mrs Joanne Elizabeth Walters, Ms Patricia Howse CBE, Mr Wayne Stuart Humphreys, Mr David Muir Nesbit, Mr Ian Carruthers, Mr Michael John Dawe, David James Fowler
Income: £2,488,310 [2017]; £2,199,240 [2016]; £2,074,408 [2015]; £1,940,873 [2014]; £1,180,496 [2013]

Positive East

Registered: 18 Jan 1991 *Employees:* 20 *Volunteers:* 180
Tel: 020 7791 9307 *Website:* positiveeast.org.uk
Activities: Education, training; advancement of health or saving of lives; disability; prevention or relief of poverty; economic, community development, employment
Address: The Stepney Centre, 159 Mile End Road, London, E1 4AQ
Trustees: Graham Stoner, Mr Peter McDonnell, Rebecca Wilkins, Ms Kirsty Jane Cornell, Miss Genoveffa Noschese, Mrs Sarah Malcolm-Shearer, Marigold Chirisa, Ravi Ravindran, Nena Foster, Mr Simon Killick, Mr Mark Butcher
Income: £1,322,658 [2017]; £1,530,170 [2016]; £1,662,254 [2015]; £1,736,105 [2014]; £1,710,309 [2013]

Positive Steps Oldham

Registered: 9 Feb 1993 *Employees:* 180 *Volunteers:* 149
Tel: 0161 621 9463 *Website:* positive-steps.org.uk
Activities: Education, training; economic, community development, employment
Address: Positive Steps, 80 Union Street, Oldham, Lancs, OL1 1DJ
Trustees: Mr Muzahid Khan, Mrs Veronica Carolyn Devonport, Ms Hannah Jane Roberts, Miss Joanne Marie Taylor, Mrs Nicola Kirkham, Mr Garth Harkness, Mrs Julie Anne Edmonson, Ms Amanda Chadderton, Mr Paul Jean Jacques
Income: £7,164,233 [2017]; £7,318,594 [2016]; £7,132,578 [2015]; £7,378,020 [2014]; £6,521,065 [2013]

Possability People Limited
Registered: 31 May 2006 *Employees:* 57 *Volunteers:* 94
Tel: 01273 323828 *Website:* possabilitypeople.org.uk
Activities: Disability
Address: Ground Floor Flat, 27 Brunswick Place, Hove, E Sussex, BN3 1ND
Trustees: Mrs Katherine Ann Goddon, Miss Shoshana Ruth Pezaro, Mr Stan Pearce, Dr Jon Hastie, Mr Nicholas Simpson, Miss Sophie Reilly, Miss Maddy Hamp, Mrs Linda Joyce Elisha, Samantha Oakley
Income: £1,281,998 [2017]; £1,173,764 [2016]; £801,742 [2015]; £817,403 [2014]; £682,602 [2013]

Postal Heritage Collection Trust
Registered: 26 Feb 2004 *Employees:* 48
Tel: 0300 030 0700 *Website:* postalmuseum.org
Activities: General charitable purposes; education, training; arts, culture, heritage, science; environment, conservation, heritage
Address: The Postal Museum, 15-20 Phoenix Place, London, WC1X 0DA
Trustees: Rick Wills, Dr Adrian Steel, Mr Julian Barker, Jayne Billam, Mr David Gold, Ms Susan Claire Raikes, Mr Jonathan Evans, Ms Paola Barbarino, Mike Russell, Mr Errol Bishop, Mr Nicholas Kennett
Income: £5,447,485 [2016]; £4,798,326 [2015]; £1,398 [2014]; £1,163 [2013]; £2,298 [2012]

Postal Heritage Trust
Registered: 26 Feb 2004 *Employees:* 28 *Volunteers:* 8
Tel: 0300 030 0700 *Website:* postalmuseum.org
Activities: General charitable purposes; education, training; arts, culture, heritage, science; environment, conservation, heritage
Address: The Postal Museum, 15-20 Phoenix Place, London, WC1X 0DA
Trustees: Mr Richard Wills, Dr Adrian Steel, Mr Julian Barker, Jayne Billam, Mr David Gold, Ms Susan Claire Raikes, Mr Jonathan Evans, Ms Paola Barbarino, Mike Russell, Mr Errol Bishop, Mr Nicholas Kennett
Income: £4,553,187 [2016]; £3,932,571 [2015]; £8,723,746 [2014]; £4,326,319 [2013]; £2,163,189 [2012]

The Potters House Christian Fellowship Walthamstow
Registered: 5 Nov 1997 *Employees:* 6
Tel: 020 8520 9626 *Website:* pottershouse.co.uk
Activities: Religious activities
Address: Potters House, Christian Centre, Folkestone Road, London, E17 9SD
Trustees: Mr Nigel James Brown, Mr Ronald Wilkie, Mr Paramjeet Sahota, Mr Richard Humphrey
Income: £1,476,737 [2016]; £1,386,585 [2015]; £1,336,046 [2014]; £1,159,286 [2013]; £1,342,097 [2012]

The Power of Nutrition
Registered: 6 Feb 2015 *Employees:* 9
Tel: 020 7783 3563 *Website:* powerofnutrition.org
Activities: The advancement of health or saving of lives; prevention or relief of poverty
Address: Bircham Dyson Bell, 50 Broadway, London, SW1H 0BL
Trustees: Jonathan Brinsden, David Neill Bull CBE, Ertharin Cousin, Dr Siobhan Patricia Crowley, Phyllis Costanza, Hon Michael David Rann, Mr Mark Cutifani
Income: £22,083,189 [2016]; £19,870,748 [2015]

Power to Change Trust
Registered: 16 Jan 2015 *Employees:* 21
Tel: 020 3857 7274 *Website:* thepowertochange.org.uk
Activities: General charitable purposes; education, training; prevention or relief of poverty; economic, community development, employment
Address: The Clarence Centre, 6 St Georges Circus, London, SE1 6FE
Trustees: Power To Change Trustee Limited
Income: £4,520,000 [2016]; £150,695,000 [2015]

Pownall Hall School Trust Limited
Registered: 26 Sep 1966 *Employees:* 39 *Volunteers:* 9
Tel: 01625 523141 *Website:* pownallhallschool.co.uk
Activities: Education, training
Address: Pownall Hall School, Carrwood Road, Wilmslow, Cheshire, SK9 5DW
Trustees: Mr Stephen Coyne, Mr Graham Dawber, Mrs Eileen MacAulay, Mrs Susan Catherine Levy, Mr Terence Frederick Barnes, Mr Michael Morris, Mr Stuart Butler Smith, Mr Thomas James Wareham
Income: £1,467,715 [2016]; £1,228,572 [2015]; £1,068,114 [2014]; £828,935 [2013]; £894,054 [2012]

Powys Association of Voluntary Organisations Cymdeithas Mudiadau Gwirfoddol Powys
Registered: 14 May 1998 *Employees:* 46 *Volunteers:* 103
Tel: 01686 626220 *Website:* pavo.org.uk
Activities: General charitable purposes
Address: PAVO, Plas Dolerw, Milford Road, Newtown, Powys, SY16 2EH
Trustees: Mr Ieuan Williams, Rev Ian Peter Charlesworth, Mrs Ruth Elvira Wright, Mr Keith Rollinson, Mrs Sian Rosalind Dulfer, Mrs Gloria Jones Powell, Mr Martin Nosworthy, Mr William Denston Powell, Mrs Sally Shiels, Mrs Patricia Anne Buchan
Income: £1,782,976 [2017]; £1,704,460 [2016]; £1,855,362 [2015]; £1,647,336 [2014]; £1,810,514 [2013]

Practical Action
Registered: 26 Apr 1966 *Employees:* 541
Tel: 01926 634408 *Website:* practicalaction.org
Activities: Education, training; advancement of health or saving of lives; prevention or relief of poverty; overseas aid, famine relief; environment, conservation, heritage; other charitable purposes
Address: Practical Action, Bourton, Rugby, Warwicks, CV23 9QZ
Trustees: Ms Helena Molyneux, Ms Valerie Celia Jolliffe, Ms Veronica Walford, Prof James Smith, Ms Brenda Ann Lipson, Ian Thornton, Ms Joanne Smith, Dr Roger Clarke, Mr Graham David Young, Mr Nigel Saxby-Soffe, Mr Imran Khan, Ms Helena Wayth, Mr Elwaleed Mohamed Elbasir Elobeid
Income: £33,187,000 [2017]; £29,688,000 [2016]; £25,949,000 [2015]; £30,252,000 [2014]; £26,237,000 [2013]

Pramacare
Registered: 20 Dec 1989 *Employees:* 257 *Volunteers:* 100
Tel: 01202 207300 *Website:* pramacare.co.uk
Activities: The advancement of health or saving of lives; disability
Address: Pramacare Ltd, Unit 1, Holes Bay Park, Sterte Avenue West, Poole, Dorset, BH15 2AA
Trustees: Mr Nicholas Charles Johnson, Dr Andrew James Morris, Mr Robert Keith Allam, John Simmons, Mrs Norma Lee
Income: £3,608,523 [2017]; £3,314,591 [2016]; £3,279,674 [2015]; £3,187,412 [2014]; £3,313,776 [2013]

Praxis Community Projects
Registered: 13 Jan 2000 *Employees:* 23 *Volunteers:* 32
Tel: 020 7729 7985 *Website:* praxis.org.uk
Activities: General charitable purposes; education, training; prevention or relief of poverty; accommodation, housing; arts, culture, heritage, science; amateur sport; economic, community development, employment
Address: Praxis, Pott Street, London, E2 0EF
Trustees: Mr David Mark Carrigan, Dylan Matthews, Ms Pasha Coupet Michaelsen, Ms Jumana Rahman, Mr Tony Wright, Mr Martin Cosarinsky Campos, Mrs Barbara Maureen Roche, Mr Elijah Agwom Sambo, Mr Nicholas Richard Pilkington, Mr Colin Cormack, Mr Raphael Perret
Income: £1,601,507 [2017]; £1,580,779 [2016]; £1,181,882 [2015]; £1,304,500 [2014]; £1,200,176 [2013]

Pre-School Learning Alliance
Registered: 14 Mar 2003 *Employees:* 2,237 *Volunteers:* 927
Tel: 020 7697 2500 *Website:* pre-school.org.uk
Activities: Education, training
Address: Pre School Learning Alliance, 50 Featherstone Street, London, EC1Y 8RT
Trustees: Sophie Ross, Graham McMillan, Lisa Maidment, Sarah Presswood, Mr Raymond Peter Smith, Mrs Simonetta McKenzie, Valerie Chadwick, David Gilbert, Mark Hart, Mrs Lorna Jane Pendred, Claire Stebbings
Income: £34,351,000 [2017]; £36,108,000 [2016]; £35,275,000 [2015]; £36,110,000 [2014]; £36,732,000 [2013]

The Prebendal School
Registered: 8 Jul 2014 *Employees:* 48 *Volunteers:* 12
Tel: 01243 772224 *Website:* prebendalschool.org.uk
Activities: Education, training; religious activities
Address: 9 Eastgate Street, Winchester, Hants, SO23 8EB
Trustees: Mrs Charlotte Pexton, Dr Anthony Cane BA MPhil, Mr Charles Freeman, Mr Andrew Wilkinson, Mr Michael Camps, Mr Dominic Oliver, The Rev Canon Tim Schofield, Mr William Neville, The Very Revd Stephen Waine, Mr John Attwater, Mrs Yvonne Thomson
Income: £2,453,792 [2016]

Premier Christian Media Trust
Registered: 8 Aug 1983 *Employees:* 102 *Volunteers:* 180
Tel: 020 7316 1300 *Website:* premier.org.uk
Activities: The prevention or relief of poverty; religious activities
Address: 22 Chapter Street, London, SW1P 4NP
Trustees: Lord Leslie Griffiths, Roger Bolton, Mr Carl Hughes, Mr Sandy Muirhead, Mr John Lawrence Pritchard, Mr Michael Wakelin, Mr Dominic Schofield
Income: £9,600,521 [2016]; £9,634,987 [2015]; £7,679,919 [2014]; £7,001,283 [2013]; £6,772,405 [2012]

The Premier League Charitable Fund
Registered: 30 Jul 2010 *Employees:* 6
Tel: 020 7864 9000 *Website:* premierleague.com
Activities: General charitable purposes; education, training; advancement of health or saving of lives; disability; prevention or relief of poverty; amateur sport; economic, community development, employment
Address: The Premier League Charitable Fund, 30 Gloucester Place, London, W1U 8PL
Trustees: William Bush, Mr David Oswald Barnes, Mrs Christine Carole Ann Davies CBE, Mrs Gail McKay, Mr Thomas Finn, Mr Timothy John Godwin
Income: £35,135,723 [2017]; £17,793,666 [2016]; £17,481,394 [2015]; £14,737,534 [2014]; £9,884,355 [2013]

The Presence Charitable Trust
Registered: 4 Jul 2007 *Volunteers:* 12
Activities: Religious activities; economic, community development, employment
Address: 50 Cassiobury Drive, Watford, Herts, WD17 3AE
Trustees: Mrs Katy Cardell, Ms Elizabeth Pembroke, Stephen Cardell
Income: £3,557,241 [2016]; £320,592 [2015]; £306,525 [2014]; £367,294 [2013]; £404,067 [2012]

The President and Fellows of Murray Edwards College, Founded as New Hall, in the University of Cambridge
Registered: 17 Aug 2010 *Employees:* 158 *Volunteers:* 25
Website: murrayedwards.cam.ac.uk
Activities: Education, training
Address: Murray Edwards College, Huntingdon Road, Cambridge, CB3 0DF
Trustees: Dr Juliet Louise Hallam Foster, Dr Martha Kate Peters, Dr Paola Filippucci, Dr Ruchira Sinnatamby, Professor Martin Roland, Dr Charlotte Lee, Professor Sarah Anne Coakley, Miss Lylaah Lakshmi Bhalerao, Dame Barbara Stocking, Dr Lucy Delap, Mr Robert Geoffrey Gardiner, Miss Fiona Duffy, Dr Holly Krieger, Dr Evaliela Pesaran, Ms Tamzin Byrne
Income: £8,372,000 [2017]; £7,429,000 [2016]; £7,695,414 [2015]; £7,349,006 [2014]; £6,949,536 [2013]

The President and Fellows of Wolfson College in the University of Cambridge
Registered: 22 Sep 2010 *Employees:* 101
Tel: 01223 335900 *Website:* wolfson.cam.ac.uk
Activities: Education, training
Address: Wolfson College, Cambridge, CB3 9BB
Trustees: Dr Jane McLarty, Mr Christopher Lawrence, Professor Jane Clarke FMedSci FRS, Mr Graham Allen, Dr Jamie Trinidad, Dr Lesley MacVinish, Mr Paul Mylrea, Mrs Margaret Westbury, Mr Ibrahim Mohammed, Professor George Salmond, Professor James Wood, Ms Sian Cook, Dr Anna Bagnoli, Dr Joanna Dekkers, Mr Michael O'Sullivan CMG, Dr Steven Watson, Mr Brian Robertson, Mr Jack Sharp
Income: £8,484,950 [2017]; £7,813,801 [2016]; £6,623,899 [2015]; £6,166,681 [2014]; £5,903,742 [2013]

Presidents Club Charitable Trust
Registered: 11 Feb 1993
Tel: 020 7625 4545
Activities: General charitable purposes
Address: M G R Weston Key, 55 Loudoun Road, St Johns Wood, London, NW8 0DL
Trustees: Mr David Robert Meller, Mr Bruce Ritchie, Mr Harvey Soning
Income: £2,052,816 [2016]; £1,349,082 [2015]; £1,080,341 [2014]; £595,865 [2013]; £370,885 [2012]

Prestfelde School Limited
Registered: 29 Mar 2004 *Employees:* 81 *Volunteers:* 18
Tel: 01743 245400 *Website:* prestfelde.co.uk
Activities: Education, training
Address: Prestfelde Preparatory School, London Road, Shrewsbury, Salop, SY2 6NZ
Trustees: Mr T Parsons, Mr William Lamplugh, Mr Mark Turner, Mrs Jane Mary Stein, Mr Stuart Hay, Mr Adrian Richards, Mrs Sally Varley, Rev Mark Rylands, Mr Matthew John Vavasour Sandford, Mr Gordon Campbell Woods MA PGCE
Income: £3,200,662 [2016]; £3,203,529 [2015]; £3,303,651 [2014]; £2,730,740 [2013]; £2,683,487 [2012]

Pret Foundation Trust
Registered: 26 Oct 1995 *Employees:* 4
Tel: 020 8827 8814 *Website:* pret.com
Activities: The prevention or relief of poverty
Address: Pret a Manger, 75B Verde Building, 10 Bressenden Place, London, SW1E 5DH
Trustees: Mr Clive Edward Benedict Schlee, Pano Christou, Mrs Andrea Wareham
Income: £1,780,512 [2016]; £1,707,131 [2015]; £1,470,359 [2014]; £1,154,265 [2013]; £1,007,656 [2012]

Prifysgol Aberystwyth
Registered: 19 Dec 2011 *Employees:* 1,290
Tel: 01970 622037 *Website:* aber.ac.uk
Activities: Education, training
Address: Aberystwyth University, Visualisation Centre, Penglais, Aberystwyth, Ceredigion, SY23 3BF
Trustees: Ms Gwerfyl Pierce Jones, Professor Christopher James Thomas, Mr Ian James Ogilvie Maceachern, Ms Anne Caroline Davies, Dr Emyr Gordon Roberts, Dr Hazel Davey, Mr Bruce Fraser Wight, Ms Anne Kathleen Williams, Mr Evan John Keith Evans, Professor Elizabeth Tulip Treasure, Mr Richard Stuart John, The Rt Hon Elfyn Llwyd, Mr George Smith Salmond Ashworth, Professor Reyer Zwiggelaar, Mr Gwion Llwyd Williams
Income: £126,264,000 [2017]; £122,452,000 [2016]; £131,085,000 [2015]; £127,923,000 [2014]; £119,224,000 [2013]

Prifysgol Cymru / The University of Wales
Registered: 22 Mar 2012 *Employees:* 104
Tel: 029 2037 6999 *Website:* wales.ac.uk
Activities: Education, training
Address: University of Wales, Registry, King Edward VII Avenue, Cardiff, CF10 3NS
Trustees: The Venerable Randolph Thomas, Dr Ann Rhys MB BCh MRCPsych MFCM(RCP) DPM, Mrs Margaret Evans, Mr Arwel Ellis Owen BA MPhil, Mr Tony Ball, Dr Liz Siberry, Mr Alun Thomas BA FCA, Mrs Elsa Davies, His Honour Judge Eifion Roberts, Mrs Hilary Neagle BSc (Hons) MBA FIPD, Professor Catrin Thomas
Income: £5,537,000 [2017]; £6,489,000 [2016]; £7,830,000 [2015]; £9,067,000 [2014]; £10,346,000 [2013]

The Primrose Hospice Limited
Registered: 23 May 1988 *Employees:* 34 *Volunteers:* 470
Tel: 01527 875333 *Website:* primrosehospice.org
Activities: The advancement of health or saving of lives
Address: The Primrose Hospice, St Godwalds Road, Bromsgrove, Worcs, B60 3BW
Trustees: Mr Ian Robert Marshall, Mr Mark William Leech, Mr Rodney James Laight, Mrs Samantha Carter, Mrs Lynne Chapman, Dr Brian Nyatanga, Mr Jason Manning, Mr Philip Richard Chapman, Miss Joanne Baldwin, Ms Jill Dorothy Edge, Mr Michael John Mushen, Mrs Alison Harrison
Income: £1,591,812 [2017]; £1,443,105 [2016]; £1,673,089 [2015]; £1,926,681 [2014]; £1,611,201 [2013]

The Prince Andrew Charitable Trust
Registered: 31 Aug 1984 *Employees:* 13
Tel: 020 3375 7000
Activities: General charitable purposes; education, training; advancement of health or saving of lives
Address: Buckingham Palace, London, SW1A 1AA
Trustees: Richard Parry, Mrs Nicola Maria Mitchell, Mrs Amanda Thirsk LVO
Income: £1,000,430 [2017]; £765,946 [2016]; £258,953 [2015]; £382,991 [2014]; £638,942 [2013]

Derek Prince Ministries (UK)
Registered: 20 Mar 2008 *Employees:* 6
Tel: 01462 492100 *Website:* dpmuk.org
Activities: Religious activities
Address: P O Box 393, Hitchin, Herts, SG5 9EU
Trustees: Mr Neil Cornick, Mr Dg Selby, Mr Mark Devito, Mr Rd Paterson, Miss R Kolaneci, Mr Ross Paterson
Income: £1,457,659 [2017]; £801,224 [2016]; £978,839 [2015]; £811,035 [2014]; £665,851 [2013]

The Prince of Wales's Charitable Foundation
Registered: 22 Dec 2008 *Employees:* 24
Website: princeofwalescharitablefoundation.org.uk
Activities: General charitable purposes; environment, conservation, heritage; other charitable purposes
Address: Clarence House, St James's, London, SW1A 1BA
Trustees: Sir Ian Michael Cheshire, Dr Kenneth Brockington Wilson, Mr Clive Alderton LVO, Dame Julie Moore DBE
Income: £12,892,000 [2017]; £13,454,000 [2016]; £12,601,000 [2015]; £6,278,000 [2014]; £14,456,000 [2013]

The Prince's Countryside Fund
Registered: 24 May 2010
Tel: 020 7024 5625 *Website:* princescountrysidefund.org.uk
Activities: Education, training; prevention or relief of poverty; environment, conservation, heritage; economic, community development, employment
Address: Clarence House, St James's, London, SW1A 1BA
Trustees: Lord Curry of Kirkharle, Edwin Booth, Paul Murphy, Mr Steven James McLean, Mat Roberts, John Wilkinson, Rob Collins, Elizabeth Buchanan CVO, Mark Allen, Mr Andrew Wright, Ms Sara Philippa Bennison, Mark Duddridge, Mark Pendlington, Lord Jamie Lindsay
Income: £2,439,513 [2017]; £1,825,432 [2016]; £1,521,188 [2015]; £1,822,513 [2014]; £1,869,632 [2013]

The Prince's Foundation for Building Community
Registered: 8 Jun 1998 *Employees:* 39
Website: princes-foundation.org
Activities: Education, training; arts, culture, heritage, science; environment, conservation, heritage; economic, community development, employment
Address: The Prince's Foundation, 19-22 Charlotte Road, London, EC2A 3SG
Trustees: Mr Doglas Connell, Mr Ian Marcus, Mr Benjamin James
Income: £2,460,859 [2017]; £4,160,829 [2016]; £3,684,846 [2015]; £5,002,483 [2014]; £8,588,712 [2013]

The Prince's School of Traditional Arts
Registered: 14 Jan 2004 *Employees:* 20
Tel: 020 7613 8500 *Website:* psta.org.uk
Activities: General charitable purposes; education, training; arts, culture, heritage, science; environment, conservation, heritage; economic, community development, employment
Address: Prince's School of Traditional Arts, 19-22 Charlotte Road, London, EC2A 3SG
Trustees: Professor David William Cadman, Mr Mohammed Abdul Latif Jameel, Mr Michael Fowle CBE, Mr Johnson Chang, Mr Rajiv Bendre OBE, Mr James Hooper, Mr Ivan Massow, Mr Mark Mansell, Mr Syed Mohamad Albukhary, Sir David Green, Mrs Kavita Chellaram, Mr Paul Kanareck, Ms Anahita Gharabaghi, The Hon Mrs Alka Bagri, Mr David Matthews
Income: £1,725,088 [2017]; £1,640,163 [2016]; £1,930,336 [2015]; £2,424,434 [2014]; £1,808,251 [2013]

The Prince's Teaching Institute
Registered: 26 Sep 2006 *Employees:* 12 *Volunteers:* 1
Tel: 020 7289 1042 *Website:* princes-ti.org.uk
Activities: Education, training
Address: 2nd Floor, The Prince's Teaching Institute, 40 Grosvenor Gardens, London, SW1W 0EB
Trustees: Professor Helen Cooper, Jon Coles, Mr Keith K'theil M Breslauer, Peter Wallace, Mr Sushil Kumar Saluja, Mr Raj Kumar
Income: £1,209,107 [2017]; £2,188,026 [2016]; £2,336,393 [2015]; £2,937,874 [2014]; £1,755,806 [2013]

Prince's Trust International
Registered: 6 Jan 2015 *Employees:* 14 *Volunteers:* 3
Tel: 020 7543 1234 *Website:* princes-trust.org.uk
Activities: Education, training; prevention or relief of poverty; economic, community development, employment
Address: The Princes Trust, Princes Trust House, 6-9 Eldon Street, London, EC2M 7LS
Trustees: Martina Milburn DCVO CBE, Lloyd Dorfman CBE, Rupert Goodman DL, Miss Michelle Pinggera, Mohamed Amersi
Income: £1,597,506 [2017]; £766,701 [2016]

The Prince's Trust
Registered: 2 Mar 2000 *Employees:* 1,186 *Volunteers:* 9,000
Tel: 020 7543 1234 *Website:* princes-trust.org.uk
Activities: General charitable purposes; education, training; prevention or relief of poverty; amateur sport; economic, community development, employment; other charitable purposes
Address: The Princes Trust, Princes Trust House, 6-9 Eldon Street, London, EC2M 7LS
Trustees: Michael Marks CVO CBE, Mr Lloyd Dorfman CBE, Ian Mukherjee, Sir Nigel Knowles, Thierry Henry, Mr The Trust, Wendy Becker, Blondel Cluff, Ms Michelle Pinggera, Shabir Randeree CBE, Mrs Alison Brittain
Income: £70,894,000 [2017]; £69,983,000 [2016]; £66,026,000 [2015]; £60,583,000 [2014]; £57,699,000 [2013]

Princes Mead School Trust
Registered: 22 Feb 1984 *Employees:* 76 *Volunteers:* 35
Tel: 01962 888000 *Website:* princesmeadschool.org.uk
Activities: Education, training
Address: Worthy Park House, Kings Worthy, Winchester, Hants, SO21 1AN
Trustees: Mr Brian Welch, Mrs Sue Annesley, Mrs Melanie Jane Renwick, Mrs Emma Sheppard, Mrs Susan Dryden, Mr Martin Kelly, Mr Andrew McMillan, Mrs Ann Hauser, Mrs Sarah Tice, Rt Revd David Williams, Mr William Pattisson
Income: £3,341,154 [2017]; £3,336,472 [2016]; £3,547,341 [2015]; £3,491,797 [2014]; £3,068,529 [2013]

Princess Alice Hospice
Registered: 15 May 1992 *Employees:* 318 *Volunteers:* 1,200
Tel: 01372 468811 *Website:* pah.org.uk
Activities: Education, training; advancement of health or saving of lives
Address: Princess Alice Hospice, West End Lane, Esher, Surrey, KT10 8NA
Trustees: Jane Formby, Mr Andrew James McIntosh, Mr Christopher Roshier, Jeannine Nolan, Ann Duncan, Peter West, Mrs Despina Don-Wauchope, Mr Andrew Wybergh Sesemann, Ms Karen Suzanne Roberts, Mr Peter Jeffrey Quest, Ms Jane Hogg, Professor Fiona Mary Ross, Professor Sean Hilton, Sean Watson, Gail Cookson, Mr Nigel Haig-Brown, Mr Andrew Jennings
Income: £15,061,484 [2017]; £16,459,592 [2016]; £15,289,389 [2015]; £14,782,180 [2014]; £12,477,549 [2013]

Princess Helena College
Registered: 18 Oct 1963 *Employees:* 56
Tel: 01462 443870 *Website:* princesshelenacollege.co.uk
Activities: Education, training
Address: The Princess Helena College, Preston, Hitchin, Herts, SG4 7RT
Trustees: Mr Peter Roberts, Mr Nigel Terry, Mrs Helen Bourne BA QTS, Mr Ian Chambers BSc (Hons) FCA, Dr Helen Barefoot, Dr Sue Parkins, Mr David Dixon, Mrs Louise Smith, Mrs Felicity Wright, Mrs Verity White BEd (Hons), Mr Richard Genichio MA (Cantab) CertEd FRSA, Mr Manfred Kuerten LLB, Mr Michael Beare, Mr David Prosser, Mr Adam Nicoll
Income: £3,532,979 [2016]; £3,455,998 [2015]; £3,740,435 [2014]; £3,686,602 [2013]; £3,731,260 [2012]

The Princethorpe Foundation
Registered: 22 Jun 2001 *Employees:* 282 *Volunteers:* 26
Tel: 01926 634204 *Website:* princethorpe.co.uk
Activities: Education, training
Address: Princethorpe College, Leamington Road, Princethorpe, Rugby, Warwicks, CV23 9PX
Trustees: Mr Kieron Dermot Shaw, Sister Mary Jude Bogie, Mr David George Jackson, Mr Colin James Russell, Commodore Bernard John Warner, Mrs Cecilia Mary Lane, Mrs Elizabeth Clare Kenward, Mr Michael William Fletcher, Mrs Patricia Mary Lines, Mr Athelstance Quintin David Cornforth, Mrs Mary Theresa O'Farrell, Mrs Teresa Mary McNamara, Mrs Elizabeth Mary Frances Griffin, Mr Charles Henry Jenkinson, Mrs Caroline Maria McGrory
Income: £15,222,106 [2017]; £12,456,002 [2016]; £10,927,225 [2015]; £10,136,294 [2014]; £9,185,196 [2013]

Princeton Charitable Foundation Limited
Registered: 29 Apr 2008
Tel: 020 7502 2813
Activities: Education, training
Address: 19 Norcott Road, London, N16 7EJ
Trustees: Mr Stephen Eugene Fiamma, Sara Morgan, Ms Genevieve Mary Muinzer
Income: £2,417,680 [2017]; £7,519,484 [2016]; £3,841,624 [2015]; £1,730,170 [2014]; £1,256,610 [2013]

Principal Fellows and Scholars of Hertford College in the University of Oxford
Registered: 17 Aug 2010 *Employees:* 136
Tel: 01865 279414 *Website:* hertford.ox.ac.uk
Activities: Education, training
Address: Hertford College, Catte Street, Oxford, OX1 3BW
Trustees: Dr Jieun Kiaer, Prof Nick Barton, Prof Charlotte Brewer, Dr David Hopkin, Dr Katherine Lunn-Rockliffe, Professor Peter Millican, Prof Pat Roche, Prof David Thomas, Professor Claire Vallance, Professor Alison Woollard, Professor L F Alday, Professor Arnaud Doucet, Professor Giora Sternberg, Ms Julia Thaxton, Professor Manolis Chatzis, Dr David Dwan, Professor Michael Wooldridge, Professor Siddharth Ashok Parameswaran, Professor Elizabeth Baldwin, Mr Jamie Clark, Prof Hagan Bayley, Prof Zhanfeng Cui, Dr Alan Lauder, Prof Martin Maiden, Dr Steve New, Professor Emma Smith, Professor Christopher Tyerman, Prof Tony Wilson, Dr Radoslaw Zubek, Mr Will Hutton, Dr Jamie Lorimer, Professor Bjarke Frellesvig, Professor David Greaves, Professor Rebecca Sitsapesan, Dr Catherine Redford, Professor Ian McBride, Dr Oliver Noble Wood, Dr Benedict Coxon
Income: £11,418,000 [2017]; £10,865,000 [2016]; £10,340,000 [2015]; £10,372,000 [2014]; £9,523,000 [2013]

The Principal and Fellows of Mansfield College in the University of Oxford
Registered: 20 Sep 2011 *Employees:* 86
Tel: 01865 270996 *Website:* mansfield.ox.ac.uk
Activities: Education, training
Address: Mansfield College, Mansfield Road, Oxford, OX1 3TF
Trustees: Baroness Helena Kennedy QC, Dr Andrew Gosler DPhil, Dr Chris Martin DPhil, Professor Jocelyn Bell-Burnell, Professor Stephen Blundell DPhil, Dr Kathryn Gleadle DPhil, Dr Helen Lacey PhD, Dr James Marrow, Dr Michelle Mendelssohn DPhil, Dr Alison Salveson DPhil, Dr Steve Biller, Dr Jon Chapman, Dr David Leopold, Dr Vicente Grau Colomer, Professor Peter Keevash, Professor Catherine O'Regan, Ms Lucinda Rumsey MA, Dr Katherine Morris DPhil, Professor Rosalind Ballaster DPhil, Dr Pavlos Eleftheriaids DPhil, Dr Marina Galano DPhil, Mr Derek Goldrei MA, Dr Paul Lodge DPhil, Dr Derek McCormack DPhil, Dr Joel Rasmussen, Dr Jason Smith, Professor Helen Margetts DPhil, Mr Allan Aynsley Dodd, Dr Colin Peter Please, Ms Helen Jones, Dr Dino Sejdinovic
Income: £7,314,000 [2017]; £9,904,000 [2016]; £5,791,000 [2015]; £4,863,000 [2014]; £4,703,000 [2013]

The Principal and Fellows of Newnham College
Registered: 17 Aug 2010 *Employees:* 140
Tel: 01223 335786 *Website:* newnham.cam.ac.uk
Activities: Education, training
Address: Newnham College, Cambridge, CB3 9DF
Trustees: Dame Carol Black, Dr Judith Quinn, Dr Barbara Blacklaws, Professor Liba Taub, Miss Maya Bailey-Braendgaard, Ms Ka Chuen Doris Mok, Miss Asia Mobeen Hussein, Dr Elizabeth Watson, Dr Rachael Padman, Professor Christine Watson, Professor Katarzyna Jaszczolt, Dr Sheila Watts, Prof Laura Itzhaki
Income: £11,772,735 [2017]; £17,308,583 [2016]; £9,321,819 [2015]; £9,597,019 [2014]; £8,798,178 [2013]

The Principal and Fellows of Somerville College
Registered: 22 Dec 2010 *Employees:* 173
Tel: 01865 270627 *Website:* some.ox.ac.uk
Activities: Education, training
Address: Somerville College, Woodstock Road, Oxford, OX2 6HD
Trustees: Professor Stephen Weatherill, Ms Joanna Innes, Dr Philip West, Dr Benjamin Thompson MA PhD, Dr Annie Sutherland, Professor Richard Stone, Professor Charles Spence PhD, Professor Stephen Roberts, Dr Natalia Nowakowska, Dr Simon Kemp, Dr Beate Dignas, Dr Jonathan Burton, Professor Jonathan Marchini, Mr Andrew Parker, Professor Christopher Hare, Professor Bhaskar Choubey, Professor Karen Nielsen, Professor Renier Van Der Hoorn, Ms Sara Kalim, Professor Damian Tyler, Professor Louise Mycock, Professor Renaud Lambiotte, Professor Aditi Lahiri, Dr Matthew Wood BM BCh MA MPhil, Dr Roman Walczak, Professor Rajesh Thakker, Dr Almut Suerbaum, Professor Fiona Sparkes FRSE, Professor Alex Rogers, Dr Luke Pitcher BA MA MSt DPhil PGCert, Professor Lois McNay, Dr Michael Hayward, Dr Julie Dickson, Dr Daniel Anthony, Dr Anne Manuel, Professor Guido Ascari, Dr Steve Rayner, Charlotte Potts, Julian Duxfield, Professor Dan Ciubotaru, Baroness Janet Royall, Dr Francesca Southerden, Professor Mari Mikkola, Professor Elena Seiradake
Income: £12,175,000 [2017]; £10,373,000 [2016]; £10,219,000 [2015]; £11,013,000 [2014]; £9,456,000 [2013]

The Principal and Fellows of St Hugh's College in the University of Oxford
Registered: 6 Jan 2011 *Employees:* 124
Tel: 01865 274913 *Website:* st-hughs.ox.ac.uk
Activities: Education, training; accommodation, housing; religious activities; environment, conservation, heritage
Address: St Hughs College, St Margarets Road, Oxford, OX2 6LE
Trustees: Mrs Shelagh Vainker, Dr Philip Blunsom, Professor John Chalker, Professor Stephen Duncan, Professor Joshua Getzler, Dr Roy Grainger, Professor Adrian Harris, Professor Elizabeth Leach, Dr Michael MacNair, Professor David Marshall, Dr James Martin, Professor Adrian Moore, Dr Rafael Perera-Salazar, Professor Kim Plunkett, Dr Timothy Rood, Dr Christopher Stevens, Professor Roy Westbrook BA PhD, Dr Luet Wong, Dr Tom Sanders, Dame Elish Angiolini DBE QC, Dr Edward Matthew Husband, Professor Dora Biro, Professor Oriel Sullivan, Professor Harald Oberhauser, Professor Erin Saupe, Professor Michael McMahon, Dr Ruth Baker, Dr Cristian Capelli, Dr Stuart Conway, Dr George Garnett, Professor Michael Giles, Dr Anthony Harnden, Dr Tom Kuhn, Mr Glen Loutzenhiser, Professor Peter McDonald, Mr Peter Marshall, Professor Peter Mitchell, Dr Senia Paseta, Dr Nicholas Perkins, Professor Thomas Powell, Dr Giuseppe Stellardi, Professor Ian Walmsley, Dr Clive Wilson, Dr Edward Mann, Vicki Stott, Dr Jonathan Parkin, Professor David Doyle, Professor Chistopher John Ballentine, Professor Horst Eidenmuller, Professor Antoinne Jerusalem, Professor Eve Morisi
Income: £9,459,000 [2017]; £9,632,000 [2016]; £12,508,000 [2015]; £12,179,000 [2014]; £9,121,000 [2013]

The Principal and Fellows of The College of The Lady Margaret in the University of Oxford
Registered: 6 Jul 2011 *Employees:* 139
Tel: 01865 274322 *Website:* lmh.ox.ac.uk
Activities: Education, training; accommodation, housing
Address: Lady Margaret Hall, Norham Gardens, Oxford, OX2 6QA
Trustees: Mr Alan Rusbridger, Professor Michael Broers, Professor Antony Galione, Prof Robert Adlington, Prof Helen Barr, Prof Xon De Ros, Professor Christine Gerrard, Prof Jose Goicoechea, Professor Brian Todd Huffman, Prof Jochen Koenigsmann, Professor David MacDonald, Dr Mary Fiona Spensley, Dr Natalie Quinn, Dr Grant Tapsell, Professor Robert Stevens, Dr Sophie Louise Ratcliffe, Professor Hiram Samel, Prof Jan Westerhoff, Professor Pawan Kumar Mudigonda, Mr Timothy Mark Pottle, Professor Anna Sapir Abulafia, Prof Kyle Jaros, Prof Gascia Ouzounian, Dr Hanne Eckhoff, Prof Helen Scott, Mr Bartholemew Ashton, Prof Philip Charles Biggin, Dr Ann Childs, Professor Li He, Professor Nigel Arden, Dr Joanne Begbie, Reverend Dr Allan Doig, Professor Vincent Gillespie, Professor Nicholas Hankins, Dr Marie-Chantal Killeen, Professor Christina Kuhn, Professor Michael Monoyios, Professor Adrian Thomas, Prof Christina Goldschmidt, Prof Abdul Aziz Aboobaker, Dr Mohamed Amin Benaissa, Prof Gianluca Gregori, Dr James Studd, Professor Robin Francis Hope Harding, Professor Dominic Scott, Mr Andrew Kenneth MacDonald, Prof Paul Chleboun, Prof Jill O'Reilly, Prof Sanja Bogojevic, Dr Varun Kanade, Dr Michael Fraser
Income: £11,067,000 [2017]; £9,751,000 [2016]; £11,139,000 [2015]; £9,951,000 [2014]; £8,427,000 [2013]

The Principal and Fellows of The Manchester Academy and Harris College in the University of Oxford

Registered: 26 Jul 2011 *Employees:* 45
Website: hmc.ox.ac.uk
Activities: Education, training
Address: Harris Manchester College, Mansfield Road, Oxford, OX1 3TD
Trustees: Reverend Dr Ralph Waller, David Matthews, Mr Harry Henderson, Terezinha Nunes, George Hudson, Bee Leng Wee, Louise Gullifer, Eric Eve, Brian Fidler, Isabel Ruiz Olaya, Dr Joshua Horden, Dr Alexandra Alvergne, Professor Alister McGrath, Professor Catherine McLoughlin, Dr Crispin Jenkinson, Richard Hobbs, Revd Dr Arthur Stewart, William Mander, Patrik Rorsman, Lesley Smith, Annette Duffell, Susan Killoran, Alex Nicholls, Dr Kristin Van Zwieten, Victoria Lill, Dr Ronald Roy, Dr Bjorn Saven, Professor Jan-Emmanuel De Neve, Dr Sina Ober-Blobaum, Dr Ross McAdam
Income: £4,133,016 [2017]; £5,153,202 [2016]; £2,244,623 [2015]; £2,998,586 [2014]; £3,929,304 [2013]

The Printing Charity

Registered: 16 May 1963 *Employees:* 21
Tel: 01293 649360 *Website:* theprintingcharity.org.uk
Activities: General charitable purposes; education, training; prevention or relief of poverty; accommodation, housing
Address: The Printing Charity, Underwood House, 235 Three Bridges Road, Crawley, Surrey, RH10 1LS
Trustees: Mr James Povey, Mr Steve Sibbald, Mr Alan Thorburn, Mrs Julia Cole, Mr Brett Lawrence, Mr Jon Wright, Mr Peter Coley, Mr Raffiq Moosa, Miss Pauline Blake
Income: £1,773,430 [2016]; £1,657,054 [2015]; £1,672,488 [2014]; £1,659,654 [2013]; £1,453,700 [2012]

Prior Park Educational Trust

Registered: 20 Oct 1980 *Employees:* 355 *Volunteers:* 1
Tel: 01225 835353 *Website:* priorparkschools.com
Activities: Education, training; religious activities
Address: Prior Park College, Ralph Allen Drive, Bath, BA2 5AH
Trustees: Mr Simon Eliot, Michael King, Mr Peter O'Donoghue, Mr Tony Bury, Mr J M Shinkwin, Mrs Nancy Freeman, Mrs Jane Singleton, Mr Joey Garcia, Mrs Ann Lloyd, Rear Admiral NJF Raby, Mr John Webster, Mrs Nicola Pearson, Ms Anne Shepherd, Dr Judy Haworth, Mr Julian Jarvis
Income: £16,998,296 [2017]; £15,626,244 [2016]; £14,547,637 [2015]; £14,226,266 [2014]; £13,437,438 [2013]

The Prior's Field School Trust Limited

Registered: 4 Sep 1963 *Employees:* 145 *Volunteers:* 20
Tel: 01483 810551 *Website:* priorsfieldschool.com
Activities: Education, training
Address: Prior's Field School Trust Ltd, Priorsfield Road, Hurtmore, Godalming, Surrey, GU7 2RH
Trustees: Mr Richard Paul Green, Mr Neale Andrews, Mr Richard Michael Hughes, Mr Robert John Southey BA FCA, Mr Alec Jeremy Sanderson, Mr John Mark Evans, Ms Tracy Anne Cook, Mr Julien Jensen-Humphreys, Mrs Caroline Colvin, Mr Paul Grinham, Mr Stephen Anthony James, Mr Andrew John Gough, Mrs Hazel Elizabeth Morris, Mrs Elizabeth Ann Gillingham
Income: £8,697,096 [2017]; £8,613,779 [2016]; £8,766,668 [2015]; £8,415,972 [2014]; £7,833,224 [2013]

Priors Court Foundation

Registered: 26 Jun 1998 *Employees:* 461 *Volunteers:* 5
Tel: 01635 245902 *Website:* priorscourt.org.uk
Activities: Education, training; disability
Address: Prior's Court School, Priors Court Road, Hermitage, Thatcham, Berks, RG18 9NU
Trustees: Mrs Alison Margaret Bateson, Mr Gordon Bull, Mrs Susan Duncan, Dr Catherine Tissot Demidoff, Mr John Byrne, Mr Christopher Morley, Mr Clive Nickolds, Mr Kenneth Bisset, Mr William Powlett Smith, Mrs Margaret Jean Shirman, Miss Claire Benita Miller, Mr Thomas James Buchan Scott
Income: £16,782,930 [2016]; £16,825,473 [2015]; £17,489,392 [2014]; £14,007,814 [2013]; £12,006,587 [2012]

The Priory Charity

Registered: 15 Aug 1979 *Employees:* 13 *Volunteers:* 10
Tel: 01920 460316
Activities: General charitable purposes
Address: Ware Priory, High Street, Ware, Herts, SG12 9AL
Trustees: Ware Town Council
Income: £1,235,979 [2017]; £910,354 [2016]; £606,873 [2015]; £585,369 [2014]; £554,859 [2013]

Priory School (Banstead) Trust Limited

Registered: 20 Jan 1965 *Employees:* 51
Tel: 01832 864477 *Website:* unitedlearning.org.uk
Activities: Education, training
Address: United Learning, Worldwide House, Thorpe Wood, Peterborough, PE3 6SB
Trustees: Jon Coles, Steve Whiffen
Income: £3,412,540 [2017]; £2,099,839 [2015]; £1,861,864 [2014]; £1,745,725 [2013]; £1,546,325 [2012]

Priory School Edgbaston Trustees Limited

Registered: 6 Oct 1986 *Employees:* 107
Tel: 0121 440 4103 *Website:* prioryschool.net
Activities: Education, training
Address: Priory School, Sir Harrys Road, Edgbaston, Birmingham, B15 2UR
Trustees: Mr Stephen Gilmore, Mr Christopher Joseph Beesley, Dr Ruth Abercrmcie Howard MA, Heather Somerfield, Mr Malcolm Hunt BSc ACIB, Mr Vishal Naik, Mr Timothy Ryan, Sr Monica Matthews, Mr Ian Naylor, Rev Jeremy Howard, Ms Deidre Mattison BA ACA MA, Mr Neil Upton
Income: £4,865,416 [2017]; £4,308,152 [2016]; £4,238,939 [2015]; £4,013,192 [2014]; £3,888,207 [2013]

The Priory for Wales of The Most Venerable Order of The Hospital of St John of Jerusalem

Registered: 15 Dec 1966 *Employees:* 150 *Volunteers:* 3,799
Tel: 029 2044 9600 *Website:* stjohnwales.org.uk
Activities: Education, training; advancement of health or saving of lives
Address: Priory House, Beignon Close, Ocean Way, Cardiff, CF24 5PB
Trustees: Sir Paul Williams, Dr Akram Baig, Miss Gwyneth Rees, Mr Gareth Wayne Chapman, Proffessor Donna Mead, Ms Caryn Laura Cox, Ms Sheelagh Lloyd Jones, Rev Desmond Robert Kitto, Mr Alastair Lyndhurst Lord Aberdare, Mr Andrew David Mitchell, Mr Richard James Paskell, Mr Derek Anthony Howell, Mr Kevin Davies
Income: £6,455,999 [2016]; £6,453,177 [2015]; £6,148,440 [2014]; £5,514,361 [2013]; £4,714,780 [2012]

The Priory of England and The Islands of The Most Venerable Order of The Hospital of St. John of Jerusalem
Registered: 2 Sep 1999 *Employees:* 1,767 *Volunteers:* 33,700
Tel: 020 7324 4000 *Website:* sja.org.uk
Activities: Education, training; advancement of health or saving of lives; religious activities; environment, conservation, heritage
Address: Richard Sims, St John's Gate, Clerkenwell, London, EC1M 4DA
Trustees: The Very Revd Dr N Frayling, Dr D Hempleman-Adams LVO OBE DL, Mr SJ Frost, Mrs A Boyes, Surgeon Rear Admiral Lionel John Jarvis CBE KSTJ MB BS FRCR, Mrs Ann Cable, Dr Acn Borg CBE, Mr Michael Messinger QPM, Mrs J Wright, Mrs Janet Gough OBE, Mr Neil Wood MBE
Income: £102,500,000 [2016]; £106,900,000 [2015]; £99,300,000 [2014]; £91,400,000 [2013]; £90,581,000 [2012]

Prism The Gift Fund
Registered: 25 Sep 2003
Tel: 020 7224 2528
Activities: General charitable purposes
Address: 20 Gloucester Place, London, W1U 8HA
Trustees: Lord Stone of Blackheath, Ms Tracey Reddings, Mr Michael Ridley, Ms Joanne Winston, Mr James Libson, Mr Charles Mesquita, Ms Penny Lovell
Income: £22,128,676 [2017]; £27,128,038 [2016]; £16,688,920 [2015]; £16,508,728 [2014]; £18,763,929 [2013]

Prison Advice and Care Trust (PACT)
Registered: 13 May 1963 *Employees:* 124 *Volunteers:* 546
Tel: 020 7735 9535 *Website:* prisonadvice.org.uk
Activities: General charitable purposes; education, training; advancement of health or saving of lives; prevention or relief of poverty; human rights, religious or racial harmony, equality or diversity
Address: PACT, The Employment Academy, 29 Peckham Road, London, SE5 8UA
Trustees: Mrs Margaret Hodgson, Mr Wilf Weeks, Mr Francis Galliano, Mrs Carolyn Swain, Miss Laura Jayne Brocklesby, Mr Chris Garside, Michael Page, Ms Sarah Mann, Mr Phil Taylor, Mr Nicholas Joseph Hamer Smart, Mr Grahame Hawkings
Income: £4,868,000 [2017]; £4,513,000 [2016]; £4,212,000 [2015]; £3,614,000 [2014]; £2,897,886 [2013]

Prison Fellowship
Registered: 23 Feb 2004 *Employees:* 10 *Volunteers:* 2,500
Tel: 020 7799 2500 *Website:* prisonfellowship.org.uk
Activities: General charitable purposes; education, training; prevention or relief of poverty; religious activities
Address: P O Box 68226, London, SW1P 9WR
Trustees: Ms Frances Mary Beckett, Ms Christine Margaret Leong, Mr Edward David Cox, Rev Martin Kettle, Rev Paul Foster, Mr Tony Watson, Mr John Gloster, Rev Kevin Andrew Dawkins
Income: £1,345,805 [2017]; £571,584 [2016]; £925,097 [2015]; £1,063,815 [2014]; £1,036,300 [2013]

Prison Reform Trust
Registered: 23 Mar 1994 *Employees:* 22 *Volunteers:* 6
Tel: 020 7251 5070 *Website:* prisonreformtrust.org.uk
Activities: Education, training
Address: Prison Reform Trust, 15 Northburgh Street, London, EC1V 0JR
Trustees: Mr Rex Bloomstein, Dr Adrian Thomas Grounds, Dame Ruth Runciman, Mr Jim Monahan, Mr Geoffrey Arnold Dobson, Miss Carlene Emma Firmin MBE, Ms Elizabeth Rantzen, Mr Osmond Junior Smart, Lord Keith John Charles Bradley, Ann Hagell, Mr Colin John Allen, Michelle Nelson, Dame Audrey Frances Glover, Sir Edward Garnier, Mr James Timpson
Income: £1,280,826 [2017]; £975,566 [2016]; £935,460 [2015]; £700,029 [2014]; £1,071,047 [2013]

Prisoners Abroad
Registered: 4 Sep 2002 *Employees:* 25 *Volunteers:* 217
Tel: 020 7561 6820 *Website:* prisonersabroad.org.uk
Activities: Other charitable purposes
Address: Prisoners Abroad, 89-93 Fonthill Road, London, N4 3JH
Trustees: Ms Fiona Shaw, Ms Vivienne Nathanson, Mr Stuart Cole, Ms Christine Ashley, Mary Catterall, Mr Wayne Murray, Mr Toby Rogers, Mr Richard Price, Ms Lynn Saunders, Mr Matthew Rhodes, Mr Mark James Atkinson, Mr Nicholas Hardwick, Mr Martin Atkinson, Lord David Neuberger
Income: £1,526,552 [2017]; £1,598,578 [2016]; £1,614,822 [2015]; £1,539,328 [2014]; £1,336,798 [2013]

Prisoners Education Trust
Registered: 26 Jan 2001 *Employees:* 19 *Volunteers:* 50
Tel: 020 3752 5680 *Website:* prisonerseducation.org.uk
Activities: Education, training
Address: Prisoners Education Trust, 17 Oval Way, London, SE11 5RR
Trustees: Mr Vanni Treves, Ms Alexandra Marks, Mr Geoffrey Wolfson, Mrs Emily Milburn, Catherine Dawkins, Mr Patrick Diamond, Dr Angela Herbert MBE, Mr Philip Deer, Mr Graham Ziegler, Mr Hugh Lenon, Ms Hilary Janet Cross, Mr Robin Peter Collins, Mr Mark Welsh, Mr Simon Scott
Income: £2,454,094 [2017]; £1,260,186 [2016]; £1,702,746 [2015]; £1,363,519 [2014]; £986,136 [2013]

Privacy International
Registered: 28 May 2012 *Employees:* 17 *Volunteers:* 6
Tel: 020 3422 4321 *Website:* privacyinternational.org
Activities: Human rights, religious or racial harmony, equality or diversity
Address: Privacy International, 62 Britton Street, London, EC1M 5UY
Trustees: Ms Eve Salomon, Ms Heather Brooke, Mr Peter Noorlander, Ms Susan Gardner, Mr David Viney, Mr Barry Kernon, Mrs Natalie Carsey, Mr Benjamin Elihu Wizner, Mrs Helena Marttila-Bridge
Income: £2,421,192 [2017]; £1,405,439 [2016]; £1,398,207 [2015]; £1,576,682 [2014]; £864,676 [2013]

Pro Mo-Cymru
Registered: 18 Nov 2002 Employees: 10 Volunteers: 5
Website: promo.cymru
Activities: Education, training; disability; prevention or relief of poverty; arts, culture, heritage, science; economic, community development, employment
Address: 18 Harrowby Street, Cardiff, CF10 5GA
Trustees: Mr Michael Bowden, Ms Elizabeth Andrews, Mr Owen Derbyshire, Ms Louise Kingdom, Mr Meirion Morgan, Mr David Martin, Ms Siobhan Corria, Ms Louise Carter
Income: £1,201,845 [2017]; £1,574,383 [2016]; £1,432,316 [2015]; £1,756,464 [2014]; £2,134,050 [2013]

Processors and Growers Research Organisation
Registered: 11 Jun 1982 Employees: 19
Tel: 01780 782858 Website: pgro.org
Activities: Environment, conservation, heritage
Address: The Research Station, Great North Road, Thornhaugh, Peterborough, PE8 6HJ
Trustees: Mr Steven Paul Marx, Mr Stephen William Bumstead, Mr Bram Van Der Have, Mr John Powell Fenton, Professor Michael Jonathan Gooding, Miss Aimee Dawson, Mr David John Sedgley, Stephen Portas, Mr John Richard Stanton Ward, Mr Stephen John Francis, Mr Andrew Bury, Mr Charles Sargent Stowe, Mr Christopher Graham Renner, Mr Franciszek Graham Smith, Mr Christopher Romer Collings
Income: £1,281,658 [2016]; £1,244,207 [2015]; £1,181,505 [2014]; £1,033,873 [2013]; £955,236 [2012]

Professional Association for Childcare and Early Years
Registered: 27 Jan 1987 Employees: 70 Volunteers: 65
Website: pacey.org.uk
Activities: Education, training; economic, community development, employment
Address: 13 Westmount Avenue, Chatham, Kent, ME4 6DA
Trustees: Mrs Jane Susan Comeau, Mr Hakeem Adebiyi, Mr Christopher Arthur John Glennie, Ms Patricia Suarez, Mrs Helen Cazaly, Ms Vicky Clow, Mr David Burch, Ms Jo-Anne Elizabeth Cullen, Ms Nicola Jane Williams, Ms Susan Meekings, Ms Amy Page, Mr Dominic White
Income: £4,056,500 [2017]; £4,782,257 [2016]; £5,848,016 [2015]; £7,739,961 [2014]; £10,222,013 [2013]

The Professional Footballers' Association Charity
Registered: 11 Jan 2013
Tel: 0161 236 0575 Website: pfa.com
Activities: General charitable purposes; education, training; advancement of health or saving of lives; disability; prevention or relief of poverty; accommodation, housing; arts, culture, heritage, science; amateur sport; human rights, religious or racial harmony, equality or diversity; recreation
Address: 20 Oxford Court, Manchester, M2 3WQ
Trustees: Mr Garth Crooks OBE, Mr Gordon Taylor BSc (Econ) Hon Dart Hon MA OBE, Mr Brendon Batson MBE, Mr Gareth Griffiths, Paul Elliot, Darren Wilson BA Hons ACA, Mr David Weir, Mr Christopher Powell, Mr Simon Charles Morgan
Income: £27,887,320 [2017]; £20,552,554 [2016]; £19,521,885 [2015]; £13,125,272 [2014]

The Proforest Initiative
Registered: 17 Aug 2010
Tel: 01865 243439 Website: proforestinitiative.org
Activities: Education, training; prevention or relief of poverty; environment, conservation, heritage; economic, community development, employment
Address: South Suite, Frewin Chambers, Frewin Court, Oxford, OX1 3HZ
Trustees: Mr Cooper, Mr Mario Abreu, Dr Ines Alessandra Riccardi Smyth, Mr Ishmael Dodoo, Miss Emily Jane Fripp
Income: £1,939,961 [2016]; £2,003,443 [2015]; £2,240,299 [2014]; £1,625,499 [2013]; £745,934 [2012]

Progress to Change
Registered: 3 Nov 1997 Employees: 52
Tel: 0113 245 6772 Website: progresstochange.co.uk
Activities: Other charitable purposes
Address: Progress to Change, 20 New Market Street, Leeds, LS1 6DG
Trustees: Mr David Edward Burgess, Mr Nigel Appleyard Wainman, Mrs Diana Favre, Mrs Lynn Hague, Prof Alastair Watt MacIntyre Hay, Mrs Jill Dilks, Mr Adrian John Armitage Lodge, Rev Michael Anthony Whatmough, Mrs Carol Cochrane
Income: £1,440,118 [2017]; £1,452,143 [2016]; £1,419,358 [2015]; £1,428,752 [2014]; £1,444,878 [2013]

Progressive Farming Trust Limited
Registered: 6 Nov 1980 Employees: 26 Volunteers: 7
Tel: 01488 658298 Website: organicresearchcentre.com
Activities: Education, training; environment, conservation, heritage
Address: Progressive Farming Trust Ltd, The Organic Research Centre, Hamstead Marshall, Newbury, Berks, RG20 0HR
Trustees: Mrs Alice Astor, Mr Timothy Mark Bennett, Mr Vikas Agrawal MA ACA, Ms Margaret Wagner, Mrs Andrea Claire Stewart, Mr Donald MacInnes Peck, Mr Michael Richard Turnbull, Christine Watson, Mr Adrian James Michael Blackshaw, Mr Ned Jonathan Westaway
Income: £1,740,825 [2017]; £1,000,422 [2016]; £882,740 [2015]; £1,017,887 [2014]; £968,245 [2013]

Project S.E.E.D. Limited
Registered: 24 Jan 2014 Employees: 37 Volunteers: 400
Tel: 020 8903 5122 Website: seed.uk.net
Activities: Education, training; prevention or relief of poverty; religious activities
Address: 370-386 High Road, Wembley, Middlesex, HA9 6AX
Trustees: Mr Marcel Bordon, Mr David Rosenthal, Dayan Henry Ehrentreu, Mr Misha Zeev Morris
Income: £1,722,038 [2017]; £1,861,003 [2016]; £1,515,285 [2015]

Project Space Leeds
Registered: 28 Aug 2012 Employees: 32 Volunteers: 26
Tel: 0113 320 2323 Website: thetetley.org
Activities: Education, training; arts, culture, heritage, science
Address: The Tetley, Hunslet Road, Leeds, LS10 1JQ
Trustees: Mr Adrian Friedli, Mr Jonathan Straight, Jean Dent OBE, Deborah Green, Ms Rosemary Lister, Mr Joseph Hill, Bob Lewis, Gerald R Jennings, Phil Beeston, Dawn Camerson, Ms Rehana Zaman
Income: £1,672,743 [2017]; £1,560,426 [2016]; £1,521,680 [2015]; £954,950 [2014]; £404,045 [2013]

Promote Mifumi Project
Registered: 20 Jun 1994 *Employees:* 5 *Volunteers:* 3
Tel: 0117 916 6457 *Website:* mifumi.org
Activities: Education, training; advancement of health or saving of lives; disability; prevention or relief of poverty; economic, community development, employment; human rights, religious or racial harmony, equality or diversity
Address: Mifumi UK, 42 Bell Hill Road, Bristol, BS5 7LU
Trustees: Mrs Perry Lucas Treasurer, Dr Ravi Thiara, Ms Jackie Otunnu Secretary, Miss Arlene Manyange
Income: £1,195,664 [2017]; £1,570,084 [2016]; £1,097,987 [2015]; £1,061,783 [2014]; £1,780,279 [2013]

Promoting Equality in African Schools
Registered: 4 Nov 2008 *Employees:* 989 *Volunteers:* 10
Tel: 020 3096 7700 *Website:* peas.org.uk
Activities: Education, training; overseas aid, famine relief
Address: Peas, 7-14 Great Dover Street, London, SE1 4YR
Trustees: Dr Peter Colenso, Catherine Brien, Dr Robin Horn, Mr Lee Robertson, Ms Sharon Ring, Mr Matthew Goldie-Scot, Erica Stuart
Income: £5,823,713 [2017]; £5,331,655 [2016]; £4,769,247 [2015]; £3,018,000 [2014]; £2,507,935 [2013]

Prospect Education Trust
Registered: 11 Apr 1995 *Employees:* 28 *Volunteers:* 100
Activities: Education, training
Address: Berkeley Campus, Wanswell, Berkeley, Glos, GL13 9RS
Trustees: Alastair Leflaive, Gerard Mark Leflaive, Mr Andy Mitchell, Marcus Smith, Douglas Lloyd Turner, Barry Small, Mr Lloyd Hamilton
Income: £2,293,104 [2016]; £1,896,048 [2015]; £1,544,950 [2014]; £1,249,969 [2013]; £1,152,861 [2012]

Prospect Hospice Limited
Registered: 23 Jun 1980 *Employees:* 190 *Volunteers:* 917
Tel: 01793 813355 *Website:* prospect-hospice.net
Activities: Education, training; advancement of health or saving of lives
Address: Prospect Hospice, Moormead Road, Wroughton, Swindon, Wilts, SN4 9BY
Trustees: Mrs Angela Gillibrand, David Barrand, Caroline Hallatt, Penny Tidbury, Dr Fiona Baskett, Eleanor Collins, Mr Timothy Willis, Clive Bassett, Douglas Looman, Lindsay Whittam, Ms Mandy Casavant
Income: £7,556,000 [2017]; £8,178,000 [2016]; £7,677,000 [2015]; £7,380,000 [2014]; £7,830,000 [2013]

Prospects for People with Learning Disabilities
Registered: 7 Feb 1997 *Employees:* 444 *Volunteers:* 1,500
Tel: 020 7452 2124 *Website:* livability.org.uk
Activities: Education, training; disability; accommodation, housing; religious activities
Address: Livability, 6 Mitre Passage, London, SE10 0ER
Trustees: Mrs Caroline Armitage, Livability, Mr David Bentley
Income: £8,264,435 [2017]; £9,822,468 [2016]; £11,698,108 [2015]; £12,424,189 [2014]; £11,184,920 [2013]

Prostate Cancer Research Centre
Registered: 5 Mar 2014 *Employees:* 4 *Volunteers:* 1
Website: prostate-cancer-research.org.uk
Activities: Education, training; advancement of health or saving of lives
Address: 16 Kent Road, Windlesham, Surrey, GU20 6JF
Trustees: Mr Timothy Schroder, Professor Prokar Dasgupta, Mr Geoffrey Ian Bowman, Mr Shaun Grady, Mr Ben Monro-Davies, Mrs Michele Hunter, Mr James Christopher Miller, Sir Robert Anthony Francis, Mr Matthew Ellis
Income: £1,360,235 [2017]; £1,195,510 [2016]; £2,928,468 [2015]

Prostate Cancer UK
Registered: 12 Nov 1991 *Employees:* 180 *Volunteers:* 2,401
Tel: 020 3310 7000 *Website:* prostatecanceruk.org
Activities: Education, training; advancement of health or saving of lives
Address: Fourth Floor, The Counting House, 53 Tooley Street, London, SE1 2QN
Trustees: Professor Jonathan Hugh Waxmanbsc MD FRC, Mr Steve Ford, Professor David Neal, Mr Robert Griffith Humphreys, Mr Michael Tye, Professor Sara Faithful, Marion Leslie, Lynne Robb, Mr Andrew Mitchell, Mr Martin Roland, Mr Charles Packshaw, Mr Tom Shropshire, Mr Simon Peter Hammett, Simon Peck
Income: £20,747,000 [2017]; £20,027,000 [2016]; £24,076,000 [2015]; £31,125,000 [2014]; £29,377,000 [2013]

Providence Row
Registered: 2 Feb 2011 *Employees:* 31 *Volunteers:* 37
Tel: 020 7422 6386 *Website:* providencerow.org.uk
Activities: Education, training; advancement of health or saving of lives; prevention or relief of poverty; economic, community development, employment
Address: Providence Row, Dellow Centre, 82 Wentworth Street, London, E1 7SA
Trustees: Elizabeth Canning, Richard Solomon, Paul Strange, Mr Simon Cribbens, Mr Gavin Mullen, Linda McHugh, Sister Evelyn Gallagher, Rita Chakraborty, Jonathan Rhodes, Right Reverend Nicholas Hudson
Income: £1,825,855 [2017]; £1,816,010 [2016]; £1,166,374 [2015]; £1,051,513 [2014]; £985,014 [2013]

The Province of Great Britain of The Institute of The Brothers of The Christian Schools (The de la Salle Brothers)
Registered: 16 Jun 1964 *Employees:* 48 *Volunteers:* 91
Tel: 01865 311332 *Website:* delasalle.org.uk
Activities: Education, training; religious activities
Address: 140 Banbury Road, Oxford, OX2 7BP
Trustees: Rev Br Paul Joseph Foy, Rev Laurence Hughes BR, Rev Br Bernard Hayward, Rev Br John Deeney, Rev Br James Kilty, Brother Nicholas Sellors
Income: £2,617,125 [2016]; £10,548,753 [2015]; £13,272,130 [2014]; £8,698,190 [2013]; £8,565,632 [2012]

The Provost and Scholars of the House of the Blessed Mary the Virgin in Oxford, commonly called Oriel College, of the Foundation of Edward the Second of famous memory, sometime King of England
Registered: 18 May 2011 *Employees:* 174
Tel: 01865 276555 *Website:* oriel.ox.ac.uk
Activities: Education, training; religious activities; amateur sport; environment, conservation, heritage; recreation
Address: Oriel College, Oriel Square, Oxford, OX1 4EW
Trustees: Edward Wilfrid Stephenson, Oliver Pooley, Kristine Krug, Michael Peter Devereux, John Armour, Christopher Bowdler, Lynne Cox, Nicholas Eyre, Pedro Ferreira, David Hodgson, John Huber, Brian Leftow, Kevin Maloy MA PhD, Teresa Morgan, Sandra Robertson, Richard Scholar, Annette Volfing, William Wood, Dr Paul Yowell, Dr Justin Coon, Dr Luca Castagnoli, Dr Maike Bublitz, Dr Andrew Wells, John Michael Spivey, Prof Lyndal Roper, Juliane Kerkhecker, Ian Forrest, Andrew Boothroyd, Christopher Peter Conlon, Bruno Currie, Lucinda Anne Ferguson, Lars Fugger, Ian Horrocks, Yakov Kremnitzer, Yadvinder Malhi, Julia Mannherz, Kathryn Murphy, Gonzalo Rodriguez-Pereyra, James Frank Sparks, Mungo Wilson, Mr Sean Power, Ms Moira Wallace OBE, Dr Teresa Bejan, Prof Hindy Najman, Dr Julien Devriendt, Dr Victor Mattellan
Income: £11,514,000 [2017]; £10,793,000 [2016]; £12,023,000 [2015]; £13,435,000 [2014]; £18,607,000 [2013]

Public Service Broadcasting Trust
Registered: 29 Feb 1988 *Employees:* 51 *Volunteers:* 2,183
Tel: 01962 810977 *Website:* psbt.co.uk; www.fixers.org.uk
Activities: General charitable purposes; education, training; prevention or relief of poverty
Address: Cheriton Mill, Cheriton, Alresford, Hants, SO24 0NG
Trustees: Ralph Bernard, Nick Fisk, Dirk Anthony, Clare Westcott, Dr Rys Farthing, Mr Jonathan Richard Peppiatt, Mr Julian Delisle Burns, Nathan Adams, Nick Finch, Ms Sarah Catherine Reynolds, Mr Robin Pieter Elias
Income: £2,188,470 [2017]; £2,783,966 [2016]; £3,413,816 [2015]; £3,070,151 [2014]; £2,089,104 [2013]

Pump Aid
Registered: 21 Oct 1999 *Employees:* 46 *Volunteers:* 2
Tel: 0845 504 6972 *Website:* pumpaid.org
Activities: The prevention or relief of poverty; overseas aid, famine relief
Address: Pump Aid Limited, Development House, 56-64 Leonard Street, London, EC2A 4LT
Trustees: Ms Megan Bingham-Walker, Mr Benjamin John Nealon, Ms Ashley Marie Lopez, Mr Gerald Peter Tyler, Mr Stefan Allesch-Taylor, Mr Alan David Duerden, Mr David Francis Waller, Mr Spencer Mahony
Income: £1,350,914 [2017]; £1,364,412 [2016]; £1,146,735 [2015]; £760,802 [2014]; £865,634 [2013]

Punchdrunk
Registered: 10 Apr 2006 *Employees:* 13 *Volunteers:* 40
Tel: 020 7655 0940 *Website:* punchdrunk.com
Activities: Arts, culture, heritage, science
Address: Cannon Factory, Ashley Road, London, N17 9LH
Trustees: Mr Sandeep Dwesar, Mr Royce Michael James Bell, Ms Amanda Fulmor Good, Mr Ben Connah, Dr Josephine Machon, Mr Marc Mathieu, Mr Paul Davies
Income: £1,832,512 [2017]; £2,221,633 [2016]; £4,462,271 [2015]; £8,867,133 [2014]; £1,674,325 [2013]

The Purcell School
Registered: 24 Feb 1964 *Employees:* 142
Tel: 01923 331100 *Website:* purcell-school.org
Activities: Education, training; arts, culture, heritage, science
Address: The Purcell School, Aldenham Road, Bushey, Herts, WD23 2TS
Trustees: Professor Colin Lawson, Mr James Christopher Fowler, Mr Charles Beer, Roger Tustin Jackling, Mr Jonathan Eley, Mr Ian Odgers, Dr Rebecca Mooney, Ms Janice Graham, Ms Joanna Van Heyningen, Mr Mark Racz, Mrs Kirsty von Malaise, Mr Timothy James Blinko, Mr William McDonnell
Income: £6,062,981 [2017]; £6,094,899 [2016]; £5,654,918 [2015]; £5,703,994 [2014]; £5,313,234 [2013]

Pure Innovations Limited
Registered: 12 Sep 2005 *Employees:* 291 *Volunteers:* 7
Tel: 0161 804 4417 *Website:* pureinnovations.co.uk
Activities: Disability; economic, community development, employment
Address: 5 Station View, Hazel Grove, Stockport, Cheshire, SK7 5ER
Trustees: Mr David Lennie, Mr Tim Cornes, Miss Nina Hinton, Mrs Nicola Dean, Mr Alan Allman
Income: £5,168,641 [2017]; £5,149,032 [2016]; £8,569,931 [2015]; £6,963,067 [2014]; £6,403,878 [2013]

The Pure Land Foundation
Registered: 8 Jan 2016
Website: purelandfoundation.com
Activities: Education, training; advancement of health or saving of lives; arts, culture, heritage, science
Address: Harbottle & Lewis, 14 Hanover Square, London, W1S 1HP
Trustees: Mr Chia Hsing Wang, Mr Luca Bozzo, Mr Glen Atchison
Income: £1,238,339 [2017]

The Puri Foundation
Registered: 28 Jun 1988
Tel: 0115 901 3000
Activities: General charitable purposes; education, training; advancement of health or saving of lives; disability; prevention or relief of poverty; overseas aid, famine relief; amateur sport
Address: Environment House, 6 Union Road, Nottingham, NG3 1FH
Trustees: Mr Nathu Ram Puri, Mr A Puri, Miss Mary Katherine McGowan
Income: £1,111,650 [2017]; £733,036 [2016]; £499,902 [2015]; £345,106 [2014]; £324,763 [2013]

Purley Park Trust Limited
Registered: 29 Oct 1970 *Employees:* 135
Tel: 0118 942 7608 *Website:* purleyparktrust.org
Activities: Disability; accommodation, housing
Address: Purley Park Trust Ltd, 12 Huckleberry Close, Purley on Thames, Reading, Berks, RG8 8HU
Trustees: Mr Leslie Jones OBE, Mrs Karen Samantha Robinson, Mr Stephen Barstow, Miss Rachel Keeling, Mrs Susan Vandersteen, Mr Christopher David Trickey, Ms Angela Cullimore-Todd
Income: £3,916,246 [2017]; £3,906,859 [2016]; £3,480,784 [2015]; £3,207,830 [2014]; £2,979,968 [2013]

Mr and Mrs J A Pye's Charitable Settlement
Registered: 17 Jun 1965
Tel: 01865 721269 *Website:* pyecharitablesettlement.org
Activities: General charitable purposes; education, training; advancement of health or saving of lives; disability; prevention or relief of poverty; arts, culture, heritage, science; amateur sport; environment, conservation, heritage; economic, community development, employment
Address: Leander Cottage, 30 East Street, Oxford, OX2 0AU
Trustees: Mr David Seymour Tallon, Mr Patrick Mulcare, Simon Stubbings
Income: £1,300,188 [2016]; £746,794 [2015]; £538,648 [2014]; £495,240 [2013]; £654,261 [2012]

QPR in the Community Trust
Registered: 30 Jan 2009 *Employees:* 66 *Volunteers:* 34
Tel: 020 8743 0262 *Website:* qpr.co.uk
Activities: Education, training; advancement of health or saving of lives; disability; prevention or relief of poverty; amateur sport
Address: Loftus Road Stadium, South Africa Road, London, W12 7PJ
Trustees: Ms Joanna Kennedy, Mr John Richard Devine, Mr Charles Lee Hoos, Mr Mohammed Khaliel, Mr Kevin McGrath, Mr Euan Inglis, Mr Ruben Emir Gnanalingam
Income: £1,542,603 [2017]; £1,293,118 [2016]; £1,255,345 [2015]; £1,086,063 [2014]; £1,031,952 [2013]

QVSR
Registered: 30 Sep 2004 *Employees:* 41 *Volunteers:* 1
Tel: 020 7987 5466 *Website:* qvsr.org.uk
Activities: The prevention or relief of poverty; accommodation, housing; religious activities; other charitable purposes
Address: 121-131 East India Dock Road, Poplar, London, E14 6DF
Trustees: Mr Ian Pattison, Miss Jean Thomas, Mr Philip Sheppard, Rev Michael Long, Mrs Mathilda Small-Byam, Rev Nigel Cowgill, Mr Terence John Simco, Mr Barry L Vaughan, Rev Alexander Cameron Kirkwood, Mrs Geraldine Enid Pearce, Mr Roy Wadeson, Colonel Derek Bristow OBE DL
Income: £2,381,826 [2016]; £2,480,284 [2015]; £2,043,195 [2014]; £2,061,692 [2013]; £1,978,654 [2012]

A M Qattan Foundation
Registered: 2 Dec 1993 *Employees:* 99
Tel: 020 7370 9990 *Website:* qattanfoundation.org
Activities: General charitable purposes; education, training; arts, culture, heritage, science
Address: Tower House, 226 Cromwell Road, London, SW5 0SR
Trustees: Mr Omar Al-Qattan, Nadia Hijab, Dr Khalil Hindi, Professor Najwa Al-Qattan, Ms Abla Maayah, Dr Raef Zreik
Income: £9,999,826 [2017]; £10,133,117 [2016]; £5,690,124 [2015]; £4,000,907 [2014]; £4,149,375 [2013]

Qi Partners
Registered: 10 Nov 2016
Tel: 07960 959840
Activities: General charitable purposes; education, training; advancement of health or saving of lives; arts, culture, heritage, science
Address: Norwich Research Park, Colney Lane, Colney, Norwich, NR4 7UH
Trustees: Mr David John Richardson, Mr Timothy Brears, Mr David Leslie Parfrey, Mr Philip Mark Redvers Davies
Income: £31,628,000 [2017]

Quadram Institute Bioscience
Registered: 7 Oct 1996 *Employees:* 139
Website: quadram.ac.uk
Activities: Education, training
Address: Institute of Food Research, Colney Lane, Colney, Norwich, NR4 7UA
Trustees: Dr Duncan Maskell, Mr Stephen West, Professor Christine Williams, Dr Celia Ann Caulcott, Prof Peter John Morgan, Mr Ian Black, Dr Tim Brears, Professor Steven Walker, Dr Benedicte Flambard
Income: £15,284,318 [2017]; £15,176,000 [2016]; £22,505,000 [2015]; £19,993,000 [2014]; £16,569,000 [2013]

Quaggy Development Trust
Registered: 26 May 2005 *Employees:* 56 *Volunteers:* 46
Tel: 020 8465 9785 *Website:* quaggydevelopmenttrust.org.uk
Activities: Education, training; advancement of health or saving of lives; prevention or relief of poverty; economic, community development, employment
Address: Quaggy Childrens Centre, Orchard Hill, London, SE13 7QZ
Trustees: Mr Simon Riley, Miss Naomi Frances Delap, Susan Jacqueline McKee, Mrs Kathryn Klaentschi
Income: £2,028,658 [2017]; £2,157,472 [2016]; £1,688,998 [2015]; £1,161,483 [2014]; £1,044,688 [2013]

Quaker International Educational Trust (Quiet)
Registered: 3 Nov 1998 *Employees:* 201
Activities: Education, training
Address: Millbrook Way, Dovecote Lane, Tetford, Horncastle, Lincs, LN9 6QD
Trustees: Mr Paul High, Mr John Crosfield, Mr William David Adams Haire, Antoine Wakim, Mr Hani Aboul Jabine, Digby Swift, Ms Philippa Neave, Averil Armstrong, Juhaina Albert Khalil, Mr David F Hickok
Income: £5,707,144 [2016]; £5,211,323 [2015]; £4,786,397 [2014]; £5,327,323 [2013]; £4,682,900 [2012]

Quaker Social Action
Registered: 16 Apr 1998 *Employees:* 23 *Volunteers:* 102
Tel: 020 8983 5030 *Website:* quakersocialaction.org.uk
Activities: Education, training; prevention or relief of poverty; accommodation, housing
Address: 17 Old Ford Road, London, E2 9PJ
Trustees: Ms Loveday Elizabeth Shewell, James Robertson MA FCA MIPA FABRP, Mr Peter Rivers, Mr Colin Charles Kinlock, Dr David John Robson, Mr Robert Anarfi, Caroline Tisdall, Miss Sandie Finn, Ms Laura Jane Roling, Ms Gillian Margaret Ashmore, Mr Nicholas Salman Tyabji, Ms Sara Elizabeth Feilden
Income: £1,007,656 [2017]; £997,639 [2016]; £994,218 [2015]; £1,097,404 [2014]; £1,609,432 [2013]

The Quality Assurance Agency for Higher Education
Registered: 9 Jun 1997 *Employees:* 122
Tel: 01452 557078 *Website:* qaa.ac.uk
Activities: Education, training
Address: Southgate House, Southgate Street, Gloucester, GL1 1UB
Trustees: Professor Andrew Wathey, Professor Joy Carter, Professor Timothy McIntyre-Bhatty, Professor John Grattan, Ms Sara Kaye Drake, Mr Robert Cashman, Mr Oliver William Johnson, Mr Stephen Melville Criddle, Mr Philip Alan Stuart Wilson, Professor Craig Mahoney, Dr Vanessa Louise Davies, Mr Christopher Nigel Banks, Professor Philip Winn, Professor Denise McAlister, Professor Maria Hinfelaar, Ms Linda Duncan, Mr Amatey Victor Doku, Mr Craig Alyn Watkins
Income: £12,393,637 [2017]; £15,443,840 [2016]; £14,851,971 [2015]; £15,279,697 [2014]; £13,614,426 [2013]

Quartet Community Foundation
Registered: 25 Apr 2000 *Employees:* 12 *Volunteers:* 7
Tel: 0117 989 7700 *Website:* quartetcf.org.uk
Activities: General charitable purposes
Address: Royal Oak House, Royal Oak Avenue, Bristol, BS1 4GB
Trustees: Ms Bina Shah, Mr Ben Silvey, Mr Julian Telling, Mr Jonathon Baker, Mr Robert Bourns, Mr Pat Meehan, Mr Christopher Johnson, Mrs Sue Elizabeth Blatchford, Mr John David Cullum, Mr William Lee, Mr Trevor Leonard, Mrs Merlyn Ipinson-Fleming, Ms Annie Kilvington, Mrs Helen Wilde, Mrs Joanna Turner
Income: £3,210,555 [2017]; £3,034,425 [2016]; £5,579,777 [2015]; £3,524,262 [2014]; £2,925,728 [2013]

Queen Alexandra College
Registered: 13 Nov 1997 *Employees:* 371 *Volunteers:* 30
Tel: 0121 428 5022 *Website:* qac.ac.uk
Activities: Education, training
Address: Queen Alexandra College, 49 Court Oak Road, Birmingham, B17 9TG
Trustees: Mr Christopher James Bradshaw, Prof John Edward Tyrrell Penny, Mr Ian Richards, William Houle, Dr Ewan Hamnett, Mr Andrew Charles Morris, Julie Reed, Ms Jane Morel, Prof John Hilbourne, Steve McCall, Mrs Janet McCall, Mrs Amanda McGeever, Ms Anne Green, Mr Gareth David Robinson, Mr Andrew John Curtis, Mrs Lorraine Maxine Moses-Copeman
Income: £10,225,263 [2017]; £10,238,854 [2016]; £9,805,005 [2015]; £10,911,910 [2014]; £10,517,214 [2013]

The Queen Alexandra Cottage Homes
Registered: 29 Oct 1962 *Employees:* 75 *Volunteers:* 2
Tel: 01323 737816 *Website:* qach.co.uk
Activities: Accommodation, housing
Address: 557 Seaside, Eastbourne, E Sussex, BN23 6NE
Trustees: Mr Ian Michael Alexander Stewart, Mr Peter Austin, Mr Robert Hugh Fovargue, Mrs Stephanie Eileen Parkes-Crick
Income: £1,874,741 [2017]; £1,797,209 [2016]; £2,351,319 [2015]; £1,552,258 [2014]; £1,550,366 [2013]

The Queen Elizabeth Diamond Jubilee Trust
Registered: 26 Jan 2012 *Employees:* 12
Tel: 020 3358 3386 *Website:* jubileetribute.org
Activities: The advancement of health or saving of lives; other charitable purposes
Address: 128 Buckingham Palace Road, London, SW1W 9SA
Trustees: The Rt Rev and Rt Hon Richard John Carew Chartres, Sir Christopher Geidt, The Rt Hon Lord Robertson of Port Ellen, Baroness Sarah Elizabeth Mary Hogg, Mr Simon Walker, Sir Trevor McDonald, The Rt Hon Sir John Major KG CH, Mr John Andrew Spence, Baroness Patricia Janet Scotland
Income: £3,973,943 [2017]; £8,472,305 [2016]; £15,132,426 [2015]; £36,198,455 [2014]; £22,410,866 [2013]

The Queen Elizabeth Prize for Engineering Foundation
Registered: 19 Jun 2012 *Employees:* 6 *Volunteers:* 10
Tel: 020 7766 0600 *Website:* qeprize.org
Activities: Education, training; arts, culture, heritage, science; other charitable purposes
Address: Prince Philip House, 3 Carlton House Terrace, London, SW1Y 5DG
Trustees: Mala Gaonkar, The Lord Browne of Madingley, Dame Ann Dowling, Sir Paul Nurse, Sir John Beddington
Income: £1,887,118 [2017]; £4,486,818 [2016]; £5,693,116 [2015]; £5,183,612 [2014]; £10,437,631 [2013]

Queen Elizabeth Scholarship Trust Limited
Registered: 14 May 2013 *Employees:* 4
Tel: 020 7798 1531 *Website:* qest.org.uk
Activities: General charitable purposes; education, training; arts, culture, heritage, science; environment, conservation, heritage
Address: Queen Elizabeth Scholarship Trust, 1 Buckingham Place, London, SW1E 6HR
Trustees: Mr Alec Richard McQuin, Mr Nicholas Crean, Mr Mark Henderson, Mr Matthew Ingle, Dr Nicholas Morgan, Mr Neil Edward John Stevenson, Mr Steve MacLeod
Income: £1,194,804 [2016]; £558,025 [2015]; £509,265 [2014]; £126,433 [2013]

Queen Elizabeth's Foundation for Disabled People
Registered: 20 Jan 1967 *Employees:* 234 *Volunteers:* 250
Tel: 01372 841105 *Website:* qef.org.uk
Activities: Education, training; disability
Address: Queen Elizabeth's Foundation For Disabled People, Leatherhead Court, Woodlands Road, Leatherhead, Surrey, KT22 0BN
Trustees: Ms Lynn Scotcher Srot, Mr Peter Gordon, Mrs Moira Bowie, Mr John Denning, Mrs Victoria Parnell, Mr Timothy Jason Davies
Income: £11,650,000 [2017]; £14,275,000 [2016]; £12,682,000 [2015]; £12,592,000 [2014]; £11,546,000 [2013]

Queen Elizabeth's Grammar School Blackburn Limited
Registered: 29 Sep 1994 *Employees:* 30
Tel: 01254 686300 *Website:* qegs.blackburn.sch.uk
Activities: General charitable purposes; education, training
Address: Queen Elizabeth's Grammar School, West Park Road, Blackburn, BB2 6DF
Trustees: Mr Brian Howard Stott, Mr Gregory Turner, Mr David Alan Peat, Mr Alan Sagar, Mr Jeremy Gorick, Mr Iain Duncan Hamilton, Mr John Joseph Riley
Income: £1,525,522 [2016]; £645,044 [2015]; £7,163,241 [2014]; £5,519,323 [2013]; £7,930,826 [2012]

Queen Elizabeth's Hospital
Registered: 13 Jul 2004 Employees: 145
Tel: 0117 930 3048 Website: qehbristol.co.uk
Activities: Education, training
Address: Queen Elizabeths Hospital, Berkeley Place, Clifton, Bristol, BS8 1JX
Trustees: Mr David Smart, Mr Richard Hill, Mrs Sarah Cosgrove, Mr Timothy Davis, Mr John Buchanan, Mrs Caroline Bateson, Mr Edward Corrigan, Mr Paul Keen, Mrs Sallie Blanks, Mr Kevin Riley, Mr Clive Woodford
Income: £9,206,451 [2017]; £8,804,546 [2016]; £8,478,770 [2015]; £7,903,600 [2014]; £7,837,204 [2013]

Queen Margaret's School, York Limited
Registered: 13 May 1986 Employees: 187 Volunteers: 1
Tel: 01904 728261 Website: queenmargarets.com
Activities: Education, training
Address: Queen Margarets School, Escrick Park, Escrick, York, YO19 6EU
Trustees: Mrs Caroline Jane Bayliss, Mr Robert Morse, Professor David Parker, Mrs Anna Morley, Dr Emma Peart, Mrs Sue King, The Hon Mrs Bel Forbes, Miss Emily Pearson, Brigadier David James Husband Maddan, Mrs Katherine Preston, Mr Nigel Corner, Mrs Clare Granger, Mr John Hoddinott
Income: £8,485,528 [2017]; £8,632,439 [2016]; £8,599,677 [2015]; £9,278,769 [2014]; £8,378,725 [2013]

Queen Mary's School (Baldersby) Ltd
Registered: 8 Jul 2003 Employees: 60 Volunteers: 8
Tel: 01845 575002 Website: queenmarys.org
Activities: Education, training
Address: Queen Marys School, Baldersby Park, Topcliffe, Thirsk, N Yorks, YO7 3BZ
Trustees: Mrs Susan Elizabeth Ford, Mrs Charlotte Alexandra Lucy Strickland, Mr Edward David Theakston, Mr Stuart James Brown, Mr Thomas Edward Fielden, Mr Nevil John Pearce, Mr Nicholas Andrew Morgan, Mr Tomothy Guy Hartley LLB, Mr Andrew James Fallows, Mrs Melanie Antoinette Crouch, Mrs Maria Claire Wike, Mrs Rosanna Elizabeth Bryant
Income: £3,482,996 [2017]; £3,424,733 [2016]; £3,539,978 [2015]; £3,524,503 [2014]; £3,521,266 [2013]

Queen Mary's Schools Foundation
Registered: 21 Feb 1964 Employees: 48 Volunteers: 26
Tel: 07803 710154
Activities: Education, training
Address: Whitehouse Ridsdale, 26 Birmingham Road, Walsall, W Midlands, WS1 2LZ
Trustees: Mr J N Punch, Mrs V M Fairbank, Mr J Vallance, Mrs S Blakemore, Miss R E Hearsey, His Honour P J Stretton, Mr W A Stephens, Mrs J Aubrook, Mr P J Sturrock
Income: £1,891,487 [2017]; £1,736,455 [2016]; £1,692,727 [2015]; £1,698,704 [2014]; £2,097,018 [2013]

Queen Mary, University of London Students' Union
Registered: 21 Jun 2012 Employees: 230 Volunteers: 1,514
Tel: 020 7882 8045 Website: qmsu.org
Activities: Education, training; amateur sport; recreation
Address: Students' Union Hub, 329 Mile End Road, London, E1 4NT
Trustees: Mr Edward Moses, Mr William James Boisonnade Atkins, Mr Mohamed Redwan Shahid, Mr Yasir Abid Yeahia, Mr Ahmed Muntaqim Mahbub, Ms Sally Pearman, Mr Andreas Richard Gaitzsch, Mr William Marcus Atkins, Mr Rakin Rownak Choudhury, Ms Mary Taiwo Funke Ojo, Ms Renad Khundakji, Mr Richard Kuti
Income: £6,596,006 [2017]; £6,172,309 [2016]; £6,029,487 [2015]; £5,578,077 [2014]; £6,252,252 [2013]

The Queen's College, Oxford
Registered: 23 Jun 2011 Employees: 176
Tel: 01865 279163 Website: queens.ox.ac.uk
Activities: Education, training; religious activities
Address: The Queens College, High Street, Oxford, OX1 4AW
Trustees: Professor John Hyman, Mr Nicholas Bamforth, Professor Peter Alistair Robbins, Dr John Harry Davis, Professor Jane Langdale, Dr Nicholas James Owen, Professor Owen Lewis Rees, Dr Charlie Louth, Professor Jonathan Doye, Professor Simon Aldridge, Dr Andrew Timms, Dr Laura Rosemary Lonsdale, Dr Charles Crowther, Professor Ritchie Robertson, Dr Paolo Tammaro, Dr Lindsay Ann Turnbull, Dr Ludovic Phalippou, Dr Christopher Metcalf, Professor Paul Madden, Professor William John Blair, Dr Richard Bruce Nickerson, Professor Robert Taylor, Professor Elizabeth Jane Claire Mellor, Prof Sir John Ball, Dr Keyna Anne Quenby O'Reilly, Professor Christopher Norbury, Professor Mark Buckley, Dr Yves Capdeboscq, Dr Panagiotis Papazoglou, Dr Rebecca Beasley, Professor Christopher O'Callaghan, Dr Dirk Meyer, Dr Anthony Gardner, Dr Jennifer Guest, Prof Richard Parkinson, Professor Seth Whidden
Income: £15,357,000 [2017]; £11,578,000 [2016]; £10,593,000 [2015]; £10,657,000 [2014]; £13,409,000 [2013]

Queen's College, Taunton
Registered: 25 Nov 1981 Employees: 328 Volunteers: 15
Tel: 020 7935 3723 Website: queenscollege.org.uk
Activities: Education, training; religious activities
Address: Methodist Church House, 25 Marylebone Road, London, NW1 5JR
Trustees: Queen's College Taunton Trustee Company Limited, Methodist Independent Schools Trust
Income: £11,766,459 [2016]; £11,613,480 [2015]; £11,286,933 [2014]; £10,769,119 [2013]; £10,324,482 [2012]

Queen's College
Registered: 7 Jan 1964 Employees: 106
Tel: 020 7291 7002 Website: qcl.org.uk
Activities: Education, training
Address: Queen's College London, 43-49 Harley Street, London, W1G 8BT
Trustees: Rev Charlotte Bannister-Parker, Professor Alison While, Mrs Rhiannon Wilkinson MA MEd, Mr Matthew Hanslip-Ward, Mr Richard Ford, Ms Alexandra Gregory, Mrs Danielle Salem BA, Mr John Jacob, Mrs Alexia Bolton, Ms Holly Porter, Mr Paul Reeve, Mr Seth Bolderow
Income: £10,284,280 [2017]; £9,769,700 [2016]; £8,873,616 [2015]; £8,324,285 [2014]; £7,892,213 [2013]

The Queen's Foundation for Ecumenical Theological Education
Registered: 1 Nov 2005 Employees: 45 Volunteers: 1
Tel: 0121 454 1527 Website: queens.ac.uk
Activities: Education, training; religious activities
Address: Queens College, Somerset Road, Edgbaston, Birmingham, B15 2QH
Trustees: Mr John Anthony Bell, Rev Lucy Winkett, Mrs Marilyn Hull, Dr Rachel M E Jepson, Rev Kenneth Howcroft, Mrs Julia Tozer, The Venerable Simon Heathfield, Rev Elizabeth Smith, Mr Paul Stewart, Rev Stephen Wigley, Mrs Mavis Jones
Income: £2,271,521 [2017]; £2,431,529 [2016]; £1,963,334 [2015]; £2,347,685 [2014]; £1,832,885 [2013]

Queen's Gate School Trust Limited

Registered: 9 Oct 1962 *Employees:* 89 *Volunteers:* 45
Tel: 020 7589 3587 *Website:* queensgate.org.uk
Activities: Education, training
Address: 131-133 Queen's Gate, London, SW7 5LE
Trustees: Mr William Gillen, Mrs Manina Weldon, Mr Gary Li, Mrs Reica Gray, Mr Joseph McNeila, Mrs Laura Marani, Mr Michael Cumming, Mr Peter Trueman, Mr Jonathan Dobson, Dr Jill Harling
Income: £9,986,177 [2017]; £9,700,336 [2016]; £9,133,407 [2015]; £8,545,108 [2014]; £7,862,743 [2013]

The Queen's School Chester

Registered: 18 Mar 1963 *Employees:* 110
Tel: 01244 312078 *Website:* thequeensschool.co.uk
Activities: Education, training
Address: The Queen's School, City Walls Road, Chester, CH1 2NN
Trustees: Elizabeth Jane Brown BA CPFA, The Lord Bishop of Chester, Euan Andrew Elliott, Rev David Nigel Chesters OBE, Mrs Caroline Mary Mosley MA LLB BA Hons Dip, Mr Nicholas Canning, Ms Sara Caroline Shepheard-Walwyn BA Hons MSc, Mrs Julia Samarji LLB Hons, Mrs Kirsty Elizabeth Dunlap, Lady Julia Margaret Eileen Spencer BA, Christine Helen Laine MSc FRCR, Mr Mark Arthur Heber Fearnall FNAEA FICBA, Mrs Anna Louise Unett MA Cantab TEP, Mr David Mason, Dr Mary McDonald BSc PhD, Mrs Marion Evelyn Ardron BA Hons Oxon, Mr Adrian Peter Walmsley FCIPD, Reverend Canon Rosemary Jane Brooke, Mrs Samantha Jane Piddington ACA
Income: £7,774,326 [2017]; £7,571,514 [2016]; £7,244,689 [2015]; £6,959,701 [2014]; £6,291,177 [2013]

Queenscourt Hospice

Registered: 4 Jun 1987 *Employees:* 157 *Volunteers:* 650
Tel: 01704 517926 *Website:* queenscourt.org.uk
Activities: Education, training; advancement of health or saving of lives
Address: Queenscourt Hospice, Town Lane, Southport, Merseyside, PR8 6RE
Trustees: Dr Pa Downham, Mrs Margaret Tarpey, Mr Christopher Leather, Tom Fairclough, Mr Keith Mitchell, Mr Anthony Damian Crewe, Mr Christopher Paul Cutner, Dr David Unwin, Mr Richard Jacklin, Ms Yvonne Burns, Mr Steven Simpson, Mrs Carol Bernard, Dr Geraldine Rose Boocock
Income: £3,882,452 [2017]; £4,437,304 [2016]; £5,151,821 [2015]; £3,816,948 [2014]; £3,275,223 [2013]

Queenswood School Limited

Registered: 1 Aug 1962 *Employees:* 179 *Volunteers:* 10
Tel: 01707 602671 *Website:* queenswood.org
Activities: Education, training
Address: 3 Chapel Close, Brookmans Park, Hatfield, Herts, AL9 6NY
Trustees: Miss Patricia May Wrinch, Mr Timothy Claude Garnham BSc, Mr H James De Sausmarez BA FCIS, Rev Timothy Swindell ACA, Mr Andrew Poppleton, Mr Simon Morris, Mrs Victoria Neale, Mr Edmund Mark Sautter MA, Mrs Jo Sotiriou, Mr Ralph Baines, Mrs Oonagh McGuinness, Rev David Chapman
Income: £12,067,171 [2016]; £12,480,643 [2015]; £11,905,187 [2014]; £9,425,196 [2013]; £9,863,941 [2012]

Questscope

Registered: 26 Oct 1990 *Employees:* 54
Website: questcope.org
Activities: Education, training; prevention or relief of poverty; economic, community development, employment
Address: P O Box 910729, Amman, 11191, Jordan
Trustees: Dr Curtis Neal Rhodes, Dr Mowafak Al Yafi, Mrs Sheila Tayback Leatherman, Ms Vilma Qahoush Tyler, Mr John Allen Gappa, Dr Heather Cordell
Income: £5,867,617 [2017]; £2,960,285 [2016]; £1,859,976 [2015]; £985,624 [2014]; £810,738 [2013]

Quintessentially Foundation

Registered: 9 Nov 2011 *Employees:* 2
Tel: 0845 388 7985 *Website:* quintessentiallyfoundation.org
Activities: General charitable purposes; education, training; advancement of health or saving of lives; prevention or relief of poverty; economic, community development, employment
Address: Quintessentially Foundation, 29 Portland Place, London, W1B 1QB
Trustees: Mr Aaron Simpson, Mr Benjamin Elliot, Mr Kevin Burke, Miss Olivia Beth Brafman, Mr Andrew Crawley, Dr Peter Crowther, Ms Caroline Villamizar Duque, Mr Sebastian Lee, Miss Emma McCarthy, Mr Geordie Greig
Income: £1,963,151 [2016]; £2,822,831 [2015]; £1,074,819 [2014]; £1,044,056 [2013]; £649,019 [2012]

Quo Vadis Trust

Registered: 22 Sep 2006 *Employees:* 49 *Volunteers:* 11
Tel: 020 8778 4546 *Website:* qvt.org.uk
Activities: The advancement of health or saving of lives; disability; accommodation, housing
Address: Quo Vadis Trust, 92 Brownhill Road, London, SE6 2EW
Trustees: Dr Stephen Dellar, Mr William Puddicombe, Mr Stephen Wells, Mr Adebaya Oyeniyi, Ms Lorraine Ash, Ms Tayvanie Nagendran, Mr Mark Lemmon, Ms Tina Paul
Income: £3,046,817 [2017]; £3,135,567 [2016]; £2,947,428 [2015]; £2,637,166 [2014]; £2,443,208 [2013]

Quwwat-Ul-Islam Society Newham London

Registered: 14 Apr 1977 *Employees:* 113 *Volunteers:* 11
Tel: 020 8475 0126 *Website:* quwwatulislam-london.com
Activities: General charitable purposes; education, training; religious activities
Address: Quwwat-Ul-Islam Society, 62-66 Upton Lane, London, E7 9LN
Trustees: Mr Saeed Yusuf Mohmed, Mr Yakub Vali Omar, Mr Zubair Alibhai Ahmed Patel, Mr Ismail Mohmed Khankhara, Mr Ismail Patel
Income: £1,427,432 [2017]; £1,278,733 [2016]; £1,181,548 [2015]; £1,075,657 [2014]; £1,035,980 [2013]

R.E.A.L. Foundation Trust

Registered: 5 May 2010 *Employees:* 37 *Volunteers:* 12
Tel: 01623 423411 *Website:* realft.org
Activities: Education, training; amateur sport; recreation
Address: Real Foundation Trust, Kingsmill House, Unit 1 Kingsmill Way, Mansfield, Notts, NG18 5ER
Trustees: Mrs Caroline Francis Ryan, Sean Ryan, Judy Keely, Mrs Nicky Bailey, Dave Collins, Jenny Egglestone
Income: £2,266,626 [2016]; £30,000 [2015]; £700 [2013]

R.I.S.E. (Refuge, Information, Support and Education)
Registered: 17 Nov 1997 *Employees:* 59 *Volunteers:* 31
Website: riseuk.org.uk
Activities: Education, training; advancement of health or saving of lives; prevention or relief of poverty; accommodation, housing
Address: 3rd Floor, Shaftsbury Court, 95 Ditchling Road, Brighton, BN1 4ST
Trustees: Ms Angie Uglow, Hazel McLeod, Ms Rosemary Friggens, Ms Karen James, Jeanette Ashton, Mrs Anne-Marie Harrison, Jean Spray, Ms Bridie Iveson, Ms Beverly Sawyers, Ms Helen Carpenter
Income: £2,172,802 [2017]; £2,010,232 [2016]; £1,828,682 [2015]; £1,581,353 [2014]; £1,559,670 [2013]

The RAF Benevolent Fund Housing Trust Limited
Registered: 24 Nov 1972
Tel: 020 7307 3301 *Website:* rafbf.org
Activities: Accommodation, housing
Address: Royal Air Force Benevolent Fund, 67 Portland Place, London, W1B 1AR
Trustees: Mr John Michael Elsworth Scott, Ms Victoria Fakehinde, Air Vice-Marshal David Murray, Air Commodore Paul Hughesdon MA FInstD FCMI, Air Vice Marshal Simon Dougherty
Income: £2,485,221 [2016]; £2,857,337 [2015]; £1,830,878 [2014]; £2,306,870 [2013]; £2,166,911 [2012]

RAF Sports Federation
Registered: 19 Jul 2016 *Employees:* 7
Tel: 01296 657045 *Website:* rafsportsfederation.uk
Activities: General charitable purposes; amateur sport; armed forces, emergency service efficiency
Address: Room 43, Kermode Hall, Royal Air Force Halton, Halton Camp, Aylesbury, Bucks, HP22 5PG
Trustees: Alan Opie MDA MA BSc FCIPD, Warren James CBE MA CMgr CCMI FRAeS RAF, Richard Stephen Faulkner, Christina Reid Elliot CBE MA BSc RAF, Geraldine Angela Watterson MCSI ACol TEP MICA
Income: £1,990,281 [2017]

RAFT - Restoration of Appearance and Function Trust
Registered: 9 Aug 1988 *Employees:* 15 *Volunteers:* 5
Website: raft.ac.uk
Activities: The advancement of health or saving of lives
Address: Mount Vernon Hospital, Rickmansworth Road, Northwood, Middlesex, HA6 2RN
Trustees: Raft Trustees Limited
Income: £1,338,520 [2017]; £1,443,410 [2016]; £1,162,862 [2015]; £1,235,696 [2014]; £836,034 [2013]

The RBS Peoplecharity
Registered: 17 Oct 2013
Tel: 020 3873 8535 *Website:* bwcharity.org.uk
Activities: The prevention or relief of poverty
Address: Bank Workers Charity, Suite 686-695, Salisbury House, Finsbury Circus, London, EC2M 5QQ
Trustees: The Bankers Benevolent Fund
Income: £1,208,590 [2017]; £1,079,541 [2016]; £1,037,564 [2015]; £912,645 [2014]

The RCJ and Islington Citizens Advice Bureaux
Registered: 3 Nov 1995 *Employees:* 43 *Volunteers:* 208
Tel: 020 7947 6974 *Website:* rcjadvice.org.uk
Activities: General charitable purposes; education, training; disability; prevention or relief of poverty
Address: Royal Courts of Justice, Strand, London, WC2A 2LL
Trustees: Bob Nightingale MBE, Mr David Lindsay Mackie QC, Mr Kevin John Perry, The Rt Hon Sir Richard George Bramwell McCombe, Mr Roger George Leese, Ms Ali Sallaway, Mr Alexander Stevens Carruthers, Mr Paul Thwaite, Ms Christine Howard, Mr Patrick William Robinson, Mr John Hine LLB FCIArb, Mr Graham Paul Kingsby Huntley, Mr Nicholas Mark Atkins, Ms Mona Bina Ann Mary Vaswani, Ms Sarah Tien Mee Lee, Mr Robin Knowles CBE QC, Mr James Robert Levy, Mr Nicholas Medniuk, Mr James William Gilbey, Ms Paula Hodges
Income: £2,242,916 [2017]; £2,207,041 [2016]; £2,522,726 [2015]; £2,348,161 [2014]; £2,738,492 [2013]

The RCN Foundation
Registered: 2 Mar 2010 *Volunteers:* 25
Tel: 020 7647 3599 *Website:* rcnfoundation.org.uk
Activities: Education, training; advancement of health or saving of lives; prevention or relief of poverty
Address: Royal College of Nursing, 20 Cavendish Square, London, W1G 0RN
Trustees: Mr David Jones, Tony Butterworth, Ian Norris, Mrs Vanessa Martin, Miss Moya Kate Kirmond, Mr Atulkumar Bhogilal Patel, Mr Robert Sowney, Mr Nicholas Pearson OBE, Mrs Christine Perry, Ms Denise Katherine Llewellyn, Mr Gordon Robert Hull
Income: £1,524,000 [2016]; £1,192,000 [2015]; £1,044,000 [2014]; £998,000 [2013]; £857,000 [2012]

READ - The Reading Agency
Registered: 8 Mar 2001 *Employees:* 30
Tel: 01727 817031 *Website:* readingagency.org.uk
Activities: General charitable purposes; education, training; arts, culture, heritage, science
Address: Free Word Centre, 60 Farringdon Road, London, EC1R 3GA
Trustees: Thomas Moody-Stuart, Jane Marriott, Derek O'Gara, Matthew Littleford, Mark Seaman, Alix Langley, Tony Durcan OBE, Miss Sarah Jane Mears
Income: £2,628,614 [2017]; £3,012,859 [2016]; £2,963,629 [2015]; £2,802,435 [2014]; £2,298,288 [2013]

REALL Limited
Registered: 10 Feb 1993 *Employees:* 21
Website: reall.net
Activities: The prevention or relief of poverty; overseas aid, famine relief; accommodation, housing; economic, community development, employment
Address: 8-14 Harnall Row, Coventry, Warwicks, CV1 5DR
Trustees: Alison Brown, David Orr, Shantanu Bhagwat, Ms Kate Wareing, Suzanne Forster, Amy Becker, Mr Steven Geoffrey Troop
Income: £15,131,004 [2017]; £18,552,590 [2016]; £16,976,006 [2015]; £11,656,544 [2014]; £8,503,424 [2013]

REDR UK
Registered: 8 Mar 2000 Employees: 79 Volunteers: 12
Tel: 020 7840 6039 Website: redr.org.uk
Activities: The prevention or relief of poverty; overseas aid, famine relief
Address: RedR, 250a Kennington Lane, London, SE11 5RD
Trustees: Mrs Isobel Hunter, Mr Peter Greeves, Dr Timothy Healing, Prof Paul Douglas Sherlock, Miss Caroline Patricia Lassen, Mr Timothy Hayward, Mrs Isobel Byrne Hill, Dr Aidan McQuade, Mr Ian Kingsley Smout, Andrew David Lamb, Ms Jane Smallman, Mr Geoff French, Mrs Linda Richardson, Dr Parneet Paul
Income: £4,809,562 [2017]; £4,419,294 [2016]; £4,923,974 [2015]; £5,485,677 [2014]; £5,034,335 [2013]

RFEA Limited
Registered: 13 Mar 1997 Employees: 108
Tel: 0845 873 7163 Website: rfea.org.uk
Activities: Economic, community development, employment; armed forces, emergency service efficiency
Address: RFEA Ltd, Mountbarrow House, 12 Elizabeth Street, London, SW1W 9RB
Trustees: Mr James Mill, Major General Andrew Ritchie, Mr Ali McKay, Mr Robert McPherson MBE, Ms Liz Cassidy, Air Commodore Stuart Burdess BEng CEng FRAeS, Mr Giles Robert Peel, Sarah Bunting
Income: £3,956,375 [2017]; £3,639,071 [2016]; £3,620,880 [2015]; £3,173,825 [2014]; £2,533,102 [2013]

RFU Injured Players Foundation
Registered: 31 Dec 2007 Volunteers: 12
Tel: 020 8831 6506 Website: rfuipf.org.uk
Activities: Education, training; advancement of health or saving of lives; disability; prevention or relief of poverty
Address: Rugby Football Union, 200 Whitton Road, Twickenham, Middlesex, TW2 7BA
Trustees: Nigel Henderson, Paul Murphy, Stephen Duckwork, Mrs Judith Metcalfe, Dr Margaret Mary Emer McGilloway, Nigel Tarrant, Dr Fred Middleton, Mr Robert Fraser Udwin, Mr Stephen Pearson
Income: £1,729,130 [2017]; £1,695,225 [2016]; £1,420,613 [2015]; £2,180,113 [2014]; £1,816,514 [2013]

The RMIG Endowment Trust
Registered: 21 Jan 1985
Tel: 020 8393 3685
Activities: Education, training
Address: 6 Briarwood Road, Epsom, Surrey, KT17 2LY
Trustees: Mr Jonathan Gary Knopp, Dr John Thompson, Dr Michael Woodcock, Mr David Thompson
Income: £1,605,075 [2015]; £2,150,244 [2014]; £2,094,446 [2013]; £2,127,265 [2012]

RNH Synagogue & College Ltd
Registered: 15 Apr 2008 Employees: 10
Activities: General charitable purposes; education, training; prevention or relief of poverty; religious activities
Address: 59 Kings Road, Prestwich, Manchester, M25 0LQ
Trustees: Mr David Neuwirth, Mr Benjamin David Hassan, Mr Benny Stone
Income: £1,403,527 [2017]; £1,257,003 [2016]; £1,337,049 [2015]; £1,425,676 [2014]; £1,171,925 [2013]

RNIB Charity
Registered: 10 Apr 2014 Employees: 820 Volunteers: 5,000
Website: rnib.org.uk
Activities: Education, training; advancement of health or saving of lives; disability; accommodation, housing
Address: Royal National Institute for The Blind, 105 Judd Street, London, WC1H 9NE
Trustees: Mr Derek Child, Margaret Bennett, Eleanor Southwood
Income: £38,644,000 [2017]; £41,511,000 [2016]; £25,116,000 [2015]

ROKPA Trust
Registered: 19 Nov 1996 Employees: 6 Volunteers: 25
Tel: 013873 73285 Website: samyeling.org
Activities: Education, training; advancement of health or saving of lives; prevention or relief of poverty; overseas aid, famine relief; religious activities
Address: Samye Ling Tibetan Centre, Eskdalemuir, Langholm, Dumfries & Galloway, DG13 0QL
Trustees: Ani Lhamo, Mrs Karma Lhamo Cosgrove, Lama Zangmo, John Maxwell, Lama Yeshe Losal Rinpoche, Mr Tsultim Palbar Lama
Income: £3,667,230 [2016]; £3,059,739 [2015]; £3,004,245 [2014]; £4,816,434 [2013]; £4,110,186 [2012]

RP Fighting Blindness
Registered: 18 Sep 2013 Employees: 15 Volunteers: 100
Tel: 01280 821334 Website: rpfightingblindness.org.uk
Activities: The advancement of health or saving of lives; disability; economic, community development, employment; other charitable purposes
Address: P O Box 350, Buckingham, MK18 1GZ
Trustees: Mrs Lynda Cantor MBE, Dr Elizabeth Graham, Mr Don Grocott, Mr Roger Charles Francis Backhouse, Rachael Stevens, Professor John Marshall MBE, Mr Colin McArthur, Mr Stephen Falconer Jones, Mrs Janet Crookes FCA, Ms Lucy Withington
Income: £1,613,502 [2016]; £1,152,994 [2015]; £919,277 [2014]

RSA (The Royal Society for The Encouragement of Arts, Manufactures and Commerce)
Registered: 23 Mar 1963 Employees: 99 Volunteers: 80
Tel: 020 7930 5115 Website: thersa.org
Activities: Education, training; arts, culture, heritage, science; environment, conservation, heritage; economic, community development, employment
Address: Royal Society for The Encouragement of Arts, Manufactures & Commerce, 8 John Adam Street, London, WC2N 6EZ
Trustees: Ms Vikki Heywood CBE, Ms Sarah Ebanja, Kully Thiarai, Mr Rhoderick Hyde, Ms Jan Portillo, Ms Tatjana Hine OBE, Mr Saleh Saeed, Mr Peter Fell, Ms Philippa Wilson, Mr Stephen Gleadle, Ms Susan Siddall, Ian Coleman
Income: £11,188,000 [2017]; £10,337,000 [2016]; £7,952,000 [2015]; £9,730,000 [2014]; £9,361,000 [2013]

RSPCA South East and West Devon Branch
Registered: 28 Mar 1962 Employees: 33 Volunteers: 85
Tel: 01392 439898 Website: rspca-littlevalley.org.uk
Activities: Animals
Address: RSPCA, Black Hat Lane, Bakers Hill, Exeter, EX2 9TA
Trustees: Mrs Beryl Gooding, Mrs Jackie Williams, Miss Elaine McPhail, Ms Johanna Westgate, Mrs Angie Eyles, Mrs Linda Stewart-Crowley, Carol Allan, Mrs Wendy Diane Brookes, Mrs Margaret Hardy, Mr Philip Brush, Mrs Evelyn Mundy
Income: £1,211,294 [2016]; £1,344,059 [2015]; £1,531,756 [2014]; £1,228,248 [2013]; £819,307 [2012]

RZIM Zacharias Trust
Registered: 9 Jan 1998 *Employees:* 53
Tel: 01865 302900 *Website:* rzim.eu
Activities: Education, training; religious activities
Address: 76 Banbury Road, Oxford, OX2 6JT
Trustees: Mr Martin David Kitcatt, Mr Francis Wright, Ms Sarah Zacharias Davis, Mr Andrew Corley, David Lilley, Mrs Caroline Santer, Mr David Reeves Taylor, Mr James Charles Exton Gardner, Mr Michael James Patrick O'Neill, Guen Soo Senn
Income: £4,221,656 [2017]; £3,870,373 [2016]; £3,613,224 [2015]; £3,099,424 [2014]; £7,197,387 [2013]

Rachel Charitable Trust
Registered: 14 Sep 1978
Tel: 020 7846 3036
Activities: General charitable purposes
Address: 30 Market Place, London, W1W 8AP
Trustees: Mr Simon Kanter, Mrs Susan Noe, Mr Leo Noe
Income: £15,347,928 [2017]; £8,492,083 [2016]; £4,596,395 [2015]; £6,935,250 [2014]; £2,219,227 [2013]

The Racing Foundation
Registered: 6 Jan 2012 *Employees:* 2
Tel: 07741 035907 *Website:* racingfoundation.co.uk
Activities: General charitable purposes; education, training; advancement of health or saving of lives; disability; prevention or relief of poverty; accommodation, housing; arts, culture, heritage, science; amateur sport; animals; environment, conservation, heritage; recreation
Address: 161 Blackpool Road, Lytham St Annes, Lancs, FY8 4AA
Trustees: Mr Ian Barlow, Mr William Rucker, Mr Mark Steven Johnston, Susannah Gill, Miss Katherine Jane Keir, Linda Bowles
Income: £1,886,000 [2016]; £1,876,000 [2015]; £50,932,301 [2014]; £9,461,729 [2013]; £19,123,355 [2012]

Racing Industry Accident Benefit Scheme
Registered: 9 Jan 1981
Tel: 01488 71719 *Website:* racehorsetrainers.org
Activities: Disability
Address: The National Trainers Federation, 9 High Street, Lambourn, Hungerford, Berks, RG17 8XL
Trustees: Mr Michael Henriques, Mr George McGrath, Mr Jonathan Lancelot Eddis, Mrs Serena Geake, Dr John Disney
Income: £1,257,950 [2017]; £1,245,932 [2016]; £1,296,977 [2015]; £1,295,612 [2014]; £1,221,697 [2013]

Racing Welfare
Registered: 8 Dec 2000 *Employees:* 28 *Volunteers:* 7
Tel: 01638 560763 *Website:* racingwelfare.co.uk
Activities: Education, training; prevention or relief of poverty; accommodation, housing
Address: Racing Welfare, 20b Park Lane, Newmarket, Suffolk, CB8 8QD
Trustees: Mr Gary Middlebrook, Mr Patrick Russell, Mr Richard Charles Farquhar, Mr Simon Clarke, Mr John William Marshall Barlow, Mrs Nicky Lyon, Mr Rod Street, Mrs Venetia Wrigley, Baroness Ann Mallalieu QC, Mr Joey Newton, Mr Jonathan Lancelot Eddis, Mr Patrick James Russell, Mrs Morag Graham Gray
Income: £1,772,000 [2016]; £1,869,000 [2015]; £1,779,000 [2014]; £1,490,000 [2013]; £1,958,000 [2012]

Radha Soami Satsang Beas British Isles
Registered: 22 Jul 1992 *Volunteers:* 25
Tel: 01234 381234 *Website:* rssb.org
Activities: Education, training; advancement of health or saving of lives; religious activities; human rights, religious or racial harmony, equality or diversity
Address: Church End, Haynes, Bedford, MK45 3BL
Trustees: Mr Ravinder Dhaliwal, Mr Nirbail Singh Dhariwal, Mr John George Sewell, Mrs Sunita Naidoo, Mr Santosh Singh Vaswani
Income: £7,435,741 [2016]; £3,761,037 [2015]; £5,642,863 [2014]; £3,496,515 [2013]

Radius Trust Limited
Registered: 3 Aug 1994 *Employees:* 168 *Volunteers:* 15
Tel: 01483 891100 *Website:* radiustrust.org
Activities: Education, training
Address: Grafham Grange, Horsham Road, Grafham, Bramley, Guildford, Surrey, GU5 0LH
Trustees: David Hope, Allan Davidson, Martin Coles, Dr Alison Smith, Jennifer Williams
Income: £8,111,308 [2016]; £8,697,763 [2015]; £7,969,355 [2014]; £5,605,915 [2013]; £6,810,173 [2012]

The Radley Foundation
Registered: 10 Feb 1977
Tel: 01235 543000 *Website:* radley.org.uk
Activities: Education, training
Address: Radley College, Radley, Abingdon, Oxon, OX14 2HR
Trustees: Mr Thomas Oliver Seymour MA, Mr Michael Guy Hilliard Heald, Mr Rupert Henson, Mr Richard Huntingford, Mr William Maydon, Mr Mark Soundy, Mr David Craig Shaw Smellie, Mr Gerald Kaye BSc FRICS, Mr Simon Melluish, Mr Simon Eccles-Williams, Mr Simon J B Shaw
Income: £3,284,123 [2017]; £2,069,452 [2016]; £2,369,000 [2015]; £992,968 [2014]; £1,004,093 [2013]

The Raf100 Appeal
Registered: 1 Jun 2016
Tel: 020 7307 3301
Activities: General charitable purposes; armed forces, emergency service efficiency
Address: Royal Air Force Benevolent Fund, 67 Portland Place, London, W1B 1AR
Trustees: Mr Stephen Andrew Armstrong, Mr James French, Mr Simon Jeremy Collins, Air Vice-Marshal David Murray CVO OBE, Air Chief Marshal Sir Glenn Torpy, Mr Nick John Bunting, Air Marshal Sir Graham Anthony Miller, Mr David Cheyne, Ms Margaret Mary Appleton, Air Marshal Sean Keith Paul Reynolds, Sir Kevin James Leeson, Air Vice-Marshal Michael Wigston
Income: £2,459,500 [2016]

Raghuvanshi Mahajan London Rama
Registered: 28 Jun 2004 *Employees:* 16 *Volunteers:* 100
Tel: 020 8578 8088 *Website:* jalarammandir.co.uk
Activities: Education, training; prevention or relief of poverty; religious activities; arts, culture, heritage, science; amateur sport
Address: 39-41 Oldfield Lane South, Greenford, Middlesex, UB6 9LB
Trustees: Cllr Rajnikant Chhotalal Khiroya, Dr Mansukh Morjaria, Mr Rashmi Jamnadas Chatwani, Mrs Asmita Masrani, Mr Amritlal Jethalal Rajani, Mr Laxmidas Tulsidas Popat, Mr Shaneel Hirani, Mr Prakash Gandecha, Mr Sharad Trikamlal Bhimjiyani, Mr Rajnikant Samji Davda, Mr Jayendrakumar Hansraj Morjaria, Mr Praful Radia, Mr Kishorkumar Dayalal Ghelani
Income: £1,436,816 [2016]; £1,082,820 [2015]; £677,531 [2014]; £672,095 [2013]; £620,438 [2012]

Rahma (Mercy)

Registered: 23 May 2003 *Employees:* 10 *Volunteers:* 30
Tel: 0116 251 6959 *Website:* rahmamercy.org.uk
Activities: General charitable purposes; education, training; advancement of health or saving of lives; disability; prevention or relief of poverty; overseas aid, famine relief; accommodation, housing; religious activities; amateur sport; economic, community development, employment; human rights, religious or racial harmony, equality or diversity; recreation; other charitable purposes
Address: 56 Hartington Road, Leicester, LE2 0GN
Trustees: Mr Salim Daud Valli, Abdulaziz Moti, Mr Mohammed Asif Vhora, Mr Abdul Raoof Kali, Mr Imtiaz Sadik Mahetar
Income: £1,514,603 [2017]; £1,417,569 [2016]; £1,292,139 [2015]; £1,790,953 [2014]; £1,586,521 [2013]

The Railway Children

Registered: 4 Nov 1996 *Employees:* 63 *Volunteers:* 41
Tel: 01270 757596 *Website:* railwaychildren.org.uk
Activities: Education, training; advancement of health or saving of lives; prevention or relief of poverty; overseas aid, famine relief; accommodation, housing; economic, community development, employment
Address: 1st Floor, 1 The Commons, Sandbach, Cheshire, CW11 1EG
Trustees: Henry Clarke, Ms Christine Taylor, Mr Haydn Abbott, Mr Trevor Winter, Anita Brook, Mr Malcolm Brown, James Horsman, Judith Lister, Mr Michael Holden BA Hons FIRO, Rob Brighouse, Mr Timothy Hartley, Mrs Dyan Crowther, Mr Arun Muttreja, Mr Jacob Kelly, Tricia Wright
Income: £3,682,890 [2017]; £3,038,879 [2016]; £3,558,855 [2015]; £3,008,042 [2014]; £2,988,296 [2013]

Railway Housing Association and Benefit Fund

Registered: 4 Jun 1963 *Employees:* 29
Tel: 01325 482125 *Website:* railwayha.co.uk
Activities: The prevention or relief of poverty; accommodation, housing; economic, community development, employment
Address: Railway Housing Association, Bank Top House, Garbutt Square, Neasham Road, Darlington, Co Durham, DL1 4DR
Trustees: Alistair Brown, June Grimes, Fiona Coleman, Stuart Blackett, Pat Wanless, David Goodman, Berni Whitaker
Income: £7,049,163 [2017]; £7,009,966 [2016]; £6,408,688 [2015]; £6,166,170 [2014]; £5,882,092 [2013]

The Rainbow Centre (Marham)

Registered: 5 Nov 2008 *Employees:* 78
Tel: 01760 446161 *Website:* marhamhub.co.uk
Activities: Education, training
Address: The Rainbow Centre, Elm Road, Upper Marham, King's Lynn, Norfolk, PE33 9NF
Trustees: Mrs Dee Gent, Mr Stewart Anthony Geary, Mr Vincent Andrew Jackson, Mr Gary James Walker, Mrs Joanne Michelle Townsend, Sqn Ldr David Smith BSc RAF, Mr Kevin Lee Gatland, Mrs Helen Deborah Hobson, Squadron Leader James David Poynton
Income: £1,545,940 [2017]; £1,323,894 [2016]; £1,385,740 [2015]; £1,275,731 [2014]; £721,979 [2013]

Rainbow Trust Children's Charity

Registered: 14 Jul 1998 *Employees:* 100 *Volunteers:* 429
Tel: 01372 363438 *Website:* rainbowtrust.org.uk
Activities: The advancement of health or saving of lives
Address: 6 Cleeve Court, Cleeve Road, Leatherhead, Surrey, KT22 7UD
Trustees: Mr Michael Wainwright, Dr Jonathan Rabbs MBChB MSc MRCPCH, Mrs Celia Jane Woollett, Mr Andrew Honnor, Mr Tim Bunting, Mr Mark Richardson, Mr Mark Victor Cunningham, Mr Howard Dyer
Income: £4,623,891 [2017]; £4,239,452 [2016]; £5,067,880 [2015]; £4,652,556 [2014]; £4,236,597 [2013]

The Rainforest Foundation (UK)

Registered: 6 Oct 2010 *Employees:* 23 *Volunteers:* 8
Website: rainforestfoundationuk.org
Activities: Education, training; environment, conservation, heritage; economic, community development, employment; human rights, religious or racial harmony, equality or diversity
Address: The Rainforest Foundation UK, 2-4 The Atelier, The Old Dairy Court, 17 Crouch Hill, London, N4 4AP
Trustees: Dr John Hemming, Ms Louise Julia Morriss, Mr Ben Kitchen, Dr Louise Erskine, Dr Helen Sarah Newing, Mr Mark Campanale, Mr Joseph Howes
Income: £3,322,466 [2016]; £2,810,358 [2015]; £2,445,845 [2014]; £2,255,298 [2013]; £1,870,630 [2012]

Raleigh International Trust

Registered: 30 Jun 1995 *Employees:* 124 *Volunteers:* 1,200
Tel: 020 7183 1270 *Website:* raleighinternational.org
Activities: General charitable purposes; education, training; economic, community development, employment
Address: Third Floor, Dean Bradley House, 52 Horseferry Road, London, SW1P 2AF
Trustees: Mr Stan Chan, Mr Jeremy Fish, Ms Mavis Owusu-Gyamfi, Mr Jack Newnham, Mr Ben Robinson, Dr Khalid Kosser MBE, Miss Amy Holmes, Miss Polly McGivern, Mr Sam Parker, Ms Karen Betts, Ms Meg Kneafsey, Alexander Nathan Lubar
Income: £7,977,000 [2016]; £7,388,000 [2015]; £6,867,000 [2014]; £6,049,030 [2013]; £4,100,282 [2012]

Rambert School of Ballet and Contemporary Dance

Registered: 8 Aug 2003 *Employees:* 21
Tel: 020 8892 9960 *Website:* rambertschool.org.uk
Activities: Education, training; arts, culture, heritage, science
Address: Rambert School of Ballet & Contemporary Dance, Clifton Lodge, St Margarets Drive, Twickenham, Middlesex, TW1 1QN
Trustees: Mrs Frances Prenn, Hon Jane Pleydell-Bouverie, Mr David Cazalet, Ms Rachel Avery, Ms Assis Carreiro, Mrs Sarah Campbell, Richard Devereux Burcombe Cooper, Miss Hope Keelan, Ms Holly Larrett, Ms Katie Thorpe, Ms Sophie Caruth
Income: £2,028,460 [2017]; £1,975,098 [2016]; £1,888,868 [2015]; £1,843,135 [2014]; £1,534,308 [2013]

The Ramblers' Association

Registered: 29 Aug 2002 *Employees:* 68 *Volunteers:* 25,000
Tel: 020 7339 8533 *Website:* ramblers.org.uk
Activities: Education, training; advancement of health or saving of lives; amateur sport; environment, conservation, heritage; recreation
Address: Ramblers Association, Camelford House, 87-90 Albert Embankment, London, SE1 7TW
Trustees: Sophie Clissold-Lesser, Dr Peter Rookes, Paul Rhodes, Alison Mitchell, Chris Hodgson, Rebecca Dawson, Malcolm McDonnell, Aynsley Jardin, Richard May, Teri Moore, Kate Ashbrook, Peter Carr, Michael Penny, Ronnie Forbes
Income: £9,617,000 [2016]; £10,184,000 [2015]; £8,906,000 [2014]; £8,120,000 [2013]; £7,699,000 [2012]

The Rank Foundation Limited

Registered: 11 Dec 1978 *Employees:* 36
Website: rankfoundation.com
Activities: General charitable purposes; education, training; disability; prevention or relief of poverty; accommodation, housing; religious activities; economic, community development, employment
Address: 12 Warwick Square, London, SW1V 2AA
Trustees: Joey Newton, Mr Andrew Edward Cowen MRICS, Mrs Lucinda Caroline Onslow MA, Mrs Johanna Louise Ropner, Mr Daniel Simon, Mr Jason Chaffer, Mr Andrew Fleming, Mr Mark Edward Trehearne Davies, The Hon Caroline Twiston Davies, Lord St Aldwyn, Ms Rose Mary Fitzpatrick, Mr Nicholas Buxton, Mr William Wyatt, Lindsey Anne Clay
Income: £2,951,000 [2016]; £3,258,000 [2015]; £2,012,000 [2014]; £820,000 [2013]; £1,350,000 [2012]

Arthur Rank Hospice Charity

Registered: 21 Dec 2009 *Employees:* 152 *Volunteers:* 300
Tel: 01223 675777 *Website:* arhc.org.uk
Activities: The advancement of health or saving of lives
Address: Arthur Rank Hospice Charity, Arthur Rank Hospice, Cherry Hinton Road, Shelford Bottom, Cambridge, CB22 3FB
Trustees: Mr Stephen Barry Kay, Mrs Jennifer Mary Brook, Ms Katherine Elizabeth Kirk, Mr Rosemary Ann Stamp, Mr Lee Foster Maughan, Mr John Richard Short, Ms Isabel Josephine Napper, Mr Alexander Geoffrey V Manning, Mr Graeme Vaughan Jones, Dr Arnold Fertig
Income: £7,638,699 [2017]; £6,369,623 [2016]; £2,023,196 [2015]; £1,858,420 [2014]; £2,953,070 [2013]

Ranyard Charitable Trust

Registered: 14 Oct 2004 *Employees:* 100
Tel: 020 8318 1119 *Website:* ranyard.org
Activities: The advancement of health or saving of lives; disability; accommodation, housing
Address: 2B Brandram Road, London, SE13 5EA
Trustees: Mr Nicholas Lines, Lady Stone, Mr Robert Cunningham, Mrs Monica Margaret Blake
Income: £3,930,652 [2014]; £4,033,659 [2013]

Rape and Sexual Abuse Support Centre

Registered: 21 Feb 2001 *Employees:* 17 *Volunteers:* 45
Tel: 020 8683 3311 *Website:* rasasc.org.uk
Activities: General charitable purposes; education, training; advancement of health or saving of lives; other charitable purposes
Address: P O Box 383, Croydon, Surrey, CR9 2AW
Trustees: Ms Diane Ovenden, Dr Carol McNaughton-Nicholls, Ms Lucy Aitkens, Ms Nicki Fraser, Ruth Tedros, Ms Saima Hirji
Income: £1,022,676 [2017]; £1,336,942 [2016]; £840,343 [2015]; £415,595 [2014]; £501,463 [2013]

The Raphael Freshwater Memorial Association

Registered: 12 Mar 1962
Tel: 020 7836 1555
Activities: General charitable purposes; education, training; prevention or relief of poverty; religious activities
Address: Freshwater Group of Companies, Freshwater House, 158-162 Shaftesbury Avenue, London, WC2H 8HR
Trustees: Mr Benzion Schalom Eliezer Freshwater, Mr Richard Fischer, Mr D Davis, Mr Solomon Israel Freshwater
Income: £15,359,000 [2017]; £8,372,000 [2016]; £3,370,000 [2015]; £4,000,000 [2014]; £3,722,000 [2013]

Rapport Housing and Care

Registered: 6 Dec 1967 *Employees:* 242 *Volunteers:* 67
Tel: 01634 723007 *Website:* rapporthousingandcare.co.uk
Activities: The advancement of health or saving of lives; accommodation, housing
Address: Abbeyfield Kent Society, Station Road, Cuxton, Rochester, Kent, ME2 1AB
Trustees: Mr S Tomlinson, Mr R Caven, Mrs M Low BSc Econ, Miss D Bride BA RSW, Mr J Townend BSc Hons, Mr Z Miles BA Hons MA FCA, Mr T Searles, Ms Cathy Deplessis
Income: £12,098,232 [2017]; £15,381,466 [2016]; £12,131,234 [2015]; £12,867,056 [2014]; £11,876,555 [2013]

Raspberry Pi Foundation

Registered: 5 May 2009 *Employees:* 61 *Volunteers:* 2,153
Tel: 01223 322633 *Website:* raspberrypi.org
Activities: Education, training
Address: Raspberry Pi Foundation, 30 Station Road, Cambridge, CB1 2JH
Trustees: Mr Jonathan Drori, David Braben, David Cleevely, Sherry Coutu, Mr Christopher John Mairs, Pete Lomas, Louis Glass, Matilda Blyth
Income: £7,272,901 [2016]; £4,193,771 [2015]; £2,019,972 [2014]; £2,297,382 [2013]; £1,152,637 [2012]

Ratcliffe College

Registered: 31 Aug 2006 *Employees:* 202 *Volunteers:* 10
Tel: 01509 817000 *Website:* ratcliffecollege.com
Activities: General charitable purposes; education, training
Address: Ratcliffe College, Fosse Way, Ratcliffe on the Wreake, Leicester, LE7 4SG
Trustees: Mrs Joan Margaret Smidowicz, Father Philip Sainter, Father David John Myers, Mr Louis Paul Massarella, Rev Anthony Furlong, Father Anthony Desmond Meredith, Mrs Mary Goldstraw, Father Brian Cuddihy, Mr Richard William Gamble, Mr Paul Raymond Francis Rudd, Rev Joseph O'Reilly, Rev Tom Thomas, Dr Sheelagh Brigid Bolt
Income: £11,640,004 [2016]; £10,776,085 [2015]; £9,561,386 [2014]; £9,110,956 [2013]; £8,816,692 [2012]

Rathbone Training

Registered: 19 Dec 2011 *Employees:* 225 *Volunteers:* 2
Tel: 07734 875055 *Website:* rathboneuk.org
Activities: Education, training; economic, community development, employment
Address: Newcastle College, Scotswood Road, Newcastle upon Tyne, NE4 7SA
Trustees: Christopher Roberts, Joe Docherty, Ian Webber, Mr Christopher Payne, Mr Graeme Dodd
Income: £20,928,000 [2017]; £18,341,000 [2016]; £23,673,000 [2015]; £26,832,000 [2014]; £34,949,000 [2013]

The Rayne Foundation
Registered: 8 Sep 1965 *Employees:* 6
Website: raynefoundation.org.uk
Activities: General charitable purposes; education, training; advancement of health or saving of lives; arts, culture, heritage, science
Address: Office 107, 239 Kensington High Street, London, W8 6SN
Trustees: Lady Jane Rayne, Robert Rayne, Professor Sir Anthony Newman Taylor, Nicholas Rayne, Rabbi Baroness Neuberger, Lady Browne-Wilkinson, Natasha Rayne, Sir Emyr Jones Parry
Income: £1,746,994 [2016]; £1,473,360 [2015]; £1,461,131 [2014]; £1,411,421 [2013]; £1,199,058 [2012]

The Rayners Special Educational Trust
Registered: 20 Jan 1999 *Employees:* 89
Activities: Education, training; disability
Address: c/o Stone King LLP, Boundary House, 91 Charterhouse Street, London, EC1M 6HR
Trustees: Mr Timothy Layfield, Mr Hugh Forsyth, Mrs Dara Galic, Mr Paul Ricketts, Ms Caroline Allen, Mr Robert Walther
Income: £3,227,733 [2014]; £3,279,295 [2013]

Rays of Sunshine
Registered: 8 Mar 2004 *Employees:* 25 *Volunteers:* 200
Tel: 020 8782 1171 *Website:* raysofsunshine.org.uk
Activities: General charitable purposes; advancement of health or saving of lives
Address: 1 Olympic Way, Wembley, Middlesex, HA9 0NP
Trustees: Mr Justin Randall, Mr Nicholas Davis, Mr Daniel Coleman, Mr Stephen David Allan, Mr David Joseph
Income: £4,420,453 [2016]; £4,180,813 [2015]; £3,865,704 [2014]; £3,101,226 [2013]; £2,272,099 [2012]

The Raystede Centre for Animal Welfare Limited
Registered: 3 Dec 1964 *Employees:* 90 *Volunteers:* 140
Tel: 01825 880472 *Website:* raystede.org
Activities: Animals
Address: Orchid Cottage, The Broyle, Ringmer, Lewes, E Sussex, BN8 5AJ
Trustees: Dr Jean O'Neill, Ms Margaret Roberts, Susan Margaret Walton, Mr Jonathan Vine-Hall, Mr John Amies
Income: £3,218,183 [2017]; £2,467,573 [2016]; £2,196,148 [2015]; £1,821,045 [2014]; £2,088,311 [2013]

Re - Bourne
Registered: 4 Aug 2008 *Employees:* 89
Tel: 01252 597050 *Website:* new-adventures.net
Activities: General charitable purposes; education, training
Address: c/o Farnham Maltings, Bridge Square, Farnham, Surrey, GU9 7QR
Trustees: Ms Helen Protheroe, Mr Sean Egan, Ms Jeanette Siddall CBE, Mr Kenneth Tharp CBE, Mrs Kaneez Shaid MBE, Ms Brenda Emmanus
Income: £9,358,199 [2017]; £6,447,952 [2016]; £999,364 [2015]; £402,937 [2014]; £252,041 [2013]

Re:Vision North Limited
Registered: 6 Mar 2014
Tel: 0303 030 0030
Activities: General charitable purposes; education, training; prevention or relief of poverty; economic, community development, employment
Address: Procure Plus, The Lancastrian Office Centre, Talbot Road, Stretford, Manchester, M32 0FP
Trustees: Prof Michael Alan Brown CBE DL, Mr Jonathan Paul Drake, Saf Arfan, Mick Smith, Mr Paul Andrew Roberts, Mr Darren Cormack, Mr Paul Martin Webb
Income: £2,334,337 [2017]; £2,098,976 [2016]; £2,281,050 [2015]

Reach Learning Disability
Registered: 29 Jun 1999 *Employees:* 38 *Volunteers:* 100
Tel: 01636 819066 *Website:* reachuk.org
Activities: Education, training; disability; accommodation, housing; economic, community development, employment
Address: Prebend Passage, Southwell, Notts, NG25 0JH
Trustees: Mr David Thompson, Mrs Madeline Oliver, Mrs Daphne Hughes, Mr Michael Norman Davidson, Mrs Patricia Colman, Mrs Rachel Lannon, Mrs Ann Best, Mr Nicholas Andrew Turner, Keith Harding, Mr Adam Peter McQuilkin, Mrs Julie Payne
Income: £1,669,832 [2017]; £1,409,963 [2016]; £976,354 [2015]; £708,405 [2014]; £649,544 [2013]

Reach to Teach
Registered: 8 Oct 2007 *Employees:* 39
Tel: 020 3167 3202 *Website:* reach-to-teach.org
Activities: Education, training
Address: Reach to Teach, 10 Barley Mow Passage, London, W4 4PH
Trustees: Mr Sanjeev Ramesh Gandhi, Mr Matthew Symonds, Ms Mahalakshmi Ramadorai, Mr Vaibhav Manek, Dr Richard Broyd, Mr Richard Meredith, Mr Soumya Rajan, Ms Maya Swaminathan Sinha
Income: £4,887,239 [2017]; £3,556,705 [2016]; £1,989,314 [2015]; £1,438,481 [2014]; £1,706,438 [2013]

Read Foundation
Registered: 30 Jan 2015 *Employees:* 15 *Volunteers:* 70
Tel: 0161 224 3334 *Website:* readfoundation.org.uk
Activities: General charitable purposes; education, training; prevention or relief of poverty
Address: 628 Stockport Road, Manchester, M13 0SH
Trustees: Mr Mohammed Farooq, Mr Tahir Begg, Mr Rizwan Rashid, Mr Haroon Rashid, Dr Yaqub Hussain, Dr Usman Choudry
Income: £2,228,746 [2017]; £2,300,830 [2016]

The Read School, Drax
Registered: 16 Jan 1968 *Employees:* 63
Tel: 01757 618248 *Website:* readschool.co.uk
Activities: General charitable purposes; education, training
Address: Read School, Drax, Selby, N Yorks, YO8 8NL
Trustees: The Read School Drax Trustee Limited
Income: £3,131,047 [2016]; £2,749,718 [2015]; £2,702,086 [2014]; £2,777,239 [2013]; £2,912,804 [2012]

Read for Good
Registered: 24 Jun 2009 *Employees:* 6 *Volunteers:* 4
Tel: 0845 606 1151 *Website:* readforgood.org
Activities: Education, training; advancement of health or saving of lives; disability
Address: Read for Good, Nailsworth Mills Estate, Avening Road, Nailsworth, Stroud, Glos, GL6 0BS
Trustees: Ms Debs Paproska-Cole, Ms Terri Passenger, Mr Stephen Morgan, Mr Michael Walker
Income: £1,148,277 [2017]; £812,464 [2016]; £1,013,700 [2015]; £1,214,653 [2014]; £1,041,417 [2013]

The Reader Organisation
Registered: 19 Nov 2008 *Employees:* 128 *Volunteers:* 280
Tel: 07807 106770 *Website:* thereader.org.uk
Activities: Education, training; advancement of health or saving of lives; prevention or relief of poverty; arts, culture, heritage, science; other charitable purposes
Address: The Reader Organisation, The Mansion House, Calderstones Park, Liverpool, L18 3JB
Trustees: Rosemary Hawley, John Flamson, Mr Giles Robert Brand, Mr Hugh John Biddell, Dr Shyamal Mukherjee, Mrs Kathy Anstey, Ms Jacqueline Anne Tammenoms Bakker, Ms Geethanjali Rabindrakumar
Income: £3,044,142 [2017]; £3,678,504 [2016]; £2,813,854 [2015]; £2,067,242 [2014]; £1,624,897 [2013]

ReadiBus
Registered: 21 Jan 1986 *Employees:* 67 *Volunteers:* 35
Tel: 0118 931 3406 *Website:* readibus.co.uk
Activities: Disability
Address: ReadiBus, Cradock Road, Reading, Berks, RG2 0JT
Trustees: Dr Sophia Bowlby, Cllr Bet Tickner, Mr Gul Muwaz Khan, Mr Guy Grandison, Cllr Charles Edward Hopper, Mrs Shirley Beggs, Trevor Bottomley, Cllr Brian Wedge, Mr Jeffrey Beck, Mr Dan Dennett, Cllr Rose Williams, Mr Martijn Gilbert
Income: £1,291,444 [2017]; £1,255,012 [2016]; £1,298,387 [2015]; £1,245,707 [2014]; £1,318,710 [2013]

Reading Blue Coat School
Registered: 2 Aug 2001 *Employees:* 164
Tel: 0118 933 5808 *Website:* rbcs.org.uk
Activities: Education, training
Address: Mr S A Jackson BSc MBA, Holme Park, Sonning Lane, Sonning, Reading, Berks, RG4 6SU
Trustees: Mr Charles Hubbard, Mr David John Few, Mrs Elaine Morgan, Rev Stephen James Pullin, Professor Jonathan Marchini, Mrs Louise Elaine Hague, Doctor Andrew Francis Worrall, Mr Clive Litten, Mr Peter Anthony Smith, Mr Peter Michael Bertram, Rev John Alexander Franklyn Taylor, Mrs Fiona Eleanor Dawson, Mr Stephen George Mount, Mrs Laura Hyde
Income: £11,549,328 [2016]; £11,196,006 [2015]; £10,618,473 [2014]; £9,967,387 [2013]; £9,102,811 [2012]

Reading FC Community Trust
Registered: 10 Sep 2008 *Employees:* 58 *Volunteers:* 20
Tel: 0118 968 2157 *Website:* community.readingfc.co.uk
Activities: Education, training; amateur sport
Address: Reading Football Club PLC, Madejski Stadium, Reading, Berks, RG2 0FL
Trustees: Bryan Stabler, Mr Richard Eric Holliday, Mr Craig Parker, Mr Ronald Gourlay, Mr James Carter, Mr David Downs, Mr Andrew Reaney, Mr Stuart Roach, Mr Neil Coupe, Mrs Diana Anthony
Income: £1,116,461 [2017]; £979,728 [2016]; £1,036,671 [2015]; £927,732 [2014]; £762,718 [2013]

Reading Gospel Hall Trust
Registered: 15 Jan 2015 *Volunteers:* 170
Tel: 07848 451716
Activities: Religious activities; other charitable purposes
Address: c/o Shinfield Court, Church Lane, Three Mile Cross, Reading, Berks, RG7 1HB
Trustees: Mr Charles Andrew White, Mr Howard Tennent, Mr Roger David Humphreys, Mr Richard James Hearn, Mr Andrew Keith Parsons
Income: £1,108,214 [2017]; £870,357 [2016]

Reading University Students' Union
Registered: 10 Sep 2014 *Employees:* 80 *Volunteers:* 232
Tel: 0118 378 4143 *Website:* rusu.co.uk
Activities: Education, training
Address: Reading University Students' Union, P O Box 230, Whiteknights, Reading, Berks, RG6 6AZ
Trustees: Mr Robert Dwyer, Mr Iain Franklin, Ms Jemima Maple Tabeart, Mr Tristan Spencer, Ed White, Mr Eliot George Thomas Smith, Ms Francess McConnell, Mr Mark Stoddart, Ms Holly Cottingham, Ms Leen Alnajjab, Ms Charlotte O'Leary, Ms Rose Lennon, Millie Farquhar
Income: £6,515,229 [2017]; £6,042,077 [2016]; £5,497,029 [2015]

Reading YMCA
Registered: 8 Mar 2011 *Employees:* 26 *Volunteers:* 20
Tel: 0118 957 5746 *Website:* ymcareading.org
Activities: General charitable purposes; education, training; prevention or relief of poverty; accommodation, housing; amateur sport; economic, community development, employment
Address: Reading YMCA, Milward Centre, 34 Parkside Road, Reading, Berks, RG30 2DD
Trustees: Mr Lindsey Edwards, Mr Ray'Jones, Mr George Nowacki, Mr Roger Fleming, Mr Stephen Sherwood
Income: £1,029,953 [2017]; £965,535 [2016]; £1,077,522 [2015]; £918,165 [2014]; £940,804 [2013]

Real Life Options
Registered: 19 Mar 2014 *Employees:* 1,485
Tel: 01977 525635 *Website:* reallifeoptions.org
Activities: Education, training; advancement of health or saving of lives; disability; accommodation, housing; economic, community development, employment
Address: Real Life Options, David Wandless House, A1 Business Park, Knottingley Road, Knottingley, W Yorks, WF11 0BU
Trustees: Mr David Wilkin, Mr Gregg Collingham, Mrs Vivien Simon, Mr John McDonald, Dr Robert Hendry, Mr Ian David Hardcastle
Income: £33,872,000 [2017]; £34,625,000 [2016]; £36,321,000 [2015]

The Sir James Reckitt Charity
Registered: 12 Feb 1964 *Employees:* 2
Tel: 01482 655861 *Website:* thesirjamesreckittcharity.org.uk
Activities: General charitable purposes; advancement of health or saving of lives; disability; prevention or relief of poverty; overseas aid, famine relief; accommodation, housing; religious activities; arts, culture, heritage, science; amateur sport; environment, conservation, heritage; economic, community development, employment
Address: 7 Derrymore Road, Willerby, Hull, HU10 6ES
Trustees: Mr William Upton, Mr Robert Martin Gibson, Mrs Caroline Jennings, Mr Robin Upton, Mr Charles Maxsted, Mr Simon Edward Upton, Miss Rebecca Holt, Mr James Patrick Atherton, Mr James Holt, Ms Ondine Elizabeth Upton, Mr Philip Holt, Mrs Sarah Craven, Mr Simon James Upton, Mr Edward Upton, Andrew Palfreman, Mr Oliver James Jennings
Income: £1,507,355 [2017]; £1,527,879 [2016]; £1,306,889 [2015]; £1,473,918 [2014]; £1,263,455 [2013]

The Rector and Scholars of Exeter College in the University of Oxford
Registered: 12 Apr 2011 *Employees:* 157
Tel: 01865 279600 *Website:* exeter.ox.ac.uk
Activities: Education, training
Address: Exeter College, Turl Street, Oxford, OX1 3DP
Trustees: Sir Richard Hughes Trainor KBE, Professor Jonathan Thacker, Simon Clarke, Cornelia Drutu Badea, Michael Hart, Jane Hiddleston, Jeri Johnson, Marc Lauxtermann, Zhongmin Qian, Helen Spencer, Maureen Taylor, Philipp Kukura, Christopher Ballinger, Michael Osborne, Karin Sigloch, Martin Davy, Professor Keith Channon, Dr Garret Cotter, Dr Barnaby Taylor, Ms Oreet Ashery, Dr Imogen Choi, Dr Asli Niyazioglu-Djasalov, Christopher Fletcher, Dr Catherine Green, Christina De Bellaigue, Andrew Farmer, Jonathan Herring, William Jensen, James Kennedy, Nigel Portwood, Carol Robinson, Andrew Steane, Ervin Fodor, Christoph Tang, Jared Tanner, James Grant, Rachel Taylor, Andrew Allen, Dr Gail Hayward, Professor Conall MacNiocaill, Dr Michael Glover, Prof Giuseppe Marcocci, Dr Natasha Simonova
Income: £11,262,000 [2017]; £8,363,000 [2016]; £12,374,000 [2015]; £12,945,000 [2014]; £15,779,000 [2013]

Red House School Limited
Registered: 3 Jul 1966 *Employees:* 51
Tel: 01642 553370 *Website:* redhouseschool.co.uk
Activities: Education, training
Address: Red House School, 36 The Green, Norton, Stockton on Tees, Cleveland, TS20 1DX
Trustees: Miss Victoria Duncan, Mr Gavin David Cordwell-Smith, Mr Simon Jonathon Asforth, Mr Sean Costigan, Mrs Kate Huddart, Mr Sven Wright, Mrs Amy Witham, Dr Amar Rangan, Ms Amanda Louise Mallen-Beadle, Mr Mark Stephen Craggs, Mr Jeremy Henning, Mr Guy Taylor, Mr Paul Card, Mr Neil Simpson
Income: £3,597,588 [2017]; £3,824,403 [2016]; £4,044,260 [2015]; £4,025,400 [2014]; £3,962,706 [2013]

Redbridge Sports Centre Trust Limited
Registered: 18 Feb 1971 *Employees:* 165 *Volunteers:* 398
Tel: 020 8498 1000 *Website:* rslonline.co.uk
Activities: Amateur sport
Address: Redbridge Sports Centre Trust Ltd, Forest Road, Ilford, Essex, IG6 3HD
Trustees: Ms Joyce Ryan, Mrs Wendy Spencer, Mrs Carolynne Spencer, Mr Clive Rippon, Cllr Robert Littlewood, Mrs Rasmita Gohil, Mr Lloyd Jacob Duddridge, Ms Jayna Jogia, Mr Paul Clarke, Miss Jane Kelloe, Mr Eric William Brown, Mr Ken Leggate, Mr John Fortescue, Mr Martin Lawrence, Mr John Norman
Income: £2,512,669 [2017]; £2,400,319 [2016]; £2,221,692 [2015]; £2,146,411 [2014]; £2,328,863 [2013]

Redbridge, Epping and Harlow Crossroads - Caring for Carers
Registered: 24 Oct 1991 *Employees:* 75
Tel: 01708 757242 *Website:* carerstrustcrossroadsehhr.org
Activities: Disability
Address: Harrow Lodge House, Hornchurch Road, Hornchurch, Essex, RM11 1JU
Trustees: Mr Ian Turnbull, Mr Richard Thomas
Income: £1,292,108 [2017]; £1,616,591 [2016]; £1,780,272 [2015]; £1,281,635 [2014]; £1,319,479 [2013]

Redcliffe School Trust Ltd
Registered: 7 Nov 1973 *Employees:* 29 *Volunteers:* 1
Tel: 020 7352 9247 *Website:* redcliffeschool.com
Activities: Education, training
Address: Redcliffe School, 47 Redcliffe Gardens, London, SW10 9JH
Trustees: Dr Gerard Silverlock, Mr Roger Flynn, Mrs Sarah Smith, Mr Mark Levine, Mrs Geraldine Engelhart, Mr Harry Biggs-Davison, Mrs Georgina Harris, Mrs Vanessa Lee Perrin, Mrs Rosaynd Kamaryc
Income: £2,418,721 [2016]; £2,585,446 [2015]; £2,262,185 [2014]; £2,024,283 [2013]; £2,005,097 [2012]

The Reddiford School Charitable Trust
Registered: 18 May 1973 *Employees:* 78
Tel: 020 8866 0660 *Website:* reddiford.co.uk
Activities: Education, training
Address: 36-38 Cecil Park, Pinner, Middlesex, HA5 5HH
Trustees: Peter Hamilton, Mrs Diana Rose, Mr Atul Doshi, Mr Caroline Ojo, Reddiford School Trustee, Graham Jukes, Mrs Valerie Coltman, Fr Dan Bond, Miss Lauren Mercurius Taylor
Income: £3,439,224 [2016]; £3,434,215 [2015]; £3,235,959 [2014]; £2,768,116 [2013]; £2,696,915 [2012]

Redeemed Christian Church of God ('RCCG') Royal Connections Network
Registered: 29 Jan 2001 *Employees:* 9 *Volunteers:* 350
Tel: 020 8525 1555 *Website:* royalconnections.org.uk
Activities: General charitable purposes; education, training; prevention or relief of poverty; religious activities
Address: The Hub, RCCG Royal Connections, 90 Monier Road, London, E3 2ND
Trustees: Dr Francis Oladimeji, Mrs Roseline Bella, Ms Modupe Bello, Dr David Olusola Oludoyi, Mr Samuel Akpan
Income: £1,429,317 [2016]; £1,421,159 [2015]; £1,632,163 [2014]; £1,404,143 [2013]; £1,359,517 [2012]

Redeemed Christian Church of God ('RCCG') Victory House
Registered: 18 Jan 2001 *Employees:* 9
Tel: 020 7252 7522 *Website:* rccgvictoryhouse.com
Activities: Education, training; religious activities
Address: 5 Congreve Street, off Old Kent Road, London, SE17 1TJ
Trustees: Mrs Abimbola Odufisan, Mr Stephen Bello, Dr Adebisi Akinde
Income: £1,409,195 [2016]; £1,432,752 [2015]; £1,516,365 [2014]; £1,343,529 [2013]; £1,480,764 [2012]

Redeemed Christian Church of God (RCCG) Trinity Chapel
Registered: 15 Jan 2001 *Employees:* 11 *Volunteers:* 150
Website: trinitychapel.org.uk
Activities: Education, training; prevention or relief of poverty; overseas aid, famine relief; religious activities; economic, community development, employment
Address: Trinity Chapel, The Discovery Centre, Jenkins Lane, Barking, Essex, IG11 0AD
Trustees: Agu Irukwu, Mr Sola Ewedemi, Mr Nick Bakare, Dr Shola Adeaga
Income: £1,063,353 [2016]; £1,374,070 [2015]; £1,839,061 [2014]; £1,591,685 [2013]; £1,574,394 [2012]

Redeemed Christian Church of God
Registered: 29 Jan 2001 *Employees:* 34 *Volunteers:* 30
Tel: 020 8171 1030 *Website:* rccguk.church
Activities: General charitable purposes; prevention or relief of poverty; overseas aid, famine relief; religious activities
Address: Redeemed Christian Church of God, Redemption House, Gunnels Wood Park, Gunnels Wood Road, Stevenage, Herts, SG1 2TA
Trustees: Pastor Femi Popoola, Pastor K Bamigbade, Pastor Andrew Adeleke, Pastor Agu Irukwu, Pastor Adeleke Sanusi, Pastor Wunmi Oladunjoye
Income: £4,760,734 [2016]; £4,577,217 [2015]; £4,401,006 [2014]; £4,186,343 [2013]; £3,846,186 [2012]

Redemptorist Publications
Registered: 28 Oct 1996 *Employees:* 37 *Volunteers:* 1
Tel: 01420 88222 *Website:* rpbooks.co.uk
Activities: Religious activities
Address: Redemptionist Publications, Wolfs Lane, Chawton, Alton, Hants, GU34 3HQ
Trustees: Rev Richard Reid, Rev Charles Corrigan, Father Andrew Thomas Burns CSsR, Rev Gerard Mulligan CSsR, Provincial Superior Ronnie McAinsh, Rev Timothy Joseph Buckley CSsR
Income: £2,799,429 [2016]; £2,631,743 [2015]; £2,645,607 [2014]; £2,704,156 [2013]; £3,013,445 [2012]

The Redland High School for Girls
Registered: 3 Nov 1966 *Employees:* 89
Tel: 0117 924 5796 *Website:* redlandhigh.com
Activities: Education, training
Address: Redmaids High School, Redland Court, Bristol, BS6 7EF
Trustees: Mrs Susan Mary Perry, Mrs Phyllida Lucy Noel Pyper Ma Hons Oxford, Mrs Yvonne Craggs, Ms Sally MacDonald Dore, Mrs Rosemary Heald, Mr Richard Page, Miss Anne Marcelle Ebery BA (Hons), Dr John Littler, Mr Michael James Henry, Ms Elizabeth Clarson, Mr Timothy Phillips
Income: £4,625,206 [2015]; £4,560,119 [2014]; £4,163,728 [2013]; £3,917,019 [2012]

Redmaids' High School
Registered: 21 Jul 2004 *Employees:* 245
Tel: 0117 962 2641 *Website:* redmaidshigh.co.uk
Activities: Education, training
Address: Redmaids' High School, Westbury Road, Westbury on Trym, Bristol, BS9 3AW
Trustees: Mr Christopher Sanford Martin, Mr Andrew George Aldridge Hillman, Mrs Thelma Howell, Mr Michael James Henry, Mr Timothy Coulson Phillips, Mrs Anne Denise Taylor, Mr Andrew Charles Hardwick BSc Hons MRICS, Mr Richard John Page, Mrs Gillian Barbara Rowcliffe, Dr John Samuel Littler, Mrs Valerie Dixon, Ms Elizabeth Spanton Clarson, Mr Michael Davies, Mr James Robert Fox, Ms Sally MacDonald Dore, Mrs Rosemary Anne Heald
Income: £11,594,396 [2017]; £18,887,538 [2016]; £6,956,282 [2015]; £6,930,645 [2014]; £6,618,649 [2013]

Redthread Youth Limited
Registered: 8 Dec 1995 *Employees:* 25
Tel: 020 3744 6888 *Website:* redthread.org.uk
Activities: Education, training; advancement of health or saving of lives
Address: Redthread Youth Ltd, Third Floor, 18 Buckingham Palace Road, London, SW1W 0QP
Trustees: Mr Simon Robert Charlick, Louisa Mann, Ms Lucie Rae Russell, Caroline Havers, Dr Vanessa Skelton
Income: £1,018,063 [2017]; £611,005 [2016]; £957,279 [2015]; £156,978 [2014]; £354,184 [2013]

Redwings Horse Sanctuary
Registered: 27 Mar 1998 *Employees:* 280 *Volunteers:* 29
Tel: 01508 481001 *Website:* redwings.org.uk
Activities: Animals
Address: Redwings Horse Sanctuary, Hapton, Norwich, NR15 1SP
Trustees: Mrs Ann Polley, Mr Stephen Clark, Mr Andrew Fryer, Mr Paul Fileman, Mr Mark Little, Mr Peter Graham Horrocks, Mr David Buckton
Income: £12,858,589 [2016]; £12,007,813 [2015]; £9,078,590 [2014]; £9,963,178 [2013]; £9,819,084 [2012]

The Reed Educational Trust Limited
Registered: 19 Sep 1989 *Employees:* 26
Tel: 01608 674224 *Website:* reedbusinessschool.co.uk
Activities: Education, training
Address: Reed Business School, The Manor, Little Compton, Moreton in Marsh, Glos, GL56 0RZ
Trustees: Sir Alec Edward Reed CBE, Mrs Stella Shaw, Mr James Andrew Reed, Mr Peter Gordon Green, Mr Asad Fazal Noorani
Income: £1,734,222 [2016]; £1,687,262 [2015]; £1,805,773 [2014]; £1,832,659 [2013]; £1,746,335 [2012]

The Reed Foundation
Registered: 20 Oct 1972
Tel: 020 7201 9980 *Website:* thebiggive.org.uk
Activities: General charitable purposes; education, training; advancement of health or saving of lives; prevention or relief of poverty; overseas aid, famine relief; arts, culture, heritage, science; environment, conservation, heritage; other charitable purposes
Address: First Floor, The Peak, 5 Wilton Road, London, SW1V 1AN
Trustees: Mr Richard Reed, Mr James Reed, Sir Alec Edward Reed CBE, Mrs Alex Chapman
Income: £4,320,778 [2016]; £45,830 [2015]; £211,649 [2014]; £672,295 [2013]; £783,041 [2012]

Richard Reeve's Foundation
Registered: 14 Jun 2010 *Employees:* 1
Tel: 020 7726 4230 *Website:* richardreevesfoundation.org.uk
Activities: Education, training; prevention or relief of poverty
Address: 13 Elliott's Place, London, N1 8HX
Trustees: Mr John Tickle, Mr Michael Hudson, Mrs Shannon Clare Farrington, Rev David Ingall, Ms Jo Emmerson, Mr Michael Bennett, Mr Mark Jessett, Gerald Rothwell, Miss Lorna Jane Russell, Dr Sotonye Odugbemi
Income: £1,109,864 [2017]; £805,820 [2016]; £643,447 [2015]; £486,919 [2014]; £625,587 [2013]

Reform Research Trust
Registered: 13 May 2004 *Employees:* 15
Tel: 020 7799 6699 *Website:* reform.co.uk
Activities: Education, training
Address: Reform Research, 5-6 St Matthew Street, London, SW1P 2JT
Trustees: Mr Stephen Thomas Hargrave, Mr Jeremy Sillem, Mr James Palmer
Income: £1,439,426 [2016]; £1,080,638 [2015]; £1,257,775 [2014]; £1,318,458 [2013]; £1,388,344 [2012]

Refuge
Registered: 13 Mar 1979 *Employees:* 215 *Volunteers:* 67
Tel: 020 7395 7700 *Website:* refuge.org.uk
Activities: Education, training; advancement of health or saving of lives; prevention or relief of poverty; accommodation, housing; human rights, religious or racial harmony, equality or diversity
Address: Refuge, International House, 1 St Katharines Way, London, E1W 1UN
Trustees: Baroness Helena Kennedy QC, Ms Manel De Silva, Ms Maggie Rae, Dame Stella Rimington, Ms Shelagh McKibbin, Ms Janice Pamela Panton MBE, Ms Ruth Margaret Harding, Ms Dianne Gwenllian Nelmes, Ms Barbara Donoghue Vavalidis
Income: £13,292,538 [2017]; £11,266,272 [2016]; £10,148,011 [2015]; £11,099,596 [2014]; £11,372,947 [2013]

Refugee Action
Registered: 10 Dec 1981 *Employees:* 79 *Volunteers:* 275
Website: refugee-action.org.uk
Activities: The prevention or relief of poverty; economic, community development, employment
Address: Refugee Action, 11 Belgrave Road, London, SW1V 1RB
Trustees: Ms Rosalind Lucas, Mr Christopher Walter Randall, Mr Thomas Skrinar, Mr Joseph Jenkins, Mr Amaf Yousef, Mr Andrew Gregg, Ms Stefanie Pfeil, Mrs Irmani Smallwood, Mr Jonathan Quinn
Income: £5,152,000 [2017]; £10,544,000 [2016]; £12,370,000 [2015]; £20,240,000 [2014]; £17,655,000 [2013]

The Regent (Christchurch) Limited
Registered: 26 Oct 2001 *Employees:* 12 *Volunteers:* 120
Tel: 01202 499199 *Website:* regentcentre.co.uk
Activities: Education, training; arts, culture, heritage, science
Address: Regent Centre, 51 High Street, Christchurch, Dorset, BH23 1AS
Trustees: Mr John Alastair George Hoare, Mrs Linda Kirkman, Mr David Roper, Mr Arthur Wardle, Mrs Maxine Davenport, Mrs Susan Lewis, Mrs Valerie Gillard, Mrs Jennet Lambert, Mrs Carole Toothill, Ms Susan Woodward, Mr Dominic Wong
Income: £1,378,104 [2017]; £1,202,093 [2016]; £1,093,748 [2015]; £954,453 [2014]; £883,194 [2013]

Regent's Park College
Registered: 23 Oct 1967 *Employees:* 36 *Volunteers:* 41
Tel: 01865 288120 *Website:* rpc.ox.ac.uk
Activities: Education, training; religious activities
Address: Regents Park College, Pusey Street, Oxford, OX1 2LB
Trustees: Keith Riglin, Mrs Enid King, Dr Carroll Stevens, Professor Paul Stuart Fiddes, Dr Robert Anthony Ellis, Mr Anthony John Clarke, Dr Paul Julian Thompson, Rev Mark Ord, Rev Stephen Keyworth, Rev Paul Robert George Burnish, Ms Julie Reynolds, Dr Nicholas John Wood, Professor Sir Malcolm Evans OBE, Mr Stephen Cowburn, Rev Alison MacKay, Dr Myra Neill Blyth, Dr Larry Joseph Kreitzer, Mr Anthony William Harris, Rev Carol Anne Murray, Mr Peter Bernard Bond, Mr Stephen McGlynn, Rev Andrew John Bevan
Income: £2,362,581 [2017]; £2,164,408 [2016]; £3,960,554 [2015]; £1,904,889 [2014]; £1,875,786 [2013]

Regent's Park Theatre Limited
Registered: 13 Jan 1964 *Employees:* 73
Tel: 0844 375 3460 *Website:* openairtheatre.com
Activities: Arts, culture, heritage, science
Address: Stage Door Gate, Open Air Theatre, Inner Circle, Regent's Park, London, NW1 4NU
Trustees: Robert Davis DL MA Cantab, Sir Peter Rogers, Ms Samantha Spiro, Mr Martin Wilkinson, Mr Stuart Griffiths, Ms Toni Rochelle Racklin, Mr James Reed
Income: £6,991,315 [2016]; £6,728,239 [2015]; £4,763,880 [2014]; £6,287,421 [2013]; £2,806,154 [2012]

Regent's University London
Registered: 24 Apr 1985 *Employees:* 439
Tel: 020 7487 7813 *Website:* regents.ac.uk
Activities: Education, training
Address: Regents University, Careers & Business Relations, Inner Circle, Regents Park, London, NW1 4NS
Trustees: Sir Graeme Davies, Mrs Carole Diane Baume, Ms Vimmi Singh, Mrs Marguerite Dennis, Mr Matthias Thomas Harald Feist, Dr Diana Walford, Ms Amanda Bringans, David Barker, Elizabeth Jenkins, Ms Mary Ann Kerr, Mr Dominic James O'Rourke, Miss Alison Jean Allden, Mr David Lionel Barnes, Mrs Rosalyn Sharon Schofield, Aldwyn John Richard Cooper, Mr Dominic Laffy, Carol Burns, Ms Rachel Anne Clarke, Ken Batty, Carl Lygo, Mr Martin Potter
Income: £46,070,000 [2017]; £50,889,000 [2016]; £51,830,000 [2015]; £53,170,000 [2014]; £48,196,000 [2013]

Rehabilitation Services Trust for Oxfordshire Re-Employment Limited
Registered: 23 Sep 1977 *Employees:* 47 *Volunteers:* 176
Tel: 0845 250 0518 *Website:* restore.org.uk
Activities: Education, training; advancement of health or saving of lives; disability
Address: Restore, Manzil Way, Cowley Road, Oxford, OX4 1YH
Trustees: Ms Anne James, Mary Robertson, Stuart Haigh, David Thurston, Trisha Andrew, Mr Godfrey Cole, Mr Robert Wilkes, Samantha Mostyn, Louise Wheeler, Dr Akiko Watanabe
Income: £1,662,596 [2017]; £1,649,576 [2016]; £1,449,652 [2015]; £1,308,323 [2014]; £1,254,391 [2013]

The Rehabilitation Trust
Registered: 2 Mar 1984 Volunteers: 3
Tel: 020 8806 1548
Activities: General charitable purposes; education, training; advancement of health or saving of lives; prevention or relief of poverty; overseas aid, famine relief; religious activities
Address: 35 Ashtead Road, London, E5 9BJ
Trustees: Rabbi Shimon Rothstein, Mr Joseph Alexander Goldstein, Mr David Birnbaum
Income: £2,598,386 [2016]; £815,694 [2015]; £492,619 [2014]; £475,209 [2013]; £1,452,606 [2012]

Reigate Grammar School
Registered: 7 Aug 2000 Employees: 289
Tel: 01737 222235 Website: reigategrammar.org
Activities: Education, training
Address: Reigate Grammar School, Reigate Road, Reigate, Surrey, RH2 0QS
Trustees: Sir Colin Chandler, Professor Sarah Louise Sayce, Mr James Dean, Mr Colin Cobain, Mr Roger Charles Newstead, Miss Lisa Page, Mr David Cole, Mr Mark Joseph O'Dwyer, Mr David Adams, Mr Mark Philip Elsey, Mr Christopher Mark Dixon, Mr Luke Herbert, Mr Marc Robert Benton, Mr Brian Vernon Day, Mrs Maxine Julie Hulme
Income: £22,344,525 [2016]; £17,623,843 [2015]; £18,095,333 [2014]; £17,149,223 [2013]; £17,127,471 [2012]

The Debra Reiss Foundation
Registered: 22 Sep 2016 Employees: 4
Tel: 020 7291 6227
Activities: Education, training; advancement of health or saving of lives; prevention or relief of poverty; animals; economic, community development, employment
Address: Reiss, 12 Picton Place, London, W1U 1BW
Trustees: Mr Darren Russell Reiss, Mrs Rosemary June Reiss, Mr David Anthony Reiss, Mrs Alison Jane Jacobs
Income: £6,032,497 [2017]

Relate
Registered: 22 Sep 1962 Employees: 78
Tel: 01302 347467 Website: relate.org.uk
Activities: General charitable purposes; education, training; advancement of health or saving of lives
Address: Relate, Premier House, Carolina Court, Doncaster, S Yorks, DN4 5RA
Trustees: Teresa Cresswell, Professor Janet Anne Walker, Sally Procopis, Ms Sue Maplesden, Ms Vineeta Manchanda, Jo Turnbull, Mr Simon Wilson, Mr David Rees Evans, Mr Ben Wealthy, Mr Gil Hilleard, Michael Anderson, Karen Railton, Juliana Lacey, Patricia Whiteside
Income: £4,690,106 [2017]; £4,688,490 [2016]; £5,549,000 [2015]; £5,478,000 [2014]; £4,084,000 [2013]

Release International
Registered: 19 Aug 1980 Employees: 27 Volunteers: 200
Tel: 01689 823491 Website: releaseinternational.org
Activities: Religious activities
Address: Release International, Priory Buildings, The Priory, Church Hill, Orpington, Kent, BR6 0HH
Trustees: Mr David Adeney, Mr Peter Colin Ewins, Mr Andrew Wayland, Mr Geoffrey Daplyn, Dr Mary Anne Print, Mr Robert Ashurst, Mr Wachuku Johnson
Income: £2,479,899 [2016]; £2,026,167 [2015]; £2,002,113 [2014]; £1,834,119 [2013]; £1,776,786 [2012]

Releasing Potential 2002 Limited
Registered: 9 May 2003 Employees: 27 Volunteers: 3
Tel: 023 9247 9762 Website: releasingpotential.com
Activities: Education, training; disability; amateur sport
Address: 8 Kingscroft Court, Ridgway, Havant, Hants, PO9 1LS
Trustees: Mr Paul Suter, Mrs Katherine Palmer, Mrs Sheilia Roberts, Mrs Elise Marguerite Claire Eminson
Income: £1,064,742 [2016]; £1,036,828 [2015]; £842,631 [2014]; £637,251 [2013]; £412,109 [2012]

Relief International UK
Registered: 19 Jun 2003 Employees: 15
Tel: 020 3457 0665 Website: ri.org
Activities: General charitable purposes; education, training; advancement of health or saving of lives; disability; prevention or relief of poverty; overseas aid, famine relief; accommodation, housing; economic, community development, employment
Address: 4th Floor, Albert House, 256-260 Old Street, London, EC1V 9DD
Trustees: Mrs Debra Davis, Ms Amanda Barnes, Mr Daniel Bader, Ms Ellen Frost, Mr Steven Hansch, Ms Dana Freyer, Ms Eden Collinsworth, Mrs Beverly Morris Armstrong, Mr Rob Cope, Paul Levengood, Ms Irene Wurtzel, Mr John Gage, Mr Leon Irish, Mrs Julia Guth, Dave Hardman
Income: £47,021,550 [2016]; £28,871,697 [2015]; £19,198,159 [2014]; £11,439,602 [2013]; £10,122,231 [2012]

Religious of The Assumption
Registered: 23 Jun 1964 Employees: 17 Volunteers: 11
Tel: 020 7361 4750 Website: assumptionreligious.org
Activities: General charitable purposes; education, training; religious activities; other charitable purposes
Address: Convent of The Assumption, 20 Kensington Square, London, W8 5HH
Trustees: Sister Maureen Connor, Sister Patricia T Mitchell, Sister Cathy Jones, Sister Sylvia Swift
Income: £4,329,000 [2016]; £1,122,000 [2015]; £1,135,000 [2014]; £1,127,000 [2013]; £1,019,000 [2012]

The Reme Charity
Registered: 4 Mar 2016 Employees: 16
Website: remecharity.org
Activities: General charitable purposes; amateur sport; armed forces, emergency service efficiency
Address: RHQ Reme, Lyneham, Chippenham, Wilts, SN15 4XX
Trustees: Major General Stephen Andrews CBE, Colonel Paul Gordon Mitchell, Colonel Daniel Gordon Scott ADC, Miss Catherine Colleen Robinson, Colonel Clare Phillips, Colonel Michael Jeremy Ainslie Bullard MBE, Colonel Ian Gibson, Colonel Mark Andrew Simpson TD, Mr Alastair Paul Graham, WO1 CASM Paul Charles Dennis Hembery
Income: £2,033,015 [2017]; £2,029,405 [2016]

Remedi - Restorative Services
Registered: 20 Mar 2002 Employees: 126 Volunteers: 47
Tel: 0114 253 6669 Website: remediuk.org
Activities: Education, training
Address: The Circle, 33 Rockingham Lane, Sheffield, S1 4FW
Trustees: Ms Beverly Ann Cross, Mrs Margaret Ann Payling, Mrs Denise Casbolt, Terry Gee, Mr David George Pidwell, Mr Robert Dudley Unwin, Mrs Annette Dews, Ms Jacky Smith
Income: £2,815,605 [2017]; £2,247,831 [2016]; £2,130,755 [2015]; £1,830,750 [2014]; £1,484,455 [2013]

Remodifyz Trust

Registered: 22 Aug 2016 *Volunteers:* 3
Tel: 020 8731 6885
Activities: Education, training; disability; prevention or relief of poverty; religious activities
Address: 13 Courtleigh Gardens, London, NW11 9JX
Trustees: Mrs Anna Noe, Mr Robert Noe, Mr David Joseph Bloom
Income: £6,338,100 [2017]

The Renal Association

Registered: 10 Jan 1989 *Employees:* 32
Tel: 0117 414 8150 *Website:* renal.org
Activities: The advancement of health or saving of lives
Address: Third Floor, L & R Building, Southmead Hospital, Southmead Road, Westbury on Trym, Bristol, BS10 5NB
Trustees: Dr Paul Cockwell, Dr Graham William Lipkin, Professor Donal O'Donoghue, Dr Philip Anil Kalra, Professor Bruce Hendry, Prof Neil Sheerin, Dr David Alexius Hughes, Dr Indranil Dasgupta
Income: £2,377,734 [2016]; £2,046,971 [2015]; £2,286,030 [2014]; £3,038,400 [2013]; £1,878,646 [2012]

Rendcomb College Foundation

Registered: 4 Aug 1966 *Employees:* 159
Tel: 01727 738284 *Website:* rendcombcollege.org.uk
Activities: Education, training; arts, culture, heritage, science; amateur sport
Address: Strutt & Parker, 15 London Road, St Albans, Herts, AL1 1LA
Trustees: Dr Catherine Wills, Mr Henry Robinson, Mrs Linda Hamilton Singer, Mr Richard Wills, Mr Shaun Parsons
Income: £7,615,000 [2016]; £8,375,000 [2015]; £7,537,000 [2014]; £6,632,000 [2013]; £6,064,000 [2012]

Rendcomb College

Registered: 22 Aug 2006 *Employees:* 166
Tel: 01285 832301 *Website:* rendcombcollege.org.uk
Activities: Education, training
Address: Rendcomb College, Cirencester, Glos, GL7 7HA
Trustees: The Venerable Hedley Ringrose, Sir Francis Richards, Mr Shaun Parsons, Mrs Prue Hornby, Mrs Sara Arkle, Mr Anthony Marchand, Mr Simon Hanbury, Mr R Wills, Mr Henry Robinson, Mrs Linnie Singer, Mr Edward Daniels, Major General Peter Williams, Mrs Imogen Ormerod, Mrs Beverley Clare Sinfield
Income: £7,598,781 [2016]; £8,333,851 [2015]; £6,749,986 [2014]; £6,577,625 [2013]; £6,025,580 [2012]

Renew Leeds Limited

Registered: 16 Apr 2002 *Employees:* 46
Tel: 0113 383 3920 *Website:* renew-leeds.co.uk
Activities: General charitable purposes; education, training; prevention or relief of poverty; accommodation, housing; amateur sport; economic, community development, employment; other charitable purposes
Address: Osmondthorpe Community, Education & Learning Centre, Osmondthorpe Lane, Leeds, LS9 9EG
Trustees: Andrew Taylor, Mr Christopher Jones, Mr William Lindsay Ross, Mr Asghar Khan Cllr, Mr Christopher Mark Billington, Ms Margaret Heath, Mrs Kellie Jayne McLoughlin
Income: £1,746,223 [2016]; £2,033,403 [2015]; £2,351,074 [2014]; £2,175,450 [2013]; £3,944,030 [2012]

Renewal Christian Centre

Registered: 28 Nov 2006 *Employees:* 39 *Volunteers:* 500
Tel: 0121 711 7300 *Website:* renewalcc.com
Activities: Education, training; advancement of health or saving of lives; prevention or relief of poverty; religious activities
Address: Renewal Christian Centre, Lode Lane, Solihull, W Midlands, B91 2JR
Trustees: Dr David Edward Carr, Mr Philip Joseph Lane, Dr Cheron Byfield, Mr Dean Smith, Rev Niall Alan Cluley, Mr David John Russell, Miss Deborah Millett, Mr Matthew Douglas
Income: £1,881,341 [2016]; £2,191,341 [2015]; £2,008,075 [2014]; £1,888,553 [2013]; £2,080,337 [2012]

The Representative Body of The Church in Wales

Registered: 11 Jul 2011 *Employees:* 97 *Volunteers:* 2,500
Tel: 029 2034 8200 *Website:* churchinwales.org.uk
Activities: Religious activities
Address: The Representative Body of The Church in Wales, 4th Floor, 2 Callaghan Square, Cardiff, CF10 5BT
Trustees: Nick Griffin, The Venerable Jonathan Simon Williams, Most Reverend John David Edward Davies, Peter Lea, Rev Canon Bob Griffiths, Mr Thomas Owen Saunders Lloyd OBE DL FSA, Mr Lyn James, Venerable Alan Neil Jevons, The Venerable Paul Mackness, Mrs Helen Jones, Sir Paul Silk, The Very Reverend Kathy Jones, Dr Hywel Parry-Smith, Miss Paulette Rosemary Brown, Mr John James Turner, Mr Roderick Davies, Mr Geoffrey Ian Moses, Tim Davenport, Mrs Hilary May Wiseman, Mrs Jane Heard, Venerable Christopher Blake Walters Smith, Mr Michael Lawley, Mrs Margaret West, Mrs Lis Perkins, Mr Peter Duncan Kennedy
Income: £19,652,000 [2016]; £19,052,000 [2015]; £19,053,000 [2014]; £19,647,000 [2013]; £19,019,000 [2012]

Reprieve

Registered: 27 Jun 2006 *Employees:* 31 *Volunteers:* 51
Tel: 020 7553 8140 *Website:* reprieve.org.uk
Activities: Human rights, religious or racial harmony, equality or diversity
Address: P O Box 72054, London, EC3P 3BZ
Trustees: Dr Andrew Graham, Mrs Ursula Margaret Owen, Ms Tanya Steele, Nasir Asad Ahmad, Mrs Nadege Vanessa Rejane Genetay, Mr Adrian Leon Cohen, Lady Susan Mary Hollick, Samir Shah, Mary Fitzgerald, Lord James Robert Wallace of Tankerness
Income: £2,126,418 [2016]; £2,242,554 [2015]; £2,527,304 [2014]; £2,224,763 [2013]; £2,290,954 [2012]

Repton Preparatory School

Registered: 26 Jul 2002 *Employees:* 158
Tel: 01283 559200 *Website:* foremarke.org.uk
Activities: Education, training
Address: The Bursar, Repton School, Willington Road, Repton, Derby, DE65 6FH
Trustees: Mr Robert John Richard Owen MA, Mrs Anne Elisabeth Hill JP, Mr Martin Wimbush, Dr Katherine Julia Dell, Professor Alistair Mitchell Buchan, Mr David Nigel Vardon Churton, Mr Matthew James Charles Needham, Mr Edward Mark Shires, Mr Andrew Michael Bock, Mrs Dawn Patricia Ward, Mr Roger Anthony Litchfield ACMA, Mr Roy Bates, Sir Henry John Michaelevery Bt, Mr Ian Richard Davenport, Mr William Tucker, Ms Kathryn Elizabeth Stone, Mr Andrew James Churchill, Mr Timothy James Hannam, Mrs Daphne St Clair Cawthorne
Income: £6,369,352 [2016]; £5,990,554 [2015]; £5,293,605 [2014]; £4,961,180 [2013]; £5,041,830 [2012]

Repton School Trust

Registered: 22 Aug 1966
Tel: 01283 559200 *Website:* repton.org.uk
Activities: Education, training
Address: The Bursar, Repton School, Willington Road, Repton, Derby, DE65 6FH
Trustees: Sir John Port's Charity
Income: £4,102,783 [2016]; £4,157,350 [2015]; £5,377,858 [2014]; £3,703,711 [2013]; £3,382,021 [2012]

Repton School

Registered: 26 Jul 2002 *Employees:* 386
Tel: 01283 559200 *Website:* repton.org.uk
Activities: Education, training
Address: The Bursar, Repton School, Willington Road, Repton, Derby, DE65 6FH
Trustees: Mr Robert John Richard Owen MA, Dr Katharine Julia Dell, Mr Roy Bates, Sir Henry John Michaelevery Bt, Professor Alistair Mitchell Buchan, Mr David Nigel Vardon Churton, Mr Matthew James Charles Needham LLB, Mr Edward Mark Shires, Mr Andrew Michael Bock, Mrs Dawn Patricia Ward, Mr Roger Anthony Litchfield ACMA, Mrs Anne Elisabeth Hill JP, Mr Martin Wimbush, Mr Ian Richard Davenport, Mr William Tucker, Ms Kathryn Elizabeth Stone, Mr Andrew James Churchill, Mr Timothy James Hannam, Mrs Daphne St Clair Cawthorne
Income: £16,055,138 [2016]; £15,802,339 [2015]; £15,214,072 [2014]; £14,546,818 [2013]; £14,104,386 [2012]

The Resolution Trust

Registered: 7 Mar 2008 *Employees:* 1
Tel: 020 3372 2960
Activities: General charitable purposes; education, training; prevention or relief of poverty
Address: 2 Queen Annes Gate, London, SW1H 9AA
Trustees: The Resolution Trust (Trustee) Limited
Income: £1,785,346 [2016]; £327,546 [2015]; £259,026 [2014]; £282,741 [2013]; £301,643 [2012]

The Resource Alliance Limited

Registered: 7 Oct 2003 *Employees:* 15 *Volunteers:* 50
Tel: 020 7065 0812 *Website:* resource-alliance.org
Activities: Education, training
Address: 5th Floor, Development House, 56-64 Leonard Street, London, EC2A 4LT
Trustees: Mr Pesh Framjee, Mr Michael Johnston, Mr Sukich Udindu, Ms Justina Mutale, Mr Atallah Kuttab, Mrs Caroline Emerton, Mr Marco Kuntze, Mr William Toliver
Income: £1,927,996 [2017]; £1,968,899 [2016]; £1,863,257 [2015]; £2,022,535 [2014]; £2,044,452 [2013]

Resource for London

Registered: 23 Nov 1992
Tel: 020 7606 6145 *Website:* resourceforlondon.org
Activities: General charitable purposes
Address: Trust for London, 6-9 Middle Street, London, EC1A 7PH
Trustees: Lynda Stevens, Mrs Denise Nicole Joseph, Mr Julian Rouse, Wilf Weeks, Mr Stephen Eric Burns, Mr Kevin Pease
Income: £1,250,464 [2016]; £1,213,138 [2015]; £1,179,617 [2014]; £841,590 [2013]; £656,845 [2012]

Resources for Autism

Registered: 13 Mar 1997 *Employees:* 71 *Volunteers:* 120
Tel: 020 8458 3259 *Website:* resourcesforautism.org.uk
Activities: Disability
Address: 858 Finchley Road, London, NW11 6AB
Trustees: Mrs Doreen Montgomery, Brian Linden, Hartley Booth, Ruth Rainbow, Mr Raymond Esdaile, Kit Hunter Gordon, Mr Edward Stourton
Income: £1,776,185 [2017]; £2,494,862 [2016]; £1,601,334 [2015]; £1,566,518 [2014]; £1,358,822 [2013]

Response Organisation

Registered: 8 Dec 2003 *Employees:* 190
Tel: 01865 397940 *Website:* response.org.uk
Activities: Education, training; disability; prevention or relief of poverty; accommodation, housing
Address: Response Organisation, A G Palmer House, Morrell Crescent, Littlemore, Oxford, OX4 4SU
Trustees: Peter Agulnik, Ben Lloyd-Shogbesan, Mrs Pat Armstrong, Roger Harwood, Mr John Taylor, Mrs Tania Amelia Wilson, David Boswell, Dr Kate Chalmers, Mr Paul O'Hare, Mrs Patricia Ross, Mrs Kathryn Elizabeth James, Mrs Ellen Hazel Nicholson
Income: £7,872,935 [2017]; £7,521,486 [2016]; £6,738,110 [2015]; £5,764,010 [2014]; £5,466,163 [2013]

Restless Development

Registered: 13 Jan 2009 *Employees:* 406 *Volunteers:* 448
Tel: 020 7633 3365 *Website:* restlessdevelopment.org
Activities: General charitable purposes; education, training; advancement of health or saving of lives; prevention or relief of poverty; overseas aid, famine relief; amateur sport; environment, conservation, heritage; economic, community development, employment; other charitable purposes
Address: Fourth Floor, Restless Development, 35-41 Lower Marsh, London, SE1 7RL
Trustees: Mr James Patrick Toyne Sewell, Jon Gorrie, Matthew Otubu, Affan Cheema, Anand Aithal, Miss Carol Monoyios, Myles Wickstead, Hannah Bronwin, Miss Charlotte Claire Eaton, Ms Bella Mosselmans
Income: £14,730,000 [2016]; £15,655,000 [2015]; £10,172,722 [2014]; £8,896,647 [2013]; £8,244,473 [2012]

Restore Our Planet

Registered: 11 Dec 2009 *Employees:* 2
Tel: 01737 355458 *Website:* restoreuk.org
Activities: Animals; environment, conservation, heritage; human rights, religious or racial harmony, equality or diversity
Address: P O Box 310, Epsom, Surrey, KT17 3YY
Trustees: Mr Michael Robert Edge, Mr Phillip Ronald Cartwright, Mr Christopher John Shaw, Mr Peter Russell Cole
Income: £1,261,961 [2017]; £493,234 [2016]; £140,156 [2015]; £196,135 [2014]; £116,109 [2013]

Results Education

Registered: 18 Nov 1992 *Employees:* 21 *Volunteers:* 120
Tel: 020 7793 3970 *Website:* results.org.uk
Activities: General charitable purposes; education, training; advancement of health or saving of lives; prevention or relief of poverty; overseas aid, famine relief
Address: Results Education, 31-33 Bondway, London, SW8 1SJ
Trustees: Mr Richard John Phipps BSc MIEE CEng, Mr Thomas Kenneth Baker, Ms Gillian Rosemary Clare Thomas, Mr Jan Willem Adriaan Van Houwelingen, Mrs Katherine Jill Hargreaves, Mr Nigel Howard Clarke Ward, Mr Reginald John Davis, Ms Victoria Elizabeth Burns, Dr Sohasini Sudtharalingam
Income: £1,230,675 [2016]; £808,168 [2015]; £648,582 [2014]; £553,961 [2013]; £513,235 [2012]

Resurgo Trust

Registered: 25 Nov 2003 Employees: 47 Volunteers: 250
Tel: 020 3327 2070 Website: resurgo.org.uk
Activities: General charitable purposes; education, training; prevention or relief of poverty; economic, community development, employment
Address: St Pauls Place, Macbeth Street, London, W6 9JJ
Trustees: Mr Nigel Mapp, Mr Jolyon Froud, Mr Thomas Shippey, Mrs Clemmie Briance
Income: £2,026,332 [2016]; £2,050,840 [2015]; £1,735,700 [2014]; £1,129,878 [2013]; £1,040,239 [2012]

Resuscitation Council (UK)

Registered: 25 Aug 2016 Employees: 17 Volunteers: 50
Tel: 020 7388 4678 Website: resus.org.uk
Activities: Education, training; advancement of health or saving of lives
Address: Resuscitation Council (UK), Entrance A, Tavistock House North, Tavistock Square, London, WC1H 9HR
Trustees: Ian Bullock, Dr Jonathan Peter Wyllie, Vanessa McKinlay, Dr Andrew Lockey, Prof Charles Deakin, Janine Roberts
Income: £6,664,147 [2017]

The Resuscitation Council (United Kingdom)

Registered: 23 Feb 1983 Employees: 19 Volunteers: 50
Tel: 020 7388 4678 Website: resus.org.uk
Activities: The advancement of health or saving of lives
Address: 5th Floor, Tavistock House North, Tavistock Square, London, WC1H 9HR
Trustees: Dr Andrew Steven Lockey, Dr Carl Leonard Gwinnutt, Dr David Anthony Gabbott, Dr Jonathan Wyllie
Income: £2,539,931 [2016]; £2,295,384 [2015]; £2,228,616 [2014]; £2,160,750 [2013]; £2,337,738 [2012]

Retail Trust

Registered: 17 Jan 2002 Employees: 109 Volunteers: 30
Tel: 020 8358 7225 Website: retailtrust.org.uk
Activities: Education, training; prevention or relief of poverty; accommodation, housing; other charitable purposes
Address: Marshall Hall, Marshall Estate, Hammers Lane, London, NW7 4DQ
Trustees: Mrs Katherine Payne, Ms Sally Hopson, Mr Nigel Duxbury, Ms Helena Feltham, Mr Simon Richard Ledsham, Ms Amanda Cox, Mr Richard Newman, Mr Terry Duddy, Mr Lindsay Page, Mr Guy Hipwell, Mrs Maria Philomena Thompson
Income: £8,225,808 [2017]; £9,672,404 [2016]; £9,462,699 [2015]; £11,788,744 [2014]; £10,277,444 [2013]

The Retired Nurses National Home

Registered: 23 Jan 2002 Employees: 46
Tel: 07484 039167 Website: rnnh.co.uk
Activities: The advancement of health or saving of lives; disability; prevention or relief of poverty; accommodation, housing
Address: Friends of The Elderly, 40-42 Ebury Street, London, SW1W 0LZ
Trustees: Mrs Soo Smith, Mrs Jennifer Griffiths, The Right Honourable Viscount Devonport, Mr Steve Allen
Income: £1,168,593 [2017]; £1,524,266 [2016]; £1,238,854 [2014]; £1,389,403 [2013]; £1,354,905 [2012]

Retrak

Registered: 15 Feb 2008 Employees: 124 Volunteers: 3
Tel: 0161 485 6685 Website: retrak.org
Activities: Education, training; advancement of health or saving of lives; prevention or relief of poverty; overseas aid, famine relief; accommodation, housing; religious activities; amateur sport; economic, community development, employment
Address: Metropolitan House, Station Road, Cheadle Hulme, Cheadle, Cheshire, SK8 7AZ
Trustees: Mr Martin Warner, Mr Gareth Henderson, Mr Paul Davis, Mrs Wendy Taylor, Mr Ian Pettigrew, Mr Peter Elson, Mr Allan Gibson, Mr Christopher Dacre
Income: £2,108,600 [2016]; £1,297,611 [2015]; £1,266,892 [2014]; £1,248,955 [2013]; £943,409 [2012]

The Retreat York

Registered: 18 Dec 2001 Employees: 376 Volunteers: 37
Tel: 07483 028513 Website: theretreatyork.org.uk
Activities: The advancement of health or saving of lives
Address: 13 West Ella Road, Kirk Ella, Hull, HU10 7QD
Trustees: Jennifer Claire Barraclough, Mr James Eddington, Dr David John Robson, Robert Griffiths, Sallie Ashe, John Miles, Michael Wash
Income: £12,675,233 [2016]; £11,863,944 [2015]; £13,380,046 [2014]; £13,153,953 [2013]; £12,858,406 [2012]

Reuben Foundation

Registered: 10 Oct 2002
Tel: 020 7802 5014 Website: reubenfoundation.com
Activities: General charitable purposes; education, training; advancement of health or saving of lives; disability; prevention or relief of poverty; overseas aid, famine relief; accommodation, housing; arts, culture, heritage, science; other charitable purposes
Address: 4th Floor, Millbank Tower, 21-24 Millbank, London, SW1P 4QP
Trustees: Mrs Annie Benjamin, Mr Malcolm Turner, Ms Dana Lisa Reuben, Mr Patrick Colin O'Driscoll, Mr Simon Reuben, Mr James Adam Reuben, Mr Richard Anthony Stone
Income: £5,088,284 [2016]; £4,597,288 [2015]; £4,201,674 [2014]; £3,848,726 [2013]; £3,978,746 [2012]

Nancy Reuben Primary School

Registered: 8 Jan 2007 Employees: 31
Tel: 020 7802 5000 Website: nrps.co.uk
Activities: Education, training
Address: 4th Floor, Millbank Tower, 21-24 Millbank, London, SW1P 4QP
Trustees: Mr Dayan Abraham David, Reuben Foundation
Income: £1,203,891 [2016]; £1,299,871 [2015]; £1,013,005 [2014]; £1,129,082 [2013]; £666,070 [2012]

Revelation Foundation

Registered: 6 Nov 2003 Employees: 2 Volunteers: 20
Tel: 020 8972 1400 Website: revelationtv.com
Activities: General charitable purposes; religious activities
Address: Revelation TV, P O Box 16833, Sutton Coldfield, W Midlands, B73 9XD
Trustees: Gordon Pettie, Alan Craig, Dr Richard Kent, Mrs Lorna Pettie, Mr Peter Darg, John Odell, Mrs Lesley Ann Conder
Income: £2,456,785 [2016]; £2,092,426 [2015]; £3,061,733 [2014]; £1,669,635 [2013]; £1,593,547 [2012]

Revitalise Respite Holidays
Registered: 20 Nov 1986 *Employees:* 217 *Volunteers:* 1,460
Tel: 020 7288 6861 *Website:* revitalise.org.uk
Activities: Disability
Address: Vitalise, 212 Business Design Centre, 52 Upper Street, London, N1 0QH
Trustees: Ms Mindy Sawhney, Mr Philip Trevor White, Mr Gavin David Wright, Mr Simon John Law, Mr Peter Cheer, Ms Linda Beaney, Mr Richard John Poxton, Ms Victoria Schneider, Mr Michael Kenneth Ashton, Mrs Lesley Lindberg
Income: £9,427,000 [2017]; £8,634,000 [2016]; £7,795,000 [2015]; £7,724,000 [2014]; £7,252,000 [2013]

Revival Church Europe
Registered: 3 Feb 2005 *Employees:* 27
Tel: 020 7265 0030 *Website:* crclondon.com
Activities: Education, training; prevention or relief of poverty; overseas aid, famine relief; religious activities
Address: Coopersale Hall, Flux's Lane, Theydon Garnon, Epping, Essex, CM16 7PE
Trustees: Mr at Boshoff, Mr Izak Christoffel Marais, Mr Rikus Harmse, Miss Ninette Heyneke, Mr Alberto Gava, Mr Conrad Pieter Nel
Income: £2,125,106 [2017]; £2,485,469 [2016]; £2,249,754 [2015]; £1,955,843 [2014]; £1,753,601 [2013]

The Rhoda Jessop Educational Charity
Registered: 24 Apr 1979 *Employees:* 55 *Volunteers:* 7
Tel: 0115 958 0596 *Website:* hollygirt.co.uk
Activities: Education, training
Address: Hollygirt School, Elm Avenue, Nottingham, NG3 4GF
Trustees: Mrs Beryl Rimmer, Mr David Overton, Mrs Deborah Joy Anderton, Mrs Rachael Ann Archer, Mr Robert John Dunmore, Dr Michael Heath, Mr Julian Patrick Townsend, Mrs Claire Wood
Income: £1,514,640 [2016]; £1,398,570 [2015]; £1,485,646 [2014]; £1,625,282 [2013]; £1,871,826 [2012]

Rhodes Trust - Public Purposes Fund
Registered: 24 Feb 1966 *Employees:* 34
Tel: 01865 270916 *Website:* rhodeshouse.ox.ac.uk
Activities: Education, training
Address: Rhodes House, South Parks Road, Oxford, OX1 3RG
Trustees: Dame Helen Ghosh, Mr Julian Ogilvie Thompson, Mr Glen James, Professor Margaret Macmillan, Prof Elleke Boehmer, Mr Donald Gogel, Ms Karen Stevenson, Dame Carol Robinson, Mr Nicholas Oppenheimer, Professor Sir John Bell, Dr John Hood, Mr Michael G McCaffery, Professor Ngaire Woods, Mr Dominic Barton, Mr John McCall MacBain, Mr John Wylie, Mr Andrew Banks, Dr Tariro Makadzange
Income: £15,127,489 [2017]; £32,382,669 [2016]; £28,055,358 [2015]; £7,197,459 [2014]; £6,573,066 [2013]

The Rhodes Trust Horizon Fund
Registered: 16 Dec 2014
Tel: 01865 270916 *Website:* rhodeshouse.ox.ac.uk
Activities: General charitable purposes; education, training
Address: Rhodes House, South Parks Road, Oxford, OX1 3RG
Trustees: Dame Helen Ghosh, Dr John Hood, Mr Michael G McCaffery, Professor Ngaire Woods, Mr Dominic Barton, Mr John McCall MacBain, Mr John Wylie, Mr Andrew Banks, Mr Nicholas Oppenheimer, Prosfessor Sir John Bell GBE FRS PMedSci, Mr Glen James, Professor Margaret Macmillan, Prof Elleke Boehmer, Mr Donald Gogel, Ms Karen Stevenson, Dame Carol Robinson DBE FRS, Mr Julian Ogilvie Thompson, Dr Tariro Makadzange
Income: £1,588,832 [2017]; £910,372 [2016]; £1,469,667 [2015]

Rhondda Cynon Taff Citizens Advice Bureau
Registered: 23 Mar 1999 *Employees:* 43 *Volunteers:* 48
Tel: 01443 409284 *Website:* citizensadvice.org.uk
Activities: The prevention or relief of poverty; other charitable purposes
Address: Pontypridd Citizens Advice Bureau, 5 Gelliwastad Road, Pontypridd, Rhondda Cynon Taf, CF37 2BP
Trustees: Cllr John Watts, Mrs Sali Elizabeth Davis, Mrs Dilys Jouvenant, Ms Nicola Redfern Willams, Mr Kelvin Granville Jones, Mr Michael James Woodington, Mr Michael Haydn Bryan, Stephen Barlow, Mr Lewis Brencher
Income: £1,149,484 [2017]; £1,123,151 [2016]; £1,080,873 [2015]; £1,093,491 [2014]; £845,189 [2013]

Ribble Catchment Conservation Trust Limited
Registered: 24 Jul 1998 *Employees:* 16 *Volunteers:* 600
Tel: 01254 686600 *Website:* ribbletrust.com
Activities: Education, training; environment, conservation, heritage
Address: Central Buildings, Richmond Terrace, Blackburn, Lancs, BB1 7AP
Trustees: Mr Alan Thomas Rowntree, Mr Philip Lord, Mr David John Wilmot, Mr Vincent Edmondson, Mr John Francis Bleasdale, Mr Colin Harvey Marchbank, Dr Michael William Horner BSc PhD MRSC CChem, Mr Dominic William Bradley, Mr Jeffrey Alan Cowburn, Mr Michael John Ellacott
Income: £2,175,925 [2017]; £736,846 [2016]; £1,290,791 [2015]; £1,674,214 [2014]; £749,303 [2013]

The Ricard Foundation
Registered: 9 Mar 2015
Activities: General charitable purposes; prevention or relief of poverty; economic, community development, employment; other charitable purposes
Address: c/o Withers LLP, 16 Old Bailey, London, EC4M 7EG
Trustees: Candice Ricard, Emily Ricard, Mr Claudio Ali, Charlotte Ricard, Mr Owen Francis Lynch
Income: £2,659,504 [2017]; £1,431,922 [2016]

Rich Mix Cultural Foundation
Registered: 31 Oct 2001 *Employees:* 49
Tel: 020 7613 7665 *Website:* richmix.org.uk
Activities: Education, training; arts, culture, heritage, science; environment, conservation, heritage; economic, community development, employment
Address: 35-47 Bethnal Green Road, London, E1 6LA
Trustees: Cllr Denise Jones, Professor Michael Keith, Mr Niranjan Kamatkar, Mr Joseph Ogbonna, Mr Mohammed Mukit, Mrs Shamim Azad, Ms Chila Kumari Burman, Ms Candida Ronald, Miss Tandeep Kaur Minhas, Mr Steve Douglas, Mrs Shazia Ali-Webber, Mrs Jackie O'Sullivan
Income: £2,602,215 [2017]; £2,950,365 [2016]; £3,365,030 [2015]; £2,738,080 [2014]; £3,024,323 [2013]

Richard House Trust
Registered: 7 Nov 1996 *Employees:* 62 *Volunteers:* 150
Tel: 020 7540 0201 *Website:* richardhouse.org.uk
Activities: The advancement of health or saving of lives; disability
Address: Richard House, Childrens Hospice, Richard House Drive, London, E16 3RG
Trustees: Mr James Joly, Ms Katrina McNamara-Goodger, Ms Wendy Pritchard, Mr Mizan Abdulrouf, Mr Derek John Lovelock, Mrs Sara Hazzard, Mr Quentin Humberstone, Ms Nicola Ukiah, Mr Robin Knowles CBE QC, Dr Meng Tan, Mrs Gowhar Shaikh, Mr David John Bickerton
Income: £3,088,559 [2017]; £3,057,840 [2016]; £3,791,519 [2015]; £3,024,840 [2014]; £2,582,493 [2013]

The Richard Ormonde Shuttleworth Remembrance Trust
Registered: 26 Mar 1963 *Employees:* 80 *Volunteers:* 100
Tel: 01767 627979 *Website:* shuttleworth.org
Activities: Education, training; environment, conservation, heritage
Address: The Shuttleworth Trust, Old Warden, Biggleswade, Beds, SG18 9EP
Trustees: Richard Shuttleworth Trustees
Income: £4,124,000 [2016]; £3,815,716 [2015]; £5,640,782 [2014]; £4,620,159 [2013]; £4,383,675 [2012]

Richmond Charities
Registered: 8 Aug 1961 *Employees:* 13
Tel: 020 8948 4188 *Website:* richmondcharities.org.uk
Activities: Accommodation, housing
Address: 8 The Green, Richmond, Surrey, TW9 1PL
Trustees: Mr Serge Lourie, Mrs Margaret Marshall, Rev Wilma Roest, Mrs Emma Davis, Mr Jeremy Williams, Cllr Robert S Thompson, Mrs Frances Bouchier, Mr Peter Marr, Mrs Susan John, Mr Stephen John King, Mrs Katherine Theresa Maxwell, Dr Nicholas Ramscar
Income: £3,449,597 [2016]; £3,133,638 [2015]; £3,028,441 [2014]; £2,756,697 [2013]; £2,654,193 [2012]

The Richmond Fellowship
Registered: 20 Sep 1961 *Employees:* 1,181 *Volunteers:* 267
Tel: 020 7697 3300 *Website:* richmondfellowship.org.uk
Activities: Education, training; advancement of health or saving of lives; disability; accommodation, housing; economic, community development, employment
Address: 80 Holloway Road, London, N7 8JG
Trustees: Geoffrey Bland, Alan Powell, Raj Lakhani, Ms Helen Edwards, Peter Molyneux, Mary Wishart, Tracey Bell, David Brindle, Stephanie De La Haye, Derek Caren, Anne Tansi Harper, Dr Michael Holland, Albert Edward Joseph Fletcher
Income: £39,101,000 [2017]; £32,973,000 [2016]; £30,947,000 [2015]; £29,314,000 [2014]; £33,854,000 [2013]

The Richmond Foundation
Registered: 28 Nov 1983
Website: richmond.ac.uk
Activities: Education, training
Address: Richmond University, Queens Road, Richmond, Surrey, TW10 6JP
Trustees: Sir Cyril Taylor, Mr Clifford Joseph, Mr Peter Williams, Dr Kevin Everett, Dr John Annette, Mr Neil Meadows, Nick Tate, Mrs Allison Cole-Stutz
Income: £10,370,769 [2017]; £504,106 [2016]; £205,116 [2015]; £1,424,732 [2014]; £473,119 [2013]

Richmond Gymnastics Association
Registered: 18 Oct 1988 *Employees:* 59
Tel: 020 8878 8682 *Website:* richmondgymnastics.co.uk
Activities: Education, training; amateur sport
Address: 1 Townmeads Road, Richmond, Surrey, TW9 4EL
Trustees: Mrs Chris Brockbank, Mrs Christine Jane Cason, Ms Kay Taylor, Mrs Helen Gilbert, Mrs Sarah Campbell, Mrs Carol Ann Bailey, Mrs Sally Wilson, Mr Philip Jeffcock, Mr Simon Kimberley
Income: £1,090,195 [2017]; £1,006,976 [2016]; £856,168 [2015]; £794,852 [2014]; £787,527 [2013]

Richmond House School
Registered: 13 Oct 1976 *Employees:* 38 *Volunteers:* 2
Tel: 0113 275 2670 *Website:* rhschool.org
Activities: Education, training
Address: Richmond House School, 168-170 Otley Road, Leeds, LS16 5LG
Trustees: Ms Catherine Shuttleworth, Mr Peter Jolly, Mr James Watson, Mr Simon Brazier, Mrs Emma Slater, Mr Martin Grange, Ms Vanessa Monnickendam, Ms Samantha Stephens, Mrs Gill Galdins, Mr Paul Julian Fox
Income: £1,971,410 [2017]; £1,882,547 [2016]; £1,849,099 [2015]; £1,815,757 [2014]; £1,684,677 [2013]

Richmond Parish Lands Charity
Registered: 12 Aug 1968 *Employees:* 3
Tel: 020 8948 5701 *Website:* rplc.org.uk
Activities: Education, training; advancement of health or saving of lives; prevention or relief of poverty; accommodation, housing
Address: Richmond Parish Lands Charity, Vestry House, 21 Paradise Road, Richmond, Surrey, TW9 1SA
Trustees: Mr Paul Velluet, Mr Paul Cole, Ms Rosie Dalzell, Ms Ashley Casson, Ms Lisa Blakemore, Roger Clark, Mr Owen Carew-Jones, Paul Lawrence, Mr Ian Durant, Ms Ros Sweeting, Mr Tim Sketchley, Ms Kate Ellis, Gill Moffett, Mr Peter Buckwell, Rachel Holmes
Income: £2,089,856 [2017]; £2,172,640 [2016]; £2,520,115 [2015]; £1,860,587 [2014]; £3,532,320 [2013]

Richmond and Hillcroft Adult and Community College
Registered: 30 Aug 1966 *Employees:* 49 *Volunteers:* 5
Tel: 020 8399 2688 *Website:* hillcroft.ac.uk
Activities: Education, training
Address: Parkshot, Richmond, Surrey, TW9 2RE
Trustees: Ms Theresa Hoenig, Ms Christine Louise Fluker, Mr Nigel Ware, Mr Mark Desmond Albrow, Ms Gabrielle Nina Flint, Mr Gavin Arthur Hardcastle-Jones, Ms Lisa Claire Sharp, Mr Graham John Tharp, Mr Richard David Brewster, Ms Linda Jones, Mrs Farah Rachlin, Mrs Helen Patricia Darracott, Professor Andrew John Tinothy George CBE, Ms Nicola Jane O'Shea, Mr Daniel Andrew Kemp
Income: £2,267,347 [2017]; £2,056,472 [2016]; £2,382,303 [2015]; £2,296,115 [2014]; £2,258,867 [2013]

Richmond upon Thames Music Trust Company Limited
Registered: 15 Feb 2002 *Employees:* 115 *Volunteers:* 4
Tel: 020 8538 3866 *Website:* richmondmusictrust.org.uk
Activities: Education, training; arts, culture, heritage, science
Address: 7 Briar Road, Twickenham, Middlesex, TW2 6RB
Trustees: Mr Alan Price, Mrs Elizabeth Rowley, Mr Peter Willan, Mrs Christine Purdy, Mr Christopher Cull, Kate Jane Howard, Mrs Susan Griffin, Lady Camilla Ruth Panufnik, Mrs Hilary Dodman, Mr Nicholas Gerard Peter Whitfield, Ms Jane Harnden, Mr Glenn Sutcliffe, Mrs Amanda Jane Letch
Income: £1,710,058 [2017]; £1,642,588 [2016]; £1,561,905 [2015]; £1,448,382 [2014]; £1,367,542 [2013]

Ridgesave Limited
Registered: 3 Nov 1983
Activities: General charitable purposes; education, training; prevention or relief of poverty
Address: 141b Upper Clapton Road, London, E5 9DB
Trustees: Mr E Englander, Mr Joseph Leib Weiss, Mrs Zelda Weiss
Income: £2,848,740 [2017]; £2,271,015 [2016]; £2,273,510 [2015]; £406,093 [2014]; £1,239,497 [2013]

Riding for The Disabled Association incorporating Carriage Driving
Registered: 18 Nov 1965 *Employees:* 24 *Volunteers:* 600
Tel: 01926 492915 *Website:* rda.org.uk
Activities: Education, training; advancement of health or saving of lives; disability; amateur sport
Address: Norfolk House, 1A Tournament Court, Edgehill Drive, Warwick, CV34 6LG
Trustees: Sam Orde, Jacqui Scott, Judi Singer, Sally Godley-Maynard, Neil Goldie-Scot, Jess Cook, Sally Anne O'Neill, Lindsay Correa, Julie Jordan, Sheila Saner, Emma Wells, Julianne Jessup, Lynda Whittaker
Income: £2,156,554 [2017]; £1,962,846 [2016]; £1,998,739 [2015]; £1,614,340 [2014]; £1,290,695 [2013]

Ridley Hall, Cambridge
Registered: 12 May 2014 *Employees:* 31
Tel: 01223 741073 *Website:* ridley.cam.ac.uk
Activities: Education, training; religious activities
Address: Ridley Hall, Ridley Hall Road, Cambridge, CB3 9HG
Trustees: The Revd Canon Frederick Kilner, Mr Simon McGuire, Dr Margaret Masson, Mr Stephen Tromans, The Rt Revd David Williams, Mrs Diane Palmer, Mr Keith George Wood, The Rt Revd David Urquhart, The Ven Hugh McCurdy, Mr Mark Gerald Spelman, Mrs Sibella Laing, Revd John Irvine, The Revd Dr Joanne Bailey, Rev Dr Jonathan Andrew Linebaugh
Income: £1,534,071 [2016]; £6,367,246 [2015]

The Rifles Benevolent Trust
Registered: 3 May 2007 *Employees:* 1
Tel: 01962 828530
Activities: Education, training; prevention or relief of poverty; accommodation, housing
Address: Regimental Headquarters, The Rifles, Peninsula Barracks, Romsey Road, Winchester, Hants, SO23 8TS
Trustees: Maj Gen Nicholas Welch OBE, Mr Andrew Wimble, Capt Jeremy Michael Archer MA, Mr Andrew George Wycliffe Jackson, Lieutenant Colonel Simon David Gray MBE, Colonel Simon Charles Chapman TD, General Sir Nicholas Patrick Carter KCB CBE DSO ADC Gen, Lieutenanat General Timothy Buchan Radford CB DSO OBE, Lieutenant Colonel Peter Dominick Browne MBE, Lieutenant Colonel John Alexander Poole-Warren MBE, Colonel David Alfred John Brown OBE, Mr Simon Charles Hazlitt, Mr Ollie Marsh, Brigadier Rupert Timothy Herbert Jones MBE, Brigadier Rupert John Thompson CBE DSO, Lieutenant General Patrick Nym Sanders CBE DSO
Income: £2,110,053 [2016]; £663,980 [2015]; £678,733 [2014]; £667,638 [2013]; £878,515 [2012]

Rift Valley Research Limited
Registered: 27 Sep 2011 *Employees:* 15
Tel: 07462 130035 *Website:* riftvalley.net
Activities: Education, training; arts, culture, heritage, science; environment, conservation, heritage; human rights, religious or racial harmony, equality or diversity
Address: Unit 107 Belgravia Workshops, 159-163 Marlborough Road, London, N19 4NF
Trustees: Ann Grant, Lindsey Hilsum, Dr Comfort Ero, Mohamed Osman, Mr Christopher Maynard
Income: £1,691,380 [2016]; £1,714,887 [2015]; £1,257,292 [2014]; £1,163,137 [2013]; £1,085,474 [2012]

Rigby Foundation
Registered: 19 May 1992
Tel: 01789 610008
Activities: General charitable purposes; other charitable purposes
Address: Bridgeway House, Bridgeway, Stratford upon Avon, Warwicks, CV37 6YX
Trustees: Sir Peter Rigby, Mr James Peter Rigby, Ms Patricia Ann Rigby, Mr Steven Paul Rigby
Income: £1,014,368 [2017]; £1,135,144 [2016]; £384,031 [2015]; £382,973 [2014]; £782,220 [2013]

Right to Play UK Limited
Registered: 5 Dec 2005 *Employees:* 8 *Volunteers:* 60
Tel: 020 3752 5640 *Website:* righttoplay.org.uk
Activities: General charitable purposes; education, training; advancement of health or saving of lives; disability; prevention or relief of poverty; overseas aid, famine relief; economic, community development, employment; human rights, religious or racial harmony, equality or diversity
Address: The Foundry, 17-19 Oval Way, London, SE11 5RR
Trustees: Ms Maria Driano, Mr Simon Holden, Mr Olivier Gers, Ms Marijana Kolak, Mrs Leslie McCormack Gathy, Mr James Garman, Mr Aki Temiseva, Delaney Brown
Income: £1,949,947 [2016]; £2,214,537 [2015]; £2,483,327 [2014]; £2,000,859 [2013]; £1,894,417 [2012]

Rikkyo School in England Trust
Registered: 7 Dec 1971 *Employees:* 98
Tel: 01403 822107 *Website:* rikkyo.co.uk
Activities: Education, training
Address: The Rikkyo School in England, Guildford Road, Rudgwick, Horsham, W Sussex, RH12 3BE
Trustees: Bishop Yutaka Minabe, Mr Tomoya Yoshioka, Mr Katsuichi Hirota, Mr Yasuo Kashiwagi, Mr Kiyoshi Sunobe, Mr Takeji Suzuki, Mr Naoya Iwashita, Mr Hajime Yamanaka, Ms Tokiko Shimizu, Mr Shigeya Kusano, Mr Tadahiro Sato, Mr Yoshisuke Kimura, Mr Shinichi Ogawa, Mr Kazuo Okamoto, Mr Roger Munechika, Mr Koichiro Nakada, Mr Haruki Hayashi, Mr Kazumi Wakabayashi, Mr Hiroshi Suzuki, Mr Akio Kamiya, Mr Yoshitaka Ihokibe, Mr Hiroyuki Tsubai, Mr Masahiro Kuwahara, Mr Koichiro Tominaga, Mr Noburu Okabe, Mrs Hiromi Bunday, Mr Keiji Kubota, Mr Toshihiko Suzuki
Income: £4,463,785 [2017]; £4,181,932 [2016]; £4,141,035 [2015]; £3,867,849 [2014]; £3,753,518 [2013]

Ringwood Waldorf School
Registered: 25 Sep 2014 *Employees:* 50 *Volunteers:* 200
Tel: 01425 472664 *Website:* ringwoodwaldorfschool.org.uk
Activities: Education, training
Address: Ringwood Waldorf School, Folly Farm Lane, Ashley Heath, Ringwood, Hants, BH24 2NN
Trustees: Mr Esbjorn Roderick Wilmar, Mr Thomas Lister, Mrs Pernille Constantine, Mr Alistair Keith Walker, Mr Lars Wilmar
Income: £4,358,088 [2016]

Ripley Court Educational Trust Limited
Registered: 27 May 1969 *Employees:* 65 *Volunteers:* 2
Tel: 01483 225217 *Website:* ripleycourt.co.uk
Activities: Education, training
Address: Ripley Court School, Rose Lane, Woking, Surrey, G23 6NE
Trustees: Lady Jenny Wicks, Mr Desmond McCann, Dr Sara Coe, Mrs Joanna Denham, Carolynn Davies-Shatz, Mr John Simpson, Mr John Evans, Mrs Stephanie Webster, Mr Jonathan Searle, Ms Caroline Frances St-Gallay
Income: £3,210,664 [2017]; £3,065,708 [2016]; £2,776,791 [2015]; £2,762,553 [2014]; £2,615,119 [2013]

Ripon College Cuddesdon
Registered: 20 Oct 1966 *Employees:* 44
Tel: 01865 877421 *Website:* rcc.ac.uk
Activities: Education, training; religious activities
Address: Ripon College, Cuddesdon, Oxford, OX44 9EX
Trustees: Philip Gee, Rev Canon Dr Janet Patricia Williams, The Rt Revd Christopher Foster, Revd Canon Dr Simon John Taylor, Rev Neil Sydney Patterson, Canon Prof Mark Chapman, Revd Professor Jennifer Strawbridge, Sorrel Wood, Mrs Judith Knight, The Rt Revd Humphrey Ivo John Southern, Sir Tony Baldry, Mr Patrick Nicholas Charles Walker, Very Revd Rogers Govender, The Venerable Guy Charles Elsmore, The Very Revd Dr David Michael Hoyle, Revd Canon Dr Andrew Jonathan Braddock, Mr Matthew Renshaw
Income: £2,223,508 [2017]; £2,046,984 [2016]; £2,370,060 [2015]; £2,353,064 [2014]; £2,314,780 [2013]

The Rise Trust
Registered: 31 May 2006 *Employees:* 61 *Volunteers:* 95
Tel: 01249 721706 *Website:* therisetrust.org
Activities: General charitable purposes; education, training; prevention or relief of poverty; religious activities; economic, community development, employment
Address: 3 Manor Farm Close, Upper Seagry, Chippenham, Wilts, SN15 5FB
Trustees: Pauline Monaghan, Mr Kevin Purkiss, Mrs Julia Dorothy Evelyn Harle, Geoffrey Monaghan, Rev Simon David Dunn, Mr Alan Kenneth Homersley, David Powell
Income: £1,304,388 [2017]; £727,883 [2016]; £733,440 [2015]; £711,809 [2014]; £609,497 [2013]

Rishworth School
Registered: 25 Jul 2006 *Employees:* 120 *Volunteers:* 18
Tel: 01422 822217 *Website:* rishworth-school.co.uk
Activities: Education, training
Address: Rishworth School, Oldham Road, Sowerby Bridge, W Yorks, HX6 4QA
Trustees: Dr Andrew Brooks, Mrs Dilys Whitaker, Mr Tom Wheelwright, Mr Philip Hudson, Ms Valerie Isabel Stevens, Mrs Maxine Garbett, Mrs Jean Slim, Rev Hilary Barber, Mrs Fiona Jayne Ellam, Mr Christopher Bell
Income: £5,603,481 [2017]; £5,876,255 [2016]; £5,739,801 [2015]; £5,702,532 [2014]; £5,907,963 [2013]

The River Farm Foundation
Registered: 28 Feb 2006
Tel: 01508 480100
Activities: General charitable purposes; education, training; advancement of health or saving of lives; disability; prevention or relief of poverty; overseas aid, famine relief
Address: The Old Coach House, Bergh Apton, Norwich, NR15 1DD
Trustees: Mr Mark Haworth, Mrs Deborah Fisher, Mr Nigel Jeremy Langstaff
Income: £2,305,987 [2017]; £1,305,804 [2016]; £197,016 [2015]; £183,064 [2014]; £237,183 [2013]

River and Rowing Museum Foundation
Registered: 7 Dec 1990 *Employees:* 21 *Volunteers:* 40
Tel: 01491 415617 *Website:* rrm.co.uk
Activities: Education, training; arts, culture, heritage, science; amateur sport; environment, conservation, heritage
Address: The River & Rowing, Museum Foundation, Mill Meadows, Henley on Thames, Oxon, RG9 1BF
Trustees: Mrs Annabel Nicoll, Mr Thomas Eliot Weil, Mr David Buckley, Cllr Lorraine Hillier, Mrs Fiona Dennis, Lord Bichard of Nailsworth, Mr David Howard Worthington, Mr Howard Jacobs, Cllr Kellie Hinton, Mr Paul Adam Reynolds
Income: £1,070,343 [2017]; £1,046,738 [2016]; £1,158,564 [2015]; £1,068,286 [2014]; £1,285,049 [2013]

The Rivers Trust
Registered: 7 Dec 2004 *Employees:* 13
Tel: 01579 372142 *Website:* theriverstrust.org
Activities: Education, training; environment, conservation, heritage
Address: The Rivers Trust, Rain Charm House, Kyl Cober Parc, Stoke Climsland, Callington, Cornwall, PL17 8PH
Trustees: Mr David Brown, Dr Geoff Brighty, Mr Jonathan Mark White, Professor Angela Mary Gurnell, Andrew Wallace, Dr Laurence Couldrick, Mrs Charlotte Lucy Hitchmough, Mr Jack William Arthur Spees
Income: £1,293,945 [2016]; £1,156,958 [2015]; £1,070,549 [2014]; £1,626,881 [2013]; £3,175,316 [2012]

Riverside Estuary Limited
Registered: 20 May 2013
Tel: 0151 295 6134 *Website:* riverside.org.uk
Activities: Disability; accommodation, housing
Address: 3 Sandy Lane, Dobcross, Oldham, Lancs, OL3 5AG
Trustees: Mrs Ingrid Fife, Mr Simon Ketteridge, Mrs Judith Crowther, Mr Andy Deutsch
Income: £26,691,000 [2017]; £36,754 [2016]; £6,490,000 [2015]

The Riverside Trust
Registered: 22 Sep 1983 *Employees:* 6
Tel: 020 8237 1000 *Website:* riversidestudios.co.uk
Activities: Arts, culture, heritage, science
Address: Riverside Trust Ltd, 65 Aspenlea Road, London, W6 8LH
Trustees: Mr Charles Edwin Mawer, Mr Farrukh Dhondy, Mr Greg Smith, Mr Alan Morgan, John Woodward, Mr Ajay Chowdhury, Chris Powell, Mr Dan Large, Mr Tim Simon, Mr Timothy Lefroy, Andrew Griffith, Mr Peter Archer
Income: £1,288,724 [2017]; £702,047 [2016]; £23,268,583 [2015]; £3,214,352 [2014]; £3,379,402 [2013]

The Road Safety Trust
Registered: 20 Mar 2014 *Employees:* 11
Tel: 01908 569971 *Website:* roadsafetytrust.org.uk
Activities: Education, training; advancement of health or saving of lives
Address: 11 Crosshills, Stony Stratford, Milton Keynes, Bucks, MK11 1HD
Trustees: Mr James Millar, Dr Claire Corbett, Mr Ashton West, Mr David Jamieson, Ms Jo Clift, Mr Anthony Bangham, Mrs Catherine McMahon, Mr Oliver Carsten, Mr Gary Walker, Ms Philippa Jane Young, Mr Tony Fuller
Income: £3,342,362 [2017]; £602,117 [2016]; £1,500,000 [2015]

The E C Roberts Centre
Registered: 3 Dec 1997 *Employees:* 50 *Volunteers:* 43
Tel: 023 9229 6919 *Website:* robertscentre.org.uk
Activities: Education, training; prevention or relief of poverty; accommodation, housing; other charitable purposes
Address: The E C Roberts Centre, 84 Crasswell Street, Portsmouth, PO1 1HT
Trustees: Professor John Craven, Mrs Linda Davies Her Honour Judge, Mike Davidson, Mr Graham Brombley, Mr Andrew Peter Sayer, Reverend Bob White, Malcolm Childs, Miss Margaret Geary, Mr Charles Edward Haviland Ackroyd, Jennifer Bennett
Income: £1,632,971 [2017]; £1,671,566 [2016]; £1,780,795 [2015]; £1,493,033 [2014]; £1,775,539 [2013]

Robinson College in the University of Cambridge
Registered: 16 Aug 2010 *Employees:* 191
Website: robinson.cam.ac.uk
Activities: Education, training
Address: Robinson College, Cambridge, CB3 9AN
Trustees: Prof Judith Lieu, Dr Jeremy Robert Thurlow, Dr Brian Sloan, Dr Michael Shin, Ms Helen Cornish, Prof Anthony David Yates, Mr Ross Reason, Dr William Nolan, Dr Paul Griffiths, Dr Kevin Chalut
Income: £10,549,000 [2017]; £12,780,000 [2016]; £8,954,000 [2015]; £8,547,000 [2014]; £8,167,000 [2013]

Rochdale Boroughwide Cultural Trust
Registered: 29 Mar 2007 *Employees:* 252 *Volunteers:* 150
Tel: 01706 626319 *Website:* link4life.org
Activities: General charitable purposes; education, training; advancement of health or saving of lives; disability; arts, culture, heritage, science; amateur sport; environment, conservation, heritage; economic, community development, employment
Address: Link4life, Floor 3, No 1 Riverside, Smith Street, Rochdale, OL16 1ZL
Trustees: Mr Mohammed Sarwar, Cllr Billy Sheerin, Ms Janine Partington, Mr Roger Platt, Mr Steven Cooke, Mrs Rina Paolucci-Escobar Cllr, Elizabeth White, Mr Stephen Griffiths, Julia Heap, Ms Anne Taylor, Cllr Neil Butterworth, Mr Miah Mohammed, Mr Martin Walker, Christopher Davison
Income: £10,433,647 [2017]; £10,540,572 [2016]; £10,743,080 [2015]; £10,636,314 [2014]; £9,978,043 [2013]

Rochdale Gateway Leisure Limited
Registered: 1 Sep 1995 *Employees:* 59 *Volunteers:* 14
Tel: 01706 515800 *Website:* gatewayleisure.co.uk
Activities: Education, training; disability
Address: Rochdale Gateway Leisure Ltd, Gateway Centre, 2 Kenion Street, Rochdale, OL16 1SN
Trustees: Steve Ellis, Miss Susan Teresa Mary Burke, Ms Sheila Hussain, Mr Anthony Collinson, Mrs Jean Barlow, Mr Graeme Terence Hill
Income: £1,272,269 [2017]; £1,285,510 [2016]; £1,198,943 [2015]; £1,137,914 [2014]; £1,197,040 [2013]

Rochdale Training Association Limited
Registered: 5 May 1969 *Employees:* 57
Tel: 01706 631417 *Website:* rochdaletraining.co.uk
Activities: General charitable purposes; education, training; economic, community development, employment
Address: Rochdale Training Association, Fishwick Street, Rochdale, OL16 5NA
Trustees: Mr Nigel Bradley, Mr Robert James Beetham, Ms Mary McGrath, Mr Neil Hickford, Mrs Susan Lindsey Cryer
Income: £4,467,969 [2017]; £4,189,415 [2016]; £3,467,852 [2015]; £3,156,719 [2014]; £2,912,959 [2013]

Rochdale and District Mind
Registered: 25 Feb 1988 *Employees:* 41 *Volunteers:* 41
Tel: 01706 752333 *Website:* rochdalemind.org.uk
Activities: Education, training; advancement of health or saving of lives; disability; economic, community development, employment; other charitable purposes
Address: The Mind Wellbeing Centre, 3-11 Drake Street, Rochdale, Lancs, OL16 1RE
Trustees: Mrs Marilyn Aldred, Mr Barry Windle, Dr David John Mossley, Mrs Margaret Stoneman, Mr Keith Marsland, Ms Kate Davies Poole
Income: £1,184,076 [2017]; £1,204,003 [2016]; £1,233,975 [2015]; £1,242,392 [2014]; £1,281,816 [2013]

The Rochester Diocesan Society and Board of Finance
Registered: 26 Sep 1966 *Employees:* 47 *Volunteers:* 200
Tel: 01634 560000 *Website:* rochester.anglican.org
Activities: Religious activities
Address: Rochester Diocesan Society & Board of Finance, St Nicholas Church, Boley Hill, Rochester, Kent, ME1 1SL
Trustees: The Ven Doctor Paul Wright PhD, The Very Reverend Dr Philip Hesketh, Mrs Lela Weavers, Mr Christopher Huish Gallico, Mr Jeremy James King, Rev Dylan Lawrence Turner, Miss Christine Bostock, Rev James Henry Langstaff, Rev Canon Julie Ann Conalty, Rev Mark Barker, Rev Simon David Burton-Jones, Mr Gordon Andrew Hunt, Mrs Sarah Penelope Poole, Rev Alyson Elizabeth Davie, Mr Philip French, Mrs Judith Jane Armitt, Dr Jeffrey Vincent Blyth
Income: £14,771,000 [2016]; £14,766,799 [2015]; £11,837,513 [2014]; £11,826,713 [2013]; £11,169,664 [2012]

Rock UK Adventure Centres Limited
Registered: 20 Jan 2005 *Employees:* 90
Tel: 01933 654103 *Website:* rockuk.org
Activities: General charitable purposes; education, training; religious activities; amateur sport; other charitable purposes
Address: Rock UK Adventure Centre, Frontier Centre, Addington Road, Irthlingborough, Wellingborough, Northants, NN9 5UH
Trustees: Mr Derek William Adams, Mrs Margaret Wooding Jones, Mr Huw Alwyn Ellis, Mr Alistair Fraser, Mr Alan David Belcher, Miss Nicola Dawn Foot
Income: £2,818,704 [2016]; £3,035,098 [2015]; £3,371,038 [2014]; £3,048,566 [2013]; £4,628,807 [2012]

Rockingham Forest Trust
Registered: 26 Oct 1995 *Employees:* 40 *Volunteers:* 50
Tel: 01933 625527 *Website:* rockingham-forest-trust.org.uk
Activities: Education, training; arts, culture, heritage, science; amateur sport; environment, conservation, heritage; economic, community development, employment; recreation
Address: Stanwick Lakes, Stanwick, Wellingborough, Northants, NN9 6GY
Trustees: Mr Harry Ford, Mr David Charles Watson, Mr Gerald Mark Couldrake, Mrs Jane Charlton-Jones, Lord John Gorell, Mr Joseph John Richardson MBE, Mrs Priscilla Padley, Mr John William Green OBE, Mrs Amanda Keys
Income: £1,230,213 [2017]; £1,002,780 [2016]; £996,796 [2015]; £850,271 [2014]; £794,660 [2013]

Roedean School

Registered: 4 Aug 1966 *Employees:* 266
Tel: 01273 667512 *Website:* roedean.co.uk
Activities: Education, training
Address: Roedean School, Roedean Way, Brighton, BN2 5RQ
Trustees: Lady Lavender Patten of Barnes BA, Dr Jean Peacey MB BS MRCGP, Ms Delva Patman FRICS, Ms Cecilia Oram MA Cantab ACIB Dip Trans, Ms Anne Whitaker, Dr Anne Edwards, Mrs Fleur Cook, Mrs Katherine Margery Cowell, Mr Andrew John Pianca FCA, Miss Victoria Jane Tait Jenkins, Ms Jennifer Mary Barnard-Langston, Mrs Sheila Fowler-Watt, Dr Henry Olufemi Fajemirokun PhD, Ms Anne-Marie Martin MBE BSc MSc, Dr Gary John Savage MA Cantab PhD FRSA, Mr Roger William Sanders, Mrs Teresa Outhwaite BA PgDip, Mrs Camilla Sarah Nightingale BA MBA, Mrs Vivien Louise Smiley BA, Ms Toyin Fani-Kayode
Income: £12,896,768 [2016]; £13,608,470 [2015]; £12,679,692 [2014]; £11,826,152 [2013]; £11,682,221 [2012]

Roehampton Students' Union

Registered: 14 Jan 2011 *Employees:* 26 *Volunteers:* 20
Tel: 020 8392 3221 *Website:* roehamptonstudent.com
Activities: General charitable purposes; education, training
Address: Froebel College, Roehampton Lane, London, SW15 5PJ
Trustees: Mr Tessa Willy, David Martin, Mr Chukwuemeka Nwagu, Mr Guy Drury, Mr Ian Robinson, Mr Jack Wilcock, Mr Joanna Briggs, Mr Jeffrey Arthur
Income: £1,101,159 [2016]; £1,070,370 [2015]; £933,904 [2014]; £726,595 [2013]

Roffey Park Institute Limited

Registered: 7 Feb 1968 *Employees:* 75
Tel: 01293 851644 *Website:* roffeypark.com
Activities: Education, training
Address: Roffey Park Institute, Forest Road, Colgate, Horsham, W Sussex, RH12 4TB
Trustees: Mr Charles Horton, Mrs Caroline Waters OBE, Mr Andrew Talbot, Mr Sebastian Michael Humfrey Ling, Mr Jabbar Sardar, Ms Alison Ritchie, Mrs Caroline Waddington, Ms Sian Harrington, Mr Roger Leek, Matthew Haworth
Income: £5,514,165 [2017]; £6,181,402 [2016]; £6,702,258 [2015]; £7,435,972 [2014]; £6,800,800 [2013]

The Roger de Haan Charitable Trust

Registered: 28 Sep 1978
Website: rdhct.org.uk
Activities: Education, training; advancement of health or saving of lives; disability; prevention or relief of poverty; overseas aid, famine relief; arts, culture, heritage, science; amateur sport; environment, conservation, heritage; recreation
Address: Strand House, Pilgrims Way, Monks Horton, Ashford, Kent, TN25 6DR
Trustees: Mr Benjamin De Haan, Sir Roger De Haan, Mr Joshua De Haan, Lady De Haan
Income: £2,624,000 [2017]; £795,000 [2016]; £5,980,000 [2015]; £644,000 [2014]; £2,710,000 [2013]

Dame Hannah Roger's School

Registered: 26 Sep 1962 *Employees:* 420 *Volunteers:* 263
Tel: 01752 898100 *Website:* discoverhannahs.org
Activities: Education, training; advancement of health or saving of lives; disability; accommodation, housing; arts, culture, heritage, science; human rights, religious or racial harmony, equality or diversity; recreation
Address: Dame Hannah Rogers School, Woodland Road, Ivybridge, Devon, PL21 9HQ
Trustees: Dame Hannah Rogers Trustees
Income: £9,288,519 [2017]; £8,785,353 [2016]; £9,063,165 [2015]; £10,394,693 [2014]; £8,975,487 [2013]

Rokeby Educational Trust Limited

Registered: 16 Mar 1966 *Employees:* 91
Tel: 020 8949 2908 *Website:* rokebyschool.co.uk
Activities: Education, training
Address: Rokeby Educational Trust Ltd, Rokeby School, George Road, Kingston upon Thames, Surrey, KT2 7PB
Trustees: Mr Robert Webster, Mr David Viles, Mr Stephen Bruce Chatterton Allen RIBA, Mrs Anna Priest, Mr James Courtney Thompson, Ms Deirdre Davidson, Dr Andrew James Mayfield, Mrs Annabel Henriette Evans-Tovey, Mrs Janice Lynne Price
Income: £5,907,175 [2016]; £5,645,114 [2015]; £5,197,950 [2014]; £5,039,100 [2013]; £4,757,790 [2012]

Roland Callingham Foundation

Registered: 22 Oct 1975 *Employees:* 62
Tel: 020 7566 4000
Activities: General charitable purposes; other charitable purposes
Address: Devonshire House, 60 Goswell Road, London, EC1M 7AD
Trustees: Peter Holgate, Mark Callingham, Mr Norman James Heaton, Mrs Sandra De Lord
Income: £1,386,744 [2016]; £1,261,429 [2015]; £1,232,142 [2014]; £1,143,107 [2013]; £1,158,847 [2012]

Roman Catholic Diocese of Hallam Trust

Registered: 16 Nov 1981 *Employees:* 48 *Volunteers:* 500
Tel: 0114 256 6430 *Website:* hallam-diocese.com
Activities: Religious activities
Address: Hallam Pastoral Centre, St Charles Street, Sheffield, S9 3WU
Trustees: Diocese of Hallam Trustee
Income: £5,837,599 [2016]; £6,109,937 [2015]; £5,928,349 [2014]; £6,330,179 [2013]; £6,127,409 [2012]

Roman Catholic Purposes Administered in Connection with the Society of African Missions

Registered: 12 May 1964 *Employees:* 13
Tel: 0161 224 4949 *Website:* sma-gb.org
Activities: Religious activities
Address: S M A Fathers, 378 Upper Brook Street, Manchester, M13 0EP
Trustees: Rev Patrick Nicholas McGuire SMA, Rev Robert Morland SMA, Rev Dermot McCaul SMA, Rev Thomas Joseph Ryan SNA
Income: £1,184,075 [2016]; £3,131,057 [2015]; £1,536,518 [2014]; £2,269,399 [2013]; £1,414,868 [2012]

Roman Catholic Purposes in Connection with the Congregation of The Most Holy Redeemer
Registered: 10 May 1967 Employees: 26 Volunteers: 100
Tel: 01738 587907 Website: redempt.org
Activities: Religious activities
Address: St Marys Monastery, Hatton Road, Kinnoull, Perth, PH2 7BP
Trustees: Rev Timothy Buckley CSsR, Rev Father Gerald Mulligan CSsR, Reverend Ronald McAinsh CSsR, Rev Father Richard Reid CSsR, Rev Father Charles Corrigan, Rev Andrew Burns Cssr The Rev'd Father
Income: £1,371,353 [2017]; £5,318,024 [2016]; £2,087,598 [2015]; £3,776,815 [2014]; £1,892,304 [2013]

Romsey Mill Trust
Registered: 4 Jun 1998 Employees: 30 Volunteers: 103
Tel: 01223 213162 Website: romseymill.org
Activities: General charitable purposes; education, training; prevention or relief of poverty; religious activities
Address: Romsey Mill, Hemingford Road, Cambridge, CB1 3BZ
Trustees: Reverend Stewart Taylor, Mr Tim Phipps, Mrs Angela Single, Mrs Tolulope Anifalaje, Mr Kim Pearson, Mr Malcolm Wylie, Mr Alistair Barry, Mrs Marion Saunders, Mr Nigel Taylor, Mr Julian Robert Hildersley
Income: £1,044,339 [2017]; £1,022,788 [2016]; £977,339 [2015]; £900,237 [2014]; £848,424 [2013]

Rontades Limited
Registered: 19 Mar 2003
Tel: 020 8880 8910
Activities: Education, training; prevention or relief of poverty; religious activities
Address: First Floor, 94 Stamford Hill, London, N16 6XS
Trustees: Mr Norman Bleier, Mr Itschak Mett, Mr Joshua Bleier
Income: £2,395,378 [2017]; £2,342,430 [2016]; £2,264,603 [2015]; £2,394,834 [2014]; £2,038,858 [2013]

Rookwood School Trust Limited
Registered: 3 Jul 1964 Employees: 73 Volunteers: 3
Tel: 01264 325901 Website: rookwoodschool.org
Activities: Education, training
Address: Rookwood School Trust Ltd, 35-39 Weyhill Road, Andover, Hants, SP10 3AL
Trustees: Miss Carole Machin, Mr David Drew, Mrs Carolyn Hardiman, Mrs Victoria Wickens, Mrs Fiona Penfold, Mr Michael Lower, Mr Kevin Knight, Mrs Victoria Rutherford, Mrs Rowena Thorne, Mr Lee Bedborough
Income: £3,564,300 [2016]; £3,546,004 [2015]; £3,531,529 [2014]; £3,453,303 [2013]; £3,443,880 [2012]

Room To Read UK Limited
Registered: 10 Sep 2008 Employees: 5 Volunteers: 50
Tel: 020 7873 3603 Website: roomtoread.org
Activities: Education, training; prevention or relief of poverty
Address: 1 Southwark Bridge, London, SE1 9HL
Trustees: Mr Martyn Christopher Gowar, Mr Douglas Hill, Mrs Geetha Murali, Mr Dean Chan, Ms Shari Freedman
Income: £2,679,778 [2016]; £2,651,351 [2015]; £3,477,923 [2014]; £2,356,858 [2013]; £2,127,102 [2012]

Wayne Rooney Foundation
Registered: 28 Jul 2015 Employees: 1
Tel: 0845 901 0229 Website: officialwaynerooney.com
Activities: General charitable purposes
Address: Great Oak Farm Offices, Mag Lane, Lymm, Cheshire, WA13 0TF
Trustees: Mr Colin Massie, Mr Michael Askew, Rob Cotton
Income: £2,173,286 [2016]

Mrs L D Rope's Third Charitable Settlement
Registered: 5 Dec 1984 Employees: 5
Tel: 01473 333288
Activities: General charitable purposes
Address: Lucy House, St William Court, Kesgrave, Ipswich, Suffolk, IP5 2QP
Trustees: Crispin Rope, Ellen Jolly, Catherine Scott, Mr Jeremy Philip Winteringham Heal, Paul Jolly
Income: £1,581,967 [2017]; £1,471,124 [2016]; £1,526,695 [2015]; £1,486,797 [2014]; £1,445,496 [2013]

Rosa Fund
Registered: 7 Jul 2008 Employees: 3 Volunteers: 5
Tel: 020 7697 3466 Website: rosauk.org
Activities: General charitable purposes
Address: Rosa, 4th Floor, United House, North Road, London, N7 9DP
Trustees: Mrs Marilyn List, Prof Ruth Pearson, Ms Sharon Mahli, Miss Kay Ali, Mrs Catherine Jane Uttley Dovey, Mr David Aeron-Thomas, Sheila Jane Malley, Linda McDowell, Ms Niamh Grogan
Income: £2,423,656 [2017]; £422,337 [2016]; £363,286 [2015]; £408,171 [2014]; £129,377 [2013]

Rose Bruford College of Theatre and Performance
Registered: 9 Jan 1964 Employees: 130
Tel: 020 8308 2612 Website: bruford.ac.uk
Activities: Education, training
Address: Rose Bruford College of Theatre And Performance, Lamorbey Park, Burnt Oak Lane, Sidcup, Kent, DA15 9DF
Trustees: Colin Campbell, Ms Cara Turtington, Ms Jennifer Sims, Ms Helen Bowles, Mr Don Massey, Professor Mike Saks, Mr Paul Dale, Mr Hassan Mahamdallie, Mr Rogan Dixon, Mr George Littlejohn, Mr Thomas Wilson, Mrs Monisha Shah, Mr Rod Brown, Mr Mike McCart, Ms Kathryn Southworth, Mr Kevin Wallace, Ms Samantha Perez-Lumbreras, Mr Andrew Exeter
Income: £9,251,000 [2017]; £9,456,000 [2016]; £8,147,000 [2015]; £7,609,000 [2014]; £7,444,000 [2013]

M.K. Rose Charitable Trust
Registered: 29 Jul 1994
Tel: 01562 882433
Activities: General charitable purposes; education, training; advancement of health or saving of lives; disability; prevention or relief of poverty; overseas aid, famine relief; accommodation, housing; religious activities; arts, culture, heritage, science; amateur sport; economic, community development, employment; armed forces, emergency service efficiency; human rights, religious or racial harmony, equality or diversity; other charitable purposes
Address: 40 Lodge Crescent, Hagley, Stourbridge, W Yorks, DY9 0NB
Trustees: Mrs Sharon Gould, Mr Alan Herbert Freeman
Income: £3,007,047 [2016]; £3,015 [2015]; £2,678 [2014]; £4,033 [2013]; £5,398 [2012]

The Rose Road Association

Registered: 20 Jul 1970 *Employees:* 191 *Volunteers:* 45
Website: roseroad.org.uk
Activities: Disability
Address: Rose Road Association, 300 Aldermoor Road, Southampton, SO16 5NA
Trustees: Mr Timothy Burbidge, Mrs Diana Gay Heatly, Mr Douglas Miller, Mrs Sarah Parker, Ms Paula Porter, Con Attridge, Mr Christopher John Cundy, Mrs Jane Lyon Maris, Tim Waldron, Dr Roxanne Marion Magdalena
Income: £3,070,737 [2017]; £3,061,482 [2016]; £2,944,822 [2015]; £2,779,709 [2014]; £2,991,026 [2013]

Rosehill Arts Trust Limited

Registered: 30 Jan 1967 *Employees:* 8 *Volunteers:* 20
Tel: 01946 62635 *Website:* rosehilltheatre.co.uk
Activities: Education, training; arts, culture, heritage, science; economic, community development, employment
Address: Waygates, Harras Road, Harras Moor, Whitehaven, Cumbria, CA28 6SG
Trustees: Mr Roger John Wilson, Yvonne Clarkson, Mrs Lucy Gallagher, Mr Andrew Smith, Mrs Joan Fisher, Peter Mann, Mr Paul Terry, Mr Richard Elder
Income: £1,956,278 [2017]; £812,400 [2016]; £649,388 [2015]; £215,586 [2014]; £378,311 [2013]

The Rosemere Cancer Foundation

Registered: 11 Sep 2009 *Volunteers:* 100
Tel: 01772 243454 *Website:* rosemere.org.uk
Activities: The advancement of health or saving of lives
Address: Royal Preston Hospital, Sharoe Green Lane, Fulwood, Preston, Lancs, PR2 9HT
Trustees: Lancashire Teaching Hospitals NHS Foundation Trust
Income: £1,292,000 [2017]; £1,187,000 [2016]; £998,000 [2015]; £699,000 [2014]; £746,000 [2013]

Roses Theatre Trust

Registered: 2 Jan 1996 *Employees:* 21 *Volunteers:* 9
Tel: 01684 290734 *Website:* rosestheatre.org
Activities: Arts, culture, heritage, science
Address: Roses Theatre Trust Ltd, Sun Street, Tewkesbury, Glos, GL20 5NX
Trustees: Mr Peter Cottingham, Miss Elaine Hancox, Mr Colin Wells, Ms Susanne Jane Hillier, Mr Paul Nicholas Johnson, Mr Keith Richard Norton, Mr Peter James Antill, Dr Adele Carter, Ms Sarah Anne Blowers
Income: £1,289,392 [2017]; £1,875,712 [2016]; £1,445,956 [2015]; £1,390,137 [2014]; £1,139,515 [2013]

The David Ross Foundation

Registered: 7 Dec 2007
Tel: 020 7534 1557 *Website:* davidrossfoundation.co.uk
Activities: General charitable purposes
Address: 10SJP Limited, 10 St James's Place, London, SW1A 1NP
Trustees: Mr Mark Bolland, Ms Anita Josephine Bott, Lady Caroline Mary Ryder, Mr David John Peter Ross, Mrs Marcia Mercier
Income: £3,974,037 [2017]; £327,026 [2016]; £5,854,525 [2015]; £2,996,146 [2014]; £5,731,775 [2013]

Rossall School

Registered: 6 May 1965 *Employees:* 236 *Volunteers:* 4
Tel: 01253 774201 *Website:* rossallschool.org.uk
Activities: Education, training
Address: Rossall School, Broadway, Fleetwood, Lancs, FY7 8JW
Trustees: Mrs Lillian Croston, Mr James Frederick Parr, Mr Martin Robert Dillon Craven, Mrs Christine Preston BSc ARICS, Mr Clive Littler, Mr David Hamilton Ewart MA PGCE DMS, Mr Chris Holt, Dr David M Elliott BSc MB ChB, Mrs Katherine Jane Thomas MIFST BSc RSCI, Canon John Michael Hall, Mr Martin Richard Mosley, Mr Michael John Reece MA, Dr Henry Fajemirokun, Mrs Michelle Anne Smith MSc FCA JP, Mr S J Fisher, Mr Nicholas Kevin Ward, The Reverend Grant Ashton
Income: £10,069,223 [2016]; £11,772,779 [2015]; £12,034,062 [2014]; £12,096,582 [2013]; £11,694,978 [2012]

The Rossendale Trust Limited

Registered: 3 Apr 2012 *Employees:* 180 *Volunteers:* 180
Tel: 01260 252500 *Website:* rossendaletrust.org
Activities: Disability
Address: Rossendale Hall, Hollin Lane, Sutton, Macclesfield, Cheshire, SK11 0HR
Trustees: Maggie Harwood, Michael J B Smith, Mr Simon Heapy, Mr Anthony Burton, Mrs M Beswick, Mr M Jones, Mr Andrew Richards, Mrs Marion Goddard
Income: £3,670,759 [2017]; £3,064,429 [2016]; £3,082,592 [2015]; £3,113,071 [2014]; £2,725,846 [2013]

Rotary Foundation of The United Kingdom

Registered: 27 Feb 1991
Tel: 01789 765411 *Website:* rotarygbi.org
Activities: Education, training; advancement of health or saving of lives; disability; prevention or relief of poverty; overseas aid, famine relief; economic, community development, employment
Address: Rotary International, Old Council Offices, Kinwarton Road, Alcester, Warwicks, B49 6PB
Trustees: Mr Michael Parry, Michael Webb, Mr John Dunkley
Income: £4,916,899 [2017]; £3,082,790 [2016]; £3,050,919 [2015]; £3,062,450 [2014]; £2,920,762 [2013]

Rothamsted Research Limited

Registered: 18 Sep 1989 *Employees:* 410
Tel: 01582 763133 *Website:* rothamsted.ac.uk
Activities: Education, training
Address: Rothamsted Research, West Common, Harpenden, Herts, AL5 2JQ
Trustees: Professor Sir David Charles Baulcombe, Professor Richard Bardgett, Sir John Beddington CMG FRS, Professor Michael Winter, Mr Stuart Jarvis, Dr Oliver Doubleday, Mr Paul Leonard, Professor Charles Godfray, Ms Sally Smith, Mr Russell Brooks, Dr Alastair Leake
Income: £34,121,000 [2017]; £32,892,000 [2016]; £42,603,000 [2015]; £37,644,000 [2014]; £42,769,000 [2013]

Rotherham Crossroads - Caring for Carers

Registered: 5 Jun 1997 *Employees:* 117 *Volunteers:* 27
Tel: 01709 360272 *Website:* crossroadsrotherham.co.uk
Activities: The advancement of health or saving of lives; disability
Address: Unit H, The Point, Bradmarsh, Rotherham, S Yorks, S60 1BP
Trustees: Mr John Hacon, Mr Thomas Martin Ensor, Mr Esrald George Bennett MBE, Mrs Monica Hudson, Dr Mary Elizabeth Holt, Mrs Angela Murray, Mrs Lorraine Wainwright, Miss Jean Dearden, Mr David Lisgo, Ms Siobhan Doran, Lois Crooke, Mrs Shelly Garlington
Income: £2,264,991 [2017]; £2,195,113 [2016]; £2,226,309 [2015]; £1,871,797 [2014]; £1,791,328 [2013]

The Rotherham Hospice Trust
Registered: 15 Jun 1988 *Employees:* 158 *Volunteers:* 414
Tel: 01709 308902 *Website:* rotherhamhospice.org.uk
Activities: The advancement of health or saving of lives
Address: The Rotherham Hospice, Broom Road, Rotherham,
S Yorks, S60 2SW
Trustees: Professor Bob Rees, Bronwen Watson, Richard Finney,
Mrs Jackie Saunders, Ian Norris, Mr John Whaling, Dr Richard
Francis Daly, Robert Bloomer
Income: £5,873,078 [2017]; £5,713,643 [2016]; £5,637,757 [2015];
£5,110,557 [2014]; £4,669,850 [2013]

The Rothermere Foundation
Registered: 2 Jan 1964
Tel: 01233 740641
Activities: General charitable purposes; education, training
Address: Beech Court, Canterbury Road, Challock, Ashford, Kent,
TN25 4DJ
Trustees: Mr Vyvyan Peter Wilfred Harmsworth LVO, The
Viscountess Claudia Rothermere, Rt Hon Viscount Jonathan
Rothermere
Income: £1,126,135 [2017]; £1,089,915 [2016]; £1,041,849 [2015];
£973,024 [2014]; £898,679 [2013]

The Rothschild Archive Limited
Registered: 4 May 1999
Tel: 020 7280 5874 *Website:* rothschildarchive.org
Activities: Education, training; arts, culture, heritage, science
Address: The Rothschild Archive, New Court, St Swithins Lane,
London, EC4N 8AL
Trustees: The Honorable Emma Rothschild CMG, Mr Anthony
Leonard Chapman, Eric De Rothschild, Ariane De Rothschild,
Mr John Grimond, Alice Rothschild, David Cannadine, Mr Lionel
De Rothschild, Julien De Beaumarchais, Mr Nigel Higgins, David
Todd
Income: £1,335,636 [2017]; £1,215,847 [2016]; £157,819 [2015];
£244,982 [2014]; £443,238 [2013]

The Rothschild Foundation
Registered: 22 Sep 2010 *Employees:* 220 *Volunteers:* 330
Tel: 01296 653208 *Website:* rothschildfoundation.org.uk
Activities: General charitable purposes; education, training;
advancement of health or saving of lives; disability; prevention or
relief of poverty; accommodation, housing; religious activities; arts,
culture, heritage, science; environment, conservation, heritage;
economic, community development, employment; other charitable
purposes
Address: The Dairy, Queen Street, Waddesdon, Bucks, HP18 0JW
Trustees: Lord Rothschild OM GBE, The Marquess of
Cholmondeley, The Hon Hannah Rothschild, Lord David John
Ogilvy, The Hon Emily Magda Freeman-Attwood, The Hon Mrs
Janet De Botton CBE, Mr Francesco Goedhuis, S J P Trust
Corporation Limited
Income: £37,775,210 [2017]; £31,148,615 [2016]; £27,534,895
[2015]; £30,551,752 [2014]; £24,491,660 [2013]

The Eranda Rothschild Foundation
Registered: 22 Apr 1968 *Volunteers:* 1
Tel: 01296 689157 *Website:* erandarothschild.org
Activities: General charitable purposes; education, training;
advancement of health or saving of lives; prevention or relief
of poverty; overseas aid, famine relief; religious activities; arts,
culture, heritage, science; amateur sport; animals; environment,
conservation, heritage; economic, community development,
employment
Address: Eranda Foundation, P O Box 6226, Wing, Leighton
Buzzard, Beds, LU7 0XF
Trustees: Sir Graham Hearne, Sir Evelyn De Rothschild, Lady De
Rothschild, Mr Benjamin Elliot, Anthony De Rothschild, Jessica De
Rothschild, Sir John Wilfred Peace
Income: £5,096,016 [2017]; £4,091,601 [2016]; £4,257,227 [2015];
£3,967,432 [2014]; £4,419,072 [2013]

Rougemont School Trust Limited
Registered: 24 Oct 1974 *Employees:* 132
Tel: 01633 820800 *Website:* rougemontschool.co.uk
Activities: Education, training
Address: Rougemont School, Llantarnam Hall, Malpas Road,
Newport, NP20 6QB
Trustees: Mrs Christine Thomas, Ms Jennifer Sollis, Mrs Jayne
Clark, Prof David Lawerence Fone MD, Mr Howard Clark,
Mr Richard Green, Mr Michael Cordner, Mr Ieuan Short, Mr Martin
Keith Tebbutt, Mrs Shilpa Desai, Mr Ian Hoppe, Mr Paul Harris,
Dr Jonathan Nicholas Tribbick
Income: £6,074,848 [2017]; £6,302,851 [2016]; £5,959,629 [2015];
£5,809,752 [2014]; £5,781,703 [2013]

The Round Square
Registered: 26 Jun 1986 *Employees:* 6
Tel: 01753 862032 *Website:* roundsquare.org
Activities: General charitable purposes; education, training;
prevention or relief of poverty; overseas aid, famine relief;
environment, conservation, heritage; economic, community
development, employment
Address: Swan House, Madeira Walk, Windsor, Berks, SL4 1EU
Trustees: Mr Rod Fraser, His Majesty King Constantine,
Mr Christopher Shannon, Mrs Papri Ghosh, Mrs Johana Christina
Ashton, Mr Nicholas Adam Richardson, Mrs Susan Redelinghuys,
Mr Hugh MacDonnell, Mr John O'Connor, Mr Murray Guest,
Mr Richard Bradley, Mrs Simona Diana Baciu, Mr Richard
McDonald, Mr Siddarth Singh Girnar
Income: £1,012,614 [2017]; £966,540 [2016]; £830,189 [2015];
£783,323 [2014]; £771,926 [2013]

Roundabout Limited
Registered: 15 Mar 1997 *Employees:* 65 *Volunteers:* 53
Tel: 0114 253 6789 *Website:* roundabouthomeless.org
Activities: Education, training; accommodation, housing
Address: Roundabout Ltd, 13-17 St Barnabas Road, Sheffield,
S2 4TF
Trustees: Mrs Ann Elisabeth Jane Arundale, Mr Kevin Docherty,
Mr Scott Bailey, Mrs Brenda Worsdale, Ms Karen Moxham, Mr John
Christopher Caldwell, Mr Zahid Hamid, David Ward, Mrs Caroline
Woffenden
Income: £2,442,172 [2017]; £1,875,944 [2016]; £1,915,265 [2015];
£1,957,029 [2014]; £2,071,232 [2013]

The Roundhouse Trust
Registered: 11 Sep 1998 *Employees:* 290 *Volunteers:* 151
Tel: 020 7424 2967 *Website:* roundhouse.org.uk
Activities: Education, training; arts, culture, heritage, science; environment, conservation, heritage; economic, community development, employment
Address: The Roundhouse Trust, Chalk Farm Road, London, NW1 8EH
Trustees: Mr Nicholas Allott, Mr Tony Elliott, Mr Caspar Joe Norman, Mr Johnson Etienne, Bob Shennan, Mr Simon Turner, Mr Michael Wornell, Mr Anthony Gutman, Mr Sanjeev Bhaskar, Marcus Davey, Ms Ella Bennett, Ms Pauline Tambling, Ms Sally O'Neil, Mrs Sarah Wood, Ms Sophie Kilburn, Mr Ade Adepitan, Mr Jonathan Badyal
Income: £12,403,223 [2017]; £11,455,523 [2016]; £12,276,799 [2015]; £11,609,466 [2014]; £15,905,021 [2013]

Rowan Organisation
Registered: 2 Mar 1993 *Employees:* 49
Tel: 024 7632 2860 *Website:* therowan.org
Activities: Disability
Address: Eliot Park Innovation Centre, Barling Way, Nuneaton, Warwicks, CV10 7RH
Trustees: Mrs Anne Forwood, Miss Denise Elizabeth Cambray, Cllr Denise Clews, Mrs Jacqueline Taylor, Ms Jacqui Caldwell
Income: £1,299,664 [2017]; £1,721,788 [2016]; £1,929,526 [2015]; £1,861,021 [2014]; £1,936,455 [2013]

The Rowans Hospice
Registered: 20 Jul 1988 *Employees:* 263 *Volunteers:* 1,200
Website: rowanshospice.co.uk
Activities: The advancement of health or saving of lives
Address: Purbrook Lodge, Purbrook Heath Road, Purbrook, Waterlooville, Hants, PO7 5RU
Trustees: Mr David Brindley, Mrs Lisa Dickens, Mr Roger Harrison, Mrs Wendy Greenish, Mrs Vivien West, Ms Eva Dixon, Mr Ian Young, Mrs Elizabeth Emms, Mrs Anne Powell, Mrs Caroline Willett BA ACA, Dr Roger Sutton, Mr Anthony Saunders
Income: £9,719,587 [2017]; £9,466,351 [2016]; £7,158,738 [2015]; £6,934,438 [2014]; £5,514,655 [2013]

Rowanville Limited
Registered: 9 Apr 1974
Tel: 020 8458 9266
Activities: Education, training; prevention or relief of poverty; accommodation, housing; religious activities
Address: 8 Highfield Gardens, London, NW11 9HB
Trustees: Joseph Pearlman, Mr Allan Becker, Mrs Ruth Pearlman
Income: £1,186,135 [2017]; £3,188,729 [2016]; £1,451,710 [2015]; £1,126,289 [2014]; £1,006,736 [2013]

Rowcroft House Foundation Limited
Registered: 30 Jun 1981 *Employees:* 166 *Volunteers:* 413
Tel: 01803 210826 *Website:* rowcrofthospice.org.uk
Activities: Education, training; advancement of health or saving of lives
Address: Rowcroft Hospice, Avenue Road, Torquay, Devon, TQ2 5LS
Trustees: Mr Richard John Sheridan Brinsley, Dr Cathryn Edwards, Mr Anthony Dee, Sally Bryant, Dr Richard William George Ward, Mr Colin Michael William Pincombe, Liz Allen
Income: £8,192,216 [2017]; £7,689,290 [2016]; £8,468,948 [2015]; £7,203,511 [2014]; £7,392,510 [2013]

The Royal Academy of Arts
Registered: 6 Aug 2008 *Employees:* 338 *Volunteers:* 196
Tel: 020 7300 8017 *Website:* royalacademy.org.uk
Activities: Education, training; prevention or relief of poverty; arts, culture, heritage, science
Address: Burlington House, Piccadilly, London, W1J 0BD
Trustees: Ms Anne Desmet RA RE, Mr Brendan Finucane QC, Fiona Rae RA, Hughie O'Donoghue RA, Mali Morris RA, Mr William Woodrow RA, Professor Gordon Benson OBE RA, Louisa Hutton OBE RA, Rebecca Salter RA, Mr Christopher Mark Le Brun PRA, Eric Parry RA, Mr Tony Bevan RA, Mr Julian Heslop, Ms Helen Boaden, Bob and Roberta Smith RA, Richard Wilson RA, Yinke Shonibare MBE RA
Income: £49,716,124 [2017]; £58,382,491 [2016]; £39,626,371 [2015]; £33,146,825 [2014]; £36,281,856 [2013]

Royal Academy of Dance
Registered: 12 Feb 1963 *Employees:* 240 *Volunteers:* 180
Tel: 020 7326 8000 *Website:* royalacademyofdance.org
Activities: Education, training
Address: 36 Battersea Square, London, SW11 3RA
Trustees: Ms Penny Parks RAD RTS, Miss Deborah Coultish RAD RTS, Ms Ida Levine, Mrs Sarah Dickinson ARAD AdvTchDip, Mr Guy Perricone, Mrs Joanna Binder, Ms Justine Berry, Ms Imogen Knight, Mrs Lynne Reucroft-Croome BA(Hons) LRAD, Miss Julia Bond, Ms Therese Cantine ARAD Dip PDTC, Ms Aliceson Robinson, Mr Michael Day, Ms Catherine Jane Margaret Weate, Ms Hilary Clark
Income: £22,301,000 [2017]; £19,912,000 [2016]; £19,726,000 [2015]; £20,463,000 [2014]; £18,577,943 [2013]

The Royal Academy of Dramatic Art
Registered: 30 Oct 1962 *Employees:* 157
Tel: 020 7908 4893 *Website:* rada.ac.uk
Activities: Education, training; arts, culture, heritage, science; economic, community development, employment
Address: Royal Academy of Dramatic Art, 62-64 Gower Street, London, WC1E 6ED
Trustees: Mr Stephen Waley-Cohen Sir, Mr Mike Leigh, Catherine Bailey, Mr Richard Wilson OBE, Miss Chipo Chung, Mr Stephen Greene, Mr Geoff Locker, Paul Pyant, Michelle Terry, Mr Paul Clay, Laurence Issacson CBE, Ms Tanya Moodie, Ros Haigh, Andrew Sutch, Fiona Shaw CBE, Professor Michael Worton, Mr Zac Barratt, Mr Glen Moreno, Mr Simon Berry, Mr Matthew Byam Shaw, Judy Grahame, Imogen Stubbs, Mr Joshua Berger, Mr Buster Dover, Robin Soans, Mr Rishi Madlani, Sir Martin Donnelly
Income: £11,148,000 [2017]; £9,620,000 [2016]; £9,381,000 [2015]; £8,697,000 [2014]; £7,910,000 [2013]

The Royal Academy of Engineering
Registered: 22 Nov 1985 *Employees:* 83
Tel: 020 7766 0600 *Website:* raeng.org.uk
Activities: Education, training; economic, community development, employment
Address: The Royal Academy of Engineering, 3-4 Carlton House Terrace, London, SW1Y 5DG
Trustees: Mr Norman David Haste OBE FREng, Professor Geoffrey Colin Maitland FREng, Mr Colin Gareth Bailey FREng, Professor Richard Andrew Williams OBE FREng, Professor Elaine Barbara Martin OBE FREng, Liz Tanner OBE FREng FRSE, Professor Iain Gilmour Gray CBE FREng FRSE, Mr Paul Stephen Westbury CBE FREng, Ms Naomi Climer FREng, Dr Frances Carolyn Saunders CB FREng, Professor Dame Ann Patricia Dowling DBE FREng FRS, Mr David John Hughes FREng, Mr Robert Simon Joyce FREng, Professor Steohen John Young FREng
Income: £27,410,424 [2017]; £29,248,147 [2016]; £32,144,065 [2015]; £25,882,377 [2014]; £25,007,701 [2013]

Royal Academy of Music

Registered: 4 Jan 1973 *Employees:* 548 *Volunteers:* 107
Tel: 020 7873 7309 *Website:* ram.ac.uk
Activities: Education, training
Address: Royal Academy of Music, Marylebone Road, London, NW1 5HT
Trustees: Jonathan Sumption, Mr Matthew Ferrey, Mr John Burgess, Professor Sir Richard Trainor, Mr Timothy Parker, Mr William Michael Jefferies De Winton, Mrs Lucy Crowe, Mrs Rehmet Kassim Lakha De Morixe, Dame Jennifer Gita Abramsky CBE DBE, Mr John Willan ARAM, Lady Sainsbury, Mr Robin Butler, Ms Amanda Lorraine Hill, Mr Damian Wisniewski, Lord Blackwell
Income: £24,252,675 [2017]; £26,438,778 [2016]; £21,441,127 [2015]; £19,613,068 [2014]; £18,937,589 [2013]

Royal Aeronautical Society

Registered: 13 Jun 1963 *Employees:* 42 *Volunteers:* 1,000
Tel: 020 7670 4331 *Website:* aerosociety.com
Activities: General charitable purposes; education, training; arts, culture, heritage, science; environment, conservation, heritage; other charitable purposes
Address: Royal Aeronautical Society, 4 Hamilton Place, London, W1J 7BQ
Trustees: Ms Jane Middleton, Mr Martin Broadhurst OBE FRAeS, ACM Sir Stephen Dalton, Dr Thurai Rahulan, Mr Simon Michael Henley FRAeS, Ms Sarah Jane Moynihan, Sir John O'Reilly FRAeS, Prof Chris Atkin, Mr Richard Malcolm Gearing
Income: £4,780,407 [2017]; £5,036,898 [2016]; £4,630,568 [2015]; £4,958,289 [2014]; £4,314,294 [2013]

The Royal Agricultural Benevolent Institution

Registered: 22 Sep 1963 *Employees:* 102 *Volunteers:* 860
Tel: 01865 724931 *Website:* rabi.org.uk
Activities: Education, training; disability; prevention or relief of poverty; accommodation, housing; other charitable purposes
Address: Shaw House, 27 West Way, Botley, Oxford, OX2 0QH
Trustees: Mr Christopher D'Olley, Mrs Jeanette Elizabeth Dawson, Mr James Orme, Mr Stephen Miles, Mrs Jo Turnbull, Mr John Hoskin, Mr Jeremy Lewis, Mr John Stanley, Mr Malcolm Thomas, Mr Joshua Hosier, Mr Richard Binning, Sue Lister
Income: £8,446,000 [2017]; £6,036,000 [2016]; £5,680,000 [2015]; £6,464,000 [2014]; £6,340,000 [2013]

Royal Agricultural University

Registered: 3 Jun 1964 *Employees:* 200
Website: rau.ac.uk
Activities: Education, training
Address: The Royal Agricultural College, Stroud Road, Cirencester, Glos, GL7 6JS
Trustees: The Rt Honorable Michael Jack, Mr Colin Pett FCA BSc, Mrs Jean Roberts, Mrs Alison Bernays, Mr James Townshend, Mr Alexander Lawson, Mr Christopher Musgrave FRAgS, Prof Patricia Broadfoot CBE DSC ACSS PhD, Professor Jonathan G Kydd, Mr Mohamed Amersi, Mr Ian Stuart Cooper
Income: £19,692,189 [2017]; £18,254,098 [2016]; £18,154,741 [2015]; £17,267,465 [2014]; £17,773,347 [2013]

The Royal Air Force Benevolent Fund

Registered: 2 Jun 2000 *Employees:* 173
Website: rafbf.org
Activities: Education, training; disability; prevention or relief of poverty; accommodation, housing; arts, culture, heritage, science; armed forces, emergency service efficiency; other charitable purposes
Address: Royal Air Force Benevolent Fund, 67 Portland Place, London, W1B 1AR
Trustees: Air Vice-Marshal Simon Dougherty, Mr Alastair Irvine, Mr Stephen Critchley, Ms Marie-Noelle Orzel, Air Commodore Simon Harper, Ms Kathryn Adamson, Mr Graeme Craig, Mr Lawrie Haynes, Mr David Cheyne, Ms Frances Brindle, Air Vice-Marshal Elaine West, Mr Richard Ingham, Mr Graeme Shankland
Income: £23,352,000 [2016]; £24,214,000 [2015]; £21,675,000 [2014]; £19,253,000 [2013]; £17,301,000 [2012]

The Royal Air Force Central Fund

Registered: 24 Jun 2013 *Employees:* 8
Tel: 01494 496458 *Website:* rafcf.org.uk
Activities: General charitable purposes
Address: RM 1E CR1 Hurricane Building, HQ Air Command, RAF High Wycombe, Naphill, High Wycombe, Bucks, HP14 4UE
Trustees: Group Captain John Michaelson, Mr Peter Allen, Air Marshal Sean Reynolds, Dr Eamonn Molloy, Air Commodore Alison Mardell
Income: £3,330,821 [2016]; £1,802,890 [2015]; £4,146,997 [2014]

The Royal Air Force Charitable Trust

Registered: 17 Oct 1962 *Employees:* 49 *Volunteers:* 2,500
Tel: 01285 713300 *Website:* rafct.com
Activities: General charitable purposes; education, training; armed forces, emergency service efficiency
Address: Douglas Bader House, Horcott Hill, Fairford, Glos, GL7 4RB
Trustees: Alan Smith, Air Marshal Sir Kevin Leeson KCB CBE FREng CEng FIET, Mr Peter Brown MBE BSc, Kate Wigston, Delia Thornton, Mr Ian Beresford MBE FRAeS CEng FIOD CDir, Andy Sudlow
Income: £10,561,232 [2017]; £9,007,314 [2016]; £8,143,933 [2015]; £7,487,757 [2014]; £232,339 [2013]

The Royal Air Force Club

Registered: 24 Feb 2005 *Employees:* 126
Tel: 020 7399 1040 *Website:* rafclub.org.uk
Activities: Education, training; accommodation, housing; armed forces, emergency service efficiency
Address: Royal Air Force Club, 128 Piccadilly, London, W1J 7PY
Trustees: Group Captain Ian Frank Bruton BA MINST, Mark Heffron, Mr John Fisher, Air Commodore Barbara Cooper, Miss Jo Salter, Flight Lieutenant Ian Melia, Air Commodore Dai Whittingham, Sqn Ldr John Peters, Wing Commander Michael John Gilbert, Wing Commander Wendy Rothery BA FCIPD MCMI RAF, Air Cdre Rick Peacock-Edwards CBE AFC FRAeS FCIM, Mr Sean O'Brien, Wing Commander James Hill, Air Vice Marshal Sue Gray, Sqn Ldr James Poynton
Income: £7,761,987 [2016]; £7,290,073 [2015]; £7,440,043 [2014]; £6,561,523 [2013]; £6,169,153 [2012]

Royal Air Force Museum
Registered: 9 May 1968 *Employees:* 172 *Volunteers:* 313
Tel: 020 8538 4839 *Website:* rafmuseum.org
Activities: Education, training; arts, culture, heritage, science; environment, conservation, heritage
Address: Royal Air Force Museum, Grahame Park Way, Hendon, London, NW9 5LL
Trustees: Mr Richard Holman FCA, Dr Rodney Eastwood PhD BSc, Mr John Michaelson BA MA MBA, Mr Robin Southwell, Mr Michael Schindler, ACM Sir Glenn Torpy GCB CBE DSO FRAeS FCGI, Mr Peter Bateson, Mrs Catriona Kempson, Mr Malcolm White OBE FRAeS, Mr Gerry Grimstone, Mr Alan Spence, Dr Carol Cole, Mr Andrew Reid LLB MCIArb, Mr Alan Coppin, Ms Laurie Benson, Ms Julie McGarvey
Income: £17,211,111 [2017]; £15,323,470 [2016]; £13,090,536 [2015]; £13,420,901 [2014]; £12,177,791 [2013]

The Royal Air Forces Association - Corporate Body
Registered: 1 Nov 1963 *Employees:* 160 *Volunteers:* 3,509
Tel: 0116 464 5027 *Website:* rafa.org.uk
Activities: The advancement of health or saving of lives; disability; accommodation, housing
Address: Atlas House, Wembley Road, Leicester, LE3 1UT
Trustees: Michael Blackman, Doctor Bryan Pattison OBE, Flt Sgt Wayne Swiggs RAF, Dave Chappell, Geoff Bridgman, Philip Tagg, Air Commodore Alan Opie, Taff Rees, Air Marshal Sir Baz North KCB OBE MA FRAeS, Pauline Bearblock, Fiona Barber, Beryl Dennett Stannard, Brian Darke MBE, Ian McEnnis, Chris Goss MA, Frank Barrett MBE, Squadron Leader Dean Gibson, Bob Chandler, Squadron Leader Ady Morris, Samantha Barber, Air Vice Marshal John Cliffe CB OBE, Mark Neal, Heather Little
Income: £12,852,000 [2016]; £9,846,000 [2015]; £9,644,000 [2014]; £8,839,000 [2013]; £9,484,000 [2012]

Royal Albert Dock Trust
Registered: 14 Apr 1992 *Employees:* 12
Tel: 020 7511 6622 *Website:* radt.org.uk
Activities: The advancement of health or saving of lives; disability; amateur sport; recreation
Address: Director of Adaptive Rowing, London Regatta Centre, Dockside Road, London, E16 2QT
Trustees: Stephen Timms MP, Mr Martin John Coles, Mr Mike Luddy, Mr Daniel Bridge, Mr Alan Leslie Laws, Mr Gary Harris, Mr Eric Kenneth Sorensen, Ms Guin Batten
Income: £1,065,126 [2017]; £2,284,313 [2016]; £548,943 [2015]; £470,170 [2014]; £451,109 [2013]

The Royal Albert Hall Trust
Registered: 28 Jul 1982
Tel: 020 7959 0505 *Website:* royalalberthall.com
Activities: Education, training; arts, culture, heritage, science; environment, conservation, heritage
Address: Royal Albert Hall, Kensington Gore, London, SW7 2AP
Trustees: Mr Jon Moynihan OBE, Mrs Lin Craig, Mr Ian McCulloch, Mr Leon Baroukh, Mr Michael Jackson
Income: £2,917,000 [2016]; £4,089,621 [2015]; £1,013,850 [2014]; £1,196,466 [2013]; £406,954 [2012]

The Royal Alexandra and Albert School
Registered: 26 Nov 1963 *Employees:* 169 *Volunteers:* 86
Tel: 01737 649050 *Website:* gatton-park.org.uk
Activities: Education, training
Address: Gatton Lodge, The Royal Alexandra & Albert School, Gatton Park, Reigate, Surrey, RH2 0TW
Trustees: Mr Graham Williams, Mr Richard Wells, Mr William Tennant Gillen, Mr John Billingham, Jon White, Mr Timothy Redburn, Mr Edward Winter, Mr Adrian Smart, Ms Frances Wadsworth, Dame Mary Richardson, David Frank, Angela Baker, Mr Charles Wates
Income: £9,302,000 [2017]; £9,296,000 [2016]; £8,747,000 [2015]; £13,449,000 [2014]; £9,320,000 [2013]

Royal Alfred Seafarers' Society
Registered: 22 Sep 1962 *Employees:* 113 *Volunteers:* 15
Tel: 01737 353763 *Website:* royalalfredseafarers.com
Activities: The advancement of health or saving of lives; disability; accommodation, housing
Address: Weston Acres Lodge, Woodmansterne Lane, Banstead, Surrey, SM7 3HA
Trustees: Commodore Ian Gibb MBE FNI FRSA FRGS, Captain Duncan Colin Glass OBE MNM, Doctor Richard Reubin, Mr Jeremy Wedge, Mr Andrew Parker, Lt Cdr Cedric Philip Wake OBE RD FNI RNR, Mrs Ann Gibb BEM, Councillor Mrs Dorothy Ross-Tomlin, Captain Adrian McCourt, Cdr Susan Lochner JP DL
Income: £3,593,661 [2016]; £3,505,797 [2015]; £3,436,351 [2014]; £3,237,875 [2013]; £3,013,742 [2012]

Royal Anthropological Institute of Great Britain and Ireland
Registered: 4 Oct 1966 *Employees:* 12 *Volunteers:* 14
Website: rai.anthropology.org.uk
Activities: Education, training
Address: Royal Anthropological Institute, 50 Fitzroy Street, London, W1T 5BT
Trustees: Professor Wendy James, Professor Roland Martin Littlewood BSc MB BS DPhil DLit DSC DipSocAnth FRCPsych, Professor Alan Bilsborough MA DipHumBiol, Prof Michael Herbert Day, Professor Ann MacLarnon, Dr James Staples, Professor Paul Basu, Prof Raymond James Apthorpe, Mr Andre Singer, Prof Christina Toren, Professor John Morgan, Dr Fiona Bowie, Dr Liana Cheng Lian Chua, Professor Robert Foley, Professor Paul Henley, Professor David Parkin, Dr Robert Storrie, Professor Jean La Fontaine BA PhD, Professor RoyFrank Ellen BSc PhD FLS FBA, Prof Adrian Curtis Mayer, Prof Michael Parker Banton, Professor Paul Sillitoe, Dr Simon Underdown, Prof Clive Gamble, Dr Christopher Morton, Dr Michael W Scott, Professor Paul Lane, Dr Nadine Beckmann, Dr Joseph Calabrese, Dr Gillian Margaret Evans, Professor Joy Hendry, Dr Catherine Palmer, Dr Emily Rousham, Dr Maya Unnitham
Income: £1,016,618 [2016]; £959,687 [2015]; £959,113 [2014]; £964,932 [2013]; £886,730 [2012]

The Royal Artillery Centre for Personal Development
Registered: 31 Aug 2005 *Employees:* 63
Tel: 01980 845482 *Website:* racpd.org.uk
Activities: Education, training
Address: RACPD, Royal Artillery Barracks, Larkhill, Salisbury, Wilts, SP4 8QT
Trustees: Mr Neil Hopkins, Maj Gen William Bramble, Col Michael Kelly, Colonel John Brian Musgrove, Dr John Bruce Knowles, Col Stephen Ellison, Brig John Mead, Mrs Amanda Jane Storey
Income: £2,523,753 [2017]; £2,578,381 [2016]; £2,469,010 [2015]; £3,917,183 [2014]; £2,679,315 [2013]

Royal Artillery Charitable Fund
Registered: 29 Apr 1964 *Employees:* 5
Tel: 01980 845698 *Website:* theraa.co.uk
Activities: Education, training; prevention or relief of poverty; other charitable purposes
Address: Artillery House, Royal Artillery Barracks, Larkhill, Salisbury, Wilts, SP4 8QT
Trustees: Mr C Fletcher-Wood, Colonel Christopher Comport OBE TD DL, Major General David Cullen CB OBE, Colonel William George Prior, Colonel Michael Relph MBE, Colonel Hugh Baker, Major Andrew Dines, Brigadier Mark Nicholas Pountain CBE, Major James Oliver Leighton TD, Colonel Michael James Kelly, Colonel John Musgrave, Colonel Giles Harry Malec
Income: £1,569,512 [2016]; £1,826,958 [2015]; £1,285,796 [2014]; £1,243,932 [2013]; £1,105,696 [2012]

The Royal Association for Deaf People
Registered: 9 Aug 2000 *Employees:* 70 *Volunteers:* 10
Tel: 0845 688 2525 *Website:* royaldeaf.org.uk
Activities: General charitable purposes; education, training; disability
Address: Century House, Riverside Office Centre, North Station Road, Colchester, Essex, CO1 1RE
Trustees: Revd Dr Margaret Joachim, Ms Sarah Reed, Mrs Shana Joanne Weimbaum, Mr Patrick Sheill, Mr Toby Burton, Mr Mark Napier, Mr David Cattermole, Mr Thomas John Mulloy
Income: £3,022,721 [2017]; £3,335,828 [2016]; £6,968,958 [2015]; £3,557,142 [2014]; £3,046,294 [2013]

Royal Astronomical Society
Registered: 23 Sep 1963 *Employees:* 18
Tel: 020 7292 3967 *Website:* ras.org.uk
Activities: Education, training
Address: Royal Astronomical Society, Burlington House, Piccadilly, London, W1J 0BQ
Trustees: Dr Ian Andrew Crawford, Professor Adrian Michael Cruise, Ms Mandy Bailey, Dr Nigel Berman, Prof Giovanna Tinetti, Prof Mark Lester, Mr Mark Woodland, Prof Steven Miller, Prof Lorraine Hanlon, Mr Kevin Kilburn, Dr Stacey Habergham-Mawson, Dr Sheila Peacock, Dr Lyndsay Fletcher, Mr Charles Barclay, Dr Paul Daniels, Prof Michael Watson, Dr Megan Argo, Dr Clare Watt, Prof William Chaplin, Dr Claire Foullon, Prof Anton Ziolkowski
Income: £4,299,415 [2016]; £4,139,808 [2015]; £4,505,168 [2014]; £3,997,609 [2013]; £3,662,047 [2012]

Royal Ballet School Endowment Fund
Registered: 10 Feb 1983
Tel: 020 7845 7052 *Website:* royalballetschool.org.uk
Activities: Education, training; arts, culture, heritage, science
Address: Royal Ballet School, 46 Floral Street, London, WC2E 9DA
Trustees: Mr Jonathan Chenevix-Trench, Mr Richard Cunis, Mr Kenneth Steele, Mr Suneel Bakhshi, Ms Menna McGregor, Ms Zita Saurel
Income: £3,294,000 [2017]; £203,000 [2016]; £3,237,000 [2015]; £1,219,000 [2014]; £930,000 [2013]

The Royal Ballet School
Registered: 12 Nov 1962 *Employees:* 187 *Volunteers:* 15
Tel: 020 7845 7057 *Website:* royalballetschool.org.uk
Activities: Education, training; arts, culture, heritage, science
Address: Royal Ballet School, 46 Floral Street, London, WC2E 9DA
Trustees: Mr Jonathan Chenevix-Trench, Ms Clarissa Farr, Ms Madeleine Plaut, Mrs Candida Hurst-Brown, Mr Suneel Bakhshi, Mr Kenneth Steele, Dr Genevieve Davis, Mr Kevin O'Hare, Ms Zita Saurel, Mrs Ricki Gail Conway, Ms Janet Lambert, Dr Stephen Spurr, The Duchess of Wellington, Mr David Fletcher, Ms Sarah Dorfman, Mrs Menna McGregor, Ms Nancy Marks
Income: £12,373,000 [2017]; £16,296,000 [2016]; £16,486,000 [2015]; £11,643,000 [2014]; £10,641,000 [2013]

The Royal Bath and West of England Society
Registered: 19 Jul 1994 *Employees:* 23 *Volunteers:* 600
Tel: 01749 822205 *Website:* bathandwest.com
Activities: Education, training; arts, culture, heritage, science; animals; environment, conservation, heritage; economic, community development, employment
Address: The Royal Bath & West of England Society, The Bath & West Showground, Shepton Mallet, Somerset, BA4 6QN
Trustees: Robert Drewett, Mr Anthony Alan Gibson OBE, Mrs Angela Betty Yeoman, Mr John Alvis MBE, Mr Richard Thomas Calver, Dr Lance Moir, Mr Richard William John Ash, Sir David James Vernon Wills Bt, Miss Nell Matheson DL, Mr Michael John Felton, Mr Martin Thatcher
Income: £3,780,989 [2016]; £4,089,675 [2015]; £3,849,364 [2014]; £3,217,982 [2013]; £3,383,523 [2012]

Royal Borough of Greenwich Heritage Trust
Registered: 22 May 2014 *Employees:* 20 *Volunteers:* 35
Tel: 020 8856 3951 *Website:* greenwichheritage.org
Activities: General charitable purposes; education, training; arts, culture, heritage, science; environment, conservation, heritage
Address: Charlton House, Charlton Road, Charlton, London, SE7 8RE
Trustees: Mr Roden Richardson, Mr Malcolm Woods, Cllr Gary Parker, Mr Richard Goodwin, Mr Philip Croall, Councillor Denise Scott-Mcdonald, Mr William Thomas Edgerley, Mr Jonathan Charles Louth, Nicky Snook, Tony Mitton, Mr Len Duvall
Income: £1,597,484 [2017]; £1,071,189 [2016]; £777,167 [2015]

The Royal Bournemouth & Christchurch Hospitals NHS Foundation Trust Charitable Fund
Registered: 6 Aug 1996 *Volunteers:* 100
Tel: 01202 704060 *Website:* bhcharity.org
Activities: The advancement of health or saving of lives
Address: Royal Bournemouth Hospital, Castle Lane East, Bournemouth, BH7 7DW
Trustees: RBCH Ft Board of Directors
Income: £1,644,724 [2017]; £1,509,000 [2016]; £1,155,000 [2015]; £1,259,000 [2014]; £2,061,000 [2013]

Royal British Legion Industries Ltd.
Registered: 18 Oct 1962 *Employees:* 371 *Volunteers:* 208
Tel: 01622 795949 *Website:* rbli.co.uk
Activities: Disability
Address: Royal British Legion Industries Ltd, Hall Road, Royal British Legion Village, Aylesford, Kent, ME20 7NL
Trustees: Mrs Nadra Ahmed OBE DL, Mr Arthur Blair Gulland, Mr Stephen William Kingsman, Mrs Kate Bosley, Mr Desmond Crampton, Brigadier Harold Hamilton Kerr OBE, Mr Frank Martin DL, Mr David Wyndham Montgomery
Income: £17,245,000 [2017]; £17,410,000 [2016]; £21,547,000 [2015]; £15,479,172 [2014]; £12,761,501 [2013]

Royal British Legion Poppy Factory Limited
Registered: 11 May 1964 *Employees:* 75 *Volunteers:* 94
Tel: 020 8939 1827 *Website:* poppyfactory.org
Activities: Economic, community development, employment
Address: The RBL Poppy Factory, 20 Petersham Road, Richmond, Surrey, TW10 6UR
Trustees: Steven Monger-Godfrey, Andrew Sharpe, Mr Peter Richard Gill, Mr Michael Francis Bustard, Mr Clifford Roderick Stanton Dare, Andrew Truscott, Dr Sridevi Kalidindi, Julius Wolff-Ingham, Mr Simon Anthony Taylor
Income: £3,946,476 [2017]; £4,157,856 [2016]; £4,046,151 [2015]; £3,801,461 [2014]; £3,799,138 [2013]

Royal British Legion Poppy Lottery Limited
Registered: 12 Dec 2011
Tel: 020 3207 2324 *Website:* poppylottery.org.uk
Activities: Armed forces, emergency service efficiency
Address: Royal British Legion Poppy Lottery, Haig House, 199 Borough High Street, London, SE1 1AA
Trustees: Charles Byrne, The Royal British Legion
Income: £6,820,189 [2016]; £7,190,309 [2015]; £7,408,462 [2014]; £6,936,435 [2013]; £6,224,717 [2012]

The Royal British Legion
Registered: 10 Jul 1977 *Employees:* 1,414 *Volunteers:* 120,000
Tel: 020 3207 2100 *Website:* britishlegion.org.uk
Activities: General charitable purposes; education, training; advancement of health or saving of lives; disability; prevention or relief of poverty; accommodation, housing; economic, community development, employment
Address: The Royal British Legion, 199 Borough High Street, London, SE1 1AA
Trustees: Mr Terry Whittles, Mr Adrian Burn FCA, Mrs Denise Edgar, Major General David Jolliffe CB FRCP, Mr Jason Coward, Mr Philip Moore, Mr Roger Garratt, Mrs Pat Chrimes, Ms Catherine Quinn, Ms Una Cleminson, Mr Anthony MacAulay, Lt Col Joe Falzon OSJ BEM, Mr Colin Kemp, Lt Col David Whimpenny, Ms Anny Reid, Mr Rod Bedford
Income: £151,256,000 [2016]; £161,317,000 [2015]; £133,472,000 [2014]; £124,558,000 [2013]; £132,816,000 [2012]

Royal Brompton and Harefield Hospitals Charity
Registered: 8 Mar 1996 *Employees:* 15 *Volunteers:* 25
Tel: 020 7351 8879 *Website:* www2.rbht..nhs.uk
Activities: The advancement of health or saving of lives
Address: Royal Brompton Hospital, Sydney Street, London, SW3 6NP
Trustees: Royal Brompton and Harefield Charity Trustee
Income: £7,560,000 [2017]; £8,110,000 [2016]; £7,806,000 [2015]; £6,873,000 [2014]; £6,375,000 [2013]

The Royal Cambridge Home
Registered: 11 Mar 1964 *Employees:* 39
Tel: 020 8979 3788 *Website:* royalcambridgehome.org
Activities: Accommodation, housing
Address: Royal Cambridge Home, 82-84 Hurst Road, East Molesey, Surrey, KT8 9AH
Trustees: Mr Robert Henry Dowler, Major John Tatham, Colonel Nigel Gilbert, Mr Alan Bott, Mr John Ross, Mr Robert S Morton, Mr George Fitzgeorge-Balfour, Mr Jeremy Michael Lloyd Williams
Income: £1,073,893 [2017]; £1,061,143 [2016]; £1,049,012 [2015]; £975,121 [2014]; £917,897 [2013]

The Royal Collection Trust
Registered: 2 Feb 1993 *Employees:* 731 *Volunteers:* 10
Website: royalcollection.org.uk
Activities: Education, training; arts, culture, heritage, science; environment, conservation, heritage
Address: York House, St James's Palace, London, SW1A 1BQ
Trustees: HRH The Prince of Wales, Vice Admiral Charles Anthony Johnstone-Burt CB OBE DL, The Duke of Buccleuch and Queensberry KBE DL, Sir Michael Stevens KCVO, The Hon James Leigh-Pemberton CVO, The Rt Hon The Earl Peel, The Rt Hon Edward Young CVO, Dr Anna Julia Keay, Mr Marc Jan Bolland
Income: £61,995,000 [2017]; £52,085,000 [2016]; £48,846,000 [2015]; £54,991,000 [2014]; £50,818,000 [2013]

The Royal College of Anaesthetists
Registered: 25 Aug 1992 *Employees:* 94 *Volunteers:* 2,415
Tel: 020 7092 1610 *Website:* rcoa.ac.uk
Activities: Education, training
Address: The Royal College of Anaesthetists, Churchill House, 35 Red Lion Square, London, WC1R 4SG
Trustees: Dr Jeremy Adam Langton, Professor John Robert Sneyd, Dr Alan William Harrop-Griffiths, Professor Ellen O'Sullivan, Dr John Russell Colvin, Dr Simon James Fletcher, Professor Judith Hall OBE, Dr Jaideep Jagdeesh Pandit, Professor Michael Grocott, Dr David Bogod, Dr Fiona Donald, Dr Russell Perkins, Dr Anna Marija Batchelor, Professor Ravi Prakash Mahajan, Dr Liam Brennan, Dr Nigel William Penfold, Dr Erica Janice Fazackerley, Professor Michael Gerard Mythen, Dr John-Paul Lomas, Dr Kirstin May, Dr Lucy Williams, Dr Krishnaswami Ramachandran, Dr Christopher Carey, Dr Jenny Cheung
Income: £13,599,819 [2017]; £12,271,732 [2016]; £11,260,949 [2015]; £10,812,438 [2014]; £9,300,232 [2013]

The Royal College of Emergency Medicine
Registered: 7 Feb 2008 *Employees:* 35 *Volunteers:* 550
Tel: 020 7404 1999 *Website:* rcem.ac.uk
Activities: Education, training; advancement of health or saving of lives
Address: Royal College of Emergency Medicine, 7-9 Breams Buildings, London, EC4A 1DT
Trustees: Mr Graham Johnson, Dr Tajek Hassan, Dr Ian Higginson, Prof Suzanne Mason, Dr Adrian Boyle, Dr Christopher Moulton, Dr Stephen Crowder, Dr Katherine Henderson, Dr Jon Bailey, Dr Robin Roop, Dr Nick Athey, Mrs Lisa Munro-Davies, Dr James Crawfurd, Miss Julia Harris, Dr Gillian Bryce, Dr Cliff Mann, Mr Derek Prentice, Dr Jason Long, Dr Carole Gavin, Dr Martin McKechnie, Dr Simon Hunter, Prof Alasdair Gray, Dr Adel Aziz, Dr Bill Bailey, Dr Peter Ahee, Dr Sean McGovern, Dr Dominic Williamson
Income: £5,638,226 [2016]; £6,094,540 [2015]; £4,385,862 [2014]; £4,124,242 [2013]; £3,346,472 [2012]

The Royal College of General Practitioners
Registered: 1 Apr 1963 *Employees:* 274
Tel: 020 3188 7400 *Website:* rcgp.org.uk
Activities: Education, training; advancement of health or saving of lives
Address: 30 Euston Square, London, NW1 2FB
Trustees: Dr Colin Hunter OBE FRCGP, Dr Stephen Mowle, Dr Helen Jayne Stokes-Lampard PhD FRCGP, Dr Christine Johnston FRCGP, Mr David Alan Pendleton, Dr Miles Mack, Professor Simon Gregory, Dr John Chisholm CBE FRCGP, Mr Edward Dove, Jonathan Leach, Mr Simon Sapper, Mr Ian Jeffrey
Income: £43,072,164 [2017]; £43,531,954 [2016]; £41,883,022 [2015]; £39,727,747 [2014]; £36,171,632 [2013]

The Royal College of Music
Registered: 11 Mar 1964 *Employees:* 457 *Volunteers:* 20
Tel: 020 7591 4363 *Website:* rcm.ac.uk
Activities: Education, training
Address: Royal College of Music, Prince Consort Road, London, SW7 2BS
Trustees: Professor Colin Lawson, Mr Ashley Solomon, Ms Victoria Robey, The Hon Richard Lyttelton, Ms Alethea Siow, Mr Rhoderick Voremberg, Mr John Nickson, Miss Ann Somerville, Mr Douglas Gardner, Mr Peter Dart, Ms Gillian Moore MBE FRCM, Professor Lord Robert Winston, Mrs Jane Barker, Mr Andrew Haigh, Lord Black of Brentwood, Geoff Richards, Sir George Iacobescu, Mr Robert Wigley, Mr Andrew Ratcliffe, Ms Ruth Keattch
Income: £35,931,028 [2017]; £22,473,133 [2016]; £22,228,860 [2015]; £21,628,267 [2014]; £20,491,109 [2013]

Royal College of Obstetricians and Gynaecologists
Registered: 28 Nov 1962 *Employees:* 181
Website: rcog.org.uk
Activities: Education, training; advancement of health or saving of lives
Address: Royal College of Obstetricians & Gynaecologists, 27 Sussex Place, London, NW1 4RG
Trustees: Professor Sir Eric Jackson Thomas, Professor Mary Ann Lumsden, Dr D Rajasingam MRCOG, Mr Roy Martin, Mr Patrick Finch, Miss Mary Felicity Ashworth, Professor Lesley Regan, Ms Linda Nash, Dr David Ian Malcolm Farquharson, Ms Kate Ellen Mathers, Mr Edward Patrick Morris
Income: £58,302,226 [2017]; £15,517,162 [2015]; £15,778,599 [2014]; £13,774,094 [2013]; £13,171,896 [2012]

Royal College of Occupational Therapists
Registered: 20 Jan 1978 *Employees:* 67 *Volunteers:* 450
Tel: 020 7450 2302 *Website:* rcot.co.uk
Activities: Other charitable purposes
Address: College of Occupational Therapists, 106-114 Borough High Street, London, SE1 1LB
Trustees: Mrs Sara Ann Forster, Dr Patricia McClure, Professor Priscilla Ann Harries, Dr Lyn Patricia Westcott, Mrs Fiona Mary Warrender, Mrs Linda Agnew, Mr David Martin Davies, Mrs Sandra Marie Rowan, Miss Lena Canavan
Income: £8,058,000 [2017]; £8,286,000 [2016]; £7,861,000 [2015]; £7,653,348 [2014]; £7,310,871 [2013]

The Royal College of Ophthalmologists
Registered: 2 Aug 1988 *Employees:* 30
Tel: 020 7935 0702 *Website:* rcophth.ac.uk
Activities: Education, training; advancement of health or saving of lives
Address: Royal College of Ophthalmologists, 18 Stephenson Way, London, NW1 2HD
Trustees: Mr Michael Anthony Burdon FRCOphth, Ms Anne Spencer FRCOphth, Mr Christopher SC Liu FRCOphth, Mr Brian Smith, Dr David Miller, Prof Stephen Vernon, Mr Gordon Cropper, Mr Nicholas Wilson-Holt, Mr Mohit Gupta FRCOphth, Lord Philip Hunt, Mr Robert Taylor, Prof Stephen Kaye
Income: £4,584,000 [2017]; £4,482,000 [2016]; £4,328,000 [2015]; £4,418,765 [2014]; £4,155,006 [2013]

Royal College of Paediatrics and Child Health
Registered: 22 Aug 1996 *Employees:* 167 *Volunteers:* 1,100
Tel: 020 7092 6000 *Website:* rcpch.ac.uk
Activities: Education, training; advancement of health or saving of lives; other charitable purposes
Address: Royal College of Paediatrics & Child Health, 5-11 Theobalds Road, London, WC1X 8SH
Trustees: Dr Lisa Kauffmann, Dr David Vickers, Mr Jon Foster, Professor Russell Viner, Mr Mark Devlin, Ms Gillian Budd, Dr Carol Roberts, Dame Mary Marsh, Dr Mike Linney, Dr John Jenkins CBE, Mr Anthony Dunnett CBE, Dr John Williams
Income: £15,065,000 [2016]; £15,868,000 [2015]; £16,342,481 [2014]; £13,664,895 [2013]; £11,906,412 [2012]

The Royal College of Pathologists
Registered: 28 Apr 1970 *Employees:* 58 *Volunteers:* 1,000
Tel: 020 7451 6700 *Website:* rcpath.org
Activities: Education, training; advancement of health or saving of lives
Address: 4th Floor, 21 Prescot Street, London, E1 8BB
Trustees: Professor Kenneth Ian Mills, Dr Bernard Lewis Croal, Professor Joanne Elizabeth Martin, Ms Avril Margaret Owen Wayte, Dr Esther Youd, Professor Shelley Ray Heard, Dr Rachael Dorothy Liebmann, Dr David Michael Cassidy, Dr Lance Nigel Sandle, Mr Tommy McIlravey, Dr Timothy James Littlewood, Mr Robert William Smith
Income: £4,968,619 [2017]; £4,843,354 [2016]; £26,766,458 [2015]; £5,061,620 [2014]; £4,495,041 [2013]

The Royal College of Physicians of London
Registered: 25 Jul 1963 *Employees:* 418
Tel: 020 3075 1649 *Website:* rcplondon.ac.uk
Activities: General charitable purposes; education, training; advancement of health or saving of lives; disability; environment, conservation, heritage
Address: Royal College of Physicians, 11 St Andrews Place, London, NW1 4LE
Trustees: Professor Jane Dacre, Lady Estelle Wolfson, Mr Tom Vyner, Dr David Cohen, Dr Rowan Mary Hillson, Professor Margaret Anne Johnson, Professor Chuka Nwokolo, Royal College of Physicians, Mr Graham Meek, Dr David Oliver, Dr Andrew Goddard, Mr Andrew Frank Chandler, Dr Gerrard Phillips, Dr David Nicholl, Dr John Firth
Income: £40,711,000 [2016]; £40,735,000 [2015]; £40,683,000 [2014]; £37,953,000 [2013]; £35,133,000 [2012]

The Royal College of Psychiatrists
Registered: 21 Aug 1963 *Employees:* 223
Tel: 020 7235 2351 *Website:* rcpsych.ac.uk
Activities: General charitable purposes; education, training; advancement of health or saving of lives
Address: 21 Prescot Street, London, E1 8BB
Trustees: Dr Wendy Katherine Burn, Mr Adrian John Boste James, Dr Louise Sell, Mr Malcolm Basing, Ms Anita Bharucha, Mr Nigel Jones, Dr Jan Falkowski, Dr Gwynnyth Mary Johanna Adshead, Dr Kate Lovett, Dr Dasha Nicholls
Income: £20,942,000 [2016]; £18,954,000 [2015]; £17,173,000 [2014]; £30,490,000 [2013]; £17,165,000 [2012]

The Royal College of Radiologists
Registered: 18 Jan 1963 *Employees:* 60 *Volunteers:* 250
Tel: 020 7406 5914 *Website:* rcr.ac.uk
Activities: Education, training; advancement of health or saving of lives
Address: 63 Lincoln's Inn Fields, London, WC2A 3JW
Trustees: Dr Roger Douglas Errington, Dr Julian Elford, Dr Nicola Hilary Strickland, Dr David James Bloomfield, Dr Ian David Pedley, Dr William Hugh Ramsden, Dr Patricia Niblock, Dr Jane Margaret Young, Dr Stephen Peter D'Souza, Dr Jeanette Dickson, Dr Fraser Andrew Smethurst, Dr David Gilligan, Dr Caroline Moira Elizabeth Rubin, Dr Andrew Mark Beale, Professor Peter John Hoskin, Dr Sanjay Vydianath, Dr Frances Anne Pascoe Yuille, Dr Robert Hywel Thomas
Income: £7,118,033 [2017]; £6,872,307 [2016]; £7,766,472 [2015]; £7,538,623 [2014]; £11,485,253 [2013]

Royal College of Speech and Language Therapists
Registered: 10 Aug 1977 *Employees:* 42 *Volunteers:* 1
Tel: 020 7378 3018 *Website:* rcslt.org
Activities: General charitable purposes; education, training; advancement of health or saving of lives; disability
Address: Royal College of Speech & Language Therapists, 2-3 White Hart Yard, London, SE1 1NX
Trustees: Mrs Ann Whitehorn, Mrs Morag Jane Dorward, Mrs Catherine Dunnet, Ms Mary Heritage, Dr Rebecca Palmer, Mrs Christine Dowle, Ms Rosalind Kyle, Ms Nikki Richardson, Mrs Lorna Caroline Bailey, Dr Della Money, Mrs Margaret Ann Cooper, Ms Helen Sylvia Rae, Mr John Humphrey, Dr Caroline Pickstone
Income: £4,191,000 [2017]; £4,064,000 [2016]; £3,853,000 [2015]; £3,536,605 [2014]; £3,508,202 [2013]

Royal College of Surgeons of England
Registered: 15 Mar 1963 *Employees:* 306 *Volunteers:* 108
Website: rcseng.ac.uk
Activities: Education, training; advancement of health or saving of lives
Address: 35-43 Lincoln's Inn Fields, London, WC2A 3PE
Trustees: Professor Neil Mortensen FRCS, Mr Peter Kay FRCS, Professor Derek Alderson FRCS, Miss Susan Marion Hill FRCS, Professor Michael Escudier, Mr Mike Hussey, Mr John Abercrombie FRCS, Mr Ian Eardley FRCS, Mr David Whitney, Sir Amyas Morse, Miss Fiona Myint FRCS, Dr Mick Horton, Mr John Robinson
Income: £33,361,000 [2017]; £32,521,000 [2016]; £32,102,000 [2015]; £29,856,000 [2014]; £29,817,000 [2013]

Royal College of Veterinary Surgeons Trust
Registered: 11 Feb 1964 *Employees:* 10 *Volunteers:* 3
Tel: 020 7222 2001 *Website:* rcvsknowledge.org
Activities: Education, training; advancement of health or saving of lives; animals; environment, conservation, heritage
Address: RCVS Trust, Belgravia House, 62-64 Horseferry Road, London, SW1P 2AF
Trustees: Mr Brian Henry Pound FCIM, Mrs Jacqui Molyneux FRCVS, Dr Bradley Phillip Viner FRCVS, Dr Timothy Stephen Mair BVSc PhD DEIM DipECEIM DESTS FRCVS, Amanda Karen Boag MA VetMB DipACVIM DipACVECC DipECVECC FHEA MRCVS, Dr Danny Chambers, Mrs Jean Turner RVN, Mr Peter Charles Jinman OBE BVetMed DipArb FCIArb MRCVS, Dr Graham Dick MRCVS, Mr Richard L Berry, Lucie Victoria Goodwin BVetMed DipACVIM MRCVS
Income: £1,135,697 [2016]; £1,221,123 [2015]; £1,132,120 [2014]; £724,762 [2013]; £572,809 [2012]

Royal Commission for The Exhibition of 1851
Registered: 22 Sep 1962 *Employees:* 4 *Volunteers:* 25
Tel: 020 7594 8790 *Website:* royalcommission1851.org.uk
Activities: Education, training
Address: 453 Sherfield Building, Imperial College, London, SW7 2AZ
Trustees: Professor Sir Christopher Frayling FCSD FRSA FRIBA, Mr Jim Eyre OBE RIBA, Mr Bernard Taylor DL FRSC, Professor Lord Mair CBE HonDSC FREng FRS FICE, Professor Lynn Gladden CBE FREng FRS, Professor Dame Kay Davies DBE FRS FMedSci, Mr Stuart Corbyn FRICS, Sir William Castell LVO, Professor Sir Richard Brook OBE FREng, Sir John O'Reilly DSC FREng FLSW
Income: £2,600,909 [2016]; £2,603,902 [2015]; £2,714,294 [2014]; £2,339,376 [2013]; £2,451,676 [2012]

Royal Commonwealth Society for the Blind
Registered: 22 Sep 1962 *Employees:* 476 *Volunteers:* 25
Tel: 01444 446601 *Website:* sightsavers.org
Activities: Education, training; advancement of health or saving of lives; disability; prevention or relief of poverty; overseas aid, famine relief; economic, community development, employment
Address: 35 Perrymount Road, Haywards Heath, W Sussex, RH16 3BW
Trustees: Mr Howard Dalzell, Mr Michael Chilton, Ms Mavis Owusu-Gyamfi, Ms Uche Amazigo, Dr Manoj Parulekar, Mr Barry Hoffman, Mr William Kendall, Professor Christopher John Whitty, Mr Stephen King, Dr Robert Chappell, Mr Martin John Dinham, Mr Christopher Kinder, Ms Maryanne Diamond, Ms Elaine Lee, Ms Abia Akram, Ms Heather Jane De Haes
Income: £302,017,000 [2016]; £198,303,000 [2015]; £187,578,000 [2014]; £199,688,000 [2013]; £158,629,000 [2012]

The Royal Cornwall Agricultural Association

Registered: 14 Nov 1966 *Employees:* 18 *Volunteers:* 600
Tel: 01208 812183 *Website:* royalcornwall.co.uk
Activities: Education, training; animals; environment, conservation, heritage
Address: Molesworth House, Whitecross, Wadebridge, Cornwall, PL27 7JE
Trustees: Mrs Alison Mary Melhuish, Mr Nicholas John Trefusis, The Hon Evelyn Boscawen DL, Sir Richard Carew Pole Bt OBE DL, Mr David Elliott, Mr Arthur Michael Johnstone Galsworthy CVO CBE DL, Lady Carew Pole CVO JP, Colonel Edward Bolitho OBE, Mr Robert Knowles, The Rt Hon The Viscount Falmouth, Mr Jonathan Coode DL, Mr Richard Gilbert, Mrs Mary Andrew, The Rt Hon The Lord St Levan, Sir Ferrers Vyvyan Bt DL, Mr James Eustice, Mr William Richard Davey, Mr Anthony Lionel Pascoe, Bishop Tim Thornton, Mr Eric Sleep, Mr Trevor Burley, Mr Richard Olds, Mr Mike Roberts, Mr Peter John Sobey, Iona Lady Molesworth-St Aubyn DL, Mr Paul Vincent, Mr Graham William Tucker, Mr Andrew Bunt, Mrs Liz Bowden, Mr Robert Osborne, Lady St Levan JP DL, Mrs Helen Claire Eustice, Mr Nicholas Phillips, Mrs Shirley Borton, Mr Patrick Lobb, Mr Lee David Pengilly, Mr Christopher John Benney, Miss Rachael Mary Eustice, Mr Robert John Thomson, Sir Nicholas Bacon Bt OBE DL, Bishop Bill Ind, Major Charles Edward-Collins DL, Mr Michael Latham DL, Mr Bevil Bunt, Mr Charles Paul Richards, Mr Simon Francis Knowles, Mrs Elizabeth Bolitho DL, Mr Julian Williams CBE JP DL, Mr Michael Williams DL, Mr Peter Bickford-Smith, The Earl Peel GCVO DL, Mr Peter Prideaux-Brune, Mr James Williams DL, Lady Banham MBE JP, Mr David Selley, Mr Peter Derek Hardaker, Mr Mark Pryor, Mr Philip Roose, Mr George Blight, Mr Alan Edmond, Mr Stephen Williams, Mr Roger Biddick, Mrs Rebecca Shute, Mr Robert Sloman, Mr Brian Trewin, Mr Edward Bailey, Mr Julian Stanbury, Mrs Vivienne Daniel, Mr Alan Snow, Mr Nicholas John Bersey, Mr Andrew Harvey Oatey, Mr Michael John Simmons, Mr Mark Stephen Hoskin, Mr Jeremy Paul Oatey, Mr James Andrew Eustice, Mr Andrew Geoffrey Jamees, Mr Andrew Trezise, Mr Peter John Olds
Income: £2,253,259 [2017]; £2,292,199 [2016]; £2,296,176 [2015]; £2,117,709 [2014]; £2,092,072 [2013]

The Royal Corps of Signals Benevolent Fund

Registered: 24 Jun 1982 *Employees:* 9
Tel: 01258 482081 *Website:* royalsignals.org
Activities: The prevention or relief of poverty; amateur sport; environment, conservation, heritage; armed forces, emergency service efficiency; recreation; other charitable purposes
Address: RHQ Royal Signals, Griffin House, Blandford Camp, Blandford Forum, Dorset, DT11 8RH
Trustees: The Royal Signals Trustee Limited
Income: £1,406,973 [2016]; £1,580,958 [2015]; £1,702,908 [2014]; £1,502,969 [2013]; £1,534,527 [2012]

Royal Court Liverpool Trust Limited

Registered: 3 Apr 2009 *Employees:* 3 *Volunteers:* 10
Tel: 0151 702 5892 *Website:* royalcourttrust.org
Activities: General charitable purposes; education, training; arts, culture, heritage, science; environment, conservation, heritage
Address: Royal Court Theatre, Roe Street, Liverpool, L1 1HL
Trustees: Mr Maurice Bessman, Max Steinberg, Councillor Wendy Ann Simon, Mr Martyn James Best, Mr Nigel Weatherill FREng DSC, Mr Mark Philip Featherstone-Witty, Mr Jonathan Mark Falkingham, Mr John Harry Godber, Mrs Sara Wilde, Ms Heather Summers
Income: £2,107,992 [2016]; £3,078,556 [2015]; £495,171 [2014]; £318,526 [2013]; £1,138,910 [2012]

Royal Docks Trust (London)

Registered: 21 Mar 1995
Tel: 01304 853465 *Website:* royaldockstrust.org
Activities: Education, training; disability; arts, culture, heritage, science; amateur sport; economic, community development, employment
Address: Olive Cottage, Station Road, St Margarets-at-Cliffe, Dover, CT15 6AY
Trustees: Mr Eric Sorensen, Sid Keys, Mr Kayar Raghavan, Katie Carter, Mr James Andrew John Kenworth, Gary Quashie, Ms Shani Thomas, Mr Stephen William Nicholas, Ms Amanda Williams, Councillor Forhad Hussain, Ken Clark, Ms Belinda Joanne Vecchio, Ms Giovanna Grandoni, Ms Sandra Erskine
Income: £1,497,432 [2017]; £257,832 [2016]; £324,786 [2015]; £299,712 [2014]; £282,031 [2013]

The Royal Drawing School

Registered: 14 Jan 2004 *Employees:* 20
Tel: 020 7613 8527 *Website:* royaldrawingschool.org
Activities: General charitable purposes; education, training; arts, culture, heritage, science
Address: 19-22 Charlotte Road, London, EC2A 3SG
Trustees: Ms Andrea Rose OBE CMG, Ms Linda Heathcoat-Amory, Mrs Manuela Wirth, Dr Alexander John Sturgis, The Hon Lady Roberts, Mr Stephen David John Davis, Hon David Maurice Benjamin Macmillan, Professor Eileen Hogan, Mrs Nancy Marks, Mr Evy Piers George Hambro, Howard Marks, Ms Laura Lindsay, Professor Humphrey Ocean, Ms Bettina Ilse Friederike von Hase
Income: £2,773,002 [2016]; £3,903,989 [2015]; £8,983,221 [2014]; £2,451,822 [2013]; £1,568,776 [2012]

The Royal Economic Society

Registered: 8 May 1964
Tel: 020 3137 6301 *Website:* res.org.uk
Activities: Education, training
Address: Royal Economic Society, 2 Dean Trench Street, Westminster, London, SW1P 3HE
Trustees: Prof James Peter Neary, Professor Robin Andrew Naylor, Prof Sarah Louise Smith, Prof Stephen Jonathan Machin, Professor Denise Osborn, Prof Andrew Douglas Chesher FBA, Professor Morten Overgaard Ravn, Prof Mary S Morgan, Prof Beata Javorcik, Prof Neil Rickman, Professor Eric John Pentecost, Prof Lord Nicholas Herbert Stern, Professor Frank Windmeijer, Mrs Susan Mary Holloway, Prof Jaap Abbring, Prof Sarah Brown
Income: £1,146,489 [2016]; £1,141,689 [2015]; £1,163,985 [2014]; £1,191,201 [2013]; £1,230,020 [2012]

Royal Engineers Association

Registered: 3 Jun 1969 *Employees:* 4
Tel: 01634 847005 *Website:* reahq.org.uk
Activities: General charitable purposes; advancement of health or saving of lives; disability; prevention or relief of poverty; armed forces, emergency service efficiency
Address: The Royal Engineers Association, Ravelin Building, Brompton Barracks, Chatham, Kent, ME4 4UG
Trustees: Brigadier Andy Craig OBE, Lt Gen Sir Mark Mans KCB CBE DL, Lt Col Adrian Bunting, Maj Gen A S Dickinson CBE, Wo2 Simon Tolley, Mr John Bell, Lt Col Larry Inge, Brigadier Matthew Bazeley, Major Peter Luscombe, Mr Brian Simm, Colonel Matthew Quare MBE ADC, Colonel Chris Davies MBE, Major Philip Gill MBE JP, Mr Bob Prosser BEM, Mr Eric Hargreaves, Lt Col Martin Heffer RE TD, Mr Garrie Owens, Mr Wal Thomas, WO1 Steven Webster
Income: £1,225,795 [2016]; £1,283,398 [2015]; £1,147,143 [2014]; £1,102,000 [2013]; £1,219,485 [2012]

Royal Engineers Central Charitable Trust
Registered: 28 May 1991 *Employees:* 6
Tel: 01634 822355
Activities: General charitable purposes; prevention or relief of poverty; amateur sport
Address: HQRE, Brompton Barracks, Dock Road, Chatham, Kent, ME4 4UG
Trustees: Major General Keith Cima CB, Colonel M Quare MBE ADC, Major General T R Urch CBE, Major General Sa Burley CB MBE, Major General C L Tickell CBE, Brigadier M T G Bazeley, WO1 Sa Webster, Lieutenant General Sir Mark Mans KCB CBE DL, Brigadier K M Copsey OBE, Major General Rr Davis CB CBE, Brig Ens Millar MBE, Major General A S Dickinson CBE, Colonel D Gray VR, Major General Nj Cavanagh
Income: £1,270,527 [2016]; £1,348,030 [2015]; £1,178,463 [2014]; £1,195,179 [2013]; £1,158,030 [2012]

Royal Exchange Theatre Company Limited
Registered: 3 May 1968 *Employees:* 136 *Volunteers:* 100
Tel: 0161 833 9333 *Website:* royalexchange.co.uk
Activities: Arts, culture, heritage, science
Address: Royal Exchange Theatre Co Ltd, St Anns Square, Manchester, M2 7DH
Trustees: Mr Geoffrey Shindler OBE, Mrs Jean Oglesby, Mr Anthony Noel Gordon, Tania Black, Mr Martyn Torevell, Mr David Roscoe, Councillor Bernard Sharp, Ms Davina Shah, Mr James Benedict Caldwell, Mrs Caroline Roberts-Cherry, Jennifer Raffle, Ms Sinead Greenaway, Cllr Ann-Marie Humphreys MS, Mr Aziz Rashid, Ms Sally Penni, Ms Nicole May
Income: £8,340,000 [2017]; £7,838,000 [2016]; £7,929,000 [2015]; £8,522,000 [2014]; £7,413,000 [2013]

The Royal Foundation of St Katharine
Registered: 4 May 1964 *Employees:* 45
Tel: 0300 111 1147 *Website:* rfsk.org.uk
Activities: Education, training; religious activities
Address: Royal Foundation of St Katharine, 2 Butcher Row, London, E14 8DS
Trustees: The Revd John H Tattersall, Rev Christopher William Mark Aitken, Mr Geoffrey Richards, Dr Joy Hinson, David Swanney, Dame Annabel Whitehead, Sir Stephen Mark Jeffrey Lamport KCVO DL, Mrs Elizabeth Ann Marshall, Andrew Grigson, The Rt Revd and Rt Hon Dame Sarah Elisabeth Mullally DBE, Mr Ian Graham, Scott Furssedonn-Wood
Income: £1,931,344 [2017]; £1,688,983 [2016]; £1,525,157 [2015]; £1,437,656 [2014]; £1,342,252 [2013]

The Royal Foundation of The Duke and Duchess of Cambridge and Prince Harry
Registered: 8 Oct 2009 *Employees:* 25
Tel: 020 7101 2963 *Website:* royalfoundation.com
Activities: General charitable purposes; education, training; advancement of health or saving of lives; disability; prevention or relief of poverty; environment, conservation, heritage; economic, community development, employment
Address: Kensington Palace, Palace Green, London, W8 4PU
Trustees: Mrs Theresa Mary Green OBE, Mr Anthony James Moxon Lowther-Pinkerton, Mr Charles Stuart Mindenhall, Mr Simon Iain Patterson, Mr Miguel Nunes Head LVO, Mr Edward Harley, Mr Guy Monson, Sir Keith Edward Mills GBE DL, Lady Demetra Aikaterini Pinsent
Income: £10,061,577 [2016]; £4,276,534 [2015]; £4,038,756 [2014]; £3,887,009 [2013]; £3,593,390 [2012]

The Royal Free Charity
Registered: 22 Feb 2016 *Employees:* 33 *Volunteers:* 650
Tel: 020 7472 6677 *Website:* royalfreecharity.org
Activities: The advancement of health or saving of lives
Address: Royal Free Charity, Royal Free Hospital, Pond Street, London, NW3 2QG
Trustees: Ms Caroline Clarke, Miss Liz Cleaver, Professor Stephen Powis, Mr Russell Brooks, Mr Robert Leak, Mr Steve Shaw, Mrs Janet Enid Morgan, Dr Russell Gilbert, Ms Christine Alexandra Fogg, Mr Michael Luck, Mrs Judy Frances Dewinter
Income: £16,507,000 [2017]

Royal Geographical Society (with The Institute of British Geographers)
Registered: 4 Feb 1963 *Employees:* 60 *Volunteers:* 2,800
Website: rgs.org
Activities: Education, training; arts, culture, heritage, science; environment, conservation, heritage
Address: Royal Geographical Society, 1 Kensington Gore, London, SW7 2AR
Trustees: Dr Vanessa Lawrence CB, Miss Laura Stone, Mr Mark Humphreys, Dr Simon Carr, Dr Jenny Balfour-Paul, Dr Michael Firth, Professor Christopher Philo, Dr David Anderson, Professor Sarah Radcliffe, Professor Jamie Woodward, Mr Daniel Casey, Professor Dame Judith Rees, Dr Nicola Thomas, Professor Joanna Bullard, Professor Adrian Smith, Professor Sarah Metcalfe, Mr Nicholas Crane, Mr David Pyle, Miss Felicity Aston, Professor Katie Willis, Mr Christopher Speight, Mrs Claire Allen
Income: £5,845,000 [2016]; £5,407,000 [2015]; £7,129,000 [2014]; £4,318,997 [2013]; £4,282,338 [2012]

Royal Grammar School Worcester
Registered: 22 Aug 2007 *Employees:* 208
Tel: 01905 613391 *Website:* rgsw.org.uk
Activities: Education, training
Address: Royal Grammar School Worcester, Upper Tything, Worcester, WR1 1HP
Trustees: Sir Roger Gordon Fry CBE, Mr Quentin Poole, Ms Kay Meredith, Mr Bryan William Radford, Mr Nicholas Fairlie, Mr Andrew Hampden Greenway, Mrs Sally Anne Mills, Mrs Rosemary Frances Ham, Mr Howard Kimberley, Mr John Gyart Peters, Mrs Lesley Cook, Dr Emma Robinson, Mr Philip John Lee
Income: £13,361,000 [2017]; £13,105,000 [2016]; £12,350,000 [2015]; £11,263,000 [2014]; £11,755,000 [2013]

The Royal Grammar School, Guildford
Registered: 1 Feb 2001 *Employees:* 235
Tel: 01483 880604 *Website:* rgs-guildford.co.uk
Activities: Education, training
Address: Royal Grammar School, High Street, Guildford, Surrey, GU1 3BB
Trustees: Reverend Robert Lloyd Cotton, Mr David John Counsell, Mr Christopher Trevor Shorter CEng MIStructE FConsE, HHJ Critchlow, Cllr Sarah Kathleen Creedy, Mr Clive Durac Barnett, Mr Brian Jeffrey Creese, Dr Henry Pearson OBE, Mr Simon George Gimson, Mr Patrick William Fell, Mrs Catherine Frances Cobley, Mrs Jennifer Jordan, Dr Lorraine Susan Kendrick Linton, Mr Peter Graham Peel, Professor Shirley Price, Mr Nicholas Edward John Vineall QC, Mr John David Fairley, Lord Rupert Charles William Bullard Onslow, Mrs Heather Styche-Patel, Mrs Julie Anne Stott
Income: £22,065,452 [2017]; £20,681,592 [2016]; £19,571,984 [2015]; £38,194 [2014]; £42,575 [2013]

The Royal Horticultural Society
Registered: 31 Jul 1963 *Employees:* 783 *Volunteers:* 1,321
Tel: 020 7821 3034 *Website:* rhs.org.uk
Activities: Education, training; arts, culture, heritage, science; environment, conservation, heritage; economic, community development, employment
Address: The Royal Horticultural Society, 80 Vincent Square, London, SW1P 2PE
Trustees: Mr Neil Lucas, Dr David Rae, Sir Nicholas Bacon, Mr Christopher James Blundell, Mr James Alexander-Sinclair, Mr Jon Wheatley, Lady Tollemache, Dame Mary Keegan, Dr Sarah Raven, Prof Michael J Crawley, Mr Alastair William Muirhead, Mr Mark Fane, Professor Peter Gregory, Mr Dennis Espley, Mr Mark Porter, Ms Lorna Parker, Mr Matthew Lindsey-Clark, Kate Lampard
Income: £82,462,948 [2017]; £76,450,230 [2016]; £73,157,000 [2015]; £71,937,000 [2014]; £81,310,000 [2013]

Royal Hospital Chelsea Appeal Limited
Registered: 6 Jul 1999 *Volunteers:* 85
Tel: 020 7881 5300 *Website:* chelsea-pensioners.org.uk
Activities: General charitable purposes; arts, culture, heritage, science
Address: Royal Hospital Chelsea, Royal Hospital Road, London, SW3 4SR
Trustees: Mr Richard Hugh Hunting BEng MBA, Mr Mark Gallagher, Mr David Rosier
Income: £5,100,971 [2017]; £5,134,908 [2016]; £3,859,096 [2015]; £3,631,157 [2014]; £3,736,762 [2013]

Royal Hospital for Neuro-Disability
Registered: 2 Dec 1963 *Employees:* 615 *Volunteers:* 196
Tel: 020 8780 4500 *Website:* rhn.org.uk
Activities: The advancement of health or saving of lives; disability
Address: Royal Hospital for Neuro-Disability, West Hill, London, SW15 3SW
Trustees: Michael Hornsby, Laurence Oates, Anne Chamberlain, James Gemmell, Mr Terence John Hanafin CBE, Des Benjamin, Mr Leslie Hurst, Peter John Siddall, Jenny Sharp, The Rt Revd Christopher Herbert, Dr Dipak Datta, Les Broude, Dr David McKenzie Mitchell
Income: £38,287,000 [2017]; £38,198,000 [2016]; £36,511,000 [2015]; £31,867,000 [2014]; £30,664,000 [2013]

Royal Institute of British Architects
Registered: 14 Aug 1962 *Employees:* 496 *Volunteers:* 500
Tel: 020 7307 3750 *Website:* architecture.com
Activities: Education, training; arts, culture, heritage, science; environment, conservation, heritage
Address: RIBA, 66 Portland Place, London, W1B 1AD
Trustees: Richard Murphy, Ralph Carpenter, Mr Anthony Lloyd, Jane Duncan, Richard Parnaby, Mr Graham Devine, John Assael, Dominic Kramer, Nicholas Mills, Flora Samuel, Christopher Williamson, Mark Hodson, Mark Jermy, Simeon Shtebunaev, Andrew Bourne, Jennifer Forakis, Ewan Miller, Richard Wooldridge, Alan Jones, Helen Taylor, Ms Yemi Aladerun, Ms Simone De Gale, Mr Christopher Hampson, Mr Patrick Lynch, Ms Carolyn Merrifield, Mr John Wilde, Ms Alice Asafu-Adjaye, Ms Despina Flevotomou, Ms Abigail Patel, Ms Catherine Eaton Davis, Tim Bailey, Elsie Owusu, Elena Tsolakis, Caroline Buckingham, Roger Shrimplin, Geoff Alsop, Benjamin Derbyshire, Julia McLoughlin, Kerr Robertson, Philip Waddy, John Cole, Paul Crowe, Fraser Middleton, Nicola Watson, Ruth Donelly, Saul Golden, Lisa Raynes, Jonathan Ball, Mark Percival, Mr Jason Bill, Ms Wendy Curtis, Mr Lanre Gbolade, Mr Stewart Henderson, Mr Michael Martin, Ms Valeria Passetti, Mr Roger Tsan-Sum Wu, Ms Stephanie Anne Edwards, Ms Alia Beyg Javed, Selasi Awo Setufe, Mr Inderpaul Singh Johar
Income: £42,306,000 [2016]; £38,167,000 [2015]; £36,595,000 [2014]; £34,139,000 [2013]; £33,333,000 [2012]

The Royal Institute of International Affairs
Registered: 22 Sep 1962 *Employees:* 158
Tel: 020 7957 5700 *Website:* chathamhouse.org
Activities: Education, training; other charitable purposes
Address: Royal Institute of International Affairs, Chatham House, 10 St James's Square, London, SW1Y 4LE
Trustees: Mr Martin Fraenkel, Lord Jim O'Neill, Ms Catherine Brown, Sir Jeremy Greenstock, Mr Alistair Burnett, Mr Mark Spelman, Ms Jasmine Zerinini, Ms Heide Baumann, Mr Tim Willasey-Wilsey, Mr Jawad Iqbal, Mr Stuart Popham, Ms Ann Cormack, Sir Richard Lambert, Mr Peter Montagnon, Mrs Barbara Ridpath, Ms Mimi Ajibade, Sir Simon Fraser, Mr Kenneth Cukier, Mr John Berriman, Ms Kate Gibbons
Income: £17,872,000 [2017]; £16,582,000 [2016]; £15,880,000 [2015]; £12,766,000 [2014]; £9,845,000 [2013]

The Royal Institution of Chartered Surveyors' Benevolent Fund Limited
Registered: 10 Jun 1970 *Employees:* 17 *Volunteers:* 14
Tel: 0845 603 9057 *Website:* lionheart.org.uk
Activities: General charitable purposes; advancement of health or saving of lives; prevention or relief of poverty; other charitable purposes
Address: Royal Institution of Chartered Surveyors Benevolent Fund Lionheart, Ground Floor, 55 Colmore Row, Birmingham, B3 2AA
Trustees: Mr James Allan FRICS MCIArb, Mr Alan Day MRICS, Mr Andrew Carrick, Miss Dayle Bayliss MRICS, Miss Katie Jane Leppard MRICS, Mr Charles Follows MBA BSc FRICS, Mr James Grierson MRICS, Mrs Jayne MacLennan, Mr Peter Daniel McCrea FRICS, Mr Richard Anthony Serra MRICS
Income: £2,520,000 [2017]; £2,049,000 [2016]; £1,891,000 [2015]; £1,848,000 [2014]; £2,744,000 [2013]

The Royal Institution of Great Britain

Registered: 4 Oct 1963 *Employees:* 52 *Volunteers:* 1,250
Tel: 020 7670 2930 *Website:* rigb.org
Activities: Education, training; arts, culture, heritage, science; environment, conservation, heritage
Address: 21 Albemarle Street, Mayfair, London, W1S 4BS
Trustees: Lord Robert Winston, Ms Sarika Patel, Dr Martin Knight, Professor Sir Peter Knight, Dr Fergus Boyd, Prof Chris Toumazou, Mr Geoffrey Potter, Sir Richard Sykes, Mr Hugh Harper, Lord Julian Hunt CB MA PhD FIMA FRS, Mrs Louise Terry
Income: £4,183,000 [2016]; £3,514,000 [2015]; £4,158,000 [2014]; £7,836,000 [2013]; £4,025,000 [2012]

Royal Institution of Naval Architects

Registered: 4 Feb 1964 *Employees:* 23 *Volunteers:* 200
Tel: 020 7235 4622 *Website:* rina.org.uk
Activities: Education, training
Address: 8-9 Northumberland Street, London, WC2N 5DA
Trustees: Mr Nicholas Pattison, Mr Robin Charles Gehling, Mr Adrian Robert Richens Pattison, Professor Paul Geoffrey Wrobel, Mr John Edward Charles De Rose, Professor Catriona Louise Savage, Mr Andrew David King, Mr Jeffrey Derrick Frier, Captain Herbert Franklin Spencer OBE, Professor Richard Walter Birmingham BEng PhD, Mr Christopher Cooper
Income: £2,296,306 [2017]; £2,287,519 [2016]; £2,282,162 [2015]; £2,236,835 [2014]; £8,218,253 [2013]

The Royal Leicestershire Rutland and Wycliffe Society for the Blind

Registered: 12 Mar 1963 *Employees:* 264 *Volunteers:* 310
Website: vistablind.org.uk
Activities: Education, training; advancement of health or saving of lives; disability; accommodation, housing; economic, community development, employment
Address: Vista, 1A Salisbury Road, Leicester, LE1 7QR
Trustees: Michael Pearson, Roy Hill, Mr Paul Ryb, Mrs Patricia Cyhan, Tony Harrop, Mohammed Bhojani, Dr Tom Pey, Mrs Urvashi Dattani, Ms Ruth Ingman, Ms Susan Disley, John Godber, Mrs Louisa Hosegood
Income: £7,694,000 [2017]; £7,438,000 [2016]; £5,777,000 [2015]; £5,697,000 [2014]; £5,731,000 [2013]

The Royal Life Saving Society - U.K.

Registered: 26 Apr 1995 *Employees:* 64 *Volunteers:* 10,000
Tel: 0300 323 0096 *Website:* rlss.org.uk
Activities: Education, training; advancement of health or saving of lives; amateur sport
Address: Royal Life Saving Society UK, Red Hill House, 227 London Road, Worcester, WR5 2JG
Trustees: Mr Bryan Finlay, Mr Cavell Burchell, Mr Dan Graham, Mr Mark Smith, Mrs Emma Davids, Ian Hutchings, Mrs Deborah Hunt, Mrs Dawn Whittaker, Mrs Rhyan Christine Barry
Income: £5,469,608 [2016]; £4,534,435 [2015]; £4,436,156 [2014]; £2,947,382 [2013]; £3,053,730 [2012]

The Royal Literary Fund

Registered: 15 Apr 1964 *Employees:* 4
Tel: 020 7353 7159 *Website:* rlf.org.uk
Activities: Education, training; prevention or relief of poverty
Address: 3 Johnson's Court, off Fleet Street, London, EC4A 3EA
Trustees: Mr Simon Brett, Ms Frances Fyfield, Mr Nick Hern, Mr Michael Ridpath, Ms Maura Dooley, Mr Richard Davenport-Hines, Professor Richard Holmes OBE, Mr Colin Luke, Ms Tracy Chevalier, Mr Dan Franklin, Mr Bruce Hunter, Ms Hilary Hale, Mr Mark Le Fanu OBE, Ms Paula Johnson, Ms Susan Hitch, Mr Michael Symmons Roberts, Mr Philip Gwyn Jones, Miss Joanna Trollope OBE, Mr Terence Blacker
Income: £2,226,192 [2017]; £2,957,014 [2016]; £2,619,713 [2015]; £2,225,955 [2014]; £3,190,139 [2013]

The Royal Liverpool Philharmonic Society

Registered: 14 Oct 1963 *Employees:* 223
Tel: 0151 210 2895 *Website:* liverpoolphil.com
Activities: Arts, culture, heritage, science
Address: Royal Liverpool Philharmonic Society, Philharmonic Hall, Hope Street, Liverpool, L1 9BP
Trustees: Ms Wendy Simon, Michael Eakin, Mr Martin Richardson, Mr John Corner, Mr Alexander Holliday, Ms Vanessa Reed, Dr Tony Harvey, Prof Nigel Weatherill, Mr David Nicholls, Mr Mel Grodner
Income: £10,251,000 [2017]; £14,046,000 [2016]; £15,398,000 [2015]; £12,790,000 [2014]; £10,488,000 [2013]

Royal Liverpool and Broadgreen University Hospitals NHS Trust Charitable Funds

Registered: 14 Jul 1995 *Volunteers:* 10
Tel: 0151 706 3142
Activities: Education, training; advancement of health or saving of lives; disability
Address: Deputy Chief Exec & Director of Finance, Royal Liverpool and Broadgreen University Hospitals, Royal Liverpool University Hospital, Precott Street, Liverpool, L7 8XP
Trustees: Royal Liverpool + Broadgreen University
Income: £1,541,427 [2017]; £1,463,939 [2016]; £882,397 [2015]; £755,412 [2014]; £828,064 [2013]

Royal Logistic Corps Association Trust

Registered: 22 Jul 1993 *Employees:* 9
Tel: 01252 833334 *Website:* army.mod.uk
Activities: General charitable purposes; education, training; disability; prevention or relief of poverty; arts, culture, heritage, science; amateur sport; environment, conservation, heritage; armed forces, emergency service efficiency; recreation
Address: RHQ The RLC, Dettingen House, Princess Royal Barracks, Deepcut, Camberley, Surrey, GU16 6RW
Trustees: Major General David John Shouesmith, Major General Malcolm David Wood CBE, Brig Paul Evans, Brigadier Simon Tony Hutchings OBE, Colonel Neil Llewellyn, Brig Christopher Murray CBE, Colonel Colin John Francis MBE ADC, WO1 Dean Burditt, Maj Gen Shumas Kerr, Col Alex Barnes, Major General Mark Poffley OBE, Colonel Stephen Rayson, Maj Gen Adrian Lyons CBE, Lt Col Nigel Shepherd, Brigadier Stephen John Shirley MBE, WO1 Shaun Owen
Income: £3,203,889 [2016]; £2,831,855 [2015]; £2,911,767 [2014]; £2,737,655 [2013]; £2,521,391 [2012]

The Royal Marines Charity
Registered: 8 Feb 2010 Employees: 11 Volunteers: 24
Website: theroyalmarinescharity.org.uk
Activities: Disability; armed forces, emergency service efficiency; recreation; other charitable purposes
Address: Commando Training Centre, Royal Marines, Exmouth Road, Lympstone, Exmouth, Devon, EX8 5AR
Trustees: Mr William John Stocks, Mr Richard Weaver, Mr Keith Breslauer, Corps Regimental Sergeant Major, Paul Richard Denning, Lieutenant Colonel Ian William Grant, Mr Daniel Cox, Mr James Zuppinger, Deputy Commandant General Royal Marines
Income: £2,660,662 [2016]; £2,756,830 [2015]; £5,339,768 [2014]; £3,088,869 [2013]; £3,050,340 [2012]

Royal Marines Museum
Registered: 11 Sep 1969
Tel: 023 9272 7582 Website: royalmarinesmuseum.co.uk
Activities: General charitable purposes; education, training; arts, culture, heritage, science; environment, conservation, heritage
Address: Defence Mail Centre, Stoney Lane, HM Naval Base, Portsmouth, PO1 3NH
Trustees: National Museum of The Royal Navy
Income: £6,988,198 [2017]

The Royal Marsden Cancer Charity
Registered: 31 Dec 2002 Employees: 79 Volunteers: 76
Website: royalmarsden.org
Activities: Education, training; advancement of health or saving of lives
Address: Ground Floor, Stewarts House, Stewarts Grove, London, SW3 6PB
Trustees: Mr Robin Shedden Broadhurst, Professor Martin Gore, Caroline Palmer, Lady Helen Taylor, Sir Terry Leahy, Richard Oldfield, Mr Douglas Jardine Flint, Richard Turnor, Mr Charles Edward Alexander
Income: £19,150,000 [2017]; £16,165,953 [2016]; £22,776,000 [2015]; £15,535,900 [2014]; £13,961,749 [2013]

The Royal Masonic Benevolent Institution Care Company
Registered: 21 Aug 2015 Employees: 1,008 Volunteers: 250
Tel: 020 3146 3304 Website: rmbi.org.uk
Activities: The advancement of health or saving of lives; disability; accommodation, housing
Address: RMBICC, Freemasons Hall, 60 Great Queen Street, London, WC2B 5AZ
Trustees: Mr John Boyington CBE, Mr Christopher George White, Dr Kevin Rhydderch Williams, Mr Ian Charles Arthur Newby, Mr Randall Wayne Marks, Mrs Sylvia Short OBE, Mr David William Snowdon, Mr David Watson, Dr John William Arthur Reuther, Mr David Southern, Sir Paul Williams OBE CStJ DL, Mr Sushikumar Chandulal Radia, Mrs Sara Sheppard
Income: £46,971,000 [2017]; £46,440,000 [2016]

The Royal Masonic Benevolent Institution
Registered: 6 Mar 1964
Tel: 020 3146 3304 Website: rmbi.org.uk
Activities: The advancement of health or saving of lives; prevention or relief of poverty; accommodation, housing
Address: Royal Masonic Benevolent Institution, 60 Great Queen Street, London, WC2B 5AZ
Trustees: Masonic Charitable Foindation
Income: £3,921,000 [2017]; £46,440,000 [2016]; £45,497,000 [2015]; £40,250,000 [2014]; £37,849,000 [2013]

The Royal Masonic School for Girls
Registered: 15 Nov 1978 Employees: 285
Tel: 01923 725306 Website: royalmasonic.herts.sch.uk
Activities: Education, training
Address: The Royal Masonic School for Girls, Rickmansworth Park, Rickmansworth, Herts, WD3 4HF
Trustees: Mr Jonathan Gary Knopp, Mr Nicholas Springer, Mr David Ellis, Mr Keith Emmerson, Prof John Brewer, Mr Simon Staite, Mr Sean Brew, Mrs Peta Dyke, Mr James Flecker, Mr Christopher Hayward, Miss Abigail Chloe Gray, Dr Mike Woodcock, Mrs Fiona Richards
Income: £14,504,312 [2017]; £14,357,657 [2016]; £15,212,802 [2015]; £13,803,815 [2014]; £12,952,447 [2013]

The Royal Masonic Trust for Girls and Boys
Registered: 21 Dec 1982
Tel: 020 3146 3304 Website: rmtgb.org
Activities: Education, training; prevention or relief of poverty
Address: Royal Masonic Trust for Girls & Boys, 60 Great Queen Street, London, WC2B 5AZ
Trustees: Masonic Charitable Foundation
Income: £4,574,000 [2017]; £6,262,000 [2016]; £8,784,000 [2015]; £5,400,000 [2013]; £7,579,000 [2012]

The Royal Medical Foundation of Epsom College
Registered: 30 Jun 1965 Employees: 405
Tel: 01372 821011 Website: epsomcollege.org.uk
Activities: Education, training; advancement of health or saving of lives; disability; prevention or relief of poverty
Address: Epsom College, College Road, Epsom, Surrey, KT17 4JQ
Trustees: Lord Carlile, Mr George Pincus, Dr Jeremy Bolton, Sir John Scarlett, Mr Edward Chandler, Mrs Karen Thomas, Mr Clive Watson, Mr Andrew Pianca, Dr Andrew Vallance-Owen, Dr Hywel Bowen-Perkins, Dr Alastair Wells, Dr Sundeep Dhillon, Mr Dej Mahoney, Mr Richard Bruce, Mr John Hay
Income: £23,997,000 [2017]; £21,251,000 [2016]; £20,551,000 [2015]; £19,664,000 [2014]; £18,598,000 [2013]

Royal Mencap Society
Registered: 23 Jul 1964 Employees: 8,181 Volunteers: 1,240
Tel: 020 7696 5614 Website: mencap.org.uk
Activities: Education, training; disability; accommodation, housing; economic, community development; employment; recreation
Address: 123 Golden Lane, London, EC1Y 0RT
Trustees: Ms Linda Redford, Mr Geoff Alltimes, Ms Elaine Hindal, Mr Graham Williams, Mr Andrew Wilson, Mr Derek Lewis, Mr David Wolverson, Ms Katie Hollier, Mr Stephen Jack
Income: £191,941,000 [2017]; £191,328,000 [2016]; £191,651,000 [2015]; £201,195,000 [2014]; £196,584,000 [2013]

Royal Microscopical Society
Registered: 26 Jul 1965 Employees: 12 Volunteers: 100
Website: rms.org.uk
Activities: Education, training
Address: 6 Taylor Close, Faringdon, Oxon, SN7 7GG
Trustees: Professor Chris Hawes, Dr Peter O'Toole, Dr Terence McMaster, Professor Michelle Peckham, Dr Ricardo Morilla, Mr Derek Davies, Dr Paul Verkade, Dr Lynne Joyce, Professor Martin Leahy, Professor Beverley Inkson, Dr Lucy Collinson, Dr Debbie Stokes, Dr Susan Anderson, Dr Philippa Catherine Hawes, Professor Peter David Nellist, Dr Rik Drummond-Brydson, Mr Eric Bennett, Dr Richard Grenfell, Dr Sarah Haigh, Dr Kesara Anamthawat-Jonsson, Dr Claire Wells, Mr Alex Sossick
Income: £1,360,903 [2016]; £1,639,504 [2015]; £1,619,802 [2014]; £1,264,564 [2013]; £2,353,357 [2012]

Royal Military Academy Sandhurst Commandant's Fund
Registered: 8 Mar 2010 *Volunteers:* 2
Tel: 01276
Activities: Education, training; other charitable purposes
Address: The Royal Military Academy, Sandhurst, Haig Road, Camberley, Surrey, GU15 4PQ
Trustees: Commandant
Income: £4,963,998 [2017]; £161,828 [2016]; £143,769 [2015]; £147,217 [2014]; £142,782 [2013]

Royal National Children's Springboard Foundation
Registered: 6 Jun 2016 *Employees:* 8 *Volunteers:* 15
Tel: 020 3405 3630 *Website:* royalspringboard.org.uk
Activities: Education, training
Address: 7 Grosvenor Gardens, London, SW1W 0BD
Trustees: Mr Patrick Derham, Mr Ric Lewis, Mrs Helen Starkie, Mr Patrick Smulders, Douglas De Brule, Mr Clive Paul Marshall, Mr Timothy Bunting, Mr Robert Swannell, Mr Andrew Corbett, Mr Eraj Shirvani, Kevin Parry, Mr William De Winton
Income: £1,725,531 [2017]

The Royal National College for the Blind
Registered: 20 Sep 1990 *Employees:* 168 *Volunteers:* 42
Tel: 01432 265725 *Website:* rncb.ac.uk
Activities: Education, training; disability
Address: c/o The Clerk, Royal National College for The Blind, Venns Lane, Hereford, HR1 1DT
Trustees: Ms Kerry Ann Diamond, Mr John Ryan, Mr Jeremy Clarke-Morris, Mr Peter Flynn, Mr Mark Fisher, Mr Paul Smith, Simon Hairsnape, Ms Tirion Hughes, Mr Jonathan Brew, Professor Tamar Thompson, Mr Edward Nicolas Lloyd, Mr Christopher Mill, Mrs Lucy Proctor, Mr Sean Davies, Mr Benjamin Adam Rendle
Income: £6,709,000 [2017]; £6,608,000 [2016]; £6,845,000 [2015]; £6,960,000 [2014]; £7,465,000 [2013]

The Royal National Institute for Deaf People
Registered: 30 Nov 1962 *Employees:* 893 *Volunteers:* 1,400
Tel: 020 7359 4442 *Website:* actiononhearingloss.org.uk
Activities: Disability
Address: Action on Hearing Loss, 1-3 Highbury Station Road, London, N1 1SE
Trustees: Mr Eric Roux, Ms Carol Cole, Prof Quentin Summerfield, Mrs Louise Caroline Craddock, Professor Brian Cecil Joseph Moore, Mr John Christopher Morgan, Mrs Ingrid Elizabeth Gallen, Mr Richard Jones, Ms Caroline Ashley, Dr Gerhard Heiner Werner May, Jacqueline Press, Ms Margaret Elizabeth Hampton, Dr Brian Patrick Caul
Income: £40,293,000 [2017]; £38,380,000 [2016]; £37,131,000 [2015]; £47,090,000 [2014]; £37,426,000 [2013]

The Royal National Institute of Blind People
Registered: 21 Mar 1963 *Employees:* 2,335 *Volunteers:* 5,000
Website: rnib.org.uk
Activities: Education, training; advancement of health or saving of lives; disability; accommodation, housing; arts, culture, heritage, science; amateur sport; economic, community development, employment
Address: Royal National Institute for The Blind, 105 Judd Street, London, WC1H 9NE
Trustees: Derek Child, Michael Nussbaum, Margaret Bennett, Simon Finnie, Sandi Wassmer, Terry Moody, Eleanor Southwood, Heather Giles, Alan Tinger, Ozzie Clarke-Binns
Income: £119,199,000 [2017]; £114,450,000 [2016]; £114,465,000 [2015]; £118,647,000 [2014]; £117,023,000 [2013]

The Royal National Lifeboat Institution
Registered: 27 Mar 1963 *Employees:* 2,103 *Volunteers:* 34,947
Website: rnli.org
Activities: General charitable purposes; education, training; advancement of health or saving of lives; arts, culture, heritage, science
Address: RNLI, West Quay Road, Poole, Dorset, BH15 1HZ
Trustees: Mr Stuart Popham QC, Vice Admiral Sir Timothy Laurence KCVO, Mr Eddie Donaldson, Mr David Delamer, Mrs Sonia Ann Modray, Ms Rosemary Francis Norris, Ms Janet Cooper, Mr Mark Byford, Sir Peter James Housden KCB, Mr Chris Walters MEng MBA DIC MRINA, Mr Mike Sturrock, Rear Admiral Roger Graham Lockwood CB
Income: £197,690,779 [2016]; £191,334,622 [2015]; £190,016,265 [2014]; £191,034,250 [2013]; £174,681,644 [2012]

Royal National Mission to Deep Sea Fishermen
Registered: 28 May 1970 *Employees:* 54
Tel: 01489 566910 *Website:* fishermensmission.org.uk
Activities: General charitable purposes; advancement of health or saving of lives; prevention or relief of poverty; accommodation, housing; religious activities
Address: Royal National Mission to Deep Sea Fishermen, Mather House, 4400 Parkway, Whiteley, Fareham, Hants, PO15 7FJ
Trustees: Mr Trevor Ernest James FCA DChA, Venerable Simon Jefferies Golding CBE, Professor Glyn Tonge, Rear Admiral Sir Jeremy De Halpert KCVO CB, David Lacy, Mr Edward James Whittle, Mr Steven Maurice Bloor, Mr Michael Vlasto OBE, Mrs Jill Henderson, Mr Ian Gatt, Mrs Elizabeth Ann Woodhatch, Mrs Alison Fowlie, Dr Jonathan Christopher Shepherd, Mr Thomas Nicholas Maier
Income: £3,178,872 [2017]; £2,735,562 [2016]; £3,597,051 [2015]; £3,208,079 [2014]; £2,901,613 [2013]

The Royal National Theatre
Registered: 17 Apr 1963 *Employees:* 1,173 *Volunteers:* 32
Tel: 020 7452 3361 *Website:* nationaltheatre.org.uk
Activities: Education, training; arts, culture, heritage, science
Address: Royal National Theatre, Upper Ground, London, SE1 9PX
Trustees: Sir Damon Buffini, Ms Katharine Louise Mosse, Mrs Elizabeth Offord, Mr Simon Warshaw, Mr Timothy Score, Mr Alan Charles Rusbridger, Mrs Ursula Brennan, Sir Lenny Henry, Mrs Sabine Chalmers, Mrs Victoria Mary Heywood
Income: £104,700,000 [2017]; £121,600,000 [2016]; £137,900,000 [2015]; £124,100,000 [2014]; £97,600,000 [2013]

The Royal Naval Benevolent Trust (Grand Fleet and Kindred Funds)
Registered: 5 Feb 1963 *Employees:* 109 *Volunteers:* 38
Tel: 023 9269 0112 *Website:* rnbt.org.uk
Activities: Education, training; advancement of health or saving of lives; disability; prevention or relief of poverty; accommodation, housing
Address: Castaway House, 311 Twyford Avenue, Portsmouth, PO2 8RN
Trustees: Mr Owen Shread, Cpl Philip Barnes, Mr Kenneth Lambert BEM, Mrs Pauline Shaw, Mrs Sarah Clewes, Mr Darren Hedges, Mr Ian Ranscombe, Captain Andy Jordan, Mr James Moulson MBE, Mr Nicholas John Gartside, Mrs Julie Behan, Lieutenant Commander Tim Forer, Brigadier Mike Ellis OBE, Colour Sergeant Ian Michelsen, WO1 Simon Tripp, Captain Nick Fletcher
Income: £5,556,003 [2017]; £4,621,485 [2016]; £5,993,391 [2015]; £5,251,268 [2014]; £5,318,263 [2013]

Royal Navy Rugby Union
Registered: 13 Jan 2016 *Employees:* 5
Tel: 023 9257 3040 *Website:* navyrugbyunion.co.uk
Activities: General charitable purposes; amateur sport; armed forces, emergency service efficiency
Address: HMS Temeraire, Burnaby Road, Portsmouth, PO1 2HB
Trustees: Rear Admiral Neil Morisetti CB, Mr James Michael Ross Saunders-Watson, Mr Michael Henry Connolly, Colonel Ewen Alexander Murchison Royal Marines DSO MBE, Mr Angus Roch Bujalski, Commander John Gavin Cunningham Royal Navy Commander, Mr John Inverdale, Commander David Mark George Royal Navy MA, Rear Adm Matthew John Parr CB
Income: £1,347,198 [2017]; £1,532,058 [2016]

The Royal Navy Submarine Museum Trust
Registered: 27 Sep 2016 *Volunteers:* 20
Tel: 023 9272 7562 *Website:* submarine-museum.co.uk
Activities: Education, training; disability; arts, culture, heritage, science; armed forces, emergency service efficiency
Address: HM Naval Base, Portsmouth, PO1 3NH
Trustees: National Museum of The Royal Navy
Income: £18,995,073 [2017]

The Royal Navy and Royal Marines Charity
Registered: 2 Feb 2007 *Employees:* 46 *Volunteers:* 83
Website: rnrmc.org.uk
Activities: General charitable purposes; armed forces, emergency service efficiency
Address: HMS Excellent, Whale Island, Portsmouth, PO2 8ER
Trustees: Mr William John Stocks, Commodore Annette Picton Royal Navy, The Honorable Stephen Watson, Mr James Pitt, Mr William Gennydd Thomas, Mr Michael John Tanner, Mr Jamie Webb, Sub Lieutenant Harriet Mary Delbridge, Ms Jennifer Rowe CB, WO1 Gary Kenneth Nicolson, Mr James Parkin, Ms Oona Muirhead, Mr Roderic Aidan Birkett, Mr Mark Lewthwaite, Mr Mark Dowie
Income: £11,697,979 [2016]; £16,097,507 [2015]; £13,746,242 [2014]; £10,996,102 [2013]; £7,389,668 [2012]

The Royal Navy and Royal Marines Children's Fund
Registered: 27 Jan 2015 *Employees:* 4
Tel: 023 9263 9536 *Website:* rnrmchildrensfund.org.uk
Activities: General charitable purposes; education, training; advancement of health or saving of lives; disability; prevention or relief of poverty; armed forces, emergency service efficiency
Address: The Royal Naval Benevolent Trust, Castaway House, 311 Twyford Avenue, Portsmouth, PO2 8RN
Trustees: Cllr Dr Miranda Nialla Whitehead, Commander David Bridger, Lt Col Ed Musto, Sheila Owens-Cairns, Mr Ian Pitts, Ian William Grant, Mrs Anne Binnie, Mr Alistair Sheppard OBE, Cdr Heather Rimmer, Cpo Claire Robson
Income: £1,217,160 [2017]; £10,272,373 [2016]

Royal Norfolk Agricultural Association
Registered: 12 Jun 1984 *Employees:* 25 *Volunteers:* 325
Website: royalnorfolkshow.co.uk
Activities: General charitable purposes; education, training; animals; environment, conservation, heritage; other charitable purposes
Address: Royal Norfolk Agricultural Association Showground, Dereham Road, New Costessey, Norwich, NR5 0TT
Trustees: Sir Nicholas Bacon Bt, Mr Grant Pilcher, Mr Roly Beazley, Mrs Belinda Rosanna Clarke, Mrs Catherine Scott, David Hill, Mr Robert John More, Mr Steffan Daniel Anderson Griffiths, Mrs Francesca Lois Broom, Mr Robert Collison Alston
Income: £2,340,321 [2016]; £2,283,611 [2015]; £2,319,772 [2014]; £2,274,307 [2013]; £2,260,086 [2012]

The Royal Northern College of Music Awards Fund
Registered: 24 Feb 1976
Tel: 0161 907 5401 *Website:* mcm.ac.uk
Activities: Education, training
Address: Royal Northern College of Music, 124 Oxford Road, Manchester, M13 9RD
Trustees: Royal Northern College of Music
Income: £1,662,370 [2017]; £1,411,226 [2016]; £1,566,311 [2015]; £1,491,620 [2014]; £1,642,690 [2013]

The Royal Northern College of Music Endowment Fund
Registered: 24 Feb 1976
Tel: 0161 907 5401 *Website:* rncm.ac.uk
Activities: Education, training
Address: Royal Northern College of Music, 124 Oxford Road, Manchester, M13 9RD
Trustees: Royal Northern College of Music
Income: £2,233,245 [2017]; £1,936,577 [2016]; £2,004,507 [2015]; £2,054,064 [2014]; £2,085,216 [2013]

Royal Opera House Covent Garden Foundation
Registered: 17 Oct 1962 *Employees:* 1,077 *Volunteers:* 71
Tel: 020 7240 1200 *Website:* roh.org.uk
Activities: Education, training; arts, culture, heritage, science; environment, conservation, heritage; economic, community development, employment
Address: Royal Opera House, Covent Garden, London, WC2E 9DD
Trustees: Mr Paul Dring Morrell, Mr Timothy Brian Bunting, Mr Ian Taylor, Lady Suzanne Heywood, Ms Laura Wade-Gery, Mr Julian Metherell, Mr Roger William Wright, Dame Vivien Louise Duffield, Ms Susan Linda Hoyle, Mr Daniel Charles Wyler, Sir Nicholas Hytner, Mr Andrew Hamish Forsyth, Dr Munira Mirza, Dr Genevieve Davies, Mr John Kingman, Mr Lloyd Dorfman CBE, Mrs Kirstine Ann Cooper
Income: £141,026,000 [2017]; £139,277,000 [2016]; £141,586,000 [2015]; £127,532,000 [2014]; £113,976,000 [2013]

The Royal Opera House Endowment Fund 2000
Registered: 2 Jan 2002
Tel: 020 7212 9664 *Website:* roh.org.uk
Activities: Education, training; arts, culture, heritage, science; environment, conservation, heritage; economic, community development, employment
Address: Royal Opera House, Covent Garden, London, WC2E 9DD
Trustees: Sir David Bryan Lees, Dame Vivien Duffield DBE, Sir Stuart Lipton, Mr Julian Metherell, Sir Simon Robertson, Mr Peter Troughton, Baroness Fiona Shackleton, Sir Simon Christopher Robey
Income: £2,314,568 [2017]; £1,795,808 [2016]; £1,726,101 [2015]; £3,328,092 [2014]; £3,085,731 [2013]

Royal Papworth Hospital Charity
Registered: 15 Sep 1995 *Employees:* 5 *Volunteers:* 16
Tel: 01480 364555 *Website:* papworthhospitalcharity.org.uk
Activities: General charitable purposes; education, training; advancement of health or saving of lives
Address: Papworth Hospital, Papworth Everard, Cambridge, CB23 3RE
Trustees: Papworth Hospital NHS Foundation Trust
Income: £3,084,000 [2017]; £2,523,000 [2016]; £1,815,000 [2015]; £1,711,000 [2014]; £1,789,000 [2013]

Royal Philharmonic Orchestra Limited
Registered: 29 Dec 1966 *Employees:* 27
Tel: 020 7608 8800 *Website:* rpo.co.uk
Activities: Education, training; arts, culture, heritage, science
Address: The Company Secretary, 16 Clerkenwell Green, London, EC1R 0QT
Trustees: Mr Charles Fairweather, Mr Benjamin Cunningham, Mr Peter Lumley, Mr James Williams, Mr Chian Lim, Mr Adam Wright, Mr Jonathan Hallett, Mr Fraser Gordon, Mr Matthew Knight, Mrs Elizabeth Case Liz Kirstruck
Income: £10,329,393 [2017]; £8,386,517 [2016]; £8,911,704 [2015]; £9,012,530 [2014]; £8,000,860 [2013]

The Royal Photographic Society of Great Britain
Registered: 27 Jan 2005 *Employees:* 18 *Volunteers:* 380
Tel: 01225 325730 *Website:* rps.org
Activities: Education, training; arts, culture, heritage, science
Address: The Royal Photographic Society, Fenton House, 122 Wells Road, Bath, BA2 3AH
Trustees: Mr Derek Trendell ARPS, Vanessa Elaine Slawson, Mr Barry Hoffman LRPS, Mr Alan Hodgson ASIS FRPS, Mr Robert Albright FRPS, Mr Richard Tucker, Dr Del Barrett
Income: £2,101,532 [2016]; £2,076,553 [2015]; £2,433,180 [2014]; £1,653,042 [2013]; £1,587,320 [2012]

The Royal School Haslemere
Registered: 19 Oct 2007 *Employees:* 213
Tel: 01428 605805 *Website:* royal-school.org
Activities: Education, training
Address: The Royal School, Farnham Lane, Haslemere, Surrey, GU27 1HQ
Trustees: Mrs Amanda Haddon-Cave, Mr Ian Fraser Robert Much, Mr Christopher William Sprague, Mr Peter James Gordon Young, Mr Charles Scott, Venerable Ian Wheatley, Ms Stephanie Pattenden, Mrs Alison Margaret Titchmarsh, Mr Robert Justin Manley-Cooper, Dr Annalisa Claire Alexander, Mrs Susan Pepper
Income: £8,704,863 [2016]; £6,759,339 [2015]; £10,475,959 [2014]

Royal School for The Deaf Derby
Registered: 21 May 1997 *Employees:* 88 *Volunteers:* 3
Tel: 01332 547664 *Website:* rsd-derby.org
Activities: Education, training; disability
Address: Royal School for The Deaf, 180 Ashbourne Road, Derby, DE22 3BH
Trustees: Alan Lamplough Passmore, David Du Celliee Muller, Mr James Alexander Bruce Ottewell, Mrs Tracy Pepper, James Richardson, Ms Lynn Elizabeth Senior, Mr Douglas Edward Bulger, Samantha Killian
Income: £4,590,000 [2016]; £4,306,346 [2015]; £4,229,569 [2014]; £4,121,821 [2013]; £3,945,064 [2012]

The Royal School for the Blind, Liverpool
Registered: 5 Sep 1963 *Employees:* 54
Tel: 0151 733 1012 *Website:* rsblind.com
Activities: Education, training; disability
Address: Royal School for the Blind-Liverpool, Church Road North, Liverpool, L15 6TQ
Trustees: Mr Brian Lawlor, Mr Geoffrey Morrow QC, Colonel Martin Graham Clive Amlot, Mrs Susan Isabel George, Mr Mark Taylor, Miss Jane Woosey, Mr David Withey, Mr John Sylvester Brown, Dr Sandra Lesley Winchester, Mr Allan Perry, Miss Marilyn MacCoss, Rev John Phillips
Income: £1,544,943 [2017]; £1,554,100 [2016]; £1,521,942 [2015]; £1,787,785 [2014]; £1,928,200 [2013]

The Royal School for the Blind
Registered: 5 Aug 1968 *Employees:* 449 *Volunteers:* 200
Tel: 01372 755000 *Website:* seeability.org
Activities: Disability; accommodation, housing
Address: Newplan, 41 East Street, Epsom, Surrey, KT17 1BL
Trustees: Mr James Deeley, Mr Gordon Ilett, Ms Tania Fitzgerald, Mrs Mary Campbell Syme Heathcote, Ms Mary Moore, Ms Rona Nicholson, Mr Gareth Mostyn, Mr Paul Ursell, Mr Jon Sparkes, Mr Francois Delbaere ACA, Deborah Hale MBE
Income: £17,690,986 [2017]; £17,064,601 [2016]; £16,281,657 [2015]; £15,122,538 [2014]; £14,581,831 [2013]

The Royal School of Church Music
Registered: 10 Apr 1963 *Employees:* 25 *Volunteers:* 500
Tel: 01722 424852 *Website:* rscm.com
Activities: Education, training; religious activities; arts, culture, heritage, science
Address: The Royal School of Church Music, 19 The Close, Salisbury, Wilts, SP1 2EB
Trustees: Dr David Price, Mr Ian Church, Lord Gill, Mrs Brigid May Frances Parkin, Mr Robin Thomas, Mrs Elizabeth Mary Evans, Mr Peter John Connor, Mr Michael Joseph Perrier, Mrs Rowan Isabella Morton Gledhill, Mr Phil Taylor
Income: £1,705,718 [2016]; £1,618,535 [2015]; £1,591,421 [2014]; £1,767,075 [2013]; £1,536,039 [2012]

The Royal School of Needlework
Registered: 7 Jul 1964 *Employees:* 24 *Volunteers:* 20
Tel: 020 3166 6930 *Website:* royal-needlework.org.uk
Activities: Education, training; arts, culture, heritage, science; environment, conservation, heritage
Address: Royal School of Needlework, 12a Hampton Court Palace, East Molesey, Surrey, KT8 9AU
Trustees: Mr Christopher MacDonald Stooke, Mrs Sharan Janet Elizabeth Wicks, Ms Deborah Lamb, Mrs Morgan Hixon Seidler Fowles, Mrs Elizabeth Ann Braakenburg Dyce, Mrs Stephanie Jane Wright, Mr Andrew William Palmer, Mrs Caroline Claire De Guitaut, Miss Samantha Jane Hoe-Richardson, Ms Nicola Ashley Clarke, Professor John Miles
Income: £1,917,802 [2017]; £1,758,317 [2016]; £1,867,656 [2015]; £1,470,971 [2014]; £1,360,881 [2013]

Royal Scot Locomotive & General Trust
Registered: 30 Dec 2010 *Employees:* 47 *Volunteers:* 15
Tel: 07950 682646 *Website:* royalscot.org.uk
Activities: Education, training; environment, conservation, heritage
Address: 2 Whiteheads Lane, Bradford on Avon, Wilts, BA15 1JU
Trustees: Denis Dunstone, Mr Jeremy John Hosking, Mr Rupert Drury, Mr Richard William Abbey, Mr Guy Richard Greenhous, Mr Peter Nigel Greenwood, Mr Peter Adds
Income: £6,179,099 [2017]; £2,592,054 [2016]; £9,366,623 [2015]; £3,501,517 [2014]; £2,761,691 [2013]

The Royal Shakespeare Company, Stratford-upon-Avon
Registered: 10 Apr 1963 *Employees:* 1,131 *Volunteers:* 84
Tel: 01789 296655 *Website:* rsc.org.uk
Activities: General charitable purposes; education, training; arts, culture, heritage, science
Address: Royal Shakespeare Theatre, Waterside, Stratford upon Avon, Warwicks, CV37 6BB
Trustees: Sir Anthony Seldon, Mr Mark Thompson, Mr Mark Smith, Ms Catherine Mallyon, Baroness McIntosh of Hudnall, Mr Gregory Doran, Ms Patsy Rodenburg OBE FGS, Ms Clare Reddington, Mr Nigel Hugill, Mr Simon Russell Beale CBE, Sir William Atkinson, Mr David Tennant, Ms Miranda Curtis, Mr James Shapiro, Mr Ian Squires, Mr Paapa Essiedu
Income: £105,137,000 [2017]; £92,639,000 [2016]; £63,947,000 [2015]; £61,740,000 [2014]; £62,790,000 [2013]

The Royal Society for Blind Children
Registered: 25 Apr 1963 *Employees:* 96 *Volunteers:* 152
Tel: 020 7808 6170 *Website:* rsbc.org.uk
Activities: Education, training; disability; economic, community development, employment
Address: RSBC, 52-58 Arcola Street, London, E8 2DJ
Trustees: William Ramsay, John Heller, Mr Ian Frederick Stephenson, Ian Godwin, Patrick Plant, Peter Knott, Stuart Ritchie, Mr Michael Brignall, Mrs Valerie Marlene May, Shalni Sood, Martin Doel
Income: £5,152,000 [2016]; £4,609,000 [2015]; £5,411,000 [2014]; £8,507,000 [2013]; £5,532,000 [2012]

Royal Society for Public Health
Registered: 18 Sep 2008 *Employees:* 47
Tel: 020 7265 7370 *Website:* rsph.org.uk
Activities: Education, training; advancement of health or saving of lives
Address: John Snow House, 59 Mansell Street, London, E1 8AN
Trustees: Ms Anne Heughan, Mr Malcolm Robert Wright OBE, Professor Carol Wallace, Professor Lisa Ackerley, Ms Jill Turner, Professor Kate Ardern, Professor Derek Ward, Dr Nigel Carter OBE, Mr Vijith Randeniya OBE, Mr Phillip Woodward, Professor Sian Meryl Griffiths OBE JP, Mr Joe Stringer, Mr Tony Vickers-Byrne, Ms Wilma Reid
Income: £3,357,203 [2016]; £3,757,481 [2015]; £3,593,772 [2014]; £3,594,957 [2013]; £2,936,738 [2012]

The Royal Society for The Prevention of Accidents
Registered: 22 Sep 1962 *Employees:* 110
Tel: 0121 248 2100 *Website:* rospa.com
Activities: Education, training; advancement of health or saving of lives
Address: ROSPA, 27-28 Calthorpe Road, Edgbaston, Birmingham, B15 1RP
Trustees: Dr Julian Redhead, Dr Donald James Lloyd, Mr Robert Ian Kenneth Bucknell, Mr Peter Roger Brown, Mrs Harpreet Kondel, Dr Mary O'Mahony, Mr Michael Parker, Mrs Yvonne Doyle, Mrs Jocelyn McNulty
Income: £8,197,321 [2017]; £7,629,136 [2016]; £8,093,820 [2015]; £7,759,788 [2014]; £7,373,177 [2013]

Royal Society for The Prevention of Cruelty To Animals Bath and District Branch
Registered: 11 Jul 1962 *Employees:* 50 *Volunteers:* 200
Tel: 01225 787325 *Website:* bcdh.org.uk
Activities: Animals
Address: Bath Cats & Dogs Home, The Avenue, Claverton Down, Bath, BA2 7AZ
Trustees: Ms Liz Oldroyd, Ms Sue Scott-Curtis, Ms Laura Andrews, Ms Kim Simpkins-Jenkins
Income: £2,408,516 [2016]; £1,539,312 [2015]; £1,739,573 [2014]; £2,084,540 [2013]; £1,236,567 [2012]

Royal Society for The Prevention of Cruelty To Animals Bristol and District Branch
Registered: 11 May 1963 *Employees:* 53 *Volunteers:* 350
Tel: 0117 300 3961 *Website:* bristolarc.org.uk
Activities: General charitable purposes; education, training; animals
Address: RSPCA Bristol & District Branch, 48 Albert Road, St Philips, Bristol, BS2 0XA
Trustees: Mr Jonathan Parker, Philippa Carey, Mr Steve Crossman, Mr Daniel Elder, Mrs Sue Lomax, Mrs Linda Harper, Mr Tom Whittaker, Ms Jayne Michelle Meacham
Income: £2,967,498 [2016]; £2,120,659 [2015]; £1,472,859 [2014]; £1,611,772 [2013]; £1,381,852 [2012]

Royal Society for The Prevention of Cruelty To Animals Bury Oldham and District Branch
Registered: 1 Nov 1963 *Employees:* 38 *Volunteers:* 75
Tel: 0161 624 4725 *Website:* rspca-buryoldham.org.uk
Activities: Education, training; animals
Address: The Strinesdale Centre, Holgate Street, Oldham, Lancs, OL4 2JW
Trustees: Miss Angela Garvin, Mr David Haigh, Mr Trevor Jones, Mrs Diane Peart, Mrs Susan Walker, Mr Keith Walker, Mr Christopher Peart
Income: £1,239,964 [2016]; £1,382,771 [2015]; £1,349,272 [2014]; £1,118,109 [2013]; £1,258,753 [2012]

Royal Society for The Prevention of Cruelty To Animals Central, West & North East London Branch
Registered: 26 Jul 1966 *Employees:* 23 *Volunteers:* 190
Tel: 07710 294180 *Website:* rspcacentrallondon.org.uk
Activities: Animals
Address: Mrs Chris Beaumont-Kerridge, Box 145, 2 Lansdowne Row, London, W1J 6HL
Trustees: Mrs Christine Beaumont-Kerridge, Miss Amanda Perry, Fraser Wright, Mrs Mary-Jane Kirkby, Mrs L R A Bowran, Ms Vicki Watson, Ms Jennifer Cranston
Income: £1,371,206 [2016]; £1,305,166 [2015]; £1,308,773 [2014]; £1,174,551 [2013]; £1,144,571 [2012]

Royal Society for The Prevention of Cruelty To Animals Halifax, Huddersfield and District Branch
Registered: 31 Oct 1963 *Employees:* 43 *Volunteers:* 257
Website: rspca-halifaxandhuddersfield.org.uk
Activities: Education, training; animals
Address: RSPCA Animal Home, Wade Street, Halifax, W Yorks, HX1 1SN
Trustees: Mrs Cathryn Harris, Ms Vivien Aspey, Mrs Liz Lindsay, Ms Nichi Lindsay, Ms Jo Sykes, Mrs Kath Airey, Mr Tim Bray FCA, Mrs Emma Harvey-Kitching, Ms Caroline Mears, Ms Jennifer MacDougall
Income: £1,237,199 [2016]; £1,305,803 [2015]; £1,256,040 [2014]; £1,183,195 [2013]

Royal Society for The Prevention of Cruelty To Animals Hillingdon, Slough, Windsor, Kingston and District Branch
Registered: 30 Mar 1972 *Employees:* 31 *Volunteers:* 260
Tel: 01895 833417 *Website:* rspcahillingdonclinic.org.uk
Activities: Animals
Address: 16 Crescent Parade, Uxbridge Road, Hillingdon, Middlesex, UB10 0LG
Trustees: Celia Kirkby, Mrs Julie White-Cole, Mr Philip Battle, Mrs Irene Hansford, Mrs Margaret Webb, Mrs Freda Longhurst
Income: £1,018,559 [2016]; £1,057,595 [2015]; £1,172,833 [2014]; £1,119,084 [2013]; £1,069,761 [2012]

Royal Society for The Prevention of Cruelty To Animals Isle of Wight Branch
Registered: 10 Jan 1969 *Employees:* 26 *Volunteers:* 121
Tel: 01983 840287 *Website:* rspca.org.uk
Activities: Animals
Address: The Isle of Wight Animal Centre, Bohemia Corner, Godshill, Isle of Wight, PO38 3NA
Trustees: Mr Richard Booker, Mr Paul David Baxter, Mr Michael Stuart Tomlinson
Income: £1,270,575 [2016]; £1,390,385 [2015]; £618,891 [2014]; £628,191 [2013]; £874,995 [2012]

Royal Society for The Prevention of Cruelty To Animals Leicestershire Branch
Registered: 28 Aug 1963 *Employees:* 38 *Volunteers:* 150
Tel: 0116 232 4933 *Website:* rspcaleicester.org.uk
Activities: Education, training; animals
Address: RSPCA, Woodside Animal Centre, 190 Scudamore Road, Leicester, LE3 1UQ
Trustees: Mr Michael Tomlinson, Ms Ruth Lane, Dave Morrish, Sue Stephens, Mr Jeff Kennington, Mrs Sue Dewick, Shirley Jones
Income: £1,332,608 [2016]; £1,208,352 [2015]; £909,849 [2014]; £922,071 [2013]; £947,900 [2012]

Royal Society for The Prevention of Cruelty To Animals Middlesex North West Branch
Registered: 22 Sep 1962 *Employees:* 25 *Volunteers:* 200
Website: rspca-middlesex.org.uk
Activities: General charitable purposes; animals
Address: 1 Flora Close, Stanmore, Middlesex, HA7 4PY
Trustees: Mrs Maureen Biscoe, Loes Berns, Caroline Bach, Jose Gresa, Jane Thompson, Mr Gary Blatt, Mr David Young, Miss Irene Ling, Carole Holton, Mrs Jean Gardner
Income: £1,204,106 [2016]; £910,051 [2015]; £833,474 [2014]; £783,076 [2013]; £776,728 [2012]

Royal Society for The Prevention of Cruelty To Animals Norwich and Mid-Norfolk Branch
Registered: 3 Feb 1964 *Employees:* 17 *Volunteers:* 40
Tel: 0303 040 1565 *Website:* rspcanorwich.org
Activities: Education, training; animals; economic, community development, employment
Address: RSPCA Norwich & Mid-Norfolk Branch, William Frost Way, New Costessey, Norwich, NR5 0JS
Trustees: John Pinnington, Jenn Parkhouse, Susan Brockhurst, Lynn Yallop-Treasurer, Wendy Dowding, Suzanne O'Connor, Darren Henderson
Income: £1,099,405 [2016]; £669,665 [2015]; £747,702 [2014]; £828,051 [2013]; £648,644 [2012]

Royal Society for The Prevention of Cruelty To Animals Sheffield Branch
Registered: 16 Oct 1963 *Employees:* 45 *Volunteers:* 100
Tel: 0114 289 8050 *Website:* rspcasheffield.org
Activities: Animals
Address: 2 Stadium Way, Attercliffe, Sheffield, S9 3HN
Trustees: Ms Deborah Jayne White, Mrs Wendy Wilkinson, Sandra Swift, Kate Payton, Mrs Gillian Thompson, Mrs Sally Parkin, Mr Daniel Hitchen
Income: £1,504,103 [2016]; £847,931 [2015]; £1,001,332 [2014]; £742,670 [2013]; £706,526 [2012]

Royal Society for The Prevention of Cruelty To Animals Solent Branch
Registered: 16 Mar 1962 *Employees:* 49 *Volunteers:* 250
Tel: 07717 738722 *Website:* stubbingtonark.org.uk
Activities: General charitable purposes; animals
Address: 6 Hayling Close, Fareham, Hants, PO14 3AE
Trustees: Mr Richard Booker, Mr Paul David Baxter, Mr Michael Stuart Tomlinson
Income: £1,273,172 [2016]; £1,103,894 [2015]; £1,553,867 [2014]; £1,169,380 [2013]; £1,308,392 [2012]

Royal Society for The Prevention of Cruelty To Animals Sussex Brighton and East Grinstead Branch
Registered: 10 Jan 1969 *Employees:* 22 *Volunteers:* 100
Tel: 01273 554218 *Website:* rspca-brighton.co.uk
Activities: Animals
Address: RSPCA, Braypool Lane, Patcham, Brighton, BN1 8ZH
Trustees: Miss Jeanette Brazier, Mr Doug Taylor, Mrs Julie Oakley, Mrs Ann Bolton, Mrs Rosemary Anne Bond, Mrs Helen Lilley, Ms Anna Mutter, Mrs Emily Bedford
Income: £1,415,301 [2016]; £623,776 [2015]; £638,087 [2014]; £554,273 [2013]; £431,193 [2012]

Royal Society for The Prevention of Cruelty To Animals, Llys Nini Branch - Cardiff To Swansea
Registered: 21 Aug 1963 *Employees:* 49 *Volunteers:* 250
Tel: 01792 899460 *Website:* rspca-llysnini.org.uk
Activities: Education, training; animals; environment, conservation, heritage; economic, community development, employment
Address: Llys Nini Animal Centre, Penllergaer, Swansea, SA4 9WB
Trustees: Mrs Catherine Thomas, Ms Sally Hyman, Chris Moss, Elaine Jenkyns, Mrs Rebecca Miles Harpwood, Ms Kathryn Smaldon, Mr Robert Upton, Ms Jean Catherine Rawlings, Claire Chappell, Mr Alain David Thomas, Stephen Jenkyns, Ms Trish Flint, Mr Steven Wilson, Ms Helen Deirdre Magoris
Income: £1,339,671 [2016]; £1,482,328 [2015]; £1,454,886 [2014]; £1,377,617 [2013]; £1,103,356 [2012]

Royal Society for The Prevention of Cruelty To Animals
Registered: 16 Jul 1964 *Employees:* 1,695 *Volunteers:* 6,628
Tel: 0300 123 0396 *Website:* rspca.org.uk
Activities: Animals
Address: RSPCA, Wilberforce Way, Southwater, Horsham, W Sussex, RH13 9RS
Trustees: Jo Piccioni, Mr Timothy Bray, Mr Richard Booker, Mr David Douglass Canavan, Dr Richard Dudley Ryder PhD MA DCP, Mrs Christine Beaumont-Kerridge, Ms Jane Marie Tredgett, Mr Paul Baxter, Mr David Thomas, Mrs Jose Parry, Terry Pavey, Mr Paul Draycott, Mrs Margaret Ann Baker, Mrs Daphne Brenda Harris, Mr Michael Tomlinson, Mr Robert Baylis, Mr Ray Ings, Ms Linda Shirley Rimington, Mrs Wendy Dowding, Dr Daniel Lyons, Liz Lindsay
Income: £143,541,000 [2016]; £124,403,000 [2015]; £125,890,000 [2014]; £121,245,000 [2013]; £132,803,000 [2012]

Royal Society for The Protection of Birds

Registered: 22 Sep 1962 *Employees:* 2,409 *Volunteers:* 12,560
Tel: 01767 693372 *Website:* rspb.org.uk
Activities: Education, training; animals; environment, conservation, heritage
Address: RSPB, The Lodge, Potton Road, Sandy, Beds, SG19 2DL
Trustees: Mr David Baldock, Mr Graeme Wallace, Mr Kevin John Cox, Professor Andrew Balmford, Professor Colin Galbraith, Mr Neil Ransome, Mr Clive Mellon, Professor Rosemary S Hails, Prof Sir Adrian Leonard Webb, Helen Mary Browning OBE, Viscount Christopher Philip Roger Mills, Mr David Cramp, Mr Nick Cross, Mr John Bullock, Ms Jennifer Ullman, Mr Stephen Moss, Mr Martin Stuart Saunders
Income: £134,179,000 [2017]; £136,994,000 [2016]; £132,872,000 [2015]; £127,045,000 [2014]; £122,114,000 [2013]

The Royal Society of Biology

Registered: 4 Jul 1979 *Employees:* 33 *Volunteers:* 500
Website: rsb.org.uk
Activities: Education, training; arts, culture, heritage, science; environment, conservation, heritage
Address: The Society of Biology, Charles Darwin House, 12 Roger Street, London, WC1N 2JU
Trustees: Professor Patricia Kuwabara, John Coggins, Dr Kim Rachael Hardie, Professor Dame Julia Goodfellow, Professor Nigel Brown, Dr Paul Hoskisson, Professor Claire Wathes, Professor Yvonne Barnett, Professor Patrick Hussey, Dr Paul Charles Brooker FSB, Professor Caroline Austin, Professor Richard Reece, Professor Jackie Hunter, Dr Louise Leong, Professor Hilary MacQueen
Income: £2,490,000 [2016]; £2,430,700 [2015]; £2,689,400 [2014]; £2,646,100 [2013]; £1,805,300 [2012]

The Royal Society of Chemistry

Registered: 24 Dec 1963 *Employees:* 544 *Volunteers:* 1,500
Tel: 01223 432521 *Website:* rsc.org
Activities: General charitable purposes; education, training
Address: The Royal Society of Chemistry, 290-292 Science Park, Milton Road, Cambridge, CB4 0WF
Trustees: Professor Geoffrey Maitland MA DPhil CChem FRSC, Professor Michael Ashfold BSc PhD CChem FRSC FRS, Professor Ben Feringa CChem HonFRSC, Professor Sir John Holman BA MA CChem FRSC, Professor Sabine Flitsch DPhil MA DipChem CChem FRSC, Professor Andrew Bell BA PhD CChem FRSC, Ms Julia Hatto BEM BSc CSci CChem FRSC, Professor Thomas Simpson BSc PhD CChem FRSC FRSE FRS, Dr Janette Waterhouse BSc MSc PhD EurChem CChem FRSC, Dr David Rees PhD CChem FRSC, Professor Thomas Welton OBE BSc DPhil CChem FRSC, Professor Polly Arnold OBE BA MA DPhil CChem FRSC FRSE, Professor Melissa Hanna-Brown BSc PhD CChem FRSC, Dr Paul W Satchell BSc PhD CChem FRSC, Dr Elizabeth Rowsell FRSC, Professor Dame Carol Robinson DBE MSc PhD HonFRSC FRS
Income: £55,689,000 [2016]; £53,989,000 [2015]; £53,940,000 [2014]; £51,602,000 [2013]; £49,126,000 [2012]

The Royal Society of London for Improving Natural Knowledge (commonly known as the Royal Society)

Registered: 22 Jan 1963 *Employees:* 167
Website: royalsociety.org
Activities: Education, training; other charitable purposes
Address: 6-9 Carlton House Terrace, London, SW1Y 5AG
Trustees: Dame Bridget Ogilvie AC DBE FMedSci FRS, Sir John Skehel FMedSci FRS, Professor Richard Catlow FRS, Professor Cheryll Tickle CBE FMedSci FRS, Professor Russell Foster CBE FRS, Dame Carol Robinson DBE FMedSci FRS, Professor Gillian Bates FMedSci FRS, Professor George Efstathiou FRS, Sir Venki Ramakrishnan PRS, Professor Eleanor Campbell FRS, Dame Sue Ion DBE FREng FRS, Professor Julia Yeomans FRS, Professor Andrew Hopper CBE FREng FRS, Mr Keith Burnett Sir, Professor Ulrike Tillmann FRS, Professor Brian Foster OBE FRS, Prof Alex Halliday, Sir Leszek Borysiewicz FMedSci FRS, Sir Richard Treisman FMedSci FRS, Professor Simon White FRS, Professor Jean Beggs CBE FRS, Dr Mariann Bienz FMedSci FRS, Professor Karen Steel FMedSci FRS
Income: £83,920,435 [2017]; £77,467,931 [2016]; £75,072,000 [2015]; £70,577,000 [2014]; £70,626,000 [2013]

The Royal Society of Medicine

Registered: 22 Sep 1962 *Employees:* 236
Tel: 020 7290 2900 *Website:* rsm.ac.uk
Activities: Education, training; advancement of health or saving of lives; arts, culture, heritage, science
Address: 1 Wimpole Street, London, W1G 0AE
Trustees: Professor Sir Andrew Haines, Professor Nadey Hakim KCJSJ MD PhD FRCS FRCSI FACS, Dr Rachel Hargest MD FRCS, Dr Susan Horsewood-Lee MB BS MRCGP, Mr Adrian Beckingsale, Dr Rashmi Patel, Rev Hilary De Lyon, Dr Natasha Robinson MA MBBS FRCA FRCP PGCert Oxon, Mr Babulal Sethia MB BS FRCS, Sir David Clementi, Mr Martin Bailey BSc FRCSEd, Dr Gillian Leng, Professor Emeritus James Spencer Malpas MB BSc DPhil FRCP FRCR FFPM FRCP, Mr Peter Richardson, Professor Roger Motson MS FRCS, Professor John Axford DSC MD FRCP FRCPCH
Income: £15,907,000 [2017]; £16,049,000 [2016]; £16,173,000 [2015]; £16,630,000 [2014]; £19,127,000 [2013]

Royal Society of Wildlife Trusts

Registered: 22 Sep 1962 *Employees:* 58 *Volunteers:* 5
Tel: 01636 677711 *Website:* wildlifetrusts.org
Activities: Environment, conservation, heritage
Address: The Wildlife Trusts, The Kiln, Waterside, Mather Road, Newark, Notts, NG24 1WT
Trustees: Mr Stewart Goshawk, Carole Nicholson, Bill Stow, Prof Rod Aspinwall OBE, Mrs Anne Selby, Jennifer Fulton, Mr Ian Brown, Mr Michael Power, Mrs Ruth Elizabeth Sutherland, Mr Peter Young, Peta Foxall, Mr Jonathan Hughes
Income: £14,918,000 [2017]; £11,818,000 [2016]; £9,226,000 [2015]; £15,754,000 [2014]; £23,082,000 [2013]

The Royal Star & Garter Homes

Registered: 22 Sep 1962 *Employees:* 245 *Volunteers:* 70
Tel: 020 8481 7667 *Website:* starandgarter.org
Activities: Disability; accommodation, housing; armed forces, emergency service efficiency
Address: The Royal Star & Garter Homes, 15 Castle Mews, Hampton, Surrey, TW12 2NP
Trustees: Surgeon Rear Admiral M Farquharson-Roberts CBE PhD MA MB FRCS, Malcolm Chapple Barrister at Law BSc FCIArb, Mr Christopher Harrison, Major General Timothy Tyler CB MA, Professor Suzanna Rose JP DL PhD MA RN, Matt Petersen MA, Colonel Alison McCourt, Air Vice-Marshal Simon Dougherty MSc MBBS FRCP FFOM DAvMed, Mr Mark Wills BSc FRGS DipAIBD MInstRE, Ms Amanda Francis DSS BSc ACA, Ms Susan J Bush RRC MBA BA, Captain Julie Thain-Smith MSc BSc RN, William Reid BA Chartered FCSI FRSA, Mr Digby Flower BSc MRICS
Income: £15,870,000 [2016]; £20,928,000 [2015]; £67,642,000 [2014]; £15,972,000 [2013]; £17,764,000 [2012]

Royal Statistical Society

Registered: 25 Feb 1964 *Employees:* 27 *Volunteers:* 1,400
Tel: 020 7638 8998 *Website:* rss.org.uk
Activities: General charitable purposes; education, training
Address: Royal Statistical Society, 12 Errol Street, London, EC1Y 8LX
Trustees: Professor Peter Diggle, Dr Paul Baxter, Dr Karen Facey, Mr Simon Briscoe, Dr Kimberley Kavanagh, Professor Sandra Eldridge, Dr James Tucker, Professor Giuliana Battisti, Dr Malcolm Hall, Professor Guy Nason, Dr Lucinda Billingham, Dr Claire Gormley, Dr Andrew Sutherland, Professor Gareth Roberts, Professor Christl Donnelly, Dr Simon White, Dr Mark Briers, Professor Emma McCoy, Professor Robin Henderson, Mr Blaise Egan, Mr Stephen Penneck, Dr Moira Musgglestone, Ms Daniela De Angelis, Dr Jennifer Doherty-Nee Rogers, Mr Trevor Llanwarne, Mr Apostolos Fakis, Dr Jennifer Mehew, Professor David Spiegelhalter, Professor Arnoldo Frigessi, Dr Lisa Hampson, Mr Phil Woodward, Professor Deborah Ashby, Professor John Kent, Ms Sharon Witherspoon, Professor Ruth King, Miss Sara Hilditch
Income: £2,352,855 [2016]; £2,051,291 [2015]; £2,065,687 [2014]; £2,087,062 [2013]; £2,103,410 [2012]

The Royal Surgical Aid Society

Registered: 13 Jul 1964 *Employees:* 6
Activities: Education, training; advancement of health or saving of lives
Address: CAN Mezzanine, 7-14 Great Dover Street, London, SE1 4YR
Trustees: Mr Alan Cogbill, Mrs Elizabeth Amanda Houlihan, Christine Ann Bailey, Mrs Caroline Denise Stevens, Dr Richard David Drummond, Mr Darren Lee Garner, Mr David James Goodridge, Miss Danota Anna Woda, Mr Lee Richard Marple, Dr Anthony Burch, Mr Daniel Lopes Carrico
Income: £1,422,000 [2016]; £5,851,000 [2015]; £7,767,000 [2014]; £6,468,000 [2013]; £6,909,000 [2012]

Royal Television Society

Registered: 29 Apr 1965 *Employees:* 21 *Volunteers:* 900
Tel: 020 7822 2815 *Website:* rts.org.uk
Activities: Education, training; arts, culture, heritage, science
Address: Royal Television Society, 3 Dorset Rise, London, EC4Y 8EN
Trustees: David Lowen, Ms Jane Lighting, Mr John Hardie, Graham McWilliam, Tim Davie, Mr Graeme Thompson, Mr David Huw Jones, Mike Green, Simon Pitts, Jane Turton
Income: £3,421,000 [2016]; £2,941,000 [2015]; £2,730,210 [2014]; £2,850,589 [2013]; £2,452,243 [2012]

The Royal Town Planning Institute

Registered: 17 Sep 1971 *Employees:* 64 *Volunteers:* 600
Tel: 020 7929 9494 *Website:* rtpi.org.uk
Activities: General charitable purposes; education, training; environment, conservation, heritage; economic, community development, employment
Address: The Royal Town Planning Institute, 41-42 Botolph Lane, London, EC3R 8DL
Trustees: Mr John Powell, Mr Andrew Taylor, Mr Graham Stallwood, Tony Crook, Sue Bridge, Miss Lucy Seymour-Bowdery, Tom Venables, Mr David Frank Stovell, Mr John Fenna, Mr Colin Haylock, Dr Peter Geraghty, Mr Ian Angus, Mr Stephen Wilkinson, Mr Ian Tant, Mr John Acres, Ms Bernadette Celeste Hillman, Ms Janet Mary Askew
Income: £6,206,000 [2016]; £7,067,000 [2015]; £7,158,000 [2014]; £6,437,000 [2013]; £6,050,000 [2012]

Royal Trinity Hospice

Registered: 28 Aug 1992 *Employees:* 232 *Volunteers:* 581
Website: royaltrinityhospice.london
Activities: Education, training; advancement of health or saving of lives
Address: Royal Trinity Hospice, 30 Clapham Common North Side, London, SW4 0RN
Trustees: Mrs Alison Elizabeth Petit, Dr Geraldine Walters, Adrian Williams Chairman, James Hibbert, Felicity Harvey, Mr James Anthony Piper, David Clarson, Mrs Katharine Jackson, Mrs Tessa Howard, Dr Naveen Puri, Mr William Buller
Income: £12,427,649 [2017]; £12,672,970 [2016]; £11,061,241 [2015]; £10,802,632 [2014]; £10,320,154 [2013]

Royal United Hospital Charitable Fund

Registered: 27 Sep 1996 *Employees:* 13 *Volunteers:* 100
Tel: 01225 825613 *Website:* ruh.nhs.uk
Activities: General charitable purposes; education, training; advancement of health or saving of lives; arts, culture, heritage, science
Address: Royal United Hospital, Combe Park, Bath, BA1 3NG
Trustees: Royal United Hospitals Bath NHS Foundation Trust
Income: £2,181,548 [2017]; £2,332,590 [2016]; £1,596,651 [2015]; £5,349,814 [2014]; £1,684,045 [2013]

The Royal United Kingdom Beneficent Association

Registered: 11 Aug 1962 *Employees:* 109 *Volunteers:* 1,131
Tel: 020 7605 4206 *Website:* independentage.org
Activities: General charitable purposes; prevention or relief of poverty
Address: 18 Avonmore Road, London, W14 8RR
Trustees: Professor Martin Green OBE, Mr Richard Gutch, Ms Estelle McCartney, Ms Tracey Bleakley, Dame Helena Shovelton, Mr Paul Richardson, Mr Noel Shanahan, Ms Denise Wilkinson OBE, Dr Justine Frain, Mr James Steel, Ms Vivienne Dews, Mr John Hannaford, Mr Mike Craston, Mr Simon Inchley
Income: £7,181,000 [2016]; £14,343,000 [2015]; £8,122,000 [2014]; £8,168,000 [2013]; £9,443,000 [2012]

The Royal United Services Institute for Defence and Security Studies
Registered: 4 Oct 1962 *Employees:* 63 *Volunteers:* 10
Website: rusi.org
Activities: Other charitable purposes
Address: RUSI, Whitehall, London, SW1A 2ET
Trustees: Sir Roger Bone, Sir John Scarlett KCMG OBE, Mr Andrew Jamieson, The Rt Hon The Lord Hague of Richmond, General Sir Nick Houghton GCB CBE ADC, Mr John Dowdy, Mr Stephen Phipson CBE, Mr Ian Willis, Baroness Catherine Ashton, Mr Nik Gowing, His Grace The Duke of Wellington Charles Wellesley OBE DL, Ms Alison Levitt QC
Income: £6,699,460 [2017]; £5,564,575 [2016]; £5,535,501 [2015]; £4,110,053 [2014]; £3,175,642 [2013]

Royal Variety Charity
Registered: 22 Sep 1962 *Employees:* 62 *Volunteers:* 2
Tel: 020 8898 8164 *Website:* royalvarietycharity.org
Activities: General charitable purposes; advancement of health or saving of lives; prevention or relief of poverty; accommodation, housing
Address: 72 Staines Road, Twickenham, Middlesex, TW2 5AL
Trustees: Mr Laurie Mansfield, Mr Ian Anthony Freeman, Mr Nilesh J Ruparel, Mr Philip Dale, Mr Giles Cooper
Income: £2,560,552 [2016]; £2,936,641 [2015]; £2,458,110 [2014]; £2,464,147 [2013]; £2,681,178 [2012]

The Royal Veterinary College Animal Care Trust
Registered: 15 Dec 1980 *Employees:* 6 *Volunteers:* 5
Tel: 01707 666237 *Website:* rvc.ac.uk
Activities: Education, training; arts, culture, heritage, science; animals; environment, conservation, heritage
Address: Royal Veterinary College, Hawkshead House, Hawkshead Lane, North Mymms, Hatfield, Herts, AL9 7TA
Trustees: The Council
Income: £1,308,762 [2017]; £2,005,954 [2016]; £1,488,000 [2015]; £1,143,000 [2014]; £941,000 [2013]

Royal Voluntary Service
Registered: 31 Dec 1992 *Employees:* 1,283 *Volunteers:* 25,000
Tel: 029 2073 9119 *Website:* royalvoluntaryservice.org.uk
Activities: General charitable purposes
Address: Royal Voluntary Service, Cardiff Gate Beck Court, Cardiff Gate Business Park, Pontprennau, Cardiff, CF23 8RP
Trustees: Mr Richard Greenhalgh, Ms Fiona Joyce, Miss June Patricia Mulroy, Ms Tracey Julie McNeill, Ms Sophie Elizabeth Livingstone, Mr David Anthony Rose, Miss Rosemary Helen Brook, Mr Martin Smith, Dr Alison Margaret Fielding PhD, Mrs Josephine Sarah Swinhoe, Mr Andrew John Moys, Mr Ian Peter Cranna
Income: £64,453,000 [2017]; £64,730,000 [2016]; £68,613,000 [2015]; £71,028,000 [2014]; £73,217,000 [2013]

Royal Wanstead School
Registered: 4 Nov 1963 *Employees:* 8
Tel: 020 3405 3630 *Website:* rncf.org.uk
Activities: Education, training; human rights, religious or racial harmony, equality or diversity
Address: RNCSF, 7 Grosvenor Gardens, London, SW1W 0BD
Trustees: Mr Kevin Allen Huw Parry MA FCA, Mr Patrick Derham, Mr Tim Bunting, Mrs Helen Starkie, Mr Eraj Shirvani, Mr Clive Marshall, Douglas J De Brule, Mr Richard Lewis, Mr Robert Swannell CBE, Andrew Corbett, Mr William De Winton, Mr Patrick Smudlers
Income: £1,725,531 [2017]; £1,502,583 [2016]; £1,087,244 [2015]; £1,219,835 [2014]; £908,121 [2013]

The Royal Welsh Agricultural Society Limited
Registered: 21 Feb 1967 *Employees:* 46 *Volunteers:* 800
Tel: 01982 553683 *Website:* rwas.co.uk
Activities: General charitable purposes; education, training; arts, culture, heritage, science; animals; environment, conservation, heritage; economic, community development, employment
Address: The Royal Welsh Agricultural Society Limited, Llanelwedd, Builth Wells, Powys, LD2 3SY
Trustees: Mr Edward Morgan, Mr Brian Davies, Mr Alun Evans CBE DL FRAgS, Mr Gwynne Davies ARAGS, Mr Edward Llewellyn Evans BSc FRAgS, Mr Harry Fetherstonhaugh OBE DL FRAgS, Mr John Derek Rees, Mr Arthur Ellis Davies FRAgS, Mr David Lewis DL FRICS FLAA FRAgS, Mr John Clive Alexander, Mr Alwyn Rees FRAgS, Mrs Nicola Davies, Mr John Thomas FRAgS, Mr Roger Perkins FRAgS, Mr John Thomas Davies, Mr Richard Stephen Gwilliam, Mr John R Davies FRAgS, Miss Susan Nia Lloyd, Mr Eric Jones, Mrs Rhian Duggan, Edward Owen, Mrs Susan Jones, Mrs Karen Spencer MBE ARAGS, Mr David Thomas James Powell, Dr Fred Slater, Mr John Vaughan DL JP FRAgS, Mr William Isaac Cyril Davies BSc FRAgS, Mr Richard Davies, Mr Gareth Roberts FRAgS, Mr Howard Nixon, Mr Hywel Lloyd, Mr Selwyn Evans, Mr Peter Evans BSc CEng MICE, Mrs Janet Phillips, Mr Allan Evans, Mr William Hanks, Mrs Menna Evans, Prof E Wynne Jones, Mr Len Bigley, Mr Dafydd Jones
Income: £6,088,754 [2016]; £5,953,570 [2015]; £5,945,790 [2014]; £5,540,978 [2013]; £5,228,464 [2012]

Royal Welsh College of Music and Drama
Registered: 9 Dec 2010 *Employees:* 176
Tel: 01443 654171 *Website:* rwcmd.ac.uk
Activities: Education, training; arts, culture, heritage, science
Address: University of South Wales, Treforest, Pontypridd, Rhondda Cynon Taf, CF37 1DL
Trustees: Professor George Caird, Mr Brian Weir, Ms Clare Hudson, Mrs Jemma Terry, Professor Julie Lydon, Mr John Derrick, Mr Jonathan Frost, Mr Lloyd Pearce
Income: £13,579,000 [2017]; £13,006,000 [2016]; £11,769,000 [2015]; £12,964,000 [2014]; £11,675,000 [2013]

The Royal Wolverhampton School
Registered: 27 May 2002 *Employees:* 238
Tel: 01902 341230 *Website:* theroyalschool.co.uk
Activities: Education, training
Address: The Royal Wolverhampton School, Penn Road, Wolverhampton, W Midlands, WV3 0EG
Trustees: Mr Peter Hill, Mr Mike Masters, Mr Abdul Kashem Muhammad Harunar Rashid
Income: £8,826,750 [2016]; £7,769,167 [2015]; £6,897,880 [2014]; £5,842,106 [2013]; £5,562,549 [2012]

Ruach City Church
Registered: 9 May 1995 *Employees:* 29 *Volunteers:* 1,000
Tel: 020 8678 6888 *Website:* ruachcitychurch.org
Activities: General charitable purposes; prevention or relief of poverty; religious activities; arts, culture, heritage, science
Address: Ruach Ministries, 122 Brixton Hill, London, SW2 1RS
Trustees: Mrs Carol Campayne, Miss Dorothea Hodge, Paul Brightly-Jones, Miss Sarah Herbert
Income: £2,770,494 [2017]; £3,025,510 [2016]; £2,962,505 [2015]; £3,914,618 [2014]; £3,552,963 [2013]

The Ruddock Foundation for The Arts
Registered: 17 Mar 2010
Tel: 020 7313 9350
Activities: General charitable purposes; arts, culture, heritage, science; environment, conservation, heritage
Address: 10 Colville Mews, London, W11 2DA
Trustees: Sir Paul Ruddock, Michael Fullerlove, Miss Isabella Shaw Ruddock, Lady Jill Shaw Ruddock, Sophie Ruddock
Income: £1,532,505 [2017]; £1,228,549 [2016]; £1,294,288 [2015]; £779,253 [2014]; £296,684 [2013]

The Rufford Foundation
Registered: 15 Dec 2006 *Employees:* 5
Tel: 020 7436 8604 *Website:* rufford.org
Activities: Animals; environment, conservation, heritage
Address: 6th Floor, The Rufford Foundation, 250 Tottenham Court Road, London, W1T 7QZ
Trustees: Robert Kenneth Reilly, Mr Iain Smailes, Hugo Benjamin Edwards, John Hedley Laing, Elizabeth Sarah Brunwin, Sarah Margaret Elizabeth Barbour
Income: £4,894,798 [2017]; £4,564,505 [2016]; £3,575,027 [2015]; £3,656,366 [2014]; £68,983,707 [2013]

Rugby Football Foundation
Registered: 23 Oct 2003
Tel: 020 8831 7790 *Website:* rugbyfootballfoundation.org
Activities: Education, training; amateur sport
Address: Rugby Football Union, 200 Whitton Road, Twickenham, Middlesex, TW2 7BA
Trustees: Mr Malcolm Wharton CBE, Peter Grace, Neil Hagerty, Mr Philip Robert Johnson, Sheila Pancholi, Richard Daniel
Income: £30,811,707 [2017]; £28,630,185 [2016]; £25,822,359 [2015]; £17,707,270 [2014]; £23,041,305 [2013]

The Rugby Free Church Homes for the Aged
Registered: 14 Feb 1963 *Employees:* 62 *Volunteers:* 15
Tel: 01788 813147 *Website:* biltonhouse.org.uk
Activities: Accommodation, housing
Address: Bilton House, 5 Bawnmore Road, Bilton, Rugby, Warwicks, CV22 7QH
Trustees: Mrs Catherine Howard, Mrs Madeleine Joyce Prager, Mrs Rachel Millward, Mrs Hilary Cox, Mr Kelvin Beer-Jones BA, Mr Stanley Raymond Bird, Mr Doug Wells, Rev Robert John Maloney, Mrs Rosemary Pugh
Income: £1,210,922 [2017]; £1,160,896 [2016]; £1,070,046 [2015]; £1,056,116 [2014]; £1,175,292 [2013]

Rugby School
Registered: 22 Jan 1971 *Employees:* 558 *Volunteers:* 20
Tel: 01788 556260 *Website:* rugbyschool.co.uk
Activities: Education, training
Address: Rugby School Bursary, 10 Little Church Street, Rugby, Warwicks, CV21 3AW
Trustees: David Urquhart, Mr Anthony Thomas, Mr Barry O'Brien, Dr E Wood, Christopher Howe, Mr Patrick Smulders, Miss Janet Eastwood, Mr Gareth Lloyd-Jones, Lieutenant General Tim Radford, Mr Simon Lebus, Mrs L Holmes BA, Ms Gemma Woodward, Mr R Hingley, Mr David Bennett, Ms Charlotte Marten, Mrs Helen Jackson, Mr John Moreland, Mr Jake Elmhirst
Income: £34,784,326 [2017]; £31,779,395 [2016]; £32,336,709 [2015]; £31,653,952 [2014]; £30,144,569 [2013]

The Rumi Foundation
Registered: 7 Jul 2006 *Volunteers:* 3
Tel: 020 7227 7000 *Website:* rumifoundation.com
Activities: General charitable purposes; education, training; advancement of health or saving of lives; prevention or relief of poverty; accommodation, housing; arts, culture, heritage, science; amateur sport; environment, conservation, heritage
Address: Bircham Dyson Bell, 50 Broadway, London, SW1H 0BL
Trustees: Mr David Murithi, Mr Jehad Verjee, Mr Brent Pollard
Income: £5,272,571 [2017]; £33,437,953 [2016]; £941,482 [2015]; £4,186,210 [2014]; £11,368,169 [2013]

Rupert House School
Registered: 2 Jan 1964 *Employees:* 51
Tel: 01491 635792 *Website:* ruperthouse.org
Activities: Education, training
Address: Rupert House School, 90-92 Bell Street, Henley on Thames, Oxon, RG9 2BN
Trustees: Mrs Anne Collinson, Mrs Rosanne Murison, Jim Hamilton-Smith, Mr Edward Hellings, Mrs Vanessa Moira Pilgerstorfer, Mr Jonathan Michael Phillips, Dr M Brennan, Neil Boddington, Ms Beverley Cecilia McKenzie, Mrs Gillian Little, Mr Paul Edward Falinski
Income: £2,142,577 [2016]; £2,097,677 [2015]; £1,990,838 [2014]; £1,908,156 [2013]

The Rural Community Council of Essex
Registered: 11 Apr 2003 *Employees:* 34 *Volunteers:* 30
Tel: 01277 353605 *Website:* essexrcc.org.uk
Activities: General charitable purposes; education, training; prevention or relief of poverty; accommodation, housing; economic, community development, employment
Address: 17 North Court, Summerfields, Ingatestone, Essex, CM4 0BD
Trustees: Mr Martyn Drain, Mr Simon Lyster, Mr Ralph Bray, Mrs Mary St Aubyn, Mr Peter James Martin, Mr Roger Brice, Mr Nicholas Spencer Charrington, Mr Simon Michael Walsh, Gillian Hayter, Mr Simon Robert Brice, Mr Martin Stuchfield MBE, Ms Sarah Pinkerton
Income: £1,264,444 [2017]; £1,229,942 [2016]; £1,300,672 [2015]; £762,236 [2014]; £615,405 [2013]

Rushmoor School Limited
Registered: 25 Oct 1965 *Employees:* 156 *Volunteers:* 20
Tel: 01234 305669 *Website:* rushmoorschool.co.uk
Activities: Education, training
Address: 96 Winchester Road, Bedford, MK42 0SB
Trustees: Hon Alderman Graham Bates, Mr Clive Simmonds, Mr Brian Thompson, Mr David Eyton-Williams, Tricia Lennie, Mr James Leydon, Mr Ivan Flack, Mr Stephen John Williamson, Mr John Wilkinson, Mrs Mary Burt, Mr Michael Grafton
Income: £5,325,506 [2017]; £4,787,145 [2016]; £5,014,838 [2015]; £5,135,221 [2014]; £2,736,751 [2013]

Ruskin College
Registered: 7 Mar 1963 *Employees:* 65
Tel: 01865 759600 *Website:* ruskin.ac.uk
Activities: Education, training
Address: Ruskin Hall, Dunstan Road, Headington, Oxford, OX3 9BZ
Trustees: Doug Nicholls, Pearl Ryall, Mr Roger McKenzie, Mr Alan Shepherd, Mr Peter Gerard Dwyer, Dr Bridget Ng'andu, Mr Christopher James Baugh, Mr Ed Hart, Mr Jordan Smith, Ms Carole-Pauline Orgell-Rosen, Mr Kieron Winters, Ms Elizabeth Anne Hock, Ms Wendy Hope Dawson, Mr Paul Inman, Mr Neil Crew, Mr Paul Di Felice, Ms Chloe Elizabeth Walsh
Income: £5,507,413 [2017]; £5,449,906 [2016]; £5,087,481 [2015]; £4,686,769 [2014]; £3,980,639 [2013]

Ruskin Mill Land Trust
Registered: 11 Mar 1996 *Employees:* 16
Tel: 01453 837537
Activities: Education, training
Address: Ruskin Mill, Millbottom, Nailsworth, Stroud, Glos, GL6 0LA
Trustees: Ruskin Mill Land Trust Limited
Income: £2,798,111 [2017]; £4,535,912 [2016]; £2,611,588 [2015]; £2,386,677 [2014]; £2,309,245 [2013]

Ruskin Mill Trust Limited
Registered: 29 Jul 2010 *Employees:* 1,159 *Volunteers:* 10
Website: rmt.org
Activities: Education, training; disability; environment, conservation, heritage
Address: Ruskin Mill, Millbottom, Nailsworth, Stroud, Glos, GL6 0LA
Trustees: Vivian Griffiths, Aonghus Gordon, Nick Stuart, Dr Peter Gruenewald, Mrs Kerry Ann Shillito, Tara Gratton, Guy Vassall-Adams QC, Mr Phillip Forder, Mrs Helen Kippax, Brian Simpson, Ms Victoria Watts, Chloe Amber Hindmarsh, Jorunn Barane
Income: £28,296,575 [2017]; £20,745,912 [2016]; £20,323,140 [2015]; £20,900,684 [2014]; £20,485,512 [2013]

Russell School Trust
Registered: 16 Aug 1976 *Employees:* 215 *Volunteers:* 25
Tel: 020 8657 9702 *Website:* royalrussell.co.uk
Activities: Education, training
Address: Russell School Trust, Coombe Lane, Croydon, Surrey, CR9 5BX
Trustees: Mr Simon Henry Kolesar FRICS, Mr Andrew Merriman, Mrs Anne Martin, Mrs Lisa Jane Jessup, Mrs Jane Victoria Burton, Mr Andrew Lorie, Mr Nicholas Cobill, Dr Agnelo Fernandes, Mr James Penny ACIB FSI, Sir Philip Drury Moor QC, Mrs Jane Ellen Ann Stevens, Mr James Douglas Lacey, Mr Rohit Mathur
Income: £17,106,776 [2017]; £16,114,444 [2016]; £14,963,391 [2015]; £14,022,835 [2014]; £13,893,737 [2013]

Russell-Cotes Art Gallery and Museum
Registered: 30 Jul 1962 *Employees:* 15 *Volunteers:* 35
Tel: 01202 451812 *Website:* russellcotes.com
Activities: Education, training; arts, culture, heritage, science
Address: Russell-Cotes Art Gallery & Museum, East Cliff, Bournemouth, BH1 3AA
Trustees: Bournemouth Borough Council
Income: £1,268,879 [2017]; £1,198,912 [2016]; £1,449,410 [2015]; £1,721,511 [2014]; £1,161,808 [2013]

Rustington Convalescent Home (Carpenters Company)
Registered: 17 Jul 1968 *Employees:* 49
Tel: 020 7588 7001 *Website:* rustcon.co.uk
Activities: The advancement of health or saving of lives
Address: Carpenters' Hall, 1 Throgmorton Avenue, London, EC2N 2JJ
Trustees: The Worshipful Company of Carpenters
Income: £1,367,338 [2016]; £1,455,087 [2015]; £1,350,410 [2014]; £1,249,459 [2013]; £1,217,336 [2012]

Ruthin School
Registered: 1 Sep 1976 *Employees:* 91 *Volunteers:* 5
Tel: 01824 702543 *Website:* ruthinschool.co.uk
Activities: Education, training
Address: Ruthin School, Ruthin, Denbighshire, LL15 1EE
Trustees: Mrs Tracey Oriole Kerrigan, His Honour Judge Ian Trigger, Rev John Stuart Evans, Dr Glyn Hywel Roberts, Mr John Edward Sharples, Mrs Julie Oldbury, Mr Christopher William Conway
Income: £7,472,128 [2017]; £5,854,159 [2016]; £4,778,506 [2015]; £3,768,448 [2014]; £3,278,758 [2013]

Rydal Penrhos Limited
Registered: 17 Jul 1997 *Employees:* 170
Tel: 01492 532728 *Website:* rydalpenrhos.com
Activities: Education, training
Address: Rydal Penrhos, Pwllycrochan Avenue, Colwyn Bay, Conwy, LL29 7BT
Trustees: Mr John Payne, Mr John Maxwell Ashby Wilford, Mr Ralph Whitaker Dransfield, Mr Nigel Bickerton, Mr Julian Barnes, Mrs Christine Evans Lunt, Mr John Edward Waszek, Mr David Charles Humphreys, Mrs Bessie Anne Mary Watson, Mr John Paul Burgess, Stephen Wigley, Mr Iwan Meurig Williams, Mrs Nicola Rutherford, Mr Stephen David Scarff, Dr Della Fazey, John Tiernay
Income: £7,921,587 [2016]; £8,125,517 [2015]; £7,710,297 [2014]; £7,721,929 [2013]; £7,781,518 [2012]

Ryde School
Registered: 4 Mar 1964 *Employees:* 180 *Volunteers:* 30
Tel: 01983 562229 *Website:* rydeschool.org.uk
Activities: Education, training
Address: Ryde School, 7 Queens Road, Ryde, Isle of Wight, PO33 3BE
Trustees: Mr Anthony McIsaac MA DPhil, Mrs Joanna Minchin, Dr Michelle Legg, Mrs Dawn Kirsten Haig-Thomas, Mrs Annabel Harvey, Mrs Jane Bland CertEd, Stephen Drew, Dr Michael Wilson, Dr Christopher Martin DPhil BSc MBA FIChemE CEng, Mr Nicholas Wakefield, Mrs Emma Millett, Dr Christoph Lees MB BS BSc MD MRCOG, Miss Chantal-Aimee Doerries QC, Mr Philip Weeks, Mrs Joanna Wallace-Dutton
Income: £8,947,370 [2017]; £8,611,259 [2016]; £8,649,193 [2015]; £8,409,962 [2014]; £8,230,295 [2013]

Sue Ryder
Registered: 17 Jan 1996 *Employees:* 3,157 *Volunteers:* 15,842
Website: suerydercare.org
Activities: The advancement of health or saving of lives; disability; environment, conservation, heritage; other charitable purposes
Address: 16 Upper Woburn Place, London, WC1H 0AF
Trustees: Mr John Michael Wythe, Mr Michael John Attwood, Neil Goulden, Helen Thomson, Jason Davies, Jeremy Chataway, Mr Keith Gordon Cameron, Mr Murray Crombie Duncanson, Ms Margaret Anne Moore, Stuart James Hudson, Nicola Josephine Hayes
Income: £98,865,000 [2017]; £99,876,000 [2016]; £95,431,000 [2015]; £90,347,000 [2014]; £83,881,000 [2013]

Rydes Hill School Guildford
Registered: 6 Jun 1988 *Employees:* 44 *Volunteers:* 28
Tel: 01483 563160 *Website:* rydeshill.com
Activities: Education, training
Address: Rydes Hill House, Aldershotn Road, Guildford, Surrey, GU2 8BP
Trustees: Fr Robin Farrow, Mr Patrick Gloyens, Mrs Mary Robinson, Mr Dermot Gleeson, Mr Paul Jay, Mrs Jenny Shaw, Mr Mike Wagstaff, Mr Giles Delaney, Katie Cardona, Mr Stuart McPherson
Income: £1,748,746 [2017]; £1,791,933 [2016]; £1,704,658 [2015]; £1,630,050 [2014]; £1,499,968 [2013]

Rye St Antony School Limited
Registered: 25 Jan 1968 *Employees:* 120 *Volunteers:* 1
Tel: 01865 229204 *Website:* ryestantony.co.uk
Activities: Education, training
Address: Rye St Antony School, Pullens Lane, Headington, Oxford, OX3 0BY
Trustees: Mr Timothy John Morton, Mrs Hilary Jane Carless Stafford Northcote, Sean Calnan, The Revd John Jackson, Dr Eleanor Lowe, Mr Ray Potts, Mr Andrew Robert Rattue, Mr David John Parke, Ian Callaghan, Dr Tomasz Marian Maksymilia Czepiel, Mrs Susan Hampshire, Mrs Shuna Helen McGregor, Mr Simon Jacques Hugh Detre
Income: £4,962,428 [2016]; £4,933,708 [2015]; £5,075,184 [2014]; £5,218,020 [2013]

The Ryleys School Limited
Registered: 11 Jan 1967 *Employees:* 59
Tel: 01625 583241 *Website:* theryleys.com
Activities: Education, training
Address: Ryleys Lane, Alderley Edge, Cheshire, SK9 7UY
Trustees: Mr Ian Brown, Mrs Anne-Marie Hudson, Mr Daniel Slack, Mr Michael Sellars, Mrs Jennifer Limond, Mr Michael Benson
Income: £2,091,285 [2016]; £2,107,857 [2015]; £2,273,110 [2014]; £2,016,369 [2013]; £1,891,790 [2012]

S L G Charitable Trust Limited
Registered: 29 Oct 1970 *Employees:* 15 *Volunteers:* 20
Tel: 01865 241849 *Website:* slg.org.uk
Activities: Religious activities
Address: Convent of The Incarnation, Parker Street, Oxford, OX4 1TB
Trustees: Sister Avis Mary SLG, Sister Susan SLG, Sister Rosemary Kemsley, Sister Eve SLG, Sister Clare Louise SLG
Income: £1,123,483 [2017]; £1,137,962 [2016]; £1,102,274 [2015]; £1,205,730 [2014]; £1,067,371 [2013]

S W Durham Training Limited
Registered: 24 Nov 1986 *Employees:* 28 *Volunteers:* 1
Tel: 07545 930255 *Website:* swdt.co.uk
Activities: Education, training
Address: 77 Burnie Gardens, Shildon, Co Durham, DL4 1NB
Trustees: Mr S J Rose, Mr Andrew Arthur Dunn, Mr A Scott
Income: £1,843,621 [2016]; £1,353,228 [2015]; £1,992,611 [2014]; £1,863,311 [2013]

S. Anselm's School Trust Limited
Registered: 21 Sep 1970 *Employees:* 83 *Volunteers:* 8
Tel: 01629 812734 *Website:* sanselms.co.uk
Activities: Education, training
Address: St Anselms School, Stanedge Road, Bakewell, Derbys, DE45 1DP
Trustees: Mr Richard Tarbatt, Mr Robert Howard, Mr Charles Bostock, Mr William Mark David Twelves, Mr John Guy Weaving Walker, Mrs Katrina Emma Blandy Mayson, Mrs Fiona Jane Barton
Income: £2,879,000 [2016]; £2,594,000 [2015]; £2,980,398 [2014]; £3,552,008 [2013]; £3,105,111 [2012]

S4E Limited
Registered: 5 Sep 2012 *Employees:* 275
Website: servicesforeducation.co.uk
Activities: General charitable purposes; education, training; advancement of health or saving of lives; arts, culture, heritage, science
Address: Unit 2 Holt Court, Holt Street, Birmingham Science Park, Aston, Birmingham, B7 4AX
Trustees: Mr Eric Williams, Mr Selwyn Calvin, Mr Matthew Clements-Wheeler, Mr Martin Edward Chitty, Ms Sarah Elizabeth Smith
Income: £8,128,210 [2017]; £8,143,830 [2016]; £8,352,987 [2015]; £7,425,121 [2014]; £9,876,404 [2013]

SANE
Registered: 10 Apr 1987 *Employees:* 22 *Volunteers:* 60
Tel: 020 3805 1756 *Website:* sane.org.uk
Activities: General charitable purposes; education, training; advancement of health or saving of lives; disability; human rights, religious or racial harmony, equality or diversity; other charitable purposes
Address: First Floor, St Marks Studios Business Centre, 14 Chillingworth Road, Islington, London, N7 8QJ
Trustees: David Gladstone, Mr Robert Anthony Matthews, Mr John Crocket Bowis, Prof Dinesh Kumar Bhugra, Mr Charles Edward Bracken, Mr Patrick Lorn MacDougall, Ms Veronica Russell Hon, Mr Mark Davison
Income: £1,326,148 [2017]; £1,361,054 [2016]; £1,000,448 [2015]; £1,074,891 [2014]; £1,295,050 [2013]

SF Foundation
Registered: 13 Sep 2004
Tel: 020 8802 5492
Activities: General charitable purposes; education, training; prevention or relief of poverty; religious activities
Address: 143 Upper Clapton Road, London, E5 9DB
Trustees: Mrs Rivka Niederman, Ms Hannah Jacob, Mrs M Schreiber
Income: £5,729,532 [2017]; £9,536,204 [2016]; £6,980,561 [2015]; £6,999,305 [2014]; £5,763,860 [2013]

SHAP Ltd
Registered: 15 Apr 1999 *Employees:* 130 *Volunteers:* 8
Tel: 01744 454056 *Website:* shap.org.uk
Activities: General charitable purposes; advancement of health or saving of lives; prevention or relief of poverty; accommodation, housing; human rights, religious or racial harmony, equality or diversity; other charitable purposes
Address: SHAP Ltd, 2nd Floor, Lakeside Building, Prescot Road, St Helens, Merseyside, WA10 3TT
Trustees: Mr David Tighe, Claire Ingle, Ms Mary Milton
Income: £3,887,982 [2017]; £3,811,516 [2016]; £3,466,380 [2015]; £3,327,641 [2014]; £3,160,297 [2013]

SIM International (UK)
Registered: 6 Sep 1963 *Employees:* 23 *Volunteers:* 25
Tel: 01892 824051 *Website:* sim.co.uk
Activities: Education, training; advancement of health or saving of lives; overseas aid, famine relief; religious activities
Address: Wetheringsett Manor, Wetheringsett, Stowmarket, Suffolk, IP14 5QX
Trustees: Mr Anthony Brian Harris, Dr Tim Cudmore, Miss Claire Newman, Mr Stephen Paul Smith, Mr Nigel Younge, Mr Yoseph Mengistu Woldegebreal, Mr Mark Heasman, Mr Peter Shelley, Miss Morag Gillies, Jonny Dyer, Miss Anja Lijcklama A Nijeholt
Income: £3,282,418 [2016]; £3,353,917 [2015]; £3,044,677 [2014]; £3,364,699 [2013]; £3,289,589 [2012]

SKT Welfare
Registered: 9 Sep 2013 *Employees:* 13 *Volunteers:* 631
Tel: 0300 302 0786 *Website:* sktwelfare.org
Activities: General charitable purposes; education, training; advancement of health or saving of lives; prevention or relief of poverty; overseas aid, famine relief; economic, community development, employment
Address: 652 Huddersfield Road, Dewsbury, W Yorks, WF13 3HP
Trustees: Asif Hussain, Majid Butt, Zubair Sharif
Income: £4,386,106 [2016]; £2,934,396 [2015]; £2,465,499 [2014]

SOAR Community
Registered: 10 Nov 2005 *Employees:* 33 *Volunteers:* 112
Tel: 0114 213 4065 *Website:* soarcommunity.org.uk
Activities: General charitable purposes; education, training; advancement of health or saving of lives; prevention or relief of poverty; accommodation, housing; environment, conservation, heritage; economic, community development, employment
Address: SOAR, Soar Works Enteprise Centre, 14 Knutton Road, Sheffield, S5 9NU
Trustees: Mr Peter Price, Mr Abdul Khayum, Mr Anthony Whiting, Sioned-Mair Richards, Ms Jayne Michel Hawley, Mr Michael Leslie Chaplin Cllr, Mr Chris Lewis, Bill Moloney, Mrs Eleanor Jane Houlston, Paul Howard, Miss Claire Marie Lane, Mr Benjamin James West, Ms Frances Belbin, Mr Andrew Denis Bainbridge Cllr, Mr Simon Peter Rippon, Mr Rafik Mohammed Al-Sakkaf
Income: £1,188,067 [2017]; £1,062,206 [2016]; £1,050,779 [2015]; £1,015,534 [2014]; £766,232 [2013]

SOS Children's Villages UK
Registered: 21 Apr 1998 *Employees:* 16 *Volunteers:* 3
Tel: 01223 222970 *Website:* soschildrensvillages.org.uk
Activities: Overseas aid, famine relief
Address: SOS Children's Villages UK, Terrington House, 13-15 Hills Road, Cambridge, CB2 1NL
Trustees: Ms Mary Cockcroft, The Earl of St Andrews, Mr Matthew De Villiers, Mr Don Haszczyn, Mr Michael Roger Brewer, Mrs Ayesha Khan MA Oxon, Mr Graham Budd
Income: £7,299,115 [2016]; £7,133,074 [2015]; £5,631,537 [2014]; £5,872,983 [2013]; £6,191,330 [2012]

SOS Sahel International UK
Registered: 16 Mar 1987 *Employees:* 3 *Volunteers:* 1
Tel: 01865 403305 *Website:* sahel.org.uk
Activities: Education, training; prevention or relief of poverty; overseas aid, famine relief; environment, conservation, heritage; economic, community development, employment
Address: SOS Sahel International UK, The Old Music Hall, 106-108 Cowley Road, Oxford, OX4 1JE
Trustees: Mr Jake Bharier, Mr Ian Barry, Dr Sara Pantuliano, Mr Brendan Bromwich, Mr Ian Cliff, Ms Karen Evelyn Twining Fooks, Mr Adam Nicholas Cooke, Ms Sheila McKenzie, Dr Elise Dufief
Income: £2,095,050 [2017]; £546,358 [2016]; £2,376,014 [2015]; £1,185,449 [2014]; £1,824,040 [2013]

SS Great Britain Trust
Registered: 25 Feb 1971 *Employees:* 87 *Volunteers:* 152
Tel: 0117 926 0680 *Website:* ssgreatbritain.org
Activities: Education, training; arts, culture, heritage, science; environment, conservation, heritage
Address: Great Western Dock, Gas Ferry Road, Bristol, BS1 6TY
Trustees: Sam Mullins, Mr Colin Green CBE, Mr James McKenna, Mrs Peaches Golding, Mr Jan Stam, Mrs Dinah Moore, James Whistler Berresford, Mr Kerry Lock, Dr Helen Doe, Professor Rosamund Jane Sutherland
Income: £6,106,498 [2017]; £5,257,314 [2016]; £4,922,469 [2015]; £4,177,985 [2014]; £3,832,950 [2013]

SS. John and Elizabeth Charity
Registered: 27 Aug 1964 *Employees:* 643 *Volunteers:* 120
Tel: 020 7432 8240 *Website:* hje.org.uk
Activities: The advancement of health or saving of lives
Address: 123 Beacon Hill Road, Newark, Notts, NG24 2JN
Trustees: The Hospital of St John & St Elizabeth
Income: £57,448,000 [2016]; £55,587,000 [2015]; £52,163,000 [2014]; £48,767,000 [2013]; £48,645,000 [2012]

STC Research Foundation
Registered: 5 Nov 2004 *Employees:* 35 *Volunteers:* 6
Tel: 01757 268275 *Website:* stockbridgeonline.co.uk
Activities: General charitable purposes; education, training; economic, community development, employment
Address: Stockbridge House, Cawood, Selby, N Yorks, YO8 3TZ
Trustees: Professor Carlo Leifert, Mr John Michael Richardson, Professor William Davies, Mr Martin Meredith Evans, Mr Nigel John Patrick, Mr Phillip Howard Effingham, Mr Colin Malcolm Frampton, Mr Peter Richard Branfield, Prof Janet Mary Bainbridge, Mr Julian Hargreaves, Mrs Janet Godfrey, Mr Andrew Stanley Burgess, Mr Nigel D Bartle, Mr Stephen Guy Poskitt
Income: £1,684,159 [2017]; £1,554,012 [2016]; £1,338,808 [2015]; £1,402,294 [2014]; £332,675 [2013]

The Sackler Trust
Registered: 13 Oct 2009
Tel: 020 7930 4944
Activities: General charitable purposes; education, training; advancement of health or saving of lives; overseas aid, famine relief; arts, culture, heritage, science; environment, conservation, heritage
Address: 9th Floor, New Zealand House, 80 Haymarket, London, SW1Y 4TQ
Trustees: Dame Theresa Sackler, Mr C B Mitchell, Mrs Sophia Davina Dalrymple, Ms Marianne Karin Mitchell, Mr Peter Stormonth Darling, Ms Marissa Theresa Sackler, Mr Michael Daniel Sackler, Anthony Collins
Income: £5,339,843 [2016]; £7,825,616 [2015]; £2,520,072 [2014]; £13,387,046 [2013]; £7,457,372 [2012]

Sacred Heart School Beechwood Trust Ltd
Registered: 3 Sep 1974 *Employees:* 119
Tel: 01892 532747 *Website:* beechwood.org.uk
Activities: Education, training
Address: 12 Pembury Road, Tunbridge Wells, Kent, TN2 3QD
Trustees: Sister Moira O'Sullivan, Mrs Penelope Susan Edgar, Mr Jonathan Paul Emery, Mrs Gillian Anne Hill, Mr Robert Graham Park, Mr Michael Francis Stevens, Mr Michael Southern, Dr Amanda Jenny Turner, Mrs Constance Ann Williams, Mr Gerrard Garcia
Income: £5,224,713 [2017]; £5,131,269 [2016]; £5,198,181 [2015]; £4,312,649 [2014]; £4,459,791 [2013]

The Sacred Hearts Sisters 1983 Charitable Fund
Registered: 22 Jun 1983 *Employees:* 235 *Volunteers:* 1
Tel: 020 8504 1624 *Website:* sacredheartsjm.org
Activities: Education, training; advancement of health or saving of lives; disability; prevention or relief of poverty; overseas aid, famine relief; religious activities
Address: Chigwell Convent, 803 Chigwell Road, Woodford Green, Essex, IG8 8AU
Trustees: Sr Catherine Collins, Sister Kathleen Corbett, Sr Mary Mangan, Sister Ellen McLoughlin, Sr Nora Emperor, Sr Lorna Walsh
Income: £11,135,202 [2017]; £9,424,668 [2016]; £10,085,805 [2015]; £10,539,039 [2014]; £8,765,044 [2013]

Sadler's Wells Trust Limited
Registered: 30 Apr 1980 *Employees:* 216
Website: sadlerswells.com
Activities: Education, training; arts, culture, heritage, science
Address: Sadlers Wells Theatre, Rosebery Avenue, London, EC1R 4TN
Trustees: Mrs Sarah Evans, Mr Nigel Higgins, Ms Sue Butcher, Mr Sanoke Viswanathan, Mr David Ripert, Ms Sharon White, Mr David Lan, Mr Robert Glick, Mr Tim Marlow, Ms Farah Golant, Mr Humphrey Battcock
Income: £26,802,000 [2017]; £27,558,000 [2016]; £23,654,000 [2015]; £26,836,000 [2014]; £25,668,000 [2013]

Safe Child Thailand
Registered: 6 Mar 2001 *Employees:* 10 *Volunteers:* 2
Tel: 020 7602 6203 *Website:* safechildthailand.org
Activities: General charitable purposes; education, training; advancement of health or saving of lives; disability; prevention or relief of poverty; overseas aid, famine relief; accommodation, housing
Address: 72 Venn Street, London, SW4 0AT
Trustees: Mr Crispian Collins, Mrs Saipin Lee, Ms Rachel Perowne, Ms Ananthinee Krishnan Tatparanandam, Mr Mike Parnwells, Mr Frederick Leslie Cramer, Mr Mark Patterson, Mr Anut Chatikavanij, Mr Steve Buckley
Income: £1,315,495 [2017]; £1,476,240 [2016]; £1,031,760 [2015]; £1,290,332 [2014]; £1,323,908 [2013]

Safe Families for Children
Registered: 9 Jan 2013 *Employees:* 52 *Volunteers:* 2,841
Tel: 0191 707 0031 *Website:* safefamiliesforchildren.com
Activities: General charitable purposes; education, training; advancement of health or saving of lives; prevention or relief of poverty; accommodation, housing
Address: 4 Diamond Court, Kingston Park, Newcastle upon Tyne, NE3 2EN
Trustees: Sir Peter Vardy, Rev Paul Roger Butler, Mr John David Gillam, Mr John Joseph Phillipson, Dr David Karl Anderson
Income: £1,630,136 [2017]; £2,056,277 [2016]; £1,094,197 [2015]; £515,151 [2014]; £250,000 [2013]

Safe Haven London
Registered: 29 Jul 2005
Activities: Accommodation, housing
Address: Safe Haven London, Thorncroft Manor, Thorncroft Drive, Leatherhead, Surrey, KT22 8JB
Trustees: Nicholas Francis Markham, Edward John Chesterman
Income: £3,785,378 [2017]; £4,167,304 [2016]; £4,038,908 [2015]; £3,963,678 [2014]; £3,869,307 [2013]

Safe Haven for Donkeys in the Holy Land
Registered: 17 Nov 2000 *Employees:* 20 *Volunteers:* 10
Tel: 01444 470136 *Website:* safehaven4donkeys.org
Activities: Animals
Address: Unit 23 More House Farm, Ditchling Road, Wivelsfield, Haywards Heath, W Sussex, RH17 7RE
Trustees: Safe Haven For Donkeys in The Holy Land Trustee Limited
Income: £1,260,635 [2016]; £743,780 [2015]; £1,056,695 [2014]; £570,861 [2012]; £795,894 [2011]

Safe in Tees Valley Limited
Registered: 9 Jan 2006 *Employees:* 142 *Volunteers:* 25
Tel: 01642 66440 *Website:* safeinteesvalley.org
Activities: General charitable purposes
Address: Safe in Tees Valley Ltd, Corvette House, Falcon Court, Preston Farm Industrial Estate, Stockton on Tees, Cleveland, TS18 3TX
Trustees: Ms Amanda Skelton, Ms Wendy Balmain, Mr Michael Home, Mr John Paul Bury, Mr Ian Hayton
Income: £2,199,175 [2017]; £1,899,047 [2016]; £1,451,570 [2015]; £1,369,865 [2014]; £2,674,028 [2013]

Safelives
Registered: 18 Nov 2004 *Employees:* 61 *Volunteers:* 20
Tel: 0117 403 3220 *Website:* safelives.org.uk
Activities: General charitable purposes; education, training; economic, community development, employment; other charitable purposes
Address: Suite 2A, Whitefriars, Lewins Mead, Bristol, BS1 2NT
Trustees: Mr Andrew John May, Mrs Caroline Mason, Mr Uzair Patel, Mrs Olivia Pinkney, Mr Roger Taylor, Isabel Boyer
Income: £4,594,419 [2017]; £5,344,548 [2016]; £3,682,505 [2015]; £2,736,606 [2014]; £2,278,462 [2013]

Safenet Domestic Abuse and Support Services Ltd
Registered: 5 Apr 2002 *Employees:* 58 *Volunteers:* 41
Tel: 01282 414130 *Website:* elwra.org.uk
Activities: Accommodation, housing
Address: P O Box 9, Burnley, Lancs, BB11 2RP
Trustees: Karen Ainsworth, Mrs Rachel Sylvia Horman, Dr Annie Huntington, Miss Saba Iftikhar, Miss Sharon Elizabeth Jane Livesey, Mrs Kelly Shaw
Income: £2,007,184 [2017]; £1,397,000 [2016]; £1,089,000 [2015]; £1,067,000 [2014]; £933,000 [2013]

Safer London
Registered: 11 May 2005 *Employees:* 66
Tel: 020 7021 0301 *Website:* saferlondon.org.uk
Activities: General charitable purposes; education, training; prevention or relief of poverty; economic, community development, employment
Address: 3rd Floor, Skyline House, 200 Union Street, London, SE1 0LX
Trustees: Ms Jenny Oklikah, Mr Craig Mackey, Mr Jeremy John Hall, Ms Janine Marcelle McDowell, Mr Francis Duku, Mr Bruce Melizan, Mr Tim Jones, Ms Sally Rachel Hamwee, Ms Fiona Margaret Hazell, Dr Robin Bhairam
Income: £2,531,509 [2017]; £2,047,588 [2016]; £2,062,347 [2015]; £1,563,870 [2014]; £1,973,870 [2013]

Safer Places
Registered: 16 Mar 1993 *Employees:* 65 *Volunteers:* 9
Tel: 0845 074 3216 *Website:* saferplaces.co.uk
Activities: Accommodation, housing
Address: P O Box 2489, Harlow, Essex, CM18 6WZ
Trustees: Miss Ruth Parmenter, Mr Jon Chapman, Ms Sandra Mary Johnson, Professor Erica Bowen, Mr Doug Wildey, Mr Paul Nosa Samuel, Dr Emma Howarth, Ms Alexandra Jane Hallam
Income: £3,718,884 [2017]; £3,588,194 [2016]; £3,038,138 [2015]; £2,969,978 [2014]; £2,924,965 [2013]

Safer Roads Foundation
Registered: 19 Jan 2009 *Employees:* 2
Website: saferroadsfoundation.org
Activities: The advancement of health or saving of lives; other charitable purposes
Address: c/o Bates Wells & Braithwaite, 10 Queen Street Place, London, EC4R 1BE
Trustees: Mr Michael Christopher Woodford, Mrs Anunciacion Somavilla
Income: £1,470,685 [2017]; £569,604 [2016]; £1,462,629 [2015]; £196 [2014]; £1,284 [2013]

Safer Wales
Registered: 27 Aug 1998 *Employees:* 28 *Volunteers:* 35
Tel: 029 2022 0033 *Website:* saferwales.com
Activities: Economic, community development, employment
Address: 1st Floor, Castle House, 1-7 Castle Street, Cardiff, CF10 1BS
Trustees: Professor Mike Maguire, Ms Margaret McLaughlin, Terry Flynn, Ms Kathryn-Ann Slade, Mr Woolley Christopher John, Professor Jacqueline Jones FRSA
Income: £1,171,265 [2017]; £976,625 [2016]; £837,928 [2015]; £985,665 [2014]; £962,866 [2013]

Saferworld
Registered: 2 Feb 1995 *Employees:* 153
Tel: 020 7324 4646 *Website:* saferworld.org.uk
Activities: General charitable purposes; education, training
Address: Saferworld, The Grayston Centre, 28 Charles Square, London, N1 6HT
Trustees: Dr Owen Greene, Professor Georg Erwin Frerks, Mr Jeremy Peter Lester, Mr Ismayil Tahmazov, Dr Stephanie Anne Blair, Ms Vicky Marye Knight, Mr Godfrey Charles Allen, Mr Golam Morshed, Mr Mark Robert Ross, Dr Lars-Eric Lundin, Ms Theresa Hanley, Mr David Charles Norman
Income: £15,422,000 [2017]; £12,301,000 [2016]; £10,352,000 [2015]; £11,069,000 [2014]; £9,061,000 [2013]

Saffron Hall Trust
Registered: 5 Sep 2013 *Employees:* 44 *Volunteers:* 66
Tel: 01799 588530 *Website:* saffronhall.com
Activities: Education, training; arts, culture, heritage, science
Address: Saffron Hall Trust, Council Offices, London Road, Saffron Walden, Essex, CB11 4ER
Trustees: Mr David Barrs, Professor Sir Barry William Ife CBE, Dr Nigel Wooldridge Brown OBE, Ms Caroline Derbyshire, Mr Mark Hayes, Mr Hugh Robert Parnell, Mr Geoffrey Maurice Lewis, Mrs Polly Lankester
Income: £1,498,446 [2016]; £1,331,748 [2015]; £471,500 [2014]

The Said Business School Foundation
Registered: 30 Apr 1998
Activities: Education, training; economic, community development, employment
Address: Said Business School, Park End Street, Oxford, OX1 1HP
Trustees: The Said Business School Foundation Trustee Limited
Income: £1,427,054 [2016]; £2,000,175 [2015]; £1,273,867 [2014]; £1,662,012 [2013]; £747,394 [2012]

The Said Foundation
Registered: 14 Aug 2008 *Employees:* 7
Tel: 020 7593 5420 *Website:* saidfoundation.org
Activities: General charitable purposes; education, training; advancement of health or saving of lives; arts, culture, heritage, science; economic, community development, employment
Address: 24 Queen Anne's Gate, London, SW1H 9AA
Trustees: Mrs Rosemary Said, Lord Powell of Bayswater, Sir Michael Peat, Mr Wafic Rida Said, Mrs Rasha Said Khawaja, Ms Ita Gallagher, Mrs Sirine Idilby, Ms Catherine Roe, Mr Khaled Said, Mr Jonathan Aitken, Mrs Nadine Zakaria
Income: £6,082,000 [2017]; £10,685,687 [2016]; £3,205,672 [2015]; £4,732,292 [2014]; £3,432,192 [2013]

The Saigon Children's Charity CIO
Registered: 8 Jul 2014 *Employees:* 29
Website: saigonchildren.com
Activities: Education, training; prevention or relief of poverty; economic, community development, employment
Address: 59 Tran Quoc Thao, District 3, Ho Chi Minh City, Vietnam
Trustees: Ms Diana Simone Wells, Mr Mark Anthony Fraser, Mr Alain Xavier Cany, Ms Truc Thi Thanh Nguyen, Tri-Mai Hoang, Mr Jonathon Ralph Alexander Waugh, Mr Paul Graham Cleves, Mr Paul Theodore McGee, Mr David Huw Appleton, Ms Jacqueline Lydall
Income: £1,237,700 [2016]; £1,083,642 [2015]

Sail Training International
Registered: 4 Apr 2003 *Employees:* 12 *Volunteers:* 2
Tel: 023 9258 6367 *Website:* sailtraininginternational.org
Activities: Education, training; amateur sport; environment, conservation, heritage; human rights, religious or racial harmony, equality or diversity
Address: Charles House, Gosport Marina, Mumby Road, Gosport, Hants, PO12 1AH
Trustees: Mr Douglas Allan Prothero, Mr Jonathan Cheshire, Mr Ross MacDonald, Mrs Lillian Westerberg, Mr Albert Paul Van Ommen, Lena Maekler, Mr Carlos Possollo, Mr Murray Henstock, Mr Einar Corwin
Income: £1,744,257 [2017]; £1,438,545 [2016]; £536,053 [2014]; £354,720 [2013]; £383,438 [2012]

Sailors' Society

Registered: 17 Dec 1964 *Employees:* 155 *Volunteers:* 1,400
Website: sailors-society.org
Activities: General charitable purposes; education, training; prevention or relief of poverty; accommodation, housing; religious activities
Address: Seafarer House, 74 St Annes Road, Southampton, SO19 9FF
Trustees: Mr Peter Henry Goldberg, Mr Shyam Sharma, Mr Michael Kenneth Drayton, Mr Colin Andrew McMurray, Captain Jonathan Stoneley, Mr Alastair Fischbacher, Dr Peter Michael Swift, Mr Jonathan Holloway
Income: £3,725,000 [2016]; £3,768,000 [2015]; £3,709,000 [2014]; £4,332,000 [2013]; £1,886,000 [2012]

The Sainsbury Laboratory

Registered: 5 Nov 1997 *Employees:* 78
Tel: 01603 450420 *Website:* tsl.ac.uk
Activities: Education, training
Address: The Sainsbury Laboratory, Norwich Research Park, Colney, Norwich, NR4 7UH
Trustees: Dr Roger Prester Freedman, Professor Dale Sanders, Prof Neil Gow, Professor Nicholas Jose Talbot, Mr Peter Hesketh, Dr Dylan Edwards
Income: £7,186,662 [2017]; £7,413,577 [2016]; £6,717,855 [2015]; £6,480,655 [2014]; £7,979,806 [2013]

Saint Catherine's Hospice Trust

Registered: 19 May 1982 *Employees:* 190 *Volunteers:* 550
Tel: 01723 356041 *Website:* saintcatherines.org.uk
Activities: The advancement of health or saving of lives
Address: St Catherines Hospice, Throxenby Lane, Scarborough, N Yorks, YO12 5RE
Trustees: Dr James Francis Philip Garnett, Mr Tim Boyes, Mrs Christine Mary Wilson, Mr Malcolm Chell, Mr John Cyril Stevenson, Mr Simon Peter Ward, Mrs Margaret Middlebrook, Mrs Diane Patricia Flint, Mr David Clarke Chapman, Mrs Susan Carole Standard-Sheader
Income: £5,517,666 [2017]; £5,898,099 [2016]; £5,309,765 [2015]; £6,952,778 [2014]; £4,878,785 [2013]

Saint Felix Schools

Registered: 16 Sep 1966 *Employees:* 125
Tel: 01502 722175 *Website:* stfelix.co.uk
Activities: Education, training
Address: Halesworth Road, Reydon, Southwold, Suffolk, IP18 6SD
Trustees: Rev Barrie Slatter, Mr Richard John Turvill, Dr Leslie William Dawson OBE, Mrs Linda Le Versha, Mr Kevin Dobson, Mr Graham John Hillier, Mr John William Whyte, Mrs Hazel Anthony, Dr John Francis Kelly, Mr Robert Stephens, Mr Rupert Wise
Income: £3,807,556 [2016]; £3,586,986 [2015]; £3,618,686 [2014]; £4,082,626 [2013]; £4,321,870 [2012]

Saint Francis Hospice

Registered: 22 Jun 1978 *Employees:* 297 *Volunteers:* 650
Tel: 01708 753319 *Website:* sfh.org.uk
Activities: Education, training; advancement of health or saving of lives
Address: St Francis Hospice, The Hall, Broxhill Road, Havering-Atte-Bower, Romford, Essex, RM4 1QH
Trustees: Mr Robin Wright, Dr Robert MacKenzie Weatherstone MA FRCP, Peter Crutchett, Mr Paul Gwinn, Mr Malcolm Paul Miller, Neville A Brown JP, Mr Peter Adams, Dr Gurdev Saini, Mr Peter John Batt
Income: £11,268,000 [2017]; £11,175,000 [2016]; £10,590,000 [2015]; £10,845,000 [2014]; £9,028,000 [2013]

Saint John of God Hospitaller Services

Registered: 4 Mar 2005 *Employees:* 706 *Volunteers:* 25
Tel: 01325 373700 *Website:* sjog.org.uk
Activities: General charitable purposes; education, training; advancement of health or saving of lives; disability; prevention or relief of poverty; accommodation, housing; recreation; other charitable purposes
Address: St John of God Hospitaller Service, Morton Park Way, Darlington, Co Durham, DL1 4XZ
Trustees: Mr Gerald Edward Kidd, Brother Robert Moore OH, Mr Anthony David Moore, Michael Francis, Brother Donatus Forkan OH, Br Malachy Brannigan
Income: £21,356,000 [2016]; £23,103,360 [2015]; £23,522,000 [2014]; £23,595,000 [2013]; £24,604,000 [2012]

The Saint John's School Foundation

Registered: 2 Nov 1964 *Employees:* 206
Tel: 01372 385446 *Website:* stjohnsleatherhead.co.uk
Activities: Education, training
Address: St Johns School, Epsom Road, Leatherhead, Surrey, KT22 8SP
Trustees: Mr Andrew Peake, Mrs Judy Harris, Mr John Willis, Mr Alexander Duma, Mrs Sarah Dickinson, Mr John Gravett, Mrs Clare Davies, Mrs Sandra Phillips, Mr Ed Sanderson, Ms Tracey Fantham, Mr Anthony Airey, Mr Tim Beckh, Mr Nick Teunon, Mr Bruce Shaw, Mr Peter Thorne, Mr Simon Williams, Mrs Ruth Marshall, Mrs Lesley Hume, Mrs Clare Turnbull
Income: £15,827,389 [2017]; £14,303,478 [2016]; £13,930,762 [2015]; £13,523,181 [2014]; £13,231,985 [2013]

Saint Margaret's Convent (Chiswick)

Registered: 9 Apr 1964 *Employees:* 109
Tel: 020 8994 4641
Activities: The advancement of health or saving of lives; disability; religious activities
Address: St Marys Convent & Nursing Home, Burlington Lane, London, W4 2QE
Trustees: Sister Barbara SSM, Sister Mary Paul SSM, Sister Raphael Mary SSM, Sister Cynthia Clare SSM, Sister Francis Anne SSM, Sister Jennifer Anne SSM, Sister Rita Margaret SSM, Sister Sarah SSM, Sister Mary Clare SSM
Income: £3,893,224 [2017]; £3,294,128 [2016]; £5,089,028 [2015]; £154,231 [2014]; £126,676 [2013]

Saint Martin's (Solihull) Ltd

Registered: 7 Jan 1964 *Employees:* 124
Tel: 0121 705 1265 *Website:* saintmartins-school.com
Activities: Education, training
Address: Malvern Hall, Brueton Avenue, Solihull, W Midlands, B91 3EN
Trustees: Mr John Shepherd, Mrs Fenella De Minckwitz, Mrs Gillian Tillman, Dr Anne Susan Houghton, Mr Keith Lewis, Mrs Carol McNidder, Mr Nigel Manley, Mrs Helen Ellis, Mr Ian Ralph, Mrs Anne Wilson
Income: £4,893,584 [2017]; £4,590,235 [2016]; £4,027,280 [2015]; £3,811,270 [2014]; £3,863,119 [2013]

Saints Foundation (SFC)
Registered: 4 Mar 2002 *Employees:* 56 *Volunteers:* 15
Tel: 023 8071 1994 *Website:* saintsfoundation.co.uk
Activities: General charitable purposes; education, training; advancement of health or saving of lives; disability; prevention or relief of poverty; amateur sport; economic, community development, employment; recreation
Address: 36 Clifton Gardens, West End, Southampton, SO18 3DA
Trustees: Toni Shaw, Tina Croucher, Mark Abrahams, Paul Bolwell, Rod Jackson
Income: £2,256,228 [2017]; £2,397,207 [2016]; £1,683,679 [2015]; £1,344,514 [2014]; £999,756 [2013]

Salesian College Farnborough Limited
Registered: 16 Jun 2009 *Employees:* 83
Tel: 01252 893000 *Website:* salesiancollege.com
Activities: Education, training; religious activities; amateur sport
Address: Salesian College, 119 Reading Road, Farnborough, Hants, GU14 6PA
Trustees: Mrs Tracy Jones, Mr Clayton Almeida, Mr Paul Page-Tickell LLB Euro, Mrs Anne Catherine Nash, Mr Mark Ian Henry Chatterton, Rev Christopher Michael Heaps, Mrs Elizabeth Jane Desmidt, Rev James Gallagher, Mr Paul Turrell BSc (Hons) CMIOSH MCIOB, Rev Daniel O'Riordan, Mr Anthony Gribbon, Mr Gerard Thomas Owens, Ms Melissa Jane Day, Mr Miroslaw Gliniecki
Income: £7,083,293 [2016]; £6,687,767 [2015]; £6,395,650 [2014]; £5,946,382 [2013]; £5,763,345 [2012]

Salesians of Don Bosco UK
Registered: 8 May 1964 *Employees:* 46 *Volunteers:* 14
Tel: 01204 600720 *Website:* salesians.org.uk
Activities: General charitable purposes; education, training; overseas aid, famine relief; religious activities
Address: Salesian Provincial Office, Thornleigh House, Sharples Park, Bolton, Lancs, BL1 6PQ
Trustees: Rev Mervyn Williams SDB, Rev Anthony Fernandes SDB, Rev James Gerrard Briody SDB, Rev Martin Poulsom SDB, Rev Bob Gardner SDB, Andrew Ebrahim
Income: £4,780,409 [2016]; £5,140,978 [2015]; £6,140,087 [2014]; £3,216,782 [2013]; £4,395,726 [2012]

The Salford Diocesan Trust
Registered: 4 Apr 1967 *Employees:* 138 *Volunteers:* 1,500
Tel: 0161 817 2222 *Website:* dioceseofsalford.org.uk
Activities: Religious activities
Address: The Diocese of Salford, Cathedral Centre, 3 Ford Street, Salford, M3 6DP
Trustees: Rev Michael Quinlan, Mr Edward Nally, Rev Monsignor Canon Anthony Kay, Rev Peter Hopkinson, Ms Winifred Goggins, Sir Peter Fahy, Rev Michael Cooke, Rev Christopher Dawson, Bishop John Stanley Kenneth Arnold
Income: £17,287,055 [2016]; £18,888,838 [2015]; £20,330,396 [2014]; £26,072,178 [2013]; £19,397,216 [2012]

Salford Foundation Limited
Registered: 10 Apr 1991 *Employees:* 37 *Volunteers:* 60
Tel: 0161 787 8500 *Website:* salfordfoundation.org.uk
Activities: Education, training; prevention or relief of poverty; economic, community development, employment
Address: Salford Foundation, Foundation House, 3 Jo Street, Salford, M5 4BD
Trustees: Mr Leonard Collinson, Mr Nicholas Abbott, Mr Kevin Brady, Mrs Charlotte Ramsden, Miss Elizabeth Potier, Ms Helen Louise Foulkes, Mr Stewart Almond, Mr Peter Openshaw, Mr Andrew Povey, Mrs Sarah Wilson-Gibbons, Mrs Katharine Selina Francis, Mr Stuart William Barton
Income: £2,233,315 [2017]; £2,029,413 [2016]; £2,475,711 [2015]; £2,164,408 [2014]; £1,921,760 [2013]

Salford and Trafford Engineering Group Training Association Limited
Registered: 13 Jan 1981 *Employees:* 22
Tel: 0161 877 4078 *Website:* stegta.co.uk
Activities: Education, training; economic, community development, employment
Address: 4th Floor, c/o Stegta Ltd, Duckworth House, Lancastrian Office Suite, Talbot Road, Stretford, Manchester, M32 0FP
Trustees: Mr Brian Travis, Mr Richard Morris Nuttall, Mr Graham Michael Smith, Mr Ian McDonald, Mr Trevor Philip Cosby
Income: £1,941,291 [2017]; £1,579,523 [2016]; £1,011,844 [2015]; £852,063 [2014]; £866,115 [2013]

Salisbury Cathedral School Limited
Registered: 27 Aug 2002 *Employees:* 88
Tel: 01722 555302 *Website:* salisburycathedralschool.com
Activities: Education, training; religious activities
Address: Salisbury Cathedral School, 1 The Close, Salisbury, Wilts, SP1 2EQ
Trustees: Mr Martin Gordon Cooke, Rev James Woodward, Mrs Christine Mary Cooper, Mrs Jacqueline Monro-Higgs, Rev Edward Probert, Mrs Liisa Wallace, Mr James Fletcher DPhil MA FCA, Yury Beylin, Mr Timothy Michael Olliff-Lee, Mr Nicholas Wood-Roe, Mr Stephen Darke
Income: £3,069,080 [2017]; £2,994,855 [2016]; £2,216,114 [2015]; £2,117,720 [2014]; £2,257,322 [2013]

Salisbury City Almshouse and Welfare Charities
Registered: 19 Jul 1979 *Employees:* 22
Tel: 01722 325640 *Website:* salisburyalmshouses.co.uk
Activities: The prevention or relief of poverty; accommodation, housing
Address: Salisbury City Almshouse And Welfare Charities, Trinity Hospital, Trinity Street, Salisbury, Wilts, SP1 2BD
Trustees: Mr Rodney Walter Shipsey, Mr Alan Corkill, Mr Peter Moss, Mr Thomas Frederick Clay, Mr Alastair James Brain, Mrs Alison Roser Hatton, Mr Trevor Austreng, Mrs Gillian Ann Ellis, Mrs Anna Taylor, Mrs Patricia Margaret Lush, Mrs Fiona Green
Income: £2,149,548 [2016]; £1,580,319 [2015]; £1,696,224 [2014]; £1,620,417 [2013]; £1,575,787 [2012]

The Salisbury Diocesan Board of Education
Registered: 13 Nov 1996 *Employees:* 27
Website: salisbury.anglican.org
Activities: Education, training
Address: Salisbury Diocese Board of Education, Diocesan Education Centre, The Avenue, Wilton, Salisbury, Wilts, SP2 0FG
Trustees: Canon Harold Stephens, Mrs Lucinda Herklots, Lady Kate Hunloke, Mrs Joy Tubbs, Mr Martin McLeman, Mr Timothy Balmforth, Ven Antony MacRow-Wood, Rev Jonathan Triffitt, Mrs Mercedes Henning, Mrs Margaret Pearson
Income: £4,698,012 [2017]; £4,607,835 [2016]; £7,064,853 [2015]; £5,908,520 [2014]; £6,389,051 [2013]

The Salisbury Diocesan Board of Finance
Registered: 4 Mar 1966 *Employees:* 37 *Volunteers:* 60
Tel: 01722 411922 *Website:* salisbury.anglican.org
Activities: Religious activities
Address: Church House, 99 Crane Street, Salisbury, Wilts, SP1 2QB
Trustees: The Very Revd June Osborne DL, The Ven Alan Paul Jeans, The Ven Paul Stanley Taylor, Mrs Margaret Morrissey OBE FRSA, The Rt Rev Nicholas Holtam, Rev Claire Maxim, Mrs Gillian Mary Clarke, Mrs Elena Oderstone, Mrs Janet Jackson, Ms Rosemary Karen Veronica Cook, The Ven Sue Groom, Rev Canon David Baldwin, The Ven Antony Charles MacRow-Wood, The Rt Rev Canon Dr Edward Francis Condry, The Rev Canon Thomas Mark Bews Woodhouse, The Rev Canon Andrew Nicholas Perry BA MA, Mr Derek Howshall, Mr Richard Chitty, Mrs Debrah Agnes McIsaac, Mr Nigel Salisbury, The Rt Rev Karen Gorham
Income: £13,463,000 [2016]; £13,461,000 [2015]; £13,023,000 [2014]; £12,626,000 [2013]; £12,324,000 [2012]

Salisbury District Hospital Charitable Fund
Registered: 26 Jan 1996 *Employees:* 3 *Volunteers:* 60
Website: starsappeal.org
Activities: The advancement of health or saving of lives
Address: Salisbury District Hospital, Odstock Road, Salisbury, Wilts, SP2 8BJ
Trustees: Salisbury NHS Foundation Trust Board
Income: £2,151,000 [2017]; £2,535,000 [2016]; £1,906,000 [2015]; £3,072,000 [2014]; £2,342,000 [2013]

Salisbury Hospicecare Trust Limited
Registered: 25 Mar 2008 *Employees:* 10 *Volunteers:* 100
Tel: 01722 416353 *Website:* salisburyhospicecharity.org.uk
Activities: The advancement of health or saving of lives
Address: Liz Bacon, Finance Manager, Salisbury Hospice Charity, Salisbury Hospice, Odstock Road, Salisbury, Wilts, SP2 8BJ
Trustees: Mr Ceri Hurford-Jones, Mr Ian Downie, Mr David Hugh Charles Pardoe, Dr Andrew Jonathan Hall, Mrs Nicola Spicer, Mr Mark Merrill, Mrs Victoria Bracey, Mrs Stella Valentine Margaret Sykes, Mrs Denise Eleanor Major
Income: £1,564,954 [2017]; £1,592,108 [2016]; £1,089,931 [2015]; £1,571,941 [2014]; £2,170,724 [2013]

The Salmon Youth Centre in Bermondsey
Registered: 11 Jul 1980 *Employees:* 9 *Volunteers:* 60
Tel: 020 7394 2444 *Website:* salmonyouthcentre.org
Activities: Education, training; advancement of health or saving of lives; disability; prevention or relief of poverty; accommodation, housing; religious activities; amateur sport; recreation; other charitable purposes
Address: 43 Old Jamaica Road, London, SE16 4TE
Trustees: Rev Robert Mayo, Ms Sara Manwell, Mr Peter Knight, Mr Carl Gunther Bauer, Mr Dean Anthony Pusey, Mr Adrian Greenwood, Mr Mike Askwith, Mr Robert Gleaves, Marie Skelton
Income: £1,100,383 [2017]; £795,588 [2016]; £741,543 [2015]; £880,004 [2014]; £717,075 [2013]

Saltbox
Registered: 5 Dec 2007 *Employees:* 38 *Volunteers:* 41
Tel: 01782 207200 *Website:* saltbox.org.uk
Activities: General charitable purposes; prevention or relief of poverty; accommodation, housing; religious activities; economic, community development, employment; other charitable purposes
Address: Saltbox, Gitana Street, Hanley, Stoke on Trent, Staffs, ST1 1DY
Trustees: Mr Geoffrey David-Gideon Bond, Mr Philip Jeremy Barber, Mrs Teresa Phillips, Mr David Alan Brewer, Mr Brian Barber, Rev David Street, Mrs Evelyn Carter
Income: £1,159,156 [2016]; £1,426,311 [2015]; £1,305,998 [2014]; £1,305,948 [2013]; £1,141,819 [2012]

Salters Hill Charity Limited
Registered: 3 Jan 1984 *Employees:* 72 *Volunteers:* 21
Tel: 01594 563533 *Website:* saltershill.org.uk
Activities: Disability; accommodation, housing
Address: 1 Hill Park, George Road, Yorkley, Lydney, Glos, GL15 4TL
Trustees: Lal Heaton, Ms Elizabeth Edwards
Income: £2,421,592 [2017]; £1,804,223 [2015]; £1,675,124 [2014]; £1,717,682 [2013]; £1,590,161 [2012]

The Salvation Army International Trust
Registered: 18 Oct 1990 *Employees:* 150
Tel: 020 7332 8116 *Website:* salvationarmy.org
Activities: General charitable purposes; education, training; advancement of health or saving of lives; prevention or relief of poverty; overseas aid, famine relief; religious activities; human rights, religious or racial harmony, equality or diversity
Address: Salvation Army International Headquarters, 101 Queen Victoria Street, London, EC4V 4EH
Trustees: The Salvation Army International Trustee Company
Income: £56,441,000 [2017]; £59,131,000 [2016]; £68,482,000 [2015]; £40,985,000 [2014]; £35,328,000 [2013]

The Salvation Army Officers' Pension Fund
Registered: 16 Jun 1964
Tel: 020 7367 4669
Activities: Other charitable purposes
Address: The Salvation Army Officers Pension Fund, 101 Newington Causeway, London, SE1 6BN
Trustees: Lieut-Colonel Alan Read, Lieut-Colonel George Pilkington, Commissioner Clive Adams, Commissioner John Wainwright, Lieut-Colonel Paul Main, Colonel David Hinton, Major James Williams, Commissioner D Marianne Adams, Ms Caroline Emerton
Income: £16,495,981 [2017]; £17,323,070 [2016]; £16,343,989 [2015]; £13,157,173 [2014]; £14,509,221 [2013]

The Salvation Army Retired Officers Allowance Scheme
Registered: 5 Sep 2013
Tel: 020 7332 8116 *Website:* salvationarmy.org
Activities: The prevention or relief of poverty; other charitable purposes
Address: Salvation Army International Headquarters, 101 Queen Victoria Street, London, EC4V 4EH
Trustees: The Salvation Army International Trustee Company
Income: £3,108,985 [2017]; £2,594,073 [2016]; £2,173,518 [2015]; £34,203,202 [2014]

The Salvation Army Social Work Trust
Registered: 13 Feb 1963 *Employees:* 2,087 *Volunteers:* 500
Tel: 020 7367 6593 *Website:* salvationarmy.org.uk
Activities: Education, training; prevention or relief of poverty; accommodation, housing; economic, community development, employment; other charitable purposes
Address: The Salvation Army, 101 Newington Causeway, London, SE1 6BN
Trustees: The Salvation Army Trustee Company
Income: £177,037,000 [2017]; £108,805,000 [2016]; £112,434,000 [2015]; £104,579,000 [2014]; £102,189,000 [2013]

The Salvation Army
Registered: 15 Feb 1963 *Employees:* 2,826 *Volunteers:* 10,000
Tel: 020 7367 6593 *Website:* salvationarmy.org.uk
Activities: General charitable purposes; education, training; advancement of health or saving of lives; disability; prevention or relief of poverty; overseas aid, famine relief; religious activities; economic, community development, employment; other charitable purposes
Address: The Salvation Army, 101 Newington Causeway, London, SE1 6BN
Trustees: The Salvation Army Trustee Company
Income: £209,659,000 [2017]; £209,008,000 [2016]; £194,080,000 [2015]; £196,099,000 [2014]; £181,516,000 [2013]

Samaritan's Purse International Limited
Registered: 20 Dec 1990 *Employees:* 62 *Volunteers:* 108
Tel: 020 8559 0342 *Website:* samaritans-purse.org.uk
Activities: The advancement of health or saving of lives; prevention or relief of poverty; overseas aid, famine relief; religious activities
Address: Victoria House, Victoria Road, Buckhurst Hill, Essex, IG9 5ES
Trustees: Mr James Arnold Barrett, The Rev William Franklin Graham, Mr John Gallagher, Mr Andrew Lawrence, Mr Mark Thomas, Mr Roger Chilvers, Mr Paul Saber
Income: £18,603,255 [2017]; £24,319,417 [2016]; £18,522,749 [2015]; £19,129,643 [2014]; £19,029,029 [2013]

Samaritans
Registered: 28 Aug 1963 *Employees:* 164 *Volunteers:* 20,454
Tel: 020 8394 8258 *Website:* samaritans.org
Activities: Education, training; advancement of health or saving of lives
Address: The Samaritans, The Upper Mill, Kingston Road, Epsom, Surrey, KT17 2AF
Trustees: Michael Rogerson, Terry Holland, Keith Walker, Mrs Ana Laing, Amanda Perrin, Jenni McCartney, Michele McClung, Mr Giles Wilmore, Jayne Finch, Ms Monica Turner, Rosemary Howell, Gillian Leo, Jackie Craissati, Mr Simon Salem, David Gunnell
Income: £19,142,000 [2017]; £16,173,000 [2016]; £13,246,000 [2015]; £12,507,000 [2014]; £12,943,000 [2013]

Samjo Limited
Registered: 30 Oct 2002
Tel: 0161 832 8721
Activities: General charitable purposes; education, training; advancement of health or saving of lives; disability; prevention or relief of poverty; overseas aid, famine relief; accommodation, housing; religious activities
Address: 6th Floor, Cardinal House, 20 St Marys Parsonage, Manchester, M3 2LG
Trustees: Mr Joshua Halpern, Rabbi Yisroel Friedman, Samuel Halpern
Income: £1,691,650 [2017]; £1,280,269 [2016]; £1,251,689 [2015]; £1,223,888 [2014]; £1,275,932 [2013]

Samlesbury Hall Trust
Registered: 3 Oct 1963 *Employees:* 49 *Volunteers:* 10
Tel: 01254 812010 *Website:* samlesburyhall.co.uk
Activities: Environment, conservation, heritage
Address: Samlesbury Hall, Preston New Road, Samlesbury, Preston, Lancs, PR5 0UP
Trustees: Mrs Lillian Croston, Mr Duncan Isherwood, Mr Gregory Turner, Mrs Catherine Mallord, Mr Geoffrey Cunliffe, Peter Clancy, Ms Karen Lawrenson, Mrs Lesley Anne Yates
Income: £1,192,302 [2016]; £186,787 [2015]; £854,755 [2014]; £965,225 [2013]; £842,970 [2012]

Sanbri Ltd
Registered: 30 Jun 2016 *Volunteers:* 3
Tel: 020 8731 8666
Activities: Education, training; disability; prevention or relief of poverty; religious activities
Address: 1 Golders Manor Drive, London, NW11 9HU
Trustees: Mr Charles Lerner, Mr Israel Grossnass, Mrs Frances Rosalind Lerner, Mr Irving Marc Lerner
Income: £3,606,159 [2017]

Sanctuary Student Homes Limited
Registered: 9 Jul 2004
Website: sanctuary-group.co.uk
Activities: General charitable purposes; education, training; prevention or relief of poverty; accommodation, housing
Address: Sanctuary Housing Association, Chamber Court, Castle Street, Worcester, WR1 3ZQ
Trustees: Mr Craig Moule, Mr Simon Clark, Ms Hilary Gardner, Mr Anthony King, Mr Alan Findlay West
Income: £18,512,000 [2017]; £29,319,000 [2016]; £19,058,000 [2015]; £15,480 [2014]; £11,461 [2013]

Sanctuary Student Properties Limited
Registered: 1 Aug 2014
Tel: 01905 334400 *Website:* sanctuary-group.co.uk
Activities: Education, training; accommodation, housing
Address: Sanctuary Housing Association, Chamber Court, Castle Street, Worcester, WR1 3ZQ
Trustees: Craig Moule, Peter Williams, Anthony King
Income: £3,323,000 [2017]; £3,253,000 [2016]; £1,557,000 [2015]

Sandroyd School Trust Limited
Registered: 4 Oct 1963 *Employees:* 105
Tel: 01725 516329 *Website:* sandroyd.org
Activities: Education, training
Address: Sandroyd School, Rushmore Park, Tollard Royal, Salisbury, Wilts, SP5 5QD
Trustees: Mrs Emma McKendrick, Mrs Karon Fuller, Mr Oliver Stanley, Mr Peter John Castleman Bourke, Mr Simon Barber, Mrs Philippa Louise Zingg, Mr George Whitefield, Mrs Elizabeth Brierley, Mr Rhodri Thomas BSc MRICS FAAV, Mrs Hannah Bell, Mr Charles McVeigh, Mrs Felicity Wilson, Mr Jaideep Barot, Mrs Laura Miles
Income: £4,061,289 [2016]; £4,107,074 [2015]; £3,764,779 [2014]; £3,794,949 [2013]; £3,666,369 [2012]

Sandwell Citizens Advice Bureaux
Registered: 10 May 1989 *Employees:* 40 *Volunteers:* 95
Tel: 0121 569 2998 *Website:* citizensadvicesandwell.org.uk
Activities: The prevention or relief of poverty
Address: 22 Lombard Street, West Bromwich, W Midlands, B70 8RT
Trustees: Mr Farooq Hussain, Mrs Loraine Furness, Ms Katherine Chung Ying Gordon, Mr Christopher Tranter, Colin Stevens, Iris Boucher, Mr Donald Harris, Mr Parminder Hayre
Income: £1,166,930 [2017]; £1,004,182 [2016]; £1,017,813 [2015]; £1,185,443 [2014]; £1,383,419 [2013]

The Sandwell Community Caring Trust
Registered: 17 Apr 2001 *Employees:* 485 *Volunteers:* 8
Tel: 0121 553 2722 *Website:* sandwellcct.org.uk
Activities: Disability
Address: Sandwell Community Caring Trust, 9th Floor, West Plaza, 144 High Street, West Bromwich, W Midlands, B70 6JJ
Trustees: Mr Frank Betteridge, Mr Ray Alsop, Mrs Sheila Anne Rogers
Income: £12,697,166 [2017]; £14,213,534 [2016]; £14,681,906 [2015]; £15,283,186 [2014]; £14,546,228 [2013]

The Sandwell Crossroads Care Attendant Scheme Limited
Registered: 9 Sep 1994 *Employees:* 62
Tel: 0121 553 8483 *Website:* sandwellcrossroads.org
Activities: The advancement of health or saving of lives; disability
Address: Grenville House, New Swan Lane, West Bromwich, W Midlands, B70 0NG
Trustees: Mr Ivan Wyle, Mr Howard Noel Painter JP BSc FCA, Wendy Bodenham, Mrs Caroline Rhonda Murrain, Mr Matthew Kelly
Income: £1,629,832 [2017]; £1,569,347 [2016]; £1,436,355 [2015]; £1,115,194 [2014]; £1,194,076 [2013]

Sandwell Leisure Trust
Registered: 2 Mar 2004 *Employees:* 171 *Volunteers:* 30
Tel: 0121 521 4423 *Website:* slt.leisure.co.uk
Activities: Arts, culture, heritage, science; amateur sport
Address: Carnegie Building, Victoria Road, Tipton, W Midlands, DY4 8SR
Trustees: Mrs Valerie McFarland, Mr Peter Hughes, Mrs Veronica Nembhard, Mrs Penelope Jane Venables, Mrs Lynda Bateman, Mr Neil Griffiths, Mrs Miriam Sharma
Income: £10,459,530 [2017]; £9,917,409 [2016]; £9,680,186 [2015]; £11,121,227 [2014]; £10,146,868 [2013]

Sandwell Training Association Limited
Registered: 27 Oct 1982 *Employees:* 21
Tel: 01384 566981
Activities: Education, training; economic, community development, employment
Address: Providence Group Services, Grainger House, Cradley Road, Cradley Heath, W Midlands, B64 6AG
Trustees: Mr Phillip Vincent Purkiss, Mr Anthony Walter Creed
Income: £1,019,038 [2016]; £1,064,149 [2015]; £1,062,329 [2014]; £1,084,957 [2013]

Sandwell and West Birmingham Hospitals NHS Trust Charities
Registered: 13 Jun 1996 *Volunteers:* 225
Tel: 0121 507 4871 *Website:* swbh.nhs.uk
Activities: General charitable purposes; education, training; advancement of health or saving of lives
Address: Sandwell & West Birmingham Hospitals NHS Trust, City Hospital, Dudley Road, Birmingham, B18 7QH
Trustees: Sandwell & West Bham Hospitals NHS Trust-Trust Board
Income: £1,246,000 [2017]; £569,000 [2016]; £1,683,000 [2015]; £1,547,000 [2014]; £1,275,000 [2013]

Sangha Tri-National Trust Fund Limited
Registered: 20 Mar 2008 *Employees:* 4
Website: fondationtns.org
Activities: Environment, conservation, heritage
Address: B.P. 35372, Yaounde, Cameroun
Trustees: Mr Samuel Makon Wehiong, Mr Rubens Nambai, Mr Roger Fotso, Mr Hanson Njiforti, Mr Marcel Ondele, Mr Thomas Breuer, Mr Djogo Toumouksala, Mrs Jacqueline Madozein, Mr Emmanuel Fourmann, Mrs Blanche Yengue, Mr Jan Frolich
Income: £1,568,043 [2016]; £1,580,205 [2015]; £1,734,993 [2014]; £1,283,332 [2013]; £973,512 [2012]

Santander UK Foundation Limited
Registered: 17 Jun 1990 *Volunteers:* 8
Website: santanderfoundation.org.uk
Activities: General charitable purposes
Address: Santander UK PLC, Santander House, 201 Grafton Gate East, Milton Keynes, Bucks, MK9 1AN
Trustees: Jennifer Scardino, Keith Moor, Rachel MacFarlane, Sue Willis, Christopher Fallis
Income: £5,809,130 [2016]; £5,550,838 [2015]; £5,577,540 [2014]; £5,803,253 [2013]; £5,347,327 [2012]

Sarcoma UK
Registered: 17 Jan 2011 *Employees:* 12 *Volunteers:* 50
Tel: 020 7250 8271 *Website:* sarcoma.org.uk
Activities: General charitable purposes; advancement of health or saving of lives; other charitable purposes
Address: 49-51 East Road, London, N1 6AH
Trustees: Mr Glyn Wilmshurst, Mrs Sharon Elizabeth Reid, Mr Richard Ian Meredith Hughes, Mr Andrew John Eckles, Miss Sarah Bartholomew, Mrs Anjula Thompson, Professor Robert John Grimer, Miss Samantha Abigail Whittam, Dr Jeffrey David White, Professor Ian Robert Judson, Miss Johanne Vass, Mrs Louisa Nicoll
Income: £1,369,014 [2017]; £1,202,498 [2016]; £964,709 [2015]; £760,967 [2014]; £438,463 [2013]

Sarjudas Foundation
Registered: 5 May 1977 *Employees:* 67 *Volunteers:* 100
Activities: Overseas aid, famine relief; religious activities
Address: 105-119 Brentfield Road, Neasden, London, NW10 8LD
Trustees: Mr Arvindkumar Patel, Mr Dineshkumar Maganbhai
Patel, Mr Amar Parekh, Mr Jitendrakumar Maganbhai Patel,
Mr Mukesh Patel
Income: £11,973,267 [2016]; £9,794,210 [2015]; £7,015,646
[2014]; £9,242,819 [2013]; £6,152,465 [2012]

Paul Sartori Foundation Limited
Registered: 15 Sep 1982 *Employees:* 39 *Volunteers:* 350
Tel: 01437 763223 *Website:* paulsartori.org
Activities: The advancement of health or saving of lives
Address: Paul Sartori Foundation, Paul Sartori House, Winch Lane,
Haverfordwest, Pembrokeshire, SA61 1RP
Trustees: Mr Charles Clewett, Mrs Rosalind Raymond, Dr Liz
Mozdiak, Mr David Evans, Mr Paul Lister, Dr John Finlay
Mackintosh, Mrs Sara Alderman, Mr Phil Thompson, Mr Jason
Tomlin
Income: £1,736,809 [2017]; £1,378,164 [2016]; £1,500,103 [2015];
£1,012,305 [2014]; £936,602 [2013]

Sarum College
Registered: 13 Apr 2015 *Employees:* 51 *Volunteers:* 27
Tel: 01722 424800 *Website:* sarum.ac.uk
Activities: Education, training; religious activities
Address: Sarum College, 19 The Close, Salisbury, Wilts, SP1 2EE
Trustees: Mr Anthony Philip Weale, Mr Roy James Bentham,
Mr Nicholas Stewart Stiven, Canon Dr Hazel Whitehead,
Rev Rachel Naomi Noel, Mr Stephen John Lamdin, Ms Clare
Fiona Sellars, Rt Revd Nicholas Roderick Holtam, Rev Dr Andrew
David Wood, Canon Dr Robert John Titley, Rt Revd Peter Hancock,
Ven Dr Susan Ann Groom, Prof David Branscombe Peter Sims,
Ms Beverley Ann Flanagan
Income: £1,710,920 [2017]; £1,737,401 [2016]

Sarum Hall School Trust Limited
Registered: 12 Jun 1963 *Employees:* 34 *Volunteers:* 18
Tel: 020 7794 2261 *Website:* sarumhallschool.co.uk
Activities: Education, training
Address: Sarum Hall School, 15 Eton Avenue, London, NW3 3EL
Trustees: Mr Blake Nicholas Gorst FRICS, Mr Phillip Ashton BSc
(Hons) ACA, Mrs Sophie Carter, Mrs Katrien Roppe, Mr Peter F
B Beesley LLB, Mr Sebastian Rice BA LLB, Mrs Sharon Martin,
Mr Vivian Thomas
Income: £2,527,935 [2017]; £2,444,813 [2016]; £2,418,614 [2015];
£2,252,905 [2014]; £2,164,787 [2013]

Sat-7 UK Trust Limited
Registered: 11 Feb 1997 *Employees:* 13 *Volunteers:* 38
Tel: 01249 765865 *Website:* sat7uk.org
Activities: Education, training; religious activities; arts, culture,
heritage, science; human rights, religious or racial harmony,
equality or diversity
Address: 2nd Floor, Sat-7 UK Trust, 3-4 New Road, Chippenham,
Wilts, SN15 1EJ
Trustees: Mr John Clark, Stephen P Dengate, Mr Richard P Giles,
Dr Onsy K Morris, Mr R Kemp, Mr Christopher Miles, Mr Mark C
Haines
Income: £1,716,851 [2016]; £1,612,849 [2015]; £1,416,228 [2014];
£1,710,850 [2013]; £1,103,509 [2012]

Cicely Saunders International
Registered: 27 Jun 2001
Tel: 020 8661 1826 *Website:* cicelysaundersinternational.org
Activities: The advancement of health or saving of lives
Address: Sixth Floor, Times House, Throwley Way, Sutton, Surrey,
SM1 4JQ
Trustees: Sir Cyril Chantler, Dr Kathleen Foley, Mr Howell James
CBE, Hugh Henderson Taylor, Mr John McGrath, Sir Richard
Vincent Giordano KBE, Mrs Kate Kirk
Income: £1,662,471 [2016]; £1,122,110 [2015]; £1,405,747 [2014];
£821,972 [2013]; £489,387 [2012]

Savannah Wisdom
Registered: 27 Apr 2011
Tel: 0161 980 4531 *Website:* savannahwisdom.org
Activities: General charitable purposes; prevention or relief of
poverty
Address: Dingle Hall, South Downs Drive, Hale, Altrincham,
Cheshire, WA14 3HR
Trustees: Mr Simon Arora, Mr Bobby Aroroa, Shalni Arora
Income: £1,253,221 [2017]; £1,253,793 [2016]; £526 [2015];
£110,170 [2014]; £8,647 [2013]

Save An Orphan Global Trust
Registered: 2 Aug 2005 *Employees:* 10 *Volunteers:* 15
Tel: 020 8472 0733 *Website:* saveanorphanglobal.org
Activities: General charitable purposes; education, training;
advancement of health or saving of lives; prevention or relief
of poverty; overseas aid, famine relief; economic, community
development, employment
Address: 55 Penge Road, Upton Park, London, E13 0SL
Trustees: Aslim Gill, Mr Mohammed Saeed
Income: £4,883,982 [2016]; £3,371,725 [2015]; £446,287 [2014];
£360,731 [2013]; £339,302 [2012]

The Save The Children Fund
Registered: 10 Oct 1962 *Employees:* 1,209 *Volunteers:* 13,000
Tel: 020 7012 6400 *Website:* savethechildren.org.uk
Activities: Education, training; advancement of health or saving of
lives; disability; prevention or relief of poverty; overseas aid, famine
relief
Address: Save The Children, 1 St John's Lane, London, EC1M 4AR
Trustees: Peter Bennett-Jones, Naomi Eisenstadt, Sebastian
James, Diana Carney, Mark Swallow, Ms Lisa Rosen, Arabella
Elizabeth Duffield, Dianna Melrose, Mr Babatunde Soyoye, Tamara
Ingram, Sophia McCormick, Jamie Cooper, Gareth Davies, Fiona
McBain, Ms Anne Kathleen Fahy, Mr David Ripert, Charles Steel
Income: £404,525,000 [2016]; £389,717,000 [2015]; £370,290,000
[2014]; £342,594,000 [2013]; £283,748,000 [2012]

Save The Children International
Registered: 30 Jul 1999 *Employees:* 17,528 *Volunteers:* 10
Tel: 020 3272 0300 *Website:* savethechildren.net
Activities: General charitable purposes; education, training;
advancement of health or saving of lives; prevention or relief
of poverty; overseas aid, famine relief; economic, community
development, employment; other charitable purposes
Address: Save The Children, St Vincent House, 30 Orange Street,
London, WC2H 7HH
Trustees: Ms Inger Ashing, Pernille Lopez, Ms Anne Fahy, Thomas
Heilmann, Elizabeth Lule, Sigrun Moegedal, Debra Fine, Mr Harpal
Singh, Mr Jonathan Powell, Peter John Hodgson, Dona Young,
Bradley Irwin, Roy Caple Hernandez
Income: £905,509,004 [2016]; £785,578,950 [2015]; £656,844,834
[2014]; £559,141,304 [2013]; £213,478,892 [2012]

Save The Elephants
Registered: 13 Apr 2007 *Employees:* 38
Tel: 020 7783 3537 *Website:* savetheelephants.org
Activities: General charitable purposes; education, training; animals
Address: Bircham Dyson Bell, 50 Broadway, London, SW1H 0BL
Trustees: Ms Marlene McCay, Mr Peter Henderson, Miles Geldard, Professor Fritz Vollrath, Mr Ambrose Carey
Income: £2,234,602 [2016]; £1,619,017 [2015]; £1,576,653 [2014]; £1,193,949 [2013]; £683,531 [2012]

Save The Rhino International
Registered: 15 Mar 1994 *Employees:* 7 *Volunteers:* 43
Tel: 020 7357 7474 *Website:* savetherhino.org
Activities: Education, training; animals; environment, conservation, heritage; economic, community development, employment
Address: Save The Rhino International, Unit 5, Coach House Mews, 217 Long Lane, London, SE1 4PR
Trustees: Mr George Stephenson, Mr Dave Stirling, Ms Samantha Fletcher, Mr Alistair Martin Weaver, Mr Henry Chaplin, Mr Timothy Holmes, Mr James Richard Hearn
Income: £1,718,661 [2017]; £1,711,433 [2016]; £1,373,172 [2015]; £1,026,286 [2014]; £944,978 [2013]

The Savitri Waney Charitable Trust
Registered: 10 Aug 2001 *Employees:* 4
Tel: 020 7725 0230 *Website:* savitri.org.uk
Activities: General charitable purposes; education, training; advancement of health or saving of lives; disability; prevention or relief of poverty; overseas aid, famine relief; economic, community development, employment
Address: 122 Wigmore Street, London, W1U 3RX
Trustees: Mrs Devika Mokhtarzadeh, Mr Azad Shivdasani, Mrs Judith Waney, Mr Pritam Waney, Mrs Rina Bijur, Mr Arjun Waney, Mr Edward Bond, Mr Gulu Waney, Mr Jai Waney
Income: £1,851,803 [2017]; £783,189 [2016]; £8,310,311 [2015]; £1,539,202 [2014]; £673,504 [2013]

The Savoy Educational Trust
Registered: 23 Mar 2015 *Employees:* 1
Tel: 020 7849 3001 *Website:* savoyeducationaltrust.org.uk
Activities: General charitable purposes; education, training
Address: Savoy Educational Trust, Room 160, 90 Long Acre, London, WC2E 9RZ
Trustees: Mr Ramon Pajares OBE FIH, Mr Howard Field FCA FIH FHospA, Councillor Robert Davis MBE DL MA Cantab, Dr Sally Messenger
Income: £1,480,708 [2017]; £54,182,515 [2016]

Saxon Weald Homes Limited
Registered: 11 May 2006 *Employees:* 182
Tel: 01403 226010 *Website:* saxonweald.com
Activities: Disability; prevention or relief of poverty; accommodation, housing; economic, community development, employment
Address: Saxon Weald Homes Ltd, Saxon Weald House, 38-42 Worthing Road, Horsham, W Sussex, RH12 1DT
Trustees: Mr Norman Hill, Mrs Vanessa Williams, Mr Martin Loates, Mr Richard Perry, Ms Charlotte Frances Moore, Mr Mark Slater, Mr David John Standfast, Mr Simon Ross Turpitt, Ms Stephanie Jane White, Mr Richard Stevens, Ms Deborah Jane Joseph, Mrs Elizabeth Ann Nicolls
Income: £45,098,192 [2017]; £45,673,403 [2016]; £43,635,481 [2015]; £36,574,231 [2014]; £38,391,771 [2013]

The Scar Free Foundation
Registered: 17 Dec 1999 *Employees:* 4 *Volunteers:* 27
Tel: 020 7869 6920 *Website:* scarfree.org.uk
Activities: Education, training; advancement of health or saving of lives
Address: The Healing Foundation, Royal College of Surgeons of England, 35-43 Lincoln's Inn Fields, London, WC2A 3PE
Trustees: Mr David Allen OBE, Lieutenant General Richard Edward Nugee, Professor Nichola Rumsey, Professor Jonathan Sandy, Lord James Bethell, Mr Nicholas Kenneth James, Professor Tim Davis, Mr Douglas McGeorge, Mr Naiem Moiemen El-Kashef, Mr Timothy James Streatfeild, Mr Simon Boadle, Bruce Keogh, Professor Peter Weissberg, Ms Alison Clarke
Income: £1,262,328 [2017]; £1,516,021 [2016]; £804,236 [2015]; £952,590 [2014]; £1,062,168 [2013]

Scarborough College
Registered: 15 Oct 1962 *Employees:* 98
Tel: 01723 380608 *Website:* scarboroughcollege.co.uk
Activities: Education, training
Address: Scarborough College, Filey Road, Scarborough, N Yorks, YO11 3BA
Trustees: Dr John Renshaw, Mr John Marcus Green, Mrs Gillian Braithwaite, Michael Baines, Mr John Rowlands, Mr Richard Guthrie, Mr Neil Gardner, Dr Ian Renwick, Mr Richard Marshall, Mr Anthony Stephen Green, Mrs Victoria Gillingham, Mr Simon Fairbank, Mr Jeremy Cook
Income: £4,680,163 [2017]; £3,905,742 [2016]; £3,981,473 [2015]; £3,637,044 [2014]; £3,276,319 [2013]

Scarborough Theatre Trust Limited
Registered: 18 Sep 1967 *Employees:* 61 *Volunteers:* 1
Website: sjt.uk.com
Activities: Education, training; arts, culture, heritage, science
Address: 30 Deepdale Avenue, Scarborough, N Yorks, YO11 2UF
Trustees: Mr John Gerald Herbert Lewis Armistead, Ms Helen Swiers, Mr Clive Groom, Mrs Christine Fitzpatrick, Mr Michael Wilkinson, Mr Archie Pheby McGarvey, Mr Martin Hyde, Helen Boaden, Mr Richard Grunwell, Mrs Kathryn Carmichael, Mr Alexander Smith, Mrs Susan Truefitt, Mr Jonathan Lee
Income: £2,499,496 [2017]; £2,781,991 [2016]; £2,613,414 [2015]; £2,393,560 [2014]; £2,330,108 [2013]

Scarborough and District Mencap
Registered: 22 Feb 1965 *Employees:* 53 *Volunteers:* 15
Tel: 01723 374819 *Website:* scarboroughanddistrictmencap.co.uk
Activities: Disability
Address: Brookleigh, Valley Road, Scarborough, N Yorks, YO11 2JE
Trustees: Mr Christopher Thomas Lumley, Mrs Jennifer Stamford, Mr John Simpson
Income: £1,051,502 [2015]; £1,230,437 [2014]; £1,124,520 [2013]

Scargill Movement
Registered: 3 Feb 2009 *Employees:* 31 *Volunteers:* 204
Tel: 01756 761236 *Website:* scargillmovement.org
Activities: Religious activities
Address: Scargill House, Kettlewell, Skipton, N Yorks, BD23 5HU
Trustees: Tony Hesselwood, Mr Stephen Weatherley, Mr John Fell, Reverend Hilary Young, Miss Susie Mapledoram, Sister Jocelyn, Revd Canon Felicity Lawson, Paul Ayers, Rev Caroline Hewlett, Rev Christopher Paul Edmondson, Mr John Wilson
Income: £1,050,868 [2016]; £924,411 [2015]; £880,025 [2014]; £823,290 [2013]; £794,069 [2012]

Sceptre Education
Registered: 6 Oct 1998 *Employees:* 45 *Volunteers:* 464
Website: dunstable.focus-school.com
Activities: Education, training
Address: Focus School - Dunstable Campus, Ridgeway Avenue, Dunstable, Beds, LU5 4QL
Trustees: Mr Brendon Tunley, Mr Russell Kingston, Mr Alvin Clarke, Mr Hans Purdom, Mr Morgan Doouss, Mr Jake Douglass, Mr Simon Calder
Income: £3,161,035 [2016]; £2,566,659 [2015]; £2,561,561 [2014]; £2,109,018 [2013]; £2,139,096 [2012]

School for Social Entrepreneurs
Registered: 9 Mar 2001 *Employees:* 26 *Volunteers:* 337
Tel: 020 7089 9120 *Website:* sse.org.uk
Activities: Education, training; economic, community development, employment
Address: School for Social Entrepreneurs, 133-139 Tooley Street, London, SE1 2HZ
Trustees: Mr Richard Collier-Keywood, Ms Luljeta Nuzi, Steve Johnson, Dr Gurnek Bains, Mr Michael David Robert Phillips, Ms Charlotte Young, Bertram Leslie, John Brown, Miss Naomi Mwasambili, Mr Joel Davis
Income: £3,916,423 [2017]; £3,935,763 [2016]; £4,138,586 [2015]; £3,710,847 [2014]; £2,620,974 [2013]

The School of Artisan Food
Registered: 31 Dec 2010 *Employees:* 15 *Volunteers:* 1
Website: schoolofartisanfood.org
Activities: Education, training; economic, community development, employment
Address: School of Artisan Food, Welbeck, Whitwell, Worksop, Notts, S80 3LR
Trustees: Ms Susan Amaku, Miss Daisy Margharita Amelia Parente, Dr Sarah Rawlinson, Mr Joseph John Schneider, Mr Daniel Jessel, Ms Alison Jane Swan Parente, Mr John Anthony Kirk
Income: £1,114,405 [2017]; £654,121 [2016]; £777,110 [2015]; £733,236 [2014]; £664,110 [2013]

The School of St Helen and St Katharine Trust
Registered: 5 May 1983 *Employees:* 208 *Volunteers:* 15
Tel: 01235 520657 *Website:* shsk.org.uk
Activities: Education, training
Address: Faringdon Road, Abingdon, Oxon, OX14 1BE
Trustees: Mr Jeremy Wormell, Miss Jane Cranston, Ms Alison Allden, Mrs Diana May, Mr Ian Todd, Mr Ian Mason, Mrs Hazel Knott, Mrs Rebecca Kashti, Mrs Pauline Elizabeth Cakebread, Mr David Lea, Mr Jon Gabitass, Mr Graham Steinsberg, Mr Kevan Leggett
Income: £12,032,703 [2017]; £11,726,950 [2016]; £11,019,524 [2015]; £10,590,033 [2014]; £9,817,545 [2013]

School-Home Support Service (UK)
Registered: 24 Jan 2001 *Employees:* 78
Tel: 0845 337 0850 *Website:* shs.org.uk
Activities: Education, training
Address: 3rd Floor, Solar House, 1-9 Romford Road, Stratford, London, E15 4LJ
Trustees: Inigo Woolf, Mr Richard Evans, Mr David Vaughan, Ms Claire Brinkman, Mr Paul Frederick Sharrock, Mr Colin Richard Horswell, Ms Liz Wolverson, Mr Andrew Dowell, Mr David Jack Marriage, Ms Sara Luder, Miss Lisa Claire Robinson, Mr John Philip Harold Patience Jeffcock
Income: £2,549,157 [2017]; £2,773,433 [2016]; £2,697,549 [2015]; £3,343,027 [2014]; £3,686,019 [2013]

Schools and Teachers Innovating for Results
Registered: 28 Sep 2012 *Employees:* 99
Tel: 07738 257761 *Website:* stireducation.org
Activities: Education, training
Address: c/o Ark, 65 Kingsway, London, WC2B 6TD
Trustees: Jo Owen, Paulo Alexandrew Pisano, Mr Andrew Hanson, Mr David Michael Rothschild
Income: £3,899,268 [2017]

The Schools of King Edward VI in Birmingham
Registered: 21 Nov 1963 *Employees:* 343 *Volunteers:* 3
Tel: 0121 472 1147 *Website:* schoolsofkingedwardvi.co.uk
Activities: Education, training
Address: Foundation Office, Edgbaston Park Road, Edgbaston, Birmingham, B15 2UD
Trustees: Mr Peter Christopher, Mr Barry Matthews, Mrs Gillian Ball, Mr Barnaby Lenon, Mr David John Wheeldon, Mrs Sharon Roberts, Dr Jane Sherwood, Mr Ian Metcalfe, Mrs Jog Hundle, Professor Hywel Thomas, Councillor Robert Alden, Dr Beverly Adab, Geoffrey Thomas, Patrick Burns, Ms Erica Conway, Mr Tim Clarke, Mr George Andronov, Mr Gurdeep Chahal, Councillor Dr Barry Henley, Mr George Marsh, Mr Fazle Kinkhabwala, Dr Neil Shastri-Hurst
Income: £23,198,817 [2016]; £23,198,817 [2015]; £18,448,204 [2014]; £19,711,747 [2013]; £17,952,056 [2012]

The Schroder Foundation
Registered: 6 Jan 2005 *Employees:* 1
Activities: General charitable purposes
Address: The Schroder Foundation, 81 Rivington Street, London, EC2A 3AY
Trustees: Bruno Lionel Schroder, Leonie Fane, Mrs Claire Fitzalan Howard, Mr Richard Robinson, Charmaine Brenda von Mallinckrodt, Mr Edward Gustav Paul Mallinckrodt, Mr Michael May OBE, Mr Philip Stephen Arnold Mallinckrodt
Income: £1,900,439 [2017]; £2,020,596 [2016]; £2,270,816 [2015]; £1,703,984 [2014]; £418,204 [2013]

SciDev.Net
Registered: 30 Nov 2001 *Employees:* 14 *Volunteers:* 8
Tel: 020 7292 9910 *Website:* scidev.net
Activities: Education, training; overseas aid, famine relief; other charitable purposes
Address: Office 7, 35-37 Ludgate Hill, London, EC4M 7JN
Trustees: Mr Robert Sloley, Mr Myles Runham, Dr Trevor John Nicholls, Mr Andrew John Jack, Mrs Caroline Anne Stanley
Income: £1,157,445 [2016]; £1,899,297 [2015]; £2,011,040 [2014]; £2,120,235 [2013]; £1,564,311 [2012]

The Science Engineering Technology Mathematics Network
Registered: 16 Sep 1996 *Employees:* 26 *Volunteers:* 33,000
Tel: 020 3206 0450
Activities: Education, training
Address: 5th Floor, Woolgate Exchange, 25 Basinghall Street, London, EC2V 5HA
Trustees: Sir David Grant CBE, Julia Waters, Mrs Riffat Wall, Professor Julia Buckingham, Professor Matthew Harrison
Income: £1,987,955 [2017]; £6,829,436 [2016]; £6,910,340 [2015]; £4,667,558 [2014]; £3,808,747 [2013]

Science Projects

Registered: 2 Feb 1988 *Employees:* 47 *Volunteers:* 10
Tel: 020 8741 2305 *Website:* science-projects.org
Activities: Education, training
Address: Science Projects Ltd, 3 Stirling Road, London, W3 8DJ
Trustees: Mrs Jill Carnie Allen, Mr Richard Leonard Allsop, Mrs Amy Derbyshire, Mr Richard Browne Scholefield, Mr Stephen Pizzey, Ms Sheila Snowden
Income: £2,487,913 [2016]; £1,649,230 [2015]; £1,327,952 [2014]; £1,666,986 [2013]; £1,753,938 [2012]

Science of The Soul - British Isles

Registered: 25 Jan 2011 *Volunteers:* 1,000
Tel: 01234 381234
Activities: General charitable purposes; education, training; religious activities; human rights, religious or racial harmony, equality or diversity
Address: Haynes Park, Church End, Haynes, Bedford, MK45 3BL
Trustees: Mr Roger French, Douglas Cameron, Mr Darshan Paul, Brian Bocking, Narinder Johal, Joga S Atwal, Mrs Elizabeth Harrison, Mrs Diana Wojewodzki
Income: £1,656,760 [2016]; £1,913,884 [2015]; £1,739,065 [2014]; £1,564,486 [2013]

Science, Engineering and Manufacturing Technologies Alliance

Registered: 11 Sep 1990 *Employees:* 124
Tel: 01923 652329 *Website:* semta.org.uk
Activities: Education, training
Address: Semta, Unit 2, The Orient Centre, Greycaine Road, Watford, Herts, WD24 7GP
Trustees: Mr Martin Hottass, Mr Mark Stewart, Mr Arthur John Connelly, Mr Jose Lopes, Dr Hayaatun Sillem, Mrs Selma Hunter, Dame Judith Hackitt, Mr I Mukerjee, Mr Ian Waddell, Professor Alison Fuller, Mr John Whelan, Mr Michael Evans
Income: £13,698,000 [2017]; £15,858,000 [2016]; £17,688,000 [2015]; £16,854,000 [2014]; £18,056,000 [2013]

Scope

Registered: 22 Sep 1962 *Employees:* 2,136 *Volunteers:* 9,000
Tel: 020 7619 7398 *Website:* scope.org.uk
Activities: General charitable purposes; education, training; disability; accommodation, housing; human rights, religious or racial harmony, equality or diversity
Address: Scope, 2nd Floor, Here East, Press Centre, 14 East Bay Lane, London, E15 2GW
Trustees: Mr Robin Charles Hindle Fisher, Andrew McDonald, Alexander Massey, Mr Joseph Barrell, Celia Atherton OBE, Mr Andrew Maitland Hooke, Ms Rebecca Simmonds, Ms Claire Flint
Income: £97,849,000 [2017]; £99,523,000 [2016]; £101,068,000 [2015]; £102,635,000 [2014]; £102,961,000 [2013]

The John Scott Charitable Trust

Registered: 30 Jan 2009
Tel: 01388 881065
Activities: Education, training; prevention or relief of poverty
Address: Torrie House, Newmills, Dunfermline, Fife, KY12 8HH
Trustees: Mr Andrew Henry Scott, David Robinson, Andrew Wemyss, Dr Alan Gray Rutherford
Income: £1,378,057 [2017]; £100,396 [2016]; £88,254 [2015]; £1,299,360 [2014]; £1,273,842 [2013]

The Scott Creative Arts Foundation

Registered: 1 Aug 2016
Tel: 07790 525384 *Website:* scotts-gallery.co.uk
Activities: Arts, culture, heritage, science
Address: The Studio, Arthington Lane, Otley, W Yorks, LS21 1JZ
Trustees: Mrs Susan Elizabeth Armstrong, Dr William Tomkiss, Dr Wendy McGrandles
Income: £1,865,156 [2017]

The Scottish Hospital of The Foundation of King Charles The Second (Royal Scottish Corporation)

Registered: 7 Dec 1962 *Employees:* 14 *Volunteers:* 68
Tel: 020 7240 3718 *Website:* scotscare.com
Activities: Education, training; prevention or relief of poverty; accommodation, housing
Address: The Royal Scottish Corporation, 22-24 City Road, London, EC1Y 2AJ
Trustees: Mr Stuart James Steele MA FRCS FRCOG, Mr Peter Hay, Mr Angus Gilroy, Brian Griffin, Mr James Elliott Chestnut, Dr Graeme Wilson, James Grieve, Mr P J M Scott, Mr Wylie Graham Crawford White, Fred Gray, Mr David Tait Coughtrie, Ms Joyce Harvie, Mr David Guild
Income: £2,323,848 [2017]; £2,252,114 [2016]; £2,174,301 [2015]; £2,035,820 [2014]; £2,189,657 [2013]

Scotts Project Trust

Registered: 12 Jan 1996 *Employees:* 33 *Volunteers:* 14
Tel: 01732 367917 *Website:* scottsproject.org.uk
Activities: Education, training; disability; accommodation, housing
Address: Scotts Project Trust, Delarue Close, Shipbourne Road, Tonbridge, Kent, TN11 9NN
Trustees: Nicholas Ward, Sara Tozzi, Sue Bourne, Martin Miles, Caroline Becher, Andrew Blevins, Jill Scott, Tom Hoppe, Derek McMenamin, Ian Storey, Raj Bhamber
Income: £1,539,508 [2017]; £1,314,891 [2016]; £1,454,113 [2015]; £1,494,783 [2014]; £1,297,485 [2013]

Scout Association County of Birmingham

Registered: 25 Mar 1964 *Employees:* 23 *Volunteers:* 2,007
Website: birminghamscouts.org.uk
Activities: General charitable purposes; education, training; disability; religious activities; arts, culture, heritage, science; amateur sport; environment, conservation, heritage; economic, community development, employment
Address: Scout Association, 89-91 Hatchett Street, Birmingham, B19 3NY
Trustees: Mr Peter Oldham, Mr Simon Cardall, David Allen, Mr Paul Little, Andrew Lloyd, Mr Sean Kelly, Mr Alex Harverson, Mr David Gilburn, Mrs Maggie Jones, Mrs Abigail McMillan, Mrs Heidi Guest, Amanda Cardall, Mr Adam Brinkworth, Linda Gurmin, Mr James Holmes, Mr Harry Fowler, Mr Daryl Holloway, Miss Sophie Bourne, Mr David Archer, Mr Gerald Peel
Income: £1,500,299 [2016]; £1,159,505 [2015]; £1,128,636 [2014]; £930,766 [2013]; £1,266,944 [2012]

The Scout Association
Registered: 21 Jan 1964 *Employees:* 314 *Volunteers:* 154,001
Tel: 020 8433 7182 *Website:* scouts.org.uk
Activities: Education, training; amateur sport; economic, community development, employment
Address: The Scout Association, Gilwell Park, Chingford, London, E4 7QW
Trustees: Dr Ann Limb, Mr Gareth Davies, Mr Matt Mills, Mr Byron Chatburn, Mr Matthew Thomas Hyde, Mr Ashley Russell, Mrs Elizabeth Jack, Ms Jane Simpson, Mr Jack Bullon, Miss Hannah Kentish, Ms Susan Harris, Ms Lexie Sims, Mr Stuart Howells, Mr Gordon Boyd, Mr John Kennedy, Miss Nicola Gamlen, Mr Kieron Moir, Mr Timothy Kidd, Mrs Frances Craven, Mr David Branagh
Income: £32,681,000 [2017]; £43,385,000 [2016]; £29,993,000 [2015]; £28,754,000 [2014]; £26,615,000 [2013]

Scripture Gift Mission (Incorporated)
Registered: 23 Oct 1964 *Employees:* 13
Tel: 020 7730 2155 *Website:* sgmlifewords.com
Activities: Education, training; prevention or relief of poverty; religious activities
Address: SGM Lifewords, Unit 1A The Chandlery, 50 Westminster Bridge Road, London, SE1 7QY
Trustees: Mr David Morgan, Mr Keith Alexander Douglas Bintley, Ms Elisabeth Louise Heyburn, Mr Frederick Kenneth Slack, Mrs Lynn Fraser Caudwell, Mr Mark Robert William Hurley
Income: £1,565,168 [2016]; £1,422,954 [2015]; £1,694,800 [2014]; £1,389,889 [2013]; £1,531,231 [2012]

Scripture Union
Registered: 3 Jan 1966 *Employees:* 78 *Volunteers:* 2,358
Tel: 01908 856000 *Website:* scriptureunion.org.uk
Activities: Education, training; religious activities
Address: Scripture Union, Trinity House, Opal Court, Opal Drive, Fox Milne, Milton Keynes, Bucks, MK15 0DF
Trustees: Mr Timothy Warren, Rev Dr Edward Fraser Austin Longmer Scrase-Field, Mr Keith Basil Civval, Clive Beard, Ms Kim Barbara Hurst, Mr Derek Adams FCA, Mrs Clare Walker, Mr Stephen Jonathan Hallett
Income: £7,360,000 [2017]; £8,456,000 [2016]; £7,381,000 [2015]; £5,840,000 [2014]; £6,369,000 [2013]

SeAp
Registered: 11 May 2000 *Employees:* 135 *Volunteers:* 43
Tel: 0330 440 9000 *Website:* seap.org.uk
Activities: Education, training; advancement of health or saving of lives; disability
Address: Town Hall, Queens Square, Hastings, E Sussex, TN34 1TL
Trustees: Mandy Heslop, Ms Avril Chester, Mr Adam Chambers, Ms Verna Connolly, Mr Andrew Voyce, Ms Jane Dodson
Income: £5,163,530 [2017]; £4,291,067 [2016]; £3,440,474 [2015]; £3,147,633 [2014]; £5,086,728 [2013]

Seafarers UK (King George's Fund for Sailors)
Registered: 28 Mar 1969 *Employees:* 18 *Volunteers:* 100
Tel: 020 7932 0000 *Website:* seafarers.uk
Activities: General charitable purposes; education, training; advancement of health or saving of lives; disability; prevention or relief of poverty; accommodation, housing; amateur sport; armed forces, emergency service efficiency
Address: Seafarers UK, 8 Hatherley Street, London, SW1P 2QT
Trustees: Mr Mark Carden, Mrs Christine Gould, Mr Simon Rivett-Carnac, Mr Mark Dickinson, Captain Roger Barker, Surgeon Commodore Peter J Buxton OBE QHP RN, Mrs Evelyn Anne Strouts, Ms Natalie Shaw, Mr Paul Gerard Butterworth, Mr Robert John Greenwood, Mr Gerald Edward Kidd, Mr Christian Marr, Alderman The Lord Mountevans, Vice Admiral Peter Wilkinson CB CVO BA, Ms Dyan M Sterling, Mr Jeremy Monroe, Mr Duncan Bain, Mr Peter Dawson Tomlin, Mr William Ernest Lawes
Income: £2,833,000 [2016]; £2,735,000 [2015]; £2,719,000 [2014]; £2,862,000 [2013]; £3,360,286 [2012]

Seashell Trust
Registered: 27 Jun 2002 *Employees:* 501 *Volunteers:* 200
Tel: 0161 610 0100 *Website:* seashelltrust.org.uk
Activities: Education, training; advancement of health or saving of lives; disability; accommodation, housing; amateur sport
Address: Seashell Trust, Stanley Road, Cheadle Hulme, Cheadle, Cheshire, SK8 6RQ
Trustees: Mr David Shipley, Mr Nic Gower, Mr Edward Baines, Mr Stephen Gillingham, Mrs Julie Vanessa Besbrode, Dr David Sanders, Mrs Gwen Carr, Dr Afshan Kawaja, Mr Christopher Luke Smale
Income: £13,726,000 [2017]; £12,608,000 [2016]; £17,892,000 [2015]; £11,403,000 [2014]; £12,544,000 [2013]

Seaton House School Limited
Registered: 10 Jan 1989 *Employees:* 24
Tel: 020 8642 2332 *Website:* seatonhouse.sutton.sch.uk
Activities: Education, training
Address: 67 Banstead Road South, Sutton, Surrey, SM2 5LH
Trustees: Mrs Judith Evans, Mr Steven John Frank Zammit, Mr Prashant Patel, Barbara Grant, Mrs Michelle Smith, Mr Mark Graham Russell
Income: £1,372,515 [2017]; £1,345,101 [2016]; £1,335,660 [2015]; £1,208,767 [2014]; £1,111,327 [2013]

Sebastian's Action Trust
Registered: 7 Mar 2013 *Employees:* 21 *Volunteers:* 477
Tel: 01344 622500 *Website:* sebastiansactiontrust.org
Activities: The advancement of health or saving of lives
Address: The Woodlands, Upper Broadmoor Road, Crowthorne, Berks, RG45 7DG
Trustees: Miss Candida Hazard, Mrs Ann Hunter Stokes MBA MSc, Mr Mark Courage, Mrs Linda Patterson, Mr Arthur Leonard Rose, Mr Brendan Dean, Mrs Sheila Elizabeth Stranks, Mrs Fiona Anne Parsons
Income: £1,065,269 [2017]; £1,144,830 [2016]; £971,487 [2015]; £474,827 [2014]

Sam and Bella Sebba Charitable Trust
Registered: 5 Sep 1967 *Employees:* 2
Tel: 020 7723 6028
Activities: General charitable purposes; education, training; advancement of health or saving of lives; disability; religious activities; environment, conservation, heritage; economic, community development, employment; human rights, religious or racial harmony, equality or diversity
Address: Office 19, 5th Floor, Sam & Bella Sebba Charitable Trust, 63-66 Hatton Garden, London, EC1N 8LE
Trustees: Mr Victor Klein, Ms Odelia Sebba, Mrs Leah Hurst, Mr Yoav Tangir, Mrs Tamsin Doyle, Dr Varda Shiffer
Income: £1,032,406 [2016]; £1,159,823 [2015]; £1,201,013 [2014]; £785,890 [2013]; £6,314,617 [2012]

The Seckford Foundation
Registered: 22 Aug 2005 *Employees:* 537 *Volunteers:* 19
Tel: 01394 615000 *Website:* seckford-foundation.org.uk
Activities: Education, training; prevention or relief of poverty; accommodation, housing; religious activities; economic, community development, employment
Address: The Seckford Foundation, Marryott House, Burkitt Road, Woodbridge, Suffolk, IP12 4JJ
Trustees: Mr Roger John Finbow, Mr James Dermot Wellesley Wesley, Professor Jane Elizabeth Anne Wright, Mr Martin Sylvester, Mr Geoff Holdcroft, Mrs Judi Newman, Ms Jill Gibbs, Mr Graham Kill, Emily Skinner, Rev Canon Kevan S McCormack, Mrs Wendy Susan Evans-Hendrick, Mr Bryan Laxton, Inga Grimsey, Jude Chin, Mr Jeston Na Nakhorn, Mrs Sarah Holsgrove, Neil Alderton
Income: £19,767,428 [2017]; £20,155,536 [2016]; £25,535,198 [2015]; £26,883,003 [2014]; £18,936,748 [2013]

Secret World Wildlife Rescue
Registered: 17 Apr 2003 *Employees:* 27 *Volunteers:* 200
Tel: 01278 783250 *Website:* secretworld.org
Activities: Education, training; animals; environment, conservation, heritage
Address: Secret World, New Road Farm, New Road, East Huntspill, Highbridge, Somerset, TA9 3PZ
Trustees: Michelle Barrows, Dr Bel Deering, Mr Roger Neil Branton, Mrs Joanne Gilbert
Income: £1,426,152 [2016]; £907,196 [2015]; £1,151,565 [2014]; £907,343 [2013]; £974,569 [2012]

Secular Clergy Common Fund
Registered: 16 Dec 1965 *Employees:* 17
Tel: 020 8969 1145
Activities: The prevention or relief of poverty; religious activities
Address: St Mary's Cemetery, Harrow Road, Kensal Green, London, NW10 5NU
Trustees: Rev Canon John Kavanagh, Rev Thomas Egan, Reverend Patrick Tansey, Rev Jonathan How, Rev John Joseph Harvey, Rev Phelim Rowland
Income: £1,745,705 [2017]; £1,770,586 [2016]; £1,654,222 [2015]; £1,587,225 [2014]; £1,381,746 [2013]

Sedbergh School
Registered: 11 May 2000 *Employees:* 302 *Volunteers:* 12
Tel: 015396 20303 *Website:* sedberghschool.org
Activities: Education, training
Address: Lofthouse Barn, Busk Lane, Sedbergh, Cumbria, LA10 5HF
Trustees: Mrs Claire Hensman, Sir Andrew Gregory, Mr Jeremy Bedford BA, The Venerable Nicholas Barker, Mr Richard Gledhill MA, Ian Durrans, Mr Richard Papworth, Mr Michael Piercy, Sir Roger Gifford, Mrs Louise Denney, Mr Hugh Blair, Mrs Louise Bates, Dr Emma Waring PhD MA LLM, Mr John Warburton-Lee, Mr John Campbell
Income: £17,691,000 [2017]; £16,406,000 [2016]; £15,063,000 [2015]; £18,536,877 [2014]; £13,320,027 [2013]

Seedbed Christian Community Trust Limited
Registered: 2 Mar 2005 *Employees:* 10
Tel: 07886 499891
Activities: General charitable purposes; prevention or relief of poverty; religious activities; arts, culture, heritage, science; economic, community development, employment; human rights, religious or racial harmony, equality or diversity
Address: 86 Granville Street, Peterborough, PE1 2QJ
Trustees: Mike Love, Ms Susan Alison Barnard Hoey, Chris Erskine
Income: £5,300,834 [2016]; £5,301,258 [2015]; £5,300,925 [2014]; £5,332,363 [2013]; £7,327,408 [2012]

Seely Hirst House
Registered: 2 Mar 2015 *Employees:* 58 *Volunteers:* 2
Tel: 0115 960 6610 *Website:* seelyhirsthouse.co.uk
Activities: Accommodation, housing
Address: Seeley Hirst House, 62-68 Mapperley Road, Nottingham, NG3 5AS
Trustees: Mrs Maureen Evans, Mrs Diane O'Malley, Mr Peter Hands, Mr Imran Sadiq, Rev Michael Richard Knight, Mrs Maryvonne Hands, Mr Christopher Allison
Income: £1,808,059 [2017]

Sefton Council for Voluntary Service
Registered: 4 Aug 1993 *Employees:* 77 *Volunteers:* 86
Tel: 0151 920 0726 *Website:* seftoncvs.org.uk
Activities: General charitable purposes; education, training; advancement of health or saving of lives; disability; prevention or relief of poverty; environment, conservation, heritage; economic, community development, employment; human rights, religious or racial harmony, equality or diversity; other charitable purposes
Address: 3rd Floor, Sefton CVS, North Wing, Burlington House, Crosby Road North, Waterloo, Liverpool, L22 0LG
Trustees: Mr Paul Cummins, Mr David Roscoe, Rev Peter Hendry Spiers, Mrs Elizabeth Barnett, Mr Mark Sonne, Mrs Valerie Elson, Mr Brian Thomas, Mr Simon Sharman, Ms Paulette Lappin, Mr David McGregor, Dr Michael Homfray, Ms Nicola Ronan, Mrs Brenda Porter
Income: £1,954,324 [2017]; £2,253,747 [2016]; £2,761,132 [2015]; £2,741,555 [2014]; £3,168,699 [2013]

The Segelman Trust
Registered: 28 Jan 2000
Activities: General charitable purposes; education, training; prevention or relief of poverty; arts, culture, heritage, science; human rights, religious or racial harmony, equality or diversity
Address: 25 Moorgate, London, EC2R 6AY
Trustees: Mr Timothy Douglas White, Mrs Rebecca Eastmond, Mr Wilson Peter Cotton, Mr Christopher Graves
Income: £1,329,466 [2016]; £1,187,158 [2015]; £932,684 [2014]; £862,423 [2013]; £837,513 [2012]

Self Help Africa (UK)
Registered: 9 Mar 1988 *Employees:* 12 *Volunteers:* 25
Tel: 01743 277170 *Website:* selfhelpafrica.org
Activities: Education, training; prevention or relief of poverty; overseas aid, famine relief
Address: Self Help Africa, Second Floor, Westgate House, Dickens Court, 25 Hills Lane, Shrewsbury, Salop, SY1 1QU
Trustees: Mr Michael R Hoevel, Ms Sheila Walsh, Mr Thomas Kitt, Ms Dervla Owens
Income: £3,777,801 [2016]; £3,215,845 [2015]; £2,651,184 [2014]; £3,570,214 [2013]; £2,192,274 [2012]

Self Help Services
Registered: 19 Dec 2007 *Employees:* 113 *Volunteers:* 125
Tel: 0161 848 2423 *Website:* thebiglifegroup.com
Activities: The advancement of health or saving of lives
Address: Big Life Group, Kath Locke Community Centre, 123 Moss Lane East, Manchester, M15 5DD
Trustees: Ms Fay Selvan, Mrs Edna Robinson, Mr Mark James Fitzgibbon
Income: £3,797,946 [2017]; £3,284,994 [2016]; £3,320,307 [2015]; £2,834,950 [2014]; £2,337,968 [2013]

Self Management UK Limited
Registered: 30 Mar 2012 *Employees:* 31 *Volunteers:* 29
Tel: 07545 609387 *Website:* selfmanagementuk.org
Activities: General charitable purposes; education, training; advancement of health or saving of lives; disability
Address: CAN Mezzanine, 32-36 Loman Street, London, SE1 0EH
Trustees: Ms Miriam McKee, Ms Catherine James, Mrs Jane Brooks, Mr Anthony Levy FEI, Mrs Alpana Malde, Ms Lisa Quinlan-Rahman
Income: £1,039,023 [2017]; £1,225,996 [2016]; £1,464,886 [2015]; £72,495 [2014]; £850,092 [2013]

Selwood Housing Society Limited
Registered: 4 Apr 2011 *Employees:* 250 *Volunteers:* 63
Tel: 01225 715903 *Website:* selwoodhousing.com
Activities: Education, training; advancement of health or saving of lives; disability; prevention or relief of poverty; accommodation, housing; economic, community development, employment; human rights, religious or racial harmony, equality or diversity
Address: Selwood Housing Society Ltd, Bryer Ash Business Park, Bradford Road, Trowbridge, Wilts, BA14 8RT
Trustees: Lee O'Bryan, Mrs Bridget Wayman, Mrs Margaret Anne Haylock, Mr Martin Willard Pain, Mr Brian Cosstick, Mr Richard Britton, Ian Harries, Ms Claudia Bailey
Income: £37,111,000 [2017]; £36,030,000 [2016]; £32,139,000 [2015]; £29,695,103 [2014]; £28,309,000 [2013]

Selwyn College Cambridge
Registered: 17 Aug 2010 *Employees:* 158
Tel: 01223 335892 *Website:* sel.cam.ac.uk
Activities: Education, training
Address: Selwyn College, Cambridge, CB3 9DQ
Trustees: Dr David Lawrence Smith, Ms Sarah MacDonald MA FRCO, Prof Patrick Baert, Dr John Benson, Professor Nicholas Butterfield, Prof Robert Stewart Cant, Prof William Clegg, Prof John Dennis, Dr James Keeler, Dr Sarah Meer, Dr Nikolaos Nikiforakis, Dr Amer Rana, Dr Michael Joseph Sewell, Dr Rupert John Ernest Thompson, Dr Charlotte Woodford, Dr Christopher Daniel Briggs, Dr Gavin Edward Jarvis, Dr Roddy O'Donnell, Dr Yu Ye, Dr Asif Hameed, Dr Chander Velu, Dr Marta Halina, Dr Filipe Carreira Da Silva, Dr Anita Faul, Dr Kirsty McDougall, Professor Ian Alexander McFarland, Dr Paul David Upton, Dr Dacia Viejo Rose, Dr Elena Filimonova, Dr Victoria Young, Dr Charlotte Summers, Mr Yuning Zhou, Mr Oliver Black, Professor Katharine Ellis, Mr Roger Mosey, Dr Daniel Beauregard, Dr Uradyn Erden Bulag, Dr Jack Oliver Button, Prof Daping Chu, Dr Philip Connell, Mr Nicholas James Anthony Downer, Mr James Michael Raistrick Matheson, Dr James Moultrie, Dr Janet O'Sullivan, Dr Stewart Sage, Rev'd Canon Hugh David Shilson-Thomas, Dr David Willis, Dr Fabian Grabenhorst, Dr George Kolios, Dr Stuart Eves, Dr Bonnie Lander Johnson, Mr Michael Nicholson, Dr Heather Mariah Webb, Dr Emily Jane Charnock, Dr Bryan Stanley Cameron, Dr Lauren Beth Wilcox, Dr Alan Howard, Dr Jennifer Bates, Dr Joseph William Sampson, Mr Oleg Kitov, Dr Gilad Antler, Dr Jessica Gardner, Dr Shaun Thomas Larcom, Dr Bjorn F N Wallace, Mr Harry Gibbins
Income: £14,225,874 [2017]; £10,685,000 [2016]; £9,150,228 [2015]; £9,206,341 [2014]; £7,426,153 [2013]

Send A Cow
Registered: 25 Oct 1988 *Employees:* 248 *Volunteers:* 3
Tel: 01225 874222 *Website:* sendacow.org
Activities: Education, training; disability; prevention or relief of poverty; overseas aid, famine relief; animals; environment, conservation, heritage; economic, community development, employment
Address: The Old Estate Yard, Newton St Loe, Bath, BA2 9BR
Trustees: Mr Peter Hinton, Rev Gerald Osborne, Mr John Geake, Mr Philip Mounstephen, Stephanie Dennison, Dr Alan Kerbey, Mr Chris Egitto, Ms Isabella Wemyss, Fiona Crisp, Dr Andrew Mubeezi-Magoola
Income: £6,908,960 [2017]; £6,523,164 [2016]; £6,711,801 [2015]; £6,276,132 [2014]; £4,830,211 [2013]

Sense International
Registered: 12 Jul 1999 *Employees:* 28 *Volunteers:* 2
Tel: 020 7014 9322 *Website:* senseinternational.org.uk
Activities: Education, training; advancement of health or saving of lives; disability; prevention or relief of poverty; economic, community development, employment; human rights, religious or racial harmony, equality or diversity
Address: 101 Pentonville Road, London, N1 9LG
Trustees: Ms Sue Turner, Mr Pankaj Shah, Paul Feeney, Ms Verity Stiff, Nicholas Corby, Richard Cooper, Mr Sunil Sheth, Robin Heber Percy, Dean Lumer, Sunil Shah, Ms Maria Arce Moreira
Income: £1,733,293 [2017]; £1,691,956 [2016]; £1,830,799 [2015]; £1,421,778 [2014]; £1,748,944 [2013]

Sense, The National Deafblind and Rubella Association
Registered: 26 Jul 1984 *Employees:* 3,349 *Volunteers:* 2,350
Tel: 020 7014 9322 *Website:* sense.org.uk
Activities: Education, training; advancement of health or saving of lives; disability; accommodation, housing; arts, culture, heritage, science; amateur sport
Address: Sense, 101 Pentonville Road, London, N1 9LG
Trustees: Gillian Wood, Dr Justin Molloy, Mr David Reeves, Mr Nicholas Keegan, Desmond Lucy, Graham Callister, Mythily Katsaris, Brian Symington, Ms Susan Turner, Benedict Leigh, Mr Duncan Tannahill, Natalie Assad, Simon Armstrong, Ashling Barve, Andrew Pearson
Income: £88,206,108 [2017]; £84,686,453 [2016]; £82,964,881 [2015]; £81,807,742 [2014]; £80,007,020 [2013]

Sentebale
Registered: 4 Apr 2006 *Employees:* 37
Tel: 020 7730 0226 *Website:* sentebale.org
Activities: Education, training; advancement of health or saving of lives; disability; prevention or relief of poverty; overseas aid, famine relief
Address: 4th Floor, 136 Sloane Street, London, SW1X 9AY
Trustees: Mr Damian West, Baroness Lynda Chalker of Wallasey, Mrs Nicola Brewer, Dr Tsitsi Chawatama, Mr Mark Dyer, Mr Johnny Hornby, Mr Tim Boucher
Income: £3,550,000 [2017]; £4,361,000 [2016]; £3,432,000 [2015]; £3,373,000 [2014]; £2,601,000 [2013]

Sentinel Leisure Trust
Registered: 29 Jun 2012 *Employees:* 280 *Volunteers:* 6
Tel: 01502 532542 *Website:* waterlanelc.co.uk
Activities: Recreation
Address: Waterlane Leisure Centre, Water Lane, Lowestoft, Suffolk, NR32 2NH
Trustees: Mr Michael Jeal, Ms Kathleen Grant, Mr Jamie Starling, Mr Andy Cook, Mr Joe Annis, Mr Andy Wilson-Sutter, Mr Keith Ibbetson, Mr Bernard Williamson, Mrs Jane Murray
Income: £5,873,517 [2017]; £5,376,511 [2016]; £2,975,248 [2015]; £2,882,271 [2014]; £2,723,403 [2013]

The Sequoia Trust
Registered: 8 Sep 2015
Tel: 020 7925 7723
Activities: General charitable purposes
Address: Marshall Wace Asset Management, George House, 131 Sloane Street, London, SW1X 9AT
Trustees: Mr Paul Roderick Clucas Marshall, Ms Deborah Jane Afdhal, Ms Claire Musgrave, Ms Sabine Marie Cynthia Jeanne Marshall
Income: £39,894,497 [2017]; £62,323,602 [2016]

Seren Ffestiniog Cyf.
Registered: 7 Mar 2005 *Employees:* 65 *Volunteers:* 3
Tel: 01766 832378 *Website:* serencyf.org
Activities: General charitable purposes; education, training; disability; prevention or relief of poverty
Address: Unit 2 Llwyn Gell Industrial Estate, Blaenau Ffestiniog, Gwynedd, LL41 3NE
Trustees: Mr Gwilym Price, Mr Aled Ellis, Mr William Anthony Evans, Mrs Adelyn Ellis, Mrs Gaenor Powell Grabowski, Mrs Linda Ann Wyn Jones, Mr John Elwyn Ellis, Mr Eifion Jarrett Lewis, Mr Edward Myrfyn Jones, Miss Meinir Angharad Williams
Income: £1,496,914 [2017]; £1,288,103 [2016]; £1,469,472 [2015]; £2,018,107 [2014]; £1,170,857 [2013]

The Serpentine Trust
Registered: 21 Mar 1988 *Employees:* 76
Website: serpentinegalleries.org
Activities: Education, training; arts, culture, heritage, science
Address: Serpentine Gallery, Kensington Gardens, London, W2 3XA
Trustees: Mr Barry Townsley CBE, Mr David Adjaye, Mr Jonathan Paul Wood, The Hon Michael R Bloomberg, Mr Michael Sidney Sherwood, Ms Amanda Miriam Sharp, Maja Hoffman, The Hon Mrs Felicity Waley-Cohen, Mr Marcus Boyle, Ms Ruth MacKenzie OBE, Miss Lynette Yiadom-Boakye, Mr Pierre Philippe Alexandre Lagrange, Mr Andrew Cohen
Income: £9,395,483 [2017]; £8,092,539 [2016]; £7,004,979 [2015]; £7,049,855 [2014]; £5,790,603 [2013]

Servants Fellowship International
Registered: 25 Mar 1982
Tel: 01672 564938
Activities: Education, training; prevention or relief of poverty; accommodation, housing; religious activities; human rights, religious or racial harmony, equality or diversity
Address: The Old Rectory, River Street, Pewsey, Wilts, SN9 5DB
Trustees: Miss Caroline Julia Chenevix Kerslake, Mrs Rosmarie Margrith Hauser, Rev Albrecht Bernhard Hauser
Income: £1,258,346 [2016]; £695,274 [2015]; £617,193 [2014]; £1,061,187 [2013]; £784,818 [2012]

Service to the Aged
Registered: 13 Feb 1991 *Employees:* 113 *Volunteers:* 30
Tel: 020 7863 1555
Activities: Education, training; advancement of health or saving of lives; accommodation, housing; religious activities; economic, community development, employment
Address: Freshwater Group of Companies, Freshwater House, 158-162 Shaftesbury Avenue, London, WC2H 8HR
Trustees: Dr Michael Jeffrey Sinclair, Mr Solomon Israel Freshwater, Mr Stephen Jonathan Goldberg, Mr Benzion Schalom Eliezer Freshwater, Mr Adrian Mark Jacobs
Income: £3,221,231 [2017]; £2,809,653 [2016]; £2,846,090 [2015]; £3,150,823 [2014]; £3,350,882 [2013]

The Services Sound and Vision Corporation
Registered: 11 May 1964 *Employees:* 213
Tel: 01494 878370 *Website:* ssvc.com
Activities: Education, training; other charitable purposes
Address: SSVC, Chalfont Grove, Narcot Lane, Chalfont St Peter, Gerrards Cross, Bucks, SL9 8TN
Trustees: Mr Howard Stephen Perlin, Air Vice-Marshal Andrew Vallance, Major General Christopher Colin Wilson, Mrs Margaret Adela Miriam Carver, Mr Anthony John Rix, Captain Graham David Brice Robinson RN, Mr Tony Hales, Mr Stephen Graham Mitchell, Mr Mark Browning, Mrs Deborah Jane Loudon
Income: £24,739,000 [2017]; £25,227,000 [2016]; £29,518,000 [2015]; £30,283,000 [2014]; £33,818,000 [2013]

Services for Independent Living
Registered: 15 Aug 2003 *Employees:* 98 *Volunteers:* 3
Tel: 01568 616653 *Website:* s4il.co.uk
Activities: General charitable purposes; education, training; advancement of health or saving of lives; disability; economic, community development, employment
Address: 1 Bacho Hill Cottages, Vowchurch, Herefords, HR2 9PF
Trustees: Mrs Margaret O'Neill, Mr Tom Misselbrook, Mrs Sylvie Nicholls, Mr Geoff Hopper, Mr John Rogers, Mrs Angela Higham
Income: £1,827,239 [2017]; £1,772,582 [2016]; £1,911,578 [2015]; £1,996,743 [2014]; £1,859,376 [2013]

N Sethia Foundation
Registered: 27 Sep 1995
Website: nirmalsethiafoundation.com
Activities: Education, training; advancement of health or saving of lives; prevention or relief of poverty
Address: 105 St John Street, London, EC1M 4AS
Trustees: Ms Richa Sethia, Mr Chhatar Singh Jain, Mr Arun Bhattacharya, Mr Nirmal Sethia, Mr Amrao Jain
Income: £2,702,279 [2017]; £1,475,476 [2016]; £1,275,589 [2015]; £2,283,294 [2014]; £280,831 [2013]

Seven Locks Housing Limited
Registered: 22 Oct 2007 Employees: 26 Volunteers: 9
Tel: 0800 435016 Website: sevenlockshousing.co.uk
Activities: Accommodation, housing; other charitable purposes
Address: Waterloo Housing Group, Unit 1700, Solihull Parkway, Birmingham Business Park, Birmingham, B37 7YD
Trustees: Prof Janet Ford, Mr Jeffrey Richard Sharnock, Mr David John Pickering, Ms Joanne Brodrick, Mr Dennis William Sleath
Income: £10,836,000 [2017]; £10,837,000 [2016]; £10,634,000 [2015]; £10,201,000 [2014]; £10,265,000 [2013]

Seven Stories, The National Centre for Children's Books
Registered: 15 Jul 1996 Employees: 62 Volunteers: 43
Tel: 0300 330 1095 Website: sevenstories.org.uk
Activities: Education, training; arts, culture, heritage, science
Address: Seven Stories, The Centre for Childrens Books, 30 Lime Street, Newcastle upon Tyne, NE1 2PQ
Trustees: Mr Nick Kemp, Sarah Pelham, Mr Mark Robinson, Mr Matthew Grenby, Ms Julia Morrison, Ms Manohari Saravanamuttu, Miss Catriona Nicholson, Ms Deirdre McDermott, Mrs Linda Moore, Mr Douglas Dodds, Ms Anthony Pierce, Mr Matthew McWhinnie
Income: £1,683,902 [2017]; £2,171,824 [2016]; £2,472,353 [2015]; £1,775,625 [2014]; £1,771,787 [2013]

Sevenoaks Preparatory School Limited
Registered: 13 Oct 2003 Employees: 80 Volunteers: 8
Tel: 01732 762274 Website: theprep.org.uk
Activities: Education, training
Address: Sevenoaks Preparatory School, Godden Green, Sevenoaks, Kent, TN15 0JU
Trustees: Mr E Oatley, Mrs Sally-Anne Huang, Mr Nicholas Courtenay Robinson, Mr Timothy Clive Dickinson, Mr Robert Burgess, Mr Richard Risino, Mr Peter Derry Wiltshire, Mr Christopher John Sutton-Mattocks, Mrs Janette Susan Berry, Dr Marius Carboni, Mr Gi Fernando, Mr Alex Durtnell
Income: £4,190,857 [2017]; £4,086,652 [2016]; £4,016,458 [2015]; £3,652,001 [2014]; £3,354,155 [2013]

Sevenoaks School Foundation
Registered: 18 Nov 1970 Employees: 8
Tel: 01732 455133 Website: sevenoaksschool.org
Activities: Education, training
Address: Sevenoaks School, High Street, Sevenoaks, Kent, TN13 1HU
Trustees: Mr Colin Robert Harris, Mr Derick Royaards Walker MA, Mr David Andrew Rees Williams, Robert Sackville-West, Mr David McEuen, Mr Timothy John Child, Mr Julian Patrick
Income: £6,694,670 [2017]; £4,347,939 [2016]; £2,870,945 [2015]; £2,879,619 [2014]; £2,217,249 [2013]

Sevenoaks School
Registered: 5 Jan 2004 Employees: 422 Volunteers: 22
Tel: 01732 455133 Website: sevenoaksschool.org
Activities: Education, training
Address: Sevenoaks School, High Street, Sevenoaks, Kent, TN13 1HU
Trustees: Mr Pratap Shirke MBA, Professor Susan Iversen, Mrs Sarah Dunnett BA(Hons), Mr David Michael Phillips BA ACA, Mr Ian Doherty MA, James London, Ms Alison Beckett, Mr Christopher Gill, Mr Roger Nicholas Hayward Gould BA, Professor Ian Wilson, Mrs Sian Carr, Mrs Eliza Ecclestone LLB Dip LP, Andrew Timms, Mr Adam Boulton, Lord Alastair Colin Leckie Colgrain, Mr John Graham Davies
Income: £29,824,153 [2017]; £28,988,933 [2016]; £27,239,905 [2015]; £26,069,991 [2014]; £24,575,718 [2013]

Severn Hospice Limited
Registered: 11 Mar 1982 Employees: 442 Volunteers: 1,400
Tel: 01743 236565 Website: severnhospice.org.uk
Activities: Education, training; advancement of health or saving of lives
Address: Severn Hospice Ltd, Bicton Heath, Shrewsbury, Salop, SY3 8HS
Trustees: Mr John Michael Fairclough, Dr Wendy-Jane Walton, John Wardle, Mrs Ann Tudor, Mr Antony Cordery, Declan Ryan, Zara Oliver, Mrs Gabrielle De Wet, Mrs Sarah Broomhead, Mr Francis Yates, Mrs Judith Beard, Mrs Barbara-Ann Tweedie, Paul Donohue
Income: £10,701,106 [2017]; £10,910,542 [2016]; £10,851,969 [2015]; £10,282,578 [2014]; £9,198,847 [2013]

The Severn Trent Water Charitable Trust Fund
Registered: 24 Feb 2005 Employees: 59
Tel: 0121 355 7766 Website: sttf.org.uk
Activities: The prevention or relief of poverty
Address: 12-14 Mill Street, Sutton Coldfield, W Midlands, B72 1TJ
Trustees: Elizabeth Ann Pusey, Ms Alexandra Gribbin, Mr Clive Jonathan Mottram, Mr Paul Clive Stone, Jane Catherine Bleach, David James Vaughan, Mrs Lowri Williams, Mr Andrew Kenneth Phelps, Mr Craig Simmons
Income: £5,294,781 [2017]; £4,816,596 [2016]; £4,242,356 [2015]; £4,644,857 [2014]; £4,429,101 [2013]

Severn Wye Energy Agency
Registered: 27 Nov 2000 Employees: 40
Tel: 01452 835060 Website: severnwye.org.uk
Activities: Education, training; advancement of health or saving of lives; prevention or relief of poverty; environment, conservation, heritage; economic, community development, employment
Address: Unit 15 Highnam Business Centre, Highnam, Gloucester, GL2 8DN
Trustees: Ms Heather Jane Watts, Mr Andrew Lichnowski, Mr Dafydd Thomas, Mrs Rowena Louise Kay, Mr Douglas Coombs, Mr David Hardie, Mr Peter Clegg, Mr Daniel Clegg
Income: £2,591,998 [2017]; £2,252,865 [2016]; £1,724,061 [2015]; £1,929,708 [2014]; £2,042,715 [2013]

Severnside Housing

Registered: 1 Apr 2016 *Employees:* 216
Tel: 01743 285073 *Website:* severnsidehousing.co.uk
Activities: General charitable purposes; education, training; disability; prevention or relief of poverty; accommodation, housing; environment, conservation, heritage; economic, community development, employment; recreation
Address: Severnside Housing, Severnside House, Brassey Road, Shrewsbury, Salop, SY3 7FA
Trustees: Mr Peter Sean Phillips, Mr Rory O'Byrne, Ms Catherine Sushma Dass, Mr Anthony Pate, Mr Malcolm Thomas Price, Mr Steven Edward Jennings, Mr Philip Ingle
Income: £30,964,869 [2017]

The Shaare Hayim Congregation

Registered: 27 Jan 1998 *Employees:* 6 *Volunteers:* 13
Tel: 0161 830 4606
Activities: General charitable purposes; education, training; prevention or relief of poverty; religious activities; other charitable purposes
Address: Horwich Cohen Coghlan, Quay House, Quay Street, Manchester, M3 3JE
Trustees: Mr Victor Hassan, Mr Anthony Leon, Mr Daniel Betesh, Mr Michael Edward Mesrie, Mr David Peppi, Mr Anthony Morris Sultan, Mr Reuben Sami Solomon
Income: £1,220,878 [2016]; £351,741 [2015]; £392,579 [2014]; £527,452 [2013]; £1,458,080 [2012]

Shaarei Rachamim Limited

Registered: 26 Sep 1996
Activities: General charitable purposes; education, training; prevention or relief of poverty; religious activities; other charitable purposes
Address: New Burlington House, 1075 Finchley Road, London, NW11 0PU
Trustees: Mr Abraham Klein, Mrs Sarah Rachel Klein, Mr Joshua Sternlicht
Income: £3,060,000 [2016]; £1,440,835 [2015]; £1,482,225 [2014]; £275,600 [2013]; £379,300 [2012]

The Shaftesbury Homes and Arethusa

Registered: 13 Aug 1965 *Employees:* 64 *Volunteers:* 9
Tel: 01634 719933 *Website:* shaftesburyyoungpeople.org
Activities: Education, training; accommodation, housing
Address: Shaftesbury Homes & Arethusa, Lower Upnor, Upnor, Rochester, Kent, ME2 4XB
Trustees: Ms Jennifer Thewlis, Mr Brian Scott, Mr Elliot Mark Bancroft, Ms Clare Louise Searle, Ms Zoe Brown, Mr David Bunce, Mr Roger Black
Income: £2,899,000 [2017]; £4,177,000 [2016]; £2,720,000 [2015]; £2,346,000 [2014]; £4,493,000 [2013]

The Shakespeare Birthplace Trust

Registered: 7 Feb 1963 *Employees:* 273 *Volunteers:* 150
Tel: 01789 201810 *Website:* shakespeare.org.uk
Activities: General charitable purposes; education, training; arts, culture, heritage, science; environment, conservation, heritage
Address: Shakespeare Birthplace Trust, Shakespeare Centre, Henley Street, Stratford upon Avon, Warwicks, CV37 6QW
Trustees: Mr Peter Kyle, Professor Carol Chillington Rutter MA PH, Mr John Russell BSc, Mrs Rosaleen Mary Haigh, Ms Kathryn Gee MBE, Professor Lena Cowen Orlin, Mr Nicholas Quilter Abell, Mr Ralph Bernard CBE, Lady Penelope Cobham CBE, Mr Colin Christopher Bennett, Ms Rebecca Ysabel Dobbs, Mr Alberto Leon
Income: £12,062,000 [2016]; £10,459,000 [2015]; £9,781,000 [2014]; £9,046,000 [2013]; £8,096,000 [2012]

The Shakespeare Globe Trust

Registered: 14 Feb 1974 *Employees:* 288 *Volunteers:* 650
Website: shakespearesglobe.org
Activities: Education, training; arts, culture, heritage, science
Address: Shakespeare Globe Trust Ltd, 21 New Globe Walk, London, SE1 9DT
Trustees: Joanna Mackle, Ms Emma Stenning, Professor Laurie Maguire, Mr Martin Clarke, Mr Danny Witter, Lady Cynthia Hall, Dame Rachel De Souza, Dame Anne Pringle, Mr Alex Beard, Mr Philip Kirkpatrick, Mr Iraj Ispahani, Mr Neil Constable, Ms Jenny Topper, Margaret Casely-Hayford, Mr David Ralph Butter, Mr Daniel Heaf, Ms Neil Leyshon, Mr Gaurav Kripalani
Income: £24,605,000 [2017]; £27,051,000 [2016]; £23,039,000 [2015]; £22,017,000 [2014]; £21,662,000 [2013]

The Shakespeare Hospice

Registered: 22 Aug 1997 *Employees:* 76 *Volunteers:* 350
Tel: 01789 266852 *Website:* theshakespearehospice.org.uk
Activities: Education, training; advancement of health or saving of lives
Address: The Shakespeare Hospice, Church Lane, Shottery, Stratford upon Avon, Warwicks, CV37 9UL
Trustees: Mr Richard Barrett, Mrs Fiona Murphy, Miss Sophie Gilkes, Mrs Miranda McCormick, Mrs Kathryn Williams, Mr Charles Horton, Mrs Elizabeth Mary Spencer, Dr Emert O'Brian White, Mr Mark Haselden, Mrs Gill Thomas, Dr Cristina Ramos, Mr James Richards, Ms Deborah Marie Smith, Mr Adrian Peter Knott
Income: £1,889,475 [2017]; £1,820,459 [2016]; £1,810,100 [2015]; £2,942,808 [2014]; £2,188,779 [2013]

Shakespeare Schools Foundation

Registered: 3 Dec 2015 *Employees:* 37 *Volunteers:* 5
Tel: 020 7601 1800 *Website:* shakespeareschools.org
Activities: Education, training; arts, culture, heritage, science
Address: 140 London Wall, London, EC2Y 5DN
Trustees: Mrs Menna Lyn McGregor, Mrs Judith Ragan, Mr Andrew Jackson, Miss Petrina De Gouttes, Mrs Vicki Margaret Wienand, Mr Geraint Talfan Davies, Mr Guy Davies, Mr James Hadley, Ms Laura Elizabeth King
Income: £2,046,359 [2017]

The Shanly Foundation

Registered: 27 Oct 1997
Tel: 01494 683866 *Website:* shanlyfoundation.com
Activities: General charitable purposes
Address: c/o The Shanly Foundation, Sorbon, 24-26 Aylesbury End, Beaconsfield, Bucks, HP9 1LW
Trustees: Mrs Tamra Booth, Mr Donald Anthony Tucker, Mr Tim Potter, Mr Michael James Shanly
Income: £1,517,721 [2016]; £1,529,082 [2015]; £628,144 [2014]; £1,530,672 [2013]; £1,269,906 [2012]

Shape London

Registered: 20 Dec 1979 *Employees:* 16
Tel: 020 7424 7330 *Website:* shapearts.org.uk
Activities: Education, training; disability; arts, culture, heritage, science; economic, community development, employment; human rights, religious or racial harmony, equality or diversity; recreation
Address: Unit 21 Deane House Studios, 27 Greenwood Place, London, NW5 1LB
Trustees: Vidar Hjardeng, Mr Robert Leighton Davies, Ms Jackie Freeman, Ms Lois Keith, Mr Aidan Moesby, Mr Tony Heaton, Ms Sabita Kumari-Dass, Mr James Hodgson, Mr Adeolu Adesola
Income: £1,993,208 [2017]; £1,381,445 [2016]; £1,645,107 [2015]; £1,389,545 [2014]; £1,011,472 [2013]

Shared Lives Plus Limited
Registered: 23 Jan 2003 *Employees:* 26
Tel: 0151 227 3499 *Website:* sharedlivesplus.org.uk
Activities: Education, training; advancement of health or saving of
lives; disability; accommodation, housing; economic, community
development, employment
Address: G04 Cotton Exchange, Old Hall Street, Liverpool, L3 9JR
Trustees: Mr Ian Coleman, Mr Mark Andrew Howarth, Mr Mark
Sutton, Mr Martin David Vernon Thomas, Ms Mary Henrietta
Clewley, Ms Amanda Clarke, Mr Martin Ewing, Mr Richard Jones,
Mr Philip Mayne, Miss Claire Rachel Morphet, Ms Brenda Tukei
Income: £1,621,641 [2017]; £1,464,481 [2016]; £1,598,369 [2015];
£1,949,843 [2014]; £938,574 [2013]

Shared Lives South West
Registered: 1 Jul 2004 *Employees:* 30 *Volunteers:* 13
Tel: 01626 360170 *Website:* sharedlivessw.org.uk
Activities: Disability; accommodation, housing
Address: Suite 3, Zealley House, Greenhill Way, Kingsteignton,
Newton Abbot, Devon, TQ12 3SB
Trustees: Mrs Susan Margaret Joseph, Mrs Janet Mary Regan,
Cheryl Lewis, Ms Nadia Hewitt, Mr Keith Charles Richards,
Mrs Louise Beard, Edward Jackson, Ms Marilyn Minter-Newson
Income: £5,005,778 [2017]; £4,804,997 [2016]; £4,677,867 [2015];
£4,919,202 [2014]; £4,479,553 [2013]

Charles Sharland Trust
Registered: 7 Jan 2014
Tel: 0161 772 0099
Activities: General charitable purposes; education, training;
disability; prevention or relief of poverty
Address: 3 Hough Lane, Wilmslow, Cheshire, SK9 2LG
Trustees: Mr Charles Sharland, Mr Patrick Edmund Jolly, Mrs Gail
Hazley
Income: £1,466,037 [2017]

The Sharpham Trust
Registered: 29 Nov 1982 *Employees:* 16 *Volunteers:* 45
Tel: 01803 732055 *Website:* sharphamtrust.org
Activities: General charitable purposes; education, training; arts,
culture, heritage, science; environment, conservation, heritage
Address: Sharpham House, Ashprington, Totnes, Devon, TQ9 7UT
Trustees: Mrs Charlotte Rathbone MA MA CMLI, William Lana,
Mr Tony Kuhl, Mrs Elizabeth Anne Seward, Mr Martin Wright,
Mr Daniel Stokes
Income: £1,031,037 [2017]; £758,880 [2016]; £726,140 [2015];
£511,683 [2014]; £542,669 [2013]

Shaukat Khanum Memorial Trust
Registered: 8 Oct 1990 *Employees:* 2 *Volunteers:* 141
Tel: 01274 424444 *Website:* ikca.co.uk
Activities: The advancement of health or saving of lives
Address: Imran Khan Cancer Appeal, P O Box 786, 66 Little Horton
Lane, Bradford, BD5 0YE
Trustees: Mr Taher Nawaz, Mr Asmi Rashid Darr, Mr Imran Khan
Niazi
Income: £5,002,281 [2016]; £4,491,650 [2015]; £3,226,350 [2014];
£3,413,507 [2013]; £2,898,408 [2012]

The Shaw Trust Limited
Registered: 8 Sep 1983 *Employees:* 1,459 *Volunteers:* 1,400
Tel: 01225 716300 *Website:* shaw-trust.org.uk
Activities: Education, training; disability; prevention or relief of
poverty; economic, community development, employment
Address: 3rd Floor, Shaw Trust, 10 Victoria Street, Bristol, BS1 6BN
Trustees: Dr Michael Leslie Nussbaum, Mrs Janet Allen, Mr Peter
Holmes, Mr Paul Michael Baldwin, Ms Christina Mary Patterson,
Ms Rebecca Anne Sudworth, Mr John Norman, Mr Mike Hawker,
Mr Kenneth Alphunezi Olisa OBE
Income: £132,107,000 [2017]; £107,166,000 [2016]; £129,290,000
[2015]; £107,897,000 [2014]; £96,590,000 [2013]

Shebbear College
Registered: 4 Nov 1965 *Employees:* 112 *Volunteers:* 9
Tel: 020 7035 3723 *Website:* shebbearcollege.co.uk
Activities: Education, training; religious activities
Address: Methodist Church House, 25 Marylebone Road, London,
NW1 5JR
Trustees: Shebbear College Trustee Company Limited, Methodist
Independent Schools Trust
Income: £4,444,594 [2016]; £3,982,539 [2015]; £3,982,727 [2014];
£3,853,201 [2013]; £3,632,565 [2012]

Sheffcare Limited
Registered: 1 Apr 1996 *Employees:* 458 *Volunteers:* 25
Tel: 0114 280 8888 *Website:* sheffcare.co.uk
Activities: The advancement of health or saving of lives; disability;
accommodation, housing
Address: Mrs E Parkinson, Springwood House, 192 Penrith Road,
Sheffield, S5 8UG
Trustees: Mr Brian Martin James, Mr Scott Sanderson, Mrs Carole
Janet Rainbird, Mrs Anna Gailey, Mr Rod Taylor, Mr David Johnson,
Ms Fiona Miller
Income: £10,032,325 [2017]; £10,003,035 [2016]; £9,419,673
[2015]; £9,271,182 [2014]; £9,056,027 [2013]

Sheffield Citizens Advice and Law Centre
Registered: 7 Aug 2013 *Employees:* 163 *Volunteers:* 120
Tel: 0114 253 6703 *Website:* citizensadvicesheffield.org.uk
Activities: General charitable purposes; education, training;
advancement of health or saving of lives; prevention or relief of
poverty
Address: Management Team Office, The Circle, 33 Rockingham
Lane, Sheffield, S1 4FW
Trustees: Miss Hilary Jane Dawson, Ms Gillian Hutchens, Alistair
Griggs, Trevor Smith, Beatrice Burks, Mary Seneviratne, Sharon
Hirshman, Mark Smith, Mark Gamsu, Claire Holden, Callum Dixon
Income: £3,625,230 [2017]; £3,757,807 [2016]; £3,272,801 [2015];
£1,601,300 [2014]

Sheffield City Trust
Registered: 5 Aug 1988 *Employees:* 1,501
Tel: 0870 150 0100 *Website:* sheffieldcitytrust.org.uk
Activities: Education, training; advancement of health or saving
of lives; disability; prevention or relief of poverty; arts, culture,
heritage, science; amateur sport; environment, conservation,
heritage
Address: Irwin Mitchell, Riverside East, 2 Millsands, Sheffield,
S3 8DT
Trustees: Mr Jonathan Simon Parish, Ms Helen Best, Mrs Lynn
Clarke, Mr John Warner, Mr David Grey MBE, Mr Justin Andrew
Cole
Income: £42,344,029 [2017]; £43,691,000 [2016]; £48,186,000
[2015]; £162,978,000 [2014]; £61,903,000 [2013]

Sheffield Diocesan Board of Finance
Registered: 25 Nov 1965 *Employees:* 44
Tel: 01709 309117 *Website:* sheffield.anglican.org
Activities: Religious activities
Address: Diocese of Sheffield, Diocesan Church House, 95-99 Effingham Street, Rotherham, S Yorks, S65 1BL
Trustees: Mr Clive Howarth, Mr Peter Rainford, Rev Ian Smith, Rev Alan Timothy Isaacson, The Rt Revd Dr Peter Jonathan Wilcox, The Venerable Malcolm Leslie Chamberlain, Mr Ian Richard Downing, Very Rev Peter Bradley, Mr Ian Geoffrey Walker, The Right Revd Peter Burrows, Dr Jacqueline Anne Butcher, The Venerable Stephen Anthony Wilcockson, Rev Eleanor Elizabeth Mary Robertshaw, Mr Neill Andrew Birchenall
Income: £9,144,000 [2016]; £8,853,000 [2015]; £9,025,000 [2014]; £8,465,000 [2013]; £8,392,000 [2012]

Sheffield Galleries & Museums Trust
Registered: 25 Mar 1998 *Employees:* 68 *Volunteers:* 205
Tel: 0114 278 2652 *Website:* museums-sheffield.org.uk
Activities: Education, training; arts, culture, heritage, science; environment, conservation, heritage
Address: Museum & Gallery Trust, Leader House, Surrey Street, Sheffield, S1 2LH
Trustees: Mr John Cowling, Mr Peter Rippon, John Biggin, Dr Sheila Watson, Mrs Rosemary Downs, Dr Antonia Bostrum, Mr Darren Christopher Dryden Chouings, Mr Neil Andrew MacDonald, Ms Julie Taylor, Ms Maria Hanson, Mr Ian Proctor, Mr Patrick Paul Meleady, Councillor Dianne Lesley Hurst
Income: £3,708,317 [2017]; £3,907,670 [2016]; £3,810,000 [2015]; £3,516,000 [2014]; £4,913,000 [2013]

Sheffield Hallam University Students' Union
Registered: 16 May 2011 *Employees:* 72 *Volunteers:* 25
Tel: 0114 225 4138 *Website:* hallamstudentsunion.com
Activities: Education, training
Address: The Hubs, Paternoster Row, Sheffield, S1 2QQ
Trustees: Ms Isabel Hartland, Mr Chris James, Mr Luke Renwick, Ms Bethany Howden, Mr Mohammed Abdulredha, Mr Asim Mahmood, Gwyn Arnold, Mr David Silver, Mr Oliver Coppard, Mr Joshua Nimmins, Ms Gemma Anthony-Dixon, Mr Matthew Green
Income: £3,199,994 [2017]; £3,591,345 [2016]; £3,436,781 [2015]; £3,261,657 [2014]; £3,156,225 [2013]

Sheffield Industrial Museums Trust Limited
Registered: 23 Nov 1994 *Employees:* 20 *Volunteers:* 47
Tel: 01909 506295 *Website:* simt.co.uk
Activities: General charitable purposes; education, training; arts, culture, heritage, science; environment, conservation, heritage; economic, community development, employment
Address: 10 Southern Wood, Worksop, Notts, S80 3DA
Trustees: Mr Roderick Howard Maxwell Plews, Mr Nick Williams, Keith Crawshaw, Mr Anthony Swift, Mr Geoff Ernest Clifford Smith, Ms Kathryn Elizabeth Platts, Mr Richard Martin John McGloin, Mrs Lisa Anne Jean Banes, Mr Alexander William Pettifer, Mr Christopher Ingram Hill, Mr Richard Iain Abdy, Mrs Susan Gail Ransom, Mr Vivian Kenneth Lockwood, Mr David Macpherson, Ms Nicola Rawlins
Income: £1,313,533 [2017]; £1,231,216 [2016]; £1,148,386 [2015]; £1,958,491 [2014]; £914,239 [2013]

The Sheffield Media and Exhibition Centre Limited
Registered: 27 Feb 1991 *Employees:* 118 *Volunteers:* 400
Tel: 0114 279 6511 *Website:* showroomworkstation.org.uk
Activities: Education, training; arts, culture, heritage, science
Address: Showroom and Workstation, 15 Paternoster Row, Sheffield, S1 2BX
Trustees: Ms Margaret Ellis, Mr Peter John Brooks, Mr Colin Michael Pons, Mr Dean Brian Gormley, Mr Antony Davenport, Mr Brian Hamilton-Tweedale, Ms Sylvia Harvey, Mr Richard Best, Ms Sara Jane Sanderson, Mrs Lisa Rowley, Mr Mike Drabble
Income: £4,952,634 [2017]; £4,722,531 [2016]; £4,886,047 [2015]; £4,021,354 [2014]; £3,572,411 [2013]

Sheffield Methodist Circuit
Registered: 5 Feb 2010 *Employees:* 27
Tel: 0114 272 6561 *Website:* sheffieldcircuit.org.uk
Activities: Religious activities
Address: The Furnival, 199 Verdon Street, Sheffield, S3 9QQ
Trustees: Mrs Stella Mate, Mrs Pat Bolland, Mr David Burton, Rev Timothy John Crome BA, Rev Julie Upton, Rev Gareth Peter Jones MA Oxon, Mr Keith Blinston, Mrs Jennifer Hilary Woolf Teaching Certificate, Rev Jonathan Haigh MA, Rev Debora Karen Marschner, Mr John Joseph Whittington, Mr David Alan Hurrell, Mr David Alan Kennell, Mrs Jane Offord, Mrs Marcia Avril Banks, Mrs Elsie Cundy, Mr David Christopher Humphreys MA MIMMM, Mrs Susan Mary Monaghan Teachers Certificate, Rev Sandra Karen Marshall BD Hons, Mrs Heather Irene Rotherham, Mr Simon Digby Etty, Mr John Charles Wilkins, Mrs Melissa Ann Quinn, Margaret Egginton, Mr David Blackburn OBE, Mr Jonathan Charles Dilks, Mrs Joyce Wiles, Mrs Pamela Eaton, Mr Michael Charles Thoday, Mr Stephen Cowley, Drummond Gillespie, Rev Gill Tutt, Mrs Judith McDonald BEd, Mr Paul Rotherham, Mr Nigel P Thomas, Mrs Andrea Richardson, Mrs Della Muriel Bullas, Mrs Sheila Lomas RGN, Mr Graham Wilkinson BMus, Rev Christopher Stebbing, Mr David Luke Whitaker, Mr Harry John Burroughes BEng CEng MIET, Mr Nicholas John Waterfield, Mr Brian Totty, Mr Jacob Magowan, Mrs Janet Williamson, Ms Tina Anderson MDiv, Mr William David Bingham, Mr Brian Chapman, Mrs Patricia Ann Garmory, Rev Katherine Anne Leonowicz, Mr Trevor Williamson, Rev Will Fletcher, Mr John Almond, Mr Philip John Rowland, Mrs Judith Margaret Hartley, Mrs Christine Margaret Jackson, Dr Anne Hollows BA PhD, Mrs Margaret Garlick, Mr Nigel Disbury, Rev Henry Chilemeze Ohakah, Mr Chris Jones, Mr Jonathan Richard Buckley, Mrs Iris Robins, Rev Carla Saraid Hall Quenet, Mrs Doris Stubbs CertEducation DipEducation Advanc, Mr Arthur Lyons, Mrs Audrey Mann, Rev Ruth Turner, Mrs Jennifer Mary Carpenter BA MRTPI, Ms Heather Morris BEd MSc, Rev Jill Margaret Pullan, Rev Phillip George Borkett MBA MA, Mr Glyn William Jones, Mrs Valerie Ann Gordon, Rev James Huntley Grayson PhD, Rev Judith Jessop, Miss Elizabeth Ann Taylor, Mrs Sheila Mappin, Miss Anne Clark, Mrs Anne Humphreys, Mrs Pamela Gwendoline Meek RSCN SRN, Miss Aileen Wendy Treloar, Mrs Brenda Adams, Mr John Booler, Mrs Kay Gilbert, Mrs Susan Lesley Stanworth, Rev Joy Adams MDCR MBA MA, Mrs Carole Irene Baker, Mrs Rita Blackwell, Mrs Susan Ann Dilks, Mr Nigel Leslie Wiles, Mr John Anthony Eaton, Rev Mark Goodhand, Rev Sally Ann Coleman, Mrs Julie Talbot, Rev Dr Catrin Lyn Harland, Mr Alan Glossop BA, Mrs Katrin Hackett, Mrs Beverley Dale, Mr Michael Frederick Bullas, Mrs Elizabeth Brook, Mrs Val Smith, Mr Sean Ashton, Mr Matthew James Irons, Mrs Ann Lyons, Rev Ian Gilchrist Lucraft BA MBA DipAD Ed, Mrs Helen Roberta Elliott, Miss Louise Claire Rowbotham, Mrs Eileen Edith Woodthorpe, Mrs Rachel Amos, Mr Alan Bettison, Mr Alexander Cartwright HND, Mrs Christine Freeman, Mrs Barbara Harvey MSc BEd, Mr Richard Wells, Mr Donald Anthony King, Rev David Markay BA MDiv, Mr Paul Krzok, Mrs Bridget Kellett, Mrs Liz Jenkinson, Mr Geoffrey Flower, Mrs Kathy Smith, Mrs Janet Elizabeth Wilshaw, Mrs Jean Cookson, Ms Siggy Parratt-Halbert, Mrs Wendy Ann Atkinson, Dr Jenny Bywaters, Mrs Joan Margaret Sharp
Income: £1,647,484 [2017]; £1,312,471 [2016]; £1,629,256 [2015]; £9,615,349 [2014]; £117,870 [2013]

Sheffield Mind Ltd
Registered: 27 Jul 1978 *Employees:* 54 *Volunteers:* 36
Website: sheffieldmind.co.uk
Activities: The advancement of health or saving of lives; economic, community development, employment
Address: Sheffield Mind Ltd, Lawton Tonge House, 57 Wostenholm Road, Sheffield, S7 1LE
Trustees: Mr Stephen Richard Jones, Mr Mark Shea, Gill Holt, Andy Cain, Mr Robert Heathcote, Mr David Henry, Ms Diane Green, Jess Harrison, Sinead Rollinson-Hayes, Ms Christie Rossiter
Income: £1,160,192 [2017]; £1,228,333 [2016]; £772,829 [2015]; £543,947 [2014]; £441,971 [2013]

The Sheffield Royal Society for the Blind
Registered: 15 Jun 1995 *Employees:* 57 *Volunteers:* 170
Tel: 0114 272 2757 *Website:* srsb.org.uk
Activities: Disability
Address: Sheffield Royal Society for The Blind, 5 Mappin Street, Sheffield, S1 4DT
Trustees: Mr Peter Lee CBE DL, Mr David Shepherd, Mr Norman Wragg OBE, Mr Tony Cooper, Catherine Pattison, Stephen Blacksell, Mr Brian Campbell, Miss Julie Smethurst, Mr Richard Anthony Frost, Mr Euin Hill, Katrina Hulse
Income: £1,822,012 [2017]; £1,508,480 [2016]; £1,413,342 [2015]; £1,287,678 [2014]; £1,367,317 [2013]

Sheffield Theatres Crucible Trust
Registered: 22 Aug 2007
Tel: 0114 249 6000 *Website:* sheffieldtheatres.co.uk
Activities: Education, training; arts, culture, heritage, science
Address: 55 Norfolk Street, Sheffield, S1 1DA
Trustees: Mr Robert Noble, Mr Neil Adleman, Lord Robert Kerslake, Mr Matthew James Byam Shaw, Mr Richard Huntrods, Ms Mojisola Kareem
Income: £4,831,043 [2017]; £4,553,899 [2016]; £4,561,887 [2015]; £4,399,557 [2014]; £4,705,782 [2013]

Sheffield Theatres Trust
Registered: 2 Dec 1968 *Employees:* 144 *Volunteers:* 2
Tel: 0114 249 6000 *Website:* sheffieldtheatres.co.uk
Activities: Education, training; arts, culture, heritage, science; economic, community development, employment
Address: Crucible Theatre, 55 Norfolk Street, Sheffield, S1 1DA
Trustees: Mr Neil Adleman, Ms Holly Kendrick, Ms Claire Pender, Mrs Julie Ann Kenny, Mr Michael John Rooney, Mrs Surriya Falconer, Lord Robert Kerslake, Mr Neil MacDonald, Ms Carol Evelyn Pickering, Mrs Patricia Anne Midgley, Ms Jackie Marie Labbe, Mr John Steven Cowling, Mr Giles Dominic Searby, Mr Clive Skelton
Income: £13,999,566 [2017]; £13,253,314 [2016]; £12,515,510 [2015]; £11,364,040 [2014]; £10,862,618 [2013]

Sheffield United Community Foundation
Registered: 10 Nov 2008 *Employees:* 29 *Volunteers:* 19
Tel: 0114 261 9883 *Website:* sufc-community.com
Activities: Education, training; disability; prevention or relief of poverty; amateur sport; economic, community development, employment; recreation
Address: Sheffield United FC, Bramall Lane, Sheffield, S2 4SU
Trustees: Miss Suzanne Claire Liversidge, Mr Andrew Birks, Mr Darren Baker, Mr Carl Forrest Shieber, Mr Tanwer Khan, Mr Michael Anthony Blundell, Mr Steve Brown, Mrs Jane Ford
Income: £1,100,078 [2017]; £1,236,966 [2016]; £1,030,786 [2015]; £716,223 [2014]; £433,621 [2013]

Sheffield Wednesday Football Club Community Programme

Registered: 11 Mar 2005 *Employees:* 56 *Volunteers:* 25
Tel: 0114 324 0523 *Website:* swfccp.co.uk
Activities: General charitable purposes; education, training; advancement of health or saving of lives; disability; arts, culture, heritage, science; amateur sport; economic, community development, employment; human rights, religious or racial harmony, equality or diversity; recreation; other charitable purposes
Address: SWFC Community Programme, Sheffield Wednesday Football Club, Hillsborough Football Stadium, Leppings Lane, Sheffield, S6 1SW
Trustees: Mr John Dean, Mr John Roddison, Mr Rob Wilson, Mr John Redgate, Mr Dejphon Chansiri
Income: £1,704,437 [2017]; £1,594,507 [2016]; £1,364,628 [2015]; £1,031,326 [2014]; £923,344 [2013]

Sheffield Wildlife Trust

Registered: 22 Sep 1988 *Employees:* 47 *Volunteers:* 100
Tel: 0114 263 4335 *Website:* wildsheffield.com
Activities: Education, training; environment, conservation, heritage; economic, community development, employment
Address: Sheffield Wildlife Trust Headquarters, Victoria Hall, 37 Stafford Road, Sheffield, S2 2SF
Trustees: Mr David Bird, Mr Frazer Snowdon, Mrs Krystyna Craik, Mrs Claire Lea, Mr Andrew Perrins, Mr Thomas Dodd, Alison Holt, Miss Alice Puritz, Mr Christopher Pennell, Barry Higgins, Mr Andrew Parker, Ms Suzanne Leckie, Mark Ridler
Income: £1,326,119 [2017]; £1,118,615 [2016]; £1,283,700 [2015]; £1,924,073 [2014]; £1,481,248 [2013]

Sheffield Young Women's Christian Association

Registered: 30 Mar 2000 *Employees:* 54 *Volunteers:* 8
Tel: 01709 703471 *Website:* sheffieldywca.co.uk
Activities: Accommodation, housing; other charitable purposes
Address: 11 Fleming Gardens, Flanderwell, Rotherham, S Yorks, S66 2EY
Trustees: Mr Duncan Grant Shepherd, Mrs Wendy Diane Peake, Mrs Lynn Kemp, Mr Steven Dudley Knowles, Mrs Janet Jesper, Mr David Forrester
Income: £1,512,367 [2017]; £1,541,980 [2016]; £1,528,229 [2015]; £1,551,765 [2014]; £1,412,124 [2013]

The Sheiling Special Education Trust

Registered: 9 Oct 2012 *Employees:* 205
Tel: 01425 482483 *Website:* thesheilingringwood.co.uk
Activities: Education, training; disability
Address: The Sheiling Ringwood, Horton Road, Ashley Heath, Ringwood, Hants, BH24 2EB
Trustees: Mr J Freeman, Mr J Morris, Mrs M Rigg, Mr Peter Edwards, Mr David Keeton, Mr J Pyzer, Mrs K Desmond, Mrs Janet Kenward, Mr Mark Gleed
Income: £6,366,294 [2016]; £5,249,433 [2015]; £4,225,869 [2014]; £569,699 [2013]

Shekinah Mission (Plymouth) Limited

Registered: 8 May 2003 *Employees:* 51 *Volunteers:* 60
Tel: 01752 872886 *Website:* shekinah.co.uk
Activities: Education, training; prevention or relief of poverty
Address: Flat 4 Heron Creek, 67 Yealm Road, Newton Ferrers, Plymouth, PL8 1BJ
Trustees: Marion Luckhurst, Dr James Robert Butler, Mr Anthony John Arthur Thomas, Rev Kenneth Charles Bromage, Mr R Morgan, Mr Stephen Canham, Dr Richard Bruce Yarwood, Miss Christine Little
Income: £1,232,284 [2017]; £1,096,078 [2016]; £1,269,706 [2015]; £1,192,242 [2014]; £1,438,020 [2013]

The David Sheldrick Wildlife Trust

Registered: 20 May 2004 *Employees:* 5 *Volunteers:* 35
Tel: 01372 378321 *Website:* sheldrickwildlifetrust.org
Activities: Animals; environment, conservation, heritage; economic, community development, employment
Address: 2nd Floor, 3 Bridge Street, Leatherhead, Surrey, KT22 8BL
Trustees: Dr Dame Daphne Sheldrick, Mrs Angela Sheldrick, Mr Robert Carr-Hartley, Mr Henry Pitman
Income: £5,090,051 [2017]; £4,065,548 [2016]; £3,455,721 [2015]; £2,509,234 [2014]; £1,776,330 [2013]

Shell Foundation

Registered: 2 Jun 2000 *Employees:* 17
Website: shellfoundation.org
Activities: Education, training; advancement of health or saving of lives; prevention or relief of poverty; environment, conservation, heritage; economic, community development, employment
Address: Shell Centre, London, SE1 7NA
Trustees: Mr Malcolm Brinded, Mr Maxime Verhagen, Mr Andy Brown, Mr Maarten Wetselaar, Ms Sinead Lynch, Ms Diane Lisa Carney, Prof Maggie Kigozi, Ms Alice Georgina Chapple
Income: £27,480,106 [2016]; £11,560,265 [2015]; £18,899,474 [2014]; £16,288,679 [2013]; £13,650,632 [2012]

Shelter, National Campaign for Homeless People Limited

Registered: 16 Mar 1972 *Employees:* 1,273 *Volunteers:* 1,765
Tel: 0300 330 1234 *Website:* shelter.org.uk
Activities: Education, training; prevention or relief of poverty; economic, community development, employment
Address: Shelter, 88 Old Street, London, EC1V 9HU
Trustees: Mr Manpreet Dillon, Ms Joanna Simons, Ms Kamena Dorling, Mr Jonathan Simmons, Helen Baker, Mr Shaun Kenneth Prime, Ms Ruth Hunt, Ms Ros Micklem, Mr Rob Hayward, Ms Antoinette Byrne, Mr Goi Ashmore, Ms Laurice Tania Ponting
Income: £60,902,000 [2017]; £57,427,000 [2016]; £69,565,000 [2015]; £57,540,000 [2014]; £53,537,000 [2013]

Shelterbox Trust

Registered: 12 Mar 2003 *Employees:* 104 *Volunteers:* 641
Tel: 01872 302600 *Website:* shelterbox.org
Activities: Overseas aid, famine relief
Address: Shelter Box Trust, Falcon House, Charles Street, Truro, Cornwall, TR1 2PH
Trustees: Mr Robert John, Mr Richard Bland, Mr Robin Bayford, Mr Shekhar Mehta, Michelle Jeuken, Mr William Decker, Mr James Sinclair Taylor, Lydia Poole, Claire Goudsmit, Greg Thacker
Income: £12,361,481 [2017]; £10,232,427 [2016]; £12,672,054 [2015]; £6,741,062 [2014]; £14,057,133 [2013]

Bob and Michelle Shemtob Charitable Trust

Registered: 8 Oct 2015
Activities: Education, training; advancement of health or saving of lives; disability
Address: 13 Ashworth Road, London, W9 1JW
Trustees: Mr Robert Alan Shemtob, Mrs Michelle Shemtob, Ms Kate Goldberg
Income: £1,011,327 [2016]

The David Shepherd Wildlife Foundation
Registered: 22 Nov 2004 *Employees:* 11 *Volunteers:* 40
Tel: 020 7227 7000 *Website:* davidshepherd.org
Activities: General charitable purposes; education, training; animals; environment, conservation, heritage
Address: Bircham Dyson Bell, 50 Broadway, London, SW1H 0BL
Trustees: Mr Bruce Norris, Mr Nigel Lawrence Colne CBE, Andre Pienaar, Fiona Luck, Mr Nigel John Keen, Mr Christopher Charles Blanchard Cowdray, Lady Melanie Lamb
Income: £1,555,303 [2017]; £1,350,945 [2016]; £1,647,024 [2015]; £1,143,350 [2014]; £1,346,846 [2013]

Sherborne Preparatory School
Registered: 11 Sep 1998 *Employees:* 104
Tel: 01935 812351 *Website:* sherborneprep.org
Activities: Education, training
Address: Sherborne Preparatory School, Acreman Street, Sherborne, Dorset, DT9 3NY
Trustees: Mr Bernard Brown, Mrs Jennifer Claire Dwyer BEd, Mrs Fiona Ashley Miller, Mr Phillip Jones, Mrs Christina Cosham, Mr John Patrick Smith, Mrs Sarah Edwards, Mr D Fowler-Watt, Mr Richard Bromell Asfav, Mr Nigel Jones BSc FRICS ACIArb, Mr Timothy Hague, Dr Dominic Luckett, Mrs Sophie Harris
Income: £3,487,110 [2017]; £2,979,759 [2016]; £3,114,550 [2015]; £2,976,711 [2014]; £2,954,941 [2013]

Sherborne School for Girls
Registered: 10 Jun 1965 *Employees:* 313 *Volunteers:* 2
Tel: 01935 818206 *Website:* sherborne.com
Activities: Education, training
Address: Sherborne School for Girls, Bradford Road, Sherborne, Dorset, DT9 3QN
Trustees: Mrs Charlotte Anne Townshend, Mr Philip Charles Ward, Mr Ian Richard Davenport, Sir Robert Alan Fry, Mrs Kay Brock, Mrs Ann Simon, Mr Robin Anthony Langley Leach, Mrs Amanda Louise Harris, Mr Nicholas John Stirling Wordie, Mr Robin Timothy Bezeck Price, The Rt Revd Karen Gorham, Mrs Isabel Burke, Mr Richard W Strang, Mr Rupert De Gascoigne Pilkington, Mr Jeremy Gordon, Mrs Louise Drummond Hall, Lady Plaxy Gillian Beatrice Arthur, Mrs Maria Wingfield Digby, Dr Steven George Connors, Ms Juliet Blanch
Income: £16,558,932 [2017]; £17,582,609 [2016]; £13,497,397 [2015]; £12,814,340 [2014]; £11,847,324 [2013]

Sherborne School
Registered: 22 Jun 2000 *Employees:* 585 *Volunteers:* 8
Tel: 01935 810501 *Website:* sherborne.org
Activities: Education, training
Address: The Bursary, Abbey Road, Sherborne, Dorset, DT9 3LF
Trustees: Mr George Marsh, Mr Roger Fidgen, Mr Rupert Robson, Mr Robin Antony Leach MA, Mr Robert Temmink QC, Mrs Isabel Burke, Mr Alan Charlton, Mr Michael Wilson, Dr Max Jonas, Lt Gen David Leakey CMG CVO CBE MA Cantab, Mr Michael French, Canon Eric Woods, Mrs Angela Lane, Mr Guy Hudson, Mrs Vicki Cotter, Mr Matthew Whittell, Mrs Gilly Staley, Mr Russell Lucas-Rowe DL, Mrs Elaine Sarah Rivett Stallard JP
Income: £25,213,000 [2017]; £25,656,000 [2016]; £24,970,000 [2015]; £25,983,000 [2014]; £24,877,000 [2013]

Sherburn House Charity
Registered: 19 Sep 1963 *Employees:* 56 *Volunteers:* 2
Tel: 0191 372 2551 *Website:* sherburnhouse.org
Activities: The prevention or relief of poverty; accommodation, housing
Address: Ramsey House, Sherburn Hospital, Durham, DH1 2SE
Trustees: Ray Pye, Mr Michael Derek Laing, Councillor David Stoker, Mr Kevin Teed Cummings, Mrs Margaret Ann Jefferson, Margaret Bozic, Mrs Susan Jean Martin, Mr David Roy Thorne, Mr James Imrie
Income: £2,850,942 [2017]; £2,518,344 [2016]; £2,637,245 [2015]; £2,459,226 [2014]; £2,540,111 [2013]

The Archie Sherman Charitable Trust
Registered: 17 Oct 1968 *Employees:* 1
Tel: 020 7493 1904
Activities: General charitable purposes; education, training; advancement of health or saving of lives; disability; prevention or relief of poverty; overseas aid, famine relief; arts, culture, heritage, science; amateur sport; economic, community development, employment
Address: 274a Kentish Town Road, London, NW5 2AA
Trustees: Mr Michael J Gee FCA, Allan Henry Simon Morgenthau, Mr Eric Charles FCA, Rhona Freedman
Income: £1,431,023 [2017]; £1,402,722 [2016]; £1,413,902 [2015]; £1,426,830 [2014]; £1,465,460 [2013]

Sherman Cymru
Registered: 13 Mar 2007 *Employees:* 22 *Volunteers:* 139
Tel: 029 2064 6900 *Website:* shermancymru.co.uk
Activities: Education, training; arts, culture, heritage, science
Address: Sherman Theatre, Senghennydd Road, Cardiff, CF24 4YE
Trustees: Ms Rosamund Anne Shelley, Mr Nicholas Harry Carlton, Ms Marlies Hoecherl, Miss Rhiannon Sarah Davis, Mr Marcgeraint Simcox, Ms Ann Kellaway, Ms Helen Ramonde Vallis, Mr David John Stacey, Mr Keith Morgan, Mr Owen Wyndham Thomas, Mr Paul Clayton, Mr Clive John Davies, Mr Clive Charles Flowers
Income: £2,128,050 [2017]; £2,032,557 [2016]; £2,022,250 [2015]; £2,276,571 [2014]; £2,551,479 [2013]

Sherrardswood School
Registered: 2 Aug 1963 *Employees:* 60
Tel: 01438 714282 *Website:* sherrardswood.co.uk
Activities: Education, training
Address: Sherrardswood School, 3 Lockleys, Welwyn, Herts, AL6 0BJ
Trustees: Mr Justin Phillips, Mrs Tara Jane Petri, Mr Ali Khan, Mr Robin Stattersfield, Mr David Chapman, Mr Benjamin Kenyon, Mr Stephen Thompson, Mr Paul Buss
Income: £3,684,685 [2016]; £3,478,746 [2015]; £3,571,842 [2014]; £3,438,743 [2013]; £3,364,867 [2012]

Shift Foundation
Registered: 26 Feb 2010 *Employees:* 11
Website: shiftdesign.org.uk
Activities: General charitable purposes; education, training; arts, culture, heritage, science; environment, conservation, heritage; economic, community development, employment
Address: 71 St John Street, London, EC1M 4NJ
Trustees: Mr Stanley Philip Harris, Ms Elizabeth Anne Owen, Mr David Robinson, Mr Goodkind Graham
Income: £1,231,368 [2017]; £1,040,671 [2016]; £210,123 [2015]

Shine: Support and Help in Education

Registered: 5 Oct 2000 *Employees:* 7
Website: shinetrust.org.uk
Activities: General charitable purposes; education, training
Address: Shine Trust, Princes Exchange, 2 Princes Square, Leeds, LS1 4HY
Trustees: Mr Mark Heffernan, Mr David Wayland Blood, Lord Jim O'Neill, Stephen Shields, Ms Sarah Loftus, Mr Gavin Simon Boyle, Professor Samantha Twiselton BA PGCE PhD FRSA PFHEA, Mr Cameron Ogden, Ann Mroz, Ms Lorna Fitzsimons
Income: £1,180,830 [2017]; £2,280,830 [2016]; £1,519,939 [2015]; £2,262,159 [2014]; £2,243,966 [2013]

Shiplake Court Limited

Registered: 13 Apr 1965 *Employees:* 127 *Volunteers:* 1
Tel: 0118 940 2455 *Website:* shiplake.org.uk
Activities: Education, training; amateur sport
Address: Shiplake College, Shiplake Court, Shiplake, Henley on Thames, Oxon, RG9 4BW
Trustees: Mr Richard Charles Lester, Sir David Whitlock Tanner KCB CBE, Rt Hon Timothy John Crommelin Eggar, Mr Mark MacKenzie-Charrington, Mrs Marsha Carey-Elms, Mr Robert Dempster, Mr Peter Blewett, Mr James Sim Gordon, Mrs Susan Jean Ryan BA, Mr Ian Howell, Mr Andrew Ashton, Mr Charles Eve, Mr James Welsh
Income: £11,279,470 [2017]; £10,174,773 [2016]; £9,615,729 [2015]; £9,078,440 [2014]; £8,730,071 [2013]

The Shipwrecked Fishermen and Mariners' Royal Benevolent Society

Registered: 20 Feb 1964 *Employees:* 7 *Volunteers:* 180
Tel: 01243 789329 *Website:* shipwreckedmariners.org.uk
Activities: The prevention or relief of poverty
Address: 1 North Pallant, Chichester, W Sussex, PO19 1TL
Trustees: Captain John Wilson Hughes, Mr George Greenwood, Captain Nigel Palmer OBE, Mr Anthony Fawcett FCA, Mr Richard Coleman, Captain John Vercoe, Captain Graham Pepper, Mrs Liz Price, Mr Eamonn Delaney, Commodore Laurie Hopkins RN, Commander Rosie Wilson OBE RN, Captain Roger Barker, Mr Tim West, Michael Seymour, Rob Jardine-Brown, Cdre Mike Mansergh CBE
Income: £1,522,571 [2017]; £1,622,144 [2016]; £1,462,893 [2015]; £1,876,074 [2014]; £1,809,824 [2013]

Shlomo Memorial Fund Limited

Registered: 28 Apr 1980 *Employees:* 66
Tel: 020 8731 0777
Activities: General charitable purposes; religious activities
Address: New Burlington House, 1075 Finchley Road, London, NW11 0PU
Trustees: Mr Eliyah Kleinerman, Mr Hezkel Moses Toporowitz, Mrs Channe Lopian, Mrs Esther Hoffner, Mr Amichai Toporowitz, Mr Chaim Yehuda Kaufman, Mr Meir Yosef Sullam
Income: £9,633,301 [2016]; £8,857,389 [2015]; £8,969,654 [2014]; £7,476,950 [2013]; £10,985,980 [2012]

Shooting Star Chase

Registered: 30 Nov 1994 *Employees:* 259 *Volunteers:* 700
Tel: 01932 823100 *Website:* shootingstarchase.org.uk
Activities: The advancement of health or saving of lives
Address: Bridge House, Addlestone Road, Addlestone, Surrey, KT15 2UE
Trustees: Mr Ken Hanna, Mr Paul Boughton, Andrew Cosslett, Jonathan Kembery, Mrs Jill Ader, Dr Jayne Price, Catherine Van't Riet, Jon Craig
Income: £7,900,865 [2017]; £8,839,443 [2016]; £8,597,626 [2015]; £8,501,204 [2014]; £7,934,489 [2013]

Shoreditch Town Hall Trust

Registered: 20 May 1998 *Employees:* 12 *Volunteers:* 34
Tel: 020 7739 6176 *Website:* shoreditchtownhall.com
Activities: Arts, culture, heritage, science; environment, conservation, heritage; economic, community development, employment
Address: Shoreditch Town Hall Trust, 380 Old Street, London, EC1V 9LT
Trustees: Patrick Hammill, William Hodgson, Jonathan McShane, Ms Caroline Routh, Mr John Roberts, Michael Berg, Mr Nick Giles, Mr Stephen Neal Robertson, Ms Penny Wrout, Ms Joanna Sunita Pandya
Income: £1,608,424 [2017]; £1,807,060 [2016]; £1,429,723 [2015]; £798,360 [2014]; £357,725 [2013]

The Shoreditch Trust

Registered: 30 May 2001 *Employees:* 42 *Volunteers:* 100
Website: shoreditchtrust.org.uk
Activities: General charitable purposes; education, training; advancement of health or saving of lives; disability; prevention or relief of poverty; arts, culture, heritage, science; economic, community development, employment
Address: Shoreditch Trust Ltd, 12 Orsman Road, London, N1 5QJ
Trustees: Mr Philip Maurice Glanville, Mr Jeremy Mark Gardner, Mr Daniel Wong, Ms Claire Katerina Smith, Ms Josephine Barbara Shiach Burns, Dr Jonathon Tomlinson, Mr Andrew Charles Waugh
Income: £2,168,901 [2017]; £4,090,500 [2016]; £3,752,933 [2015]; £1,845,753 [2014]; £2,323,990 [2013]

Shree Kutch Satsang Swaminarayan Temple (Mandir) London

Registered: 1 Apr 1976 *Employees:* 5 *Volunteers:* 500
Tel: 020 8909 9899 *Website:* sksst.org
Activities: General charitable purposes; education, training; religious activities; amateur sport
Address: SKSS Temple, Westfield Lane, Harrow, Middlesex, HA3 9EA
Trustees: Mr Dhanji Shamji Patel, Mr Shivji Naran Rabadia, Mr Dhanji Parbat Patel, Mr Valji Shamji Dabasia, Mr Vishram Vaghji Patel, Mr Dhanji Karsan Varsani, Mr Devji Karsan Patel
Income: £1,386,548 [2016]; £1,811,086 [2015]; £1,127,296 [2014]; £1,133,814 [2013]; £998,295 [2012]

Shree Swaminarayan Sidhant Sajivan Mandal London

Registered: 6 Jun 1967 *Employees:* 1 *Volunteers:* 10
Tel: 020 8200 1991 *Website:* swaminarayangadi.com
Activities: General charitable purposes; education, training; prevention or relief of poverty; overseas aid, famine relief; religious activities; arts, culture, heritage, science; amateur sport
Address: Shree Swaminarayan Mandir, Shree Muktajeevan Swamibapa Complex, Kingsbury Road, London, NW9 8AQ
Trustees: Dr Mahesh Varsani, Mr Ashokkumar Velji Patel, Mr Laxmidas Premji Dabasia
Income: £2,168,733 [2016]; £1,540,337 [2015]; £2,889,228 [2014]; £6,871,279 [2013]; £2,046,583 [2012]

Shrewsbury Drapers Holy Cross Limited

Registered: 12 Nov 2009 *Employees:* 1 *Volunteers:* 25
Tel: 01743 353503 *Website:* shrewsburydrapers.org.uk
Activities: Accommodation, housing
Address: c/o Drapers Place, Horsefair, Abbey Foregate, Shrewsbury, Salop, SY2 6BP
Trustees: Mr Andrew Cross, Mr Andrew Haslewood, Mr Gareth Jenkins, Mrs Mary Rose Bone, Mrs Jan Boyd, Mr Gordon Woods, Mr Henry Milward, Mr Richard Auger, Dr Robert Hatts, Mr David Perrin, Dr Thomas Taylor
Income: £1,424,124 [2016]; £316,092 [2015]; £65,114 [2014]; £122,701 [2013]; £101,300 [2012]

Shrewsbury House School Trust Limited
Registered: 20 Feb 1979 *Employees:* 120
Tel: 020 8399 3066 *Website:* shrewsburyhouse.net
Activities: Education, training
Address: 107 Ditton Road, Surbiton, Surrey, KT6 6RL
Trustees: Mr Lawrie Lee, Mrs Joanna Le Grice, Mrs Clare Linney, Ms Charlotte Vere, Vic Laville, Mr Timothy Haynes, Mr Darren Johns, Mrs Jane Whittingham, Mr David Sanders
Income: £7,785,857 [2017]; £7,712,311 [2016]; £6,997,523 [2015]; £6,729,357 [2014]; £6,103,424 [2013]

Shrewsbury Roman Catholic Diocesan Trust
Registered: 29 Apr 1964 *Employees:* 116 *Volunteers:* 8,804
Tel: 0151 652 9855 *Website:* dioceseofshrewsbury.org
Activities: General charitable purposes; education, training; advancement of health or saving of lives; disability; prevention or relief of poverty; overseas aid, famine relief; accommodation, housing; religious activities; arts, culture, heritage, science; amateur sport; environment, conservation, heritage; economic, community development, employment; other charitable purposes
Address: Curial Office, 2 Park Road South, Prenton, Wirral, Merseyside, CH43 4UX
Trustees: Rt Rev Mark Davies, Rev Philip Joseph Moor, Mr Noel Loughrey, Rev David Roberts, Rev Jonathan Mitchell, Rev Stephen Coonan, Mr Simon Geary, Rev Michael Gannon
Income: £17,039,000 [2017]; £14,394,713 [2016]; £13,086,057 [2015]; £13,886,634 [2014]; £13,638,226 [2013]

Shrewsbury School Foundation
Registered: 31 Aug 1965
Website: shrewsburyfoundation.org.uk
Activities: Education, training
Address: 32 Lane Green Road, Codsall, Wolverhampton, W Midlands, WV8 2JU
Trustees: Mr Michael Kerr, Mr Peter St J Worth, Mr J Dickson, Mr James Cross QC, Mr Jcr Arthur
Income: £1,128,029 [2017]; £816,046 [2016]; £1,022,439 [2015]; £1,136,488 [2014]; £818,855 [2013]

Shrewsbury School
Registered: 3 Aug 1966 *Employees:* 399
Tel: 01743 280828 *Website:* shrewsbury.org.uk
Activities: Education, training
Address: The Bursary, Kingsland House, The Schools, Kingsland, Shrewsbury, Salop, SY3 7AA
Trustees: Mr T Haynes, Mr W Hunter, Mrs Diana Rosemary Flint DL, Mr J Clark, Dr F Hay, Sir P Davis, Professor A McCarthy, Councillor C Motley, Mr D Chance, Councillor T Biggins, Mr S Baker, Mr G Woods, Professor C Dobson, Mrs L O'Loughlin, Mr P Worth, Mrs C Howarth, Mr R Boys-Stones, Mr M Moir
Income: £25,051,013 [2017]; £24,275,195 [2016]; £23,782,853 [2015]; £20,718,423 [2014]; £21,206,759 [2013]

Shri Kanagathurkkai Amman (Hindu) Temple Trust
Registered: 1 Oct 1992 *Employees:* 16 *Volunteers:* 7
Tel: 020 8810 0835 *Website:* ammanealing.com
Activities: General charitable purposes; education, training; disability; overseas aid, famine relief; religious activities
Address: 5 Chapel Road, London, W13 9AE
Trustees: Dr Velupillai Paramanathan, Mr Rajaratnam Kanesarajah, Mr Shanmuganathan Srirangan, Dr Appiah Thevasagayam, Mr Sabalingam Abayalingam, Mr Sivaguru Premachandra, Mr Thuraiappah Thevarajan
Income: £1,245,104 [2017]; £1,221,486 [2016]; £1,173,707 [2015]; £1,071,001 [2014]; £1,031,689 [2013]

Shri Vallabh Nidhi - UK
Registered: 28 Jun 1979 *Employees:* 14 *Volunteers:* 21
Tel: 020 8903 7737 *Website:* svnuk.org
Activities: General charitable purposes; prevention or relief of poverty; religious activities
Address: Shri Vallabh Nidhi-UK, P O Box 700, Ealing Road, Wembley, Middlesex, HA0 4TA
Trustees: Mr Pradip Dhamecha, Mr Mahendra Patel, Mrs Rasikaben Patel, Mr Subahu Patel, Mr Ashit Roy Thakkar, Mr Narendra Thakrar, Mrs Gorande Bhatt, Mr Ajay M Jobanputra
Income: £2,088,852 [2017]; £1,015,475 [2015]; £898,044 [2014]; £1,062,760 [2013]; £891,116 [2012]

Shri Venkateswara (Balaji) Temple of The United Kingdom
Registered: 1 Nov 1984 *Employees:* 21 *Volunteers:* 100
Tel: 0121 353 6942 *Website:* venkateswara.org.uk
Activities: General charitable purposes; education, training; religious activities; arts, culture, heritage, science; amateur sport; environment, conservation, heritage
Address: Shri Venkateswara Balaji Temple UK, Dudley Road East, Oldbury, W Midlands, B69 3DU
Trustees: Mrs Paranjyothi Ramaiah, Dr Amirchetty Rajeshwar Rao, Dr Ramakrishnagupta Mudalagiri, Dr Sinnathamby Kanagaratnam, Mr Kodavoor Ramachandra Aithal
Income: £1,801,377 [2017]; £2,249,584 [2016]; £1,700,972 [2015]; £1,765,447 [2014]; £1,588,873 [2013]

Shrimad Rajchandra Mission Dharampur (UK)
Registered: 10 Nov 2010 *Volunteers:* 200
Website: shrimadrajchandramission.org
Activities: General charitable purposes; education, training; advancement of health or saving of lives; prevention or relief of poverty; overseas aid, famine relief; religious activities; animals; human rights, religious or racial harmony, equality or diversity
Address: 3 Saddlers Close, Pinner, Middlesex, HA5 4BA
Trustees: Mr Mayur Mehta BCom FCCA, Mr Maulik Shah BCom MBA (Technology Management), Mr Ashwinkumar Mehta BSc (Hons), Mr Ajay Doshi BPharm MMS (Operations), Mr Pareshkumar Udani BSc Econ (Hons) ACA, Mrs Sonal Mehta BCom Diploma Computer Science, Mr Dilipkumar Mehta MAAT, Mr Dharmesh Doshi BCom LLB ACA, Mrs Kajal Sheth BCom Master in Feng Shui
Income: £1,119,323 [2017]; £132,187 [2016]; £194,940 [2015]; £59,679 [2014]; £187,922 [2013]

The Shropshire Horticultural Society

Registered: 26 Apr 1972 *Employees:* 5 *Volunteers:* 212
Tel: 01743 234052 *Website:* shrewsburyflowershow.org.uk
Activities: General charitable purposes; education, training; environment, conservation, heritage; other charitable purposes
Address: Quarry Lodge, Shrewsbury, Salop, SY1 1RN
Trustees: Lt Col (Ret'd) B Littlejohns, Mr Stephen Charles Rogers, Mr H Wilson, Mr E T B Butcher, Mr A R Kirkham, Mrs D Hamer, Mr J McA Hodgson, Mr M Owen, Mr M W Burton BSc (Hons) TechRICS FN, Mr R J Whittingham, Mr R G Marshall, Mr C Pettener, Mr C Chew, Mr Nicholson, Mr Rhodes, Tony Bywater, Dr John Stuart Sutton, Mr Robert James Hancocks, Ms Katherine Jane Stephens, Mr Christopher Jones, Mr Richard Lester, Miss Sarah Marshall, Mr Scott Clapworthy, Mr Simon Rhys Cunningham, Mr Stephen Graham Worrall, Mrs Susan Jane Morris, Mr Jeremy Tudor, Mr A D Cross, Mr B Goodwin, Dr Malcolm Booth, Mrs Pugh, Maj B K Harper OSEJ, Mr G Parry, Mr K A Spiby FOFIG, Lt Col Mike Carver, Mr Richard Cooper, Mr R E Key, Mr S J Kynaston, Mrs Shirley Davies, Mrs D Whitney Wood, Mr Pearson, Col Mark Cuthbert-Brown, Miss Amanda Jones, Mrs Leanne Garvey, Mrs Ann Kirkham, Mr Frank Lawton Heaversedge, Mrs Briony Cooper, Mr Peter Road-Knight, Colonel Richard Clive Hambleton, Mrs Susannah Bryant, Mrs Lindsay Pearson, Mr Nicholas Robert Pitt, Mrs Margaret Hilary Fisher
Income: £1,097,201 [2016]; £1,184,389 [2015]; £1,048,613 [2014]; £1,099,222 [2013]; £1,064,819 [2012]

Shropshire Housing Alliance

Registered: 21 Jun 2008 *Employees:* 34 *Volunteers:* 1
Tel: 01952 217005 *Website:* shalliance.org.uk
Activities: Education, training; prevention or relief of poverty; accommodation, housing; environment, conservation, heritage
Address: Wrekin Housing Trust, Colliers Way, Old Park, Telford, TF3 4AW
Trustees: Mrs Alison Jane Fisher, Mr James Dickson
Income: £1,493,620 [2017]; £1,593,783 [2016]; £1,533,049 [2015]; £1,293,777 [2014]; £1,406,007 [2013]

Shropshire Wildlife Trust

Registered: 7 Jan 1963 *Employees:* 48 *Volunteers:* 581
Tel: 01743 284280 *Website:* shropshirewildlifetrust.org.uk
Activities: Education, training; advancement of health or saving of lives; animals; environment, conservation, heritage
Address: 193 Abbey Foregate, Shrewsbury, Salop, SY2 6AH
Trustees: Veronica Cossons, Mr John Brown, Rodney Aspinwall, Mrs Kate Mayne, Mr Alan Salt, Richard Carpenter, Jenny Joy, Mr R Owen, Mr Howard Trevor Thorne, Mrs Kirsten Mould, Kathryn Foster, Mr Andrew Whyle, Mr Daniel Wrench, Mr Jon King, Mr A Platt
Income: £1,786,231 [2017]; £1,822,339 [2016]; £2,214,572 [2015]; £1,705,065 [2014]; £1,543,763 [2013]

Shulem B. Association Limited

Registered: 24 Aug 1962 *Employees:* 3
Tel: 020 8731 0777
Activities: General charitable purposes; education, training; prevention or relief of poverty; religious activities
Address: New Burlington House, 1075 Finchley Road, London, NW11 0PU
Trustees: Mr Samuel Berger, Mrs Zelda Sternlicht, Mrs Sarah Rachel Klein
Income: £10,987,589 [2016]; £20,553,657 [2015]; £11,681,397 [2014]; £14,472,089 [2013]; £10,977,189 [2012]

Shumei Eiko Limited

Registered: 24 Apr 1991 *Employees:* 71
Tel: 01227 819034 *Website:* chaucercollege.co.uk
Activities: Education, training
Address: Chaucer College Canterbury, University Road, Canterbury, Kent, CT2 7LJ
Trustees: Professor John Anthony George Craven CBE, Mr Masaaki Sekiguchi, Mr Lewis Norris, Dr Mitsu Horii, Mrs Phillida Purvis MBE, Mr Koki Kawashima, Mr Patrick Anthony Todd, Ms Diane Gowland, Mr Peter John Dalton, Ms Catherine Ann Vines
Income: £3,904,094 [2017]; £3,456,623 [2016]; £3,648,169 [2015]; £3,841,027 [2014]; £3,121,864 [2013]

Sibford School

Registered: 20 Feb 1998 *Employees:* 163
Tel: 01295 781210 *Website:* sibfordschool.co.uk
Activities: Education, training
Address: The Old Dairy, Park Lane, Swalcliffe, Banbury, Oxon, OX15 5EU
Trustees: Mr Fred Sessa, Sarah Lane, Kate Merry, Mrs Margaret Shelley, Mr Stuart Fowler, Mr Leslie Ralph Robinson, Mr Richard Cziborra, Mr Roger Chapman, Sally Bicheno, Seren Wildwood, Helena Scott, Mrs Katherine Anne Davidson, Mr Richard Bee, Mr Philip Jones, Mrs Amanda Brown
Income: £6,141,526 [2017]; £6,082,755 [2016]; £5,889,085 [2015]; £5,514,360 [2014]; £5,988,042 [2013]

The Sick Children's Trust

Registered: 23 Mar 1982 *Employees:* 37 *Volunteers:* 100
Tel: 020 7638 4066 *Website:* sickchildrenstrust.org
Activities: The advancement of health or saving of lives; accommodation, housing
Address: 4th Floor, 28-30 Worship Street, London, EC2A 2AH
Trustees: Mr Peter Cunard, Mr Patrick James Rigby, Mr Soren Svend Knud Tholstrup, Dr Jack Donald Singer, Ms Polly Staveley, Ms Joanne Mier, Mr Timothy Robert Craig, Mr Stephen George Masters, Mr Gary Boom, Mr Michael Robinson, Ms Fiona Jane Conway Smart, Mr Paul Jardine, Mrs Victoria Louise Carter
Income: £2,421,399 [2017]; £2,511,674 [2016]; £3,565,392 [2015]; £2,472,572 [2014]; £1,982,706 [2013]

Sidcot School

Registered: 8 Apr 1987 *Employees:* 261 *Volunteers:* 16
Tel: 01934 843102 *Website:* sidcot.org.uk
Activities: Education, training
Address: Winscombe, Somerset, BS25 1PD
Trustees: Mr Adam Matthews, Rosemary Carr, Roger Starr, Sarah Moore, Tessa Tyldesley, Mr Tim Bond, Christopher Hobbs, Mr Andrew Flint, Duncan Pittaway, David Whiting, Timothy Niblock, Mr Nick Pyatt, Mr Andrew Ward
Income: £11,061,236 [2017]; £10,477,121 [2016]; £10,042,717 [2015]; £9,346,820 [2014]; £8,734,000 [2013]

Side By Side (Children) Limited

Registered: 28 Apr 2010 *Employees:* 109 *Volunteers:* 5
Website: sidebyside.org.uk
Activities: Education, training; disability
Address: 21 Castlewood Road, London, N16 6DL
Trustees: Mr Sidney Sinitsky, Mr Joseph Margulies, Mrs Zelda Weiss, Rabbi Abraham Pinter
Income: £2,115,599 [2017]; £1,908,451 [2016]; £1,542,177 [2015]; £1,744,239 [2014]; £1,189,159 [2013]

Signhealth
Registered: 13 May 1992 *Employees:* 143 *Volunteers:* 10
Tel: 01494 687600 *Website:* signhealth.org.uk
Activities: Education, training; advancement of health or saving of lives; disability; overseas aid, famine relief; accommodation, housing; other charitable purposes
Address: Signhealth, Falcon Mews, 46 Oakmead Road, London, SW12 9SJ
Trustees: Miss Jackie Driver, Dr Emma Ferguson-Coleman, Dr Favaad Iqbal, Clare Mitchell, Mr Philip Gerrard, Miss Susanne Rees, Mr Jonathan Gallard, Mr Andrew Sims
Income: £5,460,027 [2017]; £4,979,374 [2016]; £4,879,469 [2015]; £4,873,382 [2014]; £4,517,208 [2013]

Signposts (Luton)
Registered: 16 Sep 1994 *Employees:* 43 *Volunteers:* 14
Tel: 01582 722629 *Website:* signpostsso.com
Activities: Accommodation, housing
Address: Signposts Head Office, 106 Old Bedford Road, Luton, Beds, LU2 7PD
Trustees: Mrs Ann Hyde, Mr Les Ward, Ms Cherry Newbery, Mr Derek John Wood, Mrs Carole Ann Vanschagen, Mr Paddy Bannon, Mr David Ball, Mr Christopher Reginald Lee Slough
Income: £2,008,385 [2017]; £1,914,721 [2016]; £1,767,234 [2015]; £1,659,132 [2014]; £1,551,564 [2013]

The Sigrid Rausing Trust
Registered: 14 Jun 1995 *Employees:* 11
Tel: 020 7313 7727 *Website:* sigrid-rausing-trust.org
Activities: General charitable purposes; human rights, religious or racial harmony, equality or diversity; other charitable purposes
Address: The Sigrid Rausing Trust, 12 Penzance Place, London, W11 4PA
Trustees: Ms Sigrid Rausing, Mr Jonathan Cooper, Mr Andrew Puddephatt, Ms Margo Picken
Income: £20,185,921 [2016]; £24,643,169 [2015]; £19,315,414 [2014]; £23,680,665 [2013]; £13,424,053 [2012]

The Sikh Channel Community Broadcasting Company Limited
Registered: 2 Jun 2010 *Employees:* 15 *Volunteers:* 3
Tel: 0121 634 6708 *Website:* sikhchannel.tv
Activities: General charitable purposes; education, training; advancement of health or saving of lives; prevention or relief of poverty; religious activities
Address: Unit 3, 24 Avenue Road, Aston, Birmingham, B6 4DY
Trustees: Davinder Bal, Mrs Surinder Kaur Dhillon, Mr Karamjit Singh Dhillon, Mr Charanjit Singh Dhillon
Income: £1,363,297 [2016]; £1,513,906 [2015]; £1,479,795 [2014]; £1,176,022 [2013]; £1,239,176 [2012]

Silcoates School
Registered: 6 Oct 2014 *Employees:* 136 *Volunteers:* 2
Tel: 01924 291614 *Website:* silcoates.org.uk
Activities: Education, training
Address: Silcoates School, Silcoates Lane, Wrenthorpe, Wakefield, W Yorks, WF2 0PD
Trustees: Mr John Richard Lane, Mr David Edward Payling, Mrs Deborah Siddle Proctor, Ms Alison Christine Malecki-Ketchell, Mr Mark Vincent Willings BDS MFGDP Dip Imp Dent RCS FFGDP, Mrs Barbara Tibbetts, Mrs Mary Christine Chippendale, Mrs Rachel Margaret Copley, Rev Steven Rowland Knapton, Mrs Susan Dorothy Lee, Mr Adrian Lingard
Income: £6,528,000 [2017]; £6,906,000 [2016]; £4,703,000 [2015]

The Silver Line Helpline
Registered: 18 May 2012 *Employees:* 124 *Volunteers:* 3,000
Website: thesilverline.org.uk
Activities: General charitable purposes; advancement of health or saving of lives; disability; economic, community development, employment; other charitable purposes
Address: The Silver Line Helpline, Trade Tower, Calico Row, London, SW11 3YH
Trustees: Mrs Eileen Hammond, Dame Esther Rantzen DBE, Lorraine Jackson, Mr Ben Summerskill OBE, Mr Michael Josephson MBE, Mr Andrew Geddes, Lady Susan Chinn CBE, Mrs Jane Ashcroft CBE, Mr Piers Ricketts, Mr Christian Dingwall, Mrs Jackie Gittins
Income: £5,126,370 [2017]; £4,334,891 [2016]; £3,662,724 [2015]; £2,078,055 [2014]; £616,096 [2013]

Silverdale Gospel Hall Trust
Registered: 29 Apr 2016 *Volunteers:* 15
Tel: 07500 012943
Activities: Religious activities; other charitable purposes
Address: 2 Hatlex Hill, Hest Bank, Lancaster, LA2 6ET
Trustees: Mr Christopher James, Mr Julien Harrison, Mr William Howden, Mr Oliver Whiley, Mr Timothy Devenish
Income: £1,031,591 [2017]

The Simon Gibson Charitable Trust
Registered: 27 May 1975
Tel: 01446 775991 *Website:* sgctrust.org.uk
Activities: General charitable purposes; amateur sport; environment, conservation, heritage; armed forces, emergency service efficiency; recreation; other charitable purposes
Address: Simon Gibson Charitable Trust, P O Box 109, Cowbridge, Vale of Glamorgan, CF71 7FD
Trustees: Mr Bryan Marsh, Mr John Homfray, Mr George David Gibson, Mrs Deborah Connor ACA BA
Income: £1,169,546 [2017]; £1,074,935 [2016]; £1,070,356 [2015]; £647,224 [2014]; £644,082 [2013]

Sinfonietta Productions Limited
Registered: 4 Mar 1968 *Employees:* 13
Tel: 020 7239 9340 *Website:* londonsinfonietta.org.uk
Activities: Education, training; arts, culture, heritage, science
Address: Kings Place, 90 York Way, London, N1 9AG
Trustees: Mrs Sally Margaret Millest, Mr Ian Dearden, Mr Matthew William Pike, Regis Cochefert, Mr Jonathan Morton, Mr Ben Weston, Mr Paul John Russell Zisman, Mr Andrew Burke, Mrs Belinda Mary Matthews, Mr Alistair Andrew Mackie, Ms Annabel Graham Paul
Income: £1,561,343 [2017]; £1,334,992 [2016]; £1,508,336 [2015]; £1,463,360 [2014]; £1,553,697 [2013]

Singh Sabha London East

Registered: 31 May 1973 *Employees:* 2 *Volunteers:* 30
Tel: 020 8594 3940 *Website:* singhsabhale.org
Activities: General charitable purposes; education, training; disability; overseas aid, famine relief; religious activities; arts, culture, heritage, science; amateur sport; economic, community development, employment; human rights, religious or racial harmony, equality or diversity; recreation; other charitable purposes
Address: Singh Sabha Temple, 100 North Street, Barking, Essex, IG11 8JD
Trustees: Mr Rashpaul Singh Pawar, Mr Gurdip Singh Hundal, Surjit Singh Toot, Lehmbar Singh Lehal, Mr Hardial Singh Rai, Mr Karnail Singh Maitala, Mr Gurmail Singh Soul, Mrs Inderjit Kaur Bhatia, Mr Harbhjan Singh Mann, Mr Rajjvinder Singh Dhaliwal, Mr Kulvinder Singh Mahal, Mr Surat Singh Atwal, Mr Balbir Singh Treasurer, Mr Major Singh Basi President, Raghbir Singh Bhangal, Mr Balvinder Singh Rayat, Karnail Singh Narwal, Mr Jagdish Singh Jutle, Mr Jatinder Singh Bassan, Mr Avtar Singh Sehmbi, Mrs Mohinder Kaur, Mr Inderpal Singh Malhi, Mr Sukhdev Singh Kahlon, Mrs Nishtro Pretam Kaur Sanghera, Jaswant Singh
Income: £1,385,152 [2017]; £886,127 [2016]; £846,103 [2015]; £806,579 [2014]; £688,026 [2013]

The Single Homeless Project

Registered: 16 Sep 1983 *Employees:* 478 *Volunteers:* 80
Tel: 020 7520 8660 *Website:* shp.org.uk
Activities: Education, training; prevention or relief of poverty; accommodation, housing
Address: 245 Grays Inn Road, London, WC1X 8QY
Trustees: Mr Jonathan Senker, Ms Jasmine Cockcroft, Mr Mark Fell, Mr Peter Rowbottom, Mr Chris Clements, Ms Anna Clark, Mr David Braverman, Ms Lindsey Chiswick, Mr Jon Edwards, Mr Joao Martires
Income: £18,935,430 [2017]; £18,051,678 [2016]; £19,036,531 [2015]; £18,063,014 [2014]; £18,050,219 [2013]

The Sir Andrew Judd Foundation

Registered: 28 Sep 1966 *Employees:* 9
Tel: 020 7236 5629 *Website:* skinnershall.co.uk
Activities: Education, training
Address: Skinners Hall, 8 Dowgate Hill, London, EC4R 2SP
Trustees: The Worshipful Company of Skinners
Income: £2,461,952 [2017]; £1,990,107 [2016]; £1,990,107 [2015]; £1,223,552 [2014]; £1,121,259 [2013]

The Sir Harold Hillier Gardens and Arboretum

Registered: 12 Jan 1978 *Employees:* 45 *Volunteers:* 160
Tel: 01962 847876 *Website:* hilliergardens.org.uk
Activities: General charitable purposes; education, training; arts, culture, heritage, science; environment, conservation, heritage; recreation
Address: Culture Communities & Business Services, Three Minsters House, 76 High Street, Winchester, Hants, SO23 8UL
Trustees: Hampshire County Council
Income: £1,869,755 [2017]; £2,013,322 [2016]; £1,904,101 [2015]; £1,891,917 [2014]; £1,843,153 [2013]

The Sir John Fisher Foundation

Registered: 6 Jun 1979
Tel: 01229 580349 *Website:* sirjohnfisherfoundation.org.uk
Activities: General charitable purposes; education, training; advancement of health or saving of lives; disability; arts, culture, heritage, science
Address: Heaning Wood, Ulverston, Cumbria, LA12 7NZ
Trustees: Mrs Diane Sara Meacock, Mr Rowland Frederick Hart Jackson, Mrs Christine Mary Tomlinson, Mr Thomas Peter Meacock, Mr Daniel Purser Tindall, Mr Christopher Thomas Stafford Batten, Mr Michael John Shields
Income: £2,472,020 [2017]; £1,878,558 [2016]; £1,706,312 [2015]; £1,498,491 [2014]; £1,430,318 [2013]

Sir Robert Geffery's Almshouse Trust

Registered: 25 Jan 1975 *Employees:* 9
Tel: 020 7776 2311 *Website:* ironmongers.org
Activities: General charitable purposes; education, training; prevention or relief of poverty; accommodation, housing; arts, culture, heritage, science
Address: Ironmongers Hall, Barbican, London, EC2Y 8AA
Trustees: The Ironmongers' Trust Company
Income: £2,113,297 [2017]; £1,877,329 [2016]; £1,955,337 [2015]; £1,436,746 [2014]; £1,274,493 [2013]

Siri Guru Nanak Darbar (Sikh Temple)

Registered: 21 May 1984 *Employees:* 16 *Volunteers:* 214
Tel: 01474 350611 *Website:* gurunanakdarbar.org
Activities: Religious activities
Address: Siri Guru Nanak Darbar, Guru Nanak Marg, Gravesend, Kent, DA12 1AG
Trustees: Mr Sohan Singh Bhatti, Mr Devinder Singh Boora, Mr Ajaib Singh Cheema
Income: £1,114,933 [2017]; £1,257,703 [2016]; £1,279,479 [2015]; £1,093,353 [2014]; £1,023,797 [2013]

The Sisters Hospitallers of The Sacred Heart of Jesus

Registered: 23 Apr 1968 *Employees:* 139 *Volunteers:* 40
Tel: 020 7373 3054 *Website:* sistershospitallers.org
Activities: Education, training; advancement of health or saving of lives; overseas aid, famine relief; accommodation, housing; religious activities
Address: St Theresa's Home, 40-46 Roland Gardens, London, SW7 3PW
Trustees: Sister Encarnacion Aguayo, Sr Isabel Canton, Sr Josefa Hernandez, Sister Maria Begona Perez
Income: £5,512,329 [2016]; £5,388,631 [2015]; £5,129,528 [2014]; £4,937,831 [2013]; £4,465,455 [2012]

The Sisters of Charity of Our Lady of Evron

Registered: 16 Feb 1967 *Employees:* 2 *Volunteers:* 20
Tel: 0161 832 6954
Activities: The advancement of health or saving of lives; prevention or relief of poverty; overseas aid, famine relief; religious activities; economic, community development, employment; human rights, religious or racial harmony, equality or diversity
Address: Emnaus, Sudell Street, Manchester, M4 4JF
Trustees: Sister Clare Kelly, Sister Maura Considine, Sister Louise Gilbey, Sister Teresa West, Sister Mary Anne McCready
Income: £1,102,806 [2016]; £385,490 [2015]; £422,351 [2014]; £429,025 [2013]; £422,318 [2012]

Sisters of Charity of St Paul The Apostle
Registered: 14 Mar 1968 *Employees:* 183 *Volunteers:* 1
Website: sistersofstpaulsellypark.org
Activities: General charitable purposes; education, training; religious activities
Address: St Pauls Convent, 94 Selly Park Road, Selly Park, Birmingham, B29 7LL
Trustees: Sister Eileen Therese Browne, Sister Margaret Mattison, Sister Teresa Anne Murphy, Sister Catherine Mary Neenan, Sister Ann Sullivan, Sister Cecilia Bordea
Income: £8,738,208 [2016]; £7,086,985 [2015]; £7,079,945 [2014]; £6,766,708 [2013]; £8,295,791 [2012]

Sisters of Christ UK Development Fund Charity
Registered: 25 Mar 2004
Tel: 020 8542 3595
Activities: Religious activities
Address: Norlands, Mayfield Road, London, SW19 3NF
Trustees: Sister May Magenis, Sister Emerentienne Ramoravelo, Sister Catherine Morton, Sister Rose-Marie Perrussel, Sister Joyce Bone
Income: £1,454,875 [2016]; £65,404 [2015]; £69,541 [2014]; £79,877 [2013]; £78,067 [2012]

Sisters of Mercy Sunderland
Registered: 30 Oct 1963 *Employees:* 60
Tel: 0191 567 4653
Activities: Education, training; prevention or relief of poverty; religious activities
Address: Convent of Mercy, Oaklea, Tunstall Road, Sunderland, Tyne & Wear, SR2 7JR
Trustees: Sister Raphael, Sister Calasanctius, Sister Adrienne, Sister Aelred, Sister Stephen
Income: £2,059,177 [2016]; £3,127,288 [2015]; £2,110,018 [2014]; £2,084,463 [2013]; £2,017,878 [2012]

The Sisters of Notre Dame (of Namur)
Registered: 4 Feb 1964 *Employees:* 157
Tel: 01257 465000 *Website:* snduk.org
Activities: Education, training; advancement of health or saving of lives; prevention or relief of poverty; religious activities
Address: Flat 4, Lancaster Court, Lancaster Lane, Parbold, Wigan, Lancs, WN8 7HS
Trustees: Sister Ann Byrne, Sister Mary Josephine MacCallum, Sister Elizabeth Brady, Notre Dame Trustee Company Limited
Income: £4,301,543 [2016]; £3,730,727 [2015]; £4,366,891 [2014]; £3,834,576 [2013]; £3,734,170 [2012]

The Sisters of The Blessed Sacrament
Registered: 12 Dec 1963 *Employees:* 65 *Volunteers:* 7
Tel: 01903 812185 *Website:* thetowersconventschool.org
Activities: General charitable purposes; education, training; prevention or relief of poverty; overseas aid, famine relief; religious activities
Address: Upper Beeding, W Sussex, BN44 3TF
Trustees: Sister Mary Patrick, Sister Zita Fogarty, Sister Mary Andrew, Sister Catherine Murphy
Income: £2,889,373 [2016]; £2,889,373 [2015]; £2,804,957 [2014]; £2,840,122 [2013]; £2,767,558 [2012]

Sisters of The Cross and Passion
Registered: 14 Jun 1994 *Employees:* 334 *Volunteers:* 864
Tel: 0161 655 3184 *Website:* crossandpassion.com
Activities: General charitable purposes; education, training; advancement of health or saving of lives; prevention or relief of poverty; overseas aid, famine relief; religious activities; environment, conservation, heritage
Address: The Provincialate Sisters of The Cross & Passion, 299 Boarshaw Road, Middleton, Manchester, M24 2PF
Trustees: Sister Eileen Fucito CP, Sister Therese O'Regan, Sr Anne Hammersley, Sr Savio Steed, Sr Carmel Gorman
Income: £13,185,043 [2017]; £13,313,404 [2016]; £12,990,614 [2015]; £13,272,020 [2014]; £13,301,310 [2013]

Sisters of The Holy Cross Charitable Trust
Registered: 3 Dec 1964 *Employees:* 74
Tel: 020 8942 2703
Activities: Education, training; religious activities
Address: 41 Westbury Road, New Malden, Surrey, KT3 5AX
Trustees: Sr Ursula Eberhardt, Sister Sheila Brennan, Sr Mary Christa Stanton, Sister Margaret Mary Donovan MA, Sr Elizabeth O'Donohoe, Sr Bernadette Morey
Income: £4,782,725 [2017]; £31,480,851 [2016]; £3,794,470 [2015]; £3,774,329 [2014]; £3,611,605 [2013]

The Sixteen
Registered: 28 Aug 1985 *Employees:* 8
Tel: 020 7936 3420 *Website:* thesixteen.com
Activities: General charitable purposes; arts, culture, heritage, science
Address: Quadrant House, 10 Fleet Street, London, EC4Y 1AU
Trustees: Mr Robin John Blackmore Barda, Mr Richard Lloyd Duffield Price, Mr Anthony Smith CBE, Mary Deissler, Sir Michael Briggs, Mr Richard Henry Tudor Christophers, Mr Keith Tony Parker, Mr Christopher Robert Smith, Mr Adam Singer, Ms Claire Long
Income: £1,752,139 [2016]; £1,834,299 [2015]; £1,988,567 [2014]; £1,619,444 [2013]; £1,796,393 [2012]

Skill Force Development
Registered: 21 Jul 2004 *Employees:* 106 *Volunteers:* 29
Tel: 01623 827603 *Website:* skillforce.org
Activities: Education, training; economic, community development, employment
Address: Skillforce, Edwinstowe House, High Street, Edwinstowe, Mansfield, Notts, NG21 9PR
Trustees: Ms Abi Topley, Sir Iain McMillan, Mr Andrew John McCully, Mrs Jane Liddell, Mrs Rachel Elizabeth Hanger, Mr Patrick Trueman, Mrs Jan Richardson MBE BA JP, Mrs Shelley Collins, Mr David John Courtley, John Gellett, Mr Timothy Rennie
Income: £5,088,718 [2017]; £5,838,475 [2016]; £6,905,193 [2015]; £6,729,348 [2014]; £8,118,997 [2013]

Skills Active UK
Registered: 3 Jul 2003 *Employees:* 26
Tel: 01302 774926 *Website:* skillsactive.com
Activities: Education, training; advancement of health or saving of lives; disability; arts, culture, heritage, science; amateur sport; economic, community development, employment; human rights, religious or racial harmony, equality or diversity; recreation
Address: Styrrup Hall Golf & Country Club, Main Street, Styrrup, Doncaster, S Yorks, DN11 8NB
Trustees: Mrs Julie Ann Amies, Mrs Joan Scott, Mr Alex De Carvalho, Mr Sukhjinder Singh Kalirai, Mr William Shaw
Income: £1,076,521 [2017]; £6,489,459 [2016]; £6,706,884 [2014]; £7,521,314 [2013]; £11,679,744 [2012]

Skills and Education Group Limited
Registered: 6 Sep 1991 *Employees:* 39
Tel: 0115 854 1316 *Website:* emfec.co.uk
Activities: Education, training
Address: EMFEC, Robinswood House, Robins Wood Road, Nottingham, NG8 3NH
Trustees: Mr John Patrick Yarham, Mr Atholl Garioch Stott, Mr Leonard John Tildsley, Ms Joanne Maher, Mrs Linda Rose Houtby, Mrs Verity Anne Hancock, Mr Paul Anthony Eeles, Mrs Janet Meenaghan
Income: £1,973,227 [2016]; £3,075,924 [2015]; £2,561,942 [2014]; £3,021,488 [2013]; £1,757,678 [2012]

Skills for Care Ltd
Registered: 14 Mar 2000 *Employees:* 192
Tel: 0113 241 1243 *Website:* skillsforcare.org.uk
Activities: General charitable purposes; education, training; disability; economic, community development, employment
Address: Skills for Care, West Gate, 6 Grace Street, Leeds, LS1 2RP
Trustees: Ms Munira Thobani, Mrs Helen Wilcox, Mr Keith Mark Lever, Mrs Amanda Jillian Thorn, Ms Susan McMillan, Mrs Rachael Wardell, Ms Susan Bott, Mr Desmond Patrick Kelly, Mr Neil Taylor, Dame Moira Gibb, Mrs Louise Elizabeth Bladen, Mr Paul Snell, Dr Mahiben Maruthappu
Income: £27,048,966 [2017]; £29,698,699 [2016]; £33,848,356 [2015]; £34,720,595 [2014]; £29,432,638 [2013]

Skillshare International
Registered: 11 Dec 1989 *Employees:* 30 *Volunteers:* 165
Tel: 0116 303 3333 *Website:* skillshare.org
Activities: Education, training; advancement of health or saving of lives; disability; prevention or relief of poverty; overseas aid, famine relief; economic, community development, employment
Address: Ashcroft House, Ervington Court, Meridian Business Park, Leicester, LE19 1WL
Trustees: Mr Roger Blake, Ms Chandni Joshi, Maggie Pankhurst, Dr Maddy Gupta-Wright, Ms Clare Nagle, Mr Martin Cumella, Ms Kay Wilson, Ismayil Tahmazov, Ms Joannah Kelly
Income: £1,988,000 [2015]; £1,704,000 [2014]; £2,383,000 [2013]

The Skinners' Almshouse Charity
Registered: 29 Jan 2009
Tel: 020 7236 5629
Activities: The prevention or relief of poverty; accommodation, housing
Address: Skinners Hall, 8 Dowgate Hill, London, EC4R 2SP
Trustees: Mr Christopher Harris Doyle Everett, Mr Mark Antony Loveday, Mr Evan Price, Dr Simon John Cooper, Catherine Roe, Miss Mary Stallebrass, Mr Simon Hansell Keith, Mr Neil Francis Maltby, Mr Christopher John David Emms, Mrs Anne Dudley Buchanan, Rosemary Goad, Miss Catherine Attenborough, Mr Alexander Ifor Lloyd, Mr James Seymour Lionel Cohen
Income: £1,227,017 [2017]; £1,044,402 [2016]; £1,038,253 [2015]; £1,015,898 [2014]; £1,001,942 [2013]

Slindon College Limited
Registered: 9 Nov 1993 *Employees:* 71 *Volunteers:* 3
Tel: 01243 814647 *Website:* slindoncollege.co.uk
Activities: Education, training; religious activities; arts, culture, heritage, science; amateur sport; animals; environment, conservation, heritage; economic, community development, employment
Address: Slindon College, Slindon House, Top Road, Slindon, Arundel, W Sussex, BN18 0RH
Trustees: Mr Michael Ewart Emmerson, Ven Philip Hugh Jones, Mr Michael John Withers, Mrs Ann Aughwane, Dr Simon Orchard, Mr Stuart Lawrance, Mr Roy Iremonger, Mr David Arthur Slee, Ms Lucinda Jane Davis
Income: £2,268,561 [2017]; £2,203,550 [2016]; £2,082,046 [2015]; £2,032,535 [2014]; £1,843,846 [2013]

Slough Community Leisure
Registered: 20 May 2013 *Employees:* 301
Website: absolutely-group.co.uk
Activities: Recreation; other charitable purposes
Address: The Arena, Stafferton Way, Maidenhead, Berks, SL6 1AY
Trustees: Ms Alison Taylor, Mr Brian Doe, Ms Patrice Bendon, Mr Brett Edwards, Mrs Jacqueline Gillan
Income: £9,559,820 [2017]; £10,117,264 [2016]; £5,096,198 [2015]; £4,856,679 [2014]

Smallpeice Trust Limited
Registered: 17 Jan 1968 *Employees:* 32
Tel: 01926 333200 *Website:* smallpeicetrust.org.uk
Activities: Education, training
Address: The Smallpeice Trust, 74 Upper Holly Walk, Leamington Spa, Warwicks, CV32 4JL
Trustees: Mrs Pauline Cox, Dr Geraint Price, Mr Paul Doble OBE BSc MTech FIMechE FIET, Mr David Gavin Thompson, Mrs Rachael Warwick, Dr Malcolm Thomas, Mr Richard Folkson, Mr Trevor Michael Gill MA CEng MIET, Dr Alan Begg, Mr Ian Jess
Income: £2,411,949 [2016]; £3,026,286 [2015]; £1,986,715 [2014]; £1,745,673 [2013]; £1,673,729 [2012]

Smallwood Manor Preparatory School Limited
Registered: 29 Mar 2004 *Employees:* 61 *Volunteers:* 2
Tel: 01889 562083 *Website:* denstoneprep.co.uk
Activities: Education, training
Address: Smallwood Manor, Uttoxeter, Staffs, ST14 8NS
Trustees: Mr Simon Marlow, Mrs Pamela Yianni ACIB, Dr Pamela Priyanka Choudhury, Mr Matthew Adam Bailey, Mrs Madeleine Nicolette Ann Faulder, Mr Steven Varley, Mr Robert Thomas Eley, Mrs Jennifer Marshall, Mrs Claire Elisabeth Frost
Income: £1,753,090 [2017]; £1,688,957 [2016]; £1,442,786 [2015]; £1,422,379 [2014]; £1,365,771 [2013]

Smart Criminal Justice Services
Registered: 8 Apr 1998 *Employees:* 98 *Volunteers:* 53
Tel: 01491 571278 *Website:* smartcjs.org.uk
Activities: General charitable purposes; education, training; advancement of health or saving of lives; prevention or relief of poverty; accommodation, housing; other charitable purposes
Address: Smart CJS, 32 St Johns Street, Bedford, MK42 0DH
Trustees: Shahin Bekhradnia, Mr Richard Warwick-Saunders, Dr Patricia Barrett, Ferus Crombie, Mr David Ian Rawcliffe
Income: £3,803,904 [2017]; £2,738,151 [2016]; £3,111,458 [2015]; £2,616,957 [2014]; £2,259,988 [2013]

The Smile Train UK
Registered: 19 Jun 2006 *Employees:* 5
Tel: 0300 303 9630 *Website:* smiletrain.org.uk
Activities: Education, training; advancement of health or saving of lives; disability
Address: The Smile Train UK, Davenport House, 16 Pepper Street, London, E14 9RP
Trustees: Mr Edoardo Monopoli, Mr Roy Evan Reichbach, Susu Stinton, Mrs Catherine Margaret Teasdale, Ms Susannah Schaefer, Tatiana Poliakova, Sarah Dransfield
Income: £6,140,812 [2017]; £7,105,104 [2016]; £7,354,776 [2015]; £8,596,679 [2014]; £8,691,217 [2013]

The Henry Smith Charity
Registered: 15 Oct 1963 *Employees:* 21 *Volunteers:* 32
Tel: 020 7264 4970 *Website:* henrysmithcharity.org.uk
Activities: The advancement of health or saving of lives; disability; prevention or relief of poverty; accommodation, housing; economic, community development, employment
Address: Sixth Floor, 65-68 Leadenhall Street, London, EC3A 2AD
Trustees: Mrs Anna McNair Scott, Mrs Diana Barran, Miko Giedroyc, Mr David Allam, Vivian Hunt, Mrs Vivienne Dews, Mr Emir Feisal, Mr Noel Manns, Patrick Maxwell, Mrs Bridget Biddell, Revd Canon Paul Hackwood, Mr James Hordern, Mr Piers Feilden, The Lady Bella Colgrain DL
Income: £12,840,000 [2016]; £11,700,000 [2015]; £11,545,000 [2014]; £10,621,000 [2013]; £10,547,000 [2012]

Paul Smith Foundation
Registered: 13 Nov 1997
Tel: 0115 986 8877
Activities: Education, training; arts, culture, heritage, science
Address: Paul Smith Ltd, The Poplars, Lenton Lane, Nottingham, NG7 2PW
Trustees: Sir Paul Smith, Mr Ashley Long, Mr Jonathan Towle
Income: £26,395,904 [2017]

The Smith Foundation
Registered: 28 Jan 1974 *Employees:* 105
Tel: 01484 710123 *Website:* whsschool.org.uk
Activities: Education, training
Address: William Henry Smith School, Boothroyd Lane, Brighouse, W Yorks, HD6 3JW
Trustees: Mr Trevor Iles, Mr Liam Sutcliffe, Roger Tilbrook
Income: £4,198,934 [2017]; £3,672,902 [2016]; £3,577,126 [2015]; £3,384,872 [2014]; £3,187,268 [2013]

Snape Maltings
Registered: 23 Jul 1970 *Employees:* 198 *Volunteers:* 130
Tel: 01728 687100 *Website:* snapemaltings.co.uk
Activities: Arts, culture, heritage, science
Address: Snape Maltings Concert Hall, Snape Bridge, Snape, Saxmundham, Suffolk, IP17 1SP
Trustees: Sarah Zins, Simon Robey, Miranda Kendall, Patricia Swannell, David Robbie, Alasdair Tait, Garth Pollard, Roger Wright
Income: £11,195,333 [2017]; £6,078,012 [2016]; £4,592,223 [2015]; £6,829,788 [2014]; £5,365,022 [2013]

The R C Snelling Charitable Trust
Registered: 22 Mar 1999
Tel: 01603 711737 *Website:* rcsnellingcharitabletrust.org
Activities: General charitable purposes; education, training; advancement of health or saving of lives; disability; prevention or relief of poverty; religious activities; arts, culture, heritage, science; environment, conservation, heritage
Address: R C Snelling Ltd, Laundry Lane, Blofield, Norwich, NR13 4SQ
Trustees: Mr Philip Jan Buttinger, Mr Toby Wise, Mr Samuel Barratt, Mr Stephan Phillips, Mr Rowland Cogman, Mr Colin Jacobs, Mr Nigel Rudolf Savory
Income: £10,833,065 [2017]; £9,638,382 [2016]; £18,279,508 [2015]; £1,960,020 [2014]; £77,302 [2013]

Snowdon Trust
Registered: 2 Jul 1981 *Employees:* 3 *Volunteers:* 7
Tel: 01403 732899 *Website:* snowdontrust.org
Activities: Education, training; disability
Address: Unit 18 Oakhurst Business Park, Wilberforce Way, Southwater, Horsham, W Sussex, RH13 9RT
Trustees: Dr Renny Philip Leach, Dr Jane Deanne McLarty, Mr Dan Norris, John Rous Milligan, Dr Wendy Piatt, Lady Frances von Hofmannsthal, Dr Richard Lansdown, Ms Anji Hunter, Mr Andrew Farquhar FCIS, Mr Simon Preece, Lord Colin MacKenzie Low of Dalston CBE, Dr Paolo Subrato Dasgupta
Income: £2,622,318 [2017]; £402,976 [2016]; £247,761 [2015]; £223,034 [2014]; £223,092 [2013]

Snowflake School for Children with Autism Limited
Registered: 26 Jun 2007 *Employees:* 21 *Volunteers:* 4
Tel: 020 7370 3232 *Website:* snowflakeschool.org.uk
Activities: Education, training; disability
Address: Flat A, 46 Longridge Road, London, SW5 9SJ
Trustees: Mrs Faryaneh Akhavan, Mrs Mahnaz Kamel, Mr James Simon Cheetham, Mr Ardavan Farman Farmaian, Mr Shahrokh Bagherzadeh
Income: £1,034,263 [2017]; £1,034,600 [2016]; £929,045 [2015]; £908,446 [2014]; £836,007 [2013]

Sir John Soane's Museum Trust
Registered: 1 Mar 2012
Tel: 020 7440 4244
Activities: Education, training; arts, culture, heritage, science
Address: 13 Lincoln's Inn Fields, London, WC2A 3BP
Trustees: Basil Postan, Dr Kenneth Gray, Dr Bruce Ambler Boucher, Roderick Smith, Dr Gisela Maria Aloisia Gledhill
Income: £1,326,540 [2016]; £687,543 [2015]; £306,288 [2014]; £1,105,935 [2013]

Sir John Soane's Museum
Registered: 18 Apr 1963 *Employees:* 44 *Volunteers:* 100
Tel: 020 7440 4244 *Website:* soane.org
Activities: Education, training; arts, culture, heritage, science; environment, conservation, heritage
Address: Sir John Soanes Museum, 13 Lincoln's Inn Fields, London, WC2A 3BP
Trustees: Mrs Katrin Henkel, Guy Elliott, Sir David Chipperfield, Mr Basil Postan, Mr Vincent Thomas Keaveny, Dr Thierry Philippe Andre Morel, Professor Jonathan Ashmore, Ms Orna Nichionna, Mrs Molly Lowell Borthwick, Professor David Patrick Martin Ekserdjian, Professor Nichola Johnson OBE SFA
Income: £3,803,647 [2017]; £3,906,226 [2016]; £2,769,807 [2015]; £3,403,963 [2014]; £2,461,238 [2013]

Soas Students' Union

Registered: 6 Feb 2013 *Employees:* 43 *Volunteers:* 1,584
Tel: 020 7898 4996 *Website:* soasunion.org
Activities: Education, training; religious activities; arts, culture, heritage, science; amateur sport; environment, conservation, heritage; recreation
Address: SOAS Students' Union, Thornhaugh Street, Russell Sq, London, WC1H 0XG
Trustees: Mr Mehdi Baraka, Mr Daryan Omer, Miss Maximiliane Fanziska Gleissner, Miss Nisha Phillipps, Miss Robyn Waite, Mx Jess Kumwongpin-Barnes, Miss Pauline Ankunda, Mr Danny Edwards, Miss Rama Ramez Fuad Sabanekh, Miss Sophie Bennett, Miss Francesca Serena Floris, Miss Valeria Racu, Mr Dimitri Cautain, Miss Rachel Hau-Yu Tam, Miss Comfort Enoch-Moye, Mr Jonny Morrison, Miss Anna Gretton, Miss Halimo Hussain, Miss Lavinya Vinette Stennett, Mr Tawsin Mujtaba Ahmed, Miss Katouche Olayiwola Goll
Income: £1,294,193 [2017]; £1,330,524 [2016]; £1,331,131 [2015]; £1,264,083 [2014]

The Sobell Foundation

Registered: 3 Oct 1977
Website: sobellfoundation.org.uk
Activities: The advancement of health or saving of lives; disability; prevention or relief of poverty
Address: P O Box 2137, Lamyatt, Shepton Mallet, Somerset, BA4 6YA
Trustees: Mrs Andrea Gaie Scouller, Mr Roger Kingston Lewis, Mrs Susan Gina Lacroix
Income: £1,994,973 [2017]; £1,971,805 [2016]; £1,973,385 [2015]; £2,100,201 [2014]; £1,955,328 [2013]

Sobell House Hospice Charity Limited

Registered: 2 Apr 2007 *Employees:* 35 *Volunteers:* 188
Tel: 01865 857007 *Website:* sobellhospicecharity.org.uk
Activities: The advancement of health or saving of lives
Address: Churchill Hospital, Old Road, Headington, Oxford, OX3 7LE
Trustees: Mrs Vivienne Spurge, Mr Kenneth John McEwing Smith, Mr Hugh Fraser, Mrs Sandra Nash, Ms Gillian Nineham, Mrs Maryrose Danvers Hodgson, Mr William Couldrick, Mr Ian Miles, Mr John Holloran, Dr Rachel Starer
Income: £5,011,246 [2017]; £4,139,787 [2016]; £4,576,452 [2015]; £4,146,147 [2014]; £2,896,000 [2013]

Social Action for Health

Registered: 31 Aug 1994 *Employees:* 32 *Volunteers:* 92
Tel: 07496 170647 *Website:* safh.org.uk
Activities: Education, training; advancement of health or saving of lives; economic, community development, employment; human rights, religious or racial harmony, equality or diversity
Address: 1A Handsworth Road, London, N17 6DB
Trustees: Mrs Hannah Stranger-Jones, Ms Pooja Shah, Mr Kendall Gilmore, Miss Annette Jack, Ms Alexandra Evans, Mr Arif Hossain
Income: £1,257,713 [2017]; £1,684,497 [2016]; £1,598,135 [2015]; £1,431,181 [2014]; £1,641,445 [2013]

Social Care Institute for Excellence

Registered: 3 Jul 2002 *Employees:* 72
Tel: 020 7766 7400 *Website:* scie.org.uk
Activities: Education, training; disability; prevention or relief of poverty
Address: SCIE, Watson House, 54 Baker Street, London, W1U 7EX
Trustees: Mr John Evans OBE, Mr Peter Hay, Tina Coldham, Ms Bev Searle, Ms Annie Hudson, Ms Katie Brennan, Mr Paul Kenneth Burstow, Mr Alex Fox, Ms Mary McKenna, Ms Sally Warren, Dr Osmund Stuart, Ms Sue Gower MBE
Income: £6,492,465 [2017]; £6,672,010 [2016]; £7,057,526 [2015]; £6,567,908 [2014]; £5,433,603 [2013]

Social Care in Action

Registered: 8 Apr 2003 *Employees:* 228 *Volunteers:* 104
Tel: 023 8036 6663 *Website:* scagroup.co.uk
Activities: Education, training; advancement of health or saving of lives; disability
Address: Amplevine House, Dukes Road, Southampton, SO14 0ST
Trustees: Mr Les Judd, Mr Raymond Hallett, Mr Manoj Patel, Mr Edward Hickman, Carolyn Beech, Cllr Eamonn Keogh, Mr Peter George Farquhar Dibben, Ms Wendy Hughes, Mr Dominic Lodge, Dean Chamberlain, Mark Venables
Income: £8,791,241 [2017]; £7,897,631 [2016]; £9,068,494 [2015]; £142,743 [2014]; £171,594 [2013]

Social Interest Group

Registered: 1 Sep 2014 *Employees:* 289 *Volunteers:* 11
Tel: 020 3668 9270 *Website:* socialinterestgroup.org.uk
Activities: General charitable purposes; advancement of health or saving of lives; prevention or relief of poverty; accommodation, housing
Address: Unit 1 Waterloo Gardens, Milner Square, London, N1 1TY
Trustees: Ms Lindsey Wishart, Ms Zelda Peters, Stuart Jenkin, Mrs Gill Arukpe, Dr Karl Hemant Singh Marlowe
Income: £13,326,000 [2017]; £12,490,000 [2016]; £1,163,000 [2015]

Social Investment Business Foundation

Registered: 8 Dec 2006 *Employees:* 38
Tel: 020 3096 7903 *Website:* sibgroup.org.uk
Activities: Economic, community development, employment; other charitable purposes
Address: 2nd Floor, Social Investment Business, CAN Mezzanine, 7-14 Great Dover Street, London, SE1 4YR
Trustees: Mr Hugh Rolo, Mr Anand Shukla, Mr Richard Pelly, Ms Jenny Elizabeth North, Mr James Joseph Edward Rice, Mr Jeremy S Newman, Rt Hon Hazel Blears
Income: £4,647,000 [2017]; £4,986,000 [2016]; £14,246,000 [2015]; £16,785,000 [2014]; £17,547,000 [2013]

The Social Mobility Foundation

Registered: 22 Aug 2006 *Employees:* 19 *Volunteers:* 1,500
Tel: 020 7183 1189 *Website:* socialmobility.org.uk
Activities: Education, training
Address: 1st and 2nd Floor, Social Mobility Foundation, 43-47 Leadenhall Market, London, EC3V 1LR
Trustees: Ms Lis Astall, Dr Geoffrey Parks, Sir Terry Leahy, Mrs Theresa Loar, Fraser Nelson, Rt Hon Nick Clegg MP, Mr Trevor Phillips OBE, Mr Tom Cassels, Rt Hon Hazel Blears, Sir Victor Blank, Ms Ann Doherty, Mrs Helen Grant MP
Income: £1,161,276 [2016]; £1,043,687 [2015]; £974,369 [2014]; £784,361 [2013]; £656,124 [2012]

Social Tech Trust

Registered: 5 Sep 2008 *Employees:* 10
Tel: 01865 334000 *Website:* nominettrust.org.uk
Activities: Education, training; advancement of health or saving of lives; disability; prevention or relief of poverty; arts, culture, heritage, science; environment, conservation, heritage; economic, community development, employment
Address: Social Tech Trust, Minerva House, Edmund Halley Road, Oxford, OX4 4DQ
Trustees: Bill Liao, Elizabeth Colleen Murray, Mr Nicolas Mark Alexander Temple, Sebastien Lahtinen, Hannah Keartland
Income: £5,695,182 [2017]; £4,061,908 [2016]; £3,327,909 [2015]; £6,067,351 [2014]; £6,122,541 [2013]

The Societe Generale United Kingdom Group Charitable Trust

Registered: 27 Jun 1994
Tel: 020 7597 3065
Activities: General charitable purposes; education, training; advancement of health or saving of lives; disability; prevention or relief of poverty; overseas aid, famine relief
Address: S G Hambros Trust Company Ltd, 5th Floor, 8 St James's Square, London, SW1Y 4JU
Trustees: Mr Philippe Robeyns, Mr Ben Higgins, Ms Tara Palmer, Kathryn Stewart
Income: £4,170,303 [2016]; £548,121 [2015]; £295,159 [2014]; £313,930 [2013]; £280,679 [2012]

Society for Applied Microbiology

Registered: 3 Mar 2008 *Employees:* 5 *Volunteers:* 26
Tel: 020 7685 2596 *Website:* sfam.org.uk
Activities: Arts, culture, heritage, science
Address: Society for Applied Microbiology, Charles Darwin House, 12 Roger Street, London, WC1N 2JU
Trustees: Professor Valerie Edwards-Jones, Dr Clare Taylor, Dr Timothy Aldsworth, Mrs Claire Hill, Dr Michael Dempsey, Dr Simon Gould, Professor Ian Feavers, Professor Mark Fielder, Dr Brian Vaughan Jones, Dr Linda Thomas, Ms Charlotte Duncan, Mr Philip Wheat, Professor Stephen Forsythe
Income: £1,449,318 [2016]; £1,334,338 [2015]; £1,362,981 [2014]; £1,243,694 [2013]; £1,229,678 [2012]

Society for Endocrinology

Registered: 10 Apr 1974 *Employees:* 70 *Volunteers:* 100
Tel: 01454 642200 *Website:* endocrinology.org
Activities: General charitable purposes; education, training; advancement of health or saving of lives
Address: Society of Endocrinology Ltd, Unit 22 Apex Court, Woodlands, Bradley Stoke, Bristol, BS32 4JT
Trustees: Dr Mark Gurnell, Dr Simon Henry Schofield Pearce, Dr Melissa Gibson, Professor Eleanor Davies, Professor Martin Hewison, Dr Barbara McGowan, Prof Graham Richard Williams, Professor Waljit Dhillo, Professor Neil Anthony Hanley, Professor Ruth Andrew, Professor Karen Elizabeth Chapman, Prof Jeremy William Tomlinson
Income: £5,849,779 [2016]; £6,004,165 [2015]; £4,922,435 [2014]; £4,755,526 [2013]; £4,733,738 [2012]

The Society for Experimental Biology

Registered: 6 Dec 1977 *Employees:* 6
Tel: 020 7685 2600 *Website:* sebiology.org
Activities: Education, training; other charitable purposes
Address: Charles Darwin House, 12 Roger Street, London, WC1N 2JU
Trustees: Dr Martin Watson, Professor Craig Franklin PhD, Professor Martin Afan John Parry, Dr George Littlejohn, Sue Broom, Prof Christine Raines, Dr Lynne Sneddon, Professor Gudrun De Boeck, Professor Patrick Hussey PhD, Dr John Love, Greig D'Cruz, Eamon Ray, Profefssor Katherine Janet Denby
Income: £2,237,073 [2016]; £2,229,173 [2015]; £2,199,060 [2014]; £2,071,922 [2013]; £1,976,830 [2012]

Society for Horticultural Therapy

Registered: 27 Mar 1979 *Employees:* 41 *Volunteers:* 300
Tel: 0118 988 5688 *Website:* thrive.org.uk
Activities: Education, training; advancement of health or saving of lives; disability; environment, conservation, heritage; recreation
Address: Thrive Horticultural Therapy, Geoffrey Udall Centre, Trunkwell Park, Beech Hill Road, Beech Hill, Reading, Berks, RG7 2AT
Trustees: Mr Christopher D'Olley, Miss Rebecca Margaret Bower, Mrs Alina Nicola Lourie, Dr Sara Katharine Kelly, Mr Jeremy Nicholas Quentin Wright, Mr Rory MacKenzie, Ms Michele Tan Cheng, Mrs Faith Lesley Ramsay, Mr Raymond James Broughton, Mr Richard Rogers
Income: £1,699,266 [2017]; £1,371,462 [2016]; £1,736,537 [2015]; £1,454,922 [2014]; £1,379,382 [2013]

The Society for Mucopolysaccharide Diseases

Registered: 19 Aug 2011 *Employees:* 22 *Volunteers:* 120
Tel: 0845 389 9901 *Website:* mpssociety.org.uk
Activities: Education, training; advancement of health or saving of lives; disability
Address: MPS House, Repton Place, White Lion Road, Amersham, Bucks, HP7 9LP
Trustees: Mrs Wilma Robins, Mrs Judith Holroyd, Prof Bryan Winchester, Mr Paul Kevin Moody, Mrs Judith Evans, Mr Tim Summerton, Mr Robert Stevens, Mrs Jessica Clare Kafizas
Income: £3,553,166 [2016]; £3,576,018 [2015]; £3,348,812 [2014]; £1,537,658 [2013]; £3,279,503 [2012]

The Society for Promoting Christian Knowledge

Registered: 21 Jun 1971 *Employees:* 36 *Volunteers:* 24
Tel: 020 7592 3900 *Website:* spck.org.uk
Activities: Education, training; religious activities
Address: Society for Promoting Christian Knowledge, 36 Causton Street, London, SW1P 4ST
Trustees: Mr James Catford, Dr Cathy Ross, The Rt Revd Dr Michael Beasley, Dr Andrew Fergusson, Mr Matthew Cashmore, Mr Eric Thompson, Mr Stephen Tudway, The Rt Revd John Pritchard, The Revd Niall Sloane, Mrs Sarah Bailey, Mrs Elizabeth Renshaw-Ames, Mr Paul Burrage
Income: £5,565,525 [2017]; £5,020,000 [2016]; £3,335,000 [2015]; £3,119,000 [2014]; £2,986,000 [2013]

The Society for The Protection of Ancient Buildings
Registered: 12 Apr 2006 *Employees:* 26 *Volunteers:* 400
Tel: 020 7377 1644 *Website:* spab.org.uk
Activities: Education, training; arts, culture, heritage, science; environment, conservation, heritage
Address: Society for The Protection Ancient Buildings, 37 Spital Square, London, E1 6DY
Trustees: Ms Gillian Mary Darley OBE, Mr John Russell Sell CBE, Mr David Alexander, Mr Richard Max, Mr Ian Harper, Mrs Jessica Sutcliffe, Mrs Mildred Cookson, Dr Mark Archer, Mr Iain Patrick Boyd, Mr Stephen Bull, Dr Peter Burman MBE, Mr Charles Wagner
Income: £1,377,440 [2016]; £1,602,801 [2015]; £1,427,519 [2014]; £1,380,673 [2013]; £1,034,099 [2012]

The Society for The Protection of Animals Abroad
Registered: 23 Jan 1963 *Employees:* 52 *Volunteers:* 293
Tel: 020 7831 3999 *Website:* spana.org
Activities: Education, training; advancement of health or saving of lives; prevention or relief of poverty; overseas aid, famine relief; animals; environment, conservation, heritage; economic, community development, employment
Address: Spana, 14 John Street, London, WC1N 2EB
Trustees: The Lady Slynn, Dr Mary-Lorraine Hughes BSc PhD MBA, Brigadier John Mark Castle OBE, Colonel William Toby Browne, Dr Jacqueline Boyd, Ms Olga Johnson, Dr Jonathon Amory, Prof Timothy Robert Charles Greet BVMS MVM Cert EO DESTS Dip ECVS, Mr Gavin Helmer, Mr Robert Edward Gethen Smith MBA BEng
Income: £6,104,377 [2016]; £6,509,870 [2015]; £6,627,019 [2014]; £5,974,785 [2013]; £4,434,441 [2012]

The Society for The Study of Addiction
Registered: 17 Mar 1992 *Employees:* 5
Tel: 07759 093062 *Website:* addiction-ssa.org
Activities: The advancement of health or saving of lives
Address: Office 116, University of Northampton Innovation Centre, Green Street, Northampton, NN1 1SY
Trustees: Dr Gillian Tober, Dr Jane Marshall, Professor Eilish Gilvarry, Dr Catriona Isobel Matheson, Professor Ann McNeill, Professor John Strang, Dr Daphne Rumball, Dr Ed Day, Dr Julia Sinclair, Professor Matthew Hickman
Income: £1,016,780 [2017]; £950,316 [2016]; £861,813 [2015]; £866,135 [2014]; £885,990 [2013]

The Society for The Study of Inborn Errors of Metabolism
Registered: 23 Apr 1992
Tel: 020 7940 8990 *Website:* ssiem.org
Activities: Education, training; advancement of health or saving of lives
Address: Association for Clinical Biochemistry, 130-132 Tooley Street, London, SE1 2TU
Trustees: Ms Ann Yvonne Brown, Prof Ivo Baric, Dr Antonia Ribes, Dr Andrew Alan Myles Morris, Prof Dr Med Johannes Haberle, Dr Helen Michelakakis, Prof Gajja Sophi Salomons, Prof Katrin Ounap, Dr Eva Morava-Kozicz, Dr Manuel Schiff, Dr Fanny Mochel, Dr Maria Dulce Silva Quelhas
Income: £1,726,876 [2016]; £1,709,749 [2015]; £1,648,051 [2014]; £464,502 [2013]; £1,667,087 [2012]

The Society of All Saints Sisters of The Poor (Commonly Called Society of All Saints)
Registered: 26 Sep 1963 *Employees:* 56
Tel: 01865 255790 *Website:* allsaintssistersofthepoor.org.uk
Activities: The advancement of health or saving of lives; prevention or relief of poverty; accommodation, housing; religious activities; environment, conservation, heritage
Address: All Saints, 15a Magdalen Road, Oxford, OX4 1RW
Trustees: Alastair Cooper, Rev Dr Andrew Teal, Mr Nicholas Edward Bell, Mrs Caroline Johnson
Income: £1,072,578 [2017]; £1,827,043 [2016]; £1,915,037 [2015]; £1,629,796 [2014]; £1,661,069 [2013]

Society of Antiquaries of London
Registered: 25 Jul 1963 *Employees:* 28 *Volunteers:* 162
Tel: 020 7479 7080 *Website:* sal.org.uk
Activities: Education, training; arts, culture, heritage, science; environment, conservation, heritage
Address: Society of Antiquaries, Burlington House, Piccadilly, London, W1J 0BE
Trustees: Dr Stewart Bryant BSc MA PhD MIFA FSA, Dr Stephen Johnson MA DPhil FSA, Mrs Gillian M Andrews BA FSA, Prof Christopher Scull MA FSA, Prof John Hines BA MA DPhil FSA, Dr Jeremy Warren MA DLitt FSA, Mr Mark E Purcell BA MA FSA, Dr Dan Hicks MA PhD MIFA FSA, Dr Stephen Greep BA PhD AMA FSA, Mr Stephen Dunmore OBE BA FSA, Mr Anthony C R Davis MA MA CTA Fellow FSA, Mr Paul J Dury MRICS IHBC FSA, Prof Stephanie Moser MA PhD FSA, Mr John Cattell BA MA Hons MA IHBC FSA, Dr Holly Trusted MA PhD FSA
Income: £3,810,519 [2017]; £1,772,011 [2016]; £1,663,628 [2015]; £1,559,852 [2014]; £1,617,634 [2013]

Society of Chemical Industry
Registered: 22 Sep 1962 *Employees:* 25
Tel: 020 7598 1511 *Website:* soci.org
Activities: Education, training; other charitable purposes
Address: Society of Chemical Industry, 14-15 Belgrave Square, London, SW1X 8PS
Trustees: Prof Alan Heaton, Mrs Diane Elaine Brown, Mr John Brown, Prof Clive Thompson, Dr Mark Harrison, Dr Peter Hambleton, Dr Jan Ramakers, Prof Joe Sweeney, Prof Anne Jennifer Mordue Luntz, Dr Geoffrey Fowler, Mr Thomas Moore, Dr Inna Baigozina-Goreli, Dr Alan Baylis, Dr David Witty, Dr Robin Michael Harrison
Income: £3,139,000 [2016]; £3,383,000 [2015]; £3,255,000 [2014]; £3,168,000 [2013]; £3,488,000 [2012]

Society of Christ (Great Britain)
Registered: 4 Mar 1988 *Employees:* 28
Tel: 01484 531452 *Website:* tchr.org.uk
Activities: The advancement of health or saving of lives; religious activities
Address: 52 Fixby Road, Huddersfield, W Yorks, HD2 2JQ
Trustees: Reverend Jan Wojczynski, Rev Krzysztof Olejnik, Rev Wojciech Swiatkowski, Rev Wojciech Rozdzenski
Income: £1,293,167 [2016]; £1,357,044 [2015]; £1,332,339 [2014]; £1,115,913 [2013]; £1,116,735 [2012]

The Society of Dyers and Colourists
Registered: 8 Nov 1962 Employees: 40 Volunteers: 70
Tel: 01274 761774 Website: sdc.org.uk
Activities: Education, training
Address: The Society of Dyers And Colourists, Perkin House, 82 Grattan Road, Bradford, BD1 2JB
Trustees: Mr Geoffrey Rudkin CCol FSDC, Paul Hamilton CCol ASDC, Mr Chi Man Spike Ngai CCol ASDC, Mr Trevor Lambourne, Mr Gavin Thatcher, Debra Bamford, Mr Anjani Prasad CCol FSDC, Mr Ian John Lewis, Professor Chris Carr
Income: £5,054,041 [2016]; £3,096,189 [2015]; £2,544,231 [2014]; £2,620,897 [2013]; £2,619,888 [2012]

Society of Friends of The Torah Limited
Registered: 21 Mar 2011 Employees: 6
Tel: 020 3240 0100
Activities: Education, training; prevention or relief of poverty; religious activities
Address: 97 Stamford Hill, London, N16 5DN
Trustees: Mr Isiah Traube, Rabbi Dovid Mapper, Mr Moses Chajim Elzas
Income: £17,042,906 [2016]; £14,901,035 [2015]; £12,323,039 [2014]; £10,587,340 [2013]; £11,350,024 [2012]

Society of Jesus Trust of 1929 for Roman Catholic Purposes
Registered: 5 Dec 1963 Employees: 359 Volunteers: 275
Tel: 020 7499 0285 Website: jesuit.org.uk
Activities: Education, training; prevention or relief of poverty; overseas aid, famine relief; religious activities; human rights, religious or racial harmony, equality or diversity
Address: c/o Secretary To The Trustees, TRCP, 114 Mount Street, London, W1K 3AH
Trustees: Francis Turner Sj, Paul Nicholson Sj, Nicholas Austin Sj, Adrian Porter Sj, Roger Dawson Sj, Matthew Power Sj, Stephen Power Sj, Damian Howard Sj, Dermot O'Connor Sj, Kensy Joseph Sj
Income: £66,058,000 [2017]; £24,639,000 [2016]; £24,362,000 [2015]; £30,780,000 [2014]; £25,552,000 [2013]

The Society of Local Authority Chief Executives and Senior Managers (Solace Group) Ltd
Registered: 9 Jan 2001 Employees: 29
Website: solace.org.uk
Activities: Education, training; other charitable purposes
Address: Solace in Business Ltd, off Southgate, Pontefract, W Yorks, WF8 1NT
Trustees: Averil Price, Mark Hynes, Graeme McDonald, John Comber, Jo Miller, Gavin Jones, Terry McDougall, Andrew Muter, Rob Kenyon
Income: £5,574,363 [2017]; £958,348 [2016]; £6,808 [2015]; £24,138 [2014]; £23,502 [2013]

The Society of Missionaries of Africa (also known as the White Fathers)
Registered: 17 Aug 1964 Employees: 12
Tel: 020 8799 5011 Website: missionariesofafrica.org.uk
Activities: General charitable purposes; religious activities
Address: Society of Missionaries of Africa, 64 Little Ealing Lane, London, W5 4XF
Trustees: Fr Christopher J Wallbank MAfr, Rev Terence Madden, Fr Brian Denis Starkey MAfr
Income: £1,697,619 [2016]; £1,528,646 [2015]; £2,154,790 [2014]; £2,083,733 [2013]; £1,867,776 [2012]

The Society of Operations Engineers
Registered: 27 Jul 2000 Employees: 24 Volunteers: 200
Tel: 020 7630 1111 Website: soe.org.uk
Activities: Education, training
Address: Society of Operations Engineers, 22 Greencoat Place, London, SW1P 1PR
Trustees: Mr Stephen Aldred Catte, Mr Alexander Ian Jackson, Garry Gilby, Mr Shaun Stephenson, Mr Howard Seymour, Mr Anthony Donald Jolliffe, Mr Garry Anthony King, Mr John Samuel Parry, Mr Adam Fraser-Hitchen, Mr Walter Ian Talbot Ling, Mr Christopher Grime, Mr Gerald Roderick Fleming, Mr Michael Paul Sweetmore, Mr Vincent David Sharpe, Mr Ian Kenneth Jones, Mr John Edward Eastman, Mr Alistair Robert Reid, Mr Ian Smith
Income: £2,686,675 [2016]; £2,544,279 [2015]; £2,309,895 [2014]; £2,101,532 [2013]; £2,087,236 [2012]

Society of Petroleum Engineers Europe Limited
Registered: 19 Feb 1993 Employees: 24
Tel: 020 7299 3303 Website: speeurope.org.uk
Activities: General charitable purposes; education, training; environment, conservation, heritage; economic, community development, employment
Address: Society of Petroleum Engineers, Threeways House, 40-44 Clipstone Street, London, W1W 5DW
Trustees: Mr Leon Beugelsdijk, Mr Stephen Graham, Mrs Suzanne Lubkowska, Mr Graeme Newton, Mr James Rawes
Income: £3,136,791 [2017]; £6,197,502 [2016]; £9,443,131 [2015]; £5,907,383 [2014]; £3,849,389 [2013]

The Society of St Columban for Foreign Missions
Registered: 26 Jul 1963 Employees: 17
Tel: 01564 772096 Website: columbans.co.uk
Activities: General charitable purposes; education, training; overseas aid, famine relief; religious activities
Address: St Columban's, Widney Manor Road, Knowle, Solihull, W Midlands, B93 9AB
Trustees: Reverend Denis Carter SSC, Rev Peter Hughes, Rev Thomas O'Reilly Fr, Rev Daniel Horgan
Income: £3,385,419 [2017]; £13,363,390 [2016]; £4,439,348 [2015]; £4,447,078 [2014]; £3,479,996 [2013]

The Society of St James
Registered: 27 Jan 1995 Employees: 205 Volunteers: 56
Tel: 023 8063 4596 Website: ssj.org.uk
Activities: Education, training; prevention or relief of poverty; accommodation, housing; other charitable purposes
Address: The Society of St James's, 125 Albert Road South, Southampton, SO14 3FR
Trustees: Mr Geoffrey Barwick, Ms Jill Lovelock, Mr David Malcolm Scott, Mr Stephen Butterfill, Ms Patricia June Hillary MS, Mr Geoff Ward, Mr Timothy Rogerson, Mrs Jenny Dawes, Dr Deborah Anne Craggs
Income: £8,394,728 [2017]; £7,310,943 [2016]; £8,073,282 [2015]; £7,600,570 [2014]; £6,542,142 [2013]

The Society of St Paul The Apostle
Registered: 7 Dec 1963 Employees: 23
Tel: 020 7828 5582 Website: stpauls.org.uk
Activities: Religious activities; arts, culture, heritage, science
Address: St Pauls, Morpeth Terrace, London, SW1P 1EP
Trustees: Rev Celso Godilano, Bro Jose Jereus Bangcaya, Rev Vincenzo Santarcangelo, Rev Francy George Kochupaliath
Income: £2,027,257 [2016]; £3,604,096 [2015]; £1,847,426 [2014]; £1,916,785 [2013]; £1,848,125 [2012]

The Society of St Pius X

Registered: 7 Dec 1977 *Employees:* 21 *Volunteers:* 20
Tel: 020 7412 0050 *Website:* fsspx.uk
Activities: Education, training; religious activities
Address: Hunters, 9 New Square, London, WC2A 3QN
Trustees: Mr John Crosfield Vernor-Miles, The Very Reverend Bishop Bernard Fellay, The Reverend Pablo Suarez, Mr Wilfrid Edward Vernor-Miles, Reverend Paul Morgan, The Reverend Robert Brucciani
Income: £1,173,388 [2016]; £2,425,985 [2015]; £1,732,929 [2014]; £1,160,120 [2013]; £1,791,814 [2012]

The Society of St Stephens House

Registered: 13 Feb 1963 *Employees:* 23 *Volunteers:* 28
Tel: 01865 613502 *Website:* ssho.ox.ac.uk
Activities: Education, training; religious activities; arts, culture, heritage, science
Address: St Stephens House, 16 Marston Street, Oxford, OX4 1JX
Trustees: Archdeacon of London, Mr Gregory Jones QC, The Revd Canon Dr Robin Ward, Rt Revd Jonathan Baker, Dr Lindsay Kathleen Newcombe BEng PhD Lond, Revd Paul Armstead, Tom Crowley, The Revd Prebendary David Houlding, Mr John David Sebastian Booth, Rt Revd Dr Martin Warner, Rev Timothy Pike, Rev Charles Leonard Card-Reynolds, Dr Mark Philpott
Income: £1,798,394 [2017]; £1,256,873 [2016]; £1,465,595 [2015]; £1,700,092 [2014]; £1,421,315 [2013]

The Society of The Little Flower

Registered: 3 Mar 2008 *Employees:* 5
Tel: 01403 274242 *Website:* littleflower.eu
Activities: Religious activities
Address: Society of The Little Flower, Barclays House, 51 Bishopric, Horsham, W Sussex, RH12 1QJ
Trustees: Father Robert Colaresi, Pauline Stuart, Rev Carl Markelz Ocarm, Father Kevin Alban, Fernando Millan Romeral
Income: £1,253,658 [2016]; £1,374,498 [2015]; £1,406,001 [2014]; £1,467,718 [2013]; £1,513,812 [2012]

Society of The Sacred Heart

Registered: 31 Jan 1964 *Employees:* 52
Tel: 020 8748 9353 *Website:* societysacredheart.org.uk
Activities: Education, training; prevention or relief of poverty; religious activities; other charitable purposes
Address: Society of The Sacred Heart, 3 Bute Gardens, London, W6 7DR
Trustees: Sister Carol Condon, Sister Christine Edwards, Sister Margaret Walshe, Sister Lorraine Pratt, Sister Maureen Cunnion, Sister Christine Austin, Sister Jane Maltby, Sister Sheila McNamara
Income: £2,189,778 [2017]; £2,422,882 [2016]; £2,304,599 [2015]; £2,376,642 [2014]; £2,857,972 [2013]

The Sofa Project

Registered: 8 Jun 1983 *Employees:* 38 *Volunteers:* 3
Tel: 0117 954 7808 *Website:* sofaproject.org.uk
Activities: Education, training; prevention or relief of poverty; environment, conservation, heritage; economic, community development, employment
Address: Nicola Peck, 48-54 West Street, Bristol, BS2 0BL
Trustees: Mrs Glenda Hagger, Mrs Lynn Maxwell, Mr C Neild, Miss Marianne Reed, Mrs Ruth Snary, Mr Edward Porter, Ron Stagg, Mrs Kate Clifford
Income: £1,005,550 [2017]; £1,027,351 [2016]; £1,107,241 [2015]; £1,138,164 [2014]; £802,459 [2013]

Sofronie Foundation

Registered: 30 Mar 2007 *Employees:* 1
Tel: 020 7421 3330 *Website:* sofronie.org
Activities: General charitable purposes; education, training
Address: 16 Great Queen Street, London, WC2B 5DH
Trustees: Mr Harold Goddijn, Mr Nicholas Kaufmann, Mr Ajay Soni, Ms Corinne Goddijn-Vigreux, Mr Robert Wilne, Mr Boris Walbaum
Income: £2,115,241 [2016]; £1,810,135 [2015]; £1,557,928 [2014]; £1,679,267 [2013]; £1,679,401 [2012]

Soho Theatre Company Limited

Registered: 3 Jul 1975 *Employees:* 64
Tel: 020 7287 5060 *Website:* sohotheatre.com
Activities: Education, training; arts, culture, heritage, science
Address: Soho Theatre Co Ltd, 21 Dean Street, London, W1D 3NE
Trustees: David Aukin, Neil Mendoza, Beatrice Hollond, Jeremy King, Carolyn Ward, Fawn James, Nicholas Allott, Hani Farsi, Christopher Yu, Shappi Khorsandi, Moyra Doyle, Miss Victoria Margaret Jones
Income: £5,384,421 [2017]; £5,357,531 [2016]; £5,390,952 [2015]; £5,150,502 [2014]; £3,908,581 [2013]

The Soil Association Limited

Registered: 22 Sep 1962 *Employees:* 245 *Volunteers:* 15
Tel: 0117 314 5000 *Website:* soilassociation.org
Activities: Education, training; animals; environment, conservation, heritage
Address: Soil Association, Spear House, 51 Victoria Street, Bristol, BS1 6AD
Trustees: Rosemary Anne Radcliffe, Mr Oliver Dowding, Mr John Carson, Prof Isabel Oliver, Joanne Ingleby, Mr Gabriel John Scally, Mr Graeme Richard Matravers, Ms Rachel Martino, Mr Thomas Bourne, Martin John Nye
Income: £16,824,100 [2017]; £12,576,698 [2016]; £14,624,002 [2015]; £11,349,179 [2014]; £8,922,361 [2013]

Soka Gakkai International - UK

Registered: 22 Jun 2004 *Employees:* 39 *Volunteers:* 3,500
Tel: 01628 773163 *Website:* sgi-uk.org
Activities: General charitable purposes; education, training; religious activities; arts, culture, heritage, science; environment, conservation, heritage; human rights, religious or racial harmony, equality or diversity
Address: Taplow Court, Cliveden Road, Taplow, Maidenhead, Berks, SL6 0EP
Trustees: Mr Paul Williams, Miss Fiona Jane Harrow, Ms Sue Thornton, Mrs Sachiyo Wilson, Mrs Jennie Peters-Smith, Mr Robert Anthony Samuels, Mr Kazuo Fujii, Mr Robert Philip Harrap, Ms Stephanie Ball, Mr Graham Holman
Income: £3,453,003 [2016]; £3,488,954 [2015]; £3,712,595 [2014]; £3,497,476 [2013]; £3,694,761 [2012]

Solace Women's Aid

Registered: 16 Sep 2000 *Employees:* 152 *Volunteers:* 88
Tel: 020 7619 1350 *Website:* solacewomensaid.org
Activities: Accommodation, housing
Address: Unit 5-7 Blenheim Court, 62 Brewery Road, London, N7 9NY
Trustees: Helen Hughes, Judy Kawaguchi, Alice Ashworth, Miss Kirsty Telford, Linda Kelly, Elizabeth Rawlings, Natalia Schiffrin, Jennifer Bosiacki, Teresa Hoey, Alice Dyke, Ms Heather Mah, Ms Kerri Ann Podobnik
Income: £7,791,554 [2017]; £6,954,984 [2016]; £6,776,398 [2015]; £6,536,287 [2014]; £5,094,243 [2013]

Solar Aid

Registered: 30 Aug 2006 *Employees:* 41 *Volunteers:* 4
Tel: 020 7278 0400 *Website:* solar-aid.org
Activities: Education, training; prevention or relief of poverty; environment, conservation, heritage; economic, community development, employment
Address: 49-51 East Road, London, N1 6AH
Trustees: Mr Jeremy Kendal Leggett, Mr John Faulks, Ms Mirjana Skrba
Income: £1,830,704 [2017]; £2,563,809 [2016]; £6,191,995 [2015]; £6,332,904 [2014]; £3,590,476 [2013]

Solden Hill House Limited

Registered: 30 Dec 1963 *Employees:* 37 *Volunteers:* 9
Tel: 01327 260234 *Website:* soldenhillhouse.co.uk
Activities: Disability
Address: Solden Hill House, Banbury Road, Byfield, Daventry, Northants, NN11 6UA
Trustees: Jane Ferguson, Catherine Wardlaw, Simon Bown, Mr James Batchelor, Wendy Coleman, Liz Horton, Tom Espley
Income: £1,433,696 [2017]; £1,208,927 [2016]; £1,115,874 [2015]; £1,082,706 [2014]; £1,159,271 [2013]

Soldiers' and Airmen's Scripture Readers Association

Registered: 2 Dec 1964 *Employees:* 25 *Volunteers:* 86
Tel: 01252 310033 *Website:* sasra.org.uk
Activities: Religious activities
Address: The Soldiers & Airmens Scripture Readers Association, Havelock House, Barrack Road, Aldershot, Hants, GU11 3NP
Trustees: Major Phil Shannon MBE, Mr John Charles Allen FRCS, Squadron Leader Paddy Gallaugher MBE, Col Christopher Robert Rider, Wg Cdr Mark Bunting, Major Philip Bray, Major Rob Hoey, Flt Lt J Greenald, Major Andrew McMahon, Capt John Wooldridge, Lt Col Charles MacKenzie St George Kirke, Lt Col Noel Charles Edwin Dawes, Colonel Robbie Hall QGM, Colonel John Lewis, Major William Wells, Rev Eddy Frazer, Brigadier R Thomson, Capt A McLeod, Major Michael Claydon
Income: £1,202,079 [2016]; £1,164,805 [2015]; £1,136,580 [2014]; £961,868 [2013]; £1,241,230 [2012]

The Soldiers, Sailors, Airmen and Families Association - Forces Help

Registered: 28 Apr 1965 *Employees:* 508 *Volunteers:* 6,682
Tel: 020 7463 9412 *Website:* ssafa.org.uk
Activities: The advancement of health or saving of lives; prevention or relief of poverty; accommodation, housing
Address: SSAFA, Queen Elizabeth House, 4 St Dunstan's Hill, London, EC3R 8AD
Trustees: Mr Jonathan Jelley JP, Sarah Rutherford-Jones, Mr Robert Murphy, Kirsty Bushell, Mrs Helen Victoria Kirkland, Lieutenant Colonel Christopher Arnold Downward MC, Sir Gary Coward, Mr James Carleton, Mr David Rowe, Colonel John Goodsir CBE, Mr Don McPhie, Commodore Peter John Cowling RN, Evelyn Strouts, David McCorkell
Income: £51,808,000 [2016]; £53,819,000 [2015]; £59,655,000 [2014]; £58,246,000 [2013]; £50,365,000 [2012]

Solefield School Educational Trust Limited

Registered: 16 Jan 1986 *Employees:* 36
Tel: 01732 452142 *Website:* solefieldschool.org
Activities: Education, training
Address: Solefield School, Solefields Road, Sevenoaks, Kent, TN13 1PH
Trustees: Mr Robert Clewley, Claire Major, Mr Salim Somjee, Mr Jonathan Christopher Harber, Mr Graham Donald Malcolm, Mr Ramon Walsh, Mr Mark Patrick Wrafter
Income: £2,175,369 [2017]; £2,225,886 [2016]; £1,998,921 [2015]; £1,702,242 [2014]; £1,780,099 [2013]

Solent Mind

Registered: 14 Jun 2000 *Employees:* 163 *Volunteers:* 100
Tel: 023 8202 7810 *Website:* solentmind.org.uk
Activities: Education, training; advancement of health or saving of lives; disability; prevention or relief of poverty; economic, community development, employment; human rights, religious or racial harmony, equality or diversity
Address: Solent Mind, 15-16 The Avenue, Southampton, SO17 1XF
Trustees: Ms Ros Cassy, Mr Richard Coundley, Mr Jack Stephen Wiseman, Mrs Fiona Hartfree, Mr Peter Hanlon, Mr Bryan Palmer, Ms Julie Todd
Income: £5,934,664 [2017]; £5,931,320 [2016]; £5,135,096 [2015]; £4,673,107 [2014]; £4,345,883 [2013]

Solent Students' Union

Registered: 12 Aug 2013 *Employees:* 31 *Volunteers:* 113
Tel: 023 8031 9873 *Website:* solentsu.co.uk
Activities: Education, training
Address: Solent Students' Union, East Park Terrace, Southampton, SO14 0YN
Trustees: Mr Andrew Gameson, Miss Hanna Head, Miss Naomi Fry, Mr Darren Xiberras, Mr Tom Wood, Bonnie Southcott, Mr Lewis Cleminson, Mr Sebastian Graves-Read, Miss Eleanor Mees
Income: £1,014,377 [2017]; £1,151,163 [2016]; £1,012,275 [2015]; £1,584,500 [2014]

Solicitors Benevolent Association Limited

Registered: 16 Jun 2008 *Employees:* 5 *Volunteers:* 74
Tel: 020 8675 6440 *Website:* sba.org.uk
Activities: General charitable purposes; education, training; prevention or relief of poverty
Address: Solicitors Benevolent Association, 1 Jaggard Way, London, SW12 8SG
Trustees: Mr Anthony Cumming, Mr Michael Gillman, Mr Matthew Robbins, Mrs Christl Hughes, Ms Hazel Ann Ryan, Mrs Tanya Ingrid Dunbar, Mr Mohammad Haroon Qayum, Ms Zoe Branka Holland, Mr Timothy Cuthbertson, Mr Graham Camps, Mr Matthew Gilbert Rhodes, Ms Kirsten Mary McEwen, Karen Margaret Matthews, Ms Karen Tina South, Mr Shams-Ur Rahman, Dr Adam Parker
Income: £1,869,693 [2016]; £707,205 [2015]; £1,773,803 [2014]; £2,180,518 [2013]; £1,863,448 [2012]

Solihull School

Registered: 16 Aug 2007 *Employees:* 162 *Volunteers:* 63
Tel: 0121 705 0883 *Website:* solsch.org.uk
Activities: Education, training; prevention or relief of poverty; religious activities
Address: Solihull School, 793 Warwick Road, Solihull, W Midlands, B91 3DJ
Trustees: Mr Michael Clough Morris, Mrs Anne Lavery, Mr Paul Geoffrey Newby FRICS, Mr Damian James Kelly BA, Mr John Anthony Shackleton MA, Prof Swaren Preet Singh MBBS MD MRCPsych DM, Dr Andrew John Burtenshaw MBChB MRCP, Dr Apollo Mulira MA MB FRCS, Mr Mark Hopton FCA, Rev Jane Elizabeth Ballantyne Kenchington MA BSc PGCE, Mrs Catherine Mary Gilbert BA MBA, Dr Heather Mary Gay PhD, Mr James Adie, Mrs Judith Anita Hetherington FCA
Income: £12,797,343 [2017]; £12,168,444 [2016]; £11,853,310 [2015]; £11,298,578 [2014]; £11,108,312 [2013]

Soll (Vale)

Registered: 26 Jan 2005 *Employees:* 47
Tel: 01235 861289 *Website:* soll-leisure.co.uk
Activities: Amateur sport
Address: Soll Vale, 17 Croft Drive, Milton Park, Milton, Abingdon, Oxon, OX14 4RP
Trustees: Mr Nigel Kevin Robinson, Mr Paul Andrew Turner, Mr Paul Sambrook, Mr Timothy Allan Hampson, Roger Booker
Income: £3,531,192 [2017]; £3,502,780 [2016]; £4,630,643 [2015]; £5,776,001 [2014]; £4,320,437 [2013]

Solo Housing (East Anglia)

Registered: 10 Feb 1998 *Employees:* 17
Tel: 01379 640250 *Website:* solohousing.org
Activities: Accommodation, housing
Address: 12A St Nicholas Street, Diss, Norfolk, IP22 4LB
Trustees: Mr Malcolm Black, Gillian Brown, Mr David Sice, Mr John Dell, David John Clarke, Mr Keir Robert Hounsome, Ms Sally Hanlin, Mr Don Crossman
Income: £1,156,392 [2017]; £1,138,298 [2016]; £1,124,418 [2015]; £1,076,686 [2014]; £909,288 [2013]

Solo Life Opportunities

Registered: 25 Feb 2004 *Employees:* 70 *Volunteers:* 250
Tel: 0121 779 3865 *Website:* solihullsolo.org
Activities: Disability; arts, culture, heritage, science; amateur sport
Address: 38 Walnut Close, Chelmsley Wood, Birmingham, B37 7PU
Trustees: Mrs Lindsey Crompton, Mrs Susan Stocks, Mr Paul Beech, Henry Griffiths, Mrs Jan Prior, Mr Stephen Rowell, Mr Andrew Gilyead, Mr Jonathan Prior
Income: £1,229,155 [2017]; £1,016,487 [2016]; £1,078,621 [2015]; £930,991 [2014]; £701,878 [2013]

Solving Kids' Cancer Europe

Registered: 20 Apr 2010 *Employees:* 7 *Volunteers:* 12
Tel: 020 7284 0800 *Website:* solvingkidscancer.org.uk
Activities: Education, training; advancement of health or saving of lives
Address: CAN Mezzanine, 49-51 East Road, London, N1 6AH
Trustees: Mr Joseph Tabone, Mr Nick Bird, Bron Ellis, Mr Matthew Giles White, Mr David Francois Coulon
Income: £1,102,188 [2017]; £1,782,731 [2016]; £2,476,166 [2015]; £1,893,600 [2014]; £2,385,635 [2013]

Somerhill Charitable Trust Limited

Registered: 12 Mar 1991 *Employees:* 125 *Volunteers:* 1
Tel: 01732 352124 *Website:* somerhill.org
Activities: Education, training
Address: The Schools at Somerhill, Somerhill, Tonbridge, Kent, TN11 0NJ
Trustees: Mr Charles John Warner, Mr Jeremy Coleridge Hills, Mr Joe Davies, Mr Peter Charles Braggins, Miss Helen Patricia Tebay, Mrs Katharine Claire Lewis, Mr David Andrew Hester Wells, Mr Philip Thomas, Mr David Robert Walsh, Mr Mark Anthony Jiskoot, Mr Michael Anthony Norrie, Mrs Diane Margaret Huntingford, Mr Robert Edward Verrell, Mr Peter Robert Brooks
Income: £8,126,523 [2017]; £7,595,156 [2016]; £7,075,701 [2015]; £6,930,029 [2014]; £6,613,339 [2013]

Somerset Activity and Sports Partnership

Registered: 20 Apr 2007 *Employees:* 62 *Volunteers:* 120
Tel: 01823 653990 *Website:* sasp.co.uk
Activities: Education, training; disability; amateur sport; economic, community development, employment
Address: Somerset Activity Sports Partnership Offices, First Floor, Castle Business Centre, Castle Road, Wellington, Somerset, TA21 9JQ
Trustees: Mr Andrew Barton Maxwell Lees, Mr Graham Jones, Emma Wilkes, Mr Brendon Cleere, Mr Kevin Freedman, Andrew Cockcroft, Alice Driscoll
Income: £1,555,897 [2017]; £1,026,820 [2016]; £948,431 [2015]; £1,270,824 [2014]; £1,690,749 [2013]

Somerset House Trust

Registered: 29 Jul 1997 *Employees:* 62 *Volunteers:* 150
Tel: 020 7845 4670 *Website:* somersethouse.org.uk
Activities: Education, training; arts, culture, heritage, science; environment, conservation, heritage
Address: Somerset House Trust, Somerset House, Strand, London, WC2R 1LA
Trustees: Mr Marcus John Charles Lyon, Sir Malcolm John Grant, Mrs Melanie Hall QC, Ms Judith Gibbons, Mr Brian Peter George Eno, Mr Paul Jonathan Goswell, Mr James Nicholas Lambert, Mr Jonathan Higgins FRSA, Ms Caroline Jayne Michel, Mr Willliam Matthew Sieghart, Mr Julien Sevaux, Miss Carol Ann Fairweather
Income: £14,837,792 [2017]; £14,703,315 [2016]; £12,910,886 [2015]; £10,863,771 [2014]; £18,334,795 [2013]

Somerset Redstone Trust

Registered: 11 Dec 2000 *Employees:* 382
Tel: 01823 270694 *Website:* srtrust.co.uk
Activities: The advancement of health or saving of lives; disability; accommodation, housing
Address: Gatchell House, Gatchell Oaks, Taunton, Somerset, TA3 7EG
Trustees: Vanda Crow, Mr Tony Cooper BEM, Mrs Jill Veronica Barter, Mr Adam Rawicz-Szczerbo, Mrs Patricia Ann Walker, Mr Jim Baker, Ms Lesley Elizabeth Darts, Mr John Whittaker
Income: £8,279,350 [2017]; £10,632,957 [2016]; £11,181,331 [2015]; £8,480,615 [2014]; £6,026,834 [2013]

Somerset Wildlife Trust

Registered: 3 Dec 1964 *Employees:* 59 *Volunteers:* 411
Tel: 01823 652400 *Website:* somersetwildlife.org
Activities: Environment, conservation, heritage
Address: Somerset Wildlife Trust, 34 Wellington Road, Taunton, Somerset, TA1 5AW
Trustees: Stephen Richard Newman, Professor Valerie Brown, Mrs Helen Lawy, Mr Melville Trimble, Mr Philip Holms, Mr Matthew Trimmer, Mr Simon Hicks, Ms Patricia Stainton, Mr John Scotford, Miss Sarah Jane Nason, Mr Matthew James Bell, Mr Richard Charles Atkin
Income: £2,841,308 [2017]; £2,762,888 [2016]; £2,897,207 [2015]; £2,003,845 [2014]; £2,216,633 [2013]

The Sons of Divine Providence

Registered: 28 Sep 2001 *Employees:* 105 *Volunteers:* 10
Tel: 020 8977 5130 *Website:* orionecare.org
Activities: General charitable purposes; education, training; disability; overseas aid, famine relief; accommodation, housing; religious activities
Address: 13 Lower Teddington Road, Hampton Wick, Kingston upon Thames, Surrey, KT1 4EU
Trustees: Rev John Carmel Perrotta, Rev Philip Kehoe, Mrs Bernadette Griffin, Rev Stephen Peter Beale, Mrs Ursula Harrison, Rev Jose Luis Simionato
Income: £3,444,898 [2017]; £3,496,319 [2016]; £3,423,590 [2015]; £3,378,549 [2014]; £3,229,551 [2013]

The Sons of The Sacred Heart of Jesus

Registered: 24 Jun 1963 *Employees:* 4
Tel: 01344 621267 *Website:* comboni.org.uk
Activities: General charitable purposes; religious activities
Address: Verona Fathers, London Road, Sunningdale, Ascot, Berks, SL5 0JY
Trustees: Rev John Downey, Rev John Clark, Rev John Troy, Rev Robert Hicks, Rev Martin Devenish, Verona Fathers Ltd
Income: £1,222,908 [2016]; £1,054,363 [2015]; £944,026 [2014]; £877,740 [2013]; £1,125,564 [2012]

Soul Survivor

Registered: 15 May 2000 *Employees:* 18 *Volunteers:* 2,000
Tel: 0303 333 1333 *Website:* soulsurvivor.com
Activities: Religious activities
Address: Soul Survivor, Unit 16, Paramount Industrial Estate, Sandown Road, Watford, Herts, WD24 7XA
Trustees: Mr David Westlake, Mr Christopher Lane, Mr Keith Johnson, Mrs Alison Martin, Mrs Jessica Jones, Rt Rev Graham A Cray, Rev Andrew Croft
Income: £3,020,669 [2016]; £3,539,359 [2015]; £3,454,912 [2014]; £3,016,155 [2013]; £3,226,168 [2012]

South Bucks Hospice

Registered: 30 Mar 2009 *Employees:* 50 *Volunteers:* 140
Tel: 01494 552750 *Website:* sbh.org.uk
Activities: The advancement of health or saving of lives
Address: Butterfly House, Kingswood Park, High Wycombe, Bucks, HP13 6GR
Trustees: Mr Alan Harry Chandler, Mr Trevor Paul Ervin Davey, Dr James Andrew Walter, Mr David Balls, Mrs Carol Horner, Dr Michael Bowker, Mr Barry Pickersgill, Mr Snehal Rabheru, Mr Philip James Watkins, Dr Anjani Prasad
Income: £1,902,713 [2017]; £1,989,942 [2016]; £2,161,015 [2015]; £3,530,470 [2014]; £1,399,403 [2013]

South Devon Railway Trust

Registered: 8 Nov 1988 *Employees:* 45 *Volunteers:* 520
Website: southdevonrailway.co.uk
Activities: Education, training; arts, culture, heritage, science; environment, conservation, heritage
Address: South Devon Railway Trust, The Station, Dart Bridge Road, Buckfastleigh, Devon, TQ11 0DZ
Trustees: Allan Cash, Peter Treglown, Phil Parratt, David Lemar, Mrs Christine Thomas, Denver Woodward BEng, John Keohane MVO BEM, Jon Morton, Richard Elliott, Mr Geoffrey Addy
Income: £1,564,258 [2016]; £2,565,263 [2015]; £2,310,926 [2014]; £2,343,260 [2013]; £2,147,599 [2012]

South Downs Leisure

Registered: 14 Sep 2015 *Employees:* 403 *Volunteers:* 68
Tel: 01903 905050 *Website:* southdownsleisure.co.uk
Activities: Recreation
Address: Field Place, The Boulevard, Worthing, W Sussex, BN13 1NP
Trustees: Ms Joanne Rose Marie Lawrence-Hall, Mr David Rawcliffe Fleming, Mr James Edward Garner, Prince Kris von Habsburg, Mrs Sharon Smith, Ms Diane Guest, Mrs Gillian Frances Jackson, Mr Jeremy Richard Le Sueur, Mrs Zoe Kathryn Smith, Mr Lionel Harman
Income: £6,626,144 [2017]; £5,878,140 [2016]

South England Conference of Seventh Day Adventists

Registered: 4 Apr 1995 *Employees:* 197 *Volunteers:* 6,000
Tel: 01923 232728 *Website:* sec.adventist.org.uk
Activities: General charitable purposes; education, training; advancement of health or saving of lives; disability; prevention or relief of poverty; religious activities
Address: South England Conference of Seventh Day Adventists, 25 St Johns Road, Watford, Herts, WD17 1PZ
Trustees: Pastor Emmanuel Osei, Mr Dave St Marie, Miss Pam Millington, Pastor Douglas William McCormac, Mr Samuel Asamoah, Mr Dominic Gyasi, Pastor Clifford Herman, Dr Christopher Levy, Mr Stephen Weekes, Mr Derek Morrison, Mr Fred Bacon Shone, Pastor Wayne Erasmus, Mr Steve Roberts, Mrs Judith Redman, Mr Victor Barendse, Mrs Gloria Christopher, Mrs Esther Aryee, Pastor Anthony Fuller, Miss Careen Hanson, Pastor Ebenezer Jones-Lartey, Mrs Abigail Wright, Pastor James Shepley, Mrs Eulalee Marshall-Wiggan, Pastor Robin Johannes Lewis, Mr Simeon Esson
Income: £20,876,080 [2016]; £21,147,161 [2015]; £21,198,972 [2014]; £22,137,931 [2013]; £22,023,836 [2012]

South Essex Gymnastics Club Limited

Registered: 18 May 2009 *Employees:* 82 *Volunteers:* 25
Tel: 01268 722479 *Website:* southessexgym.co.uk
Activities: Education, training; amateur sport
Address: 59 Kent View Road, Basildon, Essex, SS16 4JX
Trustees: Mr Stephen Smith, Mrs Julie Ann Hickton, Mr Clive Fabb, Sue Hibbitt, Roy Short, Mr Joseph Samuel Ben-Aderet
Income: £1,257,785 [2017]; £1,162,540 [2016]; £1,115,092 [2015]; £1,047,372 [2014]; £940,676 [2013]

South Essex Rape and Incest Crisis Centre

Registered: 14 Sep 1985 *Employees:* 17 *Volunteers:* 8
Tel: 01375 381322 *Website:* sericc.org.uk
Activities: Education, training; advancement of health or saving of lives
Address: SERICC, The Church Hall, West Street, Grays, Essex, RM17 6LL
Trustees: Ms Clare Quest, Ms Alison Curnick, Ms Michelene Heine, Ms Margaret Abboyi, Ms Glenda Harrington
Income: £1,508,169 [2017]; £816,904 [2016]; £885,618 [2015]; £713,353 [2014]; £761,698 [2013]

South Hampstead Charitable Trust

Registered: 24 Jan 1996
Tel: 020 7832 0444
Activities: Education, training; religious activities
Address: Wilson Wright LLP, Thavies Inn House, 3-4 Holborn Circus, London, EC1N 2HA
Trustees: Mr John Bryan Austin, Mr Stephen Pack, Mr Danny Kay, Richard Loftus, Mr Leon Blitz
Income: £2,474,843 [2016]; £813,615 [2015]; £111,876 [2014]; £317,755 [2013]

South Hill Park Trust Limited

Registered: 10 May 1973 *Employees:* 63 *Volunteers:* 70
Tel: 01344 484858 *Website:* southhillpark.org.uk
Activities: Education, training; arts, culture, heritage, science
Address: South Hill Park Mansion, Ringmead, Bracknell, Berks, RG12 7PA
Trustees: Mr Michael O'Donovan, Mr David Morton, Mr Tony Virgo, Ms Deana Hirst, Mr Bruce McKenzie-Boyle, Lisa Renals, Mrs Jessica Jhundoo-Evans, Ms Jane Li
Income: £2,091,920 [2017]; £1,983,815 [2016]; £2,293,360 [2015]; £1,888,930 [2014]; £1,893,584 [2013]

South Lee School Limited

Registered: 5 Sep 1961 *Employees:* 43
Tel: 01284 754654 *Website:* southlee.co.uk
Activities: Education, training
Address: Rose Cottage, Euston Road, Barnham, Thetford, Norfolk, IP24 2NJ
Trustees: Mr Stephen Robert Honeywood, Mrs Legge, Mr Robert George Swiney, Jenny Scarff, Ken Watson, Mr Neil John Grigg, Mrs Holly Joanna Buckingham, Mr David Graham Ashton
Income: £1,861,261 [2016]; £2,096,495 [2015]; £2,015,902 [2014]; £2,061,067 [2013]; £2,082,400 [2012]

South Liverpool Citizens Advice Bureau

Registered: 12 Sep 2001 *Employees:* 25 *Volunteers:* 71
Tel: 0151 494 3733 *Website:* southliverpoolcab.org.uk
Activities: The prevention or relief of poverty
Address: Citizens Advice Bureau, Community House, 2 Speke Road, Garston, Liverpool, L19 2PA
Trustees: Mrs Gwenllian White, Mr Enes Senussi, Mr Stephen Rochford
Income: £1,139,006 [2017]; £896,922 [2016]; £920,552 [2015]; £561,719 [2014]; £441,393 [2013]

South London Fine Art Gallery and Library

Registered: 9 May 1966 *Employees:* 54
Tel: 020 7703 6120 *Website:* southlondongallery.org
Activities: General charitable purposes; education, training; arts, culture, heritage, science
Address: South London Gallery, 65-67 Peckham Road, London, SE5 8UH
Trustees: The Slg Trustee Limited
Income: £3,396,641 [2017]; £2,106,824 [2016]; £1,344,106 [2015]; £1,605,872 [2014]; £1,793,285 [2013]

The South Northamptonshire Leisure Trust

Registered: 18 Dec 2006
Tel: 01327 354800
Activities: General charitable purposes; amateur sport
Address: Office 6, Town Hall, 86 Watling Street East, Towcester, Northants, NN12 6BS
Trustees: Mr Brian Taylor, Mr Peter Ian Dean, Mr Andrew Wilby, Mr Roger Clarke, Mr Roy Tabb, Miss Elizabeth Soames, Mrs Linda Yuill, Mrs Nicola Flynn
Income: £1,111,752 [2017]; £2,487,555 [2016]; £2,312,696 [2015]; £2,234,544 [2014]; £2,195,284 [2013]

South Suffolk Leisure

Registered: 3 Mar 2006 *Employees:* 143 *Volunteers:* 72
Tel: 01473 823470 *Website:* ssleisure.co.uk
Activities: Amateur sport
Address: South Suffolk Leisure, Hadleigh Pool & Leisure, Stonehouse Road, Hadleigh, Ipswich, Suffolk, IP7 5BH
Trustees: Mr John Turnbull, Gerald White, Mrs Marie Catherine Mills, Mr Tim Mutum, Mrs Christina Jayne Campbell, Mrs Susan Maria Ayres, Brian Lazenby, Mrs Janetta Byrne, Mrs Judith Rosemary Blatch, Mrs Jessica Janas, Mrs Lisa Jane Dagnall
Income: £2,611,223 [2017]; £2,357,951 [2016]; £2,171,273 [2015]; £2,044,663 [2014]; £1,857,550 [2013]

South Tees Hospitals Charity and Associated Funds

Registered: 11 Jun 1996 *Employees:* 6 *Volunteers:* 10
Tel: 01642 854154 *Website:* southtees.nhs.uk
Activities: General charitable purposes; education, training; advancement of health or saving of lives; other charitable purposes
Address: James Cook University Hospital, Marton Road, Middlesbrough, Cleveland, TS4 3BW
Trustees: Mr Adrian Clements, Mrs Maxime Hewitt-Smith, Ms Ruth James, Mrs Gillian Hunt, Mr David John Chadwick, Mr Richard James Carter-Ferris, Mrs Maureen Rutter, Mrs Amanda Hullick, Mr David Heslop, Mrs Siobhan McArdle, Mr Satyajit Nag, Jake Tompkins
Income: £2,692,000 [2017]; £2,818,000 [2016]; £1,705,000 [2015]; £2,444,000 [2014]; £1,907,000 [2013]

South Tynedale Railway Preservation Society

Registered: 10 Feb 1986 *Employees:* 8 *Volunteers:* 70
Tel: 01744 752397 *Website:* south-tynedale-railway.org.uk
Activities: Education, training; environment, conservation, heritage; economic, community development, employment
Address: 7 Windle Street, St Helens, Merseyside, WA10 2BZ
Trustees: Brian Craven, Jim Harper, Mr John Roger Moore, Mr Philip Aveyard, Mr Kevin Bernard Simon Malone, Richard Graham, Mr Alan Richard Farrar, Ian Hughes, Mrs Kathy Aveyard
Income: £2,482,363 [2017]; £1,484,868 [2016]; £1,469,168 [2015]; £437,040 [2014]; £278,053 [2013]

South Warwickshire NHS Foundation Trust Charitable Fund
Registered: 27 Jun 1996 *Volunteers:* 60
Tel: 01926 495321 *Website:* swft.nhs.uk
Activities: General charitable purposes; education, training; advancement of health or saving of lives
Address: Warwick Hospital, Lakin Road, Warwick, CV34 5BW
Trustees: South Warwickshire NHS Foundation Trust
Income: £1,040,000 [2017]; £725,000 [2016]; £797,000 [2015]; £328,000 [2014]; £405,000 [2013]

South West Environmental Parks Limited
Registered: 3 Apr 1964 *Employees:* 359 *Volunteers:* 225
Tel: 01803 697500 *Website:* paigntonzoo.org.uk
Activities: Education, training; animals; environment, conservation, heritage; recreation
Address: Paignton Zoo, Totnes Road, Paignton, Devon, TQ4 7EU
Trustees: Mr Andrew Charles John Cooper BSc, Mrs Sylvia Jo-Ann Greinig, Mr Richard William John Ford, Mrs Sarah Barr, Dr Judy Ravenscroft, Mr Richard Alexander Rowe, Dr Paul Robert Francis Chanin MA PhD, Mr Stephen Kings, Mrs Rachael Hill BA, Peter Stevens, Mrs Beth Kathleen McLaughlin, Mr Mark Salmon
Income: £12,750,554 [2017]; £12,692,405 [2016]; £12,123,691 [2015]; £11,491,262 [2014]; £11,607,417 [2013]

South West Grid for Learning Trust
Registered: 30 Jul 2007 *Employees:* 29
Website: swgfl.org.uk
Activities: Education, training
Address: SWGFL Trust, Belvedere House, Woodwater Park, Pynes Hill, Exeter, EX2 5WS
Trustees: Sheila Smith, Mr Simon Wainwright, Mr Paul Fletcher, Mr Christopher McDonald, Mr Neil Goddard, Mr Andrew Coghlan, Mr Jonathan Bishop, Mr Robert Bond, Mr Peter David Nathan, Mr Steven Paul Taylor
Income: £6,889,695 [2017]; £7,512,631 [2016]; £9,912,196 [2015]; £11,676,983 [2014]; £15,109,019 [2013]

The South West Heritage Trust
Registered: 6 Oct 2014 *Employees:* 78 *Volunteers:* 150
Tel: 01823 278805 *Website:* swheritage.org.uk
Activities: Education, training; arts, culture, heritage, science; environment, conservation, heritage
Address: Somerset Heritage Centre, Brunel Way, Norton Fitzwarren, Taunton, Somerset, TA2 6SF
Trustees: Lt Col Michael John Richard Motum, Prof Henry Richards French, Mr Peter John Gunner, Cllr Roger Frederick Croad, Simon Hugh D'Aquilar, Anthony Miles Dartnell Smallwood, Ms Sandra Vivien Maberley, Cllr Anna Groskop, Mr David Hugh Gwyther, Mr Terence Makewell, Peter Martyn Beacham, Ms Nicola Mary Nuttall
Income: £3,900,716 [2016]; £3,893,886 [2015]

South West Lakes Trust
Registered: 22 Mar 2000 *Employees:* 115 *Volunteers:* 264
Tel: 01566 771930 *Website:* swlakestrust.org.uk
Activities: Education, training; arts, culture, heritage, science; amateur sport; environment, conservation, heritage
Address: Lidn Park, Quarry Crescent, Pennygillam Industrial Estate, Launceston, Cornwall, PL15 7PF
Trustees: Mr Roger Preston, Mrs Monica Susan Read, Ms Dinah Nichols, Mr Ed Mitchell, Mr David Robertson, Mr John Lee, Mr Malcolm Bell
Income: £3,582,649 [2017]; £3,858,767 [2016]; £3,727,827 [2015]; £3,543,715 [2014]; £3,414,367 [2013]

South West London Law Centres
Registered: 2 Mar 2004 *Employees:* 30 *Volunteers:* 500
Tel: 020 8772 7051 *Website:* swllc.org
Activities: Education, training; prevention or relief of poverty
Address: 5th Floor, South West London Law Centres, Davis House, Robert Street, Croydon, Surrey, CR0 1QQ
Trustees: Mr Derek Sutton, Mr Peter Greig, Ms Carol Mary O'Donnell, Mrs Florence Ann Frankland Brocklesby, Ms Marion Frances Edge, Mr James Joseph Banks, Mr Davendra Singh, Mr John William Linwood, Miss Sarah Ann Towler, Mrs Clara Clint
Income: £1,629,450 [2017]; £1,204,740 [2016]; £1,119,879 [2015]; £1,242,014 [2014]; £1,308,501 [2013]

South Yorkshire Community Foundation Limited
Registered: 18 Mar 2011 *Employees:* 8 *Volunteers:* 62
Tel: 0114 242 4857 *Website:* sycf.org.uk
Activities: General charitable purposes; education, training; advancement of health or saving of lives; disability; prevention or relief of poverty; accommodation, housing; arts, culture, heritage, science; amateur sport; environment, conservation, heritage; economic, community development, employment; human rights, religious or racial harmony, equality or diversity; recreation; other charitable purposes
Address: South Yorkshire Community Foundation, Unit 9-12 Jessops Riverside, 800 Brightside Lane, Sheffield, S9 2RX
Trustees: Mr John Raymond Holt, Mr Alex Pettifer MBE, Mr Zaidah Ahmed MBE, Dr Julie MacDonald, Mr Charles William Hugh Warrack, The Earl of Scarbrough Richard Scarbrough, Mr Paul Benington, Mr Craig McKay, Mr Yiannis Koursis, Mr Melvyn Lunn, Mr James Henry Newman, Mr Nigel Brewster, Mr Martin Ross, Michele Wightman, Mr Roderick Plews, Ms Shahida Siddique, Mr Nicholas Anthony Kitchen, Mr John Pickering
Income: £1,125,531 [2016]; £1,531,101 [2015]; £1,159,902 [2014]; £888,449 [2013]; £1,019,682 [2012]

The South of England Agricultural Society
Registered: 26 Feb 1965 *Employees:* 15 *Volunteers:* 300
Tel: 01444 892700 *Website:* seas.org.uk
Activities: Education, training
Address: South of England Agricultural Sociey, The Showground, Selsfield Road, Ardingly, Haywards Heath, W Sussex, RH17 6TL
Trustees: Dr Susan Linda Greener, Mrs Eileen Carole Hayward, Mrs Mandy May Thomas-Atkin, Mr Thomas Henry Gribble, Mr Douglas Piotr Jackson, Mr Iain Craig Nicol, Mr Michael Martin, Mr Charles Peter Burgoyne, Mrs Jacquelyn Marion Appleton, Mr Roger Philip Hentsch, Mr Jeremy Stephen Gosney, Mr Duncan Andrew Rawson
Income: £2,278,288 [2017]; £2,116,915 [2016]; £2,086,235 [2015]; £1,904,371 [2014]; £2,010,018 [2013]

South of England Foundation
Registered: 25 Feb 2003 *Employees:* 193 *Volunteers:* 65
Website: cact.org.uk
Activities: Education, training; advancement of health or saving of lives; disability; prevention or relief of poverty; arts, culture, heritage, science; amateur sport; economic, community development, employment; human rights, religious or racial harmony, equality or diversity; other charitable purposes
Address: Charlton Athletic Training Ground, Sparrows Lane, New Eltham, London, SE9 2RJ
Trustees: Mr Paul Marcellous Elliott MBE, Mr Peter Cousins, Marilyn Toft, Mr Luke Christopher Ashworth, Roger Duncan Godsiff, Mr David White, Mr Paul Richard Statham, Mr Ken Francis Palmer
Income: £6,956,000 [2017]; £5,513,000 [2016]; £5,643,000 [2015]; £4,946,489 [2014]; £4,969,583 [2013]

Southampton Engineering Training Association Ltd
Registered: 16 Jun 1970 *Employees:* 34
Tel: 01489 584259 *Website:* seta-training.co.uk
Activities: Education, training; economic, community development, employment
Address: 5 Regents Gate, Sarisbury Green, Southampton, SO31 7LB
Trustees: Mr Andrew John Thornton, Mr Christopher John Savage, Mr Tony White, Mr Dean Hyde, Mr Glyn Edward Mason, Tim Millard, Jason Bonnett
Income: £2,049,903 [2017]; £1,928,314 [2016]; £2,018,486 [2015]; £2,101,743 [2014]; £1,964,485 [2013]

Southampton Hospital Charity
Registered: 19 Dec 1995 *Employees:* 12 *Volunteers:* 500
Tel: 023 8120 8881 *Website:* southamptonhospitalcharity.org
Activities: Education, training; advancement of health or saving of lives; disability
Address: Charity Fund Office, Mailpoint 135, Southampton General Hospital, Tremona Road, Southampton, SO16 6YD
Trustees: University Hospital Southampton NHS Foundation Trust
Income: £3,387,000 [2017]; £2,736,000 [2016]; £2,604,000 [2015]; £2,351,000 [2014]; £2,364,000 [2013]

The Southampton Nuffield Theatre Trust Limited
Registered: 27 Jul 1983 *Employees:* 56 *Volunteers:* 80
Website: nstheatres.co.uk
Activities: Education, training; arts, culture, heritage, science
Address: NST City, 142-144 Above Bar Street, Southampton, SO14 7DU
Trustees: Ms Vidya Thirunarayan, Mr Matthew Taylor, Ms Helen Mary Keall, Mr Jeremy Simon Meadow, Councillor Derek John Burke, Mr David Furnell, The Hon Peter Benson LVO MA FCA, Mr Edward James Rochead, Mr Adrian Antony Jackson, Professor Rosalind Cherry King, Mr Jonathan Mark Ward, Mr Donald Albert John
Income: £3,686,620 [2017]; £2,810,219 [2016]; £2,703,436 [2015]; £1,885,995 [2014]; £1,788,289 [2013]

Southampton Row Trust Limited
Registered: 20 Jan 2000
Tel: 0300 012 3088 *Website:* cafonline.org
Activities: General charitable purposes
Address: Charities Aid Foundation, 25 Kings Hill Avenue, Kings Hill, West Malling, Kent, ME19 4TA
Trustees: Dr John Menzies Low, Mr Theodore Richard Hart, Mr Mike Dixon, Mr David Charles Stead
Income: £64,715,000 [2017]; £39,619,000 [2016]; £45,746,000 [2015]; £35,709,000 [2014]; £27,302,000 [2013]

Southbank Centre
Registered: 6 May 1988 *Employees:* 411
Website: southbankcentre.co.uk
Activities: Education, training; arts, culture, heritage, science
Address: 7 Kelvin Court, 24-26 Marlborough Road, Richmond, Surrey, TW10 6JS
Trustees: Southbank Centre Limited
Income: £68,081,000 [2017]; £46,699,000 [2016]; £46,842,000 [2015]; £48,381,000 [2014]; £50,118,000 [2013]

Southbank Sinfonia Foundation
Registered: 7 Oct 2016
Tel: 020 7921 0370 *Website:* southbanksinfonia.co.uk
Activities: Education, training; disability; arts, culture, heritage, science
Address: St Johns Church, Waterloo Road, London, SE1 8TY
Trustees: Mr John Michael Berman, Mr Duncan Sutherland, Mr Julius Peregrine Harold Shepherd Wolff-Ingham, Mrs Mary Cicely Florence Monfries
Income: £2,389,981 [2017]

Southbank Sinfonia
Registered: 14 Jun 2002 *Employees:* 13 *Volunteers:* 1
Tel: 020 7921 0370 *Website:* southbanksinfonia.co.uk
Activities: Education, training; arts, culture, heritage, science
Address: St Johns Waterloo, Waterloo Road, London, SE1 8TY
Trustees: Michael Berman, Baroness McIntosh of Hudnall, Mr Sean Finnan, Ms Katharine Verney, Mr Duncan Sutherland, Mr Simon Timothy Over, Lord David Geoffrey Nigel Filkin CBE, Ms Sarah Derbyshire, Mark Payne, Ms Mindy Kilby
Income: £1,376,102 [2016]; £1,192,647 [2015]; £1,115,270 [2014]; £982,882 [2013]; £1,120,618 [2012]

The Southend on Sea Darby and Joan Organisation Limited
Registered: 20 Sep 2002 *Employees:* 65
Tel: 07951 127270 *Website:* darbyandjoan.org
Activities: The advancement of health or saving of lives; disability; accommodation, housing
Address: 59 Imperial Avenue, Westcliff on Sea, Essex, SS0 8NQ
Trustees: Mrs Anne Elizabeth Andrews, Graham Jones, Tony Lemasurier, Mr Peter Rothwell, Mr John William Anderson, Mrs Joyce Lambert, Mr Oliver Rowe
Income: £1,327,070 [2017]; £1,181,500 [2016]; £1,346,421 [2015]; £1,807,607 [2014]; £2,243,175 [2013]

Southend-on-Sea Young Mens Christian Association
Registered: 24 Mar 2004 *Employees:* 52 *Volunteers:* 60
Tel: 01702 301301 *Website:* southendymca.org.uk
Activities: General charitable purposes; education, training; prevention or relief of poverty; accommodation, housing; religious activities; amateur sport; economic, community development, employment
Address: Newlands, 85 Ambleside Drive, Southend on Sea, Essex, SS1 2FY
Trustees: Mr Ronald Wright, Mr James Brooks, Rev Simon Roscoe, Mrs Kerry Bland, Mr Simon Ling-Locke, Ms Susan Carr, Mr Stephen Phillip Onslow
Income: £1,809,181 [2016]; £4,122,304 [2015]; £2,703,075 [2014]; £1,641,283 [2013]; £1,377,248 [2012]

The Southern Counties Baptist Association
Registered: 13 Mar 2002 *Employees:* 6
Tel: 01235 517673 *Website:* scba.org.uk
Activities: Religious activities
Address: Baptist House Ltd, 129 Broadway, Didcot, Oxon, OX11 8XD
Trustees: Rev Nigel Douglas Cox, Mrs Melvina Janet Mildred Fawcett, Mrs Ann Andrews, Dr Michael John Mortimer, Rev Simon Andrew Ford, Rev Anthony Clarke, Rev Colin Michael Norris, Mrs Anne Catherine Lane BEd
Income: £1,260,818 [2016]; £361,884 [2015]; £403,771 [2014]; £160,450 [2013]; £226,888 [2012]

Southern Domestic Abuse Service
Registered: 3 Apr 2012 *Employees:* 49 *Volunteers:* 5
Tel: 023 9248 0246 *Website:* southerndas.org
Activities: General charitable purposes; education, training; accommodation, housing; other charitable purposes
Address: P O Box 53, Havant, Hants, PO9 1UA
Trustees: Mrs Gill Butler, Mrs Wendy Osgood, Ms Claire Godwin, Miss Margaret Ann Poil, Ms Donna Cullimore, Mrs Julia Munday, Mrs Samantha Lee, Ms Julia Standen, Ms Rachel Williams
Income: £1,426,679 [2017]; £1,353,010 [2016]; £747,602 [2015]; £617,655 [2014]; £784,599 [2013]

Southern Universities Management Services
Registered: 18 Nov 1994 *Employees:* 22
Tel: 0118 935 7056 *Website:* sums.org.uk
Activities: Education, training
Address: Sums, Science & Technology Centre, Earley Gate, Whiteknights Road, Reading, Berks, RG6 6BZ
Trustees: Mr Dennis Hopper, Rex Knight, Mrs Susan Carol Grant, William Liew, Mrs Jeannette Sandra Strachan, Mr Brendan Casey
Income: £1,926,908 [2017]; £2,235,645 [2016]; £1,816,600 [2015]; £1,723,469 [2014]; £1,573,164 [2013]

Southmead Development Trust
Registered: 21 Mar 1997 *Employees:* 38 *Volunteers:* 85
Tel: 0117 950 3335 *Website:* southmead.org
Activities: General charitable purposes; education, training; disability; prevention or relief of poverty; arts, culture, heritage, science; amateur sport; economic, community development, employment
Address: Southmead Development Trust, Greenway Centre, Doncaster Road, Bristol, BS10 5PY
Trustees: Mr Geoffrey Williams, Mr Kevin Sweeney, Mrs Trenna Joanne Blundell, Mr Lee Mark Gardiner, Sheralyn Fowler, Mrs Jillian Hoggans, Mrs Helen Godwin Teige, Mrs Holly Jean Maurice, Mr Peter Mansfield, Mrs Marion Elaine Baynes, Mr Billy Joe Cotterell, Mrs Brenda Margaret Massey, Mr John Woolcock, Mr Tim Temple, Mr David Vivian Roderick
Income: £1,074,822 [2017]; £808,568 [2016]; £757,473 [2015]; £564,023 [2014]; £503,636 [2013]

Southport Flower Show
Registered: 30 Oct 1990 *Employees:* 13 *Volunteers:* 145
Tel: 01704 547147 *Website:* southportflowershow.co.uk
Activities: Education, training; arts, culture, heritage, science; amateur sport; environment, conservation, heritage
Address: Southport Flower Show, Rotten Row, Southport, Merseyside, PR8 2BZ
Trustees: Mr Robert Michael Ratcliffe, Mrs Margaret Tarpey, Mr Andrew Edwards, Mr Richard James Peter McKeever, Mr Robert Anderson, Mrs Alison Pope, Mr Tim Fleming, Alan Adams
Income: £1,184,458 [2016]; £1,226,584 [2015]; £1,136,779 [2014]; £1,087,241 [2013]; £1,032,005 [2012]

Southside Partnership
Registered: 30 Mar 1992 *Employees:* 514 *Volunteers:* 50
Tel: 020 8772 6222 *Website:* certitude.org.uk
Activities: The advancement of health or saving of lives; disability; accommodation, housing
Address: Southside Partnership, 31-33 Lumiere Court, 209 Balham High Road, London, SW17 7BQ
Trustees: Mrs Sally Ann Glen, Ms Catherine James, Mrs Laura Sullivan, Mr George Venus, Ms Sue Wickerson
Income: £15,814,000 [2017]; £13,871,000 [2016]; £11,744,878 [2015]; £10,648,075 [2014]; £10,834,226 [2013]

Southwark Citizens Advice Bureaux Service
Registered: 29 Jun 1998 *Employees:* 37 *Volunteers:* 104
Tel: 020 7740 1744 *Website:* citizensadvicesouthwark.org.uk
Activities: Education, training; prevention or relief of poverty; economic, community development, employment
Address: Southwark CABX Service, 8 Market Place, Southwark Park Road, London, SE16 3UQ
Trustees: Ms Cordelia Richman, Ms Martina O'Sullivan, Mr Ayaz Manji, Ms Patricia Boyer, Mr Aleksandr Al-Dhahir, Ms Kathleen Fox
Income: £1,767,926 [2017]; £1,874,281 [2016]; £1,398,649 [2015]; £1,382,036 [2014]; £1,192,407 [2013]

The Southwark Diocesan Board of Education (Incorporated)
Registered: 30 Jan 1967 *Employees:* 18
Tel: 020 7234 9200 *Website:* education.southwark.anglican.org
Activities: Education, training
Address: Southwark Diocesan Board of Educ, 48 Union Street, London, SE1 1TD
Trustees: Fr Darren Miller, Rev Peter Organ, Ms Pamela Dorothy Davies, Mr Robert Sidney Love, Rev Ariadne Rolanda Van Den Hof, Ms Penny Smith-Orr, Rev Andrew John Williams, Rev Erica Mielle Wooff, Dr Catharina Stibe-Hickson, Mrs Emma Hart-Dyke, Rev Peter Farley-Moore, Rev Jonathon Dunnett Clark Bishop of Croydon, Miss Maria McBean, Rev Dr Sharon Moughtin-Mumby, Mrs Eileen Margaret Perryer, Mr Martin Brecknell, Mr Malcolm John Edwards CBE, Canon Gary John Jenkins, Rev Christopher Thomas James Chessun, Ven Dr Jane Elizabeth Steen, Rev Carol Coslett, Mrs Jane Christine Marwood, Dr Mark Garner, Rev Pamela Ann Kurk, Mr Niall Gallagher, Mrs Virginia Eaton, Ms Riana Gouws, Dr Nicholas Mark Shepherd, Mrs Alison Joy Hooper Venn, Mr Edundayo Olomu
Income: £1,932,469 [2016]; £1,971,206 [2015]; £1,626,724 [2014]; £1,519,214 [2013]; £1,576,521 [2012]

Southwark Diocesan Welcare
Registered: 31 Jan 2005 *Employees:* 21 *Volunteers:* 209
Tel: 020 7820 7910 *Website:* welcare.org
Activities: General charitable purposes; education, training; advancement of health or saving of lives; disability; prevention or relief of poverty
Address: Lambeth Welcare, 19 Frederick Crescent, London, SW9 6XN
Trustees: Moira Astin, Sara Drake, Mary Evans, Cherry Murdoch, Anne Coates, Megan Pacey, Debbie Haith, Ms Sarah Harty
Income: £1,025,182 [2017]; £961,421 [2016]; £866,576 [2015]; £1,090,475 [2014]; £1,691,080 [2013]

Southwark Disablement Association
Registered: 29 Jun 1989 *Employees:* 65 *Volunteers:* 15
Tel: 020 7701 1391 *Website:* sdail.org
Activities: Disability
Address: Southwark Disablement Association, 10 Bradenham Close, London, SE17 2QB
Trustees: Mr Mark Duke, Janet Jackson, Mrs Adele Carden, Mr Samba Coker, Gwen Nicholson, Mr Eric Segoh, Dolly Mace
Income: £1,036,995 [2017]; £1,030,824 [2016]; £992,978 [2015]; £1,000,341 [2014]; £1,023,847 [2013]

Southwell Leisure Centre
Registered: 11 Sep 1964 *Employees:* 71
Tel: 01636 642882
Activities: Amateur sport
Address: Tom Geraghty, 38 Northgate, Newark on Trent, Notts, NG24 1EZ
Trustees: Mr John Bruce Ashworth, Mr Peter Harris, Mr Andrew Phillip Gregory, Mr Tim Wendels, Ms Penny Rainbow, Mr Paul Handley, Mr Andrew Philip Gregory, Mrs Lyn Harris, Mr Roger Adley
Income: £1,293,592 [2017]; £1,283,787 [2016]; £1,260,518 [2015]; £1,296,287 [2014]; £1,257,904 [2013]

Southwell and Nottingham Diocesan Board of Finance
Registered: 5 Oct 1966 *Employees:* 70
Tel: 01636 814331 *Website:* southwell.anglican.org
Activities: Religious activities
Address: Jubilee House, Westgate, Southwell, Notts, NG25 0JH
Trustees: Bishop of Southwell and Nottingham, Mr Peter Vincent Stanley, Mr Michael Arlington, Rt Revd The Suffragan Bishop of Southwell & Nottingham, Ven Sarah Elizabeth Clark, Mrs Anne Walters, Revd Canon John Bentham, Mrs Elizabeth Marshall, Mr Michael Wilson, Rev Stephen Silvester, Revd Canon Tony Walker, Mr Colin Stuart Slater, Ven David Anthony Picken, Rev Phil Williams, Miss Susan Waterston, Marlene Simpson, Mrs Sarah Holt, Mr Stephen Gelsthorpe, Mrs Jennifer Hempstead
Income: £10,499,000 [2016]; £9,840,000 [2015]; £9,663,000 [2014]; £9,732,000 [2013]; £10,512,000 [2012]

Sova
Registered: 9 Feb 1999 *Employees:* 125 *Volunteers:* 802
Tel: 0114 270 9170 *Website:* sova.org.uk
Activities: Education, training; accommodation, housing; economic, community development, employment; other charitable purposes
Address: The Corner, 91 Division Street, Sheffield, S1 4GE
Trustees: Mr Nicholas Ernest Burstin, Mr Mike Pringle, Dr Andreas Raffel, Mr Stuart Russell McMinnies, Ms Sheena Nadine Marie Asthana, Ms Jean Margaret Daintith, Ms Gillian Parker, Mr John Howard Harris, Ms Hilary Jackson, Mr Wilfred John Bardsley, Ms Rachel Atkinson
Income: £3,739,951 [2017]; £3,796,215 [2016]; £4,517,924 [2015]; £4,099,825 [2014]; £4,991,034 [2013]

Peter Sowerby Foundation
Registered: 10 May 2013
Tel: 020 3909 1600 *Website:* petersowerbyfoundation.com
Activities: General charitable purposes; education, training; advancement of health or saving of lives; disability; prevention or relief of poverty; overseas aid, famine relief; arts, culture, heritage, science; environment, conservation, heritage; economic, community development, employment
Address: Aspinalls, 1 King William Street, London, EC4N 7AF
Trustees: Mr David Benjamin Harold Aspinall, Dr Peter Redmore Sowerby, Professor Carole Margaret Longson, Dr David Lindsay Stables, Mrs Sara Poulios, Aspinalls Fiduciary Limited
Income: £1,045,000 [2016]; £582,837 [2015]; £33,125,519 [2014]

Space for Giants
Registered: 17 Nov 2014 *Employees:* 19
Tel: 020 7710 5408 *Website:* spaceforgiants.org
Activities: General charitable purposes; education, training; animals; environment, conservation, heritage
Address: 80-83 Long Lane, London, EC1A 9ET
Trustees: Lord Timothy Francis Clement-Jones, Mrs Janice Elizabeth Hughes, Mr Thomas Peter William Brunner, Mr Michael Andrew Count, Mr Peter James Bacchus, Mrs Emilia Keladitis
Income: £1,016,435 [2016]

The Spanish and Portuguese Jews Home for the Aged
Registered: 3 Aug 2015 *Employees:* 71
Tel: 020 8908 4151 *Website:* edinburghhouse.org.uk
Activities: General charitable purposes
Address: Edinburgh House, 36-44 Forty Avenue, Wembley, Middlesex, HA9 8JP
Trustees: Mr Bernard Mocatta, Mrs Gina Raquel Riese, Mr Sabah Daoud Zubaida, Ms Lesley Temple, Mr Paul Francis Greek, Mrs Vivianne Ettinghausen
Income: £5,583,862 [2016]

Spear Housing Association Limited
Registered: 7 Jan 2008 *Employees:* 55 *Volunteers:* 85
Tel: 020 7036 9772 *Website:* spearlondon.org
Activities: Education, training; prevention or relief of poverty; accommodation, housing; economic, community development, employment
Address: 89 Heath Road, Twickenham, Middlesex, TW1 4AW
Trustees: Mr Charles Barrie Hatch, Mr Grant Healy, Charlotte Campanale, Rachel Smith, Mr Jack Stephen, Katy Keily, Duncan Richford, Alex Doig
Income: £1,930,335 [2017]; £2,011,289 [2016]; £1,696,913 [2015]; £1,759,493 [2014]; £1,402,625 [2013]

Special Olympics Great Britain
Registered: 2 Nov 1988 *Employees:* 15 *Volunteers:* 4,000
Tel: 020 7247 8891 *Website:* specialolympicsgb.org.uk
Activities: Disability; amateur sport
Address: Special Olympics, 6-8 Great Eastern Street, London, EC2A 3NT
Trustees: Mr Philip Charles Nathan, Mr Murton Mann, Mr Leonard Joseph Dunne, Laura Smith, Mr Robert Andrew Powell, Mr Anthony Abbott, Mr Andrew Reed, Mr Gregory Silvester, Mr Miles MacKinnon, Kathryn McColl, Professor Jan Burns MBE, Mr Tom Smith
Income: £2,385,275 [2016]; £2,454,784 [2015]; £1,431,858 [2014]; £2,845,650 [2013]; £1,924,527 [2012]

Specialeffect Org UK
Registered: 28 Sep 2007 *Employees:* 17 *Volunteers:* 50
Tel: 01608 810055 *Website:* specialeffect.org.uk
Activities: Education, training; disability; amateur sport
Address: Specialeffect, The Stable Block, Cornbury Park, Charlbury, Chipping Norton, Oxon, OX7 3EH
Trustees: Mrs Louise Mary Wiltshire, Mr Simon Bennett, Mr Paul Cross, Mrs Caroline Vlieland Friend, Mr Nick Moglia, Mr Simon John Read
Income: £2,116,391 [2017]; £1,080,901 [2016]; £1,325,587 [2015]; £619,444 [2014]; £371,535 [2013]

Spectrum Care, Resources and Education in Autism Management
Registered: 26 Aug 2015
Tel: 020 7430 7150
Activities: Disability
Address: 22 Chancery Lane, London, WC2A 1LS
Trustees: Louise Stoten, The Honourable Theresa Catherine Roxanne Boteler, Miss Katherine Laing, The Honourable Leopold Harold Hamar John Amery, Mr Christopher De Bellaigue
Income: £1,138,708 [2017]; £229,855 [2016]

Cynthia Spencer Hospice Charity
Registered: 15 May 1991 *Employees:* 5 *Volunteers:* 150
Tel: 01604 973343 *Website:* cynthiaspencer.org.uk
Activities: The advancement of health or saving of lives; disability
Address: Cynthia Spencer Hospice Charity, Pondwood House, Pond Wood Close, Moulton Park Industrial Estate, Northampton, NN3 6RT
Trustees: Mrs Pamela Nock, Mr Steve Potter, Mr Roger Wood, Mrs Catherine Shirley, Mrs Michelle Myers, Ms Danielle Soto, Mrs Paula Lucille Ollive, Mr Peter Nock, Mr Peter Hannon, Mr Russell Douglas, Mrs Claire Taylor
Income: £1,374,132 [2016]; £1,280,126 [2015]; £974,760 [2014]; £557,898 [2013]; £448,875 [2012]

Spice Innovations Limited
Registered: 24 Mar 2010 *Employees:* 32 *Volunteers:* 12
Tel: 020 8980 2691 *Website:* justaddspice.org
Activities: Education, training; advancement of health or saving of lives; prevention or relief of poverty; economic, community development, employment
Address: 15 Old Ford Road, London, E2 9PJ
Trustees: Ms Mihiri Jayaweera, Ms Lucie Stephens, Tom Ebbutt, Mr Neal Hounsell, Mr Chris Sherwood, Mr Andrew Fox, Anna Lewis
Income: £1,784,725 [2017]; £1,582,856 [2016]; £1,593,568 [2015]; £1,108,712 [2014]; £1,024,432 [2013]

Spike Island Artspace Limited
Registered: 19 Jul 1991 *Employees:* 21 *Volunteers:* 180
Tel: 0117 954 4002 *Website:* spikeisland.org.uk
Activities: General charitable purposes; education, training; arts, culture, heritage, science
Address: Spike Island, 133 Cumberland Road, Bristol, BS1 6UX
Trustees: Mr Andrew Cooper, Mrs Alice Workman, Mr Andy Braithwaite, Mr Gavin Marshall, Mrs Jacqueline Kingsley, Mr Benjamin Owen, Jane Therese Jackson, Dr Dorothy Price
Income: £1,568,679 [2017]; £1,215,754 [2016]; £988,208 [2015]; £1,004,148 [2014]; £969,011 [2013]

Spina Bifida, Hydrocephalus, Information, Networking, Equality - Shine
Registered: 1 Oct 1966 *Employees:* 45 *Volunteers:* 100
Tel: 01733 555988 *Website:* shinecharity.org.uk
Activities: The advancement of health or saving of lives; disability
Address: Shine, 42 Park Road, Peterborough, Cambs, PE1 2UQ
Trustees: Mr Aidan Kehoe, Mr Gregory Stewart Smith, Mrs Sallly Hesling, Mrs Patricia Adley, Mr Mark Richard Noakes, Dr Roger Bayston, Mr Peter Serjent, Mr Michael Brown, Mrs Joanne Frances Williams, Ms Lisa Rodan
Income: £2,313,492 [2017]; £2,462,700 [2016]; £2,397,069 [2015]; £2,429,345 [2014]; £2,550,575 [2013]

Spinal Injuries Association
Registered: 29 Mar 1996 *Employees:* 45 *Volunteers:* 163
Tel: 01908 604191 *Website:* spinal.co.uk
Activities: Disability
Address: The Spinal Injuries Association, 2 Trueman Place, Oldbrook, Milton Keynes, Bucks, MK6 2HH
Trustees: Miss Michelle Howard, Mr Darren Hughes, Dr Rupert Timothy Earl, Miss Raquel Sigianporia, Peter Hamilton, Dr Barbara Anne Todd, Mr Andrew Davies, Mr Faisal Hussain, Mrs Margaret Deane, Dr Kidangalil Mathew, Mrs Alison Lyon, Mrs Christina Dyson, Mr Martin Lewis Pollard, Mr Paul Davies MBE, Mr Marcus James Rhodes
Income: £2,228,971 [2017]; £1,870,086 [2016]; £2,261,254 [2015]; £2,151,617 [2014]; £2,929,455 [2013]

Spire (Preston) Limited
Registered: 27 Oct 2010 *Employees:* 57
Tel: 01772 524567 *Website:* spirepreston.org.uk
Activities: Education, training; disability; recreation
Address: Spire (Preston) Ltd, Ground Floor, West Wing, Derby House, Lytham Road, Fulwood, Preston, Lancs, PR2 8JE
Trustees: Mr John David Prince, Mrs Eileen Clarkson, Mr Robert James Clarkson, Mrs Doreen Prince, Mr Peter Sullivan
Income: £1,069,167 [2017]; £1,403,505 [2016]; £849,438 [2014]; £880,058 [2013]; £801,000 [2012]

Spire Homes (LG) Limited
Registered: 29 Mar 2011 *Employees:* 75 *Volunteers:* 4
Website: spire-homes.org.uk
Activities: General charitable purposes; education, training; advancement of health or saving of lives; disability; prevention or relief of poverty; accommodation, housing; environment, conservation, heritage; economic, community development, employment
Address: c/o Friendship Care and Housing, 50 Newhall Hill, Birmingham, B1 3JN
Trustees: Karen Preece, Julie Doyle, Peter Oliver, Derek Doran, Lynn Stubbs, Stephen Wenman
Income: £33,320,000 [2017]; £33,830,000 [2016]; £31,262,000 [2015]; £29,562,000 [2014]; £24,269,000 [2013]

Spirit of 2012
Registered: 20 Dec 2013 *Employees:* 11
Tel: 020 3701 7440 *Website:* spiritof2012trust.org.uk
Activities: Education, training; disability; religious activities; arts, culture, heritage, science; amateur sport; economic, community development, employment; human rights, religious or racial harmony, equality or diversity; recreation
Address: Room S100, New Wing, Somerset House, Strand, London, WC2R 1LA
Trustees: Spirit of 2012 Trustee Limited
Income: £1,175,065 [2017]; £1,423,515 [2016]; £5,481,446 [2015]

Spirit of Soccer
Registered: 9 Jun 1997
Tel: 01702 715559 *Website:* spiritofsoccer.net
Activities: Education, training; disability; overseas aid, famine relief; amateur sport
Address: 67 Chalkwell Avenue, Westcliff on Sea, Essex, SS0 8NL
Trustees: Henry Peirse, Mr Trevor Toulmin, Mr Michael Geddes
Income: £1,415,651 [2017]; £975,079 [2016]; £775,187 [2015]; £553,963 [2014]; £439,843 [2013]

The Spiritualists' National Union
Registered: 3 Mar 1971 *Employees:* 69 *Volunteers:* 160
Tel: 01279 816363 *Website:* snu.org.uk
Activities: Religious activities
Address: Spiritualist National Union, Redwoods, Burton End, Stansted, Essex, CM24 8UD
Trustees: David Bruton, June English, Mr Timothy Coombe, Min Lynda Bradley, Suzanne Gibson Foy, Miss Julia Almond, Minister Alan Rawnsley, Mr Adrian Alv Hirst, Min Carol Ellis
Income: £3,294,977 [2016]; £3,862,190 [2015]; £3,510,890 [2014]; £5,664,827 [2013]; £4,223,154 [2012]

Spitalfields Crypt Trust
Registered: 11 Jun 1999 *Employees:* 84 *Volunteers:* 55
Tel: 020 7613 5677 *Website:* sct.org.uk
Activities: General charitable purposes; education, training; advancement of health or saving of lives; prevention or relief of poverty; accommodation, housing; religious activities; economic, community development, employment
Address: Spitalfields Crypt Trust, 116-118 Shoreditch High Street, London, E1 6JN
Trustees: Mr David Charles Ely JP, Mr Andrew David Enga, Mr Corin Kingsley Pilling, Sarah Brufal, Mr Philip Young, Mrs Amelia Walker, Mr Jean-Baptiste Petard, Mr Matthew Ubogagu
Income: £2,480,000 [2017]; £2,315,000 [2016]; £2,355,235 [2015]; £2,313,808 [2014]; £2,055,989 [2013]

Splitz Support Service
Registered: 9 Oct 1997 *Employees:* 62 *Volunteers:* 19
Website: splitz.org
Activities: General charitable purposes; prevention or relief of poverty; accommodation, housing
Address: Oak House, Epsom Square, White Horse Business Park, Trowbridge, Wilts, BA14 0XG
Trustees: Annette Foster, Cindy Ervine, Ann Cornelius, Sue Eley, Stephen Foster, Alison Craddock, Alan MacKenzie, Mark Lake
Income: £2,192,184 [2017]; £2,128,897 [2016]; £2,347,985 [2015]; £1,358,290 [2014]; £1,112,345 [2013]

Sported Foundation
Registered: 25 Mar 2008 *Employees:* 32 *Volunteers:* 311
Tel: 020 3848 4670 *Website:* sported.org.uk
Activities: Education, training; advancement of health or saving of lives; disability; amateur sport; economic, community development, employment
Address: 4th Floor, House of Sport, 190 Great Dover Street, London, SE1 4YB
Trustees: Sir Keith Edward Mills, Mr Richard Wayne Lewis, Nicola Walker, Mr Trevor Watkins, Mr Alexander James Eaton Mills, Mr Alan Pascoe MBE BEd DUniv, Mr Carnegie Smyth, Timothy Wood
Income: £1,177,798 [2016]; £1,548,672 [2015]; £729,811 [2014]; £746,164 [2013]; £230,727 [2012]

Sports Aid Trust
Registered: 10 Oct 2005 *Employees:* 11 *Volunteers:* 59
Tel: 020 7273 1976 *Website:* sportsaid.org.uk
Activities: Amateur sport
Address: Sports Aid Trust, 21 Bloomsbury Street, London, WC1B 3HF
Trustees: Mr Mark Lillie, Baroness Tanni Grey-Thompson, Ms Michelle Moore, Mr David Faulkner, Mr Ronald Denholm, Ms Alison Odell CBE, Mr Ian Braid, Mr Mark Davies, Mr Mike Westcott, Mr Richard Glasson
Income: £4,688,339 [2017]; £4,690,000 [2016]; £3,804,135 [2015]; £4,020,001 [2014]; £4,103,140 [2013]

The Sports Council Trust Company
Registered: 25 Jul 1990
Tel: 020 7273 1678
Activities: Amateur sport; recreation
Address: Sport England, 21 Bloomsbury Street, London, WC1B 3HF
Trustees: Mr Peter Rowley, Mr David Joseph Cove, Mr Graeme Dell, Mr Andrew Watson, Ms Helen Martin, Mrs Vivien Margaret Blacker
Income: £3,463,454 [2017]; £4,074,043 [2016]; £5,537,557 [2015]; £11,382,420 [2014]; £9,874,779 [2013]

Spratton Hall School Trust Limited
Registered: 6 Jul 1973 *Employees:* 101
Tel: 01604 847292 *Website:* sprattonhall.com
Activities: Education, training
Address: Spratton Hall School, Smith Street, Spratton, Northampton, NN6 8HP
Trustees: Mr Timothy John Blades, Mr Jonathan Belbin, Mr Robin Green, Mr Roger Victor Peel, Mrs Nicola Pert, James Coley, Mr John Beynon, Mrs P Long, Mr Roger Outwin-Flinders, Mrs Sarah Anne Bennett, Mr Alistair Storrar Gough
Income: £4,713,620 [2017]; £4,582,341 [2016]; £4,492,166 [2015]; £4,412,061 [2014]; £4,230,082 [2013]

Spring Grove School 2003
Registered: 3 Oct 2003 *Employees:* 45 *Volunteers:* 2
Tel: 01233 812337 *Website:* springgroveschool.co.uk
Activities: Education, training
Address: Mrs Sarah Peirce, Harville Road, Wye, Ashford, Kent, TN25 5EZ
Trustees: Mr Hugo Mark Fenwick, Mr Andrew Henderson, Mr Bruce Grindlay, Mr Dominic Urand, Mr Andrew John Martin, Mr Graham Wethered, Mrs Dawne Sweetland, Ms Tanya Lee, Mrs Winifred Forrest, Mrs Suzanne Fox, Mrs Carine Borg
Income: £1,559,195 [2017]; £1,400,084 [2016]; £1,691,026 [2015]; £1,536,630 [2014]; £1,470,176 [2013]

Spring Housing Association Limited
Registered: 11 Aug 2015 *Employees:* 37 *Volunteers:* 5
Tel: 0121 663 1443 *Website:* springhousing.org.uk
Activities: General charitable purposes; accommodation, housing
Address: Spring Housing Association, 22 Old Walsall Road, Birmingham, B42 1DT
Trustees: Mrs Preet Kaur Gill, Kathryn Lucy Moore, Mr Neil Vernon De-Costa, Mr David Saunders, Tonia Clark, Paul Brian Hibbert, Mr Darren Roy Bindert, Ms Neelam Sunder
Income: £4,319,013 [2017]; £2,433,043 [2016]

Spring Impact
Registered: 30 Jul 2013 *Employees:* 13 *Volunteers:* 12
Tel: 020 7239 4929 *Website:* springimpact.org
Activities: General charitable purposes; education, training; advancement of health or saving of lives; prevention or relief of poverty; other charitable purposes
Address: Phoenix Yard, 65 Kings Cross Road, London, WC1X 9LW
Trustees: Chris Underhill, Simon Myers, Peter Freedman, Christopher Cuthbert, Alix Zwane, Neil Marshall, Kate Wareing, Peter Weiss, Emma Cooper
Income: £1,482,157 [2017]; £1,075,210 [2016]; £480,878 [2015]; £401,410 [2014]

The Springboard Bursary Foundation
Registered: 3 Jul 2012 *Employees:* 3
Tel: 020 3405 3630 *Website:* springboardbursary.org.uk
Activities: Education, training
Address: The Springboard Bursary Foundation, Buckingham Suite, 7 Grosvenor Gardens, London, SW1W 0BD
Trustees: Mr Patrick Sibley Jan Derham, Mr Timothy Brian Bunting, William De Winton, Mr Robert William Ashburnham Swannell, Mr Richard Wayne Lewis, Mr Patrick Smulders
Income: £1,324,440 [2017]; £1,287,085 [2016]; £1,064,434 [2015]; £234,655 [2014]; £480,391 [2013]

The Springboard Charity
Registered: 30 Mar 1995 *Employees:* 56 *Volunteers:* 13
Website: springboard.uk.net
Activities: Education, training; disability; prevention or relief of poverty; economic, community development, employment
Address: Springboard Charity, 44 Copperfield Street, London, SE1 0DY
Trustees: Stephen David Moss, Mr David Noble, Mr Paul Galvin, Mrs Angela Vickers, Mr Robert Silk, Miss Kay Harriman, Mrs Mina Dimitrova, Mr Frederick Edwin John Gedge Brackenbury CBE, Mr Christopher Noel Mahony, Mr Matthew Johnson, David Walker, Mr James Thomson, Mrs Aisling Zarraga, Mr Daniel Wilson
Income: £3,023,539 [2017]; £3,198,208 [2016]; £3,096,271 [2015]; £2,595,959 [2014]; £2,065,025 [2013]

Springboard Sunderland Trust
Registered: 21 Dec 1987 *Employees:* 84 *Volunteers:* 2
Tel: 07711 232243 *Website:* springboard-ne.org.uk
Activities: Education, training; economic, community development, employment
Address: 12 Etherley Close, Durham, DH1 5XQ
Trustees: Mrs Denise Wilson, Mr Jonathan Nicholson, Mr John Colin Wilson
Income: £5,544,936 [2017]; £4,430,960 [2016]; £6,179,733 [2015]; £7,197,487 [2014]; £10,946,059 [2013]

The Springfield Project
Registered: 16 Mar 2010 *Employees:* 60 *Volunteers:* 100
Website: springfieldproject.org.uk
Activities: Education, training; advancement of health or saving of lives; religious activities; amateur sport; economic, community development, employment
Address: 325 Rednal Road, Birmingham, B38 8EE
Trustees: Ms Yvonne Carolene Gordon, Dr Simon James Slater, Rev Thomas Thomas, Ms Alison Roper-Hall, Ms Elizabeth Mary Corrie, Mrs Caroline Louise Minchin, Mrs Sarah Elizabeth Smith, Dr Andreas Michael Melchior, Mr Gregor Leslie Moss, Mr Peter John Hunt
Income: £1,098,387 [2017]; £1,080,713 [2016]; £1,169,086 [2015]; £1,182,720 [2014]; £1,065,713 [2013]

The Springhead Trust Limited
Registered: 16 Nov 2005 *Employees:* 3 *Volunteers:* 36
Tel: 01747 811853 *Website:* springheadtrust.org.uk
Activities: General charitable purposes; education, training; arts, culture, heritage, science; environment, conservation, heritage
Address: Mill Street, Fontmell Magna, Shaftesbury, Dorset, SP7 0NU
Trustees: Mr Ian Scott, Mr Lee Vincent Smith, Mr Nikolaus David Sean Boulting, Ms Catherine Anne Partridge
Income: £1,632,238 [2016]; £125,487 [2015]; £106,685 [2014]; £87,191 [2013]; £122,123 [2012]

Springhill Hospice (Rochdale)
Registered: 28 Jul 1989 *Employees:* 105 *Volunteers:* 430
Tel: 01706 649920 *Website:* springhill.org.uk
Activities: Education, training; advancement of health or saving of lives
Address: Springhill Hospice, Broad Lane, Rochdale, OL16 4PZ
Trustees: Councillor Robert Clegg, Mrs Ratna Mukherjee, Mr Steven Charles Price, Rt Rev'd Mark Davies Bishop of Middleton, Miss Kitsa Efthymiadis, Dr Robert Namushi, Sultan Ali, Mr John Frederick Dafforne, Mrs Carol Hopkins, Ms Jennifer Anne Ransome, Mrs Susan Blundell, Ms Lesley Ann Mort
Income: £5,415,926 [2017]; £4,634,520 [2016]; £4,373,891 [2015]; £3,461,367 [2014]; £3,425,723 [2013]

Spurgeons College
Registered: 26 Mar 2003 *Employees:* 31 *Volunteers:* 108
Tel: 020 8683 8460 *Website:* spurgeons.ac.uk
Activities: Education, training; religious activities
Address: Spurgeons College, 189 South Norwood Hill, London, SE25 6DJ
Trustees: Rev Stuart Davison, Mrs Sarah Bridget King, Rev Philip McCormack, Rev Hillary Nyika, Mr Edward Woods, Mrs Rosemary Chandler, Rev David Kerrigan, Mrs Suzie Leveson, Angela Murray, Mrs Joanne Gale
Income: £2,008,000 [2016]; £1,606,286 [2015]; £1,544,396 [2014]; £1,470,160 [2013]

Spurgeons
Registered: 19 Jun 2000 *Employees:* 495 *Volunteers:* 227
Tel: 01933 417405 *Website:* spurgeons.org
Activities: General charitable purposes; education, training; overseas aid, famine relief
Address: Spurgeons, 74 Wellingborough Road, Rushden, Northants, NN10 9TY
Trustees: Mr Andrew Caplen, Mr Stuart Cornwell, Ms Safron Rose, Mr Simon Beresford, Ms Helen Watson, Ms Sarah Powley, Mrs Ruth Vincent, Mrs Natalie Cronin, Miss Romaine Thompson
Income: £13,209,575 [2017]; £15,164,428 [2016]; £16,272,000 [2015]; £17,115,000 [2014]; £18,161,000 [2013]

The Square Chapel Trust
Registered: 13 Dec 1988 *Employees:* 45 *Volunteers:* 80
Tel: 01422 353073 *Website:* squarechapel.co.uk
Activities: Arts, culture, heritage, science; environment, conservation, heritage
Address: The Square Chapel Arts Centre, 10 Square Road, Halifax, W Yorks, HX1 1QG
Trustees: Professor Erik Knudsen, Mr Neil Walter Horsfield, Mr Martin West, Mr David Liam McQuillan, Elizabeth Kathleen Dugdale, Ms Jennifer Lynn, Mr Nicholas Charles Worsnop, Ms Jacqueline Newman, Ms Britt Harwood, Miss Miriam Selma Razaq
Income: £5,094,865 [2017]; £2,314,791 [2016]; £1,222,166 [2015]; £1,322,758 [2014]; £4,196,489 [2013]

James Square Plymouth Limited
Registered: 18 Apr 2006
Tel: 020 7398 7200
Activities: Education, training; other charitable purposes
Address: UPP, 40 Gracechurch Street, London, EC3V 0BT
Trustees: Clive Wilson Crawford, Mrs Sarah Nancy Jones, Mr Martin Blakey, Mr Trevor Alan Wills
Income: £1,220,000 [2017]; £1,231,000 [2016]; £1,258,000 [2015]; £1,259,000 [2014]; £1,264,633 [2013]

Sri Guru Singh Sabha Southall
Registered: 14 Nov 1980 *Employees:* 42 *Volunteers:* 28
Tel: 020 8574 8901 *Website:* sgsss.org
Activities: General charitable purposes; education, training; advancement of health or saving of lives; overseas aid, famine relief; religious activities; arts, culture, heritage, science; amateur sport; environment, conservation, heritage; economic, community development, employment; recreation
Address: 2-8 Park Avenue, Southall, Middlesex, UB1 3AG
Trustees: Mr Surinder Singh Purewal, Mr Surjit Singh Bilga, Surinder Singh Dhatt, Mr Didar Singh Randhawa, Mr Sohan Singh Sumra, Mrs Surjit Kaur Bassi, Navraj Singh Cheema, Harjit Singh Sarpanch, Mr Prem Singh Dhandi, Himat Singh Sohi, Davinderpal Singh Kooner, Tej Kaur Grewal, P B Singh Johal, Mr Balwant Singh Gill, Parvinder Singh Garcha, Mr Gurmail Singh Malhi, Mr Jitpal Singh Sihota, Mr Gursharan Singh Mand, Mr Kulwant Singh Bhinder, Mr Prabhjot Singh Thind, Mr Sukhdeep Singh Gill, Harmeet Singh Gill, Sukhdev Singh Aujla, Darshan Singh Dokal, Amarjit Singh Dassan
Income: £2,792,917 [2017]; £2,717,574 [2016]; £2,820,982 [2015]; £2,745,519 [2014]; £2,701,898 [2013]

The St Albans Diocesan Board of Finance
Registered: 26 Sep 1966 *Employees:* 48
Tel: 01727 854532 *Website:* stalbans.anglican.org
Activities: Education, training; overseas aid, famine relief; religious activities; environment, conservation, heritage
Address: Holywell Lodge, 41 Holywell Hill, St Albans, Herts, AL1 1HE
Trustees: Mrs H Potter, Hon Richard Oakley Pleydell-Bouverie DL, Mr Colin Graham Bird FCA, Dr R Southern, Mr C B Gage, The Venerable J P Smith The Archdeacon of St Albans, Mr J W Butler, Mrs E J Gogarty, Mr D Clout, Mr D J Edmundson, Mrs Jayne Elizabeth Hale, Mr Martyn John Gates, Mrs Kerry Smith, Rev Graham Cappleman, The Venerable P V Hughes The Archdeacon of Bedford, Edmund Wood, Mr D W Nye, Mr S H C Baynes, Rev Kenneth Peter Joseph Padley, Dr D W Dallinger, Mr G W Nicholson, Mr R J Lyne, The Rt Revd Dr Alan G C Smith The Bishop of St Albans, Mr Timothy Russell Fleming, Mrs Patricia Elizabeth Easterbrook, Mr Philip Richard Lindley, The Venerable J MacKenzie The Archdeacon of Hertford
Income: £17,451,303 [2016]; £17,129,112 [2015]; £17,286,827 [2014]; £17,513,930 [2013]; £15,473,040 [2012]

St Albans High School for Girls
Registered: 13 Sep 1966 *Employees:* 191 *Volunteers:* 57
Tel: 01727 853800 *Website:* stahs.org.uk
Activities: Education, training
Address: Townsend Avenue, St Albans, Herts, AL1 3SJ
Trustees: Mr Robert Harvey Ward, Dr Jeffrey John, Mrs Heather Greatrex, Mr Timothy David Gardam, Miss Dorothy Henderson, Mr David Alterman, Mr Paul Anthony Brewster, Mrs Moira Ellen Darlington, Mr Kenneth Matthew Keen, Miss Rosanne Musgrave, Mr Bruce Kettle, Mr John Stewart Thomson, Mrs C R Callegari, Mr Simon Richard Martin, Mr Neil James Enright, Mr Daniel Mark Roe, Ms Eleanor Alice De Galleani
Income: £16,298,000 [2017]; £14,550,000 [2016]; £13,622,000 [2015]; £13,726,000 [2014]; £12,469,000 [2013]

St Albans School
Registered: 12 Jul 2002 *Employees:* 145
Tel: 01727 515149 *Website:* st-albans.herts.sch.uk
Activities: Education, training
Address: Abbey Gateway, St Albans, Herts, AL3 4HB
Trustees: Mr Peter Brown, Dr M Pegg, Mr Anthony Dalwood, Mr S Majumdar, Mrs Carole Pomfret, Sir Roy Gardner, Prof John Luzio, Mr Derek Foster, Mr Nigel Moore, Mr Chris McIntyre, Mr Stephen Patrick Eames, Mr Alastair Woodgate, Mr Robert Lucas, Miss L Ainsworth, Mrs A Hurst, Mr Michael Punt, Mr Matthew William Southworth Cawthorne
Income: £15,894,007 [2016]; £14,973,926 [2015]; £14,321,774 [2014]; £14,059,418 [2013]; £13,146,510 [2012]

St Andrew's (Woking) School Trust
Registered: 28 Aug 1987 *Employees:* 70
Tel: 01483 760943 *Website:* st-andrews.woking.sch.uk
Activities: Education, training
Address: St Andrews School, Church Hill House, Wilson Way, Woking, Surrey, GU21 4QW
Trustees: Mr Derek Taylor, Major James Gordon, Mr Mark Neil, Mr Kenneth Bray, Dr Claire McShane, Mr Alexis Christodoulou, Mrs Jenny Way, Mr John Kerr, Miss Rebecca Ross, Dr David Livingstone, Mr Lukas Pytel, Mr John Speed
Income: £3,674,038 [2017]; £3,542,153 [2016]; £3,480,061 [2015]; £3,307,100 [2014]; £3,021,641 [2013]

St Andrew's College, Bradfield
Registered: 19 Jul 1965 *Employees:* 527
Tel: 0118 964 4530 *Website:* bradfieldcollege.org.uk
Activities: Education, training
Address: Bradfield College, Bradfield, Reading, Berks, RG7 6AU
Trustees: Mrs Janet Aniela Scarrow, Mr Ian Davenport, Mr Peter Banfield Saunders, Mr Ian M Wood-Smith, Sophia Bergqvist, Mrs Sarah Patricia Scrope, Professor Robert Van De Noort FSA PFHEA, Mrs Emma Barker, Dr Nicola Hodson, Dr Sarah Fane, Mr Michael Jones, Dr Bruce Tomlinson, Mr Hans Peter Gangsted, Mr Simon Beccle, Mr Simon Clarkson-Webb, Mr David Mundy, Mrs Catherine Hartz
Income: £27,325,169 [2017]; £25,684,655 [2016]; £23,660,899 [2015]; £24,033,265 [2014]; £21,298,522 [2013]

St Andrew's Healthcare
Registered: 16 Jul 2004 *Employees:* 4,174 *Volunteers:* 143
Tel: 01604 616250 *Website:* standrewshealthcare.co.uk
Activities: Education, training; advancement of health or saving of lives
Address: St Andrews Hospital, Cliftonville Road, Northampton, NN1 5DG
Trustees: Mrs Frances Jackson, Stuart John Richmond-Watson, Mrs Jane Forman-Hardy, Mr Paul Thomas Serge Parsons, Mr Dean Howells, Mr Michael Harris, Peter Winslow, Mr Martin Kersey, Mr Martin Beer, Dr Sanjith Kamath
Income: £205,600,000 [2017]; £199,100,000 [2016]; £190,900,000 [2015]; £189,400,000 [2014]; £178,000,000 [2013]

St Andrew's House
Registered: 18 Feb 1963 *Employees:* 43
Tel: 024 7671 3210 *Website:* standrewshouse.org.uk
Activities: The advancement of health or saving of lives; disability; accommodation, housing
Address: 29 Spencer Avenue, Coventry, Warwicks, CV5 6NQ
Trustees: Mr David William Mills, Mrs Margaret Audrey Dunwoody, Mr Robert Frank Kemble, Verity Tiff, Joan Vera Wilkins, Mr Kenneth Leonard Holmes, Mr Rod Drew, Mr Richard Perry, Simon Paul Pudsey
Income: £1,017,090 [2017]; £974,968 [2016]; £1,086,169 [2015]; £1,158,512 [2014]; £896,574 [2013]

St Andrew's School (Bedford) Limited
Registered: 16 Feb 1966 *Employees:* 73 *Volunteers:* 10
Tel: 01234 05669 *Website:* standrewsschoolbedford.com
Activities: Education, training
Address: 96 Winchester Road, Bedford, MK42 0SB
Trustees: Mr Ivan Flack, John Wilkinson, Mrs Mary Burt, Mr Graham Bates, Mr Mike Grafton, Brian Thompsn, Mr Clive Simmonds, Mr David Eyton-Williams, Tricia Lennie, Mr Stephen Williamson, Mr James Leydon
Income: £1,871,933 [2017]; £1,893,619 [2016]; £2,294,046 [2015]; £2,105,781 [2014]; £2,212,078 [2013]

The St Andrew's School Trust
Registered: 21 Apr 2009 *Employees:* 34
Tel: 01263 837927
Activities: Education, training
Address: St Andrew's School, Aylmerton Hall, Holt Road, Aylmerton, Norfolk, NR11 8QA
Trustees: Ms Sheila Goldsmith, Mr Rex Wheeler, Mrs Veronica Ann Jones, Mrs Barbara Joan Emery, Mr John Garner, Mr John Roebuck, Mr David William Bullard, Mr Nicholas Conrad Brayne
Income: £1,214,042 [2016]; £786,681 [2015]; £720,058 [2014]; £597,875 [2013]; £361,955 [2012]

St Andrews (Pangbourne) School Trust Limited
Registered: 16 Aug 1963 *Employees:* 93 *Volunteers:* 6
Tel: 0118 974 4276 *Website:* standrewspangbourne.co.uk
Activities: Education, training
Address: St Andrews School, Buckhold, Pangbourne, Reading, Berks, RG8 8QA
Trustees: Mrs Felicity Rutland, Mr Neil McIntosh, Mr Philip Waite, Mrs Joanne Wood, Mr Geoffrey William Claude Eversfield, Mrs Jennifer Kingsland, Mr Michael John Windsor, Mrs Rachel Dent, Mr Timothy James Clark, Mr David John Binney
Income: £4,418,689 [2017]; £3,999,255 [2016]; £3,819,456 [2015]; £3,689,047 [2014]; £3,341,763 [2013]

St Andrews Hospice Limited
Registered: 13 May 1992 *Employees:* 137 *Volunteers:* 493
Tel: 01472 350908 *Website:* standrewshospice.com
Activities: The advancement of health or saving of lives; disability
Address: St Andrews Hospice, Peaks Lane, Grimsby, N E Lincs, DN32 9RP
Trustees: Mr Geoffrey Enoch Hirst, Mr Colin Ellis, Mr Stephen Alexander Oldridge, Mr John Scaife, Mr Steven Parker, Mr Nigel Tranter, Mr Leslie Jones, Mr David Hatfield, Mr Andrew Kenneth North, Dr Anne Spalding, Mr Ian Hargreaves
Income: £4,299,841 [2017]; £4,269,682 [2016]; £4,958,274 [2015]; £4,279,035 [2014]; £3,072,698 [2013]

St Ann's Hospice
Registered: 5 Mar 1969 *Employees:* 241 *Volunteers:* 772
Tel: 0161 498 3637 *Website:* sah.org.uk
Activities: The advancement of health or saving of lives
Address: St Anns Hospice, St Anns Road North, Heald Green, Cheadle, Cheshire, SK8 3SZ
Trustees: Mr Alan Bond, Mr Michael Brown, Mr Allan William Beardsworth, Ms Anna Fryer, Ms Kate Squire, Mr Luke Dillon, Ms Helen Thompson, Dr Stephanie Gomm, Ms Jacqueline Oldham, Ms Fiona Taylor
Income: £12,727,479 [2017]; £12,738,000 [2016]; £12,555,105 [2015]; £11,869,495 [2014]; £9,708,015 [2013]

St Anne's College in the University of Oxford
Registered: 30 Jun 2011 *Employees:* 109
Tel: 01865 274800 *Website:* st-annes.ox.ac.uk
Activities: Education, training
Address: St Annes College, Woodstock Road, Oxford, OX2 6HS
Trustees: Roger Crisp, Prof Patricia Rice, Martyn Harry, Peter Jeavons, Robert Chard, Gareth Davies, Bent Flyvbjerg, Andrew Goodwin, Sian Gronlie, Ben Hambly, David Harris, Howard Hotson, Freya Johnston, Liora Lazarus, Terry Lyons, Patrick McGuinness, Terence O'Shaughnessy, Dr David Pyle, Budimir Rosic, Francis Szele, Kate Watkins, Dr Johannes Abeler, Dr Dmitry Belyeav, Dr Todd Hall, Dr Jonathan Katz, Dr Graham Nelson, Professor Christopher Holmes, Prof Alex Rogers, Ms Clare White, Prof Charlotte Dean, Prof Sarah Wordsworth, Prof Stuart Robinson, Dr Simon Park, Roger Firth, Mr John Ford, Helen Christian, Andrew Briggs, Alan Cocks, Peter Donnelly, Peter Ghosh, Imogen Goold, Christopher Grovenor, Neville Harnew, Geraldine Hazbun, Patrick Irwin, Andrew Klevan, Matthew Leigh, Neil MacFarlane, David Murray, Don Porcelli, Matthew Reynolds, Sally Shuttleworth, Sarah Waters, Peter Wilshaw, Prof Jo-Anne Baird, Prof Paresh Vyas, Dr Antonios Tzanakopoulos, Mr Jim Meridew, Professor Roger Reed, Dr Elias Koustoupias, Dr Tim Schwanen, Prof Victoria Murphy, Dr Samina Khan, Dr Shannon McKellar Stephen, Ms Helen King, Professor Yaacov Yadgar
Income: £12,912,000 [2017]; £13,618,000 [2016]; £14,096,000 [2015]; £11,856,000 [2014]; £10,492,000 [2013]

St Anne's Community Services
Registered: 15 Mar 1973 *Employees:* 1,400 *Volunteers:* 12
Tel: 0113 243 5151 *Website:* st-annes.org.uk
Activities: Accommodation, housing; other charitable purposes
Address: St Annes Community Services, 6 St Marks Avenue, Leeds, LS2 9BN
Trustees: Mr Terence Moran, Mr James Dunmore, Mr Philip Brown, Mr Karl Lloyd Beckett, Mr Paul Roberts, Mr Steven Durham, Mr Ian McIntosh, Ms Rebecca Susan Farren, Mr Mark Andrew Westwood
Income: £43,792,404 [2017]; £43,232,090 [2016]; £40,974,075 [2015]; £40,425,576 [2014]; £36,462,838 [2013]

St Anthony of Padua Community Association
Registered: 2 Sep 1986 *Employees:* 124 *Volunteers:* 8
Tel: 0191 234 5775 *Website:* anthonycareservices.org.uk
Activities: Education, training; advancement of health or saving of lives; disability; prevention or relief of poverty; accommodation, housing; economic, community development; employment
Address: 25 Cliftonville Gardens, Whitley Bay, Tyne & Wear, NE26 1QJ
Trustees: Mr Michael Donnelly, Mr James McLaughlin, Mrs Julie Campbell, Mr Benjamin David Nixon, Mr Tim O'Grady, Mrs Catherine Attwell, Mr Roy Edward Stanley, Mr Daryn Robinson
Income: £1,840,411 [2017]; £1,832,629 [2016]; £1,944,086 [2015]; £1,612,907 [2014]; £1,002,494 [2013]

St Antony's College in the University of Oxford
Registered: 11 Apr 2011 *Employees:* 154
Tel: 01865 284742 *Website:* sant.ox.ac.uk
Activities: Education, training; accommodation, housing
Address: St Antonys College, 62 Woodstock Road, Oxford, OX2 6JF
Trustees: Dr Simon Quinn, Paul Collier, Timothy Garton Ash, David Johnson, Sho Konishi, Ian Neary, David Pratten, Phillip Robins, Diego Sanchez-Ancochea, Jan Zielonka, Leigh Ann Payne, Ms Kirsten Gillingham, Dr Laurent Mignon, Dr Ramon Sarro, Professor Dominic Johnson, Dr Matthew Walton, Dr Timothy Power, Dr Thomas Hale, Prof Adewale Adebanwi, Prof Christopher John Gerry, Dr Blessing Tendi, Paul Chaisty, Faisal Devji, Nandini Gooptu, Takehiko Kariya, Rachel Murphy, Kalypso Nicolaidis, Tariq Ramadan, Eugene Rogan, Michael Willis, Walter Tice Armbrust, Dr Cathryn Costello, Dr Roy Allison, Dr Paul Betts, Mr Douglas Gollin, Professor Daniel Domenic Benedict Healey, Dr Miles Larmer, Hugh Whittaker, Dr Moritz Matthiesen, Dr Eric Justin Chaney, Dr Katie Helen Sullivan De Estrada
Income: £7,912,000 [2017]; £7,018,000 [2016]; £8,154,000 [2015]; £7,168,000 [2014]; £11,121,000 [2013]

The St Asaph Diocesan Board of Finance
Registered: 19 Mar 1964 *Employees:* 14 *Volunteers:* 42
Website: dioceseofstasaph.org.uk
Activities: Religious activities
Address: St Asaph DBF, Diocesan Office, High Street, St Asaph, Denbighshire, LL17 0RD
Trustees: Mr Clive Myers, The Very Revd Nigel Howard Williams, Mr Philip Williams, Rev Huw Butler, The Venerable Dr Peter John Pike, Revd Canon Robert Griffiths, The Venerable John Derrick Percy Lomas, Dr Lynne Ashe, Trevor Trevor, Professor John Last CBE, Rt Revd Gregory Cameron, Mrs Helen Jones, Ms Carol Jones, Mr Bernard Harris MBE, Rev Hermione Jane Morris, Rev Sally Jean Rogers
Income: £5,976,034 [2016]; £5,772,146 [2015]; £5,307,350 [2014]; £5,123,531 [2013]; £5,166,704 [2012]

St Aubyn's (Woodford Green) School Trust
Registered: 20 Oct 1975 *Employees:* 89 *Volunteers:* 5
Tel: 020 8504 1577 *Website:* staubyns.com
Activities: Education, training
Address: St Aubyns School, Woodford New Road, Woodford Green, Essex, IG8 9DU
Trustees: Mr Dilip Shah, Mrs Patricia Bridget Russell, Mrs Mo Lalude, Ms Sue Evans, Mrs Debra Davidson-Smith, Mr Kenneth Farmer, Mrs Liz Ruff, Mr Abraham Jacobus Botha, Mr Michael Foster
Income: £5,291,646 [2017]; £5,058,267 [2016]; £4,961,143 [2015]; £4,782,301 [2014]; £4,572,315 [2013]

St Augustine's Priory School Limited
Registered: 2 Jun 2003 *Employees:* 92 *Volunteers:* 10
Tel: 020 8997 2022 *Website:* sapriory.com
Activities: Education, training; religious activities; amateur sport
Address: St Augustines Priory, Hillcrest Road, London, W5 2JL
Trustees: Caroline Phillips, Anthony Clark, Floyd Steadman, Hemant Parmar, Cathryn Copeland, Dr Tim Donovan, Frances Baker, Patrick D'Arcy, Jennifer Burbury, Benedict Cassidy, James Davies
Income: £7,404,659 [2017]; £5,987,654 [2016]; £5,711,215 [2015]; £5,203,999 [2014]; £4,977,853 [2013]

St Barnabas Hospice Trust (Lincolnshire)
Registered: 15 Mar 1996 *Employees:* 272 *Volunteers:* 1,100
Tel: 01522 511566 *Website:* stbarnabashospice.co.uk
Activities: Education, training; advancement of health or saving of lives; other charitable purposes
Address: St Barnabas Hospice, 36 Nettleham Road, Lincoln, LN2 1RE
Trustees: Mr Graham Dawson, Mr Robert Neilans, Mr Anthony John Martin Maltby, Dr David Boldy, Mrs Amanda Legate, Mrs Sylvia Knight, Phillip Hoskins, David Libiszewski, Mr Paul John Banton, Karen Rossdale, Mr Alan Graham Henderson
Income: £12,142,786 [2017]; £11,177,211 [2016]; £11,046,738 [2015]; £10,708,236 [2014]; £7,256,597 [2013]

St Basil's
Registered: 31 Mar 2000 *Employees:* 246 *Volunteers:* 20
Tel: 0121 772 2483 *Website:* stbasils.org.uk
Activities: Education, training; prevention or relief of poverty; accommodation, housing
Address: Heath Mill Lane, Deritend, Birmingham, B9 4AX
Trustees: Ms Jean Templeton, Rev Adam John Aidan Romanis, Ms Maddy Bunker, Mr Steve Guyon, Mr Sean Marsay, Mr Fazal Hajat OBE, Ms Amelia McCann, Ms Sara Fowler, Mr Christopher Thomas Miller, Miss Gina Reid, Mr Christopher John Todd
Income: £10,319,000 [2017]; £9,578,000 [2016]; £8,662,721 [2015]; £8,321,198 [2014]; £8,464,928 [2013]

St Bede's Childcare Limited
Registered: 7 Sep 2010 *Employees:* 122
Tel: 01204 61899
Activities: Education, training; economic, community development, employment
Address: St Bedes C of E Primary School, Morris Green Lane, Bolton, Lancs, BL3 3LJ
Trustees: Mr Jack Hatch, June Roberts, Mrs Kimberley Dearden, Mr Michael Caine, Mrs Sarah Bagshaw
Income: £2,404,737 [2016]; £2,247,390 [2015]; £1,908,259 [2014]; £1,721,102 [2013]; £2,048,802 [2012]

St Bede's College Limited
Registered: 8 Nov 1988 *Employees:* 149 *Volunteers:* 30
Website: stbedescollege.co.uk
Activities: Education, training
Address: St Bedes College, Alexandra Road South, Manchester, M16 8HX
Trustees: Rev Paul Daly, Mr Terence Walsh, Mr James Brendan Ainscough, Mr Desmond Timothy Coffey, Mrs Jennifer Johnson, Mr Paul Francis Heaps, Mr Philip Lanigan, Mrs Rebecca Mary Kennedy, Mr Trevor Allan Richards, Mr George John Comrie Macmillan, Mrs Zofia Kwiatkowska
Income: £6,376,802 [2017]; £5,811,473 [2016]; £5,692,129 [2015]; £5,752,631 [2014]; £6,303,503 [2013]

St Bede's School Trust Sussex
Registered: 17 Jan 1980 *Employees:* 347 *Volunteers:* 45
Tel: 01323 356623 *Website:* bedes.org
Activities: Education, training
Address: St Bedes School, Upper Dicker, Hailsham, E Sussex, BN27 3QH
Trustees: Major General Anthony Leslie Meier OBE, Mr Jeremy David Courtney FRAgS, Mr Mark Scanlan McFadden, Mr Ian Hunt BSc, Mr Xavier Van Hove BSc, Mr Andrew Stuart Reginald Corbett, Mr John Warwick Burbidge, Mr Christopher Paul Yates BA MBA, Mr Dermot Keegan, Mr Christopher James Bean, Mr Christopher John Doidge, Mr Peter Denison OBE CQSW, Mrs Kate Nash BEd, Prof Andrew William Lloyd MA PhD, Mrs Geraldine Patricia Watkins, Mr Nicholas Andrew Mercer BA, Mr Matthew Crummack, Mrs Katharine Lees-Jones
Income: £26,742,000 [2017]; £24,427,000 [2016]; £24,654,000 [2015]; £25,050,000 [2014]; £24,340,000 [2013]

St Bees School
Registered: 12 May 2009 *Employees:* 18 *Volunteers:* 5
Tel: 01946 828006 *Website:* stbeesschool.co.uk
Activities: Education, training
Address: St Bees School, St Bees, Cumbria, CA27 0DS
Trustees: Mark Roberts, Mr Alastair Lord, Mrs Sara Jane Calvin, Mr Mark George, Mr Peter Garth Lever, Mr Thomas Kelly, Mr Shaun Kelso, Dr Adrian Simper, Mr Robert Miller, Mr Robin Frederick Lacey, Mrs Helen Claire Miller
Income: £1,399,732 [2017]; £280,459 [2016]; £4,696,990 [2015]; £4,701,505 [2014]; £4,068,686 [2013]

St Benedict's School Ealing
Registered: 13 Aug 2012 *Employees:* 309 *Volunteers:* 20
Tel: 020 8862 2183 *Website:* stbenedicts.org.uk
Activities: Education, training; religious activities
Address: St Benedicts School, 54 Eaton Rise, London, W5 2ES
Trustees: Mr Christopher Field, Revd Dominic Taylor, Rt Revd Martin Gerald Shipperlee, Ms Susan Vale, Dr Philip Hopley, Mr Jonathan Walsh, Mr John Watson, Mrs Mary Boyle, Mr Brian Taylor, Ms Marian Doyle, Mr Patrick Murphy-O'Connor, Mr Jonathan Berger, Mr Michael Ainslie, Rev Ambrose McCambridge, Mrs Elizabeth Pilgrim, Mr Paul Keyte
Income: £16,013,997 [2016]; £15,050,076 [2015]; £14,596,504 [2014]; £14,277,296 [2013]

The St Benet's Trust
Registered: 15 Aug 2011 *Employees:* 20
Tel: 01439 766710 *Website:* st-benets.ox.ac.uk
Activities: Education, training; religious activities
Address: Ampleforth Abbey, York, YO62 4EN
Trustees: Dr Ralph Waller, Rev Michael Wulstan Peterburs, Mr Joseph MacHale, Mr Allan Dodd, Dr Susan Doran, Rt Rev James Cuthbert Madden, Rev Oswald McBride OSB, Professor Werner Jeanrond, Mr Peter Tufano
Income: £1,027,000 [2016]; £885,000 [2015]; £736,000 [2014]; £681,000 [2013]

St Catherine's - Speech and Language
Registered: 21 Nov 1983 *Employees:* 89 *Volunteers:* 10
Tel: 01983 852722 *Website:* stcatherines.org.uk
Activities: Education, training; disability
Address: St Catherine's, Grove Road, Ventnor, Isle of Wight, PO38 1TT
Trustees: Ms Pauline James, Mr Graham John Pengelly, Linda Pratley, Mrs Catherine Miller, Ms Samantha Jayne Rooney, Mrs Sally Moore, Mr Daniel Kitcher, Mrs Paddie Collyer, Mr John Metcalfe, Mr Anthony Flower, Mrs Kim Marie Williams, Miss Elizabeth Bowen, Mrs Nadine Marie Short
Income: £2,589,955 [2017]; £2,550,019 [2016]; £2,148,356 [2015]; £2,350,418 [2014]; £2,598,054 [2013]

St Catherine's British School
Registered: 8 Jun 1966 *Employees:* 162
Website: stcatherines.gr
Activities: Education, training
Address: Apollonos 19, Lofos Nymphon, Aghios Stefanos, Athens, Greece
Trustees: Mr Maurice Jean Dheere, Mr Stavros P Taki, Dr Platon Tinios, Mr George Andreas Paleokrassas, Mrs Eugenie Coumantaros, Mr Roger Outwin-Flinders, Mr Roger Victor Peel, Mrs Loukia Nicola, Dr Kyriacos G Sabatakakis, Richard Charles Sutton, Mrs Sarah Kinney Contomichalos, Mrs Nathalie Isabelle Contomichalos Coulon
Income: £10,874,546 [2016]; £9,057,098 [2015]; £9,327,969 [2014]; £10,097,235 [2013]; £9,520,868 [2012]

St Catherine's College in the University of Oxford
Registered: 15 Sep 2011 *Employees:* 138
Tel: 01865 271822 *Website:* stcatz.ox.ac.uk
Activities: Education, training
Address: St Catherines College, Manor Road, Oxford, OX1 3UJ
Trustees: Dr Fram Eduljee Dinshaw, Professor Tommaso Pizzari, Professor Peter Battle, Professor Richard Berry, Professor Byron Walter Byrne, Professor Louise Fawcett De Posada, Professor Penelope Ann Handford, Dr Robert Leese, Professor Gervase Rosser, Professor Adrian Smith, Dr Bart Van Es, Dr Justine Pila, Dr Duncan Andrew Robertson, Dr Ben Bollig, Professor John Foord, Professor Patrick Grant, Professor Peter Ireland, Professor Andreas Muench, Professor Christoph Reisinger, Professor Heidi De Wet, Professor Philipp Elias Koralus, Dr Samuel Wolfe, Professor Anna Christina De Ozorio Nobre, Professor Ian Peter Joseph Shipsey, Dr Amanda Power, Dr Alexander Teytelboym, Professor Roger William Ainsworth, Dr Richard Bailey, Mr James Leslie Bennett, Professor Andrew Bunker, Miss Cressida Elizabeth Chappell, Professor David Gillespie, Professor Marc Lackenby, Dr Marc Mulholland, Dr Kirsten E Shepherd-Barr, Professor Richard Todd, Professor David Womersley, Professor Pekka Hamalainen, Professor Eleanor Stride, Professor Peter Philip Edwards, Professor Alain Goriely, Professor Ashok Handa, Professor Gavin Lowe, Professor Udo Oppermann, Professor Gaia Scerif, Professor Andrew Dickinson, Dr Fiona McConnell, Dr Jessica Mary Goodman, Professor Laura Tunbridge, Dr Thomas Adams, Professor Shimon Whiteson, Dr Alessandro Iandolo
Income: £13,852,000 [2017]; £10,118,000 [2016]; £14,988,000 [2015]; £11,806,000 [2014]; £10,558,000 [2013]

St Catherine's Hospice Limited
Registered: 2 Nov 1980 *Employees:* 203 *Volunteers:* 808
Tel: 01293 447333 *Website:* stch.org.uk
Activities: Education, training; advancement of health or saving of lives
Address: Malthouse Road, Crawley, W Sussex, RH10 6BH
Trustees: Dr Christopher Anthony Shearn, Mr Terence John O'Leary, Miss Catherine Blackburn, Miss Nicola Wiltshire, Mr John Alan Vickers, Mr Thiomas Crowley, Mrs Christine MacLean, Mr Torben Nils Harris, Mrs Alison Livesley, Mrs Janice Anita Dowding, Ms Lisa Jane Compton, Dr Alison Crombie
Income: £10,807,000 [2017]; £9,679,000 [2016]; £10,844,000 [2015]; £13,372,452 [2014]; £8,765,246 [2013]

St Catherine's School Bramley
Registered: 4 Aug 1998 *Employees:* 238 *Volunteers:* 40
Tel: 01483 899701 *Website:* stcatherines.info
Activities: Education, training
Address: 15 Glebe Road, Ashtead, Surrey, KT21 2NU
Trustees: Dr Janet McGowan, Mr Peter James Martin, Mrs Susan Shipway, Mrs Clare Johnstone, Mrs Penelope Crouch, Mr Michael Francis Bustard, Mr Denis Brian Ulyet, Mr Jonathan Tippett, Prof Finbarr Cotter, Mr Albert Domingo Reloj Alonzo, Dr Michael John Jordan, Mr Andrew John Pianca, Mrs Karen Farrell
Income: £17,531,212 [2017]; £16,290,000 [2016]; £15,735,429 [2015]; £15,490,100 [2014]; £15,193,388 [2013]

St Catherine's School, Twickenham
Registered: 12 Oct 1992 *Employees:* 78 *Volunteers:* 25
Tel: 020 8891 2898 *Website:* stcatherineschool.co.uk
Activities: Education, training
Address: St Catherines School, Cross Deep, Twickenham, Middlesex, TW1 4QJ
Trustees: Mr Edward Sparrow Qualified Solicitor, Mr Alan Perrier, Mr Sean Skehan, Pauline Alldridge, Mr Michael John Edwards, Paul Clifford, Mr Stephen Jefferson, Mrs Elizabeth Morris, Ms Sylvia Hamilton
Income: £5,199,838 [2017]; £5,490,448 [2016]; £5,120,412 [2015]; £4,669,429 [2014]; £4,565,663 [2013]

St Catherines Hospice (Lancashire) Limited
Registered: 14 Jan 1982 *Employees:* 127 *Volunteers:* 750
Tel: 01772 629171 *Website:* stcatherines.co.uk
Activities: Education, training; advancement of health or saving of lives
Address: St Catherines Hospice, Lostock Lane, Lostock Hall, Preston, Lancs, PR5 5XU
Trustees: Mr Joseph Clifford Hughes, Mr Anthony Ernest Harrison, Dr Stephen Thomas Ward, Dr Fiona Margaret Duncan, Mr Michael James Lough, Mr Jonathan Jospeh Holden, Rev Peter David Taylor, Mr Philip Jones, Mr John Anthony Bonser, Mrs Lesleyanne Doxsey, Mr John George Chesworth
Income: £6,405,000 [2017]; £7,879,000 [2016]; £5,819,000 [2015]; £6,012,891 [2014]; £6,140,745 [2013]

St Cedd's School Educational Trust Limited
Registered: 14 Oct 1964 *Employees:* 66
Tel: 01245 392810 *Website:* stcedds.org.uk
Activities: Education, training
Address: 178 New London Road, Chelmsford, Essex, CM2 0AR
Trustees: Mrs Jane Dagg, Mr Frederick Michael Hargreaves, Mr Gareth Rhys Aubrey Davies, Mrs Frances Marshall, Dr Sibel Peck, Mr Malcolm Kenneth Bryant, Mr Paul Copeland, Mr Geoffrey Charles Allen, Mr Daniel Attridge
Income: £3,449,254 [2017]; £3,357,218 [2016]; £3,485,645 [2015]; £3,310,030 [2014]; £3,435,049 [2013]

St Chad's College Durham
Registered: 19 Jul 2011 *Employees:* 37 *Volunteers:* 50
Tel: 0191 334 3365 *Website:* stchads.ac.uk
Activities: Education, training; accommodation, housing; religious activities
Address: St Chads College, 18 North Bailey, Durham, DH1 3RH
Trustees: Mr Cyril Winskell, Mr Paul Geoffrey Chandler, Mr Jonathan Blackie, Mr Richard Taylor, Ms Elisabeth Rowark, Prof Howell Martyn Evans, Mr Alan Arthur Buckle, Mr John Patrick Angers, Venerable Dr Richard David Pratt, Prof Sarah Banks, Ms Susan Shaw, Mr Sean Power, Ms Jenny Haworth, Miss Elizabeth May Hoyt, Mr Craig Bateman, Dr Margaret Jane Masson
Income: £2,756,153 [2016]; £2,666,510 [2015]; £2,509,898 [2014]; £2,320,201 [2013]; £2,314,684 [2012]

St Christopher School (Letchworth) Limited
Registered: 19 Feb 1963 *Employees:* 171 *Volunteers:* 25
Tel: 01462 650904 *Website:* stchris.co.uk
Activities: Education, training
Address: St Christopher School, Barrington Road, Letchworth Garden City, Herts, SG6 3JZ
Trustees: Mr Bertie Leigh, Mr John Simmonds, Mrs Sarah Kilcoyne, Mrs Sophie Nolan, Dr Dasha Nicholls, Mr Peter McMeekin, Rabinder Singh, Mr Benjamin Walker, Mrs Emma-Kate Henry
Income: £8,554,500 [2017]; £8,326,950 [2016]; £7,780,908 [2015]; £7,174,038 [2014]; £7,120,720 [2013]

St Christopher's Fellowship
Registered: 17 Nov 1962 *Employees:* 329 *Volunteers:* 15
Tel: 020 8780 7800 *Website:* stchris.org.uk
Activities: Education, training; disability; prevention or relief of poverty; accommodation, housing; other charitable purposes
Address: St Christophers Fellowship, 1 Putney High Street, London, SW15 1SZ
Trustees: Mr Hanif Barma, Mr Bert O'Donoghue, Ms Sally O'Neill, Mr David Taylor BEng Hons MBA, Miss Angela Jennifer Anne Dakin, Dr David Brown, Mr Dinesh Visavadia, Mr Daniel Hobbs, Mr Wadham Downing BSc ACA, Mr Thomas Wilson
Income: £16,933,000 [2017]; £17,576,000 [2016]; £16,528,000 [2015]; £15,738,000 [2014]; £15,075,000 [2013]

St Christopher's Homes
Registered: 22 Sep 1962 *Employees:* 110 *Volunteers:* 27
Tel: 01604 637125 *Website:* stchristopherscofehome.co.uk
Activities: The advancement of health or saving of lives; disability; accommodation, housing; religious activities
Address: St Christophers Home, Abington Park Crescent, Northampton, NN3 3AD
Trustees: Mr Roger Keith Cobley, Mrs Elizabeth Loe, Mr Ashley Stuart Dunkley, Rev Beverley Hollins, Mr Tony Allen, Miss Gail Smith, Ms June-Elizabeth White-Smith-Gulley, Mr Stephen Vincent Billings, Mr David Earle, Mr John Kidney, Rev Phillip Ball, Mr Michael Clarke, Mr Martin Carnell, Rev Canon Anne Davis
Income: £1,872,965 [2016]; £1,797,559 [2015]; £1,797,733 [2014]; £1,714,979 [2013]; £1,706,961 [2012]

St Christopher's School (Hampstead) Limited
Registered: 12 Dec 1973 *Employees:* 41
Tel: 020 7433 6901 *Website:* stchris.co.uk
Activities: Education, training
Address: St Christophers School, 32 Belsize Lane, London, NW3 5AE
Trustees: Mr Warren Alan Finegold, Rachel Lewis, Mrs Claudia Arney, Mr Ion Dagtoglou, Liza Coutts, Mrs Sallie Christina Salvidant, Mr Nick Green, Mr James Twining, Dr Frances Ramsey, Mr Andrew Sandars
Income: £3,420,131 [2017]; £3,512,198 [2016]; £3,244,263 [2015]; £3,135,732 [2014]; £2,943,742 [2013]

St Christopher's School Trust (Epsom) Limited
Registered: 5 Oct 1965 *Employees:* 44 *Volunteers:* 3
Tel: 01372 721807 *Website:* st-christophers.surrey.sch.uk
Activities: Education, training
Address: St Christophers School, 6 Downs Road, Epsom, Surrey, KT18 5HE
Trustees: Mr Adam Goldman, Mrs Jacqueline Raggett, Mr Nigel Field, Mr Richard Harris, Mr Colin Lott, Miss Sarah Ann King, Mrs Helen Crossley, Mrs Kirsty Park
Income: £1,489,560 [2017]; £1,458,648 [2016]; £1,289,754 [2015]; £1,230,821 [2014]; £1,022,766 [2013]

St Christopher's The Hall School, Limited
Registered: 10 Apr 1963 *Employees:* 51 *Volunteers:* 15
Tel: 020 8650 2200 *Website:* stchristophersthehall.co.uk
Activities: Education, training
Address: 49 Bromley Road, Beckenham, Kent, BR3 5PA
Trustees: Dr Anne Sykes, Dr Christopher Martin, Mrs Lindsay Margaret Curtis, Rev Timothy John Hide, Mrs Tracy Sell-Peters, Mrs Claire Jane Coulson
Income: £2,447,322 [2016]; £2,335,814 [2015]; £2,221,251 [2014]; £2,093,862 [2013]; £1,992,942 [2012]

St Christophers (Glossop) Limited
Registered: 10 Jan 1967 *Employees:* 86
Tel: 01457 891072 *Website:* stchristopherstrust.org
Activities: Disability
Address: St Christophers Trust, Redcourt, Hollincross Lane, Glossop, Derbys, SK13 8JH
Trustees: Mr Anthony Wilkinson, Mrs Joan Roebuck, Mrs Tina Susan Owen, Mrs Christine Lobley
Income: £1,612,205 [2017]; £1,535,674 [2016]; £1,741,002 [2015]; £1,909,426 [2014]; £1,916,188 [2013]

St Christophers Hospice
Registered: 23 Oct 1962 *Employees:* 465 *Volunteers:* 1,200
Tel: 020 8768 4500 *Website:* stchristophers.org.uk
Activities: Education, training; advancement of health or saving of lives
Address: 51-59 Lawrie Park Road, Sydenham, London, SE26 6DZ
Trustees: Vivian Bazalgette, Dr Tyrrell George John Robert Evans, Mr Richard Raeburn, Mrs Barbara Noble, Mrs Gillian Ellen Baker, Eleanor Brown, Professor Ian Judson, Mr Morgan Lewis Jones, Mr Terrence Collis, Mr Richard Saunders, Mrs Jane Walters, Ms Joanna Mary Donaldson, Catherine McDonald
Income: £20,080,000 [2017]; £20,931,000 [2016]; £19,496,000 [2015]; £19,170,000 [2014]; £17,644,000 [2013]

St Clare West Essex Hospice Care Trust
Registered: 28 Jul 1997 *Employees:* 134 *Volunteers:* 518
Tel: 01279 773700 *Website:* stclarehospice.org.uk
Activities: The advancement of health or saving of lives
Address: St Clare Hospice, Hastingwood Road, Hastingwood, Harlow, Essex, CM17 9JX
Trustees: Mr Patrick Charles Stephen Foster, Mr Brian George Moore, Dr Ronald Frank Morgan, Mrs Jennifer Ann Minihane, Mr Graham James Randall, Mrs Wendy Ann Adams, Mr Philip Antony Quincey, Mr David Fraser Thomson, Mr David John Dunkley, Mr Andrew John Skelton, Mr Philip Thomas Birch
Income: £6,012,899 [2017]; £5,165,678 [2016]; £4,825,166 [2015]; £4,901,870 [2014]; £3,950,015 [2013]

St Clare's Hospice
Registered: 3 Dec 2014 *Employees:* 52 *Volunteers:* 181
Tel: 0191 529 7100 *Website:* stclareshospice.co.uk
Activities: The advancement of health or saving of lives
Address: St Clares Hospice, Primrose Terrace, Jarrow, Tyne & Wear, NE32 5HA
Trustees: Ms Samantha Pritchard, Mrs Carol Sara Singleton, Mr Wayham Moran, Mrs Elaine Kilgannon MBE, Mrs Janet Ridley, Mrs Kathryn Elizabeth Foley
Income: £1,814,920 [2017]; £2,023,299 [2016]

St Clement and St James Community Development Project
Registered: 12 Mar 1992 *Employees:* 26 *Volunteers:* 200
Website: clementjames.org
Activities: Education, training; prevention or relief of poverty; arts, culture, heritage, science; economic, community development, employment
Address: St Clement & St James Community Development Project, 95 Sirdar Road, London, W11 4EQ
Trustees: Mrs Sophie Lewisohn, Mrs Joanna Gardner, Mrs Belinda Davie, Mrs Vanessa Casey, Ms Katherine Soanes, Mr Manuel De Souza-Girao, Mr Setor Lassey, Revd Dr Alan Everett, Mr Julian Knott, Mr Robert Thompson, Richard Ryan
Income: £1,047,433 [2017]; £771,019 [2016]; £686,036 [2015]; £677,002 [2014]; £766,468 [2013]

St Columba's College and Preparatory School
Registered: 19 Sep 2001 *Employees:* 165 *Volunteers:* 38
Website: stcolumbascollege.org
Activities: Education, training; religious activities
Address: 42 South Drive, Warley, Brentwood, Essex, CM14 5DL
Trustees: Brother Daniel St Jacques, Mr Christopher Cleugh, Mr Robert Duigan, Mr Christian Savvides, Mrs Angela Gray, Mrs Joanne Goddard, Mr Edward Caddle, Mr Bradley Hutchinson, Mrs Jackie Harrison, Mr Stephen Watson, Brother Ivy Le Blanc, Mr Christopher Cook, Mrs Rachel McHattie, Rober Croteau, Mr Kevin McGovern
Income: £11,326,573 [2016]; £10,736,386 [2015]; £10,592,269 [2014]; £10,057,208 [2013]; £9,946,589 [2012]

St Cuthbert's Care

Registered: 28 Jul 1982 *Employees:* 331 *Volunteers:* 27
Tel: 0191 228 0111 *Website:* stcuthbertscare.org.uk
Activities: General charitable purposes; advancement of health or saving of lives; disability; prevention or relief of poverty; accommodation, housing; economic, community development, employment; other charitable purposes
Address: St Cuthberts Care, St Cuthberts House, West Road, Newcastle upon Tyne, NE15 7PY
Trustees: Miss Moira Helen Ashman, Mr Michael George Dickson, Mr Nicholas Alexander Gilbert, Rev Dermott James Donnelly, Mr John Devine, Dr Jeremiah Joseph Kelliher, Mr Paul Moran, Mrs Kathleen Urwin
Income: £10,413,452 [2017]; £9,534,909 [2016]; £9,689,204 [2015]; £9,304,250 [2014]; £8,182,430 [2013]

St Cuthbert's Hospice, Durham

Registered: 28 Jan 1988 *Employees:* 92 *Volunteers:* 480
Tel: 0191 386 1170 *Website:* stcuthbertshospice.com
Activities: The advancement of health or saving of lives
Address: Park House Road, Durham, DH1 3QF
Trustees: Mr Ian Roberts Dewhirst, Dr Angela Galloway, Mrs Janet Ann Brown, Mrs Sandra Ann Ruskin, Ms Angela Lamb, Mr Simon Paul Jefferson, Dr Patricia Anne Flanagan, Mrs Eunice Sneddon, Mr Kevin Whitfield, Mr John Graydon, Mrs Sheila Chapman, Dr James McMichael, Mrs Gillian Louise MacArthur
Income: £2,587,235 [2017]; £2,524,939 [2016]; £3,856,578 [2015]; £2,866,093 [2014]; £2,398,727 [2013]

St David's (Purley) Educational Trust Limited

Registered: 2 Oct 1962 *Employees:* 23 *Volunteers:* 5
Website: stdavidsschool.co.uk
Activities: Education, training
Address: 165 Pembroke Close, Banstead, Surrey, SM7 2BH
Trustees: Mr Douglas Brown FCA, Mr Ian Mitchell, Mrs Shirley Thompson, Mrs J Strudwick, Mrs Amanda Baxter, Mrs Ann Stranack, Mrs Kate Haden-Scott, Mr Christopher Hutchinson, Mrs Michelle Grant
Income: £1,509,485 [2017]; £1,503,126 [2016]; £1,275,247 [2015]; £1,238,746 [2014]; £1,115,579 [2013]

St David's College Trust

Registered: 27 May 1999 *Employees:* 152
Tel: 01492 876702 *Website:* stdavidscollege.co.uk
Activities: Education, training
Address: St Davids College, Gloddaeth Hall, Llandudno, Conwy, LL30 1RD
Trustees: Mr David John Rawlinson, Viscount Chelsea, Mr Robert McArthur Dunigan, Rev Keith Sinclair, Mr Paul Silvester, Lord Gregory Mostyn, Miss Charlotte Hart, Mr Timothy James Vince, Mr Robert Kenwell, Revd Dr Peter John Gaskell, Mrs Belinda Hutchinson-Smith, Mr Simon Greaves, Mrs Alice Seddon
Income: £5,739,623 [2016]; £4,625,611 [2015]; £5,155,302 [2014]; £4,941,442 [2013]; £4,708,611 [2012]

St David's Diocesan Council for Social Responsibility

Registered: 13 Sep 1965 *Employees:* 35 *Volunteers:* 200
Tel: 01267 221551 *Website:* plantdewi.org.uk
Activities: General charitable purposes; education, training; advancement of health or saving of lives; disability; prevention or relief of poverty; environment, conservation, heritage; economic, community development, employment
Address: Plant Dewi, St Davids DCSR, Dark Gate Buildings, 3 Red Street, Carmarthen, SA31 1QL
Trustees: Right Reverend Joanna Susan Penberthy, Mrs Delyth Anne Wilson, Rev Christopher Robin Lewis-Jenkins, Mrs Cynthia Lawrence, Rev Nicola Rachel Skipworth
Income: £1,032,432 [2017]; £1,115,277 [2016]; £962,707 [2015]; £897,656 [2014]; £841,376 [2013]

St David's Foundation Hospice Care

Registered: 21 Apr 1992 *Employees:* 273 *Volunteers:* 500
Tel: 01633 851051 *Website:* stdavidshospicecare.org
Activities: Education, training; advancement of health or saving of lives
Address: St Davids Hospice Care, Blackett Avenue, Newport, NP20 6NH
Trustees: Mr Michael Hine, Mrs Patricia Ann White MBE, Dr Christopher Charles Gaffney, Mrs Penny Davies, Mrs Judith Elizabeth Child, Mrs Margaret Van De Weyer, Mr Jeremy Llewellyn Morgan Felvus, Mr Simon Hugh Patrick Boyle, Dr John William Holland, Rev Elaine Hills, Mr James Osborne Thompson, Mr Malgwyn Davies, Dame Rosemary Janet Mair Butler DBE
Income: £11,860,000 [2017]; £8,700,000 [2016]; £7,691,000 [2015]; £7,376,000 [2014]; £6,058,708 [2013]

St David's Home for Disabled Soldiers, Sailors and Airmen

Registered: 19 Jun 1963 *Employees:* 120 *Volunteers:* 6
Tel: 020 8997 5121 *Website:* stdavidshome.org
Activities: The advancement of health or saving of lives; disability
Address: 12 Castlebar Hill, Ealing, London, W5 1TD
Trustees: Miss Elizabeth Sunley, Rev Timothy Charles Richard Hutton, Mr David Searle, Mr David James Hayward, Rev Martin Shipperlee OSB, Mr Philip James Young, Mr Mark Turner Col
Income: £4,017,089 [2017]; £3,859,166 [2016]; £3,301,907 [2015]; £3,284,692 [2014]; £3,041,135 [2013]

St Davids Diocesan Board of Finance

Registered: 19 Mar 1961 *Employees:* 6
Website: stdavidsdiocese.org.uk
Activities: Education, training; accommodation, housing; religious activities
Address: The Vicarage, Water Street, Ferryside, Carmarthenshire, SA17 5RT
Trustees: Mr Nicholas Griffin, The Venerable Dr William Anthony Strange, Mrs Jane Heard, Revd Canon Paul Mackness, Venerable Dorrien Paul Davies, Mr Nigel Roberts, Revd Ainsley Griffiths, Mrs Teresa Alice Hatfield, Mrs Judith Anne Prior Hayward, Mrs Hazel Evans, Mr Anthony Jenkins, Rt Revd Joanna Susan Penberthy, Revd Canon Brian Witt, Mr Daniel Gurnos Jones, Rev Mounes Anton Farah, Rev Christopher Charles Brown, Mr Nigel Evans, Mr David William James Thomas
Income: £5,558,049 [2016]; £5,749,566 [2015]; £5,634,649 [2014]; £5,899,856 [2013]; £5,761,294 [2012]

St Dominic's Priory School (Stone)

Registered: 5 Apr 2011 *Employees:* 42
Tel: 01785 814181 *Website:* stdominicspriory.co.uk
Activities: Education, training
Address: St Dominics Priory School, 21 Station Road, Stone, Staffs, ST15 8EN
Trustees: Mr Martin Richard Melling, Mrs Amy Glover, Mr Mark Christopher Burton, Miss Ellie Cosgrove, Mrs Karen Champ, Catharine Diana Gill, Mrs Georgina Brian, Mr Martyn Corfield
Income: £2,030,483 [2016]; £3,571,470 [2015]; £1,768,179 [2014]; £1,512,581 [2013]; £1,558,529 [2012]

St Dunstan's Educational Foundation

Registered: 20 Feb 1963 *Employees:* 173 *Volunteers:* 1
Website: stdunstans.org.uk
Activities: Education, training
Address: St Dunstans College, Stanstead Road, London, SE6 4TY
Trustees: Mr Peter Coling, Mr Nicholas Lyons, Mrs Victoria Alexander, Mr Ken Marshall, Mr Ian Davenport, Mr Paul Durgan, Miss Di Robertshaw, Mr Navdeep Sheera, Ms Judy Clements OBE, Mrs Linda Kiernan, Professor Paul Leonard, Dr Yvonne Burne OBE JP, Mr David Probert, Mr Shams Rahman, Mrs Shahnaz Ahmed
Income: £13,770,677 [2017]; £13,081,547 [2016]; £12,026,953 [2015]; £11,414,702 [2014]; £10,825,627 [2013]

St Edmund Hall in the University of Oxford

Registered: 13 Aug 2010 *Employees:* 123
Website: seh.ox.ac.uk
Activities: Education, training
Address: St Edmund Hall, Queens Lane, Oxford, OX1 4AR
Trustees: Prof Stuart John Ferguson, Dr Karma Nabulsi, Prof Adrian Briggs, Prof Keith Gull, Prof Andrew Kahn, Prof David Eusthatios Manolopoulos, Prof Philipp Podsiadlowski, Prof Oliver Riordan, Dr Dimitrios Tsomocos, Dr Robert Wilkins, Dr Jonathan Robert Yates, Dr Amy Zavatsky, Dr Richard Willden, Prof Gordon Clark, Professor Ian Douglas Pavord DM FRCP, Dr Climent Quintana-Domeque, Prof Peter Bruce, Professor Heidi Johansen-Berg, Dr Mauro Pasta, Dr Michael Gill, Mr David Bannerman, Prof N E Cronk, Mr Simon Costa, Mr Nicholas Davidson, Prof Paul Johnson, Dr Aileen Kavanagh, Prof Philip Mountford, Dr David Priestland, Dr Jeffrey Tseng, Prof Robert Whittaker, Dr Christopher Wesley Charles Williams, Dr Linda Yueh, Dr Richard Thomas Walker, Dr Roger Benson, Dr Jason Matthew Gaiger, Professor Peter Malcolm Rothwell MA MBChB MD PhD FRCP FMedSci, Dr Luc Le Nguyen, Professor Paul James Goulart, Professor Henrike Laehnemann, Dr Erica McAlpine, Leslie Ann Goldberg
Income: £9,937,000 [2017]; £11,139,000 [2016]; £12,771,843 [2015]; £8,549,181 [2014]; £9,155,721 [2013]

St Edmund's College in the University of Cambridge

Registered: 12 Aug 2010 *Employees:* 50 *Volunteers:* 1
Website: st-edmunds.cam.ac.uk
Activities: Education, training
Address: St Edmund's College, Cambridge, CB3 0BN
Trustees: Ms Edna Murphy, Prof Michael Edward Herrtage, Father Alban McCoy Fr, Dr Folma Buss, Dr Philip McCosker, Dr Ann Kaminski, Mr Matthew Bullock, Dr Judith Collis, Mr Gordon Chesterman, Dr Katharina Brett, Dr Suzanne Paul, Dr Antonina Kruppa
Income: £5,285,000 [2017]; £5,010,000 [2016]; £5,300,057 [2015]; £5,362,502 [2014]; £5,130,838 [2013]

St Edmund's College

Registered: 3 Nov 1969 *Employees:* 195 *Volunteers:* 32
Tel: 01920 824201 *Website:* stedmundscollege.org
Activities: Education, training
Address: St Edmunds College, Old Hall Green, Ware, Herts, SG11 1DS
Trustees: Mr Patrick John Mitton MSc, Mr Neville Ransley, Mrs Madeline Roberts, Mrs Jane Emma Ranzetta, Dr Frances Macintosh, Mr John Malcolm Cornelius Bryant BA, Rev Alban McCoy OFM Conv BA MLitt, Dr Stephen Grounds BSc DPhil PGCE
Income: £15,420,107 [2016]; £12,825,451 [2015]; £13,156,379 [2014]; £12,546,337 [2013]; £11,584,082 [2012]

St Edmund's School Canterbury

Registered: 25 Jun 1996 *Employees:* 144
Website: stedmunds.org.uk
Activities: Education, training
Address: Corondale, Preston Hill, Wingham, Canterbury, Kent, CT3 1BY
Trustees: Mr Michael Charles William Terry, Mr Quentin Leonard Roper MA NPQH, Mr Christopher Harbridge, Mrs Nichola Jane Leatherbarrow, Air Marshal Christopher Mark Nickols CB CBE MA FRAeS, Mr Philip St John-Stevens, Dr Phillip Eichorn, Mr Patrick Anthony Todd, Dr Louise Naylor BSc PhD, Mr Steve Maxwell Sutton BA FCA, Dr Margaret Rosamond Carnegie MBBS
Income: £10,568,636 [2017]; £9,702,280 [2016]; £9,305,215 [2015]; £9,119,348 [2014]; £8,537,649 [2013]

St Edmund's School Trust Limited

Registered: 6 Aug 1979 *Employees:* 89 *Volunteers:* 6
Website: saintedmunds.co.uk
Activities: Education, training
Address: 3 Wildacres, West Byfleet, Surrey, KT14 6PT
Trustees: Mr Bryan Eyre Farley, Mr Nigel William Kaula, Mr Gareth Doodes, Miss Isobel Victoria Maier, Mrs Jacqueline Anne Alliss, Mr Peter Richard Clutterbuck, Dr Toby Giles Anderson Griffiths, Mr Luke Gerald Michael
Income: £4,850,826 [2017]; £3,850,297 [2016]; £3,262,775 [2015]; £2,861,595 [2014]; £2,493,552 [2013]

St Edmundsbury and Ipswich Diocesan Board of Finance

Registered: 8 Sep 1966 *Employees:* 39 *Volunteers:* 207
Website: cofesuffolk.org
Activities: Education, training; religious activities
Address: Diocese of St Edmundsbury & Ipswich, 4 Cutler Street, Ipswich, Suffolk, IP1 1UQ
Trustees: Rev Malcolm Eric Osborne, Canon M Wilde, Mr Anthony Robert Allwood, Mr David Lamming, The Revd Sharon Jane Potter, Mr Stephen West, The Revd Canon C A Collins, Mark Pendlington, The Right Revd Dr Mike Harrison, The Ven Dr D H Jenkins, The Venerable Idj Morgan, Canon T E Allen, Rev Jonathan Laurence Alderton-Ford, Mrs Margaret Condick, Mr Ian Wigston, The Rt Revd Martin Alan Seeley
Income: £8,681,000 [2016]; £8,074,000 [2015]; £7,972,000 [2014]; £8,257,000 [2013]; £8,012,000 [2012]

St Edward's School Cheltenham Trust
Registered: 30 Jan 1986 *Employees:* 156 *Volunteers:* 3
Tel: 01242 538620 *Website:* stedwards.co.uk
Activities: Education, training
Address: St Edwards School, Cirencester Road, Charlton Kings, Cheltenham, Glos, GL53 8EY
Trustees: Dr Sarah Jane Welch, Mrs Elizabeth Turner, Dr Susan Honeywill, Mr Andrew Newland, Mr Christopher Roy Pearson, Mr Peter Goatley, Mrs Caroline Findlay, Mr Paul Potts, Mr Ray McGrath, Mrs Gillian Margaret Greenwell
Income: £6,522,000 [2017]; £6,634,000 [2016]; £7,136,000 [2015]; £7,001,000 [2014]; £7,105,000 [2013]

St Edward's School
Registered: 23 Dec 2014 *Employees:* 76
Tel: 01794 885252 *Website:* st-edwards.hants.sch.uk
Activities: Education, training
Address: St Edwards School, Melchet Court, Sherfield English, Romsey, Hants, SO51 6ZR
Trustees: Nick Vaughan, Carole Healy, Liam Taylor, Sylvia Peach, Rev C Pettet, Mr M H Tennant, Bernadette Cherry, Mr Robin Digby Bruce-Gardner BA ACIB, Jon Livingstone
Income: £3,299,891 [2017]; £6,841,455 [2016]

St Edward's School
Registered: 7 Mar 1963 *Employees:* 471 *Volunteers:* 131
Tel: 01865 319321 *Website:* stedwardsoxford.org
Activities: Education, training; arts, culture, heritage, science
Address: St Edwards School, Woodstock Road, Oxford, OX2 7NN
Trustees: Mr Michael Paul Stanfield, Dr Alexandra Holloway, Mr George Richard Ian Fenton, Mr Kenneth MacRitchie, Mr David Jackson, Rev Martyn William Percy, Mrs Georgina Arabella Sarah Dennis, Dr Clare Robertson, Mr Edward Wilfrid Stephenson, Mr Chris Jones, Dr Jo Peach, Dr Louise L'estrange Fawcett Posada, Mr Michael Roulston, Mrs Carloine Mary Baggs, Mr Oliver Anthony Cochrane Watson
Income: £21,797,000 [2017]; £21,480,000 [2016]; £20,321,733 [2015]; £19,459,010 [2014]; £18,130,194 [2013]

St Elizabeth Hospice (Suffolk)
Registered: 1 May 1984 *Employees:* 210 *Volunteers:* 1,200
Tel: 01473 707023 *Website:* stelizabethhospice.org.uk
Activities: Education, training; advancement of health or saving of lives; disability
Address: St Elizabeth Hospice, 565 Foxhall Road, Ipswich, Suffolk, IP3 8LX
Trustees: Mr Terence Hunt, Mr William David Barnes, Mr Paul Woodward, Mrs Cynthia Conquest, Mrs Ann Hogarth, Mrs Elizabeth Lauderdale Wellesley Wesley, Mr Mark William Nicholls, Dr Nigel Gibbons, Mrs Grainne Drummond, Mr Ian Turner, Mr Michael David Cooper, Dr Anthony David Joseph Nicholl
Income: £9,550,412 [2017]; £9,005,218 [2016]; £8,511,388 [2015]; £9,104,525 [2014]; £7,191,544 [2013]

St Francis' Children's Society
Registered: 3 Nov 1962 *Employees:* 21 *Volunteers:* 23
Tel: 01908 572700 *Website:* sfcs.org.uk
Activities: General charitable purposes
Address: St Francis Childrens Society, Collis House, 48 Newport Road, Woolstone, Milton Keynes, Bucks, MK15 0AA
Trustees: John Wallace, Kate Graves, Miss Kim Opszala, Mrs Safia Boot, Mrs Carol Elaine Jarvis, Mrs Anna Christina Saunders, Mrs Sheena Gail Marsh
Income: £1,259,373 [2017]; £1,268,024 [2016]; £1,248,442 [2015]; £1,243,371 [2014]; £1,399,225 [2013]

St Francis' College Trust
Registered: 24 Jul 1983 *Employees:* 116
Website: st-francis.herts.sch.uk
Activities: Education, training
Address: St Francis' College, Broadway, Letchworth Garden City, Herts, SG6 3PJ
Trustees: Mr John Procter, Mr Clive Gilbert Nott, Mrs Priscilla Barlow, Dr Victoria McNicholas, Professor Della Freeth, Mrs Sarah Jane Styles, Mr Martin John Dingemans, Mrs Susan Boardman, Miss Eileen Ismay, Mr Alan Goodwin, Mr George Ritchie, Dr Suzanne Margaret Richardson, Mr Jonathan William James Mitchell
Income: £6,072,561 [2017]; £5,756,438 [2016]; £6,113,707 [2015]; £6,171,600 [2014]; £5,395,475 [2013]

The St Gabriel Schools Foundation
Registered: 9 Jun 1997 *Employees:* 154 *Volunteers:* 9
Tel: 01635 555680 *Website:* stgabriels.co.uk
Activities: Education, training
Address: St Gabriels School, Sandleford Priory, Newtown Road, Newtown, Newbury, Berks, RG20 9BD
Trustees: Mr Michael William Scholl, Mrs Sarah Anne Bowen, Mr Sean Ryan, Rev John Toogood, Mrs Joanne Heywood, Mr Nigel Charles Garland, Mr Simon Ralph Barrett, Mr Derek Peaple, Mrs Jane Whitehead, Mrs Sarah Victoria Hutton
Income: £6,476,423 [2017]; £6,457,751 [2016]; £5,877,628 [2015]; £5,590,152 [2014]; £5,789,709 [2013]

St Gemma's Hospice
Registered: 23 Dec 1992 *Employees:* 212 *Volunteers:* 850
Tel: 0113 218 5521 *Website:* st-gemma.co.uk
Activities: Education, training; advancement of health or saving of lives; disability
Address: St Gemmas Hospice, 329 Harrogate Road, Moortown, Leeds, LS17 6QD
Trustees: Mrs Kuldeep Bajwa, Mrs June Toovey, Sr Eileen Fucito, Mr Angus Martin, Sr Therese O'Regan, Sr Anne Hammersley, Mrs Hilary Barrett, Professor Julia Newton-Bishop, Dr Peter Belfield, Dr Elizabeth Carmody, Ms Susan Ansbro, Ms Debra Fairley, Sr Carmel Gorman, Sr Savio Steed, Mr Christopher Schofield
Income: £9,375,866 [2017]; £9,518,055 [2016]; £9,662,572 [2015]; £9,682,073 [2014]; £9,273,132 [2013]

St George's - Augustinian Care
Registered: 10 Sep 2004 *Employees:* 3
Tel: 01444 235874
Activities: The advancement of health or saving of lives
Address: The Lodge Administration Building, St George's Park, Ditchling Common, Burgess Hill, W Sussex, RH15 0SF
Trustees: Sr Thomas, Sr Mary Clement, Sr Mary Stephen, Sister Mary Luke
Income: £17,022,796 [2016]; £7,727 [2013]; £5,680,454 [2012]

St George's Bristol
Registered: 28 Oct 1986 *Employees:* 44 *Volunteers:* 100
Tel: 0117 929 4929 *Website:* stgeorgesbristol.co.uk
Activities: Education, training; arts, culture, heritage, science
Address: Great George Street, Bristol, BS1 5RR
Trustees: Dr Marie-Annick Gournet, Mrs Sandra Teresa Foxall-Smith, Mr Richard Bacon, Dr John Manley, Mrs Caroline Hagen, Mrs Jennifer Ann Hemming, Mr Robert Boardley Suttie, Mr Ben Heald, Prof Nicholas Andrew John Lieven, Mr Robert O'Leary
Income: £2,345,000 [2017]; £1,610,000 [2016]; £2,267,000 [2015]; £1,308,000 [2013]; £2,965,000 [2012]

St George's Crypt
Registered: 28 Oct 2011 *Employees:* 77 *Volunteers:* 125
Tel: 0113 245 9061 *Website:* stgeorgescrypt.org.uk
Activities: General charitable purposes; education, training; disability; prevention or relief of poverty; accommodation, housing; religious activities; economic, community development, employment
Address: St Georges Crypt, Great George Street, Leeds, LS1 3BR
Trustees: Rt Hon John Battle, Dr Nicholas Bishop, Mrs Ann Marie Broadhead, Ms Tracey Greig, Ian Pickup, Ms Jane Elizabeth Cooper, Paul Ayers, Mr Duncan Milwain, Mr Christopher Stuart Burford, Peter Gillions, Revd Elizabeth Woolf
Income: £2,107,541 [2017]; £2,153,081 [2016]; £1,832,143 [2015]; £1,749,783 [2014]; £1,641,976 [2013]

St George's Lupset Ltd
Registered: 24 Oct 2002 *Employees:* 70 *Volunteers:* 32
Tel: 01924 369631 *Website:* stgeorgeslupset.org.uk
Activities: Education, training; advancement of health or saving of lives; economic, community development, employment
Address: St Georges Community Project, Broadway, Lupset, Wakefield, W Yorks, WF2 8AA
Trustees: Mrs Ann Elizabeth Tosta, Mr Mike Holt, Mr Edward Joseph Woodhouse, Mrs Judith Colquhoun, Mrs Sandra Elliott, Mrs Freda Jackson, Mr Michael Tattersall, Viv Hughes, Mr Christopher Peter Marsden Brown, Mrs Jane Irvine Mc Gill
Income: £1,163,895 [2017]; £1,098,166 [2016]; £1,054,309 [2015]; £916,571 [2014]; £656,349 [2013]

St George's School Ascot Trust Limited
Registered: 3 Apr 1968 *Employees:* 137
Website: stgeorges-ascot.org.uk
Activities: Education, training
Address: St Georges School, Wells Lane, Ascot, Berks, SL5 7DZ
Trustees: Mr Peter James, Mr Gerald William Priestman Barber, Mr Andrew Miles BSc, Mrs Deirdre Brown MBE, Mr Paul Sedgwick, Dr James Gibbons, Mrs Anna Laurie-Walker, Mr Edward Luker, Mr Alistair Mackintosh, Mrs Ruth Niven-Hirst, Ms Amanda Triccas
Income: £6,664,493 [2017]; £7,051,395 [2016]; £6,652,067 [2015]; £6,426,158 [2014]; £7,372,414 [2013]

St George's School Windsor Castle
Registered: 29 Oct 2003 *Employees:* 86 *Volunteers:* 2
Tel: 01753 836548 *Website:* stgwindsor.org
Activities: Education, training
Address: St Georges School, Windsor Castle, Windsor, Berks, SL4 1QF
Trustees: The Rt Revd David Conner KCVO, Mrs Helen Victoria Sandom, Canon Dr Mark Powell, Mr Stephen Charles Ion Jones, Mr Stephen MacKenzie, Mr Guy Martin Stanford, The Reverend Canon Dr Hueston Edward Finlay, Rev Martin George Poll, Mrs Julie Cornell, Mrs Barbara Ann Salisbury
Income: £4,410,177 [2017]; £4,243,344 [2016]; £3,765,298 [2015]; £4,176,397 [2014]; £4,116,147 [2013]

St George's School, Edgbaston
Registered: 1 Mar 2000 *Employees:* 130
Tel: 0121 625 0398 *Website:* sgse.co.uk
Activities: Education, training
Address: 31 Calthorpe Road, Edgbaston, Birmingham, B15 1RX
Trustees: Mr Barry Kicks, Sir Robert Dowling, Ed Smedmore, Mr Kishen Hawkins, Surinder Dhillon
Income: £5,038,087 [2016]; £4,750,807 [2015]; £5,020,948 [2014]; £4,797,856 [2013]; £3,980,350 [2012]

St George's Weybridge
Registered: 1 Mar 1993 *Employees:* 390 *Volunteers:* 70
Tel: 01932 839312 *Website:* stgeorgesweybridge.com
Activities: Education, training
Address: St Georges College, Weybridge Road, Addlestone, Surrey, KT15 2QS
Trustees: Rev Muir, Mr David Bicarregui, Mrs Diane Lesley Ewart, Professor Ann Helen Muggeridge, Mrs Catherine Isabella McCormick, Mr Charles Stanley William Prescott, Mrs Sarah Helen Conrad, Mr Christopher Trevor Peter Jansen, Mr Michael Davie, Mr John Michael Lewin, Mr David Anderson, Mrs Karen Lacovara Patterson, Mr Jason Hood
Income: £25,412,258 [2017]; £25,132,692 [2016]; £22,617,206 [2015]; £21,922,271 [2014]; £20,775,477 [2013]

St Gerard's School Trust
Registered: 10 Dec 1990 *Employees:* 33
Tel: 01248 351656 *Website:* st-gerards.org
Activities: Education, training; religious activities
Address: Ffriddoedd Road, Bangor, Gwynedd, LL57 2EL
Trustees: Mrs Angela Jane Pethig, Miss Catherine Beighton, Mr Dominic Breslin, Mrs Karen Elizabeth Fairburn, Brian Pigott, Dr Patsy Thomas, Mr Alalstair Chinery, Mr Michael Robert Jones, Mrs Wendy Eastwood, Mrs Maureen Benson
Income: £1,377,356 [2017]; £1,352,326 [2016]; £1,484,845 [2015]; £1,488,110 [2014]; £1,573,570 [2013]

St Giles Hospice
Registered: 25 Jul 1979 *Employees:* 454 *Volunteers:* 1,151
Tel: 01543 434537 *Website:* stgileshospice.com
Activities: Education, training; advancement of health or saving of lives
Address: St Giles Hospice, Fisherwick Road, Lichfield, Staffs, WS14 9LH
Trustees: Doctor Robert Maxwell Horton, Mr Charles William Theaker, Alison Fowler, Ms Lindsey Williams, Margaret Wood, Mr Robert Andrew Donald, Mr Adrian Charles Thompson, Simon Fisher, Mrs Joanne Maidment BA Hons JP, Mr Stephen John Ridler, Mrs Bernadette Creaven
Income: £14,420,309 [2017]; £12,940,870 [2016]; £13,646,894 [2015]; £13,350,843 [2014]; £12,383,480 [2013]

St Giles Trust
Registered: 2 May 1989 *Employees:* 188 *Volunteers:* 100
Tel: 020 7703 7000 *Website:* stgilestrust.org.uk
Activities: Education, training; prevention or relief of poverty; accommodation, housing
Address: St Giles Trust, Georgian House, 64-68 Camberwell Church Street, London, SE5 8JB
Trustees: Peter Little, Mrs Denise Nichola Jagger, Mr David Jonathan Pinto-Duschinsky, Mr Charles Hugh Pitts-Tucker, Alfy Hayson, Mr Duncan Alastair Gibson, Mr Steve Bending, Mr Gary Jones, Mr Philip Martin Wheatley, Ms Julie Rice, Monica Ali, Mr Terence Learmouth, Miss Philippa Cara Murray
Income: £7,933,663 [2017]; £8,532,012 [2016]; £7,602,947 [2015]; £7,792,915 [2014]; £5,413,129 [2013]

St Helen's School, Northwood
Registered: 21 Mar 1963 *Employees:* 310
Tel: 01923 843220 *Website:* sthelens.london
Activities: Education, training
Address: St Helens School, Eastbury Road, Northwood, Middlesex, HA6 3AS
Trustees: Mrs Monica Bhandari, Mrs Michelle Weerasekera, Dr Susan Pitts, Mr Nadeem Boghani, Mrs Phillipspon Alison, Ms Suzi Woolfson, Ms Puneeta Mongia, Mr Vivek Sapra, Mrs Elizabeth Radice, Dr Sara R Gordon
Income: £17,252,000 [2016]; £16,420,000 [2015]; £15,707,000 [2014]; £14,715,000 [2013]; £14,139,000 [2012]

St Helena Hospice Limited
Registered: 22 Oct 1980 *Employees:* 336 *Volunteers:* 1,200
Tel: 01206 845566 *Website:* sthelenahospice.org.uk
Activities: Education, training; advancement of health or saving of lives; disability
Address: St Helena Hospice, Barncroft Close, Highwoods, Colchester, Essex, CO4 9JU
Trustees: Andrew Dickerson, Mrs Margaret Mary Sparke, Roger Sirman, Mr Kenneth John Aldred, Mr Kenneth Nigel Rolls, Mr Clive Bull, Ms Mary Northrop, Dr Sarah Maan, Dr Milne, Prof Vergo, John Hawkins, Mrs Tracey Dickens, Mr David Cresswell, Dr Joshua Arkley, Mr Gerry Mordaunt
Income: £12,459,041 [2017]; £12,065,280 [2016]; £10,926,440 [2015]; £9,092,127 [2014]; £7,062,222 [2013]

St Helens Carers Centre
Registered: 5 Dec 2001 *Employees:* 43 *Volunteers:* 5
Tel: 01744 675615 *Website:* sthelenscarers.org.uk
Activities: General charitable purposes; education, training; disability; prevention or relief of poverty
Address: 31-35 Baldwin Street, St Helens, Merseyside, WA10 2RS
Trustees: Mrs Jane Dearden, Mrs Alma Sisson, Mrs Joyce Wilcock, Mrs Sheila Whalley, Canon Geoffrey Almond, Mrs Theresa Ann Butler
Income: £1,286,936 [2017]; £1,349,248 [2016]; £1,278,904 [2015]; £1,189,509 [2014]; £1,057,793 [2013]

St Helens and Knowsley Caring Association
Registered: 8 Dec 1988 *Employees:* 90
Tel: 0151 480 5505 *Website:* stbartholomewscourt.co.uk
Activities: General charitable purposes; advancement of health or saving of lives; disability; accommodation, housing
Address: St Helens & Knowsley Caring Association, St Bartholomews Court, Woodfield Road, Huyton, Liverpool, L36 4PJ
Trustees: Mr John Yearsley, Ms Beverley Ann Handley, Mr James Michael Peter Scragg, Mr Mark Worden, Dr Joyce Abrams, Mrs Natalie Jane Myers, Mr Martin Twist
Income: £1,921,993 [2017]; £1,816,916 [2016]; £1,792,946 [2015]; £1,787,261 [2014]; £1,764,371 [2013]

St Hilary's School Trust Limited
Registered: 20 Jan 1966 *Employees:* 55
Website: sthilarysschool.com
Activities: Education, training
Address: 9 Oxford Avenue, London, SW20 8LS
Trustees: Mrs Veronica Powell, Mr Richard Thompson Chairperson, Mrs Jane Elizabeth Alldritt, Mrs Sue Sims, Mrs Jackie Nickson, Mr Ken Ratcliff, Miss Fiona McNair Reid, Mr Francis John Sullivan, Mr Simon Allen, Dr Claire McShane
Income: £2,711,122 [2017]; £2,659,822 [2016]; £2,525,940 [2015]; £2,260,888 [2014]; £2,193,119 [2013]

St Hilda's College in the University of Oxford
Registered: 17 Aug 2010 *Employees:* 115
Tel: 01865 276815 *Website:* st-hildas.ox.ac.uk
Activities: Education, training
Address: Cowley Place, Oxford, OX4 1DY
Trustees: Dr Anita Avramides, Professor Julia Mary Yeomans MA DPhil, Dr Helen Jane Swift, Dr Rebecca Margaret Armstrong, Ms Maria Frances Jane Croghan, Dr Maike Glitsch, Professor Susan Jones, Professor Irene Margaret Moroz, Dr Petra Schleiter, Dr Hannah Elizabeth Smith, Ms Bronwyn Milner Travers, Professor Julia Alison Noble, Dr Stephen Benedict McHugh, Dr Rachel Condry, Dr Elinor Payne, Dr Dev Gangjee, Professor Sir Gordon Duff FRCP FMedSci FRSE, Dr Jane Barlow, Dr Daniel Peter Bulte, Dr Sarah Jane Norman, Prof Amanda Margaret Cooper Sarker, Professor Fiona Macintosh, Professor Selina Todd, Dr Katherine Jane Clarke, Dr Dmitry Filatov, Dr Kerstin Hoge, Dr Margaret Kean, Dr Georgina Louise Brentnall Paul, Prof Grigory Alexander Seregin, Dr Lorna Joyce Smith, Dr David Alastair Howey, Dr Robert Scott Paton, Professor Daniel Leslie Wakelin, Dr Aris Katzourakis, Dr Philippa Anne Hulley, Mr Frank Gargent, Professor John Santercole Gibbons, Dr Catherine Elizabeth Swales, Dr Lorraine Wild, Dr Anders Bredahl Kock
Income: £10,494,000 [2017]; £10,338,000 [2016]; £11,558,000 [2015]; £10,768,000 [2014]; £7,540,000 [2013]

St Hilda's East
Registered: 31 Oct 1962 *Employees:* 54 *Volunteers:* 247
Tel: 020 7739 8066 *Website:* sthildas.org.uk
Activities: Education, training; prevention or relief of poverty
Address: St Hildas East Community Centre, 18 Club Row, London, E2 7EY
Trustees: Dennis Twomey, Mrs Suzette Barry, Ms Nandini Basuthakur, Ms Arifa Akhtar Choudhury, Jean Locker, Ms Alison Klarfeld, Ms Harriet Edwards, Ms Fawziyah Rahman
Income: £1,703,184 [2017]; £1,764,977 [2016]; £1,825,123 [2015]; £1,903,247 [2014]; £1,941,848 [2013]

St Hugh's School (Carswell) Trust Limited
Registered: 30 Oct 1967 *Employees:* 99
Tel: 01367 870705 *Website:* st-hughs.co.uk
Activities: Education, training
Address: St Hughs School, Carswell Manor, Carswell, Faringdon, Oxon, SN7 8PT
Trustees: Mrs Judy Forrest, Mr James Montague Guillum Scott, Mr Paul Daffern, Mr Peter Chambers, Mr Christopher Davies, Graham James Varney, Mr Antony Clark, Mr Peter Frank Boggis, Mr Ted Sandbach, Mr Andrew Ashton, Mrs Anna Coull, Mrs Virginia Gill
Income: £5,686,195 [2017]; £5,206,701 [2016]; £4,957,189 [2015]; £4,687,610 [2014]; £4,620,280 [2013]

St Hugh's School (Woodhall Spa) Limited
Registered: 10 Jul 1964 *Employees:* 61 *Volunteers:* 3
Tel: 01526 352169 *Website:* st-hughs.lincs.sch.uk
Activities: Education, training
Address: St Hughs School, Cromwell Avenue, Woodhall Spa, Lincs, LN10 6TQ
Trustees: Mrs Louise Reynolds, Mr Lionel Mason, Mr Sam Dewhurst, Mr Thomas Bogg, Mrs Cathy Twigg, Mr Jonathan Merritt, Mr Simon Herring, Mr Richard Bussell, Mr John Harris
Income: £1,979,938 [2017]; £2,016,996 [2016]; £1,990,444 [2015]; £2,021,594 [2014]; £2,222,246 [2013]

St James' School Grimsby Ltd
Registered: 19 Aug 2003 *Employees:* 73 *Volunteers:* 6
Tel: 01472 503260 *Website:* saintjamesschool.co.uk
Activities: Education, training
Address: St James School, 22 Bargate, Grimsby, N E Lincs, DN34 4SY
Trustees: Mrs Rachael Lea Haith, Mr Paul Lynch, Mr Ian Richard Sanderson, Mr Robert Donald England, Mr David Charles Palmer, Mrs Judith Bass, Mr John H Pridgeon, Mr Jeremy Miles Woolner, Mr B G Hannington, Mr Andrew Major, Mr Andrew Whitworth, Mr James Lockwood, Mr John James Marron Shaw, Mr Alexander Easton Baxter, Mr Thomas Graeme Rook
Income: £2,053,306 [2017]; £2,102,710 [2016]; £1,909,366 [2015]; £1,676,378 [2014]; £1,753,896 [2013]

St John's Approved Premises
Registered: 20 May 2009 *Employees:* 33 *Volunteers:* 2
Tel: 0113 275 5702 *Website:* stjohnsap.co.uk
Activities: Education, training; advancement of health or saving of lives; accommodation, housing; other charitable purposes
Address: St John's Approved Premises, 263 Hyde Park Road, Leeds, LS6 1AG
Trustees: Mr John Grainger, Mr Terence Anthony Conneely, Mr Neville Thompson, Mr Mark Davison, Mr Manuel Joaquin Montoro-Blanch, Mr Colin George Spiller, Mr James Richard Johnson
Income: £1,123,861 [2017]; £883,560 [2016]; £730,791 [2015]; £707,473 [2014]; £649,291 [2013]

St John's Catholic School for The Deaf
Registered: 21 May 1964 *Employees:* 62
Tel: 01937 842144 *Website:* stjohns.org.uk
Activities: Education, training
Address: St Johns Catholic School for The Deaf, Church Street, Boston Spa, Wetherby, W Yorks, LS23 6DF
Trustees: Diocese of Leeds Trustee
Income: £3,555,520 [2016]; £2,696,405 [2015]; £2,800,972 [2014]; £2,700,732 [2013]; £2,973,950 [2012]

St John's College Cambridge
Registered: 11 Aug 2010 *Employees:* 468
Tel: 01223 338600 *Website:* joh.cam.ac.uk
Activities: Education, training
Address: St Johns College, Cambridge, CB2 1TP
Trustees: Miss Tomaselli, Professor Dobson, Dr Gowers, Professor Tombs, Professor Burton, Dr Robinson, Professor Ni Mhaonaigh, Dr Salmon, Mr Ewbank, Dr Watson, Dr Hynes, Professor Simons, Mr Teal
Income: £38,262,000 [2017]; £33,868,000 [2016]; £32,403,000 [2015]; £29,554,000 [2014]; £31,794,000 [2013]

St John's College Limited
Registered: 3 May 1989 *Employees:* 116
Tel: 029 2077 8936 *Website:* stjohnscollegecardiff.com
Activities: Education, training; religious activities; arts, culture, heritage, science; amateur sport
Address: St Johns College, Newport Road, St Mellons, Cardiff, CF3 5YX
Trustees: Mr John Charles Rees QC, Mrs P Jayne Smerald, Mrs Samantha Jane Dimond, Mr Michael Joseph Prior, Mr Simon Henry James
Income: £5,410,749 [2017]; £5,159,559 [2016]; £4,710,689 [2015]; £4,482,691 [2014]; £4,486,973 [2013]

St John's College Nottingham Limited
Registered: 1 Oct 1993 *Employees:* 24 *Volunteers:* 1
Tel: 0115 968 3206 *Website:* stjohns-nottm.ac.uk
Activities: Education, training; religious activities
Address: St Johns College, Chilwell Lane, Bramcote, Nottingham, NG9 3DS
Trustees: The Ven David Newman, Mr Colin Slater MBE, Rev Rachel Phillips, Mr Christopher John Addison Smith, Mr Philip David Carver, Rev Dr David Henry Hilborn, Ven Malcolm Chamberlain, Rev Gill Ruth Turner-Callis, Mr Peter Ellis, The Rt Revd Pete Broadbent, Rev Dr Sally Ann Nash, The Venerable David Picken, Mrs Susan Witts, Prof Alison Rodger, Rev Amanda Lees
Income: £1,020,780 [2016]; £1,589,980 [2015]; £1,733,059 [2014]; £1,696,874 [2013]; £1,906,500 [2012]

St John's College, Durham
Registered: 4 May 2011 *Employees:* 67
Tel: 0191 384 1740 *Website:* dur.ac.uk
Activities: Education, training
Address: 49 The Avenue, Durham, DH1 4ED
Trustees: Mr Ian Richard Harris, Mrs Margaret Sentamu, Rev Philip James John Plyming, Mrs Bridget Marye Cass, Professsor David Wilkinson, Dr James Harrison Canon, Mr Richard Mayland, Miss Amy Frances Ward, Mrs Susanne Mai Bradley, Mr Kevin Shoton, Dr Rebecca Bouveng, Professor Geoffrey Alastair Moore, Rt Rev James William Scobie Newcombe, Rt Revd Elizabeth Jane Holden Lane, Mr Nigel Robson, Rev Canon Sarah Bullock, Dr Michael Gilmore, Mrs Angela Cook, Miss Jessica Florence Rackham, Professor Michel Anthony Higton, Mrs Sarah Lynn Bowers
Income: £4,873,522 [2017]; £4,347,469 [2016]; £9,655,095 [2015]; £3,644,784 [2014]; £3,700,253 [2013]

St John's College, Southsea
Registered: 29 Jul 2015 *Employees:* 153
Tel: 023 9281 5118 *Website:* stjohnscollege.co.uk
Activities: Education, training; religious activities
Address: St John's College, Grove Road South, Southsea, Hants, PO5 3QW
Trustees: Mr Ronald Staker, Ms Zenna Hopson, Mr Christopher Riley, Mr Philip Holmes, Miss Rebecca Rothman, Mr David Chapman BA Dunelm FCollP FRSA, Mrs Charlotte Butterworth, Mr Stephern Fairclough
Income: £10,015,330 [2016]

St John's Home
Registered: 14 Jan 2014 *Employees:* 38 *Volunteers:* 7
Tel: 01604 755110 *Website:* stjohnsreshome.co.uk
Activities: The advancement of health or saving of lives; accommodation, housing
Address: 10 Hamlet Green, Northampton, NN5 7AR
Trustees: Rev David Graham Kirby, Mr Peter Mair, Dr Alan Sutton, Mrs Anne Goodman MBE, Mr Richard Leslie Pestell, Mr John Charles Fazackerley, Mr David John Harding, Mrs Mary Jane Huffadine-Smith
Income: £1,526,755 [2016]; £1,486,618 [2015]; £1,404,236 [2014]

St John's School
Registered: 31 Jul 1997 Employees: 65
Tel: 01923 845513 Website: st-johns.org.uk
Activities: Education, training
Address: St Johns School, Wieland Road, Northwood, Middlesex, HA6 3QY
Trustees: Mr Martin Andrew Lewis Robb, Lady Patricia Anne Harding, Mr Simon Everson, Mr Peter Ramsay MacDougall, Mrs Nicola Walker, Mr James Christopher Fowler, Mrs Elizabeth Kate Fenwick, Mr Paul Robert Henson, Mr Richard Sullivan
Income: £4,879,574 [2017]; £4,674,179 [2016]; £4,528,923 [2015]; £4,431,208 [2014]; £4,383,920 [2013]

St Joseph's College Limited
Registered: 5 Jan 1996 Employees: 151
Tel: 01473 690281 Website: stjos.co.uk
Activities: Education, training
Address: St Josephs College, Belstead Road, Ipswich, Suffolk, IP2 9DR
Trustees: Mr Perry Glading, Mr Paul Clement, Mr Simon Andrew Goulborn, Mr Antony Basset Newman, Prof P Cavenagh, Mr J Button, Mrs Josephine Lea, Mr Richard Stace LLB, Mr Matthew Potter, Mr Malcolm Arthur Earl, Mrs R Chester, Mr Philip Dennis
Income: £8,265,464 [2016]; £7,729,320 [2015]; £7,417,933 [2014]; £7,549,884 [2013]

St Joseph's College Reading Trust
Registered: 26 Feb 1979 Employees: 122
Tel: 0118 966 1000 Website: sjcr.org.uk
Activities: Education, training
Address: St Josephs College, 64 Upper Redlands Road, Reading, Berks, RG1 5JT
Trustees: Sister Helen-Marie, Mr David Halle, Mrs Hilary Buckle, Mr Charles Anthony D'Cruz, Mr Paul Adrian Barras, Miss Julia Feeney, Dr Margaret Elizabeth Cross, Mr Jonathan Hennah, Mr Giles Peter Francis Watson
Income: £5,602,500 [2017]; £5,140,213 [2016]; £4,864,769 [2015]; £4,305,033 [2014]; £3,735,521 [2013]

St Joseph's Convent Preparatory School Gravesend
Registered: 10 May 2007 Employees: 43
Tel: 01474 533012 Website: sjcps.org
Activities: General charitable purposes; education, training; religious activities
Address: St Joseph's Convent Prep School, 46 Old Road East, Gravesend, Kent, DA12 1NR
Trustees: Sr Magdalene Reilly, Mrs Bridget Busfield, Miss Margaret Doherty, Mrs Alison Knight, Mr Brett Ley, Mr Gregory Thompson, Sr Anne O'Connell, Sr Paula Thomas, Mr Joseph McCarthy, Mr Neil Rhys Edwards, Mrs Susan Lawless, Mrs Caroline Stanley, Miss Ellen Ryan
Income: £1,305,703 [2016]; £1,357,481 [2015]; £1,177,972 [2014]; £1,065,501 [2013]

St Joseph's Hospice Association
Registered: 18 Jan 2002 Employees: 119 Volunteers: 220
Tel: 0151 924 3812 Website: jospice.org.uk
Activities: The advancement of health or saving of lives; overseas aid, famine relief; religious activities
Address: St Joseph's Hospice, Ince Road, Thornton, Merseyside, L23 4UE
Trustees: David Bricknell, George Foster, Judith Welch, Mrs Jane Daly, Yvonne Atkinson, Mr Peter Morgan
Income: £3,377,265 [2017]; £3,088,943 [2016]; £3,124,639 [2015]; £3,304,317 [2014]; £3,420,875 [2013]

St Joseph's Hospice Hackney
Registered: 1 Mar 2006 Employees: 279 Volunteers: 540
Website: stjh.org.uk
Activities: General charitable purposes; advancement of health or saving of lives; disability; prevention or relief of poverty
Address: St Josephs Hospice, Mare Street, London, E8 4SA
Trustees: Mr Peter Robert Edmund Pledger, Sister Geraldine O'Connor RSC, Mr Francis Martin Campbell, Michael Moran, Mr Patrick Joseph McGuinness CMG OBE, Sister Rita Dawson MBE DL RSC MSc BSc RGN RSCN, James McManus, Mr Edward Brian McGuigan, Miss Margaret Mary Doherty
Income: £13,976,000 [2017]; £13,794,407 [2016]; £15,303,000 [2015]; £13,135,000 [2014]; £13,879,000 [2013]

St Joseph's School Nottingham
Registered: 16 Aug 1991 Employees: 38 Volunteers: 1
Tel: 0115 941 8356 Website: st-josephs.nottingham.sch.uk
Activities: Education, training
Address: St Josephs School, 33 Derby Road, Nottingham, NG1 5AW
Trustees: Mr Nigel Chapman, Mrs Paula Hemsley, Mr Martin Whitaker, Mrs Victoria Bonython Henderson, Mr Austin Kelly, Mrs Victoria Elizabeth Trafford
Income: £1,119,404 [2016]; £1,091,464 [2015]; £973,117 [2014]; £819,272 [2013]; £808,163 [2012]

St Joseph's School, Launceston
Registered: 5 Apr 1984 Employees: 65
Tel: 01566 772580 Website: stjosephscornwall.co.uk
Activities: Education, training
Address: 11 St Stephens Hill, Launceston, Cornwall, PL15 8HN
Trustees: Mr Neil Pockett, Mr David Jasper, Ms Sara Graybow, Mr Andy Gillies, Mr Paul Hicks, Mr Jason Thorns, Mrs Margaret Joan Warren, Mr Trevor Watkins, Ms Susan Lewis, Mrs Susan Rowe, Mrs Louise Holmes
Income: £2,165,811 [2017]; £2,124,754 [2016]; £2,035,421 [2015]; £1,832,260 [2014]; £1,718,100 [2013]

St Joseph's in the Park School
Registered: 26 Aug 2005 Employees: 45 Volunteers: 30
Tel: 01992 513810 Website: stjosephsinthepark.co.uk
Activities: Education, training
Address: St Josephs in the Park, St Marys Lane, Hertingfordbury, Hertford, SG14 2LX
Trustees: Mrs Jane Kemp, Mrs Anna Paula Bayford, Mr Andrew John Holden, Miss Caroline Elizabeth May, Mr Martin Porter, Mrs Charlotte Norman, Ms Claire Elizabeth Sharp, Mrs Jennifer Anne Susan Longbourne, Mrs Pauline Averil Maile, Mr Angus John Henry Head, Mrs Susan Jean Coley, Mrs Susan Wallace-Woodroffe
Income: £1,849,147 [2016]; £1,822,265 [2015]; £1,730,062 [2014]; £1,791,422 [2013]; £1,748,324 [2012]

St Kentigern Hospice
Registered: 29 Feb 1988 Employees: 50 Volunteers: 425
Tel: 01745 585221 Website: stkentigernhospice.org.uk
Activities: The advancement of health or saving of lives
Address: St Kentigern Hospice, Upper Denbigh Road, St Asaph, Denbighshire, LL17 0RS
Trustees: Mrs Gwynne Roose Thompson, Mrs Susan England, Mrs S J Last, Mrs Judith Owen, Mr James Peter O'Toole, Mrs Noelle Clare Sheppard Porter, Professor Mari Lloyd Williams, Mr Stephen Dudley Cheshire, Dr Uday Bisarya, Rev Michael Williams, Mr Jonathan Edward Osborne, Mr John Randal Owen
Income: £2,284,095 [2017]; £2,642,478 [2016]; £2,223,856 [2015]; £2,612,392 [2014]; £2,253,817 [2013]

St Laurence Education Trust
Registered: 6 Aug 1997 *Employees:* 253 *Volunteers:* 8
Tel: 01439 766710 *Website:* college.ampleforth.org.uk
Activities: Education, training; religious activities
Address: Ampleforth Abbey, York, YO62 4EN
Trustees: Rev Charles Gabriel Everitt, Mr Matthew Craston, Mrs Claire Smith, Mrs Elizabeth Berner, Right Rev James Cuthbert Madden OSB, Mr James O'Neill, Mr Christopher Adams
Income: £18,315,000 [2016]; £20,966,000 [2015]; £19,611,000 [2014]; £19,764,000 [2013]; £19,747,000 [2012]

St Leonard's Hospice York
Registered: 20 Dec 1979 *Employees:* 197 *Volunteers:* 541
Tel: 01904 708553 *Website:* stleonardshospice.org.uk
Activities: The advancement of health or saving of lives
Address: St Leonards Hospice, 185 Tadcaster Road, Dringhouses, York, YO24 1GL
Trustees: Mr David Dickson, Dr Kate Flemming, Mr Alistair Duncan, Mr David Miller, Ms Juliette Healey, Mr Michael Sturge, Dr Christine Kirk, Mr David Alexander, Dr Lavinia Norton, Ms Jacqueline Myers
Income: £5,835,684 [2017]; £5,699,569 [2016]; £5,712,332 [2015]; £5,117,058 [2014]; £5,406,134 [2013]

St Luke's Cheshire Hospice
Registered: 1 Oct 1984 *Employees:* 184 *Volunteers:* 901
Tel: 01606 551246 *Website:* stlukes-hospice.co.uk
Activities: Education, training; advancement of health or saving of lives
Address: Grosvenor House, Queensway, Winsford, Cheshire, CW7 1BH
Trustees: Dr Robert Pugh, Mr John Colclough, Mr Andrew Roberts, Mr Anthony John Baxter, Mr Kevin Highfield, Mrs Alexis Redmond, Mr Colin Peter Norman, Miss Andrea Jane Holland, Mr Antony Nicholas Hoy, Mike Ridley
Income: £4,820,137 [2017]; £4,884,910 [2016]; £4,831,021 [2015]; £3,632,193 [2013]; £3,277,731 [2012]

St Luke's Hospice (Basildon and District) Limited
Registered: 24 May 1984 *Employees:* 164 *Volunteers:* 300
Tel: 01268 524973 *Website:* stlukeshospice.com
Activities: The advancement of health or saving of lives
Address: St Lukes Hospice, Fobbing Farm, Nethermayne, Basildon, Essex, SS16 5NJ
Trustees: Mrs Ruth Margaret Booth, Dr Jeanne Marie Therese D'Mello, Mrs Marlene Moura, Mr Robert Smith, Mrs Patricia Stone, Mr Gerald William Peaty, Mrs Madeline Patricia Bartlett, Dr Robert Maunder, Mr Brian Wellman
Income: £8,208,272 [2017]; £7,029,558 [2016]; £5,844,131 [2015]; £4,848,006 [2014]; £4,280,861 [2013]

St Luke's Hospice (Harrow and Brent) Ltd
Registered: 15 Feb 1988 *Employees:* 147 *Volunteers:* 900
Tel: 020 8382 8000 *Website:* stlukes-hospice.org
Activities: Education, training; advancement of health or saving of lives
Address: St Lukes Hospice, Kenton Grange, Kenton Road, Harrow, Middlesex, HA3 0YG
Trustees: Mr Sushil Radia, Mr Christopher John Boon, Dr Gillian Schiller, Mr Rajesh Bhatia, Ms Julia Newland, Ms Carolyn Bennett, Mr Ajay Rawal, Mrs Norma Brier, Ms Christine Glenn, Ms Gemma Dawson, Mrs Sharon Aldridge-Bent, Mr Robert Samuel Elkeles, Mrs Cheryl Brodie, Dr Reena Zivia Majus
Income: £9,374,000 [2016]; £7,876,000 [2015]; £6,937,000 [2014]; £6,299,000 [2013]; £5,716,000 [2012]

St Luke's Hospice Plymouth
Registered: 25 Sep 1980 *Employees:* 271 *Volunteers:* 800
Tel: 01752 401172 *Website:* stlukes-hospice.org.uk
Activities: Education, training; advancement of health or saving of lives
Address: St Lukes Hospice, Stamford Road, Plymouth, PL9 9XA
Trustees: Professor Stephen Edward Newstead, Dr Stephen Hobbs, Mr Christopher John Cavanagh, Ms Christina Quinn, Ms Julie Anne Hendry, Mr Charles Oliver Maunsell Hackett, Mrs Fiona Field, Mrs Carol Mary Postle-Hacon, Mrs Clare Baker, Mr Richard Mark James, Mr Michael Francis Risdon
Income: £9,390,872 [2017]; £8,821,951 [2016]; £9,076,730 [2015]; £9,988,531 [2014]; £8,729,386 [2013]

St Luke's Hospice
Registered: 24 Nov 1967 *Employees:* 236 *Volunteers:* 700
Tel: 0114 235 7450 *Website:* stlukeshospice.org.uk
Activities: Education, training; advancement of health or saving of lives
Address: St Lukes Hospice, Little Common Lane, Sheffield, S11 9NE
Trustees: Mr Laurence Michael Gavin, Mr Neil Andrew MacDonald, Professor Sarah Elizabeth Thomas, Professor Robert Edward Coleman, Professor Diana Greenfield, Mrs Susan Inglis, Mr Andrew Snelling, Dr Toni Schwarz, Mrs Petra Billing
Income: £9,853,812 [2017]; £8,905,330 [2016]; £8,905,730 [2015]; £9,682,292 [2014]; £10,602,058 [2013]

St Luke's Oxford
Registered: 26 Feb 1986 *Employees:* 79 *Volunteers:* 4
Tel: 01865 228800 *Website:* stlukeshosp.co.uk
Activities: The advancement of health or saving of lives
Address: Latimer Road, Headington, Oxford, OX3 7PF
Trustees: Mr Nigel Talbot Rice MA DipEd, Mr Martin Wilkinson, Mr Rodney Mann, Mr Graham Candy, Dr Helen Van Oss, Mr Robert John Spencer Hawes, Mr Guy Wareing, Mr Luke Ponsonby, Lady Juliet Norman
Income: £2,708,111 [2017]; £2,591,276 [2016]; £2,402,383 [2015]; £2,153,109 [2014]; £2,091,560 [2013]

St Luke's Parochial Trust
Registered: 22 Sep 1962 *Employees:* 34 *Volunteers:* 60
Tel: 020 7549 8181 *Website:* slpt.org.uk
Activities: General charitable purposes; education, training; prevention or relief of poverty; arts, culture, heritage, science; economic, community development, employment
Address: St Lukes, 90 Central Street, London, EC1V 8AJ
Trustees: St Luke's Trustee Limited (Charity No 1141334)
Income: £1,975,830 [2016]; £1,672,584 [2015]; £1,658,900 [2014]; £8,000,611 [2013]; £929,624 [2012]

St Margaret's School (Hampstead) Ltd
Registered: 16 Mar 1965 *Employees:* 37
Tel: 020 7794 5140 *Website:* st-margarets.co.uk
Activities: Education, training
Address: St Margarets School, 18 Kidderpore Gardens, London, NW3 7SR
Trustees: Mr Edmund Grower, Mr Adrian Wayne BSc MBBS DCH DRCOG MRCGP, Ms Carol Gay, Mrs Lisa Harriman, Mr Dugald MacNeill, Mrs Michelle Wayne, Mr Faarid Patel, Mr Gabriel Leung, Mrs Emily Brettle, Mr Nicholas Gifford
Income: £2,202,205 [2016]; £2,013,852 [2015]; £1,927,274 [2014]; £1,846,771 [2013]; £1,760,755 [2012]

St Margaret's School Bushey
Registered: 17 Jun 1996 Employees: 168
Tel: 020 8416 4406 Website: stmargaretsbushey.co.uk
Activities: Education, training
Address: St Margarets School, Merry Hill Road, Bushey, Herts, WD23 1DT
Trustees: Mr Brian Coulshed, Rev William Gibbs, Ms Judith Elizabeth Fenn, Ms Ellen Hill, Mr Justin Alford, Mr David Clout, Mr Jamie Hill, Mrs Rachel Floretta Hodgson, Mr Malcolm Spooner
Income: £7,052,913 [2017]; £17,304,517 [2016]; £7,001,596 [2015]; £7,147,995 [2014]; £6,496,585 [2013]

St Margaret's Somerset Hospice
Registered: 5 Mar 1980 Employees: 393 Volunteers: 1,200
Tel: 01823 365603 Website: st-margarets-hospice.org.uk
Activities: The advancement of health or saving of lives
Address: St Margarets Somerset Hospice, Heron Drive, Bishops Hull, Taunton, Somerset, TA1 5HA
Trustees: Mr Alan MacDonald Large, Dr Deborah Stalker, Mr Tom Samuel, Mr Patrick Joseph Colton, Dr Julia Dominique Janine Thomas, Mrs Elizabeth Edwards, Mr Jonathan Langdon, Ms Jennifer Board, Dr Alison Grove, Mr John Douglas Martin, Mr Andrew Glass
Income: £12,152,251 [2017]; £12,142,881 [2016]; £10,040,843 [2015]; £10,924,084 [2014]; £8,872,512 [2013]

St Martin's (Northwood) Preparatory School Trust Limited
Registered: 8 Aug 1962 Employees: 72
Tel: 01923 825740 Website: stmartins.org.uk
Activities: Education, training
Address: 40 Moor Park Road, Northwood, Middlesex, HA6 2DJ
Trustees: Mr Neil Hinds MRICS, Mr James Fowler, Mr Richard Howard Evans, Mr Vernon William Hales, Mr Jeremy Richards, Dr Rabia Yaqoob MBBS MRCGP, Mr Mark Jordan, Mr Simon John Everson, Mr Andrew Simon Harris, Christopher Scott, Mrs Christine Marks
Income: £5,394,786 [2016]; £5,205,498 [2015]; £4,884,180 [2014]; £4,744,765 [2013]; £4,581,456 [2012]

St Martins Housing Trust
Registered: 29 Aug 1989 Employees: 100 Volunteers: 15
Tel: 01603 667706 Website: stmartinshousing.org.uk
Activities: General charitable purposes; prevention or relief of poverty; accommodation, housing
Address: 35 Bishopgate, Norwich, NR1 4AA
Trustees: Mrs Catherine Mary Ward, Dr Jenny Blyth, Mr Kevin Long, Mr Colin Bland, Mr David John Hoy, Mr Nicholas Trevor Williams, Mr David Brief, Mr Brian Walker, Mrs Kate Daynes, Dr Janka Rodziewicz
Income: £4,252,063 [2017]; £5,031,903 [2016]; £3,656,161 [2015]; £3,495,356 [2014]; £3,107,818 [2013]

St Mary Magdalene and Holy Jesus Trust
Registered: 19 Nov 1963 Employees: 14
Tel: 0191 269 7920 Website: mmhjtrust.com
Activities: The prevention or relief of poverty; accommodation, housing
Address: St Mary Magdalene And Holy Jesus Trust, Claremont Road, Newcastle upon Tyne, NE2 4NN
Trustees: Councillor Susan Pearson, Mr Paul Anderson, Mr Alan Bainbridge, Rev Peter Strange, Councillor Catherine Walker, Mr Keith Hall, Sir Leonard Fenwick CBE, Alderman Margaret Carter, Mr John Paul Lee OBE
Income: £1,396,600 [2017]; £1,446,000 [2016]; £1,731,800 [2015]; £2,071,800 [2014]; £1,865,700 [2013]

St Mary's College (Oscott College)
Registered: 24 Mar 1966 Employees: 33 Volunteers: 50
Tel: 0121 321 5030 Website: oscott.org
Activities: Education, training; religious activities; environment, conservation, heritage
Address: Oscott College, Chester Road, Sutton Coldfield, W Midlands, B73 5AA
Trustees: Incorporated Trustees of St Mary's College Oscott
Income: £2,780,000 [2017]; £2,579,000 [2016]; £2,408,000 [2015]; £2,256,000 [2014]; £2,247,000 [2013]

St Mary's College Crosby Trust Limited
Registered: 5 Jul 2005 Employees: 141 Volunteers: 19
Website: stmarys.ac
Activities: Education, training; prevention or relief of poverty; religious activities
Address: 10 Westwood Road, Prenton, Birkenhead, Merseyside, CH43 9RQ
Trustees: Father Michael O'Dowd, Mr Christopher Cleugh, Professor Charles Mills, Mr Henry Bond Hitchen, Mr Michael Mansour
Income: £5,317,702 [2017]; £4,838,439 [2016]; £5,117,203 [2015]; £4,983,493 [2014]; £5,016,070 [2013]

St Mary's Hare Park School
Registered: 12 May 1988 Employees: 39
Tel: 01708 761220
Activities: Education, training; economic, community development, employment
Address: 61 Roxy Avenue, Romford, Essex, RM6 4AW
Trustees: Glenda Spencer, Mr Vick Fellows, Paul Doman, Mr Nicholas Kevin Murray
Income: £1,376,588 [2016]; £1,327,388 [2015]; £1,263,066 [2014]; £1,035,953 [2013]; £990,611 [2012]

St Mary's Hospice Limited
Registered: 9 Jul 1974 Employees: 216 Volunteers: 366
Tel: 0121 472 1191 Website: birminghamhospice.org.uk
Activities: Education, training; advancement of health or saving of lives
Address: 176 Raddlebarn Road, Selly Oak, Birmingham, B29 7DA
Trustees: Mike Russell, Stan Leyland, Colin Graham, Salma Ali, Mrs Denise McLellan, Simon Jarvis, Niel De Vos, Gabrielle Stanley, Jonathan Crawford, Gurinder Mandla, Karen Dowman, Andy Williams, Sharon Benton, Dr Sabena Jameel
Income: £8,166,107 [2017]; £7,645,213 [2016]; £6,937,551 [2015]; £7,571,850 [2014]; £6,950,074 [2013]

St Mary's Independent School
Registered: 5 Feb 2014 Employees: 55
Tel: 023 8067 1267 Website: stmarysindependentschool.co.uk
Activities: Education, training; religious activities
Address: St Mary's Independent School, 57 Midanbury Lane, Bitterne Park, Southampton, SO18 4DJ
Trustees: Nick Vaughan, Mrs Sharon Bailey, Mrs Heather Eyers, Mrs Julia Elisabeth Alys Husband, Mrs Claire Elizabeth Charlemagne, Mr John Anthony Reginald Thompson, Brother Patrick Edward John Patterson, Mr Patrick McCarthy, Mrs Kay Hoile, Mr Jonathan Charles Barnes, Mr David John Cheeseman
Income: £2,527,115 [2016]; £2,108,088 [2015]; £1,119,302 [2014]

St Mary's School (Calne)
Registered: 23 May 1963 *Employees:* 253 *Volunteers:* 8
Tel: 01249 857300 *Website:* stmaryscalne.org
Activities: Education, training; religious activities; arts, culture, heritage, science; amateur sport; environment, conservation, heritage; economic, community development, employment
Address: St Mary's School, 63 Curzon Street, Calne, Wilts, SN11 0DF
Trustees: Mrs Victoria Jane Wilson, Dr Simon Turton, Mr Jonathan Stephen Smith, Prof Ann Fitz-Gerald, Mrs Cate Bell, Mrs Christine McGregor Lough, The Ven Hedley Ringrose, Dr Linda Ashton, Mr Martin Harris
Income: £15,506,231 [2017]; £15,078,450 [2016]; £14,293,715 [2015]; £13,583,457 [2014]; £12,560,047 [2013]

St Mary's School (Colchester) Limited
Registered: 20 Oct 1970 *Employees:* 67
Tel: 01206 572544 *Website:* stmaryscolchester.org.uk
Activities: Education, training
Address: St Marys School, 91 Lexden Road, Colchester, Essex, CO3 3RB
Trustees: Ms Marguerite Haddrell, Mrs L Carmel, Mrs E C Waters, Mr W Magill, Miss N Cannon MRICS, Mrs J Triggs, Mrs Sheila Foakes, Mr R G Lambert, Mrs K Loxley, Mrs L Gray, Mrs V Francis, Mrs E Bevan
Income: £4,416,875 [2016]; £4,326,217 [2015]; £4,122,978 [2014]; £3,910,658 [2013]; £3,794,241 [2012]

St Mary's School Ascot
Registered: 10 Oct 1984 *Employees:* 252
Tel: 01344 293621 *Website:* st-marys-ascot.co.uk
Activities: Education, training; religious activities
Address: St Marys School, St Marys Road, Ascot, Berks, SL5 9JF
Trustees: Rev Dermot Power, Mr Patrick Gaynor, Professor Richard John Parish, Mrs Annoushka Ayton MBE, Mr Edward Francis Horswell, Ms Clementine Mary Vaughan, Mr Peter Joseph McKenna, The Hon Martin John Hunt, Mrs Clare Elizabeth Vivienne Colacicchi, Mr Gerald Bodenham Thompson, Sister Anne Mary Robinson CJ, Miss Joana Ebner, Mr Gordon James Moore
Income: £15,333,000 [2017]; £15,107,000 [2016]; £14,520,000 [2015]; £13,045,000 [2014]; £12,771,000 [2013]

St Mary's School Cambridge
Registered: 2 Oct 1984 *Employees:* 148 *Volunteers:* 4
Website: stmaryscambridge.co.uk
Activities: Education, training
Address: St Marys School, Bateman Street, Cambridge, CB2 1LY
Trustees: Mr Stuart Westley, Mr Ronald Haynes, Professor Judith Driscoll, Mr Colin Jones, Mr Alistair Milne, Mr Andrew Grant, Mr Jeremy Pyne, Mrs Sarah Squire, Dr Nessa Ward, Sister Frances Orchard, Ms Judy Clements OBE, Mr Michael Ledzion, Mr Raymond Burch
Income: £10,478,098 [2016]; £10,200,683 [2015]; £9,986,794 [2014]; £9,228,289 [2013]

St Mary's School Shaftesbury Trust
Registered: 22 Oct 1985 *Employees:* 201
Tel: 01747 851188 *Website:* stmarys.eu
Activities: Education, training
Address: St Marys School, Donhead St Mary, Shaftesbury, Dorset, SP7 9LP
Trustees: Sr Gemma Simmonds CJ, Mr Philip Conrath, Dr Kathryn Mounde, Janet Watts, Mr Peter Geikie-Cobb, Mr Michael Farmer, Miss Victoria Younghusband, Major-General Nicholas Borton
Income: £5,981,110 [2016]; £6,257,307 [2015]; £6,637,693 [2014]; £6,765,117 [2013]; £6,451,003 [2012]

St Mary's School, Hampstead
Registered: 27 Nov 1991 *Employees:* 58 *Volunteers:* 15
Tel: 020 7435 1568 *Website:* stmh.co.uk
Activities: Education, training
Address: St Marys School, 47 Fitzjohns Avenue, London, NW3 6PG
Trustees: Mr Patrick Minns, Mr Keith Wilkins, Mrs Susan Ann McCarron, Mr Robert Carlysle, Mr D H Rands, Mr Kevin Andrew Murphy, Mr Sean Dermot Murphy
Income: £4,205,669 [2017]; £4,096,509 [2016]; £3,764,326 [2015]; £3,737,560 [2014]; £3,532,121 [2013]

St Mary's Trust
Registered: 11 Mar 1971
Tel: 020 7720 4655
Activities: Religious activities
Address: 27A Rozel Road, London, SW4 0EY
Trustees: Mr David Lawrence Marchese, The Hon Thomas Hunter Vere Cochrane, Mr Keith Leuchars, Mr Kris Romanski, Mr Shane Fletcher
Income: £1,100,655 [2016]; £144,389 [2015]; £118,626 [2014]; £125,467 [2013]; £133,387 [2012]

St Mary's University, Twickenham
Registered: 23 Jul 2007 *Employees:* 738
Tel: 020 8240 4267 *Website:* stmarys.ac.uk
Activities: Education, training
Address: St Marys University, Waldegrave Road, Twickenham, Middlesex, TW1 4SX
Trustees: Ms Noreen Doyle, Mrs Susan Kathleen Handley Jones, Mr Francis Martin Campbell, Mr David Anthony Hartnett CB, Professor Edward Joseph Acton, Mr Conal Baxter, Ms Claire McDonnell, Rt Rev Charles Phillip Richard Moth, Fr Richard Damian Finn OP, Miss June Patricia Mulroy MBE, Mr Jeffery William Cottle, Professor Anne Moran OBE, Mrs Kristen Pilbrow
Income: £52,328,415 [2017]; £50,940,537 [2016]; £45,890,000 [2015]; £41,552,000 [2014]; £38,670,000 [2013]

St Marys School Gerrard Cross Limited
Registered: 12 Dec 1963 *Employees:* 74
Tel: 01753 883370 *Website:* stmarysschool.co.uk
Activities: Education, training; religious activities
Address: St Marys School, 92-94 Packhorse Road, Gerrards Cross, Bucks, SL9 8JQ
Trustees: Mr Derek Wilson, Mr Nicholas Moss, Mr Nicholas Hallchurch, Mrs Christine Bayliss, Mrs Marina Hall, Sam Machin, Mrs Carin Eilerts De Haan, Mr David Campkin, Mrs Rosemary Martin
Income: £4,445,234 [2017]; £3,746,301 [2016]; £3,395,738 [2015]; £3,294,382 [2014]; £3,245,632 [2013]

St Mellitus College Trust
Registered: 11 Oct 2002 *Employees:* 19 *Volunteers:* 25
Tel: 020 7052 0587 *Website:* stmellitus.ac.uk
Activities: Education, training; religious activities
Address: St Jude's Church, 24 Collingham Road, London, SW5 0LX
Trustees: Revd Dr Jane Freeman, Dr Graham Stuart Tomlin, Mrs Polly Rebecca Stewart, Rt Revd Stephen Geoffrey Cottrell, Mr Jeremy Jennings, Mr John Peter Ball
Income: £2,297,131 [2017]; £2,078,812 [2016]; £1,621,532 [2015]; £1,123,945 [2014]; £930,894 [2013]

St Michael's Hospice (North Hampshire)
Registered: 10 May 1991 *Employees:* 175 *Volunteers:* 780
Tel: 01256 844744 *Website:* stmichaelshospice.org.uk
Activities: Education, training; advancement of health or saving of lives; disability
Address: St Michaels Hospice, Basil de Ferranti House, Park Prewett, Aldermaston Road, Basingstoke, Hants, RG24 9NB
Trustees: Mr John Wilkes, Mr Andrew Finney, Mr Andrew Chancellor, Mrs Suzie Scott-Malden, Miss Anne Stebbing, Mr Anthony Marten FBII, Mrs Christian De Ferranti, Mr Mike Reynolds, Mr Mark Lane, Dr Hugh Freeman
Income: £5,340,313 [2017]; £4,855,245 [2016]; £5,043,583 [2015]; £4,645,849 [2014]; £4,159,678 [2013]

St Michael's Hospice (incorporating The Freda Pearce Foundation)
Registered: 23 Jun 1982 *Employees:* 206 *Volunteers:* 1,000
Tel: 01432 851000 *Website:* st-michaels-hospice.org.uk
Activities: Education, training; advancement of health or saving of lives
Address: Bartestree, Hereford, HR1 4HA
Trustees: Alister Walshe, Tricia Greenwood, David Campion, Jane Winney, Kay Garlick, Kate Duffett, David Teague, John Dalziel, Ian Entwisle, David Hammond, George Nairn, Dr Jane Jones
Income: £7,323,103 [2017]; £7,865,265 [2016]; £8,904,397 [2015]; £8,511,020 [2014]; £4,665,692 [2013]

St Michael's Hospice Hastings and Rother
Registered: 20 Jan 1984 *Employees:* 197 *Volunteers:* 858
Tel: 01424 445177 *Website:* stmichaelshospice.com
Activities: The advancement of health or saving of lives; disability
Address: 25 Upper Maze Hill, St Leonards on Sea, E Sussex, TN38 0LB
Trustees: Mrs Irene Dibben, Mr Cliff Wallis, Mr Nigel Gaymer, Mr Michael Foster, Mr Steve Barnes, Mr Nigel Gresham Kirby-Green, Mr Bernard Hibbs, Mrs Angela Chivers, Mr Charles Everett, Dr Rosie Guy, Dr Peter Duncan Dewhurst, Mrs Evelyn Margaret Bignell
Income: £6,948,510 [2017]; £9,257,811 [2016]; £5,451,427 [2015]; £5,757,493 [2014]; £5,018,310 [2013]

St Michael's School (Leigh-on-Sea) Limited
Registered: 15 Dec 1980 *Employees:* 76
Tel: 01702 478719 *Website:* stmichaelsschool.com
Activities: Education, training
Address: St Michaels Preparatory School, 198 Hadleigh Road, Leigh on Sea, Essex, SS9 2LP
Trustees: S Mills, Mrs Jane Attwell, Mrs Susan Bird, Dr Pamela Edmonds, Mrs Faye Evans, Mr Mark Harwood Stennett, Mr Julian Barrett, Fr David Wylie
Income: £2,494,142 [2017]; £2,312,538 [2016]; £2,341,196 [2015]; £2,170,030 [2014]; £2,176,610 [2013]

St Monica Trust
Registered: 5 Dec 1962 *Employees:* 707 *Volunteers:* 116
Tel: 0117 949 4006 *Website:* stmonicatrust.org.uk
Activities: Accommodation, housing
Address: St Monica Trust, Cote Lane, Bristol, BS9 3UN
Trustees: St Monica Trustee Company Limited
Income: £29,817,000 [2016]; £28,569,000 [2015]; £26,134,000 [2014]; £24,569,000 [2013]; £23,747,000 [2012]

St Mungo Community Housing Association
Registered: 24 Sep 2012 *Employees:* 1,357 *Volunteers:* 912
Tel: 020 3856 6168 *Website:* mungos.org
Activities: General charitable purposes; education, training; advancement of health or saving of lives; prevention or relief of poverty; accommodation, housing
Address: 5th Floor, St Mungo's, 3 Thomas More Square, London, E1W 1YW
Trustees: Mr Robert Napier, Ms Rolande Anderson, Dr Helen Walters, Sir Leigh Lewis, Ms Alexandra Beidas, Mrs Tracy Allison, Mrs Yvonne Arrowsmith, Mr John Maxted, Mr Timothy Gadd, Mr Daniel Corry, Mr John Watts
Income: £86,536,000 [2017]; £82,874,000 [2016]; £69,134,000 [2015]; £53,832,000 [2014]; £49,120,000 [2013]

St Neots (Eversley) Limited
Registered: 28 Oct 1963 *Employees:* 72
Tel: 0118 973 9945 *Website:* st-neots-prep.co.uk
Activities: Education, training; amateur sport
Address: St Neots Preparatory School Ltd, St Neots Road, Eversley, Hook, Hants, RG27 0PN
Trustees: Mrs Louise Axton, Wendy Berry, Barbara Elizabeth Stanley, Mr Jonny Saunders, Mr Roger Woodbridge, Mr David Bailey, Mr Nigel Stoate, Mr Stephen Scott, Michael David Nash, Dr Raffi Assadourian, Ms Kay Price, Mr James Dahl, Mrs Gillian Empringham
Income: £4,003,600 [2017]; £6,976,198 [2016]; £3,619,884 [2015]; £3,373,836 [2014]; £3,433,278 [2013]

St Nicholas Hospice Suffolk
Registered: 4 Nov 1983 *Employees:* 170 *Volunteers:* 616
Tel: 01284 766133 *Website:* stnicholashospice.org.uk
Activities: The advancement of health or saving of lives
Address: St Nicholas Hospice Care, Macmillan Way, Hardwick Lane, Bury St Edmunds, Suffolk, IP33 2QY
Trustees: Mr Ian Calder Morgan, Mrs Marion Miles, Rev Canon Matthew Vernon, Mr Malcolm Leith, Ms Diane Elizabeth Buddery, Mr Christopher James Minett, Mr Charles Haddon McBratney Simpson, Ms Tessa Jane Wright, Mrs Susan Hayter, Ms Ann Langdon, Mrs Michelle Masson, Ms Karen Chandler-Smith
Income: £6,306,179 [2017]; £6,235,100 [2016]; £5,959,244 [2015]; £5,856,381 [2014]; £5,788,410 [2013]

St Nicholas School (Harlow) Limited
Registered: 27 Oct 1965 *Employees:* 78
Tel: 01279 429910 *Website:* saintnicholasschool.net
Activities: Education, training
Address: St Nicholas School, Hillingdon House, Hobbs Cross Road, Harlow, Essex, CM17 0NJ
Trustees: Mr Robert Ellice, Mr Simon Penney, Mr Andrew Johnson, Ms Kirsty Palmer, Mrs Jane Templeton-Knight, Mrs Diana Spellman, Mrs Lisa Saggers
Income: £3,931,311 [2017]; £3,438,868 [2016]; £3,573,376 [2015]; £3,345,729 [2014]; £3,464,054 [2013]

St Nicholas' School (Fleet) Educational Trust Limited
Registered: 23 Dec 1966 *Employees:* 49
Tel: 01252 850121 *Website:* st-nicholas.hants.sch.uk
Activities: Education, training
Address: St Nicholas School, Redfields Lane, Church Crookham, Fleet, Hants, GU52 0RF
Trustees: Mrs Susan Louise Raynsford, Mr Nicholas William Gradidge, Mrs Susan Isaacson, Mr Toby Aldrich, Mr Chris Tickell, Rev Tara Hellings, Mrs Shelia Cooper
Income: £4,305,927 [2017]; £4,384,575 [2016]; £4,376,108 [2015]; £4,297,863 [2014]; £4,243,835 [2013]

651

St Nicholas' Training Centre for The Montessori Method of Education Limited
Registered: 25 Apr 1963 *Employees:* 53
Tel: 020 7493 8300 *Website:* montessori.org.uk
Activities: Education, training
Address: Marlborough House, 38 Marlborough Place, London, NW8 0PJ
Trustees: Mr Kevin Coyne, Andrew Ling, Ms Misbah Mann, Mr Simon Thwaites, Patrick Melville, Felicity Marrian, Ms Jean Tsang, Dr John Siraj-Blatchford, Daniel Miller
Income: £2,327,856 [2017]; £2,621,485 [2016]; £3,732,298 [2015]; £3,621,481 [2014]; £3,244,868 [2013]

St Olave's School Trust
Registered: 1 Jul 1970 *Employees:* 68
Tel: 020 8294 8930 *Website:* stolaves.org.uk
Activities: Education, training
Address: St Olaves Preparatory School, 106-110 Southwood Road, London, SE9 3QS
Trustees: Mr Peter M Houillon, Mr Alan Mundy, Mrs Sarah Durham, Mrs Jane Willmott, Mr Michael D Ireland, Mrs Joan Smith, Dr Nuyen Raju, Mr Stephen Welch
Income: £2,353,532 [2016]; £2,148,892 [2015]; £2,026,793 [2014]; £1,893,483 [2013]; £1,818,789 [2012]

St Olave's and St Saviour's Schools Foundation
Registered: 13 Apr 1964 *Employees:* 2
Tel: 020 7945 6007 *Website:* stolavesfoundationfund.org.uk
Activities: Education, training
Address: St Olaves & St Saviours Schools Foundation, Europoint House, 5 Lavington Street, London, SE1 0NZ
Trustees: The Very Rev Andrew Nunn, Venerable Paul Wright, Mr Malcolm Edwards MA ACA, Lady Harding, Cllr Robert John Evans, Miss Debra Reiss, Mr Stephen Parry, Dr Emma Victoria Sanderson-Nash, Rev Neil McKinnon, Rev Jane Steen, Mr Ian Gordon Rankine FSA, Mr Edwin Langdown, Mr Laurence Johnstone FRICS, Mrs Elizabeth Edwards, Mr Robert Highmore, Cllr Stephen Wells
Income: £1,407,351 [2017]; £1,378,070 [2016]; £1,663,723 [2015]; £1,145,103 [2014]; £1,274,594 [2013]

St Oswald's Hospice Limited
Registered: 28 Jun 1974 *Employees:* 277 *Volunteers:* 1,100
Tel: 0191 285 0063 *Website:* stoswaldsuk.org
Activities: The advancement of health or saving of lives
Address: St Oswalds Hospice, Regent Avenue, Newcastle upon Tyne, NE3 1EE
Trustees: Mrs Dorothy Clasper, Mr Michael Paul Robson, Mrs Janet Clarke, Mrs Julie Harrison, Mrs Marie Liston, Mrs Kim Jobson, Mr Brian Hedley, Dr Stephen Michael Blades, Mr Kersi Fanibunda, Mrs Helen Lucraft, Mrs Christine English
Income: £12,152,294 [2017]; £10,813,788 [2016]; £10,113,742 [2015]; £10,767,680 [2014]; £9,946,935 [2013]

St Patrick's Missionary Society
Registered: 3 Jul 1975 *Employees:* 4
Tel: 020 8979 1890 *Website:* kilteganfathers.org
Activities: The prevention or relief of poverty; overseas aid, famine relief; religious activities; human rights, religious or racial harmony, equality or diversity
Address: St Patricks Missionary Society, 20 Beauchamp Road, East Molesey, Surrey, KT8 0PA
Trustees: St Patrick's Missionary Society Trustee Limited
Income: £1,495,978 [2016]; £1,571,935 [2015]; £1,232,812 [2014]; £1,465,890 [2013]; £1,263,109 [2012]

St Paul's Cathedral Choir School
Registered: 26 Oct 1962 *Employees:* 71
Website: spcs.london.sch.uk
Activities: Education, training
Address: St Pauls Cathedral School, 2 New Change, London, EC4M 9AD
Trustees: The Rev'd Canon Jonathan Brewster, The Rev'd Canon Michael Hampel, The Rev'd Canon Mark Oakley, The Rev'd Canon Tricia Hilas, The Venerable Sheila Watson, The Rev'd Dr David Ison, Mr Gavin Ralston, Ms Pim Baxter
Income: £3,938,098 [2016]; £4,007,086 [2015]; £3,905,063 [2014]; £3,742,858 [2013]; £3,673,992 [2012]

St Paul's Community Development Trust
Registered: 14 Jun 1979 *Employees:* 94 *Volunteers:* 51
Tel: 0121 464 4376 *Website:* stpaulstrust.org.uk
Activities: Education, training; advancement of health or saving of lives; arts, culture, heritage, science; amateur sport; animals; environment, conservation, heritage; economic, community development, employment
Address: St Pauls Community Development Trust, 73 Hertford Street, Birmingham, B12 8NJ
Trustees: Gill Coffin, Mr Rizvan Sadikot, Mr Patrick Wing, David Lane, Miss Judith Millington, Mr Mark Philip Riley, Tony Kennedy, Mr Nicholas Shepherd
Income: £2,151,458 [2017]; £2,263,979 [2016]; £2,836,997 [2015]; £3,572,105 [2014]; £2,930,563 [2013]

St Paul's Girls' School
Registered: 12 Jun 2007 *Employees:* 239 *Volunteers:* 44
Tel: 020 7605 1125 *Website:* spgs.org
Activities: Education, training
Address: St Pauls Girls School, Brook Green, London, W6 7BS
Trustees: Mrs Gillian Low, Nicholas Buxton, Dr Julia Riley, Miss Cally Palmer CBE, Professor Jane Ridley, Timothy Haywood, Mrs Geeta Khehar, Ms Kate Bingham, The Hon Timothy Palmer, Mr Nicolas Chisholm MBE, Mrs Dervilla Mary Mitchell, Zeina Bain, Mr Robert Henry Palmer, Ms Lisa Barclay
Income: £19,188,000 [2016]; £18,061,000 [2015]; £17,078,000 [2014]; £16,320,000 [2013]; £14,881,000 [2012]

St Paul's School
Registered: 12 Jun 2007 *Employees:* 303 *Volunteers:* 34
Tel: 020 8748 9162 *Website:* stpaulsschool.org.uk
Activities: Education, training
Address: St Pauls School, 80 Lonsdale Road, London, SW13 9JT
Trustees: Earl St Aldwyn, Mr Alistair Gerald Summers, Mr Adam Fenwick, Professor Rosemary Helen Luckin, Mr Ben Thomas, Ms Sarah Barker, Mrs Nicola Doyle, Ms Alison MacLeod, Mr Christopher John Vermont, Johnny Robertson, Mrs Alison Palmer, Lord Anthony Stephen Grabiner QC, Sir Simon Fraser GCMG
Income: £41,077,000 [2017]; £42,393,000 [2016]; £40,092,000 [2015]; £35,090,000 [2014]; £32,603,000 [2013]

St Paul's Schools Foundation
Registered: 3 Aug 1966 *Volunteers:* 66
Tel: 020 7726 4991 *Website:* mercers.co.uk
Activities: Education, training
Address: Worshipful Company of Mercers, Becket House, 36 Old Jewry, London, EC2R 8DD
Trustees: The Mercers Company
Income: £3,631,000 [2017]; £3,657,000 [2016]; £3,513,000 [2015]; £3,586,000 [2014]; £3,300,000 [2013]

St Paul's Theological Centre
Registered: 10 Oct 2005 *Employees:* 21 *Volunteers:* 20
Tel: 0845 644 7533 *Website:* sptc.htb.org
Activities: Education, training; religious activities
Address: Holy Trinity Brompton, Brompton Road, London, SW7 1JA
Trustees: Reverend Nicky Gumbel, Revd Simon Downham, Mr David Orton, Mr Angus Winther, Mr Jeremy Allan Jennings, Mr Buddy Zamora, Mr Andrew Edward Brydon, Mrs Rebecca Stewart
Income: £1,619,980 [2016]; £1,306,304 [2015]; £1,158,506 [2014]; £1,136,097 [2013]; £948,921 [2012]

The St Peter and St James Charitable Trust
Registered: 13 Jun 1996 *Employees:* 138 *Volunteers:* 430
Tel: 01444 471598 *Website:* stpeter-stjames.org.uk
Activities: Education, training; advancement of health or saving of lives; disability
Address: North Common Road, North Chailey, Lewes, E Sussex, BN8 4ED
Trustees: Mr Tim Hancock, Mr David Crudge, Ms Julie Madeleine Burgess, Mrs Deirdre Prower, Mr Andrew Richard Cook, Ms Katherine Ann Birrell, Mrs Christine Gibbons, Mrs Jo July, Mr Keith Banbury, Mrs Harriet Lucy Creamer, Dr Nicholas James Barrie
Income: £3,632,935 [2017]; £3,911,373 [2016]; £4,242,108 [2015]; £3,934,620 [2014]; £4,204,480 [2013]

The St Peter and St Paul School Trust
Registered: 14 Feb 1985 *Employees:* 31 *Volunteers:* 2
Website: spsp.org.uk
Activities: Education, training
Address: St Peter & St Paul School, Brambling House, Hady Hill, Chesterfield, Derbys, S41 0EF
Trustees: Mr Adrian Cedric Bonell, Mr Paul Webber, Neil Green, Mrs Dawn Graham, Mr Peter Pollard
Income: £1,087,752 [2016]; £1,114,875 [2015]; £1,091,110 [2014]; £988,640 [2013]; £987,136 [2012]

St Peter's College (otherwise known as Westminster School)
Registered: 8 Jul 1964 *Employees:* 341
Tel: 020 7963 1027 *Website:* westminster.org.uk
Activities: Education, training
Address: Westminster School, Little Deans Yard, London, SW1P 3PF
Trustees: Dr Priscilla Chadwick MA FRSA, Michael Baughan Esq, The Very Reverend Dr John Hall, Professor Sir Christopher Edwards, Dr Alan Borg CBE FSA, Ms Joanna Reesby LLB LLM, Dame Judith Mayhew Jonas DBE, Sir Gregory Winter, E M Cartwright Esq, Mr Mark Batten BA ACA, Mr Tony Little, Christopher Foster Esq, The Very Revd Professor Martyn Percy, Sir Peter Ogden, Mrs Ina De, Richard Neville-Rolfe MA Esq, The Reverend Canon Sinclair, The Reverend Canon Stanton, Ms Emily Reid, Professor Margaret Dallman
Income: £29,666,000 [2017]; £29,546,000 [2016]; £31,966,000 [2015]; £28,027,000 [2014]; £31,873,000 [2013]

St Peter's College, Radley
Registered: 22 Jul 1967 *Employees:* 440
Tel: 01235 543000 *Website:* radley.org.uk
Activities: Education, training
Address: Radley College, Radley, Abingdon, Oxon, OX14 2HR
Trustees: Mr Robert Warner, Mr Mark Justin Wells Rushton MA, Mrs E McKendrick BA, Mr David Craig Shaw Smellie, Mr Gerald Kaye BSc FRICS, Mr John Bridcut MA, Mr Richard Huntingford, Sir John Holmes, Mrs Jane Martineau, Mr Simon J B Shaw, Revd Dr Stephen W P Hampton, Mrs Deborah Pluck, Mr Thomas Oliver Seymour MA, Mr Michael Edward Hodgson MA, Mr Nigel Henderson MA FRCS, Mr William Sam H Laidlaw, Mr Tom Durie BA ACA FSI, Mr Charlie Mayfield MBA, Mr Peter Edward Foote Watson, Mr Hugh J R Willis MA, Ms L F Nixon
Income: £28,614,000 [2017]; £27,377,000 [2016]; £26,227,000 [2015]; £24,021,000 [2014]; £28,836,000 [2013]

St Peter's Hospice
Registered: 7 Apr 1975 *Employees:* 419 *Volunteers:* 1,500
Tel: 0117 915 9400 *Website:* stpetershospice.org
Activities: Education, training; advancement of health or saving of lives
Address: St Peters Hospice, Charlton Road, Brentry, Bristol, BS10 6NL
Trustees: Professor Karen Forbes, Mark Campbell, Dr Nicholas Peter Goyder, Ms Helen Staines, Dr Shaheen Shahzadi Chaudhry, Dr James William Dodd, Mr Roger Isaacs, Ms Alison Jean Moon, Mr Martin James Mohan, Mr Paul Burridge Montague, Ms Claire Buchanan, Mr Darren Alan Spicer
Income: £15,736,000 [2017]; £13,293,000 [2016]; £12,967,000 [2015]; £13,645,000 [2014]; £11,942,000 [2013]

St Philip's School Trust Limited
Registered: 14 Mar 1984 *Employees:* 21
Tel: 020 7373 3944 *Website:* stphilipschool.co.uk
Activities: Education, training
Address: St Philips School, 6 Wetherby Place, London, SW7 4NE
Trustees: Mr Thomas MacFarlane, Mr John Dean, Mr Simon Day, Ms Francesca Lawton Deacy, Mrs Mary Breen, Mrs Harriet Mould, Aedan MacGreevy, Mr David Rhidian Llewellyn
Income: £1,579,158 [2017]; £1,428,780 [2016]; £1,553,260 [2015]; £1,520,647 [2014]; £1,525,136 [2013]

St Piran's School Limited
Registered: 6 Apr 1972 *Employees:* 80 *Volunteers:* 10
Tel: 01628 594300 *Website:* stpirans.co.uk
Activities: Education, training
Address: Gringer Hill, Maidenhead, Berks, SL6 7LZ
Trustees: Mr Andrew Kennedy, Mr Christopher Lambert, Mrs Helen Ness-Gifford, Mrs Kate Jennifer Snowden Taylor, Mr Christopher David Kendall, Mr Michael Windsor, Rev William Stileman, Mrs Sandra Pellat, Mrs Elaine Marriner, Mrs Claire Robinson, Mr Olivier Subramanian
Income: £5,803,988 [2016]; £5,235,910 [2015]; £4,652,134 [2014]; £4,266,640 [2013]

St Richard of Chichester Christian Care Association Ltd
Registered: 9 Nov 1990 *Employees:* 37 *Volunteers:* 174
Tel: 01243 537934 *Website:* stonepillow.org.uk
Activities: Education, training; advancement of health or saving of lives; disability; prevention or relief of poverty; accommodation, housing; economic, community development, employment
Address: Stonepillow, St Josephs, Hunston Road, Chichester, W Sussex, PO20 1NP
Trustees: Clare Apel, Iain MacLeod, Mrs Shelagh Legrave, Mr Gregory Mahon, Mr Martyn John Bell, Mr Anthony Fawcett, Mr Peter Stevens, Mrs Yvonne Thomson
Income: £1,893,123 [2017]; £1,918,149 [2016]; £1,898,390 [2015]; £1,620,137 [2014]; £1,632,878 [2013]

St Richard's School Bredenbury Court
Registered: 8 Mar 2006 *Employees:* 47 *Volunteers:* 20
Tel: 01885 482491 *Website:* st-richards.org.uk
Activities: General charitable purposes; education, training; religious activities
Address: St Richards School, Bredenbury Court, Bredenbury, Bromyard, Herefords, HR7 4TD
Trustees: Mrs Tessa Norgrove, Mr Richard Green, Mr Jonathan Jackson, Father Aidan Doyle, Mr Duncan Byrne, Mrs Zinnia Wilkinson, Mrs Helen Cotterell, Mr David Jones, Mr Charles De Rohan, Mrs Anne Sharp, Mr Jonathan Forster
Income: £1,162,787 [2015]; £1,046,389 [2014]; £1,136,499 [2013]

St Richards Hospice Foundation
Registered: 22 Oct 1984 *Employees:* 230 *Volunteers:* 1,000
Tel: 01905 763963 *Website:* strichards.org.uk
Activities: Education, training; advancement of health or saving of lives; disability
Address: Wildwood Drive, Worcester, WR5 2QT
Trustees: Prof Richard Alexander Lewis, Mrs Jennifer Patricia Cowpe, Mr John MacLaine Bawden, Mr Peter Leslie Flagg, Mrs Andrea Palmer, Mrs Hannah Eve Edwards, Professor Tamar Judith Thompson, Ms Brenda Sheridan, Anthony Glossop, Mr Richard Gardner Shaw, Mr Simon Alexander Armstrong Hyslop, Mr John Galen Bartholomew, Cllr Andrew Roberts
Income: £8,281,837 [2017]; £8,388,625 [2016]; £7,441,324 [2015]; £7,707,943 [2014]; £7,288,855 [2013]

St Rocco's Hospice
Registered: 2 Nov 1981 *Employees:* 123 *Volunteers:* 672
Tel: 01925 575780 *Website:* stroccos.org.uk
Activities: The advancement of health or saving of lives
Address: St Roccos Hospice, Lockton Lane, Bewsey, Warrington, Cheshire, WA5 0BW
Trustees: The Venerable Roger Preece, Mrs Deborah Webb, Mr David Kendrick, Mrs Jennifer Sophie Elizabeth Roulston-Parry, Mr Andrew William Mellor, Mrs Mary Rudkin, Dr Catherine E Walshe, Mr Zac Clements, Mr Guy Hindle, Mr Michael Watson
Income: £3,881,606 [2017]; £3,984,918 [2016]; £4,034,770 [2015]; £4,118,063 [2014]; £3,660,128 [2013]

St Ronan's School (Hawkhurst)
Registered: 28 Nov 1997 *Employees:* 84 *Volunteers:* 45
Tel: 01580 754318 *Website:* saintronans.co.uk
Activities: Education, training
Address: St Ronans School, Water Lane, Hawkhurst, Cranbrook, Kent, TN18 5DJ
Trustees: Mr Jeremy Charles Belgrave Lucas, Dr Kathleen Dacre, Mr Stephen Langer BSc DipArch RIBA IHBC, Mr Nicholas Phillis, Mr Simon Alistair Bennie, Dominic Oliver, Mr Bruce Alexander Seton BSc, Colin Charles Willis Esq MA, Dr Robert Blundell MBBS, Sara Butler-Gallie, Andrew Ross, Julie Lowe
Income: £5,581,620 [2016]; £4,790,174 [2015]; £4,634,509 [2014]; £3,967,022 [2013]

St Swithun's School (Winchester)
Registered: 26 Sep 1966 *Employees:* 296
Tel: 01962 835713 *Website:* stswithuns.com
Activities: Education, training
Address: St Swithun's School, Alresford Road, Winchester, Hants, SO21 1HA
Trustees: Ms Margaret Rudland, Professor Natalie Lee, Mrs Frances Robinson, Mrs Julia Eager, Mr Andrew Lilley, Mrs Emma Clancey, Dr Heather Mycock, Cllr David McLean, Mr Thomas Bremridge, Mr Jonathan Russell, Mrs Sarah Parrish, Mrs Anna-Louise Peters, Dr Claire Thorne, Dr T R Hands, Richard Tyson
Income: £15,287,072 [2017]; £14,973,078 [2016]; £13,751,216 [2015]; £12,828,352 [2014]; £11,478,660 [2013]

St Teresa's Catholic School (Princes Risborough) Trust Ltd
Registered: 3 Jul 1973 *Employees:* 40 *Volunteers:* 30
Tel: 01844 345005 *Website:* st-teresas.bucks.sch.uk
Activities: Education, training
Address: St Teresas Catholic School, Aylesbury Road, Princes Risborough, Bucks, HP27 0JW
Trustees: Mrs Celia Sparkes, Mrs Margaret Cripps, Mr William Toby Bucknall, Mrs Deborah Stephanie Helen Main, Jane Morris, Mrs Anne Marie Harding, Mr Chris Doran, Mrs Jean O'Brien, Nick Jepson, Jeremy Edmund
Income: £1,228,533 [2016]; £1,196,419 [2015]; £1,094,146 [2014]; £1,064,251 [2013]

St Vincent de Paul Society (England and Wales)
Registered: 25 Mar 1996 *Employees:* 176 *Volunteers:* 10,000
Tel: 020 7703 3030 *Website:* svp.org.uk
Activities: General charitable purposes; prevention or relief of poverty
Address: St Vincent de Paul Society, Romero House, 55 Westminster Bridge Road, London, SE1 7JB
Trustees: Mrs Helen O'Shea, Ann Harris, Mr Michael Willcock, Mrs Josephine Regan, Mr Sebastian Muir, Ms Christine Knight, Mr Ian Kempsell, Mr James Bellamy, Richard Palmi, Mr Raymond John Daley, Mrs Elaine Heyworth, Mr Vincent McCallister, Mrs Ann Marie Towey
Income: £8,865,630 [2017]; £9,032,408 [2016]; £9,535,974 [2015]; £8,440,091 [2014]; £8,156,447 [2013]

St Vincent's Charitable Trust
Registered: 23 Oct 1992 *Employees:* 79 *Volunteers:* 24
Tel: 020 8872 4900 *Website:* svnh.co.uk
Activities: The advancement of health or saving of lives
Address: 153 Bartholomew Close, London, SW18 1JG
Trustees: Mr Alan Joseph Edmondson, Mr John Charles Steinitz, Rev John Patrick Deehan, Mr Neville Ransley, Mrs Patricia Kathleen Black, Ms Linda Ann Martin
Income: £3,439,144 [2017]; £3,245,521 [2016]; £3,141,190 [2015]; £3,024,127 [2014]; £2,980,739 [2013]

St Vincent's and St George's Association

Registered: 21 Sep 2005 *Employees:* 74 *Volunteers:* 9
Tel: 01242 511237 *Website:* stvsandstgs.co.uk
Activities: General charitable purposes; education, training; advancement of health or saving of lives; disability; prevention or relief of poverty; accommodation, housing
Address: Well Close, Lansdown Parade, Cheltenham, Glos, GL50 2LH
Trustees: Mr Derek Draper, Mrs Jean Gregory, Mr Les Bonney, Mrs Lauren Adler, Mrs Maralyn Reynolds, Mr Alan Winwood, Mr Peter Ireland, Mr Peter Sayers, Jo Bewley
Income: £1,460,950 [2017]; £1,709,569 [2016]; £1,624,716 [2015]; £1,351,015 [2014]; £1,658,426 [2013]

St Wilfrid's Hospice (Eastbourne)

Registered: 23 Feb 1982 *Employees:* 197 *Volunteers:* 564
Tel: 01323 434200 *Website:* stwhospice.org
Activities: Education, training; advancement of health or saving of lives
Address: St Wilfrids Hospice, 1 Broadwater Way, Eastbourne, E Sussex, BN22 9PZ
Trustees: David Turner, Mrs Karen Planterose, Ms Fiona MacIntyre, Mrs Vicki Morrey, Mrs Jane Butler, Mr Alan Breeze, Dr Janet McGowan, Mr Paul Slide, Mr Duncan Adams
Income: £4,442,603 [2017]; £7,024,378 [2016]; £5,472,567 [2015]; £5,709,529 [2014]; £5,485,514 [2013]

St Wilfrid's Hospice (South Coast) Limited

Registered: 29 Oct 1981 *Employees:* 209 *Volunteers:* 508
Tel: 01243 775302 *Website:* stwh.co.uk
Activities: Education, training; advancement of health or saving of lives
Address: Grosvenor Road, Chichester, W Sussex, PO19 8FP
Trustees: Dr Alec Graeme Dewhurst MA FRCP, Dr Alan Copsey, Mrs Angela Patricia Wormald, Ursula Watt, Mr Nicholas Fox, Ms Hilary Keenlyside, Mr Michael George Bevis, Mrs Elisabeth Anne Spence, Ms Amanda Susan Granville Sharp, Mr Christopher Joseph Dicks, Soline Jerram, Mr Julian John Clayton
Income: £9,799,335 [2017]; £7,464,903 [2016]; £5,494,352 [2015]; £5,250,934 [2014]; £7,476,656 [2013]

St. Albans School Woollam Trust

Registered: 4 Aug 1965 *Employees:* 11
Tel: 01727 515149 *Website:* st-albans.herts.sch.uk
Activities: Education, training; amateur sport
Address: St Albans School, Abbey Gateway, St Albans, Herts, AL3 4HB
Trustees: St Albans School Woollam Trustee Company Limited
Income: £1,109,418 [2016]; £1,030,983 [2015]; £1,620,179 [2014]; £1,010,155 [2013]; £759,618 [2012]

St. Barnabas Hospices (Sussex) Ltd

Registered: 3 Oct 1968 *Employees:* 320 *Volunteers:* 2,476
Tel: 01903 706303 *Website:* stbarnabas-hospice.org.uk
Activities: General charitable purposes; education, training; advancement of health or saving of lives; disability
Address: St Barnabas Hospice, St Barnabas House, 2 Titnore Lane, Goring-by-Sea, Worthing, W Sussex, BN12 6NZ
Trustees: Mr Mike Rymer, Mrs Maureen Chowen, Mr Mark Milling, Mr David Bunce, Mr Anthony Clark, Mr Patrick Neil Gatley, Mr Stephen Hollamby, Mr Derwyn Jones, Mrs Ruth Taylor, Mrs Patricia Woolgar, Mr David Brian Pegler, Mr Martin Godsmark, Mr Neil Blanchard
Income: £18,127,000 [2017]; £15,029,000 [2016]; £14,401,000 [2015]; £15,420,000 [2014]; £12,866,000 [2013]

St. Clare's, Oxford

Registered: 2 Mar 1987 *Employees:* 236
Tel: 01865 517327 *Website:* stclares.ac.uk
Activities: Education, training
Address: Mr Nicholas Paladina, 139 Banbury Road, Oxford, OX2 7AL
Trustees: Mr Peter Morris Oppenheimer, Ann Lewis, Mr John Church, Mr Jens Tholstrup, Mrs Moira Ellen Darlington, Mr Bartholomew David Ashton, Mr C R Dick, Laurence Whitehead, Yao-Su Hu, Ian Ashcroft, Mary Louise Culpepper
Income: £15,641,000 [2017]; £14,121,000 [2016]; £13,536,000 [2015]; £13,967,000 [2014]; £14,012,000 [2013]

St. David's Children Society

Registered: 5 Mar 1981 *Employees:* 21 *Volunteers:* 6
Tel: 029 2066 7007 *Website:* stdavidscs.org
Activities: General charitable purposes
Address: 28 Park Place, Cardiff, CF10 3BA
Trustees: Mr Arfon Jones, Mrs Mandy McGowan, Ms Katherine Shelton, Mr Frank Moloney, Mr Andrew Scott Lusk, Mr Phillip Chick, Mr Terry Connor, Mr Terence Champken
Income: £1,283,997 [2017]; £1,363,204 [2016]; £1,110,081 [2015]; £1,231,327 [2014]; £822,696 [2013]

St. David's Hospice

Registered: 10 Jun 1994 *Employees:* 104 *Volunteers:* 350
Tel: 01492 879058 *Website:* stdavidshospice.org.uk
Activities: The advancement of health or saving of lives
Address: St David's Hospice, Abbey Road, Llandudno, Conwy, LL30 2EN
Trustees: Victoria MacDonald, Mrs Gladys Harrison, Mr David Rhys Williams, Mr Mike Mason, Mr Roy Drinkwater, Miss Eleri Jones, Mr Alan Martin Thomas, Mr Anthony Neville, Mr Chris Davies, Mrs Amanda Jane Hughes, Mr David Richard Matthew Thomas, Dr Lyndon Miles
Income: £3,844,039 [2016]; £3,315,349 [2015]; £2,741,717 [2014]; £2,698,477 [2013]; £2,823,572 [2012]

St. George's Students' Union

Registered: 21 Jul 2011 *Employees:* 10 *Volunteers:* 42
Tel: 020 8725 2709 *Website:* sgsu.org.uk
Activities: General charitable purposes; education, training; religious activities; arts, culture, heritage, science; amateur sport; recreation
Address: St Georges Students' Union, Cranmer Terrace, London, SW17 0RE
Trustees: Mark Lubbock, Mr Corey Briffa, Mr Sam Khavandi, Miss Bethany Louise Agnew, Miss Chantal Liu, Miss Yuna Kishimoto, Dr Judith Ibison, Dr Aileen O'Brien, Mr Vafie Sheriff, Mr Anass Nuur Ali, Miss Bukola Ogunjinmi, Mr John Anthony McDonagh
Income: £1,522,326 [2017]; £1,455,254 [2016]; £1,463,749 [2015]; £1,446,625 [2014]; £1,284,789 [2013]

St. James's Place Charitable Foundation

Registered: 9 Nov 2011 *Employees:* 8 *Volunteers:* 100
Tel: 01285 878562 *Website:* sjp.co.uk
Activities: General charitable purposes
Address: St James's Place PLC, St James's Place House, 1 Tetbury Road, Cirencester, Glos, GL7 1FP
Trustees: Mr David Bellamy, Mr Malcolm Cooper-Smith, Mr David Lamb, Mr Jonathan Neil McMahon, Mr Ian Gascoigne, Mr Andrew Croft, Mrs Sonia Gravestock
Income: £7,312,760 [2016]; £7,846,924 [2015]; £6,804,577 [2014]; £5,378,666 [2013]; £5,937,779 [2012]

The St. John and Red Cross Defence Medical Welfare Service
Registered: 28 Jun 2001 *Employees:* 40
Tel: 01264 774006 *Website:* dmws.org.uk
Activities: The advancement of health or saving of lives; armed forces, emergency service efficiency
Address: The Old Stables, Redenham Park, Andover, Hants, SP11 9AQ
Trustees: Mrs Maryanne Burton, Mr Paul Taylor, Andrew Buckham, Mrs Barbara Cooper, Mr Michael Trevor Griffiths, Mr David Keenan, Mr Stephen Cowden, Mr James McNamara
Income: £1,277,217 [2017]; £2,765,178 [2016]; £2,525,109 [2015]; £3,562,686 [2014]; £2,526,840 [2013]

St. John of Jerusalem Eye Hospital Group
Registered: 29 Dec 2010 *Employees:* 239 *Volunteers:* 8
Website: stjohneyehospital.org
Activities: Education, training; advancement of health or saving of lives
Address: St Johns of Jerusalem Eye Hospital Group, 4 Charterhouse Mews, London, EC1M 6BB
Trustees: Mr Guy Morton, Ms Nicolette Shaw, Dr Anne Coleman, Ms Susan Dingwall, Mr John MacAskill, Mr Robert James Ingham Clark, Mr Nicholas Goulding, Mr Herbert von Bose, Mr David Verity, Mr Maged Abu Ramadan, Mr Philip Hall
Income: £10,811,000 [2016]; £8,521,000 [2015]; £9,290,000 [2014]; £8,100,000 [2013]; £8,220,000 [2012]

St. John of Jerusalem Eye Hospital
Registered: 31 Mar 2000 *Employees:* 54
Website: stjohneyehospital.org
Activities: Education, training; advancement of health or saving of lives
Address: St Johns of Jerusalem Eye Hospital Group, 4 Charterhouse Mews, London, EC1M 6BB
Trustees: Mr Guy Morton, Ms Nicolette Shaw, Dr Anne Coleman, Ms Susan Dingwall, Mr John MacAskill, Mr Robert James Ingham Clark, Mr Nicholas Goulding, Mr Herbert von Bose, Mr David Verity, Mr Maged Aburamadan, Mr Philip Hall
Income: £1,299,000 [2016]; £1,458,000 [2015]; £1,580,000 [2014]; £1,779,000 [2013]; £1,507,000 [2012]

St. John's Foundation Est. 1174
Registered: 31 Oct 1984 *Employees:* 57 *Volunteers:* 15
Tel: 01225 486400 *Website:* stjohnsbath.org.uk
Activities: The prevention or relief of poverty; accommodation, housing; economic, community development, employment
Address: St Johns Hospital, 4-5 Chapel Court, Bath, BA1 1SQ
Trustees: St John's Hospital Trustee Limited
Income: £5,495,000 [2016]; £5,151,000 [2015]; £5,583,000 [2014]; £5,147,000 [2013]; £5,246,000 [2012]

St. John's Hospice North Lancashire and South Lakes
Registered: 13 May 2014 *Employees:* 117 *Volunteers:* 530
Tel: 01524 382538 *Website:* sjhospice.org.uk
Activities: Education, training; advancement of health or saving of lives; disability; other charitable purposes
Address: St Johns Hospice, Slyne Road, Lancaster, LA2 6ST
Trustees: Dr Michael Robert Warren, Mrs Caroline Anne Bocking Redhead, Mr Andrew Moore Severn, Mr Richard Jan Tulej, Mrs Fiona Inglis, Mrs Fiona Ward, Mrs Jo Spencer, Mr Robert William Meacock, Mrs Christine Mary Heginbotham, Mr Mark Cullinan, Dr Simon James Nicholas Gardner, Mr John Sharples, Mrs Sue Smith
Income: £6,011,042 [2017]; £4,877,343 [2016]; £9,798,146 [2015]

St. John's School and College
Registered: 28 Feb 1997 *Employees:* 420 *Volunteers:* 10
Website: st-johns.co.uk
Activities: Education, training
Address: Walpole Road, Brighton, BN2 0AF
Trustees: Mr Richard Stewart, Mr Charles Harrison, Mr Len Parkyn, Mr William Charles Catchpole, Mrs Jill Elizabeth Gray, Mrs Linda Mary McMillan, Mrs Jean Marshall, Mrs Barbara Ann Bland, Mrs Alison Braunston, Mrs Anna Thatcher
Income: £10,822,482 [2017]; £9,364,480 [2016]; £8,342,779 [2015]; £6,710,918 [2014]; £6,640,431 [2013]

St. John's, Smith Square Charitable Trust
Registered: 30 Mar 1995 *Employees:* 12 *Volunteers:* 2
Tel: 020 7222 2168 *Website:* sjss.org.uk
Activities: Arts, culture, heritage, science; environment, conservation, heritage
Address: St Johns Church, Smith Square, London, SW1P 3HA
Trustees: The Countess of Chichester, Mr Robert Collingwood, Mr Peter Holgate, Mr Vivek Singh, Lady Brewer, Martin Smith, Ms Jessica Simor
Income: £1,000,242 [2016]; £951,156 [2015]; £933,064 [2014]; £642,767 [2013]

St. Mark's Hospital Foundation
Registered: 16 Mar 2011 *Employees:* 8 *Volunteers:* 50
Website: stmarksfoundation.org
Activities: Education, training; advancement of health or saving of lives
Address: St Mark's Hospital, Watford Road, Harrow, Middlesex, HA1 3UJ
Trustees: Mr Sharad Rathke, Ms Catherine Boardman, Mr Paul Bernard Bouscarle, Sir Thomas Richard Troubridge, Dr Michele Mary Marshall, Ms Margaret Burgess, Dr Andrew Latchford
Income: £1,667,246 [2017]; £2,107,474 [2016]; £2,070,146 [2015]; £1,225,083 [2014]; £1,203,028 [2013]

St. Martin-in-the-Fields Charity
Registered: 21 Mar 2014 *Employees:* 4 *Volunteers:* 78
Tel: 020 7766 1125 *Website:* smitf.org
Activities: The prevention or relief of poverty
Address: 6 St Martin's Place, London, WC2N 4JH
Trustees: Mr Christopher Smith CBE, Mr Jonathan Burdett, Ms Catherine Murray, Mr Mike Wooldridge, Ms Olivia Frances Harris, Mrs Helen Simpson, Rev Sam Wells, Ms Caroline Wiertz, Ms Patricia Castana
Income: £3,028,785 [2017]; £2,489,769 [2016]; £2,128,688 [2015]

St. Mary's Convent and Nursing Home (Chiswick)
Registered: 16 May 2000 *Employees:* 109 *Volunteers:* 20
Tel: 020 8994 4641 *Website:* saintmarysconventchiswick.org
Activities: The advancement of health or saving of lives; disability; religious activities
Address: St Marys Convent & Nursing Home, Burlington Lane, London, W4 2QE
Trustees: Sister Jennifer Anne SSM, Mr John Barrie Randle, Sister Cynthia Clare SSM, Sir Graham Morgan, Sister Mary Paul SSM, Mr Robert Ian Turner, Mr Colin MacKay, Sister Mary Clare
Income: £3,189,606 [2017]; £3,170,707 [2016]; £4,457,222 [2015]; £2,560,263 [2014]; £2,356,020 [2013]

St. Michael's Fellowship
Registered: 31 Mar 1994 Employees: 81 Volunteers: 5
Tel: 020 8835 9570 Website: stmichaelsfellowship.org.uk
Activities: General charitable purposes; accommodation, housing
Address: St Michaels Fellowship, 136 Streatham High Road, London, SW16 1BW
Trustees: Will Anderson, Philippa Owen, Corina Forman, Mary Gibson, Mrs Alison Jane Dixon, Annie Brough, Richard Barron, Stephen Hair, Dr Valerie Jean Wass
Income: £2,366,088 [2017]; £2,635,535 [2016]; £2,397,396 [2015]; £2,074,384 [2014]; £2,330,926 [2013]

St. Michael's School Trust
Registered: 12 Aug 1999 Employees: 103
Tel: 01959 522137 Website: stmichaels.kent.sch.uk
Activities: Education, training
Address: St Michaels School, Otford Court, Otford, Sevenoaks, Kent, TN14 5SA
Trustees: St Michael's Trust Association Ltd
Income: £5,086,854 [2017]; £5,014,203 [2016]; £4,868,300 [2015]; £4,629,039 [2014]; £4,477,338 [2013]

St. Pauls Steiner Project Two
Registered: 8 Jul 1999 Employees: 37
Tel: 020 7226 4454 Website: stpaulssteinerschool.org
Activities: Education, training
Address: 1 St Pauls Road, London, N1 2QH
Trustees: Mrs Miranda Nunhofer, Mrs Sarah Alexander, Mr Jeffrey Baker, Mr Anton Dell, Mr James MacDonald Wright, Mr Alexander Wolpert
Income: £1,348,600 [2016]; £1,284,020 [2015]; £1,222,746 [2014]; £1,160,586 [2013]; £926,253 [2012]

St. Stephen's Aids Trust
Registered: 8 Feb 2010 Employees: 60
Website: ssat.org.uk
Activities: Education, training; advancement of health or saving of lives
Address: Chelsea Chambers, 262a Fulham Road, London, SW10 9EL
Trustees: Mr John Davidson OBE BA, Dr Simon Barton, Dr David Hawkins, Dr Rachael Jones, Mr John Corneille, Professor Frances Gotch, Professor Mark Bower, Prof Brian Gazzard, Dr Anton Pozniak, Wendy Fisher, Mr Paul Catchpole
Income: £6,537,013 [2017]; £5,947,501 [2016]; £5,590,339 [2015]; £1,871,527 [2014]; £2,625,603 [2013]

St. Teresa's School Effingham Trust
Registered: 18 Dec 2002 Employees: 148
Tel: 01372 452037 Website: st-teresas.com
Activities: Education, training; religious activities
Address: St Teresas School, Effingham Hill, Dorking, Surrey, RH5 6ST
Trustees: Mr Michael Bray, Mr Graham Paulson, Mrs Heather Brennan, Mrs Annette Turner, Mr Richard Wynne-Griffith, Mr Iain Morgan, Mrs Rachel Owen, Mr Ian Sherrington, Rev Alexander Hill, Mrs Sally Hayes, Mrs Maureen Wilkinson
Income: £8,034,483 [2016]; £7,431,554 [2015]; £6,709,329 [2014]; £6,127,949 [2013]; £5,518,570 [2012]

St.Peter's School, York
Registered: 11 Apr 2011 Employees: 267 Volunteers: 45
Tel: 01904 527401 Website: stpetersyorkorg.uk
Activities: Education, training
Address: St Peters School, Clifton, York, YO30 6AB
Trustees: Dr Ann Lees, Mr James Edward Bradshaw Burdass, Mrs Daryl Margaret Hayward, Mr Phillip B Hilling, Ms Pervinder Kaur, Mr Adrian Taylor, Carol Bailey, Dr Simon Hinchcliffe, Rev'd Canon Dr Christopher Paul Collingwood, Mr Stephen Town, Miss Susan Palmer, Mr William Woolley, Professor Martin Matravers, Mr Paul Widdicombe, Mrs Jenny Copley-Farnell
Income: £16,372,133 [2016]; £15,621,223 [2015]; £15,080,581 [2014]; £14,404,902 [2013]; £14,720,753 [2012]

The Stable Family Home Trust
Registered: 3 Sep 2002 Employees: 72 Volunteers: 25
Tel: 01425 478043 Website: sfht.org.uk
Activities: Education, training; disability; accommodation, housing
Address: Stables Family Home Trust, The Stables, Bisterne, Ringwood, Hants, BH24 3BN
Trustees: Mr John Hatchard, Mrs Susan Pepper, Mr Simon Frederick Farrow, Mr John Mason, Mr Clive Anthony Graham Clifford, Mr Frederick Leslie Graham Tucker, Mr Mike Thacker, Mrs Anne Rippon-Swaine
Income: £3,031,705 [2017]; £2,575,401 [2016]; £2,384,014 [2015]; £2,140,546 [2014]; £2,112,567 [2013]

Stafford & Rural Homes Limited
Registered: 22 Dec 2005 Employees: 179
Tel: 01785 216741 Website: sarh.co.uk
Activities: Education, training; disability; prevention or relief of poverty; accommodation, housing; economic, community development, employment; other charitable purposes
Address: Stafford & Rural Homes, 1 Parker Court, Staffordshire Technology Park, Stafford, ST18 0WP
Trustees: Ms Angela Loughran, Mr Gareth Jones, Ms Gillian Parminder Kaur Pardesi, Alison Hadden, Mr Craig Royall, Ms Joy Street, Ms Tina Swani, Tim Harris, Mr Philip Green, Mr Richard Brian Lawrence
Income: £32,794,000 [2017]; £28,547,000 [2016]; £27,549,000 [2015]; £26,205,000 [2014]; £24,628,000 [2013]

Stafford Independent Grammar School
Registered: 7 Sep 1982 Employees: 126
Tel: 01889 207018 Website: staffordgrammar.co.uk
Activities: Education, training
Address: 1 The Green, Weston, Stafford, ST18 0JH
Trustees: Mr John Cunningham Lotz MB BS FRCS, Mrs Pauline Pearsall, Mr Alan Wright, Mrs Helen Louise Watson Jones, Rev John James Davis, Mrs Julia Causer, Mr Brian Karl Hodges, Mr David Michael Pearsall JP, Mr Barry John Baggott, Mr Colin Sproston, Mrs Judith Coleman
Income: £4,713,456 [2017]; £4,627,967 [2016]; £4,773,176 [2015]; £4,720,139 [2014]; £4,598,020 [2013]

Staffordshire & Birmingham Agricultural Society
Registered: 4 Jan 1999 Employees: 12 Volunteers: 200
Tel: 01785 258060 Website: staffscountyshowground.co.uk
Activities: Environment, conservation, heritage
Address: County Showground, Weston Road, Stafford, ST18 0BD
Trustees: George Alfred Greaves, Mr Michael Thompstone, Mr Anthony Winterton
Income: £1,779,121 [2017]; £1,742,617 [2016]; £1,714,968 [2015]; £1,660,020 [2014]; £701,686 [2013]

Staffordshire North and Stoke-on-Trent Citizens Advice Bureaux

Registered: 10 Dec 1990 *Employees:* 107 *Volunteers:* 100
Tel: 01782 408650 *Website:* snscab.org.uk
Activities: General charitable purposes; disability; prevention or relief of poverty
Address: Citizens Advice Bureau, 13-15 Cheapside, Stoke on Trent, Staffs, ST1 1HL
Trustees: Mr Bertram Cedric Lawton Bert Lawton, Mr James Davies, Mr Reginald John Pemberton, Ms Madelaine Mary Lovatt, Mrs Angela Jayne Wilshaw, Mrs Emor Porteous, Lesley Haines, Mrs Jacqueline Seaman, Mr Ahmad Mlouk, Mr Robert John Holt, Mr Trevor Watkins
Income: £2,970,542 [2017]; £2,579,048 [2016]; £2,433,141 [2015]; £2,454,447 [2014]; £2,202,556 [2013]

Staffordshire South West Citizens Advice Bureau

Registered: 13 Feb 2013 *Employees:* 31 *Volunteers:* 75
Tel: 01785 283472 *Website:* staffswcab.org.uk
Activities: Education, training; prevention or relief of poverty
Address: Citizens Advice Bureau, 17 Eastgate Street, Stafford, ST16 2LZ
Trustees: Mr Peter Wilkinson, Mrs E Robinson, Mr John Davies, Mr David Mee, Mrs Bev Jocelyn, Mr Ian James, Mr Martin Cumberlidge, Mr Martin Charles Wallbank, Mr Gerry Hindley, Mrs Isabella Davies, Mrs Jane Alison Matthewman, Mrs Patricia Mary Rowlands, Mr John Clifford Preston, Mr Paul Thomas Weetman
Income: £1,233,572 [2017]; £1,471,914 [2016]; £1,227,617 [2015]; £843,067 [2014]

Staffordshire University Students' Union

Registered: 28 Nov 2012 *Employees:* 230 *Volunteers:* 250
Tel: 01782 294377 *Website:* staffsunion.com
Activities: General charitable purposes; education, training; arts, culture, heritage, science; amateur sport; economic, community development, employment; human rights, religious or racial harmony, equality or diversity; recreation
Address: Faculty of Arts, Staffordshire University, College Road, Stoke on Trent, Staffs, ST4 2XW
Trustees: Swetha Reddy, Amy Smith, Andy Wright, Zenu Mirza, Tash Crump, Darren Clarke, Danny Smith, Charlene De La Cruz, Sam Pillow, Sabaat Nadeem
Income: £3,870,084 [2017]; £4,141,875 [2016]; £3,968,680 [2015]; £4,507,024 [2014]; £4,046,136 [2013]

Staffordshire Wildlife Trust Limited

Registered: 23 Sep 1969 *Employees:* 65 *Volunteers:* 428
Tel: 01889 880100 *Website:* staffs-wildlife.org.uk
Activities: Education, training; environment, conservation, heritage
Address: The Wolseley Centre, Wolseley Bridge, Stafford, ST17 0WT
Trustees: Bernard Price, Mr Richard Charles Higgs, Dr Ruth Green, Mr Michael Thomas Walker, Mr Ian Downing, Mrs Julia Hagan, Mr Paul Andrew Hackney, Miss Suzanne Margaret Carr, Sir Philip John Hunter, Mr Nicholas Andrew Young, Ms Rachel Kelsall, Lisa Stephenson
Income: £2,484,000 [2016]; £2,704,173 [2015]; £2,543,776 [2014]; £2,797,973 [2013]; £2,816,705 [2012]

Staffordshire Winter Sports Club

Registered: 11 Dec 2012 *Employees:* 100 *Volunteers:* 30
Tel: 01922 419594
Activities: Education, training; advancement of health or saving of lives; disability; amateur sport; economic, community development, employment
Address: Silverblades Ice Rink, Unit 8-10, Walkmill Business Park, Walkmill Way, Cannock, Staffs, WS11 0XE
Trustees: Mr Darren Green, Mr Heath Rhodes, Mr Tim Fife
Income: £1,819,379 [2017]; £1,561,679 [2016]; £1,292,774 [2015]; £354,656 [2014]

Stag Community Arts Centre

Registered: 11 Aug 2010 *Employees:* 21 *Volunteers:* 100
Tel: 01732 450175 *Website:* stagsevenoaks.co.uk
Activities: Education, training; religious activities; arts, culture, heritage, science; economic, community development, employment; recreation
Address: Stag Community Arts Centre, London Road, Sevenoaks, Kent, TN13 1ZZ
Trustees: Pam Walshe, Merilyn Canet, Anthony Styles Clayton, Simon Raikes, Nicolas Busvine OBE, Rachel Parry, Maxine Chakowa, Richard Parry, Robert Piper, Roderick Hogarth, Stephen Arnold, Mr Edward Parson, Oliver Schneider, Edward Waite
Income: £1,119,410 [2017]; £1,095,103 [2016]; £1,026,840 [2015]; £1,105,919 [2014]; £1,077,643 [2013]

Staines Preparatory School Trust

Registered: 28 Apr 1987 *Employees:* 81
Tel: 01784 450909 *Website:* stainesprep.co.uk
Activities: Education, training
Address: Staines Preparatory School, 3 Gresham Road, Staines upon Thames, Middlesex, TW18 2BT
Trustees: Mr Richard Howard Chadburn, Mr Robert Davies, Mrs Wendy Ransom, Mrs Mary Robinson, Mrs Penelope Anne Austin, Mrs Sarah Caulfield, Mrs Jennifer Margaret Sice, Mr Michael Bannister, Mr Richard Adams, Mr Matthew Hall, Mr Anthony Madigan
Income: £3,823,335 [2017]; £3,797,012 [2016]; £3,824,274 [2015]; £3,452,894 [2014]; £3,044,719 [2013]

Stakeholder Democracy Network

Registered: 16 Jul 2012 *Employees:* 29
Tel: 020 7065 0845 *Website:* stakeholderdemocracy.org
Activities: Education, training; prevention or relief of poverty; arts, culture, heritage, science; environment, conservation, heritage; economic, community development, employment; human rights, religious or racial harmony, equality or diversity
Address: Stakeholder Democracy Network, 56-64 Leonard Street, London, EC2A 4LT
Trustees: Josie D'Angelo, Marc Nekaitar
Income: £1,239,364 [2017]; £660,616 [2016]; £3,262,544 [2015]; £2,660,269 [2014]; £1,195,544 [2013]

Stallcombe House

Registered: 14 Jan 1982 *Employees:* 73 *Volunteers:* 9
Tel: 01392 877200 *Website:* stallcombehouse.co.uk
Activities: Disability
Address: c/o Redwoods, 2 Clyst Works, Clyst Road, Topsham, Exeter, EX3 0DB
Trustees: Mr John Michael Sillett, Mr Christopher Mark Retallack, Mr Geoffrey Douglas Hall Pook, Mrs Anne Elizabeth Liverton, Mrs Eileen Elizabeth Wragg
Income: £2,343,300 [2016]; £2,238,468 [2015]; £2,151,617 [2014]; £2,125,638 [2013]; £2,073,481 [2012]

Stamford Endowed Schools
Registered: 17 Nov 1966 *Employees:* 503 *Volunteers:* 77
Tel: 01780 750340 *Website:* ses.lincs.sch.uk
Activities: Education, training
Address: Stamford School, Bursars Office, 16 St Pauls Street, Stamford, Lincs, PE9 2BE
Trustees: Stamford Endowed Schools Trustee Limited
Income: £22,731,000 [2017]; £22,371,000 [2016]; £21,396,000 [2015]; £21,826,000 [2014]; £20,802,000 [2013]

The Stanborough Press Limited
Registered: 9 Jun 1969 *Employees:* 25
Tel: 01476 591700 *Website:* stanboroughpress.org.uk
Activities: Religious activities
Address: Stanborough Press Ltd, Londonthorpe Road, Grantham, Lincs, NG31 9SL
Trustees: Mr Graham Marcus Barham, Mr Earl Jude Ramharacksingh, Pastor John Charles Surridge, Mr Julian Hibbert, Pastor Richard Sebastian Jackson, Mr John Middleditch, Mr Victor Pilmoor, Rev Emmanuel Osei, Pastor Ian Walter Wellington Sweeney, Miss Elisabeth Sanguesa Abenia, Mr Paul Wesley Thompson, Mr Trevor Johnson
Income: £2,791,194 [2016]; £2,282,738 [2015]; £3,029,554 [2014]; £2,730,058 [2013]; £2,952,455 [2012]

Stand By Me
Registered: 30 Mar 1995 *Employees:* 11 *Volunteers:* 8
Tel: 01708 442271 *Website:* standby.me
Activities: Education, training; advancement of health or saving of lives; prevention or relief of poverty; overseas aid, famine relief; accommodation, housing; religious activities; economic, community development, employment
Address: 13-15 Butts Green Road, Hornchurch, Essex, RM11 2JR
Trustees: Mr James Laing, Mr Edward Carpenter, Mr Richard Irwin, Mr Peter Newall
Income: £1,644,230 [2017]; £1,697,625 [2016]; £1,250,769 [2015]; £1,334,602 [2014]; £1,282,829 [2013]

Standing Together Against Domestic Violence
Registered: 11 Oct 2001 *Employees:* 22 *Volunteers:* 2
Tel: 020 8748 5717 *Website:* standingtogether.org.uk
Activities: General charitable purposes
Address: Room 44d, 4th Floor, Standing Together, Polish Centre, 238-246 King Street, London, W6 0RF
Trustees: Mr James Anthony Reilly, Ms Rosemary Joy Farrar, Mr Andrew MacApline, Ceryse Nickless, Mr Simon Martin Letchford, Ms Dale Simon, Mrs Anne Elizabeth Wilkinson, Miss Kruti Patel, Ann Marie Corbett
Income: £1,285,241 [2017]; £962,285 [2016]; £891,828 [2015]; £802,778 [2014]; £719,807 [2013]

Stanford Trust
Registered: 24 Jun 1993
Tel: 020 7502 2813
Activities: Education, training; arts, culture, heritage, science
Address: 19 Norcott Road, London, N16 7EJ
Trustees: Mrs Jennifer Good, Mr Eric Carl Jonsson, Mr Howard Pearson
Income: £2,609,080 [2017]; £3,043,945 [2016]; £3,677,832 [2015]; £857,947 [2014]; £720,655 [2013]

Stansted Park Foundation
Registered: 17 Dec 2003 *Employees:* 17 *Volunteers:* 80
Tel: 023 9241 2265 *Website:* stanstedpark.co.uk
Activities: Education, training; arts, culture, heritage, science; environment, conservation, heritage
Address: Stansted Park Foundation, Stansted Park, Rowland's Castle, Hants, PO9 6DX
Trustees: Mr Yanni Petsopoulos, The Earl of Bessborough, Mrs Claire Fitzalan Howard, Mr James Royston Kenroy DL, Mr Max Davies
Income: £1,429,165 [2016]; £1,391,715 [2015]; £1,069,230 [2014]; £1,078,185 [2013]; £990,511 [2012]

Stapely Jewish Care Home Ltd
Registered: 27 Mar 2007 *Employees:* 90
Tel: 0151 724 3260 *Website:* merseyside-jewish-community.org.uk
Activities: The advancement of health or saving of lives; accommodation, housing
Address: Stapeley Residential & Nursing Home, North Mossley Hill Road, Liverpool, L18 8BR
Trustees: Mr Philip Saul Ettinger, Mr Robert Joel Ettinger
Income: £2,514,993 [2017]; £1,747,772 [2016]; £1,468,242 [2014]; £1,312,625 [2013]

Starlight Children's Foundation
Registered: 18 Feb 1987 *Employees:* 29 *Volunteers:* 2,000
Tel: 020 7262 2881 *Website:* starlight.org.uk
Activities: General charitable purposes; advancement of health or saving of lives
Address: Starlight Childrens Foundation, 227 Shepherd's Bush Road, London, W6 7AU
Trustees: Nick Mustoe, Major Christopher Hanbury, Richard Cook, Alasdair Hadden Paton, Mark Tasker, Zahra Lucas
Income: £7,243,740 [2017]; £8,626,901 [2016]; £8,261,877 [2015]; £9,862,482 [2014]; £9,946,947 [2013]

Starlow Charities Limited
Registered: 30 Jun 2000
Tel: 020 8802 9517
Activities: General charitable purposes; education, training; advancement of health or saving of lives; disability; prevention or relief of poverty; religious activities; amateur sport; environment, conservation, heritage
Address: 9 Craven Walk, London, N16 6BS
Trustees: Abraham Low, Mr Avraham Shwarts, Eve Low
Income: £2,913,743 [2017]; £3,097,237 [2016]; £1,073,617 [2015]; £270,626 [2014]; £194,723 [2013]

The Stars Foundation
Registered: 13 Aug 2001 *Employees:* 15
Tel: 020 7242 2022 *Website:* starsfoundation.org.uk
Activities: General charitable purposes
Address: Farrer & Co, 65-66 Lincoln's Inn Fields, London, WC2A 3LH
Trustees: The Honourable Mark Thomas Bridges, Mrs Sally Tennant, Professor Spyro Marcus St John Alexander, Mr Amr Dabbagh, Mr Mohamed H Jazeel, Ms Lynn Taliento
Income: £3,148,025 [2016]; £2,609,697 [2015]; £2,302,408 [2014]; £3,029,986 [2013]; £1,376,273 [2012]

Staying First
Registered: 29 Jul 1985 Employees: 31 Volunteers: 40
Tel: 020 8996 8890 Website: stayingfirst.co.uk
Activities: Disability; prevention or relief of poverty
Address: Staying Put Services, Mulliner House, Flanders Road, London, W4 1NN
Trustees: Mr Stephen Bashorun, Mr Roy Clark, Mr John Andrew Sparke, Ms Ruth Barnes, Mrs Helen Cox
Income: £4,106,327 [2017]; £2,934,854 [2016]; £4,356,201 [2015]; £4,581,627 [2014]; £2,671,342 [2013]

Staying Put
Registered: 21 Sep 2006 Employees: 19
Tel: 0113 287 1155 Website: stayingput.uk.net
Activities: Other charitable purposes
Address: Staying Put, 125 Main Street, Garforth, Leeds, LS25 1AF
Trustees: Ms Shelley Elaine Black, Mrs Laura Margaret Chapman, Ms Marilyn Susan Bryan, Oliver O'Leary
Income: £1,016,276 [2017]; £662,425 [2016]; £442,520 [2015]; £455,459 [2014]; £446,485 [2013]

The Steel Charitable Trust
Registered: 25 Nov 1976 Employees: 1
Tel: 01582 240601 Website: steelcharitabletrust.org.uk
Activities: General charitable purposes
Address: Suite 411, Jansel House, Hitchin Road, Luton, Beds, LU2 7XH
Trustees: Mr Anthony William Hawkins, Mrs Wendy Elizabeth Bailey, Mr Philip Cazenove Lawford, Mr Nicholas Edward Weatherley Wright, Dr Mary Natalie Patricia Briggs
Income: £1,242,276 [2017]; £2,251,298 [2016]; £1,177,450 [2015]; £1,136,275 [2014]; £1,089,538 [2013]

The Steinberg Family Charitable Trust
Registered: 23 Mar 1995 Employees: 1
Tel: 0161 903 8854
Activities: General charitable purposes; education, training; advancement of health or saving of lives; disability; prevention or relief of poverty; religious activities
Address: 16 Bollinway, Hale, Altrincham, Cheshire, WA15 0NZ
Trustees: Lady Beryl Steinberg, Mrs Lynne Rochelle Attias, Mr Jonathan Steinberg
Income: £2,446,973 [2017]; £3,027,220 [2016]; £5,850,121 [2015]; £3,110,073 [2014]; £6,579,671 [2013]

Rudolf Steiner School (South Devon) Limited
Registered: 3 Mar 1983 Employees: 46 Volunteers: 300
Tel: 07450 581936 Website: steiner-south-devon.org
Activities: Education, training
Address: 29 Chapel Court, St Vincents Road, Torquay, Devon, TQ1 4HQ
Trustees: Mr Christopher Cooper, Paul Mark Drewell Chairperson, Joshua Paul Malkin, Juliet Crittenden, Mrs Catherine Mary Day, Jacqueline Elizabeth Bagnall
Income: £1,223,637 [2016]; £1,222,952 [2015]; £1,232,930 [2014]; £1,182,640 [2013]; £1,123,157 [2012]

Rudolf Steiner School King's Langley Limited
Registered: 20 May 1964 Employees: 66 Volunteers: 25
Tel: 01923 262505 Website: rsskl.org
Activities: Education, training
Address: Rudolf Steiner School, Langley Hill, Kings Langley, Herts, WD4 9HG
Trustees: Jacob Tas, Mr Reinout Michael Koopmans, Peter Harrington, Laurence Chester, Veronica Held, Mr James Edmund Wesley Peacock, Mr John Leary-Joyce, Andree Piperides, Cordelia Bryan
Income: £3,096,770 [2017]; £2,872,218 [2016]; £2,983,110 [2015]; £3,094,688 [2014]; £2,834,445 [2013]

Elmfield Rudolf Steiner School Limited
Registered: 6 Dec 1973 Employees: 67 Volunteers: 80
Tel: 01384 394633 Website: elmfield.com
Activities: Education, training
Address: Elmfield School, Love Lane, Stourbridge, W Yorks, DY8 2EA
Trustees: Mr Maarten Ekama, Gertraud Soukup, Mrs Ursula Maria Werner, Rainer Klocke, Miss Jenny Susan Thorne, Mr Nicholas William Godwin, Mrs Janet Klaar, Mrs Sharon Rose, Mrs Ruth Lynne Beachim-Ratcliffe, Miss Sara Vivien Hunt, Mr Timothy Matthrw Roberts
Income: £1,304,957 [2016]; £1,232,817 [2015]; £1,221,653 [2014]; £1,259,348 [2013]; £1,254,076 [2012]

Stelios Philanthropic Foundation
Registered: 6 Apr 2011 Employees: 2
Tel: 056 0367 7488 Website: stelios.org
Activities: General charitable purposes; education, training; disability; prevention or relief of poverty; overseas aid, famine relief; environment, conservation, heritage; economic, community development, employment; other charitable purposes
Address: 10 Sydney Place, London, SW7 3NL
Trustees: Mr Malcolm Peter Barton, Mr Marios Eliades, Mr Donald Michael Manasse, Mr David Watson, Sir Stelios Haji-Ioannou, Mr Jean-Claude Louis Eude, Mr Nikolaos Mourkogiannis
Income: £3,172,015 [2016]; £2,481,606 [2015]; £1,465,730 [2014]; £1,601,990 [2013]

Step (UK) Ltd
Registered: 24 Jul 2008 Employees: 154
Website: step-uk.com
Activities: Education, training; prevention or relief of poverty; economic, community development, employment
Address: P O Box 801, Southsea, Hants, PO1 9EJ
Trustees: Mr Paul Susans, Andy Elliott, Mr Peter Richardson, Mrs Megan Dalton
Income: £1,695,269 [2017]; £1,498,559 [2016]; £981,652 [2015]; £37,340 [2013]; £14,200 [2012]

Step By Step Partnership Limited
Registered: 25 Jan 1990 Employees: 91 Volunteers: 15
Tel: 01252 346100 Website: stepbystep.org.uk
Activities: Education, training; accommodation, housing
Address: Step by Step Partnership Ltd, 36 Crimea Road, Aldershot, Hants, GU11 1UD
Trustees: John Devlin, Keith Gathergood, Ms Sarah Hamiduddin, Mr Philip Kent, Russell James, Mr Anthony John Murphy, Mr Paul Cummins
Income: £3,095,001 [2017]; £2,861,212 [2016]; £2,107,024 [2015]; £1,863,838 [2014]; £1,447,255 [2013]

Step By Step School Limited
Registered: 21 Mar 2002 *Employees:* 53
Tel: 01342 811852 *Website:* stepbystepschool.org.uk
Activities: Education, training; disability
Address: Grinstead Lane, Sharpthorne, E Sussex, RH19 4HP
Trustees: Mr Stuart King, Mr Daniel Horan, Ms Athene Burdge, Mr Bob Marsh, Dr Catherine Elizabeth James
Income: £1,851,808 [2017]; £1,749,952 [2016]; £1,620,692 [2015]; £1,455,090 [2014]; £1,289,848 [2013]

Step One Charity
Registered: 2 Jul 1964 *Employees:* 159
Tel: 01392 255428 *Website:* steponecharity.co.uk
Activities: Education, training; disability
Address: St Loye's Foundation, Beaufort House, 51 New North Road, Exeter, EX4 4EP
Trustees: Mr Graham Faulkner, Mr David Vaughan Hodgetts, Mr Imran Beider, Mr Peter McCann, Edmund Probert, Ms Diane Bassett, Mr Mark Rusbrooke Forbes Taylor, Mr Robert David Williams
Income: £3,945,099 [2017]; £5,623,307 [2016]; £4,071,110 [2015]; £4,736,707 [2014]; £4,043,302 [2013]

Stepping Stone Projects
Registered: 3 Oct 1991 *Employees:* 57 *Volunteers:* 4
Tel: 01706 353000 *Website:* stepping-stone.org.uk
Activities: General charitable purposes; accommodation, housing
Address: Stepping Stone Project, P O Box 153, Rochdale, Lancs, OL16 1FR
Trustees: Ms Susan Ashby, Ms Paula Du Plessis, Mrs Jane Allen, Mr Stephen McGuckian, Kay Owen, Mr David Berry, Mrs Diane Laming
Income: £3,091,308 [2017]; £2,690,967 [2016]; £2,804,044 [2015]; £2,574,786 [2014]; £2,637,513 [2013]

Stepping Stones School Hindhead Limited
Registered: 22 Jul 1994 *Employees:* 35 *Volunteers:* 10
Tel: 01428 609083 *Website:* steppingstones.org.uk
Activities: Education, training; disability; prevention or relief of poverty
Address: Stepping Stones School, Tower Road, Hindhead, Surrey, GU26 6SU
Trustees: Mr Sullivan, Mrs Anne Hayes, Mr James Dickson, Mr Timothy Armitage, Dr Ellie Clayden, Richard Norman, Mr David Forbes-Nixon, Mr Norman Stromsoy, Mrs Joanne Pickford, Mrs Jane Rudlin-Jones, Mr Danny Leeds, Mr Ryan Campbell
Income: £1,475,473 [2017]; £921,278 [2016]; £796,576 [2015]; £498,893 [2014]; £434,773 [2013]

Steps To Work (Walsall) Limited
Registered: 30 Oct 2003 *Employees:* 56
Tel: 01922 892007 *Website:* stepstowork.co.uk
Activities: Education, training; economic, community development, employment
Address: 105 Furzebank Way, Willenhall, W Midlands, WV12 4BZ
Trustees: Mr Ninder Johal, Mrs Susan Meryl Wood, Ged Jones, Miss Naheed Gultasib, Mr Paul Cadman, Mrs Eileen Schofield, Bob Thomas, Mr Manjit Singh Jhooty, Chris Towe, Mr Mike Gahir, Mr Andy Woodall
Income: £12,821,000 [2017]; £13,587,375 [2016]; £15,226,474 [2015]; £3,100,999 [2014]; £3,520,244 [2013]

The Sterry Family Foundation
Registered: 23 Sep 2011
Activities: Education, training; advancement of health or saving of lives; disability; prevention or relief of poverty; overseas aid, famine relief; arts, culture, heritage, science; amateur sport; recreation
Address: RSM, 5th Floor, Central Square, 29 Wellington Street, Leeds, LS1 4HG
Trustees: Mr David William Edmund Sterry, Miss Nicola Kate Clatworthy, Mr James William Sterry, Wendy Ann Sterry
Income: £2,568,352 [2017]; £40,323 [2016]; £25,651 [2015]; £51,689 [2014]; £45,738 [2013]

The Steve Morgan Foundation
Registered: 19 Jun 2001 *Employees:* 2
Tel: 01829 782800 *Website:* stevemorganfoundation.org.uk
Activities: Education, training; advancement of health or saving of lives; disability; prevention or relief of poverty; accommodation, housing; economic, community development, employment
Address: The Steve Morgan Foundation, P O Box 3517, Chester, CH1 9ET
Trustees: Mr Stephen Peter Morgan, Rhiannon Walker, Ms Sally Julia Morgan, Mr Vincent William Fairclough, Mr Ashley Martin Lewis, Mr Jonathan Roderick Charles Masters
Income: £204,257,541 [2017]; £936,013 [2016]; £1,897,037 [2015]; £1,165,741 [2014]; £1,678,504 [2013]

Stevenage Haven
Registered: 19 Sep 1997 *Employees:* 42 *Volunteers:* 20
Website: stevenagehaven.org.uk
Activities: Accommodation, housing
Address: 5 Ditchmore Lane, Stevenage, Herts, SG1 3LJ
Trustees: Mr Alan Stuart Curtis, Ms Ruth Margaret Paterson, Mr Robert Robinson, Mrs Teresa Callaghan, Miss Rosa Manning, Mrs Angela Corsbie Smith, Ms Lorna Copeland, Ms Sharon Forde, Ms Jess Dollimore
Income: £1,628,765 [2017]; £1,438,652 [2016]; £934,731 [2015]; £674,764 [2014]; £580,611 [2013]

Stevenage Leisure
Registered: 11 Nov 2011 *Employees:* 1,047 *Volunteers:* 40
Tel: 01438 242233 *Website:* sll.co.uk
Activities: General charitable purposes; arts, culture, heritage, science; recreation
Address: Stevenage Leisure Ltd, Stevenage Leisure Centre, Lytton Way, Stevenage, Herts, SG1 1LZ
Trustees: Mr Ian Dennis Paske, Mr Derek Michael Williams, Mr Zayd Al-Jawad, Mrs Jacqueline Marie Salisbury, Mrs Yolanda Rugg, Jo Ransom
Income: £22,403,102 [2017]; £19,995,566 [2016]; £18,938,264 [2015]; £18,035,668 [2014]; £17,006,121 [2013]

Stewards Company Ltd
Registered: 26 Jan 1965 *Employees:* 3
Tel: 01225 427236
Activities: The prevention or relief of poverty; religious activities
Address: 124 Wells Road, Bath, BA2 3AH
Trustees: Mr Alexander Lindsay McIlhinney, Dr John Henry Burness, Mr David Roberts, Mr Alan Paterson, Mr Andrew Bartholomew Griffiths, Mr John Gamble, Mr Simon Tomlinson, Mr Keith Bintley, Mr David Crawford Bingham, Mr Philip Symons, Mr Paul Young, Mr Denis Cooper, Mr Glyn Davies, Mr Ian Childs, Mr Andrew Mayo, Mr J Aitken, Dr Jonathan Loose, Mr Joshua Michael Fitzhugh
Income: £2,298,239 [2016]; £3,898,885 [2015]; £1,826,325 [2014]; £2,211,186 [2013]; £2,137,580 [2012]

Stewardship Services (UKET) Limited
Registered: 28 Apr 1965 *Employees:* 43
Tel: 020 8502 5600 *Website:* stewardship.org.uk
Activities: Education, training; prevention or relief of poverty; religious activities
Address: Stewardship, Unit A, 1 Lamb's Passage, London, EC1Y 8AB
Trustees: Ram Gidoomal, Antony Barnes, Mr Simon Blake ACA CF, Sandra Cobbin, Mr Gareth Burns, Mrs Helen Alice Senior CA, Mr Michael Wright, Miss Stephanie Clare Biden, Mr Jeremy Marshall, Mrs Heather Grizzle, Ritz Steytler
Income: £71,922,000 [2016]; £64,706,000 [2015]; £66,308,000 [2014]; £62,893,000 [2013]; £54,406,000 [2012]

Sir Halley Stewart Trust
Registered: 28 Jan 1963 *Employees:* 1
Tel: 020 8144 0375 *Website:* sirhalleystewart.org.uk
Activities: General charitable purposes; advancement of health or saving of lives; disability; religious activities; economic, community development, employment
Address: Secretary To The Trustees, BM Sir Halley Stewart Trust, London, WC1N 3XX
Trustees: Professor Phyllida Parsloe Emeritus Trustee, Professor John Wyatt BSc MBBS FRCP FRCPCH, Professor John Lennard-Jones Emeritus Trustee, Mr W Kirkman Mbe Ma Emeritus Trustee, Mrs Theresa Bartlett BSc Hons, Dr James Bunn, Mrs Amy Isabella Holcroft BA, Ms Celia Atherton OBE, Mr Andrew Graystone, Mrs Joanna Womack, Dr Duncan Stewart, Professor Philip Whitfield BA MA PhD, Professor Gordon Wilcock, Mr Andrew Wauchope, Mrs Louisa Elder, Mrs Jane Gilliard BA CQSW, Revd Professor David Wilkinson, Mr Paul Harrod
Income: £1,134,000 [2017]; £1,028,000 [2016]; £964,000 [2015]; £1,063,000 [2014]; £948,000 [2013]

Stillbirth and Neonatal Death Society
Registered: 26 Jul 1988 *Employees:* 42 *Volunteers:* 1,000
Tel: 020 7436 7940 *Website:* sands.org.uk
Activities: Education, training; advancement of health or saving of lives
Address: Suite GF2, Ground Floor, Victoria Charity Centre, 11 Belgrave Road, London, SW1V 1RB
Trustees: Mr Derek Neale Jenkins, Mr Michael Smith, Mrs Sarah-Jane Evans, Dr Alyson Hunter, Mr Joel Mitchell, Mrs Susanna Speirs, Mrs Angela McCafferty, Mr Edward Ford, Mrs Stephanie Frearson, Mrs Mary Catherine Roberts, Mrs Zoe Eleanor Renton
Income: £3,873,534 [2017]; £3,483,850 [2016]; £2,934,193 [2015]; £2,739,791 [2014]; £2,463,457 [2013]

Stobart Newlands Charitable Trust
Registered: 20 Dec 1989
Tel: 016974 78631
Activities: Religious activities
Address: Millcroft, Newlands, Hesket Newmarket, Wigton, Cumbria, CA7 8HP
Trustees: Ronnie Stobart, Peter Stobart, Mrs Linda Elizabeth Rigg, Richard Stobart
Income: £1,056,861 [2016]; £1,087,299 [2015]; £1,460,608 [2014]; £1,837,790 [2013]; £2,276,858 [2012]

Stockdales of Sale, Altrincham and District Ltd
Registered: 30 Sep 1980 *Employees:* 122 *Volunteers:* 25
Tel: 0161 973 2296 *Website:* stockdales.org.uk
Activities: Disability; accommodation, housing
Address: 34 Harboro Road, Sale, Cheshire, M33 5AH
Trustees: Mrs Dorothy Anne Watkins, Mr Anthony Gresty, Mrs Deborah Leigh, Mr Peter Vick Gazely Wall, Mr Nigel Mather
Income: £3,264,504 [2017]; £2,614,980 [2016]; £2,419,570 [2015]; £2,195,926 [2014]; £2,061,943 [2013]

The Stockport Engineering Training Association
Registered: 13 Aug 1980 *Employees:* 28
Tel: 0161 480 9822 *Website:* setatraining.com
Activities: Education, training
Address: 2 Hall Cottages, Manchester Road, Carrington, Manchester, M31 4BD
Trustees: Mr James Raymond Moss, Ms Susan Arslan, Mr Robert Graham Howarth, Dr Moray Kidd
Income: £1,683,431 [2017]; £1,778,657 [2016]; £1,616,726 [2015]; £1,542,169 [2014]; £1,494,661 [2013]

Stockport Grammar School
Registered: 23 Jul 2007 *Employees:* 216 *Volunteers:* 12
Tel: 0161 419 2401 *Website:* stockportgrammar.co.uk
Activities: Education, training
Address: Stockport Grammar School, Buxton Road, Stockport, Cheshire, SK2 7AF
Trustees: Mr Roger Paul Yates, Mr Philip Adrian Cuddy, Mr Peter Locke, Mr John Shackleton, Professor John Dainton, Mr Paul Milner, Mrs Samantha Lansbury, Mr Jonathan Lee, Mr Anthony Carr, Dr Elizabeth Margaret Morris, Mr Keith Lansdale, Mr Frank Andrew Booth, Miss Sarah Jane Carroll, Mr Peter Laban Giblin, Mr Christopher Frank Dunn, Mr Philip John Britton, Mrs Christine Muscutt, Mr Adrian Simpson
Income: £16,709,690 [2016]; £14,705,035 [2015]; £13,659,210 [2014]; £13,266,513 [2013]; £12,603,481 [2012]

Stockport Plaza Trust Limited
Registered: 12 Jul 1999 *Employees:* 14 *Volunteers:* 100
Website: stockportplaza.co.uk
Activities: Arts, culture, heritage, science; environment, conservation, heritage
Address: Plaza Theatre, Mersey Square, Stockport, Cheshire, SK1 1SP
Trustees: David Blake, Nigel Anderton, Linda Weekes-Holt, Melanie Spooner, Ian Hodgkiss, Richard Gray, Mr Chris Jeffries, Terry Carnes
Income: £1,005,098 [2016]; £869,704 [2015]; £1,461,388 [2014]; £1,435,671 [2013]; £1,948,365 [2012]

Stockport Sports Trust
Registered: 18 Oct 2002 *Employees:* 238
Website: lifeleisure.net
Activities: General charitable purposes; education, training; amateur sport
Address: Company Registrations Online Ltd, Maple Road, Bramhall, Stockport, Cheshire, SK7 2DH
Trustees: Mr Mike Atkinson, Mr Jason Pate, Mr Melvyn James Pomfret, Mr Bernard James Lupton, Mrs Val Cottam MBE, Ms Charlene Nunn, Mr Andrew Robert Cawley
Income: £11,548,312 [2017]; £11,486,432 [2016]; £11,622,347 [2015]; £11,521,684 [2014]; £11,015,990 [2013]

Stockport, East Cheshire, High Peak, Urmston & District Cerebral Palsy Society
Registered: 13 Mar 1992 *Employees:* 225 *Volunteers:* 33
Tel: 0161 432 1248 *Website:* stockportcp.co.uk
Activities: Disability
Address: Granville House, 20 Parsonage Road, Heaton Moor, Stockport, Cheshire, SK4 4JZ
Trustees: Mrs Nicole Guy, Mr Jonathan Bloom, Mr Roy Malcolm Dudley-Southern, Miss Natalie Grace Jackson, Miss Maria Repanos, Mr Michael Francis Bailey, Rachel Creamer
Income: £3,834,957 [2017]; £4,446,146 [2016]; £4,499,249 [2015]; £4,242,704 [2014]; £4,074,337 [2013]

Stockton Arts Centre
Registered: 17 Jan 2003 *Employees:* 58 *Volunteers:* 10
Tel: 01642 525181 *Website:* arconline.co.uk
Activities: Education, training; arts, culture, heritage, science
Address: Arc, 60 Dovecot Street, Stockton on Tees, Cleveland, TS18 1LL
Trustees: Mr Godfrey James Worsdale, Mr Ishy Din, Mrs Lynne Snowball, Mr Aaron Bowman, Ms Kate Craddock, Ms Jane Robinson, Mr Patrick Masheder, Mr John McCann
Income: £2,628,876 [2017]; £2,189,486 [2016]; £2,045,505 [2015]; £1,119,961 [2014]; £1,206,564 [2013]

Stoke City Community Trust
Registered: 28 May 2004 *Employees:* 50
Website: stokecityfc.com
Activities: General charitable purposes; education, training; disability; amateur sport
Address: Stoke City Football Club, Bet365 Stadium, Stanley Matthews Way, Stoke on Trent, Staffs, ST4 4EG
Trustees: Mr Anthony John Scholes, Mr Gary Mellor, John Pelling, Mr Robert Flello, Mr Dennis Smith
Income: £1,663,394 [2017]; £1,340,416 [2016]; £1,342,742 [2015]; £1,178,301 [2014]; £547,532 [2013]

Stoke College Educational Trust Ltd
Registered: 16 Jul 1968 *Employees:* 60 *Volunteers:* 20
Tel: 01787 279407 *Website:* stokecollege.co.uk
Activities: Education, training; environment, conservation, heritage
Address: Stoke College, Stoke by Clare, Sudbury, Suffolk, CO10 8JE
Trustees: Mr Simon Packford, Mr Jonathan Burchell, Mrs Jennifer Mary Burrett, Mrs Lydia Roe, Mr David Anthony Cardle
Income: £1,709,187 [2016]; £1,843,447 [2015]; £1,761,670 [2014]; £1,536,516 [2013]; £2,070,016 [2012]

Stoke-on-Trent and North Staffordshire Theatre Trust Limited
Registered: 31 Jul 1967 *Employees:* 116 *Volunteers:* 130
Tel: 01782 717954 *Website:* newvictheatre.org.uk
Activities: Education, training; arts, culture, heritage, science
Address: New Victoria Theatre, Etruria Road, Newcastle-under-Lyme, Staffs, ST5 0JG
Trustees: Cllr Anthony Munday, Mr Ian Parry, Mr Colin Ian Barcroft, Mr Jonathan Mark Stansfield Shepherd, Ms Susan Violet Honeyands, Miss Gabriella Kervelle Avilon Gay, Professor David Amigoni, Mr Mark Holland, Mr Bryan Carnes, Ms Sara Louise Gilroy Williams, Ms Iona Mary Jones, Mr Christopher John Lewis, Mrs Ann Elizabeth Fisher, Mr John Edwin Sambrook, Ms Gwendalyn Jane Hughes
Income: £3,776,939 [2017]; £6,472,854 [2016]; £4,028,960 [2015]; £3,617,233 [2014]; £3,285,950 [2013]

The Sir Oswald Stoll Foundation
Registered: 22 Sep 1962 *Employees:* 41
Tel: 020 7385 2110 *Website:* stoll.org.uk
Activities: Accommodation, housing
Address: Stoll, 446 Fulham Road, London, SW6 1DT
Trustees: Mrs Uta Hope, Mr John James Tomalin, Mrs Diana Hodson, Mr Shaun Cooper FCMA, Mrs Clare Hughes, Mr Simon Patrick Philips, Brigadier David Godsal MBE, Air Commodore Andrew Fryer, Mr Patrick Aylmer, Mr Alexander Gordon Hamilton, Mr Roger Shrimplin, Mr George Thronton
Income: £3,681,269 [2017]; £3,649,709 [2016]; £2,711,220 [2015]; £2,475,261 [2014]; £2,421,517 [2013]

The Stoller Charitable Trust
Registered: 29 Sep 1982
Activities: General charitable purposes; education, training; advancement of health or saving of lives; disability; prevention or relief of poverty; arts, culture, heritage, science; economic, community development, employment
Address: 24 Low Crompton Road, Royton, Oldham, Lancs, OL2 6YR
Trustees: Roger Gould, Lady Stoller, Ksl Trustees Limited, Sir Norman Stoller CBE KSTJ DL, Andrew Dixon
Income: £2,362,284 [2017]; £1,878,104 [2016]; £2,034,748 [2015]; £47,505,750 [2014]; £194,895 [2013]

The Stone Family Foundation
Registered: 3 Dec 2015 *Employees:* 2
Tel: 020 7663 6825 *Website:* thesff.com
Activities: General charitable purposes; education, training; advancement of health or saving of lives; prevention or relief of poverty; overseas aid, famine relief; environment, conservation, heritage; economic, community development, employment
Address: Stone Family Foundation, 22 Upper Ground, London, SE1 9PD
Trustees: Mr John Kyle Stone, Mr David Steinegger, Mr Charles Hugh Edwards
Income: £55,927,129 [2016]

The Stonebridge Trust
Registered: 24 Nov 1977 *Employees:* 4
Tel: 01623 822301 *Website:* thoresby.com
Activities: Environment, conservation, heritage
Address: c/o Estate Office, Thoresby Park, Newark, Notts, NG22 9EJ
Trustees: Mr Hugh Patrick Matheson, Ms Claire Van Cleave Brainerd, Mr William James Emlyn Price
Income: £2,367,667 [2016]; £263,737 [2015]; £847,394 [2014]; £345,182 [2013]; £425,361 [2012]

Stonewall Equality Limited
Registered: 17 Dec 2003 *Employees:* 114 *Volunteers:* 40
Tel: 020 7593 1850 *Website:* stonewall.org.uk
Activities: General charitable purposes; education, training; prevention or relief of poverty; human rights, religious or racial harmony, equality or diversity
Address: Stonewall, 192 St John Street, London, EC1V 4JY
Trustees: Oliver Rowe, Sheldon Mills, Jan Gooding, Tim Toulmin, Katie Cornhill, Mr Simon Blake, Lisa Pinney, Phyllis Opoku-Gyimah, Mr Richard Beavan
Income: £7,245,714 [2017]; £7,015,809 [2016]; £6,319,119 [2015]; £5,387,006 [2014]; £4,334,054 [2013]

Stonyhurst

Registered: 5 Feb 2009 *Employees:* 378
Tel: 01254 827345 *Website:* stonyhurst.ac.uk
Activities: Education, training; religious activities
Address: Stonyhurst College, Stonyhurst, Clitheroe, Lancs, BB7 9PZ
Trustees: Mr Richard Brumby, Mr John Edmund Stoer, Mr Michael Davis, Mr Anthony Chitnis, Dr Nuala Mellows, Mr Stephen Edward Withnell, Mr Simon Glassbrook, Mr John Cowdall, Mr Mark Belderbos, Father Matthew Power Sj, Dr Maria Guzkowska, Mr David Finn, Fr Roger Dawson, Mrs Christine Kuenen
Income: £16,547,575 [2017]; £16,533,323 [2016]; £15,171,427 [2015]; £14,451,688 [2014]; £13,859,102 [2013]

Stop Ivory

Registered: 7 Jun 2013 *Employees:* 2
Website: stopivory.org
Activities: Education, training; animals; environment, conservation, heritage
Address: Mishcon de Reya Solicitors, Summit House, 12 Red Lion Square, London, WC1R 4QD
Trustees: Mr I Craig, Mr Ali Akber Kaka, Mr D Stulb, Mr M Joseph
Income: £1,438,699 [2017]; £767,136 [2016]; £235,866 [2015]; £278,150 [2014]

Marie Stopes International

Registered: 9 May 1973 *Employees:* 12,357
Website: mariestopes.org.uk
Activities: The advancement of health or saving of lives; prevention or relief of poverty; human rights, religious or racial harmony, equality or diversity
Address: Marie Stopes, 1 Conway Street, London, W1T 6LP
Trustees: Ms Suzanna Taverne, Mr Timothy Morton Rutter, Dr Kristin Anne Rutter, Ms Jess Search, Philip Dow Harvey Esq, Claire Emma Morris, Dr Mohsina Ahsan Bilgrami, Mr Franki Nicolas Braeken
Income: £289,962,000 [2016]; £266,297,000 [2015]; £242,004,000 [2014]; £211,928,000 [2013]; £173,412,000 [2012]

Stormont School

Registered: 16 Sep 1964 *Employees:* 48 *Volunteers:* 32
Tel: 01707 654037 *Website:* stormontschool.org
Activities: Education, training
Address: Stormont School, The Causeway, Potters Bar, Herts, EN6 5HA
Trustees: Mr John Howard Salmon, Mrs Carolyn Gedye, Mr Andrew James Newland, Dr Sophie Harriet Pattison, Mrs Joanna Louise Sandra Cameron, Mr Kevin John Douglas, Dr Alison Frances Ritchie, Stuart Dench, Mr Ajay Rajpal, Mrs Victoria Jane Gocher
Income: £1,993,990 [2017]; £1,937,783 [2016]; £1,922,657 [2015]; £1,899,230 [2014]; £1,814,758 [2013]

The Story Museum

Registered: 26 Jan 2005 *Employees:* 17 *Volunteers:* 150
Tel: 01865 790050 *Website:* storymuseum.org.uk
Activities: Education, training; arts, culture, heritage, science; environment, conservation, heritage
Address: Rochester House, 42 Pembroke Street, Oxford, OX1 1BP
Trustees: Mr David Fickling, David Wood, Dr Will Bowen, Mr Roland Fuggle, Maggie Whitlum, Ms Maggie Farrar, Mr Ewen Cameron-Watt, John Belk Lange, Mrs Jill Hudson, Mr Michael Heaney, Mr Brian Buchan, Mr Timothy John Suter, Ms Shirin Welham
Income: £1,160,555 [2016]; £793,434 [2015]; £929,467 [2014]; £998,972 [2013]; £466,068 [2012]

Stover School Association

Registered: 4 Oct 1963 *Employees:* 117
Tel: 01626 354505 *Website:* stover.co.uk
Activities: Education, training
Address: Stover School, Stover, Newton Abbot, Devon, TQ12 6QG
Trustees: Rear Admiral Benjamin John Key BSc RN, Mr Timothy Peter Synge, Mr Stewart Killick, Mr Craig Oliver, Lt Colonel Richard David Hourahane, Mr Michael Roberts, Lynda Jones, Mrs Margaret Batten BSc RHC, Mrs Victoria Bamsey, Mr Darren Wilson ACIB, Ms Belinda Louise Atkinson, Mrs Jacqueline Milstead, Mrs Katie Bann
Income: £4,367,539 [2017]; £4,380,276 [2016]; £4,184,496 [2015]; £4,684,646 [2014]; £4,904,056 [2013]

The Stowe School Foundation

Registered: 4 Sep 1998
Tel: 01280 818222 *Website:* stowe.co.uk
Activities: Education, training
Address: Stowe School, Stowe, Buckingham, MK18 5EH
Trustees: Mr Christopher Tate, Dr Anthony Kurt Wallersteiner, Lady Stringer, Mr D W Cheyne, Mr Nicholas Verney, Mr Jonathan Bewes, Mr Patrick John Richard Stopford, Mr S C Creedy Smith, Mr Mark John Greaves
Income: £1,572,276 [2017]; £1,863,051 [2016]; £2,430,582 [2015]; £2,101,792 [2014]; £2,610,863 [2013]

Stowe School Limited

Registered: 26 Mar 1963 *Employees:* 500 *Volunteers:* 35
Tel: 01280 818222 *Website:* stowe.co.uk
Activities: Education, training; arts, culture, heritage, science; environment, conservation, heritage
Address: Stowe School, Buckingham, MK18 5EH
Trustees: Peter Ackroyd, Mr Jonathan Bewes, Mr Robert Lankester, Admiral Sir James Burnell-Nugent, Mr John Arkwright, Ms Juliet Colman, Mr John Philip Cardain Frost, Mrs Andrea Johnson, Mrs Catriona Helen Lloyd, Miss Elizabeth Joy De Burgh Sidley, Mr Christopher Tate, Lady Stringer, Mr Simon Creedy Smith, Mr David Cheyne, Mrs Joanne Hastie-Smith, Professor Guy Manning Goodwin, Ms Julie Brunskill, Mrs Elizabeth Phillips, Mr David Carr, Mrs Vanessa Stanley
Income: £26,029,855 [2017]; £27,304,645 [2016]; £23,674,371 [2015]; £25,408,251 [2014]; £24,499,730 [2013]

The Charlotte Straker Project

Registered: 17 May 1993 *Employees:* 61 *Volunteers:* 19
Tel: 01434 633999 *Website:* charlottestraker.org.uk
Activities: The advancement of health or saving of lives; accommodation, housing
Address: Mr William Cunningham, Cookson Close, Corbridge, Northumberland, NE45 5HB
Trustees: Mr Peter Wood, Mrs Margaret Ann Wagstaff, Dr William Francis Cunningham, Mr Neil Braithwaite, Mrs Lesley Woodcock, Mrs Berenice Groves, Lady Anna Margaret Blackett, Mrs Mary Elizabeth Angela Jones, Mr Gavin MacFarlane Black, Mr Michael Pottage, Mr Richard Dixon, Mr Gordon Parfitt
Income: £1,389,992 [2017]; £1,152,488 [2016]; £1,046,297 [2015]; £1,097,324 [2014]; £1,030,512 [2013]

Stratford Arts Trust
Registered: 21 Dec 2011 *Employees:* 21 *Volunteers:* 10
Tel: 020 8270 1004 *Website:* stratford-circus.com
Activities: Education, training; disability; arts, culture, heritage, science; environment, conservation, heritage; economic, community development, employment; recreation
Address: Stratford Circus, Theatre Square, London, E15 1BX
Trustees: Mr Olivier Beroud, Mr David Kohn, Clarie Middleton, Ms Sukwinder Samra, Mr Linden Neil, Mr Nigel Hinds, Mr David McNeil, Ms Lucy Atkinson, Mr Paul Deery
Income: £1,309,529 [2017]; £1,146,934 [2016]; £1,342,310 [2015]; £1,053,021 [2014]; £851,687 [2013]

Stratford-upon-Avon Town Trust
Registered: 21 Sep 2001 *Employees:* 8
Tel: 01789 207111 *Website:* stratfordtowntrust.co.uk
Activities: General charitable purposes; education, training; advancement of health or saving of lives; disability; prevention or relief of poverty; accommodation, housing; religious activities; arts, culture, heritage, science; amateur sport; environment, conservation, heritage; armed forces, emergency service efficiency; human rights, religious or racial harmony, equality or diversity; recreation; other charitable purposes
Address: 14 Rother Street, Stratford upon Avon, Warwicks, CV37 6LU
Trustees: Mrs Carole Taylor, Julia Lucas, Alan Haigh, Clive Snowdon, Tessa Bates, Matthew MacDonald, Charles Bates, Clarissa Roberts MBE, Mr Richard Lane, Quentin Willson, Tony Jackson
Income: £1,942,298 [2016]; £1,818,314 [2015]; £3,203,557 [2014]; £3,413,198 [2013]; £3,293,844 [2012]

Street (UK) Foundation
Registered: 8 Aug 2000 *Employees:* 56
Tel: 0330 024 9843 *Website:* streetuk.foundation
Activities: Education, training; prevention or relief of poverty; economic, community development, employment
Address: Metro Building, 50 Cliveland Street, Birmingham, B19 3SH
Trustees: Mr John Tackaberry QC, Mr Patrick Tyrrell, Steve Johnson, Ms Eileen Kelliher
Income: £4,565,438 [2017]; £3,121,432 [2016]; £3,165,651 [2015]; £2,642,719 [2014]; £1,989,197 [2013]

Street Child
Registered: 13 Mar 2009 *Employees:* 33 *Volunteers:* 21
Tel: 020 7614 7696 *Website:* street-child.co.uk
Activities: Education, training; advancement of health or saving of lives; prevention or relief of poverty; overseas aid, famine relief; accommodation, housing
Address: 206-208 Stewart's Road, London, SW8 4UB
Trustees: Rev David Zachary Lloyd, Mrs Jannah Britt-Green, Mr Peter James Garratt, Mr Alex Scott-Barrett, Mr Edward Creasy, Mr Nicholas Mason
Income: £3,854,314 [2017]; £2,058,783 [2016]; £3,508,335 [2015]; £811,634 [2013]; £963,443 [2012]

Street League
Registered: 22 Dec 2003 *Employees:* 124 *Volunteers:* 350
Tel: 0800 331 7600 *Website:* streetleague.co.uk
Activities: Education, training; advancement of health or saving of lives; amateur sport; economic, community development, employment
Address: Suite 1.05, The Courtyard Royal Mills, 17 Redhill Street, Manchester, M4 5BA
Trustees: Mr Mike Parker, Andy Ransom, Ms Lesley Giddins, Mr Tim Kiddell, Stuart Beaver, Mr David Ian Reilly
Income: £5,667,438 [2017]; £5,496,660 [2016]; £4,602,741 [2015]; £3,420,406 [2014]; £2,665,716 [2013]

Streetgames UK
Registered: 3 Apr 2006 *Employees:* 49 *Volunteers:* 2,250
Tel: 0161 707 0782 *Website:* streetgames.org
Activities: Education, training; advancement of health or saving of lives; disability; prevention or relief of poverty; amateur sport; economic, community development, employment; human rights, religious or racial harmony, equality or diversity; recreation
Address: Woolwich House, 61 Mosley Street, Manchester, M2 3HZ
Trustees: Mr Peter Rowley, Mrs Amanda Jacqueline Sater, Mr John Cove, Ms Karen Creavin, Dame Helena Shovelton, Miss Rosie Duckworth, Professor Susan Capel, Mr Mark Taylor, Mr Jonathan Hughes, Miss Margaret Bowler, Mrs Helen Marie McGrath
Income: £7,215,574 [2017]; £8,595,630 [2016]; £9,231,050 [2015]; £6,151,245 [2014]; £4,752,038 [2013]

Streetscene Addiction Recovery
Registered: 12 Apr 2007 *Employees:* 59 *Volunteers:* 16
Tel: 01202 540337 *Website:* streetscene.org.uk
Activities: Education, training; advancement of health or saving of lives
Address: Streetscene, 108 Cobham Road, Ferndown Industrial Estate, Wimborne, Dorset, BH21 7PQ
Trustees: Mrs Hazel Maureen Corner, Mr John Alasdair Hutton, Mr Neil Houlton, Ms Matilda Venter
Income: £2,170,136 [2017]; £1,993,622 [2016]; £2,142,917 [2015]; £2,134,566 [2014]; £2,045,927 [2013]

Paul Strickland Scanner Centre
Registered: 16 Jun 1988 *Employees:* 56 *Volunteers:* 97
Tel: 01923 844353 *Website:* stricklandscanner.org.uk
Activities: The advancement of health or saving of lives
Address: Mount Vernon Hospital, Rickmansworth Road, Northwood, Middlesex, HA6 2RN
Trustees: Paddy Kelly, Dr Terence Wright, Dr Roberto Alonzi, Mr Dilip Manek, Mrs Catherine Williams, Mr Daniel Jonathan Ross, Mrs Palvi Shah, Mrs Lynn Roberts
Income: £7,559,237 [2017]; £7,401,355 [2016]; £7,056,216 [2015]; £6,286,101 [2014]; £5,721,928 [2013]

Strode Park Foundation for People with Disabilities
Registered: 9 Jan 1963 *Employees:* 354 *Volunteers:* 150
Tel: 01227 373292 *Website:* strodepark.org.uk
Activities: Disability
Address: Strode Park House, Herne, Herne Bay, Kent, CT6 7NE
Trustees: Nicholas Wells, Mrs Virginia McCarthy, Judith Clifford, Mr Suresh Gadhia, Mrs Dawn Allaway, Mrs Patricia Unwin, Mr Ray Cordell, Mr Russell Clark, Ms Nicola August
Income: £8,258,929 [2017]; £8,133,998 [2016]; £7,966,211 [2015]; £8,109,269 [2014]; £6,197,371 [2013]

Stroke Association

Registered: 14 Jan 1963 *Employees:* 671 *Volunteers:* 3,296
Tel: 020 7566 0300 *Website:* stroke.org.uk
Activities: Education, training; advancement of health or saving of lives; disability
Address: Stroke Association, Stroke Stroke House, 240 City Road, London, EC1V 2PR
Trustees: Mr Eric Frank Tracey, Dr Martin Anthony James, Mr Ian Black, Mr Stuart Barron Fletcher OBE, Sir Charles Cockburn, Mr Peter Troy MBE, Mr Niraj Shah, Mr Mark Smith, Mr Stephen King, Professor Marion Fraser Walker MBE, Professor Philippa Jane Tyrrell, Mr Robert James Empson, Professor Tom Robinson, Dr Anne Gordon, Ms Helen Sanders
Income: £37,322,000 [2017]; £36,493,000 [2016]; £37,496,000 [2015]; £33,546,000 [2014]; £31,051,000 [2013]

Stroud & District Homes Foundation Limited

Registered: 22 Dec 2000 *Employees:* 50
Tel: 01453 753299 *Website:* stroudhomes.co.uk
Activities: Disability; accommodation, housing
Address: Barn Lodge, Lovedays Mead, Stroud, Glos, GL5 1SB
Trustees: Mrs Carol Gilbert, Mr Michael Cyril Cartledge, Mr Richard Antony Stone, Mrs Susan Margaret Cartledge, Mrs Rosemary Gadd, Mrs Janet Bearman-Mills
Income: £1,234,387 [2017]; £1,142,513 [2016]; £1,092,722 [2015]; £1,119,945 [2014]; £1,386,376 [2013]

Stroud Court Community Trust Limited

Registered: 30 Nov 1993 *Employees:* 69 *Volunteers:* 5
Tel: 01453 834020 *Website:* stroudcourt.org
Activities: Education, training; disability; accommodation, housing
Address: Stroud Court, Minchinhampton, Stroud, Glos, GL6 9AN
Trustees: Judy Lusty, Geoff Slade, Joanna Lewis, Miss Molly Laura Bruton-Cox, Tony Bateson, Jane Fenwick, Mr Paul David Cadle, Mrs Eve Blundell
Income: £2,464,724 [2017]; £2,418,456 [2016]; £2,323,545 [2015]; £2,364,483 [2014]; £2,369,823 [2013]

Structural Genomics Consortium

Registered: 29 May 2003
Website: thesgc.org
Activities: Education, training; advancement of health or saving of lives
Address: Mars Centre, South Tower, Suite 712, 101 College Street, Toronto, Ontario, Canada, M5G 1L7
Trustees: Cindy Lea Bell, Dr Saul Howard Rosenberg, Dr Adrian Carter, Dr Anke Mueller-Fahrnow, Dr Stephen Hitchcock, Dr John Mathias, Dr Michael Dunn, Dr Tetsuyuki Maruyama, Dr Trevor Howe, Dr Ronan O'Hagan, Dr Nils Ostermann
Income: £11,393,000 [2017]; £11,640,000 [2016]; £19,796,000 [2015]; £3,273,000 [2014]; £8,922,000 [2013]

Stubbers Adventure Centre

Registered: 31 May 2000 *Employees:* 52 *Volunteers:* 6
Tel: 01708 256700 *Website:* stubbers.co.uk
Activities: Education, training; amateur sport
Address: Stubbers Cottage, Ockendon Road, Upminster, Essex, RM14 2TY
Trustees: Mr Jonathan Douglas-Hughes OBE DL, Mr Martin Denis Solder, Mr Michael John Dyer, Mr David Springett
Income: £2,019,710 [2016]; £1,947,490 [2015]; £1,921,585 [2014]; £1,873,658 [2013]; £1,554,977 [2012]

Students Union University of Greenwich

Registered: 19 Oct 2012 *Employees:* 44 *Volunteers:* 1,105
Tel: 020 8331 8593 *Website:* suug.co.uk
Activities: Education, training
Address: University of Greenwich Students Union, Cooper Building, King William Walk, London, SE10 9JH
Trustees: Michael Hughes, Mr Prakash Pattni, Mr Luke Ellis, Miss Vivian Catharina Van Lent, Miss Meike Imberg, Miss Adiya Aimanova, Dr Elizabeth Jones, Mr Paul Gareth Butler, Mr Louis Hale, Mr Nicholas Sall Hopwood, Mr Vasileios Manikos
Income: £2,620,119 [2017]; £2,561,462 [2016]; £2,687,760 [2015]; £2,718,779 [2014]; £2,832,148 [2013]

Students' Union Royal Holloway University of London

Registered: 19 May 2011 *Employees:* 223 *Volunteers:* 1,185
Tel: 01784 276713 *Website:* su.rhul.ac.uk
Activities: Education, training
Address: Royal Holloway University of London, Egham Hill, Egham, Surrey, TW20 0EX
Trustees: Mr Andrew McMenamin, Mrs Kirsten Daswani, Ms Pippa Gentry, Ms Zhoufang Wei, Mr Luke Tibbetts, Mr Peter Elliot, Mr Josip Martincic, Ms Jane Broadbent, Ms Natasha Barrett, Ms Stephanie Milne, Ms Yi Thong Wong, Ms Rachelle Jiongco, Mr Clement Jones
Income: £5,769,842 [2017]; £4,608,688 [2016]; £2,780,382 [2015]; £2,613,658 [2014]; £2,533,463 [2013]

The Students' Union at Bournemouth University

Registered: 2 Dec 2011 *Employees:* 120 *Volunteers:* 352
Tel: 01202 965765 *Website:* subu.org.uk
Activities: Education, training
Address: SUBU, Talbot Campus, Fern Barrow, Poole, Dorset, BH12 5BB
Trustees: Ms Karen Churchill, Ms Geneva Guerrieri, Ms Elizabeth Howe, Mr Robert Garza, Mr Arthur Richier, Martin James, Gabriela Alexandra Cazacu, Catriona Cannon, Mr Daniel Asaya, Mr Mark Smith, Mrs Sophie Nott, Devon Biddle, Jennifer Winter
Income: £5,158,661 [2017]; £4,769,147 [2016]; £4,057,725 [2015]; £3,746,561 [2014]; £3,663,400 [2013]

Studio Wayne McGregor Limited

Registered: 11 Jan 2002 *Employees:* 13
Tel: 020 7278 6015 *Website:* waynemcgregor.com
Activities: Education, training; arts, culture, heritage, science
Address: Studio Wayne McGregor Ltd, Broadcast Centre, Here East, 10 East Bay Lane, Queen Elizabeth Olympic Park, London, E15 2GW
Trustees: Ms Caroline Miller, Miss Cordelia Barker, Ms Aleksandra Krotoski, Mr Anupam Ganguli, Mr Peter Kenyon, Ms Dominique Laffy
Income: £3,913,691 [2017]; £1,953,135 [2016]; £2,589,462 [2015]; £1,392,948 [2014]; £1,309,065 [2013]

The Study (Wimbledon) Limited

Registered: 29 Mar 1976 *Employees:* 60
Tel: 020 8947 6969 *Website:* thestudyprep.co.uk
Activities: Education, training
Address: The Study Prep School, Camp Road, London, SW19 4UN
Trustees: Mrs Kate Greenhalgh, Mr James Barnes, Mrs Christine Facon, Mrs Amanda Elysee, Mr Simon Pole, Mrs Tracy Pritchard-Drummond, Mr John Tucker
Income: £4,322,187 [2017]; £4,177,456 [2016]; £3,975,796 [2015]; £3,764,441 [2014]; £3,607,189 [2013]

Sturts Community Trust
Registered: 23 May 2013 *Employees:* 49 *Volunteers:* 26
Tel: 01202 870338 *Website:* sturtscommunitytrust.org.uk
Activities: Education, training; disability; prevention or relief of poverty; accommodation, housing; environment, conservation, heritage
Address: St Francis House, Sturts Farm, West Moors, Ferndown, Dorset, BH22 0NF
Trustees: Mr David Harvey Taylor, Prof Umut Turksen, Mrs Katherine Mary Jones, Ms Morag Margaret Doyle, Mr Michael Crutchley, Mr Timothy David Cook, Mr Simon Beckett, Mrs Caroline Rosemary Darby-Jenkins, Mrs Gabrielle Mary Gray
Income: £2,444,166 [2017]; £1,978,240 [2016]; £1,501,719 [2015]; £1,241,438 [2014]

Style Acre
Registered: 20 Jan 2004 *Employees:* 145 *Volunteers:* 36
Website: styleacre.org.uk
Activities: Education, training; advancement of health or saving of lives; disability; prevention or relief of poverty
Address: Field Seymour Parkes, Solicitors, No 1 London Street, Reading, Berks, RG1 4QW
Trustees: Dr Tony Vernon, Mr Robert Thornton, Mr Ian Boulton, Mr Paul Townsend, Mrs Sarah-Ann Nye, Philippa Chalmers, Mrs Alison Elliott, Mr Keith Tibbs
Income: £6,828,814 [2017]; £5,601,717 [2016]; £6,217,273 [2015]; £4,986,432 [2014]; £4,348,948 [2013]

Style for Soldiers
Registered: 30 Mar 2015
Tel: 020 7930 9980 *Website:* styleforsoldiers.com
Activities: General charitable purposes; advancement of health or saving of lives; armed forces, emergency service efficiency; other charitable purposes
Address: Emma Willis, 66 Jermyn Street, London, SW1Y 6NY
Trustees: Major General Sir George Norton, Ms Emma Ramsay Corfield, Ms Lisa Armstrong, Maria Witchell
Income: £1,625,408 [2017]; £122,946 [2016]

Success for All Foundation
Registered: 18 Aug 1999 *Employees:* 12
Tel: 01733 490222 *Website:* successforall.org.uk
Activities: Education, training
Address: 1 Sweetbriars, Stamford, Lincs, PE9 4BZ
Trustees: Mr Michael Fischer, Dr Nancy Madden, Mr Edward Patrick Austin, Dr Robert Slavin, Mr Vagn Nedergaard Hansen
Income: £1,060,919 [2017]; £1,089,518 [2016]; £1,479,967 [2015]; £1,771,011 [2014]; £1,186,145 [2013]

Suffolk Agricultural Association
Registered: 1 Mar 1984 *Employees:* 35 *Volunteers:* 300
Tel: 01473 707111 *Website:* suffolkshow.co.uk
Activities: Education, training; environment, conservation, heritage; economic, community development, employment
Address: Trinity Park, Felixstowe Road, Ipswich, Suffolk, IP3 8UH
Trustees: Mr David Nunn, Mr Chris Clarke, Mr Robert Baker, Mr Eric C Morton, Ms Elizabeth Kemball, Mr Peter Over, Mr Loudon Greenlees, Mr Jonathan Lawsell Edward Long
Income: £3,139,598 [2017]; £2,872,422 [2016]; £2,871,045 [2015]; £2,807,674 [2014]; £2,492,452 [2013]

Suffolk Community Foundation
Registered: 12 May 2005 *Employees:* 13 *Volunteers:* 120
Tel: 01473 602602 *Website:* suffolkcf.org.uk
Activities: General charitable purposes; education, training; advancement of health or saving of lives; disability; prevention or relief of poverty; accommodation, housing; arts, culture, heritage, science; amateur sport; environment, conservation, heritage; economic, community development, employment; other charitable purposes
Address: The Suffolk Foundation, The Old Barn, Peninsula Business Centre, Wherstead, Ipswich, Suffolk, IP9 2BB
Trustees: Mr James Kennedy Buckle, Mr William Bruce Kendall, Mr Terence Alan Ward, Jonathan George Shelton Agar, The Hon Selina Hopkins, Susan Gull, Gulshan Kaur Kayembe, Iain David Jamie, David Hughes, Mr Neil Roderick Walmsley, Peter George Newnham
Income: £2,884,297 [2017]; £3,209,850 [2016]; £5,225,411 [2015]; £4,078,504 [2014]; £3,069,647 [2013]

Suffolk Family Carers
Registered: 5 Jun 1998 *Employees:* 79 *Volunteers:* 111
Tel: 01473 835400 *Website:* suffolkfamilycarers.org
Activities: Education, training; advancement of health or saving of lives; disability; other charitable purposes
Address: Unit 8 Hill View Business Park, Old Ipswich Road, Claydon, Ipswich, Suffolk, IP6 0AJ
Trustees: Mr Terry Ward, Ms Susan Thomas, Mrs Janet Dillaway, Mr James Robert Tucker, Mrs Carole Burman, Mr Dennis Henry Weston, Dr Donald James McElhinney, Mrs Susan Brooks, Mrs Jane Ann Millar
Income: £2,118,478 [2017]; £2,201,473 [2016]; £2,726,915 [2015]; £2,790,811 [2014]; £2,498,839 [2013]

Suffolk Mind
Registered: 4 Jun 1991 *Employees:* 81 *Volunteers:* 60
Tel: 0300 111 6000 *Website:* suffolkmind.org.uk
Activities: Education, training; advancement of health or saving of lives; disability; accommodation, housing
Address: Quay Place, Key Street, Ipswich, Suffolk, IP4 1BZ
Trustees: Mr Tim Mutum, Mr Nigel Suckling, Dr Emma Brierly, Ian White, Mr Julian Tyndale-Biscoe, Mr Alan Hanson, Ms Ciara Scallon
Income: £2,593,387 [2017]; £2,316,680 [2016]; £2,666,737 [2015]; £2,153,362 [2014]; £2,836,091 [2013]

Suffolk Wildlife Trust Limited
Registered: 13 Aug 1971 *Employees:* 67 *Volunteers:* 1,400
Tel: 01473 890089 *Website:* suffolkwildlifetrust.org
Activities: Education, training; environment, conservation, heritage
Address: Brooke House, The Green, Ashbocking, Ipswich, Suffolk, IP6 9JY
Trustees: Mr John Cousins, Mr Nigel Farthing, Mr Ian Brown, Mr Peter Holborn, Mr David Bryony Alborough, Ms Anna Saltmarsh, Mr Simon Roberts, Mr James Alexander, Mrs Denise Goldsmith, Ms Philippa Goodwin, Ms Rachel Jane Eburne
Income: £4,339,000 [2017]; £3,895,000 [2016]; £3,712,000 [2015]; £3,074,000 [2014]; £2,815,000 [2013]

Summer Fields' School Trust Limited
Registered: 3 Oct 1966 Employees: 139
Tel: 01865 459203 Website: summerfields.com
Activities: Education, training
Address: Summer Fields School, Mayfield Road, Oxford, OX2 7EN
Trustees: Mr Andrew Edward Reekes MA FRSA, Mrs Tessa Gaisman, Mrs Suzette Ray Peake BSc, Justin Nolan, Mrs Carole Marie Aleth Sweetnam, Mr Roger Shaw, Mr Alex Snow, Mr Edward Alan Davidson QC, Dr Anthony Kurt Wallersteiner, Mr John Henry Chatfield-Roberts BA, Right Rev David Wilfred Michael Jennings, Jeremy Rooth, Mr Alistair Beor-Roberts, Mrs Diana Sichel
Income: £7,109,284 [2016]; £7,762,199 [2015]; £7,603,293 [2014]; £6,956,694 [2013]

Suncroft Donations Trust
Registered: 4 May 2012
Activities: The prevention or relief of poverty; religious activities
Address: 13 Overlea Road, London, E5 9BG
Trustees: Mr Heinrich Feldman, Mrs Dwora Feldman, Mr Judah Feldman
Income: £2,891,186 [2017]; £957,328 [2016]; £1,582,636 [2015]; £904,177 [2014]; £771,675 [2013]

Sunderland Carers' Centre
Registered: 23 Mar 2007 Employees: 28 Volunteers: 7
Tel: 0191 549 3768 Website: sunderlandcarers.co.uk
Activities: The advancement of health or saving of lives
Address: Sunderland Carers Centre, Thompson Road, Sunderland, Tyne & Wear, SR5 1SF
Trustees: Mr John Colin Wilson, Diane Kirtley, Ken Morris, Mr Michael Leslie Brewster, Ms Julie Dawn Gray, Mr Stewart Gee, Venerable Stuart Bain, Carol Freeman, Miss Elaine Cruikshanks, Norman Hildrew, Mrs Jane Tunmore, Mrs Sylvia Stoneham
Income: £1,130,368 [2017]; £1,037,983 [2016]; £980,841 [2015]; £798,816 [2014]; £749,721 [2013]

Sunderland Counselling Service
Registered: 3 Nov 2014 Employees: 87 Volunteers: 24
Tel: 0191 514 7007 Website: sunderlandcounselling.org.uk
Activities: General charitable purposes; advancement of health or saving of lives
Address: 51 John Street, Sunderland, Tyne & Wear, SR1 1QN
Trustees: Rev David Hands, Mr Carl Sketchley, Mrs Eileen Watt, Laura Bruton, Mr Bernard Greener, Mrs Anne Loadman, Mrs Linda Morris
Income: £2,402,420 [2017]; £1,858,965 [2016]

Sunfield Children's Homes Limited
Registered: 28 Feb 1963 Employees: 307
Tel: 01453 837604 Website: sunfield.org.uk
Activities: Education, training; disability; accommodation, housing
Address: Ruskin Mill, Millbottom, Nailsworth, Stroud, Glos, GL6 0LA
Trustees: Mr Vivian Frederick Blenheim Griffiths, Mr Martin Hermann Wood, Mr Aonghus Coinn Huntly Gordon, Mrs Helen Kippax
Income: £8,756,628 [2017]; £10,495,999 [2016]; £10,502,216 [2015]; £10,260,384 [2014]; £10,338,322 [2013]

The Bernard Sunley Charitable Foundation
Registered: 18 Apr 2005 Employees: 3
Website: bernardsunley.org
Activities: Education, training; advancement of health or saving of lives; disability; prevention or relief of poverty; amateur sport; environment, conservation, heritage; armed forces, emergency service efficiency; recreation
Address: Bernard Sunley Charitable Foundation, 20 Berkeley Square, London, W1J 6LH
Trustees: Brian Wardley Martin, Mrs Bella Sunley MBE, Mr William Tice FRCS, Mrs Lucy Pauline Alexandra Evans, Mrs Joan Tice OBE DL, Mrs Anabel Knight, Mr Inigo Paternina
Income: £4,040,000 [2017]; £3,950,000 [2016]; £4,201,000 [2015]; £3,802,000 [2014]; £3,553,000 [2013]

Sunninghill Preparatory School Limited
Registered: 9 Aug 1993 Employees: 38 Volunteers: 5
Tel: 01305 262306 Website: sunninghillprep.co.uk
Activities: Education, training
Address: Sunninghill Preparatory School Ltd, South Court, South Walks Road, Dorchester, DT1 1EB
Trustees: Mr John William Chittenden, Mr R Miller, Mr Trevor Blackburn, Dr Rupert Turberville-Smith, Mr Ian Jefferis, Mr Philip George Fry, Mrs Rosemary Lewis, Mr Duncan Perks, Ms Penny Graham, Miss Jean Rosemary Walker
Income: £1,923,314 [2016]; £1,934,063 [2015]; £1,780,164 [2014]; £1,754,548 [2013]; £1,597,810 [2012]

Sunnylands Limited
Registered: 27 May 1964 Employees: 32 Volunteers: 1
Tel: 01536 512066 Website: st-peters.org.uk
Activities: Education, training
Address: St Peters School, 52 Headlands, Kettering, Northants, NN15 6DJ
Trustees: Edward Lamb, Mrs Anne-Marie Bowers, Rev Lesley McCormack, Mr Steven Bowers, Mrs Fiona Kilsby, Mrs Elizabeth Bell, Mr Tom Fray
Income: £1,040,822 [2017]; £1,028,534 [2016]; £914,913 [2015]; £863,495 [2014]; £840,035 [2013]

Support Adoption for Pets
Registered: 4 Jun 2004 Employees: 4
Tel: 0161 486 3774 Website: supportadoptionforpets.co.uk
Activities: The prevention or relief of poverty; accommodation, housing; animals
Address: Pets at Home Ltd, Epsom Avenue, Stanley Green Trading Estate, Handforth, Wilmslow, Cheshire, SK9 3RN
Trustees: Mrs Louise Stonier, Jill Naylor, Dan Laurence, Andrew Bickerton, Mr George Lingwood, Brian Hudspith, Adrian Bates
Income: £3,945,194 [2017]; £3,665,574 [2016]; £3,442,706 [2015]; £2,814,233 [2014]; £2,152,863 [2013]

Support Staffordshire
Registered: 26 Mar 2015 Employees: 62 Volunteers: 250
Tel: 0300 777 1207 Website: supportstaffordshire.org.uk
Activities: General charitable purposes; education, training; advancement of health or saving of lives; prevention or relief of poverty; economic, community development, employment
Address: Support Staffordshire, Mansell House, 22 Bore Street, Lichfield, Staffs, WS13 6LL
Trustees: Janet Martyna Wilson, John Downie, Christine Thomas, Helen Titterton, Christopher Stuart Mayor, Christopher Shaun Elliott, Martin Chadwick
Income: £1,433,783 [2017]; £1,270,683 [2016]

The Supported Fostering Services Charitable Trust
Registered: 10 Jul 2001 *Employees:* 58
Tel: 01474 365500 *Website:* fostering.com
Activities: Education, training; advancement of health or saving of lives; disability; accommodation, housing
Address: Supported Fostering Services, 26-27 The Hill, Northfleet, Gravesend, Kent, DA11 9EU
Trustees: Ms Carole Troote, Mr Ronald St Louis, Mr Derek Clode, Ms Kathleen Greenwood, Mrs Theresa Jeapes, Ms Gloria Griffith
Income: £4,618,971 [2017]; £4,828,571 [2016]; £5,480,125 [2015]; £5,714,484 [2014]; £5,970,247 [2013]

Supporting Wounded Veterans Ltd.
Registered: 13 Nov 2012 *Employees:* 7 *Volunteers:* 200
Tel: 020 7720 4934 *Website:* supportingwoundedveterans.com
Activities: General charitable purposes; education, training; advancement of health or saving of lives; disability
Address: 38 Connaught Square, London, W2 2HL
Trustees: Colonel John Kirkwood, Mr Frank Akers-Douglas, Lord Archibald Hamilton of Epsom, Mr James Charrington
Income: £1,276,518 [2017]; £466,439 [2016]; £238,713 [2015]; £215,925 [2014]; £283,060 [2013]

Supportive SRC Ltd
Registered: 14 Jan 2003 *Employees:* 117 *Volunteers:* 138
Tel: 01740 658888 *Website:* supportive.org.uk
Activities: General charitable purposes; advancement of health or saving of lives; disability
Address: Chapter House, 7a Dean & Chapter Industrial Estate, Ferryhill, Co Durham, DL17 8LH
Trustees: Brian Meek, Bob Evans, Mr Ian Brown, Jo Hall, Mrs Alison Schreiber, Mr David Rayner, Mrs Kathleen Conroy, Mr Andrew Munro, Mike Smith, Mr Wayne Hall, Mrs Jill Lax, Mrs Linda Tyman
Income: £2,842,745 [2017]; £2,924,975 [2016]; £2,891,512 [2015]; £3,089,638 [2014]; £3,553,048 [2013]

Surfers Against Sewage
Registered: 13 Feb 2012 *Employees:* 13 *Volunteers:* 25,000
Tel: 01872 553001 *Website:* sas.org.uk
Activities: Education, training; environment, conservation, heritage
Address: Unit 2 Wheal Kitty Workshops, Wheal Kitty, St Agnes, Cornwall, TR5 0RD
Trustees: Lesley Kazan-Pinfield, Alex Wade, Lauren Davies, Jon Khoo, Chris Hides, Ben Hewitt, Peter Crane, Heather Koldewey
Income: £1,009,846 [2016]; £943,321 [2015]; £816,514 [2014]; £641,029 [2013]; £514,046 [2012]

Surgo Foundation UK Limited
Registered: 17 Jun 2014
Tel: 020 7597 6427
Activities: General charitable purposes
Address: Withers Ltd, 16 Old Bailey, London, EC4M 7EG
Trustees: Mala Gaonkar, Oliver Haarmann, Emmanuel Roman, Malcolm Gladwell
Income: £5,033,409 [2016]; £3,260,735 [2015]

Surrey Association for Visual Impairment
Registered: 12 Dec 2007 *Employees:* 109 *Volunteers:* 220
Tel: 01372 377701 *Website:* sightforsurrey.org.uk
Activities: The advancement of health or saving of lives; disability
Address: SAVI, Rentwood, School Lane, Fetcham, Leatherhead, Surrey, KT22 9JX
Trustees: Mrs Cecilia Power, Mrs Judy Anne Sanderson, Mr Andrew Taylor, Mr Steven Wherry, Mrs Christine Wilmshurst, Mr Bob Turnbull, Mrs Carol Miller, Mr Russell Gilmore, Mr Michael Jordan, Mrs Mary Da-Silva-Skinner
Income: £2,422,952 [2017]; £1,740,259 [2016]; £1,854,909 [2015]; £1,613,188 [2014]; £1,575,510 [2013]

Surrey County Football Association Limited
Registered: 7 Sep 2016 *Employees:* 20 *Volunteers:* 50
Tel: 01372 387096 *Website:* surreyfa.com
Activities: Education, training; advancement of health or saving of lives; disability; amateur sport
Address: Surrey County Football Association, Connaught House, 36 Bridge Street, Leatherhead, Surrey, KT22 8BZ
Trustees: Mr Jeremy Taylor, Mr John Alan Young, Mr Nick Drew, Mr Roderick Reginald Wood, Mr Soye Briggs, Mr Brian James Carroll, Mr Leslie Stuart William Pharo, Mr Raymond Sydney Lewis, Mrs Sheila Ann Pink, Mr Victor Michael Rolland
Income: £1,376,995 [2017]

The Surrey Cricket Board
Registered: 11 Apr 2007 *Employees:* 35
Tel: 020 7820 5637
Activities: Education, training; disability; amateur sport
Address: Surrey County Cricket Club Ltd, The Kia Oval, Kennington Oval, London, SE11 5SS
Trustees: Mr Richard Laudy, Mr Paul Bedford, Mr Steve MacDonald, Mr David Gill, Ms Lucy Donovan, Ms Ann Cottis, Mr Michael Barford, Mr Simon Dyson, Mr David Kingsmill, Mr Barbar Qureshi, Ms Julie O'Hara
Income: £1,063,480 [2016]; £975,820 [2015]; £689,211 [2014]; £981,963 [2013]; £805,584 [2012]

Surrey Crossroads
Registered: 17 Jul 2008 *Employees:* 191 *Volunteers:* 34
Tel: 01372 869970 *Website:* crossroadscaresurrey.org.uk
Activities: The advancement of health or saving of lives; disability
Address: Crossroads Care Surrey, 121 Kingston Road, Leatherhead, Surrey, KT22 7SU
Trustees: Mr Leslie Hutchinson, Alastair Paterson, Mrs Linda Jean Friend, Ms Melanie Loizou, Ms Elizabeth Taylor, Mr Raymond Anthony Brian Smedy, Mr Mehboob Dharamsi, Professor James Marfell Scudamore, Susan Hickson, Mrs Barbara Everett, Dr Julia Stephanie Goddard
Income: £2,826,607 [2017]; £3,012,000 [2016]; £2,713,000 [2015]; £2,804,000 [2014]; £2,694,000 [2013]

Surrey Disabled People's Partnership
Registered: 8 May 2014 *Employees:* 19 *Volunteers:* 48
Tel: 01483 541686 *Website:* sdpp.org.uk
Activities: Disability
Address: Surrey Disabled Peoples Partnership, 4 Thames Street, Staines upon Thames, Middlesex, TW18 4SD
Trustees: Anna Sartori, Mrs Angela Cooper, Jason Levy
Income: £1,235,275 [2017]; £1,614,999 [2016]; £1,096,784 [2015]

Surrey Independent Living Council

Registered: 21 Mar 2012 *Employees:* 34 *Volunteers:* 30
Tel: 01483 458111 *Website:* surreyilc.org.uk
Activities: Disability
Address: Surrey Independent Living Council, Astolat, Coniers Way, Guildford, Surrey, GU4 7HL
Trustees: Mrs Brenda Griffiths, Mr Neville Hinks, Mr David Bernard Fairweather Campling, Ms Sharon Johanna Komisarczuk, Mr Steve Peckham, Mr Jason Vaughan, Miss Leonie Riddett, Mr Michael Moorwood, Ms Milena Krasovec
Income: £1,154,149 [2017]; £1,331,833 [2016]; £1,396,629 [2015]; £1,189,424 [2014]; £1,346,742 [2013]

The Surrey Wildlife Trust Limited

Registered: 31 Jul 1962 *Employees:* 90 *Volunteers:* 1,911
Tel: 01483 795440 *Website:* surreywildlifetrust.org
Activities: Education, training; environment, conservation, heritage
Address: Surrey Wildlife Trust, School Lane, Pirbright, Woking, Surrey, GU24 0JN
Trustees: Ms Christine Howard, Mr Chris Wilkinson, Mr Gordon Vincent, Mr Peter Smith, Mr Andrew Beattie, Mrs Pamela Whyman, Mr Ian Smith, Mr Gerard Bacon, Ms Meryl Wingfield, Mr Mark Slater, Mr Nicholas Baxter, Mr Matthew Stanton, Mr Jason Paul Gaskell, Ms Angela Swarbrick
Income: £5,539,105 [2017]; £6,093,409 [2016]; £5,139,844 [2015]; £5,203,145 [2014]; £4,723,526 [2013]

Survival International Charitable Trust

Registered: 26 Apr 1974 *Employees:* 26 *Volunteers:* 6
Tel: 020 7687 8700 *Website:* survivalinternational.org
Activities: Education, training; prevention or relief of poverty; environment, conservation, heritage; human rights, religious or racial harmony, equality or diversity; other charitable purposes
Address: 6 Charterhouse Buildings, London, EC1M 7ET
Trustees: Mr James Cameron Wilson, Mr Robin-Hanbury Tenison, Ms Sue Edith Branford, Mr James L N Wood, Miss Caroline Pearce, Mr Thomas Joseph Fraine, Mr Herve Chandes, Ms Juliet Walker, Mr Michael John Davis, Ms Clare Catherine Dixon, Mrs Jessica Mary Sainsbury, Mr Tom Yeba Hugh-Jones, Ms Ghislaine De Give, Mrs Clara Braggio
Income: £2,287,191 [2017]; £1,255,348 [2016]; £1,731,634 [2015]; £1,168,083 [2014]; £1,236,873 [2013]

The Sussex Archaeological Society

Registered: 30 May 1962 *Employees:* 152 *Volunteers:* 200
Tel: 01273 486260 *Website:* sussexpast.co.uk
Activities: Education, training; arts, culture, heritage, science; environment, conservation, heritage
Address: Bull House, 92 High Street, Lewes, E Sussex, BN7 1XH
Trustees: Mr Peter Benjamin Vos, Mr Michael Pierre Chartier, Mrs Jane Elizabeth Ann Vokins, Mr John Manley, Mrs Janet Deborah Oldham, Joe Sullivan, Mr David Russell Rudling, Mrs Lys Drewett, Mr Tony Reid, Dr Jamie Kaminski, Mr Allan Course, Ms Christine Lesley Medlock BA Hons
Income: £2,096,528 [2016]; £1,729,821 [2015]; £1,830,491 [2014]; £1,736,033 [2013]; £1,553,750 [2012]

The Sussex Beacon

Registered: 21 Jan 1988 *Employees:* 38 *Volunteers:* 80
Tel: 01273 694222 *Website:* sussexbeacon.org.uk
Activities: General charitable purposes; education, training; advancement of health or saving of lives; disability
Address: Sussex Beacon Hospice, 10 Bevendean Road, Brighton, BN2 4DE
Trustees: Dr Duncan Churchill, Ms Jane Waterman, Mr David Fray, Paul Hilly, Mr Norman Hill, Ms Lynette Mary Lowndes, Jayne Phoenix
Income: £1,964,036 [2017]; £2,643,262 [2016]; £2,348,477 [2015]; £2,030,616 [2014]; £2,023,652 [2013]

Sussex Community Development Association

Registered: 3 Dec 2002 *Employees:* 118 *Volunteers:* 659
Tel: 01273 517250 *Website:* sussexcommunity.org.uk
Activities: General charitable purposes; education, training; advancement of health or saving of lives; disability; prevention or relief of poverty; arts, culture, heritage, science; amateur sport; environment, conservation, heritage; economic, community development, employment; human rights, religious or racial harmony, equality or diversity
Address: Highfield, Newhaven Road, Swanborough, Lewes, E Sussex, BN7 3PJ
Trustees: Mr Graham Amy, Mrs Maria Aguilar, Mr Sean Williams, Ms Ioni Anne Sullivan, Mrs Helen MacAulay, Mr John Cornish, Mr Kenneth John Alexander MacKenzie, Mr John Edwin Bell
Income: £3,820,637 [2017]; £3,531,905 [2016]; £3,445,538 [2015]; £2,127,560 [2014]; £1,464,497 [2013]

The Sussex Community Foundation

Registered: 9 Mar 2006 *Employees:* 8 *Volunteers:* 20
Tel: 01273 409440 *Website:* sussexgiving.org.uk
Activities: General charitable purposes; education, training; advancement of health or saving of lives; disability; prevention or relief of poverty; accommodation, housing; arts, culture, heritage, science; amateur sport; environment, conservation, heritage; economic, community development, employment; human rights, religious or racial harmony, equality or diversity; recreation; other charitable purposes
Address: Sussex Community Foundation, 15 Western Road, Lewes, E Sussex, BN7 1RL
Trustees: Mrs Pamela Stiles, Mr Martin Roberts, Mr Michael Martin, Mrs Consuelo Brooke, Mrs Jonica Fox, Mrs Margaret Ann Burgess, Ms Julia Helen Carrette, Mr Mark Spofforth, Mr Rodney Buse, Mr Patrick Stevens, Mr Charles Drayson, Mr Colin Field JP DL, Mrs Patricia Woolgar, His Honour Keith Hollis, Mrs Nicola Glover
Income: £2,820,921 [2017]; £2,549,814 [2016]; £1,565,175 [2015]; £4,539,172 [2014]; £2,936,161 [2013]

Sussex County Sports Partnership Trust

Registered: 20 Dec 2007 *Employees:* 11
Tel: 01273 643869 *Website:* activesussex.org
Activities: Education, training; amateur sport; economic, community development, employment; recreation
Address: University of Brighton, Village Way, Falmer, Brighton, BN1 9PH
Trustees: Miss Lucy Gail McCrickard, Melanie Kinnear, Karen Burrell, Carol Grant, Ms Jane Schofield, Mr Paul Edward Millman, Jonathan Hughes, Stephanie Maurel, Carrie Reynolds, Anthony Davy
Income: £1,099,724 [2017]; £1,061,657 [2016]; £931,187 [2015]; £1,027,383 [2014]; £870,473 [2013]

Sussex Emmaus

Registered: 28 Feb 1996 *Employees:* 11 *Volunteers:* 42
Tel: 01273 426473 *Website:* emmausbrighton.co.uk
Activities: The prevention or relief of poverty; accommodation, housing; economic, community development, employment
Address: Sussex Emmaus, Drove Road, Portslade, Brighton, BN41 2PA
Trustees: Dr Glynn Jones, Mr John McLean, Fiona Morris, Mr Philip Daniel, Mrs Frances Sally Harrison, Mr Gwyn Price, Pat Mernagh-Thompson
Income: £1,132,789 [2017]; £1,059,570 [2016]; £1,081,586 [2015]; £1,026,665 [2014]; £822,651 [2013]

Sussex House School

Registered: 29 Mar 1994 *Employees:* 38
Website: sussexhouseschool.co.uk
Activities: Education, training
Address: Sussex House School, 68 Cadogan Square, London, SW1X 0EA
Trustees: Mr Nicholas Paul Kaye, Mr Michael Arnold Johannes Goedhuis, Mr John Anthony Crewe, Mr Alexander Brunton Badenoch
Income: £3,810,625 [2017]; £3,790,069 [2016]; £3,652,625 [2015]; £3,550,194 [2014]; £3,387,391 [2013]

Sussex Interpreting Services

Registered: 27 Jun 2000 *Employees:* 11 *Volunteers:* 21
Tel: 01273 702005 *Website:* sussexinterpreting.org.uk
Activities: The advancement of health or saving of lives; other charitable purposes
Address: Community Base, 113 Queens Road, Brighton, BN1 3XG
Trustees: Ms Farangiz Mohebati, Ms Jen Henwood, Ms Lucy Bryson, Mr Sidi Mohamed El-Alami, Ms Althea Wolfe, Ms Julia Encarnacao, Dr Hanno Koppel
Income: £1,082,938 [2017]; £1,033,456 [2016]; £906,862 [2015]; £720,001 [2014]; £809,991 [2013]

Sussex Wildlife Trust

Registered: 26 Jun 1962 *Employees:* 63 *Volunteers:* 450
Tel: 01273 492630 *Website:* sussexwildlifetrust.org.uk
Activities: Education, training; environment, conservation, heritage
Address: Sussex Wildlife Trust, Woods Mill, Shoreham Road, Henfield, W Sussex, BN5 9SD
Trustees: Mr Christopher John Warne, Mrs Susan Walton, Mr David Green, Dr Alan John Anthony Stewart, Mr Michael King, Ms Linda Mary Clark, Ms Sarah Bonnot, Mrs Carole Nicholson, Mrs Claire Elizabeth Kerr, Ms Emma Montlake, Mr Simon Linnington, Mr Crispin Robert Scott, Mr Sean Ashworth
Income: £4,522,605 [2017]; £4,643,818 [2016]; £3,462,568 [2015]; £3,236,180 [2014]; £3,055,362 [2013]

Sustain: The Alliance for Better Food & Farming

Registered: 12 Mar 1993 *Employees:* 18 *Volunteers:* 30
Tel: 020 8318 6824 *Website:* sustainweb.org
Activities: The advancement of health or saving of lives; prevention or relief of poverty; environment, conservation, heritage; economic, community development, employment
Address: 56-64 Leonard Street, London, EC2A 4LT
Trustees: Mike Rayner, David Barling, Mr Keith Frank Tyrell, Mr Shaun Mark Spiers, Ms Victoria Williams, Clare Horrell, Dr Modi Mwatsama, Catherine Fookes, Alison Jane Swan Parente, Chris Stopes, Ms Katharine Helen Boyd, Ms Stephanie Wood, Bridget Jennifer Henderson, Laura MacKenzie, Clare Oxborrow
Income: £1,196,006 [2017]; £1,195,560 [2016]; £1,439,103 [2015]; £1,506,706 [2014]; £2,094,720 [2013]

Sustrans Limited

Registered: 10 Apr 1984 *Employees:* 539 *Volunteers:* 4,000
Tel: 0117 926 8893 *Website:* sustrans.org.uk
Activities: The advancement of health or saving of lives; environment, conservation, heritage
Address: Information Team, 2 Cathedral Square, College Green, Bristol, BS1 5DD
Trustees: Mark Edgell, Fiona Westwood, Ilanora Kirsty Lewin, Claire Louise Addison, The Reverend Canon Dr Edward Condry, Lynne Berry, Richard Stephen Morris
Income: £48,644,000 [2017]; £50,057,000 [2016]; £43,774,000 [2015]; £49,576,000 [2014]; £78,694,000 [2013]

Sutton Borough Citizens' Advice Bureaux

Registered: 2 Apr 1997 *Employees:* 24 *Volunteers:* 84
Tel: 020 8405 3535 *Website:* suttoncabx.org.uk
Activities: General charitable purposes; education, training; advancement of health or saving of lives; disability; prevention or relief of poverty; accommodation, housing; economic, community development, employment; other charitable purposes
Address: Sutton Borough CAB, 68 Parkgate Road, Wallington, Surrey, SM6 0AH
Trustees: Mr Andrew Burchell, Ms Shirley Mason, Mr Jason Gold, Mr Ashley Thomas, Mr Andrew Theobald, Mr Nigel Quinney, Mr Peter Honour, Mrs Doris Richards, Ms Heather Jones
Income: £1,303,295 [2017]; £1,136,004 [2016]; £943,955 [2015]; £822,195 [2014]; £820,483 [2013]

Sutton Coldfield Charitable Trust

Registered: 7 Apr 1982 *Employees:* 8
Tel: 0121 351 2262 *Website:* suttoncoldfieldcharitabletrust.com
Activities: General charitable purposes; education, training; advancement of health or saving of lives; disability; prevention or relief of poverty; accommodation, housing; religious activities; arts, culture, heritage, science; amateur sport; environment, conservation, heritage
Address: Sutton Coldfield Charitable Trust, Linguard House, Fox Hollies Road, Sutton Coldfield, W Midlands, B76 8RJ
Trustees: Honorary Alderman Margaret Waddington MBE JP, Mrs Carole L Hancox, Dr S C Martin, Rev John Routh, Mr Andrew Charles Morris, Sanjay Sharma, Mrs Ranjan Hoath, Mrs Christine Anne Brown, Mr Keith M Dudley, Mr Neil Andrews, Mr Malcolm I Cornish, Mr Andrew F Burley, Ms Inge Kettner, Cllr Diane Donaldson, Mrs Laurie Kennedy
Income: £1,923,076 [2017]; £1,805,073 [2016]; £1,741,413 [2015]; £1,764,345 [2014]; £1,718,080 [2013]

The Sutton Pendle Charitable Trust

Registered: 22 Apr 2016
Tel: 07775 661114
Activities: General charitable purposes
Address: The Cliff, Red Lane, Colne, Lancs, BB8 7JR
Trustees: Mrs Ruth Sutton, Mr Richard Sutton, Mr James Robert Sutton
Income: £1,950,000 [2016]

The Sutton Trust

Registered: 5 Mar 2012 *Employees:* 19
Website: suttontrust.com
Activities: Education, training
Address: The Sutton Trust, Millbank Tower, 21-24 Millbank, London, SW1P 4QP
Trustees: Sir Peter Oliver Gershon, Lady Susan Lampl, Sir Peter Lampl, Mr Oliver Anthony Carruthers Quick
Income: £8,899,489 [2017]; £6,491,883 [2016]; £4,321,357 [2015]; £3,088,396 [2014]; £2,991,554 [2013]

Sutton's Hospital in Charterhouse
Registered: 26 Nov 1962 *Employees:* 76 *Volunteers:* 50
Tel: 020 3818 8872 *Website:* thecharterhouse.org
Activities: The advancement of health or saving of lives; disability; prevention or relief of poverty; accommodation, housing
Address: Sutton's Hospital in Charterhouse, Charterhouse Square, London, EC1M 6AN
Trustees: The Right Hon Lord John Wakeham, Lord Simon Glenarthur DL FCILT FRAeS, Mr Daniel Hodson, Sir John Banham DL, Marquess Robert Salisbury PC DL, Mr Peter Hodgson CBE DL FCA, Baroness Kay Andrews OBE FSA, Caroline Cassels, Air Chief Marshal Sir Michael Graydon GCB CBE FRAeS RAF (Rtd), Lord Richard Dannatt GCB CBE MC DL, Mr Paul Double BSc LLM MRSC, Dr Clare Heath MA MB BS MRCGP, Mr Michael Power, Mr Timothy Boxell, Mr Simon Kitching, Mr Wilf Weeks
Income: £6,062,765 [2017]; £4,305,217 [2016]; £4,339,971 [2015]; £3,470,042 [2014]; £3,042,772 [2013]

Swalcliffe Park School Trust
Registered: 31 Mar 1965 *Employees:* 74
Tel: 01295 780302 *Website:* swalcliffepark.co.uk
Activities: Education, training
Address: Swalcliffe Park School, Swalcliffe, Banbury, Oxon, OX15 5EP
Trustees: Rev John Hartley Tattersall, Mr Ivor Hopkyns, Mr Nat Parsons, Mr Raymond Sancroft-Baker, Mr Douglas Seymour, Ms Cathy Stoertz, Mr Peter Beddowes
Income: £4,459,451 [2017]; £4,587,454 [2016]; £4,842,928 [2015]; £4,723,289 [2014]; £5,614,823 [2013]

Swan Advocacy Network
Registered: 1 Sep 2008 *Employees:* 42 *Volunteers:* 16
Tel: 0333 344 7928 *Website:* swanadvocacy.org.uk
Activities: General charitable purposes; disability; other charitable purposes
Address: Crown Chambers, Bridge Street, Salisbury, Wilts, SP1 2LZ
Trustees: Ms Irene Margaret Kohler, Mr Alan Mitchell, Mr Alan Guyver, Mr Peter Curbishley, Mr Ken Howard, Mrs Elizabth Ellen Garrett
Income: £1,004,246 [2017]; £1,055,742 [2016]; £598,836 [2015]; £621,020 [2014]; £366,406 [2013]

The Swanage Railway Trust
Registered: 3 Jul 2001 *Employees:* 49 *Volunteers:* 450
Tel: 01929 425800 *Website:* swanagerailwaytrust.org.uk
Activities: Environment, conservation, heritage
Address: Swanage Railway Co Ltd, Station House, Railway Station Approach, Swanage, Dorset, BH19 1HB
Trustees: Mr Andrew Leslie Moore, Bill Trite, Mrs Elizabeth Maureen Sellen, Mrs Beryl Rita Ezzard, Mr Paul Trevor Clements, Mr Gavin Christopher Johns, Mr Daniel John Bennett, Mr Stuart Irving Magnus, Mr Matthew McManus, Mr Michael Alan Whitwam, Mr David Anthony Budd, Mr Peter Nicholas Sills, Mr Mark Robert Woolley, Mr Trevor John Parsons, Mr Nicholas Stephen Chillcot Coram, Miss Jacqueline Ann Hagger, Mr Geoffrey Carter
Income: £3,757,781 [2016]; £4,886,460 [2015]; £3,173,477 [2014]; £2,934,763 [2013]; £2,839,659 [2012]

Swanbourne House School Trust Limited
Registered: 7 Sep 1970 *Employees:* 174 *Volunteers:* 5
Tel: 01296 722810 *Website:* swanbourne.org
Activities: Education, training; religious activities
Address: Swanbourne House School, Swanbourne, Milton Keynes, Bucks, MK17 0HZ
Trustees: Mr Mark Justin Wells Rushton MA, Mr Peter Rushforth, Susan Tyler, Mr Jonathan Sykes, Mr Matthew Deer, Mr John Willmott, Mr William Martin Alastair Land, Mrs Katherine Langston, George Masters, Mrs Tara O'Neill
Income: £6,216,999 [2017]; £6,123,103 [2016]; £5,681,812 [2015]; £5,436,536 [2014]; £5,413,524 [2013]

Swansea C V S
Registered: 5 Jul 1997 *Employees:* 42 *Volunteers:* 192
Tel: 01792 54001 *Website:* scvs.org.uk
Activities: General charitable purposes; education, training; disability; economic, community development, employment
Address: 7-8 Walter Road, Swansea, SA1 5NF
Trustees: Mr Alun Evans, Chris Mann, Mrs Cherrie Bija, Mr Lloyd Williams, Mr Lloyd Jones, Mrs P J Morgan, Mrs Jane Harris, Mr Patrick McNamara, Mrs Saskia Hamer, Ms Anna Tippett
Income: £1,438,287 [2017]; £1,644,040 [2016]; £1,976,081 [2015]; £1,873,218 [2014]; £1,548,272 [2013]

Swansea University Students' Union
Registered: 27 Nov 2012 *Employees:* 200 *Volunteers:* 1,165
Tel: 01792 513395 *Website:* swansea-union.co.uk
Activities: Education, training; arts, culture, heritage, science; amateur sport; recreation
Address: Swansea University, Singleton Park, Swansea, SA2 8PP
Trustees: Howard J Morgan, Miss Shona Johnson, Miss Emily Rees, Mr Riaz Hussan, Miss Chisomo Phiri, Mr Christopher Freestone, Mr Gwyn Rennolf, Ms Sara Correia
Income: £7,185,531 [2017]; £6,602,646 [2016]; £7,510,968 [2015]; £7,265,920 [2014]; £6,002,633 [2013]

Swansea University
Registered: 11 Oct 2010 *Employees:* 3,045
Website: swan.ac.uk
Activities: Education, training
Address: Swansea University, Singleton Park, Swansea, SA2 8PP
Trustees: Mrs Gaynor Marie Richards, Sir Roger Jones OBE BSc MSc, Professor Iwan Rhun Davies, Mrs Jill Burgess, Professor Richard Davies, Dr Simon Hoffman, Mr John Francis Mahoney, Mr Bleddyn Glynne Leyshon Phillips, Professor Steve Wilks, Dr Tessa Elisabeth Watts, Dr Kerry Beynon, Mr Michael Draper, Mr Gwyn Aled Rennolf, Professor Hilary Lappin-Scott, Professor Dame Jean Olwen Thomas, Mrs Valerie Jean Mills, Mrs Rosemary Morgan LLB, Mr Gordon Quintin Anderson, Sir Roderick Evans, Ms Debra Williams, Professor Jane Thomas, Ms Elin Rhys, Dr Angus Muirhead, Professor Joy Merrell, Miss Chisomo Phiri, Professor Kathryn Anne Monk
Income: £278,024,000 [2017]; £295,835,000 [2016]; £228,671,000 [2015]; £205,205,000 [2014]; £181,755,000 [2013]

Swansea Young Single Homeless Project
Registered: 22 May 1991 *Employees:* 37 *Volunteers:* 5
Tel: 01792 537530 *Website:* syshp.org.uk
Activities: General charitable purposes; education, training; prevention or relief of poverty; accommodation, housing
Address: 52 Walter Road, Swansea, SA1 5PW
Trustees: Mrs Susan Prosser, Mr Paul Wales, Mr Mark Adrian Sheridan, Miss Rhian Jones, Mr Owen Thomas Burt, Mr Lynn Davies, Miss Lowri Angharad Rees
Income: £1,231,391 [2017]; £1,190,550 [2016]; £1,237,905 [2015]; £1,259,624 [2014]; £1,278,201 [2013]

Swansea and Brecon Diocesan Board for Social Responsibility
Registered: 13 Dec 2002 *Employees:* 43 *Volunteers:* 22
Tel: 01792 588487 *Website:* faithinfamilies.wales
Activities: General charitable purposes; education, training; prevention or relief of poverty; religious activities; economic, community development, employment
Address: Eastmoor Centre, St Barnabas Church, Hawthorne Avenue, Uplands, Swansea, SA2 0LP
Trustees: Mr Raymond John Winchester, Mr Nigel King, Mr Julian Lovell, Dr Sian Miller, Mrs Esther Searle, Rev Alan Neil Jevons, Rev Robert John Davies-Hannen
Income: £1,755,136 [2017]; £948,764 [2016]; £1,035,306 [2015]; £1,332,333 [2014]; £1,612,527 [2013]

Swansea and Brecon Diocesan Board of Finance
Registered: 17 Apr 1968 *Employees:* 9 *Volunteers:* 2,000
Tel: 01874 623716 *Website:* churchinwales.org.uk
Activities: Religious activities
Address: Diocesan Centre, Cathedral Close, Brecon, Powys, LD3 9DP
Trustees: Mr Gwyn Lewis, Rev Alan Neil Jevons, The Venerable Jonathan Byron Davies, Sir Paul Silk, Mrs Louise Pearson, The Most Revd John Davies The Archbishop of Wales, Mrs Sonia Jones, Very Revd Dr Albert Paul Shackerley, Sir Andrew Large
Income: £3,842,197 [2016]; £3,804,475 [2015]; £3,646,827 [2014]; £3,585,064 [2013]; £3,516,834 [2012]

Swanswell Charitable Trust
Registered: 26 Mar 1999 *Employees:* 250 *Volunteers:* 6
Tel: 020 8335 1830 *Website:* swanswell.org
Activities: The advancement of health or saving of lives
Address: The Swanswell Charitable Trust, Thames Mews, Portsmouth Road, Esher, Surrey, KT10 9AD
Trustees: Mr Richard Pertwee, Mr Andy Furlong, Mr Tom Rutherford
Income: £8,529,018 [2017]; £11,403,324 [2016]; £9,529,085 [2015]; £11,181,113 [2014]; £10,996,549 [2013]

Swarovski Foundation
Registered: 2 Sep 2013
Tel: 020 7255 8400 *Website:* swarovskifoundation.org
Activities: General charitable purposes; education, training; advancement of health or saving of lives; prevention or relief of poverty; overseas aid, famine relief; arts, culture, heritage, science; environment, conservation, heritage; human rights, religious or racial harmony, equality or diversity
Address: 2nd Floor, 21 Sackville Street, London, W1S 3DN
Trustees: Dr Helen Elizabeth Jenkins, Mr Paul Van Zyl, Ambassador Helene Antonia Vondamm, Dean Teri Ellen Schwartz, Ms Nadja Swarovski, Ms Lorenza aka Mimma Viglezio, Professor Jonathan Edward Michener Baillie
Income: £1,837,423 [2016]; £983,160 [2015]; £1,955,681 [2014]

Swarthmore Education Centre
Registered: 31 Oct 2002 *Employees:* 78 *Volunteers:* 9
Tel: 0113 243 7985 *Website:* swarthmore.org.uk
Activities: Education, training; arts, culture, heritage, science
Address: Swarthmore Education Centre, 2-7 Woodhouse Square, Leeds, LS3 1AD
Trustees: Mrs Freda Matthews, May Belt, Hugh Hubbard, Mark Woodhead, Ms Kathryn Julie Badon, Marge Ellis, Mr Malcolm Walters, Patrick Hall, Ms Clare Wigzell, Dr Elizabeth Watkins, Mr Robert James Mcara, Ian Greenwood
Income: £1,532,981 [2017]; £1,332,576 [2016]; £1,347,254 [2015]; £1,122,770 [2014]; £1,052,408 [2013]

The Swedish Church in London Ltd
Registered: 12 Feb 2014 *Employees:* 12 *Volunteers:* 200
Tel: 020 7616 0263 *Website:* swedishchurch.com
Activities: General charitable purposes; education, training; prevention or relief of poverty; religious activities; arts, culture, heritage, science
Address: Swedish Church, 6-11 Harcourt Street, London, W1H 4AG
Trustees: Ms Madelaine Mason, Mrs Linda Maria Peanberg King, Mr Per Anders Jonsson, Johan Auren, Mr Mike Christopherson, Mr Henrik Hansson, Mr Eric Stefan Muhl, Christian Bjarnam
Income: £1,162,665 [2016]; £3,069,753 [2015]; £995,934 [2014]

The Swedish Folk High School
Registered: 12 Aug 1980 *Employees:* 25
Tel: 01273 414973 *Website:* loxdale.com
Activities: Education, training
Address: The Swedish Folk High School, Loxdale, Locks Hill, Portslade, Brighton, BN41 2LA
Trustees: Mr Peter Sanders, Mr Nick Wescombe, Bo Forkman, Ms Eva Maria Arnek
Income: £1,001,497 [2017]; £848,019 [2016]; £886,442 [2015]; £775,628 [2014]; £755,589 [2013]

The Swedish School Society in London
Registered: 19 Nov 1969 *Employees:* 47
Tel: 020 8741 1751 *Website:* swedishschool.org.uk
Activities: Education, training
Address: 82 Lonsdale Road, London, SW13 9JS
Trustees: Mr Rickard Jonsson, Mr Peter Burman, Mr Hans Otterling, Mrs Malin Viktoria Hagberg, Mr Johan Rafael Liljefors, Mr Andrew Craig Beaver, Mr Thomas Paulsson, Ms Kristina Andreasson, Mrs Lotti Eva Charlotte Elisabeth Kierkegaard
Income: £3,786,907 [2017]; £3,539,224 [2016]; £3,492,777 [2015]; £3,658,273 [2014]; £3,317,198 [2013]

Swimathon Foundation
Registered: 24 Apr 2008
Tel: 020 7043 0575 *Website:* swimathonfoundation.org
Activities: General charitable purposes
Address: c/o Cox Costello & Horne, 4th & 5th Floor, 14-15 Lower Grosvenor Place, London, SW1W 0EX
Trustees: Mr Anthony Kendall, Mr Philip Stinson, Mrs Deana Radice, Mr Ralph Riley, Miss Donna Notaro, Mr Grant Pearce
Income: £1,477,231 [2016]; £3,245,559 [2015]; £1,368,044 [2014]; £3,012,206 [2013]; £2,886,831 [2012]

The Swimming Teachers Association Limited
Registered: 22 Dec 1995 *Employees:* 43
Tel: 01922 645097 *Website:* sta.co.uk
Activities: Education, training; advancement of health or saving of lives; amateur sport
Address: Swimming Teachers Association, Anchor House, Birch Street, Walsall, W Midlands, WS2 8HZ
Trustees: Mrs Myra Catherine Lee Robinson, Mr Robert Phillips, Mr Mike Walters, Mr Richard Timms, Mr David Lewis, Mrs Dana Wells-Bryant
Income: £2,433,918 [2017]; £2,454,175 [2016]; £2,421,423 [2015]; £2,231,982 [2014]; £2,162,706 [2013]

John Swire 1989 Charitable Trust
Registered: 25 Sep 1989
Tel: 020 7834 7717
Activities: General charitable purposes
Address: John Swire 1989 Charitable Trust, Swire House, 59 Buckingham Gate, London, SW1E 6AJ
Trustees: Mr B Swire, Mr Michael Cradock Robinson, Mr J S Swire
Income: £1,359,760 [2016]; £1,260,322 [2015]; £3,677,871 [2014]; £1,163,100 [2013]; £2,286,860 [2012]

Swire 2765
Registered: 18 Dec 2012
Tel: 020 7834 7717
Activities: General charitable purposes
Address: Swire 2765, Swire House, 59 Buckingham Gate, London, SW1E 6AJ
Trustees: Mr Barnaby Nicholas Swire, Dr Clare Isacke, Mr John Samuel Swire
Income: £1,374,983 [2016]; £1,405,851 [2015]; £4,280,702 [2014]; £13,302,089 [2013]

The Swire Charitable Trust
Registered: 2 Feb 1976
Tel: 020 7834 7717 *Website:* swirecharitabletrust.org.uk
Activities: General charitable purposes
Address: The Swire Charitable Trust, Swire House, 59 Buckingham Gate, London, SW1E 6AJ
Trustees: Mr B Swire, Sir Adrian Swire, Mr James Wyndham John Hughes-Hallett, Mrs Martha Allfrey, Mr J S Swire, Merlin Swire, Mr Samuel Swire
Income: £2,759,389 [2016]; £2,234,993 [2015]; £1,450,739 [2014]; £1,100,353 [2013]; £750,280 [2012]

The Adrian Swire Charitable Trust
Registered: 30 Nov 1988
Tel: 020 7834 7717
Activities: General charitable purposes
Address: The Adrian Swire Charitable Trust, Swire House, 59 Buckingham Gate, London, SW1E 6AJ
Trustees: Sir Martin Dunne, Mrs Martha Virginia Allfrey, Mr Richard Leonard, The Lady Judith Swire, Merlin Swire, Samuel Swire
Income: £1,328,577 [2016]; £1,535,731 [2015]; £1,168,895 [2014]; £773,058 [2013]; £969,842 [2012]

The Valeria Sykes Charitable Foundation CIO
Registered: 6 May 2016
Tel: 0113 280 2000
Activities: Education, training; arts, culture, heritage, science; economic, community development, employment
Address: Lupton Fawcett Solicitors, Yorkshire House, East Parade, Leeds, LS1 5BD
Trustees: Mr Peter Foskett, Mr Richard Sykes, Mr Colin Little, Mrs Valeria Sykes
Income: £100,000,087 [2017]

Syracuse University (USA) London Program
Registered: 10 Sep 2001 *Employees:* 86
Tel: 020 7597 6173 *Website:* sulondon.syr.edu
Activities: Education, training
Address: Withers Ltd, 16 Old Bailey, London, EC4M 7EG
Trustees: Mr David Julian Buchler, Mr Richard Kortright, Professor Margaret Himley, Mr Michael Edward Harris, Mr Amir Rahnamay-Azar, Mr Richard Alexander Cassell, Mr Rani Raad, Ms Susan Dean Harding, Michele Wheatly
Income: £5,049,470 [2017]; £3,903,483 [2016]; £3,597,970 [2015]; £3,636,475 [2014]; £4,832,499 [2013]

Syria Relief
Registered: 14 Sep 2011 *Employees:* 89 *Volunteers:* 10
Tel: 0161 860 0163 *Website:* syriarelief.org.uk
Activities: General charitable purposes; education, training; advancement of health or saving of lives; prevention or relief of poverty; other charitable purposes
Address: British Muslim Heritage Centre, College Road, Manchester, M16 8BP
Trustees: Mr Tamim Estwani, Dr Ayman Jundi, Dr Ghanem Tayara, Dr Molham Entabi, Dr Mounir Hakimi, Dr Mohammad Anas Nashawi, Mr Louai Al-Abed, Mrs Abeer Zabadne
Income: £20,828,126 [2017]; £12,889,138 [2016]; £10,957,759 [2015]; £3,333,198 [2014]; £2,496,999 [2013]

T E D S
Registered: 17 Mar 1997 *Employees:* 41 *Volunteers:* 20
Tel: 01685 880090 *Website:* teds.org.uk
Activities: Education, training; advancement of health or saving of lives; accommodation, housing
Address: Taff Ely Drug Support, Engine House, Depot Road, Aberdare, Rhondda Cynon Taf, CF44 8DL
Trustees: Mr Glyn Evans, Ms Katherine Lenaghan, Mrs Christine Dodd, Mr Alan Watts, Mr John Lloyd
Income: £1,385,145 [2017]; £1,470,572 [2016]; £1,439,589 [2015]; £1,552,908 [2014]; £1,579,681 [2013]

T.H.O.M.A.S (Those on the Margins of a Society)
Registered: 1 Jun 2006 *Employees:* 35 *Volunteers:* 30
Tel: 01254 59240 *Website:* thomasonline.org.uk
Activities: General charitable purposes; education, training; advancement of health or saving of lives; prevention or relief of poverty; accommodation, housing
Address: St Annes RC Presbytery, France Street, Blackburn, BB2 1LX
Trustees: Mrs Anne Cunliffe BEd MA, Mr Thomas Kennedy, Mr Leo Flood, Mr John Malowana-Murphy, Mr Christopher Porter, Dr Jacob Skaria
Income: £1,493,814 [2017]; £1,606,998 [2016]; £1,641,184 [2015]; £1,293,071 [2014]; £1,271,775 [2013]

TEAM Wearside Limited
Registered: 13 Apr 2000 *Employees:* 42
Tel: 0191 404 6836 *Website:* teamwearside.co.uk
Activities: Education, training
Address: KRE (NE) Ltd, The Axis Building, Maingate, Kingsway North, Team Valley Trading Estate, Gateshead, Tyne & Wear, NE11 0NQ
Trustees: Sandy Ogilvie, Mr George Pattison FCIS, Dave Ritchie, Ms Karen Langdon
Income: £1,900,677 [2016]; £1,975,238 [2015]; £1,892,296 [2014]; £1,826,190 [2013]

TLC: Talk, Listen, Change

Registered: 26 May 1982 *Employees:* 82 *Volunteers:* 60
Tel: 0161 872 1100 *Website:* talklistenchange.org.uk
Activities: Education, training; advancement of health or saving of lives
Address: 20 Whitelow Road, Heaton Moor, Stockport, Cheshire, SK4 4BY
Trustees: Mrs Barbara Shuttleworth, Mr John Sless, Rosemary Agarwala, Mr Gerard Drugan, Mr Christopher Callaghan, Mr Keith William Marsland, Ms Margaret Shannon, Mr Michael Gaskell
Income: £1,119,483 [2017]; £781,869 [2016]; £603,915 [2015]; £515,052 [2014]; £520,404 [2013]

TNB Garrison Early Years and Play

Registered: 15 Feb 2000 *Employees:* 83
Tel: 01980 633962 *Website:* tnbearlyyears.org
Activities: Education, training
Address: 1-2 St Andrews Road, Tidworth, Wilts, SP9 7EP
Trustees: Mrs Vicky Harker, Mrs Victoria Seth, Mrs Sarah Simpson, Carol May Morris
Income: £1,650,725 [2017]; £1,555,920 [2016]; £1,537,150 [2015]; £1,629,927 [2014]; £1,216,254 [2013]

The TTE Technical Training Group

Registered: 2 Jan 1991 *Employees:* 121
Tel: 01642 770314 *Website:* tte.co.uk
Activities: Education, training; economic, community development, employment
Address: The TTE Technical Training Group, Edison House, Middlesbrough Road East, Middlesbrough, Cleveland, TS6 6TZ
Trustees: Mr Keith Mutimer, Mr Ainsley Cheetham, Mr John Philip Arbuckle, Mr Keith Leslie, Mrs Lynn Perry
Income: £9,560,945 [2016]; £17,686,908 [2015]; £21,307,159 [2014]; £16,919,826 [2013]; £13,021,641 [2012]

Tagmarsh Charity Limited

Registered: 15 Dec 1980
Tel: 020 8731 0777
Activities: General charitable purposes; education, training; advancement of health or saving of lives; disability; prevention or relief of poverty; overseas aid, famine relief; accommodation, housing; religious activities
Address: New Burlington House, 1075 Finchley Road, London, NW11 0PU
Trustees: Mr Robert Berkovits, Mr Sidney Sinitsky, Mr Chaim Shimen Lebrecht, Mr B Bard, Shalom Ervin Berkovits, Mr Asher Warmberg
Income: £2,015,312 [2017]; £2,943,686 [2016]; £2,784,156 [2015]; £190,586 [2014]; £2,292,822 [2013]

Take A Break Warwickshire Limited

Registered: 25 May 2001 *Employees:* 175 *Volunteers:* 15
Tel: 024 7651 1621 *Website:* tabw.org.uk
Activities: The advancement of health or saving of lives; disability
Address: 7 Lea Walk, Ryton on Dunsmore, Coventry, Warwicks, CV8 3QD
Trustees: Mr Richard Jonathon Harris, Miss Laura May Swanborough BA, Mrs Lesley Ellen Hines, Ms Rizwana Banu Pathan
Income: £1,609,140 [2017]; £1,801,529 [2016]; £1,813,230 [2015]; £1,835,172 [2014]; £1,680,381 [2013]

Talbot Heath School Trust Limited

Registered: 14 Dec 1981 *Employees:* 119
Tel: 01202 755419 *Website:* talbotheath.org
Activities: Education, training
Address: 448 New Road, Ferndown, Dorset, BH22 8EX
Trustees: Mrs Christine Mary Norman, Dr Richard Day, Mr Andrew Main, Mrs Claire Saunders, Mrs Clodie Sutcliffe, Mr James Paget, Mr David Anthony Townend, Canon Christopher Rutledge, Mrs Rachel Small, Mrs Diana Leadbetter, Mrs Cherry Edwards
Income: £7,062,815 [2017]; £6,770,798 [2016]; £6,238,543 [2015]; £5,898,806 [2014]; £5,583,082 [2013]

Talbot House Trust North East

Registered: 29 Jun 1999 *Employees:* 45
Tel: 0191 229 0111 *Website:* talbothousetrust.co.uk
Activities: Education, training; accommodation, housing
Address: Talbot House Trust, Hexham Road, Walbottle, Newcastle upon Tyne, NE15 8HW
Trustees: Rev Allison Joan Harding, Mrs Linda Tarbit, Mrs Louise Cannell-Mirza, Mr Christopher Denys Matthews, Mr Benjamin Ross Henderson
Income: £1,930,075 [2017]; £1,772,602 [2016]; £1,533,404 [2015]; £1,271,585 [2014]; £1,144,523 [2013]

Talbot Village Trust

Registered: 7 Jul 1967 *Employees:* 1
Tel: 01202 338551 *Website:* talbotvillagetrust.co.uk
Activities: General charitable purposes; disability; prevention or relief of poverty; accommodation, housing
Address: Talbot Village Trust, c/o Trethowans, 5 Parkstone Road, Poole, Dorset, BH15 2NL
Trustees: Sir Thomas Michael John Salt Bart, Mr Christopher James Lees, Earl of Shaftesbury, James Randolf Gibson Fleming, Mr Russell Lucas Rowe, Mr George William Owen Tapps Gervis Meyrick
Income: £2,750,614 [2016]; £4,197,975 [2015]; £2,247,309 [2014]; £2,146,020 [2013]; £2,177,329 [2012]

Talkback-UK Ltd

Registered: 6 Sep 2002 *Employees:* 60
Tel: 01494 434448 *Website:* talkback-uk.com
Activities: Education, training; advancement of health or saving of lives; disability; economic, community development, employment
Address: Amersham Community Centre, Chiltern Avenue, Amersham, Bucks, HP6 5AH
Trustees: Ms Bridget Campbell, Mr Paul Osborne, Mr David Gerard, Ms Janice Campbell, Mr Mikkel Togsverd, Mrs Elizabeth Anne Cutler
Income: £1,602,648 [2017]; £1,446,748 [2016]; £992,615 [2015]; £518,084 [2014]; £346,188 [2013]

The Talking Trust

Registered: 21 Sep 1967 *Employees:* 202 *Volunteers:* 3
Tel: 01424 730740 *Website:* stmarysbexhill.org
Activities: Education, training; advancement of health or saving of lives; disability
Address: St Marys Wrestwood Childrens Trust, Wrestwood Road, Bexhill on Sea, E Sussex, TN40 2LU
Trustees: Ms Liz Lash, Ms Amanda Croft-Pearman, Mrs Mary Briggs, Mrs Sally Wickens, Ms Sarah Arrowsmith, Mr Andrew Hodson, Mr Gerald Cooper, Mr Simon Alford, Ms Catherine Baart, Ms Sarah Doherty
Income: £4,854,350 [2017]; £5,368,198 [2016]; £6,963,445 [2015]; £8,257,586 [2014]; £7,899,006 [2013]

Tall Ships Youth Trust
Registered: 20 Jun 1963 *Employees:* 13 *Volunteers:* 2,500
Tel: 023 9283 2055 *Website:* tallships.org
Activities: Education, training; disability; amateur sport
Address: 2A The Hard, Portsmouth, PO1 3PT
Trustees: Mr Richard Graham Melly, Dr Charlotte Griffiths RN, Mr Robert Jonathan Evans, Mr Stephen Alexander Hartigan, Mr Michael Broughton, Mr John Fyfe Lennox, Mr Philip Neil McDanell, Mr Michael P Aiken MBE
Income: £2,522,356 [2016]; £2,428,564 [2015]; £2,224,795 [2014]; £2,387,515 [2013]; £3,248,657 [2012]

Tall Stories Theatre Company Limited
Registered: 30 Oct 2007 *Employees:* 6
Tel: 020 8348 0080 *Website:* tallstories.org.uk
Activities: Education, training; arts, culture, heritage, science; economic, community development, employment
Address: Somerset House, West Wing, Strand, London, WC2R 1LA
Trustees: Ms Annabel Clare Arndt, Ms Penelope Daly, Mr Tobias Park, Mr Stephen Cowton
Income: £2,199,905 [2017]; £2,225,831 [2016]; £788,130 [2015]; £897,758 [2014]; £774,247 [2013]

Talmud Torah Education Limited
Registered: 20 May 1994 *Employees:* 99
Activities: Education, training
Address: 79 Darenth Road, London, N16 6ES
Trustees: Mr Berish Berger, Mr Shalom Cik, Mr Avigdor Frankl
Income: £1,709,371 [2017]; £1,492,361 [2016]; £1,430,821 [2015]; £1,235,362 [2014]; £1,097,497 [2013]

The Talmud Torah Machzikei Hadass Trust
Registered: 7 Jan 1976
Activities: Education, training; religious activities
Address: 28 Leadale Road, London, N16 6DA
Trustees: Mr Jehudah Baumgarten, Mr Mordechaj Jaakow Wind, Mr Yitzchok Menachem Sternlicht
Income: £6,324,680 [2017]; £2,662,357 [2016]; £3,175,498 [2015]; £1,637,567 [2014]; £244,243 [2013]

Tamba, Twins & Multiple Births Association
Registered: 9 Jul 1999 *Employees:* 25 *Volunteers:* 120
Tel: 01252 332344 *Website:* tamba.org.uk
Activities: Education, training; advancement of health or saving of lives; disability; prevention or relief of poverty
Address: Tamba, The Manor House, Manor Park, Church Hill, Aldershot, Hants, GU12 4JU
Trustees: Mrs Anna Varela-Raynes, Miss Rachel Barber, Mr Duncan Moffett, Mr Oliver Gell, Ms Saira Uppal, Mr Tim Dulley, Krista Pound, Ms Heather Dembitz, Mrs Sarah Perris, Mr Simon Berney-Edwards
Income: £1,011,899 [2017]; £838,322 [2016]; £670,571 [2015]; £685,065 [2014]; £562,022 [2013]

Tameside Sports Trust
Registered: 24 Mar 1999 *Employees:* 353 *Volunteers:* 353
Tel: 0161 393 2206 *Website:* activetameside.com
Activities: Amateur sport
Address: Hattersley Road East, Hattersley, Cheshire, SK14 3NL
Trustees: Mr Ian Hamilton Munro, Mr Martin Collett, Mr Jon Keating, Mr John Charles Taylor, Mrs Yvonne Harrison, Dr Eddie Thornton-Chan
Income: £10,446,175 [2017]; £8,524,195 [2016]; £8,166,192 [2015]; £7,884,100 [2014]; £7,009,094 [2013]

Tameside and Glossop Hospice Limited
Registered: 29 Nov 1993 *Employees:* 108 *Volunteers:* 627
Tel: 0161 652 2000 *Website:* willowwood.info
Activities: The advancement of health or saving of lives
Address: 1 Alderwood Fold, Lees, Oldham, Lancs, OL4 5RW
Trustees: Patrick Eugene McCloskey, Mr John Hadfield Maltby, Mr Michael Davies, Mrs Claire Dunphy, Mr Mark Thorley, Mr Martin John Willescroft, Mr Brian Wild, Mr Philip Thomas Cowper, Mr Stephen Flanagan, Dr Andrew Parham
Income: £3,123,128 [2017]; £2,946,941 [2016]; £2,940,377 [2015]; £2,539,291 [2014]; £2,812,786 [2013]

Tameside, Oldham and Glossop Mind
Registered: 10 Apr 2008 *Employees:* 76 *Volunteers:* 97
Website: togmind.org
Activities: Education, training; advancement of health or saving of lives; disability; arts, culture, heritage, science; amateur sport
Address: Tameside Oldham & Glossop Mind, 216-218 Katherine Street, Ashton under Lyne, Lancs, OL6 7AS
Trustees: Mr Bob Mercer, Mr David Hutton, Ms Cheryl Eastwood, Ms Victoria Jane Murcott, Ms Lynn Jones, Matt Hall, Mr Gareth Paul Chadwick
Income: £1,746,048 [2017]; £1,196,842 [2016]; £820,620 [2015]; £784,215 [2014]; £577,397 [2013]

The Tank Museum Limited
Registered: 16 Mar 2004 *Employees:* 67 *Volunteers:* 100
Tel: 01929 405096 *Website:* tankmuseum.org
Activities: General charitable purposes; education, training; arts, culture, heritage, science; environment, conservation, heritage
Address: Tank Museum, Bovington, Wareham, Dorset, BH20 6JG
Trustees: Ms Kathryn Adie, Mr Richard Wigley, Mr Steven Rowbotham, Mr William Kenneth Suttie, Colonel Guy Hugh John Deacon, Mr David Webb, Mr Jeremy Pope, Lt Gen Sir Andrew Ridgway KBE CB, Mr William Bannister, Brigadier Ian Gibb, Mr Fraser Mark Stafford-Charles, Dr Christopher Brynley Hammond
Income: £4,559,426 [2016]; £4,519,187 [2015]; £3,565,316 [2014]; £4,504,456 [2013]; £3,828,342 [2012]

David Tannen Charitable Trust
Registered: 8 Mar 1981
Tel: 020 8202 1066
Activities: General charitable purposes
Address: c/o Sutherland House, 70-78 West Hendon Broadway, London, NW9 7BT
Trustees: Mr David Tannen, Mr Jonathan Mark Miller
Income: £2,712,104 [2017]; £2,035,121 [2016]; £1,607,982 [2015]; £1,657,135 [2014]; £1,014,904 [2013]

Tapestry Care UK
Registered: 23 Mar 2000 *Employees:* 109 *Volunteers:* 68
Tel: 01708 796600 *Website:* tapestry-uk.org
Activities: General charitable purposes; advancement of health or saving of lives
Address: Scottish Mutual House, Hornchurch, Essex, RM11 1RS
Trustees: Ms Gill Botwright, Ms Susan Fey, Mr Mark Peter Burton, Mrs B Olufemi Otukoya, The Reverand Hugh Dibbens, Lesley Buckland, Mrs Frances Ellen Pennell-Buck
Income: £2,206,002 [2017]; £2,271,125 [2016]; £2,146,964 [2015]; £2,152,742 [2014]; £2,148,532 [2013]

Target Housing Limited
Registered: 18 Feb 1993 *Employees:* 77 *Volunteers:* 10
Tel: 0114 281 5888 *Website:* targethousing.org.uk
Activities: Education, training; accommodation, housing
Address: 134 Upperthorpe, Sheffield, S6 3NF
Trustees: Rick Plews, Mr Shaun Needham, Ms Ellie Staniforth, Mr Steven Crane, Mrs Jacqueline Dyer, Mr Ian David Brownlee
Income: £5,536,707 [2017]; £5,137,042 [2016]; £4,863,906 [2015]; £4,540,279 [2014]; £3,578,247 [2013]

Target Learning Trust
Registered: 12 Aug 1997 *Employees:* 28 *Volunteers:* 15
Tel: 01302 892822
Activities: Education, training
Address: 8 The Sycamores, Scawthorpe, Doncaster, S Yorks, DN5 7UH
Trustees: Mr Russell Long, Edward Layton, Doug Smith, Trevor West, Mr Warren Bricknell, Sam Mallinson, James Cuckson
Income: £1,487,756 [2016]; £1,215,912 [2015]; £1,097,378 [2014]; £1,083,930 [2013]; £890,807 [2012]

Target Ovarian Cancer
Registered: 17 Jul 2008 *Employees:* 19 *Volunteers:* 150
Tel: 020 7923 5470 *Website:* targetovariancancer.org.uk
Activities: The advancement of health or saving of lives
Address: 2 Angel Gate, London, EC1V 2PT
Trustees: Emma Kane, Shona Spence, Andrew Harrison, Margaret Chamberlain, Alexandra Cran-McGreehin
Income: £1,889,091 [2017]; £1,609,840 [2016]; £1,637,948 [2015]; £1,421,037 [2014]; £1,553,367 [2013]

Taste for Adventure
Registered: 19 Oct 1993 *Employees:* 2 *Volunteers:* 5
Tel: 01432 761398 *Website:* tasteforadventure.co.uk
Activities: General charitable purposes; education, training; advancement of health or saving of lives; disability; prevention or relief of poverty; amateur sport
Address: 1 Orchard Close, Holmer, Hereford, HR4 9QY
Trustees: Mrs Kristy Gillispie, Mrs Audrey Apperley, Mr Les Davies, Amy Jones
Income: £1,043,340 [2016]; £78,631 [2015]; £218,205 [2014]; £239,309 [2013]; £226,596 [2012]

Tate Foundation
Registered: 28 Feb 2001
Tel: 020 7887 8888 *Website:* tate.org.uk
Activities: General charitable purposes; arts, culture, heritage, science
Address: Tate Gallery, Millbank, London, SW1P 4RG
Trustees: Lord Stevenson, Mr Anthony Michael Vaughan Salz, Mr Emmanuel Roman, Mr Edward Eisler, Mr Simon Daw Palley, Dr Maria Balshaw CBE, Mr John Botts CBE, Mr Edward Mead, Franck Petitgas, Mr Joseph Patrick Baratta, Mr George Economou
Income: £13,415,653 [2017]; £30,933,205 [2016]; £41,933,946 [2015]; £36,318,852 [2014]; £44,764,782 [2013]

Taunton School Educational Charity
Registered: 4 Jul 2000 *Employees:* 390 *Volunteers:* 22
Tel: 01823 703128 *Website:* tauntonschool.co.uk
Activities: Education, training; religious activities; arts, culture, heritage, science; amateur sport; other charitable purposes
Address: 16 The Point, Compass Hill, Taunton, Somerset, TA1 4AG
Trustees: Mr Christopher Butters FCA, Mrs Hilary Quantick LLB, Mr Richard Kennedy LLB FCA, Mrs Marilyn Trask BEd MA, Rev Nigel Carl Manges, Mr Philip Michael Cooper BA Hons MSc, Mr Robert Charles Aldrich, Mrs Elaine Mary Waymouth, Rear Admiral Ian Moncrieff, Mr Henry C V Keeling, Mr Tim Hayden LLB, Mr Mark Julian Hallas OBE, Mr Keith R Moore, Mr David Hugh Hebditch
Income: £21,071,300 [2017]; £21,902,100 [2016]; £21,925,300 [2015]; £21,260,900 [2014]; £20,706,500 [2013]

Taverham Hall Educational Trust Limited
Registered: 16 Nov 1967 *Employees:* 81 *Volunteers:* 1
Tel: 01603 868206 *Website:* taverhamhall.co.uk
Activities: Education, training
Address: Taverham Hall, Taverham, Norwich, NR8 6HU
Trustees: Mr Charles Edward Birch, Mrs Sharon Leigh Turner, Mr Brett William Burton, Mr Graham Ernest Watson, Mr Matthew Newnham, Mr John Hamilton Miller
Income: £2,976,603 [2016]; £2,874,513 [2015]; £2,725,561 [2014]; £2,477,105 [2013]; £2,308,557 [2012]

The Tavistock Institute of Human Relations
Registered: 16 Aug 1963 *Employees:* 32
Website: tavinstitute.org
Activities: Education, training
Address: 30 Tabernacle Street, London, EC2A 4UE
Trustees: Dr Eliat Aram, Professor Cliff Oswick, Mrs Alice Mary Charlotte Long, Mr Simeon Louis Joel Featherman, Ms Joanna Hill, Mrs Julie Anne Newlan, Professor Christopher Warhurst, Mr Robert John Branagh, Ms Chukwuemeka Golding
Income: £2,369,014 [2017]; £2,877,119 [2016]; £2,314,353 [2015]; £2,044,541 [2014]; £2,046,048 [2013]

The Tavistock Institute of Medical Psychology
Registered: 29 Oct 1962 *Employees:* 52
Website: tavistockrelationships.org
Activities: General charitable purposes; education, training; advancement of health or saving of lives
Address: 70 Warren Street, London, W1T 5PB
Trustees: Ms Mavis MacLean, Mrs H K Wright, Dr Jezzard, Dr Ros Bryar, Mr Rupert Harrison, Lizzie Insall, Patricia Key, Ms Jane Smith, Mr Nick Pearce, Mr Robert Rowland Smith, Stan Ruszczynski, Stuart Brough, Katharine Pinney, Carmel Bamford
Income: £4,514,536 [2017]; £5,096,803 [2016]; £4,994,445 [2015]; £4,150,409 [2014]; £2,604,849 [2013]

The Cyril Taylor Charitable Foundation
Registered: 16 May 2013
Tel: 020 7457 3000
Activities: General charitable purposes
Address: 125 Wood Street, London, EC2V 7AW
Trustees: Mr Robert William Maas, Mr Clifford Derek Joseph, Mr William Gertz, Mr Thomas Otto Kiechle, Mr John A Burg, Mr Clive Tucker, Mrs Elizabeth Hawksworth, Mrs Penny Egan CBE, Mr Jonathan Michael Berry, M Stephen Rasch, Ms Ailsa Brookes, Mr Christopher Archer-Lock, Mr James Husband, Ms D G Wilson
Income: £10,514,806 [2017]; £280,671 [2016]; £617,528 [2015]; £250,062 [2014]

The Taylor Family Foundation
Registered: 20 Feb 2007 *Employees:* 2
Tel: 020 8605 2629 *Website:* thetaylorfamilyfoundation.co.uk
Activities: General charitable purposes; education, training; advancement of health or saving of lives; prevention or relief of poverty; arts, culture, heritage, science; amateur sport
Address: Hill Place House, 55a High Street, Wimbledon, London, SW19 5BA
Trustees: Mr Ian Taylor, Mr Neville Philip Shepherd, Mrs Cristina Alicia Taylor
Income: £3,145,235 [2017]; £2,520,212 [2016]; £1,270,210 [2015]; £1,250,210 [2014]; £1,875,841 [2013]

Stephen Taylor Foundation
Registered: 5 Jul 2016
Tel: 020 3375 7000
Activities: General charitable purposes
Address: Farrer & Co, 65-66 Lincoln's Inn Fields, London, WC2A 3LH
Trustees: Mrs Lisa Joanne Taylor, Mr Richard James Walker, Mr Martin Edward Taylor
Income: £25,937,572 [2017]

The Helen Taylor Thompson Foundation Limited
Registered: 28 May 1999 *Employees:* 30
Tel: 020 3096 7659 *Website:* can-online.org.uk
Activities: General charitable purposes; education, training; economic, community development, employment; other charitable purposes
Address: 105 Marguerite Drive, Leigh on Sea, Essex, SS9 1NN
Trustees: Mrs Helen Taylor Thompson OBE FRSA, Mr Alistair Fraser, Mr Robin Pauley, Mr Clive Robert Dove-Dixon
Income: £5,718,860 [2017]; £4,545,595 [2016]; £3,637,483 [2015]; £3,477,478 [2014]; £3,194,176 [2013]

Tchabe Kollel Limited
Registered: 1 Nov 2006 *Employees:* 9
Tel: 020 8809 0393 *Website:* tchabe.com
Activities: General charitable purposes; education, training; religious activities
Address: 23 Portland Avenue, London, N16 6HD
Trustees: Mr Gerald Raymond Conrad, Mr Simcha Kraushar, Mrs Rachel Devries
Income: £3,214,932 [2017]; £2,197,152 [2016]; £1,694,455 [2015]; £1,490,187 [2014]; £1,250,161 [2013]

Teach First
Registered: 2 Jul 2003 *Employees:* 543 *Volunteers:* 1,582
Tel: 020 3862 8000 *Website:* teachfirst.org.uk
Activities: Education, training; human rights, religious or racial harmony, equality or diversity
Address: Teach First, 6 Mitre Passage, Greenwich Peninsula, London, SE10 0ER
Trustees: Mr Robert William Ashburnham Swannell, Mr Glenn Earle, Ms Lorna Rachel Gratton, Ms Alison Magaret Peacock, Ms Alison Duncan, Lord Jonathan Hill, Julianne Ilebode-Akisanya, Dame Mary Elizabeth Marsh, Mr Paul Drechsler, Mr James Daniel Bilefield, Mr Richard Meddings, Ally Eynon, Ms Tulsi Naidu, Jason Arthur
Income: £61,011,000 [2017]; £63,976,000 [2016]; £60,568,000 [2015]; £50,089,000 [2014]; £25,292,395 [2013]

Team Army Sports Foundation
Registered: 27 Sep 2011
Tel: 01425 403609 *Website:* teamarmy.org
Activities: Amateur sport; armed forces, emergency service efficiency
Address: Wilderhope, Southfield Lane, Burley, Ringwood, Hants, BH24 4AX
Trustees: Brigadier Richard William Dennis, Mr Nicolas Charles Anderson, Mr Andrew Stuart McMorran, Mr Graham Beal, Major General Richard Semple CBE, Brigadier David Neil Sexton
Income: £1,020,147 [2016]; £984,537 [2015]; £711,497 [2014]; £540,515 [2013]; £814,666 [2012]

Team Rubicon UK
Registered: 19 Aug 2015 *Employees:* 8 *Volunteers:* 1,344
Tel: 0300 330 9488 *Website:* teamrubiconuk.org
Activities: The advancement of health or saving of lives; overseas aid, famine relief; economic, community development, employment; armed forces, emergency service efficiency
Address: Team Rubicon UK, Chilmark, Wilts, SP3 5DU
Trustees: Mr Andrew James Hamilton Purvis, Mr Nicholas Henry Fothergill, David Michael Wiseman, Ms Sara George, Wes Turbeville, Mark Sedwill, Mr William Barker McNulty, Sir Nicholas Ralph Parker, Mr John McDonough CBE, Ms Kate Holt
Income: £1,148,704 [2017]; £512,514 [2016]

The Teamwork Trust
Registered: 15 Nov 1996 *Employees:* 30 *Volunteers:* 115
Tel: 01536 511993 *Website:* teamworktrust.co.uk
Activities: Education, training; disability; economic, community development, employment
Address: Teamwork Trust, 1 Stanier Close, Kettering, Northants, NN16 9XW
Trustees: Mr Jim Noble, Mr William Donald Clark, Miss Shirley Jayne Marshall, Mr Anthony Dady, Mr David Owens, Mr Desmond Charles Glen, John Hill, Mr Raymond Boswell, Miss Racheal Collins
Income: £1,008,653 [2017]; £602,084 [2016]; £610,063 [2015]; £464,929 [2014]; £425,925 [2013]

Tearfund
Registered: 6 Mar 1973 *Employees:* 996 *Volunteers:* 5,700
Tel: 020 8943 7807 *Website:* tearfund.org
Activities: The prevention or relief of poverty; overseas aid, famine relief; religious activities
Address: 100 Church Road, Teddington, Middlesex, TW11 8QE
Trustees: Mr Deepak Mahtani BA AIMC FRSA, Ms Stephanie Clare Biden, Mr Craig Rowland, Mrs Sally Jones-Evans, Reverand Mark Melluish, Ian Curtis, Rt Rev Anthony Dangasuk Poggo, Ms Rosemary Winifred Nuamah Williams, Mr John Davidson, Mr H C Mather, Mrs Jillian Mills, Mr John Shaw, Mrs Stephanie Heald, Right Rev Harold Creeth Miller, Mr Philip Duncan Loney
Income: £72,768,000 [2017]; £72,162,000 [2016]; £62,206,000 [2015]; £59,372,000 [2014]; £60,046,000 [2013]

The Tech Partnership
Registered: 17 Apr 2015 *Employees:* 27
Tel: 020 7963 8963 *Website:* thetechpartnership.com
Activities: Education, training; economic, community development, employment; other charitable purposes
Address: 1 Castle Lane, London, SW1E 6DR
Trustees: Mr Philip Patrick Smith, Mr David William Lister, Mr Andrew James Green, Gayna Hart
Income: £2,452,657 [2017]; £7,153,811 [2016]

Tech Trust

Registered: 8 Dec 2009 *Employees:* 12
Tel: 020 7324 3290 *Website:* tech-trust.org
Activities: General charitable purposes
Address: East Coast, East Side, Kings Cross Station, Kings Cross, London, N1C 4AX
Trustees: Mr Charles Mindenhall, Ms Delia Bushell, Ms Emma Thomas, Ian James, Mr Daniel Cobley, Mr John Wilfred Lazar, Mr Steven Dunne
Income: £1,680,340 [2017]; £2,100,536 [2016]; £1,978,042 [2015]; £2,243,014 [2014]; £2,024,043 [2013]

Technion UK

Registered: 24 May 2002 *Employees:* 3
Tel: 020 7495 6824 *Website:* technionuk.org
Activities: Education, training; overseas aid, famine relief
Address: 62 Grosvenor Street, London, W1K 3JF
Trustees: Mr Daniel Peltz OBE, Sir Michael Heller, Mrs Lois Peltz, Mr Gary Monnickendam
Income: £1,808,076 [2016]; £437,939 [2015]; £736,172 [2014]; £587,738 [2013]; £1,095,859 [2012]

Techniquest

Registered: 4 Aug 1986 *Employees:* 94
Tel: 029 2047 5475 *Website:* techniquest.org
Activities: Education, training
Address: Stuart Street, Cardiff, CF10 5BW
Trustees: Mr Stephen Best, Mrs Heather McNabb, Virginia Chambers, Mrs Julia Mortimer, Dr Grahame Guilford, Mr Stephen Thomas Bowden, Mrs Karen Elizabeth Harris, Mr Lee Sharma
Income: £4,232,848 [2017]; £3,240,153 [2016]; £3,353,814 [2015]; £3,258,125 [2014]; £3,453,640 [2013]

Teen Challenge UK

Registered: 14 Apr 1988 *Employees:* 73 *Volunteers:* 600
Tel: 01664 822221 *Website:* teenchallenge.org.uk
Activities: The prevention or relief of poverty; accommodation, housing; religious activities
Address: Teen Challenge UK, Willoughby House, Station Road, Upper Broughton, Melton Mowbray, Leics, LE14 3BH
Trustees: David Williams, Rev John Wellavize, Mr Thomas Michael McCurry, George McKim, Rev Philip Andrew Hills, Mr Steven Reilly
Income: £2,619,167 [2017]; £2,768,252 [2016]; £2,951,233 [2015]; £2,256,423 [2014]; £2,520,723 [2013]

Teenage Cancer Trust

Registered: 29 May 1997 *Employees:* 149 *Volunteers:* 600
Tel: 020 7612 0370 *Website:* teenagecancertrust.org
Activities: Education, training; advancement of health or saving of lives
Address: Teenage Cancer Trust, 93 Newman Street, London, W1T 3EZ
Trustees: Mr Ronnie Harris, Mr David Hoare, Andrew Hughes, Mrs Varda Shine, Dr Kamaljit Kaur Hothi, Mr Richard Barry Rosenberg, Paul Spanswick, Ms Caren Ayre Hindmarsh, Mr Jeremy Harmsworth Shute
Income: £16,021,823 [2017]; £15,254,514 [2016]; £16,018,445 [2015]; £19,799,351 [2014]; £13,529,241 [2013]

Teens and Toddlers Trading as Power2 Ltd

Registered: 1 Oct 2003 *Employees:* 49 *Volunteers:* 10
Tel: 020 7089 6180 *Website:* teensandtoddlers.org.uk
Activities: Education, training; economic, community development, employment
Address: 92-94 Tooley Street, London Bridge, London, SE1 2TH
Trustees: Mr Anthony Clinch, Jane Hinchliffe, Ms Georgia Hart, Mr Chris Mulrooney, Mr Marc St John
Income: £2,003,500 [2017]; £1,986,376 [2016]; £1,588,572 [2015]; £1,549,488 [2014]; £1,289,260 [2013]

Teesside High School Limited

Registered: 22 Jan 1963 *Employees:* 90
Tel: 01642 782095 *Website:* teessidehigh.co.uk
Activities: Education, training
Address: Teesside High School, The Avenue, Eaglescliffe, Stockton on Tees, Cleveland, TS16 9AT
Trustees: Mr Charles Geoffrey Watson, Mr Robert Ralph Tindle, Mr Charles Atha, Mr Robert James Stone, Mr Andrew Warrior, Mr Trevor Cook, Mr Dennis Henry Lister, Mrs Alison Lesley Greenwood, Mr Trevor George Watson, Anna Guest
Income: £3,906,293 [2017]; £3,974,902 [2016]; £3,941,663 [2015]; £4,159,683 [2014]; £4,005,516 [2013]

Teesside Hospice Care Foundation

Registered: 12 Jul 1982 *Employees:* 125 *Volunteers:* 440
Tel: 01642 811060 *Website:* teessidehospice.org
Activities: The advancement of health or saving of lives
Address: Teesside Hospice, 1 Northgate Road, Middlesbrough, Cleveland, TS5 5NW
Trustees: Mr Paul Everett Whitaker, Mr William Richard Pickersgill, Mr Les Fysh, Mrs Erica Marie Turner, Dr Maxine Craig, Mr Paul McGrath, Mr Thomas Anthony Waites, Professor Brian Footitt OBE, Mrs Ann O'Hanlon, Mr Robert Morgan Jewell, Mr David Swallow, Mrs Elaine Claire Criddle
Income: £4,578,958 [2017]; £4,408,868 [2016]; £4,671,293 [2015]; £4,270,225 [2014]; £3,632,777 [2013]

Teesside University Students' Union

Registered: 14 Jul 2010 *Employees:* 57 *Volunteers:* 750
Tel: 01642 342234 *Website:* tees-su.org.uk
Activities: Education, training
Address: Teesside University Students' Union, Borough Road, Middlesbrough, Cleveland, TS1 3BA
Trustees: Mark Fishpool, Ms Linda Maughan, Amy Preston, Tom Platt, Heather Ashton, Professor Paul Harrison BSc PhD FInstP FHEA, Georgina Arksey, Jill Mortimer
Income: £2,952,714 [2017]; £3,027,796 [2016]; £2,581,748 [2015]; £2,304,286 [2014]; £2,364,362 [2013]

Teign Housing

Registered: 21 Nov 2005 *Employees:* 82
Tel: 01626 322714 *Website:* teignhousing.co.uk
Activities: The prevention or relief of poverty; accommodation, housing
Address: Teign Housing, Millwood House, Collett Way, Newton Abbot, Devon, TQ12 4PH
Trustees: Mr Gareth Bourton, Mrs Anne-Marie Henderson, Mrs Angela Edwards-Jones, Mr Andrew Jones, Mr James O'Dwyer, Mr Alan Soper, Mrs Maureen Robinson, Mrs Joanna Reece
Income: £18,765,000 [2017]; £18,988,000 [2016]; £19,171,678 [2015]; £17,391,211 [2014]; £16,975,798 [2013]

Teikyo Foundation (UK)
Registered: 12 Dec 1990 *Employees:* 51
Tel: 01753 663756 *Website:* teikyofoundation.com
Activities: Education, training; amateur sport
Address: Teikyo Foundation (UK) Ltd, Fulmer Grange, Framewood Road, Wexham, Slough, SL2 4QS
Trustees: Mr Yoshihito Okinaga, Mr Yuji Yoshida, Dr Hiroko Okinaga, Tomoki Nakatani
Income: £2,422,492 [2017]; £2,688,547 [2016]; £2,784,656 [2015]; £2,977,367 [2014]; £3,009,765 [2013]

Tel Aviv University Trust
Registered: 3 Mar 1969 *Employees:* 5
Tel: 020 7446 8790 *Website:* tau-trust.co.uk
Activities: Education, training
Address: 126 Albert Street, London, NW1 7NE
Trustees: Mr David Robert Meller, Mr Daniel Lewin, Mr David Benaim, Mr Warner Colin Mandel, Mr Edwin Wulfsohn, Mr Anthony H Yadgaroff, Mr Richard Philip Anton, Ms Anne Joseph
Income: £8,999,075 [2017]; £8,527,562 [2016]; £1,130,034 [2015]; £860,136 [2014]; £986,637 [2013]

Telford Christian Council Supported Housing
Registered: 18 Dec 1997 *Employees:* 44
Tel: 01952 291904 *Website:* staytelford.co.uk
Activities: The prevention or relief of poverty; accommodation, housing; economic, community development, employment
Address: Southwater Square, Town Centre, Telford, Salop, TF3 4HS
Trustees: Mrs Jacqueline Osmund-Smith, Mr Andrew McAdam, Mrs Patricia Fanthorpe, Mrs Linda Haynes, Mr Benjamin Harper, Mr Brian Keates, Mr David Balderston, Mr David Gill, Ms Kerry Coley, Mr Christopher Hill
Income: £1,632,302 [2017]; £16,832,816 [2016]; £1,540,767 [2015]; £1,221,272 [2014]; £1,205,015 [2013]

The Tellus Mater Foundation Limited
Registered: 20 Aug 1999 *Employees:* 2
Tel: 020 3011 1100 *Website:* tellusmater.org.uk
Activities: General charitable purposes; education, training; environment, conservation, heritage
Address: 61 Grosvenor Street, London, W1K 3JE
Trustees: Mr James Ashley Arbib, Mr Bengt Henrik Olof Olsen
Income: £1,336,568 [2017]; £233,993 [2016]; £763,436 [2015]; £249,814 [2014]; £288,823 [2013]

The Telz Talmudical Academy and Talmud Torah Trust
Registered: 4 Aug 1988 *Volunteers:* 2
Tel: 020 8806 2666
Activities: Education, training; religious activities
Address: 18 Woodlands Close, London, NW11 9QP
Trustees: Rabbi Yaacov Chanoch Baddiel, Mr Chaim Lopian, Mr Alfred Hercz
Income: £1,827,250 [2017]; £1,490,750 [2016]; £1,158,410 [2015]; £1,308,250 [2014]; £1,914,125 [2013]

The Tennis Foundation
Registered: 29 Dec 1987 *Employees:* 40 *Volunteers:* 150
Tel: 0845 872 0522 *Website:* tennisfoundation.org.uk
Activities: General charitable purposes; education, training; disability; amateur sport; economic, community development, employment; recreation
Address: Tennis Foundation, National Tennis Centre, 100 Priory Lane, London, SW15 5JQ
Trustees: Mr James John Jordan, Mr Barry Horne, Baroness Margaret Ford, Mr Martin Corrie, Ms Cynthia Muller, Ms Funke Elizabeth Sade Awoderu, Ms Karen Keohane, Baroness Tanni Grey-Thompson, Mr Nick Fuller
Income: £12,406,000 [2017]; £11,300,000 [2016]; £11,259,000 [2015]; £14,750,000 [2014]; £12,923,000 [2013]

Tenovus Cancer Care
Registered: 25 Mar 1996 *Employees:* 218 *Volunteers:* 2,013
Website: tenovuscancercare.org.uk
Activities: The advancement of health or saving of lives; prevention or relief of poverty
Address: Gleider House, Ty Glas Road, Llanishen, Cardiff, CF14 5BD
Trustees: Mr Hugh Neil Paul O'Sullivan, Professor John Henry Lazarus, Mr Simon Evans, Dr Melanie Elizabeth Anne Goward, Dr Ann Marie Procter, Mr Iestyn Sion Morris, Mr Michael Borrill, Professor Malcolm Mason, Mr Wyn Mears, Mrs Paula Marie Kathrens, Professor Deborah Fitzsimmons, Professor Gerraint Trefor Williams, Mrs Anne-Marie Koukourava
Income: £9,026,692 [2017]; £9,310,824 [2016]; £9,303,834 [2015]; £9,222,813 [2014]; £8,539,853 [2013]

Tenterden Leisure Centre Trust Limited
Registered: 13 Apr 2004 *Employees:* 101
Tel: 01233 330215 *Website:* tenterdenleisure.com
Activities: Education, training; amateur sport
Address: Ashford Borough Council, Civic Centre, Tannery Lane, Ashford, Kent, TN23 1PL
Trustees: Mrs Suzanne Newick, Mr Justin Philip Huntly Nelson, Dr Lisa Lovelidge, Mrs Joanne West, Mrs Susan Joy Ferguson, Mr Nicholas David Clapp
Income: £1,319,228 [2017]; £1,320,077 [2016]; £1,280,453 [2015]; £1,215,749 [2014]; £1,139,088 [2013]

The Teresa Rosenbaum Golden Charitable Trust
Registered: 3 Feb 1988 *Employees:* 5
Tel: 020 8952 1414 *Website:* rosetreestrust.co.uk
Activities: General charitable purposes; education, training; advancement of health or saving of lives; disability; arts, culture, heritage, science; environment, conservation, heritage; economic, community development, employment
Address: 140 High Street, Edgware, Middlesex, HA8 7LW
Trustees: Richard Ross, Mr Lee Robert Mesnick, Mr Clive Melvyn Winkler, Mr Sam Howard
Income: £3,794,852 [2017]; £2,868,821 [2016]; £16,947,529 [2015]; £20,501,972 [2014]; £2,596,414 [2013]

Terra Nova School Trust Limited
Registered: 23 Jan 1963 *Employees:* 65 *Volunteers:* 8
Tel: 01477 571056 *Website:* tnschool.co.uk
Activities: Education, training
Address: Terra Nova Preparatory School, Jodrell Bank, Holmes Chapel, Crewe, Cheshire, CW4 8BT
Trustees: Mr Carl Bilson, Mr Andrew Arthur Fleck, Mr William Sillar
Income: £3,136,599 [2017]; £2,967,104 [2016]; £2,845,071 [2015]; £2,841,718 [2014]; £2,839,039 [2013]

The Terrence Higgins Trust
Registered: 26 Jan 1984 *Employees:* 317 *Volunteers:* 311
Tel: 020 7812 1600 *Website:* tht.org.uk
Activities: Education, training; advancement of health or saving of lives; prevention or relief of poverty
Address: 314-320 Gray's Inn Road, London, WC1X 8DP
Trustees: Rt Hon Ben Bradshaw MP, Mr William George Roberts, Mr Randeep Singh Sidhu, Dr Bilal Ali, Dr Jake David Bayley, Mr Gordon Mundie, Mr Robert Alan Glick, Mr Gavin Anthony Wills, Dr Samantha Jane Westrop, Mr Jonathan Dominic McShane, Dr Laura Jane Waters
Income: £15,588,089 [2017]; £17,747,421 [2016]; £19,399,000 [2015]; £19,646,000 [2014]; £20,107,000 [2013]

Terrington Hall Trust Limited
Registered: 3 Mar 1975 *Employees:* 45 *Volunteers:* 3
Tel: 01653 648227 *Website:* terringtonhall.com
Activities: Education, training
Address: Terrington Hall School, Terrington, York, YO60 6PR
Trustees: Mrs Wendy Machin, Mr Roger Hobson, Mr Rodney Lawrence Cordingley, Miss Zoe Anne Bannister, Mr Richard Smyth, Mr Kenelm Storey, Mr William John Patten Derby, Mrs Jessica Mary Miles
Income: £1,730,280 [2016]; £1,577,070 [2015]; £1,566,168 [2014]; £1,540,106 [2013]; £1,322,105 [2012]

Teshuvoh Tefilloh Tzedokoh
Registered: 22 Sep 2003
Tel: 0161 721 4846
Activities: General charitable purposes; education, training; advancement of health or saving of lives; disability; prevention or relief of poverty; overseas aid, famine relief; accommodation, housing; religious activities
Address: 2 Cheltenham Crescent, Salford, M7 4FP
Trustees: Mr Jacob Boruch Wolff, Mrs Ruth Wolff
Income: £3,766,106 [2016]; £3,568,659 [2015]; £2,650,370 [2014]; £2,137,498 [2013]; £1,701,039 [2012]

Tetbury Hospital Trust
Registered: 27 Feb 1992 *Employees:* 28 *Volunteers:* 20
Tel: 01666 502336 *Website:* tetburyhospital.co.uk
Activities: The advancement of health or saving of lives
Address: Tetbury Hospital Trust Ltd, Malmesbury Road, Tetbury, Glos, GL8 8XB
Trustees: Mr Stephen Hirst, Dr Anthony Walsh, Mr Tony Pooley, Mrs Kathy Callaghan, Mr Jeremy Lodwick, Mr Derek Johnson, Mr Gerard Barnes, Mrs Lesley Kunzler
Income: £2,640,810 [2017]; £2,699,671 [2016]; £2,509,481 [2015]; £2,404,926 [2014]; £1,884,081 [2013]

Tettenhall College
Registered: 6 Sep 1966 *Employees:* 106 *Volunteers:* 5
Tel: 01902 793033 *Website:* tettenhallcollege.co.uk
Activities: Education, training
Address: Tettenhall College, Wood Road, Tettenhall, Wolverhampton, W Midlands, WV6 8QX
Trustees: Mrs Jill Parker, Mrs Catharine L Hammond, Mrs Linda Cook, Mr Simon Maddox, Mr Stephen Jones, Mr Matthew Caffrey, Rev Preb Geoffrey Wynne, Mr Jeremy F Woolridge, Mr Andrew Wynne, Mrs Sarah Jane Isbister, Prof Sammy Cheung
Income: £6,709,971 [2017]; £4,265,334 [2016]; £4,072,121 [2015]; £3,210,657 [2014]; £3,576,580 [2013]

Textile Reuse and International Development
Registered: 13 Aug 1987 *Employees:* 103 *Volunteers:* 71
Tel: 020 8733 2580 *Website:* traid.org.uk
Activities: Education, training; prevention or relief of poverty; overseas aid, famine relief; environment, conservation, heritage; economic, community development, employment
Address: 51-53 High Road, London, N22 6BH
Trustees: Ms Lekha Klouda, Mr Ian Hagg, Mr Stephen Neal Robertson, Mr Rik Williams, Mr Andy Rutherford, Mrs Mary McWarren
Income: £5,197,633 [2016]; £5,182,519 [2015]; £4,945,851 [2014]; £4,959,479 [2013]; £4,589,652 [2012]

Thackray Medical Museum Company Limited
Registered: 12 Jan 1993 *Employees:* 27 *Volunteers:* 30
Tel: 0113 244 4343 *Website:* thackraymedicalmuseum.co.uk
Activities: Education, training; arts, culture, heritage, science; environment, conservation, heritage
Address: Thackray Museum, 141 Beckett Street, Leeds, LS9 7LN
Trustees: John Roles, Mark Goldstone, Keith Ramsay, Steven Clegg, Mr Andrew Fotherby, Mrs Annette Lyons, Jane Walton, Dorothy Isabel Hunt, Jake Timothy, Prof Philip Quirke, Mr David Jaynes, Mr Dean Jowett
Income: £1,111,362 [2016]; £923,296 [2015]; £858,127 [2014]; £928,767 [2013]; £759,870 [2012]

The Thalidomide Trust
Registered: 7 Aug 1973 *Employees:* 11 *Volunteers:* 29
Tel: 01480 474074 *Website:* thalidomidetrust.org
Activities: Disability
Address: Thalidomide Trust, 1 Eaton Court Road, Colmworth Business Park, Eaton Socon, St Neots, Cambs, PE19 8ER
Trustees: Thalidomide Trust Company
Income: £22,975,000 [2016]; £24,344,000 [2015]; £39,151,000 [2014]; £20,759,273 [2013]; £20,942,845 [2012]

Thames Christian College
Registered: 20 Jul 2000 *Employees:* 36 *Volunteers:* 1
Tel: 020 7228 3933 *Website:* thameschristiancollege.org.uk
Activities: Education, training; religious activities
Address: 8-10 South Street, Epsom, Surrey, KT18 7PF
Trustees: Mr Michael William Burgess, Mr Christian Elliot, Mrs Mary Okenwa
Income: £1,491,561 [2017]; £1,454,270 [2016]; £1,385,941 [2015]; £1,428,844 [2014]; £1,226,264 [2013]

Thames Hospice
Registered: 25 Feb 2005 *Employees:* 145 *Volunteers:* 523
Tel: 01753 848958 *Website:* thameshospice.org.uk
Activities: The advancement of health or saving of lives
Address: Pine Lodge, Hatch Lane, Windsor, Berks, SL4 3RW
Trustees: Mr Bruce Montgomery, Mr Martin Jervis, Mr Kenneth Coppock, Mr Stephen Moore, Mrs Jacinta Ashworth, Mr Andy Ka, Dr Judith Kinder, Mr Robert Dwyer, Mr Jonathan Jones, Mr Christopher Aitkin, Ms Margaret Neal, Mr Craig Linton, Mrs Lesley Rudd
Income: £6,679,000 [2017]; £6,612,000 [2016]; £8,179,000 [2015]; £5,380,000 [2014]; £11,478,445 [2013]

Thames Reach Charity
Registered: 1 Apr 2016 *Employees:* 297 *Volunteers:* 450
Tel: 020 3617 6079 *Website:* thamesreach.org.uk
Activities: Education, training; prevention or relief of poverty; accommodation, housing
Address: Thames Reach, The Employment Academy, 29 Peckham Road, London, SE5 8UA
Trustees: Mr Peter Davey, Mr Tony McBrearty, Mr Crispin O'Brien, Ms Joanna Wade, Mr Vasim Ul Huq, Mr Stephen Howard, Ms Rebecca Louise Taber, Mr Jeremy Swain, Ms Caroline Tulloch, Mr David Ashley John Ford, Mr Michael Scorer, Mr William Flenley, Ms Elizabeth Chapman-Clowes
Income: £15,821,934 [2017]

Thames Valley Air Ambulance
Registered: 7 Feb 2001 *Employees:* 18 *Volunteers:* 220
Tel: 0300 999 0135 *Website:* tvairambulance.org.uk
Activities: The advancement of health or saving of lives
Address: TVAA, Stokenchurch House, Oxford Road, Stokenchurch, Bucks, HP14 3SX
Trustees: Sir Timothy Ivo Jenner, Mr Roland Lawrence, Michael Ward, Mr Christopher Bannister, Ms Victoria George, Mr John Gaffney, Rick Pearce, Ms Amanda Poole, Keith Ifould, Tim Pollock, Ms Claire Dobbs, Ms Erica Moon, Ms Sarah Roberts
Income: £6,647,190 [2017]; £6,567,131 [2016]; £6,693,821 [2015]; £6,579,467 [2014]; £5,449,684 [2013]

Thames21 Limited
Registered: 27 May 2004 *Employees:* 26 *Volunteers:* 34,924
Tel: 020 7248 7175 *Website:* thames21.org.uk
Activities: General charitable purposes; education, training; arts, culture, heritage, science; amateur sport; environment, conservation, heritage; economic, community development, employment
Address: Thames 21, Corporation of London, Walbrook Wharf, Upper Thames Street, London, EC4R 3TD
Trustees: Miss Celia Hensman MBE, Ms Mary Louise Moore, Mr Alistair Gale, Mr Richard McIlwain, Mr Nicholas Tennant, Mr Charles Edward Green, Mr Simon David Moody, Mr Jeremy Lewis Simons, Mr Howard Timothy Davidson, Mr Michael John Hamilton, Mr Robin John David Mortimer, Mr Peter Anton Gerstrom, Martin Wayne4 Baggs
Income: £2,311,209 [2017]; £2,022,546 [2016]; £1,777,186 [2015]; £1,739,946 [2014]; £1,672,568 [2013]

Theatr Genedlaethol Cymru
Registered: 24 Sep 2004 *Employees:* 11
Tel: 01267 233882 *Website:* theatr.cymru
Activities: Education, training; arts, culture, heritage, science; recreation
Address: Y Llwyfan, Heol Y Coleg, Caerfyrddin, SA31 3EQ
Trustees: Ms Gwerfyl Pierce Jones, Mrs Gwenda Griffith, Ms Catrin Eurwen Beard, Arwel Edwards, Mr Gwyn Jones, Mr Elwyn Jones, Mr Alan Gwynant, Carys Edwards, Mrs Catrin Jones-Hughes, Mr Arwel Glyn Griffiths
Income: £1,257,581 [2017]; £1,212,829 [2016]; £1,532,299 [2015]; £1,304,647 [2014]; £1,161,638 [2013]

Theatr Mwldan
Registered: 21 Jul 1993 *Employees:* 20 *Volunteers:* 35
Tel: 01239 623923 *Website:* mwldan.co.uk
Activities: Arts, culture, heritage, science
Address: Bath House Road, Cardigan, Ceredigion, SA43 1JY
Trustees: Mr Philip John Layton, Mr Gareth Johnson, Judith Jones, Ms Ann Elaine Evans, David Grace, Mr Duncan Halliday, Ms Diane Llewhelin, Mr Wyn Jones
Income: £1,277,765 [2017]; £1,495,583 [2016]; £1,162,142 [2015]; £1,344,625 [2014]; £1,400,561 [2013]

Theatre Royal (Norwich) Trust Limited
Registered: 12 May 1971 *Employees:* 193 *Volunteers:* 2
Website: theatreroyalnorwich.co.uk
Activities: Education, training; arts, culture, heritage, science
Address: Theatre Royal, Theatre Street, Norwich, NR2 1RL
Trustees: Mrs Brenda Arthur, Tessa Haskey, Angela Robson, Mr Christopher Moscrip-Coubrough, Mr Stephen Michael Jaggard, Mr Stephen Askew, Ms Michelle Jarrold, Mrs Charlotte Crawley, Tom Blofeld, Mr Han Yang Yap, Mr Michael Clive Newey
Income: £16,874,313 [2017]; £14,981,356 [2016]; £12,777,874 [2015]; £13,157,837 [2014]; £13,360,208 [2013]

Theatre Royal (Plymouth) Limited
Registered: 31 Mar 1982 *Employees:* 176 *Volunteers:* 20
Tel: 01752 230366 *Website:* theatreroyal.com
Activities: Education, training; arts, culture, heritage, science
Address: Theatre Royal, Royal Parade, Plymouth, PL1 2TR
Trustees: Mrs Bronwen Lacey, Mr Francis Desmond Drake, Mr James Thomas Pidgeon, Mr Nicholas Brian Buckland, Mr Paul Lewis Woods
Income: £17,011,139 [2017]; £16,770,000 [2016]; £12,738,000 [2015]; £22,789,000 [2014]; £18,474,000 [2013]

The Theatre Royal Bath Limited
Registered: 29 May 1979 *Employees:* 67 *Volunteers:* 39
Tel: 01225 448815 *Website:* theatreroyal.org.uk
Activities: Education, training; arts, culture, heritage, science
Address: Theatre Royal, St Johns Place, Bath, BA1 1ET
Trustees: Dr Anthony Keith Clarke, Mr Philip John Addis, Ms Vicky Moffatt, Leonard Charles Pearcey, Mr Dominic Jerome Eaton, Mrs Melanie Macer, Mr Paul Bentley Heal, Mr Cosmo Joseph Fry, Mrs Charlotte Lucy Walker, Mr John Richard Monohan, Mr Nicholas Hall
Income: £12,526,000 [2017]; £11,500,778 [2016]; £13,501,943 [2015]; £10,699,633 [2014]; £7,885,941 [2013]

Theatre de Complicite Education Limited
Registered: 6 Jul 1992 *Employees:* 7
Tel: 020 7485 7700 *Website:* complicite.org
Activities: Education, training; arts, culture, heritage, science
Address: 14 Anglers Lane, London, NW5 3DG
Trustees: Tom Morris, Stephen Taylor, Mr Nitin Sawhney, Frances Hughes, Roger Graef, Sarah Coop, Lady Sue Woodford-Hollick OBE, Mrs Chetna Kishorechandra Pandya
Income: £2,219,554 [2017]; £1,599,839 [2016]; £1,029,310 [2015]; £1,252,164 [2014]; £2,079,608 [2013]

Theatre for a Change Limited
Registered: 21 Jun 2004 *Employees:* 3
Tel: 01753 857484 *Website:* tfacafrica.com
Activities: Education, training; overseas aid, famine relief; arts, culture, heritage, science
Address: 43 High Street, Eton, Windsor, Berks, SL4 6BD
Trustees: Bernard Harborne, Mr Dominic Bailey, Mr Emil Levendoglu, Mr Timothy Fassam, Ms Anne-Marie Harris, Jo Confino, Ms Jo Feather, Mr Michele Rosato, Kay Chaston, Mrs Michelle Montgomery
Income: £1,281,255 [2017]; £1,263,629 [2016]; £1,582,569 [2015]; £829,698 [2014]; £313,230 [2013]

Theirworld
Registered: 31 May 2002 *Employees:* 28
Tel: 020 3116 2735 *Website:* theirworld.org
Activities: General charitable purposes; education, training; advancement of health or saving of lives; disability; prevention or relief of poverty
Address: The Broadgate Tower, 20 Primrose Street, London, EC2A 2RS
Trustees: Mr David John Boutcher, Mrs Lucy Doughty, Ian Laing, Ms Arabella Helen Weir, Sarah Brown
Income: £3,770,105 [2016]; £3,503,715 [2015]; £2,198,815 [2014]; £2,051,913 [2013]; £968,205 [2012]

Thera Trust
Registered: 18 Jan 2002 *Employees:* 2,919 *Volunteers:* 82
Tel: 0300 303 1280 *Website:* thera.co.uk
Activities: Disability
Address: Thera Trust, The West House, Alpha Court, Swingbridge Road, Grantham, Lincs, NG31 7XT
Trustees: Mrs Jennifer Garrigan, Mr Simon Laurence Conway, Mr Mike Morgan, Mr Peter Martin Jones, Mr Martin Clifford Pilkington, Jill Parker, Mr William Begg Carter, Mr Matthew James Smith, Mrs Karen Tracy Boyce-Dawson, Mr Brian Young, Mrs Christine Chang
Income: £64,591,798 [2017]; £56,235,945 [2016]; £53,724,682 [2015]; £46,850,198 [2014]; £44,549,844 [2013]

Thetford Educational Foundation Trust
Registered: 28 Jul 1966 *Employees:* 80
Activities: Education, training
Address: c/o Bridge House, Bridge Street, Thetford, Norfolk, IP24 3AA
Trustees: Mr Terrance John Lamb BSc(Econ), Mrs Jenny Sinclair, Mr John Brown, Mr Steven McGrath, Mrs Karen Colborn, Mr Roy Frederick William Brame, Mrs Maureen Eade, Mr Jo Pearson, Mrs Brenda June Canham
Income: £2,959,107 [2016]; £3,459,225 [2015]; £3,533,719 [2014]; £3,384,543 [2013]; £3,182,720 [2012]

The Think Ahead Organisation
Registered: 18 Apr 2016 *Employees:* 17
Tel: 020 7470 6197 *Website:* thinkahead.org
Activities: Education, training; advancement of health or saving of lives; disability; prevention or relief of poverty; other charitable purposes
Address: The Think Ahead Organisation, 4th Floor, 14 Buckingham Street, London, WC2N 6DF
Trustees: Mr Donald MacInnes Peck, Lord Henry Dennistoun Stevenson, Professor Sir Julian Le Grand, Dr Ruth Allen, Mrs Sharon Rice-Oxley, Professor David Croisdale-Appleby, Professor Dame Carol Mary Black, Mr James Barrington Huw Darley, Mr Norman Peter Lamb, Mr Nicholas James Maxwell Timmins
Income: £4,165,983 [2017]

Thinkforward (UK)
Registered: 15 Jul 2013 *Employees:* 36 *Volunteers:* 140
Tel: 020 3559 8390 *Website:* thinkforward.org.uk
Activities: Education, training; prevention or relief of poverty; economic, community development, employment
Address: Thinkforward (UK), 337 City Road, London, EC1V 1LJ
Trustees: Mr Charles Edward Seager Green, Mr Matthew Grinnell, Mr David Vaughan, Ms Barbara Storch
Income: £1,929,701 [2016]; £1,360,604 [2015]; £575,269 [2014]

Thinktank Trust
Registered: 17 Apr 1997
Tel: 0121 202 2294 *Website:* birminghammuseums.org.uk
Activities: Education, training; arts, culture, heritage, science
Address: Thinktank Trust, Birmingham Museum and Art Gallery, Chamberlain Square, Birmingham, B3 3DH
Trustees: Councillor Randal Anthony Maddock Brew, Mohammed Rahman, Deborah De Haes
Income: £1,409,000 [2017]; £1,493,000 [2016]; £1,418,000 [2015]; £1,672,000 [2014]; £2,349,000 [2013]

The Third Age Trust
Registered: 14 Nov 1983 *Employees:* 8 *Volunteers:* 120
Tel: 020 8466 6139 *Website:* u3a.org.uk
Activities: Education, training
Address: 52 Lant Street, London, SE1 1RB
Trustees: Mrs Pamela Jones, Mrs Hilary Sarah Jones, Sue Stokes, Mrs Elizabeth Porter, Mrs Gillian Russell, Miss Barbara Jane Pavier, Mr Edward David Link, Jill Nicholls, Mrs Auriol Ainley, Robert John Ellison, Mrs Michaela Anne Moody, Mr Ian McCannah, Mr John Bent, Mrs Rose Marie Bradley, Mr Jeffrey Alan Carter, Bob Duckmanton
Income: £2,582,488 [2017]; £2,371,255 [2016]; £2,249,065 [2015]; £2,142,345 [2014]; £1,780,869 [2013]

Thistledown Education Trust
Registered: 3 May 1995 *Volunteers:* 7
Tel: 01935 470704
Activities: Education, training
Address: 38 Wraxhill Road, Yeovil, Somerset, BA20 2JX
Trustees: Mr Timothy Wyatt Barter, Mr Stephen M Diffey, Mr Robert Tuffin, Mr Stephen Pester, Mr Gaius Claude Dible, Mr Anthony Darren Packer, Mr Clive Pavey
Income: £1,218,974 [2017]; £216,000 [2016]; £463,200 [2015]; £387,878 [2014]; £294,335 [2013]

The Thompson Family Charitable Trust
Registered: 27 Feb 1985
Tel: 01608 676789
Activities: General charitable purposes
Address: 15 Totteridge Common, London, N20 8LR
Trustees: Mr David Brian Thompson, Mrs Katharine Patricia Woodward, Mrs Patricia Thompson
Income: £8,043,773 [2017]; £8,180,319 [2016]; £7,938,617 [2015]; £6,714,340 [2014]; £6,167,226 [2013]

The Thomson Foundation
Registered: 4 Dec 1962 *Employees:* 10
Tel: 020 3440 2438 *Website:* thomsonfoundation.org
Activities: Education, training
Address: Thomson Foundation, 46 Chancery Lane, London, WC2A 1JE
Trustees: Thomson Foundation (Trustee) Limited
Income: £2,594,000 [2016]; £1,661,000 [2015]; £1,517,000 [2014]; £1,353,000 [2013]; £1,071,000 [2012]

Thomson Reuters Foundation
Registered: 23 Aug 2000 *Employees:* 82
Tel: 020 7542 4148 *Website:* trust.org
Activities: General charitable purposes; education, training; human rights, religious or racial harmony, equality or diversity
Address: Thomson Reuters Building, 30 South Colonnade, Canary Wharf, London, E14 5EP
Trustees: Sir Crispin Tickell GCMG KCVO, Mr Geert Linnebank, Mr David Craig, Mr Peter Warwick, Mr Stephen Adler, Mr Manvinder Singh Banga, Ken Olisa, Mrs Lawton Fitt, Mr David Binet, Miss Eileen Lynch, Ms Susan Taylor Martin
Income: £11,203,000 [2016]; £9,469,000 [2015]; £8,230,000 [2014]; £8,371,000 [2013]; £8,684,000 [2012]

Sir Jules Thorn Charitable Trust
Registered: 19 Jun 1964 *Employees:* 4
Tel: 020 7487 5851 *Website:* julesthorntrust.org.uk
Activities: General charitable purposes; advancement of health or saving of lives; disability
Address: Sir Jules Thorn Charitable Trust, 24 Manchester Square, London, W1U 3TH
Trustees: Mr John Rhodes, Professor David Russell-Jones, Mrs Elizabeth Charal, Mr Mark Lever, Professor Sir Ravinder Maini, Sir Bruce MacPhail, Mr William Sporborg, Julian Ide
Income: £1,589,004 [2016]; £2,591,687 [2015]; £2,909,953 [2014]; £2,438,336 [2013]; £2,463,236 [2012]

Thorne Lodge Charitable Trust
Registered: 15 Jul 1988
Tel: 020 8458 4529
Activities: General charitable purposes
Address: 41 Norrice Lea, London, N2 0RD
Trustees: Mr Anthony Selby, Mr Phillip Selby, Mrs Zara Brooks, Mrs Rochelle Deborah Selby, Mrs Estelle Isaacson
Income: £1,473,722 [2017]; £40,503 [2016]; £49,920 [2015]; £16,765 [2014]; £36,734 [2013]

Thorngate Almshouse Trust
Registered: 8 May 1981 *Employees:* 55 *Volunteers:* 6
Tel: 023 9253 4999 *Website:* thorngate.org.uk
Activities: Accommodation, housing
Address: Administration Office, Clare House, Melrose Gardens, Station Road, Gosport, Hants, PO12 3BZ
Trustees: Thorngate Churcher Trust
Income: £1,909,116 [2017]; £1,963,112 [2016]; £1,867,853 [2015]; £1,782,928 [2014]; £1,619,776 [2013]

Thornleigh Camphill Communities Limited
Registered: 26 Oct 1962 *Employees:* 167
Tel: 01454 412194
Activities: Education, training; disability; accommodation, housing; environment, conservation, heritage; economic, community development, employment
Address: Sheiling School, Thornbury Park, Thornbury, Bristol, BS35 1HP
Trustees: Rosie Phillpot, Mr Graham Howard Snell, Mr John Southcombe, Mr William Anthony Nowlan, Nick Pike, Mr Ian Stanley Bailey, Mr Paul James Glover, Miss Sarah Anne Compson
Income: £5,154,749 [2017]; £3,838,191 [2016]; £3,366,162 [2015]; £3,346,116 [2014]; £3,166,276 [2013]

The Thoroughbred Breeders Association
Registered: 15 Feb 2010 *Employees:* 7
Tel: 01638 661321 *Website:* thetba.co.uk
Activities: Education, training; amateur sport; animals
Address: Thoroughbred Breeders Association, Stanstead House, 8 The Avenue, Newmarket, Suffolk, CB8 9AA
Trustees: Mr Paul Greeves, Mr Peter Mendham, Mr Philip Newton, Miss Anthea Gibson Fleming, Mr Robert Waley-Cohen, Mr Sam Bullard, Mr Julian Richmond-Watson, Mr Edmond Mahony, Mr Bryan Mayoh, Mr Edward John Antony Voute, Mr Nicholas Jones
Income: £1,113,415 [2016]; £1,231,154 [2015]; £1,105,260 [2014]; £1,036,505 [2013]; £982,899 [2012]

Thorpe Hall School Trust
Registered: 16 Dec 1987 *Employees:* 77
Tel: 01702 582340 *Website:* thorpehall.southend.sch.uk
Activities: Education, training
Address: Thorpe Hall School, Wakering Road, Southend on Sea, Essex, SS1 3RD
Trustees: Dr David William Sills, Mark Ian Brudenell, Sheila Joy Goldsworthy, Marc Miller, Mrs Loretta Lucy Andrews, Mr Michael Reddan, Jonathan Gorridge, Julie Catherine Turner
Income: £3,822,625 [2017]; £3,451,841 [2016]; £3,384,827 [2015]; £2,779,897 [2014]; £2,571,281 [2013]

Thorpe House School Trust
Registered: 8 Oct 1985 *Employees:* 73
Tel: 01753 882474 *Website:* thorpehouse.co.uk
Activities: General charitable purposes; education, training
Address: Thorpe House School Ltd, 29 Oval Way, Gerrards Cross, Bucks, SL9 8QA
Trustees: Mr David Forrest Hoy, Mr Christopher Gorner, Mr Gerard Paul McCarthy, Mr Henri Botha, Mr David Stanning, Mr Roy McMillan, Mr Roger George Marris, Mrs Fiona Wise, Mr Richard Coward, Mr Peter Millins, Mrs Ruth Helen Webber, Mrs Amanda Myers, Mrs Michelle Frost, Mr Andrew Charles Bannister, Mrs Deborah Jane Raven
Income: £4,165,071 [2017]; £3,776,871 [2016]; £3,600,209 [2015]; £3,534,056 [2014]; £3,222,857 [2013]

Three C's Support
Registered: 24 Jul 1995 *Employees:* 153 *Volunteers:* 53
Tel: 020 8269 4340 *Website:* threecs.co.uk
Activities: Disability
Address: Unit 4, 82-84 Childers Street, Deptford, London, SE8 5FS
Trustees: Ms Lisa Lye, Mr Paul Craven, Mr Andrew Meyer, Mr John Goodwin, Mr Divyajeevan Sahoo, Ms Sheona St Hilaire, Mr Ian Wilson, Mr Brian Akintokun, Mrs Anusha Everson, Mr Jim Collins, Ms Vijaya Sree, Mr Neville Pardi
Income: £5,007,628 [2017]; £4,707,291 [2016]; £4,669,794 [2015]; £4,438,383 [2014]; £4,289,967 [2013]

The Three Choirs Festival Association Ltd
Registered: 8 May 1962 *Employees:* 11 *Volunteers:* 155
Tel: 01452 768928 *Website:* 3choirs.org
Activities: Arts, culture, heritage, science
Address: 7C College Green, Gloucester, GL1 2LX
Trustees: Professor Michael Clarke, Mr Jeremy Wilding MBE, Mrs Clare Wichbold MBE, Mrs Myn Cotterill, Mr William Armiger, Mr David Whelton OBE HonFRAM HonRCM, Dr Timothy Brain OBE QPM, Douglas Dale, Mr Christopher Barron OBE, Mr Edwin Buckhalter
Income: £1,138,653 [2017]; £918,130 [2016]; £1,040,578 [2015]; £1,101,992 [2014]; £838,557 [2013]

Three Counties Agricultural Society
Registered: 21 Sep 1981 *Employees:* 89 *Volunteers:* 100
Tel: 01684 584900 *Website:* threecounties.co.uk
Activities: Education, training; animals; environment, conservation, heritage; recreation
Address: Three Counties Agricultural Society, The Showground, Malvern, Worcs, WR13 6NW
Trustees: Mr Michael Blandford, Mr Richard Alan Bradstock, Mr Michael David Warner, Mr Roger Head OBE, Mr Adrian Hope, Mrs Cathryn Anne Morris, Mr David Thomas Owens, Mr Patrick Stephen Downes, Mr Michael John Weaver, Mr Christopher Bailey, Mrs Lindsey Victoria Craddock, Mr David Smart
Income: £5,528,504 [2016]; £4,995,000 [2015]; £4,692,000 [2014]; £4,618,000 [2013]

Three Counties Education Trust
Registered: 10 Feb 2004 *Employees:* 40 *Volunteers:* 15
Tel: 01428 601800
Activities: Education, training
Address: Three Counties Education Trust, c/o Highcombe Edge School, Highcombe Edge, Tilford Road, Hindhead, Surrey, GU26 6SJ
Trustees: Mr David John Moggach, Mr Glenn Nigel Devenish, Mr Chester William White, Mr Bryan Philip Young, Mr Benjamin Peter White, Mr Simon Garth Napthine, Mr Gareth Paul Spencer
Income: £3,080,295 [2017]; £2,408,216 [2016]; £2,136,838 [2015]; £1,740,575 [2014]; £1,764,620 [2013]

The Three Guineas Trust
Registered: 9 Dec 1996 *Employees:* 1
Tel: 020 7410 0330
Activities: General charitable purposes; disability; environment, conservation, heritage
Address: Sainsbury Family Charitable Trusts, The Peak, 5 Wilton Road, London, SW1V 1AP
Trustees: Mr Dominic Brendan Flynn, Mr David Wood, Miss Clare Natasha Sainsbury
Income: £1,631,901 [2017]; £860,928 [2016]; £760,814 [2015]; £1,191,347 [2014]; £1,027,919 [2013]

Threshold Housing Link
Registered: 23 Feb 1993 *Employees:* 29 *Volunteers:* 15
Tel: 01793 524661 *Website:* thl.org.uk
Activities: The prevention or relief of poverty; accommodation, housing
Address: 2nd Floor, 1 John Street, Swindon, Wilts, SN1 1RT
Trustees: Mr Jez Rice, Mrs Lin Cattelain, Ms Annie Anderson, Mr Michael O'Shea, Mr Bryan Saunders
Income: £1,006,405 [2017]; £1,041,249 [2016]; £1,123,268 [2015]; £1,100,799 [2014]; £1,004,978 [2013]

Threshold Housing Project Limited
Registered: 25 Mar 1996 *Employees:* 81 *Volunteers:* 12
Tel: 0161 331 2000 *Website:* thp.org.uk
Activities: The prevention or relief of poverty; accommodation, housing
Address: Jigsaw Homes Group Limited, 249 Cavendish Street, Ashton under Lyne, Lancs, OL6 7AT
Trustees: Mr Mark Ian Dunford, Mr Steven Normansell, Tony Powell, Carole Green, Geoff Durbin, Mr Paul Hoey, Paul Woodcock, Mrs Gillian Brown, Michael Taylor
Income: £4,099,000 [2017]; £5,460,000 [2016]; £5,519,000 [2015]; £4,842,202 [2014]; £3,234,555 [2013]

The Thrombosis Research Institute
Registered: 8 Nov 1988 *Employees:* 33
Tel: 020 7404 0606 *Website:* tri-london.ac.uk
Activities: The advancement of health or saving of lives
Address: Goodman Derrick LLP, 10 St Bride Street, London, EC4A 4AD
Trustees: Patrick Burgess MBE, Mr Guy Howard Weston, Sir Martin Stuart Sorrel, Miss Joanna Zelma Kaye, Dr Jeffrey William Herbert
Income: £18,107,189 [2017]; £19,349,015 [2016]; £16,679,126 [2015]; £15,086,657 [2014]; £9,850,348 [2013]

Thurlow Educational Trust
Registered: 13 Nov 1974 *Employees:* 65 *Volunteers:* 9
Tel: 020 8670 5865 *Website:* rosemeadprepschool.org.uk
Activities: Education, training
Address: 70 Thurlow Park Road, London, SE21 8HZ
Trustees: Mr Benjamin Jones, Mrs Catherine Gardiner, Mrs Alison Morgan, Allen Lai, Tim Balaam, Mrs Anne Elizabeth Crane, Gavin Knott, Dr Emer Sutherland, Louisa Passmore, Tim Lello
Income: £3,876,361 [2016]; £3,793,411 [2015]; £3,786,575 [2014]; £3,506,437 [2013]; £3,191,656 [2012]

Thurrock Community Leisure Limited
Registered: 31 Mar 2000 *Employees:* 195
Website: impulseleisure.co.uk
Activities: Education, training; advancement of health or saving of lives; arts, culture, heritage, science; amateur sport; recreation
Address: Blackshots Leisure Centre, Blackshots Lane, Grays, Essex, RM16 2JU
Trustees: Chris Seamark, Mrs Charlotte Rose Turnbull, Mr Aaron Shaun Watkins, Mrs Thanusinthiya Jerenus Croos, Wayne Warner, Mr Omer Farooq Khwaja, Mr Carl David Black
Income: £6,504,034 [2017]; £5,640,334 [2016]; £5,504,173 [2015]; £5,223,413 [2014]; £5,157,167 [2013]

The Thursford Collection
Registered: 18 Nov 1976 *Employees:* 19
Tel: 01328 878477 *Website:* thursford.com
Activities: Education, training; arts, culture, heritage, science; environment, conservation, heritage
Address: Thursford Collection, Laurel Farm, The Street, Thursford, Fakenham, Norfolk, NR21 0AS
Trustees: Mr Andrew Wells, Mr Robert Edward Russell Carter, Mr Mark Jonathan Hazell, Mr Christopher Edward Self, Ms Mary Caroline Rudd, Mr Andrew Jonathan Barnes, Mrs David Clayton Matthews, Mr Colin Mark Wilson
Income: £5,571,350 [2016]; £5,406,418 [2015]; £4,688,959 [2014]; £4,563,058 [2013]; £4,464,520 [2012]

Tigers Sport and Education Trust
Registered: 30 May 2002 *Employees:* 62 *Volunteers:* 16
Tel: 01482 659299 *Website:* tigerstrust.co.uk
Activities: General charitable purposes; education, training; disability; amateur sport
Address: 7 Braids Walk, Kirk Ella, Hull, HU10 7PA
Trustees: Mr Trevor Boanas, Ms Diane Hayden, Ms Anita Joy Foy, Mr Sean Michael Royce, Mr Neil James Cavill, Mrs Jennifer Louise Kirby
Income: £1,200,374 [2016]; £1,218,094 [2015]; £1,014,261 [2014]; £707,976 [2013]; £704,935 [2012]

Tikva UK
Registered: 13 May 2013 *Employees:* 3
Tel: 020 8209 9100 *Website:* tikvaodessa.org.uk
Activities: Education, training; prevention or relief of poverty; overseas aid, famine relief; accommodation, housing; religious activities
Address: 2 Barham Avenue, Elstree, Borehamwood, Herts, WD6 3PN
Trustees: Mr Adam Bloom, Dr Anthony Bernard Moshal, Mr Refael Kruskal
Income: £2,754,330 [2016]; £2,298,427 [2015]; £2,138,125 [2014]; £163,076 [2013]

The Titus Trust
Registered: 9 Dec 1997 *Employees:* 18 *Volunteers:* 939
Tel: 01865 760944 *Website:* titustrust.org
Activities: Education, training; religious activities; recreation
Address: 12 Lime Tree Mews, 2 Lime Walk, Headington, Oxford, OX3 7DZ
Trustees: Mr Paul Richard Houghton, Mrs Sarah Farrar-Bell, Dr Garry John Williams, Miss Sarah Too, Rev Philip Vernon Parker, Rev Adrian Douglas John May, Miss Caroline Louisa Rose Hole, Mrs Claire O'Donoghue, Mr David William Neville Aston, Mr Richard Jonathan Dryer, Mr Edward Charles Patrick Crossley, Mrs Susan Bryony Beardsley, Rev Simon Niel Austen, Michael Paterson
Income: £1,980,248 [2017]; £2,109,327 [2016]; £2,151,363 [2015]; £1,872,677 [2014]; £1,631,444 [2013]

Tobacco Factory Arts Trust
Registered: 15 May 2003 *Employees:* 17 *Volunteers:* 30
Tel: 0117 902 0345 *Website:* tobaccofactorytheatres.com
Activities: Education, training; arts, culture, heritage, science
Address: Tobacco Factory Arts Trust, The Tobacco Factory, Raleigh Road, Bristol, BS3 1TF
Trustees: Chris Sims, Ms Anna Southall, Mr Andrew Allan Jones, Mr Mark Paney, Ms Sarah Smith, Mr Bertel Karll Martin, Katherine McGrath, Mr John Retallack
Income: £2,211,585 [2017]; £2,116,356 [2016]; £2,277,970 [2015]; £2,111,788 [2014]; £1,726,191 [2013]

Tockington Manor School Limited
Registered: 18 Jan 1967 *Employees:* 45 *Volunteers:* 12
Tel: 01454 613229 *Website:* tockingtonmanorschool.com
Activities: Education, training; arts, culture, heritage, science; amateur sport
Address: Tockington Manor School, Washingpool Hill Road, Tockington, Bristol, BS32 4NY
Trustees: Mr Peter Ernest Hart Smith, Mr Julian Wheldon, Mrs Helen Margaret Holloway, Dr Andrew John Daniel, Mrs Andrea Jane Ballance, Mr Andrew Turrell, Mr Gary Sheppard, Mr Robert Caul, Mr Andrew Charles Allan-Jones
Income: £2,359,489 [2017]; £2,120,981 [2016]; £1,928,161 [2015]; £1,932,823 [2014]; £1,847,749 [2013]

Together Against Cancer
Registered: 15 Apr 2008 *Employees:* 3 *Volunteers:* 3
Tel: 0116 246 0195 *Website:* togetheragainstcancer.org.uk
Activities: The advancement of health or saving of lives
Address: Unit S1, Troon Way Business Centre, Humberstone Lane, Leicester, LE4 9HA
Trustees: Mr Lawrence MacKay, Mr Edwin Bulaon, Miss Sarah Jayne Jackson, Joy MacKay, Mrs Merra Bacos Tabay
Income: £2,355,609 [2016]; £2,056,608 [2015]; £2,112,254 [2014]; £2,769,305 [2013]; £2,140,936 [2012]

Together Trust Limited
Registered: 5 Apr 1963 *Employees:* 811 *Volunteers:* 307
Tel: 0161 283 4848 *Website:* togethertrust.org.uk
Activities: General charitable purposes; education, training; disability
Address: The Together Trust, The Together Trust Centre, Schools Hill, Cheadle, Cheshire, SK8 1JE
Trustees: Mr Roger Anthony Horne, Mr John Rylands, Mr Simon Lees-Jones, Mr Robert Stevenson, Lady Paula Doone Gilbart, Ms Rosamund Hughes, Mr Paul Adams, Mrs Wendy Coomer JP Lib, Mr Ralph Ellerton, Ms Janet Heath, Ms Kirsteen Atkinson, Mr George Herbert, Mr Sangam Mishra, Mr Roger Bagguley
Income: £25,731,000 [2017]; £23,941,635 [2016]; £22,983,411 [2015]; £21,995,803 [2014]; £20,623,652 [2013]

Together Women Projects (Yorkshire and Humberside)
Registered: 30 Mar 2009 *Employees:* 42 *Volunteers:* 64
Tel: 0113 380 8900 *Website:* togetherwomen.org
Activities: Education, training; advancement of health or saving of lives; prevention or relief of poverty; accommodation, housing
Address: 13 Park Square East, Leeds, LS1 2LF
Trustees: Mrs Elizabeth Mary Bavidge, Ms Alison Lowe, Ms Janice Marian Colley, Alison Fisher, Dr Imogen Brown, Ms Anne Mace, Mrs Claire Vilarrubi
Income: £1,135,699 [2017]; £1,262,463 [2016]; £1,367,030 [2015]; £833,000 [2014]; £874,000 [2013]

Together for Mental Wellbeing
Registered: 22 Sep 1962 *Employees:* 587 *Volunteers:* 101
Website: together-uk.org
Activities: Education, training; advancement of health or saving of lives; disability; accommodation, housing
Address: Together Working for Wellbeing, 12 Old Street, London, EC1V 9BE
Trustees: Mr Keith Marsden, Ms Carole Murray, Miss Lisa Goodwin, Mrs Jenny Reynolds, Mr John Banks, Professor Benjamin Lawrance Thomas, Mr Christopher David Munday, Ms Helen Davies, Ms Alison Faulkner, Mr Mark Hardcastle, Ms Beth Lawton, Mrs Kimberley Radford, Dr Carol Cole
Income: £18,704,389 [2017]; £17,881,229 [2016]; £18,408,252 [2015]; £18,465,818 [2014]; £18,225,749 [2013]

Together for Short Lives
Registered: 28 Sep 2011 *Employees:* 42 *Volunteers:* 4
Tel: 0117 989 7820 *Website:* togetherforshortlives.org.uk
Activities: Education, training; advancement of health or saving of lives; disability
Address: 2nd Floor, Together for Short Lives, New Bond House, Bond Street, Bristol, BS2 9AG
Trustees: Mr Christopher Roys, Mr David Widdas, Mrs Heather Wood, Miss Maria McGill, Dr Richard David William Hain, Mr Richard Strawson, Mr Paul Obey, Ms Alaana Linney, Ms Nuala Mary O'Kane, Ms Rosalind Britton, Dr Hilary Cass, Mr Douglas John Morris, Mr David Anthony Butcher, Mrs Arlene Honeyman, Mrs Anna Ceridwen Gill
Income: £3,000,944 [2017]; £2,747,841 [2016]; £3,823,898 [2015]; £3,346,969 [2014]; £4,448,108 [2013]

The Tolkien Trust

Registered: 13 Feb 2013
Tel: 01865 339330 *Website:* tolkientrust.org
Activities: General charitable purposes
Address: Maier Blackburn, Prama House, 267 Banbury Road, Oxford, OX2 7HT
Trustees: Miss Priscilla Mary Anne Reuel Tolkien, Mr Michael George Reuel Tolkien, Mrs Baillie Jean Tolkien
Income: £1,824,300 [2016]; £2,496,161 [2015]; £1,860,312 [2014]; £1,942,814 [2013]

Tomchei Yotzei Anglia

Registered: 15 Sep 2005
Tel: 020 8802 4373
Activities: The prevention or relief of poverty
Address: 2 Paget Road, London, N16 5NQ
Trustees: Mr David Margulies, Mr Mark Bodner, Mr Pinchas Benedikt
Income: £1,115,959 [2017]; £690,933 [2016]; £484,103 [2015]; £584,588 [2014]; £582,746 [2013]

Jane Tomlinson Appeal

Registered: 25 Apr 2006 *Employees:* 19 *Volunteers:* 3,000
Tel: 0113 826 7766 *Website:* janetomlinsonappeal.com
Activities: The advancement of health or saving of lives
Address: The Jane Tomlinson Appeal, P O Box 314, Rothwell, Leeds, LS25 1BY
Trustees: Ms Suzanne Tomlinson, Mr Mark Mills, Mr Stephen Whiteside, Mr Craig Maher, Mr Robert Shaw, Adrian John Fitzpatrick
Income: £2,692,970 [2016]; £2,322,367 [2015]; £2,234,085 [2014]; £1,324,974 [2013]; £1,179,130 [2012]

Tommy's

Registered: 6 Feb 1997 *Employees:* 29
Tel: 020 7398 3400 *Website:* tommys.org
Activities: The advancement of health or saving of lives
Address: Tommy's, Nicholas House, 3 Laurence Pountney Hill, London, EC4R 0BB
Trustees: Mr Dominic Francis Proctor, Mrs Anita Rose Charlesworth, Mr Bjorn Saven, Ms Trudi Boardman, Dr Anna David, Ms Aedamar Comiskey, Mr Steve Russell, Hayley Marie Tatum, Ms Kate Smaje, Mr Joe Chambers, Mr Robert Woodward Sterling, Mr Steve Edge
Income: £6,166,228 [2017]; £5,995,025 [2016]; £4,997,599 [2015]; £4,352,800 [2014]; £3,765,890 [2013]

Tomorrow's People Trust Limited

Registered: 22 Mar 2004 *Employees:* 135 *Volunteers:* 55
Tel: 01323 418165 *Website:* tomorrows-people.co.uk
Activities: Education, training; prevention or relief of poverty; economic, community development, employment; other charitable purposes
Address: Tomorrow's People Trust Ltd, Unit 3.39 Canterbury Court, Kennington Park, 1-3 Brixton Road, London, SW9 6DE
Trustees: Mr Neil Berkett, Mr Jonathan Sobczyk, Victoria McKenzie-Gould, Ms Andrea Montague, Mr Christopher Grace, Sharon Brown, Mr John Tizzard, Mr Adam Dakin, Ms Laura Frances Bennett Kelly, Ms Nicola Joanne McCabe, Mr Nikolas Mark Powell
Income: £4,767,038 [2017]; £8,723,351 [2016]; £9,073,003 [2015]; £9,000,085 [2014]; £7,025,122 [2013]

The Tonbridge School Foundation

Registered: 28 Aug 2003 *Volunteers:* 26
Tel: 01732 365555 *Website:* development.tonbridge-school.co.uk
Activities: Education, training
Address: Tonbridge School, High Street, Tonbridge, Kent, TN9 1JP
Trustees: Tonbridge School
Income: £2,076,182 [2017]; £1,946,847 [2016]; £742,407 [2015]; £339,092 [2014]; £499,872 [2013]

Tonbridge School

Registered: 12 Jun 2003 *Employees:* 656 *Volunteers:* 30
Tel: 01732 365555 *Website:* tonbridge-school.co.uk
Activities: Education, training
Address: Tonbridge School, High Street, Tonbridge, Kent, TN9 1JP
Trustees: Mr Robert Elliott, Mrs Sally-Anne Huang, Mr Andrew Mayer, Mr Desmond Devitt, Mr Matthew Frederick Dobbs, Mr Timothy Attenborough, The Earl of Woolton, Dr Stephen Spurr, Mrs Josephine Naismith, Mrs Katherine Mary Wheadon, Mr Gavin Mark Rochussen, Dr George Taggart
Income: £31,719,402 [2017]; £30,909,230 [2016]; £28,682,804 [2015]; £25,829,034 [2014]; £24,703,461 [2013]

Tonbridge and Malling Leisure Trust

Registered: 2 Dec 2013 *Employees:* 313 *Volunteers:* 3
Tel: 01732 876062 *Website:* tmactive.co.uk
Activities: The advancement of health or saving of lives; recreation
Address: 1-5 Martin Square, Larkfield, Aylesford, Kent, ME20 6QL
Trustees: Mr Alan Charles Nicholl, Mrs Kimberley Victoria Bennett, Mr Neil Graham Salisbury, Mrs Sarah Jane King, Mrs Isabel Forsyth Garden, Mr Mark Osmond Davis, Mr Robin Patrick Betts, Mr Simon White
Income: £6,543,985 [2017]; £6,181,901 [2016]; £5,701,086 [2015]

Tone Leisure (Taunton Deane) Limited

Registered: 5 Aug 2005 *Employees:* 367 *Volunteers:* 70
Tel: 01823 217111 *Website:* gll.org
Activities: Amateur sport
Address: Prockters Farm, West Monkton, Taunton, Somerset, TA2 8QN
Trustees: Ms Juliette Dickinson, Miss Anne Priscott, Miss Karen Arnold
Income: £5,856,414 [2016]; £5,414,632 [2015]; £4,874,428 [2014]; £5,082,318 [2013]; £4,952,051 [2012]

Torah Vodaas Limited

Registered: 29 May 2002 *Employees:* 55
Tel: 020 8731 0777
Activities: Education, training
Address: 15 Alba Gardens, London, NW11 9NS
Trustees: Mr Julian Bamberger, Mr Solomon Klor, Mr Arieh Leib Levison
Income: £1,317,454 [2017]; £1,204,250 [2016]; £1,132,638 [2015]; £924,098 [2014]; £845,561 [2013]

Torbay Coast and Countryside Trust
Registered: 27 Sep 1999 *Employees:* 41 *Volunteers:* 225
Tel: 01803 520022 *Website:* countryside-trust.org.uk
Activities: Education, training; arts, culture, heritage, science; amateur sport; environment, conservation, heritage; recreation
Address: Torbay Coast & Countryside Trust, Occombe Farm, Preston Down Road, Preston, Paignton, Devon, TQ3 1RN
Trustees: Robert Newman, Anita Carolyn Newcombe, John Stocks, Jillian Ward, Janet Rallison, Andra Johnstone, Alan Tyerman, Claire Rugg, Roger Knight
Income: £2,484,463 [2017]; £2,281,263 [2016]; £1,574,204 [2015]; £2,425,153 [2014]; £1,682,868 [2013]

Torbay Community Development Trust Ltd
Registered: 28 Mar 2011 *Employees:* 31 *Volunteers:* 25
Tel: 01803 212638 *Website:* torbaycdt.org.uk
Activities: General charitable purposes; economic, community development, employment
Address: 4-8 Temperance Street, Torquay, Devon, TQ2 5PU
Trustees: Tanny Stobart, Ms Helen Jane Harman, Mr Jim Parker, Mr Martin Neil Oxley, Mr Roger Michael Ede, Mr Christopher Michael Forster, Mr Andrew Leslie Wade, Julian Summerhayes
Income: £1,167,929 [2017]; £1,525,476 [2016]; £480,307 [2015]; £112,791 [2014]; £118,089 [2013]

The Torbay Hospital League of Friends
Registered: 22 Dec 1961 *Employees:* 2 *Volunteers:* 100
Tel: 01803 298170 *Website:* thlof.co.uk
Activities: The advancement of health or saving of lives
Address: 6 Haldon Close, Torquay, Devon, TQ1 2NA
Trustees: Mrs Christine Margaret Piper, Mrs Julia Hearne, Miss Patricia Alice Roberts, Mrs Lynne Hookings, Mr Georges Adroit, Mrs Elizabeth Welch, Mr David Rogers, Mrs Shirley Cox, Mr Roy Tuttle, Lyn McCaig, Mr Philip White, Mr Mike Evans, Mr Trevor Brown ACIB, Mr Michael Hookings, Mrs Jennifer Mary Berry, Mrs Barbara Lawton, Mr Anthony Cox, Mrs Kathryn Nanette Westaway, Mrs Heather Gargette, Mrs Linda Dewis
Income: £1,426,740 [2016]; £797,438 [2015]; £697,934 [2014]; £637,882 [2013]; £766,272 [2012]

Torbay and South Devon NHS Charitable Fund
Registered: 24 Jan 1996 *Employees:* 22
Tel: 01803 654556
Activities: The advancement of health or saving of lives
Address: Regents House, Regent Close, Torquay, Devon, TQ2 7AN
Trustees: Torbay and South Devon NHS Foundation Trust
Income: £2,779,000 [2017]; £1,145,000 [2016]; £1,791,000 [2015]; £1,454,000 [2014]; £1,494,983 [2013]

The Torch Theatre Company Limited
Registered: 25 Jul 1979 *Employees:* 22 *Volunteers:* 80
Tel: 01646 694192 *Website:* torchtheatre.co.uk
Activities: Education, training; arts, culture, heritage, science
Address: Torch Theatre, St Peters Road, Milford Haven, Pembrokeshire, SA73 2BU
Trustees: Carol Garrett, Simon Hancock, Mrs Nia Marshall, Mr David Ainsworth, Dr Geoff Elliott, Mr Joshua Beynon, Mr Tim Arthur, Rhys Sinnett, Mrs Yvonne Grace Southwell, Mrs Philippa Elizabeth Davies, Mrs Alison Mary Tudor, Mr John West
Income: £1,428,366 [2017]; £1,444,056 [2016]; £1,458,514 [2015]; £1,405,932 [2014]; £1,365,402 [2013]

Torfaen Leisure Trust Limited
Registered: 5 Jun 2013 *Employees:* 218
Tel: 01633 624190 *Website:* torfaenleisuretrust.co.uk
Activities: General charitable purposes; advancement of health or saving of lives; disability; recreation
Address: 8 Augusta Park, Victoria, Ebbw Vale, Blaenau Gwent, NP23 8DN
Trustees: Mr Alun Wlliams, Mr David Bassett, Mr Keith Thorne, Helen Humphrey, Mrs Sharon Crockett, Mr Barry Jones, Mr David Reynolds, Mrs Rosemarie Seabourne, Mrs Lorna Jayne Virgo, Ms Fiona Claire Cross
Income: £4,609,246 [2017]; £4,930,032 [2016]; £4,081,127 [2015]; £3,320,505 [2014]

Torfaen and Blaenau Gwent Mind
Registered: 24 Mar 2004 *Employees:* 26 *Volunteers:* 29
Tel: 01495 768833 *Website:* torfaenmind.co.uk
Activities: The advancement of health or saving of lives
Address: 24 George Street, Pontypool, Gwent, NP4 6BY
Trustees: Mr Andy Charles, Mr David Cook, Mrs Jan Davies, Mr Dean Piper
Income: £1,041,266 [2017]; £888,818 [2016]; £860,926 [2015]; £905,005 [2014]; £856,836 [2013]

Tormead Limited
Registered: 18 Apr 1963 *Employees:* 112 *Volunteers:* 2
Tel: 01483 575101 *Website:* tormeadschool.org.uk
Activities: Education, training
Address: Tormead School, Cranley Road, Guildford, Surrey, GU1 2JD
Trustees: Mrs Rosemary Harris BA ACA, Dr Caroline Mary Kissin, Mr R Jewkes, Miss Anna Ruth Spender, Mr Mark Dixon, Mr Matthew Howse, Mr Peter O'Keefe RIBA Mgt, Mrs Anne Cullum, Mrs Jennifer Mary Wicks, Mrs Sheila Anne Geary, Mr John Watkins, Ms Suzanne Newnes-Smith
Income: £9,946,184 [2017]; £9,986,649 [2016]; £9,719,791 [2015]; £9,381,214 [2014]; £8,980,694 [2013]

Torus62 Limited
Registered: 9 Sep 2014 *Employees:* 174
Tel: 01744 418135 *Website:* wearetorus.co.uk
Activities: General charitable purposes; education, training; prevention or relief of poverty; accommodation, housing; economic, community development, employment
Address: Bank Park House, Kendrick Street, Warrington, Cheshire, WA1 1UZ
Trustees: Mr Ian Duncan Clayton, Mr Duncan James Craig, Mr Philip Pemberton, Mr Robert Clive Young, Mrs Christine Fallon, Mr Robert Charles Hepworth, Mr Roy Alfred Smith, Mr John Fulham, Mr Graham William Burgess, Mr Anthony Vincent Williams
Income: £14,709,000 [2017]; £8,055,000 [2016]

Tottenham Hotspur Foundation
Registered: 10 Apr 2006 *Employees:* 74 *Volunteers:* 120
Tel: 020 8365 5138 *Website:* tottenhamhotspur.com
Activities: Education, training; advancement of health or saving of lives; disability; amateur sport; economic, community development, employment
Address: 49 Wellington Terrace, Falmouth, Cornwall, TR11 3BL
Trustees: Mr Selwyn Tash, Miss Donna Cullen, Mr Matthew John Collecott
Income: £4,310,077 [2017]; £3,234,455 [2016]; £3,400,023 [2015]; £2,838,114 [2014]; £2,670,379 [2013]

Touareg Trust
Registered: 6 Apr 2006
Tel: 020 8357 5000 *Website:* nhhg.org.uk
Activities: General charitable purposes; education, training; accommodation, housing
Address: Notting Hill Genesis, Bruce Kenrick House, 2 Killick Street, London, N1 9FL
Trustees: Mr Andrew Belton, Mr Paul Phillips, Ms Elizabeth Froude, Mr Jeremy Stibbe, Mr John Hughes, Ms Kate Davies, Mr Mark Vaughan, Mr Vipulchandra Thacker
Income: £5,822,000 [2017]; £16,354,000 [2016]; £8,241,000 [2015]; £8,355,000 [2014]; £8,377,000 [2013]

Touchstone-Leeds
Registered: 19 Jun 1992 *Employees:* 106 *Volunteers:* 129
Tel: 0113 271 8277 *Website:* touchstonesupport.org.uk
Activities: Education, training; advancement of health or saving of lives; accommodation, housing; economic, community development, employment; human rights, religious or racial harmony, equality or diversity
Address: Touchstone-Leeds, Touchstone House, 2-4 Middleton Crescent, Leeds, LS11 6JU
Trustees: Mr Nick Brown, Ms Janet Mary Reynolds, Mr Andrew Goodchild, Ms Christine Baines, Mr Jeremy Horsell, Ms Katie Gleghorn, Dr Ramindar Singh MBE DL, Ms Julie Laxton, Dr Satwant Rait, Ms Sue Timothy, Mr Khizar Hayat
Income: £4,289,984 [2017]; £3,924,514 [2016]; £3,634,970 [2015]; £3,260,789 [2014]; £2,653,763 [2013]

Tower Hamlets Community Housing Limited
Registered: 30 Nov 1999 *Employees:* 71
Tel: 020 7780 3070 *Website:* thch.org.uk
Activities: Accommodation, housing
Address: Tower Hamlets Community Housing, 285 Commercial Road, London, E1 2PS
Trustees: Mr Nicholas John Abbey, Mr Stuart Madewell, Mr Ruediger Kloss, Mr Faisal Butt, Ms Jennifer Simnett, Mr Giancarlo Gibbs, Mr Charles Edward Moran, Mr Mark Thrasher, Ms Clare Harrisson, Mr Karanjit Randhawa
Income: £25,435,000 [2017]; £24,866,000 [2016]; £22,109,000 [2015]; £25,985,000 [2014]; £17,075,000 [2013]

Tower Hamlets Education Business Partnership Limited
Registered: 22 Sep 1994 *Employees:* 20 *Volunteers:* 4,500
Tel: 020 7655 0305 *Website:* thebp.org
Activities: Education, training
Address: Tower Hamlets Education Business Partnership, 45-55 Commercial Street, London, E1 6BD
Trustees: Mr Richard Foley, Mr Mark Campbell, Ms Michelle Quest, Mrs Esra Turk, Mrs Christine McInness, Mr David Pack, Mr Gerard Paul McDonald, Mr Michael Furtado, Mrs Jemima Reilly
Income: £1,259,976 [2017]; £821,699 [2016]; £1,107,872 [2015]; £1,010,733 [2014]; £998,398 [2013]

The Tower House School Charitable Foundation
Registered: 25 Mar 1998 *Employees:* 35 *Volunteers:* 5
Tel: 020 8876 3323 *Website:* thsboys.org.uk
Activities: Education, training
Address: Tower House School, 188 Sheen Lane, London, SW14 8LF
Trustees: Mr C L Pike, James Forsyth
Income: £2,550,472 [2017]; £2,417,086 [2016]; £2,356,011 [2015]; £2,243,806 [2014]; £2,169,511 [2013]

The Tower Project
Registered: 1 Apr 1997 *Employees:* 122 *Volunteers:* 16
Tel: 020 7790 9085 *Website:* towerproject.org.uk
Activities: General charitable purposes; education, training; disability; accommodation, housing
Address: Tower Project, 45-55 White Horse Road, London, E1 0ND
Trustees: Mrs Pamela June Mason JP, Mr Kumar Kotecha, Mrs Gaynor Tenen, Miss Samantha Walker, Mrs Julia Mason, Mr David Barnett, Mrs Jill Sullivan, Miss Kelly Dee
Income: £3,390,892 [2017]; £3,239,722 [2016]; £3,251,887 [2015]; £2,995,936 [2014]; £2,824,736 [2013]

Town Close House Educational Trust Limited
Registered: 4 Jul 1969 *Employees:* 127
Tel: 01603 624709 *Website:* townclose.com
Activities: Education, training
Address: 14 Ipswich Road, Norwich, NR2 2LR
Trustees: Mr David John Hargreaves Bolton, Mrs Clare Rosina Costello, Mr Paul Taylor, Mrs Nicola Ovenden, Mr Alec Kingham, Mrs Sarah Anthony, Ms Susan Jack, Dr Simon Carroll, Mr Peter Davies, Mrs Sarah Waddington, Mr Alistair Fish
Income: £6,036,429 [2017]; £5,391,118 [2016]; £5,009,214 [2015]; £4,761,147 [2014]; £4,631,446 [2013]

Towner
Registered: 22 Apr 2014 *Employees:* 40 *Volunteers:* 40
Website: townereastbourne.org.uk
Activities: Arts, culture, heritage, science
Address: Flat 6, Denton Court, 20 Denton Road, Eastbourne, E Sussex, BN20 7ST
Trustees: Mr David Dimbleby, Mr Henry Wyndham, Mr Mark Moorton, Mr Gyr King, Mr Timothy James William Ashdown, Ms Kay Cadell, Mr Colin McKenzie, Ms Dinah Casson, Ms Hillary Bauer, Mr Colin Swansborough, Dr Flora Dennis
Income: £1,828,149 [2017]; £1,399,188 [2016]; £1,236,714 [2015]

The Toybox Charity
Registered: 21 Dec 2000 *Employees:* 13 *Volunteers:* 20
Tel: 01908 360050 *Website:* toybox.org.uk
Activities: Education, training; prevention or relief of poverty; overseas aid, famine relief; accommodation, housing; economic, community development, employment
Address: The Toybox Charity, G4 Challenge House, Sherwood Drive, Bletchley, Milton Keynes, Bucks, MK3 6DP
Trustees: Mrs Gaynor Joan Derham, Ms Joanna Rachel Watson, Ms Nicola Battle, Mr Fernando Caicedo, Mr Ian Richard Gray, Mrs Joanna Catherine Hytner, Mr Alan David De Sousa Caires, Mr Francis Jack Goss
Income: £1,578,348 [2017]; £1,527,465 [2016]; £1,661,005 [2015]; £1,638,491 [2014]; £1,647,441 [2013]

Toynbee Hall
Registered: 4 Dec 1962 *Employees:* 62 *Volunteers:* 335
Tel: 020 7392 2984 *Website:* toynbeehall.org.uk
Activities: General charitable purposes; education, training; prevention or relief of poverty; accommodation, housing; arts, culture, heritage, science
Address: The Community Centre, 52 Old Castle Street, London, E1 7AJ
Trustees: Mr Richard Bellerby Allan, Ms Clare Katharine Corbett, Mrs Emma Davies, Mr Hanif Osmani, Mr David Timothy Warner, Ms Kate Swade, Ms Annette Zera, Mr Julian Corner, Ms Sarah Squires, Mr Kawsar Zaman
Income: £7,730,000 [2017]; £14,124,000 [2016]; £6,770,000 [2015]; £6,734,000 [2014]; £6,530,000 [2013]

Traffic International
Registered: 23 Jul 1999 Employees: 50 Volunteers: 9
Tel: 01223 277427 Website: traffic.org
Activities: Environment, conservation, heritage
Address: Traffic International, The David Attenborough Building, Pembroke Street, Cambridge, CB2 3QZ
Trustees: Dr Penelope Jane Smart, Dr Margaret Field Kinnaird, Mr Jon Paul Rodriguez, Ms Lin Li, Mr Mark Halle, Dr Joshua Ginsberg, Ms Ginette Hemley, Dr Aime Joseph Nianogo, Mr Jeremy Eppel
Income: £8,050,139 [2017]; £6,896,659 [2016]; £4,592,937 [2015]; £5,497,620 [2014]; £4,174,047 [2013]

Trafford Housing Trust Limited
Registered: 24 Nov 2004 Employees: 429
Tel: 070 0333 3333 Website: traffordhousingtrust.co.uk
Activities: Accommodation, housing; economic, community development, employment
Address: Trafford Housing Trust, 126-150 Washway Road, Sale, Cheshire, M33 6AG
Trustees: Alastair Findlay, John Verbickas, Angela Bolton, Gordon Perry, Sheila Mary Tolley, John Lamb, Mrs Edna Robinson, Sean Anstee, Nigel Mark McGurk
Income: £54,214,991 [2017]; £53,289,000 [2016]; £52,048,000 [2015]; £46,398,011 [2014]; £41,682,310 [2013]

The Traidcraft Exchange
Registered: 21 Aug 1995 Employees: 43
Tel: 0191 491 0591 Website: traidcraft.org.uk
Activities: Education, training; prevention or relief of poverty
Address: Traidcraft PLC, Kingsway, Team Valley Trading Estate, Gateshead, Tyne & Wear, NE11 0NE
Trustees: Mr Ram Gidoomal, Chris Moorhouse, Mrs Elizabeth Cotton, Mr Mathew Edmundson, Robin Roth, Mrs Margaret Sentamu, Mrs Jennifer Borden, Mr David Huw Neale, Ms Sarah Hughes
Income: £3,406,000 [2017]; £2,978,000 [2016]; £3,373,000 [2015]; £3,428,000 [2014]; £3,028,000 [2013]

Training 2000 Limited
Registered: 11 Jul 1989 Employees: 244
Tel: 01254 54659 Website: training2000.co.uk
Activities: Education, training
Address: Unit 1 Harwood Street, Blackburn, BB1 3BD
Trustees: Mr Oliver McCann, Mr Tim Webber, Mr Stephen Gray, Dr Lynne Livesey
Income: £11,278,839 [2017]; £12,239,305 [2016]; £13,000,459 [2015]; £12,411,240 [2014]; £12,115,407 [2013]

Training and Development Resource Limited
Registered: 27 Mar 1997 Employees: 74
Tel: 0191 491 1505 Website: tdrtraining.co.uk
Activities: Education, training; economic, community development, employment
Address: Q1, Quorum Business Park, Benton Lane, Newcastle upon Tyne, NE12 8EX
Trustees: Mr David Trotter, Mr Ronald Dodd, Mr Lawrence Joseph Brown, Mrs Tracey Ann Wilson, Mr Ian Young, Mr Barrie Stuart Hensby
Income: £3,001,575 [2017]; £2,612,522 [2016]; £2,759,018 [2015]; £2,606,005 [2014]; £3,806,441 [2013]

The Tramway Museum Society
Registered: 2 Apr 1963 Employees: 49 Volunteers: 187
Tel: 01922 452384 Website: tramway.co.uk
Activities: Education, training; arts, culture, heritage, science; environment, conservation, heritage
Address: 36 Seven Acres, Walsall, W Midlands, WS9 0EY
Trustees: Mr Ian Ross, Mr Roger Michael, Mrs Karen Rita Rigg, Mrs Lynda Margaret Wright, Mr William John Lane, Mr Andrew Mark Pendleton, Mr Malcolm Charles Wright, Mr Colin Heaton, Mr Andrew John Willis, Mr Michael Vivian Ballinger, Mr David Frodsham
Income: £2,443,824 [2017]; £2,287,448 [2016]; £1,781,808 [2015]; £1,844,453 [2014]; £1,786,496 [2013]

Transaid Worldwide Services Limited
Registered: 24 Oct 1998 Employees: 14 Volunteers: 10
Tel: 020 7387 8136 Website: transaid.org
Activities: Education, training; advancement of health or saving of lives; prevention or relief of poverty
Address: Transaid, 137 Euston Road, London, NW1 2AA
Trustees: Paul Orme, Mr William Howie, Julia Mary Maeve Magner, Clare Bottle, James Keeler, Suzanne Green, Mr Richard Cawston, Mr Robert John Goundry, Mr Jeffrey Turner, Ms Harriet Dodd, Mr Graham Inglis, Joanna Godsmark, Helen Varma
Income: £1,722,788 [2017]; £1,927,395 [2016]; £2,095,430 [2015]; £1,255,676 [2014]; £1,167,513 [2013]

Transform Housing & Support
Registered: 2 Oct 1972 Employees: 107 Volunteers: 137
Tel: 01372 387100 Website: transformhousing.org.uk
Activities: Education, training; disability; prevention or relief of poverty; accommodation, housing; economic, community development, employment; other charitable purposes
Address: 1st Floor, Bradmere House, Brook Way, Leatherhead, Surrey, KT22 7NA
Trustees: Mrs Sally Dubery, Mr David John Turner, Mr Christopher James Deacon, Mr Lee Harris, Miss Amanda Michelle Colman, Mr Edward Moseley, Mr Christopher John Relleen, Mr Mark Edward Austen, Mr Robert Mills, Mrs Jane Bolton, Mrs Nicola Harrison
Income: £7,486,000 [2017]; £6,587,000 [2016]; £6,145,000 [2015]; £6,448,000 [2014]; £6,685,000 [2013]

Transforming Education in Norfolk
Registered: 29 Aug 2012 Employees: 1,076
Tel: 01603 773308 Website: tengroup.org.uk
Activities: Education, training
Address: Norwich City College, St Andrews House, St Andrews Street, Norwich, NR2 4TP
Trustees: Mr Christopher Maw, Mr John Fry, Mr Richard Proctor, Mrs Susan Elizabeth Guest, Mr James McAtear, Mr Matthew Rupert Colmer
Income: £59,757,000 [2017]; £59,941,000 [2016]; £63,279,000 [2015]; £80,346,000 [2014]; £52,604,000 [2013]

Transforming Lives for Good (TLG) Ltd
Registered: 19 Feb 1999 Employees: 50 Volunteers: 295
Tel: 01274 900376 Website: tlg.org.uk
Activities: General charitable purposes; education, training; economic, community development, employment
Address: Centre of Excellence, Hope Park, Bradford, BD5 8HH
Trustees: Mr Andrew Burton, Mrs Sheron Delloris Kantor, Mr Mark Wrangles, Mr John Kirkby, Mr Dan Lane, Mr Michael Royal
Income: £2,175,347 [2016]; £2,255,159 [2015]; £2,214,921 [2014]; £1,952,647 [2013]; £2,268,805 [2012]

Transparency International UK
Registered: 27 Jan 2006 *Employees:* 35 *Volunteers:* 14
Tel: 020 3096 7675 *Website:* transparency.org.uk
Activities: Education, training; prevention or relief of poverty; economic, community development, employment
Address: CAN Mezzanine, 7-14 Great Dover Street, London, SE1 4YR
Trustees: Mrs A Fiona Thompson, Ms Shalni Arora, Mr Graham Baxter, Mr Michael Bowes QC, Natasha Clayton, Mr Seymour Arthur Miles Eastwood, Tamara Davies, Professor Paul Heywood
Income: £1,932,000 [2017]; £2,861,000 [2016]; £2,117,679 [2015]; £1,579,837 [2014]; £1,249,797 [2013]

Transport Benevolent Fund (CIO)
Registered: 16 Mar 2015 *Employees:* 20 *Volunteers:* 431
Tel: 0300 333 2000 *Website:* tbf.org.uk
Activities: General charitable purposes; prevention or relief of poverty
Address: Transport Benevolent Fund CIO, 3.1 The Loom, 14 Gowers Walk, London, E1 8PY
Trustees: Mr Ian Anthony Richard Wilson, Ms Ravinder Kaur Kalsi, Mr Christopher John Sullivan, Mr Robert Howard Jones, Mr Peter Sloan, Mrs Cheryl O'Brien, Mr David Craig Phillips
Income: £3,523,000 [2017]; £1,635,000 [2016]

The Travel Foundation
Registered: 19 Nov 1997 *Employees:* 17
Tel: 0117 927 3049 *Website:* thetravelfoundation.org.uk
Activities: Environment, conservation, heritage; economic, community development, employment
Address: The Travel Foundation, The Create Centre, Smeaton Road, Bristol, BS1 6XN
Trustees: John De Vial, Mr Rodney Brian Anderson, Debbie Hindle, Mr Noel Christie Luciano Josephides, Mr Alistair Rowland
Income: £1,294,381 [2016]; £1,230,072 [2015]; £1,374,410 [2014]; £1,160,326 [2013]; £1,172,959 [2012]

Tree Aid
Registered: 24 Mar 2010 *Employees:* 50 *Volunteers:* 3
Website: treeaid.org
Activities: Education, training; prevention or relief of poverty; environment, conservation, heritage; economic, community development, employment
Address: Brunswick Court, Brunswick Square, Bristol, BS2 8PE
Trustees: Ms Annie Moreton, Mr John Paul Collenette, Mrs Judith Twentyman, Alex Rees, Mr Terence Jagger, Ms Carol Mack, Trevor Reaney, Ms Shireen Chambers
Income: £1,914,873 [2017]; £1,843,457 [2016]; £2,503,281 [2015]; £4,050,480 [2014]; £2,157,234 [2013]

Tree of Hope
Registered: 9 Oct 2012 *Employees:* 8 *Volunteers:* 10
Tel: 01892 535525 *Website:* treeofhope.org.uk
Activities: The advancement of health or saving of lives
Address: Salford House, 19-21 Quarry Hill Road, Tonbridge, Kent, TN9 2RN
Trustees: Mrs Alexandra Noble, Mr Philip Lightbody, Mr Tim Daplyn, Mr Kevin Werry, Mr Robert Lay, Mrs Charlotte Eberlein
Income: £2,377,581 [2016]; £5,146,747 [2015]; £5,175,427 [2014]; £4,465,100 [2013]

Treebeard Trust
Registered: 12 Oct 2011 *Employees:* 1
Website: treebeardtrust.org
Activities: General charitable purposes
Address: 11 Hackney Road, Peasenhall, Saxmundham, Suffolk, IP17 2HS
Trustees: Mr Barnaby Mark Wiener, Mrs Cassandra Wiener
Income: £2,044,017 [2017]; £2,000,000 [2016]; £2,002,693 [2015]; £1,254,125 [2014]; £1,000,000 [2013]

Trees for Cities
Registered: 27 Jan 1994 *Employees:* 23 *Volunteers:* 9,800
Tel: 020 7587 1320 *Website:* treesforcities.org
Activities: Education, training; environment, conservation, heritage; economic, community development, employment
Address: Trees for Cities, Prince Consort Lodge, Kennington Park Place, London, SE11 4AS
Trustees: Mr James Bevan, Mr Graham Simmonds, Mrs Janine Capon, Mr Steven William Workman, Professor Selena Gray, Mr Anant Shah, Mr Christopher James Harper, Mr Bryan Miller
Income: £1,500,642 [2017]; £1,172,708 [2016]; £1,140,853 [2015]; £1,335,310 [2014]; £1,403,936 [2013]

Treetops Hospice Trust
Registered: 28 Jan 1988 *Employees:* 144 *Volunteers:* 650
Tel: 0115 949 1264 *Website:* treetopshospice.org.uk
Activities: Education, training; advancement of health or saving of lives; disability
Address: Treetops Hospice, Derby Road, Risley, Derby, DE72 3SS
Trustees: Mrs Julie Heath, Dr Helen Godridge, Mr Jonathan Davis, Dr Stephen John Miller, Mr Allan Perkins, Mr Anil Sarda, Dr Ruth Elizabeth Aldridge, Mr David John Millington, Mr Martin Fox, Alan Wardle, Mr Robert Wallace Jones, Mr Steve Beeley, Miss Sara-Jayne Ansley, Dr Maelie Victoria Swanwick, Mr Stephen Anthony Mitchell
Income: £3,550,710 [2017]; £3,375,974 [2016]; £3,323,308 [2015]; £3,064,311 [2014]; £2,413,102 [2013]

Treloar Trust
Registered: 9 Jul 2002 *Employees:* 597 *Volunteers:* 80
Tel: 01420 547400 *Website:* treloar.org.uk
Activities: Education, training; advancement of health or saving of lives; disability
Address: Treloar Trust, Powell Drive, Holybourne, Alton, Hants, GU34 4GL
Trustees: Mr Michael Chadwick, Mr Alistair Mackintosh, Dr Helen Harvey, Mr Rhys Calvin Iley, Mr David Victor Matthews, Mrs Jane Lesley Cooke, Sir Alexander Allan, Mr James Bateson, Mr Brian McNamara, Mrs Christine Slaymaker
Income: £20,796,000 [2017]; £21,168,000 [2016]; £20,808,000 [2015]; £18,896,000 [2014]; £17,086,000 [2013]

Trent College Limited
Registered: 22 Jun 1964 *Employees:* 294 *Volunteers:* 53
Tel: 0115 849 4921 *Website:* trentcollege.net
Activities: Education, training
Address: Trent College, Derby Road, Long Eaton, Nottingham, NG10 4AD
Trustees: Mrs Louise Ann Gray, Mr Ian Bowness, Mrs Gill Hinks, Mrs Sally Anne Rosser, Dr Richard Field, Mr Matthew Hannah, Dr Glenn Crocker, Dr Timothy Gardiner Hammond, Rev Nicola Jane Fenton, Mr Gary John Bates, Mr Mark Edward Ronan, Mr Andrew Gordon Crompton LLB MBA, Mr Chris Swallow, Mr Stephen Anelay, Miss Jennifer Ellis, Mr Anthony Nicholas Doleman, Mr Aidan Edward Butler, Mr Ian Richard Griffin, Mr Neil David Finlay
Income: £15,273,000 [2016]; £16,827,000 [2015]; £16,031,000 [2014]; £16,868,000 [2013]; £14,519,000 [2012]

Trent Valley Education Trust
Registered: 29 Jul 1996 *Employees:* 23 *Volunteers:* 25
Tel: 01332 872763
Activities: Education, training
Address: 14 Poplar Road, Breaston, Derby, DE72 3BH
Trustees: Mr P Groombridge, Mr J Ashmore, Mr C T Dallow, Mr D Wilson, Mr P South, Mr G J Bedford, Mr R South
Income: £2,205,004 [2016]; £1,375,123 [2015]; £1,162,905 [2014]; £1,104,585 [2013]; £1,212,682 [2012]

Trent Vineyard
Registered: 20 Feb 1995 *Employees:* 121 *Volunteers:* 700
Tel: 0115 988 7060 *Website:* trentvineyard.org
Activities: Education, training; prevention or relief of poverty; religious activities
Address: Trent Vineyard Nottingham, Unit 1, Easter Park, Lenton Lane, Nottingham, NG7 2PX
Trustees: Tony Simmons, Mr Clifford John Wright, Mr Paul Tomkins, Paul Bryce, Mr Clive Sillito
Income: £3,696,100 [2017]; £2,876,200 [2016]; £2,856,000 [2015]; £2,655,100 [2014]; £2,631,200 [2013]

Trialogue Educational Trust
Registered: 20 Jul 1999 *Employees:* 25 *Volunteers:* 10
Website: strategicdialogue.org
Activities: General charitable purposes; education, training; human rights, religious or racial harmony, equality or diversity; other charitable purposes
Address: Montrose Associates Ltd, 97 Jermyn Street, London, SW1Y 6JE
Trustees: Lord Turner of Ecchinswell, Mr Rowan Barnett, Mr Michael MacLay
Income: £2,167,511 [2016]; £2,151,526 [2015]; £3,285,736 [2014]; £2,977,177 [2013]; £2,902,320 [2012]

Triangle Community Services Limited
Registered: 19 Jan 1993 *Employees:* 329 *Volunteers:* 35
Tel: 020 7730 8263 *Website:* triangle.care
Activities: General charitable purposes; education, training; advancement of health or saving of lives; disability
Address: Triangle Community Services, 40-42 Ebury Street, London, SW1W 0LZ
Trustees: Miss E S Campbell, Mr Jonathan Passman, Mr James Ross, Mr Jeremy Withers Green, Chris Maidment, Mrs Joannie Ann Andrews JP MA, Mr Kerry Rubie, Mr Robert Chapman, Mr Rikki Garcia
Income: £5,686,697 [2017]; £5,570,089 [2016]; £4,668,109 [2015]; £4,489,867 [2014]; £3,766,006 [2013]

Trident Reach The People Charity
Registered: 16 Apr 2009 *Employees:* 635 *Volunteers:* 55
Tel: 0121 633 2195 *Website:* reachthecharity.org.uk
Activities: General charitable purposes; education, training; advancement of health or saving of lives; disability; prevention or relief of poverty; accommodation, housing; economic, community development, employment; other charitable purposes
Address: 239 Holliday Street, Birmingham, B1 1SJ
Trustees: Mr John Morris, Robert Turton, Andrew Neil Ballard, Nathan Talbott, Brian Cormack Carr, Yvonne Leishman, Katie Kershaw, Colin Small, Rosemarie Anderson
Income: £13,866,872 [2017]; £13,252,084 [2016]; £13,291,722 [2015]; £13,556,956 [2014]; £13,884,681 [2013]

The Trinitarian Bible Society
Registered: 4 May 1964 *Employees:* 45 *Volunteers:* 25
Tel: 020 8417 8851 *Website:* tbsbibles.org
Activities: Religious activities
Address: Trinitarian Bible Society, William Tyndale House, 29 Deer Park Road, London, SW19 3NN
Trustees: Mr Gerald Buss, Mr Roland Burrows, Mr Richard Alan Clarke, Mr Alun Jones, Rev Robert Gordon Ferguson, Rev Aaron Lewis, Rev David Silversides, Rev John Thackway, Pastor Michael John Harley, Rev Trevor Kirkland, Mr Matthew Vogan
Income: £3,269,730 [2016]; £7,618,391 [2015]; £3,162,312 [2014]; £3,846,205 [2013]; £3,443,676 [2012]

Trinity Baptist Church
Registered: 19 Oct 2009 *Employees:* 9 *Volunteers:* 9
Tel: 020 8766 7732
Activities: Religious activities
Address: 2 Thornlaw Road, London, SE27 0SA
Trustees: Pastor Kingsley Appiagyei, Mr Alexander Kwaku Appiah, Rev Cynthia Appiagyei, Ms Grace Catherine Amponsah, Dr Bernard Aisar Davis, Mr Kweku Asare Amosah, Mr Stephen William Asibuo, Mr George Senyo Appeah, Mr Samuel Noye Narh
Income: £1,084,618 [2017]; £1,270,549 [2016]; £1,198,730 [2015]; £1,013,209 [2014]; £902,430 [2013]

Trinity Church, Brentwood
Registered: 13 Jan 2006 *Employees:* 42 *Volunteers:* 60
Tel: 01277 392996 *Website:* trinitychurchbrentwood.org
Activities: Education, training; religious activities
Address: Trinity Church, 49 Coxtie Green Road, Pilgrims Hatch, Brentwood, Essex, CM14 5PS
Trustees: Mr David Ian Atter, Christine Exediuno, Mrs Lesley Elizabeth Ann Walker, Dr Juan David Esquivel, Mr Casian Virgil Sala, Mr Andrew Christopher Whealy, Miss Fiona Green, Mr David James Coleman, Mr Krish Joshua Jeremiah, Mr Simon Merrick Cleminson, Rev Michael Eric Sherwood
Income: £1,486,918 [2016]; £1,520,764 [2015]; £1,539,536 [2014]; £1,404,723 [2013]; £1,550,087 [2012]

Trinity College Bristol Limited
Registered: 30 Nov 1972 *Employees:* 50
Tel: 0117 968 2803 *Website:* trinitycollegebristol.ac.uk
Activities: Education, training; religious activities
Address: Trinity College, Stoke Hill, Bristol, BS9 1JP
Trustees: Rev Roger Driver, Mr David Mills, Rev John Dunnett, Rev Bridget Shepherd, Rev Stephen Hollinghurst, Rev Helen Fraser, Mr Anthony Miles, Rev Christopher Jolyon Trickey, Rt Revd Richard Jackson, Dr Margaret Clark, The Rt Revd Peter Hancock
Income: £1,939,715 [2016]; £1,888,331 [2015]; £2,534,458 [2014]; £2,132,059 [2013]; £1,991,315 [2012]

Trinity College Cambridge

Registered: 26 Aug 2010 *Employees:* 532
Tel: 01223 338400 *Website:* trin.cam.ac.uk
Activities: Education, training; religious activities; arts, culture, heritage, science; other charitable purposes
Address: Trinity Street, Cambridge, CB2 1TQ
Trustees: Professor Paul Brakefield, Professor Sir David Baulcombe, Dr Peter Sarris, Dr Nicolas Bell, Dr Emma Kathrine Widdis, Professor Lynn Gladden, Professor Pelham Wilson, Sir Gregory Winter, Professor Michael Grae Worster, Rory Landman, Mr Andrew Jonathan Paul Bourne, Professor Catherine Sarah Barnard, Professor Didier Queloz, Dr Ross Wilson
Income: £74,915,000 [2017]; £72,420,000 [2016]; £67,455,000 [2015]; £67,712,000 [2014]; £60,234,000 [2013]

Trinity College London

Registered: 16 Oct 1992 *Employees:* 274
Tel: 020 3752 4701 *Website:* trinitycollege.com
Activities: Education, training
Address: Trinity College London, Blue Fin Building, 110 Southwark Street, London, SE1 0TA
Trustees: Mr Mike Hildesley, Mr Mike Butcher, Ms Susanna Eastburn, Mr James Mullan, Prof John Charles Alderson, Mr Geoffrey Joseph Smith, Mr Mike Esplen, Dr Geoffrey Copland, Mr Mike Saunders, Mr Rajiv Jaitly, Ms Sarah Jane Carter
Income: £48,752,000 [2017]; £42,489,000 [2016]; £37,861,000 [2015]; £32,535,000 [2014]; £30,564,000 [2013]

The Trinity College of Music Trust

Registered: 17 Jan 1984
Activities: Education, training; arts, culture, heritage, science
Address: c/o Chiene & Tait, 15 Old Bailey, London, EC4M 7EF
Trustees: Prof Anthony Bowne, Mr James Furber, Michael Butcher, Prof Derek William Aviss, Lord Lipsey
Income: £1,045,626 [2016]; £1,040,135 [2015]; £964,438 [2014]; £936,981 [2013]

Trinity Hall Cambridge

Registered: 12 Aug 2010 *Employees:* 214 *Volunteers:* 12
Tel: 01223 332500 *Website:* trinhall.cam.ac.uk
Activities: Education, training
Address: Trinity Hall, Cambridge, CB2 1TJ
Trustees: Dr Isabelle Miranda McNeill, Lorand Bartels, Dr John Bradley, Prof Peter John Clarkson, Prof Simon David Guest, Prof Michael Hobson, Dr Clare Jackson, Dr Edmund Richard Stephan Kunji, Dr William O'Reilly, Dr Lucia Prauscello, Dr Cristiano Andrea Ristuccia, Prof Ian Boden Wilkinson, Dr Alexandra Turchyn, Dr Louise Haywood, Dr Robert Asher, Dr Kylie Richardson, Dr Stephen Watterson, Dr Tamsin O'Connell, Dr Thomas Bennett, The Revd Dr Jeremy Morris, Dr Nicholas Guyatt, Dr Thomas Dougherty, Dr Adam Branch, Mr Colm McGrath, Dr Jasmin Fisher, Dr Andrew Sanchez, Prof David Runciman, Dr Eugenio Giannelli, Dr Nicola Kozicharow, Dr Daniel Tyler, Dr Guillermo Burgos Barragan, Revd Dr Stephen John Plant, Dr Nick Bampos, Prof Brian Cheffins, Mr Paul Ffolkes Davis, Miss Alison Hennegan, Prof Florian Hollfelder, Prof Ramaithandran Vasaws Kumar, Dr Andrew James Murray, Dr Jane Partner, Dr Graham Pullan, Dr Jan-Melissa Schramm, Dr David Erdos, Prof James Montgomery, Prof Simon Moore, Dr Jerome Jarrett, Dr Alexander John Marr, Dr John Biggins, Dr Ramji Venkataramanan, Dr Pedro Ramos Pinto, Mr Andrew Arthur, Dr Jack Thorne, Dr William John Skylark, Dr Vladimir Brljak, Ms A Boyle, Dr Heather Inwood, Dr Nichol Furey, Mr Glen Sharp, Dr Koen Jochmans, Dr Goncalo Lopes Bernardes, Dr Ronald Reid-Edwards
Income: £12,656,000 [2017]; £12,089,000 [2016]; £23,126,000 [2015]; £11,309,455 [2014]; £10,731,614 [2013]

Trinity Homeless Projects

Registered: 5 Mar 2007 *Employees:* 18 *Volunteers:* 10
Tel: 020 8797 9500 *Website:* wearetrinity.org.uk
Activities: Education, training; accommodation, housing; economic, community development, employment
Address: Trinity Homeless Projects, Redford House, Redford Way, Uxbridge, Middlesex, UB8 1SZ
Trustees: Mr James Andrew Cannon, Mr Michael Crane, William Alan Madge, Mr Donald Graham, Mr John Hicklin, Mr Raymond Waite, Paula Soares
Income: £1,441,630 [2017]; £1,308,999 [2016]; £961,018 [2015]; £955,207 [2014]; £764,630 [2013]

Trinity Hospice and Palliative Care Services Ltd

Registered: 9 Feb 1981 *Employees:* 163 *Volunteers:* 900
Tel: 01253 358881 *Website:* trinityhospice.co.uk
Activities: Education, training; advancement of health or saving of lives
Address: Trinity Hospice and Palliative Care Services Ltd, Low Moor Road, Blackpool, Lancs, FY2 0BG
Trustees: Miss Maureen McDermott, Mr William Anthony Holmes, Dr Mansel Jones, Miss Kathryn Burn, Mr Tom Inman, Dr Helen Grenier, Doctor Mary Cathrine Geraldine Wren-Hilton, Mr Alan Hunter, Mr Nigel Law, Mr Christopher Beverley, Mr Peter Jackson
Income: £8,966,755 [2017]; £7,587,728 [2016]; £8,806,362 [2015]; £9,376,493 [2014]; £7,038,664 [2013]

Trinity Laban Conservatoire of Music and Dance

Registered: 11 Aug 1966 *Employees:* 314
Website: trinitylaban.ac.uk
Activities: Education, training
Address: Trinity Laban, King Charles Court, Old Royal Naval College, King William Walk, London, SE10 9JF
Trustees: Prof Anthony Bowne, John Crompton, Bill Robinson, Sam Jackson, Dr Aleksander Josef Szram, Laura Witt, Luke Faber, Jocelyn Prudence, Dr Geoffrey Malcolm Copland CBE, Professor Nirmala Rao, Mr Martin James Kettle, Deborah Harris, Mrs Rebecca Allen, Ms Harriet Harman QC MP, Lydia Touliatou, Narind Singh
Income: £25,399,508 [2017]; £24,125,107 [2016]; £23,444,387 [2015]; £23,492,294 [2014]; £22,220,648 [2013]

Trinity School Teignmouth

Registered: 21 Dec 1978 *Employees:* 127 *Volunteers:* 14
Tel: 01626 774138 *Website:* trinityschool.co.uk
Activities: Education, training
Address: Trinity School, Buckeridge Road, Teignmouth, Devon, TQ14 8LY
Trustees: Richard King, Mr Simon Brookman, Mr Nigel David Walkey, June Cohen, Mr Neil Gamble, The Venerable Christopher Futcher, Victoria Kennington, Paul Foster
Income: £4,453,634 [2017]; £4,746,845 [2016]; £4,931,967 [2015]; £5,162,674 [2014]; £5,124,431 [2013]

Tropical Health and Education Trust

Registered: 27 Feb 2006 *Employees:* 34 *Volunteers:* 2
Tel: 07908 455228 *Website:* thet.org
Activities: Education, training; advancement of health or saving of lives; disability
Address: Tropical Health and Education Trust, 1 Wimpole Street, London, W1G 0AE
Trustees: Professor Gerard John Byrne, Dr Irene May Leigh, David Alexander, Mr Jonathan Roland, Prof Judith Ellis, Morounke Akingbola, Frances Day-Stirk, Mr Hugh Risebrow
Income: £7,355,433 [2016]; £9,973,427 [2015]; £10,642,049 [2014]; £10,801,133 [2013]; £8,322,640 [2012]

Tros Gynnal Plant
Registered: 7 Oct 2003 *Employees:* 72 *Volunteers:* 27
Tel: 029 2039 6974 *Website:* trosgynnalplant.org.uk
Activities: General charitable purposes; human rights, religious or
racial harmony, equality or diversity
Address: 12 North Road, Cardiff, CF10 3DY
Trustees: Mrs Diane Daniel, Mrs Emma Jane Marshman,
Miss Angharad Mary Price, Dr Anne Catherine Crowley,
Ms Penelope Newman, Mr Richard Hibbs, Mr Hugh Russell
Income: £2,104,556 [2017]; £2,185,659 [2016]; £2,121,292 [2015];
£2,031,695 [2014]; £1,530,942 [2013]

The Troutsdale Charitable Trust
Registered: 19 Jan 2016
Tel: 01723 360361
Activities: General charitable purposes; education, training;
arts, culture, heritage, science; amateur sport; environment,
conservation, heritage
Address: Moore Stephens, 12-13 Alma Square, Scarborough,
N Yorks, YO11 1JU
Trustees: Mr John Guthrie, Mr Peter John Guthrie, Mrs Leslie Faith
Guthrie, Mr Richard Guthrie
Income: £1,552,322 [2017]

The True Colours Trust
Registered: 21 Dec 2001 *Employees:* 14
Tel: 020 7410 0330 *Website:* truecolourstrust.org.uk
Activities: General charitable purposes; disability; prevention or
relief of poverty; other charitable purposes
Address: The Peak, 5 Wilton Road, London, SW1V 1AP
Trustees: Mr Dominic Brendan Flynn, Mr Bernard John Christian
Willis, Ms Lucy Anya Sainsbury, Mr T G Price
Income: £2,172,684 [2017]; £1,125,979 [2016]; £1,952,956 [2015];
£2,250,852 [2014]; £1,975,947 [2013]

Trumros Limited
Registered: 20 Jan 1983
Tel: 020 7431 3282
Activities: Education, training; prevention or relief of poverty;
religious activities
Address: 282 Finchley Road, London, NW3 7AD
Trustees: Mrs Hannah Hofbauer, Mr Ronald Hofbauer
Income: £1,134,005 [2016]; £1,259,750 [2015]; £1,305,034 [2014];
£1,071,507 [2013]; £962,439 [2012]

The Truro Diocesan Board of Finance Limited
Registered: 21 Jun 1966 *Employees:* 27 *Volunteers:* 20
Tel: 01872 274351 *Website:* trurodiocese.org.uk
Activities: Religious activities
Address: Truro Diocesan Board of Finance Ltd, Church House,
Woodland Court, Truro Business Park, Threemilestone, Truro,
Cornwall, TR4 9NH
Trustees: The Venerable Roger Bush, The Revd Alan Bashforth,
Rt Revd Christopher David Goldsmith, Mr Andrew Keast,
Mrs Sheridan Jane Sturgess, Mr Roger Edward Hygate,
Mrs Charlotte Elisabeth Irwin, Mr Robin Clinton West, Rev Paul
Robert Holley, Mr Michael James Sturgess, Mr Robert John Perry,
Rev David Keith Barnes, Revd Canon Kenneth Paul Arthur, The
Venerable Audrey Elkington, Mr Nicolas Corin John Herian, Revd
Canon Anne Elizabeth Brown, Dr Andrew Gibb Thompson
Income: £7,680,134 [2016]; £7,102,043 [2015]; £7,057,190 [2014];
£6,475,901 [2013]; £6,122,886 [2012]

Truro High School for Girls
Registered: 4 Apr 1963 *Employees:* 65 *Volunteers:* 30
Tel: 01872 242997 *Website:* trurohigh.co.uk
Activities: Education, training
Address: Truro High School for Girls, Falmouth Road, Truro,
Cornwall, TR1 2HU
Trustees: Truro High School For Girls Trustees
Income: £3,821,335 [2017]; £3,401,806 [2016]; £3,779,781 [2015];
£3,999,816 [2014]; £4,016,675 [2013]

Truro School
Registered: 17 Nov 1965 *Employees:* 307 *Volunteers:* 23
Tel: 020 7935 3723 *Website:* truroschool.com
Activities: Education, training; religious activities
Address: Methodist Church House, 25 Marylebone Road, London,
NW1 5JR
Trustees: Truro School Trustee Company Limited, Methodist
Independent Schools Trust
Income: £11,904,000 [2016]; £11,661,000 [2015]; £11,167,000
[2014]; £11,136,000 [2013]; £11,203,000 [2012]

The Trussell Trust
Registered: 21 Jul 2005 *Employees:* 104 *Volunteers:* 2,000
Tel: 01722 580180 *Website:* trusselltrust.org
Activities: General charitable purposes; education, training;
prevention or relief of poverty; overseas aid, famine relief;
economic, community development, employment
Address: The Trussell Trust, Unit 9, Ashfield Trading Estate,
Ashfield Road, Salisbury, Wilts, SP2 7HL
Trustees: Miss Elizabeth Pollard, Ms Alison Inglis-Jones, Mr Robert
Lanyon, Rt Revd John Packer, Mr Stephen Dominic Hicks
Income: £6,625,173 [2017]; £6,778,510 [2016]; £6,800,545 [2015];
£3,397,289 [2014]; £1,884,086 [2013]

Trust Property Held By Trustees of St Augustine's Priory
Registered: 16 Dec 1965 *Employees:* 1
Tel: 07754 967885
Activities: Education, training; prevention or relief of poverty;
accommodation, housing; religious activities
Address: 38 Beaufort Road, London, W5 3EA
Trustees: Miss Claire McIntyre, Mr Colin Nelson Bennett, Alexis
Fitzgerald, Mrs Clare Mary Murphy, Mr David Percival Allen Murphy
Income: £1,227,937 [2017]; £172,684 [2016]; £453,394 [2015];
£158,751 [2014]; £163,804 [2013]

**Trust Property Held ICW The English Province of The
Congregation of The Sisters of The Presentation of The
Blessed Virgin Mary**
Registered: 9 Feb 1987 *Employees:* 58 *Volunteers:* 59
Tel: 01629 582416 *Website:* presentationsisters.co.uk
Activities: General charitable purposes; education, training;
advancement of health or saving of lives; disability; prevention or
relief of poverty; overseas aid, famine relief; religious activities; arts,
culture, heritage, science; environment, conservation, heritage;
human rights, religious or racial harmony, equality or diversity
Address: Presentation Convent, Chesterfield Road, Matlock,
Derbys, DE4 3FT
Trustees: Sister Eileen Keating, Sister Eleanor O'Gorman, Sister
Janette Brown, Sister Mary O'Halloran, Sister Bernadette Healy,
Sister Catherine O'Neill
Income: £2,717,655 [2017]; £2,798,619 [2016]; £2,728,784 [2015];
£2,683,350 [2014]; £2,599,825 [2013]

Trust Property Held in Connection with the English Province of The Congregation of Christian Brothers
Registered: 15 Nov 1967 *Employees:* 115 *Volunteers:* 100
Tel: 0161 904 0786
Activities: General charitable purposes; education, training; prevention or relief of poverty; overseas aid, famine relief; accommodation, housing; religious activities; other charitable purposes
Address: Woodeaves, Wicker Lane, Hale Barns, Altrincham, Cheshire, WA15 0HF
Trustees: Brother Patrick George Gordon, Brother Eamon O'Brien, Brother Dominic Sassi, Brother Martin O'Flaherty, Brother Edmund Garvey
Income: £5,202,285 [2016]; £5,535,068 [2015]; £5,478,445 [2014]; £5,316,470 [2013]; £6,889,693 [2012]

Trust Property Held in Connexion with the Sisters of The Holy Family of Bordeaux
Registered: 27 May 1965 *Employees:* 87 *Volunteers:* 180
Tel: 020 7624 7573 *Website:* holyfamilybordeaux.org
Activities: The advancement of health or saving of lives; religious activities
Address: 2 Aberdare Gardens, London, NW6 3PX
Trustees: Sr Josephine Carmel Bateson, Provincialate Trustees Ltd
Income: £7,451,627 [2016]; £3,549,651 [2015]; £4,719,248 [2014]; £9,809,566 [2013]; £4,462,008 [2012]

Trust for London
Registered: 2 Oct 1962 *Employees:* 20
Tel: 020 7606 6145 *Website:* trustforlondon.org.uk
Activities: The prevention or relief of poverty; economic, community development, employment; human rights, religious or racial harmony, equality or diversity
Address: Trust for London, 6-9 Middle Street, London, EC1A 7PH
Trustees: Trust For London Trustee
Income: £8,483,398 [2016]; £9,023,725 [2015]; £9,131,351 [2014]; £9,090,334 [2013]; £9,391,534 [2012]

The Trust of St Benedict's Abbey Ealing
Registered: 2 Mar 1966 *Employees:* 40 *Volunteers:* 50
Website: ealingabbey.org.uk
Activities: Education, training; prevention or relief of poverty; religious activities
Address: Ealing Abbey, Charlbury Grove, London, W5 2DY
Trustees: Rev Martin Shipperlee OSB, Rev Dominic Taylor OSB, Rev Ambrose McCambridge OSB, Rev Alexander Bevan OSB, Rev Timothy Gorham OSB
Income: £1,554,259 [2017]; £1,782,953 [2016]; £1,400,716 [2015]; £1,351,616 [2014]; £1,431,885 [2013]

Trustees of The Charity of The Bernardine Sisters
Registered: 28 Apr 1965 *Employees:* 51 *Volunteers:* 24
Website: bernardine.org
Activities: Education, training; religious activities
Address: Monastery of Our Lady of Hyning, Warton, Carnforth, Lancs, LA5 9SE
Trustees: Sister Catherine Boyle, Sister Elizabeth Mann, Sister Josephine Miller, Sister Colette Jordan
Income: £2,993,974 [2017]; £2,945,951 [2016]; £2,740,902 [2015]; £2,352,647 [2014]; £6,864,627 [2013]

Trustees of The London Clinic Limited
Registered: 19 Nov 1962 *Employees:* 1,196
Tel: 020 3219 3310 *Website:* thelondonclinic.co.uk
Activities: The advancement of health or saving of lives
Address: 20 Devonshire Place, London, W1G 6BW
Trustees: Lady Helen Otton, Mr Ian Hamish Leslie Melville, Mr Nicholas James Anthony Melhuish, Mr Manish Jayantilal Chande, Professor John Gribben
Income: £136,341,000 [2017]; £144,374,000 [2016]; £141,793,000 [2015]; £144,700,000 [2014]; £136,654,000 [2013]

The Trusthouse Charitable Foundation
Registered: 13 Aug 1997
Tel: 020 7264 4990 *Website:* trusthousecharitablefoundation.org.uk
Activities: General charitable purposes; education, training; advancement of health or saving of lives; disability; prevention or relief of poverty; overseas aid, famine relief; accommodation, housing; arts, culture, heritage, science; amateur sport; environment, conservation, heritage; economic, community development, employment
Address: Sixth Floor, 65 Leadenhall Street, London, EC3A 2AD
Trustees: Mr Crispian Collins, The Hon Mrs Olga Polizzi CBE, Mr Patrick Reeve, Rev Rose Hudson-Wilkin, Ms Philippa Hamilton, Mrs Charlie Polizzi Peyton, Ms Carole Milner, The Lady Janet Balfour of Burleigh, Sir John Nutting QC, Lady Anthony Hamilton, Mr Nicholas Melhuish
Income: £2,062,000 [2017]; £2,039,000 [2016]; £2,128,000 [2015]; £1,895,000 [2014]; £1,294,000 [2013]

The James Tudor Foundation
Registered: 16 Sep 2004 *Employees:* 2
Tel: 0117 985 8715 *Website:* jamestudor.org.uk
Activities: General charitable purposes; education, training; advancement of health or saving of lives; disability; overseas aid, famine relief
Address: The James Tudor Foundation, West Point, 78 Queens Road, Clifton, Bristol, BS8 1QU
Trustees: Mr Cedric Nash, Mrs Susan Evans, Stephanie K Wren, Mr Richard Esler, Miss Anne McPherson
Income: £1,163,803 [2017]; £1,155,921 [2016]; £1,040,579 [2015]; £968,443 [2014]; £1,049,341 [2013]

Tudor Hall School
Registered: 13 Dec 1994 *Employees:* 228 *Volunteers:* 4
Website: tudorhallschool.com
Activities: Education, training
Address: Tudor Hall School, Wykham Park, Banbury, Oxon, OX16 9UR
Trustees: Mrs Alison Darling, Ms Sarah Maxted, Mrs Rosalind Hayes, Miss Mary Kinnear, Mr Babak Lari, Mrs Sally Bowie, Mr John Gloag, Mrs Victoria Harley, Mrs Kathy Fidgeon, Mr John Elliot, Mr Duncan Bailey
Income: £11,655,210 [2017]; £10,722,864 [2016]; £10,795,869 [2015]; £10,925,289 [2014]; £10,428,810 [2013]

The Tudor Trust
Registered: 20 Aug 2004 Employees: 18
Tel: 020 7727 8522 Website: tudortrust.org.uk
Activities: General charitable purposes
Address: The Tudor Trust, 7 Ladbroke Grove, London, W11 3BD
Trustees: James Long, Ms Monica Anne Barlow PhD, Mrs Louise Katherine Collins, Mr Ben Dunwell, Mr Christopher Graves, Ms Rosalind Helen Dunwell, Amy Collins, Holly Baine, Mrs Catherine Mary Antcliff, Mrs Nell Buckler, Mrs Elizabeth Helen Crawshaw, Mr Matt Dunwell, Francis Arthur Runacres, Ms Shilpa Shah, Carey Buckler, Jonathan Bell
Income: £6,645,000 [2017]; £6,336,000 [2016]; £6,552,000 [2015]; £6,898,000 [2014]; £7,694,000 [2013]

The Tuixen Foundation
Registered: 15 Jun 2000
Tel: 020 7649 2903
Activities: Education, training; advancement of health or saving of lives; disability; prevention or relief of poverty
Address: 440 Strand, London, WC2R 0QS
Trustees: Mr Stephen Michael Rosefield, Mr Peter Englander, Mr Simon Jonathan Englander, Dr Leanda Abigail Kroll, Mr Paul Clements
Income: £2,678,132 [2017]; £14,691,907 [2016]; £1,033,010 [2015]; £1,114,551 [2014]; £1,311,308 [2013]

Tullie House Museum and Art Gallery Trust
Registered: 3 Aug 2011 Employees: 55 Volunteers: 43
Tel: 01228 618740 Website: tulliehouse.co.uk
Activities: Education, training; arts, culture, heritage, science; environment, conservation, heritage
Address: Tullie House, Museum & Art Gallery, Castle Street, Carlisle, Cumbria, CA3 8TP
Trustees: Cllr Jessica Riddle, Cllr Leslie Tickner, Andrew Smith, Ms Marcia Reid Fotheringham, Professor Peter Strike, Prof Julie Mennell, Sir Mark Ellis Powell Jones, Roger Cooke, Ms Caroline Thomson, Mr Eric Bell Robson, Mr Paul Croft
Income: £1,815,312 [2017]; £1,954,709 [2016]; £2,105,346 [2015]; £2,300,266 [2014]; £2,028,108 [2013]

The Alan Turing Institute
Registered: 6 Jul 2015 Employees: 25
Tel: 0300 770 1912 Website: turing.ac.uk
Activities: Education, training; arts, culture, heritage, science; other charitable purposes
Address: British Library, 96 Euston Road, London, NW1 2DB
Trustees: Professor Thomas Frederick Melham, Mr Neil Graham Viner, Mr Howard John Covington, Wendy Tan White, Professor Francis Kelly, Dr Julie Maxton, Professor Richard Donovan Kenway, Professor Pamela Thomas, Professor Patrick Jason Wolfe
Income: £15,747,248 [2017]; £7,726,079 [2016]

Turkish Cypriot Community Association
Registered: 30 May 2000 Employees: 53 Volunteers: 4
Tel: 020 8826 1080 Website: tcca.org
Activities: General charitable purposes; education, training; advancement of health or saving of lives; disability; prevention or relief of poverty; arts, culture, heritage, science; amateur sport; environment, conservation, heritage; economic, community development, employment
Address: Turkish Cypriot Community Association, 628-630 Green Lanes, London, N8 0SD
Trustees: Mrs Turkay Hadji-Filippou, Suleyman Fuat, Osman Ercan, Mr Yasar Ismailglu, Mr Mustafa Korel, Ismail Karamustafa, Mr Niyazi Enver, Mrs Behiye Karaman-Naci
Income: £1,324,095 [2017]; £1,284,898 [2016]; £1,245,056 [2015]; £1,216,686 [2014]; £1,170,911 [2013]

The Roger & Douglas Turner Charitable Trust
Registered: 5 Nov 2013 Employees: 28 Volunteers: 20
Tel: 01299 861368 Website: arleyarboretum.co.uk
Activities: General charitable purposes
Address: Arley House, Lion Lane, Upper Arley, Bewdley, Worcs, DY12 1SQ
Trustees: Mr Stephen Luing Preedy, Mr Geoffrey Patterson Thomas, Mrs Dawn Emma Long, Mr Ronald Alfred Wilson Middleton FCA, Mr Peter John Millward, Mrs Amanda Jane McGeever
Income: £1,706,000 [2017]; £1,565,000 [2016]; £1,562,687 [2015]; £907,327 [2014]

Turner Contemporary
Registered: 3 Jun 2009 Employees: 35
Tel: 01843 233000 Website: turnercontemporary.org
Activities: General charitable purposes; education, training; arts, culture, heritage, science
Address: Rendezvous, Margate, Kent, CT9 1HG
Trustees: Clive Stevens, Ms Laura Wright, Mr Martin Cook, Mr Kemet Hawthorne Pink, Mr Michael Armitage, Prof Simon Ofield-Kerr, Mr James Page, Ms Sara Woodward, Mrs S Hohler, Mr Piers Robert Sanders, Ms Vivienne Bennett, Ms Caroline Alton, Ms Jill Constantine, Ms Caroline Randall
Income: £2,799,073 [2017]; £3,038,138 [2016]; £3,659,169 [2015]; £2,777,830 [2014]; £4,112,983 [2013]

Turner Home
Registered: 16 Jun 1993 Employees: 62
Tel: 0151 727 4177 Website: turner-home.com
Activities: The advancement of health or saving of lives; disability; accommodation, housing
Address: The Turner Home, Dingle Lane, Dingle, Liverpool, L8 9RN
Trustees: Mr Peter Rawlinson, Mr Keith Housley, Donna Kirwan, Mrs Susan Newton, Mr Eric Tomlinson, Ms Brenda Edith Waterson
Income: £2,130,042 [2017]; £1,940,169 [2016]; £1,852,004 [2015]; £1,818,568 [2014]; £1,711,209 [2013]

Turning Lives Around Ltd
Registered: 30 Jul 1984 Employees: 85 Volunteers: 3
Tel: 0113 276 0616 Website: leedshc.org.uk
Activities: General charitable purposes; education, training; advancement of health or saving of lives; prevention or relief of poverty; accommodation, housing
Address: 4 Ashbrooke Business Park, Parkside Lane, Leeds, LS11 5SF
Trustees: Mr Ian Livingstone, Mr Martin Ford, Mr Mike White, Mr Daniel Penman, Mr Matt Seward, Mrs Janice Chattaway, Mr Chris Wright
Income: £3,521,698 [2017]; £3,545,620 [2016]; £3,459,658 [2015]; £3,665,303 [2014]; £3,616,997 [2013]

Turning Point

Registered: 26 May 1964 *Employees:* 2,982 *Volunteers:* 46
Tel: 020 7481 7681 *Website:* turning-point.co.uk
Activities: Education, training; advancement of health or saving of lives; disability; economic, community development, employment
Address: Turning Point, 21 Mansell Street, London, E1 8AA
Trustees: Lord Victor Adebowale CBE, Mrs Sarah Wood OBE, Mrs Nicola Gilham, Mr Paul Picknett, Ms Helen Spice, Chris Parker, Mrs Caroline Bailey, Mrs Julie Bass, Dr Alison Paice Hill
Income: £131,035,000 [2017]; £112,345,804 [2016]; £100,480,496 [2015]; £93,522,000 [2014]; £80,195,000 [2013]

Tusk Trust

Registered: 4 Apr 1990 *Employees:* 8 *Volunteers:* 20
Tel: 01747 831005 *Website:* tusk.org
Activities: Education, training; overseas aid, famine relief; animals; environment, conservation, heritage; economic, community development, employment
Address: 4 Cheapside House, High Street, Gillingham, Dorset, SP8 4AA
Trustees: Hon Stephen Harting Willoghby Watson, Mr Timothy Robert Gwinnett Jackson, Mark Tyndall, Alexander Rhodes, Mr Philip Ihenacho, Deborah Meaden, Nick Tims, Susan Canney, Patrick Harveson
Income: £4,641,239 [2016]; £4,255,884 [2015]; £2,722,906 [2014]; £2,145,146 [2013]; £2,465,931 [2012]

Twickenham Preparatory School

Registered: 20 Jan 1998 *Employees:* 59 *Volunteers:* 12
Tel: 020 8979 6216 *Website:* twickenhamprep.co.uk
Activities: Education, training
Address: Beveree, 43 High Street, Hampton, Surrey, TW12 2SA
Trustees: Mr Harry Bates, Mr Andrew John Murray, Mrs Martha Blyth, Miss Barbara Flight, Mrs Ruby Jones, Mr Thomas Owens, Mr Mike Fisher, Mr Nigel Rickard, Mr Mike Michael, Mr Brian Jones BA FCA, Mr Gavin John Donaldson BA Hons FCMA FGMA, Mrs Elizabeth Ferguson
Income: £3,227,256 [2017]; £3,181,128 [2016]; £2,997,889 [2015]; £2,885,633 [2014]; £2,734,546 [2013]

Twin

Registered: 20 May 1985 *Employees:* 16
Tel: 020 7422 0794 *Website:* twin.org.uk
Activities: Education, training; environment, conservation, heritage; economic, community development, employment
Address: Twin and Twin Trading, 1 Curtain Road, London, EC2A 3LT
Trustees: Dr Camilla Toulmin, Ms Sally Smith, Ms Kim Elena Ionescu, Mr Patrick Barker, Mr Richard Graham, Mr Ian Fnlayson, Mr David McCullough, Mr Elmer Pena Silva
Income: £3,001,981 [2017]; £1,920,889 [2016]; £1,423,095 [2015]; £1,326,960 [2014]; £1,518,090 [2013]

Twining Enterprise

Registered: 25 Jul 1995 *Employees:* 37
Tel: 020 8840 8833 *Website:* twiningenterprise.org.uk
Activities: Education, training; disability; economic, community development, employment
Address: Twining Enterprise, 84 Uxbridge Road, London, W13 8RA
Trustees: Navroop Kullar, Alison Deeth, Thomas Brunwin, Liz Meek, Christian Mazzi, Mr Alaster Stewart
Income: £1,210,589 [2017]; £1,004,029 [2016]; £864,890 [2015]; £878,507 [2014]; £515,847 [2013]

Two Ridings Community Foundation

Registered: 11 Apr 2016 *Employees:* 8 *Volunteers:* 15
Tel: 01904 435277 *Website:* trcf.org.uk
Activities: General charitable purposes; education, training; prevention or relief of poverty; economic, community development, employment
Address: Suite 1.34, Innovation Centre, York Science Park, Innovation Way, York, YO10 5DG
Trustees: Mrs Venetia Wrigley, Miss Hannah Purkis, Mrs Harriet Kate Reid, Ms Marie Johnstone, Mr Andrew Wilson, Mr James Naylor, Mr Joe Leigh, Mrs Alison Pearson, Miss Tracey Smith, Mr Paul Downey, Mr Daniel Yates, Mr John Furness
Income: £1,168,753 [2017]

Two Rivers Housing

Registered: 2 Jul 2004 *Employees:* 125
Tel: 01531 829340 *Website:* tworivershousing.org.uk
Activities: Disability; prevention or relief of poverty; accommodation, housing; economic, community development, employment
Address: Rivers Meet, Cleeve Mill Lane, Newent, Glos, GL18 1DS
Trustees: Mrs Susan Holmes, Mr David Leslie Powell, Mr Neil Sutherland, Mr Christopher Hillidge, Mr Alan John Blundell, Mr John Bloxsom, Mr Jonathan Richards, Mrs Rita Jones
Income: £21,913,000 [2017]; £22,540,000 [2016]; £21,530,000 [2015]; £21,758,000 [2014]; £20,482,000 [2013]

Twycross Zoo-East Midland Zoological Society Limited

Registered: 21 Sep 1972 *Employees:* 129
Tel: 01827 883122 *Website:* twycrosszoo.org
Activities: Animals
Address: Twycross Zoo, Burton Road, Twycross, Atherstone, Warwicks, CV9 3PX
Trustees: Mr Liam Wall, Mr John Peter Helas, Mr Martin Brewer, Mr Gary Alan Middleton, Mr Geoffrey William Hoon, Dr David John Chivers, Mr Douglas John Keep, Professor Gary England, Mrs Joanna Thornell
Income: £10,769,093 [2016]; £9,838,707 [2015]; £8,558,211 [2014]; £8,641,847 [2013]; £8,059,618 [2012]

Twyford School

Registered: 2 May 1962 *Employees:* 113 *Volunteers:* 1
Tel: 01962 717094 *Website:* twyfordschool.com
Activities: Education, training
Address: Twyford School, High Street, Twyford, Winchester, Hants, SO21 1NW
Trustees: Julian Thould, Dr James Hodgins, Mrs Carol Chaplin-Rogers, Mrs Sonia Watson, Mr Colin Howman, Mrs Joanne Phillips, Mr Gerald Barber, Mrs Fiona Dunger, Mrs Emma Hattersley, Mrs Janine Natalie Naismith, Richard Hammond
Income: £6,797,912 [2017]; £6,601,395 [2016]; £6,383,105 [2015]; £6,311,215 [2014]; £6,330,522 [2013]

Ty Hafan

Registered: 12 Jul 1995 *Employees:* 237 *Volunteers:* 602
Website: tyhafan.org
Activities: The advancement of health or saving of lives; disability
Address: Ty Hafan, Hayes Road, Sully, Penarth, Vale of Glamorgan, CF64 5XX
Trustees: Mr Martin Davies, Mr Peter Francis Maggs, Ms Helen Anne Lentle, Ms Samantha Brown, Dr Huw Jenkins, Ms Kath Palmer, Mrs Amanda Thomas, Dr Keith Holgate, Ms Karen Healey
Income: £9,147,774 [2017]; £8,922,410 [2016]; £9,283,217 [2015]; £8,305,159 [2014]; £8,085,216 [2013]

Tyddyn Mon
Registered: 19 Oct 1998 *Employees:* 54 *Volunteers:* 5
Tel: 01248 410580 *Website:* tyddynmon.co.uk
Activities: Education, training; disability; accommodation, housing
Address: Tyddyn Mon, Hendy, Brynrefail, Dulas, Amlwch, Anglesey, LL70 9PQ
Trustees: Mrs Eileen Clarke, Mr Jon Graham Webster, Dr Emma Roberts, Mrs Janet Nicol Spilman, Mrs Christine Michelle MacKay, Mrs Tracy Ann Davies, Mr Michael Ian Hawkes
Income: £1,672,404 [2017]; £1,539,894 [2016]; £1,605,853 [2015]; £1,524,626 [2014]; £1,595,734 [2013]

Tydfil Training Consortium Limited
Registered: 2 Mar 1990 *Employees:* 29 *Volunteers:* 5
Tel: 01685 371747 *Website:* tydfil.com
Activities: Education, training; prevention or relief of poverty; economic, community development, employment
Address: William Smith Building, High Street, Merthyr Tydfil, Mid Glamorgan, CF47 8AP
Trustees: Mr Alan Bush, Mr Robert Owen Wilding, Mr Martin Howell, Mr Terence Patrick Collins MBE, Mr Peter Brill, Mr Colin Albert Parker
Income: £1,117,884 [2017]; £1,165,924 [2016]; £1,817,109 [2015]; £1,607,365 [2014]; £1,875,624 [2013]

Tyndale House
Registered: 23 Apr 2015 *Employees:* 22 *Volunteers:* 3
Tel: 01223 566604 *Website:* tyndale.cam.ac.uk
Activities: Education, training; religious activities
Address: Tyndale House, 36 Selwyn Gardens, Cambridge, CB3 9BA
Trustees: Mr David Vardy, Professor John Wyatt, Dr Andrew Clarke, Dr Desmond Alexander, Rev Dr Alistair Donald, Mr Peter Loose, Mr Keith Bintley, Dr Daniel Strange, Dr Steffen Jenkins
Income: £1,457,169 [2017]; £485,376 [2016]

Tyne North Training Limited
Registered: 8 Feb 1973 *Employees:* 20
Tel: 0191 262 6860 *Website:* tynenorthtraining.co.uk
Activities: Education, training; economic, community development, employment
Address: Tyne North Training, Embleton Avenue, Wallsend, Tyne & Wear, NE28 9NJ
Trustees: Mr Thomas Ian Selkirk, Colin Pratt, Mr Stanley Armstrong
Income: £1,839,580 [2016]; £1,573,327 [2015]; £1,445,739 [2014]; £1,246,679 [2013]

Tyneside Cinema
Registered: 7 Aug 1973 *Employees:* 76 *Volunteers:* 19
Tel: 07989 877992 *Website:* tynesidecinema.co.uk
Activities: Education, training; arts, culture, heritage, science; environment, conservation, heritage; recreation
Address: 9 Briarwood Avenue, Newcastle upon Tyne, NE3 5DA
Trustees: Lucy Armstrong, Ms Murphy Cobbing, Mr Steven Kyffin, Mr Nick Shottel, Mr Keith Proudfoot, Ms Heather Markham, Mr Timothy James Neil Davies-Pugh, Mrs Clare Binns
Income: £4,088,755 [2017]; £3,592,349 [2016]; £3,345,363 [2015]; £2,454,263 [2014]; £2,484,572 [2013]

Tzedokoh Vechesed Limited
Registered: 18 Jan 2001
Tel: 020 8455 6789
Activities: Education, training; prevention or relief of poverty; religious activities
Address: 13 Glaserton Road, London, N16 5QU
Trustees: Mr Menachem Margalit, Mr Zvi Zeivald
Income: £1,046,614 [2016]; £1,111,668 [2015]; £846,485 [2014]; £852,715 [2013]; £790,774 [2012]

U K Med
Registered: 4 May 1995 *Employees:* 10 *Volunteers:* 2,062
Tel: 0161 275 8232 *Website:* uk-med.org
Activities: Education, training; advancement of health or saving of lives; overseas aid, famine relief
Address: UK-MED, c/o HCRI, C1.54 Ellen Wilkinson Building, The University of Manchester, Oxford Road, Manchester, M13 9PL
Trustees: Mr Mark Vincent Prescott FRCSEd, Mr John Philip Shuker, Professor Alistair Mitchell Ulph, Professor Bertrand Taithe, Mrs Lynn Charmain May
Income: £1,360,147 [2017]; £1,081,193 [2016]; £2,883,886 [2015]; £1,035,184 [2014]; £249,642 [2013]

UBS Optimus Foundation UK
Registered: 27 Aug 2013
Tel: 020 7567 8000 *Website:* ubs.com
Activities: Education, training; advancement of health or saving of lives; prevention or relief of poverty
Address: UBS, 5 Broadgate, London, EC2M 2QS
Trustees: Mr James Broderick, Ms Jo Ensor, Simone Thompson, Mr Nicholas Perryman, Ms Phyllis Kurlander Costanza
Income: £8,087,877 [2016]; £5,731,945 [2015]; £2,515,738 [2014]

UBS UK Donor Advised Foundation
Registered: 28 Aug 2013
Tel: 020 7567 8000
Activities: General charitable purposes
Address: UBS, 5 Broadgate, London, EC2M 2QS
Trustees: Mr Christopher Houlding, Mr David Rowe, Mr Richard Hardie, Mr Nicholas Anthony Perryman, Mr Nicholas Wright
Income: £31,823,000 [2016]; £22,300,000 [2015]; £31,562,000 [2014]

UCLU
Registered: 14 Jun 2011 *Employees:* 233
Website: uclu.org
Activities: Education, training; arts, culture, heritage, science; amateur sport; recreation; other charitable purposes
Address: UCLU, 25 Gordon Street, London, WC1H 0AY
Trustees: Ms Mary Margaret Basterfield, Mr Zakariya Mohran, Mr Sohail Akber Badat, Mr Mohammad Hamza Jamshaid, Miss Aiysha Tahseen Qureshi, Ms Magdalene Akosua Foda Bayim-Adomako, Miss Sarah Issa Al-Aride, Mr Farooq Dean, Mr Ilyas Morrison, Mr Mohammad Dinar Saddiqur Rahman
Income: £11,079,759 [2017]; £11,126,379 [2016]; £10,649,037 [2015]; £10,283,689 [2014]; £9,928,132 [2013]

UCS Pre-Prep Limited
Registered: 21 Jul 2003 *Employees:* 25
Tel: 020 7433 2140 *Website:* ucs.org.uk
Activities: Education, training
Address: Frognal, Hampstead, London, NW3 6XH
Trustees: Mr Robert Gullifer MA, Ms Elizabeth Bingham MIPA MABRP DBA
Income: £1,796,645 [2017]; £1,844,103 [2016]; £1,750,573 [2015]; £1,710,335 [2014]; £1,615,159 [2013]

UFI Charitable Trust
Registered: 6 Jun 2000 *Employees:* 4
Tel: 020 7969 5500 *Website:* ufi.co.uk
Activities: Education, training; economic, community development, employment
Address: Haysmacintyre, 26 Red Lion Square, London, WC1R 4AG
Trustees: Mr Tom Wilson, Valerie Michelle Dias, Dominic Gill, Mr Brynley John Davies, Bob Harrison, Professor Rosemary Helen Luckin
Income: £1,160,000 [2016]; £1,022,000 [2015]; £1,060,000 [2014]; £1,223,000 [2013]; £496,000 [2012]

UFM Worldwide
Registered: 1 Feb 1965 *Employees:* 13
Tel: 01793 610515 *Website:* ufm.org.uk
Activities: Religious activities
Address: U F M Worldwide, 145 Faringdon Road, Swindon, Wilts, SN1 5DL
Trustees: Rev Richard Myerscough, Mr Jason Elliot Duffin, Rev Steven Curry, Rev Geraint Bryn Jones, Mrs Deborah Woolley, Mrs Linda Lewis, Mr Graeme Huw Morgan Powell, Rev David Carmichael, Mr Brian Edward Mitchener, Mr Albert Smyth, Miss Kirsten Mary Wynn, Mr Matthew Dafydd Evans, Rev Iain Shaw
Income: £3,238,716 [2017]; £2,856,261 [2016]; £2,778,177 [2015]; £2,754,829 [2014]; £2,680,133 [2013]

UK Biobank Limited
Registered: 30 Dec 2003 *Employees:* 110
Website: ukbiobank.ac.uk
Activities: The advancement of health or saving of lives
Address: UK Biobank Ltd, Unit 1-2, Spectrum Way, Stockport, Cheshire, SK3 0SA
Trustees: Sir Michael Rawlins, Sir Alex Markham, Professor Andrew Hattersley, Professor Ruth Gilbert, Dr Joseph McNamara, Mr Jonathan Tross, Professor Bill Ollier, Ms Sara Elizabeth Farha Marshall, Professor Martin Bobrow
Income: £17,168,583 [2016]; £11,763,551 [2015]; £16,100,634 [2014]; £21,785,291 [2013]; £4,616,142 [2012]

UK Care for Children
Registered: 10 Jul 2008
Website: ukc4c.org
Activities: General charitable purposes; education, training; prevention or relief of poverty; overseas aid, famine relief
Address: 21 Chandos Crescent, Edgware, Middlesex, HA8 6HH
Trustees: Mr Mohamad Kozbar, Mr Riad Zaidani, Mr Ahmad Abdallah
Income: £2,309,596 [2016]; £2,786,259 [2015]; £1,552,168 [2014]; £184,663 [2013]; £45,582 [2012]

The UK Career Academy Foundation
Registered: 10 Jul 2002 *Employees:* 39 *Volunteers:* 4,000
Tel: 020 7986 5494 *Website:* careerready.org.uk
Activities: Education, training; economic, community development, employment
Address: 25 Canary Wharf, London, E14 5LB
Trustees: Mr James David Kempster Bardrick, Mr Jeremy David Fletcher Palmer, Mr Maurice Benisty, Ms Olivia Louise Cole, Mr David Richard Trott, Mr David James Bucknall, Mr Alexander Hugh McCormack Begbie
Income: £2,333,689 [2017]; £2,390,397 [2016]; £2,117,264 [2015]; £1,752,691 [2014]; £1,581,461 [2013]

UK Cat Consortium
Registered: 21 Jan 2010
Tel: 0115 823 0041 *Website:* ukcat.ac.uk
Activities: Education, training
Address: B Floor, Courses Office, Medical School, Queens Medical Centre, Nottingham, NG7 2UH
Trustees: Dr Kathleen Margaret Petty-Saphon, Dr Sandra Nicholson, Dr Robert McAndrew, Dr Fiona Stewart, Dr Christine Kay, Dr Amanda Jayne Hampshire, Dr Ruth Alison Valentine, Mr Nigel Paul Siesage, Lyndon Cabot, Professor Jennifer Mary Higham, Mr Paul Teulon, Dr Angela Kubacki, Professor Kim Mary Piper
Income: £1,762,569 [2017]; £1,789,249 [2016]; £1,844,458 [2015]; £1,924,530 [2014]; £1,892,764 [2013]

UK Citizens Online Democracy
Registered: 1 Jul 1999 *Employees:* 25 *Volunteers:* 6
Tel: 020 3239 0725 *Website:* mysociety.org
Activities: Other charitable purposes
Address: UK Citizens Online Democracy, 483 Green Lanes, London, N13 4BS
Trustees: James Cronin, Manar Hussain, Ms Rachel Emily Rank, Jonathan Flowers, Owen Blacker, Tony Burton, Nanjira Sambuli
Income: £1,384,948 [2017]; £1,258,866 [2016]; £1,391,297 [2015]; £1,574,152 [2014]; £840,781 [2013]

UK Community Foundations
Registered: 11 Oct 1991 *Employees:* 10
Tel: 020 7841 4380 *Website:* communityfoundations.org.uk
Activities: General charitable purposes; education, training; economic, community development, employment
Address: Unit 1.04, Piano House, 9 Brighton Terrace, London, SW9 8DJ
Trustees: Mr Trevor Ernest James, Mr Colin John Seccombe, Mr Arthur Roberts, Mr Stephen Parsons, Mr John Robert Williamson, Mr Tom Ward, Mrs Laura Margaret Keen, Ms Jan Garrill, Mrs Jane Alicia Moss, Mr David Sheepshanks, Mr John Denis Nickson, Mr Stephen Singleton, Ms Victoria Miles, Mr Alun Evans, Ms Martha Wilkinson-Browne, Ms Niamh Goggin
Income: £10,245,000 [2017]; £10,000,000 [2016]; £7,271,000 [2015]; £11,427,000 [2014]; £7,737,000 [2013]

UK Friends of Yale University Limited
Registered: 25 May 2007
Tel: 020 7502 2813
Activities: Education, training; arts, culture, heritage, science
Address: 19 Norcott Road, London, N16 7EJ
Trustees: Mr Richard Jacob Burston, Ms Dina Dommett, Mr Benjamin Polak, Mr Charles Lubar, Mrs Joan O'Neill
Income: £1,409,491 [2017]; £624,789 [2016]; £456,424 [2015]; £1,172,028 [2014]; £1,129,142 [2013]

UK Health Forum
Registered: 27 Apr 1990 *Employees:* 18
Tel: 020 7832 6920 *Website:* ukhealthforum.org.uk
Activities: The advancement of health or saving of lives
Address: UK Health Forum, Fleetbank House, 2-6 Salisbury Square, London, EC4Y 8JX
Trustees: Lord Nic Rea MD DCH FRCGP, Ms Katharine Jenner, Mr Oliver William Smith, Mr Declan Cunnane, Professor Joy Townsend, Dom Ahern, Dr Fiona Adshead, Mr Robin Ireland
Income: £1,867,522 [2017]; £1,360,739 [2016]; £1,714,765 [2015]; £2,096,458 [2014]; £1,978,366 [2013]

UK Online Giving Foundation
Registered: 16 Dec 2015
Tel: 01285 719592 *Website:* ukogf.org
Activities: General charitable purposes
Address: The UK Online Giving Foundation, 6 Trull Farm Buildings, Trull, Tetbury, Glos, GL8 8SQ
Trustees: Mrs Johanna Tompsett, Mrs Andrea Cutler, Mrs Maria-Magdalena Duddridge
Income: £7,665,805 [2017]

UK Sailing Academy
Registered: 6 May 1988 *Employees:* 110 *Volunteers:* 3
Tel: 01983 203004 *Website:* uksa.org
Activities: Education, training; advancement of health or saving of lives; disability; amateur sport
Address: UKSA, Arctic Road, Cowes, Isle of Wight, PO31 7PQ
Trustees: Mr David John Lister MBE, Mr Anthony Greener, Ms Claudia Margaret Suckling MA, Dawn Haig-Thomas, Mrs Claire E B Locke, Mr David Royce, Mr Richard Lawrence Palmer, Mr William Michael Maxwell Garnett, Mr Marc Giraudon
Income: £6,287,227 [2017]; £5,919,469 [2016]; £5,100,913 [2015]; £5,372,832 [2014]; £5,650,531 [2013]

UK Youth
Registered: 27 Jul 2005 *Employees:* 80 *Volunteers:* 100
Tel: 020 3137 3817 *Website:* ukyouth.org
Activities: Education, training; disability; amateur sport; environment, conservation, heritage
Address: 483 & 485 Liverpool Road, London, N7 8PG
Trustees: Mark Wakefield, Mrs Anne Stoneham, Duncan MacIntyre, Asif Noorani, Mr Graeme Swan, Miss Rebecca Lianne McCartney, Mr Alexander Edward Edge, Mr Iain Rodney McDougall, Mr Yui Chit Daniel Chan, Mr Wayne Bulpitt, Mrs Diana Organ, Kate Boddington, Chris Hindley, Miss Kamara Natalie Bennett, Mr Aaron Anthony Jose Hasan D'Souza, Mr Benjamin Peter Jessup, Mr Matthew John Price
Income: £5,707,000 [2017]; £5,334,000 [2016]; £8,557,000 [2015]; £7,902,122 [2014]; £5,187,543 [2013]

UKCISA
Registered: 8 Jan 2003 *Employees:* 17
Tel: 020 7288 4330 *Website:* ukcisa.org.uk
Activities: Education, training
Address: UKCISA, 9-17 St Albans Place, London, N1 0NX
Trustees: Dr Nora Henriette De Leeuw, Mr Paul Angelo Rossi, James Kennedy, Mrs Katherine Clare Dodd, Mr Alexander John Semple Proudfoot, Mr Mark Collier, Dr Sonal Minocha, Ms Sharon Bell, Mrs Laura Rose-Troup, Mr Mark Allen, Mr Timothy Scott Benford, Mr Yinbo Yu, Miss Marianne Julie Davies, Professor Koen Lamberts, Mr Alan MacKay, Ms Elizabeth Huckle, Ms Lynsey Benton, Miss Ruth Sweeney
Income: £1,446,232 [2017]; £1,438,780 [2016]; £1,367,336 [2015]; £1,378,775 [2014]; £1,344,769 [2013]

UKGBC
Registered: 24 Mar 2010 *Employees:* 22
Tel: 020 7580 0623 *Website:* ukgbc.org
Activities: Education, training; environment, conservation, heritage
Address: The Building Centre, 26 Store Street, London, WC1E 7BT
Trustees: Sunand Prasad, Ms Stephanie Hilborne, Alison Nimmo, Alexandra Willey, Ms Claire Elizabeth Battles, Mr Richard John Willmott, Mr William Hughes, Victoria Quinlan, Mr Alastair Thomas Graham Bell, Mr David John Gratiaen Partridge
Income: £1,976,065 [2017]; £1,969,971 [2016]; £2,018,647 [2015]; £1,778,886 [2014]; £1,817,984 [2013]

UKH Foundation
Registered: 16 Feb 2015 *Employees:* 11
Activities: The advancement of health or saving of lives; disability; other charitable purposes
Address: Lancashire Gate, 21 Tiviot Dale, Stockport, Cheshire, SK1 1TD
Trustees: Mr Andrew Redfern, Mrs Julie Hulme, Mr David Charles Udall, Mr Stephen Bell
Income: £3,480,823 [2016]; £6,167,765 [2015]

UOHC Foundation Ltd
Registered: 12 Nov 2015 *Employees:* 50
Tel: 020 8782 1600
Activities: General charitable purposes; religious activities
Address: York House, Empire Way, Wembley, Middlesex, HA9 0FQ
Trustees: Mr Jacob Schonberg, Mr Michael Lobenstein, Mr Henri Konig, Mr Yehudah Baumgarten
Income: £8,140,463 [2016]

UOHC Properties Ltd
Registered: 12 Nov 2015
Tel: 020 8782 1600
Activities: General charitable purposes; religious activities
Address: York House, Empire Way, Wembley, Middlesex, HA9 0FQ
Trustees: Mr Jacob Stern, Mr Samuel Sinitsky, Mr Morris Lobenstein, Mr Robert Grussgot
Income: £1,260,052 [2016]

UOHC Supervision Ltd
Registered: 12 Nov 2015 *Employees:* 47
Tel: 020 8782 1600
Activities: Religious activities
Address: York House, Empire Way, Wembley, Middlesex, HA9 0FQ
Trustees: Mr David Lobenstein, Mr Sydney Samuel Sinitsky, Mr Alexander Hochhauser, Mr Gerald Sinitsky
Income: £2,782,198 [2016]

USWSU
Registered: 29 Aug 2013 *Employees:* 172 *Volunteers:* 900
Tel: 01443 483500 *Website:* uswsu.com
Activities: General charitable purposes; education, training; advancement of health or saving of lives; prevention or relief of poverty; accommodation, housing; amateur sport
Address: University of South Wales, Students Union, Forest Grove, Treforest, Pontypridd, Rhondda Cynon Taf, CF37 1UF
Trustees: Miss Kim Louise Brown, Mrs Anna Elizabeth Morgan, Mr Oliver Douglas Kennedy-Britten, Mr Daniel Bowen, Miss Megan Rachael Wilson, Miss Charlotte Rose Billinghurst
Income: £2,817,054 [2017]; £2,700,160 [2016]; £2,942,328 [2015]; £2,608,223 [2014]

UTRY
Registered: 12 Nov 2013
Tel: 07971 487438
Activities: General charitable purposes; education, training; religious activities
Address: 79 Darenth Road, London, N16 6ES
Trustees: Mr Alta Mordechai Fogel, Mr Shulum Cik, Mr Berish Berger
Income: £2,016,181 [2017]; £2,236,486 [2016]; £1,138,511 [2015]; £443,002 [2014]

UW Giving
Registered: 27 Jun 1985
Tel: 0151 227 5177 *Website:* lcvs.org.uk
Activities: General charitable purposes
Address: 151 Dale Street, Liverpool, L2 2AH
Trustees: Mr Harry Williams, Liverpool Charity and Voluntary Services, Prof Hilary Enid Russell
Income: £2,171,704 [2017]; £1,918,438 [2016]; £2,263,890 [2015]; £2,276,763 [2014]; £2,321,907 [2013]

UWE Students' Union
Registered: 25 Jul 2011 *Employees:* 363 *Volunteers:* 1,045
Tel: 07958 784732 *Website:* thestudentsunion.co.uk
Activities: General charitable purposes; education, training; prevention or relief of poverty; accommodation, housing; amateur sport
Address: Yew Tree Cottage, Newland, Coleford, Glos, GL16 8NP
Trustees: Mrs Clare Davidson, Ms Sian Hampson, Mr Zain Choudhry, Miss Erin Mills, Ms Mariam Amini, Mr Christopher Clements, Mr Jamie Thomas Jordon, Mr Bahkai Wynter, Mr William Omoma
Income: £6,051,079 [2017]; £5,905,208 [2016]; £5,543,194 [2015]; £5,231,224 [2014]; £5,183,575 [2013]

The Ufton Court Educational Trust
Registered: 7 Nov 2006 *Employees:* 38 *Volunteers:* 125
Tel: 0118 983 2099 *Website:* uftoncourt.co.uk
Activities: Education, training; arts, culture, heritage, science; animals; environment, conservation, heritage
Address: Ufton Court, Green Lane, Ufton Nervet, Reading, Berks, RG7 4HD
Trustees: Mr Nicholas Burrows, Mr Jason Chaffer, Mrs Mary Riall, Mr G Morris, Charlie Clare, Edward Crookes, Geoffrey Eversfield
Income: £1,568,634 [2017]; £1,446,478 [2016]; £1,145,236 [2015]; £1,117,139 [2014]; £1,683,259 [2013]

The Ulverscroft Foundation
Registered: 13 Dec 1972 *Employees:* 130
Tel: 0116 236 1595 *Website:* ulverscroft-foundation.org.uk
Activities: The advancement of health or saving of lives; disability
Address: The Ulverscroft Foundation, The Green, Bradgate Road, Anstey, Leicester, LE7 7FU
Trustees: John Sandford-Smith, Mr Robert Paul Gent, Mr John Laccohee Bush, Mr Roger John Crooks, Pat Beech, Mr Rupert Anthony Clarke
Income: £11,389,916 [2016]; £11,598,477 [2015]; £12,053,497 [2014]; £11,696,292 [2013]; £11,669,882 [2012]

The Underfall Yard Trust
Registered: 2 Nov 1994 *Employees:* 3 *Volunteers:* 55
Website: underfallboatyard.co.uk
Activities: General charitable purposes; arts, culture, heritage, science; environment, conservation, heritage; economic, community development, employment
Address: Bristol Marina Ltd, Hanover Place, Bristol, BS1 6UH
Trustees: Ian Wilkinson, Mr Richard Mark Rothwell, Nicola Watt, Mr Richard Michael Peter Holden, Mr Andrew Louis King, Mr James Durie, Mr Nils Arne Goran Ringer
Income: £1,156,200 [2017]; £1,618,789 [2016]; £1,064,031 [2015]; £73,247 [2014]; £92,225 [2013]

The Unicorn School Ltd
Registered: 4 Feb 1971 *Employees:* 30
Tel: 020 8948 3926 *Website:* unicornschool.org.uk
Activities: Education, training
Address: Unicorn School, 238 Kew Road, Richmond, Surrey, TW9 3JX
Trustees: Fiona Timmis, Mrs Elizabeth Ann McGinn, Mrs Sonya Branch, Mr Philip Hinton, Mr Geoffrey Bayliss, Mrs Jo Webbern, Mr Adrian Floyd, Mr Tony Julius, Mrs Victoria Woodhatch-Stuart, Mr Nicholas Jeffrey Wright, Mr John Paul O'Neill, Mr Paul Aubery
Income: £1,949,441 [2017]; £1,847,274 [2016]; £1,794,808 [2015]; £1,742,382 [2014]; £1,695,838 [2013]

The Unicorn School for The Dyslexic Child
Registered: 31 Jul 1998 *Employees:* 36 *Volunteers:* 6
Tel: 01235 530222 *Website:* unicornoxford.co.uk
Activities: Education, training
Address: 20 Marcham Road, Abingdon, Oxon, OX14 1AA
Trustees: Ms Natalie MacDonald, Mr Andrew Strivens, Ms Sophie Langdale, Mr Robin Askew, Mr Mark Chambers, Mr David Anderson, Ms Annie McNeile
Income: £1,537,254 [2017]; £1,295,894 [2016]; £1,198,864 [2015]; £1,191,977 [2014]; £1,202,452 [2013]

Union Chapel Project
Registered: 27 Mar 1992 *Employees:* 53 *Volunteers:* 65
Tel: 020 7101 0090 *Website:* unionchapel.org.uk
Activities: General charitable purposes; prevention or relief of poverty; arts, culture, heritage, science; environment, conservation, heritage; economic, community development, employment
Address: 19B Compton Terrace, London, N1 2UN
Trustees: Mr Philip Ian Walker, Ms Angela Cooper, Ms Kathryn Louise Dixon, Rev Karen Stallard, Mr Gordon Montgomery, Mr Thomas Linton-Smith
Income: £1,550,098 [2017]; £1,312,491 [2016]; £1,180,406 [2015]; £1,161,177 [2014]; £1,192,325 [2013]

The Union Jack Club
Registered: 14 Dec 1962 *Employees:* 154
Tel: 020 7902 6050 *Website:* ujclub.co.uk
Activities: Accommodation, housing
Address: Union Jack Club, Sandell Street, London, SE1 8UJ
Trustees: Air Commodore Colin Adams CBE AFC, Mrs Rachel Garside, Mr David Edward Peter Albert, Vice Admiral Sir Fabian Malbon KBE, Mrs Susanne V Swan, Mr John Jeremy Brown MBE, Vice Admiral Sir David George Steel KBE DL, Lieutenant Commander Nick Ashford FCA FS, Air Commodore Michael Barnes, Mr William Cowpe, Mr Peter E Davidson, Captain Timothy Martin OBE, Mr David Arthur Cooper MBA FCA, Air Commodore James E Linter OBE
Income: £8,912,739 [2016]; £7,858,778 [2015]; £7,819,651 [2014]; £7,395,973 [2013]; £6,846,092 [2012]

Union of Kingston Students
Registered: 23 Nov 2011 *Employees:* 40
Tel: 020 8417 6396 *Website:* kingstonstudents.net
Activities: Education, training; amateur sport; recreation; other charitable purposes
Address: 4 Roymount Court, Lovelace Road, Surbiton, Surrey, KT6 6NW
Trustees: Mr David Miles, Patrick Tatarian, Humah Akram, Mr Petar Lachev, Miss Kristina Bajoraite, Daisy Bow Du Toit, Ashley Smith, Miss Alayna Zangie, Mr Imad Ui Din Nazir, Mr Feisal Daud Haji
Income: £1,507,782 [2017]; £1,390,054 [2016]; £3,115,368 [2015]; £3,114,531 [2014]; £2,489,538 [2013]

The Union of The Sisters of Mercy of Great Britain
Registered: 30 Nov 1983 *Employees:* 87 *Volunteers:* 80
Tel: 020 7723 3221 *Website:* sistersofmercyunion.org.uk
Activities: Education, training; prevention or relief of poverty; religious activities
Address: Mercy Union Generalate, 11 Harewood Avenue, London, NW1 6LD
Trustees: Sister Philomena Bowers, Sister Geraldine Lawlor-Aka Mary Philomena, Sister Monica Killeen, Sister Evelyn Gallagher-Aka Ellen Kate, Sister Mary Horgan
Income: £5,271,273 [2017]; £4,925,149 [2016]; £11,922,848 [2015]; £6,300,106 [2014]; £6,136,622 [2013]

Union of UEA Students Limited
Registered: 28 Jul 2015 *Employees:* 545 *Volunteers:* 3,300
Tel: 01603 592181 *Website:* ueastudent.com
Activities: Education, training
Address: Union House, University of East Anglia, Norwich Research Park, Colney, Norwich, NR4 7TJ
Trustees: Kemi Watchorn, Mary Leishman, Ben Gibbins, Jack Robinson, Ravon Chhay, Stefano Asciana, Ian Gibson, Madeleine Colledge, Chris Ball, India Edwards, Camille Koosiyal, Euan Scott, Ruth Flaherty, Mae Kabore
Income: £12,275,000 [2017]; £10,433,000 [2016]

Unipol Student Homes
Registered: 17 Jul 1997 *Employees:* 51
Tel: 0113 243 0169 *Website:* unipol.org.uk
Activities: Education, training; accommodation, housing
Address: Unipol, 155-157 Woodhouse Lane, Leeds, LS2 3ED
Trustees: Paul Rogerson, Diane Pedder, Mr Andy Welsh, Ms Jenny Share, Rachael Elliott, Robert Sladdin, Meri Braziel, Mr Michael Lees, Ms Chloe Ivy Sparks, Mike Wilkinson, David Collett, Mr Ian Robertson, Mr Martin Rushworth, Ms Kelly-Anne Godkin, Priscilla Preston, Mr George Thomas David Bissett, Ms Rosalyn Sewell, Mr Chris James Warrington
Income: £10,778,894 [2017]; £9,184,498 [2016]; £8,838,659 [2015]; £8,785,318 [2014]; £11,012,569 [2013]

Unison Welfare
Registered: 12 Jul 1993 *Employees:* 8 *Volunteers:* 800
Tel: 020 7121 5620 *Website:* unison.org.uk
Activities: General charitable purposes; advancement of health or saving of lives; disability; prevention or relief of poverty
Address: Unison Centre, 130 Euston Road, London, NW1 2AY
Trustees: Ms Maureen Le Marinel, John Gray, Karen Poole, Karen Worsley, Lesley Discombe, Mr Andrew Douglas, Gordon McKay, Christine Tanner, Sian Stockham, Anthony Dockray
Income: £1,336,602 [2017]; £1,351,061 [2016]; £1,273,804 [2015]; £1,277,135 [2014]; £1,277,964 [2013]

The Unite Foundation
Registered: 21 May 2012 *Employees:* 2 *Volunteers:* 8
Tel: 0117 302 7241 *Website:* unitefoundation.co.uk
Activities: Education, training; accommodation, housing
Address: Unite Foundation, South Quay House, Temple Back, Bristol, BS1 6FL
Trustees: Jenny Shaw, Joe Lister, Mr Darren Ellis, Mr Harvey Gallagher, Mr Nicholas James Miller, Becca Bland, Sir Tim Wilson
Income: £1,403,672 [2017]; £1,494,748 [2016]; £1,193,118 [2015]; £851,502 [2014]; £500,000 [2013]

United Christian Broadcasters Limited
Registered: 26 Apr 1988 *Employees:* 107 *Volunteers:* 2,859
Tel: 01782 764954 *Website:* ucb.co.uk
Activities: General charitable purposes; education, training; religious activities
Address: United Christian Broadcasters, Westport Road, Stoke on Trent, Staffs, ST6 4JF
Trustees: Rev Alan Keith Scotland, Rev David Edwards, Mr Neil Elliott, Rev Diana Avlerey Stacey, Mr Simon McCrossan
Income: £8,055,790 [2016]; £9,139,823 [2015]; £8,616,052 [2014]; £8,845,767 [2013]; £8,835,937 [2012]

United Church Schools Foundation Ltd
Registered: 23 Dec 1973 *Employees:* 8,236
Tel: 01832 864477 *Website:* unitedlearning.org.uk
Activities: Education, training
Address: United Learning, Worldwide House, Thorpe Wood, Peterborough, PE3 6SB
Trustees: Mr Richard Greenhalgh, Mr Michael Litchfield, Dr Stephen Critchley, Mr Neil Davidson, Mr Ben Gordon, Mr Michael George, Mr Nigel Rhyl Robson
Income: £387,890,000 [2016]; £336,342,000 [2015]; £359,179,000 [2014]; £322,727,000 [2013]; £302,614,000 [2012]

The United Church Schools Trust
Registered: 21 Jan 1993 *Employees:* 2,405 *Volunteers:* 737
Tel: 01832 864477 *Website:* unitedlearning.org.uk
Activities: Education, training
Address: United Learning, Worldwide House, Thorpe Wood, Peterborough, PE3 6SB
Trustees: Mr Richard Greenhalgh, Mrs Sarah Squire, Mr Michael John Litchfield, Mr Ben Gordon, Dr Rosalind Given-Wilson, Ms Mary Curnock Cook
Income: £105,284,000 [2016]; £97,741,000 [2015]; £91,994,000 [2014]; £88,560,000 [2013]; £84,932,000 [2012]

United Counties Agricultural and Hunters Society
Registered: 4 Dec 1973 *Employees:* 3
Tel: 01267 232141 *Website:* unitedcounties.co.uk
Activities: Education, training; disability; arts, culture, heritage, science; amateur sport; animals; environment, conservation, heritage
Address: United Counties Agricultural & Hunters Society, The Showground, Llysonnen Road, Carmarthen, Dyfed, SA33 5DR
Trustees: Mr David Lloyd, Mr Robert Evans, Mr Alex Warlow, Mr Hywel Griffiths, Mr David Davies, Mr Jeremy John, Mr Lynn Davies, Mr John James, Mr Norman Evans, Mr Daniel John Bryan Thomas, Mr Roger Evans
Income: £1,201,715 [2016]; £197,544 [2015]; £323,215 [2014]; £211,546 [2013]; £207,644 [2012]

United Jewish Israel Appeal

Registered: 10 Jan 1997 *Employees:* 60 *Volunteers:* 134
Tel: 020 7424 6400 *Website:* ujia.org
Activities: General charitable purposes; education, training; advancement of health or saving of lives; prevention or relief of poverty; religious activities; arts, culture, heritage, science
Address: 1 Torriano Mews, London, NW5 2RZ
Trustees: Jonathan Morris, Mr Robert Randall, Warren Persky, Miss Samantha Leek QC, Mrs Louise Jacobs, Mr Brian May, Mr Marc Cave, Mrs Nicola Wertheim, Mr Stuart Levy, Ruth Green, Marc Lester, Melvin Berwald, Mrs Karen Goodkind, Hilton Nathanson, Mr Steven Kaye, Mr Miles Webber
Income: £9,916,000 [2017]; £10,241,000 [2016]; £10,130,000 [2015]; £10,745,000 [2014]; £10,180,000 [2013]

The United Kingdom Committee for Unicef

Registered: 26 Nov 1998 *Employees:* 359 *Volunteers:* 150
Tel: 020 7375 6009 *Website:* unicef.org.uk
Activities: General charitable purposes; education, training; advancement of health or saving of lives; disability; prevention or relief of poverty; overseas aid, famine relief; economic, community development, employment; human rights, religious or racial harmony, equality or diversity
Address: Unicef UK, Unicef House, 30a Great Sutton Street, London, EC1V 0DU
Trustees: Baroness Brinton, Ms Ilse Howling, Sir Tony Redmond, Margaret Cund, Baroness Worthington, Justin Cooke, Alex Connock, Professor Surinder Sharma, Sarah Davis, Professor Martin Woodhead, Steven Day, Caroline Underwood, Cosette Reczek
Income: £102,837,000 [2016]; £100,708,000 [2015]; £93,729,000 [2014]; £79,120,000 [2013]; £62,326,000 [2012]

The United Kingdom Council for Psychotherapy

Registered: 8 Oct 1996 *Employees:* 26 *Volunteers:* 300
Website: ukcp.org.uk
Activities: General charitable purposes; advancement of health or saving of lives
Address: United Kingdom Council for Psychotherapy, 2nd Floor, America House, 2 America Square, London, EC3N 2LU
Trustees: Mr Martin Pollecoff, Mr Keith Carlton, Mr Andy Cottom, Mr John Loughrey, Suzy Greaves, Ms Jacqueline McCouat, Ms Pat Hunt, Mr Neil Robertson, Mr Bob Cooke, Ms Nasima Khanom
Income: £2,166,865 [2017]; £2,104,172 [2016]; £2,033,405 [2015]; £2,051,616 [2014]; £1,491,517 [2013]

The United Kingdom Islamic Mission

Registered: 6 Feb 1967 *Employees:* 48 *Volunteers:* 1,480
Tel: 020 7387 2157 *Website:* ukim.org
Activities: Education, training; prevention or relief of poverty; overseas aid, famine relief; religious activities
Address: 202 North Gower Street, London, NW1 2LY
Trustees: Mr Mohammad Afzal, Mr Jamshed Khan, Mr Maqsood Anwar, Mr Ziaul Haq, Mr Mohammed Riaz, Mr Abdul Hamid Bhatti, Mr Mohammad Sajjad Amin, Dr Irfan Jehangir, Sakander Mirza, Mr Amar Khan, Mr Muhammad Saqib, Mr Mahboob Ur Rasul Qamar, Dr Fiaz Hussain, Mr Mujahid Hussain, Mr Nafis Ahmed Lodhi, Mr Abdul Hamid, Mr Abdul Haq Mian, Mr Ghufran Mehmood, Mr Mahmood Hussain, Mr Zamir Ahmad, Mrs Rabia Sadique, Mr Waqar Ahmad, Mr Syed Shaukat Ali, Mr Shafqat Mahmood, Mr Mohammad Afzal Malik, Mrs Nasreen Saiad, Mr Rohan Bin Shams, Mr Tariq Ali, Dr Javed Hussain Gill
Income: £9,693,330 [2017]; £8,137,883 [2016]; £7,652,278 [2015]; £5,808,082 [2014]; £5,526,801 [2013]

United Kingdom Mathematics Trust

Registered: 11 Nov 1996 *Employees:* 12 *Volunteers:* 400
Tel: 0113 343 2339 *Website:* ukmt.org.uk
Activities: Education, training
Address: Secretary, UK Mathematics Trust, School of Mathematics, University of Leeds, Leeds, LS2 9JT
Trustees: Dr Christopher Budd, Geoff Smith, Professor Alastair Rucklidge, Dr Vicky Neale, Mr Gerald Leversha, Mr Fraser Ross Heywood, Mr Graham Keniston-Cooper, Mr Mark Knapton, Dr David Crawford, Mrs Anne Baker, Mr Steve Mulligan, Mr Robert James Gazet, Mrs Rachel Mary Dorris, Dr Calum Kilgour, Miss Jenny Ramsden
Income: £1,251,129 [2017]; £1,193,224 [2016]; £1,151,348 [2015]; £1,254,950 [2014]; £988,646 [2013]

United Kingdom Sepsis Trust Limited

Registered: 10 Oct 2014 *Employees:* 9 *Volunteers:* 250
Tel: 0800 389 6255 *Website:* sepsistrust.org
Activities: The advancement of health or saving of lives
Address: 36 Bennetts Hill, Birmingham, B2 5SN
Trustees: Mr Richard John Harris, Mr David Coleman, Mark Cawley, Mr Julian Hull, Mr Philip Harrold, Mr Nicholas Randle
Income: £1,445,765 [2017]; £423,275 [2016]

United Lincolnshire Hospitals NHS Trust Charitable Fund

Registered: 17 Sep 1996
Tel: 01522 597584 *Website:* ulh.nhs.uk
Activities: The advancement of health or saving of lives
Address: United Lincolnshire Hospitals NHS, Lincoln County Hospital, Greetwell Road, Lincoln, LN2 5QY
Trustees: Mr Keith Darwin, Mr John Barber, Mrs Penny Owston, Mrs Kathleen Truscott, Professor Steve Barnett, Mr David Pratt, Mr Timothy Staniland, Mrs Gillian Ponder, Dr Suneil Kapadia, Mr Paul Boocock, Mrs Michelle Rhodes, Mr Martin Rayson, Mr Jan Sobieraj, Mr Kevin Turner, Mrs Sarah Dunnett, Professor Dean Fathers, Mr Ron Buchanan, Mr Geoffrey Hayward, Dr Paul Grassby, Ms Elizabeth Jane Lewington, Miss Pauleen Pratt, Mr Ian Warren, Mr Mark Brassington, United Lincolnshire Hospitals NHS Trust
Income: £1,356,751 [2017]; £1,174,909 [2016]; £848,680 [2015]; £736,724 [2014]; £742,964 [2013]

United Methodist Church (UK)

Registered: 11 Nov 2002 *Employees:* 11 *Volunteers:* 120
Tel: 07869 107083
Activities: Religious activities
Address: Joseph Creighton Close, Coventry, Warwicks, CV3 2QF
Trustees: Mr Justice K L Nyakatawa, Mr Tapiwa Muchenje, Miss Mwazvita Marange, Mrs Angeline Ishemunyoro, Mrs Karen Manyika, Mr Jacques Muranda, Mr Robert Humphrey Mutungamiri
Income: £1,042,243 [2016]; £834,895 [2015]; £849,866 [2014]; £634,868 [2013]; £937,872 [2012]

United Nations Association International Service
Registered: 17 Apr 1998 *Employees:* 43 *Volunteers:* 23
Tel: 01904 647799 *Website:* internationalservice.org.uk
Activities: Education, training; advancement of health or saving of lives; disability; prevention or relief of poverty; accommodation, housing; environment, conservation, heritage; economic, community development; employment; human rights, religious or racial harmony, equality or diversity
Address: Second Floor, Rougier House, 5 Rougier Street, York, YO1 6HZ
Trustees: Mrs Naomi Anne Passman, Mr Robert Dignen, Professor Paul Richard Gready, Mr Callum Grant Northcote, Mrs Nancy Redpath, Miss Kay Francis Hyde, Mr Liam Conlon, Rev Lukas Njenga, Professor Jean Grugel, Miss Carla Michal Sayer MA, Mr Brian Keith Rockliffe
Income: £2,260,043 [2017]; £2,615,911 [2016]; £2,697,238 [2015]; £2,578,453 [2014]; £2,099,396 [2013]

United Purpose
Registered: 15 Dec 1976 *Employees:* 686 *Volunteers:* 43
Tel: 029 2022 0066 *Website:* united-purpose.org
Activities: Education, training; advancement of health or saving of lives; prevention or relief of poverty; overseas aid, famine relief
Address: United Purpose, 14 Cathedral Road, Cardiff, CF11 9LJ
Trustees: Ms Nicola Mary Mushet, Mr Peter Ayres, Mr Adam Wynne, Mr Steven Marshall, Mrs Ceri Briggs, Mr Alan Davies, Mr Martin Davidson, Mr Hadi Husani, David Bull
Income: £30,272,470 [2017]; £20,704,634 [2016]; £19,252,682 [2015]; £23,182,149 [2014]; £14,469,971 [2013]

The United Reformed Church (Eastern Province) Trust
Registered: 25 Jul 1966 *Employees:* 5 *Volunteers:* 26
Website: urc-eastern.org.uk
Activities: Accommodation, housing; religious activities
Address: United Reformed Church, 36 Duxford Road, Whittlesford, Cambridge, CB22 4ND
Trustees: Professor David Thompson, Rev Janet Elizabeth Tollington, Mr Keir Hounsome, Mr Clifford Patten, Mr Gilbert Heathcote, Rev Paul Whittle, Mr Andrew East
Income: £1,890,742 [2016]; £1,941,258 [2015]; £2,181,548 [2014]; £1,048,362 [2013]; £677,757 [2012]

The United Reformed Church (Northern Province) Trust Ltd.
Registered: 16 Oct 2009 *Employees:* 7 *Volunteers:* 12
Tel: 0191 232 1168 *Website:* urc-northernsynod.org
Activities: Religious activities
Address: 4 College Lane, Newcastle upon Tyne, NE1 8JJ
Trustees: John Forrest, David Grosch-Miller, Peter Matthew, Tony Haws, Jane Tomlin, Carol Hogg, Mike Louis, Jo Kennedy, Andrew Hamnett, Ian Buchanan, Heather Finlayson
Income: £1,551,810 [2016]; £1,054,043 [2015]; £1,016,469 [2014]; £1,221,362 [2013]; £483,119 [2012]

The United Reformed Church (South Western Synod) Incorporated
Registered: 21 Mar 1978 *Employees:* 10 *Volunteers:* 10
Tel: 01392 876744 *Website:* urcsouthwest.org.uk
Activities: Religious activities
Address: 21 Barton Close, Exton, Exeter, EX3 0PE
Trustees: Mr David John Hayden, Mrs Maria Mills, Dr Ian Harrison, Rev Ruth Josephine Whitehead, Rev Christopher Charles Baillie, Rev Donald MacAlister, Rev Dick Gray, Mrs Gwen Margaret Jennings, Rev Lythan Elisabeth Nevard, Sandra Lloydlangston, Jill Stidson
Income: £2,461,637 [2016]; £384,058 [2015]; £736,271 [2014]; £805,906 [2013]; £428,457 [2012]

The United Reformed Church (Southern Synod) Trust Limited
Registered: 14 Apr 1981 *Employees:* 8 *Volunteers:* 14
Tel: 020 8688 3730 *Website:* urcsouthern.org.uk
Activities: Religious activities
Address: Synod Office, East Croydon URC, Addiscombe Grove, Croydon, Surrey, CR0 5LP
Trustees: Revd Michael Davies, Mr David Henry Walters, Rev Nicola Furley-Smith, Rev Derrick Dzandu-Hedidor, Mr John Denison, Mr Alan David Kirby, Rev Helen Amy Elizabeth Warmington, Rev George Donald Watt, Rev Bridget Jane Banks, Miss Linda Margaret Austin
Income: £2,034,017 [2016]; £4,644,254 [2015]; £2,611,180 [2014]; £5,512,041 [2013]; £3,014,664 [2012]

The United Reformed Church (Wessex) Trust Limited
Registered: 7 Jul 1981 *Employees:* 9
Tel: 023 8067 4515 *Website:* urcwessex.org.uk
Activities: Religious activities
Address: 120 Alma Road, Southampton, SO14 6UW
Trustees: Dr David Richard Page, Mrs Margaret Rose Carrick Smith, Mr Colin Forbes MacBean, Mr Raymond Michael Dunnett, Reverend Nigel John William Appleton, Mr Michael Stewart Liddle, Mrs Susan Anne Brown, Mr Gerald Prosser, Reverend Julian James Macro, Mr Peter James Stevenson, Mr Peter Malcolm Pay, Mr Andrew Naysmith Gibb, Reverend Clare Downing, Dr Christopher David Evans, Reverend Dr Romilly Wakefield Micklem
Income: £1,288,187 [2016]; £1,538,348 [2015]; £1,076,453 [2014]; £3,418,574 [2013]; £1,823,568 [2012]

The United Reformed Church (West Midlands) Trust Limited
Registered: 14 Dec 1977 *Employees:* 10
Tel: 0121 783 1177 *Website:* urcwestmidlands.org.uk
Activities: General charitable purposes; religious activities
Address: Synod Office, Digbeth in the-Field URC, Moat Lane, Yardley, Birmingham, B26 1TW
Trustees: Rev Steven Mark Faber, Mr Keith James Thomas, Mr Stephen Mark Powell, Mr Terence Richard Dicker, Dr Anthony Frederick Jeans, Mr David Black, G William Potter, Mr Anthony Mottram, Mrs Margaret Marshall, Rev David Michael Walton
Income: £1,874,300 [2016]; £1,186,427 [2015]; £1,687,790 [2014]; £622,589 [2013]; £1,481,058 [2012]

United Reformed Church Thames North Synod Charities
Registered: 13 Apr 2010 *Employees:* 7
Tel: 020 7799 5000 *Website:* urcthamesnorth.org.uk
Activities: General charitable purposes; education, training; prevention or relief of poverty; religious activities
Address: St Paul's URC, Newton Road, London, W2 5LS
Trustees: Mr Brian Michael Hosier, Rev Dr Andrew Prasad, Rev John Danso, Rev Ann Woodhurst, Mr Anthony Alderman, Mr Anthony Obi-Ezekpazu, Mrs Tina Ashitey, Bim Oniwinde
Income: £2,999,000 [2016]; £976,000 [2015]; £1,319,000 [2014]; £2,791,000 [2013]; £1,023,000 [2012]

United Reformed Church Trust
Registered: 22 Dec 2009 *Employees:* 98
Website: urc.org.uk
Activities: Religious activities
Address: United Reformed Church, 86 Tavistock Place, London, WC1H 9RT
Trustees: Neil MacKenzie, Rev Michael Hopkins, Rev Michael Davies, Rev Richard Gray, Val Morrison, Mr Ian Harrison, Mrs Jane Baird, Mr Peter Pay, Mr Alan Yates, Mr Emmanuel Osae, Kevin Watson, Mr Ian Hardie, Margaret Thompson, Alastair Forsyth, Rev John Proctor, Mr Andrew Summers, Ms Catriona Wheeler, Mr Andrew Weston
Income: £26,693,000 [2016]; £28,638,000 [2015]; £27,701,000 [2014]; £27,286,000 [2013]; £29,954,000 [2012]

United Response
Registered: 2 Oct 1973 *Employees:* 3,877
Tel: 020 8246 5200 *Website:* unitedresponse.org.uk
Activities: Disability; accommodation, housing
Address: United Response, Highland House, 165 The Broadway, Wimbledon, London, SW19 1NE
Trustees: Dr Katherine Rake, Mrs Sandra Beryl Hannington, Mrs Karie Clifford, Mr David Charles Aitman, Miss Bronagh Mary Scott, Mr Alastair Ian Ballantyne, Mr Malcolm McCaig, Mr Charles Martin Garthwaite, Mrs Jagelman, Mr Maurice Edward Rumbold, Mr David Arthur Willis, Mrs Helen Margaret England, Mr William Richard Hodson
Income: £93,703,000 [2017]; £79,077,000 [2016]; £77,206,000 [2015]; £76,992,000 [2014]; £76,776,000 [2013]

The United Society
Registered: 26 Aug 1964 *Employees:* 25 *Volunteers:* 100
Tel: 020 7921 2200 *Website:* uspg.org.uk
Activities: General charitable purposes; education, training; advancement of health or saving of lives; prevention or relief of poverty; overseas aid, famine relief; religious activities; other charitable purposes
Address: Harling House, 47-51 Great Suffolk Street, London, SE1 0BS
Trustees: The Revd Canon Christopher Chivers, Dr Jane Watkeys, Revd Joabe Gomes Cavalcanti, Revd Dr Daphne Mary Green, Bishop Francis John McDowell, Ms Leah Skouby, The Revd Dr Olubunmi Ayobami Fagbemi, Mrs Rosemary Kempsell, Mr John Chilver, Mr Martin Canning, Mr Richard Mark Barrett, Mr Christopher Thomas Rogers
Income: £4,028,000 [2016]; £3,976,000 [2015]; £3,364,000 [2014]; £3,752,000 [2013]; £3,816,000 [2012]

United St Saviour's Charity
Registered: 13 May 2004 *Employees:* 8
Tel: 020 7089 9014 *Website:* ustsc.org.uk
Activities: The prevention or relief of poverty; accommodation, housing
Address: United St Saviour's Charity, St Saviours House, 39-41 Union Street, London, SE1 1SD
Trustees: Ms Emma Snow FCA, Mrs Camilla McGibbon, Mr Richard Heaton CB, Lord Roy Kennedy, Ms Claire Treanor, Mr Shane Holland, Mrs Julia Tybura, Mr Stephen Burns, Ms Nicola Steuer, Dr Ben Johnson
Income: £1,974,022 [2017]; £1,596,602 [2016]; £1,476,115 [2015]; £1,432,249 [2014]; £1,512,301 [2013]

United Synagogue
Registered: 2 Jun 1965 *Employees:* 803 *Volunteers:* 1,000
Tel: 020 8343 8989 *Website:* theus.org.uk
Activities: Religious activities
Address: 305 Ballards Lane, North Finchley, London, N12 8GB
Trustees: Mr Michael Howard Goldstein, Prof Andrew Howard Eric Eder, Ms Fleurise Luder, Mrs Leonie Lewis, Mr Barry Clive Shaw, Mrs Doreen Samuels, Mr Maxwell John Nisner, Dr Claire Lemer, Mr Saul David Tayor
Income: £41,478,000 [2016]; £50,627,000 [2015]; £33,100,000 [2014]; £35,605,000 [2013]; £33,308,000 [2012]

United Talmudical Associates Ltd
Registered: 18 Mar 1987 *Employees:* 3 *Volunteers:* 2
Tel: 020 8806 8283
Activities: General charitable purposes; education, training; advancement of health or saving of lives; prevention or relief of poverty; religious activities
Address: 33 Oldhill Street, London, N16 6LR
Trustees: Mr J Weinberger, Mr S Seidenfeld, Mr Simcha Dov Joseph
Income: £23,150,996 [2017]; £15,715,929 [2016]; £12,830,303 [2015]; £11,533,695 [2014]; £10,553,026 [2013]

United Utilities Trust Fund
Registered: 24 Feb 2005
Tel: 0845 179 1791 *Website:* uutf.org.uk
Activities: The prevention or relief of poverty
Address: United Utilities Trust Fund, Emmanuel Court, 12-14 Mill Street, Sutton Coldfield, W Midlands, B72 1TJ
Trustees: Mrs Deborah Morton, Mr Simon Dewsnip, Lynne Jane Heath, Mr Alastair Richards, Robert Thomas Harrison, Sandra McCaughley
Income: £5,026,410 [2017]; £6,212,655 [2016]; £6,801,683 [2015]; £7,001,894 [2014]; £5,022,513 [2013]

United Westminster Schools Foundation
Registered: 25 May 1971 *Employees:* 383
Tel: 020 7828 3055 *Website:* westminstergreycoat.org
Activities: Education, training
Address: United Westminster Schools, 57 Palace Street, London, SW1E 5HJ
Trustees: Mr Christopher Saunders MA, Mr Francis Abbott BA, Mrs Jill Clark, Mr Christopher Vyse, Mrs Carol Rider BSc, Alderman Robert Howard MA MSc, Vice-Admiral Peter Dunt CB DL, Elizabeth Lady Vallance JP PhD, Mr Tara Douglas-Home, Mrs Pat Sales JP BA MSc FCollP HonFCollT, Mr Jonathan Noakes MA, Mrs Gill Swaine BSc MEd, Mr Markus Jaigirder MA FRGS
Income: £29,506,000 [2017]; £27,981,000 [2016]; £26,704,000 [2015]; £23,850,000 [2014]; £22,720,000 [2013]

The United World College of The Atlantic Limited
Registered: 4 Oct 1962 *Employees:* 137 *Volunteers:* 10
Tel: 01446 799014 *Website:* atlanticcollege.org
Activities: Education, training
Address: United World College of The Atlantic Ltd, St Donat's Castle, St Donat's, Llantwit Major, Vale of Glamorgan, CF61 1WF
Trustees: Lady Joanna Knatchbull, Ms Jill Longson, Mr David John Stacey, Mr Manfred Johan Schepers, Mr Oscar Strugstad, Mr Driek Desmet, Mr Michael John Hilary Trickey, Professor Sir Adrian Webb, Professor Jonathan Michie, Mrs Sian Jones MRICS, Mr Ian Stuart Cooper, Mr Lutfey Siddiqi
Income: £13,234,000 [2017]; £14,832,000 [2016]; £12,734,000 [2015]; £11,553,000 [2014]; £11,165,081 [2013]

The United World Colleges (International)
Registered: 8 Nov 1967 *Employees:* 20 *Volunteers:* 10
Website: uwc.org
Activities: General charitable purposes; education, training
Address: United World College, 17-21 Emerald Street, London, WC1N 3QN
Trustees: Mr Christopher James Edwards, Mr Paul Brynsrud, Ms Veronika Zonabend, Mr Ulhas Yargop, Mr Laurence Nodder, Mrs Eva Eschenbruch, Mr Colin Habgood, Mr Peter Howe, Sir John Daniel, Ms Maria Ines Kavamura, Marco Provencio, Mr Christian Hodeige, Mrs Laura Carone
Income: £4,727,000 [2017]; £2,958,000 [2016]; £2,397,000 [2015]; £2,272,000 [2014]; £1,680,000 [2013]

United World Schools
Registered: 12 May 2009 *Employees:* 7 *Volunteers:* 20
Tel: 020 3735 9181 *Website:* unitedworldschools.org
Activities: Education, training; prevention or relief of poverty; economic, community development, employment
Address: Unit 138 South Bank House, Black Prince Road, London, SE1 7SJ
Trustees: Mr John Alun Siebert, Mr Stephen Burford Warshaw, Mr Fergus Stuart Brownlee, Mr Stuart Fletcher, Mr Christopher David Outram, Mrs Victoria Unwin, Mr Ronald Stewart Graham, Mr Matthew Lester
Income: £1,929,605 [2016]; £937,252 [2015]; £519,024 [2014]; £123,243 [2013]; £86,954 [2012]

Unity Leisure
Registered: 25 Jan 2012 *Employees:* 450
Tel: 01604 837341 *Website:* trilogyleisure.co.uk
Activities: Education, training; advancement of health or saving of lives; amateur sport; recreation
Address: 78 Robert Street, Northampton, NN1 3BJ
Trustees: Will Pope, Mr Christopher James Holmes, Mr Andrew Ellis, Mr Richard Aveling, Mr Simon John Denny, Mr Ashley Riley, Mr Paul Joseph Joyce, Mr Ian Leather, Mr Martin Thomas Sawyer, Mr Douglas Iles, Mr Peter John Windatt, Mrs Anna King, Mrs Anne Maarit Bland
Income: £6,546,238 [2017]; £6,097,136 [2016]; £5,565,168 [2015]; £5,503,368 [2014]; £5,304,968 [2013]

Unity Theatre
Registered: 19 May 1997 *Employees:* 19 *Volunteers:* 61
Tel: 0151 702 7361 *Website:* unitytheatreliverpool.co.uk
Activities: Arts, culture, heritage, science
Address: Unity Theatre, 1 Hope Place, Liverpool, L1 9BG
Trustees: Mr Richard Morgan, Mr Christopher Bliss, Christopher Hulme, Ms Marcia Jennings, Ms Kirsteen Connell, Ms Catrina Hewitson, Miss Ngunan Adamu, Mr Michael James Cavanagh
Income: £1,256,772 [2017]; £582,034 [2016]; £555,002 [2015]; £595,274 [2014]; £614,498 [2013]

The Universal Church of The Kingdom of God
Registered: 7 Feb 1995 *Employees:* 207 *Volunteers:* 2,376
Tel: 020 7686 6006 *Website:* uckg.org
Activities: General charitable purposes; education, training; prevention or relief of poverty; religious activities
Address: UCKG Help Centre, Rainbow Theatre, 232-238 Seven Sisters Road, London, N4 3NX
Trustees: Mr Rui Pedro Da Cunha Silva, Tiago De Jesus Silva Marques, Mr Paulo Alexandre Duarte Monteiro, Guilherme Munhoz, Mrs Audrey Tung De Medeiros, The Incorporated Trustees of The Univers
Income: £14,952,607 [2017]; £14,992,405 [2016]; £16,708,355 [2015]; £15,350,718 [2014]; £13,717,748 [2013]

Universal Pentecostal Church
Registered: 23 Sep 1985 *Volunteers:* 200
Tel: 020 7738 5566
Activities: Religious activities
Address: 20 Acre Lane, Brixton, London, SW2 5SG
Trustees: Sister Rachel George, Pastor Vaithialingam Rudran, Brother Asharoshan Selvarajah Chandradarshan, Mr Mark Jeyaseelan Abraham, Mrs Folasade Olayinka Lawson
Income: £1,354,882 [2017]; £1,385,518 [2016]; £1,279,125 [2015]; £1,240,766 [2014]; £1,793,011 [2013]

Universal Prayer Group Ministry
Registered: 13 Jan 1988 *Employees:* 16 *Volunteers:* 15
Tel: 020 8829 0080 *Website:* dominionchapel.org.uk
Activities: General charitable purposes; education, training; religious activities
Address: 9 The Broadway, High Road, London, N22 6DS
Trustees: Mr Jonah Kofi Mensah, Dr Sampson Kweku Boafo DD, Dr Kojo Menyah PhD, Mr Emmanuel Okhuegbe Oloke FCCA, Mr Joseph Kwadu Kwaw, Mr George Amoako-Prempeh FCCA, Dr Augustine Sibina Obaro RCPG
Income: £1,980,220 [2017]; £1,945,817 [2016]; £2,011,656 [2015]; £1,807,108 [2014]; £2,012,309 [2013]

Universities & Colleges Christian Fellowship
Registered: 26 Sep 1962 *Employees:* 97 *Volunteers:* 70
Tel: 01438 831163 *Website:* uccf.org.uk
Activities: Education, training; religious activities
Address: UCCF, Blue Boar House, 5 Blue Boar Street, Oxford, OX1 4EE
Trustees: Mr David Lilley, Mrs Joanne McKenzie, Rev John L Samuel, Rev Dafydd Job, Rev Raymond Brown, Mr Jacob Lucas, Dr Christopher Willmott, Miss Mary Currie, Rev Dr Robin Sydserff, Rev A W John Stevens, Mr Stephen Rigby
Income: £3,762,208 [2017]; £4,621,977 [2016]; £4,939,552 [2015]; £4,607,957 [2014]; £4,338,704 [2013]

Universities UK
Registered: 7 Dec 1990 *Employees:* 134
Tel: 020 7419 5473 *Website:* universitiesuk.ac.uk
Activities: Education, training
Address: Universities UK, Woburn House, 20-24 Tavistock Square, London, WC1H 9HQ
Trustees: Professor Alistair David Fitt, Professor Paul Joseph Boyle, Mr Nigel Martyn Carrington, Professor Janet Beer, Professor David Eastwood, Professor Paul O'Prey, Professor Andrea Mary Nolan, Professor David John Maguire, Professor Julie Elspeth Lydon, Baroness Valerie Amos, Mr Bill Rammell, Professor Gaoqing Max Lu, Professor Robert Alan Langlands, Professor Glynis Breakwell, Professor Julia Buckingham, Professor Anton Muscatelli, Professor Sally Louise Mapstone, Sir David Robert Bell, Professor Louise Mary Richardson, Professor Sir Steven Murray Smith, Professor Quintin Archibald McKellar, Debra Humphris, Professor Rama Shankaran Thirunamachandran, Professor Patrick Arthur Nixon
Income: £13,398,082 [2017]; £11,577,621 [2016]; £12,505,495 [2015]; £12,514,345 [2014]; £12,217,716 [2013]

The Universities and Colleges Admissions Service
Registered: 13 Aug 1993 *Employees:* 498
Tel: 01242 544842 *Website:* ucas.com
Activities: Education, training
Address: Rosehill, New Barn Lane, Cheltenham, Glos, GL52 3LZ
Trustees: Professor Sir Ian Diamond, Professor Bob Cryan, Sian Carr, David Ashton, Andy Forbes, Rob Behrens, Professor Joy Carter, Professor Colin Riordan, Steve Smith, Gerry Pennell, Professor Karen Stanton, Thomas Chambers
Income: £37,139,705 [2017]; £35,023,142 [2016]; £32,299,672 [2015]; £32,495,606 [2014]; £30,403,651 [2013]

Universities and Colleges Information Systems Association
Registered: 9 Apr 2015
Tel: 01865 283425 *Website:* ucisa.ac.uk
Activities: Education, training
Address: UCISA, University of Oxford, 13 Banbury Road, Oxford, OX2 6NN
Trustees: Adrian Ellison, Mr Drew Cook, Mr Dean Owen Phillips, Mr David Telford
Income: £1,322,483 [2016]

University College School, Hampstead
Registered: 23 Sep 1963 *Employees:* 294 *Volunteers:* 30
Tel: 020 7433 2140 *Website:* ucs.org.uk
Activities: General charitable purposes; education, training
Address: Frognal, Hampstead, London, NW3 6XH
Trustees: Professor Philippe Sands QC, Mr Simon Lewis, Dr Yogi Amin BSc MB ChB DA FRCA, Mr Rupert Bondy, Mr Sam Grodzinski QC, Ms Shirley Soskin, Mr Christopher Spooner, Mr Robert Gullifer MA, Professor Christopher Tyerman MA DPhil FRHist, Ms Elizabeth Bingham MIPA MABRP DBA, Mr Giovanni Spinella BA, Ms Smita Bora, Mr Eden Riche, Dr Saima Rana
Income: £23,968,000 [2017]; £23,072,000 [2016]; £23,001,000 [2015]; £21,349,689 [2014]; £20,564,000 [2013]

University College of Estate Management
Registered: 24 May 1963 *Employees:* 289
Tel: 0118 921 4682 *Website:* ucem.ac.uk
Activities: Education, training
Address: UCEM, Horizons, 60 Queen's Road, Reading, Berks, RG1 4BS
Trustees: Mr James Garwood Michael Wates CBE, Mr Adam Marks LLB (Hons), Mr Ashley Wheaton BA, Dr Stephen Jackson, Mr Andrew Hynard BSc FRICS, Mrs Bridget Bartlett, Ms Jatinder Kaur Brainch, Mr David Larkin FRICS, Mr Alastair Gilbert Martin FRICS, John Gellatly, Professor Kenneth Miller, Mr David Mason, Mrs Helen Edwards, Mr Christopher David Costigan
Income: £11,688,081 [2017]; £14,909,388 [2016]; £8,310,308 [2015]; £7,980,204 [2014]; £7,919,582 [2013]

University Hospitals Birmingham Charity
Registered: 23 Feb 2016 *Employees:* 9 *Volunteers:* 410
Tel: 0121 371 4852 *Website:* qehb.org
Activities: The advancement of health or saving of lives; prevention or relief of poverty; armed forces, emergency service efficiency
Address: 5th Floor, QEHB Charity, Nuffield House, Queen Elizabeth Hospital, Edgbaston, Birmingham, B15 2TH
Trustees: Mr David Robert Ritchie, Mr David Michael MacKay, Mr Mark Justin Godwin Watkins, Dr Peter Paul Mayer, Mr Michael Richard Seabrook, Mr Andrew Philip Pemberton, Mr Brian Huntley Hanson
Income: £4,070,000 [2017]

University Hospitals of North Midlands Charity
Registered: 24 Apr 1996
Tel: 01782 679012 *Website:* uhns.nhs.uk
Activities: General charitable purposes; education, training; advancement of health or saving of lives; disability
Address: 4 Ashbrook Lane, Abbots Bromley, Rugeley, Staffs, WS15 3DW
Trustees: Mrs Elizabeth Rix, Mr John Marlor, Mrs Ro Vaughan, Mr Stephen Burgin, Mrs Sarah Preston, Mr Andrew Smith, Mr Nicholas Young
Income: £2,069,000 [2017]; £1,841,145 [2016]; £2,313,094 [2015]; £1,431,391 [2014]; £4,077,413 [2013]

University of Bath Students' Union (BUSU)
Registered: 29 Jul 2011 *Employees:* 49 *Volunteers:* 3,000
Tel: 01225 383071 *Website:* thesubath.com
Activities: Education, training
Address: The Students Union, University of Bath, Claverton Down, Bath, BA2 7AY
Trustees: Ms Marian McNeir, Paul Freeston, Mr Ben Davies BSc, Ms Kimberley Pickett-Mcatackney, Mr Ben Palmer, Rob Clay, Mr Will Galloway, Mr Liam Emery, Ms Chloe Page
Income: £4,823,919 [2017]; £4,561,112 [2016]; £4,402,057 [2015]; £3,988,353 [2014]; £3,661,796 [2013]

University of Bedfordshire Students' Union
Registered: 9 Apr 2013 *Employees:* 72 *Volunteers:* 799
Tel: 01582 489367 *Website:* bedssu.co.uk
Activities: Education, training; recreation; other charitable purposes
Address: Beds SU, Campus Centre, Park Sqaure, Luton, Beds, LU1 3JU
Trustees: Mr Timothy Stone, Miss Sue Lowe, Ms Rachael Firth, Ms Nicola Hemmings
Income: £1,571,283 [2017]; £1,506,600 [2016]; £1,533,440 [2015]; £1,523,491 [2014]

University of Birmingham Guild of Students
Registered: 19 Aug 2010 *Employees:* 377 *Volunteers:* 8,089
Tel: 0121 251 2300 *Website:* guildofstudents.com
Activities: Education, training; accommodation, housing; religious activities; arts, culture, heritage, science; amateur sport; environment, conservation, heritage; economic, community development, employment; recreation
Address: Edgbaston Park Road, Edgbaston, Birmingham, B15 2TU
Trustees: Mr Robert John Smeath, Miss Krisztina Maria Mair, Mrs Christine Davies, Mr Lyndon Wyn Williams, Miss Eleanor Keiller, Miss Helena Bailey, Miss Shannon Farmer, Mr Adam Michael Goldstone, Miss Laura Brindley, Mr Robert Henry Saunders, Mr Richard Graeme Evans, Mr Christopher Granger, Miss Tanya Nikhila Chadha, Mr Ryan James Bennett, Miss Jessica Charlotte Levy, Miss Henrietta Green, Mr Kristen Ali, Ms Mayya Konovalova
Income: £5,890,540 [2017]; £5,595,523 [2016]; £5,361,997 [2015]; £5,147,340 [2014]; £4,335,560 [2013]

University of Bradford Union
Registered: 17 Aug 2012 *Employees:* 46 *Volunteers:* 1,091
Tel: 01274 233282 *Website:* ubuonline.co.uk
Activities: Education, training
Address: Student Central, Richmond Road, Bradford, W Yorks, BD7 1DP
Trustees: Professor Arthur Williams, Mr Hamza Yousaf, Ms Chioma Michael-Ononugbo, Ms Beth Stanfield, Mr Inshaal Ahmad, Maria Battul, Mr Ram Saroop, Dr Mumtaz Kamala, Ms Sharon Tariro Kunaka, Mr Faiz Ilyas, Ms Fatouma Sanyang, Ms Zainab Garba-Sani, Deborah Cross
Income: £1,808,193 [2017]; £1,621,167 [2016]; £1,666,719 [2015]; £1,666,700 [2014]; £1,480,833 [2013]

University of Brighton Students' Union
Registered: 20 Oct 2015 *Employees:* 47 *Volunteers:* 450
Tel: 01273 642873 *Website:* brightonsu.com
Activities: Education, training; amateur sport
Address: University of Brighton Students' Union, Watts Building, Lewes Road, Brighton, BN2 4GJ
Trustees: Joshua Dawson, Catherine Bach, Emma Kay, Ebun Azeez, Amy Jaiteh, Frank Dankwa, Amarbeer Singh Gill, Mr John Willson, Calum McNally
Income: £3,665,609 [2017]; £4,394,474 [2016]

University of Bristol Students' Union
Registered: 4 Jan 2011 *Employees:* 56 *Volunteers:* 3,034
Tel: 0117 331 8600 *Website:* bristolsu.org.uk
Activities: Education, training
Address: University of Bristol, The Richmond Building, 105 Queens Road, Clifton, Bristol, BS8 1LN
Trustees: Ms Noelle Rumball, Mrs Tamar-Ellen Beech, Mr John House, Mr Mazen Ammar, Mr Adam Stanford, Mr Lucky Dube, Mr Samuel March, Mr Ian Robinson, Miss Lea Hampton O'Neil, Miss Noha Abu El Magd, Des Ibekwe, Mr Mehul Pasari, Mr Shubham Singh, Mr Lawrence Woolridge
Income: £4,369,199 [2017]; £4,170,311 [2016]; £4,292,707 [2015]; £3,614,197 [2014]; £3,249,183 [2013]

The University of Buckingham
Registered: 4 May 2011 *Employees:* 328
Tel: 01280 820254 *Website:* buckingham.ac.uk
Activities: Education, training
Address: The University of Buckingham, Yeomanry House, Hunter Street, Buckingham, MK18 1EG
Trustees: Sir Anthony Seldon, Mr John McIntosh, Julian Stafford, Ms Lorinda Long, Suzanna Tomassi, Mr Charles Jackson, Lady Tessa Keswick, Mr Brandon Lewis, Professor John Drew, Dr Claire Stocker, Mr Brian Kingham, Mr Joe Harrison, Mark Rushton, Mr Warren Whyte, Dr Keith Elliott, Ken Siddle, Mr Mark Appleyard, Miss Felicity Lusk, Professor Alistair Alcock, Professor Susan Edwards, Dr Kenneth Langlands, Ms Pearl Lewis, Mr James Baker, Mrs Bethany Janes
Income: £34,727,000 [2016]; £27,101,000 [2015]; £25,155,000 [2014]; £24,967,000 [2013]; £21,599,000 [2012]

University of Central Lancashire Students' Union
Registered: 28 Jun 2011 *Employees:* 186 *Volunteers:* 288
Tel: 01772 893000 *Website:* uclansu.ac.uk
Activities: Education, training; amateur sport; recreation
Address: UCLAN Students' Union, 24 Fylde Road, Preston, Lancs, PR1 2TQ
Trustees: Mr Edward Julian Graham-Hyde, Mr Peter Andrew Hyett, Miss Jamie-Leigh Bellerby, Ms Suntosh Kaur, Miss Nyanar Jasmine Dombek DEng, Sana Iqbal, Miss Caitlin Rose McLaren, Miss Lily Green, Mrs Johanna Marie Scott
Income: £3,733,975 [2017]; £3,905,045 [2016]; £4,488,940 [2015]; £4,169,860 [2014]; £4,782,501 [2013]

University of Chester
Registered: 3 Jan 1963 *Employees:* 1,504
Tel: 01244 511454 *Website:* chester.ac.uk
Activities: Education, training; religious activities; arts, culture, heritage, science; amateur sport; economic, community development, employment; human rights, religious or racial harmony, equality or diversity
Address: University of Chester, Parkgate Road, Chester, CH1 4BJ
Trustees: Mr Jeffrey Turnbull, The Bishop of Chester, Dr Liane Smith, Mrs Cathy Maddaford, Mrs Christine Allen, Mrs Sandra Verity, Sandra Rudd, Mr Nick Jenkins, Miss Cherelle Mitchell, Mrs Karen Howell, Mr Ian Davies, Colin Daniels, Professor Timothy Wheeler, Mr Meredydd David, Ms Anna Sutton, Mr Francis Ball, Mr David Munt, Mrs Jeannie France-Hayhurst, Dr Martin Degg, Miss Anna MacKenzie, Dr Ian Graham, Dr Charles Forsdick
Income: £121,266,000 [2017]; £119,403,000 [2016]; £119,954,375 [2015]; £104,464,363 [2014]; £87,808,855 [2013]

The University of Chicago Booth School of Business
Registered: 9 Mar 2005 *Employees:* 23
Tel: 020 7070 2200 *Website:* chicagobooth.edu
Activities: Education, training
Address: Woolgate Exchange, 25 Basinghall Street, London, EC2V 5HA
Trustees: Mr Philip Gary Berger, Mr Daniel Diermeier, Ms Kimberly Taylor
Income: £9,591,896 [2017]; £8,469,424 [2016]; £9,998,234 [2015]; £7,896,393 [2014]; £8,475,980 [2013]

The University of Chicago Foundation Limited
Registered: 2 Jan 2007
Tel: 020 7502 2813 *Website:* uchicago.edu
Activities: Education, training
Address: 5th Floor, Alder Castle, 10 Noble Street, London, EC2V 7QJ
Trustees: Kimberly Taylor, Ivan Samstein, Mr John R Kroll, Sharon Marine
Income: £4,508,730 [2017]; £680,989 [2016]; £573,296 [2015]; £874,750 [2014]; £401,465 [2013]

University of Chichester Students' Union
Registered: 7 Dec 2011 *Employees:* 19 *Volunteers:* 250
Tel: 01243 816398 *Website:* ucsu.org
Activities: Education, training; other charitable purposes
Address: UCSU, Bishop Otter Campus, College Lane, Chichester, W Sussex, PO19 6PE
Trustees: Karen Velasco, Mr Jordan Sloan, Miss Lauren Ellis, Miss Daisy Smale, Rebecca Vagg, Miss Sophie Blanks, Mr Gregory Unitt
Income: £1,842,648 [2017]; £1,640,455 [2016]; £1,527,574 [2015]; £1,477,516 [2014]; £1,378,895 [2013]

University of Derby Students' Union
Registered: 20 Sep 2016 *Employees:* 138 *Volunteers:* 1,100
Tel: 01332 591520 *Website:* udsu.co.uk
Activities: General charitable purposes; education, training
Address: University of Derby, Kedleston Road, Derby, DE22 1GB
Trustees: Mr A Buss, Miss Grace Suszek, Miss Megan Hill, Miss Charlotte Gauja, Mr Muhammad Ali, Ms J A Hallam, Miss Abby Wilson, Mr Tom Surrell Fdeng Engtech Mimeche, Mr Connor Todd, Miss Melanie Welaratne, Mr M Spencer
Income: £2,399,593 [2017]

University of Derby Theatre Limited
Registered: 3 Apr 2009 *Employees:* 37
Tel: 01332 591913 *Website:* derby.ac.uk
Activities: Education, training; arts, culture, heritage, science; economic, community development, employment; recreation
Address: University of Derby, Kedleston Road, Derby, DE22 1GB
Trustees: Hari Punchihewa, Mr Keith Andrew John McLay, Mr Christopher Carl Hughes, Jane Claire, Dawn Elizabeth Foote, Mrs Kathryn Mary Mitchell
Income: £3,139,713 [2017]; £2,936,509 [2016]; £2,369,998 [2015]; £2,291,371 [2014]; £1,963,420 [2013]

University of Essex Students' Union
Registered: 8 Feb 2011 *Employees:* 312 *Volunteers:* 742
Tel: 01206 878988 *Website:* essexstudent.com
Activities: Education, training; amateur sport
Address: University of Essex, Wivenhoe Park, Colchester, Essex, CO4 3SQ
Trustees: Mr Lee Rodwell, Miss Zoe Garshong, Mr Tancrede Chartier, Miss Mariam Solomon, Mr Arran Barrett, Mr Barry Van Eupen, Mr Samuel Miles, Miss Daniela-Andrea Stan, Miss Sharifah Hani Yasmin Syed Abdullah, Mr Ernest Nyarko, Ms Christina Parthenidou
Income: £9,236,479 [2017]; £8,683,997 [2016]; £8,011,263 [2015]; £7,055,055 [2014]; £6,671,778 [2013]

University of Exeter Students' Guild
Registered: 18 Jun 2010 *Employees:* 79 *Volunteers:* 1,000
Tel: 01392 263542 *Website:* exeterguild.org
Activities: Education, training
Address: Students' Guild, Devonshire House, Stocker Road, Exeter, EX4 4PZ
Trustees: Mr Keith Eales, Miss Malaka Shwaikh, Mr Azhar Chaudhry, Miss Rebecca Hanley, Miss Bryony Loveless, Ms Deborah Lee Watson, Miss Talin Aslanian, Mr John Hindson, Miss Katalina Karmani, Miss Shraddha Chaudhary
Income: £6,315,000 [2017]; £6,630,618 [2016]; £5,851,909 [2015]; £5,130,642 [2014]; £4,972,577 [2013]

The University of Haifa UK
Registered: 3 Feb 1976 *Employees:* 2
Tel: 020 7580 3479 *Website:* haifa-univ.org.uk
Activities: Education, training
Address: 26 Mortimer Street, The White House, London, W1W 7RB
Trustees: Professor Sir Walter Bodmer PhD FRCPath FRS, Prof Simon Baron-Cohen, Mr Russell Jacobs, Dr Efrat Sopher, Mrs Hana Smouha, Peter Kadas, Lady Irene Hatter
Income: £1,219,482 [2017]; £1,193,022 [2016]; £1,580,875 [2015]; £1,110,479 [2014]; £850,214 [2013]

University of Hertfordshire Students' Union
Registered: 26 Jul 2011 *Employees:* 165 *Volunteers:* 950
Tel: 01707 285000 *Website:* hertfordshire.su
Activities: Education, training; arts, culture, heritage, science; amateur sport; recreation; other charitable purposes
Address: University of Hertfordshire, College Lane, Hatfield, Herts, AL10 9AB
Trustees: Mr Simon Petar, Miss Bethel Haimanot, Mrs Ugonna Nwachuku-Rowell, Mrs Sarah Fuell, Adil Ur Rehman, Miss Rosanna Vega, Miss Shelby Loasby, Mr Ahmad Alshemari, Mr Stephen Isaacs, Mr David Ball, Mr Mansoor Hakimyar, Miss Sarah Kwedi
Income: £5,492,580 [2017]; £5,705,040 [2016]; £5,928,109 [2015]; £6,394,574 [2014]; £13,928,138 [2013]

University of Huddersfield Students' Union
Registered: 10 Aug 2010 *Employees:* 55 *Volunteers:* 42
Tel: 01484 473555 *Website:* huddersfield.su
Activities: Education, training; recreation
Address: University of Huddersfield, Queensgate, Huddersfield, W Yorks, HD1 3DH
Trustees: Ms Jane Glaister, Professor David Butcher, Mr Jacob Oliver Rodgers, Mr Jonathan Stephen, Mr Wael Alenezi, Ms Karen O'Neill, Professor Mike Kagioglou, Mr Bright Justice Asogu, Mr Thomas Craig Bowden, Ms Rubina Rashid
Income: £2,592,226 [2017]; £2,722,965 [2016]; £2,700,904 [2015]; £2,488,601 [2014]; £2,502,595 [2013]

University of Leicester Students' Union
Registered: 6 Sep 2010 *Employees:* 34 *Volunteers:* 1,600
Tel: 0116 223 1200 *Website:* leicesterunion.com
Activities: Education, training; accommodation, housing; arts, culture, heritage, science; amateur sport
Address: 69 Stanfell Road, Leicester, LE2 3GE
Trustees: Mr H James Hunt, Mr Gary Dixon, Mrs Helen Sachdev, Miss Azza Abdulla, Mr Kennedy Adamu, Mr Jamie John Carruthers, Mr Keith Julian MA Hon LLD, Mr Stuart Anthony Knowles, Miss Amy Moran, Miss Mollie Henstock, Miss Carrie Young
Income: £4,983,416 [2017]; £5,074,047 [2016]; £5,017,848 [2015]; £4,897,224 [2014]; £4,809,270 [2013]

University of Lincoln Students Union
Registered: 27 Sep 2010 *Employees:* 76 *Volunteers:* 2,421
Tel: 01522 886730 *Website:* lincolnsu.com
Activities: General charitable purposes; education, training; advancement of health or saving of lives; disability; prevention or relief of poverty; accommodation, housing; religious activities; arts, culture, heritage, science; amateur sport; environment, conservation, heritage; economic, community development, employment; human rights, religious or racial harmony, equality or diversity; recreation; other charitable purposes
Address: University of Lincoln Students' Union, Brayford Pool, Lincoln, LN6 7TS
Trustees: Mr Paul Tatton, Ms Hester Suzannah Davies, Mr Kudzai Muzangaza, Mr Tommy George, Mr Connor Delany, Mr James Thomas Rayner, Ms Victoria Langer, Ms Beverley Anne Purdy, Mr Luke Exton, Miss Jiachen Liu, Mr Christian Cowdell, Mr Chris Bateman
Income: £4,427,680 [2017]; £3,532,904 [2016]; £3,033,977 [2015]; £1,186,507 [2014]; £833,068 [2013]

University of Manchester Students' Union
Registered: 5 Oct 2011 *Employees:* 81 *Volunteers:* 3,972
Tel: 0161 275 2930 *Website:* manchesterstudentsunion.com
Activities: Education, training; recreation
Address: University of Manchester, Students' Union, Oxford Road, Manchester, M13 9PR
Trustees: Mr Jan Henryk Sowa, Mr Daniel Lashley-Johnson, Alexander Tayler, Jack Houghton, Sara Heddi, Miss Hannah Murray, Ms Elizabeth Cameron, Miss Sara Khan, Kitty Bartlett, Riddi Viswanathan, Vicii Kirkpatrick, Miss Yuk Kwan Ng
Income: £7,012,599 [2017]; £7,417,118 [2016]; £7,029,209 [2015]; £6,575,085 [2014]; £5,169,224 [2013]

The University of Newcastle upon Tyne Development Trust
Registered: 26 Jul 1972 *Employees:* 1
Tel: 0191 208 3914 *Website:* ncl.ac.uk
Activities: Education, training
Address: University of Newcastle upon Tyne, Claremont Road, Newcastle upon Tyne, NE1 7RU
Trustees: Professor Chris Day, Dr Va Hammond, Mr Simon Dobson, Professor David John Burn, Mrs H Parker, Dr Karen Beacham, Mr Paul Woods
Income: £2,180,440 [2017]; £2,489,328 [2016]; £1,782,924 [2015]; £1,876,004 [2014]; £2,036,638 [2013]

The University of Northampton Students' Union
Registered: 28 Nov 2011 *Employees:* 47 *Volunteers:* 912
Tel: 01604 892819 *Website:* northamptonunion.com
Activities: Education, training
Address: Park Campus, Boughton Green Road, Northampton, NN2 7AL
Trustees: Mr Wray Irwin MSt FRSA, Richard Aveling, Danjie Zhong, Mr Artemis Artemiou, Mr Inderjeet Nagra, Mr Jevon Corbett, Graham Gannaway, David Lewis, Mr Matthew Storr, Mr Rafael Garcia-Krailing
Income: £3,582,538 [2017]; £3,351,733 [2016]; £2,500,739 [2015]; £2,188,080 [2014]; £1,871,898 [2013]

The University of Notre Dame (USA) in England
Registered: 21 Jul 2003 *Employees:* 57
Website: international.nd.edu
Activities: General charitable purposes; education, training; arts, culture, heritage, science
Address: University of Notre Dame, Controllers Office, 805 Grace Hall, Notre Dame, IN 46556, USA
Trustees: Mr Robert Michael Conway, Mr John Carl Hahn, Mr Andrew M Paluf, Mr William James Kennedy, Dr John Felix Affleck-Graves, Mr Alberto Piedra, Dean Nell Newton JD, Mr Michael Edwin Pippenger
Income: £6,941,168 [2017]; £9,182,499 [2016]; £8,280,136 [2015]; £5,701,721 [2014]; £4,412,401 [2013]

The University of Nottingham Students' Union
Registered: 21 Jul 2010 *Employees:* 216 *Volunteers:* 212
Tel: 0115 846 8800 *Website:* su.nottingham.ac.uk
Activities: Education, training; amateur sport
Address: University of Nottingham, University Park, Nottingham, NG7 2RD
Trustees: Mrs Carole Harvey, Mr Hugh Jacques, Mr Mark Andrew Peel, Mr Martin Nguyen, Miss Laura Bealin-Kelly, Mr George Thomas Bailey, Mr Colman O'Cathail, Miss Camilla May Porter Babbage, Mr Alan Richmond Holey, Miss Catherine O'Boyle, Mr John Lim, Mr David Peter Ellis
Income: £10,324,976 [2017]; £9,780,978 [2016]; £9,847,436 [2015]; £10,585,830 [2014]; £8,655,266 [2013]

University of Pennsylvania (USA) Foundation Limited
Registered: 11 Nov 2002
Tel: 020 7597 6173
Activities: Education, training
Address: 16 Old Bailey, London, EC4M 7EG
Trustees: Mr Paul J Burger, Mr Alexandros Haidas, Mrs Bonnie Miao Bandeen, Mr Simon Dan Palley, Mr John Zeller
Income: £13,456,055 [2017]; £3,591,060 [2016]; £4,047,211 [2015]; £2,887,143 [2014]; £4,304,263 [2013]

University of Plymouth Students' Union
Registered: 31 Aug 2011 *Employees:* 182
Tel: 01752 342021 *Website:* upsu.com
Activities: Education, training
Address: Drake Circus, Plymouth, PL4 8AA
Trustees: Mr Matthew James Horton LLB, Miss Nuria Bonet Filella, Miss Lowri Haf Jones, Miss Hadiza Adah, Mr Alex Doyle, Ms Jane Hopkinson, Dr Graham Stirling, Miss Phillipa Williams, Mr James Warren
Income: £5,414,353 [2017]; £5,592,610 [2016]; £5,664,666 [2015]; £5,465,723 [2014]; £5,407,223 [2013]

University of Portsmouth Students Union
Registered: 1 Jun 2010 *Employees:* 59 *Volunteers:* 2,185
Tel: 023 9284 3666 *Website:* upsu.net
Activities: Education, training; accommodation, housing; arts, culture, heritage, science; amateur sport; environment, conservation, heritage; human rights, religious or racial harmony, equality or diversity; recreation; other charitable purposes
Address: University of Portsmouth Student Union, Unit 4, Cambridge Road, Portsmouth, PO1 2EF
Trustees: Ms Rhian Johns, Mr James Andrew Thompson, Miss Amber Mathurin, Miss Angel Wanjiru Layer, Miss Adele Rosa Benson, Dr Jason Nathaniel Oakley, Mr Marcus Campopiano, Mrs Anita Joanne Butler, Thea Noli, Mr Benjamin Swiergon
Income: £2,351,673 [2017]; £2,127,054 [2016]; £2,055,843 [2015]; £1,973,412 [2014]; £1,854,233 [2013]

University of Salford Students' Union
Registered: 16 Sep 2010 *Employees:* 31 *Volunteers:* 500
Tel: 0161 351 5400 *Website:* salfordstudents.com
Activities: General charitable purposes; education, training; amateur sport
Address: University of Salford, University House, The Crescent, Salford, M5 4WT
Trustees: Mr Stephen Anthony Westgarth, Miss Brown Lucy, Mr Jon-Connor Lyons, Mr Kwabena Offori Ntow Anoff, Miss Temiloluwa Adebayo, Mr Stocks Lanjul, Mr Andreas Patsalos, Mr Christopher Costigan, Miss Harriet Ruddick, Miss Emily Voss-Bevan, Mr Famous Akhalumeh Dekeri, Miss Samsam Ibrahim
Income: £1,849,056 [2017]; £2,350,658 [2016]; £3,193,521 [2015]; £2,170,682 [2014]; £2,276,245 [2013]

The University of Sheffield Union of Students

Registered: 27 Jun 2012 *Employees:* 252 *Volunteers:* 4,500
Tel: 0114 222 8659 *Website:* sheffieldsu.com
Activities: Education, training; arts, culture, heritage, science; amateur sport; recreation; other charitable purposes
Address: University of Sheffield, Students Union, Western Bank, Sheffield, S10 2TG
Trustees: Mr John O'Leary, Ms Helen MacKenzie, Robbie Morgan, Mr Michael Nicholas Barge, Ms Florence Brookes, Ms Celeste Jones, Ms Megan Catherine McGrath, Ms Reena Staves, Ms Mayeda Tayyab, Ms Anita Chib, Mark Simpson, Cate O'Brien, Mr Thomas Edward Jolin Brindley, Ms Santhanavathana Gopalakrishnan, Mr Kieran Peter Maxwell, Mr Stuart McMillan, Mr Benjamin James Hawker
Income: £11,433,326 [2017]; £11,108,736 [2016]; £10,498,245 [2015]; £10,466,192 [2014]; £9,449,856 [2013]

University of South Wales/Prifysgol de Cymru

Registered: 9 Feb 2011 *Employees:* 2,134
Tel: 01443 654171 *Website:* southwales.ac.uk
Activities: Education, training
Address: University of South Wales, Treforest, Pontypridd, Rhondda Cynon Taf, CF37 1DL
Trustees: Sandra Spray, Professor Julie Lydon, Mr Tony Morgan, Mr David Baker, Mr John Derrick, Professor Michael Gunn, Mr Graham Edwards, Chris Sutton, Mr Michael Stevens, Ms Megan Wilson, Ms Angela Lewis, Mr Ollie Britten, Mr Gareth Williams, Ms Helene Mansfield OBE, Mr Huw Williams, Ms Louise Evans, Professor Helen Langton, Mr Chris Freegard, Ms Clare Hudson, Mrs Jemma Terry, Professor Diana Wallace, Ms Alison Phillips, Ms Debra Jones
Income: £184,168,000 [2017]; £190,907,000 [2016]; £196,941,000 [2015]; £195,680,000 [2014]; £192,541,000 [2013]

University of Southampton Students' Union

Registered: 22 Aug 2012 *Employees:* 306 *Volunteers:* 15,700
Tel: 023 8059 5215 *Website:* susu.org
Activities: Education, training; arts, culture, heritage, science; amateur sport; economic, community development, employment; human rights, religious or racial harmony, equality or diversity; recreation; other charitable purposes
Address: University of Southampton, University Road, Southampton, SO17 1BJ
Trustees: Nigel Coopey, Miss Flora Jane Noble, Miss Rebecca Louise James, Miss Samantha Higman, Mr Arun Aggarwal, Mr Thomas Brown, Miss Katie Duke, Mr M Beattie, Miss Hadeeka Taj, Mr Liibaan Mohamed, Miss Evie Reilly, Mr Samuel Dedman, Mr Stephen Gore, Mr James Anderson
Income: £7,633,919 [2017]; £7,764,297 [2016]; £7,541,375 [2015]; £7,512,448 [2014]; £7,321,269 [2013]

University of Sunderland Students' Union

Registered: 19 Jul 2012 *Employees:* 27 *Volunteers:* 35
Tel: 0191 515 3030 *Website:* sunderlandsu.co.uk
Activities: Education, training; prevention or relief of poverty; arts, culture, heritage, science; human rights, religious or racial harmony, equality or diversity; recreation
Address: Ground Floor, Edinburgh Building, University of Sunderland, Chester Road, Sunderland, Tyne & Wear, SR1 3SD
Trustees: Ms Laura Pike, Sarah Kirton, Mr Deonte Bibobra Jam, Mrs Marie Foalle, Mr Colin Ranshaw, Miss Jelena Pascenko, Mr Peter Tosan Velor
Income: £1,245,448 [2017]; £1,540,277 [2016]; £1,958,663 [2015]; £1,692,215 [2014]; £1,584,833 [2013]

University of Surrey Students' Union

Registered: 20 Jun 2011 *Employees:* 55 *Volunteers:* 2,200
Tel: 01483 683261 *Website:* ussu.co.uk
Activities: Education, training; amateur sport; recreation
Address: University of Surrey, Guildford, Surrey, GU2 7XH
Trustees: Mr Harri Ap Rees, Miss Saskia Louise Cochrane, Mrs Amanda Jane Emilia Massie, Mr Alastair Kenneth Douglass, Miss Jessica Chloe Wreford, Mr Matthew Michael Dutton, Mr Jeremy Edward Pattison, Mr Anthony Julian Crampton, Mr Alexander Charles Harden, Miss Helena Mary Mason, Mr Sam Anson Bryanton
Income: £2,445,577 [2017]; £2,906,529 [2016]; £3,398,701 [2015]; £3,493,914 [2014]; £3,525,651 [2013]

University of Sussex Students' Union

Registered: 14 May 2012 *Employees:* 55 *Volunteers:* 2,000
Tel: 01273 678555 *Website:* sussexstudent.com
Activities: Education, training; amateur sport; recreation
Address: University of Sussex, Falmer House, Falmer, Brighton, BN1 9QF
Trustees: Ms Eleanor Grainne Gahan, Mr Mena Harbi, Ms Frida Gustafsson, Ms Lucy Williams, Miss Ivayla Bodurova, Mr Daniel Richard Higgins, Ms Chloe Strathearn Brady, Ms Sarah McIntosh, Ms Aisling Lyle, Mr Lindsay Neville Powell Thomas
Income: £5,821,247 [2017]; £5,584,872 [2016]; £5,293,378 [2015]; £4,956,402 [2014]; £4,501,504 [2013]

University of The Arts London Students' Union

Registered: 29 Jul 2011 *Employees:* 77 *Volunteers:* 400
Tel: 020 7514 6270 *Website:* arts-su.com
Activities: Education, training; amateur sport; recreation
Address: 272 High Holborn, London, WC1V 7EY
Trustees: Mr Martin Bailey, Miss Leah Kahn, Miss Katayoun Jalilipour, Miss Sarah Jaarfar, Miss Hansika Jethnani, Miss Sahaya James, Mr Lachlan Marshall
Income: £3,477,561 [2017]; £3,296,214 [2016]; £3,328,816 [2015]; £3,013,878 [2014]; £2,958,855 [2013]

University of Wales:Trinity Saint David

Registered: 29 Oct 2012 *Employees:* 1,778
Tel: 01792 481019 *Website:* trinitysaintdavid.ac.uk
Activities: Education, training; arts, culture, heritage, science; environment, conservation, heritage
Address: UOW Trinity Saint David, Mount Pleasant Campus, Mount Pleasant, Swansea, SA1 6ED
Trustees: Professor Medwin Hughes, Dr Geoffrey Thomas, Ven A J Randolph Thomas, Ms Ann Maria Stedman, Mr Eifion Griffiths, Mr Philip Owen, Mr Andrew Curl, Mrs Pam Berry
Income: £119,340,000 [2017]; £104,650,000 [2016]; £104,605,000 [2015]; £108,823,000 [2014]; £35,652,000 [2013]

University of Westminster Students' Union

Registered: 19 Jul 2012 *Employees:* 63 *Volunteers:* 3,500
Tel: 020 3506 7061 *Website:* uwsu.com
Activities: Education, training
Address: 309 Regent Street, London, W1B 2HW
Trustees: Chris Smith, Freya Thompson, Dan Seamarks, Ethel Tambudzai, Joseph Ikebudu, Michael Olatokun, Ludo Siniscalchi, Lydia Blundell, Ahmed Mahfuz Talukder
Income: £2,151,333 [2016]; £2,000,896 [2015]; £1,889,218 [2014]; £1,558,432 [2013]

University of Wolverhampton Students' Union
Registered: 18 Jun 2010 *Employees:* 48 *Volunteers:* 1,042
Tel: 01902 322021 *Website:* wolvesunion.org
Activities: Education, training; amateur sport
Address: Wulfruna Street, Wolverhampton, W Midlands, WV1 1LY
Trustees: Ms Rajinder Mann, Dr Anthea Gregory, Issic Romel, Miss Anisah Khalid, Mr Michael Alan Ager, Ms Sarah Bishop, Mr Mohammed Majid Akhtar
Income: £1,038,877 [2017]; £1,087,617 [2016]; £1,159,986 [2015]; £1,183,950 [2014]; £1,215,773 [2013]

The University of York Students' Union (YUSU)
Registered: 3 Jan 2012 *Employees:* 73 *Volunteers:* 644
Tel: 01904 323722 *Website:* yusu.org
Activities: Education, training; amateur sport; recreation; other charitable purposes
Address: The Student Centre, James College, Heslington, York, YO10 5DD
Trustees: Mr Eran Cohen, Mr Jamie Sims, Mr James Alexander Urquhart, Miss Mia Shantana Chaudhuri-Julyan, Mr Michael Collinson, Mrs Ingrid Jenner, Mr Robin Brabham, Miss Laura Carruthers, Mr Julian Porch
Income: £5,164,775 [2017]; £5,010,897 [2016]; £4,709,415 [2015]; £4,346,871 [2014]; £4,338,299 [2013]

Unseen (UK)
Registered: 20 Jan 2009 *Employees:* 49 *Volunteers:* 41
Tel: 0303 040 2888 *Website:* unseenuk.org
Activities: General charitable purposes; education, training; advancement of health or saving of lives; prevention or relief of poverty; accommodation, housing; human rights, religious or racial harmony, equality or diversity; other charitable purposes
Address: Deben House, 1-5 Lawrence Hill, Bristol, BS5 0BY
Trustees: Mr Steve Daykin, Mrs Caroline Green, Dr Janice Birtle, Mr Daniel Morris, Mrs Amanda Hamilton-Stanley, Mr Rob Taylor, Mr Steven Jeffries, Mrs Fiona Elliott Boobbyer, Mr Jonathan Frank, Ms Samantha Jo Burt
Income: £1,710,672 [2016]; £755,838 [2015]; £727,085 [2014]; £588,445 [2013]; £438,345 [2012]

Up - Unlocking Potential
Registered: 12 Oct 2015 *Employees:* 35 *Volunteers:* 46
Tel: 020 3375 7000 *Website:* up.org.uk
Activities: General charitable purposes; education, training; advancement of health or saving of lives; prevention or relief of poverty; recreation
Address: Farrer & Co, 65-66 Lincoln's Inn Fields, London, WC2A 3LH
Trustees: Ms Jan Tallis, Mr Brian Andrew Linden, Mrs Tatiana Rose Amory, Ms Emily Meeyoung Sun, Mr Jonathan Clark, Mr Thomas William Bible, Mr Stuart Roden, Mr William Michael Jefferies De Winton, Ms Chiku Sinha Bernardi
Income: £3,322,196 [2016]

The Uphill Ski Club of Great Britain
Registered: 27 Jun 1983 *Employees:* 20 *Volunteers:* 225
Tel: 01479 861272 *Website:* disabilitysnowsport.org.uk
Activities: Education, training; disability; amateur sport
Address: Glenmore Lodge, Glenmore, Aviemore, Highland, PH22 1QU
Trustees: Mrs Claire Pimm, Miss Fiona Jane Fleming, Mrs Helen Clatworthy, Mr Edward Jones, Ms Carmel Mary Teusner, Miss Suzanne Higham, John Dickinson-Lilley, Donald McCutchan, Mrs Jessica Brown, Mrs Shona Margaret Tate, Mr Gordon Ritter, Mr Gareth Roberts
Income: £1,468,494 [2016]; £1,010,562 [2015]; £906,276 [2014]; £986,853 [2013]; £870,078 [2012]

Uplands Educational Trust
Registered: 13 Jul 2012 *Employees:* 46 *Volunteers:* 17
Tel: 01793 493916 *Website:* swindon.schooljotter.com
Activities: Education, training; advancement of health or saving of lives; disability; economic, community development, employment; recreation
Address: Uplands School, The Learning Campus, Tadpole Lane, Swindon, Wilts, SN25 2NB
Trustees: Mr Derek Alan Dinsey, Mr Jeff Smith, Mrs Susan Dinsey, Ms Jacqueline Anita Smith, Mr Anthony Griffiths, Mr Kevin John Gwilliam
Income: £1,198,306 [2016]; £932,351 [2015]; £308,931 [2014]; £26,590 [2013]

Uppingham School
Registered: 16 May 2012 *Employees:* 649
Tel: 01572 820626 *Website:* uppingham.co.uk
Activities: Education, training
Address: Uppingham School, 20-24 High Street West, Uppingham, Oakham, Rutland, LE15 9QD
Trustees: Very Reverend Christopher Dalliston, Ms Barbara Matthews, Mr Richard Tice, Mr Alasdair Locke MA, Dr Stephen Goss MA DPhil, Mrs Sophie Mason, Mrs Dora Thornton, Alan Duncan The Rt Hon Sir, Mr Christopher Ewbank, Dr Priscilla Chadwick MA FRSA, Dame Carol Black, Mr David Ross, Rt Rev Donald Allister The Lord Bishop of Peterborough, Mr Jonathan Scott, Mr Russell Price, Ms Sandra Humphrey, Mrs Katherine Gaine
Income: £28,605,643 [2016]; £27,910,826 [2015]; £27,110,886 [2014]; £27,093,959 [2013]

Uprising Leadership
Registered: 26 Nov 2012 *Employees:* 26 *Volunteers:* 450
Tel: 020 3745 7960 *Website:* uprising.org.uk
Activities: Education, training; economic, community development, employment
Address: 2nd Floor, Tayside House, 31 Pepper Street, London, E14 9RP
Trustees: Ms Rushanara Ali, Mr Stephen Colegrave, Mr Jay Bobby Seagull, Mr Myles Emmerson Charles Bradshaw, Peter Kellner, Ms Jane Margaret Earl, Mr Oluwaseye Odukogbe, Ms Lisa Soraya Aziz
Income: £1,194,836 [2017]; £635,834 [2016]; £1,568,489 [2015]; £1,071,077 [2014]

Upton House School Limited
Registered: 28 Dec 1962 *Employees:* 73 *Volunteers:* 5
Tel: 01753 862610 *Website:* uptonhouse.org.uk
Activities: Education, training
Address: Upton House School, 115 St Leonards Road, Windsor, Berks, SL4 3DF
Trustees: Mrs Emma Sarah May Wigzell, Mrs Susan Claire Cairns, Mr Rory David Lee Smyth, Mrs Barbara Elizabeth Stanley, Mr Robert Mark Stewart, Mr Anthony William Warf, Giles Delaney, Dr Peter Maciej Warwicker, Jonathan Story, Mr Carlos Vilares, Mrs Virginia Barker, Miss Sarah Elizabeth Mason
Income: £2,825,822 [2016]; £2,818,454 [2015]; £2,805,634 [2014]; £2,319,801 [2013]; £2,306,823 [2012]

Urban Partnership Group

Registered: 29 May 2002 *Employees:* 24 *Volunteers:* 90
Tel: 020 7605 0800 *Website:* upg.org.uk
Activities: General charitable purposes; education, training; prevention or relief of poverty; economic, community development, employment
Address: The Urban Partnership Group, Masbro Centre, 87 Masbro Road, London, W14 0LR
Trustees: Miss Eunice Sutherland, Mrs Maria Camacho, Ms Hope Hanalan, Franco Chen, Mrs Asmat Nadeem, Grace Poku, Ms Cristina Tragni, Mr Bo Ai, Mrs Maria Rooney, Ms Kamini Sanghani
Income: £1,183,061 [2017]; £1,059,729 [2016]; £1,238,611 [2015]; £1,171,994 [2014]; £989,401 [2013]

The Michael Uren Foundation

Registered: 9 Oct 2002
Activities: General charitable purposes; education, training; advancement of health or saving of lives; animals; environment, conservation, heritage; armed forces, emergency service efficiency
Address: Haysmacintyre, 26 Red Lion Square, London, WC1R 4AG
Trustees: Mr John Michael Leal Uren OBE, Mr David Richard Uren, Mrs Janis Bennett, Mr Roger Nicholas Hayward Gould, Mrs Anne Gregory-Jones, Mr Robert Mark Uren
Income: £2,485,792 [2017]; £7,721,847 [2016]; £5,419,665 [2015]; £4,512,749 [2014]; £2,623,714 [2013]

The Urology Foundation

Registered: 19 Mar 2009 *Employees:* 5 *Volunteers:* 18
Tel: 020 7713 9538 *Website:* theurologyfoundation.org
Activities: Education, training; advancement of health or saving of lives
Address: 1-2 St Andrew's Hill, London, EC4V 5BY
Trustees: Mr Christopher Smith, Mr John Tiner, Mr Roger Plail, Mr Andrew John Moss, Mr Mark Becker, Mr Roland Morley, Mr Ben Challacombe, Ms Laura Wyld, Professor John Daniel Kelly, Mr Adrian Joyce, Ms Susan Sayer OBE CBE, Professor Krishna Kumar Sethia, Mr David Richardson, Mr Kieran O'Flynn, Ms Giovanna Forte
Income: £1,189,268 [2016]; £1,375,783 [2015]; £1,025,878 [2014]; £698,286 [2013]; £758,376 [2012]

The Ursuline Preparatory School Ilford

Registered: 17 Jun 2009 *Employees:* 30
Tel: 020 8518 4050 *Website:* urspsi.org.uk
Activities: Education, training; religious activities
Address: Ursuline Preparatory School Ilford, 2-4 Coventry Road, Ilford, Essex, IG1 4QR
Trustees: Sister Maureen Moloney OSU, Ms Elizabeth Murphy, Mr Peter Nicholson, Mr Paul Dobson, Miss Suzanne Ward, Sister Kathleen Colmer OSU
Income: £1,442,469 [2017]; £1,463,295 [2016]; £1,552,543 [2015]; £1,689,994 [2014]; £1,705,355 [2013]

Ursuline Preparatory School Wimbledon Trust

Registered: 8 Mar 2000 *Employees:* 52
Tel: 020 8942 5981 *Website:* ursuline-prep.merton.sch.uk
Activities: Education, training
Address: 184 West Barnes Lane, New Malden, Surrey, KT3 6LS
Trustees: Sister Kathleen Colmer OSU, Mr Thomas Paul Bolland CA, Mr Mark Leclerq, Mr Gerard Smith, Ms Ann Thimont
Income: £2,750,043 [2017]; £2,727,364 [2016]; £2,658,936 [2015]; £2,403,020 [2014]; £2,057,623 [2013]

The Ursuline Preparatory School

Registered: 26 Sep 1996 *Employees:* 34
Website: ursulineprepwarley.co.uk
Activities: Education, training
Address: Warley Elms, Great Warley Street, Great Warley, Brentwood, Essex, CM13 3JP
Trustees: Mr Jason O'Shea, Mrs Angela Hyams, Mr Gavin Moule, Mrs Fiona East
Income: £1,806,758 [2017]; £1,619,700 [2016]; £1,488,299 [2015]; £1,433,561 [2014]; £1,366,596 [2013]

User Voice

Registered: 21 May 2010 *Employees:* 43 *Volunteers:* 300
Tel: 020 3137 7471 *Website:* uservoice.org
Activities: Education, training; other charitable purposes
Address: 20 Newburn Street, London, SE11 5PJ
Trustees: Mr Mark Johnson, Mr David John Harrison, Mr Noel Anthony Gordon, Mrs Patricia Hamzahee, Mr Max Warren Kelly, Jane Pound
Income: £1,508,592 [2017]; £1,586,002 [2016]; £1,272,684 [2015]; £948,763 [2014]; £816,597 [2013]

The Utley Family Charitable Trust

Registered: 10 Jun 2014
Tel: 01277 821338
Activities: General charitable purposes
Address: 199 Nine Ashes Road, Nine Ashes, Ingatestone, Essex, CM4 0JY
Trustees: Melvyn Sims, Neil Utley, Nicky Utley, Mr Raja Balasuriya
Income: £1,841,034 [2017]; £5,019,039 [2016]; £10,973,236 [2015]

The V&A Foundation

Registered: 2 Nov 2011
Tel: 020 7942 2771
Activities: Education, training; arts, culture, heritage, science; environment, conservation, heritage
Address: 35 Foxes Dale, London, SE3 9BH
Trustees: Dame Theresa Sackler, The Rt Hon Sir Timothy Alan Davan Sainsbury, Sir Paul Ruddock, Mr Manfred Stanley Gorvy, Dr Edwin Davies, Dr Genevieve Rachel Davies, Mr Ali Reza Sarikhani, Mr Michael Nicholas Snowman OBE, Jill Shaw Ruddock, Ms Lydia Ruth Gorvy, Dr Susan Weber, Nicholas David Coleridge, Mr Bernard Selz
Income: £6,870,845 [2017]; £8,654,607 [2016]; £6,835,674 [2015]; £7,607,092 [2014]; £19,241,405 [2013]

Vale House Oxford

Registered: 20 Jul 1988 *Employees:* 55 *Volunteers:* 30
Tel: 01865 718467 *Website:* valehouse.org.uk
Activities: The advancement of health or saving of lives
Address: Sandford Road, Littlemore, Oxford, OX4 4XL
Trustees: Dr Catherine Oppenheimer, Mrs Alison Rosemary Rooke, Mrs Olga Florence Senior, Mrs Jacqueline Connelly, Miss Jane Elizabeth Cranston, Mr John Henry Barneby, Ms Helen Louise Carter, Mr Robert Foster
Income: £2,099,705 [2017]; £2,120,590 [2016]; £2,046,265 [2015]; £1,962,231 [2014]; £1,949,738 [2013]

Vale House Stabilisation Services
Registered: 22 May 1996 *Employees:* 22 *Volunteers:* 5
Tel: 020 7421 3100 *Website:* stabilisationservices.org
Activities: The advancement of health or saving of lives; disability
Address: 18 Dartmouth Street, London, SW1H 9BL
Trustees: Ms Yasmin Batliwala, Mr James Saunders, Ms Gillian Benning
Income: £1,072,929 [2017]; £1,088,839 [2016]; £979,901 [2015]; £1,152,237 [2014]; £1,391,523 [2013]

Vale of Aylesbury Housing Trust Limited
Registered: 2 Jun 2006 *Employees:* 245
Tel: 01296 732600 *Website:* vaht.co.uk
Activities: Disability; prevention or relief of poverty; accommodation, housing; economic, community development, employment
Address: Vale of Aylesbury Housing Trust, Fairfax House, 69 Buckingham Street, Aylesbury, Bucks, HP20 2NJ
Trustees: Mr Stephen Bright, Mr David Briercliffe, Mr Stephen Stringer, Ms Olivia Clymer, Mr Kevin Hewson, Mrs Barbara Richardson, Mr Steven Lambert, Mr David Keeling, Mr Julian Blundell-Thompson, Mrs Angela Macpherson, Mr John Balshaw, Miss Kelly Marie Webster
Income: £45,224,000 [2017]; £44,615,000 [2016]; £42,995,000 [2015]; £41,445 [2014]; £38,919 [2013]

Vale of Rheidol Railway Limited
Registered: 16 Jun 1999 *Employees:* 31 *Volunteers:* 4
Tel: 01483 208209 *Website:* rheidolrailway.co.uk
Activities: Environment, conservation, heritage
Address: Markwick Farm, Markwick Lane, Loxhill, Godalming, Surrey, GU8 4BE
Trustees: Mr Rampton Peter John, Mr Charles Langer, Clive Higgs, Mr Philip John Neville Ellis, Mr Llyr Ap Iolo
Income: £1,156,295 [2016]; £1,221,477 [2015]; £926,171 [2014]; £889,140 [2013]; £567,395 [2012]

Valley CIDS and Related Charities
Registered: 12 Mar 2008 *Employees:* 130 *Volunteers:* 200
Website: valleycids.co.uk
Activities: Education, training; prevention or relief of poverty; religious activities; economic, community development, employment
Address: Christians Involved in Derbyshire Schools, 13-14 The Green, Swanwick, Alfreton, Derbys, DE55 1BL
Trustees: Mr Brian John Cupples, Peter Richard Whitaker, Mrs Roz Marston, Mr Jonathan Brook, Mrs Dorothy Whitaker, Dr Nicola Joy Hambley, Mr John F Turner
Income: £2,898,835 [2017]; £2,902,441 [2016]; £2,724,022 [2015]; £2,007,107 [2014]; £1,685,074 [2013]

Valley House
Registered: 5 Mar 1999 *Employees:* 74 *Volunteers:* 10
Website: valleyhouse.org.uk
Activities: Education, training; accommodation, housing
Address: 55-57 Bell Green Road, Coventry, Warwicks, CV6 7GQ
Trustees: Mr Barry Peter Whittington, Mr John Briffitt, Mr Dexter Du Boulay, Mrs Julie Linda Bradley, Mrs Surinder Kasli, Mr Graham Ernest Common, Mrs Geraldine Parker
Income: £1,977,536 [2017]; £2,207,097 [2016]; £1,854,080 [2015]; £1,599,158 [2014]; £1,533,847 [2013]

Valley Leisure Limited
Registered: 21 Mar 1989 *Employees:* 278
Tel: 01264 568240 *Website:* valleyleisure.com
Activities: The advancement of health or saving of lives; amateur sport; recreation
Address: Alexandra House, St Johns Street, Salisbury, Wilts, SP1 2SB
Trustees: Dr Keith Blacker, Mr Gavin Alan Scott Duncan, Mr Kieran David Humphrey, Mr Nicholas Howard Bone, Mr Peter James Horne, Mrs Susan Elizabeth Mills
Income: £6,025,106 [2017]; £5,942,489 [2016]; £5,723,303 [2015]; £5,644,520 [2014]; £5,261,782 [2013]

Valleys Kids
Registered: 24 Mar 1999 *Employees:* 39 *Volunteers:* 101
Tel: 01443 420870 *Website:* valleyskids.org
Activities: Education, training; arts, culture, heritage, science; amateur sport; economic, community development, employment
Address: Valleys Kids, 1 Cross Street, Penygraig, Tonypandy, Rhondda Cynon Taf, CF40 1LD
Trustees: Mrs Audrey Boyce, Mr Phillip Evans, Dr Rhiannon Howells, Ceri Assiratti, Mrs Marion Stokes, Dr Howell Edwards, Ms Rebecca Booth
Income: £1,996,467 [2017]; £1,360,670 [2016]; £1,707,083 [2015]; £1,775,522 [2014]; £2,008,364 [2013]

Values Academy
Registered: 6 Oct 2009 *Employees:* 49
Website: valuesacademy.org.uk
Activities: Education, training
Address: 19 Mill Court, Alvechurch, Birmingham, B48 7JY
Trustees: Mr Paul Vincent Roberts, Dr Anna Molony, Mr Simon Livings, Mrs Margaret Ann Henman, Mr Robert Warman
Income: £1,115,159 [2017]; £1,076,874 [2016]; £1,251,255 [2015]; £1,178,537 [2014]; £955,889 [2012]

The Vardy Foundation
Registered: 14 Nov 1989 *Employees:* 2
Tel: 0191 501 8555
Activities: General charitable purposes; education, training; advancement of health or saving of lives; disability; prevention or relief of poverty; overseas aid, famine relief; accommodation, housing; religious activities; arts, culture, heritage, science; environment, conservation, heritage; economic, community development, employment; armed forces, emergency service efficiency; human rights, religious or racial harmony, equality or diversity; other charitable purposes
Address: The Vardy Foundation, 4 Admiral Way, Doxford International Business Park, Sunderland, Tyne & Wear, SR3 3XW
Trustees: Sir Peter Vardy, Mr Peter Daniel David Vardy, Mrs Victoria Helen Vardy, Lady Margaret Barr Vardy, Mr Richard Vardy
Income: £1,808,103 [2017]; £1,199,525 [2016]; £1,126,185 [2015]; £17,856,159 [2014]; £2,749,035 [2013]

Variety The Children's Charity
Registered: 19 Jul 1962 *Employees:* 38 *Volunteers:* 373
Website: variety.org.uk
Activities: General charitable purposes; disability
Address: The Variety Club Children's Charity, Variety Club House, 93 Bayham Street, London, NW1 0AG
Trustees: Mr Stanley Anthony Salter, Mr Anthony Peter Hatch, Mr Ronald Nathan, Mr Jonathan Shalit, Mr Malcolm Brenner, Mr Ronald Neil Sinclair, Mr William James Sangster, Mr Tushar Pradhu, Mr Duncan Syers, Mrs Dilaram Williamson, Mr Anthony Leonard Harris, Mrs Pamela Sinclair, Mr Trevor Green, Mr Laurence Howard Davis, Mr Jason Grant Rees Lewis, Mr Nicholas Simon Shattock, Mr Rodney Victor Natkiel, Mr James Oliver Martin, Mr Jonathan Gold
Income: £7,633,516 [2016]; £6,729,520 [2015]; £6,970,425 [2014]; £6,526,337 [2013]; £6,199,759 [2012]

The Varkey Foundation
Registered: 16 Dec 2011 *Employees:* 59
Tel: 020 7593 4040 *Website:* varkeyfoundation.org
Activities: Education, training; prevention or relief of poverty
Address: 2nd Floor, St Albans House, 57-59 Haymarket, London, SW1Y 4QX
Trustees: Mr Sunny Varkey, Sir Michael Vernon Lockett, Ms Harsha Varkey, Mr Jay Sunny Varkey, Mr David Phillimore Clifford, Ms Vijita Patel
Income: £17,071,142 [2017]; £14,692,694 [2016]; £3,075,450 [2015]; £2,383,336 [2014]; £520,768 [2013]

The Varrier-Jones Foundation
Registered: 25 Sep 1997 *Employees:* 1
Tel: 01480 357200
Activities: Disability
Address: Varrier Jones Foundation, Ermine Street North, Papworth Everard, Cambridge, CB23 3UY
Trustees: Mr Peter Agar, Mr Richard Norton, Ms Stacey Navin, Mr Steven Beach, Mr David John Atkinson, Mr Peter Richard Denison Gutteridge, Mr Wes Cuell, Mr Michael Peter Alexander, Mr Andrew Thompson
Income: £1,197,030 [2017]; £1,159,628 [2016]; £1,148,695 [2015]; £1,152,807 [2014]; £907,334 [2013]

Vast Services (1920)
Registered: 5 Oct 1995 *Employees:* 55 *Volunteers:* 15
Website: vast.org.uk
Activities: General charitable purposes; education, training; economic, community development, employment
Address: VAST, The Dudson Centre, Hope Street, Stoke on Trent, Staffs, ST1 5DD
Trustees: Mr John Beech, Mr Neil Dawson, Mr Peter Leslie Twilley, Ms Dawn Wickham, Ms Lesley Morrey, Mrs Helena Pilkington, Mr Mark Barnish, Mr Timothy John Edwards, Mr David Holton, Mrs Susan Mary Meredith, Mr Nicholas Maslen
Income: £1,826,377 [2017]; £2,038,698 [2016]; £2,124,331 [2015]; £2,471,737 [2014]; £1,462,177 [2013]

The Vegan Society
Registered: 27 Dec 1979 *Employees:* 26 *Volunteers:* 104
Website: vegansociety.com
Activities: Education, training; advancement of health or saving of lives; animals; environment, conservation, heritage; human rights, religious or racial harmony, equality or diversity
Address: Church Hall House, Cowbridge Road, St Nicholas, Vale of Glamorgan, CF5 6SH
Trustees: Mr Graham James Neale, Jenifer Vinell, Mr Salim Akbar, Patricia Mary Fairey, Robert Masters, Ms Menna Myfanwy Jones, Stephen Walsh, Mr David Hedley Gore, Ali Ryland, Jane McKears
Income: £1,072,614 [2016]; £935,776 [2015]; £1,105,600 [2014]; £533,313 [2013]; £390,124 [2012]

The Vegetarian Society of The United Kingdom Limited
Registered: 9 Sep 1969 *Employees:* 26 *Volunteers:* 120
Tel: 0161 925 2003 *Website:* vegsoc.org
Activities: Education, training; advancement of health or saving of lives; animals; environment, conservation, heritage
Address: Vegetarian Society UK Ltd, Parkdale, Dunham Road, Altrincham, Cheshire, WA14 4QG
Trustees: Ms Deborah Jones, Mr Peter Morrall, Mr Michael Harriott, Mr Dale Hoyland, Mr Andrew Johnson, Ms Clare Crowther, Mr David Richard Mason Bennett, Ms Katharine Bagshaw, Ms Cathryn Bradley
Income: £1,038,909 [2017]; £949,788 [2016]; £1,094,000 [2015]; £1,306,000 [2014]; £851,000 [2013]

Velindre NHS Trust Charitable Fund
Registered: 1 Feb 1996
Tel: 029 2031 6952 *Website:* velindre-tr.wales.nhs.uk
Activities: General charitable purposes; education, training; advancement of health or saving of lives
Address: Velindre NHS Trust Headquarters, Unit 2 Charnwood Court, Heol Billingsley, Parc Nantgarw, Cardiff, CF15 7QZ
Trustees: Velindre NHS Trust
Income: £2,446,000 [2017]; £4,364,000 [2016]; £2,921,000 [2015]; £2,934,000 [2014]; £2,414,380 [2013]

The Venture Trust
Registered: 16 Mar 1983 *Employees:* 61 *Volunteers:* 8
Tel: 0131 228 7700 *Website:* venturetrust.org.uk
Activities: Education, training; disability; prevention or relief of poverty; economic, community development, employment; armed forces, emergency service efficiency
Address: Venture Trust, Argyle House, 3 Lady Lawson Street, Edinburgh, EH3 9DR
Trustees: Mr Pete Higgins, Ms Gillian Frances Gray, Miss Susan Margaret Davies, Mel Sangster, Ms Nicola Thomson, Ms Mairi Brackenridge, Jennifer Elizabeth Lambert, Mr Thomas Alexander Mallows, Mr Alastair Clarkson
Income: £2,661,397 [2017]; £2,507,132 [2016]; £2,574,781 [2015]; £2,312,067 [2014]; £2,904,673 [2013]

The Veolia Environmental Trust
Registered: 28 Aug 1997 *Employees:* 7
Tel: 020 3567 6805 *Website:* veoliatrust.org
Activities: Environment, conservation, heritage; economic, community development, employment; recreation
Address: Ruthdene, Station Road, Four Ashes, Wolverhampton, W Midlands, WV10 7DG
Trustees: Mr Oswald Dodds MBE, Mrs Caroline Schwaller MBE, Mr Malcolm Marshall, Mr John Brown, Ms Maggie Durran, Mr Donald MacPhail, Mr Tom Spaul, Mr Derek Goodenough, Mr Mike Smith, Mr Robert Hunt, Mr Ben Slater
Income: £4,012,000 [2017]; £4,028,000 [2016]; £5,946,000 [2015]; £5,351,000 [2013]; £4,286,000 [2012]

The Vernon Educational Trust Limited
Registered: 24 Jun 1975 *Employees:* 161
Tel: 01372 849291 *Website:* daneshillschool.co.uk
Activities: Education, training
Address: Vernon Educational Trust, Leatherhead Road, Oxshott, Leatherhead, Surrey, KT22 0JG
Trustees: Mr A H Monro, Mr R Mansfield, Mr Anthony John Lunn, Dr Marc Van Grondelle, Mrs Alex Hutchinson, Dr H Patel, Mrs Sandra Collard, Mr Timothy Jones, Mr Ian Michael Hunt
Income: £15,134,627 [2017]; £14,577,651 [2016]; £13,921,643 [2015]; £12,588,729 [2014]; £12,331,459 [2013]

Veterans Aid
Registered: 9 Jan 2003 *Employees:* 22 *Volunteers:* 5
Tel: 020 7828 2468 *Website:* veterans-aid.net
Activities: General charitable purposes; prevention or relief of poverty; accommodation, housing; other charitable purposes
Address: Veterans Aid, 27 Victoria Square, London, SW1W 0RB
Trustees: Mr Ray Evans DipArch RIBA, Colonel Paul Cummings, General The Lord Michael Walker GCB CMG CBE DL, Mr Paul Dyer, Mr Gilbert Holbourn, Mr Robert Clinton, Mr Andrew Gerard Wallis
Income: £2,035,500 [2017]; £3,418,704 [2016]; £4,974,259 [2015]; £1,696,964 [2014]; £1,915,461 [2013]

Vibrance
Registered: 24 May 2013 *Employees:* 383 *Volunteers:* 3
Tel: 020 8477 1800 *Website:* vibrance.org.uk
Activities: The advancement of health or saving of lives; disability; accommodation, housing
Address: RCHL, 2 Caxton Place, Roden Street, Ilford, Essex, IG1 2AH
Trustees: Mr Adrian Hull, Mr Michael George Atkins, Ms Anne Lyons, Mr Robert William Jarvis, Mr Paul Allen, Mr Iain Sim, Mrs Shaminder Ubhi
Income: £11,112,232 [2017]; £11,008,386 [2016]; £11,139,521 [2015]; £11,105,576 [2014]

Victim Support
Registered: 17 Nov 1987 *Employees:* 1,224 *Volunteers:* 1,287
Tel: 020 7269 0259 *Website:* victimsupport.org.uk
Activities: Education, training; prevention or relief of poverty; other charitable purposes
Address: Victim Support, Octavia House, 50 Banner Street, London, EC1Y 8ST
Trustees: Sarah Miller, Mr Christopher Digby-Bell, Mr Geoff Pollard, Ms Elizabeth Dymond, Mr Andrew David Tivey, Mr William Luke Sandbrook, Mr Les Mosco, Mrs Jo Cumbley, Ms Moyna Wilkinson, Mr Roger Harding
Income: £36,409,000 [2017]; £41,037,000 [2016]; £53,074,000 [2015]; £50,200,000 [2014]; £48,071,000 [2013]

The Victoria Foundation
Registered: 13 Nov 1985 *Employees:* 261
Tel: 020 8949 9001 *Website:* thevictoriafoundation.org.uk
Activities: The advancement of health or saving of lives
Address: The Victoria Foundation, St Davids House, 15 Worple Way, Richmond, Surrey, TW10 6DG
Trustees: Mr Graham Arthur Ridgeway Ball, Mr John Alan Hamblin, Mr Christopher Lyons, Mr Peter Hope, Mr Martin Anthony Matthews, Mr Anthony R Cooke
Income: £15,614,000 [2017]; £15,215,000 [2016]; £15,190,000 [2015]; £14,585,000 [2014]; £14,400,000 [2013]

The Victory (Services) Association Limited
Registered: 24 Jun 1970 *Employees:* 127
Tel: 020 7616 8310 *Website:* vsc.co.uk
Activities: General charitable purposes; prevention or relief of poverty; accommodation, housing
Address: 63-79 Seymour Street, London, W2 2HF
Trustees: Major General Seumas Kerr CBE, Mr Richard Ward, Colonel Phillippe Rossiter, Mr Paul Brackley, WO1 Philip Gilby, Wing Commander Tracey Farndon, Lieutenant Colonel Tim Wood, Mr Paul Higgins, Mrs Catherine Newhall-Caiger, Mr Nicholas Sharland, Mrs Sue Bonney, Rear Admiral Mike Kimmons CB, Major Charles Verrior Marment, Air Vice-Marshal Steven Chisnall CB, Vice Admiral Sir Alan Massey KCB CBE, WO1 Nicholas Wright, Warrant Officer Jonathan Crossley, Mrs Amanda Hickson, Mr Richard Harris
Income: £7,812,092 [2017]; £7,709,558 [2016]; £7,616,690 [2015]; £7,090,875 [2014]; £6,695,063 [2013]

Victory Housing Trust
Registered: 3 Feb 2006 *Employees:* 79
Tel: 0330 123 1860 *Website:* victoryhousing.co.uk
Activities: Accommodation, housing; economic, community development, employment
Address: Victory Housing Trust, Cromer Road, North Walsham, Norfolk, NR28 0NB
Trustees: Mr Stephen Burke, Mrs Doris Jamieson, Mr Keith Dixon, Mr Stephen Charles Udberg, Mr Philip Burton, Mr Peter Baynham, Miss Zoe Slater, Mr Michael Gates
Income: £29,895,000 [2017]; £29,858,000 [2016]; £28,286,000 [2015]; £28,237,000 [2014]; £22,990,000 [2013]

Videre Est Credere
Registered: 26 Jun 2009 *Employees:* 9
Tel: 0845 337 4483 *Website:* videreonline.org
Activities: General charitable purposes; human rights, religious or racial harmony, equality or diversity; other charitable purposes
Address: 4 Old Park Lane, London, W1K 1QW
Trustees: Mr John Sauven, Mrs Fiona Napier, Mr David Goldsworthy, Mr Uri Fruchtman, Ms Katy Cronin
Income: £1,843,491 [2016]; £996,059 [2015]; £867,528 [2014]; £901,728 [2013]; £825,910 [2012]

Villa Scalabrini
Registered: 26 Mar 2004 *Employees:* 55 *Volunteers:* 2
Tel: 020 8207 5713 *Website:* villascalabrini.co.uk
Activities: Accommodation, housing; religious activities
Address: Villa Scalabrini, Green Street, Shenley, Radlett, Herts, WD7 9BB
Trustees: Mr Michael Polledri, Rev Giuseppe Bortolazzo, Rev Giovanni Borin, Marco Fiori, Rev Francesco Butazzo, Rev Ronan Jotojot Ayag, Rev Lorenzo Prencipe, Dung Luc
Income: £1,761,054 [2017]; £1,635,248 [2016]; £1,538,054 [2015]; £1,389,553 [2014]; £1,292,463 [2013]

Villiers Park Educational Trust
Registered: 29 Oct 1963 *Employees:* 36 *Volunteers:* 209
Tel: 01223 872809 *Website:* villierspark.org.uk
Activities: Education, training
Address: Villiers Park, Royston Road, Foxton, Cambridge, CB22 6SE
Trustees: John Tizard, Dr Ian McEwan, Ms Tamara Sword, Heleana Blackwell, Dr Richard James Barnes, Dame Alice Hudson, Adrian Ball
Income: £1,396,352 [2017]; £998,186 [2016]; £717,445 [2015]; £1,412,252 [2014]; £1,048,278 [2013]

Vincentian Care Plus
Registered: 9 Dec 2005 *Employees:* 95 *Volunteers:* 10
Tel: 020 3870 1880 *Website:* vincentiancareplus.org.uk
Activities: General charitable purposes; education, training; advancement of health or saving of lives; disability
Address: Vicentian Care Plus, 2 Grosvenor Gardens, London, SW1W 0DH
Trustees: Mr Glen von Malachowski, Sister Evelyn Warnock, Sister Bernadette Ryder, Sister Mary O'Connor, Mr Mark Hibberd
Income: £1,598,620 [2017]; £1,094,615 [2016]; £864,978 [2015]; £681,383 [2014]; £697,862 [2013]

The Vindolanda Trust
Registered: 6 Jan 2015 *Employees:* 33 *Volunteers:* 500
Tel: 01434 344277 *Website:* vindolanda.com
Activities: Education, training; arts, culture, heritage, science; environment, conservation, heritage
Address: The Vindolanda Trust, Chesterholm Museum, Westwood, Hexham, Northumberland, NE47 7JN
Trustees: Mr Lawrence John Thompson, Mrs Elspeth Fiona Gordon Standfield, Professor Ian Haynes, Professor David Mattingly, Mrs Veryan Johnston, Mr Terry Carroll, Mr Hans Christian Andersen, Mr Gary Calland, Dr Peter Richard Wilson, Mrs Helen Woodford
Income: £1,401,230 [2016]; £1,303,308 [2015]

The Vine Trust Walsall
Registered: 17 Sep 2002 *Employees:* 82 *Volunteers:* 1
Tel: 01922 621951 *Website:* thevinetrust.co.uk
Activities: General charitable purposes; education, training; prevention or relief of poverty; religious activities; economic, community development, employment; recreation; other charitable purposes
Address: The Vine Trust, 33 Lower Hall Lane, Walsall, W Midlands, WS1 1RR
Trustees: Mr Jeremy Peter Sargent, Mr Joseph Raymond Tipper, Miss Lorraine Attwood, Mr David Lomax, Mr Philip Brian James Powell, Mr Mark Harland, Ms Jacqueline Reid
Income: £2,444,264 [2016]; £2,204,655 [2015]; £865,889 [2013]; £1,607,949 [2012]

Vinehall School Limited
Registered: 22 Mar 1967 *Employees:* 73
Tel: 01580 880413 *Website:* vinehallschool.com
Activities: Education, training
Address: Vinehall School Ltd, Vinehall Road, Mountfield, Robertsbridge, E Sussex, TN32 5JL
Trustees: Mr John Malcolm Gordon MA, Mrs Angela Jane Monro JP, Dr Caroline Moore MA PhD, Mr Paul Redstone MA, Mrs Vanessa Everett BA PGCE, Mr Jonathan Mark Gilbert, Mrs Deanne Thomas, Mr Timothy Hugh Penzer Haynes BA Hons, Mrs Elizabeth Anne Goodman, Mr David Chivers LLB, Mr William Foster-Kemp LLB ACA, Mr Michael Kenneth Scott, Mrs Helen Kremer
Income: £3,925,612 [2016]; £3,987,070 [2015]; £4,132,872 [2014]; £3,945,400 [2013]; £3,871,577 [2012]

Vineyard Christian Fellowship of St Albans
Registered: 15 Dec 1997 *Employees:* 13 *Volunteers:* 900
Tel: 01727 812765 *Website:* thevineyardchurch.co.uk
Activities: General charitable purposes; education, training; prevention or relief of poverty; overseas aid, famine relief; religious activities
Address: 7 Brick Knoll Park, Ashley Road, St Albans, Herts, AL1 5UG
Trustees: Dr Mark Bevis, Mr John Eke, Mr Mark Andrew Helvadjian, Rev Chris Lane, Tim Winfield
Income: £1,349,984 [2016]; £1,137,543 [2015]; £1,380,054 [2014]; £744,130 [2013]; £666,312 [2012]

Vineyard Churches UK and Ireland
Registered: 30 Sep 2003 *Employees:* 7
Tel: 01482 462690 *Website:* vineyardchurches.org.uk
Activities: Religious activities
Address: Vineyard Centre, Vulcan Street, Hull, HU6 7PS
Trustees: Mr Jeremy Cook, Rev Clifford John Wright, Mr Robert Adam Byk, Kim Barbara Hurst, Mr Clive Sillito
Income: £1,000,814 [2016]; £1,001,909 [2015]; £921,415 [2014]; £723,043 [2013]; £754,847 [2012]

Vinspired
Registered: 13 Mar 2006 *Employees:* 63 *Volunteers:* 52
Tel: 020 7960 7026 *Website:* vinspired.com
Activities: General charitable purposes
Address: Vinspired, Dean Bradley House, 52 Horseferry Road, London, SW1P 2AF
Trustees: Mr Sanjeev Gandhi, Mr Rupert Levy, Ms Elizabeth Beale, Mary McKenna MBE, Ms Joanna Killian, Ms Joan Watson, Mr David Harris, Mr Nathaniel Hawley, James Cotter, Mrs Caroline Rookes CBE
Income: £9,262,000 [2017]; £8,158,000 [2016]; £6,665,000 [2015]; £7,305,000 [2014]; £6,700,000 [2013]

Vintage Trains
Registered: 19 Sep 1994 *Employees:* 20 *Volunteers:* 100
Tel: 07748 636481 *Website:* vintagetrains.co.uk
Activities: Environment, conservation, heritage
Address: 8 Armour Close, Burbage, Hinckley, Leics, LE10 2QW
Trustees: Mr Christopher Michael Whitehouse, Mr Anthony John Lambert, Mr Adrian Shooter, Mr Michael George Gilbert BSc FCA, Mr Vic Michel, Mr David William Keay
Income: £1,362,293 [2016]; £1,430,341 [2015]; £1,535,120 [2014]; £1,472,285 [2013]; £1,316,684 [2012]

The Virgin Foundation
Registered: 25 Aug 1987 *Employees:* 38
Website: virgin.com
Activities: General charitable purposes; education, training; advancement of health or saving of lives; prevention or relief of poverty; overseas aid, famine relief; environment, conservation, heritage; economic, community development, employment; human rights, religious or racial harmony, equality or diversity
Address: 179 Harrow Raod, London, W2 6NB
Trustees: Ms Vanessa Branson, Holly Katie Templeman Branson, Mr Peter Norris, Ms Nathalie Jamila Richards, Ms Jane Tewson, Mr Ajaz Ahmed, Ms Jean Marie Oelwang, Ms Jillian Anne Brady
Income: £11,658,000 [2016]; £12,444,000 [2015]; £13,313,000 [2014]; £9,525,000 [2013]; £10,570,000 [2012]

The Virgin Money Foundation
Registered: 15 Apr 2015
Tel: 0191 279 2047 *Website:* virginmoneyfoundation.org.uk
Activities: General charitable purposes; other charitable purposes
Address: 29 Turnpike Walk, Sedgefield, Stockton on Tees, Cleveland, TS21 3NP
Trustees: Sir Thomas Andrew Shebbeare, Mr Edward Wakefield, Mr Timothy James Neil Davies-Pugh, Mr Tim Arthur, Ms Ruth Ibegbuna, Mrs Joanne Curry, Stephen Pearson, Miss Emma Margaret Morris
Income: £3,309,600 [2017]; £2,403,600 [2016]; £1,985,300 [2015]

Viridor Credits Environmental Company
Registered: 14 Mar 2003 *Employees:* 10 *Volunteers:* 52
Tel: 01823 476476 *Website:* viridor-credits.co.uk
Activities: Arts, culture, heritage, science; amateur sport; animals; environment, conservation, heritage; recreation
Address: Aintree House, Blackbrook Park Avenue, Taunton, Somerset, TA1 2PX
Trustees: Mr David Balfour Robertson, Mr Simon Leslie Catford, Mr Peter Renshaw, Mrs Mary Prior CVO MBE
Income: £6,963,707 [2017]; £10,267,232 [2016]; £11,500,972 [2015]; £14,874,203 [2014]; £10,816,151 [2013]

Virunga Foundation
Registered: 25 Oct 2005 *Employees:* 392
Tel: 020 3319 3700
Activities: Education, training; animals; environment, conservation, heritage
Address: 48 Chancery Lane, London, WC2A 1JF
Trustees: Dr Emmanuel De Merode, Mr Francois Xavier De Donnea, Ms Clare Back, Mr Jan Bonde Nielson, Ms Joanna Natasegara
Income: £39,202,087 [2016]; £10,208,219 [2015]; £5,558,588 [2014]; £7,283,313 [2013]; £2,760,050 [2012]

Vishnitz Girls School Limited
Registered: 29 Mar 2010 *Employees:* 75 *Volunteers:* 3
Tel: 020 8800 8541
Activities: Education, training; prevention or relief of poverty; religious activities
Address: 196 Lordship Road, London, N16 5ES
Trustees: Mr Benzion Steiner, Rabbi Mordechai Steren, Mr Israel Zieg
Income: £1,565,627 [2017]; £1,069,398 [2016]; £1,118,631 [2015]; £1,357,320 [2014]; £322,220 [2013]

Vision 21 (Cyfle Cymru)
Registered: 28 Apr 1995 *Employees:* 55 *Volunteers:* 50
Tel: 029 2062 1194 *Website:* v21.org.uk
Activities: Education, training; disability; environment, conservation, heritage; economic, community development, employment
Address: Unit 10-12 Field Way, Cardiff, CF14 4HY
Trustees: Mr Alan Pursell, Mr Michael John Peter Winter, Mr Barry Shiers, Mr John Grimes, Mrs Clare Cooze, Mr Mike Clarke, Mrs Elaine Gee, Mr Leigh Gripton
Income: £1,829,692 [2017]; £1,799,278 [2016]; £1,859,268 [2015]; £1,946,753 [2014]; £1,825,185 [2013]

Vision Aid Overseas
Registered: 21 Jul 2000 *Employees:* 13 *Volunteers:* 93
Website: visionaidoverseas.org
Activities: Education, training; advancement of health or saving of lives; disability; prevention or relief of poverty; overseas aid, famine relief; economic, community development, employment
Address: Vision Aid Overseas, Unit 12-13 The Bell Centre, Newton Road, Crawley, Surrey, RH10 9FZ
Trustees: Mr David Scott-Ralphs, Mrs Laura Bennett, Ms Lucy Carter, Mr Peter Gerard Beverley-Smith, Mr Ronnie Graham, Mr Geoffrey Ballantine, Mrs Vera Wilton, Mr Peter Michael Corbett, Ms Kajal Shah
Income: £1,146,536 [2017]; £1,239,714 [2016]; £795,009 [2015]; £995,809 [2014]; £1,013,717 [2013]

Vision Enhancement Services
Registered: 11 Mar 1998 *Employees:* 72 *Volunteers:* 95
Tel: 01244 381515 *Website:* visionsupport.org.uk
Activities: Disability
Address: Units 1 & 2, The Ropeworks, Whipcord Lane, Chester, CH1 4DZ
Trustees: Mr Peter Curtis, Mr Carl Pierce, Mr Alex Wilson, Mrs Marie Dean, Mrs Bethan Wyn Roberts, Mr John Graham, Mrs Linda Davies, Mr Miles Tutton, Mr Timothy Hall
Income: £2,499,215 [2017]; £2,583,258 [2016]; £2,755,130 [2015]; £2,846,470 [2014]; £2,388,931 [2013]

Vision Homes Association
Registered: 4 Mar 1993 *Employees:* 100
Tel: 0121 434 4644 *Website:* visionhomes.org.uk
Activities: Disability; accommodation, housing
Address: Trigate, 210-222 Hagley Road West, Oldbury, W Midlands, B68 0NP
Trustees: Mr Brian Clamp, James Inglis, Bobbie Petford, Eric Woodhead, Mrs Gillian Louise Jones
Income: £2,128,941 [2017]; £2,194,722 [2016]; £2,159,761 [2015]; £2,091,453 [2014]; £1,908,859 [2013]

Vision Redbridge Culture and Leisure
Registered: 11 Feb 2008 *Employees:* 288 *Volunteers:* 630
Website: vision-rcl.org.uk
Activities: General charitable purposes; advancement of health or saving of lives; arts, culture, heritage, science; amateur sport; environment, conservation, heritage; recreation
Address: 3rd Floor, Central Library, Clements Road, Ilford, Essex, IG1 1EA
Trustees: Mr Brian Spinks, Mrs Linda Perham, Mr Kevin Jon Pittman, Cllr Robin Turbefield, Cllr Dev Raj Sharma, Mrs Caroline Janet Ward, Mr Martin Denis Solder, Ms Catherine Jane Rowan, Mr David Charles Thorogood, Cllr Debbie Kaur-Thiara, Mr Stephen John Wilks
Income: £21,039,000 [2017]; £17,517,000 [2016]; £16,612,000 [2015]; £17,979,000 [2014]; £17,627,000 [2013]

Vision for a Nation Foundation
Registered: 31 Jan 2011 *Employees:* 17
Website: visionforanation.net
Activities: General charitable purposes; education, training; advancement of health or saving of lives; disability; prevention or relief of poverty; overseas aid, famine relief
Address: Vision for a Nation Foundation, 27 Old Gloucester Street, London, WC1N 3AX
Trustees: John Rhodes, Francis Alexander Scott, Mr Arnold Ekpe, James Chen, Catherine Colloms, Mr Paul Tomasic
Income: £1,087,950 [2016]; £2,523,611 [2015]; £462,472 [2014]; £722,128 [2013]; £118,649 [2012]

Vita et Pax School (Cockfosters) Limited
Registered: 9 Dec 1980 *Employees:* 24
Tel: 020 3909 4530 *Website:* vitaetpax.co.uk
Activities: Education, training; prevention or relief of poverty; overseas aid, famine relief; religious activities; amateur sport; human rights, religious or racial harmony, equality or diversity
Address: Vita et Pax Preparatory School, 6a Priory Close, London, N14 4AT
Trustees: Mr Christopher Edward Howell MBE, Mr Amit Patel, Mrs Anna Westcott, Mrs Helena Christine Casbolt, Mrs Seema Mehta, Mrs Mary Margaret O Connor
Income: £1,724,867 [2016]; £1,637,089 [2015]; £1,554,017 [2014]; £1,429,876 [2013]; £1,323,241 [2012]

Vital Regeneration
Registered: 16 Aug 2005 *Employees:* 16 *Volunteers:* 15
Tel: 020 7598 1751 *Website:* vitalregeneration.org
Activities: Education, training; arts, culture, heritage, science; amateur sport; environment, conservation, heritage; economic, community development, employment
Address: Vital Regeneration, 31 Plympton Street, London, NW8 8AB
Trustees: Margaret Pollock, Hugh McGeever, Ms Joni O'Sullivan, Lyndon Sly, Mr Christopher Charles Allner, Ms Madhu Rajesh
Income: £1,241,954 [2015]; £1,385,120 [2014]; £1,491,361 [2013]; £1,227,385 [2012]

Viva Network
Registered: 28 Feb 1996 *Employees:* 17 *Volunteers:* 11
Tel: 01865 811660 *Website:* viva.org
Activities: Education, training; prevention or relief of poverty; overseas aid, famine relief; economic, community development, employment
Address: Unit 8 The Gallery, 54 Marston Street, Oxford, OX4 1LF
Trustees: Mr Martin Henry Brian Hull, Mr Miles Buttrick, Stuart Pascall, Mrs Sarah Elizabeth Powley, Mrs Amanda McCalla-Leacy, Mr Nicholas Charles Bamber, Mr Roy Huang, Mrs Minakhi Chowdury-Westlake, Mr David Jonathan Bright, Mr Michael Sloane
Income: £2,047,736 [2017]; £2,311,843 [2016]; £1,669,421 [2015]; £1,654,608 [2014]; £1,401,128 [2013]

Vivacity Culture and Leisure
Registered: 4 Oct 2010 *Employees:* 407 *Volunteers:* 376
Tel: 01733 864285 *Website:* vivacity.org
Activities: General charitable purposes; education, training; arts, culture, heritage, science; amateur sport; recreation
Address: Peterborough Central Library, Broadway, Peterborough, PE1 1RX
Trustees: Mr Stewart Francis, Mr Keith Marriott, Mr Theo Anderton, Councillor Steve Allen, Mr Ian Templeton, Mr David Bath, Mrs Rachel Brownlow, Mrs Sarah Sewell, Councillor June Bull
Income: £10,065,864 [2017]; £10,172,985 [2016]; £10,275,756 [2015]; £10,877,018 [2014]; £8,266,173 [2013]

Vocational Training Charitable Trust
Registered: 30 Sep 1986 *Employees:* 121
Tel: 023 8068 4500 *Website:* vtct.org.uk
Activities: Education, training
Address: VTCT, Aspire House, 10 Annealing Close, Eastleigh, Hants, SO50 9PX
Trustees: Mr Stephen Dennison, Dr Christopher Laws, Mr Julian Glicher, Mrs Jennifer Sworder, Mrs Laraine Mary Morris, Mr Anthony Lau-Walker, Mrs B Mitchell, Mrs Stephanie Barnett, Ms Isabel Sutcliffe
Income: £9,162,479 [2017]; £5,645,217 [2016]; £5,822,850 [2015]; £5,609,736 [2014]; £5,991,944 [2013]

Yad Voezer Limited
Registered: 2 Feb 1994 *Employees:* 60
Tel: 020 8809 4303 *Website:* yadvoezer.com
Activities: Disability; accommodation, housing
Address: 9 Amhurst Park, London, N16 5DH
Trustees: Rabbi Ephraim Landau, Rabbi Solomon Singer, Mr Refoel Spitzer
Income: £1,895,985 [2017]; £1,731,978 [2016]; £1,609,129 [2015]; £1,518,770 [2014]; £1,574,953 [2013]

Voiceability Advocacy
Registered: 19 Jul 1999 *Employees:* 240 *Volunteers:* 136
Website: voiceability.org
Activities: Education, training; disability
Address: Voiceability Ltd, The Old Granary, Westwick, Oakington, Cambridge, CB24 3AR
Trustees: Mr Peter Anthony Letley, Mr Meredith Nicholas Vivian, Ms Kate Markey, Philip Tatt, Mr Cliff Broadhurst, Ms Susan Catherine Brown
Income: £9,161,024 [2017]; £9,771,726 [2016]; £9,605,981 [2015]; £9,051,344 [2014]; £6,922,897 [2013]

Voluntary Action Leicester
Registered: 31 Oct 1979 *Employees:* 76 *Volunteers:* 25
Tel: 0116 258 0666 *Website:* valonline.org.uk
Activities: General charitable purposes; education, training; economic, community development, employment
Address: Leicestershire Mediation Service, 9 Newarke Street, Leicester, LE1 5SN
Trustees: Mr Evan Rees, Mr Anil Majithia, Mr Narendrakumar Lalji Bhagwanji Waghela, Mr Stephen Martin Peatfield, Mr Duncan Cullen, Mr Ajay Aggarwal, Mohamed Salim, Mr Cleto Mudhefi, Ms Joanna Moore, Caro Hart
Income: £3,371,852 [2017]; £3,475,194 [2016]; £3,071,388 [2015]; £3,245,160 [2014]; £3,291,491 [2013]

Voluntary Action Merthyr Tydfil
Registered: 15 Mar 2007 *Employees:* 22 *Volunteers:* 3
Tel: 01685 353900 *Website:* vamt.net
Activities: General charitable purposes; economic, community development, employment
Address: TRI County Play Association, Voluntary Action Merthyr Tydfil, 89-90 Pontmorlais, Merthyr Tydfil, CF47 8UH
Trustees: Mr Brian Lewis, Mrs Ruth Eryl Hopkins, Mr Paul Gray, Mrs Ceinwen Statter, Mr Huw Williams, Ms Helen Thomas, Mrs Nicola Mahoney, Mrs Maria Kovacevic Thomas, Mrs Laura Guard, Mrs Anne Roberts
Income: £1,841,674 [2017]; £1,618,962 [2016]; £1,578,204 [2015]; £1,211,458 [2014]; £1,181,957 [2013]

Voluntary Action Rotherham
Registered: 14 Jun 1999 *Employees:* 33 *Volunteers:* 26
Tel: 01709 829821 *Website:* varotherham.org.uk
Activities: General charitable purposes; education, training; economic, community development, employment; other charitable purposes
Address: The Spectrum, Coke Hill, Rotherham, S Yorks, S60 2HX
Trustees: Mrs Margaret Oldfield, Mrs Lesley Dabell, Mr Neil Leatherland, Mr Geoff Link, Mrs Sarah Whittle, Ms Judy Robinson, Mr Stuart Walls, Mrs Stephanie Mary Hryschko, Mrs Joan Maureen Brier, Mr David Selman, Ms Jean Flanagan
Income: £1,314,095 [2017]; £1,892,629 [2016]; £1,363,459 [2015]; £1,477,890 [2014]; £1,798,172 [2013]

Voluntary Action Sheffield
Registered: 7 Oct 1963 *Employees:* 48 *Volunteers:* 88
Tel: 0114 253 6607 *Website:* vas.org.uk
Activities: General charitable purposes; education, training; economic, community development, employment
Address: VAS, The Circle, 33 Rockingham Lane, Sheffield, S1 4FW
Trustees: Ms Nicola Smith, Miss Kay Dickinson, Andy Buck, Mr Efe Eruero, Mr Rob Walton, Mr Mark Swales, Sarah Williamson, Mr Uriah Rennie, Mr Neil Booth, Ms Debbie Mathews, Ms Rachel Boyce, Mr James Lock
Income: £2,099,113 [2017]; £1,395,216 [2016]; £1,479,020 [2015]; £1,584,243 [2014]; £1,770,935 [2013]

Voluntary Norfolk
Registered: 11 Nov 2005 *Employees:* 48 *Volunteers:* 550
Tel: 01603 883810 *Website:* voluntarynorfolk.org.uk
Activities: General charitable purposes; education, training; advancement of health or saving of lives; disability; prevention or relief of poverty
Address: Voluntary Norfolk, St Clements House, 2-16 Colegate, Norwich, NR3 1BQ
Trustees: Mrs Helen Johnson, Mr David Walker, Mr John Kirkwood Archibald, Ms Vivienne Helen Clifford-Jackson, Ms Penelope Ann Seligman, Mr Colin Robert Bland, Mr Robert Hetherington
Income: £1,791,145 [2017]; £1,923,102 [2016]; £1,523,502 [2015]; £1,445,119 [2014]; £1,673,468 [2013]

Voluntary Service Overseas
Registered: 14 Feb 1962 *Employees:* 799 *Volunteers:* 5
Tel: 020 8780 7500 *Website:* vsointernational.org
Activities: The prevention or relief of poverty
Address: VSO International, 100 London Road, Kingston upon Thames, Surrey, KT2 6QJ
Trustees: Mr Stephen Pidgeon, Ms Mari Simonen, Mr James Samuel Younger, Mr Christopher Merry, Mr Charles Abani, Ms Amanda Rowlatt, Dr Noerine Kaleeba, Ms Hardeep Jhutty, Ms Hilary Arnstrong, Mr Gustaaf Teunis Franciscus Eskens
Income: £78,430,000 [2017]; £81,232,000 [2016]; £77,012,000 [2015]; £68,713,000 [2014]; £57,080,000 [2013]

The Voluntary and Community Sector Learning and Skills Consortium
Registered: 6 Sep 2004 *Employees:* 16
Website: enable.uk.net
Activities: Education, training; economic, community development, employment
Address: 26 The Orchard, Belper, Derbys, DE56 1DF
Trustees: Mr Michael Henry, Mr Bovell Anthony Palmer, Mr Alan Stuart Bunn, Mrs Teresa Cullen, Mr Safdar Azam, Mrs Nicola Alexandra Hufton
Income: £1,724,804 [2017]; £1,640,511 [2016]; £2,381,516 [2015]; £3,362,119 [2014]; £3,539,333 [2013]

Voluntary and Community Services Peaks and Dales
Registered: 7 Jan 1998 *Employees:* 150 *Volunteers:* 280
Tel: 01298 23970 *Website:* vcspd.org
Activities: General charitable purposes; other charitable purposes
Address: Voluntary and Community Services PE, 16 Eagle Parade, Buxton, Derbys, SK17 6EQ
Trustees: Mr Jonathan Charles Wood, Mr Alan Thompson, Mr Robert Shaw Treasurer, Mrs Helen Ruth Hazelhurst, William Burton, Mr David Brindley, Mike Starzec, Tina Sullivan
Income: £1,536,923 [2017]; £1,205,953 [2016]; £971,615 [2015]; £865,487 [2014]; £773,751 [2013]

Volunteer Cornwall
Registered: 8 Jun 1998 *Employees:* 34 *Volunteers:* 214
Tel: 01872 265305 *Website:* volunteercornwall.org.uk
Activities: General charitable purposes; education, training; economic, community development, employment
Address: Volunteer Cornwall, Acorn House, Heron Way, Newham, Truro, Cornwall, TR1 2XN
Trustees: The Rt Revd Timothy Martin Thornton, Mr Scott Bennett, Ms Kim Mundy, Mr Philip John McVey, Dr Michael Leyshon, Mrs Linda Emmett, Dr Peter McGregor, Miss Janet Popham, Professor Catherine Sylvia Leyshon, Ms Emma Louise Rowse
Income: £1,598,575 [2017]; £1,779,218 [2016]; £2,055,396 [2015]; £1,947,303 [2014]; £1,863,150 [2013]

Volunteer Reading Help
Registered: 4 Jul 1991 *Employees:* 121 *Volunteers:* 3,005
Tel: 020 7749 7961 *Website:* beanstalkcharity.org.uk
Activities: Education, training
Address: 3rd Floor, 6 Middle Street, London, EC1A 7JA
Trustees: Mr Jamie Pike, Mrs Jill Patricia Pay, Mr Ian Mecklenburg, Mr Viral Mehta, Mrs Sarah Jacqueline Macpherson, Mr Jared Brading, Mr Paul Dean, Mrs Magdalene Bayin-Adomako, Dr Roberta Anne Jacobson, Mrs Saana Elizabeth Johanna Karki
Income: £3,790,152 [2017]; £3,269,489 [2016]; £2,919,603 [2015]; £2,815,139 [2014]; £2,185,287 [2013]

Volunteering Matters
Registered: 22 Feb 1985 *Employees:* 160 *Volunteers:* 29,709
Tel: 020 3780 5870 *Website:* volunteeringmatters.org.uk
Activities: General charitable purposes; education, training; environment, conservation, heritage; economic, community development, employment
Address: The Levy Centre, 22-24 Lower Clapton Road, London, E5 0PD
Trustees: Mr Brian Smouha, Mr David Lindow Wilkinson, Satyen Dhana, Ms Anne Heal, Mr Patrick Luong, Mr Peter Bailey, Ms Iona Wyn, Mr Andrew Hudson, Mr Mitan Patel, Ms Katerina Rudiger, Ms Julie Kirkbride
Income: £7,723,000 [2017]; £7,079,000 [2016]; £7,100,000 [2015]; £19,481,000 [2014]; £17,825,000 [2013]

Vulcan to the Sky Trust
Registered: 6 Feb 2004 *Employees:* 36 *Volunteers:* 50
Tel: 01302 623300 *Website:* vulcantothesky.org
Activities: General charitable purposes; education, training; environment, conservation, heritage
Address: Vulcan to the Sky Trust, Hanger 3, Fourth Avenue, Doncaster Sheffield Airport, Doncaster, S Yorks, DN9 3GE
Trustees: Mr Ken Smart CBE, Mr John Nicholas Sharman, Dr Stephen Liddle CEng MRAeS, Air Commodore Thomas Edward Lawson Jarron, Sir Donald Spiers KCB TD FRAeS, Sir Gerald Howarth MP, Richard Clarke, Mr Philip Spiers
Income: £2,400,471 [2016]; £4,557,645 [2015]; £2,845,491 [2014]; £2,750,623 [2013]; £2,233,368 [2012]

W G S Trust
Registered: 13 May 1976
Tel: 0161 224 1077
Activities: Education, training
Address: Withington Girls School, 100 Wellington Road, Fallowfield, Manchester, M14 6BL
Trustees: Mr Ian Goulty, Mrs Janet Pickering, Mr David Illingworth BA FCA, Mrs Sarah Haslam, Lord John Lee, Mr Richard Bailey, Mrs Susan Marks, Mr Allan Beardsworth
Income: £1,052,765 [2017]; £729,393 [2016]; £823,971 [2015]; £1,618,647 [2014]; £694,139 [2013]

WABIL

Registered: 12 Jun 1985 *Employees:* 2 *Volunteers:* 10
Tel: 020 8459 8475 *Website:* wabil.com
Activities: General charitable purposes; education, training; prevention or relief of poverty; religious activities; economic, community development, employment
Address: 19 Chelmsford Square, London, NW10 3AP
Trustees: Sayyed-Mohammed Musawi, Dr Gulam Hadi Kadiwal, Mr Emad Dean Hilli
Income: £2,234,443 [2017]; £1,649,323 [2016]; £3,139,565 [2015]; £2,004,804 [2014]; £619,401 [2013]

WAC Arts

Registered: 18 Mar 1974 *Employees:* 95 *Volunteers:* 40
Tel: 020 7692 5800 *Website:* wacarts.co.uk
Activities: General charitable purposes; education, training; disability; arts, culture, heritage, science
Address: Old Town Hall, 213 Haverstock Hill, London, NW3 4QP
Trustees: Mr Peter Lewis Hodges, Mr Mark Malcomson, Mr Richard Gold, Ms Julieanne Gilbert, Ms Christine Kinnear, Elizabeth Cleaver, Mr Andrew Shaw, Ms Rosie Hytner, Mr Jolyon Brewis, Mr Paul McMahon
Income: £2,064,881 [2017]; £1,694,854 [2016]; £1,620,501 [2015]; £1,916,465 [2014]; £2,002,851 [2013]

WCMC

Registered: 9 Jan 1989 *Employees:* 125 *Volunteers:* 26
Tel: 01223 277314 *Website:* wcmc.org.uk
Activities: Environment, conservation, heritage
Address: WCMC, 219 Huntingdon Road, Cambridge, CB3 0DL
Trustees: Mr Alasdair David Poore, Dr Robin Bidwell, Mr Robin Mortimer, Dr Jennifer Zerk, Ms Idunn Eidheim, Mr Patrick John Haighton, Mr Robert Powell, Professor William Adams, Dr Kathleen MacKinnon, Ms Charlotte Wolff-Bye
Income: £8,941,051 [2016]; £9,051,605 [2015]; £10,042,190 [2014]; £9,797,487 [2013]; £8,575,220 [2012]

WCS Care Group Limited

Registered: 13 Jul 1992 *Employees:* 676 *Volunteers:* 12
Tel: 01926 864242 *Website:* wcs-care.co.uk
Activities: The advancement of health or saving of lives; disability; accommodation, housing
Address: Head Office 1st Floor, Newlands Whites Row, Kenilworth, Warwicks, CV8 1HW
Trustees: Mr Roger Leonard Merchant, Mr Karl Demian, Mrs Patricia Jane Southeard, Mr Keith Jon Nurcombe, Mr Mark Ronald Andrews, Mr Simon Peter Miller, Mr Barrie Christopher Cressey, Mr Lee Eamon Middleburgh, Mr Adrian Frederick Levett, Mrs Alison Last
Income: £18,696,000 [2017]; £14,116,000 [2016]; £12,987,000 [2015]; £11,214,000 [2014]; £11,200,000 [2013]

WEC International

Registered: 6 Jan 1965 *Volunteers:* 103
Tel: 01753 884631 *Website:* wec-uk.org
Activities: Education, training; religious activities
Address: WEC International, The Scala Offices, 115a Far Gosford Street, Coventry, Warwicks, CV1 5EA
Trustees: Mr Vivian Whitton, Mr Neil Wardrope, Mr Christopher Ellis, Mr Paul Hammond, Mr Andrew Bowker, Mr Stephen Banner, Mrs Carolyn Davey
Income: £3,088,053 [2017]; £3,070,678 [2016]; £3,298,935 [2015]; £2,533,760 [2014]; £2,590,839 [2013]

WECIL Ltd

Registered: 5 Mar 1996 *Employees:* 33 *Volunteers:* 102
Tel: 0117 947 9911 *Website:* wecil.co.uk
Activities: Disability
Address: Unit E, Link House, Britton Gardens, Kingswood, Bristol, BS15 1TF
Trustees: Mrs Jayne Carr, Ruth Pickersgill, Vicki Kaye, Mr Steve Strong, Ms Michelle Parfitt, Collette Fox
Income: £1,009,329 [2017]; £1,649,203 [2016]; £999,312 [2015]; £1,071,950 [2014]; £1,015,790 [2013]

WESC Foundation - The Specialist Centre for Visual Impairment

Registered: 30 Oct 1996 *Employees:* 267 *Volunteers:* 52
Website: wescfoundation.ac.uk
Activities: Education, training; advancement of health or saving of lives; disability; accommodation, housing; economic, community development, employment; other charitable purposes
Address: 27 Sweetings Road, Godmanchester, Huntingdon, Cambs, PE29 2JS
Trustees: Andrew Leadbetter, Derek Fargher, Tim Williams, Angus McNicol, James Heslop, Mr Noel Paul Fowler, Chris Knee, Mrs Susie Murray, Jules Jeffreys, Tracie Linehan
Income: £7,570,865 [2017]; £7,925,394 [2016]; £8,136,916 [2015]; £7,028,620 [2014]; £7,504,996 [2013]

WHAG

Registered: 6 Jun 2000 *Employees:* 48 *Volunteers:* 23
Tel: 01706 718180 *Website:* whag.info
Activities: Education, training; advancement of health or saving of lives; prevention or relief of poverty; accommodation, housing
Address: Womens Housing Acton Group, Rose Court, 677-679 Manchester Road, Castleton, Rochdale, OL11 3AA
Trustees: Mrs Julie Herd, Ms Elizabeth Mary Rustchynskyj, Ms Hazel Waddington, Mrs Angela Oakley, Ms Siobhan Nugent, Ms Amy Beth Rothwell
Income: £1,546,915 [2017]; £1,560,236 [2016]; £1,224,519 [2015]; £930,368 [2014]; £866,896 [2013]

WIZO.UK

Registered: 16 Jul 2008 *Employees:* 15 *Volunteers:* 120
Tel: 020 7319 9169 *Website:* wizouk.org
Activities: Education, training; disability; prevention or relief of poverty; overseas aid, famine relief; accommodation, housing
Address: Wizo, Charles House, 108-110 Finchley Road, London, NW3 5JJ
Trustees: Mrs Jill Henrietta Shaw, Mrs Johanna Marion Seifert, Mrs Loraine Warren, Mrs Danielle Sara Shane, Mrs Annabel Rachel Stelzer, Mr D Ashton, Mrs Michele Vogel, Mrs Jacqueline Carol Ellert, Mrs Michele Gloria Pollock, Mr Russell Andrew Cohen, Mrs Ronit Ribak-Madari
Income: £1,740,573 [2017]; £2,025,815 [2016]; £2,080,012 [2015]; £2,261,669 [2014]; £2,146,658 [2013]

WJEC CBAC Limited

Registered: 15 Jan 1999 *Employees:* 386
Website: wjec.co.uk
Activities: Education, training; arts, culture, heritage, science
Address: WJEC, 245 Western Avenue, Cardiff, CF5 2YX
Trustees: Mr Michael Thomas Evans, Councillor Edward Thomas, Mr Alan Richard Lockyer, Councillor Sarah Merry, Ms Beverley Frances Downes, Eryl Williams, Mrs Elizabeth Mary Williams, Ms Jessica Leigh Jones, Councillor Gail Giles, Ms Joanna Patricia Moonan
Income: £41,363,948 [2016]; £40,704,029 [2015]; £39,312,000 [2014]; £39,896,000 [2013]; £40,670,000 [2012]

WPF Therapy Ltd
Registered: 2 Jun 1977 *Employees:* 84 *Volunteers:* 20
Tel: 020 7378 2000 *Website:* wpf.org.uk
Activities: General charitable purposes; education, training
Address: 23 Magdalen Street, London, SE1 2EN
Trustees: Mr Clive Bowman, Mrs Jennifer Peart, Ms Evita Chiang Zanuso, Ms Rosalind Louisa Ramsay, Mr Stephen Elliot Davidson, Mr Philip Cambria Lee, Mrs Bernice Rook, Ms Dympna Margaret Ellen Cunnane, Miss Carol Anne Rue
Income: £1,822,404 [2016]; £1,760,043 [2015]; £1,861,494 [2014]; £1,842,778 [2013]

WST Charity Limited
Registered: 22 Sep 2000 *Volunteers:* 6
Activities: General charitable purposes; prevention or relief of poverty
Address: 1 Boyne Avenue, London, NW4 2JL
Trustees: Mr Irvine Sidney Jay, Mr Alan Nevies, Mr Maurice Wiesenfeld, Mr Abraham Ephraim David Rosenberg, Mr Gershon Joel Fraenkel, Mr Nachman Dov Heller
Income: £1,590,430 [2016]; £1,467,135 [2015]; £1,455,503 [2014]; £1,497,746 [2013]; £1,553,093 [2012]

WWF - UK
Registered: 23 Jun 2000 *Employees:* 333 *Volunteers:* 28
Website: wwf.org.uk
Activities: Environment, conservation, heritage
Address: WWF-UK, The Living Planet Centre, Rufford House, Brewery Road, Woking, Surrey, GU21 4LL
Trustees: Dr Michael Dixon BSc ARCS DPhil FCGI, Sir Andrew Cahn, Professor Eleanor Jane Milner-Gulland, Mr Christopher Mark Richardson, Mrs Jane Cotton, Professor Malcolm Press, Professor Richard Sambrook, Mr Andrew James Green, Professor Georgina Mary Mace, Ms Natalie Gross, Mr Ila Kasem, Mrs Catherine Thea Dugmore
Income: £60,795,000 [2017]; £71,088,000 [2016]; £63,203,000 [2015]; £62,952,000 [2014]; £59,980,000 [2013]

Wadham College
Registered: 6 Jan 2011 *Employees:* 194 *Volunteers:* 70
Tel: 01865 277966 *Website:* wadham.ox.ac.uk
Activities: Education, training
Address: Wadham College, Parks Road, Oxford, OX1 3PN
Trustees: Professor Richard Sharpe FBA, Prof Colin Mayer, Prof Alex Halliday, Professor Darren Dixon, Professor Paolo Radaelli, Dr Peter Thonemann, Dr Andrew Farmery, Dr Mark Thompson, Dr Stephen Heyworth, Dr Michael Bannon, Dr Carolin Duttlinger, Dr Benjamin Berks, Dr Oren Sussman, Dr Claudia Pazos Alonso, Mr Alan Beggs, Professor Fiona Powrie, Professor Philip Candelas, Dr Matthew Kempshall, Dr Giulia Zanderighi, Dr David Conlon, Lord Ken MacDonald, Dr Alexander Ritter, Dr Jane Griffiths, Dr Jack Miller, Dr Jonathan Service, Dr Lydia Gilday, Dr Thomas Sinclair, Dr Judy Stephenson, Dr Alexander Kilpatrick, Professor Karl Kugle, Dr Sakura Schafer-Nameki, Dr Sara Motta, Dr Christina Sophia Maria Benninghaus, Dr Scott Blumenthal, Mr Philip Bullock, Dr Dominic Brookshaw, Dr Margaret Hillenbrand, Dr Christopher Summerfield, Professor Eric Clarke, Dr Martin Bureau, Dr Alexander Paseau, Dr Elizabeth Jane Garnett, Professor Edmund Herzig, Dr Ankhi Mukherjee, Dr Caroline Mawson, Dr Paul Martin, Ms Laura Hoyano, Professor Paul Beer, Professor Sallie Lamb, Prof Susan Lea, Dr Nathalie Seddon, Professor Nicholas Athanasou, Dr Ian Moore, Mrs Frances Lloyd, Dr Francesco Zanetti, Dr Emma Cohen, Mrs Julie Christiane Hage, Dr Olivia Vasquez-Medina, Dr Alexander Steel, Prof Ekaterina Shamonina, Dr Thomas Simpson, Dr Peter Alsop, Professor Ursula Martin, Mr Samuel Williams, Dr Alfonso Castrejon-Pita, Mr Oliver Butler, Dr Emily McLaughlin, Dr Andrew Princep
Income: £12,899,000 [2017]; £19,634,000 [2016]; £10,998,000 [2015]; £10,765,000 [2014]; £11,291,000 [2013]

Wakefield Grammar School Foundation
Registered: 13 Sep 2001 *Employees:* 478 *Volunteers:* 25
Tel: 01924 231600 *Website:* wgsf.org.uk
Activities: Education, training
Address: Wakefield Grammar School Foundation, Governors Office, 158 Northgate, Wakefield, W Yorks, WF1 3UF
Trustees: Mr John McLeod, Dr Mahendra Gilabbhai Patel, Mr Michael Hird, Mr Simon Chamberlain, Mrs Diane Carole Watson, Mrs Penelope Jane Plumpton, Miss Alison Jane Tetley, Mr Jonathan David Jeffries, Mrs Helen Massey Janette, Mr Malcolm Golightly, Mr Jason Brook, Mr Martin John Shevill, Dr Deven Vani, Professor David Gareth Jenkins, Mr Timothy George Welton, Rev Leah Beverley Vasey-Saunders, Mrs Caroline Gorton
Income: £20,906,096 [2017]; £22,771,948 [2016]; £19,860,337 [2015]; £19,369,447 [2014]; £19,327,481 [2013]

Wakefield Hospice
Registered: 25 Nov 1988 *Employees:* 140 *Volunteers:* 365
Tel: 01924 331400 *Website:* wakefieldhospice.org
Activities: The advancement of health or saving of lives
Address: Wakefield Hospice, Aberford Road, Wakefield, W Yorks, WF1 4TS
Trustees: Mr Terry Elms, Mr David Melia, Mr Alistair Paul Howatson, Dr Jane Elizabeth Senior, Mr David James Barker, Mr Mark David Ashton, Mr Gary Mortimer, Mr David John Martindale, Mr Guy William Cattell, Ms Nichola Frances Esmond, Mr Daniel James Lumb, Ms Nina Gunson
Income: £3,797,792 [2017]; £4,311,082 [2016]; £4,567,192 [2015]; £4,105,049 [2014]; £3,598,408 [2013]

Wakefield Theatre Trust
Registered: 18 Sep 1974 *Employees:* 26 *Volunteers:* 108
Tel: 01924 334112 *Website:* theatreroyalwakefield.co.uk
Activities: Education, training; arts, culture, heritage, science; economic, community development, employment
Address: 29 Bayheath House, 20 Market Street, Wakefield, W Yorks, WF1 1DH
Trustees: Claire Lawton, Susan Williams, John Horvath, Lindsey Davies, Mr Jon Ingham, Jacquie Speight, Ms Susan Slassor, Olivia Rowley, John Godber, Pat Hanley, Gill Galdins, Tim Welton, Mrs Kathryn Morgan
Income: £2,106,864 [2017]; £1,657,375 [2016]; £1,653,370 [2015]; £1,769,737 [2014]; £1,435,362 [2013]

Walcot Educational Foundation
Registered: 4 Oct 1973 *Employees:* 6
Tel: 020 7735 1925 *Website:* walcotfoundation.org.uk
Activities: Education, training; prevention or relief of poverty
Address: Walcot Foundation, 127 Kennington Road, London, SE11 6SF
Trustees: The Walcot & Hayle's Trustee
Income: £2,255,000 [2017]; £2,387,000 [2016]; £2,129,000 [2015]; £2,198,000 [2014]; £2,217,000 [2013]

Walden School
Registered: 20 Nov 1990 *Employees:* 155
Website: waldenschool.co.uk
Activities: Education, training
Address: Grant Thornton UK LLP, 4 Hardman Square, Manchester, M3 3EB
Trustees: Mr Richard Bloomfield, Mr Stephen Portal Tomkins, Celia James, Mr Colin Winston South, Mrs Finola O'Sullivan, Mr Peter Brindle, Mrs Pauline Brindle, Dr Rory McCrea, Mrs Susan Garratt, Mr Andrew Deller, Mrs Delia Suffling, Mr Tony Penman, Mr Richard Harry Braun, Mr Adrian Sharp, Mr Andrew Clark
Income: £5,993,586 [2015]; £5,645,538 [2014]; £5,919,098 [2013]; £11,081,829 [2012]

Waldorf School (Bristol) Limited
Registered: 12 Nov 1973 *Employees:* 49 *Volunteers:* 10
Tel: 0117 933 9990 *Website:* bristolsteinerschool.org
Activities: Education, training
Address: Bristol Steiner School, Redland Hill House, Redland Hill, Redland, Bristol, BS6 6UX
Trustees: Mr James Wetz, Mr Daniel Stuart Black, Mrs Anna Rajkumar, Mr Michael Luxford, Ms Rachael Mary Philips
Income: £1,536,713 [2017]; £862,650 [2016]; £952,635 [2015]; £978,076 [2014]; £1,044,725 [2013]

Wales Council for Voluntary Action
Registered: 24 May 1963 *Employees:* 92
Tel: 029 2043 1734 *Website:* wcva.org.uk
Activities: General charitable purposes
Address: Wales Council for Voluntary Action, Baltic House, Mount Stuart Square, Cardiff, CF10 5FH
Trustees: Mrs Lydia Mair Stephens, Mrs Pauline Young, Fran Targett, Mrs Cherrie Bija, Ms Lindsay Ann Cordery-Bruce, Mr Jonathan Robert Evans, Mr Christopher Peter Lines, Mrs Catriona Williams, Mr Peter Roger Davies, Mr Simon Harris, Mrs Catherine Mair Gwynant, Dr Mark Llewellyn, Mr Richard Andrew Williams
Income: £12,154,050 [2017]; £12,803,345 [2016]; £20,033,970 [2015]; £23,364,155 [2014]; £20,855,366 [2013]

Wales Millennium Centre
Registered: 30 Jan 1997 *Employees:* 260
Tel: 029 2063 6400 *Website:* wmc.org.uk
Activities: Education, training; arts, culture, heritage, science
Address: Bute Place, Cardiff Bay, CF10 5AL
Trustees: Dr Carol Bell, Ms Fiona Elizabeth Morris, Ms Mererid Hopwood, Mr Geraint Anderson, Ms Lizz Munday, Bleddyn Phillips, Mr Peter Swinburn, Professor Ian Hargreaves, Ms Michelle Pearce, Ms Rita Singh
Income: £24,667,000 [2017]; £18,146,000 [2016]; £28,090,000 [2015]; £19,461,000 [2014]; £22,054,000 [2013]

Wales Pre-School Providers Association
Registered: 25 Jun 1996 *Employees:* 51
Website: walesppa.org
Activities: Other charitable purposes
Address: Wales Pre-School Providers Association, Unit 1 The Lofts, Hunter Street, Cardiff, CF10 5GX
Trustees: Ms Louise Bell, Miss Lisa Marie Owen, Mr Michael Frank Thorne, Mrs Alison Kitchen
Income: £1,204,297 [2017]; £1,202,464 [2016]; £1,349,237 [2015]; £1,465,438 [2014]; £1,468,439 [2013]

Walhampton School Trust Ltd.
Registered: 28 Jun 1966 *Employees:* 100 *Volunteers:* 4
Tel: 01590 613306 *Website:* walhampton.com
Activities: Education, training
Address: Walhampton School Trust Ltd, Walhampton School, Walhampton, Lymington, Hants, SO41 5ZG
Trustees: Ms Sarah Joan Thomas BA PGCE, Mr Jeremy John Leonard Bennett, Mr Matthew Winter, Mrs Kristine Host-Verbraak, Dr Mark Sopher, Mr David Ian Rawllinson, Mr Neil Alexander McGrigor, Mr Charles Nicholson, Mr Derek Shakespeare, Mrs Samantha Keen, Mrs Heidi Leavesley, Mr David Whately-Smith
Income: £5,179,355 [2017]; £4,879,275 [2016]; £4,342,792 [2015]; £3,665,827 [2014]; £3,494,867 [2013]

Walk The Plank
Registered: 27 Apr 1995 *Employees:* 16
Tel: 0161 736 8964 *Website:* walktheplank.co.uk
Activities: Education, training; arts, culture, heritage, science
Address: Cobden Works, 37-41 Cobden Street, Salford, M6 6WF
Trustees: Ms Sandra Green, Mr Simon Glinn, Ms Shona Mary McCarthy, Mrs Catrina Page, Chris Paul, Ms Angela Bhaseen, Cath Ralph, Mr Liam Naughton
Income: £1,815,127 [2016]; £3,317,017 [2015]; £1,917,954 [2014]; £2,835,034 [2013]; £2,601,903 [2012]

The Walker 597 Trust
Registered: 12 Oct 1978
Tel: 01564 792261
Activities: Animals
Address: Lodders, 16 High Street, Henley in Arden, Warwicks, B95 5BW
Trustees: Mr Kenneth Hughes, Ms Helen Rowett, Mrs Judith Helen Middleton, Mrs Sheila Ann Kitchen, Mr David Ansell
Income: £1,638,508 [2017]; £6,005 [2016]; £16,556 [2015]; £6,967 [2014]; £6,765 [2013]

Walking with the Wounded
Registered: 21 Aug 2013 *Employees:* 23 *Volunteers:* 195
Tel: 01263 863900 *Website:* walkingwiththewounded.org.uk
Activities: Education, training; advancement of health or saving of lives; disability; prevention or relief of poverty; economic, community development, employment; armed forces, emergency service efficiency; recreation
Address: Walking with the Wounded, Stody Hall Barns, Stody, Melton Constable, Norfolk, NR24 2ED
Trustees: Mr Simon Daglish, Mr Neil Greenberg, Mrs Flora Joyce McLean, Ms Emma Peters, Mr Guy Disney, Dick Turpin, Mr Darryl Eales, Mr James Alistair Hibbert, Mr William Medlicott, Mr Damian Beeley
Income: £2,608,387 [2016]; £2,127,360 [2015]; £2,629,248 [2014]

Wallace & Gromit's Children's Foundation
Registered: 24 Jan 1995 *Employees:* 37 *Volunteers:* 30
Tel: 0117 927 3888 *Website:* grandappeal.org.uk
Activities: The advancement of health or saving of lives; disability; accommodation, housing
Address: 30-32 Upper Maudlin Street, Bristol, BS2 8DJ
Trustees: Mr Jocelyn Handley Moule, Mike Norton, Simon Cooper, Angie Last
Income: £3,086,016 [2017]; £6,845,788 [2016]; £5,059,867 [2015]; £7,370,771 [2014]; £1,275,510 [2013]

The Charlie Waller Memorial Trust
Registered: 13 Jun 2005 *Employees:* 5 *Volunteers:* 75
Tel: 01635 869754 *Website:* cwmt.org.uk
Activities: Education, training; advancement of health or saving of lives
Address: 16A High Street, Thatcham, Berks, RG19 3JD
Trustees: Mrs Susan Mary Shenkman, Mr Richard Beaumont Waller, Mr George Charles Robin Booth, Mr Mark Durden-Smith, Professor Rosamund Shafran, Mr Iain Weatherby, Mr Michael Colquhoun Cole-Fontayn, Mr Gordon Leslie Black, The Rt Hon Sir George Mark Waller, Mr William Patrick De Laszlo, Mr Robert Gordon Beaumont, Mr Philip George Waller, Dr Nicholas Irwin Broughton, Mr Charles Patrick St John Lytle
Income: £1,153,735 [2016]; £713,442 [2015]; £577,368 [2014]; £515,139 [2013]; £353,777 [2012]

Wallich-Clifford Community
Registered: 11 Sep 1991 *Employees:* 316 *Volunteers:* 73
Website: wallichclifford.com
Activities: Accommodation, housing
Address: The Wallich Centre, Cathedral Road, Cardiff, CF11 9JF
Trustees: Mr Malcolm John Thomas, Dr R P Dubrow-Marshall, Mrs H C Phillips, Mr G A Hughes, Mrs Sian Davies, Mr Steve Sanders, Mr Thomas Howard Bennett, Mrs S E Cleverley, Ms Sarah Lindsay Botterill, Mr Winston Jacob
Income: £12,899,313 [2017]; £10,685,849 [2016]; £10,351,499 [2015]; £9,803,625 [2014]; £9,976,864 [2013]

Wallscourt Foundation
Registered: 8 Nov 1995
Tel: 0117 328 6695
Activities: Education, training; arts, culture, heritage, science
Address: University of The West of England, Frenchay Campus, Coldharbour Lane, Bristol, BS16 1QY
Trustees: Mrs K J Morgan, Mr David James Hider, Professor S G West, Mr Christopher Arthur Booy, Mr Simon Alick Moore, Mr John Steven Laycock, Mr Nicholas Charles Bacon, Mr Raymond Noel Burton, Mrs Gillian Elizabeth Camm
Income: £1,100,459 [2017]; £25,329,049 [2016]; £712,852 [2015]; £1,097,945 [2014]; £1,101,751 [2013]

Walsall Housing Group Limited
Registered: 1 Apr 2005 *Employees:* 630 *Volunteers:* 93
Tel: 0300 555 6666 *Website:* whg.uk.com
Activities: Education, training; advancement of health or saving of lives; disability; prevention or relief of poverty; accommodation, housing; environment, conservation, heritage; economic, community development, employment
Address: Walsall Housing Group Ltd, 100 Hatherton Street, Walsall, W Midlands, WS1 1AB
Trustees: Mike Hew, Eddie Hughes, Noel Maxwell, Ian Gardner, Mr Jatinder Sharma OBE, Greg Warner-Harris, Terry Mingay, Linda Cole, Lee Glover, Dr Amanze Ejiogu, Gary Fulford
Income: £105,561,860 [2017]; £104,050,766 [2016]; £106,085,725 [2015]; £98,553,625 [2014]; £90,016,701 [2013]

Walsingham College (Affiliated Schools) Limited
Registered: 10 Apr 1963 *Employees:* 44 *Volunteers:* 1
Tel: 07939 580397 *Website:* quaintonhall.org.uk
Activities: Education, training; religious activities
Address: Quinton Hall School, 91 Hindes Road, Harrow, Middlesex, HA1 1RX
Trustees: Mr Andrew Lee, Richard Abraham, Rev Vanessa Baron MA Cantab MA London BSc City, Mr Alan Ruddy, Mrs Ruth Suzanne Ward, The Right Revd Jonathan Mark Baker, Mr Timothy Stephen Day
Income: £1,721,807 [2016]; £1,607,831 [2015]; £1,597,536 [2014]; £1,501,300 [2013]; £1,370,610 [2012]

The Walsingham College Trust Association Ltd
Registered: 16 Jan 1963 *Employees:* 75 *Volunteers:* 134
Website: walsinghamanglican.org.uk
Activities: Religious activities
Address: The Shrine Office, 2 Common Place, Walsingham, Norfolk, NR22 6EE
Trustees: Mr John David Sebastian Booth, Mrs Ruth Ward, Rt Revd Philip North, Miss Amanda McIntyre, Bishop of Fulham, Mr A Roberts, Rev Howard Stoker, The Revd Prebendary Graeme Rowlands
Income: £2,690,023 [2016]; £2,669,236 [2015]; £1,851,224 [2014]; £3,132,203 [2013]; £2,961,382 [2012]

Walsingham Support
Registered: 23 Jul 1986 *Employees:* 918
Tel: 020 8343 5600 *Website:* walsingham.com
Activities: Disability
Address: Suite 500, Building 4, North London Business Park, Oakleigh Road South, London, N11 1GN
Trustees: Ms Maddy Thomson, Ms Janine Sturgeon, Mr Richard Keagan-Bull, Mrs Alison Margaret Heaton, Mr Mark Best, Mrs Heather Benjamin, Ms Donna Clark, Mrs Jeanette Barrowcliffe, Ms Elizabeth Edwards
Income: £22,902,405 [2017]; £20,390,973 [2016]; £18,704,336 [2015]; £18,057,151 [2014]; £15,259,402 [2013]

Walsingham Trust
Registered: 23 May 1973 *Employees:* 42 *Volunteers:* 7
Tel: 01328 820217 *Website:* walsingham.org.uk
Activities: General charitable purposes; prevention or relief of poverty; religious activities
Address: Basilica of Our Lady of Walsingham, R C National Shrine, Pilgrim Bureau, Friday Market Place, Walsingham, Norfolk, NR22 6EG
Trustees: The Rt Rev Anthony Rogers, Rt Rev Alan Stephen Hopes, Mr John Robert Montgomery Pitt
Income: £3,063,303 [2016]; £1,447,236 [2015]; £1,183,430 [2014]; £1,176,405 [2013]; £1,218,788 [2012]

Waltham Forest Noor Ul Islam Trust

Registered: 1 Mar 1993 *Employees:* 73 *Volunteers:* 100
Tel: 020 8558 0786 *Website:* noorulislam.org.uk
Activities: General charitable purposes; education, training; advancement of health or saving of lives; prevention or relief of poverty; overseas aid, famine relief; religious activities; arts, culture, heritage, science; amateur sport; environment, conservation, heritage; economic, community development, employment; human rights, religious or racial harmony, equality or diversity; recreation; other charitable purposes
Address: 711 High Road, London, E10 6RA
Trustees: Mr Hassam Maherally, Mr Mamode Hossen Gogah, Mr Ubaid Hansa, Mr Hassan Iqbal, Mr Issop Sulliman Hansa, Mr Reshad Joomun, Mr Amin Laher
Income: £2,109,346 [2016]; £2,330,629 [2015]; £1,967,481 [2014]; £1,788,897 [2013]; £1,418,659 [2012]

Walthamstow Hall

Registered: 3 Oct 1996 *Employees:* 121 *Volunteers:* 25
Tel: 01732 454227 *Website:* walthamstow-hall.co.uk
Activities: Education, training
Address: Walthamstow Hall, Holly Bush Lane, Sevenoaks, Kent, TN13 3UL
Trustees: Alun Grant Evans BSc MSI, Mrs Jayne Adams, Roger Evernden, Mr Andrew Martin Baddeley, Mr Simon Craig Heather, Mrs Janet Joynes, Mr Jonathan Wayne Lewis BSc FCA, Mr Peter Gloyne, Clare Kevis, Mrs Belinda Rattray, Dr Nigel Wolfe Jepps, Mr Graham Lacey, Professor Alastair Pearce LRAM BMus MMus PhD FRSA FBC, Mrs Sarah Alison Lewis-Davies BA
Income: £10,602,778 [2017]; £11,022,608 [2016]; £9,565,529 [2015]; £8,275,532 [2014]; £7,607,659 [2013]

Walthamstow and Chingford Almshouse Charity

Registered: 11 Oct 2006 *Employees:* 7
Tel: 020 8520 0295 *Website:* wcac.org.uk
Activities: The prevention or relief of poverty; accommodation, housing
Address: Monoux Hall, Church End, Walthamstow, London, E17 9RL
Trustees: Walthamstow and Chingford Almshouse Trustee Company
Income: £1,916,610 [2017]; £710,757 [2016]; £705,112 [2015]; £697,926 [2014]; £737,692 [2013]

The Walton Centre Charity

Registered: 20 Oct 1995 *Employees:* 3 *Volunteers:* 53
Tel: 0151 529 5516 *Website:* thewaltoncentre.nhs.uk
Activities: Education, training; advancement of health or saving of lives
Address: The Walton Centre, Lower Lane, Liverpool, L9 7LJ
Trustees: The Walton Centre NHS Foundation Trust
Income: £2,591,009 [2017]; £428,427 [2016]; £589,000 [2015]; £471,012 [2014]; £295,094 [2013]

Walton on Thames Charity

Registered: 2 Apr 1984 *Employees:* 57 *Volunteers:* 5
Tel: 01932 220242 *Website:* waltoncharity.org.uk
Activities: General charitable purposes; prevention or relief of poverty; accommodation, housing
Address: Walton on Thames Charity, Charities House, 2 The Quintet, Churchfield Road, Walton on Thames, Surrey, KT12 2TZ
Trustees: Chris Sadler, Mrs Elizabeth Kennedy, Mr Timothy Mark Armstrong Hewens, Mr Nicolas Stuart, Mr Paul Tajasque, Mr Graham Victor Mann, David Nash, Mr Robert Douglas, Mrs Juliet Hobbs, Mr Steve Wood, Mr James Vizzini
Income: £3,199,282 [2017]; £3,115,289 [2016]; £3,169,275 [2015]; £2,786,804 [2014]; £2,650,537 [2013]

Wandsworth Citizens Advice Bureaux Limited

Registered: 19 Aug 1994 *Employees:* 27 *Volunteers:* 88
Tel: 020 8682 3766 *Website:* cawandsworth.org
Activities: General charitable purposes
Address: 116 St Alphonsus Road, London, SW4 7BN
Trustees: Mr Borge Andreassen, Mr Makoto Takano, Mr James Spybey, Ms Teresa Susan Wilson Marshall, Mr Jonathan Mogford, Lucy Harmer, Mr Guy Conway
Income: £1,134,200 [2017]; £922,096 [2016]; £880,592 [2015]; £825,388 [2014]; £809,470 [2013]

War Child

Registered: 22 Sep 1998 *Employees:* 212 *Volunteers:* 3
Website: warchild.org.uk
Activities: Education, training; prevention or relief of poverty; overseas aid, famine relief
Address: War Child, Studio 320, 53-79 Highgate Studios, Highgate Road, London, NW5 1TL
Trustees: Mr Jacob Tas, Ms Penny Richards, Nabila Jiwaji, Ms Heather Francis, Mr Roderick MacLeod, Mr Sacha Deshmukh, Julie Weston, Mr Guy Gibson, Mr Tom Scourfield
Income: £13,254,250 [2016]; £8,997,000 [2015]; £6,668,000 [2014]; £5,535,000 [2013]; £4,971,000 [2012]

War Memorials Trust

Registered: 7 May 1997 *Employees:* 11 *Volunteers:* 122
Tel: 020 7834 0200 *Website:* warmemorials.org
Activities: Education, training; arts, culture, heritage, science; environment, conservation, heritage
Address: 1st Floor, War Memorials Trust, 14 Buckingham Palace Road, London, SW1W 0QP
Trustees: Mr John Peat, Mr Roger Bardell, Mr David Seymour MA MPhil PGCE, The Lord Rupert De Mauley TD, Mr Peter McCormick OBE, Mr Russell Walters, Mr Randolph Churchill, Lady Caroline Dalmeny
Income: £1,190,293 [2017]; £1,703,713 [2016]; £699,294 [2014]; £447,050 [2013]; £503,865 [2012]

War on Want

Registered: 22 Sep 1962 *Employees:* 20
Tel: 020 7324 5040 *Website:* waronwant.org
Activities: The prevention or relief of poverty; overseas aid, famine relief; human rights, religious or racial harmony, equality or diversity
Address: War on Want, 44-48 Shepherdess Walk, London, N1 7JP
Trustees: Mr Roger Andrew McKenzie, Mr Mike Cushman, Mr Mario Novelli, Elisabeth Mary Theresa Pritchard, Dr Anna Stone, Mr Hugh Anthony McMullan, Norah Rosina O'Hare, Susan Edith Branford, Marilyn Joyce Tyzack
Income: £1,941,052 [2017]; £2,055,300 [2016]; £2,114,087 [2015]; £1,816,009 [2014]; £2,058,647 [2013]

Mary Ward Settlement

Registered: 12 Jul 1963 *Employees:* 191 *Volunteers:* 166
Tel: 020 7269 6334 *Website:* marywardcentre.ac.uk
Activities: Education, training
Address: Mary Ward Centre, 42 Queen Square, London, WC1N 3AQ
Trustees: Margaret Wheeler, Ms Kim Duong, Mr Andrew Peck, Dr Austin Hill, Frances Bates, Emma Wyatt, Beatriz Montoya, Mr Brian Gerald Chandler, Mr Gerard Darby, Ms Andrea Williams, Alex Horsup, Kate Watters, Mr Stephen Gerald Carlill, Mr Graham Keith Collins, Ms Nadine Cartner, Ms Rachel Elizabeth Wright
Income: £4,634,039 [2017]; £4,587,000 [2016]; £4,630,000 [2015]; £3,531,000 [2014]; £4,775,000 [2013]

The Warden and Scholars of St Mary College of Winchester
Registered: 12 Nov 2010 *Employees:* 365 *Volunteers:* 24
Tel: 01962 621206 *Website:* winchestercollege.org
Activities: Education, training; environment, conservation, heritage
Address: Winchester College, College Street, Winchester, Hants, SO23 9NA
Trustees: Mr Charles Sinclair, Mr Miles Young, Andrew Sykes, Dr Magnus Jerome Ryan, Mr Robert Sutton, Major-General Jonathan Shaw, Mr Andrew Joy, The Hon Sir Stephen Cobb, Dr Peggy Frith, Mr Nicholas Ferguson, Miss Jean Harris Ritchie QC, Professor Christopher Sachrajda, Dr William Poole, Ms Clarissa Farr, Mr William Holland
Income: £27,880,000 [2017]; £26,005,000 [2016]; £26,542,000 [2015]; £26,279,000 [2014]; £25,440,000 [2013]

The Warden and Scholars of The House or College of Scholars of Merton in the University of Oxford
Registered: 15 Nov 2010 *Employees:* 191
Tel: 01865 276310 *Website:* merton.ox.ac.uk
Activities: Education, training
Address: Merton College, Merton Street, Oxford, OX1 4JD
Trustees: Professor Richard McCabe, Professor Peter Holland FRS, Dr Daniel Grimley, Professor Judith Armitage, Mr John Gloag, The Reverend Dr Simon Jones, Dr Patricia Thornton, Professor Gail Fine, Dr Alexander Schekochihin, Prof David Paterson, Professor Peter Neary FBA, Ms Mindy Chen-Wishart, Professor Tim Guilford DPhil, Professor Chih-Hao Ong, Professor Alexander Scott, Professor Alan Morrison, Professor Jennifer Payne, Dr Michael Whitworth, Dr Minhyong Kim, Dr Mark Williams, Mr Charles Alan Heathcote Alexander, Mr Andrew Mackie, Dr Roderick Craig MacLean, Mr Anthony Ashmore, Dr William Bowers, Professor Ehud Hrushovski, Professor Lorna Hutson, Mr Tim Lightfoot, Dr Kate Orkin, Dr Kate Blackmon, Dr Duncan Barker, Ms Isabel Garcia Garcia, Dr Carlas Smith, Dr Evert Van Emde Boas, Jonathan Ralph Warburg Prag, Professor Hugh Watkins, Dr Matthew Grimley, Professor Ulrike Tillmann, Dr Simon Wolfe Saunders PhD, Dr Steven Gunn, Professor Sir Martin Taylor FRS, Professor James Binney FRS, Professor Artur Ekert, Dr Alan Barr, Dr Rhiannon Ash, Professor Veronique Gouverneur PhD FRSC, Professor Simon Hooker, Professor Irene Lemos, Dr Ian MacLachlan, Professor Bela Novak, Dr Julia Walworth, Dr Rachel Buxton, Professor Sir Andrew Wiles, Frater John Eidinow, Dr Ralf Michael Bader, Dr Sergi Pardos-Prado, Dr Bassel Tarbush, Dr Helen Barron, Mr Yegor Grebnev, Dr Matt Hosty, Professor Julian Knight, Professor Ej Milner-Gulland, Dr Micah Muscolino, Professor Matthew Higgins, Dr Joshua Firth, Dr Emma Loftus, Dr Matthew Thomson, Ms Hatice Yildiz
Income: £13,363,000 [2017]; £13,477,000 [2016]; £14,118,793 [2015]; £11,700,000 [2014]; £13,740,000 [2013]

The Wardens and Assistants of Rochester Bridge in the County of Kent
Registered: 30 May 1962 *Employees:* 4
Tel: 01634 846706 *Website:* rbt.org.uk
Activities: General charitable purposes; environment, conservation, heritage
Address: The Bridge Chamber, 5 Esplanade, Rochester, Kent, ME1 1QE
Trustees: Mr Russell John Race, Anne Frances Helen Logan, Mr Alan Leslie Jarrett, Mr Peter John Homewood, Mr Raymond Peter Harris, Mrs Sarah Hohler, Mr Richard George Thornby, Mr Paul Edward James Harriott, Mr Russell Graham Cooper, Mr Philip Filmer, Mr Derek Butler, Mr Lars Lemonius
Income: £3,650,030 [2017]; £3,271,174 [2016]; £3,259,535 [2015]; £3,487,348 [2014]; £2,554,949 [2013]

Wargrave House Limited
Registered: 2 Jul 2004 *Employees:* 108
Tel: 01925 224899 *Website:* wargravehouse.com
Activities: Education, training; disability
Address: Wargrave House School, Wargrave Road, Newton-le-Willows, St Helens, Merseyside, WA12 8RS
Trustees: Mr Charles David Banks, Mrs Helen Whitehead, Mr Stephen Whalley, Mr John Thumpassery, Mrs Melanie Peake, Miss Jennifer Warner, Mr John Hawkins, Mr William Duncan, Mr Simon Brook, Mrs Rachelle Russell
Income: £3,406,476 [2016]; £3,721,649 [2015]; £3,733,540 [2014]; £3,372,586 [2013]; £3,257,844 [2012]

Warminster School
Registered: 18 Nov 1994 *Employees:* 166
Tel: 01985 210105 *Website:* warminsterschool.org.uk
Activities: Education, training
Address: Warminster School, Church Street, Warminster, Wilts, BA12 8PJ
Trustees: Mr Charles Goodbody, Mr David Stratton OBE DL, Mr Timothy Moore, Ms Caroline Drennan, Mr Andrew Waters, Mr Tyrone Richard Urch, Mr Jeremy Edwin Montague Pakenham, Ian McComas, Sir David Latham, Andrew Kennett, Mr Duncan James Wilson
Income: £8,534,816 [2017]; £8,415,408 [2016]; £8,259,207 [2015]; £8,788,817 [2014]; £8,302,058 [2013]

Warren House Group at Dartington
Registered: 1 Sep 2003 *Employees:* 21
Tel: 01803 762400 *Website:* dartington.org.uk
Activities: General charitable purposes; education, training; advancement of health or saving of lives; prevention or relief of poverty
Address: Lower Ground Floor, Higher Mills, Buckfast Abbey, Buckfast, Buckfastleigh, Devon, TQ11 0EE
Trustees: Ms Naomi Eisenstadt, Mr Vagn Nedergaard Hansen, Dr Patrick Diamond, Dr Deborah Cohen, Ms Elizabeth Joyce Moseley, Mr John Jeremy Hope Drew, Ms Sandra Di Vito, Ms Ruth Dobson
Income: £1,594,921 [2017]; £1,742,866 [2016]; £2,256,422 [2015]; £2,782,614 [2014]; £1,112,154 [2013]

Warrington Community Living
Registered: 23 May 1991 *Employees:* 269 *Volunteers:* 9
Tel: 01925 246870 *Website:* wcliving.org.uk
Activities: Disability; accommodation, housing
Address: The Gateway Resource Centre, 89 Sankey Street, Warrington, Cheshire, WA1 1SR
Trustees: Mr Terry Ennis, Mr Gordon Spenley, Mr Ian Fairbrother, Richard Gore, Mrs Hilda Whitfield, Ms Janice Lorraine Wycherley, Jan Preece, Kath Robinson
Income: £5,834,690 [2017]; £4,924,848 [2016]; £4,532,607 [2015]; £2,888,050 [2014]; £4,218,804 [2013]

Warrington Disability Partnership

Registered: 5 Apr 2006 *Employees:* 48 *Volunteers:* 220
Tel: 01925 240064 *Website:* disabilitypartnership.org.uk
Activities: General charitable purposes; education, training; disability; amateur sport; economic, community development, employment
Address: Warrington Disability Partnership, Unit 1, Beaufort Street, Warrington, Cheshire, WA5 1BA
Trustees: Mrs Pat Kitto, Mrs Janice Mary Prichard, Cllr Maureen McLaughlin, Mr Adrian Derbyshire, Mrs Cynthia Ann Salluyts, Mr Michael Dawbarn, Mr Graeme Hindley, Mr Gary Skentelbery, Eileen Campbell MacDonald, Mr David Williams, Mark Wilson, John Gartside OBE DL JP, Mr Latham Parry
Income: £1,476,502 [2017]; £1,253,707 [2016]; £1,278,058 [2015]; £1,185,289 [2014]; £1,437,904 [2013]

The Warrington Homes Limited

Registered: 29 Apr 1977 *Employees:* 83
Tel: 01249 280050 *Website:* warringtonresidentialcare.org.uk
Activities: The advancement of health or saving of lives; prevention or relief of poverty
Address: 23 Luker Drive, Petersfield, Hants, GU31 4SN
Trustees: Mr James Graham Brown FCA ATII, Malcolm Chatwin, Mrs Christine Reid, Dr Nicholas John Rutherford Davis, Mr Paul Sexton, Dr Rupert Drummond, Mrs Kate Hoffman, Mrs Gillian Stafford, Mr Michael Canty, Mrs Dina McAlpine
Income: £2,025,505 [2016]; £1,797,017 [2015] £1,913,748 [2014]; £1,825,288 [2013]; £1,780,570 [2012]

Warrior Preservation Trust Limited

Registered: 3 Oct 1968 *Employees:* 37 *Volunteers:* 61
Tel: 023 9277 8600 *Website:* hmswarrior.org
Activities: Education, training; arts, culture, heritage, science; environment, conservation, heritage
Address: HMS Warrior 1860, Victory Gate, Main Road, HM Naval Base, Portsmouth, PO1 3QX
Trustees: Mr Michael Bedingfield, Councillor Donna Jones, Rear Admiral Neil Degge Latham, Mr James Edwin Priory, Professor Dominic Tweddle, Professor Isobel Pollock
Income: £2,794,105 [2017]; £2,201,564 [2015]; £2,048,421 [2014]; £1,601,547 [2013]; £1,038,620 [2012]

Warwick Independent Schools Foundation

Registered: 15 Aug 2001 *Employees:* 656 *Volunteers:* 6
Tel: 01926 735400 *Website:* warwickschool.org
Activities: Education, training
Address: Warwick School, Myton Road, Warwick, CV34 6PP
Trustees: Mrs Gillian Low, Mrs M-A Grainger, Mr David Stevens, Miss Kathryn Alison Parr, Mr N F Keegan, Mrs E J Lillyman, HM Lord Lieutenant of Warwickshire, Mr R Griffiths, Mrs S M Austin, Mr A C Firth BSc MBA, Ms C A I Sawdon, Mr J P Cavanagh QC MA (Oxon) LLM (Cantab), Mrs P A Snape, Mr C R Gibbons, Mrs Marie-Bernadette Ashe, Mr A D Cocker, Mr T H Keyes, Mr J N Wallis
Income: £31,002,000 [2016]; £29,023,000 [2015]; £27,675,000 [2014]; £27,113,000 [2013]; £25,718,000 [2012]

Warwick Students' Union

Registered: 15 Jul 2010 *Employees:* 652
Website: warwicksu.com
Activities: Education, training; amateur sport; recreation
Address: University of Warwick, Gibbet Hill Road, Coventry, Warwicks, CV4 7AL
Trustees: Mr Graham Parker, Ms Emma Cox, Ms Dammy Sokale, Miss Sophie Isabelle Stistrup Worrall, Miss Hope Elizabeth Worsdale, Mr Niall Johnson, Miss Ellen Elizabeth Holmes, Mr Benjamin Richard Hayday, Ms Marta Gonzalez, James Hunt, Miss Nyasha Carmen Pitt, Ms Jill Finney, Ms Emily Victoria Dunford, Miss Eleanor Elizabeth Martin, Mr Michael Morris Kynaston, Mr Liam James Jackson, Mr Robert Blagov, Mr Brendan Tan
Income: £8,650,050 [2017]; £7,984,774 [2016]; £7,715,583 [2015]; £7,479,189 [2014]; £7,059,300 [2013]

Warwickshire Community and Voluntary Action

Registered: 1 Apr 2008 *Employees:* 54 *Volunteers:* 120
Tel: 01788 574258 *Website:* wcava.org.uk
Activities: Education, training; advancement of health or saving of lives; disability; prevention or relief of poverty; environment, conservation, heritage; economic, community development, employment
Address: c/o Warwickshire Cava, Rugby District Office, 19 & 20 North Street, Rugby, Warwicks, CV21 2AG
Trustees: Mrs Judith Mary Morley, Mrs Carole Ann Shuttleworth, Mr Jatinder Singh Birdi, Ms Sonya Ellen Johnson, Mr Derek Norman Cake, Mr Ralph Philip Robson, Mr George Anthony Guy, Mrs Kathleen Elizabeth Harper, Miss Bryony Smith, Ms Sheila Anne Hammond, Ms Catherine Anne Mulkern, Mr Andrew Arnold Gabbitas
Income: £1,842,967 [2017]; £1,120,281 [2016]; £861,188 [2015]; £1,073,026 [2014]; £1,333,067 [2013]

The Warwickshire Wildlife Trust Limited

Registered: 14 Aug 1962 *Employees:* 121 *Volunteers:* 987
Tel: 024 7630 2912 *Website:* warwickshire-wildlife-trust.org.uk
Activities: Education, training; environment, conservation, heritage
Address: Warwickshire Wildlife Trust, Brandon Marsh Nature Centre, Brandon Lane, Coventry, Warwicks, CV3 3GW
Trustees: Dr Helen Brittain, Mr Ronald William Hill, Mr Michael Bunney, Mr Andrew Gabbitas, Dr Martin Randall, Mr Laurence Wilbraham, Mr Duncan McArdle, Mrs Kathryn May Reeve, Susan Juned, Mr Luke Hamer, Mrs Crishni Waring, Mr John Duncan McKenzie, Mr Francis Almond, Mr Geoff Litterick
Income: £6,534,239 [2016]; £6,407,808 [2015]; £5,272,122 [2014]; £4,920,116 [2013]; £4,130,031 [2012]

The Waste and Resources Action Programme

Registered: 5 Dec 2014 *Employees:* 184
Tel: 01295 819605 *Website:* wrap.org.uk
Activities: Environment, conservation, heritage
Address: 2nd Floor, Wrap, Blenheim Court, 19 George Street, Banbury, Oxon, OX16 5BH
Trustees: Mr James Oatridge, Mrs Anne Caroline Jenkin, Robert Longley-Cook, Ms Sophie Lysandra Thomas, Dr Marcus Gover, Ms Julie Elizabeth Hill, Ms Susan Noelle Corbett, Dr Marc Timothy Stephens
Income: £27,136,064 [2017]; £26,827,000 [2016]

Watch Tower Bible and Tract Society of Britain
Registered: 27 Oct 1999 *Volunteers:* 50
Tel: 020 8906 2211
Activities: Overseas aid, famine relief; religious activities
Address: Ibsa House, The Ridgeway, London, NW7 1RN
Trustees: Jonathan Rastall, Mr Giosue Maraia, Andrew J Llewellyn, Mr Peter Phillip Bell, Stephen J Morice, Robert Li
Income: £89,598,492 [2017]; £50,478,154 [2016]; £82,049,332 [2015]; £44,582,617 [2014]; £30,560,270 [2013]

Wateraid
Registered: 22 Feb 1984 *Employees:* 739 *Volunteers:* 600
Tel: 020 7793 4500 *Website:* wateraid.org
Activities: The prevention or relief of poverty; overseas aid, famine relief
Address: Wateraid, 47-49 Durham Street, London, SE11 5JD
Trustees: Mr Manuel Alvarinho, Ms Heidi Mottram, Mr Christopher Loughlin, Mr Peter Newman, Ms Myriam Sidibe, Professor Mala Rao, Mr Timothy Clark, Mrs Rosemary Carr, Ms Anna Segall, Mr Steve Vaid, Ms Heather Skilling
Income: £81,077,000 [2017]; £85,475,000 [2016]; £83,600,000 [2015]; £73,695,000 [2014]; £65,648,000 [2013]

Waterloo 200 Ltd
Registered: 5 Oct 2009
Tel: 01935 851207 *Website:* waterloo200.org
Activities: Education, training
Address: Wales Barn, Queen Camel, Yeovil, Somerset, BA22 7PA
Trustees: Lady Jane Wellesley, Mr Timothy John Cooke, Major General Sir Evelyn John Webb-Carter KCVO OBE
Income: £1,309,469 [2017]; £1,309,469 [2016]; £111,697 [2015]; £118,319 [2014]; £27,057 [2013]

The Waterloo Foundation
Registered: 10 Jan 2007 *Employees:* 9
Tel: 029 2083 8980 *Website:* waterloofoundation.org.uk
Activities: General charitable purposes; advancement of health or saving of lives; disability; prevention or relief of poverty; overseas aid, famine relief; environment, conservation, heritage
Address: c/o 46-48 Cardiff Road, Llandaff, Cardiff, CF5 2DT
Trustees: Mrs Heather Stevens, Janet Victoria Alexander, Mr David Graham Stevens, Mrs Caroline Ann Oakes
Income: £9,503,237 [2016]; £8,241,929 [2015]; £8,344,892 [2014]; £11,534,383 [2013]; £4,964,016 [2012]

Watermill Theatre Limited
Registered: 11 Aug 1970 *Employees:* 45 *Volunteers:* 70
Tel: 01635 45834 *Website:* watermill.org.uk
Activities: Education, training; arts, culture, heritage, science
Address: Mill House, Watermill Theatre, Bagnor, Newbury, Berks, RG20 8AE
Trustees: Mr Andrew Tuckey, Mr Patrick Charles Lake Griffin, Mr David Grindrod, Mr Thomas Rossiter, Mrs Margaret Whitlum-Cooper, Ms Susan Foster, Mr Andrew Greig McKenzie, Mrs Carole Anne Armstrong, Mr Colin Farrant, Mr Simon Kenneth Parsonage
Income: £2,957,678 [2017]; £3,183,291 [2016]; £3,481,073 [2015]; £2,661,985 [2014]; £3,192,343 [2013]

The Watershed Arts Trust Limited
Registered: 18 Mar 1982 *Employees:* 92
Tel: 0117 927 6444 *Website:* watershed.co.uk
Activities: Education, training; arts, culture, heritage, science
Address: Watershed Arts Trust Ltd, 1 Canons Road, Bristol, BS1 5TX
Trustees: Sherrie Eugene, Ms Lisa Michelle Gardner, Ms Diane Bunyan, Mr Steven Wilson, Ms Estella Tincknell, Sue Cooper, Mr Syed Shamil Ahmed, Mr James George Touzel, Mr Paul Appleby, Mr John Durrant, Donna Whitehead, Mr Stephen Gatfield, Shahina Johnson
Income: £5,208,104 [2017]; £6,255,095 [2016]; £4,971,750 [2015]; £4,513,908 [2014]; £4,184,788 [2013]

Wates Family Enterprise Trust
Registered: 23 Sep 2008 *Employees:* 3
Tel: 01372 861250 *Website:* watesgiving.org.uk
Activities: General charitable purposes; education, training; advancement of health or saving of lives; disability; accommodation, housing; arts, culture, heritage, science; amateur sport; environment, conservation, heritage; economic, community development, employment; armed forces, emergency service efficiency; recreation
Address: Wates Family Charities, Wates House, Station Approach, Leatherhead, Surrey, KT22 7SW
Trustees: Mr Andrew Wates, Tim Wates, Andy Wates, Charles Wates, Paul Wates, James Wates, Michael Wates, Jonathan Wates
Income: £1,100,850 [2016]; £1,001,079 [2015]; £1,009,722 [2014]; £1,317,759 [2013]; £1,053,275 [2012]

Watford FC's Community Sports & Education Trust
Registered: 20 Feb 2004 *Employees:* 87 *Volunteers:* 37
Tel: 01582 873131 *Website:* watfordfccsetrust.com
Activities: Education, training; disability; amateur sport; economic, community development, employment; recreation
Address: 11 Oakway, Studham, Dunstable, Beds, LU6 2PE
Trustees: Mr Christopher John Norton, Professor Stuart Read Timperley, Mr Paul Anthony Clark, Mr Simon James MacQueen, Mr Edmund James Coan, Dr Justin Davis Smith CBE, Mr Christopher John Luff
Income: £3,034,604 [2017]; £2,384,752 [2016]; £1,629,645 [2015]; £1,542,679 [2014]; £1,464,816 [2013]

Watford New Hope Trust
Registered: 18 May 2000 *Employees:* 44 *Volunteers:* 200
Tel: 01494 765428 *Website:* newhope.org.uk
Activities: The prevention or relief of poverty; accommodation, housing
Address: Cansdales, Bourbon Court, Nightingales Corner, Amersham, Bucks, HP7 9QS
Trustees: Keith Stevens, Mr David Stephen Evans, Hugh Lloyd, Dr Tim Robson OBE, Mr John Neville Stuart, John Ford, Melanie Sills, Mr Ian Peck, Mrs Aileen Laura Johnson
Income: £2,098,957 [2017]; £2,144,953 [2016]; £2,223,993 [2015]; £2,268,390 [2014]; £2,092,959 [2013]

Watford and District Mencap Society
Registered: 15 Oct 1991 *Employees:* 70 *Volunteers:* 89
Tel: 01923 713620 *Website:* watfordmencap.org.uk
Activities: Education, training; advancement of health or saving of lives; disability; accommodation, housing; amateur sport; human rights, religious or racial harmony, equality or diversity; recreation
Address: The Old Town Hall, 105 High Street, Rickmansworth, Herts, WD3 1AN
Trustees: Mrs Pauline Joy, Mrs Pam Robertson, Nick Clark, Mr Russ Teague, Mrs Lynn Green, Roger Jones
Income: £2,344,846 [2017]; £2,323,454 [2016]; £2,274,355 [2015]; £2,054,007 [2014]; £2,089,883 [2013]

Watoto Child Care Ministries
Registered: 27 Feb 2002 *Employees:* 7
Website: watoto.com
Activities: Education, training; advancement of health or saving of lives; prevention or relief of poverty; overseas aid, famine relief; accommodation, housing; religious activities; economic, community development, employment
Address: P O Box 64946, London, E4 0EF
Trustees: Mr Stephen Matthew, Mr Peter Jordan, John Morris, Mr Ken Williamson, Gary Skinner, Alan Penry
Income: £1,150,280 [2016]; £1,179,900 [2015]; £1,272,511 [2014]; £1,084,911 [2013]; £1,044,580 [2012]

Watts Gallery
Registered: 7 Sep 1967 *Employees:* 60 *Volunteers:* 300
Tel: 01483 810235 *Website:* wattsgallery.org.uk
Activities: Education, training; arts, culture, heritage, science
Address: The Flat, Watts Gallery, Down Lane, Compton, Guildford, Surrey, GU3 1DQ
Trustees: Leonee Ormond, Rob Dickins, Emma Verey, Isabel Goldsmith, Mr Matthew Bowcock, Mr Martin Beisly, Ms Maryanne Stevens, Sir Mark Jones, Richard Dorment CBE, Mr George Anson, Mrs Deborah Brice, Robert Napier, Mr Alistair Burtenshaw, Thea Adair
Income: £3,650,867 [2017]; £3,253,736 [2016]; £3,909,979 [2015]; £2,487,795 [2014]; £1,855,053 [2013]

Richard Watts and The City of Rochester Almshouse Charities
Registered: 1 Dec 1962 *Employees:* 27 *Volunteers:* 4
Tel: 01634 842194 *Website:* richardwatts.org.uk
Activities: The prevention or relief of poverty; accommodation, housing
Address: The Office, Watts Almshouses, Maidstone Road, Rochester, Kent, ME1 1SE
Trustees: Mr Donald Alexander Gordon Troup OBE, Mr Roger Kenneth Hawkes, Mr Terence James Burton, Mr Brian Peter Cox, Mrs Catherine Gore, Ms Alex Clarabut, Mrs Sharon Elisabeth Howell, Mrs Kamaldeep Tesse, Mr Michael Robin Bailey, Mr Peter Smith, Mr Anthony William Clayton, Mrs Hilary Harwood, Mr Martin Cook, Liz Janz, Mr Colin McCarthy, Mrs Linda Reay
Income: £1,306,934 [2017]; £1,267,767 [2016]; £1,246,594 [2015]; £1,203,144 [2014]; £1,149,725 [2013]

Antur Waunfawr
Registered: 6 Aug 1984 *Employees:* 113 *Volunteers:* 6
Tel: 01286 650721 *Website:* anturwaunfawr.org
Activities: Education, training
Address: Bryn Pistyll, Waunfawr, Caernarfon, Gwynedd, LL55 4BJ
Trustees: Mr Huw Ynyr, Mr Kevin Hughes, Geraint Wyn Strello, Mrs Mererid Llwyd, Mrs Sara Mair Tomas, Mr Rhys Evans, Mrs Anna Lloyd Williams, John Gwynedd, Norman Williams, Mr Daron Harris, Dr John Prys Morgan Jones, Ms Lowri Huws Jones
Income: £2,294,170 [2017]; £2,189,088 [2016]; £2,334,312 [2015]; £2,211,754 [2014]; £2,171,653 [2013]

Wave Leisure Trust Limited
Registered: 29 Mar 2006 *Employees:* 292 *Volunteers:* 74
Website: waveleisure.co.uk
Activities: Amateur sport; recreation
Address: Sutton Cottage, Eastbourne Road, Seaford, E Sussex, BN25 3PJ
Trustees: Mr David Hearn, Mr Mark Beaumont, Dr Karl Heinirch Van Wyk, Mrs Elizabeth Boorman, Mr Marcel Philippe Miller, Mr Mike Price, Mr Philip James Clarke, Mr Alan Jurek Charles Edward Wisniewski, Mrs Lisa Fry
Income: £4,931,124 [2017]; £4,862,794 [2016]; £4,667,274 [2015]; £4,583,393 [2014]; £4,460,860 [2013]

Wavendon All Music Plan Limited
Registered: 17 Nov 1970 *Employees:* 24 *Volunteers:* 279
Tel: 01908 280808 *Website:* stables.org
Activities: Education, training; arts, culture, heritage, science
Address: The Stables Theatre Ltd, Stockwell Lane, Wavendon, Milton Keynes, Bucks, MK17 8LU
Trustees: Dr Ann Limb CBE, Mrs Donna Harrington, Mr Robert French, Dr Philip Henry Smith, Mrs Hazel Coomber, Mr Stephen Hasson, Ms Clare Teal, Mr James Rice
Income: £3,589,779 [2017]; £2,796,961 [2016]; £3,716,369 [2015]; £2,616,623 [2014]; £3,204,518 [2013]

Waverley School (Crowthorne) Limited
Registered: 20 May 1969 *Employees:* 59
Tel: 0118 973 1121 *Website:* waverleyschool.co.uk
Activities: Education, training
Address: Waverley School, Waverley Way, Wokingham, Berks, RG40 4YD
Trustees: Mr Blair Ashley Bedford Jenkins, Mr Nigel Woolnough, Mrs Joanna Duncan, Mr Andrew Mitchell, Mrs Angela Roke
Income: £1,932,197 [2017]; £1,657,009 [2016]; £1,689,267 [2015]; £1,432,195 [2014]; £1,151,168 [2013]

Waymarks Limited
Registered: 21 Jan 2010 *Employees:* 130 *Volunteers:* 8
Tel: 0300 303 9001 *Website:* waymarks.org.uk
Activities: Education, training; disability; accommodation, housing
Address: Dimensions Group, 1430 Arlington Business Park, Theale, Reading, Berks, RG7 4SA
Trustees: Mr Kevin John Lewis, Mr Martin Boniface, Mrs Jacqueline Fletcher, Alexis Acosta-Armas, Ms Anne Barnard, Mr Andrew Britton, Mr John Charles Lish
Income: £4,268,000 [2017]; £3,800,000 [2016]; £2,214,000 [2015]; £1,413,000 [2014]; £671,000 [2013]

We Are Beams

Registered: 29 Mar 1996 *Employees:* 66 *Volunteers:* 10
Tel: 01322 668501 *Website:* wearebeams.org.uk
Activities: Education, training; disability
Address: Allsworth Court, 40 St Davids Road, Swanley, Kent, BR8 7RJ
Trustees: Mrs Lesley Dyball, Mr Neil Henrik Johnston, Mrs Rosemarie Neale, Mr Garry Ratcliffe, Mr Sanjit Singh, Mrs Clare Marie Norman, Mrs Sarah Jane Redpath, Miss Joanna Ruth Burton, Mr Jason Jarvis, Mr Andrew Garrett
Income: £1,415,924 [2017]; £1,472,476 [2016]; £1,472,476 [2015]; £1,265,308 [2014]; £1,005,602 [2013]

We Are IVE Ltd

Registered: 8 Mar 1999 *Employees:* 16
Tel: 0113 322 3050 *Website:* weareive.org
Activities: Education, training; arts, culture, heritage, science; economic, community development, employment
Address: 31 The Calls, Leeds, LS2 7EY
Trustees: Sue Horner, Mrs Caroline Watson, Ms Isobel Mills, Mr Jonathan Straight, Sue Lynas, Rashik Parmar
Income: £1,454,994 [2017]; £1,318,090 [2016]; £1,324,365 [2015]; £1,336,606 [2014]; £1,302,036 [2013]

We The Curious Limited

Registered: 17 Oct 1995 *Employees:* 98 *Volunteers:* 150
Tel: 0117 915 7108 *Website:* wethecurious.org
Activities: Education, training; arts, culture, heritage, science
Address: At Bristol, Anchor Road, Bristol, BS1 5DB
Trustees: Mr Simon Cooper, Mr Nick Jones, Mr Michael David May, Mr Chris Sims, Mr Geoff Gollop, Ms Helen Godwin, Mr David Sproxton, Mr Alan Parsons, Dr Kathreena Kurian, Mrs Joanna Stringer, Mr Thomas Stringer
Income: £6,069,000 [2017]; £6,989,000 [2016]; £7,784,000 [2015]; £6,588,000 [2014]; £6,948,000 [2013]

WeSeeHope

Registered: 15 Feb 2000 *Employees:* 7 *Volunteers:* 1
Tel: 020 8288 1196 *Website:* weseehope.org.uk
Activities: Education, training; disability; prevention or relief of poverty; economic, community development, employment
Address: WeSeeHope, 79 Craven Gardens, London, SW19 8LU
Trustees: Mr Adrian Gosling, Mrs Wendy Susan Wall, James Kliffen, Mr Joseph Francis, James Meldrum, Mr Michael Charles Adams, Philip Wall, Ms Rachel Helen Madeiros-Mhende, Chris Welsh, Mrs Christianne Williamson
Income: £1,304,299 [2017]; £1,535,392 [2016]; £1,095,613 [2015]; £1,432,324 [2014]; £1,470,076 [2013]

Weald and Downland Open Air Museum Limited

Registered: 18 Feb 1969 *Employees:* 35 *Volunteers:* 500
Tel: 01243 811893 *Website:* wealddown.co.uk
Activities: Education, training; environment, conservation, heritage
Address: Weald & Downland Open Air Museum, Singleton, Chichester, W Sussex, PO18 0EU
Trustees: Dr John Godfrey DL MA, Mr Neil Hart DL LLB, Mr Paul Rigg DL, Dr John Jarvis BSc PhD, Ms Catherine Frances Hampson BSc Hons MBA FCCA MBACP, Mrs Jennie Peel, Matthew Lewis, Mr Simon Knight DL, Mr Maurice Pollock, Mr Garret Francis Turley, Ms Deborah Chiverton, Ms Elaine Sansom, Mr Sam Howes, Jo Pasricha
Income: £4,741,848 [2016]; £3,063,454 [2015]; £2,389,305 [2014]; £1,860,618 [2013]; £1,848,674 [2012]

Weaver Vale Housing Trust Limited

Registered: 9 Sep 2004 *Employees:* 302 *Volunteers:* 138
Tel: 01606 813312 *Website:* wvht.co.uk
Activities: Education, training; disability; prevention or relief of poverty; accommodation, housing; economic, community development, employment
Address: Weavervale Housing Trust, Gadbrook Point, Rudheath Way, Rudheath, Northwich, Cheshire, CW9 7LL
Trustees: Mr Donald Beckett, Miss Rachael Radway, Mrs Barbara Dean, Mr Andrew Stafford, Mr Christopher Michael Gaskell Mike Gaskell, Mr James Anthony Bolton, Mrs Jacqueline Ann Chatwood, Mr Paul Waring, Mr Peter Ronald Shaw
Income: £32,067,000 [2017]; £32,252,000 [2016]; £31,495,000 [2015]; £30,915,000 [2014]; £31,195,000 [2013]

Weidenfeld-Hoffmann Trust

Registered: 20 Oct 2014 *Employees:* 3
Website: whtrust.org
Activities: Education, training; human rights, religious or racial harmony, equality or diversity
Address: Said Business School, Park End Street, Oxford, OX1 1HP
Trustees: Mr Michael Lewis, Mrs Alina Barnett, Mr Andre Hoffmann
Income: £2,452,974 [2017]; £2,399,280 [2016]; £6,002,374 [2015]

The Weizmann Institute Foundation

Registered: 20 Mar 1964 *Employees:* 5
Tel: 020 7424 6860 *Website:* weizmann.org.uk
Activities: General charitable purposes; education, training
Address: Weizmann Institute Foundation, Unit 9 Hampstead Gate, 1A Frognal, London, NW3 6AL
Trustees: Mr Martin Paisner CBE, Dame Vivien Duffield DBE, Lord Leslie Arnold Turnberg FRS, Mr Dean Anthony Lush, Mr Michael Sandler, Mr Denis Graham Raeburn, Professor Alan David Dangour, Mrs Hayley Sieff, Mr Howard Terence Stanton, Mr Jonathan Ronald Kropman, Professor Benny Chain, Mr Maxwell Nisner, Mr Barry S Townsley, Mr Julian Dwek, Dr Arabella Duffield, Mr Charles Wolfson Townsley
Income: £6,889,619 [2017]; £9,077,318 [2016]; £2,839,534 [2015]; £5,947,030 [2014]; £3,177,477 [2013]

Weldmar Hospicecare Trust

Registered: 28 Sep 1990 *Employees:* 224 *Volunteers:* 1,228
Tel: 01305 756944 *Website:* weld-hospice.org.uk
Activities: The advancement of health or saving of lives
Address: Hammick House, Bridport Road, Poundbury, Dorchester, DT1 3SD
Trustees: The Viscount Fitzharris, Mr James David Edward Joicey-Cecil, Mr Stephen Baynard, Mrs Davina Smith, Mr Mervyn Edgecombe, Mrs Sue Davies, Dr Clare Heath, Mr Ian Richard Stone, Ms Susan Hawkett, Mrs Tanya Grant
Income: £7,612,224 [2017]; £7,968,145 [2016]; £7,785,492 [2015]; £8,238,462 [2014]; £6,264,887 [2013]

The Welfare Association

Registered: 26 Apr 1993 *Employees:* 2 *Volunteers:* 10
Tel: 020 7259 2454 *Website:* welfareassociation.org.uk
Activities: General charitable purposes; education, training; advancement of health or saving of lives; disability; prevention or relief of poverty; overseas aid, famine relief; accommodation, housing; arts, culture, heritage, science; environment, conservation, heritage; economic, community development, employment
Address: The Welfare Association, Tower House, 226 Cromwell Road, London, SW5 0SW
Trustees: Mrs Hanan Al-Afifi, Baroness Tonge, Mr John McHugo, Mr Shrenik Davda, Mrs Julia Helou, Clare Short, Dr Louise Arimatsu, Mr Martin Linton
Income: £1,266,082 [2016]; £1,760,919 [2015]; £1,272,929 [2014]; £1,307,562 [2013]; £885,640 [2012]

WellChild

Registered: 7 Jul 1984 *Employees:* 28 *Volunteers:* 777
Tel: 01242 530007 *Website:* wellchild.org.uk
Activities: The advancement of health or saving of lives
Address: 16 Royal Crescent, Cheltenham, Glos, GL50 3DA
Trustees: Mr Paul Richardson, Mr Trevor Jones, Mrs Rosemary Rogers, Ms Lisa Avellini, Ms Elizabeth Anne Morgan, Dr Huw Ritchie Jenkins, Mr John Evans, Mr Andrew Osborne, Ms Fiona Macpherson, Ms Sian Elizabeth Taylor, Mr Nicholas Fisher, Mrs Rosalind Charlotte Futter
Income: £2,344,327 [2017]; £2,435,724 [2016]; £3,390,700 [2015]; £2,533,153 [2014]; £2,209,803 [2013]

Wellbeing of Women

Registered: 27 Jan 1965 *Employees:* 13 *Volunteers:* 200
Website: wellbeingofwomen.org.uk
Activities: The advancement of health or saving of lives
Address: Wellbeing of Women, 78 New Oxford Street, London, WC1A 1HB
Trustees: Sir Maurice Victor Blank MA Hon FRCOG, Mr David Muirhead Moffat, Ms Jackie Gittins, Lynn Hiestand, Professor Peter Brocklehurst, Miss Claire Mellon, Ms Michelle Dawn Feeney, Mr Philip Eric Rene Jansen, Ms Eve Pollard, Ms Gay Huey-Evans, Professor Mary Ann Lumsden, Professor Steve Thornton, Mrs Debra White, Mr Ian Powell
Income: £1,824,138 [2016]; £2,015,349 [2015]; £2,139,248 [2014]; £2,125,273 [2013]; £2,130,229 [2012]

Wellcome Trust

Registered: 4 Oct 1962 *Employees:* 1,784
Tel: 020 7611 8888 *Website:* wellcome.ac.uk
Activities: Education, training; advancement of health or saving of lives; arts, culture, heritage, science
Address: Wellcome Trust, Gibbs Building, 215 Euston Road, London, NW1 2BE
Trustees: The Wellcome Trust Limited
Income: £425,285,020 [2017]; £390,300,298 [2016]; £438,687,590 [2015]; £337,962,640 [2014]; £281,489,136 [2013]

Wellesley House and St Peter Court School Education Trust Ltd

Registered: 9 Aug 1966 *Employees:* 77
Website: wellesleyhouse.org
Activities: Education, training
Address: Wellesley House School, 114 Ramsgate Road, Broadstairs, Kent, CT10 2DG
Trustees: Mr James Bruce Hawkins, Mr Philip John Woodhouse, Mrs Kate Fenwick, Mrs Burge Burge, Mr David Royds, John Jackson, Mr Jonathan Michael Walker Sale, Mr Ben Moorhead, Mr Gareth Mann, Mrs Louise Martine, Alice Harber, Mrs Charlotte Evans
Income: £2,978,267 [2016]; £3,219,733 [2015]; £2,980,286 [2014]; £2,892,046 [2013]; £2,914,437 [2012]

Wellgrove Education

Registered: 4 Jun 1996 *Employees:* 31
Tel: 01707 664662
Activities: Education, training
Address: 14 Fordwich Rise, Hertford, SG14 2BE
Trustees: Mr Matthew J Harvey, Mr Laurie P Smith, Mr Gordon Fleck, Mr Julian Remmington, Mr Ross S Stacey, Mr Anthony Fryer, Mr Piers Moggach
Income: £1,635,152 [2016]; £5,208,522 [2015]; £1,321,649 [2014]; £1,235,424 [2013]

Wellingborough School

Registered: 13 Jan 2004 *Employees:* 259 *Volunteers:* 8
Tel: 01933 233413 *Website:* wellingboroughschool.org
Activities: Education, training
Address: Wellingborough Prep School, London Road, Wellingborough, Northants, NN8 2BX
Trustees: Mr David Kenah Exham, Mr Jerry Higgins, Mr Simon Marriott, Mrs Dorothy Line, Mr David Waller, Mr Rajesh Haridas Thakrar, Mrs Lorna Pape, Mr Clive Alan Westley, Mrs Anne Coles, Dr Jonathan Cox, Mr Trevor Baldry, Mr Peter Tyldesley, Mr Ian Michael Cantelo
Income: £11,783,679 [2017]; £11,391,869 [2016]; £10,957,438 [2015]; £10,599,668 [2014]; £10,447,760 [2013]

The Wellington College

Registered: 11 Nov 1963 *Employees:* 780 *Volunteers:* 30
Tel: 01344 444000 *Website:* wellingtoncollege.org.uk
Activities: Education, training
Address: Wellington College, Crowthorne, Berks, RG45 7PU
Trustees: Mr Peter Glyn Chartris Mallinson BA MBA, Mr Tim Bunting, Mr Robert Perrins, Mr John Alan Claughton, Mr Edward Graham Mellish Chaplin BA MA CMG OBE, Mr Nigel Howard Jones, Mrs Gabriela Galceran Ball, Mrs Felicity Ann Kirk, Mr William Jackson MA, Dr Peter Frankopan MA DPhil FRSA, Mr Ronald Dennis CBE, Mr Howard Veary, Lord Thomas Strathclyde, Mr Duncan Stuart Ritchie FCA, The Duke of Wellington Arthur Wellesley KG LVO OBE MC DL, Mrs Virginia Elizabeth Rhodes BA, Ms Helen Stevenson MSc
Income: £57,450,000 [2017]; £52,804,000 [2016]; £49,558,000 [2015]; £46,348,000 [2014]; £42,512,000 [2013]

Wellington School 1837
Registered: 27 Apr 2015 *Employees:* 269 *Volunteers:* 35
Tel: 01823 668806 *Website:* wellington-school.org.uk
Activities: Education, training; arts, culture, heritage, science; amateur sport
Address: Wellington School, South Street, Wellington, Somerset, TA21 8NT
Trustees: Mrs Vivienne Stock-Williams, Ms Anna Govey, Ms Linda Wyeth, Mrs Samantha Vigus-Hollingsworth, Mr Peter Tait, Mr John Vick, Mrs Alison Wilson, Dr David Lungley, Mrs Linda La Velle, Mr James Hester, Mr Robert Palfrey
Income: £10,154,909 [2016]

Wellow House School Limited
Registered: 18 Jan 1971 *Employees:* 46
Tel: 01623 861054 *Website:* wellowhouse.notts.sch.uk
Activities: Education, training
Address: Newark Road, Wellow, Newark, Notts, NG22 0EA
Trustees: Kathryn Blow, Mr Michael Bingham Hawley, Keith Rodgers, Mr Steven Cooling, Mr Jonathan Brealey
Income: £1,414,149 [2016]; £1,391,787 [2015]; £1,255,732 [2014]; £1,026,060 [2013]; £960,440 [2012]

Wells Cathedral School Limited
Registered: 28 Jan 1967 *Employees:* 261 *Volunteers:* 10
Tel: 01749 834282 *Website:* wellscathedralschool.org
Activities: Education, training
Address: The Bursary, Wells Cathedral School, College Road, Wells, Somerset, BA5 2SX
Trustees: The Very Rev John Davies, Mr Jonathan Vaughan, The Reverend Canon Andrew Featherstone, Mr Martin Smout, Mrs Barbara Bates, Mrs Sarah Flannigan, Prebendary Helen Ball OBE, Mr Robert Powell, Mr Timothy William Hunt Lewis, Mr David Brown, Rev Canon Nicholas Jepson-Biddle, Andrew Campbell-Orde
Income: £13,892,000 [2016]; £12,572,402 [2015]; £12,393,820 [2014]; £12,747,000 [2013]

Welsh Air Ambulance Charitable Trust
Registered: 24 Nov 2000 *Employees:* 95 *Volunteers:* 600
Tel: 0300 015 2999 *Website:* walesairambulance.com
Activities: The advancement of health or saving of lives
Address: Wales Air Ambulance, Ty Elusen, Ffordd Angel, Llanelli Gate, Dafen, Llanelli, Dyfed, SA14 8LQ
Trustees: Des Kitto, Dr Kyle Jacques, Mr James Wagstaffe, Mr David Gilbert, Dr Bridget Kirsop, Mrs Lisa Dafydd, Mark James, Mr Dafydd Jones-Morris, Mr Stephen John Curtis, Mr Owain Spencer Davies, Mr Richard Locke
Income: £10,919,187 [2017]; £9,146,593 [2016]; £9,224,763 [2015]; £8,564,546 [2014]; £6,894,917 [2013]

Welsh Centre for Action on Dependency and Addiction Ltd
Registered: 25 Jul 2001 *Employees:* 96 *Volunteers:* 36
Tel: 01792 646421 *Website:* wcada.org
Activities: Education, training; advancement of health or saving of lives
Address: 41 St James Crescent, Swansea, SA1 6DR
Trustees: Mrs Ann Price, Mr Howard Jones, Mrs Anne Craven, Mrs Maggie Dix, Mr Dean Pulling, Ms Mary Sherwood
Income: £2,605,225 [2017]; £2,140,682 [2016]; £2,396,531 [2015]; £2,662,575 [2014]; £2,834,528 [2013]

Welsh Centre for International Affairs / Canolfan Materion Rhyngwladol Cymru
Registered: 28 Apr 2014 *Employees:* 22 *Volunteers:* 253
Tel: 029 2082 1057 *Website:* wcia.org.uk
Activities: General charitable purposes; education, training; arts, culture, heritage, science; environment, conservation, heritage; economic, community development, employment; human rights, religious or racial harmony, equality or diversity
Address: Welsh Centre for International Affairs, Temple of Peace, King Edward VII Avenue, Cardiff, CF10 3AP
Trustees: Mr Colin Williams OBE, Mr Chrishan Kamalan, Peter Sargent, Mr Darren W Raplh, Amy McGlinchy, Mr Daniel Davies, Ms Claire Cunliffe, Mr Simon Pickard, Sian Stephen
Income: £1,037,816 [2017]; £988,946 [2016]; £335,881 [2015]

Welsh Housing Aid Limited
Registered: 12 Dec 1984 *Employees:* 104 *Volunteers:* 52
Tel: 01792 469400 *Website:* sheltercymru.org.uk
Activities: Education, training; accommodation, housing
Address: Shelter Cymru, 25 Walter Road, Swansea, SA1 5NN
Trustees: Mr Nick Colbourne, Mr Shayne Hembrow, Mr Trystan Jones, Mr Martin Britton, Mr John Daniel Charles Millington, Sarah Lloyd-Jones, Mr David Jeffrey Phillip Childs, Mr Andrew Lea Weltch, Ms Nuria Zolle
Income: £3,293,480 [2017]; £3,339,032 [2016]; £3,409,425 [2015]; £3,439,685 [2014]; £3,913,813 [2013]

Welsh National Opera Limited
Registered: 6 Aug 1963 *Employees:* 200 *Volunteers:* 12
Tel: 029 2063 5000 *Website:* wno.org.uk
Activities: Arts, culture, heritage, science
Address: Welsh National Opera, The Wales Millennium Centre, Bute Place, Cardiff, CF10 5AL
Trustees: Fflur Jones, Mr Martyn Ryan, Mr Antony Hales, Mr Daniel Evans, Mr Matthew Dada, Elen Ap Robert, Mrs Menna Richards, Mr William Wyatt, Mark Molyneux
Income: £18,014,000 [2016]; £17,747,000 [2015]; £18,123,000 [2014]; £16,999,000 [2013]; £17,780,000 [2012]

The Welsh Water Elan Trust
Registered: 20 Dec 1990 *Employees:* 9 *Volunteers:* 15
Tel: 01597 810449 *Website:* elanvalley.org.uk
Activities: Environment, conservation, heritage
Address: Elan Valley Trust, Elan Estate Office, Elan Village, Elan Valley, Rhayader, Powys, LD6 5HP
Trustees: Mr Andrew Leonard, Mr David Evans FRICS, Dr Ieuan Joyce, Wyn Evans, Dr Norman Lowe OBE, Robert Vaughan
Income: £1,358,692 [2017]; £1,340,492 [2016]; £1,177,979 [2015]; £1,014,840 [2014]; £1,008,568 [2013]

Welsh Women's Aid
Registered: 31 Mar 2011 *Employees:* 46 *Volunteers:* 14
Tel: 029 2054 1551 *Website:* welshwomensaid.org.uk
Activities: Education, training; advancement of health or saving of lives; accommodation, housing; human rights, religious or racial harmony, equality or diversity
Address: Pendragon House, Caxton Place, Pentwyn, Cardiff, CF23 8XE
Trustees: Ms Morgan Fackrell, Miss Charlotte Arthur, Mrs Rachel Eagles, Mrs Danielle Dolby, Mrs Sian James, Ms Joy Dyment, Mrs Paula Walters, Mrs Julia Hobbs, Ms Jessica Taylor
Income: £1,870,943 [2017]; £1,864,944 [2016]; £1,756,688 [2015]; £1,628,814 [2014]; £1,866,060 [2013]

Wembley National Stadium Trust
Registered: 11 Nov 1998 *Volunteers:* 2
Tel: 020 7332 1055 *Website:* wnst.org.uk
Activities: Education, training; amateur sport
Address: Stewart Goshawk, Wembley National Stadium Trust, P O Box 270, Guildhall, London, EC2P 2EJ
Trustees: Sir Rodney Myerscough Walker, Lord Toby Harris, Ms Dinah Cox OBE, Mr Peter Ackerley, Ann John OBE, Gordon Haines MBE, Baroness Tanni Grey-Thompson DBE
Income: £1,054,732 [2017]; £952,054 [2016]; £930,824 [2015]; £961,949 [2014]; £852,570 [2013]

Wesleyan Holiness Church - British Isles District
Registered: 10 Jun 2015 *Employees:* 15 *Volunteers:* 50
Tel: 01902 374756 *Website:* wesleyanchurch.co.uk
Activities: General charitable purposes; religious activities
Address: Wesleyan Holiness Church, Holyhead Road, Birmingham, B21 0LA
Trustees: Mr John Duberry, Mrs Angeline C Richardson, Mrs Glenda Peters, Mr Andrew Clarke, Rev Melford Roberts, Mrs Dorrett Lemon, Rev Ruth Lowe, Ms Diane Wallace
Income: £1,374,446 [2016]; £105,095 [2015]

Wessex Archaeology Limited
Registered: 16 Sep 1983 *Employees:* 271 *Volunteers:* 30
Website: wessexarch.co.uk
Activities: Education, training; arts, culture, heritage, science; environment, conservation, heritage
Address: Wessex Archaeology Ltd, The Portway House, Old Sarum Park, Old Sarum, Salisbury, Wilts, SP4 6EB
Trustees: Anthony M Fry, Dr Ian Selby, Mrs Rosemary Karen Veronica Cook, Dr Rowan Whimster, Sarah Voaden, Nichola Johnson, Mr Christopher Mark Brayne, Mr Chris Watson, Mr Parvis Jamieson
Income: £13,109,400 [2017]; £10,644,216 [2016]; £7,939,324 [2015]; £6,778,420 [2014]; £6,115,644 [2013]

Wessex Cancer Trust
Registered: 27 Jun 2005 *Employees:* 38 *Volunteers:* 230
Tel: 023 8067 2200 *Website:* wessexcancer.org
Activities: The advancement of health or saving of lives
Address: 91-95 Winchester Road, Chandler's Ford, Eastleigh, Hants, SO53 2GG
Trustees: Miss Asha Senapati MBBS FRCS MRCS LRCP PhD, Mrs Janice Gabriel, Mr Nick Hawkins, Mr Michael Southgate, Barry Rinaldi, Cllr Janet Warwick, Mrs Janet Freeman
Income: £1,518,734 [2017]; £1,317,557 [2016]; £1,747,984 [2015]; £1,545,790 [2014]; £996,711 [2013]

Wessex Children's Hospice Trust
Registered: 9 May 1991 *Employees:* 179 *Volunteers:* 900
Tel: 01962 760060 *Website:* naomihouse.org.uk
Activities: The advancement of health or saving of lives
Address: Wessex Childrens Hospice Trust, Naomi House, Stockbridge Road, Sutton Scotney, Winchester, Hants, SO21 3JE
Trustees: Mr David Charles Holmes, Dr Michael Miller, Mrs Faith Ramsay, Mrs Samantha Jane Curd, Mr Julian Fredrick Charles Cracknell, Professor Alison Richardson, Mrs Liz Wallace, Mr Nicholas Allen, Mr Steve Radjen, Mr Julian Francis Scutts Walker TD BSc MRICS, Mr Shaun Southern
Income: £8,030,640 [2017]; £7,777,602 [2016]; £8,797,851 [2015]; £7,304,656 [2014]; £6,909,568 [2013]

Wessex Schools Trust
Registered: 2 Jun 1999 *Employees:* 43 *Volunteers:* 10
Activities: Education, training
Address: Wessex Schools Trust, c/o Focus School Wilton Campus, The Hollows, Wilton, Salisbury, Wilts, SP2 0LE
Trustees: Mr Nathanael Diffey, Mr Terry Mitchell, Mr Julian Aris, Mr Jody Meek, Mr Marcus Gill, Mr James Farrant, Mr Ben Tuffin, Mr Nathan Fowler
Income: £2,534,581 [2016]; £2,577,327 [2015]; £2,730,734 [2014]; £2,924,430 [2013]; £2,773,431 [2012]

West Anglia Crossroads Caring for Carers
Registered: 4 Apr 2002 *Employees:* 234 *Volunteers:* 47
Tel: 01480 499090 *Website:* carerstrustcambridgeshire.org
Activities: General charitable purposes; advancement of health or saving of lives; disability
Address: 4 Meadow Park, Meadow Lane, St Ives, Huntingdon, Cambs, PE27 4LG
Trustees: Miss Ann Braithwaite, Alison Griffiths, Mrs Christina Wells, Mr Stuart McLellan Evans, Mr Wayne Weedon, Matthew Lester, Mr David Stewart Hipple
Income: £4,265,060 [2017]; £3,733,638 [2016]; £2,812,602 [2015]; £2,463,128 [2014]; £2,233,971 [2013]

West Anglia Training Association Limited
Registered: 5 Jul 1977 *Employees:* 22
Tel: 01480 435544 *Website:* wata.co.uk
Activities: Education, training
Address: West Anglia Training Association, Old Houghton Road, Hartford, Huntingdon, Cambs, PE29 1YB
Trustees: Mr Richard Collman, Terri Jones, Mr Christopher James Robert Bennet
Income: £2,773,521 [2016]; £2,370,814 [2015]; £2,163,503 [2014]; £2,163,503 [2013]; £2,821,821 [2012]

West Berkshire Mencap
Registered: 20 Jul 1999 *Employees:* 45 *Volunteers:* 100
Tel: 01635 41464 *Website:* wbmencap.org
Activities: Disability
Address: Mencap, Enborne Gate, Enborne Road, Newbury, Berks, RG14 6AT
Trustees: Mr Julian Swift-Hook, Mr Paul Christopher Pointer, Mr Stuart Robert Durrant, Mrs Gillian Claire Leech, Mr Tom Rossiter, Ms Louise Rachel Thompson, Mr Darren Anderson, Mr Stephen Luff Smith
Income: £1,952,637 [2017]; £1,922,577 [2016]; £1,943,047 [2015]; £1,922,622 [2014]; £1,789,934 [2013]

West Berkshire Training Consortium
Registered: 5 Sep 1989 *Employees:* 28
Tel: 01635 35975 *Website:* wbtc-uk.com
Activities: Education, training
Address: WBTC, Consortium House, 7 Cheap Street, Newbury, Berks, RG14 5DD
Trustees: Tammera Easterling, Colin Heslop, Mrs Sally Johnson, Christopher Moore, Mr Iain Cox, Ms Anne Millar
Income: £3,596,404 [2017]; £3,362,245 [2016]; £3,406,587 [2015]; £3,056,127 [2014]; £3,055,021 [2013]

West Buckland School

Registered: 8 Jun 2016 Employees: 159 Volunteers: 12
Tel: 01598 760270 Website: westbuckland.com
Activities: Education, training
Address: West Buckland School, West Buckland, Barnstaple, Devon, EX32 0SX
Trustees: Mr Robert Ingram, Mr Andrew Jackson, Mr Kevin Ronald Underwood, Mr Neil Kingdon, Mr John Light, Mrs Maureen Read, Mr Simon Fox, Mrs Naomi Jane Wild, Mr Andrew Boggis, Ms Loraine Cairns, Mr Peter Stucley, Mr Colin Browne, Mr Jonathan Palk, Mrs Sallie Salvidant, Dr Rosalind Joan Fisher-Smith BA MA PhD PGCE, Christopher James
Income: £23,195,493 [2017]

West Ham Park

Registered: 22 Sep 1962 Employees: 17 Volunteers: 195
Tel: 020 7332 3519
Activities: Amateur sport
Address: Corporation of London, P O Box 270, London, EC2P 2EJ
Trustees: The Mayor & Community & Citizen of The City of London
Income: £1,473,435 [2017]; £1,680,680 [2016]; £1,417,935 [2015]; £1,558,783 [2014]; £1,430,079 [2013]

West Ham United Foundation

Registered: 1 Jun 2006 Employees: 120 Volunteers: 122
Tel: 020 8548 2768 Website: whufc.com
Activities: Education, training; disability; prevention or relief of poverty; amateur sport; recreation
Address: Boleyn Ground, Green Street, London, E13 9AZ
Trustees: Ms Marie Gabriel, Mr Ben Illingworth, Mr Jeremy Crook, Mr Andy Mollett, Mr Umesh Desai, Mr Henri Brandman
Income: £2,605,242 [2017]; £1,671,900 [2016]; £1,365,487 [2015]; £904,237 [2014]; £519,764 [2013]

West Heath 2000

Registered: 21 May 1998 Employees: 129
Tel: 01622 884283 Website: westheathschool.com
Activities: Education, training
Address: 6 Bicknor Court Cottages, Bicknor Lane, Bicknor, Sittingbourne, Kent, ME9 8AX
Trustees: Mr Stuart Crookshank OBE, Don Crawford, Mr Leigh Harris, Mrs Pauline Louise Knutton, Mr Andrew Morgan, Merilyn Canet, Glenn Campbell, Miss Victoria Furneaux, Mr Dougal Philps, Mrs Nishka Mary Smith
Income: £6,821,276 [2016]; £6,249,369 [2015]; £5,873,840 [2014]; £6,443,895 [2013]

West Hill School Trust Limited

Registered: 7 Nov 1963 Employees: 105 Volunteers: 4
Tel: 01329 842356 Website: westhillpark.com
Activities: Education, training; arts, culture, heritage, science; amateur sport
Address: West Hill Park School, West Hill Park, Fareham, Hants, PO14 4BS
Trustees: Mr Andrew Sears, Peter Taylor, Mr M A Waldron, Miss Michelle Young, Mrs Bridgetta Worsley, Mr Kevin Murphy, Mr Robert Jempson, Mr Alastair Bell
Income: £4,156,453 [2017]; £3,823,698 [2016]; £3,470,946 [2015]; £3,322,235 [2014]; £3,167,804 [2013]

West House School

Registered: 10 Apr 1963 Employees: 58
Tel: 0121 440 4097 Website: westhouseprep.com
Activities: Education, training
Address: 24 St James Road, Edgbaston, Birmingham, B15 2NX
Trustees: Mr Steven Trevor Heathcote, Mrs Celia Lesley Bell, Mr Clive Stuart Naisby Smith, Ann Tonks, Mr James Gittins, Edward Rutledge, Ms Sarah Hauldys Evans, Mr Ronald Alfred Wilson Middleton, Mr Keith Derek Philips BA
Income: £2,831,497 [2016]; £2,557,428 [2015]; £2,394,262 [2014]; £2,233,981 [2013]; £2,036,763 [2012]

West Kent Extra Limited

Registered: 29 Jun 2004 Volunteers: 500
Tel: 01732 749418 Website: westkent.org
Activities: Education, training; prevention or relief of poverty; economic, community development, employment
Address: West Kent Housing Association Ltd, 101 London Road, Sevenoaks, Kent, TN13 1AX
Trustees: Mr Frank Czarnowski, Mr Brian James Horton, Mr Rosie Elizabeth Serpis, Mrs Angela George, Mr Colin Wilby, Mrs Joanne Frawley, Dr Jo Simpson
Income: £1,292,059 [2016]; £1,854,644 [2015]; £2,062,949 [2014]; £1,493,362 [2013]; £750,681 [2012]

West Kent YMCA

Registered: 30 Jun 1990 Employees: 36 Volunteers: 30
Tel: 01892 542209 Website: westkentymca.org.uk
Activities: Education, training; prevention or relief of poverty; accommodation, housing; religious activities; arts, culture, heritage, science; amateur sport; environment, conservation, heritage; economic, community development, employment; other charitable purposes
Address: Chief Executive, West Kent YMCA Head Office, c/o KCC Pagoda Centre, St Johns Road, Tunbridge Wells, Kent, TN4 9TX
Trustees: Mrs Gerry Wenham, Mrs Heather Evernden, Mr Jonathan Lineker, Mark Farrar, Lady Evans, Mr Jan Smith, Mr Jack Buckley
Income: £1,632,069 [2017]; £1,163,484 [2016]; £1,241,168 [2015]; £1,396,487 [2014]; £1,395,989 [2013]

West Kirby Residential School

Registered: 22 Sep 1962 Employees: 120 Volunteers: 8
Tel: 0151 632 3201 Website: wkrs.co.uk
Activities: Education, training
Address: c/o West Kirby Residential School, West Kirby, Wirral, Merseyside, CH48 5DH
Trustees: Mr John Melville Wylie, Mr Neville Lumb, Mr Stephen Mark Dickinson, Mr Brian Boumphrey, Mrs Geraldine Moore, Mr Edward Billington
Income: £4,943,944 [2017]; £4,627,651 [2016]; £4,702,021 [2015]; £4,890,719 [2014]; £4,573,345 [2013]

West Lincolnshire Domestic Abuse Service

Registered: 11 Jul 2002 Employees: 40 Volunteers: 39
Tel: 01427 616219 Website: westlindseydomesticabuse.org.uk
Activities: General charitable purposes; accommodation, housing
Address: Unit 2, 9 Lord Street, Gainsborough, Lincs, DN21 2DD
Trustees: Mrs Sylvia Morgan, Mrs Daryl Jane Summers, Mr Philip David Dubut, Mrs Beth Tyrrel, Mrs Michelle Katie Allen ACA CTA, Tania Hings, Mrs Nicolla Gibson
Income: £1,289,582 [2017]; £1,033,183 [2016]; £940,286 [2015]; £527,009 [2014]; £216,419 [2013]

West Lodge School Limited
Registered: 18 Dec 1981 *Employees:* 44 *Volunteers:* 44
Tel: 020 8300 2489 *Website:* westlodge.org.uk
Activities: Education, training
Address: 36 Station Road, Sidcup, Kent, DA15 7DU
Trustees: Ms Caroline Graves, Mrs Margaret Frances Rohan, The Reverend Stephen Sealy, Mrs Nicolette Gaskin, Mrs Jane Davies, Miss Katherine Louise Perrior, Mr Gerald Francis Standing, Mrs Christine Head-Rapson, Mr Chris Heayberd, Mrs Penelope Martin, Mrs Gillian Frances Murray
Income: £1,448,010 [2016]; £1,418,094 [2015]; £1,406,106 [2014]; £1,345,797 [2013]; £1,318,702 [2012]

West London Mission Housing Association Limited
Registered: 1 May 1981 *Employees:* 28 *Volunteers:* 10
Tel: 020 7935 6179 *Website:* wlm.org.uk
Activities: Accommodation, housing
Address: West London Mission Offices, 19 Thayer Street, London, W1U 2QJ
Trustees: Mr Gordon Trevor Slater, Mr John Charles Hicks, Mr Rodney Geoffrey Ovenden, John Neilson, Rev Paul Jeffrey Weary, Mr Jeremy Marc Furniss, Mr Martin John Single, Ms Alethea Chia Jung Siow, Rev Andrew John Dart, Rev Susan Keegan von Allmen
Income: £1,307,931 [2017]; £1,317,552 [2016]; £1,251,680 [2015]; £1,148,676 [2014]; £1,008,612 [2013]

West London Mission Methodist Circuit
Registered: 25 Jan 2010 *Employees:* 46 *Volunteers:* 15
Tel: 020 7935 6179 *Website:* wlm.org.uk
Activities: General charitable purposes; religious activities
Address: West London Mission Offices, 19 Thayer Street, London, W1U 2QJ
Trustees: Rev David Cruise, John Charles Hicks, Lisa Warren, Gillian Books, Sallie Choate, Stephen Lee, Daniel Lai, Rev Valerie Reid, Rev Nigel Cowgill, Andrew Hoban, Deacon Linda Gilson, Nicholas Novak, Amy Tang, Daniel Chu, Gordon Trevor Slater, Martin John Single, Rev Susan Keegan von Allmen, Rev Kong Ching Hii, Roger Cotterrell, Val Halstead, Edna Wijeratna, Alethea Siow, Christine Robson, Rev James Cruddas, Rayman Wong, Sam Walker, William Wong, Judith Secker
Income: £2,162,000 [2016]; £2,130,000 [2015]; £2,133,000 [2014]; £2,106,000 [2013]; £1,925,000 [2012]

West London Students' Union
Registered: 16 Aug 2012 *Employees:* 91
Tel: 020 8231 2276 *Website:* uwlsu.com
Activities: General charitable purposes; education, training; amateur sport; other charitable purposes
Address: Students Union, North Builidng, Ealing, London, W5 5RF
Trustees: Andrea Miller, Mr Anthony Coad, Miss Katherine Hackshaw, Miss Rafiga Hersi, Mr David Evan Titley, Miss Zahra Choudry, Maddalena Ruzzene, Miss Zhane Bailey
Income: £2,856,882 [2017]; £1,984,342 [2016]; £1,700,904 [2015]; £1,531,605 [2014]; £1,073,915 [2013]

The West London Synagogue of British Jews
Registered: 17 Feb 2014 *Employees:* 30 *Volunteers:* 400
Tel: 020 7535 0280 *Website:* wls.org.uk
Activities: General charitable purposes; education, training; religious activities
Address: West London Synagogue of British Jews, 33 Seymour Place, London, W1H 5AU
Trustees: Mr Michael John Lewis, Mr Michael Israel, Mr David Norman Marks, Mr James Rennie Fletcher, Mr Adam Marc Sonin, Mr Patrick Mocatta, Ms Margaret Thurer, Dr Henrietta Hughes, Mr Paul Michael Jaffa, Mr Andrew Stone, Mrs Eleanor Sarah Angel, Mrs Monica Lesley Jankel, Mrs Naomi Katherine Ter-Berg, Mrs Marie Van Der Zyl, Mr Henry Dyson, Mrs Katie Hyman, Miss Joan Karen Arnold, Mrs Michelle Eve Susan Ross
Income: £3,131,000 [2016]; £2,932,000 [2015]; £2,989,000 [2014]

West London YMCA
Registered: 10 Oct 1996 *Employees:* 163 *Volunteers:* 25
Website: ymcawestlondon.org
Activities: Education, training; accommodation, housing; religious activities; amateur sport; economic, community development, employment
Address: 9-15 St James Road, Surbiton, Surrey, KT6 4QH
Trustees: Edward Louis Samuel Weiss, Kenneth John Youngman, David Morrow, Louise Hedges, Katherine Helen Morrissey, Albin Stadtmiller, Helen Posner, Andrew John Palmer, Howard Peter Dawson, Gerald Chifamba
Income: £6,735,814 [2017]; £6,669,384 [2016]; £5,752,854 [2015]; £6,467,952 [2014]; £6,712,344 [2013]

West London Zone
Registered: 17 Mar 2015 *Employees:* 10
Tel: 020 7998 4044 *Website:* westlondonzone.org
Activities: General charitable purposes; education, training; economic, community development, employment
Address: 140-144 Freston Road, London, W10 6TR
Trustees: Sir David Verey, Mr Nicholas Wilkie, Mrs Joanna Mary Gillum, Sir Harvey McGrath, Ms Katharine Hill, Ms Jocelyn James
Income: £1,201,027 [2017]; £618,740 [2016]

West Mercia Women's Aid
Registered: 8 Dec 1999 *Employees:* 47 *Volunteers:* 15
Website: westmerciawomensaid.org
Activities: Education, training; prevention or relief of poverty; accommodation, housing
Address: West Mercia Womens Aid, Berrows Business Centre, Bath Street, Hereford, HR1 2HE
Trustees: Ms Nicola Cheryl Griffiths, Ms Carol Louise Dover, Ms Sue Gorbing, Ms Stephanie Stanesby, Ms Rachel Emma Cotterill, Ms Lucy Proctor, Dr Joanna Margaret Liddle, Ms Stephanie Caroline Cope, Ms Linda Jane Pedrick
Income: £1,368,281 [2017]; £1,343,784 [2016]; £1,389,518 [2015]; £1,407,201 [2014]; £1,396,682 [2013]

West Midlands Winter Sports Club Limited
Registered: 25 Oct 2012 *Employees:* 60 *Volunteers:* 20
Activities: Education, training; advancement of health or saving of lives; disability; amateur sport; economic, community development, employment
Address: The Sky Dome, Croft Road, Coventry, Warwicks, CV1 3AZ
Trustees: Mr Darren Green, Mr Heath Rhodes, Mr Tim Fife, Mr Dominic McDermott
Income: £1,793,584 [2016]; £1,247,304 [2015]; £880,552 [2014]; £150,215 [2013]

West Norfolk Community Transport Project
Registered: 17 Apr 1998 *Employees:* 104 *Volunteers:* 10
Tel: 01553 776971 *Website:* wnct.co.uk
Activities: Disability; prevention or relief of poverty; other charitable purposes
Address: St Augustines, Healthy Living Centre, Columbia Way, King's Lynn, Norfolk, PE30 2LB
Trustees: Mrs Dorothy Dane, Mr Peter Brown, Mr Benjamin Colson, Mr Keith Leslie Shayshutt, Mr Nicholas Clive Smith, Mrs Pat French, Mr Derek George Howlett, Mr Carl Edward Suckling
Income: £2,488,231 [2017]; £1,824,413 [2016]; £1,736,013 [2015]; £1,680,189 [2014]; £1,338,102 [2013]

West Sussex Music Trust
Registered: 3 Jul 2013 *Employees:* 136 *Volunteers:* 36
Tel: 0845 208 2182 *Website:* westsussexmusic.co.uk
Activities: Education, training; prevention or relief of poverty; arts, culture, heritage, science; economic, community development, employment; recreation
Address: West Sussex Music, Herbert Shiner School, South Grove, Petworth, W Sussex, GU28 0EE
Trustees: Leon Nettley, Mr Peter Colin Evans, Mr Edward George Rodriguez-Molinero, Terence Chapman, Tim Riches
Income: £2,969,528 [2017]; £3,081,204 [2016]; £2,649,210 [2015]; £3,359,338 [2014]

West Wickham Common and Spring Park Wood
Registered: 27 Feb 1964 *Employees:* 12 *Volunteers:* 15
Tel: 020 7332 3519
Activities: Amateur sport
Address: Corporation of London, P O Box 270, London, EC2P 2EJ
Trustees: The Mayor & Community & Citizens of The City of London
Income: £1,287,520 [2017]; £1,285,181 [2016]; £1,448,643 [2015]; £1,108,101 [2014]; £1,355,775 [2013]

Westbank Community Health and Care
Registered: 7 Jun 2007 *Employees:* 132 *Volunteers:* 600
Tel: 01392 824752 *Website:* westbank.org.uk
Activities: The advancement of health or saving of lives; disability; amateur sport
Address: Westbank, Farm House Rise, Exminster, Exeter, Devon, EX6 8AT
Trustees: Mrs Sonia Anne Barton, Mrs Diana Lynne White, Mr Ian William Whyte, Mr John David Bewick OBE, Mr James Masters, Ms Ann Bond, Mr Ian Paul Tearle
Income: £3,995,083 [2017]; £5,558,648 [2016]; £7,396,508 [2015]; £6,151,816 [2014]; £4,275,252 [2013]

Westbourne House School Educational Trust Limited
Registered: 17 May 1967 *Employees:* 103
Tel: 01243 770750 *Website:* westbournehouse.org
Activities: Education, training; amateur sport
Address: Westbourne House School, Coach Road, Shopwhyke, Chichester, W Sussex, PO20 2BH
Trustees: Mrs Juliet Patricia Matthews, Mrs Gillian Mary Hooker BA, Mr John Ashworth BSc, Mr Christopher Keville, Mr Russell Anthony Justin Hill, Mr Nicholas Paul Backhouse MA FCA, Mr Keith William Langmead, Mr Christopher Edward Melville Snell, Mrs Deborah Alun-Jones MA, Miss Leah Kate Hamblett MA, Mr Benjamin Alistair Martin Vessey
Income: £5,833,354 [2016]; £5,972,077 [2015]; £5,715,171 [2014]; £5,462,011 [2013]; £5,228,057 [2012]

Westbourne School Trust Limited
Registered: 26 Sep 1968 *Employees:* 85 *Volunteers:* 15
Tel: 0114 266 0374 *Website:* westbourneschool.co.uk
Activities: Education, training
Address: Westbourne School, 60 Westbourne Road, Sheffield, S10 2QT
Trustees: Ms Claire Louise Lawton, Andrew Eaton, Mr Jonathan Paul Kenworthy, Mr Ian Wileman, Mrs Julia Wroth, Mr Stephen Downing Goodhart, Mr David Scott Hinchliffe, Mr David Peter Merifield, Mrs Susan Natalie Kay, Mr Glenn Kenneth Day
Income: £3,602,517 [2017]; £3,605,536 [2016]; £3,312,515 [2015]; £3,199,961 [2014]; £3,328,314 [2013]

Westbrook Hay Educational Trust Limited
Registered: 3 Sep 1985 *Employees:* 64
Tel: 01442 256143 *Website:* westbrookhay.co.uk
Activities: Education, training
Address: 100 Carnation Way, Aylesbury, Bucks, HP21 8TX
Trustees: Mrs Diana Elizabeth Deborah Robinson, Mr Michael Woolf, Mr Andrew McKenzie Newland, Mr Matthew O'Donnell, Mr Stephen Hampstead, Mr Stephen James, Mr Maurice Godden, Mr Tony Platt
Income: £3,763,419 [2017]; £3,630,015 [2016]; £3,631,075 [2015]; £3,059,709 [2014]; £2,898,500 [2013]

Westcott House
Registered: 29 May 1964 *Employees:* 34
Tel: 01223 272962 *Website:* westcott.cam.ac.uk
Activities: Education, training; religious activities
Address: 74 de Freville Avenue, Cambridge, CB4 1HU
Trustees: The Rt Revd Adrian Newman, Mr David Scott, Mr Simon Summers, Mr David Ball, Dr Nathan MacDonald, Dr Stewart Davies, Mr Thomas Mumford, Rev Dr Matt Bullimore, Dr Elizabeth Phillips, Rt Revd Stephen Conway The Bishop of Ely, Dr John Perumbalath, Mrs Morag Bushell, The Revd Canon Chris Chivers, Professor Catherine Pickstock, Ms Roxanne Harriet Liddell, Mr Andrew Peter Richard Coates, Rev Alexandra Mary Barrett
Income: £1,467,674 [2016]; £1,605,926 [2015]; £1,662,682 [2014]; £1,520,217 [2013]; £1,187,788 [2012]

Westcountry Rivers Trust
Registered: 17 Mar 2010 *Employees:* 31 *Volunteers:* 99
Tel: 01579 372140 *Website:* wrt.org.uk
Activities: Education, training; environment, conservation, heritage; recreation
Address: Westcountry Rivers Trust, Rain Charm House, Kyl Cober Parc, Stoke Climsland, Callington, Cornwall, PL17 8PH
Trustees: Lord Clinton, Mr Andrew Southall, Mr Henry Llewellyn, Sir David Hoare Bt, M D Martin MBE, Hon Mrs Sarah Lopes, Mrs Jenny Ingham Clark, Mr Paul Arnott, Mr William Robert Thomas Darwall, Mr Graeme Mason Hart, Sir Simon Day, Mr Huntington-Whiteley, William Wyldbore Smith, R A E Simpson, Dr A Torrance, Adam Fox-Edwards, Dr Keith Lancaster, Mr Andrew John Gray, Mr David Butler
Income: £1,958,534 [2016]; £2,021,896 [2015]; £2,843,753 [2014]; £3,930,213 [2013]; £3,541,519 [2012]

The Western Charitable Foundation
Registered: 22 Jun 2012 *Employees:* 10
Tel: 020 7724 7702 *Website:* westerncharitablefoundation.com
Activities: Education, training; prevention or relief of poverty; religious activities
Address: 1 Wallenberg Place, London, W1H 7TN
Trustees: Michael Ziff, Colin Jaque, Richard Mintz, Suzanne J Goodman, David Winton, Eldred Tabachnik, Paul Rayden, David Sage, Anthony Yadgaroff, Harold Pasha, Philip Kremen
Income: £1,017,799 [2016]; £914,746 [2015]; £838,079 [2014]; £1,266,767 [2013]; £282,652 [2012]

Western Sussex Hospitals Charity and Related Charities
Registered: 14 Sep 1995 *Employees:* 6 *Volunteers:* 1
Tel: 01243 831799 *Website:* loveyourhospital.org
Activities: General charitable purposes; education, training; advancement of health or saving of lives; disability; other charitable purposes
Address: Love Your Hospital Charity, Charity Management Office, Western Sussex Hospitals NHS Trust, Spitalfield Lane, Chichester, W Sussex, PO19 6SE
Trustees: Western Sussex NHS Foundation Trust
Income: £1,077,000 [2017]; £755,000 [2016]; £1,078,250 [2015]; £1,032,362 [2014]; £840,246 [2013]

Westholme School Limited
Registered: 20 Feb 1968 *Employees:* 213
Tel: 01254 506070 *Website:* westholmeschool.com
Activities: Education, training
Address: Westholme Senior School, Wilmar Lodge, Meins Road, Pleasington, Blackburn, BB2 6QU
Trustees: His Honour Judge Edward Slinger, Mr James Richard Yates, Mr David John Berry, Mr Jonathon Backhouse, Mr Michael Abraham, Dr Richard Dobrashian, Mr Brian Christopher Marsden, Mr Peter Graham Forrest, Mr Oliver McCann, Mrs Julie Meadows, Mr Stephen Anderson, Mrs Louise Anne Robinson
Income: £8,070,675 [2017]; £7,549,799 [2016]; £7,097,803 [2015]; £7,031,864 [2014]; £7,208,543 [2013]

The Westminster Abbey Trust
Registered: 12 Oct 2006
Tel: 020 7654 4966 *Website:* westminster-abbey.org
Activities: Religious activities; arts, culture, heritage, science
Address: The Chapter Office, 20 Deans Yard, London, SW1P 3PA
Trustees: Mr John O'Brien, Sir Thomas Hughes-Hallett, Rev David Stanton, Dr Julian Litten, The Very Reverend John Robert Hall
Income: £5,148,984 [2016]; £2,462,263 [2015]; £1,305,348 [2014]; £1,009,529 [2013]; £802,869 [2012]

Westminster Cathedral Choir School
Registered: 4 Aug 1997 *Employees:* 53
Tel: 020 7798 9394 *Website:* choirschool.com
Activities: Education, training; religious activities
Address: Ambrosden Avenue, London, SW1P 1QH
Trustees: Westminster Roman Catholic Diocese Trustee
Income: £3,173,237 [2016]; £3,064,117 [2015]; £2,883,242 [2014]; £2,692,183 [2013]; £2,446,463 [2012]

Westminster Chapel
Registered: 28 Nov 2011 *Employees:* 11 *Volunteers:* 100
Tel: 020 7105 7066 *Website:* westminsterchapel.org.uk
Activities: Religious activities
Address: Westminster Chapel, Buckingham Gate, London, SW1E 6BS
Trustees: Ben Chan, Paul Gardner, Howard Satterthwaite, James Edwards, Stephen Sloan
Income: £21,768,117 [2016]

Westminster Citizens Advice Bureau Service
Registered: 2 Dec 1996 *Employees:* 24 *Volunteers:* 97
Tel: 020 7706 6010 *Website:* westminstercab.org.uk
Activities: General charitable purposes; prevention or relief of poverty
Address: 21A Conduit Place, London, W2 1HS
Trustees: Ms Rosemary Gallagher, Mr Alan Gorringe, Ms Dee Conaghan, Mrs Gwyneth Angela MacAulay, Ms Nina Fletcher, Ms Georgia Helen Ackland, Mr Neil Reeder, Mr Stephen Grave, Stephanie Tyrer, Mr Joseph Anthony Haji-Hannas, Mrs Clemence Hermann, Mr Richard Geller
Income: £1,111,171 [2017]; £1,208,464 [2016]; £1,289,778 [2015]; £1,204,918 [2014]; £806,141 [2013]

Westminster College Cambridge
Registered: 15 Mar 1965 *Employees:* 35 *Volunteers:* 14
Tel: 01223 330624 *Website:* westminster.cam.ac.uk
Activities: Education, training; accommodation, housing; religious activities
Address: 39 Highfield Drive, Littleport, Ely, Cambs, CB6 1GA
Trustees: Professor David Thompson, Mr Mark Hayes, Rev Neil Thorogood, Mr Christopher Preston Wheldon Wright, Dr Rick Mearkle, Rev Nigel Philip Uden, Dr Jean Francis Stevenson, Rev Nigel Appleton, Mr William McVey
Income: £1,451,191 [2016]; £3,637,186 [2015]; £1,819,308 [2014]; £3,552,696 [2013]; £3,631,678 [2012]

Westminster Drug Project
Registered: 17 Jan 1994 *Employees:* 298 *Volunteers:* 162
Tel: 020 7421 3100 *Website:* wdp.org.uk
Activities: Other charitable purposes
Address: 18 Dartmouth Street, London, SW1H 9BL
Trustees: Ms Yasmin Batliwala JP, Mr Mark Eaton, His Honour John Graham Boal, Mr Richard Paul, Mr James Saunders, Ms Gillian Benning, Mr Leckraz Boyjoonauth
Income: £18,439,214 [2017]; £20,125,884 [2016]; £16,756,923 [2015]; £19,764,933 [2014]; £15,766,781 [2013]

The Westminster Foundation
Registered: 7 Apr 1975
Tel: 020 7312 6157 *Website:* westminsterfoundation.org.uk
Activities: The prevention or relief of poverty; economic, community development, employment; armed forces, emergency service efficiency; other charitable purposes
Address: Grosvenor, 70 Grosvenor Street, London, W1K 3JP
Trustees: Mark Preston, The Duke of Westminster, Mrs Jane Sandars
Income: £2,690,324 [2016]; £3,168,048 [2015]; £3,303,067 [2014]; £2,628,664 [2013]; £2,814,305 [2012]

Westminster Roman Catholic Diocesan Trust and Other Trust Funds Administered By The Westminster Roman Catholic Diocesan Trustee
Registered: 26 May 1964 *Employees:* 330 *Volunteers:* 40,000
Tel: 020 7798 9174 *Website:* rcdow.org.uk
Activities: Religious activities
Address: Diocese of Westminster, Vaughan House, 46 Francis Street, London, SW1P 1QN
Trustees: Westminster Roman Catholic Diocese Trustee
Income: £55,894,000 [2016]; £55,520,000 [2015]; £50,445,000 [2014]; £44,016,000 [2013]; £40,332,000 [2012]

The Westminster Society for People with Learning Disabilities
Registered: 27 Feb 1989 *Employees:* 471 *Volunteers:* 64
Website: wspld.org.uk
Activities: Disability
Address: The Westminster Society, 16a Croxley Road, London, W9 3HL
Trustees: Mr Lynne Brooke, Mrs Shirley Rodwell, Mrs Catherine Mandrama Slater, Ms Christina Susan Mary Hallett, Mr David Harry Ive, Mrs Lynne Peacock, Mr Graham Thorn, Mrs Anne Virginia Villiers Vice Chair, Mrs A Caro, Mrs Hilary Bach, Dr Steven Philip Martin, Mr Simon Jarrett, Mr Mark Corfield, Mr Michael Webber
Income: £14,726,714 [2017]; £12,295,820 [2016]; £9,211,750 [2015]; £8,522,826 [2014]; £8,160,678 [2013]

Westminster Synagogue
Registered: 8 Dec 2009 *Employees:* 11 *Volunteers:* 45
Tel: 020 7584 3953 *Website:* westminstersynagogue.org
Activities: Religious activities
Address: Kent House, Rutland Gardens, Knightsbridge, London, SW7 1BX
Trustees: Mrs Ann Patricia Mary Fischer, Mr Jeffrey David Ohrenstein, Mr Edward Glover, Mr Nick Stalbow, Mr Abel Halpern, Mr Lance David Christopher Rees, Mrs Valery Ruth Rees, Mr David Goldberg, Ms Janet Mernane, Ms Venetia Willson
Income: £1,357,782 [2016]; £738,324 [2015]; £1,003,886 [2014]; £786,354 [2013]; £854,800 [2012]

Weston Hospicecare Limited
Registered: 14 Feb 1990 *Employees:* 146 *Volunteers:* 609
Website: westonhospicecare.org.uk
Activities: The advancement of health or saving of lives
Address: Weston Hospicecare Ltd, Jackson Barstow House, 28 Thornbury Road, Uphill, Weston-Super-Mare, Somerset, BS23 4YQ
Trustees: Mr John Davey, Mrs Angela Smythe, Mrs Hilary Emery, Mr Tony Roche, Miss Elizabeth Turner, Ms Michelle Michael, Dr David Evans, Mr John Katsouris, Ms Judi Driscoll, Mr Simon Price
Income: £4,128,769 [2017]; £3,941,485 [2016]; £4,355,343 [2015]; £4,918,945 [2014]; £4,308,070 [2013]

Weston Park Foundation
Registered: 19 Dec 1986 *Employees:* 35 *Volunteers:* 130
Tel: 01952 852103 *Website:* weston-park.com
Activities: General charitable purposes; education, training; arts, culture, heritage, science; environment, conservation, heritage; economic, community development, employment; recreation
Address: Weston Park, Weston under Lizard, Shifnal, Salop, TF11 8LE
Trustees: Rose Paterson, Mr Andrew William Orlando Kenyon, Mr Mark George Orlando Bridgeman, Mrs Selina Lucy Graham, Mrs Christina Kenyon-Slaney
Income: £2,176,693 [2016]; £2,075,509 [2015]; £2,660,593 [2014]; £2,908,846 [2013]; £3,345,185 [2012]

The Weston Park Hospital Cancer Care and Research Fund
Registered: 1 Aug 1994 *Employees:* 12 *Volunteers:* 40
Tel: 0114 226 5370 *Website:* wphcancercharity.org.uk
Activities: Education, training; advancement of health or saving of lives
Address: Weston Park Hospital Cancer Charity, Whitham Road, Sheffield, S10 2SJ
Trustees: Barry Hancock, Professor Robert Coleman, Mr Niall David Baker, Dr Kash Purohit, Mr David John Whitney, Dr Patricia Fisher, Pat McGrath, Neil Riley
Income: £2,683,365 [2016]; £1,953,358 [2015]; £1,690,070 [2014]; £2,479,240 [2013]; £1,818,846 [2012]

Westonbirt Schools Limited
Registered: 3 Feb 1964 *Employees:* 171
Tel: 01666 881357 *Website:* westonbirtschools.co.uk
Activities: Education, training
Address: Westonbirt School, Westonbirt, Tetbury, Glos, GL8 8QG
Trustees: Mr Charles John Calcraft Wyld, Ms Alison Rosemary Morris, Mrs Henrietta Metters, Mr Dermot McMeekin, Ms Tamsyn Christian Luggar, Mr Thomas Gaffney, Mr Simon Smith, Ms Jacqueline Margaret Erskine-Crum, Mr Martin Barrow, Mrs Philippa Leggate, Miss Jenefer Greenwood, Mrs Susan Whitfield, Mr Mark Pyper, Mrs Karen Broomhead, Mr Duncan Battishill
Income: £5,879,527 [2016]; £6,113,314 [2015]; £6,838,951 [2014]; £6,364,750 [2013]; £6,139,399 [2012]

Westville House School
Registered: 22 May 2001 *Employees:* 31
Tel: 01943 608053 *Website:* westvillehouseschool.co.uk
Activities: Education, training
Address: West Hall, Nesfield, Ilkley, W Yorks, LS29 0BX
Trustees: Ms Helen Pattinson-James, Mr James Mundell, Mr Strewart McGuffie, Mrs Alison Schmidt, Mr William Eddison, Mr Adam Holdsworth, Dr Karen Ellison
Income: £1,065,288 [2016]; £1,054,250 [2015]; £1,089,070 [2014]; £1,022,892 [2013]; £955,132 [2012]

Westway Trust
Registered: 7 Mar 2008 *Employees:* 84 *Volunteers:* 120
Tel: 020 8962 5720 *Website:* westway.org
Activities: Education, training; advancement of health or saving of lives; arts, culture, heritage, science; amateur sport; environment, conservation, heritage; economic, community development, employment; recreation
Address: Westway Trust, 1 Thorpe Close, London, W10 5XL
Trustees: Cllr Anne Cyron, Ms Karen Bendell, Ms Angela Spence, Mr Howard Richards, Ms Thomasin Renshaw, Mr Christopher Ward, Alan Brown, Cllr Monica Press, Ms Jeannette Davidson, Mrs Tanya Thompson
Income: £7,147,000 [2017]; £8,078,000 [2016]; £8,161,744 [2015]; £7,747,488 [2014]; £7,291,340 [2013]

Whale and Dolphin Conservation
Registered: 12 Oct 1992 *Employees:* 63 *Volunteers:* 300
Tel: 01249 449500 *Website:* whales.org
Activities: Education, training; animals; environment, conservation, heritage
Address: Whale & Dolphin Conservation, 38 St Paul Street, Chippenham, Wilts, SN15 1LJ
Trustees: Mr Adrian John Reed, Mr John Gerard Leigh, Mr Phil Smith, Mr Percy Kelland, Mr George Miles Bramston Adams, Dr Lisa Drewe
Income: £3,542,446 [2016]; £4,235,592 [2015]; £4,569,545 [2014]; £2,977,818 [2013]; £4,357,552 [2012]

When You Wish upon a Star
Registered: 26 Feb 1997 *Employees:* 28 *Volunteers:* 20
Tel: 0115 979 1720 *Website:* whenyouwishuponastar.org.uk
Activities: The advancement of health or saving of lives; other charitable purposes
Address: Ground Floor, Futurist House, Valley Road, Basford, Nottingham, NG5 1JE
Trustees: Miss Barbara Susan White, Mrs Mandy Sims, Mrs Davinder Jaspal, Mr Carl Bradley, Dr Trevor Mills, Mr Paul McCormiuck
Income: £2,495,354 [2016]; £2,366,736 [2015]; £2,079,640 [2014]; £1,801,098 [2013]; £1,572,169 [2012]

Whinfield Study Trust
Registered: 10 Nov 1998 *Employees:* 19 *Volunteers:* 60
Tel: 01524 824751 *Website:* hornby.focus-school.com
Activities: Education, training
Address: 2 Whitendale Drive, Bolton-le-Sands, Carnforth, Lancs, LA5 8LY
Trustees: Mr Edward Fishwick, Mr Christopher Lawrence James, Mr Antony Devenish, Mr Greig Burwood, Mr Simon Whiley, Mr James Simpson, Mr Alan Lovell
Income: £2,190,804 [2016]; £1,091,847 [2015]; £956,000 [2014]; £763,636 [2013]

Whirlow Hall Farm Trust Limited
Registered: 10 Jul 1979 *Employees:* 36 *Volunteers:* 150
Tel: 0114 225 0165 *Website:* whirlowhallfarm.org
Activities: Education, training; advancement of health or saving of lives; disability; arts, culture, heritage, science; animals; environment, conservation, heritage; economic, community development, employment
Address: Whirlow Hall Farm Trust, Whirlow Lane, Sheffield, S11 9QF
Trustees: Mr Norman Farmer, Mr Nicholas Robert Brown Robinson, Mr Keith Lilley, Mrs Emma Stevenson, Mr Martin McKervey, Mrs Gill Ellis, Mrs Louisa Harrison-Walker, Mr Derek Henry Dawson, Mrs Olubukola Oshin, Mr Hugh Facey
Income: £1,450,626 [2017]; £1,102,583 [2016]; £906,039 [2015]; £974,832 [2014]; £878,914 [2013]

The White Eagle Lodge
Registered: 24 Mar 2014 *Employees:* 13 *Volunteers:* 20
Tel: 01730 893300 *Website:* whiteagle.org
Activities: Religious activities
Address: The White Eagle Lodge, Newlands, Brewells Lane, Liss, Hants, GU33 7HY
Trustees: Mr Paul Brenig-Jones, Mrs June Golton, Mr Christopher Sangster, Mr Jason Adam Wilson, Mrs Linda Cohen
Income: £1,213,360 [2017]; £922,557 [2016]

The White Horse Care Trust
Registered: 24 Jul 1990 *Employees:* 283
Tel: 01793 846000 *Website:* whct.co.uk
Activities: The advancement of health or saving of lives; disability; accommodation, housing
Address: White Horse Care Trust, 77a High Street, Wroughton, Swindon, Wilts, SN4 9JU
Trustees: Mr Malcolm Morrison, Mr Ken Price, Mr Phillip Simpson, Mrs M McConnell, Mr Ian Spalding, Mrs Jeanne Perons, Ms Mary Gladman, Ray Norman, Peter Swinburne
Income: £6,074,158 [2017]; £5,377,400 [2016]; £5,353,041 [2015]; £5,252,510 [2014]; £5,045,221 [2013]

White Lodge Centre
Registered: 14 Feb 1983 *Employees:* 76 *Volunteers:* 105
Tel: 01932 567131 *Website:* whitelodgecentre.co.uk
Activities: Disability
Address: 560 Woodham Lane, Woking, Surrey, GU21 5SH
Trustees: Mr Grant James Logan, Mr Tim Bevans, Mr Dave Brian Meller, Mr Patrick Draycott, Ms Alison Sarah Raw, Mrs Kathleen Taylor, Mrs Jean Choules, Mr Clive Bolton, Ms Sarah Louise Dade
Income: £2,390,000 [2017]; £2,208,000 [2016]; £2,228,000 [2015]; £2,267,000 [2014]; £2,235,000 [2013]

Sir Thomas White's Charity
Registered: 29 Nov 1963
Tel: 024 7622 6684 *Website:* charitycommission.gov.uk
Activities: Other charitable purposes
Address: Godfrey Payton & Co, Old Bablake, Hill Street, Coventry, Warwicks, CV1 4AN
Trustees: Mr Peter Wartnaby, Mr Christopher Peter Trye, Mr Peter Beddoes, Mr Paul Derek Meredith, Mr Roger Wiglesworth, Mr Richard Michael Hardy, Mr Anthony Edward Tyre Forsyth
Income: £2,369,666 [2017]; £2,134,161 [2016]; £2,183,145 [2015]; £2,449,307 [2014]; £2,077,091 [2013]

Whitechapel Centre
Registered: 21 Jul 1992 *Employees:* 93 *Volunteers:* 130
Tel: 0151 207 7617 *Website:* whitechapelcentre.co.uk
Activities: Education, training; prevention or relief of poverty; accommodation, housing; economic, community development, employment
Address: Langsdale Street, Everton, Liverpool, L3 8DU
Trustees: Ms Margaret Mary Brown, Ms Valerie Metcalf, Mr Brian Kearsley OBE, Mr Anthony Walsh, Mr David Green, Terence Crolley, Mrs Collette McGuire, David Antrobus, Mr Rowland Moore, Mr Steve Collett
Income: £2,778,686 [2017]; £2,755,241 [2016]; £2,634,970 [2015]; £2,394,577 [2014]; £2,269,104 [2013]

Whitechapel Gallery
Registered: 8 Feb 1963 *Employees:* 64 *Volunteers:* 23
Tel: 020 7522 7888 *Website:* whitechapelgallery.org
Activities: Education, training; arts, culture, heritage, science
Address: 77-82 Whitechapel High Street, Whitechapel, London, E1 7QX
Trustees: Alex Sainsbury, Ms Swantje Conrad, Ms Farshid Moussavi, Mrs Ann Gallagher, Ms Maryam Homayoun Eisler, Ms Alice Rawsthorn, Mr Daniel Hassell, Mr Anupam Ganguli, Ms Catherine Petitgas, Ms Nicola Mary Kerr
Income: £4,164,822 [2017]; £3,937,301 [2016]; £4,164,112 [2015]; £4,097,243 [2014]; £4,463,033 [2013]

The Whitehall and Industry Group
Registered: 26 Mar 1997 *Employees:* 25
Tel: 020 7222 1166
Activities: Education, training
Address: The Whitehall & Industry Group, 80 Petty France, London, SW1H 9EX
Trustees: Ms Rachel Sandby-Thomas, Mr Howard Davies, Ms Debbie Alder, Ms Eleanor Sealy Kelly, Mr Alex James Chisholm, Mr Charles Eales, Ms Pippa Greenslade, Mr David John Dinsdale, Ms Janette Anita Durbin, Mr Philip Christpher Thomson
Income: £2,298,846 [2017]; £2,179,230 [2016]; £1,864,707 [2015]; £1,735,454 [2014]; £1,745,990 [2013]

The Whiteley Homes Trust
Registered: 5 Apr 2004 *Employees:* 186 *Volunteers:* 166
Tel: 01932 842360 *Website:* whiteleyvillage.org.uk
Activities: The advancement of health or saving of lives; prevention or relief of poverty; accommodation, housing
Address: Whiteley Homes Trust, Octagon Road, Whiteley Village, Hersham, Walton on Thames, Surrey, KT12 4EH
Trustees: Roger Formby, Mr Mg Sadler, Mr Duncan Straughen BA, Mr Jason Shaw, Mr Keith Hiscock, Dr Beverly Ann Castleton, Mr Stuart James Shilson LVO BA MSc MPhil, Aileen Woollhead, Mr Michael Pomery CVO MA FIA, Mr Peter Wilkinson CBE FRSA BA, Mr Mike Tolley, Prof David William Perry, Ms Jackie Stevens
Income: £11,302,117 [2016]; £9,102,588 [2015]; £9,106,030 [2014]; £8,297,682 [2013]; £7,901,988 [2012]

The Whitgift Foundation
Registered: 16 Mar 1965 *Employees:* 737
Tel: 020 8680 8499 *Website:* whitgiftfoundation.co.uk
Activities: Education, training; accommodation, housing
Address: Whitgift Foundation, North End, Croydon, Surrey, CR9 1SS
Trustees: Mr Christopher Houlding, Mr Ian Harley, Mrs Pauline Davies BSc PGCE MEd, The Viscountess Stansgate OBE MA, Mr Michael Proudfoot, Mr David Seymour, Mr Asif Patel, Lt Colonel Geoffrey Wright TD DL FCIOB, Dudley Mead FCCA, Mr David Hudson, Rev Jonathan Clark, Mr Dean Sutton, Dr Anand Mehta
Income: £61,334,861 [2017]; £58,793,342 [2016]; £56,755,107 [2015]; £52,284,213 [2014]; £49,791,459 [2013]

The Whitley Fund for Nature
Registered: 6 Jul 2000 *Employees:* 6 *Volunteers:* 20
Tel: 020 7221 9752 *Website:* whitleyaward.org
Activities: Animals; environment, conservation, heritage; economic, community development, employment
Address: 110 Princedale Road, London, W11 4NH
Trustees: Mr Edward John Whitley, Sir David Attenborough, Mr Francis John Sullivan, Lady Catherine Faulks, Mr Ian Kenneth Lazarus
Income: £1,583,607 [2017]; £1,903,313 [2016]; £1,139,860 [2015]; £1,480,171 [2014]; £811,690 [2013]

The Whitley Wildlife Conservation Trust
Registered: 1 Jul 1963 *Employees:* 364 *Volunteers:* 237
Tel: 01803 697502 *Website:* wwct.org.uk
Activities: Education, training; animals; environment, conservation, heritage; recreation
Address: WWCT, Paignton Zoo, Totnes Road, Paignton, Devon, TQ4 7EU
Trustees: Mr Andrew Charles John Cooper, Mrs Sylvia Jo-Ann Greinig, Mr Richard William John Ford, Mrs Sarah Barr, Dr Judy Ravenscroft, Mr Richard Alexander Rowe, Dr Paul Robert Francis Chanin, Mr Stephen Kings, Mrs Rachael Hill BA, Dr Peter Michael Collinson Stevens MBE BSc DSC, Mrs Beth Kathleen McLaughlin, Mr Mark Salmon
Income: £12,892,657 [2017]; £12,811,172 [2016]; £12,180,841 [2015]; £11,646,822 [2014]; £11,665,684 [2013]

Charity of Sir Richard Whittington
Registered: 26 Jun 2001 *Volunteers:* 78
Tel: 020 7726 4991 *Website:* mercers.co.uk
Activities: The prevention or relief of poverty; accommodation, housing
Address: Worshipful Company of Mercers, Becket House, 36 Old Jewry, London, EC2R 8DD
Trustees: The Mercers' Company
Income: £3,210,000 [2017]; £2,971,000 [2016]; £2,639,000 [2015]; £2,615,000 [2014]; £2,784,000 [2013]

Wicksteed Charitable Trust
Registered: 25 May 2011 *Employees:* 271 *Volunteers:* 82
Tel: 01536 512475 *Website:* wicksteedpark.org
Activities: General charitable purposes; amateur sport; environment, conservation, heritage
Address: 8 Codlin Close, Little Billing, Northampton, NN3 9TG
Trustees: Mr Robert Hunt, Mr Oliver Charles Wicksteed, Mr Christopher Bowen, Mr John Richard Pegg, Mr Nicholas Peter Vaughan, Mr Christopher John Pykett, Mr Graham Douglas Keevill, Mrs Linden Groves, Mr Paul John Clarke
Income: £5,338,424 [2017]; £4,943,804 [2016]; £4,483,063 [2015]; £4,872,305 [2014]; £10,631,132 [2013]

Widehorizons Outdoor Education Trust
Registered: 13 Sep 2004 *Employees:* 89 *Volunteers:* 275
Tel: 020 8294 8160 *Website:* widehorizons.org.uk
Activities: Education, training; prevention or relief of poverty; amateur sport; environment, conservation, heritage
Address: Wide Horizons Environment Centre, 77 Bexley Road, London, SE9 2PE
Trustees: Mr John Francis Russell, Peter Brooks, Mr Toby Farmer, Mr Tom James Bremner, Mr Sebastian Taylor, Cllr Christine May, Irene Hickford, Mr Robert Edmund Hilyer
Income: £3,122,000 [2016]; £2,912,233 [2015]; £2,791,614 [2014]; £2,637,104 [2013]

Wigan Athletic FC Community Trust
Registered: 3 Sep 2007 *Employees:* 53 *Volunteers:* 56
Tel: 01942 318090 *Website:* laticscommunity.org
Activities: General charitable purposes; education, training; disability; amateur sport
Address: Montrose Skills Hub, Montrose Avenue, Pemberton, Wigan, Lancs, WN5 9XN
Trustees: Mrs Claire Evans, Mr Philip Ivory, Mr David Molyneux, Miss Jenny Meadows, Mr Phillip Williams, Mr Jonathan Jackson, Mr Emmerson Boyce, Mrs Catherine Robinson
Income: £1,094,197 [2017]; £641,494 [2016]; £845,177 [2015]; £746,064 [2014]; £680,125 [2013]

Wigan Boys and Girls Club
Registered: 23 Feb 2010 *Employees:* 160 *Volunteers:* 120
Website: wiganyouthzone.org
Activities: General charitable purposes; education, training; advancement of health or saving of lives; disability; arts, culture, heritage, science; amateur sport; economic, community development, employment; recreation
Address: Wigan Youth Zone, Parsons Walk, Wigan, Lancs, WN1 1RU
Trustees: Martin Ainscough, William Ainscough, Clare Higham, David Whelan, Mr A Hitchen
Income: £2,403,643 [2017]; £2,079,099 [2016]; £4,044,196 [2015]; £2,393,008 [2014]; £4,199,782 [2013]

Wigan Leisure and Culture Trust

Registered: 3 Aug 2004 *Employees:* 541 *Volunteers:* 500
Tel: 01942 828513 *Website:* wlct.org
Activities: General charitable purposes; education, training; advancement of health or saving of lives; arts, culture, heritage, science; amateur sport; environment, conservation, heritage; recreation; other charitable purposes
Address: Wigan Leisure & Culture Trust, Loire Drive, Robin Park, Wigan, Lancs, WN5 0UL
Trustees: Councillor Eunice Smethurst, Mr David Newman, Mrs Della Bartle, Mr David Lythgoe, Mrs Catherine Jane Wilks, Mr Paul Thomas Moss, Ms Jennifer Brenda Meadows, Mr Michael Weston, Mr David Arthur Lea BSc MA, Mr Gareth Cross, Mr Paul Graham Farrington, Mr Jeremy David Charles Noott, Mr Stephen Dawber
Income: £21,709,021 [2017]; £20,868,968 [2016]; £29,269,985 [2015]; £30,707,237 [2014]; £32,306,867 [2013]

Wigan Link

Registered: 14 Dec 1994 *Employees:* 101
Tel: 01942 202054 *Website:* wiganlink.co.uk
Activities: Disability
Address: 47 Oak Avenue, Hindley Green, Wigan, Lancs, WN2 4LZ
Trustees: Mr Robert Short, Mr Nigel Robinson, Mrs Marysia Magdalena J Welch MEd
Income: £1,745,304 [2017]; £1,635,801 [2016]; £1,466,393 [2015]; £1,545,541 [2014]; £1,627,561 [2013]

Wigan and Leigh Hospice

Registered: 10 Dec 1982 *Employees:* 89 *Volunteers:* 773
Tel: 01942 525566 *Website:* wlh.org.uk
Activities: The advancement of health or saving of lives
Address: Wigan & Leigh Hospice, Kildare Street, Hindley, Wigan, Lancs, WN2 3HZ
Trustees: Mr David Peter Mayes, Doctor Shelagh Elaine Kenward, Mr Walter Brown, Mrs Margaret Sarah Evans, Mr Paul Francis Carroll, Miss Mary Reid, Mr Phillip Williams, Mrs Pauline Payne, Mr Christopher Morley, Mrs June Christine Law
Income: £5,010,062 [2016]; £4,329,891 [2015]; £4,874,013 [2014]; £4,877,808 [2013]; £5,453,385 [2012]

The Wigmore Hall Trust

Registered: 11 Aug 1993 *Employees:* 37
Tel: 020 7258 8254 *Website:* wigmore-hall.org.uk
Activities: General charitable purposes; education, training; arts, culture, heritage, science
Address: The Wigmore Hall Trust, 36 Wigmore Street, London, W1U 2BP
Trustees: Mr Anthony Allen, Mr Alan Leibowitz, Lady Julia Boyd, Lady Mary Alexandra Stirrup, Mr Aubrey John Adams, Mr Mark Hawtin, Dame Felicity Lott
Income: £6,913,850 [2017]; £6,723,628 [2016]; £5,851,557 [2015]; £5,756,933 [2014]; £5,861,688 [2013]

The Wigoder Family Foundation

Registered: 30 May 2001
Activities: General charitable purposes
Address: 9 Hyde Park Gardens, London, W2 2LT
Trustees: Mr Martin Rose, Mrs Elizabeth Sophia Wigoder, Mr Charles Francis Wigoder
Income: £1,463,009 [2016]; £1,270,798 [2015]; £1,109,686 [2014]; £963,953 [2013]; £2,342,323 [2012]

The Wilberforce Trust

Registered: 20 Jun 2001 *Employees:* 86 *Volunteers:* 30
Tel: 01904 760037 *Website:* wilberforcetrust.org.uk
Activities: Education, training; disability; accommodation, housing
Address: The Wilberforce Trust, Wilberforce House, 49 North Moor Road, Huntington, York, YO32 9QN
Trustees: Mr Keith Goodey, Mrs Elizabeth Grierson, Mr Stephen James Cluderay, Mrs Sue Hawkesworth, Mr John Kennedy, Mr Colin Aspinall, Mr Simon Cowell, Mr Keith Larcum
Income: £2,821,731 [2017]; £2,646,352 [2016]; £2,631,211 [2015]; £2,557,546 [2014]; £2,580,603 [2013]

Wildfowl and Wetlands Trust

Registered: 23 Dec 1993 *Employees:* 858 *Volunteers:* 925
Tel: 01453 891900 *Website:* wwt.org.uk
Activities: Education, training; animals; environment, conservation, heritage
Address: The Wildfowl & Wetlands Trust, Bowditch, Slimbridge, Gloucester, GL2 7BT
Trustees: Pamela Castle, Mr Simon Tonge, Mr Simon Henzell-Thomas, Barnaby Briggs, Mr Andrew David Beer, Mr Peter Day, Ms Anna Carragher, Mr Alastair Driver, Martin Birch
Income: £22,414,000 [2017]; £23,766,000 [2016]; £20,788,000 [2015]; £24,363,000 [2014]; £17,203,000 [2013]

The Wildlife Aid Foundation

Registered: 11 Nov 2010 *Employees:* 5 *Volunteers:* 300
Tel: 01372 377332 *Website:* wildlifeaid.org.uk
Activities: Education, training; animals; environment, conservation, heritage
Address: Randalls Farm House, Randalls Road, Leatherhead, Surrey, KT22 0AL
Trustees: Simon Cowell, Mr Robert Leftwich, Mr Nicholas Harding, Mark Cuthbert, Mr Brian Cardy, Mr Mandip Singh Sahota
Income: £1,230,666 [2016]; £755,228 [2015]; £646,993 [2014]; £646,993 [2013]; £599,650 [2012]

Wildlife Heritage Foundation Ltd

Registered: 17 Jun 2004 *Employees:* 26 *Volunteers:* 20
Tel: 01992 470490 *Website:* whf.org.uk
Activities: Education, training; animals; environment, conservation, heritage
Address: 7 Victoria Road, Waltham Abbey, Essex, EN9 1HE
Trustees: Mr Peter Sampson, Mr Matt Brady, Mrs Lynn Kathleen Whitnall, Sir Eric Peacock
Income: £1,239,580 [2016]; £997,365 [2015]; £773,271 [2014]; £534,785 [2013]

The Wildlife Hospital Trust

Registered: 5 Apr 1983 *Employees:* 42 *Volunteers:* 50
Tel: 01844 282292 *Website:* sttiggywinkles.org.uk
Activities: Animals
Address: The Wildlife Hospital Trust, St Tiggywinkles, Aston Road, Haddenham, Aylesbury, Bucks, HP17 8AF
Trustees: Mr Alfred William Davis, Miss Louise Melanie Secker, Mr Glenn Gavin, Mrs Joan Elizabeth Davis, Mr Michael Groth, Mr Michael Joseph Brown
Income: £2,156,300 [2017]; £2,004,889 [2016]; £2,075,960 [2015]; £1,916,742 [2014]; £1,231,784 [2013]

The Wildlife Trust for Bedfordshire Cambridgeshire Northamptonshire
Registered: 28 Sep 1990 *Employees:* 91 *Volunteers:* 1,172
Tel: 01954 713520 *Website:* wildlifebcn.org
Activities: Education, training; animals; environment, conservation, heritage
Address: The Wildlife Trust, The Manor House, Broad Street, Great Cambourne, Cambridge, CB23 6DH
Trustees: Professor William Stephens, Sir Graham Holbrook Fry, Dr Matthew Walpole, Dr Sharon Wynne Erzinclioglu, Dr Samuel Fraser Brockington, Rebecca Jarrett, Ananya Mukherjee, Ms Rebecca Stock, Mr Paul Christopher Mark Solon, Dr Jennifer Bishop, Dr Edgar Clive Turner, Mr James Fanshawe, Anne Bland, Christopher Lewis, Margaret White
Income: £4,259,850 [2017]; £4,518,431 [2016]; £5,113,430 [2015]; £6,902,889 [2014]; £5,102,183 [2013]

The Wildlife Trust of South and West Wales Limited
Registered: 8 Apr 2002 *Employees:* 50 *Volunteers:* 600
Tel: 01656 724100 *Website:* welshwildlife.org
Activities: Education, training; animals; environment, conservation, heritage; economic, community development, employment; recreation
Address: The Wildlife Trust of S & W Wales, Nature Centre, Tondu, Bridgend, Mid Glamorgan, CF32 0EH
Trustees: Mr Trevor Theobald, Mr Robert Laurence Pickford, Mrs Alexis Kirsten, Mr Spencer Gammond, Mr Michael Alexander, Rosey Grandage, Sash Tusa, Mr Ian Thomas, Shirley Matthews, Ms Sally Weale, Mark Brian
Income: £1,872,283 [2017]; £2,175,304 [2016]; £1,907,196 [2015]; £1,902,881 [2014]; £2,148,296 [2013]

Wildwood Trust
Registered: 4 Sep 2002 *Employees:* 108 *Volunteers:* 247
Tel: 01227 712111 *Website:* wildwoodtrust.org
Activities: Education, training; animals; environment, conservation, heritage
Address: Herne Common, Herne Bay, Kent, CT6 7LQ
Trustees: Mr Andrew Price, Mr Paul James Nicoll, Mr Paul John Mallion, Mr Richard Alan Griffiths, Ms Lisa Whiffen, Mr David Butcher
Income: £2,815,515 [2017]; £2,263,316 [2016]; £1,823,155 [2015]; £1,652,922 [2014]; £1,536,484 [2013]

The Wilf Ward Family Trust
Registered: 22 Mar 2011 *Employees:* 917 *Volunteers:* 2
Tel: 01751 474740 *Website:* wilfward.org.uk
Activities: Disability; accommodation, housing; economic, community development, employment
Address: Westgate House, 5 Westgate, Pickering, N Yorks, YO18 8BA
Trustees: Mr William Linton Denness, Mr Malcolm Bruce Smith, Mrs Stephanie Yvonne Lacey, Dr Jamie Adamson, Mr Philip Fletcher, Mr Nicholas John Shaw, Mrs Laura Rawnsley, Ms Helen Marie Burke
Income: £18,618,022 [2017]; £18,409,413 [2016]; £18,880,549 [2015]; £18,988,381 [2014]; £18,210,231 [2013]

Willen Hospice
Registered: 6 Nov 1975 *Employees:* 125 *Volunteers:* 600
Tel: 01908 663636 *Website:* willen-hospice.org.uk
Activities: The advancement of health or saving of lives
Address: Milton Road, Willen Village, Milton Keynes, Bucks, MK15 9AB
Trustees: Graham Ball, Mr Paul Davis, Mr Michael Stevenson, Dawn Bentley, Derek Bell, Dr Madeline Rogers, Jan-Denise Wood, Ivan Philpott, Mrs Joni Hawkes, Robert Gilbert, Charlotte Dunn, Dr Chris Herman, Susan Carbert
Income: £6,022,776 [2017]; £10,226,811 [2016]; £5,002,813 [2015]; £6,008,832 [2014]; £5,184,872 [2013]

The William Frederick Haines Foundation
Registered: 7 Apr 2011 *Employees:* 2
Tel: 020 7101 1960
Activities: General charitable purposes
Address: 1A Burnsall Street, London, SW3 3SR
Trustees: Mr Qais Zakaria, Mr Nicholas Blain, Mrs Maureen Zakaria
Income: £2,500,953 [2016]; £84,631 [2015]; £19,091,185 [2014]; £2,955,883 [2013]

Willington School Foundation Limited
Registered: 24 Apr 1963 *Employees:* 59 *Volunteers:* 18
Tel: 020 8944 7020 *Website:* willingtonschool.co.uk
Activities: Education, training
Address: Willington School, Worcester Road, Wimbledon, London, SW19 7QQ
Trustees: Mr Robert Angus Stewart, Mrs Meredith Brickwood, Mrs Beverley Jane Davis, Mr Jim Brown, Mr Jeremy Hugh Lingard, Dr Naomi Potter, Dr Timothy Richard Squires MA MSc
Income: £3,318,594 [2017]; £3,389,547 [2016]; £3,255,159 [2015]; £2,945,577 [2014]; £2,693,224 [2013]

Willow Foundation
Registered: 12 Nov 2004 *Employees:* 78 *Volunteers:* 423
Tel: 01707 259777 *Website:* willowfoundation.org.uk
Activities: The advancement of health or saving of lives; disability
Address: Willow Foundation Ltd, Gate House, Fretherne Road, Welwyn Garden City, Herts, AL8 6NS
Trustees: Mr David Waddington, Mrs Gina Tress, Mr Stewart Bennett, Rachel Jones, Mr Daniel Hunter, Mr Richard King, Mr Oliver Peterken, Nick Aldridge, Mr Andrew Harvey, Ms Elena Ciallie
Income: £4,287,196 [2016]; £2,415,196 [2015]; £2,151,578 [2014]; £2,315,791 [2013]; £2,109,294 [2012]

Willow Park Housing Trust Limited
Registered: 2 Mar 1999 *Employees:* 338 *Volunteers:* 222
Tel: 0161 946 9552 *Website:* willow-park.co.uk
Activities: General charitable purposes; education, training; prevention or relief of poverty; accommodation, housing; amateur sport; economic, community development, employment
Address: Willow Park Housing Trust, Willow Park House, 8 Poundswick Lane, Wythenshawe, Manchester, M22 9TA
Trustees: Mr Nigel Sedman, Ms Sarah Jayne Judge, Ms Bernadette Mary Heanue, Ms Eula Maude Mesquita, Ms Sarah Alison Russell, Mr Robert William Cressey
Income: £40,439,000 [2017]; £38,204,000 [2016]; £37,043,000 [2015]; £36,846,000 [2014]; £34,880,510 [2013]

Willowbrook Hospice
Registered: 27 Apr 1993 *Employees:* 93 *Volunteers:* 565
Tel: 0151 430 8736 *Website:* willowbrook.org.uk
Activities: The advancement of health or saving of lives
Address: Willowbrook Hospice, Portico Lane, Eccleston Park, Prescot, Merseyside, L34 2QT
Trustees: Mr Kenneth Stringer, Mr Geoffrey Slater, Dr Karen Beeby, Mr Philip Nee, Mr Kevin Gallimore, Ms Nikki Ellison, Mr Alan Chick, Derek Corf Esq, Ms Elaine Inglesby, Dr Michael Van Dessel, Mr Terence Hankin, Ms Melanie Simmonds
Income: £4,548,441 [2017]; £5,063,962 [2016]; £4,434,156 [2015]; £3,861,142 [2014]; £3,588,638 [2013]

The HDH Wills 1965 Charitable Trust
Registered: 30 Jan 2007 *Employees:* 9
Tel: 01608 678051 *Website:* hdhwills.org
Activities: General charitable purposes
Address: H D H Wills 1965 Charitable Trust, Henley Knapp Barn, Fulwell, Chipping Norton, Oxon, OX7 4EN
Trustees: Dr Catherine Wills, Mr Charles Philip Liell Francklin, Mr Thomas Michael Nelson, Mr John Seton Burrell Carson, Martin Fiennes, Richard Tulloch
Income: £2,980,041 [2017]; £2,773,103 [2016]; £3,008,475 [2015]; £3,244,376 [2014]; £3,668,992 [2013]

The Wilton House Trust
Registered: 8 Jul 1983 *Employees:* 31
Tel: 01722 746700 *Website:* wiltonhouse.com
Activities: Environment, conservation, heritage
Address: The Estate Office, Wilton Estate, Wilton, Salisbury, Wilts, SP2 0BJ
Trustees: Dr John Martin Robinson, Mr Stuart Wyndham Murray Threipland, William George Verdon-Smith
Income: £7,584,928 [2016]; £1,523,110 [2015]; £1,353,863 [2014]; £1,288,287 [2013]; £1,204,619 [2012]

Wiltons Music Hall
Registered: 28 May 1991 *Employees:* 16 *Volunteers:* 36
Website: wiltons.org.uk
Activities: Education, training; arts, culture, heritage, science; environment, conservation, heritage; economic, community development, employment
Address: 1 Graces Alley, London, E1 8JB
Trustees: George Marsh, Mark Rhodes, Kathleen Herron, Menna Lyn McGregor, Dr John Gayner, Lucy Porten
Income: £1,565,375 [2016]; £1,222,755 [2015]; £1,464,315 [2014]; £4,388,472 [2013]; £1,825,503 [2012]

Wiltshire Air Ambulance Charitable Trust
Registered: 3 Oct 2011 *Employees:* 17 *Volunteers:* 90
Website: wiltshireairambulance.co.uk
Activities: The advancement of health or saving of lives
Address: Carlton Business Centre, Carlton House, Maundrell Road, Calne, Wilts, SN11 9PU
Trustees: Mrs Anna Karen Cole, Mr Christopher Lear, Mr Michael Fellows, Mr Peter James Foskett, Mr David Richard Youens
Income: £6,200,948 [2016]; £3,124,102 [2015]; £2,685,129 [2014]; £2,478,451 [2013]; £1,747,713 [2012]

Wiltshire Citizens Advice
Registered: 6 May 1997 *Employees:* 55 *Volunteers:* 133
Tel: 01225 617879 *Website:* cabwiltshire.org.uk
Activities: The prevention or relief of poverty
Address: Citizens Advice Bureau, 1 Mill Street, Trowbridge, Wilts, BA14 8BE
Trustees: Fiona Johnson, Mr Andrew Perry, Sharon Conner, Anna Symonds, Nigel Christopher Jackson, Mr Keith Johnston, Mr Nigel Clarke, Michael Stanton Foster, Louise Simpson, Richard Ramsden
Income: £1,989,828 [2017]; £1,538,882 [2016]; £1,467,131 [2015]; £1,266,601 [2014]; £1,372,563 [2013]

Wiltshire Creative
Registered: 14 Oct 1966 *Employees:* 69 *Volunteers:* 200
Tel: 01722 320117 *Website:* salisburyplayhouse.com
Activities: Education, training; arts, culture, heritage, science
Address: Corner Cottage, The Street, Dennington, Woodbridge, Suffolk, IP13 8JF
Trustees: Mrs Helen Judith Birchenough, Mrs Rosemary Ellen MacDonald, Mr Doric Alfred Howard Bossom, Ms Katharine Lois Barker, Ms Pauline Scott-Garrett, Mr Timothy Crarer, Mr John Grenfell Russell Perry, Mr Nick Frankfort, Ms Kathryn Louise Dalton
Income: £3,666,694 [2017]; £3,504,755 [2016]; £3,198,163 [2015]; £3,140,805 [2014]; £3,020,816 [2013]

Wiltshire Wildlife Trust Limited
Registered: 3 Sep 1973 *Employees:* 81 *Volunteers:* 1,531
Tel: 01380 725670 *Website:* wiltshirewildlife.org
Activities: Education, training; environment, conservation, heritage
Address: Elm Tree Court, Long Street, Devizes, Wilts, SN10 1NJ
Trustees: Maurice Avent, Mr Michael James Hodgkins, Mr James Ravine, Mrs Rosemary Collingborn, Mr Mark Street, Professor Penelope Endersby, Col Richard Edward Henry Aubrey-Fletcher, Mrs Denise Plummer, Mr Alan Willis
Income: £3,279,064 [2017]; £3,156,142 [2016]; £2,967,531 [2015]; £3,504,837 [2014]; £3,362,994 [2013]

The Wilverley Association
Registered: 30 Oct 1964 *Employees:* 76
Tel: 01590 645244 *Website:* newforestcarehomes.co.uk
Activities: The advancement of health or saving of lives; accommodation, housing
Address: 47 Shorefield Way, Milford on Sea, Lymington, Hants, SO41 0RW
Trustees: Mr Philip Horner, Mr John Anthony Trundle, Mr Peter Thomas Griffiths, Mrs Catherine Brenda Boynton, Mr Geoff Jennings, John Brace, Mr Martin Cooper Wilson, Mrs Joanne Rosalind Husband
Income: £3,937,305 [2017]; £3,664,181 [2016]; £3,485,393 [2015]; £3,288,223 [2014]; £2,838,124 [2013]

The Wimbledon Foundation
Registered: 9 May 2014 *Employees:* 5
Tel: 020 8971 2702 *Website:* wimbledon.com
Activities: General charitable purposes; education, training; prevention or relief of poverty; amateur sport
Address: The Wimbledon Foundation, Church Road, Wimbledon, London, SW19 5AE
Trustees: Sir Nicholas Young, I L Hewitt, Ashley J K Tatum, Mr Henry Bruce Weatherill The Hon, Mr Nicholas Andrew Bitel, P G H Brook, Sir Keith Onyema Ajegbo OBE
Income: £1,276,000 [2017]; £992,000 [2016]; £785,000 [2015]

Wimbledon Guild of Social Welfare (Incorporated)
Registered: 9 Aug 1961 *Employees:* 40 *Volunteers:* 270
Tel: 020 8946 0735 *Website:* wimbledonguild.co.uk
Activities: General charitable purposes; education, training; advancement of health or saving of lives; disability; prevention or relief of poverty; accommodation, housing
Address: Wimbledon Guild of Social Welfare, Guild House, 30-32 Worple Road, London, SW19 4EF
Trustees: Amir Siddiqui, Susan Cooke, Mr Simon Leathes MA FCA, Ms Karen Biggs, Mrs Theresa Zlonkiewicz, Mr Richard Andrew Steele, Ms Caroline Mawhood, Mr Clive Handford, Mr Roger Morris
Income: £1,723,047 [2017]; £1,965,873 [2016]; £14,803,015 [2015]; £1,814,827 [2014]; £2,866,950 [2013]

Wimbledon and Putney Commons Conservators
Registered: 14 Apr 1972 *Employees:* 22 *Volunteers:* 62
Tel: 020 8788 7655 *Website:* wpcc.org.uk
Activities: General charitable purposes; education, training; amateur sport; animals; environment, conservation, heritage; recreation
Address: Rangers Office, Windmill Road, London, SW19 5NQ
Trustees: Mr Michael Rappolt, Mr Nigel Ware, Mrs Shirley Gillbe, Mr Peter Hirsch, Diane Neil Mills, Dr Rosalind Taylor, Mrs Sarah-Jane Holden, Mr David Hince
Income: £1,598,206 [2017]; £1,576,954 [2016]; £1,756,235 [2015]; £1,424,868 [2014]; £1,455,364 [2013]

Winchester Cathedral Trust
Registered: 29 Sep 1983 *Employees:* 2
Tel: 01962 857220 *Website:* winchester-cathedral.org.uk
Activities: Religious activities; environment, conservation, heritage
Address: 9 The Close, Winchester, Hants, SO23 9LS
Trustees: Mr John Robert Steel, The Very Revd Catherine Ogle, Bruce Parker, Mr Alan Lovell, Duke of Wellington, Dame Mary Fagan, Mr Michael Campbell MBE DL, Mr Nigel Atkinson VLL, Mr Nigel McNair Scott
Income: £1,629,038 [2017]; £1,154,044 [2016]; £897,227 [2015]; £1,668,986 [2014]; £1,325,070 [2013]

Winchester Diocesan Board of Finance
Registered: 4 Oct 1966 *Employees:* 40 *Volunteers:* 101
Tel: 01962 737336 *Website:* winchester.anglican.org
Activities: Religious activities
Address: The Diocesan Office, Old Alresford Place, Old Alresford, Alresford, Hants, SO24 9DH
Trustees: The Right Reverend Timothy John Dakin, Mrs Alison Jane Coulter, The Revd Angela Karen Nutt, Rev Jane Bakker The, Mrs Esther Clift, Mr Ian Newman, Mr Alistair Barron, The Reverend Andrew Mark Micklefield, Mr Mark Ward
Income: £12,030,000 [2016]; £11,748,000 [2015]; £12,550,000 [2014]; £13,302,000 [2013]; £13,158,000 [2012]

Winchester House School Trust Limited
Registered: 8 Jul 1966 *Employees:* 132
Tel: 01280 846461 *Website:* winchester-house.org
Activities: Education, training
Address: Winchester House School, 44 High Street, Brackley, Northants, NN13 7AZ
Trustees: Mr Arthur Robert Heygate, Dr Anthony Wallersteiner, Mr George Seligman, Mr Rupert Patrick Fordham, Mr Patrick Bradshaw, Mrs Louise Brownhill, Mr Richard Greaves, Mr Thomas Edward Purton, Mr Martin Wetherill FRCS, Mr John Moule, Alan Ruddy, Mr John Floyd
Income: £5,061,614 [2017]; £5,279,295 [2016]; £4,855,039 [2015]; £5,028,820 [2014]; £4,465,016 [2013]

Winchester Science Centre
Registered: 4 Jun 1986 *Employees:* 55 *Volunteers:* 1,825
Tel: 01962 863791 *Website:* winchestersciencecentre.org
Activities: Education, training; environment, conservation, heritage
Address: Telegraph Way, Winchester, Alresford, Hants, SO21 1HZ
Trustees: Mr Colin Harry Brook, Mrs Liz Wallace, Mr Barry David Lipscomb, Prof Diane Newell, Mr Richard Peckham, Mr Jeremy Booker, Dr Ian Crozier Jenkins, Dr Martin Peter Read MA Cantab, Mr Paul Miles Wilton, Mr John Francis Clarke, Professor Malcolm Coe, Dr Toby StJohn King, Ms Janet Preston, Mrs Doleres Byrne OBE
Income: £2,050,000 [2017]; £1,872,917 [2016]; £1,556,168 [2015]; £1,448,403 [2014]; £1,494,760 [2013]

Winchester Student Union
Registered: 27 Jun 2012 *Employees:* 88 *Volunteers:* 815
Tel: 01962 827429 *Website:* winchesterstudents.co.uk
Activities: Education, training
Address: Winchester Student Union, Sparkford Road, Winchester, Hants, SO22 4NR
Trustees: Mr Steven Vear, Mr Jordan Rudge, Mr Tali Atvars, Mr William Richards, Mrs Danielle Hutchins, Miss Rosie Lewis
Income: £1,702,252 [2017]; £1,608,555 [2016]; £1,570,421 [2015]; £1,573,154 [2014]; £1,542,068 [2013]

Windermere Educational Trust Limited
Registered: 28 Nov 1967 *Employees:* 137 *Volunteers:* 21
Tel: 015394 46164 *Website:* windermereschool.co.uk
Activities: Education, training
Address: Windermere St Annes School, Browhead, Patterdale Road, Windermere, Cumbria, LA23 1NW
Trustees: Mrs Michelle Karen Rothwell, Mrs Joanne Harris, Mr Jason Dearden, Mr Michael Dwan, Mrs Alison Claire Hodson, Mrs Carol Julie Burrow
Income: £6,557,897 [2017]; £6,465,413 [2016]; £6,489,853 [2015]; £6,384,685 [2014]; £6,274,859 [2013]

Windle Trust International
Registered: 8 Jul 2002 *Employees:* 4
Tel: 01865 712900 *Website:* windle.org.uk
Activities: Education, training; prevention or relief of poverty; overseas aid, famine relief; economic, community development, employment
Address: Windle Trust International, 37a Oxford Road, Cowley, Oxford, OX4 2EN
Trustees: Mrs Cynthia Rumboll, Dr Oliver Bakewell, Mr Stuart Wilson, Dr Lucy Hovil, Mr Sam Bickersteth, Ms Eleanor Horne, Mr Malcolm McNeil, Dr Samuel Bekalo, Dr Elizabeth McNess
Income: £3,049,185 [2016]; £2,467,937 [2015]; £2,015,798 [2014]; £3,187,525 [2013]; £2,173,053 [2012]

Windlesham School Trust Limited
Registered: 16 Mar 1974 *Employees:* 55 *Volunteers:* 1
Tel: 01273 553645 *Website:* windleshamschool.co.uk
Activities: Education, training
Address: Windlesham School, 190 Dyke Road, Brighton, BN1 5AA
Trustees: Mr Graham Rowlands Hempel, Mrs Therese England, Mr John Patching, Mr Neil Baxter, Mrs Christine Mannion Watson
Income: £1,629,759 [2017]; £1,707,933 [2016]; £1,634,510 [2015]; £1,715,187 [2014]; £1,748,041 [2013]

Windmill Hill City Farm Limited
Registered: 2 Feb 1979 *Employees:* 82 *Volunteers:* 400
Tel: 0117 963 3252 *Website:* windmillhillcityfarm.org.uk
Activities: General charitable purposes; education, training; animals; environment, conservation, heritage; economic, community development, employment; recreation
Address: Windmill Hill City Farm, Philip Street, Bedminster, Bristol, BS3 4EA
Trustees: Mr Christopher Heaton, Mr Jamie Darwen, Ms Melissa Louise Denwood, Ms Emma Luke, Ms Josie Forsyth, Mrs Sally Jones, Ms Emily Talbot, Beccy Golding, Mr Harry Christopher Kauntze
Income: £1,723,639 [2017]; £1,482,111 [2016]; £1,326,342 [2015]; £1,187,498 [2014]; £1,002,978 [2013]

Wine and Spirit Education Trust
Registered: 27 Nov 1969 *Employees:* 94 *Volunteers:* 5
Tel: 020 7089 3824 *Website:* wsetglobal.co.uk
Activities: Education, training
Address: 39-45 Bermondsey Street, London, SE1 3XF
Trustees: Mr Simon McMurtrie, Mr Nicholas Andrew Hyde, Mr Simon Thorpe, Mrs Susan McCraith, Mr Jonathan Driver, Mr Troy Christensen, Mr Michael Turner, Mr Richard Connor
Income: £11,077,568 [2017]; £9,408,616 [2016]; £8,207,996 [2015]; £7,634,091 [2014]; £6,750,788 [2013]

Wings for Life UK Spinal Cord Research Foundation
Registered: 3 Nov 2010 *Employees:* 4 *Volunteers:* 200
Tel: 07772 549065 *Website:* wingsforlife.com
Activities: Education, training; advancement of health or saving of lives; disability
Address: 155-171 Tooley Street, London, SE1 2JP
Trustees: Ms Anita Gerhardter, Mr Dominik Mitsch, Mr Seth Marthinsson, Mr Andy Shaw, Mr Paul Stewart, Mr Jamie Rake
Income: £2,867,919 [2016]; £918,121 [2015]; £990,578 [2014]; £715,367 [2013]; £305,604 [2012]

The Winston Churchill Memorial Trust
Registered: 8 Feb 1965 *Employees:* 10
Tel: 020 7799 1660 *Website:* wcmt.org.uk
Activities: General charitable purposes; education, training; advancement of health or saving of lives; disability; accommodation, housing; religious activities; arts, culture, heritage, science; amateur sport; animals; environment, conservation, heritage; economic, community development, employment; armed forces, emergency service efficiency; human rights, religious or racial harmony, equality or diversity; recreation; other charitable purposes
Address: Chief Executive, Winston Churchill Memorial Trust, 29 Great Smith Street, London, SW1P 3BL
Trustees: Prof Brian Clarke, The Hon Jeremy Soames, Mr David Taylor-Smith, Viscount Brookeborough, Mr John Baker, Ms Joanne Thompson, Mr Harry Henderson, Ms Merlyn Lowther, Mr David Sheepshanks CBE DL, Mrs Anne Boyd, Mr John Armitage, Mr Jacob Polny
Income: £2,435,457 [2016]; £1,521,389 [2015]; £1,157,976 [2014]; £1,195,347 [2013]; £1,045,555 [2012]

Winston's Wish (A Grief Support Programme for Children)
Registered: 18 Mar 1997 *Employees:* 58 *Volunteers:* 316
Website: winstonswish.org.uk
Activities: Education, training; advancement of health or saving of lives
Address: 19 Eldorado Crescent, Cheltenham, Glos, GL50 2PY
Trustees: Mr Mark Winston Smith, Ms Caroline Keen, Samantha Anne Carruthers MS, Mr Christian Cullinane, Mr Benjamin Malcolm Quentin Cosh, Ms Barbara Want, Mr Nigel Purveur, Mrs Clare Louise Gallie, Professor Jane McCarthey
Income: £2,396,316 [2017]; £2,206,088 [2016]; £2,457,275 [2015]; £1,906,373 [2014]; £1,817,431 [2013]

Winterfold House School Trust Limited
Registered: 30 Jun 1997 *Employees:* 77
Tel: 01562 777234 *Website:* winterfoldhouse.co.uk
Activities: Education, training
Address: Rylands Farm, Rylands Lane, Elmley Lovett, Droitwich, Worcs, WR9 0PT
Trustees: Mrs Morag Eleanor Chapman MA, Mr John Eaton
Income: £3,022,347 [2016]; £2,682,772 [2015]; £2,976,716 [2014]; £2,949,352 [2013]; £2,909,923 [2012]

Winton Philanthropies
Registered: 21 Jun 2005
Activities: General charitable purposes; arts, culture, heritage, science; economic, community development, employment
Address: Grove House, 27 Hammersmith Grove, London, W6 0NE
Trustees: Mr David Winton Harding, Mrs Claudia Harding, The Hon Martin John Hunt
Income: £8,862,935 [2016]; £821,144 [2015]; £1,313,981 [2014]; £1,907,979 [2013]; £300,064 [2012]

Wirral Christian Centre Trust Limited
Registered: 25 May 1988 *Employees:* 115 *Volunteers:* 3
Tel: 0151 653 8307 *Website:* wirralchristiancentre.com
Activities: General charitable purposes; accommodation, housing
Address: Wirral Christian Centre, 1 Woodchurch Road, Birkenhead, Merseyside, CH41 2UE
Trustees: Paul Anthony Epton, Robert Fisher, Richard Dixon, Dr Abel Kehinde Adegoke, Simeon Kehinde, Rev Gregory Epton
Income: £1,699,974 [2017]; £1,782,129 [2016]; £2,006,390 [2015]; £1,716,930 [2014]; £1,342,135 [2013]

Wirral Churches' Ark Project
Registered: 24 Jan 2000 *Employees:* 30 *Volunteers:* 30
Tel: 0151 649 0111 *Website:* wirralark.org.uk
Activities: Accommodation, housing
Address: The Ark, Mary Cole House, 7 Sidney Street, Birkenhead, Merseyside, CH41 1BF
Trustees: Dr Ian Cubbin, Mr Peter Ashley-Mudie, Norman Jones, Revd Robert Nelson, Mr Derek Hughes, Mr Melvin Godfrey
Income: £1,001,646 [2016]; £1,009,351 [2015]; £1,275,138 [2014]; £1,036,292 [2013]; £964,192 [2012]

Wirral Hospice St John's
Registered: 11 Nov 1980 *Employees:* 163 *Volunteers:* 500
Tel: 0151 334 2778 *Website:* wirralhospice.org
Activities: Education, training; advancement of health or saving of lives
Address: Wirral Hospice, St John's, Mount Road, Higher Bebington, Wirral, Merseyside, CH63 6JE
Trustees: Mr Stephen Burrows, Graham Ridgway, Dr Susan Brennan, Mr Phillip Stephen Shepherd, Annie Johnson, Chris Pope, Paul Cuthbertson, Dr Beverly Claire Oates, Steve Schroeder, Marie Granby
Income: £5,177,605 [2017]; £4,983,611 [2016]; £5,090,234 [2015]; £5,519,207 [2014]; £4,598,053 [2013]

Wirral Independent Living and Learning
Registered: 3 Jun 1999 *Employees:* 95 *Volunteers:* 8
Tel: 0151 649 9393 *Website:* willwirral.org.uk
Activities: Disability
Address: Unit 18-20 Tower Quays Business Park, Tower Road, Birkenhead, Merseyside, CH41 1BP
Trustees: Mr John Engwall, Mr Kemal Houghton, Mrs Heather Solomon, Mrs Julie Murphy, Ms Joan Price, Mrs Catherine Hood, Mrs Marlene Hawthorne, Mrs Karen Jane Hynes
Income: £1,467,794 [2017]; £1,340,664 [2016]; £1,330,546 [2015]; £1,278,898 [2014]; £1,096,527 [2013]

Wirral Mind
Registered: 19 Aug 1997 *Employees:* 38 *Volunteers:* 60
Tel: 0151 512 2200 *Website:* wirralmind.org.uk
Activities: Education, training; advancement of health or saving of lives; disability; accommodation, housing
Address: Wirral Mind, 90-92 Chester Street, Birkenhead, Merseyside, CH41 5DL
Trustees: Mr Stephen Maddox, Mr Jonathan Ben Adams, Mrs Gaynor Mould, Mr Michael Jarvis, Mr Kenneth Henshaw, Mr Anthony Michael Mould DL JP, Mr Richard William Nicholas, Mr Nicholas Hewitt, Mrs Margaret Davies, Dr Catherine O'Brien
Income: £1,199,824 [2017]; £1,185,826 [2016]; £1,139,184 [2015]; £1,123,456 [2014]; £1,129,144 [2013]

Wirral Partnership Homes Limited
Registered: 24 Nov 2004 *Employees:* 473
Tel: 0151 606 3151 *Website:* magentaliving.org.uk
Activities: Education, training; advancement of health or saving of lives; disability; prevention or relief of poverty; accommodation, housing; economic, community development, employment
Address: Wirral Partnership Homes, Partnership Building, Hamilton Street, Birkenhead, Merseyside, CH41 5AA
Trustees: Mr Stephen Penlington, Mr Stephen Foulkes, David Clark, Ms Muriel Doreen Wilkinson, Mr Philip Gandy, Mrs Sharon Grover, Mr Stuart Whittingham, Mr Jeffrey Edwin Green, Mr Michael James Larsen, Mr Matthew Brown, Mr Nicholas Gerrard, Mr Gordon Ronald
Income: £65,327,000 [2017]; £62,963,000 [2016]; £64,373,000 [2015]; £59,060,000 [2014]; £55,189,000 [2013]

Wirral Youth Zone
Registered: 18 Aug 2015 *Employees:* 6 *Volunteers:* 50
Tel: 01204 362128 *Website:* thehiveyouthzone.org
Activities: Education, training; advancement of health or saving of lives; disability; arts, culture, heritage, science; amateur sport; recreation
Address: Onside Youth Zones, Atria, Spa Road, Bolton, Lancs, BL1 4AG
Trustees: Peter Bibby, John Syvret, Sara Stephens, Mr Allan John Wood, Cllr Phil Davies, Phil Garrigan, Matt Noon, Fiona Norcross
Income: £5,339,097 [2017]; £773,000 [2016]

Wirrelderly
Registered: 19 Apr 1988 *Employees:* 108 *Volunteers:* 9
Tel: 0151 334 0200 *Website:* elderholme.co.uk
Activities: The advancement of health or saving of lives
Address: Elderholme Nursing Home, Clatterbridge Road, Bebington, Wirral, Merseyside, CH63 4JY
Trustees: Mr Brian Rourke, Aled Cadwallader, Mr Mark Duckworth, Mr Malcolm Ayers, Mrs Rosemary Lloyd, Dr Kenneth Edwardson, Mrs Suzanne Jenkin
Income: £2,244,125 [2016]; £2,103,746 [2015]; £2,021,067 [2014]; £1,917,557 [2013]; £1,818,940 [2012]

Wisbech Grammar School
Registered: 31 Jul 2001 *Employees:* 129
Tel: 01945 583631 *Website:* wisbechgrammar.com
Activities: Education, training
Address: Wisbech Grammar School, North Brink, Wisbech, Cambs, PE13 1JX
Trustees: Dr Dennis Barter MD, Hugh McCurdy, Mr Rupert Calleja, Mrs Catherine Rebecca Mair, Mrs Judith Alison Bodger, Mrs Karina Simonne Albertine Hart, Mrs Elizabeth Christine Morris, Mr Christopher Mark Stephen Goad, Mr Ian MacLachlan, Prof James Russell Raven, Dr Quintin Wong
Income: £5,263,992 [2017]; £5,731,106 [2016]; £5,238,234 [2015]; £5,272,265 [2014]; £5,710,240 [2013]

Wisdom School
Registered: 18 Jul 2011 *Employees:* 25 *Volunteers:* 20
Tel: 020 8205 0052 *Website:* northlondongrammar.com
Activities: General charitable purposes; education, training; amateur sport
Address: North London Grammar School, 110 Colindeep Lane, London, NW9 6HB
Trustees: Mr Armagan Dursun, Mr Rustam Aliyev, Mr Ziya Kocabiyik
Income: £1,352,021 [2016]; £1,694,427 [2015]; £4,640,619 [2014]; £3,630,864 [2013]; £1,361,572 [2012]

Wise Ability Limited
Registered: 9 Oct 2009 *Employees:* 86
Website: wiseability.co.uk
Activities: Education, training; disability; prevention or relief of poverty; economic, community development, employment
Address: 552 Victoria Street, North Melbourne, Victoria, Australia
Trustees: Mr Alistair Buxton Urquhart, Mrs Anna Leyden, Ms Ernestine Rozario, John Bateup, Professor Joseph Graffam, Ms Patricia Fay Toop, Mr Zane Maurice Duff
Income: £2,729,913 [2017]; £2,037,784 [2016]; £5,660,594 [2015]; £3,598,947 [2014]; £2,791,158 [2013]

Wiseheights Limited
Registered: 29 May 1986
Tel: 020 8731 0777
Activities: General charitable purposes; education, training; prevention or relief of poverty; religious activities; other charitable purposes
Address: New Burlington House, 1075 Finchley Road, London, NW11 0PU
Trustees: Mr Abraham Klein, Mr Joshua Sternlicht
Income: £2,360,164 [2017]; £5,511,110 [2016]; £2,596,557 [2015]; £1,390,285 [2014]; £2,647,010 [2013]

Witham Hall School Trust Limited
Registered: 20 Jan 1978 *Employees:* 86 *Volunteers:* 1
Tel: 01778 590702 *Website:* withamhall.com
Activities: Education, training
Address: Witham Hall School, Witham on the Hill, Bourne, Lincs, PE10 0JJ
Trustees: Rev Andrew Hawes, Mr Charles John Urquhart Applegate, Mr Jeremy William Sharman, Mrs Katherine Robertson, Mrs Louise Hobbs, Mr David Allsop, Mrs Helen Mary Banks, Mr Algy Smith-Maxwell, Mrs Sarah Kerr-Dineen, Mr Barry James Holdsworth
Income: £4,031,903 [2017]; £4,007,623 [2016]; £3,597,697 [2015]; £3,465,543 [2014]; £3,251,076 [2013]

Withington Girls' School
Registered: 12 Aug 2014 *Employees:* 115 *Volunteers:* 100
Tel: 0161 249 3469 *Website:* wgs.org
Activities: Education, training; other charitable purposes
Address: 36 Robert Moffat, High Legh, Knutsford, Cheshire, WA16 6PS
Trustees: Malcolm Pike, Mrs Diane Hawkins, Mrs Jo Kinney, Mr Mark Adlestone, Mrs Gwen Marie Bryom, Mrs Sally Stuffins, David Illingworth, Dr Jane Allred, Mr Howard Sinclair, Mr Ashvin Pathak, Professor Irina Grigorieva, Ms Melanie Michael
Income: £7,923,892 [2017]; £7,608,095 [2016]

Witton Lodge Community Association
Registered: 27 Jun 1994 *Employees:* 16 *Volunteers:* 19
Tel: 0121 382 1930 *Website:* wittonlodge.org.uk
Activities: General charitable purposes; prevention or relief of poverty; accommodation, housing; economic, community development, employment
Address: 87 Witton Lodge Road, Birmingham, B23 5JD
Trustees: Mr Paul Michael Tomlinson, Mrs Linda Susan Hines, Mrs Sophie Allison, Mr Andrew Winmill, Councillor Ronald Keith Storer, Mrs Teresa Beryl Compton, Mary Marshall Harvey, Mr Michael Davis, Mrs Ebere Benson-Ezeh
Income: £1,535,179 [2017]; £1,893,065 [2016]; £1,014,016 [2015]; £1,004,038 [2014]; £996,597 [2013]

The Wixamtree Trust
Registered: 22 Sep 1962
Tel: 020 8777 4140 *Website:* wixamtree.org
Activities: General charitable purposes
Address: 6 Trull Farm Buildings, Trull, Tetbury, Glos, GL8 8SQ
Trustees: Sir Samuel Whitbread KCVO, Mr Harry Francis Whitbread, Mr Charles Edward Samuel Whitbread, Mr Geoff McMullen, Lady Whitbread, Mrs Elizabeth Anne Bennett, Mr Ian Alan Douglas Pilkington, Paul Patten
Income: £1,053,220 [2017]; £1,012,624 [2016]; £6,176,267 [2015]; £885,069 [2014]; £803,132 [2013]

Wodson Park Trust
Registered: 10 Dec 2003 *Employees:* 29
Tel: 01920 487091 *Website:* wodsonpark.com
Activities: Amateur sport
Address: Wodson Park Leisure Centre, Wadesmill Road, Ware, Herts, SG12 0UQ
Trustees: Cllr Phyllis Ballam, Dr Michael James Tucker, Mrs Jan Wing, Mrs Linda Elizabeth Radford, S E Storey, John Wing, Mr David Andrews, Mrs Janet Heather Goodeve
Income: £1,022,844 [2017]; £957,709 [2016]; £1,135,437 [2015]; £884,514 [2014]; £621,761 [2013]

The Maurice Wohl Charitable Foundation
Registered: 16 Sep 1965 *Employees:* 4
Tel: 020 7383 5111 *Website:* wohl.org.uk
Activities: General charitable purposes; education, training; advancement of health or saving of lives; disability; prevention or relief of poverty; religious activities; arts, culture, heritage, science; animals; other charitable purposes
Address: 2nd Floor, Fitzrovia House, 153-157 Cleveland Street, London, W1T 6QW
Trustees: Mrs Ella Latchman, Prof David Latchman, Mr Daniel Isaac Dover BA (Hons) FCA, Mr Martin Paisner CBE, Sir Ian Gainsford
Income: £1,674,887 [2016]; £1,941,923 [2015]; £2,059,633 [2014]; £1,642,345 [2013]; £1,703,372 [2012]

Woking Homes
Registered: 3 Aug 2007 *Employees:* 60 *Volunteers:* 8
Website: woking-homes.co.uk
Activities: The advancement of health or saving of lives; accommodation, housing
Address: Woking Homes, Oriental Road, Woking, Surrey, GU22 7BE
Trustees: Mr Jim Dorward, Mrs Sheila Coles, Mr Ian Christie, Jonathon Elliott, Mrs Angela Richardson, Andy Pulfer, Mr Stewart Palmer, Mr Richard Evans, John Curley, Michael Riley, Mr Simon John Brazier
Income: £1,964,098 [2017]; £1,908,776 [2016]; £1,784,039 [2015]; £1,747,503 [2014]; £1,561,047 [2013]

Woking Hospice
Registered: 9 Oct 2000 *Employees:* 168 *Volunteers:* 800
Tel: 01483 881750 *Website:* wsbhospices.co.uk
Activities: The advancement of health or saving of lives
Address: Woking Hospice, 5 Hill View Road, Woking, Surrey, GU22 7HW
Trustees: Mr Rhodney Hayden Bray Lofting, Mr David Perry, Mr Timothy Andrew Stokes, Mr Marc Leslie Riggs, Mr Peter Goodyear, Sian Wicks, Mr Roy Anthony Jarvis, Mr Simon Oxley, Mrs Susan Mary Jones, Dr Christopher John Douglas Dunstan, Mr Piers Meadows, Peter Lovibond, Mr Richard Michael Roberts, Mr Jon Richard Jagger
Income: £9,236,000 [2017]; £8,351,000 [2016]; £7,537,709 [2015]; £8,689,378 [2014]; £6,976,266 [2013]

Woldingham School
Registered: 6 Aug 2008 *Employees:* 208
Tel: 01883 654202 *Website:* woldinghamschool.co.uk
Activities: General charitable purposes; education, training; religious activities
Address: Woldingham School, Marden Park, Woldingham, Caterham, Surrey, CR3 7YA
Trustees: Mr Martin Louis Redman, Ms Marie-Ange Bouchard, Mr Tim Woffenden, Mrs Alexandra Maule, Mr Robert Henry Parkinson, Ms Ciara Mary Brown, Mr William Crothers, Mr Nicholas Crapp, Mr Ian P Tyler, Mr Simon Collins, Mr James Nicholas Wright, Mrs Heather Hanbury
Income: £15,793,483 [2017]; £15,326,967 [2016]; £15,033,124 [2015]; £14,396,317 [2014]; £13,908,998 [2013]

Wolfson College in the University of Oxford

Registered: 14 Apr 2011 *Employees:* 195 *Volunteers:* 20
Tel: 01865 274104 *Website:* wolfson.ox.ac.uk
Activities: Education, training; accommodation, housing; arts, culture, heritage, science; amateur sport
Address: Wolfson College, Linton Road, Oxford, OX2 6UD
Trustees: Professor Jan Fellerer, Professor Julie Curtis, Professor Samson Abramsky, Dr Imre Bangha, Dr James Benson, Professor Lucie Cluver, Mr William Conner, Professor Frances Gardner, Professor Paul Harrison, Professor Jeremy Johns, Professor Bettina Lange, Professor William McKenna, Dr Philomen Probert, Professor Rosalind Rickaby, Professor Rick Schulting, Professor Vlatko Vedral, Professor Zeynep Yurekli-Gorkay, Professor Michael Chappell, Professor Matthew Howard McCartney, Professor Nikita Sud, Professor Paul Jarvis, Professor Moritz Riede, Professor Feliciano Giustino, Ms Catriona Cannon, Mr Richard Morin, Professor Jonathon Wolff, Ms Emily Victoria Eastham, Dr Nayanika Mathur, Mr Timothy Mark Hitchens, Dr Erica Charters, Dr Ellen Rice, Professor Jonathan Austyn, Professor Marcus Banks, Professor Elleke Boehmer, Professor Bob Coecke, Professor Janet Delaine, Professor Martin Goodman, Professor Christopher Howgego, Dr Geraint Jones, Dr James Lewis, Professor Jonathan Pila, Professor Christina Redfield, Professor Ulrike Roesler, Professor David Taylor, Professor Marc Ventresca, Professor Jonathan Barrett, Professor De Melo Wolfgang, Professor Peter Charles Stewart, Professor Paul Aveyard, Professor Tarje Nissen-Meyer, Professor Jacob Dahl, Professor Paul Roberts, Professor Matthew Costa, Prof Ruben Andersson, Professor Christopher Woodruff, Professor Alain Fouad George, Dr Yuhan Sohrab-Dinshaw Vevaina
Income: £7,149,489 [2017]; £7,949,701 [2016]; £7,246,243 [2015]; £7,695,312 [2014]; £12,136,235 [2013]

The Wolfson Foundation

Registered: 10 Mar 2014 *Employees:* 9
Tel: 020 7323 5730 *Website:* wolfson.org.uk
Activities: Education, training; advancement of health or saving of lives; disability; religious activities; arts, culture, heritage, science; environment, conservation, heritage
Address: The Wolfson Foundation, 8 Queen Anne Street, London, W1G 9LD
Trustees: Lord McColl of Dulwich MS FRCS FACS FRCSE, The Hon Mrs Laura Wolfson Townsley, Dame Janet Wolfson De Botton DBE, Lord Turnberg of Cheadle MD FRCP FMedSci, Dame Hermione Lee DBE FRSL FBA, The Hon Mrs Deborah Wolfson Davis MA, Sir Eric Ash CBE FRS FREng, Sir David Cannadine DPhil LittD FRHistS FBA FSA FRSL, Mrs Rebecca Sarah Marks, Dame Jean Thomas DBE ScD FMedSci FRS, Sir Michael Pepper FRS FREng, Sir Peter Ratcliffe
Income: £19,631,000 [2017]; £19,467,000 [2016]; £18,310,000 [2015]

Wolverhampton Citizens Advice Bureaux

Registered: 16 Oct 1985 *Employees:* 51 *Volunteers:* 55
Tel: 01902 572222 *Website:* citizensadvicewolverhampton.org.uk
Activities: General charitable purposes; education, training; advancement of health or saving of lives; prevention or relief of poverty
Address: Citizens Advice Wolverhampton, 26 Snow Hill, Wolverhampton, W Midlands, WV2 4AD
Trustees: Ms Louise Mary Jones, Dr Frank Reeves, Mr Bernard Cysewski, Mr Jonathan Crockett, Mr Nicholas William Cheesewright, Dr Stephen Iafrati, Mr James Michael Smith, Brian Chindindere, Ms Primula Paul, Geeta Patel, Mrs Gem Elaine Lopez, Mr Rob Marris
Income: £1,355,406 [2017]; £1,511,831 [2016]; £1,298,572 [2015]; £1,450,608 [2014]; £1,299,141 [2013]

Wolverhampton Grammar School Limited

Registered: 30 Jul 2008 *Employees:* 121 *Volunteers:* 100
Tel: 01902 421326 *Website:* wgs.org.uk
Activities: Education, training
Address: Wolverhampton Grammar School, Compton Road, Wolverhampton, W Midlands, WV3 9RB
Trustees: Mr Keith Madelin, Mr Philip Sims, Mr Peter Hawthorne, Mr James Sage, Mr Rodney Grainger, Mr Jitendra Patel, Mr Nicholas Berriman, Mr Mervyn Brooker, Rev Sarah Cawdell, Dr Carol Griffiths, Mr Christopher Bill, Mr Yusuf Malik
Income: £9,056,000 [2017]; £8,885,000 [2016]; £8,277,931 [2015]; £7,697,292 [2014]; £7,587,796 [2013]

The Wolverhampton Grand Theatre (1982) Limited

Registered: 24 May 1984 *Employees:* 120
Tel: 01902 573300 *Website:* grandtheatre.co.uk
Activities: Arts, culture, heritage, science
Address: Grand Theatre, Lichfield Street, Wolverhampton, W Midlands, WV1 1DE
Trustees: Councillor Peter Bilson, Ms Tracy Worthington, Mr Ian Morrison, Mrs Nuala O'Kane, Sir Geoffrey Hampton, Mr Philip Barnett, Ms Hayleigh Lupino
Income: £8,350,463 [2017]; £9,828,328 [2016]; £6,543,624 [2015]; £6,457,889 [2014]; £6,060,973 [2013]

Wolverhampton Voluntary Sector Council

Registered: 24 Nov 1988 *Employees:* 37 *Volunteers:* 30
Tel: 01902 773761 *Website:* wolverhamptonvsc.org.uk
Activities: General charitable purposes; education, training; advancement of health or saving of lives; economic, community development, employment; other charitable purposes
Address: WVSC, 16 Temple Street, Wolverhampton, W Midlands, WV2 4AN
Trustees: Ms Janet Clarke-Lewis, Pamela Cole-Hudson, Anne-Marie Harrison, Mr Mike Hastings, Mr Stephen Clay, Mr James Alexander Fox, Lesley Davies, Ms Anna Place
Income: £4,473,482 [2017]; £3,043,541 [2016]; £1,990,426 [2015]; £1,535,141 [2014]; £1,291,158 [2013]

Wolverhampton Youth Zone

Registered: 14 Mar 2013 *Employees:* 58 *Volunteers:* 98
Tel: 01902 393000 *Website:* thewayyouthzone.org
Activities: General charitable purposes; education, training; advancement of health or saving of lives; disability; arts, culture, heritage, science; amateur sport; economic, community development, employment; recreation
Address: Muras Baker Jones, Regent House, Bath Avenue, Wolverhampton, W Midlands, WV1 4EG
Trustees: Mrs Ann Sarah Gough, Mr William Robert John Clowes, Mr John Gough, Mr Paul Horton, Mr Andrew James Wolverson, Mr Vincent William Fairclough LLB, Mr Delisser Roy Bernard, Mr Oliver Ross, Mr Kevin Manning, Ms Helen Elizabeth Taylor
Income: £1,127,177 [2017]; £3,772,390 [2016]; £2,057,572 [2015]; £371,743 [2014]

Wolverton Leisure Trust

Registered: 19 Nov 2001 *Employees:* 70
Tel: 01908 562257 *Website:* wolvertonpool.com
Activities: Amateur sport
Address: Wolverton and Watling Way Pools, Watling Way Middle School, Stony Stratford, Milton Keynes, Bucks, MK11 1PA
Trustees: Mrs Hilary Monica Saunders, Mrs Maureen Higgins, Mr Norman Miles, Mr John Eric Haynes, Mr Michael Leslie Levitt
Income: £1,631,546 [2017]; £1,641,300 [2016]; £1,517,188 [2015]; £1,161,835 [2014]; £224,447 [2013]

Wolves Community Trust

Registered: 19 Nov 2008 *Employees:* 61 *Volunteers:* 41
Tel: 01902 687033 *Website:* wolvescommunitytrust.org.uk
Activities: Education, training; advancement of health or saving of lives; disability; amateur sport; economic, community development, employment
Address: Molineux Stadium, Waterloo Road, Wolverhampton, W Midlands, WV1 4QR
Trustees: Mr Richard Ian Skirrow, Mr Ian Stuart Millard, Mr Matthew David Wild, Neeraj Malhotra, Laurie Edgar Dalrymple
Income: £1,004,164 [2017]; £1,019,554 [2016]; £918,188 [2015]; £597,355 [2014]; £788,399 [2013]

Womancare Global International

Registered: 9 Nov 2010 *Employees:* 21
Tel: 020 7783 3563 *Website:* womancareglobal.org
Activities: General charitable purposes; education, training; advancement of health or saving of lives; other charitable purposes
Address: 50 Broadway, London, SW1H 0BL
Trustees: Professor Stephen Howard Kennedy, Mr Bryan Gerard Noonan, Ms Ellen Thomas
Income: £10,065,416 [2016]; £15,771,800 [2015]; £6,517,403 [2014]; £8,379,038 [2013]; £7,720,899 [2012]

Womankind Worldwide

Registered: 25 Jul 1989 *Employees:* 23 *Volunteers:* 9
Tel: 020 3567 5930 *Website:* womankind.org.uk
Activities: General charitable purposes; education, training; prevention or relief of poverty; overseas aid, famine relief; economic, community development, employment; human rights, religious or racial harmony, equality or diversity
Address: Womankind Worldwide, Wenlock Studios, 50-52 Wharf Road, London, N1 7EU
Trustees: Miss Tania Cohen, Ms Sally Baden, Dr Fenella Porter, Roshana Arasaratnam, Lia Larson, Ms Alphonsine Kabagabo, Ms Noelia Serrano, Laura Hucks, Christina Gordon-Henderson
Income: £3,046,536 [2017]; £3,526,998 [2016]; £3,631,130 [2015]; £3,792,649 [2014]; £4,712,826 [2013]

Women and Children First UK

Registered: 21 Feb 2001 *Employees:* 3
Tel: 020 7700 6309 *Website:* womenandchildrenfirst.org.uk
Activities: Education, training; advancement of health or saving of lives; prevention or relief of poverty; overseas aid, famine relief
Address: Women and Children First, United House, North Road, London, N7 9DP
Trustees: Mr Peter Clokey, Ms Margaret Irene Braddock, Mr Jaiprakash Agrawal, Ms Carol Eileen Bradford, Ms Audrey Gabrielle Pauline Prost, Ms Joanna Dorothea Torode, Ms Patricia Croll, Ms Deborah Jane Botwood Smith, Ms Sarah Grace Edith Blakemore, Ms Meera Mukeshchandra Dodhia, Ms Laura Salisbury
Income: £1,309,170 [2016]; £1,674,862 [2015]; £807,657 [2014]; £361,233 [2013]; £948,579 [2012]

Women and Girls Network

Registered: 7 Jan 2013 *Employees:* 25 *Volunteers:* 30
Tel: 020 7610 4678 *Website:* wgn.org.uk
Activities: Education, training; advancement of health or saving of lives; human rights, religious or racial harmony, equality or diversity
Address: P O Box 13095, London, W14 0FE
Trustees: Ms Donna Carty, Ms Sabrina Qureshi, Ms Rani Selvarajah, Ms Katherine Ruth Whidborne Taylor, Ms Kyhati Rawal, Ms Amanda Hill-Dixon, Ms Asma Bhol, Ms Sally Ann Thomas
Income: £1,131,579 [2017]; £1,067,677 [2016]; £972,449 [2015]; £791,981 [2014]

Women for Women International (UK)

Registered: 5 Jul 2006 *Employees:* 17 *Volunteers:* 39
Tel: 020 7922 8002 *Website:* womenforwomen.org.uk
Activities: Education, training; advancement of health or saving of lives; prevention or relief of poverty; overseas aid, famine relief; economic, community development, employment; human rights, religious or racial harmony, equality or diversity
Address: Women for Women International (UK), 32-36 Loman Street, London, SE1 0EH
Trustees: Martin Thomas, Alex Duncan, Michelle Yue, Hikari Yokoyama, Erik Berglof, Amy Towers, Laurie Adams, Lyndsey Posner, Lady Penelope Holmes, Stephanie Wong, Paula Laird, Tony Gambino, Alison Deighton
Income: £3,682,000 [2016]; £3,304,000 [2015]; £2,874,690 [2014]; £2,205,465 [2013]; £1,730,592 [2012]

Women in Informal Employment: Globalizing and Organizing (Wiego) Limited

Registered: 23 Aug 2011 *Employees:* 5
Tel: 0161 819 1200 *Website:* wiego.org
Activities: Education, training; prevention or relief of poverty; economic, community development, employment
Address: 521 Royal Exchange, Manchester, M2 7EN
Trustees: William F Steel, Renana Jhabvala, Professor Sanjiv Madhwarao Kanbur, Professor Jeemol Unni, Ms Juliana Brown Afari, Debra Davis, Ms Barbro Margareta Budin, Dr Lin Lean Lim, Professor Carmen Aurora Marcela Vildoso Chirinos, Mrs Vicky Kanyoka
Income: £4,842,678 [2017]; £3,850,938 [2016]; £2,395,184 [2015]; £2,068,476 [2014]; £6,310,970 [2013]

Women in Prison Limited

Registered: 10 Apr 2007 *Employees:* 53 *Volunteers:* 8
Tel: 020 7840 6703 *Website:* womeninprison.org.uk
Activities: General charitable purposes; education, training; prevention or relief of poverty; accommodation, housing; human rights, religious or racial harmony, equality or diversity
Address: Women in Prison, 2nd Floor, Elmfield House, 5 Stockwell Mews, London, SW9 9XG
Trustees: Sue Wilson, Ms Martine Lignon, Ms Mary Pimm, Mrs Yvonne Roberts, Ms Naima Sakande, Ms Grace Elanor Stevens, Ms Lynne Laidlaw, Ms Joanne Ryan, Dianne Nelmes, Ms Paramjit Ahluwalia, Ms Aisling Wootten, Ms Harriet Johnson
Income: £1,956,540 [2017]; £2,306,262 [2016]; £1,406,670 [2015]; £1,148,751 [2014]; £1,122,960 [2013]

Women in Sport

Registered: 21 Jan 1997 *Employees:* 11
Website: womeninsport.org
Activities: General charitable purposes; education, training; advancement of health or saving of lives; amateur sport
Address: House of Sport, 4th Floor, 190 Great Dover Street, London, SE1 4YB
Trustees: Ms Sue Wicks, Ms Jayne Haines, Ms Elie Barnes, Ms Jane Martinson, Mrs Zoe Collins, Ms Karen Wilson, Ms Cathy Leanne Woods, Mrs Susan Young, Prof Simon Malcolm Chadwick
Income: £1,212,385 [2017]; £919,522 [2016]; £1,131,481 [2015]; £962,815 [2014]; £747,031 [2013]

Women's Aid Integrated Services (Nottingham and Region)
Registered: 3 Oct 2002 *Employees:* 82 *Volunteers:* 59
Tel: 0115 822 1775 *Website:* wais.org.uk
Activities: Education, training; advancement of health or saving of lives; prevention or relief of poverty; accommodation, housing; animals
Address: Nottingham Womens Centre, 30 Chaucer Street, Nottingham, NG1 5LP
Trustees: Chris Cutland, Ms Joyce Buchan, Sue Tongue, Mrs Susan Bryant, Mrs Nikola Halse, Ms Shane Morgan, Ms Christina Pamplin, Ms Sue Gregory, Mrs Lucia Swift
Income: £2,093,795 [2017]; £2,075,383 [2016]; £2,091,377 [2015]; £1,652,471 [2014]; £1,449,179 [2013]

Women's Aid Leicestershire Limited
Registered: 17 Jun 2010 *Employees:* 36 *Volunteers:* 3
Website: wa-leicester.org.uk
Activities: Education, training; accommodation, housing
Address: P O Box 26, Leicester, LE1 1AA
Trustees: Mrs Marea Roberts, Ms Kari Mellon, Ms Nicola Meskimmon, Ms Sandra Parkinson, Ms Mary Jill Tyler, Ms Rajveer Kaur, Ms Harjeet Chakira, Ms Patricia Scholes-Noble
Income: £1,136,473 [2017]; £894,650 [2016]; £882,838 [2015]; £751,525 [2014]; £858,612 [2013]

Women's Aid in Rhondda Cynon Taf
Registered: 22 Jan 2014 *Employees:* 29 *Volunteers:* 18
Tel: 01685 879673 *Website:* warct.co.uk
Activities: Education, training; advancement of health or saving of lives; prevention or relief of poverty; accommodation, housing
Address: Cwm Cynon Womens Aid, 215 Cardiff Road, Aberdare, Rhondda Cynon Taf, CF44 6RG
Trustees: Mrs Margaret Abraham, Mrs Beverley Channon, Ms Stella Millward, Mrs Ruth Eryl Hopkins, Mrs Margaret Ann Green, Mr Philip Bevan
Income: £1,041,776 [2017]; £1,030,670 [2016]; £1,131,062 [2015]

The Women's Organisation
Registered: 20 Jan 2009 *Employees:* 27 *Volunteers:* 2
Tel: 0151 236 6601 *Website:* thewomensorganisation.org.uk
Activities: Education, training; advancement of health or saving of lives; prevention or relief of poverty; economic, community development, employment; human rights, religious or racial harmony, equality or diversity; other charitable purposes
Address: 54 St James Street, Liverpool, L1 0AB
Trustees: Ms Gillian Anne Moglione, Ms Alex Morgan, Miss Jayne Croft, Ms Susan Oshikanlu, Ms Mona Mealey, Mrs Angela Cain
Income: £1,284,750 [2016]; £2,094,798 [2015]; £1,546,561 [2014]; £1,314,676 [2013]; £1,048,541 [2012]

Women's Technology Training Limited
Registered: 3 Apr 1984 *Employees:* 34 *Volunteers:* 1
Tel: 0151 709 4356 *Website:* blackburnehouse.cfo.uk
Activities: Education, training
Address: Blackburne House, Centre for Wome, Blackburne Place, Liverpool, L8 7PE
Trustees: Ms Elizabeth Cross, Ms Sally-Anne Watkiss, Ms Maureen Kathleen Mellor, Ms Collette Russell, Ms Jennifer Sanderson, Ms Jude Robinson
Income: £1,744,098 [2017]; £1,161,991 [2016]; £1,348,729 [2015]; £1,360,341 [2014]; £1,305,633 [2013]

Womencentre Limited
Registered: 13 Mar 2007 *Employees:* 31 *Volunteers:* 107
Tel: 01422 386500 *Website:* womencentre.org.uk
Activities: General charitable purposes; education, training; advancement of health or saving of lives; economic, community development, employment; other charitable purposes
Address: 23 Silver Street, Halifax, W Yorks, HX1 1JN
Trustees: Judith Gannon, Ms Juliet Clark, Ms Rosette Kamche, Ms Marilyn Bryan, Ms Tamsin Courtney Walker, Mrs Sarah Simi Khanna, Ms Andrea Wardell, Ms Maura Wilson, Ms Ann Dower, Hilary Turley, Ms Lucy Simmonds, Ms Lisa Dawn McGorrigan
Income: £1,168,122 [2017]; £1,373,031 [2016]; £1,142,421 [2015]; £1,362,018 [2014]; £1,262,966 [2013]

Andrew Wommack Ministries-Europe
Registered: 17 Jun 2008 *Employees:* 40 *Volunteers:* 16
Tel: 01922 473300 *Website:* awme.net
Activities: General charitable purposes; education, training; religious activities
Address: Grace International Centre, Leamore Lane, Walsall, W Midlands, WS2 7PS
Trustees: Mr Andrew Wommack, Mr John Donnelly, Karen Conrad, Mrs Jamie Wommack, Gary Luecke
Income: £2,990,778 [2017]; £2,890,323 [2016]; £2,480,519 [2015]; £2,378,970 [2014]; £2,260,609 [2013]

Wood Green Animal Shelters
Registered: 13 Jan 1988 *Employees:* 266 *Volunteers:* 630
Tel: 0300 303 9333 *Website:* woodgreen.org.uk
Activities: Animals
Address: Wood Green Animal Shelters, London Road, Godmanchester, Huntingdon, Cambs, PE29 2NH
Trustees: Mrs Janet South, Mrs P L Gee, Mrs Angela Au, Dr Jo Lawton, Dr S Carden, Mr John Cousins, Mr Colin Peter Alder, Mr Jonathan Younger, Mr Duncan Canney
Income: £12,515,638 [2017]; £10,288,039 [2016]; £10,110,429 [2015]; £8,981,370 [2014]; £8,094,675 [2013]

The Woodard Corporation
Registered: 27 Feb 2003 *Employees:* 3,044 *Volunteers:* 146
Tel: 01283 840120 *Website:* woodard.co.uk
Activities: Education, training; religious activities
Address: Woodard Corporation, High Street, Abbots Bromley, Rugeley, Staffs, WS15 3BW
Trustees: Mrs Margaret Holman, Mr Brian Morley Newman, Reverend Prebendary Lynda Mary Barley, Mrs Patricia Pritchard, Mr Richard South Morse, Rt Rev Dr John Inge, Miles Hedges, Mr Peter Henry William Southern, Dr Irene Bishop CBE, Mr Anthony Prince
Income: £173,932,000 [2016]; £178,517,000 [2015]; £175,282,000 [2014]; £169,160,000 [2013]; £224,468,000 [2012]

Woodard Schools (Nottinghamshire) Limited
Registered: 21 Apr 2004 *Employees:* 247
Tel: 01909 537100 *Website:* wsnl.co.uk
Activities: Education, training; religious activities
Address: Worksop College, Enquiry Office, Sparken Hill, Worksop, Notts, S80 3AP
Trustees: Mr David Wilson FCA CTA, Mr Richard Steel BSc (Lond), Ms Sara Cundy, Mr Stephen Derek Armstrong, Professor Patricia Joan Sikes, Mr Colin Anderson MA, Mrs Alison Natasha Hurton, Mr Kumar Muthukumarappan, Mrs Caroline Jane Peake, Mr Andrew Mark Pepper
Income: £9,374,032 [2017]; £9,398,065 [2016]; £9,429,517 [2015]; £9,100,092 [2014]; £9,030,310 [2013]

Woodbrooke Quaker Study Centre

Registered: 24 Apr 1963 *Employees:* 57 *Volunteers:* 200
Website: woodbrooke.org.uk
Activities: Education, training; religious activities
Address: Tregear House, 1046 Bristol Road, Selly Oak, Birmingham, B29 6LJ
Trustees: Robert Gibson, Peter Allen-Williams, Dorothy Carson, David Pulford, Anne Bennett, Michael Hutchinson, Margaret Mortimer, Jenny Routledge, Terry Oakley, Joycelin Dawes, Averil Armstrong, Martina Weitsch, John Dash, Jennifer MacLennan, Barbara Sharrock
Income: £1,867,586 [2016]; £1,835,961 [2015]; £2,104,348 [2014]; £2,013,228 [2013]; £2,632,569 [2012]

Woodcraft Folk

Registered: 18 Jul 2012 *Employees:* 12 *Volunteers:* 2,558
Tel: 020 7703 4173 *Website:* woodcraft.org.uk
Activities: General charitable purposes; education, training; economic, community development, employment; human rights, religious or racial harmony, equality or diversity; other charitable purposes
Address: Unit 9, 83 Crampton Street, London, SE17 3BQ
Trustees: Jack Brown, Tom Gower, Tom Brooks, Stuart Walker, Millie Mae Burgh, Holly Carter-Rich, Sonia Kelly, Lucy Faircloth, Sapna Agarwal, Iolo Walker, Ralph Sleigh, Pat Hunter, Roland Susman, Claire Slocombe, Brynn Alred, Philip Sayers, Jack Walker, Nadia Asri, Lara Taylor, Zeph-Formerly Faye - Deakin
Income: £1,180,487 [2016]; £1,701,778 [2015]; £1,413,440 [2014]; £3,989,601 [2013]

Wooden Spoon Society

Registered: 22 Oct 1984 *Employees:* 16 *Volunteers:* 400
Tel: 01252 773720 *Website:* woodenspoon.org.uk
Activities: Education, training; advancement of health or saving of lives; disability; amateur sport; economic, community development, employment
Address: Sentinel House, Harvest Crescent, Fleet, Hants, GU51 2UZ
Trustees: Mr Nigel Timson, Mr Martin Sanders, Mr Richard Smith, Mr Mark McCafferty, Miss Joanna Elizabeth Coombs, Mr David Allen OBE, Ms Alison Natalie Kay Lowe, Mr John Gibson, Mr Quentin Paul Graham Smith
Income: £2,804,913 [2017]; £3,703,841 [2016]; £3,192,441 [2015]; £3,819,022 [2014]; £3,711,493 [2013]

Woodford Green Preparatory School Limited

Registered: 8 Apr 1963 *Employees:* 50 *Volunteers:* 14
Tel: 020 8504 5045 *Website:* wgprep.co.uk
Activities: Education, training
Address: Woodford Green Preparatory School, 23 Snakes Lane, Woodford Green, Essex, IG8 0BZ
Trustees: Mr Michael Townsend, Mrs Jacqueline Deeks, Mrs E Hare, Mrs Gurinder Chahal, Mr Ranan Dasgupta, Mr Christopher Parkinson, Anne Elizabeth Quaife-O'Donnell, Mr Jason Whiskerd, Mrs Paula Fisher, Mr Peter Kempe, Mrs Lydia Shamrakov, Mr R Patel
Income: £3,393,452 [2016]; £3,113,340 [2015]; £3,099,969 [2014]; £2,980,225 [2013]; £2,908,261 [2012]

The F Glenister Woodger Trust

Registered: 8 Jan 1990
Tel: 01243 513116
Activities: General charitable purposes; education, training; advancement of health or saving of lives; disability; prevention or relief of poverty; accommodation, housing; religious activities; arts, culture, heritage, science; amateur sport; environment, conservation, heritage; economic, community development, employment; recreation
Address: Wicks Farm Caravan Park, Redlands Lane, West Wittering, Chichester, W Sussex, PO20 8QE
Trustees: Mr Stuart Francis Dobbin, Mr Richard Shrubb, Mrs Rosamund Jane Gentle, Mrs Maxine Pickup, Mrs Rosamund Champ, Mr William Henry Craven
Income: £1,499,899 [2017]; £1,334,540 [2016]; £1,324,824 [2015]; £1,277,472 [2014]; £1,357,626 [2013]

Woodhorn Charitable Trust

Registered: 19 May 2009 *Employees:* 111 *Volunteers:* 59
Tel: 01670 624451 *Website:* experiencewoodhorn.com
Activities: General charitable purposes; education, training; arts, culture, heritage, science; environment, conservation, heritage; economic, community development, employment
Address: Woodhorn Museum Archives & Country Park, Queen Elizabeth II Country Park, Ashington, Northumberland, NE63 9YF
Trustees: Mr Ian Lavery, The Venerable Peter John Alan Robinson, Mr Philip Ashley Browell, Mr John Browne-Swinburne, Mrs Mai Lai Chun Mak, John Carr-Ellison, Mr Jeffrey George Watson, Ms Penelope Jane Wilkinson, Mr Peter John Atkinson
Income: £3,074,638 [2017]; £3,148,315 [2016]; £2,554,211 [2015]; £3,023,580 [2014]; £2,353,262 [2013]

Woodhouse Grove School

Registered: 11 Jan 1965 *Employees:* 213 *Volunteers:* 10
Tel: 020 7935 3723 *Website:* woodhousegrove.co.uk
Activities: Education, training; religious activities
Address: Methodist Church House, 25 Marylebone Road, London, NW1 5JR
Trustees: Woodhouse Grove School Trustee Company Limited, Methodist Independent Schools Trust
Income: £11,607,128 [2016]; £10,676,567 [2015]; £10,501,379 [2014]; £10,240,629 [2013]; £9,873,049 [2012]

Woodland Heritage Limited

Registered: 21 Oct 1994 *Employees:* 8 *Volunteers:* 20
Tel: 01428 641702 *Website:* woodlandheritage.org.uk
Activities: Education, training; environment, conservation, heritage
Address: P O Box 168, Haslemere, Surrey, GU27 1XQ
Trustees: Mr L J Scott, Geraint Richards, Mr Simon Burvill, Dr Hugh Williams, Mr Roger Richardson, Mr Graham Taylor, Dr James Walmsley, Mr Thomas Edward Christian
Income: £1,506,884 [2017]; £1,530,040 [2016]; £773,328 [2015]; £164,333 [2014]; £254,386 [2013]

The Woodland Trust

Registered: 20 May 1986 *Employees:* 377 *Volunteers:* 2,600
Tel: 01476 581111 *Website:* woodlandtrust.org.uk
Activities: Environment, conservation, heritage
Address: The Woodland Trust, Kempton Way, Grantham, Lincs, NG31 6LL
Trustees: Barbara Scott Young of Old Scone, Mr Mike Greenwood, Mr Richard Sykes, Miss Julia Smithies, David Babbs, Mr Humphrey Battcock, Mr Patrick MacDonald, Mrs Sally Benthall, Paul Nevett
Income: £49,587,000 [2016]; £37,502,000 [2015]; £38,139,000 [2014]; £33,397,000 [2013]; £31,878,000 [2012]

Woodlands Group of Churches
Registered: 16 Jul 2008 *Volunteers:* 600
Tel: 0117 946 6807 *Website:* woodlandschurch.net
Activities: Religious activities
Address: Woodlands Christian Centre, Belgrave Road, Bristol, BS8 2AA
Trustees: Mr Robert Lawrence Scott-Cook, Mr Timothy John Dobson, Mrs Louise Hughes, Mr Edward James Marsh FCA DChA, Mr David John Mitchell, Mr Bradley Askew
Income: £1,396,756 [2017]; £1,411,260 [2016]; £1,300,787 [2015]; £1,152,566 [2014]; £1,127,750 [2013]

Woodlands Hospice Charitable Trust
Registered: 6 Sep 1995 *Employees:* 102 *Volunteers:* 180
Tel: 0151 529 2299 *Website:* woodlandshospice.org
Activities: The advancement of health or saving of lives
Address: Woodlands Hospice Charitable Trust, Fazakerley Hospital, Longmoor Lane, Liverpool, L9 7LA
Trustees: Dr Cathy Hubbert MRCGP DRCOG, Rev Nicholas Wilde, Mrs Edna McDonald, Mrs Annette Johnson, Mrs Susan Ollerhead, Mr Colin Brennand FCA, John Wood, Dr Barbara Lynne Roberts, Mr Barry James Bartlett, Mrs Angela Keith
Income: £3,812,677 [2017]; £3,747,552 [2016]; £3,594,957 [2015]; £3,948,500 [2014]; £3,363,694 [2013]

Woodlands Quaker Home
Registered: 27 Apr 2011 *Employees:* 66 *Volunteers:* 9
Tel: 01902 341203 *Website:* woodlandsquakerhome.org
Activities: Disability; accommodation, housing
Address: The Woodlands Quaker Home, 434 Penn Road, Wolverhampton, W Midlands, WV4 4DH
Trustees: Dr Richard Taylor, Mr Peter Collard, Mrs Julia Southard Furminger, Mr Robert Jeays, Mrs Claire Susan Bowman, Ms Dorothy Hull, Mr Nicholas Paton Philip
Income: £1,535,951 [2017]; £1,416,403 [2016]; £1,347,097 [2015]; £1,308,722 [2014]; £1,264,377 [2013]

Woodside Animal Welfare Trust
Registered: 27 Jul 2011 *Employees:* 76 *Volunteers:* 200
Tel: 01752 347503 *Website:* woodsidesanctuary.org.uk
Activities: Animals
Address: c/o Woodside Animal Welfare Trust, Elfordleigh, Plympton, Plymouth, PL7 5ED
Trustees: Mrs Carole Bowles MBE, Mrs Janet Mary Gorman, Mrs Jennifer Margaret Rogers, Mrs Anne Marshall, Mrs Clare Smith, Mrs Amanda Ann McArthur, Mrs Anne Taylor, Mrs Miranda Mary MacLean
Income: £1,527,082 [2016]; £1,123,808 [2015]; £1,675,898 [2014]; £2,513,985 [2013]

Woolf Institute
Registered: 18 May 1998 *Employees:* 15
Tel: 01223 741048 *Website:* woolf.cam.ac.uk
Activities: Education, training
Address: Woolf Institute, Madingley Road, Cambridge, CB3 0UB
Trustees: Mr Robert Glatter FCA, Mr Timothy Stevens CBE, Lord Ian Blair, Julius Lipner, Professor Waqar Ahmad, Lady Marguerite Leah Woolf, Mr Edward John Williams, Ms Sarah Yamani, Mr Martin Paisner, Mr David Leibowitz, Dr Edward David Kessler, Mr Peter Halban, Rev Dr Martin Forward, Mrs Beatrix Brenninkmeijer-Schuerholz, Mr Shabir Ahmed Randeree
Income: £2,166,879 [2016]; £2,811,047 [2015]; £1,680,983 [2014]; £511,158 [2013]; £699,313 [2012]

The Woosnam Foundation
Registered: 16 Jan 2017
Tel: 020 7842 8000
Activities: General charitable purposes; education, training; advancement of health or saving of lives; disability; prevention or relief of poverty
Address: Laytons Solicitors, 2 More London Riverside, London, SE1 2AP
Trustees: Mr Ian Anthony Burman, Mr Michael Stewart Feldman
Income: £3,505,326 [2017]

Worcester Citizens Advice Bureau and Whabac
Registered: 11 Mar 2009 *Employees:* 39 *Volunteers:* 76
Tel: 01905 744582 *Website:* cabwhabac.org.uk
Activities: The prevention or relief of poverty; accommodation, housing
Address: Worcester Citizens Advice Bureau & WHABAC, 11a The Hopmarket, Worcester, WR1 1DL
Trustees: Mr Graham Hughes, Mr Ian Pugh, Mrs Helen Fenton, Mr Bryn Griffiths, Mr Ronald Justinian Tyler, Mr Paul Y Griffith, Mr Simon John Lister, Mrs Anita Mobberley, Mr Matthew Jenkins
Income: £1,174,874 [2017]; £1,338,682 [2016]; £1,387,532 [2015]; £1,367,923 [2014]; £1,486,002 [2013]

Worcester College Oxford Endowment Trust
Registered: 4 Dec 2012
Tel: 01865 278362
Activities: Education, training; religious activities; arts, culture, heritage, science; environment, conservation, heritage
Address: Worcester College, Walton Street, Oxford, OX1 2HB
Trustees: Mr Martin Paisner CBE, Professor Jonathan Bate, Professor Lady Judith Anne Freedman CBE FBA, The Right Honourable Sir Timothy Alan Davan Sainsbury FSA, Mr Barrie Wigmore
Income: £1,255,800 [2016]; £2,449,363 [2015]; £2,013,437 [2014]; £2,958,814 [2013]

Worcester College, Oxford
Registered: 19 Aug 2011 *Employees:* 137
Tel: 01865 278335 *Website:* worc.ox.ac.uk
Activities: Education, training
Address: Worcester College, Walton Street, Oxford, OX1 2HB
Trustees: Mr Donal Nolan, Professor Sir Jonathan Bate CBE FBA, Professor Heather Viles, Professor Ernesto Macaro, Dr Gabriel Stylianides, Professor Andrew Carr, Dr Laura Ashe, Professor Susan Gillingham, Dr Mark Howarth, Dr Benjamin Morgan, Professor Andrew Price FRCS (Orth), Dr David Steinsaltz, Dr Nir Vulkan, Dr Peter Darrah, Dr Josephine Mary Crawley Quinn, Professor Endri Suli, Professor Robert Saxton, Dr Zofia Stemplowska, Dr James Edwards, Dr Alifi Al-Akiti, Dr Steven James Methven, Mr Mark Bainbridge, Professor Deborah Cameron, Dr John Parrington, Professor Robert Gildea FBA, Professor Julian Roberts, Dr Rory Bowden, Dr Simon George Brook Cowan, Professor Kim Dora, Professor Robert Harris, Dr Conrad Leyser, Dr Antonis Papachristodoulou MA MEng PhD, Dr Grant Ritchie, Dr Kate Tunstall, Professor Andreas Willi Kaufmann, Dr Richard Earl, Dr John Scott Scullion, Professor Judith Freedman, Dr Michail Peramatzis, Dr Felix Parra-Diaz, Professor Sadie Creese Professor, Dr Josephine Van Zeben, Mrs Coleen Linda Hunter
Income: £12,993,000 [2017]; £14,017,000 [2016]; £17,215,000 [2015]; £18,126,000 [2014]; £9,539,000 [2013]

Worcester Diocesan Board of Finance Limited
Registered: 13 May 1966 *Employees:* 47 *Volunteers:* 70
Tel: 01905 20537 *Website:* cofe-worcester.org.uk
Activities: Religious activities
Address: The Old Palace, Deansway, Worcester, WR1 2JE
Trustees: John Inge, Rev Stephen Mark Agnew, Mr John Keith Layton, Mr Eric Allen Wiles, Ven Robert Jones, Rev Alan Ronald Norman Williams, Mr Robin Christopher Lunn, Mr David Stuart Hargreaves, Mr Bryan William Allbut, The Venerable Nicola Jane Groarke, Mr David Southall, Rev Vincent Wyn Beynon, Mr Paul Blackham, Mr David Nicholas Hawkins, Mr Alastair Findlay, Rev Richard Martin Clark, Rev Mark Badger, The Very Revd Peter Atkinson, Mr John Anthony Lovesy, Rev David James Hoskin, Mr Michael Ernest Hancox, Dr Andrew David Quinn, The Rt Revd Graham Barham Usher, Ms Victoria Day, Rev Anne Mary Potter, Rev Beverley Joyce Jameson
Income: £7,610,000 [2016]; £8,919,000 [2015]; £7,755,000 [2014]; £8,083,000 [2013]; £7,872,000 [2012]

Worcester Live Charitable Trust Ltd
Registered: 15 Mar 1989 *Employees:* 26 *Volunteers:* 160
Tel: 01905 612822 *Website:* worcesterlive.co.uk
Activities: Arts, culture, heritage, science
Address: 22 Sansome Walk, Worcester, WR1 1LS
Trustees: Mr John Anthony Yelland, Mr Paul West, Mr Stephen John Boffy, Lord Richard Oliver Faulkner of Worcester, Sir Michael Sydney Perry GBE, Mrs Dawn Emma Long, Mr John Julius Murfin, Mr Toby Julien Anderson Hooper
Income: £1,226,886 [2017]; £1,132,990 [2016]; £1,196,999 [2015]; £1,139,902 [2014]; £1,159,698 [2013]

Worcester Municipal Charities (CIO)
Registered: 4 May 2016 *Employees:* 6
Tel: 01905 317117 *Website:* wmcharities.org.uk
Activities: Education, training; prevention or relief of poverty; accommodation, housing
Address: Kateryn Heywood House, Berkeley Court, The Foregate, Worcester, WR1 3QG
Trustees: Paul Y Griffith, Mrs Margaret Jones, Martyn Saunders, Roger Berry, Sue Osborne, Margaret Panter, Mr Richard Boorn, Alan Feeney, Mr Geraint Thomas, Brenda Sheridan, Robert Peachey, Paul Denham, Ron Rust, Graham Hughes, Mel Kirk, Roger Knight, Geoff Williams
Income: £3,949,476 [2016]

Worcestershire Wildlife Trust
Registered: 31 Jul 1969 *Employees:* 29 *Volunteers:* 500
Tel: 01905 754919 *Website:* worcswildlifetrust.co.uk
Activities: Education, training; animals; environment, conservation, heritage
Address: Lower Smite Farm, Smite Hill, Hindlip, Worcester, WR3 8SZ
Trustees: Bob Gillmor, Mervyn Needham, Peter Holmes, Sandra Young, Linda Butler, David Mortiboys, Peter Scriven, Julia Letts, Harry Green, Geoff Trevis, Graham Martin, Roger Pannell, Richard Cory, Poppy Morris, John Blakiston, Chris Greensmith
Income: £1,741,783 [2017]; £1,950,071 [2016]; £1,932,243 [2015]; £2,075,024 [2014]; £2,503,495 [2013]

Worcestershire YMCA Limited
Registered: 16 Oct 1985 *Employees:* 127 *Volunteers:* 105
Tel: 01905 423197
Activities: General charitable purposes; education, training; advancement of health or saving of lives; prevention or relief of poverty; accommodation, housing; religious activities; arts, culture, heritage, science; amateur sport; economic, community development, employment
Address: Worcestershire YMCA Ltd, Gordon Anstis House, Loxley Close, Redditch, Worcs, B98 9JS
Trustees: Mr Michael Peter Higley, Mr Philip James Simpson, Mrs Jacintha Margaret Hodgson, Dr Juliet Horne, Mr Simon Robert Hill
Income: £3,451,338 [2017]; £3,674,215 [2016]; £3,703,337 [2015]; £4,074,225 [2014]; £3,295,007 [2013]

The Wordsworth Trust
Registered: 24 Nov 1997 *Employees:* 39 *Volunteers:* 11
Tel: 015394 63509 *Website:* wordsworth.org.uk
Activities: Education, training; arts, culture, heritage, science
Address: The Wordsworth Trust, Dove Cottage, Grasmere, Ambleside, Cumbria, LA22 9SH
Trustees: Mrs Diana Ruth Matthews, Mr Drummond Bone, Dr Seamus Perry, Mrs Jennifer Uglow OBE, Judith Helen Cooke, Dr Lynn Barbara Shepherd, Mr Charles Adam Laurie Sebag-Montefiore, Mr John Collier FCA, Dr Lucy Peltz, Mrs Mary Chuck, Mr David Michael Heal
Income: £1,430,000 [2016]; £1,364,000 [2015]; £1,432,000 [2014]; £1,576,000 [2013]; £1,497,000 [2012]

Workers' Educational Association
Registered: 20 Jan 2006 *Employees:* 2,331 *Volunteers:* 3,000
Tel: 020 7426 3485 *Website:* wea.org.uk
Activities: Education, training; advancement of health or saving of lives; disability; prevention or relief of poverty; economic, community development, employment; human rights, religious or racial harmony, equality or diversity
Address: WEA Corporate Services, 4 Luke Street, London, EC2A 4XW
Trustees: Mr Michael Crilly, Mr Peter Threadkell, Mr Hugh Humphrey, Ms Narinder Uppal, Mr Lindsay Pearson, Mr Colin Hughes, Mrs Lynne Smith, Mr Trevor Phillips, Dr Cliff Allum, Mr Jon Gamble, Ms Marion Flett
Income: £27,350,000 [2017]; £26,658,000 [2016]; £30,737,000 [2015]; £29,210,000 [2014]; £28,047,000 [2013]

The Workforce Development Trust Limited
Registered: 4 Aug 2011 *Employees:* 169
Tel: 0117 922 1155 *Website:* skillsforhealth.org.uk
Activities: Education, training; advancement of health or saving of lives; economic, community development, employment
Address: 4th Floor, Skills for Health, 1 Temple Way, Bristol, BS2 0BY
Trustees: Mr Robert Abberley, Mr John Rogers, Mr Rory Cassian Love, Dr Kathleen Janet Fallon, Mr Iain Fraser MacDonald, Mr David Leonard Wood, Mr Julian Hartley, Mr Hugh Henry McCaughey, Mr Robert Calderwood, Mr Gerald Robert Howe Davies, Ms Allison Jane Williams, Mr Jeremy Newman
Income: £16,364,891 [2016]; £15,605,177 [2015]; £14,765,035 [2014]; £15,524,757 [2013]; £2,952,359 [2012]

Working Men's College Corporation
Registered: 27 May 1963 *Employees:* 102 *Volunteers:* 7
Website: wmcollege.ac.uk
Activities: Education, training
Address: Working Mens College, 44 Crowndale Road, London, NW1 1TR
Trustees: Mr David Malcolm Offenbach, Ms Kate Olivier Bell, Tom Erskine Schuller, Ms Jean Esnard, Helen Hammond, Mr Chris Percy, Mr Ahsan Akbar, Mr Gerry Munnelly, Ms Amanda Blinkhorn, Ms Paula Whittle, Ms Barbara Anne Byrne, Ms Alexi Ferster Marmot, Ms Samata Khatoon, Mr Paul Graham Smith, Ms June Viviana Jarrett, Mr Guy Shackle
Income: £5,767,000 [2017]; £5,559,000 [2016]; £5,418,000 [2015]; £5,809,000 [2014]; £5,172,490 [2013]

World Animal Protection
Registered: 4 Aug 2000 *Employees:* 230 *Volunteers:* 2
Tel: 020 7239 0525 *Website:* worldanimalprotection.org
Activities: Education, training; overseas aid, famine relief; animals; environment, conservation, heritage
Address: 5th Floor, 222 Gray's Inn Road, London, WC1X 8HB
Trustees: Mr Dominique Bellemare, Mr Paul Baldwin, Ms Nesta Hatendi, Ms Mwikali Nzioka, Anna Lemessany, Mr John Thomas Jones, Mr Mark Watts, Ms Christine Lloyd, Mr Carter Luke, Ms Sarah Ireland, Karen Winton
Income: £34,106,000 [2016]; £30,892,000 [2015]; £34,480,000 [2014]; £27,892,000 [2013]; £24,991,000 [2012]

World Association of Girl Guides and Girl Scouts
Registered: 18 Nov 2014 *Employees:* 100 *Volunteers:* 15
Tel: 020 7794 1181 *Website:* wagggs.org
Activities: Education, training
Address: World Association of Girl Guides & Girl Scouts, World Bureau, Olave Centre, 12c Lyndhurst Road, London, NW3 5PQ
Trustees: Ana Maria Mideros Gadea, Connie L Matsui, Nadine Kaze, Mrs Marjolein Sluijters, Mrs Zoe Rasoaniaina, Marybelle Marinas, Mrs Jayne Kabue Wachira, Ms Tashia Batstone, Mrs Aikaterini Agorogianni, Anne-Therese Guyaz, Haifa Ourir, Dr Natasha Hendrick, Joey Carter, Ms Heidi Jokinen, Mrs Raeda Bader Ismael Issa, Mrs Ntombizine Velma Madyibi, Miss Normala Baharudin
Income: £7,381,000 [2016]; £7,511,535 [2015]

World Cancer Research Fund
Registered: 30 Oct 1990 *Employees:* 44 *Volunteers:* 1
Tel: 020 7343 4200 *Website:* wcrf-uk.org
Activities: Education, training; advancement of health or saving of lives
Address: World Cancer Research Fund, 22 Bedford Square, London, WC1B 3HH
Trustees: Mr Jeffrey Hall Bunn, Mr Peter Crowley McCarty, Professor Ashley Cooper, Mr Laurence Isaacson CBE, Ms Susan Anderson Pepper, Alison Sinclair
Income: £8,237,563 [2017]; £8,423,990 [2016]; £8,443,176 [2015]; £8,043,620 [2014]; £8,622,905 [2013]

World Child Cancer UK
Registered: 26 Jan 2001 *Employees:* 16 *Volunteers:* 150
Website: worldchildcancer.org
Activities: The advancement of health or saving of lives
Address: Unit 2.3, Lafone House, Leather Market, 11-13 Weston Street, London, SE1 3ER
Trustees: World Child Cancer Trustees
Income: £2,096,699 [2017]; £2,074,235 [2016]; £2,374,356 [2015]; £1,956,361 [2014]; £44,398 [2013]

The World Children's Fund
Registered: 27 Jan 2000 *Employees:* 1
Tel: 020 8464 4602 *Website:* worldchildrensfund.org.uk
Activities: The prevention or relief of poverty; overseas aid, famine relief
Address: 34 High Street, Bromley, Kent, BR1 1EA
Trustees: Mr Joseph Lam, Yevgen Yakushev, Mrs Ruth Kendrick, Natalia Yakusheva
Income: £3,247,363 [2017]; £3,016,059 [2016]; £2,951,546 [2015]; £3,026,654 [2014]; £3,302,514 [2013]

The World Community for Christian Meditation
Registered: 1 Jul 1986 *Employees:* 5 *Volunteers:* 15
Tel: 020 7278 2070 *Website:* wccm.org
Activities: Education, training; religious activities
Address: St Marks Church, Myddelton Square, London, EC1R 1XX
Trustees: Mr Clement Sauve, Father Laurence Freeman, Mr Bertrand Bouhour, Mr Mathias Beiswenger, Ms Susan Spence, Mr Charles Posnett, Ms Celina Chan
Income: £1,091,292 [2016]; £691,172 [2015]; £545,111 [2014]; £980,156 [2013]; £517,279 [2012]

World Energy Council
Registered: 14 May 2001 *Employees:* 30 *Volunteers:* 1
Tel: 020 7734 5996 *Website:* worldenergy.org
Activities: Education, training; environment, conservation, heritage; other charitable purposes
Address: 49 Rectory Road, Oxford, OX4 1BU
Trustees: Dr Christoph Frei, Dr Leonhard Birnbaum, Mr Nuer Baikeli, Mr Shigeru Muraki, Dr Elham Mahmoud Ibrahim, Ms Claudia Cronenbold, Mr Oleg Budargin, Mr Younghoon David Kim, Mr Jose Da Costa Carvalho Neto, Dr Klaus-Dieter Barbknecht, Dr Matar Al Neyadi, Dr Ibrahim Al-Muhanna, Mr Robert Hanf, Dr Jose Antonio Vargas Lleras, Mr Jean-Marie Dauger
Income: £5,633,000 [2016]; £4,828,000 [2015]; £4,401,000 [2014]; £4,659,000 [2013]; £3,810,000 [2012]

The World Federation of Khoja Shia Ithna-Asheri Muslim Communities
Registered: 1 Jun 1982 *Employees:* 11 *Volunteers:* 7
Tel: 020 8954 9881 *Website:* world-federation.org
Activities: General charitable purposes; education, training; advancement of health or saving of lives; disability; prevention or relief of poverty; overseas aid, famine relief; accommodation, housing; religious activities; economic, community development, employment; other charitable purposes
Address: Islamic Centre, Wood Lane, Stanmore, Middlesex, HA7 4LQ
Trustees: Mr Shan-E-Abbas Sadik Hassanali Hassam, Mr Anwarali Rajabali Dharamsi, Mr Mohamedkazim Shabbir Bhaloo, Mr Shabbar Yusuf Dhalla, Mr Mahmood Ahmed Musa G Dhala, Mr Muntazir Zulfikar Bhimji
Income: £17,397,671 [2016]; £17,644,151 [2015]; £12,485,837 [2014]; £7,752,395 [2013]; £6,830,822 [2012]

World Habitat
Registered: 5 Apr 1976 *Employees:* 13
Tel: 01530 510444 *Website:* world-habitat.org
Activities: Education, training; accommodation, housing; economic, community development, employment
Address: Building & Social Housing Foundation, Memorial Square, Coalville, Leics, LE67 3TU
Trustees: Mr Alan Pearson, Ms Jill Gibbs, Mr John Strange, Professor Joanna Richardson, Mrs Patricia Elderfield, Dr Angus Kennedy, Mr Stuart Keith MacDonald
Income: £1,226,820 [2016]; £1,105,932 [2015]; £816,004 [2014]; £740,931 [2013]; £678,150 [2012]

World Horse Welfare
Registered: 25 May 1979 *Employees:* 120 *Volunteers:* 200
Tel: 01953 497218 *Website:* worldhorsewelfare.org
Activities: Education, training; animals
Address: World Horse Welfare, Anne Colvin House, Snetterton, Norwich, NR16 2LR
Trustees: Mr Geoffrey Hughes, Mr Michael Baines, Mr Michael Duff, Miss Carly Dimes, Mrs Julie Ross, Mr Richard Davison, Sam Bullard, Mrs Sally Godley-Maynard, Mrs Carol Mitchell, Mrs Sarah Louise Coombs-Girling, Mr Tom Morrison, Ms Caroline Nokes MP, Mr Christopher Keith Price CBE, Mr John Jarvis QC
Income: £9,159,000 [2016]; £8,253,000 [2015]; £7,615,000 [2014]; £8,369,000 [2013]; £7,115,000 [2012]

World Land Trust
Registered: 14 Dec 1990 *Employees:* 25 *Volunteers:* 1
Tel: 01986 874422 *Website:* worldlandtrust.org
Activities: Education, training; animals; environment, conservation, heritage
Address: World Land Trust, Blyth House, 3b Bridge Street, Halesworth, Suffolk, IP19 8AB
Trustees: Mrs Rohini Finch, Dr Mark Stanley Price, Ms Nicola Davies, Mr Nick Brown, Pauline Harrison, Dr Miranda Stevenson, Mr Myles Archibald, Alistair Gammell, Dr Mark Avery
Income: £3,366,000 [2016]; £4,002,808 [2015]; £3,202,446 [2014]; £2,818,461 [2013]; £2,455,951 [2012]

World Mission Agency - Winners Chapel International
Registered: 22 Feb 2010 *Employees:* 42 *Volunteers:* 23
Website: winners-chapel.org.uk
Activities: Education, training; religious activities
Address: World Mission Agency, Green Street Green Road, Dartford, Kent, DA1 1QE
Trustees: Mr Adebayo Arowolo, Mr Olumuyiwa Olufote, Mrs Christine Ogunkanmi, Mrs Abosede Obanobi, Mr Alakoro Abaya
Income: £9,984,540 [2016]; £8,870,249 [2015]; £8,284,709 [2014]; £6,572,958 [2013]; £5,280,262 [2012]

World ORT Trust
Registered: 1 Dec 1994 *Employees:* 3
Tel: 020 7446 8506 *Website:* ort.org
Activities: Education, training
Address: 14 Fitzalan Road, London, N3 3PD
Trustees: Mr Peter Sussmann, Lady Irene Hatter, Mr Richard Hatter, Mr Anthony Brittan
Income: £1,696,080 [2016]; £1,421,900 [2015]; £1,146,000 [2014]; £1,145,000 [2013]; £2,340,000 [2012]

World Villages for Children
Registered: 1 Nov 1996 *Employees:* 2
Tel: 020 7629 3050 *Website:* worldvillages.org.uk
Activities: General charitable purposes; education, training; advancement of health or saving of lives; disability; prevention or relief of poverty; overseas aid, famine relief; accommodation, housing; religious activities; arts, culture, heritage, science; amateur sport; economic, community development, employment
Address: World Villages for Children, Sackville House, 40 Piccadilly, London, W1J 0DR
Trustees: Ms Nicola Lawson, Duk Lim Cho, Elena Grengia Belarmino, Yongsook Cheong
Income: £3,568,238 [2016]; £3,649,668 [2015]; £6,571,161 [2014]; £4,507,290 [2013]; £4,641,566 [2012]

World Vision UK
Registered: 6 Jan 1983 *Employees:* 323 *Volunteers:* 9
Tel: 01908 841000 *Website:* worldvision.org.uk
Activities: Education, training; advancement of health or saving of lives; disability; prevention or relief of poverty; overseas aid, famine relief; religious activities; economic, community development, employment; human rights, religious or racial harmony, equality or diversity; other charitable purposes
Address: World Vision UK, World Vision House, Opal Drive, Fox Milne, Milton Keynes, Bucks, MK15 0ZR
Trustees: Mr Simon Burne, Miss Jennie Collins, Mr Richard Izard, Marie-Eve Coulomb, Rev David Richards, Marcus Manuel, Mr Julian Thomas, Mrs Linda Emery, Mr Mark Parsons, Ms Serena Brown, Douglas Millican
Income: £95,372,000 [2016]; £90,938,000 [2015]; £71,825,000 [2014]; £66,742,000 [2013]; £68,789,000 [2012]

Worldwide Veterinary Service
Registered: 3 Nov 2003 *Employees:* 10
Tel: 01725 557225 *Website:* wvs.org.uk
Activities: Education, training; overseas aid, famine relief; animals
Address: 4 Castle Street, Cranborne, Wimborne, Dorset, BH21 5PZ
Trustees: Mr Robert Lowe, Mr Les Ward, Mr Craig Rutland, Mr John Gaye, Mr Nicholas Bell, Mr Clive Munns, Mr Richard Mellanby
Income: £1,227,570 [2016]; £1,362,561 [2015]; £1,292,810 [2014]; £932,195 [2013]; £468,889 [2012]

Worth Abbey
Registered: 24 Sep 2002 *Employees:* 217
Tel: 01342 710225 *Website:* worthabbey.net
Activities: Education, training; disability; prevention or relief of poverty; overseas aid, famine relief; religious activities; other charitable purposes
Address: Worth Abbey, Paddockhurst Road, Turners Hill, Crawley, Surrey, RH10 4SB
Trustees: The Reverend Aidan Murray, Rev John Douglas Mark Barrett, Rev Martin McGee MA MSt, The Reverend Luke Jolly, Rev Patrick Vincent Fludder, Brother Anthony Brockman BSc BTh
Income: £13,805,829 [2017]; £13,532,551 [2016]; £13,786,390 [2015]; £13,903,024 [2014]; £13,336,478 [2013]

Worth School
Registered: 24 Sep 2002 *Employees:* 193
Tel: 01342 710200 *Website:* worthschool.org.uk
Activities: Education, training; religious activities
Address: Worth School, Paddockhurst Road, Turners Hill, Crawley, Surrey, RH10 4SD
Trustees: Mr Ralph Townsend, Miss Alda Andreotti, The Reverend Mark Barrett, Mrs Fiona Newton, Peter Green, Mr Jeremy Fletcher, Mrs Helen Paula Parry, Mr Timothy Pethybridge, The Reverend Luke Jolly, Mr David Richard Buxton, Mr Benedict James Elwes, David Jarmy, Mrs Minette Fudakowski, Dr Bridget Dolan
Income: £12,889,592 [2017]; £12,797,431 [2016]; £13,132,647 [2015]; £13,086,132 [2014]; £12,468,772 [2013]

Worthing Churches Homeless Projects
Registered: 29 Oct 1993 *Employees:* 69 *Volunteers:* 234
Tel: 01903 680740 *Website:* wchp.org.uk
Activities: The prevention or relief of poverty; accommodation, housing
Address: WCHP, Town Hall, Chapel Road, Worthing, W Sussex, BN11 1HA
Trustees: Geoff Wheeler, Dr Linda Jane Rockall, Mr Matthew Hodson, Mr Ian Mintram, Mrs Richenda Margaret Kullar, Mr David Standing, Rev Benjamin Eadon, Ms Moira James
Income: £2,864,179 [2017]; £2,518,702 [2016]; £2,085,493 [2015]; £1,495,937 [2014]; £1,739,510 [2013]

Worthing Homes Limited
Registered: 4 Mar 1999 *Employees:* 97 *Volunteers:* 107
Tel: 01903 703160 *Website:* worthing-homes.org.uk
Activities: Accommodation, housing
Address: Worthing Homes Ltd, Davison House, North Street, Worthing, W Sussex, BN11 1ER
Trustees: Mrs Helen Rice, Miss Amy Dewey, Ms Louise Murphy, Mrs Celia Rowe, Mrs Jeni Graham, Mr Colin Goodwin, Mr Paul Smith, Mr Chris Simpson, Steve Wills, Mr Nigel Perryman
Income: £28,256,000 [2017]; £20,368,000 [2016]; £19,343,000 [2015]; £18,873,000 [2014]; £16,725,000 [2013]

The Wrekin Housing Trust Limited
Registered: 17 Mar 1999 *Employees:* 480
Tel: 01952 217005 *Website:* wrekinhousingtrust.org.uk
Activities: The prevention or relief of poverty; accommodation, housing
Address: Chris Horton, Colliers Way, Old Park, Telford, Salop, TF3 4AW
Trustees: Ms Esther Leonie Wright, Mr Desmond Gerard Hudson, Mrs Jacqueline Aminoritse Esimaje-Heath, Mr James Dickson, Mrs Deborah Pauline Griffiths, Mrs Anne Marie Ward, Ms Danielle Oum, Mrs Alison Jane Fisher, Mrs Angela Diane McClements, Mrs Annette Marie Shipley, Mr Paul Weston, Mr John Philip Broadhead
Income: £71,442,000 [2017]; £73,678,000 [2016]; £58,856,000 [2015]; £56,772,000 [2014]; £54,591,000 [2013]

The Wrekin Old Hall Trust Limited
Registered: 1 Sep 1963 *Employees:* 232 *Volunteers:* 20
Tel: 01952 265000 *Website:* wrekincollege.com
Activities: Education, training
Address: Wrekin College, Bursars Office, Sutherland Road, Wellington, Telford, TF1 3BH
Trustees: Mr Anthony Lock, Mrs Pauline Dorothy Mack, Mrs Victoria Hughes-Hines, Mr Andrew Huxley, Mr Toby Shaw BSc MRICS, Mr Christopher Jones, Mr Anthony Herber-Davies, Mr Richard Pearson, Mrs Alison Dixon, Mrs Penny Hunt, Mr Michael Halewood, Mr Robert Mottram, Mr Jonathan Alan Grant, Mr Duncan Malyon
Income: £9,715,670 [2017]; £9,132,064 [2016]; £8,674,059 [2015]; £8,691,015 [2014]; £8,497,312 [2013]

Wrexham Diocesan Trust
Registered: 30 Jun 1988 *Employees:* 23 *Volunteers:* 150
Tel: 01978 352404 *Website:* wrexhamdiocese.org.uk
Activities: Religious activities
Address: The Coach House, 25 Rhosddu Road, Wrexham, LL11 1EB
Trustees: Wrexham Diocesan Trustees Registered
Income: £2,530,037 [2017]; £3,896,251 [2016]; £2,570,359 [2015]; £2,797,556 [2014]; £2,596,663 [2013]

Wrexham Hospice and Cancer Support Centre Foundation
Registered: 24 Mar 1994 *Employees:* 85 *Volunteers:* 700
Tel: 01978 316800 *Website:* nightingalehouse.co.uk
Activities: Education, training; advancement of health or saving of lives
Address: Wrexham Hospice & Cancer Support Centre, Nightingale House, Chester Road, Wrexham, LL11 2SJ
Trustees: Mrs Eluned Griffiths, Dr Neil William Braid, Mr Andrew Morse, Mrs Joan Lowe, Dr Helen Paterson, Vicky Davies, Mr Paul Maddocks, Mr Graham Gilmour Greasley, Dr Jennifer Duguid, Mr Christopher Burgoyne, His Honour Philip Hughes, Mr Robert Cole
Income: £3,750,324 [2016]; £3,689,838 [2015]; £3,754,134 [2014]; £3,856,436 [2013]; £3,553,966 [2012]

The Eric Wright Charitable Trust
Registered: 17 May 1991 *Employees:* 647
Tel: 01772 694698 *Website:* ericwright.co.uk
Activities: General charitable purposes; education, training; disability; amateur sport
Address: Eric Wright Group Ltd, Sceptre House, Sceptre Way, Bamber Bridge, Preston, Lancs, PR5 6AW
Trustees: Mr Alan Douglas Sturrock, Mr Hugh MacDonald, Mr Bernard Whewell, Mr Michael Edward Collier, Mrs Alison Wright
Income: £35,026,000 [2016]; £358,544 [2015]; £869,376 [2014]; £838,873 [2013]; £891,065 [2012]

Writers' Centre Norwich
Registered: 4 Aug 2005 *Employees:* 16 *Volunteers:* 20
Tel: 01603 877177 *Website:* writerscentrenorwich.org.uk
Activities: Education, training; arts, culture, heritage, science
Address: Dragon Hall, 115-123 King Street, Norwich, NR1 1QE
Trustees: Mr David Bryan, Dr Christopher Gribble, Mr David Gilbert, Ms Pamela Henderson, Mr George Szirtes, Ms Helen Dawson, Mr Andrew Yuill, Mr James Slinger, Ms Helen Wilson, Professor Sarah Barrow
Income: £1,474,890 [2017]; £1,518,488 [2016]; £1,064,580 [2015]; £806,402 [2014]; £940,870 [2013]

Writhlington Trust
Registered: 29 Sep 2005 *Employees:* 45 *Volunteers:* 15
Tel: 01761 433581 *Website:* writhlingtonsportscentre.co.uk
Activities: General charitable purposes; education, training; advancement of health or saving of lives; amateur sport
Address: Writhlington School, Knobsbury Lane, Writhlington, Radstock, Somerset, BA3 3NQ
Trustees: David Jeremy Howard Pilling, Mr Mark Everett, Johnathan Pike, Mr Clive Sampson, Mr Richard Akers, Miss Alison Victoria Weeks
Income: £2,719,881 [2017]; £2,187,694 [2016]; £1,491,623 [2015]; £1,362,560 [2014]; £1,268,406 [2013]

Wychwood School for Girls
Registered: 11 Sep 1963 *Employees:* 66
Tel: 01865 557976 *Website:* wychwoodschool.org
Activities: Education, training
Address: Wychwood School, 72-74 Banbury Road, Oxford, OX2 6JR
Trustees: Mr Paul Hall, Mrs Deborah Pluck, Ms Alysoun Stewart MA ACA, Mrs Nicola King, Mrs Anna Hunter, Mr Richard Briant, Mrs Rosalind Hayes, Miss Michele Crawford, Mrs Katherine Rogers, Dr Ann Sharpley
Income: £1,895,331 [2016]; £1,883,567 [2015]; £1,739,359 [2014]; £1,584,673 [2013]; £1,683,325 [2012]

Wycliffe College (Incorporated)
Registered: 28 Jul 1966 *Employees:* 270 *Volunteers:* 15
Website: wycliffe.co.uk
Activities: Education, training
Address: Finance Department, Wycliffe College, Stonehouse, Glos, GL10 2AD
Trustees: Mr Jeremy Robert Ellis Williams, Mrs Susan Joy Lacey BA MEng, Dr Geoffrey Reid MB ChB FRCPysch RAF, Mr Ian Hamilton Paling BMet MMet, Mr Simon Kinnaird Collingridge BA Hons LLB, Mr William Robert Garrard MBA BSc Hons, Mrs Lynn Carol Duncan BSc PGCE, Mrs Sophie Melanie Pudge BSc Hons FCA, Mr Nicholas John Hughes, Brigadier Retd Robin John Bacon MBA Chartered FCIPD FCMI CMILT, Mr James Slater FRICS, Mrs Caroline Duckworth MA Hons, Mr Simon Frederick Modlin Lloyd BSc Hons MRICS, Mrs Andrea Louise Palk MBE BA Hons, Mr Graeme May BA MA Oxon
Income: £13,234,211 [2016]; £13,203,951 [2015]; £13,152,123 [2014]; £12,917,016 [2013]; £13,278,710 [2012]

Wycliffe Hall
Registered: 1 May 2014 *Employees:* 29
Tel: 01865 274216 *Website:* wycliffehall.ox.ac.uk
Activities: Education, training; religious activities
Address: Wycliffe Hall, 52-54 Banbury Road, Oxford, OX2 6PW
Trustees: The Revd Canon Frederick Kilner, The Revd Ann Templeman, Mr Nigel Christopher Tinker, Mr Peter Doyle, Rev James Edward Kennedy, Ms Sarah Finch, Ms Emma Coley, Ms Alison Coulter, Very Revd John Dudley Irvine, Mr Simon McGuire, The Rt Revd Alistair Magowan, Rt Revd Julian Tudor Henderson, Dr Philip Giddings, Professor Nigel Biggar, Ms Katrina Clare Hancock
Income: £2,478,673 [2017]; £2,349,422 [2016]; £2,171,118 [2015]

Wycliffe UK Limited
Registered: 22 Feb 1967 *Employees:* 21 *Volunteers:* 43
Website: wycliffe.org.uk
Activities: Education, training; prevention or relief of poverty; religious activities
Address: 71 Great Russell Street, London, WC1B 3BP
Trustees: Mrs Jane Meryl Showell-Rogers, Rev Roger William Welch, Mr Joseph Kelly, David Steinegger, Mr Robert Martin Peake, Mr Kenneth MacAngus MacKenzie, Mr Kevin Stewart Ashman, Mr Keith Civval, Dr Ian Kenneth Kirby, Mrs Rebecca Helen Benton
Income: £6,528,592 [2017]; £5,968,364 [2016]; £7,319,027 [2015]; £7,007,895 [2014]; £10,798,047 [2013]

The Wye and Usk Foundation
Registered: 13 Apr 2000 *Employees:* 20 *Volunteers:* 91
Tel: 01874 711714 *Website:* wyeuskfoundation.org
Activities: Education, training; arts, culture, heritage, science; amateur sport; animals; environment, conservation, heritage; economic, community development, employment; recreation
Address: The Right Bank, The Square, Talgarth, Brecon, Powys, LD3 0BW
Trustees: Mr Michael Ross Murray, Mr Roger William Blears, Mr Anthony James Norman, Mr Andrew John Rattray Sayer, Mr Kim Waters, Mr Christopher Morley, Mr Charles Newington-Bridges, Major Patrick James Auchinleck Darling, Mr Michael Andrew Timmis, Miss Elizabeth Passey, Mr Patrick Lloyd, Mrs Helen Natalie Harrison, Mr Peter John Horsburgh
Income: £1,287,607 [2016]; £1,228,878 [2015]; £2,138,591 [2014]; £1,686,805 [2013]; £1,470,092 [2012]

Wynstones Limited
Registered: 20 Dec 1962 *Employees:* 48 *Volunteers:* 80
Tel: 01452 429222 *Website:* wynstones.com
Activities: Education, training
Address: Wynstones School, Church Lane, Whaddon, Gloucester, GL4 0UF
Trustees: Mr Edward William Yates, Mr Graham Kennish, Mr David Rowson, Ms Anna Caroline Stephenson, Mr Peter Alexander Cooke, Mr Martin Sharp, Ms Susanna Perry, Mr Duncan McCanlis
Income: £1,567,817 [2017]; £1,592,347 [2016]; £1,507,949 [2015]; £1,451,064 [2014]; £1,450,093 [2013]

Wythenshawe Community Housing Group Limited
Registered: 5 Mar 2013 *Employees:* 498 *Volunteers:* 413
Tel: 0161 946 9552 *Website:* wchg.org.uk
Activities: General charitable purposes; education, training; prevention or relief of poverty; accommodation, housing; amateur sport; economic, community development, employment; other charitable purposes
Address: Wythenshawe House, 8 Poundswick Lane, Manchester, M22 9TA
Trustees: Bishop David Walker, Ms Sarah Alison Russell, Ms Bernadette Heanue, Mr Robert William Cressey
Income: £65,461,000 [2017]; £63,662,000 [2016]; £62,423,000 [2015]; £60,569,000 [2014]

XCEL County Durham
Registered: 17 Oct 2013 *Employees:* 36 *Volunteers:* 50
Tel: 01325 300614
Activities: General charitable purposes; education, training; prevention or relief of poverty; religious activities
Address: 43 Youens Crescent, Newton Aycliffe, Co Durham, DL5 4ZE
Trustees: Ms Rosemary Ann Laxton, Ms Jean Carter, Mr John James Greenow, Mr Paul Benger, Ms Kerina Lucy Clark
Income: £2,178,184 [2017]; £777,360 [2016]; £756,510 [2015]

XLP
Registered: 9 Dec 2003 *Employees:* 41 *Volunteers:* 200
Tel: 020 7256 6240 *Website:* xlp.org.uk
Activities: Education, training; prevention or relief of poverty; overseas aid, famine relief; religious activities; arts, culture, heritage, science; amateur sport; economic, community development, employment; other charitable purposes
Address: XLP, 83 London Wall, London, EC2M 5ND
Trustees: Mr Simon Philip Thomas, Ms Elizabeth Ursula Constance Biddulph BA Jt Hons, Eddie Donaldson, Mrs Andi Russell, Mr Denis Michael Wade, Sam Miller, Ms Rosemary Winifred Nuamah
Income: £1,893,695 [2017]; £1,575,878 [2016]; £1,387,468 [2015]; £1,246,878 [2014]; £1,078,220 [2013]

Xtend Global
Registered: 14 Nov 2011 *Employees:* 18 *Volunteers:* 2
Website: arabworldmedia.org
Activities: Education, training; prevention or relief of poverty; religious activities; other charitable purposes
Address: 51-63 St Dunstan's Road, Worthing, W Sussex, BN13 1AA
Trustees: Mr David Paul Milligan, Mr Jonathan Graham Black, Mr Chi-Chung Keung, Don Little, Mr Hugo Wolmarans, Mr Walter Alexander Jones
Income: £1,183,409 [2016]; £1,121,821 [2015]; £861,922 [2014]; £815,704 [2013]; £967,383 [2012]

Y Care International
Registered: 1 Jun 2005   *Employees:* 33   *Volunteers:* 211
Tel: 020 7549 3166   *Website:* ycareinternational.org
Activities: Education, training; prevention or relief of poverty; overseas aid, famine relief; economic, community development, employment
Address: Y Care International, 67-69 Cowcross Street, London, EC1M 6BP
Trustees: Mr David French, Mr Timothy James Fallon, Ms Grace Conacher, Peter Liu, Mel Zuijdam, Miss Adwoa Darko, Mr James Holian, Miss Sarah Sansom, Mr Terence Waite CBE, Ms Sally Hartley, Ms Kerry Reilly, Ms Michaela Kelly, Mr Brian Murtagh, Mr Benjamin Tucker, Mr James Ernest Helm
Income: £5,916,459 [2017]; £6,288,233 [2016]; £5,572,896 [2015]; £3,998,550 [2014]; £3,871,829 [2013]

Y Coleg Cymraeg Cenedlaethol
Registered: 24 Aug 2011   *Employees:* 22
Tel: 01267 610402   *Website:* colegcymraeg.ac.uk
Activities: Education, training; arts, culture, heritage, science
Address: Y Coleg Cymraeg Cenedlaethol, Y Llwyfan, Heol y Coleg, Caerfyrddin, SA31 3EQ
Trustees: Dr Thomas Hefin Jones, Dr Haydn Ellis Edwards, Yr Athro Thomas Gerald Hunter, Yr Athro Hywel Rhys Thomas, Dr Gwyn Lewis, Mr Gwilym Dyfri Jones, Mr Ieuan Wyn, Yr Athro Iwan Rhun Davies, Pedr Ap Llwyd, Dr Rhodri Llwyd Morgan, Mr William Callaway, Llinos Roberts
Income: £5,988,000 [2017]; £8,913,000 [2016]; £8,615,000 [2015]; £6,957,000 [2014]; £5,721,000 [2013]

YHA (England and Wales)
Registered: 13 Aug 1963   *Employees:* 1,223   *Volunteers:* 3,116
Tel: 01629 592751   *Website:* yha.org.uk
Activities: General charitable purposes; education, training; accommodation, housing; amateur sport; environment, conservation, heritage
Address: Youth Hostels Association, Trevelyan House, Matlock, Derbys, DE4 3YH
Trustees: Dr Vishaal Virani, Mrs Barbara Kasumu, Anthony Peter Gaines, Mr Ian Maginnis, Mr Graham Turnock, Mr Marcus Holburn, Ms Cathryn Hayhurst, Paul Wright, Mr Christopher Roberts, Ms Josephine Murray, Mrs Margaret Hart, Mrs Fiona Steggles
Income: £50,316,000 [2017]; £51,477,000 [2016]; £48,018,000 [2015]; £45,233,000 [2014]; £44,094,000 [2013]

YMCA Bath Group
Registered: 20 Oct 2004   *Employees:* 176   *Volunteers:* 45
Tel: 01225 325900   *Website:* bathymca.co.uk
Activities: General charitable purposes; accommodation, housing; religious activities; amateur sport
Address: YMCA, International House, Broad Street Place, Bath, BA1 5LH
Trustees: Mr John Davis, Mr Mike Bendrey, Mr Matthew Palfrey, Sarah Beresford-Smith, Mrs Teresa Spencer, Mr Mark Pitman, David Pendle, Mr Richard Caddick, Jonathan Webb-Peploe, Mrs Noreen Finnamore
Income: £3,929,376 [2016]; £3,108,204 [2015]; £2,857,619 [2014]; £2,790,219 [2013]; £2,487,887 [2012]

YMCA Bedfordshire
Registered: 22 Feb 1989   *Employees:* 61
Tel: 01234 307040   *Website:* ymcabedfordshire.org.uk
Activities: Education, training; accommodation, housing; religious activities; amateur sport; economic, community development, employment; other charitable purposes
Address: 1st Floor, YMCA Bedfordshire, 43 Bromham Road, Bedford, MK40 2AA
Trustees: Mrs Lisa Hunt, Ms Deborah Maggs, Mr Andrew McKean, Miss Sue Bean
Income: £2,793,312 [2017]; £2,331,577 [2016]; £2,390,298 [2015]; £2,229,381 [2014]; £1,363,001 [2013]

YMCA Black Country Group
Registered: 26 Apr 2001   *Employees:* 186   *Volunteers:* 25
Tel: 01902 371550   *Website:* ymcabc.org.uk
Activities: General charitable purposes; education, training; prevention or relief of poverty; accommodation, housing; religious activities; economic, community development, employment; recreation
Address: YMCA, 29-31 Temple Street, Wolverhampton, W Midlands, WV2 4AN
Trustees: Mr Geoffrey Malcolm Stonyer, Mr Eric Moore, Mrs Hazel Margaret Bloxham, Mr Walker Philip Wilfred Leonard, Mr Jonathan Robert Rowe, Mr Brenda May Moore, Rev Jeremy Steven Oakley, Mr John Welsby
Income: £6,778,251 [2017]; £7,246,259 [2016]; £5,816,328 [2015]; £5,558,520 [2014]; £5,357,704 [2013]

YMCA Derbyshire
Registered: 16 Oct 1995   *Employees:* 100   *Volunteers:* 20
Tel: 01332 579550   *Website:* ymcaderbyshire.org.uk
Activities: Education, training; accommodation, housing; other charitable purposes
Address: YMCA, 770 London Road, Alvaston, Derby, DE24 8UT
Trustees: Mr David Connor, Mary Gordon, Rev David Ayling, Mr Neil Graydon White, Mr Howard Blacksmith, Mrs Joanne Robinson, Mrs Helen Michele Wigglesworth, Richard Swainson, Peter Posner, Mr Timothy John Penter, Miss Elizabeth Mills
Income: £2,891,000 [2017]; £2,956,000 [2016]; £3,564,000 [2015]; £2,330,000 [2014]; £3,260,000 [2013]

YMCA Downslink Group
Registered: 28 Feb 2000   *Employees:* 346   *Volunteers:* 168
Tel: 01273 222550   *Website:* ymcadlg.org
Activities: Education, training; accommodation, housing; religious activities; amateur sport; economic, community development, employment
Address: YMCA Downslink Group, Reed House, 47 Church Road, Hove, W Sussex, BN3 2BE
Trustees: Mr Peter Jeffrey, Mr John Andrew Duncan Slater, Mr Robert Stephen Wilkinson, Mrs Ingrid Beatty, Mr John Eric Holmstrom, Mrs Caroline Stearman, Mr Andrew Wilson, Rev Simon Braid, Mr James Lister, Mrs Deborah Pepper, Mr Richard David Nerurkar
Income: £14,472,573 [2017]; £11,291,258 [2016]; £12,558,687 [2015]; £8,878,813 [2014]; £8,837,594 [2013]

YMCA East Surrey
Registered: 9 Apr 1999 *Employees:* 152 *Volunteers:* 140
Tel: 01737 779979 *Website:* ymcaeastsurrey.org.uk
Activities: General charitable purposes; advancement of health or saving of lives; disability; prevention or relief of poverty; accommodation, housing; amateur sport; economic, community development, employment; recreation
Address: YMCA East Surrey, Princes Road, Redhill, Surrey, RH1 6JJ
Trustees: Mrs Freda Clark BA (Hons), Mrs Penelope Horsfall, Mr Phil Baker, Rev David Martin McLellan Skitt, Mrs Caroline Fisher, Mr Paul Byrne, Mr Ian Thomas, Mr Christopher Brewer, Mrs Ann Woodford, Mr Richard Mantle, Mrs Amanda McNeil, Mr Jeff Travis, Mr Nigel Clifford, Dr Diane Louise Empain Bullock
Income: £3,846,659 [2017]; £3,035,379 [2016]; £2,978,060 [2015]; £3,021,423 [2014]; £2,393,900 [2013]

YMCA Essex
Registered: 26 Mar 1996 *Employees:* 70 *Volunteers:* 20
Website: chelmsfordymca.co.uk
Activities: General charitable purposes; education, training; accommodation, housing
Address: YMCA, Victoria Road, Chelmsford, Essex, CM1 1NZ
Trustees: Mr David Clarke, Rev Ray Gibbs, Mrs Helen Robinson, Mrs Elspeth Johnson, Mr Roger McFarland, Sir Bob Russell, Mrs Dahlia Wilkinson, Rev Edward John Carter, Ms Dawn Bostock, Ms Beverley Strutt, Mrs Joanna Elsey, Mr Darren Vythilingum
Income: £1,183,031 [2017]; £1,052,081 [2016]; £1,071,210 [2015]; £1,096,341 [2014]; £1,006,141 [2013]

YMCA Fairthorne Group
Registered: 7 Mar 2002 *Employees:* 375 *Volunteers:* 350
Tel: 023 8214 5453 *Website:* ymca-fg.org
Activities: Education, training; advancement of health or saving of lives; disability; accommodation, housing; amateur sport; economic, community development, employment; recreation
Address: YMCA Fairthorne Group, Bugle House, 53 Bugle Street, Southampton, SO14 2LF
Trustees: Mrs Sheila Clark, Mr Ian William Creek, Mr Timothy Titheridge, Professor Chris Laws, Mrs Judy Hillier
Income: £9,237,763 [2016]; £9,120,802 [2015]; £8,258,016 [2014]; £6,664,960 [2013]; £6,281,258 [2012]

YMCA Indian Student Hostel
Registered: 17 Oct 2013 *Employees:* 32
Tel: 020 7387 0411 *Website:* indianymca.org
Activities: Accommodation, housing
Address: YMCA, Indian Students Hostel, 41 Fitzroy Square, London, W1T 6AQ
Trustees: Mrs Anne-Marie Rogan, Mr Raja Pratap Mani Kumar Challapalli National General Secretary, Mr Raviraj Sathyapal Shettian, Mr Pradeep Mathew Johns, Rev Madhu Smitha Prasadam, Dr Lebi Philip Mathew, Mr Mammen Zachariah, Mr Richard Anthony Leonard Lees
Income: £2,072,325 [2017]; £2,014,437 [2016]; £1,976,175 [2015]

YMCA Norfolk
Registered: 24 Aug 1989 *Employees:* 90 *Volunteers:* 53
Tel: 01603 621263 *Website:* ymcanorfolk.org
Activities: Accommodation, housing
Address: YMCA Norfolk, 35-37 Exchange Street, Norwich, NR2 1DP
Trustees: Richard Pennington, Rebecca Gascoyne-Richards, Philip MacDonald, John Lee, Anne Aves, John Rockliff, James Shelton, Gillian Duffy
Income: £3,778,724 [2017]; £3,595,412 [2016]; £3,415,425 [2015]; £3,375,453 [2014]; £3,194,898 [2013]

YMCA North Staffordshire Ltd.
Registered: 17 Nov 2003 *Employees:* 132 *Volunteers:* 23
Tel: 01782 864500 *Website:* ymcans.org.uk
Activities: General charitable purposes; education, training; advancement of health or saving of lives; prevention or relief of poverty; accommodation, housing; religious activities; arts, culture, heritage, science; amateur sport; recreation
Address: YMCA, Edinburgh House, Harding Road, Stoke on Trent, Staffs, ST1 3AE
Trustees: Rev Sally Smith, Mr Michael Jonathon Toohey, Mr Glenn Handforth, Rev Darren McIndoe, Peter Dartford, Paul Franklin, Mr Norman George Prophett, Mrs Lynn Tindale, Mrs Steph Poulter, Mrs Barbara Sumner, Mr Andrew Robinson, Paul Williams
Income: £3,699,886 [2017]; £4,016,393 [2016]; £3,218,188 [2015]; £2,736,747 [2014]; £3,078,150 [2013]

YMCA North Tyneside
Registered: 29 May 1992 *Employees:* 45 *Volunteers:* 50
Tel: 0191 257 5434 *Website:* ymcanorthtyneside.org
Activities: General charitable purposes; education, training; advancement of health or saving of lives; disability; accommodation, housing; religious activities; arts, culture, heritage, science; amateur sport; recreation
Address: YMCA, Church Way, North Shields, Tyne & Wear, NE29 0AB
Trustees: Mr David Hodgson, Mrs Carol Ann Groombridge, Mr Russell Hall, Mrs Barbara Morris, Mr John Hawksworth, Mrs Louise Stewart, Ms Louise Snelders, Mrs Samantha Kleis Meredith
Income: £1,953,275 [2017]; £1,945,887 [2016]; £1,183,948 [2015]; £959,061 [2014]; £1,071,739 [2013]

YMCA St Helens
Registered: 19 Jun 1986 *Employees:* 58 *Volunteers:* 10
Tel: 01744 455038 *Website:* ymcasthelens.org.uk
Activities: Education, training; accommodation, housing; amateur sport
Address: St Helens YMCA, North Road, St Helens, Merseyside, WA10 2TJ
Trustees: Elaine Stanley, Mr Kenneth Jackson, Mr Louis Frederick Rigby FRICS, Mr John Frodsham, Sheila Whitton, Mr Frank Grayson, Mr Leslie David Hickman, Mr Richard Ian Tully MRTPI FRSA, Jane Gallimore-Griffiths
Income: £2,291,573 [2017]; £2,248,600 [2016]; £1,977,377 [2015]; £2,059,801 [2014]; £2,111,610 [2013]

YMCA St Pauls Group
Registered: 8 Nov 1994 *Employees:* 348 *Volunteers:* 200
Tel: 020 8399 5427 *Website:* ymcalsw.org
Activities: General charitable purposes; education, training; disability; prevention or relief of poverty; accommodation, housing; religious activities; amateur sport; economic, community development, employment; recreation; other charitable purposes
Address: St James House, 9-15 St James Road, Surbiton, Surrey, KT6 4QH
Trustees: Edward Weiss, Howard Dawson, David Morrow, Kenneth Youngman, Helen Posner, Andrew Palmer, Albin Stadtmiller, Kathy Morrissey, Louise Hedges, Gerald Chifamba
Income: £17,089,802 [2017]; £10,177,461 [2016]; £9,633,723 [2015]; £9,337,179 [2014]; £8,771,904 [2013]

YMCA Suffolk

Registered: 19 Aug 1999 *Employees:* 120 *Volunteers:* 31
Website: ymcasuffolk.org.uk
Activities: General charitable purposes; accommodation, housing; religious activities; amateur sport
Address: 2 Wellington Street, Ipswich, Suffolk, IP1 2NU
Trustees: Mrs Linda Sheppard, Mr David Swanney, Mr Peter Day, Mr Gareth Millen, Mr Stephen Arthur Smith, Mr Geoffrey Probert, Mr Derek Grant Forder
Income: £2,924,796 [2017]; £2,797,847 [2016]; £2,608,514 [2015]; £2,210,300 [2014]; £2,503,025 [2013]

YMCA Thames Gateway

Registered: 11 Dec 2009 *Employees:* 194 *Volunteers:* 69
Tel: 01708 766211 *Website:* ymcatg.org
Activities: Education, training; accommodation, housing; religious activities; arts, culture, heritage, science; amateur sport; economic, community development, employment; recreation
Address: YMCA, Rush Green Road, Romford, Essex, RM7 0PH
Trustees: Father Martin David Howse, Mrs Cheryl Burden, Mr Damon Thomas, Mrs Gaggandip Sandhu-Nelson, Mr Edward Galgano, Mr Andrew Dyckhoff, Mr Desmond Lee Potter, Mrs Susan Unsworth-Tomlinson, Mr Dominic Scott-Malden
Income: £4,827,095 [2017]; £4,802,858 [2016]; £3,242,999 [2015]; £3,258,769 [2014]; £3,131,337 [2013]

YMCA Training

Registered: 12 Apr 2002 *Employees:* 141
Tel: 020 7343 1844 *Website:* ymcatraining.co.uk
Activities: Education, training; economic, community development, employment
Address: Central YMCA, 112 Great Russell Street, London, WC1B 3NQ
Trustees: Ms Philippa Campbell, Mrs Janice Lloyd, Ms Susan Ross Morton
Income: £10,183,000 [2017]; £13,777,000 [2016]; £10,499,000 [2015]; £11,465,000 [2014]; £13,617,000 [2013]

YMCA Trinity Group

Registered: 29 May 1998 *Employees:* 95 *Volunteers:* 114
Tel: 01733 373176 *Website:* theymca.org.uk
Activities: General charitable purposes; education, training; disability; accommodation, housing; amateur sport; other charitable purposes
Address: YMCA, Queen Anne House, Gonville Place, Cambridge, CB1 1ND
Trustees: Mrs Mary Sanders MBE, Mr Ian Dow, Mr William David Reid Swanney, Mrs Julie Horne, Mrs Kay Elizabeth Hoggett, Mr Simon Pickering, Revd Anthony Chandler, Mrs Antonia Karen MacLean, Mr Derek Grant Forder, Mr Andy Lucas, Mr Dominic Bowles
Income: £5,761,613 [2017]; £5,072,665 [2016]; £3,574,842 [2015]; £3,025,981 [2014]; £2,903,489 [2013]

YMCA Wearside Ltd

Registered: 27 Nov 1996 *Employees:* 33 *Volunteers:* 5
Tel: 0191 567 6160 *Website:* sunderlandymca.org.uk
Activities: General charitable purposes; education, training; accommodation, housing; religious activities; economic, community development, employment
Address: 2-3 Toward Road, Sunderland, Tyne & Wear, SR1 2QF
Trustees: Mr Kenneth Taylor, Mr J Swan, Mr John Lambton, Mr John Damian Waugh, Mr Alex Scullion, Mrs Winifred Lundgren, Mr Aiden Bell, Mrs Anne Lawson
Income: £1,494,993 [2016]; £1,162,299 [2015]; £1,209,559 [2014]; £1,221,825 [2013]; £948,422 [2012]

YMCA Wolverhampton

Registered: 31 Jan 1995 *Employees:* 63
Tel: 01902 371550 *Website:* ymcabc.org.uk
Activities: General charitable purposes; education, training; prevention or relief of poverty; accommodation, housing; religious activities; economic, community development, employment; recreation
Address: YMCA, 29-31 Temple Street, Wolverhampton, W Midlands, WV2 4AN
Trustees: Mr Geoffrey Malcolm Stonyer, Mr Eric Moore, Mr John Welsby, Mrs Brenda Moore, Mr Jonathan Robert Rowe, Rev Jeremy Steven Oakley, Mrs Hazel Bloxham, Mr Philip Wilfred Leonard Walker
Income: £1,848,403 [2017]; £2,057,855 [2016]; £1,976,766 [2015]; £2,053,749 [2014]; £2,221,497 [2013]

YSS Ltd

Registered: 11 Aug 2000 *Employees:* 59 *Volunteers:* 118
Tel: 01905 730780 *Website:* yss.org.uk
Activities: General charitable purposes; education, training
Address: YSS Ltd, Polysec House, Blackpole Trading Estate West, Worcester, WR3 8TJ
Trustees: Mr David John Chantler, Mr Ronald George Whitfield, Mr Ian Warwick Richards, Ms Sandra Diane Kelley, Lady Susanna Jane McFarlane, Mrs Fiona Elizabeth Charny, Mrs Helen Mary Barker, Mr Graham Andrew Brotherton
Income: £1,701,986 [2017]; £1,852,636 [2016]; £1,806,425 [2015]; £1,792,008 [2014]; £1,728,648 [2013]

YWCA England & Wales

Registered: 4 Aug 1969 *Employees:* 20 *Volunteers:* 30
Tel: 020 7600 7451 *Website:* youngwomenstrust.org
Activities: General charitable purposes; prevention or relief of poverty; economic, community development, employment
Address: Young Women's Trust, Unit D, 15-18 White Lion Street, London, N1 9PD
Trustees: Mr Ryan Paul Shorthouse, Baroness Susan Jane Nye, Martin Pilgrim, Laura Blake, Ms Anushka Asthana, Miss Noor Kalumba, Ms Jo-Ann Robertson, Ms Tara Leathers, Ms Alexandra Catherine Hewitt Birtles, Deirdra Moynihan, Mr John Andrew Hitchin, Mrs Danielle Marie Papagapiou, Miss Leanne Naomi Hall
Income: £1,178,000 [2017]; £1,016,000 [2016]; £1,092,000 [2015]; £2,092,000 [2014]; £3,384,000 [2013]

Yad Shlomo Trust

Registered: 17 Dec 2007
Tel: 020 8800 5860
Activities: General charitable purposes; education, training; prevention or relief of poverty; religious activities
Address: 86 Amhurst Park, London, N16 5AR
Trustees: Mr F Getter, Mr Benjamin Katz, Mr Benjamin Stern
Income: £1,554,830 [2017]; £1,284,926 [2016]; £1,183,845 [2015]; £836,737 [2014]; £944,869 [2013]

Yale University Press London

Registered: 17 Jul 1984 *Employees:* 47
Tel: 020 7079 4900 *Website:* yalebooks.co.uk
Activities: General charitable purposes; education, training; arts, culture, heritage, science
Address: Yale University Press, 47 Bedford Square, London, WC1B 3DP
Trustees: Mr Angus William McPhail, Mr Timothy Aidan John Knox, Ms Fionnuala Duggan, Ms Dorothy Robinson, Mrs Susan Lynn Gibbons, Mr John Francis Callahan Jr, Mr John Donatich, Ms Katherine Brown, Mr Richard Fisher, Mrs Mary Cannam, Mr Timothy Haire
Income: £9,207,746 [2017]; £7,414,931 [2016]; £7,658,862 [2015]; £7,309,272 [2014]; £7,246,793 [2013]

W J Yapp Bequest

Registered: 17 May 1965 *Employees:* 41 *Volunteers:* 6
Tel: 01509 852531 *Website:* derbyshirehouse.org.uk
Activities: General charitable purposes; prevention or relief of poverty; accommodation, housing
Address: Derbyshire House, Station Road, East Leake, Loughborough, Leics, LE12 6LQ
Trustees: Mr Peter Moore FCA, Mrs Georgina Raffle, Mr Jeffrey Hooley, Mr Tony Kelly, Tim Parker
Income: £1,068,066 [2017]; £996,778 [2016]; £858,485 [2015]; £746,551 [2014]; £700,426 [2013]

Yardley Grange Care Services

Registered: 9 May 2002 *Employees:* 57
Tel: 0121 784 7889 *Website:* ygtrust.org.uk
Activities: The advancement of health or saving of lives; accommodation, housing
Address: 102 Burman Road, Shirley, Solihull, W Midlands, B90 2BQ
Trustees: Reverend John Richards, Mrs Joy Olive Kathleen Holt, Mr Robert Charles Jones, Mrs Iris June Ann Aylin, Reverend Andrew Bullock, Rev William Sands
Income: £1,767,650 [2017]; £1,771,342 [2016]; £1,622,429 [2015]; £1,562,969 [2014]; £1,507,019 [2013]

Yardley Great Trust

Registered: 18 Feb 1987 *Employees:* 65 *Volunteers:* 1
Tel: 0121 784 7889 *Website:* ygtrust.org.uk
Activities: The prevention or relief of poverty; accommodation, housing
Address: Yardley Great Trust, 31 Old Brookside, Birmingham, B33 8QL
Trustees: Mr Stewart Stacey, Mrs Joy Olive Kathleen Holt, Reverend Andrew Timothy Bullock, Mr Basharat Dad, Mr Andrew Veitch, Mrs Iris June Ann Aylin, Mr Robert Jones, Reverend John George Richards, Rev William Sands, Rev Lydia Gaston
Income: £2,681,027 [2017]; £2,799,477 [2016]; £2,265,414 [2015]; £2,312,178 [2014]; £2,329,531 [2013]

The Yarlet Trust

Registered: 18 May 1970 *Employees:* 34 *Volunteers:* 20
Tel: 01785 286568 *Website:* yarletschool.org
Activities: Education, training
Address: Yarlet School, Yarlet, Stafford, ST18 9SU
Trustees: Mrs A Fisher, Mr Steven Bane, Mrs Judy Anne Teather, Mrs Giulia Mitchell, Benson Greatrex, Mrs Sarah Ann Baker Tennant, Mr Peter Middleton, N D Tarling, Mrs Pauline Sharratt, Mr Paul Richard Vicars, Mrs Rachel Bullock, Mr Paul Teeton, Mr Keith Robins
Income: £1,370,787 [2016]; £1,263,512 [2015]; £1,269,714 [2014]; £1,171,216 [2013]; £1,206,650 [2012]

Yarlington Housing Group

Registered: 1 Apr 2005 *Employees:* 315
Tel: 01935 404534 *Website:* yhg.co.uk
Activities: Education, training; disability; prevention or relief of poverty; accommodation, housing
Address: Yarlington Housing Group, Lupin Way, Yeovil, Somerset, BA22 8WN
Trustees: Mr Wayne Morris, John Coutts, Mr Gary Orr, Mrs Joanna Makinson, Ms Lindy Morgan, Mr Ray Thompson, Mrs Caroline Moore, Mr Michael Stancombe
Income: £58,210,000 [2017]; £63,357,105 [2016]; £54,946,735 [2015]; £50,610,524 [2014]; £51,170,855 [2013]

Yarm School

Registered: 15 Aug 2002 *Employees:* 218 *Volunteers:* 5
Tel: 01642 786023 *Website:* yarmschool.org
Activities: Education, training
Address: Yarm School, The Friarage, Yarm, Cleveland, TS15 9EJ
Trustees: Mr Mark Thompson, Mrs Sarah Helen Anderson, Mrs Olufemi Omoyoola Ajekigbe BSc PGCE MEd NPQH, Mr Liam Dickinson Gamble, Dr Paul Michael Chapman, Mr Ian Frances Lovat, Mr Kevin Shotton, Mr Stephen Robert Davidson, Mr Alastair Provan Thomson, Mrs Ruth Margaret Langford, Mr Alexander Martin Turner, Mrs Elizabeth Lynn Longstaff, Dr Penelope Sarah Ann Jones
Income: £12,980,000 [2016]; £12,312,000 [2015]; £11,875,000 [2014]; £11,534,000 [2013]; £10,921,000 [2012]

Yateley Industries for The Disabled Limited

Registered: 14 Oct 1963 *Employees:* 106 *Volunteers:* 2
Tel: 07766 204086 *Website:* yateleyindustries.uk
Activities: Education, training; disability; accommodation, housing; economic, community development, employment
Address: 11 Robin's Meadow, Fareham, Hants, PO14 4JL
Trustees: Mr Frederick James England McCrindle OBE, Mrs Julie Clare Cable, Mr Michael Steel, Mrs Sejal Patel, Mr Roy O'Shaughnessy, Mrs Maria Thomas, Mr Nick Carey, Mr Stanley Alden
Income: £1,447,299 [2017]; £1,246,373 [2016]; £1,120,758 [2015]; £1,125,081 [2014]; £1,074,911 [2013]

Yateley Manor School Ltd

Registered: 11 Dec 1969 *Employees:* 88
Tel: 01252 405500 *Website:* yateleymanor.com
Activities: Education, training
Address: c/o Yateley Manor School, 51 Reading Road, Yateley, Hants, GU46 7UQ
Trustees: Mr Stephen Gorys, Mrs Tracy Squirrell, Mr Tom Li, Mrs Jacqueline Davies, Mrs Caroline Rosemary Good, Mr John Ashworth, Mr John Kirkpatrick, Mrs Elisabeth Noble
Income: £4,345,645 [2016]; £4,530,783 [2015]; £4,491,023 [2014]; £4,346,146 [2013]; £4,252,911 [2012]

Yavneh Foundation Trust

Registered: 4 Feb 2003
Tel: 020 8736 5580 *Website:* yavnehcollege.org
Activities: Education, training
Address: 74 Deacons Hill Road, Elstree, Borehamwood, Herts, WD6 3JG
Trustees: Mr Benjamin Eliezer Perl MBE, Mr Daniel Album, Rabbi Chaim Kanterovitz, Mrs S Nyman, Mr A Rubenstein
Income: £3,848,029 [2016]; £1,172,292 [2015]; £1,117,461 [2014]; £1,745,116 [2013]; £1,644,001 [2012]

Yehudi Menuhin School Limited
Registered: 14 Oct 1964 *Employees:* 39
Website: yehudimenuhinschool.co.uk
Activities: Education, training; arts, culture, heritage, science
Address: The Beeches, Beech Avenue, Effingham, Leatherhead, Surrey, KT24 5PJ
Trustees: Mr Oscar Lewisohn, Mr Richard Francis Maxwell Morris, Mr John Ellis Everett, Mrs Alice Mary Phillips MA, Ms Veronica Wadley, Mr John Clovis Pagella, Mr Geoffrey Richards, Mr Stuart Mitchell, Ms Anna Joseph, Mr Peter Willan, Lord Blackwell, Mr Jonathan Willcocks, Mr Andrew Hunter Johnston, Mr Jonathan Deakin, Dr John William Scadding, Ms Vanessa Richards, Mr Dominic Benthall
Income: £3,774,420 [2017]; £5,858,535 [2016]; £4,208,279 [2015]; £4,230,327 [2014]; £4,208,279 [2013]

Yeldall Christian Centres
Registered: 8 Aug 1990 *Employees:* 23 *Volunteers:* 5
Tel: 0118 940 1093 *Website:* yeldall.org.uk
Activities: Education, training; advancement of health or saving of lives; accommodation, housing; economic, community development, employment
Address: Yeldall Manor, Bear Lane, Hare Hatch, Reading, Berks, RG10 9XR
Trustees: Mr Roger Howard, Mr Ian Myerscough, Mr James Douglas Toyne Herring, Mr Alan Francis Beauchamp Tower, Mr Michael Phillips, Peter Emms, Ms Heidi Lynn Yoder, Mr Samy Fouad Guirguis Mansour, Mr Jeffrey Mark Whitton, Dr John Peter William Stone
Income: £1,098,754 [2017]; £1,070,479 [2016]; £1,019,515 [2015]; £736,191 [2014]; £788,143 [2013]

Yeovil District Hospital NHS Foundation Trust Charitable Fund
Registered: 14 Aug 1996 *Employees:* 2
Tel: 01935 475122 *Website:* yeovilhospital.nhs.uk
Activities: General charitable purposes; education, training; advancement of health or saving of lives
Address: NHS Foundation Trust, Yeovil District Hospital, Higher Kingston, Yeovil, Somerset, BA21 4AT
Trustees: Mrs Jane Henderson, Paul von der Heyde, Mrs Caroline Moore, Mr Martyn Scrivens, Mrs Shelagh Meldrum, Mr Simon Sethi, Mr Maurice Dunster, Mr Timothy Newman, Mr Graham Hughes, Mr Jonathan Higman, Mr Tim Scull
Income: £4,050,000 [2017]; £483,000 [2016]; £363,000 [2015]; £382,000 [2014]; £376,000 [2013]

Yesamach Levav
Registered: 10 Feb 2009 *Employees:* 5
Tel: 020 8800 8788 *Website:* yesamachlevav.com
Activities: Education, training; prevention or relief of poverty; religious activities
Address: 160 Holmleigh Road, London, N16 5PY
Trustees: Mr Mordechai Hersh Bindinger, Rabbi Nathan Benjamin Bindinger, Mr Reuben Spitzer
Income: £8,057,095 [2016]; £8,018,701 [2015]; £7,575,580 [2014]; £5,584,222 [2013]; £4,831,510 [2012]

Yesodey Hatorah Nursery
Registered: 6 Mar 1987 *Employees:* 97
Activities: Education, training
Address: 2-4 Amhurst Park, London, N16 5AE
Trustees: Mr Zalman Rabinowitz, Rabbi Chaim Pinter, Mr Sidney Sinitsky
Income: £1,076,048 [2016]; £801,844 [2015]; £732,850 [2014]; £673,778 [2013]

Yesodey Hatorah Primary Girls School Trust
Registered: 22 Nov 2006 *Employees:* 133
Tel: 020 8800 8612
Activities: Education, training; prevention or relief of poverty; religious activities
Address: 153 Stamford Hill, London, N16 5LG
Trustees: Mr Arieye Rand, Mr Kahn Aaron Solomon, Rabbi Chaim Pinter
Income: £1,680,566 [2016]; £1,381,256 [2015]; £1,254,859 [2014]; £963,048 [2013]; £871,244 [2012]

Yishaya Adler Memorial Fund
Registered: 25 Jul 2006 *Volunteers:* 1
Tel: 0191 420 2050
Activities: General charitable purposes; education, training; prevention or relief of poverty; accommodation, housing
Address: 172 Whitehall Road, Gateshead, Tyne & Wear, NE8 1TP
Trustees: Mrs Haddassah Adler, Mr Leo Prijs
Income: £1,646,793 [2017]; £1,422,053 [2016]; £1,406,736 [2015]; £1,236,786 [2014]; £999,159 [2013]

Ymddiriedolaeth Clough Williams-Ellis Foundation
Registered: 4 Mar 2016 *Employees:* 4
Tel: 01743 241181 *Website:* brondanw.org
Activities: General charitable purposes; education, training; environment, conservation, heritage
Address: Balfours, New Windsor House, Holsworth Park, Oxon Business Park, Bicton Heath, Shrewsbury, Salop, SY3 5HJ
Trustees: Mr Julian Clough Wallace, Miss Menna Angharad, Mr David Heneage Wynne Finch, Dr Rachel Carys Garden, Mr Dafydd Iwan, Mr Richard Merfyn Jones, Mr Gwilym Iwan Huws, Miss Seran Arianwen Dolma
Income: £18,446,246 [2017]

Ymddiriedolaeth Nant Gwrtheyrn
Registered: 10 Dec 1999 *Employees:* 25 *Volunteers:* 50
Tel: 01758 750334 *Website:* nantgwrtheyrn.org
Activities: Education, training; arts, culture, heritage, science; environment, conservation, heritage
Address: Canolfan Iaith A Threftadaeth Cymru, Llithfaen, Pwllheli, Gwynedd, LL53 6NL
Trustees: Mr Carl Iwan Clowes, Mr Gareth Jones OBE, Mr Jeffrey Williams-Jones, Phyl Brake, Miss Phyllis Mary Ellis, Mr Clive Wolfendale, Ms Gwenda Griffith, Mr Huw Jones
Income: £1,040,682 [2016]; £1,554,498 [2015]; £986,372 [2014]; £943,384 [2013]; £879,892 [2012]

Michael Yoakley's Charity
Registered: 22 Sep 1962 *Employees:* 55 *Volunteers:* 2
Tel: 01843 223652 *Website:* yoakleycare.co.uk
Activities: Accommodation, housing
Address: Yoakley House, Drapers Close, Margate, Kent, CT9 4AH
Trustees: Yoakley Care Trustee Ltd, Yoakley Care Share Ltd
Income: £1,194,901 [2016]; £1,154,799 [2015]; £1,128,680 [2014]; £1,110,915 [2013]; £1,079,524 [2012]

York Arc Light Limited
Registered: 7 Mar 2006 *Employees:* 34 *Volunteers:* 7
Tel: 0191 273 8891 *Website:* york-arclight.co.uk
Activities: The prevention or relief of poverty; accommodation, housing
Address: Changing Lives, Dukesway, Team Valley Trading Estate, Gateshead, Tyne & Wear, NE11 0LF
Trustees: Mr Dean Andrew Fielding, Ms Katrina Lawson, Mr Stephen Bell
Income: £1,171,804 [2017]; £1,168,561 [2016]; £1,082,186 [2015]; £1,086,235 [2014]; £994,499 [2013]

York Archaeological Trust for Excavation and Research Limited
Registered: 4 Sep 1982 *Employees:* 208 *Volunteers:* 300
Tel: 01904 663008 *Website:* yorkarchaeology.co.uk
Activities: Education, training; arts, culture, heritage, science; environment, conservation, heritage
Address: York Archaeological Trust, Cuthbert Morrell House, 47 Aldwark, York, YO1 7BX
Trustees: Professor Richard Morris, Professor Anthony William Robards, Mrs Helen Dobson, Professor Stephen Driscoll, Professor Ellen Roberts, Dr David Richard Joseph Neave, Mr Michael Richard Watson, Ms Susan Palmer, Ms Elizabeth Heaps, Mr Peter Wheatcroft
Income: £11,872,548 [2017]; £6,547,562 [2016]; £6,546,070 [2015]; £6,407,004 [2014]; £5,992,055 [2013]

York Childcare Ltd
Registered: 20 Feb 1992 *Employees:* 64
Tel: 01904 409763 *Website:* yorkchildcare.co.uk
Activities: Education, training; prevention or relief of poverty
Address: York Childcare Ltd, The Pavilion, Rawcliffe Lane, York, YO30 6NP
Trustees: Mr Christopher Jenkins, Mrs Suzanne Claire Lawson, Mrs Diane Turner, Ms Jo Armistead, Mr David Streather, Michael Douglas Richardson
Income: £1,112,109 [2017]; £986,998 [2016]; £952,622 [2015]; £1,005,552 [2014]; £976,330 [2013]

York Citizens' Theatre Trust Ltd
Registered: 28 Oct 1963 *Employees:* 125 *Volunteers:* 488
Tel: 01904 715464 *Website:* yorktheatreroyal.co.uk
Activities: Education, training; arts, culture, heritage, science
Address: York Theatre Royal, St Leonards Place, York, YO1 7HD
Trustees: Cllr Carol Runciman, Mr Richard Smith, Mr John Short, Mrs Ann Green, Mr Richard Jagger, Mr Avijit Datta, Mr Colin Parkin, Mrs Julie Rebbeck, Ms Tiggy Clifford, Ms Annette Barker, Mr Paul Smith, Ms Prema Mehta
Income: £4,978,086 [2017]; £4,503,635 [2016]; £4,274,333 [2015]; £4,515,836 [2014]; £3,901,235 [2013]

York Conservation Trust Limited
Registered: 20 Oct 1975 *Employees:* 4
Tel: 01904 651880 *Website:* yorkconservationtrust.org
Activities: Accommodation, housing; environment, conservation, heritage
Address: York Conservation Trust, 92 Micklegate, York, YO1 6JX
Trustees: Mr John Bowes Morrell, Mr Jeremy Spence Morrell, Professor Peter Spence Morrell, Miss Olivia Holden Morrell, Ms Vanessa Rachel Morrell Butler, Dr Ruth Isobel Morrell, Mr N C Morrell, Mrs Margaret Anne Morrell, Mr James Robert Morrell, Mrs Patricia Anne Butler, Dr Charles Hedley Esdon Butler
Income: £2,619,386 [2017]; £4,845,455 [2016]; £2,657,862 [2015]; £1,932,812 [2014]; £1,893,992 [2013]

The York Diocesan Board of Finance Limited
Registered: 8 Oct 1965 *Employees:* 256 *Volunteers:* 6
Tel: 01904 699500 *Website:* dioceseofyork.org.uk
Activities: Religious activities
Address: Diocese of York, Amy Johnson House, York, YO30 4XT
Trustees: Mrs Maureen Loffill, The Rt Rev Paul Ferguson, Dr Nick Land, Rev John Ford, Rev Matthew Porter, Rev Canon Dr Neal Duncan Barnes, Venerable Sarah Ruth Bullock, Venerable Samantha Jayne Rushton, Rev Timothy James Robinson, Miss Hilda Margaret Cowling, Mr Ben Hudson, Mr Charles Rodney Barton, The Very Reverend Vivienne Faull, Most Reverend John Tucker Mugabi Sentamu, Mrs Rosalind Brewer, Canon Richard Liversedge, Rev Fiona Ruth Mayer-Jones, Mr Daniel Brookes, The Rt Rev John Thomson, Ven Andrew Clifford Broom, Rt Rev Alison Mary White, Dr Neill Andrew Burgess, Mr Philip Priestley Ashton, Mr Michael Oswald Stallybrass
Income: £14,244,000 [2016]; £14,029,000 [2015]; £14,401,000 [2014]; £13,653,000 [2013]; £12,992,000 [2012]

York House School Trust Limited
Registered: 22 May 1963 *Employees:* 65 *Volunteers:* 17
Tel: 01923 772395 *Website:* york-house.com
Activities: Education, training
Address: York House School, Sarratt Road, Croxley Green, Rickmansworth, Herts, WD3 4LW
Trustees: Mr Patrick Atkinson, Dr Ken Young BSc (Hons) PhD, Mrs Julia Ginger MRPharmS, Mr Jimmy Scragg, Barry Porter, Mr Raj Khiroya, Mrs Leigh Keating BA (Hons) Law, Ms Helen Regan, Mrs Mary Ward
Income: £3,814,831 [2017]; £3,502,134 [2016]; £3,066,307 [2015]; £2,757,047 [2014]; £2,703,239 [2013]

York Methodist Circuit
Registered: 18 Feb 2010 *Employees:* 3 *Volunteers:* 40
Tel: 01904 499661 *Website:* yorkmethodist.org.uk
Activities: Religious activities
Address: Strensall Methodist Church, The Village, Strensall, York, YO32 5XS
Trustees: W Brian Taylor, Rev Keith Albans, Mr Timothy Bernard Duffy, Rev Elizabeth Jane Cushion, Rev Andrew John Lindley, Mrs Freda Mary Taylor, Mrs Elizabeth Ross Griffiths, Miss Geraldine Conn, Mr Graham Langton, Mrs Christine Stephenson, Malcolm Whinray, Mr John Ernest Lancaster, Mrs Jeanette Anne Free, Mrs Alison White, Miss Elisabeth Aida Jefferson, Mr Jonathan Morley, Mrs Susan Lindsay Gill, Mr Philip John Barber, Mrs Anne Hysted, Dr David George Thompson, Mr John Middleton, Mr Malcolm Parker, Mrs Rosamond Carter, Rev Rachel Muthoni, Mrs Joyce Jinks, Ms Jean Preston, Mr Peter John Metcalf, Mr Martyn Holman, Rev Ian Colin Hill, Mr Stephen Anthony John Leah, Mrs Rosemary Freeborn, Mr Robin Jackson, Mrs Dorothy Godfrey, Professor Edward Royle, Mrs Karen Jane Valentine, Mrs Kathryn Wright, Mrs Carole Smith, Rev Rory James Dalgliesh, Rev Julia Skitt, Peter Halls, Mr David Anderson, Mrs Sylvia Pauline Bunting, Mr John Morrison, Rev John Charles Schofield, Mrs Heather Rosemary Revett, Mr Vic Paylor, Mr Russ Smallwood, Deacon Judith Stoddart, Mr Michael Jinks, Mr Mark Bevan
Income: £1,328,321 [2017]; £1,626,714 [2016]; £1,069,750 [2015]; £791,480 [2014]; £3,205,399 [2013]

York Minster Fund
Registered: 18 Apr 1967 *Employees:* 3
Tel: 01904 623247 *Website:* yorkminster.org
Activities: Environment, conservation, heritage
Address: Church House, 10-14 Ogleforth, York, YO1 7JN
Trustees: York Minster Fund Ltd
Income: £1,261,583 [2016]; £998,625 [2015]; £1,264,776 [2014]; £1,661,326 [2013]; £1,582,881 [2012]

York Museum & Gallery Trust
Registered: 14 Jun 2002 *Employees:* 195 *Volunteers:* 410
Tel: 01904 687687 *Website:* yorkmuseumstrust.org.uk
Activities: Education, training; arts, culture, heritage, science; environment, conservation, heritage
Address: St Mary's Lodge, Marygate, York, YO30 7DR
Trustees: Professor Sir John Lawton, Mr Stephen Eric Lusty, Mr Philip Ashton, Mr Zulfi Hussain, Mrs Julia Bell, Mr David Andrews, Ms Mary Haworth, Ms Sita Brand, Cllr Ian Cuthbertson, Ms Angela Dean, Mr James Grierson, Mr Richard Jagger, Miss Sarah Drummond, Cllr Keith Myers, Ms Dianne Willcocks
Income: £7,386,224 [2017]; £7,374,136 [2016]; £11,375,116 [2015]; £7,685,635 [2014]; £6,805,530 [2013]

York RI
Registered: 10 Feb 2016 *Employees:* 27 *Volunteers:* 50
Website: yorkri.org.uk
Activities: Amateur sport; recreation
Address: 98 Malvern Avenue, York, YO26 5SG
Trustees: Mr Brian Smith, Mr John McCarthy, Mr Sean Heslop, Mr Hugh Brazier, Mr Samuel Stow, Mr David Chapman, Mr Peter Hope, Mr Christopher Smith, Mr Granville Miller
Income: £2,313,527 [2017]

York St John Students' Union
Registered: 15 Jul 2010 *Employees:* 20 *Volunteers:* 241
Tel: 01904 629816 *Website:* ysjsu.com
Activities: Education, training
Address: York St John University, Lord Mayors Walk, York, YO31 7EX
Trustees: Mr Michael Wilkinson, Lewis Bretts, Mr George Ronald Coombs, Miss Annie Victoria Severn, Mr William Fade, Amy Roberts, Richard Quayle, Miss Stephanie Cecilia Foxton, Mr Joseph Thomas Lynch
Income: £1,145,532 [2017]; £1,040,212 [2016]; £1,011,810 [2015]; £942,700 [2014]; £980,608 [2013]

York Teaching Hospital Charity
Registered: 11 Apr 1996
Tel: 01904 724138 *Website:* york.nhs.uk
Activities: General charitable purposes; advancement of health or saving of lives
Address: York Teaching Hospital NHS, Foundation Trust, Unit 1 Centurion Office Park, Tribune Way, York, YO30 4RY
Trustees: York Teaching Hospital NHS Foundation Trust
Income: £1,673,000 [2017]; £1,245,401 [2016]; £1,126,897 [2015]; £1,537,821 [2014]; £1,520,581 [2013]

Yorkshire Agricultural Society
Registered: 21 Dec 1982 *Employees:* 119 *Volunteers:* 300
Tel: 01423 541000 *Website:* yas.co.uk
Activities: General charitable purposes; education, training; environment, conservation, heritage
Address: Yorkshire Agricultural Society, Regional Agricultural Centre, Great Yorkshire Showground, Railway Road, Harrogate, N Yorks, HG2 8NZ
Trustees: Mr Charles David Forbes Adam, Mr Charles Edwin Mills, Mr Robert Copley, Mrs Christine Anne Thompson, Mr George Charles Nicholas Lane-Fox, Mr John Steven Andrew Crabtree, Paul Russell
Income: £10,940,093 [2017]; £9,627,474 [2016]; £9,018,519 [2015]; £9,085,827 [2014]; £8,810,315 [2013]

Yorkshire Air Ambulance Limited
Registered: 2 Jan 2001 *Employees:* 25 *Volunteers:* 201
Tel: 01422 237900 *Website:* yaa.org.uk
Activities: The advancement of health or saving of lives
Address: Yorkshire Air Ambulance, 10 South Lane, Elland, W Yorks, HX5 0HQ
Trustees: Mr Peter Sunderland, Mr Kevin Hynes, Mrs Sandra Marson, Mr Amarjit Singh, Mr Vivian John Lewis, Mr James Eastwood, Mr Brian Chapman, Mr Peter Howard Kerr Smith, Mrs Sarah Jane Moore, Mr John Samuel, Mrs Judith Alison Parker
Income: £8,251,041 [2017]; £8,173,685 [2016]; £7,423,900 [2015]; £6,470,390 [2014]; £5,197,815 [2013]

Yorkshire Cancer Research
Registered: 23 Oct 1985 *Employees:* 32 *Volunteers:* 450
Tel: 01423 877214 *Website:* ycr.org.uk
Activities: The advancement of health or saving of lives
Address: Yorkshire Cancer Research, 7 Grove Park Court, Harrogate, N Yorks, HG1 4DP
Trustees: Mrs Sandra Jane Dodson, Mr Alan Mark Sidebottom, Ms Catherine Rustomji, Mrs Janet Mary Myers, Dr Alan Suggett, Mr Graham Michael Berville, Mrs Margaret Kitching, Dr Yvette Alison Oade
Income: £20,891,423 [2017]; £6,818,405 [2016]; £17,778,107 [2015]; £5,139,520 [2014]; £4,199,978 [2013]

Yorkshire Coast Homes Limited
Registered: 20 Jul 2004 *Employees:* 256
Tel: 0345 065 5656 *Website:* ych.org.uk
Activities: Education, training; disability; prevention or relief of poverty; accommodation, housing; economic, community development, employment
Address: Yorkshire Coast Homes, Brook House, 4 Gladstone Road, Scarborough, N Yorks, YO12 7BH
Trustees: Jane Mortimer, Rosalyn Fox, Sharon Markham, Andy Gambles, James Hayward, Martyn Broadest, Bill Chatt, Graham Priestley, Judith Jones, Fay Yeomans, Andy Reynoldson
Income: £23,291,000 [2017]; £20,929,000 [2016]; £20,286,000 [2015]; £19,374,000 [2014]; £19,308,000 [2013]

The Yorkshire Dales Millennium Trust
Registered: 7 Apr 1997 *Employees:* 24 *Volunteers:* 81
Tel: 015242 51002 *Website:* ydmt.org
Activities: Education, training; environment, conservation, heritage; economic, community development, employment
Address: Yorkshire Dales Millennium Trust, Clapham, Lancaster, LA2 8DP
Trustees: Professor Christine Mary Leigh BA PhD, Mr Mark Cunliffe-Lister, His Honour Peter James Charlesworth, Mr Thomas Wheelwright, Mr David Shaw, Mrs Eileen Spencer, Miss Tracy Ann Louise Walker, Mr Carl Lis OBE, Mrs Jane Anne Roberts, Mr Stephen Macare, Mr Andrew Neville Campbell QC, Mrs Karen Cowley, Mrs Heather Lee McQue, Miss Eloise Brown
Income: £1,774,222 [2017]; £1,056,781 [2016]; £1,098,077 [2015]; £1,240,913 [2014]; £880,233 [2013]

Yorkshire Mesmac

Registered: 24 Aug 1994 *Employees:* 46 *Volunteers:* 135
Tel: 0113 244 4209 *Website:* mesmac.co.uk
Activities: Education, training; advancement of health or saving of lives; prevention or relief of poverty; economic, community development, employment
Address: Yorkshire Mesmac, 22-23 Blayds Yard, Leeds, LS1 4AD
Trustees: Mr Colin Lea, Mr Kenneth Leigh, Mr David William Eales, Mr Stephen William Hopker, Ms Penelope Jane Brown, Mr Eric Smith, Mr Andrew Howard Goodchild, Mr Stephen Craig Bridge, Mr Craig Jonathan Hassall, Ms Susan Pascoe
Income: £1,967,525 [2017]; £1,860,734 [2016]; £1,319,495 [2015]; £1,395,426 [2014]; £1,035,374 [2013]

Yorkshire Sculpture Park

Registered: 2 Feb 1998 *Employees:* 227 *Volunteers:* 110
Tel: 01924 832519 *Website:* ysp.co.uk
Activities: General charitable purposes; arts, culture, heritage, science; environment, conservation, heritage; economic, community development, employment
Address: Yorkshire Sculpture Park, Bretton Hall, Bretton, Wakefield, W Yorks, WF4 4LG
Trustees: Sir Rodney Walker, Mr Greville Worthington, Professor Peter Alexander Clegg, Mr Magnus von Wistinghausen, John Foster CBE, Mr Rupert Gerald Nunes Nabarro, Councillor Peter Box CBE, The Rt Hon Alan Milburn, Ms Maria De Peverelli Luschi, Ms Susan Wilkinson
Income: £7,033,772 [2017]; £7,852,825 [2016]; £6,049,798 [2015]; £5,698,235 [2014]; £5,651,298 [2013]

Yorkshire Sport Foundation

Registered: 2 Sep 2011 *Employees:* 42 *Volunteers:* 194
Tel: 0330 202 0280 *Website:* yorkshiresport.org
Activities: General charitable purposes; education, training; advancement of health or saving of lives; disability; amateur sport; recreation
Address: Nepshaw Lane South, Morley, Leeds, LS27 7JQ
Trustees: Anthony Rogers, Ms Linda Tully, Brian Richards, Ms Gwendolyn Smith, Mr Andrew Watson, Mr Paul William Reid, Ms Merran McRae
Income: £3,066,734 [2017]; £3,006,541 [2016]; £2,718,184 [2015]; £2,418,131 [2014]; £1,840,308 [2013]

Yorkshire Wildlife Trust

Registered: 16 Mar 1964 *Employees:* 117 *Volunteers:* 600
Tel: 01904 659570 *Website:* ywt.org.uk
Activities: Environment, conservation, heritage
Address: Yorkshire Wildlife Trust, 1 St Georges Place, York, YO24 1GN
Trustees: Dr David Counsell, Andrew Mendus, Mrs Christine Packer, Mr Richard Edward Tripp, Mr Mike Cooke, Mrs Joanne Webb, Mr Robert Missin, Mr Hugh Williamson, Mr Alastair Fitter, Ms Louise Farnell, Mr Paddy Hall, Mr Martin Randle, Mr Gurdev Singh, Professor John MacArthur, Miss Joanna Royle
Income: £5,775,413 [2017]; £5,353,763 [2016]; £5,869,853 [2015]; £5,724,598 [2014]; £5,032,960 [2013]

The You Trust

Registered: 10 Apr 1985 *Employees:* 264 *Volunteers:* 19
Tel: 01329 821911 *Website:* theyoutrust.org.uk
Activities: Education, training; advancement of health or saving of lives; disability; prevention or relief of poverty; accommodation, housing; economic, community development, employment; other charitable purposes
Address: You Trust, 43 High Street, Fareham, Hants, PO16 7BQ
Trustees: Mrs Tessa Ann Short, Mr James Fullarton, Ann Ridley, Graeme Quar, Ms Louise Randall, Mr Derek Stanley Marshall, Mr Christopher Jake Wynn, Mr Norman John Rowlinson, Mrs Penelope Ann Rowlinson, Steve Pitt, Miss Sara Rose Langston, Canon Nicholas Paul Fennemore, Mr Jonathan Hugh Crutchfield
Income: £9,254,000 [2017]; £8,153,000 [2016]; £7,951,000 [2015]; £8,311,000 [2014]; £11,129,000 [2013]

Young Devon

Registered: 10 Sep 1996 *Employees:* 137 *Volunteers:* 104
Tel: 01752 691511 *Website:* youngdevon.org
Activities: Education, training; accommodation, housing; other charitable purposes
Address: Young Devon, 10 Erme Road, Ivybridge, Devon, PL21 0AB
Trustees: Mrs Dianne Alice Conduit, Ms Philippa Knott, Dr Poppy Elizabeth Harrison, Mrs Alison Bernadette Hannaford, Mr Roscoe Hastings, Mr Ross Martin Johnston, Mr Steve Warren-Brown, Mr Christopher Vincent Coward
Income: £3,258,204 [2017]; £2,937,164 [2016]; £2,976,052 [2015]; £2,878,855 [2014]; £4,472,617 [2013]

Young Enterprise

Registered: 1 May 1962 *Employees:* 148 *Volunteers:* 5,317
Tel: 020 7549 1980 *Website:* young-enterprise.org.uk
Activities: Education, training; economic, community development, employment
Address: Mrs Liz Crossley, Yeoman House, Sekforde Street, London, EC1R 0HF
Trustees: Mr Grey Denham, Mr Jaswinder Rayet, Mr Alan Williams, Ms Elizabeth Kitcatt, Mr Johaan Leslie Roy Wiggins, Mrs Judith Felton, Mr David Walter, Ms Helen Mary Nixseaman, Miss Alicia Navarro
Income: £6,566,101 [2017]; £6,762,000 [2016]; £9,361,000 [2015]; £6,304,000 [2014]; £6,404,000 [2013]

The Young Foundation

Registered: 11 Nov 1977 *Employees:* 34 *Volunteers:* 200
Tel: 020 8980 6263 *Website:* youngfoundation.org
Activities: General charitable purposes; education, training; advancement of health or saving of lives; prevention or relief of poverty; economic, community development, employment; human rights, religious or racial harmony, equality or diversity; other charitable purposes
Address: The Young Foundation, 18 Victoria Park Square, London, E2 9PF
Trustees: Mr Pete Gladwell, Dame Julie Mellor, Ms Vidhya Alakeson, Mrs Abigail Rotheroe, Mr Gareth Williams, Prof Michael Antony Savage
Income: £5,318,446 [2016]; £3,811,856 [2015]; £3,558,442 [2014]; £2,741,752 [2013]; £5,104,978 [2012]

Young Gloucestershire

Registered: 27 Mar 1981 *Employees:* 33 *Volunteers:* 60
Tel: 01452 501008 *Website:* youngglos.org.uk
Activities: General charitable purposes; education, training; prevention or relief of poverty
Address: Greyfriars House, Greyfriars, Gloucester, GL1 1TS
Trustees: Mr Hugh Gladman, Robin Bevan, Mr Martin Moule, Mr John Reilly, Mark Sheridan, Mrs Camille Stallard
Income: £1,049,875 [2017]; £1,067,301 [2016]; £1,040,186 [2015]; £1,122,615 [2014]; £1,420,081 [2013]

Young Life International

Registered: 11 Feb 2002 *Employees:* 32 *Volunteers:* 313
Tel: 07803 505221 *Website:* ylinternational.org
Activities: Religious activities
Address: Kestin House, 45 Crescent Road, Luton, Beds, LU2 0AH
Trustees: Mr Paul Sherrill, Mr Kevin Smith, Mr Chad Edwards, Sundeep Salins, Mr Liam McCormick
Income: £1,265,152 [2017]; £1,410,381 [2016]; £1,175,751 [2015]; £741,525 [2014]; £621,692 [2013]

Young Minds Trust

Registered: 2 Feb 1993 *Employees:* 71 *Volunteers:* 107
Tel: 020 7089 5063 *Website:* youngminds.org.uk
Activities: Education, training; advancement of health or saving of lives
Address: Youngminds, Suite 11 Baden Place, Crosby Row, London, SE1 1YW
Trustees: Dame Elizabeth Mary Vallance, Ms Jennifer Ann Clayton, Mr Robert Leslie William Mack, Ms Julie Dodd, Ms Meryl Davies, Mr Peter Lewis Jenkins, Ms Rebecca Mary Baird, Mr Simon Charles Major, Ms Caroline Hope
Income: £2,911,389 [2017]; £2,418,458 [2016]; £2,197,561 [2015]; £2,459,008 [2014]; £3,371,173 [2013]

Young Persons Advisory Service

Registered: 26 Apr 1991 *Employees:* 53 *Volunteers:* 4
Tel: 0151 707 1025 *Website:* ypas.org.uk
Activities: General charitable purposes; education, training; prevention or relief of poverty
Address: Young Persons Advisory Service, 36 Bolton Street, Liverpool, L3 5LX
Trustees: Ms Helen Fessey, Ms Alison Jane Herdman, Miss Nicole Konigs Balfry, Mr Jake Mills, Mr Andrew Kerr, Mrs Ann Brigid Jones, Ms Anna Mary O'Hare
Income: £2,204,307 [2017]; £1,560,274 [2016]; £898,333 [2015]; £655,302 [2014]; £462,341 [2013]

The Young Vic Company

Registered: 20 Feb 1975 *Employees:* 56
Tel: 020 7922 2800 *Website:* youngvic.org
Activities: Education, training; arts, culture, heritage, science
Address: 66 The Cut, London, SE1 8LZ
Trustees: Mr Ivan Lewis, Mr Sean Egan, Mr Rory Kinnear, Mr Steve Tompkins, Ms Nicola Ann Dunn, Ms Anna Elizabeth Williams, Ali Hossaini, Mr Patrick Anthony McKenna, David Fletcher, Miss Anna Lane, Mrs Rita Skinner, Ms Fiona Mary Shaw, Dr Robert James Campbell Easton, Kwame Kwei-Armah
Income: £7,191,675 [2017]; £7,432,926 [2016]; £7,627,559 [2015]; £7,544,585 [2014]; £5,950,593 [2013]

Youth Aliyah - Child Rescue

Registered: 23 Oct 1999 *Employees:* 4 *Volunteers:* 4
Tel: 020 8371 1580 *Website:* youthaliyah.org.uk
Activities: Education, training; overseas aid, famine relief
Address: Trojan House, 34 Arcadia Avenue, London, N3 2JU
Trustees: Mr Melvin Robinson, Mr Daniel Jeremy Polden, Mr Grahame David Roth, Mrs Lorraine Robinson, Mr Aron Joseph Taylor, Mr Anton David Curtis, Mr Steven Strauss, Mrs Bettina Curtis, Mrs Anna Joy Shields
Income: £1,421,772 [2017]; £1,571,537 [2016]; £1,110,921 [2015]; £1,897,371 [2014]; £1,385,147 [2013]

Youth Business International

Registered: 1 May 2008 *Employees:* 30 *Volunteers:* 5
Tel: 020 3326 2060 *Website:* youthbusiness.org
Activities: Education, training; prevention or relief of poverty; economic, community development, employment
Address: 11 Belgrave Road, London, SW1V 1RB
Trustees: Sir George Malcolm Williamson, Mr Fadi Sarkis, Ms Ramanie Kunanayagam, Mr Timothy Copnell, Mr John Downie, Mr Crispin William Rapinet, Ms Jeannie Helen Arthur
Income: £4,498,023 [2016]; £6,347,104 [2015]; £5,103,363 [2014]; £3,644,074 [2013]; £3,429,598 [2012]

Youth Enquiry Service (Plymouth) Limited

Registered: 4 Jan 1996 *Employees:* 55 *Volunteers:* 46
Tel: 01752 206626 *Website:* thezoneplymouth.co.uk
Activities: Education, training; advancement of health or saving of lives; prevention or relief of poverty; accommodation, housing; environment, conservation, heritage
Address: 14-16 Union Street, Plymouth, PL1 2SR
Trustees: Mr Shaun Patrick Walbridge FCCA, Mr David Page Davies, Mr Stuart Higgs, Ms Stephanie Kenyon, Mrs Sarah Jane Davey
Income: £1,192,216 [2017]; £1,107,154 [2016]; £1,051,577 [2015]; £1,461,018 [2014]; £1,348,507 [2013]

Youth Federation Limited

Registered: 3 Aug 2011 *Employees:* 85 *Volunteers:* 50
Tel: 0151 356 1971 *Website:* youthfed.org.uk
Activities: General charitable purposes; education, training; environment, conservation, heritage; economic, community development, employment; recreation; other charitable purposes
Address: 20 Rossmore Business Village, Inward Way, Ellesmere Port, Cheshire, CH65 3EY
Trustees: Alastair Stoddart, James Bisset, Jacqui Sinnott-Lacey, Glyn Carter, Mr Peter Bibby, Mrs Amanda Jean Kiddle
Income: £2,246,072 [2017]; £2,075,243 [2016]; £2,078,079 [2015]; £1,800,149 [2014]; £1,044,283 [2013]

Youth Music Theatre UK

Registered: 6 Apr 2004 *Employees:* 6 *Volunteers:* 6
Tel: 020 8241 4922 *Website:* youthmusictheatreuk.org
Activities: Education, training; arts, culture, heritage, science
Address: 26 Orme Road, Kingston upon Thames, Surrey, KT1 3SA
Trustees: Mr Alastair Roberts, Mrs Laura Jeanne Palmer, Mr Jonathan Church, Mr Philip Matthew Siddle, Mr James Jewell, Ms Olenka Drapan, Mr Anthony Fisher, Mr Royce Bell, Ms Sara Bingham, Miss Fern Stoner, Mr David Warburton MP
Income: £1,229,295 [2017]; £1,180,863 [2016]; £945,746 [2015]; £1,372,074 [2014]; £783,714 [2013]

Youth Options

Registered: 27 Jun 1996 *Employees:* 47 *Volunteers:* 30
Tel: 01794 525510 *Website:* youthoptions.co.uk
Activities: Education, training; recreation
Address: 2 Eastwood Court, Broadwater Road, Romsey, Hants, SO51 8JJ
Trustees: Ms Caroline Horrill, Mrs Lucy Varcoe, Mr James Spencer John Fillingham, Mrs Natalie Lumby, Mr Richard Coleman, Mr Peter Edwin Davidson, Charles David Blackmore, Dr Martyn David Diaper MBBS MRCGP MBA
Income: £1,536,272 [2017]; £1,358,514 [2016]; £1,290,228 [2015]; £2,003,233 [2014]; £1,256,278 [2013]

Youth Sport Trust

Registered: 5 Jun 2001 *Employees:* 99
Tel: 01509 226657 *Website:* youthsporttrust.org
Activities: Education, training; disability; amateur sport
Address: Youth Sport Trust, 3 Oakwood Drive, Loughborough, Leics, LE11 3QF
Trustees: Denise Gladwell, Mr Timothy Philip Hollingsworth, Dr Katherine Jane Grainger, Billy Downie, Mr Richard Colin Neil Davidson, Mrs Belinda Richards, Sally Munday, Mrs Melanie Beth Honnor, Mr Ben Stimson, Dr Paula Catherine Heather Franklin, Mr Adrian Malcolm Simpson, Mr David John Gilbey
Income: £13,694,041 [2017]; £18,389,947 [2016]; £19,290,200 [2015]; £17,948,997 [2014]; £15,175,729 [2013]

The Youth Sport UK Charitable Trust

Registered: 22 Aug 1994 *Employees:* 23
Tel: 01509 226661
Activities: Education, training; disability; amateur sport
Address: Loughborough University, Loughborough, Leics, LE11 3TU
Trustees: Sir John Beckwith CBE, Mr Geoffrey Rees CBE MA, Mr Duncan Goodhew, Viscount Mackintosh of Halifax, Debbie Lye, Sally Holder
Income: £1,705,048 [2017]; £2,441,206 [2016]; £3,139,360 [2015]; £2,845,575 [2014]; £3,137,202 [2013]

Youth with a Mission Limited

Registered: 16 May 1972
Tel: 01582 463210 *Website:* ywamengland.org
Activities: Education, training; religious activities
Address: Highfield Oval, Harpenden, Herts, AL5 4BX
Trustees: Mr Dale Lambert, Lynn Green, Mr Mark Anthony Simon Vening, Mr Carl Tinnion, Mrs Edwina Clare Waddell, Mr Stephen Charles Mayers, Mr Henry Benwell Clarke, Peter Irwin-Clark, Ms Jemimah Wright
Income: £2,274,507 [2016]; £3,008,066 [2015]; £3,367,932 [2014]; £2,300,235 [2013]; £3,170,745 [2012]

YouthNet UK

Registered: 4 Sep 1995 *Employees:* 38 *Volunteers:* 180
Tel: 020 7009 2500 *Website:* themix.org.uk
Activities: General charitable purposes; education, training; other charitable purposes
Address: The Mix, 30 Binney Street, London, W1K 5BW
Trustees: Henny Braund, Lorraine Harper, Mr Edward Wray, Gearoid Lane, Jessica Burley, Mr James Scroggs, Mr Luke Taylor, Mr Christian Jennings, Mr Andrew Harrison, Mr Rakesh Shah
Income: £2,759,395 [2017]; £1,857,585 [2016]; £1,750,868 [2015]; £2,188,934 [2014]; £2,675,789 [2013]

Youthscape

Registered: 27 Jul 2000 *Employees:* 18 *Volunteers:* 42
Tel: 01582 877220 *Website:* youthscape.co.uk
Activities: Education, training; religious activities; other charitable purposes
Address: Youthscape, 74 Bute Street, Luton, Beds, LU1 2EY
Trustees: Mr Andrew Edward Beale MHCIMA FRGS, Rev John Good BTh, Dr Nenadi Adamu, Christine Boyd, Rev Andrew Neil Gardner
Income: £1,021,042 [2017]; £1,145,202 [2016]; £2,437,130 [2015]; £1,803,215 [2014]; £684,205 [2013]

Yusuf Islam Foundation

Registered: 25 Feb 2010 *Employees:* 61
Tel: 020 7372 2171 *Website:* yif.org.uk
Activities: General charitable purposes; education, training; prevention or relief of poverty; religious activities; arts, culture, heritage, science; economic, community development, employment; other charitable purposes
Address: The Yusuf Islam Foundation, 131b Salusbury Road, London, NW6 6RG
Trustees: Dr Abdulkarim Khalil, Mr Muhammad Adamos, Mrs Fawziah Islam, Mr Shabir Randeree
Income: £2,983,601 [2017]; £9,336,072 [2016]; £3,072,666 [2015]; £15,451,660 [2014]; £2,436,791 [2013]

ZANE: Zimbabwe A National Emergency

Registered: 7 Feb 2006 *Volunteers:* 1
Tel: 020 7060 6643 *Website:* zane.uk.com
Activities: The advancement of health or saving of lives; disability; prevention or relief of poverty; overseas aid, famine relief
Address: P O Box 451, Witney, Oxon, OX28 9FY
Trustees: Mrs Clare Hayns, Mr Christopher Compston, Mr John Broadley, Prof Richard Ekins, Mrs Georgina Ann Knaggs, Mrs Olivia Jane Benyon, Mr Mark Harris, Mrs Nicola Mary Gayner, Mr Robert Richardson, Mrs Judith Mellor
Income: £2,418,587 [2017]; £2,084,694 [2016]; £1,717,790 [2015]; £1,962,041 [2014]; £1,662,060 [2013]

Zabludowicz Art Projects

Registered: 12 Jul 2007 *Employees:* 22
Tel: 020 7629 6636 *Website:* zabludowiczcollection.com
Activities: Arts, culture, heritage, science
Address: Tamares R E Investments (UK) Ltd, 41 Dover Street, London, W1S 4NS
Trustees: Mrs Anita Zabludowicz, Mr David Halpern FCA, Mr Chaim (Aka Poju) Zabludowicz, Dr Fabio Botterini De Pelosi
Income: £1,208,458 [2016]; £1,312,558 [2015]; £1,067,535 [2014]; £783,244 [2013]; £772,468 [2012]

Zetetick Housing

Registered: 24 Apr 2007 *Employees:* 8
Tel: 01424 858312 *Website:* zetetickhousing.org.uk
Activities: Disability; accommodation, housing; amateur sport
Address: Zetetick Housing Ltd, Innovation Centre, Highfield Drive, St Leonards on Sea, E Sussex, TN38 9UH
Trustees: Mr Ray Wilkinson, Mr Leonard Melvin Stevens, Mr Roger Lomax, Mr Gary Malcolm Scott, Mr Stuart Cakebread, Miss Delia Bedis
Income: £3,467,565 [2017]; £3,422,920 [2016]; £3,326,577 [2015]; £3,148,516 [2014]; £2,905,996 [2013]

Zichron Meir Limited
Registered: 24 Jun 2004
Tel: 020 8802 7211
Activities: Education, training; prevention or relief of poverty; religious activities
Address: 26 Leweston Place, London, N16 6RH
Trustees: Mr Marcus Landau
Income: £1,683,137 [2017]; £1,511,530 [2016]; £479,183 [2015]; £594,161 [2014]; £204,542 [2013]

The Zochonis Charitable Trust
Registered: 27 Jan 1978 *Employees:* 1
Tel: 0161 435 1005
Activities: General charitable purposes
Address: The Zochonis Charitable Trust, Manchester Business Park, 3500 Aviator Way, Manchester, M22 5TG
Trustees: Archibald Graham Calder, Mr Paul Milner, Mr Christopher Nigel Green
Income: £4,929,423 [2017]; £4,500,621 [2016]; £4,399,604 [2015]; £4,382,459 [2014]; £3,423,444 [2013]

Zoe's Place Trust
Registered: 20 Jun 2002 *Employees:* 120 *Volunteers:* 75
Tel: 01926 889633 *Website:* zoes-place.org.uk
Activities: The advancement of health or saving of lives; disability
Address: Zoe's Place Trust, 15 Dormer Place, Leamington Spa, Warwicks, CV32 5AA
Trustees: John J Scarisbrick, Mrs Joan Stainsby, Mr Christopher Greenall, Peter McGuire, Professor Sunil Sinha
Income: £3,945,170 [2017]; £3,606,898 [2016]; £3,606,898 [2015]; £3,375,624 [2014]; £2,719,259 [2013]

The Zoological Society of East Anglia Limited
Registered: 13 Dec 2012 *Employees:* 215 *Volunteers:* 120
Tel: 01953 715308 *Website:* banhamzoo.co.uk
Activities: Education, training; arts, culture, heritage, science; animals; environment, conservation, heritage
Address: Wash Farm, Wash Lane, Banham, Norwich, NR16 2HD
Trustees: Mr T W Stevenson, Mr Michael Owen Brown, Miss Wendy Fenwick, Dr Andrew Hassan, Mr Frederic Edouard Barrelet, Mr Jonathan Charles Pearson, Mr Gerard Smith, Mr Jonathan James Goodson
Income: £6,059,983 [2016]; £5,772,158 [2015]; £5,535,388 [2014]; £4,885,706 [2013]

The Zoological Society of London
Registered: 8 Apr 1963 *Employees:* 906 *Volunteers:* 530
Tel: 020 7449 6207 *Website:* zsl.org
Activities: Education, training; animals; environment, conservation, heritage
Address: Zoological Society of London, Regent's Park, London, NW1 4RY
Trustees: Mr Paul Johannes Rutteman CBE BSc (Econ), Mr Ray Heaton, Dr Brian Bertram MA PhD FIBiol, Dr Anna Meredith MA VetMB CertLAS DZooMed MRCVS, Mr Andrew Kitchener, Sir John Beddington CMG FRS, Ms Shiela Anderson MBE BSc, Ms Victoria Wilson, Martin Rowson, Ms Elizabeth Passey, Professor Geoff Boxshall Professor, Mr Sean Rovai, Mr Robert Wingate, Ken Sims, Mr Paul Wilson
Income: £85,609,000 [2017]; £55,550,000 [2015]; £55,202,000 [2014]; £52,076,407 [2013]; £44,630,148 [2012]

The Zurbaran Trust
Registered: 16 Mar 2012
Tel: 01388 743750 *Website:* aucklandcastle.org
Activities: General charitable purposes; education, training; prevention or relief of poverty; arts, culture, heritage, science; environment, conservation, heritage; economic, community development, employment
Address: Auckland Castle, Market Place, Bishop Auckland, Co Durham, DL14 7NR
Trustees: Mr Jonathan Garnier Ruffer, Dr Jane Mary Ruffer, Dr Jose Luis Colomer, Dr Lindsay Stainton, Anthony Mould, Sir Stephen Wright
Income: £3,864,912 [2017]; £4,752,755 [2016]; £1,126,801 [2015]; £1,019,355 [2014]; £9,121,161 [2013]

Zurich Community Trust (UK) Limited
Registered: 7 Mar 1974 *Employees:* 24 *Volunteers:* 3,620
Tel: 01793 502450 *Website:* zct.org.uk
Activities: General charitable purposes
Address: Zurich Community Trust (UK) Ltd, P O Box 1288, Swindon, Wilts, SN1 1FL
Trustees: Mr Ian Lovett, Mr Vinicio Cellerini, Mrs Anne Torry, Mr Conor Brennan, Mr Richard Peden, Mr Tim Culling, Mr Wayne Myslik, Mr Andrew Jepp, Mrs Tulsi Naidu
Income: £3,855,000 [2016]; £4,025,000 [2015]; £3,753,000 [2014]; £3,697,000 [2013]; £2,833,000 [2012]

Income League Table

The British Council	£1,076,893,479	Walsall Housing Group Limited	£105,561,860
Lloyd's Register Foundation	£908,172,000	The United Church Schools Trust	£105,284,000
Save The Children International	£905,509,004	Royal Shakespeare Company, Stratford-upon-Avon	£105,137,000
Nuffield Health	£839,600,000	Charity Projects	£104,718,000
The Arts Council of England	£724,215,000	The Royal National Theatre	£104,700,000
Cancer Research UK	£679,281,449	Alzheimer's Society	£103,596,000
The Charities Aid Foundation	£604,747,000	The English Heritage Trust	£102,995,000
The National Trust for Places of Historic Interest	£591,742,000	The United Kingdom Committee for Unicef	£102,837,000
Cardiff University	£505,123,000	The Priory of England and The Islands	£102,500,000
Wellcome Trust	£425,285,020	Consumers' Association	£101,147,000
The Children's Investment Fund Foundation (UK)	£412,318,816	The Grace Trust	£100,723,956
Oxfam	£408,600,000	The Valeria Sykes Charitable Foundation CIO	£100,000,087
The Save The Children Fund	£404,525,000	Cardiff Metropolitan University	£99,871,000
United Church Schools Foundation Ltd	£387,890,000	Methodist Independent Schools Trust	£99,557,000
Anchor Trust	£329,387,000	The Leverhulme Trust	£99,383,000
Barnardo's	£312,847,000	National Association of Citizens Advice Bureaux	£99,110,000
CITB	£310,570,000	Sue Ryder	£98,865,000
British Heart Foundation	£310,500,000	Scope	£97,849,000
Royal Commonwealth Society for the Blind	£302,017,000	The National Autistic Society	£97,290,000
Marie Stopes International	£289,962,000	Christian Aid	£97,030,000
Swansea University	£278,024,000	International Planned Parenthood Federation	£95,875,735
The Girls' Day School Trust	£260,919,000	The British Film Institute	£95,724,000
The British Red Cross Society	£251,700,000	World Vision UK	£95,372,000
Macmillan Cancer Support	£247,441,000	The People's Dispensary for Sick Animals	£94,213,002
Oasis Charitable Trust	£210,393,000	United Response	£93,703,000
The Salvation Army	£209,659,000	Care International UK	£93,414,000
Methodist Homes	£207,089,000	Great Ormond Street Hospital Children's Charity	£93,290,056
St Andrew's Healthcare	£205,600,000	Historic Royal Palaces	£91,497,000
The Steve Morgan Foundation	£204,257,541	Watch Tower Bible and Tract Society of Britain	£89,598,492
Canal & River Trust	£202,900,000	Sense, The National Deafblind & Rubella Association	£88,206,108
Caryl Jenner Productions Limited	£200,694,484	St Mungo Community Housing Association	£86,536,000
The Royal National Lifeboat Institution	£197,690,779	Nursing and Midwifery Council	£86,155,000
Royal Mencap Society	£191,941,000	Fusion Lifestyle	£85,927,000
University of South Wales/Prifysgol de Cymru	£184,168,000	The Zoological Society of London	£85,609,000
The Salvation Army Social Work Trust	£177,037,000	The Archbishops' Council	£85,077,000
The Woodard Corporation	£173,932,000	The Royal Society	£83,920,435
AQA Education	£169,091,000	The Extracare Charitable Trust	£82,624,000
Church Commissioners for England	£167,327,468	The Royal Horticultural Society	£82,462,948
Leonard Cheshire Disability	£161,339,000	Wateraid	£81,077,000
The Francis Crick Institute Limited	£160,609,000	Addaction	£78,857,000
Action for Children	£159,830,000	Voluntary Service Overseas	£78,430,000
Marie Curie	£159,122,000	HF Trust Limited	£78,257,000
Change, Grow, Live	£155,970,000	Trinity College Cambridge	£74,915,000
The Royal British Legion	£151,256,000	Eton College	£73,378,000
Age UK	£149,697,000	New Charter Homes Limited	£72,808,000
RSPCA	£143,541,000	Tearfund	£72,768,000
Bangor University	£143,380,000	Stewardship Services (UKET) Limited	£71,922,000
International Rescue Committee, U.K	£142,618,000	The Wrekin Housing Trust Limited	£71,442,000
Royal Opera House Covent Garden Foundation	£141,026,000	The Prince's Trust	£70,894,000
The City and Guilds of London Institute	£137,371,289	The Gatsby Charitable Foundation	£69,941,000
Trustees of The London Clinic Limited	£136,341,000	Helena Partnerships Limited	£68,689,000
Genome Research Limited	£135,336,000	The Football Foundation	£68,399,000
Canterbury Christ Church University	£135,054,000	Southbank Centre	£68,081,000
Royal Society for The Protection of Birds	£134,179,000	Education Development Trust	£68,020,000
Jisc	£132,967,000	BBC Children in Need	£67,718,000
The Shaw Trust Limited	£132,107,000	The Institute of Physics	£67,448,000
George Peabody Donation Fund	£131,254,000	Masonic Charitable Foundation	£67,008,000
Turning Point	£131,035,000	Elim Foursquare Gospel Alliance	£66,291,442
LifeArc	£128,967,000	Society of Jesus Trust of 1929	£66,058,000
NSPCC	£127,407,530	Garfield Weston Foundation	£65,939,000
Prifysgol Aberystwyth	£126,264,000	The Challenge Network	£65,792,000
International Medical Corps (UK)	£123,658,942	Knowsley Housing Trust	£65,620,000
University of Chester	£121,266,000	Wythenshawe Community Housing Group Limited	£65,461,000
University of Wales:Trinity Saint David	£119,340,000	Cross Keys Homes Limited	£65,434,000
The Royal National Institute of Blind People	£119,199,000	Wirral Partnership Homes Limited	£65,327,000
The Orders of St John Care Trust	£116,156,620	Southampton Row Trust Limited	£64,715,000
Community Integrated Care	£114,909,000	Thera Trust	£64,591,798
Liverpool School of Tropical Medicine	£111,496,000	Royal Voluntary Service	£64,453,000
Islamic Relief Worldwide	£110,395,914	Plan International UK	£64,262,000
The Guide Dogs for the Blind Association	£107,000,000	Chelmer Housing Partnership Limited	£62,627,000
General Medical Council	£106,958,176	The Royal Collection Trust	£61,995,000
Dogs Trust	£106,446,000	Lifeline Project	£61,812,600

The Whitgift Foundation	£61,334,861	Harper Adams University	£42,685,000
Teach First	£61,011,000	The Helping Foundation	£42,499,341
Shelter The National Campaign for Homeless People	£60,902,000	Sheffield City Trust	£42,344,029
WWF - UK	£60,795,000	Royal Institute of British Architects	£42,306,000
ActionAid	£60,406,000	New Linx Housing Trust	£42,061,000
Transforming Education in Norfolk	£59,757,000	The North of England Zoological Society	£42,052,000
John Lyon's Charity	£59,571,000	Charities Trust	£42,043,807
Alternative Futures Group Limited	£59,157,000	Church of England Children's Society	£41,614,000
The Institution of Engineering and Technology	£58,453,000	United Synagogue	£41,478,000
Royal College of Obstetricians and Gynaecologists	£58,302,226	WJEC CBAC Limited	£41,363,948
Yarlington Housing Group	£58,210,000	Mind (The National Association for Mental Health)	£41,329,000
The Wellington College	£57,450,000	Battersea Dogs' and Cats' Home	£41,323,547
SS. John and Elizabeth Charity	£57,448,000	The Overseas Development Institute	£41,320,000
The Kentown Wizard Foundation	£57,191,953	St Paul's School	£41,077,000
The Disabilities Trust	£57,093,000	Care South	£41,022,000
The Salvation Army International Trust	£56,441,000	The HALO Trust	£40,903,000
Jewish Care	£56,089,000	The Babraham Institute	£40,901,000
The Stone Family Foundation	£55,927,129	The Royal College of Physicians of London	£40,711,000
Westminster Roman Catholic Diocesan Trust	£55,894,000	John Innes Centre	£40,506,163
The Royal Society of Chemistry	£55,689,000	Willow Park Housing Trust Limited	£40,439,000
Cats Protection	£55,546,000	The Royal National Institute for Deaf People	£40,293,000
Malaria Consortium	£55,031,000	The London Diocesan Fund	£40,100,000
The Abbeyfield Society	£54,653,000	Chartered Institute of Personnel and Development	£40,042,000
Trafford Housing Trust Limited	£54,214,991	Compassion UK Christian Child Development	£39,944,000
Medecins Sans Frontieres (UK)	£54,118,000	The Sequoia Trust	£39,894,497
Disasters Emergency Committee	£54,053,000	Christ's Hospital Foundation	£39,768,000
Motability	£53,325,000	Heritage Care Limited	£39,693,000
Marlborough College	£53,192,000	The British Academy	£39,539,475
The Harpur Trust	£52,794,000	Golden Gates Housing Trust	£39,520,000
St Mary's University, Twickenham	£52,328,415	Virunga Foundation	£39,202,087
The Soldiers, Sailors, Airmen & Families Association	£51,808,000	Garden Bridge Trust	£39,196,316
Anthony Nolan	£51,335,000	The Richmond Fellowship	£39,101,000
Liverpool Hope University	£51,307,062	The Church of Jesus Christ of Latter-Day Saints	£39,072,000
The Brandon Trust	£50,669,790	The London Diocesan Board for Schools	£39,019,000
Livability	£50,334,000	The Corporation of Oundle School	£38,648,000
YHA (England and Wales)	£50,316,000	RNIB Charity	£38,644,000
Catholic Agency for Overseas Development	£50,115,000	The British Computer Society	£38,586,000
HCT Group	£49,904,932	Keble College in the University of Oxford	£38,352,000
Cyngor Celfyddydau Cymru	£49,864,000	The Donkey Sanctuary	£38,343,000
The Royal Academy of Arts	£49,716,124	Royal Hospital for Neuro-Disability	£38,287,000
The Woodland Trust	£49,587,000	St John's College Cambridge	£38,262,000
Foundation for Credit Counselling	£49,487,000	Bromsgrove School	£37,860,642
The Fremantle Trust	£49,440,000	The Rothschild Foundation	£37,775,210
Millfield	£49,278,000	Eastlands Homes Partnership Limited	£37,625,000
Associated Board of The Royal Schools of Music	£49,168,000	Stroke Association	£37,322,000
English National Opera	£49,061,000	Congregation of The Daughters of Cross of Liege	£37,289,000
Trinity College London	£48,752,000	The Kennedy Trust for Rheumatology Research	£37,282,000
Sustrans Limited	£48,644,000	The Universities and Colleges Admissions Service	£37,139,705
Brighton College	£47,944,392	Selwood Housing Society Limited	£37,111,000
MacIntyre Care	£47,846,000	Engineering Construction Industry Training Board	£37,035,000
Autism Initiatives (UK)	£47,558,000	The Blagrave Trust	£36,812,995
Relief International UK	£47,021,550	Help for Heroes	£36,514,568
The Royal Masonic Benevolent Institution Care Co	£46,971,000	Human Appeal	£36,493,079
Nacro	£46,940,000	The British Diabetic Association	£36,474,000
The Mines Advisory Group	£46,879,000	King Edward VII's Hospital Sister Agnes	£36,436,000
Catch 22 Charity Limited	£46,818,000	Choice Support	£36,435,605
BRE Trust	£46,747,000	Victim Support	£36,409,000
Regent's University London	£46,070,000	King's College School	£36,348,000
The Methodist Church in Great Britain	£46,035,000	The Against Malaria Foundation	£36,192,981
The Black Stork Charity	£45,661,664	The London Marathon Charitable Trust Limited	£36,132,990
The Avenues Trust Group	£45,653,000	The Royal College of Music	£35,931,028
Affinity Trust	£45,237,885	Huo Family Foundation (UK) Limited	£35,876,540
Vale of Aylesbury Housing Trust Limited	£45,224,000	Glyndwr University	£35,716,000
Saxon Weald Homes Limited	£45,098,192	Blue Cross	£35,294,000
Dulwich College	£44,765,391	Family Fund Trust for Severely Disabled Children	£35,279,000
Haberdashers' Aske's Charity	£44,552,000	Crisis UK	£35,208,000
The American School in London Educational Trust Ltd	£44,199,000	Framework Housing Association	£35,182,000
BBC Media Action	£44,151,000	The Premier League Charitable Fund	£35,135,723
Christian Vision	£43,929,201	The Eric Wright Charitable Trust	£35,026,000
St Anne's Community Services	£43,792,404	The Havebury Housing Partnership	£34,992,000
The Katherine Martin Charitable Trust	£43,704,000	Rugby School	£34,784,326
The Royal College of General Practitioners	£43,072,164	The University of Buckingham	£34,727,000

Focus Learning Trust	£34,617,633	4children	£29,482,285
The Pirbright Institute	£34,495,000	British Pregnancy Advisory Service	£29,376,000
King's School of The Cathedral Church of Canterbury	£34,435,000	Norwood Schools Ltd	£29,253,000
The Federation of Groundwork Trusts	£34,389,680	BH Live	£29,139,918
Pre-School Learning Alliance	£34,351,000	Multiple Sclerosis Society	£29,023,000
The Ashridge (Bonar Law Memorial) Trust	£34,314,000	The Association of Accounting Technicians	£28,974,629
Rothamsted Research Limited	£34,121,000	Girl Effect	£28,882,698
World Animal Protection	£34,106,000	Arthritis Research UK	£28,877,000
Acis Group Limited	£34,105,899	Greensleeves Homes Trust	£28,805,759
Bridge House Estates	£34,100,000	Friends of The Elderly	£28,801,050
Moondance Foundation	£34,031,548	Bolton School	£28,780,000
Real Life Options	£33,872,000	The Law Family Charitable Foundation	£28,777,342
Sir Roger Cholmeley's School at Highgate	£33,829,005	St Peter's College, Radley	£28,614,000
Allchurches Trust Limited	£33,730,000	Blind Veterans UK	£28,613,000
National Schizophrenia Fellowship	£33,717,000	Uppingham School	£28,605,643
National Museum of Wales	£33,580,000	Loughborough Schools Foundation	£28,575,000
Royal College of Surgeons of England	£33,361,000	Milestones Trust	£28,477,867
Spire Homes (LG) Limited	£33,320,000	The Church of England Pensions Board	£28,437,000
Practical Action	£33,187,000	Breast Cancer Now	£28,318,000
National Centre for Social Research	£33,108,712	Ruskin Mill Trust Limited	£28,296,575
MCCH	£33,073,000	Worthing Homes Limited	£28,256,000
MyTime Active	£33,059,355	Clifton College	£28,254,000
Brunelcare	£33,012,000	Aga Khan Foundation (United Kingdom)	£27,983,000
JTL	£32,996,775	The Professional Footballers' Association Charity	£27,887,320
Parkinson's Disease Society of The United Kingdom	£32,864,000	Warden & Scholars of St Mary College of Winchester	£27,880,000
Stafford & Rural Homes Limited	£32,794,000	Depaul International	£27,856,000
The Scout Association	£32,681,000	National Energy Action	£27,853,956
Leeds Trinity University	£32,657,987	Nectar Trust	£27,850,434
The Healthcare Management Trust	£32,635,771	Birmingham Hippodrome Theatre Trust Limited	£27,772,000
The Corporation of The Hall of Arts and Sciences	£32,616,000	The Eden Trust	£27,707,000
Centrepoint Soho	£32,586,000	The Chartered Institute of Procurement and Supply	£27,696,000
Liverpool Roman Catholic Archdiocesan Trust	£32,400,052	Abingdon School	£27,530,000
Our Lady of Charity of The Good Shepherd	£32,320,749	Oakham School	£27,500,000
The Education and Training Foundation	£32,192,000	CLIC Sargent Cancer Care for Children	£27,490,713
Nazareth Care Charitable Trust	£32,186,243	Shell Foundation	£27,480,106
Cornwall Care Limited	£32,163,000	The Order of St. Augustine of The Mercy of Jesus	£27,417,304
Weaver Vale Housing Trust Limited	£32,067,000	The Royal Academy of Engineering	£27,410,424
Hult International Business School Ltd	£32,048,744	Fitzroy Support	£27,351,438
The Benenden Hospital Trust	£32,005,582	Workers' Educational Association	£27,350,000
Berkhamsted Schools Group	£31,916,000	St Andrew's College, Bradfield	£27,325,169
UBS UK Donor Advised Foundation	£31,823,000	Brentwood School CIO	£27,179,859
Tonbridge School	£31,719,402	Mission Aviation Fellowship International	£27,141,743
Horder Healthcare	£31,638,000	The Waste and Resources Action Programme	£27,136,064
Qi Partners	£31,628,000	Guy's and St Thomas' Charity	£27,103,000
Norwood Ravenswood	£31,534,000	Skills for Care Ltd	£27,048,966
Christ Church, Oxford	£31,229,000	Helpage International	£26,979,000
Charterhouse School	£31,140,000	Sadler's Wells Trust Limited	£26,802,000
Warwick Independent Schools Foundation	£31,002,000	St Bede's School Trust Sussex	£26,742,000
Coleg Sir Gar	£30,971,000	United Reformed Church Trust	£26,693,000
Severnside Housing	£30,964,869	Riverside Estuary Limited	£26,691,000
Ahmadiyya Muslim Jamaat International	£30,944,000	Achisomoch Aid Company Limited	£26,671,948
The Hospital Saturday Fund	£30,850,204	Coastline Housing Limited	£26,612,000
Rugby Football Foundation	£30,811,707	Concern Worldwide (UK)	£26,498,915
The Institution of Civil Engineers	£30,778,000	Merchant Taylors' Educational Trust	£26,492,618
Cheltenham Ladies College	£30,749,000	Paul Smith Foundation	£26,395,904
Futures Homescape Limited	£30,748,000	The David Lewis Centre	£26,389,000
Alzheimer's Research UK	£30,456,941	Action Against Hunger	£26,382,148
Elizabeth Finn Care	£30,397,000	Ben - Motor and Allied Trades Benevolent Fund	£26,331,000
Herefordshire Housing Limited	£30,349,000	Business in the Community	£26,315,582
Latymer Foundation at Hammersmith	£30,322,635	The Licensed Trade Charity	£26,289,950
United Purpose	£30,272,470	Alleyn's School	£26,240,000
Amanat Charity Trust	£30,230,349	Developing Initiatives for Support in the Community	£26,188,168
Legacy Leisure Limited	£30,219,843	Aston Student Village	£26,178,738
Bournville Village Trust	£30,139,000	East End Homes Limited	£26,067,000
Victory Housing Trust	£29,895,000	Stowe School Limited	£26,029,855
Sevenoaks School	£29,824,153	Stephen Taylor Foundation	£25,937,572
St Monica Trust	£29,817,000	Cranleigh School	£25,895,000
Glyndebourne Productions Limited	£29,733,397	London Grid for Learning Trust	£25,841,000
St Peter's College (known as Westminster School)	£29,666,000	The Grammar School at Leeds	£25,809,145
International Bible Students Association	£29,591,385	The Percy Hedley Foundation	£25,759,000
Camfed International	£29,577,988	Together Trust Limited	£25,731,000
United Westminster Schools Foundation	£29,506,000	The Mill Hill School Foundation	£25,692,000

Cheltenham College and Preparatory School	£25,664,000	The Auckland Castle Trust	£22,255,274
Arundel and Brighton Diocesan Trust	£25,559,000	William Jones's Schools Foundation	£22,229,000
The National Centre for Young People with Epilepsy	£25,510,000	Cothill Trust	£22,166,000
The Oxford Diocesan Board of Finance	£25,436,000	Museum of London	£22,157,000
Tower Hamlets Community Housing Limited	£25,435,000	Prism The Gift Fund	£22,128,676
St George's Weybridge	£25,412,258	Bishop Grosseteste University	£22,113,286
Trinity Laban Conservatoire of Music and Dance	£25,399,508	The Power of Nutrition	£22,083,189
Sherborne School	£25,213,000	The Royal Grammar School, Guildford	£22,065,452
Shrewsbury School	£25,051,013	Birmingham Diocesan Trust	£22,009,000
NIAB	£25,044,000	The Institution of Mechanical Engineers	£21,941,000
Hampton School	£25,027,407	Family Action	£21,930,000
Parkway Green Housing Trust	£25,021,000	Friends of The Royal Botanic Gardens, Kew	£21,921,000
The Perse School	£24,921,000	Two Rivers Housing	£21,913,000
Nesta	£24,908,000	St Edward's School	£21,797,000
Christ's Hospital	£24,890,000	Westminster Chapel	£21,768,117
Making Space	£24,824,000	The Adolescent and Children's Trust	£21,762,808
The Services Sound and Vision Corporation	£24,739,000	L.E.A.D. Academy Trust	£21,750,000
Sir John Port's Charity	£24,733,222	Wigan Leisure and Culture Trust	£21,709,021
Ampleforth Abbey	£24,713,000	Eastbourne College (Incorporated)	£21,650,000
Wales Millennium Centre	£24,667,000	The Mayflower Theatre Trust	£21,646,261
The Leys and St Faith's Schools Foundation	£24,609,521	Bishop's Stortford College Association	£21,573,000
The Shakespeare Globe Trust	£24,605,000	The Dean Close Foundation	£21,448,697
African Agricultural Technology Foundation	£24,547,499	New Hall School Trust	£21,417,552
The Act Foundation	£24,472,915	Saint John of God Hospitaller Services	£21,356,000
Newman University	£24,451,477	New College, Oxford	£21,353,000
Leeds Diocesan Board of Finance	£24,445,771	King Edward VI School Southampton	£21,187,535
Healthcare Quality Improvement Partnership	£24,435,466	The Manchester Grammar School Foundation	£21,179,597
Hestia Housing and Support	£24,338,487	James Allen's Girls' School	£21,144,468
Royal Academy of Music	£24,252,675	Phoenix House	£21,095,000
King's College, Cambridge	£24,052,802	Taunton School Educational Charity	£21,071,300
Church Communities UK	£24,010,992	Vision Redbridge Culture and Leisure	£21,039,000
The Royal Medical Foundation of Epsom College	£23,997,000	International Institute for Environment & Development	£21,030,675
University College School, Hampstead	£23,968,000	The Camphill Village Trust Limited	£21,028,000
Girls' Education Company Ltd	£23,900,000	Dulwich Preparatory Schools Trust	£20,996,146
Avante Care and Support Limited	£23,887,041	The Royal College of Psychiatrists	£20,942,000
The Chelmsford Diocesan Board of Finance	£23,859,000	Rathbone Training	£20,928,000
The North London Collegiate School	£23,834,570	Headington School Oxford Limited	£20,915,221
Chartered Institute of Public Finance & Accountancy	£23,623,000	Wakefield Grammar School Foundation	£20,906,096
Haileybury and Imperial Service College	£23,589,000	Yorkshire Cancer Research	£20,891,423
Calico Homes Limited	£23,502,000	National Star Foundation	£20,891,172
The Royal Air Force Benevolent Fund	£23,352,000	South England Conference of Seventh Day Adventists	£20,876,080
Yorkshire Coast Homes Limited	£23,291,000	Coventry School Foundation	£20,854,901
International Finance Facility for Immunisation Co	£23,235,077	Forest School, Essex	£20,852,975
The Children's Trust	£23,219,000	Syria Relief	£20,828,126
Bryanston School Incorporated	£23,214,895	The Central Young Men's Christian Association	£20,808,000
Ambitious About Autism	£23,209,000	Treloar Trust	£20,796,000
Goldman Sachs Gives (UK)	£23,201,944	The Portsmouth Grammar School	£20,789,697
The Schools of King Edward VI in Birmingham	£23,198,817	Benenden School (Kent) Limited	£20,760,000
West Buckland School	£23,195,493	Magdalen College, Oxford	£20,751,000
United Talmudical Associates Ltd	£23,150,996	Prostate Cancer UK	£20,747,000
Felsted School	£23,149,155	Mental Health Concern	£20,643,000
The Institute of Development Studies	£23,071,000	Ardingly College Limited	£20,634,465
The Thalidomide Trust	£22,975,000	Downe House School	£20,509,000
Walsingham Support	£22,902,405	The Brendoncare Foundation	£20,448,000
Bromsgrove District Housing Trust Limited	£22,797,000	International HIV/Aids Alliance	£20,412,051
Congregation of The Brothers of Charity	£22,783,367	IVCC	£20,369,000
Hinxton Hall Limited	£22,768,000	The Oxfordshire Care Partnership	£20,358,984
Hurstpierpoint College Limited	£22,743,000	City South Manchester Housing Trust Limited	£20,306,000
Stamford Endowed Schools	£22,731,000	The Conservatoire for Dance and Drama	£20,271,000
Cartrefi Cymru Co-operative Limited	£22,690,000	The Lowry Centre Trust	£20,270,000
Action for Blind People	£22,567,000	NCFE	£20,255,000
The National Deaf Children's Society	£22,525,000	The Sigrid Rausing Trust	£20,185,921
Merchant Taylors School	£22,512,190	Francis Holland (Church of England) Schools Trust	£20,165,000
In Kind Direct	£22,501,427	The Normandy Memorial Trust Ltd	£20,150,468
King Edward VI's Grammar School, Guildford	£22,477,815	Al-Khair Foundation	£20,146,030
NMRN Operations	£22,477,516	Autism Together	£20,138,000
Malvern College	£22,476,544	International Fund for Animal Welfare (IFAW)	£20,117,783
Wildfowl and Wetlands Trust	£22,414,000	Active Northumberland	£20,090,541
Stevenage Leisure	£22,403,102	Hertsmere Leisure	£20,089,265
Reigate Grammar School	£22,344,525	St Christophers Hospice	£20,080,000
Royal Academy of Dance	£22,301,000	Churchill College in the University of Cambridge	£20,039,000
Accessible Transport Group Limited	£22,281,438	The Guide Association	£19,984,726

Marine Stewardship Council	£19,942,284	Futures Homeway Limited	£17,701,000
Canford School Limited	£19,896,038	Sedbergh School	£17,691,000
National Council of YMCAs	£19,888,000	The Royal School for the Blind	£17,690,986
The National Museum of The Royal Navy	£19,873,323	Gonville and Caius College, Cambridge	£17,679,338
The Seckford Foundation	£19,767,428	Hillsong Church London	£17,605,867
The Gurkha Welfare Trust	£19,711,000	The Architectural Association (Incorporated)	£17,558,655
The Bell Concord Educational Trust Ltd	£19,710,000	St Catherine's School Bramley	£17,531,212
Lancing College Limited	£19,700,415	The King's School Worcester	£17,486,000
Royal Agricultural University	£19,692,189	The St Albans Diocesan Board of Finance	£17,451,303
NPT (UK) Limited	£19,656,798	World Federation of Khoja Shia Ithna-Asheri Muslim	£17,397,671
The Representative Body of The Church in Wales	£19,652,000	Barts and The London Charity and Related Charities	£17,375,000
The Wolfson Foundation	£19,631,000	The Salford Diocesan Trust	£17,287,055
Cranstoun	£19,560,000	Congregation of The Little Sisters of The Poor	£17,285,131
The British and Foreign Bible Society	£19,537,000	King Edward The Sixth Grammar School, Norwich	£17,267,000
The Brooke Hospital for Animals	£19,517,525	St Helen's School, Northwood	£17,252,000
Bridewell Royal Hospital	£19,506,000	The Lady Eleanor Holles School	£17,249,122
Paul Hamlyn Foundation	£19,409,654	Royal British Legion Industries Ltd.	£17,245,000
ABF The Soldiers' Charity	£19,371,465	Royal Air Force Museum	£17,211,111
National Children's Bureau	£19,354,000	UK Biobank Limited	£17,168,583
International Health Partners (UK) Limited	£19,268,456	Chichester Festival Theatre	£17,165,300
The Duke of Edinburgh's Award	£19,256,000	Bristol Grammar School	£17,125,618
St Paul's Girls' School	£19,188,000	Russell School Trust	£17,106,776
The Royal Marsden Cancer Charity	£19,150,000	YMCA St Pauls Group	£17,089,802
Samaritans	£19,142,000	Godolphin and Latymer School	£17,080,667
People Potential Possibilities	£19,130,773	The Varkey Foundation	£17,071,142
Innovate Trust Ltd	£19,120,095	The National Society for Epilepsy	£17,056,000
Caterham School Limited	£19,012,000	The Cyrenians Ltd	£17,047,445
The Dolphin Square Charitable Foundation	£19,009,242	Society of Friends of The Torah Limited	£17,042,906
The Royal Navy Submarine Museum Trust	£18,995,073	Shrewsbury Roman Catholic Diocesan Trust	£17,039,000
The Single Homeless Project	£18,935,430	Ambition School Leadership Trust	£17,028,496
Outward Housing	£18,911,529	St George's - Augustinian Care	£17,022,796
Lichfield Diocesan Board of Finance (Inc)	£18,873,000	Theatre Royal (Plymouth) Limited	£17,011,139
Teign Housing	£18,765,000	Kingswood School	£17,001,515
Together for Mental Wellbeing	£18,704,389	Prior Park Educational Trust	£16,998,296
WCS Care Group Limited	£18,696,000	The Papworth Trust	£16,940,800
Gresham's School	£18,675,127	The John Black Charitable Foundation	£16,936,554
The Constance Travis Charitable Trust	£18,652,050	St Christopher's Fellowship	£16,933,000
Penny Appeal	£18,629,628	Kingston Grammar School	£16,930,000
The Wilf Ward Family Trust	£18,618,022	The NHS Confederation	£16,922,618
Samaritan's Purse International Limited	£18,603,255	Ibstock Place School	£16,914,729
Ahmadiyya Muslim Association United Kingdom	£18,557,799	The Newcastle upon Tyne Royal Grammar School	£16,899,197
Chapter 1 Charity Ltd	£18,551,000	Breast Cancer Care	£16,899,000
Nugent Care	£18,550,000	Theatre Royal (Norwich) Trust Limited	£16,874,313
Sanctuary Student Homes Limited	£18,512,000	Perthyn	£16,864,623
Chichester Diocesan Fund and Board of Finance	£18,448,137	Parish Giving Scheme	£16,829,775
Ymddiriedolaeth Clough Williams-Ellis Foundation	£18,446,246	The Soil Association Limited	£16,824,100
Westminster Drug Project	£18,439,214	The King's School, Ely	£16,789,835
North Devon Homes Limited	£18,428,148	Priors Court Foundation	£16,782,930
International Baccalaureate Organization (UK) Ltd	£18,382,300	The Aldenham Foundation	£16,778,042
The London Early Years Foundation	£18,336,086	The Anna Freud Centre	£16,747,436
St Laurence Education Trust	£18,315,000	The National Childbirth Trust	£16,723,000
The London Symphony Orchestra Limited	£18,271,794	Stockport Grammar School	£16,709,690
The Pears Family Charitable Foundation	£18,263,232	Keren Association Limited	£16,697,528
The Forward Trust	£18,255,000	The Heart of England Forest Ltd	£16,683,633
Dauntsey's School	£18,217,418	Motor Neurone Disease Association	£16,683,000
Dragon School Trust Limited	£18,209,000	Amnesty International UK Section Charitable Trust	£16,565,000
English National Ballet	£18,175,060	Sherborne School for Girls	£16,558,932
St. Barnabas Hospices (Sussex) Ltd	£18,127,000	The Marine Society and Sea Cadets	£16,548,000
The Thrombosis Research Institute	£18,107,189	Stonyhurst	£16,547,575
Bedales School	£18,097,361	Lempriere Pringle 2015	£16,524,567
The Football League (Community) Limited	£18,066,805	Children with Cancer UK	£16,524,416
North East Autism Society	£18,038,440	The Royal Free Charity	£16,507,000
Welsh National Opera Limited	£18,014,000	The Salvation Army Officers' Pension Fund	£16,495,981
The City Literary Institute	£17,943,000	Local Solutions	£16,467,385
Opera North Limited	£17,933,027	St.Peter's School, York	£16,372,133
International Alert	£17,921,000	The Workforce Development Trust Limited	£16,364,891
Farm Africa Limited	£17,900,000	London Transport Museum Limited	£16,359,000
Emmanuel College, Cambridge	£17,877,531	The Air Ambulance Service	£16,306,000
The Royal Institute of International Affairs	£17,872,000	St Albans High School for Girls	£16,298,000
Field Studies Council	£17,795,408	Magdalen College School Oxford Limited	£16,252,525
The International Institute for Strategic Studies	£17,772,783	The Institute of Grocery Distribution	£16,184,840
The National Foundation for Educational Research	£17,753,000	The Merchant Taylors' Schools Crosby	£16,179,835

The Leri Charitable Trust	£16,101,467	The Vernon Educational Trust Limited	£15,134,627
The Gloucestershire Care Partnership	£16,064,789	REALL Limited	£15,131,004
Repton School	£16,055,138	Rhodes Trust - Public Purposes Fund	£15,127,489
Jesus College in the University of Cambridge	£16,049,345	The Dr Mortimer and Theresa Sackler Foundation	£15,099,421
The Abbey School, Reading	£16,045,105	Open Society Foundation	£15,097,093
Health Limited	£16,045,101	Royal College of Paediatrics and Child Health	£15,065,000
Teenage Cancer Trust	£16,021,823	Princess Alice Hospice	£15,061,484
Birdlife International	£16,021,184	ISSA Foundation	£15,045,257
St Benedict's School Ealing	£16,013,997	Career Connect	£15,033,494
Newcastle Theatre Royal Trust Limited	£16,011,703	Eduserv	£15,027,200
Bloodwise	£15,971,000	A W Charitable Trust	£15,023,560
Pembroke College, Cambridge	£15,926,000	The Forest Trust	£14,963,477
Channing House Incorporated, Highgate	£15,924,600	Hampstead Heath	£14,957,608
Barnabas Aid International	£15,923,340	The Universal Church of The Kingdom of God	£14,952,607
The Royal Society of Medicine	£15,907,000	The Health Foundation	£14,939,000
St Albans School	£15,894,007	Aid to The Church in Need (United Kingdom)	£14,926,432
The Royal Star & Garter Homes	£15,870,000	Royal Society of Wildlife Trusts	£14,918,000
Poor Servants of The Mother of God	£15,867,926	The Chester Diocesan Board of Finance	£14,915,000
Kirklees Active Leisure	£15,852,553	CDP Worldwide	£14,900,000
Community Lives Consortium	£15,845,967	Ezer V' Hatzalah Ltd	£14,856,568
The Saint John's School Foundation	£15,827,389	Barnsley Premier Leisure	£14,856,060
Thames Reach Charity	£15,821,934	Somerset House Trust	£14,837,792
The Independent Educational Association Limited	£15,818,791	Golden Lane Housing Ltd	£14,830,748
Southside Partnership	£15,814,000	Homerton College Cambridge	£14,829,046
Nottingham High School	£15,804,000	Cheadle Hulme School	£14,827,000
Muslim Hands	£15,797,759	Everybody Sport & Recreation	£14,821,232
Woldingham School	£15,793,483	Lord Wandsworth College	£14,815,101
Fauna & Flora International	£15,782,969	Rochester Diocesan Society and Board of Finance	£14,771,000
Bancroft's School	£15,777,778	Restless Development	£14,730,000
Animal Health Trust	£15,748,000	Westminster Society People with Learning Disabilities	£14,726,714
The Alan Turing Institute	£15,747,248	King's School, Bruton	£14,718,737
St Peter's Hospice	£15,736,000	Torus62 Limited	£14,709,000
Combat Stress	£15,709,000	The Exeter Diocesan Board of Finance	£14,586,261
The London Orphan Asylum (Reed's School)	£15,708,000	Kimbolton School	£14,530,287
Bauer Radio's Cash for Kids Charities	£15,699,876	Portsmouth Roman Catholic Diocesan Trust	£14,526,470
The Landmark Trust	£15,699,000	Guildford Diocesan Board of Finance	£14,509,000
Chetham's Hospital School and Library	£15,676,781	The Royal Masonic School for Girls	£14,504,312
Demelza House Childrens Hospice	£15,648,427	International House Trust Limited	£14,494,000
St. Clare's, Oxford	£15,641,000	The National Army Museum	£14,487,000
The Outward Bound Trust	£15,631,325	The Christie Charitable Fund	£14,482,000
The Victoria Foundation	£15,614,000	YMCA Downslink Group	£14,472,573
Kathleen and Michael Connolly Foundation (UK) Ltd	£15,599,256	Mirus - Wales	£14,444,514
The Terrence Higgins Trust	£15,588,089	St Giles Hospice	£14,420,309
Nightingale Hammerson	£15,586,000	The Bell Educational Trust Limited	£14,397,000
Gedling Homes	£15,556,000	Alexandra Park and Palace	£14,389,000
Circle Care and Support	£15,530,000	Guild Care	£14,385,499
St Mary's School (Calne)	£15,506,231	University College, Oxford	£14,372,766
M J Camp Charitable Foundation	£15,476,785	The Chartered Institute for Securities and Investment	£14,356,401
Book Aid International	£15,460,412	The National Gallery Trust	£14,309,591
Colfe's School	£15,430,000	Monkton Combe School	£14,308,445
Saferworld	£15,422,000	LHA London Ltd	£14,270,372
St Edmund's College	£15,420,107	NYU in London	£14,249,860
Ipswich School	£15,408,396	The York Diocesan Board of Finance Limited	£14,244,000
Groundwork London	£15,365,476	Selwyn College Cambridge	£14,225,874
The Raphael Freshwater Memorial Association	£15,359,000	Active Nation UK Ltd	£14,158,021
The Queen's College, Oxford	£15,357,000	DEBRA	£14,136,343
Rachel Charitable Trust	£15,347,928	Clare College Cambridge	£14,097,000
St Mary's School Ascot	£15,333,000	The London Institute of Banking & Finance	£14,073,000
Albert Memorial College	£15,308,282	Manchester Diocesan Board of Finance	£14,048,000
St Swithun's School (Winchester)	£15,287,072	Barnabas Fund	£14,039,126
Quadram Institute Bioscience	£15,284,318	Community Sports Arts and Leisure Trust	£14,034,212
Trent College Limited	£15,273,000	Halo Leisure Services Limited	£14,032,056
Acorns Children's Hospice Trust	£15,271,000	Ronald McDonald House Charities (UK)	£14,027,000
EMH Care and Support Limited	£15,257,629	Sheffield Theatres Trust	£13,999,566
The Land Restoration Trust	£15,240,000	Merthyr Tydfil College Limited	£13,988,000
The National Film and Television School	£15,235,374	St Joseph's Hospice Hackney	£13,976,000
Avenues South East	£15,231,000	The British Academy of Film and Television Arts	£13,960,000
The Princethorpe Foundation	£15,222,106	Claysmore School	£13,921,980
Foundation of Sir John Percyvale in Macclesfield	£15,215,000	Pilgrims Hospices in East Kent	£13,915,000
National Art Collections Fund	£15,192,000	Wells Cathedral School Limited	£13,892,000
Leicester Grammar School Trust	£15,157,224	The Oratory Schools Association	£13,888,569
The New Victoria Hospital Limited	£15,157,000	The Collegiate Charitable Foundation	£13,886,491

Trident Reach The People Charity	£13,866,872	Jesus College, Oxford	£12,923,000
St Catherine's College in the University of Oxford	£13,852,000	St Anne's College in the University of Oxford	£12,912,000
The Leprosy Mission International	£13,836,520	Brighton Housing Trust	£12,903,196
Lloyds Bank Foundation for England & Wales	£13,835,000	Performances Birmingham Limited	£12,901,000
Birmingham Royal Ballet	£13,827,845	Wallich-Clifford Community	£12,899,313
Caudwell Children	£13,822,914	Wadham College	£12,899,000
North Music Trust	£13,812,077	Roedean School	£12,896,768
PSS (UK)	£13,808,840	The Whitley Wildlife Conservation Trust	£12,892,657
Worth Abbey	£13,805,829	The Prince of Wales's Charitable Foundation	£12,892,000
Free Grammar School of King Charles II at Bradford	£13,796,997	Worth School	£12,889,592
Place2Be	£13,791,000	Redwings Horse Sanctuary	£12,858,589
The Bath and Wells Diocesan Board of Finance	£13,774,000	The Royal Air Forces Association - Corporate Body	£12,852,000
St Dunstan's Educational Foundation	£13,770,677	The Henry Smith Charity	£12,840,000
Chigwell School	£13,765,957	St Catharine's College, Cambridge	£12,833,000
Lloyd's Register International	£13,754,000	The Guy Pilkington Memorial Home Limited	£12,822,182
Education and Services for People with Autism Ltd	£13,750,718	Steps To Work (Walsall) Limited	£12,821,000
Seashell Trust	£13,726,000	East Anglian Air Ambulance	£12,815,652
Sidney Sussex College, Cambridge	£13,717,000	King Edward's School Bath	£12,812,056
Science, Engineering and Mfg Technologies Alliance	£13,698,000	Buckinghamshire Learning Trust	£12,803,503
Blundell's School	£13,695,000	Solihull School	£12,797,343
Youth Sport Trust	£13,694,041	South West Environmental Parks Limited	£12,750,554
Orchard Hill College	£13,685,126	St Ann's Hospice	£12,727,479
Ability Housing Association	£13,671,352	British Gas Energy Trust	£12,719,275
Earlham Institute	£13,602,000	Children's Hospice South West	£12,708,206
The Royal College of Anaesthetists	£13,599,819	Grimsthorpe and Drummond Castle Trust Limited	£12,707,909
The Border Consortium	£13,599,500	Leeds Grand Theatre and Opera House Limited	£12,707,508
Royal Welsh College of Music and Drama	£13,579,000	The Sandwell Community Caring Trust	£12,697,166
Justice & Care	£13,559,830	The British Psychological Society	£12,684,000
The Linkage Community Trust Limited	£13,545,519	Anglo Australian Christian & Charitable Fund	£12,680,999
International NGO Safety Organisation	£13,519,942	Loughborough Students' Union	£12,680,525
Eltham College	£13,509,277	Christ's College, Cambridge	£12,675,774
Drive	£13,505,626	The Retreat York	£12,675,233
Lamda Ltd	£13,498,285	Trinity Hall Cambridge	£12,656,000
Museum of London Archaeology	£13,479,248	Bury Grammar Schools Charity	£12,619,000
The Salisbury Diocesan Board of Finance	£13,463,000	Federation of Synagogues	£12,615,113
University of Pennsylvania (USA) Foundation Ltd	£13,456,055	Brentwood Roman Catholic Diocesan Trust	£12,586,599
Tate Foundation	£13,415,653	Institute of Our Lady of Mercy	£12,580,775
Universities UK	£13,398,082	The Theatre Royal Bath Limited	£12,526,000
The Pony Club	£13,388,383	Wood Green Animal Shelters	£12,515,638
Armed Forces Education Trust	£13,380,581	St Helena Hospice Limited	£12,459,041
Merton College, Oxford	£13,363,000	Essex & Herts Air Ambulance Trust	£12,450,330
Royal Grammar School Worcester	£13,361,000	Depaul UK	£12,444,000
The Gloucester Diocesan Board of Finance	£13,328,000	Creative Skillset - Sector Skills Council Limited	£12,442,270
Social Interest Group	£13,326,000	The Howletts Wild Animal Trust	£12,429,617
Mission Aviation Fellowship UK	£13,314,000	CXK Limited	£12,428,665
The Dartington Hall Trust	£13,301,000	Royal Trinity Hospice	£12,427,649
British Union Conference of Seventh-Day Adventists	£13,292,710	Kent, Surrey & Sussex Air Ambulance Trust	£12,426,673
Refuge	£13,292,538	JNF Charitable Trust	£12,417,000
War Child	£13,254,250	The Tennis Foundation	£12,406,000
Chartered Management Institute	£13,253,000	Enham Trust	£12,404,000
Wycliffe College (Incorporated)	£13,234,211	The Roundhouse Trust	£12,403,223
The United World College of The Atlantic Limited	£13,234,000	The Quality Assurance Agency for Higher Education	£12,393,637
Spurgeons	£13,209,575	The Royal Ballet School	£12,373,000
Chatsworth House Trust	£13,203,000	Holy Trinity with Saint Paul Onslow Square	£12,371,876
Sisters of The Cross and Passion	£13,185,043	Shelterbox Trust	£12,361,481
Cystic Fibrosis Trust	£13,182,000	Church of England Central Services	£12,356,000
King's Schools Taunton Ltd	£13,129,765	The Blackburn Diocesan Board of Finance Limited	£12,354,000
Kent College, Canterbury	£13,114,114	The Johnson Trust Limited	£12,351,620
Wessex Archaeology Limited	£13,109,400	Culford School	£12,332,390
Peterhouse, Cambridge	£13,089,000	East Anglia's Children's Hospices	£12,292,695
The Institution of Occupational Safety and Health	£13,042,000	The Old Vic Theatre Trust 2000	£12,290,567
Leics & Rutland Organisation for Relief of Suffering	£13,032,903	Ashville College	£12,290,256
Midlands Air Ambulance Charity	£13,028,129	The Claremont Fan Court Foundation Limited	£12,280,883
Lincoln College Oxford	£13,028,000	Farleigh Hospice	£12,280,000
The Norwich Diocesan Board of Finance Limited	£13,027,000	The February Foundation	£12,275,570
Worcester College, Oxford	£12,993,000	Union of UEA Students Limited	£12,275,000
Yarm School	£12,980,000	National Library of Wales	£12,255,000
King's School	£12,972,000	The Charles Kalms, Henry Ronson Immanuel College	£12,249,046
Absolutely Cultured Limited	£12,965,101	Beamish Museum	£12,233,000
The Dorothy House Foundation Limited	£12,959,738	People's Health Trust	£12,212,836
The Design Museum	£12,939,609	The Elton John Aids Foundation	£12,177,230
Absolute Return for Kids (Ark)	£12,938,000	The Principal and Fellows of Somerville College	£12,175,000

All Souls College, Oxford	£12,168,000	The Liverpool Diocesan Board of Finance	£11,283,667
Wales Council for Voluntary Action	£12,154,050	L'Arche	£11,280,380
St Oswald's Hospice Limited	£12,152,294	Shiplake Court Limited	£11,279,470
St Margaret's Somerset Hospice	£12,152,251	Training 2000 Limited	£11,278,839
Balliol College, Oxford	£12,149,000	Saint Francis Hospice	£11,268,000
Goodenough College	£12,149,000	Exeter College, Oxford	£11,262,000
St Barnabas Hospice Trust (Lincolnshire)	£12,142,786	Brook Young People	£11,261,264
Kaleidoscope Project	£12,134,740	European Society of Cataract & Refractive Surgeons	£11,244,832
Goal (International)	£12,123,366	The Mike Gooley Trailfinders Charity	£11,239,584
Rapport Housing and Care	£12,098,232	Lingfield College	£11,233,513
Circadian Trust	£12,078,976	Birmingham Repertory Theatre Limited	£11,210,000
Queenswood School Limited	£12,067,171	Thomson Reuters Foundation	£11,203,000
The Shakespeare Birthplace Trust	£12,062,000	Snape Maltings	£11,195,333
Hollybank Trust	£12,051,421	Royal Society of Arts	£11,188,000
The School of St Helen and St Katharine Trust	£12,032,703	Leeds Diocesan Trust	£11,183,000
Winchester Diocesan Board of Finance	£12,030,000	Fair Ways Foundation	£11,168,042
The British Museum Trust Limited	£12,008,697	Marwell Wildlife	£11,164,279
Langley House Trust	£12,000,000	ADS (Addiction Dependency Solutions)	£11,161,405
Kent Union	£11,999,586	Kingsway International Christian Centre	£11,153,588
The Grange School Hartford Limited	£11,993,365	The Royal Academy of Dramatic Art	£11,148,000
The Cambridge Mosque Trust	£11,979,104	The Sacred Hearts Sisters 1983 Charitable Fund	£11,135,202
Leighton Park Trust	£11,977,794	Christadelphian Care Homes	£11,134,272
Sarjudas Foundation	£11,973,267	The Pocklington School Foundation	£11,134,117
Morden College	£11,921,000	Cokethorpe Educational Trust Limited	£11,134,056
Truro School	£11,904,000	POhWER	£11,120,393
York Archaeological Trust for Excavation & Research	£11,872,548	Vibrance	£11,112,232
St David's Foundation Hospice Care	£11,860,000	The Friends of The Royal Academy	£11,104,299
Magdalene College, Cambridge	£11,813,104	Doncaster Culture and Leisure Trust	£11,097,613
Wellingborough School	£11,783,679	The King's Hall and College of Brasenose in Oxford	£11,092,000
The Principal and Fellows of Newnham College	£11,772,735	Malvern St James Limited	£11,084,636
Queen's College, Taunton	£11,766,459	UCLU	£11,079,759
Milton Keynes Parks Trust Limited	£11,765,000	Wine and Spirit Education Trust	£11,077,568
London Cyrenians Housing Limited	£11,759,148	Academy of Medical Sciences	£11,077,414
Open Doors with Brother Andrew	£11,758,414	Lady Margaret Hall, Oxford	£11,067,000
The Fairtrade Foundation	£11,755,000	Chailey Heritage Foundation	£11,063,000
The Federation of London Youth Clubs	£11,739,868	Sidcot School	£11,061,236
Leicester Theatre Trust Limited	£11,728,000	The Chartered Institute of Building	£11,056,000
Master Fellows and Scholars of Pembroke College	£11,727,000	Northamptonshire Arts Management Trust	£11,047,068
The Royal Navy and Royal Marines Charity	£11,697,979	The Myton Hospices	£11,043,496
University College of Estate Management	£11,688,081	The Derby Diocesan Board of Finance Limited	£11,030,281
The Virgin Foundation	£11,658,000	Mary Hare	£11,008,000
Tudor Hall School	£11,655,210	The Mittal Foundation	£11,000,000
The Frontline Organisation	£11,650,000	Shulem B. Association Limited	£10,987,589
Queen Elizabeth's Foundation for Disabled People	£11,650,000	Mission Care	£10,969,489
Diocese of Hexham and Newcastle	£11,644,748	Infant Jesus Sisters (Nicolas Barre) Generalate CIO	£10,963,443
Ratcliffe College	£11,640,004	Yorkshire Agricultural Society	£10,940,093
Bristol Clifton & West of England Zoological Society	£11,608,000	The Corporation of St Lawrence College	£10,925,906
Woodhouse Grove School	£11,607,128	Welsh Air Ambulance Charitable Trust	£10,919,187
Redmaids' High School	£11,594,396	London Philharmonic Orchestra Limited	£10,919,136
Downing College in the University of Cambridge	£11,563,045	Quakers in Britain	£10,902,000
Reading Blue Coat School	£11,549,328	Birmingham Museums Trust	£10,900,000
Stockport Sports Trust	£11,548,312	Haig Housing Trust	£10,887,000
Oxford Archaeology Limited	£11,519,831	St Catherine's British School	£10,874,546
King Alfred School Society	£11,517,549	Devon and Cornwall Autistic Community Trust	£10,867,459
Oriel College, Oxford	£11,514,000	Leeds Castle Foundation	£10,851,000
Bootham School	£11,497,761	Seven Locks Housing Limited	£10,836,000
The Birmingham Diocesan Board of Finance	£11,493,000	The R C Snelling Charitable Trust	£10,833,065
Grey Coat Hospital Foundation	£11,453,000	Exeter School	£10,828,871
The University of Sheffield Union of Students	£11,433,326	St. John's School and College	£10,822,482
Autism East Midlands	£11,426,153	St. John of Jerusalem Eye Hospital Group	£10,811,000
Autism Wessex	£11,420,562	St Catherine's Hospice Limited	£10,807,000
Hertford College, Oxford	£11,418,000	Unipol Student Homes	£10,778,894
Structural Genomics Consortium	£11,393,000	Twycross Zoo-East Midland Zoological Society Ltd	£10,769,093
Nuffield College in the University of Oxford	£11,392,000	Break	£10,766,000
The Ulverscroft Foundation	£11,389,916	Kent College, Pembury	£10,764,385
Foundation	£11,387,000	The King's Fund	£10,754,000
Philharmonia Ltd	£11,353,790	Fitzwilliam College in the University of Cambridge	£10,752,184
Nottingham Roman Catholic Diocesan Trustees	£11,350,000	Derwen College	£10,741,646
St Columba's College and Preparatory School	£11,326,573	The Conservation Volunteers	£10,717,000
Christians Against Poverty	£11,313,000	Severn Hospice Limited	£10,701,106
Friends of Mercaz Hatorah Belz Macnivka	£11,302,559	Plymouth Marine Laboratory	£10,681,000
The Whiteley Homes Trust	£11,302,117	North Country Leisure	£10,676,911

Lincoln Diocesan Trust and Board of Finance Ltd	£10,655,000	World Mission Agency - Winners Chapel International	£9,984,540
Eleven Arches	£10,637,450	The Peterborough Diocesan Board of Finance	£9,975,144
Douglas Macmillan Hospice	£10,613,634	Lancaster Roman Catholic Diocesan Trust	£9,967,378
Leeds University Union	£10,607,354	People in Action	£9,966,413
Walthamstow Hall	£10,602,778	Helen & Douglas House	£9,958,000
The Dulwich Estate	£10,597,835	Ellesmere College Limited	£9,957,608
Delapage Limited	£10,590,718	League Football Education	£9,957,597
The Gordon Foundation	£10,573,901	The Kingham Hill Trust	£9,948,122
St Edmund's School Canterbury	£10,568,636	Tormead Limited	£9,946,184
The Royal Air Force Charitable Trust	£10,561,232	Corpus Christi College, Cambridge	£9,938,154
Robinson College in the University of Cambridge	£10,549,000	St Edmund Hall in the University of Oxford	£9,937,000
7 Hills Leisure Trust	£10,542,697	The Hintze Family Charitable Foundation	£9,936,306
The Cyril Taylor Charitable Foundation	£10,514,806	Hand in Hand for Aid and Development	£9,920,670
British Province of The Unitas Fratrum	£10,506,361	Hospice in the Weald	£9,916,973
Evolve Housing + Support	£10,499,125	United Jewish Israel Appeal	£9,916,000
Southwell & Nottingham Diocesan Board of Finance	£10,499,000	The Engineering and Technology Board	£9,906,000
St Hilda's College in the University of Oxford	£10,494,000	Phyllis Tuckwell Memorial Hospice Ltd	£9,902,366
Autism Anglia	£10,492,977	Pangbourne College Limited	£9,892,235
Downside Abbey General Trust	£10,488,022	The James Dyson Foundation	£9,856,326
St Mary's School Cambridge	£10,478,098	St Luke's Hospice	£9,853,812
Kids	£10,468,714	Cobalt Health	£9,839,733
London Emergencies Trust	£10,465,878	The Edgbaston High School for Girls	£9,829,012
Sandwell Leisure Trust	£10,459,530	The Northampton Theatres Trust Limited	£9,827,081
Tameside Sports Trust	£10,446,175	Gatsby Africa	£9,819,000
Rochdale Boroughwide Cultural Trust	£10,433,647	St Wilfrid's Hospice (South Coast) Limited	£9,799,335
Dame Allan's Schools	£10,415,356	The Emmanuel Community Charitable Trust Limited	£9,798,746
St Cuthbert's Care	£10,413,452	Al-Ayn Social Care Foundation	£9,733,067
New Testament Church of God	£10,394,159	The Rowans Hospice	£9,719,587
Mental Health Matters	£10,380,943	The Wrekin Old Hall Trust Limited	£9,715,670
Morley College Limited	£10,377,000	The Coventry Diocesan Board of Finance Ltd	£9,711,064
The Richmond Foundation	£10,370,769	The Durham Diocesan Board of Finance	£9,699,646
Buckfast Abbey Trust	£10,356,827	The United Kingdom Islamic Mission	£9,693,330
Manchester High School for Girls	£10,346,395	Design Council	£9,670,947
The Camden Society	£10,341,040	Asser Bishvil Foundation	£9,656,906
Portsmouth Diocesan Board of Finance	£10,340,771	The Leicester Diocesan Board of Finance	£9,645,000
Portland College	£10,336,000	The Edward James Foundation Limited	£9,640,159
Royal Philharmonic Orchestra Limited	£10,329,393	Shlomo Memorial Fund Limited	£9,633,301
Operation Mobilisation	£10,325,725	The London City Mission	£9,628,093
The University of Nottingham Students' Union	£10,324,976	The National Coaching Foundation	£9,621,838
St Basil's	£10,319,000	The Ramblers' Association	£9,617,000
Llamau Limited	£10,297,922	Bloxham School Limited	£9,603,563
The British Horse Society	£10,291,480	Premier Christian Media Trust	£9,600,521
Queen's College	£10,284,280	FARA Foundation	£9,599,624
Cardiff Educational Endowment Trust	£10,260,881	Chabad Lubavitch UK	£9,598,284
The Liverpool Institute for Performing Arts	£10,259,510	Sir William Perkins's Educational Foundation	£9,592,234
Find A Future	£10,253,185	The University of Chicago Booth School of Business	£9,591,896
The National Foundation for Youth Music	£10,253,082	The Martlets Hospice Limited	£9,573,422
The Royal Liverpool Philharmonic Society	£10,251,000	Lambrook School Trust Limited	£9,572,025
UK Community Foundations	£10,245,000	Pipers Corner School	£9,569,057
Queen Alexandra College	£10,225,263	Holstein UK	£9,566,320
YMCA Training	£10,183,000	Langley School	£9,561,129
Wellington School 1837	£10,154,909	The TTE Technical Training Group	£9,560,945
Community Foundation Serving Tyne & Wear	£10,148,027	Slough Community Leisure	£9,559,820
Canterbury Diocesan Board of Finance	£10,146,000	Newcastle-Under-Lyme School	£9,552,882
The Brenley Trust	£10,141,818	Fylde Coast YMCA	£9,551,216
Bochasanwasi Shri Akshar Purushottam Swaminarayan	£10,137,863	St Elizabeth Hospice (Suffolk)	£9,550,412
Movember Europe	£10,108,984	Henshaws Society for Blind People	£9,544,000
Havens Christian Hospice	£10,085,000	Institute of Integrated Systemic Therapy	£9,530,240
The Ely Diocesan Board of Finance	£10,078,000	Active Luton	£9,519,772
Rossall School	£10,069,223	International Society for Krishna Consciousness Ltd	£9,515,945
Vivacity Culture and Leisure	£10,065,864	Hope and Homes for Children	£9,511,899
Womancare Global International	£10,065,416	Mayfield School Ltd	£9,506,966
Royal Foundation of Duke & Duchess of Cambridge	£10,061,577	Church Extension Association (Incorporated)	£9,504,300
Keech Hospice Care	£10,051,000	The Waterloo Foundation	£9,503,237
Sheffcare Limited	£10,032,325	British Limbless Ex-Service Men's Association	£9,496,641
Faithful Companions of Jesus	£10,025,698	Association of Commonwealth Universities	£9,463,000
Cwmni Urdd Gobaith Cymru (Corfforedig)	£10,021,162	St Hugh's College, Oxford	£9,459,000
St John's College, Southsea	£10,015,330	British Refugee Council	£9,457,000
Burghley House Preservation Trust Limited	£10,008,416	Adult Placement Services	£9,455,221
A M Qattan Foundation	£9,999,826	Thomas Coram Foundation for Children	£9,433,364
Queen's Gate School Trust Limited	£9,986,177	Revitalise Respite Holidays	£9,427,000
Ashgate Hospicecare	£9,984,583	Hymers College	£9,424,536

Box Hill School Trust Limited	£9,408,500	Tenovus Cancer Care	£9,026,692
The Corporation of Trinity House of Deptford Strond	£9,403,000	Heythrop College	£9,023,935
The Serpentine Trust	£9,395,483	Money Advice Trust	£9,015,029
St Luke's Hospice Plymouth	£9,390,872	Girton College	£9,015,000
St Gemma's Hospice	£9,375,866	Moreton Hall Educational Trust Limited	£9,013,147
Woodard Schools (Nottinghamshire) Limited	£9,374,032	Bell House Dulwich	£9,010,792
St Luke's Hospice (Harrow and Brent) Ltd	£9,374,000	City of Birmingham Symphony Orchestra	£9,006,000
Kidney Research UK	£9,372,872	Tel Aviv University Trust	£8,999,075
Re - Bourne	£9,358,199	Autism Plus Limited	£8,984,025
The Chartered Institute of Housing	£9,333,000	Trinity Hospice and Palliative Care Services Ltd	£8,966,755
Advance HE	£9,326,000	Farringtons School	£8,958,402
German School Association Limited	£9,302,887	Ryde School	£8,947,370
The Royal Alexandra and Albert School	£9,302,000	WCMC	£8,941,051
Compton Care Group Limited	£9,299,218	The Union Jack Club	£8,912,739
ActiveNewham	£9,293,018	The Sutton Trust	£8,899,489
Dame Hannah Roger's School	£9,288,519	AKO Foundation	£8,897,072
Badminton School Limited	£9,287,909	Hereford Cathedral School	£8,882,575
Bespoke Supportive Tenancies Ltd	£9,287,839	Federation of Jewish Services	£8,880,409
Halle Concerts Society	£9,279,000	Giggleswick School	£8,878,778
The Mount Kelly Foundation	£9,278,481	St Vincent de Paul Society (England and Wales)	£8,865,630
Alpha International	£9,278,220	Winton Philanthropies	£8,862,935
The Master Charitable Trust	£9,273,500	Newport Live	£8,861,876
Denstone College Limited	£9,264,906	Hospiscare	£8,861,320
Vinspired	£9,262,000	Imagine Act and Succeed	£8,844,518
Cornwall Hospice Care Limited	£9,259,703	The Royal Wolverhampton School	£8,826,750
The You Trust	£9,254,000	The Malden Trust Limited	£8,816,096
Rose Bruford College of Theatre and Performance	£9,251,000	Oak Foundation	£8,797,000
The Institute of Leadership and Management	£9,250,000	Social Care in Action	£8,791,241
Northern Ballet Limited	£9,240,588	North West Air Ambulance	£8,784,495
YMCA Fairthorne Group	£9,237,763	Lumos Foundation	£8,773,767
University of Essex Students' Union	£9,236,479	Leeds Theatre Trust Limited	£8,762,746
King's School, Rochester	£9,236,041	Sunfield Children's Homes Limited	£8,756,628
Woking Hospice	£9,236,000	The Daughters of Charity of St Vincent de Paul	£8,744,306
Durham Aged Mineworkers' Homes Association	£9,233,000	Sisters of Charity of St Paul The Apostle	£8,738,208
Cotswold Archaeology Ltd	£9,221,711	Hearing Dogs for Deaf People	£8,730,662
Community Links (Northern) Limited	£9,216,865	Lycee International de Londres	£8,716,032
BookTrust	£9,212,017	The Royal School Haslemere	£8,704,863
Yale University Press London	£9,207,746	The Prior's Field School Trust Limited	£8,697,096
Queen Elizabeth's Hospital	£9,206,451	Ellen MacArthur Foundation	£8,694,235
Blenheim CDP	£9,202,481	Eurocentres UK	£8,693,040
Governance Ministries	£9,200,950	St Edmundsbury & Ipswich Diocesan Board of Finance	£8,681,000
One YMCA	£9,195,175	Porchlight	£8,679,980
Higher Education Statistics Agency Ltd	£9,194,349	The Lolev Charitable Trust	£8,660,267
London's Air Ambulance Limited	£9,193,909	Warwick Students' Union	£8,650,050
Novalis Trust	£9,185,816	Cardiff University Students' Union	£8,638,471
Churches Conservation Trust	£9,184,283	National Examination Board in Occupational Safety	£8,630,211
Imperial College Union	£9,178,608	GambleAware	£8,621,499
The Fleet Air Arm Museum	£9,177,172	The Brain Tumour Charity	£8,600,686
AECC University College	£9,167,799	The Diana Forty Memorial Trust	£8,595,065
Barnard Castle School	£9,165,946	Poole Hospital NHS Foundation Trust Charitable Fund	£8,594,460
Frensham Heights Educational Trust Limited	£9,163,000	British Association for Counselling and Psychotherapy	£8,587,937
Vocational Training Charitable Trust	£9,162,479	Medical Foundation for The Care of Victims of Torture	£8,560,808
The Morrisons Foundation	£9,162,394	Life Leisure Trust	£8,560,383
Voiceability Advocacy	£9,161,024	St Christopher School (Letchworth) Limited	£8,554,500
World Horse Welfare	£9,159,000	Lilian Faithfull Homes	£8,553,762
Ty Hafan	£9,147,774	Abbeycroft Leisure	£8,540,295
Sheffield Diocesan Board of Finance	£9,144,000	Blenheim Palace Heritage Foundation	£8,535,684
Donisthorpe Hall	£9,138,941	Warminster School	£8,534,816
The AES Tring Park School Trust	£9,131,049	Swanswell Charitable Trust	£8,529,018
Moor House School & College	£9,129,385	North England Conference of Seventh-Day Adventists	£8,496,356
Friends of the Earth Trust	£9,126,746	Queen Margaret's School, York Limited	£8,485,528
The Baptist Union of Great Britain	£9,120,000	Wolfson College, Cambridge	£8,484,950
British Safety Council	£9,107,624	Trust for London	£8,483,398
Guideposts Trust Limited	£9,098,953	Harrogate Ladies' College Limited	£8,453,592
St Peter's College, Oxford	£9,086,000	The Royal Agricultural Benevolent Institution	£8,446,000
Migrant Helpline	£9,074,000	Birtenshaw	£8,410,596
Avenues London	£9,064,000	Lincs Inspire Limited	£8,408,410
Contemporary Dance Trust Limited	£9,059,601	Dacorum Sports Trust	£8,408,025
Wolverhampton Grammar School Limited	£9,056,000	Chartered Institute of Environmental Health	£8,403,000
The British Paralympic Association	£9,048,030	The Society of St James	£8,394,728
Plymouth College & St Dunstan's Abbey Schools Charity	£9,032,605	Lhasa Limited	£8,376,000
Greenwich and Bexley Community Hospice Limited	£9,028,306	The Horniman Public Museum and Public Park Trust	£8,375,223

Murray Edwards College, Cambridge	£8,372,000	Rydal Penrhos Limited	£7,921,587
The Cathedral School (Llandaff) Limited	£8,369,906	Northampton Roman Catholic Diocesan Trust	£7,920,594
Farleigh School Trust Limited	£8,358,943	Asthma UK	£7,920,000
Margaret Green Animal Rescue	£8,355,310	St Antony's College in the University of Oxford	£7,912,000
Brighton Dome and Festival Ltd	£8,354,175	Groundwork North East	£7,911,930
The Wolverhampton Grand Theatre (1982) Limited	£8,350,463	Orphans in Need	£7,909,414
Hughes Travel Trust	£8,347,643	Shooting Star Chase	£7,900,865
The Ffestiniog and Welsh Highland Railways Trust	£8,342,746	The Congregation of Marie Auxiliatrice CIO	£7,888,030
Royal Exchange Theatre Company Limited	£8,340,000	John Lyon's Charity	£7,886,000
The Harrow Development Trust	£8,335,513	Response Organisation	£7,872,935
Carlisle Diocesan Board of Finance	£8,335,346	The Arts Educational Schools	£7,870,802
The African Institute for Mathematical Sciences	£8,331,726	County Air Ambulance Trust	£7,865,801
Birkdale School	£8,322,048	Durham School	£7,840,891
North London Hospice	£8,315,354	A C O R D	£7,833,000
International Water Association	£8,309,912	Edhi International Foundation UK	£7,828,410
The Bristol Diocesan Board of Finance Limited	£8,290,000	Christ College, Brecon	£7,826,873
Greenham Trust Ltd	£8,288,430	Lakeland Arts	£7,825,344
St Richards Hospice Foundation	£8,281,837	Future Leaders Charitable Trust Limited	£7,824,496
Somerset Redstone Trust	£8,279,350	Rennie Grove Hospice Care	£7,823,307
Dawat-E-Hadiyah Trust (United Kingdom)	£8,273,126	Fairfield Residential Home	£7,822,187
The Frank Litchfield General Charitable Trust	£8,270,792	The Victory (Services) Association Limited	£7,812,092
St Joseph's College Limited	£8,265,464	Oasis Care and Training Agency (OCTA)	£7,808,561
Prospects for People with Learning Disabilities	£8,264,435	Azure Charitable Enterprises	£7,808,037
Birkenhead School	£8,261,666	The Charity of The Order of The Marist Sisters	£7,805,515
Strode Park Foundation for People with Disabilities	£8,258,929	FIA Foundation	£7,802,238
Yorkshire Air Ambulance Limited	£8,251,041	ICAN Charity	£7,793,000
World Cancer Research Fund	£8,237,563	Solace Women's Aid	£7,791,554
KKL Charity Accounts	£8,229,733	Shrewsbury House School Trust Limited	£7,785,857
Retail Trust	£8,225,808	Mayheights Limited	£7,783,684
The National Council for Voluntary Organisations	£8,210,000	The Queen's School Chester	£7,774,326
St Luke's Hospice (Basildon and District) Limited	£8,208,272	The Beacon Educational Trust Limited	£7,764,888
International Agency for The Prevention of Blindness	£8,198,557	The Royal Air Force Club	£7,761,987
The Royal Society for The Prevention of Accidents	£8,197,321	Film Nation UK	£7,758,521
Rowcroft House Foundation Limited	£8,192,216	Hope House Children's Hospices	£7,739,805
Keychange Charity	£8,188,391	Toynbee Hall	£7,730,000
Housing for Women	£8,174,704	The Leprosy Mission England, Wales, CI and IoM	£7,728,234
Donmar Warehouse Projects Limited	£8,174,603	Volunteering Matters	£7,723,000
Devon Air Ambulance Trust	£8,167,000	The Asda Foundation	£7,702,112
St Mary's Hospice Limited	£8,166,107	Claire House	£7,696,237
The Hall School Charitable Trust	£8,157,866	Royal Leics Rutland and Wycliffe Society for The Blind	£7,694,000
International Foundation for Aids To Navigation	£8,148,428	The Farnborough Hill Trust	£7,681,442
UOHC Foundation Ltd	£8,140,463	The Truro Diocesan Board of Finance Limited	£7,680,134
International Students House	£8,137,859	Muscular Dystrophy Group of Great Britain and NI	£7,675,000
Fire Fighters Charity	£8,129,788	Pickering and Ferens Homes	£7,673,374
S4E Limited	£8,128,210	Hulme Grammar Schools	£7,670,688
Somerhill Charitable Trust Limited	£8,126,523	UK Online Giving Foundation	£7,665,805
General Optical Council	£8,113,113	Colston's School	£7,663,691
Radius Trust Limited	£8,111,308	The Game and Wildlife Conservation Trust	£7,662,798
UBS Optimus Foundation UK	£8,087,877	Nilkanth Estates	£7,654,803
Westholme School Limited	£8,070,675	Arthur Rank Hospice Charity	£7,638,699
Royal College of Occupational Therapists	£8,058,000	Notre Dame School Cobham	£7,634,003
Yesamach Levav	£8,057,095	University of Southampton Students' Union	£7,633,919
Gard'ner Memorial Limited	£8,056,193	Variety The Children's Charity	£7,633,516
Compassion in World Farming	£8,055,852	The National Federation of Women's Institutes	£7,626,663
United Christian Broadcasters Limited	£8,055,790	Bristol Music Trust	£7,625,404
Trinity College, Oxford	£8,055,000	The Institute for Fiscal Studies	£7,617,608
Traffic International	£8,050,139	The Dorset and Somerset Air Ambulance Charity	£7,615,257
The Thompson Family Charitable Trust	£8,043,773	Rendcomb College Foundation	£7,615,000
St. Teresa's School Effingham Trust	£8,034,483	Weldmar Hospicecare Trust	£7,612,224
Wessex Children's Hospice Trust	£8,030,640	Worcester Diocesan Board of Finance Limited	£7,610,000
Abbot's Hill Limited	£8,027,387	Rendcomb College	£7,598,781
Doncaster Deaf Trust	£8,013,000	The Baptist Missionary Society	£7,598,552
Cambridge in America (UK) Limited	£8,004,754	Orbis Charitable Trust	£7,597,915
The Godolphin School	£7,999,553	Paypal Giving Fund UK	£7,594,474
Kirkham Grammar School	£7,991,768	The Wilton House Trust	£7,584,928
Raleigh International Trust	£7,977,000	Opera Holland Park	£7,574,946
Essex Wildlife Trust Limited	£7,971,574	WESC Foundation	£7,570,865
ESCP Europe - Business School	£7,955,971	Royal Brompton and Harefield Hospitals Charity	£7,560,000
The Institution of Chemical Engineers	£7,954,000	Paul Strickland Scanner Centre	£7,559,237
The English Stage Company Limited	£7,947,317	Alabare Christian Care Centres	£7,558,967
St Giles Trust	£7,933,663	Prospect Hospice Limited	£7,556,000
Withington Girls' School	£7,923,892	Great Commission Ministries	£7,552,701

The Chartered Institute of Taxation	£7,541,372	The Royal United Kingdom Beneficent Association	£7,181,000
The Fidelity UK Foundation	£7,534,482	Positive Steps Oldham	£7,164,233
The Jack Petchey Foundation	£7,517,383	The Hinrichsen Foundation	£7,153,540
1610 Limited	£7,514,029	Wolfson College in the University of Oxford	£7,149,489
Christian Blind Mission (United Kingdom) Limited	£7,508,696	Westway Trust	£7,147,000
British Lung Foundation	£7,507,000	Orley Farm School Trust	£7,141,179
Age UK Leicester Shire and Rutland Limited	£7,493,597	Holmewood House School	£7,137,065
Hampshire Cultural Trust	£7,489,740	Energy Institute	£7,136,000
Integrate (Preston and Chorley) Limited	£7,488,951	The Royal College of Radiologists	£7,118,033
Transform Housing & Support	£7,486,000	Summer Fields' School Trust Limited	£7,109,284
The Old Dart Foundation	£7,484,722	CAIS Limited	£7,103,895
The Claude and Sofia Marion Foundation	£7,480,412	International Centre for Life Trust	£7,095,750
Cheam School Educational Trust	£7,475,634	Isabel Hospice Limited	£7,095,000
Midland Mencap	£7,473,785	Broadening Choices for Older People	£7,094,358
Ruthin School	£7,472,128	Castel Froma Neuro Care Limited	£7,093,809
Church Mission Society	£7,471,000	The Army Museums Ogilby Trust	£7,091,960
Methodist Central Hall Westminster	£7,468,537	Larkfield with Hill Park Autistic Trust Limited	£7,085,842
Sisters of The Holy Family of Bordeaux	£7,451,627	Salesian College Farnborough Limited	£7,083,293
Benesco Charity Limited	£7,450,791	Talbot Heath School Trust Limited	£7,062,815
Caritas Care Limited	£7,448,883	The Fetal Medicine Foundation	£7,055,602
The Company of Biologists Limited	£7,448,131	St Margaret's School Bushey	£7,052,913
Society of the Holy Child Jesus	£7,441,640	Railway Housing Association and Benefit Fund	£7,049,163
Radha Soami Satsang Beas British Isles	£7,435,741	The Movement for Non-Mobile Children (Whizz-Kidz)	£7,047,000
Magna Vitae	£7,433,130	Heathfield School	£7,038,297
The Oaklea Trust	£7,431,854	The Chartered Institute of Arbitrators	£7,037,058
The Reginald M Phillips Charitable Foundation	£7,424,468	Earl Mountbatten Hospice	£7,034,455
OMF International (UK)	£7,415,174	Kings House School Trust (Richmond) Limited	£7,033,834
Compass - Services To Tackle Problem Drug Use	£7,408,823	Yorkshire Sculpture Park	£7,033,772
Ackworth School	£7,406,422	Make-a-Wish Foundation UK	£7,031,367
St Augustine's Priory School Limited	£7,404,659	University of Manchester Students' Union	£7,012,599
York Museum & Gallery Trust	£7,386,224	The Great North Air Ambulance Service	£7,008,666
International Federation of Gynecology and Obstetrics	£7,381,456	Dove House Hospice Limited	£6,998,884
World Association of Girl Guides and Girl Scouts	£7,381,000	Regent's Park Theatre Limited	£6,991,315
The National Fund	£7,369,726	Chartered Institution of Building Services Engineers	£6,990,660
Katharine House Hospice	£7,368,550	Royal Marines Museum	£6,988,198
D&AD	£7,366,545	The Civil Service Benevolent Fund	£6,983,000
Corpus Christi College	£7,363,000	Imagine Independence	£6,981,426
Scripture Union	£7,360,000	Birmingham Women's and Children's Hospital Charity	£6,964,000
London School of Economics Students' Union	£7,357,951	Viridor Credits Environmental Company	£6,963,707
The King's School, Gloucester	£7,356,016	South of England Foundation	£6,956,000
Tropical Health and Education Trust	£7,355,433	Kirkwood Hospice	£6,949,461
Gofal Cymru	£7,343,264	St Michael's Hospice Hastings and Rother	£6,948,510
The Nuffield Foundation	£7,343,000	Bethany School	£6,945,887
The Council of Milton Abbey School Ltd	£7,338,765	The University of Notre Dame (USA) in England	£6,941,168
Hymns Ancient and Modern Limited	£7,328,886	Adviza Partnership	£6,934,233
St Michael's Hospice (inc The Freda Pearce Foundation)	£7,323,103	The Joseph Rowntree Foundation	£6,934,000
The Newcastle Diocesan Board of Finance	£7,318,824	Moorfields Eye Charity	£6,919,000
Marymount International School	£7,315,782	Hazelwood School	£6,916,774
Mansfield College, Oxford	£7,314,000	The Wigmore Hall Trust	£6,913,850
St. James's Place Charitable Foundation	£7,312,760	Send A Cow	£6,908,960
ClientEarth	£7,311,514	South West Grid for Learning Trust	£6,889,695
SOS Children's Villages UK	£7,299,115	The Weizmann Institute Foundation	£6,889,619
Raspberry Pi Foundation	£7,272,901	EMIH Limited	£6,887,510
Millennium Point Trust	£7,272,000	The College of Optometrists	£6,882,706
Healthcare Financial Management Association	£7,266,000	The V&A Foundation	£6,870,845
Luton Cultural Services Trust	£7,262,310	Ellenor	£6,852,775
Stonewall Equality Limited	£7,245,714	Bletchley Park Trust Limited	£6,849,138
Starlight Children's Foundation	£7,243,740	Sir John Cass's Foundation	£6,847,988
The Institute of Advanced Motorists Limited	£7,239,000	Hill House School Limited	£6,843,184
Addysg Oedolion Cymru / Adult Learning Wales	£7,229,000	Plymouth Diocesan Trust	£6,838,000
Bristol Old Vic and Theatre Royal Trust Limited	£7,224,114	Style Acre	£6,828,814
The London Community Foundation	£7,219,000	The Loddon Foundation Ltd	£6,826,121
Streetgames UK	£7,215,574	Burgess Hill School for Girls Company	£6,823,969
Exeter Royal Academy for Deaf Education	£7,208,840	The Clothworkers' Foundation	£6,823,832
Penrose Options	£7,205,000	Action Medical Research	£6,822,953
North York Moors Historical Railway Trust Limited	£7,202,377	West Heath 2000	£6,821,276
European Renal Association-European Dialysis	£7,200,111	Royal British Legion Poppy Lottery Limited	£6,820,189
Fashion Retail Academy	£7,198,000	The Cochrane Collaboration	£6,805,399
The Young Vic Company	£7,191,675	The Hereford Diocesan Board of Finance	£6,805,334
Hughes Hall in the University of Cambridge	£7,188,270	The Iceland Foods Charitable Foundation	£6,798,817
The Sainsbury Laboratory	£7,186,662	Twyford School	£6,797,912
Swansea University Students' Union	£7,185,531	Dawat-E-Islami UK	£6,785,518

College Francais Bilingue de Londres Ltd	£6,784,722	The Langdon Foundation	£6,493,093
British Motor Industry Heritage Trust	£6,781,696	Social Care Institute for Excellence	£6,492,465
YMCA Black Country Group	£6,778,251	Fairfield (Croydon) Limited	£6,490,141
Newbury and Thatcham Hospital Building Trust	£6,776,279	Mathematics in Education and Industry	£6,489,172
The City of Sheffield Theatre Trust	£6,774,912	Congregation of Sisters of Nazareth Charitable Trust	£6,485,026
Encompass (Dorset)	£6,770,000	Jewish Futures Trust Limited	£6,476,882
Diverse Abilities Plus Ltd.	£6,767,628	The St Gabriel Schools Foundation	£6,476,423
Darwin College, Cambridge	£6,763,364	Charlton Triangle Homes Limited	£6,465,000
The Fostering Network	£6,748,208	Bournemouth Symphony Orchestra	£6,463,941
The Certified Accountants Educational Trust	£6,746,999	National Space Centre	£6,463,321
Moreshet Hatorah Ltd	£6,744,135	The British Trust for Ornithology	£6,461,812
East Anglia Roman Catholic Diocesan Trust	£6,744,086	Priory for Wales of Most Venerable Order of St John	£6,455,999
Global Charities	£6,743,443	The National Youth Advocacy Service	£6,454,136
Peace Hospice Care	£6,740,397	Battersea Arts Centre	£6,448,916
West London YMCA	£6,735,814	Humanitarian Leadership Academy	£6,432,629
Hampshire and Isle of Wight Air Ambulance	£6,735,559	Dyslexia Institute Limited	£6,432,000
Imperial Society of Teachers of Dancing	£6,727,844	Robert Owen Communities	£6,430,646
The Tony Blair Governance Initiative	£6,712,000	The MacDaibhidh Charitable Trust	£6,429,039
Help for Heroes Recovery	£6,710,308	The Llandaff Diocesan Board of Finance	£6,425,450
Tettenhall College	£6,709,971	King's College London Students' Union	£6,418,064
The Royal National College for the Blind	£6,709,000	Poole Arts Trust Limited	£6,413,011
Cyngor Llyfrau Cymru-Welsh Books Council	£6,707,598	Heath Mount School Trust Ltd	£6,409,421
Royal United Services Institute for Defence	£6,699,460	The Hawthorns Educational Trust Limited	£6,408,498
Sevenoaks School Foundation	£6,694,670	Beaudesert Park School Trust Limited	£6,408,409
Daughters of Charity of St. Vincent de Paul Services	£6,687,627	St Catherines Hospice (Lancashire) Limited	£6,405,000
Clifton High School	£6,684,000	East Midlands Crossroads-Caring for Carers	£6,397,394
Thames Hospice	£6,679,000	Autism.West Midlands	£6,391,000
Impetus - The Private Equity Foundation	£6,678,625	Nottinghamshire YMCA	£6,387,716
Highclare School	£6,670,689	St Bede's College Limited	£6,376,802
St George's School Ascot Trust Limited	£6,664,493	The Hall for Cornwall Trust	£6,369,645
Resuscitation Council (UK)	£6,664,147	Repton Preparatory School	£6,369,352
Loftus Charitable Trust	£6,654,743	The Sheiling Special Education Trust	£6,366,294
Thames Valley Air Ambulance	£6,647,190	Help The Needy Charitable Trust	£6,357,778
Greenhouse Sports Limited	£6,646,695	Cumnor House School Trust	£6,351,552
The Tudor Trust	£6,645,000	The Cinnamon Trust	£6,348,744
Cardiff Roman Catholic Archdiocesan Trust	£6,643,849	Derby High School Trust	£6,344,078
Brooklands Museum Trust Limited	£6,634,429	Father Hudson's Society	£6,342,621
Julia's House Limited	£6,633,798	MQ: Transforming Mental Health	£6,341,449
South Downs Leisure	£6,626,144	Mount St Mary's	£6,339,642
The Trussell Trust	£6,625,173	Remodifyz Trust	£6,338,100
Greenwich Foundation for The Old Royal Naval College	£6,619,159	Kosher Outlet Assistance Ltd	£6,333,215
The Institution of Structural Engineers	£6,615,707	The Chatham Historic Dockyard Trust	£6,327,688
Ewell Castle School	£6,600,893	The Talmud Torah Machzikei Hadass Trust	£6,324,680
Crosfields School	£6,599,381	The Bloom Foundation	£6,321,853
Internews Europe	£6,598,638	University of Exeter Students' Guild	£6,315,000
Queen Mary, University of London Students' Union	£6,596,006	St Nicholas Hospice Suffolk	£6,306,179
Beechwood Park School Limited	£6,594,846	The Christian Conference Trust	£6,303,282
British Friends of The Hebrew University of Jerusalem	£6,583,934	The Lord's Taverners	£6,301,655
Lewes Old Grammar School Trust	£6,573,517	The Aldingbourne Trust	£6,299,818
Young Enterprise	£6,566,101	The Federation of European Biochemical Societies	£6,297,793
Windermere Educational Trust Limited	£6,557,897	The British Asian Trust	£6,296,279
The Kent Autistic Trust	£6,552,962	Ironbridge Gorge Museum Trust Limited	£6,295,267
Kisharon	£6,549,331	Ormiston Families	£6,295,000
Unity Leisure	£6,546,238	The Central British Fund for World Jewish Relief	£6,290,822
Tonbridge and Malling Leisure Trust	£6,543,985	UK Sailing Academy	£6,287,227
E D P Drug & Alcohol Services	£6,541,500	ECFR	£6,285,584
St. Stephen's Aids Trust	£6,537,013	Norfolk Wildlife Trust	£6,274,477
The Warwickshire Wildlife Trust Limited	£6,534,239	The Blue Coat School Birmingham Limited	£6,274,034
Afghanaid	£6,530,430	Equinox Care	£6,256,000
Wycliffe UK Limited	£6,528,592	The Martin Foundation	£6,255,251
Silcoates School	£6,528,000	Edge Grove School Trust Ltd	£6,251,687
Arch Initiatives	£6,525,745	Martin House	£6,251,324
St Edward's School Cheltenham Trust	£6,522,000	Iglesia ni Cristo (Church of Christ)	£6,248,113
Newham Training and Education Centre	£6,519,195	The Peterborough School Limited	£6,245,499
Our Lady's Abingdon Trustees Limited	£6,518,295	Avocet Trust	£6,238,363
Reading University Students' Union	£6,515,229	Barod Project	£6,234,959
Almeida Theatre Company Limited	£6,512,223	Nottingham Trent Students' Union	£6,231,801
Greater Manchester Arts Centre Limited	£6,507,079	Halliford School Limited	£6,231,794
The Godstowe Preparatory School Company Ltd	£6,505,359	The Leadership Foundation for Higher Education	£6,225,030
Thurrock Community Leisure Limited	£6,504,034	Caldecott Foundation Limited	£6,223,821
Life Path Trust Limited	£6,498,165	Swanbourne House School Trust Limited	£6,216,999
Chelsea FC Foundation	£6,493,857	Hospice of St Francis (Berkhamsted) Ltd	£6,207,000

The Royal Town Planning Institute	£6,206,000	National Rifle Association	£5,982,619
Wiltshire Air Ambulance Charitable Trust	£6,200,948	St Mary's School Shaftesbury Trust	£5,981,110
Epping Forest	£6,199,946	The St Asaph Diocesan Board of Finance	£5,976,034
Pinewood School Ltd	£6,192,416	The Marcela Trust	£5,968,958
Handicap International UK	£6,190,748	Furniture Resource Centre Limited	£5,937,722
The Black Country Living Museum Trust	£6,188,002	The English Dominican Congregation (Stone) Fund	£5,936,416
Fairley House School	£6,182,078	Solent Mind	£5,934,664
Chartered Institution of Wastes Management	£6,180,710	National College for Digital Skills	£5,925,505
HCPT (Hosanna House & Children's Pilgrimage Trust)	£6,180,219	Y Care International	£5,916,459
Royal Scot Locomotive & General Trust	£6,179,099	The Apostolic Church	£5,911,222
Caldicott Trust Limited	£6,174,103	The Church of Pentecost - UK	£5,911,171
The Linbury Trust	£6,172,000	Hull University Union Limited	£5,908,825
Tommy's	£6,166,228	Local Trust	£5,908,285
Global Alliance for Livestock Veterinary Medicines	£6,162,552	Rokeby Educational Trust Limited	£5,907,175
The Cremation Society of Great Britain	£6,160,091	The Cheltenham Trust	£5,904,524
Middlesbrough Diocesan Trust	£6,158,002	Big Local Trust	£5,900,792
Options for Supported Living	£6,157,683	British Small Animal Veterinary Association	£5,895,637
Thomas Pocklington Trust	£6,152,000	University of Birmingham Guild of Students	£5,890,540
Sibford School	£6,141,526	Westonbirt Schools Limited	£5,879,527
The Smile Train UK	£6,140,812	NIAB EMR	£5,879,000
Borough of Havant Sport and Leisure Trust	£6,138,080	Hospice UK	£5,876,000
Hornsby House Educational Trust	£6,129,501	Outreach 3 Way	£5,874,000
European Association for Cardio-Thoracic Surgery	£6,120,413	Sentinel Leisure Trust	£5,873,517
Celtic Leisure	£6,120,366	The Rotherham Hospice Trust	£5,873,078
Forest Young Men's Christian Assoc of East London	£6,120,018	Questscope	£5,867,617
Feltonfleet School Trust Limited	£6,111,380	Bolton Community Leisure	£5,866,032
SS Great Britain Trust	£6,106,498	The Clocktower Foundation	£5,864,652
The Education and Training Trust of The CII	£6,106,000	Good Things Foundation	£5,859,991
The Goodman Foundation	£6,105,740	Tone Leisure (Taunton Deane) Limited	£5,856,414
The Society for The Protection of Animals Abroad	£6,104,377	International Fellowship of Evangelical Students	£5,855,206
National Grocers Benevolent Fund	£6,101,947	Society for Endocrinology	£5,849,779
Green Templeton College	£6,101,000	The Injured Jockeys Fund	£5,847,662
Malvern Theatres Trust Limited	£6,093,357	Royal Geographical Society with IBG	£5,845,000
The Royal Welsh Agricultural Society Limited	£6,088,754	Roman Catholic Diocese of Hallam Trust	£5,837,599
The Church Army	£6,086,000	St Leonard's Hospice York	£5,835,684
Juvenile Diabetes Research Foundation Limited	£6,084,517	Warrington Community Living	£5,834,690
Peabody Community Foundation	£6,083,848	Westbourne House School Educational Trust Ltd	£5,833,354
The Said Foundation	£6,082,000	Film London	£5,833,005
Palestinians Relief and Development Fund	£6,077,075	The Children's Family Trust	£5,829,657
Canterbury Oast Trust	£6,076,149	Promoting Equality in African Schools	£5,823,713
Meath Epilepsy Charity	£6,075,481	Chevras Mo'oz Ladol	£5,823,258
The King Fahad Academy Limited	£6,074,933	Touareg Trust	£5,822,000
Rougemont School Trust Limited	£6,074,848	University of Sussex Students' Union	£5,821,247
The White Horse Care Trust	£6,074,158	Santander UK Foundation Limited	£5,809,130
St Francis' College Trust	£6,072,561	Euro Charity Trust	£5,804,513
We The Curious Limited	£6,069,000	St Piran's School Limited	£5,803,988
Hallfield School Trust	£6,068,849	Cope Childrens Trust	£5,802,269
The Purcell School	£6,062,981	CLC International (UK)	£5,797,491
Sutton's Hospital in Charterhouse	£6,062,765	The Grace Eyre Foundation	£5,794,273
The Zoological Society of East Anglia Limited	£6,059,983	Hoe Bridge School Limited	£5,792,770
UWE Students' Union	£6,051,079	Mercy Ships - U.K Ltd	£5,790,410
Berkshire, Buckinghamshire and Oxon Wildlife Trust	£6,050,000	Hand in Hand International	£5,784,344
Catholic Trust for England and Wales	£6,049,966	Newground Together	£5,784,258
Oswestry School	£6,048,212	Greenpeace Environmental Trust	£5,781,932
Town Close House Educational Trust Limited	£6,036,429	The Corporation of The Church House	£5,780,409
The Debra Reiss Foundation	£6,032,497	Yorkshire Wildlife Trust	£5,775,413
Port Regis School Ltd	£6,028,743	Hampstead Theatre Limited	£5,775,038
Humberside Engineering Training Association Ltd	£6,027,766	The Benjamin Foundation	£5,773,802
Valley Leisure Limited	£6,025,106	Students' Union Royal Holloway University of London	£5,769,842
Cranmore School	£6,024,258	Kabbalah Centre	£5,769,262
Willen Hospice	£6,022,776	Working Men's College Corporation	£5,767,000
Action on Addiction	£6,020,808	The Britford Bridge Trust	£5,764,913
King/Cullimore Charitable Trust	£6,020,454	YMCA Trinity Group	£5,761,613
Belgrade Theatre Trust (Coventry) Limited	£6,018,431	B A S School Limited	£5,752,151
Daughters of Mary and Joseph Congregation Fund	£6,017,615	Everychild	£5,752,000
St Clare West Essex Hospice Care Trust	£6,012,899	The Geological Society of London	£5,750,171
St. John's Hospice North Lancashire and South Lakes	£6,011,042	Pilgrims' Friend Society	£5,749,000
Article 19	£6,005,309	Khoo Teck Puat UK Foundation	£5,748,189
The Mulberry Bush Organisation Ltd	£5,999,952	The Amar International Charitable Foundation	£5,745,549
Walden School	£5,993,586	Honourable Artillery Company	£5,742,000
Embrace The Middle East	£5,990,789	St David's College Trust	£5,739,623
Y Coleg Cymraeg Cenedlaethol	£5,988,000	Police Now	£5,739,204

SF Foundation	£5,729,532	Sisters Hospitallers of The Sacred Heart of Jesus	£5,512,329
Intouni	£5,728,993	Ruskin College	£5,507,413
National Learning and Work Institute	£5,727,000	Musicians Benevolent Fund	£5,504,000
The Helen Taylor Thompson Foundation Limited	£5,718,860	Eric and Salome Estorick Foundation	£5,500,582
Missio	£5,714,629	Garsington Opera Limited	£5,497,908
Quaker International Educational Trust (Quiet)	£5,707,144	Freeways	£5,497,000
UK Youth	£5,707,000	Imperial College Healthcare Charities	£5,496,000
London Sport	£5,706,950	St. John's Foundation Est. 1174	£5,495,000
Birmingham Association for Mental Health	£5,704,081	University of Hertfordshire Students' Union	£5,492,580
The Association for Cultural Exchange Limited	£5,698,052	The Haddad Foundation	£5,486,963
Deeside House Educational Trust Limited	£5,696,554	Aquarius Action Projects	£5,486,072
Social Tech Trust	£5,695,182	Ludgrove School Trust Limited	£5,486,018
Family for Every Child	£5,688,342	The Royal Life Saving Society - U.K.	£5,469,608
Triangle Community Services Limited	£5,686,697	Maudsley Charity	£5,469,000
St Hugh's School (Carswell) Trust Limited	£5,686,195	Signhealth	£5,460,027
Great Walstead Limited	£5,680,356	Hafal	£5,459,306
Derwen Cymru Limited	£5,679,000	Illuminated River Foundation	£5,456,662
Portsmouth Naval Base Property Trust	£5,672,285	Postal Heritage Collection Trust	£5,447,485
Street League	£5,667,438	Fareshare	£5,446,000
The Nordoff-Robbins Music Therapy Centre	£5,666,966	Carers Trust	£5,443,875
Ecole Jeannine Manuel UK	£5,664,579	The New Beacon Educational Trust Limited	£5,443,283
Cambridge Live	£5,663,000	The Exilarch's Foundation	£5,442,077
Human Relief Foundation	£5,650,169	Dementia UK	£5,430,887
The American School in London Foundation (UK) Ltd	£5,644,000	Cambridge Centre for Sixth Form Studies	£5,430,231
Coleg Ceredigion	£5,644,000	Medical Aid for Palestinians	£5,430,000
Diagrama Foundation-Psychosocial Intervention	£5,642,992	Lantra	£5,425,229
The Royal College of Emergency Medicine	£5,638,226	Cyclists' Touring Club	£5,418,879
World Energy Council	£5,633,000	St Martin-in-the-Fields, London	£5,418,541
The Army Cadet Force Association	£5,624,766	Springhill Hospice (Rochdale)	£5,415,926
Aldwickbury School Trust Ltd	£5,622,919	University of Plymouth Students' Union	£5,414,353
The Community of The Religious of Jesus and Mary	£5,619,362	Mountview Academy of Theatre Arts Limited	£5,412,580
The Foundation for Social Entrepreneurs	£5,616,900	St John's College Limited	£5,410,749
Cranford House School Trust Limited	£5,614,119	Liverpool and Merseyside Theatres Trust Limited	£5,409,000
Living Streets (The Pedestrians Association)	£5,611,388	Age UK Northumberland	£5,407,416
The Northern College for Residential Adult Education	£5,610,835	The Charles Wolfson Charitable Trust	£5,405,062
Keep Britain Tidy	£5,607,812	Newells School Trust Limited	£5,398,063
Church Urban Fund	£5,605,000	Hadras Kodesh Trust	£5,396,599
Rishworth School	£5,603,481	St Martin's (Northwood) Preparatory School Trust Ltd	£5,394,786
St Joseph's College Reading Trust	£5,602,500	Ealing Community Transport	£5,390,900
The Polish Catholic Mission	£5,596,575	Holme Grange Ltd	£5,389,624
The Fellowship of The School of Economic Science	£5,594,000	The Drinkaware Trust	£5,387,003
Bethphage	£5,587,887	The Gosling Foundation Limited	£5,386,362
Spanish and Portuguese Jews Home for the Aged	£5,583,862	Soho Theatre Company Limited	£5,384,421
St Ronan's School (Hawkhurst)	£5,581,620	Institute of Fundraising	£5,375,957
The Mary Stevens Hospice	£5,578,778	Greater Manchester Accessible Transport Limited	£5,374,456
Cheltenham Festivals	£5,574,578	Autism Sussex Limited	£5,372,785
Society of Local Authority Chief Executives	£5,574,363	Forest Peoples Programme	£5,372,246
The Children's Food Trust	£5,573,000	Amabrill Ltd	£5,362,944
The Thursford Collection	£5,571,350	Bible and Gospel Trust	£5,359,921
The Society for Promoting Christian Knowledge	£5,565,525	Khodorkovsky Foundation	£5,356,214
Alive Leisure	£5,559,270	Northamptonshire Music and Performing Arts Trust	£5,348,212
Al-Shirkatul Islamiyyah	£5,558,823	Esmee Fairbairn Foundation	£5,344,000
St Davids Diocesan Board of Finance	£5,558,049	St Michael's Hospice (North Hampshire)	£5,340,313
Durston House School Educational Trust Limited	£5,556,096	The Sackler Trust	£5,339,843
The Royal Naval Benevolent Trust	£5,556,003	Leweston School Trust	£5,339,140
The Angel Foundation	£5,555,530	Wirral Youth Zone	£5,339,097
The Police Rehabilitation Centre	£5,549,212	Wicksteed Charitable Trust	£5,338,424
Springboard Sunderland Trust	£5,544,936	The Education Endowment Foundation	£5,333,867
The Surrey Wildlife Trust Limited	£5,539,105	Dontchev Foundation	£5,331,204
Prifysgol Cymru / The University of Wales	£5,537,000	The Ormerod Home Trust Limited	£5,328,341
Target Housing Limited	£5,536,707	Rushmoor School Limited	£5,325,506
Bedstone Educational Trust Limited	£5,534,288	Farmland Reserve UK Limited	£5,324,000
The David Hockney Foundation (UK) Limited	£5,533,418	Headway - The Brain Injury Association	£5,321,761
Lyric Theatre Hammersmith Limited	£5,533,101	The Young Foundation	£5,318,446
Three Counties Agricultural Society	£5,528,504	St Mary's College Crosby Trust Limited	£5,317,702
Catholic Blind Institute	£5,528,041	The Chartered Quality Institute	£5,316,000
Jaffray Care Society	£5,520,225	Action Housing and Support Limited	£5,312,910
The Police Treatment Centres	£5,518,323	The Becht Family Charitable Trust	£5,303,222
Saint Catherine's Hospice Trust	£5,517,666	Seedbed Christian Community Trust Limited	£5,300,834
Maltman's Green School Trust Limited	£5,515,594	The Severn Trent Water Charitable Trust Fund	£5,294,781
Roffey Park Institute Limited	£5,514,165	St Aubyn's (Woodford Green) School Trust	£5,291,646
Alton Convent School Charity	£5,512,592	Institute for Public Policy Research	£5,288,160

Arthritis Care	£5,287,000	St George's School, Edgbaston	£5,038,087
St Edmund's College in the University of Cambridge	£5,285,000	Surgo Foundation UK Limited	£5,033,409
The Rumi Foundation	£5,272,571	United Utilities Trust Fund	£5,026,410
The Union of The Sisters of Mercy of Great Britain	£5,271,273	Nuneaton & Bedworth Leisure Trust	£5,023,478
DKMS Foundation	£5,265,831	All Hallows Healthcare Trust Ltd	£5,019,902
Wisbech Grammar School	£5,263,992	Centre for Effective Dispute Resolution Limited	£5,015,000
Papplewick Educational Trust Limited	£5,263,204	Sobell House Hospice Charity Limited	£5,011,246
Bolton Hospice	£5,262,878	The Manor Preparatory School Trust	£5,010,754
The Cambridge Crystallographic Data Centre	£5,258,749	The Common Purpose Charitable Trust	£5,010,652
Northamptonshire Association of Youth Clubs	£5,253,680	Wigan and Leigh Hospice	£5,010,062
Conservation Education & Research Trust	£5,251,906	Mudiad Meithrin	£5,010,010
Clarion Futures	£5,250,000	Crimestoppers Trust	£5,008,846
Life Opportunities Trust	£5,249,968	Three C's Support	£5,007,628
Active Life Limited	£5,241,520	Shared Lives South West	£5,005,778
Oshwal Association of The UK	£5,231,614	Bologna Center of The Johns Hopkins University	£5,005,361
The Nelson Trust	£5,228,208	The Naked Heart Foundation	£5,003,613
Sacred Heart School Beechwood Trust Ltd	£5,224,713	Shaukat Khanum Memorial Trust	£5,002,281
Ashorne Hill Management College	£5,223,419	Lepra	£5,001,352
Dover College	£5,220,504	Finton House Educational Trust	£4,999,568
The Watershed Arts Trust Limited	£5,208,104	The Motability Tenth Anniversary Trust	£4,995,000
The Congregation of Christian Brothers	£5,202,285	Coquet Trust	£4,992,060
The I T F Seafarers Trust	£5,200,255	Chesham Preparatory School Trust Limited	£4,986,503
St Catherine's School, Twickenham	£5,199,838	BeyondAutism	£4,984,553
Textile Reuse and International Development	£5,197,633	University of Leicester Students' Union	£4,983,416
The Forum for The Future	£5,193,278	Anheddau Cyf	£4,982,728
Compton Verney House Trust	£5,187,298	The Penderels Trust Limited	£4,981,897
Walhampton School Trust Ltd.	£5,179,355	Eisteddfod Genedlaethol Cymru	£4,981,000
Wirral Hospice St John's	£5,177,605	Crohn's and Colitis UK	£4,978,196
Pure Innovations Limited	£5,168,641	York Citizens' Theatre Trust Ltd	£4,978,086
Institute of Biomedical Science	£5,165,874	The Royal College of Pathologists	£4,968,619
The University of York Students' Union (YUSU)	£5,164,775	Butterwick Limited	£4,967,091
SeAp	£5,163,530	Phenomen Trust	£4,965,117
The Students' Union at Bournemouth University	£5,158,661	Greater Manchester Centre for Voluntary Organisation	£4,964,690
Humber Learning Consortium	£5,157,961	Royal Military Academy Sandhurst Commandant's Fund	£4,963,998
The British Museum Friends	£5,155,682	Rye St Antony School Limited	£4,962,428
Thornleigh Camphill Communities Limited	£5,154,749	Carers UK	£4,962,123
Arnold House School Ltd	£5,152,172	Bader International Study Centre	£4,958,773
Refugee Action	£5,152,000	Bournemouth Young Men's Christian Association	£4,957,000
The Royal Society for Blind Children	£5,152,000	IES London	£4,955,480
The Westminster Abbey Trust	£5,148,984	After Adoption	£4,954,026
Medical Mission International (UK)	£5,147,040	Hope City Church	£4,952,734
Moulsford Preparatory School Trust Limited	£5,146,912	The Sheffield Media and Exhibition Centre Limited	£4,952,634
The Brilliant Club	£5,130,037	Pact Educational Trust Limited	£4,951,878
Brathay Trust	£5,128,000	West Kirby Residential School	£4,943,944
The Silver Line Helpline	£5,126,370	BRS Education Limited	£4,943,665
Diabetes Research & Wellness Foundation	£5,123,885	Citizens UK Charity	£4,942,816
Newbold College	£5,118,192	Jesus House	£4,940,587
Northumbria Students' Union	£5,111,547	Elmhurst Ballet School	£4,939,602
Acorn Early Years Foundation	£5,109,977	Alder Hey Children's Charity	£4,937,000
Royal Hospital Chelsea Appeal Limited	£5,100,971	Harlow and District Sports Trust	£4,936,541
The Dulverton Trust	£5,100,416	Borough Market (Southwark)	£4,932,574
Goodwin Development Trust	£5,100,000	The Heart of Kent Hospice	£4,932,413
Islamic Help	£5,097,320	Wave Leisure Trust Limited	£4,931,124
The Eranda Rothschild Foundation	£5,096,016	The Zochonis Charitable Trust	£4,929,423
The Square Chapel Trust	£5,094,865	Nottingham Playhouse Trust Limited	£4,922,873
The Edmund Trust	£5,091,854	The Paul Mellon Centre for Studies in British Art	£4,919,990
The David Sheldrick Wildlife Trust	£5,090,051	Rotary Foundation of The United Kingdom	£4,916,899
Skill Force Development	£5,088,718	NABS	£4,915,455
Reuben Foundation	£5,088,284	City Catering Southampton	£4,914,507
Betel of Britain	£5,087,537	The Berkshire Young Musicians Trust	£4,911,801
St. Michael's School Trust	£5,086,854	The Mary Rose Trust	£4,911,072
Chance To Shine Foundation Ltd	£5,084,000	Avenues East	£4,909,000
Alderley Edge School for Girls	£5,082,923	Jewish Secondary Schools Movement	£4,908,076
The Asfari Foundation	£5,080,103	Blind Children UK	£4,908,000
Ballard School Limited	£5,077,192	Beachborough School Trust Limited	£4,906,089
Bilton Grange Trust Limited	£5,066,585	Gosling Sports Park	£4,904,106
Winchester House School Trust Limited	£5,061,614	Newland House School Trust Limited	£4,902,000
Autism Hampshire	£5,056,696	The Mercers Charitable Foundation	£4,901,000
The Society of Dyers and Colourists	£5,054,041	The Doreen Bird Foundation	£4,897,618
Syracuse University (USA) London Program	£5,049,470	The Rufford Foundation	£4,894,798
Borletti-Buitoni Trust	£5,046,804	Saint Martin's (Solihull) Ltd	£4,893,584
Autism at Kingwood	£5,038,477	Lincolnshire Bomber Command Memorial	£4,889,754

Apasen	£4,887,983	The Institute for War and Peace Reporting (IWPR)	£4,710,779
Reach to Teach	£4,887,239	Quintin Hogg Trust	£4,707,079
Save An Orphan Global Trust	£4,883,982	The Alnwick Garden Trust	£4,701,680
Harrogate District Hospice Care	£4,881,247	The Salisbury Diocesan Board of Education	£4,698,012
St John's School	£4,879,574	Bradford Trident Limited	£4,698,011
Bristol Drugs Project Limited	£4,879,351	The Onside Foundation	£4,697,000
Manchester Metropolitan University Students' Union	£4,879,187	Kingsley School, Bideford	£4,691,373
Phoenix Sports and Recreation (Rotherham)	£4,877,771	Clacton Family Trust Limited	£4,690,323
Beaconsfield Educational Trust Ltd	£4,874,026	Relate	£4,690,106
St John's College, Durham	£4,873,522	Sports Aid Trust	£4,688,339
Cruse Bereavement Care	£4,871,356	The Hammond School Limited	£4,684,202
Prison Advice and Care Trust (PACT)	£4,868,000	The Mental Health Foundation	£4,683,430
Priory School Edgbaston Trustees Limited	£4,865,416	Christ Embassy	£4,681,905
The Mount School (York)	£4,861,343	Scarborough College	£4,680,163
Halifax Opportunities Trust	£4,860,079	Keele University Student Union	£4,679,126
Austin Friars	£4,855,921	Dudley and West Midlands Zoological Society Ltd	£4,672,503
The Talking Trust	£4,854,350	Amphibian and Reptile Conservation Trust	£4,669,506
St Edmund's School Trust Limited	£4,850,826	The Biochemical Society	£4,669,000
Incorporated Council of Law Reporting for E&W	£4,846,608	Grace and Compassion Benedictines	£4,667,961
N-Compass North West Limited	£4,843,817	Coventry Sports Foundation	£4,665,175
Women in Informal Employment Globalizing	£4,842,678	ASCB Charitable Fund	£4,662,945
National Osteoporosis Society	£4,841,209	Contact A Family	£4,661,873
Orwell Park School Educational Trust Ltd	£4,836,775	Kennedy Independent School Trust Limited	£4,659,128
Merthyr Tydfil Leisure Trust Limited	£4,834,310	Conciliation Resources	£4,655,383
NECA	£4,833,258	Franciscan Missionaries of The Divine Motherhood	£4,653,328
The Motivation Charitable Trust	£4,832,854	Elstree School Limited	£4,652,704
New College Worcester	£4,832,049	The National Memorial Arboretum Company Limited	£4,650,656
Sheffield Theatres Crucible Trust	£4,831,043	Amana Trust	£4,647,056
Awen Cultural Trust	£4,830,768	Social Investment Business Foundation	£4,647,000
The Climate Change Organisation	£4,830,524	Heart of England Mencap	£4,644,127
YMCA Thames Gateway	£4,827,095	Tusk Trust	£4,641,239
Chain of Hope	£4,826,504	The Anvil Trust Limited	£4,640,638
University of Bath Students' Union (BUSU)	£4,823,919	CVQO Ltd	£4,639,445
Midlands Arts Centre	£4,820,708	Mary Ward Settlement	£4,634,039
St Luke's Cheshire Hospice	£4,820,137	Manchester University NHS Foundation Trust Charity	£4,634,000
Essential Christian	£4,819,854	The Little Princess Trust	£4,632,951
The Gloucestershire Everyman Theatre Company Ltd	£4,817,140	The Cambridge Arts Theatre Trust Limited	£4,631,882
The New Wolsey Theatre Company Limited	£4,813,883	The Redland High School for Girls	£4,625,206
Bute House Preparatory School for Girls Limited	£4,811,668	Leasowe Community Homes	£4,624,000
Leicestershire Independent Educational Trust	£4,811,108	Rainbow Trust Children's Charity	£4,623,891
REDR UK	£4,809,562	The Supported Fostering Services Charitable Trust	£4,618,971
Birmingham and Solihull Women's Aid	£4,809,397	China Fleet Trust	£4,617,146
Exceed Worldwide	£4,799,870	Community Links Trust Limited	£4,613,276
Roy Castle Lung Cancer Foundation	£4,795,618	Manor Lodge School	£4,612,102
Care for Veterans	£4,786,078	Torfaen Leisure Trust Limited	£4,609,246
Baltic Flour Mills Visual Arts Trust	£4,786,024	Mayfair Charities Limited	£4,607,000
Sisters of The Holy Cross Charitable Trust	£4,782,725	Groundwork Cheshire Lancashire & Merseyside	£4,599,746
Newcastle upon Tyne Hospitals NHS Charity	£4,781,191	Picker Institute Europe	£4,599,000
Salesians of Don Bosco UK	£4,780,409	International Development Enterprises (UK)	£4,598,504
Royal Aeronautical Society	£4,780,407	Safelives	£4,594,419
North Herts Hospice Care Association	£4,772,012	The Field Lane Foundation	£4,594,002
Tomorrow's People Trust Limited	£4,767,038	Duke of Edinburgh's International Award Foundation	£4,592,000
Durham High School for Girls	£4,764,018	Norwich City Community Sports Foundation	£4,591,659
Gwent Association of Voluntary Organisations	£4,761,240	Royal School for The Deaf Derby	£4,590,000
Redeemed Christian Church of God	£4,760,734	The Royal College of Ophthalmologists	£4,584,000
The Alexander Mosley Charitable Trust	£4,759,871	The National Youth Agency	£4,582,000
DFN Charitable Foundation	£4,755,131	Teesside Hospice Care Foundation	£4,578,958
Abbotsholme School	£4,752,235	Int Network for the Availability of Scientific Publications	£4,576,926
Bridgewood Trust Limited	£4,751,652	The Royal Masonic Trust for Girls and Boys	£4,574,000
Coventry and Warwickshire Mind	£4,748,390	Buttle UK	£4,574,000
Weald and Downland Open Air Museum Limited	£4,741,848	The Connection at St Martin-in-the-Fields	£4,573,247
Humbercare Limited	£4,738,689	People for The Ethical Treatment of Animals (PETA)	£4,572,284
Chartered Institute of Library & Info Professionals	£4,738,350	Centre 404	£4,571,558
Age UK North Tyneside	£4,733,668	Achievement for All (3as)	£4,571,496
The Charitable Trusts for University Hospitals Bristol	£4,732,000	Lichfield Cathedral School	£4,571,102
Linacre College	£4,730,000	Street (UK) Foundation	£4,565,438
The Message Trust	£4,729,571	Locality (UK)	£4,561,000
North Devon Hospice	£4,727,205	The Generation Foundation	£4,560,671
The United World Colleges (International)	£4,727,000	The Tank Museum Limited	£4,559,426
Blackheath Preparatory School	£4,722,974	Postal Heritage Trust	£4,553,187
Spratton Hall School Trust Limited	£4,713,620	Gilmoor Benevolent Fund Limited	£4,552,281
Stafford Independent Grammar School	£4,713,456	The Hospital of God at Greatham	£4,550,285

Willowbrook Hospice	£4,548,441	New Kadampa Tradition - Kadampa Buddhist Union	£4,367,319
GamCare	£4,541,970	Aspire Living Limited	£4,359,300
Midland Group Training Services Limited	£4,539,109	Culture Coventry	£4,359,000
Martha Trust	£4,535,738	Ringwood Waldorf School	£4,358,088
Magen David Adom UK	£4,534,708	Office of The Independent Adjudicator for HE	£4,357,795
Gayhurst School Trust	£4,534,013	Fylde Community Link Limited	£4,357,294
The Bowes Museum	£4,530,058	The Crossrail Art Foundation	£4,355,952
The Electrical Safety Council	£4,524,000	The Jubilee Sailing Trust	£4,355,936
Lucton Pierrepoint School Educational Trust	£4,523,105	Gatehouse Educational Trust Limited	£4,354,600
Sussex Wildlife Trust	£4,522,605	The Engineering Development Trust	£4,348,300
Power to Change Trust	£4,520,000	Yateley Manor School Ltd	£4,345,645
The British Institute of Innkeeping	£4,519,909	East Cheshire Hospice	£4,345,121
NUS Students' Union Charitable Services	£4,517,030	Hospice of The Good Shepherd Ltd	£4,345,099
Developing Health and Independence	£4,516,758	The Foundation Trust Network	£4,344,242
The Tavistock Institute of Medical Psychology	£4,514,536	The Born Free Foundation	£4,341,533
The University of Chicago Foundation Limited	£4,508,730	Suffolk Wildlife Trust Limited	£4,339,000
Opportunity International United Kingdom	£4,507,509	British Dressage	£4,337,363
Cornwall Air Ambulance Trust	£4,503,932	Bransby Horses	£4,333,974
Maharishi Foundation	£4,503,024	The Centre for Economic Policy Research	£4,333,763
Absolutely Leisure	£4,502,622	Echoes of Service	£4,333,565
Kings Place Music Foundation	£4,502,489	Religious of The Assumption	£4,329,000
Youth Business International	£4,498,023	The Maynard School	£4,328,543
The Drapers' Charities Pooling Scheme	£4,494,663	Akshar Educational Trust	£4,325,382
The Pilgrims' School	£4,493,901	Mayville High School Limited	£4,325,324
JW3 Trust Limited	£4,491,272	The AIM Foundation	£4,322,949
Medical Research Foundation	£4,481,993	The Study (Wimbledon) Limited	£4,322,187
Keren Hatzolas Doros Alei Siach	£4,478,433	Babington House School Ltd	£4,321,999
Wolverhampton Voluntary Sector Council	£4,473,482	The Reed Foundation	£4,320,778
Cundall Manor Limited	£4,472,349	Spring Housing Association Limited	£4,319,013
Gardeners' Royal Benevolent Society	£4,470,141	The Greenbank Project	£4,312,560
Calico Enterprise Limited	£4,469,654	Keyring-Living Support Networks	£4,311,000
Rochdale Training Association Limited	£4,467,969	Tottenham Hotspur Foundation	£4,310,077
The Millennium Awards Trust	£4,464,041	The Lancashire Wildlife Trust	£4,308,000
Rikkyo School in England Trust	£4,463,785	St Nicholas' School (Fleet) Educational Trust Limited	£4,305,927
Swalcliffe Park School Trust	£4,459,451	Kingston Theatre Trust	£4,304,951
Mitcham Lane Baptist Church CIO	£4,458,347	Homefield Preparatory School Trust Limited	£4,301,818
The Mission To Seafarers	£4,458,000	The Sisters of Notre Dame (of Namur)	£4,301,543
The Chaseley Trust	£4,456,121	British Association of Dermatologists	£4,300,529
Trinity School Teignmouth	£4,453,634	St Andrews Hospice Limited	£4,299,841
Bournemouth War Memorial Homes	£4,450,313	Age Concern Essex	£4,299,677
Polam Hall Darlington Limited	£4,450,299	Royal Astronomical Society	£4,299,415
Bid Services	£4,450,234	Chapter (Cardiff) Limited	£4,294,779
St Marys School Gerrard Cross Limited	£4,445,234	The Gregg and St Winifred's Schools Trust	£4,293,758
Shebbear College	£4,444,594	Leazes Homes Limited	£4,292,000
Chartered Institute of Logistics and Transport in UK	£4,443,000	Northamptonshire Independent Grammar School Charity	£4,290,370
St Wilfrid's Hospice (Eastbourne)	£4,442,603	Devon Wildlife Trust	£4,290,203
The Tony Blair Faith Foundation	£4,440,000	Touchstone-Leeds	£4,289,984
Kingshott School Trust Limited	£4,438,477	Willow Foundation	£4,287,196
Homeless Link	£4,436,492	Our Kids	£4,284,142
University of Lincoln Students Union	£4,427,680	The Coalfields Regeneration Trust	£4,284,000
Amref Health Africa	£4,424,240	International Liberty Association	£4,283,327
Rays of Sunshine	£4,420,453	Crafts Council	£4,279,395
St Andrews (Pangbourne) School Trust Limited	£4,418,689	King's College Hospital Charity	£4,278,630
St Mary's School (Colchester) Limited	£4,416,875	The Presbyterian Church of Wales	£4,274,000
Ashdown Medway Accommodation Trust	£4,415,646	The Bridget Espinosa Memorial Trust	£4,272,452
The L G S General Charitable Trust	£4,413,774	People 1st	£4,272,000
St George's School Windsor Castle	£4,410,177	Waymarks Limited	£4,268,000
Havencare (South West) Limited	£4,409,887	Abbots Bromley School for Girls Limited	£4,266,935
Northwick Park Institute for Medical Research Ltd	£4,407,485	West Anglia Crossroads Caring for Carers	£4,265,060
New Roots Limited	£4,406,988	M and R Gross Charities Limited	£4,263,991
Lochinver House School	£4,404,493	The Lincs and Notts Air Ambulance Charitable Trust	£4,263,797
The Mare and Foal Sanctuary	£4,403,549	Cardiff YMCA (1910) Trust	£4,261,166
Legatum Institute Foundation	£4,398,079	Wildlife Trust for Beds Cambs Northants	£4,259,850
The Kingsley School	£4,398,028	Passage 2000	£4,254,654
London Central Young Men's Christian Association	£4,396,128	Child Action Northwest	£4,252,632
Institute for Government	£4,387,284	St Martins Housing Trust	£4,252,063
Glendower School Trust Limited	£4,386,162	Mifal Hachesed Vehatzedokoh	£4,250,490
SKT Welfare	£4,386,106	Alternative Theatre Company Limited	£4,244,878
Everton in the Community	£4,385,340	Mountain of Fire and Miracles Ministries International	£4,244,840
The Bromley By Bow Centre	£4,373,000	The Ditcham Park School Charity Association	£4,244,661
University of Bristol Students' Union	£4,369,199	CAYSH	£4,241,267
Stover School Association	£4,367,539	Techniquest	£4,232,848

Dogs for Good	£4,232,040	Fundacao Focus Assistencia Humanitaria Europa	£4,056,782
The Pennies Foundation	£4,228,680	Professional Association for Childcare and Early Years	£4,056,500
The National Garden Scheme	£4,228,340	The Hetton Charitable Trust	£4,056,388
RZIM Zacharias Trust	£4,221,656	Yeovil District Hospital NHS Foundation Trust	£4,050,000
Birmingham Young Men's Christian Association	£4,221,246	Murray Hall Community Trust	£4,049,268
The Carmelite Charitable Trust	£4,218,573	Coleg Llanymddyfri	£4,045,108
Brambletye School Trust Limited	£4,213,974	Penny Brohn Cancer Care	£4,045,105
Eothen Homes Limited	£4,210,870	Duke of Kent School	£4,042,982
Homefield College Limited	£4,207,585	The Bernard Sunley Charitable Foundation	£4,040,000
Bickley Park School Ltd	£4,206,098	Gads Hill School	£4,038,938
St Mary's School, Hampstead	£4,205,669	The Malvernian Society Limited	£4,035,281
The Physiological Society	£4,205,000	Arch (North Staffs) Limited	£4,034,880
Microbiology Society	£4,202,000	Ahavat Shalom Charity Fund	£4,033,545
Islamic Aid	£4,200,168	Witham Hall School Trust Limited	£4,031,903
The Smith Foundation	£4,198,934	The Foundation for Liver Research	£4,031,373
Community Foundation for Leeds	£4,194,000	Order of Malta	£4,031,281
Royal College of Speech and Language Therapists	£4,191,000	The CH Foundation (UK)	£4,030,600
Sevenoaks Preparatory School Limited	£4,190,857	The United Society	£4,028,000
Farlington School Trust Limited	£4,189,694	Energy 4 Impact	£4,027,502
Hampshire and Isle of Wight Wildlife Trust	£4,189,290	Age UK Northamptonshire	£4,027,457
Michael Hall School	£4,186,170	Lucy Cavendish College, Cambridge	£4,020,695
Hertford British Hospital Corporation, Paris	£4,185,671	Moira House School Limited	£4,019,686
The Royal Institution of Great Britain	£4,183,000	Centre for Effective Altruism	£4,019,637
Foundation of Light	£4,181,865	Canterbury Cathedral Trust Fund	£4,018,437
Art Services Grants Limited	£4,179,635	St David's Home for Disabled Soldiers, Sailors & Airmen	£4,017,089
Sons and Friends of The Clergy	£4,177,820	Imperial Health Charity	£4,013,000
London Film School Limited	£4,177,436	The Veolia Environmental Trust	£4,012,000
New Wine Trust	£4,173,395	Norfolk Community Foundation	£4,012,000
Charity of The Roman Union of The Order of St Ursula	£4,173,296	Yvonne Arnaud Theatre Management Limited	£4,010,459
Societe Generale UK Group Charitable Trust	£4,170,303	National Cancer Research Institute	£4,005,764
The Think Ahead Organisation	£4,165,983	St Neots (Eversley) Limited	£4,003,600
Thorpe House School Trust	£4,165,071	Amesbury School Trust Limited	£4,000,710
Whitechapel Gallery	£4,164,822	One Nation	£3,999,599
Institute of Contemporary Arts Limited	£4,164,027	Westbank Community Health and Care	£3,995,083
The Gaudio Family Foundation (UK) Limited	£4,162,442	The Charleston Trust (Bloomsbury in Sussex)	£3,993,334
The Magdalen College Development Trust	£4,162,365	Parkhaven Trust	£3,992,383
The Macular Disease Society	£4,161,000	Abbeyfield The Dales Limited	£3,992,173
Newcastle School for Boys	£4,160,847	Kent Wildlife Trust	£3,989,000
Lohana Charitable Foundation Ltd	£4,159,965	Aberdour School Educational Trust	£3,988,681
Emuno Educational Centre Limited	£4,159,724	Jah-Jireh Charity Homes	£3,985,623
The Gloucester Charities Trust	£4,158,588	Bath Abbey with St James, Bath	£3,979,729
West Hill School Trust Limited	£4,156,453	Lady Barn House School Limited	£3,976,958
Francis House Family Trust	£4,155,764	Jubilee Sailing Trust (Tenacious) Limited	£3,974,950
International Society for Krishna Consciousness	£4,142,777	Liverpool Charity and Voluntary Services	£3,974,263
Greyhound Trust	£4,135,511	The David Ross Foundation	£3,974,037
Harris Manchester College, Oxford	£4,133,016	The Queen Elizabeth Diamond Jubilee Trust	£3,973,943
Overgate Hospice	£4,129,488	Abbeyfield Wey Valley Society Limited	£3,970,223
Council for World Mission (UK)	£4,129,303	The Legal Education Foundation	£3,969,000
Weston Hospicecare Limited	£4,128,769	The E P A Cephalosporin Fund	£3,966,796
Ascentis	£4,125,749	Bruton School for Girls	£3,966,740
Richard Ormonde Shuttleworth Remembrance Trust	£4,124,000	BBC Media Action (India) Limited	£3,965,735
British Friends of Ezrat Yisrael Kiryat Sefer	£4,118,650	Church of God of Prophecy Trust	£3,956,761
Marlborough House School	£4,118,177	Al-Imdaad Foundation UK	£3,956,742
Forward in Faith Ministry U.K.	£4,117,640	RFEA Limited	£3,956,375
Castle Court School Educational Trust Limited	£4,116,851	Pendleside Hospice	£3,955,835
AAGBI Foundation	£4,115,747	The ABC Trust	£3,954,385
Netherhall Educational Association	£4,107,366	Holocaust Educational Trust	£3,951,562
Staying First	£4,106,327	Brighton and Hove Seaside Community Homes Ltd	£3,950,127
Repton School Trust	£4,102,783	Worcester Municipal Charities (CIO)	£3,949,476
Bluebell Wood Children's Hospice	£4,102,000	Royal British Legion Poppy Factory Limited	£3,946,476
John Ellerman Foundation	£4,100,000	Support Adoption for Pets	£3,945,194
The Grange Centre for People with Disabilities	£4,099,290	Aspire	£3,945,183
Threshold Housing Project Limited	£4,099,000	Zoe's Place Trust	£3,945,170
Coleg Elidyr Camphill Communities	£4,094,489	Step One Charity	£3,945,099
Birmingham Voluntary Service Council	£4,093,426	Big Life Centres	£3,943,485
Bishopsgate School Limited	£4,088,873	Crossroads Care Cheshire, Manchester & Merseyside	£3,942,667
Tyneside Cinema	£4,088,755	The Mall School Trust	£3,942,006
The London Library	£4,077,447	Ballet Rambert Limited	£3,939,257
University Hospitals Birmingham Charity	£4,070,000	St Paul's Cathedral Choir School	£3,938,098
Burnley Leisure	£4,066,356	The Wilverley Association	£3,937,305
Aurora Options	£4,062,301	Cambridge Tutors Educational Trust Limited	£3,937,304
Sandroyd School Trust Limited	£4,061,289	The Dunhill Medical Trust	£3,936,920

Greenfield Gospel Hall Trust	£3,933,612	Society of Antiquaries of London	£3,810,519
St Nicholas School (Harlow) Limited	£3,931,311	The Cecil and Alan Pilkington Trust Fund	£3,810,266
Ranyard Charitable Trust	£3,930,652	National Spiritual Assembly of The Baha'is of UK	£3,809,506
YMCA Bath Group	£3,929,376	Saint Felix Schools	£3,807,556
Brighton YMCA	£3,929,122	Llanthony Secunda Priory Trust	£3,806,609
Empowering People Inspiring Communities Limited	£3,926,277	Smart Criminal Justice Services	£3,803,904
Vinehall School Limited	£3,925,612	British Society for Rheumatology	£3,803,685
Grange Park Opera	£3,923,381	Sir John Soane's Museum	£3,803,647
The Royal Masonic Benevolent Institution	£3,921,000	Self Help Services	£3,797,946
The British Ecological Society	£3,918,000	Wakefield Hospice	£3,797,792
School for Social Entrepreneurs	£3,916,423	Newcastle University Students' Union	£3,795,000
Purley Park Trust Limited	£3,916,246	The Teresa Rosenbaum Golden Charitable Trust	£3,794,852
The Oxford Playhouse Trust	£3,914,133	New Marston Limited	£3,794,699
Studio Wayne McGregor Limited	£3,913,691	Bury Metropolitan Arts Association	£3,793,331
Chafyn Grove School	£3,911,266	The Ace Centre-North	£3,792,532
Teesside High School Limited	£3,906,293	British Eye Research Foundation	£3,792,000
Shumei Eiko Limited	£3,904,094	The 29th May 1961 Charity	£3,791,323
The South West Heritage Trust	£3,900,716	One Heart - Lev Echod	£3,791,061
Schools and Teachers Innovating for Results	£3,899,268	East of England Agricultural Society	£3,790,552
CAN Mezzanine	£3,893,389	Volunteer Reading Help	£3,790,152
Saint Margaret's Convent (Chiswick)	£3,893,224	The Swedish School Society in London	£3,786,907
Bromley, Lewisham & Greenwich Mind Ltd	£3,891,455	Katharine House Hospice Trust	£3,785,677
One Young World Limited	£3,890,000	Safe Haven London	£3,785,378
Yvonne Arnaud Theatre Trust	£3,888,887	Little Bookham Manor House School	£3,783,527
Manchester United Foundation	£3,888,468	The Chicken Shed Theatre Trust	£3,783,145
The Fred Hollows Foundation (UK)	£3,888,389	The Grand Charity	£3,781,000
SHAP Ltd	£3,887,982	The Royal Bath and West of England Society	£3,780,989
Queenscourt Hospice	£3,882,452	Coram Children's Legal Centre Limited	£3,780,887
St Rocco's Hospice	£3,881,606	County Durham Community Foundation	£3,779,677
Adcote School Educational Trust Limited	£3,879,384	YMCA Norfolk	£3,778,724
Gilbert Deya Ministries	£3,876,583	Pioneer Theatres Limited	£3,778,262
Thurlow Educational Trust	£3,876,361	The East Lancashire Hospice	£3,777,926
Stillbirth and Neonatal Death Society	£3,873,534	Self Help Africa (UK)	£3,777,801
British Universities and Colleges Sport Limited	£3,871,082	The Book Trade Charity	£3,777,287
Staffordshire University Students' Union	£3,870,084	Stoke-on-Trent and North Staffordshire Theatre Trust	£3,776,939
East London Business Alliance	£3,869,711	Yehudi Menuhin School Limited	£3,774,420
Dumpton School	£3,869,300	Crossroads Care Kent	£3,773,775
East Lancashire Railway Holdings Company Limited	£3,868,217	Liverpool Guild of Students	£3,773,304
Cloverleaf Advocacy 2000 Ltd	£3,865,151	Theirworld	£3,770,105
The Zurbaran Trust	£3,864,912	The British School of Alexandria	£3,769,923
Our Lady of Sion School, Worthing	£3,863,513	Magpas	£3,766,387
Pancreatic Cancer UK	£3,862,963	Teshuvoh Tefilloh Tzedokoh	£3,766,106
Aspire Sussex Limited	£3,859,056	Julian Support Limited	£3,765,508
Zurich Community Trust (UK) Limited	£3,855,000	Friends of Beis Chinuch Lebonos Trust	£3,764,774
Street Child	£3,854,314	Bible Churchmen's Missionary Trust Limited	£3,764,037
Yavneh Foundation Trust	£3,848,029	Westbrook Hay Educational Trust Limited	£3,763,419
YMCA East Surrey	£3,846,659	Universities & Colleges Christian Fellowship	£3,762,208
St. David's Hospice	£3,844,039	Middlesbrough and Stockton Mind Limited	£3,760,999
Hackney Council for Voluntary Service	£3,843,372	Care for The Family	£3,759,061
Coeliac UK	£3,842,633	Bridgwater Young Men's Christian Association	£3,758,636
Swansea and Brecon Diocesan Board of Finance	£3,842,197	British Epilepsy Association	£3,758,239
Abbeyfield South Downs Limited	£3,841,846	The Swanage Railway Trust	£3,757,781
City Year UK	£3,836,809	Aldro School Educational Trust Limited	£3,755,211
Stockport, E Cheshire, High Peak, Cerebral Palsy	£3,834,957	Foundation of the Society of Retina Specialists	£3,753,467
Abberley Hall Ltd	£3,827,913	My Space Housing Solutions	£3,753,081
Chalfords Limited	£3,826,483	The Calleva Foundation	£3,751,001
Cobham Hall	£3,826,095	JMWM Hussain Foundation	£3,750,674
Staines Preparatory School Trust	£3,823,335	Wrexham Hospice & Cancer Support Centre Foundation	£3,750,324
Kahal Chassidim Bobov	£3,823,123	All Hallows (Cranmore Hall) School Trust Limited	£3,742,253
Thorpe Hall School Trust	£3,822,625	Sova	£3,739,951
Truro High School for Girls	£3,821,335	University of Central Lancashire Students' Union	£3,733,975
Sussex Community Development Association	£3,820,637	Great Western Air Ambulance Charity	£3,733,910
Aysgarth School Trust Limited	£3,820,555	Martha Trust Hereford Limited	£3,732,933
Basingstoke and Deane Community Leisure Trust	£3,819,827	Ashfold School Trust Limited	£3,732,769
Bristol Charities	£3,819,606	Harbour Support Services	£3,731,937
The Downs School (Charlton House) Limited	£3,819,184	Gateways Educational Trust Limited	£3,729,605
Anthony and Elizabeth Mellows Charitable Settlement	£3,818,620	Sailors' Society	£3,725,000
The Performing Right Society Foundation	£3,818,218	Kingsgate Community Church	£3,723,228
Mind in the City, Hackney and Waltham Forest Ltd	£3,815,551	Colchester Mercury Theatre Limited	£3,720,769
York House School Trust Limited	£3,814,831	The Oakhaven Trust	£3,720,092
Woodlands Hospice Charitable Trust	£3,812,677	Safer Places	£3,718,884
Sussex House School	£3,810,625	Copthorne School Trust Limited	£3,717,296

British Pharmacological Society	£3,716,676	The Basingstoke and District Sports Trust Limited	£3,604,977
Age UK Lincoln and Kesteven	£3,715,070	Westbourne School Trust Limited	£3,602,517
Luckley House School Limited	£3,714,684	Red House School Limited	£3,597,588
FAW Football in the Community Limited	£3,709,960	West Berkshire Training Consortium	£3,596,404
Jewish Blind & Physically Handicapped Society Ltd	£3,708,984	Brain Tumour Research	£3,594,251
Langdon Community	£3,708,890	Royal Alfred Seafarers' Society	£3,593,661
Sheffield Galleries & Museums Trust	£3,708,317	Autistica	£3,593,349
Centre for Engineering and Manufacturing Excellence	£3,708,291	David & Ruth Lewis Family Charitable Trust	£3,591,714
Age UK Lancashire	£3,704,099	Wavendon All Music Plan Limited	£3,589,779
Barnwood Trust	£3,703,490	South West Lakes Trust	£3,582,649
YMCA North Staffordshire Ltd.	£3,699,886	The University of Northampton Students' Union	£3,582,538
East London Mosque Trust	£3,698,348	English- Speaking Union of The Commonwealth	£3,580,392
Hamelin Trust	£3,697,317	World Villages for Children	£3,568,238
Trent Vineyard	£3,696,100	British Home and Hospital for Incurables	£3,565,318
Gloucestershire Wildlife Trust	£3,695,828	Mifal Tzedoko V'chesed Limited	£3,564,869
Alliance Family Foundation Limited	£3,692,885	Rookwood School Trust Limited	£3,564,300
Butterfly Conservation	£3,691,959	The Photographers' Gallery Ltd	£3,558,145
Grange Rose Hill School Limited	£3,690,303	The Presence Charitable Trust	£3,557,241
The Southampton Nuffield Theatre Trust Limited	£3,686,620	Clare Hall in the University of Cambridge	£3,556,314
Sherrardswood School	£3,684,685	St John's Catholic School for The Deaf	£3,555,520
Liverpool Young Men's Christian Association	£3,683,919	Arundel Castle Trustees Limited	£3,554,787
The Railway Children	£3,682,890	Peterborough Winter Sports Club	£3,554,732
Women for Women International (UK)	£3,682,000	The Society for Mucopolysaccharide Diseases	£3,553,166
Parkside School Trust	£3,681,723	Treetops Hospice Trust	£3,550,710
The Sir Oswald Stoll Foundation	£3,681,269	Monmouth Diocesan Board of Finance	£3,550,024
PLUS (Providence LINC United Services)	£3,674,812	Sentebale	£3,550,000
Gellideg Foundation Community Association	£3,674,622	Nottingham Community Transport Ltd	£3,544,416
St Andrew's (Woking) School Trust	£3,674,038	Whale and Dolphin Conservation	£3,542,446
Animals Asia Foundation	£3,672,401	The Institute of Materials, Minerals & Mining	£3,542,000
Barnsley Hospice Appeal	£3,670,778	Fair Play (Workforce) Limited	£3,539,728
The Rossendale Trust Limited	£3,670,759	The Five Towns Plus Hospice Fund Limited	£3,539,719
The Lankellychase Foundation	£3,669,039	Birmingham City Students' Union	£3,536,748
Dogs Trust Worldwide	£3,668,379	Hamilton Lodge (Brighton)	£3,535,757
Edgeborough Educational Trust Limited	£3,667,365	The Movement for Reform Judaism	£3,534,996
ROKPA Trust	£3,667,230	The Bacit Foundation	£3,533,765
Wiltshire Creative	£3,666,694	Old Buckenham Hall (Brettenham) Educational Trust	£3,533,737
University of Brighton Students' Union	£3,665,609	The Co-Mission Churches Trust	£3,533,266
The Mortimer Society	£3,661,528	Princess Helena College	£3,532,979
Derian House Childrens Hospice	£3,658,916	Soll (Vale)	£3,531,192
Africa Educational Trust	£3,657,617	Connection Oxford	£3,530,539
Media Legal Defence Initiative	£3,657,453	Age Concern Manchester	£3,528,673
Eden Valley Hospice, Carlisle	£3,655,837	Longridge Towers School	£3,525,843
Acorn Villages Limited	£3,654,920	The Mothers' Union	£3,525,687
The Campden Charities Trustee	£3,654,368	Transport Benevolent Fund (CIO)	£3,523,000
Caring for Life	£3,652,961	Independent Options (North West)	£3,521,993
Watts Gallery	£3,650,867	The Forget Me Not Children's Hospice	£3,521,971
Leicester High School Charitable Trust Limited	£3,650,817	Turning Lives Around Ltd	£3,521,698
AbilityNet	£3,650,394	Mola Northampton	£3,520,822
Wardens and Assistants of Rochester Bridge in Kent	£3,650,030	Global Partners (UK)	£3,520,659
The Cornwall Trust for Nature Conservation Limited	£3,635,296	Catholic Care (Diocese of Leeds)	£3,520,465
Leeds Jewish Welfare Board	£3,634,818	New Economics Foundation	£3,519,786
Ahavath Chessed Charitable Association Limited	£3,633,612	Eureka The National Children's Museum	£3,517,194
The St Peter and St James Charitable Trust	£3,632,935	Congregation of La Sainte Union des Sacres Coeurs	£3,513,095
St Paul's Schools Foundation	£3,631,000	Onside Youth Zones	£3,511,705
Cancer Research Wales	£3,630,274	National Animal Welfare Trust	£3,511,348
The Dorothy Kerin Trust	£3,629,000	Nottingham University Hospitals Charity	£3,511,000
Aquaculture Stewardship Council	£3,628,719	Congregation of The Sisters of Saint Martha	£3,510,809
Florida State University International Programs Assoc	£3,627,887	Albion in the Community	£3,507,315
The Lee Abbey Movement	£3,627,601	The Woosnam Foundation	£3,505,326
National Marine Aquarium Limited	£3,627,593	The Marian Elizabeth Trust	£3,505,000
Forres Sandle Manor Educational Trust Limited	£3,625,917	Fusion Housing Kirklees Ltd	£3,504,129
Sheffield Citizens Advice and Law Centre	£3,625,230	The Havering Theatre Trust Limited	£3,503,856
Harlaxton College	£3,623,314	Jeremy Coller Foundation	£3,502,557
CWR	£3,620,206	Christian Publishing and Outreach	£3,501,190
Localgiving Foundation	£3,619,181	Pepperdine University (USA)	£3,498,414
Nautilus Welfare Fund	£3,618,506	Backstage Trust	£3,497,561
Aspire Sports and Cultural Trust	£3,618,295	Duchesne Trust	£3,493,358
Hasmonean High School Charitable Trust	£3,617,340	Mildmay Mission Hospital	£3,490,000
Manor Gospel Trust	£3,609,000	Sherborne Preparatory School	£3,487,110
Pramacare	£3,608,523	The Children's Hospital Charity	£3,486,908
The Henry Moore Foundation	£3,606,212	Jubilee Sailing Trust Limited	£3,485,906
Sanbri Ltd	£3,606,159	The Metanoia Institute	£3,484,984

Queen Mary's School (Baldersby) Ltd	£3,482,996	World Land Trust	£3,366,000
Community Advice and Law Service Ltd	£3,482,778	The NGT Foundation	£3,365,865
UKH Foundation	£3,480,823	Cardiac Risk in the Young	£3,364,109
The Complete Works Limited	£3,480,633	Education Support Partnership	£3,362,491
Life Church UK	£3,480,245	Bernard Lewis Family Charitable Trust	£3,357,337
The Gemmological Association	£3,479,762	Royal Society for Public Health	£3,357,203
University of The Arts London Students' Union	£3,477,561	English Touring Opera Limited	£3,355,265
The Jigsaw Trust	£3,477,468	Church Pastoral Aid Society	£3,354,435
Biala Synagogue Trust	£3,475,074	Forces Support Limited	£3,350,046
OM International Services (Carlisle) Ltd	£3,474,967	Greater Nottingham Groundwork Trust	£3,348,143
Oxfordshire Mind	£3,474,161	The Road Safety Trust	£3,342,362
Zetetick Housing	£3,467,565	Independent Training Services Limited	£3,342,151
Packwood Haugh School Limited	£3,466,192	Princes Mead School Trust	£3,341,154
The Sports Council Trust Company	£3,463,454	National Theatre of Wales	£3,337,012
Cambridge Malaysian Education & Development Trust	£3,462,499	The Orchard Trust	£3,336,447
Lady Verdin Trust Limited	£3,458,706	The Marine Biological Association of the UK	£3,331,758
Homeless Action Resource Project	£3,458,602	The Royal Air Force Central Fund	£3,330,821
More House Trust Ltd	£3,456,983	The English Province of The Order of Preachers	£3,326,944
Ategi Limited	£3,455,733	Sanctuary Student Properties Limited	£3,323,000
Soka Gakkai International - UK	£3,453,003	Gideons UK	£3,322,835
Cerebra - for Brain Injured Children and Young People	£3,452,480	The Rainforest Foundation (UK)	£3,322,466
Operation Smile United Kingdom	£3,452,428	The Coal Industry Social Welfare Organisation 2014	£3,322,252
Peaceful Change Initiative	£3,451,841	Up - Unlocking Potential	£3,322,196
Blackpool Grand Theatre (Arts and Entertainments)	£3,451,685	The Charles Dunstone Charitable Trust	£3,322,058
Canine Partners for Independence	£3,451,392	Willington School Foundation Limited	£3,318,594
Worcestershire YMCA Limited	£3,451,338	Fairfield Farm Trust	£3,317,199
Richmond Charities	£3,449,597	The Built Environment Trust	£3,313,758
St Cedd's School Educational Trust Limited	£3,449,254	Derby Grammar School Trust Limited	£3,313,191
Muntham House School	£3,447,775	Expectations (UK)	£3,313,060
The Cavendish School Charitable Trust Limited	£3,445,176	British Overseas NGOs for Development (Bond)	£3,311,982
The Sons of Divine Providence	£3,444,898	The Virgin Money Foundation	£3,309,600
New Covenant Church	£3,443,443	Open Road Visions	£3,307,709
National Zakat Foundation (NZF)	£3,439,880	Free The Children UK	£3,306,363
The Reddiford School Charitable Trust	£3,439,224	Breckenbrough School Limited	£3,303,464
St Vincent's Charitable Trust	£3,439,144	Manchester Islamic Educational Trust Ltd	£3,303,291
Northern Stage (Theatrical Productions) Limited	£3,432,031	Dorset Wildlife Trust	£3,301,000
The Kessler Foundation	£3,424,239	St Edward's School	£3,299,891
Children's Links	£3,423,000	Orchestra of The Age of Enlightenment	£3,297,222
Longfield Hospice Care	£3,421,418	The National Football Museum	£3,297,129
Royal Television Society	£3,421,000	Individual Care Services	£3,295,717
Merseyside Youth Association Limited	£3,420,999	The Spiritualists' National Union	£3,294,977
Kolyom Trust Limited	£3,420,677	Royal Ballet School Endowment Fund	£3,294,000
St Christopher's School (Hampstead) Limited	£3,420,131	National Coal Mining Museum for England Trust Ltd	£3,293,521
Great Hospital	£3,419,295	Welsh Housing Aid Limited	£3,293,480
Nekton Foundation	£3,418,715	Dame Alice Owen's Foundation	£3,287,551
Priory School (Banstead) Trust Limited	£3,412,540	Include	£3,286,722
Wargrave House Limited	£3,406,476	P F Charitable Trust	£3,284,669
The Traidcraft Exchange	£3,406,000	The Radley Foundation	£3,284,123
Moor Park Charitable Trust Limited	£3,405,786	Cumbria Theatre Trust	£3,282,605
Haven House Foundation	£3,404,332	SIM International (UK)	£3,282,418
Campaign To Protect Rural England	£3,403,946	Wiltshire Wildlife Trust Limited	£3,279,064
The Elmhurst Foundation	£3,403,871	The Coal Industry Social Welfare Organisation	£3,277,832
Focus Birmingham	£3,400,473	CHK Charities Limited	£3,276,034
South London Fine Art Gallery and Library	£3,396,641	Kew College	£3,275,109
Woodford Green Preparatory School Limited	£3,393,452	The Trinitarian Bible Society	£3,269,730
Palmers Green High School Limited	£3,390,899	The Donna Louise Trust	£3,268,440
The Tower Project	£3,390,892	The Academy of Youth Limited	£3,266,215
St Helen, Bishopsgate	£3,390,541	The Hands Up Foundation	£3,265,269
Black Country Women's Aid	£3,389,196	Stockdales of Sale, Altrincham and District Ltd	£3,264,504
The Hepworth Wakefield	£3,387,917	Barca - Leeds	£3,259,315
Southampton Hospital Charity	£3,387,000	Young Devon	£3,258,204
The Society of St Columban for Foreign Missions	£3,385,419	Coventry Sports Trust Ltd	£3,252,923
Haberdashers' Charities Investment Pool	£3,385,000	The Maurice Hatter Foundation	£3,252,345
Age UK Hertfordshire	£3,383,044	The Bridge Project	£3,252,255
Kew Community Trust	£3,380,730	Plantlife International-Wild Plant Conservation	£3,250,355
St Joseph's Hospice Association	£3,377,265	The Officers' Association	£3,250,000
Peta Limited	£3,376,565	Mountain Training Trust	£3,248,729
Bridgewater School	£3,372,800	The Port Sunlight Village Trust	£3,248,353
Voluntary Action Leicester	£3,371,852	The World Children's Fund	£3,247,363
Charity for St Joseph's Missionary Society (Generalate)	£3,369,487	Asda Tickled Pink	£3,245,313
The Friends of The V & A	£3,368,633	Caring for Communities and People Ltd	£3,244,530
The Garden Museum	£3,367,149	The Little Way Association	£3,238,980

UFM Worldwide	£3,238,716	Suffolk Agricultural Association	£3,139,598
Harrogate (White Rose) Theatre Trust Ltd	£3,237,489	Society of Chemical Industry	£3,139,000
CMZ Ltd	£3,237,072	Home-Start UK	£3,137,954
Newham Foundation	£3,236,000	Age UK Suffolk	£3,137,818
Central School of Ballet Charitable Trust Limited	£3,232,258	Society of Petroleum Engineers Europe Limited	£3,136,791
British Orthopaedic Association	£3,230,326	Minchinhampton Centre for the Elderly Limited	£3,136,751
European Society for Paediatric Endocrinology	£3,228,525	Terra Nova School Trust Limited	£3,136,599
Low Cost Living Limited	£3,228,126	Doctors of the World UK	£3,136,246
The Rayners Special Educational Trust	£3,227,733	Institute for European Environmental Policy, London	£3,134,405
Twickenham Preparatory School	£3,227,256	The National Literacy Trust	£3,134,328
The Jane Hodge Foundation	£3,226,295	The Read School, Drax	£3,131,047
Homeless Oxfordshire Limited	£3,223,570	The West London Synagogue of British Jews	£3,131,000
Service to the Aged	£3,221,231	Brookvale	£3,129,657
The Minchinhampton Centre for the Elderly	£3,219,952	The Jerusalem Foundation	£3,128,979
The Ballinger Charitable Trust	£3,218,774	Longacre School	£3,127,913
The Raystede Centre for Animal Welfare Limited	£3,218,183	Community Foundations for Lancashire & Merseyside	£3,127,420
Kent Music	£3,218,167	The London Wildlife Trust	£3,126,000
Tchabe Kollel Limited	£3,214,932	Littlegarth School Limited	£3,123,732
Ripley Court Educational Trust Limited	£3,210,664	Tameside and Glossop Hospice Limited	£3,123,128
Quartet Community Foundation	£3,210,555	National Day Nurseries Association	£3,122,076
Charity of Sir Richard Whittington	£3,210,000	Widehorizons Outdoor Education Trust	£3,122,000
The Metro Centre Ltd	£3,207,754	Cornwall Food Foundation	£3,119,893
Dame Kelly Holmes Trust	£3,204,969	Parish of Wimbledon	£3,118,321
The Hartlepool Hospice Limited	£3,204,561	Age Concern Hampshire	£3,118,256
Royal Logistic Corps Association Trust	£3,203,889	Nottinghamshire Wildlife Trust	£3,117,778
Lessons for Life Foundation	£3,202,994	The National Forest Company	£3,109,468
Community Transport Association UK	£3,202,299	Age Concern Camden	£3,109,406
The Crusaders' Union	£3,201,103	Salvation Army Retired Officers Allowance Scheme	£3,108,985
Prestfelde School Limited	£3,200,662	Horris Hill Preparatory School Trust Limited	£3,107,226
Sheffield Hallam University Students' Union	£3,199,994	Moon Hall Schools Educational Trust	£3,104,826
Walton on Thames Charity	£3,199,282	Hackney Empire Limited	£3,104,050
The Monteverdi Choir and Orchestras Limited	£3,198,571	All Souls, Langham Place, London	£3,103,848
Halcyon London International School	£3,198,069	Oxford Diocesan Council for Social Work Inc	£3,101,894
Artichoke Trust	£3,197,939	Belvedere Trust	£3,101,131
Gardens of Peace Muslim Cemetery	£3,197,904	Age UK Warwickshire	£3,098,104
Caerphilly County Borough Citizens Advice Bureau	£3,197,154	Missing People Limited	£3,097,979
Cymdeithas Caer Las	£3,196,143	Rudolf Steiner School King's Langley Limited	£3,096,770
The Monastery of St Francis Gorton Trust Ltd	£3,189,990	NWL Jewish Day School	£3,096,412
No Limits (South)	£3,189,981	Step By Step Partnership Limited	£3,095,001
St. Mary's Convent and Nursing Home (Chiswick)	£3,189,606	Eversfield Preparatory School Trust Limited	£3,094,169
Hoffmann Foundation for Autism	£3,187,049	Christian Schools Limited	£3,093,859
Meningitis Now	£3,182,586	The Orr Mackintosh Foundation Limited	£3,092,520
Cumbria Community Foundation	£3,182,258	Stepping Stone Projects	£3,091,308
Link-Ability	£3,182,226	Richard House Trust	£3,088,559
Age Concern in Cornwall and The Isles of Scilly	£3,181,253	Carers First	£3,088,542
The Film and Television Charity	£3,181,000	WEC International	£3,088,053
Help and Care	£3,180,920	Big Change Charitable Trust	£3,087,562
One Trust	£3,179,600	Age Concern Cheshire	£3,087,221
Bangor Diocesan Board of Finance	£3,179,188	Friends of Achiezer Arad	£3,086,523
Royal National Mission to Deep Sea Fishermen	£3,178,872	Life 2009	£3,086,506
The Gevurath Ari Torah Academy Trust	£3,177,063	Wallace & Gromit's Children's Foundation	£3,086,016
ASDAN	£3,175,536	Bishop Challoner School	£3,084,280
The Michael Bishop Foundation	£3,174,658	Royal Papworth Hospital Charity	£3,084,000
Westminster Cathedral Choir School	£3,173,237	Three Counties Education Trust	£3,080,295
Stelios Philanthropic Foundation	£3,172,015	Norwich and Central Norfolk Mental Health Resources	£3,079,052
Mid-Hants Railway Preservation Society Limited	£3,170,238	Farney Close School Ltd	£3,078,916
Disability Challengers	£3,165,475	The Pious Society of The Daughters of St Paul	£3,078,319
Leeds Mind	£3,164,977	Clarendon Trust Limited	£3,077,068
Macmillan Caring Locally	£3,163,372	Handmaids of The Sacred Heart of Jesus	£3,076,611
Launchpad Reading	£3,162,287	The Downs, Malvern College Prep School	£3,075,993
Sceptre Education	£3,161,035	Coventry Citizens Advice	£3,075,138
Keble Preparatory School (1968) Ltd	£3,160,616	Woodhorn Charitable Trust	£3,074,638
The Matthew Project	£3,158,000	Pennthorpe School Trust Limited	£3,073,569
Consumers International	£3,149,355	Mencap in Kirklees	£3,073,453
The Stars Foundation	£3,148,025	Child Poverty Action Group	£3,071,805
Community Housing and Therapy	£3,147,134	London School of Theology	£3,070,984
Dudley Lodge	£3,145,679	The Rose Road Association	£3,070,737
The Taylor Family Foundation	£3,145,235	Salisbury Cathedral School Limited	£3,069,080
The Monument Trust	£3,144,000	Chai-Lifeline Cancer Care	£3,068,662
Carers in Hertfordshire	£3,140,406	Institute for Employment Studies	£3,067,336
Expect Ltd	£3,140,198	Yorkshire Sport Foundation	£3,066,734
University of Derby Theatre Limited	£3,139,713	Walsingham Trust	£3,063,303

Shaarei Rachamim Limited	£3,060,000	Taverham Hall Educational Trust Limited	£2,976,603
The Copsewood Education Trust	£3,058,882	The Five Lamps Organisation	£2,976,462
Girls Not Brides	£3,058,512	Heart Research UK	£2,975,653
Adur Community Leisure Limited	£3,056,772	The Hollick Family Charitable Trust	£2,973,169
The Community Foundation in Wales	£3,053,069	Community Transport	£2,972,566
Action with Communities in Rural England (Acre)	£3,050,082	The National Motor Museum Trust Limited	£2,971,609
Windle Trust International	£3,049,185	Staffordshire North and Stoke-on-Trent CAB	£2,970,542
The Jerusalem Trust	£3,049,000	The London Mathematical Society	£2,970,370
Carers Trust Heart of England	£3,048,948	Deafblind UK	£2,969,660
Quo Vadis Trust	£3,046,817	West Sussex Music Trust	£2,969,528
Womankind Worldwide	£3,046,536	Darlington and District Hospice Movement	£2,968,516
Age UK Nottingham and Nottinghamshire	£3,045,254	The Nottinghamshire Hospice Limited	£2,968,472
The Nautical Institute	£3,045,132	Global Canopy Foundation	£2,968,110
The Reader Organisation	£3,044,142	RSPCA Bristol and District Branch	£2,967,498
Octagon Theatre Trust Limited	£3,042,762	Caritas - Anchor House	£2,967,175
The Methodist Relief and Development Fund	£3,039,542	Thetford Educational Foundation Trust	£2,959,107
The Engineering Council	£3,037,106	Alliance Learning Ltd	£2,958,511
New Philanthropy Capital	£3,036,911	Watermill Theatre Limited	£2,957,678
The Association of Jewish Refugees (AJR)	£3,036,583	Teesside University Students' Union	£2,952,714
The Friends of Ohr Someach	£3,035,441	The Rank Foundation Limited	£2,951,000
Watford FC's Community Sports & Education Trust	£3,034,604	The Barrow Cadbury Trust	£2,950,000
Effective Intervention	£3,033,738	Bolton Lads and Girls Club Limited	£2,945,736
Kusuma Trust UK	£3,032,355	Meningitis Research Foundation	£2,944,689
Forward Housing SW	£3,031,751	Durlston Court School Trust Limited	£2,939,978
The Stable Family Home Trust	£3,031,705	Berkhampstead School (Cheltenham) Trust Limited	£2,939,288
Bridge 86 Limited	£3,030,673	The Grange Festival	£2,936,797
The Sir Joseph Hotung Charitable Settlement	£3,029,980	Foundation for Integrated Transport	£2,936,438
Marlborough College Foundation	£3,029,931	The Orpheus Centre Trust	£2,936,373
St. Martin-in-the-Fields Charity	£3,028,785	The Camelia Botnar Foundation	£2,934,026
BRAC UK	£3,027,845	The Roger and Sarah Bancroft Clark Charitable Trust	£2,931,781
The Springboard Charity	£3,023,539	NOCN	£2,931,144
Hospice of St Mary of Furness	£3,023,531	The Big C Appeal Limited	£2,931,133
The Royal Association for Deaf People	£3,022,721	Citizens Advice Manchester Ltd	£2,930,015
Arab World Ministries	£3,022,653	Central Lancashire Age Concern Ltd	£2,929,484
Winterfold House School Trust Limited	£3,022,347	The Cunmont Charitable Trust	£2,929,368
Soul Survivor	£3,020,669	Deeper Christian Life Ministry	£2,927,780
British Association for The Advancement of Science	£3,019,381	Aish Hatorah UK Limited	£2,925,805
The Christian Trust	£3,019,280	International Society of Ultrasound in Obstetrics	£2,925,509
Childhope (UK)	£3,014,627	YMCA Suffolk	£2,924,796
The Chalk Cliff Trust	£3,014,565	The Courtyard Trust	£2,924,541
Inspire Community Trust	£3,012,526	Nuffield Trust for Research in Health Services	£2,922,000
Mayday Trust	£3,008,479	Age UK Oxfordshire	£2,919,944
M.K. Rose Charitable Trust	£3,007,047	Age UK Cambridgeshire and Peterborough	£2,919,793
Blue Ventures Conservation	£3,006,982	The Royal Albert Hall Trust	£2,917,000
The Kendal Brewery Arts Centre Trust Limited	£3,006,813	Polesworth Group Homes Limited	£2,916,596
The Greggs Foundation	£3,003,105	Henry Oldfield Trust	£2,916,155
Twin	£3,001,981	Age Cymru	£2,914,122
Training and Development Resource Limited	£3,001,575	Starlow Charities Limited	£2,913,743
Together for Short Lives	£3,000,944	Lincolnshire Y.M.C.A. Ltd	£2,913,128
United Reformed Church Thames North Synod Charities	£2,999,000	Young Minds Trust	£2,911,389
Dolphin School Trust	£2,996,211	European Society of Endocrinology	£2,907,698
Perrott Hill School Trust Limited	£2,995,024	British Society of Gastroenterology	£2,907,138
Teresa Ball International Solidarity Fund	£2,994,481	Pioneering Care Partnership	£2,907,084
Trustees of The Charity of The Bernardine Sisters	£2,993,974	Gosfield School Limited	£2,905,942
Milton Keynes Community Foundation Limited	£2,993,740	Bridge To The Future	£2,903,178
Bawso Ltd	£2,993,080	Child Bereavement UK	£2,903,078
The League Against Cruel Sports	£2,991,877	Dr Kershaw's Hospice	£2,903,001
Andrew Wommack Ministries-Europe	£2,990,778	The Albany 2001 Company	£2,902,886
Action on Disability and Development	£2,990,112	Greyfriars, Reading	£2,900,513
Chartered Institute of Credit Management	£2,990,091	The Shaftesbury Homes and Arethusa	£2,899,000
Global New Car Assessment Programme	£2,989,842	Valley CIDS and Related Charities	£2,898,835
International Animal Rescue	£2,989,582	Beit Halochem UK	£2,898,010
England and Wales Cricket Trust	£2,986,828	The National Botanic Garden of Wales	£2,898,000
Independent Housing UK Ltd	£2,985,182	Suncroft Donations Trust	£2,891,186
Building Crafts College	£2,984,043	YMCA Derbyshire	£2,891,000
Yusuf Islam Foundation	£2,983,601	Kairos Community Trust	£2,890,656
Family Lives	£2,983,000	The Sisters of The Blessed Sacrament	£2,889,373
Friends of Beis Soroh Schneirer	£2,982,842	Internet Watch Foundation	£2,887,298
Disablement Association of Barking and Dagenham	£2,982,032	Centre for Alternative Technology Charity Limited	£2,887,042
The HDH Wills 1965 Charitable Trust	£2,980,041	Lindsey Lodge Limited	£2,886,372
Wellesley House and St Peter Court School Trust	£2,978,267	Suffolk Community Foundation	£2,884,297
North Cestrian Grammar School Limited	£2,977,690	The Elms (Colwall) Limited	£2,883,734

Congregation of Jesus Charitable Trust	£2,883,204	The Hilary Craft Charitable Foundation Limited	£2,804,596
Leicester YMCA	£2,882,040	Liverpool FC Foundation	£2,802,078
S. Anselm's School Trust Limited	£2,879,000	Oakhill Education Trust	£2,801,577
The Lloyd Park Children's Charity	£2,878,685	Keswick Foundation Limited	£2,799,927
Assemblies of God Incorporated	£2,878,367	Redemptorist Publications	£2,799,429
Clydpride Limited	£2,876,782	Turner Contemporary	£2,799,073
Peter Harrison Foundation	£2,876,431	The Golden Bottle Trust	£2,798,777
Empower - The Emerging Markets Foundation Ltd	£2,876,153	Ruskin Mill Land Trust	£2,798,111
The Beit Trust	£2,871,296	Leehurst Swan Limited	£2,797,794
Cumberland Lodge	£2,870,997	Order of The Sisters of St Joseph of The Apparition	£2,796,664
Instructus	£2,870,871	The Jewish Leadership Council	£2,795,331
Lockers Park School Trust Limited	£2,870,757	Warrior Preservation Trust Limited	£2,794,105
Metropolitan Police Benevolent Fund	£2,870,116	YMCA Bedfordshire	£2,793,312
Lancaster Foundation	£2,869,358	Sri Guru Singh Sabha Southall	£2,792,917
Gingerbread, The Charity for Single Parent Families	£2,868,561	The Stanborough Press Limited	£2,791,194
Oxfordshire Community Churches	£2,867,935	Breast Cancer Haven	£2,790,014
Wings for Life UK Spinal Cord Research Foundation	£2,867,919	The Aspinall Foundation	£2,786,000
Guru Nanak Nishkam Sewak Jatha (Birmingham)	£2,867,410	UOHC Supervision Ltd	£2,782,198
Worthing Churches Homeless Projects	£2,864,179	City YMCA, London	£2,780,396
Jamie Oliver Food Foundation	£2,864,102	St Mary's College (Oscott College)	£2,780,000
Alleyn Court Educational Trust	£2,861,105	Torbay and South Devon NHS Charitable Fund	£2,779,000
Farnham Maltings Association Limited	£2,860,730	Old Vicarage School Trust	£2,778,852
Bristol Old Vic Theatre School Limited	£2,858,827	Whitechapel Centre	£2,778,686
Manchester International Festival	£2,858,738	The Foyle Foundation	£2,777,329
Cardinal Hume Centre	£2,857,000	Monday Charitable Trust	£2,776,825
West London Students' Union	£2,856,882	West Anglia Training Association Limited	£2,773,521
Institute of Marine Engineering, Science & Technology	£2,855,206	The Criterion Theatre Trust	£2,773,226
Sherburn House Charity	£2,850,942	The Royal Drawing School	£2,773,002
Leverhulme Trade Charities Trust	£2,850,000	Petans Limited	£2,772,835
De La Warr Pavilion Charitable Trust	£2,849,534	Brent, Wandsworth and Westminster Mind	£2,772,305
Pate's Grammar School Foundation	£2,849,426	Aman Foundation UK	£2,771,520
Ridgesave Limited	£2,848,740	International Service Fellowship Trust	£2,770,790
The Army Central Fund	£2,848,726	Ruach City Church	£2,770,494
Buckinghamshire Healthcare NHS Trust	£2,848,000	Clarity - Employment for Blind People	£2,770,486
The Horse Trust	£2,846,469	Charity for St Joseph's Missionary Society	£2,765,412
Academy Concerts Society	£2,845,412	The Langham Partnership (UK and Ireland)	£2,764,606
Africa Inland Mission International	£2,845,406	Institute for Human Rights & Business Limited	£2,762,608
Kaleidoscope Plus Group	£2,845,268	The Newcastle Preparatory School Trust Limited	£2,760,939
Kiln Theatre Limited	£2,843,965	YouthNet UK	£2,759,395
Caritas Diocese of Salford	£2,843,225	The Swire Charitable Trust	£2,759,389
Supportive SRC Ltd	£2,842,745	The Cherie Blair Foundation for Women	£2,759,370
Somerset Wildlife Trust	£2,841,308	The Big Church Day Out	£2,758,850
The Lantern Community	£2,834,155	New Directions (Rugby) Limited	£2,757,476
The Abbeyfield Ilkley Society Limited	£2,833,648	St Chad's College Durham	£2,756,153
Seafarers UK (King George's Fund for Sailors)	£2,833,000	Tikva UK	£2,754,330
Noah's Ark - The Children's Hospice	£2,832,090	The Latvian Welfare Trust	£2,752,487
West House School	£2,831,497	Lincolnshire Agricultural Society	£2,752,331
The Frewen Educational Trust Limited	£2,831,087	Freedom Food Limited	£2,751,593
The Christian Institute	£2,830,908	Talbot Village Trust	£2,750,614
The Invesco Cares Foundation	£2,829,233	Ursuline Preparatory School Wimbledon Trust	£2,750,043
Lauderdale House Trust	£2,827,139	North West Training Council	£2,749,305
Surrey Crossroads	£2,826,607	Nottingham Media Centre Limited	£2,747,002
Upton House School Limited	£2,825,822	Beis Chinuch Lebonos Limited	£2,746,574
Laureus Sport for Good Foundation	£2,825,181	Jamie's Farm	£2,746,391
The Brainwave Centre Limited	£2,823,608	The Littlegate Trust	£2,743,826
The Wilberforce Trust	£2,821,731	Langstone Society	£2,734,371
The Sussex Community Foundation	£2,820,921	Chartered Accountants' Benevolent Association	£2,730,927
Northpoint Wellbeing Limited	£2,819,577	Wise Ability Limited	£2,729,913
Rock UK Adventure Centres Limited	£2,818,704	The Geffrye Museum Trust	£2,727,653
USWSU	£2,817,054	The Berkeley Charitable Foundation	£2,723,621
Remedi - Restorative Services	£2,815,605	The Marchig Animal Welfare Trust	£2,723,333
Wildwood Trust	£2,815,515	English Touring Theatre Limited	£2,722,884
Afrikids Limited	£2,815,318	Ashford Leisure Trust Limited	£2,722,466
Lincolnshire Wildlife Trust	£2,812,266	The Case Centre Limited	£2,721,902
Broom Foundation	£2,812,085	The Hadley Trust	£2,721,828
Adoption Matters	£2,810,799	National Institute of Economic and Social Research	£2,721,084
Derby Museums	£2,810,431	Dementia Care	£2,720,179
Access Community Trust	£2,809,821	Enthuse Charitable Trust	£2,719,926
Association of Masters in Business Administration	£2,807,921	Writhlington Trust	£2,719,881
Habitat for Humanity Great Britain	£2,805,890	Sisters of The Presentation of Blessed Virgin Mary	£2,717,655
Wooden Spoon Society	£2,804,913	Beacon Centre for the Blind	£2,717,434
Micklefield School (Reigate) Limited	£2,804,656	Carers Support West Sussex	£2,717,426

Hamilton Lodge Trust Limited	£2,717,100	The Beatrice Laing Trust	£2,622,798
Age Concern Norfolk	£2,714,559	Agape Ministries Ltd	£2,622,345
The British Music Experience	£2,713,885	Snowdon Trust	£2,622,318
JW3 Development	£2,712,354	The National Small-Bore Rifle Association	£2,621,866
David Tannen Charitable Trust	£2,712,104	Students Union University of Greenwich	£2,620,119
Commonwealth Parliamentary Association	£2,712,083	The Pleasance Theatre Trust	£2,619,500
The Machzikei Hadass Communities	£2,711,971	York Conservation Trust Limited	£2,619,386
Celia Hammond Animal Trust	£2,711,824	Teen Challenge UK	£2,619,167
Newcastle United Foundation	£2,711,266	The Garwood Foundation	£2,617,780
St Hilary's School Trust Limited	£2,711,122	The de la Salle Brothers	£2,617,125
St Luke's Oxford	£2,708,111	The Association of Taxation Technicians	£2,615,631
Acorn Recovery Projects	£2,707,500	The Jericho Foundation	£2,613,036
N Sethia Foundation	£2,702,279	The Carers' Resource	£2,613,027
Active Communities Network Limited	£2,702,018	Cord Global	£2,612,340
The Arisaig Partners Foundation	£2,698,302	South Suffolk Leisure	£2,611,223
Hipperholme Grammar School Foundation	£2,697,058	Clifton Suspension Bridge Trust	£2,609,986
Challenge Partners	£2,696,352	Stanford Trust	£2,609,080
Devonport & Western Counties Assoc Welfare of Blind	£2,695,739	Walking with the Wounded	£2,608,387
Hazrat Sultan Bahu Trust (UK)	£2,694,493	City Gateway Limited	£2,607,043
Jane Tomlinson Appeal	£2,692,970	Bellview Charitable Trust	£2,606,402
South Tees Hospitals Charity and Associated Funds	£2,692,000	West Ham United Foundation	£2,605,242
The Westminster Foundation	£2,690,324	Welsh Centre for Action on Dependency and Addiction	£2,605,225
ATG Training	£2,690,281	The National Youth Theatre of Great Britain	£2,605,122
City Hearts (UK)	£2,690,087	The Fortune Centre of Riding Therapy	£2,604,925
The Walsingham College Trust Association Ltd	£2,690,023	The British Institute of Non-Destructive Testing	£2,604,559
Gardners Lane and Oakwood Federation	£2,689,134	Rich Mix Cultural Foundation	£2,602,215
Manchester City F.C. City in the Community Foundation	£2,686,799	Age Concern Wirral	£2,601,922
The Society of Operations Engineers	£2,686,675	Royal Commission for The Exhibition of 1851	£2,600,909
Weston Park Hospital Cancer Care & Research Fund	£2,683,365	English Federation of Disability Sport	£2,600,112
Medway Youth Trust	£2,681,841	PAC-UK Ltd	£2,599,858
Elephant Family	£2,681,112	The Henry Doubleday Research Association	£2,599,654
Yardley Great Trust	£2,681,027	HMC (UK)	£2,599,560
Room To Read UK Limited	£2,679,778	The College of Radiographers	£2,598,847
The Link Day School Ltd	£2,678,664	The Rehabilitation Trust	£2,598,386
The Tuixen Foundation	£2,678,132	The Thomson Foundation	£2,594,000
Harvard Global UK	£2,676,648	Suffolk Mind	£2,593,387
CTVC Limited	£2,673,000	Customs House Trust Limited	£2,592,446
Energise Me	£2,669,234	University of Huddersfield Students' Union	£2,592,226
Maria Montessori Training Organisation	£2,665,602	Chartered Institution of Highways and Transportation	£2,592,129
Groundwork East	£2,663,381	Severn Wye Energy Agency	£2,591,998
Hoylake Cottage	£2,662,551	The Walton Centre Charity	£2,591,009
The Venture Trust	£2,661,397	Four Paws	£2,589,977
The Royal Marines Charity	£2,660,662	St Catherine's - Speech and Language	£2,589,955
The Ricard Foundation	£2,659,504	Independence Trust	£2,589,879
Age UK West Sussex	£2,658,599	A New Direction London Limited	£2,589,751
Green Lane Masjid and Community Centre	£2,657,626	Bootstrap Company (Blackburn) Limited	£2,588,925
Keighley & Worth Valley Railway Preservation Society	£2,656,903	St Cuthbert's Hospice, Durham	£2,587,235
Home-Start Greenwich	£2,652,607	Age Concern Kensington and Chelsea	£2,586,283
Maidwell Hall School	£2,650,762	The Hearth Foundation	£2,584,012
Chatham Maritime Trust	£2,650,463	The Catholic Children's Society (Westminster)	£2,583,453
The Norfolk Hospice	£2,648,030	The Third Age Trust	£2,582,488
The Jewish Museum London	£2,647,677	Aston Students' Union	£2,581,962
Broadreach House	£2,647,363	The Helen Hamlyn Trust	£2,579,168
Cardiff Met Students' Union	£2,647,248	The King's Foundation	£2,578,885
Kent County Agricultural Society	£2,645,580	Grace Dieu Manor School	£2,578,451
Oakwood School	£2,642,110	British Editorial Society of Bone and Joint Surgery	£2,574,817
The Nationwide Foundation	£2,641,746	Culture Warrington	£2,574,523
Commutual	£2,641,000	Hull Truck Theatre Company Limited	£2,573,472
Tetbury Hospital Trust	£2,640,810	Ethiopiaid	£2,572,426
Leicestershire and Rutland Wildlife Trust Limited	£2,640,009	Halstead (Educational Trust) Limited	£2,570,230
East Northamptonshire Cultural Trust	£2,639,568	The Sterry Family Foundation	£2,568,352
Audacious Church	£2,638,891	Policy Exchange Limited	£2,567,901
The Boys' Brigade	£2,636,705	Build Africa	£2,565,195
Eastbrook Education Trust	£2,635,382	Birmingham Education Partnership Limited	£2,562,250
Intensive Care National Audit and Research Centre	£2,631,437	Royal Variety Charity	£2,560,552
Stockton Arts Centre	£2,628,876	Exeter Cathedral School	£2,557,952
READ - The Reading Agency	£2,628,614	Betsi Cadwaladr University Health Board Charity	£2,555,000
The Don Miller Charitable Trust CIO	£2,626,415	The Chamber Orchestra of Europe	£2,554,461
B E Perl Charitable Trust	£2,625,095	Kids Out UK	£2,551,680
The Birmingham Dogs Home	£2,624,091	The Tower House School Charitable Foundation	£2,550,472
The Roger de Haan Charitable Trust	£2,624,000	School-Home Support Service (UK)	£2,549,157
Foscote Court (Banbury) Trust Limited	£2,622,817	Age UK Oldham Limited	£2,548,832

Pilgrim Homes (formerly Aged Pilgrims' Friend Society)	£2,548,000	The Forum Trust Limited	£2,479,947
Nene Park Trust	£2,546,000	Release International	£2,479,899
Northumberland Wildlife Trust Limited	£2,545,287	Wycliffe Hall	£2,478,673
Morthyng Limited	£2,544,176	Brentwood Leisure Trust	£2,478,251
EMLC	£2,543,235	The Medaille Trust Limited	£2,475,526
Herefordshire Group Training Association Limited	£2,541,167	Menevia Diocesan Trust	£2,474,956
The Resuscitation Council (United Kingdom)	£2,539,931	South Hampstead Charitable Trust	£2,474,843
The ABDO College of Education	£2,539,378	The Federation of European Microbiological Societies	£2,473,904
Osteopathic Education and Research Limited	£2,538,468	Kent Community Foundation	£2,473,529
Charities ICW Spanish & Portuguese Jews Synagogue	£2,537,042	The Sir John Fisher Foundation	£2,472,020
The Pace Centre Ltd	£2,536,902	Cumbria Wildlife Trust Ltd	£2,470,674
Chartered Institution of Water & Environment Mnmgt	£2,535,877	The Creative Foundation	£2,470,197
Wessex Schools Trust	£2,534,581	Hospice of Hope Romania Limited	£2,468,617
Safer London	£2,531,509	The Evangelical Alliance	£2,467,059
Alexis and Anne- Marie Habib Foundation	£2,531,474	Entindale Limited	£2,465,647
Christian Care Homes	£2,530,791	Stroud Court Community Trust Limited	£2,464,724
Wrexham Diocesan Trust	£2,530,037	The George Muller Charitable Trust	£2,462,060
Belmont School (Feldemore) Educational Trust Ltd	£2,529,866	The Sir Andrew Judd Foundation	£2,461,952
The Landscape Institute	£2,528,899	The Keswick Convention Trust	£2,461,842
Sarum Hall School Trust Limited	£2,527,935	United Reformed Church (South Western Synod)	£2,461,637
St Mary's Independent School	£2,527,115	Drapers Charitable Fund	£2,461,025
National Centre for Circus Arts	£2,526,620	The Prince's Foundation for Building Community	£2,460,859
The Royal Artillery Centre for Personal Development	£2,523,753	Citizens Advice County Durham	£2,460,490
Equality Challenge Unit	£2,522,689	Marine Conservation Society	£2,460,369
Tall Ships Youth Trust	£2,522,356	The Raf100 Appeal	£2,459,500
Lonia Limited	£2,520,581	Friends Therapeutic Community Trust	£2,457,809
The Leaders of Worship and Preachers Homes	£2,520,482	CCCU UK	£2,456,840
The RICS' Benevolent Fund Limited	£2,520,000	Revelation Foundation	£2,456,785
The English Language Centre Limited	£2,519,053	The Henley Festival Trust	£2,455,939
Halton Haven Hospice	£2,518,755	Access for Living	£2,455,936
The Harbour Centre (Plymouth)	£2,518,580	Greenfield School	£2,454,858
Derby Quad Limited	£2,515,107	Prisoners Education Trust	£2,454,094
Stapely Jewish Care Home Ltd	£2,514,993	The Prebendal School	£2,453,792
Home for Aged Jews (Liverpool and District)	£2,514,993	New Wine International	£2,453,435
Redbridge Sports Centre Trust Limited	£2,512,669	Edward Penley Abraham Research Fund	£2,453,425
Forever Manchester	£2,511,296	Birmingham Methodist Circuit	£2,453,292
The Alcohol and Drug Service	£2,510,649	Weidenfeld-Hoffmann Trust	£2,452,974
The Grand Lodge of Mark Master Masons' Fund	£2,507,835	The Tech Partnership	£2,452,657
Goodheart Animal Sanctuaries	£2,506,193	The Ena Makin Educational Trust	£2,452,230
Newark and Nottinghamshire Agricultural Society	£2,504,854	Denville Hall 2012	£2,450,444
The British Thoracic Society	£2,504,115	Essex County Scout Council	£2,449,824
Lench's Trust	£2,503,272	Gloucestershire Engineering Training Limited	£2,449,765
Naima JPS	£2,501,507	St Christopher's The Hall School, Limited	£2,447,322
The William Frederick Haines Foundation	£2,500,953	Chester Performing Arts Centre Limited	£2,447,190
Al-Muntada Al-Islami Trust	£2,500,853	The Steinberg Family Charitable Trust	£2,446,973
The Samuel Tak Lee Charitable Trust	£2,500,175	Velindre NHS Trust Charitable Fund	£2,446,000
Scarborough Theatre Trust Limited	£2,499,496	University of Surrey Students' Union	£2,445,577
Vision Enhancement Services	£2,499,215	ALRA	£2,445,082
When You Wish upon a Star	£2,495,354	Bikur Cholim Limited	£2,444,836
St Michael's School (Leigh-on-Sea) Limited	£2,494,142	The Vine Trust Walsall	£2,444,264
Padworth College Trust Limited	£2,494,028	Sturts Community Trust	£2,444,166
The Directory of Social Change	£2,493,541	The Tramway Museum Society	£2,443,824
The Jewish Association for Mental Illness	£2,491,354	Bowdon Preparatory School	£2,443,754
Natural Breaks Limited	£2,490,679	Roundabout Limited	£2,442,172
The Royal Society of Biology	£2,490,000	National Maritime Museum Cornwall Trust	£2,439,642
CISV International Limited	£2,488,467	The Prince's Countryside Fund	£2,439,513
Portsmouth Royal Maritime Club	£2,488,310	The Media Trust	£2,437,305
West Norfolk Community Transport Project	£2,488,231	The Winston Churchill Memorial Trust	£2,435,457
Science Projects	£2,487,913	The Swimming Teachers Association Limited	£2,433,918
The Michael Uren Foundation	£2,485,792	The Institute of Franciscan Missionaries of Mary	£2,429,231
Great Yarmouth Community Trust	£2,485,338	Lee Abbey Fellowship	£2,426,446
The RAF Benevolent Fund Housing Trust Limited	£2,485,221	Cartref Limited	£2,424,876
Torbay Coast and Countryside Trust	£2,484,463	Rosa Fund	£2,423,656
Oasis Aquila Housing	£2,484,114	Calan DVS	£2,423,175
Staffordshire Wildlife Trust Limited	£2,484,000	Surrey Association for Visual Impairment	£2,422,952
The Chief Fire Officers' Association	£2,483,608	Teikyo Foundation (UK)	£2,422,492
South Tynedale Railway Preservation Society	£2,482,363	Lichfield Garrick Theatre	£2,421,791
New Schools Network	£2,482,053	Salters Hill Charity Limited	£2,421,592
Masonic Samaritan Fund	£2,482,000	The Sick Children's Trust	£2,421,399
Junction CDC Limited	£2,480,790	Privacy International	£2,421,192
Spitalfields Crypt Trust	£2,480,000	Redcliffe School Trust Ltd	£2,418,721
The Oldham Coliseum Theatre Limited	£2,479,974	ZANE: Zimbabwe A National Emergency	£2,418,587

Princeton Charitable Foundation Limited	£2,417,680	Heart of England Community Foundation	£2,346,119
Age Concern Kingston upon Thames	£2,414,718	St George's Bristol	£2,345,000
Norfolk and Norwich Festival Trust	£2,414,317	Age Concern Isle of Wight	£2,344,910
The Palace Theatre Watford Limited	£2,413,924	Watford and District Mencap Society	£2,344,846
The New Room/John Wesley's Chapel	£2,412,729	WellChild	£2,344,327
Smallpeice Trust Limited	£2,411,949	Alt Valley Community Trust Limited	£2,343,821
The Northumbrian Educational Trust Limited	£2,410,613	Stallcombe House	£2,343,300
Impact Initiatives	£2,410,115	The Headley Trust	£2,343,000
RSPCA Bath and District Branch	£2,408,516	The Knightland Foundation	£2,341,396
Oxford Russia Fund	£2,407,052	The Clink Charity	£2,341,329
The Guild Estate Endowment	£2,406,789	Assemblies of God Property Trust	£2,341,000
Age UK South Staffordshire	£2,405,935	Royal Norfolk Agricultural Association	£2,340,321
St Bede's Childcare Limited	£2,404,737	John James Bristol Foundation	£2,338,636
Wigan Boys and Girls Club	£2,403,643	Leeds Autism Services	£2,335,297
Sunderland Counselling Service	£2,402,420	Re:Vision North Limited	£2,334,337
The Haynes International Motor Museum	£2,401,903	The UK Career Academy Foundation	£2,333,689
Vulcan to the Sky Trust	£2,400,471	Lifeworks Charity Limited	£2,333,474
University of Derby Students' Union	£2,399,593	Manchester Young Men's Christian Association	£2,332,552
Winston's Wish (Grief Support Programme for Children)	£2,396,316	City and Guilds of London Art School Limited	£2,331,141
Rontades Limited	£2,395,378	Honourable Society of Gray's Inn Trust Fund	£2,329,497
Kent Association for the Blind	£2,394,003	Commonwealth Parliamentary Association (UK)	£2,328,527
The T. S. Eliot Foundation	£2,393,380	St Nicholas' Training Centre for The Montessori Method	£2,327,856
Bucks Students' Union	£2,392,819	Early Intervention Foundation	£2,327,767
Broadway Lodge Limited	£2,392,777	Brighton & Sussex University Hospitals NHS Trust	£2,325,518
London Skills for Growth Limited	£2,390,660	London Business School Student Association	£2,325,287
White Lodge Centre	£2,390,000	Scottish Hospital of The Foundation of King Charles II	£2,323,848
Southbank Sinfonia Foundation	£2,389,981	Action Homeless (Leicester) Limited	£2,323,119
Hyndburn Leisure	£2,389,765	The Goldsmiths Centre	£2,321,345
PAS Housing Association	£2,389,550	Communities First Wessex	£2,319,981
NETA Training Trust	£2,388,529	Heathfield Educational Trust	£2,317,658
Anglican Consultative Council	£2,386,499	Kingswood House School Trust Limited	£2,317,101
Special Olympics Great Britain	£2,385,275	The Royal Opera House Endowment Fund 2000	£2,314,568
The Novak Djokovic Foundation (UK) Limited	£2,383,010	The National Hospital for Neurology and Neurosurgery	£2,314,396
QVSR	£2,381,826	King's Church London	£2,314,119
The British Cardiovascular Society	£2,381,084	York RI	£2,313,527
Cartref NI Limited	£2,381,064	Shine - Spina Bifida, Hydrocephalus, Information	£2,313,492
The Elders Foundation	£2,381,000	Thames21 Limited	£2,311,209
1st Place Children and Parents' Centre Ltd	£2,379,848	UK Care for Children	£2,309,596
The Renal Association	£2,377,734	Exeter Northcott Theatre Company	£2,308,516
Tree of Hope	£2,377,581	Bowel Cancer UK	£2,307,222
The EY Foundation	£2,375,947	The Courtauld Institute of Art Fund	£2,306,566
The Foundation of Edward Storey	£2,374,395	The River Farm Foundation	£2,305,987
Manchester Great New & Central Synagogue	£2,373,356	King David Schools (Manchester)	£2,304,330
Bolton Middlebrook Leisure Trust	£2,372,553	Minhaj-Ul-Quran Welfare Foundation	£2,303,673
The Museums Association	£2,371,449	Northern Land Trust	£2,303,635
The English Schools' Football Association	£2,370,111	Minstead Trust	£2,301,341
Sir Thomas White's Charity	£2,369,666	Mind in Bexley Limited	£2,300,816
The Tavistock Institute of Human Relations	£2,369,014	The Drug Safety Research Trust	£2,300,251
The Stonebridge Trust	£2,367,667	The Whitehall and Industry Group	£2,298,846
St. Michael's Fellowship	£2,366,088	Anglo American Group Foundation	£2,298,451
Pancreatic Cancer Research Fund	£2,365,668	Stewards Company Ltd	£2,298,239
Regent's Park College	£2,362,581	The Lewis-Manning Trust	£2,297,670
The Stoller Charitable Trust	£2,362,284	St Mellitus College Trust	£2,297,131
Age UK Shropshire Telford & Wrekin	£2,361,007	Congregation of The Sisters of Nazareth Generalate	£2,296,469
Multiple Sclerosis Trust	£2,360,991	Royal Institution of Naval Architects	£2,296,306
Wiseheights Limited	£2,360,164	The Big Give Trust	£2,294,866
Tockington Manor School Limited	£2,359,489	Antur Waunfawr	£2,294,170
Oxfordshire Crossroads	£2,359,133	Prospect Education Trust	£2,293,104
English UK Limited	£2,357,188	Bible Reading Fellowship	£2,291,898
Duchenne UK	£2,356,582	YMCA St Helens	£2,291,573
Together Against Cancer	£2,355,609	Devon County Agricultural Association	£2,289,309
The Ethiopian Christian Fellowship (UK)	£2,354,707	Survival International Charitable Trust	£2,287,191
St Olave's School Trust	£2,353,532	Chesterfield Society for People with a Learning Disability	£2,286,540
Royal Statistical Society	£2,352,855	Cambridge Community Church	£2,286,203
Carers Trust Thames	£2,352,803	The Corn Exchange (Newbury) Trust	£2,286,000
Anglia Care Trust	£2,351,969	Northbourne Park School Limited	£2,285,258
East Cheshire Housing Consortium Limited	£2,351,908	St Kentigern Hospice	£2,284,095
University of Portsmouth Students Union	£2,351,673	Age UK West Cumbria	£2,283,372
British Journal of Anaesthesia	£2,351,397	British American Drama Academy	£2,281,260
Cwmni Cynnal	£2,347,928	The South of England Agricultural Society	£2,278,288
The Charity of The Sisters of Christ	£2,346,786	Bridge Estate	£2,277,916
Our Daily Bread Ministries Trust	£2,346,734	The Amber Foundation	£2,277,240

The Harlow Health Centres Trust Limited	£2,276,696	Alexian Brothers of The Province of The Sacred Heart	£2,220,269
Jacobs Well Appeal	£2,275,802	Theatre de Complicite Education Limited	£2,219,554
Youth with a Mission Limited	£2,274,507	The Liversage Trust	£2,219,002
St Barnabas, Woodside Park	£2,273,576	Council for Advancement and Support of Education	£2,218,786
Global Action Plan	£2,273,211	Age UK Milton Keynes	£2,217,242
The British School at Rome	£2,273,000	Ashden Sustainable Solutions, Better Lives	£2,215,673
Chiltern College	£2,272,995	The Sisters of Loreto	£2,213,294
Durham Students' Union	£2,272,606	Tobacco Factory Arts Trust	£2,211,585
Feed The Hungry, UK	£2,272,383	The Council for Industry and Higher Education	£2,210,961
Age Concern Liverpool & Sefton	£2,272,290	Age UK Lewisham and Southwark	£2,210,817
Queen's Foundation for Ecumenical Education	£2,271,521	Lakshmi-Narayana Trust	£2,208,961
The Audience Agency	£2,271,331	The Childwick Trust	£2,206,498
Faculty of Sexual & Reproductive Healthcare RCOG	£2,271,243	Age UK Sunderland	£2,206,215
Chevras Tsedokoh Limited	£2,270,609	Tapestry Care UK	£2,206,002
Mission Without Borders	£2,269,205	Health for All (Leeds) Ltd	£2,205,108
Environmental Justice Foundation Charitable Trust	£2,268,743	Community Family Care	£2,205,066
Slindon College Limited	£2,268,561	Trent Valley Education Trust	£2,205,004
Cornwall Community Development Limited	£2,268,269	Young Persons Advisory Service	£2,204,307
Housing Pathways	£2,267,534	Christian Solidarity International	£2,204,158
Cedars Castle Hill	£2,267,490	Larchcroft Education Trust	£2,203,346
Richmond and Hillcroft Adult and Community College	£2,267,347	Childreach International	£2,203,205
R.E.A.L. Foundation Trust	£2,266,626	Dominican Sisters (Third Order) of Newcastle Natal	£2,202,522
Minority Rights Group	£2,266,224	St Margaret's School (Hampstead) Ltd	£2,202,205
The Abbeyfield (Maidenhead) Society Limited	£2,266,218	Clatterbridge Cancer Charity	£2,202,000
Rotherham Crossroads - Caring for Carers	£2,264,991	British Society for Antimicrobial Chemotherapy	£2,200,228
Andover and District Mencap	£2,264,433	Tall Stories Theatre Company Limited	£2,199,905
John Laing Charitable Trust	£2,263,000	London Board for Shechita	£2,199,369
Gateshead Talmudical College	£2,262,154	Safe in Tees Valley Limited	£2,199,175
Children in Crisis	£2,261,637	The Central Foundation Schools of London	£2,199,000
Dance East	£2,261,486	The Mayhew Home	£2,197,123
Derby Hospitals Charitable Trust	£2,261,000	Hayfran Trust	£2,195,767
United Nations Association International Service	£2,260,043	Splitz Support Service	£2,192,184
The Albion Foundation	£2,258,456	Lifeline Community Projects	£2,191,288
Saints Foundation (SFC)	£2,256,228	Whinfield Study Trust	£2,190,804
Options for Life	£2,255,720	Cripplegate Foundation	£2,190,665
Walcot Educational Foundation	£2,255,000	The Friendly Almshouses	£2,190,144
Essex Community Foundation	£2,253,317	The Newspaper Press Fund	£2,190,000
The Royal Cornwall Agricultural Association	£2,253,259	Society of The Sacred Heart	£2,189,778
The Kirby Laing Foundation	£2,252,407	Nottingham Contemporary	£2,188,682
Artsadmin	£2,247,223	Public Service Broadcasting Trust	£2,188,470
Youth Federation Limited	£2,246,072	Downs Syndrome Association	£2,186,863
Ealing Mencap	£2,245,760	Community Care Trust (South West) Limited	£2,184,708
The Bishopsgate Foundation	£2,245,508	Advice UK	£2,182,751
Wirrelderly	£2,244,125	Archange Lebrun Trust Limited	£2,182,000
The RCJ and Islington Citizens Advice Bureaux	£2,242,916	Royal United Hospital Charitable Fund	£2,181,548
The Cadogan Charity	£2,238,285	The Institute of Brewing & Distilling	£2,181,104
The Society for Experimental Biology	£2,237,073	University of Newcastle upon Tyne Development Trust	£2,180,440
Action for Kids Charitable Trust	£2,236,161	Creative and Cultural Industries Limited	£2,179,994
Humberside Offshore Training Association	£2,234,702	The Council of European Jamaats	£2,179,966
The Bournemouth Healthcare Trust	£2,234,663	XCEL County Durham	£2,178,184
Save The Elephants	£2,234,602	Eurovision Mission To Europe	£2,177,451
WABIL	£2,234,443	Bikur Cholim and Gemiluth Chesed Trust	£2,176,904
The Lucy Faithfull Foundation	£2,233,408	Weston Park Foundation	£2,176,693
Salford Foundation Limited	£2,233,315	Fortunatus Housing Solutions	£2,176,033
Royal Northern College of Music Endowment Fund	£2,233,245	MAC AIDS Fund	£2,176,000
The Access To Justice Foundation	£2,232,516	Ribble Catchment Conservation Trust Limited	£2,175,925
Keep Wales Tidy	£2,230,967	Solefield School Educational Trust Limited	£2,175,369
Landaid Charitable Trust Limited	£2,229,769	Transforming Lives for Good (TLG) Ltd	£2,175,347
Spinal Injuries Association	£2,228,971	Merseycare Transport Services Ltd	£2,173,784
Read Foundation	£2,228,746	Wayne Rooney Foundation	£2,173,286
The Arvon Foundation	£2,228,725	R.I.S.E. (Refuge, Information, Support and Education)	£2,172,802
AG Bell International	£2,226,935	The True Colours Trust	£2,172,684
Learning Disability Wales - Anabledd Dysgu Cymru	£2,226,526	Crossroads in Herts (N and NE) Caring for Carers	£2,172,398
The Royal Literary Fund	£2,226,192	The Bais Rochel Dsatmar Charitable Trust	£2,172,379
Ark UK Programmes	£2,226,083	Fircroft College Trust	£2,172,310
Lewisham Nexus Service	£2,225,723	Leicestershire Education Business Company Ltd	£2,172,053
Friends of Wiznitz Limited	£2,225,149	IOM Communications Ltd	£2,171,908
The C Alma Baker Trust	£2,223,766	UW Giving	£2,171,704
Ripon College Cuddesdon	£2,223,508	Leeds Beckett Students' Union	£2,171,661
Age UK Calderdale & Kirklees	£2,222,944	Joyce Meyer Ministries	£2,170,144
Cure Leukaemia	£2,222,720	Streetscene Addiction Recovery	£2,170,136
Countryside Restoration Trust	£2,222,586	The Shoreditch Trust	£2,168,901

Shree Swaminarayan Sidhant Sajivan Mandal London	£2,168,733	Sofronie Foundation	£2,115,241
King's Church Enfield	£2,167,943	Sir Robert Geffery's Almshouse Trust	£2,113,297
Trialogue Educational Trust	£2,167,511	The Biswas Foundation	£2,111,406
Northern Racing College	£2,167,468	Business Disability Forum	£2,111,351
Woolf Institute	£2,166,879	Jewish Teachers' Training College	£2,110,684
The United Kingdom Council for Psychotherapy	£2,166,865	Groundwork Oldham and Rochdale	£2,110,459
St Joseph's School, Launceston	£2,165,811	Leeds Citizens Advice Bureau	£2,110,360
Advance Advocacy & Non-Violence Community Ed	£2,164,289	The Rifles Benevolent Trust	£2,110,053
Age UK Coventry	£2,163,811	Care (Christian Action Research and Education)	£2,109,940
Harrow Mencap	£2,163,336	Chaigeley Educational Foundation	£2,109,850
The Jewish Community Secondary School Trust	£2,162,588	Waltham Forest Noor Ul Islam Trust	£2,109,346
West London Mission Methodist Circuit	£2,162,000	Retrak	£2,108,600
Henry Lonsdale Charitable Trust	£2,159,878	Paddington Development Trust	£2,108,077
British Institute of International and Comparative Law	£2,159,039	Royal Court Liverpool Trust Limited	£2,107,992
Sam Beare Hospice	£2,158,000	St George's Crypt	£2,107,541
Adref Ltd	£2,157,376	Wakefield Theatre Trust	£2,106,864
Riding for The Disabled Association	£2,156,554	The Hertfordshire and Middlesex Wildlife Trust Ltd	£2,106,000
The Wildlife Hospital Trust	£2,156,300	National Children's Centre	£2,105,874
Northease Manor School Ltd	£2,154,806	Tros Gynnal Plant	£2,104,556
Abu Bakr Trust	£2,153,858	Independent Lives (Disability)	£2,103,778
Grange Farm Centre	£2,152,685	Mercaz Torah Vechesed Limited	£2,103,289
St Paul's Community Development Trust	£2,151,458	The Royal Photographic Society of Great Britain	£2,101,532
Ordinary Life Project Association	£2,151,392	Great Britain Wheelchair Basketball Association	£2,101,002
University of Westminster Students' Union	£2,151,333	Artswork Limited	£2,100,798
Salisbury District Hospital Charitable Fund	£2,151,000	Vale House Oxford	£2,099,705
Salisbury City Almshouse and Welfare Charities	£2,149,548	Voluntary Action Sheffield	£2,099,113
The British Sports Trust	£2,148,909	Watford New Hope Trust	£2,098,957
Catalyst Support	£2,148,872	The John Horseman Trust	£2,098,257
Avon Wildlife Trust	£2,148,802	Addiction Recovery Agency Ltd	£2,098,224
ICC Missions	£2,147,886	Camden Arts Centre	£2,098,015
Beth Jacob Grammar School for Girls Limited	£2,147,615	Bury Hospice	£2,097,060
The Henry Barber Trust	£2,147,511	The NIA Project	£2,096,802
All Aboard Shops Limited	£2,147,061	World Child Cancer UK	£2,096,699
Community Foster Care	£2,147,024	Cheshire Deaf Society	£2,096,610
Newstraid Benevolent Fund	£2,146,350	The Sussex Archaeological Society	£2,096,528
Age UK Medway	£2,145,824	Lancashire Women's Centres	£2,096,440
Cheshire Centre for Independent Living	£2,143,018	LGBT Foundation Ltd	£2,096,378
Rupert House School	£2,142,577	Polka Children's Theatre Limited	£2,096,043
Kaleidoscope South Hams Limited	£2,142,032	The Mulberry Trust	£2,095,854
Bliss -The National Charity for The Newborn	£2,140,953	SOS Sahel International UK	£2,095,050
German Young Men's Christian Association in London	£2,140,368	Women's Aid Integrated Services (Nottingham & Region)	£2,093,795
Kenneth Copeland Ministries	£2,139,663	Brahma Kumaris World Spiritual University (UK)	£2,093,272
The Ethnic Minority Foundation	£2,139,370	KFC Foundation	£2,093,081
Nofit State Community Circus Ltd	£2,133,643	Greater London Fund for the Blind	£2,092,991
Central England Law Centre Limited	£2,133,636	The Norfolk and Norwich Association for the Blind	£2,092,235
Education for Health	£2,133,454	South Hill Park Trust Limited	£2,091,920
Greater Manchester Sports Partnership	£2,132,409	The Ryleys School Limited	£2,091,285
Magic Breakfast	£2,131,219	National Association of Decorative & Fine Arts Societies	£2,090,842
Turner Home	£2,130,042	The House of St Barnabas	£2,090,562
Vision Homes Association	£2,128,941	Christ for All Nations (U.K.)	£2,090,557
Gateway Qualifications Limited	£2,128,587	Richmond Parish Lands Charity	£2,089,856
The Mayor's Fund for London	£2,128,147	Age Concern Slough and Berkshire East	£2,089,070
Sherman Cymru	£2,128,050	Shri Vallabh Nidhi - UK	£2,088,852
Crossroads Care Staffordshire Limited	£2,127,054	The Liz and Terry Bramall Foundation	£2,084,831
Reprieve	£2,126,418	Hampton Fuel Allotment	£2,084,735
Kirkdale Industrial Training Services Limited	£2,126,310	Crossroads Sir Gar Limited	£2,083,137
Hospital of William Wyggeston & The Hospital Branch	£2,125,990	The National Youth Orchestra of Great Britain	£2,080,235
Goldsmiths Students' Union	£2,125,680	IM01 Limited	£2,079,995
Palestine Assoc for Childrens Encouragement of Sports	£2,125,501	Central G H Trust	£2,079,097
Age Concern East Sussex	£2,125,495	The Northam Care Trust	£2,077,627
The Linnean Society of London	£2,125,241	Marchant-Holliday School Limited	£2,077,054
Revival Church Europe	£2,125,106	Deafway	£2,076,891
Interact Chelmsford Limited	£2,122,254	The Herefordshire Wildlife Trust Limited	£2,076,314
Bison in the Community	£2,122,020	The Tonbridge School Foundation	£2,076,182
Arnolfini Gallery Limited	£2,120,872	The William Harvey Research Foundation	£2,075,740
Suffolk Family Carers	£2,118,478	Kerem Schools	£2,073,084
Countess Mountbatten Hospice Charity Limited	£2,117,954	Dodderhill School	£2,072,969
Manchester and District Home for Lost Dogs Limited	£2,117,763	YMCA Indian Student Hostel	£2,072,325
Specialeffect Org UK	£2,116,391	Ovarian Cancer Action	£2,072,195
CAPITB Trust	£2,116,149	General Assembly Unitarian & Free Christian Churches	£2,071,735
Side By Side (Children) Limited	£2,115,599	Cymryd Rhan	£2,071,271
East Kent Mencap	£2,115,264	Birmingham Jewish Community Care	£2,070,959

The John Armitage Charitable Trust	£2,069,734	The Minack Theatre Trust CIO	£2,016,229
University Hospitals of North Midlands Charity	£2,069,000	Milton Keynes Christian Centre	£2,016,193
The Duke's Playhouse Limited	£2,067,174	UTRY	£2,016,181
Norfolk Coalition of Disabled People	£2,066,311	Tagmarsh Charity Limited	£2,015,312
WAC Arts	£2,064,881	The Cheshire Wildlife Trust Limited	£2,015,128
Pontesbury Project for People with Special Needs	£2,064,501	DM Thomas Foundation for Young People	£2,014,661
Pallant House Gallery	£2,064,269	G G S Khalsa College	£2,013,453
Hethersett Old Hall School Limited	£2,064,095	The New Forest Agricultural Show Society	£2,013,007
Mohs Workplace Health Limited	£2,064,080	Age UK South Lakeland	£2,011,373
International Food Information Service (IFIS Publishing)	£2,063,462	Cambridgeshire Community Foundation	£2,010,896
The Trusthouse Charitable Foundation	£2,062,000	The Hanford School Charitable Trust Limited	£2,010,893
Beeston Hall School Trust Limited	£2,061,627	Eastbourne and District Mencap Limited	£2,008,957
Greenbank School Limited	£2,061,504	Liverpool Student Union	£2,008,482
The Japanese School Limited	£2,061,368	Signposts (Luton)	£2,008,385
The East Malling Trust	£2,061,176	Kingsmead School Hoylake Trust Ltd	£2,008,197
Sisters of Mercy Sunderland	£2,059,177	Spurgeons College	£2,008,000
Petrus Community	£2,058,032	Latin Link	£2,007,791
The J Van Mars Foundation	£2,056,882	Safenet Domestic Abuse and Support Services Ltd	£2,007,184
Parish of Howell Hill with Burgh Heath	£2,055,497	The Constable Educational Trust Limited	£2,007,113
Action for Deafness	£2,054,338	New Israel Fund	£2,006,063
St James' School Grimsby Ltd	£2,053,306	Lambeth and Southwark Mencap	£2,005,720
Presidents Club Charitable Trust	£2,052,816	Microloan Foundation	£2,005,564
Moorlands College	£2,052,753	Carers Gloucestershire	£2,004,152
The Millby Foundation	£2,052,683	Teens and Toddlers Trading as Power2 Ltd	£2,003,500
Northamptonshire Association for the Blind	£2,051,982	Citizens Advice Bradford & Airedale & Bradford Law	£2,003,442
Friends International Ministries	£2,051,806	Ana Leaf Foundation	£2,002,594
Andrews Charitable Trust	£2,051,600	Pompey in the Community	£2,002,549
Winchester Science Centre	£2,050,000	Hull and East Yorkshire Medical Research Centre	£2,002,356
Southampton Engineering Training Association Ltd	£2,049,903	Kneehigh Theatre Trust Limited	£2,001,857
The MacFarlane Trust	£2,048,836	Global Giving UK	£2,001,481
IHG Foundation (UK) Trust	£2,048,431	The Sisters of Saint Joseph of Annecy	£2,001,035
Viva Network	£2,047,736	The Mereside Education Trust	£2,000,924
British Society for Immunology	£2,046,871	Hull Community and Voluntary Services Ltd	£2,000,806
Shakespeare Schools Foundation	£2,046,359	Bury Manor School Trust Ltd (Dorset House School)	£1,999,984
Treebeard Trust	£2,044,017	R L Glasspool Charity Trust	£1,999,962
Muslim Charity Helping The Needy	£2,041,346	Citizens Advice Gateshead	£1,999,108
Anglia Ruskin Students' Union	£2,040,331	Brain Research Trust	£1,998,000
Alexander Devine Children's Cancer Trust	£2,039,869	Coventry University Students' Union Limited	£1,997,805
Groundwork South Tyneside and Newcastle-upon-Tyne	£2,037,558	Valleys Kids	£1,996,467
D T F Limited	£2,036,742	Eckling Grange Limited	£1,995,435
DDRC Healthcare	£2,036,201	The Sobell Foundation	£1,994,973
The Arts Depot Trust Limited	£2,035,649	Stormont School	£1,993,990
Veterans Aid	£2,035,500	Shape London	£1,993,208
Forest of Dean Crossroads Caring for Carers	£2,035,458	The Anglo-American Charity Limited	£1,993,081
United Reformed Church (Southern Synod) Trust	£2,034,017	Adventist Development and Relief Agency - UK	£1,992,962
Baxendale	£2,033,454	International Road Assessment Programme	£1,992,610
Medway Education Trust	£2,033,404	RAF Sports Federation	£1,990,281
The Reme Charity	£2,033,015	The Oundle School Foundation	£1,990,000
Norwich Consolidated Charities	£2,031,631	Wiltshire Citizens Advice	£1,989,828
St Dominic's Priory School (Stone)	£2,030,483	De Montfort University Students' Union Limited	£1,989,614
Age Concern Newcastle upon Tyne	£2,030,213	Independent Domestic Abuse Services	£1,988,497
MK Gallery	£2,029,156	Orange Tree Theatre Ltd	£1,988,275
Genesis America (UK) Limited	£2,029,057	The Costa Foundation	£1,988,241
Quaggy Development Trust	£2,028,658	Skillshare International	£1,988,000
Rambert School of Ballet and Contemporary Dance	£2,028,460	Science Engineering Technology Mathematics Network	£1,987,955
The Society of St Paul The Apostle	£2,027,257	CASP	£1,982,599
Faculty of Public Health of The RCP of UK	£2,027,026	International NGO Training and Research Centre	£1,981,814
The Cure Parkinson's Trust	£2,026,924	The Cheshire Residential Homes Trust	£1,981,109
Malaria No More United Kingdom	£2,026,811	The Titus Trust	£1,980,248
Resurgo Trust	£2,026,332	Universal Prayer Group Ministry	£1,980,220
The Warrington Homes Limited	£2,025,505	St Hugh's School (Woodhall Spa) Limited	£1,979,938
Blue Marine Foundation	£2,024,158	Inner City Music Limited	£1,979,544
Leicester Arts Centre Limited	£2,024,149	Norfolk and Norwich University Hospitals NHS	£1,978,016
Jubilee Hall Trust Limited	£2,023,961	Valley House	£1,977,536
Barnet Education Arts Trust	£2,023,891	UKGBC	£1,976,065
The Lake District Calvert Trust	£2,022,050	The Brook Trust	£1,975,988
Hilden Oaks School Educational Trust Limited	£2,021,201	St Luke's Parochial Trust	£1,975,830
Christian Education Movement	£2,020,907	Jamiyat Tabligh-Ul-Islam	£1,975,275
Modern Electric Tramways Limited	£2,020,551	Bow Arts Trust	£1,974,524
African Prisons Project	£2,020,312	United St Saviour's Charity	£1,974,022
Stubbers Adventure Centre	£2,019,710	Azhar Academy	£1,973,979
Morris Cerullo World Evangelism	£2,017,237	Skills and Education Group Limited	£1,973,227

Huggard	£1,971,476	Camphill Milton Keynes Communities Limited	£1,923,116
Richmond House School	£1,971,410	Sutton Coldfield Charitable Trust	£1,923,076
National Justice Museum	£1,970,167	Foundation for Environmental Education	£1,922,838
Age UK East London	£1,968,827	Northumbria Calvert Trust	£1,922,582
Off Centre Limited	£1,968,257	St Helens and Knowsley Caring Association	£1,921,993
Yorkshire Mesmac	£1,967,525	The Rodney Aldridge Charitable Trust	£1,921,508
The British Psychoanalytical Society	£1,966,087	Portsmouth Cultural Trust	£1,921,142
Woking Homes	£1,964,098	Bluecoat Sports	£1,919,692
The Sussex Beacon	£1,964,036	National Society (CoE & CiW) for Promotion of Education	£1,919,437
Quintessentially Foundation	£1,963,151	Imago Community	£1,918,556
Ansbury	£1,962,967	Foundation for The Parks and Reserves of Cote D'Ivoire	£1,918,350
Fulham Football Club Foundation	£1,961,055	Canterbury Archaeological Trust Limited	£1,917,895
Westcountry Rivers Trust	£1,958,534	Children North East	£1,917,892
The Froebelian School (Horsforth) Limited	£1,957,899	The Royal School of Needlework	£1,917,802
Women in Prison Limited	£1,956,540	Islamia Schools Limited	£1,917,609
Rosehill Arts Trust Limited	£1,956,278	St. Andrew and St. Mary Magdalene, Maidenhead	£1,916,996
The Hobson Charity Limited	£1,955,932	Walthamstow and Chingford Almshouse Charity	£1,916,610
Mahdlo (Oldham Youth Zone)	£1,955,515	Tree Aid	£1,914,873
Elam Ministries	£1,954,819	The Institute of Economic Affairs Limited	£1,913,000
Community of St Mary at The Cross	£1,954,587	Bristol Aero Collection Trust	£1,911,640
Sefton Council for Voluntary Service	£1,954,324	Frimley Health Charity	£1,910,000
Frankgiving Limited	£1,954,226	Thorngate Almshouse Trust	£1,909,116
YMCA North Tyneside	£1,953,275	Creative Youth Network	£1,908,392
Designability Charity Limited	£1,952,924	Devon and Exeter Spastics Society	£1,908,325
West Berkshire Mencap	£1,952,637	The Arsenal Foundation	£1,908,139
The Kimmeridge Trust	£1,951,417	Amicus Trust	£1,907,989
Blue Sky Development and Regeneration	£1,950,061	Action for Carers (Surrey)	£1,907,473
The Sutton Pendle Charitable Trust	£1,950,000	Florence Nightingale Hospice Charity	£1,906,187
Modiano Charitable Trust	£1,950,000	Daisy Chain Project Teesside	£1,906,033
Doteveryone	£1,949,955	Congregation of Sisters of Charity of Jesus and Mary	£1,905,123
Right to Play UK Limited	£1,949,947	Manor and Castle Development Trust Limited	£1,904,930
The Unicorn School Ltd	£1,949,441	Harewood House Trust Limited	£1,904,695
Disability Rights UK	£1,949,353	Capernwray Missionary Fellowship of Torchbearers	£1,903,845
The Bluecoat	£1,946,743	Latch Welsh Children's Cancer Charity	£1,902,915
The Golf Foundation	£1,945,118	Centre for Sustainable Energy	£1,902,749
Fulmer Education Trust	£1,944,894	South Bucks Hospice	£1,902,713
Stratford-upon-Avon Town Trust	£1,942,298	Harvey's Foundry Trust	£1,902,532
Salford and Trafford Engineering Group Training Assoc	£1,941,291	The British Society for Haematology	£1,901,533
Hull and East Yorkshire Mind	£1,941,255	Mendip Young Mens Christian Association	£1,901,465
War on Want	£1,941,052	The Harbour Foundation	£1,901,222
ARP Charitable Services	£1,940,000	ECI Schools	£1,901,184
The Proforest Initiative	£1,939,961	The Order of The Daughters of Mary and Joseph	£1,901,002
Eton End School Trust (Datchet) Limited	£1,939,816	TEAM Wearside Limited	£1,900,677
Trinity College Bristol Limited	£1,939,715	The Schroder Foundation	£1,900,439
British Wireless for the Blind Fund	£1,939,687	Kings Church International	£1,899,473
Emmaus U.K.	£1,939,065	Krishnamurti Foundation Trust Ltd	£1,898,038
Doncaster Performance Venue Limited	£1,937,145	Hertfordshire County Scout Council	£1,896,185
Natural Resource Charter Limited	£1,936,769	Yad Voezer Limited	£1,895,985
Outreach Community and Residential Services	£1,934,201	Dance Consortium Limited	£1,895,953
The Caxton Foundation	£1,932,513	The Association for Real Change	£1,895,896
Southwark Diocesan Board of Education (Inc)	£1,932,469	Wychwood School for Girls	£1,895,331
Waverley School (Crowthorne) Limited	£1,932,197	Anti-Slavery International	£1,894,632
Transparency International UK	£1,932,000	Lyonsdown School Trust Ltd	£1,893,859
The Royal Foundation of St Katharine	£1,931,344	XLP	£1,893,695
Spear Housing Association Limited	£1,930,335	St Richard of Chichester Christian Care Association	£1,893,123
Talbot House Trust North East	£1,930,075	Near Neighbours	£1,893,000
Community Action Suffolk	£1,929,704	Queen Mary's Schools Foundation	£1,891,487
Thinkforward (UK)	£1,929,701	The Architectural Heritage Fund	£1,890,978
United World Schools	£1,929,605	Melton Mowbray Town Estate	£1,890,877
Hulme Hall Educational Trust Limited	£1,928,895	United Reformed Church (Eastern Province) Trust	£1,890,742
Gaddum Centre	£1,928,047	The Shakespeare Hospice	£1,889,475
The Resource Alliance Limited	£1,927,996	Crossroads Together Ltd.	£1,889,447
Cosmetic Toiletry and Perfumery Foundation	£1,927,282	Target Ovarian Cancer	£1,889,091
Southern Universities Management Services	£1,926,908	The Queen Elizabeth Prize for Engineering Foundation	£1,887,118
Highfield Priory School Limited	£1,926,738	Museum of Modern Art Limited	£1,887,082
Essex Boys and Girls Clubs	£1,926,668	East Lindsey Information Technology Centre	£1,886,410
Ashburnham Christian Trust	£1,926,604	The Racing Foundation	£1,886,000
The National Horseracing Museum	£1,926,352	The Al-Khoei Benevolent Foundation	£1,885,110
College of St Barnabas	£1,926,000	CACDP	£1,884,904
GFA World	£1,924,616	J Paul Getty Jr General Charitable Trust	£1,884,547
The Mayfield Trust	£1,923,878	The Foundation for Art and Creative Technology	£1,884,301
Sunninghill Preparatory School Limited	£1,923,314	Humentum UK	£1,884,000

Library & Museum Charitable Trust of Grand Lodge	£1,883,892	The Utley Family Charitable Trust	£1,841,034
Hestercombe Gardens Trust Limited	£1,883,442	St Anthony of Padua Community Association	£1,840,411
The Haramead Trust	£1,881,823	Tyne North Training Limited	£1,839,580
Renewal Christian Centre	£1,881,341	Druglink Limited	£1,838,772
Access - The Foundation for Social Investment	£1,881,000	The Joseph Storehouse Trust	£1,838,184
Mooji Foundation Ltd	£1,879,722	Swarovski Foundation	£1,837,423
East End Citizens' Advice Bureaux	£1,879,016	Enhanceable	£1,837,239
The Kent and East Sussex Railway Company Ltd	£1,878,769	Age Concern Hillingdon	£1,837,130
Emmanuel Bristol	£1,878,506	Krizevac Project	£1,837,086
International Psychoanalytical Association	£1,878,499	The Margaret Thatcher Scholarship Trust	£1,836,883
The Linda and Gordon Bonnyman Charitable Trust	£1,878,405	The Care Forum	£1,836,685
East and North Herts NHS Trust Charitable Fund	£1,877,338	Medway League of Friends	£1,835,465
CoppaFeel	£1,877,314	Groundwork West Midlands	£1,834,392
Harpenden Mencap	£1,875,919	Crescent Purchasing Limited	£1,833,531
The Queen Alexandra Cottage Homes	£1,874,741	The Baily Thomas Charitable Fund	£1,833,528
The United Reformed Church (W Midlands) Trust Ltd	£1,874,300	Durrell Wildlife Conservation Trust - UK	£1,833,000
Middlesbrough Football Club Foundation	£1,873,998	Action Together CIO	£1,832,967
The British Kidney Patient Association	£1,873,646	Punchdrunk	£1,832,512
Fulham Palace Trust	£1,873,219	The PWC Foundation	£1,831,754
St Christopher's Homes	£1,872,965	Asia House	£1,831,677
The Wildlife Trust of South and West Wales Limited	£1,872,283	Solar Aid	£1,830,704
Area 51 Education	£1,872,093	Al Badr Islamic Trust	£1,830,446
St Andrew's School (Bedford) Limited	£1,871,933	Gemach Ltd	£1,830,307
Derby County Community Trust	£1,871,771	Vision 21 (Cyfle Cymru)	£1,829,692
The Charity Finance Group	£1,871,464	42nd Street - Resource for Young People Under Stress	£1,829,058
Welsh Women's Aid	£1,870,943	The Lord Mayor's Appeal	£1,828,967
The Sir Harold Hillier Gardens and Arboretum	£1,869,755	Orchard Vale Trust Limited	£1,828,310
Solicitors Benevolent Association Limited	£1,869,693	Crossroads Care North West	£1,828,273
The Leathersellers' Company Charitable Fund	£1,868,000	Towner	£1,828,149
Morgan Stanley International Foundation	£1,867,698	Hull and East Riding Citizens Advice Bureau Ltd	£1,827,805
The Aimwell Charitable Trust	£1,867,620	The Telz Talmudical Academy and Talmud Torah Trust	£1,827,250
Woodbrooke Quaker Study Centre	£1,867,586	Services for Independent Living	£1,827,239
UK Health Forum	£1,867,522	BW Foundation	£1,827,008
Methodist Action (North West) Limited	£1,867,203	Missionaries of Charity of Mother Teresa of Calcutta	£1,826,386
The Lisieux Trust Limited	£1,866,732	Vast Services (1920)	£1,826,377
North East Theatre Trust Limited	£1,866,088	The Melow Charitable Trust	£1,826,150
The Scott Creative Arts Foundation	£1,865,156	Providence Row	£1,825,855
Christian Witness To Israel	£1,864,479	Dance North	£1,825,782
Medical Detection Dogs	£1,861,691	The Tolkien Trust	£1,824,300
The British Dyslexia Association	£1,861,562	Wellbeing of Women	£1,824,138
South Lee School Limited	£1,861,261	The Electrical Industries Charity Limited	£1,824,000
The Isle of Wight Railway Company Limited	£1,861,254	Aberystwyth University Students' Union	£1,823,394
The Ashmolean Museum Endowment Trust	£1,860,346	The Lodge Trust CIO	£1,823,178
The Children's Cancer and Leukaemia Group	£1,858,536	WPF Therapy Ltd	£1,822,404
The Manchester Young People's Theatre Limited	£1,857,306	The Sheffield Royal Society for the Blind	£1,822,012
Doorstep of Hull	£1,856,951	The Clockmakers' Charity	£1,821,513
The Army Dependants' Trust	£1,855,920	Peace Direct	£1,821,399
Christians in Sport	£1,855,678	Staffordshire Winter Sports Club	£1,819,379
The Incorporated Catholic Truth Society	£1,852,367	Holy Trinity and St Peter Le Bailey, Oxford	£1,819,164
French Education Charitable Trust	£1,852,000	Delphside Ltd	£1,817,452
Step By Step School Limited	£1,851,808	Festival of Life	£1,817,232
The Savitri Waney Charitable Trust	£1,851,803	The Manufacturing Institute	£1,816,974
Huddersfield Community Trust	£1,849,398	Jubilee House Care Trust Ltd	£1,815,607
Dr. Vivian Child Charitable Trust	£1,849,367	BCNO Limited	£1,815,391
Hope for Justice	£1,849,246	Tullie House Museum and Art Gallery Trust	£1,815,312
St Joseph's in the Park School	£1,849,147	Burgess Autistic Trust	£1,815,267
University of Salford Students' Union	£1,849,056	Walk The Plank	£1,815,127
YMCA Wolverhampton	£1,848,403	Grimsby Cleethorpes and Humber Region YMCA	£1,815,103
Coram Cambridgeshire Adoption Limited	£1,847,521	St Clare's Hospice	£1,814,920
Age Concern London	£1,847,025	East London Advanced Technology Training	£1,813,824
The Pilgrim Trust	£1,846,313	North Staffs Mind	£1,813,332
Collage Arts	£1,845,820	Contact The Elderly Limited	£1,812,027
British Olympic Foundation	£1,844,833	Apostleship of the Sea	£1,810,937
S W Durham Training Limited	£1,843,621	Southend-on-Sea Young Mens Christian Association	£1,809,181
Domestic Violence Intervention Project	£1,843,501	The Banner of Truth Trust	£1,808,901
Videre Est Credere	£1,843,491	Impact Foundation	£1,808,875
GrantScape	£1,843,158	University of Bradford Union	£1,808,193
Warwickshire Community and Voluntary Action	£1,842,967	The Vardy Foundation	£1,808,103
University of Chichester Students' Union	£1,842,648	Technion UK	£1,808,076
North Kent Mind	£1,842,195	Seely Hirst House	£1,808,059
Bolton Young Persons Housing Scheme	£1,841,828	Bootstrap Company Limited	£1,807,901
Voluntary Action Merthyr Tydfil	£1,841,674	The Disability Resource Centre	£1,807,685

The Ursuline Preparatory School	£1,806,758	Mothers2mothers (UK) Limited	£1,758,683
Lewes Community Screen	£1,802,978	The British Institute of Florence	£1,758,000
Dawliffe Hall Educational Foundation	£1,802,880	Derbyshire Wildlife Trust Limited	£1,757,000
Leicester Hospitals Charity	£1,802,000	The Cote Charity	£1,756,263
Shri Venkateswara (Balaji) Temple of The UK	£1,801,377	The Karuna Trust	£1,755,809
BFI Trust	£1,800,693	Church of England Soldiers', Sailors' & Airmen's Clubs	£1,755,605
Credit Suisse EMEA Foundation	£1,800,395	Swansea & Brecon Diocesan Board for Soc Resp	£1,755,136
Chartered Surveyors Training Trust	£1,799,783	Herts Mind Network Ltd	£1,754,357
Petworth Cottage Nursing Home	£1,798,698	Imperial College Trust	£1,753,401
The Society of St Stephens House	£1,798,394	Smallwood Manor Preparatory School Limited	£1,753,090
Advocacy Support in Cymru Ltd	£1,797,843	Kollel and Co Limited	£1,752,344
UCS Pre-Prep Limited	£1,796,645	Manchester Mind	£1,752,265
British Friends of Igud Hakolelim B'yerushalayim	£1,795,262	The Sixteen	£1,752,139
Kirklees Music School	£1,795,000	Metal Culture Limited	£1,751,639
Mancroft Advice Project (MAP)	£1,794,005	Cambridge House and Talbot	£1,751,396
Abertawe Bro Morgannwg University LHB	£1,794,000	Age UK Doncaster	£1,750,759
The Artangel Trust	£1,793,881	Coram Voice (formerly Voice for The Child in Care)	£1,750,341
West Midlands Winter Sports Club Limited	£1,793,584	The Clore Duffield Foundation	£1,750,157
Changing Faces	£1,792,784	European College of Business and Management	£1,750,020
The Academy of Medical Royal Colleges	£1,792,187	The Abbeyfield Newcastle upon Tyne Society Limited	£1,749,788
Voluntary Norfolk	£1,791,145	Jo's Cervical Cancer Trust	£1,749,644
The Ashley Foundation	£1,790,403	The New Rachmistrivke Synagogue Trust	£1,749,549
The Antiquarian Horological Society	£1,789,143	Bury St Edmunds Theatre Management Limited	£1,749,033
Huddersfield Christian Fellowship	£1,788,183	Rydes Hill School Guildford	£1,748,746
The Apax Foundation	£1,787,309	Medeshamstede Education Trust	£1,747,730
Shropshire Wildlife Trust	£1,786,231	The Rayne Foundation	£1,746,994
The Resolution Trust	£1,785,346	Renew Leeds Limited	£1,746,223
Spice Innovations Limited	£1,784,725	Tameside, Oldham and Glossop Mind	£1,746,048
The Evolution Education Trust	£1,784,652	Secular Clergy Common Fund	£1,745,705
English National Ballet School Limited	£1,783,599	The Humane Society International (UK)	£1,745,654
Hetton Home Care Services	£1,783,352	Wigan Link	£1,745,304
Powys Association of Voluntary Organisation	£1,782,976	The Great Dixter Charitable Trust	£1,745,269
Merthyr Tydfil Institute for the Blind	£1,782,297	C P S Preston Ltd	£1,744,377
Avenue House Estate Trust	£1,780,790	Sail Training International	£1,744,257
Greenwich + Docklands Festivals	£1,780,654	Women's Technology Training Limited	£1,744,098
Pret Foundation Trust	£1,780,512	The Kays Foundation	£1,743,193
Samuel Lewis Foundation	£1,780,000	Mid Warwicks Society for Mentally Handicapped	£1,741,912
Staffordshire & Birmingham Agricultural Society	£1,779,121	Worcestershire Wildlife Trust	£1,741,783
Age UK Faversham and Sittingbourne	£1,776,736	Derwentside Hospice Care Foundation	£1,741,667
Resources for Autism	£1,776,185	Groundwork Wales	£1,741,633
JCD Foundation	£1,776,102	Progressive Farming Trust Limited	£1,740,825
Our Lady of Fidelity Established at Upper Norwood	£1,775,760	WIZO.UK	£1,740,573
Gisda Cyfyngedig / Arfon Young Single Homeless Group	£1,775,563	New Tribes Mission	£1,740,269
DENS Limited	£1,775,080	Family Care Trust	£1,739,989
The Yorkshire Dales Millennium Trust	£1,774,222	The Loyola Preparatory School	£1,739,264
Adoption UK Charity	£1,774,153	Cardiff and Vale Citizens Advice Bureau	£1,738,339
Debenhams Foundation	£1,774,100	Beva Limited	£1,738,253
Brentford FC Community Sports Trust	£1,773,663	International Spinal Research Trust	£1,738,000
The Printing Charity	£1,773,430	The Institute for Optimum Nutrition	£1,737,540
The Children's House School	£1,773,222	Bnos Yisroel School Manchester	£1,736,866
Magna Trust	£1,772,693	Paul Sartori Foundation Limited	£1,736,809
Racing Welfare	£1,772,000	Marina Theatre Trust	£1,736,707
Northamptonshire Health Charitable Fund	£1,772,000	Medair UK	£1,736,436
Keren Chochmas Shloma Trust	£1,771,979	Hawk Conservancy Trust Limited	£1,736,363
Sir Josiah Mason's Almshouse Charity	£1,771,717	Hurdale Charity Limited	£1,735,986
MV Balmoral Fund Limited	£1,771,567	Holy Trinity, Cambridge	£1,734,832
The 5BEL Charitable Trust	£1,771,313	Plymouth Argyle Football in the Community Trust	£1,734,285
Advanced Life Support Group	£1,770,022	The Reed Educational Trust Limited	£1,734,222
Southwark Citizens Advice Bureaux Service	£1,767,926	Landmarks	£1,733,887
Yardley Grange Care Services	£1,767,650	BalletBoyz Ltd	£1,733,827
Hull Trinity House Charity	£1,765,750	North Western Reform Synagogue	£1,733,533
The Haven Wolverhampton	£1,765,706	Sense International	£1,733,293
Lincolnshire House Association	£1,765,336	Carers Trust Mid Yorkshire	£1,731,299
Community Housing Cymru	£1,765,137	The Oxford Trust	£1,731,062
The Joseph Rowntree Charitable Trust	£1,764,000	Beechwood Education Trust	£1,730,966
The MedicAlert Foundation	£1,763,999	The Kenelm Youth Trust Limited	£1,730,695
AIM Awards	£1,763,274	The Park School (Yeovil) Limited	£1,730,283
UK Cat Consortium	£1,762,569	Terrington Hall Trust Limited	£1,730,280
Anawim - Women Working Together	£1,761,719	Church Burgesses Trust	£1,729,279
Club Peloton	£1,761,538	RFU Injured Players Foundation	£1,729,130
Villa Scalabrini	£1,761,054	Beth Shalom Limited	£1,728,111
Camphill Devon Community Limited	£1,760,077	Brighton, St Peter	£1,728,097

Society for The Study of Inborn Errors of Metabolism	£1,726,876	Glebe House School Trust Ltd	£1,694,108
Action Deafness	£1,726,461	Global Dialogue	£1,692,642
Royal National Children's Springboard Foundation	£1,725,531	Samjo Limited	£1,691,650
Royal Wanstead School	£1,725,531	Churches Child Protection Advisory Service	£1,691,549
Memhay Limited	£1,725,376	British Record Industry Trust	£1,691,523
The Prince's School of Traditional Arts	£1,725,088	Rift Valley Research Limited	£1,691,380
Vita et Pax School (Cockfosters) Limited	£1,724,867	The Broomgrove Trust	£1,690,907
Voluntary and Community Sector Learning and Skills	£1,724,804	Multiple Sclerosis International Federation	£1,690,382
The Live Theatre Winchester Trust	£1,723,886	Bromley Youth Music Trust	£1,690,138
Cliff College	£1,723,690	Gerald Leigh Charitable Trust	£1,689,546
Windmill Hill City Farm Limited	£1,723,639	Clarets in the Community Limited	£1,689,334
The Dancexchange Limited	£1,723,528	The Rosemarie Nathanson Charitable Trust	£1,688,874
Wimbledon Guild of Social Welfare (Incorporated)	£1,723,047	Mary Feilding Guild	£1,688,739
The Candlelighters Trust	£1,722,839	National Zoological Society of Wales	£1,688,308
Transaid Worldwide Services Limited	£1,722,788	The Jesmond Trust	£1,687,638
The Hounslow Arts Trust Ltd	£1,722,069	General Federation of Trade Unions Educational Trust	£1,687,433
Project S.E.E.D. Limited	£1,722,038	Camden Garden Centre Charitable Trust	£1,687,201
The Garden Tomb (Jerusalem) Association	£1,722,033	Doncaster Rotherham and District Motor Trades	£1,686,952
Walsingham College (Affiliated Schools) Limited	£1,721,807	Founders for Good Ltd	£1,685,072
History of Parliament Trust	£1,721,288	Islington Law Centre	£1,684,676
Age Cymru Gwent	£1,721,208	Herne Hill Velodrome Trust	£1,684,330
Help for Carers	£1,719,342	STC Research Foundation	£1,684,159
The Sir Alister Hardy Foundation for Ocean Science	£1,719,253	Seven Stories, National Centre for Children's Books	£1,683,902
Fyling Hall School Trust Limited	£1,719,000	Achieve Lifestyle	£1,683,807
Save The Rhino International	£1,718,661	The Stockport Engineering Training Association	£1,683,431
Beis Yaakov Primary School Foundation	£1,716,876	Zichron Meir Limited	£1,683,137
Sat-7 UK Trust Limited	£1,716,851	Ichthus Christian Fellowship	£1,681,651
Noor Trust	£1,716,589	Yesodey Hatorah Primary Girls School Trust	£1,680,566
Centre of Life Church International	£1,715,424	Tech Trust	£1,680,340
Groundwork Wakefield Limited	£1,713,831	Aldeburgh Music Endowment Fund	£1,679,264
Dacorum Council for Voluntary Service	£1,712,154	Beating Bowel Cancer	£1,679,119
Age UK Derby & Derbyshire	£1,712,069	The Pankhurst Trust	£1,678,779
The Citizens Foundation (UK)	£1,710,920	The Art Academy	£1,678,526
Sarum College	£1,710,920	Birmingham Citizens Advice Bureau Service Ltd	£1,678,029
Unseen (UK)	£1,710,672	Lymphoma Action	£1,677,351
Richmond upon Thames Music Trust Company Ltd	£1,710,058	Estate Charity of William Hatcliffe	£1,676,891
Talmud Torah Education Limited	£1,709,371	The Arnold Foundation for Rugby School	£1,676,499
Stoke College Educational Trust Ltd	£1,709,187	The Clore Leadership Programme	£1,676,017
The H B Allen Charitable Trust	£1,709,174	The Actors' Benevolent Fund	£1,675,230
Groundwork Manchester Salford Stockport Tameside	£1,708,307	The Maurice Wohl Charitable Foundation	£1,674,887
The Bradgate Park and Swithland Wood Charity	£1,707,530	Intercountry Adoption Centre	£1,674,554
The Federation of British Artists	£1,707,374	York Teaching Hospital Charity	£1,673,000
New North London Synagogue	£1,706,380	Project Space Leeds	£1,672,743
The Roger & Douglas Turner Charitable Trust	£1,706,000	Tyddyn Mon	£1,672,404
The Royal School of Church Music	£1,705,718	International Youth Hostel Federation	£1,672,237
The Youth Sport UK Charitable Trust	£1,705,048	Baker Dearing Educational Trust	£1,672,202
The JMCMRJ Sorrell Foundation	£1,704,510	The Clare Milne Trust	£1,671,786
Chess in Schools and Communities	£1,704,510	Cool Earth Action	£1,671,616
Sheffield Wednesday FC Community Programme	£1,704,437	M.G.S. Trust	£1,671,538
Khoja Shia Ithnaasheri Muslim Community of London	£1,703,232	Belmont-Birklands School Trust Limited	£1,670,614
St Hilda's East	£1,703,184	Reach Learning Disability	£1,669,832
Christ Faith Tabernacle International	£1,702,763	Dreams Come True Charity	£1,669,786
Winchester Student Union	£1,702,252	The Navigators UK Limited	£1,669,190
YSS Ltd	£1,701,986	British Deaf Association	£1,668,932
Palace for Life Foundation	£1,700,688	Eleanor Palmer Trust	£1,668,873
Battersea Methodist Mission	£1,700,456	St. Mark's Hospital Foundation	£1,667,246
Haringey Advisory Group on Alcohol	£1,700,103	Bendrigg Trust	£1,666,546
Bernhard Baron Cottage Homes	£1,700,000	Cransley School Limited	£1,664,761
Wirral Christian Centre Trust Limited	£1,699,974	Birmingham Rathbone Society	£1,664,540
Diverse Excellence Cymru	£1,699,925	City College Nottingham	£1,664,502
Society for Horticultural Therapy	£1,699,266	British Sign Language Broadcasting Trust	£1,663,755
Manchester Care and Repair	£1,699,017	Brandon Centre for Counselling and Psychotherapy	£1,663,666
Herts Young Homeless Group	£1,698,948	Stoke City Community Trust	£1,663,394
London Oratory Charity	£1,698,302	Families for Children Trust	£1,662,970
The Society of Missionaries of Africa	£1,697,619	Rehabilitation Services Trust for Oxon Re-Employment	£1,662,596
Britten Sinfonia Ltd	£1,697,360	Cicely Saunders International	£1,662,471
English Speaking Board (International) Limited	£1,697,044	The Royal Northern College of Music Awards Fund	£1,662,370
The Merlin Magic Wand Children's Charity	£1,696,753	Carers Federation Ltd	£1,662,156
World ORT Trust	£1,696,080	William Blake House Northants	£1,662,000
Northamptonshire Carers	£1,695,371	Child Dynamix	£1,661,761
Step (UK) Ltd	£1,695,269	St Aldates, Oxford	£1,660,987
National Governance Association	£1,695,118	The Kenneth & Susan Green Charitable Foundation	£1,660,843

Age Concern Islington	£1,660,799	South West London Law Centres	£1,629,450
Adults Supporting Adults (ASA Lincs)	£1,660,726	Winchester Cathedral Trust	£1,629,038
The Matt Hampson Foundation	£1,659,715	Itzchok Meyer Cymerman Trust Limited	£1,628,827
Magdalen & Lasher Charity - Old Hastings House	£1,659,615	Stevenage Haven	£1,628,765
Curious Minds	£1,658,204	National Confidential Enquiry Into Patient Outcome	£1,628,715
Community Leisure Services Partnership	£1,657,625	New Horizon Youth Centre	£1,627,804
Headway Suffolk Ltd	£1,657,422	Community Childcare Centres	£1,627,735
NEPACS	£1,657,301	High Peak Theatre Trust Limited	£1,627,392
Mylnhurst Limited	£1,656,871	Maritime + Engineering College North West	£1,626,649
Science of The Soul - British Isles	£1,656,760	Style for Soldiers	£1,625,408
Community Forest Trust	£1,656,587	Age UK Surrey	£1,625,000
Gospel Standard Bethesda Fund	£1,656,381	The Rory McIlroy Foundation Limited	£1,624,813
Healthcare Infection Society	£1,655,993	BHT Early Education and Training	£1,624,688
Centre for Mental Health	£1,655,374	The Albert Hunt Trust	£1,624,516
Northumbria Health Care National Health Service Trust	£1,655,000	Nottingham and District Citizens Advice Bureau	£1,624,024
The Island Project	£1,654,858	Fulwood Christ Church, Sheffield	£1,623,694
Bedfordshire Rural Communities Charity	£1,654,851	Community First	£1,623,124
Link Community Development International	£1,654,432	Driving Mobility	£1,623,075
The Institution of Gas Engineers and Managers	£1,654,087	Open Age	£1,622,939
The Franciscan Missionary Sisters (Littlehampton)	£1,653,507	Action for Family Carers	£1,622,367
Plymouth Citizens Advice Bureaux	£1,652,622	Shared Lives Plus Limited	£1,621,641
International Society for Krishna Consciousness London	£1,651,892	The King's School Development Trust	£1,621,237
Benny Hinn Ministries Limited	£1,651,513	Mind in Croydon Ltd	£1,620,654
TNB Garrison Early Years and Play	£1,650,725	St Paul's Theological Centre	£1,619,980
The Charis Trust	£1,650,457	Leeway Domestic Violence and Abuse Services	£1,619,222
Ecole Francaise de Londres Jacques Prevert Ltd	£1,650,278	The Community of The Resurrection	£1,619,000
Headway East London	£1,650,204	Age UK Wakefield District	£1,617,523
Active Lancashire Limited	£1,648,423	Liverpool Biennial of Contemporary Art Limited	£1,617,201
Sheffield Methodist Circuit	£1,647,484	East Street Arts	£1,616,441
Croft Care Trust	£1,647,367	Involve Northwest	£1,616,399
Yishaya Adler Memorial Fund	£1,646,793	Centre for Advanced Welsh and Celtic Studies	£1,616,000
Community Drug and Alcohol Recovery Services	£1,645,931	Learning Foundation	£1,614,402
Mission Direct Limited	£1,645,427	RP Fighting Blindness	£1,613,502
Royal Bournemouth & Christchurch Hospitals NHS	£1,644,724	Local Information Unit Limited	£1,612,871
Eveson Charitable Trust	£1,644,637	Parchment Trust	£1,612,632
Stand By Me	£1,644,230	St Christophers (Glossop) Limited	£1,612,205
Off The Record (Bristol)	£1,643,755	Gerald Palmer Eling Trust Company	£1,612,107
Colleges Wales / Colegau Cymru	£1,643,567	The Learning Through Landscapes Trust	£1,609,380
Childcare and Business Consultancy Services	£1,643,504	Take A Break Warwickshire Limited	£1,609,140
British Humanist Association	£1,643,329	Artists Studio Company	£1,609,093
Aquaterra Leisure	£1,643,000	The British Institute of Radiology	£1,608,611
Fassnidge Memorial Trust	£1,642,991	Shoreditch Town Hall Trust	£1,608,424
Changes Health & Wellbeing	£1,642,721	Liberal Judaism (ULPS)	£1,607,296
Child Light Limited	£1,642,610	Age Concern Herefordshire & Worcestershire	£1,607,248
Orwell Mencap	£1,642,084	First Step Trust	£1,606,616
Feba Radio	£1,641,280	Cardiff and Vale University Local Health Board	£1,605,678
Children's Discovery Centre East London	£1,639,828	The Liberal Jewish Synagogue	£1,605,438
Advonet	£1,638,834	The RMIG Endowment Trust	£1,605,075
The Walker 597 Trust	£1,638,508	Buxton Arts Festival Limited	£1,605,001
The Sir James Knott Trust	£1,638,004	Chance for Childhood	£1,604,544
Kirklees Theatre Trust	£1,637,734	Catholic Marriage Care Limited	£1,603,950
Northamptonshire Industrial Training Association Ltd	£1,637,655	The Back-Up Trust	£1,603,708
The Portland Trust	£1,637,380	Talkback-UK Ltd	£1,602,648
International Cat Care	£1,637,199	Hill Valley & Vale Children's Centres	£1,601,855
The Baring Foundation	£1,636,185	The Heart Research Institute (UK)	£1,601,774
Wellgrove Education	£1,635,152	Headlong Theatre Limited	£1,601,741
If...	£1,634,237	Praxis Community Projects	£1,601,507
The British School at Athens	£1,633,467	Kehal Yisroel D'Chasidei Gur	£1,601,412
The E C Roberts Centre	£1,632,971	Manchester Pride Limited	£1,601,385
Telford Christian Council Supported Housing	£1,632,302	Bedfordshire and Luton Community Foundation	£1,599,352
The Springhead Trust Limited	£1,632,238	Vincentian Care Plus	£1,598,620
West Kent YMCA	£1,632,069	Volunteer Cornwall	£1,598,575
Lavant House School Educational Trust Limited	£1,631,905	Wimbledon and Putney Commons Conservators	£1,598,206
The Three Guineas Trust	£1,631,901	The Bradley Family Charitable Foundation	£1,597,552
Wolverton Leisure Trust	£1,631,546	Prince's Trust International	£1,597,506
The Harlington Area Schools Trust	£1,630,611	Royal Borough of Greenwich Heritage Trust	£1,597,484
English Folk Dance and Song Society	£1,630,573	The Dudley Council for Voluntary Service	£1,595,780
Club Doncaster Community Sports & Ed Foundation	£1,630,547	Association for Cultural Advancement Through Visual Art	£1,595,755
Glasallt Fawr - Camphill Centre	£1,630,243	The Galilee Foundation	£1,595,641
Safe Families for Children	£1,630,136	Warren House Group at Dartington	£1,594,921
The Sandwell Crossroads Care Attendant Scheme Ltd	£1,629,832	Ordinary Lifestyles	£1,594,646
Windlesham School Trust Limited	£1,629,759	Midstream (West Lancs) Ltd	£1,593,349

Partnership for Growth	£1,593,236	Campaign Against Living Miserably	£1,564,759
Kingdom Faith Church	£1,592,965	South Devon Railway Trust	£1,564,258
Inter-Varsity Press	£1,592,069	East Lancashire Deaf Society Limited	£1,563,701
Children in Wales-Plant Yng Nghymru	£1,592,049	Halas Homes	£1,563,601
The Primrose Hospice Limited	£1,591,812	Oasis Domestic Abuse Service Ltd	£1,563,282
Kemp House Trust Ltd	£1,591,170	Sinfonietta Productions Limited	£1,561,343
Christadelphian Bible Mission	£1,590,822	The Howe Green Educational Trust Limited	£1,560,691
WST Charity Limited	£1,590,430	Alpha Preparatory School, Ltd	£1,560,412
Open University Students Association	£1,590,280	The Parachute Regiment Charity	£1,560,171
The Honeypot Children's Charity	£1,590,008	Leaden Hall School Limited	£1,559,978
The National Churches Trust	£1,589,700	Spring Grove School 2003	£1,559,195
The Central England Area Quaker Meeting Charities	£1,589,540	Migrants Resource Centre	£1,558,141
British Youth for Christ	£1,589,039	Cransley Hospice Trust	£1,557,992
Sir Jules Thorn Charitable Trust	£1,589,004	The Joshua Trust	£1,557,352
The Rhodes Trust Horizon Fund	£1,588,832	The George Edward Smart Homes	£1,556,581
Bethshan Sheltered Housing Association	£1,588,727	Somerset Activity and Sports Partnership	£1,555,897
Cardiff Third Sector Council (C3SC)	£1,588,579	Anjuman-E-Burhani (London)	£1,555,840
Business and Human Rights Resource Centre	£1,586,801	The Inland Waterways Association	£1,555,811
Firstsite Limited	£1,586,733	The British Friends of The Bar-Ilan University	£1,555,407
Denise Coates Foundation	£1,586,556	The David Shepherd Wildlife Foundation	£1,555,303
Charity Assets Trust	£1,586,000	Yad Shlomo Trust	£1,554,830
The Caxton Trust	£1,584,776	The John Booth Charitable Foundation	£1,554,311
Education & Employers Taskforce	£1,584,447	The Trust of St Benedict's Abbey Ealing	£1,554,259
King's Arms Trust (Bedford)	£1,584,096	The Troutsdale Charitable Trust	£1,552,322
The Bat Conservation Trust	£1,584,049	United Reformed Church (Northern Province) Trust	£1,551,810
The Whitley Fund for Nature	£1,583,607	The Allen & Overy Foundation	£1,551,582
Mercy in Action	£1,582,680	The Kelmarsh Trust	£1,551,045
Mrs L D Rope's Third Charitable Settlement	£1,581,967	Nene Valley Railway	£1,550,735
The Beis Malka Trust	£1,581,409	Union Chapel Project	£1,550,098
The Fitzwilliam Wentworth Amenity Trust	£1,581,330	New Servol	£1,549,116
International P.E.N.	£1,581,131	Oxford Diocesan Board of Education	£1,549,000
All Nations Christian College Limited	£1,580,863	Key House Project	£1,547,591
Age Concern Bromley	£1,580,225	Folkestone Sports Centre Trust Limited	£1,547,513
Carn Brea Leisure Centre Trust	£1,579,413	The Museum of Army Flying Limited	£1,547,233
St Philip's School Trust Limited	£1,579,158	WHAG	£1,546,915
The Toybox Charity	£1,578,348	The Florence Nightingale Foundation	£1,546,826
Milton Keynes YMCA Limited	£1,577,263	The Magdi Yacoub Institute	£1,546,021
National Coastwatch Institution	£1,577,175	The Rainbow Centre (Marham)	£1,545,940
The Abbeyfield Southend Society Limited	£1,576,997	International Learning Movement (Ilm)	£1,545,504
The Northumbria Education Trust	£1,575,982	Inaura	£1,545,222
The Church of The Holy Ghost Crowthorne Trust	£1,575,644	The Royal School for the Blind, Liverpool	£1,544,943
Frontiers	£1,573,511	The Abbeyfield (St Albans) Society Limited	£1,543,760
Care for Children	£1,573,174	Roald Dahl's Marvellous Children's Charity	£1,543,634
Parks Options Limited	£1,572,984	QPR in the Community Trust	£1,542,603
Beauland Limited	£1,572,822	Age UK Stockport	£1,542,474
Buglife The Invertebrate Conservation Trust	£1,572,352	Co-operative Community Investment Foundation	£1,541,462
Green Pastures	£1,572,325	Royal Liverpool & Broadgreen Univ Hospitals NHS Trust	£1,541,427
The Stowe School Foundation	£1,572,276	O.F.M. Capuchin GB Charitable Trust	£1,541,028
The Fellowship of St Nicholas	£1,572,131	Impact Giving UK Trust	£1,540,610
Coworth-Flexlands School Limited	£1,572,107	New Pathways Family Friendly Therapeutic Centre	£1,540,490
Christchurch London	£1,572,022	Lighthouse Construction Industry Charity	£1,540,257
University of Bedfordshire Students' Union	£1,571,283	Scotts Project Trust	£1,539,508
Holbeach and East Elloe Hospital Trust	£1,570,088	British Friends of the Rabbi Meir Baal Haness Charity	£1,539,346
Age UK Croydon	£1,569,872	Age Concern Durham County	£1,539,028
Royal Artillery Charitable Fund	£1,569,512	The Counselling Foundation	£1,538,994
Hospitality Action	£1,569,384	Age Concern York	£1,538,765
Foundation for Women's Health R & D	£1,569,381	Plymouth Young Men's Christian Association - YMCA	£1,538,601
St Mary Abbots, Kensington	£1,569,363	Broughton House - Home for Ex-Service Men & Women	£1,537,530
Camp Simcha	£1,568,731	The Unicorn School for The Dyslexic Child	£1,537,254
Spike Island Artspace Limited	£1,568,679	Voluntary and Community Services Peaks and Dales	£1,536,923
The Ufton Court Educational Trust	£1,568,634	Waldorf School (Bristol) Limited	£1,536,713
Sangha Tri-National Trust Fund Limited	£1,568,043	Youth Options	£1,536,272
Berkshire Health Charitable Fund	£1,568,000	Woodlands Quaker Home	£1,535,951
Wynstones Limited	£1,567,817	The Embroiderers' Guild	£1,535,922
Care & Repair Cardiff and The Vale	£1,567,768	Witton Lodge Community Association	£1,535,179
Age Concern East Cheshire	£1,566,084	Greenfields Educational Trust	£1,535,133
The British Association of Urological Surgeons Ltd	£1,566,062	KT Educational Charitable Trust	£1,535,000
Vishnitz Girls School Limited	£1,565,627	Ridley Hall, Cambridge	£1,534,071
Knighton House School Limited	£1,565,583	The Lullaby Trust	£1,533,489
Wiltons Music Hall	£1,565,375	Gatsby Technical Education Projects	£1,533,039
Scripture Gift Mission (Incorporated)	£1,565,168	Swarthmore Education Centre	£1,532,981
Salisbury Hospicecare Trust Limited	£1,564,954	Partners of Prisoners and Families Support Group	£1,532,562

The Ruddock Foundation for The Arts	£1,532,505	Woodland Heritage Limited	£1,506,884
Huntingtons Disease Association	£1,531,987	The Leeds Groundwork Trust	£1,506,248
The Norwegian School in London Limited	£1,531,936	The Ampersand Foundation	£1,505,065
Everyday Church	£1,531,280	RSPCA Sheffield Branch	£1,504,103
Coram's Fields & Harmsworth Memorial Playground	£1,530,557	Plymouth Society for Mentally Handicapped	£1,503,380
Birmingham Industrial Therapy Association Limited	£1,530,203	Brent Community Transport	£1,503,312
Booker Prize Foundation	£1,529,783	The Carpenters Company Charitable Trust	£1,502,701
The Kenward Trust	£1,529,767	Age UK Sheffield	£1,502,672
Music in Hospitals and Care	£1,527,842	Dollond Charitable Trust	£1,502,236
Kerith Community Church	£1,527,365	Carers Leeds	£1,501,737
Woodside Animal Welfare Trust	£1,527,082	The Chelsea Physic Garden Company	£1,501,081
East End Community Foundation	£1,526,836	The Maritime Educational Foundation	£1,501,058
St John's Home	£1,526,755	Camphill Communities East Anglia	£1,500,769
Prisoners Abroad	£1,526,552	The Dover Counselling Centre	£1,500,693
Harlington Hospice Association Limited	£1,526,544	Trees for Cities	£1,500,642
Queen Elizabeth's Grammar School Blackburn Limited	£1,525,522	Dallaglio Rugbyworks	£1,500,381
The Goldman Sachs Charitable Gift Fund (UK)	£1,524,203	Scout Association County of Birmingham	£1,500,299
Headway Birmingham & Solihull	£1,524,081	North Liverpool Regeneration Company Ltd	£1,500,150
The RCN Foundation	£1,524,000	The Ernest Kleinwort Charitable Trust	£1,500,112
Boarbank Hall Convalescent Home, Grange-Over-Sands	£1,523,011	The Emerald Foundation	£1,500,000
Mushkil Aasaan Limited	£1,522,806	The F Glenister Woodger Trust	£1,499,899
Future First Alumni Limited	£1,522,595	The National Energy Foundation	£1,499,243
Shipwrecked Fishermen and Mariners' Society	£1,522,571	Birchfield Educational Trust Limited	£1,498,843
St. George's Students' Union	£1,522,326	Saffron Hall Trust	£1,498,446
The Britten-Pears Foundation	£1,522,264	Royal Docks Trust (London)	£1,497,432
Lattitude Global Volunteering	£1,521,743	Seren Ffestiniog Cyf.	£1,496,914
The Adventure Learning Charity	£1,521,476	ICAEW Foundation	£1,496,577
Blyth Star Enterprises Limited	£1,521,003	Citizens Advice Leicestershire	£1,495,995
Congregation of The Holy Spirit and Heart of Mary	£1,519,407	St Patrick's Missionary Society	£1,495,978
Lime Walk Gospel Hall Trust	£1,519,082	Cheltenham YMCA	£1,495,914
Wessex Cancer Trust	£1,518,734	YMCA Wearside Ltd	£1,494,993
Carlisle Mencap Limited	£1,518,609	The City Hospice Trust Limited	£1,494,547
Council for At-Risk Academics	£1,518,427	City of London Sinfonia Limited	£1,494,110
British Exploring Society	£1,517,966	T.H.O.M.A.S (Those on the Margins of a Society)	£1,493,814
The McPin Foundation	£1,517,855	Shropshire Housing Alliance	£1,493,620
The Shanly Foundation	£1,517,721	Living Options Devon	£1,493,281
Open College of The Arts	£1,517,522	Eritrea and The Horn of Africa Relief Ethar	£1,493,118
The Community Foundation for Wiltshire & Swindon	£1,517,440	Caia Park Partnership Limited	£1,491,572
Oxford Philharmonic Orchestra Trust	£1,517,088	Thames Christian College	£1,491,561
Hartlepool and East Durham Mind	£1,516,984	The Independent Schools' Bursars Association	£1,491,421
The Jewish Day Primary School	£1,516,519	Hebron Hall Limited	£1,491,190
Age Concern Birmingham	£1,516,377	Croydon Voluntary Action	£1,490,525
Northamptonshire Community Foundation	£1,515,941	The Equal Rights Trust	£1,490,522
The International Youth Foundation	£1,515,076	Lambeth Elfrida Rathbone Society	£1,490,148
The Hampstead Garden Suburb Trust Limited	£1,514,660	The Access Project	£1,489,917
The Rhoda Jessop Educational Charity	£1,514,640	St Christopher's School Trust (Epsom) Limited	£1,489,560
Rahma (Mercy)	£1,514,603	London Higher	£1,489,449
The Battersea Power Station Foundation	£1,514,500	The Kings Theatre Trust Limited	£1,488,694
The Davis Foundation	£1,514,195	Target Learning Trust	£1,487,756
Anglia Region of The Guide Association	£1,514,087	Hammersmith United Charities	£1,487,333
Charitworth Limited	£1,513,855	Exeter Phoenix Ltd	£1,486,926
Mind in Cambridgeshire Ltd	£1,513,807	Trinity Church, Brentwood	£1,486,918
The Grand at Clitheroe Ltd	£1,513,805	The Chartered Association of Business Schools	£1,486,066
Blackburne House	£1,513,151	ITEC North East Limited	£1,484,477
East Surrey Rural Transport Partnership	£1,513,108	The Newbury and District Agricultural Society	£1,483,756
The Morley Agricultural Foundation	£1,512,875	The Menorah Primary School	£1,483,387
Sheffield Young Women's Christian Association	£1,512,367	The D'Oyly Carte Charitable Trust	£1,482,677
British Muslim Heritage Centre	£1,511,835	Dover Sholem Community Trust	£1,482,545
Grammar School of King Edward VI at Stratford	£1,511,501	Spring Impact	£1,482,157
Community Transport for Town and County	£1,511,055	Age Cymru Swansea Bay Limited	£1,481,169
Gateshead Crossroads Caring for Carers	£1,510,859	Hubbub Foundation UK	£1,480,921
About with Friends	£1,510,037	Harvington School Educational Trust Ltd	£1,480,723
St David's (Purley) Educational Trust Limited	£1,509,485	The Savoy Educational Trust	£1,480,708
Gilbert White & The Oates Collections	£1,508,763	International Baccalaureate Fund UK	£1,480,229
User Voice	£1,508,592	Menorah Foundation	£1,479,320
South Essex Rape and Incest Crisis Centre	£1,508,169	Berkshire Community Foundation	£1,478,547
The Arkwright Society Limited	£1,507,828	Swimathon Foundation	£1,477,231
Union of Kingston Students	£1,507,782	The Potters House Christian Fellowship Walthamstow	£1,476,737
Donating Charity Limited	£1,507,710	Congregation of Our Lady of The Missions	£1,476,735
The Sir James Reckitt Charity	£1,507,355	Warrington Disability Partnership	£1,476,502
Choices (formerly North Kent Women's Aid)	£1,507,324	Gloucestershire Group Homes Limited	£1,476,477
Bnos Zion D'Bobov Limited	£1,507,074	North Bristol NHS Trust Charitable Funds	£1,476,280

The British Allergy Foundation	£1,475,813	Westminster College Cambridge	£1,451,191
Stepping Stones School Hindhead Limited	£1,475,473	People for Animal Care Trust (PACT)	£1,450,799
The Air Training Corps General Purposes Fund	£1,475,332	Whirlow Hall Farm Trust Limited	£1,450,626
Community Action Isle of Wight	£1,475,199	The Guildhall School Trust	£1,450,354
National Aquarium Limited	£1,474,963	Community Foundation for Surrey	£1,449,700
Writers' Centre Norwich	£1,474,890	The Liverpool Merchants' Guild	£1,449,462
The Pharo Foundation	£1,474,292	Society for Applied Microbiology	£1,449,318
Newham Community Renewal Programme Limited	£1,473,960	Institute for Strategic Dialogue	£1,449,273
Floris Books Trust Limited	£1,473,796	The Marsh Christian Trust	£1,448,782
Thorne Lodge Charitable Trust	£1,473,722	West Lodge School Limited	£1,448,010
West Ham Park	£1,473,435	Birkenhead Young Men's Christian Association	£1,447,749
Newpier Charity Limited	£1,472,711	Yateley Industries for The Disabled Limited	£1,447,299
The Mount Camphill Community Limited	£1,471,950	Advocacy Focus	£1,446,469
Carnival Village Trust	£1,470,874	UKCISA	£1,446,232
Safer Roads Foundation	£1,470,685	The Community Foundation for Staffordshire	£1,446,104
One Community Eastleigh	£1,470,109	Derbyshire Districts Citizens Advice Bureau	£1,446,053
Commission Apostolic Trust Ltd	£1,469,816	Edge Hill Students' Union Limited	£1,445,932
Force Cancer Charity	£1,469,240	BASIS (Registration) Limited	£1,445,796
The Uphill Ski Club of Great Britain	£1,468,494	United Kingdom Sepsis Trust Limited	£1,445,765
Wirral Independent Living and Learning	£1,467,794	The National Council for Palliative Care	£1,444,230
The North of England Horticultural Society	£1,467,757	The Bevern Trust	£1,443,823
Pownall Hall School Trust Limited	£1,467,715	Botanic Gardens Conservation International	£1,443,656
Westcott House	£1,467,674	Oxford Brookes Students' Union	£1,443,501
Longleigh Foundation	£1,467,356	The Ursuline Preparatory School Ilford	£1,442,469
Lindley Educational Trust Limited	£1,467,013	Mosaic: Shaping Disability Services	£1,442,285
Charles Sharland Trust	£1,466,037	Trinity Homeless Projects	£1,441,630
EDF Energy Trust	£1,465,946	The Edgware and District Reform Synagogue	£1,441,622
Lawes Agricultural Trust	£1,465,277	Beenstock Home Management Co. Ltd	£1,440,953
Park School for Girls (Ilford) Limited	£1,465,277	The Friars, Aylesford	£1,440,735
HENRY	£1,464,883	Kirklees Citizens Advice and Law Centre	£1,440,676
Age UK Lambeth	£1,464,847	Progress to Change	£1,440,118
Human Capability Foundation	£1,464,628	The Drapers' Almshouse Charity	£1,439,693
Basildon Women's Aid	£1,464,220	Reform Research Trust	£1,439,426
Age UK Bristol	£1,464,133	Stop Ivory	£1,438,699
British Dental Association Trust Fund	£1,463,649	Muntada Aid	£1,438,564
The Hunslet Club	£1,463,521	Swansea C V S	£1,438,287
Keystone Accountability	£1,463,208	Bridport and West Dorset Sports Trust Limited	£1,437,629
Bethany Homestead	£1,463,141	Children and Families Limited	£1,437,099
Beis Soroh Schenierer Seminary	£1,463,090	Raghuvanshi Mahajan London Rama	£1,436,816
The Wigoder Family Foundation	£1,463,009	The Finchley Charities	£1,436,080
Country Holidays for Inner City Kids	£1,462,483	Construction Industry Trust for Youth	£1,435,686
Aston - Mansfield	£1,462,409	Brentry and Henbury Childrens Centre Limited	£1,435,416
The British Geriatrics Society	£1,461,868	Climate Bonds Initiative	£1,435,138
St Vincent's and St George's Association	£1,460,950	Community & Voluntary Support Conwy	£1,434,923
LICC Limited	£1,460,712	Chapter of the Order of The Holy Paraclete	£1,434,056
Longborough Festival Opera	£1,460,662	B. O. Education Limited	£1,434,020
The British Occupational Hygiene Society	£1,459,974	Support Staffordshire	£1,433,783
Burton upon Trent and District YMCA	£1,459,295	Solden Hill House Limited	£1,433,696
The Lady Fatemah (A.S.) Charitable Trust	£1,459,224	Bridge Care Limited	£1,431,425
Delta-North Consett Limited	£1,459,101	Inspiration Ministries UK	£1,431,416
Hastings and St Leonards Foreshore Charitable Trust	£1,459,009	Family Care	£1,431,222
The British Nutrition Foundation	£1,457,722	The Archie Sherman Charitable Trust	£1,431,023
Derek Prince Ministries (UK)	£1,457,659	First Rung Ltd	£1,430,774
Nutley Hall	£1,457,257	Comet Charities Ltd	£1,430,508
Tyndale House	£1,457,169	Cardiff City FC Community Foundation	£1,430,491
National Youth Choirs of Great Britain	£1,456,831	Metropolitan Tabernacle	£1,430,244
Islington Play Association	£1,456,789	The Wordsworth Trust	£1,430,000
Open Youth Trust	£1,456,752	Redeemed Christian Church of God Royal Connections	£1,429,317
The Child Beale Trust	£1,456,617	Cornwall Music Service Trust	£1,429,239
Circles Network	£1,456,407	Stansted Park Foundation	£1,429,165
Ellen MacArthur Cancer Trust	£1,456,390	European Orthodontic Society	£1,429,144
Pennine Camphill Community	£1,456,343	The British Sociological Association	£1,428,513
All Nations	£1,456,083	The Torch Theatre Company Limited	£1,428,366
Chester Students' Union	£1,455,329	JRoots Limited	£1,428,242
We Are IVE Ltd	£1,454,994	Quwwat-Ul-Islam Society Newham London	£1,427,432
Lindfield Christian Care Home	£1,454,910	Hywel DDA Health Charities	£1,427,379
Sisters of Christ UK Development Fund Charity	£1,454,875	The Said Business School Foundation	£1,427,054
Narconon Trust	£1,454,142	Old Oak Housing Association Limited	£1,427,000
Friends of Highgate Cemetery Trust	£1,453,354	The Handel House Trust Limited	£1,426,809
Lancashire Environmental Fund Limited	£1,453,075	The Torbay Hospital League of Friends	£1,426,740
Mayfield Fellowship	£1,452,943	The London Playing Fields Society	£1,426,700
Essex Coalition of Disabled People	£1,451,494	Pathways To Independence Ltd	£1,426,685

Southern Domestic Abuse Service	£1,426,679	ICE Benevolent Fund	£1,401,738
European Society of Thoracic Surgeons	£1,426,353	Highgate Wood and Queens Park Kilburn	£1,401,374
Connexions Buckinghamshire	£1,426,248	The Vindolanda Trust	£1,401,230
Secret World Wildlife Rescue	£1,426,152	Blackpool Carers Centre Limited	£1,400,711
The London International Festival of Theatre Limited	£1,425,638	St Bees School	£1,399,732
The Friends of The Bobover Yeshivah	£1,424,284	Barnet Mencap	£1,399,591
The British Institute of Learning Disabilities	£1,424,247	Love Jesus Fund	£1,399,523
Above The Stag Theatre	£1,424,207	The London Buddhist Centre	£1,398,701
Shrewsbury Drapers Holy Cross Limited	£1,424,124	Integrated Neurological Services	£1,398,210
Leap Confronting Conflict	£1,423,886	Friends of The Eastbourne Hospital	£1,397,166
National Children's Orchestras of Great Britain	£1,423,254	Congregation of The Sisters of Saint Anne	£1,397,120
Debate Mate Schools Limited	£1,422,822	Woodlands Group of Churches	£1,396,756
Northumbrian Citizens Advice Bureau	£1,422,321	The National Forest Charitable Trust	£1,396,681
Crewe YMCA Limited	£1,422,089	St Mary Magdalene and Holy Jesus Trust	£1,396,600
The Royal Surgical Aid Society	£1,422,000	Villiers Park Educational Trust	£1,396,352
Youth Aliyah - Child Rescue	£1,421,772	Nanaksar Thath Isher Darbar (Guru Nanak Sikh College)	£1,396,005
The Harborne Parish Lands Charity	£1,421,354	Advocacy for All	£1,395,792
National Examining Board for Dental Nurses	£1,420,500	The Norman Laud Association	£1,395,504
James Paget University Hospitals Charitable Fund	£1,420,235	Hampshire and Isle of Wight Community Foundation	£1,395,493
Congregation of Missionary Oblates of Mary Immaculate	£1,417,736	The English Concert	£1,393,710
The Near East Foundation UK	£1,417,627	Family Society	£1,393,706
Durham Wildlife Trust	£1,417,470	Greater Together	£1,393,426
Gateshead Jewish Primary School	£1,417,311	Association for Behavioural & Cognitive Psychotherapies	£1,393,194
Oxfordshire Community Foundation	£1,416,160	Kings Community Church (Southampton)	£1,393,000
Alcoholics Anonymous (Great Britain) Limited	£1,415,933	Age UK Leeds	£1,392,385
We Are Beams	£1,415,924	Institute of Sacred Heart of Mary Immaculate Virgin	£1,391,718
Spirit of Soccer	£1,415,651	Family Planning Association	£1,390,342
RSPCA Sussex Brighton and East Grinstead Branch	£1,415,301	ABC Awards	£1,390,112
Philo Trust	£1,415,234	The Charlotte Straker Project	£1,389,992
Jimmy's Cambridge	£1,415,174	Action 4 Youth	£1,389,767
Emmanuel Evangelical Church	£1,415,139	Healthworks Newcastle	£1,389,445
The Monkey Business Foundation Limited	£1,415,070	Neuromuscular Centre	£1,388,920
Wellow House School Limited	£1,414,149	The Cat and Rabbit Rescue Centre	£1,388,488
The English Sangha Trust Limited	£1,413,617	Age UK Exeter	£1,388,209
Age UK Bradford & District	£1,412,132	Genetic Disorders UK	£1,387,960
Activate Community and Education Services	£1,412,120	The Daiglen School Trust Limited	£1,387,604
Horseworld Trust	£1,412,040	Roland Callingham Foundation	£1,386,744
The Harington Scheme Limited	£1,410,763	Shree Kutch Satsang Swaminarayan Temple	£1,386,548
North Wales Wildlife Trust	£1,410,384	Charity of Richard Cloudesley	£1,386,109
Charlotte House School Limited	£1,410,195	Age UK North West Kent	£1,385,873
Mary Ann Evans Hospice	£1,410,120	Association of Graduate Careers Advisory Services	£1,385,230
Chinthurst School Educational Trust Limited	£1,409,702	Singh Sabha London East	£1,385,152
UK Friends of Yale University Limited	£1,409,491	T E D S	£1,385,145
Redeemed Christian Church of God Victory House	£1,409,195	UK Citizens Online Democracy	£1,384,948
Eating Disorders Association	£1,409,131	Agored Cymru	£1,384,547
Thinktank Trust	£1,409,000	Age Concern Solihull	£1,384,212
Cullum Family Trust	£1,408,685	Army Rugby Union Trust	£1,383,799
The Indigo Trust	£1,408,531	Parayhouse School	£1,382,688
Groundwork Creswell, Ashfield and Mansfield	£1,408,303	Camden School Foundation of Frances Mary Buss	£1,380,952
Meadowhall Education Centre	£1,407,929	Hope for Children	£1,380,505
Exmoor Calvert Trust	£1,407,891	The Abbeyfield Loughborough Society Limited	£1,379,924
The Noah Enterprise (New Opportunities and Horizons)	£1,407,672	The Ferne Animal Sanctuary	£1,379,436
Evangelical Fellowship of Congregational Churches Trust	£1,407,535	National Association of Almshouses	£1,378,881
Ikon Gallery Limited	£1,407,400	Employers Network for Equality and Inclusion	£1,378,874
The A1 Steam Locomotive Trust	£1,407,373	The Batsford Foundation	£1,378,705
St Olave's and St Saviour's Schools Foundation	£1,407,351	Changing Lives Housing Trust	£1,378,656
Families Health and Well-Being Consortium	£1,407,180	Kehal Charedim Trust	£1,378,315
The Foundation of Lady Katherine Leveson	£1,406,988	The Regent (Christchurch) Limited	£1,378,104
The Royal Corps of Signals Benevolent Fund	£1,406,973	The John Scott Charitable Trust	£1,378,057
Headway Shropshire	£1,406,768	Four Towns and Vale Link Community Transport	£1,377,820
CASE Training Services	£1,406,428	Donnington House Care Home Limited	£1,377,659
Friends of Michael Sobell House	£1,406,065	Family Federation for World Peace and Unification	£1,377,486
Meriden Sports and Recreation Trust	£1,405,938	The Society for The Protection of Ancient Buildings	£1,377,440
Pallottine Missionary Sisters of The Catholic Apostolate	£1,403,959	European Society for Vascular Surgery	£1,377,395
The Unite Foundation	£1,403,672	St Gerard's School Trust	£1,377,356
RNH Synagogue & College Ltd	£1,403,527	Surrey County Football Association Limited	£1,376,995
Architects Benevolent Society	£1,403,454	Keystone Education Trust	£1,376,720
Epilepsy Research UK	£1,402,998	St Mary's Hare Park School	£1,376,588
The Persula Foundation	£1,402,967	Southbank Sinfonia	£1,376,102
Lord Crewe's Charity	£1,402,480	Human Aid UK	£1,375,604
The Construction Sector Transparency Initiative	£1,402,280	The Charles Hayward Foundation	£1,375,349
The Blackpool Fylde and Wyre Society for the Blind	£1,402,017	Mid Essex Hospitals NHS Trust Charitable Fund	£1,375,000

The Insurance Charities	£1,375,000	Age UK Leicester Shire & Rutland Home Help Ltd	£1,344,379
Swire 2765	£1,374,983	East Midlands Christian Fellowships	£1,343,104
The Heritage Trust for The North West	£1,374,982	Bristol and South Glos Circuit of The Methodist Church	£1,342,968
The Lighthouse Chapel International	£1,374,765	Norfolk and Norwich Scope Association	£1,342,460
Groundwork South Yorkshire	£1,374,690	Osprey Quay Management Services Company Limited	£1,342,127
Oakdene Education Trust	£1,374,516	London Youth Games Limited	£1,341,624
Wesleyan Holiness Church - British Isles District	£1,374,446	Learning on Screen - Film and Video Council	£1,341,432
Cynthia Spencer Hospice Charity	£1,374,132	Bows and Arrows	£1,341,245
Burnley Pendle & Rossendale Council for Vol Service	£1,373,599	The Chinese Overseas Christian Mission	£1,340,634
The One Foundation	£1,373,123	Hospice at Home Carlisle and North Lakeland	£1,340,439
Seaton House School Limited	£1,372,515	The Franciscan Missionaries of St. Joseph	£1,340,116
One Community Foundation Limited	£1,372,508	The Council of The Inns of Court	£1,339,732
Paul Foundation	£1,371,522	Emmaus South Lambeth Community	£1,339,727
Chorley Youth Zone	£1,371,487	RSPCA Llys Nini Branch - Cardiff To Swansea	£1,339,671
The Congregation of The Most Holy Redeemer	£1,371,353	The Simon Mark Lazarus Foundation	£1,339,486
RSPCA Central, West & North East London Branch	£1,371,206	Claridge House	£1,339,455
Abilities Limited	£1,370,905	Jigsaw +	£1,339,067
The Yarlet Trust	£1,370,787	North West Cancer Research	£1,338,957
The Duchenne Research Fund	£1,370,532	RAFT - Restoration of Appearance and Function Trust	£1,338,520
Sarcoma UK	£1,369,014	The Horizon Foundation	£1,338,183
King's Arms Project (Bedford)	£1,368,819	Blyth Valley Disabled Forum Limited	£1,337,617
The Lind Trust	£1,368,635	Hedley Foundation Limited	£1,337,359
Greenbelt Festivals	£1,368,568	Hyelm	£1,337,151
West Mercia Women's Aid	£1,368,281	The Forest of Marston Vale Trust	£1,336,730
Rustington Convalescent Home (Carpenters Company)	£1,367,338	Arcola Theatre Production Company	£1,336,681
The Harper Adams University Students' Union	£1,367,240	Unison Welfare	£1,336,602
First Steps (Bath)	£1,366,866	The Tellus Mater Foundation Limited	£1,336,568
Parity for Disability	£1,366,353	The JD Foundation	£1,336,558
The Basil Larsen 1999 Charitable Trust	£1,366,293	The Family Holiday Association	£1,336,416
Mid and North Essex Mind	£1,365,355	The Rothschild Archive Limited	£1,335,636
Cherry Trees	£1,363,318	Newark Preparatory School Company Limited	£1,335,077
The Sikh Channel Community Broadcasting	£1,363,297	CHUF	£1,335,056
British Friends of The Art Museums of Israel	£1,362,745	Koinonia Christian Care	£1,334,361
Vintage Trains	£1,362,293	Home-Start Lincolnshire	£1,334,220
Royal Microscopical Society	£1,360,903	Links International Trust	£1,333,991
Bolton Wise Limited	£1,360,707	Beis Chaye Rochel (The Gateshead Jewish Academy)	£1,333,650
Luther King House Educational Trust	£1,360,588	North London Asian Care	£1,333,254
Prostate Cancer Research Centre	£1,360,235	RSPCA Leicestershire Branch	£1,332,608
U K Med	£1,360,147	Harris (Belmont) Charity	£1,331,773
Newport Mind	£1,360,143	Limmud	£1,331,712
La Scuola Italiana a Londra	£1,360,023	The Congregation of The Dominican Sisters of Malta	£1,331,092
John Swire 1989 Charitable Trust	£1,359,760	Woking Christ Church	£1,330,493
Derwent Rural Counselling Service	£1,359,570	Ellingham Employment Services	£1,329,995
GMDN Agency	£1,359,451	Christian Medical Fellowship	£1,329,874
The Burberry Foundation	£1,359,230	The Coventry Refugee and Migrant Centre	£1,329,709
The Borrow Foundation	£1,359,207	The Segelman Trust	£1,329,466
Keelman Homes Limited	£1,359,000	Newcastle upon Tyne Council for Voluntary Service	£1,328,981
The Welsh Water Elan Trust	£1,358,692	The Adrian Swire Charitable Trust	£1,328,577
Parentkind	£1,357,863	Isha Foundation	£1,328,538
Westminster Synagogue	£1,357,782	York Methodist Circuit	£1,328,321
The Careers Research and Advisory Centre	£1,357,262	Abbeyfield Wessex Society Limited	£1,327,831
United Lincolnshire Hospitals NHS Trust Charitable Fund	£1,356,751	The Alice Ellen Cooper-Dean Charitable Foundation	£1,327,738
IOL Educational Trust	£1,356,732	Southend on Sea Darby and Joan Organisation	£1,327,070
The British Orthodontic Society	£1,355,777	Sir John Soane's Museum Trust	£1,326,540
Wolverhampton Citizens Advice Bureaux	£1,355,406	SANE	£1,326,148
Universal Pentecostal Church	£1,354,882	Sheffield Wildlife Trust	£1,326,119
Governors for Schools	£1,353,527	Court Based Personal Support	£1,325,923
The Borne Foundation	£1,353,353	The Federation of Disability Sport Wales Limited	£1,325,551
Hampshire Hospitals Charity	£1,352,524	Downe House Foundation	£1,325,000
Wisdom School	£1,352,021	The Springboard Bursary Foundation	£1,324,440
Age UK Richmond upon Thames	£1,351,536	Friends of The National Libraries	£1,324,401
Pump Aid	£1,350,914	Basingview Trust Limited	£1,324,343
The Hudson Foundation	£1,350,653	Turkish Cypriot Community Association	£1,324,095
Vineyard Christian Fellowship of St Albans	£1,349,984	Parham Park Limited	£1,323,867
Network for Social Change Charitable Trust	£1,349,954	Charterhouse Club	£1,323,486
St. Pauls Steiner Project Two	£1,348,600	Dudley District Citizens Advice Bureaux	£1,323,213
Highfield Preparatory School Limited	£1,348,275	Positive East	£1,322,658
Birmingham Botanical and Horticultural Society Ltd	£1,348,228	Commonwork Trust	£1,322,638
Royal Navy Rugby Union	£1,347,198	Universities & Colleges Information Systems Assoc	£1,322,483
Downside Up Limited	£1,346,560	Care After Combat	£1,322,251
The Egmont Trust	£1,345,811	Frampton Park Baptist Church	£1,322,182
Prison Fellowship	£1,345,805	Institute of Physics and Engineering in Medicine	£1,321,930

Genesis Research Trust	£1,321,499	Carers Trust Bucks and Milton Keynes	£1,301,131
Ipswich Housing Action Group Limited	£1,320,777	Aegis Trust	£1,301,069
Christian Broadcasting Network (UK)	£1,320,739	British Plumbing Employers Council (Training) Ltd	£1,300,814
Durham County Carers Support	£1,320,413	Notre Dame Preparatory School (Norwich) Limited	£1,300,341
The Helen Arkell Dyslexia Centre	£1,320,025	Mr and Mrs J A Pye's Charitable Settlement	£1,300,188
King's Church in Greater Manchester	£1,319,906	Maharishi School Trust Limited	£1,299,715
Plymouth Hospitals General Charity	£1,319,718	Rowan Organisation	£1,299,664
Minhaj-Ul-Quran International	£1,319,626	The BASW Trust	£1,299,192
Elite Supported Employment Agency Limited	£1,319,581	St. John of Jerusalem Eye Hospital	£1,299,000
Hampshire Christian Education Trust	£1,319,349	Cymunedau'n Ymlaen Mon Communities Forward	£1,298,877
Tenterden Leisure Centre Trust Limited	£1,319,228	Centre for Cities	£1,298,658
The Bulldog Trust Limited	£1,319,084	Bioregional Development Group	£1,298,618
Peacehaven House	£1,319,032	Faculty of Pharmaceutical Medicine of The RCP of UK	£1,298,092
Daybreak Family Group Conferences	£1,318,599	Lebara Foundation	£1,298,007
Farms for City Children Limited	£1,318,504	The Nesta Trust	£1,298,000
Motiv8 South	£1,318,333	Bangor Students' Union	£1,297,876
Jackson's Lane	£1,318,309	International Glaucoma Association Limited	£1,297,666
Manchester Camerata Limited	£1,318,211	Doncaster Refurnish	£1,297,239
Improving Lives Plymouth	£1,318,171	Coventry Cyrenians Limited	£1,296,841
Parish of Uxbridge	£1,318,122	The Jessie May Trust	£1,296,785
E Ivor Hughes Educational Foundation	£1,317,626	Ashiana Network	£1,296,446
Torah Vodaas Limited	£1,317,454	Howgill Family Centre	£1,296,265
Human Care Foundation Worldwide	£1,317,454	The East Lancashire Masonic Charity	£1,295,974
NLT Training Services Limited	£1,317,162	Benevolent Fund of Institution of Mechanical Engineers	£1,295,514
The Burdett Trust for Nursing	£1,316,727	Age Concern Cardiff and The Vale of Glamorgan	£1,294,990
Dair House School Trust Limited	£1,316,519	Airedale Voluntary Drug and Alcohol Agency	£1,294,533
Hackney Joint Estate Charity	£1,316,038	The Travel Foundation	£1,294,381
Safe Child Thailand	£1,315,495	North London Bikur Cholim Limited	£1,294,376
Cyfle Building Skills Limited	£1,315,097	Soas Students' Union	£1,294,193
The Contemporary Art Society	£1,314,755	Northmoor Educational Trust	£1,294,027
The Mighty Creatives	£1,314,596	The Rivers Trust	£1,293,945
Great Western Society Limited	£1,314,545	Southwell Leisure Centre	£1,293,592
Voluntary Action Rotherham	£1,314,095	Society of Christ (Great Britain)	£1,293,167
The Open College Network South East Region Ltd	£1,313,707	Milton Keynes Dons FC Sports & Education Trust	£1,292,710
Sheffield Industrial Museums Trust Limited	£1,313,533	Plymouth Age Concern	£1,292,649
The Henry Jackson Society	£1,313,156	Compass Disability Services	£1,292,566
Adventure Hyndburn	£1,312,306	Redbridge, Epping and Harlow Crossroads	£1,292,108
Carleton House Preparatory School Limited	£1,311,785	West Kent Extra Limited	£1,292,059
North Notts Crossroads Caring for Carers	£1,311,725	Arlington Futures	£1,292,000
Foresight North East Lincolnshire Ltd	£1,311,617	The Rosemere Cancer Foundation	£1,292,000
The General Conference of The New Church	£1,311,441	The Chabad Jewish Community of Central London	£1,291,962
The Breadsticks Foundation	£1,310,967	The Leadership Centre for Local Government	£1,291,895
Age UK Birmingham Limited	£1,310,807	Centre for Ageing Better Limited	£1,291,751
Camden Citizens Advice Bureaux Service Limited	£1,310,082	Autograph ABP	£1,291,462
Bowles Rocks Trust Limited	£1,309,969	ReadiBus	£1,291,444
Stratford Arts Trust	£1,309,529	Mercy Ministries UK	£1,291,210
Waterloo 200 Ltd	£1,309,469	The Benenden School Trust	£1,290,383
Women and Children First UK	£1,309,170	Dhammakaya International Society of UK	£1,290,029
The Royal Veterinary College Animal Care Trust	£1,308,762	National Playing Fields Association	£1,290,000
Care & Repair Cymru 2015	£1,308,430	BF Adventure	£1,289,773
The Muslim Academic Trust	£1,308,229	Age Concern Tyneside South	£1,289,710
West London Mission Housing Association Limited	£1,307,931	West Lincolnshire Domestic Abuse Service	£1,289,582
Richard Watts and Rochester Almshouse Charities	£1,306,934	Roses Theatre Trust	£1,289,392
Masorti Judaism	£1,306,811	Hounslow Jamia Masjid and Islamic Centre	£1,289,284
Double Impact Services	£1,305,932	The Alternative Animal Sanctuary	£1,288,776
St Joseph's Convent Preparatory School Gravesend	£1,305,703	The Riverside Trust	£1,288,724
Elmfield Rudolf Steiner School Limited	£1,304,957	Georgetown University (USA) UK Initiatives Organisation	£1,288,609
The Intensive Care Society	£1,304,783	The United Reformed Church (Wessex) Trust Ltd	£1,288,187
The Rise Trust	£1,304,388	The Association for Perioperative Practice	£1,287,933
WeSeeHope	£1,304,299	Just for Kids Law	£1,287,759
London Youth Rowing Ltd	£1,304,216	Creative Kernow Limited	£1,287,631
Operational Research Society Limited	£1,303,899	The Wye and Usk Foundation	£1,287,607
Childline	£1,303,625	West Wickham Common and Spring Park Wood	£1,287,520
Sutton Borough Citizens' Advice Bureaux	£1,303,295	St Helens Carers Centre	£1,286,936
Extonglen Limited	£1,303,142	Standing Together Against Domestic Violence	£1,285,241
Pioneers UK Ministries	£1,303,011	The London Central Mosque (Algame) Fund	£1,285,229
Jewish Joint Burial Society	£1,302,372	Formby Pool Trust	£1,284,940
Brake	£1,302,197	The Ironmongers Common Investment Fund	£1,284,898
NMRN Services	£1,302,107	The Women's Organisation	£1,284,750
Paines Plough Limited	£1,301,952	Northorpe Hall Child & Family Trust	£1,284,290
Guerrand Hermes Foundation for Peace	£1,301,467	St. David's Children Society	£1,283,997
Gynaecology Cancer Research Fund	£1,301,424	Body and Soul	£1,283,791

Blackburn Diocesan Board of Education	£1,282,000	The Grocers' Charity	£1,261,176
Possability People Limited	£1,281,998	The Southern Counties Baptist Association	£1,260,818
Mentor Foundation UK	£1,281,855	Cornwall Old People's Housing Society	£1,260,793
Processors and Growers Research Organisation	£1,281,658	The Mudchute Association	£1,260,784
E B M Charitable Trust	£1,281,303	Safe Haven for Donkeys in the Holy Land	£1,260,635
Theatre for a Change Limited	£1,281,255	UOHC Properties Ltd	£1,260,052
Prison Reform Trust	£1,280,826	The Gateshead Jewish Nursery	£1,260,028
Family Links (Educational Programmes)	£1,280,642	Tower Hamlets Education Business Partnership Ltd	£1,259,976
Disability Direct	£1,280,067	Anne Frank Trust UK	£1,259,798
The Park Theatre	£1,279,000	My Life Legacy	£1,259,666
Animals in Distress (Torbay and Westcountry)	£1,278,106	M B Foundation	£1,259,431
Theatr Mwldan	£1,277,765	St Francis' Children's Society	£1,259,373
Ibad-Ur-Rahman Trust	£1,277,699	Cumberland and Westmorland Convalescent Institution	£1,258,775
Dartmoor Zoological Society	£1,277,522	Coventry & Warwickshire YMCA	£1,258,562
St. John and Red Cross Defence Medical Welfare	£1,277,217	Fleet Baptist Church	£1,258,410
International Justice Mission UK	£1,276,711	Notts County F.C. Community Programme	£1,258,387
Supporting Wounded Veterans Ltd.	£1,276,518	Servants Fellowship International	£1,258,346
Carer Support Wiltshire	£1,276,003	London South Bank University Students' Union	£1,258,127
The Wimbledon Foundation	£1,276,000	Bede House Association	£1,258,076
Nottinghamshire Miners Welfare Trust Fund Scheme	£1,275,531	The Oxford Centre for Mission Studies	£1,257,995
Advising Communities	£1,275,324	Racing Industry Accident Benefit Scheme	£1,257,950
Belper Leisure Centre Limited	£1,275,000	South Essex Gymnastics Club Limited	£1,257,785
The Derbyshire Environmental Trust Limited	£1,274,685	Social Action for Health	£1,257,713
The Elm Foundation Ltd	£1,274,519	Congregation of The Daughters of The Holy Ghost	£1,257,711
Earth Trust	£1,274,428	Theatr Genedlaethol Cymru	£1,257,581
Bosence Farm Community Limited	£1,274,326	The Eikon Charity	£1,257,016
Oakhyrst Grange Educational Trust at Caterham	£1,274,052	Unity Theatre	£1,256,772
Charity of John Marshall	£1,273,918	Latate Limited	£1,256,093
Al-Mahdi Institute	£1,273,865	Worcester College Oxford Endowment Trust	£1,255,800
Cintre	£1,273,654	The Henfrey Charitable Trust	£1,255,715
The Nutrition Society	£1,273,370	Essex Blind Charity	£1,254,763
The Elizabeth Creak Charitable Trust	£1,273,227	Harrogate International Festival Limited	£1,254,564
RSPCA Solent Branch	£1,273,172	Blackburn Youth Zone	£1,254,341
AOUK	£1,273,014	The Blackheath Halls	£1,254,120
African Foundation for Development Afford	£1,272,953	Ivy Manchester Limited	£1,253,840
Bounce Back Foundation	£1,272,706	The Society of The Little Flower	£1,253,658
Rochdale Gateway Leisure Limited	£1,272,269	Kingdom Education Limited	£1,253,278
The Birmingham Settlement	£1,271,908	The Fifth Trust	£1,253,232
Chinese Church in London	£1,271,151	Savannah Wisdom	£1,253,221
Age UK Brighton & Hove	£1,271,118	G & K Boyes Charitable Trust	£1,253,025
Emmaus Turvey	£1,270,595	The Piece Hall Trust	£1,252,348
RSPCA Isle of Wight Branch	£1,270,575	Age Concern Salford	£1,252,026
Royal Engineers Central Charitable Trust	£1,270,527	Middlesex University Students' Union	£1,251,526
Newcastle upon Tyne Dog and Cat Shelter	£1,270,043	United Kingdom Mathematics Trust	£1,251,129
The Palace Trust	£1,269,953	Resource for London	£1,250,464
The Jerwood Charitable Foundation	£1,269,860	The Centre for Literacy in Primary Education	£1,250,382
The Crescent School Trust	£1,269,006	Painshill Park Trust Limited	£1,250,095
Russell-Cotes Art Gallery and Museum	£1,268,879	The Newbury Community Resource Centre Limited	£1,250,088
William Morris (Camphill) Community Limited	£1,268,697	Basingstoke Community Churches	£1,249,880
Independent Living Alternatives	£1,268,072	Children & The Arts	£1,249,152
Birmingham Sport and Physical Activity Trust	£1,267,833	LPW Limited	£1,248,460
The Carers Centre (Bristol and South Gloucestershire)	£1,267,774	Mountain Rescue England and Wales	£1,248,226
Mind in Brighton & Hove	£1,267,573	British HIV Association	£1,248,049
Oasis Community Partnerships	£1,266,587	Bedford Hospital NHS Trust Charitable Fund	£1,248,000
The Welfare Association	£1,266,082	Housing Pathways Trust	£1,247,136
Young Life International	£1,265,152	Open Awards	£1,246,962
The Cambrian Education Trust	£1,264,739	Sandwell & W B'ham Hospitals NHS Trust Charities	£1,246,000
The Rural Community Council of Essex	£1,264,444	Crossroads Care South Central Ltd	£1,245,503
GIA England	£1,264,324	University of Sunderland Students' Union	£1,245,448
Mount Zion Christian Ministries International	£1,264,321	Shri Kanagathurkkai Amman (Hindu) Temple Trust	£1,245,104
Congregation of Servants of Mary (London)	£1,264,225	Kent Association for Spina Bifida and Hydrocephalus	£1,244,968
Crossways Community	£1,263,910	Great Britain Wheelchair Rugby Limited	£1,244,709
The National Museum of Labour History	£1,263,842	The Sisters of Charity of St Jeanne Antide	£1,244,242
ComputerAid International	£1,263,668	The Ashden Trust	£1,244,085
Burnie's Foundation	£1,263,320	Charnwood 20:20	£1,242,831
The Scar Free Foundation	£1,262,328	Leeds Women's Aid	£1,242,640
Community Southwark	£1,262,288	The Steel Charitable Trust	£1,242,276
The Police Dependants' Trust Limited	£1,262,137	The Heathside Charitable Trust	£1,242,011
Restore Our Planet	£1,261,961	Hampshire Advocacy Regional Group	£1,241,959
The International Schools Theatre Association	£1,261,923	Vital Regeneration	£1,241,954
Linskill and N Tyneside Community Development Trust	£1,261,754	European Social Network	£1,241,902
York Minster Fund	£1,261,583	The Lichfield Diocesan Board of Education	£1,241,000

Aberglasney Restoration Trust	£1,239,993	The Sons of The Sacred Heart of Jesus	£1,222,908
RSPCA Bury Oldham and District Branch	£1,239,964	Jewish Child's Day	£1,221,981
Ataxia UK	£1,239,813	CPotential Trust	£1,221,878
Home of Comfort for Invalids	£1,239,725	The Shaare Hayim Congregation	£1,220,878
Wildlife Heritage Foundation Ltd	£1,239,580	Cardboard Citizens	£1,220,758
Stakeholder Democracy Network	£1,239,364	PESGB	£1,220,646
Essential Drug and Alcohol Services	£1,239,323	Plunkett Foundation	£1,220,644
Abbeyfield Bristol and Keynsham Society	£1,239,262	New Hackney Education Business Partnership Ltd	£1,220,261
Oxford Institute for Energy Studies	£1,238,940	Ace Africa (UK)	£1,220,222
The Pure Land Foundation	£1,238,339	James Square Plymouth Limited	£1,220,000
Freedom Church Hereford	£1,238,287	Centre Ministries	£1,219,782
The Saigon Children's Charity CIO	£1,237,700	Ferring Country Centre Limited	£1,219,751
The Croydon Almshouse Charities	£1,237,626	The Marcia and Andrew Brown Charitable Trust	£1,219,667
RSPCA Halifax, Huddersfield and District Branch	£1,237,199	The University of Haifa UK	£1,219,482
Age Concern Cambridgeshire	£1,237,042	The Institute of Family Therapy	£1,219,010
Moorlands School Ltd	£1,236,955	Thistledown Education Trust	£1,218,974
Libury Hall	£1,236,594	Open College Network London Region	£1,218,946
East Bedlington Community Centre	£1,236,239	The Conversation Trust (UK) Limited	£1,218,631
The Pennine Acute Hospitals Charity	£1,236,000	Cornwall Community Foundation	£1,218,340
Amnesty International Charity Limited	£1,236,000	Fairshare Educational Foundation	£1,217,433
The Priory Charity	£1,235,979	Manchester Young Lives Ltd	£1,217,257
Mezzanine 2 Limited	£1,235,844	The Royal Navy and Royal Marines Children's Fund	£1,217,160
Surrey Disabled People's Partnership	£1,235,275	Ealing Educational Resources Trust	£1,216,472
Board of Deputies Charitable Foundation	£1,235,183	Barnet Carers Centre	£1,215,932
The Llangollen International Musical Eisteddfod Ltd	£1,234,388	The D-Day Revisited Society	£1,214,474
Stroud & District Homes Foundation Limited	£1,234,387	The St Andrew's School Trust	£1,214,042
The Joseph Cox Charity	£1,233,611	Galloway's Society for the Blind	£1,213,741
Staffordshire South West Citizens Advice Bureau	£1,233,572	The White Eagle Lodge	£1,213,360
Alzheimer's and Dementia Support Services	£1,232,811	The Pathological Society of Great Britain and Ireland	£1,213,001
Shekinah Mission (Plymouth) Limited	£1,232,284	Women in Sport	£1,212,385
Gnanam Foundation	£1,232,114	Business Education Partnership (UK) Ltd	£1,212,352
Citizens Advice Merton and Lambeth	£1,232,096	The Luton and Dunstable Hospital Charitable Fund	£1,212,000
Bobath Childrens Therapy Centre Wales	£1,232,075	Central and South Sussex Citizens Advice Bureau	£1,211,743
International Institute of Risk and Safety Management	£1,232,013	Elrahma Charity Trust	£1,211,470
Hull Resettlement Project Limited	£1,231,521	RSPCA South East and West Devon Branch	£1,211,294
Swansea Young Single Homeless Project	£1,231,391	National Sheep Association	£1,211,226
Shift Foundation	£1,231,368	The Rugby Free Church Homes for the Aged	£1,210,922
BS3 Community Development	£1,231,122	Malvern Hills Conservators	£1,210,674
Results Education	£1,230,675	Twining Enterprise	£1,210,589
The Wildlife Aid Foundation	£1,230,666	The Battle of Britain Memorial Trust	£1,210,392
The Ferry Project	£1,230,384	Anatomical Society	£1,210,051
The Mustard Tree	£1,230,347	The Hamlet Centre Trust	£1,210,017
Rockingham Forest Trust	£1,230,213	Liverpool Citizens Advice Partnership	£1,209,967
The Emerson College Trust Limited	£1,229,969	European Society for Sexual Medicine	£1,209,407
Hammersmith and Fulham Association for Mental Health	£1,229,452	The Prince's Teaching Institute	£1,209,107
Chescombe Trust Limited	£1,229,437	The RBS Peoplecharity	£1,208,590
The Bluebell Railway Trust	£1,229,429	The Focolare Trust	£1,208,510
Youth Music Theatre UK	£1,229,295	Zabludowicz Art Projects	£1,208,458
Solo Life Opportunities	£1,229,155	The Highcombe Edge Trust	£1,208,351
Leeds Mencap	£1,228,969	Clinks	£1,208,317
Independent Cinema Office	£1,228,854	Generate Opportunities Ltd	£1,208,072
St Teresa's Catholic School (Princes Risborough) Trust	£1,228,533	The North West Police Benevolent Fund	£1,207,744
Nottingham Forest Community Trust	£1,228,385	Age Concern Mid Mersey	£1,206,476
Trust Property Held By Trustees of St Augustine's Priory	£1,227,937	Age Concern Gloucestershire	£1,205,988
Worldwide Veterinary Service	£1,227,570	Greek and Greek Cypriot Community of Enfield	£1,205,926
The Skinners' Almshouse Charity	£1,227,017	The Bentley Priory Battle of Britain Trust	£1,205,267
Worcester Live Charitable Trust Ltd	£1,226,886	The Daughters of Divine Charity (Swaffham, Norfolk)	£1,205,117
World Habitat	£1,226,820	Charity Right	£1,204,742
Dewis Centre for Independent Living	£1,226,469	Wales Pre-School Providers Association	£1,204,297
The Next Step Trust	£1,226,430	Llenyddiaeth Cymru - Literature Wales	£1,204,282
Army Families Federation	£1,226,291	RSPCA Middlesex North West Branch	£1,204,106
Emergency Nutrition Network	£1,225,956	The Philadelphia Network Limited	£1,204,082
Institution of Engineering and Technology Fund	£1,225,931	Action on Disability	£1,203,995
Royal Engineers Association	£1,225,795	Nancy Reuben Primary School	£1,203,891
Freshfields Animal Rescue	£1,225,494	Association of Coloproctology of GB and Ireland	£1,203,802
Merlin MS Centre Ltd	£1,224,890	Fynvola Foundation	£1,203,470
Manchester Cathedral Development Trust	£1,224,345	Northumberland Aged Mineworkers' Homes Association	£1,203,226
Age Cymru Gwynedd A Mon	£1,224,233	The Minster Centre	£1,203,221
St Michael & All Angels, Summertown	£1,224,214	Alive Church Lincoln	£1,202,935
Rudolf Steiner School (South Devon) Limited	£1,223,637	Soldiers and Airmens Scripture Readers Association	£1,202,079
Cae Post Limited	£1,223,451	Citizens Advice Cheshire West	£1,201,876
Association of Voluntary Organisations in Wrexham	£1,223,298	Pro Mo-Cymru	£1,201,845

United Counties Agricultural and Hunters Society	£1,201,715	Friends of Mir	£1,182,758
The National Rheumatoid Arthritis Society	£1,201,455	The Foundling Museum	£1,182,643
Founders4schools	£1,201,240	Heart Church	£1,181,907
The Frontiers Charitable Trust	£1,201,098	Cambridge Sports Hall Trust Limited	£1,181,898
The National League Trust	£1,201,081	Benslow Music Trust	£1,181,480
West London Zone	£1,201,027	Mens Accommodation and Support	£1,181,232
Halton Tennis Centre	£1,200,814	Manchester Alliance for Community Care	£1,181,080
Living Coasts	£1,200,676	Shine: Support and Help in Education	£1,180,830
The Lady Nuffield Home	£1,200,530	Woodcraft Folk	£1,180,487
Tigers Sport and Education Trust	£1,200,374	Hartcliffe and Withywood Ventures	£1,178,340
Bradnet	£1,200,361	YWCA England & Wales	£1,178,000
The Noam Primary School Limited	£1,200,004	The Great Britain Sasakawa Foundation	£1,177,834
The Green Alliance Trust	£1,199,829	Canbury School Limited	£1,177,812
Wirral Mind	£1,199,824	Calibre Audio Library	£1,177,807
Falmouth & Exeter Students' Union	£1,199,271	Sported Foundation	£1,177,798
Jerry Green Dog Rescue	£1,198,781	Kensington and Chelsea Social Council	£1,177,654
Age Concern Bedfordshire	£1,198,513	Hyperlipidaemia Education & Atherosclerosis Research	£1,177,560
Uplands Educational Trust	£1,198,306	Age Concern Enfield	£1,176,974
Haringey Citizens Advice Bureaux	£1,198,097	The Haemophilia Society	£1,176,886
The Divine Healing Mission	£1,198,069	Barrow and Districts Society for the Blind Limited	£1,176,183
The Varrier-Jones Foundation	£1,197,030	Cancercare (North Lancashire & South Cumbria)	£1,175,740
The Congregation of The Daughters of Wisdom	£1,196,246	Greenpower Education Trust	£1,175,460
Sustain: The Alliance for Better Food & Farming	£1,196,006	Glen Carne	£1,175,256
New Life Christian Centre (Croydon)	£1,195,991	Spirit of 2012	£1,175,065
Community Law Service (Northampton and County)	£1,195,754	Worcester Citizens Advice Bureau and Whabac	£1,174,874
Promote Mifumi Project	£1,195,664	The Greensand Trust	£1,174,259
The Advocacy Project	£1,195,560	Bradford Women's Aid	£1,173,643
The Kadas Prize Foundation	£1,195,460	Construction Industry Relief	£1,173,505
Freedom Festival Arts Trust	£1,195,225	The Society of St Pius X	£1,173,388
Michael Yoakley's Charity	£1,194,901	Cardiff Women's Aid	£1,173,068
Uprising Leadership	£1,194,836	Nazarene Theological College	£1,172,975
Queen Elizabeth Scholarship Trust Limited	£1,194,804	Gloucestershire Rural Community Council	£1,172,764
The Belsize Square Synagogue	£1,194,220	Honeywood House Nursing Home	£1,172,369
Christ Church Students' Union	£1,193,646	Horatio's Garden	£1,171,954
Berkshire Women's Aid	£1,192,752	Lighthouse Women's Aid Limited	£1,171,947
Samlesbury Hall Trust	£1,192,302	York Arc Light Limited	£1,171,804
Youth Enquiry Service (Plymouth) Limited	£1,192,216	Orison Charitable Trust	£1,171,792
ACE (Action in Caerau and Ely)	£1,191,705	Oizer Charitable Trust	£1,171,707
Crawley Open House	£1,191,262	Institute of School Business Leadership	£1,171,369
War Memorials Trust	£1,190,293	Safer Wales	£1,171,265
Emmaus Cambridge	£1,190,051	Lincolnshire Sports Partnership	£1,171,128
Everyday Language Solutions	£1,190,016	CPA Studios	£1,170,076
The Arboricultural Association	£1,189,554	Go Run for Fun Foundation	£1,169,946
The Urology Foundation	£1,189,268	The Simon Gibson Charitable Trust	£1,169,546
Jewish Lads' and Girls' Brigade	£1,189,249	Le Platon Home, Guernsey	£1,169,484
St Paul, Hammersmith	£1,189,212	St Nicholas, Sevenoaks	£1,168,935
Greenwich Steiner School Initiative	£1,188,744	Two Ridings Community Foundation	£1,168,753
The PSP Association	£1,188,291	The Retired Nurses National Home	£1,168,593
SOAR Community	£1,188,067	The Factory Youth Zone (Manchester) Limited	£1,168,209
Clybiau Plant Cymru Kids Clubs	£1,187,319	Womencentre Limited	£1,168,122
Disabled Living	£1,186,853	Friends of Westonbirt Arboretum	£1,168,122
Great Western Hospital NHS Foundation Trust	£1,186,392	Torbay Community Development Trust Ltd	£1,167,929
Rowanville Limited	£1,186,135	Formission Ltd	£1,167,342
Malawi Relief Fund UK	£1,185,989	Langdon Housing	£1,167,148
The Graeae Theatre Company Limited	£1,185,868	Sandwell Citizens Advice Bureaux	£1,166,930
Durand Education Trust	£1,185,718	Holland House School	£1,166,743
Ely Cathedral Trust	£1,185,678	Northern Broadsides Theatre Company	£1,166,672
Listening Books	£1,185,565	Association of Charitable Foundations	£1,165,978
Bayis Sheli Ltd	£1,185,262	Media Diversity	£1,165,706
Barrowmore Limited	£1,185,142	Cymdeithas Gofal The Care Society	£1,165,584
High Peak Hospicecare	£1,185,000	Colchester League of Hospital & Community Friends	£1,164,690
Over The Wall	£1,184,963	The Music in Secondary Schools Trust	£1,164,649
Southport Flower Show	£1,184,458	Bipolar UK Ltd	£1,164,485
Rochdale and District Mind	£1,184,076	Fairstead House School Trust Ltd	£1,163,955
Society of African Missions	£1,184,075	St George's Lupset Ltd	£1,163,895
Frantic Theatre Company Ltd	£1,183,701	The James Tudor Foundation	£1,163,803
Demos Limited	£1,183,425	St James Gerrards Cross with St James Fulmer	£1,163,484
Xtend Global	£1,183,409	Museum of Brands, Packaging and Advertising	£1,163,340
Hofesh Shechter Company Ltd	£1,183,243	St Richard's School Bredenbury Court	£1,162,787
Urban Partnership Group	£1,183,061	Falcon Support Services E.M Ltd	£1,162,694
YMCA Essex	£1,183,031	The Swedish Church in London Ltd	£1,162,665
Netherthorpe and Upperthorpe Community Alliance	£1,182,837	Alzheimers Support	£1,162,504

Congregation of The Ursulines of Jesus	£1,162,321	Marks Hall Estate	£1,140,025
The Apuldram Centre	£1,161,660	Age UK Lindsey	£1,139,777
Hertfordshire Community Foundation	£1,161,605	Jews' College	£1,139,700
The Social Mobility Foundation	£1,161,276	South Liverpool Citizens Advice Bureau	£1,139,006
Fordham University UK Charitable Trust	£1,161,197	Spectrum Care, Resources and Education in Autism	£1,138,708
The Story Museum	£1,160,555	The Three Choirs Festival Association Ltd	£1,138,653
The Chipping Norton Theatre Limited	£1,160,526	Christ Church Oxford United Clubs	£1,138,432
Hopscotch Asian Women's Centre	£1,160,407	Carers' Support - Canterbury,Dover & Thanet	£1,137,890
Sheffield Mind Ltd	£1,160,192	Palfrey Community Association	£1,137,808
UFI Charitable Trust	£1,160,000	Women's Aid Leicestershire Limited	£1,136,473
Holy Trinity (Hull) Development Trust	£1,159,829	First Light South West Ltd	£1,136,289
English Benedictine Order of Oulton Abbey	£1,159,399	One Dance UK	£1,136,027
Disability Action Yorkshire	£1,159,262	Jewish Philanthropic Assoc for Israel and Middle East	£1,136,000
Saltbox	£1,159,156	The Barbican Centre Trust Limited	£1,135,950
The Friends of The Wisdom Hospice Limited	£1,158,594	Together Women Projects (Yorkshire and Humberside)	£1,135,699
One Awards	£1,157,458	Royal College of Veterinary Surgeons Trust	£1,135,697
SciDev.Net	£1,157,445	The Greenwich Theatre Limited	£1,135,425
Friends of Animals League	£1,156,921	The DHL UK Foundation	£1,135,185
The Lohana Mahajan (UK) Trust	£1,156,884	Open College Network West Midlands	£1,135,083
Great Yarmouth & Waveney Mind	£1,156,768	Devon Community Foundation	£1,134,948
Solo Housing (East Anglia)	£1,156,392	The New Art Exchange Ltd	£1,134,862
Bethany Care Trust	£1,156,373	Mind BLMK	£1,134,518
Vale of Rheidol Railway Limited	£1,156,295	Wandsworth Citizens Advice Bureaux Limited	£1,134,200
The Underfall Yard Trust	£1,156,200	Trumros Limited	£1,134,005
High House Production Park Limited	£1,156,076	Sir Halley Stewart Trust	£1,134,000
London Legal Support Trust	£1,155,636	At Home in the Community Limited	£1,133,725
Mission Rabies Limited	£1,155,546	Brent Citizens Advice Bureaux	£1,133,625
Hornsey Y.M.C.A.	£1,155,180	Greendown Trust	£1,133,427
Kensington & Chelsea Citizens Advice Bureau Service	£1,154,960	Indochina Starfish Foundation	£1,133,123
The Metropolitan Masonic Charity	£1,154,792	Middlesbrough Environment City Trust Limited	£1,133,051
Brent Mind (Association for Mental Health)	£1,154,415	Derbyshire Carers Association	£1,133,012
Surrey Independent Living Council	£1,154,149	Community Equality Disability Action	£1,132,883
Dalaid	£1,154,111	Sussex Emmaus	£1,132,789
The Dohnavur Fellowship Corporation	£1,153,762	Batus General Fund	£1,132,568
Thomas Heatherley Educational Trust	£1,153,743	New World Mission Association UK	£1,132,482
The Charlie Waller Memorial Trust	£1,153,735	Manchester and Warrington Area Quaker Meeting	£1,132,362
The Little Angel Theatre	£1,153,446	Lamport Hall Preservation Trust Limited	£1,132,282
Friends of The United Institutions of Arad	£1,153,379	Funding Fish	£1,132,161
Hounslow Music Service	£1,152,959	Lee Abbey International Students' Club	£1,132,124
Hope for Tomorrow	£1,152,460	Get Kids Going	£1,131,976
The Association for Science Education	£1,151,532	Pestalozzi International Village Trust	£1,131,655
Fight for Peace International	£1,151,228	Women and Girls Network	£1,131,579
Watoto Child Care Ministries	£1,150,280	Mirza Sharif Ahmad Foundation	£1,131,000
Rhondda Cynon Taff Citizens Advice Bureau	£1,149,484	Park Families Limited	£1,130,852
Pilotlight	£1,149,145	Newbridge Preparatory School Limited	£1,130,547
Team Rubicon UK	£1,148,704	Sunderland Carers' Centre	£1,130,368
Read for Good	£1,148,277	Ongo Communities Limited	£1,129,754
Glastonbury Abbey	£1,147,700	Blackburn Rovers Community Trust	£1,128,992
New Community Network	£1,146,937	The Daphne Jackson Memorial Fellowships Trust	£1,128,684
Children on the Edge	£1,146,819	Dementia Concern	£1,128,537
Vision Aid Overseas	£1,146,536	Shrewsbury School Foundation	£1,128,029
The Royal Economic Society	£1,146,489	Christadelphian Meal A Day Fund	£1,127,796
The Frederick Hugh Trust	£1,145,994	Exeter City Community Trust	£1,127,601
Nottinghamshire Women's Aid Limited	£1,145,699	The Fairlight Charitable Company	£1,127,471
York St John Students' Union	£1,145,532	Exbury Gardens Limited	£1,127,244
Bollington Health & Leisure	£1,145,433	Wolverhampton Youth Zone	£1,127,177
The Geographical Association	£1,145,237	The Rothermere Foundation	£1,126,135
The Academy of Ancient Music	£1,144,873	Carers in Bedfordshire	£1,125,976
The Catherine Cookson Charitable Trust	£1,144,667	Genesis Trust Bath	£1,125,761
Clean Break Theatre Company	£1,144,590	South Yorkshire Community Foundation Limited	£1,125,531
The American Museum in Britain	£1,144,099	National Council for The Training of Journalists	£1,125,239
Augustinians of The Assumption	£1,144,010	The Davidson Family Charitable Trust	£1,125,173
CMSS	£1,143,579	Blackheath Conservatoire of Music and The Arts	£1,124,738
Excellent Development Limited	£1,143,573	One To One Children's Fund	£1,124,072
PHAB Limited	£1,143,420	St John's Approved Premises	£1,123,861
Action Against Medical Accidents	£1,143,296	Harrison Housing	£1,123,680
J J Charitable Trust	£1,143,234	S L G Charitable Trust Limited	£1,123,483
Girls' Brigade Ministries	£1,143,179	The North London Conservatoire	£1,123,422
LHR Airport Communities Trust	£1,142,765	The Braunstone Foundation	£1,123,367
Access Sport CIO	£1,142,622	Assoc of Chief Executives of Voluntary Organisations	£1,123,341
The British Skin Foundation	£1,141,799	Paul O'Gorman Lifeline	£1,121,226
Coastal West Sussex Mind	£1,140,256	Moreton Hall School Trust Limited	£1,121,036

The Order of St John	£1,120,636	Norfolk Carers Support	£1,102,451
Oxford University Student Union	£1,120,417	Solving Kids' Cancer Europe	£1,102,188
The Brian Mercer Charitable Trust	£1,120,199	The Bronte Society	£1,101,969
TLC: Talk, Listen, Change	£1,119,483	Bromley and Croydon Women's Aid	£1,101,869
Stag Community Arts Centre	£1,119,410	The FIEC (Legacy) Charity	£1,101,612
St Joseph's School Nottingham	£1,119,404	Biblica Europe Ministries Trust	£1,101,330
Alfurqan Education Trust	£1,119,324	National Operatic and Dramatic Association	£1,101,210
Shrimad Rajchandra Mission Dharampur (UK)	£1,119,323	Roehampton Students' Union	£1,101,159
Development Through Challenge	£1,119,305	The Change Foundation	£1,101,122
The Institute of Mathematics and Its Applications	£1,119,198	Wates Family Enterprise Trust	£1,100,850
Off The Record Youth Counselling Croydon	£1,119,071	St Mary's Trust	£1,100,655
British Friends of The Bible Lands Museum, Jerusalem	£1,118,859	MYBNK	£1,100,619
Ort UK Foundation	£1,118,761	Wallscourt Foundation	£1,100,459
E and E Kernkraut Charities Limited	£1,118,282	The Salmon Youth Centre in Bermondsey	£1,100,383
Cosgarne Hall Ltd.	£1,118,202	Sheffield United Community Foundation	£1,100,078
Tydfil Training Consortium Limited	£1,117,884	Lancaster Training Services Limited	£1,099,922
Hill Holt Wood	£1,117,675	Bumblebee Conservation Trust	£1,099,801
The Muath Trust	£1,117,655	Sussex County Sports Partnership Trust	£1,099,724
Learning Links (Southern) Limited	£1,117,645	RSPCA Norwich and Mid-Norfolk Branch	£1,099,405
Reading FC Community Trust	£1,116,461	Emmanuel, South Croydon	£1,099,403
Guide Association London and South East England	£1,116,385	Gables Farm Dogs and Cats Home	£1,099,218
Gordon Moody Association	£1,116,044	Digartref Cyf	£1,099,078
Tomchei Yotzei Anglia	£1,115,959	Bury St Edmunds Heritage Trust	£1,099,056
The Dr Hadwen Trust	£1,115,697	British Psychotherapy Foundation	£1,098,979
Cyfannol Women's Aid	£1,115,682	Yeldall Christian Centres	£1,098,754
Lordswood Leisure Centre Limited	£1,115,578	The Springfield Project	£1,098,387
Values Academy	£1,115,159	Jami Mosque and Islamic Centre (B'ham) Trustees	£1,097,770
Siri Guru Nanak Darbar (Sikh Temple)	£1,114,933	People's Trust for Endangered Species	£1,097,455
The Citizenship Foundation	£1,114,510	Community Foundation for Calderdale	£1,097,270
The School of Artisan Food	£1,114,405	The Shropshire Horticultural Society	£1,097,201
The Creswell Heritage Trust	£1,113,878	MapAction	£1,097,155
Atma Vignani Dada Bhagwan Foundation	£1,113,817	The Independent Schools Association	£1,097,133
National Health Service Retirement Fellowship	£1,113,744	Dina Perelman Trust Limited	£1,096,233
The King Henry VIII Endowed Trust, Warwick	£1,113,680	Bristol Sheltered Accommodation & Support Limited	£1,095,972
The Thoroughbred Breeders Association	£1,113,415	Direct Help & Advice Ltd.	£1,095,407
The New Theatre Royal-Trustees (Portsmouth) Ltd	£1,113,289	Alliance Francaise de Londres Limited	£1,095,121
Money Advice and Community Support Service	£1,112,923	Wigan Athletic FC Community Trust	£1,094,197
Glebe House (Charnwood) Limited	£1,112,879	East Cleveland M S Home	£1,094,068
Hospice at Home West Cumbria	£1,112,797	One Plus One Marriage and Partnership Research	£1,093,814
Canon Collins Educational and Legal Assistance Trust	£1,112,539	Freshwater Biological Association	£1,093,623
International Society for Influenza	£1,112,535	Medical Schools Council	£1,093,540
York Childcare Ltd	£1,112,109	New Forest Quaker Care Home	£1,093,377
The South Northamptonshire Leisure Trust	£1,111,752	The Metropolitan and City Police Orphans Fund	£1,092,383
The Puri Foundation	£1,111,650	C.A.B. Cornwall	£1,092,256
All Saints Woodford Wells	£1,111,490	African Enterprise International	£1,092,179
Thackray Medical Museum Company Limited	£1,111,362	The Cinnamon Network	£1,092,071
European Christian Mission (Britain)	£1,111,173	Give It Forward Today	£1,091,927
Westminster Citizens Advice Bureau Service	£1,111,171	Farming and Wildlife Advisory Group South West Ltd	£1,091,694
Age Concern Wigan Borough	£1,111,026	Carmel Ministries International	£1,091,480
British Association of Plastic Reconstructive Surgeons	£1,110,959	The World Community for Christian Meditation	£1,091,292
Maryvale Institute	£1,110,730	Blackfriars Settlement	£1,091,216
The King Edward's School Birmingham Trust	£1,110,502	The Leukaemia Care Society	£1,091,213
Adventure Plus	£1,110,067	Lyng Community Association	£1,091,072
Actes Trust	£1,109,894	The Hereford Cathedral Perpetual Trust	£1,090,253
Richard Reeve's Foundation	£1,109,864	Richmond Gymnastics Association	£1,090,195
Pembrokeshire Agricultural Society Limited	£1,109,596	The Bowland Charitable Trust	£1,089,908
St. Albans School Woollam Trust	£1,109,418	Forward Thinking	£1,089,840
Age Concern (Herne Bay)	£1,108,849	Michael Batt Charitable Trust	£1,089,798
Portsmouth Hospitals Charity	£1,108,260	Centre for Ageing Better Trust	£1,089,751
Reading Gospel Hall Trust	£1,108,214	The Brain and Spine Foundation	£1,089,385
Odstock Charitable Trust	£1,107,245	The Multiple Sclerosis Research and Relief Fund	£1,088,962
The Parenting Project	£1,106,141	NEWCIS	£1,088,463
International Association of Teachers of TOEFL	£1,106,125	Noah's Ark Children's Hospital Charity	£1,088,325
Burton Albion Community Trust	£1,105,353	The Credit Union Foundation	£1,088,208
Bolton NHS Charitable Fund	£1,105,000	Congregational Federation	£1,088,079
Manor Gardens Welfare Trust Ltd	£1,104,139	Newham Music Trust	£1,088,031
The End of Life Partnership Limited	£1,104,126	Nexus Institute of Creative Arts	£1,087,986
Age UK Maidstone	£1,104,019	Vision for a Nation Foundation	£1,087,950
Emmaus St Albans	£1,103,643	The St Peter and St Paul School Trust	£1,087,752
Finchley Reform Synagogue	£1,103,293	The British Society for Surgery of The Hand	£1,087,576
Pembrokeshire Association of Voluntary Services	£1,103,041	The Poetry Society	£1,087,351
The Sisters of Charity of Our Lady of Evron	£1,102,806	Leicester Cathedral Charitable Trust	£1,086,877

Beis Aharon Trust Ltd	£1,086,496	Pavilion Dance South West Limited	£1,068,014
Oxford Centre for Hebrew and Jewish Studies	£1,085,985	Castle Supported Living Limited	£1,067,994
Merton Music Foundation	£1,085,674	Grandparents Plus	£1,067,949
Empower Global	£1,084,730	Impact Family Services	£1,066,673
Trinity Baptist Church	£1,084,618	Aquaid Lifeline Fund	£1,066,589
Play Adventures & Community Enrichment	£1,084,454	Westville House School	£1,065,288
Lorenden School	£1,084,326	Sebastian's Action Trust	£1,065,269
Sussex Interpreting Services	£1,082,938	London Cycling Campaign	£1,065,157
Heathrow School of Gymnastics & Dance Ltd	£1,082,547	Royal Albert Dock Trust	£1,065,126
Orchestras Live	£1,082,368	Barnsley Community Build	£1,065,105
GFS Community Enterprise	£1,082,000	E Hayes Dashwood of Aston Rowant House Oxon	£1,064,971
Bhaarat Welfare Trust	£1,081,300	Releasing Potential 2002 Limited	£1,064,742
Ipswich Hospital NHS Trust Charitable Funds	£1,081,000	Leicester Charity Organisation Society	£1,064,709
ICW The Honourable Society of the Middle Temple	£1,081,000	Mosaic Clubhouse	£1,064,404
Hendon Mosque & Islamic Centre	£1,080,826	The Housing Associations' Charitable Trust	£1,064,230
The National Communities Resource Centre Limited	£1,080,781	Bourneheights Limited	£1,064,215
Bristol Islamic Schools Trust	£1,080,741	Birmingham City Mission	£1,063,675
Concordis International Trust	£1,080,604	City and Guilds of London Art School Property Trust	£1,063,659
Knowle West Media Centre	£1,080,489	Faith in Families	£1,063,483
Foundation for Conductive Education	£1,080,255	The Surrey Cricket Board	£1,063,480
Citizens Advice Shropshire	£1,080,185	Redeemed Christian Church of God Trinity Chapel	£1,063,353
Cardiff Mind Ltd	£1,079,890	The League of Friends of The Royal United Hospital	£1,063,012
BJU International	£1,079,779	Jaamiatul Imaam Muhammad Zakaria Muhajir Madani	£1,062,321
National Association for Special Educational Needs	£1,079,746	Bath Festivals	£1,062,082
Centre for London	£1,079,328	North Eastern YWCA Trustees Ltd	£1,061,985
Education Policy Institute	£1,079,200	Oral Health Foundation	£1,061,727
The Clore Social Leadership Programme	£1,078,326	BFCVDFF Limited	£1,061,448
British Emunah Fund	£1,077,921	Success for All Foundation	£1,060,919
Age UK Blackburn with Darwen	£1,077,187	King George's Field, Mile End	£1,060,604
Darlington Association on Disability	£1,077,126	China Dialogue Trust	£1,060,387
Western Sussex Hospitals Charity & Related Charities	£1,077,000	The College of Osteopaths	£1,060,244
October Gallery Trust	£1,076,884	Catalyst Stockton on Tees Limited	£1,059,269
Paces Sheffield	£1,076,599	Herefordshire Mind	£1,058,960
Skills Active UK	£1,076,521	B.T.D.A. Limited	£1,058,332
The Boparan Charitable Trust	£1,076,473	Fegans	£1,058,312
Institute of Export and International Trade (The)	£1,076,210	Community Ventures (Middlesbrough) Ltd	£1,058,259
Holy Trinity, Cheltenham	£1,076,106	The Douglas Bader Foundation	£1,058,116
Yesodey Hatorah Nursery	£1,076,048	The Nuclear Institute	£1,057,401
The Locker Foundation	£1,075,902	Stobart Newlands Charitable Trust	£1,056,861
Churches Conservation	£1,075,863	Children's Scrapstore	£1,056,686
The Earley Charity	£1,075,636	Chance (UK) Ltd	£1,056,479
St James, Westminster	£1,075,340	Coutts Charitable Foundation	£1,056,074
Southmead Development Trust	£1,074,822	Fosse Bank New School	£1,055,810
The Genesis Charitable Trust	£1,074,514	The Association of Dental Implantology Limited	£1,055,644
Ashoka UK	£1,074,487	Classquote Limited	£1,055,543
Lupus UK	£1,074,479	Baron Davenport's Charity	£1,054,878
The JGW Patterson Foundation	£1,074,211	Wembley National Stadium Trust	£1,054,732
The Royal Cambridge Home	£1,073,893	London Christian School Ltd	£1,054,595
Abbeyfield Reading Society Ltd	£1,073,552	Diana Award	£1,054,465
The Open School Trust	£1,073,170	The Oasis Partnership UK	£1,053,917
Nottingham Diocesan Sick and Retired Priests Fund	£1,073,000	The Wixamtree Trust	£1,053,220
Vale House Stabilisation Services	£1,072,929	Dorset Natural History and Archaeological Society	£1,052,812
The Vegan Society	£1,072,614	W G S Trust	£1,052,765
Onside Independent Advocacy	£1,072,592	Free Word	£1,052,069
The Society of All Saints Sisters of The Poor	£1,072,578	Oglesby Charitable Trust	£1,051,963
Above Bar Church	£1,072,049	Bromley Y	£1,051,860
Abbeyfield Southern Oaks	£1,071,511	Scarborough and District Mencap	£1,051,502
Care England	£1,071,332	The Housing Link (2003)	£1,051,251
Lincolnshire Integrated Voluntary Emergency Service	£1,070,616	Centre for Counselling & Psychotherapy Education Trust	£1,051,071
The Howard League for Penal Reform	£1,070,386	Climate Parliament	£1,050,972
River and Rowing Museum Foundation	£1,070,343	Scargill Movement	£1,050,868
Oakfield (Easton Maudit) Limited	£1,070,198	Cheshire Agricultural Society CIO	£1,050,057
The Order of Friars Minor	£1,069,879	Young Gloucestershire	£1,049,875
Hospice of The Valleys	£1,069,361	Care 4 All (North East Lincolnshire) Ltd	£1,049,868
Spire (Preston) Limited	£1,069,167	The British Limousin Cattle Society Limited	£1,049,180
Danish Young Women's Christian Association in London	£1,068,973	Girton Town Charity	£1,049,000
Emmaus Gloucestershire	£1,068,832	KH Theatre Limited	£1,048,722
Helen Bamber Foundation	£1,068,816	Genetic Alliance UK Ltd	£1,048,394
Millwall Community Trust	£1,068,528	Exeter Community Initiatives	£1,048,098
Acre Housing	£1,068,436	The Makaton Charity	£1,047,612
William Rowan Hamilton Trust	£1,068,353	The Fleet Air Arm Museum CLG Limited	£1,047,557
W J Yapp Bequest	£1,068,066	The Institute of Acoustics Limited	£1,047,490

St Clement and St James Community Dev Project	£1,047,433	The William Scott Abbott Trust	£1,032,963
The Carningli Trust	£1,047,269	Lewisham Citizens Advice Bureaux Service Limited	£1,032,959
Mind in Harrow	£1,047,098	Groundwork North Wales	£1,032,490
Basingstoke Gymnastics Club	£1,047,058	St David's Diocesan Council for Social Responsibility	£1,032,432
The Nurture Group Network Limited	£1,046,733	Sam and Bella Sebba Charitable Trust	£1,032,406
Tzedokoh Vechesed Limited	£1,046,614	Bath Spa University Students' Union	£1,031,834
St Mary Magdalene, Richmond with St Matthias	£1,046,396	Bromsgrove Arts Centre Trust	£1,031,673
The Children's Adventure Farm Trust Ltd	£1,046,007	Silverdale Gospel Hall Trust	£1,031,591
The Trinity College of Music Trust	£1,045,626	The Badur Foundation	£1,031,490
Peter Sowerby Foundation	£1,045,000	The Sharpham Trust	£1,031,037
High Hilden Limited	£1,044,718	International Seafarers' Welfare & Assistance Network	£1,030,654
The Dickens House and The Dickens House Fund	£1,044,603	Friends of The Lake District	£1,030,616
Romsey Mill Trust	£1,044,339	Age UK Portsmouth	£1,030,602
Afghan Ekta Cultural/Religious Community Centre	£1,044,185	Anjuman-E-Badri (Birmingham)	£1,030,304
Taste for Adventure	£1,043,340	Reading YMCA	£1,029,953
Donnington Hospital	£1,043,004	Multiple System Atrophy Trust	£1,029,755
Gloucestershire Assoc of Secondary Headteacher	£1,042,552	Chiltern Student Villages Limited	£1,029,490
The Big Issue Foundation	£1,042,513	East and West Looe Harbour and Bridge Charities	£1,029,369
National Dance Company Wales	£1,042,357	Family and Childcare Trust	£1,029,145
United Methodist Church (UK)	£1,042,243	Obstetrics Anaesthetists Association	£1,029,138
Guildford City Swimming Club	£1,042,131	Abbeyfield Braintree, Bocking and Felsted Society Ltd	£1,028,556
The Band Trust	£1,041,996	Gloucestershire Hospitals NHS Foundation Trust	£1,028,000
Groundwork Northamptonshire	£1,041,862	Active Humber Ltd	£1,027,757
Women's Aid in Rhondda Cynon Taf	£1,041,776	Central and East Northamptonshire CAB	£1,027,264
The Organisation for New Music and Sound	£1,041,719	Hillingdon Community Trust	£1,027,150
Guides Cymru	£1,041,328	The St Benet's Trust	£1,027,000
Torfaen and Blaenau Gwent Mind	£1,041,266	Halcrow Foundation	£1,026,183
Beechwood Cancer Care Centre	£1,040,930	The Earl of Northampton's Charity	£1,026,000
Chrysalis (Cumbria) Ltd	£1,040,901	Crossroads Care Central & East Gloucestershire Ltd	£1,025,627
Sunnylands Limited	£1,040,822	The Greenfields Centre Limited	£1,025,429
Ymddiriedolaeth Nant Gwrtheyrn	£1,040,682	The Methodist Church - Chester and Stoke-on-Trent	£1,025,426
Huntingdon Mencap Society Limited	£1,040,604	Birmingham Multi-Care Support Services Ltd	£1,025,345
Cornell University Foundation (UK) Limited	£1,040,441	Southwark Diocesan Welcare	£1,025,182
Dawatul Islam UK and Eire	£1,040,109	Academy for Contemporary Circus & Physical Theatre	£1,024,888
BasicNeeds	£1,040,081	Papyrus Prevention of Young Suicide	£1,023,936
South Warwickshire NHS Foundation Trust	£1,040,000	Build It International	£1,023,493
Christian Life Ministries	£1,039,130	Wodson Park Trust	£1,022,844
Self Management UK Limited	£1,039,023	Rape and Sexual Abuse Support Centre	£1,022,676
Bakewell and Eyam Community Transport	£1,038,930	The City of London Charities Pool	£1,021,998
The Vegetarian Society of The United Kingdom Ltd	£1,038,909	The Message Enterprise Centre	£1,021,926
University of Wolverhampton Students' Union	£1,038,877	The Ahoy Centre	£1,021,874
Beaumont House Community Hospice	£1,038,623	Create London	£1,021,436
Leicester City Football Club Trust Limited	£1,038,613	Youthscape	£1,021,042
Compaid Trust	£1,038,402	Citizens Advice Bureaux (Salford)	£1,020,817
Linking Environment and Farming	£1,038,119	St John's College Nottingham Limited	£1,020,780
Adult Training Network Limited	£1,037,995	The Migraine Trust	£1,020,619
Welsh Centre for International Affairs	£1,037,816	Avon Autistic Foundation Limited	£1,020,541
The Bosco Centre	£1,037,709	Team Army Sports Foundation	£1,020,147
Dorset Advocacy	£1,037,335	Polish Social and Cultural Association Limited	£1,019,747
Southwark Disablement Association	£1,036,995	Cockpit Arts	£1,019,334
The Abbeyfield Hoylake and West Kirby Society Ltd	£1,036,892	Sandwell Training Association Limited	£1,019,038
National Heart and Lung Institute Foundation	£1,036,259	The Edward Cadbury Charitable Trust	£1,018,710
Masschallenge	£1,036,127	International Aid Trust	£1,018,646
Cleveland Youth Association	£1,036,122	RSPCA Hillingdon, Slough, Windsor, Kingston	£1,018,559
The Albert Kennedy Trust	£1,035,814	Dreamflight	£1,018,435
Breakthrough (Deaf-Hearing Integration)	£1,035,648	Headway Worcestershire	£1,018,073
Carers Trust South East Wales	£1,035,623	Redthread Youth Limited	£1,018,063
Birkenhead School Foundation Trust	£1,035,233	The Institution of Railway Signal Engineers	£1,018,007
Hadassah Medical Relief Association U.K.	£1,035,105	The Western Charitable Foundation	£1,017,799
Guildford Baptist Church	£1,035,088	Chartered Institution of Civil Engineering Surveyors	£1,017,405
BT Benevolent Fund	£1,035,064	St Andrew's House	£1,017,090
St Marylebone with Holy Trinity St Marylebone	£1,034,974	Herries Educational Trust Limited	£1,017,051
Leo Baeck College	£1,034,968	Lancing College Preparatory School at Worthing Ltd	£1,016,903
Avalon School Educational Trust	£1,034,821	The Society for The Study of Addiction	£1,016,780
The Norden Farm Centre Trust Limited	£1,034,558	Cambridge Science Centre	£1,016,757
Age UK Sutton	£1,034,400	Royal Anthropological Institute of GBn and Ireland	£1,016,618
Gwasanaeth Ysgolion William Mathias Cyf	£1,034,381	Space for Giants	£1,016,435
Snowflake School for Children with Autism Limited	£1,034,263	Philadelphia Church of God	£1,016,343
Keswick Enterprises Holdings Charitable Trust	£1,034,250	Staying Put	£1,016,276
Khalsa Aid	£1,034,205	The Aurum Charitable Trust	£1,015,486
Bridgend Association of Voluntary Organisations	£1,033,314	Congregation of Sisters of Our Lady of Sion	£1,015,483
Bleakholt Animal Sanctuary	£1,033,235	Helen Rollason Heal Cancer Charity Limited	£1,015,018

Concordia (UK) Limited	£1,014,711	Grey Gables	£1,006,204
Gabrieli	£1,014,559	The Bath Preservation Trust Ltd	£1,006,154
Hawthorne Trust Limited	£1,014,509	Godolphin International Leadership Programme	£1,005,991
The Oxford School of Drama Trust	£1,014,389	Cornerstone Evangelical Church	£1,005,869
Solent Students' Union	£1,014,377	Gillingham Football Club Community Trust	£1,005,784
Rigby Foundation	£1,014,368	The Diocese in Europe Board of Finance	£1,005,697
Edge Hotel School Limited	£1,014,179	The Sofa Project	£1,005,550
The Booth Charities	£1,014,000	Hampshire County Scout Council	£1,005,442
Branwood School Trust Limited	£1,013,187	Global One 2015	£1,005,108
The Round Square	£1,012,614	Stockport Plaza Trust Limited	£1,005,098
Mr Willats' Charity	£1,012,395	The London Irish Centre	£1,004,783
Tamba, Twins & Multiple Births Association	£1,011,899	The Godinton House Preservation Trust	£1,004,567
Multiple Sclerosis-UK Limited	£1,011,508	Swan Advocacy Network	£1,004,246
Business Launchpad	£1,011,342	Wolves Community Trust	£1,004,164
Bob and Michelle Shemtob Charitable Trust	£1,011,327	The Innocent Foundation	£1,003,864
Maccabi GB	£1,011,216	Community360	£1,003,714
IBM United Kingdom Trust	£1,011,000	The Co-operative College	£1,003,647
Child Brain Injury Trust	£1,010,907	Hope Consultants International Ltd	£1,003,256
Alfanar	£1,010,821	Blackpool FC Community Trust	£1,002,999
ASIST	£1,010,537	Dance 4 Limited	£1,002,646
Pentreath Limited	£1,010,157	Family Support Centre [Kings Lynn]	£1,002,577
Irshad Trust	£1,009,946	Medical Missionary News Fund	£1,002,467
Surfers Against Sewage	£1,009,846	Autism Research Trust	£1,002,450
WECIL Ltd	£1,009,329	Kings Church Centre Norwich	£1,002,423
The Ovo Charitable Foundation	£1,009,019	Wirral Churches' Ark Project	£1,001,646
The Design and Technology Association	£1,008,976	The New Phytologist Trust	£1,001,505
The Teamwork Trust	£1,008,653	Parish of Great Chesham	£1,001,503
Order of Hermit Friars of St Augustine	£1,008,390	The Swedish Folk High School	£1,001,497
Hope Worldwide	£1,008,352	BHA for Equality	£1,001,012
Changing Lives in Cheshire	£1,007,687	Vineyard Churches UK and Ireland	£1,000,814
Quaker Social Action	£1,007,656	Age UK Barnet	£1,000,477
William Harding's Charity	£1,007,422	Approach Supporting Your Life Your Way	£1,000,437
Breadline Africa	£1,007,383	The Prince Andrew Charitable Trust	£1,000,430
Hatzola Trust Limited	£1,006,868	Middlesbrough Voluntary Development Agency	£1,000,400
Maidstone YMCA	£1,006,410	Bromley Mencap	£1,000,333
Threshold Housing Link	£1,006,405	St. John's, Smith Square Charitable Trust	£1,000,242
The Not Forgotten Association (NFA)	£1,006,271	City Hospitals Sunderland NHS Foundation Trust	£1,000,098

This page is intentionally left blank

Printed in 8pt Nimbus Sans L

Designed by URW++ Design and Development GmbH

Dellam Publishing Limited

2 Heath Drive, Sutton, Surrey, SM2 5RP

Fax: 020 8770 7478   email: enquiries@dellam.com

9 781912 736003